Encyclopædia
of
Religion and Ethics

Encyclopædia
of
Religion and Ethics

EDITED BY

JAMES HASTINGS

WITH THE ASSISTANCE OF

JOHN A. SELBIE, M.A., D.D.

PROFESSOR OF OLD TESTAMENT LANGUAGE AND LITERATURE IN THE UNITED FREE CHURCH COLLEGE, ABERDEEN

AND

LOUIS H. GRAY, M.A., Ph.D.

SOMETIME FELLOW IN INDO-IRANIAN LANGUAGES IN COLUMBIA UNIVERSITY, NEW YORK

VOLUME XII
SUFFERING–ZWINGLI

EDINBURGH: T. & T. CLARK, 38 GEORGE STREET
NEW YORK: CHARLES SCRIBNER'S SONS, FIFTH AVENUE AT 48TH STREET
1921

Printed by MORRISON & GIBB LIMITED

FOR

T. & T. CLARK, EDINBURGH

LONDON: SIMPKIN, MARSHALL, HAMILTON, KENT, AND CO. LIMITED

NEW YORK: CHARLES SCRIBNER'S SONS

TO

SIR JOHN MAURICE CLARK, BARONET

PUBLISHER

AND

FRIEND

PREFACE

IN issuing this, the twelfth, volume of THE ENCYCLOPÆDIA OF RELIGION AND ETHICS, I wish to thank those who have assisted me in the work.

And first let me name the Publishers, Messrs. T. & T. CLARK, and their Staff, above all Sir JOHN M. CLARK, Bart., to whom I have taken the liberty of dedicating it. The Printers also, Messrs. MORRISON & GIBB LTD., deserve the thanks of all concerned, and mine most of all; and especially must their able and accurate Readers be remembered.

What shall I say of my accomplished and loyal Staff? Besides Dr. Selbie and Dr. Gray, whose names are on the title-page, I must mention Mr. J. F. Grant and Mr. T. Riach. Not less deserving than these are the two sisters Miss M. C. Macdonald (now Mrs. Laburn) and Miss D. R. Macdonald (now Mrs. Dow), to whom most of all is due the minute accuracy of the ENCYCLOPÆDIA. With them let me name my Secretary, Miss H. Robertson, who was with me at the planning of the Work and has guided its course to the end. I must also mention our indispensable Librarian, Miss E. M. Mitchell, and Miss B. Wisely, the Typist, whose work has often won the admiration of the authors of articles.

Many scholars have aided with their contributions and with their counsel. I cannot name them. But I must say one thing. The ENCYCLOPÆDIA would not have been what it is if I had not had in every department of study covered by it at least one man upon whom I could rely for advice.

The names of the translators have never appeared. The translations from the French have for the most part been made by my assistants. The German translations are almost all due to the Rev. ALEXANDER GRIEVE, M.A., D.Phil. Mr. ALBERT BONUS, M.A., has translated nearly all the Italian work. Either Professor W. R. MORFILL or Dr. E. H. MINNS has been responsible for the Russian translations. A few articles written in Danish were translated by the Rev. JOHN BEVERIDGE, B.D.

The editing of a work like THE ENCYCLOPÆDIA OF RELIGION AND ETHICS is undoubtedly difficult, but it has brought me into touch with so many men of ability and generosity, and has enabled me to make so many friendships, that the pleasure of it has far outweighed its pain.

An Index Volume is in course of preparation.

THE EDITOR.

AUTHORS OF ARTICLES IN THIS VOLUME

ABELSON (JOSHUA), M.A., D.Lit. (London).
Rabbi, Cardiff; author of *Immanence of God in Rabbinical Literature, Jewish Mysticism, Maimonides on the Jewish Creed.*
Usury (Jewish).

ABRAHAMS (ISRAEL), M.A. (Lond. and Camb.), D.D. (Heb. Union Coll., Cincin.).
Reader in Talmudic and Rabbinic Literature in the University of Cambridge; formerly Senior Tutor in the Jews' College, London; editor of the *Jewish Quarterly Review*, 1888–1908.
Symbolism (Jewish), **Talmud, Targums.**

ADAM (DAVID STOW), M.A., D.D.
Professor of Church History and Systematic Theology in Ormond College, University of Melbourne.
Theology.

ADENEY (WALTER FREDERIC), M.A., D.D.
Late Principal of Lancashire College, and Lecturer on History of Doctrine in Manchester University; author of *The Greek and Eastern Churches*, and other works.
Toleration, Waldenses.

ALEXANDER (ARCHIBALD BROWNING DRYSDALE), M.A., D.D. (Glas.).
Minister of the United Free Church at Langbank; formerly Lecturer on Ethics and present Assessor to Chair of Ethics and Practical Theology in the United Free Church College, Glasgow; author of *A Short History of Philosophy*, and other works.
Wealth.

ALEXANDER (HARTLEY BURR), Ph.D.
Professor of Philosophy in the University of Nebraska; author of vol. x. (*North American*) of *The Mythology of All Races.*
Worship (Primitive).

ANESAKI (MASAHARU), M.A., D.Litt., LL.D.
Professor of the Science of Religion in the Imperial University of Tokyo; Professor of Japanese Literature and Life in the University of Harvard, 1913–15; author of *Buddhist Art in its Relation to Buddhist Ideals; Nichiren, the Buddhist Prophet.*
Sun, Moon, and Stars (Japanese), **Tathagata, Transmigration** (Buddhist), **Vows** (Buddhist).

ANGUS (SAMUEL), M.A., Ph.D.
Professor of New Testament and Historical Theology in St. Andrew's College, University of Sydney; author of *The Environment of Early Christianity* (1915).
Zealots.

ARNOLD (THOMAS WALKER), C.I.E., Litt.D., M.A.
Professor of Arabic, University of London, University College; author of *The Preaching of Islam*; English editor of *The Encyclopædia of Islām.*
Toleration (Muhammadan).

BALL (JAMES DYER), I.S.O., M.R.A.S., M. Ch. Br. R.A.S.
Late of the Hongkong Civil Service; author of *Things Chinese, The Chinese at Home.*
Tonsure (Chinese).

BARNS (THOMAS), M.A. (Oxon.).
Vicar of Hilderstone, Staffordshire.
Trees and Plants.

BARTLET (JAMES VERNON), D.D.
Professor of Church History in Mansfield College, Oxford; author of *The Apostolic Age* (1900); joint-author of *Christianity and History* (1917).
Worship (Christian).

BARTON (GEORGE AARON), A.M., Ph.D., LL.D.
Professor of Biblical Literature and Semitic Languages in Bryn Mawr College, Pennsylvania; author of *A Sketch of Semitic Origins*, 'Ecclesiastes' in the *International Critical Commentary, The Origin and Development of Babylonian Writing, Archæology and the Bible.*
Suicide (Semitic and Egyptian).

DE BEAUMONT (LOUIS-LEOPOLD MARTIAL BAYNARD), D.Sc.
Sometime Fellow and Examiner of the Royal University of Ireland; Fellow of the Linnean Society; Member of the 'Société Astronomique de France.'
Swedenborg.

BENNETT (WILLIAM HENRY), M.A. (Lond.), D.D. (Aberd.), Litt.D. (Camb.).
Late Principal of Lancashire College, Manchester; sometime Fellow of St. John's College, Cambridge; author of *The Religion of the Post-Exilic Prophets*, and other works.
Usury (Hebrew).

BESANT (ANNIE).
President of the Theosophical Society; author of *Reincarnation*, and other works.
Theosophical Society.

BLACKMAN (AYLWARD MANLEY), D.Litt.
Formerly Laycock Student of Egyptology at Worcester College, Oxford; Oxford University Nubian Research Scholar, 1910; formerly Scholar of Queen's College.
Worship (Egyptian).

BOX (GEORGE HERBERT), M.A., D.D.
Professor of Hebrew and Old Testament Exegesis, King's College, London; Hon. Canon of St. Albans; author of *The Book of Isaiah translated in accordance with the results of Modern Criticism* (1908), *The Ezra Apocalypse* (1912), *The Virgin Birth of Jesus* (1916), *The Gospel according to St. Matthew*, revised ed. ('Century Bible,' 1920).
Worship (Hebrew).

BRASH (WILLIAM BARDSLEY), B.D. (London), B.Litt. (Oxon.).
Minister of the Wesleyan Methodist Church at Southport.
Wesley.

BROAD (CHARLES DUNBAR), M.A., Litt.D.
Professor of Philosophy in the University of Bristol; formerly Fellow of Trinity College, Cambridge.
Time.

BRYANT (Mrs. SOPHIE), D.Sc. (London), Litt.D. (Dublin).
Formerly Headmistress of the North London Collegiate School; author of *Educational Ends, How to read the Bible in the Nineteenth Century, Moral and Religious Education*, and other works.
Sympathy.

CABATON (ANTOINE).
Professeur à l'École des Langues orientales vivantes et à l'École Coloniale, Paris; Ancien Membre de l'École Française d'Extrême-Orient.
Tongking.

CANNEY (MAURICE A.), M.A. (Oxon.).
Professor of Semitic Languages and Literatures in the University of Manchester; editor of the *Journal of the Manchester Egyptian and Oriental Society*.
Sun, Moon, and Stars (Hebrew).

CARNOY (ALBERT JOSEPH), Docteur en Philosophie et Lettres (Louvain).
Professor of Greek and General Linguistics in the University of Louvain; Professor in the University of California, 1918.
Yezidis, Zoroastrianism.

CARPENTER (J. ESTLIN), M.A., D.Litt., D.D., D.Theol.
Wilde Lecturer in Natural and Comparative Religion in the University of Oxford; formerly Principal of Manchester College, Oxford; author of *The Bible in the Nineteenth Century*, and other works; joint-editor of *The Hexateuch according to the Revised Version*.
Unitarianism.

CARROLL (JOHN SMYTH), M.A., D.D.
Minister of the United Free Church at Glasgow; author of an Exposition of Dante's *Divina Commedia*.
Tolstoy.

CLARKE (Mrs. DAISY EMILY MARTIN).
Cambridge Mediæval and Modern Languages Tripos, Class I.; Marion Kennedy Student, Newnham College, 1920–21.
Teutonic Religion.

COE (GEORGE ALBERT), Ph.D., LL.D.
Professor of Religious Education and Psychology in the Union Theological Seminary, New York; author of *The Spiritual Life, The Religion of a Mature Mind, Education in Religion and Morals*.
Suggestion.

CROOKE (WILLIAM), B.A., D.Sc.
Ex-Scholar of Trinity College, Dublin; Fellow of the Royal Anthropological Institute; President of the Anthropological Section of the British Association, 1910; President of the Folklore Society, 1911–12; late of the Bengal Civil Service.
Tanjore, Thanesar, Tirupati, Travancore, United Provinces of Agra and Oudh, Vaisnavism, Water, Water-gods (Indian).

CZAPLICKA (MARIE ANTOINETTE), F.R.A.I., F.R.G.S.
Late Lecturer in Anthropology in the University of Bristol; formerly Mary Ewart Lecturer in Ethnology in the University of Oxford; author of *Aboriginal Siberia, My Siberian Year, Turks of Central Asia*.
Tungus, Turks, Yakut.

DARBYSHIRE (JOHN RUSSELL), M.A.
Canon Residentiary of Manchester Cathedral; Rector of S. George's Hulme; Examining Chaplain to the Bishops of Manchester and Bradford.
Typology.

DAVIDS (T. W. RHYS), LL.D., Ph.D., D.Sc., F.B.A.
Formerly Professor of Comparative Religion, Manchester; President of the Pāli Text Society; author of *Buddhism* (1878), *Questions of King Milinda* (1890–94), *American Lectures on Buddhism* (1896), *Buddhist India* (1902), *Early Buddhism* (1908), *Dialogues of the Buddha* (1899, 1910).
Tonsure (Buddhist), **Wheel of the Law, Wisdom Tree.**

DICKINS (BRUCE), M.A.
Lecturer in English in the University of Edinburgh; sometime Donaldson Bye-Fellow of Magdalene College, Cambridge; author of *Runic and Heroic Poems of the Old Teutonic Peoples*.
Transmigration (Teutonic).

DORNAN (SAMUEL SHAW), F.R.A.I.
Superintendent of Missions, in Orange Free State, for the Presbyterian Church of South Africa.
Tati Bushmen.

DOTTIN (GEORGES), Docteur ès-Lettres.
Professeur de langue et littérature grecques à l'Université de Rennes.
Sun, Moon, and Stars (Celtic), **Transmigration** (Celtic), **War, War-gods** (Celtic).

DOW (JOHN), M.A.
Minister of the United Free Church at Montrose.

Usury (Christian).

EDWARDS (EDWARD), B.A. (Wales and Cantab.), M.R.A.S.
Member of the Board of Archæology and the Board of Oriental Studies, and Examiner in Persian to the University of London; Assistant in the Department of Oriental Printed Books and Manuscripts in the British Museum.

Worship (Parsi).

EDWARDS (JAMES F.).
Wesleyan Minister at Bombay; author of *The Holy Spirit the Christian Dynamic* (1918), and Marathi works on this subject (1919–20); joint-author of *The Life and Teaching of Tukārām* (1921).

Tukaram.

FALLAIZE (EDWIN NICHOLAS COLLINGFORD), B.A. (Oxon.).
Late King Charles Exhibitioner, Exeter College, Oxford.

Sun, Moon, and Stars (Primitive).

FARBRIDGE (MAURICE HARRY), M.A.
Langton and Faulkner Fellow, and Assistant Lecturer in Oriental Studies, in the University of Manchester.

Swine, Symbolism (Semitic).

FARQUHAR (JOHN NICOL), M.A., D.Litt. (Oxon.).
Literary Secretary of the Young Men's Christian Association in India; author of *Gita and Gospel, A Primer of Hinduism, The Crown of Hinduism, Modern Religious Movements in India.*

Thags.

FU (TUNG), M.A.
Professor of Philosophy in The Teacher's College, Peking, China; editor of the *Philosophia.*

Sun, Moon, and Stars (Chinese).

FULTON (WILLIAM), D.D., D.Sc.
Professor of Systematic Theology in the University of Aberdeen.

Teleology, Theodicy, Trinity, Tritheism, Validity.

GAMBLE (JOHN), B.D.
Vicar of Leighwoods, Clifton.

Symbolism (Christian).

GARBE (RICHARD), Ph.D.
Professor des Sanskrit und der allgemeinen Religionsgeschichte an der Universität zu Tübingen.

Transmigration (Indian), **Vaisesika, Vedanta, Yoga, Yogis.**

GARDNER (ALICE), F.R.Hist.S.
Lecturer and Associate of Newnham College, Cambridge; author of *Julian, Philosopher and Emperor; Theodore of Studium.*

Superstition.

GARDNER (ERNEST ARTHUR), Litt.D.
Yates Professor of Archæology in University College, London; Public Orator and Dean of the Faculty of Arts in London University; formerly Fellow of Gonville and Caius College, Cambridge, and Director of the British School of Archæology at Athens.

War, War-gods (Greek and Roman), **Water, Water-gods** (Greek and Roman), **Wings** (Greek and Roman).

GARDNER (PERCY), Litt.D., LL.D., F.S.A.
Professor of Classical Archæology in the University of Oxford; Vice-President of the Hellenic Society; author of *Exploratio Evangelica* (1899), *Principles of Greek Art* (1913), and other works.

Symbolism (Greek and Roman).

GASTER (MOSES), Ph.D.
Chief Rabbi, Spanish and Portuguese Congregations, London; formerly President of the Folklore Society; Vice-President of the Royal Asiatic Society.

Transmigration (Jewish), **Water** (Hebrew and Jewish), **Zohar.**

GEDEN (ALFRED S.), M.A. (Oxon.), D.D. (Aberd.).
Formerly Professor of Old Testament Languages and Literature and of Comparative Religion in the Wesleyan College, Richmond, Surrey; author of *Studies in the Religions of the East, Introduction to the Hebrew Bible, Comparative Religion*; translator of Deussen's *Philosophy of the Upanishads.*

Sun, Moon, and Stars (Hindu), **Symbolism** (Hindu), **Tantras, Upanisads.**

GEIKIE-COBB (WILLIAM FREDERICK), D.D.
Rector of the Church of St. Ethelburga the Virgin, London; author of *Origines Judaicæ, The Book of Psalms, Mysticism and the Creed, Spiritual Healing.*

Vivisection.

GLAZEBROOK (MICHAEL GEORGE), D.D.
Canon Residentiary of Ely Cathedral; formerly Headmaster of Clifton College.

Sunday.

GOODMAN (PAUL).
Secretary to the Spanish and Portuguese Jews' Congregation, London; author of *The Synagogue and the Church.*

Zionism.

GORDON (ALEXANDER REID), D.Litt., D.D.
Professor of Hebrew in McGill University, and of Old Testament Literature and Exegesis in the Presbyterian College, Montreal; author of *The Early Traditions of Genesis, The Poets of the Old Testament.*

Wisdom.

GRAY (LOUIS HERBERT), M.A., Ph.D. (Columbia).
Editor of *Mythology of All Races*; author of *Indo-Iranian Phonology* (1902).

Tushes and other Pagan Tribes of the Caucasus.

GRIERSON (Sir GEORGE ABRAHAM), K.C.I.E., Ph.D. (Halle), D.Litt. (Dublin), I.C.S. (retired).
Fellow of the British Academy; Honorary Member of the American Oriental Society; Honorary Fellow of the Asiatic Society of Bengal; Foreign Associate Member of the Société Asiatique de Paris; Hon. Secretary of the Royal Asiatic Society; Superintendent of the Linguistic Survey of India.
Tulasi-Dasa.

GRIERSON (HERBERT JOHN CLIFFORD), M.A., LL.D.
Professor of Rhetoric and English Literature in the University of Edinburgh; editor of *The Poems of John Donne.*
Vondel.

GRIEVE (ALEXANDER JAMES), M.A. (Oxon.), B.A., D.D. (Lond.).
Principal of the Lancashire Independent College, Manchester; assistant-editor of *Peake's Commentary on the Bible.*
Vows (Christian).

HAGAR (STANSBURY), B.A., LL.B.
Counsellor at Law; Fellow of the American Association for the Advancement of Science, and the American Anthropological Association; Executive Officer of the Departments of Ethnology and Astronomy in the Brooklyn Institute of Arts and Sciences.
Sun, Moon, and Stars (American).

HALDANE (ELIZABETH SANDERSON), C.H., LL.D.
Author of *The Life of James Ferrier* (1899), *Life of Descartes* (1905); joint-translator of *Hegel's History of Philosophy* (1892), and *The Philosophical Works of Descartes* (1911–12).
Voltaire.

HARADA (TASUKU), D.D., LL.D.
Formerly President of the Doshisha University, Kyoto, Japan.
Suicide (Japanese).

HARRISON (JANE ELLEN), LL.D. (Aberd.), D.Litt. (Durham).
Staff Lecturer and sometime Fellow of Newnham College, Cambridge; author of *The Religion of Ancient Greece* (1905), *Prolegomena to the Study of Greek Religion* (1907), *Themis: a Study of the Social Origins of Greek Religion* (1912).
Titans, Under World (Greek).

HARTLAND (EDWIN SIDNEY), LL.D., F.S.A.
President of the Folklore Society, 1899; President of the Anthropological Section of the British Association, 1906; President of Section I (Religions of the Lower Culture) at the Oxford International Congress for the History of Religions, 1908; author of *The Legend of Perseus, Primitive Paternity, Ritual and Belief.*
Totemism, Twins.

HASTINGS (ANNE WILSON), M.A.
H.M. District Inspector of Factories, Leeds.
Utilitarianism.

HENKE (FREDERICK GOODRICH), M.A., Ph.D.
Truman D. Collins Professor of Philosophy and Education in Allegheny College, Meadville, Pennsylvania; Member of the Royal Asiatic Society (North China Branch); author of *A Study in the Psychology of Ritualism, The Philosophy of Wang Yang-ming.*
Wang Yang-ming.

HILL (GEORGE FRANCIS), M.A., (Oxon.), F.B.A.
Keeper of the Department of Coins and Medals in the British Museum.
Token, Treaties.

HILLEBRANDT (A. F. ALFRED), Ph.D. (Munich), LL.D.
Ord. Professor of Sanskrit and Comparative Philology in the University of Breslau; Corresponding Member of the Königliche Gesellschaft der Wissenschaften zu Göttingen, and of the Royal Bavarian Academy of Sciences; Geheimer Regierungsrat.
Worship (Hindu).

INGE (WILLIAM RALPH), D.D.
Dean of St. Paul's; author of *Christian Mysticism* (1899), *Studies of English Mystics* (1906), *Personal Idealism and Mysticism* (1907), *Faith and its Psychology* (1908).
Synderesis.

JACKSON (A. V. WILLIAMS), Ph.D., L.H.D., LL.D.
Professor of Indo-Iranian Languages in Columbia University, New York; author of *Zoroaster, the Prophet of Ancient Iran; Persia, Past and Present.*
Sun, Moon, and Stars (Iranian).

JAMES (EDWIN OLIVER), B.Sc., B.Litt. (Oxon.), F.C.S. (Lond.).
Vicar of Holy Trinity, Reading; Fellow of the Royal Anthropological Institute; Member of Council of the Folklore Society; Secretary of the Anthropological Section of the British Association; author of *Primitive Ritual and Belief, An Introduction to Anthropology,* and other works.
Tutelary Gods and Spirits, Water, Water-gods (Primitive and Savage), **Yawning.**

JENKINSON (Mrs. CONSTANCE), F.R.A.I.
Somerville College, Oxford; Diploma in Anthropology, Oxford.
Tatuing.

JOHNS (CLAUDE HERMANN WALTER), M.A., Litt.D., D.D.
Late Master of St. Catharine's College, Cambridge, and Canon Residentiary of Norwich; author of *Assyrian Deeds and Documents of the 7th Century B.C., Babylonian and Assyrian Laws, Contracts and Letters,* the Schweich Lectures on *The Relations between the Laws of Babylonia and the Laws of the Hebrew Peoples.*
Usury (Babylonian).

JOHNSON (HUMPHREY JOHN T.), B.A. (Oxon.).
Fellow of the Royal Anthropological Institute.
Sweat, Sweat-house.

JOHNSTON (REGINALD FLEMING), C.B.E., M.A. (Oxon.).
Tutor to H.M. the Emperor Hsüan T'ung; formerly District Officer and Magistrate, Weihaiwei (administered the Government 1917–18); author of *From Peking to Mandalay* (1908), *Lion and Dragon in Northern China* (1910), *Buddhist China* (1913), *Letters to a Missionary* (1918).
Vows (Chinese), **War, War-gods** (Chinese), **Worship** (Chinese).

JOLLY (JULIUS), Ph.D. (Munich), Hon. M.D. (Göttingen), Hon. D.Litt. (Oxford).
Ord. Professor of Sanskrit and Comparative Philology in the University of Würzburg; formerly Tagore Professor of Law in the University of Calcutta; Geheimer Hofrat.
Tonsure (Hindu), **Vows** (Hindu).

JONES (RUFUS M.), M.A., D.Litt.
Professor of Philosophy in Haverford College, Haverford, Pennsylvania; author of *Social Law in the Spiritual World* (1904), *Studies in Mystical Religion* (1909), *Spiritual Reformers* (1914), *The Inner Life* (1916).
Theurgy.

JOSEPH (MORRIS).
Senior Minister of the West London Synagogue; author of *Judaism as Creed and Life* (1910).
Vows (Jewish).

KEITH (ARTHUR BERRIEDALE), D.C.L., D.Litt.
Barrister-at-Law; Regius Professor of Sanskrit and Comparative Philology in the University of Edinburgh.
Suicide (Hindu), **Trimurti.**

KENNETT (ROBERT HATCH), D.D.
Regius Professor of Hebrew in the University of Cambridge; Canon of Ely; Fellow of Queens' College, Cambridge; Examining Chaplain to the Bishops of Ely and Manchester.
Tophet.

KERSHAW (NORA).
Newnham College, Cambridge; formerly Lecturer in English in the University of St. Andrews.
Teutonic Religion.

KILPATRICK (THOMAS B.), M.A., B.D., D.D.
Professor of Systematic Theology in Knox College, Toronto; author of the articles 'Conscience' and 'Philosophy' in the *Dictionary of the Bible*, and of 'Character of Christ' and 'Incarnation' in the *Dictionary of Christ and the Gospels*.
Suffering.

KINNAIRD (Hon. EMILY), C.B.E.
Acting Vice-President of the Y.W.C.A. of Great Britain, and Vice-President of the World's Y.W.C.A.
Young Women's Christian Association.

KROEBER (A. L.), A.M., Ph.D.
Assistant Professor of Anthropology in the University of California.
Zuni.

LAIRD (JOHN), M.A.
Professor of Logic and Metaphysics in the Queen's University of Belfast; author of *Problems of the Self, A Study in Realism.*
Will.

LANGDON (STEPHEN HERBERT), M.A., B.D., Ph.D.
Professor of Assyriology and Comparative Semitic Philology in the University of Oxford; Member of Council of the Royal Asiatic Society; author of *Neo-Babylonian Royal Inscriptions* (V.A.B. vol. iv.), *Sumerian and Babylonian Psalms, A Sumerian Grammar, Babylonian Liturgies.*
Word (Sumerian and Babylonian), **Worship** (Babylonian).

LESTER-GARLAND (LESTER V.), M.A., F.L.S.
Formerly Fellow of St. John's College, Cambridge.
Trade Unions.

LOEWE (HERBERT MARTIN JAMES), M.A.
Lecturer, Exeter College, Oxford; sometime Curator of Oriental Literature in the University Library, Cambridge, and Director of Oriental Studies, St. Catharine's College, Cambridge.
Worship (Jewish).

LYTTELTON (Hon. E.), M.A., D.D., D.C.L.
Dean of Whitelands College, Chelsea; formerly Headmaster of Eton College.
Vegetarianism.

MACCULLOCH (JOHN ARNOTT), Hon. D.D. (St. Andrews).
Rector of St. Saviour's, Bridge of Allan; Hon. Canon of the Cathedral of the Holy Spirit, Cumbrae; Examiner in Comparative Religion and Philosophy of Religion, Victoria University, Manchester; Examining Chaplain to the Bishop of St. Andrews; author of *The Religion of the Ancient Celts.*
Teeth, Temples, Tithes, Tonsure, Under World, Vampire, Virgin Birth.

MACDONELL (ARTHUR ANTHONY), M.A. (Oxon.), Ph.D. (Leipzig).
Boden Professor of Sanskrit in the University of Oxford; Fellow of Balliol College; Fellow of the British Academy; Fellow of the Royal Danish Academy; Keeper of the Indian Institute, Oxford.
Vedic Religion.

MCFADYEN (JOHN EDGAR), B.A. (Oxon.), M.A., D.D.
Professor of Old Testament Language, Literature, and Theology in the United Free Church College, Glasgow; author of *Messages of the Prophetic and Priestly Historians*, and other works; editor of Davidson's *Hebrew Grammar.*
Vows (Hebrew).

MCINTYRE (JAMES LEWIS), M.A. (Edin. and Oxon.), D.Sc. (Edin.).
Anderson Lecturer in Comparative Psychology to the University of Aberdeen; Lecturer in Psychology, Logic, and Ethics to the Aberdeen Provincial Committee for the Training of Teachers; formerly Examiner in Philosophy to the Universities of Edinburgh and London; author of *Giordano Bruno* (1903).
Temperament.

MACKENZIE (DONALD), M.A.
Minister of the United Free Church at Tain; Assistant Professor of Logic and Metaphysics in the University of Aberdeen, 1906-1909.
Synergism, Transcendentalism.

MACKICHAN (D.), M.A., D.D., LL.D. (Glas.), LL.D. (Bombay).
Formerly Principal of Wilson College, Bombay, and Vice-Chancellor of the University of Bombay.
Vallabha, Vallabhacharya.

MACLAGAN (P. J.), M.A., D.Phil.
Foreign Mission Secretary of the Presbyterian Church of England; formerly of the English Presbyterian Mission, Swatow.

Suicide (Chinese), **Taoism.**

MACLEAN (ARTHUR JOHN), D.D. (Camb.), Hon. D.D. (Glas.).
Bishop of Moray, Ross, and Caithness; author of *Dictionary and Grammar of Vernacular Syriac, Ancient Church Orders*, and other works; editor of *East Syrian Liturgies.*

Syrian Christians, Unction (Christian).

MACLER (FRÉDÉRIC).
Ancien Attaché à la Bibliothèque Nationale; Lauréat de l'Institut; Professeur d'Arménien à l'École des Langues orientales vivantes.

Syrians.

MAIR (ALEXANDER WILLIAM), M.A. (Aberd. and Camb.), Litt.D. (Aberd.).
Sometime Fellow of Gonville and Caius College, Cambridge; Professor of Greek in the University of Edinburgh; editor of *Hesiod.*

Suicide (Greek and Roman), **Worship** (Greek).

MARETT (ROBERT RANULPH), M.A., F.R.A.I.
Fellow of Exeter College, and Reader in Social Anthropology in the University of Oxford; author of *The Threshold of Religion.*

Supernaturalism, Tabu.

MARGOLIOUTH (DAVID SAMUEL), M.A., D.Litt., F.B.A.
Fellow of New College, and Laudian Professor of Arabic in the University of Oxford; author of *Mohammed and the Rise of Islam, Mohammedanism, The Early Development of Mohammedanism.*

Symbolism (Muslim), **Wahhabis, Zaidi.**

MARGOLIOUTH (GEORGE), M.A. (Cantab.).
Member of the Board of Studies in Theology and Examiner in Hebrew and Aramaic in the University of London; formerly Senior Assistant in the Department of Oriental Printed Books and MSS in the British Museum.

Suicide (Jewish).

MÉNÉGOZ (EUGÈNE), Docteur en Théologie.
Professeur honoraire de la Faculté de Théologie protestante et de l'Université de Paris; auteur de *Théologie de l'Epître aux Hébreux.*

Symbolo-Fideism.

MERCER (SAMUEL ALFRED BROWNE), M.A., Ph.D., D.D.
Professor of Hebrew and Old Testament in the Western Theological Seminary, Chicago; author of *Extra Biblical Sources for Hebrew and Jewish History, The Ethiopic Liturgy, Sumero-Babylonian Sign List, Ethiopic Grammar, Assyrian Grammar*; editor of the *Anglican Theological Review*, the *Journal of the Society of Oriental Research*, and the *Biblical and Oriental Series.*

War, War-gods (Semitic), **Water, Water-gods** (Babylonian, Egyptian).

MOFFATT (JAMES), D.D., D.Litt., Hon. M.A. (Oxon.).
Professor of Church History in the United Free Church College, Glasgow; author of *Critical Introduction to New Testament Literature*, and other works.

Syncretism, Therapeutæ.

MORGAN (WILLIAM), D.D.
Professor of Systematic Theology and Apologetics in Queen's Theological College, Kingston, Canada.

Trust.

MOULTON (JAMES EGAN), D.D.
Late President of Tubou College, Tonga.

Tongans.

MUTCH (WILLIAM JAMES), A.M. (Wisconsin), B.D., Ph.D. (Yale).
Professor of Philosophy and Education in Ripon College, Ripon, Wisconsin; formerly Minister of the Congregational Church at New Haven, Connecticut; Lecturer on Religious Education in Yale University; author of *Christian Teaching*, and other works.

Training (Religious).

NALLINO (CARLO ALFONSO).
Rome; author of *Sulla costituzione delle tribu arabe prima dell' islamismo.*

Sun, Moon, and Stars (Muhammadan).

NEILSON (GEORGE), LL.D.
The Stipendiary Magistrate of Glasgow; author of *Trial by Combat.*

Torture.

NICHOLSON (REYNOLD ALLEYNE), M.A., Litt.D., LL.D.
Lecturer in Persian in the University of Cambridge; sometime Fellow of Trinity College; author of *A Literary History of the Arabs* (1907), the *Tarjuman al-Ashwaq* of Ibn al-Arabi, with translation and commentary (1911), *The Mystics of Islam* (1914).

Sufis, Suhrawardi, 'Umar al-Khayyam.

ODGERS (JAMES EDWIN), M.A., D.D.
Fellow of University College, London; formerly Lecturer and Tutor, Manchester College, Oxford.

Universalism.

OEFELE (Baron FELIX VON).
Neuenahr, Germany.

Sun, Moon, and Stars (Introduction).

OLTRAMARE (PAUL).
Professor of the History of Religions in the University of Geneva.

Theosophy.

ORR (JAMES), M.A., D.D.
Late Professor of Systematic Theology and Apologetics in the United Free Church College, Glasgow; author of *The Christian View of God and the World, David Hume* in the 'Epoch Makers' series.

Supralapsarianism.

OTTLEY (ROBERT LAURENCE), D.D.
Regius Professor of Pastoral Theology, and Canon of Christ Church, Oxford; author of *The Doctrine of the Incarnation* (1895), *Aspects of the Old Testament* (1905), and other works.

Temperance.

OWEN (MARY ALICIA).
President of the Missouri Folklore Society; Councillor of the American Folklore Society; admitted to Tribal Membership with the Indians, 1892.
Voodoo.

PATERSON (WILLIAM P.), D.D., LL.D.
Professor of Divinity in the University of Edinburgh.
War.

PATTON (WALTER MELVILLE), M.A., Ph.D., D.D.
Professor of Biblical Literature and History of Religion, and Director of the Library, Carleton College, Northfield, Minnesota.
Suicide (Muhammadan), **Sunnites.**

PEARSON (A. C.), M.A., Litt.D.
Regius Professor of Greek in the University of Cambridge; editor of *Fragments of Sophocles*, Euripides' *Helena*, *Heraclidæ*, and *Phœnissæ*, *Zeno and Cleanthes: Fragments*.
Transmigration (Greek and Roman), **Vows** (Greek and Roman).

PETRIE (WILLIAM MATTHEW FLINDERS), D.C.L. (Oxon.), LL.D. (Edin. and Aberd.), Litt.D. (Camb.).
Fellow of the Royal Society and of the British Academy; Edwards Professor of Egyptology in the University of London.
Transmigration (Egyptian).

PINCHES (THEOPHILUS GOLDRIDGE), LL.D. (Glas.), M.R.A.S.
Lecturer in Assyrian at University College, London, and at the Institute of Archæology, Liverpool; Hon. Member of the Société Asiatique.
Sumero-Akkadians, Tammuz.

POPE (ROBERT MARTIN), M.A. (Camb. and Manchester).
Author of *Introduction to Early Church History*, and other works.
Western Church.

POUSSIN (LOUIS DE LA VALLÉE), Docteur en philosophie et lettres (Liége), en langues orientales (Louvain).
Professeur de sanscrit à l'Université de Gand; Membre de l'Académie royale de Belgique; Hibbert Lecturer (1916); Membre de la R.A.S. et de la Société Asiatique; Membre correspondant de l'Académie impériale de Petrograd; Correspondant de l'Ecole Française d'Extrême-Orient.
Suicide (Buddhist), **Tantrism** (Buddhist), **Worship** (Buddhist).

PRICE (IRA MAURICE), Ph.D., LL.D.
Professor of the Semitic Languages and Literatures in the University of Chicago; author of *The Monuments of the Old Testament*, *The Great Cylinder Inscriptions A and B of Gudea*, and other works.
Toltecs.

REID (JAMES SMITH), M.A., LL.D., Litt.D.
Fellow and late Tutor of Gonville and Caius College, Cambridge; Professor of Ancient History in the University of Cambridge; editor of the *Academica* and other works of Cicero; author of *Municipalities of the Roman Empire*.
Worship (Roman).

REVON (MICHEL), LL.D., D.Litt.
Professor of History of the Civilization of the Far East in the University of Paris; formerly Professor of Law in the Imperial University of Tokyo and Legal Adviser to the Japanese Government; author of *Le Shinntoïsme*.
Worship (Japanese).

RIVERS (W. H. R.), M.A., M.D., F.R.S., F.R.C.P.
Fellow of St. John's College, Cambridge; President of the Anthropological Section of the British Association, 1911; author of *The Todas*, *History of Melanesian Society*, *Kinship and Social Organisation*.
Todas.

ROBINSON (HENRY WHEELER), M.A. (Oxon. and Edin.).
Principal and Professor of Systematic Theology and Hebrew in Regent's Park (Baptist) College, London; author of 'Hebrew Psychology in relation to Pauline Anthropology' in *Mansfield College Essays*, *The Christian Doctrine of Man*, *The Religious Ideas of the Old Testament*.
Tongue.

ROSE (HERBERT JENNINGS), M.A. (Oxon.).
Professor of Latin, University College of Wales, Aberystwyth; sometime Fellow of Exeter College, Oxford.
Suicide (Introductory), **Thrace.**

ROSE (HORACE ARTHUR), I.C.S. (retired).
Superintendent of Ethnography, Punjab, 1901–06; author of *A Glossary of Punjab Tribes and Castes*, and other works.
Udasis.

ROSS (WILLIAM), M.A., B.D.
Minister of the United Free Church at Edinburgh.
Voluntaryism.

ROUSE (WILLIAM HENRY DENHAM), M.A., Litt.D.
Headmaster of the Perse Grammar School, Cambridge; University Teacher of Sanskrit; President of the Folklore Society, 1904–06.
Tithes (Greek), **Votive Offerings** (Greek).

SAPIR (EDWARD), Ph.D.
Chief of Anthropological Division, Victoria Memorial Museum, Ottawa, Ontario.
Vancouver Island Indians.

SCHILLER (FERDINAND CANNING SCOTT), M.A., D.Sc. (Oxon.).
Fellow and Senior Tutor of Corpus Christi College, Oxford; author of *Riddles of the Sphinx* (new ed. 1910), *Humanism* (1903, new ed. 1912), *Studies in Humanism* (1907, 1912), *Plato or Protagoras?* (1908), *Formal Logic* (1912), etc.
Telepathy, Value.

SCOTT (ERNEST FINDLAY), B.A., D.D.
Professor of New Testament Literature in Queen's University, Kingston, Canada; author of *The Fourth Gospel: its Purpose and Theology*, *The Apologetic of the New Testament*, *The Kingdom and the Messiah*.
Valentinianism.

SEATON (MARY ETHEL), M.A. (Lond.).
Sometime Lecturer at Girton College, Cambridge.
Swan-maidens.

SELIGMAN (Mrs. BRENDA Z.), London.
Veddas.

SELIGMAN (CHARLES G.), M.D., F.R.S., F.R.C.P.
Professor of Ethnology in the University of London; President of the Anthropological Section of the British Association, 1915; author of *The Melanesians of British New Guinea*; joint-author of *The Veddas*.
Veddas.

SHOREY (PAUL), Ph.D., LL.D., Litt.D.
Professor and Head of the Department of Greek in the University of Chicago; Roosevelt Professor at the University of Berlin, 1913; Member of the American Institute of Art and Letters.
Summum Bonum, Theognis.

SHOWERMAN (GRANT), Ph.D.
Professor of Latin in the University of Wisconsin; Fellow in the American School of Classical Studies at Rome, 1898–1900; author of *The Great Mother of the Gods* (Dissertation), 1901, *With the Professor*, 1910; translator of Ovid's *Heroides* and *Amores* (Loeb Classical Library), 1914.
Taurobolium.

SIKES (EDWARD ERNEST), M.A.
Fellow, Senior Tutor, and Classical Lecturer of St. John's College, Cambridge; author of *The Anthropology of the Greeks*, and *Hero and Leander, translated in verse from the Greek*; editor of Æschylus's *Prometheus Vinctus*, the *Homeric Hymns*, etc.
Torch (Greek and Roman).

SMITH (CHARLES RYDER), B.A., D.D. (Lond.).
Professor of Systematic Theology in Richmond College, Surrey; author of *The Bible Doctrine of Society in its Historical Evolution*.
Theocracy.

SMITH (VINCENT ARTHUR), M.A., Litt.D.
Late of the Indian Civil Service (retired); author of *Asoka* in 'Rulers of India,' *Early History of India, A History of Fine Art in India and Ceylon, Akbar the Great Mogul, Oxford History of India*.
Vaisali, Vikrama Era.

SOARES (THEODORE GERALD), M.A., Ph.D., D.D.
Professor of Preaching and Religious Education, and Head of the Department of Practical Theology, in the University of Chicago.
Sunday Schools.

STEVENSON (Mrs. SINCLAIR), M.A., Sc.D.
Of the Irish Mission, Rajkot, India; sometime Scholar of Somerville College, Oxford; author of *Notes on Modern Jainism, The Rites of the Twice-born*.
Svetambaras, Worship (Jain).

STOKES (GEORGE J.), M.A. (Trinity College, Dublin).
Of Lincoln's Inn, Barrister-at-Law; Professor of Philosophy and Jurisprudence in University College, Cork, National University of Ireland; author of *The Objectivity of Truth*.
Universality.

SWANTON (JOHN REED), Ph.D.
Ethnologist in the Bureau of American Ethnology, Smithsonian Institution, Washington, D.C.; President of the Anthropological Society of Washington, 1916.
Tlingit, Tsimshian, Wakashan.

TAKAKUSU (JYUN), M.A., D.Litt. (Oxford), Dr. Phil. (Leipzig).
Professor of Sanskrit in the University of Tokyo.
Yuan-Chwang, Fa-Hian, and I-Tsing.

TAYLOR (ALFRED EDWARD), M.A. (Oxon.), D. Litt. (St. Andrews).
Professor of Moral Philosophy in the United College of SS. Salvator and Leonard, St. Andrews; late Fellow of Merton College, Oxford; Fellow of the British Academy; author of *The Problem of Conduct* (1901), *Elements of Metaphysics* (1903), *Varia Socratica* (1911).
Theism.

TESSITORI (Dr. L. P.).
Late of Udine, Italy; editor of the Uvaesamala of Dharmadasa.
Yogis (Kanphata).

THOMAS (EDWARD JOSEPH), M.A. (St. And. and Camb.), B.A. (Lond.).
Under-Librarian of Cambridge University; editor of *Buddhist Scriptures*; joint-editor of *Mahāniddesa* and *Jātaka Tales*.
Sun, Moon, and Stars (Buddhist).

THOMAS (NORTHCOTE WHITRIDGE).
Élève diplômé de l'École pratique des Hautes Études; Corresponding Member of the Société d'Anthropologie de Paris; Member of Council of the Folklore Society; author of *Thought Transference, Kinship Organization and Group Marriage in Australia*.
Transmigration (Introductory and Primitive).

THURSTON (HERBERT), B.A., S.J.
Joint-editor of the Westminster Library for Priests and Students; author of *Life of St. Hugh of Lincoln, The Holy Year of Jubilee, The Stations of the Cross*.
Xavier.

URQUHART (FRANCIS FORTESCUE), M.A.
Fellow and Tutor of Balliol College, Oxford.
Ultramontanism.

URQUHART (WILLIAM SPENCE), M.A., D.Phil.
Senior Professor of Philosophy in the Scottish Churches College, Calcutta; Fellow and Member of Syndicate of Calcutta University.
Theosophy.

WADDELL (L. AUSTINE), C.B., C.I.E., LL.D., F.L.S., F.R.A.I., M.R.A.S., M.F.L.S., M.S.B.A., Lt.-Colonel I.M.S. (retired).
Formerly Professor of Tibetan in University College, London; Hon. Correspondent of the Archæological Survey of India; author of *The Buddhism of Tibet, Lhasa and its Mysteries*.
Swat or Udyāna, Tibet.

WATT (HUGH), M.A., B.D.
Professor of Church History in New College, Edinburgh.
Zwingli.

WELSFORD (ENID ELDER HANCOCK).
Fellow of Newnham College, Cambridge.
Sun, Moon, and Stars (Teutonic and Balto-Slavic).

WERNER (ALICE), L.L.A. (St. And.).
University Reader in Swahili and Bantu Languages, School of Oriental Studies, London; Goldsmiths' Scholar, Newnham College, Cambridge, 1878–80; Mary Ewart Travelling Scholar, 1911–13; formerly Associates' Fellow, Newnham College, Cambridge; author of *The Language Families of Africa, The Native Races of British Central Africa*; translator of *An Introduction to the Study of African Languages.*

Zanzibar and the Swahili People.

WHITACRE (ÆLRED), O.P., Sac. Theol. Lector.
Professor of Dogmatic Theology at the Dominican House of Studies, Hawkesyard Priory, Staffordshire.

Thomism.

WHITLEY (WILLIAM THOMAS), M.A., LL.D., F.R.Hist.S., F.T.S.
Honorary Secretary and editor of the Baptist Historical Society; Member of the American Historical Association; author of *Roman Catholic and Protestant Bibles, Missionary Achievement*; editor of *A Baptist Bibliography, The Works of John Smyth.*

Trappists.

WILDE (NORMAN), Ph.D.
Professor of Philosophy in the University of Minnesota.

Welfare.

WILLIAMS (NORMAN POWELL), M.A., B.D.
Chaplain Fellow of Exeter College, Oxford; Lecturer in Theology at Exeter and Pembroke Colleges; Examining Chaplain to the Bishop of Newcastle.

Tradition.

WOGIHARA (UNRAI), Ph.D.
Professor of Shyu-kyo-daigaku, Tokyo, Japan.

Vasubandhu.

WORKMAN (HERBERT B.), M.A., D.Lit.
Principal of Westminster Training College; Member of the Board of Studies in the Faculty of Theology, London University; author of *The Dawn of the Reformation, The Letters of John Hus, Persecution in the Early Church*, and *Christian Thought to the Reformation.*

Wyclif.

YAPP (Sir ARTHUR KEYSALL), K.B.E., Officier de l'Ordre de la Couronne (Belgium), Wen Hu (China).
National Secretary of the Y.M.C.A.

Young Men's Christian Association.

YOUNGERT (SVEN GUSTAF), Ph.D., D.D.
Professor of Philosophy and History of Religion at Augustana College and Theological Seminary, Rock Island, Ill.

Vows (Teutonic).

CROSS-REFERENCES

In addition to the cross-references throughout the volume, the following list of minor references may be useful:

Topic.	Title of Article.
Sulpicians	Religious Orders (Christian).
Supper	Eucharist.
Sutra	Literature (Vedic).
Suttee	Sati.
Svastika	Cross.
Swan	Animals.
Swastika	Cross.
Taborites	Hussites.
Tai	Ahoms, Burma.
Taimiya	Ibn Taimiya.
Taittiriya	Literature (Vedic and Classical Sanskrit).
Talaings	Burma.
Tapuyas	Brazil.
Tartarus	Eschatology, State of the Dead (Greek).
Tatars	Turks.
Teaching	Education.
Templars	Religious Orders (Christian).
Temple Society	Friends of the Temple.
Testament, New	Bible.
Testament, Old	Bible.
Thankfulness	Gratitude.
Theodoret	Antiochene Theology.
Theriomorphism	Lycanthropy.
Thomas à Kempis	Brethren of the Common Life.
Thomas, St. (Christians of)	Nestorianism.
Thread (Sacred)	Initiation (Hindu, Parsi).
Tobacco	Smoking.
Tuatha Dé Danann	Celts.
Vajapeya	Abhiseka.
Vegetation	Agriculture.
Vijaya	Durga.
Vikings	Teutonic Religion.
Virgines Subintroductæ	Agapetæ.
Vision	Ecstasy.
Washing	Feet-washing, Purification.
Week	Calendar.
Wends	Slavs.
Wergeld	Blood-feud.
Westminster Assembly	Councils and Synods.
Westminster Catechism	Catechisms.
Westminster Confession	Confessions.
Wills	Inheritance.
Wills (Muslim)	Law (Muhammadan).
Word of God	Logos.
Work	Economics, Employment.
Works (Good)	Merit.
Yuga	Ages of the World (Indian).
Zeus	Greek Religion.
Zoar Society	Communistic Societies of America.
Zodiac	Sun, Moon, and Stars.

LISTS OF ABBREVIATIONS

I. General

A.H. = Anno Hijrae (A.D. 622).
Ak. = Akkadian.
Alex. = Alexandrian.
Amer. = American.
Apoc. = Apocalypse, Apocalyptic.
Apocr. = Apocrypha.
Aq. = Aquila.
Arab. = Arabic.
Aram. = Aramaic.
Arm. = Armenian.
Ary. = Aryan.
As. = Asiatic.
Assyr. = Assyrian.
AT = Altes Testament.
AV = Authorized Version.
AVm = Authorized Version margin.
A.Y. = Anno Yazdagird (A.D. 639).
Bab. = Babylonian.
c. = *circa*, about.
Can. = Canaanite.
cf. = compare.
ct. = contrast.
D = Deuteronomist.
E = Elohist.
edd. = editions or editors.
Egyp. = Egyptian.
Eng. = English.
Eth. = Ethiopic.
EV, EVV = English Version, Versions.
f. = and following verse or page.
ff. = and following verses or pages.
Fr. = French.
Germ. = German.
Gr. = Greek.
H = Law of Holiness.
Heb. = Hebrew.
Hel. = Hellenistic.
Hex. = Hexateuch.
Himy. = Himyaritic.
Ir. = Irish.
Iran. = Iranian.
Isr. = Israelite.
J = Jahwist.
J″ = Jehovah.
Jerus. = Jerusalem.
Jos. = Josephus.
LXX = Septuagint.
Min. = Minæan.
MSS = Manuscripts.
MT = Massoretic Text.
n. = note.
NT = New Testament.
Onk. = Onkelos.
OT = Old Testament.
P = Priestly Narrative.
Pal. = Palestine, Palestinian.
Pent. = Pentateuch.
Pers. = Persian.
Phil. = Philistine.
Phœn. = Phœnician.
Pr. Bk. = Prayer Book.
R = Redactor.
Rom. = Roman.
RV = Revised Version.
RVm = Revised Version margin.
Sab. = Sabæan.
Sam. = Samaritan.
Sem. = Semitic.
Sept. = Septuagint.
Sin. = Sinaitic.
Skr. = Sanskrit.
Symm. = Symmachus.
Syr. = Syriac.
t. (following a number) = times.
Talm. = Talmud.
Targ. = Targum.
Theod. = Theodotion.
TR = Textus Receptus, Received Text.
tr. = translated or translation.
VSS = Versions.
Vulg., Vg. = Vulgate.
WH = Westcott and Hort's text.

II. Books of the Bible

Old Testament.

Gn = Genesis.
Ex = Exodus.
Lv = Leviticus.
Nu = Numbers.
Dt = Deuteronomy.
Jos = Joshua.
Jg = Judges.
Ru = Ruth.
1 S, 2 S = 1 and 2 Samuel.
1 K, 2 K = 1 and 2 Kings.
1 Ch, 2 Ch = 1 and 2 Chronicles.
Ezr = Ezra.
Neh = Nehemiah.
Est = Esther.
Job.
Ps = Psalms.
Pr = Proverbs.
Ec = Ecclesiastes.
Ca = Canticles.
Is = Isaiah.
Jer = Jeremiah.
La = Lamentations.
Ezk = Ezekiel.
Dn = Daniel.
Hos = Hosea.
Jl = Joel.
Am = Amos.
Ob = Obadiah.
Jon = Jonah.
Mic = Micah.
Nah = Nahum.
Hab = Habakkuk.
Zeph = Zephaniah.
Hag = Haggai.
Zec = Zechariah.
Mal = Malachi.

Apocrypha.

1 Es, 2 Es = 1 and 2 Esdras.
To = Tobit.
Jth = Judith.
Ad. Est = Additions to Esther.
Wis = Wisdom.
Sir = Sirach or Ecclesiasticus.
Bar = Baruch.
Three = Song of the Three Children.
Sus = Susanna.
Bel = Bel and the Dragon.
Pr. Man = Prayer of Manasses.
1 Mac, 2 Mac = 1 and 2 Maccabees.

New Testament.

Mt = Matthew.
Mk = Mark.
Lk = Luke.
Jn = John.
Ac = Acts.
Ro = Romans.
1 Co, 2 Co = 1 and 2 Corinthians.
Gal = Galatians.
Eph = Ephesians.
Ph = Philippians.
Col = Colossians.
1 Th, 2 Th = 1 and 2 Thessalonians.
1 Ti, 2 Ti = 1 and 2 Timothy.
Tit = Titus.
Philem = Philemon.
He = Hebrews.
Ja = James.
1 P, 2 P = 1 and 2 Peter.
1 Jn, 2 Jn, 3 Jn = 1, 2, and 3 John.
Jude.
Rev = Revelation.

III. For the Literature

1. The following authors' names, when unaccompanied by the title of a book, stand for the works in the list below.

Baethgen = *Beiträge zur sem. Religionsgesch.*, 1888.
Baldwin = *Dict. of Philosophy and Psychology*, 3 vols. 1901–05.
Barth = *Nominalbildung in den sem. Sprachen*, 2 vols. 1889, 1891 (²1894).
Benzinger = *Heb. Archäologie*, 1894.
Brockelmann = *Gesch. d. arab. Litteratur*, 2 vols. 1897–1902.
Bruns-Sachau = *Syr.-Röm. Rechtsbuch aus dem fünften Jahrhundert*, 1880.
Budge = *Gods of the Egyptians*, 2 vols. 1903.
Daremberg-Saglio = *Dict. des ant. grec. et rom.*, 1886–90.
De la Saussaye = *Lehrbuch der Religionsgesch.*³, 1905.
Denzinger = *Enchiridion Symbolorum*¹¹, Freiburg im Br., 1911.
Deussen = *Die Philos. d. Upanishads*, 1899 [Eng. tr., 1906].
Doughty = *Arabia Deserta*, 2 vols. 1888.
Grimm = *Deutsche Mythologie*⁴, 3 vols. 1875–78, Eng. tr. *Teutonic Mythology*, 4 vols. 1882–88.
Hamburger = *Realencyclopädie für Bibel u. Talmud*, i. 1870 (²1892), ii. 1883, suppl. 1886, 1891 f., 1897.
Holder = *Altceltischer Sprachschatz*, 1891 ff.
Holtzmann-Zöpffel = *Lexicon f. Theol. u. Kirchenwesen*², 1895.
Howitt = *Native Tribes of S.E. Australia*, 1904.
Jubainville = *Cours de Litt. celtique*, i.–xii., 1883 ff.
Lagrange = *Études sur les religions sémitiques*², 1904.
Lane = *An Arabic-English Lexicon*, 1863 ff.
Lang = *Myth, Ritual, and Religion*², 2 vols. 1899.
Lepsius = *Denkmäler aus Aegypten u. Aethiopien*, 1849–60.
Lichtenberger = *Encyc. des sciences religieuses*, 1876.
Lidzbarski = *Handbuch der nordsem. Epigraphik*, 1898.
McCurdy = *History, Prophecy, and the Monuments*, 2 vols. 1894–96.
Muir = *Orig. Sanskrit Texts*, 1858–72.
Muss-Arnolt = *A Concise Dict. of the Assyrian Language*, 1894 ff.
Nowack = *Lehrbuch d. heb. Archäologie*, 2 vols. 1894.
Pauly-Wissowa = *Realencyc. der classischen Altertumswissenschaft*, 1894 ff.
Perrot-Chipiez = *Hist. de l'art dans l'antiquité*, 1881 ff.
Preller = *Römische Mythologie*, 1858.
Réville = *Religion des peuples non-civilisés*, 1883.
Riehm = *Handwörterbuch d. bibl. Altertums*², 1893–94.
Robinson = *Biblical Researches in Palestine*², 1856.
Roscher = *Lex. d. gr. u. röm. Mythologie*, 1884 ff.
Schaff-Herzog = *The New Schaff-Herzog Encyclopedia of Religious Knowledge*, 1908 ff.
Schenkel = *Bibel-Lexicon*, 5 vols. 1869–75.
Schürer = *GJV*³, 3 vols. 1898–1901 [*HJP*, 5 vols. 1890 ff.].
Schwally = *Leben nach dem Tode*, 1892.
Siegfried-Stade = *Heb. Wörterbuch zum AT*, 1893.
Smend = *Lehrbuch der alttest. Religionsgesch.*², 1899.
Smith (G. A.) = *Historical Geography of the Holy Land*⁴, 1897.
Smith (W. R.) = *Religion of the Semites*², 1894.
Spencer (H.) = *Principles of Sociology*³, 1885–96.
Spencer-Gillen[a] = *Native Tribes of Central Australia*, 1899.
Spencer-Gillen[b] = *Northern Tribes of Central Australia*, 1904.
Swete = *The OT in Greek*, 3 vols. 1893 ff.
Tylor (E. B.) = *Primitive Culture*³, 1891 [⁴1903].
Ueberweg = *Hist. of Philosophy*, Eng. tr., 2 vols. 1872–74.
Weber = *Jüdische Theologie auf Grund des Talmud u. verwandten Schriften*², 1897.
Wiedemann = *Die Religion der alten Aegypter*, 1890 [Eng. tr., revised, *Religion of the Anc. Egyptians*, 1897].
Wilkinson = *Manners and Customs of the Ancient Egyptians*, 3 vols. 1878.
Zunz = *Die gottesdienstlichen Vorträge der Juden*², 1892.

2. Periodicals, Dictionaries, Encyclopædias, and other standard works frequently cited.

AA = Archiv für Anthropologie.
AAOJ = American Antiquarian and Oriental Journal.
ABAW = Abhandlungen d. Berliner Akad. d. Wissenschaften.
AE = Archiv für Ethnographie.
AEG = Assyr. and Eng. Glossary (Johns Hopkins University).
AGG = Abhandlungen der Göttinger Gesellschaft der Wissenschaften.
AGPh = Archiv für Geschichte der Philosophie.
AHR = American Historical Review.
AHT = Ancient Hebrew Tradition (Hommel).
AJPh = American Journal of Philology.
AJPs = American Journal of Psychology.
AJRPE = American Journal of Religious Psychology and Education.
AJSL = American Journal of Semitic Languages and Literature.
AJTh = American Journal of Theology.
AMG = Annales du Musée Guimet.
APES = American Palestine Exploration Society.
APF = Archiv für Papyrusforschung.
AR = Anthropological Review.
ARW = Archiv für Religionswissenschaft.
AS = Acta Sanctorum (Bollandus).
ASG = Abhandlungen der Sächsischen Gesellschaft der Wissenschaften.
ASoc = L'Année Sociologique.
ASWI = Archæological Survey of W. India.
AZ = Allgemeine Zeitung.
BAG = Beiträge zur alten Geschichte.
BASS = Beiträge zur Assyriologie u. sem. Sprachwissenschaft (edd. Delitzsch and Haupt).
BCH = Bulletin de Correspondance Hellénique.
BE = Bureau of Ethnology.
BG = Bombay Gazetteer.
BJ = Bellum Judaicum (Josephus).
BL = Bampton Lectures.
BLE = Bulletin de Littérature Ecclésiastique.
BOR = Bab. and Oriental Record.
BS = Bibliotheca Sacra.
BSA = Annual of the British School at Athens.
BSAA = Bulletin de la Soc. archéologique à Alexandrie.
BSAL = Bulletin de la Soc. d'Anthropologie de Lyon.
BSAP = Bulletin de la Soc. d'Anthropologie, etc., Paris.
BSG = Bulletin de la Soc. de Géographie.
BTS = Buddhist Text Society.
BW = Biblical World.
BZ = Biblische Zeitschrift.

CAIBL=Comptes rendus de l'Académie des Inscriptions et Belles-Lettres.
CBTS=Calcutta Buddhist Text Society.
CE=Catholic Encyclopædia.
CF=Childhood of Fiction (MacCulloch).
CGS=Cults of the Greek States (Farnell).
CI=Census of India.
CIA=Corpus Inscrip. Atticarum.
CIE=Corpus Inscrip. Etruscarum.
CIG=Corpus Inscrip. Græcarum.
CIL=Corpus Inscrip. Latinarum.
CIS=Corpus Inscrip. Semiticarum.
COT=Cuneiform Inscriptions and the OT [Eng. tr. of *KAT*[2]; see below].
CR=Contemporary Review.
CeR=Celtic Review.
ClR=Classical Review.
CQR=Church Quarterly Review.
CSEL=Corpus Script. Eccles. Latinorum.
DAC=Dict. of the Apostolic Church.
DACL=Dict. d'Archéologie chrétienne et de Liturgie (Cabrol).
DB=Dict. of the Bible.
DCA=Dict. of Christian Antiquities (Smith-Cheetham).
DCB=Dict. of Christian Biography (Smith-Wace).
DCG=Dict. of Christ and the Gospels.
DI=Dict. of Islam (Hughes).
DNB=Dict. of National Biography.
DPhP=Dict. of Philosophy and Psychology.
DWAW=Denkschriften der Wiener Akad. der Wissenschaften.
EBi=Encyclopædia Biblica.
EBr=Encyclopædia Britannica.
EEFM=Egyp. Explor. Fund Memoirs.
EI=Encyclopaedia of Islām.
ERE=The present work.
Exp=Expositor.
ExpT=Expository Times.
FHG=Fragmenta Historicorum Græcorum (coll. C. Müller, Paris, 1885).
FL=Folklore.
FLJ=Folklore Journal.
FLR=Folklore Record.
GA=Gazette Archéologique.
GB=Golden Bough (Frazer).
GGA=Göttingische Gelehrte Anzeigen.
GGN=Göttingische Gelehrte Nachrichten (Nachrichten der königl. Gesellschaft der Wissenschaften zu Göttingen).
GIAP=Grundriss d. Indo-Arischen Philologie.
GIrP=Grundriss d. Iranischen Philologie.
GJV=Geschichte des jüdischen Volkes.
GVI=Geschichte des Volkes Israel.
HAI=Handbook of American Indians.
HDB=Hastings' Dict. of the Bible.
HE=Historia Ecclesiastica.
HGHL=Historical Geography of the Holy Land (G. A. Smith).
HI=History of Israel.
HJ=Hibbert Journal.
HJP=History of the Jewish People.
HL=Hibbert Lectures.
HN=Historia Naturalis (Pliny).
HWB=Handwörterbuch.
IA=Indian Antiquary.
ICC=International Critical Commentary.
ICO=International Congress of Orientalists.
ICR=Indian Census Report.
IG=Inscrip. Græcæ (publ. under auspices of Berlin Academy, 1873 ff.).
IGA=Inscrip. Græcæ Antiquissimæ.
IGI=Imperial Gazetteer of India[2] (1885); new edition (1908-09).
IJE=International Journal of Ethics.
ITL=International Theological Library.
JA=Journal Asiatique.
JAFL=Journal of American Folklore.
JAI=Journal of the Anthropological Institute.
JAOS=Journal of the American Oriental Society.
JASB=Journal of the Anthropological Society of Bombay.
JASBe=Journ. of As. Soc. of Bengal.
JBL=Journal of Biblical Literature.
JBTS=Journal of the Buddhist Text Society.
JD=Journal des Débats.
JDTh=Jahrbücher f. deutsche Theologie.
JE=Jewish Encyclopedia.
JGOS=Journal of the German Oriental Society.
JHC=Johns Hopkins University Circulars.
JHS=Journal of Hellenic Studies.
JLZ=Jenäer Litteraturzeitung.
JPh=Journal of Philology.
JPTh=Jahrbücher für protestantische Theologie.
JPTS=Journal of the Pāli Text Society.
JQR=Jewish Quarterly Review.
JRAI=Journal of the Royal Anthropological Institute.
JRAS=Journal of the Royal Asiatic Society.
JRASBo=Journal of the Royal Asiatic Society, Bombay branch.
JRASC=Journal of the Royal Asiatic Society, Ceylon branch.
JRASK=Journal of the Royal Asiatic Society, Korean branch.
JRGS=Journal of the Royal Geographical Society.
JRS=Journal of Roman Studies.
JThSt=Journal of Theological Studies.
KAT[2]=Die Keilinschriften und das AT[2] (Schrader), 1883.
KAT[3]=Zimmern-Winckler's ed. of the preceding (really a totally distinct work), 1903.
KB or *KIB*=Keilinschriftliche Bibliothek (Schrader), 1889 ff.
KGF=Keilinschriften und die Geschichtsforschung, 1878.
LCBl=Literarisches Centralblatt.
LOPh=Literaturblatt für Oriental. Philologie.
LOT=Introduction to Literature of OT (Driver).
LP=Legend of Perseus (Hartland).
LSSt=Leipziger sem. Studien.
M=Mélusine.
MAIBL=Mémoires de l'Acad. des Inscriptions et Belles-Lettres.
MBAW=Monatsbericht d. Berliner Akad. d. Wissenschaften.
MGH=Monumenta Germaniæ Historica (Pertz).
MGJV=Mittheilungen der Gesellschaft für jüdische Volkskunde.
MGWJ=Monatsschrift für Geschichte und Wissenschaft des Judentums.
MI=Origin and Development of the Moral Ideas (Westermarck).
MNDPV=Mittheilungen u. Nachrichten des deutschen Palästina-Vereins.
MR=Methodist Review.
MVG=Mittheilungen der vorderasiatischen Gesellschaft.
MWJ=Magazin für die Wissenschaft des Judentums.
NBAC=Nuovo Bullettino di Archeologia Cristiana.
NC=Nineteenth Century.
NHWB=Neuhebräisches Wörterbuch.
NINQ=North Indian Notes and Queries.
NKZ=Neue kirchliche Zeitschrift.
NQ=Notes and Queries.
NR=Native Races of the Pacific States (Bancroft).
NTZG=Neutestamentliche Zeitgeschichte.
OED=Oxford English Dictionary.
OLZ=Orientalische Litteraturzeitung.
OS=Onomastica Sacra.
OTJC=Old Testament in the Jewish Church (W. R. Smith).
OTP=Oriental Translation Fund Publications.
PAOS=Proceedings of American Oriental Society.

PASB = Proceedings of the Anthropological Soc. of Bombay.
PB = Polychrome Bible (English).
PBE = Publications of the Bureau of Ethnology.
PC = Primitive Culture (Tylor).
PEFM = Palestine Exploration Fund Quarterly Memoirs.
PEFSt = Palestine Exploration Fund Statement.
PG = Patrologia Græca (Migne).
PJB = Preussische Jahrbücher.
PL = Patrologia Latina (Migne).
PNQ = Punjab Notes and Queries.
PR = Popular Religion and Folklore of N. India (Crooke).
*PRE*³ = Prot. Realencyclopädie (Herzog-Hauck).
PRR = Presbyterian and Reformed Review.
PRS = Proceedings of the Royal Society.
PRSE = Proceedings Royal Soc. of Edinburgh.
PSBA = Proceedings of the Society of Biblical Archæology.
PTS = Pāli Text Society.
RA = Revue Archéologique.
RAnth = Revue d'Anthropologie.
RAS = Royal Asiatic Society.
RAssyr = Revue d'Assyriologie.
RB = Revue Biblique.
RBEW = Reports of the Bureau of Ethnology (Washington).
RC = Revue Critique.
RCel = Revue Celtique.
RCh = Revue Chrétienne.
RDM = Revue des Deux Mondes.
RE = Realencyclopädie.
REG = Revue des Études Grecques.
REg = Revue Égyptologique.
REJ = Revue des Études Juives.
REth = Revue d'Ethnographie.
RGG = Die Religion in Geschichte und Gegenwart.
RHLR = Revue d'Histoire et de Littérature religieuses.
RHR = Revue de l'Histoire des Religions.
RMM = Revue du monde musulman.
RN = Revue Numismatique.
RP = Records of the Past.
RPh = Revue Philosophique.
RQ = Römische Quartalschrift.
RS = Revue sémitique d'Épigraphie et d'Hist. ancienne.
RSA = Recueil de la Soc. archéologique.
RSI = Reports of the Smithsonian Institution.
RTAP = Recueil de Travaux rélatifs à l'Archéologie et à la Philologie.
RTP = Revue des traditions populaires.
RThPh = Revue de Théologie et de Philosophie.
RTr = Recueil de Travaux.
RVV = Religionsgeschichtliche Versuche und Vorarbeitungen.
RWB = Realwörterbuch.

SBAW = Sitzungsberichte d. Berliner Akademie d. Wissenschaften.
SBB = Sacred Books of the Buddhists.
SBE = Sacred Books of the East.
SBOT = Sacred Books of the OT (Hebrew).
SDB = Single-vol. Dict. of the Bible (Hastings).
SK = Studien und Kritiken.
SMA = Sitzungsberichte d. Münchener Akademie.
SSGW = Sitzungsberichte d. Kgl. Sächs. Gesellsch. d. Wissenschaften.
SWAW = Sitzungsberichte d. Wiener Akademie d. Wissenschaften.
TAPA = Transactions of American Philological Association.
TASJ = Transactions of the Asiatic Soc. of Japan.
TC = Tribes and Castes.
TES = Transactions of Ethnological Society.
ThLZ = Theologische Litteraturzeitung.
ThT = Theol. Tijdschrift.
TRHS = Transactions of Royal Historical Society.
TRSE = Transactions of Royal Soc. of Edinburgh.
TS = Texts and Studies.
TSBA = Transactions of the Soc. of Biblical Archæology.
TU = Texte und Untersuchungen.
WAI = Western Asiatic Inscriptions.
WZKM = Wiener Zeitschrift f. Kunde des Morgenlandes.
ZA = Zeitschrift für Assyriologie.
ZÄ = Zeitschrift für ägyp. Sprache u. Altertumswissenschaft.
ZATW = Zeitschrift für die alttest. Wissenschaft.
ZCK = Zeitschrift für christliche Kunst.
ZCP = Zeitschrift für celtische Philologie.
ZDA = Zeitschrift für deutsches Altertum.
ZDMG = Zeitschrift der deutschen morgenländischen Gesellschaft.
ZDPV = Zeitschrift des deutschen Palästina-Vereins.
ZE = Zeitschrift für Ethnologie.
ZKF = Zeitschrift für Keilschriftforschung.
ZKG = Zeitschrift für Kirchengeschichte.
ZKT = Zeitschrift für kathol. Theologie.
ZKWL = Zeitschrift für kirchl. Wissenschaft und kirchl. Leben.
ZM = Zeitschrift für die Mythologie.
ZNTW = Zeitschrift für die neutest. Wissenschaft.
ZPhP = Zeitschrift für Philosophie und Pädagogik.
ZTK = Zeitschrift für Theologie und Kirche.
ZVK = Zeitschrift für Volkskunde.
ZVRW = Zeitschrift für vergleichende Rechtswissenschaft.
ZWT = Zeitschrift für wissenschaftliche Theologie.

[A small superior number designates the particular edition of the work referred to, as *KAT*², *LOT*⁶, etc.]

ENCYCLOPÆDIA
OF
RELIGION AND ETHICS

S

SUFFERING.—I. *INTRODUCTION: THE FACT AND THE PROBLEM.*—Suffering, as a feature of life in this earth, is too obvious and too familiar to need description. Sentimentality and denunciation are alike superfluous. Suffering is all but universal. From the point where, in the evolutionary process, a brain is developed, upward through all ranks of being, suffering is an unvarying element in experience. It appears in endless variety. Some of it belongs to animals in their natural conditions as an accompaniment of their life-story or as a consequence of their predaceous habits. It is, however, in human life that suffering most abounds. A great deal of human suffering is what we term roughly 'physical pain,' though, in point of fact, the suffering of a self-conscious being must be radically distinct from that of a living creature in whose sentient life the thought of personality has not yet dawned. Physical pain is found in many degrees of intensity, from that which is easily bearable, at least by persons in normal health, to that which is appalling to look upon, and must constitute an unimaginable anguish. If we pass from physical suffering to that which is mental and moral, we are overwhelmed by the mass and the magnitude of the agonies that are the lot of mankind. From the sorrows of childhood, deeper than the observer can calculate, to the stony griefs of age, untold and ungauged, there is a range of suffering beyond all enumeration and conception, baffling the imagination, affronting the intelligence.

The worst feature of human suffering is the chaotic nature of its distribution. If strong men alone were sufferers, we would comfort ourselves by noting the gladness of little children; but children suffer, often with an intensity which seems too awful for the tender frame to endure and yet survive. If the guilty alone suffered, we might have some kind of theodicy to fit the facts; but the innocent suffer; they are the greatest sufferers. If we had to consider only our own pains, we might find a reason for them, or at least we could retreat to the fastness of our unconquerable soul. When, however, it is the pain of others that confronts us, we feel that our explanations are an impertinence. The clue to their sufferings is not to be found in any supposed rationale of our own.

The deepest element in the problem of pain is that so much suffering is meaningless, as far as our most careful thought can discern. After we have noted causes the removal of which would certainly reduce the quantity of pain in the world, after we have seen the ends which it may be supposed to serve, there remains a surplusage of pain unaccounted for by our largest theory. It is this surplusage that forms the heart of the mystery of suffering. If there is any meaningless pain in the world, it cannot, surely, be the best of all possible worlds. How can a world crossed by such a bar sinister be the expression of wisdom, power, or goodness?

> 'The dilemma of Epicurus is still with us: if God wishes to prevent evil but cannot, then he is impotent; if he could but will not, he is malevolent; if he has both the power and the will, whence then is evil?'[1]

The challenge to theism is direct. There is probably little theoretic atheism among ordinary men and women. But it is certain that in multitudes of cases faith has suffered shipwreck on the rock of meaningless pain. To this form of unbelief women are peculiarly prone. Suffering appeals to their sympathy. Their acquaintance with it is wide and intimate. They feel, more deeply than men, the waste and cruelty of it; and they are accordingly brought to doubt the existence of a God who is at once almighty and all-merciful. In their case, too, scepticism means more than it does to the majority of men. It is not merely the abandonment of a theory. It is the ruin of a life, through the loss of the hope which alone makes life endurable. In all ages the pressure of this problem of pain has been felt. It may even be said to be the driving force in all philosophy and in every great religion.

How shall man be reconciled to life? What view of the world must be taken if man is to live worthily in it? What estimate of life must be held if it is to be at least endurable? How are the facts of suffering to be adjusted to the sense of value and the inspiration of hope, which are the mainsprings of fruitful labour?

II. *THE LEADING ATTEMPTS AT SOLUTION.*—

1. **Pessimism.**—Frankly and definitely, suffering is so wide-spread and so intense that the verdict

[1] W. R. Sorley and others, *The Elements of Pain and Conflict in Human Life*, p. 48.

of open-eyed and unprejudiced observers must be that the world is an intolerable place to live in, and that life is an unendurable burden.

The classical example of this solution of the problem of pain is the doctrine of Buddha, which, in the heart of the 19th cent., was reproduced by Schopenhauer. Pessimism must always be substantially the same. It is interesting for its verdict, not for its discussions. Buddha's 'Four Noble Truths'—pain, the origin of pain, the destruction of pain, and the eightfold holy way—are the conclusion of the whole matter. The first contains the result of direct observation. Suffering prevails. Life is worthless and miserable. The second traces this universal wretchedness to its source in 'thirst,' the desire which attaches the soul to worldly objects and leads to 'becoming'—an infinite series of new existences, with a monotonous repetition of birth, pain, and despair. The third points out the means of deliverance from life and from suffering, viz. cessation of desire. Let desire cease; then the thread of life will be snapped; then the fountain of suffering will cease to flow. The fourth is Buddha's plan of salvation, containing a careful account of the steps by which the extinction of desire is to be accomplished. Among these morality has its place; and Buddhist ethic has a mild lustre of its own. The crown of the procedure, however, is contemplation. Schopenhauer's 'path' includes art, but otherwise is scarcely an improvement upon Buddha's. The issue for both is the same—the cessation of desire, the abandonment of the will to live.

To discuss the philosophy of pessimism (*q.v.*) would be wasted labour. The Buddhist psychology, with its rigidly atomistic sensationalism, has gone to the scrap-heap. Schopenhauer's dependence on Kant does not give his system commanding authority. The real strength of pessimism, or the final demonstration of its weakness, must be sought elsewhere. Pessimism pursues the empirical method. The first question to be asked is as to the validity of this method and as to the certainty of the first 'Noble Truth' reached by means of it. Can the worthlessness of life be established by any enumeration of details? The question is not as to the possibility of balancing the pessimist's instances by others of a more cheering nature. Optimism cannot be established by such means. The real question is as to the method itself. The pessimist inference from the facts of pain is not really drawn by mere generalization. It rests on a preconceived theory of values, by which all the facts of life are tested. Pessimism is simply disappointed hedonism. If the highest good is pleasure, life is certainly not worth living, for pleasure in any guise is not to be had, on any terms whatever, in human experience, to such a degree as to counterbalance the damning facts of pain. If the Creator was bound to secure for His creatures a surplusage of pleasure, He certainly has failed to do so. His power has not been equal to His good intentions. If He exists, we must conceive of Him as shorn of His omnipotence, or even 'gone mad.' Hedonism, however, is of all ethical theories the most precarious. If appeal be made to experts in living, the answer will be returned that happiness is not the chief good for man and cannot be conceived as the chief end of creation. That place of eminence belongs to moral goodness.

Our question as to the world, accordingly, must be: Is it so framed and ordered that moral goodness is being wrought out therein, not merely in spite of, but actually by means of, the suffering that is to be found in all human life? It is to be observed, however, that the answer might be enough to refute pessimism, and yet leave a crux for theism. We might be quite convinced that virtue is the highest good for man, and we might vindicate the position that virtue grows to its maturity through the discipline of pain; still, if there remains a margin of suffering that bears no relation at all to character and cannot be related to the chief end of creation, the theistic conclusion remains open to doubt. It may even become necessary to maintain that optimism cannot be established by argument at all, and that theism is warranted by some other process than that of logical demonstration. In that case the challenge of suffering may be met; but not otherwise. After we have refuted a theoretic pessimism, we have to recognize the fact of pain. Before one irrelevant pang our best theorizings sink abashed. We have nothing to say. Our speech would be a worse irrelevance.

2. Stoicism.—Another answer to the challenge of suffering is to the effect that, while pain is real and may be very acute, it is one of those indifferent things which a wise and strong man may neglect, not allowing it to disturb him in any way. The Stoic philosophy is the elaboration of this answer, by means of a full apparatus of metaphysic, psychology, and ethic. Stoicism, however, is more than a philosophical theory. It is an attitude to life. It reappears in noted personalities, when the insistent evils and disorders of the world drive men to the inner region of their own souls, to find there a refuge nowhere else discoverable. The circumstances under which classical Stoicism arose are familiar. It was an age of individualism. No relief or satisfaction could be found in any form of life open to man in the world of that day. Men could not go into the world and find the counterpart of their own moral nature. They could not lose themselves in the activities of city or nation and in the very process of such devotion achieve their own highest welfare. And this for two reasons: no city or nation was left standing in its independence; and the soul of man had grown so great in its needs and capacities that it could no longer be satisfied within the limits of civic or national activities, however intense and vivid these might be. Man had discovered himself. He knew now that nothing less than the universe would meet his need and afford a satisfying life. Here, then, is the Stoic gospel, which is at once a philosophy and a message of salvation. The ultimate reality is reason. We may speak of Nature or of God. In any case there is one principle at work in the world and in man. Stoicism is, in this aspect, optimism. It believes in a principle which underlies all phenomena and is moving through all events to complete victory. This principle is the life of all that is, both within man and beyond him. It is a principle of reason and of harmony. It is inherently good; and its supremacy is the highest welfare of the world and of man. The ethical ideal for man, accordingly, is consistency with nature or with reason; or, speaking religiously, it is harmony with the will of God. The ancient Stoic doctrine of providence has the fervour of intense religious conviction. It is strange at first sight that such a glowing optimism should have any room for a theoretic acknowledgment of the facts of pain and evil. It is to be noted, however, that the ultimate reason has been reached in Stoicism too easily. It is, after all, a negation of the vast and confusing facts of a miserable and perplexing experience. It is the bare affirmation of an abstract principle which ought to be the truth of all things and, in point of fact, is reproduced in scarcely any of them. Reason is everything; and yet reason is nowhere. Stoic optimism is a faith; but the Stoic estimate of facts is dark and pessimistic. What, then, is man to do, poised as he is between reason, which is his true nature, and a world in which man and things are so irrational? What attitude is he to take towards such brute facts as hunger and cold, oppression and cruelty, bereavement and grief? The Stoic answer is serene and hard. The wise man will choose reason. He will be absolutely sure that this choice brings him a good of which no power in man or in things can rob him. He is in indefeasible possession of the absolute best. His harmony with reason sets him in a charmed circle, into which nothing irrational and evil can ever enter. Pain racks his body; but his body is not his reason. Death robs him of wife or child; but they are not himself. Evil afflicts his friends; but that cannot invade the citadel of his own peace. We read the aphorisms and counsels of an Epictetus with a shudder. So calm, so logical, so inhuman! It ought to be noted, however, that this attitude of complete detachment towards pain and evil is an advance upon a view such as that of Aristotle, which regards them as obstacles in the way of a perfect life. To the Stoic they are not obstacles. The perfect life has simply nothing to do with them. The wise man will not court them; but he will not allow them to disturb his serenity. He will make their occurrence in his experience the occasion of manifesting his consistency with reason. He will even benefit by their presence, inasmuch as his conquest of them will invigorate his strength and enable him to gain a yet greater superiority over them. But, in themselves, they have no relation to his inner life, which is complete without them and does nothing to them. At this point our admiration for the Stoic attitude reaches its highest.

Here also our criticism begins. The reason, which is the Stoic's God, and highest good, is not positively related to the manifold experiences of life. It is not in and through them that reason is revealed in its own inner wealth, and that man attains the fullness of his being. Very specially, pain and evil serve no end of reason, and the supreme principle of the universe has no relation to them. Man, in union with that principle, has no duty with regard to them, save to repel them and to refuse to them the tribute of an emotion. It is not on these lines that the worth of life can be vindicated or an idealist construction of the universe be established. The Stoic conclusion is mere negation, abstraction, and emptiness. It is good only for defiance; but defiance is not victory over pain; and far less is it transmutation of evil into the means of a greater good.

Yet is it good, even for defiance? Stoicism has too easily assumed that man can choose the reason of the universe and identify himself with it. A painful doubt develops. What if a man's self be the main obstacle to his being identified with God? In abandoning all things finite and particular, will he not need also to surrender himself? Thus the axe is laid to the root of Stoic pride; and the Stoic gospel turns out to be a counsel of despair. In the might of my self I am to defy the world. But who am I? The very essence of finitude, the very acme of contrast with the reason which is the harmony of the universe. My utmost willing, then, is weakness. Upon my resistance falls the doom of ineptitude and impotence. Victory is turned to defeat. Self-confidence is no longer possible; for self is the secret of failure. When Stoicism has reached this point, it is ready for a philosophy, or a religion, which shall start where it ended and make the condition of man's achievement of the highest good, not his self-assertion, but his self-surrender. The challenge of suffering might now be met in a different way—not by resistance, but by acceptance. Pain might become, not an obstacle in the path of the perfect life, not even a thing indifferent to man's inner good, but the opportunity and the instrument of his death to self, and therefore, also, of his complete self-realization. Stoicism began with optimism and ended in pessimism. It might be possible to reverse the process and to lean our optimism upon a deeper view of evil than an empirical pessimism had ever reached. Such a stage beyond Stoicism is found in one direction in Neo-Platonism, and by another path in Christianity.

3. Meliorism.—A nobler answer to the challenge of suffering than that offered by Stoicism was very prevalent during the recent war. The world, it is admitted, is full of virulent evils and untold sufferings. These things are not to be explained. They are to be fought. They are not to be accepted as an irresistible fate or as the appointment of an almighty and sovereign Disposer of events. They are evil, and only evil, continually. Judged by the human conscience, they exist only to be resisted, defeated, banished from the experience of the race. They are a challenge to love, sympathy, honour, to be met by sacrifice, by service, and above all by unending war. All intelligences are summoned to take part in this war for peace, this struggle for the abolition of suffering. Among the hosts engaged in this life-and-death conflict some individuals, both human and superhuman, occupy the position of leadership, as well in strategy as in the actual fighting. Commander-in-chief of this army is God. He is not what absolutism, or orthodox theism, has conceived Him to be. He is not the inscrutable ground of all being, the omnipotent will, the omniscient mind by whose unalterable decree all things in creation are predetermined. He is a finite being, though of course His resources both in wisdom and in power are far more than human. He is in this fight, which is no shadowy and spectral combat, but is for Him as for man tragically real, a genuine life or death struggle. We can indeed scarcely imagine His being defeated ultimately; but He has not won yet. Nay, He cannot win unless He secure the co-operation of man. In this tremendous conflict human beings cannot be neutral. If they are not for Him, they are against Him, slackers, traitors, or open enemies. He sends out a great call for volunteers; and all who have a spark of generosity or heroism will rally to His side. They will fight with the splendid courage which comes from sympathy with the oppressed and tortured everywhere, and with the desperate energy of those who see the issue plainly. They are fighting for their all, for the very life of humanity, and humanity's radiant and high-souled Leader. Every rookery pulled down, every disease routed, every social wrong redressed, is a battle won in the long campaign, a stage to the final, all-comprehensive victory. Suffering is being eliminated. Progress is being made. The end, if not in sight, is reasonably secure.

But the practical value of meliorism must rest ultimately on the validity of its presuppositions. If these are invalid, their results cannot be permanent. Now the presuppositions of meliorism are mainly three: (1) the universe is conceived as growing in time, its future, strictly speaking, unpredictable; (2) God Himself is avowedly a finite being, in time, sometimes described even as 'young,' with a future before Him in which He has still to make good; (3) the issue of the conflict is, in the nature of the case, uncertain, though every successive victory and the inexhaustible resources of intelligences, human and superhuman, give ground for hope. It is not too much to say that each one of these presuppositions is disputable. Not one of them has won universal consent. Together they constitute a huge hypothesis. If regarded as more than this, they become sheer dogmatism; and dogmas are but 'iron rations' at best, and are soon exhausted.

The error both of Stoicism and of meliorism lies in trying to turn what is partial into an absolute. Because a man is summoned to oppose the evil that is in the world with all his might, it is supposed that he can 'carry on' till the victory is his. Suppose, however, that this rough dualism between the good man and the wicked world does not represent the real situation. Suppose that the real source of evil is not without, but within, and that the conflict that is being waged in the world is the image and the outcome of a more devouring strife that rages in man's own soul. Then the result will be, as happened in the history of Stoicism, that self must give up its self-sufficiency and must seek the true and the good, not by self-assertion, but by self-surrender, and see in its attainment of virtue and knowledge the disclosure and the communication of One who includes the universe in His consciousness and His control. Then the fighter may 'carry on' without anxiety and without self-confidence, because the victory has been won already, not by himself, but by the Power which is working in him, whose servant and vehicle he is. The end of such a war is not uncertain, though it can be reached only through a sacrificial ministry.

It ought to be added that meliorism makes no pretension of having solved the problem of pain. It knows no more than any other theory why pain should ever be; and it cannot be blamed for refusing to face the question. A graver defect, however, is its inability to provide hope or comfort for those sufferers who are not taking part in the successive victories, or are not directly benefited by them. In this war, as in all wars, it is the non-combatants who suffer most. But really the metaphor breaks down altogether. Where time is the whole of reality, there can be no 'repatriation' of those who have been overwhelmed by the powers of evil. Some meliorists believe in immortality. But their faith is not a certain conclusion from their presuppositions; nor does meliorism require such a faith for its completeness. It is concerned only with the progress of humanity. Its soldiers get their fill of fighting, and this is all the pay they ask for. Those who have never had a chance to fight, who have been crushed by forces too great for them, have no compensatory advantages offered them. At this point meliorism lapses below Stoicism. It has no resource against pessimism. A world with such hopeless, meaningless pain in it had better never have been. The meliorist 'God' escapes the condemnation and contempt even of the most ordinary intelligence, only because, to do him justice, he is not creator of the world, and is not responsible for its blemishes. We stand, as does 'God' also, in the midst of a circumambient fate, unintelligible, inaccessible, whose blind decree can be neither modified nor served, which is liable at any moment to intervene disastrously in our affairs and turn our most brilliant victory into mockery and despair.

4. Optimism.—The most perfect optimism would be a thoroughgoing pantheism. If finitude is really an illusion which disappears from the point of view of the Absolute, evil cannot be held to exist. Ascend to the point of view of the Absolute, and forthwith evil is seen to be mere seeming. The idea that it exists is the mistake of those who attribute to things finite a reality which does not belong to them.

This sounds convincing. But two remarks immediately occur. (1) Who shall ascend to the height of the Absolute? How shall the finite leap to the Infinite? Practically, pantheism has nothing to say to the sufferer. His pain is utterly irremediable. Pain necessarily belongs to the finite. He is bound to the finite. As long as he exists he must suffer. When suffering ceases, he will have ceased to be. Pantheistic optimism is thus pessimistic in its estimate of life. (2) If evil is an illusion, because it is finite, so must good be also, for it too is finite. Good and evil are, in fact, meaningless. For the Absolute they do not exist. Optimism and pessimism, accordingly, are philosophies of the unreal, and are in the strictest sense alike nonsense. Of course this treatment of the problem of pain is due to the error which turns the unity of thought against the manifold of experience and regards the universal as the only real, while the particular is condemned as the illusory.

The philosophy of Leibniz has been dealt with in this *Encyclopædia*[1] and needs no further exposition here. Leibniz stands at the opposite pole from pantheism; yet it is pantheism to which his own ruling principle of thought constantly leads him. The principle of sufficient reason, as he interprets it, is the same as that of identity and contradiction. A complete analysis would be a perfect explanation. The principle of identity is the highest principle of truth. All appearance of difference is mere illusion, due to the disability of a finite consciousness. From this point of view the problem of evil may be solved; but the solution is really pantheistic.

The criticism of Hume, and the yet more destructive work of Kant, have made the dominance of an abstract Absolute impossible for modern thought. The finite has come to its rights. The principle of freedom is too strongly entrenched in the convictions of men ever to be relegated to the sphere of the negative and the illusory. This means that modern optimism can no longer take the position of pantheism, and so affirm the sole reality of good as to destroy the possibility of evil. Its proof must now consist in arguing that evil is inseparable from the highest good in this sense, that the highest good is attainable only through the conquest of evil. This argument consists fundamentally in a special reading of the facts of human life. It may be presented as a deduction from an idealist philosophy, or it may appear as an induction from data empirically reached. Fundamentally it is a judgment of value, as intuition of the significance of life, and is not reached by either the *a priori* or the *a posteriori* method.

'There is no evil except for a rational being, who is capable of willing a good which he identifies with the absolute good, but which is in reality in antagonism to it. But, inasmuch as the possibility of willing this lower good is inseparable from the existence of free subjects, who only come to the clear consciousness of the higher through experience of the lower, it is just the high destiny of man and the infinite perfection of God which make it inconceivable how there should be a universe, containing beings who realize what is the meaning of their own life and of the whole, unless those beings pass through the long and painful process by which the absolutely good is revealed as that which can overcome the deepest depths of evil.'[1]

Watson, from whom these words are quoted, develops them into a view of human life and history which shows that, the higher the conception of the good, the deeper will be the insight into evil. The man who knows himself a sinner knows that no sin is alien to him. He is the supreme sinner of the universe, the chief of sinners; and in the act in which he confesses and dies to his sin the violated order is rectified; and the guilt which he so profoundly acknowledges is lifted to the shoulders of Another, and he is free for ever. Watson does not in this passage explicitly apply this profound conception of an optimism, vindicated through a deeper pessimism than Buddha or Schopenhauer ever knew, to the pangs of nature and the physical woes of men. Plainly, however, the one problem lies within the other. The deepest evil man can suffer is the division within his own spirit. Let his breach with the Absolute be healed, and his breach with nature cannot fail to be healed likewise. The truth of nature is spirit. If the unity of spirit rise triumphant above the dualism that a false assertion of freedom has wrought, there can be left nowhere in the universe any element of difference, and therefore of evil, which is not in process of being transcended in the realization of the ultimate good.

Many writers who do not adhere to Watson's type of idealism base their ethical view of the universe on the facts which he emphasizes. The world was certainly not framed to produce the pleasure of all sentient creatures or the happiness of human beings. The highest good is moral good, and moral good can be attained by man only through a process of discipline. A world which made goodness easy would make true goodness impossible. By work, by suffering, and by temptation, human character is perfected. The theistic and optimistic inference is more securely drawn from a world with imperfections, in conflict with which character is ripened, than it would be from one in which neither physical nor moral evil was present. It is possible to believe that the Creator of such a

[1] See artt. LEIBNIZ and PESSIMISM AND OPTIMISM.

[1] John Watson, *The Philosophical Basis of Religion*, p. 459.

world is good and wise and almighty, whereas such a faith would be valueless if the world were a machine for turning out mechanical perfection. This does not mean, of course, that for every pain we suffer we can allege a moral purpose. Physical suffering comes to us through our place in a cosmic order whose laws operate with absolute impartiality.

Would we prefer that it were otherwise? Yet in such a world, and in such a world alone, can the highest good be realized. As matter of observed fact, the good is making progress towards a victory, which may be delayed, but which stands in no reasonable doubt. One difficulty lies in the path of such modest optimism, viz. the fate of the individual. Most upholders of this view take refuge in the idea of personal immortality. It is granted that the general optimistic estimate requires that there shall be a balance of good for the individual as well as for the race, seeing that the individual is an end in himself, and not a mere link in a chain. But in the vast majority of individuals this balance is not struck within time and space. It is necessary, therefore, to postulate another life, in which the wrongs and sufferings of this world shall be rectified and their memory lost in the realization of perfect good.

An argument such as this, which turns upon the supremacy of moral worth, and the function of pain in realizing it in the history of individuals and of the race, is intellectually unanswerable. The conclusion of the whole matter is:

> 'God's in His heaven—
> All's right with the world!'

It is to be noted, however, that, when we have solved the problem of pain from the point of view of the spectator, suffering still remains a mystery for the sufferers. No amount of argument can meet their need. What they require is an experience. Their pain cannot be transmuted into joy by telling them that, in the final result, there will be for them a preponderance of good. They will continue to suffer, and before their anguish argument sinks back ashamed. They need to be introduced to the experience of a suffering within which theirs is comprehended and of a good through which theirs is guaranteed.

Optimism must submit to the test of fact. The fact in this case is pain; and pain is insoluble by a process of reasoning. Over against every phase of the argument stands the intractable pain, or, rather, there stands the piteous army of the sufferers. Optimism appears satisfactory only when we stand back from the facts. Stand in the midst of them, and our philosophy is smitten into silence. A world, with pain in it—and such pain!—cannot be the best of all possible worlds.

Of course, Omar Khayyam's aspiration is ridiculous. We cannot 'grasp this sorry scheme of things entire,' cannot 'shatter it to bits' and 'remould it nearer to the heart's desire.' None the less, we turn from the best that the optimist can say to the contemplation of a universe which contains such 'things' in it and are conscious of a lamentable gap. The key does not fit the lock. Suffering remains a mystery and a challenge to theism.

5. The Christian doctrine of providence.—It cannot be doubted that Jesus had the whole fact of pain present to His mind. He lived in the midst of suffering. Yet it did not present itself to Him as a problem. Certainly He made no explicit reference to the questions with which Job wrestled. His compassions flowed forth unhindered by any theory of the causes of pain. He never viewed suffering as other than a great evil. He devoted a large part of His ministry to its alleviation. But He never stood before it confounded or paralyzed. If He was conscious of its challenge to theism, He never replied by argument. He lived in unbroken communion with God, and faced all the problems of life from that position of perfect acquaintance. He knew God. He knew that God's love gathers into its compass all the suffering of man and of the whole sentient creation. The good will of a God whom He knew as the Father cannot be impugned. The victory of His love cannot be doubted. In this faith Jesus lived and died. He revealed to men its divine object, and gave theism the verification of experience. Christianity is the reproduction of this proof. It is a life 'hid with Christ in God.' Its secret is an experience. This experience is not a mystic rapture, to be attained in rare moments by those who have leisure to cultivate the conditions leading to such remote and perilous heights. It may be reached by children. It can be reached only by those who consent to become as little children. It is peculiarly accessible to sufferers. It is reached in the act by which man surrenders his separateness of will and commits himself trustfully to the divine love as it meets him in the chiefest of all sufferers. Such an experience cannot be translated directly into a theory of pain. It contains more than any theory can express. All noble idealism seeks to interpret its fullness; and, apart from it, no philosophical solution can be more than an attractive speculation.

The Christian doctrine of providence (*q.v.*) articulates the leading ideas which are implicit in this experience, and by means of them seeks to exhibit the relation of God to the history of the world. It does so, however, under the distinct understanding that the experience of communion with God, while it is central and all-comprehensive, cannot be drawn upon to provide ready-made answers to the questions which intellect may raise regarding the course of nature and of human life. The divine love is the highest reason. The Logos is love incarnate in the life of the Son of God. But this does not mean that a book could be written, solving, on the whole and in every detail, the mystery of pain. No reasoning process can reach the sanctuary where God at once comforts and remakes the soul that pain has shattered. The Christian is an optimist, but not a theorist. He knows God. He has seen Him in Christ. God is love. That is the secret. There is no truth outside of love, no power that can withstand love. It dominates the universe. It is almighty. When it is reproduced in man, it is the greatest thing in the world. The doctrine of providence simply says, in different connexions, that the divine love is sure of itself, knows its own design, is baffled by no obstacles, overcomes all enemies, is moving to an end, guaranteed in Christ, which is none other than God's perfect communication of Himself in and to a universe which responds with the 'Amen' of absolute faith and unhindered devotion. Christian optimism blends the confident assertion of love's supremacy with an unashamed agnosticism. Its key unlocks the mystery of suffering. Yet the Christian does not employ this key to meet the question of why and wherefore, either as to the presence of pain in the world at large or as to any individual affliction. He bears witness to the fact of love. The acceptance of that fact introduces the sufferer to an experience in which all questionings are transcended in a great possession. Christianity accordingly stands apart from theoretic optimism. It does not, of course, impugn the function of pain, by which philosophers and poets have sought to establish their hopeful conclusions. It can use such instances of beneficial pain as illustrations of its own central truth. It doubts, however, their adequacy to establish, by intellectual demonstration, results so magnificent. It is in full sympathy with their spirit. But it rests its optimism on a different basis; and it presents its results not so much to those who contemplate suffering from without, in order to satisfy their questions, as to those who know it from within, that they may know it better and enter through it into fellowship with God.

(*a*) *The ground of Christian optimism.*—The Christian doctrine of providence stands at one point in profound and significant agreement with such an idealism as is presented in the writings of Caird and Watson. It believes that the problem of pain is part of the wider and deeper problem of moral evil. It does not stay to discuss the fact of physical evil before it has dealt with the graver problem of sin. It presses on to the tremendous fact of breach with God, confident that, if that has been met and healed, no other discord can remain finally unresolved. Nature finds its truth in man. Physical suffering has its analogue in the division which exists between the human soul and God. Reconciliation with God will be the final solution of a mystery of pain which reverberates throughout the universe. In spite of this parallelism, however, Christianity and idealism stand apart. Christianity is an idealism, no doubt. But idealism is not Christianity. The vital question for both is the reconciliation of man and God. How is it achieved? Idealism answers, In an idea. Christianity ventures its all on an historic fact. Idealism pursues the soul to its deepest consciousness of guilt and declares that there already is the reconciliation. The consciousness of guilt is possible only to a soul fundamentally at one with God. In awaking to a sense of his guilt, man knows himself reconciled at once to God and the universe. The spiritual unity is gained; the unification of all experience is thereby guaranteed. Christianity deepens the diagnosis and exhibits a different remedy. In sin man has the universe against him. It reacts to his sin in perpetual judgment, registering in his character and his career, in loss and defeat and pain, the condemnation which man's attack upon the universal order has brought upon him. This automatic reaction does not stand apart from the will of God. It reflects one aspect of the divine mind regarding sin and carries out one part of the divine dealing with it. But sin is not the ultimate reality of the moral world; and judgment is not the whole mind and will of God. The ultimate in God and in the universe is love. The reconciliation is accomplished not in an idea, but in the action of God. The love of God goes into action coincidently with the sin of man. It is true that God's experience of time must differ from ours in a manner necessarily inconceivable by us; so that it is not improper to speak of an eternal act of love and an eternal atonement. But the standpoint of Christianity is definitely historical. Sin is in time. Sin-bearing is in time also. Love can reconcile the world to God only if it pass to the world's side and in the world realize experimentally the whole meaning of sin. It must enter into the tragedy of human life in an experience more tragic than any penitent sinner ever passed through. 'Christ died for our sins' (1 Co 15^3). It is the first, the only, Christian gospel. In the action and passion of a life crowned by the Cross Christ is not another than God. He is God, in a temporal experience, manifesting an eternal fact. Love has gone to the utmost limit of sin and suffering and has returned bearing the fruits of that unimaginable agony in a world reconciled, mankind redeemed, sin and evil judged, exposed, broken. The fact of sin—that is pessimism. The fact of Christ—that is optimism. Christianity confronts the world of sin and suffering with the deeper suffering of divine sin-bearing love. All else that it has to say is an inference from that basal fact. Its doctrine of providence consists in developing the significance of that fact for the varied discipline of life.

'The Christian faith in providence is an immediate inference from the Christian experience of redemption, and it is an inference as vast and unqualified as the redeeming love on which it rests.'[1]

To be reconciled to God is to be reconciled to life. To be at one with God is to be at home in the universe. The reactions of the order with which we now live in harmony set like a tide towards our perfecting. 'All things work together for good to them that love God.' Love has taken the place of fate. Possessing it and being possessed by it, we possess all things. We cross every chasm, even the ultimate gulf of death, and find ourselves still in a region where love is king.

The NT is a lyric; but it is not a freak of poetic fancy. It is the song of a victory won, the record of an experience, not the less reliable that it is amazing, an inference which is strictly logical, from the greater to the less, though it surpass all calculation. 'He that spared not his own Son, but delivered him up for us all, how shall he not with him also freely give us all things?' (Ro 8^{32}).

(*b*) *The Christian attitude towards suffering.*—(1) Pain means obstruction of life. It is essentially evil. It is not the intention of God that any of His sentient creatures should suffer. It is not possible to say to every sufferer, 'God sent you this; He has laid this affliction upon you.' This judgment upon suffering as evil will be assailed from many points of view, scientific, ethical, and religious. Suffering, it will be said, is inevitable, as an element in the evolution of the world. It was experienced by innumerable sentient creatures millenniums before man appeared on the earth, before the first sin was committed. Suffering, it will be urged, is a splendid moral discipline. It is, therefore, a good, of which no man can complain that he has had too much. It is sufficient to reply that the Author and Object of Christian faith, the Revealer and the Organ of the infinite love, did not think so. He steadfastly set Himself to reduce the sum of pain. So far as we know, He never met a case of pain which He did not relieve, if the conditions were present for His doing so. In such action He Himself suffered exceedingly. He made no moan. He recognized such suffering to be necessary to the fulfilment of His redeeming vocation (Mt 8^{17}). But His doing so cannot be construed as an approval of pain. Rather was it a judgment upon pain as an evil to be removed at any cost of pain. This judgment, moreover, was not an implicit hedonism. It would be ridiculous to make such a suggestion regarding the teaching of Jesus. He never taught that it was a primary concern of God's love to keep His creatures immune from suffering. He absolutely denied that the crown of life was pleasure. But this cannot be construed to mean that He regarded suffering as a good, or asceticism as the ideal of life, or sorrow as the soul of religion. It does imply, however, that He regarded the condition of the world as abnormal. He occupies the point of view of the religious mind of Israel in looking upon the world as standing in intimate and vital relation with human life. There is a strict relevance between these two. If there be evil in man, there will be pain in nature. Nature stands so near to spirit that it thrills responsive to the breach that sin has wrought between the human spirit and the divine. Paul is enlarging the same idea inherited from the OT, and reinterpreted through the death and resurrection of the Redeemer, when He speaks of the 'sighing of creation,' of its subjection to ματαιότης and its share in the hope of redemption (Ro 8^{18-22}). There is suffering in nature; and there is suffering in man as part of nature. And all suffering, in nature or in little children, is the exposition and illustration of that which, in self-conscious and self-determining man, is sin. Dogmatism regarding the origin of sin and suffering is forbidden. To appeal to predestination for a theory is to bring the Eternal within the limits of time. We have nothing to do with origins. We have to do only with meanings and values. And this is the meaning which Christianity puts on pain. It means intensely; and it means evil. The first thing to be done with it is

[1] J. Denney, *Christian Doctrine of Reconciliation*, p. 330 f.; see also pp. 1, 3, 177–179.

not to discuss it or apologize for it, but to relieve it, if possible, and at least administer the healing of sympathy. This, then, is the first position of Christianity with respect to pain: it is not God's will for His creatures that they should suffer; it is His will that pain shall be abolished from His universe for evermore.

(2) Pain is not an unanswerable challenge to theism. It is not inconsistent with the supremacy of love. Love has won an eternal victory in an event which occurred in time. Love has snatched victory from defeat. It has transmuted the foulest crime of man into the instrument of the divine redemption. It has done this greatest thing. How shall it not accomplish all lesser things in the same order? He who redeems from sin will not be baffled by suffering. It is to be noted carefully that Christian thought, in claiming that God is not hindered by the obstacle of pain, is not passing from ethical to non-ethical considerations, giving up love to take up power. What Christian experience finds in the Cross of Christ is not an incident, an act over and done with, like the punishment of a criminal. It is the historic revelation of that which is in essence timeless, and endures through all time, and triumphs in all history, viz. the atoning love of God. The Cross is the supreme revelation of the divine immanence. God is present in all pain. He suffers in all suffering. He is the chief sufferer in the world.

Theology has never done justice to the surest affirmation of faith: 'In all their affliction he was afflicted.' The incarnation of God in Christ is the deepest truth of the divine relation to the world. Nicene orthodoxy is not orthodox enough. Misled by the Greek conception of the Absolute, it ascribes divinity to One who, nevertheless, has an experience of which God is incapable. But the God whom faith finds in Christ is the only God there is. He suffers in all that sin has wrought, and His suffering is the redemption of the world. Christianity meets the challenge of pain, not by anxious computations of the amount of good which may be extracted from the agonies that fill the records of time, but by the unveiling of the suffering of God. The Cross is the only Christian apologetic. Only through the suffering of God is it tolerable to suppose that a world with pain in it is His world, reconciled to Him, and carrying within its tragic history the energy of omnipotent redeeming love. We time-determined consciousnesses cannot pretend to understand God; but we know Him with an estimate that is sure and pierces the inevitable mists of time. God is love. This we know. For the rest we can afford to wait.

(3) Christianity sets out in the name and by the power of a victory already won, on its age-long vocation—the conquest of sin and suffering. To accept at God's hands the deliverance He has wrought by pain is to be committed to a perpetual war with pain. The campaign is world-wide. The battles are innumerable. The fundamental strategy is to utilize for every instance of pain the energy of love, which is the very nature of God and is available and adequate for the redemption of man. In this matter it may be that Church theology and Church policy have lagged behind the actual experience of Christians and have failed to push home the victory.

Three lines of action are prescribed by the consciousness of redemption. (i.) The employment of pain. It is here that optimism is most at home. Browning has rung out the answering challenge to pain. It is absolutely true that in a sinful world the perfecting of souls is won through suffering. We are to react on the pains we endure, and so make them subservient to the development of moral stature. We are bound to be swift and earnest in this subjection of pain to our uses; for the opportunity of so employing it passes with the passing moment. We are to lay to heart the thought which finds eloquent expression in Ugo Bassi's 'Sermon in the Hospital':

> 'While we suffer, let us set our souls
> To suffer perfectly: since this alone,
> The suffering, which is this world's special grace,
> May here be perfected and left behind.'[1]

All this is to be accepted, rejoiced in, and practised. The only reservation to be made is that such considerations do not establish optimism as a theory. The data are not broad enough. The victory over pain must first be won before specific sufferings can be attacked in detail and made to yield booty to the conqueror. This is the paradox of the higher life of man. Apart from this sure base in triumphant love, the flood of irrelevant pain in nature and history would rout the most confident optimism.

(ii.) The mastery of conditions. This is the sphere of organized ministry. All such service, whether operated by idealists or materialists, Christians or non-Christians, proceeds on the supposition that the conditions of human life are abnormal, and that, before full vigorous life can be enjoyed, these conditions must be improved. Another presupposition, however, has to be made if such ministerial aid to sufferers is to be completely successful, and is to be rendered, not merely with skill and fidelity, but with the energy of perfect confidence. We must be certified that in rendering such help we have the universe on our side, that resident within it are forces capable of carrying sentient creatures to such complete and harmonious exercise of function as shall be a perfect victory over pain. No alteration of conditions will be of any avail in social service or in medical work, unless there be this fountain of energy, discharging itself for ever through these channels. Apart from this, we shall not escape the verdict of pessimism on our most abundant efforts. Many will appeal to 'Nature'; but Christianity knows nothing of personified abstractions. It goes deep into experience, and finds the living God, triumphant over pain, and pouring the energy of His Spirit through channels of human ministry. Such an experience of God binds upon those who share it an inescapable obligation of combating pain of every kind, wheresoever it shows its desolating presence. They are the fellow-workers, without question or criticism, of all of any creed, or none, who will do this work and become conscious or unconscious instruments of love, suffering and victorious.

(iii.) The direct exhibition of the ultimate cure of pain, viz. the love of God in Christ. This is not an extravagance of unreasoning emotionalism. It is sober fact, verified in innumerable instances; God's love does heal pain. If the love of God were regnant in all human life, how much of the world's pain would remain? This is not an abstract speculation; it is a question whose answer cannot be arithmetically complete, and yet is absolutely sure, and admits of boundless practical application. We must make thorough work of the category of solidarity. Soul and body, man and man, race and race, humanity and nature: the universe is organic to the core. It lives from the centre. By the lines of solidarity pain has penetrated to the last filament of the vast web of life. By the same lines of solidarity the healing of pain will go spreading through the entire creation which now waits with eager longing for the revelation of the sons of God. Man's part in this comprehensive conquest of pain corresponds to his place and function in the world. In him the meaning and value of the world are consciously apprehended and uttered. By him too they have been grievously mistaken, and the forces which should have filled the world with the peace and joy of functions normally operating and perfectly fulfilled have been hindered, and the world of man and nature has been put to illimitable torture. It is not morbid when a man sees in the pain of innocent children, of wronged womanhood, and even of the creatures beneath our rank, the sign and seal of his own sin, the issues of a mighty evil in which he is confederate. It is the simple truth.

Therefore man has special work to do in the healing of pain. He has to receive the healing which love can bestow in his own experience, allowing it unhindered exercise as he is reconciled to God and to life. He has to become the conscious organ of that healing to all who suffer. He is never to inflict pain except in so far as pain, in the conditions under which we live (themselves abnormal), is the instrument of moral or physical benefit. He is to be ceaselessly the channel of the love of God to man. Simply by being in the communion of God, one living in the divine love becomes source and centre of healing to the souls and bodies of all around. The evidence is matter of daily experience. Yet the power of healing is not a bare physical force. It requires conscious appropriation and direction. Love that heals is not magic. It is effective as a vocation, accepted and fulfilled. The specific task of love belongs to the manifold opportunities of life, and these are innumerable. They include all ministries of help. In particular, two great obligations rest on all in whom love is doing its reconciling and healing work. One is witness, the other is prayer. The Church, called into being by love's deed, has been

[1] H. E. Hamilton King, *The Disciples*[9], London, 1887, p. 191.

slow in its recognition of these evident duties—slower, and less confident, in respect of the second than of the first. Yet it is in prayer that the function and high privilege of humanity do chiefly consist. By prayer man enters the sanctuary of the divine immanence. In prayer the indwelling love finds another home and citadel, a new centre from which to work. Prayer is the liberation of the spiritual energies that are saving the world. Prayer provides God with the conditions without which an Omnipotence that is moral, and not physical, dare not and cannot work. The question will be asked, Does this mean that any given pain can be relieved by prayer? The answer must be that dogmatism and prediction are forbidden by the organic structure of the universe. No man sins by himself or suffers by himself, and no man is redeemed for himself alone. It is impossible to cut a man out of the texture of his existence and operate on him as though he were an unrelated atom moving in empty space. We have no calculus by which to work out the measurements of the individual's sin and sufferings or to forecast the immediacy and completeness of his deliverance. At the same time, our answer must not 'limit God.' He certainly does not fling about His powers, healing at haphazard. But with equal confidence we may affirm that His healing power is available beyond any measure in which men have permitted it to operate. The *ordo salutis* here is fixed and cannot be altered: first the reconciliation, then the healing; first the faith that commits itself absolutely to God in Christ, then the faith that refuses no gift of God.

The experience recorded in the NT is normative. First, believers owned Jesus Lord, then they received the Spirit. The love to which they committed themselves lived on in them, and wrought mightily. No complete catalogue of such operations could be given. But among the lists that are given we read of healings (1 Co $12^{9.28}$). The gifts of the Spirit are not magical, and there is nothing stereotyped in the activities produced by them. It would be ridiculous to infer from the presence of a certain gift in the NT communities that it must be perpetual in the Church of all ages. The gifts were created for use. If the use ceased, the gift was withdrawn. But is it fair to regard healing as a sporadic and passing manifestation of the Spirit's presence? Healing of the world's pain is certainly part of the world's redemption. Is it proper to make a distinction here and say that we will believe in the forgiveness of sins, but draw the line at the relief of pain? It may be that sects which we justly condemn for their absurd metaphysic and their ridiculous jargon, and for faults graver still, have such influence as belongs to them because they have been bold enough to rely on a healing power which belongs to the love that was, in Christ, the reconciliation of the world. It may be that the Church has to learn in this matter from those whom, quite justifiably, it has excluded from its fellowship. In any case, the conquest of pain is the work of omnipotent atoning love; and in prayer man co-operates with God in healing the hurt of humanity and of the world.

(4) Christian faith is more than conqueror of pain and can do much more for the sufferer than relieve him of his distress. Christianity teaches the transmutation of pain. Those who love God find that all things, pain included, work together for their good. As they go deeper into the experience of suffering, they make a still more wonderful discovery. In their pain they are not alone. They meet in that sequestered place Another, and He too is a sufferer. These two pains, theirs and His, draw together into the unity of one experience—He in them, and they in Him; their pain His, His pain theirs. This is not to escape from pain. It is to take out of pain the element which makes it an evil. When the self is surrendered to the love of God in Christ, the sting of pain, which is sin, is taken out of it. It becomes straightway part of a life-fellowship with redeeming love. It undergoes a complete transmutation. It has been taken up into the pain that is the price of the world's redemption. There is no question of diminishing the value of love's redeeming deed on the Cross of Christ. But the method of triumphant love remains. The ages reproduce the method of Calvary. The sufferings of Christ rise like a tide in the souls of His people (Ph 3^{10}, Col 1^{24}). Their sufferings take on the quality of His. They are ministerial, vicarious, sacrificial. They are not on that account less hard to bear. Were shame and spitting, thorns and nails, less painful because Jesus bore them as part of His obedience? Suffering borne with Him is suffering still. It is, however, bearable, and far more than bearable. It is utterly changed. It is not a fate, but a vocation, the highest service that a soul can render to God or man. Its evil is blotted out. It is a moment in the being of the highest good. This does not mean that in every suffering a believing man will be conscious that it is good. The pain may inhibit the sense of joy, even as it did with Jesus on the Cross. But none the less is it received and retained by the servant of God as the crown of his ministry, even as Jesus refused to come down from His Cross.

Perhaps James Hinton overstrains the thought when he suggests that our feeling of pain in sacrifice is due to the lack of a perfect love in us. Sacrifice is pain; but in deepest anguish we know it preferable to the best that the world can give.

> 'Remembering these things . . . what should we consider the presence of pain in the world to mean? . . . Does it not mean that a world in which so much of pain is present, is adapted—was altogether made—to be the scene of an overpowering, an absorbing love? . . . The reason we are made, or seem as if we were made for pain, is that we are made for love. . . .
>
> What is the happiness God has meant us for, the happiness to which human nature is fitted, to which it should aspire? Should it be that from which the painful is banished, or that in which pain is latent? Should pain be merely absent, or swallowed up in love and turned to joy? . . .
>
> The pain that is latent in man's bliss is latent, too, in God's; in His most as He is highest: and that great life and death to which the eyes of men are ever turned, or wandering ever are recalled, reveals it to us. . . .
>
> All pains may be summed up in sacrifice; and sacrifice is—of course it is—the instrument of joy.'[1]

This is a nobler optimism than that which rests its case on the fruitage of benefit out of pain. Browning, who is the poet of the one, has not missed the other:

> 'I think this is the authentic sign and seal
> Of Godship, that it ever waxes glad,
> And more glad, until gladness blossoms, bursts
> Into a rage to suffer for mankind,
> And recommence at sorrow: drops like seed
> After the blossom, ultimate of all.'[2]

The mystery of pain, then, is hid with Christ in God and becomes the open secret of the universe. All pain is a symbol of the suffering of God, and fulfils the function of sacrifice. These innumerable untold and incalculable pains of nature and of humanity are drawn into the compass of the atoning suffering of God. The sign of the Cross is upon a world of sin. The ministerial, vicarious, sacrificial quality of suffering begins very early in the history of the world. Its presence is ever more closely marked as the scale of being rises. It can be traced in each stage of the 'ascent of man.' It can be followed along the whole course of that river of blood and tears which flows through human history. It is useless to make computations, and ask, Was even redemption worth such a price? It would

[1] *The Mystery of Pain*[2], pp. 37, 38, 39, 40, 52.
[2] *Balaustion's Adventure.*

not be, if the price paid were merely human pain. But within the human pain is hid the anguish of crucified love. It is part of 'the reproach of Christ.' Because the infinite love shares this pain, it is transmuted. It becomes part of the price which God pays. Nothing could apologize for God, not any benefit wrung from tortured bodies and slaughtered souls, if He merely looked on from a throne of omnipotence. But a God who suffers is immune from our criticism and does not need our defence. The suffering of love has redeemed the world and has not lost its redeeming power.

Confessedly, this is a faith, not a theory. It is not the less, but the more, sure on that account. It is not a precarious inference from insecure premisses. Its premisses are the love and suffering of God, revealed in the ministry and the Cross of Christ, and apprehended in the act which commits the soul to their redeeming power. Faith is not an act finished in a spasm of emotion. It is the assumption of an attitude towards God and towards life, warranted and established by God's redeeming action.

Faith, says a great Christian teacher, 'is the whole being and attitude of the soul as determined by the sin-bearing love of God in Christ. That love, and that love alone, evokes it, and on that love and that alone, it rests.'[1]

Therefore, Christian optimism is not a document which can be signed, sealed, and delivered to a suffering world to solve the whole problem of suffering. It is the outcome of an experience. Experience cannot be finished, gathered up, and put aside. It lives and grows from a centre. Those who will know the force of its demonstration must occupy the central standpoint. As that is reached in the act of self-commitment to the appeal of divine suffering love, it can be retained only in the continued action of communion with God. Faith in divine providence is not easy. Did any serious thinker ever imagine a state of mind in which faith would rest on an argument? Faith is a post held in the midst of a furious attack which never ceases. It can be held only in prayer. Prayer is at once communion and co-operation with God. In both aspects it carries with it confirmation of faith. Without it faith withers and dies. As we live by receiving the divine love and by acting in the power of it, even to the last limit of devotion, the world where men suffer reveals itself as still within the compass of a sovereign purpose which through pain is passing to its victory. And prayer is the concentrated power of that life, the life of receiving and of giving. Prayer, therefore, conveys the final proof of divine providence. In prayer the darkness of suffering comes into the light of divine victorious love.

(5) Lastly, the Christian view of pain is available for comfort. Comfort for such suffering as the world is full of cannot consist in words.

'The philosopher's generalisations falter, and only the professional pietist, babbling about all being for the best, keeps on talking. His observations are highly admirable. But even faith is almost ashamed of them. It is better to say nothing. There is simply nothing to be said.'[2]

The only offer of comfort that will not insult the sufferer comes from the love of a God who can and does suffer. This is the knowledge we have of Him. Where suffering is He is, in the fullness of a power won by His own pain. Outside of Him there is no comfort. A world without suffering love at the heart of it would be an atheistic world. The last word regarding it would be unrelieved pessimism.

Comfort is the work of God within the soul. It is direct, immediate, as the divine Spirit enfolds the human in the unity of a mutual indwelling. Its action is beneath the eye of the observer; and it fulfils its mission when there is no eye to see, no heart to pity. It is the privilege of creatures whose consciousness is other than human. It upholds those who are not conscious of its operations. Beneath their pain there is a divine experience of which theirs is part. Christianity is withheld from pessimism, only because it holds thus profoundly the truth of the divine immanence. Only so is it withheld from blasphemy, as it beholds the agonies of the world. Even so, it is dumb with amazement. All the more earnestly does it lay upon those who have received the Divine consolations the duty of ministering to those who suffer. Their fulfilment of this duty consists in making themselves the vehicles of redeeming love. They have nothing of their own to give. The comfort they can give is simply the comfort they have received, and that is the love of God. Whatever they say and do will be effective as it bears witness to, and is the medium of, this —the only medicine for human hurt. In many cases silence will be the most perfect human vehicle of the divine comfort.

The Christian view of pain does not warrant the conclusion that in the case of the individual all suffering will cease. The organism is disordered, and the elimination of pain cannot take place at haphazard. The doctrine of divine providence, however, rests on the eternal victory of love, of which the time-development of the world contains the progressive achievement. It, therefore, becomes a prediction of that which will emerge out of time—the complete reconciliation of the world.

Without this, comfort in suffering would be incomplete. God has no comfort to give if He is uncertain of victory. Love is triumphant over sin and suffering; therefore both sin and suffering will cease to be. The final message of Christianity to a suffering world is one of an immortal hope: 'There shall be no more death, neither sorrow, nor crying, neither shall there be any more pain; for the former things are passed away.'

LITERATURE.—See references in artt. PESSIMISM AND OPTIMISM and GOOD AND EVIL; and art. 'Pessimism' in *EBr*[11]. Almost all volumes dealing with the philosophy of religion, or with Christian apologetic or dogmatic, have discussions of the topic. A selection of English works is here appended. J. Sully, *Pessimism, a History and a Criticism*[2], London, 1892; John Tulloch, *Modern Theories in Philosophy and Religion*, Edinburgh, 1884; Robert Flint, *Anti-theistic Theories*[5], do. 1894; W. L. Davidson, *The Stoic Creed*, do. 1907; E. Naville, *Le Problème du mal*, Lausanne, 1868, Eng. tr., Edinburgh, 1871; A. M. Fairbairn, *The Philosophy of the Christian Religion*, London, 1902; J. Ward, *The Realm of Ends*, Cambridge, 1911; A. Seth Pringle-Pattison, *The Idea of God*, Oxford, 1917; John Watson, *The Philosophical Basis of Religion*, Glasgow, 1907, *The Interpretation of Religious Experience*, 2 vols., do. 1912; E. Caird, *The Evolution of Religion*, 2 vols., do. 1893, *The Evolution of Theology in the Greek Philosophers*, 2 vols., do. 1904; A. C. Fraser, *Philosophy of Theism*[2], Edinburgh, 1899; J. Oswald Dykes, *The Divine Worker in Creation and Providence*, do. 1909; Horace Bushnell, *The Moral Uses of Dark Things*, New York, 1868; Henry Jones, *Browning as a Philosophical and Religious Teacher*, London, 1891; J. Y. Simpson, *The Spiritual Interpretation of Nature*, Edinburgh, 1912; P. Carnegie Simpson, *The Facts of Life*, London, 1913; C. F. D'Arcy, *God and Freedom in Human Experience*, do. 1915; R. L. Ottley, *Christian Ideas and Ideals*, do. 1909; B. H. Streeter and others, *Concerning Prayer*, do. 1916; F. J. Foakes-Jackson and others, *The Faith and the War*, do. 1915; [L. Dougall], *The Christian Doctrine of Health*, do. 1916; W. R. Sorley and others, *The Elements of Pain and Conflict in Human Life*, Cambridge, 1916; J. Orr, *The Christian View of God and the World*[3], Edinburgh, 1897; A. K. Rogers, *The Religious Conception of the World*, New York and London, 1907; G. J. Blewett, *The Christian View of the World*, New Haven, U.S.A., and London, 1912; William James, *Pragmatism*, London, 1907; A. B. Bruce, *The Moral Order of the World*, do. 1899, *The Providential Order of the World*, do. 1897; C. C. Everett, *Theism and the Christian Faith*, New York and London, 1909; W. L. Walker, *Christian Theism and a Spiritual Monism*, Edinburgh, 1906; G. C. Workman, *At Onement*, London, 1911; Henry Drummond, *The Ascent of Man*, do. 1894; W. S. Palmer, *Providence and Faith*, do. 1917; Douglas White, *Forgiveness and Suffering*, Cambridge, 1913; W. F. Cobb, *Spiritual Healing*, London, 1914; Frank Ballard, *Why does not God intervene?*, do. 1912; James Hinton, *The Mystery of Pain*[2], do. 1907; J. H. Brookes, *The Mystery of Suffering*, New York, 1903; P.

[1] Denney, *Christian Doctrine of Reconciliation*, p. 295.
[2] Carnegie Simpson, *Facts of Life*, p. 72.

Laurent, *The Mission of Pain*, Eng. tr., London, 1910; V. C. Harrington, *Problem of Human Suffering*, New York, 1899; J. Denney, *The Christian Doctrine of Reconciliation*, London, 1917; J. E. McFadyen, *Jesus and Life*, do. 1917; G. Steven, *The Warp and the Woof*, do. 1917; W. R. Sorley, *Moral Values and the Idea of God*, Cambridge, 1918.

T. B. KILPATRICK.

SUFFERING MESSIAH. — See JESUS CHRIST, vii. 514, MESSIAH, viii. 574ª.

ṢŪFĪS. — **1. Derivation and meaning.** — The derivation of the name 'Ṣūfīs' (Muḥammadan mystics) was long a subject of dispute. Most Ṣūfīs favour the theory that it is derived from *ṣafā* ('purity') and that the Ṣūfī is one of the elect who have become purified from all worldly defilements. Others would connect it with *ṣaff* ('rank'), as though the Ṣūfī were spiritually in the first rank in virtue of his communion with God; or with *ṣuffa* ('bench'), referring the origin of Ṣūfism[1] to the Ahl al-ṣuffa ('people of the bench'), a title given to certain poor Muslims in the early days of Islām who had no house or lodging and therefore used to take shelter on the covered bench outside the mosque built by the Prophet at Medīna. As Qushairī and other Ṣūfīs admit, none of these explanations is etymologically defensible. There is, however, among the derivations proposed by the Ṣūfīs themselves one which does not violate the principles of etymology. The author of the oldest extant Arabic treatise on Ṣūfism, Abū Naṣr al-Sarrāj, declares that in his opinion (which, naturally, is not based on philological grounds) the word 'Ṣūfī' is derived from *ṣūf* ('wool'), 'for the woollen raiment is the habit of the prophets and the badge of the saints and elect, as appears in many traditions and narratives.'[2] Notwithstanding the facetious remark of Scaliger, 'quod quidam Sofi a flocco lanae dictum uolunt, hoc leuius est ipso flocco lanae,' it was perceived by some European Orientalists in the 18th cent. that this derivation was what Reiske pronounced it to be—'sola uera et grammaticae ipsique rei congrua.' Meanwhile its claims to acceptance were challenged by Joseph von Hammer, who in his *Gesch. der schönen Redekünste Persiens*,[3] asserted that the Ṣūfīs are related to the ancient gymnosophists of India and that 'the Arabic words Ṣūfī (mystic) and *ṣāfī* (pure) belong to the same root, like the Greek σοφός and σαφής.' This unlucky sentence might cast doubt on von Hammer's competence as a philologist, but his suggested equation of 'Ṣūfī' with σοφός was, at first sight, plausible enough. Although rejected by Tholuck,[4] it has been championed in comparatively recent times by Adalbert Merx.[5] In 1894 the question was finally settled by Th. Nöldeke, at that time Professor of Arabic in the University of Strassburg. He pointed out[6] that the word σοφός is unknown in Aramaic and therefore could scarcely be expected to occur in Arabic. On the other hand, both Aramaic and Arabic have the words σοφιστής and φιλόσοφος, and in the latter language the σ is represented by *sīn* (س), as is almost invariably the case in Greek words which have been Arabicized, not by *ṣād* (ص). If 'Ṣūfī' were of Greek extraction, its initial *ṣād* would be at least abnormal. Further, we have no positive ground for regarding the derivation from σοφός as probable in itself, whereas the derivation from *ṣūf* is confirmed by the authority of Oriental tradition. Nöldeke then cites a number of passages showing that, in the first two centuries of Islām, garments of coarse wool were worn by the common people and especially by those who followed an ascetic way of life. The words *labisa 'l-ṣūf*, 'he clad himself in wool,' occur frequently in the early literature and signify that the person to whom they are applied has renounced the world and become an ascetic; at a later period, when asceticism passed into mysticism, *labisa 'l-ṣūf* generally means 'he became a Ṣūfī.' In Persian too the ascetic is often called *pashmīna-pūsh*, *i.e.* 'wearing a woollen garment.' The old Muslim ascetics who clothed themselves in wool borrowed this practice from Christian hermits or monks. When Ḥammād b. Salama († A.D. 784) came to Baṣra, he said to Farqad al-Sanjī, who appeared before him in a woollen garment, 'Put off this (emblem of) Christianity.'[1] Such garments are described as *ziyy al-ruhbān*, 'the dress of the Christian ascetics.'[2] A *ḥadīth* put in the mouth of the Prophet states that Jesus Himself used to wear them.

We are told by Jāmī[3] that the name 'Ṣūfī' was first borne by Abū Hāshim of Kūfa, a contemporary of Sufyān al-Thaurī († A.D. 778). According to Qushairī,[4] it came into vogue before A.H. 200 (=A.D. 815). Al-Sarrāj mentions the view that it was invented by the people of Baghdād.[5] Although the circumstances of its origin are obscure, it seems to have gained currency during the period of transition from asceticism to mysticism, about the end of the 2nd cent. of the Hijrah, and may possibly mark some stage in that process. No weight can be attached to the apocryphal traditions which seek to prove that the appellation existed in the Prophet's time or even throw it back into the pre-Islāmic age. The Ṣūfīs of the 3rd and 4th centuries, who claimed to be the true spiritual descendants of Muḥammad, considered themselves fully justified in fabricating evidence in support of their assertion. So far as the present writer is aware, the first Arabic writer to use the word 'Ṣūfī' is Jāḥiẓ of Baṣra († A.D. 869), who refers to 'the Ṣūfīs amongst the pietists' (*al-Ṣūfīya mina 'l-nussāk*) and enumerates the names of several who were famous for their eloquence.[6]

In the present article the terms 'Ṣūfī' and 'Ṣūfism' are to be understood in their ordinary sense, viz. as equivalent to 'Muḥammadan mystic' and 'Muḥammadan mysticism.' Ancient Ṣūfism, however, had strong ascetic tendencies, while the mystical element might be insignificant; and there have always been Ṣūfīs of an ascetic and devotional type whom we should hesitate to describe as mystics in the proper meaning of the word. In Persian and Turkish poetry 'Ṣūfī' sometimes bears the sense of 'hypocritical pietist' or 'dissolute free-thinker' and may be used as a term of reproach by poets who are themselves Ṣūfīs of a different sort.[7]

2. Origin and early development.—The beginnings of mysticism in Islām take us back to the great ascetic movement which arose, largely under Christian influence, during the 7th cent. A.D.[8] This is reflected in the biographical works containing notices of eminent Ṣūfīs, which include the names of many of those early ascetics. The movement, though extreme in certain directions, was mainly orthodox. It is characterized by

1 'Ṣūfism' is the more correct form. 'Ṣūfiism' implies derivation from 'Ṣūfī,' whereas the corresponding Arabic words *taṣawwuf* and *ṣūfī* are collateral formations from *ṣūf*, which is the common root of both.
2 *Kitāb al-Luma'*, ed. R. A. Nicholson, London, 1916, p. 20 f.
3 Vienna, 1818, p. 346, note 1.
4 *Ssufismus*, p. 30 f.
5 *Idee und Grundlinien einer allgemeinen Gesch. der Mystik*, p. 37 f.
6 *ZDMG* xlviii. [1891] 45 f.

1 *'Iqd*, Cairo, A.H. 1293, iii. 348.
2 Sha'rānī, *Lawāqiḥ*, i. 45.
3 *Nafaḥāt al-uns*, ed. W. N. Lees, Calcutta, 1859, p. 34.
4 *Risāla*, Cairo, A.H. 1318, p. 9.
5 *Kitāb al-Luma'*, p. 22.
6 *Kitāb al-bayān*, Cairo, A.H. 1313, i. 138.
7 Cf. E. J. W. Gibb, *Hist. of Ottoman Poetry*, London, 1900–09, i. 25 f.
8 See art. ASCETICISM (Muslim).

intense religious exaltation, an overwhelming consciousness of human frailty, boundless fear of God, and utter submission to His will. There was no organized monastic life, though some ascetics wandered to and fro accompanied by a few friends or held prayer-meetings in which they studied the Qur'ān and discussed their spiritual experiences. Baṣra seems to have been the centre of an anti-ritualistic party who laid stress on the higher aspects of asceticism, regarding it as essentially an inward feeling, whereas the Syrians were more concerned with its external forms;[1] Ḥasan al-Baṣrī (*q.v.*) said that it consisted in humility and was not a matter of dress and food. Examination of what is involved in the first article of the Muslim creed—the command to associate nothing with Allāh—gradually led to the view that true asceticism is incompatible with any selfish desire, even with the desire to undergo the utmost privations and austerities for the sake of winning paradise, and that it must culminate in disinterested love of God.[2] Thus the old asceticism, rooted in fanatical exaggeration of religious observances, gave way to a doctrine which in the end threatened to make all observances unnecessary. But this consequence did not show itself immediately. The Ṣūfīs of the 2nd cent. were usually orthodox and law-abiding. They cultivated poverty, self-abasement, resignation. If they loved God, they feared Him more, and on the whole their mysticism lacked positive qualities as well as distinctive theories. They stand midway between asceticism (*zuhd*) and theosophy, or gnosis (*ma'rifat*). The word that best describes their attitude is 'quietism' (*riḍā*).

Special mention may be made of Ibrāhīm b. Adham, a prince of Balkh, whose legend is modelled on the story of Buddha;[3] Shaqīq, also of Balkh, who developed the doctrine of 'trust in God' (*tawakkul*);[4] Rābi'a al-'Adawīya, a saintly woman who was born at Baṣra and died at Jerusalem;[5] and Ma'rūf al-Karkhī, a native of Baghdād.[6] The two last-named foreshadow the ecstatic and enthusiastic mysticism which is characteristic of the succeeding age, although it may be doubted whether all the sayings and verses attributed to Rābi'a on the subject of divine love are genuine. Ma'rūf is the author of the first recorded definition of Ṣūfism, 'to grasp the verities and to renounce that which is in the hands of God's creatures.'[7]

During the 3rd cent. Ṣūfism enters decisively on a new course. The ascetic and quietistic spirit, though still strong, is overpowered by speculative and pantheistic tendencies which had hitherto remained in the background but now assert themselves with increasing boldness. Notwithstanding the dominant and vital part which these tendencies play in the future development of Ṣūfism, it is a mistake to identify their triumph with the origin of Ṣūfism. Nor is it less a mistake to describe them as an entirely foreign element which flowed into Ṣūfism from outside and rapidly transformed it, so that all at once it became different in kind. The germs of Ṣūfī pantheism are to be found in the Qur'ān:

E.g., xxviii. 88: 'Every thing is perishing (*hālik*) except the face (reality) of Allah'; lv. 26 f.: 'Every one on the earth is passing away (*fānī*), but the glorious and honoured face of thy Lord abideth for ever'; and ii. 109: 'Wheresoever ye turn, there is the face of Allah.'

Certainly the Muslim mystics might have arrived independently at the conclusion that Allāh is the only real being.

'It is conceivable that this notion may have come into Islam from outside; on the other hand, speculation on the doctrine of the divine unity appears sufficient to account for its development and indeed for its origin. Had there been more gods than one, says the Koran, the heavens and the earth must have come to grief; but if any attempt be made to define the word "god" metaphysically, speculation quickly leads to something like the truly existing or the necessarily existing; even with Homer the difference between God and man is that the former is eternal, the latter transient. The relation between God and matter immediately suggests questions: is matter independent of God, or not? The former supposition leads to polytheism, the latter only is consistent with real monotheism. If, then, God is not outside matter, He must in a way be identical with matter; and the most thoughtful of the Ṣūfis, accepting this conclusion, based on it a series of inferences as unlike the original doctrines of Islam as any that could have been evolved.'[1]

Theoretically, there is no reason why the Ṣūfīs should not have reached their pantheistic goal in some such fashion as this, and probably they often did, although in most cases it was a truth grasped intuitively from mystical experience rather than the result of philosophical reflexion. But, in seeking to explain how they advanced from quietism to pantheism, we cannot proceed on the assumption that they were wholly impervious to non-Islāmic ideas. The influence of Christianity, Neo-Platonism, and Buddhism is an undeniable fact. It was in the air and inevitably made itself felt. Of its extent and importance we have ample evidence, although the materials at our disposal seldom enable us to trace it out in detail. In short the new Ṣūfism of the 3rd cent., like Ṣūfism in every period of its history, is the product of diverse forces working together — speculative developments of the Muḥammadan monotheistic idea, Christian asceticism and mysticism, Gnosticism, Greek and Indian philosophies. Until recently the problem has been attacked on the wrong lines. Many former investigators held the view that this great movement, which drew its life and strength from all classes and races in the Muslim empire, could be adequately explained by pointing to one definite source (*e.g.*, the Vedānta or Neo-Platonism) or by formulating theories which are at best half-truths (*e.g.*, that Ṣūfism was a reaction of the Aryan mind against a Semitic religion forcibly imposed on it). It is now, the present writer thinks, recognized that, instead of searching in vain after a single cause, we should endeavour to study the various influences by which the Ṣūfī doctrine was moulded, to place them in due order and connexion, and to distinguish as far as possible what was contributed by each. These influences constitute the environment in which the doctrine developed, and among them are to be reckoned all political, social, and intellectual conditions which favoured the growth of mysticism, such as the devastating civil wars of the Umayyad period, the sceptical and rationalistic currents that ran strongly in the early 'Abbāsid age, and particularly the bitter sectarianism and barren dogmatism of the '*ulamā*.

The main features in the evolution of Ṣūfism in the 3rd cent. may be set forth as follows.

The older Ṣūfīs had sought to bring every word, act, and thought of their lives into harmony with the divine will—an ideal which expressed their conception of Allāh as a transcendent personality, 'the Lord of created beings,' and which they attained by means of asceticism. This theory and practice naturally produced (1) the doctrine of divine love, which is the highest positive form of quietism, and (2) ecstasy, which is frequently a result, either involuntary or intentional, of ascetic exercises. Although the early Ṣūfīs were more or less orthodox, their relation to Islām being not unlike that of the mediæval Spanish mystics to the Roman Catholic Church, a religion of love and ecstasy was bound to come into conflict with Islām sooner or later. Rābi'a declared that she had no

1 *Qūt al-qulūb*, Cairo, A.H. 1310, i. 129.
2 Cf. D. S. Margoliouth, *The Early Development of Mohammedanism*, p. 167 f.
3 See art. 'Ibrāhīm b. Adham' in *EI*; Goldziher, in *JRAS*, 1904, p. 132 f.; Nicholson, in *ZA* xxvi. [1911] 215 f.
4 See art. ASCETICISM (Muslim).
5 See von Kremer, *Gesch. der herrschenden Ideen des Islams*, p. 64 f.; R. Dozy, *Essai sur l'hist. de l'islamisme*, tr V. Chauvin, Leyden, 1879, p. 318 f.; Nicholson, *A Literary Hist. of the Arabs*, London, 1907, p. 233 f.
6 See *JRAS*, 1906, p. 306 f.
7 *Ib.* p. 331.

1 Margoliouth, *The Early Development of Mohammedanism*, p. 180 f.

fear of hell or hope of paradise, and that she could not love the Prophet because her love of God absorbed her so entirely that neither love nor hate of any other thing remained in her heart. The barrier between Allāh and His creatures was gradually broken down. The definition of divine unity (*tauḥīd*) became pantheistic; the unique personality of Allāh, far above and beyond human reach, was transformed into the one real Being (*al-Ḥaqq*) revealed in all created things, the mystic's true self, which he finds by losing his individual consciousness in ecstatic self-abandonment. This doctrine, however it may be disguised, is the essence of Ṣūfism, and the historical circumstances of its origin justify the statement that it was at least partially derived from sources outside of Islām. Merx, indeed, seems to go too far when he calls it 'Greek' and connects it specifically with the writings attributed to Dionysius the Areopagite,[1] though it may well have been influenced both by them and by the so-called *Theology of Aristotle*, a Neo-Platonic treatise of which an Arabic version appeared before the end of the 3rd century. But at this epoch little can have been borrowed directly from books. What makes the influence of Hellenism certain is the fact that in Western Asia and Egypt the Ṣūfī theosophy arose on a soil long saturated with Hellenistic culture, while some of its leading exponents were non-Arab Muslims belonging to the subject nationalities.[2]

One example will suffice. The mystical knowledge of God peculiar to the Ṣūfīs is denoted by the term *ma'rifat* = γνῶσις, *i.e.* immediate knowledge resulting from apocalyptic vision. It is defined in this sense by several Ṣūfīs of the 3rd cent., but we owe the first important speculations on its nature to Dhu 'l-Nūn of Egypt († A.D. 859), of whom his Persian biographer says: 'He is the head of this sect [the Ṣūfīs]: they all descend from and are related to him.'[3] That, no doubt, is an exaggeration; yet it shows the significance of the man. Now, Dhu 'l-Nūn was a Copt or Nubian by race; he is described as a philosopher and alchemist—*i.e.* a student of Greek wisdom; during his life he was regarded by many as a *zindīq* (free-thinker). Here we have plain indications that, as soon as Islāmic mysticism began to develop, it drew inspiration from the doctrine concerning 'a gnosis or higher knowledge which can be taught with safety'—as Dhu 'l-Nūn also says—'only to the "perfect" or "fully initiated."'[4] While Dhu 'l-Nūn conceived the Ṣūfī's supreme experience as a super-intellectual God-given knowledge, peculiar to those who 'see God with their hearts' and ultimately involving complete unconsciousness ('the more a man knows God, the more is he lost in Him'), he never makes use of the term *fanā*, which is associated with the name of his contemporary, Abū Yazīd, or Bāyazīd, of Bisṭām. *Fanā* is best rendered by 'passing-away'; it may be applied to the disappearance of evil qualities or, in its pantheistic sense, to the passing-away of the whole individual self in union with God. Possibly the term was derived by Muslim mystics from a verse in the Qur'ān[5] quoted above, but in Eastern Persia, where it first came into prominence, it must have been deeply coloured by Perso-Indian ideas.[6] The definition of *fanā* as a moral state, and of the means by which the extinction of all passions and desires is brought about, agrees so exactly with the definition of *nirvāṇa* that Buddhistic influence cannot be denied. As regards the pantheistic aspect of *fanā*, the Vedānta and similar forms of Indian thought readily suggest themselves. Here again the lives and sayings of representative Ṣūfīs, in conjunction with other historical evidence, provide the only trustworthy clue. Bāyazīd was a native of Khurāsān. His grandfather was a Zoroastrian and his master in Ṣūfism a Kurd. He learned the mystical doctrine of passing-away (*fanā*) in the divine unity from Abū 'Alī of Sind. He knew the Indian practice of 'watching the breaths' (*pās-i anfās*) and described it as the gnostic's worship of God.[7] The character of his pantheism is probably reflected in the utterances which his legend records, even if their authenticity may be questioned—for example,

[1] *Idee und Grundlinien*, p. 18 f.

[2] Many illustrations of the close parallelism existing between the leading ideas of Hellenistic religious philosophy and those of early Ṣūfism will be found in the introduction to *Bar Hebræus's Book of the Dove*, tr. A. J. Wensinck, Leyden, 1919, p. xxxix f.

[3] Jāmī, *Nafaḥāt al-uns*, p. 36.

[4] W. R. Inge, *Christian Mysticism* (*BL*), London, 1899, p. 81.

[5] lv. 26.

[6] See Goldziher, *Vorlesungen über den Islam*, p. 163; Nicholson, *The Mystics of Islam*, p. 16 ff.

[7] *Tadhkirat al-auliyā*, i. 162, 10; cf. T. W. Rhys Davids, *The Yogāvacara's Manual* (*PTS*), London, 1896, p. x.

'I went from God to God, until they cried from me in me, "O Thou I!"'

'Verily, I am God, there is no God except me, so worship me. Glory to me! How great is my majesty!'

'Nothing is better for man than to be without aught, having no asceticism, no theory, no practice. When he is without all, he is with all.'

'Creatures are subject to states, but the gnostic has no state, because his vestiges are obliterated and his individuality (*huwyīat*) passes away in the individuality of Another and his traces are effaced by Another's traces.'

At this time earnest Ṣūfīs did not habitually and openly indulge in the language of 'deification.' The doctrine underlying it was esoteric, reserved for adepts in theosophy, who usually were more discreet than Bāyazīd and Ḥallāj. They saw the necessity of keeping their mystical theories in close touch with the religion which they professed. Consequently the Qur'ān and the Sunna were proclaimed to be the standard to which not only speculation but also spiritual feelings and states must conform.

Let us now consider the methods whereby a reconciliation was effected and take a general survey of the relations existing between Ṣūfism and Islām.

3. The Law, the Path, and the Truth.—The Qur'ān contains a few passages from which it can fairly be argued that Muḥammad had in him something of the mystic, but that book as a whole is no better fitted than the Pentateuch to form the basis of a system of mysticism. Nevertheless, the Ṣūfīs, adopting the Shī'ite principle of allegorical interpretation (*ta'wīl*), were able to prove to their own satisfaction that every verse and word of the sacred text hides treasures of meaning which God reveals to the elect[1]—meanings which flash upon the inward eye in moments of rapt meditation. So much being granted, one can imagine that it was easy to show Qur'ānic authority for any mystical doctrine whatsoever and to maintain that Ṣūfism was really the esoteric teaching of the Prophet communicated by him to his son-in-law, 'Alī b. Abī Ṭālib. From the same principle it follows that the Ṣūfī interpretation of Islām admits an endless variety of divergent and even contradictory beliefs and practices, all of which *ex hypothesi* are equally valid in kind, though not in degree, since the meanings of the Qur'ān are infinite and reveal themselves to each mystic in proportion to the spiritual capacity with which he is endowed. Hence the Ṣūfīs are not a sect, and there is no uniform body of doctrine constituting what is called 'Ṣūfism.' The many-sidedness of the term is exemplified by the innumerable attempts made to define it.[2] Similarly, the attitude of the Ṣūfīs towards Muḥammadan religious law depends on a subjective criterion. Some punctiliously fulfilled their ritual obligations, while at the same time they recognized that forms of worship have only a relative value in comparison with 'the works of the heart,' or are altogether worthless except as symbols of spiritual realities. To make the pilgrimage, *e.g.*, is to journey away from sin; to put on the pilgrim's garb (*iḥrām*) is to cast off with one's every-day clothes all sensual thoughts and feelings. This is a well-known doctrine of the Ismā'īlīs, from whom the Ṣūfīs seem to have borrowed it.[3] Others are antinomian, whether they be free-thinking and free-living dervishes, genuine mystics like the Malāmatīs described by Hujwīrī,[4] whose fear of men's praise caused them deliberately to act in such a way as to incur reprobation, or gnostics supremely indifferent to the shadow-shows of religion and

[1] Cf. *Kitāb al-Luma'*, p. 72 f.

[2] See *JRAS*, 1906, p. 330 ff.; Goldziher, *Vorlesungen*, p. 166.

[3] Cf. *Kitāb al-Luma'*, p. 172 f. (Nicholson, *Mystics of Islam*, p. 91 f.) with Browne's *Literary Hist. of Persia*, ii. 241 f.

[4] *Kashf al-Maḥjūb*, tr. Nicholson, p. 66; cf. M. Hartmann, *Der islamische orient. Berichte und Forschungen*, Berlin, 1899–1910, i. 156 f.

morality in a phantom world. Many Ṣūfīs, however, insist that, normally at any rate, perfect realization of the Truth (*ḥaqīqat*)—*i.e.* the consummation of the mystical life—is not only compatible with observance of the Law (*sharī'at*) but includes it as a facet or aspect of the whole. This view will be better explained if we give a brief account of its ethical and psychological basis.

The Ṣūfīs regarded themselves as a peculiarly favoured class, possessing an esoteric knowledge of the Qur'ān and the apostolic traditions, and using technical expressions which no ordinary Muslim could understand. This fostered a feeling of brotherhood, and it was not long before traces of organization began to appear. Eminent mystics gathered round them groups of disciples (small at first) for private instruction and in course of time became recognized teachers, heads of mystical schools, and abbots presiding over convents where Ṣūfīs were trained. It was generally held that for those entering on the religious life a teacher was indispensable. A self-trained mystic, who had not passed through the discipline prescribed by a spiritual director (*shaikh, pīr, murshid*), was looked upon with suspicion. The authority of the *shaikhs* was absolute. It lay with them to decide whether the novice, after his probationary period, should be granted leave to take the vow of obedience to his master which was exacted from all candidates for initiation. Hujwīrī mentions a three years' probation.

'The first year is devoted to service of the people [*i.e.* the Ṣūfīs], the second year to service of God, and the third year to watching over his own heart. He can serve the people, only when he places himself in the rank of servants and all others in the rank of masters, *i.e.*, he must regard all, without exception, as being better than himself and must deem it his duty to serve all alike. And he can serve God, only when he cuts off all his selfish interests relating either to the present or to the future life, and worships God for God's sake alone. . . . And he can watch over his heart, only when his thoughts are collected and every care is dismissed, so that in communion with God he guards his heart from the assaults of heedlessness.'[1]

On taking the vow of initiation, the novice was invested by his *shaikh* with the *khirqa* or *muraqqa'a*, a garment made of pieces of cloth stitched together, which in later times superseded the woollen dress worn by the original Ṣūfīs. This ceremony marked his admission to the Ṣūfī brotherhood. Occasionally a Ṣūfī might be invested with two *khirqas* by different *shaikhs*, as happened to Abū Sa'īd ibn Abi 'l-Khair. The veneration which the *shaikhs* inspired in their disciples is well known. Dhu 'l-Nūn went so far as to say that the true disciple should be more obedient to his master than to God Himself.[2] The rule, method, and religious practice inculcated by the *shaikh* and followed by the disciple constitute the Path (*ṭarīqa*). Accordingly, the Path has no fixed and uniform character; its details are determined by the individuality of the teacher. The *ṭarīqas* of the dervish orders exemplify this divergence. Broadly speaking, the Path corresponds to the *via purgativa* of mediæval Christian mysticism. Hunger, solitude, and silence are the chief weapons employed in the war against 'the flesh' (*nafs*). The ascetic and ethical discipline is divided into a progressive series of 'stations' (*maqāmāt*), which the learner must traverse, making himself perfect in every one of them before advancing to the next. They vary in number and order, but the first place is usually occupied by 'repentance' or 'conversion' (*tauba*), *i.e.* turning away from sin towards God. The moral ideal of the Ṣūfīs is unselfishness, whether it take the form of renouncing worldly possessions and desires, sincerity in word and deed without regard for the good opinions of others,

[1] *Kashf al-Maḥjūb*, tr. Nicholson, p. 54.
[2] *Tadhkirat al-auliyā*, i. 131, 7.

patience, humility, charity, or trust in God and single-hearted devotion to His will.[1] These are the fruits of the Path, but its true end is attained by means of exercises in spiritual meditation and recollection which predispose and prepare the disciple for ecstatic experiences. It may be that he will never reach that end; ecstasy is an incalculable gift of divine grace and cannot be extorted. But the Ṣūfīs had a method of their own for producing the state of mind in which 'revelation' of the unseen was most likely to occur. They called it *dhikr* ('recollection'), set the highest value upon it, and deemed it the corner-stone of practical religion.[2] The simplest form of *dhikr* is the continual repetition of the name Allāh or of some short litany, accompanied with intense concentration on the thought of God.[3] Concentration might be assisted by other means, such as flagellation and holding the breath, until the sense of personality gradually disappeared in a state of trance.

'The first stage of *dhikr* is to forget self, and the last stage is the effacement of the thinker in the act of thought, without consciousness of thought, and such absorption in the object of thought as precludes return to the subject thereof.'[4] Concerted performances of *dhikr*, with music and dancing, were introduced at an early date, and their demoralizing effect on neophytes is noted by Hujwīrī.[5] Such prayer-services, as is well known, play an important part in the ritual of the dervish orders.[6]

A general view of Ṣūfī psychology, so far as it bears on the ecstatic life, may be obtained from Qushairī[7] or from the more systematic treatment of the subject by Ghazālī in the second half of his *Iḥyā*.[8]

There are four terms which, taken together, comprise the sensual, spiritual, and intellectual nature of man: (1) *nafs*, the appetitive soul; (2) *rūḥ*, the spirit; (3) *qalb*, the heart; (4) *'aql*, the intelligence. The *nafs*, being the seat of the passions, is wholly evil; its mortification by means of asceticism is the Ṣūfī's holy war (*jihād*). The *qalb* and the *rūḥ* (to which Qushairī adds the *sirr*, the inmost ground of the *qalb*) are the proper organs of the mystical life and are not clearly distinguished from one another. *Qalb*, as used by Ṣūfīs, does not signify the heart of flesh, but 'a transcendental subtlety' or non-material essence whereby the realities of all things are perceived and reflected as in a mirror. Hence the phrase *oculus cordis* has equivalents in Arabic, Persian, and Turkish. But the power of the heart to perceive and reflect spiritual realities depends on its purity. It is veiled in greater or less degree by sensuous impressions—sin, egoism, book-learning, traditional faith, etc.; and, in proportion as these veils are removed, its vision of reality becomes more perfect. God alone can purify it, but the need for co-operation with the act of divine grace is asserted by those Ṣūfīs who follow the Path and attach particular importance to the methods of recollection (*dhikr*) and meditation (*murāqabat*), by which the heart is purged of everything except the thought of God. The 'stations' (*maqāmāt*) of the Path, which belong to the mystic's practical religion, are subordinate to the 'states' (*aḥwāl*), which belong to his inner life. The term 'state' (*ḥāl*) denotes a mood of feeling, a spiritual disposition or experience, which God causes to pass over the heart; it is not subject to human control, but comes and goes as God wills; usually it is transient, but it may abide permanently. The classification of *aḥwāl* in pairs of opposites —*e.g.*, hope and fear, expansion and contraction, presence and absence—answers to psychological facts familiar to students of mysticism. Passively yielding to the divine influences which swing him to and fro in an ascending scale, the Ṣūfī is 'the son of his time,' dominated by the 'state' in which he finds himself at the moment, oblivious of the past and without thought of the future. The highest 'states' are ecstatic, and the term *ḥāl* is often synonymous with ecstasy, though it had not this special sense originally.

Here we come back to the point at issue between Ṣūfism and Islām. Through ecstasy the Ṣūfī reaches the plane of the Truth (*ḥaqīqat*), where he is one with God. The person thus enraptured

[1] See R. Hartmann, *Das Ṣūfītum nach al-Ḳuschairī*, p. 44 ff.
[2] See art. ASCETICISM (Muslim).
[3] Cf. D. B. Macdonald, *Religious Attitude and Life in Islam*, p. 255 f.
[4] *Nafaḥāt al-uns*, 161, 18. [5] *Kashf al-Maḥjūb*, 420.
[6] Cf. E. W. Lane, *An Account of the Manners and Customs of the Modern Egyptians*[5], London, 1871, i. 309; Macdonald, *Aspects of Islam*, New York, 1911, p. 160 ff.; J. P. Brown, *The Dervishes, or Oriental Spiritualism*, London, 1868.
[7] R. Hartmann, *Das Ṣūfītum nach al-Ḳuschairī*, p. 69 f.
[8] Summarized in Macdonald, *Religious Attitude and Life in Islam*, p. 220 ff.

(*majdhūb*) is a saint (*walī*); no further testimony is required, since the doctrine that a saint who violates the Law is thereby shown to be an impostor applies only when the ecstatic fit has subsided. And in any case, it was argued, a divinely inspired man must not be judged by appearances; his knowledge of unseen things may justify him in doing what religion and morality condemn: the story of Moses and Khaḍir[1] illustrates this. Ecstasy not being confined to one sex, the Ṣūfī legend includes a long roll of women, to whom a separate section is sometimes allotted in standard hagiographical works. In accordance with the theopathetic character of Muslim saints, their miracles (*karāmāt*=χαρίσματα) are described, not as wrought by them, but as granted or manifested to them; and, while the higher Ṣūfism declares that 'reliance on miracles hinders the elect from penetrating to the inmost shrine of the Truth,' and that 'the greatest miracle is the substitution of a good quality for a bad one,' the popular *walī* cannot, even if he wishes, avoid the reputation of being gifted with powers which Muslims call 'extraordinary' and Europeans 'supernatural.' The saints form an invisible hierarchy by which the order of the world is maintained. At their head stands the *quṭb* ('axis'), under him inferior grades of sanctity—*nuqabā, autād, abrār, abdāl* or *budalā*, etc.—the numbers of each class increasing in proportion to its distance from the *quṭb*.[2] Probably this idea was taken over by the Ṣūfīs from the Shī'ites and Ismā'īlīs.[3]

The Ṣūfī theory of ecstasy recognizes two aspects of the experience of oneness with God. These aspects are symbolized by such negative terms as *fanā* ('passing-away' from individuality), *faqd* ('self-loss'), *sukr* ('intoxication'), with their positive counterparts *baqā* ('abiding in God'), *wajd* ('finding God'), and *ṣaḥw* ('sobriety'). In the controversy which arose as to the relative values of the ecstatic state and the subsequent return to consciousness[4] it is easy to discern the same motives as ranged Ṣūfīs on opposite sides in regard to the question, Were they antinomian or not? From the standpoint of pure Ṣūfism there is nothing beyond the supreme negation of self, when 'the mortal disappears' and religion no longer exists; but logic compels those Ṣūfīs who are more than nominal Muslims to set the life in God against and above the death to self, and to find the highest mystical experience in the state of conscious clairvoyance which succeeds the moment of ecstasy.

'The full circle of deification must comprehend both the inward and outward aspects of Deity—the One and the Many, the Truth and the Law. It is not enough to escape from all that is creaturely without entering into the eternal life of God the Creator as manifested in His works. To abide in God (*baqā*), after having passed away from selfhood (*fanā*), is the mark of the Perfect Man, who not only journeys *to* God, *i.e.* passes from plurality to unity, but *in* and *with* God, *i.e.* continuing in the unitive state, he returns with God to the phenomenal world from which he set out, and manifests unity in plurality. In this descent . . . he brings down and displays the Truth to mankind while fulfilling the duties of the religious law.'[5]

Such a compromise could not restore the balance effectually. The Ṣūfīs might do homage to the Law, but they ranked it below the Truth and even below the Path. And, if the Truth is above the Law, yet not in contradiction with it, the view was plausible that, when a man has attained to the Truth, all his acts and words are holy and in harmony with the spirit of the Law, however they may seem to clash with its letter. Still, a *via media* had to be secured, even at the price of illogical concessions on both sides.

A Persian Ṣūfī, writing in the 5th cent., laments that his contemporaries 'give the name of "law" to their lusts, call their own senseless fancies "divine knowledge," the motions of the heart and affections of the animal soul "divine love," heresy "poverty," scepticism "purity," disbelief in positive religion "a passing away from self," neglect of the Law of the Prophet "the mystic path."'[1]

In A.D. 1045 Qushairī published his famous 'Epistle on Ṣūfism' (*Risāla fī 'ilm al-taṣawwuf*), recalling to his fellow-mystics how in past times great Ṣūfīs spoke and behaved as good Muslims and set an example of piety which their unworthy successors had almost forgotten. That these protests were not made in vain was due above all to Ghazālī.[2] He fused the traditional and mystical elements into one mass. His work was lasting because it took shape not so much from the force of his mind as under the pressure of a searching spiritual experience: he had worked out and solved the problem in himself before he gave the result in his books. Fifty years after the appearance of Qushairī's *Risāla* Ghazālī resigned the professorship of theology and canon law which he held in the Niẓāmīya college at Baghdād and went into retirement as a Ṣūfī. He has told us in pages as fascinating as Newman's *Apologia* how his studies and meditations at last made his conversion inevitable, through what struggles he shed off philosophy, scholasticism, and legalism, and gained the certainty that the central truth of religion lies in the inner life of the soul.[3] By frankly accepting the main Ṣūfī position Ghazālī gave a new meaning to Islām and an assured place within its fold to many earnestly religious men and women whom the formalists would have driven out if they could. Henceforth Islām is in large measure a mystical faith. But Ghazālī always remained a Muslim in two essential points: (1) his reverence for the religious law, (2) his view of the nature of God. He shut the door against pantheism by insisting on the dogma that the Divine Being is personal, unique, distinct from all other beings. In so far as the human soul has these attributes, it is capable of knowing God; but it can never be identified with God. Our knowledge of God depends on His will to make Himself known through revelation to prophets and saints whom He created. This left Allāh spiritualized and brought near to men's hearts, but still Allāh, not the All in One. It may be said that Ghazālī belongs to Islām rather than to Islāmic mysticism, and that, inasmuch as he is not a pantheist, he is not a typical Ṣūfī. This seems true. On the other hand, while Ṣūfīs who are pantheists often use language implying belief in a personal God, such belief is by no means inconsistent with the full theory of *fanā*, or at least may be sincerely combined with it.

4. God, man, and the universe.—Upon the foundation of experimental mysticism the Ṣūfīs built a theology and a philosophy of which the forms are as various in content and expression as the materials are diverse in origin. It is a notable fact that the oldest scheme of this kind—which has recently been made accessible through the publication of the *Kitāb al-Ṭawāsīn* of Ḥallāj[4]—was derived from the Christian doctrine of two natures in God.

According to Ḥallāj (*q.v.*), the essence of God's essence is love. Before the creation God loved Himself in absolute unity and through love revealed Himself to Himself alone. Then, desiring to behold that love-in-aloneness, that love without otherness

1 *Qur'ān*, xviii. 64–80.
2 Cf. E. Blochet, 'Etudes sur l'ésoterisme musulman,' *JA*, 9th ser., xx. [1902] 49 ff.; Hujwīrī, *Kashf al-Maḥjūb*, p. 214.
3 Ibn Khaldūn, *Prolegomena*, tr. M. de Slane, Paris, 1862–68, iii. 104 ff.; cf. H. S. Nyberg, *Kleinere Schriften des Ibn al-'Arabī*, Leyden, 1919, introd., p. 113.
4 Cf. Hujwīrī, *Kashf al-Maḥjūb*, p. 184 f.
5 Nicholson, *The Mystics of Islam*, p. 163.

1 Hujwīrī, *Kashf al-Maḥjūb*, p. 8.
2 See art. ETHICS AND MORALITY (Muslim).
3 See *al-Munqidh min aḍ-ḍalāl*, tr. Barbier de Meynard, *JA* VII. ix. 5 ff.; D. B. Macdonald, *Development of Muslim Theology, Jurisprudence and Constitutional Theory*, London, 1903, p. 215 f.
4 See Literature.

and duality, as an external object, He brought forth from non-existence an image of Himself, endowed with all His attributes and names. This divine image is Adam, in and by whom God is made manifest. Ḥallāj, however, maintains a certain distinction between the divine and human natures. Even in their mystical union some personality survives: divinity (*lāhūt*) is infused in—not confused with—humanity (*nāsūt*), as wine in water; hence the 'deified' man cries, '*Ana 'l-Ḥaqq*,' '*I* am God.'[1] The markedly Christian flavour of the Ḥallājian doctrine, together with its author's use of the heretical term *ḥulūl* ('infusion' or 'incarnation'), condemned it in Muslim eyes, and later Ṣūfīs take care to give it a monistic interpretation; Ibn al-'Arabī, *e.g.*, reduces the *lāhūt* and *nāsūt* to correlative and interchangeable aspects of the one reality. Yet the magnitude of the debt which Ṣūfism owes to Ḥallāj can hardly be overestimated. His doctrine, though formally rejected, introduced and established in Islām the revolutionary idea that there is a principle of difference in the Absolute itself.

An important school of Ṣūfīs, whose watchword is 'the unity of being' (*waḥdat al-wujūd* or *ittiḥād*), hold that reality is one, that all apparent multiplicity is a mode of unity, and that the phenomenal is the outward manifestation of the real. Their views may be illustrated by giving some account of a work entitled *The Man perfect in Knowledge of the Last and First Things* by 'Abd al-Karīm al-Jīlī, a mystic of the 15th century A.D.[2]

The essence of God is unknowable *per se*; we must seek knowledge of it through its names and attributes. It is a substance with two accidents, eternity and everlastingness; with two qualities, creativeness and creatureliness; with two descriptions, uncreatedness and origination in time; with two names, Lord and slave (*i.e.* God and man); with two aspects, the outward or visible, which is the present world, and the inward or invisible, which is the world to come. Pure being, as such, has neither name nor attribute; only when it gradually descends from its absoluteness and enters the realm of manifestation do names and attributes appear imprinted on it. The sum of these attributes is the phenomenal universe, which is phenomenal in the sense that it shows reality under the form of externality. Although the distinction of essence and attribute must be admitted if we are to think of the universe at all, the two are ultimately one, like water and ice. The so-called phenomenal world—the world of attributes—is no illusion; it really exists as the self-revelation or other self of the Absolute. It expresses God's idea of Himself; for, as Ibn al-'Arabī says,

> 'We ourselves are the attributes by which we describe God: our existence is merely an objectification of His existence. God is necessary to us in order that we may exist, while we are necessary to Him, in order that He may be manifested to Himself.'

The simple essence, apart from all qualities and relations, Jīlī calls 'the darkness' (*al-'amā*). It develops consciousness by passing through three stages which modify its purity and simplicity. The first stage is oneness (*aḥadīyat*), the second is 'He-ness' (*huwīyat*), the third is 'I-ness' (*anīyat*). By this process of descent absolute being becomes the subject and object of all thought and reveals itself as divinity with distinctive attributes embracing the whole series of existence. While every appearance displays some attribute of reality, man is the microcosm in which all these attributes are united, and in him alone does the Absolute become conscious of itself in all its diverse aspects. This can only mean that the Absolute, having completely realized itself in human nature, returns into itself through the medium of human nature, or, in mystical language, that God and man become one in the perfect man—the divinely rapt prophet or saint—whose religious function as a mediator between man and God corresponds with his metaphysical function as the unifying principle by which the opposed terms of reality and appearance are harmonized. Therefore the upward movement of the Absolute, from the sphere of manifestation back to the unmanifested essence, takes place in and through the unitive experience of the soul; and so we have exchanged metaphysics for mysticism. Jīlī recognizes three phases of this experience running parallel, as it were, to the three stages—oneness, He-ness, and I-ness—traversed by the Absolute in its descent to consciousness, viz. the illumination of the names, the illumination of the attributes, and the illumination of the essence. The perfect man is the final cause of creation, the preserver of the universe, the *quṭb* ('axis') on which all the spheres of existence revolve. He is a copy made in the image of God—a type of the essence with its two correlated attributes, divinity and humanity. Hence his real nature is threefold, as Jīlī expressly declares in the following verses:

> 'If you say that it (the essence) is One, you are right; or if you say that it is Two, it is in fact Two;
> Or if you say, "No, it is Three," you are right, for that is the real nature of man.'[1]

Coming from a Muslim, who identifies the absolutely perfect man with the prophet Muḥammad, this Trinitarian doctrine is very remarkable; but we must remember that the Ṣūfīs generally regard Muḥammad as the Logos, the Light of God which existed before the creation of the world, and for the sake of which all things were made.[2] The Logos is manifested in every age by the prophets and saints, who alone are actually perfect, though all men are potentially so.

Other Ṣūfīs enumerate 'five different planes of existence (*ḥaẓarāt-i khamsa*), which loses in true Being as it descends,'[3] and many adopt the Neo-Platonic scheme of emanation.[4]

The theory that all existence, thought, and action are really divine leads to consequences from which the Ṣūfīs do not shrink. In the first place, the universe must be essentially good. Even infidelity and sin are effects of the divine activity and belong to the divine perfection. Satan himself glorifies God, inasmuch as his disobedience is subordinate to the eternal will. Yet some attributes, *i.e.* some aspects in which God shows Himself, such as majesty and wrath, are relatively less perfect than others, such as beauty and mercy. What men call evil is privation, not-being. In relation to the One, who has no opposite, it is nothing; it appears only in the phenomenal world, where things are manifested *per contraria*. Similarly, all religious beliefs must be essentially true. God, as Ibn al-'Arabī says, is not limited by any one creed.

To summarize Jīlī once more: the different forms of worship result from the variety of names and attributes by which God reveals Himself in creation. Every name and attribute produces its own characteristic effect; *e.g.*, God is the true Guide (*al-Hādī*); but He is also the Misleader (*al-Muḍill*), for the Qur'ān says: 'Allāh shall lead the wicked into error.' If any one of His names had remained ineffectual and unrealized, His self-manifestation would not have been complete. Therefore He sent His prophets, in order that those who followed them might worship Him as the One who guides mankind to salvation, and that those who disobeyed them might worship Him as the One who leads mankind to perdition. He is the truth or essence of every belief. Idolaters worship the being who permeates each atom of the material world; dualists adore the Creator and creature in one; magians (fire-worshippers) the unity in which all names and attributes pass away, just as fire destroys all natural properties and transmutes them to its own nature; those who deny the existence of a Creator really worship Him in respect of His He-ness, in which He is potentially but not actually creative. It follows that all men are saved at the last. But Jīlī, as a Muslim, is obliged to make distinctions.

1 *Kitab al-Ṭawāsīn*, ed. Massignon, p. 129 f.
2 See Shaikh Muhammad Iqbāl, *The Development of Metaphysics in Persia*, p. 150 ff.; Nicholson, 'The Ṣūfī Doctrine of the Perfect Man,' in *The Quest*, viii. [1917] 545 ff. A more adequate account of Jīlī's work will be found in the present writer's *Studies in Islamic Mysticism* (in the press).

1 *Al-insān al-kāmil*, Cairo, A.H. 1300, p. 10, l. 21 f.
2 Tor Andrae, *Die person Muhammads*, Stockholm, 1918, p. 333 ff.
3 See E. J. W. Gibb, *Hist. of Ottoman Poetry*, i. 54 f.
4 Cf. Nicholson, *Selected Poems from the Divāni Shamsi Tabriz*, Cambridge, 1898, p. xxxii f.

The more completely and universally the idea of God is presented in any form of worship, the more perfect that form must be. Religions revealed through a prophet contain the fullest measure of truth, and among these the most excellent is Islām. Non-Muslims, although their felicity is ultimately assured, suffer retribution: in the case of those who acknowledge no prophet, because they invented forms of worship for themselves; and, in the case of Jews and Christians, because they altered the one revelation brought by all the prophets from Adam to Muḥammad. Jīlī finds in Christianity the nearest approach to his own monistic interpretation of Islām. Christians (he says) recognize the two complementary sides of true belief concerning God, viz. that from one point of view He is above all likeness, while from the other point of view He reveals Himself in the forms of His creatures. Their mistake lies in the limitation to which they have subjected the principle that God becomes manifest in this way. God said in the Qur'ān, 'I breathed my spirit into Adam'; and here the name Adam signifies every human individual. The worship of those who behold God in man is the highest of all. Something of this vision Christians possess, and their doctrine about Jesus is a bridge that will lead them at last to the knowledge that mankind are like mirrors set face to face, each of which contains what is in all; and so they will behold God in themselves and declare Him to be absolutely One.

5. Ṣūfī poetry.—Among the practices devised by the Ṣūfīs for the purpose of stimulating religious emotion there is none more potent than that which they name 'audition' (*samā'*), *i.e.* listening to music and song.[1] Countless stories are told of Ṣūfīs who were thrown into ecstasy on hearing a few lines of verse chanted inadvertently by a singing-girl or with intention by one of themselves. Such verses were usually erotic, but not mystical; the allegorical sense was not given by the poet but was supplied by the hearer. In Ṣūfī poetry, of course, it is otherwise; here the poet's meaning is mystical, however sensuous may be the form in which it lurks. And often the two kinds are so like each other superficially that, unless we have some clue to the intention of the writer, we cannot easily decide whether we are reading an ode of human love or a hymn addressed to the Deity.[2] If it be asked why the Ṣūfīs make such large use of erotic and bacchanalian symbolism, the answer is that they could find no analogy more suggestive and better adapted to shadow forth the states of enthusiasm and ecstasy which their poets describe.

'Wine, torch, and beauty are epiphanies of Verity,
For it is that which is revealed under all forms soever.
Wine and torch are the transport and light of the knower;
Behold The Beauty, for it is hidden from none.

. . . .

Wine, torch, and beauty, all are present;
Neglect not to embrace that Beauty.
Quaff the wine of dying to self, and for a season
Peradventure you will be freed from the dominion of self.
Drink wine, for its cup is the face of the Friend;
The flagon is His eye drunken and flown with wine.'[3]

This poetry is the chief glory of Persian literature. It may be studied in the quatrains attributed to Abū Sa'īd b. Abi'l-Khair,[4] in the poems of Farīdu'ddīn 'Aṭṭār,[5] Jalāl al-dīn Rūmī (*q.v.*), and Jāmī,[6] or in the *Gulshani Rāz* of Maḥmūd Shabistarī. Whinfield's edition of the last-named work[7] is provided with explanatory notes and may be recommended as the best introduction to the subject. In Arabic this *genre* of poetry takes a more conventional form, which is not so attractive to Western readers, but the odes of Ibn al-Fāriḍ[8] are exceedingly fine, while those

1 Cf. D. B. Macdonald, 'Emotional Religion in Islam as affected by Music and Singing,' *JRAS*, 1901, pp. 195 ff., 705 ff.; Hujwīrī, *Kashf al-Maḥjūb*, p. 393 ff.
2 See Nicholson, *Mystics of Islam*, p. 102 ff.
3 *Gulshani Rāz*, ed. and tr. E. H. Whinfield, London, 1880, p. 78 f.
4 Text and Germ. tr. by H. Ethé in *Sitzungsberichte der k. bayer. Akad. der Wissenschaften*, Philos.-philol. Classe, lxxix. pt. 2 [1875] p. 145 f., lxxxix. pt. i. [1878] p. 38 f.; cf. E. G. Browne, *Lit. Hist. of Persia*, ii. 261 ff.
5 *La Poésie philosophique et religieuse chez les Persans, d'après le Mantic uttair, ou le Langage des oiseaux*[4], ed. and tr. Garcin de Tassy, Paris, 1864.
6 *Yūsuf und Zulaikha*, tr. R. T. H. Griffith, London, 1882.
7 London, 1880.
8 Cf. Grangeret de Lagrange, *Anthologie arabe*, Paris, 1828, p. 25 ff.; Nicholson, *Lit. Hist. of the Arabs*, p. 393 ff.

of Ibn al-'Arabī,[1] in spite of their recondite style, contain some passages of great beauty. Of the Turkish Ṣūfī poets the most interesting is Nesīmī,[2] a fervent admirer of Ḥallāj and a member of the sect known as Ḥurūfīs, who derive their title from the mystic significations which they attach to the letters of the alphabet and to combinations of these.[3]

The Ṣūfī poet is not directly concerned with metaphysics.

He 'lets his heart be wholly filled by the sublime conceptions of all-embracing Unity and all-conquering Love which form the real basis whereon all the rest is built. . . . He sees how the Truth is the one source of all existence, diffused throughout the universe through emanation after emanation; how the Primal Intelligence, itself rayed out from the One, rays out in turn the Primal Soul; how the Divine Names cast their light upon the darkness of not-being, each atom of which mirror-like reflects one. He sees how the Awful Attributes of the Truth are reflected in the existence of hell and the devils, and how the Beautiful Attributes are reflected in that of Paradise and the angels. He further sees how Man reflects all the Attributes, Awful and Beautiful alike, and is thus the Microcosm, summing up the universe in himself. He thus sees how it is the Truth alone that is acting through all things, and moreover how this action is a never-ceasing, never-pausing process, every existent atom being each instant clothed with a fresh phenomenal efflux radiated from the Source of Existence, and being again stripped of it, so that the whole contingent universe is momentarily being annihilated and re-created, though the successive acts of destruction and renewal follow one another in such swift succession that they are wholly imperceptible, and all appears as one uninterrupted line, even as an unbroken circle of fire is seen if a single spark shall be whirled quickly round. But the poet may not rest content with the mere perception of these high mysteries; indeed that very Love which has revealed them to him impels him to seek reunion with the Truth.'[4]

God, as the poets conceive Him, is the eternal Beauty which by the necessity of its nature desires to be loved, manifests itself for the sake of love, and is the real object of all love. Even earthly love is a type of spiritual, a bridge leading to reality.[5] The soul, being divine in its essence, longs for union with that from which it is separated by the illusion of individuality, and this longing aspiration, which urges it to pass away from selfhood and to rise on the wings of ecstasy, is the only means whereby it can return to its original home. Love transmutes into pure gold the base phenomenal alloy of which every creature partakes. While reason is dualistic, love unifies by transcending thought.

'He comes, a moon whose like the sky ne'er saw, awake or dreaming,
Crowned with eternal flame no flood can lay.
Lo, from the flagon of thy love, O Lord, my soul is swimming,
And ruined all my body's house of clay!

When first the Giver of the grape my lonely heart befriended,
Wine fired my bosom and my veins filled up,
But when his image all mine eye possessed, a voice descended:
"Well done, O sovereign Wine and peerless Cup!"

Love's mighty arm from roof to base each dark abode is hewing
Where chinks reluctant catch a golden ray.
My heart, when Love's sea of a sudden burst into its viewing,
Leaped headlong in, with "Find me now who may!"'[6]

The following passages further illustrate the manner in which this principle is applied by Ṣūfī poets.

Love is the final cause of creation:

'In solitude, where Being signless dwelt,
And all the universe still dormant lay
Concealed in selflessness, One Being was,
Exempt from "I"- or "Thou"-ness, and apart
From all duality; Beauty Supreme,
Unmanifest except unto Itself
By Its own light, yet fraught with power to charm
The souls of all . . .
But Beauty cannot brook
Concealment and the veil, nor patient rest
Unseen and unadmired: 'twill burst all bonds
And from its prison-casement to the world
Reveal Itself . . .

1 *Tarjumān al-Ashwāq*, ed. and tr. Nicholson, London, 1911.
2 Gibb, i. 336 ff.
3 See E. G. Browne, in *JRAS*, 1898, p. 61 ff.; C. Huart and Feylesouf Riẓā, *Textes persans relatifs à la secte des Houroûfîs*, London, 1909.
4 Gibb, i. 65 f.
5 See Gibb, i. 20 f., 63 f.
6 *Dīvāni Shamsi Tabrīz*, p. 342.

Wherever Beauty dwells,
Such is its nature and its heritage
From Everlasting Beauty, which emerged
From realms of purity to shine upon
The worlds, and all the souls which dwell therein.
. . . .
Each speck of matter did He constitute
A mirror, causing each one to reflect
The beauty of His visage. From the rose
Flashed forth His beauty, and the nightingale,
Beholding it, loved madly. From that fire
The candle drew the lustre which beguiles
The moth to immolation . . .
Beware! say not, "He is All-Beautiful,
And we His lovers." Thou art but the glass,
And He the face confronting it, which casts
Its image on the mirror. He alone
Is manifest, and Thou in truth art hid.
Pure love, like beauty, coming but from Him
Reveals itself in thee. If steadfastly
Thou canst regard, thou wilt at length perceive
He is the mirror also; He alike
The Treasure and the Casket. "I" and "Thou"
Have here no place, and are but phantasies
Vain and unreal.'[1]

Love is the essence of all religions:

'Soul of mine, thou dawning Light: be not far, O be not far!
Love of mine, thou Vision bright: be not far, O be not far!
. . . .
See how well my Turban fitteth, yet the Parsee Girdle binds me;
Cord and Wallet I bear light: be not far, O be not far!
True Parsee and true Brahman, a Christian, yet a Mussulman,
Thee I trust supreme by Right: be not far, O be not far!
In all Mosques, Pagodas, Churches, I do find one Shrine alone;
Thy Face is there my sole delight: be not far, O be not far!'[2]

The same principle enables the Ṣūfī poet to solve the problems of evil and predestination.

'The more a man loves, the deeper he penetrates the divine purposes. Love is "the astrolabe of heavenly mysteries," the eye-salve which clears the spiritual eye and makes it clairvoyant.'[3]

Through love we can discern that evil, so far as it has any real existence—and in relation to God it has none—is a good in disguise or, at the worst, a necessary condition for the manifestation of good.[4] As regards predestination, perfect love implies identity of will and thus abolishes the conflict between freedom and necessity.

'The word "compulsion" makes me impatient for love's sake;
'Tis he who loves not that is fettered by compulsion.
This is close communion with God, not compulsion,
The shining of the sun, and not a dark cloud.'[5]

The lyric poetry of Ṣūfism reaches its highest mark in pantheistic hymns describing the states of *fanā* (negation of individuality) and *baqā* (affirmation of universal consciousness).

'Lo, for I to myself am unknown, now in God's name what must I do?
I adore not the Cross nor the Crescent, I am not a Giaour nor a Jew.
East nor West, land nor sea is my home, I have kin nor with angel nor gnome,
I am wrought not of fire nor of foam, I am shaped not of dust nor of dew.
I was born not in China afar, not in Saqsīn and not in Bulghār;
Not in India, where five rivers are, nor 'Irāq nor Khorāsān I grew.
Not in this world nor that world I dwell, not in Paradise, neither in Hell;
Not from Eden and Rizwān I fell, not from Adam my lineage I drew.
In a place beyond uttermost Place, in a tract without shadow of trace,
Soul and body transcending I live in the soul of my Loved One anew!'[6]

Though many of these poems are exquisite in form and elaborate in style, it is difficult to regard them as products of conscious literary art, and the present writer is inclined to accept the statement that the odes of Jalāl al-Dīn Rūmī, Ibn al-Fāriḍ, Ibn al-'Arabī, and other Ṣūfī poets were often composed under the influence of ecstasy and are in fact analogous to what is known as 'automatic writing.'[1] Their rhythm and melody, combined with the symbolic form in which they are clothed, give them a strange power of communicating to the reader the same feeling of rapture by which their composer was inspired; and the effect is greatly enhanced when they are chanted with an accompaniment of music, as is customary among Ṣūfīs engaged in *dhikr*. While students of this poetry cannot ignore the conventional rules of interpretation which assign a fixed allegorical meaning to a large number of words that are commonly used in a different sense, such a method may easily be pushed too far. Ibn al-'Arabī's commentary on the *Tarjumān al-Ashwāq* shows that even the author of a mystical ode is sometimes unable to explain its meaning. The ecstatic element appears only at intervals and seldom with its first intensity in narrative romances, which depict the soul's love of God and its ultimate union with Him as the story of two human lovers—*e.g.*, Yūsuf and Zulaikhā, Lailā and Majnūn, Salāmān and Absāl—and didactic poems, of which the *Masnavī* is the most celebrated.

LITERATURE.—This art. is supplementary to, and should be read in connexion with, the art. ASCETICISM (Muslim). In the present writer's opinion, it would be premature to aim at giving a historical conspectus of the subject, since adequate materials are not yet available. Further information concerning the doctrines of individual Ṣūfīs will be found in the artt. 'ABD AL-QĀDIR AL-JĪLĀNĪ, 'ABD AR-RAZZĀQ, ḤALLĀJ, IBN ṬUFAIL, JALĀL AL-DĪN RŪMĪ, MUḤYĪ AL-DĪN IBN AL-'ARABĪ, ASH-SHA'RĀNĪ, and SUHRAWARDĪ. See also artt. BLESSEDNESS (Muhammadan), COMMUNION WITH DEITY (Muslim), DERVISH, and LOVE (Muhammadan).

(1) *General.*—F. A. G. Tholuck, *Ssufismus sive Theosophia Persarum pantheistica*, Berlin, 1821; E. H. Palmer, *Oriental Mysticism*, Cambridge, 1867; E. G. Browne, art. 'Ṣūfiism,' in *Religious Systems of the World*, London, 1892, p. 314 ff.; I. Goldziher, *Vorlesungen über den Islam*, Heidelberg, 1910, pp. 139–200; D. B. Macdonald, *The Religious Attitude and Life in Islam*, Chicago, 1909; R. A. Nicholson, *The Mystics of Islam*, London, 1914; Hujwīrī, *Kashf al-Maḥjūb*, tr. R. A. Nicholson, do. 1911.

(2) *Origin and early development.*—A. von Kremer, *Gesch. der herrschenden Ideen des Islams*, Leipzig, 1868, p. 52 ff.; E. G. Browne, *Literary Hist. of Persia*, London, 1902–06, i. 296 ff., 416 ff.; A. Merx, *Idee und Grundlinien einer allgemeinen Gesch. der Mystik*, Heidelberg, 1893, p. 25 ff.; I. Goldziher, 'Materialien zur Entwickelungsgesch. des Ṣūfismus,' *Vienna Oriental Journal*, vol. xiii. [1899] no. 1, p. 35 ff.; R. A. Nicholson, 'An Historical Enquiry concerning the Origin and Development of Ṣūfiism,' *JRAS*, 1906, p. 303 ff.; D. S. Margoliouth, *The Early Development of Mohammedanism (HL)*, London, 1913, p. 167 ff.; Shaikh Muhammad Iqbāl, *The Development of Metaphysics in Persia*, do. 1908, p. 96 ff.; H. Frank, *Beitrag zur Erkenntniss des Sufismus nach Ibn Khaldūn*, Leipzig, 1884; L. Massignon, *Kitāb al-Ṭawāsīn*, Paris, 1913; D. S. Margoliouth, 'Notice of the Writings of al-Ḥārith al-Muḥāsibī, the first Ṣūfī Author,' in *Trans. of the Third Internat. Congress for the Hist. of Religions*, Oxford, 1908, i. 292 ff.; R. Hartmann, *Das Ṣūfītum nach al-Ḳuschairī*, Hamburg, 1914; *Al-Kuschairī's Darstellung des Ṣūfītums*, Berlin, 1914; I. Goldziher, 'Neuplatonische und gnostische Elemente im Ḥadīth,' *ZA* xxii. [1908] 317 ff., *A Buddhismus hatása az Iszlamra*, Budapest, 1903, tr. T. Duka, in *JRAS*, 1904, p. 125 ff.; E. H. Whinfield, 'Hellenism and Muhammadanism,' *JRAS*, 1905, p. 527 ff.; R. A. Nicholson, 'The Goal of Muhammadan Mysticism,' *JRAS*, 1913, p. 55 ff.

(3) *Doctrine.*—Most of the important European books and papers on Ṣūfism have already been mentioned in the present art. or in the various artt. enumerated above. These titles are not repeated in the list which follows. M. Schreiner, 'Beiträge zur Gesch. der theologischen Bewegungen im Islam,' *ZDMG* lii. [1898] 513 ff.; E. Blochet, 'Etudes sur l'ésoterisme musulman,' *JA*, 9th ser., xix. [1902] 489 ff. and xx. [1902] 49 ff. (concerning the different grades of Ṣūfīs, the *quṭb*, and the inferior saints); I. Goldziher, *Muhammedanische Studien*, Halle, 1888-90, pt. ii. pp. 277–378 (worship of Muslim saints); H. Ethé, 'Der Sūfismus und seine drei Hauptvertreter,' in *Morgenländische Studien*, Leipzig, 1870, p. 95 ff.; W. H. T. Gairdner, 'Al-Ghazālī's Mishkāt al-Anwār and the Ghazālī-Problem,' in *Der Islam*, v. [1914] 121 ff., "*The Way*" *of a Mohammedan Mystic*, Leipzig, 1912; E. H. Whinfield, *Lawā'iḥ* of Jāmī, Persian text with Eng. tr., London, 1906; F. A. G. Tholuck, *Blüthensammlung aus der morgenländischen Mystik*, Berlin, 1825.

REYNOLD A. NICHOLSON.

[1] Jāmī, *Yūsuf ū Zulaikhā*, tr. E. G. Browne, in art. 'Ṣūfiism' in *Religious Systems of the World*, p. 328 f.
[2] Tr. after Rückert by W. Hastie in *The Festival of Spring, from the Divan of Jelâleddîn*, Glasgow, 1903, p. 3.
[3] Whinfield, *Masnavi-i Ma'navi: the Spiritual Couplets of Maulana Jalālu-'d-dīn Muhammad-i Rūmī*[2], London, 1898, Introd. p. 28.
[4] Nicholson, *Mystics of Islam*, p. 96 f.
[5] Whinfield, *Masnavi-i Ma'navi*, p. 26.
[6] *Dīvāni Shamsi Tabrīz*, p. 344.

[1] Cf. the testimony of Madame Guyon and Blake, cited in E. Underhill, *Mysticism*[4], London, 1912, p. 78 ff.

SUGGESTION.—Suggestion is the production of a reaction by an ideational process, but without deliberation on the part of the subject thereof. The term applies also to any attempt by the subject or by another person to produce such a reaction. 'A' suggestion is any idea that determines, or is used for the purpose of determining, the outcome of such a non-deliberative process.

The qualification 'by an ideational process' is intended to differentiate suggestion from primary instinct-acts. Such acts, though they may be secondarily initiated by an idea or mental image (as when a letter makes me angry with the writer of it), require as their primary stimulus nothing but an appropriate sense-presentation. Suggestion, on the other hand, is primarily ideational. The most typical suggestions are those that are conveyed by language. Gesture, in the broad sense of significant bodily motions, postures, and inarticulate vocalization, comes next. Natural phenomena act suggestively only when they have antecedently acquired a meaning, as when one avoids poison ivy, or quickens one's pace upon hearing distant thunder.

The term 'reaction,' as here used, refers to both psychical and bodily responses. It includes beliefs, hallucinatory perceptions, attitudes (with their affective and emotional aspects), stimulation of involuntary muscles and of certain glands, particular contractions of voluntary muscles and muscle-systems, even extended chains of such contractions, and finally, in all these fields, inhibitions and functional paralyses as well as stimulations.

A reaction is 'deliberate' when it is made after attention has been given to alternatives, and with the alternatives in view. Associated with the idea that defines any alternative is a tendency towards something beyond itself as merely this idea now present. Because of these associated tendencies ideas may be said to compete with one another and therefore to involve inhibitions as well as positive stimulations. In deliberation there is mutual inhibition of two or more competing ideas, wherefore popular thought correctly conceives that pause or postponement is a mark of deliberate conduct and of deliberate believing. Suggestion, on the other hand, implies the absence, or relative lack, of such competition, inhibition, and pause. All that is necessary is that attention should be withheld from some of the ideas appropriate to the given situation, and focused or 'narrowed down' to some one idea or coherent chain of ideas. Thereupon the associated tendency that has just been referred to is automatically instated.

How such associated tendencies should be conceived has been a matter of debate. W. McDougall, emphasizing the subconscious character of the connexions here involved, and also the close relation of suggestion in general to 'psychic phenomena,' is of the opinion that any adequate analysis of suggestion must rest at last upon a theory of the subconscious.[1] William James used the phrase 'ideo-motor action' to designate what he regarded as a mental law, namely:

'Every representation of a movement awakens in some degree the actual movement which is its object; and awakens it in a maximum degree whenever it is not kept from so doing by an antagonistic representation present simultaneously to the mind.'[2]

On the other hand, E. L. Thorndike opposes to the 'ideo-motor' theory, and by implication to McDougall also, the following far simpler theory: an idea may produce a movement in either of two ways—by imaging an object that awakens an instinctive response, or, under the ordinary law of habit, by reinstating something that has previously been associated in the subject's experience with the suggestive idea. The reason why the idea of bending my first finger produces actual bending, according to Thorndike, is that the two—the idea of the bending and the actual bending—have been experienced together heretofore. The very first flexions of the finger, it may be added, occurred reflexly, without any antecedent idea thereof. Just so, if the sight of a glass of water upon my dinner-table induces me to drink water that I do not want, habit is clearly the explanation.[1]

This theory enables us to bring all the psychical and physical manifestations of suggestion under the same two heads, habit and instinct.

Both are found in Antony's handling of the Roman rabble. The opinion of the artisans concerning Cæsar's death was quickly reversed, not by the weighing of pros and cons, but by bringing attention back again and again to essentially the same point, *i.e.* by narrowing attention so that the old attitude of admiration for Cæsar the conqueror was reinstated. In addition, Antony arouses various instincts, as when he works upon curiosity until the crowd demands to hear the will that he pretends to withhold.

It is evident that suggestion is not an exceptional, rare, or abnormal phenomenon, but an omnipresent fact of all mind whenever its reactions are upon the ideational level. In hypnosis competing ideas may be inhibited to an extraordinary degree, but there is no fixed line of division between the incipient stages of hypnosis gradually brought on and fully normal mental action. Similarly the ordinary effects of cheerful or of gloomy expectation are merely heightened in the extreme and truly remarkable facts of suggestive therapeutics.[2]

The process of suggestion has, as such, no particular relation to the truth or the falsity of what is suggested. One may arrive by suggestion at true beliefs or false, and at ethically correct or incorrect attitudes and conduct. Suggestion is an ordinary device of oratory and of preaching, as it is also of advertising and of salesmanship. Recent works on 'business psychology' present what may fairly be called a technic that is parallel to that of physicians who employ psycho-therapy. Thus far the ethical aspects of influencing buyers by suggestion have not been examined as carefully as the technic.

If any one should doubt whether the deliberate influencing of men to act without deliberation is ever justifiable, the following three considerations would have a bearing. (1) There are numerous cases in which the ends of deliberation are defeated by the process of deliberation itself, as when too meticulous weighing of possible consequences or an overwrought insistence upon complete certainty prevents the action that a situation calls for. One way to get such a person over his 'dead centre' is precisely to narrow his attention to one of the alternatives until action ensues. (2) When an instinctive capacity for noble emotions and attitudes has become dull from disuse, one simply lacks considerations that are needed for deliberation. A psychological pre-condition of all deliberation is appreciation of the pertinent alternatives. What is to be done for a man, then, whose habits preclude any feeling of the force of a pertinent alternative? The obviously rational procedure is by processes of suggestion to narrow his attention upon some object that may awaken an instinctive response of the desirable sort, and then to lead him to include this fresh experience among the data of his deliberate thinking. (3) Whether we will or not, a large factor in education, particularly in the development of standards and ideals in the young, is suggestion emanating from adults, especi-

[1] See art. HYPNOTISM.
[2] *Principles of Psychology*, ii. 526.

[1] See Thorndike, 'Ideo-Motor Action,' *Psych. Rev.* xx. [1913] 91-106.
[2] See artt. DISEASE AND MEDICINE, HYPNOTISM, PSYCHOTHERAPEUTICS.

ally parents and teachers. A purely rationalistic education is a psychological impossibility. Hence it is a custom of educators to take at least some measures for determining the sorts of suggestion to which pupils shall be exposed. M. W. Keatinge argues for careful, deliberate planning of this part of teaching.[1]

On the other hand, suggestion is, on the whole, a process of repetition or of maintaining some *status quo ante* rather than a process of criticism and revision. Under the influence of suggestion alone one merely drifts with social currents, or follows a leader, or imitates one's own past, or at best applies a recognized standard or sets free a disused instinctive capacity. To judge a standard, on the other hand, one must attend to alternatives. It would be a mistake, nevertheless, to suppose that truly ethical action requires nothing but deliberation. Ethical situations are made real to us, especially situations that call for reform, by some kindling of elemental processes that include strong satisfactions or their opposites. Thus it comes to pass that great sermons commonly interweave strong suggestions with analysis and even argument.

To exhibit the whole significance of suggestion in religion would require an historical catalogue of practically all forms of deeply felt experience. Primitive fears connected with tabu and with spiritism were propagated from individual to individual and from generation to generation by suggestion. The same is true of the rejoicing that accompanied some of the ceremonies. Priesthoods acquired and retained their power by narrowing the attention of worshippers by means of sense stimuli of various sorts focused upon some point that required no deliberation. The mystics of all ages have practised auto-suggestion under the name of contemplation or interior prayer. Modern revivals have produced a sense of sin, conversion (reversal of attitudes and of likes and dislikes), and 'assurance' or the 'witness of the Spirit' chiefly by suggestion. Indeed, managers of revival campaigns at the present day are accustomed to organize preaching, singing, personal work, and advertising of various kinds upon a strictly suggestive basis. Not the least item is the careful preparation of the public mind, sometimes for weeks in advance of the first public meeting. Finally, such experiences as 'the jerks,' 'the power,' 'speaking in tongues,' and 'interpretation of tongues' present as a whole cases of suggestion. They are usually initiated by a spontaneous automatism which is then imitated (by oneself and by others) without deliberation, but often with support from passages of Scripture. The idea of a baptism 'with fire' has similarly fulfilled itself here and there.[2]

The phenomena of suggestion reach their climax in human masses, whether crowds (which involve spatial propinquity) or a public whose opinions and attitudes are formed by common reading matter or even by statements passing from mouth to mouth. It is a fact of common observation that in a crowd one may act 'like a different person,' accepting as truth what one could not ordinarily believe, and conducting oneself contrary to one's ordinary standards. The mechanism whereby crowd suggestion acquires this remarkable power is as follows. (1) Certain instinctive capacities are strongly stirred by the massing of appropriate stimuli. Man has a gregarious instinct, is peculiarly interested in the movements of his fellows, and is sensitive to their approvals and disapprovals. Here is the basis for a quickening or excitement of the mind through the mere presence of others, as also for watching and following others, and for subordinating, even forgetting, one's own ideas in the presence of a sentiment generally held by the mass. (2) A crowd usually assembles under the influence of some common thought. Even when this is not the case, conversation tends to produce a common thought. Moreover, under the stimulus of the excitement already referred to, some individual—either one with relatively few inhibitions or one with strong convictions, or even a designing demagogue—is likely to speak aloud. This often precipitates the thinking of the entire mass. It is now as if each one were suggesting to every other one the idea that has come to expression. Thus sentiment rolls up like a snowball. (3) This narrowing of attention, as already indicated, involves an equally strong inhibition upon ideas that would ordinarily appear as competitors. Therefore strong, impulsive action occurs spontaneously and appears to the subject to be natural and justifiable. A crowd is incapable of fine discriminations and of skill; its acts tend towards the simplicity and crudity of instinct; and therefore, in this case, a human association easily acts less socially (as far as ends and consequences are concerned) than its members would do if they faced the same moral issue severally.

All that has just been said applies also to masses that are unified by means of the public press. Our present means of communication are so swift and so all-pervasive that men feel the presence of one another almost the world over at almost the same instant. Communities that are a thousand miles apart get the same news, often word for word, at about the same hour; the effect of the news in one community now becomes an item of news in the other; action as well as idea thus spreads. This is the process whereby a whole nation rises to succour sufferers from earthquake or from fire, or to repel an invader. Thus, too, political opinions as well as fashions of dress and of speech spread with great rapidity.

A study of suggestion as a means of governing men in the State as well as in the Church will show that one of the basal differences between types of organization lies in the degree to which suggestion, as compared with deliberation, is officially used. At the tribal level of organization common action is secured to a great extent by suggestion of the crowd type, as in dances and other ceremonies, and in the personal leadership of the chief. In the monarchical State, as in sacerdotal religion, men are ruled partly by direct command (which is, under some conditions, a potent mode of suggestion), and partly by pageantry and other sensuous or sentimental appeal that ever reawakens a traditional attitude of loyalty. The underlying psychical principle of democracy, on the other hand, is deliberate group action. A deliberative group is one in which unity is sought, not by withdrawing attention from alternatives, but by mutual incitement to pause and weigh alternatives before acting. This type is most fully developed in bodies that have formal rules of order. Here, as a preliminary to each common act, the entire group pauses, the chairman saying, 'Are there any remarks?' Then, as if challenging each individual to full, deliberate self-expression, he asks, 'Are you ready for the question?' This procedure has been devised so as to prevent action under suggestion. Whereas the crowd becomes a unit by the suppression of individual inhibitions, the deliberative group achieves its unity precisely by inviting the expression of competing ideas, and by spreading them out for inspection and unforced selection. The ballot, in popular government, is an organ for essentially

[1] *Suggestion in Education*[2].

[2] See H. S. Dyer, *Revival in India*, London, 1907, ch. iv. and p. 76.

the same type of deliberation on the scale of the local community or of the nation.[1]

LITERATURE.—A. Binet, *La Suggestibilité*, Paris, 1900; Warner Brown, 'Individual and Sex Differences in Suggestibility,' *University of California Publications in Psychology*, 1916, ii., no. 6, pp. 291–430; G. A. Coe, *The Psychology of Religion*, Chicago, 1916, chs. viii. and x.; A. S. Edwards, 'An Experimental Study of Sensory Suggestion,' *AJPs* xxvi. [1915] 99–129; H. L. Hollingworth, *Advertising and Selling*, New York and London, 1917, ch. xii.; W. James, *The Principles of Psychology*, 2 vols., New York and London, 1890 and later editions, ii. 522–530, and ch. xxvii.; M. W. Keatinge, *Suggestion in Education*², London, 1911; W. D. Scott, *The Psychology of Advertising*, Boston, 1908, ch. vi., *Influencing Men in Business*, New York, 1911, chs. v. and vi.; E. L. Thorndike, 'Ideo-Motor Action,' *Psych. Rev.* xx. [1913] 91–106; C. L. Tuckey, *Treatment by Hypnotism and Suggestion*⁶, London, 1913; W. Wundt, *Hypnotismus und Suggestion*, Leipzig, 1892, reprinted from *Philosophische Studien*, vol. viii. pt. i. The *Psychological Bulletin* publishes annually an annotated list of new publications on suggestion. See also the annual *Psychological Index* under division VIII. 2.

GEORGE A. COE.

SUHRAWARDĪ.—Suhraward, a small town in the Jibāl province of Persia, has given its name to two celebrated mystics whose lives, characters, and opinions present a remarkable contrast, though both were born in the same decade. Of Shihāb al-dīn 'Umar b. 'Abdallah al-Suhrawardī (A.D. 1144–1234) it is enough to say that he was a Ṣūfī of the conventional type, that he lectured and preached in Baghdād under court patronage, and that his writings include a well-known treatise on Ṣūfism—the *'Awārif al-ma'ārif*—and a polemical work directed against the study of Greek philosophy, which he dedicated to the khalīfah al-Nāṣir.[2] His contemporary, Shihāb al-dīn Yaḥyā b. Amīrak al-Suhrawardī (A.D. 1153–91), after studying jurisprudence and theology at Marāgha, devoted himself to mystical philosophy, led the wandering life of a dervish, and finally settled in Aleppo. While some of his earlier books were written under the influence of Aristotle, he was at heart a Platonist, as is shown by the title and contents of his chief work, the *Ḥikmatu 'l-ishrāq* ('Philosophy of Illumination')—whence the school of mystics who follow him are called Ishrāqīs (*al-ishrāqīyūn*). Being an enthusiast as well as a bold and original thinker, he made no attempt to disguise the anti-Islāmic tendency of his doctrines. It cannot be denied that from the orthodox standpoint they were detestable; and, though at first he found an admirer in al-Malik al-Ẓāhir, the son of Saladin, he was condemned and executed by order of that prince in 1191. The name of 'martyr' (*shahīd*) was refused to him; he is generally known as Suhrawardī al-maqtūl ('Suhrawardī the slain') or al-Shaikh al-maqtūl.

In his theory of illumination he combines Neo-Platonic and Persian ideas. The source of all things is the Absolute Light (*al-nūr al-qāhir*). That which is visible requires no definition, and nothing is more visible than light, whose very nature consists in manifestation.

'The Primal Light, therefore, has no reason of its existence beyond itself. All that is other than this original principle is dependent, contingent, possible. The "not-light" (darkness) is not something distinct proceeding from an independent source. It is an error of the representatives of the Magian religion to suppose that Light and Darkness are two distinct realities created by two distinct creative agencies. . . . The relation between them is not that of contrariety, but of existence and non-existence. The affirmation of Light necessarily posits its own negation—Darkness, which it must illuminate in order to be itself. This Primordial Light is the source of all motion. But its motion is not change of place; it is due to the *love* of illumination which constitutes its very essence. . . . The number of illuminations which proceed from it is infinite. Illuminations of intenser brightness become in their turn the sources of other illuminations; and the scale of brightness gradually descends to illuminations too faint to beget other illuminations. All these illuminations are mediums, or in the language of theology angels through whom the infinite varieties of being receive life and sustenance from the Primal Light.'[1]

We may distinguish two illuminations, *i.e.* modes of being, of the Primal Light: (1) pure, abstract, formless; (2) accidental, derivative, possessing form. The pure light is self-conscious substance (spirit and soul), knowing itself through itself, for 'whatever knows itself must be pure light.' The accidental light is related to the pure light as effect to cause and only exists as an attribute in association with the illuminated object (body), which is not matter in Aristotle's use of the term, but merely the negation necessarily implied in the nature of light.

'The experimental fact of the transformation of the primary elements[2] into one another points to this fundamental Absolute matter which, with its various degrees of grossness, constitutes the various spheres of material being.'[3]

It is of two kinds: (*a*) dark substance, (*b*) dark forms, *i.e.* qualities; and the combination of these two makes up a material body. Since darkness is nothing but the absence of light, and light is identical with reality, the substance and forms of the universe consist of illuminations diffused from the Primal Light in infinite gradations of intensity. It follows that everything partakes of reality in proportion to the radiance which it receives and towards which it ever moves 'with a lover's passion, in order to drink more and more of the original fountain of Light.' This perpetual flow and ebb of desire produces the revolutions of the heavenly spheres, the processes of nature, and all human activities. The abstract light (First Intelligence) is less perfect than the Primal Light (God), in contemplating which it becomes conscious of its imperfection, whence there arises in it a darkness that is the ground of plurality in the sensible world. While the entire universe is eternal as emanating from the eternal Light, but contingent if regarded as the object of irradiation, some illuminations are simple, others compound and therefore inferior. The intelligences, the celestial spheres, the souls of the heavens, time, motion, and the archetypes of the elements belong to a higher world, which may be called eternal in contrast with all below it, though in the relation existing between them not posteriority but parallelism is implied. Suhrawardī, like Plato, conceives a world of Ideas—he declares that it was revealed to him mystically—in which every kind of sublunary thing exists as a substance in itself.[4] The wise men of Persia (Zoroastrians), he says, gave names to many of these pure lights (Ideas); *e.g.*, they named the Idea of water Khurdād (May), that of trees Murdād (July), and that of fire Ardībihisht (April).

As each species is endowed with its distinctive qualities and preserved by its guardian Idea—'the lord of the species' (*rabbu 'l-nau'*)—so the Idea of the human body is 'the holy spirit' or universal Reason, while bodies individually are types of rational souls. The soul does not exist before the body. Being pure light, it imparts illumination to the body through the medium of the animal soul. It operates with the five external and the five internal senses, which correspond to powers residing in the ideal archetype. Thus vision, knowledge, memory, imagination, etc., are essentially not passive functions but illuminative acts of the soul. Obeying the principle that what is lower in the scale of being loves what is higher, the soul longs to be united with the formless

[1] Cf. G. A. Coe, *Psychology of Religion*, ch. viii.

[2] Brockelmann, *Gesch. der arab. Litteratur*, i. 440; von Kremer, *Gesch. der herrschenden Ideen des Islams*, p. 99.

[1] Shaikh Muhammad Iqbāl, *The Development of Metaphysics in Persia*, London, 1908, p. 127 f.

[2] Suhrawardī recognizes only three elements, fire being regarded as hot air.

[3] Iqbāl, p. 133.

[4] Carra de Vaux, 'La Philosophie illuminative d'après Suhrawerdi Meqtoul,' *JA*, 9th ser., vol. xix. [1902] p. 72.

world of light, and it advances towards this end according as it seeks to become perfect in philosophy and the practice of virtue. By so doing it develops a mystical perception (*dhauq*) which clears all doubts away. *Dhauq*, as Suhrawardī tells us, forms the basis of the speculations set forth in the *Ḥikmatu 'l-ishrāq*. In one passage he seems to hint that he himself is the *quṭb*, the mysterious head of the Ṣūfī hierarchy,[1] for he asserts that the philosophy of illumination was taught by Empedocles, Pythagoras, Plato, and the Zoroastrian sages, and that the world is never without some one who possesses the doctrine and can expound it with authority; that person, he adds, is God's vicegerent (*khalīfat Allah*) on the earth.[2] Attainment of *fanā*[3] unites the soul with God, but does not mean that one substance is absorbed in another. No two souls can be completely alike.

'The individual souls, after death, are not unified into one soul, but continue different from each other in proportion to the illumination they received during their companionship with physical organisms. . . . Some souls probably come back to this world in order to make up their deficiencies. The doctrine of transmigration cannot be proved or disproved from a purely logical standpoint, though it is a probable hypothesis to account for the future destiny of the soul. All souls are thus constantly journeying towards their common source, which calls back the whole universe when this journey is over, and starts another cycle of being to reproduce in almost all respects the history of the preceding cycles.'[1]

Suhrawardī agrees with Ghazālī in holding that the world could not be better than it is. Evil is a negation depending on the motion and darkness which, as we have seen, are involved in the nature of light; it is associated with the effects and does not proceed *per se* from the First Cause; if it existed *per se*, it would not be evil. In his clear and sympathetic exposition of the Ishrāqī philosophy Shaikh Muhammad Iqbāl calls attention to Suhrawardī's intellectual independence and to the skill with which he moulded his Neo-Platonic materials into a thoroughly Persian system of thought, uniting speculation and emotion in perfect harmony. Mystic and (in a sense) pantheist as he was, he regards the external world as real and never loses touch with it.

'No Persian thinker is more alive to the necessity of explaining all the aspects of objective existence in reference to his fundamental principles.'[2]

LITERATURE.—Besides the references given in the art., M. Horten, *Die Philosophie der Erleuchtung nach Suhrawardī* (*Abhandlungen zur Philosophie und ihrer Geschichte*, xxxviii.), Halle, 1912; A. von Kremer, *Gesch. der herrschenden Ideen des Islams*, Leipzig, 1868, p. 89 ff.; C. Brockelmann, *Gesch. der arab. Litteratur*, Berlin, 1898–1902, i. 437.

REYNOLD A. NICHOLSON.

SUICIDE.

SUICIDE (Introductory).—Before attempting any discussion of suicide from the standpoint of ethics or religion, we should note that in many cases — probably the majority, among civilized peoples—either no moral judgment can be passed upon the act or at least great allowance must be made for the mental condition of the agent. Lunacy not infrequently involves such complete loss of the instinct of self-preservation that the patient, even where analgesia is not present, will mutilate or kill himself, apparently without any idea of what he is doing. So in *dementia præcox* 'self-respect, modesty and the instinct of self-preservation are quite absent'; and the result is various absurd, criminal, or indecent acts, including suicide for a trivial reason or none at all.[4] Again, *dementia paralytica*, or chronic periencephalitis, although like many forms of mental diseases it generally produces intense and unreasoning attachment to life,[5] often involves accesses of wild, self-directed fury, such as that in which Guy de Maupassant tried to kill himself.[6] But the most typical examples are those of melancholia. We quote part of Tanzi's admirably lucid account:

'In some cases of melancholia scenes of the most horrible and sanguinary nature, which are represented to the patient's mind as simple possibilities, and repeated as favourite images on account of their hideousness, become transformed into a *motor obsession*. The obsession, meeting with but slight resistance in an exhausted and abulic brain (*i.e.* one almost if not quite deprived of will-power), becomes so imperative as to drive the patient inexorably to the commission of acts corresponding to it, such as . . . suicide in its most horrible forms.'[7]

The state in which these acts occur—the *raptus melancholicus*—is quasi-unconscious. But suicide often takes place in less advanced cases than this, when the patient is not wholly irresponsible, but is actuated by motives the importance of which his disease greatly exaggerates. A preliminary symptom of the *raptus* is precordial anxiety—a sort of horrible intensification of that uneasy 'sinking feeling in the pit of the stomach' which often attacks a healthy man when frightened or anxious.[3] Now, as a normal subject may be tempted, by the depression arising out of a real misfortune, to take his own life, so a melancholiac suffering from this intense and abnormal feeling of anxious misery is not infrequently driven in a quasi-normal way to commit suicide. Objectively he has no sufficient motive, but subjectively his hopeless depression, the morbid nature of which he is unable to realize, presents itself as a good reason for wishing to be dead and fulfilling his wish.[4] Still more typical are those suicides of melancholiacs which are inspired by altruistic motives, the patient believing that his death will in some way greatly benefit his friends—*e.g.*, that he is miserably poor and must relieve his family of the burden of supporting him,[5] or that his life is demanded in expiation of a fancied crime, or the like. Such unfortunates are well aware of what they are doing; their delusion consists simply in believing that they have an adequate motive. Often their action has a kind of perverted nobility, arising from a devotion to an ideal which in itself is lofty enough, although the ideal is imaginary and the form which the devotion takes morbid. It has been suggested that in these cases the disease has exaggerated and distorted the instinct of self-sacrifice,[6] which is a normal constituent of the

1 See art. ṢŪFĪS. 2 Carra de Vaux, p. 68 f.
3 See art. ṢŪFĪS.
4 Tanzi (*A Text-book of Mental Diseases*, p. 640) gives a case (p. 641) of a patient who believed that he was invulnerable and killed himself in trying to prove it. An apparently unmotived suicide is described on p. 662.
5 Tanzi, p. 231. 6 *Ib.* p. 519. 7 *Ib.* p. 513.

1 Iqbāl, p. 147 f. 2 *Ib.* p. 149.
3 This is merely a rough description of the nature of the two sensations. Physiologically they are quite distinct, one being precordial, the other epigastric.
4 Tanzi, p. 514; Mercier, *Sanity and Insanity*[2], p. 350.
5 Mercier, p. 351; this suicide was in reality very well off.
6 It might also be described as a distortion of the social sense, or herd-instinct, which some would regard as primary (like self-preservation, etc.). See W. Trotter, *Instincts of the Herd*[2], London, 1919, especially p. 18 ff.

sexual emotions, especially in women. Hence such suicides are particularly common among adolescents. As there is admittedly a close connexion between sexual and religious emotions, especially in their more exaggerated and morbid forms, we may put some at least of the religious suicides (see below) in this category.[1]

In most cases of this kind the patient's insanity is easily recognizable; and even in those instances where a melancholiac supposed to be cured relapses and ends his life in a suicidal fit—or possibly feigns recovery in order to carry out, when left unguarded, his purpose of self-destruction—we need have no hesitation in pronouncing him at least partly irresponsible.[2] It is less easy to pass judgment on the numerous class of neurasthenics. A characteristic feature of the mental state of these sufferers is that impulses, often of the most absurd or criminal nature, haunt and obsess the imagination; and, while the patient knows perfectly well that these impulses are not rational—thus differing from the melancholiac—he is not always strong-minded enough to control them.

The most vivid description known to us of this condition occurs, not in a technical work at all, but in two of the stories of one who seems himself to have been a neurasthenic and clearly regarded such impulses as part of the normal human mentality—Edgar Allan Poe.[3] This author represents two men, one as betraying a fatal secret, the other as killing a pet animal, for no other reason than that the acts are insanely devoid of motive; and the writings of alienists[4] give many actual cases of the same kind. Clearly, then, when a neurasthenic's obsession is suicidal, if he yields to it, he cannot either be regarded as an ordinary lunatic who does not know what he is doing or imagines that he has good reasons for his act, or be judged like a normal man who decides, on more or less rational grounds, that he wishes to end his life.

It is still harder to pass satisfactory moral judgments on the rather numerous persons, apparently sane but perhaps really neurasthenic, whose suicides have a motive, but an inadequate one—a small injury, real or supposed, to honour, or even so trivial a cause as a wager.

Suicides of this kind sometimes amount to a sort of epidemic. When one member of a family has ended his life, the recurrence of the anniversary of his death, the sight of the weapon that he used, or some such casual association has been known to drive a relative to follow his example, until as many as seven of one household have died by their own hands.[5] Larger epidemics, extending through an entire city, or even wider,[6] have not been unknown in ancient or modern times, and are frequently associated with religious mania. These are probably hysterical, as hysteria is easily communicated and often produces, especially among women, 'theatrical attempts at suicide.'[7]

To all these classes of more or less non-moral acts of self-destruction should be added the very large number of instances of persons who are sane for the greater part of their lives, but, as a result of violent nervous shock, disease, grief, excesses of one sort or another, etc., become temporarily unbalanced to a slight degree. These causes are so many that it is questionable whether any one whose life is of normal length is absolutely sane during every waking moment of it.[8] We need not doubt that the charitable verdict of the average coroner's jury, 'suicide while of unsound mind,' is in a large percentage of cases quite in accordance with medical facts.

But our primary interest is in the act of one who, being perfectly sane, takes his own life. The question whether such a deed is justifiable, and, if so, when and under what circumstances, has been answered in the most various ways by peoples of

[1] See Mercier, pp. 354–357.

[2] For other forms of mental disease resulting in suicide during more or less complete irresponsibility see Tanzi, pp. 321 (alcoholism), 603 f. (epilepsy).

[3] See 'The Imp of the Perverse' and 'The Black Cat' in *Tales of the Grotesque and Arabesque*, especially the opening paragraphs of the former.

[4] Several examples in Tanzi, p. 540 f.

[5] Tanzi, p. 231.

[6] *E.g.*, at Miletos; see Plutarch, *de Mulierum Virtutibus*, p. 249 *b*, *c* (wholesale suicide by hanging of the young women 'from some obscure cause'); cf. Aulus Gellius, xv. x. 1 f.

[7] Tanzi, p. 585.

[8] Mercier, p. 131.

different degrees of culture, from the lowest savages to members of the highest civilizations, ancient and modern. Some account of these answers has been given elsewhere.[1] We propose now to consider the attitude taken by religions, savage and civilized, and by the leading schools of moral philosophy.

1. Religion.—Various faiths have taken every conceivable view of suicide, from recommending it to resolutely and uncompromisingly opposing it. As the grounds for the former view are less obvious to us, it is well to begin by briefly discussing them. First in the list stand those fanatic beliefs, including degraded forms of Christianity, whose votaries have been impelled to kill themselves, often in most painful ways, to attain a blissful immortality or to avoid something which they regarded as polluting.

Russia furnishes us with some remarkable examples. Thus at Tiraspol, in 1897, twenty-eight persons buried themselves alive to escape the census, which apparently they regarded as sinful. But a more wide-spread epidemic occurred in 1666, in which year many Russian zealots looked for the appearance of Antichrist. To escape him and enter heaven, suicide was strongly urged by certain wrong-headed and often wholly criminal persons, clerical and lay. 'Whole communities hailed with enthusiasm the gospel of death, and hastened to put its precepts into practice. . . . At first the favourite mode of death was by starvation. . . . (But) death by famine was attended by some obvious disadvantages. It was slow: it opened the door to repentance: it occasionally admitted of rescue. Accordingly death by fire was preferred as surer and more expeditious. . . . The mania in its most extreme form died away towards the end of the seventeenth century, but during the eighteenth and nineteenth centuries cases of collective suicide from religious motives occurred from time to time.'[2]

Many of these people, and other such religious suicides, were undoubtedly in a condition of hysteria, if not actual paranoia. We have a parallel to such self-destruction in the most horrible of the rites of Kybele—that which took place on the *dies sanguinis*, at least in its earlier form.[3] On this occasion the devotees of the goddess, wrought up to a pitch of frenzy by an exciting and elaborate ritual, not only wounded themselves, but performed the act of self-emasculation, thereafter joining the ranks of the *Galli*. Turning now to medical evidence, we find[4] such mutilation named along with suicide and manslaughter as typical of some forms of lunacy. We have thus two closely related acts, both involving loss of the instinct of self-preservation, arising, not from ordinary mania, but from a temporary insanity artificially produced and due to a perverted or degraded religious instinct.

But religious suicides are not always maniacs. We need only allude in passing to the innumerable cases, familiar from Frazer, of divine kings and other incarnate deities who kill themselves or are killed, either after a fixed period has elapsed or when their bodily vigour begins to fail. Indeed, these can hardly be called suicides in the strict sense, since the killing is, in intent, merely the first act of a process of reincarnation. That the god should be destroyed is never thought of; it is simply desired to provide him with a new and more desirable fleshly covering. Nor can one justly class as maniacs those persons who hold that by killing themselves they can attain future happiness—an idea not uncommon in some forms of Buddhism—or will return to life in this world stronger or wiser than before.[5] However erroneous their belief may be from the point of view of any sound theological or metaphysical system, it is not a delusion in the medical sense, but often the perfectly logical result of their tenets. In the

[1] See art. EUTHANASIA.

[2] Frazer, *GB*³, pt. iii., *The Dying God*, London, 1911, p. 44 f., quoting I. Stchoukine, *Le Suicide collectif dans le Raskol russe*, Paris, 1903; cf. Tanzi, p. 731 f.

[3] Vividly described by Frazer, *GB*³, pt. iv., *Adonis, Attis, Osiris*, London, 1914, i. 223 ff.; cf. Wissowa, *Rel. und Kultus der Römer*², Munich, 1912, p. 321 ff.

[4] Tanzi, p. 513.

[5] Examples of both in *GB*³, pt. iii., *The Dying God*, p. 42 ff.

lower strata of human history we have numerous examples of savages who regard suicide as perfectly justifiable (*a*) because the deceased will in the next world have a body in the same state as his present one.[1] This naturally leads to the conclusion that voluntary death is much preferable to mutilation or long and wasting illness, since it will avoid a maimed or helpless life after death. Such suicides are practically examples of euthanasia (*q.v.*). Or (*b*) suicide may, at least in some cases, be reputed as honourable and therefore as procuring a more than usually pleasant lot in the next world, not merely avoiding an unpleasant one. Obviously such ideas are not wide-spread or unqualified, or they would result in the extinction of the peoples holding them. They mostly take this form: a dependent — wife, vassal, or slave—is so closely bound to his or her superior that death cannot sever the tie; therefore, just as in any earthly journey the vassal will faithfully attend his lord, so, when his lord dies, the most honourable course is to follow and continue to serve him. Such fidelity will, it may be expected, result in due honour among the dead.

So at the death of a king of Benin 'his favourites and servants used to compete with each other for the privilege of being buried alive with his body in order that they might attend and minister to him in the other world,' and 'the first to die was deemed the happiest,'[2] no doubt as being the most prompt and willing. Similarly among the early Germans 'infame in omnem uitam ac probrosum superstitem principi suo ex acie recessisse';[3] and in a higher civilization Persian nobles were capable of similar devotion to their king.[4]

But this is hardly a religious idea; more definitely connected with religious belief is the Hindu *satī* (*q.v.*).

Religious opposition to suicide is to be found in all, or nearly all, strata of civilization. Probably the chief, if not the only, reason for this among primitive races is simply the dread of the ghost. The self-destroyer must have been greatly wronged or troubled in some way, or he would not have acted as he did; therefore his ghost will be an unusually troublesome and revengeful spirit, like that of all βιαιοθάνατοι—to borrow the convenient Greek term. Hence, either he must be appeased by the death of his enemy, if known, or by offerings of some kind, or else he must be rendered harmless.

A natural way to accomplish this is to mutilate or destroy the corpse—in fact, to treat it much as mediæval Europe did a supposed vampire. Well-known survivals of this are the Athenian practice of severing its right hand,[5] and the custom, not long discontinued in England, of driving a stake through the body. Such treatment, originally a mere precautionary measure, would easily enough generate the belief that the act of the deceased was something extraordinarily wicked, *i.e.* strongly displeasing to whatever deity the community worshipped. It should be noted, however, that among some peoples in a not very advanced stage of culture suicide is objected to on religious grounds, but no such drastic methods of treating the corpse are in vogue. The Kayans of North Borneo hold that those who die by their own hands live miserably in the next world; but the bodies are not burned or mutilated, nor is any fear of them shown,[6] unless their unceremonious burial on the spot where they are found may be taken to be a precautionary measure indicating fear.[7]

This vague idea of suicide as a crime has been taken over by several higher religions and explained by them in the light of their ethical and eschatological beliefs. Thus for any uncorrupted and logical form of Buddhism it is clearly forbidden, since it violates the first of the five fundamental precepts, 'Kill not any living thing.'[1] A religion—it can scarcely be called a philosophy—which presents certain striking parallels to that of Gautama gave an elaborate justification of its prohibition of suicide. To the Orphic-Pythagorean the present life was a penance which took the form of imprisonment; therefore to kill one's self was to attempt, quite vainly, to shirk a deserved penalty.[2] This view, with various modifications, was taken up by Plato, and reappears in the theological teachings of later philosophy.[3]

The native Roman religion perhaps condemned suicide originally and in theory at least. Servius[4] tells us that the *libri pontificales* bade the body of one who had hanged himself to be cast forth unburied; and the later *Seruius Danielis* adds on the authority of Cassius Hemina that the idea of the disgracefulness of suicide dates from the time of Tarquinius Superbus. More noteworthy is a quotation from Varro,[5] confirming the statement that *suspendiosi* were denied the regular funeral rites. We have no hint, however, that the various suicides of legend and history were otherwise than honourably treated. Possibly the objection was not to suicide in general, but to hanging, regarded as *informis*. At any rate, the rhetorical discussions of the subject[6] quote no native religious scruple.

The opposition of Christianity has from an early date been of the most determined kind. It is true that nothing in the NT directly justifies such an attitude, but certain Patristic writings make it obvious that by their time the discussion had taken the form of an inquiry whether self-destruction was ever allowable. Thus St. Augustine[7] deliberates at considerable length whether such a crime (*scelus*), as he repeatedly calls it, may be condoned in the case of a woman whose honour is in danger, or in any case; and he arrives at a negative conclusion. His reasons are chiefly: (*a*) that suicide is an act which precludes the possibility of repentance,[8] and (*b*) that it is a form of homicide, and therefore a violation of the sixth commandment,[9] not justified by any of the exceptions, general or special to that commandment, which have been divinely established,[10] and aggravated by the fact that the person thus killed has done nothing worthy of death.[11] Hence suicide to avoid violation is at best the commission of a greater sin to escape a lesser.[12] But even St. Augustine himself was obliged to admit the possibility of exceptions, since in his day several persons who had taken their own lives were recognized officially as martyrs—an indication, even if other proofs were lacking, that the opposition to suicide was of gradual growth. He suggests[13] that in such cases as in that of Samson a special divine ordinance superseded the general law, which nevertheless remains in full force for all ordinary persons. This remains in substance the position of orthodox Catholicism. It is not insignificant that in the most splendid of all mediæval works on eschatological subjects, although the possibility of repentance at the very moment of a violent death is admitted, the examples are chosen from persons killed in battle or by assassins.[14] Nor has orthodox Protestantism been any less emphatic; indeed, its rejection of the doctrine of purgatory makes it still more uncompromising in condemnation of suicide and less hope-

1 See, *e.g.*, T. C. Hodson, *Nāga Tribes of Manipur*, London, 1911, p. 159; W. B. Grubb, *An Unknown People in an Unknown Land*, do. 1911, p. 120; for these and other examples cf. *GB*[3], pt. iii., *The Dying God*, p. 10 ff.; and for classical survivals of this belief see Verg. *Æn.* vi. 427, 446 ff., 494 ff.; Lucian, *Menippus*, 470, 472, and elsewhere.

2 *GB*[3], pt. iii., *The Dying God*, p. 139 f.

3 Tacitus, *Germ.* 14.

4 Xen. *Anab.* I. viii. 29; Herod. viii. 118.

5 Æschines, *in Ctes.* 244.

6 C. Hose and W. McDougall, *The Pagan Tribes of Borneo*, London, 1912, ii. 40, 201.

7 Cf. the reluctance to have anything to do with the dangerous corpse of a woman dying in child-birth (*ib.* p. 155).

1 See Monier-Williams, *Buddhism*, London, 1889, p. 126.

2 See Plato, *Phædo*, 62 B; cf. Philolaos, *ap.* Clem. Strom. iii. 433 (fr. 23 Mullach), and artt. PYTHAGORAS, THRACE.

3 Plato, *Phædo*, *loc. cit.*; cf. Cicero, *de Senect.* xx. 73, *pro Scauro*, iii. 4.

4 On Verg. *Æn.* xii. 603.

5 *Ib.*

6 *E.g.*, Cic. *pro Scauro*, iii. 2 ff., *Tusc. Disp.* I. xxxiv. 83 f., etc.

7 *De Civ. Dei*, I. xvii. ff.

8 Ch. xvii. 'Quoniam (Iudas) Dei misericordiam desperando exitiabiliter paenitens, nullum sibi salubris paenitentiae locum reliquit: quanto magis a sua nece se abstinere debet qui tali supplicio quod in se puniat non habet.'

9 Ch. xx.

10 Ch. xxi.

11 Ch. xvii.

12 Ch. xxv. 'Quis ita desipiat ut dicat: "Iam nunc peccemus, ne postea forte peccemus"? . . . Nonne satius est flagitium committere quod paenitendo sanetur, quam tale facinus ubi locus salubris paenitentiae non relinquitur?'

13 Ch. xxvi.

14 Dante, *Purgatorio*, v. 52 ff.

ful with regard to the future destiny of suicides. Judaism in its later forms strongly denounces self-destruction,[1] but the OT says nothing which could reasonably be held to justify this, unless we adopt the Augustinian view of the meaning of the sixth commandment. Probably the Hebrews, until late post-Exilic times, must be counted among those races to whom suicide is simply one of the various possible forms of death and calls for no special comment.[2]

2. Ethics.—All the different views of suicide taught by various religions re-appear, with additions and re-statements, in various ethical systems. The religious side of Plato's views has already been mentioned. Both he and Aristotle[3] objected to self-destruction as cowardly and an offence against the State, which thus loses a citizen. Plato also declares it unnatural, since a man is his own closest friend. But both are willing to allow it in some cases—incurable pain, or disgrace so great as to make life no longer worth living. The flood of individualism which resulted from the overthrow of the old political life by the Macedonian conquest swept away the second of the above arguments; and consequently we find much discussion of suicide in the later schools, notably Stoicism, and a decided tendency to condone or even commend it. Its most whole-hearted upholders are those who deny immortality, or at least personal immortality; for they readily embrace the idea—as old as Homer and frequently appearing in poetry—that death is the cure for all ills.[4] A thoroughgoing exponent of this view and insister upon the miseries of life was Hegesias the Cyrenaic, who, according to Cicero, was 'forbidden by King Ptolemy to lecture on that topic, owing to the number of suicides which took place among his hearers.'[5] Less extreme doctrines were prevalent among the Stoics, who before the time of Posidonios generally denied personal immortality and without exception refused to admit that death was an evil or life a good. Both being 'indifferent,' since neither is a virtue or a vice, it follows that sometimes one and sometimes the other is 'preferable' (*προηγμένον*); hence it is 'reasonable' for even the perfectly wise man to kill himself if it will benefit his friends or his country, or will free him from great pain or incurable disease.[6] Suicide for trifling reasons, however, was condemned.

Epiktetos, perhaps the most lovable member of this school, puts the matter thus in an imaginary dialogue with his pupils: 'Epiktetos, we can no longer endure to be bound to this wretched body! . . . Let us go whence we came; let us at length get free of these chains that weight us down.' . . .

'Wait for God, sirs; when He gives the signal and sets you free from this your service, you shall depart to Him; for the present, endure to live in the place where He has stationed you. . . . Wait, do not depart unreasonably.'[7]

Another passage indicates what he means by a 'reasonable' departure:[8] 'The room is smoky. If only moderately, I will stay; if there is too much smoke, I will go. Remember this, keep fast hold on it—the door is open. . . . "You must live in Gyara."[9] Very well. But Gyara seems to me a very smoky room. So I will depart to a habitation in which no one can prevent me dwelling; a habitation which is open to everyone.'

The Epicureans did not indeed recommend suicide in general; but that death, although an evil, is not one which can touch or harm us is one of their fundamental principles. 'When we are, death is not present; when death is present, then we are not,' says the founder of the sect.[10]

The suicide of the ordinary unphilosophical man, Lucretius stigmatizes as self-contradictory, since it is caused by fear of the very death which it courts.[1] The Cynics professed to be absolutely indifferent to life and death as to everything else and are accused of killing themselves by extraordinary methods for little or no reason,[2] while some Skeptics were equally insensible.[3] In Rome, where originally suicide appears to have been rare,[4] the famous deaths of Cato, Thrasea, and others were for the most part inspired by Greek teaching, generally Stoic. Mediæval ethics added nothing new.

Perhaps the greatest contribution of modern times to the rational treatment of the matter is the consideration noticed in the opening paragraphs of this article, that many suicides are non-moral and entirely the affair of the specialist in mental diseases. Apart from this, and considering only cases where the agent is fully rational, the characteristic feature of the ethical discussions of the subject is their elimination of the theological elements in the arguments, Hume's famous essay 'Of Suicide'[5] being the last important work to pay them much attention. Perhaps the school most nearly favourable to suicide is Utilitarianism; for, starting from its definition of a good act as one which increases the sum total of human happiness (identified with pleasure),[6] one can easily imagine cases where the death of a man by his own hand would cause little or no pain to any one and would be more or less completely a source of pleasure to many. The more metaphysical schools discountenance it, either as an insult to humanity in general as embodied and exemplified in oneself (Kant) or as a final assertion of the will to live (Schopenhauer). There is also a tendency, arising from a contemplation of such medical facts as those already mentioned, to remove it altogether from the field of ethics—a view which we believe to be an exaggeration of a truth. The general trend of non-theological thought on the part of the ordinary educated man is towards a compromise between the extreme laxitude towards suicide represented by Stoicism and the extreme rigidity of the Kantians. That self-destruction is now and then justified by circumstances is admitted by most; and it is quite as widely admitted that those circumstances must be of an extreme and unusual kind to make the act anything else than cowardly and otherwise immoral.

LITERATURE.—Besides the works given under EUTHANASIA, the following may be cited: E. Tanzi, *A Text-book of Mental Diseases*, Eng. tr., London, 1909; C. Mercier, *Sanity and Insanity*², do. 1905 (short popular account); J. G. Frazer, *GB*³, do. 1911–14; J. S. Mill, *Utilitarianism*, do. 1863 (many subsequent edd.).

H. J. ROSE.

SUICIDE (Buddhist).

1. Introduction.—We are concerned only with 'religious suicide' and the Buddhist views thereon, not with the various kinds of suicide mentioned in Buddhist literature, interesting as they may be.[7] The position of the old Indian ascetics in regard to suicide may be summarized as follows. While the majority of sects were addicted to rapid methods of suicide—throwing oneself down from a mountain, etc.—the Jains (and probably also the disciples of Gosāla) considered those methods vulgar and evil.[8] Men

1 Josephus, *BJ* III. viii. 5. This view probably had great influence on early Christianity.

2 See art. EUTHANASIA.

3 Plato, *Laws*, 873 C, D; Aristotle, *Eth. Nic.* v. 1138ᵃ7, with J. Burnet's note.

4 Homer, *Il.* v. 61 ff.; Soph. *Philoct.* 797; cf. *Oed. Col.* 1225 ff.; Eur. *Heracl.* 595 f.

5 *Tusc. Disp.* I. xxxiv. 83. Hegesias's teachings won him the surname of *πεισιθάνατος*.

6 Diog. Laert. vii. 130.

7 *Dissert.* I. ix. 16.

8 *Ib.* I. xxv. 18.

9 A rocky islet in the Ægean—the Roman Siberia.

10 Diog. Laert. x. 125; cf. Lucr. iii. 830 ff.

1 *De Rer. Nat.* iii. 79 ff.

2 Luc. *Vit. Auct.* 10 [p. 550], *καὶ τέλος, ἤν σοι δοκῇ, πολύποδα ὠμὸν ἢ σηπίαν φαγὼν ἀπόθανε.*

3 Pyrrhon, *ap.* Stob. *Flor.* cxxi. 28.

4 See art. SUICIDE (Greek and Roman) and note the clumsiness of the Latin, as compared with the Greek, expressions for suicide. The word 'suicide' itself, although of Latin derivation, is impossible as a Latin compound.

5 First published in his *Essays and Treatises*, London, 1777.

6 'Actions are right in proportion as they tend to promote happiness, wrong as they tend to produce the reverse of happiness. By happiness is intended pleasure, and the absence of pain; by unhappiness, pain, and the privation of pleasure' is the famous dictum of J. S. Mill, *Utilitarianism*, ch. ii.

7 See, *e.g.*, *Majjhima*, ii. 109; a husband, threatened with separation from his wife, kills her and commits suicide, in order that they may be husband and wife in their next birth.

8 See *Kathākośa*, tr. C. H. Tawney, London, 1895, p. 8.

who thus kill themselves are reborn as demons.[1] While practising starvation, the Jain must avoid any desire for death (*maraṇāśaṃsā*):[2] 'Renouncing all food and drink, I patiently wait for my end.'

2. Buddhism condemns asceticism.—Any austerity which is likely to weaken body or mind is forbidden. The Jains and many others saw in asceticism and physical pain (*duḥkha*, *tapas*) a force that makes for purification from sin: suicide by starvation is the ascetic act *par excellence*.[3] While vocal sins are destroyed through silence (*mauna*) and mental sins through 'respiratory-restraint,' bodily sins are destroyed through starvation (*abhojana*)[4] and lust is crushed through mortification. Buddhism had better methods of crushing lust and destroying sin—the realization of the impermanence of pleasure and of the non-substantiality of the Ego, the experience in trance (*dhyāna*) of a happiness which has nothing to do with pleasure and destroys in a man any infatuation for pleasure. It was thus enabled to disqualify ascetic methods.

3. Buddhism condemns suicide. — There is a celebrated text:

'A monk who preaches suicide, who tells man: "Do away with this wretched life, full of suffering and sin; death is better," in fact preaches murder, is a murderer, is no longer a monk.'[5]

A man must live his allotted span of life. He cannot avoid, by suicide, the sufferings which are the result of his former evil deeds; nor can he win sooner, by a voluntary death, the reward of his good deeds. Everything comes to him who waits. To that effect Buddha employs to Pāyāsi the simile of the woman who cuts open her body in order to see whether her child is a boy or a girl.[6]

It seems also that suicide from religious motives is not effective. Buddhists object to 'thirst for non-existence' (*vibhavatṛṣṇā*), as they object to 'thirst for existence' (*bhavatṛṣṇā*). A saint must abide in indifference, without caring for life, without caring for death. He will not commit suicide in order to reach *nirvāṇa* sooner. Is not suicide a desperate act of disgust and desire, disgust of existence, desire of rest?

4. Buddhism admits suicide.—We have therefore good reason to believe (1) that suicide is not an ascetic act leading to spiritual progress and to *nirvāṇa*, and (2) that no saint or *arhat*—a spiritually perfect being—will kill himself. But we are confronted with a number of stories which prove beyond dispute that we are mistaken in these two important conclusions. On the one hand, suicide may be in certain cases the actual cause or the occasion of the attainment of *arhat*ship, although in other cases it may be premature and sinful. On the other hand, *arhats* commit suicide.

In illustration of the first point, we may quote the stories of the attempted suicide of (1) Sīhā, (2) Sappadāsa, and (3) Vakkali; for the second the suicide of (4) Vakkali and (5) Godhika.

[1] The *giripadana* or *bhṛgupāta* is *pāgayajanacheṭṭhiya* (H. Jacobi, *Ausgewählte Erzählungen in Mahārāṣṭrī*, Leipzig, 1886, p. 2; A. Weber, *Fragment der Bhagavati*, Berlin, 1865–66, p. 206).

[2] On Jain suicide see J. J. Meyer, *Hindu Tales*, Eng. tr., London, 1909; Uvāsagadasāo, ed. and tr. A. F. R. Hoernle, Calcutta, 1888–90, §§ 57, 89; *Ăchārāṅgasūtra*, i. 7. 5–8, tr. H. Jacobi, *SBE* xxii. [1884] 74–78; E. W. Hopkins, *The Religions of India*, London, 1896, p. 291; G. Bühler, *Ueber die indische Sekte der Jaina*, Vienna, 1887, p. 12. As concerns Gosāla, see Uvāsagadasāo, app. ii. p. 23 (suicide is permitted to ascetics who have reached the highest degree of perfection).

[3] Violent death, voluntary or not, destroys sin (see J. J. Meyer, *Hindu Tales*).

[4] See, *e.g.*, *Majjhima*, i. 93; *SBE* 1. [1910], *s.v.* 'Suicide,' the references to vols. xxii. and xlv.

[5] *Pārājika*, iii.; see *SBE* xiii. [1881] 4.

[6] *Dīgha-Nikāya*, ii. 331; *Dialogues of the Buddha*, ii. 350 (*SBB* iii. [London, 1910]).

(1) Sīhā was distressed at not obtaining spiritual progress after seven years of endeavour. She said: 'What have I to do with this wretched life (*pāpajīvita*)? I will die through hanging.' But, just as the rope was tied round her neck, she was turning her thought towards enlightenment (*vipassanā*), as was her former habit. She attained *arhat*ship, and at this very moment the rope loosened from her throat and fell.[1]

(2) The story of Sappadāsa is to the same effect. This monk was overpowered by passion (*kilesa*) and never obtained concentration. This distressed him so much that he was about to commit suicide with a razor or a sword, when he suddenly realized the inward vision.[2]

(3) Vakkali was fond of looking at the Buddha, and the excessive importance which he attached to the physical body—a putrid body (*pūtikāya*)—of the Master was an obstacle to his spiritual advance. In order to create in him a 'holy fear' (*saṃvega*), the Buddha commanded him to go. Desperate at being no longer able to see the Master, Vakkali decided to commit suicide by throwing himself down from a mountain, saying: 'What have I to do with this life, if I can no longer see Him?' At this moment the Master appeared and prevented him from thus 'destroying the conditions of his reaching the Path (*maggaphala*).'[3]

(4) Vakkali was suffering from a painful illness. Bhagavat came to comfort him and said: 'Your death will be a holy one, an auspicious one (*apāpika*).' When the Master had gone, Vakkali uttered for the last time the Buddhist profession of faith (universal transitoriness) and took the sword.[4]

(5) Godhika was unable because of disease to remain in a certain state of meditation. He thought: 'If I were to take a sword.' Māra approached the Buddha and told him: 'Your disciple wants to die; he has resolved to die. Prevent him. How could one of your disciples die while he is not yet an *arhat*?' But, as it is explained in the *Abhidharmakośavyākhyā*, Godhika reached *arhat*ship just after he had begun cutting his throat.[5] It is said: 'Those who take the sword are without regard for life; they achieve insight (*vipassanā*) and reach *nirvāṇa*.' 'Thus act the strong ones (*dhīra*); they desire not life; having removed thirst and the root of thirst (that is, ignorance), Godhika is at rest.'[6]

5. The nirvāṇa of the great saints.—Vakkali was an *arhat*, but, as he did not possess the power of 'loosening the *saṃskāras* of life,' he had, in order to die, to take the sword. On the other hand, Śākyamuni and, in later sources, a number of saints — *e.g.*, Mahāpajāpatī Gotamī in the *Apadāna*—possess such a power. The Sanskrit *Abhidharma*[7] teaches that it belongs to the saints who have reached the *nirupadhiśeṣanirvāṇa* ('*nirvāṇa* without rests').

In the case of Śākyamuni we have to deal with a voluntary death; in the case of Mahāpajāpatī, who has to obtain permission of Śākyamuni before she resolves to die, we have to deal with a voluntary death of a slightly different character. The Pratyekabuddhas, like Śākyamuni, decide for themselves when the 'time' has arrived; their method is to rise a few cubits above the ground and burn themselves.

We can easily understand that a Buddha, when he has set in motion the wheel, when he has elected two chief disciples—briefly, 'when he has done what he had to do'—is duly authorized to enter into the final rest. The case of an *arhat* is not different; the *arhat* also has achieved what he had to achieve—*i.e.* he has removed the slightest kind of desire. If he is not, like a Buddha, capable of abandoning life in a quiet way, there is no reason why he should not have recourse to more drastic methods.

6. Mahāyāna praises and deprecates suicide as self-surrender and worship.—The saint of the new Buddhism must, before reaching *nirvāṇa*, spend millions of lives in charity, worship, and meditation. 'Abandoning one's existence' (*ātmanas tyāgaḥ*, *ātmabhāvatyāga*) is to be looked upon as the best self-sacrifice, for to give one's body is better than to give alms; and also as the best

[1] *Therīgāthā*, 77. [2] *Theragāthā*, 408.

[3] *Ib.* 350; Dhammapada's Commentary, 381; also Aṅguttara's Commentary.

[4] *Saṃyutta*, iii. 123. [5] Cf. *Kathāvatthu*, i. 2.

[6] The *Milindapañha* deals with suicide (see *SBE* xxxv. [1890] 273 ff.), but does not mention Godhika and Vakkali. See J. P. Minayeff, *Recherches sur le bouddhisme*, tr. R. H. Assier de Pompignan, Paris, 1894, p. 223; *Saṃyutta*, i. 120, iii. 123; Dhammapada's Commentary, v. 57 (i. 431); Kathāvatthu's Commentary, *ad* i 2.

[7] *Abhidharmakośa*, ch. vi.

worship, for to burn one's body as an offering is certainly more meritorious than to kindle lamps at a shrine. We may refer (1) to the story of the future Śākyamuni giving his body to feed a starving tigress,[1] and (2) to the legend of Bhaiṣajyarāja, who, dissatisfied with his previous worship although painful and extravagant, filled his body with all sorts of oil and set it on fire.[2]

The *bodhisattvas* of the past have practised in that way many heroic deeds (*duḥkara*), some of which are told in the canon of ancient Buddhism (*Chariyapiṭaka, Jātaka*); the new scriptures are inexhaustible on this topic.

In accordance with the principles of the new Buddhism and the *Légende dorée* of the eternal Buddhism, self-surrender culminating in voluntary death has been held in honour in various Buddhist countries. It happens (or it used to happen) that Chinese monks beg for fuel, build a funeral pyre, sit cross-legged on it, cover their head with linen soaked in oil, and set themselves on fire. With some branches of the Chinese Mahāyāna, the 'burning of the skull' is an essential part of ordination as a 'future Buddha'—a symbol of the holocaust for which human courage is nowadays inadequate.[3]

The pilgrim I-tsing says that Indian Buddhists abstain from suicide and, in general, from self-torture.[4] Whether this statement be accurate or not—A. Barth did not believe it to be quite accurate—the theologians of the Great Vehicle strongly deprecate such practices. One of the chief aims of Śāntideva in his *Śikṣāsamuchchaya*,[5] 'A Compendium of the Rules of the Disciple of the Great Vehicle,' is to elucidate this point: In what measure is a disciple—a beginner—to imitate the heroic deeds of the *bodhisattvas* of old? The disciple is ready, willing, and resolved even to commit sin and to burn in hell for the sake of another, not to mention sacrificing his limbs and body; but he must avoid any mistake in the realization of his resolve. The question is whether in such and such a case sacrifice or self-denial is really useful to our fellow-creatures; whether there is not some other means of procuring universal welfare. To sum up, the sacrifice of one's body is not in accordance with a wise estimate of the spiritual needs of a beginner.

LITERATURE.—See, in addition to the sources cited in the footnotes, L. de la Vallée Poussin, 'Quelques Observations sur le suicide dans le Bouddhisme ancien,' *Bulletin de la Classe des Lettres de l'Académie de Belgique*, 1919, pp. 685-693; A. Rémusat, *Foĕ Kouĕ Ki*, Paris, 1836, p. 272; J. Legge, *Fâ-hien's Record of Buddhistic Kingdoms*, Oxford, 1836, p. 86; *Divyāvadāna*, ed. E. B. Cowell and R. A. Neil, Cambridge, 1886, p. 39; E. Chavannes, *Cinq cents contes et apologues, extraits du Tripitaka chinois et traduits en français*, Paris, 1910, i. 207, 265, *passim*; E. Huber, *Le Sutralamkara de Açvaghoṣa*, French tr., Paris, 1908, pp. 126, 440; *Abhidharmakośa*, ii. 10, v. 7.

L. DE LA VALLÉE POUSSIN.

SUICIDE (Chinese).—Suicide is at least not uncommon in China. Literature and history supply illustrations. In a Chinese novelette the heroine commits suicide on the grave of her betrothed lover to avoid the marriage arranged for her with his rival, and that rival thereupon takes his own life in order to pursue in the other world at once his quest for his bride and vengeance on her lover. Among some eight hundred biographical notices in W. F. Mayers's *Chinese Readers' Manual*,[1] 27 instances of suicide are recorded—generals after defeat, a tyrant to escape his impending doom, a dethroned ruler, statesmen whose advice, like Ahithophel's, has been rejected, or who desired to enforce their counsel by this last proof of their earnestness, a captive to avoid exile, hopeless prisoners, ministers who, having incurred imperial displeasure, were allowed to die thus rather than by the hands of the executioner, a rebel whose plot was discovered, women to avoid a marriage deemed by them to be shameful, an upright servant rather than commit a murder enjoined on him, a minister of justice under whose subordinates capital punishment was unduly frequent, those moved by loyalty to a deceased master, by grief for the death of father or son, or by shame for a son's treachery.

In addition to suicides on such occasions as these, some of which will be noted as peculiarly Chinese, cases also occur in which misery (*e.g.*, hopeless leprosy) drives to suicide. More frequent are cases in which suicide is committed in an access of passion, sometimes with the view of involving one's adversary in legal proceedings in this world, or less frequently with the hope of harassing him by visitations of the vengeful ghost.

Hanging, leaping down a well, and opium poisoning have been perhaps the most common methods of suicide; the last may diminish in frequency under the present opium restrictions.

In the absence of accurate statistics it is impossible to estimate the ratio of deaths by suicide to the total population. The general impression, probably well founded, is that suicide is much more frequent than in Great Britain. This greater frequency, if it is assumed as fact, may be accounted for by the low value put on individual life, a tendency to ungovernable rage, and the fact that social and religious feelings do not rigorously inhibit suicide, but rather in certain circumstances (*e.g.*, where marriage is being urged on a widow or a bride whose betrothed bridegroom has died) approve it.

LITERATURE.—*The Encyclopædia Sinica*, Shanghai, 1917, London, 1918; J. Doolittle, *Social Life of the Chinese*, New York, 1865, London, 1866; A. H. Smith, *Village Life in China*, Edinburgh, 1900; *Records of the General Conference of Protestant Missionaries*, Shanghai, 1890, pp. 329-333.

P. J. MACLAGAN.

SUICIDE (Greek and Roman).—I. *GREEK*.—Under the name 'suicide' we here include all forms in which the individual kills himself intentionally, whether he acts of his own free will or under compulsion, and whether the end of his action be selfish or altruistic.

1. Legendary suicides.—The earliest definite mention of suicide in Greek literature is the case of Epikaste (Iokaste), the mother of Oidipus of Thebes, in the *Nekyia*.[2]

Odysseus tells how in Hades 'I saw the mother of Oidipodes, fair Epikaste, who wrought an awful deed in ignorance of mind, marrying her own son. And he had slain his father and he married her. And presently the gods made it known to men. Then he in lovely Thebe endured sorrow and ruled over the Kadmeans by the grievous counsels of the gods. But she went to the house of Hades, fastening a high noose from the lofty hall, holden by her woe. And to him she left sorrows in the aftertime full many, even all that the Erinyes of a mother bring to pass.'

The precise motive for suicide is not very clearly indicated here, or rather Homer does not distinguish clearly between the horror of Epikaste at the revolting nature of the situation in which she unwittingly finds herself and her shame in the face of her deed becoming known. But the essential points are that (1) suicide presents itself to Homer as the natural and fitting act when life has lost all that makes life worth living, and (2) no blame attaches to suicide in itself.

1 *Jātakamālā*, i., tr. J. S. Speyer, *SBB* i. [1895].

2 *Saddharmapuṇḍarīka*, xxii., tr. H. Kern, *SBE* xxi. [1884].

3 See J. J. M. de Groot, *Le Code du Mahāyāna en Chine*, Amsterdam, 1893, pp. 50, 217, 227. It is recorded that in the Japanese sect of Sukhāvatī religious suicide was not unknown. In 1422 a large company of persons, after hearing a stirring sermon by a zealot to the effect that paradise may be gained solely by calling on the name of Amitābha, committed suicide by walking into the sea while repeating the 'Namu Amida Butsu.'

4 *A Record of the Buddhist Religion*, tr. J. Takakusu, Oxford, 1896, p. 197 f. (ch. xxxviii. f.); A. Barth, *Journ. des Savants*, 1898, p. 541.

5 *Bibl. Buddhica*, i. [Petrograd, 1902].

1 New ed., London, 1910.

2 Hom. *Od.* xi. 271 ff.

But the most famous and indeed the typical heroic suicide is that of Aias. Homer does not mention his suicide explicitly, but it is clearly alluded to in *Od.* xi. 548 ff., where Odysseus expresses his regret at having obtained the arms of Achilles:

ὡς δὴ μὴ ὄφελον νικᾶν τοιῷδε ἐπ' ἀέθλῳ·
τοίην γὰρ κεφαλὴν ἕνεκ' αὐτῶν (the arms of Achilles) γαῖα κατέσχεν,
Αἴανθ', ὃς κτλ.

His suicide was recounted in the *Aithiopis* of Arktinos in connexion with the award of the arms of Achilles to Odysseus.[1] It is to be noted that so far there is no mention of madness or of an attack by Aias upon the herds. These incidents were, however, recounted in the *Little Iliad* of Lesches.[2] Also, whereas in *Od.* xi. 555 it is emphasized that the death of Aias was mourned by the Greeks equally with that of Achilles, the *Little Iliad*[3] told of the withholding of burial honours. But even so there is nothing to indicate that the suicide in itself was considered blameworthy. It is an act quite in accordance with the haughtiness and self-sufficiency which characterize Aias in Homer, and of which the famous 'silence of Aias' in *Od.* xi. 553 ff., so admired by the author of the treatise *On the Sublime*,[4] is a fitting expression. The suicide of Aias is the typical act of a great soul which cannot brook dishonour.

A motive of a less heroic kind which prompts to suicide is excess of sorrow for the dead. The feeling is one familiar to Homer. 'If I lose thee, it were better for me to go beneath the earth,' says Andromache to Hektor,[5] in the same spirit in which David cries, 'Would God I had died for thee, O Absalom, my son, my son!'[6] There is not in Homer any express mention of suicide for this reason, but Antikleia is referred to in terms which are hardly consonant with any other explanation than that she died by her own hand.

Eumaios says to the disguised Odysseus: 'Laertes still lives, but evermore he prays to Zeus that life may perish from his limbs within his halls; for he mourns exceedingly for his son that is gone and for his wedded wife, whose death beyond all else hath grieved him and brought him to untimely age. She in grief for her glorious son perished by a miserable death (λευγαλέῳ θανάτῳ): so may none perish who dwells here friendly to me and doing friendly deeds.'[7]

The natural inference from these words is strongly confirmed by the reference to her in *Od.* xi. 84 ff. and 197 ff. The later story said frankly that she hanged herself.[8]

The list of such suicides is a long one.

Aigeus, father of Theseus, had arranged with his son when he left for Crete, carrying the annual tribute of the Athenians to the Minotaur, that, if Theseus were successful in slaying the monster, a white sail should be hoisted upon the returning vessel. Theseus forgot to take down the black sail which the ship was flying, and Aigeus, thinking that his son had perished, threw himself from the rock on which he was keeping watch into the sea (Ægean) which thenceforth bore his name.[9] Erigone, daughter of Ikarios, hanged herself when she found the dead body of her father.[10] Skedasos committed suicide when his daughters had hanged themselves.[11] When Evadne throws herself on the funeral pyre of her husband, her father Iphis threatens to commit suicide by starvation.[12]

A special case of suicide to avoid shame is that to escape sexual dishonour.

Legend told how the Leukadian rock received its name from Leukatas, who, to escape the unwelcome attentions of Apollo, plunged into the sea off the island of Leukas.[13] Pausanias tells us[14] how the daughters of Skedasos of Leuktra hanged themselves to escape the violence offered them by certain Lacedæmonians.

[1] Cf. Proclus in *Epicorum Græc. Fragmenta*, ed. G. Kinkel, Leipzig, 1877, p. 34, 8 ff.
[2] Cf. Proclus, *Ep. Gr. Fr.* p. 36.
[3] *Ep. Gr. Fr.* p. 40; Eustath. *Il.* p. 285, 34.
[4] [Longinus] ix. 2: ἡ τοῦ Αἴαντος ἐν Νεκυίᾳ σιωπὴ μέγα καὶ παντὸς ὑψηλότερον λόγου.
[5] *Il.* vi. 410.
[6] 2 S 18[33].
[7] *Od.* xv. 353 ff.
[8] Hygin. *Fab.* 243.
[9] Plut. *Thes.* 22; Diod. iv. 60 f.; Hygin. *Fab.* 242; Suidas, *s.v.* Αἰγαῖον πέλαγος; Serv. on Verg. *Æn.* iii. 74.
[10] Apollod. iii. 14, etc.
[11] Paus. IX. xiii. 3.
[12] Eurip. *Suppl.* 1105 f.
[13] Serv. on Verg. *Æn.* iii. 279.
[14] IX. xiii. 3.

Suicide, in the sense of self-devotion for one's country, has always occupied a prominent place in patriotic saga. Kodros, the last king of Athens, is a famous example.

The Lacedæmonians, under pressure of famine, resolved to invade Attica. But first they consulted the Delphic oracle as to their prospects of taking Athens and, receiving an answer that they would be successful if they did not kill the Athenian king, marched on the city. Cleomantis, a Delphian, secretly communicated to the Athenians the purport of the oracle. Kodros thereupon dressed himself as a beggar and stole out of the besieged city and proceeded to gather firewood. When two enemy scouts approached him, he slew one of them with his hatchet, whereupon the other, taking him for a beggar, drew his sword and slew him, thus rendering the capture of Athens impossible.[1]

There is the similar story of Makaria, daughter of Herakles and Deianeira.[2] That such a death was deemed a glorious one is sufficiently attested.[3]

2. Heroic suicide.—The motives which in the Homeric poems seem mainly to be regarded as prompting to suicide are of a heroic nature—the sense of dishonour suffered or impending, the devotion of a high purpose, or the intolerable sorrow of a personal bereavement. The sense of the common ills of humanity is by no means ignored—τλητὸν γὰρ Μοῖραι θυμὸν θέσαν ἀνθρώποισιν.[4] But there is no pessimism. Whatever the evils that darken human life, at least it is a good thing to enjoy the sun, and the darkest shadow that falls athwart Homeric life is the sense not of its burden but of its brevity. Life at any level is to be preferred to the sunless realms of Hades.[5]

But with the rise of reflexion, as witnessed in the poetry of the age succeeding the Homeric, we have a view of life which is frankly pessimistic. Hesiod conceives the present to be an age of iron, thrown into darker relief by the picture of a happier golden age gone by.[6]

That life is an evil has become a commonplace. πάντων μὲν μὴ φῦναι ἐπιχθονίοισιν ἄριστον[7] is a doctrine which becomes a hackneyed phrase of later poetry—τὸ μὲν δὴ πανταχοῦ θρυλούμενον, κράτιστον εἶναι φημὶ μὴ φῦναι βροτῷ.[8] The logical consequence of this view of life is that man is justified in ending what he cannot mend. Whether, in fact, this pessimistic view of life actually induced an increased practice of suicide is more difficult to establish. But in any case motives of a less heroic kind seem now to be recognized as worthy causes of suicide. Thus poverty is expressly recognized by Theognis[9] as a sufficient cause.

3. The historians.—In the historians of the 5th cent. suicide is not a particularly prominent feature, and belongs in general to one or other of the types already noticed.

Herodotus relates the legend of Nitokris, who, in order to escape punishment for her misdeeds, committed suicide by leaping into a room full of ashes.[10] Arion is compelled by the ferrymen either to commit suicide, with the prospect of being buried ashore, or to jump into the sea.[11] The daughter of Mykerinos, being violated by her father, hanged herself from grief.[12] Shame was the motive for the suicide of Spargapises, leader of the Massagetai, who in a state of intoxication were surprised and killed or captured by the Persians.[13] And we have the parallel stories of Othryades, who, ashamed to return to Sparta when his company was killed, slew himself at Thyreai,[14] and of Pantites, who, having survived the disaster at Thermopylai, 'on his return to Sparta, being held in dishonour, hanged himself.'[15]

[1] Lycurg. *c. Leokrat.* 84 ff.
[2] Paus. I. xxxii.; Eurip. *Herakleidai.*
[3] Paus. IX. xvii. 1.
[4] *Il.* xxiv. 49.
[5] *Od.* xi. 488 ff.
[6] *Works*, 174 ff.
[7] Theognis, 435 ff.
[8] Eurip. *Bellerophon*, frag. 287. 1 f. (A. Nauck); cf. Soph. *Oed. Col.* 1227 f.
[9] 173 ff.
[10] ii. 100.
[11] *Ib.* i. 24.
[12] *Ib.* ii. 131.
[13] *Ib.* i. 213.
[14] *Ib.* i. 82.
[15] *Ib.* vii. 232.

In Thucydides we read how in 427 B.C. the Corcyrean democrats 'went to the temple of Hera and, persuading some fifty of the suppliants (belonging to the oligarchic party) to stand their trial, condemned them all to death. The majority refused to come out, and, when they saw what was going on, destroyed one another in the enclosure of the temple where they were, except a few who hanged themselves on trees or put an end to their lives in any other way they could.'[1] Again in 425 B.C. the oligarchs of Corcyra were entrapped into a large building from which they were led forth in groups of twenty for execution. When those in the building got to know what was happening, they refused to come out. Then the Corcyrean populace broke a hole in the roof through which they showered tiles and arrows at those within. 'The prisoners tried to shelter themselves as best they could. Most of them put an end to their own lives. Some thrust into their throats arrows which were shot at them; others strangled themselves with cords taken from beds which they found in the place, or with strips torn from their own clothes. This went on during the greater part of the night, until in one way or another, by their own hands or by missiles from the roof, they all perished.'[2] Thucydides knows, too, the story that Themistokles poisoned himself: λέγουσι δέ τινες καὶ ἑκούσιον φαρμάκῳ ἀποθανεῖν αὐτόν.[3]

In Xenophon, *Hell.* VI. ii. 36, we have the familiar motive of shame. Krinippos, when the Syracusan fleet under his command was captured by Iphikrates (373 B.C.), ὑπὸ λύπης θανάτῳ αὐθαιρέτῳ ἀποθνήσκει. So *Hell.* VII. iv. 9, when the invading Arkadians were attacked in camp by the Eleans, whom they defeated, the Elean hipparch, who was held responsible for the attack, committed suicide (364 B.C.).

But the suicide which is more prominent in Xenophon is of the romantic type, described as ἐπαποθανεῖν, ἐπισφάξαι ἑαυτόν, where love faithful unto death refuses to be comforted otherwise than by sharing the fate of the beloved. 'Cyrus himself died, and eight of his best followers fell over him (ἔκειντο ἐπ' αὐτῷ). And Artapates, the most faithful of his staff, when he saw that Cyrus had fallen, is said to have leapt from his horse and thrown himself upon him. And some say that the king ordered him to be slain over Cyrus (ἐπισφάξαι αὐτὸν Κύρῳ); but others say that he drew his sword and killed himself over him (ἑαυτὸν ἐπισφάξασθαι).'[4] We have the same motive in the story of Pantheia, so beautifully told by Xenophon.[5]

The emotional value of this motive has made it very prominent in literature, as, indeed, it has everywhere and at all times been actually a very common cause of suicide.

It is familiar to the OT.[6] Already in Homer Antilochos holds the hands of Achilles, lest in his grief for Patroklos he should cut his throat;[7] and, even if suicide is not meant, Andromache's anguish for Hektor almost makes her die.[8] Most familiar perhaps of all is the case of Laodamia, the wife of Protesilaos, to whom she had been married just before his departure for Troy. There Protesilaos was the first to leap ashore and, after slaying many Trojans, was killed by Hektor. After his death his wife grieved for him so much that Hermes for pity brought back Protesilaos from the dead. At first Laodamia, thinking he had actually returned from Troy, rejoiced, but when he returned to Hades ἑαυτὴν ἐφόνευσεν.[9] As this legend is enshrined for us in the verses of Wordsworth, so Tennyson has told the story of another who was faithful unto death: Oinone, the beloved of Paris, whose story is unknown to the epic cycle and to the tragedians. When Paris died, she either hanged herself[10] or threw herself into his funeral pyre.[11]

---

1 iii. 81. 2 iv. 48. 3 i. 138.
4 *Anab.* i. 8. 5 *Cyrop.* vii. 3.
6 1 S 31[4f.]; see art. SUICIDE (Semitic and Egyptian).
7 *Il.* xviii. 33 f. 8 *Ib.* xxii. 473 f.
9 Apollod. *Epit.* iii. 30: ξίφει διεχρήσατο ἑαυτήν; Eustath. on *Il.* ii. 700; cf. Ovid, *ex Ponto*, III. i. 109 f.
10 Apollod. III. xii. 5. 4, vi. 1–3; Lycophron, 57 ff.; Konon, 23; Parthen. *Erot.* 4.
11 Q. Smyrn. x. 262, 484; Ovid, *Her.* 5.

Another late legend is that of Hero and Leander, the subject of the poem by Musaios entitled τὰ καθ' Ἡρὼ καὶ Λέανδρον. Leander of Abydos swam the Hellespont nightly to visit his beloved Hero, the priestess of Aphrodite at Sestos across the straits, being lighted by a lamp which Hero set upon her tower by the seashore. He attempted the passage one stormy night, when the lamp was extinguished by the storm. Next morning his dead body was washed ashore, and Hero threw herself from her tower to join him in death.[1] Pausanias[2] remarks of three heroines, Marpessa, Kleopatra, and Polydora, that they all committed suicide in this way: προαποθανοῦσι πᾶσαι τοῖς ἀνδράσιν ἑαυτὰς ἐπικατέσφαξαν.

The motives of such suicides are not always identical and no doubt were sometimes complex. Sometimes it was the last sacrifice of devotion, a tradition become a religion, like the Indian *satī* or our own proud tradition that the captain goes down with his ship.

Xenophon tells how in 388 B.C. Anaxibios the Spartan, falling into an ambush, said to those by him: '"Gentlemen, my duty is to die here. As for you, seek safety before we engage the enemy." Then he took his shield from his armour bearer and fell fighting at his post. But his favourites (τὰ παιδικά) abode with him, and twelve of the Lacedæmonian harmosts who had come from the cities died with him fighting.'[3] Haimon in the *Antigone* of Sophocles had all along determined to die with Antigone,[4] but the actual suicide is complicated by his futile attempt to slay his father and becomes outwardly an act of disappointed rage.[5]

Where the suicide considers himself responsible for another's death, his own death may appear to be due as an act of atonement.

Thus Kallirrhoe, having by her unkindness brought about the suicide of her lover Koresos, repented and out of pity for him and shame for her conduct killed herself,[6] precisely as Adrastos, when he accidentally killed the son of Crœsus, 'stood before the dead and submitted himself to Crœsus, holding out his hands and entreating him to slay him over the dead (ἐπικατασφάξαι τῷ νεκρῷ) since for him life was no longer tolerable (οὐδέ οἱ εἶναι βιώσιμον).'[7]

But, without any such complications, we have the devotion of those who, lovely and pleasant in their lives, in death would not be divided. When Kastor is slain by Idas, his brother Polydeukes cries: 'Our Father, Son of Kronos, what release shall there be from sorrow? Give me also to die with him, O Lord. Honour is departed for him who is bereft of friends.'[8] And the more one knows of the religious thought of the Greeks, the less is one inclined to disparage the influence of the motive to which Plato alludes—the hope of a blessed reunion hereafter: 'Ere now for human love, for dead wife, for dead son many a man has gone willingly to the house of Hades, drawn by the hope that in the world beyond they might see and be with those they loved.'[9]

4. Compulsory suicide.—A special interest attaches to Xenophon, *Hell.* II. iii. 56. In describing the execution by compulsory suicide of Theramenes in 403 B.C., he says: 'When, being compelled to die, he drank the hemlock (τὸ κώνειον ἔπιε), it was said that he threw what was left of it as in the game of *cottabos*, crying, "This for the fair Kritias!"' This is the first occurrence of the word κώνειον in the historians and the only one in Xenophon. When the practice of execution by compulsory poisoning was introduced in Athens we do not know, nor when hemlock first became the recognized medium. The use of hemlock for this purpose, we may with probability suppose, first became regular in the latter part of the 5th cent. B.C. Even in the orators, however, references to it are surprisingly rare. It is not mentioned in Antiphon. Andocides mentions it only once.[10] Lysias refers to it twice.[11] It is not found in Demosthenes, Lycurgus, Dinarchus. The advantages of hemlock-drinking over other more

---

1 Musaios, *op. cit.*; Stat. *Theb.* vi. 542; Verg. *Georg.* iii. 258; Ovid, *Her.* 17, 18.
2 IV. ii. 5; cf. the case of Skedasos (IX. xiii. 3).
3 *Hell.* IV. viii. 38 f. 4 751.
5 1234 f. 6 Paus. VII. xxi.
7 Herod. i. 45. 8 Pind. *Nem.* x. 76 ff.
9 *Phœdo*, 68 A. 10 *De Pace*, 10.
11 *C. Erastosthenem*, 17, and Περὶ δημ. τ. τ. Νικίου ἀδελφ. (*Or.* 18) 24.

cumbrous methods of suicide are referred to in the *Frogs*[1] of Aristophanes (405 B.C.).

It was by drinking hemlock that Socrates died in 399 B.C.[2] It was the method used by the Athenian women whom the shameful conduct of the characters of Euripides drove to suicide, according to Aristophanes.[3] It is difficult to resist the conclusion that in the stress and excitement and anxiety of the closing years of the Peloponnesian war suicide had assumed a prominence hitherto unknown, and it would appear that this phenomenon was not unconnected with the interest in the preparation of speedy and painless modes of putting an end to life. Incidentally it may be noted that Attic hemlock was reputed to be specially effective.[4] Theophrastus tells us of the discovery by Thrasyas of Mantineia of a *ῥᾴδια καὶ ἄπονος ἀπόλυσις* in which the juices of hemlock (*κώνειον*) and poppy (*μήκων*) and other such herbs were made up in a dose of small bulk, weighing about a drachma, the effects of which were incurable and which, moreover, would keep and retain its potency for an indefinite period.[5] No doubt, also, the fact of having at their disposal a convenient and not too painful means of terminating life induced, as in our own time, many rash persons to attempt their lives. It is interesting to note that Menander wrote a play with the title Κωνειαζόμεναι. Hence there was developed the interest in antidotes of which we have evidence.[6] Theophrastus has much to say of antidotes.[7] In particular it is interesting, in view of the attitude of the people of Ceos to suicide, to notice that to them is attributed an improved method of preparing hemlock.[8]

The story of the death of Theramenes points in the same direction. When in our own country death by the axe of the headsman was a common fate, it became a point of honour with his victims that they should take leave of life like gentlemen. Montrose, we are told, went to the scaffold clad in rich attire 'more becoming a bridegroom than a criminal going to the gallows.' Such conduct is the true analogue to the dying libation of Theramenes. Socrates had the same idea:

'What about making a libation with this cup?', he says to the jailer, 'May I or not?', and, that not being feasible, he yet drank the cup of death 'easily and cheerfully' as one who toasts a friend.[9]

And, as meaner victims of the axe imitated the conduct of Montrose and others, and the grand manner degenerated into the bravado of the desperate and callous, so we have a degenerate echo of the heroic in the story told by Ælian and Athenæus of the devotees of debauchery who, having drained the cup of pleasure to the lees, ended by throwing away the cup, and concluded life's banquet with a toast.[10]

5. Legal aspect.—So long as suicide does not become so frequent as to threaten seriously the well-being of the community, the State has no motive to intervene by legislation against it. At no time does Athenian law define suicide as a penal offence. The only outbreak of which we hear in Attica suggesting an epidemic of suicide is that which legend connected with the origin of the Aiora, or swing-festival.

Legend told how, when Dionysos first came to Attica with the new gift of wine, he was hospitably entertained by Ikarios, to whom he revealed his intoxicating boon. Ikarios gave of the wine to some shepherds, who in their vinous frenzy killed their would-be benefactor. His daughter, Erigone, guided to the spot by his faithful dog Maira, hanged herself on a tree. Then there broke out among the Athenian women an epidemic of hanging, which abated only when the Athenians discovered the cause and instituted the Aiora festival in honour of Erigone.[1]

Plutarch tells of a similar outbreak at Miletos which, obscure in origin, was generally attributed to atmospheric conditions:

'A strange and terrible affliction once came upon the maidens of Miletos, from some obscure cause—mostly it was conjectured that some poisonous and ecstatic temperament of the atmosphere produced in them a mental upset and frenzy. For there fell suddenly upon all of them a desire of death and a mad impulse towards hanging. Many hanged themselves before they could be prevented. The words and the tears of their parents, the persuasions of their friends, had no effect. In spite of all the ingenuity and cleverness of those who watched them, they succeeded in making away with themselves. The plague seemed to be of an unearthly character and beyond human remedy, until on the motion of a wise man a resolution was proposed that women who hanged themselves should be carried out to burial through the market-place. The ratification of this resolution not only checked the evil but altogether put an end to the passion for death. A great evidence of the high character and virtue of the women was this shrinking from dishonour and the fact that they who were fearless in face of the two most awful things in the world—death and pain—could not support the appearance of disgrace nor bear the thought of shame after death.'[2]

Theramenes, in whose time hemlock as a means of suicide appears to have come into vogue, was a native of Ceos, and we have seen above that Theophrastus[3] ascribes to the Ceans certain improvements in the method of preparing that poison. There is evidence that at some period suicide by drinking hemlock was a recognized practice—if not a legal regulation—in Ceos for persons who had passed the age of 60. Strabo[4] (63 B.C.–A.D. 23), speaking of Iulis, the chief town in Ceos, birthplace of Simonides and his nephew Bacchylides, says:

παρὰ τούτοις δὲ δοκεῖ τεθῆναί ποτε νόμος, οὗ μέμνηται καὶ Μένανδρος [342–291 B.C.] "*καλὸν τὸ Κείων νόμιμόν ἐστι, Φανία· ὁ μὴ δυνάμενος ζῆν καλῶς, οὐ ζῇ κακῶς.*" *Προσέταττε γάρ, ὡς ἔοικεν, ὁ νόμος τοὺς ὑπὲρ ἑξήκοντα ἔτη γεγονότας κωνειάζεσθαι, τοῦ διαρκεῖν τοῖς ἄλλοις τὴν τροφήν· καὶ πολιορκουμένους δέ ποτε ὑπ' Ἀθηναίων, ψηφίσασθαί φασι τοὺς πρεσβύτας τοὺς ἐξ αὐτῶν ἀποθανεῖν, ὁρισθέντος πλήθους ἐτῶν· τοὺς δὲ παύσασθαι πολιορκοῦντας.*

Stephanus of Byzantium[5] writes to the same effect.[6] So too Ælian.[7] Valerius Maximus, who wrote under Tiberius, attests a similar practice for Massilia and tells of the Cean practice as he had actually witnessed it.[8]

In Thebes, too, the treatment of suicides attracted some remark.[9] In Athens such differential treatment as we hear of is of a religious rather than of a legal nature. The suicide as a victim of violence belongs to the class of those whose spirits 'walk.'[10] According to a statement in Suidas,[11] suicides and other victims of violent and untimely death were buried in a special place. We find a similar ordinance given by Plato.[12] To the same order of ideas belongs the Athenian custom of burying the hand which wrought the

---

1 116 ff.

2 Plato, *Phædo*, 57 A: *τὸ φάρμακον ἔπιεν*; cf. 57 B, 116 D, 117 A. Though Plato does not name the poison, it is clear from the symptoms described that it was hemlock. Ælian, *Var. Hist.* i. 16, calls it merely *τὸ φάρμακον*; Diodor. xiv. 37: *πιὼν κώνειον ἐτελεύτησεν*; Diog. Laert. ii. 42.

3 *Frogs*, 1050 f.

4 Plutarch, *Dio*, 58.

5 Theophr. *Hist. Plant.* IX. xvi. 8.

6 Plato, *Lysis*, 219 E: 'I mean, for example, if a father knew that his son had drunk hemlock and thought that wine would save him, he would value the wine.' Cf. Nicander, *Alexipharmaca*, 186.

7 IX. xvi. 6.

8 *Ib.* 9.

9 Plato, *Phædo*, 117.

10 Ælian, *Var. Hist.* iv. 23; Athen. XII. 537 C.

1 Servius and Probus on Vergil, *Georg.* ii. 389; Hygin. *Fab.* 130, *Astron.* ii. 4; Pollux, iv. 55; Hesych. *s.vv.* Αἰώρα and Ἀλῆτις; *Etymologicon Magnum*, ed. F. Sylburg, Leipzig, 1816, *s.v.* Αἰώρα; schol. Hom. *Il.* xxii. 29; Athen. xiv. 618 E, F. For this and other swinging rites cf. *GB*3, pt. iii., *The Dying God*, London, 1911, Note B, p. 277 ff.

2 Plut. *Mulierum Virtutes*, 249 B–D.

3 *Hist. Plant.* IX. xvi.

4 x. 486.

5 *De Urbibus*, *s.v.* Ἰουλίς.

6 Cf. Heracleid. *Polit.* 9, and the epigram of Meleager, *Anthologia Palatina*, vii. 470, where the deceased is made to say that at an advanced age (*κάρτα πρέσβυς*) *ἤλυθον Ἀΐδαν αὐτοθελεί, Κείων γευσάμενος κυλίκων.*

7 *Var. Hist.* iii. 37.

8 Val. Max. ii. 6.

9 Zenob. *Prov.* vi. 17; Phot. *Lex.* s. *Τί οὐκ ἀπήγξω ἵνα Θήβησιν ἥρως γένῃ;*

10 See Plato, *Laws*, 865.

11 *S.v.* Κυνήγιον: *ὅτι ἐν τῷ Κυνηγίῳ καλουμένῳ ἐρριπτοῦντο οἱ βιαιοθάνατοι.*

12 *Laws*, 873 C.

deed apart from the suicide's body.[1] Josephus, in mentioning the custom, adds the unsatisfactory reason that the hand was regarded as alien to the body.[2] It is more natural to connect the practice with the idea of the soul of the suicide 'walking'—'perhaps to prevent his ghost from attacking the living.'[3]

6. Philosophy.—As regards the attitude of the philosophic schools, the teaching of the Pythagoreans condemned suicide. According to Orphic or Pythagorean doctrine, the soul is undergoing in the body a penitential discipline for ante-natal sin.[4] Hence suicide is an unwarranted rebellion against the will of God on the part of the individual, whom it behoves to wait until it please God to set him free.

Plato, if we may infer his position from the *Phædo* and the *Laws*, condemns suicide on grounds which we would characterize as religious. Religious, too, are the grounds on which Aristotle appears to regard suicide as reprehensible.[5] Aristotle treats suicide as an offence not against the individual, but against the State, and that of a religious kind, as involving the city in pollution and requiring therefore penalties of a religious nature. No doubt Aristotle had in view such ceremonial observances as the severance of the right hand and the like, to which we have referred above.

Stoic teaching was decidedly favourable to suicide. Life and death being for the wise man indifferent (*ἀδιάφορα*), morally neither good nor evil, the question of suicide resolves itself for him into a decision whether life or death is in a given case preferable. Life in accordance with nature being the Stoic ideal,[6] when the conditions essential to that ideal are no longer fulfilled, suicide becomes a reasonable deliverance (*εὔλογος ἐξαγωγή*).

Thus suicide may be demanded by a man's duty to his country or his friends or by a condition of severe pain or of physical disablement or incurable disease.[7] The paradox of the Stoic position is that the question of 'to be or not to be' is decided not with regard to virtue or vice, but with regard to the *ἀδιάφορα*, the 'indifferent' things. It is a question of *τὰ καθήκοντα* and *τὰ παρὰ τὸ καθῆκον*.[8] Hence it may be proper (*καθῆκον*) for the happy to commit suicide, for the unhappy to remain in life.[9] Goodness or badness *per se* has no bearing on the question.[10] There is, indeed, little that differs from the Platonic position in the statement of their doctrine in Diogenes Laertius.[11] But the danger of the Stoic doctrine lay in the facility with which comparatively trivial discomforts might be held to justify suicide.

Zeno (*c.* 300 B.C.), the founder of the Stoic school, is said, according to one account, to have taken his own life because he had stumbled and wrenched his finger.[12] Cleanthes, his successor, having developed a gum-boil, refrained from food by the advice of his doctors for two days. The treatment was successful, and the doctors relaxed the regime and allowed him *πάντα τὰ συνήθη*, all the usual foods. But Cleanthes, having gone so far in the path of death, persisted to the end.[13]

For the Stoic the length or brevity of life was a matter of indifference.[14]

The Cynics, too, favoured suicide. Antisthenes seems to have used the term, afterwards so familiar in the Stoics, *ἐξαγωγή*, to denote suicide.[1] Diogenes is said to have recommended suicide to Antisthenes.

According to Diog. Laert. vi. 18, when Antisthenes was lying upon his deathbed, Diogenes visited him, carrying a dagger; and, when Antisthenes said, 'Who will deliver me from this trouble?', Diogenes, showing him the dagger, said, 'This.' There is a similar story in Diog. Laert. iv. 3, that on one occasion Speusippos, driving in his carriage to the Academy, met Diogenes and wished him good-day (*χαῖρε εἰπεῖν*), to which he replied that he would not wish him the same *ὅστις ὑπομένεις ζῆν τοιοῦτος ὤν*.

On the other hand, the Academic, Peripatetic, and Epicurean schools were all opposed to suicide, at any rate in theory.

With regard to the Academics it may suffice to quote the story of Carneades, who, when he heard that the Stoic Antipater had committed suicide by drinking poison, exclaimed, 'Then give me too to drink!' And, when his friends said, 'What?' 'Athol brose' (*οἰνόμελι*), he said.[2]

The Peripatetics hold that the excellences of the soul are superior to the excellences of the body and other external excellences, yet they aim at the other excellences, first, as desirable for their own sakes, and, next, as being useful *πρός τε τὸν πολιτικὸν καὶ τὸν κοινωνικὸν βίον καὶ δε καὶ πρὸς τὸν θεωρητικόν. παραμετρεῖσθαι γὰρ τὸν βίον ταῖς πολιτικαῖς καὶ ταῖς κοινωνικαῖς πράξεσι καὶ ταῖς θεωρητικαῖς.*[3] Their attitude to suicide is thus in sharp contrast to that of the Stoics.

As regards the Epicureans, believing as they did in the extinction of the soul at dissolution, it might well seem that life at any level was at least worth something, and it were folly to cast that away for the nothingness of the grave. It would seem that they occupied themselves particularly in pointing out the folly of committing suicide through fear of the terrors of death.

'Death, that most dreaded of ills, is nothing to us. For while we are, death is not; and when death has come, we are not. Death, then, is nothing to the living nor yet to the dead, since it does not affect the former, and the latter no longer exist. The crowd, to be sure, at one time shrink from death as the worst of evils, at another choose it as a refuge from the miseries of life. But the wise man neither declines life nor shrinks from death, since life is not distasteful to him, nor does he think it an evil not to live.'[4]

The Cyrenaics seem in general to have been opposed to suicide. Theodoros, counting the world his country and disbelieving in friendship, held that even self-sacrifice for one's country was unjustifiable.[5] Hegesias, on the other hand, preached suicide so frankly as to earn the title of ὁ Πεισιθάνατος,[6] and with such success as to provoke the interference of Ptolemy.[7]

7. Religion.—From the religious point of view suicide was regarded always as a crime, a violation of the social order. We have seen that Orphic teaching condemned suicide. But it is impossible to regard this condemnation as limited to so confined a circle. The more one reflects on the evidence, the more one is forced to the conclusion that much which we ascribe to the Orphics is really part of the general tradition—part of the popular belief. The sort of doctrine which Plato ascribes at one moment to the mystics he at another ascribes to popular belief. In any case the belief in immortality is described in the *Apology* as among *τὰ λεγόμενα*, among the popular beliefs. And popular belief certainly differentiated between the fortune after death of the suicide and of those who died a natural death (*θανάτῳ εἰμαρμένῳ*, *morte sua*). Already in Homer it is difficult to account for the position of Antikleia, the mother of Odysseus, on any other supposition than that

[1] Aischin. *c. Ktes.* 244: *ἐάν τις αὐτὸν διαχρήσηται, τὴν χεῖρα τὴν τοῦτο πράξασαν χωρὶς τοῦ σώματος θάπτομεν.*
[2] *BJ* III. viii. 5.
[3] *GB*3, pt. iii., *The Dying God*, p. 220 n.
[4] Philolaos, *ap.* Clem. *Strom.* iii. 3, p. 186. Cf. Plato, *Gorg.* 493 A, *Cratyl.* 400 C.
[5] *Eth. Nic.* v. 11 (1138a).
[6] *τέλος ἐστὶ τὸ ὁμολογουμένως τῇ φύσει ζῆν* (Cleanthes, *ap.* Stob. *Ecl.* ii. 132).
[7] Diog. Laert. vii. 130.
[8] Stob. ii. 226; Plut. *de Stoic. Repugn.* 1042 D.
[9] Plut. *loc. cit.*
[10] Plut. *de Stoic. Repugn.* 1039 E, *de Comm. Not.* 1163 C–D; Cicero, *de Fin.* iii. 18.
[11] vii. 130. [12] *Ib.* vii. 28 ff. [13] *Ib.* vii. 176.
[14] Cic. *de Fin.* iii. 14.

[1] Cf. Athen. iv. 157 B; Plutarch, *de Stoic. Repugn.* 1039 E, 1040 A, and *de Comm. Not.* 1063 C, D; Diog. Laert. vi. 24.
[2] Diog. Laert. iv. 64 f.; Stob. *Flor.* cxix. 19.
[3] See Stobæus, ii. 264–266.
[4] H. Usener, *Epicurea*, Berlin, 1887–1908, iii. 60, tr. A. E. Taylor; cf. Seneca, *Ep.* xxiv. 22, lxx. 8; and the eloquent protest of Lucretius, iii. 79 ff.
[5] Diog. Laert. ii. 98. [6] *Ib.* 86.
[7] Cicero, *Tusc.* i. 34; cf. Plutarch, *de Amore Prolis*, 497 D.

she is a suicide and thus not admitted immediately to the realm of Hades.[1] We have seen above that, according to one tradition, the dead Aias was deprived of certain rites of burial. The same feeling is at the bottom of the practice of severing the right hand of the suicide and burying it apart from the rest of the body. So in our own country suicides used to be buried at the marches in a no man's land: or, if in the churchyard, the body must be passed over the wall and not enter by the gate.

As popular religion regarded with horror all shedding of blood, all interference with the natural bounds of life, so it regarded with a peculiar horror the shedding of kindred blood (αἷμ' ἐμφύλιον). Ixion, who first introduced this crime—ἐμφύλιον αἷμα πρώτιστος οὐκ ἄτερ τέχνας ἐπέμιξε θνατοῖς—won for himself a choice woe.[2] The supreme case of 'kindred blood'—which is the term used by Sophocles to denote the patricide of Oidipus[3]—is suicide. The Greek language hardly distinguishes between self-murder and murder of kin. The suicide belongs to the class of the victims of violent and untimely death—ἄωροι βιαιοθάνατοι (or, in late usage, βιοθάνατοι)—the murdered, the dead on birth or in nonage,[4] the unborn victim of abortion,[5] regarding the fate of whom the popular mind was peculiarly sensitive. It seems probable that these religious grounds, and not any speculative theories, were the really active motives at all periods of ancient Greece in condemning the practice of suicide.

II. *ROMAN.*—**1. Heroic suicide.**—What we may call the heroic type of suicide—committed either to escape intolerable shame or for great causes which seem to demand the sacrifice of the individual life—was thoroughly consonant with the character of Republican Rome. Such suicides were a prominent feature in the early history of Rome, and the tradition of them undoubtedly exercised a powerful influence upon later conduct.[6]

The typical example of self-sacrifice for the fatherland is that of the Decii. According to modern authorities, the story is true only of the younger Decius. But, in any case, both are enshrined in Livy's matchless prose. The elder, P. Decius Mus, devoted himself in 337 B.C. in a battle with the Latins near Mount Vesuvius, when he was in command of the left wing. A precisely similar story is told of the younger Decius, who at the battle of Sentinum in 295 B.C. devoted himself to death, charging into the densest ranks of the Gauls, where he fell.[7]

Suicide to escape intolerable dishonour is illustrated by the story of Lucretia, the victim of the *mala libido*[8] of Sextus Tarquinius. Her story is too familiar to be told here.[9]

2. Penalties of suicide.—We have seen that suicide by hanging was regarded by the Greeks as a shameful type of death. When Oidipus discovers the nature of his sin, he can find no stronger words to describe his deeds than to say that they are κρείσσον' ἀγχόνης, *i.e.* such as even suicide by hanging could not expiate. The Roman feeling seems to have been precisely similar. If we quote the case of Amata, wife of King Latinus, it is mainly on account of the interesting matter preserved by Servius in his commentary on the passage. Vergil tells us that

> 'Regina ut tectis venientem prospicit hostem,
> Incessi muros, ignes ad tecta volare:
> Nusquam acies contra Rutulas, nulla agmina Turni:
> Infelix pugnae iuvenem in certamine credit
> Exstinctum; et, subito mentem turbata dolore,
> Se causam clamat, crimenque, caputque malorum:
> Multaque per moestum demens effata furorem,
> Purpureos moritura manu discindit amictus,
> Et nodum informis leti trabe nectit ab alta.'[1]

Servius on this passage tells us that certain posthumous penalties attached to this form of suicide:

'Sane sciendum quia cautum fuerat in pontificalibus libris ut qui laqueo vitam finisset, insepultus abiceretur. . . Cassius autem Hemina [the oldest Roman annalist] ait: "Tarquinium Superbum cum cloacas populum facere coegisset et ob hanc iniuriam multi se suspendio necarent, iussisse corpora eorum cruci affigi: tunc primum turpe habitum est mortem sibi consciscere." Et Varro ait: "Suspendiosis quibus iusta fieri ius non sit, suspensis oscillis[2] veluti per imitationem mortis parentari."'

It is clear in any case that the grounds on which this particular kind of suicide was condemned were religious or mystical rather than ethical.

3. Suicide under the Empire.—That suicide was extremely prevalent under the Empire, at any rate among the higher ranks of society, cannot be doubted. Nor are the causes which contributed to this state of affairs difficult to conjecture. The most important were probably chiefly two: on the one hand the decay of religious belief and on the other hand the great popularity of a school of philosophy which was favourable to suicide. With regard to the first, however, it is to be remarked that it does not appear that even in Republican times suicide, for sufficient cause, was considered to be inconsistent with piety. The Stoic teaching suited in general the typical Roman character, and, in particular, the Stoic teaching in regard to suicide found ready acceptance among the educated classes under the Empire. In this matter the Stoic position appealed even to men who in other respects were at variance with the Stoics. In one sense the Stoic doctrine was merely a logical development from the position taken up by Plato. Even Plato had admitted suicide when some compelling ἀνάγκη—some ineluctable constraint of circumstances—forced a man to end what he could not mend. The nature of this ἀνάγκη, or, as the Romans called it, *necessitas*[3] or *necessitudo*, was so indefinite as to be capable of a very various interpretation. It only remained for later Stoics like Panaitios (*c.* 140 B.C.) and Posidonios (*c.* 130–46 B.C.) to interpret it in the sense not of an external compulsion, but of an inner overmastering impulse. By this interpretation the whole philosophic anti-suicide position was undermined. It was no longer felt to be a disgraceful thing to commit suicide: the only thing worth considering was how to commit suicide with such bravery or bravado, such fortitude or such parade of fortitude, as would most appeal to the imagination. The morality of suicide was no longer in dispute: given such a situation as either from the individual point of view or from the point of view of his relation to the State appeared intolerable, then suicide was the obvious and expected course of action.

The pages of the writers of the Empire teem with suicides, and a glance at some of these will help to illustrate what was the current view of voluntary death.

Pliny the younger,[4] writing of Titus Aristo, an eminent lawyer whom he describes as inferior to none of the philosophers 'castitate, pietate, iustitia, fortitudine,' tells how, being afflicted by 'longa et pertinax valetudo,' he contemplated taking his own life: 'You would be surprised, were you present, at the patience with which he bears this illness, holding out against pain, resisting the temptation to quench his thirst, enduring the unbelievable heat of fever while motionless and warmly covered. He lately summoned me and a few other special

[1] *Od.* xi. 85 f. [2] Pind. *Pyth.* ii. 30 ff.
[3] *Oed. Tyr.* 1406.
[4] Plato, *Rep.* 615 C: τῶν δὲ εὐθὺς γενομένων καὶ ὀλίγον χρόνον βιούντων.
[5] See S. Reinach, 'Ἄωροι βιαιοθάνατοι, in *ARW* ix. [1906] 312–322, and S. Wide, in *ARW* xii. [1909].
[6] See Cic. *Pro Sestio*, 48, *pro Scauro*, iii. 1 ff.
[7] Livy, viii. 9 f., x. 28. [8] *Ib.* i. 57.
[9] *Ib.* 57 f.; Ovid, *Fasti*, ii. 741 ff.

[1] *Æn.* xii. 595 ff.
[2] The meaning of these *oscilla* we have seen above in connexion with the Athenian festival of the Aiora; cf. Verg. *Georg.* ii. 387 ff.
[3] Tac. *Ann.* vi. 23. [4] *Ep.* i. 22.

friends and requested us to consult his physicians about the issue of his illness, with the intention of voluntarily departing from life, if his illness were incurable, while on the other hand, if it were merely to be difficult and tedious, he would bear up and bide his time; for so much, he thought, was due to the entreaties of his wife, the tears of his daughter, even to us his friends, that he should not by voluntary death abandon our hopes, if only they were not vain. Such conduct I consider eminently high and praiseworthy. For to rush to death under the influence of an impulse and an instinctive feeling is no more than what many have done: but deliberately to weigh the motives for and against and then, as reason advises, to accept or reject the policy of life or death, that is the conduct of a great soul.'

In A.D. 101 the poet Silius Italicus committed suicide by abstention from food. Pliny says: 'It has just been announced that Silius Italicus has ended his life by starvation (*inedia*) in his Neapolitan villa. Bad health was the cause. He had developed an incurable tumour and, weary of it, he betook himself to death with irrevocable firmness. Up to his last day he had been happy and fortunate, with the exception of the death of the younger of his two children.'[1]

In *Ep.* iii. 16 Pliny celebrates the heroic conduct of Arria, who, when her husband Cæcina Pætus was condemned for his share in the conspiracy of Scribonianus against Claudius in A.D. 42, encourages her husband to commit suicide, first stabbing herself and then handing the dagger to her husband with the words 'Paete, non dolet.' This famous suicide is the subject of an epigram of Martial.[2]

A somewhat similar story is told in Pliny.[3]

A special interest attaches to the type of suicide mentioned by Pliny in *Ep.* iii. 9.

Cæcilius Classicus, proconsul of Bætica A.D. 98-99, was accused of extortion and anticipated judgment by death—presumably suicide: 'Ille accusationem vel fortuita vel voluntaria morte praevertit; nam fuit mors eius infamis, ambigua tamen: ut enim credibile videbatur, voluisse exire de vita, cum defendi non posset; ita mirum pudorem damnationis morte fugisse, quem non puduisset damnanda committere.'

References are frequent under the Empire to the forestalling of judgment by suicide. In a well-known passage[4] Tacitus explains the motives, referring to the year A.D. 34, as being dread of the executioner and the desire to secure certain posthumous advantages which the suicide had over the condemned in respect of the disposal of his person and his property. Normally, it appears, the goods of a condemned person were confiscated, and he forfeited the rites of burial. The suicide, on the other hand, did not forfeit the rites of burial, and his testamentary dispositions remained valid. These advantages constitute what Tacitus calls the 'pretium festinandi.'[5] In practice, however, there seems to have been considerable variation in the treatment of the goods of such a suicide. In the time of the Republic apparently his goods were confiscated as a matter of course.[6] It is clear from the evidence of Tacitus himself that even under the Empire suicide before sentence did not always save the suicide's goods from confiscation.[7]

The perplexities of the question and the various distinctions made may be seen in Justinian, *Dig.* xlviii. 21: 'DE BONIS EORUM QUI ANTE SENTENTIAM VEL MORTEM SIBI CONSCIVERUNT VEL ACCUSATOREM CORRUPERUNT,' where § 3 forms an important document with regard to suicide:

'Persons accused of or caught in crime who, through fear of the charge hanging over them commit suicide, have no heirs. Papinianus,[8] however, writes that, when guilty persons who have not been accused commit suicide, their goods are not forfeited to the *fiscus*. For it is not the fact of guilt that is liable, but the fear of the guilty conscience is held in the case of an accused person as tantamount to a confession of guilt. Therefore, for the confiscation of the goods of suicides, it is required that they must either have been accused or caught in the criminal act. According, however, to the rescript of the emperor Pius, the goods of a person who, lying under an accusation, commits suicide are confiscated only if the crime of which he was accused was such that, if condemned, he would have suffered either death or deportation. He likewise held that a person who was accused of a petty theft, even if he committed suicide by hanging, was not in such case that his goods should be taken away from his heirs, any more than they would have been taken from himself, had he been convicted of theft. Therefore the goods of a suicide are to be forfeited only if the charge in which he was implicated were of such a nature that conviction would have entailed the loss of his property. If, on the other hand, a person committed suicide from weariness of life or impatience of pain or the like, he was entitled, according to Antoninus, to have a successor. According to a rescript of the emperor Hadrian, if a father, accused of killing his son, committed suicide, it must be held that his suicide was due rather to grief for the loss of his son, and therefore his goods were not to be confiscated. This distinction is on the same level as the inquiry whether a person who commits suicide without being guilty is liable to any penalty on the ground that he has passed sentence on himself. For in any case suicide is punishable save when it is due to weariness of life or intolerance of some grief. And rightly so: for, if a man did not spare himself, much less will he spare another. It is forbidden by imperial mandates to confiscate the goods of persons who have died in prison or on bail, while the issue of their case is still uncertain. We have to consider, in the case of a person who has died by his own hand without reasonable cause while under accusation, whether, if his heirs are prepared to take up his case and maintain the innocence of the deceased, they are to be heard and his goods not to be confiscated until the charge is proved; or whether in any case they are to be confiscated. But a rescript of the emperor Pius to Modestus Taurinus laid down that, if the heirs are prepared to undertake the defence, the goods are not to be confiscated, until the charge is proved.'

Other examples of this type of suicide in Tacitus are P. Vitellius,[1] M. Æmilius Scaurus,[2] Plancina.[3] L. Piso died before his trial by a *mors opportuna* which was probably suicide.[4]

A notable feature of the Empire is the use of compulsory suicide as a means of execution. Intimation is conveyed, more or less explicitly, to the party concerned that his death is desired. The advantages of this form of compulsory death over actual execution were apparently partly æsthetic, but probably the main advantage was that it seemed to make the guilty person his own judge and executioner and thus relieved the emperor of the *invidia* which necessarily attached to an actual execution. This method left to a man his 'choice of death'—what was known as 'liberum mortis arbitrium,'[5] or merely 'mortis arbitrium.'[6]

Other examples of compulsory suicide recorded in the *Annals* of Tacitus are Silanus,[7] Poppæa Sabina,[8] Silvanus,[9] Narcissus,[10] Iulius Montanus,[11] Thrasea Pætus, Soranus Barea and his daughter,[12] Valerius Asiaticus,[13] Arruntius,[14] Anteius.[15]

Three examples may be selected as being the suicides of notable men with regard to whose last moments we possess detailed records—the poet Lucan, the emperor Nero, and Seneca.

The suicide of Lucan in A.D. 65 is thus described by Tacitus:[16]

'Exim M. Annaei Lucani caedem imperat [sc. Nero]. Is, profluente sanguine, ubi frigescere pedes manusque, et paulatim ab extremis cedere spiritum, fervido adhuc et compote mentis pectore, intellegit; recordatus carmen a se compositum, quo vulneratum militem, per eiusmodi mortis imaginem obisse tradiderat, versus ipsos rettulit [*Pharsal.* iii. 635-646?], eaque illi suprema vox fuit.'[17]

The suicide of Nero has often been described. The account given by Suetonius[18] is too long to quote. The story of Seneca's death is told in Tacitus, *Ann.* xv. 60-63.

It appears that in those times every suicide was more or less a *poseur*, who was expected to make his suicide remarkable by some notable word or act. Hence Tacitus remarks: 'Senecio . . . et

1 *Ep.* iii. 7. 2 i. 14. 3 *Ep.* vi. 24.
4 *Ann.* vi. 29. 5 *Ib.* 6 Cf. Livy, iii. 58.
7 Tac. *Ann.* iv. 19 f., ii. 31 f., iii. 15, 17.
8 *Digesta Responsa*, bk. xvi.

1 *Ann.* v. 8. 2 *Ib.* vi. 29. 3 *Ib.* 26.
4 *Ib.* iv. 21; cf. Livy, vi. 1: 'iudicio eum mors adeo opportuna, ut voluntariam magna pars crederet, subtraxit.'
5 Suet. *Domit.* 8. 6 Tac. *Ann.* xvi. 33.
7 *Ib.* xv. 32. 8 *Ib.* xi. 2. 9 *Ib.* xv. 71.
10 *Ib.* xiii. 1. 11 *Ib.* xiii. 25. 12 *Ib.* xvi. 33.
13 *Ib.* xi. 3. 14 *Ib.* vi. 48. 15 *Ib.* xvi. 14.
16 *Ib.* xv. 70.
17 Cf. Sueton. *Vit. Luc.*: 'Impetrato autem mortis libero arbitrio, codicillos ad patrem de corrigendis quibusdam versibus suis exaravit: epulatusque largiter, brachia ad secandas venas medico praebuit.'
18 *Nero*, 49.

Quinctianus et Scaevinus . . . mox reliqui coniuratorum periere, nullo facto dictove memorando.'[1]

A notable feature of those suicides is the frequency with which the wife shares the suicide of the husband or even by example prompts him to death—*e.g.*, Sextia,[2] Pompilia,[3] Seneca's wife, as just mentioned, and Arria, wife of Pætus.

Suetonius, as the historian of the emperors, naturally has numerous suicides, some of which present interesting features.

In his life of Augustus[4] we have a curious case (in 42 B.C.): 'patrem et filium pro vita rogantes sortiri vel dimicare [i. 9, trial by combat] iussisse [sc. Augustus] ut alterutri concederetur; ac spectasse utrumque morientem, cum patre, qui se obtulerat occiso, filius quoque voluntaria occubuisset nece.'

'Quin et Artabani, Parthorum regis, laceratus est literis, parricidia et caedes et ignaviam et luxuriam obicientis, monentisque, ut voluntaria morte maximo iustissimoque civium odio quam primum satisfaceret.'[5]

'Alios [other senators], cum clam interemisset, citare nihilo minus ut vivos perseveravit, paucos post dies voluntaria morte periisse mentitus.'[6]

The attitude of at least the educated world of the time may be described as an advanced Stoicism, and the permissibility of suicide under certain circumstances was accepted at Rome not merely by professed Stoics but also by adherents of other philosophical schools. We cannot do more here than summarize and illustrate the chief aspects of the question of suicide as it presented itself to the chief exponents of later Stoicism.

In the first place, whereas to Plato suicide had seemed to be permissible only, if at all, under compulsion (ἀνάγκη) of an external nature, this compulsion is now so interpreted that suicide becomes in fact not so much the involuntary act of the unwilling victim of circumstances as the voluntary assertion by the individual of his freedom. The liberty of the 'wise' man consists precisely in this that he is entitled to 'withdraw himself' (ἐξάγειν ἑαυτόν) when he finds his liberty hampered by his environment. Already Cicero had interpreted for the Romans this phase of later Stoicism:

'Et constat Stoicos, praesertim inter Romanos, in eo quod vitae se subducere liceat morte voluntaria (ἐξαγωγήν dicere solebant) vel libertatem sapientis cerni putasse.'[7]

This is the prevalent doctrine under the Empire.[8]

Hence the man who finds it no longer possible to obey God, or, in other words, to live as his nature requires, is to perceive precisely in this fact an intimation from God that it is time to depart from life.[9]

Again, Plato had felt the difficulty that, while on the one hand it was better for man to depart and be with God, it was yet held to be unlawful to hasten that departure by one's own voluntary act. Now the conviction of the nothingness of this present life as compared with the after life for which it is a preparation has become an additional motive for suicide, no longer hampered by any other restraint than that the individual must convince himself that God gives the signal for him to depart.[10]

In the end, then, to be or not to be becomes purely a question for the individual. Suicide is not to be the rash act of a momentary impulse, a temporary confusion of values. It is to be determined upon or rejected after due deliberation. Nothing indeed is more striking in the accounts of suicides under the Empire than precisely this formal weighing of the considerations for and against.

1 *Ann.* xv. 70. 2 *Ib.* vi. 29. 3 *Ib.* xv. 63.
4 Ch. 13. 5 *Tiberius*, 66.
6 *Caligula*, 26. For other cases of suicide cf. *Galba*, 3, *Jul. Cæs.* 36, *Claud.* 31.
7 *De Fin.* iii. 60.
8 Cf. Seneca, *Ep.* xii. 10; Epictetus, *Dissert.* i. 24: τὸ δὲ κεφάλαιον· μέμνησο ὅτι ἡ θύρα ἤνοικται.
9 Cf. Epictetus, *Diss.* iii. 24. 101.
10 Cf. *Ib.* i. 9. 16; Seneca, *Ep.* cii. 23.

The individual point of view was much insisted upon in the later Stoicism. The same set of circumstances might in a given case demand suicide, in another not. A situation of intolerable shame, for instance, might be for an ordinary man a sufficient ground for suicide. Yet it might be the duty of another man, whose life was essential to the State, to reject the temptation. A man's death must be in consonance with his life.

Peregrinus, according to Lucian, ἔφη βούλεσθαι χρυσῷ βίῳ χρυσῆν κορώνην ἐπιθεῖναι· χρῆναι γὰρ τὸν Ἡρακλείως βεβιωκότα, Ἡρακλείως ἀποθανεῖν.[1]

This doctrine of 'propriety' is expounded in a well-known passage of Cicero's *de Officiis*, which is of course based upon Panætius.[2]

III. *CONCLUSION.*—Our review, then, of the history of suicide among Greeks and Romans shows that at all times the only valid motives against the practice of suicide have been, in the main, not ethical but religious. And consequently the penalties attached to suicide are not so much civil as religious. They affect a man's condition not here but in the hereafter. The withholding of the rites of burial, the severance of the right hand, and so forth, all belong to the religious circle of ideas. When religious values ceased to have any meaning and were not replaced by other values, then, as in the case of the Cynics, there was no antagonism to suicide. When, on the other hand, the life hereafter was so emphasized that in comparison with that after life the life here seemed of little account, there was an obvious impulse to suicide. But that impulse was resisted and decried —by Plato on the ground of a higher law, a great mystery which demands that we remain in our prison-house till God shall please to set us free; by the Neo-Platonists because suicide is *ipso facto* detrimental to the soul. The whole question is admirably put in Macrobius, *Comm. in Somn. Scip.* i. 13:

'Haec Platonicae sectae semina altius Plotinus exsequitur. Oportet, inquit, animam post hominem liberam corporeis passionibus inveniri. Quam qui de corpore violenter extrudit, liberam esse non patitur. Qui enim sibi sua sponte necem comparat, aut pertaesus necessitatis aut metu cuiusquam ad hoc descendit aut odio; quae omnia inter passiones habentur; ergo etsi ante fuit his sordibus pura, hoc ipso tamen, quod exit extorta, sordescit. Deinde mortem debere ait animae a corpore solutionem esse, non vinculum, exitu autem coacto animam circa corpus magis magisque vinciri. Et revera ideo sic extortae animae diu circa corpus eiusve sepulturam vel locum, in quo iniecta manus est, pervagantur: cum contra illae animae, quae se in hac vita a vinculis corporia philosophiae morte dissolvunt, adhunc extante corpore caelo et sideribus inserantur.'

LITERATURE.—K. A. Geiger, *Der Selbstmord im klassischen Altertum*, Augsburg, 1888; E. Durkheim, *Le Suicide*, Paris, 1897; R. Hirzel, 'Der Selbstmord,' in *ARW* xi. [1908]; A. Buonafede, *Histoire critique et philosophique de suicide*, Paris, 1762.

A. W. MAIR.

SUICIDE (Hindu).—I. **Vedic.**—In view of the devotion to life and its pleasures which marks the *Rigveda*, and which is reflected in the disapproval therein implied of the practice of *satī*, it is not surprising that no trace of the custom of religious suicide can be found in that text. Nor in the later *Saṁhitās* and the *Brāhmaṇas* is there any clear recognition of such a usage, unless we accept the suggestion of Hillebrandt[3] that the consecration ceremony (*dīkṣā*),[4] which is an essential preliminary to the most important rites, is in reality a faded form of the older practice of suicide by fire. While it is true that the generation of heat in the man who undergoes the rite is an important feature of it, the purpose of this practice, as of the fasting which constitutes even a more essential

1 Lucian, *Peregrin.* 33.
2 Cicero, *de Officiis*, i. 111 ff., tr. G. B. Gardiner, London, 1899.
3 *Rituallitteratur* (=*GIAP* iii. 2), Strassburg, 1897, p. 125.
4 See B. Lindner, *Die Dikṣâ oder Weihe für das Somaopfer*, Leipzig, 1878.

element of the ceremony, may much more naturally be deemed to be to produce the psychological condition best suited for the performance of the sacrifice. There are, however, in the *Brāhmaṇas* two doctrines which undoubtedly pave the way for the approval of suicide from religious motives. In the first place, there is developed the conception that the proper sacrifice is that of a man's self, and that other forms of offering are substitutes;[1] in the second place, in the latest of the great *Brāhmaṇas*, the *Śatapatha*,[2] the closing act of both the *puruṣamedha* and the *sarvamedha*, the human and the universal sacrifices, is the giving away by the performer of the whole of his possessions, including in the latter case even the land, and his wandering into the forest, doubtless as a preliminary to an early death. The teaching of the *Upaniṣads*, which emptied empirical life of all true reality, held out union with the infinite as the result of knowledge, and glorified the cessation of existence, must have tended to the same result, but the logical conclusion of their thought is not expressed in any of the older *Upaniṣads*, and it is only in such late works as the *Jābāla*[3] and *Kaṇṭhaśruti*[4] *Upaniṣads* that it is expressly laid down that the *sannyāsin*, who has acquired full insight, may enter upon the great journey, or choose death by voluntary starvation, by drowning, by fire, or by a hero's fate. Earlier evidence (and better proof of usage) is afforded by notices in the *Dharmasūtras*: in Vasiṣṭha[5] it is expressly stated that the world of *Brahman* is obtained by entering the fire; and in Āpastamba,[6] in an interesting discussion which ends with a defence of secular life and aims, it is admitted that in one view the ideal was for an ascetic first to live on fruits, roots, grass, and leaves only, then on those things alone which become spontaneously detached, then on water, then on air, and finally on ether alone. With the testimony of Vasiṣṭha accords the record of the death on a pyre erected by his own wish of Kalanos, an Indian follower and friend of Alexander, who fell ill at Pasargadæ and decided on death, despite the opposition of the king, rather than alter his mode of life.[7]

2. Buddhism and Jainism.—It is characteristic of the general sanity of Buddhism in its earliest form that the Buddha appears to have disapproved of suicide, as he disapproved of all excesses of ascetic fervour. But it would be surprising if the influence both of Brāhmanism and of Jainism had not had its effect in making suicide reputable in certain communities. Not only is the duty of self-sacrifice deemed to excuse the action of the *bodhisattva* in committing suicide with the definite aim of being reborn as the fish whose flesh alone can save the people from disease, but self-destruction appears to be approved if undertaken with the desire of securing rebirth in such a condition as will permit entry into the Buddhist order.[8]

While this attitude is exceptional in Buddhism, Jainism frankly recognizes and commends religious suicide. It is dealt with at length in the *Āyāra*,[9] the first *Aṅga*, and its preliminaries are described in detail in the *Āurapachchakkhāṇa* and the *Saṁthāra*, the second and fourth of the *Painnas* in one reckoning. But suicide is not permitted promiscuously; it is allowed to those ascetics who have acquired the highest degree of perfection, and it in essence consists of giving up begging, and lying down in a duly chosen place to await death by hunger and thirst. Frequent mention is made of death being thus brought about by a month's abstinence (*kālamāse*); this fate is recorded of the Tīrthakaras Pārśva and Ariṣṭanemi,[1] of the monk Khandaga,[2] of the layman Ambaḍa,[3] and of all those celebrated in the *Uvāsagadasāo*. At this supreme moment of his career the ascetic must not long after rebirth in this world or as a god; he must not wish to live on or desire sensual pleasures, but equally he must not seek for death to come more swiftly. The final condition thus reached by the sage (*samāhipatte*) is one of complete mental and physical collapse. Practically identical with it appears to be the *pannabhūmi*, the last of the eight stages of man's existence as taught by Gosāla Maṅkhaliputta.[4] The popularity of the practice is attested throughout the whole history of Jainism: in 1172 thus died the great scholar and statesman Hemachandra, followed in a short time by his patron Kumārapāla;[5] in 1912 a monk at Aḥmadābād, though in perfect health, starved himself to death by a fast of 41 days; and in the following year a nun at Rājkot, having previously weakened herself by austerities, died after two or three days' fast. Suicide, however, is still not permitted to others than ascetics, and non-religious suicide is regarded with especial horror by the Jains, as they disapprove of all taking of life. The problem of reconciling these two views is solved as little by the Jains as by the Brāhmanical schools.

3. Hinduism, mediæval and modern.—Hinduism stands firmly on the position reached in the *Dharmasūtras*, which permits religious suicide, while censuring ordinary forms of self-murder. Manu[6] expressly permits a Brāhman, in circumstances explained (doubtless correctly) by his commentators as disease or great misfortunes, to walk straight on in a north-easterly direction subsisting on water and air until his body sinks to rest, and declares that a Brāhman who has got rid of his body by any of the means practised by ancient sages obtains the world of *Brahman*; and Medhātithi interprets the methods in question as drowning oneself in a river, leaping from a height, burning, or starvation. The *Mahābhārata*[7] fully recognizes the wickedness of suicide; nevertheless the prince Duryodhana himself resolves to die by starvation, and for this purpose, as the ceremony is a religious rite, dons old garments and holy grass, drinks water, and applies his mind to devotion, though his purpose is eventually defeated.[8] An interesting tale,[9] which appears also in the *Pañchatantra*,[10] is that of the hunter for whom a pigeon roasts itself as a guest-offering; the wife of the bird declines to survive her husband, and the hunter, saddened by their sacrifice, repents and himself ends his life by fire. A new aspect of suicide appears in connexion with the development of the devotion paid to the sectarian deities which is characteristic of Hinduism, for suicide now means not so much absorption in an impersonal absolute as union with a very personal deity. The idea is reflected in the mythical account of the history of Mīrā Bāī, the

1 A. B. Keith, tr. of *Taittirīya Saṁhitā*, pt. i. p. cvi ff.
2 xiii. vi. 1 ff.
3 5; cf. P. Deussen, *The Philosophy of the Upanishads*, Eng. tr., Edinburgh, 1906, p. 382.
4 See F. O. Schrader, *The Minor Upaniṣads*, Madras, 1912, i. 39, 390 f. The great journey is probably wandering on without food until death takes place.
5 xxix. 4.
6 ii. ix. 23. 2.
7 Arrian, *Anab.* vii. 3. A similar deed is recorded of an Indian sage who formed part of an embassy to Augustus in 20 B.C., and accompanied his court to Athens; but he had not the excuse of disease (Dio, liv. 9; Strabo, xv. i. p. 720).
8 J. S. Speyer, *Die indische Theosophie*, p. 276 f. Cf. art. SUICIDE (Buddhist).
9 i. vii. 6 ff.

1 *Kappa Sutta*, 168, 182.
2 *Bhagavatī*, ed. A. Weber, Berlin, 1866, p. 300.
3 *Ovavāiya Sutta*, 100.
4 Buddhaghoṣa's comm. on *Dīgha Nikāya*, ii. 20.
5 G. Bühler, *Über das Leben des Jaina Mönches Hemachandra*, Vienna, 1889, p. 50 f.
6 vi. 31 f.
7 xii. ccxcvii. 31 f.
8 iii. ccli. 20 ff.
9 *Mahābhārata*, xii. cxliii. 10 ff.
10 T. Benfey's tr., Leipzig, 1859, ii. 247 ff.

devotee of Kṛṣṇa in the time of Akbar, who is recorded to have disappeared into a fissure which showed itself for a moment in the image of her chosen divinity when she was paying homage to him at Dvārakā. Similar considerations doubtless prompted some of the comparatively rare suicides which took place during the *yātrās* of Viṣṇu as Jagannātha at Purī. Neither Chaitanya, to whose teaching the fame of the shrine was largely due, nor any of his followers appears to have encouraged or approved this form of worship; no allusion is made to it in the elaborate account of the car-procession by Kṛṣṇadāsa or by Abu-l Faẓl. It is not impossible that the conception may have been borrowed from a Śaiva sect, some fusion of the two cults having taken place at Purī, but Chaitanya's own end was mysterious, and in his lifetime he had sought mystic union with the god in ecstatic trance, so that the occasional suicides of ardent devotees beneath the wheels of the car of Jagannātha can hardly be deemed unnatural or surprising.[1]

The wide-spread nature of the custom, and its prevalence both with and without Brāhmanical sanction, are attested by H. T. Colebrooke from personal observation just at the opening of the 19th century. In 1802 the legislature intervened to prevent the practice of suicide on the island of Sāgar, at the mouth of the Ganges, where, in pursuance of vows, not only were children cast into the sea to be devoured by sharks but grown-up persons voluntarily underwent the same fate. This practice was confined to the lower castes, as was also the custom by which men used annually to hurl themselves from a precipice in the mountains south of the Narmadā, sacred to Kālbhairo, in fulfilment of vows undertaken at an earlier period. This rite was carried out by mountaineers; great concourses gathered at the place on the new moon of Phālguna, the day appointed for the ceremony, and it is significant of the passion for public recognition as part of the motive of such suicides that the man meditating this fate was wont to proclaim his intention publicly and, attended by a band of musicians, to promenade in the neighbouring towns collecting alms. On the other hand, not only did the practice of *satī* (*q.v.*) flourish under Brāhmanical auspices, but the custom of suicide by drowning at the specially holy spot of the junction of the Jumna and the Ganges was approved, while the practice of lepers consenting to burial alive was promoted by the grant of obsequies which were otherwise denied. The Śaivas also allowed suicide by cutting the throat before the image of Bhavānī in the temple of Vindhyāvāsinī, near Mirzapur. Interference with these rites was gradual, but the final adoption of the principle of treating as a criminal offence participation in a ritual suicide has deprived the act of much of its religious character, though it is of course impossible to prevent suicide on the part of those who regard such a fate as a logical outcome of the religious convictions which they hold.

So far as religious suicide has been approved in India, it is significant that it has been in cases of men who have lived a full life and acquired a high measure of ascetic power, and that suicide in other cases has never been authorized and has instead been strongly condemned. There is obviously comparatively little essential distinction between the practice of austerities to a pitch which deprives the ascetic of all mental and physical activity, and the actual termination of life; an intermediate stage is furnished by the cataleptic condition which the Yogi seeks to induce, and of which the most famous case is that of Haridās, who even survived burial for considerable periods.[1] But in its essence the practice can hardly be traced to any origin other than the effort to supply a rationale for the old and inhuman usage by which the aged head of a family might be cast out to die, when he became too old to rule or be of service to his kindred—a usage for which there is clear evidence in the *Rigveda*.[2] In place of the violent removal of the elders there was substituted the doctrine that in old age it was the duty and privilege of a man to adopt a hermit's life, unless he preferred to terminate of his own will an existence which had become burdensome. The essentially popular character of the practice is proved conclusively by the pertinacity with which the Jains have maintained it from the earliest period, though the doctrine of the sanctity of life as adopted by them would otherwise have forbidden approval of the custom.

LITERATURE.—For the question of the *dīkṣā* see A. Hillebrandt, *Vedische Mythologie*, Breslau, 1891–1902, i. 482 f., *Deutsche Litteraturzeitung*, xvi. [1895] 74; H. Oldenberg, *Die Religion des Veda*, Berlin, 1894, p. 398 f., *ZDMG* xlix. [1895] 176; A. B. Keith, tr. of *Taittirīya Saṅhitā*, Cambridge, Mass., 1914, p. cxiv f. For Buddhism see L. de la Vallée Poussin, *Bouddhisme: Opinions sur l'histoire de la dogmatique*, Paris, 1909, p. 325 ff. The Jain views are given and explained by H. Jacobi, *Gaina Sutras*, pt. i. [*SBE* xxii.], Oxford, 1884, p. 68 ff., pt. ii. [*SBE* xlv.], do. 1895, p. 24; A. F. R. Hoernle, in his ed. of the *Uvāsagadasāo*, Calcutta, 1890; Lewis Rice, *Inscriptions at Śravaṇa Belgoḷa*, Bangalore, 1889, p. 15 ff.; A. K. Forbes, *Rās Mālā*, London, 1856, ii. 331 ff.; Margaret Sinclair Stevenson, *The Heart of Jainism*, Oxford, 1915. For Hinduism generally see A. Barth, *The Religions of India*, Eng. tr., London, 1882; H. H. Wilson, *Essays and Lectures on the Religion of the Hindus*, do. 1862, vol. i.; E. W. Hopkins, *The Religions of India*, do. 1896, *Epic Mythology* (=*GIAP* iii. 1*b*), Strassburg, 1915; J. S. Speyer, *Die indische Theosophie*, Leipzig, 1914. The facts as to the *yātrā* of Jagannātha are examined in detail by W. W. Hunter, *Orissa*, London, 1872, i. 132 ff., 306 ff., *The Indian Empire*³, do. [1893], p. 276 ff. The observations of H. T. Colebrooke are given in a paper quoted by T. E. Colebrooke, *The Life of H. T. Colebrooke*, London, 1873, p. 178 ff.

A. BERRIEDALE KEITH.

SUICIDE (Japanese).—Japan is known as a country in which an unusually large number of people commit suicide. According to the latest statistics, compiled by the Bureau of Statistics of the Japanese Government, the number of deaths by suicide in the ten years preceding 1915 was as follows:

Year.	Population.[3]	Number of Deaths.	Deaths by Suicide.	Number of Suicides per One Million Inhabitants.
1905	47,678,396	1,004,661	9,413	197
1906	48,164,761	955,256	8,906	184
1907	48,819,630	1,016,798	9,180	188
1908	49,588,804	1,029,447	9,595	193
1909	50,254,471	1,091,264	10,553	210
1910	50,984,844	1,064,234	10,773	213
1911	51,753,934	1,043,906	10,753	207
1912	52,522,753	1,037,016	11,128	212
1913	53,362,862	1,027,257	11,942	223
1914	54,142,441	1,101,815	12,705	234

The same returns give the number of deaths by suicide according to sex and age, as shown on Table 1.

According to the methods employed, the number of deaths is as shown on Table 2.

Some of the principal causes of suicide are shown on Table 3.

Among the methods of suicide used by Japanese the following three are unique and worthy of description:

(1) *Harakiri* ('belly-cutting'), more commonly

[1] See art. JAGANNATH.

[1] R. Garbe, *Sāṁkhya und Yoga* (=*GIAP* iii. 4), Strassburg, 1896, p. 47.

[2] VIII. li. 2; H. Zimmer, *Altindisches Leben*, Berlin, 1879, p. 328; cf. A. A. Macdonell and A. B. Keith, *Vedic Index*, London, 1912, i. 395.

[3] Populations in Korea, Formosa, and Saghalien are not included.

TABLE 1.

Age.	Sex.	Year.									
		1905.	1906.	1907.	1908.	1909.	1910.	1911.	1912.	1913.	1914.
1–16	Male	82	84	83	79	135	131	135	108	122	141
	Female	108	64	90	80	103	115	116	91	111	100
16–20	Male	201	244	258	309	299	316	345	379	344	388
	Female	383	381	373	440	409	405	399	356	449	413
20–30	Male	1105	1277	1318	1494	1568	1527	1597	1683	1767	1855
	Female	929	971	1019	1015	1069	1021	1058	1102	1213	1231
30–40	Male	825	785	909	894	965	1019	1022	1015	1131	1214
	Female	480	461	515	504	573	543	587	560	580	641
40–50	Male	903	774	773	821	918	881	834	861	998	1049
	Female	402	365	406	398	388	418	408	485	479	479
Over 50	Male	2607	2252	2122	2296	2608	2756	2569	2657	2913	3210
	Female	1379	1241	1308	1261	1383	1428	1421	1452	1592	1724
Unknown	Male	9	6	5	4	94	171	209	212	206	221
	Female	—	1	1	—	41	42	53	67	37	39

TABLE 2.

Method.	Sex.	Year.									
		1905.	1906.	1907.	1908.	1909.	1910.	1911.	1912.	1913.	1914.
Hanging	Male	3593	3337	3296	3427	3861	3909	3666	3769	4123	4376
	Female	1591	1516	1573	1517	1637	1616	1578	1621	1791	1814
Drowning	Male	1148	984	921	1087	1183	1247	1222	1245	1318	1516
	Female	1685	1510	1536	1574	1698	1693	1746	1770	1810	1927
Stab-cut	Male	186	193	201	239	265	243	269	276	325	343
	Female	95	87	112	108	117	118	86	103	127	126
Fire-arms	Male	117	127	121	143	150	158	132	136	149	144
	Female	8	13	9	12	16	12	8	9	13	10
Poison	Male	124	137	170	171	223	260	349	346	347	375
	Female	58	68	103	112	107	137	186	206	190	226
Railway	Male	—	—	—	—	698	804	821	930	1017	1105
	Female	—	—	—	—	294	307	343	403	465	436
Otherwise	Male	564	644	759	830	207	190	252	213	202	219
	Female	244	290	379	380	98	89	95	101	65	88
Total	Male	5732	5422	5468	5897	6587	6811	6711	6915	7481	8078
	Female	3681	3484	3712	3703	3967	3972	4042	4213	4461	4627

TABLE 3.

Cause.	Year.									
	1905.	1906.	1907.	1908.	1909.	1910.	1911.	1912.	1913.	1914.
Mental disease	4563	4312	4298	4174	3784	3622	3421	3358	3276	3453
Physical pain	1676	1514	1640	1835	2109	2155	2146	2224	2460	2669
Poverty	1192	984	1005	1017	891	824	771	837	897	875
Jealousy	340	373	428	485	327	257	264	234	232	235
Remorse	274	271	226	232	230	165	156	173	157	193
Family trouble	248	278	334	330	227	251	248	268	321	382
Fear of punishment	86	64	102	91	167	185	195	213	219	214
Anxiety	42	65	68	55	163	229	238	219	232	199
Business failure	162	116	128	136	177	187	184	189	252	304
Dissipation	51	81	86	95	203	147	184	215	185	197

called *seppuku*, was, until the promulgation of the new criminal code in 1873, a method of punishment frequently required of offenders from the nobility and the military class. The laws of the Tang period in China, which for several hundred years had been the model of the Japanese legal system, recognized three forms of capital punishment: beheading, strangulation, and self-execution. The last was allowed to offenders of rank, that they might escape the shame of public death at the hands of others. The criminal laws of Japan allowed self-execution to members of the royal family and to others above the fifth court-rank, except in case of high treason. *Harakiri* dates from the Taira and Minamoto period in the 12th cent. and was widely practised during the Sengoku period of internal strife. During the Tokugawa period the practice developed into a complicated system with much etiquette and formality.

'It was not mere suicide. It was an institution, legal and ceremonial, invented in the middle ages, by which warriors could expiate their crimes, apologize for error, escape from disgrace, redeem their friends or prove their sincerity.'[1]

The most notable historical case of *harakiri* is that of the 47 Ronin, in 1703. The *daimyo* Asano had been obliged to commit *harakiri* to atone for an unjustifiable attack upon Kira, a nobleman in the Shogun's palace. A band of devoted followers, after long effort, avenged their master by assassinating Kira. They gave themselves up to justice and, under sentence, committed *harakiri* at the

[1] T. Harada, *Faith of Japan*, New York, 1914, p. 129.

homes of the *daimyos* to whom, in groups, they had been entrusted. Their bodies were buried with respect at a Buddhist temple in Tokyo; and to this day many admirers of their chivalrous loyalty pay homage at their tomb.

For the purpose of *harakiri* a site was usually selected in some garden facing a residence, sheltered at the back and sides by curtains of white cotton. Within the curtained enclosure were placed two mats covered with a mattress of light blue. The condemned seated himself upon the mattress in the presence of superintending witnesses, with a kinsman or special friend to act as an assistant. He was clothed in special garments, and, after certain formal ceremonies, was handed a short sword with which to make the horizontal cut through the abdomen. The cut having been made, it was the duty of the assistant to behead the sufferer, that the agony of death might be short.

Though *harakiri* is no longer recognized as a form of public execution, the method is still not uncommon among those who seek to avoid the humiliation of public condemnation and punishment or the supposed disgrace of capture by the forces of an enemy in battle.

(2) *Shinju* or *aitaishi* ('dying between two parties') is the death together of unhappy lovers who seek escape from the difficulties of their earthly lot and entrance upon a happier life in the next world. For the accomplishment of *shinju* drowning has been the most frequent method, the lovers often tying themselves together with a strong rope. So common was this form of suicide among the lower classes during the Tokugawa period that in 1723 the Shogunate issued special regulations forbidding it, refusing formal burial to the bodies, and condemning to shame or exile any one who might survive the attempt. At present *shinju* is of frequent occurrence; and in recent years other forms of death, such as poison or mutilation beneath trains, have been employed.

(3) *Junshi* is suicide upon the death of one's lord or master with the idea of following him into the next world. In ancient times this was an act of loyalty required by custom, until the emperor Suinin (29 B.C.–A.D. 70) ordered the substitution of clay images for the bodies of attendants and favourite animals. *Junshi* was revived during the feudal period, not as a requirement, but as a voluntary custom whereby loyal followers, through *harakiri*, expressed their devotion to their masters. The drowning of almost the entire Taira clan in the western sea at the downfall of that clan and the *junshi* of hundreds of the family of Hojo Takatoki at the end of his career are among the most striking manifestations of this *junshi* spirit. The custom was forbidden by the Shogunate in 1744, and, before the opening of the Meiji era, had become uncommon; but solitary cases have occurred from time to time. Of these the most startling in recent times was the death by *harakiri* of General Nogi and his wife, at the time of the funeral of the emperor Meiji, in Sept. 1912.

LITERATURE.—*Encyclopædia Japonica*, vol. vi., *s.v.* 'Seppuku (in Japanese), Tokyo, 1914; B. H. Chamberlain, *Things Japanese*[4], London, 1902; *Annual Report of Statistics of the Japanese Imperial Government* (in Japanese), Tokyo, 1917.

TASUKU HARADA.

SUICIDE (Jewish).—Only a very few cases of suicide are recorded in the OT. The ancient Hebrews were, on the whole, a naive people, joyously fond of life, and not given to tampering with the natural instinct of self-preservation. Nor are all of the few instances recorded on the ordinary level of suicidal occurrences. The case of Ahithophel (2 S 17^{23}) is the only one which, in the modern mind at any rate, excites loathing and reprobation. The suicide of Zimri (1 K 16^{18}) and of Abimelech (killed at his own request by his armour-bearer [Jg 9^{54}]) only leaves us cold; whilst, on the other hand, the death of Samson (Jg $16^{26ff.}$) and of Saul and his armour-bearer (1 S $31^{4f.}$) inspire us with a sense of awe and a certain kind of admiration rather than any other feeling.

But, when later the people of the Dispersion became more and more affected by some of the evil influences around them, and the difficulties and perplexities of existence kept on increasing, a much less wholesome attitude towards life made itself perceptible. And, as cases of suicide became more frequent, it was at last found necessary to give a name to the evil. A suicide was thus, in exact legal terminology, described as 'one who purposely destroys himself.'[1] In accordance with a general Rabbinic principle of legislation, an effort was, moreover, made to find support in the Scriptures for the new ideas and enactments which the practice of suicide brought in its train. In *Midrash Rabbāh*, 34, the prohibition of suicide is thus derived from the wording of Gn 9^5, the little word את in ואך את דמכם ('and surely your blood') being taken to include self-destruction. Dt 4^9 ('Only take heed to thyself, and keep thy soul diligently') has been considered capable of a similar interpretation, and some[2] would even include suicide in 'Thou shalt not kill,' contained in the Ten Commandments. An indignantly rejected suggestion to commit suicide rather than suffer is also by some discovered in Job 2^{9-10} (cf. 7^{15}).

Considering some confusion of ideas which the elaborate treatment of the subject by J. Hamburger[3] may produce in the reader's mind, it seems necessary to state that the Rabbinic, like the Christian and general, conception of the act entirely excludes submission to a death of martyrdom from even the category of condoned or permissible suicide, so long as the victims do not, under the stress of fear or suffering, lay violent hands on themselves (or, by mutual consent, on one another).

The difference between an act of self-destruction during martyrdom and martyrdom pure and simple is illustrated by the striking case of Ḥananiah b. Tĕradyon, who, whilst suffering the pangs of death by fire during the Hadrianic persecutions, is reported to have replied to his disciples' suggestion that he should open his mouth, so that the fire should enter it and consume him more quickly, in these words: 'It is right that he who has given life should take it away, but let not a man destroy himself' (though, on the other hand, he allowed the executioner to heap up the flames and otherwise hasten his end).[4]

We must, therefore, limit ourselves to cases in which the act of death is, in the literal sense of the term, self-inflicted, though a division into different categories is at the same time necessary. Concerning suicide induced by the martyr spirit of patriotism we find instructive information in Josephus, where both sides of the argument are forcibly stated from the points of view of warriors, philosophers, and men of the world.

In the speeches addressed to the Jewish garrison of Masada[5] their commandant Eleazar lays special stress on their resolve, made long ago, 'never to be servants to the Romans, nor to any other than God himself,' and then exhorts them to receive their punishment for their past sins from none other than the Deity, 'as executed by our own hands'; and, on finding that his words had not yet produced the desired effect, he adds, among other things, the further argument that death 'affords our souls their liberty, and sends them by a removal into their own place of purity, where they are to be insensible to all sorts of misery,'

---

[1] המאבד עצמו לדעת (*e.g.*, at the beginning of *Sĕmāḥoth*, ii.). The terms החונק את עצמו ('one who strangles himself') and ההורג את עצמו ('one who kills himself') are also used. The act of suicide is represented by איבוד עצמו לדעת.

[2] See J. L. Saalschütz, *Das mosaische Recht*, Berlin, 1846–48, p. 550.

[3] Art. 'Selbstmord,' in *Realencyclopädie*, Talmudic part.

[4] T.B. '*Abōdāh Zārāh*, 18*a*.

[5] *BJ* VII. viii. 6 f.

the final result being that 960 persons (*i.e.* the whole garrison, including women and children, with the exception of two women and five children) consented to die rather than yield themselves up to the Romans. (The spirit of the act is, of course, the same as caused the self-destruction of Razis, as related in 2 Mac 14[37-46]; and with the occurrence at Masada may be fitly compared the typical mediæval instance of the death of a large number of Jews in York in the year 1190.)

Josephus's own attitude towards suicide, under similar conditions, is revealed in *BJ* III. viii.

In the speech which, after the fall of Jotapata, he addressed to the men who had taken refuge with him in a cave, he compares a suicide to a pilot 'who, out of fear of a storm, should sink his ship of his own accord,' reminds them that it is a wicked and perfidious act to cast out of one's body the soul which God had committed to it, and exhorts them not to endeavour, by an act of self-destruction, 'to run away from God, who is the best of all masters.'[1]

A somewhat analogous, though much more pitiable, class is well represented by the case[2] of 400 captive boys and girls who, when they understood that they were being carried off for a life of shame, determined to end their lives by drowning. To quite another category belong a certain number of persons who are reported to have committed suicide under the stress of acute remorse for certain acts of theirs.[3] A different case, again, is that of the executioner of Ḥananiah b. Tĕradyon, already referred to, who, on receiving from the dying martyr the promise of future bliss, is said to have destroyed himself in the flames in which the saint had died, in order to enter at once on his inheritance. Rabbinic leniency by way of accepting excuses for young suicides is shown in the cases of certain children who had destroyed themselves because they lay under a threat of punishment from their respective fathers.[4]

The judgment of a person who, in our own legal phraseology, has been proved a *felo de se* is, in the main, left to God (לשמים),[5] though a person who recklessly endangers his life is subject to judicial chastisement (מכת מרדות).[6] With regard to the treatment of the body of a suicide, there is a mention in the speech of Josephus referred to of the custom which demanded that the remains should lie exposed till sunset. In *Sĕmāḥoth*, ii. 1,[7] it is enacted that one should neither rend one's garments for a suicide nor bare the shoulder or engage in any other formal mode of mourning. Care is taken, however, not to offend the feelings of the relatives of the dead. Those present at the funeral, therefore, form themselves in a row and recite the necessary order of service. The general rule, indeed, is that one does everything required by respect for the living, but omits all the rest. There has also been a rule of burying a suicide away from the regular line of graves, but this is not always observed.[8]

It should be mentioned in conclusion that statistics comparing the prevalence of cases of suicide among modern Jews with those of other races and denominations are given in *JE*, *s.v.* 'Suicide.'

LITERATURE.—The literature has been indicated in the article.

G. MARGOLIOUTH.

SUICIDE (Muhammadan).—There is no specific text of the Qur'ān which forbids suicide, though it would seem that the texts which bear upon the taking of human life in general are sufficiently clear as to their purpose to include any kind of wilful killing in private life. The following verses will indicate the bearing of the Qur'ān upon the subject:[1]

'It is not for any soul to die, save by God's permission written down for an appointed time' (iii. 139; the reference is to him who 'dies or is killed'). 'It is not for a believer to kill a believer save by mistake' (iv. 93). 'And whoso kills a believer purposely, his reward is hell, to dwell therein for aye; and God will be wroth with him, and curse him, and prepare for him a mighty woe' (iv. 95). 'He respites them until a stated time; and when their time comes they cannot put it off an hour, nor can they bring it on' (xvi. 63).

The attitude of Muhammad has no doubt been correctly interpreted by *hadīths* which Bukhārī accepts as genuine:

'Whosoever shall kill himself shall suffer in the fire of hell,' and 'shall be excluded from heaven for ever.'[2]

At the present time, and for many centuries past, there has been unanimity of opinion throughout Islām that suicide is a violation of a divine command contained in the Qur'ān and the Sunnah of the Prophet. A tradition relates that Muhammad refused to bury a suicide, and his example has established a law to that effect in Islām. In spite of the law, however, it is customary to accord the funeral rites in such cases.

It is difficult to obtain statistics covering suicide in Muhammadan countries, but all authorities who treat of suicide in an exhaustive way agree that in those countries the practice is almost unknown. It is clear from the statistics presented in scientific works on suicide that the physical environment of different peoples offers no adequate explanation of the varying ratio of suicides among them, while difference of religious belief as between groups always results in a varying proportion of suicides. The regions of Islām show few suicides precisely because of the nature of the Muslim's belief in God and the future life. The right attitude for the Muslim is *islām*, an acceptance of life's events as settled by divine appointment, of death as fixed as to both time and manner, and of the hereafter as a pre-arranged order of retributive rewards and penalties distributed according to the individual's attitude of acquiescence in the arrangement of life and destiny or of revolt against it. Suicide is an act of revolt against God, and the perpetrator of the act risks the wrath of God and the indescribable penalties of the Fire. Whatever else Islām may lack in the way of ethical influence, its sense of obligation to make acceptance of Providence the cardinal factor in obedience to God has been an effective determinant of conduct, and its doctrine of future retribution has been efficacious in strengthening this virtue of active resignation to the will of God.

LITERATURE.—Most of the leading treatises on suicide contain a brief reference to the Muslim attitude on the subject. In none of these works is there any attempt really to cope with the question, the available materials not permitting any well-founded conclusions as to the extent and causes of the phenomenon. The most useful general discussion is found in *RGG* v., *s.v.* 'Selbstmord.' See also *DI*, *s.v.* 'Suicide.'

WALTER M. PATTON.

SUICIDE (Semitic and Egyptian).—Among the ancient Hamito-Semitic peoples the love of life was strong. They were (with the possible exception of the Egyptians) still in the earlier and less reflective stages of civilization, and consequently showed little of that melancholy which leads to frequent suicide.

1. Semitic.—Among the Semites not only was the love of life strong, but their primitive religion was a worship of the goddess of life. Most of their deities of later time were gods that were in some form closely associated with the idea that life was divine. Their general attitude towards life was one of joyous interest in objective things. Their philosophical and reflective powers never attained any great degree of vigour. There are, accordingly, no cases of suicide on record except where

---

[1] The manner in which Josephus finally escaped death, whilst all his companions save one lay slain around him, will be found described in *BJ* III. viii. 7.

[2] Recorded in T.B. *Giṭṭin*, 57*b*.

[3] See, *e.g.*, *Genesis Rabbāh*, ch. 40; T.B. *Qiddushin*, 81*b*; Rashi in the mention of Beruriah (a doubtful case, however) in T.B. *'Abōdāh Zārāh*, 18*b*.

[4] *Sĕmāḥoth*, ii. 4 f.

[5] Maimonides, *Mishneh Tōrah*, *Hilkhōth Rōṣēaḥ*, ch. ii.

[6] *Ib.* ch. xi.

[7] Also embodied in, *e.g.*, *Yōrēh Dē'ah*, § 345.

[8] See Hamburger, end of art. 'Selbstmord,' where references relating to this point are given.

[1] The translation is E. H. Palmer's, *SBE* vi. [1900].

[2] See *DI*, *s.v.* 'Suicide.'

the deed was committed in order to avoid a form of death that was considered particularly disgraceful.

An early and classical example of this is the suicide of King Saul of Israel (1 S 31[4]). Israel's armies had been defeated by the Philistines. Saul said to his armour-bearer: 'Draw thy sword, and thrust me through therewith; lest these uncircumcised come and thrust me through, and abuse me.' Naturally the armour-bearer was afraid to do this, so Saul fell upon his own sword and ended his life. Clearly the deed would not have been committed but for the desperate straits in which the king found himself. To him, as to many in all parts of the world, the foreigner was unclean. Philistine foreigners did not bear the sacred mark of circumcision; they were doubly unclean. He took his own life in order to avoid dying by such unholy hands after having been tortured by them.

A second case is that of Saul's armour-bearer. When he saw that his king had committed suicide, he followed the example of his master. His motive may have been in part the same as Saul's; it may have been in part despair at the death of his chief. At all events the armour-bearer, like Saul, took his own life only when a death which he regarded as disgraceful was inevitable.

Closely analogous to the suicide of Saul was the death of Abimelech, the son of Gideon (Jg 9[54]). Abimelech had made himself king of Shechem and a small territory about it; he sought to enlarge his dominion by the conquest of Thebez, a city some miles to the north-east of Shechem. In attacking the city he drew near to the wall, whence a woman threw a millstone on his head and broke his skull. He thereupon commanded his armour-bearer to thrust him through, lest it should be said of him that a woman slew him, and the armour-bearer obeyed. Abimelech did not actually die by his own hand, but, since the death-wound was inflicted by his own command, it was practically suicide.

A similar case in the Maccabæan period is reported in 2 Mac 14[37-46]. A certain Razis, imprisoned in a tower in Jerusalem, which Nicanor was besieging, when he saw that resistance was useless, fell upon his sword. As the wound thus inflicted was not fatal, he threw himself from the tower. When that did not kill him, he disembowelled himself.

At least two instances are recorded among the Hebrews in which traitors committed suicide.

Ahithophel, one of David's trusted advisers, betrayed his master and conspired with Absalom. When he saw that David had eluded the traitors and that civil war would follow, he hanged himself (2 S 17[23]). Similarly Judas Iscariot, the betrayer of Jesus Christ, when he saw that, as a consequence of his deed, Jesus was arrested and condemned, went and hanged himself (Mt 27[5]). Possibly his effort to end his life in this manner failed, for another account (Ac 1[18]) implies that he, like Razis, died from being disembowelled.

Conscience, then as now, sometimes drove traitors to end their own lives. Both the reasons for suicide which can be traced in ancient Israel operated in the case of Shamash-shum-ukin, king of Babylon, 668–648 B.C.

He headed an extensive conspiracy against his brother and suzerain, Ashur-bani-pal, king of Assyria. When Ashur-bani-pal, having defeated Shamash-shum-ukin's army and the forces of his allies, besieged him, Shamash-shum-ukin, reduced to extremity, threw himself into a burning pit rather than fall into the hands of his brother.[1] His rebellion had exposed him, in case of capture, to the kind of barbarous torture inflicted by the Assyrians on rebels—a prospect that might well drive a man to the less painful death of a burning pit. Shamash-shum-ukin might, however, have faced this, as many another had done, had it not been for an accusing conscience.

The cases cited sufficiently reveal the ancient Semitic attitude towards suicide. It was resorted to only in extreme cases.

2. Egyptian. — The attitude of the ancient Egyptians towards suicide was in general like that of the Semites. The love of life was strong in them, and their conception of the life beyond such that it presented to them deterrents of various kinds. The inscriptions present us with two sources of information on the subject, one practical, the other theoretical.

In the reign of Ramses III. (1198–1167 B.C.) a conspiracy against the life of the king was formed in the *harīm*, in which a number of high officials were implicated. The king appointed a commission to investigate the matter and to try the criminals. From the records of this commission we learn that at least seventeen persons, who were found guilty, were left to themselves and permitted to take their own lives.[2] It was in a way compulsory suicide.

[1] Cf. *KB* ii. 191.

[2] See J. H. Breasted, *Ancient Records of Egypt*, iv. §§ 444–454.

Death by their own hands was, however, apparently regarded as less humiliating than death at the hands of an executioner. An eighteenth person, when found guilty, committed suicide, apparently to the regret of the commission.[1] It appears from this record that the punishment of high and formerly trusted officials was probably accomplished by the ancient Egyptian government in this way.

An interesting document written during the Middle Kingdom (2100–1800 B.C.), which has been entitled by Erman and Breasted 'The Dialogue of a Misanthrope with his Own Soul,'[2] indicates that, in the *mêlée* of Egyptian feudal development, as the failure of old religious forms to satisfy increased and a sense of the injustices of life attained power, suicide was contemplated by some as an escape from life's ills.

The beginning of the papyrus is lost, but from what remains it is clear that a certain man of gentle spirit (his name is lost) fell sick. He was forsaken by his friends; even his brothers left him uncared for. Deserted by all, he was robbed by his neighbours. His former good deeds were forgotten. Although a wise man, when he would plead his own cause, he was thrust aside. His name, which should have been revered, was defamed. He then determined to take his own life, but, as he stood on the brink of the grave, his soul shrank back in horror and refused to accompany him. The dialogue then began. The soul's first reason for not going with him was the fear that there would be no tomb to dwell in after death. This afforded the misanthrope an opportunity to expose to his soul the utter futility of all such preparations. The soul had counselled death by burning, but had then shrunk from that, as there would be no surviving friend to stand by the bier and make the mortuary offerings. He urged his soul to undertake these duties itself, but then the soul refused death in any form, declaring that, even when the great built pyramids and endowed mortuary services, their tombs were in time neglected and permitted to fall into ruins, so that they were in no better case than the poor. His soul urged that it was good for men to 'follow the glad day and forget care.' The misanthrope then proceeds to demonstrate that life, instead of being an opportunity for pleasure, is far more intolerable than death. The demonstration is embodied in four poems addressed to his soul. The first of these pictures the unjust abhorrence in which the speaker's name was held by the world. The second sets forth the corruption of society. The third, which speaks of death as a glad release, justifies suicide. It runs as follows:[3]

'Death is before me to-day
[Like] the recovery of a sick man,
Like going forth into a garden after sickness.

Death is before me to-day
Like the odour of myrrh,
Like sitting under a sail on a windy day.

Death is before me to-day
Like the odour of lotus flowers,
Like sitting on the shore of drunkenness.

Death is before me to-day
Like the course of a freshet,
Like the return of a man from the war-galley to his house.

Death is before me to-day
Like the clearing of the sky,
Like a man ⌜fowling therein toward⌝ that which he knew not.

Death is before me to-day
As a man longs to see his house
When he has spent years in captivity.'

The fourth poem contributes to the argument in favour of suicide by expressing the conviction that in the 'beyond' that justice which is unattainable in this world will be experienced.

'He who is yonder
Shall seize (the culprit) as a living god,
Inflicting punishment of wickedness on the doer of it.

He who is yonder
Shall stand in the celestial barque,
Causing that the choicest of the offerings there be given to the temples.

He who is yonder
Shall be a wise man who has not been repelled,
Praying to Re when he speaks.'[4]

This document shows how world-weary Egyptians looked at suicide 4000 years ago. An interesting feature of the point of view is that it betrays no

[1] *Ancient Records of Egypt*, iv. § 456.

[2] For a more complete account of it see J. H. Breasted, *Development of Religion and Thought in Ancient Egypt*, pp. 188–198.

[3] As translated by Breasted, p. 195.

[4] *Ib.* p. 197.

consciousness that self-destruction is wrong. In this respect it is in striking contrast to the Talmud. Rabbi Eleazar says that Gn 9[5] means that 'I [God] will require your own blood from you'[1]—a clear recognition of the sinfulness of suicide. The Egyptian misanthrope, so far from betraying any such consciousness, seems to hold that the fact that in the world beyond he can not only attain the justice that is denied him here, but also assist in the establishment of justice, is a reason for hastening by his own hand his release from life's intolerable conditions.

LITERATURE.—K. Kohler, *Jewish Theology*, New York, 1918, p. 484; J. H. Breasted, *Ancient Records of Egypt*, Chicago, 1905–07, iv. 217–221; A. Erman, *Gespräch eines Lebensmüden mit seiner Seele*, in *ABAW*, Berlin, 1896; J. H. Breasted, *Development of Religion and Thought in Ancient Egypt*, New York and London, 1912. GEORGE A. BARTON.

SUKHARS.—See RUKHARS.

SUMATRA.—See JAVA, BALI, AND SUMATRA.

SUMERO-AKKADIANS.—**1. The term.**—The ethnic expression 'Sumero-Akkadian' does not occur in the inscriptions, but, as the compound *Kengi-Ura*, translated by the Semitic *Šumer u Akkad*, 'Šumer and Akkad,' is found, it is a perfectly legitimate name for the mixed population which of old occupied the alluvial plain of the Tigris and the Euphrates, where they flowed into the Persian Gulf.

2. Probable derivation of the names.—Many suggestions have been made as to the origin and meaning of *Kengi* (or *Kingi*)-*Ura* and *Šumer u Akkad*, but it must be admitted that both these points are doubtful even now.

J. D. Prince[2] suggests that it may be a combination of *kên* (long form of *ki*), 'land,' and *gi*, 'reed,' 'land of reeds' being 'an appropriate designation of Babylonia.' In the lists, however, *Kengi* or *Kingi* is rendered simply by *mâtu*, 'country,' and here stands for 'the country' in the sense of 'our native land.'[3] This being the case, it is probable that the above forms are nasalized from *kigu*, the name of the first character, suggesting that *kiki* may have been the unweakened form. As to *Ura*, that is the pronunciation given to the characters *bur* / *bur*, superimposed, when they are used for *Akkad*. This group also stands for the highlands of Armenia and of Palestine, and therefore indicated a mountainous region.[4] That the Akkadian Semites (not, as formerly supposed, the Sumerians) came from some highland district is quite possible, and that may be the meaning of *Ura*. *Akkad*, however, is probably shortened from *Agadé*, one of the names of the old capital of the northern district of Babylonia. In Gn 10[10] *Accad* is named as one of the cities of Nimrod's kingdom, after Babel (Babylon), but *Agadé* seems to have come into prominence before the great capital city. In addition to *Kingi*, Šumer is also expressed by the characters *Eme-ku ki*, which have, perhaps, to be pronounced *Eme-laḫ*, '(the land of) the holy tongue (or language),' meaning the idiom used in the religious services of the Babylonian temples, and esteemed as sacred from pre-historic times. The connexion of Šumer with the OT Shinar (*Shin'ar*) is still uncertain. Suggestions will be found in *HDB* iv. 503 f., that which makes it a changed form of *Shingi-Ura*, for *Kingi-Ura*, being the best.

3. The earthly paradise.—The tract wherein lay Êridu, 'the good city,' and the land of Tilmun,[5] which traditionally enjoyed, in the beginning, the happiness and the innocence of the golden age, seemingly always appealed to the imagination of the Babylonians as being at that time the most desirable abode on earth. It was this, apparently, which led to the designation of Adam's first dwelling-place as 'a garden eastward, in Eden' (Gn 2[8])—*i.e.* in the *êdinnu* (Sumerian *edina*)—which, however, seems not to occur as a place-

[1] *Baba Qamma*, 91*b*.

[2] *Materials for a Sumerian Lexicon*, Leipzig, 1905–08, pt. ii. p. 206.

[3] There is apparently another (variant) form for *Kingi*, viz. *Kibēgi*, but this may be due to a pun (see *PSBA* xxxv. [1913] 155).

[4] If, however, *Bur* stands for a reservoir or waterway, *bur* / *bur* would indicate the watershed of the Tigris and the Euphrates—see § 6 (*b*).

[5] See below, § 6 (*c*).

name except in the compound Sippar-edina ('Sippar of the *eden*') and in the river-name *id edina*, 'the river of Eden (or of the plain).' Nevertheless, the idea always existed, and probably increased among the Babylonians, that their land was the site of the paradise of old time. This theory, moreover, is in a measure supported by the fact that Ê, which often stands for Babylon or Babylonia, may be an abbreviation of *Êridu*, and *Tin-dir*, 'the abode' or 'the grove of life,' probably refers to the wonderful vine therein. Many things, in fact, support the theory advocated by Friedrich Delitzsch,[1] and treated of by scholars and theologians before and since.[2]

4. Ethnic position.—As remarked above, it is probable that the Akkadians (the Semitic section of the inhabitants) came from some mountainous district, and it may have been originally an early stream from the west (the Amorite or Palestinian highlands) which preceded that of Ḫammurabi, who, having installed himself at Babylon, made that city the capital of the land. But both races were apparently, in their origin, mountaineers, as is suggested by the fact that the Sumerian word *kura* is the common word for both 'mountain' and 'country.' If de Lacouperie's contention[3] (afterwards followed up by C. J. Ball[4]) is correct, that Sumerian, both tongue and writing, is an early form of Chinese, then their Mongolian origin would seem to be proved. The likeness of certain Sumerian words to Turkish suggests that they may have been a pre-historic race from the Far East, of Turko-Mongolian origin. Traces of oblique eyes are to be found in the small head from Tel-loh (Lagaš in S. Babylonia), given in de Sarzec;[5] and another example is the bearded male head in relief.[6] Good grounds for the theory exist.

5. Evidence of the Syllabary as to the probable original home of the Sumerians.—It was long ago noted that the absence of a special ideograph for 'river' implies that such a thing, in the ordinary acceptation of the word, did not exist in the country of their origin. This, in fact, seems to be true, as the compound ideographic group for 'river' shows the sign for 'water' (*a*) followed by a square representing a lake or reservoir with the character for 'to run,' 'to flow,' within. The Sumerians may, therefore, have come from a mountainous region where lakes and ponds were common, and rivers were mountain-streams or torrents. The word *kur*, which stands for both 'country' and 'mountain,' and seems to be a picture of three mountains, supports this. On the other hand, the existence of a character for 'date-palm,' *gišim-mar*, 'the fruit-tree' in a special sense, somewhat negatives this evidence.

In the list of characters known as 'Syllabary *b*' we gather from the first entry that the Sumerians thought of the heavens (*ana*) as the abode of the deity (*dingir*). They believed also in spirits (*gidim*, *utuk*, etc.), and made offerings (*sigisse*) to the gods. To all appearance they lived in houses (*ê*), not tents, and those houses had doors (*giš-gal*) furnished with bolts and bars. The houses were situated in streets (*sila*), which formed cities (*uru*, dialectic *eri*). Their fields were more or less rectangular, and were protected, at least in Babylonia, by boundary-stones. It was apparently not until they had settled in their new home that their fields were called 'water-centres' (*a-šag*). They had dogs, and the dogs were faithful but quarrelsome. They also possessed goats, sheep, oxen, and swine. They did not at first know the horse, the ass (*anšu*) being the common beast of burden. Naturally they knew of wool (*sig*), and it would seem

[1] *Wo lag das Paradies?*, Leipzig, 1881.

[2] See also *PSBA* xxxiii. [1911] 161, xxxv. [1913] 154 f.; *ExpT* xxix. [1918] 181 ff., 288; and cf. art. BLEST, ABODE OF THE (Semitic), vol. ii. p. 704[b].

[3] See 'Babylonia and China,' in *Babylonian and Oriental Record*, i. [1886–87] 113, 'The Old Babylonian Characters and their Chinese Derivates,' *ib.* ii. [1887–88] 73; cf. also pp. 149 ff., 184 ff., 221 ff., 251 ff.

[4] See 'The New Accadian,' in *PSBA* xii. [1890] five papers, 'Ideograms common to Accadian and Chinese,' *ib.* xiii. [1891] three papers.

[5] *Découvertes en Chaldée*, Paris, 1884–1912, pl. 25, no. 1.

[6] *Ib.* pl. 21, no. 6.

that linen (*kat*, Semiticized as *kitû*) was one of the fabrics which they produced. They had pots (*duk, lut*) and dishes (*banšur*), and used ovens (*udun*). Apparently the only simple ideograph for a metal was *urudu*, 'copper,' silver and gold being described as the 'day-bright' and the 'reed-bright' metals respectively. It is supposed that the only iron at first known—*an-bar*, 'the heaven-metal'—was meteoric. Tin was called *nigga* or *nagga*, and was probably originally pronounced *anagga* (Semiticized as *anaku*). They knew of fire, and used braziers, and a modification of the character for 'fire,' expressing the word 'new' (*ge*), suggests the purification of the metals and the completion of pottery and the like by its means.

6. Languages and literature. — (*a*) There has been much difference of opinion as to the existence of the non-Semitic Sumerian language as distinguished from the Semitic Akkadian. Halévy and his followers have even contended that it was merely an 'allography'—an invention of the Semites for expressing their own language in another way. Such an expression as 'to pour out speech' (*gu-de*), however, for 'to call,' 'announce,' is probably too foreign to the Semitic mind to admit of such an idiom replacing the common Semitic *nabû*—so, also, 'to set the breast' (*gab-ri*) for 'to resist.' Sumerian, moreover, has an involved and more widely-differing grammatical construction. The complicated system of verbal incorporations, the absence of case-endings, the use of 'postpositions' instead of prepositions, and other peculiarities, stamp Sumerian as being a language which Semites would be most unlikely to invent. Concerning its connexion with old Chinese,[1] there seem to be many analogies with regard to both characters and words, but the theory has not been very generally accepted. Many admit, on the other hand, that Turkish contains a certain number of similar roots, such as *mal* (*wal*) and *ol* in *olmak*, 'to be'; *ara* and *yuru* in *yurumek*, 'to go'; *du* and *de* in *demek*, 'to speak,' etc. Turkish, however, with its longer history, has naturally developed many new forms, and the numerals differ, but perhaps it is recognizable as a very late relative of Sumerian in its pronouns.

(*b*) Akkadian is now accepted as the correct designation of the speech of the Semites of Babylonia, derived from what was apparently the most ancient Semitic settlement in the tract, viz. the kingdom of Agadé. Akkad, as already remarked, was called by the Sumerians *Ura*,[2] and the ideograph $\overset{bur}{bur}$, by which it is expressed, is suggested by J. D. Prince[3] as referring to the two rivers which were regarded as 'the life of the land,' viz. the Tigris and the Euphrates. There is some uncertainty as to the division in which the Akkado-Assyrian language should be placed, but it may, perhaps, be regarded as the bridge connecting the Aramaic and the Canaanitish forms of Semitic speech. Its verbal conjugations belong to the former, whilst the consonantal system of its roots resembles that of the Semitic languages to which Hebrew belongs. In the use of the words, however, Akkado-Assyrian struck out a line of its own.

Thus 'hand' is not *idu* (Heb., Arab., etc. *yad*), but *qâtu*; 'man' is not *ish*, as in Hebrew, but *âwēlu*; 'servant' is not *'ebed* or *'abd*, but *wardu*, the comparatively rare *abdu* having been borrowed at an early date from W. Semitic speech. On the other hand, the roots of the words for 'God' (*ilu*) and 'lord' (*bêlu*) are the same as in the other Semitic tongues. The Heb. *melek*, 'king,' and *sar*, 'prince,' are represented in Semitic-Akkadian by *šarru*, 'king,' and *malku*, 'petty king' respectively. 'House' (*bîtu*) and 'street' (*sûqu*) are from the same roots as in the other Semitic languages, but in Akkadian a temple was simply a 'house' (*bîtu*), whilst the other Semitic languages used the word *hêkal*, from Sum.-Akk. *(h)êkallu*, 'palace'—*(h)egala*, 'great house,' in Sumerian. Similarly the Sumero-Akkadian word for 'city' was *âlu*, but the Hebrews used the Sumerian dialectic *'ir*, which appears as *yeru* (for *êru* or *ûru*) in the name of Jerusalem.

(*c*) Most of the Sumero-Akkadian legends and mythical stories have been dealt with in the artt. BABYLONIANS AND ASSYRIANS and HEROES AND HERO-GODS (Babylonian). It is naturally difficult to distinguish the nationality of each legend, but most or all of them have a more or less Sumerian foundation. Among the distinctively Sumerian legends of Babylonia may be classed that of Alorus and his five successors, as well as those of Alaparus or Adapa, Tammuz, and Euedoreschus.[1] From their names it seems that the ancestors of the hero of the Flood were Sumerian, and the origin of the legend of the Flood itself is now proved to be so, notwithstanding that his names, Atra-ḫasis and Ut-napištim, are Semitic. This is shown by the very noteworthy earlier version in the Pennsylvania University Museum,[2] which is written in the Sumerian language, without any Akkadian rendering.

In this text the mother-goddess (Nin-tu, Aruru, and Zēr-panîtum are some of her names) speaks of certain people whom she had created. At that time—long, probably, before the Flood —five great cities existed, viz. Êridu, the paradise-city, protected by the god Êa; Dûr-Kiš, 'the fortress of Kiš,' which preceded Babylon as foremost city of the land; Larancha, allotted to the god Papil-ḫursag, who apparently became its patron; Zimbir (Sippar), which was given to the sun-god, and became the great centre of his worship; and Suruppak, now Farą, the Babylonian Noah's birthplace, allotted to the god Suruppak or Sukurru. It will be noted that in this list of primitive Babylonian (Sumero-Akkadian) cities there is no mention of 'Babel, and Erech, and Accad, and Calneh' (Gn 10^{10}). As in the case of the bilingual Creation-story,[3] in which Merodach and Aruru not only create, but also construct the cities wherein men are to dwell, it may be supposed that these deities were not only the guardians, but also the builders of the foundations of which they were now appointed patrons. A fracture of the tablet here makes an unfortunate gap, and, when the inscription is again readable, we have, instead of the Creation, an old version of the Flood-story. The mother-goddess, here called Nin-tu ('lady of reproduction'), like Maḫ in the 11th tablet of the Gilgameš-legend,[4] bewails the destruction of the people whom she had created, and the gods invoke the compound deity Ana-Enlila ('heaven and welkin') possibly to prevent the Flood from taking place. At this point Zi-û-suddu ('the being [or soul] of remote days'),[5] an anointing-priest of the god Êa, went through certain rites and ceremonies, apparently with the object of saving mankind from the threatened destruction, but without effect.

'All the powerful wind-storms as one rushed forth—a water-flood raged over the [hostile]. After the water-flood had raged over the land for seven days and seven nights—after the mighty boat had been carried away by wind-storms over the swollen waters, Utu [the sun-god] came forth again, on heaven and earth shedding day. Zi-û-suddu opened a window of the mighty boat—the hero Utu maketh his light to shine within the mighty boat. Zi-û-suddu, the king, prostrateth himself in the presence of Utu—the king sacrificeth an ox, slaughtereth a sheep.'[6]

In the final column Zi-û-suddu and his companions conjure Ana-Enlila, 'by the soul of heaven and the soul of earth,' to be well disposed towards them. This favour was duly accorded, and the twofold divinity, as in the Gilgameš Flood-story, conferred immortality upon him. Afterwards, to make good the ravages of the tempest, which had slain so many of the human race, 'the seed of mankind' was taken up, and made to live again in the land of Tilmun,[7] the district at the head of the Persian Gulf, which at that time extended much farther inland than now.

An analogous legend is that of Uttu (?)—probably one of the strangest records of the Creation and the Flood in existence. It was found at Nippur (Niffer) and was first translated by Stephen Langdon.[8]

1 See above, § 4.
2 See above, § 2.
3 Pt. iii. p. 352.

1 *ERE* vi. 642 f.
2 See Arno Poebel's ***Historical and Grammatical Texts*** in *Publications of the Babylonian Section of the University Museum*, vol. iv. no. 1 (Philadelphia, 1914), p. 7 ff.; T. G. Pinches, in the *Journal of the Transactions of the Victoria Institute*, London, 1915, pp. 307-312.
3 *ERE* ii. 314a.
4 *Ib.* iv. 551a, var. for line 10: '(The goddess) Maḫ called out, making her voice resound.'
5 The Sisythes (for Sisydes) of Lucian's *de Dea Syria*, 12 (see J. Garstang, *The Syrian Goddess*, London, 1913, p. 50).
6 The sacrifice seems to take place whilst the patriarch was still in the ark, and not after its inmates had come forth. But perhaps two acts of sacrifice were recorded.
7 See *ExpT* xxix. [1918] 181.
8 *The Sumerian Epic of Paradise, the Flood, and the Fall of Man*, Philadelphia [1915]; see notice by A. H. Sayce, *ExpT* xxvii. [1916] 88 ff.; also S. Langdon, *ib.* p. 165 ff., and Pinches in the *Journal of the Transactions of the Victoria Institute*,

It begins with a description of Tilmun, the glorious and pure (or holy). There Enki (Ea) and his spouse (Damkina) had their home, and on that account the original condition of Tilmun was that of the world during the traditional golden age of the Greeks. The people who lived in this happy land were not afflicted by sickness and old age, nor, apparently, did crime exist. This happy state of things, however, was seemingly not to last, for Enki, the water-god, announced his intention to destroy the field (probably meaning the whole district) by means of a flood. This was to last for nine periods of a month each, during which mankind would disappear like butter when it melts. There was one man, however, who was faithful to the deity, and for him, according to Langdon's translation, 'Enki the king' waited on a boat. The context seems to show that the great and pious personage whom the god thus favoured was Uttu, saved by the deity owing to his faithfulness. After the gap which occurs here Uttu seems to be engaged in gardening-work, he having become, like Noah, an agriculturist.

After another gap certain plants, possibly cultivated by Uttu, are spoken of, and it is stated which of them he (probably Uttu) might or might not eat. One of the forbidden plants Langdon regards as the cassia, but this is doubtful. The parallel between this story and the Creation-story in Genesis, where Adam is forbidden to eat of the tree of life and the tree of knowledge, is noteworthy, though what is attributed to the first man in the one is attributed to a prototype of Noah in the other. But Uttu's plants were not trees, and they apparently did not confer either life or wisdom.

Among other Sumerian legends may be noted the story of Enlil and Ninlil, the older Bel and Beltis,[1] the legends of Merodach,[2] the legend of Tammuz, and probably that of Ištar's descent into Hades to seek him.[3] The myth of Ura or Nergal, the god of plague and death, Nergal and Ereš-ki-gal,[4] Enlil, Tišpak, and the Labbu-serpent,[5] together with others[6] of which the names only are known, may be added.

But besides the legends there are many historical documents, of which the most noteworthy are the inscriptions of Ê-anna-tum (*Stèle des Vautours*), En-anna-tum II. (cone), Uru-ka-gina (cones), Gudea (statues and cylinders), with numerous others.[7] As the dynasty of Ur seems to have been Sumerian, it is probable that detailed histories of the kings existed, and a fragment of one dealing with Sur-Engur and his son Dungi is known. This is the period (2300 B.C.) when the transformation of the Sumerian states into a Sumero-Akkadian collection of nations may be said to have taken place.

There are also numerous temple-records and accounts, inventories, lists, a few letters and contracts, and chronological lists and mathematical tablets. The Sumerian lists of words are unaccompanied by Semitic-Akkadian renderings. These, as well as the lists of names (places and men), are generally classified.

(*d*) From a religious point of view, the Akkadian legends are most valuable and interesting. It seems not improbable that the accounts of the Creation and the Flood first published by George Smith were Semitic compositions, though based upon Sumerian originals. This is implied by the fact that most of the names, especially those of deities (Anu, the heaven-god, Enlil, the older Bêl, Ea and Damkina, the god and goddess of the waters, Merodach, the king of the gods, Anšar and Kišar, the host of heaven and the host of earth, etc.),[8] are Sumerian, though Tiamat (Tiawath), the dragon of chaos, Kingu, her spouse, and Mummu, their son, seem to be Semitic-Akkadian. How Sumerian dominated in the religion of the Sumero-Akkadians may be realized when it is remembered that Sumerian names in their pantheon exceeded enormously those of Semitic origin —Šamaš, the sun, Bêl and Bêltu (Beltis), which generally stand for Merodach and his spouse, Nabû, the teacher, and his spouse, Tašmêtu[m], 'she who hears,' Addu (Assyr. Adad) or Rammānu (Hadad or Rimmon), and certain other descriptive divine names which possibly came into existence only after the Sumerian cult had conquered. Everything tends to show that the Sumerian element of the population preponderated in religious matters, as in the literature and the art of the Sumero-Akkadians.

1915, p. 312 f. Instead of Uttu (?), the name was at first read as Tagtug (?), which is a transcription of the two characters by which it is expressed.

1 *ERE* vi. 644[b]; also *JRAS*, 1919, pp. 185 ff., 575 ff. (numerous additions by Langdon).

2 *Ib.* p. 644 f.

3 *Ib.* p. 645[a].

4 *Ib.*

5 *Ib.* p. 645[b].

6 *Ib.* p. 644[b].

7 See F. Thureau-Dangin, *Inscriptions de Sumer et d'Akkad*, Paris, 1905.

8 See art. SABAOTH.

7. Social life.—Sumerian influence in the land of the Sumero-Akkadians was, in fact, evident in every phase of their life.

The system of government was by a 'great man' (*lugal*) or 'king' (Sem. *šarru*), who had under him various officers, and was represented in the more important civic centres by a 'head-man' (*ig-sag*, Sem. *iššaku*, 'he who is head')—viceroy or mayor. To lighten the work of the supreme ruler, the tablets indicate that he had numerous 'servants,' or royal or vice-regal secretaries, whose cylinder-seals appear (generally beautifully-engraved specimens of intaglio art) on the documents written or drawn up on the king's or the *iššaku's* behalf. During the time of the dynasty of Babylon the *iššaku* had sunk to the position of administrative officer—probably something like a mayor.

Other officials were the superintendent (*nubanda*), often, apparently, the king's treasurer and palace-steward, and the business-agent (*damgar*), who acted sometimes as superintendent of the women's house or harim. Naturally, there were business-agents of various kinds, and belonging to the same class were apparently the messengers and ministers, political and other. These two classes of officials had to do with the transport of 'drink, food, and oil,' and apparently acted as political ministers. The number of documents referring to the transmission of goods, etc., suggests the existence of something analogous to posts as early as 2300 years B.C. Passing over the *nimgir*, 'director' or 'governor,' of whom there were several grades, and the *qa-šu-du*, 'grain-measurer' (Lau) or 'cup-bearer' (Zimmern), we have the *sag-nanga*, 'district-chief,' the *nimgir-abzu*, director of reservoirs, springs, or watercourses, the *muwe*, distributors of rations, etc. Among the humbler civil servants were the carriers, labourers, gardeners, scribes, barbers—tonsure-cutters of the religious orders and apparently also hair-dressers (Sum. *šui*, Akkadian *gallubu*)—a few of them being women. Connected with the royal and temple domains were also smiths, shoemakers, carpenters, tailors or cloth-workers, goat-herdsmen, shepherds, ass-herdsmen, boatmen, gate-keepers, and various others.

Though it may be held that these details are of but little importance, they all tend to show how highly organized were the Sumero-Akkadians at an exceedingly early date, and the social and industrial system which they had initiated naturally formed the foundation of those of the Babylonians and the Assyrians later on. One list of late date (perhaps a copy of an earlier one) from Nineveh contained, when complete, about 190 official titles or designations, some of them ethnic, like 'the Itu'ite,' 'the Assyrian secretary,' 'the Aramæan secretary,' etc. Priests and temple officials, judges and law-court officers, were also to be found with the Sumero-Akkadians, as with the Babylonians and Assyrians at all times.

8. Ethical character.—The numerous names of men compounded with those of deities show, independently of the temple worship and ceremonies, how religious the Sumero-Akkadians were. Each city had its favourite deity, and every man worshipped the form or aspect, shown by the appellation chosen, of the deity whom he regarded as his or his family's special protector. In addition to their religious tendencies, however, they were exceedingly superstitious, and fond of incantations and charms, of the efficacy of which they were never in doubt.[1] Every disease or sickness was capable of being cured by these means, and in all probability other advantages which men are accustomed to seek could be attained by the same means. Among these may be classed the destruction of one's enemy by melting away his waxen effigy, the cutting off of his life by the cutting of a string or thread symbolizing it, and the like. When seeking a sign, they generally appealed to the deities Šamaš and Hadad, whose rays and wind, penetrating everywhere, revealed to them

1 See art. CHARMS AND AMULETS (Assyro-Babylonian).

everything that passed on the earth. They were therefore the gods of judgment and justice, and appeal was made to them that the sign or pronouncement asked for might be true.

In the matter of morals the Sumero-Akkadians were probably not better than their neighbours, but there is one point which is worthy of note, viz. that in their literature, so far as we are acquainted with it (with the exception of the legend of Gilgameš and one or two others), immoral or obscene passages are exceedingly rare. Moreover, it is in the same legend of Gilgameš that the greatest hostility to the goddess Ištar or Venus is shown—hostility which brought upon that hero all the misfortunes which afterwards befell him. Slavery seems to have been in full force among the Sumero-Akkadians, but there is no proof that slaves were ever ill-treated. Ruthlessness in war was also not one of their failings, as far as their records are preserved, and they were probably the superiors of the Assyrians at all times in that respect. As a nation, whether the states be taken individually or as a whole, there is no doubt that they had a high opinion of learning and the advantages to be gained therefrom. To all appearance it was a meritorious thing to know the mythology which, to them, occupied the place of Holy Scriptures, and to be acquainted with the history of their land, which enabled them to judge of the dealings of their gods with their rulers during their long existence as a nation. In like manner, a knowledge of the methods of legal procedure enabled their scribes to employ themselves usefully by drawing up contracts; and those who made a specialty of such things could read the signs in the heavens and make known all kinds of omens, thus earning the gratitude of their fellow-citizens and their own living by the fees of those whom they served. Whatever their defects, their records exhibit them as worthy people, equal in social progress to all their contemporaries at the early age at which they flourished.

9. Early Sumerian dominion.—Whether the Sumerians or the Akkadians entered Babylonia first is another uncertain point, but it is to be noted that the earliest documents are in the Sumerian language, and the earliest records refer to Sumerian kings. Legends, ritual-texts, hymns, contracts, etc., and word-lists are all Sumerian at the earlier periods, and, when these documents came to be translated, the Sumerian text always preceded the Akkadian or Semitic. Their entry into the country must have taken place about 5000 B.C. or earlier, but the Semitic-Akkadians probably became prominent only about 2500 B.C. The Semites, however, were certainly numerous in the country at an earlier date, and were steadily growing in power. Sargon of Agadé or Akkad seems to have reigned about 2800 B.C. (Nabonidus's date for this ruler is equivalent to 3800 B.C.), and he was certainly not the first ruler of Semitic race. The presence of such Semitic-looking names as Qalumu^{m} and Zuqakip, 'the scorpion,' who reigned before the mythical Etanna,[1] notwithstanding that we have to make allowance for the inordinate lengths of their reigns, probably takes back Semitic (Akkadian) dominion in Babylonia to a date which can hardly be later than 4000 B.C. In that case we may carry back Sumerian dominion to 4500 or 5000 B.C., and even 8000 B.C. has been spoken of.

10. Babylonia under Sumero-Akkadian rule.—(*a*) *The large states.*—The number of states into which Babylonia was divided until the time of Ḫammurabi's dynasty (*c.* 2000 B.C.) is uncertain, but it can hardly have been less than 40 or 50. This, naturally, only shows that each state had its own ruler, and claimed independence from all its neighbours. As may be imagined, the total of these states varied at different times, owing to conquest of the strong by the weak and to the gradual absorption of their smaller neighbours by the larger or more predominant centres of civilization. The name of each little state was generally that of its capital, and it is thus that we have the kingdoms of Agadé or Akkad, Kiš, Unug or Erech, Uriwa or Ur, Isin, Muru, Larsa, Lagaš, Ka-dingira or Babylon, Nipri or Nippur, and many others. Apparently after the Kassite conquest of about 1700 B.C. Babylonia was called Kar-Duniaš, 'the district of the lord of the world,' but the older name of Akkad, derived from the state of which Sargon the Babylonian was the ruler about 2800 B.C., clung to it even in the time of Aššur-bani-âpli, 'the great and noble Asnappar,' about 650 B.C. The name of Chaldæa seems to have been applied to it, and that by non-Babylonians, only after the time of the Chaldæan dynasty to which Merodach-baladan belonged. As has been remarked above (§ 4), the usual word for 'country' was *kur*, but another largely used is worthy of notice, viz. *kalama*, written with the character *un*, which generally stands for 'people.' This identification of the land with its people implies a strong sense of nationality in the minds of the non-Semitic Sumerians, but was less pronounced in the minds of the Semitic-Babylonians after the time of Nebuchadrezzar.

(*b*) *The smaller foundations.* — Though the capitals and larger cities (as understood in those days) were numerous, there were many smaller centres and settlements, sometimes founded by prominent agriculturists or traders, but in many cases they were religious foundations. Among the former may be mentioned the city of Idi-Uraš (*âl Idi-^{d} Uraš*) and the 'upper city of Elnanu' (*âl Elnana êlû*) of tablet 23 of the Relph collection,[1] where also we find Larsa and Pulukku (*Larsa ^{ki}, Dûr âl Pulukku ^{ki}*, 'the fortification of the city Pulukku') mentioned. No. 26 of the same collection refers to the cities of men named Amat-îli, Sin-nûr-mâti^{m}, etc., the 'Taribu^{m}-district' (*kar taribu^{m}*), the '(god) Enki-district' (*kar ^{d} Enki*), the 'new Broad-street district' (*kar sila dagala-ge*), etc. These 'districts' were apparently instituted for the reception of the temple revenues, paid in kind.

11. The Sumero-Akkadians' view regarding their native land.—The idea gained by the study of the inscriptions is that the people of Babylonia (and probably of Assyria also) looked upon their dwelling-place as a holy land. Every state, every foundation, had its deity, and visits to the holy places were meritorious acts.[2] First and foremost, apparently, we have the paradise-city Êridu, the abode of the god Êa—the city whose ideograph was sometimes used, in later times, to express the land of Babylonia in general.[3] Next came the great capital, Bâb-îli (Sum. *Ka-dingira*), 'the gate of God'—probably a folk-etymology brought about by the name *Babila^{m}*, which was possibly (with *Babala^{m}*) the true form. Near Babylon was Gudua (Cutha), the city of the god Nergal, and Dailem, the ancient Delmu, where Uraš (one of the names of En-urta) had his seat. Other foundations were Muru, where the god Muru (Hadad or Rimmon) was worshipped, Qatan, the seat of the god Qatnu, and Lasima, that of the god Lasimu, the swift runner. These similar names of the cities and their patron-gods remind us of Aššur, the old capital of Assyria, the centre of the worship of the national god Asshur, and Nineveh,

[1] See *ExpT* xxvii. 518^{a}. For the legend of Etana see *ERE*, vol. ii. p. 315^{a}, vol. vi. p. 644^{a}.

[1] *PSBA* xxix. [1917] 90 f.

[2] See *ERE*, vol. x. p. 12.

[3] See § 3.

imitated from the Babylonian Nina, the former the city of the goddess Ištar as the goddess of war, and the latter that of Nina, her Babylonian prototype. Greatly favouring the gods, Babylonia was held to be greatly favoured by them—hence, perhaps, the reputation of the land as the district of the whilom Paradise (see § 3).

LITERATURE.—L. W. King, *A Hist. of Sumer and Akkad*, London, 1910, and the works mentioned at the end of the art. BABYLONIANS AND ASSYRIANS. See also artt. CRIMES AND PUNISHMENTS (Assyro-Babylonian), FAMILY (Assyro-Babylonian), CONSCIENCE (Babylonian), DEATH AND DISPOSAL OF THE DEAD (Babylonian).

T. G. PINCHES.

SUMMUM BONUM.—Modern ethical philosophy has at various times sought its constitutive principle in the will of God, the law of duty, the problem of the origin of the moral sense, the ideas or ideals of perfection, personality, progress, and evolution. For ancient ethics the ultimate reference was to the idea of good.

1. Definitions and early ideas of the good.—In its broadest acceptation 'good' is simply the term of general approval which no developed language lacks. Etymology cannot help us to a closer definition, for the etymology of ἀγαθός is not known and cannot be identical with that of *bonus* or of 'good.' The conjectural psychology of primitive man is of no avail, for it is uncertain, and in any case Homer was already far beyond that stage. It is obvious that primitive man did not draw our sharp distinction between moral good and other good or desirable things. There is abundant evidence in and out of Greek literature for the unmoral specification of good to courage in war, high birth, wealth, and other objects of approval or desire.[1] A unifying definition of good will always remain either a more or less plausible generalization from extant literature or an arbitrary deduction from metaphysical first principles. The Platonic *Euthyphro* and *Lysis* may serve as anticipatory illustrations of all such attempts, though the one nominally discusses holiness and the other the primal object of love or friendship (the φίλον). The *Euthyphro* leads to the *impasse* of the problem debated by scholasticism: Does God love holiness (or the good) because it is holy, or is it holy because God loves it?[2] The *Lysis* refers all particular loves to the primary love or end which seems to be the good.[3] But what intelligible motive is there for loving the good save as a remedy against evil?[4] Near the end of the dialogue the difficulty is evaded by renaming the good, in anticipation of Stoic terminology, the οἰκεῖον, the 'own,' the 'proper' (or, as Emerson sometimes renders it, the 'friendly'), and by calling evil the 'alien.'[5] The association in the *Lysis* of the good with the end or purpose dominates all later discussions and is the basis of most modern definitions from Schopenhauer to Herbert Spencer and William James. It is of course not explicit in pre-philosophic literature.

2. Homer.—In Homer we find the ethical meaning of good already existing side by side with its unmoral or half-moral use in the sense of brave or well-born. This has been and will be denied. But it is the only reasonable interpretation of such passages as Achilles' saying: 'Every good and sensible man loves and cherishes his own bride.'[6] The fact that Homer also speaks of a good meal, and of the menial services which the worse sort

1 See art. THEOGNIS.

2 10 A.

3 220 B.

4 *Lysis*, 220 E ff.; cf. T. Gomperz's observation (*Greek Thinkers*, Eng. tr., London and New York, 1901–12, ii. 149) that 'in nearly all philosophies (of any vogue the technical terms denoting "the supreme good" were words of negative import.'

5 221 E; cf. also *Symp.* 205 E.

6 *Il.* ix. 341; cf. L. Schmidt, *Die Ethik der alten Griechen*, Berlin, 1882, i. 289.

render to the good,[1] need not signify more than does our own language about a good dinner or the best citizens. The abstract use of the neuter ἀγαθόν, 'a good thing,' is also found in Homer and in Hesiod's *Theogony*.[2]

3. The pre-Socratics.—The philosophic discussion of the good begins with Socrates. But a few passages of the pre-Socratics might be regarded as anticipations. Several fragments of Heraclitus suggest the idea of the relativity of the good eloquently developed by the Platonic *Protagoras*.[3] And Aristotle says that Empedocles' use of the opposites love and hate is equivalent to the doctrine that good and evil are the causes of things.[4] Later philosophy found the beginnings of a classification or scale of goods in the famous scolium:

'Health is the best when all is done,
The gift of beauty is next in worth,
The third is riches fairly won,
To be young with comrades is the fourth.'

It is with latent reference to that that Plato affirms with emphasis that not even health takes precedence of the virtue or good of the soul.[5] It may be the highest of popular or so-called goods. It is not the good.

4. Socrates and Xenophon.—The Xenophontic Socrates identifies the good with the useful: 'If you ask me for a good that is good for nothing, I do not know it, nor have I any use for it.'[6] There is no proof that this is a genuine report of distinctive Socratic teaching and no presumption that Xenophon had any ideas on the subject which he did not pick up from Plato.

5. Plato.—Plato's doctrine of the good has been obscured by the unnecessary mystery that has been made of its allegorical elaboration in the imagery of the sun, the divided line, and the cave in the *Republic*.[7] The essential meaning of this allegory is demonstrably quite simple. It is merely the postulate that ethical, political, or social science presupposes the conscious apprehension of some co-ordinating purpose and final test of all endeavour.[8] In the lack of such a vision of the idea of good, the so-called statesman is only an empiric and a rhetorician. The statesmen of Plato's reformed republic must possess this vision and this insight.[9] They can attain it only through the scientific and philosophic education which he prescribes[10] and the practical experience of affairs with which it must be supplemented.[11] Further than this Plato does not wish to define the idea of good[12] except through the implications of the entire moral and social ideal embodied in the *Republic* and the *Laws*.[13]

Plato's is the earliest and most effective presentation of these ideas. But so obvious a thought has of course occurred to many other moralists. Locke[14] uses it to prove that moral rules are not innate or self-evident, since their 'truth . . . plainly depends upon some other antecedent . . . from which they must be deduced.' Höffding[15] expresses it thus: 'Every ethical reasoning has validity only so far as the disputants recognize a definite primordial value which determines all more

1 *Od.* xv. 324.

2 For the further pre-philosophic history of the word and its synonyms see Schmidt, *Ethik der alten Griechen*, i. 290 ff., and art. THEOGNIS. In this matter, as in all study of Greek philosophy, entire precision is attainable only by thinking in the Greek terms, if need be, transliterated.

3 *Protag.* 334 A; cf. Heraclitus, frag. 52, 57, 61, in *Heracliti reliquiæ*, ed. Ingram Bywater, Oxford, 1877.

4 *Met.* 985 a 8.

5 *Rep.* 591 C, *Laws*, 661 B, 728 D.

6 *Mem.* III. viii. 3.

7 508 A ff., 509 D ff., 514 ff.

8 See *Rep.* 519 C; and P. Shorey, in *Classical Philology*, Oct. 1914, pp. 351, 366; *Meno*, 91 A, *Euthydem.* 291 B, 291 D E, *Protag.* 318 E with *Rep.* 428 B, *Protag.* 329 D ff., *Gorg.* 455 B with 504 D, 507 D, 503 D E with *Laws*, 635 E.

9 *Rep.* 504 C, 534 D.

10 *Ib.* 533 A.

11 *Ib.* 519 B C, 539 E.

12 *Ib.* 506 D E.

13 *E.g.*, the sketch, or ὑπογραφή, of *Rep.* 504 D is the system of the definition of the virtues given in bk. iv.

14 *Essay concerning Human Understanding*, bk. i. ch. iii. § 4.

15 *Problems of Philosophy*, Eng. tr., New York, 1905, p. 165.

special goods.' In the words of G. Lowes Dickinson:[1] 'For we must live or die; and if we are to choose to do either, we must do so by virtue of some assumption about the Good.' Whether by accident or design, a witty page of G. K. Chesterton's *Heretics*[2] is an admirable statement of Plato's postulate that we must know the good before we can rightly know or do anything else. The conception pervades all Ruskin's preaching.[3]

If these and countless other modern writers still find occasion to dwell upon this elementary truth, there is no presumption that it is too simple to constitute the underlying significance of Plato's allegory. The difficulty is in the prevailing quest for subtler or more mystical interpretations to obtain a hearing for the demonstration that this in fact was Plato's essential meaning. It is then, as we shall see later, mere misapprehension when modern scholars identify the idea of good with God, confuse its plain ethical and political interpretation by the introduction of the metaphysical problems common to all Platonic ideas, or read into its ethical application in the *Republic* all the teleological developments of the *Timæus*.

Apart from this misapprehension, Plato's doctrine of the good is his entire ethical and social philosophy as collected from the minor dialogues, from the discussion of utilitarian hedonism in the *Protagoras*, *Gorgias*, and *Laws*, and from the closer psychological analysis of the same problem in the *Philebus* and the 9th book of the *Republic*, 583 B ff. Throughout the minor dialogues the undefinable good is the test that all tentative definitions of the virtues or exaggerated claims of the sophists fail to pass. The phrasing of *Republic*, 505 B f., is equivalent to a reference to these discussions. The virtue which we are trying to define, the ability of which you boast, must be a good, Socrates urges, and the interlocutor is unable to show that it is always and unconditionally good. The consistency and symmetry of this method point directly to the idea of good in the *Republic* as the symbol of such an absolute good, and to the Platonic guardians' knowledge of it as distinguishing them from the politicians, the sophists, and their pert disciples whom Socrates puts to confusion.

The other approach to the problem of the good is through the hedonistic utilitarian controversy. Is the good pleasure or is it something higher—virtue, knowledge, or communion with God?[4] The Socrates of the *Protagoras* formulates the obvious hedonistic utilitarian argument in a way that leaves nothing for Epicurus and very little for Bentham and Mill to add. The eloquent rejection of this point of view in the *Gorgias* and *Phædo* is an inconsistency only for critics who fail to observe by what nice distinctions Plato's affirmations are guarded or who refuse to interpret the apparent antinomy by the psychology of the *Philebus* and the conclusion of the whole matter in the *Laws*.[5] The measured preponderance of pleasure might arguably be the good if pleasure were really measurable and rightly measured[6] or if what the multitude call pleasures were really pleasant.[7] Plato's final feeling is aptly expressed in the words of Matthew Arnold:

> 'That joy and happiness are the magnets to which human life inevitably moves, let not the reader . . . confuse his mind by doubting. The real objection is to low and false views of what constitutes happiness. *Pleasure* and *utility* are bad words to employ because they have been so used as to suggest such views.'[8]

[1] *The Meaning of Good*, Glasgow, 1901, New York, 1907, p. 189.
[2] London, 1905, p. 33.
[3] See in particular the preface to *The Crown of Wild Olive*, and in *The Two Paths* the passage beginning: 'If you will tell me what you ultimately intend Bradford to be, perhaps I can tell you what Bradford can ultimately produce' (lect. iii. § 87).
[4] *Rep.* 505 B, *Phileb. passim*, *Theæt.* 176.
[5] 733 f.; cf. *Classical Philology*, Oct. 1914, p. 364.
[6] *Laws*, 733, 734 A B.
[7] Cf. ἄγευστος in *Rep.* 576 A, and Arist. *Eth. Nic.* 1176 b 19; *Rep.* 586 A ff., 583 B.
[8] *God and the Bible*, popular ed., New York, 1883, p. 141.

Plato did not object to the Greek equivalent of utility, but he did to ἡδονή, as Cicero did to ἡδονή, *voluptas*. In *Laws*, 733 A, Plato substitutes χαίρειν, but to make his meaning clear he, in a sentence which Epicurus might have written,[1] allows ἥδιων.[2]

To return to the idea of good, the Socratic censure of Anaxagoras in *Phædo*, 98, is sometimes misunderstood. What Plato plainly says is that a teleological explanation of the universe in terms of the good[3] would most completely satisfy his feeling. He is unable to find or to construct such an explanation[4] and so falls back upon a different thing, the safe and second best method of the ideas—a kind of working logic which renounces both the speculative physical hypotheses of the pre-Socratics[5] and the hope of a teleological interpretation.[6] In spite of this, interpreters persistently identify the doctrine of ideas with the method of teleological deduction from the good. The *Timæus* does attempt such a deduction, but avowedly in the form of poetry and as a probable tale. There is nothing to justify the transference of this line of thought to the idea of good in the *Republic*. Amid the 'demonic hyperboles' of the *Republic* passage, 509 C, there may be phrases that suggest the dependence of the physical universe on the idea of good and the subordination of all other ideas to this *summum genus*.[7] But the main emphasis and purpose of the passage is to stress the ethical and political significance of the idea of good as we have already met it in the minor dialogues. Plato does not say that all other ideas are included in the good as a logical *summum genus*, nor does he say that mathematics and the sciences are to be deduced from the idea of good. He says that, rightly studied, these disciplines will quicken the mind's eye for the apprehension of all abstract truth and so ultimately for that of the idea of good.[8] In other words, the sociologist and the statesman must be prepared for their tasks by the severest scientific and philosophical education which the age affords.

Space fails to show how every significant part of the allegory confirms our simple and rational interpretation.[9] The idea of good is the cause of both existence and knowledge because all human institutions originate in the founder's purpose or idea of good and are, as Coleridge often said, best understood in the light of their purpose—the good they were intended to accomplish. This could be extended to the physical universe by the teleology of the *Timæus* and the *Phædo*.[10] God's idea of good in the *Timæus* is the cause of the world, so far as necessity permitted; and we understand the world best when we apprehend His designs. But the *Republic* is not directly concerned with these applications, and we distort Plato's meanings when we force them into the systematic metaphysical construction from which he abstained.

The comparison of the idea of the good with the sun is of great interest for the study of the history of religion, but need not detain us here.[11] Nor can we delay for the enormous influence of this passage in the history of Neo-Platonism,

[1] 734 A; cf. H. Usener, *Epicurea*, Leipzig, 1887, pp. 64, 72; R. D. Hicks, *Stoic and Epicurean*, London and New York, 1910, p. 172.
[2] Cf. Shorey, *Unity of Plato's Thought*, p. 22, *Class. Phil.* x. 335; Jowett, introd. to his tr. of the *Philebus*; Seneca, *Epist.* lxvii. 15: 'Ego tam honestae rei ac severae numquam molle nomen imponam.'
[3] 98 B. [4] 99 C. [5] 96 A B.
[6] 100 C. [7] 509 B, 517 B, 532 A.
[8] 511 C, 534 C, 520 C, 521 D, 525 C, 527 A, 529 B.
[9] Cf. Shorey, 'Idea of Good,' p. 225 ff.
[10] 97 D E; cf. also the Platonizing passage in Aristotle, *de Cœlo*, 288 a, 1–10.
[11] Cf. Shorey, 'Idea of Good,' p. 223 f.; A. C. Pearson on Soph. frag. 752.

mysticism, and superstition. In Apuleius 'Platonis τὸ ἀγαθόν' actually occurs in a context which might cause it to be mistaken for one of a list of demons.[1]

6. The idea of good and God.—The identification of the idea of the good with God could do no harm if taken merely as religious poetry. The goodness of God is His chief attribute both as a negative criterion in the theological canons of the *Republic*[2]—so the Stoics held that God was the cause of good only, never of evil—and positively in the teleology of the *Timæus*. Plato is perhaps not unwilling to hint at the identification in such passages as *Rep.* 508 C and 517 B. God and the idea of good are both expressions of the highest ethical ideal, and the language which Plato used of both is, as Emerson and Arnold would put it, an ejaculation 'thrown out as it were at certain great objects which the human mind augurs and feels after.'[3] As Epictetus says,

> 'God is beneficent, but the good also is beneficent. It is natural therefore that the true nature of the good should be in the same region as the true nature of God.'[4]

But in fact the two terms and the two ideas came to Plato in different trains of thought and as symbols of distinct traditions, and they cannot be identified without wresting the Platonic texts from the plain purport of their contexts and attributing to him a system of metaphysics which he did not care to construct.[5] By the same methods of interpretation one could identify God and the idea of good in the philosophy of Jesus with the aid of Mt 19[17], Mk 10[18], Lk 18[19].

7. The minor Socratics.—We shall make only brief reference to the so-called minor Socratics. The fundamental theory of the Cyrenaic hedonism differed little from that of Epicurus and of the Socrates of the Platonic *Protagoras*, though special points of distinction were laboured in the schools.[6] The alleged doctrine of Aristippus, that only the pleasure of the present moment counts, perhaps because 'the next may never come,' is a temperamental attitude rather than a philosophy. This attitude was illustrated by many anecdotes, and strongly appealed to Horace.[7] Walter Pater's *Renaissance* and the chapter on the 'New Cyrenaicism' in *Marius the Epicurean* commend the Cyrenaic *summum bonum* to an æsthetic generation in the form: 'Be perfect in regard to what is here and now.' 'Burn always with this hard, gem-like flame.'

Cynicism is only a cruder, harsher anticipatory form of Stoicism. Antisthenes is said to have affirmed toil and hardship (πόνος) to be the good and to have prayed, 'Let me be mad rather than feel pleasure.'[8]

We do not know enough about the 'Megarians' to interpret Euclides' pronouncement that the one is good,[9] though Gomperz[10] undertakes to interpret it.

8. Aristotle.—The first sentence of Aristotle's *Ethics* and the first sentence of the *Politics* repeat as a truism the main thought that emerges from the Platonic quest for the good. Aristotle recognizes that the problem of ethical theory is to ascertain and define the nature of this good that all action and choice presuppose. As he proceeds, Aristotle seems to repudiate the debt to his teacher, to which every page of the *Ethics* testifies, by his insistence on metaphysical objections to the theory of ideas in general and so to the idea of good in particular.[11] The polemic has of course no relevance to the ethical problem. And, when Aristotle contemptuously asks,[1] 'How would a weaver or a carpenter be profited by knowing the absolute idea of good?', he forgets that he himself has just borrowed the Platonic imagery of the unifying σκοπός, or aim, to prove that a generalized conception of the good will be practically helpful.[2] As Sir Thomas Browne aptly puts it,

> 'Aristotle, whilst he labours to refute the ideas of Plato, falls upon one himself: for his *summum bonum* is a chimæra, and there is no such thing as his felicity.'[3]

Aristotle himself admits that the synonym happiness, εὐδαιμονία, which he substitutes for the good, is only a blank cheque.[4] Happiness is of course, as Plato said before him and Pope after, 'our being's end and aim.'[5] Cicero, while repudiating pleasure, assumed happiness to be the end as a matter of course,[6] and Leslie Stephen says:

> 'Good means everything which favors happiness . . . nor can any other intelligible meaning be assigned to the words.'[7]

It depends upon your conception of happiness or your definition of pleasure whether, with Epicurus, Bentham, and Herbert Spencer, you add pleasure as a third synonym or with Plato, Cicero, Coleridge, Hazlitt, Macaulay, Arnold, and Jowett, protest that to do so is either to confuse the right use of language or to suggest a false ideal of happiness. The definition of happiness with which Aristotle fills out the blank cheque is a somewhat lame and impotent conclusion of so elaborate a discussion. What hinders us, he asks, from pronouncing happy the man who energizes in accordance with complete virtue and is sufficiently equipped with external goods, not through any chance time, but for a complete life?[8] Later philosophers interpreted the Aristotelian definition of happiness as a trimming compromise between Epicurean hedonism and the severe idealism of Plato's *Gorgias* and the Stoics. Cicero sometimes argues that in theory there can be no adequate sanction for virtue except on the Stoic principle that nothing else is a good.[9] Sometimes he affirms that in practice the Peripatetics, who recognize external goods, give no larger place to them in their own lives than do the Stoics, who evade this concession by a change of terminology and denominate what the rest of mankind call goods not goods, but 'preferred.'[10] Otherwise Aristotle's contribution to our topic is slight. He is not deeply interested in the fundamental problem.[11] He reviews the hedonistic controversy, in substance concurring with Plato, but unable to refrain from a tone of condescending superiority to Plato's pursuit of edification.[12] The poetical allegory of the idea of the good in the *Republic* would of course be unsympathetic if not incomprehensible to him. But the statement of an eminent scholar, that he never alludes to it, overlooks the fact that Plato's distinction there between the method of pure dialectic and that of the sciences[13] is one of Aristotle's fundamental ideas recurring throughout his writings.

In the end Aristotelianism, in this matter as in others, comes back to an extreme form of the Platonism which it begins by repudiating. In Neo-Platonic interpretation and in the philosophy of the Middle Ages and the Renaissance the desire by which the Aristotelian first mover moves the heavens is the yearning of all creation towards him as the supreme good. This interpretation, supported by one metaphor and two or three ambigu-

[1] *Apol.* xxvii. [2] 379 C.
[3] *God and the Bible*, p. 22; cf. *Rep.* 505 E: ἀπομαντευομένη τι εἶναι.
[4] *Discourses*, 281.
[5] Cf. Shorey, 'Idea of Good,' p. 188 f., *Unity of Plato's Thought*, p. 17.
[6] Diog. Laert. ii. 88 f.; Cic. *de Fin.* i. 11; Gomperz, ii. 215.
[7] *Sat.* II. iii. 100 ff., ~~*Ep.* I. i. 18,~~ xvii. 14, 23.
[8] Diog. Laert. vi. 104. [9] *Ib.* ii. 106; Cic. *Acad.* i. 42.
[10] ii. 173–175. [11] *Eth. Nic.* 1096 a 11 ff.

[1] *Eth. Nic.* 1097 a 8.
[2] *Ib.* 1094 a 24; cf. Shorey, *Unity of Plato's Thought*, n. 102.
[3] *Religio Medici*, pt. ii. § 15.
[4] *Eth. Nic.* 1097 b 22. [5] Cf. *Sym.* 205 A.
[6] *De Fin.* ii. 27.
[7] *The Science of Ethics*, London, 1882, p. 42.
[8] *Eth. Nic.* 1101 a 14.
[9] *De Fin.* ii. 18 f., iii. 11, v. 26–28, *Tusc.* v. 8, 15.
[10] *De Fin.* iv. 26.
[11] See art. PHILOSOPHY (Greek).
[12] *Eth. Nic.* 1172 a 30–35. [13] *Rep.* 510.

ous verbs in the Aristotelian text, was blended with the poetical doctrine of Platonic love as the aspiration for ultimate beauty[1] identical with ultimate good. But this theme would demand a volume.

9. The post-Aristotelian schools.—The *summum bonum* was one of the two or three chief topics of debate in the post-Aristotelian schools.[2] Cicero tells an amusing story of a Roman pro-consul who proposed to convene a world's congress of philosophers and settle the question once for all.[3]

Locke[4] argues from the diversity of human tastes that 'the philosophers of old did in vain inquire whether summum bonum consisted in riches, or bodily delights, or virtue, or contemplation.' Locke's argument has been used against the utilitarian reference of all things to 'happiness' or pleasure by Coleridge, Hazlitt, Macaulay, and many others. But, as Mill[5] says, the question concerning the summum bonum is the same thing as that concerning the foundation of morality. And it is idle to expect men to cease discussing that. Horace, *e.g.*, was no metaphysician. He is interested only in

'quod magis ad nos
pertinet, et nescire malum est,'[6]

and he sums up this necessary knowledge in the three problems: (1) 'Divitiis homines, an sint virtute beati,' which was the ordinary man's conception of the difference between the Peripatetic and the Stoic good; (2) 'Quidve ad amicitias, usus rectumne, trahat nos,' the compatibility of disinterested friendship with Epicurean principles — a question much debated between the Epicureans and their opponents; [7] (3) 'Et quae sit natura boni, summumque quid ejus.'

Locke's impatience of the problem is perhaps a survival of Renaissance distaste for the scholasticism of the mediæval literature *de bonitate pura* as seen in Albert's report of the treatise of al-Farabi.

The title of Cicero's *de Finibus* exhibits the continued association of the 'good' with the 'end,'[8] and Cicero resumes for all practical purposes the net outcome and the influence on modern literature of the post-Aristotelian discussion of the *summum bonum*.[9]

10. The Epicureans.—The Epicureans revived the thesis of Plato's *Protagoras* and insisted that pleasure 'rightly understood' is the only conceivable end for a sentient creature.[10] They then, like modern utilitarians, devoted themselves to the re-valuation or the restatement in their terminology of all ethical values—what the Epicurean in Cicero[11] styles 'ad eam accommodare Torquatos nostros,' 'fit our examples of Roman virtue into the theory.' They also, like their modern analogues, complained bitterly of the critics who had misunderstood their meaning.[12] These tactics irritate Cicero, who thinks that he knows the meaning of the Greek ἡδονή, a perfect synonym of the Latin *voluptas*.[13] The Epicurean *summum bonum* may be discussed in a corner. No one would dare proclaim it to a large audience.[14] And the heroic deeds of Greek and still more of Roman worthies who gave their lives for their country[15] are sufficient proof that 'the quadruped opinion will not prevail.'[16]

11. The Stoics.—The Stoic doctrine is more sympathetic to the moralist and the orator and has the further interest of a strictly deduced and ingeniously elaborated scientific system.[17] In essence

1 Cf. Emerson, *Nature*, ch. ii.: 'God is the all-fair.'
2 Cic. *Lucullus*, 9, 42 f.
3 *De Leg.* i. 20.
4 *Human Understanding*, bk. ii. ch. xxi. § 55.
5 *Dissertations and Discussions*, New York, 1882, iii. 300.
6 *Sat.* II. vi. 71 ff.
7 Cic. *de Fin.* i. 20, ii. 26.
8 *Ib.* i. 4, 9.
9 The fragmentary Greek texts are most conveniently consulted in Usener's *Epicurea*, and von Arnim's *Stoicorum veterum fragmenta*, 3 vols., Leipzig, 1903-05. The more significant of these texts are correctly translated in R. D. Hicks, *Stoic and Epicurean*.
10 Epicurus in Hicks, p. 171.
11 *De Fin.* i. 10.
12 See, *e.g.*, Epicurus in Hicks, p. 172; Usener, pp. 64, 88; Cicero, *de Fin.* i. 11, ii. 7.
13 *De Fin.* ii. 4, 33; cf. i. 5.
14 *Ib.* ii. 22-24, iv. 9, v. 22.
15 *Ib.* i. 7, ii. 19, 35.
16 Emerson, 'Montaigne, or The Skeptic,' in *Representative Men*. Emerson, like Cicero, is thinking of the close of the *Philebus* or of *Republic*, 586 A; cf. *Acad.* i. 2; *de Fin.* i. 21, ii. 33: 'bestiis . . . quibus vos de summo bono testibus uti soletis.'
17 *De Fin.* iii. 8, 22, v. 28.

it is the old paradox of the Socrates of the *Gorgias*, that nothing is really good except the good moral will. All other so-called values are either non-existent or insignificant when weighed against this. 'Sunt enim Socratica pleraque mirabilia Stoicorum,' says Cicero in *Lucullus*, 44, and in the *Tusculans*, v. 12, he takes for the text of the entire doctrine a single sentence of Plato's *Menexenus*.[1]

In the refutation of Epicurean hedonism and the working out of the system the supreme end was variously defined and deduced, and the schools and sects of philosophy were minutely classified by the various 'ends' or principles of the supreme good which they adopted.[2] The demonstration that pleasure is not the end and the detailed deduction of Stoic ethical principles could take their start from the idea of nature and the life accordant with nature[3] or from the abbreviated formula, the consistent life.[4] The argument from nature, as set forth in Cicero,[5] presents startling analogies both with the 17th and 18th cent. philosophy of 'self-love' and with the modern logic of evolution. Pleasure is not the end, because it is not in fact the beginning, of animal or human activity.[6] The earliest and fundamental *conatus* of all sentient life is not towards pleasure as such, but towards self-preservation.[7] The pleasure is, so to speak, a by-product.[8] Upon this supervenes in the rational animal man the recognition that the true self, the higher self, is the spiritual and moral self. The conservation of this self then becomes the end. And it matters little in practice whether all other ends are annihilated or merely dwindle to insignificance in comparison with this.[9] Thus Cicero sometimes treats the entire suppression of the animal or lower self as a fallacy of Stoic paradox[10] and sometimes as a rebuke of Peripatetic compromise and as an indispensable condition of absolute and disinterested virtue.

12. The sceptics.—The various schools of sceptics impartially assailed all dogmatic systems. But they did not for that reason admit that they lacked a moral ideal or the conception of the supreme practical end. Their scepticism was a means to the end of tranquillity or imperturbability of soul and the guidance of life by reasonable probability.

13. Developments of Platonism: the ascetic ideal.—In the Græco-Roman empire the eclectic literature of moral and religious edification reproduces all these points of view and ideas, but retains little interest in the dialectic of the schools and the philosophic theory of ethics. The cumulative influence of Platonism reveals itself not only in the softening and refinement of Stoic technicality and paradox, but also in the increasing prominence of another ideal, if not idea, of good—the ideal of detachment from the world and the flesh and approximation to God through the lonely purity of a spiritual and contemplative life. Plato's *Phædo* and the eloquent digression of the *Theætetus* are the earliest explicit Greek expression of this ideal. It is a human mood or temperament of renunciation and reaction. The opposition of the theoretic and the practical life was debated in the *Antiope* of Euripides.[11] And recent conjecture attributes to Pythagoras the three types of life associated with the tripartite psychology of Plato's *Republic* and employed as an ethical commonplace in the beginning of Aristotle's *Ethics*.[12] Thenceforth philosophy was the way of life, and the *summum bonum* was the happiness embodied in or to be attained by the wise man.[13] The latent and still unresolved contradiction between the social conception of virtue and this personal ideal of salvation and happiness is apparent already in Plato and Aristotle. The artist Plato paints the two companion pictures of the Socrates of the

1 239 E.
2 Cic. *de Fin.* ii. 11; cf. *Lucullus*, 42, *de Fin.* v. 7, *Tusc.* v. 30.
3 *De Fin.* iii. 9, iv. 11.
4 Von Arnim, i. 45; Diog. Laert. vii. 89.
5 *De Fin.* v. 11, 13.
6 *Ib.* i. 16, ii. 11, iii. 5.
7 *Ib.* iii. 5, iv. 7, v. 9.
8 Diog. Laert. vii. 94: ἐπιγεννήματα; cf. Arist. *Eth. Nic.* 1174 b 32: ὡς ἐπιγιγνόμενόν τι τέλος.
9 *De Fin.* iv. 12, v. 24, 30, *Tusc.* v. 17.
10 *De Fin.* iv. 11, 14 f.
11 Reconstructed from the quotations in Plato's *Gorgias*, 485 E ff.
12 1095 B 15.
13 Cf. in von Arnim, iii. 146-71, the collections 'de sapiente et insipiente.'

Symposium and the Socrates of the *Phædo* and leaves their reconciliation to the ingenuity of modern interpretation. Will the sage take part in politics? To this question of the later schools the idealist Plato answers: 'Only in the politics of his own city, the city of God.'[1] But Plato's practical decision appears in the prescription of the *Republic* that the philosopher must descend into the cave to help his fellowman,[2] in his journeys to the court of Syracuse, and in his devotion of the last years of his life to the laborious composition of the *Laws*.

In Aristotle the contradiction is disguised, but pervades the entire *Ethics*. Happiness is activity in accordance with virtue,[3] but it finally appears that there are intellectual as well as moral virtues,[4] and the highest activity is the pure contemplation of thought which the student may enjoy interruptedly and God eternally.[5] The life in accordance with ethical virtue is secondary.[6] The Stoic sage is distinguished from the Cyrenaic and Epicurean in Horace[7] by his immersion in political activities.

Chrysippus said that Aristotle's theoretic life was only a form of hedonism.[8] The literature of Stoicism harps on the word κοινωνικός, as the literature of to-day on the words 'social' and 'socialized.' And many modern critics have taken the Stoics at their own estimate and praised Stoicism on this score as against Platonism. But Cicero points out that in fact the Academy and the Lyceum were the chief schools of oratory and political science. And Seneca says epigrammatically:

> 'Quorum tamen nemo ad rempublicam accessit, at nemo non misit.'[9]

14. Neo-Platonism.—The divorce between culture and life in the declining period of the Græco-Roman empire confirmed these tendencies, and Neo-Platonism, the predominant philosophy of the last three centuries, constructed its system and its ideal out of the eloquent passages of the *Phædo*, the *Gorgias*, the *Republic*, and the *Theætetus* that preach purification from sin or sensualism, flight from the world, concentration of the mind upon itself, and assimilation of the human to the divine as the way of salvation and of good.[1] These conceptions were blended with the doctrine, derived from the Platonic *Symposium* and Aristotle's *Metaphysics*, of the upward striving and aspiration of all creatures towards the primal source of the good and the beautiful, God.

It is not a practicable final philosophy of the supreme human good for any race of men in whom the will to live persists. It is only the beautiful legacy which the dying philosophy of Greece bequeathed to the idealism and the religious poetry of the world:

> 'If, in the silent mind of One all-pure,
> At first imagined lay
> The sacred world;
> . . . . . .
> O waking on a world which thus-wise springs!
> . . . O waking on life's stream!
> By lonely pureness to the all-pure fount
> (Only by this thou canst) the colour'd dream
> Of life remount!'[2]

With this poetic interpretation of Matthew Arnold we may compare the last words of Plotinus' *Enneades*, φυγή, with Plato, *Theæt.* 176 B, φυγὴ δὲ ὁμοίωσις θεῷ κατὰ τὸ δυνατόν, and with the closing words of Emerson's last essay, 'Illusions,' in his *Conduct of Life*: 'They alone with him alone.' But the final good of Plato and of Greece in her prime is rather that of Tennyson's *Ancient Sage*:

> 'Let be thy wail
> And help thy fellow men.'

LITERATURE.—See the works cited in the footnotes.

PAUL SHOREY

1 *Rep.* 592 A B.
2 *Ib.* 529 E, 519 B. The ingenious suggestion that this is the Orphic κατάβασις exemplifies again the danger of over-stressing Plato's imagery as against his meanings.
3 1102 a 5 ff.
4 1103 a 5, *Ethics*, bk. vi.; Plato, *Rep.* 518 D E.
5 1177 a 12, 1178 b, *de Cœlo*, 292 a 22.
6 1178 a 9.
7 *Ep.* I. i. 16 f.
8 Hicks, p. 54.
9 *De Tranquillitate Animi*, i. 7.

1 On this aspect of Plato's own philosophy cf. E. Zeller, *Plato and the Older Academy*, Eng. tr., London, 1876, p. 440 ff., and O. Apelt, *Platonische Aufsätze*, Leipzig, 1912, p. 147 ff., 'Der Wert des Lebens.'
2 Matthew Arnold, 'In Utrumque Paratus' (*Poems*, ed. London, 1881, i. 70).

SUN, MOON, AND STARS.

SUN, MOON, AND STARS (Introduction).—In every quarter of the globe the star-studded heavens have attracted the attention and challenged the scrutiny of mankind. Very especially was this the case in the low-lying plain of Babylonia, with its pellucid atmosphere, and hence the study of astrology and astronomy, while practically universal, reached a remarkably high stage of development in that region. On the one hand, the fixed stars, of various degrees of brilliance, are ranged immovably in groups that stamp themselves upon the visual organs; while, on the other, the moon, the sun, and the five visible planets seem to be constantly changing their respective positions. Such phenomena were interpreted by primitive man in a subjective and anthropomorphic fashion, and his notions regarding them were still in vogue when genuine scientific inquiry entered the field, so that until about 1500 A.D. astrology and astronomy remained an inextricable mass of confusion.

1. The seven planets.—In the northern regions of the Old World every object was regarded by the primitive mind not merely as personal, but also as sexual. In the north-east the twin concepts of *Yang* and *Yin* long survived amongst the Chinese as a philosophical formula, classifying all existing things as male (= good) or female (= evil). Persian dualism retains the twofold principle in its most incisive form. In the Middle Ages, Christian ideas were for a time excessively influenced by the antithesis of God and Satan, though here the sexual dichotomy characteristic of the primitive mind has disappeared.

Now this tendency of the aboriginal mind towards sexual personification left some of its earliest deposits upon the observation and study of the stars. Even the simplest observations of the planetary movements brought to light the striking fact that the elongations of the two inferior planets, Mercury and Venus, never reached beyond a certain limit, and that these bodies traversed the zodiac as if held within the magic circle of the sun. The moon and the three superior planets were less restricted in their motions. It was therefore quite in keeping with the imaginative and symbolizing proclivity of the primitive intellect to represent the Sun, Mercury, and Venus as a family, travelling, in relatively close company, like nomads in the ecliptic. Of this family the Sun came to be regarded as the father, Venus as the mother, and Mercury as their son. The other planets were looked upon as mere vagrant males, who on occasion, however, might act as a disturbing influence in the union of the Sun and Venus.

In speculations of a still earlier period it was the sun and moon alone that formed the marriage relationship, the sun being usually the husband and the moon the wife; only in exceptional cases were the positions reversed. Occasionally, too, the relations between sun and moon were represented as homosexual and pederastic. But in the ancient Orient and in Egypt the septet of planets had already attained to such prominence in comparison with the two greater luminaries that the idea of a marriage between sun and moon hardly left a trace behind.

Even in the most remote ages the periods of revolution peculiar to the several planets had been studied, with results which led to their being arranged in the following sequence (with the earth, of course, at the centre of the universe)—Moon, Mercury, Venus, Sun, Mars, Jupiter, Saturn. The sun's superiority in size was enough of itself to give him the median position. The planets named before the sun alternated as morning and evening stars, or in other ways; and of the twofold characteristic thus exhibited one aspect might be regarded as good and the other as evil. The three last-named, or exterior, planets formed a triad by themselves, and they appeared to the observer as less under the control of the sun than his own family or the moon. The middle place amongst them was occupied by Jupiter, who might thus be deemed their king; and the king as such, according to Oriental ideas, was good. But as the sun, the giver of life and light, was likewise good, it followed that Mars and Saturn must be evil—by the principle of alternation, namely, which is even yet resorted to, as, *e.g.*, in the counting of one's coat-buttons, in ideas about even and odd, and in other primitive superstitions. Mars with his relatively short period of revolution became the youthful turbulent demon, while the slowly-revolving Saturn was figured as the hoary-headed begetter of evil.

Not only, however, do men look upwards towards the planets, but the planets themselves look downwards upon men and events on the earth. They were even supposed to impress their own characters upon earthly affairs, intervening therein as their nature prompted. In the case of the sun and the moon such action was obvious to all, and by analogy it was attributed to the other five planets as well. These ideas were so simple and natural that, at the time when, in the oldest civilized lands, such as Babylonia and Egypt, the earliest scientific observations and records of the planetary motions were collected, they had permeated all study of the subject. The consequence was that these naive ideas continued to mingle with the subsequent results of genuine astronomical inquiry.

Aboriginal man came upon a fresh vein of ideas when he divined a mutual connexion between the lustre of the stars and that of the metals. The metals with which he was acquainted being precisely seven in number, it was natural to associate with them, not the fixed stars, but the seven planets. The parallels were as follows: the Sun with gold, the Moon with silver, Mars with iron, Mercury with quicksilver, Jupiter with tin, Venus with copper, and Saturn with lead. Hence in mediæval, and even until modern, times, the metals were indicated by the planetary symbols. Then alchemy attached special symbols to other substances; and as alchemy and astrology were intimately connected with each other throughout their entire course, it may be well to give a list of the symbols used by alchemists in the Middle Ages:—

☉ gold, ☾ silver, ♂ iron, ☿ quicksilver, ♃ tin, ♀ copper, ♄ lead, ♁ antimony, ♆ lime, 🜍 sulphur, 🜿 tartar, ⊖ salt, ⦶ saltpetre, 🜖 sulphuric acid, ✱ ammonia, -⌒- distillate and sublimate, -⌣- precipitate. As will be shown in dealing with the horoscope, the symbols of the four traditional elements were derived from the two 'houses' known as *ὑπόγειον* and *μεσουράνημα* respectively.

We have thus sketched the main lines of thought by which the planets came to have their particular significance in astrological speculation. More remote considerations must here be left aside. Suffice it to say that, in the final scheme of astrology, Mercury became the lord of wisdom, cunning, artifice, and craft, and was likewise bi-sexual; Venus became the lady of love; Mars, the lord of war and violence generally; Jupiter, the ruler of gods and men; Saturn, the lord of cruelty and truculence. The Sun, Jupiter, and Saturn were propitious by day, and the Moon, Mars, and Venus by night. The planets infected with their own qualities such as were born under their influence, but in certain situations their normal action might be completely reversed.

2. The ecliptic and the zodiac.—Civilized man is still affected by the variation of times and seasons, and in a yet higher degree this was the case with primitive man. The latter could hardly remain inattentive to changes of temperature and weather in their connexion with day and night, or with summer and winter, or, again, with the varying position of the sun in the sky. In his ingathering of marine products for daily food and his cruising expeditions off the coast he became aware of the connexion between the ebb and flow of the sea and the course of the moon. His interest in the chase and his sexual relations obliged him to take notice of the fluctuating brightness of the moon by night. He noted that the period of menstruation coincided with that of a lunar revolution. In the life of primitive man, accordingly, there was no concern of importance but was somehow related to the movements of the sun or the moon. As soon, however, as the planets came to be regarded as endowed with personality, the interventions of sun and moon in human affairs began to be thought of as the conscious and voluntary actions of higher beings, whose purpose it was to bring the fortunes of nations, monarchs, and individual human beings into continuous correlation with their own particular activities in the higher sphere.

The planets Venus and Mercury, being represented as respectively the wife and the son of the sun, must inevitably, according to human notions, exert an influence upon the actions of the being personified as husband and father. But, this being so, it was impossible to leave Mars, Jupiter, and Saturn out of account. Now these five smaller planets, equally with the larger two, confined their movements to a certain narrow belt of the firmament. The only difference between the circular paths of the sun and the moon and the paths of the smaller planets is that the latter exhibit certain peculiar convolutions, which were called epicycles, and may be illustrated by a curved line as follows : 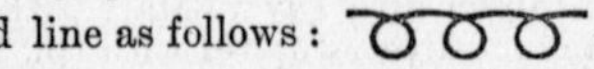. The orbits of the sun and the moon, no doubt, also showed many deviations from the path of simple revolution about the observer's own point of view. But the only change which a dweller upon the earth could discern in the smaller planets was the shifting of their several positions among the fixed stars, and their concomitant variations in apparent magnitude. Investigation of these planets, therefore, did not reach beyond investigation of their paths in the firmament.

After sunset about one-half of all the stars are visible. The great mass of these lie in the broad equatorial girdle of the heavens between the sun and a point 180° E. of the sun. The lines bounding the stars of the circumpolar vault and those of the southern hemisphere are not constant, but fluctuate inversely. The stars, however, that come into consideration in regard to the planetary orbits travel from east to west, passing below the horizon one after another, so that just before sunrise the other half of the stars, *i.e.* those lying between the sun and 180° W., are within the field of view. Thus, an examination of the sky made twice in one night, viz. shortly after sunset and shortly before sunrise, will embrace practically every important phenomenon in the starry heavens. These accordingly were the two times of astronomical observation to which prime importance was ascribed throughout antiquity, and into relation with which all observations were brought.

In the course of one night, then, primitive man could see almost all the stars visible in our latitude. One of the few exceptions was formed by the stars which happened to be situated in the sun's meridian for the time being. Their light was lost in the sun's beams, and they were meanwhile invisible. After sunset and before sunrise, moreover, there was a short period of twilight, causing a degree of obscuration such that brighter stars remained visible only when they were over 12°, and fainter stars only when over 15°, E. or W. of the sun. In virtue of the sun's movement in the zodiac, the observer of the morning and the evening sky might witness the following phenomenon. On a particular evening of the year a star, especially one situated in the zodiacal belt, would be visible for a few minutes after sunset, and on the following evening be seen no more. Now, such a star remained invisible for a certain time every year, and the astrologer spoke of it as being 'combust,' *i.e.* dissolved in the overpowering beams of the sun. Then, after a period of 24 to 30 days, according to its brilliance, the same star reappeared shortly before sunrise. The star's disappearance from the evening sky in the west was termed its heliacal setting, and its reappearance in the morning sky to the east its heliacal rising.

In the astrology and astronomy of both East and West throughout the entire ancient era the heliacal rising of various groups of stars was carefully noted, and employed in registering the date of events. So far, the earliest known instance of this, found more than once in historical records, is the heliacal rising of Sirius, the 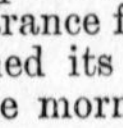 of the Egyptians, which was pronounced Σῶθις, and translated τὸ ἄστρον τὸ τῆς Ἴσιος, by the Greeks. By this means, long before the building of the pyramids, was indicated the beginning of the sidereal year, as well as a particular era of about 1500 years, at the end of which the first day of the sidereal year coincided with that of the tropical year. Half-way through the period of invisibility the star and the sun lie in the same meridian. The corresponding proximity of a star to any of the planets but the sun is called a conjunction, and every conjunction was astrologically of great importance. But when the sun is one of the coincident pair, the occurrence is known as the cosmical rising of the star in question. It is to this cosmical rising, not as in ancient times to the heliacal rising, that special prominence is attached by modern scientific astronomy.

The Egyptian sacred year was subsequently adopted by the Romans as the Julian year, with the intercalation of a day in every fourth year. This computation allowed for the fact that the sun seems to move forward some $\frac{4}{1461}$ of his orbit every day. This might have suggested a division of the ecliptic into 365 parts, only a trifling error being thus involved. What was actually done, however, was to divide the great circle into 360 parts, involving a still larger error of adjustment. The calculation of the yearly period and its division into twelve months—of which we shall treat more fully below—together with many other things, were thereby greatly simplified. But the sun's orbit of 360 degrees, with a day for each degree, left some $5\frac{1}{4}$ days of every year out of account. Now we still speak of a summer solstice and a winter solstice, meaning thereby the two points at which the sun reaches his greatest declination north and south respectively. Originally, however, the residual $5\frac{1}{4}$ days were divided between the two solstices, the sun being actually represented as pausing in his declination, so that he could still traverse the 360 degrees of the ecliptic in 360 days. In the ancient Egyptian calendar this whole redundant period was transferred to the time just anterior to the heliacal rising of Sirius, five days being inserted in ordinary, and six in leap (or temple) years. In the early Roman calendar the intercalation was made at the winter solstice. To the Babylonian calendar, which, with a displacement of the year's beginning, is still in use as the Jewish calendar, we must return when we deal with lunar computations. Be it noted here, however, that for astrological and astronomical purposes the Babylonians placed the compensatory interval for the most part at the beginning of spring, but sometimes at the beginning of autumn.

The time at which this yearly intercalation was made was dependent in the main upon the fixing of the zero meridian in the movable vault of heaven. The points through which this zero line might be conveniently drawn were, of course, many. Once it was fixed, astronomy and calendar were brought into harmony, and a definite instant established for commencing the day. The Babylonians began the day with sunrise, and the year with the spring equinox, thus placing the zero of the ecliptic upon the first point of Aries. Among the Jews the day began with sunset, and the civil year with the autumn equinox ; and, had the Jews studied astronomy independently, they would have drawn the zero of the ecliptic through Libra. In the early Roman, as in our modern, calendar the day is reckoned from midnight, and the year from the winter solstice ; here, therefore, the zero would lie in the first point of Capricornus. The Romans, however, as classical writers inform us, borrowed their astronomy and astrology from Babylonia, and accordingly it is the Babylonian zero point that is found among the Romans, as also in later developments, and even in the astronomy of the present day. The Egyptians dated their year from the rise of the Nile on the 19th of July, and the corresponding zero meridian passed through Sirius. With this, however, the beginning of the day did not harmonize, for, according to notices found in the Mantelpaviane and other hieroglyphic texts, the Egyptian day was reckoned from sunrise. This dislocation likewise is probably due to Babylonian influence of a very remote date.

We have seen that the ecliptic, and indeed the circle generally, was divided into 360 degrees, to correspond approximately with the sun's daily change of position among the stars throughout one year. These divisions, however, were found inconveniently small, and the ecliptic was then portioned out into constellations, each having an arc of 30 degrees, and three subdivisions of 10 degrees, or decanates. This division came about in two ways. In the first place, at any given time something like one-twelfth of the ecliptic was 'combust'; and, secondly, each of these twelfths was traversed by the sun in about the same time as the moon required for one complete revolution. In this way the annual course of the sun was furnished with the 12 zodiacal signs of the ecliptic. Moreover, in the earliest times the synodical period of the moon was divided into three, viz. waxing, dominant, and waning moon, and this division was adhered to by later astrology. Now to each of these synodical thirds of the moon's course corresponded a movement of the sun extending to some 10 degrees, and thus in time arose the division of the ecliptic into 36 decanates.

The trisection of the moon's period just noted probably led in very remote times to the institution of weeks of ten and five days. It does not appear, however, from what we have so far learned of ancient Eastern history, that these measurements had any practical significance. It was only in astrology and astro-mythology, with its historical legends, that the 36 decanates (or the 72 semi-decanates) were actually made use of. This chronometry, no less than that explained above, was in vogue throughout Babylonia and Egypt, if not elsewhere. A final vestige thereof was the Egyptian practice of assigning 401 *ushabti* for the dead—365 for the days of the year and 36 as guardians for the ten-day weeks. In astrology of the higher type, to the time of Kepler, calculations were made by means of the degree and, above all, of the decanate; and the moon from her tenth to her twentieth day was always spoken of as being in her domain. In general, however, the method of reckoning which superseded all others, for both astronomical observation and astrological interpretation, was that of the well-known 12 zodiacal signs, although these were variously designated in the several civilized lands of antiquity. It likewise forms the foundation of the Babylonian scheme of months, as appears from the following parallelism: Libra, *taśritu* (Bab.), Tishri (Heb.), followed by Scorpio, *araḫ-samna* (Bab.), Marcheshvan (Heb.); then Sagittarius, *kislimu* (Bab.), Kislev (Heb.), etc. The names of the months were also indicative of their meteorological conditions; thus, *e.g.*, the winter rainy season was symbolized by Capricornus (originally the marine animal *Hippocampus guttulatus*), Aquarius, and Pisces, all in some way connected with water.

Here, moreover, we again meet with the practice of portioning out good and evil, or rather male and female, alternately. Astrologically the zero point of this distribution lay between Cancer and Leo, approximating, therefore, to that of the Egyptian Sirius-year. Leo, Libra, and Sagittarius came to be regarded as male; Virgo, Scorpio, and Capricornus as female. It is worthy of remark that as a result of this law of alternation the astrologer was actually forced for thousands of years to speak of Taurus as feminine. Then the constellations of the zodiac were also allotted severally to the planets; thus Cancer was assigned to the moon, Leo to the sun, Gemini and Virgo to Mercury, Taurus and Libra to Venus, Aries and Scorpio to Mars, Sagittarius and Pisces to Jupiter, and Capricornus and Aquarius to Saturn. The particular planet was called the 'lord of the mansion' belonging to its respective sign or signs. Tradition tells us, however, that there were other 'gods (or lords) of the mansion.' Those of the Egyptians have been transmitted to us not only by the reports of Marcus Manilius, but also by an almanac notice found in the Ebers Papyrus; some of their names likewise survive in the Coptic designations of the months. A comparison of the various lists shows us that in the course of thousands of years the tradition remained unaltered, though in that of Manilius there is a dislocation to the extent of one zodiacal sign.

The ecliptic of the sun is traversed approximately also by the moon, and in relation to the latter it was measured by a unit of the sun's course, viz. the arc described by the moon in one day. In order to correspond, therefore, with the moon's period of 28 days, the ecliptic was divided afresh into 28 lunar stations. But as the sun, during the moon's sidereal period, has moved onward by about two lunar stations, astrological calculation assumed a period of about 30 lunar stations, *i.e.* the time between one new moon and another, as the measure of a month. In order to delimit these stations, however, the astrologer did not portion out the ecliptic in a fresh series of constellations, but distinguished each of the 28 by a dominant star in the ecliptic. In contradistinction to the older method of dividing the 30 days of the moon's synodical period in three, there arose subsequently the plan of dividing its sidereal period in four. Once in each of these quarters each of the seven planets was recognized as the lord of a lunar station, the order of sequence being the same as that in which, in the horoscope of the hours, the planets became lords of the ascendant at sunrise.[1] Thus came about the division of the sidereal month of 28 days into four weeks of 7 days, with Sun, Moon, Mars, Mercury, Jupiter, Venus, and Saturn as successive lords of the lunar stations in each week. This astrological scheme of naming the days of the week after the rulers of the lunar stations still survives throughout Christendom, while, on the other hand, the canonical books of the Old and New Testaments entirely avoid the use of such designations, distinguishing the days of the week by ordinal numbers alone.

The various locations of the five smaller planets were usually designated by the 12 zodiacal signs into which the sun's path is divided, as is specially shown in regard to Egypt by the Berlin Demotic Papyrus, p. 8279.

3. Spherical astronomy and the astrological houses. — Observations of the astral motions within the scope of natural vision are designated spherical, and when these have been duly adjusted they are, by way of contrast, called cosmical, while the actual occurrences themselves are spoken of as sidereal. Modern scientific astronomy likewise must always take the direct spherical observations as its starting-point, only then proceeding to elaborate its way towards the higher levels of knowledge. The astrology and astronomy of the ancient world never got beyond the spherical stage. Hence it was necessary from the outset to lay down fixed bearings for observational purposes, such as would be furnished by two lines, one run-

[1] If we take the planets, therefore, in the reverse order of their propinquity to the earth, viz. Saturn, Jupiter, Mars, Sun, Venus, Mercury, Moon, and suppose that each planet in turn presides over an hour of the day, then, if, *e.g.*, Saturn presides over the first hour of a particular day, he will also preside over the 8th, 15th, and 22nd hours; the 23rd hour accordingly will fall to Jupiter, the 24th to Mars, and the 1st hour of the new day to the Sun: hence Saturday is followed by Sunday, and so on.

ning east and west, the other north and south, through the observer's own position.

In connexion with nearly all ancient systems of religion are found sacred edifices of great age whose longitudinal axes lie exactly east and west. The determination of this east and west line, *i.e.* the parallel of latitude, was thus one of the early triumphs of the human mind. The oldest known instrument employed for the purpose was the stile, which afterwards developed into the gnomon of the sun-dial, and, indeed, the sun-dial itself. The stile was a vertical shaft fixed in the centre of a circle. In the morning, and again in the evening, the shadow of the pillar extended a considerable distance beyond the circle, while for an hour or two before, as also for an hour or two after, midday the extremity of the shadow lay within the circle. It was necessary, therefore, to mark the two points at which the shadow, forenoon and afternoon, terminated precisely upon the circle. The straight line joining these two points supplied an accurate east and west alignment, which could thus be secured on any sunny day at any season of the year. The use of the gnomon, in some form or another, seems to be common to primitive and the older civilized peoples.

Simple trial and observation showed that a stationary point was to be found in the north pole of the firmament and the star lying nearest to it. The direction of the meridian line through any given point of observation could then be ascertained by the following expedient. Two horoscopers stood face to face upon a line lying roughly north and south. The observer on the south, holding up before him the split rib of a palm leaf, moved it into such a position as enabled him through the fissure to see the pole star directly above the crown of his companion's head. Then the observer on the north, looking through the slit, saw all the then culminating stars from the southern point of the horizon upwards, and in this way projected his meridian upon the celestial vault.

The east and west points of the horizon, and the meridian of the observer, having been ascertained, the earliest facts of observation regarding the paths of the planets could be brought into relation therewith. The fixed stars, indeed, never varying in their positions relative to one another, also rose and set at constant distances from the east and west points respectively. On the other hand, the sun, the moon, and the five smaller planets rose and set at points never twice the same successively, and sometimes north, sometimes south, of due east and west. As regards the sun, the most northerly point of his rising and setting was reached as he entered Cancer, and the most southerly as he entered Capricorn, while his rising and setting were due east and due west respectively twice a year, viz. as he entered Aries and Libra. The extreme limits of his northward and southward movements in the ecliptic were called the tropical points, and the two constellations concerned came to be known in astrology and astronomy as the tropical constellations of the zodiac. Corresponding results were established with reference to the other planets.

But there is likewise an apparent daily revolution of fixed stars and planets alike around the position of the observer, each of them crossing his meridian once in every 24 hours; while if they lie in the equatorial circle the intersection takes place exactly 6 hours after they rise in the east, and 6 hours before they set in the west. Hence the observer's celestial equator, too, is always laid out in 12 segments corresponding to the 12 constellations of the zodiac; and if we disregard the sun's daily eastward movement of one degree, we find that every two hours the zodiac changes its position relatively to the equator by one whole zodiacal sign of 30 degrees. Now the intermediate positions of the signs during these two hours being left out of account, the observer's celestial equator was once for all divided into 12 apparently stationary parts, each of these having its own meridian. The illustration below shows an equatorial section traversing the horizon and the celestial sphere. These parts were called 'houses,' and all the conditions found within them were treated as if stationed in their respective middle lines. Now, as the enumeration of the houses began in the east, and then proceeded downwards under the eastern horizon, *i.e.* according to the order in which the phenomena of each successive house would appear above that horizon, the due east point fell exactly in the middle of the first house, the due west point in that of the seventh, the meridian in that of the

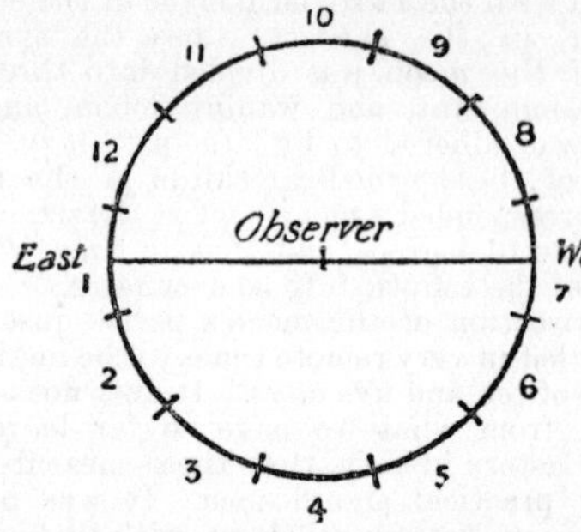

tenth, and the opposite meridian in that of the fourth. All primitive astronomical and astrological study of the sky was occupied, and indeed necessarily occupied, with the rising, culmination, and setting of the heavenly bodies, with the passage of planets, normal stars, and constellations from one house to another, and with the mutual positions of the planets as measured by the houses they happened to occupy at any given time.

It would appear that these houses were sometimes divided in two, as, *e.g.*, in Egypt in the time of King Seti; and this led quite naturally to the division of the day into 24 hours, and eventually to the arrangement of the dial-plate of our clocks. For more exact observations, however, each house was subdivided into three decanates, and each decanate into ten degrees, the advantage of this being that the sphere of the observer had the same number of parts as the ecliptic, while the boundary lines defining the parts of each coincided every four minutes.

This method of parcelling out the sun's apparent daily course must have been instituted at a very remote period, in an age indeed when the astronomer had not yet grasped the idea of a circular orbit, but still thought of the solar path as a square. In

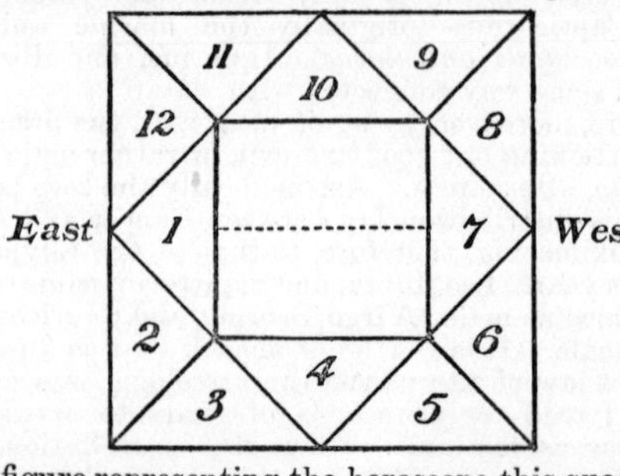

the figure representing the horoscope this quadrate form was retained, and it has remained in use till modern times, and, in fact, till the present day. To this method of delineating the stellar paths in the horoscope by means of the square we shall frequently have occasion to return, as a considerable number of symbols relating to God and the world were evolved therefrom. In interpreting the horoscope the various positions were so far as possible brought into relation with the first house, and with the latter as starting-point the astrologer, applying the principle of even and odd as in the case of the exterior planets, Sun, Mars, Jupiter, and Saturn, alternately assigned to the other houses an essential character of benefit or bane. Thus the twelfth house was unfavourable, the eleventh favourable, the tenth—apart from its special position—unfavourable, the ninth favourable, the eighth supremely unfavourable, and so with the rest. This mode of interpretation was also arrived at along another line of thought, and, being thus supported by two ostensible proofs, it was believed to be established beyond dispute. The second proof in question was that supplied by the 'aspects,' of which we shall treat presently.

The plan of indicating position by means of zodiacal signs and houses could at best give approximate results. For the sake of simplicity it was assumed that the boundary lines of the several signs always coincided with those of the several houses, and that accordingly at the end of a Babylonian double-hour each sign moved instantaneously into another house, whose number was one less than that of the house which it had vacated. For all further deductions within the limits of plane geometry, the entire contents of any particular zodiacal sign were regarded as concentrated in the middle point of the sign and the house then congruent therewith.

The enumeration of the astrological houses from the east downwards towards the west, then eastwards again above the horizon, so that account is first of all taken of the invisible regions of the stellar heavens, had its origin in the fact that the attention of the astrologer was primarily directed towards the rising of the stars, and accordingly the houses were numbered in the order in which the stars contained in them at any given time would reach the eastern horizon and become visible.

4. Aspects.—The term 'aspects' was used in astrology to denote the relative positions of the houses and zodiacal signs, or of the stars situated in the houses at any given time. Planets in the same sign and the same house were said to be in conjunction; planets in opposite signs and houses, in opposition. The other possible relations amongst the celestial phenomena were defined with reference to regular inscribed polygons. Thus, if a planet were situated in the twelfth or the second house, then the line joining the middle point of either of these houses and that of the first house would form one side of a regular inscribed dodecagon; in

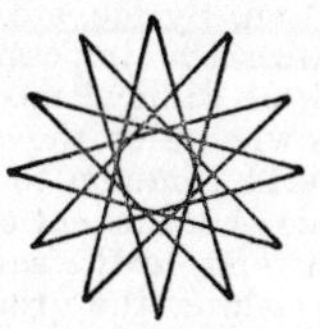

which case the planet in question was said to be in dodecagonal aspect to the east point, or 'horoscope' in the original sense. As in the same way planets in the eleventh and third houses furnished the side of a regular hexagon, their aspect towards the east or the horoscope was spoken of as sextile. Similarly planets in the tenth and fourth houses were in quartile or square, and those in the ninth and fifth were in trine. The line joining the middle point of the eighth or the sixth house with the east point was not a constituent part of any regular figure within the circle, and suggested at best a cross dodecagon, formed thus, which was regarded as the violation of all order. But as conjunction and opposition were reckoned amongst the regular aspects, the eighth was the only visible house having no aspect towards the horoscope. The principle of alternate numeration likewise pronounced this house unfavourable. In the astrological application of spherical astronomy it therefore signified the house of death.

Prior to the stage now reached, the exclusive concern of the astronomer had been to map out the heavens with such precision as would enable him to fix his observations by means of a verbal record. His conception of aspects, however, *i.e.* of the relations of the stellar positions to the horoscope, led him to assign values to the stellar positions themselves, and as soon as these came to be represented as anthropocentric or concentric, the initiative was given to the science of Judicial Astrology. Nevertheless we must emphasize the fact that the original scheme of the horoscope was depicted as a square, and that, before it became possible for astrology to speak of regular polygons, the conception of the sun's apparent diurnal motion as a circle must have come to the front. Thus the very language of astrology shows it to have been a kind of excrescence, not inherently connected with astronomy at all. Even in the Middle Ages a distinction was still maintained between Natural Astrology and Positive Astrology. The former dealt with the actual, and especially the baneful, influence of the planets upon meteorological changes—wind, storm, hurricane, thunder, flood, and earthquake. It was accordingly bound up with the naive and fantastic weather-lore of primitive man, and is to some extent still in evidence in scientific meteorology. In regard to the latter it is even yet frequently true that *sub iudice lis est*.

Positive or Judicial Astrology, on the other hand, was concerned from the earliest times with the supposed influences of the planets upon the fortunes of men and nations. It is now regarded by all sober minds as an extravagance of the human intellect, as something that the race has finally left behind. In Judicial Astrology it was no longer merely the aspect of a star to the horoscope, *i.e.* the east point, that was specified and appraised, but also the aspect of two planets with respect to each other. If one planet, for example, was situated in the eleventh house and another in the eighth, the two were said to be mutually in quartile. Here again, moreover, we find the alternate distribution of good and evil: conjunction was good; adjacent aspect or aspect in dodecagon was evil; sextile was good; quartile relatively evil; trine specially good; absence of regular aspect was specially evil, and opposition relatively good.

Since the line between the eighth or the sixth house and the east point did not form the side of a regular inscribed polygon, these two houses were deemed of inferior value. For the anthropocentric mind of the astrologer it was therefore a short step to regard them as houses of misfortune. The eighth house thus became the house of death, and the sixth the house of pains. We shall see later that in the reciprocal relations between the macrocosm and the microcosm the left arm became a synonym for the house of death and the left leg for the house of pains, and that in consequence these bodily parts themselves came to be regarded as of evil omen.

As emphasis was laid likewise upon the mutual correspondence of east and west—an idea that was corroborated by the principle of alternate numbering—the twelfth and second houses were counted unfavourable. In primitive plane geometry the inscribed triangle and hexagon were deemed pre-eminently regular figures, and once more the alternate enumeration gave the same result. Consequently the eleventh, ninth, fifth, and third houses were reckoned favourable; while the tenth and fourth, again, were relatively evil. These symbolical interpretations, however, were sometimes set aside, sometimes even reversed, especially those connected with the invisible half of the sky.

The tenth house, as that in which the stars culminated, was supposed, by a very natural symbolism, to preside over dignities and offices, while the fourth house, lying directly beneath us, came in similar fashion to be associated with parents and ancestors, as those who had passed into the under world, and inferentially with all the other ties of kinship. On the ground of a certain analogy with the eighth house, *i.e.* that of death, the twelfth became the house of enmity (*κακοδαίμων*), and, by a further analogy, the second became the house of poverty. As the second house, however, was situated in the sky belonging to the under world and therefore opposite to ours, it became the house of fortune and riches, and for the same reason the sixth house, that of pains (or, according to another interpretation, that of service), became the house of health. Next to the house of death came the ninth as the house of the tutelary deity, while the eleventh, adjacent to the house of enmity, became that of friendship (*ἀγαθοδαίμων*). On the ground of similar considerations the third became the house of brothers, and the fifth the house of children. Finally, as the first house was specially associated with the querent of the astrological oracle, the seventh belonged to the querent's counterpart, *i.e.* in the ordinary course of things, wife or husband.

The designations of the various houses were therefore as follows: (1) life, (2) riches, (3) brothers, (4) parents, (5) children, (6) health, (7) marriage, (8) death, (9) religion, (10) dignities, (11) friendship, and (12) enmity. But this arrangement gave only the general scheme of astrological prognostication, and in the course of thousands of years various changes were introduced. Our information regarding any particular era of astrological speculation is defective, and we speak only in a general sense when we assert that from first to last the system detailed above remained essentially unchanged. It was all along recognized, moreover, that the scheme must be specially adjusted to special circumstances. Thus in the case of sickness the real querent was the invalid himself, and it was about him, therefore, that the first house supplied information. The counterpart was meanwhile not the wife, but the disease itself, upon which accordingly light was cast by the seventh house. The tenth house, in which the stars culminated over the patient, symbolized the physician, while the fourth, lying directly beneath in the under world, signified medicine. Account was also taken, of course, of the eighth house as the house of death, and of the sixth as the house of health. The houses of friendship, enmity, riches, brothers, and children were not supposed to wield any influence upon the course of the disease. Nor was much importance attached, in such cases, to the symbolism of the sun's planetary family; and, in fact, according to Greek accounts of Egyptian astrology, neither Venus nor Mercury was taken into consideration at all.

5. The astrological conception of the world.—The enormous advances that have been made within modern times in the study and practical application of the natural sciences, as well as the great contrast that obtains between the ancient and the modern scientific point of view, are matters of common knowledge. It is impossible to understand the theories of nature held by the ancients without a clear conception of the difference between their fundamental standpoint and our own. According to the older view of the world, which can be traced backwards for 5000 years before Christ, and which still held unquestioned sway for 1000 years after Christ, all natural objects issued in parallel lines from certain primary causes of universal operation. Modern science, on the other hand, assumes that the various groups of physical phenomena proceed by differentiation from certain primordial forms. While the ancients, therefore, looked upon the diversity of things as original, and their common elements as due to external influences, the moderns assume that the properties which objects have in common are inherited from a single primary form, and that their differences have been produced by external conditions, such as, *e.g.*, the struggle for existence.

The two conceptions, however, are not held stringently apart, nor does history show a rigid line of demarcation between the later and the earlier. Even in Genesis (10[1ff.]), for instance, we have a table of nations which stands in complete agreement with the modern point of view, more particularly in the circumstance that it traces back the ancestry of all mankind in a series of converging lines. Much more in accordance with the ancient conception, on the other hand, is the Greek Deluge-story of Deucalion, according to which human beings were generated spontaneously from stones acted upon by the formative powers present in the air.

The theory of parallel processes may be called the 'ancient astrological,' or, again, the 'Oriental astrological' view of the universe. It had its birth amongst the early civilizations of the East, and its leading science was astrology; nor is it yet a spent force among certain Asiatic peoples of to-day. Now even our modern science, with its discovery of steam-power and its remarkable utilization of electricity, does not enter so profoundly into contemporary experience as did the ancient astrological conception into the life, thought, and feeling of the distant past.

Perhaps the most effective resistance to the more harmful issues of the astrological theory of the universe was made by the peoples living around the Mediterranean. But the Scriptures of the Old and New Testaments are likewise free from the evil outgrowths of that view. Nevertheless, we must remember that even the Biblical writers were children of their time, and could therefore hardly avoid expressing their thoughts in terms of the recognized philosophy of their age. Hence, just as we have come to recognize that the thoroughgoing study of Biblical Hebrew cannot dispense with the philological investigation of Arabic, Ethiopic, Babylonian, Syriac, etc., so we are now beginning to realize the impossibility of understanding the tenor of Biblical modes of expression apart from a knowledge of the astrological conception of the world common to the Babylonian, the Egyptian, and other ancient civilizations.

We must again refer to the square form of the horoscope, as furnishing the ground-plan of this theory of the world. The figure shows us the link which the theory had with astrology, and also with other two occult sciences, viz. Alchemy and the Kabbala.

It is of interest to note that the symbols used in astrology for the four cardinal points were simply the triangles corresponding to the first, fourth, seventh, and tenth houses respectively. But while, according to the expedient already noticed (p. 52[a]), the positions of the stars in the ecliptic were determined by the observer on the north, the fixing of the cardinal points was effected by his fellow on the south. The horoscope was therefore seen by the latter from the opposite point of view, and the four houses in question took a reverse form, so that △ came to mean north, ▽ south, ▷ east, and ◁ west. With this exception, however, all further inferences were drawn from the proper form of the horoscope, *i.e.* from the figure it presented to the observer on the north.

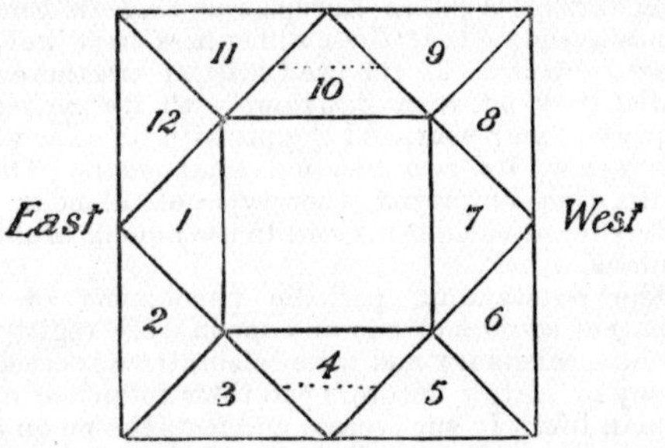

The tenth house, as the *summum cœlum*, and the fourth, as the *imum cœlum*, embraced everything in the world above and the world below respectively. The upper world as a whole, however, consists of the eighth, ninth, tenth, eleventh, and twelfth houses. In the hieroglyphic script of Egypt, accordingly, heaven is represented by the exterior boundary of these five houses, thus: , which, of course, according to the Egyptian practice in such matters, is only a contour, and really stands for 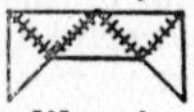. The same proportions and angles are likewise retained in the Egyptian representation of the goddess of heaven, who broods over the earth-god—a phenomenon which will meet us again when we treat of Egypt. The under world was represented, of course, by the same figure inverted. Now we find two different ideas attaching to each of the houses numbered ten and four. According to one conception the *summum cœlum* contains the heavenly upper ocean, from which rain falls (אֲרֻבֹּת הַשָּׁמַיִם in the Biblical narrative of the Deluge), while the *imum cœlum* embraces both the ocean of the under world and the subterranean water from which the fountains of the deep are fed (מַעְיְנוֹת תְּהוֹם; also the sources of the Nile in Herodotus). According to the other conception there lies above us first of all air, then fire; and beneath us, first earth, then water.

Now the latter theory furnished also the alche-

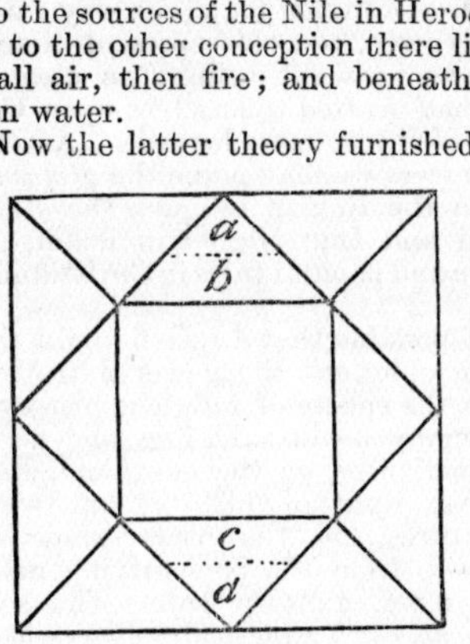

a=Fire 🜂

b=Air 🜁

c=Earth 🜃

d=Water 🜄

mistic symbols of the elements—symbols which are still written by doctors in old-fashioned mysterious receipts, and were in common use among physicians and apothecaries a hundred years ago. Thus, for example, 🜃*sigill.* signified *terra sigillata*; *lumbric.* 🜃*restr.*=*lumbrici terrestres*; 🜄*flor.* ⊙*rant.*=*aqua florum aurantiorum*; or something was to be boiled *leni* △, *i.e.* *leni calore.* Distilled alcoholic liquors were known as 'burnt water,' and were denoted by a combination of the symbols for water and fire, thus ✡. To this day the device 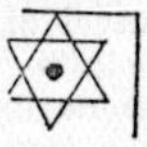 displayed upon rustic inns indicates the licence to sell brandy.

This combined symbol ✡ was used not only in alchemy but also in the Kabbala, where it represented the Star of David. It became, in fact, a symbol for God (just as the fire-eye, *i.e.* , was employed in Christian symbolism to signify the Holy Spirit); for, by the rules of the Kabbala, the combination of the principal consonants of אֵשׁ ('fire') and מַיִם ('water') yielded the word שָׁמַיִם ('heaven'), which in its turn was the cabalistic equivalent of אֱלֹהִים ('God'). Thus the term God could be expressed by the secret sign ✡ as the synthesis of fire and water. In the synagogue all pictorial representation of God was forbidden, nor was it allowable to give utterance to the tetragram יהוה unless absolutely necessary. In the same way, therefore, as the word אדני had to be resorted to as the oral designation of God, the symbol ✡ came to be used in the architecture of the synagogue as His graphic designation. This figure, moreover, not only contains within itself the symbols of the four elements, interlaced with one another, but, besides the upper and lower triangles signifying fire and water respectively, it also shows four extra-mundane triangles, which could thus be regarded on cabalistic principles as metaphysically symbolizing the four consonants of the tetragram. Hence, even in passages of ancient Christian works where we might expect some such phrase as 'with God,' we actually find the cabalistic device

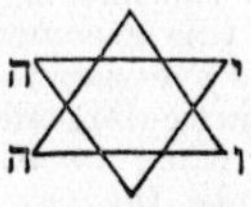

signifying יהוה.

According to the astrological theory of the world, however, not only the perpendicular section through the universe, but the surface of the earth itself, was thought of as quadrate, since the cube, as the ideal geometrical figure, was the accepted symbol of the world as a whole. This idea finds

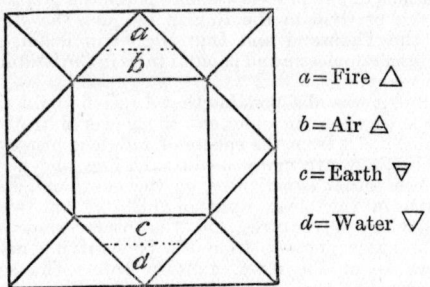

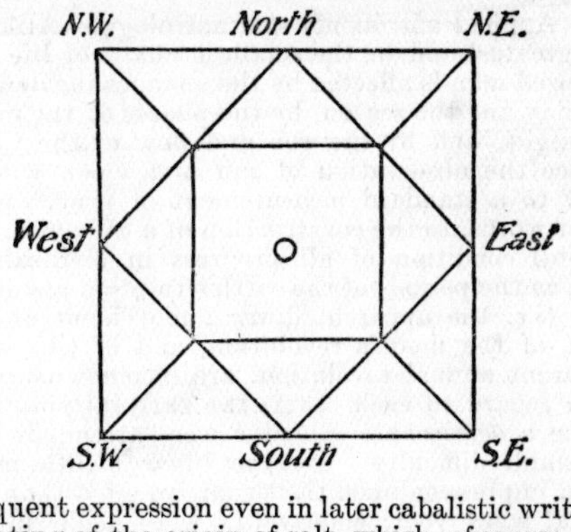

frequent expression even in later cabalistic writings treating of the origin of salt, which, of course, also crystallizes in cubes. The scheme of the horoscope, accordingly, became a comprehensive map of the world as well. As previously explained in connexion with the points of the compass, the horoscope was in this case constructed, as it were, from the opposite point of view. In the centre was the navel of the world, which every nation sought to claim for its own territory, and as the site of the national sanctuary. The figure also supplied the four pillars, viz. N.E., N.W., S.E., and S.W., upon which the heavens are supported. Of these the best known was the S.W. pillar, as it was there that Atlas had been relieved by Hercules.

6. Anthropomorphic nomenclature of the sphere.—The square horoscope was not the only expedient resorted to in setting forth the relations of the stars, as another method was also in use among the Egyptians. From a time anterior to Menes until the final period, the high priest of Heliopolis was known as , *i.e.* 'chief astrologer.' We may note in passing that this office was held by Poti-phera (of which name the literal Greek translation was Heliodoros), the father-in-law of Joseph (Gn 41[45]). Tables of observations made in Egypt during the Twentieth Dynasty are still extant, and in these are recorded the times at which the fixed stars cross the middle lines of the houses, *i.e.* the beginnings of the double-hours. The astrologer on the north found the meridian of the place of observation by looking through the slit of the palm-leaf rib above the bald crown of his companion. The middle meridians of the first and seventh houses were given by the horizontal line, while the observer found those of the eleventh and ninth houses by lines projected over his companion's right and left eyes respectively, and in similar fashion those of the twelfth and eighth houses by lines above the right and left elbows. It is probable that the sixth house was in like manner associated with the left knee, and the second house with the right.

From this point of view the left arm corresponded with the house of death and the left leg with the house of sorrows, and on this account there eventually arose a superstitious aversion to using the word 'left' at all. In particular, all actions performed by the left hand came to be regarded as unlucky. It may well be the case that mankind was right-handed rather than left-handed before astrology asserted its sway, but the ban thus laid upon the left extremities of the body undoubtedly supplied a further reason for excluding the left side and especially the left hand from all actions of great and critical moment.

7. Applied astronomy and astrology.—Alike in the greatest and in the smallest affairs of life uncivilized man is affected by the changes incident to the day and the season, by the phases of the moon by night, and by the ebb and flow of the tides. Hence the observation of sun and moon with a view to a standard measurement of time, or, in other words, to the construction of a calendar, was a vital condition of all progress in civilization. But, as the periods of the earth's rotation about its axis (*i.e.* the apparent diurnal movement of the sun), of the moon's revolution, and of the sun's apparent annual revolution, are incommensurable with regard to each other, the early attempts to frame a serviceable calendar were attended with no small difficulty. As the lunar month made more impression upon the primitive mind than the actual solar year, endeavours were made in the earliest calendars to base the latter upon an integral number of the former, and all sorts of expedients were tried in order to harmonize the two periods. At a further stage in the growth of civilization the determination of the true solar year became the subject of inquiry, the length of the true lunar month being then left out of consideration. Here again, however, the residual fraction of days provided difficulties, and the difference between the calendars of Western Europe and Eastern Europe (Russia) shows that these difficulties have not yet been overcome. In the pre-Christian era there was a disparity between Babylon, with its cyclically adjusted lunar year, and Egypt, with its solar year, or, rather, its two unequal solar years. Other civilizations employed other types of calendar. A purely lunar calendar is still in use among Muhammadans.

The outstanding periodic phenomena of the apparent courses of sun and moon were registered in these calendars, and were celebrated as occasions of joy or sorrow according to their influence upon human life. In such feasts and fasts the moon and the sun were, first of all, personified, and they still continued to be revered as divine or heroic beings even after the particular days connected with their movements by astrology and astronomy had been duly set down in the artificially corrected and adjusted calendars of ancient and modern civilized peoples.

8. Lunar, solar, and planetary deities.—The ascertainment of such varying influences of the moon and the sun as could be registered in the calendar was undoubtedly a forward step in the mental development of primitive man. But the notion that the movements of moon, sun, and planets were effected by powerful and conscious beings, more or less endowed with free will, was an open door to all illusion. The religion and mythology of the lowest races are permeated with this idea. Amongst more highly civilized peoples, again, we find a stock of myths of like purport, which, partly indigenous and partly exotic, forms a kind of illicit religion or superstition, and which shows many points of contrast with the teachings of the recognized national cult. In periods distinguished by a high state of civilization this supplementary religion finds acceptance only amongst the lowest and least enlightened ranks of the people, while at times, when culture is at a low ebb, it extends its sway over the leading classes as well.

In cases, however, where a relatively advanced and purified form of religion found its way into a region already civilized, the old representations of moon and sun as personal beings, as also the narratives that had grafted themselves upon their festivals, degenerated into mere legends. As illustrations of the process we may name the *Metamorphoses* of Ovid in the Roman religion, the stories of the Thousand and One Nights in Islām, and Grimm's domestic and popular tales in Christianized Germany.

But it was also possible that a fusion might take place between the older and the newer narratives. Thus, apart from the sphere of religious history as such, there are many mediæval kings and heroes whose actual experiences, on the one hand, stand forth in the clear light of history, but whose legendary adventures, on the other, show unmistakable deposits from the personifying narratives about the moon and the sun. The same process has been at work practically everywhere; we trace it not only in the *Nibelungenlied* and the *Iliad*, but also in connexion with all the great figures who as gods or prophets occupy the supreme place in the various systems of religion. Popular imagination, in fact, clinging as it does to the ancient legends, is quite indifferent as to the figure around which it throws them; it may fix upon Confucius, Buddha, Zarathushtra, Jesus, or Muhammad. Even the older religions, with deities unmistakably of planetary origin—the Babylonian

Shamash, the Egyptian Rê, the Greek Apollo—show such secondary deposits from various astro-mythological sources.

The disengagement of this secondary astro-mythological element from the Christian system of thought has now become one of the prime tasks of theological criticism. It is no longer possible for any earnest scholar to reject the fundamental idea of such analysis, and the extent to which the work of elimination shall be pursued depends entirely upon whether the individual theologian leans towards the more orthodox or the more liberal side. In regard to Confucius, Buddha, Zarathushtra, and Muhammad, as also in regard to the Alexander romances, the Christian theologian concedes the rights of the method without hesitation. Further, the OT and the Life of Jesus have from ancient times been the nuclei of a mass of legendary stories (the Talmud, etc.; Gospels of the Infancy, etc.), which all theologians have for centuries regarded as apocryphal; and it cannot be disputed that the study of astro-mythology has rendered valuable service in throwing light upon the origin of these spurious additions to the lives of the leading personalities of our religion. Once more, there is a group of writings which, though reckoned apocryphal by evangelical Churches, are still included in the Roman Catholic canon; and, as might be expected, the bearing of the astro-mythological theory upon these writings is estimated by the two great parties within Christianity in precisely opposite ways. And when at length the theory is applied to certain constitutive elements in the OT, and to the life of Jesus as given in the evangelical records, the theologians who concede its rights in these domains are fewer still in number. The explanation of this, of course, is that such criticism seems to undermine the historicity of the Biblical narratives, and to leave nothing but a mass of mythical stories about the planets, which have crystallized around certain more or less unreal figures in the history of Israel. The logical result of the process appears to be the subversion of every constituent of Christianity save its ethics.

Taken in this sense, the comparative study of astrology and astro-mythology rests upon an impregnable foundation. The implications of its results, as was said above, may quite well be brought into harmony alike with the most rigid orthodoxy and the broadest liberalism. Hence it cannot be non-suited by either of the warring schools; it is reconcilable even with the aims of its critics. Just as comparative philology is an ideal and impartial science, so must the comparative study of myths assume a like impartiality; and the indispensable framework of this study is formed by the planetary deities of astrology.

9. **Prophetic astrology.**—From the theological point of view, prophetic astrology must be regarded as a by-way towards superstition, and, indeed, as one of the main sources of superstition. It was evolved by gentle gradations from what we may call 'calendar astronomy.' Primitive man discerned parallelism not only in the processes of nature, but also in the State and in human life; nay, even in the forms and organs of animals he read analogies and homologies, and many other fields of observation presented similar correspondences. But by far the most obvious and unmistakable cases of parallelism were those which subsisted between the motions of the sun and the moon, on the one hand, and the periodic variation of the tides, of light and heat during the day, and of the seasons, on the other. Hence arose the notion of planetary deities or angels—beings who acted according to highly complicated laws, ordained either by themselves or by a superior power, and who sought to bring all events, great and small alike, within the range of parallel uniformities. Where the trend of thought was polytheistic, the planets were regarded as gods; where it lay towards monotheism, they were but the messengers of a Divine will beyond them; or, as the case might be, an inevitable fate was supposed to hang over the gods themselves.

From the standpoint of the ancient astrologer, the supreme function of all learning was the observation of certain simple phenomena and the drawing of inferences bearing upon a parallel series of facts otherwise veiled. The primary task of astrology was to ascertain the positions of the planets in relation to one another, to the zodiacal signs, and to the observer himself, and then to make deductions therefrom. This was astrology properly so called, and it required for every particular case a direct reading of the sky. A cloudy night, however, rendered such direct readings impossible. Now, the Kouyunjik inscriptions, dating from the time of the Assyrian king Assurbanipal, yield evidences for a continuous series of actual observations. From these we learn that, notwithstanding the complexity of the planetary movements, the periodic repetition of essential phenomena had been calculated for each particular planet. Thus the astrologer could fall back upon tabulated records covering every particular sequence of planetary movement, and could substitute these for direct observation. It is true that, owing to trifling inaccuracies in the data thus supplied, this course was avoided for thousands of years; but at length the momentous step was taken. No doubt, it still remained necessary to bring certain recorded positions to the test of actual observation; but, with these exceptions, the researches of the practical astrologer were thenceforth pursued in the study. Our earliest evidences for this procedure date from the period of the Persian monarchy.

So far as astronomy itself is concerned, this was a progressive movement; but, from the standpoint of observational science, it was a backward step. It issued finally in the determination and mathematical calculation of the planetary orbits by Kepler. But, in our estimate of Kepler's discoveries, we must always bear in mind that he was still under the spell of the astrological conception of the universe. It was his firm belief that his discoveries supplied the key to all events of history, and had exalted astrology to the level of a perfect and independent science of simple calculation, while in reality he had given the death-blow to its pretensions.

From the time of the earliest attempts to draw up a calendar—through the period of the Sumerians and Akkadians—to the days of Kepler astrology underwent no essential change, save that it gradually abandoned the method of direct observation of the heavens in favour of, first, a partial use of tables containing earlier observations, and, finally, a purely arithmetical determination of the positions occupied by the planets at any given time. Astrology, be it remembered, was a study of international importance. Wherever, therefore, in the history of any civilized country we can trace some slight advance in astronomical science, we find corresponding records, practically contemporaneous, in all the civilized countries of that epoch. Additions to men's knowledge of the stars were valued only as ancillary to the determination of the planetary positions. As all the available evidence goes to show, however, astrology, throughout its entire career, had but one method of adapting this knowledge to oracular ends—the method, namely, of symbolical interpretation, with a more or less clearly realized principle of alternation. In the main, the positions of the planets were made the basis of prognostications of the unborn future, but they were also used as a means of filling up *lacunæ* in the knowledge of the past and the present.

10. Astrology and medicine.—In the ancient Oriental view of the world, astrology, religion, and therapeutics went hand in hand. In the conviction that all things in the universe proceeded in parallel lines, men spoke of a macrocosm (primarily the stellar world as the province of Deity) and a microcosm (primarily the human body), and sought for far-reaching analogies between them. Thus—to take one of many examples found in Sanskrit literature—the Vedas and their allied texts exhibit attempts to establish an exact equivalence between the number of the bones in the human body and that of the days in a year. Simple as would have been the task of enumerating the bones accurately, they were purposely numbered wrongly, so that the desired numerical relations might be educed; the lower jaw, for instance, was said to be composed of eighteen single pieces, not including the teeth, just because this number, while purely factitious, could, as the twentieth part of 360, be used for purposes of speculation. The method was applied in every field, and things which did not harmonize in fact were arbitrarily made to do so.

In the ancient East the therapeutic art was based upon the two fundamental postulates of air in motion and liquid in motion, and it was supposed that in the human body the air passed along the arteries, while the liquid traversed the veins. The solid substance of the body (its earthy constituents) and its native heat (its igneous constituents) were regarded as forming a fixed and constant mass: earth and fire, in fact, were probably never considered in their physiological aspects until the Hellenistic period. The astrological references hitherto discovered in Babylonian and Egyptian texts show that air and liquid alone were taken into account. In the further development of these notions, special prominence was given to the air by the pneumatists, and to the blood (*i.e.* liquid, and a mixture of the four principal humours, viz. water, phlegm, yellow bile, and black bile) by the hæmatists. We cannot enter here into the particulars of the antagonism maintained between the two schools for several thousand years, an antagonism which we can trace in the period when the Pyramids were built, and which, again, moved the hæmatist Aristophanes to the mortal hatred wherewith in the *Clouds* he arraigned the pneumatism of Socrates before the Athenian populace. Suffice it to say that, in all references to the facts of nature found in the Pentateuch, the Jahwistic sections (of Genesis in particular) represent the pneumatic, and the Elohistic portions the hæmatic, point of view, whereas the Priestly Code exhibits no scientific tendency at all. The pneumatists regarded the nose as the most important organ of the body. We may recall the numerous phrases formed with אַף in the OT, and the large noses of the singers in the chorus of the *Clouds*. Even amongst the inscriptions from Nineveh, which must, on the whole, be reckoned to the hæmatic school, the present writer has found no fewer than fourteen different texts referring to divination by the nose.

According to the hæmatist, life was concentrated in the liver, the כָּבֵד, or heavy organ, which, accordingly, together with the blood, plays a prominent part in the OT and the Talmud. Among the Babylonians and Etruscans, again, as also among the various peoples influenced by them, haruspicy took the special form of divination by inspection of the liver. The cuneiform texts which treat of this hepatoscopy are without number, and have been read and translated mainly by Jastrow. In the ancient East, and even in Greece, the hæmatists were for the most part firm believers in astrology, omens, and all that we now brand with the name of superstition. To dreams, above all, they attached great importance, while the pneumatists, on the other hand, as is shown by the writings of Hippocrates, declared dreams to be unworthy of consideration. The pneumatists seem to have borne the reputation of being enlightened persons, or sometimes even atheists, as was the case with the pneumatist Socrates as delineated by Aristophanes. From certain fragmentary indications we may perhaps gather that in the main the Christians of the early centuries were pneumatists in their knowledge of nature.

From the mental standpoint of the hæmatic astrologer every actual group of relations amongst the planets mirrored itself in all synchronistic events and conditions, and thus the entire horoscope would be reproduced in the variations and peculiarities found in the liver—the central organ—of the newly-born sacrificial animal. An expert examination of the liver could therefore quite well take the place of a direct observation of the sky. The practice of hepatoscopy was extensively diffused, and diagrams illustrative of the art are still extant. The method adopted by the Babylonians was to portion out the liver in what may be called oracular squares by means of a right-angled system of ordinates, a device reminding us of the square sections shown by the extant Egyptian projection of the heavens made in the time of King Seti, and likewise of the square figure used as the ground-plan of the normal horoscope. Among the Etruscans, however, hepatoscopy employed a polar projection in its construction of oracular fields, and to this arrangement corresponds the system of regular polygons designed to represent the relative positions of the planets in the circular horoscope.

Another way of dispensing with direct observation of the heavens was to watch the forms assumed by certain substances when suddenly placed under new conditions, as it was supposed that the forms thus produced were determined by the configuration of the planets at the time. Oil or melted tallow was dropped into water, or water into oil, and the diviner took note of the resultant forms. We possess two comprehensive lists drawn up in the reign of King Ḫammurabi of Babylon for the express purpose of interpreting these formations. This mode of divination still survives in the superstitious practice of dropping molten lead upon a cold surface.

A further variety of oracle was found in dreams, to which reference has already been made. Dreams also were believed to run parallel to the facts of astrology, and might, therefore, be substituted for the latter. But, as dreams were held to have their origin in the blood, their significance was conceded by the hæmatists only.

Finally, every unaccountable phenomenon of nature—from the movement of an animal to a monstrous birth—everything, in short, that touched human life at any point, came to be associated with planetary influence, and might become the basis of divination. The library of Sardanapalus contains thousands of tablets in which such superstitious ideas and practices are expounded with the most precise casuistry. They seem to have been regarded as the supreme and final expression of wisdom, and might relate to matters a thousand years old. But these fallacious issues of man's search for knowledge, involving such a prodigal expenditure of energy in collecting data, find their ultimate explanation in the fundamental misconception of astrology, viz. that the incidents of life, being dependent upon the contemporaneous configuration of the planets, must exhibit a parallel order in their occurrence, and that accordingly valid inferences regarding either of the parallel series may be drawn from the other. The underlying conception of the whole procedure, however, was that of the astrologer, and hence we find that in the system of divination by bowls which was practised in the time of Ḫammurabi, the instantaneous formations of dropped grease were regarded as yielding actual knowledge of the planetary deities.

11. Subsidiary tables.—The various substitutes for astrological diagnosis might become, and, indeed, necessarily became, very important, as it was often difficult to determine the requisite facts concerning the planets. We must remember that the problem usually set before the astrologer was to draw the horoscope of the birth or conception of an individual at a time when years had elapsed since these events, and by this means to forecast the future. His task was, in short, to re-construct the astrological conditions of a past event, and he had in consequence to refer to tables or lists of earlier astronomical observations. As regards the sun and the moon, the information he required was furnished by the calendar, but special lists were necessary for the five smaller planets. An extensive table of this kind, written in the Demotic character of Egyptian, and dating from the reign of Augustus, has been preserved. The Julian emperors, let us remember, used to settle their retired soldiers in Egypt. Colonies of veterans thus established in the Fayum would be largely drawn from those who had been born in the reign of Augustus. It was therefore necessary that the astrologer who practised his art in this province should possess lists of the successive positions of the planets during that reign. The example before us is but the transcript of a transcript: whole lines are wanting, and figures have been misread. We may thus infer that such lists were produced in great profusion to meet the needs of astrologers in the various districts and villages. In order to make the proper entries in the horoscope required, the astrologer needed simply to know the zodiacal signs in which the several planets were situated at the time, and accordingly the information supplied by the astrological lists regarding any particular planet was confined to the day of the month on which it entered a new sign. The ancient lists of ephemerides were thus neither more nor less than astrological tables.

For predictions of a general kind the astrologer constructed 'nativities,' while for cases of sickness he drew horoscopes of the κατάκλισις, *i.e.* the inception of the disease, and otherwise adapted his art to special circumstances. He had to be informed of the day, month, and year of the critical event. The signs occupied by the smaller planets at the given date were then noted down from lists like that of the Berlin Papyrus 8279; the moon, together with the day indicating its age, was inserted in the proper sign according to the calendar of the lunar cycle, its lunar station being also fixed by established rules; the sun was placed according to the date. The next step was to arrange these particulars systematically in the twelve houses, the exact hour of the event, or, failing that, the time of sunrise, being used as the determining point. From this, again, the positions of the planets relative to one another, to the eastern point, and to the different zodiacal signs, were deduced and interpreted.

12. The horoscope of Jesus Christ.—As an illustration we shall take the horoscope of the conception of Jesus, according to the form in which we are able to re-construct it from the Demotic table of the planets in the Berlin P. 8279. The dates given are themselves products of astrological speculation, and cannot be regarded as historically established, but they are nevertheless worthy of notice. On the 24th of June, B.C. 7 (or previously), took place the conception or birth of John the Baptist. On the 15th of April, B.C. 6, 5 a.m., the annunciation to Mary (instead of the conception of Jesus), and, at the same time, the observation of this 'nativity' by the Magi. Between the 24th of June, B.C. 6, and the 25th of November, B.C. 6, occurs the visit of the Magi to King Herod. After the 25th of November, B.C. 6, the Magi notice the re-appearance of the stellar configuration at the annunciation. On the 27th of December, B.C. 6, the stellar configuration becomes stationary (ἀστὴρ ἔστη), and the Magi worship the infant at Bethlehem.

Now the horoscope of the 15th of April, B.C. 6, can be re-constructed thus:

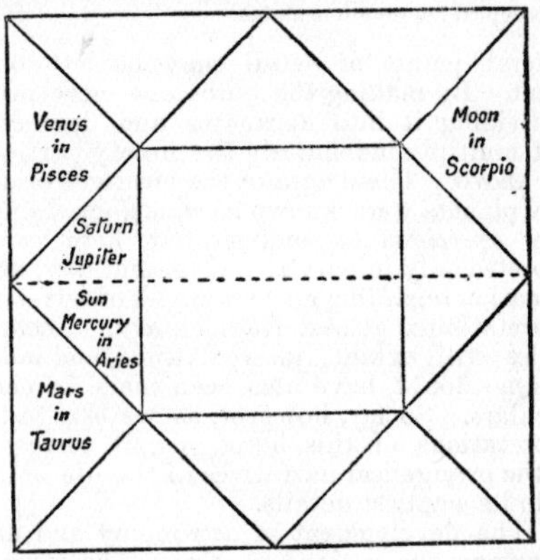

and supplies the following apotelesmata capable of interpretation:

(1) The horoscope of the day appears (with sunrise). (2) Aries is in the ascendant. (3) Mars, as lord of the house of Aries, presides over the birth. (4) The sun is in the ascendant. (5) Saturn in the ascendant. (6) Jupiter in the ascendant. (7) Mercury in the ascendant. (8) Saturn in the ascendant, and above the horizon. (9) Saturn is intercepted between the favourable planets Venus and Jupiter. (10) Mars in the second house. (11) The moon enters the eighth house. (12) Venus is in the twelfth house. (13) Mercury in the house of Mars, and likewise in immediate proximity to Mars. (14) Saturn is in his ταπείνωμα, or 'detriment.' (15) The sun in his ὕψωμα, or 'exaltation.' (16) The moon in her ταπείνωμα. (17) Venus in her ὕψωμα. (18) Venus is *matutina* (morning star). (19) Jupiter is in proximity to his house Pisces. (20) Jupiter in trine (*adspectus trigonalis*) with his house Sagittarius. (21) The sun in trine with his house Leo. (22) Saturn's motion is direct. (23) Jupiter is direct. (24) Mars is direct. (25) Venus is retrograde. (26) Mercury is direct. (27) Mercury is combust. (28) Mercury in immediate proximity to the sun. (29) Mercury is invisible. (30) Mars is not combust. (31) Mars is nevertheless invisible, and is, in fact, entering upon its invisible period of three months. (32) Mars is separated from the sun by Mercury. (33) Saturn is separated from the sun by Jupiter, though the latter is combust. (34) Jupiter is combust. (35) Jupiter is separated from the sun by small planets. (36) All the morning stars are visible. (37) All the evening stars are invisible. (38) Mars is situated in his nocturnal triangle. (39) The terrestrial triangle contains Mars only, its nocturnal lord, situated in Taurus. (40) Mars is in opposition to his house Scorpio. (41) The moon in trine with her house Cancer. (42) The moon is in her domain. (43) The trigonum of fire contains its lords conjoined in Aries. (44) The trigonum of water contains its diurnal lady Venus. (45) The trigonum of water contains its nocturnal ruler, the moon. (46) The moon and Venus are in trine. (47) The trigonum of air is empty. (48) Saturn and Jupiter are in conjunction. (49) This conjunction occurs in Aries, and is thus *conjunctio maxima*, and dominates the entire horoscope. (50) This *conjunctio maxima* was preceded by a *conjunctio magna*, occurring in Pisces (indicating the astrological necessity for the forerunner, John the Baptist). (51) Saturn is in conjunction with the sun (but cf. 33). (52) Saturn is in conjunction with Mercury. (53) Mars and Mercury are in different houses, but close together. (54) Saturn and Venus are in the same relation. (55) Jupiter is in conjunction with Mercury. (56) Venus is visible. (57) Saturn is visible. (58) Jupiter is visible. (59) Saturn has no aspect with the moon. (60) Saturn is in *adspectus confinis* with Venus. (61) Saturn is in *adspectus confinis* with Mars, but triply intercepted.

(62) Jupiter has no aspect with the moon. (63) Jupiter is in *adspectus confinis* with Venus, but intercepted by Saturn. (64) Jupiter is in *adspectus confinis* with Mars, but doubly intercepted. (65) The sun has no aspect with the moon. (66) The sun is in *adspectus confinis* with Venus, but doubly intercepted. (67) The sun is in *adspectus confinis* with Mars, but intercepted once. (68) Mercury has no aspect with the moon. (69) Mercury is in *adspectus confinis* with Venus, but triply intercepted. (70) Mercury is in *adspectus confinis* with Mars. (71) Mars is in opposition to the moon. (72) Mars is in trine aspect with Venus. (73) Full moon is just past. (74) No planets are in quartile with each other. (75) Of the tropical signs only Aries is occupied, but it contains four planets. (76) All the planets except the moon are clustered near the sun. (77) All the planets except the moon and Venus are under the influence of the sun (Mars as lord of the sun's house). (78) Jupiter emerges from the sun's beams. (79) Hence the *conjunctio maxima* also emerges. (80) All the visible planets and the moon are situated in the diurnal sky. (81) All invisible planets are in the nocturnal sky. (82) The lord of Saturn's house is Mars. (83) The lord of Jupiter's house is Mars. (84) The lord of the sun's house is Mars. (85) The lord of Mercury's house is Mars. (86) The lord of Venus's house is Jupiter. (87) The lord of the moon's house is Mars. (88) The lord of the house of Mars is Venus. (89) The horoscope, *i.e.* Aries, is masculine. (90) The other occupied houses are feminine.

Several points of detail may be left out of account. By making the horoscope more precise, and dividing it into decanates and degrees, we might multiply indefinitely the ninety particulars given above. These data of the positions occupied by the planets were known as *apotelesmata*. The ninety *apotelesmata* enumerated here can be interpreted only in part at the present day, as our information regarding ancient modes of astrological interpretation is at best fragmentary. According to rules still extant, interpolations and adjustments, no doubt, have also been made in certain particulars. So far, however, as we can test the interpretations of this horoscope, it corresponds with the evangelical narratives of the life of Jesus even in its smallest details.

13. The development of astronomy and astrology among the various peoples.—The foregoing sketch makes it evident that primitive peoples constructed their calendars by direct observation of the heavens. Similarly, it is amongst these primitive peoples, as indeed we might expect, that we find the first steps of the transition from astronomy to astrology. Thus, in the interior of some of the larger South Sea Islands, as, *e.g.*, Borneo, a primitive astronomy and astrology are found amongst the aborigines, while the inhabitants of the sea board, as also of the smaller islands, exhibit a higher development in the science of the stars, partly because their nautical interests demanded a more thoroughgoing observation of the heavenly bodies, and partly because they were influenced by the higher standard of culture attained by the Asiatic races, as is shown, for example, by the fact that the Malay language contains words borrowed from Chinese, Sanskrit, Arabic, and Persian. Of the pictorial writing of ancient Mexico, part of the calendar is all that has hitherto been deciphered; but even this suffices to show striking correspondences between the civilizations of America anterior to its discovery by Columbus and those of the ancient Asiatic races, and not least in astronomy and astrology. The development of these sciences already attained in the Babylonian period or later in the time of Alexander the Great is practically the same as now prevails throughout China, in part of Japan, and, above all, in India.

In the West, likewise, the results of astronomical inquiry were still encumbered with the old superstitious conceptions. The earliest successful attempts to eliminate these conceptions and their effects from astronomy were made about A.D. 1500. It is true that at the zenith of Roman civilization the educated classes tried to throw the lumber of astrology overboard. Certain of the Church Fathers wrought strenuously to oust it from its place. But, on the one hand, the vexed question regarding the date of Easter, which was simply a consequence of combining the lunar calendar of Babylon with the solar calendar of Egypt, and, on the other, the attempt to fix a year for the birth of Christ, gave astrology once more a certain adventitious prestige in Christian life and theology. Fresh vantage ground was also won for it in the secular learning of the Middle Ages by the Western drift of Islām and the Jewish Kabbala. As a matter of fact, the astronomy of the West, and, in particular, the coalescence of astronomy and astrology in the later culture of Western lands, is a development or an importation from the astronomy and astrology of the ancient East.

Until the time of Kepler, astronomy was always bound up with astrology, and its progress was for the most part of a meagre kind. This may seem incredible so long as we confine our investigation to a short period abounding in records, but it is always unsafe to argue from the silence of the earlier records that the apparently fresh facts set forth in the later constitute an actual advance. No candid observer in the field of astrology could fail to notice that, while this or that forecast might happen to be correct, yet in many cases the configuration of the planets, however skilfully interpreted, could not be reconciled with the facts of experience. Certain details of astrological procedure were, therefore, constantly being left behind, as in an ever-seething witches' caldron; and, on the other hand, long disused methods were once more resorted to. This was especially the case when, in periods of unrest, races and civilizations were shaken and mingled together. Detailed research in a narrowly circumscribed period may thus produce the illusion of rapid development in a science which, in its leading features, really remained unchanged from age to age.

The fundamental tenets promulgated by astrology as inviolably true were manifold. From the fourth house, as it seemed, welled up the subsoil water and the springs which fed the rivers, while from the tenth house came the rain. Now when primitive man found the moon in either of those houses he anticipated a flood. But the moon was evidently connected also with the occurrence of menstruation, which was regarded as a periodic overflow of blood. The astrological explanations of these phenomena tended to corroborate one another so fully that the sovereignty of the moon over the liquid element was deemed indisputable. An example of a different kind is furnished by the horoscope of disease, or rather of the κατάκλισις. Here the invalid was the querent, and his malady the quesited, and information regarding them was supplied by the first and seventh houses respectively. Now, in the regular horoscope the sixth house was significant of pain and the eighth of death, and thus the entire western section of the sky from 45° above the horizon to 45° below it was the region of disease. In this expanse, however, the sun, distinguished among the planets as the source of heat, is situated between three and nine o'clock p.m., and this again is the time when the invalid shows symptoms of fever. An easy explanation was thus provided for the increase of febrile temperature, while on the other hand the validity of the science was demonstrated once more. Astrology simply abounded in spurious proofs of this type.

Thus the leading principles and ideas of astrology were looked upon for centuries as incontrovertible. Its failures were attributed to points of secondary moment, save in cases where it seemed more convenient to change the time premised by a whole double-hour, and so to shift the entire horoscope by one house—an artifice which would in general quite invert the first interpretation. Corrections and alterations were thus made in matters of detail, while among the more progressive peoples the general tendency was towards over-refinement in interpretation and an ever-expanding casuistry.

Accordingly there was no real development in the astronomy and astrology of the ancient East within historic times. The extant evidences of the inscriptions go as far back as the period of Šargâni-šar-ali and Narâm-Sin. From the reign of the former eight short texts are all that have as yet been brought to light, and from that of the latter sixteen only, all of the same date. It is not to be expected, therefore, that we shall trace all the details of later astrology in such meagre records. It is surely sufficient for our purpose that the later period, the archives of which may quite well extend backwards to the monarchs just named, yields a mass of evidence to show that astronomy and astrology had by this time reached the status of a closed and rounded system. Inscriptions from the age of Ḫammurabi make it clear that full instructions had already been drawn up for the practice of divination by cups in connexion with planetary configurations. From a period about a thousand years before Christ come the inscribed boundary-stones, the dates of which are indicated by their arrangement of the planetary symbols. Thereafter the richest vein of astrological records is found in the library of Sardanapalus. We learn from these that there was a system of observatories covering the whole kingdom, that there was an established scheme of relays for the professional astrologers and of serial reports regarding their work, and that a State library had been established for the purpose of supplying all needed information in astrology and the auxiliary arts of divination. It is to be regretted that as yet only the *Reports* of the astrologers and the instructions regarding hepatoscopy have been properly edited. The cuneiform texts of the period between Sardanapalus and the beginning of the Christian era are not so rich in relevant information. The astronomical texts of this epoch, however, have found a thoroughly capable editor in Kugler, whose labours were based on the preparatory studies of Strassmaier and Epping, but who, unfortunately, engaged as he was with the productions of a relatively short period, has failed to grasp the subject in its entirety. A final residuum of Babylonian astrology was the perfunctory knowledge of 'the science of the Chaldæans' current in the days of the Roman Empire. From the beginning of our era astrology and astronomy languished on in the various Asiatic countries, but they were borne westwards by the Arabs. Mesopotamia always remained more or less of a *terra incognita* for countries influenced by Græco-Roman civilization.

On the other hand, Egypt became permanently merged in the Roman Empire, and, at a later period, in the Byzantine Empire. It was Egypt, therefore, that brought Babylonian astronomy and astrology into real contact with the West. Even in the most remote times, in a period, it may be, anterior to the First Dynasty, astrology, religion, and medicine were combined as one science at Heliopolis. The high priest of Heliopolis, officially invested with the star-spotted panther's skin, was all along the supreme State astrologer until the imperial age of Rome, and he bore the title of 'great in vision' already alluded to. A hierarch of this order is named in the Bible (Gn 41⁴⁵) as the father-in-law of Joseph—of that Joseph who was himself an interpreter of dreams (40^{5ff.} etc.), and practised the art of divination by bowls (44^{5. 15}), referred to in connexion with Ḫammurabi. On the wall of a tomb dating from the reign of Seti I. we find lists of stars, times of culmination, etc. Extensive tables of ephemerides and a fragment of planetary divination according to the different houses, together with corresponding dream-tables, have survived from the age of Augustus. We possess even horoscope-texts drawn up in the Imperial period. Our minor records of later Egyptian astrology are thus fairly numerous.

Græco-Roman civilization throughout its entire geographical and historical range, until the establishment of the world-empire and its swift decline, never produced such monuments as we find in the great empires of the East. Observatories of colossal proportions, attached to primeval temples containing archives by which the positions of the planets might be traced and tested for centuries and millenniums, were never the work of Greece and Rome. Among the Etruscans, therefore, and subsequently among the Romans, it was the surrogates of astrology that occupied the central place. Apuleius explicitly asserts that the Chaldæans were the founders of astronomy and astrology. But, so far as the Romans concerned themselves with the study, they appealed to the works of an assumed Egyptian king called Nachepso and his astrologer Petosiris of Sais. At a later period Claudius Ptolemæus (A.D. 100–178) was regarded as the final authority in our twin sciences, and beside him we catch a glimpse of the somewhat legendary Hermes Trismegistos. But, as has been already indicated, the claims of astrology were not left unchallenged in this period. About the year A.D. 200 the famous physician Sextus Empiricus wrote a work in six books πρὸς μαθηματικούς, of which the fifth was directed πρὸς ἀστρολόγους. He prefaces his confutation by a sketch of the entire system of knowledge possessed by the Χαλδαῖοι, and in this he provides valuable materials for a thoroughgoing digest of the astrological texts in the library of Sardanapalus.

In this later period, however, astrology has maintained some degree of progress in the Far East. Among the Chinese and Japanese, occult art, in the modern 'fengshui,' seems rather to have taken the form of geomancy. Just as in the Near East astrology gave birth to hepatoscopy, so in China and Japan the interpretation of the planets in the celestial vault has been transformed into divination by the carapace of the tortoise. Similarly the Gypsies have developed a system of fortune-telling from the open hand; and the designation of the convexities of the palm as 'mounts' of the various planets shows us that this practice also is a surrogate of astrology.

LITERATURE.—The significance of astronomy and astrology for the interpretation of the religious conceptions of the ancient East, as also for the exegesis of the Bible, has only recently been recognized. There is as yet no comprehensive work dealing with the subject. Contributions to the study have come mainly from the hand of H. Winckler (especially in *Im Kampfe um den alten Orient*, Leipzig, 1907), of whom A. Jeremias (*Die Panbabylonisten, der alte Orient und die aegyptische Religion*, Leipzig, 1907) has proved an able ally. Fugitive essays have appeared in considerable numbers, principally in publications of the *Vorderasiatische Gesellschaft* and the *Orientalistische Literaturzeitung*; Hinrichs (Leipzig) has also issued a number. At first the new exegetical theory encountered very strong opposition, but afterwards seemed to have won a general assent; more recently, however, the work of Kugler, already referred to and appraised, has given it a partial reverse. K. Sudhoff (*Iatromathematiker, vornemlich im 15. und 16. Jahrhundert*, Breslau, 1902) and the present writer, starting from the history of medicine, have studied the ancient astronomy and astrology, and have arrived at the same results as Winckler, though by a very different path. The present writer has also written numerous essays on the subject, and these have appeared in various periodicals, medical, philological, and theological, esp. *Die Angaben der Berliner Planetentafel*, p. 8279, Berlin, 1903, *Das Horoscop der Empfängnis Christi*, do. 1903. These publications are based upon cuneiform and hieroglyphic (or demotic) texts which have only recently become accessible.

The leading work for the discovery of the relevant cuneiform texts is C. Bezold, *Catalogue of the Cuneiform Tablets in the Kouyunjik Collection of the British Museum*, 5 vols. The shorter texts are to some extent accessible in Thompson, *Reports of the Magicians and Astronomers of Nineveh and Babylon* (1900). Outgrowths of Oriental astronomy and astrology are found in the writings of Claudius Ptolemæus, Claudius Valens, Paulus Alexandrinus, Julius Firmicus Maternus, and Marcus Manilius, and also in the works of opponents, such as Sextus Empiricus, Cicero (*de Divinatione*), Horace, Juvenal, Pliny, and, in the 15th and 16th cents., Hieronymus Cardamus and Pico de Mirandola. Boll, *Sphæra*, is a modern comprehensive work dealing with classical astrology and astronomy, but the author had not the requisite data for a corresponding treatment of the ancient East. The latest cuneiform texts from the period of the Persian kings and the Seljūks have been utilized by Kugler in vol. i. of a work to be completed in 5 vols. E. Stucken, *Astralmythen* (Leipzig, 1907), admirably depicts the process by which the myths and legends of the various races of mankind grow out of the same original astrological conceptions, and arranges the stupendous mass of materials according to their affinities with the Biblical narratives regarding Abraham, Lot, Jacob, Esau, and Moses. A short manual of astrology by Ernst Mayer, entitled *Kurzes Handbuch der Astrologie*, and giving technical information about the placing of the horoscope, was published by Dekker (Berlin, 1891). A vast aggregation of data relating to the vestiges of astrology in Asia and the South Seas may be gleaned from the *Mittheilungen der deutschen Gesellschaft für Natur- und Völkerkunde Ostasiens*, in *Der Janus* (*Archiv für Gesch. der Medicin*), and in the publications of Sanskrit scholars. The attempt to furnish a more detailed bibliography than the present is always confronted with the difficulty of knowing which of the manifold ramifications of our subject the reader is interested in. In one or other of the leading works here cited, however, the student will find a more complete list of works relating to the particular field of inquiry with which he is concerned.

F. VON OEFELE.

SUN, MOON, AND STARS (Primitive).—Knowledge of the movements of the heavenly bodies is possessed in varying degrees by most primitive peoples. In the earlier stages of civilization that continued observation which is necessary to arrive at a reasoned explanation, which is the foundation of astronomical science, is not possible through lack of proper means of recording its results, nor is it called for by the practical requirements of a population which lives chiefly by hunting. For an agricultural people, however, foreknowledge of the recurring seasons becomes essential, and it is necessary that some means should be found to mark the proper seasons for performing the operations to ensure the food supply. In the stars, with their regular motions of rising and setting, primitive man has found the earliest and most convenient calendar. In default of a theory based upon a series of observations, the supposed movement of the sun round the earth, the phases of the moon and the motion of the stars, the shape and character of the sky, have been explained by formulæ composed of material drawn from the texture of man's religious beliefs. The celestial bodies, equally with his fellows and material surroundings, he considers to be animated with a personality like his own, though more powerful. Starting from this fundamental assumption, primitive man has fashioned for himself, in his legends, a fairly complete explanation of the celestial phenomena which come under his observation.

1. Sun and moon.—It is almost universal among primitive races that both sun and moon should be regarded as alive and quasi-human in nature. Their sex differs among different races, but the moon is more commonly male and the sun female. Relation between them, varying in character, is also recognized. Among the Dieri of Australia the sun is the daughter of a Dieri woman, who after her birth sank into the earth in shame. The natives of Encounter Bay say that the sun is a woman who has a lover among the dead. Each night she descends among the dead. At her rising she appears in a red kangaroo skin, given her by her lover. A Wotjobaluk legend relates that the sun is a woman who was digging yams and reached the West; after wandering round the earth she came back to the other side, and has done the same ever since. The Wurunjerri say that the sun is the sister of every one. This may be compared with the story of the origin of the sun told by the Arunta. At Alice Springs there is a tradition that in the Alcheringa the sun came out of the earth at a spot now marked by a stone in the country of the Bandicoot people, in the form of a spirit woman, accompanied by two other Panunga women, who were sisters, the elder of whom carried a child. The spirit woman went up into the sky, and she does this every day, visiting the old spot at night and rising in the morning. A medicine-man could see her in the hole, but not a person with ordinary vision. The two women settled among the Bandicoot people, and originated a local sun totem. This totem may be compared with the sun totem of the Incas. The sun has a definite relation to each individual member of the various divisions, belonging itself to the Panunga division, as did the two women. Among these people a ceremony connected with the woman and the child is performed, in which symbols of the sun are worn.

The Masai say that the sun married the moon, and they had a fight. Each damaged the other. The sun was so ashamed that he became bright, in order that people might not be able to look at him. The moon was not ashamed, and it is possible to see that her mouth is damaged and that one eye is missing.

It is interesting to note that, while the sun is a man and the moon a woman, the Masai word for sun, *eng-oloñg*, is feminine, and *ol-apa*, 'the moon,' is masculine. The Bushman story goes that the sun was an old man, from whose armpit light radiated; some children threw him up in the sky, where he stuck.

Occasionally both sun and moon are feminine. Among the Mantras the sun is a woman, who is continually being pulled by a string held by her lord. The moon is a woman, the wife of Moyang Bertang, who sits in the moon making nooses for men.

(*a*) *Origin and movements of the sun.*—The origin of the sun, as related in the Tembeh legend of Sam-mor and his battle with Naing, has advanced beyond the anthropomorphic stage. When Sam-mor had imprisoned Naing, he rolled the fire with which he had fought into a ball, and this, as the sun, still revolves round the mountain to watch Naing. This conception of the sun as inanimate is probably due to external influence, but it has a parallel among the Gallinomeros of Central California, where the hawk and the coyote, after jostling one another painfully in the darkness which then prevailed, collected two masses of inflammable substance; the hawk then flew up into the sky with them, and lighted them with flint. They give light as the sun and the moon. The Wurunjerri believe that the sun was made by Puppu-imbul, one of the race inhabiting the earth while everything was dark. This personage, it is hardly necessary to point out, belongs to the race of demiurges of which Prometheus is the type.

The sun did not always cross the sky in the same leisurely manner as at present. The great feat of Maui, the Maori hero, was that he tamed the sun. According to one version, he beat him so unmercifully that he lamed him, and he has walked slowly ever since. In Samoa the sun had a child by a Samoan woman, who trapped the sun by a rope made of vine. Another Samoan lassoed the sun, and made him promise to go slowly. The same or an analogous explanation is found in Aztec folk-lore and in North America. On the other hand, in Australia and in Melanesia the sun did not set. In the myth of the aborigines of Victoria, Norralie decided that the sun should disappear at intervals, and addressed it in an incantation, 'Sun,

sun, burn your wood, burn your internal substance, and go down.' The sun now burns his fuel in a day, and goes below for fresh firewood (R. Brough Smyth, *Aborigines of Victoria*, iv. 430). In Melanesia Qat (the Melanesian hero) went to Qong ('night') and begged assistance. The latter put him to sleep, and, in twelve hours or so, crept up from the horizon and sent the sun crawling to the West (Codrington, *JAI*, Feb. 1881). In a Brazilian myth, a man ('the great serpent') who owned night sent it in a gourd to his daughter on her marriage; the messengers opened the gourd and let it out.

Various explanations are given of the sunset. The simplest is that the sun sinks into a hole, occasionally the hole from which he arose. The Dieri say it sinks into a hole near Lake Eyre, and in the night travels underground to the East, in the same manner as it was believed to do in ancient Egyptian belief. Not infrequently the sunset myth takes the form of a legend of a personal hero plunging into the body of a personal night. Maui was caught in the mouth of Hine-nui-te-po, 'Great Daughter of Night,' and thus brought darkness and death into the world. Since then the sun descends into the under world, and repeats the battle with Hine-nui-te-po every night. An explanation of sunset is that Maui took fire, and when it burnt him he plunged into the sea. Among the Basutos, all men but Litaolane were devoured by a monster. He also was swallowed, but cut his way out. The Zulu story of the rescue of Princess Utombende is of a similar character.

(*b*) *Origin and movements of the moon.*—The moon occupies a prominent place in primitive folklore for which her periodical growth, diminution, and disappearance, phases more marked than those of the sun, may not unreasonably be held to be responsible. Like the sun, the moon is regarded as a living person. Allusion has already been made to the variation in the attribution of sex to the moon among different peoples. One or two further instances which illustrate other points of lunar mythology may be added. Among the Aruntas the moon is a big man (*etwa oknurcha*). They say that, when there was no moon in the sky, a man died and rose again as a boy. The people ran away. He said, 'Do not run away or you will die. I shall die, but will rise again in the sky.' He grew up and died, reappearing as the moon. Since then he dies periodically. When he is not visible, he goes away to his two wives who live in the west. A second legend of the origin of the moon, which is found among the same tribes, relates that the moon was carried by a blackfellow in the hollow of his shield, who hid it in a cleft of the rocks during the day. Once it was stolen from his shield while lying on the ground. He pursued the robber but could not catch him, so he shouted that the moon should go up into the sky and give light to the people during the night. In South-East Victoria in one myth the moon is an old man who climbed a tree to pick grubs. His sons made the tree grow to the sky, where he became the moon. The Dieri say that there was once no moon; the old men held a council, and a *mura-mura* gave them a moon in order that they might know when to hold their ceremonies. The same reason for the moon's existence is given among the Todas.

The marks on the face of the moon are explained in various ways. The Eskimos say that these marks are the ashes which were smeared on his face by his sister the sun, when he tried to embrace her. Among the Besisi it is said that their chief ancestor Gaffer Engkoh once fell to earth and climbed back to the moon by means of a festoon which he plaited. His comrade Porang Aliyan ascended with Engkoh, but the latter slipped back quickly, taking his rope with him. Porang now dwells in the moon, protecting the souls of the dead who visit the moon from wild beasts. The Mantras believe the dark spots on the moon to be a tree. The Malays see in the moon a banyan tree, under which sits a hunchback plaiting a fishing line. When the line is finished, he will fish up everything on earth, but a rat always gnaws away the line. This belief also occurs in Sumatra. The Malays also say 'the moon is great with a mouse deer,' a belief possibly derived from the Sanskrit idea of the hare which was taken up into the moon for protection. In Mexico it was said that a god smote the moon in the face with a rabbit (Sahagun, viii. 2); in Zululand and Tibet a hare was translated to the moon. The connexion between the hare and the moon is also found among the Namaquas of South Africa. The hare was sent to men to confer upon them a return to life after death, but by a mistake in the message made them mortal. In Fiji the same point of human mortality was argued between the moon and the rat. The latter prevailed.

The Wotjobaluk also connect the moon with a resurrection after death. When all animals were men and women, the moon used to say, 'You up again,' and the dead came to life. An old man said, 'Let them remain dead'; none then came to life except the moon. The connexion is obviously suggested by the necessity for finding an explanation of the phases of the moon. Various explanations are current. The Masai say that the sun carries the moon in his arms when she is tired. After carrying her for two days, he leaves her in his setting-place. On the fourth day she is visible to donkeys. On the fifth day men and cattle see her again. The Wiimbaio say that the moon did not die periodically until so ordered by Nurelli. The natives of Encounter Bay held that the moon was a dissipated woman who spent her time among the men, but when she wasted away they drove her out. While she is in seclusion she feeds upon nourishing roots and becomes plump again (Brough Smyth, *op. cit.* i. 432).

(*c*) *Eclipses.*—An eclipse, whether of the sun or of the moon, is at all times regarded with dread; it is almost universally believed, at the early stages at least, to be caused by a monster who devours, or attempts to devour, the luminary. See art. PRODIGIES AND PORTENTS, vol. x. p. 368 f.

2. Stars.—The belief that the stars are great men and divinities translated to the heavens occurs among nearly every people in the world. Stars are grouped together in constellations which represent persons, many of them large, sometimes including one or more of the constellations of our astronomy. The inhabitants of Torres Straits include in their constellation Tagai—a hero who stands at the head of a canoe holding a spear and a bunch of fruit—the Southern Cross, Scorpio, Sagittarius, Corvus, and stars of Lupus and Centaurus. The 'Shark' includes the Great Bear and Arcturus and Gemma. In New Zealand Orion's Belt is Maui's Elbow, while the Southern Cross is identified with the stern of the canoe of Tamarete. Among the Wurunjerri of Australia α and β Crucis and α and β Centauri and other stars are the sons of Bunjil, the latter himself being Altair. Two stars on either side of him are his wives, who belong to the black swan totem, while his brother Nurong and his wives are Antares and adjacent stars. Bunjil and his sons were translated to the sky in a whirlwind. The whole group is intimately connected with the totemic system, Bunjil or Pund-jel being an Australian demiurge. At Alice Springs in Australia the Aruntas say the Evening Star is a woman who went into the earth at a spot marked by a white stone at Temple Bar in the Macdonnell Range, leaving her *churinga* behind. Every child conceived at this stone belongs to the Evening Star totem, although it is in the lizard totem country, and any child conceived *near* the stone is a lizard. Orion's Belt is said to be a group of young men dancing corroboree. Jupiter, the 'foot of day' (Ginabong-Bearp), was a chief among the old spirits, a race translated before the appearance of man. Among the Eskimos of Greenland, Orion's Belt is 'the Lost Ones,' a number of seal hunters who lost their way home. The Pleiades, an extremely important group of stars for primitive peoples, were known to the Indians of North America as 'the Dancers,' to the Lapps as a company of virgins, and to the Australians as a group of girls playing corroboree. The Aruntas believed them to be women who went up into the sky and have remained there ever since. A legend of the Wurunjerri runs that, when some young women were digging yams, the crow stole their yam sticks. They were swept into the air, when Bellin-Bellin let the whirlwind out of the bag, and the stars are the fire on the end of their yam sticks. Another version says that the group is Bunjil's daughter and two men who were turned into women by Bunjil's son, each receiving yam sticks from Bunjil's daughter. The almost unvarying association of the Pleiades with women among different races is remarkable. It thus appears that the legends which attribute an heroic and human origin to the stars and constellations contain the germs of conceptions which have been utilized by modern astronomy in mapping out the heavens.

Stars, however, are not always translated human, divine, and 'semi'-divine beings. Allusion has already been made to the Malay and Sakai belief that stars are clefts in a superincumbent rock. Take-mahuta, in the Polynesian story, after separating his father and his mother, stuck stars all over his father's body. Maui, after slaying his sons, placed an eye of each in the heaven as the morning and evening star respectively—a story which represents a transition stage between the two groups of animate and inanimate origin.

It is not surprising to find the stars regarded as the moon's children. The Mantras say that once the sun and moon, who were both women, had many children, the stars. They agreed to devour them. While the sun did as agreed, the moon hid her children, producing them afterwards. The sun, being very angry, now pursues the moon but cannot catch her, though sometimes she succeeds in biting her, causing an eclipse. The same story is told by the Hos of Chota Nāgpur. In this story, however, the sun threw a hatchet at the moon and cut her in two.

For practical purposes among most primitive peoples the stars perform a more important function than the sun. By their rising and setting the times of the feasts and ceremonies are determined, and among agricultural peoples their movements serve as a calendar by which the various operations in cultivating the soil are regulated. In the Torres Straits, Tagai marks the time for new yams and the migrations of turtle; Seg, the time for another kind of yam. The Murray Islanders also use Tagai as a mark in navigation. The rising of the constellation Dorgai, which coincides with the North-West Monsoon, is the time to 'make dance.' The natives of Borneo, especially the Dayaks, watch for the Pleiades to determine when to prepare their ground for planting. When it is estimated that the wet season is approaching, men are sent to the forest to watch for the rising of the Pleiades. The Kenyahs and Kayans of Borneo measure the length of the sun's shadow by means of a marked stick with the same object (C. Hose, *JRAS*, Straits Branch, Jan. 1905). The importance of such observation of sidereal phenomena is evident when it is remembered that in tropical regions the seasons bring little or no sign of change to serve as the farmer's calendar. The Masai recognize that the rainy season is approaching when they see the Pleiades, while in the Society Islands the year is divided into two halves, *Matari-i-inia* and *Matari-i-raro* according as this constellation is visible above the horizon after sunset or not. In fact, over nearly the whole world the rising of the Pleiades is the beginning of the year or a cycle, marks the time for feasts, and is an occasion of ceremonial observance. It may be recalled in passing that Penrose found that the Hecatompedon and the old Erechtheum had been ascribed to the heliacal rising of the Pleiades on May day; and in Britain, it is suggested, while Stonehenge appears to have been built in relation to the rising of the sun at the summer solstice, the 'Hurlers' in Cornwall on *prima facie* evidence seem to have been built in relation to the heliacal rising of the Pleiades on May morning B.C. 1600 approximately.

In some cases the use of the stars as a calendar is not immediately obvious, but is a matter of interpretation. In Australia, Yuree and Wanjel (Castor and Pollux) pursue the Kangaroo (Capella) and kill him at the beginning of the great heat, and the mirage is the smoke of the fire they roast him by. Marpean-Kurrk and Neilloan (Arcturus and Lyra) discovered the ant-pupa and the eggs of the loan bird and taught the aborigines to use them for food. As Tylor points out, these legends and their analogues may fairly be interpreted as indicating the seasons when the pupa and eggs may be found, the great heat expected, and so forth.

3. Signs and omens.—The train of thought underlying primitive astronomical theory would seem peculiarly adapted to foster the magical conceptions and analogies upon which astrological reasoning is based. Omens and signs, favourable and unfavourable, are and have always been the object of constant observation in the past of savage and semi-civilized people. It is, therefore, not surprising that peculiar powers in controlling human events should be attributed to those heavenly bodies which are regarded as endowed with powers similar to but greater than those possessed by human beings. Even when a stage has been reached at which the magic powers of the witch no longer gain credence, belief in the power of the moon or the first star of the evening to grant a wish remains as evidence of a time when the favour of the heavenly bodies was essential to success. Lacking the knowledge necessary for the pseudo-scientific cartography of astrology, primitive races never attained the heights of judicial astrology. Yet the belief that, for instance, a child born under Leo would possess qualities usually associated with a lion is one with which a savage would find himself in full sympathy. The Malays possess an elaborate system by which the year is mapped out into lucky and unlucky periods depending upon a rotation of days, each associated with deities, planets, and lucky and unlucky colours, and are acquainted with the use of the magic squares. But their astrological science has been borrowed from the Hindus and Arabs. In the case of races which may truly be described as primitive, the germ of the science rather than the science itself is found, while vestigial traces of these primitive beliefs linger in the popular folk-lore of civilized countries. The belief that the weather changes with the phases of the moon is found among the Ewe peoples of West Africa, where a certain number of days' rain is said to accompany each of the four changes of the moon. At these times they are forbidden to take purgatives, and children and cattle are born. At the rising of Ezā (Orion) rain falls for seven days in accordance with the number of stars in the group; three days' rain follows the rising of the group Atielo, while the star Toro is peculiarly favourable to huntsmen, who call this time *Ladorgbe*, 'animal chop grass' (P. Fr. Müller, 'Folkloristische Ewhetexte' (Gē-Dialekt), *Globus*, lxxix. Jan. 17, 1901). These beliefs, however, may be regarded as generalizations from imperfect data assisted by magic, rather than as originating in a magical connexion. A less doubtful case of intimate relation between celestial and terrestrial phenomena occurs in the widely distributed belief, still common in European folk-lore, that fertility of crops and success in an enterprise depend on an action undertaken under a waning moon. The Lithuanians wean boys on a waxing, and girls on a waning moon, believing that in the one case it provides strength, in the other, slenderness and grace.

An instance of a belief which most nearly approaches judicial astrology is quoted by Tylor (*Prim. Cult.*[4] i. 129) from Shortland. The Maoris when besieging a 'pa' believed that the result could be foretold by the relative position of Venus and the moon; if the planet were above the moon, the foe would conquer; if below, the home force would be victorious.

LITERATURE.—No comprehensive study of *primitive* astronomy on scientific lines has been made; reference to astronomical legends and a few identifications of stars known to the natives will be found scattered in works dealing with individual races. General principles of study will be found in E. B. Tylor, *Prim. Cult.*[4] 2 vols., 1904, and A. Lang, *Myth, Rit. and Relig.* 1899. See also Sir N. Lockyer, *Dawn of Astronomy*, 1894. For ceremonies connected with the Pleiades see R. Andree in *Globus*, lxiv. no. 22. Instances here quoted are taken chiefly from W. W. Skeat, *Malay Magic*, 1900; Skeat-Blagden, *Pagan Races of the Malay Peninsula*, 1906; A. W. Howitt, *Nat. Tr. of S.E. Aust.*, 1906; Spencer-Gillen, *Nat. Tr. of Cent. Aust.*, 1898; A. C. Haddon, *Head Hunters*, 1901; A. C. Hollis, *The Masai*, 1905; Sir G. Grey, *Polynesian Mythology*, 1855.

E. N. FALLAIZE.

SUN, MOON, AND STARS (American).—

1. Sources.—A large part of our knowledge of the astrology and astronomy of the American Indians is derived from their traditions as reported by early European and American missionaries and travellers. These writers had the advantage of contact with the various tribes before European influence had extensively modified their modes of thought, but they paid little attention to astronomical traditions. The few constellations mentioned by them are seldom identified, and the identifications are frequently indefinite or incorrect. A number of works by native authors give tribal tradition in authentic form, but little astronomy.

In Mexico and Yucatan a few codices, which escaped destruction at the hands of the Spanish priests, contain many complex astronomical symbols of which little is definitely known as yet, but from which, undoubtedly, much will eventually be learned. They are supplemented by hieroglyphs on structures and monuments. In Guatemala there is the *Popol Vuh*, or 'Book of the People' (ed. and tr. Brasseur de Bourbourg, Paris, 1861), and in Peru Salcamayhua's Spanish account of Aymara Quichua antiquities (tr. Markham, Hakluyt Society, 1873). These manuscripts either are of pre-Columbian origin or present pre-Columbian material with slight European modifications. They include some myths and legends having an astronomical basis (cf. also Brinton, *Annals of the Cakchiquels*, Philadelphia, 1885; and *Tres relaciones de antigüedades peruanas*, ed. Ximenez de la Espada, Madrid, 1879). Until recently even scientific travellers have often shown indifference towards astronomical traditions, but ethnologists now recognize the importance of this subject and are collecting material which, in spite of the long contact between Indians and Europeans, affords sufficient evidence of native origin.

In North America these traditions are supplemented by a few valuable star charts. Three have recently been collected amongst the Osages, Pawnees, and Huichols (Dorsey, in *9 RBEW*, p. 378; *Field Columbian Museum Report*, xi. pl. 72; Lumholtz, in *Memoirs of the American Museum of Natural History*, iii. 57 ff.). The two first are intimately associated with the ritual of the tribal secret societies. The Osage chart represents the Hyades, Pleiades, morning and evening stars, sun and moon, and probably the Milky Way and part of Scorpio. The Pawnee chart shows the Pole Star, Great and Little Bear, Northern Crown, Orion, Hyades, Pleiades, Milky Way, and probably Capella; that of the Huichols depicts as stars or constellations the Scorpion (Scorpio) and its Heart (Antares), the Deer (Taurus?), which is pursued by the Dog, a Woman bearing a child, the Crab, Beehive, Humming Bird, and other objects. The winter counts of the Western tribes represented each year by some important event, which is pictured upon a buffalo hide. Naturally they include astronomical figures. That of Lone Dog, for example, presents the meteoric shower of 1833, a comet, and a solar eclipse. The altars of Pueblo secret societies furnish numerous stellar symbols, as is shown by the researches of Cushing and Fewkes in *RBEW*, *JAFL*, and *Amer. Anthropologist.* Tablets inscribed with astronomical characters have been found at Rockford, Illinois, Mitchell Co., North Carolina, and in Missouri. Excepting the rayed solar face, crescent moon, and morning and evening stars, the characters upon these tablets have not been satisfactorily deciphered.[1]

The Mexican calendar stones present another and an elaborate source of astronomical symbolism, to which considerable study has been directed (see CALENDAR [Mexican]). Inscribed stones of astronomical significance have also been found in the Chibcha region of Colombia. The symbols seem to correspond with those ascribed to the Chibcha calendar and constellations by Duquesne (cf. Bollaert, *Antiquarian Researches*, London, 1860; also Humboldt, *Researches*, and Lemly, in *Century Mag.*, 1891, p. 885). A circular gold 'zodiac' from Cuzco presents a solar rayed face surrounded by twelve unknown symbols (Bollaert, *op. cit.* p. 146; Markham, *Cuzco and Lima*, London, 1856, pp. 107–108; Winsor, *Critical and Narrative History of America*, Boston, 1884–1889, i. 235). A wooden box from the west coast of South America figured by Kingsborough (*Mexican Antiquities*, London, 1831, iv.) presents Peruvian symbols of the sun and moon, Orion, Taurus, the Pleiades, and other constellations, but they are associated with symbols of European origin.

A most valuable source of astronomical knowledge is the Peruvian star chart of Salcamayhua, a pure-blooded Aymara of the ruling class, who wrote during the first quarter of the 17th century. With the exception of a prudential reference to the symbol of the Southern Cross, this chart presents only native concepts. It gives symbols of the sun and moon, morning and evening stars, southern pole, Coal Sack, Milky Way, and all the zodiacal asterisms (cf. Hagar, in *Compte Rendu du Congrès international des Américanistes*, Paris, 1900, p. 271 ff.).

2. Scientific knowledge.—The use of gnomons, natural and artificial, was wide-spread in America. Amongst many of the tribes there are still old men who delight in determining the seasons and the time of day by the position and direction of the solar shadows. The Pueblos have measured and named the sunrise points on the eastern horizon so as to divide the year into two periods of six months, and the time of the equinox is determined with great care. The Zuñis used as a gnomon an erect sandstone slab adorned with a solar effigy (Dellenbaugh, *North Americans of Yesterday*, New York, 1901, pp. 305–306; Fewkes, *Annual Ceremonies at Walpi*, Leyden, 1895).

At Chapultepec, in 1775, a stone was found under which three crossed arrows pointed accurately to the equinoctial and solstitial sunrise points (Bollaert, in *Memoirs of the Anthropological Society of London*, i. 210 ff.). The main doorway of the chief temple of Cuzco fronted the north-east, so that at the June solstice the rays of the rising sun would penetrate into the temple and illumine the solar plate at the opposite end, thus recalling the temples of Egypt and Greece; and the early Christian cathedrals oriented to the sunrise point on the day of the saint to whom they were dedicated. It is not unlikely that the orientation of Mexican and Peruvian structures will enable future investigators to determine the dates of their construction by means of the method so brilliantly pursued by Lockyer in Egypt and Penrose in Greece (Lockyer, *Dawn of Astronomy*, London, 1894). Beebe has shown that the monolithic gateway and a large stone platform at Tiahuanaco probably served as a solar dial. The

[1] See *Proceedings of Davenport Acad. of Sciences*; J. P. McLean, *The Mound Builders*, Cincinnati, 1879, p. 118; Short, *North Americans of Antiquity*, New York, 1880, p. 38. W. S. Beebe, who made a special study of the Davenport and Piqua tablets, attempted a full explanation of both. He makes the former wholly and the latter partly astronomical, but his interpretation of the latter stands little chance of acceptance in the present stage of our knowledge. A copy of his privately printed notes is deposited in the Davenport Academy, Davenport, Iowa. One is in the author's possession.

sides of the pyramids of Mexico and Central America are often aligned to the cardinal points. In Mexico, Nobel describes a perpendicular shaft in the pyramid of Xochicalco which permitted the rays of the zenith sun to fall upon an altar in an interior chamber. The shadows cast by the steps of the pyramid of Papantla were observed for calendar purposes (Humboldt, *Researches*, ii. 87), and tradition indicates a similar use of the steps and platforms at Cuzco known as the 'Monkeys' Dance.' Mrs. Zelia Nuttall, moreover (*Boas Anniversary Volume*, New York, 1906, pp. 290–299), points out various pictographs in the Mexican codices which represent priests observing the stars to determine the time. The different divisions of time were marked by the sounding of drums or trumpets in the temples. The priests used various methods to fix the position of the asterisms. They observed them through the doorway of the temple, which was elevated above the surrounding country, sometimes placing forked or bifurcated sticks within the doorway to define the position more exactly, and sometimes using a peculiar figure representing the drawn-up limbs of a seated man for the same purpose. A possible use of rows of upright sticks is also indicated.

The Peruvians are also said to have noted the solstices and equinoxes by means of the shadows cast by certain columns. Those on the equator were held most sacred, because at the equinox they cast no shadow (Garcilasso de la Vega, *Commentarios reales de los Incas*, vi. 22). These columns have never been found, but circular stone sun-dials, called *intihuatana*, 'the sun tied up,' exist on the Carmenca hill at Cuzco, where the 'columns' are said to have stood, and elsewhere. A shadow is cast thereon by a small erect stone, which, Squier suggests, may rightly have been known as the *inti rucana*, or 'sun-finger.'

Alleged telescopic tubes have been found in the mounds of the United States and in Peru (Bollaert, *op. cit.* pp. 213, 276; du Gourcq, in *Popular Science Monthly*, xlv. 832), but were probably used by the physicians, who in the latter country were expert in sucking poison from wounds and diseased tissues. The Mexican astronomers, however, seem to have employed obsidian mirrors in their observations (Nuttall, 'Fundamental Principles of New and Old World Civilization,' in *Peabody Museum Publications*, ii., Cambridge, Mass., 1901).

The more advanced American nations, such as the Mayas and Aztecs of Mexico, and the Aymaras and Quichuas of Peru, seem to have attained an astronomical knowledge nearly, if not fully, equal to that of any people prior to the invention of telescopes; they had learnt all that could be learnt by the unaided eye. Their principal practical incentive to stellar observation was the accurate determination of seed-time and harvest, this being elaborated into a calendar. They do not seem to have attained to the heliocentric system, but they knew the cause of the lunar phases, and distinguished the five brighter planets. The Mexicans estimated their synodic periods accurately, and the Peruvians observed the sun-spots (Humboldt, *Vues des Cordillères*, ii. 302, *Researches*, ii. 173; Salcamayhua, *op. cit.* p. 131; du Gourcq, *op. cit.* p. 825), large spots being sometimes visible to the naked eye through the mist or light cloud (*garua*) which is of common occurrence in Peru. In some myths the sun and other celestial bodies, and even the earth, are represented as balls or globes. This does not necessarily imply either European influence or exact knowledge. It may be an analogy derived from the supposed hollow ball of the sky.

3. Astrology.—A system of astrology was undoubtedly in vogue in America. The *Tonalamatl*, or book of lucky and unlucky days, included in the Mexican codices, indicates the propitious and unpropitious times for performing certain actions. In the Codex Vaticanus a human figure appears surrounded by the day signs, which have also zodiacal associations. The commentator says that the influence of month signs upon the moment of birth was an established belief.

'The Mexicans,' says Sahagun (*Historia general de las cosas de Nueva España*, iv. Introd.), 'take much care to know the day and hour of birth of each person in order to conjecture his destiny, life, and death, but they do not base their prognostications upon the positions of the stars.' Nevertheless, the stars warn a god that he must go away in five years (H. Phillips, jun., in *Proc. of American Philosophical Soc.* xxi. 617 f. [Philadelphia]). In Guatemala diviners were called upon to determine the propitious date for each monthly festival. As soon as a child was born, it was brought before the diviner, who, observing the day of birth, told what the child would be and what disposition it would show. He announced these things after consulting a book which contained the month and day signs (Ximenez, *Las Historias del origen de los Indios de Guatemala*, Vienna, 1857, pp. 158–160). In Peru one class of priests devoted themselves to divination by observation of the stars, and the chief priest dwelt away from the Inca capital that he might observe them and meditate more freely upon them. In the solitude of the mountain deserts lived priests who contemplated and adored the stars 'almost without ceasing.' People visited them to learn about lost articles, absent friends, and future events. Even the wild tribes of Eastern Peru regard some constellations as propitious to man, others as hostile (Lorente, *Hist. del Peru*, Lima, 1860, p. 229; Markham, *Cuzco and Lima*; von Tschudi, *Travels in Peru*, New York, 1854, p. 288; 'Relacion anonima,' in *Tres relaciones de antigüedades peruanas*, pp. 157, 164, 178).

It is said that the coming of the Spaniards had been predicted many times by these observations. Atahualpa's general is quoted as saying to his ruler just before the arrival of the Spaniards became known: 'My lord, I watched the stars last night, and saw in them the presage of a great calamity.' Later, Atahualpa himself declared that the appearance of a comet in the Sword of Perseus presaged the death of a man of high rank, and that a similar sign had been seen in the skies a short time before the death of his father, Huayna Ccapac. He was murdered soon after. A diviner, by observing the appearance of the moon, is said to have foretold to Huayna Ccapac the civil war between his sons and the destruction of the Inca rule. Comets and a thunderbolt which fell upon that Inca's Cuzco palace occasioned analogous predictions. Similar prophecies in Mexico were not so clearly attributed to the stars (Garcilasso, *Commentarios reales*, tr. Markham, Hakluyt Society, v. 28, ix. 14; Humboldt, *Views of Nature*, London, 1856, p. 429; Prescott, *Conquest of Peru*, bk. ii. ch. 6).

4. Ritual.—The ceremonials of the various tribes also include astronomical features; in fact many of their elements seem to have originated in the wish to imitate on earth the aspects and movements of the celestial world. The imitations of animals in the dances of the primitive tribes arise among those more advanced to elaborate figures, dances, and processions reflecting the orderly movement of the sun and stars across the sky and the progress of time and of the seasons. The American Indians as a whole are a thoughtful and religious race, much given to ceremonials. Even their games and sports, even their ordinary details of domestic life, are made part of the religious ritual to be ceremonially performed, and from the grandest to the most insignificant details of their ritual much is based upon astronomical symbolism.

In the various ball games found from one end of the continent to the other, the movement of the ball originally represented that of the sun (Brinton,

Myths of the New World, New York, 1868, *American Hero Myths*, Philadelphia, 1882, p. 119). Among the Cherokees, prior to the contest, the opposing teams were carefully instructed in the use of magic formulæ, and the issue was supposed to depend upon the amount of magic power thereby developed (Mooney, in *7 RBEW*, p. 301 ff.). In Yucatan and Central America the ball court itself represented the celestial field. The game was won by the player who drove the ball through a stone ring upon which two interlaced serpents, symbols of the eternal years, were sculptured. The *Popol Vuh* describes contests at this game, the result of which determined the control of *Xibalba*, or Shadow Land; and Mrs. Nuttall asserts that the ball courts were also used as astronomical observatories. The Araucanians saw the divine will in the result of the game, and used it to decide the fate of those accused of crime.

It is probable that the annual ceremonial hunts, once common in the South-western United States, formed a terrestrial imitation of the celestial Hunter, as in Peru, and foot-races also symbolized the solar journey. In the Mexican game of 'those who fly' the celestial revolution was symbolized by four men masked as eagles who circled about a pole at the end of four cords wound round it (Clavigero, *Historia*, ed. Mora, Mexico, 1844; Nuttall, *op. cit.* p. 24 f.). Dice games, common in North America, reflect the celestial imagery on both dice and board. The Mexican game of Patolli uses a cruciform board representing the four celestial regions, through the divisions of which a stone marker progresses like one of the celestial bodies (Sahagun, *op. cit.* vi. 8; Culin, 'American Indian Games' in *24 RBEW*; Nuttall, *op. cit.* pp. 82, 87). A serpent-dance in which the dancers imitated the motion of the serpent existed until recently among the Micmacs and other Northern tribes, and in Peru. In the North the dance symbolized the movement of the Pleiades across the sky (Hagar, in *Congrès international des Américanistes*, New York, 1902, and *JAFL* xiii. 92 ff.). The famous serpent-dance of the Hopis, figured on Mexican and Central American monuments, was a rain-making ceremonial performed in August under the sign of the Tiger Sun (Leo). The well-known mural paintings in the Temple of the Tigers at Chichen Itza represent a similar ceremony also dedicated to the Tiger Sun. In the Mandan buffalo-dance, twelve dancers divided into groups of four represented the cardinal points, and doubtless also the twelve regions and the months. Two of the middle four were painted black and dotted white to represent the night sky and the stars. The other two, painted red, personated the day (Catlin, in *Smithsonian Report*, 1885, p. 359), and the movement represented alternating day and night. The Natchez ceremonially gathered to watch the rising and setting solstitial sun through the doorway of their temple. The sun-dances of various tribes dramatize the progress of time and the seasons. The nocturnal Iroquois feast of the dead seems to have celebrated the return of the spirits to earth over the Milky Way in spring and fall.

At the end of each fifty-two years' period the Mexicans expected that the midnight culmination of the Pleiades would mark the end of the cosmos, or its renewal for a like period. All fires were extinguished, and the advance of the Pleiades towards the critical point was observed from the summit of the mountain called 'Hill of the Star.' The stars having passed the meridian, a fire was kindled upon the summit, from which fires were re-lighted elsewhere, and the people gave themselves over to rejoicing (Sahagun, *op. cit.* tom. i. lib. 4, tom. ii. lib. 7; Torquemada, *Monarquia Indiana*, tom. ii. 292–295; Boturini, *Idea*, pp. 18–21; Clavigero, *Storia antica del Messico*, tom. ii. pp. 62, 84, 85; Mendieta, *HE*, p. 101; Acosta, *Hist. de las Yndias*, pp. 398–399). In Peru as in Mexico this date marked the entrance of the sun into the sign of the dead, symbolizing death, destruction, and renewal.

The rising of the morning star, the Pleiades, and Gemini was hailed with songs and dances by many tribes. In Mexico there was an annual sacrifice of a human being, who enacted the yearly course of the sun. He ceremonially ascended the steps of the *teocalli*, or god-house, to represent the sun climbing from the south to the northern solstice. At the moment when the sun reached the meridian he was slain, and his body was hurled down the steps to represent the declining course of the sun after the northern solstice (Hagar, *Peruvian Astronomy*). Similarly, among the Chibchas a human victim fastened on a pole was annually slain by the arrows discharged by a ceremonial procession of people masked and costumed to represent the various zodiacal asterisms (Duquesne, in Bollaert, *Antiquarian Researches*, p. 47).

About the time of the December solstice, though in recent times not every year, the Skidi Pawnees sacrificed a maiden to the morning star. There is no reason to doubt the indigenous origin of this very remarkable and suggestive ritual, which is described in art. PAWNEE, vol. ix. p. 699[a].

In similar obstacle legends among the more advanced tribal families of the American Indians there are indications that the astronomical symbolism was itself used to typify as the ultimate meaning the progress of the human soul (cf. Dorsey, in *Congrès international des Américanistes, XVe session*, Quebec, 1907, ii. 66–70, and Natalie Curtis, *The Indians' Book*, New York, 1907, pp. 102, 103; the deductions are the writer's, and will be found further developed in his *Peruvian Astronomy*).

A monthly ritual is known to have existed among the Pueblos, Mexicans, Mayas, Central American tribes, Peruvians, and probably the Chibchas. Among all of them the features of these festivals referred to some attribute of the zodiacal asterism through which the sun was supposed to be passing at the time.

The plan of the Peruvian temple of Cacha, or 'the messenger,' as well as the remarkable legend connected with it, points to a ceremonial procession enacting the yearly course of the sun within the building. The importance of the stellar cult in Peru is indicated by the fact that the Peruvians made images of all their constellations.

5. Mythology and star-lore.—The arch of the sky was generally regarded as a kind of transparent roof, over which the heavenly bodies walk. The Chinooks on the north-west coast and the Peruvians represented it by two oblique lines meeting in an acute angle. Possibly the 'Maya arch' possessed a similar symbolism.[1] On the Peruvian box the sky is seen as a woman's breast. It forms the clothing of the Huichol eagle-goddess and of the wife of the Pawnee Spirit of Life, and is symbolized by the concave interior curve of some Central American and Pueblo vases (Dorsey, *op. cit.* p. xviii; Stevenson, *op. cit.* p. 24). Above the sky dwells the Sun Father, with his wife the Moon Mother (who is sometimes also his sister), attended by the divine pair of the morning and evening stars, and surrounded by their stellar children.

The sun and moon were regarded as the progenitors of the stars and of mankind, but seldom or never as the supreme celestial powers. They

[1] Collection of A. F. Chamberlain; Hagar, *Peruvian Astronomy*, Salcamayhua Chart.

were the objects of a celestial cult existing practically everywhere in America, in which, at different times and places, sun, moon, and various constellations seem to have assumed predominance without occasioning more than a relative change of influence. Nor is there much evidence of conflict between the votaries of the various aspects of the astronomical cults. Sectarianism was almost unknown in the natural religions of America; such tortures and persecutions as existed in Mexico, for example, had little or no connexion with religious or theological differences. In Mexican tradition two men, one of them leprous, threw themselves into a fire and came out respectively the sun and the moon.

The gender of the sun and moon is sometimes reversed. A legend found in almost identical form among the Eskimos, the Cherokees, and the Amazon tribes personifies the moon as a man who secretly visited his sister at night. She, desiring to identify her unknown visitor, rubbed upon his face some black substance, which produced the lunar spots. A similar legend occurs among the Caddos (Dorsey, *Traditions of the Caddo*, Washington, 1905, pp. 11–12). The Iroquois saw in these spots an old woman who each month stirs a bowl of hominy with her cat (dog?) seated beside her. The Peruvians interpreted them as resulting from the embraces of a fox enamoured of her beauty; the Mexicans as a form of a rabbit, with which the gods struck the face of the moon, wishing to lessen its light, which formerly was as great as that of the sun. According to the Mexicans, the moon is always running after the sun, but never overtakes him. The divine being Quetzalcoatl made his son the sun, the god of water made his the moon (Phillips, *op. cit.*). The Onas of Patagonia make the sun pursue the moon (his wife) because she overheard some of the secrets of the male secret society. In terror she sprang off a cliff, the sun followed, and both jumped into the sky, where the pursuit continues (Barclay, in *Geographical Journal*, xxii. 62). In Corvichan tradition the sun, moon, and stars were shut up in three boxes, which were opened by the hero Yehl, whereupon they escaped to the sky (Deans, in *AAOJ* x. 111).

In higher Peruvian symbolism, the sun was tied by an invisible cord to the invisible pole of the sky, and was driven round it like a llama by the power of the Universal Spirit, although generally, after passing over the sky, he was thought to enter a cave in the west and to proceed by a subterranean passage to emerge next morning in the east. An equally interesting explanation of the origin of night and day is found in the Wichita legend (echoed by the Caddo) of the three deer, who are three stars, pursued by a fourth, which is a hunter who will overtake them at the end of the world. One deer is white, representing day, one black, representing night, one half black and half white, representing alternate day and night. The last was wounded, whence we have day and night (Dorsey, *Myth. of the Wichita*, Washington, 1904, pp. 21, 25–26, *Traditions of the Caddo*, pp. 13–14).

Among the Peruvian coast tribes, according to Garcilasso, the sun plunged into the western ocean and dried up the waters with his heat both where he entered and where he emerged—whence, apparently, the tides. In numerous North American legends he is visited by terrestrial travellers, whom he receives kindly, and to whom he sometimes imparts supernatural powers. The Mexicans described how he was once caught in a snare which a hero had contrived for him. This legend, which is also Polynesian, probably refers to the solstices, when the Indians generally thought of him as seated or resting, since they observed that for several days at these seasons he moved neither north nor south at his rising, but appeared at the same point on the horizon. The Mayas accordingly called these days 'the bed of the sun'; and at this time the Mexicans, Mayas, and Peruvians refrained from labour in imitation of the solar repose. The Mayas symbolized the June solstice by a tortoise, that of December by a snail, because of the slow motion of these animals (Forstemann, 'Commentary on Maya MSS' in *Peabody Museum Papers*, vol. iv. no. 1, p. 45, Cambridge, 1904; Schellhas, 'Representation of Deities of the Maya Manuscripts,' *ib.* no. 2, p. 115, Cambridge, 1906).

The Peruvians represented the sun as a bearded man in the prime of life, who impressed his footprint on a rock to mark the height of his power. This affords an explanation of a world-wide type of solar legends. Throughout America the solar rays were symbolized by hair. In Peruvian art the sun becomes the conventionalized face of a man upon which appear marks called tears by some, but perhaps having a pathological meaning. The Mexican hero Citli shoots three arrows at the sun and succeeds in wounding him. The enraged sun returns one arrow, which pierces Citli's forehead (Mendieta, *op. cit.* p. 77). The sun is the Spider Woman of some western tribes, the Ojibwa Wigwam of the Great Spirit, and the Zuñi shield of burning crystal which he carries, while the Kutenai Coyote manufactures the sun out of grease made into a ball (Chamberlain, in *AAOJ* xvii. 69). In Peru an oval plate, the symbol of the All-pervading Spirit, ultimately manifested in fire, earth, air, and water, was called the image of the true sun, of which the solar orb was only the reflexion. The sun, says the Quichua, Blas Valera, was the child of the Creator, and his light was that part of his divinity which the Creator had imparted to him. It was considered sacrilegious to look at his face; but early writers give several accounts of Inca rulers (particularly Huayna Ccapac) who did so, and who declared their scepticism of the supremacy of an object which never rested, but eternally moved upon its track like a driven animal, whose face the clouds obscured. From the nature of their light, gold was sacred to the sun and silver to the moon.

Eclipses were regarded as attacks made by some insect or animal upon the object enshadowed. In accordance with a world-wide custom, a terrific noise was made to frighten away the attacking monster, although the Tlascalans believed that the sun and moon were fighting. To induce them to cease, red-skinned people were sacrificed to the sun and albinos to the moon. The Peruvians thought the sun was angry when his face became obscured, while under like conditions the moon was believed to be ill. If her light disappeared altogether, she was dead and would fall from the sky upon earth, killing every one upon it. Dogs were beaten, as the moon was thought to be fond of them because they had rendered her a certain service, and it was hoped that their cries would induce her to uncover her face. A similar custom existed in Mexico (Ixtlilxochitl, *Hist. des Chichimèques*, Paris, 1840, cap. 6; Oviedo, *Hist. gen. y nat. de las Indias*, Madrid, 1851, xxix. 5; Piedrahita, *Hist. del Nuevo Reyno de Granada*, Antwerp, 1688, v. 1, vii. 6; Garcilasso, *op. cit.* xi. 1).

The altruistic spirit of the Pueblo community may be seen in the legend that the moon was once as bright as the sun, but gave up part of her light that people might sleep at night. According to the Sioux, the diminishing of the moon is caused by the nibbling of field mice, who thus prevent it from growing too large and injuring the earth (*Red Man*, xvi. no. 45). The profile face of the woman in the moon is figured on the Salcamayhua chart. The Osages and the Mexicans seem also to have observed her. As the sun, being a male, watches over the fortunes of men, so the female moon is the guardian of women, to whom appeals for help were addressed in childbirth.

According to the Micmacs and Ojibwas, the stars are the lights of camp-fires before the wigwams of the dwellers in the land of the sky. Here and there we see them grouped in villages, and the brightest represent the largest fires before the dwellings of the chiefs. By other North American tribes they are described as birds that fly to the sky at night, by the Mexicans as eyes. Some Brazilian tribes regard them as rifts in the canopy of the eternally glowing sky-land (Seler, *Codex Vaticanus*, London, 1902, p. 44; Hagar, 'Micmac Star Lore,' MSS; Nery, *Land of the Amazons*, London and N.Y., 1901, p. 47). These simple and primitive notions existed coincidently with the division of the sky into constellations bearing the names of animals, plants, and frequently of inanimate objects.

Among the American tribes we find single stars named after individual objects, and groups forming true constellations; but probably nowhere in America is a constellation recognized which has become conventionalized like our own to such a degree that the derivation of the name is not really apparent from the alignment or other features. The morning and evening stars were naturally the most important of the stellar host. In the legends of the Cherokees, Peruvians, and others, the morning star appears before the first rising of the sun. It is the great star, the warrior, or messenger who goes in advance to announce the coming of his solar master. Its advent was hailed with incense and dances. It was widely symbolized by an equal-armed red cross. An Ojibwa legend makes it an older sister, who at her own desire was borne by the winds into the eastern sky, whilst her brother ran up a high mountain to hunt. So, according to Diodorus Siculus, the divine youth Hesperus went to the summit of a mountain at night to study the stars and a great wind carried him into the sky, where he became the evening star (Schoolcraft, *Hiawatha Legends*, Philadelphia and London, 1856, p. 90 ff.).

Among the Caddos the morning star was the errand man selected by the moon to be his assistant chief and to call the people together. He used to get up early during war expeditions, long before dawn, to go round the camps and wake the people so that the enemy would not find them. That is the reason why he gets up so early now. Morning Star has three brothers, Evening Star, North (Pole) Star, and South Star. Their father's name was Great Star, and he was the chief of the people (Dorsey, *Traditions of the Caddo*, pp. 7–8, 15).

In America the evening star was usually regarded as a woman, because it governed the time of family re-union at home, though among the Zuñis it is the twin brother of the morning star. In Mexico it is the Lord who comes with his torch to light the dwellings on high, in Peru the female maize-grinder, the torch in the west, while among the Micmacs it is leader of the stellar tribe. Its symbol is frequently a white cross. It is the mother of all things to the Skidi Pawnee, who keeps a garden in the west in which the sun rests at night, where the corn is always ripening and much buffalo meat is stored (Schoolcraft, *op. cit.* p. 90 ff.; Cushing, *Zuñi Folk Tales*, New York, 1901, p. 378; Dorsey, *Traditions of the Skidi Pawnee*, pp. xv, 5; Hagar, *Peruvian Astron.*, ch. on 'Cult and Symbol,' pp. xv, 3). As the converse of the morning star, the Caddos believe that the evening star would go back a long distance upon the trail and warn his people if the enemy approached (Dorsey, *Traditions of the Caddo*, p. 15).

The identity of the planets, whether the morning or the evening star, was recognized in Peru, Mexico, California, and parts of South America. The Peruvians made Mercury the ruler of merchants, travellers, and messengers. The Amazon tribes call it 'Deprived of Fish,' since it is believed to cause a scarcity of food fishes. Venus, in Peru, governed the daughters of the rulers, and women generally, dawn, rains, and flowers; Mars, war and soldiers; Jupiter, public matters and food supplies, and to him they offered firstfruits. The Peruvians placed Venus alone of all the stars in the dominion of the sun, evidently because it alone is sometimes visible in the full solar light. Because of its brilliant rays they called it Chasca, 'Curling Hair.' Because of its beauty they said that the sun never permitted it to wander far from his presence—a poetical interpretation of the fact that Venus never departs as far from the sun as the major planets. They also called this planet Chasqui, 'the Messenger,' because its swift passage from star to star suggested the swift running messenger upon the highways (Hagar, *Peruvian Astron.*, ch. on 'Cult and Symbol'). In the codices it is represented by numerous symbols, in the temple of Mexico by a high column, and in the myths it is identified with Quetzalcoatl. The Californian Indians say that the sun has two daughters, Mercury and Venus. Twenty men kill them, and after fifty days they return to life (Mendieta, *op. cit.* pp. 82, 83; Nuttall, *op. cit.* p. 53; Emerson, *Indian Myths, Legends, and Traditions*, Boston, 1885, p. 481; Nery, *op. cit.* p. 251; *Explication Codex Telleriano-Ramensis* in Kingsborough, *Mexican Antiquities*, 191).

The Milky Way in North America generally, and among the Guaranis of Paraguay, was the path of spirits, over which the souls of the dead pass between this world and the sky-land of the hereafter. Those of the good follow the broader and easier arm, those of the evil-doers the narrow and difficult arm. It is the Cherokee and Pueblo 'Way of Meal,' the Micmac 'Ancient Trail' and 'Way of Reeds,' the Californian 'Backbone of the Sky,' the Pawnee 'Dust raised by Buffalo Racing.' A Zuñi legend calls it the 'Great Snow Drift of the Skies' (Stevenson, *op. cit.* p. 25; Cushing, *op. cit.* p. 581; Dorsey, *Traditions of the Skidi Pawnee*, p. 57; Hagar, *Cherokee Star Lore* [in *Boas Anniversary Volume*, p. 354 ff.]). In Peru and at Zuñi, as among the ancient Sumerians, it is associated with a gigantic celestial serpent. On the Osage star chart it is figured as a river, and it appears as a celestial stream in the mythology of the Peruvian and Amazon Indians. In Peru, as in the legends of the Ojibwas and Cherokees, and as in the Euphratean region, China, and Japan, this river is associated with the passage of souls. The Cherokees and the Kutenai also call the Galaxy 'the Way of the Dog,' the tribes of Guiana 'the Way of the Tapir' and the 'Path of the Bearers of Whitish Clay' (Brett, *Indian Tribes of British Guiana*, New York, 1852, p. 107; Chamberlain, in *AAOJ* xvi. 69).

In the sand paintings of the Mission Indians of California the outer circle is called 'Our Spirit,' a name of the Milky Way. The whole represents the world resting on the Milky Way. A gate or door to the north permits the escape of the soul at death.

The Cherokees recognize two dog stars, Sirius and Antares. In spite of the identical name of the former in our tradition, this is probably a native name, for it is explained by a Cherokee legend which bears no resemblance to its Oriental analogue. In it the two dogs act as guardians of 'the Way of Souls,' at the extremities of which they are stationed, and they must be propitiated with food before they will permit the souls to pass. The Winnebagoes, Ojibwas, and Huichols also recognize a dog star, and the Hindus and Zoroastrians likewise place two dogs upon the way of souls. The Caddos say that a dog gifted with prophetic powers talked with its master, the pair becoming two bright stars in the south (Dorsey, *Traditions of the Caddo*, p. 25).

The Pleiades are the most conspicuous constellation in the star-lore and ritual of the American Indians, though in North America they share the leadership with Ursa Major. Throughout America they are known as the stars of harvest and of the propitious rains. Their Peruvian name 'Granary' is echoed by the Eskimo 'Sharing-out of Food.' In allusion to their alignment they were generally known as a group of various objects: in Peru 'the Doves,' in Guatemala 'the 400 Young Men,' and in Mexico 'the 400 Rabbits,' patrons of feasting and of intoxication. They are also the Algonquian 'Sweating-Stones,' referring to the seven stones with which the sacred bath of the medicine-man was heated. Their Maya name and Micmac symbol, the rattle of the rattlesnake, suggest an association with the group of small mounds on 'the Way of the Dead' at Teotihuacan, for these mounds are traditionally dedicated to the stars, and from some of them have been exhumed large and erect rattle figures, which were evidently used as altars.

Another important aspect of the group is that of 'the Dancers,' suggested by the twinkling of the closely grouped stars. The whole stellar world follows the group, as they perform their cosmic dance across the sky; and so on earth their rising was hailed by Brazilians, Cherokees, Micmacs, and probably many other tribes, with an imitative song and dance referring more or less directly to the eternal procession of the heavens. The Iroquois, Housatunnuks, and Cherokees have, or had, an explanatory legend which describes how a group of boys, while dancing, ascended to the sky and became the Pleiades. Among the Caddos there are seven brothers who played all day long. Being scolded by their mother and refused food, they danced round the house, gradually rising from the ground until they reached the sky. As they disliked work, they disappeared in spring, when work time begins (Dorsey, *Traditions of the Caddo*, p. 64). The Blackfeet believe that they ascended because their fathers gave to their sisters, instead of to them, the yellow skins of the buffalo calves they had slain. In revenge they determined to go away each year when the buffalo calf skins became yellow. This occurs in May, when the Pleiades are hidden in the sunlight. The Kiowas call the Pleiades 'the Star Girls,' and they are probably represented by the dancing stellar maidens who descend to earth in the poetic legend of Algon. The seventh Pleiad appears in the Cherokee and Iroquois legends, in the former as a boy who is knocked down with a pole before reaching the sky, in the latter as a star whose light is dimmed because of his desire to return to earth (James Mooney, letter to author; R. W. Wilson, *AAOJ* xv. 149; Emerson, *op. cit.* p. 72; Sergeant, *Housatunnuk Indians*, Boston, 1753; Domenech, *Deserts of North America*, London, 1860; Schoolcraft, *Hiawatha Legends*, p. 116 ff.; Mrs. Erminie Smith, in *2 RBEW*, p. 80).

Almost invariably seven stars are attributed to the group, thus including one star which, though of the sixth magnitude while its companions are of the third and fourth, may be seen by one with strong sight or in a clear atmosphere. The Cherokees also relate that the seventh Pleiad fell to earth, leaving a fiery trail. He became a bearded man, who warned them of the coming flood. So in Peru the approach of the Pleiades to the meridian enabled the llamas of Ancasmarca to warn their shepherd of the coming of the annual deluge or rainy season in November. In Mexico the six *tzontemocque*, or stars which fall at the deluge, seem to have been Taurid meteors (Mooney, in *17 RBEW*, p. 621; *Explication Codex Telleriano-Ramensis*). 'If people will look at these stars (the Pleiades),' runs the Pawnee song, 'they will be guided aright.' Many tribes actually did use them as a guide by night (Morgan, *League of the Iroquois*, Rochester, N.Y., 1857, ii. 106). Everywhere the Pleiades are a peaceful, beneficent, and friendly constellation; and there are some indications in Peru and elsewhere that they were once regarded as being (or having special influence over) the home of souls.

The pole star of the Northern hemisphere seems to have been observed by all, or nearly all, the northern tribes. It is the Ojibwa 'Man who walks behind the Loon,' a disappointed lover, who, metamorphosed into a firefly, flew to the sky; in another version a hunter of bears. The Kutenai call it a female grizzly bear; but this apparently refers also to a constellation which includes Ursa Minor and Ursa Major. The Sioux declare that 'all stars walk around the pole star, which is the star that does not walk.' The Micmacs describe it as a bear hidden in a den, about which a group of hunters (Ursa Minor) eternally circle in a vain attempt to discover it. The Pawnees call it 'the star that does not move,' and regard it as the chief of the stars. In the Southern hemisphere the pole is indicated on the Salcamayhua chart as the apex of two slanting lines, which form the sky roof of the world. To it point three stars of the Southern Cross, called the male group, and having phallic attributes. The Maya name of Vega is 'Scrotum Star,' but this star ceased to mark the north pole several thousand years ago. The Peruvians used the Southern Cross to indicate the divisions of the night, the Mayas to indicate the seasons (Emerson, *op. cit.* p. 58; La Flèche in *AAOJ* vii. 106; Chamberlain, *ib.* 1770; Copway, *Traditional History of the Ojibway Nation*, London, 1850, p. 113 ff.; Dorsey, *Traditions of the Skidi Pawnee*, pp. 3–4).

The stars of Ursa Major seem to have been called 'the Bear' by the Indians of practically the whole of British America and the United States. An accompanying legend is found in almost identical form among the various Algonquian tribes, the Housatunnuks, Iroquois, and the Cherokees, but is given most fully by the Micmacs. The four stars of the body of Charles's Wain, or the Dipper, as Americans call it, form the body of the bear. The three following stars, ϵ, ζ, η, with four trailing behind them in the form of a bow (γ, ϵ, η Bootis, and Arcturus), are seven hunters, who are pursuing the animal. The little star, Alcor, close to the second hunter, is the pot in which they intend to cook her meat. Corona Borealis and μ, δ Bootis form the den from which she climbs down in the spring. In the summer she runs across the sky with the hunters in full pursuit; in the fall she is overtaken and shot, and begins to fall over on her back. The blood from her wound causes an eternal stain upon the breast of the foremost hunter, the robin, and, dripping upon the trees of earth, it gives to the foliage its blood-red autumn hues. But the bear eternally returns to life. Through the winter she lives in her den invisible (below the horizon), to issue forth again in spring, and thus eternally to renew the celestial drama. The seasonal features of the legend correspond accurately with the actual positions of the stars in the early evening. There is good reason to believe that this is a native legend, or at least one of pre-Columbian origin, though the earliest reference to it seems to be by Le Clerq in 1691 (Hagar, in *JAFL* xiii. 92 ff.). In connexion with the hunting concept, it is noteworthy that the Wichitas regard the Great Bear as the patron of those about to engage in war expeditions (Dorsey, *Myth. of the Wichita*, p. 18).

The Blackfeet know the principal stars of Ursa Major as seven boys, all save the youngest of whom (Dubhæ) had been killed by their sister. The Sioux call the four body stars the coffin. It is borne by four men who are followed by mourners. Mizar and Alcor are called 'She who Comes with her Young One Weeping.' The Ojibwas also called these stars 'the Fisher,' and the Zuñis represented them by seven white pebbles in the rites of the 'Priesthood of the Bow.' The Pawnees described Corona Borealis as a circle of chiefs, in whose honour was founded the society of 'Chief Dancers.'

The Belt of Orion among the Point Barrow Eskimos becomes three men who were buried in the snow, the Micmac 'Three Fishermen,' the Zuñi 'Hanging Lines,' and the Patagonian 'Three Bolas,' or round stones with which animals are slain by hunters. The Peruvians, like the Basques and the people of Deccan, call it 'the Steps.' The whole constellation is the Zuñi 'Celestial Hunter' pertaining to the sun. In Peru it is symbolized by crossed arrows, and relates to hunters and hunting. A myth makes it the Promethean figure of a criminal raised aloft for punishment by two condors. It may be connected with the Mexican Citli, 'the Bowman.' The names of a few other constellations and single stars have reached us, but present no features of special interest.

In view of the similar and wide-spread symbolism associated with some constellations in America, a more or less uniform system of celestial symbolism may have existed through a large part of the continent, similar to the primitive symbolism of the eastern continent in some elements, yet unique in others.

Unquestionably many of the symbolical concepts have been transmitted from tribe to tribe for long distances. Many of them are of pre-European, or at least of pre-Columbian, origin, and the analogies which they present with Oriental symbolism must be explained either as like effects of like independent causes or by pre-Columbian intercommunication between the continents. The weakness of the former explanation lies in the complexity and conventionality of the concepts, and in the difficulty of tracing the symbolism to any natural basis. The American zodiacs, for example, reveal analogies with the ancient Oriental zodiacs in every sign, yet in few if any instances, either in the Orient or in the Occident, are we able to explain why these signs were so named or why their symbolical attributes are what they are. The zodiac is older than its seasonal associations; its origin remains unknown, yet we find it in similar form in America and in the Orient. The same argument applies, although perhaps less forcibly, to a large part of the astronomical symbolism of America.

LITERATURE.—The literature has been given throughout the article.

STANSBURY HAGAR.

SUN, MOON, AND STARS (Buddhist).—The astronomical ideas found in Buddhism do not form an independent system, but have developed in close relation with Hindu theories. The problem is rather to determine what stages of development are to be found in the canonical and later books. Thibaut[1] divides Indian astronomy into three periods: (1) that of the Vedas and *Brāhmaṇas*, (2) the middle period with a fully developed native Indian system, (3) the third period, showing Greek influence. The Buddhist scriptures cover a long time, some of the later containing references to the Greeks, but it is to the middle period, and rather to the early stages of this, that the astronomical notions of these works belong. They are in the main the same as those that we find in the *Purāṇas*. The Hindus had two important uses for astronomy: the sacrifices and astrology, neither of which was countenanced by the Buddhists. The latter had no special motive for paying close attention to astronomical theory beyond that required for determining the periods of the lunar month with its fast-days, the period of Retreat in the rainy season, and the divisions of the day. According to *Vinaya*, ii. 217, a monk who lives in the forest is to learn 'the positions of the lunar signs (*nakṣatras*), either the whole or one section, and is to know the cardinal points.'[2] At the end of the ordination service the process of 'measuring the shadow,' *i.e.* calculating the time of day, is performed in order to determine the seniority of the monk, and he is instructed in the length of the seasons and division of the day.[3]

1. Position of sun and moon.—The heavenly bodies that we see are the vehicles of gods, who have been thus reborn through their merit, and who are associated with the thirty-three gods, but below them in rank.[4] The moon, the sun, and the constellations come as gods in the retinue of Sakka to visit Buddha,[5] and in *Dharmasaṃgraha*, 10, the moon, sun, earth, and the *asura* Rāhu occur along with the guardians of the ten quarters as world-protectors. When sun and moon occur together, the moon is always mentioned first.

In the scriptures there is no systematic description of the heavenly bodies, but the account given in the *Sārasaṃgraha*[6] corresponds to scattered notices in earlier works and probably underlies them. The earth, a flat disk, is 1,203,450 leagues (*yojanas*) in diameter and 3,610,350 in circumference. In the centre is Mt. Meru, rising 84,000 leagues above the surface of the earth, and round it circle the sun, moon, and stars, shining in turn on the four continents round Mt. Meru.[7] Night is caused by the sun passing to the other side of Mt. Meru. The diameter of the moon is 49 leagues and the circumference 147; of the sun 50 and 150 respectively.[8] The sun as the vehicle (*vimāna*) of the god is one league higher in position than the moon. It is of crystal outside, gold within,[9] and hot within and without. The moon is of silver outside, of jewel within, and cool within and without. The sun has three paths—*ajavīthi*, *nāgavīthi*, and *govīthi*—according to its apparent course in the ecliptic during the seasons along the equator, and above or below.[10] This fact appears to be referred to in the *Sīlāni*,[11] where the sun and moon are spoken of as going along their paths or out of their paths. Whether there was any early theory

1 *Astronomie, Astrologie, und Mathematik*, Strassburg, 1899, p. 4.
2 *Vinaya Texts*, pt. iii. (*SBE* xx. [1885]) p. 294.
3 *Upasampadā-kammavācā*, tr. J. F. Dickson, Venice, 1875, p. 13; I-tsing, *A Record of the Buddhist Religion*, tr. J. Takakusu, Oxford, 1896, p. 100.
4 *Jātaka*, no. 450.
5 *Dīgha*, ii. 259.
6 Cosmological passages are quoted in R. S. Hardy, *Legends and Theories of the Buddhists*, London, 1866, appendix.
7 *Aṅguttara*, i. 227.
8 The ratio of the diameter and circumference of a circle is thus 1 : 3, as in *Jātaka*, v. 271. This illustrates the rudimentary character of Buddhist astronomy.
9 We should expect gold outside, but such is the text.
10 So, but more elaborately, in the *Viṣṇu Purāṇa*, bk. ii. ch. 8.
11 *Dīgha*, i. 10; cf. *Dialogues of the Buddha*, tr. T. W. Rhys Davids, London, 1899, i. 20.

of the cause of revolution, apart from the choice of the god of the luminary, is not clear. The Chinese sources of A. Rémusat state that five vortices of wind support and move the vehicle of the sun in the required directions, and five other vortices similarly move the moon.[1]

2. Eclipses.—Eclipses are due to the *asura* Rāhu, who is stationed at the moon's nodes, and periodically swallows the sun and the moon. The legend that Rāhu is the monster's head, severed when he was drinking the ambrosia produced at the churning of the ocean, appears not to be early Buddhist, nor even ancient Hindu. It is absent from the account of the churning in the *Viṣṇu Purāṇa*.[2] Buddhaghoṣa describes Rāhu not as a head, but as having a complete body, of which he gives the dimensions.[3] The Puranic notion of Ketu as the severed body of Rāhu at the descending node, although mentioned in *Mahāvyutpatti*, 164, and implied in *Abhidhānappadīpikā*,[4] 61, among the 'nine planets,' is a late borrowing from Hinduism. Two ancient *suttas* describe the moon and sun as being afflicted by Rāhu and appealing to Buddha, who commands Rāhu to let them go.[5]

3. Planets.—The stars also are said to move along and out of their paths.[6] The term here used for star is *nakkhatta* (Skr. *nakṣatra*), and probably refers to the planets, as Buddhaghoṣa understands it in this context.

The only planet distinctly mentioned in the *Suttas* is Osadhitārakā. That this is Venus may be inferred from its being described as the brightest of the luminaries next to the moon and as appearing in the morning.[7] The Sanskrit recension of the *Dīgha* passage in *Mahāvyutpatti*, 71, definitely identifies it with Venus by substituting Uśanas, one of the Sanskrit names of this planet, for Osadhi. The name Osadhitārakā is unexplained. The phrase *Osadhī viya tārakā*, 'like the star Osadhi,'[8] shows that it does not mean 'star of plants' (as in *oṣadhīpati*, 'lord of plants [or of the *soma*-plant],' a title of the moon). The possibility that *osadhī* is a corruption of *auṣasī*, 'star of dawn,' is attractive, but there is nothing in texts or commentaries to support it. The same is the case with the view of Kern that it is a corruption of *osanī*=Skr. *auśanī*, a derivative of *uśanas*.[9]

4. The lunar zodiac.—The term *nakṣatra* has been from late Vedic times applied especially to 27 or 28 constellations lying roughly along the ecliptic and forming a lunar zodiac; and from the Buddhistic use of many of them as proper names it may be inferred that they were known to the earliest Buddhists. They are as follows:

(1) Assayuja (β, γ Arietis), (2) Bharaṇī (35, 39, 41 Arietis), (3) Kattikā (Pleiades), (4) Rohiṇī (Hyades), (5) Magasira (λ, φ Orionis), (6) Addā (α Orionis), (7) Punabbasu (Gemini), (8) Phussa or Tissa (θ, δ, γ Cancri), (9) Asilesā (ε, δ, σ, η, ρ Hydræ), (10) Maghā (Regulus), (11) and (12) Pubba- and Uttara-phagguni (δ, θ, β, 93 Leonis), (13) Hattha (δ, γ, ε, α, β Corvi), (14) Chittā (Spica), (15) Sāti (Arcturus), (16) Visākhā (Libra), (17) Anurādhā (δ, β, π Scorpionis), (18) Jeṭṭhā (Antares), (19) Mūlā (λ Scorpionis, etc.), (20) and (21) Pubba- and Uttara-asāḷha (δ, ε, σ, ζ Sagittarii), [(22) Abhiji (Vega)], (23) Savaṇa (Aquila), (24) Dhaniṭṭhā or Saviṭṭhā (Delphin), (25) Satabhisaja (λ Aquarii, etc.), (26) and (27) Pubba- and Uttara-bhaddapadā or -poṭṭhapadā (the square of Pegasus), (28) Revati (ζ Piscium, etc.).[10]

No. 22 in this list is not in the *Abhidhānappadīpikā*. It was early omitted in Hindu astronomy, but the existence of Abhiji (Skr. Abhijit) in the Buddhist system may be inferred from the statement that the number of *nakṣatras* is 28[11] and from the existence of Abhijika as a proper name.[1] It also occurs in *Mahāvyutpatti*, 165, and in the list of Rémusat.[2]

References to other fixed stars than *nakṣatras* are rare in all Indian literature. The descent of the Heavenly Ganges, a myth relating to the Milky Way, is referred to in the canon, but never in any astronomical connexion. In *Jātaka*, vi. 97, seven sages are mentioned, but their names are not those which Hindu mythology gives to the seven *ṛṣis*, after whom the seven stars of Ursa Major are named. The name Sakaṭa, 'the cart,' in *Dīgha*, ii. 234, is probably a name of Rohiṇī, as suggested by S. Konow.[3] It is so named by several Hindu astronomers.[4]

5. Months.—The moon in the course of a year may be full in any of the *nakṣatras*, and we find such expressions as *Visākhapuṇṇamā*, 'full-moon when the moon is in Visākhā'; but there had been established earlier than Buddhism a system of twelve lunar months, with names derived from certain of the *nakṣatras*. These are:

(1) Chitta (Mar.–Ap.), (2) Visākhā (Ap.–May), (3) Jeṭṭha (May–June), (4) Āsāḷha (June–July), (5) Sāvaṇa (July–Aug.), (6) Poṭṭhapāda (Aug.–Sept.), (7) Assayuja (Sept.–Oct.), (8) Kattika (Oct.–Nov.), (9) Māgasira (Nov.–Dec.), (10) Phussa (Dec.–Jan.), (11) Māgha (Jan.–Feb.), (12) Phagguna (Feb.–Mar.).

These names were later applied in Hindu systems also to the twelve solar months, but in the canon the reckoning appears to be always lunar, as well as in the Ceylon chronicles.

The month is divided into two parts (*pakkha*), the dark (*kāḷa*) from full to new moon, and the light (*sukka*, *juṇha*) from new moon to full. Whether the month ended with full or new moon is not clear, but the fact that the dark half is mentioned first and that the months of Retreat began the day after a full-moon day and ended on a full-moon day, suggests that the full-moon day was the end. Both methods were in use by the Hindus in Vedic times, as they are at the present day.[5]

6. The week.—The division of the half month at the eighth and fourteenth or fifteenth day easily led to the reckoning of seven days as a usual period (*sattāha*), but there is no trace in the Pāli writings of the system (no doubt non-Indian in origin) of naming the week-days from the names of the sun, moon, and planets. These names occur in the order of the days of the week as the first seven of the nine planets in *Mahāvyutpatti*, 164.

7. The year.—In *Aṅguttara*, i. 213, where the length of a year of the gods is given, it is said to be a year of twelve months, the month being made up of 30 nights (and days). This gives a year of 360 days, and is the exact number in use in the Vedic period.[6] The number 30 is probably obtained by adding together the 15 days of each half of the lunar month. In practice the number would be sometimes 29 and sometimes 30, as the synodic lunar month is rather over 29½ days. There must have been a mode of intercalating months to bring the lunar months and solar year into harmony from time to time, as in the case of the Hindu systems, but the process is unknown. The modern Siamese have a year of 354 days, the months being alternately of 29 and 30 days. In every third or second year (seven times in 19 years) the eighth month is reckoned twice, and in every fifth or sixth year one day is added to the seventh month, bringing the lunar year into harmony with the solar year.[7]

The Hindu systems have two modes of beginning

1 *Mélanges posthumes d'hist. et de litt. orientales*, Paris, 1843, p. 83.

2 Bk. i. ch. 9.

3 Comm. on *Dīgha*, no. iv. § 6.

4 This work (of the 12th cent.) was the chief source of the astronomical items in R. C. Childers, *Dictionary of the Pali Language*, London, 1875, but it is based largely on Hindu sources, and forms no independent evidence for Buddhist astronomy. The nine planets are the moon, sun, five greater planets, Rāhu, and Ketu (*Mahāvyutpatti*, 164).

5 *Saṃyutta*, i. 50 f., tr. C. A. F. Rhys Davids, in *Kindred Sayings*, London, 1918, i. 71.

6 *Dīgha*, i. 10.

7 *Majjhima*, ii. 34.

8 *Vimānavatthu*, I. ix. 1.

9 *Verspreide Geschriften*, The Hague, 1913, ii. 250.

10 From *Abhidhānappadīpikā*, 58-60. Exact identifications of them are given by W. D. Whitney in *Sūryasiddhānta*, tr. E. Burgess, New Haven, 1860, p. 324; cf. *Nakṣatra* in A. A. Macdonell and A. B. Keith, *Vedic Index of Names and Subjects*, London, 1912.

11 *Mahānidesa*, 382; *Jātaka*, Com. vi. 476.

1 *Saṃyutta*, ii. 204.

2 P. 85.

3 *JPTS*, 1909, p. 13.

4 H. Kern, note on Varāhamihira's *Bṛhatsaṃhitā*, ix. 25, tr. in *Verspreide Geschriften*, i. 217.

5 Thibaut, p. 12; R. Sewell and S. B. Dikshit, *The Indian Calendar*, London, 1896, § 13; see art. FESTIVALS AND FASTS (Buddhist).

6 Thibaut, p. 7.

7 F. J. Wershoven, *Lehr- und Lesebuch der siames. Sprache und deutsch-siames. Wörterbuch*, Vienna, 1892.

the year: (1) with the full moon of Kattika, (2) with the month Chitta.[1] The former is implied in the usual Buddhist reckoning of the three seasons, in which the cold season is always mentioned first.[2] This period was also the end of the Retreat, in which the annual redistribution of robes took place. The second mode of beginning the year is implied in the *Dīpavaṃsa* and in the list of lunar months in the *Abhidhānappadīpikā*, which begins with Chitta.[3]

8. Seasons.—The ancient Hindu seasons are three: *hemanta*, the cold season from Māgasira to Phagguna; *gimha*, the hot season from Chitta to Āsalha; and *vassa*, the rainy season from Sāvaṇa to Kattika. These dates, however, would vary from year to year through the irregularity caused by the lunar months and occasional intercalation.[4]

Dīpavaṃsa, xii. 44, calls Jeṭṭha the last of the hot months. *Vassa* in the sense of Retreat does not correspond with the rainy season, but extends over three months of that period. The Hindu subdivisions of the three seasons into five or six[5] are not found in Pāli works, but there are occasional references to autumn (*sarada*) as the early part of *hemanta* and to spring (*vasanta*) as the early part of the hot season.[6] *Mahāvyutpatti*, 253, gives the list of six, and I-tsing[7] also describes other systems of division used in various localities.[8]

9. Astrology.—Indian astrology, as the science of omens drawn from celestial phenomena, is a branch of divination. It is stigmatized in *Dīgha*, i. 10, as a base science and false means of livelihood. In the *Sutta Nipāta*, 927, the monk is forbidden to devote himself to magic (*āthabbana*), to (the interpretation of) the dream, the sign, and the *nakṣatra*. That such a science is possible is generally taken for granted, but in the *Jātaka* there is a tendency to ridicule the belief in lucky *nakṣatras*,[9] omens,[10] names,[11] and sneezing. There is no reason to think that this sceptical attitude is primitive; it is rather the rationalizing of a single individual or of a school. The survival of the belief within orthodox Buddhism is shown in the collection of *suttas* drawn from the canonical books called the *Paritta*, which, among other formulas intended to ward off hostile powers or to win their favour, contains the two *suttas* on the eclipse of the moon and of the sun.[12]

A fragment of a MS of an astrological work in corrupt Sanskrit has recently been discovered in East Turkestan at Khotan.[13] It is shown to be Buddhist by the phraseology, as well as by the reference to the *ṛṣi* Kharuṣṭa, who makes known to the congregation the knowledge of 'nights, days, moments, planets, half-months and months.'[14] The matter is similar to that in Hindu astrological works, such as: what *nakṣatras* are effective for conception, which are causers of misfortune or success in certain undertakings. There can be little doubt that it is borrowed from some Hindu work, and, like later works of this kind, it shows the influence of Greek astronomy in the use of such terms as *hora*, and the names of the 12 signs of the zodiac (Pisces, Scorpio, etc.) along with those of the *nakṣatras*.

LITERATURE.—The sources and authorities are given throughout the article.

EDWARD J. THOMAS.

[1] Whitney, p. 270.
[2] *Vinaya*, i. 137.
[3] There is no reason for thinking that the year ever began with Sāvaṇa. The recurring phrase *Komudī chātumāsinī* does not mean the full moon of Kattika 'in the fourth month,' but 'at the Chāturmāsya festival.' See T. W. Rhys Davids and H. Oldenberg, in *Vinaya Texts*, pt. i. (*SBE* xiii. [1881]) p. 324, n. 2; *Jātaka*, vi. 221; *Dīpavaṃsa*, xv. 1. On the Chāturmāsya, or 'Four month' celebration, see art. FESTIVALS AND FASTS (Hindu).
[4] See the Commentaries on *Sutta Nipāta*, 233, p. 192, and *Vimāna Vatthu*, vii. 5, 6.
[5] Thibaut, p. 11.
[6] *Majjhima*, i. 115; *Jātaka*, i. 86; Com. on *Sutta Nipāta*, 233.
[7] Pp. 101, 219.
[8] See also art. CALENDAR (Buddhist).
[9] 49.
[10] 126, 155.
[11] 97.
[12] See artt. MAGIC (Buddhist) and DIVINATION (Buddhist), where the later developments of Buddhist astrology are given. See also, for modern Sinhalese Buddhism, E. Upham, *The History and Doctrine of Budhism popularly illustrated; with Notices of the Kappooism, or Demon Worship, and of the Bali, or Planetary Incantations of Ceylon*, London, 1829; for Tibetan, E. Schlagintweit, *Buddhism in Tibet*, Leipzig and London, 1863; for Chinese, Rémusat, *Mélanges posthumes*, p. 84 ff.
[13] *Manuscript Remains of Buddhist Literature found in Eastern Turkestan*, ed. A. F. Rudolf Hoernle and others, Oxford, 1916, i. 121.
[14] Cf. *Dīgha*, iii. 85.

SUN, MOON, AND STARS (Celtic).

—**1.** Very little is known about the astrology and astronomy of the Celts. The Druids, as we learn from Cæsar (*de Bell. Gall.* vi. 14), discussed and transmitted to their disciples many questions regarding the stars and their motion. They had observed the course of the moon, and by it they regulated their calendar. Their months and years began with the sixth day of the moon (Pliny, xvi. 95, 250); they counted by nights (Cæsar, vi. 18. 2); and their cycle was one of thirty years (Pliny, xvi. 95, 250).

The discovery of the calendar of Coligny has made it possible to determine these general ideas for the Gallo-Roman period. This calendar gives a year of 354 days, divided into twelve months of twenty-nine and thirty days alternately. To establish agreement between the lunar and the solar year a month of thirty days was intercalated every two and a half years. At the beginning of every fifth year there was complete agreement between the two methods of calculation; and probably this was the occasion, as Jullian remarks, on which were offered the quinquennial sacrifices of which Diodorus speaks (v. 32. 6).

Astrology, properly so called, does not seem to have been practised by the pagan Irish. But in the 'Lives of Saints' there are to be found some superstitious practices derived from the observation of the stars. The foster-father of Columcille goes to ask a prophet when he should begin to teach the child to read. The prophet after having examined the heavens replies that he must begin immediately (*Lives of Saints from the Book of Lismore*, l. 812). Manannan mac Lir used to know by studying the sky when there would be fine weather and when bad (*Cormac's Glossary*, p. 114).

The scientific observation of stars was also in use among the ancient Irish. Loeg observes the stars to ascertain when midnight comes (*Mesca Ulad*, 13). Some treatises on Irish astronomy dating from the early Middle Ages have been preserved. They are founded on the system of Ptolemy, and seem to be translations of foreign works. The words used to denote the sun-dial are borrowed from the Latin. Yet the Irish were particularly clever at calculating dates, and in the *Saltair na Rann* it is told that every intelligent person should know the day of the solar month, the age of the moon, the flow of the tide, the day of the week, and the chief saints' festival days. Perhaps in the ancient Irish and Welsh texts there are traces to be found of the primitive Celtic calendar. The year was divided into two halves or into four periods of three months, the month being divided into two parts. The periods of time most in use were those of three nights and three days, or nine nights and nine days, while the most common cycles were those of three years and of seven years. In Armorican Brittany and in Wales the names of the complementary days which served to convert the lunar year into a solar year (Brit. *gourdeziou*, Welsh *dyddiau dyddon*) have been preserved. Several popular superstitions are attached to them. Thus a medical manuscript mentioned by O'Curry contains a list of unlucky days, and in Irish literature there are numerous examples of births delayed in order that they may take place on a lucky day, and of disasters which might have been prevented if an undertaking had not been engaged in on an unlucky day.

2. The Gallic god Belenos had been assimilated to Apollo as a healer rather than as a sun-god. We have no evidence of worship of the stars among the Gauls except a few dedications to the sun and the moon in Gallo-Roman inscriptions (A. Holder, *Altceltischer Sprachschatz*, 3 vols., Leipzig, 1896–1913), and the mention of the worship of an image of the sun (*AS*, 4 Sept. ii. 197 C). No conclusion can be drawn from the representation of stars on the shields of the Orange-arch, from the *rouelles* dug out in so great a number, or from the wheel that is an attribute of a Gallo-Roman god assimilated to Jupiter; for the stars may be ornaments or armorial bearings, and the wheel may be a divination-wheel or a symbol of the thunder as well as a symbol of the sun. Some customs of the ancients may be connected with the beliefs relating to the stars—*e.g.* the gathering of the mistletoe and the beginning of the years and months on the sixth day of the moon (Pliny, xvi. 250), the dread of the Asiatic Galatians during an eclipse of the moon (Polyb. v. 78).

The evidences of the worship of the sun and the moon in ancient Ireland are not numerous. The most explicit text is in the *Confessio* (§ 60) of St. Patrick, in which he alludes to worshippers of the sun. G. Keating (*History of Ireland*, ed. D. Comyn and P. Dinneen, 1902–1908, bk. i. § 12) says that one of the Dê Danann was named Mac Gréine, 'Son of the Sun,' because his god was the sun. A passage of *Cormac's Glossary* (p. 54) tells us that Irish pagans used to carve some pictures—*e.g.* that of the sun—on the altars of their idols, and Keating (ii. 11) relates that in Columcille's time a priest of Tirconnel who had set up images of the sun and the moon in the church was carried off by a devil. The king of Ulster, Loegaire, swore by the name of the elements—the earth, the sun, and the wind (W. St. Boroma, *RCel* xiii. [1892] 52 f.).

LITERATURE.—J. Loth, 'L'Année Celtique' in *Revue Celtique*, xxv. (1904) 113–142; P. W. Joyce, *A Social History of Ancient Ireland*, London, 1903, i. 464–471; C. Jullian, *Histoire de la Gaule*, Paris, 1907, i. 393, ii. 124, 141.

G. DOTTIN.

SUN, MOON, AND STARS (Chinese).—I. *INTRODUCTION.*—The Chinese view of the sun, moon, and stars taken as a whole may be likened to a web woven of three different threads: the thread of astronomy, the thread of religion, and the thread of astrology. Astronomy means here the observation of the heavenly bodies and the truths deduced therefrom, chiefly for practical purposes. It may therefore be called 'observational' astronomy, as distinguished from what is called 'physical' or 'descriptive' astronomy, founded by Galileo after his invention of the telescope, and it may also be called 'practical' astronomy, as distinguished from what is called 'theoretical' astronomy, founded by Newton on the hypothesis of the law of gravitation. The religious view of the Chinese concerning the heavenly bodies may be called astrological, and their astrological view may be called religious in the comprehensive sense of the term. But a clear line of distinction can be drawn between them. The idea of deity or God is always present and predominant in the religious view, whereas it may be vague and even absent in the astrological view. The latter is concerned chiefly with the influences of the heavenly bodies upon men, while the former is concerned chiefly with the relation of God to men as revealed in the heavenly bodies—*i.e.* God's messages and warnings derived by means of the observation of the heavenly bodies.

The Chinese term for the study of the heavens is *tien wen*, literally 'the system (or order) of heaven.' The term is not limited to purely astronomical knowledge, but has been applied equally to astrological and religious beliefs or views concerning the heavens.

Chinese astronomy has been of much interest to many European scholars, its great antiquity being widely admitted.

> 'The progress of Astronomy among the Chinese,' says John Williams, 'is a subject of highest interest whether it be considered as recording observations of the heavenly bodies made by one of the most ancient and primitive races of mankind, which appears in extremely remote time to have advanced to a high degree of civilisation; peculiar, however, to itself; and which has preserved the manners and customs established by its early rulers more than two thousand years before the Christian era, in a great measure unaltered to the present day. Or whether the fact that at a period long anterior to the commencement of civilisation among the Western nations, and when almost universal barbarism prevailed among them, astronomy had been carried to a great degree of perfection by the Chinese, as manifested by their still existing records, whose authenticity is not only strongly asserted by that people, but is acknowledged by some of the most eminent European scholars of the present day.'[1]

It has been said by some of the authorities of our own century that the antiquity of Chinese astronomy is 'greater even than that of almost any other nation.'[2] But the study of the heavens in China is not pursuit of knowledge, or astronomical knowledge, for its own sake. Being a highly practical nation, the Chinese, when they seek to know anything, generally have some end or ideal in view to the attainment of which knowledge is merely a means. The present case is not an exception. Having to arrange all their religious ceremonies, social and governmental affairs, and, most important of all, their agricultural work according to the seasons, the Chinese, even at the earliest period of their history, felt the great need of a proper calendar, the formation of which required astronomical knowledge. Apart from this, there were other motives—the religious and the astrological. The latter explains itself, and the former has a double purpose. On the one hand, the Chinese sought to know the laws of the heavens, which were for them, in some sense, divine, in order to apply them to their own conduct, social as well as individual. The doctrine of the imitation of, or the conformation of men's conduct with, the laws of the heavens has been much held by Confucianists, and especially by Taoists, and can be found in most of the Chinese classics. On the other hand, as they believed the celestial phenomena to be God's revelations or warnings to men, they wanted to know them in order to re-adjust their conduct.

Both the astronomical and the religious views of the Chinese concerning the heavens are as old as their history, and it is difficult to tell which is earlier; their astrology is a later development. The Chinese term for 'astrologer' is *êrh tse* or *sing tse*, which may be translated 'the man of sun' or 'the man of stars.' According to the Chinese records, the former term did not occur until the 5th cent. B.C., and the latter is of still later date. Kepler says that astronomy is the wise mother and astrology the foolish daughter. If we may adopt this saying with a little modification, we can regard the astrology of the Chinese as the daughter of their astronomy and religion. These three different views have for thousands of years influenced the Chinese mind, and the astrological view, though the latest, has almost since its birth been the most powerful. Even at the present day among many of the Chinese astronomy has not divorced itself from religion, nor has it disowned or rid itself of astrology, as Western astronomy has since the 16th century.

II. *THE ASTRONOMICAL ASPECTS.* — The

[1] *Observations of Comets*, London, 1871, p. vii.

[2] E. B. Knobel, 'Abstract of a Lecture on Chinese Astronomy,' in *Journal of the British Astronomical Association*, xix. [1908–09] 338.

Chinese are great believers in their ancient classics, so that to deal with their ancient views and beliefs is to a great extent to deal with their modern ones as well. The great antiquity of Chinese astronomy has been admitted by many of the best European scholars of both the last and the present century. According to tradition, a sort of calendar was invented by Fu Hsi (3328 B.C.) as a result of observations of the phenomena of the heavens. The reformation of the calendar and the rectification of intercalation are attributed to Hwang Ti, or the Yellow Emperor (2698 B.C.). In the record called *Ssŭ Ki* of Ssŭ Ma Chien, China's most famous historian (2nd and 1st centuries B.C.), it is recorded:

'Hwang Ti commanded Hi Ho to take charge of the observation of the sun, Yih Chang the observation of the moon, and Yu Chu the observation of the stars.'

He is also said to have brought into use the lunar cycle of nineteen years, by which the conjunctions and oppositions of the sun and moon can be calculated, and the intercalary months regulated. This was more than 2000 years before the introduction of the same system among the Greeks by the astronomer Meton.[1] *The Annals of the Bamboo Books*[2] record that at the time of the reign of Tsuan Hsu (beginning 2513 B.C.) a conjunction of the five planets was observed by the Chinese in the constellation called Yin Shih or Shih.[3] It has been carefully calculated and asserted by the French astronomer, Jean S. Bailly, that such a conjunction did take place on 29th Feb. 2449 B.C., which would be the 65th year of Tsuan Hsu's reign. In the time of the emperor Yaou (2356 B.C.) the Chinese already knew the exact, or almost exact, number of days in a year, had a way of determining solstices and equinoxes, and had in use an intercalary system and some instruments for the survey of the heavens, and the knowledge of the five planets and of the twelve zodiacal signs, and most probably of the 28 stellar divisions.

In the 'Canon of Yaou,'[4] the first book of the *Shu King* ('The Canon of History'), we read:

'Thereupon Yaou commanded He and Ho[5] to have reverence to the great heavens, and to calculate and delineate the movements and appearances of the sun, the moon, the stars, and the zodiacal spaces; and so to deliver respectfully the seasons to the people.

He separately commanded the second brother He to reside at Ye-e, in what was called the Bright Valley, and there respectfully to receive as a guest the Rising Sun, and to adjust and arrange the labours of the Spring. "The day," he said, "is of the medium length, and the star is in Neaou;[6] you may thus exactly determine mid-spring. The people begin to disperse; and the birds and beasts breed and copulate."

He further commanded the third brother He to reside at Nankeaou, and arrange the transformations of the summer, and respectfully to observe the extreme limit of the shadow. "The day," said he, "is at its longest, and the star is Ho;[7] you may thus exactly determine mid-summer. The people are more dispersed; and the birds and beasts have their feathers and hair thin, and change their coats."

He separately commanded the second brother Ho to reside in the west, in what was called the Dark Valley, and there respectfully to convoy the setting sun, and to adjust and arrange the completing labours of the autumn. "The night," he said, "is of the medium length, and the star is Hiü;[1] you may thus exactly determine mid-autumn. The people begin to feel at ease; and birds and beasts have their coats in good condition."

He further commanded the third brother Ho to reside in the northern region, in what was called the Sombre Capital, and there to adjust and examine the changes of the winter. "The day," said he, "is at its shortest, and the star is Maou;[2] thus you may exactly determine mid-winter. The people keep their cosy corners; and the coats of birds and beasts are downy and thick."

The emperor said, "Ah! you, He and Ho, a round year consists of three hundred, sixty, and six days.[3] By means of an intercalary month do you fix the four seasons, and complete the determination of the year. Thereafter, in exact accordance with this, regulating the various officers, all the works of the year will be fully performed."'

In the 'Canon of Hsun,' the second book of the *Shu King*, it is recorded that, having accepted the throne which had been often offered to him by the emperor Yaou, the emperor Hsun examined the gem-adorned sphere and the gem transverse tube in order to regulate the seven directors or planets.

Both the commandment of Yaou and the examination of Hsun are supposed to have taken place at the beginning of their reigns. The observation of the heavens then must have been of great importance. According to another book of the *Shu King*, called 'The Punitive Expedition of the Prince Yin,' in the reign of King Tsung Kang (2159–2146 B.C.) there were astronomers who failed to foretell an eclipse of the year 2158 B.C. (?), and it was considered such a great crime that the prince of Tin, who was then commander-in-chief of the imperial armies, received orders from the king to punish them with the imperial forces.

The Chinese then commenced their observation of eclipses from a time not later than the 22nd cent. B.C., though some European scholars regard the eclipse of the sun on 29th Aug. 775 B.C., recorded in the *Shi King* ('Book of Odes'),[4] as the earliest recorded eclipse in all history. In Ma Twan Lin's *Encyclopœdia* more than 600 eclipses of the sun are recorded from 2168 B.C. to A.D. 1223. There are many other kinds of heavenly phenomena which have been keenly observed by the Chinese from a very early period as well. From 611 B.C. to A.D. 21 alone comets are recorded 372 times, as shown in Williams' *Observations of Comets*. The spots of the sun were observed and recorded by the Chinese not later than A.D. 301, *i.e.* 1308 years before the assumed first discovery of solar spots by Galileo in A.D. 1610 and 1300 years before the invention of the telescope. 48 observations of solar spots, from A.D. 301 to 1205, are recorded in Ma Twan Lin's *Encyclopœdia*, which was published in A.D. 1323, *i.e.* 288 years before Galileo's observation. In the same *Encyclopœdia* a great number of instances of the observation of moving or shooting stars are recorded from 1122 B.C. to A.D. 1230. Meteors have been observed, and recorded by the Chinese since, as early as 1578 B.C. The *Bamboo Books* record: 'In the tenth year [of the emperor Kwei of the Hia dynasty, *i.e.* 1579 B.C.] the five planets went out of their courses. In the night stars fell like rain.' Comparing it with the year A.D. 1866, remarks E. B. Knobel, when they had the great display of meteors, the interval gave 104 periods of 33·11 years. Now Leverrier's period for the November meteor is 33·25. Thus it is hardly possible to doubt that

1 See Williams, *Observations of Comets*, Introduction.

2 A large collection of ancient documents, discovered A.D. 279; see James Legge's tr. in *Chinese Classics*, Hongkong, 1861–72, vol. iii. pt. i.

3 One of the 28 stellar divisions determined by α, β, and other stars in Pegasus, extending north and south from Cygnus and Piscis Australis and east and west 17° and comprising part of Capricornus and Aquarius.

4 Legge, *Chinese Classics*, vol. iii. pt. i. [1865] pp. 15–27.

5 Names of two families which had been hereditary officers of the Board of Astronomy since the time of Hwang Ti.

6 Neaou is a space of heavens extending over 112° and embracing the seven constellations of the southern quarter. The star in Neaou is, according to the view held by Chinese scholars and adopted by many Western scholars, such as James Legge, John Williams, etc., the star Tsun Hwuo, corresponding to Cor Hydra. After an elaborate calculation Williams says (p. xi) that that star should culminate at sunset on the day mentioned in the *Shu King*. He then says: 'Thus a strong presumptive proof is again afforded of the veracity of the Chinese history as recorded in the *Shu King*.'

7 The central star of the seven constellations of the eastern quarter, corresponding to the heart of Scorpio.

1 The central star of the seven constellations of the northern quarter, corresponding to β Aquarii.

2 The culminating star of the seven constellations of the western quarter, corresponding to the Pleiades.

3 'When it it said,' says the editor of Yung Ching's *Shu King* (James Legge's tr.), 'that the year consists of 366 days, we are to understand that Yaou was speaking in round numbers. The period in question is now called the value of the years. It has been differently estimated by the astronomers of successive dynasties.'

4 II. iv. 9; Legge's tr., London, 1876, p. 229 f.

we have here the earliest record of a shower of those meteors.[1]

III. *DIVISION OF THE STARS.*—**1. The 28 siüs or shĕs.**—In common with the Hindus, Arabs, Babylonians, Persians, and Copts, the Chinese have the division of the ecliptic into 28 mansions, which are called *siüs* or *shĕs*. According to the interpretation of Ssu Ma Kuang, a great scholar of the Sung dynasty (A.D. 960–1279), *shĕ* has the meaning 'to reside (or to stop) somewhere' and *siü* means 'an abode,' and both words express the idea of the sun, the moon, and the five planets in their revolution residing in turn in the divisions of the sphere indicated as the 28 abodes. This meaning is very similar to that of the Hindu *nakṣatras* ('stars' or 'asterisms') and the Arabian *manāzil al-kamar* ('lunar mansions'). There is, according to Knobel's calculation, a concordance of the determinants of the *siüs*, the *nakṣatras*, and the *manāzils* in fifteen divisions, of the *siüs* and the *nakṣatras* in four divisions, of the *siüs* and the *manāzils* in five divisions, and of the *nakṣatras* and the *manāzils* in four divisions. This remarkable resemblance attracted the attention of many Western scholars and seemed to them a sufficient reason for presuming that all three systems sprang from a single source. The conclusions arrived at are different. Some hold that the system originated in India and the Chinese borrowed it from there; others are of opinion that the Chinese borrowed from the Arabs; another opinion is that the Babylonians were the originators; while still others say that the origin is to be found in Central Asia or some part of Persia. Unfortunately none of these conclusions is supported by satisfactory evidence.

But there are differences as well as resemblances between these three systems, and the Chinese division has its own peculiarity. The Chinese divisions are very unequal in the angular intervals and therefore cannot present the daily stations of the moon, as the Hindu divisions do. They are measured on the equator rather than on the ecliptic. According to G. Schlegel,[2] there is no connexion at all between the Chinese asterisms and the lunar zodiac. Some of the names of the 28 *siüs* were known to the Chinese as early as the time of the emperor Yaou (2356 B.C.), while the earliest Babylonian record concerning the lunar mansions and the earliest Hindu record of the *nakṣatras* named after the Vedic deities are much later than that.[3]

The *nakṣatras*, in their recent forms at least, are apparently assimilated to the Chinese *siüs*, and the whole system of junction stars is undoubtedly an imitation of them.[4]

J. B. Biot and his son were the first to demonstrate the identity of the Chinese *siüs* and the 28 lunar mansions of the Hindus and Arabs. They concluded that this arrangement of celestial divisions was invented by the Chinese and borrowed from them by the Hindus and Arabs for purely astrological purposes.

'To this day,' says J. J. M. de Groot, 'no considerations of importance have cancelled these views [of Biot], and though they have been rigorously combated by Weber, Max Müller, and other authorities of renown, yet it seems that most investigations of oriental astronomy silently subscribe to them.'[5]

2. The twelve kungs.—Besides the division of the lunar cycle into 28 unequal mansions, the Chinese, in common with the Hindus and Western nations, divide the zodiac into twelve equal parts as follows:

(1) Ta Liang, Aries-Taurus; (2) Hsi Chen, Taurus-Gemini; (3) Tsun Hseo, Gemini-Cancer; (4) Tsun Go, Cancer-Leo; (5) Tsun Vi, Leo-Virgo; (6) Hseo Sing, Virgo-Libra; (7) Ta Ho, Libra-Scorpio; (8) Ssi Mu, Scorpio-Sagittarius; (9) Sing Ki, Sagittarius-Capricorn; (10) Huan Hio, Capricorn-Aquarius; (11) Tsu Tsu, Aquarius-Pisces; (12) Hiang Lo, Pisces-Aries.

These names are found in Chinese books written several centuries B.C.—*e.g.*, *Tso Tsuan*, *Êrh Ya*, etc. The Hindu zodiac signs, which are probably of Greek origin, entered China at a much later date.

3. The four quarters and the five kungs.—The Chinese divide the heavens into four quarters. The eastern quarter is called Tsang Lung ('the Blue Dragon') and is associated for astrological purposes with the season of spring, the planet Jupiter, the element wood, the colour blue, the taste sour, and the virtue of benevolence. The southern quarter is called Chü Niaou ('the Red Bird') and is associated with the season of summer, the planet Mars, the element fire, the colour red, the taste bitter, and the virtue of propriety. The western quarter is called Pe Hwu ('the White Tiger') and is associated with the season of autumn, the planet Venus, the element metal, the colour white, the taste hot, and the virtue of righteousness. The northern quarter is called Hsüan Wu ('the Black Warrior,' or 'the Black Tortoise,' as it has also been interpreted) and is associated with the season of winter, the planet Mercury, the element water, the colour black, the taste salt, and the virtue of wisdom.

In Ssŭ Ma Chien's *Ssŭ Ki* the stars are divided into five *kungs*, or palaces—middle palace, eastern palace, southern palace, western palace, and northern palace. The middle palace consists of the northern circumpolar stars, and the other four are like the four quarters stated above. This system of division is followed by Pan Ku in his *History of the Later Han Dynasty*.

4. The three yuans and the two kuans.—The three *yuans* (palaces or stellar spaces) are (1) Tsu Vi Yuan (the Middle Palace), consisting of the northern circumpolar stars, (2) Tai Vi Yuan (the Upper Palace), consisting of stars in Leo, Virgo, Corvus, etc., and (3) Tien Ssu Yuan (the Lower Palace), bounded by two chains comprising Hercules, the upper part of Ophiuchus, etc.

The two *kuans*, or kinds of officers, are (1) *tsung kuan*, the internal officers, consisting of groups of stars inside the equator, and (2) *wusi kuan*, the external officers, consisting of groups of stars outside the equator.

This system of the division of the heavens is peculiarly Chinese and is very ancient. In the *Tien Wun*, consisting of eight chapters, written by Wu Hian, an astronomer of the Yin (or Shang) dynasty (1766–1122 B.C.), the astronomer assigned to the Middle Palace four seats or officers, consisting of eight stars, to the Upper Palace one seat, consisting of one star, to the Lower Palace four seats, consisting of eight stars, to the internal officers five seats, consisting of 24 stars, and to the external officers nineteen seats, consisting of 93 stars. In the *Tien Wen Sing Chan*, written by Kan Te, an astronomer of the state of Tsi, and the *Tien Wen*, written by Hsi Hsen, an astronomer of the state of Wui (both astronomers lived about the 4th cent. B.C.), the method of division is identical with that of Wu Hian, but the numbers of officers and stars are greatly increased. Adding these estimates together, we get 283 officers, consisting of 1464 stars.

5. The three yuans and the 28 siüs.—There is a

1 *Journ. of the British Astronomical Association*, xix. 337–345.
2 *Uranographie chinoise*, The Hague, 1875.
3 *Observatory*, xxxii. [1909] 187.
4 According to Agnes M. Clerke's art. 'Zodiac' in *EBr*[11], the *siüs* were of Chinese invention and the *manāzils* were of Indian derivation. The *nakṣatras* in their recent organization were, as far as possible, assimilated to the Chinese *siüs*. 'The whole system of junction stars,' she says, 'was doubtless an imitation of the *sieu*; the choice of them by the Hindu astronomers of the 6th century A.D. was plainly instigated by a consideration of the Chinese, compiled with a widely different intent.'
5 *The Religious System of China*, Leyden, 1892–1910, bk. i. vol. iii. p. 974, footnote.

popular book consisting of 31 songs by Tan Yuan Tsu of the Sui dynasty (589–617), called *Pu Tuen Ko*. It divides the stars into three *yuans* and 28 *siüs*. There are in all 193 *kuans*, or officers, consisting of 1457 stars. The stars which have been named by the Chinese are not many more than this, except in the book of Chang Heng, which gave 320 *kuans*, consisting of 2500 stars, and, besides these, 11,520 stars. This system of division is followed by Ma Twan Lin and others.

IV. *THE RELIGIOUS ASPECTS*.—**1. Animistic view.**—The animistic view which the Chinese took of many things in nature is seen in their attitude to the sun, moon, and stars. Many of them regard the heavenly bodies not as merely inanimate bodies, but as dwelling-places of spiritual beings or as spiritual beings themselves; *e.g.*, there is, it is said, a cock in the sun and a hare in the moon, the palace of angels; the hare is said to be sitting under a tree pounding medicine in a mortar. Those spiritual beings have superhuman powers, though the supreme power is not attributed to any of them, but to *Tien*, *Shang-ti*, or God alone. Hence the movements and appearances of the heavenly bodies are not regarded as mechanical, lifeless, or inevitable, for within or behind them there is a will which causes them. This will may be the will of the heavenly bodies, of the spiritual beings who dwell in them, or of God, the Supreme Ruler.

2. Comparison of the heavens with the earth.—In the heavens there are the sun and the moon; correspondingly on the earth there are the *yang* and the *yin*, the two contrary conceptions applied to phenomena mental and moral as well as physical. *Yang* is the male principle, associated with heat, day, etc., and *yin* is the female principle, associated with cold, night, etc. Hence the sun is called 'the great *yang*,' and the moon 'the great *yin*.' It is also said that the sun is 'the crystallization of the *yang*' and the moon 'the crystallization of the *yin*.' The five planets are said to correspond to the five elements of the earth, and therefore Mars is called 'the planet of fire,' Mercury 'the planet of water,' Venus 'the planet of metal,' Jupiter 'the planet of wood,' and Saturn 'the planet of earth.' Similarly, the different stars and constellations are believed to correspond to the various portions of the surface of the earth. In the chapter called *Tien Kwan* ('The Heavenly Officers') in Ssŭ Ma Chien's *Ssŭ-Ki*, in which all the beliefs mentioned above may be found, we read: 'The twenty-eight *siü* or constellations correspond to the twelve *chows*, or provinces. . . . The source of this (saying or belief) is of remote antiquity indeed.'

It is a popular saying in China that 'the stars of the heavens above and the configurations of the earth beneath correspond with each other.' A great number of stars—*e.g.*, the twenty stars constituting the two chains of the Tien Ssu Yuan, or the Lower Palace—are believed to correspond to certain countries in China and are given the names of those countries.

In some of the ancient books the heavens are said to be spherical and the earth square, the heavens dynamic and the earth static. There are also ancient stories or mythologies which represent the heavens as having a hollow place in the north-west round which all the stars revolve, and the earth as having a hollow place in the south-east towards which all the waters run.

3. Comparison of the heavenly bodies with men.—Heaven, earth, and men are believed to be the three great powers or genii in the universe. The heavenly bodies are regarded not merely as separate individuals, but as having a society like that of men. As the Chinese state was an empire, so the heavenly society was believed to be an empire. This can be observed in the names of the stars. The coining of significant poetical or mythological names for the heavenly bodies was probably to render easier the task of discriminating and remembering them. Many stories grew round those names, which are regarded by some as fables and by others as true. According to the names of the stars in the Tai Vi Yuan, the Upper Palace, the northern polar star (Polaris) is where the emperor is. The reason is quite plain, as Confucius said: 'He who exercises government by means of his virtue is like the northern polar star, which keeps its place, and all the other stars turn towards it.'[1] The Great Bear, or the Spoon, as it is called in China, is said to be the imperial chariot, and its motion round the northern polar star is said to be the emperor viewing his empire in all directions. Names of some of the other stars are: the Empress's Palace, Crown Prince, Prince, Princess, Guards, Civil and Military Officers, Law-Court, Prison, Armoury, Storehouse, Kitchen, Bed, Canopy, etc.

4. Relation between the heavenly and the earthly empires.—These two empires are not separated from one another without inter-communication. *Tien*, or *Shang-ti*, the Supreme Ruler, governs both, but the heavenly one more directly. The ruler of the earthly empire used to be called Tien-tsu, 'the son of Tien (or God).' Enthronement used to be regarded as the appointment of God, the rewarder of the good and the punisher of the bad. Therefore, when the Son of Heaven was good and his empire well governed, auspicious phenomena used to appear from God in the heavens, and, when he was bad and his empire in disorder, threats used to appear. There are many heavenly phenomena which are regarded as God's threats—notably eclipses. The *Canon of Odes* refers to an eclipse of the sun of the date 29th Aug. 775 B.C., which was carefully verified by John Chalmers.

> 'The sun was eclipsed—
> A thing of very evil omen,
> First the moon looked small,
> And then the sun looked small,
> Henceforth the people
> Will be pitiable indeed.
> The sun and moon presage evil
> By not keeping to their proper paths;
> All through the kingdom there is no [good] government,
> Because good men are not employed.
> For the moon to be eclipsed
> Is a small matter,
> But now the sun is eclipsed,
> How dreadful is that!'

In the Confucian classic called *Tsun Tsiu* ('Springs and Autumns') the eclipse of the sun which took place on 20th April 610 B.C. is recorded. The writer says:

> 'On the occasion of an eclipse of the sun, the Son of Heaven should not have his table spread so lavishly as usual, and should have drums beaten at the altar to the spirits of the land, while the feudal princes should present offerings of silk to the spirits of the land and have drums beaten at their courts, thus manifesting their own service of the spirits and so teaching the people to serve their rulers, according to the respective rights of each, as was customary in ancient days.'

The word 'eclipse' used here is the same as the word 'eat.' The eclipse of the sun or the moon is described, in some of the Chinese stories, as the sun or moon being eaten by a certain animal, and the beating of drums is said to frighten the animal away.

The sun in the heavens is also said to correspond to the ruler on the earth; *e.g.*, when the people wished the death of Kie, the tyrant (reigned 1818–1753 B.C.), they said: 'O sun, why expirest thou not? Let us die together with thee.' Therefore the eclipse of the sun is generally regarded as a threat from God to the emperor. There are

[1] *Analects*, bk. ii. ch. 1.

numerous examples, and the edict of the emperor Ming Ti (A.D. 227–239) after the eclipse of the sun in 233 is most illuminating:

'We have heard,' says the emperor, 'that if a sovereign is remiss in government, God terrifies him by calamities and portents. These are divine reprimands sent to recall him to a sense of duty. Thus, eclipses of the sun and moon are manifest warnings that the rod of empire is not wielded aright. Ever since We ascended the throne, Our inability to continue the glorious traditions of Our departed ancestors and carry on the great work of civilization has now culminated in a warning message from on high. It therefore behoves Us to issue commands for personal reformation, in order to avert impending calamity. The relationship, however, between God and man is that of father and son; and a Father, about to chastise his son, would not be deterred were the latter to present him with a dish of meat. We do not therefore consider it a part of Our duty to act in accordance with certain memorials advising that the Grand Astrologer be instructed to offer up sacrifices on this occasion. Do ye governors of districts, and other high officers of State, seek rather to rectify your own hearts; and if anyone can devise means to make up for Our shortcomings, let him submit his proposals to the throne.'[1]

Comets, even more than eclipses, are regarded as God's threats. When the comets appeared in 524 B.C., travelling eastward towards the Milky Way, an officer said: 'This is a broom to sweep away the old, and give us new. God often makes us such signs. The feudal princes will suffer from calamities by fire.'[2] The stars or the spiritual beings who dwell in them sometimes descend from the heavens, either by themselves or by the will of God, are born on earth, and go back to their positions in heaven after their earthly life.

In *The Annals of the Bamboo Books* there are the following legends:

'He's mother (the mother of Hwang Ti, 2968 B.C.) was called Tu Paon. She witnessed a great flash of lightning, which surrounded the star Chu (or Dubhe) of the Great Bear with a brightness that lighted all the country about her, and thereupon became pregnant.'

'His mother was called Niu Tsie. She witnessed a star like a rainbow come floating down the stream to the islet of Hwa. Thereafter she dreamed and received it, and was moved in her mind, and bore *Shaon-Haon* [the emperor Che, 2597 B.C.].'

'His mother was called Niu Chu. She witnessed the *Yaou Kwang* star (or Bemtuash) go through the moon like a rainbow, when it moved herself in the palace of Yio-Fang, after which she brought forth *Tsun Hu* [the emperor, 2513 B.C.].'

'His mother was called *Sis-Ki*. She saw a falling star which went through the constellation Maou, and in her dream her thoughts were moved till she became pregnant, after which she swallowed a spirit's pearl, . . . and gave birth to *Yu* (king 2205 B.C.) in Shih Nio.'

There are 28 heroes in Chinese history who were believed to be the 28 *siüs*, or constellations, descended. A great man on earth may become after death a spiritual being in heaven and dwell in one of the stars. Some stars are named after historical heroes. There are a great many stories, love stories, and mythologies based upon beliefs of this kind.

5. Sacrifices.—We read in the 22nd book called *Kî Tung* ('The Foundation of Sacrifices') of the *Lî Kî* ('The Book of Rites'), a collection of treatises on the rules of propriety or ceremonial usages, one of the five Confucian books or canons:

'Of all the methods for the good ordering of men, there is none more urgent than the use of ceremonies. Ceremonies are of five kinds, and there is none of them more important than sacrifices.'[3]

Among various sacrifices there are sacrifices to the sun, moon, and stars. We do not know when these rites began, but they have been performed under each dynasty from the 23rd cent. B.C. down to the time of the present Republic of China. In the 20th book of *Lî Kî*, called *Kî Fâ* ('The Laws of Sacrifices'), it is said:

'With a blazing pile of wood on the Grand altar they [the Emperors, from Emperor Shun 2255 B.C. to King Wu 1122 B.C.] sacrificed to Heaven;[4] by burying (the victim) in the Grand mound, they sacrificed to the Earth. (In both cases) they used a red victim.[1]

By burying a sheep and a pig at the (altar of) Great brightness, they sacrificed to the seasons. (With similar) victims they sacrificed to (the spirits of) cold and heat, at the pit and the altar, using prayers of deprecation and petition; to the sun, at the (altar called the) royal palace; to the moon, at the (pit called the) light of night; to the stars at the honoured place of gloom; to (the spirits of) flood and drought at the honoured altar of rain; to the (spirits of the) four quarters at the place of the four pits and altars; mountains, forests, streams, valleys, hills, and mounds, which are able to produce clouds, and occasion winds and rain, were all regarded as (dominated by) spirits.'[2]

In the 21st book of *Lî Kî*, called *Kî Î* ('The Meaning of Sacrifices'), it says:

'The sacrifice in the suburb of the capital was the great expression of gratitude to Heaven, and it was specially addressed to the sun, with which the moon was associated. The sovereigns of Hsiâ [dynasty, 2205–1766 B.C.] presented it in the dark. Under the Yin dynasty [1766–1122 B.C.] they did so at noon. Under the Kau [dynasty, 1122–255 B.C.] they sacrificed all the day, especially at daybreak, and towards evening.

They sacrificed to the sun on the altar, and to the moon in the hollow;—to mark the distinction between (the) gloom (of the one) and (the) brightness (of the other), and to show the difference between the high and the low. They sacrificed to the sun in the east, and to the moon in the west;—to mark the distinction between (the) forthcoming (of the former) and (the) withdrawing (of the latter), and to show the correctness of their (relative) position. The sun comes forth from the east, and the moon appears in the west; the darkness and the light are now long, now short; when the one ends, the other begins, in regular succession:—thus producing the harmony of all under the sky.'[3]

These are the sacrifices at the equinoxes; that to the sun at the vernal equinox in the eastern suburb, and that to the moon at the autumnal equinox in the western suburb. These had been performed under each dynasty, and can also be found in *Ta Tsing Tung Li* ('The Ritual of the Manchu Dynasty'). The former is called *Chow Zi*, 'The Morning Sun,' and the latter *Si Yüe*, 'The Evening Moon.'

In the dynasty of Chin (255–206 B.C.) they sacrificed to what they called the eight gods, *i.e.* the god of the heavens, the god of the earth, the god of war, the god of the *yin*, the god of the *yang*, the god of the sun, the god of the moon, and the god of the four seasons. In *Han Shu* ('the Book [or History] of the early Han Dynasty') [206 B.C.–A.D. 25] it is said: 'There were such eight gods in the ancient times, but their origin is unknown.'

In the dynasties after the China dynasty different temples were built for their sacrifices. Even at the present day temples connected with the sun, moon, and stars can be found in different places. In Peking there is the world-famous Tien Tan ('Temple of Heaven'), and in it there are altars of the sun, of the moon, of the 28 constellations, and of some other stars and groups of stars. In the Manchu dynasty (1644–1911) sacrifices were offered in the Temple of Heaven once every spring and once every autumn. Even since the establishment of the Republic of China (1911), a grand sacrifice was offered in the Temple of Heaven by Yuan Shi Kai, the first Chinese President.

The 15th of the eighth lunar month is a Chinese holiday called *Tsung Tsiu Tse* ('the mid-autumn holiday'). The moon is said to be always at its fullest and brightest on this evening if it is visible, whereas this need not be so on the same date of other lunar months. A family festival used to be, and in some places still is, held in Chinese houses on that evening. The offerings to the moon consist chiefly of fruits, and the ceremony is similar to that of Chinese ancestor-worship. On this holiday schools, shops, etc., are closed, and farmers cease work for a few days. Relatives and friends exchange presents, chiefly

[1] H. A. Giles, *Confucianism and its Rivals*, London, 1915, p. 180.
[2] *Ib.* p. 53.
[3] Tr. J. Legge in *The Sacred Books of China*, pt. iv. (*SBE* xxviii. [1885] 236).
[4] On the blazing pile were placed the victim and pieces of jade; in the square mound were buried the victim and pieces of silk.

[1] Red was the special colour of victims under the Chow dynasty.
[2] *SBE* xxviii. 202 f. [3] *Ib.* p. 218 f.

eatables, and invite each other to dinner on one or more of the days following the mid-autumn holiday.

With regard to the sacrifices to the stars we read in *Urh Ya*, an ancient dictionary, one of the Thirteen Confucian Classics: 'The sacrifice to the stars is called Pu.' Even in our day tablets of stars can be found in public temples and private houses in different provinces.

6. Significance or purpose of sacrifices.—The significance of these sacrifices is not merely religious, nor is their religious significance always the most prominent. Sometimes these rites were used for political purposes by the rulers. This is the case not only in ancient times; there was a time in our present century when *Shinkio Riyo Mondai* ('The Problem of the Utilization of Religions') was of great interest to statesmen and politicians in Japan, and the political significance of the sacrifices at the Temple of Heaven performed by Yuan Shi Kai was sufficiently obvious. When the sacrifices are performed by the people, their purpose is sometimes social as well as religious. In any case the idea of keeping up the custom seems to play a great part. Western scholars are apt to take these sacrifices purely as the expression of religious faith and devotion. The following passages in *Lî Kî* may show that they are not always so.

As sacrifices are the most important of ceremonies or rites, let us first indicate the purposes for which they are offered.

'The rites to be observed by all under heaven were intended to promote the return (of the mind) to the beginning (=Creator of all); to promote (the honouring of) spiritual Beings; to promote the harmonious use (of all resources and appliances) of government; to promote righteousness; and to promote humility. They promote the return to the beginning, securing the due consideration of their originator. They promote (the honouring) of spiritual Beings, securing the giving honour to superiors. They promote the (proper) use of all resources, thereby establishing the regulations (for the well-being of) the people. They promote righteousness, and thus there are no oppositions and conflictings between high and low. They promote humility, in order to prevent occasions of strife. Let these five things be united through the rites for the regulation of all under heaven, and though there may be some extravagant and perverse who are not kept in order, they will be few.'[1]

There are two other passages, one of which indicates the objects to whom sacrifices should be offered and the other the purposes of the sacrifices.

'According to the institutes of the sage kings about sacrifices, sacrifice should be offered to him who had given (good) laws to the people; to him who had laboured to the death in the discharge of his duties; to him who had strengthened the state by his laborious toil; to him who had boldly and successfully met great calamities; and to him who had warded off great evils.'[2]

'Sacrifices were for the purposes of prayer, or of thanksgiving, or of deprecation.'[3]

The sun, moon, and stars fall under none of the above five classes except that in later dynasties some stars were sacrificed to for the power of warding off evils. With regard to the three purposes that of thanksgiving seems to be the sole motive for which the Chinese sacrificed to the sun, moon, and stars.

The Chinese were grateful to the sun, moon, and stars, and expressed their gratitude by means of sacrifices, because, says a passage: 'As to the sun and moon, the stars and constellations, the people look up to them.'[4] The phrase 'look up to' (*jan yang*) in this case has an ethical meaning, as when we speak of looking up to a great man with a view to modelling our behaviour on his. The Chinese believed that they could adjust their conduct by observing the appearances and movements of the heavenly bodies, which were regarded as God's revelation.

[1] *Lî Kî*, XXI. i. 20 (*SBE* xxviii. 219 f.).
[2] *Ib.* xx. 9 (*SBE* xxviii. 207 f.).
[3] *Lî Kî*, IX. iii. 28, in *Sacred Books of China*, pt. iii. (*SBE* xxvii. [1885] 448.
[4] *Lî Kî*, xx. 9 (*SBE* xxviii. 209).

There seem to be other reasons why the Chinese should be grateful to the sun, moon, and stars—especially to the sun for its great and various benefits—but the fact is that they attribute these benefits to *Tien*, God, rather than to the heavenly bodies themselves. Indeed their sacrifices to these bodies are sometimes an indirect way of expressing their gratitude to God.

7. Sun-worship, moon-worship, and star-worship.—Is there, or has there been, sun-worship, moon-worship or star-worship in China? The answer to this question depends upon what we mean by the term 'worship.' If by worship we mean the 'adoration, sacrifice, praise, prayer, thanksgiving, or other devotional acts performed in honour of the Supreme Being or God,'[1] it is certain that there is no such worship in China, and perhaps also that such worship has never existed there. None of the heavenly bodies is conceived by the Chinese as the Supreme Being. The Supreme Being is, for them, *Tien*, God, and God only. Nor can we find such worship in China if we take the term 'worship' to mean (1) the 'prostration which arises in presence of a superior being on whom we are absolutely dependent and whom we fear or reverence,' or (2) 'the feeling and act of worship' which 'involves primarily submission and fealty,' and 'is the attitude of the weak to the strong on whom they are absolutely dependent.'[2] The Chinese do not regard themselves as absolutely dependent on any of the heavenly bodies or on the spirits dwelling in them, but they regard the heavenly bodies or their indwelling spirits as dependent on *Tien*, 'God,' as they themselves are. It is true that they believe these heavenly bodies to possess powers which do not belong to men, but they also believe that men have powers which these bodies do not possess. What is more, some of them believe that certain men have the power of subjugating the spirits of the heavenly bodies, as magicians have the power of controlling spirits.

There are certain passages which have been regarded as evidence of sun-worship in China. In the 9th book of *Lî Kî*, called *Kiâo Teh Sĕng* ('The Single Victim at the Border Sacrifices'), a passage says:

'At the (Great) border sacrifice he [the Son of Heaven] welcomed the arrival of the longest day. It was a great act of thanksgiving to Heaven, and the sun was the chief object considered in it.'

Legge, commenting on this, says:

'The sun became for the time the "spirit-tablet" of Heaven. Fang Küeh says: "(The Son of Heaven) was welcoming the arrival of the longest day, and therefore he regarded the sun as the residence (for the time) of the spirit of Heaven. That spirit could not be seen; what could be looked up to and beheld were only the sun, moon, and stars."'[3]

The present writer need not give his own translation here, but he must point out that the idea that the sun was regarded as the residence of the spirit of Heaven is not implied either in Fang Küeh's commentary or in the text.

With reference to the passage in the book[4] on the meaning of sacrifices, namely:

'The sacrifice in the suburb of the capital was the great expression of the gratitude to Heaven, and it was specially addressed to the sun, with which the moon was associated,'

Khăn Hâo, a Chinese commentator, says, according to Legge:

'Heaven is the great source of tâo (the course of nature and duty), and of all the visible bodies which it hangs out, there are none greater than the sun and moon. Therefore, while the object of the suburban sacrifice was a grateful acknowledgment of Heaven, the sun was chosen as the resting-place for its spirit (or spirits). The idea in the institution of the rite was deep and far-reaching.'[5]

[1] *The Century Dictionary of the English Language*, London, 1889, *s.v.* 'Worship.'
[2] *DPhP* ii. 822.
[3] *SBE* xxvii. 427, n. 1.
[4] *Lî Kî*, XXI. i. 18.
[5] *SBE* xxviii. 218, n. 2.

The same remark may be made on the translation of this passage, viz. that there is neither in the text nor in the commentary the idea that the sun was chosen as the resting-place of the spirit (or spirits). The ultimate purpose in both these cases was to express gratitude by means of sacrifices to Heaven, but not to the sun or the spirit of the sun. Heaven is invisible, and they thought that for the object of sacrifice something visible was required. Therefore the sun was chosen as a symbol. Neither of these two cases therefore can be regarded as an example of sun-worship. There does not seem to be any other case. Legge says concerning the last example :

'It must be borne in mind that the rites described in the text are those of former dynasties, especially of that of Kâu. I cannot bring to mind any passages in which there is mention made of any sacrifice to the sun or sun-spirit in connexion with the great sacrifice to Heaven, or Shang Ti, at the service on the day of the winter solstice in the southern suburb.'[1]

Hence it is only by taking the term 'worship' in a very comprehensive sense, and by ignoring the purpose of the sacrifices, that we may say that the fact that the Chinese sacrificed to the sun implies that they worshipped it. It is the same with regard to their worship of the moon and the stars. In whatever sense we may be justified in saying that some of the Chinese worshipped the sun, moon, and stars, such worship occupies a very insignificant position in China compared with the worship of other natural phenomena or the spirits of them. If by sun-worshipper, moon-worshipper, etc., we mean one who regards the sun or the moon as the only or the supreme object of worship, we may say with conviction that the Chinese are not, as they have never been, sun-worshippers, moon-worshippers, or star-worshippers.

LITERATURE.—See the works quoted in the footnotes.

T. FU.

SUN, MOON, AND STARS (Hebrew).—The Hebrew conception of the universe, as we find it in the OT, is not scientific in the modern sense of the term. The cosmology of the Hebrews (see art. COSMOLOGY [Hebrew]) is characterized by the simplicity and *naïveté* of primitive folk. The attitude of mind is one of awe and wonder, not of critical inquiry ; and to pry closely into the secrets of the divine government is felt to indicate a want of reverence, and even to be dangerous. Moreover, it would be natural to a people which seems to have had an innate genius for religion to think, even after it had progressed beyond the stage of quite primitive ideas of the universe, that religion itself constituted the whole of true science or knowledge.[2] We need not expect, therefore, to find in the OT any inkling of the modern science of astronomy. The Hebrew shepherds without doubt, like the Phœnician mariners (cf. Pliny, *HN* vii. 57), closely observed the sky, and learned from the scrutiny many lessons of practical value for their every-day life. It is equally likely that at an early date the Hebrews were wont to worship the stars and planets. There are later traces of this worship in the OT (cf. 2 K 17^{16}).[3] And, besides this, the figures suggested by various constellations no doubt gave rise to a number of curious fables and fancies. On the other hand, the OT, as we have it, a collection of much-edited writings, preserves few traces of the astronomical and astrological lore of the Hebrews themselves. Since in the course of their national development the study of the stars and planets became more and more associated with the idolatrous practices of surrounding nations, later editors would be anxious to avoid, or even to remove, references to astronomy and astrology (cf. Dt 18^{10}). This would account for the fact that most of the references preserved in the OT are of a very general nature.

The chief planets are, of course, alluded to frequently. The sun (*shemesh*) is spoken of as ruling by day (Ps 136^{8}), and is often referred to as coming forth (from one chamber) in the morning and going in (-to another chamber) in the evening. Its magnificence (Jg 5^{31}) and its wonderful power for good (Dt 33^{14}) or for evil (2 K $4^{18f.}$; cf. Ps 121^{6}) impressed the Hebrews, as they have impressed all peoples. Jahweh Elohim Himself might be compared to a sun (Ps 84^{11}).[1] There are four words for 'moon' in the OT. *Yārēaḥ* is used especially in poetry (Gn 37^{9}, Jos 10^{12} etc.). To this word is closely related one of the words for 'month,' *yĕraḥ*, a word which is common to all the Semitic languages, though not in frequent use in the OT. Another word, *lebhānāh*, which occurs only three times (Ca 6^{10}, Is 24^{23} 30^{26}), designates the moon as the 'white one' or the 'pale one.' Rarer still is a word *kese'* (perhaps connected with the Assyr. *kusê'u*, 'headdress' or 'cap'), which denotes the full moon (perhaps the moon-god clothed in the splendour of his tiara).[2] The most common word is *ḥōdesh*, which means 'new moon,' and also 'month.' Thus the new moon was regarded as marking a new period or month, and the use of *yārēaḥ*, *yeraḥ*, and *ḥōdesh* for both moon and month shows that among the Hebrews the month and year were lunar. The moon rules the night (Ps 136^{9}), and, like the sun, is a power for good (Dt 33^{14}) or for evil (Ps 121^{6}). Its pale brilliance made it the emblem of beauty (Ca 6^{10}). In a few passages reference seems to be made to eclipses (Am 8^{9}, Is 38^{8}, Job 9^{7} etc.). And we are once told that 'the sun stood still, and the moon stayed, until the nation had avenged itself on its enemies'[3] (Jos $10^{12f.}$). In late writings there are several allusions to the worship of the sun (Ezk $8^{16f.}$, Job $31^{26f.}$; cf. 2 K 23^{5}) and moon (Dt 4^{19}).

Other planets are mentioned more incidentally. Thus, in all probability, Venus[4] as the Morning Star is referred to in Is 14^{12} under the name הֵילֵל, *hêlēl*, or הֵילָל, *hēlāl* (lit. 'the glittering one'), though it should be mentioned that some expositors have seen in the term an Arabic name for the moon (هلال, *hilâl*). W. Lotz (*PRE*³, *s.v.* 'Sterne') indeed argues that the Arabic word means 'new moon,' which would be unsuitable ;

[1] *SBE* xxviii. 218, n. 2.

[2] On this point Laurie Magnus's '*Religio Laici*' *Judaica* (1907) will be found suggestive. It has been argued elsewhere (W. Jay Hudson, *Law of Psychic Phenomena*[10], 1907) that ignorance of, or indifference to, what we term science might co-exist with a perfect knowledge of the laws of the moral and spiritual life.

[3] It is quite unnecessary to suppose that the idea of worshipping the stars and planets was borrowed, though, of course, the Hebrews came more and more into contact with people who were addicted to this worship. Whether and to what extent they came under direct Babylonian and Egyptian influence is a disputed matter (see K. Marti, *Religion of the OT*, p. 36 ff.). Cf. the proper names שִׁמְשׁוֹן (Jg 13^{24}) and שִׁמְשַׁי (Ezr 4^{8}), derived from שֶׁמֶשׁ, 'sun']; the Palmyrene ירחי, and the Biblical ירחו, Jericho, derived from יָרֵחַ, 'moon.' Cf. also Beth-shemesh, a place sacred to the sun-god. Commentators have seen in Mal 3^{20} (4^{2}) the conception of a winged solar disk such as we find among the ancient Egyptians, Babylonians, Assyrians, and Persians. But the present writer has pointed out (*Journal of the Manch. Egyptian and Oriental Society*, 1917, pp. 67–70) that the word usually translated 'wings' will bear another meaning. The meaning may be 'skirts' rather than 'wings,' and the figure that of the glorious robe that flows from the sun.

[1] In Jg 14^{18}, Job 9^{7} the word translated 'sun' is not *shemesh*, but *ḥeres* (cf. Is 19^{18}, and the place-names in Jg 1^{35} 8^{13}). It is probable that in Jg 14^{18} the text is corrupt.

[2] The name Sinai is probably derived from Sin, the name of the moon-god in Babylonian. In Ex 3^{1} Sinai is described as 'the mountain of Elohim,' *i.e.* the sacred mountain. This suggests that it had long been sacred.

[3] The writer clearly intends a miracle to be understood (so C. Steuernagel in Nowack's *Handkommentar*, 1899). Other expositors (*e.g.* W. H. Bennett in 'Joshua,' *SBOT*, 1899) regard the passage as poetic and figurative (cf. Jg 5^{20}).

[4] Another designation of Venus is *meleketh ha-shāmayim* מְלֶכֶת הַשָּׁמַיִם, 'the queen of heaven,' mention being made of cakes which were baked for her (Jer 7^{18} $44^{17.25}$).

but, according to Zimmern and Buhl's edition of Gesenius's *Lexicon* (*Handwörterbuch*^{14}, 1905) it can denote the old moon as crescent.[1] Further, in Am 5^{26} we probably have an allusion to Saturn (סִכּוּת, *sikkuth* = סַכּוּת, *sakkuth* = Assyr. *sakkut*; and כִּיּוּן, *kiyyun* = כֵּיוָן, *kêvān* = Assyr. *kaivânu*).

The stars, again, are alluded to frequently in a general way; but there are a few references to particular stars or constellations, and these require special attention. The earliest of them is found in Am 5^{8}. Since, however, the same terms occur, with others, in passages in the late book of Job which contain more precise references to astronomy, it is best to consider the Job passages first.

In Job 9^{9}, in a description of God's almighty power as manifested in the marvels of the material world, Job is represented as pointing to God as one

'Who shaketh the earth out of her place,
  and the pillars thereof tremble.
Who commandeth the sun, and it riseth not;
  and sealeth up the stars.
Who alone spreadeth out the heavens,
  and treadeth upon the waves of the sea.
Who maketh '*āsh*, *kĕsīl*,
  and *kīmāh* and the chambers of the south.'

The context indicates that the terms in the last two lines (עָשׁ, '*āsh*; כְּסִיל, *kĕsīl*; כִּימָה, *kīmāh*; חַדְרֵי תֵמָן, *ḥadrê tēmān*) designate particular stars or constellations. We are helped, too, by the fact that three of them occur again (*kīmāh* in Am 5^{8}, Job 38^{31}; *kĕsīl* in Am 5^{8}, Is 13^{10}, Job 38^{31}; '*ayish* = '*āsh* in Job 38^{32}); but there is considerable uncertainty as to the correct interpretation of some at least of the terms.

1. עָשׁ, '*āsh*, or better עַיִשׁ, '*ayish*, as in Job 38^{32}, and better still עֲיֻשׁ, '*ăyush*, as suggested by the Syriac (Pesh. עיותא). In Job 9^{9} LXX has Ἕσπερος, Vulg. 'Hyades'; in Job 38^{32} LXX Ἕσπερος, Vulg. 'Vesper.' Modern expositors have found in the word either the Great Bear, the Pleiades, Hyades, or the Northern and Southern Crown. '*Āsh* in Job 9^{9} has to be taken in connexion with the other passage, 38^{32}, in which, according to the Massoretic text, it is said: 'or dost thou guide '*ayish* with her young?' (וְעַיִשׁ עַל־בָּנֶיהָ תַנְחֵם).[2] It is noteworthy, too, that what in Arabic corresponds to the Great Bear is called *na'sh*, 'the bier,' and that the three tail stars of Ursa Major are called *banāt na'sh*, 'children of the bier' (*i.e.*, in this case, 'mourners'). It is true that no philological connexion can be established between the two words, but the Arabic phrase 'children (or daughters) of the bier' is suggestive as regards '*ayish* and her children. It might seem natural to expect to find a striking constellation like the Great Bear mentioned in Job 9, and it would be fitting that it should be assigned the first place, though it may be mentioned in passing that possibly the Hebrews thought of this constellation not as a Great Bear, but as a lioness with her young (cf. with Ewald, Arabic '*ayuth*, and see A. Dillmann's Commentary). But there is some force in the argument that '*ayish* can hardly be Ursa Major, because the constellations in Job $38^{31f.}$ are referred to on account of their meteorological importance. Some expositors, therefore (*e.g.*, M. A. Stern, Nöldeke, Schrader), have thought that '*ayish* represents the Pleiades. The great objection to this is that there is very good reason to think another Hebrew term (see below) designates that constellation. The 'children' of '*ayish* would certainly suit the Pleiades, which are sometimes represented as a hen with its chickens. But, on the other hand, the smaller stars surrounding or adjoining a star of the first magnitude might in several cases be described as its children. The Pleiades not being probable, some scholars agree with the Vulgate of Job 9^{9} in thinking that '*ayish* represents the Hyades (so, *e.g.*, Hoffmann, Schiaparelli); and this view has the support of the Syriac (Pesh. עיותא).[1] Moreover, the constellation is suitable as being one of great meteorological importance. Elsewhere in Hebrew '*āsh* means 'moth.' Friedrich Delitzsch has suggested that it may have the same meaning here, since the name 'moth' (*sâsu*) seems to have been given to a star by the Assyro-Babylonians (see T. G. Pinches, in Hastings' *DB*, *s.v.* 'Astronomy'). Now, the Hyades, a great red star of the first magnitude (Aldebaran) and five stars of the fourth magnitude, resemble our letter V or the Greek Λ. And Schiaparelli points out (p. 58) that in the butterfly stage, when the moth is at rest, 'its wings are not held detached from the body, as happens with most other butterflies, but spread themselves over it in such a way as to form a cloak, more or less similar (according to the several species into which the animal can be divided) to an isosceles triangle.' The suggestion is that to the author of the passages in Job '*āsh* meant 'moth,' which was a name for the Hyades. In that case, assuming the identity of '*āsh* and '*ayish*, the 'children' of '*ayish* would be the minor Hyades which surround Aldebaran. Against this it might be urged that it is easier to explain '*āsh* as short for '*ayish* than to account for '*āsh* as the original form, and that 'moth' does not seem a likely name for a constellation (especially the Hyades, apart from its form). The question of identification cannot be decided definitely. But, as the Pleiades has to be excluded (see below), there are reasons for thinking that either the Great Bear or the Hyades is intended. The Great Bear was no doubt as well known to the Hebrews as to other ancient peoples; but it would not be in the least surprising to find no mention of it in the OT, the references to astronomy being so few.

2. כְּסִיל, *kĕsīl*, usually translated 'fool.' In Job 9^{9} LXX has Ἀρκτοῦρος, Vulg. 'Orion'; in 38^{31} LXX Ὠρίων, Vulg. 'Arcturus'; in Am 5^{8} LXX omits, Vulg. 'Orion'; in Is 13^{10} (כְּסִילֵיהֶם, their '*kĕsīlīm*') LXX Ὠρίων, Vulg. 'splendor earum.' Some of the Rabbis of the Middle Ages (Saadya, Abulwalid, and others) identified the word with the Arabic *Suhail* and interpreted it in its later sense, Canopus. The preponderating view of the versions is in favour of Orion, a constellation which was popularly thought of as a giant who was bound in chains to the sky. *Kĕsīl* occurs elsewhere in Hebrew with the meaning 'dullard' or 'fool,' and modern expositors commonly think of the giant (Orion) as a fool in the sense of an impious person who had rebelled against God. But the Arabic equivalent of the root (كسل, *kasala*) means 'to be thick, plump,' which suggests that *kĕsīl* itself need not mean anything more than giant (the big, burly one); and, as Cheyne says (art. 'Orion' in *EBi*), *kĕsīl* ought not to be confounded with *nābāl* ('fool' in the sense of impious person). In Job 38^{31} there seems to be a reference to some myth current among the Hebrews, the giant being spoken of as bound with cords; but what exactly the myth was is quite uncertain. In Am 5^{8} *kīmāh* (see below) and *kĕsīl* are again mentioned together ('seek him that maketh *kīmāh* and *kĕsīl*, and turneth black darkness into morning,' etc.) as well as in Job 38^{31} ('Dost thou bind the bands of *kīmāh*, or loose the cords of *kĕsīl*?'). Further, in Is 13^{10} we find the curious expression 'their *kĕsīlīm*' (often translated 'the stars of

[1] P. Jensen, however, thinks (*JE*, *s.v.* 'Astronomy') that there is little ground for supposing that any star or planet is referred to; the reference in Isaiah is too vague.

[2] For תַנְחֵם, however, it is better to read תְּנַחֵם ('and dost thou console '*ayish* for her children?'). See, further, below.

[1] It seems certain that the Syriac word does denote the Hyades or the chief star of the group (cf. Barhebræus).

heaven and the Orions thereof').[1] This seems to indicate that primarily *kěsīlīm* was used to denote stars of the first magnitude, in distinction from lesser stars (*kōkābīm*). In any case it is pretty generally agreed that *kěsīl* represents Orion. It is one of the most brilliant constellations, and did not fail to arrest the attention of the ancients.

3. כִּימָה, *kīmāh*, literally 'a group, cluster,' cognate with Arabic *kâma* (كَامَ), 'to heap up.' In Job 9[9] LXX has Πλειάς, Vulg. 'Arcturus,' Pesh. and Targ. כִּימָא; in 38[31] the renderings of the Versions differ only to the extent that the Vulg. has 'Pleiades'; in Am 5[8] LXX omits, Vulg. has 'Arcturus,' Pesh. and Targ. כִּימָא. Most of the ancient authorities, in fact, understand the Pleiades by *kīmāh*. Several modern expositors, however, prefer to think of Sirius (*e.g.*, G. Hoffmann). But the word itself suggests that we are to look for a compact cluster of stars, and, of course, we must seek for one that early attracted attention. The Pleiades, as Schiaparelli says, is the best known of such clusters, 'and also the only one which has in consequence of its conspicuous light awakened universal attention at every time and among all peoples' (p. 62).[2] The expression 'the bands of *kīmāh*' in Job 38[32] is no doubt to be understood metaphorically.[3] The Arabic name for the Pleiades, *thurayya*, also means 'cluster,' and Bar Ali mentions it as an explanation of *kīmāh*. The word *kīmāh* itself has also been connected with the Arab. *kūmat*[un], 'house,' and the Assyr. *kimtu*, 'family.' In either case the name would suit the Pleiades.

It should be noted, further, that, according to some ideas found in the Talmud (*Beṛakhōth*, 58*b*; *Rosh ha-shanah*, 11*b*), God brought the flood by causing *kīmāh* to set instead of rise in the morning, and by removing two stars from it. This is given as the explanation of Rabbi Joshua. According to R. Eliezer, the changes took place at a season when *kīmāh* is wont to set in the morning, and what God did was to make *kīmāh* rise in the morning on the day in question and lose two stars. This caused the flood. According to Stern, the dates mentioned suit exactly the morning rising and setting of the Pleiades, and seem to prove that in the time of Rabbi Joshua and Rabbi Eliezer (beginning of 2nd cent. A.D.) the Jews identified the Pleiades with *kīmāh*. It is further represented in the Talmud (*ib.*) that God afterwards set things right by taking away two stars from *'ayish* to diminish its rain-producing force.[4]

4. חַדְרֵי תֵּמָן, *ḥadrê tēmān*, lit. 'chambers of the south.' The LXX renders ταμεῖα Νότου, Vulg. 'interiora Austri.' We seem to require mention of another definite constellation. This has given rise to the suggestion that the phrase designates the bright star Canopus or the constellation to which it belongs (so Stern). Other expositors regard the text as corrupt, and, emending חדר וְתמן, see in the first word some uncertain constellation, and in the second (תאמן=תמן) Gemini, 'the Twins.' But we are not obliged to find in *ḥadrê tēmān* a special constellation. 'Chambers (or store-houses) of the South' might, as K. Budde says ('Hiob,' in W. Nowack's *Handkomm. zum AT*, 1896), denote a whole group of constellations in the southern sky. Dillmann (*loc. cit.*) thinks that the author of Job cannot have known anything of the stars of the southern hemisphere, but that it was known to him, as one who had travelled, that the farther one goes south the more stars and constellations become visible. To those who dwelt in the north these were, so to say, enclosed in the inmost chambers of the vault of heaven, and were therefore invisible. This would explain the expression 'treasure-houses of the South' (cf. Pr 24[4]; Job 37[9]). The word *ḥeder*, coming from a root meaning literally 'to conceal,' in the plural would bear the meaning 'penetralia.'[1] Schiaparelli gives reasons for thinking that the reference is to the imposing constellation found on the charts of to-day 'distributed between Argo, the Southern Cross, and the Centaur'; but whether this was visible to the author of Job depends upon the date of the book, which is uncertain.

In Job 38[31f.] we find another difficult astronomical term. The passage is as follows:

'Dost thou bind the bands of *kīmāh*,
or loose the cords of *kěsīl*?
Dost thou bring out *mazzārōth* in his season,
or dost thou lead out *'ayish* with her young?'

We have already dealt with three of the terms which occur here. We have now to consider—

5. מַזָּרוֹת, *mazzārōth*. The Vulg. has 'Lucifer'; Targ. שמרי מוליא. The word may come from זָרָה, *zārāh*, which means literally 'to scatter,' but can be applied to powder (Ex 32[20]), hair (Ezk 5[2], Is 30[20]), etc. *Mazzārōth* would then mean 'scatterers' or 'sprinklers,' the reference being to rain. On this supposition, Stern and Hoffmann understand the Hyades to be meant, since the heliacal rising of their chief star, Aldebaran, announces the season of rain.[2] Gesenius derived the word from נזר, *nāzar* (Arab. نذر), and explained it as 'astra præmonentia.' Another suggestion is that it is derived from זהר, *zāhar*, *mazzārōth* being for *mazhārōth*, and meaning the 'brilliant' stars which shine with a special lustre, the planets, either all of them or the brightest and most striking. But the word is more commonly regarded as identical with *mazzālōth* (מזלות) in 2 K 23[5], the interchange of *l* and *r* presenting little difficulty. The LXX has μαζουρώθ in both cases. In 2 K *mazzālōth* has been supposed by some expositors to mean 'the signs of the zodiac,' being apparently a loan-word from Assyr. *manzaltu* or *mazaltu*, 'station, abode (of gods),' which, again, is from *nazâzu*, 'to stand.' But in the passage in question it would be more natural to find mention of the planets, and some expositors so interpret *mazzālōth* (in Rabbinic *mazzālōth* means 'planets' as well as 'signs of the zodiac'). *Mazzālōth* would be the stars and planets regarded as 'mansions' (Assyr.) of the great gods (see *EBi, s.v.* 'Mazzaloth').[3]

[1] Kittel would read כּוֹכְבֵיהֶם, 'their stars.' But this is not necessary. Nor is it necessary to follow Cheyne in emending the whole of the beginning of the verse thus: עַיִשׁ וְכִימָה וּכְסִיל, 'the Great Bear, the Pleiades (?), and Orion.'

[2] An old English name for them is 'the seven stars' (AV in Am 5[8]).

[3] The Hebrew has מַעֲדַנּוֹת כִּימָה, *ma'dannōth kīmāh*, which AV translates 'sweet influences,' some such idea being suggested by the root as found elsewhere. It is better, however, to follow many modern expositors, and regard *ma'dannōth* as equivalent to *ma'naddōth*, 'bands' or 'fetters,' from *'ānad*, 'to bind' (so Ewald, Dillmann, Duhm, and others). It we translate 'bands,' we may think of the Oriental poets' habit of comparing the Pleiades with an ornament (Ideler, *Sternnamen*, p. 147).

[4] According to Stern, the Talmudists undoubtedly understood the Hyades by *'ayish*. May there not be references to an earlier form of this kind of legend in Job 38[31f.]? The passage might be translated thus (interchanging תקשר and תפתח in ver. 31):

Dost thou loosen the bands of the Pleiades (*kīmāh*)
or bind fast the cords of a giant (-star, *kěsīl*)?
Dost thou lead forth the rainers (*mazzārōth*) in due season
and comfort the Hyades for its children?

The 'rainers' (from זָרָה, lit. 'to scatter') would be the stars taken from the Hyades, and are referred to in the next clause as 'its children.'

[1] Cf. A. B. Davidson, 'Job' in *Cambr. Bible*, 1893: 'probably the great spaces and deep recesses of the southern hemisphere of the heavens, with the constellations which they contain.'

[2] Stern identifies *mazzārōth* with *mazzālōth*, and would derive the latter from הִזִּיל, *hizzīl*, 'to cause to flow.' This, again, would give some meaning equivalent to 'rain-producers.'

[3] P. Jensen (*JE, s.v.* 'Astronomy') says that *mazzālōth* may mean either 'planets,' 'signs of the zodiac,' or 'stations of the moon.'

It is not necessary, however, to regard *mazzārōth* and *mazzālōth* as identical. We have found reason to think that another word denotes the Hyades as a constellation. That does not prevent us from supposing that *mazzārōth* may be a further description of some of the stars in this group.[1] The word *mazzārōth* has also been identified with the Great Dog, whose chief star is Sirius. This, as the brightest of the fixed stars, and for meteorological reasons as well, everywhere attracted the notice of the ancients.

6. It should be noted further that in Job 37[9] another word occurs (מְזָרִים, *mĕzārīm*) which bears some resemblance to *mazzārōth*. The passage runs: 'Out of its chamber cometh the whirlwind, and cold out of *mezārīm*.' This word might also come from *zārāh*, 'to scatter.' On that assumption, it has been supposed to mean 'scattering' or north winds. Another suggestion, however, is that it is a corruption of the Babylonian *miśri*, 'the northern (star)' (so *EBi*, *s.v.* 'Mazzaroth'). A more recent conjecture is that of Schiaparelli (p. 69 ff.). He suggests that the correct punctuation of מזרים is *mizrīm* or *mizrayim*, *i.e.* the plural or dual of a word מִזְרֶה, *mizreh*, which is referred to in Is 30[24] and Jer 15[7] as an instrument for winnowing. Schiaparelli points out that the arrangement of the stars of the Great Bear is such that they might be thought to resemble a winnowing fan. To the ancient Chinese these stars actually suggested a ladle, which, with its cavity and handle, is very like a winnowing fan. The plural *mizrīm* would indicate more than one instrument. Schiaparelli therefore thinks that the word might designate the Great Bear and the Lesser Bear; and in that case, of course, the dual *mizrayim* would be a still more suitable description. The fact that the Phœnicians used the Lesser Bear when at sea to find the direction of the north is noteworthy in this connexion. The suggestion is very ingenious. But unfortunately *mizreh* is not the term which denotes a winnowing instrument of the shape required. The word for that is *raḥath* (the other term mentioned in Is 30[24]). *Mizreh* is apparently the *midhrā* of modern Syria, a pitch-fork with six prongs, and the Great Bear can hardly be said to resemble that.

7. Some expositors have found yet another reference to astronomy in the נָחָשׁ בָּרִחַ, *nāḥāsh bārīaḥ*, of Job 26[13]. Meaning literally 'the fleeing serpent,' the words have been supposed to refer to the Dragon between the Great and the Little Bear. There is nothing in the context, however, to indicate that the author had any star or constellation in mind.

The OT contains very few definite references to astrology, though the prohibition in Dt 18[10] shows that it was practised. We can hardly say that there was no astrology amongst the ancient Hebrews, in spite of the fact that the present allusions are late and due to Assyro-Babylonian influence. In Is 47[13] (post-Exilic) we read: 'Yea let them deliver thee, the dividers (?) of heaven (הֹבְרֵי שָׁמַיִם), the gazers on stars (הַחֹזִים בַּכּוֹכָבִים), those who make known each new moon (מוֹדִיעִים לֶחֳדָשִׁים), from the things that are coming upon thee.' The word translated 'dividers' occurs here only, and LXX has for the whole phrase *οἱ ἀστρολόγοι τοῦ οὐρανοῦ*. It has been connected with an Arabic word 'to divide' (*habara*, lit. 'to cut into large pieces'), a meaning which suits very well, since the Babylonians divided the sky for astrological purpose into signs of the zodiac. 'Those who make known each new moon' (or the 'monthly prognosticators') would be persons, like the Assyrian and Babylonian astrologers, who noted lucky and unlucky days, preparing monthly almanacs or calendars based on astrological calculations (see Cheyne, 'Isaiah,' *PB*, 1898). In Dn 5[11], according to AV, Daniel became chief of the 'astrologers' (אָשְׁפִין) in Babylon; but the correct translation of the word is 'conjurers' or 'enchanters.'

[1] See the conjecture made above on p. 82[a], note 4.

LITERATURE.—M. A. Stern, 'Die Sternbilder in Hiob 38, v. 31 und 32' in Geiger's *Jüd. Zeitschr. f. Wissensch. u. Leben*, iii. 1864–1865, pp. 258–276; Eb. Schrader, 'Sterne' in Schenkel's *Bibellexikon*, 1875; G. Hoffmann, 'Versuche zu Amos' in *ZATW* iii., 1883, pp. 107–110, 279; Ed. Riehm, 'Sterne' in Riehm's *HWB*, 1894; T. G. Pinches, 'Astronomy and Astrology' in Hastings' *DB*, vol. i. 1898; F. Hommel, *Der Gestirndienst der alten Araber und die altisraelitische Ueberlieferung*, 1901; 'Astrology' and 'Astronomy' in *JE*, vol. ii. 1902; C. F. Burney, 'Stars' in *EBi*, vol. iv. 1903; G. Schiaparelli, *Astronomy in the Old Testament* (Eng. tr.), Oxford, 1905; A. Jeremias, *Das Alte Testament im Lichte des alten Orients*[2], 1906; W. Lotz, 'Sterne' in *PRE*[3], 1907; E. W. Maunder, *The Astronomy of the Bible*[2], London, 1908.

MAURICE A. CANNEY.

SUN, MOON, AND STARS (Hindu).—**I. The sun.**—Solar worship has been described as the real religion of India. Nor is it difficult to understand how in a land flooded with sunshine, where every phase and function of life is dependent upon the kindly warmth of the sun and his destructive energy and power are felt in the uttermost extremes of heat, it should have been man's primary business to win his favour and placate his wrath. In the ancient verse of the *Gāyatrī* every Hindu begins his day with prayer and ascription of praise to the sun, the giver of light, heat, and fertility. In his mid-day devotion also he remembers and renders homage to the same deity. It is apparently true that at no period in India was the worship of the sun to any great extent exclusive. There are no distinct sects at the present time who reverence the sun alone and bear his name. The essentials of his worship, however, are present everywhere and in all the sects, more or less avowedly, or in disguise, and combined with other cults; and his practical and decisive influence on daily life is universally recognized.

In the *Ṛigveda* Sūrya, or the sun, is worshipped under many names and forms. The three chief aspects under which he presents himself to his worshipper are the rising, culminating, and setting sun. These are not separated or distinguished as three deities, but are varying forms of one and the same god, in each of which he displays himself with different attributes and as exercising different powers. Especially is he reverenced as Savitṛ, the giver and sustainer of life, who each morning wakes the universe and men from sleep. One of his most ancient cults, perhaps the most ancient of all, is under the name Mitra, the Persian Mithras; whence some have conjectured that India derived her solar religion from the West. If borrowing took place on either side, it is probable that in those early days the indebtedness was Persian. As Mitra, the sun was associated as a member with an early triad, symbolized by the sacred syllable *Om*, Agni or fire, Vāyu the wind, and Mitra. This triune aspect also was manifested in the sun as the heavenly fire, and he bore corresponding epithets or titles, as *tripād*, 'three-footed,' *trivikrama*, 'three-stepping,' and others. The last name was appropriated more particularly to Viṣṇu, the sun as the all-pervader, who in three strides traverses the three worlds, earth, heaven, and hell. He is invoked also as Pūśan, the guardian and preserver of the cattle, the companion of travellers, and guide of the soul on its perilous way to the lower world.

In the mythology Sūrya is the son of Dyaus, the wide-spreading sky, and is described as 'all-creating' and 'all-seeing.' In this aspect his most ancient and significant name is Prajāpati, the 'lord of creation.' He traverses the heavens in his golden car, drawn by seven steeds, of which Uṣas, or the Dawn, is the charioteer; and the Aśvins, twin gods of the morning, are his children. By his power he drives away the demons of sickness, and expels diseases and all the subtle and dreaded influences of darkness. The beneficent offices of physician and healer of bodily ills, which later are ascribed to the Aśvins, are in the first instance those of Sūrya himself.

There seems no reason to reject or doubt the statement of Śaṅkara in the 10th cent. that in his time there existed distinct sects of sun-worshippers, Sauryas, of one at least of which the members were accustomed to carry branded on their forehead and breast the symbol of their deity. They have, however, all died out and been forgotten.[1]

Not many temples dedicated to the worship of the sun have survived, nor is it probable that at any period in Indian history they existed in any considerable number. That at Konārak in Orissa is the best known, and architecturally of the most interest. It is, however, neglected and ruinous, and attracts no worshippers. There is another at Gayā, and a small but much-frequented shrine at Benares, where the fire-sacrifice is offered in honour of the sun.

Among the non-Aryan peoples of India and the sub-tribes, who may be described as on the borders of Hinduism, sun-worship is much more open and confessed. By the Dravidians and Kolarians the sun is widely invoked as Parameśvar, the creator and preserver, and is worshipped with prayer and sacrifice. The most popular form of offering is a white cock, whose head is struck off at the village shrine. He is Sūrāj Nārāyan (Sūrya-Nārāyaṇa), and the traders in the bazaars draw images or symbols of the sun at the entrance to their booths for good luck.[2] Similar representations or figures may be often seen on pillars. The *nīm*-tree is especially sacred to the sun, and there exists a popular legend or story which records its association with his cult. By many the *Holī* festival in the south of India is believed to have been instituted originally in order to propitiate the sun-god. He is invoked also to avert or to heal disease, and on the occasion of an eclipse the tom-toms are beaten and other ceremonies observed to rescue the deity from the powers of evil. The same conception, that worship and sacrifice are efficacious to avert disaster from the object of worship, may perhaps be recognized in the especial frequency of sun-ritual and adoration in the winter season among some northern tribes, at a time when the divinity may be supposed to be weak. A sacred meal is partaken of in his honour, and this must be eaten without salt. A similar ritual is observed when the sun enters a new sign of the zodiac. There are races and peoples in India at the present time who believe themselves to be descended from the sun.

2. The moon.—From the earliest times in India it would appear that the moon has been a popular subject of traditional story and mythology, but, so far as is known, there never existed any formal moon-cult or sectarian worship. A late work of the 17th cent. mentions 'moon-worshippers' and 'star-worshippers.' It is improbable, however, that any special sect was in the writer's mind. Worship of the moon in one or other of her aspects, either alone or in conjunction with other rites, is common in India at the present day, and such worship has in all probability never been intermitted. There are, however, no exclusive votaries or sects who make the moon their chief deity. In this respect, therefore, the popular worship of India is in contrast with the established cults of ancient Babylonia and other countries.

In the *Rigveda* and the early literature Soma (*q.v.*) is identified with the moon, and in one passage at least the waning of the moon is caused by the gods drinking up the nectar (*amṛta*).[3] The great deities Indra and Agni are identified with its phases, representing the new and full moon respectively; so also Varuṇa and Mitra are deities of the waxing and waning moon.[1] As usual among primitive peoples, the moon is a male divinity. A title of Śiva is *chandra-śekhara*, 'he whose crest is the moon,' *i.e.* the moon-bearer, and in this sense he is contrasted with Viṣṇu, who represents the sun. The ancient lunar dynasty of India (*chandravaṁśa*), whose capital was at Hastināpura, or Delhi, about 50 miles north-east of the modern city, claimed descent from the moon.

The moon also (Soma) was one of the treasures recovered at the churning of the ocean, together with the *amṛta* (nectar). Elsewhere he is enumerated among the eight *lokapālas*, or guardians of the universe. He is lord of the planets and of plants, of offerings and of penances.[2] More often he is regarded as one of the nine planets and is associated with them in worship, but especially with the sun. The departed go to the moon, and there is the abode of the *pitṛs*, 'fathers,' whither they are borne on the smoke of the funeral pyre. A more popular title or a more popular ritual for him is as Oṣadhipati, or Oṣadhīśa, 'lord of plants.' Agriculture in general is under his protection and is subject to his influence.

The phases of the moon are often decisive for the work of the fields; and the economy of the household, with its various anniversaries and important events, is similarly determined by the moon's position and aspects. The title 'lord of plants' is probably derived from the practice, common also in other countries, of collecting medicinal herbs, etc., by the light of the moon. In this character he is a god of healing, and for certain diseases—*e.g.*, leprosy—to gaze at the reflexion of the moon in *ghī* or oil is an important and efficacious remedy. The periods of new and full moon are especially dangerous owing to the increased activity of the spirits at these times. In some parts of the country the conch-shell is a symbol of the deity of the moon. Among some of the primitive Kolarian tribes, instead of being regarded as a male divinity, the moon is mythologically the wife of the sun, and the stars are their children.

3. The stars.—The principal stars and constellations are known to the Hindus by name, and are recognized as beneficent or the reverse, especially in their relation to family and individual happiness or misfortune.

Thus the Pole-star is *dhruva*, 'fixed' or 'stationary,' although the same title is given to some of the *nakṣatras* (see below). The seven stars of the Great Bear are seven *ṛṣis*, translated to the heavens. Canopus also is a *ṛṣi*, Agastya, the sage and reputed evangelist of S. India. The Pleiades are the six *kṛttikās*, 'nymphs,' the nurses of Skanda, the god of war, who bore from them the title of Kārttikeya. Orion represents the head of Brahmā in the form of an antelope's or stag's head (*mṛgaśiras*), struck off by Śiva, etc. Great regard is paid especially to the planets and the constellations or groupings of stars known as *nakṣatras*; and the star, planet, or constellation under which a man is born gives infallible indication of his future lot. In parts of N. India the stars generally are the cattle that the moon tends in the character of shepherd.

The full number of the planets is nine, but sometimes only seven or five are enumerated. There is a temple at Benares dedicated to the nine planets, where flowers and other offerings are presented. The complete number includes the sun and moon, and the others in order are Mercury, Venus, Mars, Jupiter, Saturn, with Rāhu and Ketu. The two last represent the ascending and descending nodes of the moon's orbit.

Rāhu is the cause of eclipses, when he swallows the sun or moon, and this he is said to do in revenge for the loss of his head, which was cut off by Viṣṇu as a punishment for his having stolen and drunk part of the nectar churned from the ocean. By drinking the *amṛta* he became immortal, and his wrath is perpetually exhibited in the eclipses, when the village folk seek to propitiate him with various rites. Rāhu is therefore known as the bodiless, and there exists at Benares a shrine dedicated to him under this form. Ketu is the progenitor of the numerous tribe of meteors and comets. In the *Purāṇas* they are all described as deities, each with his own car, that of Mars being golden with eight red horses. The days of the week also are named from them.

Some of the planets are favourable and some malevolent; but all need to be propitiated and their favour if possible secured before a marriage or other important event in the household. The omission of the *śānti* or *śānti-karman*, the 'propitiation' ceremony, would most certainly result in harm and disaster.

[1] See art. SAURAPĀTAS, SAURAS, OR SAURYAS.
[2] See art. SYMBOLISM (Hindu).
[3] *Rigveda*, x. lxxxv. 5.

[1] *Śatapatha Brāhmaṇa*, II. iv. 4. 17 f.
[2] *Vishṇu Purāṇa*, i. 22.

Rāhu and Ketu, with Saturn, are deities of ill omen who presage sickness and all kinds of trouble, and to be born when one of these is in the ascendant is a grave misfortune. The remaining planets are propitious, especially Mercury, Venus, and Jupiter, in whose hands are the gifts of wisdom and all knowledge and skill.

In the *Rigveda nakṣatra* is the name for a constellation in general. Universally, however, in later times and technically the *nakṣatras* are the lunar mansions, or stations, through which the moon passes, as the sun through the twelve signs of the zodiac. Originally these seem to have been 27 in number, but in the later literature and in astrological calculations more usually 28. Mythologically they are the wives of the moon and daughters of Dakṣa, one of the Ādityas. Like the planets, the *nakṣatras* are important and influential deities, whose countenance is sought before undertaking a journey or making arrangements for marriage or other domestic rites. Every Hindu boy's horoscope contains a reference to the *nakṣatra* under which he is born, and he bears a secret name other than that which is given him at the special name-giving ceremony (*nāmadheya*), which is written in the horoscope and is stated to contain always one letter at least from the name of the *nakṣatra* through which the moon was passing at the hour of his birth.

LITERATURE.—M. Monier-Williams, *Brāhmanism and Hindūism*4, London, 1891, pp. 341–346; W. Crooke, *The Popular Religion and Folk-Lore of Northern India*, 2 vols., do. 1896, *passim*; A. S. Geden, *Studies in the Religions of the East*, do. 1913, pp. 212 ff., 221 ff.; S. Reinach, *Cults, Myths, and Religions*, tr. E. Frost, do. 1912; H. Whitehead, *The Village Gods of South India*, Oxford, 1916; W. J. Wilkins, *Modern Hinduism*, London, 1887, *Hindu Mythology, Vedic and Puranic*, Calcutta, 1882.   A. S. GEDEN.

SUN, MOON, AND STARS (Iranian).—
Astronomy received much attention in ancient Persia, as is obviously implied by the current tradition that the Magi, the sacerdotal class of the Medes and Persians, were highly skilled in divination, an art which depended largely upon a knowledge of the heavenly bodies, astrology and astronomy being sister sciences in antiquity. The part which the veneration of the sun, moon, and stars played in the national religion of early Iran is well known (see art. ZOROASTRIANISM), and some of the Greeks regarded Zoroaster as much in the light of a professed astrologer and star-worshipper as in that of a wise man and prophet (cf. Diogenes Laertius, *Proœm.* i. 6, ἀστροθύτην; Scholiast on the Platonic *Alcibiades*, i. 122; *Clementine Homilies*, ix. 3–6, *Recognitiones*, iv. 27–29; Suidas, *Lexicon, s.v.* ἀστρονομία, Ζωροάστρης—all collected in Jackson, *Zoroaster, the Prophet of Ancient Iran*, New York, 1899, pp. 226–273). The Avesta and the Pahlavi books, especially the *Bundahišn* and *Dīnā-i Maīnōg-i Khraṭ*, contain frequent allusions of an astronomical nature; and Persian literature, after the Muhammadan conquest of Iran in the 7th cent., contains similar references. These three sets of sources furnish our chief supply of information, supplemented by comparisons drawn from Babylonia and Assyria, as well as by other material.

1. Conception of the universe.—The ancient Iranians naturally based their astronomical system upon a geocentric conception of the universe. It is probable that in the earliest times the shape of the earth was regarded as round and flat, although it is not altogether clear whether the Avestan word *skarna*, 'round' (cognate with the Greek σφαῖρα), signified merely circular, or whether it actually meant spherical (*Yašt*, v. 38, x. 95, xvii. 19). It is almost certain, however, that in later times the globular form of the earth was recognized by the Persian astronomers, possibly influenced by

Ptolemy, who was a great authority among the Arab-Persian scientists. The spherical shape may be inferred from two Pahlavi passages which apparently contain the idea of the cosmic egg—a wide-spread notion in antiquity. The first of these passages occurs in the *Dīnā-i Maīnōg-i Khraṭ*, xliv. 1–11 (tr. West in *SBE* xxiv. 85): 'The sky is arranged above the earth, like an egg, by the handiwork of the creator Aūharmazd; and the semblance of the earth, in the midst of the sky, is just like as it were the yolk amid the egg.' The second Pahlavi passage is found in the *Dīnkarṭ*, ii. 74. 2 (ed. Peshotan Sanjana, Bombay, 1876, ii. 72): 'The world and the other creatures are placed together in the midst of the sky, like the bird in the midst of the egg; the sky surrounds all, as the egg does the bird' (tr. Casartelli, *Mazdayasnian Philosophy*, Bombay, 1889, p. 107). In the arrangement of the universe the earth was regarded as encompassed by the atmosphere (Av. *vayu*, Phl. *vāi*; or Av. θwāša, Phl. *spihr*), above which was the sky or firmament (Av. O.P. *asman*, Phl. *Asmān*, lit. 'stone'), beyond which again rose the empyrean realm (Av. *anaγra raočā̊*, lit. 'endless lights'), the abode of Ormazd and his angels. Through a misapprehension of the true facts, moreover, the sun and moon were located beyond the sphere of the stars (cf. Phl. *Arṭā-Vīrāf*, vii. 1–x. 13; *Bundahišn*, iv. 4; *Zāṭ-Sparam*, vii. 6; *Šāyast lā-Šāyast*, xii. 5; *Gr. Iran. Bund.*, tr. Darmesteter, *Le Zend-Avesta*, ii. 310; *Dāṭistān*, ii. 1, xxxiv. 2; Av. *Vendīdād*, vii. 52; and consult Jackson, 'Die iranische Religion,' § 66, in Geiger and Kuhn, *Grundriss der iranischen Philologie*, ii. 671–672).

2. Sun and moon.—In the Zoroastrian ritual, as preserved in the Avesta, both the sun (*hvar*) and the moon (*māh*) receive high veneration individually, and each has a special hymn of praise devoted to its glorification (*Yašt*, vi. and vii.); besides, minor litanies and prayers are consecrated to their particular service (*Sīrōzah*, i. 11, ii. 11; *Yašt*, vi. 1–7, vii. 1–7; *Nyāiš*, i. 1–10, iii. 1–11). A similar degree of reverence was accorded them during Parthian and Sasanian times, as is shown by the Pahlavi texts themselves and by allusions in the Greek and Latin classics (*e.g.*, Phl. *Šāyast lā-Šāyast*, vii. 1–3; *Dīnkarṭ*, i. 51. 6, the former translated by West in *SBE* v. 297–298, and the latter by Peshotan Sanjana, Bombay, 1875, i. 47, and tr. p. 48: cf. also such classical writers as Strabo, xv. 3. 13, p. 732; Ammianus Marcellinus, *Hist.* xxiii. 6, xvii. 5; Dio Chrysostomus, *Orat. Borysthenitica*, xxxvi.; and Nicolaus Damascenus, frag. 66, p. 401, ed. Müller. The supremacy of the sun among the heavenly bodies is naturally emphasized in the Avesta (*e.g.*, *Yašt*, vi.), and its various positions in the heavens are described in *Bundahišn*, v. 1–7, and *Šāyast lā-Šāyast*, xxi. 1–7. In the latter passage there are to be found special observations of the midday and afternoon shadows with respect to the sun's altitude in the various zodiacal constellations. Solar observations were important in determining the various times of day for performing the sacrifice.

The moon, like the sun, is invoked because of its beneficent influence (*Yašt*, vii. 1–7), and there are several specific allusions to its periodic phases (*e.g.*, *Yasna*, xliv. 3; *Yašt*, vii. 2–4; *Fragment*, viii. 1; *Dāṭistān-i Dīnīk*, lxviii. 1–6, lxxi. 2, tr. West, *SBE* xviii. 210–211, 215). The connexion between the moon and the tides was fully recognized in Sasanian times, and a crude attempt was made to explain it (see *Bundahišn*, xiii. 13–14; *Zāṭ-Sparam*, vi. 14–17). Eclipses, both of the sun and of the moon, were regularly taken into account 'in the calculations of the astronomers,' at least under the Sasanians, as is shown by *Dāṭistān-i*

Dīnīk, lxix. 1–7, and the cause of these obscurations was thought to be the intervention of two bodies that revolve below the two greater lights (*Dāṭ*. lxix. 1–7; *Šikand Gūmānīg Vijār*, iv. 46, tr. West, *SBE* xviii. 212–213, xxiv. 132).

3. Stars.—There is an abundance of star-lore throughout the entire literature, and particular stars, or groups of stars, are alluded to as guarding the quarters of the heavens into which the Zoroastrians divided the firmament. The chief star in the Avesta, as elsewhere, is called Tishtrya (Av. *tištrya*, Phl. *tištr*), and it is usually identified with Sirius. Tishtrya is regent of the eastern division of the sky, an opponent of the meteors, and the bringer of rain by overcoming Apaosha, the demon of drought (*Yašt*, viii. 1 ff.; *Bundahišn*, ii. 7, v. 1, vii. 1, ix. 2). The fixed star Satavaēsa (Av. *satavaēsa*, Phl. *sat-vēs*, 'having a hundred servitors'), which is possibly to be identified with Fomalhaut, is an ally of Tishtrya, and lord of the southern heavens (*Yašt*, viii. 9, 32, 43, 44; *Bundahišn*, ii. 7, v. 1, xiii. 12; *Šāyast lā-Šāyast*, xiv. 5, vi. 16). The guardianship of the west is entrusted to Vanant (Av. *vanant*, Phl. *vanand*, 'victorious'; cf. *Yašt*, xxi. 1, viii. 12, xii. 16; *Nyāiš*, i. 8; *Bundahišn*, ii. 7, v. 1; *Maīnōg-i Khraṭ*, xlix. 12; *Šikand Gūmānīg Vijār*, iv. 28–38), while the keeping of the north is consigned to the constellation of Ursa Major, called Haptō-iringa (Av. *haptō-iringa*, Phl. *haptō-iring*, 'with seven signs'; cf. *Yašt*, viii. 12, xii. 28, xiii. 60; *Bundahišn*, ii. 7, v. 1, xiii. 12; *Maīnōg-i Khrat*, xlix. 12; *Šikand Gūmānīg Vijār*, iv. 28–38). The Pleiades (Av. *paoiryaēinī*) are mentioned in the Avesta (*Yašt*, viii. 12), and there are certain other allusions that may contain the names of special stars, though their interpretation is open to question (see Kuka, 'Stars mentioned in the Avesta' in *Zartoshti*, ii. 7–22, Bombay, 1904). In giving an account of creation, the Pahlavi book *Bundahišn* (ii. 5) sets the number of stars at 6480 (or 6,480,000, according to another reading). This figure is not uninteresting when taken in connexion with the fact that astronomers generally allow that between 5000 and 8000 fixed stars are visible to the naked eye. Regarding the identification of certain of the major stars, though some are positively sure, reference may be made to a monograph by Muncherji P. Kharegert, 'Some Heavenly Bodies mentioned in Old Iranian Writings,' in the *Sir Jamsetjee Jejeebhoy Madressa Jubilee Volume*, Bombay, 1914, pp. 116–158; see also Moulton, *Early Zoroastrianism*, London, 1913, pp. 23–27, 210–213, 279–281.

4. Planets, meteors, and comets.—In contrast to the fixed stars and regular constellations, the planets, meteors, and comets were held by Zoroastrians to be disturbers of the established order of the universe, and consequently to be of Ahrimanian origin and evil nature—a point of view directly opposed to that of Babylonia, where the planets were looked upon as distinctly beneficent in character (cf. Jastrow, *Religion of Babylonia and Assyria*, Boston, 1898, p. 373). To the planets Mercury, Mars, Jupiter, Venus, and Saturn (the only five then known, but making seven with the sun and the moon, by the side of which they were usually mentioned) there were given, respectively, in Pahlavi the euphemistic names *Tīr*, *Vahrām*, *Aūharmazd*, *Anāhid*, and *Kēvān*, derived from divine names, including the name of the god Ahura Mazda himself, because these beneficent powers curb and restrain the maleficent influence exercised by the planets (*Bundahišn*, v. 1–2; *Šikand Gūmānīg Vijār*, iv. 1–5; *Zāṭ-Sparam*, ii. 10, iv. 7–10, vi. 1–2; and consult the list in al-Bīrūnī, *Chronology*, tr. Sachau, London, 1879, p. 172). The Persian treatise *Ulamā-i Islām* (tr. Vullers, *Fragmente über die Religion des Zoroaster*, Bonn, 1831, p. 52) states that they originally bore the names of demons, but were afterwards given designations of good omen. At the same time it is not impossible that we have in their nomenclature a translation of the Babylonian names of the planets, *Nabu*, *Nergal*, *Marduk*, *Ištar*, *Ninib*, as may be surmised from the equations, Marduk (lord of the gods) = Aūharmazd = Jupiter; Nergal (god of war) = Vahrām = Mars; and Ištar = Anāhid = Venus; on the confusion between Tishtrya ('Sirius') and Tir ('Mercury') compare the note by Gray, *ERE* i. 798ᵇ; and, for the Babylonian names of the planets, consult Jensen, *Kosmologie der Babylonier*, Strassburg, 1890, pp. 134–139; Jastrow, *Religion of Babylonia and Assyria*, pp. 370, 454–466. This parallel, in any case, is of interest because the Sanskrit names given by the Hindus to the planets show no likeness to the Babylonian (cf. Weber, *Vorlesungen über indische Literaturgeschichte*[2], Berlin, 1876, p. 267 f.). Shooting stars are alluded to in the Avesta (*Yašt*, viii. 8) under the name of *kərəmā stārō*, a designation meaning, perhaps, 'worm stars'; and there are several passages, in both Avesta and Pahlavi literature, which allude presumably to comets (*Yasna*, xvi. 8; *Bundahišn*, v. 2, xxviii. 44, xxx. 17; *Dāṭistān-i Dīnīk*, xxxvii. 55, lxix. 2).[1]

5. Signs of the zodiac.—The names of the twelve signs of the zodiac, at least in Sasanian times, correspond in concept with those familiar to us through the Greek and Latin designations, and are parallel likewise with the Babylonian, from which, like the Indo-Germanic zodiac in general, they are believed to be derived, and of which their names are translations—a phenomenon precisely paralleled in India and in other Asiatic countries (see Ginzel, *Handbuch der Chronologie*, i., Leipzig, 1906, pp. 78–88). Thus in Pahlavi we find *Varak* ('Ram,' Aries), *Tōrā* ('Bull,' Taurus), *Dō-patkar* ('Two-figures,' Gemini), *Kalakang* ('Crab,' Cancer), *Šēr* ('Lion,' Leo), *Khušak* ('Maiden,' Virgo), *Tarāzuk* ('Balance,' Libra), *Gazdūm* ('Scorpion,' Scorpio), *Nēmasp* ('Half horse,' Centaur or Sagittarius), *Vahīk* ('Goat,' Capricorn), *Dūl* ('Waterpot,' Aquarius), *Mahīk* ('Fish,' Pisces). The names of the twenty-eight lunar mansions, as recognized in 'the subdivisions of the astronomers' (Phl. *xūrṭak-i hāmārīkān*), are given in the *Bundahišn* (ii. 3); but the reading of the various designations is by no means sure, and the individual identification of the names remains, therefore, uncertain, even when compared with those in the Soghdian and Khorasmian list, given about A.D. 1000 by al-Bīrūnī (*Chronology*, tr. Sachau, p. 227 f.).[2] Possibly some further light may be gained from a study of the terminology used for these asterisms by the Hindus, Chinese, and Arabs, if not by the Babylonians (see Ginzel, *op. cit.* pp. 70–76). Such an attempt has already been made from the Sanskrit side, in comparison with Avestan and Pahlavi, by a Parsi scholar named Anklesaria, in an article entitled 'Asterisms in Iranian Literature' in *Cama Memorial Volume*, Bombay, 1900, pp. 216–227.

6. Prediction of events.—Like the reference in the preceding paragraph to the minute subdivisions used by the astronomers (*Bund.* ii. 3), there are kindred allusions in Sasanian literature to 'the calculations of the astronomers' or to 'the com-

1 The Soghdian names of the planets given by Manichæan fragments discovered at Turfan, in Chinese Turkestan, correspond in general to the forms given above (see F. W. K. Müller, 'Die "persischen" Kalendarausdrücke in chinesischen Tripiṭaka,' *SBAW*, 1907, pp. 458–465).

2 The zodiacal names given by the Turfan fragments (Müller, *loc. cit.*) are identical with those of Eastern Asia, as found in China, Siam, and Cambodia, as well as in Tibet and in Old Turkish inscriptions (Ginzel, pp. 85–87, 404, 411, 452, 501), thus differing entirely from the Babylonian nomenclature.

putations made by astrologers' with regard to observing favourable or unfavourable conjunctions of the stars (*e.g.*, *Dāṭistān-i Dīnīk*, lxix. 3; *Šikand Gūmānīg Vijār*, iv. 28; *Epistles of Mānuščīhar*, II. ii. 9–11; see West, *SBE* v. 11, xxiv. 130, xviii. 212, 333–335, xxxvii. p. xlvii). Ardavān, the last of the Parthians and predecessor of Ardashīr Pāpakān, who founded the Sasanian dynasty in the 3rd cent. A.D., is represented as consulting on grave matters with his 'wise men and constellation-knowers' (*dānakān va axtar-mārān*, in the Pahlavi text *Kārnāmē-i Artakhshīr-i Pāpakān*, ii. 4–5, iii. 5–6, ed. Darab Peshotan Sanjana, Bombay, 1896, pp. 10–11, 15–16), and their knowledge of the position of the stars at the moment enabled them to predict to him future events. In a Pahlavi work dated A.D. 881 and entitled *Epistles of Mānuščīhar*, II. ii. 9–11 (re-translated by West, *SBE* xxxvii., Introd. p. xlvii), there is a specific allusion to a set of astronomical 'tables' (Phl. *zīk*, cf. Arab. *zīj*, and the Byzantine Gr. ζῆζι of Theodorus Meliteniotes, ed. Usener, *Ad historiam Astronomiæ Symbola*, Bonn, 1876, p. 14), which were constructed by 'the great Shatro-ayār.' See, more fully, art. SUN, MOON, AND STARS (Muhammadan), p. 95b below. The passage cited mentions the tables alongside of those of Ptolemy and of the Hindus.

7. Astronomical works.—Some of the works from which citations have been drawn above, like the one last quoted, actually belong to the early Muhammadan period of Persia, even though written in Pahlavi. Astronomy, influenced by Arab science, continued to flourish in Iran under Muslim rule. The notable scientific achievements of the great savant and chronologist, al-Bīrūnī of Khiva (973–1048), are sufficient to prove that fact, and it is certain that computations of the positions of the heavenly bodies must have played an important part in the reform of the calendar and establishment of the new Jalalian era, in 1079, by the Seljūk sultan, Jalāl-al-dīn Malikshāh, under the direction of a commission of scholars headed by the well-known astronomer poet, Omar Khayyam. Omar, in fact, had been summoned to Merv by the sultan, four years previously, to make observations in the royal observatory, and there he constructed the *Zīj-i Malikšāhī*, 'Astronomical Tables of Malikshāh,' which were employed in the calendar reform. The names of two of his colleagues engaged upon the reform were Abu'l Muẓaffar al-Iṣfizārī and Maimūn ibn Najīb al-Wāsiṭī (see Browne, *Literary History of Persia*, London, 1906, ii. 181, n. 2). A section of a large work composed in 1082–1083 by Kai-Kā'ūs and entitled *Qābūs-Nāmah* (ch. 34) was devoted to 'astrology and mathematics' (ed. Teheran, 1285 A.H.; tr. A. Querry, Paris, 1887; cf. Browne, *Lit. Hist. Pers.* ii. 277). The Persian poet Anvarī, of the 12th cent., was a great astrologer, and a conjunction of the planets in the sign of Libra, calculated to take place on September 16, 1186 (or in October of the preceding year, according to other accounts), led him to predict dire calamities for that day; but happily they did not occur (see Browne, *Lit. Hist. Pers.* ii. 368; Horn in *GIrP* ii. 262–263). In the 13th cent. the Mongol ruler Hulāgū Khān, grandson of Chingīz Khān, established a celebrated observatory at Marāghah, in Azarbaijan, Western Persia, the building of which was begun in 1259, and traces of its ruins are still to be seen (cf. Wilson, *Persian Life and Customs*, New York, 1895, p. 77). Hulāgū's astronomer-royal was the learned Naṣīr-al-Dīn of Ṭūs (1201–1274), whose *Zīj-i Ilkhānī*, or almanac and astronomical tables, was a notable contribution to science (see Browne, *Lit. Hist. Pers.* ii. 484–486). The names of several other mediæval Persian astronomers, with a mention of their tables, are found in the Byzantine treatise of Theodorus Meliteniotes, referred to above (ed. Usener, pp. 13–14). Best known among the astronomical tables, however, are those of Ulugh Begh, grandson of Timur and founder of the observatory at Samarkand, in which city he died in 1449. These tables, written in Arabic, were translated into Persian and were made accessible in Europe through a Latin version by Greaves (Gravius, London, 1652), and again by Hyde in Persian and Latin (Oxford, 1665), and more recently by Baily (London, 1843) in *Memoirs of the Royal Astronomical Society*, xiii. 79–125. With reference to the present status of astronomical studies in Persia itself, one of the largest meteorites in the world is preserved as a curiosity in the Shah's palace at Teheran to-day; but there is no astronomer-royal to know its true value, and Persia must still wait a renaissance before independent work in studying the heavens is done by those of native birth.

8. Influence of the heavenly bodies.—The astrological aspects of Persia's early studies of star-lore have already been indicated above. In fact, there is little reason to doubt that 'judicial astrology,' or the attempt to determine scientifically the presumed influence of the heavenly bodies upon the destiny of human events, was often regarded more highly than natural astrology, or astronomy in our sense, which confines its investigations to determining the motions and positions of the stars, sun, and moon, in order to gain more strictly scientific results, as we regard them.

In some of the paragraphs given above there have been allusions to the beneficent part played by the sun and the moon in the development of the world and in advancing the welfare of mankind (*e.g.*, *Yašt*, vi. 1–5, vi. 5; *Bundahišn*, vii. 2–4, and elsewhere), while the stars also entered into the sphere of human activity by exercising a kindly sway over the earth. Thus the great rain star Tishtrya, aided by Satavaēsa in the Avesta (*Yašt*, viii. 1–62; *Sīrōzah*, i. 13, ii. 13), combats the demon of drought, when invoked by men, and confers blessings upon his faithful worshippers. The victorious star Vanant (*Yašt*, xx. 1) repulses the influence of evil; and Haptō-iringa (Ursa Major) is effective even in tempering the torment of the souls in hell, a region located in the North (*Maīnōg-i Khraṭ*, xlix. 15–21; *Šikand Gūmānīg Vijār*, iv. 31–33). The three fixed stars or constellations just named are regarded in the Pahlavi book *Šāyast lā-Šāyast* (xiv. 5–6), which was written about the 7th cent., but contains older material, as exercising an influence upon the efficiency of the sacrifice during the time of their ascendancy. In another chapter of the same work (*Šāyast lā-Šāyast*, xxi. 1–7) a specifically fortunate character is ascribed to the shadow of the noonday and afternoon sun when occupying certain positions in the zodiacal signs; and in *Dāṭistān-i Dīnīk*, vi. 9, the stars are synonymous with destiny. The malign influence ascribed to the planets has been sufficiently indicated above, and need not be referred to again in this section.

Sufficient reference has likewise been made to the part played by astrology, astrologers, and horoscopes both in Sasanian and in Muhammadan-Persian times. We need only recall the allusion to the last of the Parthian kings, Ardavān, and his astrologers (*Kārnāmē*, ii. 4–5, iii. 5–6), and we have the authority of the great Khorasmian scientist al-Bīrūnī for the fact that the Persian astrologers, like others, held that the zodiacal sign of Cancer was 'the horoscope of the world' (al-Bīrūnī, *Chronology*, tr. Sachau, p. 55). A good illustration, in the 17th cent., of ephemerid tables that were used also for horoscopic purposes may be found in a work translated from the Arabic, Persian, and Turkish, with a Latin commentary, by Beck, in his *Ephemerides Persarum per totum annum*, Augsburg, 1696 (especially chs. iii.–iv., vi.). Even to-day the astrologer's art in casting a horoscope holds an important place in the life of the ignorant and superstitious folk of Persia, and it still survives, though it is gradually disappearing, among the Zoroastrian Parsis of India (cf. Karaka, *History of the Parsis*, London, 1884, i. 160–162).

LITERATURE.—For a translation of the Avesta and the Pahlavi books consult the versions by Darmesteter and West in *SBE*, vols. iv., xxiii.; and v., xviii., xxiv., xxxvii., and by Mills, *ib.* xxxi.; likewise the French translation by Darmesteter, *Le Zend-Avesta*, 3 vols., Paris, 1892–1893. The more important single works on the subject have been given in the course of the article.

A. V. WILLIAMS JACKSON.

SUN, MOON, AND STARS (Japanese).—In the ancient mythology of Japan the sun-goddess plays the most important rôle, while the moon-god, her brother, occupies an insignificant place, and almost nothing is told about stars. The commonly accepted story is that the sun-goddess (Amaterasu, 'the heaven-shining deity') and the moon-god (Tsuki-yomi, 'the ruler of the moonlight night') were born, together with the storm-god (Susa-no-wo, 'the swift-impetuous'), of the couple who were the progenitors of the Japanese archipelago.[1] In this story the creation of these deities is conceived evidently as a generative act, whereas another version makes the emergence of the two deities from the 'white copper' mirrors the work of the male progenitor alone. Perhaps a more interesting version of the story is that the sun and the moon were produced out of the eyes of the progenitor, when he was washing in order to purify himself from the stains with which he had been contaminated on his visit to the infernal world after the death of his consort.[2] Though there are these different versions, the common trait and predominant factor in the story is that the sun-goddess is considered to be the supreme ruler of heaven and earth, and also the progenitrix of the ruling family, who claim to have handed down from the goddess herself the three insignia of the throne (see below). Now the relation between the sun-goddess and the moon-god is based on the natural phenomenon that the two are visible alternately by day and by night. The story is as follows:

> The sun-goddess once commissioned her brother, the moon, to go down from their heavenly abode to earth to see Ukemochi, the female genius of food. When the latter entertained the moon with the food-stuffs taken out of her body, the moon became flushed with anger and slew the goddess of food. The sun-goddess was so displeased with her brother's wantonness that she said to him: 'Thou art a wicked deity. I must not see thee face to face.' Hence the sister and brother appear alternately in heaven.[3]

The intention of the story is evident, but at the same time it shows a characteristic of the sun-goddess as the matron of agriculture, which played a great part in the myths and worship of the goddess.[4] Thus, in contrast to the prominent rôle played by the sun-goddess, the moon plays a very inferior part, and a much smaller part is played by the stars. A star-god is mentioned in the ancient myth, but his rôle is quite ambiguous, while a festival in honour of certain stars (the stellar constellations called the Herdsman and the Weave-maid) was derived from China. All other stories and worship of stars are much later and were introduced chiefly through Buddhist agency, though some of them may have been derived from other sources—Hindu, Persian, or Chinese. The most prominent star-worship is that of the Pole star, together with Ursus Major. These stars, conceived as one deity, are worshipped by the Buddhists as the protector of the country as well as of individual fortune, while the Shintōists identify them with the Taoist 'palace of iridescent subtlety' (Shi-bi-kyū in Sino-Japanese), where the highest deity of Shintō, the 'eternal-ruling' (Minaka-nushi), is believed to reside. But this Shintō worship is of late origin; it was specially emphasized by a Shintō theorizer in the early part of the 19th century.

When Buddhism was introduced into Japan (6th cent.) and questions came up as to the relationship between the indigenous deities and the Buddhist pantheon, the Buddhist teachers tried to discover analogies between them and to explain that the Buddhist deities were the original noumena and the native ones their lateral manifestations. The most striking analogy was found between the sun-goddess and the aspect of Buddha's personality conceived in the sun-myth. The difference in gender concerned the syncretist but little, partly because the Japanese language had no genders and partly because the noumenon and the manifestation may take any sex. The result was an identification of the Japanese sun-goddess with Buddha Vairochana ('the illuminator'), and this conception exercised a wide influence on doctrine and worship during the sway of the syncretic Shintō from the 8th cent. down to the middle of the 19th, when the combination was dissolved by force. Among the theorizers of the syncretism we may cite one, Kanera (1402–81), who explained sun, moon, and stars as corresponding to the three insignia of the throne, *i.e.* the sun to the mirror, the moon to the jewel, and the stars to the sword.[1] This eclectic theory was backed by the popular conception of the 'three illuminating bodies' (*San-kō*) and their worship. People even nowadays regard a simultaneous appearance of the three as an auspicious occasion for worship and as a sign of special blessing to the country—*e.g.*, when on an autumn day the clear sky and the comparatively weak light of the sun cause the new moon and a certain star (Venus) to be visible to the eyes. Naturally, various configurations of the celestial bodies were used for methods of divination and predictions. In these methods Hindu, Persian, and Chinese elements may be detected, and their influence is still a living force among the mass of the people.

LITERATURE.—Besides the works cited in the footnotes, see M. Anesaki, *Japanese Mythology* (=vol. viii. of *The Mythology of All Races*), Boston, 1920.

M. ANESAKI.

SUN, MOON, AND STARS (Muhammadan).—I. *ASTROLOGY*.—1. Name.—Among the Muslims the technical name of astrology is *'ilm* (or *ṣinā'at*) *aḥkām an-nujūm*,[2] 'science (or art) of the decrees of the stars,' *'ilm al-aḥkām*, 'science of the decrees.' Sometimes, though rarely, in place of *aḥkām* its synonym *qaḍāyā* is found. Another name is *an-najāmah* (*nijāmah*) or *'ilm an-najāmah*. On the other hand, the names *'ilm* (*ṣinā'at*) *an-nujūm*, 'science (or art) of the stars,' *'ilm at-tanjīm*, mean astronomy as well as astrology, and they also mean both of these sciences taken together. The word *aḥkām* also signifies 'judgments,' 'judicial decisions'; accordingly the first of the denominations given above was in the Middle Ages translated in the Latin versions of Arabic works by *scientia judiciorum stell-*

[1] See *Nihongi: Chronicles of Japan*, tr. W. G. Aston (*Proc. Japan Soc. of London*, Suppl. to vol. i. [1896]), p. 18 f.; and, for the following stories, pp. 20, 32, etc.

[2] See *Koji-ki, or Records of Ancient Japan*, tr. B. H. Chamberlain (*TASJ*, Suppl. to vol. x. [1883]), pp. 42–44. This version is preserved also in *Nihongi*, p. 32, and, for its connexion with the conception of life and death, see art. LIFE AND DEATH (Japanese).

[3] *Nihongi*, p. 32.

[4] Aston, *Shinto*, London, 1905, p. 282 f., where the ritual to the goddess for harvest is cited.

[1] See art. PHILOSOPHY (Japanese), vol. ix. p. 870.

[2] As in the case of the other branches of scientific literature, so for astrology the Musalmān peoples made use of the Arabic language.

arum, and thence came the name of *astrologia judiciaria* or *astronomia judiciorum*, astrology, as opposed to *astrologia* (*astronomia*) *quadrivialis* (or *doctrinalis*), which is astronomy. Thus in the denomination of astrology among the Musalmāns there is a concept somewhat different from that contained in the Greek term [τέχνη] ἀποτελεσματική, 'science of the fulfilment [of astrological prognostications].' The astrologer is usually called by the same name as the astronomer, viz. *munajjim* (much more rarely *najjām*); sometimes, however, he is called by the special word *aḥkāmī* (plur. *aḥkāmiyyūn*, *aṣḥāb ṣinā'at al-aḥkām*). It was only in the 19th cent. that the distinction between *munajjim*, 'astrologer,' and *falakī*, 'astronomer,' was introduced into Arabic (at least in Egypt and in Syria).

2. Divisions.—The Muhammadans usually arrange the science of astrology under five principal heads:

(*a*) The fundamental principles of astrology, viz. the different divisions of the ecliptic, the properties of the various celestial places and of individual planets, the methods of determining the ascendant and the 12 celestial houses (*buyūt*, 'domus'), the planetary conjunctions, etc.

(*b*) Prognostics of a universal character (*al-aḥkām 'alā umūr al-'ālam*), viz. those which refer to the vicissitudes of kingdoms, dynasties, religions, and cities, to wars, epidemics, famines, winds, rains, the prices of goods, etc. This part of astrology, which Ptolemy calls ἀποτελεσματικὴ καθολική, 'universal apotelesmatics,' is usually called by the Arabs *taḥāwīl sinī al-'ālam*, 'revolutiones annorum mundi,' since a great part of these prognostics is deduced from the planet which has the dignity of 'significator' (ἀφέτης, *dalīl*, *haylāj*) at the moment when the sun enters Aries, *i.e.* at the beginning of each tropic year. This universal part of astrology is subdivided into three sections: (i.) predictions drawn from the various kinds of planetary conjunctions (*qirānāt*, *iqtirānāt*), (ii.) predictions based on the 'revolutiones annorum mundi,' (iii.) predictions relating to the 'mutationes aëris' (*taghayyur al-hawā'*), *i.e.* to meteorological phenomena, and which are deduced from the lunar stations, or from the heliacal rising of Sirius, etc.

(*c*) Individual prognostications relating to the vicissitudes of individuals, derived from the planet or other celestial place which may happen to be the 'significator' at the moment of birth, and then from the 'significator' at each revolution of successive tropic years. This part of astrology Ptolemy calls γενεθλιαλογική, and the Arabs *al-mawālīd*, 'nativitates.'

(*d*) *Masā'il*, 'interrogationes' (ἐρωτήσεις), or that part of astrology which is concerned with replies to questions, *e.g.*, the circumstances of a distant relative, the author of a theft, the hiding-place of a runaway slave, etc. The 'interrogationes' are always connected by the Muhammadan astrologers with the division of the heavens into 12 'domus.' The astrologers who follow the pure tradition of Ptolemy do not admit the 'interrogationes.'

(*e*) *Iḫtiyārāt*, 'electiones,' *i.e.* the choice of the propitious moment for doing any particular thing. The most common method is that of determining such a moment by seeking in which of the 12 celestial 'domus' the moon is found at that particular moment. This was also very probably the method employed by the Greeks; but along with this some Muhammadan astrologers use another method, of Indian origin (but also attributed to Dorotheus), which consists in deducing the fitting moment for action from the place which the moon then occupies in one of the 28 lunar stations or mansions (*manāzil*). The 'electiones' also are not admitted by the astrologers who follow Ptolemy's teaching.

3. Place among the sciences.—The science of the stars, says Ptolemy at the beginning of his *Tetrabiblos*, or *Quadripartitum*, consists of two parts: the first studies the appearances of the motions of the heavenly bodies either with respect to each other or with respect to the earth; the second seeks to deduce, from the physical qualities of those appearances, the changes which take place in the sublunar world. The first part is a science which stands by itself, and can be studied independently of the second; this, on the contrary, cannot do without the first. This conception that astrology is but the sister of astronomy, a branch, that is to say, of the 'science of the stars,' which in its turn is a part of 'mathematics' (*'ulūm riyāḍiyyah*, *'ulūm ta'līmiyyah*, *ta'ālīm*), is common to all the Musalmān astrologers and astronomers, and is accepted also by some philosophers (al-Fārābī in his *de Scientiis*, and the Iḫwān aṣ-ṣafā', or 'sincere companions' of the 10th cent. in their *Epistles*), by the author of the *Mafātīḥ al-'ulūm*, or 'Encyclopædia of the Sciences' (10th cent.), and by the great historian philosopher Ibn Ḫaldūn (*Proleg.* lib. vi. cap. 13; M. G. de Slane's Fr. tr., Paris, 1862–68, iii. 122 f.).

Astrology, however, is classified in a different way by the majority of the philosophers. Musalmān writers commonly divide all science into two great categories: (*a*) sciences which relate to religious law (*'ulūm shar'iyyah*), that is to say, in addition to theology and canon law, the learning which serves as an introduction to them, namely, grammar, lexicography, rhetoric, poetry, history, etc.; (*b*) intellectual or philosophic sciences (*'ulūm 'aqliyyah* or *ḥikmiyyah*), which the author of the *Mafātīḥ al-'ulūm*, thinking of their origin, calls *'ulūm al-'ajam*, 'foreign sciences.'[1] The intellectual or philosophical sciences in their turn are for the most part divided into the three sections[2] already fixed by the later Greek peripatetics and by the Neo-Platonic expounders of Aristotle (*e.g.*, Ammonius, Simplicius, and Johannes Philoponus), namely: (*a*) metaphysic (*al-ḥikmah al-ilāhiyyah*, θεολογία, τὰ μετὰ τὰ φυσικά); (*b*) natural sciences (*al-ḥikmah aṭ-ṭabī'iyyah*, 'natural philosophy,' φυσική); (*c*) mathematical sciences (*al-ḥikmah ar-riyāḍiyyah*, μαθηματική). These last correspond to the *Quadrivium* of Boethius, namely, arithmetic, geometry, astronomy, and music; on the other hand, the natural sciences are subdivided into eight fundamental parts, named for the most part after the titles of the corresponding Aristotelian works, namely: *Auscultatio physica*, *Generatio et corruptio*, *Cœlum et mundum*, *Meteoræ*, *Mineralia*, *Vegetalia*, *Animalia*, *de Anima*. Avicenna (*Fī aqsām al-'ulūm al-'aqliyyah*, in *Tis' rasā'il*, Constantinople, 1298 A.H. [=A.D. 1881], p. 71 ff.), Muḥammad al-Akfānī as-Saḫāwī (*Irshād al-qāṣid*, ed. A. Sprenger, Calcutta, 1849; the author died in 749 A.H. [=A.D. 1348]), Ḥājjī Ḫalīfah (in the introduction to his *Lexicon bibliographicum et encyclopædicum*),[3] and others consider astrology as one of the 7 (or 9) *furū'*, 'secondary branches' of the natural sciences, placing it, that is to say, beside medicine, physiognomy, interpretation of dreams, alchemy, the science of talismans, etc. This same classification of the natural sciences is found in al-Ghazālī († 505 A.H. [=A.D. 1111]), who, in his *Tahāfut al-*

[1] Each of these two great categories afterwards gives place to the distinction between theoretical (*naẓariyyah*) and practical (*'amaliyyah*) science—a distinction which has its origin in Aristotle (E. Zeller, *Die Philosophie der Griechen*³, Tübingen, 1875–81, II. ii. 177).

[2] Other divisions, indicated in the writings of the Iḫwān aṣ-ṣafā', in the *Mafātīḥ al-'ulūm*, etc., are useless for our present purpose.

[3] Ed. G. Flügel, 8 vols., London, 1835–58.

falāsifah, Cairo, 1319 (1901), p. 63 f., refers to it as common amongst the Musalmān peripatetics, and approves of it.

Averroës, in the *Tahāfut al-tahāfut*, Cairo, 1319 (1901), p. 121, admits, as corresponding to Aristotelian teaching, the eight fundamental parts of the natural sciences; but he denies that the so-called derived branches are sciences. Medicine, he says, is an art (*ṣinā'ah*) and not a science; it has a practical and not a theoretical character; accordingly astrology is included in the same category with divination from the flight of birds and from the movement of quadrupeds (*zajar*), with divination in the form of vaticinations (*kahānah*), with physiognomy and with the interpretation of dreams, all being arts which have as their aim the prediction of the future, but which 'are not sciences either theoretically or practically, however it may be supposed that one may sometimes derive some practical advantage from them.'

A curious classification is found at the beginning of the unedited book *de Interrogationibus* (*Fī'l-masā'il*) of the astrologer Ya'qūb al-Qaṣrānī, who lived in the 3rd cent. A.H. (9th A.D.). According to the catalogue of the Arabic MSS of Berlin (W. Ahlwardt, *Verzeichniss der arab. Handschriften*, Berlin, 1887–99, v. 275, no. 5877), he maintains three degrees (*marātib*) of science: theology, medicine, science of the stars; the last, being based not on observation, but on deduction from analogy, occupies a place between the other two.

4. Sources.[1]—(*a*) *Greek.*—These are represented by the classic (if we may call it so) astrology of the *Tetrabiblos* or *Quadripartitum* of Ptolemy; by the writings of Dorotheus Sidonius (1st cent. A.D.), which go back to the Græco-Egyptian tradition; by the great eclectic compilation of Vettius Valens (2nd cent. A.D.);[2] by the book on the 'decani,' the 'interrogationes,' and the nativities of Antiochus of Athens (2nd or 3rd cent. A.D.), which appears especially to follow the Babylonian tradition; by the Καρπός, or *Centiloquium*,[3] falsely attributed to Ptolemy; by some works ascribed to the mythical Hermes;[4] and by an author whose name (Rīmos ?, Zīmos ?) is cited by Arabic writers in a form so corrupt as to be unrecognizable. Of another Greek writer, Teucer or Teucrus of Babylon, the Arabs had knowledge through Iranian sources.

(*b*) *Indian.*—The Musalmān writers mention seven or eight Indian astrologers, whose names, however, it has not as yet been possible to identify with the corresponding Sanskrit. The most important is K.n.k.h or K.t.k.h, who, according to some Arabic writers, appears to have come to Baghdād to the court of the khalīf al-Manṣūr, bringing thither astronomical books of India, and, according to others, making known Indian arithmetic. The Arabs attribute to him writings on the *numūdār* (that is, on the method of ascertaining a factitious ascendant of the nativity), on the nativities, and on the conjunctions of the planets; it is therefore plain that he had also treated of the part of Indian astrology called in Sanskrit *horā* or *jātaka*, which arose through Greek influence. This confirms a conjecture of F. Boll (*Sphaera*, Leipzig, 1903, p. 414 f.), who, from the citations contained in the *Introductorium* of Abū Ma'shar (or Albumasar), infers that K.n.k.h had before him materials of distant Greek origin for his representation of the figures arising in the heavens together with the 'decani.' But in general, Musulmān astrologers cite simply 'the Indians' (*al-Hind*), without particular names of authors. We must further add that the influence of Indian astrology made itself felt sometimes through Iranian writings and oral teaching, as is apparent from some Indian words which have passed into Arabic terminology in an Iranian form—*e.g.*, *darījān* (Ind. *drekkāna*).

(*c*) *Iranian.*—These are in the Pahlavī language or Middle Age Persian. The writings of Teucrus of Babylon (second half of the 1st cent. A.D.) on the figures arising in the heavens together with the 'decani' reached the Arabs through a Persian version, where the name of the author, on account of the ambiguity of the Pahlavī writing, was afterwards spelt by the Persians and Arabs Tīnkalūs (also Tankalūsh or Tankalūshā); so that in the *Introductorium* of Abū Ma'shar his teachings were given as 'teachings of the Persians' (*madhhab al-Furs*) and contain also some Persian names of constellations (cf. Boll, p. 415 f.). Another source was Buzurjmihr's commentary on the astrological 'Ανθολογίαι of Vettius Valens; the Pahlavī translation of the Greek title was *vižīdhak*, 'selected,' which became in Arabic *al-bizīdhaj* and was afterwards variously and strangely corrupted by Arabic writers.[1] The Musalmāns also cited as a source of astrological teachings the mythical Zoroaster (Zarādusht in Arabic writings, Zardusht in modern Persian writings), whose name indeed was already frequently found in Greek astrology of the 4th and following centuries. A fourth source is the book on 'nativities' of [al-]Andarzghar, son of Zādānfarrūḥ; but we lack information about this personage, whose name is corrupted into Alendezgod in the Latin version of Alcabitius (al-Qabīṣī), and into Andruçagar in the Latin version of the book of the Jew Ibn 'Ezrā on nativities (which always draws on Arabic sources). Those astrological writings which are ascribed by the Arabs to Jāmāsp the Wise (the trusted counsellor of the mythic king Gushtāsp) seem to be late Muhammadan falsifications.

We do not know exactly when all these works hitherto mentioned were first translated into Arabic, but it is certain that the great majority of them were known in the second half of the 8th cent. A.D., that is, when Musalmān culture began. If the indication placed at the end of the unedited '*Arḍ miftāḥ an-nujūm* of Hermes (MS in Biblioteca Ambrosiana in Milan) is true, this book would seem to have been translated in the month Dhū 'l-qa'dah, 125 A.H., namely, in September 743 A.D., while the Umayyad khalīfs were still reigning. The first version of the *Tetrabiblos* is due to Abū Yaḥyā al-Baṭrīq, a translator of the time of al-Manṣūr, the second 'Abbāsid khalīf (136–158 A.H. [A.D. 754–775]); Dorotheus and Antiochus are already mentioned in the writings of Mā shā' Allāh (Messahala) in the second half of the 8th cent.; all the other Greek authors mentioned above are amply cited by the astrologers of the 9th century. As has already been said, the writings of the Indian K.n.k.h seem to have been known at Baghdād in the time of the khalīf al-Manṣūr; and about the middle of the 9th cent. we have already several small astrological works of al-Kindī (Alchindus) formed expressly on Indian models. It is almost certain that the Persian books were translated by members of the family

[1] For details see the present writer's Arabic lessons on the origins of astronomy among the Arabs (*'Ilm al-falak, ta'rīkhuhu fī 'l-qurūn al-wusṭā*, Rome, 1911–12), pp. 189–215 (Iranian sources), 216–220 (Greek sources), etc.

[2] Muhammadan astrologers were also acquainted with the *Anthologiæ* of Vettius Valens through an Arabic translation of a Pahlavī version; cf. below, under (*c*).

[3] The Arabic tr. is rather a paraphrase, which attempts to interpret the theories obscurely indicated in the Greek text.

[4] Some of the works attributed to Hermes seem to be Musalmān falsifications—*e.g.*, the book *de Revolutionibus nativitatum*, which has reached us in a Latin translation.

[1] In the Latin version of Albohazen Haly filii Abenragel, *De iudiciis astrorum*, Basel, 1571, the name of the book is *Yndidech* (p. 149, col. b), *Enzirech* (p. 176, col. a), *Endenadeyg Persarum* (p. 347b), *Endemadeyg Persarum* (348b), *Andilarehprosu* (404b).

Nawbaḥt, known by their translations from Pahlavī into Arabic (cf. *Kitāb al-Fihrist*, pp. 244, 274), whose head was astrologer at the court of al-Manṣūr; and in any case the antiquity of Iranian influence in astrology is attested by the fact that in the works of Mā shā' Allāh, according to the Latin translation of John of Seville, technical terms of Iranian origin are freely used: *e.g.*, *alhyleg* (*alhaylāj*), *alcochoden* (*al-kadḥudāh*), *alimbutar* (*al-jānbaḥtān*).

Side by side with the written sources there was, without doubt, the oral tradition of the peoples converted to Islām.[1] Among the Syrians Christianity had almost suffocated astrology, although Bardesanes (154–222) had reconciled Christian dogma with an attenuated form of predestination by means of the stars; all the same we know that at Ḥarrān, the ancient Carrhæ, special astrological traditions flourished along with other pagan sciences. It is further probable that Theophilus, son of Thomas, a Christian of Edessa who was astrologer of the khalīf al-Mahdī (A.D. 775–785), and who has been cited by several Musalmān astrologers as an authority on the subject of 'electiones,' again took up with Syrian oral tradition. In the same manner it is natural that there were absorbed into Musalmān culture the astrological beliefs and practices of the Aramaic centres (tending to paganism) of Mesopotamia and Babylonia, of the Egyptians, etc. Finally, we must not forget the Judaic element which had a notable part in the first ages of Musalmān astrology; in fact, among the principal writers on astrological matters in Arabic in the 2nd and 3rd centuries of the Hijra are the Jews Mā shā' Allāh, Sahl ibn Bishr, Rabban aṭ-Ṭabarī, and Sanad ibn 'Alī.

5. Special character.—The civilized peoples over whom the Arabic domination of the 7th, 8th, and 9th centuries extended, viz. Greeks, Copts, Syrians, Persians, and Indians, had already imagined all the possible fundamental combinations concerning the influence of the stars over mundane events; consequently it was impossible for the Musalmān astrologer to find out anything substantially new. On the other hand, the principal justification of astrology consisted precisely in presenting itself as the jealous preserver of that which an age-long experience had taught the wise of preceding generations. The office of the Musalmān astrologers consequently was reduced to a choosing of what seemed suitable among the many principles and methods of their predecessors, and at times to a harmonizing of elements of very diverse origin, amplifying and completing particular points on which it was easy to give free rein to fancy. All this, as we have said, was done with the widest eclecticism. But, though nothing really original is met with in the field of apotelesmatics properly so called, there is, all the same, a point on which Arabo-Musalmān astrology is far superior to other astrologies, including the Greek, and represents a real progress. This consists of a wide and continued application of spherical astronomy and of exact mathematical processes to the methods of astrological research. Among the Greek astrologers the calculations are very rough; arcs of the ecliptic are substituted for arcs of the equator, right ascensions for oblique ascensions; rough tables, useful for a determined terrestrial latitude, are also employed for different latitudes; the latitudes of the planets are neglected in the calculation of the radiations ('projectiones radiorum,' *maṭāriḥ ash-shu'ā'*). Among the Greeks we seek in vain for a clear exposition of the method of determining mathematically the 12 heavenly 'domus,' which, however, form one of the hinges of the astrological system. Ptolemy himself, teaching minutely in the *Tetrabiblos* how the 'directio' (ἄφεσις) is calculated, completely neglects the latitude of the planets. Characteristic is the fact that Ptolemy, in the *Almagest*, occupies himself with three problems useful only to astrologers (inclination of the shadow of the eclipses with respect to the ecliptic and to the horizon, position of the stars with respect to the sun in consequence of the daily motion of the sphere, appearances and occultations of the planets with respect to the solar rays), and which even in astrology are of very small importance; and, on the other hand, he does not make the slightest allusion to other problems of spherical astronomy which would be of capital importance for apotelesmatics. Musalmān astronomers, on the contrary, teach exact calculations, and often even prepare tables for all the mathematical problems required by astrology: determination of the 12 celestial houses, 'directio,' 'revolutiones annorum,' 'profectio,' 'projectio radiorum.' Thus astrology, among the Musalmāns, becomes an art which demands a solid scientific preparation, and which tends to give an ever greater mathematical complication and exactness to its methods of research among celestial phenomena. *E.g.*, the *mamarr* ('passage [of one planet over another],' *almanar*, or 'supereminentia,' of our astrologers) corresponds exactly from an apotelesmatic point of view to the καθυπερτέρησις of the Greeks; but whilst for the Greeks this takes place when a planet is situated to the west of another, viz. has a lesser longitude, for the Arabs the *mamarr* takes place when a planet in its own epicycle is distant from the apogee of the epicycle less than another planet is distant from the apogee of its own epicycle. Consequently, its calculation in Musalmān astrology is not a light matter, and requires the employment of complete planetary tables. We can understand, therefore, why the theory of the *mamarr* of the planets is not only expounded in several treatises of spherical astronomy, but has also given rise to special monographs. The importance of all this is plain: in the Hellenistic world astrology flourishes while astronomy decays; in the Musalmān world of the Middle Ages astrology becomes a potent ally of mathematical and observational astronomy.

6. Polemic concerning astrology.—From Islām astrology at first had a much less unfavourable reception than from Christianity. The latter had to combat in the teachings of astrology an entire world of pagan ideas and cults; it had to contend against the concept of necessity, which excluded Christian free will. In the 7th and 8th centuries A.D., however, the pagan elements of astrology were completely modified; they were so entirely hidden under a verbal formalism as to be no longer recognizable; and, on the other hand, orthodox Islām, with its doctrine of predestination, which excluded the freedom of human actions, was, at bottom, not very far removed from the εἱμαρμένη of the Stoics and of many astrologers of antiquity. When we consider that the first Musalmān theologians took no heed whatever of the sciences which did not appear to have any relation to the religious content of Islām, we easily understand how astrology had been able to advance unimpeded through its first stages almost up to the end of the 2nd cent. of the Hijra. It is not, therefore, astonishing that Abū Ma'shar, writing his *Introductorium* in 848 A.D., among the ten categories of persons hostile to astrological teaching, makes no mention whatever of opponents influenced by strictly religious reasons,[1] and he makes his defence of astrology to consist (*Introd.* I. 5, fol. b 2 v.–b 3 v.) only in an amplification of the arguments with which Ptolemy (*Tetrab.* I. 3)

[1] Cf. Nallino, *'Ilm al-falak*, pp. 326–332.

[1] *Introductorium*, I. 4 (Augsburg, 1489, fol. a 7 v.–b 2 v.).

had already maintained the material and moral advantages of foreseeing the future, even if this should appear to be adverse to us. The 'philosopher of the Arabs,' al-Kindī, who died a little after 870 A.D., regards astrology as an integral part of philosophy (*ḥikmah, falsafah*); he seeks its basis not only in the four mathematical, but also in the physical and metaphysical doctrines;[1] and he opposes it to many popular prejudices. Al-Kindī was perhaps the only one who endeavoured to reduce to a completely rational and systematic form the principles and the methods of astrology.

But matters soon underwent a change. Towards the end of the 2nd cent. of the Hijra the knowledge of Aristotle's teaching grew more definite and profound, and in this there was no place for astrology; hence the philosophers commenced to make war against it. On the other hand, the theologians were not slow to see in the influence attributed to the stars over human actions a menace to the severely monotheistic conception of Islām, more especially when later on there filtered into Musalmān theology an opposition to the idea of necessary causality, and the atomistic doctrine of continued creative acts became more prevalent. Moreover, the daring predictions concerning the duration of Islām[2] became an evident danger to dogma. Thus the polemic against astrology became very acute.[3]

The most ancient confutation which we possess is that of **Abū 'l-Qāsim 'Īsā ibn 'Alī**,[4] drawn up in the first half of the 10th cent.,[5] and preserved in a work of the Ḥanbalite theologian, Ibn Qayyim al-Jauziyyah, *Miftāḥ dār as-sa'ādah*.[6]

After an exordium in which he admits that the stars may have some influence on such natural phenomena as climate and temperament, but denounces the practice of foretelling the future by their means, he divides his dissertation into three distinct parts. The first has reference to the discordance among astrologers as to their fundamental principles concerning the nature of the influence of the stars, and an exposition follows of several fundamental principles for astrological calculations on which the various writers disagree—*e.g.*, the method of determining the planetary 'termini,' the 'significator' (*dalīl*, ἀφέτης), the 'pars fortunæ,' the male and female zodiacal signs. The second part consists of the examination of many principles which are affirmed by the astrologers, but which are repugnant to good sense (*mustabsha'*). In the third part 'Īsā ibn 'Alī cites some of the arguments adopted by the astrologers in favour of their science, and refutes them.

Contemporary with 'Īsā ibn 'Alī is the famous philosopher **al-Fārābī** (*q.v.*; † A.D. 950), who, as a profound student of Aristotle, could not but be opposed to astrology. We have a work of his against astrology,[7] which, however, is not so vigorous a confutation as we should have expected from such a philosopher and contains some childish reasonings. This is explained by the fact that the work is merely a series of notes, published by a disciple just as he found them.

The philosophers contemporary with al-Fārābī did not all share his hostility to astrology; in fact the schools which had been less subject to Aristotelian influence favoured it, as was already the case with al-Kindī.

With reference to this a special place is held by the Iḫwān aṣ-Ṣafā', 'Sincere Companions,' who flourished in al-Baṣrah towards A.D. 950–960, and whose writings set forth the philosophic doctrines of the heretical Bāṭinites, a branch of whom were the Carmaṭians (al-Qarāmiṭah), who towards the end of the 3rd cent. A.H. (9th cent. A.D.) caused political disorders in the 'Irāq, and who founded an independent kingdom in N.E. Arabia which lasted until after A.H. 474 (A.D. 1081–82). The Carmaṭians had reaped great advantage from astrological predictions based on the theory of the great planetary conjunctions.[1] One can therefore understand that the Iḫwān aṣ-Ṣafā' not only admitted, with Aristotle and other Arabic philosophers, that the changes (generation and corruption) of the sublunar world were consequent upon celestial movements, but also that the planets foretell the future and have a direct influence upon the will and the moral character. The great encyclopædic work of the Iḫwān is imbued with those astrological ideas, among which the theory of planetary conjunctions occupies the principal place.

Favourable to astrology also are those other philosophers who lead up to Abū Sulaimān Muḥammad ibn Ṭāhir ibn Bahrām as-Sijistānī al-Manṭiqī, who, in the second half of the 10th cent., gathered about him at Baghdād a number of learned men for the purpose of discussing various subjects. Notes and summaries of many of these discussions were collected in the *Kitāb al-muqābasāt* of Abū Ḥayyān at-Tawḥīdī, a philosopher, mystic, and jurist († after 400 A.H. [A.D. 1009–1010]), about whose orthodoxy there is some suspicion. A record of a meeting in reference to astrology is preserved almost entire in the work already cited of Ibn Qayyim al-Jauziyyah.[2] Some of those present had attacked astrology, declaring it to be useless, since, after so much study and effort on the part of its supporters, it does not succeed in modifying those events which overwhelm both the wise astrologer and the ignorant man. There then rose up several questioners to refute these accusations, and they set themselves specially to explain how predictions can fail in spite of the truth of astrology, and that, in any case, the efforts of astrologers to discover the truth are always noble. Their defence of practical astrology is somewhat weak, and is probably the last that has been made in the field of philosophy.

Avicenna (*q.v.*; † 428 A.H. [A.D. 1037]) contends against astrology, not only in his great encyclopædia, *ash-Shifā'*, 'The Recovery of the Health [of the Soul],' and in the *an-Najāh*, but also in a special work of which a full résumé was made by Mehren.[3] He demonstrates that astrology has no foundation, and proceeds to show that, even admitting its theoretical truth, it would be impossible for men to acquire a knowledge of it.

Averroës (*q.v.*), or Ibn Rushd († 595 A.H. [A.D. 1198]), is also a decided adversary of astrology, as appears from the severe judgment referred to above (§ 3) and from some passages of his comments on Aristotle. But it would be useless to continue the review of the philosophers, who after the 10th cent. A.D. are all in agreement on this question. It is more interesting to consider the position taken up by the theologians, who—from the motives indicated at the beginning of this section—engaged, towards the end of the 9th cent. A.D., in a relentless war against astrological theories.[4]

We have already seen the attitude of al-Jubbā'ī. We may add here that **Ibn Ḥazm** († 456 A.H. [A.D. 1064]), who fiercely opposed the scholastic or speculative theology of al-Ash'arī in Spain, gives his ideas on astrology in *Al-Fiṣal fī 'l-milal wa 'l-ahwā' wa 'n-niḥal*.[5] He divides those who believe that the future can be foretold by means of the stars into two classes: (1) misbelievers and polytheists, and (2) persons who are in error. The first are those who maintain that the stars and the

[1] Cf. the quotations in M. Steinschneider, *ZDMG* xviii. [1864] 134; and chs. x. and xi. of the anonymous Latin pamphlet *De erroribus philosophorum* (written in the second half of the 13th cent.), ed. P. Mandonnet, *Siger de Brabant*[2], Louvain, 1908–11, pt. ii. pp. 18–21.

[2] *E.g.*, Theophilus, son of Thomas, the astrologer of the third 'Abbāsid khalīf (see above, § 4), maintained that the reign of Islām would last only 960 years (Ibn Ḫaldūn, *Proleg.*, lib. iii. ch. liv., tr. de Slane, ii. 222 f.). The philosopher al-Kindī calculated that the duration of the kingdom of the Arabs would be 693 years (see O. Loth, 'Al-Kindī als Astrolog,' in *Morgenländische Forschungen, Festschrift an H. L. Fleischer*, Leipzig, 1875, pp. 263–309).

[3] Men like al-Jāḥiẓ († 255 A.H., 869 A.D.) and the famous theologians al-Jubbā'ī († 303 A.H., 915–916 A.D.) and al-Ash'arī († 324 A.H., 936 A.D.) were declared enemies of astrology.

[4] According to Ibn al-Qifṭī, ed. Lippert, p. 244 f., he died on Friday, 28 Rabī' ii., 395 A.H., *i.e.* 28th March, 1001 A.D.; cf. also *Fihrist*, p. 129.

[5] It is, in fact, cited in the preface of the *Libellus isagogicus ad magisterium judiciorum astrorum*, which al-Qabīṣī had written for Saif ad-daulah, prince of Aleppo, who reigned from 333 to 356 A.H. [A.D. 944–967].

[6] Cairo, 1323–25 A.H. [A.D. 1905–07], ii. 156–196.

[7] Al-Fārābī, *Philosophische Abhandlungen*, tr. F. Dieterici, Leyden, 1892, pp. 170–186 (pp. 104–114 of the text published in 1890). Dieterici at some points has not understood the meaning of some technical terms of astrology, so that his version is not always perfect.

[1] Cf. M. J. de Goeje, *Mémoire sur les Carmathes du Bahraïn et les Fatimides*[2], Leyden, 1886, pp. 115–129.

[2] ii. 185–193.

[3] A. F. Mehren, 'Vues d'Avicenne sur l'astrologie,' *Muséon*, iii. [Louvain, 1884] 383–403, reprinted in 'Homenaje á D. Francisco Codera,' *Estudios de erudición oriental*, Saragossa, 1904, pp. 235–250.

[4] See also a brief account by I. Goldziher, 'Stellung der alten islamischen Orthodoxie zu den antiken Wissenschaften' (*ABAW*, 1915), pp. 20–25.

[5] Cairo, 1317–21 A.H. (A.D. 1899–1903), v. 37–40.

heavenly spheres are intelligent beings, agents, of eternal duration, and disposing of earthly things either with or without God. The second are those who hold that the stars and the celestial spheres, whilst without intelligence, have been created and established by God as indicators of things which are to take place.

The preserver of Ash'arite dogmatic theology, **al-Ghazālī** († 505 A.H. [A.D. 1111]), opposes astrology in his *Ihyā' 'ulūm ad-dīn*, 'The Revival of Religious Sciences.'[1] And the same attitude we find in the books of the famous Ḥanbalite, Ibn Taimiyyah († 728 A.H. [A.D. 1328]).[2]

But the most vigorous and complete confutation of astrology is contained in the *Miftāḥ dār as-sa'ādah* of **Ibn Qayyim al-Jauziyyah** († 751 A.H. [A.D. 1350]),[3] one of the most noted theologians of the Ḥanbalite school. Only the famous work of Pico della Mirandola, *Adversus astrologiam*, can be compared to the 110 closely printed quarto pages of the confutation written by this Muhammadan theologian, whose impassioned polemics press upon the adversary with an infinity of subtle distinctions which prove the force of his dialectic.

In the theological world perhaps the sole defender of astrology is **Faḫr ad-dīn ar-Rāzī** († 606 A.H. [A.D. 1210]), cited above. Famous especially for his great commentary on the Qur'ān, he composed also many theological, philosophical, and astrological works, and studied medicine and mathematics. Without doubt his confidence in astrology is due to his cultivation of the sciences, and this confidence already appears in his commentary on the Qur'ān.

No theologian seems to have followed Faḫr ad-dīn ar-Rāzī in his bold interpretations of Qur'ānic passages and of religious traditions. Besides, after the writings of Ibn Qayyim al-Jauziyyah and his predecessors, polemics about astrology could no longer reckon on any novelty of argument. The considerations developed by the great philosopher of history, **Ibn Ḫaldūn** († 808 A.H. [A.D. 1406]), in his historical *Prolegomena*,[4] are alone deserving of notice.

7. Astrology in common life.—The four orthodox schools of jurisprudence and the Shī'ite school were already in existence when the war of the philosophers and theologians against astrology became fierce; accordingly, the anathema launched against it in the name of religion did not occupy much space in Muhammadan law, notwithstanding the fact that this had its chief foundation in religious doctrine. Among some jurists of a rather later age, however, we meet with open hostility to astrology. In Muhammadan law the buying and selling of useless things is forbidden; therefore some jurists[5] teach that one may not sell or buy books of astrology. Another legal prescript does not admit the testimony of misbelievers; therefore some jurists, regarding the astrologer as a misbeliever, deny him the right of acting as a witness.[6] But, before theological anathema smote it, astrology was deeply rooted among all lay classes of society. The courts of the 'Abbāsid khalīfs at Baghdād and of the numerous small dynasties which arose in the Muhammadan world after the 3rd cent. of the Hijra received astrologers with great favour and consulted them on affairs of State as well as on trifling matters of daily life. At the foundation of Baghdād in A.D. 762, and at that of al-Mahdiyyah (in Tunis) in 916, the astrologers, summoned for the purpose, indicate the propitious moment for beginning the work. Many writings on apotelesmatics are dedicated to khalīfs, sultans, and princes. In Turkey, even at the beginning of the 19th cent., one of the chief posts at court was that of *munajjim-bāshī*, or chief astrologer; and the case was similar in Persia, in India, and in Muhammadan central Asia.[1] In the *Thousand and One Nights* not only is the astrologer with his astrolabe mentioned several times (*e.g.*, Nights 28 and 50 of the Egyptian edd.), but there is also a complete dissertation on the elements of astrology (Nights 254-257, in the story of the slave girl Tawaddud). Further, the considerable number of old Arabic astrolabes still existing in the East and in South Europe would alone suffice to prove the great diffusion of astrology throughout the Muhammadan world; and it found strong support among the students of astronomy. Cases of persecution of astrologers by the State are extremely rare. Al-Ḥākim, Fāṭimid khalīf of Egypt, who in 404 A.H. (A.D. 1013-1014) prohibited the study of astrology and banished from Cairo those who cultivated it, was an astrologer himself, and that decree of his is one of many acts of madness committed in the last years of his life.

In the Muhammadan countries into which European civilization has penetrated (which with the Copernican system has destroyed the bases of apotelesmatics) astrology has lost its importance and remains the monopoly of the popular classes, among whom it has degenerated into a form of prediction without any serious mathematical and astronomical basis. On the other hand, in countries where there is little or no European influence (*e.g.*, in many parts of Morocco) apotelesmatics still flourish, but accompanied by only rudimentary astronomical knowledge. To-day in S. Arabia the function of the astrologer is exercised especially by the *qāḍī*,[2] *i.e.* by those whose duty it is to see that canon law is observed!

8. Influence on European astrology. — The astrology of the Latin Middle Ages from the beginning of the 12th to the end of the 15th cent. is really Arabic astrology. Its sole sources are Arabic (Albohali, Albohazen, Albumasar, Alcabitius, Alchindus, Almansor, Alphadol, Aomar, Gergis, Hali, Haly Heben Rodan, Messahala, Zahel, and some pseudepigraphical works), or at least translations from Arabic (*e.g.*, the *Tetrabiblos* or *Quadripartitum* of Ptolemy, and the Καρπός or *Centiloquium*); the technical terminology is literal translation or mere corruption of Arabic words. In the 16th cent. the humanists rescued from oblivion the poem of Manilius and the crude compilation of Firmicus Maternus; but this was a mere literary exercise of no importance for the astrology of the 17th century.

In the Byzantine world also Muhammadan astrology leaves deep traces in many versions from the Arabic and from the Persian;[3] so that side by side with the works derived from the classic Greek authors appear those of 'Απομάσαρ (Abū Ma'shar), 'Αχμέτ (Aḥmad ibn Yūsuf ibn ad-Dāyah), Μεσσάλα (Mā shā' Allāh), Σέχλ (Sahl ibn Bishr), and other Arabic writers. Thus there frequently occur in Byzantine astrological writings Arabic and Persian names of planets or technical terms which no longer correspond to those of classical Greek.

1 Cairo, 1302-03 A.H. (A.D. 1885-86), i. 27 f. All this passage is copied without indication of its source in ad-Damīrī, *Ḥayāt al-ḥayawān*, Cairo, 1311 A.H. (A.D. 1893), i. 12 f., *s.v.* 'Asad.'

2 *Majmū'at al-fatāwā*, Cairo, 1326-29 A.H. (A.D. 1908-11), i. 323-336.

3 Ed. Cairo, 1323-25 A.H. (A.D. 1905-07), ii. 132-240.

4 Bk. vi. ch. 26 (tr. M. G. de Slane, iii. 240-249).

5 *E.g.*, al-Bājūrī, *Ḥāshiyah 'alā Ibn Qāsim al-Ghazzī*, Būlāq, 1292 A.H., i. 445.

6 Cf. the quotations in Saḥnūn ibn 'Uthmān al-Wānsharīsī, *Mufīd al-muḥtāj fī sharḥ as-sirāj*, Cairo, 1314 A.H., p. 5.

1 Cf. *e.g.*, F. Bernier, *Evénements particuliers des états du Mogol*, Paris, 1671, p. 96. See also J. T. Reinaud, *Monumens arabes, persans, et turcs*, Paris, 1828, ii. 367 f. For Persia see *Voyages du chevalier Chardin en Perse, et autres lieux de l'Orient*, new ed., Amsterdam, 1735, i. 242, iii. 163-165, 174-183.

2 R. Manzoni, *El Yèmen*, Rome, 1884, p. 209; H. von Maltzan, *Reise nach Südarabien*, Brunswick, 1873, p. 164.

3 The Arabs and the Persians are called indifferently Πέρσαι.

Finally, the Jewish astrological literature of Europe, in which a conspicuous place is occupied by the works of Abrāhām ibn 'Ezrā († 1167), is based exclusively on Arabic sources.

LITERATURE.—There is no work setting forth the content and history of Muhammadan astrology. For biographical and bibliographical notices of individual astrologers reference may be made to H. Suter, *Die Mathematiker und Astronomen der Araber und ihre Werke*, Leipzig, 1900 (completed in 'Nachträge und Berichtigungen zu "Die Math. und Astron.,"' in *Abhandlungen zur Gesch. der mathematischen Wissenschaften*, xiv. [1902] 157–185). The mathematical side of Muhammadan astrology and the explanation of several technical terms are set forth in the present writer's annotations on al-Battānī, *Opus astronomicum*, 3 vols., Milan, 1899–1907. Beyond two or three small pseudepigraphical writings of no importance, printed or lithographed in Cairo, and the dissertation of al-Kindī published by O. Loth (see above, p. 92a, n. 2), there are no edd. of complete astrological works in the original text; there are, on the other hand, edd. of Middle Age Latin versions (15th–16th cent.), several of which have been cited in the course of the article.

II. *ASTRONOMY*.—1. **Name.**—The names *'ilm* (or *ṣinā'at*) *an-nujūm*, 'science (or art) of the stars,' *'ilm* (or *ṣinā'at*) *at-tanjīm* denote both astronomy and astrology. For the former science Averroës[1] adopts the expression *ṣinā'at an-nujūm at-ta'ālīmiyyah*, 'mathematical art of the stars,' which is found also in the original Arabic of the *de Scientiis* of al-Fārābī, where Gerard of Cremona translated it by 'astronomia doctrinalis,' misled by the double signification of the adjective *ta'ālīmī*. The astronomy of observation is designated by Averroës[2] *ṣinā'at an-nujūm at-tajrībiyyah*, 'experimental art of the stars.' Special names of astronomy are *'ilm al-hai'ah*, 'science of the form [of the universe],' and *'ilm al-aflāk*, 'science of the celestial spheres.'[3] The branch of astronomy which deals with the construction and use of instruments for determining the time, especially for the purpose of regulating the times of the religious services in the mosques, is named *'ilm al-mīqāt*, 'the science of the time appointed [for the canon prayers],' and he who cultivates it is called *muwaqqit*.

2. **Scope.**—The Greek and Muhammadan conception of astronomy does not exactly correspond to the modern conception.

Al-Fārābī says in his treatise *de Scientiis*[4] that astronomy has for its object the study of the celestial bodies and of the earth from these three points of view: (*a*) number, figure, order, and respective position of the spheres and of the celestial bodies; their magnitudes and distances from the earth; immobility of the earth; (*b*) celestial motions and their consequences with regard to the stars themselves (conjunctions and oppositions, eclipses, etc.); (*c*) magnitude of the inhabited part of the earth and its division into zones or climates; determination of geographical co-ordinates; effects of the rotation of the celestial sphere in regard to parts having different latitudes (varying length of the day, right and oblique ascensions of the points of the ecliptic, etc.). This scheme of the content of astronomy is found also in later writers,[5] with the sole difference that the study of the magnitudes and distances of the celestial bodies and spheres comes to be considered under a category (*d*) separate from (*a*).

According to Avicenna, the astronomer studies 'the parts of the universe as far as regards their figure, their respective positions, their magnitudes, and their distances from each other; he further studies the motions of the spheres and of the celestial bodies, the estimate (*taqdīr*) of the globes, of the axes (*l. quṭūb*) and of the circles [ideal] on which those motions take place. All this is contained in the *Almagest*.'[6]

The limits of astronomy are well defined by Ibn Ḫaldūn († A.D. 1406):

Astronomy consists of the study of the celestial bodies and motions as they appear to us; 'it is a most noble science, but it does not give, as is often supposed, the form of the heavens and the disposition of the spheres and of the stars as they are in reality. It only indicates that from those motions there result for the spheres these forms and these dispositions. Now, as is known, it is not strange that from one and the same thing there should result necessarily two different things; therefore, when we say that those motions give as a result [those celestial configurations], we seek to argue the mode of existence of the result by means of the necessary cause; a proceeding which does not at all guarantee the truth. Nevertheless, astronomy is an important science, indeed one of the fundamental parts of the mathematical sciences.'[1]

The diversity of criteria and of purposes by and for which the physicist ('naturalis') studies celestial phenomena, in contrast to the astronomer ('astrologus'), is shown also in a passage of Averroës.[2] This conception of the philosophers is shared by the Muhammadan astronomers, for whom astronomy embraces spherical astronomy (with the theory of instruments), mathematical chronology, spherical trigonometry, and geography as based on mathematics (like that of Ptolemy); and it excludes all that for us would enter into the field of stellar physics and celestial mechanics. This is evident from the summary[3] of the best systematic treatise on Muhammadan astronomy, viz. the unedited *al-Qānūn al-mas'ūdī*, composed in Arabic by al-Bīrūnī († A.D. 1048):

(*a*) General notions and fundamental hypotheses for the geometrical representation of celestial phenomena; (*b*) mathematical chronology, conversion of one era into another, festivals of various peoples; (*c*) spherical trigonometry; (*d*) circles of the celestial sphere and systems of co-ordinates; phenomena of the diurnal motion of the sphere with reference to the earth (amplitudes, solar altitudes, right and oblique ascensions of the points of the ecliptic, etc.); (*e*) form, dimensions, etc., of the earth; problems relating to terrestrial longitudes and latitudes; the direction of Mecca with regard to other places on the earth; geography on a mathematical-astronomical basis; (*f*) theory of the sun; (*g*) theory of the moon; solar and lunar parallaxes; (*h*) syzygies, eclipses, appearance of the new moon; (*i*) fixed stars and lunar stations; (*j*) theories of the five planets; geocentric distances and magnitudes of the celestial bodies and spheres; (*k*) problems of spherical astronomy as subserving astrology (calculation of the twelve celestial 'domus,' of the 'applicationes,' of the 'projectiones radiorum,' of the 'directiones' and 'profectiones,' of the 'revolutiones annorum,' of the *mamarr*, of the planetary conjunctions, of the millenary periods).

Muhammadan astronomical writings, almost always in Arabic, can be classified under four groups:

(*a*) General elementary introductions which represent a perfected form of what the *Isagoge* of Geminus and the *Hypotheses* of Ptolemy were for the Greeks; belonging to this category—to cite only writings translated into European languages and edited—are: the *de Imaginatione Sphæræ* of Thebit (or Thābit) ibn Qurrah († A.D. 901), the compendium of Alfraganus or al-Farghānī († after 861), and the compendium of al-Jaghmīnī († 1344–45);[4] (*b*) systematic treatises corresponding in type to the *Almagest*, but more perfect—*e.g.*, the unedited work of al-Bīrūnī cited above; the Latin translation of the *Almagest* of Geber (or Jābir) ibn Aflaḥ, printed at Nürnberg, 1534, would belong to this category if it had not omitted all the mathematical and astronomical tables; (*c*) treatises of spherical astronomy for the use of calculators and observers; these are called *zīj* (plur. *zījāt, azyāj, ziyajah*); they presuppose a knowledge of the general principles of cosmography and consist essentially of tables for calculation, illustrations of the use of the tables, and indications as to the manner of solving problems of spherical astronomy (for the most part without demonstration); the only treatise of this kind published and translated is that of al-Battānī;[5] of the Persian treatise of Ulūgh Beg only the prolegomena (explaining the use of the tables) and the stellar catalogue have been edited and translated; (*d*) writings on special subjects—*e.g.*, stellar catalogues, treatises on instruments, etc.

---

1 Ibn Rushd, *Metaphysic*, Cairo, n.d. [1902], p. 65, l. 3 from end (ed. and tr. by C. Quirós Rodríguez, Madrid, 1919, bk. iv. § 13).

2 P. 83 (Quirós, bk. iv. § 77).

3 See also above, I. 1.

4 This has reached us only in the Latin version of Gerard of Cremona († 1187), Paris, 1588. The part relating to the mathematical sciences has been translated into German by E. Wiedemann, 'Beitr. zur Gesch. der Naturwissenschaften,' xi. (*Sitzungsberichte der physik.-medizin. Sozietät in Erlangen*, xxxix. [1907] 74–101.

5 *E.g.*, Muḥammad al-Akfānī as-Saḫāwī, *Irshād al-qāṣid*, Calcutta, 1849, p. 84 f.

6 *Risālah fī-aqsām al-'ulūm al-'aqliyyah*, in the *Tis' rasā'il*, Constantinople, 1298 A.H. (1881). The same definition is found in the *Chahār Maqālah*, written in Persian about 1160 by Niẓāmī-i-'Arūḍī-i-Samarqandī (tr. E. G. Browne, Hertford, 1899 [extract from *JRAS*], p. 89).

1 *Prolegomena*, bk. vi. ch. xvi. (tr. de Slane, iii. 145 f.).

2 *Comm. de Cælo*, bk. ii. ch. 57 (*Aristotelis Opera omnia cum Averrois Cordubensis commentariis*, Venice, 1562, vol. v. fol. 136r.–v.).

3 According to the indexes of the chapters given in the catalogues of the Arabic MSS in Oxford and Berlin.

4 *Sullāḳā Haunānāyā*, the course of astronomy of Barhebræus, ed. and tr. F. Nau (*Le Livre de l'ascension de l'esprit sur la forme du ciel et de la terre*, 2 pts., Paris, 1899–1900), although written (in 1279) in Syriac by a Christian bishop, belongs to this category.

5 To which is to be added the Latin translation, made in the 12th cent. by Athelhard of Bath, of Maslamah al-Majrīṭī's recension of the tables of al-Ḫuwārizmī, ed. with an excellent German commentary by H. Suter, 1914.

3. Relation to Islām.—Muhammadan religious ritual bases some of its prescriptions on elements of an astronomical character. The hours within which each of the five daily ritual prayers is valid depend on the latitude of the place and on the epoch of the solar year; further, the legal time for the night prayer is between the end of the evening and the beginning of the morning twilight. The ritual prayer is not valid unless the face is turned in the direction of Mecca; hence the necessity of solving the astronomical-geographical problem of the azimuth of Mecca. The beginning and the end of the month assigned to the fast are determined not by the civil calendar, but by the actual appearance of the new moon; and the beginning of the daily fast is given by the morning twilight. Finally, special ritual prayers are prescribed at eclipses of the sun and moon, for which it is well to be prepared in time. All this presupposes a certain degree of astronomical knowledge; and, although the majority of theologians and jurists are not content with pure calculation for the appearance of the new moon, but require the actual sight of the phenomenon, it is evident that the religious precept must be a real stimulus to scientific study. This explains also why the Muhammadans have undertaken so much research into the complex phenomena of the twilight and of the conditions of visibility of the new moon—phenomena which were almost entirely neglected by the Greek astronomers. On the other hand, many passages of the Qur'ān set forth the benefits which God has vouchsafed to men by means of celestial bodies and motions; at least they invite reflexion on the goodness and providence of God. Astronomy thus becomes an ally of religion.

4. Sources.[1]—(*a*) *Arabian.*—A first element of an exclusively practical character is due to the Arabs before Islām. Like all other peoples who dwell in hot countries and are compelled to prefer night to day for travelling, the Bedawīn made use of the stars for guiding their wanderings and for calculating (approximately) the hours of the night; they were thus familiar with the principal appearances of Venus and of Mercury, the places of the rising and setting of the more brilliant stars, and above all the annual course of the moon determined by noting its position in relation to 28 successive groups of stars called for this reason *manāzil al-qamar*, 'lunar stations.' Further, among the sedentary agricultural tribes, the seasons and many meteorological provisions (especially those for rain) were strictly connected with the annual rising of certain fixed stars[2] or else with the cosmic setting of the lunar stations. Hence, even in the 16th and 17th centuries, Arabic writers on astronomy still occupied themselves with the lunar mansions[3] and their *anwā'*, or cosmic settings.

(*b*) *Indian.*—The Muhammadans owe the first scientific elements of astronomy to India. In 154 A.H. (A.D. 771),[4] there came to Baghdād an Indian embassy one learned member of which introduced to the Arabs the *Brāhmasphuṭasiddhānta*, composed in Sanskrit in A.D. 628 by Brahmagupta. From this work (which the Arabs called *as-Sind-hind*) Ibrāhīm ibn Ḥabīb al-Fazārī drew the elements and the methods of calculation for his astronomical tables (*zīj*) adapted to the Muhammadan lunar year. Almost contemporaneously Ya'qūb ibn Ṭāriq composed his *Tarkīb al-aflāk*, 'The Composition of the Celestial Spheres,' which was based on the elements and methods of the *Brāhmasphuṭasiddhānta* and on other data furnished by another Indian scientist (K.n.k.h), who came to Baghdād with a second embassy in 161 A.H. (A.D. 777–778). It seems that almost at the same time there was translated into Arabic under the name *al-Arkand* the *Khaṇḍakhādyaka*, written about A.D. 665 by the same Brahmagupta, but containing elements different from those of his other work. Abū 'l-ḥasan al-Ahwāzī, a contemporary of al-Fazārī and of Ya'qūb ibn Ṭāriq, probably drawing on oral teachings of learned Indians, introduced to the Arabs the planetary motions according to al-Arjabhad (a corruption of Āryabhaṭa, the name of an Indian astronomer who wrote in A.D. 500). These Indian works had many imitators in the Muhammadan world up to the end of the first half of the 5th cent. of the Hijra (11th cent. A.D.); some astronomers (*e.g.*, Ḥabash, an-Nairīzī, Ibn as-Samḥ) wrote contemporaneously books based on Indian methods and elements and books with Græco-Arabic elements; others (*e.g.*, Muḥammad ibn Isḥāq as-Saraḫsī, Abu 'l-Wafā', al-Bīrūnī, al-Ḫāzinī) adapted elements calculated by the Muhammadan astronomers to great artificial cycles of years constructed in imitation of those of the Indians. For one of the characteristics of the astronomical books of India is their representation of the mean motions of sun, moon, and planets by the number of their revolutions in cycles of millions of years, starting from the supposition that at the beginning of creation sun, moon, and planets were all in conjunction in a given degree of longitude (*e.g.*, at the first point of Aries), taken as the initial point of the celestial sphere, and that at intervals of millions of years they will all be in conjunction again at the same point.[1] Further, many treatises composed by the Arabs gave the roots of the mean motions for the meridian of Uzain (corrupted later into Azīn and Arīn, the Sanskrit Ujjayinī), supposed to be the central meridian of the inhabited earth (90° E. of the first Ptolemaic meridian). From those Indian books the Arabs also derived their first knowledge of trigonometrical sines, of course in the form employed in India, *i.e.* for arcs of 3° 45′ and for the radius of 3438′.

(*c*) *Iranian.*—A few years after the introduction of Indian astronomy, and before the end of the 8th cent. A.D., there was translated into Arabic the Pahlavī work entitled *Zīk i Shatro-ayār*, 'Astronomical Tables of the King,' a name which became in the Arabic version *Zīj ash-Shāh* or *Zīj ash-Shahriyār*. The original was certainly composed in the last years of the kingdom of the Sāsānids, since the tables were based on the epoch of Yazdagird III. (16th June, A.D. 632); its elements were derived, not from Persian observations, but from Indian books. It appears also that the roots of the mean motions were referred to the meridian of the mythical castle Kangdizh, which Persian epic legend placed in the Far East. The Arabic version met with great favour among the Muhammadans. We know that the astronomer and astrologer Mā Shā' Allāh († at the beginning of the 9th cent. A.D.) made use of it for his calculations, that in the first half of the 9th cent. Muḥammad ibn Mūsā al-Ḫuwārizmī had deduced from it the equations of the planetary motions, whilst he had drawn the mean motions from the *as-Sind-hind* and other elements from Ptolemy, and that Abū Ma'shar († A.D. 886) used it for his astronomical tables. After the 9th cent. A.D. the *Zīj ash-Shāh* rapidly fell into disuse; but a passage of az-Zarqālī (Arzachel) shows that towards the middle of the 11th cent. some astrologers in Spain still calculated the longitude of the fixed stars according to the tables of the Persians.

(*d*) *Greek.*—Last in chronological order is the influence of Greek astronomy. At the end of the 8th cent. or at the beginning of the 9th A.D. a rich patron, of the family of the Barmecids, Yaḥyā ibn Ḫālid († 191 A.H. [A.D. 807]), caused the *Almagest* to be translated for the first time into Arabic. But this book, full of difficulties and obscurities, could not, at first, compete with easier and more practical works of Indian and Persian origin. It acquired influence later, when the mathematical preparation of the Muhammadans was more advanced, and when better translations appeared. In the first half of the 9th cent. also Arabic translations were made of the *Geographia*, the *Tabulæ Manuales*, the *Hypotheses Planetarum*, the *Apparitiones* (φάσεις) *Stellarum fixarum*, and the *Planisphærium* of Ptolemy; the *Tabulæ Manuales* of Theon of Alexandria; the book of Aristarchus on the magnitudes and distances of the sun and moon; the *Isagoge* of Geminus; two tractates of Autolycus; three of Theodosius; and the little work of Hypsicles on the ascensions. To the 9th cent. also probably belongs the Arabic translation of the astronomical tables of Ammonius, of which we still find traces in the 11th cent., when they were remodelled by az-Zarqālī, to pass afterwards into mediæval Latin literature under the names of Humenus, Armanus, etc. Finally, there appear to have been translated in the same century the book of the constellations of Aratus and a book on the magnitudes and distances of the celestial bodies, which, falsely attributed to Ptolemy, is known by the Arabs under the name of *Kitāb al-manshūrāt*.

5. Some astronomical teachings.—We may here refer to some special points, which have an importance for the history of the general ideas of celestial phenomena. The only system received by the Muhammadan peoples was the geocentric. Aristotelian philosophy, the authority of Ptolemy, and the requirements of astrology were insurmountable obstacles to the conception of a heliocentric system, which, in any case, could not have been demonstrated by irrefutable reasons or, in the absence of telescopes, have procured any real advantage to practical astronomy. The lack of telescopes kept Muhammadan astronomers from becoming acquainted with other planets than those already known to the Greeks. The mode, too, of representing their motions is always that of the Greeks, viz. by means of combinations (sometimes very complicated) of eccentrics and epicycles; nor

[1] For details see Nallino, *'Ibn al-falak*, pp. 104–140, 313–323 (for Arabic sources), 149–180 (Indian), 180–188 (Persian), and 216–229 (Greek).

[2] Alois Musil and Antonin Jaussen have found this usage still in vogue among the Bedawīn of Moab. Eduard Glaser indicates it for the Yemen.

[3] These correspond only approximately to the *nakṣatras* of the Indians.

[4] So al-Bīrūnī. On the other hand, Ibn al-Qifṭī (a source of less authority) has 156 = 773.

[1] This Indian idea occurs also in some Arabic works which are not astronomical—*e.g.*, Ibn Qutaiba, *Liber poësis et poëtarum*, ed. M. J. de Goeje, Leyden, 1904, p. 503 f.

do the modifications of certain parts of the planetary theories of Ptolemy introduced by some (*e.g.*, Naṣīr ad-dīn and Quṭb ad-dīn ash-Shīrāzī) depart much from this principle. Only among writers who are philosophers rather than astronomers do we meet with theories that supersede those of eccentrics and epicycles.[1] In any case, among them all, the Aristotelian and Ptolemaic doctrine of the circular form of celestial motions reigns supreme, for the elliptic orbit indicated by az-Zarqālī for Mercury[2] is merely a graphical construction on the lamina of the astrolabe, and not a theoretical representation.

(*a*) *Number of the spheres.*—The number of the spheres, *i.e.* of what in the Middle Ages in Europe were called 'heavens,' is eight in Aristotle and Ptolemy, viz. seven for the planets (including the sun and the moon) and one for the fixed stars. This number of eight is preserved by the first Arabic astronomers—*e.g.*, al-Farghānī and al-Battānī, for whom, however, these ideal spheres, created to satisfy the requirements of physics and not those of astronomy properly so called, had no practical importance. Still the number of eight, combined with the Aristotelian theory of solid spheres in which the heavenly bodies are infixed without being able to move themselves, did not easily agree with the other teachings of the Ptolemaic system. Aristotle, who was ignorant of the motion of the precession of the equinoxes, and who consequently held that the fixed stars are really immovable, assigned to the eighth sphere the apparent diurnal motion of the celestial vault from east to west, a motion which the eighth sphere impressed also on all the others. But Ptolemy, accepting from Hipparchus the precession of the equinoxes on account of which the fixed stars have a slow and continued increase of longitude, came implicitly to attribute to the sphere of the fixed stars two motions in opposite directions—one (diurnal) from east to west, and the other from west to east. Ptolemy had no occasion to notice and correct this contradiction, which was soon perceived by the Arabic writers. The contradiction would have been easily eliminated by supposing that the fixed stars moved by the precessional motion within their own sphere, supposed accordingly to be fluid and not solid; and perhaps al-Battānī had in mind the possibility of this hypothesis when he entitled ch. li. of his book[3] thus: 'Of the motion of the fixed stars, whether they move in their sphere, or whether the sphere moves with them.' Another solution of the difficulty would have been to suppose the fixed stars to be infixed in the convexity of the sphere of Saturn, itself naturally subjected, like all the planetary apogees, to the motion of the precession; then the eighth sphere, no longer containing the stars, would only have had the office of impressing the diurnal motion on the spheres below. This solution was actually given by Muhammadan writers, some of whom indeed took advantage of it for reducing the number of the spheres to seven, to conform with the seven heavens of the Qur'ān; but this was never accepted by the astronomers.[4] Therefore, when Ibn al-Haitham († 1039) introduced into pure astronomical teaching the doctrine of the solid spheres of Aristotle, it was necessary for the physical reasons set forth above to add a ninth sphere without stars, impressing on the other spheres diurnal motion. This ninth sphere, accepted by all the later astronomers, was called 'the universal sphere,' 'the greatest sphere,' 'the sphere of the spheres,' 'the smooth sphere' (*al-falak al-aṭlas*), 'the sphere of the zodiac,' 'the supreme sphere.' In general also the philosophers—*e.g.*, Avicenna and Ibn Ṭufail—accept these nine spheres; Averroës,[1] however, under the influence of Aristotle, cannot bring himself to exceed the number of eight. In the theological camp the nine spheres did not find many opponents, in spite of 'the seven heavens' mentioned in *Qur.* ii. 27; it was held that the specification of the number seven did not imply the negation of a superior number.[2] In fact, several theologians saw in the eighth and ninth spheres respectively the 'seat' (*kursī*) and the 'throne' (*'arsh*) of God mentioned in the Qur'ān.[3]

Doubts were not wanting, however, concerning the unity of the sphere of the fixed stars. Faḫr ad-dīn ar-Rāzī[4] informs us that Avicenna, in his book *ash-Shifā'*, declared: 'Up till now it has not been clear to me whether the sphere of the fixed stars be a single sphere or be several spheres, placed one above the other.' And Faḫr ad-dīn ar-Rāzī[5] adds that the hypothesis of the single sphere for all the fixed stars rests only on the assumption of the equality of their motions, but that this equality is not at all certain. He further says that, even if the equality of the motions were a certainty, he would not deduce from it the necessity of a single sphere bearing all the stars infixed in it. In face of these criticisms, one comprehends the scepticism of Niẓām ad-dīn al-Ḥasan an-Naisābūrī: 'In conclusion, to none of the ancients or of the moderns is the number of the heavens quite certain, either by the force of reasoning or by the way of tradition.'[6]

(*b*) *Order of the planets.*—The order of the planets followed by almost all the Muhammadan astronomers is identical with that of Ptolemy, although they recognize, together with the Greek astronomers, the lack of absolute proofs in the case of the two inferior planets and the sun. Without telescopes they could not see the transits of Venus and Mercury across the sun or determine the parallaxes of the planets situated above the moon. Some Arabic authors believed that they had perceived transits of Venus or of Mercury across the sun; but what they really saw was solar spots.[7] On the other hand, the postulates of astrology continued in the Muhammadan age to guarantee, from lack of scientific reasons to the contrary, the Ptolemaic series: moon, Mercury, Venus, sun, Mars, Jupiter, Saturn. Spain alone had astronomers who departed from this order. Jābir ibn Aflaḥ (*c.* 1140) held it more probable that Mercury and Venus were above the sun on account of their analogy to the superior planets in having epicycles and eccentrics, stations and retrogradations. Al-Biṭrūjī (*c.* 1200), moved by physical reasons connected with his special system of planetary notions, placed the sun between Mercury and Venus.

(*c*) *Obliquity of the ecliptic.*—The obliquity of the ecliptic with regard to the celestial equator is one of the fundamental elements of astronomical calculation. The Greeks, from Eratosthenes (230 B.C.), had assigned to it the constant value of 23° 51′ 20″; *i.e.*, they held it to be invariable. The astonishment of the Arabic astronomers must have been great when they found by their observations an obliquity sensibly less; at first they could not decide whether the discrepancy was due to a real diminution of the obliquity or to a defect in the ancient observations. Al-Battānī leaves the ques-

[1] Cf. below, § 6.

[2] In the *Libros del saber de astronomia*, iii. 280. In any case, the earth there occupies the centre of the ellipse and not one of the foci.

[3] Ed. Nallino, i. 124.

[4] Cf. Niẓām ad-dīn al-Ḥasan an-Naisābūrī, *Tafsīr* (in marg. to the *Tafsīr* of aṭ-Ṭabarī), 1st ed., i. 205 (comm. on *Qur.* ii. 27); Faḫr ad-dīn ar-Rāzī, *Mafātīḥ al-ghaib*, Cairo, 1308–10 A.H., ii. 60 (comm. on *Qur.* ii. 159).

[1] *Metaphys.*, Cairo, n.d. [1902], p. 66 (ed. and tr. Quirós, bk. iv. § 16).

[2] Niẓām ad-dīn al-Ḥasan an-Naisābūrī, *loc. cit.*; Faḫr ad-dīn ar-Rāzī, i. 260.

[3] See al-Qazwīnī, *Cosmography*, ed. F. Wüstenfeld, Göttingen, 1848, i. 54; the glosses on *Mawāqif* of 'Aḍud ad-dīn al-Ījī; E. W. Lane, *Arabic-English Lexicon*, 8 vols., London, 1863–93, *s.v.* ''Arsh,' etc.

[4] ii. 59; cf. Avicenna, *Ash-Shifā'*, Teherān, 1303–05 A.H., i. 175 (in the 6th ch. of the 2nd *fann* of the *Ṭabī'iyyāt*).

[5] ii. 59 and i. 259 f.

[6] *Loc. cit.*

[7] See § 7 below.

tion undecided and declares that he chooses the excellent value found by himself (23° 35′), 'since this was observed by us with our own eyes; the other, on the contrary, was received through the information of others.'[1] Some, less prudent, deduced the theory of libration[2] from the discrepancies as to the obliquity of the ecliptic combined with those relative to the precession of the equinoxes. But the continued series of observations left no doubt by the 13th cent. that the obliquity of the ecliptic was subject to a very slow regular diminution,[3] which therefore came to be admitted by all the astronomers; in Europe, on the other hand, we must come down to Tycho Brahe (1546–1601) to see it affirmed in the midst of opposition which lasted through the greater part of the 17th century. The Muhammadan astronomers had no means of determining whether this diminution was continuous or periodical and within what limits it was contained.[4] Abū 'Alī al-Ḥasan (*c.* 1260), who had accepted the hypothesis of az-Zarqālī as to libration, believed that the obliquity oscillated between a maximum of 23° 53′ and a minimum of 23° 33′; Faḫr ad-dīn ar-Rāzī[5] admitted a continuous diminution on account of which the ecliptic will coincide one day with the equator and then will depart from it again, so that the Tropic of Cancer will pass to the south and that of Capricorn to the north. Naṣīr ad-dīn aṭ-Ṭūsī († 1274 A.D.) confined himself to setting forth the eight possible hypotheses as to the continuity or the periodicity of the diminution, without giving preference to any.

(*d*) *Precession of the equinoxes.*—The precession of the equinoxes, on account of which the equinoctial points retreat from east to west along the equator and cause a continuous increase in the longitude of the fixed stars (calculated precisely from the point of the vernal equinox or the first point of Aries), is one of the greatest discoveries of Hipparchus, accepted by Ptolemy. It was accepted by all the Muhammadan astronomers, who, from the first half of the 9th cent., assigned it a value much more exact than that of Ptolemy (36″ yearly), viz. 54″ 33‴; later, a continued series of observations indicated other values still more approximate to the true one. There remained a question which celestial mechanics alone has been able to solve with certainty: Is the precession to be regarded as continuous, so that in many thousands of years the retreating equinoctial points will accomplish the entire circuit of the ecliptic, or is it confined within limits so as to be reduced to one oscillation, more or less great, of the equinoctial points? The first hypothesis, which is the true one, is accepted by Ptolemy; the second was followed by some Greek astrologers after the Christian era, who held that the equinoctial points, after having advanced 8° in 640 years, retreated 8° in a similar lapse of time, returning thus to the primitive point. According to them, the precession was 45″ a year. Finally, it is necessary to note that, while some Indian writers are quite ignorant of the precession, others admit it in an oscillatory form with arcs of 54° or 48° (namely, 27° or 24° from the one part and from the other of ζ Piscium), which they imagined by gross mistakes and not for scientific reasons.

(*e*) *Hypothesis of libration or trepidation.*—The great majority of Muhammadan astronomers held that there was a continuous precession, rightly attributing the discrepancies concerning its value to the imperfection of the observations of the Greeks. We know only three writers of the second half of the 9th cent. who, through Indian influence, accepted the idea of the oscillatory precession in the empirical form of the Greek astrologers mentioned above and of the Indians. On the other hand, Thābit ibn Qurrah († 901) suggested that the discrepancies in the estimate of the annual precession were due in reality to an apparent irregularity of that motion, and that they were connected with the discrepancies relative to the obliquity of the ecliptic. In an epistle which is preserved by Ibn Yūnus he says that he had up till then kept his own calculations private, because he regarded them as uncertain and only provisional. It seems that these secret papers formed the tractate which has come down to us only in two unedited Latin translations under the title *De motu octavæ sphæræ* or *De motu accessus et recessus*.[1] In this tractate Thābit notes that, if all the known observations were exact, there would be a slackening and an acceleration in the motion of precession and in the increase and diminution of the obliquity of the ecliptic. In order to explain these apparently irregular variations, he proposes the following hypothesis:

> The eighth sphere, viz. that which contains the fixed stars, has a movable ecliptic, the extremities of whose axis rotate about the equinoctial points of an ideally fixed ecliptic inclined 23° 33′ in respect of the equator; the complete rotation on those two small circles, having 4° 18′ 43″ of radius, is accomplished in $4171\frac{1}{3}$ lunar years. In this period the equinoctial points would seem to accomplish, with a motion not uniform, an oscillation of 21° 30′ (10° 45′ forwards and the same backwards); in a similar time there will take place an unequal variation of the obliquity.

The hypothesis of Thābit was received in its entirety in Europe by Purbachius (1423–62) and by his commentators Reinhold and Nonius. The oscillation of the equinoctial points is called by the Arabs *ḥarakat al-iqbāl wa 'l-idbār*, 'motion of advance and of retreat,' whence the Latin name *motus accessus et recessus*; this was also called in Europe *motus octavæ sphæræ*, in contradistinction to the motion of the ninth sphere, to which was attributed the motion of the continuous precession; finally, since the longitude of the fixed stars underwent the same oscillations of the equinoctial points, it was often called in Europe *trepidatio fixarum*. This does not seem to have had supporters among the Muhammadans of the East after the 11th century. It had greater fortune among the Muhammadans of the extreme West (Spain and Morocco). Towards 1060–70, at Toledo, az-Zarqālī, in order to make his observations agree with those of his predecessors, suggested that the poles of the ecliptic circulated about the equatorial poles, so that the equinoxes advanced by one unequal motion towards the east about 10° and then retreated irregularly by 20°, accomplishing, *i.e.*, an oscillation of 10° forwards and 10° backwards with reference to an equinoctial point ideally fixed. Every arc of 10° would have been passed over in 750 years, so that the complete cycle of the libration would be accomplished in 3000 years. The hypothesis of az-Zarqālī, explicitly denied by Averroës,[2] was accepted by al-Biṭrūjī (*c.* 1200) in Spain and by Abū 'Alī al-Ḥasan (*c.* 1260) in Morocco; it also found great favour among the Jews and Spanish Christians and had an influence on the Hebrews, who, on a basis of Arabic sources, compiled about 1270 the *Tabulæ Alphonsinæ*.[3]

(*f*) *Motion of the solar apogee.* — Ptolemy (followed by all the later Greeks) says that he found the longitude of the solar apogee to be equal to that observed by Hipparchus, and consequently believes that it is immovable at 65° 30′, while the apogees of the five planets move with the motion of the precession. It is a merit of the Arab astronomers of the khalīf al-Ma'mūn (813–833) that they recognized that the solar apogee is subject to the

[1] Ed. Nallino, i. 12.

[2] See below, § (*e*).

[3] This was already the opinion of Ḥāmid al-Ḥujandī, about A.D. 1000.

[4] Only in the second half of the 18th cent. has celestial mechanics been able to establish the fact that it is a question of a very slow oscillation contained within limits of less than $2\frac{1}{2}$°.

[5] *Mafātiḥ al-ghaib*, i. 260, ii. 59 f.

[1] A suspicion arises, however, that this tractate may rather be by a grandson of Thābit, viz. Ibrāhīm ibn Sinān ibn Thābit, who wrote concerning libration (as al-Bīrūnī and Qāḍīzādeh attest).

[2] *Metaphys.* p. 66 (Quirós, bk. iv. § 15).

[3] It must be noticed that these Hebrews combined the hypothesis of Az-Zarqālī with fantastic elements; viz. they admitted a continuous precession accomplishing the circuit of 360° in 49,000 years (*i.e.* just about 26″ 27‴ a year), which precession was to be always corrected on the basis of an inequality accomplishing its own period in 7000 years. They evidently wished to introduce into the hypothesis of trepidation Judaic elements —a thousand jubilary periods of 49 years and a thousand sabbatical periods of 7 years!

motion of the fixed stars and of the planetary apogees, *i.e.* to the displacement of longitude due to the precession of the equinoxes. But the solar apogee has also another very small proper motion in longitude which, according to Leverrier, is only 11·464″ yearly. This motion must have escaped the Muhammadan astronomers. The determination of the longitude of the apogee is not easy and, in times when telescopes and pendulum-clocks were lacking, could not be effected with absolute certainty in the minutes of arc; on the other hand, there was no term of comparison with ancient observations. One understands, therefore, why the majority of Muhammadan astronomers did not give to the solar apogee any other motion than that of the precession, attributing the small discrepancies to the imperfection of instruments and observations. It seems that Thābit ibn Qurrah, however, had dared to affirm the existence of a *proper* motion. Al-Bīrūnī[1] informs us that Thābit, author of a tractate on the inequality of the solar year, had determined 365 days, 6 hours, 12 minutes, 9 seconds, as being the length of the year which we call anomalistic, *i.e.* the time which the sun takes to return to its own apogee. If, then, the same Thābit (if we may rely upon a piece of information which Regiomontanus and Copernicus seem to have derived from the *De motu octavæ sphæræ* cited above) determined the length of the sidereal year as 365 d., 6 h., 9 m., 12 s., it is plain that he must have attributed to the solar apogee a small proper motion added to that of the precession.[2] Certainly the values found by Thābit are excellent, since, according to the moderns, the anomalistic solar year is 365 d., 6 h., 13 m., 54·9 s., and the sidereal year 365 d., 6 h., 9 m., 10·7 s. It is beyond doubt that az-Zarqālī determined with great exactness ($12\frac{12}{299}$″ every Julian year) the proper motion of the apogee, as distinguished from that due to the precession; and he therefore supposed that the centre of the eccentric of the sun moved over a very small circle, and by this was also settled the variation of the eccentricity of the solar orbit. Among us the proper motion of the apogee was discovered only in the 16th cent. by Kepler and Longomontanus.

(*g*) *Third lunar inequality.*—We need not notice other modifications of special points of Ptolemaic doctrines. It will be enough now to make a reference to a controversy carried on from 1836 to 1871 in the Academy of Sciences of Paris without any definite conclusion being arrived at, viz.: Is the discovery of the variation or third lunar inequality to be ascribed to Abū 'l-Wafā' († 998), as L. A. Sédillot maintained, rather than to Tycho Brahe? There would have been no reason for this dispute if that part of the *Almagest* relative to the movements of the moon had been better studied, and if the analogous discussions in the works of other Arabic astronomers had been examined with care. Carra de Vaux[3] has demonstrated that the hypothetical theory of the variation was nothing else than the πρόσνευσις of Ptolemy, *i.e.* the difference between the true and the mean apogee of the epicycle by which difference the mean anomaly is corrected so as then to calculate the simple equation of the moon. Al-Battānī opportunely calls it 'equation of the anomaly.' It is curious to note that no one has observed that already in 1645 Bullialdus (I. Boulliau) had recognized that the πρόσνευσις corresponded to about half of the 'variation' of Tycho Brahe, and that consequently the tables of Ptolemy for the moon were sufficiently near to the truth.

[1] *Chronology of the Ancient Nations*, Eng. tr., London, 1879, p. 61 f.

[2] The fact that Thābit wrote a tractate to maintain that the solar apogee does move is of no importance, since it is probably merely a confutation of the Ptolemaic immobility.

[3] 'L'Almageste d'Abû 'l-Wéfa al-Bûzdjânî,' in *JA* VIII. xix. [1892] 440–471.

6. Opposition to Ptolemy.—The many modifications of the doctrines of the *Almagest* never abandon the geometrical foundation followed by Ptolemy for the representation of the motions of the sun and planets, viz. a combination of eccentric circles and epicycles. This permitted the representation of celestial motions with all the exactness of which astronomical instruments were capable before the discovery of pendulum-clocks and telescopes; it was further obedient to the Aristotelian principle that celestial motions are circular only. Practical astronomy therefore did not feel the need of theories based on different geometrical principles. The difficulty arose only from a physical point of view, since the idea of numerous circular motions round an imaginary point was repugnant to the principles of Aristotelian physics. It was precisely in the name of Aristotelian natural laws that the battle began among the Arabs of Spain in the 12th cent. against the eccentrics and epicycles of Ptolemy; but their opponents were philosophers.[1]

The first of these was Abū Bakr Muḥammad ibn aṣ-Ṣā'igh, known by the name of Ibn Bājah or Avempace († 1139), who is said to have explained the celestial motions by means of eccentrics only, rejecting the epicycles as repugnant to the physics of Aristotle; but we have no particular account of his system.[2] After him we find Abū Bakr ibn Ṭufail (*q.v.*; † 1185–86), famous in Europe for his *Philosophus autodidactus*, who said to al-Biṭrūjī that he had found a theory of those motions quite different from that of Ptolemy rejecting both eccentrics and epicycles, and that he had promised to put it in writing. But it seems that the promise was not fulfilled. The ideas of Ibn Ṭufail probably influenced his friend Averroës (*q.v.*; † 1198), who affirms[3] the physical impossibility of the geometrical hypothesis of Ptolemy. The astronomers, he continues, assign an eccentric to the moon because, since she is eclipsed now more and now less in one and the same point of the zodiac, they suppose that she traverses the cone of shade at different distances with regard to the earth. 'But this may happen also on account of the diversity of her position, if we imagine that the poles of the lunar sphere move around the poles of another sphere. If God shall prolong our life, we will investigate the astronomy of the time of Aristotle, since this seems not to contradict physics; it consists of motions which Aristotle calls *laulab* [*i.e.* spirals]. I believe that this motion consists in this, that the poles of one sphere move about the poles of another; since then the motion [resulting] is according to a line *leulebia* [*i.e.* spiral], just so is the motion of the sun [combined] with the diurnal motion [of the celestial sphere]. Perchance it is possible by means of such a motion to represent the inequalities which take place in the planetary motions.'

In his commentary on the *Metaphysic*, xii. 47,[4] Averroës does not succeed in forming a clear idea of the system of Eudoxus from the scanty allusions of Aristotle and from the commentary of Alexander of Aphrodisias, which is very defective in this part, it not being clear in what manner the 'motus gyrativi'[5] arise from two contrary motions, unless two different poles be supposed.[6] He observes that by this hypothesis one could explain all the appearances of the planets: 'et iste motus, ut mathematici Hispaniæ dicunt, existit in orbe stellato, et vocant ipsum motum processus et reversionis.'[7]

Although Averroës did not complete his exposition,[8] he had guessed a notable part of the hypothesis of Eudoxus (*c.* 409–356 B.C.), which was for the first time reconstructed by G. Schiaparelli in 1875. Averroës, like Eudoxus, allows only spheres concentric with the earth; he admits that the line *laulabī* may be the apparent result of two contrary circular motions—one of the sphere of the planets, and the other, in an opposite direction, of another sphere whose axis is inclined in respect of the axis of the first sphere; finally, the line *laulabī* corresponds to the ἱπποπέδη of Eudoxus, in the form of ∞, which, according to the Greek geometricians, belongs to the category of spiral lines (σπεῖραι), and, according to modern geometricians, would

[1] Cf. L. Gauthier, 'Une Réforme du système astronomique de Ptolémée tentée par les philosophes arabes du xiie siècle,' in *JA* x. xiv. [1909] 483–510; but this article is insufficient from a mathematical-astronomic point of view.

[2] See Maimonides, *Le Guide des égarés*, ed. and tr. S. Munk, Paris, 1856–66, ii. 185 f.

[3] *Comm. de Cœlo*, ii. 35 (*Aristotelis Opera omnia cum Averrois Cordubensis commentariis*, Venice, 1562, v. fol. 118v.–119r.).

[4] Ed. cit. viii. fol. 331v.–332r.

[5] Thus the Latin translator in the commentary on the *Metaphysic* renders the Arabic adjective *laulabī* 'spiral, in the form of a spiral or of a screw.'

[6] And, in fact, this was the hypothesis of Eudoxus.

[7] *I.e.* the motion of the libration of the fixed stars in the hypothesis of the Spaniard az-Zarqālī (see above, § 5, (*e*)).

[8] Cf. also ed. cit. viii. fol. 329v. (on *Metaphys.* xii. 45).

be a lemniscate described on a spherical superficies instead of on a plane. There naturally occur in the hypothesis of Eudoxus some special conditions, of which Averroës does not seem to have thought; one does not understand, then, how the Arabian philosopher thought to save himself from the greatest objection which could be made to the system of concentric spheres, viz. that by making the distance of the celestial bodies from the earth always equal it did not permit of an explanation of the variation of the diameters of the sun and moon.

Another friend and disciple of Ibn Ṭufail, al-Biṭrūjī (a native of Pedroche to the north of Cordova),[1] attempted a complete system as a substitute for the geometrical hypothesis of Ptolemy,[2] by placing the data of observation of the *Almagest* in agreement with the peripatetic philosophy. He says that, moved by discourses of Ibn Ṭufail to meditate on this question, he had arrived at new theories by a kind of divine revelation. He admits with Ptolemy the nine spheres concentric with the earth; on the other hand, he denies the eccentrics and the epicycles. He finds it to be contrary to natural order that, while the ninth sphere impresses on all the others the diurnal motion of rotation from east to west, the spheres below the ninth should have besides a motion of their own in an opposite direction. In order to remove this contradiction, he conceives a whimsical theory which betrays the inexperience of the author in the field of practical astronomy.

According to him, the movements of the planets and of the fixed stars in longitude take place in reality from east to west, like the diurnal motion of the rotation of the heavens; those movements which astronomers have judged to be from west to east are simply illusory appearances due to the progressive diminution of the angular velocity of the spheres, according as a gradual approach is made from the ninth sphere to the earth.[3] The ninth sphere accomplishes the 360° of circumference in 24 hours and communicates this motion to the spheres below; but the impulse grows weaker from sphere to sphere. That of the fixed stars, which is immediately under the ninth, accomplishes in 24 hours something less than 360°; and this little retardation brings it about that after 36,000 years[4] it has accomplished a whole circuit less than the ninth sphere and appears to be moving very slowly in a direction contrary to it. Under the sphere of the fixed stars comes that of Saturn, considerably slower; it accomplishes in the space of about 30 years[5] a whole circuit less than the ninth sphere. Thus Jupiter loses a whole circuit in 12 years; Mars in two; Venus, the sun, and Mercury in one; and the moon in a little more than 27 days. This, then, is the reason why all the spheres under the ninth appear to move in a direction contrary to it.

For physical reasons, therefore, al-Biṭrūjī believes that the sphere of Venus is to be placed above the sun and that of Mercury below it. There remain to be explained the inequalities of the motions of the sun, moon, and planets. He says that he drew inspiration for this from constructions analogous to that by which az-Zarqālī had imagined the motion of the libration of the fixed stars. While az-Zarqālī made the poles of the ecliptic rotate parallel with the plane of the equator, al-Biṭrūjī, in the case of the planets, made the poles of the planetary spheres move on inclined planes round the poles of the equator or of the ecliptic; from this it results that the planets describe lines *laulabinæ*, *i.e.* spiral, on a spherical superficies. Thus are also explained the stations and retrogradations of the planets. For this part, therefore, we have the partial resuscitation of the hypothesis of Eudoxus. The ideas of al-Biṭrūjī were accepted by a fair number of Christians and Jews in Spain and Provence; and they had also an echo in Italy in the 16th century.

7. Celestial physics.—As is said above,[6] celestial physics, according to Muhammadan and Greek writers, lies outside the field of astronomy; its problems are discussed in books of metaphysics, of physics in an Aristotelian sense, and of theology, or at least in special works, of which the greater part are now either lost or unedited.

Like Ptolemy, the most ancient Arabic astronomers neglect to define the idea of the celestial spheres and limit themselves to considering them in the mathematical aspect of ideal circles representing the movements of the heavenly bodies. The Aristotelian conception of solid spheres was introduced for the first time[1] into a purely astronomical treatise by Ibn al-Haitham; and he, in his unedited compendium of astronomy, gives the definition which was accepted afterwards by all the other writers of elementary treatises: 'A celestial sphere (*falak*, plur. *aflāk*) is a body completely spherical, bounded by two parallel spherical superficies having the same centre.'[2] In this, as he himself says, he drew his inspiration from the *Hypotheses Planetarum* of Ptolemy; in fact, as we see from a passage of Naṣīr ad-dīn aṭ-Ṭūsī, he followed the *Hypotheses* also in expounding how the celestial motions can be represented, and also by supposing simple equatorial zones of those complete spheres, so that the spheres of the epicycles become, as it were, tambourines (*duff*) rotating on their own axes, and the other spheres like armils.[3] This second form of representation was soon abandoned, as contrary to the principles of natural philosophy.

Muhammadan writers agree with Aristotle in holding that the spheres and the celestial bodies are a simple unique substance, different from the four elements of the sublunar world, and forming a fifth element. The solidity also of the spheres, by reason of which the stars remain infixed within them, and by which the stars are carried round, is accepted by almost all,[4] except a few theologians who, to support a strictly literal meaning of a passage of the Qur'ān,[5] maintain that the stars move within the spheres like fish swimming in water. The ideas of the majority of writers after the 4th cent. of the Hijra are those set forth in the dogmatic theology of al-Baiḍāwī († 1286) as follows:

'The spheres are transparent; since if they were coloured, our eyes could not possibly see that which is within them. They are neither hot nor cold; since otherwise the heat and cold would dominate in the elements of the sublunar world on account of their contiguity to it. They are neither light nor heavy; since otherwise in their nature there would be a tendency to rectilinear motion.[6] They are neither moist nor dry; otherwise the facility or difficulty of taking certain forms or of attaching themselves would be manifested in rectilinear motion. They are not capable of quantitative motion; since, if the convexity of the external superficies were to increase, it would be necessary that there should be a void above it, which is absurd; and the same is to be said regarding concavity, since if this were to increase it would be necessary that one sphere should enter into another or that between the two there should be a void.'[7]

So also it is proved by Aristotelian reasonings that the motion of the spheres must be circular.

The greater number of Muhammadan philosophers accept the peripatetic doctrine that the spheres and the stars are living beings, rational, operating by their own will; that the spheres have souls which exist in their bodies as our souls in our bodies; and that, as our bodies move under the impulse of our souls towards the ends we have in view, so also do the spheres, which have as their end the serving of God. This doctrine is for the most part repudiated by the theologians: al-Ghazālī († 1111) does not deny the possibility of it, but he affirms that we are incapable of knowing it; on the other hand, Ibn Ḥazm († 1064), Ibn Qayyim

[1] Alpetragius of our mediæval writers.

[2] Of the book of al-Biṭrūjī there has been published only an obscure Latin tr. (Venice, 1531) made from a Hebrew version. The Latin tr. made in 1217 at Toledo by Michæl Scotus is unedited, as is also the Arabic text.

[3] This idea was already maintained by the Iḫwān aṣ-Ṣafā' about the middle of the 10th cent. (see their *Rasā'il*, Bombay, 1305–06 A.H., ii. 22–26) and by Faḫr ad-dīn ar-Rāzī, *Mafātīḥ al-ghaib*, Cairo, 1308 A.H., ii. 60 f. (comm. on *Qur.* ii. 159) and vi. 117 f. (on *Qur.* xxi. 34). But they admit Ptolemy's eccentrics and epicycles.

[4] This is the period of time in which, according to Ptolemy, the fixed stars accomplish the circumference, proceeding towards the east.

[5] The duration of the heliocentric sidereal revolution of Saturn is a little less than 29½ years; it is, in the Ptolemaic hypothesis, the revolution of the centre of the epicycle of Saturn in the zodiac.

[6] See § I.

[1] This follows from the preface itself of Ibn al-Haitham and from the attestation of Muḥammad al-Akfānī as-Saḫāwī, *Irshād al-qāṣid*, p. 85.

[2] Only the spheres of the epicycles are full, *i.e.* are true globes.

[3] These two forms of hypothesis are always found side by side for every planet, in bk. ii. of the *Hypotheses*, published for the first time (1907) in German according to the Arabic version which takes the place of the lost Greek text (in Ptolemy, *Opera astronomica minora*, ed. Heiberg, p. 113 ff.).

[4] The ancient Arab astronomers—*e.g.*, al-Battānī (i. 124)—leave the question uncertain.

[5] xxi. 34.

[6] According to the Aristotelian theory (*de Cœlo*, i. 8 f.), heavy bodies tend in a straight line towards the centre of the world, light bodies tend to withdraw in a straight line from the centre.

[7] *Maṭāli' al-anwār*, Constantinople, 1305 A.H., p. 262.

al-Jauziyyah († 1350), and many others absolutely deny life and intelligence to the heavenly bodies. The philosophers of the peripatetic school and several theologians (*e.g.*, al-Baiḍāwī) hold that the movers of the celestial souls and consequently of the spheres are pure intelligences. Concerning their origin al-Fārābī, Avicenna, and their followers maintain a Neo-Platonic emanatory theory: from the first principle emanates the first intelligence, and from this are derived all the nine spheres by means of successive triads always composed of intelligence, soul, and body, until one arrives at the final or active intelligence from which is derived all the material of the sublunar world. This theory is vigorously opposed by al-Ghazālī and the other theologians.

The question of the marks on the moon is either neglected or only hinted at in the works hitherto published. The idea that the moon had valleys and mountains like the earth—an idea set forth by several Syriac writers—did not harmonize with the Aristotelian conception of the nature of the heavenly bodies and so could not be accepted by Muhammadan writers.

Observation of the solar spots is almost impossible to the naked eye; Faḫr ad-dīn ar-Rāzī, however, explicitly affirms: 'There are those who believe that there exist on the surface of the sun spots, in the same manner as there are marks on the surface of the moon.'[1] These spots were actually seen on some occasions, but were erroneously believed to be transits of Mercury and Venus across the sun.

The comets and the other meteors (in an Aristotelian sense) were the subjects of observations and of numerous monographs. But, judging from the little that we know about them, Muhammadan writers followed in this matter the theories set forth by Aristotle in his books on meteorology.[2]

8. Conclusion.—The importance of Muhammadan astronomy in the history of science has been variously judged; sometimes Muhammadan astronomers have received excessive praise, sometimes unjust criticism, as if they had done nothing but preserve and transmit to Europe Greek science, improving it only in minor details. This harsh verdict is due not only to very imperfect knowledge of the Arabic writings on astronomy (of which the greater part is still unedited), but also to the fact that no account has been taken of the special conditions of astronomy in the glorious period of Muhammadan culture. The system invented by the Greek geometricians, and completed by Ptolemy, for representing all the celestial motions had mathematically all the precision that could be desired or attained by the use of the best instruments; it produced no sensible discrepancy between theory and the result of observation. The elliptic orbits of Kepler would not have given the theory greater perfection than it received from the complicated system of eccentrics and epicycles; the latter indeed had the advantage of preserving the Pythagorean and Aristotelian principle, which denied any but circular movement in the heavens. One must not forget that even in the heliocentric system of Copernicus the motions of the planets were still explained by means of combinations of epicycles — combinations which were in several cases less perfect than those employed by the Ptolemaic astronomy. To change the method of geometrical representation would therefore have been whimsical—a mathematical trick, which no datum of observation would have justified; and, in fact, those Arabs who wished to eliminate the eccentrics and the epicycles[1] were philosophers rather than astronomers, and they propounded their hypotheses from data based only on Aristotelian physics.

It is thus easy to understand how it was that, *e.g.*, the astronomers of the khalīf al-Ma'mūn and their successors saw no necessity for drawing from their observations of the movement of Venus[2] the final conclusion that Venus revolved round the sun. From the point of view of such phenomena as could be observed without telescopes, this second hypothesis had no higher value than that which made Venus revolve round the earth. In a word, celestial appearances gave no cause to shake the foundations of the geocentric system, which agreed very well with every religious notion, and which was supported by the authority of both Aristotle and Ptolemy, reinforced by a very potent element in Hellenistic and mediæval culture, viz. astrology. Giovanni Schiaparelli, in one of his monographs on Greek astronomy,[3] has set forth clearly the decisive influence which astrology, brought into Greece by the Chaldæan Berosus (3rd cent. B.C.) and consequently received with great favour by the Stoics and Neo-Pythagoreans, had in the abandonment of the heliocentric system of Aristarchus. Astrological doctrine, based on the immobility of the earth in the centre of the world, was irreconcilable with any system which made the earth revolve round the sun or round any other body; astrology was thus a very powerful additional obstacle to the abandonment of the geocentric idea. Further, we must not forget that it was only in the 17th cent. that European physics reached clear proofs of the diurnal rotation of the earth and justified elliptic orbits and the heliocentric system, and that the really irrefutable argument for the revolution of the earth round the sun was furnished only in 1728 by the discovery of the aberration of the fixed stars.

An essential condition of all astronomical progress is to have at disposal a long series of methodical observations; and in this matter Muhammadan astronomers were obliged to begin, so to say, from the foundation. Ptolemy was the last Greek observer; but not even all the observations which he says he made are true. In several cases of capital importance—*e.g.*, regarding the obliquity of the ecliptic and the longitude of the solar apogee —he gave as agreeing with his own observations data found about 270 years before his time by Hipparchus, thus causing certain elements to be believed constant which are really variable. In other cases—*e.g.*, regarding the precession of the equinoxes — his observations are very rough. Theon of Alexandria (4th cent. A.D.) and Proclus (5th cent.) do no more than accept Ptolemy's elements, in some ways aggravating his errors; accordingly, during the seven centuries from Ptolemy to the first flourishing of Arabo-Muhammadan astronomy, we have not even one observation which is of use to the science. The first task, therefore, of the Arabic astronomers was to revise all the Ptolemaic elements of the celestial motions; it was a time not to form new theories but to collect the indispensable elements of fact by means of continuous observations more accurate than those of the Greeks. This task was accomplished by the Muhammadan astronomers in a marvellous manner;

[1] *Mafātiḥ al-ghaib*, i. 259, on *Qur.* ii. 27.

[2] On falling stars see present writer's art. in *Rivista degli Studi Orientali*, viii. [1920] 375–388.

[1] See above, § 6.

[2] They found (contrary to Ptolemy) that Venus has the same longitude of apogee, the same eccentricity, and the same equation of centre as the sun; and so the true longitude of the centre of the epicycle of Venus is always equal to the true longitude of the sun. This was the same as to suppose that the orbit of Venus is an epicycle whose centre is always the true place of the sun and runs over the solar orbit; in other words, it was equivalent to making Venus a satellite of the sun.

[3] *Origine del sistema planetario eliocentrico presso i Greci*, Milan, 1898, § 55.

indeed, we must come down to the time of Tycho Brahe (1546–1601) to find observers and observations comparable to those of the Muhammadan Middle Ages. Further, by founding trigonometry in a modern sense and developing it to a high degree they furnished astronomical science with an excellent instrument for its work.

The influence of Muhammadan astronomy in Europe is so far-reaching that to treat of it at length would be to give the history of some centuries of European astronomy. From the 12th cent. to the end of the 15th the compendiums used in the schools were translated from Arabic or were based on Arabic writings; the astronomical tables and the processes of calculation were derived from Arabic works, among which must be classed (from the point of view not of their language but of their contents) the celebrated tables of Alfonso which were still used by many in the 16th century. Spherical trigonometry in Europe started from Arabic treatises; the famous Regiomontanus himself (1436–76) borrows more than appears on the surface from al-Battānī. Through the influence of these Arabic sources the ancient Latin technical terminology was greatly modified, and not only do Arabic astronomical terms enter into European languages, but Latin words acquire new significations by imitation of corresponding Arabic words. The words 'degree,' 'minute,' 'equation' (in its astronomical sense), 'equation of the centre,' 'argument' (of a table), and some others, owe their technical signification to ridiculously literal translations of Arabic writings. We cannot enumerate all that European astronomy owes to Muhammadan observers; it will be enough to recall that they rendered inestimable services even to writers of the 17th cent.—*e.g.*, Halley—precisely because they offered the only certain means of checking elements determinable only by a comparison with observations separated by long intervals of time. The books of Regiomontanus, Purbachius, Copernicus, Tycho Brahe, Riccioli, etc., cite the observations which were known to them of their Oriental predecessors. The theory and practice of instruments in Europe has also Arabic sources. Finally, we must not forget the influence exercised by the Arabs in the way of example. They infused into the Christians and Jews of Spain a passion for continued observations and an idea of the perfectibility of astronomical science; from Spain this passion and idea spread through the rest of Europe, preparing the way for modern astronomy.

The conditions of the Byzantine mediæval world were not favourable to the development of the sciences. Nevertheless, Muhammadan culture, which left many traces in Byzantine astrology, had also its part in astronomical studies. In 1323 an anonymous Greek introduced the Persian astronomical tables of Shams ad-dīn al-Buḫārī (Σὰμψ Μπουχαρῆς), which were at once widely used; in 1346 George Chrysococces made a new redaction of them, preserving at the same time many Arabic-Persian technical terms; and finally, about 1361, Theodore Meliteniotes reproduced these methods and these Persian tables in the third and last book of his Ἀστρονομικὴ Τρίβιβλος, after having set forth in the first and second books the methods and the tables according to Ptolemy and Theon of Alexandria. Thus there was created at Byzantium also a new astronomical terminology different from that of the classic Greek; and sometimes even Greek proper names appeared transformed by their passage through Arabic-Persian sources, as Θαούνης in place of Θέων.

LITERATURE.—There is no satisfactory exposition of the astronomy of the Muhammadan peoples in the Middle Ages; the general histories of astronomy—*e.g.*, those of F. Hoefer, J. H. von Mädler, R. Wolf (the best of all), and Arthur Berry—are inadequate, antiquated, and often erroneous. J. B. J. Delambre, *Hist. de l'astronomie du moyen âge*, Paris, 1819, pp. 1–211, and 513–539, is not a history but an analysis (of very unequal value) of various works of Muhammadan authors; the part devoted to the unedited book of Ibn Yūnus (pp. 76–156) is especially noteworthy, but it has the usual defect of Delambre—instead of the analyzed processes of the author, it substitutes a series of formulæ found by Delambre himself. Useful, but to be used with great caution, is L. A. Sédillot, *Matériaux pour servir à l'hist. comparée des sciences mathématiques chez les Grecs et les Orientaux*, 2 vols., Paris, 1845–49; see also his *Mémoire sur les instruments astronomiques des Arabes*, do. 1841 (*MAIBL, Savants étrangers*, i.). The present writer's Arabic book quoted above, p. 90ᵃ, n. 1, concerns only the earliest period (summary of H. Suter, in *Bibliotheca Mathematica*, III. xii. [1912] 277–282). Many historical notices concerning the development of astronomical theories are to be found in the present writer's commentary on al-Battānī, *Opus astronomicum*, 3 vols., Milan, 1899–1907; short notices are to be found here and there in E. Wiedemann, 'Beiträge zur Geschichte der Naturwissenschaften,' nos. iii.–xxxviii. (in the *Sitzungsberichte der physikal.-medizinischen Sozietät in Erlangen*, 1904–1914) and in other small pamphlets by the same author. For biographical and bibliographical notices concerning individual writers see the excellent book of H. Suter, *Die Mathematiker und Astronomen der Araber und ihre Werke*, Leipzig, 1900, and 'Nachträge und Berichtigungen zu Die Math. und Astron.,' in *Abhandl. zur Gesch. der mathemat. Wissenschaften*, xiv. [1902] 157–185. For edd. and tr. of original texts see above, II. 2.

CARLO ALFONSO NALLINO.

SUN, MOON, AND STARS (Teutonic and Balto-Slavic). — I. *TEUTONIC*.—**1. Archæological evidence.**—The world-wide symbol of the sun-wheel occurs in the earliest Scandinavian rock-markings. Rude representations of horses and ships, which may have solar significance, are also found. In 1902 a curious object, apparently connected with the sun-cult, was discovered near Trundholm in Sweden. It is a representation of a disk, having gilding on one side and spiral ornamentation on the other, with a horse in front of it, both horse and disk being drawn on a waggon.

2. Solar myths.—Sun and moon, day and night, summer and winter, are personified in the poems of the older Edda. The Valkyrie Sigrdrifa invokes Day and the sons of Day, Night and her kinswoman.[1] Various passages from *Grimnismál*, *Vafþrúðnismál*, and *Völuspá* are summarized by Snorri:[2]

'Night, who was of Jotun race, married Delling, who was of Aesir race, and their son was named Day.' 'Then Allfather took Night and her son Day and set them up in heaven and gave them two steeds and two chariots and they were to drive round the earth every twenty-four hours.' The earth is bedewed by the foam which falls each morning from the bit of Hrimfaxi, the horse of Night. Day's steed is called Skinfaxi and he lights up the whole world with his mane. 'Then said Gangleri: "Who steers the course of the sun and of the moon?"' Mundilföri had a son Mani and a daughter Sol, whom the gods set up in heaven. 'They let Sol drive the steeds which drew the chariot of that sun which the gods made to light the world, from the sparks which flew out of Muspellheim [*i.e.* the world of fire and heat]. . . . These steeds are called All-Swift and Early-Awake, but under the withers of the horses, the gods set two wind-bellows to cool them, but in some old records that is called "isarnkol" [*i.e.* iron-coolness]. Mani steers the course of the Moon and rules over waxing and waning.'

The belief in the chariot and horses of the sun is very wide-spread; in Scandinavia, judging by the archæological evidence, it must have existed in very early times. We may have a reference to the same idea in Tacitus:

'Beyond the Suiones is another sea, sluggish and almost stagnant, by which the whole globe is imagined to be girt about and enclosed, from this circumstance that the last light of the setting sun continues so vivid till its rising as to obscure the stars. Popular belief adds, that the sound of his emerging from the ocean is also heard, and the forms of horses and the rays streaming from his head are beheld.'[3]

Like most other primitive people, the Scandinavians were struck by the phenomena of the eclipses, which they thought were caused by wolves.

'He who pursues her [*i.e.* the sun] is called Skoll; he frightens her and he will catch her; but he who is called Hati

[1] *Sigrdrifumál*, 2. [2] *Gylfaginning*, x.–xii.

[3] *Germ.* 45. Unfortunately the text is uncertain; some editors read *deorum* for *equorum* in the last sentence.

Hroðvitnison leaps in front of her, and he will catch the moon, and so it must be.'[1] 'Skoll is the name of the wolf, who pursues the gleaming goddess to Ironwood. Another called Hati, son of Hroðvitni, goes before the fair bride of heaven.'[2]

Sun and moon will be involved in the final world-catastrophe.

'Then said Gangleri: "Of what race are these wolves [*i.e.* Skoll and Hati]?" Hár said: . . . "The old giantess rears the sons of many Jotuns and all in the form of wolves, and it is said that of the race of these wolves, there shall come one mightier than all, called Moon-Swallower and he . . . in demon's form shall seize the moon. . . . He shall fill himself with the bodies of doomed men, he shall stain the god's abode with red blood; the sunshine shall be black, and all the weather treacherous during the following summer."'[2]

'Whence comes a sun, in the smooth sky,
When Fenrir [*i.e.* a monstrous wolf] has overtaken this one,
One daughter alone, shall the Elf-beam [*i.e.* the sun] bear,
Before Fenrir overtakes her.
The maiden shall ride on the mother's paths
After the Powers have perished.'[3]

3. Sun-worship.—Our knowledge of the religious practices of the Teutons is very meagre, and it is difficult to say how far the stories told in the two Eddas formed part of a living religion, even among the Scandinavians. We have, however, various references to the sun-cult from other sources. Procopius[4] describes how in the island of Thule [*i.e.* Scandinavia] the sun does not appear for 40 days at the winter solstice. At the end of this period messengers are sent up into the mountains to watch for the rising sun. They send word to the people below that the sun will shine upon them in five days: thereupon begins 'the greatest feast of the inhabitants of Thule.'

The positive side of Cæsar's well-known description of Teutonic religion[5] is probably true. The Teutons may well have acknowledged as gods such things as are 'objects of sight and by whose power they are apparently benefited, the sun, moon, fire,' although these were not their only deities. Observances in connexion with the sun and moon are forbidden in Christian sermons and penitentiaries. St. Eligius (588–659) tells his hearers that no Christian person 'calls sun or moon lords.' In the 11th cent. the *Decrees* of Burchard of Worms mention pagan traditions:

'Id est ut elementa coleres, id est lunam aut solem, aut stellarum cursum, novam lunam, aut defectum lunae, ut tuis clamoribus aut auxilio splendorem ejus restaurere valeres.'[6]

From Canute's Anglo-Saxon Laws[7] we learn that 'heathenship is to honour heathen gods, and sun or moon, . . . etc.' We have perhaps a trace of sun-worship in *Landnámabók*:

'Thorkell Moon, the law speaker, was of the best conversation of any heathen man in Iceland. . . . He had himself carried out into the rays of the sun in his death-sickness and commended himself to that god which had made the sun.'[8]

We know little of Anglo-Saxon paganism. Bede, however, mentions a goddess Eostur, in whose honour April was called 'Eosturmonath.'[9] The word 'Eostur' is identical with the Latin, Greek, Sanskrit, and Lithuanian names for the goddess of the dawn, or *Morgenröthe*, probably the same being who is referred to in the Lithuanian and Lettish folk-songs as the daughter of the sun.

Throughout Teutonic territory the first and second days of the week are named after the sun and moon. Sunna is mentioned with Wodan and Frûa in the Merseberg charm. Sol is counted as one of the *asynjur*.[10]

It is noteworthy that Snorri (see above) distinguishes between the physical sun and moon and the beings who rule over them and guide their movements. This distinction has been partly preserved in the Old Norse language, where the word *tungl* (A.S. *tungol*, Goth. *tuggls*, 'a star') denotes the actual moon, and Máni the supernatural being who directs his course. The same idea seems to underlie many of the Lithuanian and Lettish folk-songs.

[1] *Gylf.* xii. 15. [2] *Grimn.* xxxix. 88.
[3] *Vafþrúðnismál*, 46 f. [4] *De Bell. Goth.* ii. 15.
[5] *De Bell. Gall.* vi. 21. [6] *PL* cxl. 960.
[7] *Ancient Laws and Institutes of England*, ed. B. Thorpe, London, 1840, p. 162.
[8] i. 9. [9] *De Temp. Ratione*, 15.
[10] *Gylf.* xxxv. 45.

II. *LETTISH, LITHUANIAN, AND OLD PRUSSIAN.*—**1. Mythology.**—Our chief knowledge of the solar mythology of the Baltic peoples is derived from Lettish and Lithuanian folk-songs, the most significant of which have been translated and analyzed by W. Mannhardt.[1] In these poems the changes which pass over the face of the sky, especially at dawn and sunset, are viewed as a drama, the chief actors being sun, moon, the daughter of the sun, the sons of God, Perkun, the thunder deity, 'God' and 'dear Maria'—the last two being as frankly pagan as the rest. Often, of course, the poems are confused and inconsistent, and it must be remembered that the terms 'sun,' 'moon,' etc., sometimes stand for the presiding deity, sometimes for the actual sun, etc., personified:

'The Sun, in the apple garden,
Weeps bitterly.
The *golden apple* hath fallen
From the apple tree.'[2]

(Here there is a clear distinction between the deity and the physical sun.)

'The Sun dances over the silver mountain,
Silver shoes she hath on her feet.'[3]

(In this case sun and sun-goddess appear to be one and the same.)

'God,' who was at war with the sun for three nights and three days, is evidently a sky-deity. The sky itself is described as a 'great water' or a mountain:

'The Sun with two gold horses
Rides up the rocky mountain,
Never heated, never weary,
Never resting on the way.'

(In this and in other songs we get the wide-spread myth of the horses of the sun.)

2. The sun.—The sun is called in many of the songs 'daughter of God,' in Lettish sources *saulesmaat*, 'mother of the sun.' She is married to the moon, who is, however, an unfaithful husband.

'It happened in the spring-time
That sun and moon did wed,
But the sun rose up early
And from her the moon fled.
The morning star was loved then
By the lone wandering moon,
Who with a sword was smitten
In deep wrath by Perkun.'[4]

The children of the sun and moon are the stars, who are called orphans, because they appear only at night after their mother, the sun, has abandoned them.

3. The sons of God.—The morning and the evening stars play an important part in the folk-songs, sometimes as a single being, sometimes in dual form. In Lithuanian sources they are called Auszrine and Wakarine[5] and are described as the handmaids of the sun.

'"Dear sun, daughter of God,
Who kindles your fire in the morning?
Who spreads your bed in the evening?"
"Auszrine kindles the fire.
Wakarine spreads the bed."'[6]

In Lettish songs the morning and the evening stars are called the 'sons of God'—an epithet exactly equivalent to the Greek Dioskouroi. Like the Dioskouroi and the Aśvins of Indian mythology, the Lettish sons of God are connected with horses:

'Hither rode the dear sons of God
With steeds dripping with sweat.'[7]
'Folks say the moon has no steeds of his own.
The morning star and the evening star
They are the steeds of the moon.'[8]

[1] 'Die lett. Sonnenmythen,' *ZE* vii. 73–104, 209–244, 280–330.
[2] *Ib.* p. 91 ff. [3] *Ib.* [4] *Ib.*
[5] Nom. fem. of adjective derived from Lith. *auszra*, 'dawn,' *vakaras*, 'evening.'
[6] *ZE* vii. *loc. cit.* [7] *Ib.* [8] *Ib.*

4. The daughter of the sun.—A favourite theme of the Lettish folk-songs is the wooing of the daughter of the sun by the son of God, the sun providing the dowry, often most unwillingly.

'Why are grey steeds standing
By the house-door of the sun?
They are the grey steeds of the son of God
Who woos the daughter of the sun.
The son of God stretches out his hand
Over the great water
To the daughter of the sun.
The sun cries bitterly
Standing on the mountain.
Why should she not weep?
She sorrows for the little maiden,
She sorrows for the dowry,
For the chest which is laden
With gold and silver gifts.'[1]

This is a good example of a sunrise or sunset myth. The daughter of the sun is the red glow which is in the sky when the planet Venus appears, but soon afterwards melts into darkness or the full light of day. The 'dowry' seems to be the rays of the sun which light up the edges of the clouds and the tops of trees and mountains.

'The sun prepareth the dowry herself, gilding the edge of the forest of pines.'[2]

The daughter of the sun is almost certainly identical with the goddess mentioned by Lasicius.[3] 'Ausca dea est radiorum solis, vel occumbentis vel supra horizontem ascendentis.'[4]

5. Dear Maria.—Mannhardt considers that the name Maria has been substituted for that of various pagan deities, but it is also possible that she stands for a particular goddess, perhaps the Perkuna tete (*i.e.* the aunt of Perkun) mentioned by Lasicius: 'Perkuna tete is the mother of thunder and lightning; who receives into a bath the weary and dusty sun, and sends her out again next day washed and shining.'[5] Maria also presides over a bath-chamber:

'Behind the mountains smoke is rising.
Who is it hath kindled fire?
Dear Maria heats the bathroom
Where bathe little orphan maidens [*i.e.* stars].'[6]

'I ran down into the valley, into the bath-chamber of dear Maria.'[7]

According to Prætorius,[8] the Nadravians worshipped a star-god Szweigsdukks, who is evidently the Suaixtix worshipped by the Sudavians in Samland and equated with Sol in the *Constit. Synod. Evangel.* of 1530. Lucas David[9] calls Suaixtix the god of light and mentions him as one of the four deities who were invoked at agricultural festivals.[10] This deity seems to have been worshipped in both male and female form: 'They more commonly called this godhead Sweigsdunka, a star-goddess, whom they consider the bride of the sky and through whose power the morning and evening stars are guided.'[11] Is this perhaps 'the maiden who weaves star-coverings,' mentioned in one of the folk-songs, and also the goddess whose place has been taken by dear Maria, and who was also known as the aunt of the thunder-god? The underlying idea may be that she is a goddess of fire, light, and heat.[12]

6. Cult.—We know little of the sun-cult of the Baltic peoples, although we know from Peter von Dusburg[13] and Erasmus Stella[14] that sun, moon, and stars were worshipped as important deities. Prætorius[1] tells us that Bretkius (a historian of the 16th cent.) had observed that the Nadravians did honour to their gods by worshipping the different phases of the moon at various stages of their agricultural work.

In the course of his missionary journeys among the Lithuanians Jerome of Prague met with a people who worshipped the sun and who had a strange cult of a huge iron hammer. The priests justified this cult by telling Jerome that formerly the sun had been invisible for many months because a king had imprisoned it in a tower. 'The signs of the zodiac brought help to the sun, and broke the tower with the huge hammer, and restored the liberated sun to men, and therefore that which had been the instrument by which mortals had received light was worthy of veneration.'[2] According to Rendel Harris, the signs of the zodiac here stand for the Heavenly Twins or 'Sons of God': 'These and similar cases all arise out of the same theme, that the Sun (or the daughter of the Sun) has been carried off, or swallowed or imprisoned, and must be recovered.'[3] They use the hammer, the weapon of the thunder-god, because sacred twins are universally considered as children of the sky or thunder-god. In one of the Lettish songs they are described as 'workmen of Perkun.'

LITERATURE.—(I.) See works cited in art. NATURE (Teutonic). (II.) W. Mannhardt, 'Die lettischen Sonnenmythen,' *ZE* vii. [1875] 73–104, 209–244, 280–330; J. Rendel Harris, *The Cult of the Heavenly Twins*, Cambridge, 1906, *Boanerges*, do. 1913; see also art. OLD PRUSSIANS for further literature.

ENID WELSFORD.

SUN-DANCE.—See PHALLISM, ix. 823.

SUNDAY.—1. History of Sunday before the Christian era.

—Only three times in the NT is there any reference to a religious observance of Sunday. St. Paul urged his converts at Corinth to put aside money for charity every Sunday (1 Co 16²). Shortly after writing this he preached at a service held at Troas, which is mentioned as if it were a regular institution (Ac 20⁷). Thirty years later, perhaps, the author of the Apocalypse wrote: 'I was in the Spirit on the Lord's day' (Rev 1¹⁰). Though not quite conclusive, the evidence makes it probable that the observance of Sunday began among St. Paul's churches, which were predominantly Gentile. Now we cannot suppose that Gentile Christians, who were taught by St. Paul to protest against having the Sabbath imposed upon them, would yet accept from the Jews a whole system of reckoning time by weeks. It is important, therefore, to inquire how far the week was recognized in the Græco-Roman world independently of the Jews.

The week originated in Babylon, where it was invented for astrological reasons, but came to be used as a civil division of time. At first each month began with a fresh week, so that there were two or three odd days at the end. This was too inconvenient to last; and the weeks, emancipated from the month, ran on in an unbroken series. The gradual diffusion of Babylonian astrology carried a knowledge of the week into W. Asia, then into Egypt, and later still into E. Europe. The Israelites, when they invaded Canaan, found it established there and adopted it, as they did many other elements of Amorite culture; but the emphasis laid upon the Sabbath was their own.

In considering the recognition of the week in Europe it will be convenient to trace the evidence backwards. We may begin with Dio Cassius. Writing soon after A.D. 230, he says:

'The dedication of the days to the seven planets originated in Egypt, but has spread over all the world in comparatively

---

1 *ZE* vii. *loc. cit.* 2 *Ib.*
3 *De Diis Samagitarum*, in *Respublica sive Status regni Poloniæ, Lituaniæ, Prussiæ, Livoniæ, etc.*, Leyden, 1627, ch. viii.
4 Ausca, in Lith. Auszra, a word which is connected with Skr. *usas*, Gr. Ἠώς, Lat. *Aurora*, O.E. *Eostur*, all of which (with the possible exception of Eostur) denote goddesses of the dawn.
5 P. 300. 6 *ZE* vii. *loc. cit.* 7 *Ib.*
8 *Deliciæ Prussicæ*, ed. W. Pierson, Berlin, 1871, p. 26.
9 *Preussische Chronik*, ed. E. Hennig, Königsberg, 1812, i. 86.
10 *Ib.* p. 91. 11 Prætorius, p. 26.
12 See art. NATURE (Lettish, Lithuanian, and Old Prussian).
13 *Scriptores Rerum Prussicarum*, Leipzig, 1861–74, i. 53.
14 *Ib.* iv. 294.

1 *Deliciæ Prussicæ*, p. 18. 2 Æneas Sylvius, in *ib.* iv. 239.
3 *Boanerges*, p. 334.

recent times. The ancient Greeks, at any rate, knew nothing of it: but now it is established not only among all other peoples but even among the Romans, who already regard it as more or less a national tradition.'[1]

In the middle of the 2nd cent. Justin Martyr, writing for heathen readers, speaks of Saturday and Sunday (τὴν Κρονικήν, τὴν Ἡλίου ἡμέραν) as if they were familiar names to all.[2] Near the end of the 1st cent. Josephus boasts:

'Nor is there any city of the Greeks, nor any barbarian city, nor any nation, where our custom of resting on the seventh day has not reached.'[3]

That, no doubt, is an exaggeration; but it would have been meaningless unless division of time into weeks had been so familiar that any one might know which day was a Saturday. The belief that such was the case in the 1st cent. is supported by a picture which was found at Herculaneum, and therefore painted before A.D. 79. It contains the heads of the seven planetary deities in the order of their days—Saturn, Apollo, Diana, Mars, Mercury, Jupiter, Venus. Numerous references in Latin literature assure us that the Jewish Sabbath was well known as early as the Christian era. But only those are to our purpose which imply familiarity with the week. Such are the passages in Tibullus,[4] Ovid,[5] and Martial,[6] which mention the observance of Sabbaths by Romans. But more remarkable is the fact that Horace,[7] writing about 35 B.C., could represent an ordinary superstitious mother as making a vow for next Thursday (*Jovis dies*) and could describe how he himself attempted to escape from a bore by pleading that it was a special Saturday.[8] Neither the vow nor the plea would be intelligible without the week as a familiar background.

2. Sunday in the primitive Church.—It was therefore not only the Jewish proselytes among St. Paul's converts, but all his Greek and Roman disciples, who reckoned their time by weeks and therefore found a weekly day of worship natural. To such, again, as were Jews by race it seemed actually part of the order of nature. That is why, we may well suppose, St. Paul's protests against the observance of the Sabbath or of any fixed days[9] were but partially successful. The Sabbath, indeed, was given up by the churches which he founded. But, as a concession to his converts' habit of mind, another day of the week was chosen for worship. There could be no question what the choice should be, for the Lord's resurrection had given the first day of the week an unquestionable pre-eminence.

The name of this day which was current in the Roman Empire was 'the day of the sun' (ἡ Ἡλίου ἡμέρα, *dies solis*). The Jews, who avoided all use of heathen terms for either days or months, called it the first day of the week (μία Σαββάτων), and the earliest Christians followed their example. But a mere number was felt to lack distinction, and very soon an appropriate name was found, which contrasted alike with Sabbath and Sunday. The first day of the month, at least in Asia Minor, was usually called the 'Emperor's Day' (Σεβαστή).[10] Now the early Christians, partly by way of challenge, applied to their Lord many of the official terms which were consecrated to the emperor, the lord of the earth. So it was probably not without reference to the term Σεβαστή that they entitled the first day of the week Κυριακή, 'the Lord's Day.' So apt a name was rapidly established. The author of the Apocalypse, writing about A.D. 90, uses it without explanation. To Ignatius[11] (*c.* A.D. 110) it was a matter of course and a basis for argument. When the empire became Christian, the name entirely displaced 'the day of the sun' for all who spoke Greek or Latin. Κυριακή remains to this day in Greek; and in the Romance languages we find derivatives of *dies Dominica* — Dimanche, Domenica, and so on. But the Northern peoples, who in accepting the week from the heathen Romans had named the days after the corresponding Northern divinities, were more conservative. In England Sunday (A.S. *Sunnan Daeg*), in Germany *Sonntag*, in Sweden *Söndag*, have resisted all attempts to substitute either Lord's Day or Sabbath.

[1] *Hist. Rom.* xxxvii. 18.
[2] *Apol.* i. 67.
[3] *C. Apion.* ii. 40.
[4] I. iii. 18.
[5] *Ars Amat.* i. 415.
[6] IV. iv. 7.
[7] *Sat.* II. iii. 290.
[8] *Ib.* I. ix. 69.
[9] Ro 14[5], Gal 4[10], Col 2[16].
[10] A. Deissmann, *Light from the Ancient East*, Eng. tr., London, 1910, pp. 361-366.
[11] *Ad Magn.* 9.

3. Observance in the Church before A.D. 321.—The records tell us very little about the manner in which Sunday was observed during the first three centuries, except that it was the day on which Christians assembled for worship. After St. Paul, who is quoted above, our first witness is the younger Pliny. His famous letter, written to the emperor Trajan in A.D. 104, tells how the Christians in his province of Bithynia held a service early in the morning 'on a fixed day' (*stato die*) and a common meal late in the evening.[1] Ignatius (A.D. 110) insists upon the contrast between the Lord's Day and the Sabbath.[2] A little later the *Teaching of the Apostles* ordains:

Κατὰ κυριακὴν δὲ Κυρίου συναχθέντες κλάσατε ἄρτον καὶ εὐχαριστήσατε προεξομολογησάμενοι τὰ παραπτώματα ὑμῶν, ὅπως καθαρὰ ἡ θυσία ὑμῶν ᾖ.[3]

A simple service, before or after the day's work, was the only observance possible for a community most of whose members occupied very humble stations, while many were slaves. As the Christians advanced in numbers and in social position, they were able to command the time for a long service. Justin Martyr, writing about A.D. 170, describes one which must have occupied at least two hours; for it includes readings from the Bible, sermon, prayers, and Eucharist.[4] And, since Melito, bishop of Sardis, just about the same time published a treatise *On the Lord's Day*, we may conclude that the services were being systematized.[5] How important they were considered is partly shown by Tertullian's attack upon cowardly bishops, who excused themselves for fleeing from persecution on the ground that in such times they could not assemble a congregation or celebrate the Sunday rites: 'Sed quomodo colligemus, inquis, quomodo Dominica sollemnia celebrabimus?'[6] From that time onward the position of Sunday as a holy day was unquestioned; and we need trace its history no further.

Just at that point we find the first suggestion of a Sunday holiday. Two sentences of Tertullian are worth quoting, both written while he was still a Catholic. In Sunday worship, he says, Christians avoid every trace of gloom, and even put aside business which might interfere with prayer ('differentes etiam negotia, ne quem diabolo locum demus').[7] And, when he tells the Christians that they have more festivals in the year than the heathen, he implies that Sunday, like a Roman festival, is more or less a holiday: 'Si quid et *carni indulgendum* est, habes, non dicam tuos dies tantum, sed et plures. Nam ethnicis semel annuus dies quisque *festus est, tibi octavus quisque dies*.'[8]

It is to be observed that he compares Sunday with heathen festivals rather than with the Sabbath. So long as Jewish Christianity remained a power, or the hostility of Jews a thing to be feared, Gentile Christians were anxious to repudiate any connexion between the Sabbath and Sunday. The feeling was obviously strong when Ignatius wrote μηκέτι σαββατίζοντες ἀλλὰ κατὰ κυριακὴν ζῶντες,[9] and when the author of the *Epistle of Barnabas* described Sunday as ἄλλου κόσμου ἀρχήν.[10] Justin Martyr shows its influence when he derives the sanctity of Sunday from the creation and the Resurrection. Although Jewish Christianity disappeared from the West before the end of the 2nd cent., there is plenty of evidence that some of its traditions persisted in the Eastern Church for two hundred

[1] *Epp. ad Traj.* 96.
[2] *Ad Magn.* 9.
[3] *Didache*, xiv.
[4] *Apol.* i. 67.
[5] Eusebius, *HE* iv. 26.
[6] Tert. *de Fuga in Persecutione*, 14.
[7] *De Orat.* 18(23).
[8] *De Idol.* 14.
[9] *Ad Magn.* 9.
[10] *Ep. Barn.* 15.

years more. The *Apostolic Constitutions*,[1] *e.g.*, recognized a parallel observance of the Sabbath and Sunday. And the Council of Laodicea (363), while condemning a Judaizing observance of the Sabbath, marked it as a festival and a day of worship. Different as was the East from the West, they were in constant communication; and the maintenance of the Sabbath in the East was a reason for keeping Sunday clear of Sabbatarianism in the West. Egypt, intermediate between East and West, was Western in its observance of Sunday. Accordingly Clement of Alexandria (*c.* 200) says that the Lord's Day is celebrated by putting away evil thoughts and acquiring true knowledge;[2] and Origen (*c.* 240) apologizes for the common observance of Sunday as a concession to the feelings of the weaker brethren. They, 'being either unable or unwilling to keep every day in this manner, require some sensible memorials to prevent spiritual things from passing altogether away from their minds.'[3]

A hundred years later Athanasius wrote to much the same effect: 'We keep no Sabbath day (but) we keep the Lord's Day as a memorial of the beginning of the second new creation.'[4]

St. Jerome follows in the same line. He tells how his party of recluses at Bethlehem attended Church services on Sunday, but otherwise pursued their usual occupations.[5] St. Augustine, while insisting upon the festal character of Sunday—'Dies tamen Dominicus non Judaeis sed Christianis resurrectione Domini declaratus est, et ex illo habere coepit festivitatem suam'[6]—pronounces that the Fourth Commandment is in no literal sense binding upon Christians. His words seem framed to exclude the idea of any transference of obligation from the Sabbath to Sunday.

4. Movement in favour of a day of rest.—While the leaders of the Church gave no sanction to the idea that Sunday was the heir of the Sabbath, that idea was all the time gaining power among the mass of the Christian people in the West. Several causes combined to favour its growth. As the passage quoted above from Tertullian indicates, the numerous heathen festivals constantly suggested that a holy day should be a day of rest. Familiarity with the OT, whose authority was unchallenged, insensibly turned men's thoughts in the direction of Sabbatarianism. Increasing leisure and power enabled many Christians to command a day of rest. Greater stress was laid, as time went on, upon the duty of attendance at the Church services, which in many cases involved the abandonment of regular work. How steadily popular opinion was moving in the direction of a Sunday holiday may be inferred from a resolution passed in 305 by the Council of Illiberis in Spain, making the observance of the Lord's Day compulsory and ordaining that failure to attend the services shall be punished with excommunication. The Sabbatarian movement, therefore, like that for the worship of the saints, came from below. Theologians long resisted it, but at last yielded, and sought for reasons to justify a practice which the people had adopted. Among these we do not usually find either the duty of observing the Fourth Commandment in the spirit or the social need (recognized in Deuteronomy) of a day for rest and recreation. The reasons alleged are of a mystical and symbolical character, such as would naturally suggest themselves to theologians in difficulties. And yet the very contrasts which they draw between the Sabbath and the Lord's Day show the influence of the popular pressure, and prepare the way for the identification of the two which was to come in the 9th century.

St. Ambrose, *e.g.*, describes how the first day has succeeded to the dignity which formerly belonged to the seventh: 'Ubi enim Dominica dies coepit praecellere, qua Dominus resurrexit; Sabbatum, quod primum erat, secundum haberi coepit a primo. *Prima enim requies* cessavit, *secunda* successit.'[7] St. Chrysostom (*c.* 390) goes further. Commenting on 1 Co 16[1], he says that the first day of the week was well chosen for acts of charity, ὅτι καὶ ἄνεσιν ἔχει καὶ πόνων ἀτέλειαν. He thus actually carries back the Sunday rest into the year 57. And, when he writes about Ro 14[5], he asserts that 'esteemeth every day alike' has reference only to fasting. The reason of so strange a misconception is doubtless that he regards the observance of Sunday as a matter of course. Although, therefore, he generally contrasts Sunday and Sabbath in the manner of his time, it is not surprising to find him once coming very near to the later Sabbatarian view. In the 10th *Homily* on Gn 1 he writes: 'God from the first teaches us symbolically to set apart one whole day in the week and devote it to spiritual activities.'

Examples might be given from other writers. But these are enough to indicate the double process which was going on. While the official position of the Church was hostile to Sabbatarianism, the writers could not altogether resist the influence of popular opinion which was steadily moving towards it.

5. Constantine's decree of A.D. 321.—Parallel to the Christian movement in favour of a Sunday rest there seems to have been another, which was quite independent. The matter is obscure, and we must rely in part upon conjecture. As the social and industrial organization of the empire advanced under the Pax Romana, the sporadic festivals of the ancient calendar became more and more inconvenient. The efficiency of labour depends largely upon recreation; but holidays at irregular intervals are not effectual for recreation, and interfere sadly with organization. We can imagine that the heathen often reflected upon the contrast, to which Tertullian points, between the regular weekly festival of the Christians and their own uncertain celebrations; and that they wished that they could exchange their inconvenient holidays for a regular rest on 'the day of the sun.' Some such process of thought in the popular mind is required to explain the readiness with which the whole world, heathen as well as Christian, accepted Constantine's famous decree. Though he was doubtless influenced mainly by the wishes of his Christian supporters, it was not as 'the Lord's Day' but as 'the venerable day of the sun' that he described the new public holiday:

'Omnes judices urbanaeque plebes et cunctarum artium officia venerabili die Solis quiescant. Ruri tamen positi agrorum culturae libere licenterque inserviant, quoniam frequenter evenit ut non aptius alio die frumenta sulcis aut vineae scrobibus mandentur, ne occasione momenti pereat commoditas coelesti provisione concessa.'[1]

There has been much speculation about Constantine's motives. Eusebius would persuade us that they were wholly religious,[2] others that social and political considerations determined his action; but we have not sufficient evidence to decide the question. One thing is certain. The edict of A.D. 321 marks an epoch in the history of Sunday. It was the parent of a double series of legal enactments and conciliar decrees which exercised a great influence—both for good and for evil—upon the life of all Europe during many centuries.

6. Later imperial decrees.—With regard to the imperial decrees, it is important to remember that they affected an ever-decreasing area. The laws of Theodosius the Great, which forbade all litigation and the spectacles of the theatre and the circus on the 'dies Solis quem Dominicum rite dixere majores' (386), affected mankind from Spain to Mesopotamia. But its reiteration by Leo and Anthemius (469) was addressed only to Turkey, Greece, Asia Minor, Syria, and Egypt. The chief importance of those later decrees is that, enshrined in Justinian's Code, they set up a standard for the new nations which gradually rose out of the flood of barbarian invasion.

7. Decrees of Church Councils (300–600).—On the other hand, the decrees of Church Councils had an immediate influence not only in the areas which they represented but also to some extent throughout the former Roman Empire, for the Church maintained a large degree of unity. It is therefore worth while to record not only how the Council of Laodicea (363), ordering men to work on the Sabbath, bade them τὴν Κυριακὴν προτιμῶντες, εἴ γε δύναιντο, σχολάζειν ὡς χριστιανοί, but also how the Council of Orleans (538), while protesting

1 vii. 23, 36.
2 *Strom.* vii. 12.
3 *C. Celsum*, viii. 22 f.
4 *De Sabbat. et Circumcis.* 4.
5 *Ep.* cviii. 20.
6 *Ep. ad Jan.* 22 f.
7 *In Ps.* 47.

1 *Cod. Just.* bk. III. tit. xii. 3.
2 *Vita Const.* iv. 18–21.

against an excessive Sabbatarianism, forbade all field work under pain of censure; and the Council of Macon (585) laid down that the Lord's Day 'is the day of perpetual rest, which is suggested to us by the type of the seventh day in the law and the prophets,' and ordered a complete cessation of all kinds of business. How far the movement had gone by the end of the 6th cent. is shown by a letter of Gregory the Great[1] (pope 590–604) protesting against the prohibition of baths on Sunday.

8. Sabbatarian movement (600–800).—It was a right instinct which led the people to demand, and emperors and councils to grant, that Sunday should be a day of rest as well as of worship. Up to the end of the 6th cent. the resultant changes in law and custom, in spite of some extravagances, were on the whole beneficial. But in the darkness of the next two centuries other influences came into play. The ceaseless wars and disorders which lowered the standard of civilization both in the Eastern Empire and in Western Europe threw all initiative into the hands of military or ecclesiastical rulers. Changes were no longer made in response to the people's demand, but were imposed upon them by rulers who were guided not by a sense of practical need but by monkish theory. Thus an edict[2] of Clotaire III. (*c.* 660) forbids servile labour on Sunday.

'Quia hoc lex prohibet et sacra scriptura in omnibus contradicit.'

Among the laws of Ine, king of Wessex (*c.* 690), we find the following:

'If a "theowman" work on Sunday by his lord's command, let him be free; and let the lord pay xxx shillings as "wite." But if the "theow" work without his knowledge, let him suffer in his hide, or in "hide-gild." But if a freeman work on that day without his lord's command, let him forfeit his freedom, or sixty shillings: and be a priest doubly liable.'[3]

9. The Christian Sabbath from 800 to 1500.—(*a*) *Decrees of rulers and councils.*—Though the decrees of the 7th and 8th centuries were obviously part of a Sabbatarian movement, the term 'Sabbath' was not applied to Sunday until Alcuin had written:

'Cujus observationem mos Christianus ad diem dominicum competentius transtulit.'[4]

Under his inspiration the new feeling, long fluid in society, was crystallized in Charlemagne's decree of A.D. 789, which forbade all ordinary labour on Sunday as a breach of the Fourth Commandment. In particular it forbade agricultural labour, which Constantine had expressly permitted, and the holding of markets, which Constantine had appointed in order to encourage country people to attend the church services: 'Provisione pietatis suae nundinas die solis perpeti anno constituit.'[5] From that time onward the identification of Sunday with the Sabbath was taken for granted, and from that principle deductions of increasing severity were drawn by princes and ecclesiastics.

Among the decrees which were issued by princes for their own dominions we may mention that of the emperor Leo (*c.* 900) which forbade agricultural work in the Eastern Empire, and that of Edgar the Peaceable (A.D. 958) which extended the Lord's Day from 3 p.m. on Saturday to Monday's dawn. More interesting, because of wider influence, are the pronouncements of leading churchmen. In the 12th cent., *e.g.*, Bernard of Clairvaux maintained that the Fourth Commandment required the Sabbatical observance not only of Sundays but also of holy days. In the 13th cent. Thomas Aquinas lent his immense authority to the same principle: 'Sabbatum . . . mutatur in diem dominicam . . . Similiter aliis solennitatibus veteris legis novae solennitates succedunt.'[6] In the 15th cent. Tostatus, bishop of Avila, a learned canonist, laid down the law of the Christian Sabbath with a fullness of detail which rivals that of the Pharisees. And the precepts of the learned were enforced and illustrated for the multitude by stories of miraculous judgments—ranging from toothache to sudden death—which had fallen upon those who profaned Sunday or Saint's Day by labour.[1]

For five hundred years after Charlemagne Church Councils were much occupied with questions of Sunday observance. The following examples may perhaps be sufficient for the purpose of illustration:

A.D. 829—The Council of Paris re-enacts the prohibition of ploughing, marketing, and law business on Sunday.[2]

853—A Synod at Rome forbids markets and field labour.[3]

1009—A Council at Hexham (? Eingthamense) forbids markets, fairs, hunting, and ordinary labour.[4]

1031—The Council of Bourges forbids travelling, except in cases of necessity or charity.[4]

1050—The Council of Coyac (in Spain) forbids all 'servile work' and all travelling.[4]

1212—The Council of Pamiers commands all parishioners to hear *the whole* of the mass and preaching.[4]

1244—The Synod of Lyons found it necessary to limit the number of holy days, whose increase was causing various abuses.[5]

1322—The Synod of Valladolid ordained 'quod nullus in diebus Dominicis et Festivis agros colere audeat, aut manualia artificia exercere praesumat, nisi urgente necessitate, vel evidentis pietatis causa.'[4]

(*b*) *How Sunday was observed.*—What was the effect of all these exhortations? The constant reiteration of the same orders is general evidence that they had not been obeyed. But particular evidence is not lacking. In 1226, *e.g.*, the prior of Walsingham, who held a market on Saturday and Sunday, granted half the profits to Sir William de Clare in exchange for other rights.[6] And the records tell not only of journeys which emperors and kings made on Sunday, but also of three emperors who were crowned in St. Peter's at Rome on that day, causing thereby an immense amount of labour.[7] Sunday, therefore, was not generally observed with anything like the strictness which Church authorities enjoined. Yet it was to a large extent observed as a holiday and a day of worship. How were the hours of leisure spent? In all the decrees of Councils and pronouncements of individuals, down to the 15th cent., there is no prohibition of any recreation except dancing, the singing of ribald songs, theatrical performances, and races in the circus.[8] The last two prohibitions of the emperor Leo soon became needless, for theatre and circus ceased to exist. So from 900 till the Reformation there was practically no limit set to the amusements of the people on Sunday. What use was made of that liberty we may infer partly from the decrees of Councils in the 16th cent. and partly from the Puritan reaction which soon began in Protestant countries.

10. The Roman Catholic Sunday in the 16th century.—The Council of Cologne[9] (1536) decrees:

'Cupimus his diebus prohiberi nundinas, claudi cauponas, vitari comissationes, ebrietates, sumptus, lites, lusus improbos, choreas plenas insaniis, colloquia prava, cantilenas turpes, breviter omnem luxum.'

The Council of Milan (1573) complains that Sunday is commonly profaned by markets, open shops, hawking, dicing, sports, conjuring, and theatrical performances. The Council of Rheims (1583) decrees:

'Nemo lusibus et choreis det operam. Venditiones quarumcunque rerum, his exceptis quae ad divinum cultum et victum necessarium pertinent, nundinae publicae, mercatus et auctiones, ne fiant diebus festis. Ludos etiam theatrales, etiam praetextu consuetudinis, prohibemus.'

The Council of Narbonne (1609) protests against the profanation of Sunday by dancing, singing,

---

[1] *Ep.* xiii. 1.

[2] Heylin, *Hist. of the Sabbath*, ii. 137.

[3] A. W. Haddan and W. Stubbs, *Councils and Ecclesiastical Documents relating to Great Britain and Ireland*, Oxford, 1869–78, iii. 215. The resolution of the Council of Cloveshoo (747), which is sometimes quoted, applies only to monasteries.

[4] *Hom.* 18, *post Pentec.*

[5] J. Gruter, *Inscriptiones antiquæ*, Amsterdam, 1707, clxiv. 2.

[6] *Summa*, II. i. qu. ciii. art. 3.

[1] Concil. Parisiense, *c.* 50; H. Spelman, *Concilia*, London, 1739–64; i. 128; *Miracles de St. Benoît*, vi. 10, viii. 32.

[2] Heylin, ii. 5, § 7.

[3] *Ib.* ii. 5, § 7.

[4] Spelman, *op. cit.*

[5] *De Consecratione distinct.* iii. cap. 1.

[6] F. Blomefield, *Topographical Hist. of Norfolk* London, 1805–10, ix. 276.

[7] Heylin, ii. 5, § 9.

[8] *Ib.* ii. 5, § 10.

[9] See P. Labbe and G. Cossartius, *Sacrosancta Concilia*, Paris, 1670–72.

hunting, hawking, markets, public feasts, and revelling, and allows none but travellers to be served in the inns.

These quotations prove that the Counter-Reformation led the authorities of the countries which remained Roman Catholic to recognize a duty with regard not only to Sunday labour but also to Sunday recreations. They seriously endeavoured to check the licence which had been allowed for many ages and had doubtless increased with the advance of material prosperity in the 14th and 15th centuries. It is difficult to estimate how far they succeeded in reforming the manners of the people. Peter Heylin, sub-dean of Westminster, whose *History of the Sabbath* is the most valuable book on the subject, is an important witness, for he travelled on the Continent very soon after the close of the 16th century. He sums up his impressions in these words:

'Nor is their discipline so severe as their Canons neither. So that the Lord's Day there, for ought I could observe, when I was amongst them, is solemnised after the same manner as with us in England: repairing to the Church, both at Masse and Vespers, riding abroad or walking forth to take the ayre, or otherwise to refresh themselves, and following their honest pleasures, at such leisure times as are not destinate to the publick meetings: the people not being barred from travelling about their lawful business, as occasion is, so they reserve sometime for their devotions in the publike.'[1]

But Heylin, as an advocate, looks only on the fair side; and undoubtedly (as the decrees of the Councils imply) there were many regions in which Sunday was spoiled both by needless labours and by the coarsest amusements.

11. The Protestant Sunday in the 16th century.—The Reformers of the 16th cent. were in a difficult position, for, although they regarded both Gn 2 and Ex 20 as historical, they could not rest the institution of Sunday on either of the traditional grounds. They could not identify it with the Jewish Sabbath; nor could they admit that an ecclesiastical rule of observance, however venerable, was of unchangeable validity. Yet both feeling and reason urged them to maintain its obligation. Luther, Calvin, and the various catechisms and confessions put forward much the same view—to this effect:

The Fourth Commandment was abrogated by the New Testament: and ideally there should be no distinction between days. But human nature requires a day of rest from labour: the soul demands leisure for joint worship: therefore a day must be fixed for all. We cannot do better than follow the tradition which sets apart the first day of the week.[2]

Sound as that argument was, it had an unfortunate effect upon the minds of a generation who had been trained to rest upon absolute law and were not ready to accept reason in its place. To a vast number of Protestants Sunday appeared to have lost its authority; and there was a decided slackening of its observance. Heylin thus describes the state of things in the latter part of the century:

'There was no restraint on Sundays in the afternoone, from any kind of servile work, or dayly labours; but that men might and did apply themselves to their severall businesses, as on other days. As for the greater townes, there is scarce any of them, wherein there are not Faires and Markets (Kirk Masses, as they used to call them) upon the Sunday: and those as much frequented in the afternoone as were the Churches in the forenoone. . . . So that in generall the Lord's day is no otherwise observed with them . . . than an half holiday is with us. . . . For recreations, last of all, there is no question to be made, but that where working is permitted, and most kind of businesse, a man may lawfully enjoy himselfe and his honest pleasures; and without danger of offence pursue those pastimes by which the mind may be refreshed and the spirits quickened.'[3]

This is true, he says, of Holland, Belgium, Switzerland, France, and Germany, and part of Poland.

In England, where religious changes were far less violent, the observance of Sunday in the reigns of Henry VIII. and Elizabeth was considerably stricter.

Both *The Institution of a Christian Man* (1537) and the queen's *Injunctions* (1558) lay down excellent principles. And yet one of the *Homilies*, published in 1563, sorrowfully confesses: 'The Lord was more dishonoured and the Devill better served on Sunday than upon all the dayes in the weeke besides.' King James's proclamation of 7th May 1603 is a significant confirmation of this complaint: Having been informed 'that there had been in former times a great neglect in keeping the Sabbath day,' he ordains 'that no Bearebaiting, Bull-baiting, Enterludes, common Playes, or other like disordered or unlawful Exercises or Pastimes be frequented, kept, or used at any time hereafter upon any Sabbath day.' And this was not because James was accustomed to great strictness in Scotland, where up to 1600 observance was on the whole less precise than in England. The early Calvinists were not Sabbatarians, and John Knox himself played bowls on Sunday.

12. The 17th and 18th centuries.—(*a*) *England.*—Till the reign of James I., as we have seen, England and Scotland kept pace with the movements on the Continent. But throughout the 17th cent. our island was the scene of a dramatic struggle which had no parallel elsewhere. The extreme Protestant type of mind has a natural affinity to the OT, and the Calvinists and other Puritan sects early felt the attraction. By a process somewhat like that which took place in the 5th and 6th centuries, they turned towards the Jewish Sabbath, and their steps were hastened by repulsion from the scandals of the 16th cent. Sunday. The movement, of which the early stages are obscure, came to a head in the publication of a remarkable book.

Nicholas Bownd, a Suffolk clergyman, in his *Sabbathum Veteris et Novi Testamenti*, or the *True Doctrine of the Sabbath* (1595), boldly and crudely claimed for Sunday the authority and the observances of the Jewish Sabbath and maintained that they should be enforced by the State. The book had an immense vogue. It was translated and circulated on the Continent, where it exercised much influence. In England, accepted as an inspiration by some and as a challenge by others, it gave rise to a literary controversy which lasted for a hundred years. The first reply to it was James I.'s *Book of Sports*[1] (1618), which proclaimed liberty for the people to enjoy their traditional pastimes on Sunday except bull- and bear-baiting. This was followed by the Sunday Observance Act (1625), which forbade men to go outside their own parishes in search of amusement on Sunday. The *Book of Sports* was republished by Charles I. in 1633, with a special admonition to justices of the peace: 'Look to it, both that all disorders there may be prevented and punished, and that all neighbourhood and freedom, with manlike and lawful exercises, be used.'

In 1635 Francis White, bishop of Ely, published an official defence of this view; and in 1638 Heylin supported it with *The History of the Sabbath*, a book which shows much ability and learning. The controversy was continued, and 120 books on the subject were published in the next hundred years. Other weapons were used besides the pen. In 1643 Parliament ordered the *Book of Sports* to be burned by the hangman and imposed the Puritan Sabbath upon the ever-increasing area which their troops commanded. In 1648 they formally adopted the *Westminster Confession* and the *Longer* and the *Shorter Catechisms*. One quotation from the last-named must suffice.

'Q. 60. How is the Sabbath to be sanctified?—A. The Sabbath is to be sanctified by a holy resting all that day, even from such worldly employments and recreations as are lawful on other days; and spending the whole time in the public and private exercises of God's worship, except so much as is to be taken up in the works of necessity and mercy.'

By successive enactments (1644, 1650, 1656) the same Parliament proscribed every kind of Sunday recreation, even 'vainly and profanely' walking for pleasure. At the Restoration the pendulum swung the other way. The court, the cavaliers, and the High Church clergy led the way in a violent reaction; and the return of the Prayer-book service on Sunday morning was accompanied by trading, open theatres, and ostentatious frivolity

[1] Vol. ii. p. 191.

[2] See Luther's *Larger Catechism*, the *Augsburg Confession*, the (Calvinist) *Heidelberg Catechism*, the *Helvetic Confession*, Calvin's *Institutes*.

[3] ii. 6, § 9.

[1] The full title of this work is *The Kings Majesties Declaration to his Subjects concerning Lawfull Sports to be Used*, London, 1618.

in the afternoon and evening. To what lengths the court went may be learned from Macaulay's description of Charles II.'s last Sunday night. There were many protests; and the battle of the books continued, Bishop Pearson, John Owen, and Richard Baxter being among the combatants. In 1677 a compromise was effected. The Sunday Observance Act regulated trade, labour, and travelling in a reasonable way, making ample allowance for 'works of necessity.' At the same time the Sunday Observance Act of 1625 was revived and came to be recognized as the standard by which amusements were to be regulated. Both acts were observed with varying degrees of strictness at different times and in different places. But it is no little tribute to their reasonableness that both remained in force until the year 1871, though they were modified in some details; *e.g.*, in 1699 forty watermen were allowed to ply on the Thames, in 1710 coaches and chairs received permission to stand for hire, and in 1794 bakers to sell bread at certain hours. From the Revolution to the death of Queen Anne a higher standard prevailed, both of attendance at church and of obedience to the law. Under the Georges, though no change was made in the law, and though the same literary controversy continued, there was a steady decline in both respects. About 1780 the Evangelical Revival, following the movement led by the Wesleys, produced a considerable change in opinion and observance. How much need there was for improvement may be inferred from three actions of Bishop Porteous, who was a leader of the new school. He supported the institution of Sunday Schools, which began in 1780 and soon spread over the country. He persuaded the Prince of Wales to transfer the meetings of his rowdy 'Sunday Club' to a week day. And he drew up the Sunday Observance Act of 1781, which enacts that any place of public entertainment or debate where a charge is made for admission may be deemed a disorderly house. Passed in order to check bear-baiting and infidel propaganda, this act has been used of late to impede Sunday concerts and lectures to working-men.[1] For many years it was undoubtedly of great value, helping to restore the credit of Sunday in the public eye. But, when the rapid growth of large towns, due to the industrial revolution, presented new problems, this law combined with the restrictions of travelling to cause mischief. The mass of the industrial population, cooped up in towns which were almost destitute of churches, had no meeting-place but the street or the public-house. This evil became serious in the latter part of the 18th cent., but its full development was not seen till the 19th.

(*b*) *Scotland*.—Scotland very early in the 17th cent. adopted the theory of the 'Christian Sabbath' and applied it to social life with the ruthless logic which is characteristic of Calvinism. The *Westminster Confession* was adopted by the General Assembly of the Kirk of Scotland in 1647, before Parliament had passed it; and it has remained the formal standard of faith to the present day. So long as it was enforced by public opinion—*i.e.* till about 1870—the Scottish Sunday was observed with amazing rigour. Not only were ordinary recreations disallowed; a ban was put even upon books and music, except such as were recognized as religious in the narrow sense. No recreation remained but whisky-drinking, and a great part of the drunkenness which is still common in Scotland may be traced to an unwise Sabbatarianism. In parts of the Highlands and the Islands the old rigour remains; but in the greater part of the country, as will be explained below, the last fifty years have witnessed a great change.

[1] The present writer was threatened with prosecution in 1897 for lecturing to a Sunday Society in Bristol.

(*c*) *America*.—The American colonies differed in their practice. The more southerly States, such as Pennsylvania and Virginia, were inclined to English views of Sunday. The New England States, founded by Puritans, kept very close to the Scottish standard; but their coast towns were influenced by English practice, and their Western border by the practical necessities imposed by danger from their Indian neighbours.

(*d*) *Protestant Europe*.—Nicholas Bownd's book was translated into several Continental languages and exercised a considerable influence. In Holland and Switzerland a strong Sabbatarian party grew up; and in Protestant Germany his doctrine found rigorous advocates. But on the whole the Sabbatarians failed; and the observance of Sunday, especially in Germany, fell much below the standard in England. Sunday labour was very common, and Sunday amusements were very coarse.

(*e*) *Roman Catholic Europe*.—In Roman Catholic countries, during the same centuries, Sunday was so much eclipsed by the Saints' Days that it ceased to be observed with any kind of strictness. While the Saints' Days were real holidays, labour on Sunday was the rule rather than the exception. Till near the end of the 18th cent. the priesthood were powerful enough to secure a general attendance at mass; but the rest of the day was usually given to ordinary occupations. If in Spain Sunday was more a day of rest than in France or Italy, this was because it was the day set apart for bull-fights.

13. From the French Revolution to 1848.—The French Revolution marks an epoch in the history of Sunday observance. Its new calendar, with a week of ten days, though ephemeral and rather absurd, was a practical challenge to tradition, whose effects were permanent. The questions which it raised frightened some men into reaction, but excited others to free speculation. And it gave prominence to one fact, which no Government could afford to ignore for long. In every country there was an increasing number of citizens who did not acknowledge the Christian sanctions for Sunday, for whom, therefore, any rules for Sunday observance must rest on social rather than religious grounds. The recognition of this fact gradually affected the administration of the existing laws; and perhaps it may account for the complete absence of legislation between 1780 and 1850. In England the repulsion caused by the Revolution combined with the Evangelical Revival to render Sunday observance much stricter. The laws of 1677 and 1781 were rather rigidly enforced, and public opinion (among the minority who had votes for Parliament) was on the whole Sabbatarian. For the middle class and for all the people in country districts the movement was largely beneficial. The churches were filled; the sense of duty was strengthened; and habits of reflexion were induced. On the other hand, for the growing multitudes in the great towns the restrictions imposed by law became ever more cruel. Neglected by the Church, they had few places of worship and little will to enter them. They wanted means of getting into the country and opportunities of reasonable recreation in the town; but these were denied them, and nothing was left but the public-house. It was not till about 1850 that their needs were recognized. The active controversy which was carried on about Sunday concerned only the reasons for observing it. Several distinguished writers took part in the discussion, but they did little more than reproduce the well-worn arguments of the 17th cent. on either side.

In France, though Napoleon re-established the Church, the hold of Sunday upon the public mind could not be restored. It remained to a large extent a day of trade and of labour, as well as of social amusement. In Spain and Italy there was no striking change. In Germany, which had been penetrated with French ideas, there was a marked decline. If we may judge by the books which were published there between 1780 and 1848, public opinion was averse to strictness based on religious grounds and not yet alive to the social reasons in favour of a day of rest. Sunday observance therefore, resting mainly upon tradition, naturally failed to maintain its hold.

The United States continued the division of opinion which had existed among the colonies of N. America. New England and the Western States, which were gradually peopled by emigrants from New England, remained Sabbatarian, while the Southern States, led by the Quakers of Pennsylvania, generally adopted the more liberal view. Between 1820 and 1850 many books were published on both sides, but no legislation resulted.

14. From 1848 to 1914.—From 1848, the 'year of revolution,' we may date a new phase of the Sunday controversy. Suddenly the masses of the people, especially in manufacturing towns, acquired a new consciousness and began to be regarded with a new interest. The consequences were not long in making themselves felt. Hitherto it may be said that the churches and the legislatures had, on the whole, worked in harmony. Since 1848 there has been a gradual divergence. For, while the churches were slow to admit the possibility of change, the legislatures, more and more influenced by popular opinion, tended to favour relaxations which were supposed to be required by new social conditions. At the same time an agitation began in some countries in favour of limiting the Sunday labour which vast numbers felt to be oppressive. These two elements were mixed in very different proportions in different countries.

(*a*) *England.*—In England, where Sunday labour was already severely limited, the main question was that of relaxation. In 1851 a lively controversy arose about two points. Should railway travelling be allowed on Sunday? And should the new Crystal Palace be open to the public on Sunday afternoon? The instances could not have been better chosen, for their discussion involved all the main principles which were at stake. Twenty years passed before any legislative result came of the debate. In 1871 an Act was passed requiring the consent in writing of the chief officer of a police district, or of two magistrates, before a prosecution for Sunday trading could be instituted under the Act of 1677. Since then the Sunday Observance Act has been a dead letter. And an Act of 1875 has very much limited the application of the Act of 1781. That did not end the debate. In 1875 the Sunday League was formed to advocate the opening of museums and picture galleries and other means of rational recreation on Sundays. In spite of several societies started in opposition, the Sunday League has gradually effected a great and beneficial change.

But the real crux of the situation is connected with travelling. Nothing has done so much to alter the habits of the people as the rapid increase in means of communication. The railway, the steamer, the tramcar, and the motor-car have successively helped to empty the towns on Sunday. They have answered a real need; for the strain of modern life has created a new craving for fresh air and change of scene, which finds satisfaction in the week-end habit of the richer folk and in the excursion train for the poorer. The desire for such recreation is natural and wholesome. At the same time it is responsible for two serious evils. (1) Those who spend Sunday away from home rarely devote any part of it to worship, and those who remain at home feel themselves thereby excused from attendance at church. Consequently the number of those who enter any place of worship on Sunday forms an increasingly small percentage of the population. (2) Every added facility for travel on Sunday involves additional labour on the part of a large class of workers. The railways, the tramways, the restaurants, the bands, and the news agencies are so heavily tasked on Sunday that few of their employees enjoy anything like a day of rest.

Intent upon claiming what they considered their right to recreation and convenience, the mass of the people did not see what was involved in its satisfaction. Shops were increasingly opened, trains ran in ever-increasing numbers, and a large number of subsidiary industries were obliged to join the movement. Then contractors who were in a hurry took to Sunday work; and there was a real danger that the industrial population might lose their day of rest. About the beginning of the 20th cent. the trade unions and other bodies began to realize the danger; shop-assistants began to protest; and so a check was imposed upon the movement. In the first year (1914–15) of the Great War it seemed as if the national necessity might obliterate Sunday rest. Munition factories and many others were opened on Sunday, and double pay was offered for work on that day. But the result was uniformly a diminished output. Many of those who worked on Sunday for double pay spent the extra money in drink on Monday and Tuesday; and such as conscientiously toiled all seven days did so with rapidly failing energy. After two years Sunday work was generally abandoned; and it may be hoped that the nation has taken the lesson to heart.

(*b*) *The Continent.*—On the Continent during the latter half of the 19th cent. the same causes produced even more marked effects. In the eighties and nineties a stranger could hardly tell from the aspect of the towns whether the day was Sunday or not. But at last even the 'anti-clerical' Governments, which had looked on complacently at a change which diminished religious observance, became aware that it was causing immense social mischief; while on behalf of the overstrained workers urgent claims were made for a legal day of rest. Between the years 1895 and 1910 laws were passed, in almost every country of Europe, which were intended to secure a weekly holiday for every working-man.[1] Even in France, where the secularist influences were strongest, it was judged necessary to insist upon Sunday as the normal day of rest, all substitutes in special cases being regarded as exceptional. The general effect of this movement was a marked change in the aspect of the towns. In the year 1913 no factories were working on Sundays, and few shops were opened. Thus in a large measure Sunday observance has been restored, but with a difference. It is now popularly regarded, not primarily as a response to the religious need of worship, still less as obedience to a divine command, but as the condition of wholesome life for the labouring man.

15. The present state of the question.—The foregoing narrative should help us to discern the principles upon which Sunday observance ought to be based, and perhaps to determine the proper mode of observance, and the means by which it may rightly be enforced or encouraged.

Why is Sunday to be observed? It is easier for us to answer this question than it was for the theologians of the 17th and 18th centuries, and that for two reasons. Recent investigations into early Church history, of which the results are summarized above, have removed some prejudices which hampered our ancestors. We now know how gradually the observance of Sunday developed and how late was the theory which connected it with the Sabbath. And the modern study of the

[1] See the return made to the House of Lords on the subject in 1911.

OT has removed a difficulty which they could never fully meet. So long as the story of the creation in Gn 1 and 2 and the account of the giving of the Law on Mt. Sinai were regarded as historical, the question had to be faced: How can a divine command, directly given to men, be abrogated? The answer for us is plain: No such commands were ever given, and the stories which record them are legends. The Sabbath was made for man; and, under the guidance of Providence, it was made by man. Sunday, in its turn, was made by man and for man. Man, therefore, is lord both of the Sabbath and of Sunday. It is from the experience of men, both as individuals and in societies, that the reasons must be drawn which determine the manner in which Sunday is to be observed.

(*a*) *The new reasons for observing Sunday.*—These reasons are evidently of two kinds, answering to the conditions required for bodily vigour and spiritual health. While the former may be regarded as especially the concern of the State and the latter of the Church, the mutual influences of body and mind are so considerable and so intricate that in practice it is hard to draw a line between the sphere of politics and that of religion. It is all the harder because to ancient thought the distinction was unknown, and even in modern times is largely artificial. For the Church cannot ignore the body, nor can the State disregard the interests of the spirit. But happily no sharp division is necessary. The reasons given by the Reformers[1] are of general application and may satisfy both the Churchman and the statesman. Since three hundred years of controversy have added nothing substantial to them, we may be content with restating them in a more detailed form.

The need of bodily rest at short intervals is a fact of human nature which all civilized nations have recognized by instituting public holidays. The more complex the social and industrial organization, the more important it becomes that such holidays should recur at regular intervals. The sporadic festivals of the ancient Roman calendar and the Saints' Day system of modern Italy could not be tolerated in an industrial country; for production depends upon regularity of labour and the efficiency of labour upon regularity of recreation. Constantine's decree of A.D. 321, therefore, not only conferred a benefit upon the individual and satisfied a requirement of the Church, but also solved economic and social problems which were growing very difficult. Its wisdom is proved by the fact that, in spite of occasional protests and experiments, the Sunday holiday has remained the rule of civilized countries ever since.

The well-being of the people, which is the proper object of government, demands more than mere cessation of work at sufficient intervals. The life of the citizen is incomplete, and his value to the State is small, unless he cultivates his mind, develops family affection, and enjoys social intercourse. All these functions require leisure—not merely the tired hours after a day's work, but whole days when the time can be disposed of at will. It is in days of leisure, also, that personality has the best chance of development. The State, therefore, has a responsibility, not only for appointing holidays, but also for preventing such misuse of them as may diminish their value to the citizen and to the community. On the other hand, experience proves such responsibility to be of a negative rather than a positive character. The State can remove obstacles to a right course of action, but cannot compel the individual to walk therein. If any positive commands are laid down

[1] See above, § II.

for the weekly holiday, they must issue from a religious authority, which appeals only to spiritual sanctions, and affects only those who acknowledge its right. The Christian Church is such an authority, and has strong reasons, besides those just mentioned, for requiring its members to observe Sunday. Putting aside the mistaken claims for Sunday, which originated in the dark ages and were so hotly urged in the 17th cent., there remain some which are undeniable. The spiritual life of the individual requires a recurrent leisure time, in which he may read or meditate, may do acts of charity, and commune with his friends, with nature, or art. It requires, also, regular opportunities of joining in common worship, without which his membership of a Church becomes unreal. The former demand might be satisfied by times of leisure peculiar to himself. But the latter involves regular holidays which are common to all. Nor can it be a matter of indifference whether these holidays fall on Sundays. The power of association and tradition is enormous: no man can escape from it, and no Church can ignore it. To substitute another day would be to waste the accumulated associations and traditions of nearly 2000 years which are concentrated on Sunday. For on the Lord's Day Jesus rose from the dead; on that day, ever since, His disciples have met for worship and mutual comfort; on that day they have joined in the feast of His love. Luther did not state the whole case when he wrote: 'Because Sunday has been appointed from the earliest times, we ought to keep to this arrangement, that all things may be done in harmony and order, and no confusion be caused by unnecessary novelties';[1] for he ignored one of the strongest impulses in human nature.

(*b*) *The mode of observance.*—Assuming the above reasons for the observance of Sunday, we have to consider, from the point of view of Church and State, what ought to be the manner of its observance. The action of the State in such matters, as we have indicated already, is mainly negative. It has to protect the worker against the oppression of unbroken labour, to secure for him a regular period of recreation, and to prevent other persons from interfering, whether by force or by bribery, with his reasonable use of his leisure time. That task is not so simple as might appear. Every right, when exercised, imposes a duty upon some one else. The right to food involves the Sunday labour of the milkman; the right of the public to enjoy works of art encroaches upon the leisure of the custodians; the right to fresh air and green fields compels the toil of the railwayman. These classes also have their rights, which must somehow be safeguarded. To adjust conflicting claims in the interest of the people as a whole is a work of much insight and patience; nor can it be accomplished once for all, since every enlargement in the tastes and interests of the many involves a fresh tax upon the ministrations of a few. In Britain, happily, men seem to be approaching a general agreement about the main principles of such accommodations. No man should be required or encouraged to work on Sunday except for the benefit of a large number. The railwayman, the custodian of a picture gallery, or the musician who plays in a band, is engaged in a work of charity, if he is not adding a seventh working day to his week for the sake of profit. No such plea can be made on behalf of a manager who makes profit by the performances of others, or of a tradesman who opens his shops on Sunday. A partial exception is rightly made in the case of those who supply the public with needed refreshments. But even that requires careful watching;

[1] *Larger Catechism.*

and the Government has long recognized the duty of limiting the sale of intoxicants to certain hours of the day.

The action of the Church, on the other hand, is positive. It aspires to guide men in their use of the leisure which is secured to them by the State. The primary duty which it inculcates upon all is that of attendance at public worship, for which the Sunday rest was originally instituted. But it also indicates proper uses for the hours which are not spent in such attendance. In the past such guidance took the form mainly of prohibitions. We have seen that, when the prohibitions were few, the result was licence; and, when they were multiplied, Sunday became a day of gloom and boredom. Not to speak of the Scottish 'Sabbath,' which has become proverbial, the restraints were mischievous enough in England till past the middle of the 19th century. The children of pious parents might not play on Sunday except with a Noah's ark. Boys and girls might not take exercise, but sat wearily still. Their elders, limited to 'religious' books or 'sacred' music, took refuge in sleep. Much harm was done to the cause of religion by such observances, and still more by the opposition which Churchmen raised in Parliament to every proposal for allowing rational entertainments for the artisans of the great towns.

A better spirit now prevails. But, while there is little of coercion by Church authority, there is very little of positive suggestion. The time has come when the Christian Church as a whole must formulate something like a programme, instead of leaving Sunday progress to individual experiment. Some such statement of principles as the following, if issued by authority, would relieve many troubled consciences and prevent much revolt.

(1) Sunday is the day for Christians to join in worship. No man spends it well who does not habitually unite with his neighbours in praise and prayer.

(2) Sunday is a day of recreation. Recreation means different things for different people, since an essential feature of it is change. The manual labourer will rest his body; the brain worker will seek exercise; both alike will be the better for a visit to a picture-gallery, or a concert, or a talk with friends.

(3) Sunday is the festival of family life. It is the only day on which most fathers can see much of their children. Unless some hours of the day are employed in cultivating family affection, its ties will be dangerously relaxed.

(4) Sunday is the day for meditation. The average man, if he does not devote some part of Sunday to reading or thought about matters outside his daily occupations, becomes a slave to routine and no longer possesses his own soul.

(*c*) *How far observance can be enforced.*—By what means can the due observance of Sunday be promoted? The primitive Church punished some offenders with excommunication; the mediæval Church employed the method of penance on a large scale. Both these weapons are now out of date; and they were never of much use for promoting what is best. In proportion as her rules advance from 'thou shalt not' to 'thou shalt,' the Church is less and less able to use any kind of compulsion. She cannot, in fact, compel her members to-day; she can only persuade them through the teaching of ministers and the opinion of neighbours.

The State, on the other hand, just because its commands are nearly all prohibitions, whose object is to protect the rights and interests of the community, can and must use compulsion. Every breach of positive law can be measured and punished by fine or imprisonment. Yet the main influence is really that of public opinion; for the magistrates and police, who administer the law, will always be strict or lax according to the general feeling of the society in which they live. The best means therefore of securing a proper observance of Sunday is to educate public opinion.

LITERATURE.—Many hundreds of volumes have been written on this subject. A very good account of some 300 will be found in **Robert Cox**, *The Literature of the Sabbath Question*, 2 vols., Edinburgh, 1865. A few of them are historical, but the mass are arguments for and against the obligation of the Sabbath, in which the same ideas (very few) recur over and over again. The following short list gives specimens of the writings of different countries and denominations. The English predominate, for England has produced far more books than all the other countries put together.

(i.) *13th century.*—**Thomas Aquinas**, *Exposition of the Commandments.*

(ii.) *16th century.*—**Martin Luther**, *Larger Catechism* and other books; **John Calvin**, *Institutes*, bk. ii. ch. viii.; **Philip Melanchthon**, *The Augsburg Confession*; **Thomas Cranmer**, *A Confutation of Unwritten Verities*; **Richard Hooker**, *Ecclesiastical Polity*, v. 69–71.

(iii.) *17th century.*—**Nicholas Bownde**, *Sabbathum Veteris et Novi Testamenti* or *The True Doctrine of the Sabbath*, London, 1595, ^{4}1606; **King James I.**, *The Book of Sports*, do. 1618; **Francis White**, *A Treatise of the Sabbath Day*, do. 1635; **Peter Heylin**, *The Hist. of the Sabbath*, do. 1636; **Hugo Grotius**, *De Veritate Religionis Christianæ*, Amsterdam, 1627, reprint, Glasgow, 1745, bk. v.; *The Westminster Confession of Faith* and *Catechisms*, London, 1647, 1648; **John Cocceius**, *Indagatio Naturæ Sabbati*, Leyden, 1658; **Edward Stillingfleet**, *Irenicum*, London, 1659; **Richard Baxter**, *The Divine Appointment of the Lord's Day proved*, do. 1671.

(iv.) *18th century.* — **Thomas Morer**, Κυριακὴ Ἡμέρα, London, 1701; **Jonathan Edwards**, 'On the Perpetuity and Change of the Sabbath,' Sermons xiii., xiv., xv., in *Twenty Sermons on Various Subjects*, Edinburgh, 1804; **Isaac Watts**, *The Holiness of Times, Places and People*, London, 1733, Discourse i., 'On the Perpetuity of a Sabbath'; *An Act for preventing certain Abuses and Profanations on the Lord's Day*, 1781; *Decree of the National Convention of France appointing a new Calendar*, 1793; **Beilby Porteous**, *A Letter to the Clergy of the Diocese of London*, London, 1789.

(v.) *19th century.* — *Report of the Lord's Day Observance Society*, 1832; **'Edinensis,'** *Sunday Railway Travelling*, Edinburgh, 1847; **J. A. Hessey**, *Sunday: its Origin, Hist. and present Obligations* (*BL*), London, 1860, ^{5}1889; *Report of a Committee of Congress* (U.S.A. 1833); *Report of the Committee of the Legislature of New York, on the Judiciary*, 1838; **E. W. Hengstenberg**, *Über den Tag des Herrn*, Berlin, 1852, Eng. tr. London, 1853; **François Perennès**, *De l'Institution du dimanche*, Paris, 1844; **P. J. Proudhon**, *De la Célébration du dimanche*, do. 1848; **W. F. Crafts**, *The Sabbath for Man*, New York, 1885; **J. Lefort**, *Du Repos hebdomadaire*, etc., Paris, 1873; **C. Büttner**, *Die Sonntagsruhe im Gewerbebetrieb und im Handelsgewerbe*, Leipzig, 1895.

Heylin and Hessey treat the question historically and with much ability. Parts of the history are well treated in articles and special chapters: **Smith's** *DCA*, *s.v.* 'Lord's Day'; *EBr*^{11}, *s.v.* 'Sunday' (deals chiefly with legislation); *PRE*^{3}, *s.v.* 'Sonntagsfeier'; *HDB*, *s.vv.* 'Lord's Day' and 'Sabbath.' There is also a good chapter (ch. vii.) in **W. E. H. Lecky**, *Democracy and Liberty*, 2 vols., London, 1896.

M. G. GLAZEBROOK.

SUNDAY SCHOOLS.—**I. Origin.**—The history of the Sunday school is not the history of religious education. The latter has always existed; the former is a modern institution. The Sunday school is a voluntary lay organization conducting religious instruction in classes on Sunday, generally but not always in church buildings, generally but not always as part of a church organization. The informal instruction that was probably given by teachers in the early Christian communities was somewhat akin to the activity of the Sunday school teacher. But the catechetical schools[1] which flourished in the post-apostolic Church were entirely different. Moreover, the regular catechizing of children, which was always the duty of the minister, albeit a duty very much neglected for many centuries, was not a precursor of the Sunday school. Indeed, if it had been thoroughly effective and well developed, there might never have been a Sunday school. The failure of the clergy thoroughly to systematize and to develop the religious education of the children made the Sunday school necessary. Thus the Scottish clergy, who were more successful in the training of children, regarded the new institution at first as altogether superfluous. The origin of the Sunday school is to be sought in the sporadic efforts of earnest men and women to supply some elementary instruction to children who were neglected by the Church. The most notable instance of such effort was that of Robert Raikes at Gloucester; the name 'Sunday school' seems first to have been attached to his

[1] See art. CATECHUMEN, CATECHUMENATE.

institution; and there was genetic connexion between Raikes's enterprise and the whole Sunday school movement that succeeded.

2. The period of beginnings.—(*a*) *Robert Raikes and the first Sunday schools.*—The national duty of universal education was not fully recognized in England until fifty years ago. In the 18th cent. education was the privilege of the well-to-do. Even the many benefactions which had been provided from time to time for the education of the poor had become almost universally devoted to the children of the middle classes. Moreover, with the development of the factory system, the children had been forced into labour at a very early age, with the result that they grew up in hopeless illiteracy. Among a number of efforts to remedy this intolerable condition the most significant was that of Robert Raikes, editor of the *Gloucester Journal*. He was a man of generous sympathies, interested in various efforts to ameliorate the lot of the unfortunate. His attention was attracted to the vicious conduct of the 'young pagans' who were employed in the factories during the week, but who were at large on Sunday, and who naturally employed their single holiday in the only rough recreation which they understood. Believing that their ignorance was responsible for their depravity, he gathered a number of them into a school and secured four women at one shilling per day to instruct them 'in reading and the Church Catechism.' The date of this simple enterprise, which was soon copied in numerous towns, is usually set at 1780. Sunday schools became so popular that attention was given to them in the *Gentleman's Magazine*, and the various letters in that once influential periodical still remain our most important source of information regarding the beginning of the movement. Wesley, in his itineracy, soon came upon Sunday schools in various places, and with fine insight immediately saw their possibilities.

(*b*) *The Sunday school in America.*—The American churches were accustomed to hold services in the morning and afternoon. There was an 'intermission' of an hour or more, during which a simple lunch was eaten. Naturally this period was often used for the catechetical instruction of the children, for whom the somewhat solemn services provided little that was appropriate. There is no evidence that any such practice was at all common previous to the Revolution. The catechizing of children took place in the schools, in the family, and in connexion with the pastoral visits of the minister. A large proportion of the children were of course altogether neglected. The period of the Revolutionary War was not favourable to religious education, and the strong influence of France tended decidedly away from religion. In the general desire of the churches to meet this condition, they turned with interest to the new institution of the Sunday school, which had been introduced into the United States from England. It was not in America primarily (though it was to some extent) a school held on Sunday for illiterate children who could not be instructed on weekdays, but rather a school conducted by the Church for religious instruction on the day set apart for that purpose. Thus from the beginning the Sunday school in America was more closely related to the Church than it was for a long time in England. This is not to say that there was not considerable opposition in the one country as in the other from clergymen who felt the danger of the intrusion of inexpert laymen.

(*c*) *Sunday school organizations.*—Within a few years of the establishment of the Raikes schools organizations for propagating the institution came into existence.

William Fox, a London merchant, had had in contemplation a large plan for the gratuitous instruction of the poor. When he learned of the Raikes scheme, it seemed to him more practical than his own more ambitious project; and he took the lead in forming, in 1785, the Society for the Establishment and Support of Sunday Schools. In 1796 was organized the Edinburgh Gratis Sabbath School Society. Others were formed in other Scottish cities. In 1810 the Hibernian Sunday School Society was organized in Dublin. These societies collected funds for the establishment of new schools, for the payment of teachers, for the purchase of Bibles, spelling-books, etc. The practice of paying teachers, although continued in a few places for many years, very soon gave way to the volunteer system, with the spread of the new institution. A number of young men who were giving their services in the Sunday schools of London felt the necessity of mutual help and conference, and organized in 1803 the Sunday School Society for this purpose. This organization became the most significant means of developing the Sunday school in Great Britain.

Organization began in America with the First-Day or Sunday School Society at Philadelphia, in 1791. It was undenominational in character and philanthropic in purpose. The visit of Albert May of London in 1811 greatly stimulated interest in Sunday school organizations. Many of them were formed in American cities. After a number of federations of these had been made, the desire for a national undenominational union resulted in the organization in 1824 of the American Sunday School Union, which has continued to do effective work to the present time.

(*d*) *Lessons and methods of teaching.*—The earliest Sunday school teaching was of the most primitive sort. Many schools on both sides of the Atlantic were obliged to give much of their time to the simplest lessons in reading and spelling. Religious instruction consisted of the memorizing of Scripture, hymns, and catechism, the teacher simply listening to the recitation. Soon some simple plans of lessons were prepared, with some practical appreciation of child religion. Helps to the teacher were the *Sunday School Repository, or Teachers' Magazine*, which began in London in 1813, and the *American Sunday School Magazine*, started in 1824.

3. Development of the Sunday school in America. — (*a*) *Denominational organizations.*— The definite adoption of the Sunday school by the Church in America is seen in the steps taken by almost all the denominations subsequent to the organization of the American Sunday School Union to supervise and extend the work within their own churches. For example, in 1827 the Sunday School Union of the Methodist Episcopal Church was organized in New York City; Baptist and Congregational organizations starting in 1825 developed into the American Baptist Publication Society in 1840, and into the Congregational Sabbath School and Publishing Society in 1868. The superior church bodies of other denominations undertook similar responsibilities.

(*b*) *The Sunday School as a pioneer religious agency.*—It is easy in the light of our modern educational science to criticize the poor endeavours of early religious education, but no history of the wonderful development of the Mississippi valley would be adequate which failed to recognize the social significance of the little Sunday schools that went far ahead of the organized Church into the pioneer communities.

In 1829 the American Sunday School Union established its first western headquarters at Cincinnati, and in the following year resolved at its annual convention to undertake the organization of a Sunday school in every destitute place in the Mississippi valley. Funds were raised, lay and clerical missionaries were appointed, and a notable advance was made. A single missionary in the course of a life of arduous journeying organized over 1300 new schools. As it was said of old that where ten Hebrews lived there should be a synagogue, so it came to be the expectation in America that, wherever three or four Christian families were neighbours, a Sunday school should be started, at first in the farm-house, later in the school-house or in the court-house. Very many churches of the West had their origin in the activities of a few of the laity who had begun religious work by the organization of a little Sunday school.

(*c*) *The International Sunday School Association.*—The convention system has been characteristic of the American movement. Neighbourhood conventions were held before 1820. Springing from the annual meeting of the American

Sunday School Union, a national convention of Sunday school workers was called in 1832. After a very successful session this body adjourned to meet the following year. Numerous state and county conventions met in the succeeding years, until in 1859 a third annual convention was called. The fourth did not meet until after the Civil War, in 1869, and by that time the noted Illinois leaders, B. F. Jacobs, Edward Eggleston, J. H. Vincent, and D. L. Moody were prominent. While this convention was not called international, there were delegates from Canada and from the British Isles. The same was true of the fifth convention of 1872, at which the uniform lessons were adopted. The movement then became definitely organized as international, with delegates from all the states and provinces of North America. An official body was gradually developed, which supervised the extension of the system to state, county, and township conventions, meeting annually and leading up to the great triennial gathering. At the eleventh convention in 1905 it was resolved to incorporate under the name 'International Sunday School Association.' This was done in 1907, headquarters being established at Chicago. A completely articulated organization exists under an executive committee, with a general secretary and a corps of superintendents over the various divisions and departments.

(*d*) *The development of the lesson system.*—As an improvement on mere memorizing, the 'limited lesson' system came into vogue about 1825. Two years later Albert Judson published a question-book, which supplied some notes and explanations of the selected lessons. In the same year the American Sunday School Union issued the *Union Question-Book*, which was followed annually by others covering a considerable portion of the Bible. Various schemes followed, the result partly of private enterprise, partly of denominational zeal. There was no adequate direction, and Sunday school leaders felt the need of some unity of effort. After much discussion the convention of 1872 voted to issue a uniform system of lessons for all Sunday school pupils. A lesson committee was appointed, and great enthusiasm was developed in the scheme. The co-operation of the British Sunday School Union was secured, and the lessons became practically universal. Noted writers prepared lesson-helps and commentaries; great teachers' meetings were held for the exposition of the lesson of the forthcoming Sunday, and the public press frequently devoted a column on Saturday to this purpose.

After twenty years of great external success the educational value of the uniform lesson was seriously called in question. The subject was warmly debated in conventions. At last, in 1908, the convention decided, while continuing the uniform lesson, to authorize its lesson committee to prepare a thoroughly graded course, to be used by such schools as desired it. This has since been done, and a series of text-books has been prepared by the various denominations upon the lessons thus outlined.

(*e*) *Teacher training.*—It has been recognized that most Sunday school teaching has been very unsatisfactory. Efforts have been made almost from the beginning to effect improvement. The institutes held since 1837 for public school teachers were a challenge to the Sunday school, which was answered by the development of conferences and institutes. The normal class of J. H. Vincent in Illinois in 1857 was a model which many followed. Courses for normal training of increasing scope have been issued, until to-day those published by the various denominational societies and prepared by educational experts are of very high grade. A summer school has been established at Lake Geneva, Wisconsin, where instruction for professional and lay workers is carried on during the vacation season.

(*f*) *The Sunday School Council of Evangelical Denominations.* — The activity of the various denominations in Sunday school work has very markedly developed during the last thirty years, until there has grown up a professional body of editors and secretaries representing the more definitely Church point of view. These leaders, feeling the need of a common expression of the denominational responsibility for religious education, organized in 1910 the Sunday School Council of Evangelical Denominations. Annual meetings are held, at which important problems of educational policy and administration are discussed. The existence of such a representative body naturally raised the question of future responsibility for the making of the lessons for the Sunday school world. The lesson committee has therefore been reconstituted, and now consists of eight members selected from the international association, eight members selected by the council, and one member selected by each denomination having a lesson committee.

(*g*) *The emphasis on religious education.*—The last quarter of a century has been marked by a growing emphasis upon the more serious educational responsibility of the Church. This was seen in the demand for the graded curriculum. In addition to the international lessons, several very significant courses of study have been produced, notably the *Constructive Studies* of the University of Chicago Press, the *Completely Graded Series* of Scribner, and several series of various denominations. In 1903 was organized the Religious Education Association to promote the educational ideal in religion and the religious ideal in education. The Association holds annual conventions or conferences, conducts studies and surveys, publishes a magazine, gathers in its offices in Chicago all significant material on religious education, and conducts an extensive correspondence of advice and stimulus on problems in this field. Several denominations have established Boards of Religious Education, which are undertaking the supervision of the entire educational work of the Church. Leaders of great ability are being selected as secretaries. In some cases these boards are preparing new and specially graded curricula.

The numerous agencies of religious education are being co-ordinated in the more progressive churches under a professional director of religious education. He is becoming the educational minister of the Church. Some colleges and universities and most theological seminaries have established chairs of religious education, by means of which a trained professional force is being developed and scientific work in religious education is being undertaken. An extensive literature has already been produced, both technical and popular.

4. British developments.—(*a*) *The Sunday School Union.*—The parent society in London developed into a nation-wide enterprise. In 1821 there were four metropolitan auxiliaries and sixty provincial unions, besides the Sunday School Society of Ireland and the Sabbath School Union of Scotland. The reports of that year show 4000 schools with 36,000 teachers, and 500,000 scholars. In 1823 infant schools were added for children below the ordinary Sunday school age, as in 1811 Thomas Charles of Bala, the Welsh Methodist leader, had already established adult schools. The latter subsequently became known as senior classes, and in time both infant and senior branches became part of a completely organized school. The Union celebrated its jubilee in 1853 by inaugurating a fund for the erection of a permanent building. In 1862, at the time of the International Exhibition in London, a general Sunday school convention was held, attended by delegates from all over the British Isles, as well as from the Continent, the United States, and the Colonies. British Sunday schools were accustomed to meet in the morning and in the afternoon, and the Union had prepared annually a double series of lessons. Beginning with 1874, the British Lessons Committee co-operated with the American Committee in the production of the international series of lessons.

In 1880 was celebrated the centenary of Sunday schools throughout the United Kingdom, and a great convention was held in London to which delegates came from all over the world. As a result of this enlarged interest, the Union modified its constitution so as to become thoroughly national in character, representation to the counties being extended in 1890.

During the last thirty years the Union has developed a very significant philanthropic work, including country homes for poor scholars, a home of rest for lady teachers, a children's convalescent home, etc.

(*b*) *Educational progress.*—In the second quarter of the 19th cent. a forward movement in the science and art of pedagogy began in Scotland. David Stow organized the Glasgow Normal School for the training of teachers. Believing that the same principles could be applied to religious education, he published in 1826 a training system. The Union published in 1837 *Popular Education, or a Normal School Manual.* In 1856 a training class was organized at Pimlico. An attempt was made in 1861 to establish a college for Sunday school teachers, but it was found more feasible to develop a system of standardizing examinations. The college was finally established in 1899, and the examination system adapted to this organization. In addition to the publication of lessons and the encouragement of teacher training, the Union has developed a considerable literature for teachers and scholars, a separate building being required for this phase of its work.

5. World Sunday school work.—The Sunday school spread naturally through the English-speaking world. Various efforts were made, beginning as early as 1815, to establish it on the Continent, but with slight success. The convention in London in 1862, at the earnest solicitation of Albert Woodruff, undertook a continental propaganda. Sunday schools were established in all European countries. This movement was promoted by the world's conventions which met in London in 1889, in St. Louis in 1893, in London in 1898, in Jerusalem in 1904, in Rome in 1907, in Washington in 1910, in Zürich in 1913. At Rome the World Sunday School Association was organized, with American and British sections. Missionary work in China, India, S. Africa, and Europe was assigned to the British section; in Japan, Korea, the Philippines, S. America, and in the Muslim fields to the American section. The Association reported at Zürich the world Sunday school membership as 30,015,037, with 310,057 schools, and 2,669,630 officers and teachers.

6. Non-Protestant Sunday schools.—The Roman Catholic Church has adapted the Sunday school to its system, though without relinquishing the control to lay leadership. In the Hebrew Reformed Synagogue the Sunday school, generally under paid teachers, has become very effective. Among the Latter-Day Saints an excellent system of religious education has been developed, including the Sunday school. The Christian Science churches have established Sunday schools especially for children.

LITERATURE.—L. G. Pray, *Hist. of Sunday Schools*, Boston, 1847; 'The Sunday School and the American Sunday School Union,' *AJRPE* xv. [1865] 705 ff.; R. G. Pardee, *The Sabbath School Index*, Philadelphia, 1868; W. H. Watson, *First Fifty Years of the Sunday School*, London, 1872; *Centenary Memorial of the Establishment of Sunday Schools*, do. 1881; H. C. Trumbull, *Yale Lectures on the Sunday School*, Philadelphia, 1888; J. H. Harris, *Robert Raikes: the Man and His Work*, London and New York, 1899; J. H. Vincent, *The Modern Sunday School*, do. 1900; M. C. Brown, *Sunday School Movements in America*, do. 1901; W. H. Groser, *A Hundred Years' Work for the Children*, London, 1903; E. De Witt Burton and S. Mathews, *Principles and Ideals for the Sunday School*, Chicago, 1903; Marion Lawrance, *How to Conduct a Sunday School*, New York, 1905; A. S. Peake, *Reform in Sunday School Teaching*, London, 1906; F. Johnson, *The New Century Sunday School*, do. 1907; G. H. Archibald, *The Sunday School of To-morrow*, do. 1909; A. H. Angus, *Ideals in Sunday School Teaching*, do. 1910; H. H. Meyer, *The Graded Sunday School in Principle and Practice*, New York, 1910; H. F. Cope, *The Evolution of the Sunday School*, Boston, 1911; W. S. Athearn, *The Church School*, do. 1914; H. F. Cope, *The Sunday School and its Present-Day Task*, New York, 1916; E. W. Rice, *The Sunday School Movement and the American Sunday School Union*, Philadelphia, 1917; *Reports of the International Sunday School Association* (triennial), esp. that of 1905.

THEODORE GERALD SOARES.

SUNNITES

SUNNITES.—1. Distribution.—Islām is at present divided into two great unevenly divided sections. The Shīʿahs (*q.v.*) are found in Persia and among the masses in India; the Sunnites in the Turkish empire as it was prior to the Great War, in N. Africa, Egypt, other parts of Africa, Central Asia, Afghanistan, India, China, and the East Indies. In India the ruling class is of Sunnite faith; in the Turkish empire there are numbers of Shīʿahs of the better class who make a point of concealing their religious convictions. The Muhammadan population of the world is estimated to be about 221,000,000, and of this total it is reckoned that about 15,000,000 are Shīʿahs; the rest are Sunnīs. The Ibāḍīs (*q.v.*) of E. Arabia and N. and E. Africa are not relatively numerous and are neither Shīʿah nor Sunnite inasmuch as they claim descent from the Khārijite[1] schism of the early Umayyad period. The Zaidites (*q.v.*) of Yemen, though of Shīʿah origin, are on terms of fellowship with the Sunnites of Arabia.

2. The term 'Sunnite' and the early attitude towards the sunnah.—The Sunnite is the follower of the *sunnah* ('form,' 'outline,' 'mode,' 'usage'), or the view and usage of the Prophet. The issue implied in the use of the term is as to how new demands of thought are to be satisfied and new situations are to be met. The party of the *sunnah* contended that, where the Qur'ān did not fully and clearly provide direction, the inquirer should seek trustworthy information as to what Muhammad had said on the subject, what his action had been with relation to it, or what he had approved in others. The *sunnah* of the Prophet would be found embodied in a tradition (*ḥadīth*), and it was of the highest importance that the trustworthiness of traditions should be certified. They were tested, not by their intrinsic probability or by their consistency with other reports, but solely by the reputed reliability of the succession of persons through whom they had been handed down. If the *'isnād*, or chain of guarantors, had no unreliable members, the contents of a tradition were considered to furnish unimpeachable support for the opinion or course of action on behalf of which they had been cited. This mode of arriving at the *sunnah* of the Prophet opened the way to the wholesale fabrication and perversion of traditions to suit the needs of persons hard pressed for arguments on behalf of causes honest or dishonest. Abū Ḥanīfah († 150 A.H.) seems to have felt that tradition as a basis of support was not sufficient. Possibly, as a Persian he lacked the Arab's respect for this mode of proof and sought a more rational method, but what determined his attitude to an

[1] See art. KHAWĀRIJ.

even greater degree was probably the notoriously untrustworthy manner in which traditions were produced. He preferred to resort directly to the Qur'ān and, where it was not explicit, to decide according to his own view of what might fairly be inferred from its teaching as bearing on the question in hand. This method of obtaining direction involved two principles which the party of the *sunnah* for a long time viewed with distrust, viz. *ra'y*, or independent personal judgment, and *qiyās*, argument from the analogy of known cases to secure direction for new cases. Both of these were thought to imply disrespect towards inspired authority. Abū Ḥanīfah went farther than this in the readiness which he showed to depart from the written authority of the Qur'ān and the direction given by the *sunnah*. Even when these gave a clear decision, or where the principle of *qiyās* gave a definite instruction, the situation might suggest a better view or a wiser course of action. To follow such a suggestion was a duty. The principle here implied is termed *istiḥsān*, preference, or asking for the better thing. It involves personal independent judgment (*ra'y*) to a greater degree than the employment of *qiyās* does and is still more inconsistent with the early view of the party of the *sunnah* ('Ahlu-'s-Sunnah). Mālik ibn 'Anas († 179 A.H.) lived in the atmosphere of tradition at Medīna, and tradition had more weight with him than with Abū Ḥanīfah. Still, where traditions were being forged at the rate he knew and for the purposes of which he was aware, there was room for a principle of decision in legal and doctrinal questions which would protect Islām against injury through capricious or irrational judgments. Mālik, therefore, admitted the rule of *istiṣlāḥ*, the seeking of the public welfare, which might override the dictation of the Sacred Book and the *sunnah*. The strict party of the *sunnah* opposed this rule, as it had the liberal practice of Abū Ḥanīfah; both allowed too much room to *ra'y*. To men accustomed to earlier conditions, when the absence of a *sunnah* which might cover all cases left room for decision on other grounds, the mere multiplying of traditions did not afford a sufficient reason for surrendering methods of obtaining guidance which had been followed when traditions were not available. Meanwhile the uninformed masses of Islām were strongly inclined to the simpler method of appeal to external authority. *Qiyās*, *istiḥsān*, *istiṣlāḥ*, and *ra'y* were too human, and hence too feeble and erring. The future of Islām largely depended on whether free scholarship (*ra'y*) or authority (*sunnah*) became the ruling factor in the community, whether the need of the Muslims was to be conceived according to the view of intelligent leaders or to that of the great body of the people with its clinging to old-established ways.

3. The Mu'tazilite reaction.—The traditional and rationalistic tendencies both went on developing, and the mutual antagonism between them was intensified. The rationalistic party became recognized as a party which favoured *ra'y*, lent its approval to Greek philosophy and Christian culture, and regularly employed the Aristotelian method of arriving at truth. The earlier *khalīfahs* of the Abbāsid dynasty had been interested in these things, but they became established and officially approved under the *khalīfah* al-Ma'mūn († 218 A.H.). In the last year of his reign he instituted an inquisition against the traditionalists. This inquisition (*al-Miḥna*) went on for sixteen years (218–234 A.H.), and, while it lasted, the orthodox suffered severely and their leaders were often under peril of death. This period of persecution, with the strenuous controversies which it witnessed, settled the characteristic marks of the later Sunnī belief and also brought out and sharpened the weapons by which rationalism sought to destroy the positions of the 'Ahlu-'s-Sunnah. The latter applied to their opponents the name Mu'tazilah, 'dissenters' or 'seceders.' It was a name which had been used in a favourable sense of pious ascetics or hermits, but in the late 2nd cent. A.H. it was given an unfavourable significance and came to mean heretics. On the one side were the 'Ahlu-'s-Sunnah, and opposed to them were the 'Ahlu-'r-Ra'y, the Mu'tazilah. The fundamental question for both parties was the true conception of God. Was the view held by the one party or the other a view which did justice to the unity of the Supreme Being? Was it one which adequately set forth and protected His character as a perfect Being? The Mu'tazilah, as their orthodox antagonists called them, were proud to describe themselves as the 'party of the (divine) unity and justice' ('Ahlu-'t-Tawhīd wa'l-'adl). They charged the party of the *sunnah* with a contradiction of both these divine virtues.

Connected with these fundamental issues were others of sufficiently vital importance but subordinate to them. The question as to the source of authority for belief and conduct required to be solved. The party of the Qur'ān and *sunnah* insisted upon a literal conformity to these two sources, while the Mu'tazilah demanded that belief and conduct should be consistent with reason, and the method by which the rational view was to be tested was that of the Aristotelian logic. This science was known by the term *kalām* (*q.v.*), and those who relied upon it were designated Mutakallimūn — descriptions without intrinsic stigma, but acquiring in the hands of the orthodox Sunnites the unpleasant implication of heresy and heretics respectively. The Mu'tazilah nevertheless were proud to call themselves 'Ahlu-'l-'Aql, 'the party of reason,' and felt that only by reason could one reach a worthy view of God and of man's duty to Him. The Qur'ān was saved from absurd interpretations and became a real guide for reasonable beings only as it was subjected to a rational process of study. Literal acceptance of the text had led the orthodox to proclaim the dogma of the uncreated and eternal nature of the Qur'ān, and as a party in this early time they applied the dogma even to the letters and words of the book as written and to the sounds of the uttered recitation or reading. It was in the controversy regarding the uncreated nature of the Qur'ān that Aḥmad ibn Ḥanbal (*q.v.*) appeared as the outstanding champion of the traditional view. When pressed by the Mu'tazilite argument to the effect that the human media and the inanimate records were obviously not unlimited in either nature or duration, his answer was that the book declared itself to be (or, rather, God in the book declared it to be) *kalām Allāh*, *i.e.* the word or speech of God, which was inseparably and uninterruptedly an attribute (*ṣifa*) of God. It could not be dissociated from the thought of God and the divine reason and was therefore eternal. This polemic instantly raised the question of the divine attributes (*ṣifāt*). Was the *kalām Allāh* to be conceived as an entity independent as to essence from the being or essence of God? Were all the attributes entities in this sense? On the basis of the statements of the Qur'ān the party of the *sunnah* persistently argued for the affirmative. The Mu'tazilah charged them with giving God a partner (*shirk*). It was polytheism to assert that there were other eternal entities beside God. The Qur'ān text should not be interpreted in such a sense as to violate the unity of God and 'associate' other beings with Him. It should be explained in an allegorical sense (*ta'wīl*) where the literal sense would involve irreverence or what was irrational. The orthodox rejoinder relentlessly attacked the presumptuous setting up of *ra'y* over the *kalām Allāh*. It surely was the greater sin that the creature should venture to set aside the plain words which God had spoken because to him they seemed absurd. The ambiguity of the terms used in the controversy made agreement between the two parties impossible. 'Word of God' meant one thing for Aḥmad ibn Ḥanbal and a very different thing for his persecuting inquisitors. For him to claim that his Qur'ān was uncreated, and for them to reply that their Qur'ān was created, must necessarily have left each where he was before the argument. The *sunnah* party suffered much ridicule at the hands of their opponents because of their readiness to accept all the anthropomorphisms of the Qur'ān as precise descriptions of fact. They boldly taught that God sat on a throne, possessed sight, smell, hearing, etc., though they grew more cautious as the controversy wore on and pressed for verbal acceptance of the Qur'ān teachings, with a consent to leave questions as to how such things could be with God Himself to make plain later or not to make plain as He chose. It was to be an acceptance 'without seeing how' (*bilā kaifa*, or, contracted, *balkaifa*). Connected with this subject of the anthropomorphic attributes and acts of God in the Qur'ān is that of the possibility of actually seeing God, as the Qur'ān declares. If the saints see God, it is implied that the anthropomorphic view is literally true; if it is not true, they do not see Him.

One more element in the Mu'tazilite controversy

remains to be noticed. The party of the *sunnah* held the characteristic Arab view that the will of Allāh was the all-determining source of change and activity in the world. The 'party of *'aql*' allowed to man the capacity to initiate action and placed upon him the responsibility for his choice. Because of their attitude on this special point, the Mu'tazilah are classed as Qadarites (believers in free will). Their argument attacked the orthodox, particularly on the ground that they held man responsible for his acts and nevertheless denied that he was free. Freedom he might seem to have, but it was only illusory; in reality his acts were created by God, without whom nothing happened. This orthodox contention the Mu'tazilah repudiated as involving injustice to man and also as implying an insulting impeachment of God's justice.

4. Re-establishment of orthodoxy.—The Mu'tazilite controversy was summarily terminated by the *khalīfah* al-Mutawakkil in 234 A.H. He reversed the liberal policy of his predecessors, declared the doctrines that they had championed to be offences against the State, and proclaimed the orthodox views to represent the official opinions which alone would be tolerated in Islām. This official endorsement of the 'Ahlu-'s-Sunnah has been maintained in Islām down to the present. The dogmatic beliefs of the persecuted orthodox are held by both Sunnites and Shī'ahs, and the Sunnī khalīfate has regularly stood sponsor for them. There is no doubt that the Mu'tazilite *khalīfahs* of the Miḥna period represented a relatively small minority in the Muslim world of their time and that al-Mutawakkil was wise not to continue his support of their views in the face of an adverse popular sentiment. Tradition and Qur'ān retained their hold upon the masses, to whom their directness and their clear mandatory accent appealed as mere reflective opinion could hardly hope to do. The great body of Islām ranged itself behind the orthodox *khalīfahs*, and the Mu'tazilah tend to disappear little by little. The free-thinking teachers notwithstanding give the traditional theologians a great deal of trouble, in spite of the smallness of their numbers. It was easy to make a system based on literal interpretations appear ridiculous when attacked by means of keen dialectic, and the orthodox tenacity and insistence did not prevent their partisans from feeling an awkward discomfort when they were forced to evade rather than answer the attacks made upon them. It will be readily understood that the man who enabled them to inflict genuine defeat upon their opponents, Abū'l-Ḥasan al-Ash'arī (*q.v.*), would seem to the orthodox to be almost a prophet when he arrived.

5. Abū'l-Ḥasan al-Ash'arī.—Al-Ash'arī had been long trained in the views and arguments of the Mutakallims, and there is some plausibility in the legend which represents him as using their method against his own teacher al-Jubbā'ī to the discomfiture of the latter. He had apparently come to see that the Aristotelian logic was valuable, not for the discovery of truth, but for making explicit the significance of propositions which were taken for granted and for the confutation of false arguments. It became clear to him that religion could not be built securely upon *kalām*, a formal science. The foundation must be in revelation through inspired men and media, through prophets and sacred writings. Feeling that, in spite of their poor logic, the party of the *sunnah* had founded Islām upon the true basis, that tradition was a genuinely trustworthy means of communicating revealed guidance from age to age, and that the consensus of the Muslim community (*ijmā'*) expressed through its leaders was more reliable than the judgment of the individual Mutakallim, al-Ash'arī returned to the orthodox faith which he seems to have inherited from his forbears in the first instance. He came back converted through his own employment of *kalām* against itself, and naturally he made use of the weapon from that time (300 A.H.) forward to disprove the views of the Mu'tazilah and to develop into a system the orthodox doctrine.

6. The principle of consensus.—The principle of consensus operated more largely from the days of al-Ash'arī onward. It was Ash-Shafi'ī († 204 A.H.) who first made extensive use of it in his teaching and was prepared to accept it as a guide where the Qur'ān and *sunnah* failed to afford direction. His preference for *ijmā'* was approved only with reserve by the rigid Ḥanbalite orthodoxy of the 3rd century. Al-Bukhārī's strictness in the criticism of *ḥadīths* and his refusal to give an opinion on the human utterance of the Qur'ān are possibly alike based upon an employment of the *ijmā'*. The principle has a bearing upon the division of Islām into Sunnites and Shī'ahs. In the days of the early Ash'arite school this division, which is based, not upon dogmatic differences of a genuine religious character, but upon a divergent view of the khalīfate, had not yet taken place, and the *ijmā'* embraced the whole Muslim community. When the division came, it was recognized that the 'Ahlu-'s-Sunnah lay beyond the boundaries of the Persian empire as organized under the Ṣafawids (A.D. 1502), and that *ijmā'* had a sense and a binding force in Sunnite Islām which it did not have in Persia. The Persian Muslims readily accord the name Sunnīs to their rivals and accept Shī'ah as a proper term by which to describe themselves. *Ijmā'* is especially a Sunnite principle and has guided the leading movements and changes of Sunnite Islām during many centuries. There is no need of its use among the Shī'ahs, where appeal is made to the inspired authority of the *imāms* as it is voiced through their *mujtahids*.

In spite of the fact that the Ḥanbalite school, so powerful in the 3rd cent. of Islām, is now almost a negligible quantity, al-Ash'arī, the founder of the Sunnite theological system, was an ardent Ḥanbalite after his conversion and died in that faith (320 A.H.). It is necessary to say, however, that the views which are now held by all the Sunnite schools are the founder's views as somewhat liberalized by the Ash'arite school after his death. There is evidence to show that the cast-iron system into which the great teacher came back at the time of his conversion from Mu'tazilism was modified through the very *kalām* influence which he brought with him. It was probably al-Ash'arī's thought to employ *kalām* for purely apologetic purposes, but his followers gave much more scope to the principle of the censensus than he seems to have thought of. The 'Six Correct Books' of traditions (*Kitābu Sittah*), of which the two great *Saḥīḥs* of al-Bukhārī and Muslim are the most essential authorities, contain the only generally accepted evidence as to the *sunnah*, but in the application of the *sunnah* the principle of the *ijmā'*, used in accordance with the scholastic method introduced by al-Ash'arī, has made it possible to leave far behind the strict views of law held by the triumphant Ḥanbalite school of the 3rd Muslim century. That kind of unchanging orthodoxy would not have preserved the unity of Islām as it has been preserved among the Sunnites. Modern Ḥanbalites are the consistent successors of the early Ḥanbalite school before al-Ash'arī, but they exert little influence. Sunnite Islām is an Islām to which the liberal views of the Ḥanifites and the moderate views of the Mālikites and Shāfi'ites have had less and less difficulty in adjusting themselves as time has passed, so that in opinion and practice unity and even a large measure of uniformity have come to prevail. The Ḥanbalite domination of the Sunnī sect became at once impossible with the admission of the *kalām* method and the broader understanding of the *ijmā'*. The schools differ, as they have always differed, in the extent to which they recognize certain liberal principles and attitudes of mind. Analogy (*qiyās*) and judgment according to personal opinion (*ra'y*, and, in special relations, *istiḥsān*, or preference for a better view) play a large part in the administration of Ḥanifite law, a less important part among the N. African Mālikites, and a small part in the Shāfi'ite communities of Islām. But the difference is within the region of *fiqh* and not within that of dogmatic opinion.

7. Triumph of Ash'arite theology.—The process of liberalizing the orthodox system of al-Ash'arī must have been somewhat rapid in the century following his death. Towards the end of the 4th cent. A.H. there seems to have been a disposition to allow *kalām* to run riot in Baghdād, where we read of theologians who were willing to argue questions without reference to the traditional authorities of Islām. Even in the West the great thinkers, excluding Ibn Ḥazm (*q.v.*) as almost a sole exception, gave themselves more and more to a philosophical account of religion and at the same time realized painfully that they had parted company with accepted orthodox views. Men like Ibn Ṭufail and Averroës (*qq.v.*) in the late 6th cent. A.H. have one system for the masses and another teaching for the instructed few. Nevertheless one may say that, in spite of excesses, the Ash'arite school had definitely imposed its views and method upon the Muslim world before the end of the 11th cent. of our Christian era. The liberty of thought which al-Ash'arī had secured for Islām had developed by that time a controversial intellectualism which left no place for intuition or mysticism in religion, and orthodoxy was in serious danger of losing the sympathy of the masses. A new emphasis was called for in order to supply a corrective to the general rationalism which prevailed.

8. Al-Ghazālī.[1]—Al-Ghazālī († 505 A.H.) was by nature an intensely religious man to whom the truth was the greatest of all possessions. It was for him life's supreme concern to solve the problem of Ultimate Reality in such a way as to be satisfied that he enjoyed contact, response, and fellowship with it. He was convinced that what he sought could not be given by an acceptance of truth on mere external authority, a point to which, in spite of his dependence upon *kalām*, al-Ash'arī still held. He saw that the Mutakallims could proceed to their conclusions only as they took for granted certain propositions which they did not prove, and that, when they had said all, the seeker had in possession only a system of logical inferences and not at all an experience of the ultimately real. Not because it was a last resort or because he was in despair of finding anything better, al-Ghazālī turned to Ṣūfism. He made a full and sympathetic trial of the Ṣūfī discipline, after having tried other ways, and was convinced that the Ṣūfīs (*q.v.*) had solved the problem of the soul's quest. Man craved a satisfying revelation and a satisfying communion with God; he received both through faithful conformity to the Ṣūfī ideal and persistent openness to receive higher communications. Al-Ghazālī was a moderate Ṣūfī who was ready to give due weight to reason within its own limits, and who recognized the ethical and religious duties of the common life. His pre-eminent gifts and virtues—for he was one of the finest characters as well as one of the greatest minds which Islām has produced—have made his solution of the religious problem exceedingly influential down to our own day. Ṣūfism became a power far beyond the borders of the dervish organizations; the extreme dependence upon rationalism was checked; the emotional factors in human nature were provided for with due regard to ethical and religious conduct. Probably no teacher since the days of the Prophet has afforded to Muslims a better illustration of the possibilities of their own faith. Sunnites generally admit a great indebtedness to him, and his works are standard texts in the training of orthodox theologians (*'ulamā*).

9. Sunnites and Shī'ahs.—The distinction between Shī'ahs and Sunnīs has its roots in the dispute between the 'Alids and Umayyads in the years which followed the *khalīfah* 'Uthmān's assassination (35 A.H.). In its origin it has nothing to do with the religion founded by Muhammad, but rather is occupied with the political question of the succession to the leadership of the Muslim community. At first the 'Alids on their side claimed that they were the legitimate *khalīfahs* because they were descended from the Prophet's daughter Fāṭimah and his cousin and intimate companion, 'Alī. The Umayyads on their part claimed a nomination by the choice of the Muslims themselves and as a further title claimed kinship with the Prophet as being of the Hāshimite family. Later the 'Alids stood for the claims of descent against all claims of right to office because of the popular choice. This difference still marks off the Shī'ah political theory from that held among the Sunnites.

(*a*) *Theory of the khalīfate.*—There is, moreover, an old standing difference between the Sunnites and Shī'ahs as to the functions of the *khalīfah*. Among the Sunnites the *khalīfah* is a political ruler essentially, while from the first the 'Alid party regarded the Prophet's successor as a religious guide and therefore preferred to designate him as the *imām* of the Muslim community. It was assumed that his physical descent from the Prophet secured to him not merely divine rights, but also a divine endowment of grace and wisdom. No such assumption was held by the Sunnites with relation to their *khalīfahs*. They were chosen from among the believers and could claim no supernatural qualifications. Their authority was conferred by the Muslim community and carried with it no implication of pre-eminent saintliness or infallibility. The Sunnite attitude towards the *khalīfahs* differs greatly from that of the Shī'ahs towards the *imāms*. The personal qualities and public influence of the *khalīfahs* have been largely determinative of the respect shown to them. Among the Shī'ahs the office hallows the occupant, and the *imāms* are regarded with the deepest religious veneration. The Sunnite *khalīfahs* by law are required to be of the Prophet's tribe, the Quraish; the *imāms* were chosen from the still more narrow circle of the Prophet's immediate family.

Since the twelfth *imām*, Muhammad ibn al-Ḥasan, disappeared in the middle of the 3rd cent. A.H., the line of visible *imāms* has been suspended, but there has never been a legal reason why the Sunnī khalīfate should be interrupted, as it has always been possible for the Muslim community to find an eligible candidate and to nominate him, provided circumstances did not interpose a physical hindrance. The *sulṭāns* of Turkey have assumed to be the *khalīfahs* of the Prophet and have taken to themselves the exclusive title pertaining to that office, Emir al-Mu'minīna, 'Commander of the Faithful,' since the time of the Ottoman conquest of Egypt in A.D. 1512. As they are not of Arab race, let alone of Quraishite lineage, there is no basis in law for the Ottoman claim. The first *sulṭān* (Selīm I.) to assume the title justified his act on the ground of a surrender of his rights on the part of the last 'Abbāsid *khalīfah*, al-Mutawakkil II., who at the time of the conquest of Egypt was attached to the court of the Mamluk *sulṭāns* and was recognized by them as the spiritual head of Islām. The Ottoman *sulṭāns* have retained in their own persons the dual authority temporal and spiritual which the Mamluks had divided, and the principle of the consensus seems to have permitted the *'ulamā* to legalize the departure from the law of the khalīfate as settled by the *sunnah*. They have accepted the transfer of the 'Abbāsid rights to Sulṭān Selim as giving a title, and have regarded it as fortified by other considerations, viz. the Ottoman conquest of Muslim domain, the control of the sacred cities, and the possession of relics of the Prophet. The *sulṭān* has made a concession to traditional sentiment in constituting the chief *mufti* in Constantinople as *shaikh ul-Islām*, or highest spiritual authority over all believers. This functionary, nevertheless, derives his power from the *sulṭān* who appoints him, though it is to be admitted that the choice of the *'ulamā* practically settles the appointment. All questions affecting Islām are considered by the *shaikh ul-Islām*, and are subject to his decision as promulgated by a *fatwā* issuing from him. The other conditions recognized by Sunnite authorities as binding in the election of a *khalīfah* are that he shall be of adult years, of sane mind, of free condition, a man versed in the learning of Islām, and a capable administrator who will rule justly. In contrast to the Shī'ahs, the Sunnī doctors have always recognized Abū Bakr, 'Umar, and 'Uthmān, the first successors of the Prophet, as genuine *khalīfahs* (*al-Khulafā ar-rāshidūn*) together with the fourth *khalīfah* 'Alī, who of course is allowed to be a legiti-

[1] Cf. art. ETHICS AND MORALITY (Muslim), § 7.

mate successor by the Shī'ah sect also. For 'Alī and his successors in the imāmate the Sunnīs have much respect on account of their reputation for either piety or learning, though they do not admit the Shī'ah claim of supernatural gifts or divine rights as belonging to them.

(*b*) *Enmity between Sunnites and Shī'ahs.*—The intense hatred between Sunnīs and Shī'ahs as distinct sects dates from the time when the Shī'ahs were constituted a separate political organization by the foundation of the Ṣafawid empire of Persia in A.D. 1502. The fault in this mutual bitter feeling is greater on the Shī'ah side than on that of the Sunnites, but the treatment of Persian pilgrims to Mecca has been an enduring irritation, and in earlier times the military aggression of the Turkish *sulṭāns* gave occasion for resentment in Persia. As has been pointed out above, there are many individual Muslims of Shī'ah connexion in the Turkish empire, and, either because of an acquired indifference or oftener because of their practice of *taqīyah* (concealment of faith), they suffer no personal inconvenience at the hands of their Sunnite neighbours. The proposal of Nādir Shah in the 18th cent., that a reunion of Islām be brought about by admitting the Shī'ahs to fellowship with the Sunnīs as a fifth orthodox school, was prompted by the world-ambition of that ruler and was met by vigorous and successful opposition on the part of the Persian *mujtahids* and *mullahs.*

(*c*) *Position as to the sunnah.*—The difference between the Sunnites and the Shī'ahs does not consist in the acknowledgment of the *sunnah* of the Prophet by the former and its denial by the latter. The title of the Sunnīs to have the oldest and the most thoroughly tested body of traditions is not questioned, but the Shī'ahs also have their *sunnah*, whose authorities are the acknowledged *ḥadīth* collections of the sect. Resting upon these recognized standards, the Shī'ah teachers claim that they alone have the genuine *sunnah*, while the Sunnite version, they allege, has been perverted so as to furnish arguments against the claims of 'Alī and his sons to the succession of the Prophet. The corruption of the *sunnah* for any such purpose by the Sunnites is exceedingly unlikely, while the evidence of the manipulation of traditions by the Shī'ahs to support their own side is considered to be fairly clear. In the interpretation and adaptation of the *sunnah* to new relations the Sunnites are guided by the consensus (*ijmā'*) and analogy (*qiyās*), while the Shī'ahs claim to be alone rightly guided in their following of the *sunnah*, inasmuch as they have enjoyed the infallible instruction of the *imāms* either in person or since the line has been suspended by the inerrant communication of their word and will through the *mujtahids.* According to the *sunnah* view, there can be no *mujtahids* in Islām since the death of the last great orthodox founder in the 3rd cent. A.H. The term as employed in Sunnī circles is limited to the great *imāms* of the earlier centuries who founded the four orthodox schools and laid on indisputable foundations the theology and law of Islām. Since their day no teacher's opinions have justified themselves as a permanent basis for faith and life.

10. Changes in Sunnite Islām. — In theory Sunnite Islām is tied up to the Ash'arite system, and because of that it is thought to be fated to intellectual stagnation. The facts show that from the time of al-Ash'arī himself there was some modification of the founder's positions, and with the contribution made by al-Ghazālī one may say that the modification amounts to a materially altered view-point and the introduction of a new and revolutionary emphasis which laid stress upon intuitive and emotional factors in religious experience. The necessities of the historical situation have repeatedly rendered nugatory the theoretical requirements of Sunnite orthodoxy. Where Muslims live under Christian governments, as in India, the law of the khalīfate has to yield place to the obligations of political loyalty, the duty imposed by the *jihād* is in most cases unfulfilled, and the *zakāt* must be modified, especially as to the authority to whom it is to be turned over and the mode and purpose of its distribution. With the universal recognition of saint-worship and the cult of relics, the dogma of the unity of God and the law against idolatry (*shirk*) are violated, and the sufficiency of the canonical authorities, the Qur'ān and *sunnah*, is called in question. It may be recalled that one fruit of the modern liberal movement in India is the rise of the Aḥmadīyah sect, whose founder, Mirza Ghulam Aḥmad († 1908), recognized the logic of facts in the position of the Indian Muslims and declared that the duty of the *jihād* was not binding any longer. The practical effect of the Ṣūfī teaching when fully developed is a pantheism which is in contradiction with the hard, clear-cut monotheism of the Ash'arite theology. It is a pantheism leading to a loosening of the positive bonds of conduct which the orthodox teaching imposes. The righteousness of the Ṣūfī may become extravagantly mechanical and violently anti-social, so much so that public regulation may be called for, as is the case in Egypt. Enough has been said to show that Sunnite Islām, however immobile it may be in theory, has admitted into its system under the compulsion of facts vastly important modifications, some of which have seemed to contain unrevealed potentialities of disintegration.

11. Detailed differences between Sunnites and Shī'ahs.—A few points in which Sunnites and Shī'ahs differ require to be mentioned.

(*a*) The Sunnites do not accord to 'Alī and his sons the degree of veneration which the feast of Muḥarram implies. This holds true even if the Sunnite Muslims of India do not scruple to participate in the ceremonies of the feast along with their Shī'ah neighbours. (*b*) There is some confusion of the orthodox feast of the 'Ashūra, which falls on the tenth day of Muḥarram, with the Shī'ah feast, which extends from the first to the tenth day of that month. The motive of the respective feasts is, however, entirely different. The 'Ashūra commemorates the completion of creation by the creating of Adam and Eve on the tenth day of Muḥarram, while the tenth day of the Shī'ah ceremonies is simply the crowning day of the whole Muḥarram feast, pointing in particular to the Kerbelā massacre which is supposed to have taken place on that day. (*c*) Generally speaking, the ritual of ordinary worship differs only in the non-essential points. The mode of purification before the *ṣalāt* with the Sunnites includes the washing of the arm upwards to the elbow, while with the Shī'ahs the process is reversed. In the washing of the feet the Sunnite ritual literally washes; the Shī'ah merely rubs or wipes the feet. (*d*) To perform the *ḥājj* by proxy is not permitted by the Sunnīs, while it is not uncommon among their rivals. This permission, if granted, would violate the cardinal Sunnī requirement that a Muslim must perform the *ḥājj* at least once during his lifetime. (*e*) More far-reaching in its social effects is the permission given by the Shī'ah law to contract *mu'ta* marriages. These temporary unions, for a price agreed upon and under conditions of legal contract, are forbidden by the Sunnite codes. (*f*) The Sunnite recognition of the principle of *taqīyah* is limited to cases of extreme personal danger when it is at most permitted to dissemble one's religious convictions in order to preserve one's life. The Shī'ahs do not view *taqīyah* as limited to situations of personal risk, and, where it applies, they do not merely permit a resort to *taqīyah*, but strongly recommend the employment of it. Especially where the interests of religion may be supposed to be in jeopardy, the Muslim of Shī'ah faith will feel the use of *taqīyah* to be a moral obligation.

In all that has been said in the foregoing description of the Sunnite position and practice regard has been had to only those matters which fall within the canon law (*sharī'ah*). It must be kept in mind that in all Muslim countries, whether Sunnite or Shī'ite, there is another authority which has its constituted rights and its organized administration, viz. the customary law (*'urf* or *'adah*). This differs according to the established conventions of different places. It is not a distinctive feature of the Sunnites and need not be more fully treated in this article.

The power of the *'ulamā* among the Sunnīs is

very great, though as a class they are not viewed with the superstitious veneration or even fear which the Persian Shīʿah shows to many of the *mullahs*, to all the *mujtahids*, and to the large class of *sayyids* who are to be found in Shīʿite regions. The influence of the *'ulamā* has been conserved by their learning, which, though narrowly restricted to Muslim theology and law, is often comprehensive within those limits. This learning is constantly on call in the service of the Muslim community. Their influence, moreover, has been much greater than it might have been owing to a certain measure of accommodation which has made large room for such a phenomenon as the Ṣūfī movement—a movement whose elements of wonder and emotionalism have proved to the satisfaction of the masses that Islām was still a medium of supernatural power and divine life. Along with this they have admitted to the curriculum of theological studies in all the leading schools the works of the great mystics, particularly those of the master, al-Ghazālī. The tacit or explicit approval of the cult of saints, endowed as it is by public funds, may be an anomaly, but for the orthodox leaders it also is an instrument of power. More potent than any other factor is the fact that the consensus (*ijmāʿ*) is realized only through the *'ulamā* and that no cause has been so effective in bringing about change of policy and the initiation of new lines of action as the voice of the *'ulamā* declaring the mind of the universal Muslim community. The *ijmāʿ* is being prepared by the training which the candidates for the learned calling receive, whether it be in the Azhar University at Cairo, in the schools of Constantinople and India, or in the ancient seats of learning like Bokhāra. It is a long mechanical process aiming at fixing rigidly the positions of traditional orthodoxy in the thoughts and sympathies of the student and cultivating in him a fanatical devotion to the authority of the past, especially of the primitive age of the faith. It is natural that, when his opportunity to lead comes, he should adjust himself as an obedient part of the whole traditional system.

LITERATURE.—R. Dozy, *Het Islamisme*, Leyden, 1863, French tr., do. 1879; C. Eliot ('Odysseus'), *Turkey in Europe*², London, 1908; *EBr*¹¹, *s.vv.* 'Mahommedan Religion,' 'Mahommedan Institutions,' 'Mahommedan Law,' 'Sunnites'; I. Goldziher, *Mohammed and Islam*, New Haven, U.S.A., 1917; C. Hamilton, *The Hedaya*², London, 1870; T. P. Hughes, *DI*, London, 1895; F. A. Klein, *The Religion of Islām*, do. 1906; E. W. Lane, *An Account of the Manners and Customs of the Modern Egyptians*, 2 vols., do. 1836, and many subsequent edd.; D. B. Macdonald, *Development of Muslim Theology, Jurisprudence, and Constitutional Theory*, New York and London, 1903, *The Religious Life and Attitude in Islam*, Chicago, 1909; D. S. Margoliouth, *The Early Development of Mohammedanism*, London, 1914; A. Müller, *Der Islam im Morgenland und Abendland*, 2 vols., Berlin, 1885–87; T. Nöldeke, *Sketches from Eastern History*, Eng. tr., Edinburgh, 1892; W. M. Patton, *Aḥmed ibn Ḥanbal and the Miḥna*, Leyden, 1897; *RGG*, 5 vols., Tübingen, 1908–13, *s.vv.* 'Islam,' 'Sunniten,' 'Tradition'; E. Sell, *The Faith of Islam*², London, 1896; C. Snouck Hurgronje, *Mekka*, 2 vols., The Hague, 1888–89, *Mohammedanism*, New York and London, 1916.

W. M. PATTON.

SUPERNATURALISM.—Supernaturalism is the mental attitude that has the supernatural for its object. The term is used by anthropologists[1] to express the fact that primitive magic and primitive religion alike rest on a belief in supernatural powers. In such a context it is convenient to have a word such as 'supernatural' that may be equated now with 'magical' and now with 'divine.'[2] For the savage respects the human magician 'on account of his continual intercourse with the supernatural world,'[3] and, on the other hand, must be allowed 'to possess a rudimentary notion of certain supernatural beings who may be fittingly called gods, though not in the full sense in which we use the word.'[1] Frazer, indeed, assumes a general tendency among savages to claim 'powers which we should now call supernatural,'[2] on the ground that 'a savage hardly conceives the distinction commonly drawn by more advanced peoples between the natural and the supernatural.'[3] F. B. Jevons, on the other hand, warns us against 'the error of imagining that there was a time when man did not distinguish between the natural and the supernatural. This error may take the form of saying either that to primitive man nothing was supernatural or that everything was supernatural.' He goes on to say:

> 'Primitive man took to himself the credit of his successful attempts to work the mechanism of nature for his own advantage, but when the machinery did not work he ascribed the fault to some overruling *super*natural power.'[4]

The objection of E. Durkheim, that to recognize breaches in a habitual order does not amount to the recognition of breaches in an order conceived as necessary after the manner of modern science,[5] is surely somewhat hypercritical in such a context. An objection of another kind, since it does not dispute the facts, but merely regards convenience of terminology, is that of J. H. Leuba,[6] who in naming the belief in supernatural power would call attention to the power rather than to the supernatural quality attaching to it, and hence would substitute for 'supernaturalism' the term 'dynamism,' originally used by A. van Gennep[7] to describe the 'impersonalist' theory of *mana* as contrasted with the 'personalist' theory of animism. Now there is much to be said for the view that the positive content of supernaturalism receives its fullest conceptual expression in terms of the *mana* type.[8] But the mental attitude in question has its negative side as well as the positive side connoted by *mana*, since it is called forth by the frustration of reasonable expectation; so that, as Jevons says, 'where the natural ended, the supernatural began.'[9] Again, this mental attitude is not so predominantly intellectual that it can be suitably designated by means of any mere concept that it generates. For the rest, anthropological terminology is, happily, in a somewhat fluid condition, and may be varied without impropriety in response to the needs of different theoretical purposes. It will suffice here to give a brief account of the chief aspects of the mental attitude under consideration.

1. Emotional aspect.—The emotional constituents of the magico-religious sentiment have been subjected to psychological analysis with results that show it to be, even in its simplest forms, exceedingly complex. 'Awe' is perhaps the word in our language that expresses its many-sided nature most fully, and awe is defined by W. McDougall as 'a tertiary compound of fear, wonder, and negative self-feeling.'[10] Round the object provided by the supernatural, fear, admiration, and submissiveness in varying degrees are organized into a mood, whether, in addition, that object be on the whole hated or loved, and consequently take rank as a manifestation of evil or of good supernatural power. Thus the sentiment is excited equally by magic and religion, the sorcerer, like the god, being 'surrounded by a halo of mystery and an atmosphere of awe.'[11] To appreciate the

1 *E.g.*, J. G. Frazer, *GB*, London, 1890, i. 37, ²1900, i. 137, ³1911, pt. i., *The Magic Art*, i. 386; R. R. Marett, *The Threshold of Religion*, do. 1909, p. 11.
2 *GB*³, pt. i., *The Magic Art*, i. 366; cf. p. 374.
3 *Ib.* p. 357.

1 *GB*³, pt. i., *The Magic Art*, i. 376.
2 *Ib.* p. 386. 3 *Ib.* p. 51.
4 *Introd. to the Hist. of Religion*, London, 1896, p. 18 f.
5 *Les Formes élémentaires de la vie religieuse*, Paris, 1912, p. 36.
6 *A Psychological Study of Religion*, New York, 1912, p. 84.
7 *Les Rites de passage*, Paris, 1909, p. 17.
8 See art. MANA.
9 *Introd. to Hist. of Rel.*, p. 19.
10 *An Introd. to Social Psychology*⁷, London, 1913, p. 305; cf p. 131.
11 *GB*³, pt. i., *The Magic Art*, i. 356.

emotional attitude of primitive man towards a universe which, beyond the narrow circle of the daily routine, is almost wholly unknown, yet felt to be pregnant with immeasurable possibilities of weal or woe, one should take stock one by one of the more baffling and startling elements in his experience, as is done, *e.g.*, by W. D. Wallis in his paper 'The Element of Fear [better 'Awe'] in Religion.'[1] Confined by his ignorance to the immediate here and now, the savage attributes mystic powers alike to the stranger at a distance and to those of his own race that are dead and gone. Nor does the familiar present remain unvisited by portents. The sky above him is disturbed by thunderstorm, eclipse, shooting stars, the aurora; earth and sea about him have their haunted pools, their fantastic rocks. Then living nature teems with wonders—trees and herbs, reptiles and fishes, birds and quadrupeds, that look strange or behave unaccountably. Moreover, man is mysterious to himself, with his visions, his seizures, the power of his eye and gesture, his sheer impressiveness, ranging from the majesty of kings to the gruesomeness of witches. For the rest, life is full of accidents and coincidences. Altogether, the savage world provides plenty of scope for that interplay of primary emotions of which awe is the outcome. Be it noted, however, that the essence of supernaturalism does not consist in bare feeling, but attains to expression through every aspect of the mental life at once.[2]

2. Intellectual aspect.—Since supernaturalism has a negative as well as a positive side, embodying a cautious doubt of the unknown combined with an effort to read a meaning into it, primitive thought needs a twofold set of concepts. Negatively the supernatural is *tabu*, positively it is *mana*.[3] Among savages, of course, such notions have not been built up into any systematic theory; nor is it possible to say at what stage of mental evolution they first came into use, though perhaps it would be hard to point to any primitive people that lacks them entirely. Moreover, since the supernatural implies evil power as well as good, ministering to the purposes of the sorcerer no less than to those of the priest, it is to be expected that *mana* will sometimes split up into two notions that stand antithetically for the good and bad kinds of supernatural power.[4] Finally, it cannot be said that rudimentary thought is altogether without an idea corresponding to that of the natural or normal. It seems highly doubtful whether we can credit the savage with a belief in what we call the uniformity of nature, as some have sought to do;[5] indeed, historically, the modern concept of 'nature' would seem to have descended from *mana*, its wonder-working quality having been shed by the way.[6] But in the Polynesian *noa*, the non-sacred, common, or permitted,[7] we have the counterpart, as in the Latin *profanus*, of 'nature' so far as it stands not for mechanism but for routine. We must not, however, look for definiteness in primitive categories, since they are never subjected abstractly and as ideas to reflective examination, but merely embody such more or less arbitrary associations as custom suggests and sanctions.

3. Practical aspect.—Seeing, then, that the savage may be said to live out his ideas rather than to think them out, it is in the sphere of his actual practice as regulated by social use and wont that we are likely to meet with the clearest indications of his mental tendencies. Primitive supernaturalism will declare itself primarily in a group of traditional activities through which the appropriate feelings and thoughts find their satisfaction. The question, then, is how far there is a distinctive province of behaviour corresponding to the interest in the supernatural. Now, there can be no doubt that among some peoples of low culture the cleavage between the secular and the magico-religious sides of the social life is made 'as with a hatchet.' Thus we are told of the Central Australian:

> 'From the moment of his initiation . . . his life is sharply marked out into two parts. He has first of all what we may speak of as the ordinary life, common to all the men and women, and associated with the procuring of food and the performance of corrobborees, the peaceful monotony of this part of his life being broken every now and again by the excitement of a fight. On the other hand, he has what gradually becomes of greater and greater importance to him, and that is the portion of his life devoted to matters of a sacred or secret nature. As he grows older he takes an increasing share in these, until finally this side of his life occupies by far the greater part of his thoughts.'[1]

B. Malinowski, however, referring to this passage, raises a doubt whether such a bipartition of activities is a universal feature of primitive society. He instances Veddas and Melanesians, among whom religious and secular interests and pursuits seem to shade into each other without perceptible break.[2] But, when Durkheim states[3] that 'the division of things into sacred and profane lies at the base of all religious organization,' he can hardly be intending to affirm that a religious organization worthy of the name is to be found among all mankind. It is surely enough if the generalization hold good in the typical case. Moreover, this theory of the 'two worlds' of the sacred and the profane, though convenient in certain contexts—as, *e.g.*, to explain those 'rites of passage' whereby a man during initiation, or a woman at child-birth, enters a condition of *tabu* and passes out again into ordinary life[4]—need not be pressed too hard, seeing that sacredness is to some extent relative, so that, *e.g.*, a man may be *tabu* to strangers without being so to his friends.[5] All that need be assumed here is that certain activities tend to be organized about the interest in the supernatural as embodied in a specific tissue of feelings and beliefs. The magico-religious life is unlimited in its claim on human endeavour, and in its ulterior effects on human welfare may be well-nigh all-pervasive. But the mental attitude that it demands cannot be continuously maintained. Whenever the tension is relaxed, 'nature,' in the shape of the effortless rule of habit, is busy making good the strain.

LITERATURE.—See the works cited in the footnotes.

R. R. MARETT.

SUPERSTITION.—**I. Signification and use of the term.**—The word 'superstition' is used both in a concrete and in an abstract sense. We group together as superstitions a number of beliefs, habits, and fancies, tribal and individual, which we regard as not being founded on reasonable conceptions of the world and of human life, necessities, and obligations. The general or abstract term 'superstition' signifies the disposition to attribute occurrences to præternatural or occult influences, and to direct conduct with a view to avoiding mischief or obtaining advantages which such influences are supposed to produce. The precise connexion between the etymology of the word and its ordinary signification is not easy to trace. The prefix *super* seems to imply some excess, and this excess may generally be conceived as an exaggeration of a reasonable belief in some supernatural agents or agencies, with a readiness

1 *Journ. Rel. Psychol.*, July, 1912, pp. 257–304.
2 Cf. F. H. Bradley, *Appearance and Reality*, London, 1893, p. 453.
3 Cf. R. R. Marett, 'The *tabu-mana* Formula as a Minimum Definition of Religion,' in *ARW* xii. [1909] 186–194.
4 For examples see Marett, *The Threshold of Religion*², p. 85 f.
5 Cf. *GB*³, pt. i., *The Magic Art*, i. 51, 112, 220; A. O. Lovejoy, *Monist*, xvi. [1906] 381.
6 Cf. H. Hubert and M. Mauss, in *ASoc* vii. [1904] 72; Durkheim, p. 35.
7 See E. Tregear, *Maori-Polynesian Comparative Dictionary*, Wellington, N.Z., 1891, *s.v.*

1 Spencer-Gillen^b, p. 33.
2 *Rep. Brit. Assoc.* 1914, p. 534.
3 *ASoc* ii. [1899] 19.
4 Cf. A. van Gennep, *op. cit.*
5 *Ib.* p. 16.

to accept unverified statements as to spiritual or magical interference in the material world. The origin of the most potent and widely spread superstitions has already been discussed under various headings.[1] It seems therefore more suitable here to consider superstition as an abstract quality, and to regard it in its psychological and historical aspects.

Two points may be noted for the purpose of clearing the ground: (1) the intensely subjective way in which the word is commonly used. No man is ready to acknowledge himself as superstitious, but almost every one is ready to recognize superstition in another. We find that men of a particular race, culture, and tone of mind brand as superstitious the religious or ceremonial observances of an alien people, while charging such people with incredulity if they are unready to receive new doctrines equally superstitious from their own standpoint. 'What is religion to you is superstition to me,' and *vice versa*, is a tacit assumption against which we must be on our guard. (2) Superstition need not be in any way connected with mysticism (*q.v.*). True, the mystic who regards all things and persons as owing what reality they have to a divine and supernatural life or element is likely to have a strong desire to find traces of the spiritual and eternal manifested in or through the form of the material and temporal. But the reasonable mystic, by very reason of his belief in the spiritual nature of ultimate reality, is the less liable to give credence to fanciful and grotesque intimations from a spirit world. Plato, the greatest of mystics, was eminently sane and reasonable. If the same cannot be said of all the Neo-Platonists, the reason must be that some of them were less mystical because more material than he.[2] Some confusion, however, may arise from the circumstance that many minds (especially of a saintly or of a poetic order) attach a symbolic meaning to certain material phenomena or ceremonial acts without any excessive regard for their intrinsic value. Hence we have the interesting fact that, in the higher religions of an advanced race, we may have what seems to be identity in attachment to doctrine and ritual with far-reaching differences in fundamental religious conceptions. Hence the warnings of religious teachers, on the one hand against the sudden demolition of 'superstitions' which have, for the uneducated, been valuable from their association with religious thought and feeling, and on the other against the confusion of symbol and reality, which tends to materialize and crystallize popular religion.

The superstitious mind, then, is one that is not educated to discern the character of evidence, or that has not patience to suspend judgment in the presence of unfamiliar phenomena. If it is objected that some very powerful and (in some directions) well trained intellects have coincided with a superstitious bias, these exceptions would seem due to a want of mental balance.

2. Historical aspects.—Turning from the individual to society and to historical progress, we may say that, roughly speaking, superstition declines as the view of the universe becomes more scientific. True, the birth of many—perhaps of all—sciences is attended by crude hypotheses which lend themselves to strange vagaries of thought. This is specially evident in the pseudo-science of alchemy, whence emerged the science of chemistry.[3] Even the earliest efforts of Ionic thought were not without such vagaries, yet the Greek philosophers had in them the root of the matter—a whole-hearted desire after truth. Therefore they progressed, and their progress belonged to the Western world.

When, in May, 585 B.C., in the midst of a battle between Lydians and Medes, there occurred 'the first eclipse of which European science foretold when it should betide,' the date was to have 'a deeper interest for Europe than the warfare. . . . Thales of Miletus, the father of Greek, and thereby of European, philosophy and science, had studied astronomy in Egypt; and he was able to warn the Ionians that before such a year had passed—his lore could not tell the day or the hour—the sun would be darkened.'[4]

This does not, of course, imply that the Greeks had already become, or were ever to become, what we should call a scientific people. But to bring so uncanny an occurrence as a darkening of the sun within the range of calculable events was to cut the ground beneath many superstitions. Yet Greek religion and Greek life abounded with superstitions. The religion of the Olympians was bound up with beliefs about the gods which Plato would have excluded from his ideal city, and the old-world ritual which survived in popular ceremonies was yet more favourable to unreasonable fancies and actions. The Athenians were doubtless the most intellectual of the Greeks, yet their prosecutions for impiety show both a low standard of religious liberty and a high standard (if the expression may be used) of respect for ancestral religion. Anaxagoras, Pericles, Euripides, above all Socrates, suffered at the hands of their countrymen. True, their cause prevailed in so far that in the next century speculation was more free and scepticism had scope; and, after all, the moderation centred in the maxim μηδὲν ἄγαν seems to have checked any tendency to persecution like that of the Middle Ages and later. Nicias was, in spite of his popularity, blamed by posterity for delaying the retreat of the Athenians before Syracuse on account of an eclipse of the moon. But the point against him, most probably, was not that he was too ill-educated to know the cause of lunar eclipses (since most Athenians would then have been in his company), but that he preferred the almost certain event of annihilation for his army to the exceedingly doubtful risk of supernatural punishment if he neglected the state of the heavens.

Yet, by a kind of paradox, scepticism seems to have overshot the mark, and, by denying the possibility of all certainty, to have opened the way, for people who *must* believe something, to all manner of superstitious habits and practices.[1] The interchange of religious ideas, the foundation and migration of religious societies, and the general disintegration which followed the conquests of Alexander and the advance of Rome meant, to many individuals in many places, a remarkable development and enlightenment of the religious consciousness; but it also meant a recrudescence of Oriental and barbarous superstition. This is found even among the late philosophical sects, notably the Neo-Pythagorean.[2]

As might naturally be expected, in societies comprising men of culture considerably above the rank and file of their contemporaries, we have, from the ancient pagan world, emphatic protests against the mischief wrought by superstition. Chief among these is the great poem of Lucretius (*q.v.*), who sees in superstition, or in popular religion, the most potent source of human ill. The same missionary spirit pervades the treatise of Plutarch περὶ Δεισιδαιμονίας, in which he holds up to contempt the figure of the man who lives in perpetual fear of having, by some trivial action, offended supernatural powers. There is, however, this great difference between the two: that, whereas Lucretius would dispense with the gods altogether, Plutarch (*q.v.*) holds to a faith in the divine beneficence and to the propriety of observing ancestral rites. The most eloquent part of his essay is that in which he shows the absurdity of stigmatizing as blasphemous those who deny the existence of the gods, while tolerating those who spread evil notions as to their malignity and vindictiveness. The same contrast may be noticed in assailants of superstition at various periods: the uncompromising enthusiast would sweep away all religious beliefs and institutions, though he may, like Lucretius, entertain conceptions of the universe which may fairly be regarded as religious. The conservative reformer, however anxious to remove causes of distress and aberration due to mistaken theology, may cling to old habits of piety, and reinterpret ancient traditions in accordance with liberty of thought.

3. Superstition and Aberglaube.—It may be noted that the kinds of superstition opposed by moral reformers are generally those which arise from baseless terrors. There are, of course, other manifestations of the superstitious spirit of a comparatively innocuous kind, such as belief in fairies, superstitions concerning the weather, lucky and unlucky days, and the like. And there is a mass of what may be regarded as superstition about the accretions to almost every system of positive religion, which on the one hand changes it very

[1] See esp. artt. MAGIC, CHARMS AND AMULETS, DREAMS AND SLEEP, EVIL EYE, MYTHOLOGY, PRODIGIES AND PORTENTS.

[2] See art. NEO-PLATONISM.

[3] See M. M. Pattison Muir, *The Story of Alchemy and the Beginnings of Chemistry*, London, 1902, also artt. ALCHEMY.

[4] J. B. Bury, *A Hist. of Greece*, London, 1900, ch. vi., sect. 1.

[1] This 'overshooting of the mark' by the sceptics is suggested by E. Bevan, *Stoics and Sceptics*, London, 1913.

[2] See art. NEO-PYTHAGOREANISM.

conspicuously from its original form, and on the other hand may bring it within the reach of minds unaccustomed to deal with abstract ideas. These accretions are sometimes, in order to avoid the unpleasant connotation of 'superstition,' called by the German name of *Aberglaube*. They consist both of ritual and of dogma, and are hardly ever entirely to be distinguished from the necessary appurtenances of the religion with which they are associated.

The Middle Ages are generally regarded as pre-eminently a time of superstition. The judgment is probably justifiable, though there were as many hard-headed and constructive thinkers at most epochs of the Middle Ages as there have been earlier or later. But apart from the mixture of races and consequent multiplication of superstitions in the declining Empire, with the deficiency of mental culture in the leaders of the barbarian races, there was a great force arising to control speculation—that of ecclesiastical authority. This, however, must be considered on two sides. The worst kinds of superstitions, or at least the most conspicuous kinds, especially in Eastern Europe, were distinctly discouraged by the Church—soothsaying, necromancy, charms, and the like. And there can be little doubt that many of the heresies crushed out by the mediæval Church were accompanied by superstitious vagaries. Still, the fact is patent that the suppression of free thought, especially as directed to Church doctrine and ritual, must have tended to the growth of δεισιδαιμονία in Plutarch's sense. Of course, when we speak of the suppression of free thought, we do not necessarily mean that a very large number of persons suffered from not being allowed to think freely. Probably the number who thus suffered was comparatively very small. But many more must have lived in perpetual fear of the unseen. The terrors of the Judgment Day and of the world to come are very familiar objects of mediæval art, and it is difficult for us to see how far they were practically mitigated by the harmonious setting forth of the more comforting and spiritual elements in Christianity, with which they were, perhaps not quite consistently, associated.

The Renaissance and the Reformation are commonly regarded as having given the death-blow to superstition—so far, at least, as their influence extended. It is certain, however, that the indiscriminate cult of antiquity, which in some sections of society accompanied the Renaissance, contained or encouraged superstitious fancies and observances of a novel kind. And as to the Reformation even in Protestant countries, practically a good deal of *Aberglaube* formed part of the newly established doctrines and usages, and the sway of spiritual authority was by no means removed. The great movement towards mental and spiritual emancipation is generally taken as beginning in the 18th century.[1] It is to be noted that the battle waged on behalf of human reason was not confined to the world of thought and opinion. Political institutions, social divisions, industrial methods, and moral conventions were to be submitted to the test of right reason, and, if they failed, to be extirpated forthwith. The bitterness with which the contest was carried on, and which reached its culminating point in the excesses of the French Revolution, was partly due to the belief that superstitious practices had been maintained chiefly by those who profited by them—from the medicine-men of a savage tribe to the officers of an established church or a hereditary monarchy. Although there is, of course, some ground for such a supposition, as a partial explanation of the evil in question, its wholesale acceptance shows a very deficient comprehension of human nature. Without intelligible reasons, man is always desirous of knowing more than he can know about the spiritual world, and he will more readily submit to authority which has a traditional, if not actually a divine, sanction. And the exact nature of the government and institutions which right reason would commend has, of course, been very differently conceived by socialists or revolutionists of various types. Still, the general recognition that all beliefs and practices ought to have some rational justification was a great point gradually gained. It does not, of course, imply that nothing should be believed without strict logical proof, or that no institution should be maintained that does not evidently serve some useful object. But it does embody the Stoic principle that life should be according to nature and according to reason, and thus it tends to eliminate most of what is injurious either in superstitions with regard to religion or in tame acquiescence in existing governments.[1]

1 See artt. ENLIGHTENMENT, ENCYCLOPÆDISTS.

4. Influence of education.—The great agency making for the reduction of superstition during this century and the last is popular education. True, our elementary education can hardly as yet be called scientific, and what passes for scientific education may, after all, be superficial and narrow. But all sound teaching, at the present day, may be said to produce something like a scientific view of man and his environment—a view perfectly compatible with belief in the spiritual significance of life and even in a possible communion with non-material beings, but inconsistent with fanciful and trivial interpretations of natural phenomena as determined by præternatural agency.

If there should ever be a recrudescence of superstition in this generation or the next, it would probably be due, not to a defect in the scientific faculty, but to the expectations lately raised within the bounds of scientific investigation. Experts in psychology, especially those who have devoted themselves to what is technically called psychical research (*q.v.*), have, to many sane and scientific minds, proved the possibility of telepathy, thought-transference, and other processes which, fifty years ago, would certainly have been set down as superstitious. More than this, some persons of scientific mind and education believe that they have actually established and conducted a means of communication between living and dead.[2] When the persons engaged in these investigations are careful and scientific, we are inclined to accept their evidence, as we should on any other point of expert investigation. But in this field the 'media' used are of such uncertain character, the conditions and possibilities of communication so deeply veiled in obscurity, the desire to attain to fellowship with the departed so intense, that it is as well to approach all such problems with the most suspicious caution. There may be, as has often been said, a 'superstitious fear of superstition.' But, while suspending judgment on the result of the inquiries of experts, the non-expert may be in danger of falling into a superstitious habit of mind such as tends to upset entirely the mental balance.

LITERATURE.—For primitive superstitions see the works mentioned in the artt. here cited, esp. J. G. Frazer, *GB*³, London, 12 vols., 1911–15; E. B. Tylor, *PC*⁴, 2 vols., do. 1903. For the philosophy and history of the question see the various histories of philosophy and W. E. H. Lecky, *Hist. of Rationalism*, new ed., 2 vols., London, 1887; A. W. Benn, *Hist. of English Rationalism in the Nineteenth Century*, 2 vols., do. 1906; J. Masson, *Lucretius, Epicurean and Poet*, do. 1907; Plutarch, *Moralia*, including *de Superstitione*, tr. into very vigorous English by Philemon Holland, do. 1603; Matthew Arnold, *Literature and Dogma*, do. 1873, chs. on '*Aberglaube* invading' and '*Aberglaube* re-invading.'

ALICE GARDNER.

1 See art. RATIONALISM. 2 See art. SPIRITISM.

SUPRALAPSARIANISM.—The term supralapsarianism is used in Calvinistic theology, in contrast with sub- or infra-lapsarianism, to denote a view of the divine decrees in which, for the manifestation of His glory, God is held to destine a certain portion of mankind to eternal life, and another portion to destruction, regarding both simply as creatures, and antecedently to any consideration of the Fall and sin. It is not meant that this purpose is actually carried out without regard to character or condition; but, in the order of decrees, it is first determined who are to be embraced in the one class, and who in the other; then the means are appointed—including creation, the Fall, sin, redemption—by which the end in each case is to be attained. So harsh a view of the divine procedure has always been in the highest degree repellent to Christian minds; accordingly, the great majority of Calvinists have shrunk from it, and contented themselves with the milder sublapsarian view, which affirms an election of God from the mass of mankind, regarded as already fallen.

On its historical side, the question is raised whether Calvin himself is to be classed as a supralapsarian or a sublapsarian. Some incline to the former view, but the truth seems to be that, when Calvin wrote, the question had not distinctly emerged, and the emphasis which he continually lays on election as a choice of some from a sinful mass, and on reprobation as grounded on the sinner's own evil, fairly warrants the more usual opinion that his doctrine inclined more to sublapsarianism.[1] On the other hand, Beza, Calvin's successor, Gomar, the colleague and opponent of Arminius in Holland, Twisse, the prolocutor of the Westminster Assembly, and a few others,[2] were conspicuous for their advocacy of supralapsarianism; and the Remonstrants, in the Arminian controversy, naturally sought to fasten this view on all Calvinists. It is really, however, an extreme opinion, and the bulk of Calvinists, as already said, have wisely kept themselves aloof from it. Turretin, *e.g.*, ably states and defends the sublapsarian position in his *Institutio*.[3] The Synod of Dort, in its decision, framed its canons on sublapsarian lines.[4] The *Westminster Confession* leans, in certain of its clauses, to the stronger view of Archbishop Ussher (author of the Irish Articles), and of a few members of the Assembly, but the tone of the debates in that body sufficiently shows that the prevailing opinion was sublapsarian, and the Confessional statement, taken as a whole, is of this character. The stronger view has, indeed, no symbolical sanction.

Cunningham, in his discussion of the subject,[5] claims that the controversy is one 'of no great intrinsic importance,' but this can hardly be allowed.

'A doctrine of this kind, which bids us think of beings not yet conceived of as even created (therefore only as *possibles*)—not to say as sinful—set apart for eternal blessedness or misery, and of the fall and redemption as simply means for effecting that purpose, is one which no plea of logical consistency will ever get the human mind to accept, and which is bound to provoke revolt against the whole system with which it is associated.'[6]

It cannot even be conceded, though it has often been contended, that this *is* the most logical form of the predestinarian doctrine. The end, it is argued, comes necessarily first in order of thought; then the means are devised which are to accomplish it. In the case of moral destiny, we are disposed to say, this is the precise inversion of the fact. There can be no legitimate consigning of a moral being to wrath, save as he is in some way viewed as deserving of that wrath; even in order of thought, therefore, the consideration of moral state must precede the sentence of rejection. If the reply is made that the sin itself is viewed in Calvinism as foreordained, this is doubtless true, but only in the sense in which every event in life is foreordained, viz. by God's decreeing to admit it into His providential plan and to overrule it for the ends of His wisdom. It is a totally different thing to affirm that sin is ordained as a means to the destruction of a being already foreordained to wrath prior to consideration of his sin.

It need only be added that the whole subject assumes a different aspect when fuller justice is done to the Scriptural idea of election as aiming, not at exclusion, but at subsequent wider inclusion.[1]

LITERATURE.—P. Schaff, *A Hist. of the Creeds of Christendom*, London, 1877, pp. 453–455; W. Cunningham, *The Reformers and the Theology of the Reformation*, Edinburgh, 1862; C. Hodge, *Systematic Theology*, London and Edinburgh, 1872–73, ii. 316–320.

JAMES ORR.

SURINAM.—See GUIANA.

SURVIVALS.—See RELIGION, vol. x. p. 664, § 4.

ŚVETĀMBARAS.—**I. Origin and history.**—'We,' said a Śvetāmbara once to the present writer, 'are the Catholics amongst the Jains; the Digambaras represent the Puritans'; and that does roughly sum up the difference between the two great sects of the Jains.[2]

Even during the lifetime of Mahāvīra[3] two parties probably existed, for the great Jain hero seems to have formed his community by uniting two different orders of mendicants, the Sthavira kalpa and the Jina kalpa. The Sthavira kalpa wore clothes, but one section of the Jina kalpa did not, going about like Mahāvīra himself, clad only in the four quarters of the sky. This outward and visible difference was symbolic of the differing types of men in the community, and only a strong statesman could have held the two parties together; under any great strain the cleavage was bound to become permanent.

According to the Sthānakavāsī Śvetāmbara tradition, the first crisis arose through a great famine that occurred in the reign of Chandragupta (? 310 B.C.), when 12,000 Jain monks went to S. India under Bhadrabāhu in search of food. These, being the young and vigorous members of the order, were able to carry out their rule in its entirety and so went unclad, whilst the other members of the community, who remained at home under Sthūlabhadra, amounting also, the legend says, to 12,000, were allowed (owing perhaps to age and infirmity) to wear clothes, no matter to which of the two parties they had originally belonged. When Bhadrabāhu returned home after the famine, although he became once more head of an undivided community, he was never able to insist on nakedness as a rule of even a section of the community. The second cause of schism also arose during this famine—at least according to the Sthānakavāsī Śvetāmbara tradition; for it was then, during his leader Bhadrabāhu's absence, that the second in command, Sthūlabhadra, called a council at Pāṭaliputra to collect the sacred books. The council were able to produce only eleven *Aṅga*, but Sthūlabhadra himself supplied the missing twelfth *Aṅga*. Bhadrabāhu on his return was annoyed to find that this council had been held in his absence, and not unnaturally, though irritably, declared that the twelfth *Aṅga* was hopelessly lost. It only remained now for a leader to be found for the malcontents to hive off, and (if the legend be true) irritability had much to do with that leader's decisive action. About forty years after the great famine (according to Tapāgachchha Śvetāmbara tradition, about A.D. 142; according to Sthānakavāsī, A.D. 83; and according to Hoernle, A.D. 79 or 80) the reins of government fell into the weaker hands of a man called Vajrasena, and the community finally divided. The Śvetāmbara quote

[1] See art. CALVINISM.
[2] See Cunningham, *The Reformers and the Theology of the Reformation*, p. 366 f.
[3] Loc. iv. qu. ix.
[4] Cf. Schaff, *Hist. of the Creeds*, i. 455.
[5] *Hist. Theology*, Edinburgh, 1862, ii. 435, *Reformers and Theol. of Reformation*, p. 358.
[6] Orr, *The Progress of Dogma*, London, 1901, p. 296.

[1] See artt. CALVINISM, ELECTION, PREDESTINATION.
[2] See artt. DIGAMBARAS, JAINISM.
[3] See art. ĀJĪVIKAS, § 2 f.

the following legend to account for the actual cleavage:

A monk named Śivabhūti had been given a most beautiful blanket by the king in whose service he had been at the time of his initiation. His spiritual preceptor warned him that it was becoming a snare to him and advised him to give it away; this he refused to do, so his preceptor took the extreme step of tearing up the blanket in its owner's absence. Śivabhūti, when he discovered what had happened, was so angry that he declared that, if he could not have the one possession which he valued, he would keep nothing at all, but would wander in entire nakedness like the Lord Mahāvīra himself; and he then and there started a new sect, that of the naked Digambara.

This very human legend which the Śvetāmbara (the 'White-clothed') tell of their unclothed rivals not only accounts for their nakedness, but also goes on to explain another difference between the two sects; for, when Śivabhūti's sister wanted to join his order, seeing that it was impracticable for a woman to go about nude, he roundly told her that it was impossible for a woman to become a nun, or to obtain *mokṣa* (*q.v.*) without rebirth as a man, and thus laid down for all time a distinctive tenet of the Digambara. Important as these legends are, it must be remembered that they are quoted only as illustrative of the Jain point of view, for their confirmation is sadly to seek, and the legends connecting Chandragupta with the faith are essentially open to suspicion.

2. Distinctive tenets and practices.—We are on firmer ground when we notice the main differences between the two sects at the present day. We are already prepared for the fact that the Śvetāmbara list of sacred books is not accepted by the Digambara, and that, since they hold that no woman can attain *mokṣa*, the Digambara will not admit the Śvetāmbara tradition that Mallinātha (the nineteenth *tīrthaṅkara*) was a woman. But the two sects differ very considerably about the life-story of Mahāvīra.

The Śvetāmbara say that their great saint married and enjoyed life to the full before entering an order, and that, even when he at last decided to do so, he waited till his parents' death, and until he had gained his brother's consent, lest he should grieve any one before receiving initiation, which he obtained in his thirtieth year. The more austere Digambara tradition, however, is that their founder never married; and, having no hesitation about hurting any one's feelings, renounced the world at the mature age of eight. Even the prenatal stories differ, for the Śvetāmbara believe that Mahāvīra's mother had fourteen wonderful dreams; the Digambara say that she had sixteen; while the legend of the removal of the embryo of Mahāvīra from Devānandā to Triśalā is a Śvetāmbara one.

The lists of the heads of the community since Śivabhūti of course differ also. The Śvetāmbara generally arrange their philosophy in nine categories; the Digambara arrange very much the same philosophy under seven heads. One point of divergence on which they lay great stress is that, according to the Śvetāmbara, a *tīrthaṅkara* needs food to support him until he dies; while the Digambara believe that, once a *tīrthaṅkara* has attained omniscience, he has no further need of meals.

There are also differences in actual practice. A Śvetāmbara ascetic may keep a loin-cloth, a shoulder-cloth, and a blanket to wear. Indeed, including these and his brush, mouth-cloth, and wooden vessels, he is allowed to retain fourteen possessions in this world, whereas a Digambara is absolutely nude and, though provided with a brush and peacock's feathers, has to live entirely in the jungle. The Śvetāmbara laymen complain that their ascetics interfere too much in their conferences; this complaint is, of course, never brought against a Digambara ascetic, whose lack of clothing interns him for life in the wilderness.

There are also different rules about begging for the ascetics of the two orders, and the Digambara ascetics have no *upāsarā*. Again, the Śvetāmbara idols have glass eyes inserted in the marble, wear a loin-cloth, and are bedecked with jewels, whereas the austere Digambara idols are nude and are represented as being dead to the world, with eyes cast down. There is naturally therefore a difference in the installation ceremonies of their idols. The ordinary worship differs also. The Śvetāmbara, when performing the eightfold worship, offer flowers and fresh fruit to their idols, and so on great festivals do the Visapanthī Digambara; but the Terāpanthī Digambara never offer flowers or fresh fruit; in their stead they use cloves, dry coco-nut, sugar, and rice.[1]

There is another very interesting difference. A Digambara Jain has no private idol in his own house, but, if a Śvetāmbara is a wealthy man and lives far from a temple, he may have his own private chapel. This chapel is separate from the house and can be entered only by persons in a state of ceremonial purity. In the chapel, if he can afford it, he may have a *pratimā* (an image of any one of the twenty-four *tīrthaṅkara* that an astrologer selects for him), or he may have a *siddha chakra* (a tray on which are depicted the leading points of the Jain faith).[1] The householder offers the eightfold worship to the *pratimā*, but only washes and wipes the *siddha chakra* and marks it with sandalwood paste. An instructed Śvetāmbara would never ask a boon even of the idol in his own house: he would only stir himself up to future efforts by meditating on it. But if, as often happens, an uninstructed Śvetāmbara does ask a gift, his prayer would be answered not by the *tīrthaṅkara* (who as a matter of fact does not even hear it) but by the *yakṣa* in attendance on the *tīrthaṅkara*.

3. Śvetāmbara sects.—The main division of Śvetāmbara Jains is into Sthānakavāsī and Derāvāsī. The Sthānakavāsī are a non-idol-worshipping sect, which arose about A.D. 1474.[2] Excepting on the crucial point of idol-worship, they do not differ much from other Śvetāmbara Jains.

At the present time the chief sects among idol-worshipping (Derāvāsī) Śvetāmbara are the Tapāgachchha (whose ascetics use red alms-bowls, and whose laymen in their devotions first confess their sins of walking and later their sins of trading), the Kharataragachchha (whose ascetics use black alms-bowls, and whose laity first confess their sins of trading and later their sins of walking), and the Añchalagachchha and the Pāyachandagachchha, whose divergences are very slight.

It must be remembered that these are only spiritual distinctions and do not interfere with the freedom of marriage between different sects. The chief castes among the Jains are Osavāla, Poravāda, Śrīmālī and Śrī Śrīmāla, which are each divided into two sections, Dasā and Vīsā. It is impossible for members of these different castes to intermarry: thus an Osavāla Kharatara could marry an Osavāla Sthānakavāsī, for, though the sect differs, the caste is the same, but a Dasā Osavāla could never marry a Vīsā Osavāla, and still less could any Poravāda marry any Osavāla. It is interesting to notice, however, that any Jain could dine with any other Jain, Śvetāmbara or Digambara, whether Osavāla or Śrīmālī; but they would not interdine with any Brāhman convert to Jainism.

LITERATURE.—Through the kindness of Jain friends the writer was given an opportunity of translating this art. to the leading Tapāgachchha Śvetāmbara Sādhu in Rājkot in his *apāsaro*, when the principal Sthānakavāsī Jain *paṇḍits* were also present; the art. has thus had the advantage of criticisms and suggestions from both parties at first hand. See also A. F. R. Hoernle, *Annual Address to the Asiatic Society of Bengal*, in *JASB*, Calcutta, 1898; Mrs. Sinclair Stevenson, *Notes on Modern Jainism*, Oxford, 1910, and *The Heart of Jainism*, do. 1915.

MARGARET STEVENSON.

[1] Cf. art. WORSHIP (Jain).

[2] Stevenson, *The Heart of Jainism*, p. 87.

SWAHILIS.—See ZANZIBAR.

SWAN-MAIDENS.

—The beautiful and poetic myth of swan-maidens is of early origin and, in varying forms, of very wide diffusion. The central idea of the myth is that certain beings, half-mortal, half-supernatural, have the power of metamorphosis into bird-form; connected with this are two secondary ideas: (1) that this power is dependent on the possession of a magic attribute, which was generally a bodily covering, such as a feather coat, robe, or veil, but sometimes merely a ring or chain; (2) that either this being, when in human form, or her captor is subject to a tabu of some kind. There are so many variations on these themes that it is impossible to do more than refer briefly to some of the most significant versions.

1. In Oriental folk-lore. — Oriental folk-lore furnishes many instances of bird-maiden stories. In Indian tradition we find the very early myth of Urvaṣī embedded like a jewel in the dull ritual of the *Śatapatha-Brāhmaṇa*.

The *apsara*, or nymph, Urvaṣī loves one of the lunar race of kings, Purūravas; in wedding him she stipulates that she must never look upon him naked. By a trick played by the *gandharvas*, supernatural beings who desire the return of their former playmate, the promise is broken, and Urvaṣī vanishes. Purūravas, seeking her, finds her and her companions swimming on a lotus-lake in the shape of water-birds. They 'appear to him,' *i.e.* assume human form, but in response to his pleading Urvaṣī replies: 'I have passed away like the first of dawns. . . . I am like the wind, difficult to catch.'[1] Finally, however, she relents, and the couple are re-united.

In the *Vikramurvaṣī* of the poet Kālidāsa, a drama based upon this story, the bird-myth has almost disappeared, except for Urvaṣī's power of flying and for the constant references to swans throughout act iv. Her change into human form depends merely upon the laying aside of a veil, in itself probably a stage convention for invisibility; the marital tabu, which Lang[2] characterizes as a relic of 'a traditional Aryan law of nuptial etiquette,' assumes a quite different form.[3]

The myth re-appears in one of the finest tales of the *Thousand and One Nights*, that of Hasan of Bassorah.

Hasan is enjoying the hospitality of a family of princesses; when obliged to leave him, they enjoin him not to open a certain door. He disobeys, and finds a fair pavilion and a bathing-pool, to which come flying from the desert ten birds, one among which was pre-eminent for beauty. Each bird, as it alighted, 'rent open its neck-skin with its claws, and issued out of it, and lo, it was but a garment of feathers.' After their departure Hasan, who has become deeply enamoured of the fairest bird-maiden, confesses his disobedience to his hostess, and is told that this damsel is 'the daughter of the sovran of the Jans. He hath an army of women, smiters with swords, and lungers with lances, . . . and the plumed skins wherewith they fly are the handiwork of enchanters.' Hasan is advised to steal the feather dress and never again to let it come into the owner's hands; he does so, but after three years the wife by a ruse secures the dress, buttons it on, and flies away. Hasan tracks his wife to the islands of Wāk-Wāk, inhabited by the warrior women, and recovers her.[4]

The story of Janshāh[5] is a slighter tale that begins similarly; but the bird-maidens are only three in number, and are 'as doves, eagle-sized.' The husband's device to secure the feather coat is to place it in a chest, leaden-bound, which is built into the foundations of the palace; but in vain, for the lady traces it by scent and digs it out.[6]

The Wāk-Wāk islands of the former tale have been identified with various Melanesian islands;[7] it is not surprising, therefore, to find the tale of Hasan re-appearing in the Celebes in a modern form, which Tylor quotes in connexion with the heaven-plant myth.[1] Tatar versions of the myth are signalized as being the only ones to represent the bird-maiden as a malignant being, half-vampire, half-fury;[2] in the Tatar poem quoted by J. G. Frazer[3] to illustrate the external soul belief, the hero wrestles with the evil swan-woman for 'moons and years.'

2. In classical tradition. — Classical tradition does not seem to have preserved any swan-maiden tale in a complete form, but that the main idea was a familiar one is evident from the Cycnus myths, the bird-transformation of the comrades of Diomedes, the story of Leda, and the symbolic connexion of swans with Apollo, with the Muses, and with Aphrodite.[4] Modern Greek folk-lore represents the Nereids as flying maidens, similar in many points to swan-maidens.[5]

3. Slavic.—Slavic folk-lore bears frequent testimony to the myth. The South Slavs were naturally more influenced by late Greek and by Oriental tradition, and the Bulgarian *samodivas*, and the Serbian *vilas*, like the Greek Nereids, resemble the swan-maidens; *e.g.*, the *vilas* are associated with water and have the power of flying.[6]

The Polish fairy-tale of the prince and the twelve geese-princesses shows that the myth in its simplest form was known to the Western Slavs.[7] The most important Russian example is the tale of 'Sweet Mikāilo Ivānovitch the Rover' and Mārya the white swan; this begins in fairly conventional style, although without the feather dress, but later it diverges considerably, for Mārya dies, is magically revived, and finally forsakes her husband for another love.[8]

4. Celtic.—Old Celtic tradition has two beautiful and elaborate swan-maiden tales, as well as an episode in the story of Etain, wife of Eochaid, who is carried off by the hero-god Mider in the form of a swan.[9]

The story of the 'Children of Lêr,' one of 'the three most sorrowful tales of Erinn,' is an example, with Christian 'overlay,' of that variant of the myth in which the swan shape is enforced by malignant magic. The four royal children, metamorphosed for 900 years, retain their powers of human reasoning and speech, and have the gift of singing 'plaintive music at which the men of the world would sleep, and there shall be no music of the world its equal.'[10]

This power of song is turned to account in the Christian episode which concludes the tale.[11] 'The Dream of Oengus' conforms more closely to the regular swan-maiden type, so much so that J. A. MacCulloch[12] dismisses it as of no mythological or religious value; its artistic value, however, is very great.

The god Oengus is smitten with love for a dream-maiden, the original of whom proves to be Caer, a princess who spends every alternate year in the form of a swan. Oengus, having once seen her in mortal form, succeeds in discerning her in swan-guise from among her 150 companions 'with their silvery chains and golden caps around their heads.' He woos and wins her, and flies off with her, himself also metamorphosed, and their singing is of such beauty as to lull to sleep all its hearers for three days and three nights.[13]

5. Teutonic.—The Teutonic races bear the distinction of having developed the swan-maiden myth most elaborately, and of having enriched it by connecting it with other supernatural ideas. Traces of the symbolic importance of swans are found in the primitive myths of the life and death

---

1 This formula, 'difficult to catch,' recurs in the Welsh tale of the Van Pool, quoted by Hartland, *Science of Fairy Tales*, p. 275 ff.

2 *Custom and Myth*, p. 76.

3 Cf. *Śatapatha-Brāhmaṇa*, XI. v. 1, tr. J. Eggeling, *SBE* xliv. [1900] 68–74; *Vikramurvaṣī*, tr. E. B. Cowell, Hertford, 1851.

4 R. F. Burton, *A Plain and Literal Translation of the Arabian Nights*, Benares, 1885, viii. 7–143.

5 *Ib.* v. 329–381.

6 Contrast with this Hartland's idea (p. 308) that the swan-maiden must always employ an intermediary to obtain her robe.

7 E. W. Lane, *The Thousand and One Nights*, London, 1838–41, iii. 523, note 32.

1 *Researches into the Early History of Mankind*³, London, 1878, p. 355 f.

2 A. Schiefner, *Heldensagen der minussinischen Tataren*, St. Petersburg, 1859, p. 201.

3 *GB*³, pt. vii., *Balder the Beautiful*, London, 1913, ii. 144.

4 W. Smith, *Classical Dictionary*, *s.vv.* 'Cycnus,' 'Diomedes'; Baring-Gould, *Curious Myths of the Middle Ages*², pp. 569–572.

5 B. Schmidt, *Griechische Märchen*, Leipzig, 1877, p. 133.

6 F. S. Krauss, *Tausend Sagen und Märchen der Südslaven*, i., Leipzig, 1914, *passim*.

7 A. H. Wratislaw, *Sixty Folk-tales from exclusively Slavonic Sources*, London, 1889, p. 111 f.

8 Isabel F. Hapgood, *The Epic Songs of Russia*, New York and London, 1886, pp. 214–231.

9 H. d'Arbois de Jubainville, *Irish Mythological Cycle*, Dublin, 1903, p. 182.

10 With this sleep-bringing power may be compared the trolls' swans that sing the enchanted prince asleep in the Icelandic fairy tale (J. C. Poestion, *Isländische Märchen*, Vienna, 1884, no. vii. pp. 49–54).

11 *Atlantis*, iv. [1863] 113 ff., tr. E. O'Curry.

12 *The Religion of the Ancient Celts*, Edinburgh, 1911, p. 82

13 *RCel* iii. [1876–78] 347 ff., tr. Edward Müller.

both of the world and of individuals; thus the two swans, the progenitors of all the swan-kind, that float on the Urtharbrunnr of the old Norse cosmogony,[1] may be contrasted with the swan that lived, according to Finnish myth, on the river of Tuoni or Death.[2] In later folk-tale we find a swan living on a hidden lake, which maintains the world in equipoise by carrying a ring in its beak; when it drops it, the end of the world will come.[3] Popular saying still remembers the bird as one of omen and augury;[4] in Rügen, swans, not storks, are the bringers of new-born children,[5] while, on the other hand, the sight of a swan in flight may betoken death,[6] and swans are often leaders of the spirit-host.[7] The ideas of animal shape-changing and of the external soul favoured the development of the swan-maiden myth in folk-lore. The Scandinavian North, as one of the chief haunts in Europe of the wild swan, showed itself especially alive to the beauty and significance inherent in the myth; Grimm,[8] influenced perhaps by the legends of the 'goose-footed woman,' 'la reine pédauque,' and 'Berthe aux grands pieds,' thinks that the goose supplanted the swan in legend, but this seems hardly proved. The power of flying and the possession of a feather coat were attributes of many gods in the Norse pantheon. The swan-maiden of the Scandinavians appears to have been merged into the Norns on the one hand and the Valkyries on the other, who themselves often have traits in common. The connexion of swans with augury and with the Urtharbrunnr, the home of the Norns, prepares us for the former aspect; the power of 'riding through the air' possessed by the Valkyries prepares us for the latter; and we have already seen the bird-maidens as warrior-maidens in the story of Hasan of Bassorah.

The swan-maidens of the *Nibelungenlied* are Norns also; as swan-maidens they appear to Hagene 'like birds,' and they fall into his power when he takes their garments, but they are also 'wise women,' and one gives him prophetic warning.[9] The maidens of the *Völundarkvitha*[10] are conventional swan-maidens with their 'swan-coats,' but they are also Valkyries, for they appear helmeted. Again, the hero Helgi is helped in battle by Kāra, a rebirth of the Valkyrie Svava, who hovers singing above him.[11] Fridlevus II., king of Denmark, is given helpful warning before a battle by the song of three swans.[12] After this it is not surprising to find also traces of a connexion between swan-maidens and the *fylgja*, or female guardian-spirit; thus the *fylgja* of a beautiful woman appears as a swan.[13]

6. The swan-knight.—The swan-knight seems to have been monopolized and localized by Teutonic mythology, although there are traces of the idea in classical legend, as in the Cycnus myth already mentioned,[14] and although the Teutonic myth appears to have fused with Celtic Arthurian legend. The popularity of the charming tale of Helyas, knight of the swan, and supposed ancestor of Godfrey of Bouillon, is attested by the numerous versions of it in various languages.

In the popular German fairy-tale the enchanted brothers owe their restoration to human form, not to the prowess of their brother, as in Helyas, but to the devotion of a sister. Of the other swan-knights of Brabant, the link with the Graal legends has brought Lohengrin, son of Parsival, most into prominence and popularity. The fact that the swan-hero arrives from an unknown land in a skiff, and departs in the same way, has led Grimm[1] to trace the beginning of the Teutonic swan-knight myth to Scyld and Sceáf, semi-divine founders of the Danish race, of whom a similar tale is told, although the connexion with the bird-myth is very obscure.

7. Interpretations.—The interpretations of the swan-myths have been various; the earlier school of mythologists saw in them nature-myths, the swan-maiden being the white cloud, her captor the storm-spirit.[2] Others have explained the swan-maiden, who is subject to mysterious prohibitions and who in the end is almost always lost to her captor, and the swan-knight, who must not reveal his name or place of origin, as denizens of the world of the dead or of the islands of the blessed.[3] A more prosaic view takes into account merely the totemistic aspect which the myth shows in common with all animal shape-changing tales, points to the swan-maidens and swan-knights as founders of clans, and compares them with such figures as Mélusine of Lusignan.[4] The most modern theory brings the tabu into prominence, to the overshadowing of other aspects, and adduces the wide evidence now forthcoming of marital tabus among primitive peoples;[5] thus a curious piece of corroborative evidence on the symbolic connexion between swans and women has been found in the rites enforced on secluded girls among American Indian tribes.[6] Fortunately for the appeal of the myth, none of these theories has power to detract from, but all serve only to enhance, its elusive and poetic beauty.

LITERATURE.—J. Grimm, *Teutonic Mythology*, tr. J. S. Stallybrass, London, 1882–88, i. 426–430; W. Mannhardt, *Germanische Mythen*, Berlin, 1858, p. 340 ff.; E. H. Meyer, *Germanische Mythologie*, do. 1891, chs. vi. and vii.; J. Fiske, art. in *Atlantic Monthly*, xxviii. [1871] 129–144; S. Baring-Gould, *Curious Myths of the Middle Ages*², London, 1869, chs. xxi. and xxii.; F. Liebrecht, *Zur Volkskunde*, Heilbronn, 1879, pp. 54–65, 239–250; A. Lang, *Custom and Myth*, London, 1884, ch. iv.; E. S. Hartland, *The Science of Fairy Tales*, do. 1891, chs. x.–xii.; P. D. Chantepie de la Saussaye, *Religion of the Teutons*, tr. B. J. Vos, Boston, U.S.A., 1902, ch. xv.; W. Müller, 'Die Sage vom Schwanritter,' in *Germania*, ed. F. Pfeiffer, i. [1856] 418–440.

M. E. SEATON.

SWĀT or **UDYĀNA.**—This is a famous principality in Independent Eastern Afghanistan, between the latter country and Kashmīr, to the south of Chitral and the Pamirs. It receives the name of Swāt from the river of that name (the Svastu, in Sanskrit), which joins the Kabul branch of the Indus above Peshāwar. Its literary name of Udyāna (in Prakrit, Ujjāna) is ascribed to its 'garden or park-like' appearance; for it is an exceptionally richly cultivated and well-watered beautiful Alpine valley. Through this Indo-Scythian country Alexander descended for his invasion of India, crossing, it is generally supposed, the Malakand Pass, which is on the main route to the Indian plains; but Swāt is best known for its fame as an ancient centre of Buddhism. It is still thickly covered with the ruins of Buddhist monuments and temples, richly decorated with some of the finest sculptures of the Græco-Buddhist or so-called Gandhāra (*q.v.*) type of art. These sculptured friezes and terra-cottas date chiefly between the 2nd and 5th centuries A.D.; and a collection of several hundreds was made by the present writer during the Chitral expedition of 1895 and is now preserved in the Calcutta and Peshāwar museums.[7] The Chinese Buddhist pilgrim Fa Hian, who visited the country *c.* A.D.

1 Snorri, *Edda*, ed. E. Wilken, Paderborn, 1877, p. 24.
2 *Kalevala*, rune 14.
3 F. Gottschalck, *Sagen und Volksmärchen der Deutschen*, Halle, 1814, p. 227.
4 Cf. Grimm, i. 437, note 1.
5 E. M. Arndt, *Schriften für und an seine lieben Deutschen*, Leipzig, 1845, iii. 547; cf. in Chinese legend the fostering of the hero Hou Chi by a wild swan (C. F. R. Allen, *The Book of Chinese Ballads*, London, 1891, p. 385 f.).
6 F. F. A. Kuhn, *Märkische Sagen und Märchen*, Berlin, 1843, no. 68.
7 W. Müller, 'Die Sage vom Schwanritter,' in *Germania*, ed. F. Pfeiffer, i. 421.
8 P. 1098.
9 *Nibelungenlied*, Aventiure xxv.
10 Stanzas 1–3.
11 *Fornaldar Sögur*, ii. 375 f.
12 Saxo Grammaticus, *Hist. Danica*, vi. 178.
13 M. Bartels, 'Isländischer Brauch und Volksglaube in Bezug auf die Nachkommenschaft,' *ZE* xxxii. [1900] 70.
14 Cf. *Æneid*, x. 185–197.

1 368–370.
2 E. H. Meyer, *Germ. Mythologie*, pp. 90, 125.
3 W. Müller, *op. cit.*; Liebrecht, *Zur Volkskunde*, pp. 54–65.
4 Cf. art. ANIMALS, § 26.
5 Hartland, pp. 304–322.
6 *GB*³, pt. vii., *Balder the Beautiful*, i. 47–50, 90–92.
7 L. A. Waddell, *Report on Archæological Tour in Swat*, Calcutta, 1895, reprint in *Asiat. Quarterly Rev.*, Oct. 1895, and 'Newly Excavated Greco-Buddhist Sculptures from Swāt Valley,' *Trans. of the Oriental Congress*, 1897, sect. i. 245–247.

400, says: 'The religion of Buddha is very flourishing . . . in all there are 500 monasteries, they belong to the Little Vehicle (*Hīna-yāna*) without exception.'[1] But, when Hiuen Tsiang visited the land *c.* A.D. 630, he found that nearly all the convents, some 1400 in number with formerly 18,000 priests, were 'waste and desolate.'[2] It is a striking commentary on Fa Hian's reference to the exclusive prevalence of the 'Little Vehicle' form of Buddhism that as a fact all the sculptural remains are of the 'Great Vehicle' (*Mahā-yāna*).

It was regarded by Fa Hian as the most northerly province of India, and the food and clothing of the people were the same as in India, and this is still the case—the people dress in white. The dimensions of the Swāt country, as described by Hiuen Tsiang at 5000 *li* (about 833 miles) in circuit, show that it in those days evidently included, in addition to the valley of Swāt, also the Chitral and Dard adjoining countries and the mountains on the right bank of the Indus, even beyond the great bend of the river to the south.

It was the native country of Padma-saṁbhava (*q.v.*), the founder of Lāmaism in Tibet; and the notorious prevalence of Śaivite magical rites in the manuals ascribed to that saint in the Tibetan is somewhat in keeping with the old reputation of this country for sorcery. Hiuen Tsiang, in his visit to this land about a century before Padmasaṁbhava's period, writes: 'The science of magical formulas is become a regular professional business with them (the men of Swāt or Udyāna).'[3]

The belief in serpent-dragons of rivers and springs was especially prevalent here. It was at the source of the Swāt river that was located the legendary water-dragon or serpent Apalāla, whose conversion by Buddha is a favourite motive in Buddhist art, both north and south. Hiuen Tsiang refers especially to the 'white water' issuing from this spring, as also does al-Bīrunī about the 11th cent. A.D.,[4] which would doubtless be snow-water rather than glacial, yet it suggests that the river-name Svastu may have originally been derived from *sveta*, or *sweta*, 'white,' which approximates the modern name of that river, 'Swāt.' Confirmation of this ancient water-serpent worship was found by the present writer in a Kharoṣṭhī inscription upon a great boulder at a spring of which the record reads from a rubbing taken by the present writer: 'By the son of Dati, the Thera (Buddhist monk) Nora, a tank was caused to be made for the worship of All Serpents (in) the year 113.'[5] This date, from the palæographic details, is placed about 65 B.C.

LITERATURE.—References are cited in the article.

L. A. WADDELL.

1 Ch. viii.
2 *Si-yu-ki*, tr. S. Beal, London, 1884, i. 120.
3 S. Julien's tr. of *Hiouen Thsang*, Paris, 1853, confirmed by T. Watters, *On Yuan Chwang's Travels in India*, London, 1904–05, i. 226.
4 *Alberuni's India*, ed. E. C. Sachau, London, 1910, ii. 182.
5 Cf. J. G. Bühler, *Vienna Oriental Journ.* x. [1896] 55 f.

SWAZIS.—See BANTU AND S. AFRICA.

SWEARING.—See OATH, PROFANITY.

SWEAT, SWEAT-HOUSE.

—Sweat, a colourless fluid containing about 2 per cent of solid matter, is a secretion of the sebaceous glands. Its chief function is to regulate the heat discharge of the human body. It is connected with some curious and interesting religious and magical customs in various parts of the world.

1. Sweat in magic.—Primitive man regards sweat, like blood, saliva, hair, and nail-parings, as a medium both for setting sorcery in motion against an enemy and for working the more harmless forms of magic. Codrington says that among the Melanesians the belief prevails that a leaf with which a man has wiped the perspiration from his face may be employed to work mischief against him.[1] A like belief is found among the Negroes of N. America.[2] Some of the natives of N.E. New Guinea take elaborate precautions to prevent a drop of their sweat from being made use of by a sorcerer; on leaving a camping-place, they stab the ground all over with their spears.[3] Some of the most curious uses to which this exudation of the human body has been put are illustrated by a group of customs connected with love magic.

'A cake, an apple, or a sweetmeat impregnated with the sweat of the giver is a powerful philtre throughout the greater part of northern and central Europe, from Cairn Gorm to the Carpathians.'[4] A Hungarian girl steals meal and honey at Christmas-time, bakes a cake, takes it to bed with her for one night, and then bestows it on a youth whom she wishes to fall in love with her.[5] W. R. Paton says that in three Νομοκάνονες (confessors' manuals) of the Orthodox Church, which are, he believes, less than three centuries old, 'women are accused of rubbing dough on their bodies, and giving it to eat to men in whom they wish to arouse satanic love.'[6]

The victim of such love magic can, however, have recourse to a counter-charm of the same character. 'It was narrated that if a man who, under the influence of a philtre, was forced to love against his will, would put on a new pair of shoes, and wear them out by walking in them, and then drink wine out of the right shoe, where it could mingle with the perspiration already there, he would promptly be cured of his love, and hate take its place.'[7]

A similar idea underlies the superstition prevalent among the Negroes and Indians of N. America, and also in Belgium, that, if the owner of a dog wishes to make the animal faithful to him, he should give it some bread which has been soaked in his sweat.[8] In the island of Tutu, in the Torres Straits, men drink the sweat of renowned warriors to acquire courage.[9]

The mythology of ancient Egypt seems to have ascribed a sacramental virtue to the sweat of Osiris. In the pyramid libation-formulæ the libations appear to be his sweat; and in the ritual of Amon the incense appears to be crystallized drops of it.[10] A song quoted by A. Erman speaks of the Nile as the sweat of Osiris' hands.[11] The Negroes of Jamaica identified a man's luck with the perspiration of his hands, and believed that, if the latter were wiped away, the former would disappear.[12]

2. The sweat-house.—The ceremonial use of vapour baths is a custom of great antiquity and wide geographical distribution, being found both in N. America and in N. Europe. In the former continent it was probably known to every tribe north of Mexico, though along the north-west coast it has been superseded by sea-bathing.

'The type of the ordinary sweat-house seems to have been everywhere the same. Willow rods or other plant stems were stuck into the ground and bent or fastened with withes into a hemispherical or oblong frame-work, which generally was large enough to accommodate several persons. A hole was dug conveniently near the door into which stones, usually heated outside, were dropped by means of forked sticks. These were sprinkled with water to generate steam. A temporary cover of blankets or skins made the enclosure tight.'[13]

In each tribe there were certain prescribed rules for the construction of the sweat-house. In some cases, however, the communal ceremonial chamber was used for this purpose. Sometimes it was used as a kind of men's club like the Pueblo *kiva*,

1 R. H. Codrington, *The Melanesians*, Oxford, 1891, p. 203.
2 E. S. Hartland, *LP* ii. 74.
3 J. G. Frazer, *GB*3, pt. i., *The Magic Art*, London, 1911, i. 213.
4 *LP* ii. 123. 5 *Ib.* 6 *FL* v. [1894] 277.
7 J. G. Bourke, *Scatalogic Rites of all Nations*, Washington, 1891, p. 349, quoting S. A. Flemming, *De Remediis*, p. 19.
8 *LP* ii. 124.
9 A. C. Haddon, in *Reports of the Cambridge Anthropological Expedition to Torres Straits*, Cambridge, 1901–12, v. 301.
10 A. M. Blackman, *ZÄ* l. [1912] 69 ff.
11 *A Handbook of Egyptian Religion*, Eng. tr., London, 1907, p. 81.
12 *FL* xv. [1904] 209.
13 *Bull. 30 BE* [1910], pt. 2, p. 660.

women being permitted to enter it for certain ceremonial purposes, but not for sweating. Among certain tribes on the Pacific coast women were not even permitted to gather wood for the holy fire to be kindled in the sweat-house. In California, where sweating always had a religious significance, some of the tribes used the sweat-house as a sleeping-place for adult males. Half-an-hour was usually spent in the sweat-house, and then the bather plunged into a stream, if there was one at hand.

'Among the Eskimo, hot air was used in place of steam and in Zuñi, and probably in the Pueblos generally, hot stones near the body furnished the heat.'[1]

Some tribes lit the fire in the sweat-house in autumn and kept it alive till spring. Bancroft says of the Northern Californians:

'A fire is built in the centre [of the sweat-house] in early fall and kept alive till the following spring, as much attention being given to it as ever was paid to the sacred fires of Hestia.'[2]

Sweating in N. America was practised for three purposes: (1) *religious*—such as purification and the propitiation of spirits, preparation for war, and on arrival at puberty, when it was usually attended by scarification and mutilation; (2) *therapeutic*—prescribed by a shaman, who stood outside and invoked the spirits believed to cause the disease (among the Plains Indians shamans who officiated at these ceremonies had usually to pass through the sweat-house themselves for purposes of purification); (3) *social and hygienic*—a number of persons would enter a sweat-house for the purpose of enjoying the luxury of a bath (among certain tribes this became an almost daily practice, and was perhaps a degeneration).

The sweat-bath is also used by the Eskimos of Bering Strait, among whom the men and boys indulge in it about once a week, or once in every ten days during winter, but with this people it does not appear to possess a religious significance.[3]

Among many tribes the sweat-house had its own guardian spirit or *manitu* (*q.v.*).

Among the Lillooets of British Columbia 'men who had the spirit of the sweat-house for their guardian spirit made a sweat-house of elk-skin supported on wands, and inside it they placed four large stones, which were heated to make the steam for the bath.'[4]

It was believed among the Algonquins that a man when in the sweat-house might acquire *manitu*. A Fox Indian, relating his experiences during a sweat-bath, once said:

'Often one will cut one's self only through the skin. It is done to open up many passages for the manitou to pass into the body. The manitou comes from the place of its abode in the stone. It comes roused by the heat of the fire, and proceeds out of the stone when the water is sprinkled on it. It comes out in the steam, and in the steam it enters the body wherever it finds entrance. It moves up and down, and all over and inside the body, driving out everything that inflicts pain. Before the manitou returns to the stone, it imparts some of its nature to the body. That is why one feels so well after having been in the sweat-lodge.'[5]

Among the Thompson Indians of British Columbia, when a boy reached the age of puberty, he went through certain ceremonies to obtain a guardian spirit.

In the sweat-bath 'he prayed to the spirit of sweat-bathing under the title of "Sweat-bathing Grandfather Chief," begging that he might be strong, brave and agile, lucky, rich, a good hunter, a skilful fisherman, and so forth.'[6]

The Ojibwa (*q.v.*), an Algonquin tribe, had a secret society called the 'Midē'wiwin,' or society of the shamans. For four days before initiation into it a candidate would purify himself in the sweat-bath.

'In all ceremonies, prophetical or medico-magical, great reliance is placed on the vapor-bath. . . . It is entered with sacred feelings, and is deemed a great means of purification. Secret arts are here often disclosed between *Medais* [shamans] of high power, which could not be imparted in other places, or positions, believed to be less subject to the influence of sanctifying power.'[1]

1 *Bull. 30 BE* [1910], pt. 2, p. 661. 2 *NR* i. 356.
3 E. W. Nelson, in *18 RBEW* [1899], pt. i. p. 287.
4 J. G. Frazer, *Totemism and Exogamy*, London, 1910, iii. 420; cf. p. 414.
5 W. Jones, 'The Algonquin *Manitou*,' in *JAFL* xviii. [1905] 184.
Frazer, *Totemism and Exogamy*, iii. 414.

When we turn to the Old World, we find a striking resemblance to the American customs in Herodotus's description[2] of the use of the sweat-bath among the Scythians as a means of purification, after mourning. The construction of the sweat-house was, however, simpler than in America. Three sticks were stuck in the ground, leaning towards each other, and around them pieces of felt were tightly stretched. A dish containing red-hot stones was placed inside. Hemp seed was then thrown on to the stones. A close parallel to this custom was found among the Delaware Indians, and is described by Tylor:

'At their festival in honour of the Fire-god with his twelve attendant manitus, inside of the house a small oven-hut was set up, consisting of twelve poles tied together at the top and covered with blankets, high enough for a man to stand nearly upright within it. After the feast this oven was heated with twelve red-hot stones, and twelve men crept inside. An old man threw twelve pipefuls of tobacco on these stones, and when the patients had borne to the utmost the heat and suffocating smoke, they were taken out, generally falling in a swoon.'[3]

The sweat-bath, as used among the peasantry of Great Russia, possesses the nature of a ceremonial purification even at the present day. It is taken weekly on Saturday afternoons, and all kinds of pollution must be avoided till after the service on Sunday morning.[4] Among the northern Finns, for the *savna*, or sweat-bath, a log-hut is used. The bath is frequently taken *en famille*.[5] With this people, however, and also with the Lapps, who make use of the sweat-bath on Saturdays before putting on their clean clothes, it appears to be an entirely secular institution.[6] Vapour baths were in use among the Celtic tribes, and the sweat-house was in general use in Ireland down to the 18th,[7] and even survived into the 19th century. It was of beehive shape and was covered with clay. It was especially resorted to as a cure for rheumatism.[8]

Vapour baths were used by the Greeks and Romans; details for their construction are given by Vitruvius.[9] The sweat-bath, which in England has been miscalled the 'Turkish bath,' being in reality of Russian origin, was introduced into this country by David Urquhart, M.P. (1805–77).

3. Origin and distribution.—The presence of the sweat-bath both in N. Europe and in N. America at once raises the question whether it has originated independently in each of these continents, or whether it has reached them from a common centre of distribution. It is essentially a northern institution, and one belonging to the Mongoloid branch of the human family. M. A. Czaplicka suggests that the Slavs of Great Russia probably borrowed it from the Finns of the Middle Volga. There are many unsolved problems connected with the ethnology of the Scythians, but there appears to have existed among them a Finno-Ugrian element from which most likely the sweat-hut was derived. We should naturally expect to find the sweat-hut in N. Asia, whose inhabitants form an ethnological bridge uniting the Mongoloid peoples of Europe and N. America. We are,

1 H. R. Schoolcraft, *Indian Tribes of the United States*, Philadelphia, 1853–56, v. 423 f., quoted by Frazer, *Totemism and Exogamy*, iii. 486.
2 iv. 73–75. 3 *PC*³ ii. 417 f.
4 D. Mackenzie Wallace, *Russia*, rev. ed., London, 1905, i. 41.
5 S. Tromholt, *Under the Rays of the Aurora Borealis*, ed. C. Siewers, London, 1885, ii. 102.
6 P. B. du Chaillu, *Land of the Midnight Sun*, London, 1881, ii. 206.
7 David Urquhart, *Manual of the Turkish Bath*, London, 1865, p. 62.
8 See art. DISEASE AND MEDICINE (Celtic), vol. iv. p. 749ᵃ.
9 *De Architectura*, v. 10, 11.

however, disappointed in this expectation, since among the aborigines of N. Siberia it is not indigenous, but is in use only among those tribes which, like the Yakuts, have derived many elements in their culture from the Russians. We seem, then, to be led to the conclusion that the sweat-bath originated independently in both Europe and America, or else that it originated in a more southerly latitude than N. Siberia. The vapour-bath appears to be one of those institutions which were originally indulged in for hygienic purposes, but afterwards, owing to their beneficial results, came to be connected in the mind of primitive man with mysterious unseen powers, and hence were used in connexion with religious rites. Now, however, the sweat-bath seems to be regaining its former secular character.

LITERATURE.—This is given in the footnotes.

H. J. T. JOHNSON.

SWEATING.—See ECONOMICS.

SWEDENBORG. — **1. Life and works.** — Emanuel Swedenborg was born in Stockholm on 29th Jan. 1688. He was the second son of Jesper Swedberg, bishop of Skara and previously professor in the University of Upsala. The family was ennobled by Queen Ulrica Eleonora in 1719, when the patronymic of Swedberg was changed into the name of Swedenborg.

Little is known of Swedenborg's childhood. After completing his studies at Upsala in 1709, he started on an extended foreign tour, and he was in England in 1711, 'studying Newton daily and very anxious to see and hear him.'[1] We gather from one of his letters to his brother-in-law, Dr. Ericus Benzelius, that mathematics and astronomy absorbed at that time most of his interest. He wrote of his conversations with Flamsteed, Halley, and other well-known men of science, but his copious references to the works of Dryden, Spenser, Milton, Shakespeare, and others show that his scientific studies did not prevent him from becoming acquainted with the best English literature. Swedenborg spent nearly two years in London and Oxford. He afterwards visited Holland, France, and Germany, working all the time at a number of inventions. One of them was 'the plan of a certain ship which with its men was to go under the surface of the sea and do great damage to the fleet of the enemy.'[2] Another of his inventions was a magazine air-gun to discharge 60 or 70 shots in succession without reloading. He also devised a flying machine, but the great Swedish engineer, Christopher Polhem, expressed the opinion that, with respect to flying by artificial means, it was about the same thing as trying to make a *perpetuum mobile* or to make gold!

In 1716 Swedenborg was appointed by King Charles XII. extraordinary assessor at the Royal Board of Mines, an appointment which caused him to decline the offer of a professorship of astronomy in the University of Upsala. As the eldest son of his family, Swedenborg had a seat in the House of Nobles of the Swedish Parliament, but his interest in science, always greater than in politics, led him in 1721 to go abroad to study the mines and manufactures of other lands. It was during this journey that he published a treatise on physics and chemistry, at Amsterdam, a second edition of his *New Method of finding the Longitude*, at Leipzig, and *Miscellaneous Observations on Geology and Mineralogy*. But the work which won for Swedenborg a European reputation was his *Opera Philosophica et Mineralia* in 3 vols., with numerous copperplates, published at Dresden and Leipzig in 1734 at the expense of his patron, the Duke of Brunswick. In the first volume of that work, the *Principia*, Swedenborg gives an elaborate theory of the origin of the visible universe and propounds his nebular hypothesis. This theory has been often attributed to Kant and Laplace as the original authors, but Swedenborg's theory appeared in the *Principia* in 1734, while Kant's *Natural History of the Heavens* was published in 1755, and Laplace's *Système du Monde* in 1796, as has been shown by Arrhenius in his introduction to the Latin reprint of Swedenborg's *Cosmologia*. Soon after appeared the *Economy of the Animal Kingdom* (1740-41) and *The Animal Kingdom* (1744-45), in which are given the results of Swedenborg's extensive labours in anatomy and physiology. In 1745 his *Worship and Love of God* was published. This work marks the surprising transition of its author's mind from plain scientific and philosophical reasoning to what is generally considered a form of religious mysticism, but what the author himself would have described as spiritual perception. A great change had come over him. His mind, as he himself says, had been opened to enable him to hear and see things of the other life.

Swedenborg gives the year 1743 as the date of the opening of his spiritual sight, but it was in April 1745, according to his own statement, that he was fully admitted to intercourse with angels and spirits, not by any process analogous to what is usually termed spiritism (*q.v.*), but by speaking with them directly, while remaining normally conscious of everything about him on earth. He was quite aware of the scepticism with which such a mental state would be received, when made known to the world, and he anticipated it in his first theological work in these words: 'I am well aware that many persons will insist that it is impossible for any one to converse with spirits and angels during his life-time in the body; many will say that such intercourse must be mere fancy; some, that I have invented such relations in order to gain credit; whilst others will make other objections. For all these, however, I care not, since I have seen, heard and felt.'[1]

In 1747 Swedenborg resigned his position on the Royal Board of Mines and devoted himself to the new work to which he believed himself to have been divinely called. His vast work, the *Arcana Cœlestia*, was completed in 8 vols. in 1756. Then followed, among others, *The Earths in the Universe* (1758), *The New Jerusalem and its Heavenly Doctrine* (1758), *Heaven and Hell* (1758), perhaps the best known of all his books, *On the Intercourse between the Soul and the Body* (1769), *Divine Love and Wisdom* (1763), *Divine Providence* (1764), *The Apocalypse Revealed* (1766), *Conjugal Love* (1768), the first theological work to which Swedenborg's name is attached, and lastly *The True Christian Religion* (1771).

It is interesting, and in a sense very significant, to find that, while Swedenborg was fully occupied with the publication of so many theological works, he yet found time and freedom of mind to attend to mundane affairs. In 1763 he wrote several papers on scientific subjects in the *Transactions of the Royal Academy of Sciences of Stockholm*, and in 1766 he republished at Amsterdam his *New Method of finding the Longitude of Places on Land and Sea*. Count Höpken has stated that 'the most solid and best written memoirs at the Diet of 1761 on matters of finance were presented by Swedenborg.'[2]

The last political document bearing his signature is an address to the Diet entitled 'Frank Views concerning the Maintenance of the Country and the Preservation of its Freedom,' in which he utters a warning against the revival of an absolute monarchy.

On Christmas Eve, 1771, while in London, he had a stroke of apoplexy and was visited by the minister of the Swedish Church, E. Ferelius. He never completely recovered, and he died on 29th March 1772 in the eighty-fifth year of his age at his residence in Great Bath Street, Coldbath Fields, London. He was buried in the Swedish Church. In 1908 the Swedish Government, having made arrangements for the transfer of Swedenborg's remains to his native country, sent the frigate *Fulgia* to England to bring them home, and in due time they were deposited in the Cathedral of Upsala, close to the resting-place of Linnæus.

2. Doctrines.—The philosophical and theological doctrines professed by Swedenborg may be conveniently considered under three heads—God, the world, and man.

(*a*) *God.*—He has nowhere given any formal arguments to prove the existence of God. He starts at once from the conviction that 'all the principles of human reason unite and, as it were, concentre in this, that there is one God, the Creator of the Universe.' Two principles constitute the essence of God—love and wisdom. His infinity comprehends both immensity and eternity, His immensity having relation to space and His eternity to time. But God with respect to the created world is 'in space without space, and in time without time.' God is life, and all life is from Him. Life itself is uncreatable, but it can be communicated, lent, as it were, to finite beings. God is one absolutely in essence and in person. The Lord Jesus Christ is God, indeed, but He is not another divine person. He is Jahweh manifested in the finite garment of humanity. Yet in Him is a divine Trinity of love, wisdom, and power —the three essentials of His divine nature. Thus the Lord alone ought to be loved supremely and worshipped as our Heavenly Father. To see Him is to see the Father (Jn 12^{45} 14^{9}).

In a sense Swedenborg admits that God, in His essence, is unknowable, but he believes that there is a form of anthropomorphism which is not only permissible in speaking of God, but necessary, because it conveys a profound truth about Him. He asserts that our thinking in human symbols would be baseless and misleading if God Himself were not divinely human. Hence his startling postulate, 'God is a man.' Of course, he does not

[1] R. L. Tafel, *Documents concerning the Life and Character of Swedenborg*, 3 vols., London, 1875-77, i. 200-344 (Swedenborg's first letter from England to Benzelius, Oct. 1710).

[2] *Ib.* i. (Correspondence with Benzelius).

[1] *Arcana Cœlestia*, § 68.

[2] Tafel, ii. 408.

mean that God is a man in a physical sense. His real meaning is simply that, if we think at all about God, we must do so by means of symbols derived from our highest human experience. But, if these symbols do not correspond, in an infinite Reality, to what they represent, as finite symbols, to us, then all these conceptions are not merely imperfect and inadequate, but actually false. We are then obliged to conclude that there is a fundamental antinomy in the constitution of the human mind, so that the Power from whom it proceeds has so constructed it that it must think about that Power, and think about it falsely. Surely, Swedenborg considers, what the human mind *must* think should be, at least, an approximate symbol or representation of a fact. If we doubt this, the grounds upon which we believe any philosophical, ethical, or spiritual truth are undermined.

Thus, to think of God as a divine man would simply mean, for Swedenborg, to think of Him as being infinite love and wisdom, as He is apprehended by us by means of symbols derived from the highest of human faculties, the intellect and the will—those faculties by which we are made 'in the image of God.' But Swedenborg seems also to have discerned some profound connexion between this conception of God as a divine man in His essential nature and the rational interpretation of a possible incarnation in time. In reading Swedenborg it must always be remembered that there is an idealism, quite his own, at the basis of his philosophical views and consequently of his theology. This enables one to understand much that lies hidden behind his realistic language when he deals with spiritual matters for which our human vocabularies have only weak and inadequate expressions.

(*b*) *The world.*—This should be particularly remembered in his treatment of the creation of the world. Swedenborg has attempted to correlate two apparently irreconcilable ideas—the idea of a personal God distinct from the universe, and the idea of an immanent Creator. He has done it by means of his doctrine of 'discrete degrees.' He holds that there are substances of many orders composing the universe. The primary, self-existent substance is the infinite God from whom all finite substances originate. But those substances are related to each other in an order constituted by degrees named 'discrete degrees' in distinction from 'continuous degrees,' because they are plans of existence entirely separate from each other and incapable of being resolved one into another. A continuous degree is merely a variation of being or quality on its own plane, as from heavier to lighter, or from denser to rarer. It is only a question of more or less. Discrete degrees, on the other hand, are never of the same forms or qualities of being, and, moreover, they involve the relation of cause and effect. Hence Swedenborg says: 'Nothing, so far as I am aware, has hitherto been known of discrete degrees but only of continuous degrees; yet without a knowledge of both kinds of degrees nothing of cause can be truly known,' for 'seeing from effects alone is seeing from fallacies.'[1] He means that fallacies arise, not from a failure to distinguish between cause and effect, as, *e.g.*, between matter and spirit, but from the fact of regarding them as differing by continuous degrees only and not by discrete degrees. For thus cause is never lifted above the plane of effect, nor spirit above the plane of matter.

It is maintained therefore that in everything of which anything can be predicated there are what are called end, cause, and effect, and these three are to each other according to discrete degrees. In creation the natural or material world is the effect, of which the spiritual world is the cause, and God is the end. The first act of creation, not in time but in order, is the putting forth by the Divine of a finite emanation of love and wisdom from Himself. This is conceived as a spiritual sun of incomparable splendour, a manifestation so intense that the finite mind could not bear its ardour, were it not tempered by intermediate stages. Thus, successive discrete degrees, separated not in space but in the quality of their spiritual constitution, produce the higher and the lower heavens; other discrete degrees subsist in the angelic forms according to their receptibility of love and wisdom.

[1] *Divine Love and Wisdom*, no. 187 f.

Similarly, the affections and thoughts which constitute the life of men are not, as it seems to us, self-generated, but pass into their minds out of the spiritual world, in a clearer or more obscure manner, always according to discrete degrees and in the order of cause and effect. In the world of matter a different law operates. Matter is derived not directly from spirit, but from the natural sun, which, according to Swedenborg, is not only the centre and support of our solar system, but also the proximate cause of its existence. From the activity of this primal sun are ultimately produced, by discrete degrees, the atmospheres and matter itself out of which the physical world is formed. The material substances, conceived as inert in themselves, are nevertheless capable of being acted upon by spiritual forces. But there is nothing of God in them as the ultimate of creation, since their life has ended in no-life, and love and wisdom have ended in forms of motion. Of course, this does not mean that God is not present in this ultimate of creation.

This doctrine is intended to exclude the incomprehensible idea of a creation *ex nihilo*, whilst it is meant also to provide against a pantheistic interpretation of the universe. It inevitably presents the difficulties which are inseparable from any theory of emanation.

(*c*) *Man.* — The theology of Swedenborg, as it deals with man, his nature, and his destiny, cannot be understood apart from his view (or, as he would insist, apart from the doctrine that he was divinely commissioned to make known to the modern world) of the real meaning of God's Word as we have it in the letter of Holy Scripture. More than 150 years ago Swedenborg had foreseen the difficulties and objections which criticism might bring forward as an argument against a belief in a divine revelation. 'It is in the mouth of all,' he says, 'that the Word is from God, is divinely inspired and therefore holy. But yet it has been unknown hitherto where within it its Divinity resides. The man who worships Nature instead of God may easily fall into error concerning the Word, and say within himself when he is reading it: "What is this? Is this divine? Can God who has infinite wisdom speak thus?"'[1] Yet Swedenborg never lost his faith in a divine revelation, and one of the principal objects of his theology is to show that the difficulties which create so serious a stumbling-block in many minds are due to the fact that they are looking in the Bible for what its letter does not and cannot explicitly manifest. He affirms that the Word contains throughout a spiritual meaning which alone gives the true and full sense of God's revelation to man.

Philo, Origen, Clement of Alexandria, and others have attempted to discover a spiritual sense in the Bible, but Swedenborg's conception proceeds on entirely different lines. For him the Word is the divine truth itself as it exists in God. It is the very form of God, and the medium of communication and conjunction with Him for the

[1] *True Christian Religion*, no. 189.

angels in the heavens and for men upon earth. But truth in this divine form is utterly incomprehensible to any finite mind. To render it at least partly intelligible, it must descend through the discrete degrees already described, and assume successively lower and lower forms of expression adapted to the comprehension of the various grades of finite intelligence. On earth it presents itself to us as the letter of our Bible, or rather as the original texts from which that letter has come to us.

How then are those texts written? They are written in pure 'correspondences,' *i.e.* in symbols derived from nature. Every natural object is conceived to be the effect, and therefore the expression, of spiritual causes. Those effects 'correspond' to those causes; hence their capacity, when properly understood, to reveal the spiritual meaning contained in them.

The first result of this principle is that man is thus enabled to know the true canon of the sacred Scriptures. Those books which are so written as to present a correspondential spiritual meaning are really 'the Word.' The other books possess devotional and even doctrinal value, but they are not 'the Word.' Guided by this fact, Swedenborg declares that the only books of the Word in the Bible are, in the OT, the Pentateuch, Joshua, Judges, 1 and 2 Samuel, 1 and 2 Kings, the Psalms, and the Prophets from Isaiah to Malachi; in the NT, the four Gospels and Revelation. The Epistles form therefore no part of what Swedenborg strictly calls 'the Word.' But he valued them highly, and he frequently quotes them.

In the letter, as we have it, Swedenborg recognizes a human element manifested in the language and feelings of the writers of the various books of the Bible; it is only the spiritual sense that is entirely and solely divine. Hence many of the difficulties raised by the higher criticism would be no difficulties for him; *e.g.*, instead of a creation in six days in the book of Genesis, he reads there the earliest condition of man and the gradual development of his psychological constitution; his growth in a knowledge of good and truth, of love and faith, and of divine things; and finally his introduction to a celestial perception of divine truth itself. It is a conception of the regeneration of man, called to reach his spiritual destiny through knowledge, trial, faith, and love, and Swedenborg sees that such a conception has a sublime meaning for us which it could not have had for the men who lived when the letter was written. It would have been an unintelligible revelation for most of them. Therefore the full meaning of the letter as contained in the spiritual sense was not given to them. There is, according to Swedenborg, a grave spiritual danger in the premature disclosure to any mind of divine Truth.[1]

But what is man? He is, says Swedenborg, made to be at the same time in the spiritual world and in the natural world. He is not life, but a recipient of life from God. And God grants man a sense that the life which he feels within himself is his own, in order that he may live as of himself. In every man's soul there is an inmost or supreme degree into which the divine of the Lord proximately flows; hence it is that man can receive intelligence and wisdom and speak from reason, and from this also comes the fact that his soul is endowed with immortality.

The will rather than the understanding constitutes the man. Swedenborg rejects the idea of angels having been created as such to people the heavens. All spirits, he believes, whether in heaven or in hell, are from the human race. He also holds that there is no personal Devil or Satan, but that that name signifies the whole society of evil spirits.

[1] See *Arc. Cœlest.* no. 3398.

The life of man cannot be changed after death, for the spirit of man is such as his love is, and infernal love cannot be changed into heavenly love, 'because they are opposite.'

The problem of evil, as presented by Swedenborg, is explained by the freedom with which God has endowed man, and it is because God 'who changeth not' will not withdraw that gift that man's love remains what it was even after death. If he has deliberately made evil his good and good his evil, then he is his own hell, and does not desire heaven. He could find no ease there, and would long for his congenial surroundings and associates. He is not sent to hell; he goes there of himself, and would be happy there, if an evil soul could find permanent happiness anywhere. But he inevitably meets with sufferings and punishments, inflicted not by God or His agents, but chiefly by the evil spirits his associates. What happens under our eyes here upon earth continues in hell. For evil breeds evil always and everywhere. This conception is sad, but certainly drawn from life.

Are then those sufferings eternal? It is difficult to interpret definitely the teaching of Swedenborg on that point. How far 'those sufferings may be mitigated,' says Howard Spalding, 'we are not told, but a careful study of all that Swedenborg has said on the subject suggests that they may be so greatly modified as to cease to be acutely felt.'[1] It is remarkable that, according to Swedenborg, there is no absolute destruction of evil even in heaven, for nothing which has formed part of the spiritual nature of man can ever be annihilated. Spirits therefore—yea, angelic spirits—carry with them into heaven the perverted organic forms in which their evils resided. They are even permitted to experience from time to time a sense of their evils, but not uselessly, for by those alternations of state spirits are kept in continual spiritual progress. Thus the regeneration of man, begun on earth, continues to eternity.

Of heaven we are told that God Himself is heaven, and that His presence to each human spirit brings heaven into him, but always in a degree which depends on a certain faculty of reception acquired on earth by man's conscientious endeavour to make what he truly believes the rule of his life.[2]

There has been a tendency, more or less defined, to class Swedenborg among the mystics, but this seems to be due to an imperfect understanding of his system. His conception of life in heaven should suffice to show how little he has in common with mysticism past or present.

The fulfilment of God's purpose in creating the world is a fundamental doctrine in Swedenborg's theology. That purpose, we are told, was, by making man in His own image and endowing him with the faculties of freedom and rationality, to prepare him for that conjunction with God which constitutes the angelic heaven. In this sense, the creation means infinite love seeking by love to cause love to arise freely between the Creator and His rational creature. But the misuse of rationality and freedom has led to evil being chosen and loved instead of good; hence sin, whose effect is the weakening of true freedom, and the obscuring of that interior light within us which is rationality. Then it is that the love which had created man has also come to save him. By His incarnation the Lord did not come to reconcile His Father

[1] *The Kingdom of Heaven as seen by Swedenborg*, p. 4 f.

[2] For full details see especially Swedenborg's *Heaven and Hell*.

to man, for God in Christ, as Swedenborg says, is the one only God who is love itself and does not need to be reconciled to His creature. It is man who needs to be reconciled to God. The Lord came and, as to His human nature, was born, lived, suffered, and died 'for us,' not 'instead of us.' He came to enable man to do that which, through sin, he had almost lost all power of doing, namely, to shun evil and to do the Lord's will in a life of righteousness and true holiness. Moreover, God 'became flesh,' not only to effect this work of redemption, but also that He might visibly manifest His infinite love for man, and thereby give to him for ever a definite object of intelligent faith, worship, and love. Man is said to be saved by the blood of Christ, in this sense, that His blood is the symbol of divine truth, and the shedding of His blood is the symbol of the imparting of His spirit of truth, the Holy Spirit. The Atonement, for Swedenborg, is thus really an at-one-ment, the reconciliation of man to God by the love and power of God. It was accomplished by the Lord taking upon Himself man's nature, enslaved by sin, from the Blessed Virgin Mary, sustaining in His own person the assaults and temptations of the powers of darkness, and gradually subduing them. For this work the Lord laid down His life, *i.e.* the life in Him of all that was not in perfect agreement with the infinite perfections of His indwelling divinity. When this was done, 'consummated,' the Lord Jesus Christ was no longer, even as to His human nature, the Son of Mary. He was the 'only begotten Son of God,' the perfect manifestation of the infinite, invisible Father. This process, called glorification, was completed after His resurrection, when the Lord 'put off' from the infirm human nature all its hereditary tendencies to evil and sin, and 'put on' from the Father the divine humanity subsisting in the essential divinity within Him. This is the supreme type of man's own regeneration by which, having put off hereditary tendencies to evil and his actual sins, he puts on from the Lord, in the degree that he has thus put off evil, a new regenerated and spiritual humanity, a spiritual mind. No real regeneration can be attained except in accordance with the principle that a 'saving faith' is 'a faith which worketh by love.' Salvation by 'faith alone' is rejected and condemned by Swedenborg in innumerable passages in his works.

It is important in connexion with this subject to understand his idea of 'the Church.' The essential Church for him is constituted by a genuine love of goodness and truth and by the spiritual relation established with the Lord in the minds of men. The true Church is therefore invisible, but, so far as it is a true Church, it can never pass away. This, however, does not exclude the possibility of the disclosure by the Lord of further truths called for by new conditions in the world of human thought and experience, and needed to establish a higher level of spiritual life. Nor does it exclude the possibility of the loss or the corruption of truths previously held, rendering necessary the institution of a specific 'New Church' in order to restore what has been lost, and to incorporate new truths which the Church in the past was not ready to receive. The assertion, therefore, made by the disciples of Swedenborg that a 'New Church' has been instituted, involves, as they would insist, no disparagement of the former Christian Church 'so far as it is really the Lord's.' The members of the 'New Church' at the present time consider it an entire misconception to imagine that Swedenborg is the founder of a 'New Church.' He himself always repudiated any such pretension. He considered himself a mere instrument through whom new truths needed in the Church were communicated to the world. His chief point always is, however, that 'the Church is one thing and religion is another.' The Church is called a Church from doctrine; religion is called religion from a life according to doctrine. Hence his well-known saying: 'All religion is related to life, and the life of religion is to do Good.'

LITERATURE.—Benjamin Worcester, *The Life and Mission of Emanuel Swedenborg*[6], Boston, 1907; George Trobridge, *A Life of Emanuel Swedenborg: with a popular Exposition of his Philosophical and Theological Teachings*, London, 1912; John Howard Spalding, *The Kingdom of Heaven as seen by Swedenborg*, do. 1916; Samuel M. Warren, *A Compendium of the Theological Writings of Emanuel Swedenborg*, do. 1896 (very useful to obtain a first general idea of Swedenborg's voluminous works); *A Dictionary of Correspondences, etc., extracted from the Writings of Emanuel Swedenborg*, Boston, 1910; Frank Sewall, *The New Metaphysics*, London, 1888, *Swedenborg and Modern Idealism: a Retrospect of Philosophy from Kant to the Present Time*, do. 1902; Theophilus Parsons, *Deus-Homo*, do. 1871; Edward Madeley, *The Science of Correspondences elucidated*, new and enlarged ed., do. 1902; *Transactions of the International Swedenborg Congress*, do. 1910.

L. B. DE BEAUMONT.

SWINE.—The swine plays a prominent part in many ancient and modern religions. The word 'pig' is unlucky to the Scottish fisherman, and on hearing it he will feel for the nails in his boots and mutter 'Cauld iron.'[1] The inhabitants of certain villages on the north-east coast of Scotland consider the words 'sow,' 'pig,' and 'swine' very unlucky; should any one be so unwise as to utter these words while the line is being baited, the line will surely be lost. The Galelareese, having noticed that, whilst men suffer from itch, caused by treading on the fallen fruit of the *aren* palm-tree, the wild boar, which is fond of the fruit and runs freely among it, is not liable to such a disease, argue that the fruit treats the pig as a real friend, and, if one by grunting can impress the fruit that he is a pig, it will treat him in the same way.[2] The pig was offered by the Romans and Greeks as an expiatory sacrifice. Cato advises that, before thinning a grove, the Roman farmer should offer a pig to the god or goddess of the place.[3] The grain distributed as prizes in the Eleusinian games in Greece was grown on the Rarian plain near Eleusis; this plain was so sacred that no dead body was allowed to touch it, and, whenever a defilement occurred, a pig was offered as a sacrifice. The Caribs abstained from pig's flesh because, like most primitive races, they believed that the physical and mental qualities of the human being depend largely upon the food which he eats; therefore, if they were to eat the flesh of pigs, they would have small eyes like those of a pig. Similarly Zulu girls abstain from eating pig's flesh because they fear that by eating it they might gradually come to resemble the ugly pig in appearance. But there are other reasons why primitive man abstained from pork. The Kai of N.E. New Guinea find that pigs are the worst enemies of the crops; therefore, if a field-labourer were to eat pork, the dead pig in his stomach would attract the living pig into the field.[4] Swine's flesh was forbidden to all the Semites except the Babylonians, but it is an open question whether this was because the animal was holy or because it was unclean.[5] As early as the time of Ḫammurabi pork was a highly valued food among the Babylonians and frequently formed part of the temple offering. By

[1] J. Macdonald, *Religion and Myth*, London, 1893, p. 91.

[2] M. J. van Baarda, 'Fabelan, Verhalan, en Overleveringen der Galelareezen,' *Bijdragen tot de Taal- Land- en Volkenkunde van Nederlandsch-Indië*, xlv. [1895] 511.

[3] H. Dessau, *Inscriptiones Latinæ Selectæ*, Berlin, 1892–1914, no. 4911.

[4] C. Keysser, 'Aus dem Leben der Kaileute,' in R. Neuhaus, *Deutsch Neu-Guinea*, Berlin, 1911, iii. 125.

[5] Lucian, *de Dea Syr.* 54; cf. Antiphanes, *ap.* Athenæus, iii. 95 (A. Meineke, *Fragmenta Comicorum Græcorum*, Berlin, 1839–57, iii. 68).

the inspection of pigs various omens were derived, and in the official lists special provision is even made for the temple pigs. The heathen Harranians sacrificed swine's flesh once a year and ate the flesh.[1] By the Syrians the swine was regarded as sacrosanct, and it was specially sacred to Aphrodite.[2] To the Greeks the attitude of the Jews towards swine was difficult to understand.[3] In Is 65[4] 66[3. 17] we are told that some of the Jews used to meet secretly to eat swine's flesh; it has been suggested therefore that 'the swine was revered rather than abhorred by the Israelites,'[4] and that it was not eaten because it was divine. To the Egyptians the pig was very loathsome.[5] Swineherds were forbidden to enter a temple and even had to marry among themselves. If a man even touched a pig, he immediately stepped into a river to wash off the taint. Pig's milk caused leprosy. These prohibitions prove that the Egyptians originally regarded the pig as sacred, for the belief that the eating of a sacred animal produces leprosy and that the effect caused by touching a sacred object is removed by washing was current among many ancient tribes and religions.[6] Later, however, the pig began to be looked upon with horror and was regarded as the Egyptian devil and the embodiment of Set or Typhon and enemy of Osiris. Typhon, in the form of a pig, injured the eye of Horus, who burned him and ordained that a pig was to be sacrificed, seeing that Ra, the sun-god, had declared the pig to be an abominable beast. We find in various religions that the animal sacrificed to a god because he is the god's enemy was originally the god himself. Now, we read that Typhon was hunting a boar when he discovered and mangled the body of Osiris, and that for this reason pigs were sacrificed once a year. It has therefore been suggested that originally the pig was a god, and that he was no other than Osiris.[7] We have already seen that the Kai of New Guinea abstain from pork because they regard the pig as the enemy of the crops, so that we can understand why the Egyptians should have identified their corn-god Osiris or his enemy Typhon with a wild boar. It might also be noted that pigs were sacrificed to Osiris on the very day on which he is recorded by tradition to have been killed. Further, the pig was sacred to the corn-goddess Demeter and was often associated with her. In art she is represented as accompanied by a pig.[8] At the Thesmophoria it was customary to throw pigs into some sacred vaults, which are described as the 'caves of Demeter and Persephone.'[9] It seems that the pigs were intended to represent Persephone and her descent into the lower world. An ancient legend tells that, when Pluto carried off Persephone, Eubuleus, a swineherd, was herding his swine near the spot, and his herd were engulfed in the cave into which Pluto and Persephone had vanished. The Thesmophoria has analogies in the folk-customs of N. Europe. In certain districts of Courland the pig is the corn-spirit, whose power of

[1] En-Nedim in D. Chwolsohn, *Die Ssabier und der Ssabismus*, St. Petersburg, 1856, ii. 42.

[2] Swine were also sacrificed to Aphrodite at Argos (Athen. iii. 49) and in Pamphylia (Strabo, ix. 5. 17).

[3] Plutarch, *Symposiacon*, iv. 5.

[4] But see R. H. Kennett, *The Composition of the Book of Isaiah in the Light of History and Archæology*, London, 1910, p. 61.

[5] Plut. *de Is. et Osir.*, 8; Herodotus, ii. 47, etc.

[6] Cf. the practice of the Jews of washing their hands after reading the Scriptures, also Lv 16[23f.]; *Central Provinces Ethnographic Survey*, Allahabad, 1907–11, ii., 'Draft Articles on Uriya Castes,' p. 16.

[7] E. Lefébure, *Le Mythe osirien*, Paris, 1874–75, pt. i., 'Les Yeux d'Horus,' p. 44; E. A. Wallis Budge, *The Gods of the Egyptians*, London, 1904, i. 496 f., also *Osiris and the Egyptian Resurrection*, London and New York, 1911.

[8] J. Overbeck, *Griechische Kunstmythologie*, Leipzig, 1873–78, pt. ii.

[9] F. C. Movers, *Die Phönizier*, Berlin, 1841–56, i. 220.

fertility lies in his tail; therefore, when barley is sown for the first time in the year, the sower sticks a pig's tail into the field, believing that the ears of corn will grow as long as the tail.[1] The idea that the pig is an embodiment of the corn-spirit can further be seen from the Scandinavian custom of 'Yule boar.' This is a loaf prepared from the last sheaf in the form of a pig. It is usually prepared at Christmas and kept till sowing-time, when it is given to the plough-horses in the hope that it will be the means of securing a good harvest.[2] In this connexion it is of interest to note that Ball finds a philological connexion between Tammuz, the Assyrian god of the under world and of vegetation, and the Chinese and Turkish words for pig. He also cites the evidence of classical writers[3] that 'the Jews did not use swine's flesh because it was sacred inasmuch as by turning up the earth with its snout it taught men the art of ploughing.'[4] In some parts of White Russia it is believed that the bones of a pig preserve the corn from hail, whilst in other places the ribs are thrown into the seed-bag among the flax-seed because they cause the flax to grow well and tall. The Alfoors of Minahassa in N. Celebes believe that a pig's blood causes inspiration, and at one of their festivals the priest drinks a pig's blood and thereupon is able to prophesy as to how the rice-crop will turn out.[5] The inhabitants of Car Nicobar rub themselves over with pig's blood in order to cleanse themselves of any devils of which they may be possessed.[6] In the same way the Greeks cleansed a homicide by sprinkling him with pig's blood and beating him with a laurel bough. The Karens of Burma believe that a bad harvest is caused by adultery, and, in order to atone for this, those detected in adultery must buy a pig, scrape out furrows in the ground with each foot, and then fill them with the pig's blood.[7] Some Yabim believe that after death their souls will be turned into swine, and they therefore abstain from swine-flesh lest they should thus be eating the souls of their relatives. The people of Tamara (off the coast of New Guinea) also abstain from pork because the souls of the dead transmigrate into the bodies of pigs. The worshippers of Adonis did not eat pork because their god had been killed by a boar. It has been suggested that the cry '*Hyes Attis!*', raised by the worshippers of Attis, meant 'Pig Attis!'[8] In Fiji a huge pig is presented to those who are initiated into manhood. At Maewo, in Aurora, one of the New Hebrides, fifty days after the death of a wealthy man pigs are killed, and the point of the liver of each pig is cut off. The brother of the deceased goes to the forest and calls out the dead man's name, saying 'This is for thee to eat,' the idea being that, if pigs are not killed for the benefit of the dead man, his ghost has not proper existence.[9] It should be noted also that the pig is very often represented by a cowry-shell. Malinowski, in an

[1] W. Mannhardt, *Mythologische Forschungen*, Strassburg, 1874, p. 186 f.; also A. Witzschel, *Sagen, Sitten, und Gebräuche aus Thüringen*, Vienna, 1878, pp. 189, 218.

[2] For further details concerning this and similar customs throughout various parts of Europe see F. Panzer, *Beitrag zur deutschen Mythologie*, Munich, 1848–55, ii. 491; J. Jamieson, *Etymological Dictionary of the Scottish Language*, new ed., Paisley, 1879–82, iii. 206 f.; Mannhardt, *Antike Wald- und Feldkulte*, Berlin, 1877, p. 197 f.

[3] Callistratus, *ap.* Plut. *Symp.* iv. 5.

[4] C. J. Ball, 'Tammuz, the Swine God,' *PSBA* xvi. [1894] 195 ff.

[5] J. G. F. Riedel, 'De Minahasa in 1825,' *Tijdschrift voor Indische Taal- Land- en Volkenkunde*, xviii. [1872] 517 f.

[6] V. Solomon, 'Extracts from Diaries kept in Car Nicobar,' *JAI* xxxii. [1902] 227.

[7] F. Mason, 'On Dwellings, Works of Art, Laws, etc., of the Karins,' *JASBe* xxxvii. [1868] pt. ii. p. 147 f.

[8] J. G. Frazer, *GB*[3], pt. v., *Spirits of the Corn and of the Wild*, London, 1912, ii. 22.

[9] R. H. Codrington, *The Melanesians*, Oxford, 1891, p. 282.

account of the natives of Malu Island, off the coast of New Guinea,[1] says that at one of their feasts the natives erect a gallows and ornament it with a white shell called *moto* (the so-called white cowry, *Ovulum ovum*). This shows that they are about to offer pigs for sacrifice, and the number of pigs to be sacrificed is always the same as the number of shells. The association of this shell with pigs is important when it is remembered that cowries are widely known as pig-shells. This fact, and also the passionate tendencies of swine, would be the most plausible explanation of the abhorrence with which they have always been, and still are, regarded in the East.

LITERATURE.—The literature is contained in the article.

MAURICE H. FARBRIDGE.

SYMBOLISM.

SYMBOLISM (Christian).—It is proposed in this article to indicate the more important of the emblems and personifications in which Christian belief has found spontaneous expression. The literary images which deserve to be called symbolical, but which have not embodied themselves in pictorial or material shapes, are excluded from view. An attempt will be made, however, to connect the emblems which call for notice with the language of the New Testament.

When the subject is thus defined, the field to be surveyed is at once seen to admit of a clear division. The first four or five Christian centuries separate themselves for our purpose markedly from the centuries which follow. For the symbolism of the earlier period we have the definite and varied testimony offered by the sepulchral paintings and inscriptions of the Roman catacombs. With the light thus obtainable we are able to see the hopes with which the Christians of Rome during this formative period followed their dead into the unseen world and connected the life that now is with that to which they believed it to be the portal.

Burial in the catacombs and the symbolism to which it gave rise practically ceased before the middle of the 5th century. From that time onwards new images and ideas crowd in upon us, created by the popular imagination in response to the Church's teaching and worship, to legends of the saints, animal fables, and spiritual plays and moralities. Many of these images do not succeed in finding an emblematic expression, but those which do create a symbolism far exceeding that of the previous period in amplitude. We shall give our chief attention to the earlier period, and briefly indicate the later emblems which, either from their permanence or from their inherent significance, seem especially to claim notice.

A review of the entire field brings one decisive feature of the symbolism into prominence. The emblems will all be found to point onwards to a life beyond the tomb. The symbolism is created by a hope or, it may be, a fear whose fulfilment is not expected within the limits of our present existence. The justification of this 'other-worldliness' may readily be found in our records of the life of Christ. His ministry began with the announcement, 'The kingdom of God is at hand,' and was throughout a prophecy of good things to come (Mk 1^{15}). Some of His disciples may at first have believed that they would see these good things before they 'tasted' death (9^{1}). The mere lapse of time was enough to stamp such expectation with the mark of illusion. Every year it became more clear that the realization of the promised kingdom must needs be a slow and gradual process. In another respect also the desired consummation underwent a change. The earth ceased to be regarded, as perhaps it had at first been, as the scene of fruition. The liveliest hope cannot resist the accumulating contradictions of continuous experience. Year by year it became less likely that the kingdom could ever be localized or assume any material shape. The Crucifixion and its sequel had lifted the thoughts of the disciples from the earth and carried them into that heaven which had now become the Master's home. To this heaven they transferred their 'treasure' (Mt 6^{19}), less perhaps from deliberate apostasy than from the reluctant acceptance of undeniable experience, and to it their hearts ascended. Death thus reassumed its normal character, and what lay beyond it became an object of anxious thought or fervent longing. These thoughts and longings form the central motives of Christian symbolism. The blessedness hoped for after death, the means by which it may be reached, and the character of Him who procured and guarantees it—these will be found to be the subjects round which the Christian emblems of all periods gather. From the beginning hope has been the dominant Christian characteristic. The scene of fulfilment and the mode of realization may have shifted. Hope itself has remained.

The symbolism of the catacombs embodies the hopes of future blessedness entertained by those who used these burying-places up to the time when such subterranean burial ceased. Thus the roses, or flowery meadows and shrubs, which appear on so many tombs represent paradise. Its entrance is sometimes indicated by a curtain which is in process of being drawn aside. The Good Shepherd who appears on tomb after tomb may with greatest probability be here regarded as the Lord and Protector of the dead. It is they whom He gathers round Him in the heavenly fields. One of their number is the sheep He carries on His shoulders. The fish, one of the two articles of food with which the thousands were fed (Jn 6^{1-14}), represents the mystical union with Christ, and its fruit incorruptibility (ἀφθαρσία). The vine points to the heavenly feast, or to its earthly pledge—the Eucharist. The dove, sipping water from the basin or jar, is the soul refreshing itself from the water of life (Rev 22^{1}). The palms symbolize either the palms borne by the blessed (7^{9}) or the wreaths or crowns of those who have been victorious in the race of life (1 Co 9^{25}, 2 Ti 4^{8}). The anchor indicates the hope of He 6^{19} which enters in 'within the veil.' The ship and lighthouse typify the dangerous voyage across the ocean of life to the haven of safety. The stag is that of Ps 42^{1}, and represents the soul's thirst for God.

The paintings of the catacombs have been fully described by two recent writers. Wilpert, in his *Malereien der Katakomben Roms*, has classified the paintings, reproducing all that are important and giving his interpretations of their symbolism. Von Sybel, in his *Christliche Antike*, has reviewed the subject on the ground provided by his predecessor's labours. He also reproduces many of the paintings and states his own conclusions in a lucid style and with much wealth of learning.

The symbolism of the later centuries has the

[1] *Trans. and Proc. Royal Soc. S. Australia*, xxxix. [1915] 494 f.

same general character. As sin and misery increase on the earth, fear plays a larger part in the Church's symbolism. The torments of the lost become more conspicuous than the joys of the blessed. A final judgment of all mankind displaces the earlier individual judgment and assumes truly terrifying aspects. The figure of Christ becomes more stern and awful, and, as it does so, the person of the Virgin Mother takes His place as Protector and Advocate.[1] She is invested with steadily-growing dignity and is separated more and more from human infirmity. The Church becomes a figure of regal authority. In what has been said[2] to be 'perhaps the finest mediæval personification'—the sculpture on Strassburg Cathedral—she appears as a royal lady, with the crown upon her head and the banner of victory and the chalice in her hand. Elsewhere Christ is seen crowning her from the Cross, or she receives His blood in her chalice. Thus, whether in earlier or in later art, the symbolism alike points beyond the tomb.

We may now proceed to deal in greater detail with the separate symbols. They will be found to gather, for the most part, round two central subjects: (1) Christ, regarded as the author of eternal life, and (2) the heavenly state.

1. The author of eternal life.—Christ is represented in all our Gospels as the giver of eternal life to those who accept and follow Him. The synoptists amply confirm His declaration in the Fourth Gospel: 'He that heareth my word, and believeth him that sent me, hath eternal life, and cometh not into judgement, but hath passed out of death into life' (Jn 5^{24}; cf. Mt $10^{32f. 39}$ 19^{29}, Lk $9^{24. 26}$, etc.). There can be no doubt that, whatever the Kingdom of God may have meant to the first Jewish disciples, it represented an inseparable association with Christ, here and hereafter, as Master and Saviour. To the Gentile world Christ, we may safely say, appeared as, above all else, a deliverer from the power of death. He had taken flesh that 'through death he might . . . deliver all them who through fear of death were all their lifetime subject to bondage' (He 2^{14}). He had 'abolished death, and brought life and incorruption to light through the gospel' (2 Ti 1^{10}). These and similar passages were probably understood by the earliest believers much as they are by ordinary Christians to-day. They were taken to mean that the faithful disciple would find Christ waiting for him, when death was past, and that Christ would then lead him into a better and happier existence than he had hitherto known, better and happier because it was nearer to God. Christians generally would not perplex themselves then, any more than they do now, with questions regarding the precise nature or locality of this future existence. The 'eternal life' which in the Fourth Gospel is the equivalent of Messianic blessedness was probably understood by the great majority of readers as a life in which the disciple would 'see' God, and which would not come to an end as earthly life does. Far as this is from exhausting the meaning of the word 'eternal,' it is difficult to suppose that the word can ever have conveyed, or does even now convey, to the ordinary Christian more than this simple interpretation. Of this better life, to be known hereafter, Christ had given a foretaste or prophecy during His earthly ministry. The blind then received their sight, the lame walked, the lepers were cleansed, the deaf heard, the dead were raised, and the poor had good tidings preached to them (Mt 11^5). It is this power of God to save from death and harm that finds expression in the paintings of the catacombs. Christ appears as the son of God foretold by prophetic voices. His ministry has been heralded by many previous displays of God's saving power. He has actually shown Himself to be the raiser of the dead, the restorer of the blind, and the healer of the sick. He waits for His disciples beyond death to lead them into the heavenly pastures. Such are the subjects and implications of the symbolism.

(*a*) *OT types.*—Scenes from the OT which were especially held to typify this deliverance recur with great frequency on the tombs. These are the salvation of Isaac, when he was about to be slain in sacrifice by Abraham, the salvation of Noah in the Ark, the restoration of Job to his former prosperity (Job $42^{10. 12}$), the rescue of Jonah from the jaws of the sea-monster, and the preservation of the three Hebrew youths in the flaming furnace. Some features in the symbolism of these paintings deserve particularly to be noted. In the representations of Abraham's contemplated sacrifice it is the rescue of Isaac from death that the painter desires to symbolize. This is plain from the attitude in which Isaac is represented when the design of the picture permits. He appears with extended arms—a posture of prayer or adoration of which more is said below. This is also the attitude of Noah as he stands in the Ark, and of the three children in the furnace. There is no suggestion in the paintings of the theological meanings afterwards found in Abraham's projected sacrifice. It may also be observed that the Deity is represented here, as generally or often in the earliest Christian art, by an outstretched hand. No attempt is made to delineate His features. There are no representations of the Trinity such as we find afterwards. Of all Biblical types Jonah has been the most frequently chosen by these painters. He forms the subject of 129 separate pictures which have come to light. It is to be observed that he does not here appear as a type of the resurrection of Christ, as he does in Mt 12^{40}. Nor is it the repentance of the Ninevites at his preaching (Mt 12^{41}) that the painters wish to symbolize. He is represented as an example of God's saving power. Sometimes he forms the subject of three or four connected pictures. We first see him standing on the deck of the vessel and about to be cast into the sea. We then see the monster vomiting him out towards the land. He next appears resting under the gourd, which takes the form of an arbour like those in paradise. There may be a fourth picture where he reclines in an attitude of dejection, his head resting on his hand.[1]

(*b*) *The sacred infancy.*—The divine childhood is depicted on a number of tombs. One of the most beautiful paintings in the catacombs[2] is the picture in the Priscilla cemetery of the Christ-child on His mother's breast. The mother bends slightly forward as if to suckle the child. The child's hand is spread out over the mother's breast, but the face, with wonderful eyes, is half turned towards the spectator. Above the heads of mother and child two stars are indicated in an oblique direction. To the left stands a man in mantle and sandals who has in his left hand a written roll and with his right points to the star above. This figure probably represents, not Joseph (who, as far as is known, does not appear in early Christian art), but a prophet, either Isaiah, who pointed to the light of the Messianic age (60^{1-6}), or Balaam (Nu 24^{17}, Rev 22^{16}), who told of the star to arise out of Jacob. If this identification be correct, it is, as von Sybel says,[3] 'one more evidence that at least the earlier Catacomb painting was in no sense historical, but entirely symbolical art.' The picture belongs to the beginning of the 2nd century.

Another incident of the sacred infancy frequently

[1] See art. 'Mary,' in *HDB*.
[2] Schulze art. 'Sinnbilder,' in *PRE*³ xviii. 392.

[1] Von Sybel, p. 216 ff.
[2] *Ib.* p. 247.
[3] *Ib.* p. 249.

depicted is the visit of the Magi. They are generally represented as three in number, although the painter may be led by the exigencies of space to increase them to four or reduce them to two.

'The definite determination of their number as three, their designation as kings, the ascription to them of proper names (Kaspar, Melchior, Balthasar), the differentiation of their ages—to this legendary web antiquity only contributed the first threads. Its elaboration was the work of the Middle Ages.'[1]

The Annunciation (Lk $1^{26ff.}$) forms the subject of two paintings, one belonging to the end of the 2nd and the other to the 3rd century.[2] Mary is seated. The angel, in the form of a man, makes the announcement standing, as a visitor who has just entered the house. The relative postures of the two figures can be explained without the supposition of an intention to claim for Mary a higher dignity than for the angel. The two paintings may presuppose, but cannot be held to go beyond, the Gospel narratives.

On the other hand, Mary's perpetual virginity finds constant expression in mediæval art. The OT provides many images of inviolability which are applied to Mary. She is the 'fons signatus,' the 'hortus conclusus,' and the 'turris' of the Song of Solomon (4^{15} 4^{12} 4^{4}). The christianized *Physiologus*—a mediæval bestiary or book of animals, real and fabulous, with allegorical explanations[3]—supplied the legend of the unicorn, a fabulous animal which could be tamed only by being caught in the lap of a pure virgin. Ezk 44^{2} provided the symbol of the barred door, Jg 6^{37} that of Gideon's fleece watered by the dew from heaven. The number and variety of these symbols show the value assigned to the doctrine of Mary's perpetual virginity by the mediæval Church.[4]

(*c*) *The Divine Healer.*—The Gospel miracles, of which there are numerous representations in the catacombs, are evidences of God's desire to release humanity from its plagues. In the heavenly city of the Apocalypse there was to be neither sorrow nor death (Rev 21^{4}). To this divine purpose the healings of Christ bore emphatic witness. His ministry was a short-lived anticipation of the Messianic Age (Mt $11^{4f.}$). The beneficent power, then displayed in a few instances, would hereafter be seen in the fullness of its strength. It is an evidence of the authority rapidly acquired by the Fourth Gospel that the miracle most frequently represented in the catacombs is the raising of Lazarus (50 examples have been discovered). We remember how both the sisters greet the Saviour with the words, 'If thou hadst been here, my brother had not died' (Jn $11^{21. 32}$). We are intended to regard the presence of Christ as incompatible with death, or at least with its bereaving power. Other healings which may with certainty be identified are that of the paralytic (Mk $2^{1ff.}$ and ||), where the man appears walking with his bed on his shoulder, and that of the blind man, where we see Christ touching with His finger the man's closed eyes. Another unmistakable scene is the cure of the issue of blood (Mk 5^{25} and ||). The woman comes behind the Saviour as He walks with two disciples, and kneels that she may touch the hem of His robe. Other paintings have no distinctive features which would justify certain identification.

(*d*) *The Cross.*—The absence from the earlier catacombs of what has now become the distinctive Christian emblem is full of significance. The use of the cross as a separate symbol appears to date from the campaign of Constantine against Maxentius (A.D. 312), when Constantine put the cross upon the shields of his soldiers. Previous to this date we find the cross mentioned in one inscription

[1] Von Sybel, p. 250.

[2] Wilpert, p. 202; von Sybel, p. 252.

[3] See Cahier and Martin, *Mélanges d'archéologie*, Paris, 1847–56, 'Curiosités mystérieuses,' ch. vii. pp. 107–117.

[4] Schulze, *PRE*[3] xviii. 392.

in the catacombs, and appearing doubtfully in two ceiling-paintings. Both inscription and paintings belong to the 2nd century. The monogram of Christ 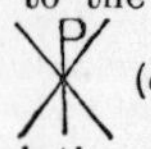 (*e.g.*, ἐν 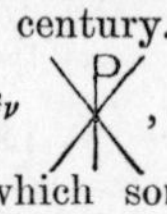, δοῦλος ) appears in inscriptions of which some may possibly be anterior to Constantine, but its general use dates from the reign of this emperor. It has accordingly become customary to regard both the cross and the monogram as indicating a date not earlier than the 4th century. It should also be observed that the only known reference to the Passion in the catacombs previous to the 4th cent. is what is believed to be a representation of the crowning with thorns in the Pretextatus cemetery.[1] The absence of any symbol of the Passion from the earlier tombs may readily be accounted for by the fact that their paintings were intended to display, not death, but the victory over death. Even when the cross does begin to appear, it seems to be introduced, not for its own sake, but as a support for the rose-leaves which gather round it. It thus becomes a beautified or transfigured cross. We are reminded of the symbolism of the Passion-narrative in the Fourth Gospel, where we see Christ reigning with sovereign authority from the Cross, and the majesty of the Divine Sufferer shining through the indignities which strive in vain to obscure it. The foliage-crosses of the catacombs—concealed or 'dissimulated' crosses—have indeed been traced to the supposed desire of the Christians to avoid observation. Apart, however, from the fact that such crosses do not begin to appear until the 4th cent., it is difficult to believe that the other emblems which do appear would not have clearly indicated these vaults as Christian burying-places. It seems more natural to suppose that the transfiguration of the Cross effected by St. Paul's theology required much reflexion before it could find emblematic expression. The Cross was at first a stumbling-block (Gal 5^{11}) and only slowly became a symbol of glory (6^{14}).[2]

It will thus have been observed that the earliest representations of the Passion were avowed symbols, suggesting, but not depicting, the sacrifice of the God-man. Realism becomes more pronounced as we travel down the centuries. The crucifix—an inevitable development of the cross—does not appear in churches till after the 7th century.[3] The implements of the Passion (hammer, claws, etc.) become independent emblems towards the end of the Middle Ages, when indulgences began to be attached to their veneration. The lamb with blood streaming from its breast, and carrying the cross or a banner upon which the cross was depicted, became a favourite symbol on the portals of Latin churches. The pelican (taken from the *Physiologus*), who tears open its breast to feed its young, was used to represent the sacrificial death of Christ.[4]

(*e*) *The Good Shepherd.*—The favourite symbol of Christ among those who constructed and used the catacombs was that of the Good Shepherd. This image takes here the place of the crucifix in later art. It appears in two different forms in the Gospels. In Lk 15^{3-7} the shepherd is seen bringing home on his shoulders, 'rejoicing,' a sheep that has been lost. In Jn 10^{1-17} the shepherd leads his sheep to and from the pastures and protects them

[1] Wilpert, p. 226; von Sybel, p. 292.

[2] For the three forms of the cross in later symbolism—*decussata*, or St. Andrew's cross, ; *commissa*, Tau or Egyptian cross, ; and *immissa*, —see art. CROSS.

[3] See *DCA*, *s.v.* 'Crucifix.'

[4] Schulze, *PRE*[3] xviii. 392.

from the wolf, even at the price of his own life. It is added by Christ in a subsequent verse (v.[27f.]): 'My sheep hear my voice, and I know them, and they follow me: and I give unto them eternal life; and they shall never perish, and no one shall snatch them out of my hand.' Both representations are of frequent occurrence on the tombs. We see the shepherd pasturing his flock, and carrying upon his shoulders a sheep, whose legs he clasps sometimes with one and sometimes with both hands. There seems to be little doubt that this favourite symbol, like the others in the catacombs, is intended to transport the mind beyond death. The painters wished to indicate the power of Christ over death. Those who died, no less than those who lived, were under His protection, 'the sheep of his pasture.' Thus, where a landscape is indicated in the paintings it is invariably that of the garden or park which typifies paradise. The image, so understood, would appear to have passed into the early burial prayers of both the Greek and the Latin liturgies.[1] Thus, when A. P. Stanley[2] points to the frequent image of the Good Shepherd as an evidence of the joyousness of early Christian feeling, we must remember that the sheep in these pictures are in all probability those who have passed from the vicissitudes of the world into the safe haven of eternal rest.

A brief reference may here be made to the emblems which early Christian art adopted from Greek and Roman mythology. We cannot measure the precise significance which these emblems possessed for the Christians who used or looked at them. They may have been little more than the current decorations of the period; or they may have had a distinct didactic purpose, and been intended to suggest that Christ was the reality to which the heathen mythology pointed in unconscious and hesitating prophecy. So Eros and Psyche appear in many of the catacomb paintings, and in five different pictures where we should have expected the Good Shepherd we find Orpheus with his lyre.

(*f*) *The Judge of the dead.*—In some paintings Christ is seen seated upon a raised platform, plainly in the character of Judge. In one of these[3] we see a male figure in the posture of an *orans* between two taller forms, who point to him as if they were his introducers or sponsors. In the background upon a raised pedestal is Christ, who stretches His open right hand over the head of the middle figure, while in His left He holds a roll. In Wilpert's opinion, the middle figure represents one of the dead who has already stood before the judgment-seat of Christ, while the two other figures represent his advocates.

These representations of judgment convey some important suggestions. The face of Christ in the picture described above is grave without being stern. It must be remembered that no authentic likeness of Christ appears to have been preserved by His disciples. The varieties given to His face and figure from the earliest times put this beyond reasonable doubt. Irenæus[4] shows that no trustworthy portrait existed in his day. To the same effect are the words of Augustine.[5] The disciples were thus left to their own insight and skill to depict His likeness. The painters of the catacombs seem to have given Him the typical male head of their time. This type was during the first two centuries a beardless face with the hair closely cut. It was followed in the 3rd cent. by a face, still beardless, but surrounded by long hair falling upon the forehead and down the back. A still later type was a bearded face framed in flowing or curling locks. If the painters were guided by the prevalent fashions of wearing the hair and beard, it is obvious that we cannot infer much from the apparently increasing seriousness of the countenance.[1] The growth of asceticism in subsequent ages had a marked influence. The early effort after beauty was abandoned. Manly beauty was associated in the mind of the monastic Church only with barbarian soldiers. The words of Is 53^2, 'There is no beauty that we should desire him,' shaped the artist's conceptions. The figure of Christ in the Church of Galla Placidia in Ravenna (*c.* A.D. 450), when compared with the portrait to be seen in the Church of Apollinaris in the same city, painted about a century later, shows the transition from the earlier ideal, shaped by the love of beauty, to the ascetic or melancholy conceptions of later art.[2]

These representations seem also to make it plain that the judgment symbolized was individual and thought of as taking place immediately after death. The departed appears at once before the judgment-seat of Christ (2 Co 5^{10}). The approving sentence of the Judge is the signal for his immediate entrance into paradise. Thus in one painting[3] we see two figures, one on either side, drawing back a curtain to admit into paradise one of the departed, who stands in the centre in the posture of an *orans*. In another painting two of the blessed move eagerly forward to welcome a new arrival, who advances in the same attitude of devotion. We find no representation in the catacombs of a general judgment of mankind. Nor do the paintings, as archæologists of all schools agree, give any indication of belief in an 'intermediate state' or a period between death and judgment. All those who die in Christ are conceived as passing at once from their death-beds into heaven.[4]

When we pass into the subsequent centuries, death and judgment assume terrifying shapes. The destructive power of death is symbolized by a man who weeds the garden of life or fells its trees, or (after Rev 6^8) as a rider with drawn bow, above all as an emaciated old man who finally reaches the form of a skeleton with scythe and hour-glass. 'The dance of death' appears to have originated in the plague known as 'the Black Death.' It quickly gained a wide popularity, which it retained far beyond the Middle Ages. The soul, leaving the body, was regularly represented as a little human figure, naked and sexless, emerging from the mouth. In pictures of the Last Judgment popular imaginations of hell took the place of the earlier representations of paradise. Hell was symbolized by the open throat of a monster (after the leviathan of Job 41), into which men and women, masters and servants, priests and people, were thrust. Devils in every shape did their work of derision and torture under the supervision of the prince of hell. To him the popular imagination transferred everything it knew of monsters, and thus there arose the being of many shapes and names with goat's horns, cloven hoof, bat's wings, and a tail. He even took the form of a blackbird, and, as such, flew into the mouth of Judas at the Last Supper, and whispered into the ear of Pilate as he sat in judgment. Popular humour may well have had its share in shaping these fancies.[5]

2. The heavenly state.—St. Paul represents Christ as the second Adam, who undid the consequences of the first Adam's transgression (Ro 5). By the early Christians heaven was pictured as a restored Eden. The word 'paradise' appears to

1 Von Sybel, p. 242; *ap.* Muratori, *Liturgia Romana Vetus*, Naples, 1760, i. 751: 'We pray God faithfully that He may grant [to the departed] that, redeemed from death, released from his sins, reconciled to the Father, brought home on the shoulders of the good Shepherd, he may enjoy the society of the blessed.'
2 *Christian Institutions*, London, 1881, ch. xiii., 'The Roman Catacombs.'
3 Wilpert, p. 394; von Sybel, p. 271.
4 *Contra Hær.* i. 25. 6.
5 *De Trin.* vii. 4 f.

1 Von Sybel, p. 281; Wilpert, p. 106; E. von Dobschütz, 'Christusbilder,' in *TU*, new ser., iii. [1899].
2 See art. 'Jesus Christ, Representations of,' in *DCA*.
3 Wilpert, p. 467; von Sybel, p. 267.
4 Wilpert, p. 430; von Sybel, p. 273.
5 Schulze, *PRE*3 xviii. 393.

have been originally Persian and to have been introduced into Greek literature by Xenophon.[1] The Greeks seem to have passed it on to the Hebrews. It appears in the OT only in writings subsequent to the Greek period (Ec 2^5, Ca 4^{13}, Neh 2^8), and bore the meaning of a park with trees, shrubs, and grass, and tenanted by wild animals, such as surrounded the residences of eastern potentates. Such parks were commonly enclosed by a wall or trellis-shaped fence. Trees, shrubs, flowers, and the trellised fencing in the catacomb paintings are invariably symbols of paradise.[2]

On the threshold we meet with the figures known as *orantes*. These are forms, male or female—the latter are much more numerous than the former—standing with arms either fully extended or bent at the elbows, and with opened hands. The *orantes* give rise to questions which are still in debate. Whom, in the first place, are these figures intended to represent? Against the supposition that they are either likenesses of the departed or intended to represent their souls[3] we have to place the fact that a female *orans* often appears painted on the tomb of a man, and also to remember that the paintings appear to have been sometimes executed before the tombs were filled. It seems therefore most natural to regard the *orantes* as ideal figures, poetic representations of the blessed dead. Again, what is the meaning of the outstretched arms and open hands? Are we to understand the attitude as one of prayer or one of adoration? And, if it be prayer that is symbolized, for what do the suppliants pray? The answers to these questions are not unaffected by dogmatic interests. According to the opinion of Wilpert, the *orantes* are praying for the salvation of their friends who still remain upon the earth. In some of the inscriptions we find the survivors asking for the prayers of the departed.[4] On the other hand, we meet with the attitude in some cases where it unquestionably symbolizes adoration, or at least the prayer in which entreaty loses itself in submission. Thus in the OT scenes of deliverance from death the rescued appear often in the attitude of *orantes*. So Noah stands in the Ark, and Daniel among the lions, and so the three children appear in the furnace. Yet in each of these cases the deliverance has already been granted. If anything is asked for, it can only be the continuance of something begun. So the new inmates of paradise seem to stand in an attitude of wondering recognition. In the highest Christian prayer entreaty ceases because the human will is one with the divine. The lifting up of the hands was a Jewish as well as a Christian practice (Is 1^{15}, 1 Ti 2^8).

3. The heavenly feast. — The Christians who buried their dead in the catacombs had two sacraments, both of which are frequently symbolized in the paintings. In baptism the believer was admitted among the number of the elect. He became a 'saint' in the original sense of that word. On the tombs we find representations both of the baptism of Christ by His forerunner and of the Church's baptism. There are also three pictures of a fisherman, seated on the bank and drawing a fish out of the water with his hook. The figure may point to baptism and to the words of Jesus addressed to the disciples: 'Come ye after me, and I will make you fishers of men' (Mt 4^{19} and ||). If this be so, it would supply an additional reason for the adoption of the fish as a Christian symbol.

In the Eucharist the believer partook of the bread which came down from heaven, and of which he who ate would not die (Jn 6^{50}). In it he had the prophecy of the heavenly feast. When Jesus took leave of His disciples, He told them of the new wine which He would drink with them in the Kingdom of God (Lk 22^{18}). The Crucifixion shattered for a brief interval the hope raised by the prophetic words. Despondency gave way to renewed confidence when it became clear that God had not 'allowed His Holy One to see corruption.' So 'day by day, continuing stedfastly with one accord in the temple, and breaking bread at home, they [the disciples] did take their food with gladness and singleness of heart' (Ac 2^{46}). It is no longer possible to mark the steps by which this early 'breaking of bread' passed into the Church's Eucharist. It is enough to recognize that what afterwards became the ecclesiastical rite originally formed part of the corporate feast of the Christian society. If the presence of the heavenly Christ was, as we can well believe, more vividly realized during these feasts than at any other time, the disciples would naturally associate them with the peace or joy which awaited them hereafter. The fellowship of the earthly feast would provide the mould for their anticipations of future happiness. They might recall the Biblical assurances: 'Blessed is he that shall eat bread in the kingdom of God' (Lk 14^{15}), 'Blessed are they which are bidden to the marriage supper of the Lamb' (Rev 19^9), 'To him that overcometh, to him will I give to eat of the tree of life, which is in the Paradise of God' (2^7). It is profitless to dwell upon the inconsistency of picturing spiritual happiness by an image which appeals only to man's bodily appetites. For in the 'new world' which, whether it be peopled by corporeal or incorporeal beings, is in any case to be the scene of fruition every earthly image, the most attenuated equally with the most material, becomes obsolete. An instrument intended for a region surrounded by an atmosphere is useless when the atmosphere is transcended. Thus the most spiritually-minded Christians, restricted by limitations from which they cannot escape, may well continue, as they do, to associate heaven with the 'shout of them that triumph, the song of them that feast.' In the catacomb paintings heavenly happiness is frequently represented by the image of festal joy. The scene of the feast is marked, by the customary indications, as paradise. The guests are to be seen, generally if not always, behind the roll which is the recognized symbol for the cushions used at feasts. Often attendants appear carrying a dish or holding a flagon or wine-cup. In one series of four pictures these attendants take the form of two female figures who are designated by inscriptions as 'Irene' and 'Agape.' They are appealed to by the guests to supply warm water or to mix the wine ('Irene, da calda'; 'Agape, misce nobis'). One of the figures seems thus to symbolize the peace of heaven, and the other the love from which the Christian love-feast derived its name, and which was one of St. Paul's three abiding things.[1] The food indicated in these pictures consists invariably of bread and fish. Sometimes a number of baskets, filled with small round loaves, appear either in front of the cushion-roll or on either side of it. The miraculous feeding of the thousands was plainly the model in the painter's mind. This miracle, connected by St. John (6^{35}) with the 'bread of life,' was an anticipation of the heavenly feast. Similarly prophetic was the Church's Eucharist, which in some of the paintings seems to be expressly depicted and made a symbol of its heavenly antitype. It need only be added that the fish, from its presence in the miracle, as well perhaps as for the reason given above, appears to have established itself as a symbol for a Christian disciple, long before the acrostic was discovered: ἰχθύς = Ἰησοῦς χριστὸς θεοῦ ὕιος σωτήρ.

It will appear from the foregoing summary that, while Christian symbolism points persistently onwards towards an ideal world, conceived as lying beyond death, the hope thus expressed is sustained by experiences which are prized for their own sake, and also as earnests of things yet to come. Eternal life, the ultimate blessing of the Fourth Gospel, is there represented as both present and future. So the Messianic kingdom of the earlier evangelists was yet to come, while it was also 'within' or 'among' the disciples who walked with Jesus and saw God in Him. The Church which continued His ministry in the ages that followed was likewise a prophet of what was yet to be, and also a teacher of men amidst the dangers and obligations of actual life. Thus in the Middle Ages, while the three theological virtues (faith, hope, charity) appear repeatedly on church porches, pulpits, and monuments, the cardinal virtues (prudence, justice, fortitude, temperance) also assume their symbolic shapes. The Church is a teacher of common-place morality, while at the same time she must bear witness to truths whose validity cannot be demonstrated by everyday experience. The Christians who built the catacombs tell us in many inscriptions of the central hope with which they consigned their dead to the tomb. Their desire was that the departed might 'see God' ('Vivat in Deo,' 'Vives in æternum,' 'Deum videre cupiens vidit'). Such is the hope, vague and yet real, changing but steadfast, which has created the Christian symbols of the past, and may be trusted to fashion new ones as the human heart becomes more proficient in the interpretation of its own language.

LITERATURE.—J. Wilpert, *Die Malereien der Katakomben Roms*, 2 vols., Freiburg i. Br., 1903; L. von Sybel, *Christliche Antike*, Marburg, 1906–09, i.; G. B. de Rossi, *La Roma sotterranea cristiana*, 3 vols., Rome, 1864–77; V. Schulze, *Archäolog. Studien über altchristliche Monumente*, Vienna, 1880, art. 'Sinnbilder,' in *PRE*³; C. Cahier and A. Martin [Jesuit Fathers], *Mélanges d'archéologie, d'histoire et de littérature . . . du moyen âge*, 4 vols., Paris, 1848–56, *Nouveaux mélanges d'archéologie, d'hist. et de litt. sur le moyen âge*, do. 1873–75; F. Cabrol, *DACL*, *s.v.*; R. St. J. Tyrwhitt, *DCA*, *s.v.*

JOHN GAMBLE.

[1] See a learned note in von Sybel, p. 161.

[2] Von Sybel, p. 167.

[3] De Rossi, *Roma sotterranea cristiana*, ii. 324, *Bull. Christ.*, 1867, 1885, quoted by von Sybel.

[4] 'In orationibus tuis roges pro nobis quia scimus te in Christo' (Wilpert, p. 211; von Sybel, p. 264).

[1] Wilpert, p. 470; von Sybel, p. 207; de Rossi, *Bull. Christ.*, 1882.

SYMBOLISM (Greek and Roman).—A symbol is a visible or audible sign or emblem of some thought, emotion, or experience, interpreting what can be really grasped only by the mind and imagination by something which enters into the field of observation.

So far as Greek and Roman religion are concerned, we need speak only of two kinds of symbols—symbolic representation by means of actions or words and symbolic representation in art.

Religion, taking its rise in experience and belief, tends, as it becomes less literal and less insistent, to give rise to symbolism; and this is true also of that lower kind of religion which is called magic. When primitive men thought that by certain actions and words they could compel spiritual powers to do their bidding, or when they thought that the painting of animal forms on the walls of their caves gave them power over the animals depicted, they had not yet reached the stage of symbolism, but had taken the first steps towards it; when they poured water on the ground to produce rain, they thought that there was an actual causal connexion between the ritual act and the fall of rain. But just as, when religious belief decays, the feelings which gave rise to it often find scope in the field of poetry, so, when actual belief in the power of sympathetic magic grows less, the actions and ceremonies to which it led are often continued in symbolism.

I. *GREEK.*—**1. In local cults.**—The local cults of Greece, which went on at a lower level, and in a more conservative key, than the religion of poetry and of philosophy, preserved a great deal of symbolism. Even in Athens the great festivals embodied such traces of primitive religion. At the Brauronian festival young girls, impersonating bears, danced a bear-dance in honour of Artemis. At the Diasia the priest who struck down the sacrificial ox was accused of murder and in turn accused his instrument, the axe, which was condemned and solemnly cast into the sea. In the worship of the dead flowers and fruits gradually took the place of the more serious offerings of an earlier time. With the dead were buried, not, as in primitive times, real armour and ornaments, but only symbolical offerings, money of gold-leaf, animals of terra-cotta, and the like. Sometimes these objects were only depicted in relief on the tombstone. The terrible human sacrifices once brought to the sterner deities were commuted into sacrifices of animals, sometimes clad in human fashion, or mere images of human beings. Naturally it was in the mysteries, where the survivals of primitive religion were most rife, that symbolism was most prominent. Mere ceremonial ablutions took the place of actual immersions as a ceremony of purification. The sacred meal which the deity shared with his votaries became a mere ceremonial tasting of some special food. At Eleusis, in the great mysteries, the votaries emptied two vessels filled with water, turning to east and west and repeating the sacred formula ὕε, κύε ('Sky pour rain; earth bear grain'), which was directed to earth and sky, and was evidently a survival of an ancient magical formula for the production of rain.

The suppliant who visited the cave and oracle of Trophonius at Lebadeia, before he went into the presence of the hero, drank from two springs, that of oblivion and that of memory, to signify that he was to forget the past and to remember the revelation which was to come to him. Originally, in all probability, the water of these springs was supposed to have some actual effect on the votary, as had the spring in the cave of the Clarian Apollo at Colophon on the priest who drank of it before soothsaying. But in the time of Pausanias[1] the action had become merely ritual and symbolical.

The sacred marriage was common to several cults in Greece. When the notion of the deity was somewhat crude, women were shut into the temple, to stand in the same sexual relation to him in which, according to tradition, Cassandra stood to Apollo. But, as time went on, such dedication became only symbolical, the place of the victim being sometimes taken by the wife of the priest.

As the mystery religions spread and their outlines hardened, a new element came in, which was destined to take further development in Christianity—the element of authority. Symbolic rites were practised, not on the ground of mere tradition, but by ordination of the recognized hierophants of each cultus, who claimed a divine communication. This element, however, scarcely belonged to the earlier religious view of either Greeks or Romans, among whom authority in religion was scarcely recognized apart from tradition. Cults had an open field and freely competed one with another, except those with which the safety of the State was supposed to be connected.

It seems that almost all ritual which does not appeal to the intelligence is in character symbolic. And the notable feature in symbolic ritual is that, since it appeals mainly to the emotions, it may be interpreted or understood in a great variety of ways. At the mysteries of Eleusis, *e.g.*, some of the votaries might regard the whole proceedings as a sort of spell to cause fertility; some might be genuine worshippers of the great goddesses Demeter and Persephone; some might, like Cicero, find in the ritual a promise and pledge of a life beyond the grave. Everything depended on the religious outlook, the exalted or materialist beliefs of the votary himself.

> 'Aristotle,' says Synesius,[2] is of opinion 'that the initiated learned nothing precisely; but that they received impressions, were put into a suitable frame of mind.'

Thus symbolic ritual has a great attraction for persons of emotional temperament, while it is distasteful to those of strongly developed intelligence, who like definite views. Compared with clear doctrine, it is like music compared with painting. It was by no means well suited to the minds of the more cultivated Greeks.

2. In art.—In early Greek art symbolism appears in two forms: in representing by some simple figure an idea such as a quality or attribute of one of the deities and in representing the whole of anything by depicting some characteristic part of it.

A few symbols of the deities seem to have been taken over by the Greeks from the pre-historic peoples whom they displaced in Crete and Hellas. Such is the double-edged axe, which is found in the palace of Cnossus in Crete in the third millennium B.C. in scenes of cultus, and which belongs to a male or female deity of the people. This axe became among the Greeks a symbol of Dionysus. The snake also appears as an attribute of a goddess of Crete frequently represented, and later was inherited by the Greek Erinyes. But most of the symbols of the gods of the Greek pantheon seem to be more immediately derived from the art of the nations of Syria and Mesopotamia. Most of these symbols were displaced by growing anthropomorphism. This statement requires some explanation. On early bronzes and terra-cottas found on Greek sites, dating from the 7th or 6th cent., the goddess Artemis is figured as winged and holding in her two hands lions, panthers, or swans. On the chest of Cypselus, a

[1] ix. xxxix.
[2] Aristotle, *Frag.*, ed. E. Heitz, Leipzig, 1869, p. 40.

7th cent. work preserved at Olympia, Pausanias[1] saw such a figure, which surprised him by its strangeness. It was strictly symbolical; the wings were not for flight, but only to typify swiftness, the lions were added to show the power of the goddess over animals, whose mistress (πότνια) she was. We can trace this representation step by step through Greek art and see how in maturer times the swiftness of the deity was indicated by her stature and slimness of build, her power over animals by the stag or dog who accompanied her. A similar transformation takes place in the case of Zeus. On early coins of Elis an eagle appears as a substitute for the god; later he bears the eagle in his hand. Later still, as in the great statue of Pheidias, a golden eagle was an adornment of the sceptre of Zeus. Thus, as time went on, merely outward symbols tended to disappear or at all events to become unimportant; and the meaning which they had conveyed was expressed in the type of the deity. Certain symbols, however, held their ground. The thunderbolt of Zeus, indicating him as the lord of storms (Ζεὺς ὑέτιος), is usual in the 5th century. To express this feature in the type of the deity would not be easy. The bow, as symbol of the rays of the sun-god,[2] is usual in the hand of Apollo in archaic representations; later the lyre is far more usual. Even wings do not altogether disappear, but they mostly lose their merely symbolic character and are used for flight, as in the case of Victory and Eros, an innovation ascribed to the sculptor Archermus of Chios (*c.* 570 B.C.). The god Hermes, even in late art, carries wings on his cap or his heels—a survival of archaic symbolism.

Coins furnish us with many examples of symbols belonging to the deities. In the 7th and 6th centuries the obverse of electrum and silver coins usually presents some very simple symbolical device—a griffin at Teos and Abdera, a thunderbolt at Olympia, a wolf at Argos, an owl at Athens; and then, after the archaic period, this type is usually banished to the reverse of the coin, and in its place we have the head of the deity to whom the type belongs. It must, however, be observed that, when numismatists speak of a symbol on a coin, they use the word in a technical sense, to indicate not a symbolical type, but one of those small and subsidiary devices often placed in the field of a coin by magistrates who were responsible for its issue—a device probably often taken from the private signet of such magistrates.

Another phase of symbolism is found when in artistic representation a part is taken to stand for the whole. This often appears on Greek vases and reliefs. Pausanias[3] observes that, in the painting representing Hades by Polygnotus at Delphi, the grove of Persephone is represented by one tree. So on vases a temple or a house is often represented by a single column, a river by a swimming fish, a sea-shore by a shell, and so forth. It is probable that this was how the scenes in tragedies were represented on the background of the stage. It is really a sort of shorthand, and altogether parallel to the process by which in Egypt and elsewhere picture-writing came into being.

Symbolical or allegorical impersonations are to be found in Greek art at all periods, though more often in archaic art and that of Hellenistic times than in the greatest period. On the chest of Cypselus, in the 7th cent., we are told by Pausanias[4] that Night was figured, carrying two boys, one white and one black, who represented Sleep and Death respectively. Justice as a beautiful figure

[1] v. xix. 9. [2] Homer, *Il.* i. 45.
[3] x. xxx. 6. [4] v. xviii.

scourged Injustice, who had the form of an ugly woman. Fate, with teeth and claws like a wild beast, claimed Polynices as a victim. Even in the great age we have such figures as Virtue, Nemesis, Opportunity (Καιρός). But it is in the Hellenistic age, in the great cities of the East, that symbolic personalities most abound. In the celebrated procession of Ptolemy II. of Egypt[1] we have figures of the Year and the Seasons; in that of Antiochus IV. of Syria[2] we find statues of Night, Day, Earth, Heaven, Morning, and Noon. On the coins of Alexandria under the Romans we find a remarkable set of fanciful figures—Euthenia (Prosperity), Kratesis (Dominion), and the like.

The great Ionian cities of Asia Minor appear on monuments of the Roman age in the persons of the legendary Amazons whom they claimed as their foundresses.[3] Smyrna on coins carries a double-axe and has a prow of a ship at her feet; Cyme holds a dolphin and a trident; Teos, a city renowned for vines, carries the thyrsus of Dionysus; Ephesus carries poppies and ears of corn, and so forth. In each case the attributes embody the situation or the produce of the city. In a noted Pompeian painting[4] we have well-characterized impersonations of Europe, Asia, and Africa. The list might be almost indefinitely lengthened.

Symbolism in Greece, in the great period, often takes fine poetic forms, as when the sun-god in his chariot on the pediment of the Parthenon represents the East in the morning, or boys plunging into the sea represent the setting stars on a fine vase in the British Museum.[5] In the same age rivers are represented by man-headed bulls, as on the coins of Gela and Catana in Sicily; nymphs have cows' horns; Alexander the Great appears on the money of his general Lysimachus with the ram's horn of Ammon.

But, in spite of such examples as these, there is a broad line of distinction between the use of symbolism in Oriental art—the art of Babylon, Assyria, Egypt, and India—and the use in Greek art. Oriental art is content with adding symbols to the human forms of deities, without caring for their beauty or appropriateness. In Egypt and Babylon we find human bodies joined to the heads of all kinds of animals—lion, bull, jackal, hawk, and so on. And Indian figures of deities represent them with several heads, many arms (each holding some attribute), necklaces of skulls, and the like. Oriental art tries to represent in this way qualities and attributes which sculpture or painting could not otherwise portray—elements of mysticism, mythological tales, or sometimes the ideas of pantheistic religion. Greek art avoids monstrous forms as a rule, though it inherits a few specially suitable for artistic development, such as the Centaur. And it does not attempt to portray, in sculpture or in painting, anything which lies outside the scope of those arts. Exquisite in form and clear in meaning, its creations do not carry us beyond sense and intellect, do not appeal to the mystical tendencies of men. Thus Greek symbolism has no wide limits.

II. *ROMAN*.—I. **In cult and law.**—In Roman religious ceremonies the symbol held a large place. This was natural, as in quite the early times of the republic there was an invasion of Greek religion and Greek deities, which caused the old rustic religion of the Roman people to survive only in the form of ritual, the meaning of which was in a great degree obscured. Hence the State cultus of Rome was divorced alike from belief and from morality, and, so long as the magistrates performed

[1] Athenæus, v. 196. [2] *Ib.* p. 194.
[3] *JHS* ix. [1888] 56.
[4] W. Helbig, *Wandgemälde Campaniens*, Leipzig, 1868, no. 1113.
[5] *Catalogue*, E 466.

exactly the ceremonies handed down by their ancestors, it mattered little what meaning they attached to those ceremonies or what beliefs they held in religion. The emperor, whether he were a Trajan or a Nero, was always *pontifex maximus* and represented to the gods the State in its religious capacity. Hence the Romans were extremely careful as to the way in which they wore the toga or the cap called *apex*, as to their exact position in relation to the points of the compass, and as to the attitude in which they stood when they were sacrificing. All these details had no doubt some meaning in their origin; but not only are we unable usually to discover what it was, but even the Romans did not know: they blindly followed the tradition, with an uneasy feeling that, unless they did so, some great calamity would overtake the State. Most of these ritual customs were probably derived from the Etruscans, a people at a low level of culture, but exact in all matters of a religion which seems scarcely to have risen above the level of magic.

When an official conducted a sacrifice, he sprinkled the victim with wine and threw over it salt meal; then he made a ritual motion symbolical of slaying it, but the actual butchering was done by attendants.[1] Like the Greeks, the Romans contrived to put in the place of human sacrifices the mere offering of substitutes and symbols.[2]

When the Greek deities migrated to Rome, they took with them their recognized symbols; and the native gods, who were largely identified with the immigrants, also adopted these outward signs of inward powers. Thus in art Greek customs went on, as in fact the artists were usually Greek. So we have on Roman monuments the symbolism of Ephesus and Alexandria. Allegorical and sym bolical figures, such as Pudicitia, Ubertas, Annona, appear abundantly on the Roman coins; but they can have had but little serious worship. In short, while symbolism is of importance in relation to Roman cultus, it is unimportant in earlier Roman art, requiring a concrete poetical imagination of which the Romans were destitute.

There was a good deal of symbolism or symbolic ritual in the customs of Roman law; *e.g.*, if a man purchased a slave, he laid hands on him (*mancipatio*) in the presence of witnesses and weighed out at the same time to the seller a piece of money which was accepted as a symbol of the price, *quasi pretii loco*, as Gaius says.[3] We need not be surprised that much symbolism made its way into Christianity in Rome, since it had become a recognized part of the routine of daily life.

2. In art.—In the time of the Roman dominion, as the religion of Mithras and other mystery cults spread from east to west through Europe, the range and power of symbolism increased. We may especially trace on tombstones of the period of the empire, alike in Italy, Gaul, and other regions, a growth of religious symbols mainly having reference to the life beyond the tomb, which was taking an ever larger place in men's thoughts and hopes. Some of the mythological scenes which the Greeks had depicted on tombs, from mere artistic and decorative motives, seem to have been re-interpreted in a more mystic fashion. Such were the rapes of women and the combats of men; and more especially scenes from the lives of Heracles and Orpheus and other heroic persons who had won immortality by great deeds, or had descended into Hades and returned. Some ordinary figures of earlier art—the griffin, the lion, the bull, the cock—became connected with the hope of immortality. The Mithraic shrines of northern Europe contain reliefs in which symbolism seems to run wild, though we know so little about Mithraism that our interpretation of such reliefs is usually conjectural. On this subject the works of Franz Cumont are authoritative. It is impossible here to discuss the question of the symbolism on later pagan tombs. A good account of it will be found in Mrs. Arthur Strong's *Apotheosis and After Life* (1915). This writer, however, goes too far in interpreting almost all the scenes and figures on such tombs in reference to the future life. It is obvious that, unless we keep in restraint the tendency to read mystic meanings into painted and sculptured scenes, we may drift back into the fancy world of Creuzer, who traced the influence of the mysteries everywhere on Greek vases and Roman reliefs. We are on safer ground in speaking of contemporary Christian art, because here we have a literature for comparison.

In the early Christian art[1] of the catacombs and of sarcophagi there is even an increase of symbolism, as compared with contemporary pagan works. This is natural, because the Christians commonly adopted pagan types, only giving them a fresh meaning; *e.g.*, the peacock, which in Greek art belonged to Hera, became to Christians a symbol of the resurrection, probably because the flesh of the peacock was supposed not to decay. Orpheus became an emblem or symbol of Christ. The fish, the sheep, the vine, all acquired a new Christian signification. Probably in many cases the meaning would not be realized by the pagan artist who was called in; and it was safer that the knowledge should be confined to the society. This symbolism is apt to degenerate into something like shorthand: a man carrying a couch refers to the miracle of the healing of the paralytic man; a cock beside Peter to his denial of his Master, and so forth.

The use of symbols in the later Neo-Platonic philosophy is so closely connected with their use in Christianity that it need not be here treated. See art. NEO-PLATONISM.

LITERATURE.—There is no recent work which deals methodically with Greek symbolism. Roman symbolism is treated in Mrs. Arthur Strong, *Apotheosis and After Life*, London, 1915.

P. GARDNER.

SYMBOLISM (Hindu).

—Of all religions of the East, the home of type and imagery, Hinduism makes the most use of symbols. It has formally declared the ultimate truth to be unknowable and indefinable. In all its scheme of practice and teaching it seeks to make definite approach to the reality by suggestive type or symbol—an approach that can never find its goal, but can only draw nearer and nearer, as it points successively, like the ancient Greek philosophers, to the symbol or likeness which most fully and faithfully reflects the true, and embodies the largest part of a reality which in its entirety is inconceivable by the human mind and inexpressible in the language of men. The symbol is the necessary and helpful intermediary between the inadequate capacity of the mind of the would-be worshipper and the incommunicable nature and fullness of the Unknown whom he adores. A complete and adequate description therefore of the Hindu use of type and symbol would require an almost complete exposition of Hindu belief in its many varieties and ramifications. Whether in creed or in practice, the symbolic in Hinduism is not far from being co-extensive with the religion itself. Of this the literature of Hinduism and its systems of doctrine are sufficient illustration. All, however, that is practicable within the limits of an article is to indicate the motive or motives that more or less consciously and avowedly have prompted the use of the symbol, to set forth in the briefest possible

1 G. Wissowa, *Religion und Kultus der Römer*, Munich, 1902, p. 352.

2 *Ib.* p. 355.

3 i. 119.

1 Cf. art. SYMBOLISM (Christian).

manner its historical relations in the religious scheme and cult, to define its necessary limits, and to select for illustration and comment a few of the more important types which have occupied a considerable place in the belief and profession of the adherents of the faith. A mere enumeration of the symbols employed would be a large and probably impossible task.

1. Use and purpose of symbols.—The use and purpose of the symbol is twofold: (1) to set forth in visible or audible likeness what cannot be really or fully expressed to the physical eye or ear, or even clearly conceived by the limited faculties of the human mind. All language is in the last resort symbolic, and religious language in an especial degree, for it endeavours to present a mystery, a reality too deep for words. The Hindu faith had at its service a language of the utmost delicacy and flexibility, with a vigorous and fertile growth and an almost unlimited vocabulary, and found itself in a world of tropical luxuriance, with a tropical wealth of beauty and suggestiveness. It was not to be wondered at that it became profuse in type and symbol and laid under contribution all the facts and phenomena of nature to serve its religious and priestly ends. All the great gods had their resemblances, animal or material forms, in which they presented themselves embodied to human sight, which served to recall to the worshipper the deity, whose mind and character they more or less inadequately reflected. Other more rare and refined symbols were presentative of qualities or attributes, as the lotus, the emblem of spotless purity preserved under the most unfriendly conditions. All idols, totems, fetishes are symbols. The wise man does not worship the symbol, the shape in clay or wood or stone, but is thereby reminded of the invisible substance or reality which they each represent.

(2) The image or symbol serves the purpose also of providing in material and suitable form a convenient object of reverence, to meet the religious need of those whose minds, through darkness and ignorance, are unable to grasp the conception of an unseen formless deity. Such men, if left without a visible object to which their reverence and fear may attach themselves, will wander in a maze of doubt, disquiet, and unbelief. It is better that they should worship erroneously, worship a thing, than that they should not worship at all. There is much that might be urged in favour of the Hindu view that regards the worship of the external symbol as a stepping-stone to higher, clearer forms of belief; it is a view unacknowledged perhaps but not unknown to other faiths. And in Hinduism, whatever may be said of or claimed by the wise and instructed thinker, the *pūjā* of the multitude to the image of the god is reverent and sincere. In some respects also and within definite limits the Indian contention has justified itself that the symbol has proved a signpost and a guide to better, higher thoughts and to a truer worship of Him whom no form can express or language describe.

2. The most important types.—(*a*) The most important symbols are those of the *Brahman*, the undefinable and unknowable origin and source of all. Of the *Brahman* only signs and types can be employed, for the primeval source and sustainer of the universe is beyond and above thought or word. His names or titles are symbolic: *hiranyagarbha*, the golden germ, that was in the beginning; *svayambhū*, the self-existent one; *viśvakarman*, the artificer of all things; and many others. The authors of the *Upaniṣads* especially attempt to set forth in symbolic terms the being and nature of that which in the last resort they are obliged to confess is beyond knowledge. *Prāṇa*, the breath, or *vāyu*, the wind, is a frequently recurring type; and it seems to have been felt that by its mysterious and elusive character the *prāṇa* was peculiarly fitted to represent that which in its essence eludes comprehension. The breath, *prāṇa*, is *Brahman*.[1] A similar type is the *ākāśa*, the all-pervading and all-surrounding ether, 'omnipresent and unchanging in the heart.'[2] *Manas* also, the mind or will, is with the *ākāśa* a symbolic form or type under which the *Brahman* is to be meditated on or worshipped.[3] The mystical syllable *Om*, the most widely venerated syllable in the world, is the highest *Brahman*, and its utterance with understanding of its significance secures the accomplishment of every wish.[4] *Om* is also a symbol of the Hindu triad, Brahmā, Viṣṇu, and Śiva, and each of the three sounds of which the word is composed represents one of these deities. To the Buddhists also the word is a symbol of much significance, forming part of the sacred six-syllabled formula which every Buddhist cherishes in his memory and makes a constant part of his invocation and prayer.

A more comprehensive and suggestive symbol of the *Brahman* is given in the compound *sachchidānanda*, a kind of triple representation in three several modes or aspects, as *sat*, 'being,' *chit*, 'thought,' and *ānanda*, 'bliss.'[5] This more refined and abstract symbolizing represents a later phase of speculative thought and marks a forward step in the progress of philosophic insight. As a type or symbol it is less inadequate than the sun in the heavens (*āditya*),[6] the material *ākāśa*, the golden *puruṣa* in the eye,[7] or even than *manas*, or the significant name *ātman* itself. In its further course, moreover, speculative thought denied that even in *sachchidānanda* any positive implication concerning the *Brahman* did or could reside. The *Brahman* transcended all symbols and assertions, comprehended both being and not-being (*sat, asat*), thought and not-thought (*chit, achit*), bliss and its contrary (*ānanda, anānanda*), or rather he was above and beyond all, the unsearchable and unknown.

(*b*) Each of the great gods has an animal or material form or object which represents him to the eyes of men, by which he is symbolically known. The more popular gods have many symbols. The 'vehicles' of the gods are practically symbols of their presence and power—the goose of Brahmā; Garuda, the monstrous eagle of Viṣṇu; the bull (Nandi) of Śiva; the fabulous sea-monster (*makara*) of Varuṇa, who is then depicted as a white man and is described as *makarāśva*, 'he whose steed is the *makara*,' riding, with the head and fore-legs of an antelope and the body and tail of a fish; the peacock of Kārttikeya, the god of war; the monkey of Hanumān; the deer of Vāyu; the elephant Airavata of Indra, produced with other sacred and marvellous objects at the churning of the ocean; the buffalo and dogs of Yama; and many others. Of the well-known Hindu triad Brahmā hardly possesses any emblem or type except his sacred goose—an indication of how little the first member of the triad attracted to himself the thought and worship of the Hindu. Of the popular Viṣṇu there were many symbols, some of which are always represented on the images or pictures of the god. The most frequent and characteristic is perhaps the *chakra*, or discus;

1 *Kauś.* ii. 1 f.

2 *Chhānd.* III. xii. 7–9 (*SBE* i. 46); *Bṛhad.* III. vii. 12, 16, iv. 1. 3.

3 *Chhānd.* III. xviii. 1 (*SBE* i. 53); *Bṛhad.* IV. i. 6.

4 *Bṛhad.* v. i. 1; *Kaṭha*, I. ii. 16; cf. Manu, ii. 83.

5 *Chhānd.* VI. ii. 1, VIII. xii. 4; *Taitt.* ii. 1, iii. 4–6; *Bṛhad.* II. i. 20, iii. 6. The formula itself as a whole is found only in late Upaniṣads; cf. Deussen, *Up.* p. 126 ff.

6 *Chhānd.* III. xix. 1 (*SBE* i. 54).

7 *Taitt.* II. viii. 5; *Chhānd.* I. vi. 8.

the club and conch-shell also which he carries are indicative of his authority and power. The auspicious mark (*śrīvatsa*) usually represented on the breast of the god, in form like a curl of hair, and the three-pronged or trident-like mark made with white or coloured earths on the foreheads of his worshippers are symbolic, the latter of devotion to the service of the deity. The sacred *tulasī* plant in the courtyard of the dwelling is the mark of the deity's presence and protection, and in it centres the worship especially of the women of the household. The *śālagrāma* also, the sacred ammonite-stone, is another mystical and well-known symbol.

The symbolic types or presentations of the rival deity, Śiva, who in almost equal degree with Viṣṇu holds the affection and regard of the Indian peoples, were equally numerous. The most important are the bull Nandi, on which he rides, and the *liṅga*, or phallus. Every Śaivite temple has its sacred bull, who roams the courtyards and streets unmolested and receives practically divine honours. The *liṅga* is the commonest emblem of the god, and the stones, great or small, which represent him have this form or are roughly shaped to it. Two of these stones are said to bear a pre-eminently holy character: that at Benares, where Śiva is worshipped as Viśveśvara, παντοκράτωρ, the lord of all; and the idol in the temple at Somnath, destroyed by Mahmud of Ghazni in his iconoclastic raid into India. The trident also is borne by Śiva, a type of government and authority; and the crescent moon depicted on his forehead has a special significance, recalling the sovereignty which was assigned to him when the moon was recovered from the depths of the ocean.

Similarly the wives of the great gods have each their symbols—the trident and skull of Kālī, the lotus of Sarasvatī, wife of Brahmā, and also of Lakṣmī, wife of Viṣṇu.

In a late writing the Gāyatrī is said to represent the triad of gods, Brahmā, Viṣṇu, and Śiva, and also the three Vedas.

(*c*) Under sacred trees in the vicinity of Indian villages will often be found the images or symbols of the *grāmadevatā*, the village divinities who watch over its interests and care for the inhabitants; and in the village fields the clay or pottery steeds of Aiyanar (*q.v.*), the tutelary deity of the fields, on which he rides by night to pursue and rout the demoniac powers.

(*d*) There are symbols also of a more general import, which are not always easy to classify. The *piṇḍa*, or ball of cooked rice, used at the commemorative services for deceased relatives and offered to the *pitṛs*, represents symbolically the share which the departed still have in the family life. The most important and widely recognized symbol of this character is probably the sacred footprint, which typifies both the presence and the authority of the god. In the courtyard or vicinity of many, perhaps most, Hindu temples there is the print of a foot on the ground, often of large size, with sacred symbols engraved on the sole, which differ according to the deity commemorated. To these there is sometimes a legend attached, which gives its supposed history and describes the occasion on which it was impressed. The well-known footprint on Adam's Peak in Ceylon is believed by Śaivites to be that of Śiva. By Buddhists also the numerous footprints of the Buddha are regarded with reverence.

(*e*) In many parts of India the symbols of the sun and moon and the planets may be seen. The two first are represented by a disk or crescent respectively, made of metal. The signs of the planets in their order are as follows: of Budha, or Mercury, a bow; of Śukra, or Venus, a square; of Maṅgala, or Mars, a triangle; of Vṛhaspati, or Jupiter, a lotus; of Śani, or Saturn, an iron scimitar or sword; of Rāhu, a *makara*; and of Ketu, a snake. The last two symbols are usually of iron; the square of Śukra is silver or silvered, and the bow of Budha is gilt.

(*f*) Hindu coins and seals also bore symbols, which were very numerous and diversified. Besides figures of gods and goddesses, the commonest emblems were the trident, denoting empire; the elephant or bull, power; the umbrella, royal dignity and right; the crescent, a lunar dynasty; a thunderbolt, spear, or other weapon, armed might. Others also with these were indicative of the authority or claims of the sovereign by whom they were designed.

LITERATURE.—W. J. Wilkins, *Hindu Mythology, Vedic and Puranic*^{2}, Calcutta and London, 1900; M. Monier-Williams, *Brāhmanism and Hindūism*^{4}, London, 1891; W. Crooke, *PR*, 2 vols., do. 1896; V. A. Smith, *A Hist. of Fine Art in India and Ceylon*, Oxford, 1911, ch. x., 'Symbols on Coins and Seals, etc.'; E. J. Rapson, 'Indian Coins,' in *GIAP* ii. 3B, Strassburg, 1898; J. A. Dubois, *Hindu Manners, Customs, and Ceremonies*, Eng. tr.^{3}, Oxford, 1906.

A. S. GEDEN.

SYMBOLISM (Jewish).—Symbolic actions as well as symbolic ideas occur in the Hebrew Bible frequently. The prophets often made use of symbolic ideas—*e.g.*, the basket of fruit in Am 8^1, the vineyard in Is 5^{1-7}, the almond-trees in Jer 1^{11}, the dry bones in Ezk 37^{1-14}, and the various figures in Zechariah. Equally frequent are symbolic actions—*e.g.*, the rending of mantles (1 S 15^{27}, 1 K 11^{30}), the discharge of arrows from a bow (2 K 13^{15-19}), the casting of shoes (Ps 60^8, Jos 5^{15}, Ru 4^7). The former type easily merges into the parable, the latter into charms; possibly we should say that they emerge from these literary and magical arts. Symbols, in any case, have frequent historical connexion with primitive culture, though they tend to transcend their origin under the transforming influence of higher conceptions. Most important, therefore, for the present article is the association of symbolic ideas with religious ceremonial. Prominently the Sabbath is described as a symbol, *ôth*;[1] similarly with the rite of circumcision (Gn 17^{11}), the phylacteries (Dt 6^8), the Passover (Ex 13^9), natural phenomena such as the rainbow (Gn 9^{12}; cf. Gn 1^{14} in the Rabbinical commentaries).

It was accordingly easy for later Judaism to apply symbolic meanings to many of the Biblical institutions. Philo, throughout his works, elaborates such interpretations, but the method is much older. Thus in the *Letter of Aristeas* (which can scarcely be later than the 2nd cent. B.C. and may well belong to a century earlier) the enactments as to the animals lawful for food are explained symbolically.[2] But by Philo's age symbolical interpretation had so fully developed that the Alexandrian allegorist felt impelled to rebuke those of his brethren who neglected the ceremonial acts because they regarded them merely as symbols of ideal things.[3] Though this is a real danger to a ceremonial religion, on the other side it can gain appreciably by idealizing institutions the original significance of which is outworn or unknown. Ancient rites may have been derived from primitive tabus, and yet they have retained permanent acceptance by the process of symbolization. In a remarkable letter Maimonides (*q.v.*) dealt with certain acts of worship, such as prostration (as practised by Muhammadans in the 12th century). Probably such acts were derived from olden customs of exposing parts of the body, but, contends Maimonides,[4] they no longer mean anything

[1] See art. SABBATH (Jewish). [2] §§ 139–166.

[3] *De Migr. Abrahami*, 16 (*Opera*, ed. T. Mangey, London, 1742, i. 450).

[4] *Teshûbôth She'elôth we-Iggarôth* ('Letters'), Constantinople, 1520, fol. 5*b*.

of the kind and have become symbols of humility. Present values do not entirely depend on past origins. A similar principle might undoubtedly be very widely applied to the history of religious ceremonial, which often becomes ennobled by the newer ideas read into it by progressive ages. And, conversely, when an institution is lost (as with the Biblical sacrifices), the whole system may be retrospectively idealized by symbolical adaptation. When, after the destruction of the Temple, prayer and charity and fasting perforce displaced sacrifice, the latter shared in the moralizing process. But the relation went deeper. Fasting *was* sacrifice: the loss of bodily tissue corresponded (in the Rabbinic conception) to the offering of a sacrificial animal on the altar.[1] The table at which the ordinary meals were eaten became a veritable altar,[2] and the partaking of food was in the Jewish home associated with a variety of customs, derived in large part from the same range of symbolism. It has often been claimed, moreover, that the dietary laws, besides being included in the law of holiness, or rather because of that inclusion, were a training in control of the appetites and restraint of desires.[3] Maimonides also offers a utilitarian view, that the forbidden food was unwholesome;[4] thus showing that, though the utilitarian and the symbolical interpretations are in a sense rival theories, they may be syncretized by a skilful moralist.[5]

Another aspect of the same phenomenon is presented by symbolic survivals. Acts which were once literal are retained as rites. Many current Jewish marriage customs are of this nature. The bridal canopy, so picturesque a feature of a Jewish wedding, was originally the marriage chamber. Then the Scriptural application of the marital state to the relation of God to Israel led to symbolic results, among them the appointment of a bridegroom of the Law on the feast of Rejoicing at the end of Tabernacles.[6] It is not quite clear why a glass is broken at Jewish weddings; it is probably a *memento mori.*[7] Funeral customs are also marked by symbolic survivals. Some of these are Kabbalistic in origin, and it is not always easy to discriminate the symbolical from the superstitious.[8] So, too, with such ceremonies as *tashlikh.*[9] Many symbolical customs arose in memory of the destruction of the Temple. Historical associations are also responsible for many a symbolic rite. Draping the synagogues in black on the fast of the 9th of Ab is an instance in point. The *shofar*, or ram's horn, was thus connected with events and anticipations, with Sinai in the past and the Messianic age in the future. According to Se'adiah, the *shofar* symbolized ten ideas: (1) creation, (2) repentance, (3) revelation, (4) prophecy, (5) destruction of the Temple, (6) the binding of Isaac, (7) imminence of danger, (8) day of judgment, (9) restoration of Israel, and (10) resurrection. In this manner many rites were saved from becoming obsolete. The phylacteries worn on the head typify service of the mind; on the hand, service of the body. The former represents the recognition of the Godhead, the latter restraint of lust.[1]

[1] *Num. Rabbāh*, 18. [2] T.B. *Ber.* 55*a*.
[3] Maimonides, *The Guide of the Perplexed*, tr. M. Friedländer, London, 1885, iii. 25.
[4] *Ib.* iii. 48.
[5] Cf. on this point M. Friedländer, *The Jewish Religion*, p. 456; M. Joseph, *Judaism as Creed and Life*, p. 194. In modern times there has been a strong tendency (often unhistorical) to explain symbols on utilitarian grounds.
[6] On greeting the Sabbath bride see *Annotated Ed. of Auth. Daily Prayer Book*, pp. cxxiv, 111 (this work may be consulted throughout for liturgical symbolism).
[7] Cf. I. Abrahams, *Jewish Life in the Middle Ages*, London, 1896, ch. x.
[8] The best collection of the customs connected with illness and death may be found in Aaron b. Moses, *Ma'abar Yabboḳ*, Mantua, 1626 (often reprinted).
[9] *JE*, *s.v.*

Jewish symbolism is also illustrated in ecclesiastical art, and in colours. Thus the blue thread on the fringes (Nu 15^{38}) is the colour of the sea, the sky, the divine throne of glory.[2] The symbolism of art was more thoroughgoing. The Crown of the Law is a frequent ornament on mantles of the scrolls, and so is the Shield of David.[3] On ancient Jewish coins, too, symbols were employed; so also with tombs.

The prevalent custom now is to avoid sepulchral emblems. This accords with the oldest rule, for the *ṣiyyun* of the Talmud was only a mark warning wayfarers against incurring ritual impurity by contact with the tomb. Yet the action of Simon, who carved panoplies and (possibly) ships on the pyramidal tombs at Modin (1 Mac 13^{29}), can scarcely have been isolated. Outside Palestine the Jews of the first centuries of the Christian era certainly adopted the Greek habit of inscriptions and introduced symbols, such as an oil vessel, the seven-branched candlestick (symbolical of the soul [Pr 20^{27}]), the ram's horn (Messianic), and an ear of corn (type of the resurrection). These emblems are parallel to those on the Maccabæan coins and to those favoured by Jews in the late mediæval period. At that late date symbols appear descriptive of the dead, as out-stretched palms as in act of benediction (for priest), ewer as in act of bathing (Levite), a harp for a musician, a crown for a goldsmith, and so forth. In the 18th cent. Jews, like their Christian neighbours, used symbolical signs for houses and businesses. Thus the Rothschild family still exemplifies the custom in its name ('Red Shield'). Ornamental coats-of-arms are found on tombs in the oldest Jewish burial-ground of the Sephardic Jews in London. Such customs are no longer in vogue. There has been a growth, however, of symbolism in synagogue decoration in the form of glass windows mostly without human or animal figures.

In the Talmud a good deal of legal symbolism was taken over from ancient Biblical as well as from Roman law.[4] Some of this is still retained.

Returning to the more religious aspect of the subject, we may say in general that in the Midrash symbolism is the soul of Jewish ceremonial. Many particulars of the sacrificial system, the ritual of the Temple, synagogue, and home, are treated in this manner. Take, *e.g.*, the rites of Tabernacles—the bearing of palm-branch, citron, myrtle, and willows of the brook (Lv 23^{40}). The palm is the spine, the citron the heart, the myrtle the eye, the willow the mouth, so that, in the synagogue liturgy, the citron atones for heart sins, the palm for stiff-necked pride, the willow for foul speech, the myrtle for lusts of the eye. In another version the old homilists[5] explain the 'four kinds' as symbolizing four types of character. The citron has both scent and taste, so there are men who study and perform; the palm-date has taste but no scent, so there are men who study but do not perform; the myrtle has scent but no taste, so there are men who perform but not on the basis of study; the willow has neither scent nor taste, so there are men who neither study the law nor perform good deeds. The Holy One did not destroy these, but bade all be united into one bundle, the better elements atoning for the less

[1] Cf. *Shulḥān 'Ārukh*, i. ch. 25.
[2] Cf. *Sifrē* on the text.
[3] On this see *JE* viii. 251 f. and *Jewish Opinion*, London, Jan. 1919. The Tree of Life (on the basis of Pr 3^{18}) was also a symbol of the life-giving power of the Law, and the Tree accordingly appears in synagogue decorations.
[4] Cf. S. Krauss, *Talmud. Archäologie*, Leipzig, 1910–12, iii. 8. On the symbolism of the shoe see *JQR*, new ser., vi. [1915–16] 1–22.
[5] *P^{e}siqtā R.*, 28, ed. M. Friedmann, Vienna, 1880, p. 178.

good. In this manner symbolism is turned to the cause of humanism.

LITERATURE.—The authorities are cited in the course of the article. See particularly M. Friedländer, *The Jewish Religion*, London, 1891, pp. 328 f., 335, 344, 356, 487; M. Joseph, *Judaism as Creed and Life*, do. 1903, Introd., ch. i. (end) and *passim; JE, s.v.* 'Symbol'; *Annotated Edition of the Authorised Daily Prayer Book*, ed. I. Abrahams, London, 1914.

I. ABRAHAMS.

SYMBOLISM (Muslim). — The Islāmic languages appear to have no exact equivalent for 'symbol.' When it signifies a badge indicative of office, party, or community, the nearest would be *shi'ār*, or in certain cases *ghiyār*; where what is meant by it is a veiled expression for an idea, the Arabic rendering would be *kināyah*.

Islām as a religious system has nothing corresponding to the Christian cross. Muhammad seems to have adopted the Roman eagle as the standard for his armies,[1] but the flag of the later ('Abbasid) khalīfahs was 'like any other, only black in colour with the legend in white, "Muhammad is the Apostle of God."'[2] Those borne by various factions and regiments differed in colour and at times in the wording of the legend; thus the 'Abbasid colour was black, the 'Alawid green, the Umayyad white; the flag of the Zanji pretender of the year 255 A.H. was a strip of silk with a Qur'ānic legend in red and green;[3] in the processions of the sultans of Tunis white, red, yellow, and green flags were carried; those of the different tribes differed in legend;[4] the flags of the different divisions of the Ottoman army were red, yellow, green, white, red and white, green and white.[5] The Muhammadan colour in India is green,[6] which by an ordinance of the Mamluk Sultan Sha'ban of 773 A.H. on the turban indicates descent from the Prophet.[7]

There is no more common error than the supposition that the crescent (or rather crescent and star) is an Islāmic symbol, and even approved writers on Oriental subjects are apt to fall into it.[8] It was certainly in pre-Turkish times sometimes used as an ornament on the minarets of mosques;[9] and on flags—*e.g.*, that of the Fāṭimids of Egypt, accompanied by a lion of red and yellow satin,[10] and that of the Almohads (A.D. 1159)[11]—and on the sedan-chair of a Zanjid princess.[12] As such the crescent had been employed on the Roman senatorial shoe—a practice for which Plutarch[13] offers a variety of reasons. The current view of its adoption by the Turks is well presented by F. T. Elworthy:

'Hera, under her old moon-name, Iö, had a celebrated temple on the site of Byzantium, said to have been founded by her daughter Keroëssa, "the horned." The crescent, which was in all antiquity and throughout the Middle Ages the symbol of Byzantium, and which is now the symbol of the Turkish Empire, is a direct inheritance from Byzantium's mythical foundress Keroëssa, the daughter of the moon goddess Iö-Hera.'[1]

Keroëssa, supposed to have been not the foundress, but the mother of the founder, of Byzantium, seems to have been an inference from the Golden Horn and so to have no place in this inquiry. Further, it seems correct to say that the crescent and star figure, though rarely, on coins of Byzantium, but as one of numerous ornaments,[2] and that no ancient author mentions any connexion between this emblem and the city. The *signa Constantinopoleos*, according to A. Geofræus,[3] who asserts that the Turks 'neque insigniis utuntur neque coronis,' were quite different. The earliest mention of it in English literature is said to be in the *Arte of English Poesie* by G. Puttenham (1589),[4] who ascribes its introduction to the sultan Selim I. (1512–20), with the notion of increase and brightness, though it has been observed[5] that the crescent is not that of the new but that of the waning moon, while rising in its wake is the morning star of hope; from Puttenham's time the antithesis between it and the cross has been common in English and French literature. F. Sansovino,[6] however, supposes it to have been the ancient emblem of Bosnia, adopted by Muhammad II. when that country was conquered in 1463. This is declared to be an error by Zinkeisen,[7] who speaks of a golden crescent inherited from the Seljuks, and displayed on all the flags and standards of viziers, beglerbegs, etc., appearing on the earliest flags of the Janissaries. With von Hammer Purgstall[8] it is a silver crescent which, with the two-pointed sword of 'Umar, gleamed on the blood-red flag of the earliest Janissaries; in the authority to which he refers[9] the Janissaries' flag displays the sword without the crescent; what appears on the flag of the cavalry is evidently a horseshoe rather than a crescent, with no star. It is worth noticing that the Seljuk chronicler Ibn Bibi[10] compares the shoe of the sultan 'Ala-addin's horse to a crescent and its nails to stars; whence the symbol may originally belong to cavalry regiments. Its occurrence, however, on certain Byzantine coins is remarkable, and seems to have some connexion with its later employment by the Turks, who have not often introduced it on coins.

The symbols of royalty in use at the Islāmic courts were similar to those found elsewhere. In Umayyad times the khalīfah on accession received a rod, a signet, and a scroll.[11] The rod was doubtless the Prophet's; in 'Abbasid times a new khalīfah received not only the Prophet's signet, which was a silver ring with a bezel of Chinese iron with the legend 'Muhammad is the Prophet of God,' but that of his predecessor, with a ruby inscribed with the khalīfah's name.[12] The 'Abbasid khalīfah also wore a crown,[13] against Arab usage;[14] and indeed the etiquette of their court was closely modelled on that of the Sasanians, as appears from the recently published handbook of it by Jāḥiẓ of Basrah.[15] A crown was worn by the Fāṭimids of

1 A. von Kremer, *Culturgesch. des Orients*, Vienna, 1875–77, i. 81.
2 Miskawaihi, tr. D. S. Margoliouth, i. 198.
3 Ṭabarī, *Chronicle*, ed. M. J. de Goeje, Leyden, 1879–1901, iii. 1748.
4 Qalqashandī, *Subḥ al-A'sha*, Cairo, 1915, v. 143.
5 J. W. Zinkeisen, *Gesch. des osmanischen Reiches in Europa*, Gotha, 1840–63, iii. 271.
6 J. W. Kaye and G. B. Malleson, *Hist. of the Mutiny*, London, 1888–89, v. 82.
7 Ibn Iyās, *History of Egypt*, Cairo, 1311, i. 227.
8 Kaye and Malleson, iii. 96: 'From the time when Mahmud of Ghazni had introduced the crescent as a sign of rule and domination in the country of the Hindus.' Al-Biruni, *Chronology of Ancient Nations*, tr. E. Sachau, London, 1879, p. 293, compares with the Christian symbolism of the cross the comparison of the name Muḥammad with the human figure.
9 See a case about A.D. 1270 in the mosque of San'a in Yemen (Khazraji, *The Pearl-Strings*, tr. J. W. Redhouse, Leyden, 1906–08, i. 189).
10 Qalqashandī, iii. 474.
11 E. Mercier, *Hist. de l'Afrique septentrionale (Berbérie)*, Paris, 1888–90, ii. 100.
12 Ibn Jubair, *Viaggio*, tr. C. Schiaparelli, Rome, 1906, p. 226.
13 *Quæst. Rom.* p. 281.

1 *The Evil Eye*, London, 1895, p. 183.
2 Provisionally collected by J. H. von Eckhel, *Doctrina Nummorum Veterum*, Vienna, 1792–98, ii. 28.
3 *Aulæ Turcicæ Descriptio*, Basel, 1577, p. 3.
4 In *English Reprints*, ed. E. Arber, London, 1868, p. 117.
5 By G. H. Lancaster, *Prophecy, the War, and the Near East*, London, 1916, p. 151.
6 *Hist. universale dei Turchi*, Venice, 1568, f. 67.
7 iii. 273.
8 *Gesch. des osmanischen Reiches*, Pest, 1827–35, i. 93.
9 Plate XVII. in Comte de Marsigli's *État militaire de l'empire ottoman*, The Hague, 1732, ii. 53.
10 Ed. M. T. Houtsma, Leyden, 1902, p. 204.
11 *Aghani*, Cairo, 1323, vi. 106.
12 Miskawaihi, i. 329. He also inherited the Prophet's cloak (*burdah*), turban, and throne or pulpit.
13 *Diwan* of Buḥturī, Constantinople, 1300, i. 70, ii. 153, etc.
14 *Mutanabbii Carmina cum Comm. Wāhidii*, ed. F. Dieterici, Berlin, 1861, p. 380.
15 *Livre de la Couronne*, ed. Ahmed Zeki, Cairo, 1914.

Egypt also.[1] In their processions there were borne a rod, a special sword (said to have been made of meteorite), an inkpot, a lance, a target (said to have belonged to the Prophet's uncle Ḥamzah), a horse-shoe-shaped ruby,[2] and a canopy or umbrella. The last of these was a common emblem of royalty, and figures, *e.g.*, at Indian courts,[3] where the sovereign in the 16th cent. was attired 'in a white *qaba*, made like a shirt tied with strings on the one side, and a little cloth on his head coloured oftentimes with red or yellow.'[4] The *qaba* appears in the attire of the Buwaihid Mu'izz al-Daulah (10th cent.),[5] and, with a black robe, a belt, and a sword, it formed the distinguishing dress of a vizier.[6] Apparently the belt symbolized some sort of subordination, as an Indian prince to whom Yamin al-Daulah gave a robe of honour had to be compelled to put on this portion of it.[7]

Homage to a newly-appointed sovereign was (at any rate in early times) indicated by a shake of the hand, the meaning of which is shown by the term employed to be agreement over a bargain. In later times homage was indicated by kissing the ground before the ruler; this practice, originally alien to Islāmic ideas, had become familiar before the end of the 4th Islāmic century.[8] To a newly-appointed vizier (or emir) food was sent in the 4th cent. from the khalīfah's table,[9] probably signifying that he had become a member of the royal household. The practice of offering such a person fragrant herbs[10] is said to have been a purely Persian or Dailemite rite, the sense of which is not clear.

Owing to Islāmic objection to the limner's art, symbolism is very scanty in its architecture, and where found appears to be borrowed. The great mosque of Cordova exhibited in the carvings of its lattices the peculiar form of the Indian cross, the meaning of which is unknown, whereas 'the cresting of the walls, originally painted scarlet, is typical of flame, and, brought from Persia, symbolized the faith of the Ghebers, worshippers of fire.'[11] Probably in such cases the Muslim worshippers and spectators were quite ignorant of the signification. The same is likely to be true of the ornaments to be found on other works of art, such as pottery and textiles. Certain creatures are indeed habitually associated with particular ideas, chiefly on etymological grounds—*e.g.*, the raven with parting—but there is little scope for their employment in art. The symbolism of magical or quasi-magical rites in use in some communities (*e.g.*, the figures representing either a double hand or the spathe of the male palm, indicative of fertility, painted in Tunis on the walls of the house where there is to be a wedding)[12] is probably not Islāmic.

The practices of Islāmic ritual are tralatitious, though taken from many different communities; their symbolic interpretation is therefore conjectural, and is the subject of considerable speculation. Several pages are devoted by the mystic Ibn 'Arabī to the meaning of the postures of prayer (*ṣalāt*):

'The raising of the hands implies that whatever was therein has fallen away; it is as though the Almighty, when He commanded this, said, "When thou standest before Me, stand as a poor mendicant, who owns nothing; fling away everything that thou possessest, and stand empty-handed, setting it behind thee; for I am in front of thee." Moreover since the hands are the seat of power, by raising his hands he confesses that the power is God's, not his own; he who raises them to the chest is thinking that God is in front of him; he who raises them to his ears is thinking that God is above him. Sitting in prayer is the attitude of the slave before his master, an attitude which he may not adopt without the master's leave,' etc.[1]

Similar speculations on the meaning of the ceremonies of the pilgrimage are to be found in the work of Ghazālī;[2] the special garments worn by the pilgrim, *e.g.*, are to remind him of the grave-clothes wherein he will meet his Maker.

Besides explaining much of the Qur'ān as elaborate symbolism the Ṣūfīs (*q.v.*) developed a system of their own, or rather a number of systems; and there are numerous collections of odes in Arabic and Persian which, ostensibly dealing with love and wine, are traditionally interpreted as dealing with the doctrines of pantheism. Illustrations of the style will be found in the commentary of H. Wilberforce Clarke on his translation of the *Divān* of Hāfiz,[3] where we are told that 'breeze' signifies the means whereby union with the Desired One is attained, 'bell' signifies the angel of death, 'dark night' the world, 'wave' the excess of divine knowledge, etc., whereas in some cases the same term is variously explained; thus 'narcissus' may signify the growth of the world, the pure existence of God, the vision of God, or inward results of joy in respect of deeds. These interpretations are not always very convincing; but in some works of the kind the symbolism is either interpreted by the author himself or is sufficiently clear or conventional to leave no doubt of the meaning; an example is to be found in the *Masnavi* of Jalāl al-Dīn Rūmī.[4]

The employment of symbolic acts, either to emphasize language or in lieu of it, is common with Oriental peoples, but not specially Islāmic. The same parable has a tendency to do duty through many centuries. Ibn al-Athir records (A.H. 442) how, when an Arab tribe proposed to take Kairawan, they selected as their commander a man who offered to pursue the following plan: taking a carpet, he unfolded it, and then said to the others, 'Which of you can get to the middle of this carpet without treading upon it?' They declared it to be impossible. He showed them that the carpet had to be rolled up from the edge, meaning that the country had gradually to be conquered and secured. According to W. G. Palgrave, Ibrahim Pasha obtained the command of an expedition against Nejd eight centuries after by solving the problem of the carpet.[5]

LITERATURE.—See the works quoted in the footnotes.

D. S. MARGOLIOUTH.

SYMBOLISM (Semitic).—The extent to which symbolism exists in OT literature is very doubtful. In the case of the Babylonians and Assyrians, however, our knowledge is much more definite and is obtained chiefly from a study of cylinder-seals, the Babylonian boundary-stones, and the monoliths of Assyrian kings. On the Babylonian *kudurrus*, or boundary-stones, the emblems of the gods are grouped together, and in one case the name of the god with whom the emblem is associated is inscribed by the side, thus giving us definite data on which to base our investigations.

The Hebrew word for symbol, *ôth*, is most probably connected with the root *āwā*, 'to describe with a mark,' and with Assyr. *ittu*. Some scholars have suggested a connexion between Assyr. *ittu* and Heb. חִידָה.[6]

---

1 Qalqashandī, iii. 472.
2 Rubies of this shape adorned the case of the supposed Qur'ān of 'Uthmān, carried before the Almohad Yūsuf (S. P. Scott, *Hist. of the Moorish Empire in Europe*, Philadelphia, 1904, ii. 304).
3 V. A. Smith, *Akbar, the Great Mogul*, Oxford, 1917, p. 37.
4 Description by Ralph Fitch, 1585, *ib.* p. 108.
5 Miskawaihi, ii. 165.
6 *Ib.* i. 166, etc.
7 Ibn al-Athir, *Chronicle*, A.H. 396.
8 See Hilal, ed. H. F. Amedroz, Beyrut, 1904, p. 456, etc. Earlier examples are *Aghāni*, vi. 20 (time of Amīn); Ṭabarī, iii. 1825 (time of Muhtadi).
9 Miskawaihi, i. 186, 223, 351, ii. 15, 82.
10 *Ib.* ii. 82.
11 Scott, i. 656.
12 A. J. N. Tremearne, *The Ban of the Bori*, London, 1914, p. 114.

---

1 *Futūḥāt Makkiyyah*, Cairo, 1293, i. 551 f.
2 *Iḥyā 'Ulum al-Din*, Cairo, 1306, i. 208 f.
3 Calcutta, 1891, i. 2 f.
4 See the tr. by E. H. Whinfield, London, 1898.
5 *Personal Narrative of a Year's Journey through Central and Eastern Arabia*, London, 1865, ii. 48.
6 *BOR* i. [1900] 130.

1. The symbolism of religious life.—The Temple as the centre of the religious life of ancient Israel should be treated first. Solomon's temple was specifically built in order that it might contain the ark, the symbol of the presence of the deity. In the second Temple, the adytum being empty, the presence of the deity was symbolized by the continuance of the altar service, the Day of Atonement ritual, and the shewbread. Among the Semites the god was symbolically represented as a nobleman dwelling in his palace, and W. M. Flinders Petrie[1] has shown that the features and routine of Egyptian temples were similar to those of large households. First came the small chamber symbolizing the mysterious dwelling of the deity himself. The larger hall in front of this could be compared to the audience-chamber where human kings receive their subjects, whilst the larger space in front of the building was primarily a meeting-place for the people. The division of the Temple into a Holy Place and Holy of Holies was also symbolical and corresponded to the heavens and the highest heaven (שָׁמַיִם and שְׁמֵי הַשָּׁמַיִם [1 K 8^{27}]), whilst the entrance may have symbolized the earth, Jahweh's footstool (Is 66^{1}). Why was the Temple built on a mountain? This really brings us to another question. Was there any connexion between the idea which represented Jahweh's home on a mountain and the 'high places' referred to in the OT? From the standpoint of the Deuteronomic historian, the high places were legitimate places of worship until the building of the Temple at Jerusalem. It is to be noted also that the high places are said to have been built on hills, and it has therefore been suggested[2] that they were artificial mounds taking the place of natural high places such as the summits of hills and mountains. The explanation of this symbolism can be learned from Babylonia. One of the most noticeable characteristics of the Babylonian temples was their enormous size. In Gn $11^{3f.}$ we read that the people meet together in the land of Shinar and decide to build a city and a tower that shall reach up to heaven. To the Babylonians a temple was above all a 'high place,' and there is a symbolic reason to account for this conception. Jensen[3] has shown that the Babylonians regarded the earth as a huge mountain. In fact the earth was actually called E-Kur, 'mountain house.' Later they began to identify one particular part of the earth —a mountain peak preferably—as the dwelling of the god, so that the temples which were built later were known as 'mountain houses.' The height of the temple thus symbolized the mountain which had formed the original home of the deity.[4] The same idea can be seen by sketching the history of Mt. Zion. The sanctuary on the mountain existed before the settlement of the Hebrews. Just as His people dispossess the early settlers of Canaan, so Jahweh dispossesses the god of Zion. Mt. Zion is now regarded as His home and He therefore reveals Himself to His people from the mountain (Ex 19^{11}). We can thus see the symbolic idea which suggested the *ziqqurats* in Babylonia, the high places in Canaan, and the sacred temple mount in Israel.

The very names 'ark of Jahweh,' 'ark of God,' suggest that the ark contained an object which in some manner symbolized the God of Israel. In the Assyrian temples a statue of the god took the place of the ark in the Holy of Holies, and it has therefore been suggested that the ark with the cherubim over it was a symbol of Jahweh. The custom of carrying about an ark as a symbol of the deity has its parallel in other Semitic religions. In Babylonia the gods were carried about in ships in solemn procession, and in Egypt the arks with their images were placed in boats. Renan[1] actually derives the Hebrew ark from the Egyptian ark-boat, but there is not sufficient evidence to warrant such a suggestion.

Cheyne[2] thinks that the symbolic meaning of the brazen serpent can be learned from Babylonia. He thinks that the brazen oxen in 1 K 7^{25} were copies of the oxen which stood in Babylonian temples as symbols of Marduk. I. Benzinger[3] has suggested that there was a serpent-clan among the Israelite tribes and that *Nehushtan* may have been its sacred symbol (Gn 49^{17}). The two pillars Jachin and Boaz which stood in front of the porch of the Temple were probably symbolical. The temple of Melkarth at Tyre and also the temple at Hierapolis had two similar pillars in front of them, and, as these were symbols of the deity and Solomon's temple was constructed on the same principle, it has been suggested that Jachin and Boaz were symbols of Jahweh. It is possible that the brazen lavers and the sea of the Temple symbolized the clouds. As to the sea and oxen, W. H. Kosters[4] finds here a symbolic trace of the Babylonian myth of the struggle of Marduk and Tiamat—the sea representing Tiamat and the oxen Marduk. Seeing that the Babylonian creation-myth determined the form of the Israelitish cosmogony, this view has received general support, although there is no direct reference to it in the OT. H. P. Smith[5] suggests that the twelve oxen were symbols of the twelve constellations and that the sea was a symbol of the great celestial reservoir from which the earth is watered. The ornamental figures on the smaller lavers he also regards as symbolical. The bull was sacred to Jahweh, the lion was sacred to Astarte, whilst the palm-tree is represented with a symbolic meaning in Phœnician art. The ornamentation therefore suggested a syncretistic purpose in building the Temple.

Although there is not the slightest reference in the OT to any symbolic meaning of the tabernacle, scholars, both ancient and modern, have suggested that both in its structure and in its appurtenances it symbolized various religious truths. The Heb. מִשְׁכָּן, 'dwelling,' expressed the idea that God dwelt among His people; אֹהֶל מוֹעֵד, 'tent of meeting,' represented the idea that God met His people there; whilst the name אֹהֶל הָעֵדוּת, 'tent of the testimony,' constantly called to mind that the decalogue inscribed on the tables of the ark bore witness to the covenant between Jahweh and His people. But there are other ideas symbolized by the tabernacle. The innermost chamber, the Holy of Holies, was the dwelling-place of the deity Himself. This could be entered by the high-priest alone, and only once a year—on the Day of Atonement. In this chamber everything was made of gold and decorated with beautifully-made fabrics, whilst the vestments of the high-priest were conspicuous by their gorgeous finery. This gave expression to the thought that God's most holy minister and His chief abode should be adorned with becoming dignity and splendour. On the other hand, in the Holy Place, which could be entered by the priesthood only, the furniture was of gold, whilst the outer pillars, which were taken, no doubt, as belonging to the court, were made of brass. The court, which was for the people, had

1 Presidential address before the Egyptian Section of the Third International Congress for the History of Religions (*Transactions*, Oxford, 1908, i. 186 f.).

2 W. Gesenius, preface to C. P. W. Gramberg, *Religionsideen des AT*, Berlin, 1829, i. xix–xxi.

3 *Die Kosmologie der Babylonier*, pp. 185–195.

4 Cf. the minarets attached to the Muhammadan mosques, and see K. Herzfeld's monograph, *Samarra*, Berlin, 1907.

1 *Hist. of the People of Israel*, Eng. ed., London, 1888, i. 123.

2 *EBi*, col. 3388.

3 *Hebräische Archäologie*, Tübingen, 1907, p. 392.

4 *Theologisch Tijdschrift*, ii. [1879] 455 ff.

5 *OT Hist.*, Edinburgh, 1903, p. 166.

only brass. The covering for the Holy of Holies was made of costly materials with figured cherubim; the curtain at the door of the Holy Place was without cherubim, and that at the court was simply made of white linen. We can thus see how the costliness of the adornments of the different apartments symbolized their sacredness; the more sacred a chamber was, the more sumptuously was it adorned.

'Together the curtains are designed to form the earthly, and, with the aid of the attendant cherubim to symbolize the heavenly, dwelling-place of the God of Israel.'[1]

The sacrificial system of the Hebrews symbolized self-surrender and devotion to the will of God, the need of forgiveness, and the blessing of divine fellowship. The peace-offering with its communion-feast showed the idea of fellowship between God and man; the *tamid*, or continual offering, symbolized Israel's pledge of unbroken service to Jahweh; whilst the sin-offering with its sprinkling of blood showed that one of the conditions of cleansing oneself from sin was to place oneself submissively before God. The care taken in the preparation of the aromatic compounds of the incense suggests a symbolic meaning. From Ps 141^{2} it appears that incense was regarded as a spiritual symbol of prayer. Bähr regards the shewbread as a symbol of the fact that Jahweh was ever present with His people and was the giver of their daily bread. Circumcision was a tribal badge and showed that the patient had been admitted a member of the tribe, whilst the Sabbath symbolized the completion of the work of creation. In Ex 31^{13} it is actually described as an everlasting symbol (אוֹת) between Jahweh and Israel. The long hair worn by the Nazirite symbolized his consecration for some special service. In ancient religions the offering of one's hair, like the offering of one's blood, symbolized the making of a covenant between the worshipper and his god. The frontlets, or *ṭôṭāphôth* (Ex 13^{16}), were badges worn upon the forehead and arm to show that the worshipper belonged to a certain religious community, and as a worshipper of the national deity was subject to His help and protection.[2] Fire occurs as a symbol of the divine presence (Ex 20^{18} 3^{2} etc.). It was also regarded as a purifying agent (Is 48^{10}), and to pass through fire was therefore a symbol of purification. Would not this explain why sacrifices were burned before they could be accepted by God? Water was another source of symbolical purification. Ablutions were so common among the Hebrews that it is difficult to distinguish washings performed for the sake of the body and those with a symbolical significance. Anointing[3] denoted the consecration of a person or even of an inanimate object (such as the tabernacle and its appurtenances or the stone at Bethel). In Ps 92^{10} it is referred to as a symbol of prosperity and joy, and the cessation of the practice was therefore a symbol of mourning (2 S 12^{20}). The word *asherāh*, which appears very often as a name for Astarte (1 K 18^{19}, 2 K 21^{7} etc.), came to be used as a name for the symbol of the goddess[4] (Dt 7^{5}, Ex 34^{13} etc.). The *hammanîm* were most probably symbols of the sun-god, who is called in Phœnician inscriptions בעל חמן,[5] whilst the *maṣṣēbhôth* were symbols expressing gratitude for a

1 A. R. S. Kennedy, art. 'Tabernacle,' in *SDB*, p. 885.

2 Cf. the custom among later Jews of fastening to the door-post a small box containing certain texts from OT, and the Babylonian custom of hanging up images of some protecting deity at the entrance to houses (L. W. King, in *ZA* xi. [1896] 50–62).

3 For the origin and significance of the rite see A. H. H. Kamphausen, art. 'Salbe,' in Riehm, *Handwörterbuch des bibl. Altertums*², 1893–94.

4 G. A. Barton, 'The Semitic Ištar Cult,' *Hebraica*, ix. [1893] 131–165, xi. [1895] 73.

5 A. Bloch, *Phön. Glossar*, Berlin, 1890, p. 22.

divine revelation (Gn 28^{22} 31^{13} etc.). As to bull symbolism, it most probably originated among the Hebrews themselves (and was not borrowed from the Egyptians, as hitherto supposed). The Hebrews being an agricultural race, it was natural that they should look upon the bull as a symbol of strength and power. The bulls on the lavers of Solomon's temple may have been due to the influence of Phœnician workmen, for among the Phœnicians Baal was represented as a bull. The horns of the altar are regarded by some scholars as symbols of ancient bull-worship. The *ziqqurats*, or temple towers, of Babylonia consisted usually of three, four, or seven stones, no doubt on account of the symbolic sacredness attached to these numbers. The quadrilateral shape of the *ziqqurats*, with the four corners towards the four cardinal points, symbolized the four quarters over which the Babylonian kings held dominion. The lions (symbols of Nergal) and the bulls (symbols of En-lil) which stood at the entrances of Assyrian temples probably symbolized the means which the gods had at their disposal for punishing man. The names of the temples symbolized the character of the gods to whom they were dedicated. Nabu's temple was known as E-pad-kalama-suma, 'the house of him who gives the sceptre of the world'—no doubt suggested by the staff which formed the symbol of Nabu. Sin's temple at Harran was called 'the house of joy,' and that of Shamash was known as 'the house of the universal judge.' The basin of the temple known as *apsu* represented the domain of Ea, the water-god. The *ziqqurats* and the basin thus became 'living symbols of current cosmological conceptions.'[1]

We may now turn to the symbols of the gods themselves.[2] The symbol of Ramman, the storm- and thunder-god, was a lightning fork, whilst an axe represented the destruction which storm and thunder bring in their wake. His nature as a solar deity was also symbolized by a bull. Sin had a crescent, either by itself or with a disk. Since the moon at certain phases suggested the appearance of a horn, he was represented as an old man with a flowing beard, and wearing a cap on which were the horns of the moon. The horn was thus regarded as his crown and came to symbolize his power. This explains why the Assyrian kings adorned themselves with a horned crown as a symbol of divinity.[3] Anu symbolized 'the abstract principle of which heaven and earth are emanations.'[4] Such expressions as 'light of heaven and earth,' by which Ninib was known, symbolized his beneficent character as a solar deity. But the fiery rays of the sun might also be destructive, and he was therefore represented also under the form of a lion. Ea's symbol consisted of a ram's head which projected from a frame. This symbol occurs on the Bavian relief and the Esarhaddon stele. But on boundary-stones his symbol is usually an animal with the head of an antelope and the lower part of a fish. As the water-god of Babylonia, fountains were sacred to him, and he was regarded as the giver of fertility. He was the Oannes of Berossus—half man, half fish—who came out of the water to instruct the people. The symbol of a fish was therefore suggested either by the idea of fertility or by the fact that he was god of the water. Nabu, as scribe of the gods, was symbolically represented as carrying the tablets of fate and recording the decision of the gods upon them.

1 M. Jastrow, *The Religion of Babylonia and Assyria*, Boston, 1898, p. 653.

2 These symbols can be studied most conveniently from the *Mémoires de la délégation en Perse*.

3 In OT the horn was a symbol of power and its exaltation signified victory (1 K 22^{11}, Jer 48^{25} etc.).

4 Jensen, p. 274.

The staff by which he is represented symbolizes either the stylus of a writer or a ruler's sceptre. The solar god Marduk symbolized the sun of spring which brings about the growth of vegetation and the revival of nature. As a warrior-god his symbol is a spear, and as a storm-god he is represented by a horned dragon. Sometimes he is represented by the symbol of a dog, and in a lexicographical tablet[1] there is a reference to four dogs of Marduk. As the goddess of love and the symbol of creation Ishtar was represented by a female figure with her breasts exposed and a child on her left arm sucking her breast. She symbolized every feminine phenomenon of the Babylonian pantheon. She was the mother of the gods and the mother-goddess, and was therefore prayed to in hymns as 'helper and heavenly midwife.' As goddess of the passions she was represented on seal-cylinders as nude, with the distinctively feminine parts particularly emphasized. In the astrological system she was identified with Venus and regarded as a symbol of light. Sometimes her symbol is a star[2] of various shapes.

Nergal, who symbolized the hot sun of midsummer, was represented by a lion; Nusku, the fire-god, by a lamp; and Nirgusu by an eagle. Hommel[3] connects the name Bau with *bohu* of Gn 1, and suggests that the goddess was a symbol of the watery depths of the universe. On one of the inscriptions of Nabu-pal-iddin Shamash is represented as seated in his shrine; before him is a table resting on a wheel, and attached to the wheel are cords held by two male figures which direct its course. These figures represent the messengers of Shamash, Malik and Bunene, who occupy the position of chariot-drivers. The sun's movement across the heavens, which is here symbolized by the wheel, was thought of as a drive[4] (cf. Ps 19^{6}). On seal-cylinders his beneficent character is symbolized by the manner in which he pours forth streams of water from jars placed on his shoulders. But the most common symbol of Shamash is a sun-disk.

The chief symbol of Ashur was a standard which consisted of a pole surrounded by a disk enclosed within two wings. Above the disk was the figure of a warrior shooting an arrow. The terra-cotta images of Bel found at Nippur[5] represent him as an old man with a flowing beard, a real 'father' of the gods. He personified the various forces of nature whose seat and sphere of action is the inhabited world. Together with Anu and Ea, therefore, he symbolized the eternal laws of the universe.

2. The symbolism of common life.—A Hebrew slave who refused to take advantage of the liberty open to him after seven years' service had one of his ears bored with an awl and pinned to the door to show that he was in future to be devoted to the service of that house[6] (Ex 21^{6}). Elevation to a position of superiority was symbolized by placing a crown on the head (2 S 1^{10}, 2 K 11^{12} etc.). The worshipper spread out his hands in prayer to show that he desired to obtain divine mercy and help (Ex $9^{29.33}$, 1 K 8^{22} etc.). Washing of the hands was a symbol of innocence. In Dt 21^{6} the heifer's neck was broken to show that the murderer deserved the punishment, whilst the elders of the city by washing their hands showed that they were free from the guilt. Hostility towards a person is shown by gaping with the mouth (Ps 35^{21}, Job 16^{10} etc.); ill-feeling by clapping the hands (Ezk 6^{11} 21^{17} 22^{13}), or by spitting in the face (Nu 12^{14}, Dt 25^{9}); and anger by gnashing the teeth (Ps 35^{16}, Job 16^{9}, La 2^{16} etc.). The key of the door was probably looked upon as a symbol of authority, and to place it upon a man's shoulder showed that he was appointed steward (Is 22^{22}). Covering a woman with one's mantle signified the intention of acting as her protector (Ezk 16^{8}). The father of a new-born child acknowledged it as his offspring by placing it upon his knees (Job 3^{12}). In a Babylonian poem describing the wickedness wrought by the evil spirits they are said to snatch the child from the knees of a man. The use of salt as a condiment and the piquancy which it gives to insipid articles of diet caused it to be regarded as a symbol of life. An abundance of salt has the effect of preventing the growth of vegetation, and therefore the ploughing of a city with salt denoted that it was condemned to eternal destruction (Jg 9^{45}). It was a mark of reverence to cast off the shoes on approaching a sacred person or place (Ex 3^{5}, Jos 5^{15}). To appear barefoot was a sign of great emotion or of mourning (2 S 15^{30}, Is 20^{2} etc.), and to draw off the shoes meant to give up a legal right (Ru 4^{7}). The taking of an oath was symbolized by placing the hand under the thigh of the adjurer (Gn 24^{2} 47^{29}), or by lifting up the hand towards heaven[1] (Gn 14^{22}). As kissing was a means by which parts of the body of different persons came into contact, it was naturally a symbol of affection and reverence (Gn 27^{26}, Ex 18^{7}, Ru 1^{9} etc.). Various symbolisms were used in mourning.[2] Sackcloth was worn to show that the mourner's grief for the departed was so great that he was ready to give up all the pleasures and conveniences of life (Gn 37^{34}, 2 S 3^{31}). The tearing of one's garment denoted that the mourner's dearest friend had been torn from him (Gn 37^{29} 44^{13} etc.). The mourner went about barefoot and bareheaded (2 S 15^{30}, Ezk 24^{17}), sat in ashes and sprinkled ashes upon his head (Jer 6^{26}, La 3^{16} etc.), and practised various mutilations of the body (Jer 16^{6} etc.). Shaving the head (as among the Arabs at the present time) was also a sign of mourning. The making of a covenant was symbolized by the person who gave the pledge passing between the parts of an animal cut into pieces, and thus showing that he was ready to be similarly treated if he failed to keep his promise (Gn $15^{9ff.}$ etc.).

Light represented to the Orientals the highest human good. The most joyful emotions and pleasing sensations are described under imagery derived from light (1 K 11^{36}, Ps 97^{11} etc.). It was only natural that there should follow a transition from corporeal to spiritual things, so that light came to typify true religion and the happiness which it brings. Sin, wickedness, chaos, were represented by darkness. The lion was a symbol of strength (Jl 1^{6}). Kneeling was a mark of homage to a superior, and is therefore referred to as an attitude of worship (2 Ch 6^{13}, 1 K 8^{54}).

In Babylonia it was customary for the suitor to present gifts to the girl's parents. According to some scholars, this symbolized the purchase of the bride—a practice which existed in earlier times. Various symbolisms were connected with the marriage ceremony, but their meaning is obscure. The officiating ministers bound sandals on the feet of the newly-wedded pair,[3] gave them a leather

1 H. C. Rawlinson, *The Cuneiform Inscriptions of Western Asia*, London, 1861–84, ii. 56, col. iii. 22–25.

2 On a Phœnician gem the gazelle is figured along with the star and dove as a symbol of Astarte (W. R. Smith, *Kinship and Marriage in Early Arabia*2, London 1903, p. 227 f.).

3 *Die semit. Völker und Sprachen*, Leipzig, 1881–83.

4 See A. Jeremias, *The OT in the Light of the Ancient East*, Eng. tr., London, 1911, i. 116.

5 H. V. Hilprecht, *Explorations in Bible Lands during the 19th Century*, Edinburgh, 1903.

6 Nowack, *Lehrbuch der heb. Arch.*, Freiburg i. B., 1894, i. 177.

1 Cf. the Babylonian expression *nish ḳate*.

2 M. Jastrow, 'Dust, Earth, and Ashes as Symbols of Mourning among the Ancient Hebrews,' *JAOS* xx. [1899] 133–150.

3 T. G. Pinches, *Notes on some Recent Discoveries in the Realm of Assyriology*, London, 1892–93.

girdle, and fastened it to a pouch of silver and gold. The first of these ceremonies may have symbolized the marriage-contract between them. We are told in the Code that, if a maid behaves insolently towards her mistress, the latter may put an *abuttu* on her and reduce her to slavery. The adoptive parent may do the same with a disobedient son. What the *abuttu* was is unknown. Jensen has suggested that it was some kind of incised mark which acted as a symbol of the person's position (cf. the mark on Cain's forehead [Gn 4^{15}]). The repayment of a debt or the dissolution of a partnership was symbolized by the breaking of a tablet. Mutilation is often referred to as a punishment for crime, and the form of mutilation was symbolical of the offence itself. For striking a father the hand was cut off; for ingratitude evidenced by speech the tongue was cut out; as a punishment for unlawful curiosity the eye was torn out; and as a mark of disobedience the ear was often cut off. The cutting short of the hair was a mark of degradation. The city walls were regarded as a symbol of shelter.[1] Swearing by the gods and the king was a means of sanctioning an agreement. When a contract was made, both parties and witnesses added their names to it. And this was authenticated by impressing their seals or making a nail-mark. The Code states explicitly that a woman was not a wife without 'bonds.' This was a marriage-contract which symbolized an official acknowledgment of the union. An artisan symbolized his adoption of a child by teaching him a trade. The penalty of breaking a contract was the payment of two or more white horses to the god. The exact meaning of this symbolism is unknown, but white no doubt suggested purification and innocence. In Babylonian magic there was a symbolical tying and loosening of knots according as the sorcerer wished to strangle his victim or to release him from any demon by which he had been captured. If a magician wished to rid himself of an object, he would burn or torture an image of it, believing that the victim would meet with the same fate as his image. By 'seizing the hands of Bel,' the Assyrian kings legitimized their claim to the Babylonian throne.

3. The symbolism of numbers and colours.—It is doubtful whether the Hebrews used numerical symbols in OT times. On the Moabite Stone and the Siloam inscription the numbers given are invariably in words. But this does not exclude the possibility that numerical symbols, which were employed by the Babylonians and Egyptians, were also used by the Israelites. In S. Arabian and Phœnician inscriptions also the numbers are partly written and partly indicated by figures. The numbers most commonly used with a symbolical meaning are three, four, and seven.[2]

White symbolized purity and innocence. It represented light, which impressed the Hebrew mind not only by its brilliance and beauty, but by its divine symbolism and profound moral connotation (Lv $16^{4.32}$, Dn 7^9, Ps 104^2). As black absorbs all colours and thus buries the light, it symbolized death, humiliation, mourning (Mal 3^{14}, La 4^8 etc.). Blue, representing the colour of an unclouded sky, symbolized revelation (Ex 24^{10}). It was the first of the colours used for the curtains of the sanctuary, and the Israelites were commanded to have a ribbon of blue fringe on the edge of their garments in order to remind them of Jahweh (Nu $15^{38f.}$). Red, as the colour of blood, represented bloodshed, war, guilt (Zec 6^2). Purple was the distinguishing mark of royalty, representing dignity and honour (Est 8^{15}, Jg 8^{26}), whilst green, as the colour of plants—growths to which people look forward in winter—symbolized hope and resurrection.[1] It was also the symbolic colour of the moon.[2]

4. Special symbolisms in OT.—Ahijah tore his garments into twelve pieces in order to show that the kingdom of Israel would be similarly divided (1 K 11^{30-32}). One of the sons of the prophets asked his comrade to smite him, and by his wound thus showed the punishment that Ahab had deserved (20^{35}). Zedekiah, a false prophet, put on horns in order to show that Ahab would push the Syrians as with horns of iron (22^{11}).

In considering the special symbolical actions of the prophetic books, we are confronted with very great difficulty. For scholars are divided in their views as to whether these actions were actually performed in their literal sense or were merely conceived as symbolic visions in the minds of the prophets. It seems almost certain that there are a number of such actions which could not have been performed literally. It is impossible, however, for the present writer to discuss in this brief article the category to which each of these many prophetic symbolisms belongs. But a brief discussion of some of these from the books of Jeremiah and Ezekiel may give some indication as to the difficulties in arriving at a definite decision. In Jer 13^{1-11} Jahweh tells the prophet to go to the Euphrates and hide his linen girdle in a rock. After a while he is told to remove the girdle, and he then finds it to be marred. The lesson is that, just as a girdle from its nature clings to a person, so Israel is closely united to Jahweh.

Now, on the one hand, it may seem unlikely that Jeremiah should have undertaken a journey from Jerusalem to Babylon—a distance of about 200 miles—in order to bring out this point to the people. But it is possible that the journey *was* actually performed. (1) We know that the prophet was absent from Jerusalem during part of Jehoiakim's reign, and, as we have no account of his whereabouts during this period, it is possible that he made the journey to Babylon then. (2) In Jer $39^{11f.}$ we are told that Nebuchadrezzar behaved in a most friendly way towards him on the capture of Jerusalem. This can be explained by the suggestion that king and prophet had met previously, and that it was on the occasion of the prophet's visit to Babylon. In Ezk 4^5 we are told that the prophet lay upon his side for 390 days. How can this be taken literally? Did any person actually count the number of days? In 4^{12} we are told that Ezekiel used human excrement for fuel in baking some barley cakes. Surely it cannot reasonably be suggested that the prophet would have inconvenienced himself by going to such extremes merely in order to bring home to the people some divine message which he could very well have preached in a much more suitable manner. There are some scholars, chief of whom is A. Klostermann, who argue that these symbolical actions *were* performed. The dumbness of Ezekiel (3^{24-27}), they suggest, was due to a temporary loss of speech, and they explain similar performances by somewhat similar suggestions. Against this it may be argued that the prophet here refers to his keeping silent from delivering any prophetic message rather than actual speechlessness. Again, the fact that the prophet had to remain at home, in order to carry out the divine command, suggests

[1] The Code says that, if a father repudiates his son, 'he shall leave house and yard.' 'Yard' simply means 'enclosure' and may refer to the city walls, as a symbol of shelter (C. H. W. Johns, *Bab. and Assyr. Laws, Contracts, and Letters*, Edinburgh, 1904, p. 42).

[2] Cf. art. NUMBERS (Semitic).

[1] Hammurabi says that he 'bedecked the grave of Malkat with green,' the colour of resurrection (introduction to his Code of Laws).

[2] Jeremias, i. 110.

that it was not loss of speech but an injunction to refrain from reproving his co-religionists any more. The present writer is therefore inclined to agree with R. Smend, A. Kuenen, and E. Hühn in regarding many of the symbolisms of Ezekiel as being merely symbolical visions in the mind of the prophet and as not having been performed externally.

LITERATURE.—Very little indeed has been written by modern scholars on OT symbolism. Among the older works the most important is C. Bähr, *Symbolik des mosaischen Cultus*, 2 vols., Heidelberg, 1837–39. For discussion of prophetic symbolism by modern scholars see F. Giesebrecht, *Die Berufsbegabung der alttest. Propheten*, Göttingen, 1897; F. E. König, 'Zur Deutung der symbolischen Handlungen des Propheten Hesekiel,' in *NKZ* iii. [1892]; E. Hühn, *Die Messianischen Weissagungen*, 2 vols., Tübingen, 1899; W. Nowack, *Die kleinen Propheten*, Göttingen, 1897, p. 29; F. Delitzsch, *Iris: Studies in Colour and Talks about Flowers*, Eng. tr., Edinburgh, 1889.

For a study of Babylonian symbolism see W. J. Hinke, *A New Boundary Stone of Nebuchadrezzar I. from Nippur*, Philadelphia, 1907; W. H. Ward, *The Seal Cylinders of Western Asia*, Washington, 1910; P. Jensen, *Die Kosmologie der Babylonier*, Strassburg, 1890; K. Frank, *Bilder und Symbole der babylonisch-assyrischen Götter*, Leipzig, 1906; J. de Morgan, *Mémoires de la délégation en Perse*, Paris, 1900–05, vii. 137–153; F. Hommel, 'Ursprung des Tierkreises,' in *Aufsätze und Abhandlungen*, Munich, 1900, ii. 236–268.

MAURICE H. FARBRIDGE.

SYMBOLO-FIDEISM.—Symbolo-fideism[1] is the name given to the theology taught in the second half of the 19th cent. at the Protestant Faculty of Paris by Professors Auguste Sabatier and Eugène Ménégoz, and disseminated since by a large number of their pupils and disciples. It has also been called the theology of the Paris school.

As its name indicates, this theology has two aspects: (*a*) symbolism, which deals with religion more particularly from the point of view of its form, and (*b*) fideism, which deals with it from the point of view of its content. Sabatier devoted himself specially to the former and Ménégoz to the latter aspect. But the two conceptions are inseparable and interdependent. Together they form a theology with a distinct character of its own.

The basis of symbolism is the psychological observation that the essence of things escapes us, and that we know only their manifestations in the form of images, figures, and symbols. We cannot, *e.g.*, know what God is in Himself. We know Him only by the more or less anthropomorphic representation which we form of Him in our thought. This we express by the terms 'Father,' 'Lord,' 'Master,' 'Captain,' 'Sovereign,' 'King,' or by emblems bringing out one or other of His attributes—*e.g.*, Lion, Rock, Banner, Fire. These symbols are without doubt the expression of a living reality, but the conformation of our brain is such that it cannot grasp that reality naked; our mind can apprehend it only when it presents itself in the garment of a more or less sensuous representation. This observation holds good in regard to all religious data, and is borne out in the most subtle dogmatic systems. The task of the theologian is to lay bare the eternal truth from under its contingent manifestations and its historical formulæ; moreover, these formulæ are subject to the laws of historical evolution.

As regards the Deity, it is the name 'Father,' habitually used by Jesus Christ, that best suits the religious man's conception of the Supreme Being—perfect, just, merciful, eternal, all-embracing; a Spirit both transcendent and immanent, on whom man feels himself absolutely dependent, while at the same time conscious of liberty and responsibility before Him. On the ideas of liberty and responsibility depend those of sin and penalty, which in turn suggest those of pardon and salvation. A lively conviction that we are created for life and not for death, for happiness and not for suffering, rouses us to aspirations after salvation. We desire life, happy life, eternal life. The whole idea of salvation is summed up in these words.

[1] In recent years the word 'fideism' has frequently been used alone.

How are we to attain this life, this salvation? Conscience replies: By the pardon of our sins. But how is pardon to be obtained? It is with this vital question that fideism is concerned. The term 'fideism' (Lat. *fides*, 'faith') was employed in the religious sense for the first time by Ménégoz in his *Réflexions sur l'Évangile du salut*.[1] Its meaning is most concisely indicated in the phrase: 'We are saved by faith, independently of beliefs.'

The distinction between faith and beliefs is one of the fundamental premisses of fideism. By faith is meant the movement of the self towards God—a movement which implies forsaking sin, repentance. The man who repents and gives his heart to God is saved, whatever his beliefs may be. This statement is opposed to the old orthodoxy, which made adherence to certain official dogmas a condition of salvation. Fideism declares that a man is saved by faith alone ('*sola fide*'). At the same time, it recognizes the value of doctrines. Doctrines are dynamic ideas which make for good when true, and for evil when false. Fideists regard them therefore as pedagogic instruments of the first order. It is for this reason that they attach so much importance to the pursuit of truth and oppose so resolutely doctrines which they consider erroneous. It is only through a great and regrettable misunderstanding that their opponents reproach them with indifference to doctrine; and it is also false to assert, as has been done, that fideists fail to appreciate the intellectual factor in religious faith. Faith, according to their teaching, is an activity of the self in its unity, and therefore must comprise all the elements of the soul's faculties—thought, feeling, and will. But the essential factor in salvation is the inward movement towards God, not intellectual adherence to some doctrinal tenet. Fideists reject the doctrine of salvation by beliefs without thereby denying the spiritual influence of beliefs, as the Reformers rejected the doctrine of salvation by works, while maintaining that good works are obligatory on Christians.

In a general way, and as a result of historical, critical, exegetical, and philosophical studies, fideists have departed from orthodox theology and returned to the simple doctrine of salvation as taught by Jesus Christ, according to their interpretation, to the multitudes in His preaching of the gospel; hence their emphasis on repentance and on consecration of the soul to God as conditions of salvation.

As regards the idea of salvation, they find it in the symbolic interpretation of the primitive Christian conception of the Kingdom of God. This idea has for them two aspects: (1) the entrance of believers at death into celestial happiness, and (2) the gradual establishment of the Kingdom of Justice and Peace on the earth. These two ideas combined constitute in their eyes the Kingdom of Heaven.

The name 'Symbolo-fideism,' which expresses the union of symbolism and fideism, gained currency from two articles by Eugène Ménégoz, signed T. P. ('Théologien protestant') in the *Eglise Libre* (1894, nos. 31 and 33). Auguste Sabatier accepted this title (*Esquisse*, p. 456). It passed into Holland with the thesis by J. Riemens entitled *Het Symbolo-fideisme: Beschrijving en kritische Beschouwing* (Rotterdam, 1900), and into Germany with Gustav Lasch's *Die Theologie der Pariser Schule: Charakteristik und Kritik des Symbolo-Fideismus* (Berlin, 1901).

Symbolo-fideism has given rise to numerous controversies, an echo of which is found in current

[1] Paris, 1879, § 44.

religious journals and theological reviews. Its adversaries have also published a number of polemical pamphlets. These are referred to in the writings mentioned below.

LITERATURE.—The two principal works of Auguste Sabatier on the subject are the *Esquisse d'une philosophie de la religion d'après la psychologie et l'histoire*, Paris, 1897 (several times re-edited), Eng. tr., London, 1897, and *Les Religions d'autorité et la religion de l'esprit*, Paris, 1904 (published from MS, after the death of the author), Eng. tr., London, 1904. The writings of E. Ménégoz are collected in *Publications diverses sur le fidéisme et son application à l'enseignement chrétien traditionnel*, 5 vols., Paris, 1900–20. The reader will find in these works references to other works of the same authors. See also Hector Haldimann, *Le Fidéisme; Etude critique de la doctrine du 'Salut par la foi, indépendamment des croyances*,' Paris, 1907; E. Ménégoz, *Religion and Theology*, London, 1908; *Le Salut par la foi, indépendamment des croyances: Anthologie du fidéisme*, by the Comité des publications religieuses libérales de Genève, Geneva and Paris, 1913; A. Delcourt, *Le Fidéisme: La notion intégrale du salut et l'essence de l'Evangile*, Paris, 1914. A. Thiébaut has given an objective and critical exposition of fideism in the *Journal religieux des Eglises indépendantes de la Suisse romande*, 1917, nos. 23–26.

EUGÈNE MÉNÉGOZ.

SYMPATHY.—Sympathy, as the etymology denotes, is 'feeling with' others. Two persons feeling alike do not, however, make a true sympathetic couple unless the feeling of one has partly caused or is reinforcing the feeling of the other. The perfection of mutual sympathy is reached when similar feelings originate spontaneously in the two and reinforce each other. Any relation, however, in which there is a mutual reinforcement of feeling, however originated, is one of mutual sympathy.

1. Emotional contagion.—The primary fact in sympathy is that the feeling of one person can, on occasion, cause similar feeling in another. In its primitive manifestations this occurs without reflective consciousness of the feeling, and certainly without distinction of persons in respect of its origin. This is shown in the contagion of popular excitement—*e.g.*, panic, war-frenzy, the intensified enthusiasm of public meetings, the wild joy, the furious hatred, the boundless affection, that mark the excited crowd. The emotion, or its manifestation in some, excites similar emotions latent in the others, and forthwith by sympathetic reinforcement the emotional disturbance in each is abnormally increased. Probably it is only those who, from the beginning, have some set against the prevalent emotion that maintain a normal level throughout. Such sympathetic outbursts must be themselves short-lived, and, as the cause of excitement is withdrawn, the persons affected by contagious feeling return to their ordinary emotional level. This may even be one of indifference to the popular frenzy in which they took part. It may, indeed, be one of revulsion if they have been drawn, as sometimes happens, into a condition of which in their normal moods they disapprove. Such revulsion would happen, *e.g.*, if an advocate of peace found that he had been drawn by fellow-feeling into a demonstration of war enthusiasm. The hot fit is followed by a cold fit. Hence the instability of popular acclamation, the apparent superficiality of feeling which appears when people liable to sympathy of this primitive unreflective kind are massed together. The most suitable material for the typical 'fickle mob' is a town population sympathetically sensitive and intellectually immature.

The short-lived character of the feeling thus contagiously aroused follows in the nature of the case, because there is no settled identification of self-conscious personality with it. I feel in a sense, but do not feel myself as feeling: I do not take the feeling into myself as mine. It is *on* me and moves me, but it does not enter into any relation to that total of ideas, impulses, feelings, and desires which is *me*. It may be a mere motive excitement, moving me blindly to action, or it may take possession of me completely with fixed idea and over-mastering mood, acting instead of me and overpowering me. In either case I come out of it, and in the latter case as one recovered from a madness. Something like this, no doubt, befell Parisians in the brief violence of the Terror.

2. Self-conscious sympathy.—When self is identified with the feeling which nevertheless is ascribed to another person as origin, we have sympathy proper. The development of self-consciousness goes hand in hand indeed with the exercise of sympathy. We learn to know ourselves, and to become all that we are capable of becoming as self-conscious persons, by our dealings with our fellows, and *pari passu* with our consciousness of them as other selves. In so far, however, as we are clearly conscious of self, we are prepared to set bounds to the operation of primitive sympathy. A new condition of feeling, discontinuous with my previous state so as to preclude its origination in me, is roused in me by sympathetic contagion. It is to the self an invasion from without. As a feeling, moving me but not mine, it must be referred to a neighbouring conscious self, who is manifesting it independently. Our first concern, however, is its treatment by the self which is invaded. Feelings that harmonize with the total state of this self enter into it as elements in its development: the sympathy of children with parents and other elders plays a large part in the building up of their personality. Confidence in the elders who give the lead to sympathy predisposes to acceptance of their guidance. The emotional being of the child is educated in this way. If of average docility, it takes the form suggested to it by its society. On the other hand, the suggested feeling may be out of harmony with the character as already formed: thus the brave man may feel the horror communicated to him by the panic-stricken multitude, but he overcomes it as no possible part of himself. When the feeling thus communicated to us takes strong hold, the repulse by a strong character is correspondingly emphatic. In sensitive natures this gives rise to a peculiar sense of revulsion, as towards something put into us against our will; and the transference of this revulsion to the source of contagion is probably the chief cause of violent personal antipathy. Between this attitude of abhorrence towards the induced emotion and willing receptiveness of it, as extremes, lie all degrees of being moved by a feeling from which, as outside the disposition of our own personality, we nevertheless withhold ourselves. Whether we admit the feeling to influence over us, or harden our will against it in a sort of self-defence, it appears to us essentially, and throughout its action, as the feeling of another person with which in a measure we feel. This definite ascription of the feeling to another is the second characteristic feature in sympathy, and gains prominence with the developing consciousness of self and of other selves.

3. Control of sympathy.—In passing it may be noted how large a part in life is played by the partial hardening of the heart against the contagion of social feeling. This control of sympathetic distraction in general belongs to the preservation of self as maintenance of character. It is not only that undesirable emotions—*e.g.*, of hatred, fear, envy—should be suppressed, as they are by the self-possessed though sensitive members of the excited crowd.[1] Experience soon reveals that the preservation of self, even in the ordinary physical

[1] Common self-possession, as in the man who is not liable to the contagion of feeling, must be distinguished from the subtle excellence of sympathy under control. Probably this is one of the qualities of the born leader.

sense, requires much systematic control of emotion, whether initiated sympathetically or otherwise. An emotional nature loosely controlled is morally unstable and makes for a nervous break-down in course of time. This is the hysteric type, so far as it depends on moral character. It is a main principle of moral health that the emotional life as it increases should be kept more and more strictly in subordination to the ends which it subserves. The precise definition of those ends belongs to the subject of ethics: the average man conceives them simply as the happiness of personal health for himself and his associates, together with some service in furtherance of the common weal. It may be that the rank and file of modern humanity suffer from lack of vitality and variety in the emotional life, but for the moment we are not concerned with them. Persons of the sympathetic cast are—under modern conditions more especially—liable to so much emotional invasion as must result in nervous exhaustion if not systematically kept in check. It is interesting to note how the habit of control over sympathy develops with experience from youth to maturity: the first great sympathetic grief overwhelms us as if it were our own; later we have learnt to throw ourselves outside the emotion into the actions required to assuage the sufferings of our friend; later still, to those who are overtried, callousness may come, with the exhaustion of either physique or morale.

Most of these observations apply to all feeling, however initiated. Sympathetic feeling differs from other feeling as being specially liable to increase of control by development of the element of otherness in it. This is of a piece with another useful psychological truth, namely that the tension of any violent feeling may be relieved by treating it as an object of imagination or thought. Tennyson's lines bear on this point:

> 'Likewise the imaginative woe,
> That loved to handle spiritual strife,
> Diffused the shock thro' all my life,
> But in the present broke the blow.'[1]

In constructing a story, an essay, or a poem which depicts the emotion as affecting imaginary persons, the sense of its personal attachment is obscured: it is projected more or less, *i.e.* thrown out of self-consciousness into the non-ego. Similarly, but as of course and instinctively, we project our sympathetic feelings back into the other self and, although still feeling them, are as a rule much relieved. This relief is no doubt chiefly due to the stop that is placed on the disturbance of the emotional personality in general by the sharp dissociation of the new feeling from those immediately pertaining to the self: it is the other person's feeling, and, though it disturbs me, I limit that disturbance by *knowing* it as something which has not its origin, and is therefore not necessarily permanent, in me. This control of the sympathetic disturbance furthers and is furthered by practical activity in relief of the other's distress.

4. Identification with the 'other.'—The exceptions indeed in this case explain the rule. When the sympathetic feeling is ascribed to a person much beloved, it may affect us more than if it were of our own origination. This, no doubt, is what is meant when it is said that another person is dearer to us than ourselves. The consciousness of the beloved person's consciousness is in this case so established as part of our own that the projection of the feeling into it does not in the least dissociate the self from the feeling. So far as we know what the beloved person feels, we go on feeling it and being further disturbed by it all the time. Indeed there appear to be, in cases of intense affection when the self identifies itself passionately with the other, two ways in which the sympathetic feeling may become more disturbing than the equivalent primary feeling would be. (1) In projecting it on the beloved other, imagination, moved by the habit of affectionate concern, may greatly exaggerate its force and significance: the finger-prick which, in spite of instinctive tears, is a trifle to the baby may bulk large in the distressed imagination of the anxious mother; and the same kind of thing happens in a thousand hidden ways when love prevails, and it happens for pleasure as well as for pain. (2) Each person has an intimate sense of the powers and resources within himself by means of which he bears his troubles and controls his emotional being generally. About the beloved other, however intimately known, he is never quite so sure, and thus, no matter how equal things may otherwise be, the sense of mystery breeds, as it were, a germ of fear that heightens pain and, by release from it, also heightens joy. This goes, moreover, with the essential fact that love at its strongest exceeds self-love in desiring the welfare of its object. The heightening in this way of feeling sympathetically experienced may perhaps be discriminated introspectively as an additional element of anxious concern about subjective consequences. Such concern is given to their own emotions by none but morbid people. And indeed even in the lover-like relation to which this tender anxiety naturally belongs it may be so exaggerated as to be morbid concern of self for the other. For this reason it is often well that persons who get too much on one another's mind—as we say—should be sometimes separated.

The absence of this intimate affection in the case of ordinary associates makes it possible to limit the sympathetic disturbance by instinctively projecting it back into the other mind, consciousness of which is only now and then associated with the consciousness of self. There are, of course, all degrees of dependence on one another in this respect. A man may go through life without one associate in whose welfare he has any genuine lasting interest, capable of sympathy but never in danger of being shaken by it. Most persons, however, have friends sympathy with whom does penetrate into them, as well as move them out of themselves. Some men are, in the absence of contrary cause, friendly to all their associates: these are universally sympathetic also, in proportion to their primary sympathetic sensitiveness. Friendliness, however, as the disposition to identify oneself with another, must be carefully distinguished from the primary capacity to feel as others feel.[1] When they are combined, we have the sympathetic nature as popularly understood. But an unfriendly man may be sensitive to another's feelings, in which case he not only projects them on the other but sharply dissociates himself from all interest in him. It is as if he said, 'I know what you feel; I feel you feeling it; but it is nothing to me.'

5. Insight and sensitiveness.—Apart from unfriendliness, however, this cool dissociation of self from interest in the other, combined with sympathetic sensitiveness, explains the gift of neutral or cold insight which plays so large a part in the intuitive knowledge of men. Intellectual constructiveness, which bodies forth an idea of the man's character as shown by his actions, is the ordinary substitute for intuition; and in some ways it is a safer guide. The intuitionist, *e.g.*, may mistake his man by overestimating the significance of a transitory mental attitude. He is also likely to eke out his intuitions by specula-

[1] *In Memoriam*, lxxxv.

[1] Friendship is in its degree the affectionate interest in another's consciousness of which the extreme has been described, and friendliness is the disposition to be so interested.

tions and imaginings into which all sorts of error may creep. If he abounds in self-confidence, he is a dangerous guide: but, if he treats his gift humbly as a useful auxiliary, it will serve him in good stead and improve with such exercise.

A person of sympathetic bent may have experiences of cool insight, but with this difference that, since in such case he does not identify himself with the other, he is moved to change the state of the other into identification with him. Thus the orator feels that his audience is puzzled or hostile: they do not convert him, but he is not indifferent, so he puts out his strength to express himself and make them feel his feeling. The mere lecturer, on the other hand, only tries to show and make them see his meaning. The orator is the speaker whom the Americans call 'magnetic': he makes his hearers feel as he does, at least for the time. But the beginning which he makes is at the other end of the coil, by insight into the feeling which is theirs but not his. This is the getting into sympathetic touch. By showing this sympathy on neutral ground or even in respectful dissent, he fixes the attention of his hearers. His interest in them interests them in him: then the position is reversed, the mind of the speaker shown, and the original attitude of the audience merged in the new state by which they are identified with him. This kind of thing happens every day on a small scale in the experience of sympathetic people. To understand, to be interested though in disagreement, to persuade—these are the means, and in this order, by which one person transforms the mental attitude of another. The more instinctive the process is, the better, sympathy operating in the pair by its natural impulse to mutual identification of mental content.

6. Affinity of character.—In so far as the sympathetic bent in the full sense turns upon friendliness of disposition, persons may be characterized as sympathetic generally, *i.e.* in relation to all sorts of other persons. In so far, however, as it depends on primary contagiousness of feeling, affinities of character must profoundly affect the relation between any pair. Racial type, *e.g.*, is a basis of such affinity, and the mutual intelligibility of two compatriots, while partly arising from like habits of expression and community of associations, turns also on functional capacity to feel alike. In whatever way we explain the prime fact of emotional contagion, it is evident that no one can communicate to another a feeling of which the latter is constitutionally incapable. The fearless man cannot feel like the coward, nor the liberal man like the mean. Each can only see that the other acts in a manner directly opposite to himself and recognize the corresponding state of mind as a mystery. To sympathize with another, we must be *able* to feel like him. Some would say, further, that we must have felt on our own origination as he now feels; but that is not so certain, though perhaps it generally happens so. Our capacity to sympathize, therefore, is at least limited by the possibilities of our character. How far these are limited, or how far they may be extended beyond our present experience of them, we never know. Certain it is that in human society we run up now and then against mysteries, persons with whom after much acquaintance we never get in touch, who always seem to us as if they were feeling their way through life at the other side of a high wall over which we cannot see, through which we cannot hear, them. At the same time, we meet others with whom, in trifling things and large alike, we find ourselves in tune, so much in tune that diversities of aim and opinion, though standing out the more clearly, do not mar the general harmony. But mental conditions are so complex that likeness of condition between two minds must generally be of a very partial kind.

7. Similarity and association.—Another influence to the same effect which enters into these cases is natural similarity in habit of expression. This is best seen in racial affinity: the stock of native gesture due to heredity, including facial expression, intonations of voice, and a multitude of tiny movements, felt rather than seen—all are available for that involuntary play of subtle signs which is the veiled language of sympathy. Whether contagion of feeling originates with instinctive imitation of feeling-signs or not, its development in relation to the complex psychoses of the adult is dependent on the swift interpretation of their secret signs. Human beings are indeed so profoundly interesting to each other when they really show themselves that an easy mutual intelligibility is often almost equivalent to friendship at first sight.

Intelligibility follows also on intimate association, and this is favourable to the sympathetic relation. A common stock of experiences, habits, and even feelings is formed by association in life, and the result is similar to that of congenital affinity, though lacking the charm of its ever-recurring unexpectedness. Congenital affinity, it should be noted, is not limited to cases of similar racial type. It is a happy accident of human development which may be encountered at any turn.

8. Sympathy in education. — The value of sympathy as an element in the development of moral life is too large a subject to be treated here. A few words, however, may be devoted to (1) the teacher's use of sympathy in education, and (2) the training of sympathy in the child.

(1) The teacher's use of sympathy, like that of the orator described above, begins in his own sympathy with the learner's state of mind and ends in the achievement of the learner's sympathy with his. The teacher's sympathy requires as a starting-point, therefore, some demonstration on the child's part, and to evoke this in as good a form as possible for his purpose—but in any form rather than none—must be his first care. By entering into the child's mind thus shown to him he establishes the contact of sympathy, and by maintaining this contact he leads where he will, provided he keeps to the possible levels of the child throughout. It is not so much in regard to the method of individual lessons as in respect of his general procedure and influence that the teacher's tact is shown. A mistake of intellectual method is a small matter compared with an error in the procedure of moral discipline. It is quite possible to keep in touch with the child's sympathies, even when punishment seems to estrange him for a time.

(2) In the training of sympathy the first requisite is to encourage its manifestations when they occur spontaneously, and to suggest conduct which is the natural expression of interest in others. The tendency to sympathize with joy as well as with sorrow—*Mitfreud* as well as *Mitleid*—should be called out. All this belongs to the development of the sympathetic nature, which, however, also stands in need of disciplinary training. This, for the most part, life supplies, and the educator should be wary lest he interfere unwisely and too much. The delicate process of control and moderation by which each self sets limits to its sympathies had better be left to itself; and, as a rule, it is dangerous to train the young to repress, otherwise than by more fully expressing, their nature. Wise discipline trains to the control of one function for the sake of fulfilling another more perfectly. Thus, emotion is in general controlled by using it to subserve the voluntary and intellectual life.

Thought and conduct are the antidotes to hysteria and emotional riot. As regards sympathy in particular, we should be chiefly concerned to develop first its voluntary and, second to that, its intellectual side. The barren sympathy with suffering, *e.g.*, which does not go on to some comforting act is morbid because it ends in useless emotional disturbance. Doing in accordance with the occasion is the habit to which sympathy should be most carefully trained. Its other requisite is that it should be intelligent, and this is often a much-needed lesson. A useful sympathy with others requires imagination and reflexion sufficient to construct a true ideal of what they want. This intelligent apprehension of another's case is of inestimable value in making the fellow-feeling, as well as the friendly action, fit.

Persons who are 'too sympathetic to be of any use in trouble' are persons who, by neglecting to help their fellows as need arose, have let themselves get into a habit of being overwhelmed by painful fellow-feeling. The remedy is to do something for the prime sufferer. This is the natural course in the case of an unspoiled will.

LITERATURE.—W. Mitchell, *Structure and Growth of the Mind*, pt. iii. London, 1907; James Mark Baldwin, *Social and Ethical Interpretations in Mental Development*, New York, 1897, ch. vi.; William McDougall, *An Introduction to Social Psychology*, London, 1908, *The Group Mind*, Cambridge, 1920; G. Tarde, *Les Lois de l'imitation*, new ed., London, 1900; James Sully, *The Human Mind*, do. 1892, vol. ii. ch. xv.; William James, *The Principles of Psychology*, 2 vols., do. 1891, ch. xxiv. f.

S. BRYANT.

SYNAGOGUE.—See WORSHIP (Hebrew) and (Jewish).

SYNAGOGUE, THE GREAT.—See JUDAISM, vii. 593 f.

SYNCRETISM.—**1. Untechnical use of term.**—The term 'syncretism' has a very curious record. It is as old as Plutarch, who seems to have coined it, or at any rate to have made it current. In his essay on brotherly love[1] he observes that even brothers and friends who have quarrelled prefer to associate with one another, in face of a common danger, rather than to fraternize with the foe; which is a Cretan precedent and principle,

'for, although the Cretans were frequently at faction and feud with one another, they became reconciled and united whenever a foreign foe attacked them. This they called "syncretism" (συγκρητισμός).'

By 'syncretism,' in this political sense, therefore, we are to understand the instinct of self-defence which sinks private differences before a threatening peril on the outside. The 'syncretists' close their ranks; they like quarrelling among themselves, but they would rather exist than indulge in fatal internecine strife at home.

After Plutarch the term became submerged. Fourteen centuries later it re-appears in the pages of Erasmus, who was in his own way, especially when the way ran through the *Adagia*, a 'syncretist' of the reconciling order, averse to feuds. Erasmus sets down the reference to Plutarch, and he also employs the term in his correspondence.

Thus we find him writing from Louvain (22nd April 1519) to Melanchthon, hoping that scholars of all parties will close their ranks against the barbarians: 'Vides quantis odiis conspirent quidam adversus bonas literas. Aequum est nos quoque συγκρητίζειν. Ingens praesidium est concordia.'[2]

During the next century and a half the term is tossed about Europe by members of the Reformed and of the Roman Church, sometimes as an appeal, more often as a taunt; theologians who endeavoured to reconcile extremists were dubbed 'syncretists,' and 'syncretism' was indifferently and acrimoniously applied to all irenical proposals, whether these were the product of a Laodicean indifference or of a genuine love for moderation. In passing from the humanists to the theologians, the term upon the whole acquired disparaging associations, which continued to cling to it. 'Syncretist' became almost a synonym for 'hybrid.' It was derived from συγκεράννυμι, and the supposed etymology corroborated the connexion of the term with all that was heterogeneous.

This is the predominant meaning of the term in ordinary French. In untechnical English it also denotes 'fusion' of a more or less illegitimate or artificial kind. Thus Hallam[1] says of Giordano Bruno: 'What seems most his own . . . is the syncretism of the tenet of a pervading spirit, an Anima Mundi, which in itself is an imperfect theism, with the more pernicious hypothesis of an universal Monad.'

2. Philosophical and ecclesiastical applications.—In the history of philosophy 'syncretistic' has been applied to the harmonizing efforts of those who, like Cardinal Bessarion in the 15th cent., refused to allow their love of Plato to be identified with any depreciation of Aristotle. The controversy between the Aristotelians and the Platonists had been sharpened by the impetus given to Platonic studies after the fall of Constantinople. Partisanship ran strong, and the more moderate men failed to draw the rival schools together.

'Throughout all the tangles of this complicated controversy, a thread of gold is interwoven by the serene and imperturbable temper of Bessarion.'[2]

What happened in 15th cent. philosophy was repeated on a larger scale in the theology of the 17th century. The 'syncretistic controversy' of that age rose out of the efforts made by G. Calixtus (1586–1656), a distinguished scholar at Helmstädt, to draw the Lutheran and the Reformed Churches together. 'A plague o' both your houses,' he cried, like Mercutio. But it was Mercutio's dying cry of indignant protest. Calixtus lived and worked to check the plague. He was acutely sensible of the harm and danger to Christianity which the sharp internal divisions within the Church produced. But his broad, catholic temper met with little response among his contemporaries. The controversy lasted even after his death, assuming political as well as theological forms. The 'syncretistic' party in the Church failed, however, to carry its principles into effect. Even well-meaning and wise attempts to emphasize the fundamental Christian principles held by various Reformed Churches, or by all the Reformed Churches in common with the Roman Church, were suspect in that age of hardening division and widening cleavage. Men were told that in view of the Roman peril they would be well advised to subordinate their private idiosyncrasies in the Reformed Church; or Christians in both Churches were reminded that the menace of outside heathenism should make them close their ranks. But 'syncretism' of this kind was generally branded as a betrayal of principles or as an attempt to secure unity at the expense of truth. The 'syncretistic controversy' was a quarrel over peace, and such quarrels are not the least bitter upon earth. What the 'syncretists,' in Plutarch's sense of the term, called a harmony, their opponents called a 'hybrid,'

The Roman Church had a 'syncretistic' controversy of its own, an eddy in the turbulent dispute over the relations between grace and free will, which poured from the last quarter of the 16th century.[3] 'Syncretic' is the term applied to the system of belief which endeavours to harmonize the conflicting views of the Thomist and the Molinist parties by assuming two sorts of efficacious grace, which are held together by prayer.

3. In comparative religion.—'Syncretism,' as men like Calixtus and Zwingli used it, still retained something of the practical sense which

[1] *De Fraterno amore*, 19.
[2] *Opus Epistolarum*, ed. P. S. Allen, Oxford, 1906–13, iii. 539.

[1] *Introd. to the Literature of Europe*, 4 vols., London, 1837–39, pt. ii. ch. iii.
[2] J. E. Sandys, *Hist. of Classical Scholarship*, Cambridge, 1903–08, ii. 75.
[3] Cf. *CE* iv. 238 f., vi. 713 f.

Plutarch had originally attached to the expression. But this is lost in the technical, modern application of the term to a phenomenon in the history of religion, *i.e.* to the fusion of various religions in doctrine or in cult. Here 'syncretism' denotes generally an unconscious, wide-spread tendency, due to or fostered by some re-adjustment of political relationships or by some clash of civilizations. There is a blending of religious ideas and practices, by means of which either one set adopts more or less thoroughly the principles of another or both are amalgamated in a more cosmopolitan and less polytheistic shape. Such movements in the religious world are often preceded and accelerated by a new philosophical synthesis as well as by a political re-arrangement, but the outcome invariably is a unification of deities, which, as J. Toutain has pointed out,[1] proceeds on one or other of two lines: either two deities of different religions are assimilated by comparison or several deities are grouped together in a fresh synthesis. The motives for this re-statement are drawn from the dawning consciousness that any particular form of religion is no longer adequate by itself, that others possess like features, possibly of superior efficacy and appeal, and that such features can be incorporated without detriment to the essential principles of the particular religion in question. The study of comparative religion exhibits this phenomenon in a variety of shapes and stages, but it is specially prominent during the first four centuries of the Christian era.[2]

The tendency to this syncretism or amalgamation of deities and cults had been in operation long before the rise of Christianity. When one tribe conquered another, or when two tribes or nations formed a political alliance, there was a strong movement towards fusing their gods. The foreign power, especially if it were dominant, fascinated many of its subject or weaker neighbours. An exchange of deities might be made, out of courtesy. Similarities in ritual were developed, and stress was laid on what was common to the two religions. Now and then the gods were identified, and this was specially easy in the primitive days when certain gods were still nameless powers;[3] men were invited to recognize their own gods under the names of foreign deities or to welcome the latter as allies. The connexion between Israel and Canaan is an illustration in point,[4] and an equally familiar one is the influence of Assyrian rites upon the religion of Israel under kings like Manasseh and Amon,[5] when syncretistic influences were specially powerful in consequence of the political situation. The phenomenon is by no means confined to the history of Israel's religion in the ancient world. For different reasons syncretism, or, as some prefer to term it, 'theocrasy' (θεοκρασία),[6] was rife at one period in Greek religion owing to Oriental influences,[7] and as late as the 8th cent. of our era a similar blending took place in Japan.[1] But it is in the history of Judaism, particularly during the two centuries preceding the Christian era, that the elements and issues of syncretism are most clearly marked.[2]

The main impetus to this rise of syncretism came from the political re-adjustment after Alexander the Great. The Seleucid period witnessed a contact between the East and the West, round the Mediterranean basin, which led not only to a fusion of Babylonian with Greek and Roman deities[3] and to a ferment of Oriental religious feeling throughout the Græco-Roman world, but also to movements which, in spite of the vigorous reaction led by the Maccabees[4] and their supporters, affected some circles in Judaism itself. The Hellenizing tendency was fostered by Jewish writers like Eupolemus and Artapanus. It went hand in hand with the allegorizing of Homer and of the OT and with the Stoic philosophy of the Logos. As the tendency to syncretism was innate in Egyptian religion[5]—the spread of the Serapis-cult is only one later instance of it—and as Alexandria formed the centre of activity not only for the amalgamation of Egyptian and Greek or Syrian cults but also for speculative Judaism under the spell of the new ideas of cosmopolitanism, it is not surprising that a step was there taken in the direction of a syncretistic Judaism, which should assimilate and employ current Greek ideas of a cosmopolitan, cosmic character. The exponent of this syncretism is Philo.

> 'Un syncrétisme dans lequel sont admis tous les éléments, en particulier péripaticiens et platoniciens, qui s' accordent avec l'idée stoïcienne fondamentale de la sympathie des parties du monde, telle serait la définition la plus exacte des vues cosmologiques de Philon.'[6]

Philo's aim was not to blend Judaism with Hellenism. He adhered to his religious inheritance. But he endeavoured to enrich and safeguard it by re-stating it in terms of the current religious philosophies of his day.

As Judaism on the whole resisted this Philonic speculative tendency,[7] so did Christianity in the main resist the later Gnostic movement with its syncretistic impulse during the 2nd and 3rd centuries.[8] Syncretism was partly an evidence of strength and partly an indication of weakness at that period. So far as it meant a readiness to set the new faith in a positive relation to the elements of truth in contemporary cults and mysteries, so far as it breathed a spirit strong enough to assimilate vital data from its new soil and yet preserve its distinctive characteristics, it was healthy. In this respect it carried on the work of the best apologists, linking the Christian tradition to the new situation and proving that the faith was too vital to remain a Semitic cult. But there was another side to syncretism, and to this the Church was keenly, if not always wisely, alert. The fascination of the movement lay in its cosmopolitan appeal—an appeal which was the more seductive that already, within paganism itself, the movement had made headway, as we see from the tone of men like Plutarch, Maximus of Tyre, and Numenius,[9] and from a specific phenomenon like the transformation which had come over a deity such as Isis[10] in the popular pieties of the age. The

1 *Les Cultes païens dans l'empire romain*, Paris, 1908–11, ii. 227 f. See J. H. Moulton, *The Christian Religion in the Study and the Street*, London, 1919, pp. 253–268 ('Syncretism in Religion').

2 Cf. *ERE* vi. 232 f.; A. Harnack, *The Mission and Expansion of Christianity*[2], Eng. tr., London, 1908, i. 33 ff., 312 ff.; J. Reville, *La Religion à Rome sous les Sévères*, Paris, 1886, ch. iv.; J. Huby, in *Christus: manuel d'hist. des religions*, do. 1912, p. 340 f.; S. J. Case, *The Evolution of Early Christianity*, Chicago, 1914, pp. 71 ff., 191 f.; S. Angus, *The Environment of Early Christianity*, London, 1914, p. 23 ff.; W. R. Inge, *The Philosophy of Plotinus*, do. 1918, i. 46 f.

3 Cf. F. B. Jevons, *An Introd. to the Hist. of Religion*, London, 1896, pp. 235 f., 255 f., 390 f.

4 Cf. *ERE* vii. 441 f., 582.

5 Cf. B. Stade, *Biblische Theologie des AT*, Tübingen, 1905–11, i. 235 f.

6 *E.g.*, recently F. Legge, *Forerunners and Rivals of Christianity*, Cambridge, 1915, ii. 32 ('the *theocrasia* which was welding all the gods of the mysteries into one great God of nature').

7 Cf. *HDB* v. 150 f., and *ERE* vi. 421 f.

1 *ERE* vii. 483; J. Dahlmann, in *Christus*, p. 122 f.

2 Cf. H. A. A. Kennedy, *St. Paul and the Mystery-Religions*, London, 1913, p. 57 ff.

3 *ERE* vii. 434[a].

4 Cf. W. O. E. Oesterley, *The Books of the Apocrypha*, London, 1914, p. 22 ff.

5 Cf. A. Menzies, *Hist. of Religion*, London, 1895, p. 145.

6 E. Bréhier, *Les Idées philosophiques et religieuses de Philon d'Alexandrie*, Paris, 1908, p. 161.

7 Elsewhere combinations of Judaism and paganism are to be detected, however—*e.g.*, in Asia Minor, in the worship of θεὸς ὕψιστος.

8 Cf. *ERE* vi. 232 f.

9 *Ib.* vi. 282[b], ix. 308[b].

10 Cf. *ib.* vi. 378 f., vii. 434 ff.

passion of the time was for a vague monotheism, which should reflect and answer the unity of the empire. A cosmopolitan syncretism, in the 3rd cent.,[1] began to overlay the earlier national religions and to embrace the Syro-Hellenic and the Western cults in a synthesis which regarded all deities as so many varied expressions of the One, and all rites as more or less acceptable forms of approach to this central, all-pervasive Deity.[2] The individual features of the separate gods and goddesses became less and less distinct. Idiosyncrasies were obliterated, and stress was laid, from the religious as well as from the philosophical and the political points of view, upon the all-embracing unity—generally conceived as a solar pantheism. A man like Macrobius voices this in the 4th century. It underlay the pagan reaction of Julian, which was its last serious challenge to a recalcitrant Christianity. For, although the Church admitted elements which were of semi-polytheistic character, in the worship of the saints, the exploiting of miracles, and even the adoration of the emperor, nevertheless formally the sense of Christianity decided against syncretism of the Gnostic and later of the Neo-Platonic shape.[3] This is the paradox of the situation. Christianity proved by its exclusiveness that it was not, and was not to be, a merely 'syncretistic' faith, in the sense of being eclectic or derivative. At the same time, it not only assimilated bravely and wisely many elements organic to its growth, but also admitted, as we see, *e.g.*, in its later Egyptian popular developments,[4] semi-pagan features which were a handicap ultimately to its successful advance.[5] The syncretistic situation was at once an opportunity and a risk for Christianity. The opportunity was often seized, and the risk was sometimes too much for the faith. Still, the environment did not mould Christianity as it moulded movements like Mithraism and Neo-Platonism. The catholicism of that age suffered from the desire to conciliate the natural man, but it had more in it than an indiscriminate selection or an anxious imitation, such as syncretism usually exhibited.

The tendency of syncretism, when broadly viewed, was to henotheism or pantheism rather than to monotheism. It is true that syncretistic movements meant a break away from polytheism.

'The first corollary of a truly pantheistic religion is not so much toleration of all forms of worship, as a tendency to embrace them all in a single syncretistic system. The one God is the same for all. What, then, does the name they give him matter?'[6]

Such is the theme of a book like the *Saturnalia* of Macrobius, and it is the principle of the religious synthesis underlying Plutarch's philosophy of things. But, as the arguments of a Neo-Platonist like Iamblichus show, this serene indifference was not incompatible with ideas which were henotheistic rather than monotheistic, and the popular cravings proved too much for even a monotheistic principle in Christianity. Pope's opening lines in 'The Universal Prayer'—

'Father of All! in ev'ry Age,
In ev'ry Clime ador'd,
By Saint, by Savage, and by Sage,
Jehovah, Jove, or Lord!'—

echo the syncretistic aspiration in its exalted and abstract form. But syncretism, like Catholicism, appealed to lower as well as higher cravings. The adoration of a Deity like this left the heavens strangely bare for those who had been accustomed to a richer variety of worship, and thus the syncretistic tendency was welcomed as it allowed these heavens to be repeopled by a host of spirits and saints. Syncretism, in practice, almost invariably fostered mythology. Sages and saints, no less than savages, yielded to its spell in this direction. It was found quite compatible, in pagan syncretism, to unite a reverence for the One with some special adoration of one or more favourite, traditional deities.[1] And it is a question how far even the Christian Church of the 4th cent., *e.g.*, which had rejected in earlier days the hospitable syncretism of a monarch like Alexander Severus, tolerated, for the sake of their associations and popular appeal, forms of adoration which were, strictly speaking, out of line with essential monotheism.

LITERATURE.—The literature has been noted during the course of the article; the 'syncretistic controversy' of the 17th cent. is discussed by I. A. Dorner, *Hist. of Protestant Theology*, Eng. tr., Edinburgh, 1871, ii. 177 f.; K. Löffler, *CE* xiv. 383 f.; P. Tschackert, *PRE*[3] xix. 243 ff., and in J. H. Blunt, *Dict. of Sects, Heresies, Ecclesiastical Parties, and Schools of Religious Thought*, London, 1874, p. 585 ff.

JAMES MOFFATT.

1 'The expansion of the imperial organisation, the mixture of nationalities in the capital, and the flooding of them by Oriental elements, the heightened intercourse, the prolonged residence of the legions in the provinces and their permeation by foreigners, finally, since the 3rd century, the advent of emperors who were foreigners and unfamiliar with the national spirit of Rome—all these produced the syncretism of religions' (P. Wendland, *Die hellen.-röm. Kultur in ihren Beziehungen zu Judentum und Christentum*[2], Tübingen, 1912, p. 152).

2 See G. Wissowa, *Religion und Kultus der Römer*, Munich, 1902, p. 80 f. 'The reconciled East and West met in Rome to exchange compliments and gods' (J. Martineau, *Essays, Reviews, and Addresses*, London, 1890–91, ii. 315).

3 *ERE* ix. 320.

4 Cf. P. D. Scott-Moncrieff, *Paganism and Christianity in Egypt*, Cambridge, 1913, pp. 126 f., 129 f., 150 f.

5 Cf. Harnack, *Hist. of Dogma*, Eng. tr., London, 1894–99, ii. 124 f.

6 G. d'Alviella, *Lectures on the Origin and Growth of the Conception of God* (*HL*), London, 1892, p. 232.

1 W. Pater notes this in Marcus Aurelius: 'To his pious recognition of that one orderly spirit, which, according to the doctrine of the Stoics, diffuses itself throughout the world . . . he had added a warm personal devotion towards the whole multitude of the old national gods, and a great many new foreign ones' (*Marius the Epicurean*[3], London, 1892, i. 198).

SYNDERESIS

SYNDERESIS.—The word συντήρησις, which has no classical authority, should mean 'preservation.' In scholastic and mystical theology it appears, often in the corrupt forms *synderesis* or *sinderesis*, in a sense which is hardly justified by the etymology of the word. Τήρησις is used in later Greek in the sense of 'observation,' and συντήρησις may have been coined on the analogy of συνείδησις. The first example is in Jerome:

'Quartamque ponunt quae super haec et extra haec tria est, quam Graeci vocant συντήρησιν, quae scintilla conscientiae in Cain quoque pectore, . . . non extinguitur, et qua . . . nos peccare sentimus.'[2]

Bonaventura[3] couples *synteresis* with *intelligentia*, as *intellectus* with *ratio*. Elsewhere he connects *synteresis* with *conscientia*.

'Benignissimus Deus quadruplex contulit ei adiutorium, scilicet duplex naturae et duplex gratiae. Duplicem enim indidit rectitudinem ipsi naturae, videlicet unam ad recte iudicandum, et haec est rectitudo conscientiae, aliam ad recte volendum, et haec est synteresis, cuius est remurmurare contra malum et stimulare ad bonum.'[4]

In the *Itinerarium* he defines *synteresis* as 'apex mentis seu scintilla.' Hermann of Fritzlar speaks of it as a power or faculty in the soul, wherein God works immediately, without means and without intermission. Ruysbroeck defines it as the natural will towards good implanted in us all, though weakened by sin. Giseler uses similar language, saying that the spark (so Eckhart speaks of a *Fünkelein* in the soul which cannot be extinguished) was created with the soul in all men, and is a clear light in them, striving in every way against sin and impelling steadily to virtue, and pressing back towards the source from which it came. In Thomas Aquinas *synteresis* is the highest activity of the moral sense. Gerson says that the cognitive power in man has three faculties—the simple intelligence or natural light, which comes from God Himself; the understanding, which is the frontier between the two worlds; and the sense-consciousness. *Synteresis* is the effective

2 *In Ezech.* i. 1.

3 *Itinerarium mentis ad Deum*, i.

4 *Breviloquium*, ii. 11.

faculty answering to the first of these, and contemplation is its corresponding activity. The word also occurs in Albertus Magnus and Alexander of Hales. Eckhart sometimes seems to identify *synteresis* with the *Fünkelein* or *Ganster*, and with the *intellectus agens* or *die oberste Vernunft*; but the tendency of his philosophy is to make the 'spark' supra-rational and uncreated; he even says: 'Diess Fünkelein, dass ist Gott.' In the earlier writers *synteresis* is usually thought of as a remnant of the sinless state of man before the fall, while in the bolder thought of the school of Eckhart it becomes the seat or organ of divine immanence and of the highest personal inspiration. The notion of an impeccable 'soul-centre' may be traced back to the Neo-Platonists.

LITERATURE.—W. Preger, *Gesch. der deutschen Mystik im Mittelalter*, 2 vols., Leipzig, 1874–81; A. Lasson, *Meister Eckhart der Mystiker*, Berlin, 1868; W. R. Inge, *Christian Mysticism*, London, 1899.

W. R. INGE.

SYNDICALISM.—See SOCIALISM.

SYNERGISM.—**1. General meaning of the term and its Scriptural support.** — The term 'synergism' (συνεργεῖν, συνεργός, 'to co-operate,' 'fellow-worker') became definitely fixed as a *terminus technicus* in theology in the 16th century. It was applied to the later views of Philip Melanchthon and his followers on the question as to the relation between the Holy Spirit (or God's grace) and man's will in regeneration. This view, broadly stated, is that the human will can and does co-operate with the grace of God as a *vera causa regenerationis*. It opposes the position expressed in the sentence 'Homo convertitur nolens.' The human will was, it is true, not regarded as the primary cause (hence synergism differs from Pelagianism or even Semi-Pelagianism); that was unreservedly assigned to God's Spirit and to the preaching of the Word, but the energy of the human will was given a place, and its assent an essential place, in the act of regeneration. The enunciation of this view caused unusual heat among theologians, because its truth or falsehood affected the whole realm of theological truth—the effects of the fall on human nature, the nature and working of God's decrees, the responsibility of the sinner, in fact all Christian anthropology and soteriology.

The term 'synergism' owes its origin to Scripture, but the Scriptural usage of the word operates in a different universe of discourse from the theological. In the NT συνεργεῖν (συνεργός) is never applied to the psychological relation, whatever that may be, whether creative or co-operative, between God's Spirit and man's will in regeneration or conversion. Its general usage is to describe the objective co-operation of Christian brethren in the furtherance of God's kingdom on earth.

In 1 Co 3[9] (θεοῦ γάρ ἐσμεν συνεργοί) the co-operation referred to is that between men in their outward labours for God, not a co-operation between them individually or unitedly with God, however true that may be in itself; and at any rate it refers to post-conversion experience, not to pre- or simul-conversion relationships. In Ph 2[13] the reference is to men already regenerated, and the same is true of Ro 8[28], if ὁ θεὸς is the true text—God works in all things for good with those who love God. It does not directly refer to what takes place in conversion, nor does it state the active elements involved therein and their relationships. Again, in Mk 16[20] the co-operation of the ascended Lord with the heralds of the gospel is spoken of in regard to miracles. But the word in Scripture is never used of man's natural faculties or capacities (before conversion) working together with the Spirit of God to effect regeneration, which is the specific and proper theological application of the term. If thus synergism is to be rejected or to be defended from Scripture, it must be by reference to the truth of Scripture, and not to its letter.

2. The origin and development of synergism in Melanchthon's doctrine.—The earlier writings of Melanchthon betray no synergistic tendencies. On the contrary, they are in some respects more rigidly deterministic than even Luther's. The religious man is profoundly conscious of his dependence on God's grace. He does not dream of co-ordinating or equating his own freedom with the grace of God as causal in his salvation. This is true even of those who are legitimately called synergists. 'Arminians usually pray like Calvinists,' said Charles Hodge, adding, what is equally true, that 'Calvinists frequently preach like Arminians';[1] *i.e.*, they appeal to men as responsible voluntary agents. The difficulty arises when one or other of these aspects of experience is made the determining factor in the elaboration of a theological system. Truth is largely a matter of proportion and balance. To begin with, Melanchthon, whose mind was eminently of a systematic cast, worked out his system under the dominating influence of the experience of divine dependence. The Holy Spirit teaches us, he says, that all things happen necessarily by predestination, and therefore there is no such thing as freedom of our will. To maintain free will was to dethrone the grace of God from its unique supremacy. This was his position in the first edition of his *Loci Communes Rerum Theologicarum*,[2] and it was even more rigidly expressed in his Commentary on Romans and Corinthians.[3] Free will he regarded as a scholastic figment emanating from carnal wisdom and obscuring the blessings brought to us by Christ. It made men arbiters of their own salvation and consequently undermined the immediacy of Christian assurance and froze the stream of personal devotion to the Redeemer. Melanchthon resolutely applied this conception of predestination to all events, physical and moral, outward and inward:

> 'Si ad praedestinationem referas humanam voluntatem nec in externis, nec in internis operibus ulla est libertas.' Since man is born a child of wrath, it follows that he is born without the Spirit of God, and therefore 'nihil nisi carnalia sapit, amat, et quaerit.'[4]

Man has no power over his inward affections, and, though Melanchthon admits that in outward things he has some freedom, even here the power of will seems to vanish. Thus Melanchthon, applying a transcendental conception, predestination, to the facts of human life, as he read them or understood them from Scripture, came to assert that no real causality existed anywhere but in God's will, and so the betrayal of Judas is as truly and as immediately an act of God as the calling of Paul. The reprobation of the damned is as properly and in the same sense the effect of God's will as the salvation of the elect. We are not to think of certain events as determined while others are allowed. All things immediately flow out of God's will necessarily. All questions as to the rightness of God's procedure he silences by regarding these questionings as issuing from man's carnal inquisitiveness.

It follows from this position that man could contribute nothing to his own conversion. He could not repent of himself, and so-called morality (pre-conversion) has no spiritual value.

> 'Homo per vires naturales nihil [potest] nisi peccare. Carnale est quidquid per naturae vires fit, Socratis constantia, Zenonis moderatio, nihil nisi carnales affectus sunt.'[5]

At this stage we see Melanchthon planted firmly on the experience of God's free grace which gave its strength to the new outlook of the Reformation, combating strongly the popular Roman Catholic view according to which man's free will aided by certain ecclesiastical rites contributed

[1] C. A. Salmond, *Princetoniana*, Edinburgh, 1888, p. 177.
[2] Originally published at Wittenberg and Basel in 1521, and ed. T. Kolde, Leipzig, 1900.
[3] Nüremberg, 1522.
[4] *Loci*, 1521, p. 97.
[5] *Ib.* pp. 97–115.

something to man's salvation—a view which cut the vital nerve of personal trust in Christ as the alone Redeemer and opened a door by which the whole mechanism of merits and of an external ecclesiastical authority as ultimate source of redemptive assurance could be reinstated. Melanchthon, however, was extravagant in his elaboration and his application of the truth of man's dependence on God for salvation. He confused in the interests of a theory natural and moral causality, and left no moral bridge between nature and grace. He raised a spiritual feeling—of supreme importance, no doubt—to a position of absolute sovereignty over man and nature and over God Himself. It was impossible that this could be the final resting-place of one like Melanchthon to whom the ethical interest was so important and who was of a mediating spirit.

> 'Ego mihi conscius sum, non ullam ob causam unquam τε θεολογηκέναι, nisi ut mores meos emendarem.'[1]

Accordingly he was soon convinced, both by the development of his own experience and by the movement of events, of the necessity of defending his position from misconceptions—not now so much from the side of Rome as from pretended followers of free grace itself—and this led him to modify his earlier views. He now came to see that there were many positions previously held by him which he would have to alter. His study of the Greek fathers, whose views on free will were determined by their hostility to Eastern fatalism, and who were very conscious of the moral continuity between nature and grace (often the two were not clearly distinguished by them), influenced his thought, and we find him frequently quoting from Chrysostom: ἕλκει μὲν ὁ θεὸς βουλόμενον δὲ ἕλκει, or from Basil: μόνον θέλησον καὶ θεὸς προαπαντά.[2]

The contentions of Erasmus as against Luther undoubtedly influenced Melanchthon also, and the result was emphasis on the will's own activity in conversion.

His increasing familiarity with the classical moralists and the Stoics, but above all his earnest ethical nature, stimulated into protest by the fanaticism of enthusiasts who regarded regeneration as an immediate unmediated *opus operatum*, led him to alter his views or, as he thought himself, to replace the emphasis. Pre-conversion morality was now given a moral valuation. Men were saying that they could do nothing, and so they defended everything that they did or felt inclined to do, however wicked or outrageous. Roman Catholics were thus given an occasion to equate Lutheranism with immoralism in personal life and anarchy in society, and the doctrines of grace had therefore to be set on an ethical basis for the benefit alike of opponents and of adherents. The result was the advocacy by Melanchthon of what became known in the Lutheran Church as synergistic views. It was in his eyes not a capitulation or a palinode, but an ethical rehabilitation of the doctrine of free grace, although it was viewed by genuine Lutherans as a reversion to Pelagianism.

> 'One egg is not liker another than his synergy is to the Pelagian,' said Matthias Flacius[3] the Illyrian, a champion of Lutheranism, concerning the views of Melanchthon's follower Victorine Strigel. 'Man, they say, can by the natural powers of his free will equip and prepare himself for the reception of God's grace—exactly the teaching of the godless sophists, Thomas of Aquino, Scotus, and their disciples,' said Nicholas Amsdorf of Johann Pfeffinger and Melanchthon.[4]

1 From a letter to Joachim Camerarius, in *Corpus Reformatorum*, ed. C. G. Bretschneider and H. E. Bindseil, Halle and Brunswick, 1834-60, i. 722.

2 *Loci*, 1535, p. 376, and elsewhere.

3 Weimar Disputation, 9th session (cf. Luthardt, *Die Lehre vom freien Willen*, p. 226).

4 *Öffentliche Bekenntnis der reinen Lehre, des Evangelii*, etc., Jena, 1558.

Synergism, however, is to be understood not from the extreme censures of its opponents, not even from the extreme statements of its advocates, but rather when we look on it as an ethical protest against positions that threatened to submerge the conscience and heart and to disarm the Church in her fight against licence and anarchy. It is therefore necessary to state Melanchthon's position more fully.

3. Melanchthon's synergism and its effect on his theological outlook.—Melanchthon's interest, we have said, was mainly practical, not theoretic. Accordingly his interest latterly in predestination was that of the custodian of morals. He desired to safeguard God's moral purity from any shadow that might be cast upon it by this dogma and at the same time to free man's moral nature from the paralysing effect of a monergistic determinism. His early statements were extravagant. Now he emphatically declared that God could in no sense be regarded as the author of sin. Evil was permitted by Him, but it was abhorrent to His nature. He therefore felt obliged to give up the dogma of an eternal decree of reprobation. The cause of man's sin was in man himself, and the hardening of his heart was due to wilful disobedience and perversity. Man's own responsibility for his spiritual state was emphasized. The offer of God's grace was universal. Original sin was a fact, yet man's will, though it could not initiate a gracious state, could yet adopt an attitude of welcome or of repugnance to God's grace offered in His Word. Accordingly we find Melanchthon editing the original *Augsburg Confession* in this interest.

> Art. 18, which originally read, '*Justitia spiritualis* is effected by the Holy Spirit which is received into the heart through the Word,' he altered to read, '*Justitia spiritualis* is effected in us when we are helped (*adjuvamur*) by the Holy Spirit.' The same alteration, *adjuvari*, is made in art. 20. He prepared the *Leipzig Interim* in the same spirit: 'Although God does not justify men through their merits, nevertheless the merciful God does not act on man as on a block but draws him so that his will co-operates, provided he has come to years of discretion.'

Melanchthon's position is clearly stated in the revised edition of his *Loci* (published in 1533) in a sentence that became famous and stereotyped in after controversy:

> 'In hoc exemplo videmus conjungi has causas, verbum, Spiritum sanctum et voluntatem non sane otiosam, sed repugnantem infirmitate suae'; or, as he expressed it in later editions: 'hic concurrunt tres causae bonae actionis, verbum Dei, Spiritus sanctus, et humana voluntas assentiens nec repugnans verbo Dei. Posset enim excutere ut excutit Saul sua sponte, sed cum mens audiens, ac se sustenans non repugnat, non indulget diffidentiae, sed adjuvante etiam Spiritu sancto conatur assentiri in hoc certamine voluntas non est otiosa.'[1]

There is little doubt that Melanchthon applies this to the act of conversion, and his view was that the positive assent of the will was essential, although, as Herrlinger[2] points out, he maintained at times that the help of the Holy Spirit was necessary to enable the will to accept the gospel.[3] While he does not make it at all times quite clear whether this assent was itself the result of the working of God's Spirit or due to the natural energy of the will, yet he seems certainly to maintain that something must be granted to the will itself, and here is the point on which the synergistic controversy hinges. This dubiety is noticeable also in some of his followers. One of them, Pezelius, interprets his master as teaching that the will was a *causa subordinata*, after the Holy Spirit in the Word had roused up the soul.[4]

Latterly he defined the will after Erasmus as *facultas applicandi ad se gratiam*, and therefore the difference between the saved and the lost is

1 *Corp. Reform.* xxi. 658.

2 *Die Theologie Melanchthons*, Gotha, 1879.

3 See I. A. Dorner, *A System of Christian Doctrine*, iv. 171.

4 See Luthardt, p. 189.

ultimately due not to election—for even God foresaw something in the elect which conditioned His election—nor to reprobation, but to man himself. The difficulty which confronted Melanchthon was just to determine what constitutes responsibility, and, even if his solution is defective and open to verbal criticism, as it certainly is, it is a merit that he recognized the problem in its seriousness and that he tried to solve it on moral grounds.

Melanchthon's synergism also affected his practical outlook. To those who defended civil and social outrage because they were sinners, and would remain sinners unless changed by a divine act which they could do nothing to initiate, he sternly said that man in spite of original sin had liberty in outward actions, the reason could control the will, and the will the bodily movements. No man could say, like the servant of Zeno, that he was compelled to sin by fate. It is clear that his soul loathed this Manichæism, as he called it, and his safeguarding of predestination from those who so understood it was clamantly demanded by the circumstances of the age and of many ages since. It is surely as immediate a datum of Christian experience that the sinner is responsible for his sin as that he ascribes his salvation to God's grace.

Melanchthon did not take a prominent part in the Majoristic controversy, which arose over George Major's statement that 'good works are necessary for holiness,' but by various utterances he indicated that, whilst maintaining the Lutheran position that justification is of grace alone, he was anxious to show that a holy life was the inevitable consequence and the test of the reality of a justified life. Amsdorf's statement that 'good works are harmful to holiness' he characterized as a 'lewd saying' (*unflätige Rede*).[1]

4. The synergistic controversy.—Melanchthon's statements concerning free will were ambiguous and so hesitating that men, accustomed to the breezy statements of Luther on the same subject, felt as if he attributed to the will more than he actually expressed, and his acceptance of Erasmus's formula gave this feeling a colour of truth. Luther on this point was definite:

'In geistlichen und göttlichen Sachen was der Seelen Heil betrifft da ist der Mensch wie die Salzsäule, wie Loth's Weib, ja wie ein Klotz und Stein, wie ein todt Bild, das weder Augen noch Mund weder Sinn noch Herz brauchet.'[2]

What Luther advocated with zeal Melanchthon admitted with reserve. Controversy was therefore inevitable, and it broke out violently, occasioned by two disputations of Pfeffinger,[3] a Leipzig professor and disciple of Melanchthon.

He tried to answer the question why one man under the preaching of the Word became converted and another did not, and the decisive factor, he maintained, was that one willingly assented and the other did not. The difference cannot be attributed to a difference in the activity of the divine will: therefore the difference lies in man himself. We must therefore attribute a certain synergy to our will. Man even now in his fallen state is not as a statue or a stone, nor is he purely passive, for, if that were the case, there would be no difference between the pious and the impious, the elect and the damned, Saul and David. God would become a respecter of persons and the author of contumacy in the impious and the damned. On the other hand, the human will has not the power to effect spiritual motions without the help of the Holy Spirit, but the Holy Spirit moving through the Word of God, and the mind thinking, and the will not resisting but complying under the Spirit's influence—these are the causes which concurrently produce conversion.

Pfeffinger's defence and explanation of Melanchthon's views called forth violent opposition especially from Amsdorf and Flacius. The former (see above) said that, according to Pfeffinger, man could prepare and equip himself for conversion by the natural powers of his free will without the aid of the Holy Spirit. Verbally this was very unjust, but essentially it had an element of truth in it. Flacius appealed to Luther's words and declared that man was worse than a stock or stone because he offered resistance to God's Spirit. The will therefore does not co-operate; it opposes and resists. Every one knows that this criticism, though infelicitously expressed, is in touch with reality and spoken out of personal experience. As regards regeneration, man is absolutely passive—he is spiritually dead; the image of God is not only wholly obliterated, but is transformed into the image of Satan. Man thus contributes nothing positive to his own conversion; any contribution of his is negative and resisting.

Pfeffinger replied to Amsdorf and incidentally mentioned Flacius. He declared himself more explicitly as holding that the unconverted will had the power of either obeying or resisting God's offer in His Word. Thus the controversy raged, the new university of Jena contending for the old position of Luther and violently opposing the synergistic movement, which was stoutly advocated by the faculties of Leipzig and Wittenberg. At last, at the instigation of Flacius, an attempt was made to silence opposition by authority. John Frederick II., Elector of Saxony, was appealed to, and by his command a *Book of Confutation and Condemnation* of all prevalent heresies was published at Jena in 1559. Of its nine divisions the sixth was devoted to the refutation of synergism. Those who taught that man had power in his will to co-operate with the grace of God in conversion were stigmatized as overthrowers of the grace of God. It was false to maintain that man can do anything by his free will in accepting or rejecting grace. Human nature is wholly adverse from God and hostile to God and is subjected to the tyranny of sin and Satan.

In a similar strain the orthodox Lutherans—Amsdorf, Wigand, Tilman Hesshusen, etc.—spoke and wrote against synergism and deduced this anthropology from their predestinarian views, the last-named saying that, in one respect,

'God did not wish that all men should be saved, for He did not elect all. God's will acts in one uniform way on men just as on stocks and stones.'[1]

Melanchthon raised his voice against this deterministic delirium and declared that it is absurd to talk of conversion until the will consents, that to reject God's grace is an act of will and not an act of God, and that human nature had at least power in outward actions. An attempt was made to make the book binding on teachers and preachers, but without success. Even in Jena, the citadel of orthodoxy, Pastor Hugel refused to read the document from the pulpit, and Strigel raised his voice on the synergistic side. Both Strigel and Hugel were imprisoned, and it looked as if synergism were doomed in Jena, for the university was strengthened in the orthodox interest by the appointments of Wigand and Judex to professorial chairs and by the recall of Musæus, all of whom were strong champions of orthodoxy. However, the prisoners were set free after an imprisonment of less than six months, and a further attempt was made to settle the dispute by public discussion. This disputation lasted from 2nd until 8th Aug. 1560, and occupied thirteen sittings. The interest for us centres in the positions defended and refuted regarding free will and God's grace.

To begin with, Strigel maintained that the substance and qualities of human nature were not obliterated by the fall nor altered, but only hindered in their activity. His position he made clear by a curious physical illustration.

A magnet, he said, cannot attract iron when smeared with onion-juice, yet it retains its magnetic properties, and it can attract though smeared with goat's blood. It is the same magnet in both cases, but its activity is hindered in the one

1 *Corp. Reform.* ix. 407.
2 *Enarr. in Ps. xc.*
3 *Propositiones de libero arbitrio* and *Quæstiones quinque de libertate voluntatis humanæ*, Leipzig, 1555.

1 See Luthardt, p. 241.

case and not in the other. So by the fall man's nature is not destroyed, but only weakened. He is like him who fell among thieves between Jerusalem and Jericho, half-dead, or like one weakened by disease but not dead like a corpse.

Strigel is here aiming at a distinction which satisfies many theologians—that between formal freedom and material freedom or that between natural ability and moral ability, a distinction largely used by Jonathan Edwards but in currency before his day.[1] According to this distinction, man does what he pleases and wills what he pleases. That is the very meaning of will—it is not compelled from without; but, though man has this natural ability, as a matter of fact he does not will the good spiritually simply because he does not want to—he lacks moral ability.

Seeberg contends that Strigel was groping after this distinction, but did not adequately express it.[2] That is certainly true of him at this Weimar disputation. He did not make his meaning clear, but afterwards he distinguished very clearly between *efficacia* (δύναμις) or *facultas*, on the one hand, and *capacitas* or *aptitudo*, on the other. Man has lost the first through the fall, and the Holy Spirit restores to the will the δύναμις or efficacy or faculty of believing, which was lost by the fall. At this disputation, however, Strigel did not go so far as that. When asked by Flacius if the human will co-operated with the Holy Spirit before conversion or only after, he hesitated and said that to him conversion was not a point but a line, not the beginning of the Christian life but the whole of it.

It is evident from reading the disputation that Strigel really wished to attribute power to the will, but at the same time to ascribe the chief place to the Holy Spirit—so that synergism is an unfortunate term to use of factors that cannot be equated. He repeated the Melanchthonian formula: 'Concurrunt in conversione haec tria: Spiritus sanctus movens corda, vox Dei, voluntas hominis quae voci divinae assentitur,' a sentence which is ambiguous; and on this point no decision could be reached. On the other hand, Flacius went so far as to say that the very substance of the soul was altered by the fall and by sin, and that therefore man was purely passive, or active only in hostility to God. Peace could not be restored by public controversy. In a few months the party of the Illyrian was driven from the country, and Flacius, a man of undoubted erudition, died in his fifty-fifth year at Frankfort-on-Main. Strigel also left and died in Heidelberg at the early age of forty-five.

5. The Formula of Concord.—After various unsuccessful attempts at a solution of this and other disputes the *Formula of Concord*[3] appeared, and, as it became an authoritative standard of the Lutheran Church, its position on this topic must be stated here.

The problem is dealt with in artt. 1 and 2 of the *Formula*, and, while no personal names are mentioned, the views of contending parties are very clearly kept in mind. In the 1st art., dealing with original sin, a clear distinction is drawn between actual transgressions (*actualia delicta*) and the hereditary sickness of the soul. Man's nature is in all its parts poisoned by inherited sin, and for this condition man is guilty and condemned by God's law, so that by nature men are the children of wrath, and from this state they can be saved only by the benefits of Christ's merit. How this corruption is transmitted is described. God creates every soul afresh, but because of physical generation from corrupted seed the hereditary disease of sin is propagated. Yet God is not the author of sin in either its origin or its development, nor is man's substance converted into sin. Original sin is not to be identified with the essence of man. A clear distinction must be made between our nature (which was created, and which is daily preserved, by God), in which original sin dwells, and that original sin itself which dwells in our nature. To teach otherwise is Manichæism, not Christianity. This is further corroborated by the fact that the Son of God, according to His human nature, is consubstantial with us, His brethren. He took our nature, but it was sinless in Him. Further, God in sanctifying men purifies them from sin, accepting them for Christ's sake. He gives them grace, but He has eternal hostility towards sin itself. Moreover, if original sin were the substance of the soul, the doctrine of the resurrection of believers would be null and void. Thus the *Formula* disposes of the Flacian error. Yet, while all this is so, man before God in his actual fallen state is truly and spiritually dead in all his faculties, as far as spiritual good is concerned. Strigel's illustration of the magnet will not do. Man is not simply surrounded by outward hindrances; he cannot do anything, however small, in his natural state in regard to spiritual things. He has not the capacity 'in rebus spiritualibus aliquid inchoandi, operandi aut cooperandi.'

In the 2nd art., in which we have an attempt at an analytical solution, the relation of man's powers to the Holy Spirit is set forth. In fallen man before conversion there does not remain the smallest spark ('ne scintillula quidem') of spiritual power by which he can prepare himself for apprehending God's grace, or for applying or accommodating it to himself. Rather he resists it. Man is capable certainly of being converted. He is still a reasonable creature, but as regards any real initiative 'hac in parte deterior est trunco, quia voluntati divinae rebellis est et inimicus.' He has a capacity for conversion, but a passive one, and his conversion is purely a work of the Holy Spirit. At the same time it is stated that man by natural reason and will has somehow power to live a decent outward life. Thus the *Formula of Concord*, while strongly opposing the strange view of Flacius as regards the substance of the soul of fallen man, at the same time as strongly opposes the view which would give any power to the will in initiating conversion. Of Melanchthon's three causes it makes the Holy Spirit alone the efficient cause, the will and nature of man being only a subject to be converted, while the Word of God preached or read is the means through which the Spirit works. Great stress is laid on the Word of God as the means of the Spirit's working. Thus God softens men's hearts, draws them, and reveals to them their sin; and, realizing His anger, they feel in their heart contrition which makes them attend to the promises of the gospel, and so faith ('scintillula fidei') is quickened in their soul and 'hoc modo Spiritus Sanctus qui haec omnia operatur in cor mittitur.'

Thus the *Formula of Concord* unhesitatingly rejects synergism. In conversion the real agent is the Holy Ghost, the assent of the will is not a cause, but is itself an effect of the Spirit's working through the Word. Co-operation may be spoken of after conversion, but even then we must not think of God's Spirit and man's will as if they were like horses drawing a load and working side by side. God's Spirit in the converted man works on and through the will.

6. The Reformed position as regards synergism.—The problem of the relation of man's nature to the grace of God was agitated in the Lutheran Church after the *Formula of Concord* and has been a subject of dispute down to the present day.

[1] It is used by Twisse, Howe, and very clearly by Isaac Watts, the famous hymn-writer.
[2] *Lehrbuch der Dogmengesch.*, Leipzig, 1895-98, ii. 356.
[3] See *ERE* iii. 849.

In the Reformed Church the same problem arose, though it was approached somewhat differently. The distinctive feature of the Calvinistic system is its logical consistency; every doctrine is discussed not only by itself but in the light of the whole. The supreme regulative principle in Calvinism is the sovereignty of God; and, when man's regeneration was viewed in the light of this principle, it was recognized that God's grace acted differently on men who are regenerated and on those who are not. That is obvious, but whence the difference? It was due to the determination of God. God, who had elected some, did so not as a bare matter of decree or quiescent foreknowledge or fortuitously waiting on their faith, but energetically through a series of efficient means—the redemptive mission of His Son, the preaching of the Word, the irresistible working of the Holy Spirit; and these were effective all along the line in the case of the elect, leading them from spiritual death to grace and glory. Now, in the case of the unregenerated it was a sufficient proof that this divine redemptive causality had no place, that it failed in this link of regeneration. It was non-existent here; therefore it was wholly non-existent. God did not elect them; the redemption of His Son was not purposively undertaken or efficaciously operative in their case. Thus the question of the will is so embedded in the logical coherence of the system that to moot it is to raise the question of the validity of the system as a whole, and that is what happened in the case of Arminius, and especially—for Arminius himself did not attribute regenerating power to the will—in the case of his followers Simon Bischop (Episcopius), Philippus van Limborch, and others. The objections to Calvinism, as far as the subject of this article is concerned, were directed mainly against what was called irresistible grace and the extent of the Atonement.

The Arminians—for we may leave the Socinians out of account; W. Robertson Smith has aptly described them as 'Pelagians of the intellect'—held that grace worked similarly on all, the difference from which conversion arose being due not to God's grace but to man's own will. To them irresistible grace (or, more properly, efficacious grace) meant necessity, and so the responsibility for the final damnation of the lost fell on God. Again, they maintained that by the Atonement the possibility of salvation was opened to all, and they vehemently rejected the doctrine of the eternal reprobation of some, as Wesley so strenuously did afterwards. The Synod of Dort attempted to settle the problem, but in the Reformed Church as in the Lutheran it keeps constantly emerging. Here even more than in the Lutheran Church, which diffidently refrained from applying predestination theories to its anthropological and eschatological views,[1] the problem is an acute one, for the question of God's moral character is raised, and it is from this quarter, rather than from the sphere of religious psychology, that the opposition emerges, and here its strength lies. Hence we find that Calvinistic apologetic has largely been a defence against what is regarded as misunderstandings, perversions, and unwarrantable inferences.

In regard to efficacious grace the Calvinist did not mean that God's grace did violence to the human will by outward or inward compulsion, or that it altered the nature of the will as such, which always has worked and does work voluntarily, but that grace affected the disposition of man in such a way that the resistance of the will was changed into obedience. It was not the obedience of the will that made grace efficacious, but much more the efficacy of grace that made the will not only in act but in disposition obedient.

Some Calvinists, notably the school of Samur, agreed with the Arminians that the Atonement was intended for all mankind; but the Arminians contended further that it is left to the free will of man either to concur with or to reject this intention. The Calvinists felt that, while this opened a possibility of salvation to all, it made salvation certain for none; the Atonement thus became itself a contingency rather than a reality, and they could not understand a purpose of God which could thus be frustrated. To leave the future of mankind hanging on the slender thread of the free will—even if that thread was not itself an illusion—seemed too precarious to be consistent with a purposive God, and rendered the salvation of the regenerate itself problematic, a denial of the perseverance of the saints. Hence the position that the Atonement was meant for those that are saved or to be saved, and that grace is efficacious in the case of the elect; and so the empirical fact that some are not saved is itself a proof that in God's secret purpose the Atonement was not meant for them.

Here also, as in the Lutheran Church, and as in the internal disputes on this question between the Jesuits and the Jansenists in the Church of Rome, as well as in the disputes between Rome and Reformers on this point, we see the question at issue in spite of many cross currents in the discussion itself. The Calvinistic and Arminian problem is even more illuminating than the Lutheran because it is more conscious of the pervasive nature of the issue. It is a matter not of anthropology simply, but of theology in all its bearings. A survey of the discussion, in spite of the changed outlook of our own day, reveals the palpable dangers on either side and at least teaches us where we are not to search for an adequate solution.

The problem is not an accident of history, but a fundamental problem of thought, perhaps the problem which goes deepest of all—the relation between God and man. It goes deeper and higher than the question of man's place in nature or man's place in history; it is the question of man's place in relation to God.

7. Conclusion.—What, then, is the significance of the synergistic controversy for modern Christianity? It is evident that many of the preconceptions accepted by both parties alike, whether we look at the discussion as handled by Augustine and Pelagius, by Flacius and Melanchthon, by Calvin and Arminius, or by Jansenist and Jesuit, are antiquated. The march of natural science has raised afresh the whole question of the nature of man, and the problem is now whether man's nature can be explained from below as a development of life in general. Alongside of the activity of science has gone a prodigious wealth of philosophical speculation dealing with the nature of man, his place in the universe, and the value of his experience and his ideals. The profound changes also in the structure of society, the emergence of democratic ideas, and the consequent application of new categories in the explanation of the significance of human life have changed the outlook considerably. The more direct activities of Christianity itself, its vast missionary ideals and efforts, the investigations into the psychology of the Christian life, the insight into what is permanent in Christian experience as distinct from what is accidental or subsidiary—in short, the main currents of modern thought and life—have poured through Christian theology till the old landmarks are submerged, and history and reflexion alone make us certain that the unity of experience is a reality and that the problems of the spirit change not,

[1] Cf. also the Thirty-nine Articles of the Anglican Church.

however much the outlook may change. It is on this changed background and in the light of these tendencies that the problem of synergism can alone be approached.

(*a*) Modern Christianity in all its schools has had to fight against a naturalistic conception of man. From this point of view we can appreciate the emphasis laid by the early Greek theologians on man's freedom. Whatever may be thought of their view of freedom, the important point is that as against fatalism Christianity asserts that freedom has a real meaning as applied to man. So all Christian schools to-day, whether they be historically affiliated with Augustine or Pelagius, emphasize freedom as against physical necessity or direct determinism. Freedom has a meaning in regard to man that it has not in regard to matter. It is necessary to be clear on this point because naturalistic necessitarians too often claim the Augustinian and the Calvinist as on their side, whereas they are working on a different level of experience altogether. This is brought out clearly by the following considerations.

(1) According to Calvinism and Arminianism alike, man was originally created in the image of God, and his final end is 'to glorify God and to enjoy Him for ever.' This is deeper than any change brought about by sin and subsists as an inalienable characteristic of human nature.

'A lady once said to me, "The more I see of myself, I see nothing so properly mine as my sin." I said to her, "Well, you do not see deep enough. There is something far more properly yours than your sin; and your sin is improperly yours. It is a blot in your being, which, if you do not get quit of it, will never cease to be *unnatural* to you. No; the image of God is more properly yours, though you had no share in the production of it."'[1]

(2) It has always been held that man is responsible for his sin. He has formal freedom, nor can he ever become a non-moral being in the sense that he can become non-voluntary in his actions or place himself beyond the claims of the moral law on his character. Whatever his actual condition due to sin, these things hold true. His reason, conscience, and will always act rationally, morally, and volitionally. Again, the question here is not whether we agree with the content of this nature as explained by different schools of Christian thought. We may consider that the Arminian view gives too much, and the Calvinistic view too little, real freedom; but the important point is that from the general Christian standpoint man is not explicable in terms of mechanism, however subtle or refined in form. The synergistic controversy has no meaning either for opponent or for defender if the naturalistic view of man is true. The theory of T. H. Green[2] as to the relation of the character to volitions is simply Calvinistic psychology in a philosophical dress, but its whole motive is to overthrow the naturalistic conception of man.

(*b*) Synergism becomes a real problem when man's freedom is viewed in the light of God's activity. We are so accustomed to defending liberty against material necessity in our age that we are apt to forget that the real problem of freedom emerges on the religious plane. What meaning and content are we to give to man's freedom, not now as against nature, but as against God Himself? Two main streams of thought emerge in history on this question.

(1) The Pelagian, looking almost exclusively at man's free power of initiative, became jealous even of God's interference. Man on this view is a bare individual and largely, if not wholly, his own creator. His sin is a bare act of will, undetermined by what went before and unaffected by what comes after. His will is his unconditionally, for the character is the result of acts of will; but an act of will can alter it easily. His merit is his own, and his salvation is his own. God never gets inside the adytum of man's free spirit, and free will is primarily the power of choosing between alternatives.

(2) To the Augustinian the problem was far more complicated. He recognized that man was organically related to the past. The influences of the past affect his will and disposition and character. He does not begin as a moral neutral or moral unit. Sin is more than a bare act of will. When a man becomes self-conscious, it is there not simply as the result of a wrong choice, but as the fruit of a vitiated disposition and itself a source of vitiation. The characteristic of moral awakening is the discovery of our bondage. We become conscious of our need of freedom more than of the fact that we are free. The interposition of God is not regarded as a violation of freedom, but welcomed as the restorer and succourer of true freedom itself, which to the Augustinian meant acting in accordance with the highest. This deeper view of man led Augustine to the certainty of pre-individual iniquity—racial evil—as it led Kant to posit a supra-temporal fall. Objections may be raised to phrases like original sin, the guilt of Adam's transgression, the fall of Adam, supra-temporal fall, and it is right to aim at verbal accuracy if possible, but it is essential that the repudiation of inadequate phraseology should not be accompanied by the rejection of the realities bodied forth by inaccurate phrases.

We have the same tendencies in philosophy in our day represented by pluralism in its many forms and by absolute idealism. The former is so alive to the importance of the individual that in its extreme and logical forms it makes the individual eternal *a parte ante*, and, if God is recognized, it is as a *primus inter pares*; the latter is so conscious of the claims of God that it tends to annihilate the personal life of the individual *a parte post*. The problem as to how a man can act against God's will is insoluble intellectually, and the Calvinist has great difficulty, in spite of his insistence on man's accountability and God's holiness, in saving himself from the pitfall of pantheism where sin is factorized into something different from what it is to the conscience. Yet, however sinful man's state may be, however the sinner may be alive to the deep-seated nature and wide extent of this disease, he accepts responsibility for it as his. He cannot devolve the responsibility on Adam or on circumstances. That is the moral attitude. The intellect may attempt to explain sin either scientifically as a residuum from our animal origin or philosophically as due to finitude or as a necessary stage in our development; but every explanation that explains away the moral attitude is itself unsatisfactory. Pantheism, material, philosophical, or theological, suffers shipwreck on the conscience. But, on the other hand, though we are compelled to recognize centres of activity acting contrary to God's will, it is impossible to give them the self-subsistence that we give to God. Even in sinning they depend on Him and are within the scope of His control. The Christian doctrine of creation—creation in time, for creation has no other meaning in regard to dependent beings — saves from pantheism and pluralism alike. While all subsist in God, personalities have a limited power of self-antagonism to God, but they do not compel God to disown His character as Source and responsible sustainer of all. He creates personalities with the capacity to create themselves. Their endowments and faculties, which vary so much as regards both individuals

[1] John Duncan, *Colloquia Peripatetica*[3], Edinburgh, 1871, p. 124.

[2] *Prolegomena to Ethics*, Oxford, 1883.

and races, which are also so clearly dependent on their historical setting, are of God. It is this inalienable immanence of God that accounts for the presence of high ideals among men however sinful, for the unrest and lack of harmony in the life of man of which Pascal speaks so eloquently, and it is this that makes salvation possible and essential. The Augustinian tended to view man's original constitutive nature as made in God's image as an affix of an ideal human ancestor, and to leave man as he now is nothing but his sinful organic relations. A logical distinction was made an absolute distinction *in rerum natura*. The divine image in man was practically regarded as a *fulgor* appearing once in Adam for a brief space, but now no more; but sin has meaning only when the inalienable immanence of God in man is fully recognized. The Church has never agreed to the Flacian view of human nature as itself sin; but its language has often been perilously near it, and, when it has, protests have been raised, as in New England, where the amiable qualities of man have been emphasized until the need of salvation has been minimized or evaporated. On the ground, then, of man's original creation, we understand that man has freedom which, alas, has been exercised against God Himself, though given by God and intended by Him to coincide joyfully with His own.

How to reconcile God's holy omnipotence and foreknowledge with this human fact seems an insoluble problem. We must give content to God's predestinating activity; it is not enough to posit a quiescent, non-interfering divine knowledge; otherwise there is no guarantee of the ultimate success of God's purposes. But, on the other hand, we must not look on God's absolute decrees as the moral cause of sin or as acting mechanically in man, and certainly not as an insurmountable barrier to the recovery of his true freedom, and that in a moral way.

The synergist fought against a view of God which made Him in the case of some men the obstacle to salvation, withholding His grace from some, and making remedial provision only for some; and in this the synergist was right. Here again the Christian doctrine of the new creation is the safeguard. God is not only inalienably immanent in man by virtue of the first creation; He is also redemptively active in man through Christ. The Calvinist is mainly right in his psychology of conversion.

God's grace is efficiently active, and the consent of the will is the result of that activity; yet He is active in harmony with man's true being, and man's consent is voluntary. Man does not simply accept the offer of grace by the power of his unaided will and so convey it into the soul. His will is never unaided; grace comes into the soul as a power of God moulding the will itself. The acceptance itself is not the cause of its presence. The supremacy of grace and its efficiency is maintained by the religious consciousness on self-examination, but the acceptance itself is an act of will.

The miracle here also is not that a man's will should be effectually motived to harmonize with God's redemptive activity; the miracle is that some men should resist even this. It is not to be thought that their resistance is due to the fact that God withholds or withdraws His gracious activity or that He uses it only gingerly. The gospel offer is to all, even the Calvinist says, and it is a *bona fide* offer; it is more, for the cost to God—what we mean by the Atonement—is so real and so great that the activity of God is an energy penetrating into man. God does not deal with the sinner simply in the way of punishing him; He deals with him in a redemptive way. How can this fact of man's resistance, again, be reconciled with God's omnipotence in grace? Many, like Schleiermacher, find refuge in final universal salvation, in a probation extending beyond this life. But God's omnipotence is a reality which recognizes now man's power of resistance because it values man's freedom. This resistance does not annihilate the divine omnipotence, nor does it rob God of His character as Creator and Redeemer, were the resistance to be eternal.

The value of synergism is in its denials. It is wrong to regard God's activity as doing violence to this initiative of man. The weakness of synergism is that it tends to regard this activity of man as separate from God to begin with and as only co-operating with God. The relation between them is more intimate. God Himself is present from the outset in this freedom; and when, as in Christian experience, the soul awakens to the presence of God, then it is felt that God has done so much in Christ, and is doing so much, that it is joyfully acknowledged that the will's power is His, and the renewal of it is His work. Salvation is not an acquisition of the will so much as the welcome deliverance and liberation of the whole personality. Religion in its strength emphasizes God, and in so doing frees man into the liberty of joyful service.

LITERATURE.—The lives of the reformers, and the general treatises on the history of the Reformation, all deal with the synergistic controversy. J. W. Richard, *Philipp Melancthon: The Protestant Preceptor of Germany, 1497–1560*, New York, 1898, gives a good account of Melanchthon in English; cf. Karl Schmidt, *Philipp Melancthon*, Elberfeld, 1861.

C. E. Luthardt, *Die Lehre vom freien Willen*, Leipzig, 1863, gives a detailed history of the controversy in its origin and development; also *Die Arbeiten Melancthons im Gebiete der Moral*, Leipzig, 1884; Flotow, *De synergismo Melancthonis*, Vratislaw, 1867, is a special handling of the subject referred to by G. Kawerau, who has written much on the various antagonists in the synergistic controversy; see Schaff-Herzog, xi. 223 ff., also *PRE*³ xix. 229 ff.; E. F. Fischer has a treatise on Melanchthon's teaching on conversion (*Melanchthons Lehre von der Bekehrung*), Tübingen, 1905; and Paul Tschackert, *Die Entstehung der lutherischen und der reformierten Kirchenlehre*, Göttingen, 1910, pp. 520–531, is an excellent summary.

The literature on the *Formula of Concord* is relevant to the discussion; cf. F. H. R. Frank, *Theologie der Konkordienformel*, vol. i., Erlangen, 1858; R. Rothe, *Dogmatik*, Heidelberg, 1870, p. 171 ff.; F. Loofs, *Leitfaden zum Studium der Dogmengeschichte*⁴, Halle, 1906. R. Seeberg, *Lehrbuch der Dogmengeschichte*, Leipzig, 1895–98, as well as other treatises on dogmatics, give relevant sections. See also H. Heppe, *Gesch. des deutschen Protestantismus*, 4 vols., Marburg, 1853–56; I. A. Dorner, *System of Christian Doctrine*, Eng. tr., Edinburgh, 1880–82, iv. 164 ff. For Reformed doctrine see literature under art. CALVINISM, and for the modern problem H. Wheeler Robinson, *The Christian Doctrine of Man*², Edinburgh, 1913. See also artt. CONVERSION, FREE WILL, GRACE.

D. MACKENZIE.

SYNODS.—See COUNCILS AND SYNODS.

SYRIANS (or Aramæans).—**I. General introduction.**—The Hebrew 'Aram' is rendered in the LXX by Συρία, 'Syria.' We may therefore take it for granted that originally the words 'Aramæans' and 'Syrians' were synonymous. At a later time 'Syrian' and 'Assyrian' were used indiscriminately: Ἀσσύριος = Σύριος = Σύρος.[1] According to Gn 10²², Aram was one of the five sons of Shem, and, according to Gn 10²³, Aram was the father of Uz, Hul, Gether, and Mash. The Aramæans, or Syrians, are therefore Semites.

A complete study of the Aramæans would include that of all the races whose languages, manners, and religions come within the Syrian scope. But our purpose here is to consider only the pagan Aramæans. We shall not touch upon Western (*i.e.* Biblical) Aramæan, represented by several quotations preserved in the OT and the NT, nor the Egyptian papyri and ostraka, particularly those of Elephantine, nor the Jewish dialects

[1] Cf. T. Nöldeke, in *Hermes*, v. [1870] 443 ff.

represented by the Targums, the Megilloths, and the Jerusalem Talmud, nor Samaritan, nor the fragments of Christo-Palestinian literature. All those are of the greatest importance from the general Aramæan point of view, religious as well as philological, but are outside the scope of this article. The same remark applies to the different branches of Eastern Aramæan, which includes the Babylonian Talmud, the literature, language, and religion of the Manichæans, Mandæans, and Harranians (*qq.v.*). We shall also leave untouched the study of Syriac (language and literature) and the chief Neo-Aramæan (Christian) dialects.

The best known of the pagan Aramæans are the Palmyrenes (*q.v.*), the Nabatæans (*q.v.*), and the Syrians of Damascus and of the region north of Syria. We get our information on these races from the OT, ancient inscriptions, and Latin and Greek coins and documents.[1]

The ethnic *arami*, אֲרַמִּי, 'Aramæan,' is found in 2 K 5^{20}, Gn 25^{20}, Dt 26^{5}. Its fem. is *aramiia*, אֲרַמִּיָּה in 1 Ch 7^{14}. The plur. is *aramim*, אֲרַמִּים in 2 K $8^{28f.}$ 9^{15}. The corresponding Greek of the LXX is respectively *βαθουὴλ τοῦ Σύρου ἐκ τῆς Μεσοποταμίας, ἀδελφὴν Λαβὰν τοῦ Σύρου* (Gn 25^{20}), etc.; *ἡ Σύρα* (1 Ch 7^{14}); *οἱ Σύροι* (2 K 8^{28}).

The adverb אֲרָמִי, *arami*, 'in Aramæan,' is translated by the LXX *Συριστί* in Is 36^{11}, 2 K 18^{26}, Dn 2^{4}, 2 Es 4^{7}.

The OT gives the following information on the pagan Aramæans.

Aram Ṣoba (*Zobah*), אֲרַם צוֹבָה (LXX *τὴν Συρίαν Σουβά*), in 1 S 14^{47}, 2 S $8^{3\text{ etc.}}$, $10^{6.8}$, 1 K $11^{23\text{ etc.}}$. This expression means an Aramæan state in the north of Canaan or its capital. The town of Zobah was situated in Lebanon, according to 1 Ch 18^{3}.

Aram Ma'aka (*Maachah*), אֲרַם מַעֲכָה (LXX *ἐκ Συριὰς Μααχὰ*), in 1 Ch 19^{6}, means a territory at the foot of Mount Hermon (Jos 13^{13}). The name of the people is Ma'akati (Maachathites), מַעֲכָתִי; according to Dt 3^{14}, the Ma'akati dwelt beyond the kingdom of Og; they were not included in the conquest of the descendants of Manasseh (cf. Jos 12^{5} 13^{11}, 2 S 23^{34}).

Aram beth Reḥob (*Beth Rehob*), אֲרַם בֵּית־רְחוֹב (LXX *Ῥοώβ*), in 2 S $10^{6\text{-}8}$, was a small Aramæan or Syrian kingdom which supplied mercenaries to the sons of Ammon when fighting against Joab, King David's general. They took to flight before Joab, who re-entered Jerusalem in triumph. Rehob is said to be in the north of Palestine, in the region of Laish, or Dan (Jg 18^{28}).[2]

Aram Naharaim (*Nahor*), אֲרַם נַהֲרַיִם (LXX *εἰς τὴν Μεσοποταμίαν*), is identified by the LXX with Mesopotamia (Gn 24^{10}, Dt 23^{5}, Jg 3^{8}, 1 Ch 19^{6}), 'Syria of the two rivers.' This is a mistake. Naharaim means 'country of the river,' and corresponds to the Nārima of the Tel el-Amarna letters and to Nahrina in the Egyptian inscriptions; it extended along the two banks of the middle Euphrates.[3] At the time of the Khati the name Naharanna was given to the country lying between the Balikh and the Orontes.[4]

Paddan Aram (*Padan-aram*), פַּדַּן אֲרָם (LXX *ἐκ τῆς Μεσοποταμίας Συρίας*), in Gn 25^{20} $28^{2.5\text{-}7}$ 31^{18} 33^{18} 39^{9} etc. This term, 'field of Aram (?),' perhaps refers to northern Mesopotamia.[5]

2. Damascus.—*Aram Damêśeq*, אֲרַם דַּמֶּשֶׂק (LXX *Συρία Δαμασκοῦ*), in 2 S $8^{5f.}$, 1 Ch $18^{5f.}$, is Syria of Damascus, which came to the help of Hadadezer, king of Zobah; David slew 22,000 Syrians and put garrisons in Syria of Damascus (Syria-Damascus).

In the course of time Syria (Aram) comprised numerous divisions, the chief of which, besides those mentioned above from the Bible, were: Batania, or country of Bashan, Commagene with its capital Samosata, Cyrrhestice with Cyrrhus as capital, Chalybonitis with its capital Chalybon (Halep = Alep), Coele-Syria with Heliopolis (Baalbek) as capital, Seleucide, or Tetrapolis, with Seleucia, Antioch, Laodicea, and Apamea as principal towns, Chalcidice with its capital Chalcis (Kinnesrin), etc. In many cases we have not enough information about these divisions to treat them separately. The best plan will be to give a résumé of the details supplied by history, inscriptions, and other documents, grouping them round Damascus and the Damascene.

The god who received most worship was Hadad, whose consort was 'the Syrian goddess,' or Atargatis. This god was also called Ramân or Rammân. These two names appear as early as 3000 B.C. in the cuneiforms. This deity does not appear in Phœnician texts. Hadad is represented in the same way in Syria and Mesopotamia. He is the god of lightning and thunder; he shakes the mountains; he is beneficent when he sends the rain which fructifies the earth; he is the destroyer when he sends floods and inundations. According to the inscriptions of Senjirli, Hadad was the first of the gods of northern Syria in the 8th cent. B.C. His chief sanctuary was at Hierapolis (Mabbog, Manbij), near the Euphrates. He was specially worshipped by the agricultural populations of Syria as the protector-god of the harvests. In time his cult became confused with that of the sun; his head was then ornamented with rays; this identification is particularly noticeable in Heliopolis (Baalbek), where the cult of Hadad and that of the sun are one and the same. In Roman times Hadad became Jupiter Optimus Maximus; he received various local denominations (Dolichenus, Hadaranes, Heliopolitanus), but he can always be recognized by the fact that he is represented with the bull or that he is mentioned along with his consort, the Syrian goddess Atargatis. A third personage is usually connected with these great gods, regarded as their son or their daughter. These three together form the triad known as the *dii syri*. They have sanctuaries in a great many Syrian towns—Rhosus, Raphaneæ on the Lebanon (in Græco-Roman times). But the principal sanctuary of the Syrian gods, after Hierapolis, was Damascus, and the Bible mentions kings of Syria in the 9th cent. B.C. with theophorous names, such as Ben-Hadad, Tabrimmôn. It is even possible that this cult of Hadad exercised a certain influence on some Israelite centres, which would explain the representation of Jahweh by a young bull. In Roman times Hadad became Jupiter Damascenus. In all probability Jupiter Heliopolitanus, the god of Heliopolis (Baalbek), should be identified with Hadad.

The consort of Hadad is Atargatis, the great Syrian goddess—also under the names Allāt and Venus—who must not be confused with Astarte, the Phœnician goddess. Coins of Hierapolis call her 'Ate or 'Atar'ate. She was represented with her head surrounded with rays. The symbol of Atargatis was composed of the crescent moon in conjunction with the solar disk.

Besides the divine couple, Hadad and Atargatis, the Syrian pantheon included other deities, of secondary rank, several of whom had a purely local character.

Reshef, or Rashuf, was the incarnation of thunder and lightning. He was often represented as a soldier armed with spear, mace, bow, and shield; he carried on his helmet a gazelle's head surmounted by two sharp horns. Reshef is also met with in Phœnicia and in Cyprus. He was in later times identified with Apollo. Some scholars regard him as a Phœnician rather than a Syrian deity.

The inscriptions also mention Rekub-El, 'the charioteer of El,' who is probably an importation into Syria of the charioteer of the sun-god of the Assyrians. El was an important deity, but did not occupy the first rank in the Syrian pantheon.

Bel was worshipped in Syria, as in Assyria and among the other Semitic races.

Alongside of sun-worship the Syrians devoted a very special cult to the moon-god. Of two

[1] Cf. Nöldeke, 'Die Namen der aram. Nation und Sprache,' in *ZDMG* xxv. [1871] 113 ff.

[2] Cf. F. de Saulcy, *Dict. topog. abrégé de la Terre Sainte*, Paris, 1877, p. 260.

[3] Cf. *La Bible du centenaire*, Paris, 1916, p. 28.

[4] Cf. G. Maspero, *Hist. ancienne des peuples de l'Orient classique*, ii.

[5] Cf. *La Bible du centenaire*, p. 32

Neirāb inscriptions (6th cent. B.C.) one mentions Sahar, Shamash, Nikkal, and Nusk, the other omits Shamash, 'the sun,' and mentions only Sahar, Nikkal, and Nusk. Sahar, the moon-god, was the chief deity of Harrān. His wife, Nikkal, corresponds to Nin-gal, 'the great lady,' wife of Sin, the Assyrian moon-god. Their son, Nusk (Nusku in Assyrian), represents fire, according to some scholars, and, according to others, he personifies the crescent moon.[1]

The stele of Teima (an oasis in the north of Arabia) names three Aramæan deities: 'Ṣalm, Singalla, and Ashira, gods of Teima.' Lagrange[2] proposes to identify Ṣalm with Salmu, the 'dark,' the dark planet, *i.e.* Saturn. According to other writers, the word *ṣalm*, 'image,' 'statue,' means the idol of the local god (*ba'al*) of Teima; Singalla is of Assyrian importation and denotes the great Sin; Ashira corresponds to the Asherah of the Canaanites.

An inscription recently discovered by Pognon in the region of Aleppo, but probably the oldest Syrian inscription, mentions not only Zakir, king of Hamath, and La'ash, but also a new deity, the god Alur (800 B.C.). He is probably a local god, the *genius loci* of Hazrak, for in the continuation of the text the important part is ascribed not to Alur but to Ba'al Shamain.

Of the three Senjirli inscriptions that of Hadad, the oldest, mentions the gods Hadad, El, Reshef, Rekub-El, Shamash, who accorded to Panammu what he asked of them. Lagrange[3] calls attention to the fact that no goddess figures in this list. The second inscription, called that of Panammu, dates from the reign of Tiglath-Pileser III. (754–727 B.C.) and mentions the gods Hadad, El, Rekub-El, Shamash, and all the gods of Jadi. The third one, called that of Barrekub, dates from the same period, but does not mention any deity, except that Barrekub declares that, on account of his loyalty, his lord Rekub-El and his lord Tiglath-Pileser have placed him on his father's throne.

When Zenobia was taken captive to Rome, the cult of the Syrian gods penetrated to the great city with her (or before her). This fact is now duly established by the discovery of a sanctuary to Janicula in the gardens of the Sciarra villa. There we read inscriptions dedicated to the Syrian god Adad (Hadad) of Lebanon on a small white marble altar. There is also an inscription dedicated 'diis syris' at Spalato.[4]

LITERATURE.—Lucian, *de Dea syria*; C. Clermont-Ganneau, *Études d'archéologie orientale*, vol. i. in 2 pts., Paris, 1880–95, *Recueil d'archéologie orientale*, do. i. [1888], v. [1902] (the remainder in course of publication); G. Maspero, *Hist. ancienne des peuples de l'Orient classique*, do. 1895–99, ii.; W. M. Ramsay, art. 'Hierapolis,' in *HDB* ii. 379 f.; M. J. Lagrange, *Études sur les religions sémitiques*², Paris, 1905, *passim*, and pp. 491–510 for the inscriptions in Aramæan dialects; F. Cumont, *Les Cultes d'Asie Mineure dans le paganisme romain*, do. 1906, *Les Religions orientales dans le paganisme romain*, do. 1906; R. Dussaud, *Notes de mythologie syrienne*, 2 pts., do. 1903–05, and artt. 'Hadad' and 'Heliopolitanus,' in Pauly-Wissowa; P. Gauckler, 'Le Bois sacré de la nymphe Furrina et le sanctuaire des dieux syriens, au Janicule, à Rome,' in *CAIBL*, Mar. 1907, pp. 135–159; H. Pognon, *Inscriptions sémitiques de la Syrie, de la Mésopotamie, et de la région de Mossoul*, Paris, 1908; R. Dussaud, 'Le Royaume de Hamat et de Lou' ouch au viiiᵉ siècle avant J.-C.,' in *RA* i. [1908] 222–235; R. Savignac, review of Pognon's work in *RB*, 1908, pp. 596–600; A. Legendre, art. 'Syrie,' in *Dictionnaire de la Bible*, ed. F. Vigouroux, Paris, 1891–1912, v. 1930–48; H. A. Strong and J. Garstang, *The Syrian Goddess*, London, 1913 (cf. R. Dussaud, in *RHR* i. [1913] 387 f.).

3. The Nabatæans.—According to some scholars, the Nabatæans were Arabs who used Aramæan as their literary language; according to others, on the contrary, they were pure Aramæans who in the course of their migrations mingled on the one side with the southern populations of Arabia, while to the north they became masters of Trans-Jordan as far as Damascus. The oldest Nabatæan inscriptions (1st cent. B.C.) contain no Arabisms; afterwards, at the beginning of the 1st cent. of our era, Arab influence makes itself clearly felt, especially in the regions of Ḥegrā and Medain Sāleh.

The Nabatæan sources now in our possession are inscriptions, which are published in the second part of *CIS*, and coins, which have been studied most recently by R. Dussaud and have revealed an almost unbroken succession of kings, from Obedas I. (90 B.C.) to Malichus III. (A.D. 106). But before these dates a Nabatæan race was known which in 312 B.C. was powerful enough to gain the victory against Antigonus. After this victory the Nabatæans, an essentially trading people, occupied the north of Arabia, the country of Edom, and the Damascene. F. H. Vincent has gathered together all that is known about the pantheon of the Nabatæans; they honoured the sun, to whom they built an altar on their houses, and to whom they offered libations and burned incense. The following are the principal deities. Dūshara (Dusarēs) seemed to occupy the first rank and to be the god of the king. Then came Allāt (fem. of Allah) and Manūthu or Manavat. The god Hobal belonged originally to Syria. Mutaba and Harisa are almost unknown. Qaysa was perhaps the ancient national god of the Edomites. The names of the goddesses Vagrah and Tada are from a doubtful reading as well as those of Nashbu and Elgē. The Syrian god Ba'al Shamin was also adopted by the Nabatæans. The Nabatæans erected temples to their gods. The temple comprised a small building to contain the statue of the god, a sacred enclosure (*ḥaram*), votive stelæ, and niches for the icons.

Whether the Nabatæans were strongly Aramaized Arabs or real Aramæans, they gave a very large place in their pantheon to the deities and cult-objects of Aramæan or Syrian origin. See, further, art. NABATÆANS.

LITERATURE.—M. de Vogüé, *Inscriptions sémitiques publiées*, Paris, 1869–77, 'Textes nabatéens,' pp. 100–124; C. Clermont-Ganneau, 'Les Noms royaux nabatéens employés comme noms divins,' in *Recueil d'archéologie orientale*, i. [1888] 39, 'Le Cippe nabatéen de D'meir et l'introduction en Syrie du calendrier romain combiné avec l'ère des Séleucides,' *ib.* 48, 'La Statue du dieu Obodas roi de Nabatène,' *ib.* ii. [1898] 366, 'Les nouvelles Inscriptions nabatéennes de Pétra,' *ib.* 370, 'Manboug-Hierapolis dans les inscriptions nabatéennes,' *ib.* iv. [1900] 99, 'Le Dieu nabatéen Chaî 'al-Qaum,' *ib.* 382; F. H. Vincent, 'Les Nabatéens' in *RB*, 1898, pp. 567–588; R. Dussaud and F. Macler, *Voyage archéologique au Safâ et dans le Djébel ed-Drûz*, Paris, 1901; R. Dussaud (in collaboration with F. Macler), *Mission dans les régions désertiques de la Syrie moyenne*, Paris, 1903 (= extract from vol. x. of *Nouvelles Archives des missions scientifiques*); E. Littmann, *Semitic Inscriptions* (*Publications of an American Archæological Expedition to Syria in 1899–1900*, iv.), New York, 1904; R. Dussaud, 'Numismatique des rois de Nabatène,' in *JA* i. [1904] 189, *Monnaies nabatéennes* (= extract from *RN*, 1905, p. 170); M. J. Lagrange, *Études sur les religions sémitiques*², Paris, 1905; G. Dalman, *Petra und seine Felsheiligtümer*, Leipzig, 1908, *Neue Petra Forschungen und der heilige Felsen von Jerusalem*, do. 1912; J. B. Chabot, *Les Langues et les littératures araméennes*, Paris, 1910, pp. 21–23; A. J. Jaussen and R. Savignac, *Mission archéologique en Arabie (mars–mai 1907)*, i., 'De Jérusalem au Hedjaz Medain-Saleh' (*Publications de la Société des fouilles archéologiques*, ii.), Paris, 1909 (see review by R. Dussaud in *Journal des Savants*, Oct. 1910, pp. 460–474, entitled 'Les Ruines de Hégra'); R. Dussaud, art. 'Pétra' in *La grande Encyclopédie*, Paris, n.d., p. 531 f. ('son importance [de Pétra] nous est surtout connue à l'époque gréco-romaine. Elle est alors la capitale des Nabatéens. . . . Les Nabatéens sont des Arabes. La langue de leurs inscriptions est araméenne, ce qui prouve simplement la diffusion de l'araméen à l'époque gréco-romaine. L'ancien idiome arabe s'est conservé dans les noms propres'); *CIS*, pt. ii. (vol. i. 1 [1893], 2 [1902], 'Inscriptiones nabateæ,' no. 157–489, vol. ii. 1 [1907], no. 1472 f.).

4. The Palmyrenes.—See art. PALMYRENES.

LITERATURE.—In addition to the Literature appended to art. PALMYRENES, see L. Double, *Les Césars de Palmyre*, Paris, 1877; L. G. Deville, *Palmyre: souvenirs de voyage et d'histoire*, do. 1894; R. Dussaud, *Notes de mythologie syrienne*, 2 pts., do. 1903–05; J. B. Chabot, *Les Langues et les littératures araméennes*, do. 1910, pp. 19–21; *Répertoire d'épigraphie sémitique* (published by the commission of the *CIS*), do. 1900 ff.

[1] Clermont-Ganneau, *Études d'archéologie orientale*, ii. 182 f.; Lagrange, *Études sur les religions sémitiques*, pp. 499–501.
[2] Pp. 501–504. [3] P. 494. [4] *CIL* iii. 1961.

5. Syrian cult.—In their pantheon, as in their religious practices, the Aramæans had naturally very close relations with the Assyro-Babylonian cults on the one hand and with those of Phœnicia and Canaan on the other. They practised the local agrarian cults, in conjunction with the worship of sun, moon, and stars, preferably on high mountains or sharp mountain-peaks, regarded as the abode of the gods. They worshipped sacred trees (the tree of life) and plants. They also rendered worship to sacred springs, and Palmyra possessed a specially consecrated river, whose Tyche was venerated. Certain sacred rivers had miraculous powers: if the offering sank to the bottom of the water, it was approved by the deity; if it floated, it was not approved.

As among the rest of the Semites, sacred enclosures have been found among the Aramæans, known as *ḥaram*, and much used among the Arabs. The boundaries of the *ḥaram* were fixed by stelæ, several of which have been recovered during the course of excavation.

We have little information concerning the after life among the Semites in general, and the Aramæans in particular. Like the ancient Hebrews, they probably had Sheol, the kingdom of the dead. From the Senjirli and Neirāb inscriptions, which are very important funerary texts, we learn that the Aramæans believed that a part of the dead person survived, called *nephesh*, 'soul.' It was a material principle, to which they had to offer food and drink.

Among the most venerated objects of worship we must mention the sacred stones, or bætyls, which assumed various aspects. The presence of the god was materialized by a stone placed in the sacred enclosure. The inscription of Hadad shows that the Aramæans worshipped the *neṣib*, a hewn stone or statue. A Palmyrenian inscription shows among the Aramæans the use of the *maṣṣēbhāh* (*q.v.*), in the sense of 'stele.' And they distinguished between the funerary stele, *nafsha*, 'soul,' of pyramidal form, and the votive stele, or *mesjida* (whence our word 'mosque,' through Arabic), which meant the place in which the deity was worshipped.

As regards the personnel of the cult, we hear of the priest, *komer*, attached to the service of such-and-such a god. It was he who offered the holocaust. Barbers played an important part, both in performing the ritual incisions and in shaving the heads of those who dedicated their hair to the deity in consequence of a vow. There were also scribes, charged more especially with keeping the accounts of the temple. Sacred prostitutes were not lacking in the Aramæan cults; and lastly we must mention the familiars of the temple, who rendered services to the faithful who came to worship or make vows, and who lived in the surroundings of the temple, finding their food in the remains of the meals offered to the gods.

6. Calendar.—The Aramæan calendar is fairly well known; the Nabatæans and Palmyrenians employed the Seleucid era, and for a very long time the Syrians made their year begin in autumn. The names of the months of the Palmyrenians are all known: Tishri, Kanun, Kslul, Ṭbt, Shbṭ, Adar, Niṣan, Ir, Sion, Qinian Ab, Elul. Those of the Nabatæans are the same, except the second and tenth, which are not known. This information refers to the Aramæans in Roman times. The ancient names of the months have not yet been brought to light by the oldest inscriptions (Senjirli and Neirāb).

LITERATURE.—Ph. Berger, *Les Inscriptions sémitiques et l'histoire* (a lecture delivered at the Sorbonne), Paris, 1883, (=extract from *Bulletin de l'Association scientifique*, 155); *CIS* I. i. [1889], ii. [1893], iii. [1902], II. i. [1907]; Ph. Berger, *La Bible et les inscriptions*. Paris, 1890; R. Duval, *Les Littératures araméennes*, do. 1895; G. Maspero, *Hist. ancienne des peuples de l'Orient classique*, do. 1895–99, ii.; A. H. Sayce, art. 'Aram, Aramæans,' in *HDB* i. 138 f.; T. Nöldeke, artt. 'Aram' and 'Aramaic Language,' in *EBi* i. 276–286; *Répertoire d'épigraphie sémitique*, ed. by the commission of *CIS* i. (Paris, 1900–05), ii. pt. i. [1907], pt. ii. [1908], pt. iii. [1912], *s.v.* 'Araméen,' 'Nabatéen,' 'Palmyrénien'; R. Dussaud, 'Les premiers Renseignements historiques sur la Syrie' (=extract from the *Revue de l'École d'anthropologie de Paris*, July, 1902, pp. 252–264), *Notes de mythologie syrienne*, 2 pts., Paris, 1903–05; M. J. Lagrange, *Études sur les religions sémitiques*[2], do. 1905; A. Lods, *La Croyance à la vie future et le culte des morts dans l'antiquité israélite*, 2 vols., do. 1906; R. Dussaud, 'Un Monument du culte syrien et d'époque perse,' in *RHR* ii. [1913] 62–68, art. 'Syrie,' in *La grande Encyclopédie*, do. n.d., xxx. 798 f.

FRÉDÉRIC MACLER.

SYRIAN CHRISTIANS.

1. Scope of this article.—Much confusion has arisen from the fact that several different bodies of Christians—Jacobite, Maronite, Nestorian, Malabarese, and others—habitually call themselves 'Syrians,' as well as from the fact that the word 'Syria' itself has meant different things at different times. It will therefore be well at the outset to define the scope of this article.

The East Syrians or Nestorians call themselves 'Sūrāyé,' said to be a corrupt form of 'Sūryāyé.'[1] The Syrian Jacobites are in the Syriac vernacular commonly called 'Siryâné,' by way of distinction (or better 'Sūryâné' or 'Seweryâné').[2]

The name 'Syria' (Syr. Sūrīyā, Gr. Συρία or Σούρ, 'e locis Palestinæ maritimis')[3] has been derived from 'Tyre' (Syr. Ṣūr), though it is spelt with a different *s*. It varied in meaning from time to time. In Roman days, at the beginning of our era, it denoted the country west of the Euphrates and north of the Arabian desert, including Palestine and Palmyra, and extending north to the Taurus; though the Roman procurators or the Herods ruled all or part of Palestine, being more or less independent of the governors of the Roman province of Syria. At a later date 'Inner Syria' meant Palestine (and the coast lands to the north thereof), and 'Outer Syria' meant Mesopotamia.[4] The modern Turkish *vilayet* of Syria is only a fraction of the old Roman province, and lies east of the Lebanon, extending from Hama on the Orontes in the north to the Hedjaz in the south, Damascus being the capital, while the *vilayet* of Beirut is west of the Lebanon, and the old Judæa is an independent *sanjak* under a *muteserif*.[5] Thus the term 'Syrian Christians' has little relation to the term 'inhabitants of Syria.' The most comprehensive definition of the former is 'those Christians who use or have used the Syriac language in their liturgical services or as a vernacular.' It thus includes the Jacobites of Mesopotamia, the Nestorians, the Maronites of the Lebanon, the Syrian and Chaldæan Uniats, and the Christians of St. Thomas in Malabar.

The history of many of these Christians has usually been considered in Europe only as far as it affects their relations with certain heresies, *i.e.* only from one episode (however important) of their annals. These doctrinal questions have already been dealt with in artt. MONOTHELETISM, MONOPHYSITISM, and NESTORIANISM, and will therefore not be referred to in this article except incidentally, and when they are necessary to explain the history or customs of the Syrian Christians.

2. Syriac-speaking Christians.—Syriac is a branch of the Aramaic family of languages. The written or classical Syriac—the Syriac of the liturgies and patristic literature—was the language spoken at Edessa, and was not very distant (though differing somewhat in grammar and vocabulary) from the Aramaic of Palmyra and that of Palestine (the Biblical Aramaic of the OT, or 'Chaldee,' as it used to be called), perhaps not more distant

[1] R. Payne Smith, *Thesaurus Syriacus*, ii. 2585.
[2] *Ib.* ii. 2586. [3] *Ib.* ii. 2585. [4] *Ib.*
[5] *The Geographical Journal*, l. [1917] 13.

than some dialects of 'English' now current in the British Isles are from one another. The Edessa Syriac was the medium of commerce in the valley of the Euphrates, and was used far and wide for literary purposes. But, though this was, and is, the written language, other dialects of Syriac were spoken vernacularly throughout a very wide district, from the Mediterranean to the eastern limits of Mesopotamia, Assyria, and Adiabene (east of the Tigris), and southwards to the borders of Egypt and Arabia.[1] There were many Syriac-speaking monks in Egypt in the 4th cent. and later.[2] Even the Armenian Christians used Syriac till the 4th century.[3] Thus there were many Syriac dialects. They were not the lineal descendants of classical Syriac, but were rather in the position of sisters or nieces of that language.[4]

Syriac gradually gave way, vernacularly and to some extent liturgically, to Arabic after the Muhammadan conquest, though it has had locally a considerable influence on the vocabulary, pronunciation, and even the grammatical forms of the Arabic which supplanted it.[5] The only Christians who now speak it habitually are the East Syrians (Nestorian and Uniat Chaldæan), among whom it is practically the only language used (though many of the Moṣul Uniats also speak Arabic), the Jacobites of Jebel Ṭūr, and the people of Ma'lūlā near Damascus. The other Jacobites and the Maronites now ordinarily use Arabic for their vernacular. The Malabarese have probably never used Syriac vernacularly—unless the immigrants from Persia used it for a while (see below, § 9)—but have always spoken an Indian dialect. It may be noted that many Jews in E. Turkey and Persia have a vernacular closely akin to the spoken Syriac of the Nestorians; and the language of the Mandæans (*q.v.*), or so-called 'Christians of St. John,' if they still exist, is another branch of Aramaic. In the early ages of Christianity the literary language of Syria proper was Greek (see below, § 3), but Syriac was the popular language there till after A.D. 500. It should be remembered that Antioch itself was a Greek, not a Syriac, centre. The city was predominantly Greek, though Syriac was the language of numerous monks in it and its neighbourhood, and of the country people.[6]

All the above-mentioned Christians use classical Syriac as their liturgical language; and many of them use it still as their literary language, as all did till the Middle Ages. It will thus be seen that the prayers in the Church services are only imperfectly, if at all, understood by the majority of the worshippers. In Syria proper, however, many of the prayers are said in an Arabic translation, so as to be intelligible to the people; they are then written in Syriac characters, and this combination of Syriac and Arabic is called Carshuni (Syr. *garshūnī*).[7] But those services which are the bishop's own—*e.g.*, ordination—are in Syriac only, as are all the prayers which are said inaudibly by the priest.

The vernaculars differ from classical Syriac in different degrees. The East Syrian vernacular dialects, which vary a good deal among themselves, differ from it perhaps as much as Italian from Latin, while the Ma'lula dialect has retained more of the older grammar and is less analytically developed.[8] This last vernacular is particularly noticeable as being preserved by those who are so far isolated from other Syriac-speaking Christians. Ma'lula (called Seleucia by the Turks) is a village of some 1000 inhabitants, situated on a high plateau about 5000 ft. above sea-level, north-east of Damascus; while two neighbouring villages, though most of their inhabitants have become Musalmāns within the last 250 years, also speak Syriac vernacularly. Ma'lula consists ecclesiastically of two divisions; half are of the Uniat Melkite rite (see below, § 6), half of the Greek Orthodox rite. Each division has an ancient monastery.[1] The local tradition is that the inhabitants are immigrants from the east, from the district of Singar or Sinjar (west of Moṣul), which is now largely inhabited by Yezīdīs, or so-called 'devil-worshippers'; but this tradition is of very doubtful value.[2]

Of all the Syrian Christians, whether they have lost their own vernacular or have retained it, it may be noted that their clergy are supposed all to be able to read and write and understand classical Syriac; and most of them can do so, and can even, with some difficulty, speak it. But this is now only as a foreign language.

There are some differences of pronunciation. The East Syrians (Nestorian and Uniat Chaldæan) say *ā* when the West Syrians (Jacobite) and the Maronites say *ō* (*e.g.*, *malkā*, *malkō*, 'a king'), the former being the older sound, preserved to us in transliterations like Talitha (Syr. *ṭlīthā*), Maranatha (Syr. Māran ethā or possibly Mārānā thā). The East Syrians hardly ever aspirate *p* (except when it is used to form a diphthong), and many of them never aspirate *t* or *d*; almost all of them pronounce the vowels Rbhāṣā (Rwāṣā) and Rwāḥā alike as *ū*, the *ō* sound being produced only by a combination of the vowel Zqāpā (Zqapha) with *w* or aspirated *b* or *p*. One point with regard to transliteration of Syriac words into Roman characters must be mentioned. European Orientalists usually write twice a medial consonant in certain verbal formations and in words derived from them, because it is said to be 'virtually doubled' (*e.g.*, 'Addai' for 'Adai'). The Syrians themselves, however, dislike doubled letters, and in their vernacular admit them only in a few (chiefly foreign) words, and in that case they pronounce each letter distinctly, like the *d*'s in 'mid-day.' On the other hand, they sometimes compensate for not doubling a medial consonant by converting a preceding short *a* into a long one. Most of them pronounce aspirated Kaph (*kh*) and Ḥeith (*ḥ*) alike.

3. Syrian Christianity in early times.—In considering the spread of Christianity in these regions before the theological controversies of the 5th cent. caused the divisions which exist to this day, we are faced with the difficulty that legends are the traditional groundwork of the religious history. It is not easy to estimate the amount of truth or falsehood that underlies the legends; but there is no doubt that all these regions were largely Christianized at an early period.

(*a*) *The Roman province of Syria.*—Here we are not troubled with legend. In the 1st cent. of our era the province extended to the Euphrates, and was conjoined with Cilicia.[3] Antioch was the civil metropolis, and was likewise the headquarters of Syrian Christianity; there the disciples were first called 'Christians' (Ac 11[26]). Greeks and Syrians were both represented at Antioch (see above, § 2). There is no evidence as to the extent to which the Church services were conducted in the Aramaic vernacular rather than in Greek; but probably, at a time when the worship was in the main extemporaneous, both languages were used. Though most of the people, perhaps, understood Greek, even if it was not their mother tongue, yet experience shows that the last sphere in which a vernacular gives way to the language of commerce and public life is that of religion. It is therefore probable that Syrian Christians in the Roman province to a large extent worshipped in their vernacular from apostolic times onwards. But Greek was the literary language. Ignatius, bishop of Antioch at the beginning of the 2nd cent., wrote in Greek (he calls himself 'bishop of Syria');[4] Lucian and Dorotheus, Diodorus, bishop of Tarsus, and Theodore, bishop of Mopsuestia (both these of Antioch), Chrysostom, Theodoret, bishop of Cyrrhus—all of the 4th and 5th centuries—did

[1] M. Parisot, in *JA* xi. [1898] 240.
[2] J. B. Lightfoot, *Apostolic Fathers*, pt ii., *Ignatius and Polycarp*², London, 1889, i. 327.
[3] F. C. Burkitt, *Early Christianity outside the Roman Empire*, p. 19.
[4] T. Nöldeke, *Grammatik der neusyrischen Sprache*, p. xxxv.
[5] Parisot, pp. 240, 246.
[6] Burkitt, *Early Eastern Christianity*, p. 45.
[7] Payne Smith, i. 790.
[8] See Parisot's sketch of this dialect.

[1] Parisot, pp. 255–261. [2] *Ib.* p. 270.
[3] W. M. Ramsay, *A Historical Commentary on St. Paul's Epistle to the Galatians*, London, 1899, p. 277; cf. Gal 1[21].
[4] τὸν ἐπίσκοπον Συρίας (*Rom.* 2; cf. 9, where he speaks of the 'church in Syria,' and God as its shepherd in his stead).

the same. The Antiochene school of theology was clearly a Greek school.[1] A trace of the mixture of the Greek and Syriac elements may be seen in the *Pilgrimage of 'Silvia'* (*'Etheria'*), a work probably of the end of the 4th cent., which describes the bishop of Jerusalem as knowing Syriac (*'siriste'*), but as always speaking Greek and having his sermons and the lections interpreted into Syriac by a presbyter who stood by.[2]

In the 4th cent., when the provincial organization of the Church was promoted, Antioch was one of the great centres, and its bishop was called a 'metropolitan'; the corresponding verb is found in canon 19 of the Council of Antioch *in encæniis* (A.D. 341), and the name itself in can. 6 of Nicæa (A.D. 325), which says that the rights formerly possessed by Antioch must be preserved to it. Thus Antioch had long exercised some sort of jurisdiction over neighbouring sees. Yet the *Apostolic Constitutions*, a Greek work written in Syria *c.* A.D. 375, does not mention metropolitans, any more than the other 'Church Orders' do.[3] This is important in connexion with the supposed dependence of Seleucia-Ctesiphon on Antioch, for which see below (*c*).

(*b*) *Edessa.*—This famous city of Mesopotamia, called in Syriac Ur-hai (now Urfa), was the capital of the kingdom of Osrhoëne (a Greek name derived from 'Ur-hai'). 'Edessa' was the Greek name for the city. The kingdom was independent till A.D. 216, when it was incorporated in the Roman empire. According to the well-known legend of Abgar and Addai, Edessa was Christianized in the middle of the 1st cent.; the legend is given in full in the *Doctrine of Addai* (see below, § 4), and in a shorter, and perhaps more original, form by Eusebius,[4] who says that his account was translated from the Syriac. Edessa is represented as a heathen city, which worshipped (the *Doctrine* tells us) Bel and Nebo,[5] though Burkitt suggests that these names come from a perusal of the OT and not from any real historical reminiscence.[6] Abgar,[7] the heathen king or toparch of Edessa, sends messengers to our Lord, and a correspondence ensues; after the Ascension the apostle 'Judas Thomas' sends Addai (called by Eusebius Thaddæus, and said to be one of the Seventy) to Abgar to teach him the faith.[8] Addai does many mighty deeds; one of his converts was Aggai, who 'made the silks and headbands of the king,' and he was made bishop[9] by Addai as his successor. Addai died a natural death at Edessa, but Aggai was afterwards martyred by the son of Abgar; and, as he could not consecrate his successor Palūṭ by reason of his sudden death, the latter was sent to Antioch and was ordained by Serapion the bishop. Narsai, king of Assyria, sent messengers to King Abgar to learn about all these matters. Such is the legend. As we have it, it is of the 4th cent., though clearly based on one that is a good deal older; R. A. Lipsius[10] concludes that the extant correspondence between our Lord and Abgar was manufactured *c.* A.D. 200. What is the substratum of truth in all this it is not easy to say. The mention of Serapion (bishop of Antioch, A.D. 190–210) gives us a date for Palūṭ, and Lipsius[11] regards the latter as the first historical bishop of Edessa. But there is no need to dismiss Addai entirely to the realms of myth. If the Edessenes were casting about for an early founder of their Church, they would be much more likely to fix on the great apostle 'Judas Thomas,' whose tomb was claimed for Edessa in the middle of the 3rd cent. (see below, § 9), than on the unknown Addai. It seems to be likely, therefore, that Addai (probably a Palestinian Jew) was the first preacher of the gospel at Edessa, perhaps early in, or about the middle of, the 2nd century. The real Abgar who favoured Christianity may have been Abgar IX., the last independent king of Edessa. Burkitt[1] suggests that the consecration of Palūṭ by Serapion of Antioch represents a movement for closer union with 'Western' (Greek) Christianity, and perhaps means a break in the episcopal succession.

1 See art. ANTIOCHENE THEOLOGY, vol. i. p. 584 ff.

2 vii. 5.

3 A. J. Maclean, *The Ancient Church Orders*, Cambridge, 1910, p. 72 f.

4 *HE* i. 13.

5 So also the *Acts of Sharbil*, for which see below, § 4.

6 *Early Eastern Christianity*, p. 17; cf. Is 46[1].

7 Most of the independent kings of Edessa were called either Abgar or Maʻnu.

8 In the Ethiopic *Preaching of Judas Thaddæus in Syria* Thaddæus is associated with St. Peter, not with St. Thomas (E. A. W. Budge, *The Contendings of the Apostles*, London, 1899–1901, text and Eng. tr., ii. 357).

9 'Guide and ruler'; so also the *Edessene Canons* (see below, § 4) call the bishop, can. 17 and (?) 24.

10 *DCB* iv. 881.

11 *Ib.* iv. 876.

In the 2nd cent. **Bardaiṣān** (Bardesanes) was born at Edessa (A.D. 155–223?);[2] he is reckoned as a Syrian Gnostic (though this is doubtful), and was a most learned man, a great hymn-writer,[3] and author of a polemic against Marcion. All his works have perished except the extant Syriac treatise *de Fato*, which is usually thought to be his; Eusebius[4] tells us that he wrote a book with that title. Burkitt[5] assigns the *de Fato* (which is called in the MS the *Book of the Laws of Countries*) to Bardaiṣān's disciple, Philip, on the strength of the work itself; but many think that the insertion of 'Philip' (a very unusual Syriac name) is only a literary device, and that Bardaiṣān himself is the real author. He certainly is the chief speaker in the dialogue, which is between a Christian and a heathen, and turns largely on the question why God allowed man to sin. Eusebius[6] and Epiphanius[7] say that Bardaiṣān was originally a follower of Valentinus, and Epiphanius makes him always a Valentinian. The fullest biography of this erratic writer is by Michael the Syrian, Jacobite patriarch of Antioch (1166–99), but his details cannot be entirely trusted. The school of Bardaiṣān survived his death, and remained in opposition to the orthodox party; Rabbula is said to have converted the remnants of it.[8]

One of the most famous of the Edessenes was **Ephraim** (Ephrem) **the Syrian** (born *c.* 308, †373). He came from Nisibis[9] to Edessa and founded or reorganized a seminary there, which became the great university of the East, though for a while after his death it fell under Arian influences. He was a deacon only, said to have been ordained by Basil of the Cappadocian Cæsarea, and to have declined advancement;[10] his own statement, that he had 'the talent of the priesthood,'[11] does not contradict this, for in Syriac 'priesthood' (*kāhnūthā*) includes all orders of the ministry. He was a most diffuse writer, and achieved a great fame in posterity.[12]

In the 5th cent. the most famous Edessenes were two of the bishops of Edessa. **Rabbūlā** (bishop from 411 to 435) was the son of a heathen priest and of a Christian mother. He was converted

1 *Early Eastern Christianity*, p. 28 ff.

2 See F. J. A. Hort, in *DCB* i. 250 ff., for the date.

3 See art. HYMNS (Syriac Christian).

4 *HE* iv. 30.

5 *Early Christianity outside the Roman Empire*, p. 14.

6 *Loc. cit.*

7 *Hær.* lvi.

8 Burkitt, *Early Eastern Christianity*, p. 189.

9 As appears both from the Syriac (Nṣibhin, pron. Nṣīwīn) and from the Greek, the middle *i* is long, contrary to the ordinary pronunciation. The word forms the end of a Greek hexameter in the epitaph of Abercius; see the restoration in Lightfoot, *Ignatius and Polycarp*[2], i. 496. Burkitt has pointed out to the present writer that the pronunciation with short *i* perhaps comes from the Armenian form of the name, 'Mtsbīn.'

10 Sozomen, *HE* iii. 16.

11 *DCB* ii. 138 n.

12 For Ephraim see also Theodoret, *HE* iv. 26, and Jerome, *de Vir. illustr.* 115; for a very unfavourable view of his intellectual powers see Burkitt, *Early Eastern Christianity*, p. 95 ff.

after he attained to manhood; and he became a great ascetic, and the friend of Cyril of Alexandria. At the end of his life he strenuously opposed Nestorius.[1] The other famous bishop was his successor, **Ibas** (bishop from 435 to 457), who was inclined to favour Nestorius (see below, § 8).

During all this period the Church seems to have made rapid progress. Eusebius [2] says that bishops from 'the whole of Syria and Mesopotamia' attended the dedication of Constantine's great church at Jerusalem in 335.

(*c*) *The Persian empire.*—A great deal of light has been thrown on early Syrian Christianity in Persia by the recent publication of the works of Nestorian writers. Formerly we had to rely mainly on the accounts of Jacobite authors like Bar Hebræus. The two sets of accounts correct one another and disprove more than one myth; and Neale's narrative in his *History of the Holy Eastern Church* [3] needs much correction in this respect.

One legend is a continuation of that of Abgar and Addai already mentioned. Mari, disciple of Addai, travelled from Edessa and evangelized 'Persia' (*i.e.* what became later the eastern part of Asiatic Turkey, as well as the modern Persia), penetrating as far as the province of Fars. Mari is not mentioned in the *Doctrine of Addai*, which, however, has a hint that Christianity extended from Edessa into Persia. Nor is Mari mentioned in the lately published and very valuable *History* of Mshīḥā Zkhā (lit. 'Christ has conquered'), of the 6th cent., which states that Addai was the apostle of Adiabene and Assyria (this apparently contradicts the *Doctrine*, which makes Addai live and die at Edessa), and that he ordained Pqīdhā as first bishop there. The Nestorian *Sūnhādhūs*, or Book of Canon Law,[4] names as the 'converters' of that region Thomas 'of the Indians and Chinese' (*Sīnāyé*), 'Bartholomew, that is Nathanael, of the Aramæans, Addai of the Seventy, the teacher of Aggai, and Mari of Mesopotamia and of all Persia.'[5] This is all clearly mythical, but is there any truth underlying the legend? Some consider that there was no Christianity, or at least no organization of Christianity, east of the Tigris before the Sasanid empire was established by a revolution, A.D. 225. This is perhaps going rather too far. If there was nothing before the third decade of the 3rd cent. to build upon, it is unlikely that so early a writer as Mshiḥa Zkha could have given us such details; he could not have invented Pqīdhā out of nothing. It is quite probable that there were Christians in Assyria in the 2nd cent., for Tatian,[6] the disciple of Justin Martyr, tells us that he was born 'in the land of the Assyrians.' This must be discounted by the fact that he probably wrote only in Greek, though many think that his *Diatessaron* (for which see below, § 4) was written in Syriac;[7] and that he may therefore have been of Greek parentage, and have been converted to Christianity when in the West. We learn from Epiphanius that he laboured in Syria and Mesopotamia.[8] In any case there was no bishop at Seleucia-Ctesiphon, the twin-capital of the Persian empire, situated on the Tigris below Baghdād, till the end of the 3rd century. Papa is the first known bishop of that city; he was consecrated *c.* 280.

Another legend is much later, and professes to account for the existence of a patriarch at Seleucia-Ctesiphon. It is given by Bar Hebræus and other writers, and in the *Sūnhādhūs*,[9] and is to the effect that two men went from Persia to Antioch to receive the episcopate in 190. According to the first writer, one of them was crucified as a Persian spy, as was Ṣlibha (pron. Ṣlīwā, lit. 'cross,' still a common name), the bishop of Antioch, while the other escaped to Jerusalem and was consecrated there, returning with a letter conferring the patriarchate on the Church in Persia. The *Sūnhādhūs* does not name Ṣlibha, but says that two patriarchs, 'one of the East and one of the West,'[10] were crucified on the doors of the church of Antioch, and it gives the pretended letter of the 'Western patriarchs' to the 'Easterns,' bestowing on the latter a patriarchate, and absolving them from the duty of sending their patriarchs to Antioch to be consecrated. The first patriarch, it says, was either Papa or Shaḥlūpā—it does not profess to be certain.[11] This Shaḥlūpā was probably the bishop of Adiabene, east of the Tigris and between the two Zabs, who was a contemporary of Papa. The letter of the 'Westerns' is a late forgery. The earlier writers, like Mshiḥa Zkha, know nothing of the story, despite the fact that that historian wrote the life of Aḥā d'abhūh, the bishop who is said to have escaped. The whole is doubtless a fiction, and it is improbable that the Persian Christians ever depended for their bishops on Antioch, though they doubtless received their Christianity from Edessa, and Edessa possibly received it from Antioch. The idea of patriarchates, it need hardly be said, belongs to a much later time than these pretended events. The East Syrian ('Persian') metropolitanates were organized *c.* A.D. 410. There is no early evidence of Antioch exercising jurisdiction over the Church in Persia. When Papa was condemned by his brother bishops, he appealed, successfully, to Edessa, and perhaps to Nisibis.[1]

An important event for the Church occurred in A.D. 297, when five Persian provinces were ceded to the Roman emperor.[2] This strengthened the ecclesiastical ties between East and 'West.' The cession made Nisibis a Roman city. Its most famous bishop at that time was **James of Nisibis,** who was born there towards the end of the 3rd century. Ephraim was his disciple, and was baptized by him. James himself was a great author of Syriac works.[3]

It is remarkable that, though James was present at Nicæa in A.D. 325, the East Syrians knew nothing officially of that council till the Synod of Seleucia-Ctesiphon in A.D. 410, when they freely accepted the Nicene decrees and creed. To this day they use a rather peculiar version of the longer form, the so-called 'Constantinople' creed, which came into general use (see below, § 9). The Arian controversy did not touch them; and an illustration of this may be seen in the fact that Aphraates, whose Homilies (see below, § 4) are a continuous exposition of the Christian faith, does not mention Arianism at all, though he lived at a time when that heresy was prevalent in the 'West.'

The principal East Syrian bishops of Seleucia-Ctesiphon after Papa and before the Nestorian period were **Simeon Bar Sabā'é** (martyred under Sapor II.), **Yahbh-alaha** I. (pron. Yāw-alāhā), and **Dādhīshū**. Of other bishops may be specially mentioned **Aphraates** (Aphrāhāṭ), in the 4th cent., whose see was perhaps Mar Mattai, near Moṣul (see below, § 5), and **Mārūthā** (early 5th cent.), bishop of Maipharqaṭ or Martyropolis, north of Nisibis, author of the *Book of Martyrs* (see below, § 4). Mārūthā often acted as adviser to the Persian king and as ambassador to the Roman emperor. The *Sūnhādhūs*[4] mentions an earlier Mārūthā, who was (it says) present at Nicæa, but it is probable that he did not exist, and that the statement is due to a confusion.

The period was marked by many personal quarrels,[5] a feature of later history also, and by the great persecution under King Sapor II. († A.D. 379), which lasted some 40 years and resulted in many martyrdoms.[6] The Persian kings at one time favoured the Church and at another persecuted it. It is important to notice that even in the early days the political conditions tended, quite apart from theological considerations, to separate the East Syrians from the rest of Christendom. It was the policy of the Persian authorities when they tolerated Christianity to separate it as much as possible from that in the rival Roman empire. Another persecution, at the instigation of the Magians, whose religion was that of the State, broke out under King Bahram (Vararanes) V., *c.* A.D. 420. Theodoret [7] makes it arise under his predecessor Yazdegerd, though continued under Bahram, but Socrates [8] says more accurately that it arose after Yazdegerd's death.

The title of the bishops of Seleucia-Ctesiphon, *c.* A.D. 400, was 'the Catholicos of the East,' and this is still preserved by their successors. The title 'Patriarch' was added a little later, at the Council of Dadhishu, held A.D. 424 at 'Markabta of the

1 For his Biblical work see below, § 4.
2 *Vit. Const.* iv. 43.
3 *Gen. Introd.* i. 139 ff.
4 This is here quoted in the MS form used by the Nestorians themselves. It is also incorporated in a larger collection given by Chabot (*Synodicon Orientale*).
5 ix. 1.
6 *To the Greeks*, 42.
7 E. Nestle, in *HDB* iv. 646.
8 *Hær.* xlvi. 1.
9 ix. 1, 5.
10 The 'West' means what we should call the 'Near East.'
11 For Papa see above.

1 W. A. Wigram, *Introd. to the Hist. of the Assyrian Church*, p. 53 f.
2 The provinces reverted to Persia in 352.
3 For notices of him see Theodoret, *HE* ii. 26, and Gennadius, *de Script. Eccles.* § 1 (continuation of Jerome's *de Vir. illustr.*).
4 i. 3, 5.
5 Wigram, ch. iii.
6 Sozomen, *HE* ii. 10 ff.
7 *HE* v. 38.
8 *HE* vii. 18.

Arabs.' This council firmly established the independence of the 'Eastern' patriarchate.

4. The Syriac Bible and early Syriac literature.—Before the doctrinal divisions of the 5th cent. there was a considerable activity in Syriac literature, all written in what we call 'classical Syriac' (see above, § 2). The Gospels were current in Syriac in five forms. (*a*) The four 'Gospels separate' (Syr. *Ewangeliyōn da-Mpharrshê*), now generally called the 'Old Syriac,' are known to us by two MSS: the Curetonian, discovered in Egypt in 1842, and ed. by Cureton in 1858; and the Sinaitic Syriac, a palimpsest discovered by Mrs. Gibson in the monastery of Mount Sinai in 1893. Both of these have the above Syriac title, which distinguishes them from the *Diatessaron* (see below). Both are perhaps of the 4th century. The Curetonian has the same type of text as the Sinaitic, but differs from it in many details.[1]

(*b*) The *Diatessaron* of Tatian (2nd cent.), sometimes called by the Syrians 'the Mixed [Gospels],'[2] is a harmony of the four Gospels, and is known to us through a commentary on it by Ephraim handed down in an Armenian translation, by quotations in Aphraates, and by an Arabic translation of the Harmony itself made in the 11th cent. by the Nestorian monk Ibn aṭ-Ṭayyib.[3] The *Diatessaron* is mentioned in the *Doctrine of Addai*.

(*c*) The Pshīṭtā,[4] or 'simple' version, so called to distinguish it from the complicated recension of Thomas of Ḥarqel (see below), is the version still used by Syrian Christians. The name is first found in the 8th or 9th century. This version, which is now often called 'the Syriac Vulgate,' contains the whole Bible, OT and NT (including the OT Apocrypha), less 2 Peter, 2 and 3 John, Jude, and Revelation. Because of its universal acceptance, it may safely be assigned to a date before the divisions of the 5th century. The Gospels in this version have been critically edited by G. H. Gwilliam.[5] It appears that Tatian's Harmony was at one time in popular use among the Syrian Christians, but early in the 5th cent. Rabbūlā, bishop of Edessa (see above, § 3), and Theodoret, bishop of Cyrrhus, were instrumental in its being abolished and destroyed in favour of the 'separate Gospels.' Burkitt's theory has been very generally accepted, viz. that the Pshīṭtā Gospels are a revision of the 'separate Gospels' made early in the 5th cent. under the direction of Rabbūlā; that the *Diatessaron* was written in Greek (but see above, § 3), probably at Rome, by Tatian, and translated into Syriac in his lifetime, *c.* A.D. 170; and that the 'separate Gospels' date from *c.* A.D. 200, the translator being familiar with the *Diatessaron*.[6] These views are combated by Gwilliam, who is inclined to assign a much earlier date to the Pshīṭtā Gospels;[7] he objects that Burkitt's theory is not adequately attested, does not explain the disappearance of the 'Old Syriac,' and does not account for the acceptance of the Pshīṭtā in the 5th cent. by Nestorians and Jacobites alike.[8] The fact that the East Syrians were not definitely Nestorian in Rabbūlā's time, or indeed for a long time after him (see below, § 8), appears to the present writer adequately to account for their being ready enough to accept such a version of the Gospels in place of the *Diatessaron*.

1 For these two MSS see F. C. Burkitt, *Evangelion da-Mepharreshe*, Cambridge, 1904. For the date see Burkitt, *Early Christianity outside the Roman Empire*, p. 54, and *Evang.* ii. 13, 28.

2 Burkitt, *Evang.* ii. 115.

3 *Ib.* ii. 4.

4 Usually written in English Peshitta, Peshitto, or Peshito, but all these forms give the ordinary reader an erroneous idea of the pronunciation of the first syllable. Also the first *t* is pronounced quite differently from the second.

5 *Tetraeuangelium Sanctum*, Oxford, 1901.

6 Burkitt, *Evang.* ii. 5.

7 *Studia Biblica et Ecclesiastica*, v. [Oxford, 1903] 189 ff.

8 On this last point see Burkitt, *Evang.* ii. 162, and *Early Eastern Christianity*, p. 59 ff.

(*d*) Recensions of the Pshīṭtā were made by **Philoxenus**, bishop of Mabug (Hierapolis, near the Euphrates), A.D. 508 (not now extant), and by **Thomas of Ḥarqel** ('Harklean' version), A.D. 616. Both of these writers were Monophysites, and it appears that the only dissatisfaction with the Pshīṭtā that made itself felt was among the Jacobites, and not among the Nestorians. But even among the Jacobites that version remained supreme.

Some characteristics of the Pshiṭtā may here be mentioned. Its MSS, unlike those of the Greek Bible in the 5th cent., all show practically the same text. Some of them are as old as the 5th cent., the oldest *c.* A.D. 450. One rather noticeable difference between the 'Old Syriac' and the Pshiṭtā Gospels occurs in the Lord's Prayer, where the former has 'our continual bread,' the latter 'the bread of our need.' Another difference is in the gender of 'Holy Spirit.' The noun 'spirit' being feminine in Syriac, the older writers make 'Holy Spirit' feminine also, and Aphraates speaks of the Holy Ghost as 'our mother,' just as the *Gospel according to the Hebrews* speaks of Him as our Lord's mother. But from the time of the Pshiṭtā onwards 'Holy Spirit' is made masculine by a grammatical revolution, though in Lk 4^{1} and Jn 7^{39} Psh there is a survival of the older usage, the feminine being retained.

Hitherto we have considered only the Gospels. There is no extant text of Acts or the Epistles older than the Pshiṭtā, but quotations in Aphraates and in Ephraim's *Commentary on the Pauline Epistles*, now extant only in an Armenian translation, are of some slight help.[1] In Aphraates and in the genuine works of Ephraim there is no clear reference to any of the Catholic Epistles. The *Doctrine of Addai* expressly confines the Scriptural canon to the Law and the Prophets, the Gospel, St. Paul's Epistles, and Acts. Thus the Pshiṭtā, admitting as it does the principal Catholic Epistles, shows an advance on the way to a fuller canon.[2] The Pshiṭtā OT was not revised by Rabbūlā, and is undoubtedly much older than his time, perhaps dating from the end of the 2nd century.[3] The translator had a good knowledge of Hebrew, though he was somewhat influenced by the Septuagint. Burkitt thinks that he must have been a Jew, and that he made his translation for the Jews, who had probably settled at Edessa before it became a Christian centre. The OT quotations of the *Acts of Judas Thomas*, the *Doctrine of Addai*, the *Edessene Canons*, Aphraates, Cyrillona, and the genuine works of Ephraim (for all these see below) agree largely with the Pshiṭtā, but their Gospel quotations do not do so, rather resembling the 'Old Syriac' and the *Diatessaron*. After Rabbūlā all the quotations but two agree with the Pshiṭtā, the 'Old Syriac' having thus almost entirely disappeared.[4] The 'Old Syriac' Gospels appear to be later than the Pshiṭtā OT, as the translator of the former, translating direct from the Greek, uses Hebrew proper names correctly transliterated from the Hebrew, as does the Pshiṭtā translator of the OT. The Old Syriac Gospel translator could hardly do this unless he had the correct forms of the proper names before him already in use.[5]

Of other early Syriac works, in addition to liturgies, some of which seem in their main features to have been written before the middle of the 5th cent., and in addition also to early Syriac translations of Greek books, the following may be mentioned. (1) *The Disputation with Manes*, by **Archelaus**, bishop of Kashkar in Mesopotamia (3rd cent.?), is now extant only in Greek fragments and in a Latin translation, but was originally written in Syriac. (2) The *Doctrine of Addai*,[6] already mentioned, is a work of the latter part, or, according to R. A. Lipsius,[7] of the beginning, of the 4th cent., giving the legend of Abgar (see above, § 3). (3) The voluminous works of **Ephraim** consist of commentaries, homilies, letters, and hymns.[8] At least one of his works, *On the Holy Spirit*, was translated into Greek before Jerome's time.[9] (4) **Aphraates**, the Persian martyr and sage, wrote his *Homilies* A.D. 337–345. Their theological attitude calls for some remark in view of their aloofness from Hellenistic influence. There is no special difference between him and 'Western' writers in the presentment of the doctrine of the Holy Trinity, and in Aphraates, as elsewhere, baptism is 'in the name of the Father and of the Son and of the Holy

1 Burkitt, *Early Eastern Christianity*, p. 48.

2 *Ib.* p. 59.

3 *Ib.* p. 70.

4 *Ib.* pp. 54–56.

5 *Ib.* p. 73.

6 Ed. G. Phillips, London, 1876.

7 *DCB* i. 31.

8 For a list of the works attributed to him of which we have pre-Muhammadan MSS, see Burkitt, *Evang.* ii. 113; but some works in later MSS may also be genuine.

9 *de Vir. illustr.* § 115.

Ghost.' Man is a temple for God to dwell in.[1] But the doctrine of the sacraments must be noticed. The teaching about the eucharist, indeed, is more or less that of the Greek-speaking Christians. The body and blood of our Lord are received by the faithful. Fasting communion is enjoined, but special stress is laid on fasting from sin. Yet this seems to be only the complement and groundwork of the literal fasting. One passage,[2] however, is thought by Burkitt[3] to show that Aphraates considered baptism, and the sacramental system generally, to be only for ascetics, and not for the married laity. This conclusion has been much disputed. At least it is certain that Aphraates favoured the postponing of baptism till after marriage, just as Constantine postponed it till the end of his life. The same tinge of ultra-asceticism is seen here that appears in the *Acts of Judas Thomas* (see below and § 9). But there is no evidence that this was more than the private opinion of individuals, or that the original East Syrian Church as a whole considered full membership to be incompatible with anything but the ascetic life. (5) The Syriac *Doctrina Apostolorum* (or *Edessene Canons*) was written *c.* A.D. 350 and is a kind of 'Church Order.' As is the case with many books of that class, it puts injunctions into the mouth of the apostles, and it is of great interest as telling us of the customs of the Edessene Church in the 4th century. It makes Addai the apostle of Edessa, and Aggai, 'a maker of silks,' the apostle of Persia, Assyria, Armenia, Media, the countries round Babylon, the 'Huzites and the Gelae, as far as the borders of the Indians and as far as the land of Gog and Magog.' This shows that the East Syrians at a very early date were a missionary body. (6) The *Syriac Martyrology* may be dated *c.* A.D. 350. It is found in the MS (dated 411) mentioned below. It mentions Ḥabbīb the deacon, as well as Shamuna and Guria (on whom a metrical homily is extant), but not Aggai, Sharbil, or Barsamya (see below). (7) **Abba** (Abha, pron. Awā), the disciple of Ephraim, wrote a commentary on the Gospels, of which only a few fragments remain. (8) **Cyrillona** wrote his poems *c.* A.D. 396.[4] (9) The *Martyrdoms of Barsamya and of Ḥabbīb*, and (10) the *Acts* or *Hypomnemata of Sharbil*, are accounts of the deaths of three Edessene heroes.[5] (11) The *de Fato* of Bardaiṣān (?) has already been mentioned (§ 3). (12) **Mārūthā** (§ 3) wrote his *Book of Martyrs* early in the 5th cent. to commemorate those who suffered in Persia in the great persecution of Sapor II. (13) The *Life of Rabbūlā* (see above) was written shortly after his death, A.D. 435. (14) The *Acts of Judas Thomas* (the apostle) is a highly interesting religious novel, written by one who was of doubtful orthodoxy, but was perhaps a pioneer missionary in E. Mesopotamia in the 3rd cent., or possibly Bardaiṣan himself, or at any rate one of his school. The Syriac origin of this work is maintained by T. Nöldeke and F. C. Burkitt[6] and others.[7] The *Acts* contain the well-known *Hymn of the Soul*, for an English translation of which see Burkitt's *Early Eastern Christianity*, p. 218 ff.; but the hymn is really an independent Syriac composition added to the *Acts*. These *Acts*, while unorthodox, are probably not Gnostic, being very different from the Greek *Acts of John*, which are thoroughly

[1] *Hom.* xvii. [2] *Ib.* vii. 20.

[3] *Early Christianity outside the Roman Empire*, p. 51 f., and so the later *Early Eastern Christianity*, p. 125 ff.

[4] Burkitt, *Evang.* ii. 150; Lightfoot, *Ignatius and Polycarp*², i. 168.

[5] For a summary of these histories of Barsamya and Sharbil see Lightfoot *op. cit.* i. 66 f. Lightfoot remarks that they must not be taken as genuine history.

[6] *JThSt* i. [1899–1900] 280 ff., ii. [1900–01] 429, iii. [1901–02] 94, and *Evang.* ii. 101.

[7] For these *Acts* see further below, § 9.

Gnostic. In the Syriac *Acts* there is no inner circle to whom alone the whole truth is taught.[1] (15) Syriac may be the original language of the Clementine story which has been reproduced in the *Clementine Homilies and Recognitions*. An earlier form of the story,[2] perhaps of the 3rd cent., has lately been discovered in Syriac.[3]

There are also several translations of Greek works into Syriac which were made before the great separation of Syrian Christians. Thus the works of Eusebius were so translated very shortly after his death; a MS of a Syriac version of the *Martyrs of Palestine* and the *Theophania* is extant, dated A.D. 411, and this is not the original autograph,[4] and another of the *Ecclesiastical History* is extant dated A.D. 462.[5] Pamphilus the martyr, Eusebius's teacher, had a society, *c.* A.D. 300, which translated Greek works into Syriac.[6] The Ignatian Epistles were translated into Syriac (the 'Curetonian Syriac Letters') at least in the 5th cent., and, if the six additional letters are not an integral part of this version, probably earlier.[7] It is noteworthy that Syrian Christians, by means of classical Syriac, made many Greek works, philosophical, scientific, and religious, known to the East. Some Greek works are known to us only in their Syriac dress; and even some works in Armenian come to us from the Greek through the Syriac. The principal era of Armenian translations from the Syriac was the 5th century.[8]

5. West Syrians or Jacobites.—We now proceed to consider the divisions of Syrian Christianity which resulted from the Christological controversies of the 5th century. It is not necessary here to repeat the accounts of those controversies which have already been given in this *Encyclopædia*; but we may discuss the general history and the customs of the different Syrian bodies which separated from one another and from the 'Western' Church of Constantinople and Rome.

The Syrian Monophysites may be considered first.[9] In Syria proper there was a constant contention between them and the Orthodox for more than a hundred years after the Council of Chalcedon (A.D. 451), and the patriarchs of Antioch were sometimes Orthodox and sometimes Monophysite. The most famous of the latter was **Severus**, who maintained possession of Antioch itself from A.D. 513 to 518; he was an author, and wrote in Greek. He was a great admirer and quoter of Ignatius's Epistles.[10] He was the leader of his party till his death *c.* A.D. 540, after which a double succession to the patriarchate was continuous; and it has been preserved to the present day. The final breach between Orthodox and Monophysites may be said to have occurred in the reign of Justin II., the successor of Justinian. He persecuted the Monophysites, and an account of these troubles may be read in the third book (the only part extant) of **John of Ephesus**, a contemporary. John was Monophysite bishop of Ephesus in the 6th cent., but he wrote in Syriac, and was the first Syriac historian. He was a native of Amida (Diarbekr). For **James of Sarug** († A.D. 521 or 522), who has been thought to have been a Monophysite (but this is very doubtful), and for other early Syrian poets, see art. HYMNS (Syriac Christian), § 1.

The Syrian Monophysites are called Jacobites from **Jacob Baradai** (Baradæus), or Zanzalus, a monk of a monastery near Edessa, who came to Constantinople *c.* A.D. 540 to plead the cause of Monophysitism. After remaining there fifteen

[1] Burkitt, *Early Christianity outside the Roman Empire*, pp. 76–79.

[2] Edited with translation by A. Mingana, *Some Early Judæo-Christian Documents*, Manchester, 1917.

[3] For most of the above works see W. Wright's *Short Hist. of Syriac Literature*; many of them appear in English in the 'Ante-Nicene Christian Library,' xx. [Edinburgh, 1871], though they cannot all claim to be ante-Nicene.

[4] *DCB* ii. 320. [5] *Ib.* p. 326.

[6] Lightfoot, *Ignatius and Polycarp*², i. 327.

[7] *Ib.* p. 326. [8] *Ib.* p. 86 f.

[9] For the struggle between Monophysitism and orthodoxy after the Council of Chalcedon, and for the alternately favourable and unfavourable attitude of the Byzantine Court towards the latter, see art. MONOPHYSITISM. With the opponents of Chalcedon in Egypt and in Armenia we are not here concerned.

[10] Lightfoot, i. 178.

years, he was consecrated bishop by the imprisoned Monophysite bishops in the capital, and sent to Syria to organize his sect. He consecrated **Sergius** to succeed Severus at Antioch, and appointed **Paul the Black** to succeed Sergius. He is said to have ordained two patriarchs, 89 bishops, and an enormous number of clergy. He is often called bishop of Edessa, but Bar Hebræus [1] says that he was a bishop with no fixed see. John of Ephesus was his panegyrist. He died in 578, and after his death the Monophysites were driven from Antioch. The term 'Jacobites' was a nickname, given by the Orthodox; but the Jacobites themselves readily accepted it, tracing it, however erroneously, to the apostle James, to whom also they ascribe their principal liturgy. Their controversy with the Greeks, like the controversy of the East Syrians with the Greeks, was not only theological; it was largely tinged with national differences. Indeed both were to a considerable extent contests between Syriac thought and Hellenistic culture.

In the 7th cent. the Muhammadans conquered Palestine, Syria, and the East; and at first the new rulers favoured the Jacobites as the rivals of the Greeks. The principal writer of this period was **James** (Jacob) **of Edessa** († 708), who was a poet, commentator, and letter-writer, and a voluminous translator of Greek works into Syriac. To him, *e.g.*, we owe the knowledge of the 'Church Order' called the *Testament of our Lord*, a Greek work of *c.* A.D. 350, now extant only in Syriac.

The Jacobite patriarchs have continued to this day (at any rate from the 13th cent., or, according to Neale,[2] from the end of the 16th cent.) to style themselves 'of Antioch,' though they transferred their residence to various places—to Malatia on the Euphrates, to Amida, and finally (in the 12th cent.) to the monastery of Deir-el-Zaʿafaran (the 'saffron monastery') near Mardin, where they have been ever since.

Perhaps the most eminent Jacobite of all history was **Gregory Bar Hebræus,** or Abulfaraj († 1286), a man of Jewish parentage, who became a convert to Christianity and afterwards *maphrian* or metropolitan of Moṣul, having formerly held other sees.[3] He wrote many works, and his *Chronicle* (which may be read in Assemani) is a valuable history. He seems to have been greatly esteemed even by his Nestorian opponents, who attended his funeral in large numbers; he died at Maragha (south of Tabriz), but was buried in the monastery of Mar Mattai on Jebel Maqlub (Syr. Elpeph), a day's ride north-east of Moṣul, and his grave is still shown there. His *Chronicle* is, for his age, fairly trustworthy, but when he deals with Nestorian matters it should be compared with the writings of that body.

A less known Jacobite writer was **Dionysius Bar-ṣalibi** (Syr. ṣlibhi, pron. ṣlīwī), also called James, metropolitan of Amida, a theologian and commentator, probably of the 11th century.[4]

We know less of Jacobite organization and customs, ecclesiastical and liturgical, than we do of those of the Nestorians, of which we have been fully informed in the last quarter of a century. For the modern Jacobites the best short account is to be found in O. H. Parry's *Six Months in a Syrian Monastery*, which has been largely drawn upon in the description which follows. The ecclesiastical hierarchy consists of the patriarch; the maphrian, who since the 12th cent. has had his see at Mar Mattai (see above) or in Moṣul itself; and bishops of Jerusalem, Damascus or Homs (Emessa), Edessa, Amida, Mardin, Nisibis, Maipharqaṭ (now Farqin; see above, § 3) and Maʿdan, Aleppo, Jezireh (on the Tigris), and Ṭur ʿAbhdin (Jebel

1 Assemani, *Bibl. Or.* ii. 327.
2 *Gen. Introd.* i. 152.
3 Assemani, ii. 244 ff.
4 Renaudot, *Lit. Or.* ii. 453.

Ṭur). There are also some bishops without sees, as at Mar Mattai, where, when the present writer visited the monastery in 1887, the establishment consisted of one bishop and one monk. The patriarch is elected by the people, and the election is confirmed by the bishops resident near Mardin; it is common for the maphrian to be promoted to the chief position. The patriarch, or more rarely the maphrian, consecrates all the bishops, who must be either monks or widowed priests; those chosen from the monks are called *maṭrān*, or 'metropolitan,' while those chosen from the widowed priests are called *asqof* (ἐπίσκοπος), and are of slightly lower rank, not being eligible for the patriarchate or maphrianate. Each bishop has the prefix 'Mār' ('my lord') before his name.[1] The patriarch and the other bishops are recognized by the State as judges for their own people, especially in minor matters, and in questions of marriage and divorce. The canonical age for the ordination of bishops is 35, of deacons 20; but this has never been kept as a fixed rule. Bar Hebræus was ordained bishop at 20; deacons are often ordained as little boys, but they must be able to read the Psalms in classical Syriac. The parish priests, who are elected by the parish councils of deacons and laymen, must be married men; if their wives die, they enter a monastery or else become *asqofs*. A second marriage is not allowed to them. The priests must let their beards grow, but they shave their heads completely. The leading priest in a large town is often made a chorepiscopus, but he is not a bishop, and cannot ordain. There are many deacons in each village—they are engaged in secular work during the week—as they are indispensable for the celebration of the eucharist. Minor orders are practically obsolete.

Several ground-plans of churches may be seen in Parry.[2] The altar, at least in most cases, stands in an apse, not (as among the Nestorians) attached to the east wall, and there are seats for bishops and clergy behind. This is also the usual Greek custom. The whole sanctuary in Syrian churches, Eastern and Western, is called 'the altar' (Syr. *madhbʿḥā*), though this name is sometimes also given to the holy table itself. The latter is usually of stone, though in some of the Jacobite churches it is of wood.[3] There are side chapels with 'altars,' north and south of the sanctuary—the churches face east—and in some cases, as at Mar Mattai, there is another chapel at the north side for the burial of bishops, called *beith qaddīshé* ('house of the saints'). Between sanctuary and nave there is a stone wall or screen, sometimes with folding doors, and always with a veil. The nave has no furniture except one or two lecterns. The altar is usually placed under a baldacchino. The Jacobites, like the Nestorians, do not allow images in their churches, but have a great veneration for the cross.

Monasteries are common; the monks are often laymen, though they are sometimes in holy orders. The monasteries are under the rule of the diocesan bishop except where they contain the tomb of a patriarch or a maphrian; in that case they are directly under the patriarch. Nunneries seem to be obsolete. The technical Syriac term for the monastic life, among both the Jacobites and the Nestorians, is 'sadness,' 'mourning.'[4]

The eucharistic liturgy ordinarily used is that of 'St. James,' a translation of which, in the Jacobite form, is given in Brightman's *Liturgies Eastern and Western*, i. 69 ff. The Syrian Jacobites, Maronites, Uniat Syrians, and Malabar Jacobites all use the same liturgy with some variations.[5] Leavened bread is used, and must be baked for each occasion. The leaven is handed down from remote ages, as among the Nestorians. The eucharist is reserved for the sick, but only for communion on the same day. Little children (who are confirmed immediately after baptism) are communicated.

1 For the forms of admission to holy orders see art. ORDINATION (Christian), § 12.
2 Pp. 328, 332, etc.
3 Neale, *Gen. Introd.* i. 181.
4 Syr. *abhīlūthā* (see the Nestorian *Sūnhādhūs*, vii. 2, can. 7, etc.).
5 For a list of other Jacobite liturgies see Brightman, i. p. lviii ff.

The antidoron or eucharistic bread not consecrated (Syr. *bŭrkthā* = εὐλογία) is distributed after the service. The celebrant wears albe, amice, undivided stole, yellow shoes, a maniple over each arm, and a chasuble split down the front and buckled with silver at the neck. The vesting takes place in the side chapel, where also the elements are prepared. There are in some churches daily eucharists. There are no special vestments (except girdles, and often, for the deacons, stoles) at the daily offices. These last have not been published, and exist in manuscript only. One of the great features of Jacobite worship is the peculiar addition of 'who wast crucified for us' to the Trisagion ('Holy God, Holy Mighty, Holy Immortal, have mercy upon us'), which is used at many of the services. The addition was first made by **Peter the Fuller** († A.D. 477), and was eagerly adopted and retained as a test of Monophysitism.[1] Baptism is not allowed to be administered in private houses. The child at baptism is signed with *moron*, or unguent (which is consecrated once a year by the patriarch), anointed all over the body with oil (which has been hallowed by the *moron*), immersed in water thrice up to the neck, clothed, and confirmed.[2] Confession before communion is recommended by the canons, but is now almost obsolete. Some of the canons[3] are more strict, and insist on confession before communion on Maundy Thursday, Christmas, and Pentecost.[4] The fasts are somewhat severe. Besides Lent and Advent, both of which are strict fasts, there are (*a*) the Fast of the Ninevites, three days in spring, said to have been instituted owing to a plague in the 6th cent.,[5] and strenuously maintained also by the East Syrians; (*b*) the Fast of the Apostles, after Pentecost; and (*c*) the Fast of Mary, August 1-15. Wednesday and Friday are fasts in each week, from sunset to sunset.

The Jacobites are to be found chiefly in Mesopotamia and northwards to Ḥarput and Diarbekr, but there are also a good many of them near Damascus and a certain number around Moṣul. The largest numbers are perhaps to be found in the hilly region of Jebel Ṭur (Arab. also Ṭūr 'Abdīn; Syr. Ṭūr 'Abhdīn), N. of the line Mardin—Nisibis—Jezireh. In this district Syriac is still spoken vernacularly. Here some of their oldest and most interesting churches are situated.[6] It is always difficult to reckon numbers in Turkey; but Gibbon's estimate[7] of from fifty to eighty thousand is certainly too low. We may perhaps put the total in Turkey at rather less than 200,000.[8]

Certain communities of Jacobites have become Uniat (see below, § 6). Jesuit missionaries first came to Mesopotamia in 1540. In 1646 the Uniat patriarchate was fixed at Aleppo, and the patriarch took his title from that place. The Syrian Christians in that neighbourhood mostly belong to that jurisdiction.

6. Melkites and Uniats.—The former name, which is derived from Syr. *malkā* ('king'), a word used also, like βασιλεύς, for an emperor, was invented in the 10th cent. by the Jacobites for those Christians who adhered to the Council of Chalcedon. It was a nickname, meaning 'royalists,' and implying that they could stand only by the support of the Roman emperor. It may be compared with the nickname 'Erastians' used in this country at the present day; both have a somewhat similar shade of meaning. But the name 'Melkites' was quite readily accepted by those to whom it had been given in derision,[1] and was applied to all those who were in communion with Constantinople, whether Syrian, Egyptian, or Greek. In comparatively recent times the name has been given, and given exclusively, to the Christians of Syria and Egypt who have been drawn from the Orthodox Eastern Church and have been united to Rome. Such, *e.g.*, are the 'Syrian Melkites,' whose liturgical language is, or was, Syriac.

The name 'Uniat' is applied to those Eastern Christians who have been united to Rome, but are allowed to keep their own liturgies, liturgical language, and ecclesiastical customs, especially as to the marriage of their clergy—though in all these respects modifications, sometimes very considerable, have been introduced. The earliest of these 'Uniats' are the Maronites (see below, § 7); but there are also four Uniat Churches of the Græco-Slavonic rite—the Bulgarian, Greek Melkite (formed of Arabic-speaking Orthodox after the Synod of Bethlehem, in 1672), Rumaic or Roumanian, and Ruthenian; there are also the Armenian Uniats; the Syrian Uniats, drawn from the Jacobites in 1646 (see above, § 5); the Chaldæan Uniats, drawn from the Nestorians (see below, § 8); and the Malabar Uniats (see below, § 9). The Uniats have nine Eastern patriarchs. Those of Constantinople, Alexandria, and Antioch live in Rome. In addition there are Uniat patriarchs of Jerusalem (Greek), Antioch (Maronite), Antioch (Greek), Antioch (Syrian), Cilicia (Armenian), Babylon (Chaldæan).[2] European readers are often confused by the fact that there are no fewer than six patriarchs who take their title from Antioch—one Greek Orthodox, four Uniats, and one Jacobite.

The Syrian Uniats use the liturgy of 'St. James'; the rubrics are often in Carshuni (Arabic in Syriac characters), the audible prayers both in Syriac and in Carshuni, the inaudible in Syriac only.[3] The Chaldæan Uniats use the liturgy of 'Addai and Mari' with some amendments; their daily services are considerably abbreviated compared with those of the Nestorians, and in the case of the long festal Night Service about six-sevenths are omitted.[4]

7. Maronites.—These Syrian Christians of the Lebanon derive their name from their teacher **John Maro**, or Maron, a learned monk, who was named patriarch of Antioch, perhaps early in the 8th century. He has often been confused with an earlier Maron, called by Gibbon[5] 'a saint or savage of the fifth century,' whose relics were greatly venerated. In the time of John Maron the Monothelete controversy was still going on, and these Lebanon Christians espoused that cause.[6] They were thus in opposition to their Christian neighbours, and later, as Christians, to the Muhammadan authorities; and they received the nickname 'Mardaites' or 'Rebels' (Syr. *marīdhé*).

In 1182 they renounced Monotheletism under the influence of their patriarch **Aimeric**, and were united with Rome, then numbering about 40,000 souls.[7] At that time the connexion with the West

[1] But the ancient and authoritative Jacobite statement of faith (the 'Creed of our Sainted Fathers'), published by the Syrian Patriarchate Education Committee in English (*The Ancient Syrian Church in Mesopotamia*, London, 1908), emphatically states that the Trisagion with this addition is addressed to 'the Only-begotten Son,' and not to 'the Three blessed Persons' (p. 10). This 'Statement of faith' is quite free from Monophysitism. It denies that the divine nature of our Lord was commingled with the human nature, or that the two natures became commixed and changed so as to give rise to a third nature, and asserts that the two natures became united in indissoluble union without confusion, mixture, or transmutation, and that they remained two natures in an unalterable unity.

[2] For early Syrian baptisms see below, § 8.

[3] Several collections of these may be read in H. Denzinger, *Ritus Orientalium*, i. 475 ff.

[4] *Ib.* p. 487.

[5] Wigram, p. 214.

[6] Parry, p. 169 ff.

[7] vi. 55.

[8] For the Jacobites in India see below, § 9.

[1] Gibbon, vi. 44, note 109.

[2] A. Riley, 'Synopsis of Oriental Christianity,' *The Guardian*, xliii. 947 (27th June, 1888), since reprinted.

[3] Brightman, *Liturgies Eastern and Western*, i. p. lvi.

[4] Conybeare-Maclean, *Rituale Armenorum*, p. 298.

[5] vi. 55.

[6] See art. MONOTHELETISM.

[7] Neale, *Gen. Introd.* i. 154.

was through the Latin kingdom of Jerusalem. After the destruction of that kingdom in the 14th cent. relations with Rome were at times broken off, but they were resumed, and still continue. In the year 1584 Pope Gregory XIII. founded a college in Rome for training their clergy, and this institution has the honour of having in the 18th cent. educated the learned brothers J. S. and J. A. Assemani, to whose literary labours scholars are so much indebted for their knowledge of Syriac Christianity. The Maronites subscribed the decrees of the Council of Trent in 1736.

They are allowed to retain their own liturgical customs, and use the Syriac 'St. James' and other anaphoras.[1] The rubrics in the printed books are in Carshuni; some of the formulæ are in Carshuni and Syriac.[2]

The Maronite clergy may marry. They also elect their own patriarch, who still takes his title from Antioch. He lives at the monastery of Qānōbīn (κοινόβιον), in the Lebanon, and has under his jurisdiction bishops at Aleppo, Tripoli (in Syria), Byblus and Botra, Baalbek or Heliopolis, Damascus, Berytus, Tyre and Sidon, and in Cyprus.[3] Their numbers are difficult to estimate. Gibbon[4] gives 150 priests and 100,000 souls, but they probably number about a quarter of a million.

They have suffered much from their feuds with their neighbours, the Druses, and in the year 1860, after great massacres of the Maronites, the British and French governments intervened for their protection.

8. East Syrians, or Nestorians.—We may now take up the history of the Church in the Persian empire from the middle of the 5th century.[5] The first great event for the East Syrians after the Council of Ephesus, A.D. 431, was their final expulsion by the emperor Zeno from the school of Edessa and the consequent founding of the school of Nisibis, A.D. 489. **Ibas** (Syr. Ihibha, pron. īhīwā, lit. 'given'), bishop of Edessa, who was strongly Dyophysite, had been condemned by the Latrocinium, or 'Robber Synod,' of Ephesus in 449, but was acquitted and restored to his see by the Council of Chalcedon two years later, after having anathematized both Nestorius and Eutyches. During his lifetime the Monophysites made no way at Edessa, but after his death in 457 they became predominant there, and after a long struggle expelled their opponents. This was a decisive event in the Persian Church. Although up to that time it had had no direct dealings with Nestorianism, its tendency was mainly Dyophysite, and the influx of Nestorians from the Roman empire greatly strengthened that tendency. Nevertheless it is a mistake to suppose that the Persian Church at some definite date in the 5th cent. espoused Nestorianism and was therefore cut off from the Catholic Church. The process was a gradual one. The principal influence in the latter half of the 5th cent. was that of **Bar Sōmā** (Barsumas, lit. 'son of the fast'), bishop of Nisibis, who had taught at Edessa, and now, in the vacancy of the catholicate, organized the East Syrian Church in a Nestorian sense; he must not be confused with his namesake of the Latrocinium, who was a Monophysite. There was some opposition to 'Nestorian' doctrine, especially from the monks of Mar Mattai (see above, § 5), who to this day are Jacobites. The catholicos **Acacius** (Syr. Aqaq), who was bishop of Seleucia-Ctesiphon from

[1] For a list of these see Brightman, *Liturgies Eastern and Western*, i. p. lviii.

[2] *Ib.* p. lvii.

[3] Neale, *Gen. Introd.* i. 154. For their forms of admission to holy orders see art. ORDINATION (Christian), § 14.

[4] vi. 57.

[5] For the doctrinal controversy which occupied the Council of Ephesus see art. NESTORIANISM.

485 to 496, went to Constantinople on a mission from the Persian king, and there declared that his Church knew nothing of Nestorius; he was admitted to communion by the Orthodox, having anathematized Bar Ṣōmā.[1] We may perhaps discount his statement as an Oriental exaggeration; but the incident shows that the separation was not yet complete. Still later, good relations with Constantinople took place in the time of **Mar Abha** (pron. Awā) **the Great**, a contemporary of Jacob Baradai (see above, § 5). This prelate, a convert from Magianism, was catholicos from 540 to 552, having been a teacher at Nisibis, and having visited Jerusalem, Egypt, Greece, and Constantinople in the time of Justinian. In his Catholicate, as it would seem, the Council of Chalcedon was accepted by the East Syrian Church.[2] The *Sūnhādhūs*[3] quotes with approval one of its canons, and dates the council as '25th October, 763 of Alexander,' *i.e.* A.D. 452 (*sic*); the session of that day was particularly solemn, and was attended by the emperor and empress: it ended the principal work of the council.[4]

One of the first matters discussed in this period was the marriage of bishops and clergy. A council was held in 484 at Beith Lapaṭ (also called Gondisapor, perhaps the modern Shiraz); it allowed them to marry, and even permitted a second marriage to clerical widowers. This was confirmed in a council held by Acacius in the following year. Several patriarchs were married: Babhai (pron. Bā-wai), catholicos from 496 to 505, his successor Silas, Elisha, Paul, and Ezekiel, all of the 6th century.[5] But Mar Abha set his face against episcopal marriage, himself declining to marry; and after his time it became rare. The present rule is that a bishop must be a *rabban* ('monk,' but see below), and may not marry or have married, and must never have eaten flesh-meat; nor must his mother have eaten meat during her pregnancy.[6] There is evidence that the rule against eating meat did not hold in the 7th century.[7] It is noteworthy that Ebedjesus (see below) in his *Sūnhādhūs* passes over the question of episcopal marriage in silence, and does not refer to the decrees which permitted it.[8]

The definite official adoption of Nestorianism, or of what was taken for such, must be dated at the beginning of the 7th cent., when the East Syrians formally repudiated the term 'Theotokos' and adopted the phrase 'two *qnomé*, one *parṣopa* (πρόσωπον), two natures' with reference to our Lord.[9] The opposition to the 'Nestorians' of the Monophysite minority in Persia was greatly strengthened by the influx of a large number of captives of the latter persuasion from Syria, in 540 and 573, under Chosroes I.; the influence of Shīrīn, the Christian queen of Chosroes II. (590–628), was latterly in their favour.[10]

Monasticism was at one time a most flourishing institution among the East Syrians. Thomas of Marga (see below) gives us a graphic description of his own monastery, and we have other sources of information in Sozomen,[11] in P. Bedjan's *Acta Martyrum et Sanctorum*, and elsewhere.[12] It seems to have been introduced into the East from Egypt by **Mar Awgin** (pron. Ōgīn; = 'Eugenius,' † 363?), who founded the famous monasteries of Mount Izla (near Nisibis) and Deir-el-Zaʿafaran (near Mardin; see above, § 5). He is said to have been the teacher of James of Nisibis. His *Life* is included in

[1] Wigram, p. 170. [2] *Ib.* p. 188. [3] v. 21.

[4] Hefele, *Hist. of the Councils of the Church*, Eng. tr., iii. 353 ff.

[5] Wigram, pp. 175, 178, 212; Budge, *Book of Governors*, i. p. cxxxii f.

[6] Cf. Jg 13[4f].

[7] Wigram, p. 249. Eusebius (*HE* ii. 23) says that James the Just 'was holy from his mother's womb . . . he did not eat flesh (ἔμψυχον)'; *i.e.* he was a Nazirite, though abstinence from flesh was not part of a Nazirite's vow.

[8] The *Sūnhādhūs* (vii. preface) says that bishops were *usually* chosen from among the monks.

[9] Wigram, p. 258. But the latest investigations show that *qnoma* (=hypostasis) is used in the earlier sense of 'substance,' not of 'person.' This makes the phrase, if redundant, at least quite orthodox.

[10] *Ib.* pp. 242, 247. [11] *HE* vi. 34, very short.

[12] For an account of the institution see Budge, *Book of Governors*, i. p. cxvii ff.

Bedjan's work, but it is remarkable that Thomas of Marga does not mention him. The great organizer of monasticism among the East Syrians was a later monk, **Abraham of Kashkar,** a town between the lower Euphrates and the Tigris. Abraham refounded Mount Izla in the 6th cent., and his canons, which are still extant,[1] are included in the Nestorian *Sūnhādhūs.*[2] His successor as abbot, **Dadhishu,** made canons accepting the doctrines of Diodorus, Theodore, and Nestorius.[3] The rules as to jurisdiction of monasteries were the same as among the Jacobites (see above, § 5); in the 'patriarchal' monasteries the diocesan bishop might not officiate nor be mentioned in the litany.[4] One of the most famous of the monasteries was that of Beith 'Abhé (pron. 'Awé), probably founded by **Jacob of Lāshūm,** a monk of Mount Izla, in the 6th cent.; its situation is uncertain, but probably it was near the Great Zab.[5] This monastery produced from the 7th to the 9th centuries many patriarchs, as well as its famous historian, Thomas of Marga. The monastery of Rabban Hormuzd, about 30 miles north of Moṣul, is close to the village of Alqosh (Elkosh), where the tomb of the prophet Nahum, in a Jewish synagogue, is still shown. The monastery was founded by **Hormuzd of Beith Laphaṭ,** *c.* 600. He spent the last 22 years of his life there and was buried within it, as were several patriarchs.[6] The number of monks had dwindled from fifty in 1820 to about ten in 1890,[7] a new monastery having been built at the foot of the hills, not far away. When the present writer visited the two monasteries in 1887, there was in the new one a large number of monks, busily engaged. Both the monasteries now belong to the Uniat Chaldæans (see above, § 6). There were also many other monasteries elsewhere.[8]

Monasteries are now quite obsolete among the Nestorians, though a few *rabbans* (monks) live in the world under a private rule, neither marrying nor eating meat, such as the late well-known Rabban Yonan (Jonah) of Qūchānīs.[9]

Among a large number of Nestorian writers the following may be mentioned. **Narsai** († *c.* 502), a poet and homilist, called 'the Harp of the Spirit,' went to Nisibis from Edessa on the expulsion of the Nestorians. Ebedjesus says that he wrote 360 homilies; of these 47 have been published in Syriac by A. Mingana, and those on the eucharist and baptism, translated into English by R. H. Connolly, are of the greatest importance for the history of the early East Syrian rite. **Mshiḥa Zkha** was the writer of a most valuable history in the 6th century (see above, § 3). **Ishu'yahbh III.** (pron. Ishūyāw), who was catholicos for ten years from 650, was the reputed author or reviser of the ordination and baptismal services, and also of the Ḥudhra (see below).[10] In the earlier Syrian rite of baptism, as evidenced by Narsai, the *Syriac Didascalia*, and some other Syriac descriptions, the anointing seems to have been only before baptism; the post-baptismal anointing was added among the Jacobites in the 5th cent., probably by Severus (see § 5), and among the Nestorians by Ishu'yahbh.[11] **Thomas of Marga,** bishop in the 9th cent. of that city (on the Zab) and metropolitan of Beith Garmai (east of the Tigris), was a monk of Beith 'Abhé (see above); his *Book of Governors*, a monastic history, is most valuable as filling a gap of 300 years in the history, otherwise hardly known. **George of Arbela,** metropolitan of Moṣul and Arbela (south-east of Moṣul) in the 10th cent., wrote a commentary on the services of the Church, which is valuable for the history of the Nestorian liturgies.[12] **Mari Ibn Suleiman** ('son of Solomon') was a chronicler of the 12th century. **Ebedjesus** (E. Syr. 'Abhdishu, pron. 'Ōdīshū, lit. 'servant of Jesus'), metropolitan of Ṣubha (pron. Ṣūwā), by some identified with Nisibis,[13] in the 13th cent. compiled the *Sūnhādhūs*, or 'Book of Canon Law,' now in constant use by the Nestorians, though many of its provisions have become obsolete.[1]

The missions of the East Syrians have been far extended. Their work in India is attested in the 6th cent. by Cosmas Indicopleustes (see below, § 9). Gibbon remarks[2] that 'the barbaric churches, from the Gulf of Persia to the Caspian Sea, were almost infinite.' The missionaries extended their labours to Socotra, Ceylon, Turkestan, and even to China, where the Nestorian monument of Si-ngan-fu, dated A.D. 781 ('1092 of the Greeks'), attests their activity, which also gave rise to the legend of Prester John (*q.v.*), a supposed priest-king in Tartary. Wherever they carried their teaching, they used Syriac as their liturgical language, even though it was not that of the people.[3] Thus the Malabarese have always used Syriac liturgies. This great activity swelled the numbers of Syrian Christians exceedingly, and the Nestorians and Jacobites together are said to have been more numerous than the Greeks and Latins together.[4]

Under Muhammadan rule East Syrian Christianity was alternately favoured and persecuted. Under Tamerlane ('Timur the Lame') in the 14th cent. it was almost annihilated. But a remnant survived and is still to be found in the mountains of Kurdistan in E. Turkey, in the upland plains of Azarbaijan in the north-west of the present Persian kingdom, especially in that of Urmi or Urumi (often called in Europe Urmia), and in the low-lying plain of Moṣul (Nineveh). The patriarch, who after the foundation of Baghdād (A.D. 762) had left Seleucia-Ctesiphon for that city, later removed to the north. But disputes as to the succession divided the patriarchate. The Nestorians themselves are now under the rule of Mār Shimūn (these two words are pronounced as one and are accented on the first and last syllables), who lives at Qūchānīs in the almost inaccessible mountains which surround the Great Zab, a beautiful retreat near the small town of Julamerk. Each successive catholicos takes the name 'Shimūn' (Simon), whatever his baptismal name. The East Syrians of the Moṣul plain, now called Chaldæans, have been united with Rome since 1680, when they were received by Pope Innocent XI. Their head ('patriarch of Babylon') bears the name Mār Elīyā (Elijah). He has several bishops, each styled metropolitan, under him. He retains the title ('of Babylon') which the Nestorian patriarchs often used when they lived at Seleucia-Ctesiphon; it is also found in the *Sūnhādhūs.*[5] There were at one time patriarchs at Amida (Diarbekr), who also were united with Rome; these bore the name Mar Joseph.

All the East Syrians speak Syriac vernacularly, though many of those in the Moṣul plain speak Arabic also. It is common to hear the sailors on the Tigris steamers talking vernacular Syriac, these being Chaldæan Uniats. The total number of Nestorians and Uniats combined is, or was till lately, perhaps about 300,000.

A detailed account of the ecclesiastical hierarchy of the Nestorians is given in Maclean-Browne, *The Catholicos of the East*, ch. ix. The patriarch, or catholicos, has under him a *maṭrān*, or metropolitan, who bears the dynastic name of Mār Ḥnān-ishū ('mercy of Jesus'), and several bishops, the number varying considerably from time to time. The present method of filling bishoprics (including the patriarchate) is for each bishop to bring up one or two boys or young men, his nephews or near relatives, as potential successors. Such a one is called in the vernacular *nāṭar kūrsī* ('keeper of the seat'), and is not allowed to eat meat or marry; the bishop ordinarily nominates the one

1 *Book of Governors*, i. p. cxxxiv. 2 vii. 3.
3 *Ib.* vii. 4. 4 *Ib.* vii. 6. 5 Budge, i. p. xli ff.
6 *Ib.* p. clvii ff. 7 *Ib.* p. clxix.
8 For the Jacobite monastery of Mar Mattai near Moṣul see § 5.
9 Maclean-Browne, *Catholicos of the East*, p. 19. The *Sūnhādhūs* forbids monks to marry 'like the rest of the clerks and laymen' or to eat meat in their monasteries (vii. 2, can. 5).
10 Cf. Budge, i. p. lvi.
11 T. Thompson, *The Offices of Baptism and Confirmation*, Cambridge, 1914, p. 31. See also art. CONFIRMATION, §§ 6, 7.
12 For an account of this book see Connolly, *Liturgical Homilies of Narsai*, p. 75 ff.
13 But see R. Payne Smith, *Thes. Syr.* ii. 3373.

1 For a list of the works of Ebedjesus see Assemani, *Bibl. Or.* i. 3 ff., 380 ff. G. P. Badger (*Nestorians and their Rituals*, ii. 380 ff.) gives an English translation of his best known work, the *Margānīthā* ('Pearl'), and (ii. 361 f.) of his catalogue of authors and their works, chiefly East Syrian. For East Syrian hymn-writers see art. HYMNS (Syriac Christian).
2 vi. 49. 3 Renaudot, *Lit. Or.* ii. 563.
4 Gibbon, vi. 50.
5 ix. 1. The above remarks and much of what follows apply to the time before the Great War.

whom he wishes to succeed, but in theory the people elect from among the 'keepers of the seat.' In the 15th cent. the catholicos made a law restricting the catholicate to members of his own family. This was an innovation, though perhaps not a very recent one. The catholicos consecrates the bishops; but the metropolitan consecrates the catholicos.[1]

In most villages there is at least one priest, in some several; and deacons are very numerous, as the eucharist cannot be celebrated without the assistance of a deacon or of a priest acting as deacon. Occasionally a priest is made an archdeacon (*arkān*), but this is now only an honour, not involving special duties. Formerly there were chorepiscopi and periodeutæ ('visitors'); these were presbyters, not bishops. The office of periodeuta is at least as old in Syrian Christianity as Rabbūlā (6th cent.), as he mentions it in his canons.[2] The East Syrian *Book of Heavenly Intelligences*[3] enumerates nine orders in three divisions; (1) the episcopate: patriarch (or catholicos), metropolitan, bishop; (2) the presbyterate: chorepiscopus, periodeuta (or archdeacon), presbyter; (3) the diaconate: deacon, subdeacon, reader. These are said to correspond to the angelic hierarchy (as given by pseudo-Dionysius Areopagita and others) of (1) cherubim, seraphim, thrones; (2) dominions, virtues, powers; (3) principalities, archangels, angels. Minor orders are now obsolete. There are no longer any deaconesses.

Many of the ecclesiastical customs of the Nestorians are those also of the Jacobites (see above, § 5). But there are some differences. The Nestorian priests and deacons may marry, and if their wives die they may marry again; but the parish priests are not obliged to be married, though as a matter of fact they are hardly ever single men. The churches, which (especially in the mountains of Kurdistan) have exceedingly narrow and low doors, sometimes only accessible by a ladder, and which are often built for security in a cleft of a rock or in some almost inaccessible place, are nearly all of the same pattern. Outwardly they show no sign of Christianity save a small cross beside the church door. They have no towers or spires, such as the Armenian churches have. Internally they have a stone wall reaching to the roof and dividing the nave from the sanctuary; a doorway in this wall is covered with a veil which is drawn back at certain parts of the service. On the nave-side of this wall is a raised pace called *bema* (a name which in other Eastern communions means the sanctuary), and this again is bounded by a dwarf wall with apertures in the middle and at the side, where the clergy stand to communicate the people. This raised pace somewhat corresponds to the Greek σωλέας.[4] Against the dwarf wall, towards the nave, are projections (said to contain relics) for the cross and for books. The altar is attached to the east wall, and is usually built into a recess therein. It is oblong, not square as among the Greeks. The people stand in the nave to worship, the men in front, and the women behind; there are no seats, and if there is any occasion for sitting, such as a sermon, the people sit on the matted floor. Two other features of the churches may be noticed: a baptistery (also used as a vestry, and usually for baking the eucharistic bread), at the south-east corner of the church next the sanctuary; and a court (often open to the air) on the south side of the nave, where the daily prayers are said in summer. This is the usual arrangement, and is that of the church of Mart Mariam (St. Mary) at Urmi in Persia, which claims to be the oldest church in the world, and to contain the tomb of one of the Wise Men of Bethlehem, built (as the most ancient tombs are) into the wall of this church—in this case at the south-east corner of the nave.[5] The people are called to worship by a wooden board (Syr. *nāqūshā*) hit by a mallet; this is the Greek σήμαντρον.[6] Bells are seldom used to summon to prayer, though there are often strings of small bells hung inside the church.

1 For the forms of admission to holy orders see art. ORDINATION (Christian), § 13.

2 Given in Burkitt, *Early Eastern Christianity*, p. 144.

3 Maclean-Browne, p. 184.

4 Neale, *Gen. Introd.* i. 201.

5 For a ground plan see Maclean-Browne, p. 301; for plans of two other famous churches see pp. 291, 296.

6 Neale, *Gen. Introd.* i. 217.

The vestments worn at the eucharist differ somewhat from those of the Jacobites. For a chasuble the Nestorians wear a kind of cope (*ma'ăprā*), which has no fastening at the neck, and is very difficult to keep in position. The priests' stoles, like those of the West, do not differ in shape from those of the deacons; maniples and amices are not worn. Private confession, though often referred to in the service-books, is now obsolete. The fasts are the same as those of the Jacobites, but the fasts of the Apostles and of Mary are almost if not quite obsolete, as are some others mentioned in the East Syrian books. The Wednesday and Friday fasts do not in practice begin on (what we call) the evening before, but they end at sunset; all Eastern Christians reckon the day as beginning and ending at sunset, and our 'Sunday evening' is their 'Monday evening.'

The chief liturgy used by the Nestorians is that of 'the apostles Addai and Mari.' This liturgy has many early features, especially a form of eucharistic invocation of the Holy Spirit which is not as fully developed as that in most of the Great Liturgies. It prays that the Holy Ghost may come and rest on the oblation, and bless and sanctify it, that it may become (or be) for us for the remission of sins, etc.; and it does not explicitly mention the change in the elements. But the most curious feature is the absence of the words of our Lord spoken at the Last Supper, when after 'blessing' or 'giving thanks' He gave the sacrament to the disciples ('This is my body,' etc.). Neale[1] argues on *a priori* grounds that 'Addai and Mari' must have originally had these words. But this is a precarious statement; there are other instances of at least the partial omission of the words.[2] This liturgy in no way refers to the Nestorian controversy. On certain days of the year the anaphora of 'Addai and Mari' is not used, but that of 'Theodore the Interpreter' (of Mopsuestia) or that of 'Nestorius' is substituted, the first part of the liturgy, and the ending, being common to all three. All these anaphoras date, in some form, from very early times; the first probably, in its earliest shape, was compiled before A.D. 431; the other two are certainly not the work of the bishops after whom they are named, but are the work of East Syrian authors. The author of 'Nestorius' must have had a Byzantine liturgy before him, as many traces of that rite are found in it. But all three anaphoras are quite distinctly of the East Syrian, not of the Byzantine, family of liturgies. All three seem to have been composed before Narsai (end of 5th cent.), though doubtless many more modern additions have been made to them.

Eucharists do not occur very often among the Nestorians—some five or six times a year as a rule, though in a few churches weekly eucharists are the custom. The people communicate, as they pray, standing, the mothers holding up the very little children in their arms to receive. All receive in both kinds separately (the species of bread in their hands), except the very little ones, for whom the celebrant dips a small portion of the consecrated bread in the chalice and then puts it in their mouth. Reservation for the sick is not allowed. The eucharistic bread is leavened.[3] All services, without exception, are sung; but no instrumental music is allowed.

The baptismal customs do not differ greatly from those of the Jacobites.[4] The service is closely modelled on the eucharistic liturgies, than which

1 *Gen. Introd.* i. 486.

2 A. J. Maclean, *Ancient Church Orders*, pp. 40, 45, *Early Christian Worship*[2], London, 1915, pp. viii, 25.

3 For a curious tradition as to the handing down of the leaven see Maclean-Browne, p. 247.

4 For a description see Maclean-Browne, p. 267 ff.

it is certainly later. There is, however, no kiss of peace. The triple immersion is absolutely total. As with all Easterns, the presbyter confirms, and lays his right hand on or over the neophytes; the use of the consecrated oil at this point is not explicitly mentioned in the service-book, but it is customary for the priest, when signing the neophytes with the sign of the cross, to do so with his thumb which he has dipped in the oil. There are now no interrogations or renunciations,[1] though they are alluded to in the 5th cent. by Narsai, where the renunciations have special reference to heresy.[2] Private baptism is not, in practice, allowed; if a village has no church, a child must be carried to another village which has one. Thus some children die unbaptized, though it is not likely that a person would grow up without baptism. Sponsors are considered as being akin to their godchildren, and the relationship is a bar to marriage.

The non-liturgical services are of great interest, and are extremely long, at least in theory. They consist mainly of hymns and anthems.[3] The great number of martyrs in the East Syrian Church is reflected in the frequent mention of them by name in these anthems. The calendar is remarkable, and in some respects unique. Most of the saints' days fall on a Friday, and suit very well with the arrangement of the ecclesiastical year, which is divided into periods of about seven weeks each, more or less—Advent, Epiphany, Lent, Easter, 'The Apostles' (after Pentecost), 'Summer,' 'Elijah,' 'Moses,' and the 'Hallowing of the Church.' A few of the holy days, however, fall on fixed days of the month, as Christmas (Dec. 25), Epiphany (Jan. 6), St. George (April 24, etc.), St. Cyriac and St. Julitta (July 15 and Dec. 22), St. Peter and St. Paul (July 29), St. Mary (Aug. 15), Holy Cross Day (Sept. 13, not 14 as elsewhere). The twelve apostles are commemorated together on a Friday before Lent, the four evangelists on another, the 'Greek doctors' (Diodorus, Theodore, Nestorius) on a third, the 'Syrian doctors' (especially Ephraim, Narsai, Abraham [of Kashkar?, see above]) on a fourth. On other Fridays are commemorated St. James the Lord's brother, St. Mary, St. John Baptist, St. Peter and St. Paul (a second commemoration), Mar Abha or else the patron saint of the church, St. Stephen, the forty martyrs of Sebaste, all the departed, the Seventy, and some others.

The choirs are divided into two parts, and according as the first or the second choir begins the anthems the week is called 'Before' or 'After,' 'Before and After' (Syr. *Qdhām ū-Wāthar*) being thus taken for the name of the ordinary book of daily services. The *propria* for Sundays, fasts, and festivals are of very great length, and are contained in the books called *Ḥūdhrā* ('cycle') and *Gazzā* ('treasure'), two enormous MS volumes, and some others. These two are not published; but the complete East Syrian service for the Epiphany is given in English in Conybeare-Maclean, *Rituale Armenorum*, p. 288 ff. (from a MS in the Library of the Propaganda Fide in Rome), with the cues all filled in, and a part of these two books is published in Syriac in the *Breviarium Chaldaicum*. The Psalms are said (at least in theory) all through twice a week, and the whole Psalter is recited on festivals of our Lord. In the litanies, which are numerous, and one at least of which is said at almost every service, the ruling patriarch, metropolitan, and bishop of the diocese are commemorated by name. The marriage-service and the burial-service for laymen (*ʿanīdhā*) have been published in Syriac.[1] The burial-service for the clergy (*kūrastā*) is much longer and more elaborate than that for laymen. These burial-services are most dramatic, and consist partly of dialogues between the departed and the mourners, or between the departed and those already in Sheol. After the funeral the kiss of peace is given, at least in the case of priests and bishops. All pass in line and kiss the hand of the departed, or a cross laid on his breast, and so take leave of him.[2] Badger gives an English translation of the baptismal-, marriage-, and ordination-services, and of the burial-service for priests.[3]

9. Christians of Malabar, or of St. Thomas.—Ancient tradition, in which, however, we can have little confidence, makes St. Thomas the apostle the first teacher of Christianity in India. The legend is told in the Syriac *Acts of Judas Thomas* (see above, § 4), which, curiously enough, makes Thomas (lit. 'twin') the twin-brother of our Lord. J. R. Harris sees here traces of the influence of the Heavenly Twins on Christian legend.[4] The Ethiopic legend of St. Thomas[5] is still fuller. Our Lord divides the world into twelve portions, and Thomas's lot is to go to India. Very unwillingly, but encouraged by our Lord, he goes, guided by Peter and accompanied by Matthias. Jesus appears in the form of a rich man, who sells Thomas as a slave, the price to be given to the poor and needy. Peter and Matthias return. Thomas is set to work as a stonemason, carpenter, and physician; but he afterwards explains that the buildings which he undertook to build were the souls which he won to Christ. He appoints a bishop, priests, and deacons, and departs in a cloud, having been miraculously clothed again in the skin which had been flayed off him. According to another account,[6] he was pierced by soldiers' spears and died. The opposition is said to have been largely due to his preaching encratism,[7] and persuading wives to forsake their husbands. The *Acts of Judas Thomas* says that the relics of the apostle were transferred to Edessa (A.D. 232?). It has been suggested by some that the name 'Christians of St. Thomas' comes from another Thomas than the apostle. This later namesake, **Thomas Cannaneo**, is variously assigned to the 4th or the 9th century.[8] Another legend connects Pantænus of Alexandria (*c.* A.D. 200) with India, where, it says, the apostle Bartholomew had already preached.[9] Pantænus is said by these writers to have found there a copy, in the Hebrew language, of St. Matthew's Gospel, and to have left it behind him.

The first certain historical testimony to the existence of Christians in India is that of the Alexandrian merchant who afterwards became a monk, and whom we know from his Indian travels as **Cosmas Indicopleustes**. He travelled far, and his *Christian Topography of the Whole World* in twelve books, still extant, is a valuable historical piece of evidence, though it is marred by the erroneous geographical conceptions of the day. The first six books may be dated *c.* A.D. 547, the rest *c.* 560. Cosmas's other works are not now extant. He travelled in India and Ceylon, and describes 'Mali' (identified with Malabar) on the Indian coast, the centre of the pepper trade. He

1 See art. ABRENUNTIO.
2 Connolly, *Liturgical Homilies of Narsai*, p. 37.
3 See art. HYMNS (Syriac Christian), § 4.

1 See under Literature at end of this article.
2 Maclean-Browne, p. 287.
3 *Nestorians and their Rituals*, ii. 195 ff.
4 *The Dioscuri in the Christian Legends*, London, 1903, p. 20 ff.
5 E. A. W. Budge, *Contendings of the Apostles*, London, 1901, Eng. tr., ii. 319 ff., Ethiopic text in vol. i.
6 *Ib.* ii. 353.
7 See art. ENCRATITES.
8 Howard, *The Christians of St. Thomas and their Liturgies*, p. 15 f.
9 Eusebius, *HE* v. 10; Jerome, *de Vir. illustr.* 36.

testifies to a large number of Christian churches on the coast of India and in Ceylon and Socotra, whose clergy, he says, were ordained by the Persian archbishop of Seleucia, and were subject to his jurisdiction; the Church there had had many martyrs and a large number of monks. Thus we may gather that the 'Christians of St. Thomas' are the fruits of the missionary activities of the Church of the Persian empire (see above, § 8), and that their Christianity had begun long before Cosmas's time, probably in the 4th century.

The subsequent history is somewhat obscure. Immigrations of Christians to Malabar from Baghdād and elsewhere occurred twice in the 8th and 9th centuries, and the immigrants intermarried with the native Christians. The later of these movements was under two Nestorian priests (bishops?), **Mar Sapor** and **Mar Peruz**. The fame of the Malabar Christianity spread to the West, and King Alfred of England sent ambassadors to that country.[1] The converts were protected by the king of Cochin. They had their bishop at Angamala, and he was styled 'Metropolitan of India,' having in his jurisdiction 1400 churches and 200,000 souls in the whole district.[2]

A theory has lately been put forward by P. T. Geevergese, a native Malabar Syrian, in a tract entitled *Were the Syrian Christians Nestorians?*, to the effect that the Malabarese were Jacobites till the 15th cent., when they became Nestorians for a hundred years. It is agreed that their Church was originally founded from Seleucia-Ctesiphon, and that they were under the Catholicos of the East in the pre-Nestorian period; but this writer maintains that thereafter they depended on the Jacobites, not on the Nestorians. The only argument of any importance adduced in favour of this theory is the existence of two inscriptions at Kottayam, a town of Travancore, in Pahlavi, the official language of the Persian empire during the Sasanian dynasty; they are said to be of the 7th or 8th century. One of the inscriptions has a line also in Syriac, in Estrangéla characters, perhaps of the 10th century. The two run thus: (*a*) 'In punishment by the cross (was) the suffering of this One, He who is the true Christ, and God above, and Guide ever pure'; (*b*) ['Let me not glory save in the cross of our Lord Jesus Christ] who is the true Messiah and God above and Holy Ghost.' The words in square brackets are in Syriac. Geevergese amends 'Holy Ghost' to 'Guide ever pure' as in the former inscription. These are said to be anti-Nestorian. But is this the case? The 'Nestorians' of the Persian empire never failed to assert that He who died upon the cross was God. The existence in Malabar of an old Jacobite Bible of the 12th cent. or earlier proves nothing in the absence of evidence as to when it was brought there. The suggestion that the Portuguese inquisitors found some liturgical practices existing which showed traces of Jacobite rather than Nestorian influence, though *ex hypothesi* the latter had been predominant for over a hundred years, will hardly bear examination. Thus the inquisitors mention a liturgy 'of Diodorus' as being in use. There is no such known Nestorian liturgy. Therefore, it is maintained, the liturgy in use was non-Nestorian, *i.e.* Jacobite. It would indeed have been remarkable if the Jacobites had named one of their liturgies after the real father of Nestorianism. Renaudot[3] supposes that 'Diodorus' is here a mistake for 'Theodorus,' but, as the Synod of Diamper mentions both Diodore and Theodore, this is very unlikely.[4] Geevergese agrees that the Nestorians of the Tigris valley at the end of the 15th cent. and the beginning of the 16th sent bishops to Malabar, on the request of deputies who had come thence, and he maintains that these converted Malabar from Jacobitism to Nestorianism. It does not appear to the present writer that Geevergese has proved his theory; but there is possibly this amount of truth in it, that certain of the Malabarese Christians, who have unfortunately always been conspicuous for quarrelsomeness (like their spiritual ancestors), may have had dealings with the dissentient Jacobites of the Tigris valley, or with the Western Jacobites, before the 15th century. Thus a deputation is said to have gone to the Monophysites of Alexandria to ask for a bishop for 'India' (Malabar?), A.D. 695.[5]

An ecclesiastical revolution was effected by the Portuguese in the 16th century. They established the Inquisition at Goa in 1560. The Synod of Diamper, in the south of Cochin, held in 1599 under **Alexius de Menezes**, archbishop of Goa, united the Malabarese, then estimated at about 200,000 souls,[6] to Rome, and rooted out all traces of Nestorianism. Celibacy of the clergy was enforced, and made retrospective. All old books

[1] Howard, p. 21. [2] Gibbon, vi. 51. [3] ii. 569.
[4] Brightman, *Liturgies Eastern and Western*, i. p. lxxx.
[5] Neale, *Patriarchate of Alexandria*, ii. 88.
[6] Howard, p. 23.

and liturgies were destroyed, or radically altered, so that probably there does not now exist a single complete copy of the liturgies as used before the synod. Renaudot remarks[1] that the Portuguese censors incautiously condemned things which had nothing to do with Nestorianism. The liturgy which they found to be principally used was closely related to, or practically the same as, the Nestorian 'Addai and Mari' (see above, § 8). An English translation of this[2] is published by J. M. Neale,[3] who says[4] that it is given as revised by Menezes and the Synod of Diamper. Yet this cannot be altogether the case, as it contains the names of Nestorius, Diodore, and Theodore, as well as of Ephraim, Abraham, and Narsai (see above, § 8), and the phrase 'Mother of Christ' for 'Mother of God' (see below). Neale gives some of the prayers in what was probably the original order, but indicates by numbers the order in the form approved at Diamper.

The change from ancient customs was effected only after great opposition on the part of the Malabarese themselves, who rallied under their bishop, **Mar Abraham** († 1597). It was his death that made the Synod of Diamper and the real union with Rome possible.[5]

It is interesting to notice the changes of custom and of liturgy effected at Diamper. Up to this time the Malabar Christians had had but a single bishop at a time; hence, perhaps, arose the custom for the chrism at confirmation to be consecrated by a priest (*catanar*) rather than, as elsewhere in the East, by a bishop; indeed, the Malabarese were accused of not having had confirmation at all,[6] though this is clearly a mistake. The chief changes in the eucharistic liturgy made at Diamper were the following. The pope's name was substituted for that of the patriarch of Babylon. For the names of Nestorius, Diodore, Theodore, and other 'Nestorian' fathers, those of Cyril (of Alexandria) and others were substituted. The phrase 'Mother of God' replaced 'Mother of Christ.' Where, before the consecration, the words 'the body,' 'the blood,' occurred (as often in Eastern liturgies by anticipation), the words 'bread,' 'wine,' were substituted. In the 'Nicene' creed the phrases 'God of God, Light of light, very God of very God,' which were said to have been wanting in the Malabar form, were inserted; probably what is meant is that the first two of these phrases were wanting in Malabar, as they do not occur in the Nestorian creed (see above, § 3). The phrase 'consubstantial with the Father' was substituted for 'Son of the essence of the Father,' the usual equivalent in Syriac (Neale unfortunately does not give the text of the creed in his Malabar liturgy). The host was ordered to be elevated at the consecration. But the chief change was a reversal of prevalent Oriental conceptions of liturgy. The epiclesis, or invocation of the Holy Ghost, was moved from its place after the narrative of the Last Supper and placed before it,[7] the wording being altered so as to make the epiclesis refer only to a good reception of the sacrament. For these changes see Howard, p. 40; but two of his statements appear to be doubtful. The Portuguese censors probably found no narrative of our Lord's words at all, as they were working on 'Addai and Mari' (see above, § 8); they probably therefore inserted them from one of the other anaphoras, though not in the place where

[1] ii. 565.
[2] From the Latin of J. F. Raulin's *Hist. eccl. Malabaricæ*.
[3] *Liturgies of St. Mark . . . and the Church of Malabar*, p. 128 ff.
[4] *Ib.* p. xvi. [5] Howard, p. 26. [6] *Ib.* p. 38.
[7] For a double invocation in the Egyptian rite, one before and one after the narrative of the Last Supper, see art. INVOCATION (Liturgical), § 6.

they are found in those anaphoras, but in the place which they thought most suitable. The other statement, that the Portuguese altered the wording of the epiclesis, is also doubtful, for, as Neale gives it,[1] it agrees exactly with the epiclesis of 'Addai and Mari,' which, as we have seen, is of a somewhat early type, throwing most of the emphasis on the effects and purpose of the consecration, for the benefit of the communicants, rather than on the change effected in the bread and wine. The history of the changes at Diamper fully justifies Renaudot's dictum quoted above, and shows that the Portuguese censors were quite ignorant of liturgical science.

The Portuguese changed the episcopal see from Angamala to Cranganor on the coast, so that it might be more accessible to them, and that they might have a greater hold on the native Church. But during the whole time of their rule in India they aroused constant opposition from the Malabarese, whom the terrors of the Inquisition were never able entirely to subdue.

In 1663, after more than 60 years of Portuguese rule, the Malabarese were enabled by the Dutch conquests in India once more to assert their independence, induced thereto by the murder of Theodore, a bishop sent from 'Babylon.' The Dutch expelled the Jesuits from Malabar soon after 1663. But the Malabarese were not united among themselves, and about half remained in obedience to the Roman see, while the rest became independent of it. These last gladly accepted **Gregorius,** Monophysite bishop of Jerusalem, who came from the Jacobite patriarch at Mardin in 1665. Gregorius consecrated **Thomas** as metropolitan, and since then the Malabarese have been in the main Jacobite. This change of front appears remarkable at first sight. Yet we must remember that in their origin neither the Malabar Church nor her mother, the East Syrian Church, was Nestorian, for they both existed before Nestorianism was propounded. And, though many East Syrians were genuinely Nestorian, it is very doubtful if their Church was consistently and officially so; still less certain is it that the Malabarese were strongly imbued with that doctrine. Hence we can understand why they grasped at the first hand that was stretched out to help them in getting rid of the Western authority which was imposed on them, but under which they had never rested content.

In the year 1700 and afterwards Nestorian bishops were sent, but they only secured the allegiance of a minority. In the 19th cent. the history is one of constant litigation between rival parties. The Nestorians of Malabar, after many lawsuits, won recognition in the courts and part of the endowments. In the year 1850 they obtained a bishop from Mar Shimun, the Nestorian catholicos (see above, § 8). Later, another was sent, but he was murdered by robbers on the journey. In 1907 Mar Shimun consecrated Mar Timotheus (Abimelech), who now holds office.[2]

There are now perhaps 300,000 Syrian Christians, all told, in India; the majority are Jacobites, and have since the 17th cent. adopted the Jacobite liturgies and customs.[3] The metropolitan usually consecrates his own successor, from the family in which the archidiaconate has been hereditary. The archdeacon is called *ramban.* The eucharist is only rarely celebrated; the laity must communicate at least three times in the year,[4] but there are often eucharists without lay communicants. The churches are plain, consisting of nave

[1] *Liturgies*, p. 149 f.
[2] Heazell-Margoliouth, *Kurds and Christians*, p. 196.
[3] An account of these may be seen in Howard, p. 55 ff.
[4] Howard, p. 147.

and chancel without transepts.[1] There is one altar, the so-called 'side altars' being used only, as in the Nestorian churches, for holding a cross, or books, or the like. The altar itself is 4 ft. high by 6 ft. long and 3½ (or 4) ft. wide, sometimes of stone and sometimes of wood. It stands out from the east wall, as in the Jacobite churches of Mesopotamia, in contrast to the Nestorian altars. At the eucharist the altar is covered with a white cloth, and has a frontal. On it are placed a wooden cross (often with the figure of our Lord painted on the wood), two candlesticks, a book-stand, a slab of wood or marble for the chalice and paten to rest upon, a 'sponge' of silk for wiping the priest's fingers and for cleansing the chalice after the service, and three veils for the chalice and paten. The bread is leavened, and must be prepared on the day when it is used; each bread is round, and stamped with a cross. It is called variously *Qōrbānā* ('Oblation'), 'first-begotten,' 'the Seal,' 'the Body,' 'the Coal' (Is 6^6). These are common Syriac names elsewhere for the eucharistic bread. The naves of the churches have earthen floors; they have no furniture except two bells inside the church; a gallery is often placed at the west side of the nave. On the nave-side of the chancel arch there is a space railed off, not unlike the Nestorian *bema* (see above, § 8), but some 12 ft. wide as compared with a 3 ft. width of the *bema.* The churches sometimes have pictures;[2] this is probably a relic of Portuguese influence. There is always a veil at the chancel arch, which is drawn back at certain parts of the service. Externally the churches have little adornment; the west front has three storeys, and is whitewashed. The roof is high-pitched, that of the chancel being always higher than that of the nave. The vestments worn seem to be much the same as those of the Jacobites of Mesopotamia (see § 5), and are more elaborate than those of the Nestorians. At the eucharist the celebrant wears special shoes, whereas the Nestorians take their shoes off; also a black serge or coarse cotton robe (perhaps a sort of cassock), a white linen albe, a stole in one piece with an opening for the head, girdle, maniples, chasuble (or cope) of silk damask, and cap.[3] At ordination the clergy receive the tonsure,[4] as do the Nestorians, the latter, however, only cutting off some of the ordinand's hair in the form of a cross. As in the worship of all Syrian Christians, much incense is used at the eucharist and other services.

In some externals, especially in the matter of vestments, the Nestorian Malabarese seem to have assimilated their customs to those of their Jacobite neighbours.

10. Modern missions. — Besides the Jesuit, Dominican, and Lazarist missions to the Uniat bodies mentioned in § 6, there have been during the last 80 years various missions to the Jacobites and Nestorians. The American Presbyterian and Congregational Boards of Missions have long had missionaries among them; the Archbishop of Canterbury's educational 'Assyrian Mission' has worked among the East Syrians since 1886; and later the Russian Church sent a mission to them. Similarly missionaries from the West have laboured among the Malabarese in India. To all these missions we are largely indebted for a knowledge of the people, and for the publication of the Bible in classical and vernacular Syriac, of patristic texts, and of other liturgical and educational works.

LITERATURE.—i. *GENERAL.*—J. S. Assemani, *Bibliotheca Orientalis*, 4 vols., Rome, 1719-28; J. M. Neale, *Hist. of the Holy Eastern Church*, pt. i., *General Introduction*, 2 vols.,

[1] Howard, p. 123 ff.
[2] *Ib.* p. 153.
[3] *Ib.* p. 132.
[4] *Ib.* p. 160.

London, 1850, *Patriarchate of Antioch*, do. 1873, a posthumous fragment; E. Gibbon, *Decline and Fall of the Roman Empire*, ed. W. Smith, do. 1862, vol. vi. ch. xlvii.; F. C. Burkitt, *Early Eastern Christianity* (the Syriac-speaking Church), do. 1904, *Early Christianity outside the Roman Empire*, Cambridge, 1899 (both for the early period).

ii. *THE JACOBITES* (for their doctrine see Literature given under art. MONOPHYSITISM).—J. W. Etheridge, *The Syrian Churches*, London, 1846; O. H. Parry, *Six Months in a Syrian Monastery*, do. 1895; J. M. Neale, *The Patriarchate of Alexandria*, 2 vols., do. 1847 (chiefly for the 'Jacobites' of Egypt, but this is scarcely a correct designation for the Egyptian Monophysites); C. J. Hefele, *A Hist. of the Councils of the Church*, Eng. tr., Edinburgh, 1872–96, iii. 449 ff.; Jacob of Edessa, *Letter to Thomas the Presbyter* (on the liturgy), the Syriac in Assemani, *Bibl. Or.* ii. 479 ff., English in Brightman, as below (vii.).

iii. *THE MARONITES* (for their former doctrine see Literature given under art. MONOTHELETISM).—J. W. Etheridge, as above (ii.); F. J. Bliss, in *PEFSt*, 1890, p. 74 ff., 1892, pp. 71 ff., 129 ff., 207 ff., 308 ff.

iv. *THE NESTORIANS* (for their doctrine see Literature given under art. NESTORIANISM).—J. Labourt, *Le Christianisme dans l'empire perse*, Paris, 1904; A. J. Maclean and W. H. Browne, *The Catholicos of the East and his People*, London, 1892; W. A. Wigram, *An Introd. to the Hist. of the Assyrian Church*, do. 1910; F. N. Heazell and Mrs. Margoliouth, *Kurds and Christians*, do. 1913; J. W. Etheridge, as above (ii.); G. P. Badger, *The Nestorians and their Rituals*, 2 vols., do. 1852; J. B. Chabot, *Synodicon orientale*, Paris, 1902; P. Bedjan, *Acta Martyrum et Sanctorum* (Syriac), do. 1892; R. H. Connolly, *The Liturgical Homilies of Narsai* (in English), Cambridge, 1909 (=*TS* viii. 1; illustrates the growth of the anaphoras); A. Mingana, *Homilies and Poems of Narsai* (in Syriac), Moṣul, 1905; E. A. W. Budge, *The Book of Governors: the Historia Monastica of Thomas of Marga* (Syriac and English), 2 vols., London, 1893.

v. *MALABAR CHRISTIANS.*—G. B. Howard, *The Christians of St. Thomas and their Liturgies*, Oxford, 1864; G. M. Rae, *The Syrian Church in India*, Edinburgh, 1892; J. F. Raulin, *Historia ecclesiæ Malabaricæ*, Rome, 1745; P. T. Geevergese, *Were the Syrian Christians Nestorians?*, Madras, n.d.

vi. *VERNACULAR SYRIAC DIALECTS.*—M. Parisot, 'Le Dialecte de Ma'lula,' in *JA* xi. [1898], xii. [1898]; P. J. Bliss, as above (iii.) (Ma'lula); A. J. Maclean, *Grammar of the Dialects of Vernacular Syriac*, Cambridge, 1895 (East Syrians, Jews of Azarbaijan, etc.), and *Dictionary of the Dialects of Vernacular Syriac*, Oxford, 1901 (the same, and Ṭur 'Abhdin, etc.); T. Nöldeke, *Grammatik der neusyrischen Sprache*, Leipzig, 1868 (East Syrians); I. Rosenberg, *Lehrbuch der neusyrischen Schrift- und Umgangssprache*, Vienna, 1901; E. Sachau, *Skizze des Fellichi-Dialekts von Moṣul*, Berlin, 1895; A. Socin, *Die neu-aramäischen Dialekte von Urmia bis Moṣul*, Tübingen, 1882; M. Lidzbarski, *Die neu-aramäischen Handschriften*, Weimar, 1896; D. J. Stoddard, *Modern Syriac Grammar* (American Oriental Society, vol. v., 1856), published separately, London, 1855; R. Payne Smith, *Thesaurus Syriacus*, 2 vols., Oxford, 1870–1901. The Bible in the Urmi dialect has been published by the American Bible Society, New York, 1893 (earlier edd. at Urmi), and many books in the same dialect have been published at Urmi by the various Mission presses there.

vii. *LITURGICAL BOOKS USED BY SYRIAN CHRISTIANS.*—(*a*) *Translations.*—F. E. Brightman, *Liturgies Eastern and Western*, i., Oxford, 1896 (has Eng. trr. of 'Syriac St. James' [West Syrian] and 'Addai and Mari' [East Syrian], and a Latin translation of an East Syrian liturgy in fragments first published by G. Bickell); J. P. Margoliouth, *Liturgy of . . . Addai and Mari* (with two other East Syrian liturgies and the baptismal service), London, 1893; E. Renaudot, *Liturgiarum Orientalium Collectio*², 2 vols., Frankfort-on-Main and London, 1847, vol. ii. (Latin tr. of several Syriac liturgies, Eastern and Western); A. J. Maclean, *East Syrian Daily Offices*, London, 1894 (Eng. tr.) and *East Syrian Epiphany Rites* (Eng. tr. in one volume, with F. C. Conybeare's *Rituale Armenorum*), Oxford, 1905; G. P. Badger, as above (iv.) (Eng. tr. of East Syrian liturgies, etc.); G. B. Howard, as above (v.) (Jacobite Malabar liturgies); H. Denzinger, *Ritus Orientalium*, 2 vols., Wurzburg, 1863–64 (baptismal-, marriage-, and ordination-services of the minor Eastern Churches, etc.; Lat. tr.); J. M. Neale, *The Liturgies of St. Mark . . . and the Church of Malabar*, London, 1859 (Eng. tr. of the Malabar Nestorian liturgy). (*b*) *Syriac texts.*—For the Nestorians the Archbishop of Canterbury's Assyrian Mission has published from the old MSS: *Ṭākhsā* (the three anaphoras, baptismal-service, etc.), London, 1890; *Qdhām ū-Wāthar* (Daily Offices), do. 1892; *Liturgical Psalter*, do. 1891; *Lectionary Tables*, do. 1889; *Sūrgādhā* (calendar tables), do. 1894; *Būrākhā* (marriage-service), do. 1892; *'Anīdhā* (burial-service for laymen), do. 1900; *Bā'ūthā* (service for the Rogation of the Ninevites), do. pt. i., 1894, pt. ii., 1902. For the Uniat Chaldæans the Lazarists have published similar works adapted to that community, especially *Liber psalmorum, Horarum Diurnarum, Ordinis Officii Divini et Homiliarum Rogationum*, Paris, 1886; *Breviarium Chaldaicum*, do. 1886; older is the *Missale Chaldaicum*, Rome, 1767 ('Addai and Mari' only). For the Uniat Malabarese see *Ordo Chaldaicus . . . juxta ritum ecclesiæ Malabaricæ*, Rome, 1775 and 1844. For the Jacobites no Syriac text of St. James appears to have been published (Brightman, i. p. lvi), but for the Syrian Uniats see *Missale Syriacum*, Rome, 1843, and *The Book of the Clerks* (in Syriac), Beirut, 1888. For the Maronites see *Missale Chaldaicum juxta ritum . . . Maronitarum*, Rome, 1592 and 1716, Qozhayya, 1816, 1838, and 1855, Beirut, 1888; *Liber ministri missæ*, Rome, 1596 and 1715; *Diaconale Syriacum*, do. 1736. An old but general collection of texts and Latin translations is J. A. Assemani's *Codex Liturgicus Ecclesiæ Universæ*, Rome, 13 vols., 1749–66 (eucharistic liturgies, baptismal offices, ordination-services, etc.). For a fuller bibliography of Syriac liturgies see Brightman, as above (Introduction).

viii. For *SYRIAC TEXTS* of early works by Syrian Christians see W. Wright, *Short Hist. of Syriac Literature*, London, 1894.

A. J. MACLEAN.

T

TABERNACLES.—See FESTIVALS AND FASTS (Hebrew).

TABU.—The word 'tabu' is properly an adjective and appears to mean literally 'marked off' (perhaps from Polynesian *ta*, 'mark,' *pu*, 'exceedingly'). Applying equally to persons and things, it signifies that casual contact with them is forbidden as being fraught with mystic danger. Custom enjoins a negative or precautionary attitude towards them because of the supernatural influence with which they are temporarily or permanently charged. In short, they are 'not to be lightly approached,' and that always for some magico-religious reason. The term is native to the Pacific region, but has been adopted, with some modification of meaning, to designate a fundamental category of comparative religion. Thus, as in regard to the cognate term *mana* (*q.v.*), it is advisable to distinguish the local from the generalized sense.

1. Local meaning of tabu.—(*a*) *Cook's discovery of tabu.*—'Taboo,' used indifferently as adjective, noun, or verb, was introduced into English by Captain Cook. He first met with the word, in 1777, at Tonga.[1] Hence, by the way, the popularization of the Tongan form *tabu*, *tapu* being usual elsewhere in Polynesia, with *kapu* in the Hawaiian group; though in Melanesia *tabu* again occurs, as also *tambu*. When Cook later on discovered the Sandwich Islands, he found the institution of tabu prevailing there with even more rigour than at Tonga, whereas it seemed to him to have been less strictly observed in the Society Islands, except as regards the tabu resulting from contact with the dead.[1] He gives a clear and consistent account of the notion involved, stating that tabu 'has a very comprehensive meaning, but in general signifies that a thing is forbidden,' being 'applied to all cases where things are not to be touched.' He also emphasizes its 'mysterious significance' and duly notes the 'mixture of religion' in a certain ceremony concerning which 'we seldom got any other answer to our inquiries but *taboo*.'[2] Moreover, he makes it clear that religion herein made common cause with law and government. In reference to the same ceremony, he says: 'When we returned to the king, he desired me to order the boat's crew not to stir from the boat; for, as every thing would, very soon, be *taboo*, if any of our people, or if their own, should be

[1] See J. Cook and J. King, *A Voyage to the Pacific Ocean, 1776–80*, London, 1784, i. 286, and *passim*.

[1] *A Voyage to the Pacific Ocean, 1776–80*, ii. 249.
[2] *Ib.* i. 286, 350, ii. 40.

found walking about, they would be knocked down with clubs, nay, *mateed*, that is, killed.'[1]

Indeed, Captain King (who carries on the story after Cook's death) is perplexed to decide how far the 'implicit and scrupulous obedience' of the natives in regard to the prohibitions laid upon them—as when Karakakooa Bay was tabued, at the request of the navigators, while the remains of Captain Cook were being committed to the deep—was due to some 'religious principle' and how far to 'the civil authority of their chiefs.'[2] The whole account, however, makes it clear that king, chiefs, priests, and the gods themselves, formed one undivided theocracy, whereof tabu constituted the chief instrument, at once spiritual and temporal in its nature and effects. More especially, it ensured a complete control of the economic situation. Thus at Tonga the special officer who 'presided over the *taboo*' was a veritable food-controller:

He and his deputies inspected all the produce of the island; taking care that every man should cultivate and plant his quota; and ordering what should be eat, and what not. By this wise regulation, they effectually guard against a famine; a sufficient quantity of ground is employed in raising provisions; and every article, thus raised, is secured from unnecessary waste.'[3]

For the rest, tabu was the corner-stone of the class-system, ensuring the subjection of women to men, of the lower orders to the chiefs, and of all to the king, whose very name was tabu on penalty of death.[4]

(*b*) *Primary connexion of Oceanic tabu with a theocratic system.*—Here, then, in this alliance of the religious with the civil forms of authority, we have the distinctive mark of tabu as understood in its local sense. R. Taylor's definition of it, as 'a religious observance established for political purposes,'[5] hits off what is at any rate its leading aspect in Oceania. In the Polynesian islands a class of chiefs with a social influence proportionate to their *mana*, or supernatural power, was everywhere recognized; and in the Eastern groups at any rate there were supreme potentates who might fairly be termed kings, though sometimes, as at Tonga in Mariner's day, the religious head of the community might be said to reign while the war-chief, his inferior in the hierarchy, actually governed.[6] On the other hand, no chieftainship proper is to be found in Melanesia. Here, however, the secret societies exercise a tumultuous, but none the less forcible, control over affairs by means of tabu; while, conversely, 'in cases where the English word taboo can be employed there is always in Melanesia human sanction and prohibition.'[7] Thus there is every reason to suppose that throughout the Pacific we have to do with customs belonging to a single type. This view is supported by the remarkable fact that, despite the diversity of tongues obtaining in this wide area, the word tabu in one of its dialectical forms, as well as the complementary term *mana*, is in general use. But, if the nature and name of the institution are uniform, so presumably will be its origin. On the strength of this argument, W. H. R. Rivers has recently tried to show that tabu in its Oceanic distribution stands everywhere alike for the prestige acquired and the authority exercised by an immigrant folk—his so-called '*kava* people'—in its dealings with an indigenous population of markedly inferior culture.[8] It is interesting to speculate how a system of tabus may have developed on the spot under stress of such

[1] *A Voyage to the Pacific Ocean, 1776–80*, i. 338.
[2] *Ib.* iii. 163. [3] *Ib.* i. 411. [4] *Ib.* ii. 170.
[5] *Te Ika a Maui*, London, 1855, p. 55.
[6] Cf. W. Mariner, *An Account of the Natives of the Tonga Islands*, ed. J. Martin, London, 1817, ii. 87.
[7] R. H. Codrington, *The Melanesians*, Oxford, 1891, p. 215.
[8] Cf. Rivers, *The Hist. of Melanesian Society*, Cambridge, 1914, pp. 239, 252, 384, 409, 485.

culture-contact—how, for instance, barbarians, already worshipping gods and respecting private property, might come to impose their will on magic-haunted communistic savages, for whom threats rather than reasons must be provided as the grounds of obedience. On the other hand, if the immigrants came from Indonesia, as the theory assumes, it is also possible that they brought some form of the custom with them ready-made, since the Indonesian *pomali* is 'exactly equivalent to the "taboo" of the Pacific islanders.'

Thus in Timor 'the custom of "tabu" called here "pomáli," is very general, fruit trees, houses, crops, and property of all kinds being protected from depredation by this ceremony, the reverence for which is very great. A palm branch stuck across an open door, showing that the house is tabooed, is a more effectual guard against robbery than any amount of locks and bars.'[1]

This mode of indicating a tabu is similar to the Oceanic. Thus, when Cook wished to set up his observatory in the Sandwich Islands, the priests tabued the place for him by setting up wands;[2] and the *soloi*, or tabu-marks, of the Banks group in Melanesia usually consist of the leaves of some plant.[3] It may well be, then, that the property-mark, with its implication of a transferable curse, came into Oceania along with the notion of private ownership. It certainly was most effective in protecting property—far more so than the guns which the early mariners discharged at the thievish islanders with a like object in view.

(*c*) *Secondary developments of tabu in Oceania.*—It remains to note that, whereas the essence of tabu in its local signification consists, as has been shown, in a theocratic form of government, which in its turn may have developed by way of an apotheosis of landlordism, the ramifications of the notion are endless and cover the whole religion of Oceania, at any rate so far as it is taken in its negative aspect, namely as a system of scruples. The theocracy could consecrate a site, or devote a victim, or appropriate a house or canoe, or betroth a woman, or proclaim a rest-day for men or a close-time for game, all these being cases of the communication of tabu by a ritual act of imposition, such as could at will be neutralized by a ceremonial removal.[4] On the other hand, many tabus were inherent rather than acquired, such as those associated permanently with women, strangers, the sick, and the dead, or for the time being with the woman in child-birth or the warrior on a campaign. The world-wide distribution of similar beliefs concerning an infectious impurity makes it extremely improbable that they can be referred in the mass to an immigrant culture or treated as mere reasons of state, the by-products of the administrative scheme. At most we may say that, in so far as the direction of affairs was centralized and deliberate, they were incorporated in the political machine and to a like extent became subject to manipulation. Thus, at Hawaii in 1819, King Rihoriho at one stroke abrogated the laws of the tabu; though only, let us note, to make way for *la tabu*, the British Sunday.[5] So much, then, for the local or Oceanic sense of tabu with its special connotation of a theocratic system of controls, a more or less consciously organized body of sanctions backed by the joint authority of Church and State.

2. Scientific meaning of tabu.—(*a*) *Tabu as an aspect of rudimentary religion.*—For the purposes of the science of comparative religion it is convenient to drop the implication of a human sanction and to insist solely on the supernatural

[1] A. R. Wallace, *The Malay Archipelago*², London, 1869, i. 196, ii. 450.
[2] Cook-King, iii. 10, 36. [3] Rivers, i. 92.
[4] Cf. Taylor, pp. 78, 91.
[5] W. Ellis, *Narrative of a Tour through Hawaii*, London, 1826, pp. 15, 52, 95.

or mystic aspect of the penalties in store for the tabu-breaker. In this way it is possible to bring together under one head a large variety of avoidances characteristic of the less advanced peoples, of whom it may broadly be said that they have no king but custom. Just as their response to traditional rules is largely automatic, so, correspondingly, the rule itself has imputed to it a no less automatic power of self-maintenance and self-vindication. Indeed, so necessary is it for general purposes to lay stress on the immanence of the sanction normally attributed to a tabu that it is safer to deny the name altogether to prohibitions deriving their force mediately from a god or his earthly representative and to distinguish these as religious interdicts or bans. Tabu, in short, is to be understood as meaning 'unlucky to meddle with' rather than forbidden by edict human or divine. It belongs to what may be termed the perceptual (Lévy-Bruhl would say 'prelogical') stage of religion, when values are massively apprehended without analysis of their grounds. At this stage emotion of the collective or mobbish order is paramount as regards both the excitatory and the inhibitive processes that govern the social life. Now of all the emotions fear is inhibitor-in-chief, having in virtue of its haunting quality a special power of sustained control. A primary source of fear is the unfamiliar or strange as such; and this kind of fear in varying degree is always present as an element in that complex emotion of awe or reverence which is the root of religion. Tabu, then, stands for the whole mass of such fear-inspired inhibitions in so far as they proceed directly from the religious emotion, as it regulates the social tradition in the relative abeyance of reasoned direction. Here we have at any rate the psychological clue to a vast variety of customary abstinences—'negative rites,' as they may be called—of which the particular conditions are a matter for historical treatment in detail.

(*b*) *Tabu and the notion of contagion.*—It may next be noted that emotions are infectious. It is, indeed, the leading principle of mob-psychology that emotions are propagated more readily than ideas, their external manifestations lending themselves to unintelligent imitation. Moreover, fear is, perhaps, the most infectious of all. Hence the fear-inhibition embodied in tabu always implies an infectious unluckiness—a transferable curse on meddlers. As A. van Gennep in his analysis of the *fady* (=*tabu*) of Madagascar shows, the institution rests on two notions, one being that of *tohina*, 'contagion.'[1] 'Everything,' says Jevons, 'which comes in contact with a tabooed person or thing becomes itself as dangerous as the original object, becomes a fresh centre of infection, a fresh source of danger to the community.'[2]

Jevons goes on to discriminate between 'things taboo,' the primary sources of such contagion, and 'things tabooed,' in which the tabu-infection is not inherent but derivative.[3] 'A single thing taboo might infect the whole universe,' as he says with pardonable exaggeration;[4] but in practice the transmissible fear is strictly limited in its possible effects, being confined to certain channels prescribed by convention. Meanwhile it is not always easy to draw the line between the two classes. The clearest cases of 'things tabooed' are those in which, as in Oceania, a divine chief tabus something hitherto common, or *noa*—say, a hunting-ground—and then after a time restores it to ordinary use. But, when Jevons accepts at its face-value the Polynesian explanation that the tabu on the sick is due to the fact that they are possessed by an *atua*, or spirit, and therefore pronounces them 'tabooed but . . . not taboo,'[1] it is at least arguable that a 'pre-animistic' basis must be sought for the belief; for what more perceptibly contagious than certain (and those precisely the stranger and more alarming) forms of disease? It is surely no mere superstition to suppose that sickness—nay, as it were, death itself—is 'catching.' On the other hand, it is hardly profitable, in deference to the theory that the emotions of man afford the best criterion of his instincts, to regard 'things taboo' as so many danger-signals to which mankind has an innate predisposition to attend. Tabus need rather to be studied in relation to their proximate conditions, which are not biological but historical. In other words, tabus are primarily matters of custom, forming part of the social inheritance, not of the individual heredity.

(*c*) *Tabu and the notion of supernatural power.*—The other notion on which the tabu of Madagascar rests, according to van Gennep,[2] is that of *hasina* =*mana*, or supernatural power. The person or thing is not to be trifled with, because liable to react with a force of unknown range and degree. There is a spiritual electricity that must be insulated lest it blast the unwary. Now, if religion were all fear, such *mana* would rank as wholly bad, since fear is a shrinking from evil. But other primary constituents of the religious mood make rather for interest, receptivity, approach, communion. For reckless self-assurance, indeed—for what the Greeks knew as ὕβρις—there is always 'the devil to pay.' But fear tempered with wonder and submissiveness, and thus transmuted into reverence, is the forerunner of love. So *mana* has its good side as well, though from the standpoint of tabu this helpfulness remains, so to say, in reserve, being a consummation that lies beyond the purview of the fear-inhibition as such. Meanwhile to an advanced theology that has clarified its concepts by the method of antithesis the savage apprehension of *mana* by way of tabu seems blurred and equivocal, an experience of something monstrous, half-devil and half-god. And that there is some such ambiguity in the value perceived cannot be denied. The sacred and the abominable, the pure and the obscene, the hallowed and the accursed pivot within the same perturbed awareness of the object. Nevertheless, rudimentary religion has gone a long way towards defining in practice, if not in theory, the good and the bad manifestations of the hidden power. Thus the novice at initiation or the warrior on a campaign is tabu that he may seek and find grace in the self-concentration that ensues after spiritual crisis overcome. On the other hand, the criminal is tabu because his very soul is attainted; wherefore, as the words of his doom, 'Sacer esto,' imply, he cannot touch water and fire lest he sully their purity with his foulness.

(*d*) *Tabu as a source of personal religion.*—At this point it may be observed that the institution of tabu is not only the main organ of social discipline at the lower levels of culture, but likewise the seed-bed of personal religion. The latter function hinges on the fact that to be tabu with respect to society is at the same time to be tabu in relation to oneself. The external signs of this self-regarding attitude of precaution are often ludicrous enough, as when a man cannot feed himself, or must scratch his head with a stick, or needs to snuff up the holiness that exudes from his fingers. But an inward-seeking view reveals a profit even in such practices. The *mana* to be conserved is just that part of a man that he feels to be most

1 *Tabou et totémisme à Madagascar*, p. 17.
2 F. B. Jevons, *An Introd. to the Hist. of Religion*, London, 1896, p. 61 f.; see the whole of ch. vi. for examples.
3 *Ib.* p. 69 f.
4 *Ib.* p. 69.

1 *An Introd. to the Hist. of Religion*, p. 70.
2 *Loc. cit.*

worth the saving—the will for power. Such power may be coveted for temporal ends. Savage shepherds of the people are not more disinterested than the rest of their kind. But at least it is proximately envisaged as a spiritual power. At least it is the sort of power that comes with and after self-abnegation and the exercise of humility. There is good evidence, too, that a sense of unworthiness consequent on the violation of his self-regarding tabus—as one might say, his 'vows' —is enough to cause voluntary resignation of office on the part of the primitive wonder-worker. There can be no doubt, then, that the experience both of the access of inspiration and of its withdrawal is often perfectly genuine; and, again, that the due safeguarding of such a gift is a lesson first acquired in the school of tabu. Further, not to lay exclusive stress on the ecstatic experience peculiar to the religious genius, the whole development of personality, so far as this comes about by way of reverie and reflexion, arises largely out of the tabu condition. No other such opportunity is afforded in the gregarious life of the savage tribesman for that self-communing whereby man eventually becomes master instead of slave of the sense-world. Self-respect, again, is nourished on privacy; the king or priest must keep his distance from the *profanum vulgus*, lest he make himself cheap not only in their eyes but also in his own.[1] For the rest, tabu stands for the etiquette of savage life, and by encouraging mutual consideration enables manners to ripen into morals, the end of which is freedom.

(*e*) *Danger of the over-development of tabu.*—Hitherto the fruitfulness, the educative value, of tabu as a factor in religion of the perceptual or rudimentary type has been chiefly signalized. After all, the inhibition of impulse affords the measure of human advance. But such inhibition may be overdone, with paralysis of the will to live as a consequence. Tabu as such represents negation, and a religion made up mostly of negations is necessarily sterile. Denial, even self-denial, cannot but be soul-destroying, if taken as an end in itself. Hence a meticulous scrupulosity is a mark of degraded religion. Nothing, *e.g.*, is so characteristic of the dairy-cult of the Todas as the web of tabus in which every action of the priest-dairyman is emmeshed, and Rivers not without good reason comments: 'The Todas seem to show us how the over-development of the ritual aspect of religion may lead to atrophy of the ideas and beliefs through which the religion has been built up.'[2]

Even a positive rite such as prayer may degenerate into formalism. Much more is this likely to happen with the negative rite or tabu, wherein the nature of the spiritual activity subserved is less immediately manifest. In the last stage of such decay—and in this also the case of the Todas is instructive[3]—the scrupulosity itself tends to become a sham, an organized hypocrisy of evasions. The function of ritual in religion is to relieve attention in regard to things indifferent, and of negative ritual to do so in regard to things actually disturbing—all this in order to set attention free for active converse with the divine. It is true that there is in many forms of religious experience —and they are perhaps especially to the fore in rudimentary religion—a characteristic prelude of apparent inaction, a spell of listening, as it were; and, so far as the tabu condition corresponds to this halt on the threshold, it is apt to seem barren of results when it is not. To judge fairly in each case, we must watch the ritual drama as a whole to see whether the passivity induced is of the pregnant order. As an incident in a 'rite of passage' to a higher plane of experience, the chrysalis stage of the soul is symptomatic of development. If, on the other hand, the will to win through be somehow asphyxiated on the way, negation has triumphed; too much safeguarding has destroyed; the husk has stifled the germinal process.

(*f*) *Methods of studying tabus in detail.*—This cursory sketch of tabu aims at no more than a generalized version of the institution as it bears on the earlier growth of the spirit of religion. A fuller treatment might be based on the study of the particular systems of tabu native to the various ethnic areas—as has here been attempted only in regard to the Pacific region—when many differences of detail and shades of local colour would doubtless come to light. In defence of the present method, however, it can be urged that to deal with tabus on the ethnological principle would well-nigh involve a survey of religions on the same distributive plan, since every savage people has a religion and every savage religion has its tabus. Nay more, savage religion tends to be co-extensive with the social life itself; so that a regular panorama of cultures may seem to be the logical outcome of such a method. Another way of dividing up the subject (but one again that must inevitably lead too far afield) would be that of distinguishing certain main departments of activity typical of primitive society as a whole and showing how each is conditioned by its own set of special tabus. The food-interest, *e.g.*, is engirdled by one vast network of ritual controls, the sex-interest by another. Indeed, the critical stages of every vital process are hung about with such customary danger-signals. Sometimes these traditional fears can be shown to correspond to facts; more often they appear arbitrary, sheer aberrations of fancy, due to false analogy or what not, that have been incorporated in the tribal lore by a historical chance. Thus, however detailed our study of tabus, we are not likely to arrive at the explanation of minor features. For these reasons it has seemed preferable here simply to enlarge on the general principle that, at the primitive level, the object of religious belief or worship is always tabu, just as it is always *mana* as well; and that, moreover, tabu forms the hither aspect of the religious experience, inasmuch as fruition is reached through fear.

(*g*) *Tabu from the standpoint of civilization.*—Tabu being properly an institution of savagery, it would hardly be in point to consider at length its ulterior consequences for civilization—as apart from its survivals in folk-lore, which indeed are numerous. But a word about such after-effects may be added by way of conclusion. We must not look for them solely within the sphere of religion as it is now. With the gradual substitution of a rational for an emotional system of controls, there has come about a decentralization of authority whereby disciplines once merged in an all-pervasive religious sanction have been invested with quasi-independent functions. Politics to-day deals with the divine right of kings, law with the sacredness of property, morals with the virtues of temperance and chastity, and so forth. In all such cases the tendency is to refuse any validity to the old-world sentiment of tabu. Reason prefers to rest its case on grounds of so-called common sense. At most the immediacy and seeming unconditionality of the tabu-feeling might enlist the sympathies of certain schools of ethical thought. As for modern religion, while it hesitates to adopt a rationalist outlook, it is naturally anxious to purge its traditional rites of the mildew of ancient superstition. On all sides, however, so far as the influence of a philosophy of man makes

[1] Cf. *kapukapu*, 'to put on airs of distance or separation from others,' with *mamana*, 'to respect oneself,' in E. Tregear, *The Maori-Polynesian Comparative Dictionary*, Wellington, N.Z., 1891, pp. 203, 473.

[2] *The Todas*, London, 1906, p. 455.

[3] *Ib.*

itself felt, there is of late manifested a deeper interest in the emotional life, more especially as it relates to conduct. Alike in social psychology with its study of the crowd and in individual psychology with its doctrine of the subconscious the conviction is growing that society and mind alike are controlled from below, as it were, as well as from above—that reason is at best a constitutional ruler whose authority rests not on force but on consent. It may be, then, that, examined from this point of view, the primitive institution of tabu will be found to embody elemental principles of order that to-day are as active as ever beneath the surface of a changed custom. Experience, which is experiment, has doubtless taught us to reject many a freakish usage dear to the old order; but this experience, which in its most critical form is science, bids us seek beneath the accidents of history for those essential laws whereby our racial sense of direction is continuously maintained.

LITERATURE.—(i.) For tabu in Oceania see the works cited above, early authorities such as Cook and Mariner being especially enlightening, since the original social system has long been gone, at any rate in Polynesia; compare also Th. Waitz and G. Gerland, *Anthropologie der Naturvölker*, Leipzig, 1859–72, vi.; W. Ellis, *Polynesian Researches*, London, 1831, iv.; G. Turner, *Samoa a Hundred Years Ago and Long Before*, do. 1884; *Old New Zealand*, by a Pakeha Maori, do. 1884; since the same cultural influences presumably extend to Indonesia and the Malay region (including Madagascar), see also W. W. Skeat, *Malay Magic*, do. 1900. A. van Gennep, *Tabou et totémisme à Madagascar*, Paris, 1904, brings the local into relation with a general interpretation.

(ii.) For a world-wide review of the facts about tabu see J. G. Frazer, *The Golden Bough*[3], 12 vols., London, 1911–15, esp. vol. iii., *Taboo and the Perils of the Soul*, and for his general theory vol. i., *The Magic Art*, i. 111 ff., also *Psyche's Task*[2], do. 1913. The subject being germane to any systematic account of primitive religion, it is hard to draw up a short list of authorities, but the following, in addition to those already quoted in the text, will be found useful: W. Robertson Smith, *Lectures on the Religion of the Semites*[2], London, 1894; E. Crawley, *The Mystic Rose*, do. 1902; E. Durkheim, *Les Formes élémentaires de la vie religieuse*, Paris, 1912, esp. p. 427 f.; and, on special aspects of tabu, Crawley, *FL* vi. [1895] 130 ff.; E. Westermarck, *Marriage Ceremonies in Morocco*, London, 1914; H. Webster, *Rest Days: a Study in Early Law and Morality*, New York, 1916. For a psychological study of tabu see R. R. Marett, *The Threshold of Religion*[2], London, 1914; E. S. Ames, *The Psychology of Religious Experience*, do. 1910.

R. R. MARETT.

TAHITIANS.—See POLYNESIA.

TALISMAN.—See CHARMS AND AMULETS.

TALMUD.—Two great works are known under the title 'Talmud'—a word (תַּלְמוּד) which denotes primarily 'teaching' and secondarily 'learning.' The two works are the Palestinian and Babylonian recensions, both of which are, in form, commentaries on the text of the Mishnāh (מִשְׁנָה). The Mishnāh ('repetition,' hence oral teaching by repeated recitation) was completed about A.D. 200. The Talmud consists of the Mishnāh with the Gemara (גְּמָרָא). It represents the scholastic activities of the Jewish Rabbis from the beginning of the 3rd to the close of the 5th century A.D.

The history of the compilation of the Talmud has been dealt with in many treatises and essays.[1] It is not the design of the present article to add to these or to reconsider the critical literary problems involved. Two practical questions will occupy us: (1) the attitude of the outside world to the Talmud,[2] and (2) the causes and nature of the permanent value of the Talmud within Judaism.

1. The Talmud in history.—The century which saw the completion of the Talmud also witnessed the beginning of interference with the normal circulation of the Rabbinical literature. In the year 553 the Emperor Justinian was called upon to arbitrate on a difference which arose between two sections of Jewry in the Byzantine realm. Whereas some were desirous of publicly reading the Scriptures both in Greek and in Hebrew, others wished to use the Hebrew only. Justinian[1] ordered the præfect Areobindus to promulgate the imperial decision in favour of the use of Greek (the Synagogue might use Aquila if it preferred it to the Septuagint), or of other vernacular tongues such as Latin in the Italian provinces. The emperor, moreover, forbade any attempt on the part of the heads of the schools or elders to prevent the use of the vernacular by devices or excommunication. Most significant of all was Justinian's interdiction of the practice of giving the Haggādic exposition (δευτέρωσις) after the reading of the Scripture. The opening words of the rescript explain Justinian's intention. The Jews, he suggested, should read their Scriptures with an eye to the hidden meaning and see in them a prophetic announcement of Christianity. Hence the emperor would naturally desire to curb the popularity of the Rabbinic exegesis, which of course would confirm the Jews in their refusal to admit Christological interpretations. Thus Justinian, who introduced drastic legislative enactments against the Jews, was also among the first to attempt interference with the free use and spread of their literature.[2]

We must here confine our attention to that phase of interference which concerns the Talmud. It was not till the 13th cent. that the attack assumed practical shape. Paris, in the year 1244, was the scene of the first public burning of copies of the Talmud. Before that date the Rabbinic doctrines had been assailed in the *de Insolentia Judæorum* of Agobard; but from the Paris incident onwards these assaults became far more frequent and dangerous. Nicholas Donin of La Rochelle had, while a Jew, been excommunicated by the Rabbi Yeḥiel of Paris because of his denial of the validity of the Rabbinic tradition. This occurred in 1225; he subsequently joined the Franciscans, and in 1239 he formally laid an accusation against the Talmud before Pope Gregory IX., who addressed bulls to many lands (including England) ordering the seizure of copies of the Talmud pending a public inquiry. In France the matter was seriously taken up. Charges of blasphemy, immorality, particularism, and absurdity were formulated; a public dispute between Donin and four Rabbis was ordered. The humours and futilities of such debates have been satirized in Heine's poem 'Disputation.' But the consequences were deplorable. The Talmud was condemned; many copies of it were burnt; and popular outbreaks against the Jews resulted.

Within a few years similar scenes were enacted in Barcelona. Here again the attack originated with a Jewish convert to Christianity, Pablo Christiani. He instigated a public debate between himself and Naḥmanides in 1263, as to the attributes and coming of the Messiah, and the Rabbi was sentenced to exile because his defence of Judaism was pronounced blasphemous. In 1264 Christiani induced Pope Clement IV. to appoint a Commission of censors, who expunged all those passages which appeared derogatory to Christianity. In particular, as time went on, Talmudic references to ancient paganism were misinterpreted as being attacks on the Church. This charge was brought forward by yet another erstwhile Jew, Geronimo de Sante Fé, who engineered a public dispute in Tortosa in 1410, and, like Christiani, submitted to the verdict of the crowd the most intricate problems of Biblical exegesis in relation to Messianic belief. The practical outcome again

[1] See 'Literature' below.

[2] Cf. art. ANTI-SEMITISM.

[1] *Novellæ Constitutiones*, 146.

[2] The view of Justinian's rescript given in the text is the one usually adopted. It is by no means the only possible explanation, for it is possible that what Justinian prohibited was the use of the traditional Aramaic translation (see art. TARGUMS).

was not a settlement as to the significance of Is 53, but the confiscation of copies of the Talmud.

Of much greater interest was the controversy which waged round the Talmud at the beginning of the 16th century. Owing to the part taken by Reuchlin (*q.v.*) in this incident, the Talmud became the battle-ground between the old and the new, between the obscurantists and the humanists. Again the protagonist in the attack on the Talmud was one who had left the Synagogue for the Church. It must not, however, be thought that the proverbial zeal of converts has invariably assumed this guise. In the recent assaults made on the Talmud by representatives of modern anti-Semitism (*q.v.*), powerful among the defenders of the fair fame of the Rabbinic system were such famous Judæo-Christian scholars as Daniel Chwolsohn and Paulus Cassel. The opponent of Reuchlin was of a different type. We know very little as to the antecedents of Johann Pfefferkorn, of whom Erasmus said that from a bad Jew he became an execrable Christian ('ex scelerato Judæo sceleratissimus Christianus'), for no reliance can be placed on the insinuations made by satirists that in his earlier days Pfefferkorn had added to the respectable calling of a butcher the disreputable career of a burglar. All that we know is that Pfefferkorn was animated by a strong animosity towards his former co-religionists, that his fanaticism far exceeded his learning, and that he found support for his campaign among the Dominicans of Cologne. Though the Jews had been excluded from that city in 1426 and only regained rights of free domicile there with the coming of the French in 1798, Cologne remained during the 15th and 16th centuries the headquarters of the campaign against Jewish books.

It would be unprofitable to repeat the details of the oft-told tale of Pfefferkorn's pamphlets and Reuchlin's rejoinders; of the seizure of Hebrew books in Frankfort-on-the-Main in 1509, their restoration, and the long-drawn-out struggle that ensued in Rome. Nor is it of any importance to us now whether or not Pfefferkorn wrote the works that bear his name. The whole incident would have been forgotten but for certain facts. In the first place, this battle of the books gave rise to a famous satire, the *Epistolæ Obscurorum Virorum*, the first part of which appeared at Tübingen towards the end of 1514. The effect of this rather savage satire was instantaneous and permanent. As an exposure of obscurantism it remains one of the most masterly efforts ever put forward on behalf of humanism. The struggle between Reuchlin and Pfefferkorn became, in short, elevated to a higher plane. Reuchlin, once for all, struck the true note when he protested against the destruction of a literature because elements of it were distasteful to certain of its critics. 'If the Talmud contains errors,' he said, 'let us render them innocuous by studying to sift the chaff from the grain. Do not burn the Talmud, but read it.' It is to Reuchlin that we owe the foundation of Hebrew chairs in the universities; the first Hebrew text printed in Germany was the edition of seven Psalms used by Reuchlin in 1512. The study of Hebrew in Christian Europe commenced with him, was taken up by his immediate successors, and has never since been relinquished.[1] Reuchlin's devotion to Rabbinism began with his interest in the Ḳabbālā. But Hebrew was the passion of his life. And there is no doubt that to him we owe that interest in the Talmud which soon led to the publication of a complete printed edition of all its tomes. There were, as we shall see, printed editions of parts of the Talmud available in 1510, when he wrote that 'he would like to pay the price for a copy of the Talmud twice over but he had not yet been able to obtain one.'[1] He was referring to MS copies. Within about a decade of the year in which Reuchlin wrote this lament it was easy to procure the Bomberg edition printed in Venice. It was fortunate for scholarship that Daniel Bomberg began to print the Talmud in 1520, before the censorship intruded its hand. Yet the censorship has this value. In 1550 the Talmud was placed on the Index. But the Tridentine Synod in 1564 provided that the Talmud might be circulated, if the passages obnoxious to Christianity were deleted. This was done, and between 1579 and 1581 there was completed the censored Basel edition which formed the model for many subsequent editions. In this form, claims the Basel editor, the Talmud may be read by Christians not only without reproach but even with profit ('etiam cum fructu a nostris legi potest'). The Inquisitor Marco Marino went through the Venice edition of 1546–50, censored it, and affixed his name to the expurgated version page by page. The expurgated passages have often been edited and commented on separately. Attacks on the Talmud, nevertheless, continued. As late as 1757 copies of the Talmud were publicly burned in Poland as a result of the Kamenetz-Podolsk disputation. Literary onslaughts have naturally continued, and modern anti-Semitism has displayed much energy in seeking in the pages of the Talmud grounds for attacks on the Jews. Those pages contain enough and to spare of superstition, narrowness, folly, and intolerance. But the faults are superficial, the merits fundamental; and it is because of the latter that the Talmud retains its permanent worth.

2. Permanent value.—In the first instance the Talmud represents more fully than any other Jewish work the lineal development of the religion of the OT. In several important particulars, the Talmud, indeed, represents an advance on the OT. The view (adopted by the school of R. H. Charles) is untenable that Rabbinism was a degeneration, while Apocalypse was an advance. On the contrary, all the nobler elements of the OT teaching were absorbed into and developed by Rabbinism, which was essentially a prophetic system. The moral life was at once the basis of religion and its ultimate outcome. The Talmud concerned itself with life. It therefore drew little or no distinction between the secular and the religious. This is not the place to discuss the Pharisaism which is assailed in the Gospels. For, however we explain the discrepancy, the Pharisaism of the Gospels is not identical with the Pharisaism of the Talmud.

Hence, though the Talmud, because it combines secular and religious into one whole, is often inclined to attach undue importance to ritual or customary trivialities, it cannot be said that it does so at the expense of the great principles. And, when all has been said, the fact remains that, difficult though it be to harmonize the daily round with the higher calls of spiritual moments, the Talmud did effect this harmonization with a considerable measure of success. The Talmud is interpenetrated with the presence of God in human life, and worship was not merely confined to the hours spent in congregational prayers. The home was sanctified as well as the synagogue. This fact constituted and constitutes the worth of the Talmud to the Judaism of all ages. The liberals who have rejected the authority of the Talmud have not rejected its spirit and its outlook.[2] They, like the conservatives, feel that the hallowing of life is the purpose of life. And, among the many attempts to effect this hallowing of life—in relation primarily to God, but also in intercourse

[1] S. R. Hirsch, *A Book of Essays*, London, 1905, p. 14.

[1] *A Book of Essays*, p. 141. [2] Cf. art. LIBERAL JUDAISM.

with man—the Talmud must be conceded a high place.

In the main, then, the Talmud retains its worth because it has so thoroughly absorbed the prophetic conception of the close interconnexion of religion and life. But life is not altogether expressible in terms of conduct. There is the intellectual side. Now, for long intervals, the Talmud was the main means by which the Jew cultivated his mind. Some of the greatest Talmudists of the Middle Ages were indeed also devoted to science and philosophy, in the technical sense of those terms. But there were masses of Jews who knew no other intellectual interest than the Talmud and the allied literature. The nature of the Talmud saved them from stagnation. For the Talmud is a work of most manifold interest. It concerns itself with every phase of human activity. To read it intelligently—and it was assuredly so read—was a liberal education in the arts and sciences and philosophies. So wide is its range that a student of the Talmud is perforce acquainted with very many subjects which nowadays are regarded as distinct disciplines. The mind of the student was kept alert; his attitude never became scholastic; at every point he was in contact with actualities. It was an essential function of the Talmud to maintain this alertness, so that to con over its pages was not identical with losing oneself in an obsolete past. The Talmud breathes with vital freshness.

This enables us to understand why the Talmud has never been superseded by the codes founded upon it even by authorities so competent and able as Moses Maimonides and Joseph Qaro. The codes omit the very element which makes the Talmud so important, so unique. The codes reduce ritual and religious conduct to rule; the decisions are stated in precise paragraphs; they are anonymous. But the Talmud presents processes as well as results; there is little of rule in it, less of precision; and the dicta are largely associated with the names of their authors. We see the religious evolution in action. And, just as it is in action in the older book, it remained in action in the modern life. The claim often put forward by recent Talmudists that their beloved tomes represent a progressive Judaism is well founded. Codes have an air of finality, while the key-note of the Talmud is continuity.

For the Talmud, after all, comes into line with the newer theory of the evolution of religion. The effect of the Talmud, it has been said, was to obscure the difference between Scripture and Tradition. This may be true, but modern criticism tends (on quite other grounds) to obliterate the distinction. The Scripture is itself a traditional evolution—so the newer theories hold. The Talmud in essence anticipated this theory, not in the direction of belittling the divine character of the written text, but in the direction of magnifying the human part in the authorization of the message. Man has his part to play in bringing the Law into operation—in interpreting it, which is often another term for expanding it.

We can here merely mention the beauties of the Talmud, its felicities of thought, its flights of fancy, its parables, its poetry. The Jew did not merely feed his mind on the wit of the Talmud or his spirit on its idealism. His heart and imagination found their nourishment there also. From its pages the liturgy derived some of its choicest prayers. In germ, the Talmud already contains the mysticism which in later ages grew up so luxuriantly in Judaism. That this mysticism rarely became antinomian was due almost entirely to the Talmud, which more than permitted—for it encouraged—individualism as well as communism in the religious life. Our present point, however, is that volumes could be compiled (volumes have been compiled) out of the fine gems presented in a literary form which is unlike that of any other work—unlike in grotesqueness as well as in efficiency.

In the presence of these merits the attacks on the Talmud failed. Partly they were theological, partly moral, partly social. Ridicule was cast on its trivialities; fault was found with its religious conceptions; objection was taken to its attitude to Gentiles. These unfavourable criticisms were not all unfounded, for the Talmud contains much of inferior value, and bears the marks of the different ages and strata of thought in which it grew up. Nevertheless, some of the attacks on the Talmud were absolutely false; in others the assailants confused the attitude towards the Rome which destroyed the Temple with the attitude to the Rome which became the seat of the papacy. Often, too, overmuch importance was attached to the *obiter dicta* of isolated Rabbis. When, however, it was protested by Donin in 1239, and by Romano in 1553, that it was the Talmud that confirmed the Jews in their obstinate fidelity to the Synagogue, the charge was largely just. But that must be assigned to the Talmud as a merit, not as a fault. At all events it explains, perhaps in the most effective manner, how it came about that a work, so curiously alien from the modern canons of excellence in literature, has maintained its position not only with those Jews who more or less order their lives in accordance with it, but also with those who, rebels against its authority, retain an affectionate regard for its spirit. Written in style far removed from modernity, the Talmud is one of the most modern of books.

LITERATURE.—S. Schechter, in *HDB* v. 57-66, with full bibliography; W. Bacher, in *JE* xii. 1-27 (also with bibliography); H. Graetz, *History of the Jews*, Eng. tr., London, 1891-92, ii. chs. xiii.-end, and elsewhere in passages indicated in detail in the Index volume (1898) to the American ed. of the translation, p. 589 ff. The well-known unfavourable view of Schürer is contained in his section on 'Life under the Law,' in his *History*, Eng. tr., II. ii. § 28. An account of the Talmud is given in I. Abrahams, *Short History of Jewish Literature*, London, 1906, ch. iii. Special attention may be drawn to the brilliant essays of E. Deutsch (*Literary Remains*, London, 1874) and J. Darmesteter (*Reliques scientifiques*, Paris, 1890).

I. ABRAHAMS.

TAMIL-SPEAKING PEOPLES.—See DRAVIDIANS.

TAMMUZ.—Tammuz was the West Semitic form of the name of the great Asiatic nature-god, typifying the changing seasons in their relation to man's needs, desires, and passions, though the last-named were far from being so pronounced in connexion therewith as the other two aspects. For its meaning, and also other names of Tammuz, see §§ 7, 10, below.

1. The old view of the legend of Tammuz.—Prior to the successful reading of the Assyro-Babylonian inscriptions the legend of Tammuz was regarded as being exclusively West Semitic, owing, apparently, to the scene of the god's activities being located, in the then extant records, in Syria. There was considerable difficulty, however, in finding an acceptable root by which the name of the god might be explained.

2. Its most familiar versions.—According to the classic legend of Tammuz, his mother had unnatural intercourse with her own father, urged thereto by Aphrodite, whom she had offended. Pursued by her father, who sought to kill her for this crime, she prayed to the gods, who changed her into a tree, from whose trunk Adonis (the Græco-Syriac name of Tammuz) was in due time born. So charmed was Aphrodite with the beauty of the infant that, placing him in a chest, she handed him to Persephone to take care of. The goddess of the under world, however, when she found what a treasure she had in her keeping, refused to part with him again. Zeus was therefore appealed to, and he decided that for four months in the year Adonis should be left to himself, four should be spent with Aphrodite, and the remaining four with Persephone. A variant account, however, agrees with the Babylonian legend in making him pass six months with Êreš-ki-gal (Persephone) and six with Ištar, or Aphrodite. The classic versions represent Adonis, or Tammuz, as being passionately fond of hunting, and undeterred therefrom by the fiercest quarry. His end was tragic, as he was slain through the tusk of a wild boar piercing his groin (see § 14).

3. The Syrian versions.—The centre of the Syrian worship of Tammuz was probably Gebal; in any case, Balthi ('the [divine] Lady,' as Aphrodite seems to have been called in the extreme west of Asia) was believed to have migrated thither from her realm of Cyprus for love of Tammuzo (Tammuz). But before Tammuzo she had loved Ares (Mars)[1] and thereby aroused the jealousy of her husband Hephæstus. In this version Tammuz is described as the son of Cuthar, king of the Phœnicians, to whom, when she fled from Cyprus, Balthi made all the villages around subject. It was not the irresponsible act of a wild boar, however, that caused the death of Tammuz, but the jealousy of either Aphrodite's husband Hephæstus or her lover Ares, who came and slew Tammuz on Lebanon whilst he was hunting wild boars.

The Syrian lexicographer Bar Bahlul also gives the legend as he had heard it: 'Tomuzo was, as they say, a hunter shepherd and chaser of wild beasts; who when Balathi loved him took her away from her husband. And when her husband went forth to seek her Tomuzo slew him,' but was himself slain later on by a wild boar which he encountered in the wilderness, and his father made a great weeping for him in the month named after him.

The Rabbinical references to Tammuz are more curious than instructive with regard to the history and development of the myths concerning him.

One (that of Rabbi Solomon Isaaki, or Rashi), commenting on Ezk 8^{14}, in order to connect the root of the name Tammuz with the Chaldæan *aza*, 'to make hot,' describes it as 'an image which the women made hot in the inside, and its eyes were of lead, and they melted by reason of the heat of the burning, and it seemed as if it wept; and they (the women) said, "He asketh for offerings."'

This and other varying traditions concerning Tammuz, however, seem to belong to the Christian era.

4. The worship of Tammuz in Syria.—In all probability the mourning for Hadadrimmon mentioned by Zechariah (12^{11}) is a reflexion of the lamentations for Tammuz, with whom this deity is said to have become identified; and in a passage in Amos (8^{10}) the Israelites lament as for 'an only son.' The most noteworthy Biblical passage, however, is seemingly that in Jeremiah (22^{18}), where it is said that they shall not lament for Jehoiakim, saying, 'Ah my brother! or, Ah sister! Ah lord! or, Ah his glory!' and where the word 'sister' suggests the sympathy of the mourners for his bereaved spouse or lover. When Belili, his sister, in the Babylonian legend, says, 'My brother, only (one), do not cause me pain'[2] (by leaving the world again to go to the regions below), we have perhaps a better parallel. Byblos, the Biblical Gebal, was the centre of the worship of Tammuz in Syria, where, in the month of June, the funeral-festival of the smitten sun-god was held, and lasted for seven days. 'Gardens of Adonis'—flower-vases planted with seeds which sprang up quickly, and as quickly, owing to lack of moisture, faded away—were prepared by the mourning women as emblems of the early death of the youthful Adonis. Throngs of wailing women filled the streets and the gates of the temple, tearing their hair, disfiguring their faces, and gashing their breasts. The Galli—emasculated priests of Ashtoreth, the spouse of Tammuz—took part in the mourning for 'the bridegroom of her youth.' These days of mourning were followed by days of rejoicing for his resurrection, during which a papyrus-head came over the waters of the Mediterranean from Alexandria—an emblem of the severed limbs of Osiris, which, gathered up by Isis, his inconsolable spouse, after he had been dismembered by Typhon, had of old arrived at Gebal. Thus did the legend of Tammuz assimilate itself with the Egyptian myth of the sun-god Osiris.

5. Tammuz in Babylonia, his birth-place.—So far Babylonian sources have furnished but few of the details of the Syrian and the Greek versions of the myth of Tammuz. To all appearance the legend had not been carried from Syria to Babylonia, as might be expected, but the reverse. In its original form it must have been of considerable antiquity. According to the archaic list of royal names[1] discovered at Nippur (*Niffer*), and now preserved in the museum of the University of Pennsylvania, Dumu-zi, as the Babylonians called Tammuz, was a king of Erech and ruled for 100 years. His predecessor was the god Lugal-banda, who reigned for no less than 1200 years, whilst his successor was the half-divine and only half-historical king of Erech Supuri, Gilgameš, who ruled for 160 or possibly 180 years. According to this record, Tammuz was a fisherman (Sumerian *šu-ḫa*) of the city Ḫa-a, a site as yet unidentified, but which one would expect to find somewhere in the neighbourhood of the Persian Gulf. Though king of Erech, Tammuz was more especially associated with Êri-du, the divine city of Êa, the god of the waters, at the head of the same waterway, and it was only natural that a maritime people, such as the southern Babylonians were, should make Tammuz a fisherman. In that part of the land he was evidently the god of the fruitfulness of the teeming waters, just as, inland, he was god of the fruitfulness of the fertile Babylonian plain.

6. Ištar's search for Tammuz in Hades.—Outlines of this legend are given in the articles BABYLONIANS AND ASSYRIANS[2] and HEROES AND HERO-GODS (Babylonian).[3] From this text we see that Tammuz was, at the time of Ištar's descent, in the under world with Êreš-ki-gal (Persephone), whither he had descended in accordance with the decision of the king of the gods (Bel-Merodach = Zeus). This legend likewise shows that Tammuz had become the lover of Ištar, or, as the record puts it, 'the husband of her youth.' The sacrifices which she was willing to make on his account are noteworthy, for at each of the seven gateways of 'the land of No-Return' she parted—under protest—with an article of apparel or adornment, until she appeared in the presence of the queen of the region perfectly naked. As things went wrong on earth owing to the absence of the goddess of love, Šamaš, Sin, and Êa bestirred themselves and secured her release. Here the subject suddenly changes, and the name of Tammuz appears in the text for the first time:

'If she [Êreš-ki-gal] hath not given thee her dismissal, return to her.
Upon Tammuz, the husband of [her] you[th],
Pour out pure water, [sprinkle] sweet oil.

[1] Mars is probably to be identified with the Bab.-Nergal rather than with En-urta (Ninip). The former was the spouse of Êreš-ki-gal (Persephone). (See § 10 below.)
[2] See § 6 below.

[1] See *ExpT* xxvii. [1915–16] 519^a.
[2] *ERE* ii. 315^b.
[3] *Ib.* vi. 645^a.

Clothe him with a festive garment, let him strike up with the flute of lapis-stone—
Let the joy-maidens dance, [let] the honoured one . . .
[Then] Belili set [down] her instrument,
[And] "eye-stones" filled [her] la[p ?]—[1]
[When] she heard her brother's voice, Belili smote her instrument . . .
Her "eye-stones"[2] filled [her] thoughts (?).
"My brother, only (one), do not cause [me] pain (?)."
On the day Tammuz plays on the lapis-flute, they will play along with him the tambour of chalcedony (?).
The men-mourners and the women-mourners will play along with him.
May the dead (?) arise and smell the incense.'

Belili, mentioned here as the sister of Tammuz, appears also in the great list of gods[3] in connexion with Alala, as forms of the deities of the heavens, Anu^{m} and Anatu^{m}. The flute of Tammuz, like the divine vine at Êridu, was of lapis-stone, emblematic of the blue sky, and it is not unlikely that the other objects mentioned—Belili's 'eye-stones' and the 'tambour'—were of precious and similarly symbolical materials.

7. Other Babylonian references to Tammuz.—The first place ought probably to be assigned to the lists of gods, which furnish us with some of his names, and the deities with whom he was identified. The transcription of the group standing, in Sumerian, for Tammuz is 'Dumu-zi,' though a longer form, 'Dumu-zida,' is often found. The commonly accepted rendering of this group into Semitic Babylonian is *mâru kênu*, 'the true (or faithful) son.' Of the lists in which the name is found the most important is probably the trilingual text (two dialects of Sumerian and Semitic Babylonian equivalents) published in *WAI* ii. pl. 59. In that inscription his character as a sun-god is indicated by the fact that his name comes towards the end of the section referring to the sun-god Šamaš, after Kêttu and Mêšaru, that deity's two attendants.[4] After this comes Ṭu-zi-zi (? from Ṭumu-zi), in standard Sumerian [Dumu]-zi, rendered by *šu-ma*—*i.e.* transferring Dumu-zi into the Semitic Babylonian column—and from the next line we see that he bore in Sumerian also the name of U-libir-si (dialectic) or Enligir-si, probably meaning 'the lord of the righteous covenant,' or the like. The next line, which begins a new section, has the name of Sir-du, dialectic Ṣir-ṭumu, the mother of Tammuz. Other deities in this section are 'the lady of the plain,' Ištar, and 'the lady of the gods.' A section giving further names of these goddesses follows, and then comes the final section of the tablet, beginning with Êreš-ki-gal and explaining her as Allatu^{m}, the Babylonian Persephone. Important as showing the feminine aspect of Tammuz, which is also visible in the Syro-Greek view of the deity, is the list[5] in which he is called Ama-ušumgal-ana, 'the peerless mother of heaven,' which may be one of the aspects of the planet Venus, described[6] as 'male at sunrise.' Another name, En-mersi, dialectic for Nin-Girsu, the god of Lagaš, identifies Tammuz with that deity and stamps him specifically as the great god of agriculture.[7]

8. The abodes of Tammuz in Babylonia.—The chronological list preserved at Philadelphia, U.S.A.,[8] makes Tammuz a king of Erech and seems to indicate that his native place was a city expressed by the characters Ḫa-a. In the incantation published in *WAI* iv. pl. 15, however, Êridu seems to have been his chief city, of which, therefore, Ḫa-a may have been a suburb or even another name:

'In Êridu a black vine grew—in a sacred spot it was made.
Its substance was white-flaked lapis-stone, planted in the Deep.
Êa's path in Êridu is filled with fruitfulness—
His seat is the [central] place of the earth.
His abode is the bed of Engur [the Abyss].
In his holy house, which is like a forest, [his] shelter is set—no man can enter therein.
In the midst of it is Samaš [and] Tammuz [Dumu-zi],
Between the mouths of the rivers [or canals] on both sides.'

Here follow the names of the waterways in question: Ka-ḫengala, Igi-ḫengala, and Ka-na-ab-ul, though the true total seems to have been four.[1]

Instead of 'the god Šamaš (and) Tammuz' we might read 'the sun-god Tammuz,' which would correctly describe his position in the Babylonian pantheon. The Sumerian original has expressed the name of Tammuz by the feminine Ama-ušumgal-ana.[2] The connexion of Tammuz with the vine of Êridu, the Paradise-city, stamps him here likewise as one of the gods of fertility, and it is owing to this that he is so closely connected with the god Êa, to whose nourishing streams the great fruitfulness of the land was due. It is noteworthy that Nin-Girsu, the god of Lagaš, who was identified with him, bore also the name of Uru, 'the husbandman.'[3]

9. Tammuz as the herdsman.—It has already been noted that Dumu-zi, or Tammuz, was called the fisherman (*šu-ḫa* = *bayaru*), but later he appeared as 'the herdsman.' This view of the deity is referred to in another incantation:

'The milk of a yellow goat which has been brought forth in the holy fold of Tammuz [Dumu-zida]—
The milk of a goat of the flock—may he give thee with his holy hand.
Pour it then into the skin of an undefiled she-goat.
Azag-suga, the uz-maḫ-Enlila ['glorious goat of the god Enlila'], has caused [it] to be eaten with his sacred hand.
Merodach, son of Êridu, has given the incantation—
May Nin-aḫa-kuddu, the lady of the limpid fountain, make him [the sick man] holy, make him pure.'

'The incantation of the milk of the yellow goat, and the flour of the undefiled she-goat's skin.'

The antiquity of the association of Tammuz with the flocks in Babylonia is shown by the noteworthy text in *The Amherst Tablets*, i. (London, 1908) no. 119, where 'fleece' is expressed by the phrase 'sheep of the sky.' This indicates that the flocks of Tammuz, the sun-god of spring, were the clouds illuminated by the setting sun, and comparable with the flocks of Helios in Greek mythology. In the same publication, nos. 110, 112, and 114 refer to the 'grain of the priest of Tammuz,' and no. 118 mentions his temple at Lagaš. The date of these inscriptions is about 2300 B.C.

10. The Babylonian hymns to Tammuz.—At least two series of these existed, and they may have formed the originals of some of those chanted by the Hebrew women[4] as well as by the Phœnicians and the other nationalities who accepted or adopted the cult. The following will show their nature:

'The ewe and her lamb he taketh;
The goat and her kid he taketh.
The ewe and her lamb he smiteth down;
The goat and her kid he smiteth down.

Arise then, go, hero, the road of "No-return."
Alas, hero! warrior, Un-azu;
Alas, hero! hero, my god Damu;
Alas, hero! son—my faithful lord;
Alas, hero! Gu-silim the bright-eyed;
Alas, hero! god Nagara, lord of the net;
Alas, hero! overseer, lord of prayer;
Alas, hero! thou who [art] my heavenly light;

1 Probably poetically put for some such idea as 'Crystal tears filled her body'; see below.
2 Probably 'crystal tears'—evidences of the grief she had felt when Tammuz descended into the under world.
3 *Cuneiform Texts from Babylonian Tablets, etc., in the British Museum*, London, 1908, pt. xxiv. pl. 1.
4 See the art. RIGHTEOUSNESS (Babylonian), §§ 1 and 4.
5 *WAI* ii. 54, 349.
6 *Ib.* iii. pl. 53, l. 31; see *ExpT* xxx. [1918–19] 167^{a}.
7 *WAI* ii. 54, ll. 34 and 36. For references to his temple at Lagaš see § 9 below.
8 See § 5 above.

1 See *ExpT* xxix. [1917–18] 182 f., 288.
2 See § 7 above.
3 Tammuz visited not only the under world, but also 'the heaven of Anu'; see *ERE* vi. 644^{a}.
4 Cf. Ezk 8^{14}.

Alas, hero! Ama-ušumgal-ana;
Alas, hero! brother, mother, heavenly vine.
He goeth, he goeth, to the bosom of the earth—
He will cause abundance for the land of the dead.[1]
For his lamentation, for the day of his fall,[2]
In an unpropitious month of his year.[3]
To the road of man's last end,
At the call of the lord,
[Go], hero, to the distant land which is not seen.'

Or, according to the Sumerian original of the last four lines:

'In an unpropitious month of thy year,
To the road of the people's end [or rest],
At the call of the lord,
The worthy one, in his distant land, is not seen.'

'The unpropitious month' is probably Du'uzu, or Tammuz; 'the road of man's last end' is that leading to the under world; 'the lord,' who calls him, is possibly Merodach, but may be Nergal, king of that region, the Babylonian Mars.[4]

After a division-line the text continues:

'Alas, my abundance which has been withheld! Alas, my produce which has been detained!
My heart is oppressed, shepherd, dwelling in exile—
Where is his city? My heart is oppressed!
From the house of gloom he shall be brought forth—
Thou who art worthy, from the house of gloom thou shalt be brought forth!
Alas, hero! warrior, Un-azu,' etc., etc., as above.

Though these lamentations may have been recited by the women and others who joined in the ceremonies, it is probable that they were originally placed in the mouth of Ištar. The abundance and plenty referred to is probably the fruit of the earth; the oppression of heart was due to the lack of these things, and also to the god's exile in the regions below.

The bearing of these hymns upon the legend is clear. We learn that (1) some accident had happened to Tammuz, by which his sojourn in the under world was brought about; (2) this accident was that in some way he 'fell'—either through an attack by a wild animal (boar) or, like Eshmun, the Phœnician deity, by his own hand; (3) the result was that he passed part of his life in the under world, whereby the earth suffered and the under world profited; (4) the under world, to which Tammuz went, was man's last abode and the place of the people's rest. Notwithstanding that he was fulfilling his mission, the exile of Tammuz was still an unpropitious event for him, the realm of Ēreš-ki-gal not being, even for the earth-dweller, that place of delight which the man looking forward to life with his god in the realms of bliss would like it to be. It may be supposed, however, that the worshipper of Tammuz, when he departed this life to dwell with his god, hoped to enjoy companionship with him not only in Hades, but also on earth when his time came to return thither.

11. The transfer of the legend to Syria.—As has already been stated,[5] the legend of Tammuz in Babylonia was of considerable antiquity—as early, in fact, as 4000 B.C. or even earlier, and it had had, therefore, ample time not only in which to spread abroad, but also to assume new forms and receive additions. Besides Byblos, the Babylonian Gublu (Gebal), Tammuz was also venerated in many intermediate states and cities—Cilicia, Cappadocia, Lycia, Lydia, Ephesus, and Pterium. Everywhere the cult was most enthusiastically adopted, falling in, as it did, so exactly with the Semitic view of the nature of things. Apart from the theories which were held as to the creation of the universe, the legendary teaching connected with Tammuz dealt only with the continuance of what had been brought into existence by the Creator. Regarded as a sun-legend, it was recognized that 'the kindly fruits of the earth' were due to his rays, and to the fact that, when these and their accompanying warmth were withdrawn or reduced, the growth of vegetation ceased.

12. The reflex-influence of the legend of Tammuz in Babylonia and Assyria.—That this enthusiastic worship of the Babylonian Dumu-zida, under the name of Tammuz, had influence in Babylonia and Assyria, sympathetically related as they were with the Western Semites, is but natural; and its greater importance in the countries of its adoption than in the land of its origin is also easily comprehensible. This was due to the fact that the Babylonians had, from the date of the rise of Babylon, accepted Merodach, who was also a sun-god, as their supreme deity. Tammuz therefore continued to represent simply one of his forms, and thus remained ineligible as chief of their pantheon, whose construction, as a philosophical system, his position of supremacy would have destroyed.

13. The development of the legend farther west.—In all probability more than one version of the legend anciently existed in Babylonia and migrated, with the worship, westwards. Representing the summer sun, with all its warmth and its vivifying and productive power, Tammuz was regarded as the god who passed the six months between the beginning of autumn and the end of winter in the under world. As the planet Venus seems to follow the course of the sun, her disappearance with him was interpreted as due to her desire to rescue him from that prison-house, but, as her movements do not coincide with the seasons, she generally had to come forth without him. When the time for his release came, therefore, he had to return to earth unaccompanied by his spouse.

In the West the legend was modified, and Tammuz-Adonis there appears as the son of the Cypriote king Kinyras and as beloved of the goddess Aphrodite. He died, it was said, in the forest of Lebanon, killed by the wild boar typifying winter; and since the time of that catastrophe the river Adonis, now the Nahr Ibrahim, 'Abraham's stream,' flows yearly, when in flood, reddened by his blood. The name Adonis is the Greek form of the Phœnician Adōn, 'lord,' which this deity, in common with many others, bore. In the Sumerian hymns (mostly in the dialect) he is constantly called the 'lord,' *un* or *uwun*, and it is probably owing to this, at least in part, that Adōn (Adonis) became one of his names.

14. Tammuz in Cyprus.—According to Ovid,[1] the scene passes, in part, from Assyria (Syria) to Cyprus. Kinyras, king of that island, had, by an incestuous relation with his daughter[2] Myrrha, a beautiful son named Adonis. The child was brought up by the nymphs and had hardly reached manhood when he became the lover of Aphrodite. One day, notwithstanding the goddess's supplications, he went hunting in the forest of Lebanon and was wounded by a boar sent by Ares (Mars), who was jealous of the divine youth. Aphrodite, hearing of this tragedy, filled the forest with her lamentations and tried to revive him, but without success. From the blood of the dying Adonis the anemone had its birth, and the river Adonis was thenceforth reddened yearly by his blood.

15. The legend of Tammuz in Greece.—According to Panyasis (5th cent.), Adonis was the son of a princess of Assyria (Syria), Myrrha or Smyrna,

1 Variant rendering: 'Šamaš will make him great in the land of the dead,' but that given above seems preferable.

2 The full rendering in Semitic is 'Filled with lamentation on the day that he fell and (was) in distress,' but the Sumerian is insufficient for all this.

3 In the calendar of lucky and unlucky days (*WAI* v. 48) the entries for the month Tammuz (col. iv.) include 'weeping' on the 2nd day, and 'lamentation' on the 10th, but it is doubtful whether these really refer to the legend.

4 See § 3 above, and § 14 below.

5 § 6 above.

1 *Metam.* x.

2 See §§ 2, 15.

whom Aphrodite had inflamed with a violent love for her father Theias. Myrrha profited by her father's drunkenness and the darkness, but, when afterwards Theias found out what had taken place, so violent was his anger that he attacked his daughter, sword in hand. Myrrha fled, praying the gods for protection, and the divinities who had been the cause of her ruin, recognizing that she was not really to blame, changed her into the tree which, since that time, has borne her name. Nine months later the tree opened and gave birth to the beautiful Adonis. Aphrodite took charge of him and, placing him in a casket, handed him to Persephone to take care of.

Other variants of the legend of Tammuz are recorded, but, as they are apparently later developments and seem not to bear upon the origin of the myth, it is needless to speak of them here. How far the above or any other variants may be founded upon further details from Babylonia is uncertain and will not be known until the Babylonian legend of Dumu-zida comes to light.

16. Why did the legend vary?—Not only was Tammuz faithful in fulfilling his fate and passing a part of his existence in the under world, but he was also faithful in bringing, as the god of agriculture, the fruits of the earth to perfection in their season. The climates of Babylonia and of Syria are so different that any legend common to both was bound, in its province, to differ; hence the variations in that of Tammuz noted here. According to G. Rawlinson,[1] increasingly heavy showers fall in Babylonia, in November and December, raising the river-levels. As spring advances, the showers become lighter and fewer until about May, when summer-weather arrives. From May to November rain is very rare indeed, and the sun's rays are only tempered at morning and evening by the grey mist. For five months, therefore, Babylonia is a land of drought. With this description the month-list of Lagaš, whose principal deity was Nin-Girsu—identified with Tammuz—seems to agree,[2] but it is the common calendar of later days[3] that is the most instructive. In this it would seem that it was the fourth month, Šu-(n)umuna, 'perfection of seed,' or the like (June–July), that ended the time of productiveness, and that this month was called Du'uzu, the West Semitic Tammuz, as the month of the god's greatest fruitfulness. The month next following, Bibi-gar, apparently means 'making heat' (=Heb. Ab), whilst the 6th month, August–September, is Kin-Innanna, 'the errand of Ištar,' generally regarded as that in which Ištar descended to Hades in search of her lover. Its Heb. name Elul (in Babylonian, Ululu) probably means 'grief' and seems to express the common Semitic sound of mourning and distress. In Marcheswan, the 8th month, the opening of the water-channels took place and was succeeded by the rain-clouds of November–December (the Heb. Chislev). The 11th month, January–February, was 'the month of seed' and probably marks the time when sowing became general. Finally came the 1st and 2nd Adars (Feb.–March), in Sumerian Še-gur-kud and Dir še-gur-kud, the two grain-plant cutting months, when the seedlings were cropped to encourage the increase of sprouts.

Roughly, the 12 months of the year fall into three groups of four each, Nisan to Tammuz marking the growth and perfection of the grain, Ab to Marcheswan practically barren owing to the great heat, and Chislev to Adar the season of irrigation by the rivers and the sprouting of the crops. It is probably to this that the three periods of the year of Tammuz—with Ištar, with Ereš-ki-gal or Persephone, and at his own disposal—are due, the division of his year into two periods of six months each being apparently Western.

17. Tammuz in the late Assyrian inscriptions.—In these documents there are certain names which testify to the popularity of the god—not, however, under the name of Dumu-zi or Tammuz, but under that of Adōn. The Assyrian form appears as Adunu, and the names containing it may be divided into the specifically Syrian and the Assyrian—the latter apparently imitations, or translations from Syrian into Assyrian. Among these are Adunu-apla-iddina, 'Adōn has given a son'; Adunu-nadin-apli, 'Adōn, giver of a son'; and Adunu-mâta-uṣur, 'Adōn, protect the land.' The purely Syrian names seem to be Adunaiz(i) or Aduna-iz(i), perhaps 'my lord hath sprinkled'; Aduni-ṭu and Aduni-ṭuri, 'my lord is my rock' (Heb. *ṣûr*); Aduni-iḫa, 'my lord liveth (?).' Aduni-ba'ali, 'Adōn is my lord,' is West Semitic and belongs to about 850 B.C. (he was king of Sianu), but all the rest fall between 680 and 660 B.C.

Whether, with Vellay, the gods of the countries into which the worship penetrated may be regarded as having become identified with Tammuz or not is doubtful. If correct, it was due to the fact that Tammuz, under the name of Adōn, 'lord,' was designated by a word which could be applied as a title to any god, whether the Merodach of the Babylonians, the Moloch of the Syrians, or the Hadad of the Amorites. It is this, in all probability, that caused Tammuz to become, in a measure, identified with the Adonai of the Hebrews—that more general divine name which, with them, replaced the all too sacred Jahweh (Jehovah) of their own monotheistic creed.

18. The Tammuz-cult and its contemporary creeds.—Naturally, the idea of a kind of martyr-god, dying, it may be, for the good of mankind, notwithstanding the difficulty of bringing Tammuz into this category, has to be taken into consideration. The most striking parallel, perhaps, is the Osiris of the Egyptians; and the Babylonian Merodach, who died in order that mankind might be produced from his divine blood, is equally noteworthy. As Merodach, the 'steer of day,' was a sun-god, it is not unlikely that he was regarded as dying daily and as being reborn that men might live. The sun as Tammuz, however, died yearly, not so much that men might live, but because he fell under the evil influences of the spouse of Nergal, the god of battle, disease, and untimely death. Vellay contends also that Jesus Christ, like Tammuz, was a sun-god and, also like him, descended into Hades; but there are so many fundamental differences in the career of the mythical sun-god of 4000 or 5000 years B.C. and the Christ of history that comparisons may well be set aside. The half-mythical Babylonian ruler, with his 100-year reign, comparing so unfavourably with his predecessor's 1200, may easily have had a misadventure in the hunting-field which gave birth to the nature-myth which the Babylonians, Syrians, and Greeks have handed down to us.

LITERATURE.—Charles Vellay, *Le Culte et les fêtes d'Adônis-Thammouz* (*AMG*, 'Bibliothèque d'Études,' xii.), Paris, 1904; M. Jastrow, Jr., *Die Religion Babyloniens und Assyriens*, Giessen, 2 vols., 1905–12 (details rather meagre); T. G. Pinches, *Hymns to Tammuz in the Manchester Museum, Owens College*, Manchester, 1904 (vol. xlviii. pt. iii. of the *Memoirs and Proceedings of the Manchester Lit. and Philosophical Society*, session 1903–04), *The Religion of Babylonia and Assyria* London, 1906, pp. 48, 69 ff.; *PSBA* xxxi. [1909] 63 (prayer to Tammuz); W. Aldis Wright, in Smith's *DB* iii. [London, 1893]; A. H. Sayce, in *HDB* iv.; T. K. Cheyne, in *EBi* iv.

T. G. PINCHES.

[1] *The Five Great Monarchies of the Ancient Eastern World*, London, 1862–67, i. 38.

[2] See *PSBA* xxxv. [1913] 20 ff., 123 ff.

[3] T. G. Pinches, *An Outline of Assyrian Grammar*, London, 1910, p. 60.

TANJORE.—**1. History.**—Tanjore (Tamil Tanjāvūr, 'city of refuge') is the capital of the District of the same name in the eastern portion of the Madras Presidency; it is situated in 10° 47′ N. lat., 79° 8′ E. long.; in 1911 the population was 60,341. The District formed part of the ancient Chola country, and the kingdom reached the zenith of its power under Rājārājā I. (A.D. 985–1011). During the 13th cent. it passed under the rule of the Hoysala Ballālas of Dorasamudra and the Pāṇḍyas of Madura. An independent Nāyak dynasty was established in the 16th cent., which was displaced by a Marāṭhā kingdom about 1674. It was occupied by the British in 1773 and finally ceded to them in 1799; the royal family, who were pensioned, became extinct in 1885.

2. The temple.—Tanjore owes much of its importance to the great temple built by King Rājārājā I., who was a devoted Śaiva, but tolerant of other religions. It is known as Brihadīśwara, Brihatīśwara, said to mean 'temple of the great god,' or Rājārājīśwara, after its founder. Fergusson writes:

'In nine cases out of ten, Dravidian temples are a fortuitous aggregation of parts, arranged without plan, as accident dictated at the time of their erection. . . . The one great exception to this rule is to be found at Tanjore. The Great Pagoda there was commenced on a well-defined and stately plan, which was persevered in till its completion.' [1]

Entered by a fine gateway (*gopuram*), which is supposed to cast no shadow on the ground, the outer court, used as an arsenal by the French in 1772, is 500 ft. long and 250 broad, and is surrounded on all sides by a cloister. The main shrine stands to the west, and above it rises to a height of about 200 ft. a magnificent tower, decorated with pillars and statues. The summit is crowned by a single block of granite, weighing 80 tons, said to have been raised to its present position up an inclined plane commencing at a village four miles distant. An interesting feature of the tower is that the carvings are generally of a Vaiṣṇava type, while the ornamentation of other parts is Śaiva. Another curious fact is that one of the figures on the north side of the tower represents a European; the popular belief is that it is the figure of a Dane who assisted in the building or that it was erected to foretell the British occupation. It is probable that both the European figure and the Vaiṣṇava ornamentation were erected by one of the Nāyak princes, and that he was helped by some Danes who acquired Tranquebar in 1620. The base of the great temple and many of the other buildings are covered with inscriptions which have been translated;[2] nearly all of them belong to Rājārājā and his successors.

Another noteworthy building is the temple of Subrahmaṇya, god of war, younger son of Śiva,[3] with a colossal figure of Nandi, the bull of Śiva, 'a perfect gem of carved stone-work, the tooling of the stone in the most exquisitely delicate and elaborate patterns is as clear and sharp as the day it left the sculptor's hands.' [4]

'The temple, though beautiful, is not considered particularly sacred. The legendary cause of this is that the Śaivite saint Appar was refused admission to it, and that therefore it was not celebrated in his hymns or those of the other three Śaivite poet-saints. A peculiarity about it is that Śūdras are admitted to the apartment next the shrine, from which in most temples in this District they are excluded, and that Valaiyans [a hunting, fishing, iron-making, and cultivating caste],[5] who are usually not admitted at all, here come as far as the great bull.' [1]

3. Tiruvādi.—Tiruvādi (Tiruvaiyāru, 'the five holy rivers'), six miles N.W. of Tanjore, is a place of great sanctity, said to be holier than Benares by one-sixteenth, where pious Hindus desire to die and where their bones are cast into the river. It has a fine temple, called Pañchanadīśwara, 'Lord of the five rivers,' which contains inscriptions of Rājārājā and his successors.[2]

LITERATURE.—The authorities have been quoted in the article. For the early Tamil history see V. Kanakasabhai, *The Tamils Eighteen Hundred Years Ago*, Madras, 1904; G. Oppert, *The Original Inhabitants of Bhāratavarṣa or India*, London, 1893.

W. CROOKE.

1 *Hist. of Indian and Eastern Architecture*, London, 1899, p. 342 f.

2 E. Hultzsch, *South Indian Inscriptions*, Madras, 1890 ff., esp. vol. ii.

3 B. Ziegenbalg, *Genealogy of the South-Indian Gods*, Madras, 1869, p. 63 ff.

4 F. R. Hemingway, *Tanjore Gazetteer*, Madras, 1906, i. 271.

5 E. Thurston, *Castes and Tribes of S. India*, Madras, 1909, vii. 272 ff.

TANNAIM.—See JUDAISM.

TANTRAS.—In the series of sacred books of the Hindus the *Tantras* occupy the fifth or sixth place. According to their character and contents they are fourth in the order of inspiration and authority, the degrees being *śruti*, *smṛti*, *Purānik*, and *Tāntrik*. They are also known as a fifth or the fifth Veda by those who regard them as authoritative and observe the ritual which they enjoin. In neither case is the series entirely chronological or consecutive. The *Tantras*, which succeed and are in part dependent on the *Purāṇas*, are also in parts unrelated to the latter and of greater antiquity. Their date, however, it is impossible to determine with any precision. The existing treatises are probably for the most part at least reproductions with additions and variations of older works which are no longer extant. In their present form they are usually ascribed to the 6th or 7th cent. of our era, but they may be considerably later. Tāntrik usages and popular formulas were current and practised in a much earlier age; they belong to a type of thought that is primitive and among primitive peoples varies little in the course of the centuries. Until recent years little was known of these works outside of India. A few have now been made accessible in translations, but the greater number are as yet unexplored.

The name *tantra* signifies a 'web' or 'warp,' then a continuous or uninterrupted series, and in religious usage an orderly rule or ritual. The word was then further applied to the doctrinal theory or system itself, and finally to the literary work or treatise in which it was set forth. In the last sense the word is not found in the *Amarakośa*, the great Sanskrit dictionary,[3] nor is it used by the Chinese pilgrims. The *Mahābhārata* also contains no reference to the *Tantras* or to any religious system founded upon them. All these facts are confirmatory of the comparatively late origin of the existing books. Śaṅkara enumerates the titles of 64 *Tantras*, comparatively few of which can be identified at the present day. The best-known of these treatises and the most worthy of study are perhaps the *Tantrakaumudī*, *Śaktisaṅgama*, *Rudrayāmala*, *Kālikā*, *Kulārṇava*, *Tantratattva*, and *Mahānirvāṇa*. Translations of the two last have been published by Arthur Avalon. Parts of the *Hitopadeśa* also are known as '*tantras*.' [4]

Traditionally the authorship of these works is attributed to Dattātreya, who was an incarnation of the Hindu trinity, Brahmā, Viṣṇu, and Śiva.

1 Hemingway, i. 271. For an account of the temple with illustrations see Fergusson, p. 342 ff.; *EBr*[11] xiv. 430; V. A. Smith, *A Hist. of Fine Art in India and Ceylon*, Oxford, 1911, p. 36 f.

2 Hemingway, i. 276 ff.; Fergusson, p. 346 f.; *EBr*[11] xiv. 431.

3 Dated by Macdonell, but with much uncertainty, *c.* A.D. 500; see *Hist. of Sanskrit Literature*, London, 1905, p. 433; cf. also T. Zachariæ, *Die indischen Wörterbücher*, Strassburg, 1897, p. 18 ff.

4 For further titles see Monier-Williams, *Sanskrit Dict.*, *s.v.*, and *Brāhmanism and Hindūism*[4], p. 207.

They are therefore to be regarded as equally the revelation of the three supreme divinities. In form, however, they are dependent on Śiva alone, who in dialogue with his wife Durgā, or Kālī, reveals the mystical doctrines and observances which are to be received and practised by his worshippers. This authoritative or 'higher tradition' is further said to have been delivered from his central or fifth mouth. As such it is pre-eminently sacred and secret and may not be revealed to the uninitiated. 'The Vedas, the Śāstras, and the Purāṇas are like a common woman, but this mystical Śaiva science is like a high-born woman,'[1] and its communication is forbidden. The real authors of the several treatises are unknown. They bear the name also of *Āgamas*, and as such are sometimes distinguished from *Nigama*, the text of the *Vedas*, *Dharmaśāstras*, and other sacred books. The Indian commentator, Kullūka Bhaṭṭa, asserts that revelation (*śruti*) is two-fold, Vaidik and Tāntrik.[2] In the popular knowledge and belief they have practically superseded the *Vedas* over a large part of India, where religious practice and ritual are guided by the teaching of the *Dharmaśāstras*, *Purāṇas*, and *Tantras*. A native writer and exponent of these works in Bengal asserts that 'two-thirds of our religious rites are Tāntrik, and almost half our medicine.' They are the *Śāstras*, the scriptural authority and rule for the present age, the *kaliyuga*, and it is therefore incumbent on all orthodox Hindus to follow their directions.

In particular, the *Tantras* are the religious text-books of the Śāktas and of their various sects. There are different Tāntrik schools, with variant traditions, the distinctions between which are little understood outside of their immediate circle of adherents. The ritual of the *Tantras* of the Dakṣinācharins, however, is said to be pure and in harmony with the *Vedas*, while that of the Vāmachārins is intended only for Śūdras. Their influence unquestionably extends far beyond those who profess to accept their authority. Wilson quotes a passage from one of these treatises which claims that 'many a man who calls himself a Śaiva or a Vaishnava is secretly a Śākta, and a brother of the left-hand.'[3] Even the Jains of N. India are said to have adopted formulæ and ritual from the *Tantras*, and the Lāmaism or corrupt Buddhism of Nepāl and Tibet owes much to the same source.

The teaching of the *Tantras*, as of the *Purāṇas*, is essentially based on the *bhakti-mārga* (*q.v.*), which is regarded as superior to the *karma-mārga* and *jñāna-mārga* of the *Brāhmaṇas* and *Upaniṣads*. Adoration of a personal deity is inculcated, especially of the wife of Śiva, who is worshipped as the source of all regenerative power. In all these writings the female principle is personified and made prominent, to the almost total exclusion of the male. Ultimately their doctrine is derived from the philosophy of the Sāṅkhya-Yoga, with its theory of *puruṣa* and *prakṛti*, with especial emphasis on the mystical side of Yoga teaching and practice. Like the *Purāṇas* also every *Tantra* should theoretically discuss in order five subjects—the creation and destruction of the universe, the worship of the gods, the attainment of supernatural power, and union with the Supreme Being. In reality their contents are almost entirely magical and mystical, but they range over a wide variety of subjects, scientific, religious, medical, speculative, etc., and are interested in all that

1 Quoted from Monier-Williams, *Brāhmanism and Hindūism*[4], p. 191.

2 *Śrutiśća dvividhā vaidihā tāntrikīća*, note on Manu, ii. 1; H. H. Wilson, *Essays and Lectures*, i. 248.

3 H. H. Wilson, *Essays and Lectures on the Religion of the Hindus*, London, 1862.

concerns human need and destiny. One at least of the more important *Tantras* expounds in metaphysical terms the nature of the Supreme Brahman, who is *nishkala* and *sakala*, *i.e.* with or without *prakṛti*, *nirguna*, and *saguna*; in the beginning only the *nishkala* Brahman existed, etc. Great use is made of mystical syllables, *om*, *ām*, *um*, *ūm*, etc., with which sometimes whole pages of writing are filled. By the repetition of these, magical and supernatural abilities may be gained. The use of *mantras* also is enjoined, and numerous examples are given; their essence consists in certain mystical and secret letters or syllables which they contain (*bīja*). The significance of the letters of the alphabet is taught, the employment of mystic diagrams (*yantra*), sacred circles (*śrīchakra*), spells, charms, and amulets (*kavacha*), symbolical movements and crossing of the fingers (*mudrā*), etc.

Together with all this, which appears to us so meaningless and puerile, there is undoubtedly much that is of historical interest in the *Tantras*, and that is of value for the interpretation and interrelation of Hindu doctrine. They are generous and broad in their sympathies, recognize no distinction of caste or sex, 'for men and women equally compose humankind,' and they forbid the practice of *satī*. According to the orthodox view, the rites and doctrine which they inculcate are to prevail until the close of the *kaliyuga*.

LITERATURE.—H. H. Wilson, *Works*, i., ii., *Essays and Lectures on the Religion of the Hindus*, London, 1862, esp. i. 248-251, iii., *Essays on Subjects connected with Sanskrit Literature*, do. 1864, p. 95 ff.; M. Monier-Williams, *Brāhmanism and Hindūism*[4], do. 1891, *Indian Wisdom*[2], do. 1875, p. 501 ff.; M. Winternitz, *Gesch. der indischen Litteratur*, Leipzig, 1908, i. 162 f., 229 n. 3, 481 f.; N. Macnicol, *Indian Theism*, Oxford, 1915; W. J. Wilkins, *Modern Hinduism*[2], London, 1900; Arthur Avalon, *Principles of Tantra* (*Tantratattva*), 2 parts, do. 1914 and 1916, *Tantra of the Great Liberation* (*Mahānirvāṇa Tantra*), do. 1913; Arthur and Ellen Avalon, *Hymns to the Goddess*, do. 1913; A. Barth, *The Religions of India*[3], Eng. tr., do. 1891; R. W. Frazer, *Indian Thought, Past and Present*, do. 1915.

A. S. GEDEN.

TĀNTRISM (Buddhist).

TĀNTRISM (Buddhist). — A complete study of Buddhist Tāntrism would include the description and the history of its rites, its deities, and its doctrines, practically the *exposé* of the many problems which confront the historian of mediæval India. Buddhist tāntrism is practically Buddhist Hinduism, Hinduism or Śaivism in Buddhist garb. The present writer intends only to provide the reader with a definition of the chief topics.

Buddhists were not quite clear as to the specific meaning of the word *tantra*, 'book.' The Tibetan canon distinguishes the *Sūtra* (*Mdo*) and the *Tantra* (*Rgyud*), but a number of texts are classified in both sections: the limits between *Sūtra* (i.e. *Mahāyānasūtra*) and *Tantra* are not fixed. On the one hand, topics which are essentially Mahāyānist—*e.g.*, hymns to *bodhisāttvas* (*stotra*), resolutions to become Buddha (*praṇidhāna*)—are met with in *Tantra*; on the other hand, *Mahāyanasūtras* include a number of fragments and often whole chapters which would constitute by themselves so many Tāntrik texts.

A good example is found in the *Saddharmapuṇḍarika*, 'Lotus of the true Law,' which contains a whole chapter[1] of *dhāraṇīs*, on talismanic words, invocations in litany form to a female deity or to a female power; 'giantesses' are mentioned as protectors of the *Sūtra* and of its readers. There are good reasons for believing that this chapter is a late addition: such an addition testifies that the spirit of Mahāyāna had become largely tinted with the spirit of Tantrism, or rather that the Tāntrik syncretism made little distinction between Mahāyānism and Tantrism properly so called.

Tāntrik books, by assuming the title of *Sūtra*, secured authority. The *Kāraṇḍavyūha* is styled *Mahāyānasūtraratnarāja*, 'the very best of the Sūtras.' As a matter of fact, the introductory section is written according to the pattern of a *Mahāyānasūtra*; it does not pretend to relate, as

1 Ch. xxi.

Tantras do, the dialogue of a god with a goddess; it preserves the old phrase, 'Thus have I heard,' followed by the mention of the place, Śrāvasti, Jetavana, and the description of an audience of *bodhisattvas*. But, when we consider the chief topic of the book, viz. the glorification of Avalokiteśvara as the owner of the 'science in six syllables,' we cannot say that the author has written what we should like to style a *Sūtra*. In many cases the Tibetan scholars were not deceived by mere titles; *e.g.*, although the *Suvarṇaprabhāsa*[1] is styled *Sūtra*, it is not in the *Mdo*, but in the *Rgyud*, that the Sanskrit and the Chinese recensions of this celebrated book are to be found. But the fact remains that *Mdo* and *Rgyud* overlap in a great number of cases.[2]

These confusions or 'overlappings' are accounted for by the fact that a number of speculations, beliefs, and practices which reach their full development in the Tāntrik or last period of Buddhism were not unknown during the former period —*e.g.*, the use of talismanic spells. Again, the Westerns establish a close connexion between the word 'Tantrism' and the worse forms of Hindu (or Buddhist) paganism—magic, theurgy, left-hand worship—and so far they are right, for the magical or left-hand practices are properly Tāntrik, and not to be found in Buddhism outside *Rgyud*; but these practices are not the whole of Tantrism. *Tantra*, with the Hindus as with the Buddhists, covers a large field. We find in the *Rgyud* the texts which are concerned with worship, whether it is 'Tāntrik' worship or Mahāyānist worship, including the building of domestic *stūpas*, the erection and the consecration of idols, the *stotras* or hymns, the daily offering. Worship, with the whole of the religious practices, is a Tāntrik topic. The *Bhadracharīpraṇidhāna*, 'Resolution of Pious Conduct,' is reckoned a *Tantra*, because the recitation of this *praṇidhāna* is one of the daily duties of a Buddhist devotee of the Great Vehicle: from the point of view of the Western definition of 'Tantra,' this text is absolutely non-Tāntrik: it is free from any tinge of idolatry, it breathes the most lofty spirit of the Great Vehicle.[3] Litanies, lists of 100 names, whether of Prajñāpāramitā, Avalokiteśvara, or Mañjuśrī, are also *Tantras*. Litanies may be used for Tāntrik or non-Tāntrik worship. We know that the *Mañjuśrīnāmasaṃgīti*, 'Collection of the Names of Mañjuśrī,' is susceptible of a twofold interpretation: the first is a gnostic or purely philosophical one, the second sees its way to give to the most decent phrases the worst Tāntrik meaning.[4]

Therefore, in order to draw a general outline of the history of Tāntrik ideas in Buddhist literature and life, we must disregard the traditional divisions as embodied in the Tibetan catalogues or the Western theories on the subject, and build a classification of our own.

I. *EARLY BUDDHISM*.—The Old Buddhism, as preserved in the Pāli canon and in the Sanskrit Hīnayāna literature, has a number of features which are not specifically Buddhist, which are alien to the noble eightfold path, which, to put it otherwise, are more or less Tāntrik or open the way to Tantrism properly so called. Let us mention a few topics. (1) There is a general belief in the mystic power of the 'statements of truth';[1] Sākyamuni praises the use of half-magical 'formulas of protection' which have a large place in the more recent Sinhalese Buddhism (*paritrā*, *paritta*, *pirit*).[2] (2) In the earliest documents respect is paid to a number of deities or non-human beings who are both powerful and unfriendly; there is an 'orthodox' way of dealing with them, but 'unorthodox' worship is the natural result of fear. Vajrapāṇi is regarded as the 'guardian angel' of Śākyamuni, as the protector of the *avoué* of the Church. He is the pattern of the 'Dharmapālas' of a later age. (3) The worship of relics, the building of *stūpas*, pilgrimages, and idolatry are old features of Buddhism. (4) Last, not least, the earliest machinery of meditation or trance is akin to the more intricate machinery which constitutes the basis of the *Yogatantras*. Buddhist 'meditation' is simply Hindu *yoga* more or less transformed. The 'insight into the truth' (*satyadarśana*), which is the only and the sufficient means to *nirvāṇa*, practically implies (*a*) the meditation on loathsomeness (*aśubhabhāvanā*), when the ascetic, often 'a dweller in the cemeteries,' 'purifies his bones' —*i.e.* fancies that his flesh is rotten and falls, and sees only the bones behind, until the whole world appears to him as full of skeletons—and thus succeeds in crushing desire; (*b*) the restraint of breath (*prāṇāyāma*), counting the expirations and inspirations, in order to render thought more tractable and to direct it towards the Buddhist truths; (*c*) the *vimokṣas*, *abhibhvāyatanas*, and *kasinas*, prolonged contemplation of disks of earth, etc., by which (*d*) a number of supernormal states are induced, the so-called *dhyānas* (*jhāna*), or 'trances' and *samāpattis*, or 'ecstasies.' According to the Pāli and Sanskrit theologians it is only when absorbed in those supernormal states that a man is susceptible of rightly understanding the four Buddhist Truths (*satyābhisamaya*) and thus progressing towards *nirvāṇa*. Now it is quite safe to state that meditations on corpses, restraint of breath, the diverse methods of inducing trance, and the trances themselves have been borrowed by Buddhism from Hindu *yoga*. Buddhism established, more or less artificially, a strong connexion between those archaic devices of *yoga* and its own spiritual aim, *nirvāṇa*. But Buddhists did not ignore, and their books do not conceal, the fact that the discipline of *yoya*, while it may be made 'supramundane' (*lokottara*), *i.e.* utilized for the conquest of *nirvāṇa*, also provides a man with many 'mundane' (*laukika*) advantages: he who lives in cemeteries acquires power over the *bhūtas* and the manifold spirits who haunt these places; he who 'restrains the breath' masters thought and the body; he who practises trance becomes the possessor of magical powers and secures rebirth amongst gods. In short, a man who practises *yoga* becomes a *yogin*, or a *siddha*, an owner of 'perfections' or 'powers' (*siddhi*). It is clear that the position of Buddhism is not a safe one. Let us state it in plain words. A monk must perform in a Buddhist spirit, *i.e.* for the sake of *nirvāṇa*, a number of rites and meditations which confer the most precious 'mundane' advantages; he must disregard these advantages—which, in India, are the surest mark of holiness—while he perfectly knows that he can enjoy them when he likes. We may be sure—even if there were no documents to this effect—that many of the monks of early

1 Fully analyzed by E. Burnouf, *Introd. à l'hist. du bouddhisme indien*, p. 528.

2 See M. C. Ridding and L. de la Vallée Poussin, *Catalogue of the Tibetan MSS of the Stein Collection in the India Office* (Manuscript).

3 *Kanjur*, *Rgyud* (Beckh), xxiv. 331; also in *Vinaya* (Dulva); B. Nanjio, *A Catalogue of the Chinese Translation of the Buddhist Tripiṭaka*, Oxford, 1883, no. 1142, ed. and tr. by Kaikioku Watanabe, *Die Bhadracari: Eine Probe Buddhistisch-religiöser Lyrik*, Leipzig, 1912.

4 *The* [*Mañjuśrī*]*nāmasaṃgīti* has been published by I. P. Minayeff together with the *Mahāvyutpatti* in *Buddhism, Researches and Materials*, Petrograd, 1887, i. sect. 2 (in Russian); we refer to the commentary called *Amṛtakaṇikā*.

1 *Satyavachana*; see E. W. Burlingame, in *JRAS*, 1917, p. 429.

2 See, *e.g.*, R. Spence Hardy, *Eastern Monachism*, London, 1860, pp. 26, 30, 240; H. C. Warren, *Buddhism in Translations*, Cambridge, Mass., 1896, pp. 302, 321. A large portion of the *Rgyud* is *paritrā*.

Christianity were not strong enough to resist so powerful a temptation; *e.g.*, they performed miracles for 'vain glory.' In such cases they acted as 'mundane' *yogis*; technically they followed the rules that later constitute the *Yoga-tantra*.

II. *MAHĀYĀNA*. — In Mahāyāna *bhakti*, or devotion, and *pūjā*, or worship in the Hindu guise, increase.

Mahāyāna is, like Hīnayāna, a thoroughly Buddhist discipline, viz. a way to *nirvāṇa*; the disciple of Mahāyāna is a candidate for Buddhahood (*bodhisattva*, future Buddha), because Buddhas alone reach *nirvāṇa*; he will become a Buddha by acquiring the wisdom and accumulating the merit of a Buddha. But an essential feature of the doctrine is that the candidate for Buddhahood cannot succeed without the help of the Buddhas and of the future Buddhas nearing Buddhahood; this help is secured through *bhakti*. The early Buddhist paid worship to Śākyamuni, to the relics, to the holy places, but there was little or no *bhakti* in his respectful behaviour. Now the objects of worship are so many living gods, so many *bhagavats*, quite different from Śākyamuni, very much like the Hindu *bhagavat*, and they are entitled to the *bhakti* of the faithful. As has been pointed out several times,[1] *bhakti* is seldom free from elements which easily take a Tāntrik shade. To mention only one point: a man will be saved by remembering at death the name of Avalokita or of Kṛṣṇa. The names of the Buddhas or the *bodhisattvas*, the mystic formulas in which they have themselves placed a wonderful force, acquire a rôle in the sanctification of the devotee. *Bhakti* has exalted the god to such a degree that *bhakti* is no longer necessary. Sāntideva, an orthodox divine of the Mahāyānist school, praises without reservation the use of *dharaṇīs* for the pardon of sins.[2] The schools of the Mahāyāna known as the Sukhāvatī sects place the highest spiritual advantages at the command of the man who knows how to worship Amitābha.[3]

Every form of *pūjā*, including the circumambulation of a *stūpa*,[4] offering flowers to a *stūpa*, giving food to the monks, etc., was considered very useful from the beginning. A treatise like the *Ādikarma-pradīpa*[5] shows us that Mahāyāna has added much to the primitive liturgy; it gives a description of the many acts of worship which a Mahāyānist devotee, a 'beginner' (*ādikārmika*), was expected to perform — recitations of formulas, symbolic offerings, wonderful advantages to be obtained by acts which easily assume a mechanical character, so many features which give to Tantrism its specific aspects. A daily observance was the eightfold high *pūjā* (*aṣṭavidhā anuttarā pūjā*), a sort of worship 'in spirit and truth': confession of sins to the Buddhas and *bodhisattvas*—to the Buddhas who have a special claim to the title of 'Buddha of confession'[6]—resolve to become a Buddha, 'application of merit' (*pariṇāmanā*), etc. That this eightfold *pūjā* often becomes a mere ritualistic performance—a special kind of *dhāraṇī* —is proved by the fact that it is a part of the *śādhanas* (see below). It is well known that Mahāyāna is prompt to admit any sort of spells

1 *E.g.*, by A. Barth, *Œuvres*, Paris, 1914, i. 190.

2 *Śikṣāsamuchchaya* (*Bibliotheca Buddhica*, i.), ed. C. Bendall, Petrograd, 1897, p. 140.

3 See *Anecdota Oxoniensia*, series III. (Aryan), pt. 2, Oxford, 1883, and *SBE* xlix. [1894].

4 See *Śikṣāsamuchchaya*, p. 297; I-Tsing, *A Record of the Buddhist Religion*, tr. J. Takakusu, Oxford, 1896, ch. xxx., 'On Turning to the Right in Worship': 'What is walking towards the right or towards the left, however, would seem a little difficult to determine' (p. 141). I-Tsing has many details on worship as practised in Mahāyānist convents.

5 Ed. and tr. L. de la Vallée Poussin, *Bouddhisme: Etudes et matériaux*, London, 1898, pp. 162–282.

6 See *Śikṣāsamuchchaya*, p. 289.

that provide 'mundane' advantages[1]—of course it objects to 'black magic.' From our point of view, it is more important to observe that Mahāyāna worships a number of beings which are no longer Buddhist in character.[2] The demoniac origins of Vajrapāṇi are not forgotten; he nevertheless obtains a high rank in the pantheon; as he is the 'destroyer of the enemies of the Law,' he is probably one of the first gods who have been worshipped under a 'choleric' aspect.[3] Female figures —*e.g.*, the Tārās—are associated with the Buddhas, but there is not in this association any tinge of 'properly so called Tantrism.' The same can be said of Hārītī, the former goddess of smallpox, the account of whose avatars is one of the most curious and the best known pages in the religious and iconographic history of Buddhism. Her worship, both in the monastic and in the popular *milieux*, gives a correct idea of the Mahāyānist and of the half-Tāntrik methods of worship.[4]

III. *TANTRISM PROPER*.—Tantrism, properly so called, bears a twofold character; on the one hand, it is a systematization of the vulgar magical rites and it has existed under this form for many centuries in India and in Buddhism itself, together with its formulas and its pantheon; on the other hand, it is a 'theurgy,' a highly developed mysticism styled Vajrayāna; under this form Tantrism is an innovation in Buddhism.

Tantrism has its professionals, the sorcerers (*yogin*, *siddha*), and its laymen, the *clientèle* of the sorcerers, also all the Hindus who worship deities or idols of the Tāntrik type. The sorcerers, who are at the same time 'mystics' or adepts of the Vajrayāna, constitute a number of schools; there are many rival secret traditions characterized by different sets of formulas, of deities, and of theories.

We shall deal with only two points which deserve special notice: (1) the methods of *sādhana*, (2) the *vajrayoga*. To be complete, it would be necessary to study a number of *vidhis*, or rites, many of which are part of the Tāntrik daily cult and have been adopted by Mahāyānist Buddhism.[5]

1. **Sādhana**.—In order to perform a *sādhana*, *i.e.* the evocation of a god, the ascetic must be duly instructed by a *guru* and duly consecrated. The ascetics who have established the manifold secret sects of Tantrism had to propitiate the gods by long austerities and meditations before being favoured with the manifestation of the god; they at last received from him the secrets they are now able to teach to their pupils. The *guru* therefore assumes great importance: he is the paramount god of his pupil and the incarnation of the Buddha himself. When he has been taught all the details of the rites, the Tāntrika must undertake the *sādhana*, by which he renders visible any god he wishes and obtains control over him. The most important items in these magical performances are the knowledge of the *bīja*, the mystic syllable which is the 'germ' or the 'seed' of the god, and the knowledge of the *vidyā* or *mantra*, which gives to its owner control over him.

On a chosen day the ascetic, after performing the regular ablutions, wearing a neat dress or a new dress, goes to a solitary place, either auspicious—a wood or the bank of a river

1 See, *e.g.*, *Ṭišastvustik* (*Bibl. Buddh.* xii.), ed. W. Radloff and A. von Staël-Holstein, Petrograd, 1910.

2 We say 'in character,' for it is difficult to say whether Amitābha, *e.g.*, is not originally a sun-god; but Amitābha is 'Buddhistic'; he is the *sambhogakāya*, a modern name for the quasi-eternal Buddha of the Docetic school.

3 The latest authority on the subject is A. Foucher, *L'Art gréco-bouddhique du Gandhâra*, Paris, 1905–18, ii. 48–64.

4 A. Foucher, *The Beginnings of Buddhist Art and other Essays*, tr. L. A. and F. W. Thomas, Paris, 1917; Noël Peri, 'Hārītī, la Mère-de-démons,' in *Bulletin de l'École française d'Extrême Orient*, xvii., fasc. 3 [1917]; cf. *JRAS*, 1895, p. 149.

5 A glance at the catalogue of the *Rgyud* will show the variety of the *vidhis*.

—or loathsome—a cemetery—according to the purpose. He sits there at ease in a purified spot and fulfils in order the different acts of a Mahāyānist *pūjā*, offering of flowers and perfumes, either mental or real, to the host of Buddhas and *bodhisattvas*, confession of sins, etc.[1] He continues in the same style by practising the virtues of friendship, pity, joy, indifference, by dwelling on the essential voidness of all things. Thus he is supposed to have acquired both merit (*punya*) and wisdom (*jñāna*): all this is only a preparation to the rite itself. The rite begins with the meditation on the *bīja* of the god who has been chosen for some technical reason (every god has his own department in mundane and supramundane affairs). If the god is Yamāntaka or Yamāri (the enemy or the destroyer of Yama, god of death), the syllable is *hūm*; it is to be written on the disk which in the magic circle (*maṇḍala*) is the symbol of the sun. The ascetic causes to arise from *hūm* the wrathful Yamāntaka, hair bristling, blue, with six faces, with six arms, with six feet, riding a bull, standing in the *ālīdha* pose, adorned with a garland of skulls, exceedingly frightful. When the god has been summoned in that way, the ascetic undertakes the second part of the rite: he fancies that he is the god; the identity of the ascetic and the god is a metaphysical truism; the ascetic does not identify himself with the god, he only realizes the identity. As soon as the ascetic knows that he is the god, he possesses all the powers that belong to the god: any wish he utters in the proper form—for his voice must be the voice of the god—will surely be accomplished.[2]

As A. Foucher, from whom this definition of *sādhana* is borrowed, rightly observes, the description of the gods as given in Tāntrik treatises must be accurate: any mistake in the mental representation of those frightful persons would be fateful. The *Sādhana* treatises have been the pattern according to which Hindu and Tibetan artists worked, and they furnish the best means to the identification of the icons or idols.

Sādhanas serve all sorts of purposes—worship, white and black magic. In many cases they are complete with their first part, the summoning of the deity, to whom worship and prayers are respectfully offered. More often, when the deities are the 'girls' or 'princesses' (*kumārī*, which is not 'virgin'), or the 'ascetic goddesses' (*yoginī*), we have to deal with the worst features of paganism.[3]

2. Vajrayāna.—But Tantrism is much more than a pagan system of rites of worship and sorcery. It is a vehicle (*yāna*, *naya*), a way to final liberation or to the *summum bonum*. Tantrism is the Tantrayāna, or the Mantrayāna (=*naya*), 'Vehicle of the Magic Formulas,' more often and more technically, the Vajrayāna. *Vajra*, 'lightning,' is originally and remains the weapon of Indra, of Vajrapāṇi, of the ascetics or *yogins*, against human or demoniac enemies. But *vajra* has assumed new meanings: (1) it designates the mystic or divine energy which is identified with 'intelligence' (*vijñāna*): there are *vajrabodhisattvas*, '*bodhisattvas* of *vajra*,' *vajrayoginīs*, 'divine female sorcerers,' *vajravarāhī*, 'the divine sow'; all divine beings are so many *vajrasattvas*, 'beings of *vajra*'; the supreme being, the Ādibuddha,[4] is the *vajrasattva par excellence*. (2) On the other hand, *vajra* (with the variant *mani*) is a decent or mystic phrase for *liṅga*, the male organ, just as *padma*, lotus, is the literary rendering of *bhaga* or *yoni*.[5]

To this twofold meaning of *vajra* correspond two Tāntrik schools, right-hand and left-hand. Both owe much to the Mahāyānist doctrines, to Madhyamaka, and to Vijñānavāda;[6] they cling

1 See art. Bodhisattva, vol. ii. p. 749b.

2 Freely translated from A. Foucher, *Étude sur l'iconographie bouddhique de l'Inde d'après des textes inédits*, Paris, 1899–1905, pt. ii. p. 8 f. See F. W. Thomas, 'Deux Collections sanscrites et tibétaines de *Sādhanas*,' *Muséon*, new ser., iv. [1903] 1.

3 On the Tāntrik pantheon see A. Grünwedel, *Mythologie du Bouddhisme au Tibet et en Mongolie*, tr. J. Goldschmidt, Leipzig, 1900. The description of the local deities of Nepāl in S. Levi, *Le Népal*, Paris, 1905, i. 316–392, practically applies to all parts of Buddhist India.

4 See *ERE* i. 93.

5 On the spell *oṃ maṇi padme hūm* see *JRAS*, 1915, p. 397, and L. A. Waddell, art. Jewel, vol. vii. p. 555. The old translation, 'Jewel in the lotus,' may be right after all.

6 See art. Philosophy (Buddhist).

to the theory of universal voidness (*śūnyatā*), but they develop the concepts of *tathatā*, *tathāgatagarbha*, etc., and result in an undisguised monism. While Mahāyāna states that all beings are 'future Buddhas,' that all beings are 'embryos of *tathāgatas*,' the two Tāntrik schools maintain that all beings are *vajrasattvas*, are the unique Vajrasattva; they also maintain that the nature of *vajra* is immanent in all beings and can be actualized by appropriate meditations and rites.

Now the left-hand school conceives the nature of *vajra* according to the Śaivite pattern; the right-hand school is nearer the Vedāntist or Yoga tradition: on the one hand the traditions of the *Mahākālatantra*, etc., on the other hand the Church of the *Mahāvairochanābhisambodhi*, the Vajraśekhara, etc.—the modern Japanese sect of Shin-gon-shū.

In the Tantras of the Śaivite type we have to deal with a Buddhist adaptation of Śaivism and Śāktism. The three traditional bodies of a Buddha are preserved, but the true nature of *vajrasattva* is his fourth body, 'the body of bliss' (*ānanda*, *sukhamaya*, *mahāsukhakāya*), the body of *vajra*; it is with that body that the eternal *tathāgata* or *bhagavat* eternally embraces his *śakti*, Tārā or Bhagavatī. From this erotic conception of the nature of being or the divine being it follows that, in order to actualize his real divine nature, the ascetic must perform the rites of union with a woman (*yoginī*, *mudrā*) who is the personification of the *bhagavati*,[1] who is Bhagavatī herself; as it is said, *buddhatvam yoṣidyonisamāśritam*, 'Buddhahood abides in the female organ.'[2] This truth was discovered by Śākyamuni, who, according to the *Chaṇḍamahāroṣaṇa*, conquered Buddhahood by practising the Tāntrik rites in the *harīm*. The most conspicuous topic of this literature is what is called the *strīpūjā*, worship of women:[3] disgusting practices, both obscene and criminal, including incest, are a part of this *pūjā*, which is looked upon as the true 'heroic behaviour' (*duḥkaracharyā*) of a *bodhisattva*, as the fulfilment of the perfect virtues. Buddhist mythology and mysticism are freely mixed with *śāktas*: the semen is the five Buddhas, etc. The leading idea that 'everything is pure to a pure man,' *omnia sancta sanctis*, is often expressed. 'Lust is to be crushed by lust. . . . Do strenuously that which is condemned by fools, united with your chosen deity, intent upon the purification of thought. Women stirred with the poisonous fire of love provide their lovers, ascetics of pure mind, with all the fruit of love. . . . Enjoy all the pleasures of love without fear. Do not fear; you do not sin.'[4]

We may add two remarks. (1) Some 'moral' rules are to be observed even in the ceremonies (*chakra*) which are provided for the thorough enjoyment of the *ma* (*māṃsa*, 'meat,' *madya*, 'alcohol,' *maithuna*, 'sexual union'). A modern Śaivite work, the *Mahānirvāṇatantra*,[5] explains that 'the ascetics should drink so long as their eyes do not roll and mind is not agitated. Beyond it, drinking is like that of a beast.' The rite of *pūrṇābhiṣeka* or *tattvachakra* must not be practised with any woman, but with one's own wife; so far, good, but there are two sorts of marriages, one for life, the other contracted for the purpose of the rite and lasting only till the completion of the rite. (2) Secret rites are the business of a few 'devotees.'

1 We meet the formula, *Bhagavān bhagavatībhageṣu vijahāra*.

2 On the *maithuna* rites see C. Bendall, 'Sabhāṣitasaṃgraha,' *Muséon*, new ser., iv.–v. [1903–04]; L. de la Vallée Poussin, 'Une Pratique des Tantras,' *ICO*, Paris, 1899, i. 241, 'Note sur le Pañcakrama,' *ICO*, Geneva, 1895, i. 137.

3 On *strīpūjā* in Hindu Tāntrism see H. H. Wilson, *Sketch of the Religious Sects of the Hindus*, Calcutta, 1846, p. 160 f. (*Select Works*, London, 1861–77, i. 256 ff.). Little has been added by modern scholars; see R. G. Bhandarkar, *Vaiṣṇavism, Śaivism and Minor Religious Systems* (=*GIAP* iii. 6), Strassburg, 1913, p. 146.

4 H. P. Shastri, 'Discovery of a Work by Āryadeva,' *JASB*, vol. lxvii. pt. i. no. 2 [Calcutta, 1898], p. 175.

5 Tr. Manmatha Nath Dutt, *Wealth of India*, Calcutta, 1899–1900, vii.–viii.

On the whole and for the largest number of its adherents, Tantrism is simply paganism.

According to the left-hand Tantrism which we have described, the rites of union (*maithuna*) are not efficacious by themselves: before practising them the candidate for *vajrasattva*-hood must be 'purified' in a threefold respect; he must possess the body, the voice, and the thought of a *tathāgata*. This threefold purification constitutes the Tantrism of the right hand.

These are 'aspersions' or 'consecrations' (*abhiṣeka*),[1] 'marking' (*nyāsa*) which consecrates the different limbs of the body, 'prayers' (*japa*) which purify the voice. The most intricate part of this discipline concerns thought. No Western scholar has yet endeavoured to understand the three mysteries of the body, the voice, and thought, the *vajradhātu* and the *garbhadhātu*, the five *tathāgatas* (the so-called *dhyānibuddhas*[2]) who are associated with five wisdoms, with the five *dhātus* (earth, etc.), etc.; the Buddha, Vajra, and Padma class of formulas, etc. We depend on the descriptions of the Shin-gon-shū sect, which are too meagre and obscure to be thoroughly intelligible.[3] The opinion of the present writer is that a number of schools are to be distinguished: there are branches which are connected with *rājayoga* (meditation and knowledge are the only means to the actualization of the nature of a *tathāgata*); some other branches praise ritualistic performances, especially 'intertwinings of the fingers' (*mudrā*);[4] some will admit the rite of union, but with a female described as a *jñāna-mudrā*, a mental female.[5]

LITERATURE.—i. *Tibetan canon.*—A. Csoma, *Asiatic Researches*, xx. [Calcutta, 1820], tr. L. Feer, *AMG* ii. [1881]; H. Beckh, *Verzeichnis der tibetischen Handschriften*, Berlin, 1914 (on which see P. Pelliot, *JA* ii. [1914] 113); Tāranātha, *Gesch. des Buddhismus in Indien*, tr. F. A. von Schiefner, Petrograd, 1869; P. Cordier, *Catalogue du fonds tibétain de la Bibliothèque nationale*, pt. ii., Paris, 1909, pt. iii., do. 1915.

ii. *Sanskrit sources.*—C. Bendall, *Catalogue of Buddhist Sanskrit MSS in the University Library*, Cambridge, 1883; R. Mitra, *The Sanskrit Buddhist Literature of Nepal*, Calcutta, 1882; H. P. Śāstri, *A Catalogue of Palm Leaf and Selected Paper MSS*, do. 1905.

iii. *Editions, translations, or descriptions of Tāntrik texts.*—E. Burnouf, *Introd. à l'hist. du bouddhisme indien*, Paris, 1845; W. Wassilieff, *Der Buddhismus*, Petrograd, 1860; L. de la Vallée Poussin, *Bouddhisme: Études et matériaux*, Brussels and London, 1898; C. Bendall, 'Meghasūtra,' *JRAS*, 1880, p. 286, 'Subhāṣitasaṃgraha,' *Muséon*, new ser., iv.–v. [1903–04]; Poussin, *Études et textes tantriques*, i. *Pañcakrama*, Ghent, 1896.

iv. *The Tāntrik literature* is supposed to be included in a fourth basket, the *Dhāraṇipiṭaka* or the *Vidyādharapiṭaka*, on which see Hiuen-Tsiang, S. Julien, *Voyages des pèlerins bouddhistes*, Paris, 1853–58, iii. 37 (S. Beal, *Si-yu-ki: Buddhist Records of the Western World*, London, 1884, ii. 165); I-tsing, *Voyages des pèlerins bouddhistes: mémoire . . . sur les religieux éminents*, tr. E. Chavannes, Paris, 1894, p. 101; L. de la Vallée Poussin, *JRAS*, 1895, p. 433.

v. *On the authors of the Tāntras.*—L. de la Vallée Poussin, *Bouddhisme: Opinions sur l'hist. de la dogmatique*, Paris, 1909, pp. 355, 384.

vi. *On the subdivision of the Tāntras*, with the data of L. A. Waddell, *The Buddhism of Tibet, or Lamaism*, London, 1895, p. 152 and H. A. Jäschke, *A Tibetan-Eng. Dict.*, do. 1881, p. 112, cf. the *Padmatāntra, Catalogue of the Sanskrit Manuscripts in the Library of the India Office*, pt. iv., *Sanskrit Literature*, by E. Windisch and J. Eggeling, London, 1894, p. 847; Sarat Chandra Das, *Tibet.-Eng. Dict.*, Calcutta, 1902, pp. 342, 396, 586, 697.

L. DE LA VALLÉE POUSSIN.

TAOISM.—Taoism is one of the three 'Teachings' (*Sam Chiao*) of China, the others being Confucianism and Buddhism. Like Confucianism, and unlike Buddhism, it claims to be a native growth.

1. Lao-tse.—The primary source for our knowledge of Taoism is the *Tao-Teh King*. This small book of about 5000 characters, usually divided into two parts, 'Concerning Tao' and 'Concerning Teh,' comprising 81 chapters, is traditionally ascribed to Lao-tse (born 604 B.C.), an older contemporary of Confucius. Lao-tse, surname Li, name Erh (= 'ear'), also known as Tan, a character which implies some aural peculiarity, is said to have been an official at the court of Chow and to have been visited on one occasion by Confucius, who after the interview compared him in his lofty incomprehensibility to a soaring dragon. Despairing of the world, Lao-tse retired from office and disappeared through the Western passes, the guardian of which induced him before leaving to compose the *Tao-Teh King* as a record of his teaching. This account of him was in later times supplemented by many marvels—*e.g.*, his prolonged gestation, which entitled him to be called 'old boy,' as his name Lao-tse might also be translated. Si-ma Ch'ien († 85 B.C.), who gives the more sober account of Lao-tse, gives also the names of his son and grandson and of the great-great-grandson of this grandson. He tells us further that about the middle of the 2nd cent. B.C. a book of Lao's was a favourite with the widowed empress of the second Han emperor. The emperor King (156–143 B.C.) is said to have made it a 'classic.' Still further back than Si-ma Ch'ien we have in Hwainan († 122 B.C.), Han Fei († 230 B.C.), and Chwang-tse (4th cent. B.C.) many quotations from Lao-tse (or Lao Tan) which are to be found in the *Tao-Teh King*. According to Legge, the first two of these authors quote the whole or parts of 71 out of the 81 chapters of that book. On a review of the evidence thus summarized, Legge concludes that he does not know of any other book of so ancient a date of which the authenticity of the origin and genuineness of the text are so well substantiated.

Criticism, however, has been busy both with Lao-tse and with his book. Founding upon the name Lao-tse, which may mean equally well 'old philosopher' or 'old philosophers,' an extreme criticism has resolved him into a number of ancient thinkers, some of whose sayings are preserved for us in the *Tao-Teh King*. For this view there is no ground except the ambiguity of the name. A less drastic criticism, of which H. A. Giles is representative, allows that at a remote period Lao-tse lived and thought and taught, and that some fragments of his teaching are preserved in the *Tao-Teh King*, in which we have those fragments pieced together by a not too skilful forger of the 2nd cent. B.C. with padding of his own. This conclusion is said to be practically certain. The criticism, however, by which it is attempted to establish this conclusion is somewhat crude. The external evidence summarized above at least does not support it; nor is it warranted by the occurrence in early Taoist writers of sayings ascribed to Lao-tse which do not appear in the *Tao-Teh King* and of sayings ascribed to Hwang-ti which do appear there, or by the evidence adduced from the *Tao-Teh King* itself (repetitions, quotations, late characters, rhyme), while the discrimination of what is admitted as genuinely from Lao-tse from what is rejected as compiler's padding is too subjective to be convincing. In favour of the earlier date of the *Tao-Teh King* it may be noted that, in its general type of teaching and in the avoidance of technical terms current in later Taoist authors it leaves on the reader the impression that it belongs to a less developed stage of Taoist thought than is found in them. The *Tao-Teh King*, however, still awaits a thorough application of sound critical principles. Indian influence on both the matter and the form of the *Tao-Teh King* has been asserted by some. The truth of this assertion cannot be considered apart from the general archæological question of the intercourse between India and China. There is a certain congruence between the mood of the *Tao-Teh King* and Buddhism, but not such as requires the dependence of one on the other as its explanation, and the present state of our knowledge hardly warrants the assumption of contact with Indian thought early enough to influence the *Tao-Teh King*, unless that book is dated later than all the other evidence seems to demand. According to D. T. Suzuki, the so-called Indian influence on the early Taoists is not probable. It is curious that in *Tao-Teh King*, ch. 39, § 3, there is an illustration taken from a chariot and its parts to which T. W. Rhys Davids[1] quotes a close parallel as having been used by Nāgasena, the founder of the Madhyamika school of Northern Buddhism, who taught about the beginning of our era. It is to be noted, however, that the same argument, only with a horse instead of a chariot as illustration, is found in Chwang-tse, bk. 25, p. 126.

It is not difficult to cull from the *Tao-Teh King* admirable ethical maxims.

[1] See INITIATION (Buddhist), vol. vii. p. 321, under 4 and 5.
[2] This phrase has never been met in any Sanskrit book.
[3] R. Fujishima, *Le Bouddhisme japonais*, Paris, 1889, pp. 81–99.
[4] See Si-do-in-dzou, 'Gestes de l'Officiant,' *AMG*, *Bibl. d'Études*, t. viii., Paris, 1899.
[5] *Mudrā* has a twofold meaning.

[1] *Buddhism*, London, 1878, p. 97.

'The highest goodness is like water. Water is good for advantaging all things and does not strive. It takes the place that all men hate' (ch. 8). 'He who raises himself on tip-toe cannot stand: he who straddles cannot walk' (14). 'He who overcomes men has force; he who overcomes himself is strong. He who knows he has enough is rich' (33). 'I have three precious things which I count and hold precious. The first is gentleness. The second is moderation. The third is not daring to take the first place under heaven' (67). To these might be added, but for the considerations mentioned below, the famous 'Recompense injury with kindness' (63).

The virtues commended lie in the line of self-suppression. For the inward state of which they are modifications the characteristic word is *hsü*, 'emptiness,' *i.e.* freedom from desires. Corresponding to this inner freedom from desires is the outward life of non-action (*wei wu wei*), *i.e.* absence of self-determined action for particular ends. Hence the world is an ethical danger (12), for it is by the world that we are drawn out into desire and action away from the stillness of our inner being, which it should be our object to keep (5), though this true type of life is unattractive except to the sage (35). He attains this life by a process of abscission of motives, by which he arrives at a childlike state of spontaneity and tenderness, in which there is also exemplified the paradoxical possession of security and strength (10, 20, 28, 55). This ethical ideal is supported by various arguments. Thus in ch. 13 the argument seems to be that to be in a position to enjoy what the world regards as honour is to be exposed to what the world regards as calamity. That which makes me a possible subject of either is just that I am an object to myself. The sage therefore treats his person as if it were alien from him. He never identifies his happiness with this or that, so never loses his happiness. Having no private ends, his private ends are realized (7). Again, it seems to be argued that as ideas suggest their contraries—*e.g.*, to know beauty is also to know ugliness—so the sage, seeing that everything is dogged by its opposite as by its shadow, refrains from all positive action (2). From the external world Lao-tse gathers illustrations, both negative and positive, of his teaching. The short-lived storm of wind and rain suggests the futility of violent action. Water in its fluidity and taking the lowest place exemplifies absence of self-determination and humility, while, as it also benefits all things and wears away that which is hard, it illustrates the paradoxical issue of *wu wei* ('Do nothing') in *wu pu wei* ('There is nothing that is not accomplished'). Specially is illustration to be found in vegetable life, which in obedience to an inner impulse or appointment passes through its cycle of growth, culminating and again subsiding (16). The Taoistic life is therefore a life of equable indifference, outwardly of non-action, devoid, *i.e.*, of action for chosen ends; moved in obedience to an inward spontaneity rather than motived by outward inducement; a life conscious, rather than self-conscious, spontaneous rather than self-determined. Hence the sage is 'simple' (19) with the simplicity of unwrought wood as contrasted with the definiteness of a carved beam; *i.e.*, he is free from self-determinateness. Again, he grasps 'the one' (22), withdrawing himself from the manifoldness of self-determination along particular lines and holding to 'the one,' *i.e.* the principle which Lao-tse knows as *Tao*.

The metaphysics of the *Tao-Teh King* centre in this conception of *Tao*. In many passages *Tao* has its common meaning of 'a way,' either the ethical way that men should follow or the method of action followed by Heaven (cf. 'course of Providence') or prescribed by Heaven for man's following. But elsewhere it is a metaphysical principle (chs. 1, 4, 14, 21, 25, 34, 37, 40, 42, 51, 62). The gist of what is stated in these chapters is as follows:

The origin of heaven and earth is nameless (1), is indeed non-existence (40), something quite indefinite, which, when we attempt to define it, becomes nothing (14, 25); if we must make a name for it, we may call it *Tao*: it may seem to be prior to God (4); it becomes nameable in relation to the universe that springs from it (1), in an order which may be partly known (42); not only is it the origin of the universe as a whole, but it presides over all beginnings (21), reaching everywhere (25, § 3) and doing everything, while it seems to do nothing (37).

Summing up what we have here, we may say: (1) as transcendent existence *Tao* is something quite indefinite, which Lao-tse struggles to express by negatives; (2) from this indefinite ground the universe of things issues by a process which is emanation from *Tao* as mother and not creation by *Tao* as agent; (3) *Tao* is immanent in the world, working in an unobtrusive way, producing and bringing to perfection individual existences. On the whole, we perhaps come nearest to the meaning of *Tao* when we say that it is pure being (most abstract of categories) endowed with spontaneity, the ultimate essence and impulse of all definite things. Obviously this conception of *Tao* excludes all idea of its equation with God. In ch. 4 Lao-tse says of *Tao*, 'I do not know whose son it is: it appears to be before God (*Ti*).' There can be no doubt that with Lao-tse *Tao* is the ultimate ground of all definite existences, *Ti* among them, while, by saying that he did not know whose son *Tao* was, he lets us see that, having arrived at his conception of *Tao*, beyond which he could not go, for in the line of logical abstraction there is no going further than 'being' which is nothing, he yet dimly felt that it did not explain itself.

The only other term in the *Tao-Teh King* capable of a theistic interpretation is *T'ien*, Heaven. In some instances of its use a near approach is made to what we mean by Heaven when we use it as equivalent to Providence. In this, its highest, use it is not merely the physical sky, but a power supreme in the world of visible things obscurely connected with the sky, which is the supreme exemplar of *Tao*, but, even so, posterior and subordinate to it. *Tao* is to Lao-tse the ultimate and determining fact.

His metaphysic, as thus explained, explains his ethic. The ground of existence being a perfectly indefinite spontaneity, a dark abysmal one from which, for no reason assigned, the multiplicity of the world emanates, by the immanence of which the world is and is moved—all this agrees with the ethical doctrine of abstention from self-determination and of sinking back on the inner ground of our being that we may be as this spontaneity in us causes us to become. Here is the justification for regarding Lao-tse's doctrine as simply a variant of 'Follow nature'; only we must remember that *Tao* is both the substantial essence and the dynamic spontaneity of all things. This, of course, brings up the difficulty of accounting for the existence in *natura naturata*, the world of concrete things, of any contrariety to *natura naturans*, *Tao*, and raises the question, neither asked nor answered by Lao-tse, why a short-lived storm is not as much an expression of *Tao* as the enduring stillness of Heaven.

Before turning again to the practical side of Lao-tse's teaching, we may refer to what may, by courtesy, be called his theory of knowledge. It is by freedom from desire that we can attain to a knowledge of the mysteries of *Tao* (1). Inasmuch as *Tao* is the principle of all existence, knowing it, we are at the heart of all knowledge. There is no need for the sage to expatiate over the world. Without moving out of doors he already knows (47). Knowing one case, he knows all, for *Tao* is the one universal principle (44).

We can best return to Lao-tse's practical teaching by the word *Teh*, which next to *Tao* is his key-word. Like *Tao*, it received from Lao-tse a new meaning, since it is the outcome of *Tao* (51). There is indeed a *Teh* which begins where *Tao* ends (38). This is the *Teh* which is the result of effort, self-conscious *teh*. *Teh* in the Taoist sense is usually distinguished by some epithet—'mysterious,' 'large,' 'lasting,' etc. As the outcome of *Tao*, it is activity devoid of self-determination, the expression of the spontaneity of the immanent *Tao*. The various virtues commended by Lao-tse are aspects of, or approximations to, this *teh*. It is in this Taoistic sense that we must take the famous maxim 'Recompense injury with *teh*,' where it is a mistake to translate *teh* by 'kindness.' The maxim is no more than a precept of indifferent self-possession: 'Be a Taoist, even though provoked' (cf. 5).

Lao-tse's practical teaching is completed by his speculations on physiology and politics. As to the former, it is asserted that the Taoist adept attains to 'lastingness' (7, 16, 44, 59). There is no place of death in him, and so he passes through dangers unscathed (50). Hints are also given of a death which is not destruction, implying a persistence in spite of death which is true long life (33). This thought, however, is not developed. With the other form of longevity appears to be associated a certain management of the breath (10, 52), and through this vein of thought there is a connexion with later Taoist developments.

In Lao-tse's politics, as in his ethics, there are attractive thoughts—*e.g.*, the protest against luxury in the court alongside misery among the people (53) and the detestation of war (31). The Taoist method of government is *laissez-faire*. The sagely king does nothing, and everything comes right of itself (32, 37, 57). Logically Lao-tse's thought implies that any sage would be the centre of a universal sway (49, 57, 77), but it is hinted that the influence of a sage becomes effective only when he has the advantage of high place (56). Here Lao-tse is in line with Confucius, who asserted that his principles would transform the world if only he could find a ruler wise enough to give him office. In describing the society which would come to being under Taoist influence, Lao-tse pictures small stay-at-home communities devoid of letters and of luxury, content with what is theirs and utterly incurious of what is not. As men within a Taoist society so societies in their relation to one another are to act Taoistically. The right way is one for men and for States (61).

There are unexplained remainders in the *Tao-Teh King*, but Lao-tse does give us a reasoned view of things. As we think back and back, we come to something which we cannot see or hear or touch, an obscure something from which all things come. It is in all things, which could not be apart from it. Yet it never parades itself. It simply is, a mysterious, ever-during, all-working existence. Let us conform ourselves to this: let us become one with it. For it is in us as in all else—our essence which would realize itself if it were not hindered by our self-will and self-seeking. If we put away these, then we know it and are and become what it tends to be. It is *Tao*, unqualified being, origin of things, and in them as essence and spontaneity.

2. Taoism before Lao-tse.—The question has been raised whether Taoism existed prior to Lao-tse. That there was such an early Taoism is argued on the grounds of quotations in the *Tao-Teh King* from earlier Taoists, the persistent reference of Taoism not only to Lao-tse but also to the at least semi-mythical Yellow Emperor (Hwang-ti, 2697 B.C.), so that 'the words of Hwang and Lao' came to be a term for Taoist teaching, and the allusions in the *Tao-Teh King* and other Taoist writings to an age when the world moved on Taoist principles. It has also been argued that, while the *I-King* is dualistic, it also contains allusions to a monistic and idealistic strain in pre-Confucian speculation, and that a doctrine of that from which the dual principles derived (*Tao*) was in various forms well known. Hence, it is claimed, the *I-King*, the doctrine of *Tao*, and some strongly held ethical principles intuitively known were the materials on which Confucius and Lao worked, Lao appropriating the monistic sayings of the *I-King* but placing his chief reliance on the doctrine of *Tao* as handed down from the Yellow Emperor.[1] In the same line E. H. Parker[2] says that there is little doubt that Lao-tse simply gave a name (*Tao*) to a floating group of ethical principles already for many centuries spread far and wide over China and already well known as the maxims of Hwang-ti, and that every single thought in the *Tao-Teh King* had been foreshadowed, usually word for word, in the *Book of History*, *Book of Rites*, *Record of Rites*, *Book of Changes*, *Book of Odes*, or other very ancient work. Among these other ancient works Parker puts the volume attributed to Kwan-tse, which he dates from the 7th cent. B.C. In spite of all that is here said, it may still be reasonably maintained that there is no conclusive evidence of an explicit Taoism previous to Lao-tse. Even Parker does not deny a certain originality to Lao-tse in developing a new quietistic conception of how human affairs once presumably were, and ideally should be, regulated. There may have been a floating group of ethical principles which Lao-tse took over, but it is the reasoned quietism of the *Tao-Teh King* based on *Tao* as metaphysical principle that alone has the right to be called Taoism, and of the earlier existence of this proof is yet lacking. In the *Tao-Teh King* itself there is no mention of Hwang-ti, and the allusions to the simpler social conditions of earlier times do not prove the existence then of a reasoned Taoism. Certainly this would be proved if we found Lao quoting 'from some sage anterior to himself who had already formulated the doctrine of inaction in the very terms we are accustomed to associate with the name and fame of Lao-tse himself.'[3] The reference is to *Tao-Teh*, ch. 57. But the introductory phrase may be translated 'Therefore the sage says,' meaning that such language is characteristic of the sage, whether actually or hypothetically existing, just as the next chapter contains a similar gnomic reference to the sage's action. Five other quotations (22, 41, 50, 69, 78) may be admitted, but they are not of a kind to prove the existence of Taoism anterior to Lao. Only if numerous other phrases introduced by the formula '*ku yüeh*' are treated as quotations, can justification be found for speaking as Legge does of 'the sentence-makers often drawn on by Lao-tsze'[4] or for saying that Lao-tse 'abounds in sentences out of some ancient lore of which we have no knowledge but for him.'[5] But these phrases may not be quotations so much as aphoristic expressions of Taoistic teaching, perhaps already current with Lao and his school. Parker's wide reference to ancient literature must be heavily discounted. It is difficult to justify his appeal to books so innocent of Taoism as the *Book of History* and *Book of Odes*. Moreover, it is one thing to find in ancient literature expressions congruent with Taoism and quite another thing to find expressions essentially Taoistic. It is true that *Tao-Teh* is a conjunction of characters

1 *Encyclopædia Sinica*, p. 433.
2 *Studies in Chinese Religion*, p. 53.
3 Giles, *China Review*, xiv. 270.
4 *The Texts of Tâoism*, pt. i. [*SBE* xxxix.] p. 2.
5 S. Johnson, *Oriental Religions: China*, Boston, U.S.A., 1877, p. 81.

long consecrated by use in the *Book of Changes* and the *Book of Rites.*[1] In the *Book of History* or elsewhere we may meet with phrases such as 'The Son of Heaven acts as the people's Father and Mother, and as such is the King of the world,' or 'That the Prince of a State should hold dirt in his mouth is the Providence (*Tao*) of Heaven.' But such things do not prove the existence of Taoism as a scheme of thought prior to Lao-tse. Nor, when we read in the *Tao-Teh King*, 'Thus we cannot say that the ancients meant nothing by the expression "Bend and survive,"' is it quite legitimate to annotate, 'Note Lao's allusion to more ancient philosophy.' There is no evidence that the ancients grounded this maxim on a metaphysical *Tao*. The *I-King* does in parts[2] contain indications of what may be called Taoist philosophy; but this very fact leads Legge to put the origin of these parts posterior to Lao-tse in the 5th or 4th cent. B.C. Kwan-tse may be dated in the 7th cent. B.C., but the work ascribed to him is suspected of being a forgery of a later date. In the present state of our knowledge it is probably right to say that the existence of a Taoist philosophy prior to Lao-tse is not proven. The *Tao-Teh King* may still be taken as the earliest example of Taoist thought.

3. Taoism after Lao-tse.—The history of Taoism immediately subsequent to Lao-tse is obscure. Somewhat later its development can be traced in a succession of authors.

(*a*) *Lieh-tse.*—The earliest of these may be Lieh-tse (=Licius, 5th cent. B.C.), but the authenticity of the work ascribed to him is doubtful. According to him, the whole of things is in perpetual transformation. The ultimate basis of all is a vague something which differentiates itself into *ch'i*, *hsing*, and *chih*. The second and third terms may be translated 'form' and 'matter' respectively, though we must beware of assuming an exact equivalence to these terms as used elsewhere (*e.g.*, in Greek philosophy). *Ch'i* is more difficult to translate. Giles[3] gives as its meanings 'the vivifying principle or aura of Chinese cosmogony: breath, vital fluid: force: influence.' The state of things when these three were in an undifferentiated and therefore imperceptible condition is called 'chaos,' whether this is or is not to be identified with the ultimate origin and basis of things. Progress is made from chaos by an evolution vaguely indicated, in the final stages of which the pure and light portions form 'heaven,' the heavy and gross form 'earth,' and 'man' appears as the vehicle of their harmonious *ch'i*. The general ethical temper is quietist, based now on ignorance, now on fatalism. Another root for it is found in the subjectivity of knowledge, and the absence of any criterion of truth and falsehood, right and wrong, though this is hinted at rather than developed. Along with this may be noted a disclaiming of any discrimination in worth between waking and dreaming experiences. Views of death are given which are perhaps not quite consistent. On the one hand is put the question, which might suggest Buddhist influence, 'When the spiritual enters its gate and the material returns to its root, where do "I" survive?' On the other hand, it is asked whether death may not be another birth. Lieh-tse makes much use of anecdotes, a good many of which seem to have been treated by Taoist writers as the stock property of their school. The magical side of Taoism shows in Lieh-tse considerable development as compared with the *Tao-Teh King*. The secret of it is such a selfless identification with the life of nature as brings the Taoist into harmony with all its forces, animate and inanimate. The alleged immunity of a drunken man from injury by accident is used to illustrate the still higher immunity which one would enjoy who was entirely under the influence of the 'heavenly' (*i.e.* 'natural' as opposed to 'self-determined') element of his constitution.

(*b*) *Chwang-tse.*—The most brilliant of the Taoist writers is Chwang-tse (*c.* 330 B.C.). In him as little as in the *Tao-Teh King* is there any systematic exposition of Taoism. In the development of his views he uses various literary devices—anecdote, allegory, and imaginary conversation. In some places he handles somewhat freely not only Confucius, but even more ancient worthies, such as Yao and Shun. How little historical accuracy or consistency is regarded is shown by the fact that Confucius is also introduced speaking in quite a Taoist vein. It is not easy to see the drift and relevance of all Chwang-tse's chapters, but the reader cannot fail to find a characteristic attitude towards reality. As in the *Tao-Teh King*, the metaphysical basis of everything is *Tao*, which as the explanation of all things is not itself a thing. It is more abstract even than non-existence, which is made definite by its opposition to existence, and so it may be called non-existing non-existence. To call it *Tao* is only a metaphor. From this absolute indifference all existences, including spirits and God, have come. No explanation is given of this coming into existence of definite things, though, to be consistent with the general scheme, the evolution must be unmotived and spontaneous. The process from unconscious indifference to the world of consciousness and of differentiated things is described in the allegory of 'Heedless' and 'Hasty' pitying insensible Chaos, and digging in him orifices of perception with the result that he died (bk. 7). *Tao* is in things, their reality and the regulator of their processes. In accordance with this view *Tao* and things are the hints of the illusory nature of all knowledge coming through the senses. The truth of things is perceived by the spirit, and Taoist adepts, when most in touch with reality, are in a trance, their bodies like rotten tree-stumps and their minds like slaked lime. One may notice also the incipient scepticism based on the relativity of knowledge and the phenomenon of dreaming. A paragraph more quoted perhaps than any other from Chwang-tse, though by no means the most central to his position, is that in which he hesitates to decide whether he is Chwang-tse dreaming that he is a butterfly or a butterfly dreaming that he is Chwang-tse. Since *Tao* alone really is, the truth of life is to be found in the above-mentioned trance when self-consciousness and self-determination are completely lost. But, as in the *Tao-Teh King*, so here, things are taken for granted, with *Tao* as their spontaneously operating essence; and in accordance with this assumption the ethical ideal is with Chwang as with Lao a life of spontaneity. There is inculcated an abscission of all definite volition and an indifferent yielding of oneself to the course of nature. Hence follows a characteristic attitude towards death, which is regarded as natural and therefore as little to be feared as birth. The Taoist is independent of all accidents, which are of no importance in comparison with the independent worth of self as an expression of *Tao*. It is only false opinion which differentiates between this and that outward state. If all self-determined effort is a departure from the truth of life, it follows that the devotee of virtue and the worker of iniquity fall under the same condemnation. Hence results a paradoxical levelling down of moral distinction. A similar strain of thought appears in Yang-tse, the heresiarch whom

[1] Parker, p. 70. [2] *E.g.*, Appendix, iii.
[3] *A Chinese-English Dict.*[2], London, 1912, *s.v.*

Mencius criticized, and is there regarded as congruent with the teaching of Lao Tan.[1]

(c) *Han Fei-tse and Hwainan-tse.*—Other writers reckoned as belonging to the Taoist school are Han Fei-tse († 230 B.C.) and Hwainan-tse († 122 B.C.). The writings of the former are preserved in 55 chapters, two of which (21 and 22) are entitled 'Explanations of Lao' and 'Illustrations of Lao.' Apparent quotations from the *Tao-Teh King* occur elsewhere in his writings. Han Fei-tse hardly discusses the metaphysical side of Taoism. His book is ethico-political, and is marked by shrewdness rather than by loftiness of tone. One sympathizes with the Chinese student who protests against his being classed as a Taoist and explains what he regards as the degenerate nature of his teaching as due to a perversion to a scheming selfishness of such sayings of Lao-tse as 'When one is about to take an inspiration, he is sure to make a previous expiration' (36) and 'The sage wishing to be above men, puts himself by his words below them' (66). Hwainan-tse is a more genuine Taoist than Han Fei, but his writings in their fanciful analogies and extravagant statements give evidence of a progressive deterioration of Taoism. Ethically he is superior to Han Fei. In at least one statement of his fundamental ethical position he shows a close verbal approximation to orthodox Confucianism: action in accordance with the nature (*hsing*) is called *Tao*, and this nature is to be distinguished from the passions (*yü*).

4. Later Taoist literature.—Later Taoist literature is voluminous and reflects that medley of subjects which make up Taoism, such as the search for immortality (which Chu Hi singles out as its main object), the conquest of the passions, alchemy, amulets, the observance of fasts and sacrifices, ritual and charms, and the multiplied objects of worship. Much of present-day popular hortatory literature may be reckoned as Taoist. Probably the most popular of all Taoist writings is *The Tractate of Actions and their Retributions*, which dates from the Sung dynasty. According to the original text, retribution takes effect in this world. The practiser of virtue indeed not only may receive earthly happiness but also may hope as the culmination of his reward to become immaterial and immortal, *hsien-jen* (=*ṛṣi* of Buddhism). As for the transgressor, he suffers in his person and fortune, and, if at his death guilt still remains unequated by punishment, judgment extends to his posterity. Of this retribution Heaven and spiritual beings are recognized as the agents. In the illustrative anecdotes added in many editions to the original text the stage of retribution includes the other world and successive rebirths in this world. The inculcated morality has many excellent details, but extends also to tabus—*e.g.*, striding over a well or leaping over food.

5. Present-day Taoism.—Chang Tao-ling (A.D. 34) has been regarded as the founder of present-day popular Taoism, which is not unfairly described as a mass of superstitious magic. The earlier literature, however, makes it evident that before his time Taoism had yielded to the love of the marvellous. Chang Tao-ling is said to have received from Lao-tse himself, who appeared to him from the realm of spirits, a sword and other apparatus in virtue of which he was able to exercise control over the spirit world. Descendants of Tao-ling, in each of whom it is said the soul of their ancestor is successively incarnate, and whose residence is at Lung-hu Shan in Kwangsi, have inherited his powers, and since A.D. 748 hold by imperial decree the hereditary dignity of 'Master of Heaven.' They are often spoken of in works on China as Taoist popes. After the introduction of Buddhism into China Taoism shows very evident traces of Buddhist influence, which was particularly potent in the 3rd and 6th centuries A.D. In its religious literature and practices it follows Buddhist models and borrows Buddhist phraseology. It has its temples, priesthood, and monasteries. Giles' statement, that the celibacy of Taoist priests has been strictly enforced since the 10th cent.,[1] is subject to qualification. Eitel says that Taoist monks or priests do not take the vow of celibacy. They may keep their families outside the cloister walls and spend the whole time between meals at home.[2] Doolittle distinguishes two classes of Taoist priests.[3] A Christian influence in the names and titles of objects of Taoist worship has also been traced by some (*e.g.*, Wieger). Many of the best known objects of popular worship are members of the Taoist pantheon; *e.g.*, Yü Hwang Shang-ti, who is the Supreme Taoist god, is also he to whom the great name Shang-ti 'sans phrase' would be most readily referred by the ordinary Chinese. Lao-tse is himself worshipped as one of the 'Three Pure Ones' whose images are prominent in every Taoist temple, the two others being Yü Hwang and Pan Ku. Taoism has produced a plentiful crop of legends and fairy-tales, the influence of which is seen in Chinese art.

The gulf between the Taoism of the *Tao-Teh King* and present-day Taoism is a wide one. It has to be remembered, however, that even in the *Tao-Teh King* there are passages which suggest a marvellous mastery of nature by the Taoist adept and provide a starting-point for that search after immortality which, according to Suzuki, first opened the door for the inrush of superstition. The suggestion has also been made that, as the opposition sharpened between Confucianism and other strains of thought, all of popular religion and superstition that found no encouragement in Confucianism took refuge in Taoism. Over and above any such accretions and any particular phrases in the *Tao-Teh King* which might provide a germ of magical developments, the general position of Taoism from the beginning exposed it to such deterioration. Starting from the assumption that man and nature are fundamentally one, its quietism obliterated the line between moral and physical, and promised its adept such a harmony with Nature as laid open to him her secrets and made him merely the vehicle of her great powers. The distinctness of the moral person was lost in the all-embracing sweep of *Tao*. Confucianism also speculated on the relation between man and nature, and thought of the sage as exercising a cosmic influence. But this influence is the issue of moral development, and the Confucian emphasis on self-determined morality prevented any sinking of man into nature.

The nobler elements of Taoism are, however, not extinct. The Taoist pope is not recognized as head by all the Taoist priesthood. There are celibate Taoists among whom the nobler Taoist strain is cherished, who disclaim any connexion with him. In some of the secret societies also elements of the higher Taoism survive. Even in Confucian circles classical Taoism has influence. The writer recalls one scholar who would not have described himself as other than Confucianist, who was well acquainted with the *Tao-Teh King*, and who used to repeat with genuine appreciation, 'The highest goodness is like water.'

6. State relations.—During its long history Taoism has experienced a considerable vicissitude of political favour and disfavour. In the pre-Ch'in

[1] J. Legge, *Chinese Classics*, London, 1861, vol. ii. *Mencius* (Prolegomena, ch. iii.).

[1] *Confucianism and its Rivals*, p. 176.
[2] *Notes and Queries of China and Japan*, Oct. 1868.
[3] *Social Life of the Chinese*, 2 vols., London, 1866, ch. ix.

times the various schools of Chinese thought seem to have been allowed free play. With the Ch'in dynasty, the first emperor of which tried to suppress Confucianism, Taoism was in favour, and it continued to enjoy imperial patronage under the early Han dynasty. Thereafter its political relations were chequered; *e.g.*, in the 6th cent. it was suppressed in favour of Buddhism, while in the 8th cent. it was honoured by the emperor Hsüan Tsung. After other such vicissitudes it was by the late Manchu dynasty reckoned along with Buddhism and Christianity as a heterodox teaching in contrast to the sacred teaching of Confucius.[1] See also art. MYSTICISM (Chinese).

LITERATURE.—J. Legge, *The Texts of Tâoism*, pts. i. and ii. [*SBE* xxxix. and xl.], Oxford, 1891, *China Review*, Jan.–Feb. 1888; F. H. Balfour, *Taoist Texts*, London [1884], *The Divine Classic of Nan-hua*, Shanghai, 1881; S. Julien, *Le Livre de la voie et de la vertu . . . par le philosophe Lao-Tseu*, Paris, 1842; H. A. Giles, *Chuang-Tzŭ*, London, 1889, *China Review*, March–April, 1886, *Confucianism and its Rivals* (*HL*), London, 1914; E. H. Parker, *Dublin Review*, Oct. 1903, Jan. 1904, *Studies in Chinese Religion*, London, 1910; R. Dvořák, *Chinas Religionen*, Münster, 1895–1903, ii., 'Lao-tsï und seine Lehre'; R. K. Douglas, *Confucianism and Taoism*, London, 1906.

P. J. MACLAGAN.

TAPAS.—See ASCETICISM (Hindu).

TARGUMS.

TARGUMS.—Though the term 'Targum' was used by Jewish authorities to designate the translation of the Hebrew Scriptures into any language, it was specifically restricted to the Aramaic renderings (cf. Ezr 4). Aramaic versions were used liturgically; the Hebrew text was read from a scroll, and this was followed by the Aramaic, recited without book by the official called *meturgeman*. This custom continued to the 10th cent., and was in parts maintained beyond that date. It is possible that the famous rescript of Justinian[2] was directed against the liturgical use of the Targum.

The most widely read of the Targums was that ascribed to Onqelos (*i.e.* Aquila), who lived in the 2nd century A.D. Aquila really rendered the Scriptures into Greek, but his name became associated also with the Aramaic version. Onqelos is a translation of the Pentateuch only, and it is known as the 'Babylonian Targum,' not so much because of its language, as because of its official adoption in the Babylonian Jewish academies. Thus, though edited in Babylonia, Onqelos is dialectically Palestinian. Onqelos probably includes elements of considerable antiquity, which were derived from oral tradition; some of it, on the other hand, is obviously of literary origin. Onqelos went through various re-editings, so that the extant text is not usually referred to an earlier period than the 4th or 5th century. The 'Palestinian Targum' (known also as the 'Targum of Jonathan'), though later than the earliest recension of Onqelos, contains elements older than the latter. The most remarkable theological characteristic of the Targums is the avoidance of anthropomorphisms. They are thus paraphrases rather than translations, though in very large part Onqelos is literal enough.

Similarly there were two Targums to the Prophets: the 'Babylonian' (ascribed to Jonathan, son of Uzziel), which originated (despite its Babylonian use) in Palestine; and the 'Palestinian,' which is fuller of homiletic elements. As selections were read from the Prophets (*haftārôth*) in the synagogues, these Targums also partook of an official character.

On the other hand, there were no such official Targums to those parts of the Bible from which no *haftārôth* were derived. Hence these Targumim to the Hagiographa form independent groups. On the whole they are freer, and in some cases (as in the Second Targum to Esther) are of greater interest for folk-lore than for exegesis. The Targum to the Song of Songs is throughout allegorical.

LITERATURE.—See full list of authorities in *HDB* iv. 683. Add W. Bacher, *Die älteste Terminologie der jüdischen Schriftauslegung*, Leipzig, 1899, p. 204 ff., and his art. in *JE*.

I. ABRAHAMS.

TARTARS.—See TURKO-TATARS.

TASMANIANS.—See AUSTRALASIA, POLYNESIA.

TATHĀGATA.

TATHĀGATA.—Whatever it may have meant originally, or from whatever source it may have been derived, Tathāgata is an epithet of Buddha used to express his very personality. It is, first of all, an appellation to specify his dignity as an enlightened being and a teacher of men and gods. He is the one who has realized the four truths according to reality (*yathābhūtam*) and, consequently, mastered the way to the realization of the truths. Sensation, perception, and thoughts are all under his own control. He is free from the bondage of the six senses and attachment to their objects, because they are not his masters, as they are with the common people, but he is master over them.[1] Thus he is beyond all the commotions and disturbances arising from contact with the objects of sense and thought. He was born a man, but has become a superhuman being in respect of and by virtue of these highest moral and intellectual attainments.[2] In order to express these superhuman excellences of Buddha's personality, the Buddhists from the earliest time used to call their master the Tathāgata with a special reverence. In this use, therefore, the appellation signifies nearly the same thing as Sugata ('the one who has gone blessed'). Here Tathāgata means the one who has gone (*gata*) from the realm of attachment to the other beyond according to reality (*tathā*, which means the same as *yathābhūtam*).

But the virtue of a Buddha does not consist in attaining this position for himself alone. He teaches the people the Way to the same attainment and guides them in its realization. He is the Master who, having himself reached the castle of fearlessness, invites and leads them to the same. The Tathāgata is not only sure that he is the perfectly enlightened one and has thoroughly overcome the miseries of existence, but also equally sure that he is the master of the Truth and the Law. With this confidence he turns the supreme wheel of the Law and roars a lion's roar in the assemblies of beings.[3] Thus the Tathāgata is the enlightened one who knows the Way and reveals that Way by treading which he himself has become the 'thus-gone.'[4] He practises as he preaches (*yathā-vādī tathā-kārī*) and *vice versa*.[5] Though this explanation of the term is, as etymology, certainly far-fetched, it is quite natural that the Buddhists saw in their Master a being without any falsehood and self-deceit. The association of the appellation with the very personality of an unerring Master of the way to final emancipation is undeniable. A stanza which is said to have been uttered by the disciples at the death of the Master is another testimony to this association. It reads:

[1] *Sacred Edict Maxim*, 7.

[2] See art. TALMUD.

[1] See *Majjhima*, nos. 102 and 123 (tr. K. E. Neumann, iii. 33, 261 f.), and *Saṃyutta*, xxii. 94, xxxv. 136 (*PTS* ed. iii. 139 f., iv. 127).

[2] See *Saṃyutta*, xxxv. 90, xliv. 2 (*PTS* ed. iv. 64, 380).

[3] See *Saṃyutta*, xii. 21 (*PTS* ed. ii. 27), and *Aṅguttara*, iv. 9 (*PTS* ed. ii. 9).

[4] See *Saṃyutta*, viii. 7 (*PTS* ed. i. 191), xxii. 58 (*PTS* ed. iii. 65); cf. *Aṅguttara*, vi. 64 (*PTS* ed. iii. 417); *Majjhima*, no. 35 (*PTS* ed. i. 372); *Saddharma-puṇḍarīka* (*SBE* xxi. [1884] 120 f.).

[5] See *Itivuttaka*, 112 (*PTS* ed. p. 122); *Aṅguttara*, iv. 23 (*PTS* ed. ii. 23 f.). Cf. below, *Lotus*, ch. ii.; and *Mahāvastu* (ed. Sénart, Paris, 1890, ii. 260, 266, 362, etc.).

'The Master, such a Master as he is (*yathā etādiso*), without any parallel in the world, the *Tathāgata* . . . is gone.'[1]

'Thus-gone' is the Master who has seen the way and revealed it to us, according to reality.

To the Buddhists their Master was the 'thus-gone' or 'thus-destined' (translation of Edmunds) to final emancipation, the 'perfected' (*der Vollendete*, Neumann) in wisdom and its realization, in short, the 'truth-winner' (Rhys Davids). The appellation was certainly a self-designation of Buddha, but it was more used by his disciples to express their confidence in the Master.

So far the empirical aspect of the concept. We must now take up the metaphysical side of the idea conveyed by or attached to the term. The Buddhists were, probably in Buddha's lifetime, nearly realizing for themselves the truth that the revealer of the Way must be at home in it, and that therefore he is the Way itself. They said:

'The laws (*dhammā*) are real and not otherwise as they are, and these are perfectly known by the Tathāgata.'[2] Here 'the laws' mean not only Buddha's teaching, but the things taught in his teaching and their essence. Hence the saying: 'He, the Blessed One, knows having known (the laws), sees having seen, born of Light, born of Wisdom, born of Truth (*dhamma-bhūto*), and born of Brhmā; He is the one who reveals and tells, the One who gives immortality, the Lord of Truth, the Tathāgata.'[3] Here we have translated the *dhamma* by 'truth,' *i.e.* the truth expressed in Buddha's laws.

The ideas here formulated cannot be called metaphysical speculations; still they show a tendency to base the faith in the Master on the transcendental entity of the Truth, not only revealed to us by him, but also represented personally by him. The foundation and elaboration of these ideas must proceed to a further development of Buddhological (so to speak, in analogy with 'Christological') speculations. The fact of the faith has been laid down by the personal influence of the Master; thought and clear conception must follow it. And it is quite natural that the Buddhological ideas were always closely associated with the appellation Tathāgata. These thoughts may be studied from three aspects or phases of their development. They are: (1) the relation of the Tathāgata to the Truth (*dhamma*) which he revealed, (2) the communion of the Tathāgata with the many other Tathāgatas, and (3) the eternity of the personality of the Tathāgata.

(1) The term *dhamma* (in both singular and plural) is a very flexible one. But the various aspects of the concept have a necessary connexion, when viewed as centring in the person of the Master. The *dhammā* (plural) are qualities of things, both physical and mental, which are transient, but subject to the laws. These laws make up existence,[4] and our attachment to and thirst for them are the causes of the miseries of life. Misery, its genesis, its extinction, and the way of release from it—these truths have been revealed by the Tathāgata according to reality (*yathābhūtam*). Thus our emancipation from the miseries is possible only by realizing to ourselves the laws according to reality. These are the laws or teachings (*dhammā*) of the Tathāgata. Therefore the laws have their root, light, and basis in the Blessed One.[5] Buddha is the king of the laws. On the other hand, however, Buddhahood is attainable only by the comprehension of the laws. Hence it is true also that Buddha is the protector of the laws, who, leaning upon the laws, reveres, honours, and adores them.[6] The Law and its revealer are mutual in their relations. He who sees the Law sees the Master, and *vice versa*.[1] The *dhamma* is not merely a phenomenon or an instruction; it is in reality the Truth, according to and by virtue of which the Master and his followers, and consequently the Buddhas of the past and future, have attained or shall attain Buddhahood.

(2) According to a commentator, as given by Burnouf, Tathāgata (*tathā-āgata*, 'thus-come') means the one who has come thus, in the same manner as his predecessors, the Buddhas of the past; it is, on the other side, *tathā* and *gata*, 'thus-gone,' and means the one who has proceeded or departed as they.[2] The oneness of enlightenment and Law among the Buddhas of the past and of the present is an idea as old as the history of Buddhism, and the development of its philosophy has always had a close relation with the idea. 'The Tathāgatā (plur.) lead men by the right law (*saddhamma*)'[3]—these are the words believed to have been spoken by Buddha himself to his temptresses. This and similar passages, speaking of the Tathāgatas and the Law, indicate the communion of the Tathāgatas, or the unity of Buddhahood in the same truth. Not only has the Law been proclaimed by the Law-born Buddhas,[4] but they all have one and the same road to tread. This one road (*ekayāna*)[5] consists in nothing but reverence towards and realization of the Law. Herein lies the very essence of the teaching of all the Tathāgatas, or, speaking metaphysically, their entity—*dhammatā*[6] or *dhammassa sudhammatā*.[7] In this concept of the essence of Buddha's teaching or Law, and consequently of his personality as the Law-born, the Buddhist philosophers have found a metaphysical basis for their faith in Buddha as the *dhamma*-born. They were to find, by the help of this idea, a metaphysical unity in the communion of all the Tathāgatas. It is quite natural that Nāgārjuna,[8] the Mahāyānist philosopher of the 2nd cent. A.D., founded his theory of Buddha's *dharmakāya*, or *dharma-ātmā*, upon this concept of *dhammatā* and the authority of the verses speaking of the *ekayāna*, above referred to.

(3) This point gives us a key to the consideration of Buddhological speculation on the eternity of the Tathāgata's life. Whether the Tathāgata exists after his bodily death or not is a question that had been asked from very early times in Buddhist history. Buddha is said to have neither affirmed nor denied it.[9] It is remarkable that every time this question is asked Buddha is named by the epithet Tathāgata. Whatever this connexion may have implied, we see that the question is affirmed on a metaphysical basis in the Mahāyāna texts, and that here again the appellation Tathāgata comes most conspicuously to the front. We have two most important texts, which devote each a whole chapter to the question of the duration of the Tathāgata's life (*Tathāgata-āyuṣ-pramāṇā*)—the *Lotus of the Law*[10] and the *Golden Light*.[11]

[1] *The Book of the Great Decease*, vi. 15 (*SBE* xi. [1900] 116 f., and ed. R. C. Childers, London, 1878, p. 62).
[2] *Dīgha*, no. 34; cf. below, ch. ii. of the *Lotus*.
[3] See *Majjhima*, no. 18 (*PTS* ed. i. 182); *Saṃyutta*, xxxv. 116 (*PTS* ed. iv. 94 f.); cf. below, ch. v. of the *Lotus*.
[4] See *Aṅguttara*, v. 57 (*PTS* ed. ii. 75), and *passim*.
[5] See *Saṃyutta*, xxiv. (*PTS* ed. iii. 202–217), etc.
[6] See *Aṅguttara*, iii. 14 (*PTS* ed. i. 109), v. 133 (*PTS* ed. iii. 150), etc.

[1] *Itivuttaka*, 92 (*PTS* ed. p. 91); *Saṃyutta*, xxii. 87 (*PTS* ed. iii. 120).
[2] *Introd. à l'hist. du bouddhisme indien*, Paris, 1845, p. 76; cf. *Mahāvastu* (ed. Sénart, ii. 266).
[3] *Saṃyutta*, iv. 3, 5 (*PTS* ed. i. 127).
[4] *Theragāthā*, verse 491 (*PTS* ed. p. 51); tr. C. A. F. Rhys Davids, *Psalms of the Early Buddhists*, London, 1913, p. 237.
[5] See *Saṃyutta*, xlvii. 18, 43 (*PTS* ed. v. 168, 186), etc.; *Aṅguttara*, vi. 26 (*PTS* ed. iii. 314); cf. the *Lotus*, esp. ch. ii. (*SBE* xxi. 49, 54, etc.).
[6] See *Saṃyutta*, vi. i. 2, lvi. 24 (*PTS* ed. i. 140, v. 434); *Aṅguttara*, iv. 21 (*PTS* ed. ii. 21); cf. *Prajñā-pāramitā* in 8000 verses (ed. Mitra, Calcutta, 1888, p. 396).
[7] *Dīgha*, no. 19.
[8] In his *Prajñā-pāramitā-śāstra* (B. Nanjio, *Catalogue of Chinese Buddhist Literature*, Oxford, 1883, no. 1169).
[9] A whole chapter called the *Avyākata*, 'Undefined,' *Saṃyutta*, xliv., is devoted to the question; cf. *Saṃyutta*, xxii. 85 f., xxiv. 15–18, xxiii. 1–10; *Majjhima*, nos. 63, 72, etc.
[10] *Saddharma-puṇḍarīka*, *SBE* xxi. ch. xvi.
[11] *Suvarṇa-prabhā* (ed. Chandra Das, Calcutta, 1898), pp. 3–9.

The first of these texts expounds at length the transcendental side of the Buddhological speculation, and the chapter above referred to may be taken as the conclusion of the exposition. Though the whole text seems to be a composite one, made up of heterogeneous elements, a definite line of argument may be found from its opening up to ch. xv. Ch. ii., entitled 'Tactfulness,' gives a view of the Buddha's personality as a skilful and tactful teacher of the Law, who, being versed himself in the deepest truth, knows how to guide men to enlightenment and how to carry out the one vehicle.[1]

The Tathāgata is a perfect being who knows all and is perfected in all virtues.[2] 'The Tathāgata only can proclaim the Tathāgata's Law, those laws which the Tathāgata knows. And the Tathāgata knows all laws, *i.e.* what are (*ye te*) the laws,[3] how (*yādṛśās*) they are, of what characteristics (*yallakṣaṇās*) they are, of what essence (*yat-svabhāvās*) they are. In these laws (*i.e.* truths) the Tathāgata is versed face to face. . . . Believe me, I speak what is real, I speak what is truthful, I speak what is not otherwise (*bhūtavādī, tathāvādī, ananyathāvādī*). . . . Having seized the one vehicle (*ekayāna*) I proclaim to beings the Law, the Buddha-vehicle; there is no second vehicle, nor a third. This is the nature of the Law (*dharmatā*) universally in the worlds in ten directions. All the Tathāgatas of the past, of the future, as well as of the present, proclaim the same one vehicle.'

After elucidating this mastership of the one vehicle by two parables, the text proceeds, in ch. v., entitled 'On Plants,' to reveal the entity of the Tathāgata's personality and his omnipotent powers. The Tathāgata who knows all *dharmas* is identified here with the *dharmas* themselves, or rather all the *dharmas* are concentrated in, and derived from, the personality of the Tathāgata. He is the king of the Law, as is stated in the *Nikāya* texts. But the king is not a mere legislator: he is the very entity of the laws.

'Whatever law for any case is laid down by the Tathāgata it becomes really so. The Tathāgata aptly ordains and lays down all laws. By the Tathāgata-wisdom he lays down the laws in such a manner that they enter into the position of omniscience.'

The Tathāgata is such a being because his omniscience, the *Tathāgata-jñāna*, is the very essence of all the laws, the real metaphysical foundation of all their manifestations. The saying that one who sees the Tathāgata sees the Law finds here a metaphysical interpretation, illustrated by a parable of rain which nourishes all plants, each according to its capacity and nature.

The discourses and dialogues following this chapter try to disclose the mysteries of Buddhahood. It is explained as of remote origin and in communion with all the enlightened of the past and future. The person of the Buddha, who was born among the Śākyas, and who has attained Buddhahood at Gayā, is nothing but a personal revelation of the eternal *dharmatā*,[4] *i.e.* the Tathāgata.[5] This faith is illustrated and supported figuratively by the issuing of innumerable saints out of the earth. The idea is that these saints cannot be the Tathāgata's disciples, unless he is Buddha from an infinite past. The argument reaches its climax in ch. xv., entitled 'The Duration of the Tathāgata's Life,' which brings to light the true measure of the Tathāgata's life. A corporal manifestation of the Tathāgata is for the benefit of those who need to be educated in that way. In reality he was perfectly enlightened long ago (*chira-abhisambuddha*), and he is everlasting (*sadā sthita*). Therefore the Tathāgata declares, at the close of the chapter, that he knows eternity. Then he proclaims to all beings: 'I am the Tathāgata' (*lect. var.* 'I am thus and thus,' *tathā tathā 'ham*).

In the *Golden Light* it is first asked why the life of Śākyamuni lasted only eighty years. Buddha answers by affirming the immeasurableness of his life. All the saints and celestial beings utter verses praising and adoring the Buddha of an immeasurable life. Here we shall give an abstract of the verses, which are indeed the statement of a metaphysics of the Tathāgata. They say:

Hearken, unimaginable is the entity of the Lord of the world, the Tathāgata, who proceeds according to reality (*yathā-ākrama*). All the Buddhas are equal in their virtue, having the same *dharmatā*. The Tathāgata is unoriginated, and our Master is not a conditioned being. The Perfectly Enlightened has the Law as his body (*dharma-kāya*),[6] the Tathāgata has the Law as his realm (*dharma-dhātu*). Neither does the Buddha vanish nor does the Law perish, yet he shows extinction, in order to bring the beings to perfection. Unimaginable is Buddha, the Blessed One; the body of the Tathāgata is eternal; for the sake of compassion towards all beings he manifests himself in various appearances.

Here, as in the *Lotus*, remains a problem to be elaborated—the question of the relations between the unchangeable entity of the Tathāgata and his manifestation. A Chinese version[7] of the text, produced by I-tsing, adds a chapter after these verses, and it treats of the three bodies (or personalities) of the Tathāgata. This may be the work of a commentator, but it indicates how the Buddhological speculations have been closely connected with the appellation Tathāgata.

[1] *SBE* xxi. 30–59.
[2] Cf. *Mahāvastu* (ed. Sénart, ii. 362).
[3] Here and in the following passage *dhammā* means the things, together with their qualities and laws.
[4] Cf. *tathatvam* (*Lotus*, v. 20), and *dharma-tathatā* (*Lalita-vistara*, ed. S. Lefmann, Halle, 1902, p. 351, l. 8).
[5] Cf. *Lalita-vistara*, ch. v. (Lefmann, p. 351).
[6] Cf. *Lalita-vistara*, ed. Lefmann, p. 436 f.; *Divyāvadāna*, ed. E. B. Cowell and R. A. Neil, Cambridge, 1886, p. 396 f.
[7] Nanjio, no. 126.

In summing up these ideas we may see that with the Buddhists the Tathāgata has meant the personal aspect of the *dharma*. To found metaphysical ideas upon faith in the person of the Tathāgata has always been the task of Buddhist orthodoxy, even in its phases of development in the East. But, in addition to this, we should consider two currents of thought which flowed beside the central one. (*a*) One of them is the theory that denies personality in the Tathāgata or anything else. It may be designated the theory of 'no-sign' (*alakṣaṇa*) and is represented by *The Diamond-cutter*[1] and other texts of the so-called Prajñā class. There the person of Buddha remains as the preacher of the sermons, and the epithet Tathāgata remains also; but nothing is allowed to be defined, any definition or qualification being thought to be a limitation, which means the same thing as illusion. Thus the texts which assert the omniscience of the Tathāgata deny to him any ascribable quality (*lakṣaṇa*). 'Tathāgata means one who does not go to anywhere, and does not come from anywhere.'[2] Here we see that the very idea of Tathāgata is put away. Nevertheless, in the midst of thorough negations, the identity of the Tathāgata and the Law is asserted.[3] This is indeed a testimony to the tenacity of the idea.

(*b*) Another current, opposite to the above, may be called the theory of 'signs' (*dharma-lakṣaṇa*). In its theoretical aspect this doctrine cannot be distinguished from orthodoxy, being founded upon the idea that all the *dharmas* are realities, which are realized in the person of the Tathāgata. But in practical aspects it looks to a Tathāgata beside the historical Buddha. Amitābha, the lord of the Sukhāvatī, or Vaiśā-jya-guru, the lord of the Eastern paradise, or Maitreya, the future Buddha in the Tusitā heaven, is the object of their adoration and their hope of salvation. The cult of the Tathāgatas in various heavens is found also in the *Lotus*,[4] and it has proved to be useful for propagandism. Buddhism of this kind, whichever may be its Tathāgata and ideal heaven, is founded upon the belief that any Buddha or saint is the manifestation of the one Tathāgata. This philosophy of the *dharma-lakṣaṇa* is a natural outcome of the early Buddhist concept of *dhamma* and is in conformity with the faith that every *dharma* is the manifestation of Buddha's wisdom (providence, so to speak). Moreover, the religion of adoring this or that Buddha as the being of compassion or as our saviour is not only in accordance with the philosophy, but also has a very sympathetic aspect of faith and piety. But the defect of this system lies in its losing concentration of faith in the historical Tathāgata and therefore in its running sometimes to an extreme pantheism.

To sum up the results: Buddhist philosophy started with the ideal of release from the miseries of life in conformity with the real nature of things (*dhammā*). As the reality, so the existence (*yathā dhammā tathā sattā*). This *yathā tathā* has been revealed by the Tathāgata, whose personality consisted in *yathā-vādī tathākārī*. This Buddha's personality is inseparable from the metaphysical entity of *dhamma*, and *vice versa*. The idea of the Tathāgata has, in this way, become the pivot around which both philosophical speculations and religious faith have moved and developed.

LITERATURE.—Besides the works quoted, see J. H. Moore, *Sayings of Buddha*, New York, 1908, p. 131; R. Chalmers, *JRAS*, 1898, p. 103; M. Anesaki, *Nichiren, the Buddhist Prophet*, Cambridge, Mass., 1916, Appendix.

M. ANESAKI.

[1] *SBE* xlix. pt. ii. [1894] pp. xii–xix, 110–144.
[2] *Ib.* xlix. pt. ii. p. 142; cf. art. DOCETISM (Buddhist).
[3] *Sarva-dharmā Buddha-dharmā* (*SBE* xlix. pt. ii. p. 134).
[4] Ch. xx.

TATI BUSHMEN.—1. Race and distribution.—The Tati Bushmen, called by the Bechuana Masarwa, and by the Matebele Amasile, are a branch of the Bush people of S. Africa, with whom they have many characteristics, both morphological and linguistic, in common.

The Bushmen in general were formerly spread over a much larger area of the continent of Africa than they occupy at present. Traces of their occupation, such as paintings, weapons, and implements, have been found far beyond their present limits. Indeed there is good reason for believing that at one time they occupied practically the whole continent and were driven by other peoples into their present territory. They are considered therefore by most anthropologists to be the true aborigines of S. Africa. In their legends they speak of a time when they were the only inhabitants of S. Africa. Paintings in the W. Sudan, in the caves of Algeria, and in Central France are strangely reminiscent of the Bushman paintings of Rhodesia or Cape Colony. The Grimaldi race, who inhabited some of the European caves in Aurignacian times, may have been either the ancestors of the Bushmen or a portion of the people who crossed over into Europe probably as slaves of the Cro-Magnon race. The Bush people are now confined to the country west of the Drakensberg Mountains and south of the Zambesi River to the Atlantic Ocean, but are principally found in the northern parts of Cape Colony, the Bechuanaland Protectorate, S.W. Protectorate, and S. Rhodesia. There are few, if any, Bushmen between the Drakensberg and the Indian Ocean, and not many in the Transvaal. So far as is known, there are none north of the Zambesi. From the Bantu traditions they must be recently extinct in N. Rhodesia and Nyasaland.

The Bushmen are divided into many different tribes and clans, speaking languages differing widely from one another, but all of the same general type. According to Meinhof,[1] the Bushman tongues are purely isolating and have their closest relations among the isolating languages of the W. Sudan. While this is true to a certain degree so far as the language of the Tati Bushmen is concerned, it is too sweeping a generalization in the present state of our knowledge. The Tati Bushmen inhabit the country between the Zambesi and the Crocodile Rivers, from the Transvaal and S. Rhodesia on the east to Lake Ngami on the west. They are fairly tall, 5 ft. 3 in. being the average stature of the men, while they are much darker in colour as a whole than the southern Bushmen. The Cape Bushmen seldom exceed 5 ft. in height, the average stature being 4 ft. 9 in., and are dirty yellow in colour. Among the Tati Bushmen some individuals attain a height of 6 ft., but they are rare. The face of the typical Bushman is triangular in outline, flat in appearance, with weak chin, depressed nose, and prominent cheek-bones. The ears usually have no lobes, the hair is thinly scattered over the skull in small tufts, there is little or no beard, and the whole appearance of the face is wild and foxy. Most of these characteristics are shared by the Tati Bushmen. Their bodies are small but tightly built, and they are seldom fat. Steatopygy is common among them, as among the southern Bushmen. The whole Bush population of S. Africa probably does not exceed 10,000, of which the Tati people may number 1000. They are a fast vanishing race.

2. Culture and organization.—The Bushmen, as their name (originally given to them by the early Dutch settlers) implies, are a people of the open country, a race of hunting savages living largely in the Stone Age. Their love of freedom amounts to a passion, and they are passionate, irresponsible, courageous, and cruel. Consequently they have practically no tribal organization, and very little clan system, except in the sense that a particular portion of country was the possession of a certain clan, the families of which, under the leadership of a man of known prowess, would combine to defend it against intruders. But usually all that obtained was that the various families combined in the face of danger, under the strongest and most capable leader, and, once that passed, the combination came to an end. They do not cultivate the soil and have no domesticated animals except dogs. They therefore depend entirely upon the chase. Their dwellings are caves or holes in rocks, or shelters made of a few branches stuck in the ground, with skins or mats thrown over them, which they carry away with them when they migrate from the district. Their material civilization is thus very meagre, being restricted to what is absolutely necessary for the capture and cooking of game. A little coarse pottery is or was made, while ostrich egg shells are used to hold water. Beads of dried wild berries and necklaces made from disks cut from ostrich egg shells are worn by both men and women. Ear-rings made from pieces of bone or wood, or—since the white man came to the country—of metal, usually brass, are common. Leather arm- and leg-rings, together with fillets of skin round the head, into which are stuck ostrich and other feathers, are also worn. Clothing is scanty and generally consists of the skin of an animal thrown over the shoulders in cold weather. The women wear a small piece of skin with fringes in front, while the men are content with a narrow piece of skin passed between the legs and tied round the waist with sinew or cord. Children of both sexes go naked. In warm weather to prevent the sun from blistering the skin, and in winter to keep out the cold, they smear the body with fat, often rancid, so that they smell very offensively. Weapons of war and the chase are spears, bows and arrows, and throwing-sticks. The tips of the arrows are smeared with poison made from the Bushman's poison bush (*Acocanthera venenata*) and the two-rowed Amaryllis (*Amaryllis distichia*), mixed with snake poison, and in some cases with poisonous ants. The food of both sexes consists of the flesh of animals, locusts, larvæ of ants, called 'Bushman rice,' gum, and various tubers and seeds. For the collection of tubers an implement called the *!kibi* or *!kwe* is employed. It is a stout stick about 3 ft. long, upon which a round flat stone with a hole in the centre is fastened about 9 ins. from the end. This is the well-known digging stick, which is also used to excavate graves.

3. Mentality; artistic and moral life.—The Bush people as a whole are low in the scale of mental acquirements. They have an extensive knowledge of the outdoor world, especially of the habits of wild animals. They are wonderful as trackers and have a remarkable sense of direction. Their reflective faculties are not highly developed, although some of their paintings, and more especially their folk-tales and songs, are not wanting in this respect. The most interesting thing about the Bushmen is their artistic ability. They have left paintings upon the walls of caves and rocks and incised figures upon boulders all over the country. Most of these paintings or chippings indicate objects of the chase, the habits of animals,

[1] C. Meinhof, 'The Language of the Hottentots,' *Addresses and Papers read at the Joint Meeting of the British and South African Associations for the Advancement of Science*, South Africa, 1905, iii. 198.

or more rarely scenes of war and domestic life. The drawings of the wild animals are in many cases really well executed, though one can trace in places the gradual evolution of the art of painting. A fresco recently discovered in the Matopo Hills near Bulawayo is remarkable for its artistic merit. There is not much perspective in most of the paintings, while the execution as a whole reminds one of the paintings of the Old Stone Age. Certain paintings of figures are supposed to have a mythological signification, as they cannot be connected with animals or circumstances of the present day. Some caves were called after particular paintings—*e.g.*, the Cave of the Great Serpent, the Cave of the Lion—and hence were held in a certain degree of reverence by the people. To such caves they would periodically return as to a rallying-point to talk over their wild adventures. It has been suggested that the art of the Bushman is due to sympathetic magic, that this was the idea underlying it—in other words, that the Bushman painted the animals on the walls of his cave-dwelling to give him power over them in the field. While this is possible, and may be probable in some cases, there is not any good evidence of it. It has been maintained that paintings usually depict animals desirable for food, and that noxious animals are conspicuous by their absence. So far as Bushman paintings are concerned, this is not true. If animals such as lions, leopards, snakes, and rhinoceroses are to be considered noxious animals, they occur often enough on the paintings. But such animals are not undesirable as food to the Bushmen, as they eat practically everything, and certainly would not refuse to eat the flesh of a lion, unless it happened to be the totem of the hunter. On the whole the paintings reflect no more than the ordinary life of the people *plus* the caprice of the particular artist. At intervals of leisure—and the Bushmen, when food was plenty, had much of that—the scenes of the past would rise up in their minds, and they would attempt to visualize them by painting them on the rock, and by constant practice the faculty of drawing improved. The colours employed were yellow, brown, red, and sometimes white, and blue. Some of these paintings are ancient, and some are quite modern, as certain of the artists are or were recently alive. The faculty of drawing and painting was said to be hereditary in certain families. The theory has been advanced that the painters and sculptors belonged to different tribes, but there is no good reason for accepting this.

The Bushmen are passionately fond of dancing, more especially at full moon and at certain seasons of the year. Fires are lit outside their caves, and dancing is kept up all night, or until the performers are exhausted. Some of these dances, in which the performers paint their faces and bodies, are of a religious nature. Some of them are more or less coarse. Songs are sung by the leaders, and the other performers join in the chorus. The motions are not at all graceful. Some dances are called after animals—*e.g.*, the eland bull dance, the baboon dance, the bee dance, and the frog dance—and each has its own peculiar tune. The dancers give very good imitations of the animal in its different attitudes. The instruments used to accompany these dances are stringed instruments similar to an ordinary bow, with a tortoise-shell as a sound-box variously called *!kopo*, *!kangen*, and *‖gora*, 'reed,' 'flutes,' and 'drums.' The dancers have rattles round their ankles, made of the skin of the inside of the springbok's ear, with small pebbles inside to make as much sound as possible. Circumcision dances are performed after the boys have undergone the ceremony. These are of a distinctly religious character. Bushman music is, as might be expected, of a very primitive character—the melancholy and monotonous repetition of a few notes. It does not usually consist of more than six tones (which do not belong to our scale), but the strangeness and wildness of the melody give it a peculiar charm. There are other tunes which show some advance, especially one by the Natal Bushmen. Harmony does not exist.

The Bushmen have an extensive range of terms for family relationships, both male and female. Some of these are connected with tabus; *e.g.*, a mother-in-law must not see her son-in-law or mention his name; he, on his part, must not mention hers. The same rule applies to some other relations also. A woman must avoid mentioning the name of her husband or any of his near relatives. There are different terms for these relationships, but the system among the Bushmen is not nearly so perfect as that among the Australians.

Marriage is usually a very simple matter among the Bushmen, some of whom are monogamists and some polygamists, according to their individual worldly position. Two young people very often simply go off and live together, but usually the young man has to prove his prowess by going into the veld and slaying some wild animal—the strongest and fiercest he can find—and presenting the whole or a selected portion to the girl's father. Among some tribes this is considered indispensable before asking the hand of a girl in marriage. If the present is accepted, the marriage is complete. Sexual intercourse before marriage, while looked upon as a crime, is very often practised. Divorce too is simple. A man or woman leaves his or her partner and goes off with some one else. The custody of the children does not cause much trouble, as the young people are accustomed to fend for themselves at an early age. Parental control is thus exceedingly weak. Marriage usually takes place within the clan, but a man cannot marry a woman of the same family as his own—*i.e.* bearing his own surname. So far as we know, a man cannot take his own sister to wife, because of his totem, but he may take his sister-in-law. Although there is much freedom in the intercourse of the sexes, incest and adultery are regarded as crimes and are punished by death, usually by retaliation on the part of the injured person. Murder, theft, abduction, and especially witchcraft, are crimes against the Bushman moral code and are punished by fines, expulsion from the tribe, or even death in the case of persistent offenders. The old people, when too infirm to follow the family in its wanderings or unable to procure food for themselves, are left to die.

4. Totemism and religion.—As has been remarked, totemism exists among the Bushmen, especially among those tribes that have had long contact with the Bantu peoples, but they are too much the children of the wild to have developed it to any extent. Some call themselves the Zebra clan, or the Eland clan, or the Duiker clan, and, while they avoid killing and eating these animals or certain portions of them, they are not at all strict about the matter when pressed by hunger. In the case of the Duiker clan, the members may eat all of the animal except the heart. Those clans whose totem was the buffalo did not scruple to eat every portion of a domestic ox, although they might not eat every portion of a wild buffalo, even though they looked upon oxen as tame buffaloes.

They believe in a spirit which the northern tribes call Thora, and the southern !Kang or ‖Kaggen.

W. H. I. Bleek,[1] J. M. Orpen,[2] and others think that ! Kang is simply the mantis insect, for which they have a great reverence, but there does not seem to be great force in this contention. While it may be true of the Bushmen of Cape Colony, it is certainly not true of the Tati Bushmen. These tribes say that Thora is a spirit, that he sends the rain, the lightning (of which they are very much afraid), good weather, bad luck, and plenty. They are not very clear as to whether he is a person or not, but he is usually spoken of with dread, as a malevolent spirit, with whom it is advisable to keep on good terms. They also say that he made the animals, but they are not sure if he made the first men. The Tati Bushmen reverence the mantis to a certain extent, and do not like killing it if they can help it. All Bushmen have a great dread of death, and in common with many peoples believe that it is due to bewitchment by an enemy. Arbousset,[3] speaking of the Bushmen of Basutoland of his day, says that they looked upon death as a sleep. It is difficult to ascertain what they do really think on the subject, as they are so unwilling to speak of it at all. They also believe in some form of future life, but do not know what it is really like. They imagine that it does not differ much from the present life. This is shown by the burial customs of some tribes. They used to drag their dead into the surrounding bush to be devoured by wild animals, but generally they bury the bodies in a hole or cleft in a rock, which they carefully wall up, or they excavate a round hole about 3 or 4 ft. deep and place the dead man at the bottom in a sitting or lying position, with the legs doubled up to the chin, and in each case place beside him some food and his weapons of war. They generally indulge in a funeral feast afterwards, desert the locality, and never mention the dead man's name. Why they keep silence regarding the departed they cannot explain. Some tribes place the dead with his face to the rising sun; others observe no such custom.

The Tati Bushmen have no regular priests, but they have certain individuals, whom they call doctors, who possess a considerable knowledge of the properties and uses of wild plants, and thus exercise great influence over the people. This knowledge is sometimes confined to certain families, who jealously guard it. They have a considerable knowledge of vegetable poisons and have antidotes for them. Malicious poisoning does not often occur among them. Bushman doctors profess to cure malaria, typhoid, blackwater fever, dysentery, and other diseases, and, according to reliable information, are often successful. Most of the plants which they use are employed in religious ceremonies or in ordeals and trials for witchcraft. In fact, much, if not all, of the Bushman practice of medicine has a religious signification.

The Tati Bushmen, in common with most other Bushmen, practise circumcision. At present they perform the rite according to the Bechuana custom. Boys are operated upon at about the age of twelve years, development being rapid with them. A stone knife was formerly employed and still is by most tribes—a matter of necessity at first, but now a matter of custom, or of hygiene, as the knife is thrown away and a new one made for each ceremony. A number of boys of approximately the same age are operated upon at once. The method is as follows. The foreskin is pulled forward over the glans as far as it will stretch and then cut off with one slash of the knife. It quickly retracts and so prevents excessive bleeding, and usually heals rapidly. It is not known for certain whether the girls underwent the rite or not. The southern Bushmen cut off the last joint of the little finger of the right hand in the case of boys, and of the left hand in the case of girls. This was also a religious ceremony, but whether it took the place of circumcision or was additional thereto is still uncertain. Cutting off the joints of one or more fingers was also practised as a sign of mourning. The Tati Bushmen, whatever they may have done in the past, do not now practise finger-cutting.

5. Omens.—The great factor in the life of the Bushmen is their divining bones, commonly but erroneously called dice. The Bushmen would undertake no expedition without consulting them. They are four and sometimes five in number, and designated male and female. The female bone is usually longer than the male. They are made from the hoofs of animals, bone, horn, wood, or even the stones of wild fruits. Sometimes they are ornamented with designs on back or front. To consult them a man would clear a small space of ground, rub the bones with various kinds of medicine, blow upon them, and then cast them upon the ground. From their positions and conjunctions he divines what he wants to know, according to certain laws. If the result is unfavourable, it is useless for him to persevere in his object. Divination is also practised by means of the shoulder-blade of a springbok, and by certain other animals, such as the mantis, lion, jackal, and snake.

6. Spirits.—The Bushmen personify some animals and look upon them as men in another state of existence. They also believe that men, especially witch-doctors, can assume animal shapes at will and compel other people to do the same. This, they say, is to 'have power' over such victims. It has been held to indicate a belief in the transmigration of souls, but the point is very doubtful. They certainly believe in transformations of animals. The Tati Bushmen thoroughly believe in the existence of spirits, usually of a malevolent character, and, when closely questioned, admit that they can change their shapes at will, but they do not seem to believe that these spirits can be born again into other animal shapes. Lightning, wind, eddies of dust, storms, and other natural phenomena are looked upon as spirits. This is probably a relic of primitive man's belief that the animals and things about him were not different from himself—certainly to some extent the Bushman view. There are spirits of rivers, fountains, and thermal springs known to the Bushmen and much reverenced by them.

7. Mythology of the heavenly bodies.—The Bushmen have no regular system of mythology in the sense that the ancient Greeks or the modern Hindus have, but they have the elements of such. They are said to have worshipped the heavenly bodies and are therefore to be included among those people who attained to sidereal worship. Among the Tati Bushmen no special ceremonies are connected with these bodies, although it is evident from numerous tales in which the sun and moon appear that a considerable degree of reverence is paid to them. The new moon figures in many of their tales.

The moon is the shoe of the mantis. Her waxing and waning is explained as her dying and coming to life again. The Tati Bushmen have some of these tales in a more or less modified form; *e.g.*, one speaks of the moon coming down to wash her face in a pool of water. The Bushmen do not know why the sun is hot, and why there is no heat in the moon. Among the southern Bushmen the sun is spoken of as a little boy by the wayside; sometimes he is said to have been thrown into the sky by some children while he was sleeping. Again, the moon is spoken of as being cut by the sun and after death

[1] *A Brief Account of Bushman Folk Lore*, p. 6 ff.

[2] 'A Glimpse into the Mythology of the Malute Bushmen,' *Cape Monthly Magazine*, July, 1874, pp. 1–13.

[3] T. Arbousset and F. Daumas, *Relation d'un voyage d'exploration au nord-est de la Colonie du Cap de Bonne-Espérance*, p. 504.

carries away the people who are dead. Some of the Tati Bushmen say that the stars were once human beings and animals, and the Cape Bushmen speak of girls as having been turned into stars and flowers by the rain. Certain prominent stars have particular names among the Bushmen; *e.g.*, Jupiter is the Dawn's Heart; the Magellanic Clouds the Male and Female Steinbok, the Southern Cross the Giraffe Star (Tati Bushmen), Aldebaran the Male Hartebeest, Procyon the Male Eland, Orion's Belt the Female Tortoises. The origin of the stars is explained in the following manner. A girl of the early race, being angry with her mother because the latter asked her for a certain kind of food which she had put to roast in the fire, threw it together with the wood ashes that were upon it into the air. The food was changed into stars, and the ashes became the Milky Way. The rising of particular stars at certain seasons of the year was noted, as they were connected with the return of the seasons. Shooting stars were considered unlucky by the Tati Bushmen, and, if they appeared in great numbers, inspired terror.

8. Folk literature.—The Bushmen have a great body of folklore, mostly relating to animals and natural objects, customs, and so on, but next to none of a historical character, certainly none that throws much light on their origin and migrations. Not a tithe of those folk-tales have been garnered, and, as the race is a fast vanishing one, they will soon be completely lost. Bleek collected a large number of tales, and a selection from his great mass of materials was published in 1911 by his niece, Miss Lloyd. Smaller collections by Schultze, Theal, and Dornan have been issued. A study of these tales throws much light on the mental and moral outlook of the Bushmen.

LITERATURE.—Peter Kolben, *The Present State of the Cape of Good Hope*, Eng. tr., 2 vols., London, 1731; A. Sparrman, *A Voyage to the Cape of Good Hope*, Eng. tr., 2 vols., do. 1785; J. Barrow, *An Account of Travels into the Interior of Southern Africa in the Years 1797 and 1798*, 2 vols, do. 1801-04; H. Lichtenstein, *Travels in Southern Africa in the Years 1803-06*, Eng. tr., 2 vols., do. 1812-15; W. J. Burchell, *Travels in the Interior of Southern Africa*, 2 vols., do. 1822-24; W. C. Harris, *Narr. of an Expedition into Southern Africa 1836-7*, Bombay, 1838; A. Sutherland, *A Memoir respecting the Kaffirs, Hottentots, and Bosjemans of S. Africa*, 2 vols., Cape Town, 1845; R. Moffat, *Missionary Labours and Scenes in Southern Africa*, London, 1842; T. Arbousset and F. Daumas, *Relation d'un voyage d'exploration au nord-est de la Colonie du Cap de Bonne-Espérance*, Paris, 1842; D. Livingstone, *Missionary Travels and Researches in S. Africa*, London, 1857; G. Fritsch, *Die Eingeborenen Süd-Afrika's*, Breslau, 1872; W. H. I. Bleek, *A Brief Account of Bushman Folk Lore and other Texts*, London, 1875; L. C. Lloyd, *A Short Account of Bushman Material collected by L. C. Lloyd*, do. 1889; L. Schultze, *Aus Namaland und Kalahari*, Jena, 1907; G. W. Stow, *Native Races of S. Africa*, London, 1905; S. Passarge, *Die Buschmänner der Kalahari*, Berlin, 1907; M. Helen Tongue, *Bushman Paintings*, Oxford, 1909; S. S. Dornan, 'The Bushmen of Basutoland,' *Transactions of the South African Philosophical Society*, xviii. [1909] 437 ff.; G. M. Theal, *The Yellow and Dark-Skinned People of Africa South of the Zambesi*, London, 1910; W. H. I. Bleek and L. C. Lloyd, *Specimens of Bushman Folklore*, do. 1911; W. J. Sollas, *Ancient Hunters and their Modern Representatives*, do. 1915; S. S. Dornan, 'The Tati Bushmen (Masarwas) and their Language,' *JRAI* xlvii. [1917] 37 ff.

S. S. DORNAN.

TATUING.—The word 'tatu' or 'tattoo,' meaning to mark or puncture the skin, is derived from the Tahitian word *tatau*, a reduplicated form of the root *ta*, 'to strike.' It was used by Captain Cook in the account of his visit to Tahiti:

'Both sexes paint their Bodys, *Tattow* as it is called in their Language. This is done by inlaying the Colour of Black under their skins in such a manner as to be indelible.'[1]

Cook was thus the first to introduce the word to the civilized world of his day. Many writers since his time have included in the general term 'tatu' the practice of marking the skin with cicatrices; the two processes are, however, very different. Tatu proper is the insertion of pigment under the skin, whereby a practically permanent stain is produced, while cicatrization is the marking of the body, either by cutting or burning the skin in such a way as to cause scars forming small depressions or by cutting into the skin and keeping the wounds open, so that keloids, or raised scars, are formed, which stand out prominently from the surrounding tissue.

[1] *Journal during his First Voyage, 1768-71*, ed. W. J. Wharton, London, 1893, p. 93.

1. Antiquity and distribution.—Both these modes of personal decoration are of considerable antiquity and of wide distribution; they have been found among people of greatly varying culture, from the aborigines of Australia, who adorn their bodies with cicatrices, to the Polynesians and Japanese, who have developed tatu proper into a fine art. At a very early stage man no doubt felt a desire for personal decoration and learnt to use pigment for this purpose; and it is possible that tatu was resorted to as a means of giving a permanent character to the designs thus made to beautify the body at a stage prior to the use of clothes. Archæological evidence can, unfortunately, give us no direct proof of the existence of such a custom as tatu in pre-historic times, but it is well known that Aurignacian man was skilful in the use of colour. Déchelette suggests that the finely pointed implements found in Magdalenian deposits may have been used for tatuing. Referring to the practice among primitive peoples of cicatrization and tatu, he says:

'Les premiers habitants de l'Europe préhistorique s'ornaient le corps à l'aide des mêmes procédés, mais en général il nous est impossible de distinguer nettement pour cette période entre la teinture corporelle simple et le tatouage. C'est là un fait établi par des preuves indirectes mais décisives pour la fin des temps quaternaires, pour l'époque néolithique et le commencement tout au moins de l'âge du bronze.'[1]

In the pre-dynastic tombs of the old Egyptians excavated by Flinders Petrie, de Morgan, Amélineau, and others, some rude human figures have been found bearing marks that suggest the use of tatu—*e.g.*, the female figure discovered at Tukh.[2] In the second Theban empire the Egyptians tatued themselves on the breast or arms with the names or symbols of deities, but decorative tatu marks are rare on Egyptian remains of the classical period.[3] The prohibition in Lv 19[28], 'Ye shall not make any cuttings in your flesh for the dead, nor print any marks upon you,' indicates that the Jews had seen these practices carried on by the heathen nations among whom their lot was cast, and perhaps had themselves adopted them.

There are many classical allusions to tatu in Europe. Herodotus writes of the Thracian women being tatued as a sign of nobility.[4] Pliny[5] says that the men of the Dacians and Sarmatians marked their bodies ('corpora sua inscribunt'). That tatu was known to the Pictones and other tribes of Gaul is shown by the evidence from coins.[6] Chinese tradition says that the great Chinese hero Tschaipe found tatu among the Ainus of Japan, who indeed practise it to this day. In China it ceased at a very early time to be a desirable mode of decoration and survives only as a method of imposing a distinctive mark. A. T. Sinclair says that 'among the ancient natives in the West Indies, Mexico and Central America, tattooing was general if not almost universal.'[7] It was also practised by the early inhabitants of S. America, as notably among the coastal tribes of Ecuador and ancient Peru.[8] G. Elliot Smith finds it along the coast-lines of a great part of the world and includes it in the culture-complex of the 'heliolithic' track.[9] Darwin, in drawing attention to the universality of the custom among primitive peoples, said: 'Not one great country can be named, from the Polar regions in the north to New Zealand in the south, in which the aborigines do

[1] *Manuel d'Archéologie*, Paris, 1908-13, i. 203.
[2] W. M. Flinders Petrie, *Naqada*, London, 1896, pl. 59. 6.
[3] J. Capart, *Les Débuts de l'art en Egypte*, Brussels, 1904, p. 32 f.
[4] v. 6.
[5] *HN* xxii. 1.
[6] T. Rice Holmes, *Ancient Britain and the Invasions of Julius Cæsar*, Oxford, 1907, p. 418 ff.
[7] 'Tattooing of the American Indians,' *American Anthropologist*, new ser., xi. [1909] 399.
[8] T. A. Joyce, *S. American Archæology*, London, 1912, p. 61 f.
[9] *The Migrations of Early Culture*, London, 1915, p. 7.

not tattoo themselves.'[1] W. Joest goes so far as to say that no race or people exists that has not had the custom of either painting or tatuing the body.[2] On the other hand, some investigators have failed to find traces of cicatrization or tatu among certain primitive tribes, such as the Vedda of Ceylon,[3] the Mafulu of British New Guinea,[4] the Tati Bushmen,[5] and others; but this negative evidence does not rule out the possibility that such practices were once known to these people and have become lost arts. Cicatrization is mainly confined to dark-skinned races, while tatu proper prevails with those of lighter colour. Thus we find cicatrization in Australia, Tasmania, New Caledonia, Fiji, and other parts of Melanesia, in Torres Straits islands, among the Papuans of New Guinea, in the Malay Peninsula (Sakai), the Andaman Islands, and in negro Africa. It has been superseded in S. America by tatu proper, but has been observed among the Caribs of Guiana and in Brazil. The light-coloured races who have practised tatu proper include the Maoris of New Zealand and the inhabitants of the other islands of Polynesia. It is also found in Melanesia, Micronesia, the Malay Archipelago, the Malay Peninsula, Burma, India, among the Tibeto-Burman peoples in general (but rare in Tibet), and in Japan. In Africa it is found in Algeria, in Egypt, among the For, the Tushilang, the Namaqua Hottentots, and other tribes, but it is by no means so widely distributed in this continent as cicatrization. On the other hand, tatu proper was very prevalent in the New World, especially among the Indian tribes of N. America, such as the Iroquois, the Pricked Pawnees, the Delawares, and others. It is used extensively at the present day by the Haida Indians of the N.W. American coast, and also by the Eskimo, and in S. America, notably among the Mundrucu and Guaycura tribes.

Tatuing is said to be one of the chief occupations of the Oriental gypsies. Sinclair found that most of the tatuing among the lower orders in Syria, Mesopotamia, Arabia, Egypt, and some parts of Persia was done by them. They also tatu themselves, and in this they differ from European gypsies, for these do not wear tatu marks. 'Hence their tattooing is an easy mode of identifying Oriental gipsies, who are often seen in all parts of Europe and America.'[6] At the present day tatuing persists in Europe among the lower classes. Lombroso made a comparative study of tatu among soldiers and criminals, and concluded that it was especially prevalent among the latter. He noted that the designs in criminal tatu are often extremely complex and of a cynical and obscene character.[7] There was a considerable revival of tatu among the soldiers and sailors serving with the British forces in the recent war. A revival, too, has been evident in Japan since 1881, when tatu ceased to be a penal offence and came once more into vogue, with the result that it is now an elaborate art.[8] Apart from these and similar isolated revivals, tatu is, on the whole, rapidly declining, especially in Polynesia, once the centre of a highly developed system of tatu. This change is due, no doubt, in a great measure to the action of the missionaries, who have discouraged the practice, because of the orgies that often accompanied the tatuing operations.

2. Methods and implements.—The methods and implements used to produce these marks on the body vary considerably in different parts of the world and often reflect the cultural conditions of the people among whom they have been found. It is impossible here to do more than indicate briefly some of the more striking variations of the processes which have been recorded and add a few examples by way of illustration.

1 *Descent of Man*, London, 1871, ii. 339.
2 *Tätowiren, Narbenzeichnen, und Körperbemalen*, Berlin, 1887, p. 45.
3 C. G. and B. Z. Seligmann, *The Veddas*, Cambridge, 1911, p. 207.
4 R. W. Williamson, *The Mafulu Mountain People of British New Guinea*, London, 1912, p. 36.
5 S. S. Dornan, 'The Tati Bushmen,' *JRAI* xlvii. [1917] 44.
6 *Amer. Anth.*, new ser., x. [1908] 361.
7 C. Lombroso, 'Criminal Anthropology,' in *20th Century Practice of Medicine*, London, 1897, xii. 382 ff.
8 B. H. Chamberlain, *Things Japanese*², London, 1891, p. 399 ff.

(*a*) *Cicatrization.*—In Central Africa prominent keloids are formed by detaching a piece of skin, which is raised and held by a pellet of tow till the wound is healed. A. L. Cureau alludes to 'dandies of the Upper Ubangi and Equatorial Congo' who undergo this operation as a means of obtaining 'the prominent crest which gives them a fierce expression.'[1] Irritant substances are sometimes rubbed into the incisions to prevent the wounds from healing too rapidly. Among the Bageshu, a Bantu people on the south and south-east slopes of Mt. Elgon, the girls use a crescent-shaped flesh hook sharpened to a needle point at one end. Scars are formed on the forehead and stomach by pinching up the flesh between the thumb and finger and running the hook through it; fine dust from a wood fire is then rubbed into the wounds.[2] Natives from the interior of Mozambique wear marked *rugæ* on the forehead.

These are formed 'by making vertical incisions in the skin, rubbing in a medicine, and then binding tightly with a cloth, so that wrinkles are formed in the line of the incision.'[3]

Cicatrization begins with the Andamanese at the age of eight and continues at intervals until the sixteenth or eighteenth year is reached. It is usually done by women, who use a flake of quartz or glass held between the forefinger and thumb. The arms and back are marked first, while fasting, and afterwards the chest, abdomen, and legs, but never the face; the special tribal marks are, in some tribes, made by men with a pig arrow. Pork is not eaten while the wounds are healing; and the northern tribes have certain ceremonies connected with the operation.[4] The aborigines of Central Australia cut the skin with flakes of flint or glass and rub in ashes or the down of the eagle-hawk.[5] At Port Essington (N. Territory of Australia) scars are formed by burning the flesh with a red-hot stick.[6] In N.W. Queensland they are made by lighting charcoal on the flesh and allowing it to burn there. The implements used in Melanesia differ in different islands; *e.g.*, in the Solomons the circular or chevron-shaped cicatrices worn by both sexes on the face are made with the claw of the flying fox,[7] while in Florida Island the pattern is 'marked out in circles with a bamboo, and the skin is cut with the bone of a bat's wing.'[8] The keloids and scars called *kotto*, which are customary in New Britain, are made with obsidian flakes.[9]

(*b*) *Tatu proper.*—A method which seems to suggest a combination of cicatrization and tatu proper is that of cutting the flesh and rubbing pigment into the wounds. Livingstone says of the Makoa (Makua) of Central Africa, who have double lines of keloids on the face: 'After the incisions are made, charcoal is rubbed in and the flesh pressed out, so that all the cuts are raised above the level of the surface.'[10] The charcoal gives a bluish tinge to the skin, 'and the ornament shows brightly in persons of light complexion, who by the by are common.'[11] The Ainu women of Yezo (Japan) cut gashes on the face with a sharp knife and rub in soot from burnt birch-bark, which

1 *Savage Man in Central Africa*, tr. E. Andrews, London, 1915, p. 169.
2 J. Roscoe, 'Notes on the Bageshu,' *JRAI* xxxix. [1909] 186.
3 G. A. Turner, 'Tribal Marks of S. African Natives,' *Transvaal Medical Journal*, Feb. 1911, p. 13.
4 E. H. Man, *Aboriginal Inhabitants of the Andaman Islands*, London, 1883, p. 112.
5 Spencer-Gillen^a, p. 41 f.
6 B. Spencer, *Native Tribes of the N. Territory of Australia*, London, 1914, p. 9.
7 C. M. Woodford, *A Naturalist among the Head-Hunters*, London, 1890, p. 31.
8 R. H. Codrington, *The Melanesians*, Oxford, 1891, p. 237.
9 R. Parkinson, *Dreissig Jahre in der Südsee*, Stuttgart, 1907, p. 145.
10 D. Livingstone, *Last Journals in Central Africa*, London, 1874, i. 33.
11 *Ib.* i. 49 f.

produces a bluish-black effect.[1] This method has also been observed in some of the islands of Micronesia.

The implements used for pricking the skin range in complexity from such simple natural objects as thorns, fish spines, cactus spikes, shells, and bones, to the elaborate metal appliance of the Burmese and the steel and electric needles of Japan and Europe in use at the present day. The Roro-speaking tribes of British New Guinea obtain the desired effect by very simple means. The operator, who is generally an old woman, applies colouring matter—soot mixed with water—with a fragment of wood frayed out at one end to form a coarse brush. The colour is pricked in by means of a pricker having one or more thorns set at right angles to its long axis; these thorns are driven into the skin by tapping the pricker gently with a small wooden mallet. The women of these tribes are tatued from head to foot, but the operation takes place at intervals, and there is a regular order in which the different parts of the body must be tatued; thus the hands and arms are done in childhood, and later the tatu is gradually increased until at marriageable age it is applied to the buttocks, legs, and last of all to the face.[2] The Polynesian method of tatuing is generally to trace the design on the skin first with charcoal and then to follow the pattern with a small adze-shaped implement furnished with a serrated bone edge. The skin is perforated by hammering or tapping this implement with another made of wood and shaped like a paddle. But the ways and means employed vary a good deal in the South Sea Islands, and the operation is often accompanied by much ceremonial and feasting, and the keeping of certain tabus; *e.g.*, brides in the Fiji, while being tatued, are *tabu siga*, and are kept in seclusion, for they must not see the sun.[3] In New Zealand a very strict tabu has to be observed by the person undergoing the ordeal; he may not communicate with any one not in the same condition, nor may he touch his food. The Maori chief had to be fed through a special funnel during the process, which entailed a good deal of ceremonial of a somewhat religious character. The Maori tatu, or *moko*, was of two kinds, of which the older method was a cutting into the skin with a small chisel-like tool made of sea-bird's wing-bones, shark's teeth, stones, or hard wood, and of different sizes and shapes. The edge of the chisel was applied to the skin and tapped by a small mallet, which sometimes had a broad flattened surface at one end used to wipe away the blood. This chiselling process was superseded by prick tatu, which was done with small-toothed or serrated implements dipped in colouring matter obtained either from charcoal mixed with oil or dog's fat or burnt and powdered resin.[4] In Borneo the design is pressed on to the skin with a tatu block dipped in pigment made from a mixture of soot and sugar-cane juice. The needle points of the pricker, which are also charged with pigment, are then driven into the skin by taps from a striker. Among the Kayans the men carve the designs on the blocks, but the tatu is done by women. The artists are under the protection of a tutelary spirit to whom sacrifices must be made, and the operator has to avoid certain foods. The women are tatued in a hut built for the purpose; their male relatives are dressed in bark-cloth and must remain indoors until the operation is completed; in fact it cannot be commenced unless their men-folk are at home.

[1] J. Batchelor, *The Ainu and their Folk-lore*, London, 1901, p. 24.
[2] C. G. Seligmann, *The Melanesians of British New Guinea*, Cambridge, 1910, p. 265.
[3] T. Williams, *Fiji and the Fijians*[3], London, 1870, p. 146.
[4] Major-Gen. Robley, *Moko: Maori Tattooing*, London, 1896, pp. 47, 62.

It is prohibited to tatu women at seed-time, or if a dead body lies unburied in the house, and bad dreams, such as 'a dream of floods, foretelling much blood-letting, will also interrupt the work.'[1] In Burma the outline of the desired pattern is roughly sketched on the skin with a camel's hair brush and is then pricked in by a series of punctures close together, which merge into a rough line. The pricker is of an unusual kind, being two feet long and weighted at the top with a brass or lead figure; the pigment is contained in a style four inches long, which fits into a hollow pipe and is thus joined to the weighted end.[2] In Japan steel needles of four different sizes are used; the effect of shading is procured by tying rows of needles together. Sepia, vermilion, and Prussian blue are used in the designs, which are very ornate.[3] In some parts of N. America the pigmented effect is obtained by running a needle-like implement through the skin threaded with some material coated in pigment.

This method was followed by the Salish tribes, who used a 'needle of fish-bone or a cactus spike, which passed a fine thread coated with charcoal under the skin,' or sometimes the charcoal was carried on an unthreaded needle, 'which was thrust under the skin in a horizontal direction.'[4]

The Eskimo use a needle and thread smeared with soot or gun-powder. Thus, speaking of the personal appearance of the Greenlanders, D. Crantz says:

'No one . . . is a finished beauty till the skin of her cheeks, chin, hands and feet, has been threaded by a string smeared with soot, which when drawn out leaves a black mark. The mother performs this painful operation on her daughter in childhood, fearful that she will else attract no husband. This custom obtains among the Indians of North America, and various Tartar tribes, where both sexes practise it; the one to heighten their charms, the other to inspire terror.'[5]

3. **Patterns.**—A detailed study of the patterns would doubtless yield results of considerable ethnological interest as pointing to the migrations and culture-contact of peoples. Flinders Petrie[6] has drawn attention to the resemblance between the Algerian patterns described by Lucien Jacquot[7] and those on the female figure found at Tukh and on the Libyans in the tomb of Seti I. (XIXth dynasty, 1300 B.C.). The dominating designs in Algeria are a cross and a figure resembling a fly, which are thought to be degenerate forms of the swastika—a device widely distributed in Africa and elsewhere, and of great antiquity, as is shown by its appearance on a leaden figure[8] in the second city of Troy (about 2500–2000 B.C.) and by its prevalence in ancient Crete. The designs in favour among the Haida tribes on the north-west coast of America are similar to those on their boats, house-fronts, pillars, and monuments, and include family crests and totemic symbols such as the thunder-bird, wolf, bear, codfish, and so on. There is a great variation in the patterns of the Polynesian tatu, for almost every island has some distinctive characteristic of its own. The Marquesans, *e.g.*, tatu in broad straight lines. Many of their signs suggest a hieroglyphic system which can be interpreted only by their priests; in Anaa, however, sea-urchins and quaint zoophytes are well represented on the leg and thigh. The Marquesan women have a design somewhat resembling a gridiron tatued on their lips.[9] In Tahiti the patterns are simpler, but of greater taste and elegance than those of the Marquesas Islands.

[1] C. Hose and W. McDougall, *The Pagan Tribes of Borneo*, London, 1912, i. 245–277.
[2] Shway Yoe (J. G. Scott), *The Burman*[2], London, 1896, pp. 39, 41.
[3] Chamberlain[2], p. 401.
[4] C. Hill-Tout, *British N. America*, i., 'The Far West,' London, 1907, p. 74.
[5] *Hist. of Greenland*, Eng. tr., London, 1820, i. 129.
[6] *L'Anthropologie*, xi. [1900] 485.
[7] 'Les Tatouages des indigènes de l'Algérie,' *L'Anthropologie*, x. [1899] 434.
[8] H. Schliemann, *Ilios*, London, 1880, p. 337 f.
[9] F. W. Christian, *E. Pacific Lands*, London, 1910, pp. 197, 199.

The coco-nut tree is a favourite object, and figures of men, animals, and flowers also occur, as well as stars, circles, and lozenges.[1] The Maori tatu stands out in striking contrast to that of the rest of Polynesia, its chief feature being the blending of spirals and sweeping curves, which follow the conformation of the human form, the face being generally completely covered. This prevalence of curved lines suggests Melanesian influence; for Polynesian tatu is generally rectilinear in character. Melanesian tatu is often asymmetrical, perhaps because it is done at different times and by different artists. Here again the patterns are very diverse and suggest, as regards some islands, Polynesian influence. Each of the three principal centres of tatu proper in New Guinea has peculiarities of design and execution; thus, curved lines prevail in Humboldt Bay instead of the broader stripes of the south coast, and in the central district the designs used in tatu resemble those on the pipes and gourds, which show a preponderance of straight lines over curves and an absence of human or animal forms. The Motu (Port Moresby) and kindred tribes are said to have a geometrical art, and their tatu is angular in character, but there seems to be good evidence that many of their designs were naturalistic in origin and became conventionalized later.[2] In the Admiralty Islands the men wear cicatrices on chest and shoulders in the form of circular spots of the size of half-a-crown. Tatu proper is mainly confined to the women, who have rings round the eyes and all over the face, and diagonal lines on the upper part of the front of the body crossing one another so as to form lozenge-shaped spaces.[3]

Complicated serial designs are worn by the women in Borneo. The fingers and feet are done at the age of ten, the forearm at eleven, the thighs partly at twelve, being finished at puberty; it is thought immodest to be tatued after motherhood. The men have isolated designs, such as the dog design, in elongated or rosette form—a device prominent in Kayan art and one that can be traced in the shoulder tatu of many of the tribes including the Barawans (Sarawak). The most primitive tatu in Borneo is that of the Uma Long women of Batang Kayan; it is stippled in—on the forearm only—in irregular dots. Indigenous patterns are done by freehand, no blocks being used for them. The thigh tatu in Borneo produces the effect of tight-fitting breeches, and resembles that found among the Burmese and some of the Naga tribes. The latter have an elaborate face tatu called *ak*, formed of continuous lines across the forehead, round and underneath the eyes, over the cheeks, to the corners of the mouth and the chin. 'Rows of spots follow the outside lines, and two fine lines mark out the nose in a large diamond space.' With the Nagas both sexes tatu, but some tribes do not mark the face, and have the tatu placed on the breast, shoulders, back, wrists, and thighs.[4] The Burmese tatu generally from the waist to the knees, but among the Shans it extends from the neck to the feet. The designs include mystic squares, triangles, and a great variety of animals. The old or jungle style was to cover the skin with tracery producing an indefinite effect; the new style is distinct in outline.[5] Perhaps the most highly developed tatu is that of the Japanese, who cover the body with fantastic figures of dragons, birds, flowers, and landscapes, in a manner that recalls the patterns on their silks.

1 W. Ellis, *Polynesian Researches*², London, 1831, i. 265 f.
2 Seligmann, *Melanesians*, p. 38.
3 H. N. Moseley, 'On the Inhabitants of the Admiralty Islands,' *JAI* vi. [1876] 401.
4 R. G. Woodthorpe, 'Notes on the Wild Tribes inhabiting the so-called Naga Hills,' *JAI* xi. [1881] 208.
5 Shway Yoe², p. 41 f.

4. Use and significance.—(*a*) *Magico-religious.*—The use and significance of these marks were manifold, and they have played an important part in the life of primitive man, since they had a magico-religious as well as a social aspect. Their wide-spread use, even at the present day, as a magical protection against sickness and other misfortunes shows a very general belief in their supernatural efficacy. The Yuin tribe of S.E. Australia wear vertical cicatrizations round the upper arm to make boomerangs glance off.[1] In Timorlaut scars are made with red-hot stones on the arms and shoulders in imitation of smallpox marks to ward off that disease.[2] The Andamanese believe that cicatrization is good for rheumatism, toothache, headache, paralysis, epilepsy, and phthisis; it is resorted to for these and other ailments when all else fails. The Todas use it to cure the pains caused by milking buffaloes. Tatu proper is a remedy for rheumatism much in favour with the men of the Halba caste, who work on the lands in the south of the Raipur District and the Kānker and Bastar States in India; its action is probably that of a counter-irritant.[3] The Gonds and Baigas have a number of designs for the protection of different parts of the body, including a figure of the monkey-god Hanuman to give strength, of Bhimsen's club to assist digestion, of the foot-god to cure pain, and so on.[4] The Burman has similar safeguards worn on all parts of the body; they are a protection against wounds and secure freedom from pain, and are sufficiently potent to procure even the favour of princes. The only tatu worn by the Burmese women is a love-charm in the form of a triangle between the eyes or on the lips or tongue; it is done with the 'drug of tenderness'—a mixture of vermilion with herbs and other ingredients such as the skin of trout-spotted lizards.[5] The Shans tatu boys as a test of courage, but special designs are added to prevent injuries or other mishaps. In Borneo the Kayan men wear a special tatu on the wrist called *lukut*, which keeps away illness. The *lukut* is a much-valued bead, which was formerly fastened on the wrist of the sick man to 'tie in' the soul; but, as the bead was liable to be lost, a tatued representation of it came to be worn instead. The Ainu women are tatued on the lips and arms to keep away the demons of disease, who are thus led to believe they are the wives of the gods, since these are all tatued in this manner. If an epidemic occurs in a village, the women must tatu each other; they also use tatuing as a remedy for failing eyesight.[6]

Many races believe that the efficacy of tatu marks extends beyond the present life to that of the next world, where they serve as marks of identification—*e.g.*, Nāgas of Manipur, Kayans of Borneo, N. American Indians, and many others—or as a guide, or as currency enabling the traveller to accomplish his journey.

The Dhanwār, who inhabit the wild hilly country adjoining Chotā Nāgpur, say that tatu marks 'remain on the soul after death, and that she shows them to God, probably for purposes of identification.'[7]

Women of the Brāhman caste believe that after death they will be able to sell the ornaments tatued on their bodies and to subsist on the proceeds. In Africa a similar belief is found among the Ekoi women, who think that in the next world they can exchange their scars for food, and that the ghost is able to remove them one by one for this

1 Howitt, p. 746.
2 H. O. Forbes, 'On the Ethnology of Timor-laut,' *JAI* xiii. [1883] 10.
3 R. V. Russell, *The Tribes and Castes of the Central Provinces of India*, London, 1916, iii. 200.
4 *Ib.* iii. 124–127.
5 Shway Yoe², p. 45.
6 Batchelor, p. 23 f.
7 Russell, ii. 386.

purpose.[1] The Eskimo and the Fijians believe in Elysium only for the tatued; the Fijian women who have not these marks are said to be served up as food for the gods. Some investigators have insisted upon a considerable religious element in tatu, since the operation is often accompanied by sacrifice, prayer, and other religious ceremonies, and the designs frequently represent sacred animals, or other objects that may be regarded as symbols of gods. These serve to express a close union between the god and his disciple; hence the need for certain tabus to avoid the dread consequences of contact with persons in this dangerous state. The priest of the Ewe-speaking people of W. Africa has special tatu marks indicating the deity whom he serves and the rank that he holds in the priestly order; the shoulder marks in this case are so sacred that they must not be touched by the laity.[2] In San Domingo the priests did not wear a distinctive dress, but had a figure of a *zemi* (idol) tatued or painted on their bodies.[3] Tatuing was regarded by many people as a sacred profession, and the artists were under the special protection of deities of the craft. In Tahiti these were the children of Taaroa, the principal deity; their images were kept in the temples of those who practised the art professionally, prayers being addressed to them by the operator before he began his work. The Tahitians say that tatuing originated among the gods, and there are legends in Samoa and elsewhere telling of its sacred origin.

(*b*) *Informatory*.—To people who do not possess a system of writing the wearing of permanent and distinctive body-marks is not merely an æsthetic advantage, but in many cases a real necessity. Used extensively by uncultured peoples, these marks became a convenient means of conveying to their fellow-men all kinds of information concerning their activities and environment. They serve as a record of achievement and a means of identifying a man's tribe, clan, totem, social status, age-grade, and so on; and they have been regarded by some authors as a primitive form of writing.[4] Thus, in Africa cicatrization is a common form of tribal mark, the scars being worn on the face or on other parts of the body and arranged in a certain pattern. The Shilluk, Dinka, Dahoman, Mxosa, Mtyopi, and Hausa tribes are among those who follow this practice. Scars are used for the same purpose in the Andaman Islands, and in Melville and Bathurst Islands of N. Australia. Ellis, writing of the Maoris of New Zealand, says that their faces were much tatued:

> 'Each chief had thus imprinted on his face the marks and involutions peculiar to his family or tribe; while the figures tatued on the faces of the dependants or retainers, though fewer in number, were the same in form as those by which the chief was distinguished.'[5]

Even individual Maoris could be identified by special marks which were tatued on the face—usually near the ear—in addition to the general pattern. These came to be used as the signature of the wearer and have been accepted as such on documents relating to transactions carried on between the Maoris and white men.

The Salish and Déné tribes of N. America have markings—generally on the breast—symbolic of the totem or *manitu* of the individual wearing them. The Haida Indians of Queen Charlotte Islands have their family totems or crests tatued on their bodies with great skill. The designs are often very elaborate and resemble those on the totem-posts that stand outside their houses. A. C. Haddon records an instance of the use of cicatrization to represent the totemic device in the Torres Straits, where he saw some women wearing it cut into their backs. He was told that the men wore it cut into the shoulder or calf of the leg.[1]

The Kavuya Indians of California formerly used the tatu designs worn by a landowner as a property mark by cutting or painting them upon trees and posts selected to indicate the boundaries. It was customary for the Maidu women to have a red spot tatued on the forehead by which, if taken prisoners in war, they could be identified by friends and so ransomed.[2]

A curious use of tatu occurs in the well-known story in Herodotus of the slave who was sent from Susa to Aristagoras of Miletus by Histiæus with instructions that he was to be shaved, and that Aristagoras should look at his head; this being done, it was found that a message had been tatued on the man's head, urging Aristagoras to revolt against the Persians.[3]

Cicatrization and tatu proper are included in the puberty rites and initiation ceremonies of many primitive peoples. In an account of one of these ceremonies in Australia Spencer and Gillen report:

> 'The final ceremony of initiation to manhood in the Urabunna tribe is called Wilyaru, and the same name is given to men who have passed through it. The most important part of the ceremony consists in making cuts on the back, one in the middle line of the neck and four or six others down each side of the backbone.'[4]

In the Marquesas Islands tatu proper was the principal initiatory rite.

> In Samoa 'until a young man was tattooed, he was considered in his minority. He could not think of marriage, and he was constantly exposed to taunts and ridicule, as being poor and of low birth, and having no right to speak in the society of men. But as soon as he was tattooed he passed into his majority and considered himself entitled to the respect and privileges of mature years.'[5]

It sometimes marked the admission to secret societies, as in the Banks Islands (Melanesia), where at the performance of the *kole-kole* ceremonies the head of the *tamate* design adopted by members of the society is tatued on the wrist, a part of the body highly valued.[6] Mary H. Kingsley says of the initiation of boys in Africa:

> 'The boy, if he belongs to a tribe that goes in for tattooing, is tattooed, and handed over to instructors in the societies' secrets and formulæ.'[7]

In New Zealand tatuing began with both sexes at puberty, the women being tatued chiefly on the lips and chin.[8] Chin tatu on women signifies marriage, not only in New Zealand, but also among the Eskimo, the Chukchi, the Indians of the Pacific Coast, and in Syria, Egypt, and Tunis. Women are usually tatued at puberty. This is not, however, always the case, for in some of the islands of Fiji and among the Todas of the Nilghiris it is deferred until they have borne children, while with some races it is begun in infancy and completed at marriage. Only women are tatued among the Chukchi, most Californian tribes, the Ainus of Japan, and in many parts of India. In the Omaha tribe of N. America tatu marks on women signified great honour and a rank equal to that of a chief. Bachofen saw in the limitation of tatu to women among the Thracians an expression of their distinction and good social position.[9] This is contrary to the view taken by Plutarch, who said that the Thracians tatued their wives as a punishment to avenge the murder of Orpheus. In

1 P. Amaury Talbot, *In the Shadow of the Bush*, London, 1912, p. 203.
2 A. B. Ellis, *The Ewe-speaking Peoples of the Slave Coast*, London, 1890, p. 146.
3 T. A. Joyce, *Central American and West Indian Archæology*, London, 1916, p. 195.
4 H. Wuttke, *Gesch. der Schrift und des Schrifttums*, i., 'Die Entstehung der Schrift,' Leipzig, 1872, p. 101.
5 *Polynesian Researches*², iii. 354.

1 *Evolution in Art*, London, 1895, p. 252.
2 W. J. Hoffman, *The Beginnings of Writing*, London, 1895, pp. 37, 39.
3 v. 35.
4 *Across Australia*, London, 1912, i. 24.
5 G. Turner, *Samoa*, London, 1884, p. 88.
6 W. H. R. Rivers, *The Hist. of Melanesian Society*, Cambridge, 1914, i. 134.
7 *Travels in W. Africa*, London, 1897, p. 530.
8 Robley, p. 33.
9 *Das Mutterrecht*, Stuttgart, 1861, p. 336.

Melanesia, where tatu is mainly confined to women, their social position is very inferior, whereas in Polynesia it is comparatively good, and they are seldom tatued. But it is questionable whether there is any necessary correlation between the tatuing of women and their position in the social scale. The limitation of tatu to one sex or the other may be due to other causes; *e.g.*, it is possible that in the South Seas it may be connected with the migrations of different peoples.[1]

The social rank and profession of men are often indicated by their tatu marks, as in the case of the Maori chief who wore a complicated face tatu, and the Creek Town king who was marked in blue with figures of the sun, moon, and stars, animals, landscapes, and even battle-scenes. It has already been noted that priests sometimes had distinctive tatu marks. In some parts of India they serve as an indication of caste. All Gowari men—a herdsman caste of the Marātha country—are tatued with a vertical line on the forehead, the possession of this mark securing admission to the caste feasts.

Among some Indians of Brazil the executioner, or *matador*, was scarified above the elbows by the chief of the clan 'so as to leave a permanent mark there; and this was the star and garter of their ambition, . . . the highest badge of honour. There were some who cut gashes in their breast, arms and thighs, on these occasions, and rubbed a black powder in, which left an indelible stain.'[2]

The wearing of tatu marks proved a convenient method of recording, among other things, great achievements demanding personal valour and skill. The Koita tribes of British New Guinea have a special tatu for homicides.[3] Those of the Baronga (Bantu) who have slain an enemy used to be decorated with special marks from one eyebrow to the other:

'Dreadful medicines were inoculated in the incisions and there remained pimples "which gave them the appearance of a buffalo when it frowns."'[4]

On the Mendalam river in Borneo, the Kayans reserve thigh tatu for head-taking braves. With the Western Eskimo the men are tatued as a sign of distinction. Those who have captured whales have marks to show this, so that their tatu becomes a kind of whale tally.[5]

In many countries it is not only a record of great events, but also a memorial of the dead. In the Saibai and Dauan Islands (Torres Straits) the women wear a shoulder scar for a brother's death; it represents his nose, and the longer the nose, the longer the scar.[6]

In New Zealand 'the women were the chief mourners at funerals. . . . The custom was, in days gone by, that they should gash their faces, neck, arms, and bodies with sharp shells until they streamed with blood; the *narahu* or moko-dye was sometimes applied to the wounds, and the stains commemorated the scenes at which the women assisted.'[7]

In Polynesia the tongue was tatued as a sign of mourning. Ellis saw this operation performed in a house where a number of chiefs had assembled for the purpose, and has described the tatuing of Queen Rihoriho's tongue after the death of her mother-in-law.

(*c*) *Decorative.*—Perhaps the most general use to which tatu has been put is that of personal adornment. Ellis, after noting that tatu was used in Polynesia as a badge of mourning and a kind of historical record, adds: 'But it was adopted by the greater number of people merely as a personal ornament; and tradition informs us that to this it owes its existence.'[8] Among the Kayans of Borneo, who have a very artistic style of tatu, the men affect it chiefly for ornament: so do the women in Greenland, New Zealand, and elsewhere. In fact both sexes in many parts of the world attach to it considerable æsthetic value. In regard to cicatrization among the Andamanese, Man says that it is primarily for ornament and secondarily to prove courage in enduring pain. It seems evident that in the Torres Straits islands it was adopted as a means of acquiring a certain accepted standard of beauty, for Haddon says that the women had a Λ-shaped scar to prevent the breasts from becoming too pendulous.[1] This fashion is also found on the neighbouring coasts of New Guinea and was observed by Seligman among the Otati, an Australian tribe on the east coast of Cape York.

In contrast with the opinions expressed in the writings of Waitz-Gerland[2] and others in reference to the religious significance of tatu, Joest and Westermarck see in it only an expression of man's vanity and love of adornment: 'At present tattooing is everywhere regarded exclusively, or almost exclusively, as a means of decoration, and Cook states expressly that, in the South Sea Islands, at the time of their discovery, it was in no way connected with religion.'[3] Westermarck admits, however, that it has been made to subserve many purposes, but adds: 'Nevertheless, it seems to be beyond doubt that men and women began to ornament, mutilate, paint, and tattoo themselves chiefly in order to make themselves attractive to the opposite sex,—that they might court successfully, or be courted.'[4] Wundt suggests that the marks at first gave magical protection against evil powers, but gradually became merely decorative, and were used to make the personality of the wearer more striking, as in the case of warriors, who wore them to increase their terrifying aspect.[5] On the other hand, E. Grosse thinks the priority should be given to the taste for embellishment, and that the marks only later came to have a tribal or social significance: 'Summarizing the results of our investigations of the significance of primitive scarification and tattooing, we find that the marks serve partly as tribal tokens and have perhaps as such sometimes a religious meaning, although this cannot be proved for a single instance. But in other and the largest number of cases the scars and tattoo marks are for ornament.'[6]

5. Origin and development.—Many theories have been put forward to account for the origin and development of the practice of thus marking the human body: as regards the origin, however, they must remain, for lack of evidence, little more than mere speculations. Instances have been known of involuntary tatu occurring among mechanics and other workmen, who have accidentally grazed or cut themselves while handling charcoal or other colouring matter. Primitive man may have arrived at the notion of tatu by accident, such as the pricking of a finger by a half-burnt splinter or thorn while kindling a fire. The unusual mark thus made might well excite his interest and so lead to an attempt at imitation and to elaboration and invention. Herbert Spencer thought that the practice arose from the custom of making blood-offerings to departed spirits, and that the marks thus made expressed subordination to or close union with them, and became in many instances tribal marks, 'as they would of course become if they were originally made when men bound themselves by blood to the dead founder of the tribe.'[7] In this connexion F. B. Jevons writes:

'The marks or scars left on legs or arms from which blood had been drawn were probably the origin of tattooing, as has occurred to various anthropologists. Like most other ideas, we may add, that of tattooing must have been forced on man; it was not his own invention, and, being a decorative idea, it must have followed the laws which regulate the development of all decorative art. . . . So the scars from ceremonial blood-letting may have suggested a figure; the resemblance was deliberately completed; and next time the scars were from the beginning designedly arranged to form a pattern.'[8]

1 Rivers, ii. 436–438.
2 R. Southey, *The Hist. of Brazil*², London, 1822, i. 232.
3 Seligmann, *Melanesians*, p. 130.
4 H. A. Junod, *The Life of a S. African Tribe*, London, 1912–13, i. 454.
5 J. Murdoch, 9 *RBEW* [1887–88], p. 139.
6 *Reports of the Cambridge Anthropological Expedition to Torres Straits*, Cambridge, 1901–12, iv. 26.
7 Robley, p. 45.
8 *Polynesian Researches*², i. 262.

1 *Rep. Camb. Anthrop. Exped. to Torres Straits*, iv. 16 f.
2 *Anthropologie der Naturvölker*, Leipzig, 1859–72, iv. 33–38.
3 E. Westermarck, *The Hist. of Human Marriage*, London, 1894, p. 171 f.
4 *Ib.* p. 172.
5 *Völkerpsychologie*, Leipzig, 1900–09, v. 174.
6 *Beginnings of Art*, Eng. tr., New York, 1897, p. 80.
7 *The Principles of Sociology*, London, 1893–96, ii.³ 71 f.
8 *An Introd. to the Hist. of Religion*, London, 1896, p. 172.

M. Neuberger regards tatu as one of the popular customs that have sprung from primitive therapeutics: 'Smearing the skin with earth led to painting the body, and scarification of wounds and rubbing in the earth or rust (according to whether the pain was to be lessened or increased) developed into tattooing.'[1] Wundt, Joest, and others see a possible causal connexion between body-painting and tatuing and suggest that the latter was a crude attempt to fix the designs once painted on the body. Wundt regards both these practices as specific stages in primitive art; and in tatu he recognizes two types, the one being a crude system of simple marks often intensifying the natural lines of the body, and the other a stage in which the skin is treated as a material to work on—just as sand or rock is used for drawing upon—when the simpler marks are replaced by fantastic symbols. Capart points out the practical importance of replacing temporary marks by permanent ones, if they have a special meaning attached to them: 'Les dessins que le primitif se peint sur la peau n'ont aucun caractère de persistence et l'on peut à volonté les faire disparaître et les remplacer par d'autres. Il peut y avoir parfois intérêt à les rendre indélébiles, lorsqu'ils sont, par exemple, des marques de tribus ou des marques religieuses. De là naît la coutume de tatouage.'[2]

Concerning the origin of *moko*, or Maori tatu, native tradition says that the first settlers marked their faces for battle with charcoal, and later these warlike decorations were made permanent to save trouble. 'Hence arose the practice of carving the face and the body with dyed incisions.'[3]

How difficult and well-nigh impossible it is to arrive at an accurate knowledge of the early history of such a custom may be gathered from the admission of W. Ellis, who, after many years of personal contact with, and careful observation of, the natives of the Polynesian islands, said in reference to their tatu: 'Although practised by all classes I have not been able to trace its origin.'[4]

LITERATURE.—This is indicated in the footnotes. In addition to the works there mentioned the following may be consulted: C. Hose and R. Shelford, 'Materials for a Study of Tatu in Borneo,' *JAI* xxxvi. [1906] 60 ff.; A. W. Buckland, 'On Tattooing,' *ib.* xvii. [1887] 318 ff.; A. Lacassagne, *Les Tatouages*, Paris, 1882; C. Marquardt, *Die Tätowierung beider Geschlechter in Samoa*, Berlin, 1899; Otto Finsch, 'Ueber Bekleidung, Schmuck und Tätowirung der Papuas der Süd-Ost Küste von Neu-Guinea,' *Mittheilungen der Anthrop. Gesellsch. in Wien*, xv. 12 [1885]; M. Haberlandt, 'Ueber die Verbreitung und den Sinn der Tätowirung,' *ib.* xv. [1885] 53; G. von Düben, *Om Tatuering*, Ymer, 1886; A. Krämer, 'Die Ornamentik der Kleidmatten und der Tatauierung auf den Marshallinseln,' *AA*, new ser., ii. 1 [1904]. Valuable information has also been obtained from an unpublished essay by W. O. Hambly on 'Tatooing as a Means of Emotional Expression.'

CONSTANCE JENKINSON.

TAUROBOLIUM.—The *taurobolium*, a sacrifice performed in connexion with the cult of the Great Mother of the Gods, but not limited to it, was one of the most peculiar and most celebrated rites of the last two centuries of paganism. A striking description of it is put by the Christian poet Prudentius, of the 4th cent., into the mouth of one of his characters, Romanus the Martyr (*Peristephanon*, x. 1006 ff.). The high priest of the Great Mother, a golden crown on his head, his temples richly bound with fillets, his toga worn *cinctu Gabino*, descends into a deep foss which is completely covered by a platform of planks pierced by a great number of fine holes. On to this platform is led a huge bull, bedecked with garlands of flowers, his front gleaming with gold. His breast is pierced by the consecrated spear, and the torrent of hot, steaming blood floods the covering of the trench, and rains through the thousand chinks and perforations on the expectant priest below, who throws back his head the better to present cheeks, ears, lips, nostrils, and even tongue and palate, to the purifying baptism. When life has fled and left cold the body of the slain bullock, and the flamens have removed it, the priest emerges and, with hair, beard, and vestments dripping with blood, presents himself to the expectant throng of worshippers, who salute and do obeisance to him as to one who has been purified.

There were two principal motives which prompted the ceremony of the *taurobolium*. In the earlier period, the 2nd and 3rd cent. A.D., it was usually a sacrifice whose object was the welfare of the Empire, Emperor, or community. An entire college, community, or even province could give it, and a frequent date for it was March 24, the *Dies Sanguinis* of the annual festival of the Mother and Attis. The more frequent motive of the rite in the late 3rd and 4th cent. was the purification and regeneration of an individual. Its efficacy lasted for twenty years, or was even eternal, the baptized person being spoken of as 'renatus in æternum' (*CIL* vi. 510, 512). It was performed by laymen as well as priests, and by persons of all ranks and both sexes. A special altar was erected for the occasion, the time occupied by the ceremony varied from one to five days, and the expense was borne by the individual or association that inaugurated it. Besides the personal and the patriotic motive, it was performed as a fulfilment of vows, or at the command of the Mother herself. In Rome it usually took place near a shrine which existed where the present church of St. Peter stands. The *criobolium*—the sacrifice of a ram—was instituted later in honour of Attis on the analogy of the *taurobolium*, in order to give him due prominence in the rites of the cult. See art. CRIOBOLIUM.

As the *taurobolium* was celebrated in honour of both the Great Mother and Attis, it probably possessed a significance regarding that part of the legend which concerned them both (see MOTHER OF THE GODS). The priest descends into the dark pit and leaves the light of day; Attis dies; the vegetation of the earth withers; the priest is bathed in blood, and rises from the pit purified; Attis is restored; the vegetation returns.

The similarity between Christian doctrine and the phrase *renatus in æternum* ('born again for eternity') is startling, and has suggested belief in some connexion between the two religions in the way of borrowing, especially as paganism vied with Christianity in later days in promising such benefits as the latter conferred. The *taurobolium*, however, is better explained as the survival of a primitive Oriental practice based upon the belief, not uncommon among rude peoples, that the strength of brute creation can be acquired by consumption of its actual substance or by contact with its blood. The spiritual meaning of the practice first came with the advance of culture and the discarding of the primitive, literal belief (see Cumont, *op. cit.* below).

Though the *taurobolium* might with reason be supposed to have come, with the cult of the Great Mother, from Asia Minor, there is no positive evidence that it was originally connected with it either in the East or in Italy. Cumont thinks that it was a rite in honour of the eastern Artemis Tauropolos, deriving from her its name *tauropolion*, which was corrupted to *taurobolium*; and that the rite, having become wide-spread in Cappadocia and the neighbouring provinces in connexion with the worship of Artemis Tauropolos and other deities closely allied or identified with her—principally Anaïtis and Bellona—naturally found its way with them into Italy early in the 2nd cent. A.D., after the annexation of that part of Asia to the Roman Empire, and was soon afterwards adopted and popularized by the priesthood of the Great Mother. Its first known celebration took place at Pozzuoli in A.D. 134, in honour of Venus Cælestis, who, Cumont thinks, was Anaïtis under a Roman name. His conclusion that it was celebrated in connexion with the worship of Bellona rests on slender evidence. Others believe it to have been a part of the Great Mother's worship in Asia Minor (Hepding, *op. cit.* below). Whatever its origin, its popularity was attained through the cult of the Great Mother.

[1] *Hist. of Medicine*, tr. E. Playfair, London, 1910, i. 2.
[2] Capart, p. 30.
[3] Robley, p. 2.
[4] *Polynesian Researches*², i. 262.

It spread throughout the Empire, and maintained its importance up to the fall of paganism, the last celebration known occurring at Rome in 394.

LITERATURE.—E. Esperandieu, *Inscriptions de Lectoure*, 1892, p. 94 ff.; Zippel, *Festschrift zum Doctorjubilæum Ludw. Friedländer*, 1895, p. 489 f.; G. Showerman, 'The Great Mother of the Gods' in *Bulletin of the University of Wisconsin*, no. xliii., Madison, 1901; F. Cumont, 'Le Taurobole et le Culte de Bellone,' in *RHLR*, vi. no. 2, 1901; H. Hepding, *Attis, seine Mythen und sein Kult*, 1903, pp. 168 ff., 201.

GRANT SHOWERMAN.

TEETH.—1. Ornament and trophy.—Among both pre-historic and savage races teeth of animals and human beings are used as an ornament, usually strung together as a necklace, headband, or girdle. Such ornaments are already found among burial remains of Solutrean, Magdalenian, and Azilian horizons, the corpses having been buried wearing them. In a ceremonial burial of thirty-three skulls in the grotto at Ofnet, on the upper Danube, the skulls were ornamented with stag's teeth and shells.[1] Among savages the custom of wearing teeth is well-nigh universal,[2] and, while it may simply serve an ornamental purpose, the intention often goes farther. The teeth are worn as a trophy. Thus, among the tribes of the N.W. Amazon, necklaces are made of the teeth of the tiger and other animals, bored and threaded, or of human teeth bound into a necklace with fibre string. These denote the skill of the wearer as a hunter, or his bravery in war, and the human teeth, which are those of an enemy, are 'a visible and abiding token of completed revenge,' and are buried with the owner. Sometimes the larger animal teeth are ornamented with lines or carved.[3] Analogous to the practice of wearing teeth as a trophy is the curse used by savages, 'Let their teeth be broken,' and the Psalmist's words, 'Break their teeth' (58^6), 'Thou hast broken the teeth of the ungodly' (3^7). The suggestion is that of enemies as ferocious beasts deprived of their power to tear and rend.[4] Men doubtless used their teeth in early times as a weapon, as savage men and maniacs still do. Divine images are known to have actual teeth set in their mouths, possibly as a trophy or offering.[5]

Possibly teeth worn by men also served the purpose of an amulet, as having a connexion with the qualities of the animal or person from whom they were taken,[6] or as protecting the wearer from similar animals in time to come.[7] On the other hand, a person's own tooth might serve as an amulet. Pliny says that the first tooth shed by a child was so used and protected him from pain.[8] Where teeth are knocked out at initiation, they are sometimes carefully preserved, or regarded as sacred, or used for magical purposes.[9]

Teeth taken from a corpse were used to cure toothache or for magic, and those of an old woman were used as a fertility charm in the yam garden by the New Caledonians.[10]

2. Mutilation of the teeth.—Filing the teeth to a point either singly or in pairs, and knocking out certain teeth as a ceremonial act, usually at initiation, and the purposes which these practices serve, have been already discussed.[1]

Staining the teeth is practised by several lower tribes—*e.g.* in S. America and Indonesia—as well as at higher levels—*e.g.* in China (applying lac to the teeth).[2]

3. Teeth as relics.—Teeth of Christian saints have often formed relics, and in early Buddhism the four canine teeth of Gautama were among his 'seven great relics.' One of these has been famous in Ceylonese Buddhism as the *Dalada*. Its miraculous preservation from every means taken to destroy it by a hostile Indian king, and its ultimate arrival in Ceylon in A.D. 312, are the subjects of a long narrative, and the Chinese traveller Fa-hian describes the procession of the relic as he saw it in 405. At a later time the Portuguese are believed to have destroyed it, though the Ceylonese allege that they only destroyed a counterfeit and that the real tooth is the one still preserved at Kandy in a shrine. It is probably not genuine.[3]

4. Teeth in myth and legend.—Greek myth told how Kadmos, having slain the dragon guardian of the spring Areia, at the suggestion of Athene scattered its teeth on the earth like grain. From the teeth sprang armed men called Spartoi ('scattered') from the manner of their birth. A similar myth was told of Jason.[4]

In the 16th cent. a report that a child had been born with a golden tooth in Silesia caused much anxiety in Germany, being regarded as a portent. The physician Horst in 1595 published the result of his astrological researches on the subject, and declared that the tooth symbolized a golden age, preceded by the expulsion of the Turks from Christendom.[5]

LITERATURE.—This is referred to in the notes.

J. A. MACCULLOCH.

TEETOTALISM.—See ALCOHOL, DRUNKENNESS.

TEINDS.—See TITHES.

TELEOLOGY.—I. *INTRODUCTORY.*—1. The term.—The word 'teleology' (Mod. Lat. *teleologia*, Germ. *Teleologie*, Fr. *téléologie*) appears to have been devised by Christian Wolff in 1728. He felt the need of a term to designate the branch of natural philosophy which had to do with ends (Aristotle's τέλος or οὗ ἕνεκα) or final causes (the *causa finalis* of the schoolmen) as distinguished from efficient causes (ἐξ οὗ γίγνεται, *causa efficiens*). For Wolff, accordingly, teleology signified the study of ends or final causes in nature, and more precisely the explanation or interpretation of natural phenomena in the light of the concept of end or final cause. In popularizing Leibniz's philosophy, he set explanation based on final cause side by side with explanation by efficient cause. Presumably Wolff derived teleology directly from τέλος, 'an end,' but, as J. Burnet has remarked,[6] the word is properly derived in the first instance from τέλειον, 'complete.' Thus, etymologically regarded, it does not bear the implication, which it has historically, of an external end; and the

1 H. F. Osborn, *Men of the Old Stone Age*², London, 1916, pp. 327, 378, 472, 477.
2 O. Stoll, *Das Geschlechtsleben in der Völkerpsychologie*, Leipzig, 1908, p. 264 ff.; E. Grosse, *Les Débuts de l'art*, tr. E. Dirr, Paris, 1902, p. 67 ff.
3 T. Whiffen, *The North-West Amazons*, London, 1915, pp. 80, 82, 124.
4 Cf. Pr 30^{14}, Job 4^{10} 29^{17}, Jl 1^6.
5 Stoll, p. 265.
6 See art. CHARMS AND AMULETS (Introductory and Primitive), vol. iii. p. 396ᵇ.
7 M. Dobrizhoffer, *An Account of the Abipones*, tr. S. Coleridge, London, 1822, i. 258.
8 Pliny, *HN* xxviii. 7.
9 Spencer-Gillenᵇ, p. 593 f.; A. W. Howitt, *The Native Tribes of S.E. Australia*, London, 1904, pp. 542, 562 ff.
10 Pliny, *HN* xxviii. 11; Stoll, p. 263; G. Turner, *Samoa, a Hundred Years Ago and Long Before*, London, 1884, p. 342.

1 See art. AUSTERITIES, vol. ii. p. 233 f.
2 Whiffen, p. 88; Stoll, p. 366; J. Deniker, *The Races of Man*, London, 1900, p. 174.
3 J. Fergusson, *Tree and Serpent Worship*, London, 1868, pp. 82, 158 f.
4 For a connexion of these myths with the preservation of the teeth knocked out at initiation rites as a possible vehicle of reincarnation, being practically imperishable, and also because they look like 'seed-corn,' see Jane E. Harrison, *Themis*, Cambridge, 1912, pp. 272, 435.
5 H. T. Buckle, *Hist. of Civilization in England*⁴, London, 1864, i. 304; K. Sprengel, *Hist. de la médecine*, tr. A. J. L. Jourdain, Paris, 1815–20, iii. 247 f.
6 *Greek Philosophy*, pt. i., *Thales to Plato*, London, 1914, p. 346, note 1.

prevalent 'organic' use of it in modern thought is justified.

2. The concept.—As already indicated, the concept is much older than the term. It attaches itself primarily to that organic view of nature which was developed in the ancient Greek philosophy as against the mechanical view. According to the mechanical view, the whole is the product of the parts by their mutual interaction. According to the organic doctrine, the whole is ideally prior to the parts and constitutes the explanation of their mechanical actions and reactions. This last was a doctrine influential not only in the sphere of natural philosophy but in the spheres of political and social philosophy as well, and it led to the teleological interpretation of nature as a realm of ends or final causes. As the whole was an unchangeable form, it gave to all movement a purpose and goal; and in the light of its purpose and goal the movement itself was most deeply interpreted. This ancient opposition between the mechanical and teleological standpoints, as represented by Democritus and Aristotle respectively, set a problem which runs through the whole history of philosophy. The fundamental question at issue is, Are natural processes subordinate to conscious rational purpose, or is the world to be explained and interpreted by mechanical principles alone? That is the deeper philosophical issue in its most clear-cut form. There is a narrower issue which has assumed increasing definiteness in modern times. The fundamental question here belongs to scientific method rather than to metaphysics, and is most prominent at the present time in the dispute between mechanism and teleology in biological theory. Are the characteristic problems of biology (*q.v.*) capable of solution by means of mechanistic categories, or must teleological factors also be postulated?

II. *HISTORICAL.* — A. ANCIENT PERIOD. — **1. Anaxagoras** (*c.* 500–428 B.C.) has been hailed as the father of teleology, but he is so only in a qualified sense.[1] His explanation of nature—to judge from the fragments of his Περὶ φύσεως preserved by Simplicius and from the references in Plato and Aristotle—appears to have been virtually a mechanical explanation on the basis of a qualitative atomism, nor is it even certain that his First Cause of motion was an immaterial or incorporeal essence. The movement and order of the universe he ascribes analogically to Νοῦς (mind, intelligence, reason), which by an initial impulse imparted a rotatory motion to the pre-existent chaos in which 'all things were together.' But, once the rotatory motion was set up, Νοῦς apparently had little else to do. It may be that a thoroughgoing teleological view of nature is logically involved in the Anaxagorean doctrine of Νοῦς, whether Νοῦς (which is represented as omniscient and omnipotent) be regarded as a spiritual or a corporeal essence, as mind or mind-stuff. On the other hand, it is altogether probable that Anaxagoras did not carry out the full implications of his doctrine. Socrates in the *Phædo*[2] complains that in actual explanations he called in only mechanical causes—'airs, æthers, waters, and such like absurdities'; and Aristotle in his *Metaphysics*[3] (in a passage reminiscent, as Burnet[4] allows, of the passage from the *Phædo*) charges him with making use of Νοῦς merely as a *deus ex machina*, to account for the formation of the cosmos or for phenomena that he could not explain on mechanical grounds. Similar objections, as J. Adam[5] reminds us, were afterwards urged against Descartes and Newton. But, however we may interpret the Anaxagorean concept, we cannot but recognize its significance in the history of thought.[1]

2. Diogenes of Apollonia.—The teaching of Anaxagoras was apparently influential upon his contemporary Diogenes, who attributes Νοῦς to his primary substance, air, inasmuch as all things are 'disposed in the best possible manner'—a phrase which sends one's mind on to Leibniz and his theological optimism. It is, however, impossible to say whether Diogenes followed up his affirmation of purpose or design in nature any farther than Anaxagoras appears to have done; and this difference between them remains, that, whereas with Anaxagoras the teleological inference is in the direction of theism, with Diogenes it is definitely pantheistic.[2]

3. Socrates.—The teleology of Socrates (*q.v.*) is to be found in the *Phædo* and the *Memorabilia*. (*a*) The Socrates of the *Phædo* expresses himself as mightily pleased with the book of Anaxagoras in which Νοῦς is affirmed to be the cause of all things, but as disappointed with the failure of Anaxagoras to transcend the mechanical view. He is dissatisfied with a philosophy that cannot show how everything finds itself as it is because it is best for it so to be. He has grasped the distinction between mechanical and final causes in nature, and discovers only in the latter a true ground of explanation. To rely upon mechanical causes alone would be as absurd as to say that the real reason or final cause of his sitting in prison was certain bodily dispositions, and not his mental resolve to abide by his sentence, as the best thing to do. Had this not seemed the best, then 'by the dog these muscles and bones would have been off to Megara or the Bœotian frontier long ago.'[3] (*b*) Consistently with this representation in the *Phædo* the Socrates of the *Memorabilia*[4] is found affirming an immanent Reason in the world, and consistently too with the general doctrine of the Platonic Socrates concerning the individual and the State (which Adam would sum up as 'noocracy,' or the supremacy of Νοῦς or Reason).[5] At the same time the Anaxagorean concept receives in the *Memorabilia* a development so one-sided that it becomes difficult, if on no other ground than this, to believe in the representations of Socrates in Plato and Xenophon respectively as both even essentially historical. W. Windelband[6] suspects the influence of Cynicism and Stoicism upon the representation in Xenophon. In any case it is an exclusively anthropocentric teleology that is here formulated. The whole world of nature is said to yield traces of design, as appears in particular from the wonderful adaptations of means to end in the structure of the human body, in man's psychical constitution, and in the phenomena of external nature; and, furthermore, all is designed towards the one end of the advantage and well-being of men. (*c*) The Socrates of the *Memorabilia* gave perhaps the first formal exposition of the 'argument from design.' Formally, and often naively, he argues from the evidences of design in nature to the existence of an intelligent and beneficent Deity (σοφοῦ τινὸς δημιουργοῦ καὶ φιλοζώου).[7] This anthropocentric teleology, with the theistic inference associated with it, impressed itself strongly upon subsequent religious thought.

4. Plato.—(*a*) The teleology of Plato (*q.v.*) is so far indicated in what has been said regarding the Socrates of the *Phædo*, but it has a deeper philosophical setting than can actually be found in

[1] See art. ANAXAGORAS and also art. PHILOSOPHY (Greek), vol. ix. p. 860b.
[2] 97 B, 8.
[3] i. 4 (985*a* 18 ff.).
[4] *Early Greek Philosophy*², London, 1908, p. 310.
[5] *The Religious Teachers of Greece* (*Gifford Lectures*), Edinburgh, 1908, p. 263.

[1] See art. ANAXAGORAS, vol. i. p. 424.
[2] See art. PANTHEISM (Greek and Roman), vol. ix. p. 614a.
[3] *Phædo*, 99 A.
[4] I. iv., IV. iii.
[5] *Religious Teachers of Greece*, p. 342.
[6] *Hist. of Ancient Philosophy*², Eng. tr., London, 1900, p. 124.
[7] *Mem.* I. iv.

Socrates. In keeping with his ethical and social philosophy, Plato seeks in his metaphysics to interpret the real in terms of the end or ideal of the Good. Ethics is for him the foundation of metaphysics, as it came to be for Lotze, and reality yields up its secrets according as its ethical meaning is apprehended. His conception, already adumbrated in the *Phædo*, of a 'Jacob's ladder of science' (as E. Caird calls it [1]), beginning with the lower principles of explanation and reaching to the highest principle of unity or the idea of the Good, by which all the others are explained, is developed more fully in the *Republic*.[2] The Good or Universal Reason (Νοῦς) is the final cause of every event and change, and to the idea of the Good all the other ideas are teleologically subordinate. The Good, as we may learn from a famous passage of the *Laws*,[3] is the perfection of the whole; and in the preservation and perfection of the whole every creature has its own proper end to fulfil. Thus it was that Plato sought by means of his theory of ideas to interpret the rational principle of Anaxagoras more adequately. He looks upon the world, says J. Hutchison Stirling, as 'a single teleological system with the Good alone as its heart.'[4]

(*b*) In applying his metaphysical principles to the interpretation of nature, Plato is hardly liable like the Socrates of the *Memorabilia* to the charges of externality and anthropocentrism. For the *Timæus*, in which such a teleology may be found, is, in its details at least, 'mythical.' In consistency with his theory of ideas, Plato could not have claimed more for his accounts of the phenomenal world than that they were 'likely tales' (εἰκότες λόγοι). In any case he does not, even in the *Timæus*, lay much stress upon particular instances of adaptation in nature, nor does he encourage the notion of adaptations as designed exclusively for human needs. (*c*) In the *Timæus*, as indeed in the *Philebus* in non-mythical form, a theological interpretation is offered of the teleological constitution of the world. In offering it, Plato would apparently overcome the dualism between the ideal and the phenomenal which is inherent in his theory of knowledge and reality. God, the Demiurge, is represented as bringing order and harmony out of the moving chaos of not-being (μὴ ὄν), in accordance with the pattern of the Good, and in so far as natural necessity (ἡ ἀνάγκη) allows. Thus natural necessity comes in when divine activity according to ends fails as a principle of explanation, and something is yielded to Democritus. But, while the teleological explanation involves a recognition of divine activity, and is so far on the lines of the theistic argument, the Demiurge of the *Timæus*—the self-moved mover who fashions the world—is not identified with the Good, nor is he to be equated with the God of modern theism.

5. Aristotle.—(*a*) While it may be allowed to Plato that no ultimate explanation of anything is possible apart from the discovery of its final cause, we have to turn to Aristotle (*q.v.*) for a more adequate recognition of mechanical causes as principles of explanation, and this although Aristotle is the protagonist of the organic and teleological view of the universe. In the endeavour to overcome the Platonic dualism of ideas and things, Aristotle gives an even more thoroughgoing interpretation of the Anaxagorean Νοῦς than is to be found in Plato. With Plato he believes in the real existence of the form or idea, but he cannot think of it as separate from the world. It exists in the world and in things. Reality is a process of development, in which the change from more imperfect to less imperfect being is to be interpreted in the light of the τέλος, which in things that are not eternal is the moving form or final state of actuality (ἐνεργεία). The moved matter, which is the primal state of potentiality (δύναμις), exists for the sake of the form.[5] The individual is both form and matter, being form in relation to what is lower in the scale of things, and matter in relation to what is higher. The marble is form in relation to the materials composing its substance, and matter in relation to the statue which is made from it. The tree is form in relation to the elements of the soil that enter into the process of its growth, and matter in relation to the house built of it. The Good is the highest form of all, being pure form without matter, and is the ultimate end or final cause of all existence and all movement. It is not actually generated in the world-process, but is eternally implied in it, as the goal of the creation.

(*b*) With this peculiar speculative idea of development which fills the central place in the *Metaphysics* Aristotle opposes Democritus (*q.v.*) and the atomists, who appeared to him as mere 'drunken stutterers' in comparison with Anaxagoras. Even in inorganic nature he finds purpose or final cause operative. Just as an army moving on the field, or a ship cleaving the sea under full sail, offers an instance of effort directed towards an end, so, wherever we observe in natural processes the regular achievement of results, we may similarly discern the presence of purpose. But it is principally the realm of organic nature that is viewed thus teleologically. How absurd, he urges, to ascribe the forms and activities of living beings to the operation merely of accident (τὸ αὐτόματον) or chance (ἡ τύχη)! Empedocles (*q.v.*) was emphatically wrong in his theory of the origin of species, in which he avers that nature produces in her prodigality every possible type of animal form, and that only those forms survive which are coherently and consistently constructed. If, as Empedocles believed, nature once produced 'man-faced cattle' (βουγενῆ ἀνδρόπρῳρα), presumably she also produced at one time or other 'olive-faced grapes'! Nature is a cause which acts purposively, and if her end is sometimes unattained, it is due to the mechanical necessity to which matter (ὕλη)—Plato's 'not-being'—is subject.

(*c*) Much more clearly than in Plato we find in Aristotle, especially in the *de Partibus Animalium* and other biological works, the recognition of the double play of mechanism and teleology in nature, especially in organic nature, which does not operate with the refractory medium of matter. As a naturalist he is content to lay stress upon only two forms of causation—material or mechanical (ἐξ ἀνάγκης) and formal or final (οὗ ἕνεκα), and the formal or final cause comes first, being the reason which determines the whole process. The mechanical causes are the servants and instruments of the final causes. Thus in Aristotle both mechanism and teleology are accepted as factors in the explanation of nature, though the Platonic principle preponderates. It is not quite true, however, to say that Aristotle has succeeded in reconciling Plato and Democritus, that by his cosmo-teleology he mediates between the onto-teleology of the theory of ideas and the mechanism associated with the atomistic hypothesis. Owing to his scientific limitations, notably in connexion with the mechanics of the heavens, Aristotle pushed explanation by final causes farther than his general principles warranted. Frequently resting upon final causes alone, he at once hindered the progress of his own scientific thought and lent his authority to the narrow and one-sided finalism of the scholastic interpretation.

(*d*) Aristotle's organic or teleological doctrine, based on the metaphysical concepts of matter and form, strikingly anticipates certain modern positions in biological and psychological science. Applied, *e.g.*, to the conception of the organism, it offers, as L. J. Henderson assures us,[1] a complete formulation of the biological principle of organization. Aristotle conceives of the living thing as an autonomous unit, having the teleological principle within, and with every part functionally related to every other and existing as the servant of the whole. That is the implication, we are told, of his comparison of the organism to a well-governed commonwealth, in which, once order is established, the individuals duly play their parts and a separate monarch is no more needed.

6. The Stoics.—(*a*) Among the so-called sects that came after Plato and Aristotle the Sceptics (*q.v.*) had no contribution to make in teleology. If causality was suspect with them, as with Hume in a later age, so also was finality. The contribution of the Epicureans (*q.v.*) was distinctly negative. Epicurus is to be classed with Leucippus and Democritus, of whom Aristotle said that they 'rejected design and referred all to necessity.'[2] But the Stoics (*q.v.*) recognize the principle of teleology. There was one philosopher indeed, an Aristotelian, who came near to Stoicism in his opposition to the mechanical explanations of the atomists; but, on the other hand, as Windelband puts it,[3] he 'threw away the keystone of the Aristotelian teleology.' This was Strato of Lampsacus, who denied the existence of pure form as of

[1] *The Evolution of Theology in the Greek Philosophers* (*Gifford Lectures*), Glasgow, 1904, i. 129.
[2] Bk. vi. [3] x. 903.
[4] *Philosophy and Theology* (*Gifford Lectures*), Edinburgh, 1890, p. 113.
[5] Cf. also R. Adamson, *The Development of Greek Philosophy*, Edinburgh, 1908, p. 155.

[1] *The Order of Nature*, Cambridge, U.S.A., 1917, p. 21.
[2] *De Generatione Animalium*, v. 18.
[3] *Hist. of Ancient Philosophy*, p. 301.

pure matter, declaring form to be always immanent in matter, and so converting the Aristotelian system into a consistent naturalism. Stoicism may also be described as naturalism, but it was at the same time a pantheistic system. The old dualism of form and matter which Plato and Aristotle had inherited from Anaxagoras, and had failed to throw off, gave place to an eclectic and somewhat facile monism, in which one eternal substance manifested itself as spirit (λόγος σπερματικός) and matter (πνεῦμα διάπυρον). It was essentially a teleological explanation of the world that was given by Stoicism, because, although every particular phenomenon was said to be determined by natural necessity, as Democritus had maintained, natural necessity was not based, as with the atomists, on quantitative differences and initial movements, but depended on the vital activity of the whole.

(*b*) In carrying out its teleology, Stoicism made much of the beauty, order, and harmony of the world and the adaptations of means to end, especially in organic nature, as manifestations of the rational unity and ideal meaning of things. The evils of the world, which offered even more difficulty on the monistic hypothesis than in the Platonic and Aristotelian systems, were optimistically explained as instruments or concomitants of the great cosmic movement, and it was said that they would be recognized as such, if the individual could take the point of view of the whole. But the Stoic appeal to order and adaptation often descended to externality and anthropocentrism, as in the teaching attributed to Socrates in the *Memorabilia*. Thus it was said that the peacock was made for the sake of its beautiful tail, and the ass to carry man's burdens. Yet an immanent or intrinsic teleology such as is characteristic of Plato and Aristotle would have been altogether congruous with Stoic principles.

(*c*) If the *Memorabilia* is possibly influenced by Stoicism, Cicero's *de Natura Deorum* indubitably is. There the inference to God from the order and beauty of the universe is eloquently set forth in a well-known passage[1]—reminiscent perhaps of Plato's story of the Cave—attributed to Aristotle, where is depicted the impression that would be made on men whose dwellings had been underground, on their first beholding the glorious spectacle of earth and sea and sky. It has been suggested[2] that in the argument for the being of God contained in the *de Natura Deorum* it is Aristotle we have chiefly before us; *e.g.*, the comparison, in several passages, of the world to a furnished or inhabited house or an adorned and decorated temple of the gods (a comparison which is to be found also in writers like Philo the Jew and Minucius Felix the Christian apologist) is said to have come from Aristotle. This suggestion is odious to philosophers who are jealous for the purity of the Aristotelian doctrine of the end, especially as Cicero in the *de Natura Deorum* furnishes the prototype, in the ancient world, of Paley's *Natural Theology* and the Bridgewater Treatises.

7. Teleology of history.—While in the ancient Greek philosophy a teleology of nature was expounded, in the religious period of the ancient world and within the early Christian Church the idea of a teleology of history gained ground. The opposition in the Gnostic view of history to the OT religion as the revelation of an inferior Deity led to the view of history which has established itself as the truly Christian. It fastened upon the Pauline doctrine of the pædagogic function of the Law, which gave to the Law a distinctive place in a teleological series of divine processes; and the whole course of the ages was interpreted in the light of the great divine plan of redemption culminating in Jesus Christ. With Irenæus the teleology of nature is ancillary to the teleology of history as thus expounded from the Christian standpoint. At the hands of Augustine the whole conception receives an impressive treatment, and the human race is regarded as a teleological unity, as being destined to receive entrance into the catholic or universal Church (*civitas Dei*). This anthropocentric view of the world as the scene of the divine redemption in Jesus Christ still prevails in Christian theology, in which the teleological principle of history is sometimes described as Christological or Christocentric.

B. MEDIÆVAL PERIOD.—Thomas Aquinas.—All through the Middle Ages, in Christian and Muhammadan countries alike, the Aristotelian teleology dominated philosophical and scientific thought. Unfortunately it was the Aristotelian teleology in its defective form of explanation by final causes alone (*i.e.* apart from mechanical causes), and it laid an arrest upon the movement of natural philosophy. Yet Archimedes and others who came after Aristotle had shown that mechanics at any rate could altogether dispense with the hypothesis of final cause. Aquinas (*q.v.*) makes use of the so-called teleological proof, which was the favourite proof in the patristic and scholastic ages, and he quotes as exponents of it John of Damascus and Averroës on Aristotle's *Physics*. There is an intelligent 'somewhat,' says Aquinas, by which all natural objects are ordered in relation to an end, and this 'somewhat' we call God—which, indeed, is the gist of the teleological argument, whether in its popular or in its more philosophical form. Aquinas also catches up the patristic idea of the teleological unity of nature and history, and through his doctrine of the State gives it a more systematic expression. The State was not with him, as with Augustine, the devil's province (*civitas huius sæculi*), but was based on natural law or right (*lex naturalis*), which has its source in God; and the life of virtue, which Aristotle said was to be realized in the political society, was the preparation for the higher life of grace in the society or community of the Church. 'Gratia naturam non tollit sed perficit.'

C. MODERN PERIOD.—1. Bruno.—The transition from ancient and mediæval to modern thought is well illustrated, in this matter of teleology, as in others, in the views of Giordano Bruno (*q.v.*). His whole philosophy represents an attempt to combine in a unitary system the Platonic and Aristotelian idealism and the modern mechanical view of nature, of which Democritus was the precursor. Like the atomists, he affirmed that only, as it were, after repeated experiments on nature's part did combinations of elements arise which, as being adapted to ends, conserved their stability. At the same time he affirmed—and here the idealistic strain appears—that there is a world-soul, or inner principle of motion in nature, which is purposive in its working, and so orders all things as to secure the world's progress. Thus the mechanical and teleological views are united in this thinker.

2. Bacon.—Though Francis Bacon (*q.v.*) may also be said to belong to the age of transition, he was more definitely on the side of the modern scientific movement. It would appear that he looked upon the philosophies of Plato and Aristotle as 'planks of lighter and less solid wood' than the physical philosophies of ancient Greece lost in the wreckage of the Roman Empire. For him philosophy was restricted to the investigation of nature, and there were certain 'idols of the tribe,' or common prejudices, to be dismissed from the mind if nature was to be explained aright. Among these was interpretation by final causes. Under the illusion that man is the measure of things (which Protagorean utterance, curiously enough, is actually become the watchword of a recent philosophical movement) we interpret things in reference to ourselves (*ex analogia hominis*) instead of universally (*ex analogia universi*). Yet Bacon does not reject the reality of final causes.

'For the cause rendered, that the hairs about the eyelids are for the safeguard of the sight, doth not impugn the cause rendered, that pilosity is incident to orifices of moisture.' Final causes in physics are, however, sterile like Vestal virgins, and, worse than that, they are 'impertinent,' being indeed 'but remoras and hindrances to stay and slug the ship from further sailing.' But final causes have their place in metaphysic and religion. The divine wisdom even appears more admirable when nature 'intendeth' one thing and providence 'draweth forth' another.[1]

[1] Bk. ii.

[2] See Hutchison Stirling, *Philosophy and Theology*, p. 170 ff.

[1] *De Augmentis*, iii. 5.

Thus Bacon throws off the two thousand years' yoke and touches hands with Democritus and Leucippus across the centuries. But, while vindicating physical causation as the one form of causation of which physical science need take cognizance, he conserves the metaphysical and religious interests which were bound up with the Platonic and Aristotelian teleology. It were incredible to him that this 'universal frame' should be 'without a Mind.'[1] He failed, however, to appreciate the scientific importance of the Aristotelian concept of organization in biology, as also—but this was the legacy of the schools—the philosophical depth of the essential Aristotelian doctrine of the end.

3. Hobbes and Descartes.—(*a*) Hobbes (*q.v.*), following Bacon and Galileo, tried to liberate philosophy from the Platonic and Aristotelian ideas and forms and to substantiate the mechanical view not only in the realm of nature but in the realms also of mind and society. He reduced all cause to motion, and philosophy to a doctrine of motion.

(*b*) Though Descartes (*q.v.*) also dispensed with final causes in nature, he did not fall like Hobbes into materialism. He explained natural phenomena by the mechanical principles of matter and motion, so founding the now orthodox systematic view of mechanics, but he dissociated himself from the ultimate positions of the ancient atomistic philosophy. Mechanical explanation was not ultimate explanation. But his rejection of final causes in nature was on theological rather than epistemological grounds. We may legitimately enough, he thought, attribute ends or purposes to God, but we cannot hope to discover these, as they are hidden 'in the inscrutable abyss of His wisdom.' Here, as in Bacon, there is a clear distinction between the scientific and the metaphysical and religious interest in final causes—a distinction which became clear only in the modern period of thought.

(*c*) For the issue between mechanism and teleology in scientific explanation Descartes possesses considerable significance, not merely because of his peculiar vitalistic theory that the *vis viva* might alter the direction of motion if unable according to the law of conservation to change its quantity, but chiefly because of his law of conservation itself. In the effort to reach the true principle of mechanical causation, he arrived at the belief that God conserved in things as a whole all the movement which He introduced into them at the creation; so that in virtue of this initial disposition the necessary world-process was at every stage teleological. His vitalism was a short-lived theory, but his principle of conservation marks a notable advance in the teleology of nature.

4. Spinoza.—(*a*) The most vigorous, as it was the most uncompromising, attack upon final causes in nature came from Spinoza (*q.v.*). In explaining a particular phenomenon we cannot, he said, go beyond the particular attribute of the one divine substance, be it the attribute of thought or of extension, under which the phenomenon appears to us. For, while the attributes are parallel to each other, there is no interaction between them. Thus material phenomena, including the movements of the human body, are only explainable in physical terms. Matter cannot be grounded in mind. There can be no ends or purposes in nature.

(*b*) Apart from the incompatibility of the doctrine with his fundamental philosophy, two main objections are urged by Spinoza against final causes. The first is Bacon's objection—that acceptance of final causes hinders the investigation of nature: recourse to the will of God in the explanation of natural phenomena, and in particular of untoward phenomena like tempests, earthquakes, and diseases, is a refuge of ignorance (*asylum ignorantiæ*). The secrets of nature are with those who abandon final causes and place their trust in mathematics, which, as dealing with the essences and properties of things, leads to rational knowledge. The other objection is that the method of explanation by final causes encourages false anthropomorphic conceptions of God. A God who works purposively, or towards ends, is subject to fate or necessity and lacks perfection of being. It implies defect in God that He should be in need of anything. Nor have we any right to infer distinctions in the divine nature analogous to the elements of the human mind. The intellect and will we may ascribe to God are no more analogous to our intellects and wills than the constellation of the Dog to the animal that barks.

(*c*) Undoubtedly Spinoza did good service in exposing the weakness and superficiality of the traditional teleology, but it should be observed that, while the denial of teleology is already involved in the doctrines of substance and parallelism with which he sets out, at the close of his thought a certain light breaks in upon his system. The *amor intellectualis Dei* with which he concludes is part of the infinite love wherewith God loves Himself, and we may learn from it that with His universe God is well pleased. The ideas of satisfaction and value which are essential to a teleological interpretation of the universe appear to be here conserved.[1]

5. Leibniz.—(*a*) Despite the able efforts of the Cambridge Platonists (*q.v.*), such as Cudworth and More, to vindicate for final causes a place in physics, the mechanical view found increasing support, being applied also as against Platonists and vitalists to the phenomena of life, and it was left to Leibniz (*q.v.*) to attempt a reconciliation of the opposing principles. Leibniz's essential position still meets with great acceptance among scientists, philosophers, and theologians. In the phenomena of nature, he says, everything happens mechanically and at the same time metaphysically, and the source of the mechanical is the metaphysical. This position finds clear expression in two sayings that may be placed side by side—one from a recently discovered fragment, and the other quite familiar: 'Omnia in tota natura demonstrari possunt tum per causas finales, tum per causas efficientes.' 'Causae efficientes pendent a finalibus.'

(*b*) While Leibniz was as 'corpuscular' as Descartes or Spinoza in the explanation of particular phenomena, he could not, for two reasons, rest in the mechanical explanation. One reason appears in his metaphysical construction of the concept of substance. Rejecting the Cartesian and Spinozan opposition of extension and thought, and affirming substance to be force (*un être capable d'action*) and force substance, he passed from an abstract to a more concrete monism. Matter was no longer to be defined as extension but as a form of force, more specifically as power of resistance; and mind was no longer to be restricted to the sphere of consciousness, and was represented as comprising subconscious states (*petites perceptions*). With this view of substance, and with the aid of the Aristotelian principle of continuity and development, Leibniz at length reached the speculative position that the real world consists of an infinite host of independent monads or individuals, at countless different stages of development, whose activity is fundamentally spiritual or perceptual. Now it is the very nature of the monad to strive after the realization of all its latent possibilities. It has to rid itself of confused perceptions and attain true ideas, and so to enter into the mind of God the Supreme Monad—an end which may only be achieved on the plane of self-consciousness and spiritual freedom. So it is, according to Leibniz, that the forces active in mechanism may be interpreted from the standpoint of teleology. Everywhere in nature purposive activity may be discerned. Take but the inward view, or, rather, take but the universal view, and the world of physical causes and effects becomes a world of means and ends.

(*c*) The second reason that led Leibniz to uphold the teleological interpretation of the world starts from his postulate of 'pre-established harmony,' which is intimately connected with his monadology. Though independent or 'windowless,' each monad 'mirrors' the rest of the universe. Though subject to its own laws, each monad is in harmony with the universal development. Geulincx and Spinoza had already applied the principle of harmony or correspondence to the two Cartesian attributes, but Leibniz applies it to the totality of substance. He compares the correspondence which he has in view to different bands of musicians who may keep perfectly together without seeing or even hearing one another. He compares it also, using a frequent analogy of the time (and with the relation of body and mind chiefly in view), to two clocks so skilfully made as never to get out of time. The pre-established harmony is not imposed upon the world from without, but belongs to the inner life of the monads; none the less it needs to be explained. The only possible explanation is to be found in the will and purpose of God. It is God alone who brings to pass the union or interconnexion of substances whereby the world is orderly and rational. Thus the order of the world, interpreted as a pre-established harmony, necessitates the teleological inference to God.

(*d*) The principle involved in the teleological inference is named by Leibniz the principle of determinant or sufficient reason, viz. that nothing can exist or be true without a sufficient reason why it should be so and not otherwise. Without such a

[1] *Essays*, xvi., 'Of Atheism.'

[1] A. S. Pringle-Pattison, *The Idea of God in the Light of Recent Philosophy* (*Gifford Lectures*), Oxford, 1917, p. 333; cf. also below, § III. C, 7 (*b*), 8.

principle, implying the complete rationality of existence, philosophy would for Leibniz have ceased to be, as indeed for Descartes or Spinoza. But Leibniz gave the principle a characteristic application. He regarded it as the foundation of the contingent truths of natural science, just as the principle of identity and contradiction was the foundation of the necessary truths of mathematics and logic. So that the conservation of force or energy and the equivalence of cause and effect in the world must be teleologically explained as dependent upon the divine wisdom and order.

(*e*) In biology, as in physics, Leibniz advanced the teleological problem. He is said to have established the truth that biological organization is compatible with the mechanistic theory, but in comparing the organism to a kind of 'divine machine' or 'natural automaton' he still comes short of the Aristotelian teleology.

6. Rationalistic theism.—(*a*) In the 18th cent. Leibniz's theology was more influential than his monadology. There appears to be a certain looseness of connexion between the two, and it was accentuated by Wolff's effort to systematize and popularize the master's doctrines. In Wolff the harmony of the world is no longer an immanent order, but an order externally imposed by God; and the world's chief end is utility and advantage for man and beast—especially utility for man. This externalism impressed itself upon the 'popular philosophy' that arose in Germany about the middle of the 18th cent., and it promoted a remarkable and many-sided growth of natural theology or teleological physics and organics, the aim of which was to multiply the evidences of design in nature in the interests of the teleological inference to creative wisdom and benevolence. There were astro-theologies, litho-theologies, phyto-theologies, insecto-theologies, ichthyo-theologies, and numerous others. As among the Stoics, the ideas of advantage and utility were often beaten out into petty trivialities (*Nützlichkeitskrämerei*).

(*b*) In France Fénelon had already written eloquently on natural theology on similar lines, although later the materialism of d'Holbach and the scepticism of Bayle were to cut at the root of the popular teleology, and Voltaire was to pour contempt upon its anthropocentrism and shallow optimism.

(*c*) In England, too, natural theology was early developed on the lines of a superficial utilitarianism, beginning in the 17th cent. with the works of the naturalist Ray (on whom Milton drew in *Paradise Lost*), and of Boyle, Barrow, and Parker, continuing with Derham and many others through the 18th cent., and receiving classical exposition in Paley's *Natural Theology*.[1] So exhaustively had the teleology of nature been discussed that the Scottish divine Thomas Chalmers, in the first Bridgewater Treatise,[2] turned to mental as distinguished from physical teleology, discoursing on the adaptation of nature to mind and on adaptations within the mind; while McCosh[3] laid the emphasis upon moral teleology, inferring from the moral order a moral Governor.

(*d*) Notice should here be taken of a universal view of teleology held by the English deist Shaftesbury,[4] who rose above the particular views that so largely prevailed in the deistic as in the orthodox circles of his time. His was an æsthetic teleology, and in the beauty and perfection of the world he found a proof of the existence of God. Not only does the unity of the world point to a universal Spirit; but beauty lies not in matter but in form or formative power, which must work with design.

7. Hume.—(*a*) The speculative sincerity of David Hume (*q.v.*) was probably not so great as

[1] London, 1802.

[2] *On the Power, Wisdom, and Goodness of God as manifested in the adaptation of external Nature to the Moral and Intellectual Constitution of Man*, 2 vols., London, 1833.

[3] *The Method of Divine Government, Physical and Moral*, Edinburgh, 1850.

[4] See art. Deism, § 3.

his speculative genius. In the *Treatise of Human Nature*[1] he reduced the world to a mere complex of sensations—not an ordered complex, which could be ascribed to a divine Author; and yet in his theological writings, notably in the *Dialogues concerning Natural Religion*,[2] we find him apparently assuming order and purposiveness in the universe. If the tendency of recent interpretations of the *Dialogues* is to be trusted, we may even regard Hume as sincerely adhering to what is there called a 'genuine theism,' and as accepting the essential core of the argument from design as its rational basis. We may hear Hume himself speaking through Cleanthes, the rationalistic theist, when it is maintained that at every turn we are obliged to have recourse to the hypothesis of design in the universe; or through Philo, who is sceptical and naturalistic in tendency, when he admits that all objections to the hypothesis of design appear mere 'cavils and sophisms' to those who realize the beauty and fitness of final causes.

(*b*) None the less the criticisms of the teleological inference which are put in the mouth of Philo are of great historical interest and importance. Cleanthes, who states the theistic argument from design (round which the discussion of natural religion mainly turns), compares the world of order to a great machine, subdivided into an infinite number of lesser machines, which, even in their most minute parts, are all adjusted to each other with marvellous accuracy. This universal adaptation of means to ends so resembles the products of human contrivance that we are led by all the rules of analogy to infer that the Author of nature is somewhat similar to the mind of man, though possessed of much larger faculties. Philo replies, in Hume's own sceptical vein, that the principle of analogy is not a sure basis of argument, especially as we depart the more from the similarity of the cases. Can we really speak, *e.g.*, of analogy between the fabric of a house and the generation of the universe? And why should thought, design, intelligence, be made the model of the whole? If it is valid to say that, because the world resembles a machine, it arose from design, is it not at least equally valid to say that, because the world resembles an animal, it arose from generation? And why go beyond nature in search of a transcendent cause? To take one step beyond the mundane system is to be forced to go on in an infinite progression. For the ideal world, into which the material world is traced, is itself to be traced into another ideal world, and so on. May it not be that there are forces in nature by means of which, even after a botching and bungling of many worlds throughout an eternity, this orderly and harmonious system was struck out? At most the argument from design can only prove the existence of a being in time and space, fashioning a given material, and all pretension to ascribe infinity to the Deity or even perfection in His finite capacity must be renounced. Can we even pretend to decide from the phenomena of nature as to whether the Deity is one or many? (A similar reference to the limitations of the argument is found in the *Enquiry concerning Human Understanding*,[3] in which the criticism is in the form adopted and made famous by Kant.)

(*c*) By the objections thus urged by Philo a strong impression is made upon Cleanthes, who is also led to admit, in view of the problem of evil, that the Deity might be described in the terms of 'benevolence, regulated by wisdom, and limited by necessity'—an old position of the Greek theology with which we have been familiarized in recent thought. The carefully formulated conclusion of the *Dialogues*, that (as Philo says) 'the cause or causes of order in the universe probably bear some remote analogy to human intelligence,' may not have represented in Hume's mind the whole of 'genuine theism,' but it dealt a destructive blow to the rationalistic theology of his time, with its deistic implications, its petty teleology, and its hedonistic view of life.

(*d*) On the scientific or philosophical side, however, Hume made a positive contribution to the problem of natural teleology. The idea goes back as far as Empedocles, and is expounded in Lucretius, that in nature the principle holds of the survival of the fit. In the *Dialogues*, as we have seen, Hume gives expression to this principle, and he does so in respect of both inorganic and organic nature. Described as the tendency towards equilibrium or equilibration, it is recognized in modern physics and biology as teleological in character; but, when Hume speaks of it further as perhaps originally contained in matter, he at least suggests the idea that there is a deeper and

[1] 3 vols., London, 1739–40.
[2] London, 1779.
[3] London, 1748.

more original teleology in nature than ordinary mechanistic theory suspects. So that with Hume the teleological appearance of nature is perhaps more than a postulate of the reflective or subjective judgment, as it is with Kant.

8. Kant.—(*a*) In his early work on *Universal Natural History and Theory of the Heavens*[1] Kant acknowledged the great value of the arguments drawn from the beauties, harmonies, and perfections of the universe, and more particularly of the starry heavens, to establish the existence of a supremely wise and powerful Creator. At the same time he rises above the popular teleology. In a later pre-critical work on *The Only Possible Proof of the Being of God*[2] he declares himself impressed with the physico-theological argument, but, like Hume's Philo, he doubts the validity of the inference to a Creator who is perfectly wise and good. In the *Critique of Pure Reason*[3] a similar criticism appears, with a famous tribute to the physico-theological argument as 'the oldest, the clearest, and that most in conformity with the common reason of humanity.'[4] The argument at the best, however, cannot take us beyond the great power and wisdom of the Author of the universe; and it can prove, not a Creator, but no more than an Architect, who is necessarily limited by the character of His material. Contingency belongs not to the matter but to the form of the world. The attempt to show that matter is contingent and dependent upon a principle of intelligence is to fall back upon the cosmological proof, which in its turn rests upon the ontological, with the consequence that the claim of the physico-theological to be a pure induction from experience is invalidated. This argument in fact originates in the propensity of the human mind to view the order and purposiveness of nature as though they were the products of intelligence and design—a propensity for which on the principles of the critical philosophy there can be no real basis.

(*b*) We need not dwell on Kant's views in his pre-critical writings of the teleological principle. It is sufficient to note that they were on the lines afterwards developed in the *Critiques*. In the *Critique of Pure Reason* he justifies, as against Hume's scepticism, the mechanical or scientific view of nature as subject to causal determination. In the *Critique of Practical Reason*[5] he vindicates the teleological view of the spiritual life as a realm of moral freedom and independence. From the critical standpoint therefore the doctrine of nature and the doctrine of morality may each be true in its own sphere, and mechanism and teleology be so far reconciled. In the *Critique of Judgment*[6] he seeks to overcome the dualism—in his own phrase, to bridge the gulf—between nature and the moral order, which he had regarded to begin with as closed systems, independent and separate. He realized that the sensible world of things and persons is but one aspect of reality, and the supersensible world of moral values but another, and that the two must be interrelated. Accordingly he draws attention to certain things belonging to the sensible world of nature which we cannot describe adequately without that notion of purpose or end which has its proper sphere in the supersensible world of spirit. One of these is the phenomenon of beauty, the other that of organic being.

(*c*) The first section of the *Critique* treats of the æsthetic judgment. In the æsthetic experience the beauty of nature, as of art, is felt to be purposive, in the sense that, while it arises out of the sensible, it is in harmony with our 'undefined idea' of the supersensible. The second section has to do with the teleological judgment, in which nature is regarded as purposive in itself, and not merely, as in the æsthetic judgment, in relation to the subject of experience.

(*d*) The purposive character of living beings raises for Kant anew the whole problem of the world as a teleological or organic system, and he now gives the notion of judgment a wider meaning than before. In its use of the principles of the understanding for the subsumption of the particular under the general (in which the faculty of judgment consists) judgment had been shown in the first *Critique* to be determinant or, as we might say, mechanical; *i.e.*, its function is to determine or specify the phenomenal world of experience as a mechanical system under inviolable principles. But judgment is also of another kind, viz. reflective. In subsuming the particular under the universal, reflective judgment makes use of the idea of subordination to purpose or end as the guide to its operations. The determinant judgment is analytical, and simply brings particular facts under the universal principles of the understanding. The reflective judgment is synthetical, and, operating with the idea of nature as a teleological or organic unity, discovers its specific laws. As Windelband[1] remarks, in this application of the category of the practical reason to the object of the theoretical, we have evidently the highest synthesis of the critical philosophy.

(*e*) But still there is no real transcendence of the dualism between the realms of nature and ends, between the factual world of experience and the ideal world of purpose and meaning. For the principle on which reflective judgment proceeds—that the form of nature implies purpose, that the specific laws of nature are to be regarded as though determined by purposive intelligence—is not constitutive of objects. Transcendental though it be, as involving an *a priori* synthetic judgment, it remains a subjective or regulative principle, serving as a rule or guide for the organization of experience and the further extension of knowledge. Yet without the conception of end or a purpose of reason, as realized in the form of organized beings, we could not make such beings intelligible to ourselves. Even a simple blade of grass is inexplicable unless we look upon it as purposive.

(*f*) The conception of the organism as purposive leads, moreover, to the view of collective nature as an organic whole or teleological unity. But it should be reiterated that we cannot affirm the principle of end or final cause as belonging to the essential constitution of nature. Could we penetrate to the hidden ground of nature, we should possibly discover that the principles of mechanical and teleological causation are assimilated in one single principle. The very limitation of our knowledge suggests to us the idea of a higher intelligence, possessed of knowledge which is direct and not mediated by a subjective principle. For such an intuitive or perceptive understanding there would be no such separation as our discursive understanding makes between means and end. As it is, the mechanical and teleological principles are at once complementary and heterogeneous, though the teleological is the final or inclusive principle.[2]

9. Hegel.—(*a*) In the course of his examination of the critical philosophy Hegel (*q.v.*) dealt with Kant's view of the physico-theological proof. He agrees with Kant as to its inadequacy as a rational or logical argument. The conception of design, like that of cause in the cosmological proof, cannot express the true nature of the relation of the world to God. At the same time the argument represents a further stage, the first stage being represented by the cosmological argument, in the process whereby in the hidden or implicit logic of religion thought reaches the full apprehension of God as spirit or self-conscious intelligence. Kant might have allowed this, but for the rigidity of the distinction he drew between the phenomenal and noumenal worlds, which made it impossible for thought to pass from the one to the other. But the distinction is only relative, and from the ultimate standpoint the two worlds are one. (*b*) As for the critique of the teleological judgment, here again Kant's doctrine is vitiated by the view of the phenomenal and the noumenal as abstract opposites. Yet Kant indicates, if indirectly, the right principle of cosmic interpretation. For it is impossible to distinguish the categories of mechanical and teleological causation as being constitutive and regulative, objective and subjective respectively. With his true apprehension of the idea of purpose as internal and immanent, Kant, but for his rationalistic prejudices, might have advanced to the recognition of the constitutive character of the organic or teleological principle. Internal

[1] Königsberg, 1755. [2] Königsberg, 1762. [3] Riga, 1781.
[4] *Critique of Pure Reason*, tr. J. M. D. Meiklejohn, London, 1860, p. 383.
[5] Riga, 1788. [6] Berlin and Libau, 1790.

[1] *A Hist. of Philosophy*, Eng. tr., New York and London, 1893, p. 561.
[2] Cf. Pringle-Pattison, *The Idea of God*, p. 330.

adaptation or design is no less constitutive than the principle of mechanical causation. To overcome, says Hegel, the opposition of phenomena and noumena, we must follow the development of the world from the realm of nature to the realm of mind and thence to the unity of nature and mind in the idea of God, in whom the world is seen to be a rational system.

10. Schelling: the philosophy of nature.—(*a*) If Kant promoted the movement of German idealism, he also promoted—perhaps indirectly rather than directly—the new German humanism. We shall take occasion later to speak of the teleological or organic view of history associated with the names of Schelling and Hegel, who carried forward the work of Bossuet and Montesquieu, of Herder (*q.v.*) and Lessing (*q.v.*). Meantime we refer to another aspect of the humanistic movement, viz. the teleological or organic view of nature which was upheld under the leadership of Schelling by the so-called philosophers of nature. For Schelling, as for Plato and others among the ancients, there was a world-soul which as an inner principle of life united all differences in nature in a single organic system. It was felt by the new humanists, as J. T. Merz[1] puts it, that in the Kantian and more particularly the Fichtean philosophy the details of the scenery of nature were forgotten in the interest of studying the attitude and the emotions of the beholder. (*b*) Under the shelter of the humanistic movement, it should be noticed, there was a recrudescence of vitalistic theories in biology (which term was first used in this period by Treviranus to cover the whole of the science of life). Though the biological implications of the *Critique of Judgment* are difficult to grasp, vitalism could readily appeal to Kant's philosophical authority against the mechanical theory of life. For, while Kant handed over the inorganic realm to the mechanical theory (in this only sanctioning a *fait accompli*), he had maintained along with the teleological unity of nature as a whole the Aristotelian concept of biological organization. So at least it was generally thought, despite the metaphysical distinction he drew between the determinant and the reflective or teleological judgment as constitutive and regulative respectively. It is a distinction indeed which science cannot but ignore. When science employs teleological concepts such as function or adaptation, it gives them the same validity as the concept of mechanical causation.[2]

11. Lotze.—(*a*) The humanistic movement soon lost its force. The vitalistic theories which had received their impulse from it, and which culminated in Johannes Müller, fell into comparative neglect, and the mechanical view of life was once more dominant. The most solid, according to H. Driesch,[3] of all the attacks upon the older vitalism was made by Lotze (*q.v.*), whom he describes as a static teleologist in physiology in that he believed in the irreducibility of the category of the organism, but a dynamic teleologist or vitalist in psychology in that he believed the soul to be productive of absolutely new mechanical movement. (*b*) But the significance of Lotze for teleology lies not so much in his work in the domain of biology as in his philosophical system. In him science and philosophy, which since Leibniz and Kant had been going separate ways, meet once more. For he combines the mechanical view of nature with a teleological metaphysics (which he holds Schelling also did). It is his aim to show, as he says in the Introduction to the *Microcosmus*, 'how absolutely universal is the extent and at the same time how completely subordinate the significance, of the mission which mechanism has to fulfil in the structure of the world.'[1] In his scientific materialism he was at one with the great body of the scientific thinkers of his age. In his speculative teleology he had affinities with Leibniz, Spinoza, Kant, and Herbart. Following Leibniz, he was led to conceive of the world as a plurality of real spiritual elements, but in mutual interaction according to the principle of immanent as distinguished from transeunt causality. In his endeavour to account for the causal relation and the reciprocal interaction of the elements, he was led, by a similar process of thought to that which Spinoza went through, to the idea of a universal all-embracing principle, which for religion has the value of God. Under the influence of Herbart and the Kantian criticism, he utilizes the principle of human analogy in interpreting the inner reality of nature, which he regards as the instrument of a purpose, viz. the purpose of supreme good, though it is by a practical conviction rather than a logical or rational process that we pass from the world of things and forms to the world of values. So it is that Lotze reaches his teleological interpretation of nature.

12. Darwin.—(*a*) At first sight it would appear that the theory of biological evolution associated with the name of Charles Darwin so strikingly vindicates the mechanical view of nature as to banish the idea of teleology altogether, not only from scientific explanation but also from philosophical interpretation. Certainly, as Darwin himself realized, the doctrine of descent by natural selection gave a fatal blow to the old argument from design as expounded by Paley.

> 'We can no longer argue,' he says, 'that the beautiful hinge of a bivalve shell must have been made by an intelligent being, like the hinge of a door by a man.'[2]

Paley had not appreciated the metaphysical difficulties involved in the notions of an external designer or contriver and of special external adaptations, and he laboured under the further limitation that he believed with the orthodox science of his time in the fixity or immutability of species. If species were not fixed and permanent forms but the results of long evolutionary processes determined by necessity or chance, then Paley's argument was still further discredited. There appeared to be no more design in the principle of natural selection than 'in the course which the wind blows.'[3]

(*b*) But, while the Darwinian theory was subversive of the teleological argument in its popular form, which was deistic or rationalistically theistic, it was not really anti-teleological in the Aristotelian and post-Kantian sense. No doubt the principle of natural selection is in itself fortuitous or non-teleological, and that despite the teleological flavour of the terms 'selection,' 'fitness,' by which it is expressed; so that J. Ward, borrowing a 'plain' term from Herbert Spencer, would describe the principle in mechanistic language as one of 'equilibration.'[4] Moreover, in the hands of ultra-Darwinians natural selection of random variations has been employed as an exclusive explanation of the modification and transformation of species, and, so employed, may be properly described as anti-teleological. But Darwin himself did not urge natural selection as an exclusive principle. He recognized in evolution other factors besides, both non-teleological and teleological; *e.g.*, in the last edition of the *Origin of Species* he makes a

[1] *Hist. of European Thought in the 19th Century*, 4 vols., Edinburgh, 1896-1914, iii. 352.
[2] Henderson, *The Order of Nature*, p. 67.
[3] *The Hist. and Theory of Vitalism*, London, 1914, pp. 127-132.

[1] *Microcosmus*, Eng. tr.[4], Edinburgh, 1894, vol. i. p. xvi.
[2] *The Life and Letters of Charles Darwin*[2], 3 vols., London, 1887, i. 309.
[3] *Ib.* i. 309.
[4] *The Realm of Ends* (*Gifford Lectures*), Cambridge, 1911, p. 101.

point of saying that natural selection is 'aided in an important manner by the inherited effects of the use and disuse of parts.'[1] Ward contends that this, the Lamarckian factor, like the factors of sexual and human selection, is strictly teleological in the sense that it presupposes psychical activity, conscious or at least sentient, directed to the end of the satisfaction of needs or desires. Whether the Lamarckian is a real or supposititious factor in evolution is a point with which we are not here concerned. It might be added, however, that the anti-Darwinian theories of evolution are more favourable to the teleological idea than the Darwinian and ultra-Darwinian theories; also that Darwin's general theory of organic evolution, like the general cosmogonic theory of Kant and Laplace, is being increasingly recognized as not inconsistent with an ultimate teleology, profounder, subtler, and less rationalistic than Paley's.

'Unless the cosmos itself,' says Ward, 'is to be regarded as a finite and fortuitous variation persisting in an illimitable chaos, we must refer its orderliness and meaning to an indwelling, informing Life and Mind.'[2]

13. Lachelier. — In Merz's opinion Lachelier's short tract, *Du Fondement de l'induction*,[3] is 'a corner-stone in the edifice of modern thought.'[4] Lachelier faces the problem of the contingent (or the collocation of things in space) which, along with that of the discontinuous, is involved in the Lotzean formula, that 'the things which surround us are the material in which, the laws of nature the forms *through* which, the world of values, or the Ideals, are, or have to be, realized.'[5] Following Cournot, he took up into his philosophy the old distinction between nature passively conceived and nature hypostatized or taken actively (*natura naturata, natura naturans*). The possibility of inductive reasoning rests, he says, on the recognition of both these aspects of nature, which are complementary. From the one standpoint nature is a mechanical or serial unity in which the antecedent determines the consequent; from the other it is a teleological, systematic, or harmonious unity in which the whole determines the existence of the parts. Efficient causes and final causes are both needed in the inductive process. Nature is at once a science, for ever producing effects from causes, and an art, for ever setting about new inventions. As there is a principle of regularity in nature, so there is a principle also of harmony or order. The contrast of mechanism with teleology, as Bosanquet has put it, 'is rooted in the very nature of totality.'[6] We shall see that this philosophical position of Lachelier has been fruitful in the scientific investigation of the problem of universal teleology.

III. *SYSTEMATIC.* — A. TELEOLOGY IN EMPIRICAL DESCRIPTION.—**1. Description, explanation, interpretation.**—(*a*) In proceeding from the historical to the systematic discussion, it will make for convenience of treatment to distinguish three aspects of teleology. Historically they have been closely associated, and it is impossible to separate them in any rigid fashion. They may be named, however, the descriptive, the explanatory, and the interpretative. If one hesitates to set up the distinctions here implied, one hesitates more as to the terms by which to designate them. For description, explanation, and interpretation are ill-defined terms in current usage, although—perhaps because—they circulate so freely in discussions of the world and its meaning. By descriptive teleology we mean the teleology which answers at once to the definition of the concept of end or purpose and is immediately recognizable. It might be otherwise named as formal, empirical, or *de facto* teleology. By explanatory teleology we mean the teleology which is postulated in scientific theory in explanation of things, processes, and events. It might be otherwise named as methodical or logical teleology. By interpretative teleology we mean the teleology which offers in philosophy and religion a spiritual interpretation of the world as a whole. It might be otherwise named as speculative, ideal, or spiritual teleology.

(*b*) It might be objected in particular to this scheme that modern physical science leaves explanation to metaphysical philosophy and claims for its formulas no more than descriptive validity. It concerns itself only with the question, 'What is it?', and hands over to metaphysics and religious philosophy the questions, 'How came it to be?', and 'Why came it to be?' But it appears to us that physical science has been suffering in the last generation from an excess of reactionary modesty. Behind its so-called descriptive formulations, which are broad generalizations, lie worlds of patient observation and experiment and a host of flashing inspirations; and, if it does not tell us all about the 'How,' it tells us a great deal about it, and is richly entitled to the larger claim involved in the term 'explanation.'

'It is an interesting point,' remarks J. Arthur Thomson, 'that just about the time when physics began to proclaim emphatically that its office was to describe and not to explain, natural history in Darwin's hands passed emphatically from description to historical explanation.'[1]

For the rest, there is in any case august and already classical authority for a certain individualism in matters of terminology.[2]

2. Descriptive teleology.—(*a*) Teleology, in the sense of purposiveness or activity directed towards an end, is immediately recognizable in the ordinary work-a-day world. Conscious striving after ends, with adaptation of means to ends, is characteristic of human life. The concept of end or purpose is itself derived from observation of the human mind, and conative activity involving ends is central in human experience. But the idea of teleology is readily extended beyond the reference to consciousness. There is a teleology below consciousness, just as there is a teleology above consciousness.

'Neither Christianity nor the coral reef,' says Bosanquet, 'were ever any design of the men or the insects who constructed them; they lay altogether deeper in the roots of things.'[3]

(*b*) As in human history teleology or purposiveness appears to be present in the process, though the individual goes forth, like Abraham, not knowing whither he goes, so it is also in the spheres of subconscious and unconscious life. Many biological processes show the appearance at least of purposiveness, and Kant was right in saying that we could not attain to the knowledge of living things except under the form of the teleological judgment. The structure of the organism, the reciprocal relation of its parts as both means and ends for each other, and its growth, in which it is at once continually self-produced and self-producing, all appeared to him to demand a teleological explanation. It may be that, as Kant's critical philosophy forced him to admit, the teleological principle is subjective and only regulative of knowledge. All we have to say here is that the phenomena of organismal life have been explained both mechanistically and teleologically, but *prima facie* they are susceptible to description in teleological terms.

[1] P. 421, quoted by J. Ward, *Naturalism and Agnosticism*[3] (*Gifford Lectures*), 2 vols., London, 1906, i. 280.
[2] *Naturalism and Agnosticism*, i. 302.
[3] Paris, 1871.
[4] *Hist. of European Thought*, iii. 620.
[5] *Ib.* iii. 616.
[6] *The Principle of Individuality and Value* (*Gifford Lectures*), London, 1912, p. 155.

[1] *The System of Animate Nature* (*Gifford Lectures*), 2 vols., London, 1920, i. 13.
[2] Cf. C. C. J. Webb, *Studies in the History of Natural Theology*, Oxford, 1915, p. 6.
[3] *The Principle of Individuality and Value*, p. 155.

(c) When we pass from organic to inorganic nature, we meet no longer with the appearance of purposiveness, because in inorganic nature there are, to the eyes of sight at least, no individual beings. Yet, if we were to indulge the 'pathetic fallacy,' we should look even upon inorganic nature, the air, the sea, a rock, as responsive to our varying moods and thus as so far teleologically constituted.

(d) But, if purposiveness may not be discerned in the inorganic world, it is recognizable in products of art and man's device that are composed of inorganic elements. To our fancy a piece of machinery is often informed with life and purpose, like the machines in Samuel Butler's satire of *Erewhon*, but the purposiveness resides not in the parts but in the processes they subserve. A machine, as Driesch[1] says, is distinguished from other human 'artefacts' as being made for processes. It is, as it were, the depository of a purpose. That is why the comparison of the world to a machine in the old natural theology, as by Cleanthes in Hume's *Dialogues*, is apt enough, especially when the Deity is deistically conceived as purely transcendent. On the other hand, it is also the reason why the comparison is inept from the standpoint of materialism or naturalism, and why from such a standpoint mechanism as applied to the world is not a particularly happy term.

(e) Nor should it be forgotten that under descriptive teleology may be included the recognition of order, beauty, and adaptations in nature as a whole. These things are upon that empirical level of reality which has been attained by the unreflective processes of common sense, and are consequently appreciated by all; and they form the sufficient basis of the traditional argument from design. For order, beauty, adaptation, all speak the language of teleology.

3. The argument from design.—The argument classically expounded in the ancient world by the Stoic Lucilius Balbus in Cicero's *de Natura Deorum*, and in the modern world by Paley in his *Natural Theology*, is doubtless made more impressive, but is not essentially strengthened, by the multiplication of curious instances of extrinsic and intrinsic adaptation derived from the scientific order of nature. It is sufficiently based, as already said, on the fact of the empirical order. As an integral part, nay the very marrow and substance, of the old natural theology of Paley and the Bridgewater Treatises, the argument is liable to criticism for its deistic flavour, its hedonism, its antiquated pre-evolutionary science, its old-fashioned teleology; and apart from its limiting historical associations it is liable, as Hume and Kant made it abundantly clear, to the charge of being essentially fallacious. In inferring divine purposeful agency from the teleological appearance of nature, it is guilty, as the logicians would say, of the fallacy of transcendent inference. Obviously it must be restated in a profounder way, if it is to retain validity. The essence of the argument, says R. Flint,[2] is that order implies intelligence. It is an argument not *from* but *to* design, and it is only to be regarded as part of a great cumulative argument. G. T. Ladd[3] admits that the argument is properly an argument from universal order, and he is careful to say that it implies the validity of the ontological argument. From the 'orderly totality' of the universe he would postulate a world-ground conceived of as absolute will and intelligence. But the 'plain man,' with his eye only upon the empirical order, uses the argument without hesitation or logical scruple. When his mind beholds

[1] *The Hist. and Theory of Vitalism*, p. 4.
[2] *Theism*², p. 131 ff.; cf. also *Agnosticism* (*Croall Lecture*), Edinburgh, 1903, pp. 182–184.
[3] *The Philosophy of Religion*, 2 vols., London, 1906, ii. 59 ff.

the chain of causes 'confederate and linked together, it must needs fly to Providence and Deity.'[1] Nor need the man of science, with his deeper appreciation of nature's order, be hesitant to follow the 'plain man.'

'The Logos,' says J. Arthur Thomson, 'is at the core of our system, implicit in the nebula, as now in the dewdrop. It slept for the most part through the evolution of plants and coral-like animals, whose dream-smiles are a joy for ever. It slept as the child sleeps before birth. It became more and more awake among higher animals,—feeling and knowing and willing. It became articulate in self-conscious Man,—and not least in his science.'[2]

'There is . . . something,' says D'Arcy W. Thompson, 'that is the order of the cosmos and the beauty of the world, that lives in all things living, and dwells in the mind and soul of man. . . . You may call it Entelechy, you may call it the Harmony of the World; you may call it the *Élan vital*, you may call it the Breath of Life. Or you may call it, as it is called in the Story-book of Creation, and in the hearts of men—you may call it the Spirit of God.'[3]

B. TELEOLOGY IN SCIENTIFIC EXPLANATION.—**1. Cosmology.**—(1) *Mechanical explanation.*—The teleological appearance of nature and the forms of life, considered above, has set a problem which science no more than philosophy can afford to ignore. In cosmology, however, narrowly interpreted as the science of inorganic nature, teleology is not required as a principle of explanation, whether the cosmos be considered in the spatial or in the temporal reference, *i.e.* from the standpoint of cosmography or from that of cosmogony. The inorganic world is not teleological, for physical science at least, in the sense of exhibiting immanent purposiveness. In its formulations of the things and processes of the inorganic world science employs only the mechanistic terms of kinematics, mechanics, physics, and chemistry; and it has amply vindicated its right to employ mechanistic terms exclusively in this sphere. Whether it may also do so in the spheres of biology, psychology, and sociology is another question. But in cosmology it has no use for the category of end or purpose, or for that matter for the categories of cause and substance, but assumes the working only of the non-spontaneous, the automatic, the mechanistic. It may possibly be that such real categories as substance and cause (whether efficient or final) are, in Mach's phrase, tinctured with 'fetishism,' but the exact sciences as such are by no means committed to a materialistic or naturalistic standpoint. Materialism and naturalism are ultimate positions, and scientific explanation is not necessarily that ultimate explanation which we would include under the term 'interpretation.' In point of fact, exact science increasingly recognizes the abstract and artificial quality of its explanations, as it realizes increasingly the distinction between conceptual formulation and perceptual reality. Its formulas have been variously characterized as symbols or counterfoils of reality, as a kind of conceptual shorthand, as economics of thought, as convenient hypothetical summations, or, in J. Royce's favourite metaphor, as the ledger entries and balances of a particular method of book-keeping. It is open to science, as he truly remarks, to enter its accounts by other methods of book-keeping.[4] Gravitation, *e.g.*, may yet be explained as a mere appearance of some more genuine process of nature.

(2) *Collocations.*—In view of the foregoing, we may allow that mechanical explanation, if abstract and hypothetical, reigns supreme and alone in the physical domain. While therefore Chalmers strengthened the case for physico-theology by reviving the Cartesian distinction between the

[1] Bacon, *Essays*, xvi., 'Of Atheism.'
[2] *The System of Animate Nature*, ii. 637.
[3] *Life and Finite Individuality* (two symposia of the Aristotelian Society), London, 1918, p. 54.
[4] *The World and the Individual* (*Gifford Lectures*), 2nd ser., New York, 1901, p. 216.

laws and the dispositions or collocations of matter, he placed his argument in jeopardy when he said that 'the main evidence for a Divinity lies, not in the laws of matter, but in the collocations.'[1] 'But what would become of this main evidence for a Divinity,' remarks J. Ward,[2] 'if the laws of matter themselves explained its collocations?' Yet, although science has been gathering the collocations within the mechanism of nature, the problem of order still remains. As in the biological sphere, so in the cosmological there is an ultimate collocation or configuration to be acknowledged which natural laws cannot explain. Says L. J. Henderson:

'The forms and states and quantities of matter and energy in the nebula determine the resulting solar system.'[3]

So that we may affirm that the universe possesses an original teleological character.

(3) *Fitness of the environment.*—(*a*) But is it possible to discover an explanation of the order of nature beyond the laws of nature's uniformity? Henderson thinks positive thought has found a clue. He points out that, if the scientific or mechanistic origin of the natural order is to be explained, it must be through principles that account not merely for the general character of orderliness in the phenomena of nature and the products of evolution, but also for that radical or fundamental diversity which Herbert Spencer declared necessary to the evolutionary process. Such principles, clearly, are to be sought not so much in the laws of nature as in the properties of matter. Accordingly Henderson has investigated the properties of the elements hydrogen, carbon, and oxygen, and of their compounds water and carbon dioxide, which have been the chief factors in both geological and organic evolution. These properties are found to constitute a unique group of singular physical and chemical characteristics, so that they are *maxima* or the fittest possible for organic life; *e.g.*—to take the compounds, which are the primary constituents of the environment—the solvent action of water is greater than the solvent action of any other liquid, and the solubility of carbon dioxide in water is such that it must always be evenly distributed between the atmosphere and aqueous liquids. Or—to take the elements themselves—hydrogen, carbon, and oxygen possess the greatest number of compounds and enter into the greatest number of reactions, involving the greatest transformations of energy known to the chemist. Further (and here a teleological consideration appears), the aforesaid unique ensemble of properties is uniquely favourable to the existence of systems—of which the world of physics and chemistry consists—of numerous, diverse, stable systems. In fitness for systems no other elements and compounds even approach hydrogen, carbon and oxygen, water and carbon dioxide. In short, the arrangement of the properties of matter among the elements makes the diversity of the evolutionary process possible.

(*b*) It is Henderson's opinion, following up these results of physico-chemical research, that, as according to the law of probabilities the connexion between the properties and the process cannot be due to mere contingency, the properties can only be regarded as a preparation for the process, or, in other words, as resembling adaptation. There must be a functional relationship between them—something like that known to physiology—which must be described as teleological. How otherwise can we express the fact that the collocation of properties unaccountably precedes that to which they are unquestionably related? Just as biological organization is teleological and non-mechanical, so with the connexion between the properties of hydrogen, carbon, and oxygen and the process of evolution. This is the positive contribution Henderson has to offer towards the vast problem of the contingent set for natural science by Lotze and Lachelier, and it goes to strengthen the philosophical position that mechanism and teleology are both at the foundation of the natural order.[4]

2. Biology.—(1) *Evolution.*—(*a*) The term 'evolution' (*q.v.*) is itself teleological in its primary meaning, and denotes more than mechanistic process; but it is possible that the mechanistic (*i.e.* physico-chemical) explanation of biological descent may be found sufficient in natural science. Possibly the evolutionary process is mechanistically determined through and through by natural selection interpreted as non-teleological (whether working upon so-called fortuitous variations or upon variations themselves subject to the law of probability), or by natural selection supplemented by other non-teleological factors, perhaps by some non-teleological factor yet to be discovered. On the other hand, we have seen that Darwin did not regard natural selection as exclusive of teleological factors, and it may well be that the psychical principles of self-conservation and subjective selection, on which J. Ward would lay stress, are required to give natural selection a *point d'appui.*[1]

(*b*) It is a searching test of the sufficiency of mechanistic explanation that H. Bergson in the rôle of biologist proposes. If it could be proved, he says, that life may manufacture the like apparatus, by unlike means, on divergent lines of evolution, then pure mechanism would be refutable and finality in a certain sense so far demonstrable. Accordingly he examines the evolutionary hypothesis in the two forms of it that have emerged from the welter of biological controversy since Darwin's time. He puts it to neo-Darwinism and neo-Lamarckism alike, What is the explanation of the structural analogy between the eye of a vertebrate and that of a mollusc like the common pecten?[2] It appears impossible on neo-Darwinian principles, which enter readily into a mechanistic philosophy of life, to account for the production of the same effect by two different accumulations of an enormous number of small causes, whether the possibility be urged, as by the stricter Darwinists, on the theory of insensible accidental variations or, as by de Vries, on the theory of sudden and simultaneous variations or, as by Eimer, on the theory that assigns a direct rather than an indirect influence to the environment, explaining the evolution of the various organs by a kind of mechanical composition of the external with the internal forces. To account for the convergence of effects we must appeal, continues Bergson, to some inner directing principle. Here Bergson's sympathy with the neo-vitalism of Driesch and Reinke appears, though he is more interested in their critical work than in their constructions. Turning to neo-Lamarckism, which explains variations not as accidental or determined but as springing from the effort of the living being to adapt itself to the environment, he declares it to be the only form of the later evolutionism capable of admitting, as it actually does with Cope, 'an internal and psychological principle of development.'[3] Weismann has shown, however, that the Lamarckian hereditary transmission of acquired characteristics is at most the exception and not the rule. How then may an organ such as the eye be developed? Is not the organic effort a deeper and more psychological thing than any neo-Lamarckian supposes? So Bergson returns to his speculative theory of life. He finds the fundamental cause of variations that accumulate and create new species, in the transmission of the *élan vital* from one generation of germs to the next through the developed organisms which bridge the interval between the generations. Life does not proceed by the association and addition of elements, which is the false anthropomorphic view both of mechanism and of finalism. Life proceeds by dissociation and division. It starts with a direction or tendency no doubt, and is in this sense finalistic, but we cannot foretell how and where it will end.

(2) *Mechanism and vitalism.*—(*a*) Leaving genetic considerations, we find ourselves still pursued by the mechanistic hypothesis, which affirms 'living matter' to be completely describable as a physico-chemical system, and organization and regulation—those distinguishing marks of living bodies—to be conceivable in physico-chemical terms. But it is also maintained as against this that the way of physico-chemical analysis and synthesis yields but an abstract product falling short of what answers to that *vue d'ensemble* which Comte advocated in the study of the living.

(*b*) Mechanistic theory in biology may be said to follow two main types, so far as regards the relation to teleology. Sometimes it has no traffic with teleology at all, and is still afflicted with what von Baer called 'teleophobia,' in its jealousy for the mechanical explanation. Sometimes again—and this represents the predominant tendency—it finds room for the teleological view, re-affirming in fact the Aristotelian doctrine of the internal teleology of the living thing, which is its self-regulation.

(*c*) But, with the more synthetic method involved in this type of mechanistic theory, vitalism has appeared once again in the history of biological theory, if in subtler and more elusive forms. The difference between the prevalent mechanistic theory and the vitalistic hypothesis may be expressed in the distinction due to Driesch between statical

[1] *On the Power, Wisdom, and Goodness of God*, i. 20, note.
[2] *Naturalism and Agnosticism*, i. 47.
[3] *Fitness of the Environment*, p. 301.
[4] Cf. *Fitness of the Environment*, *Order of Nature*, *Philosophical Review*, vol. xxv. no. 3 [1916], *Journal of Philosophy, Psychology and Scientific Methods*, vol. xiii. no. 12 [1916].

[1] *Naturalism and Agnosticism*, i. 290.
[2] *L'Évolution créatrice*, Paris, 1907, Eng. tr., London, 1911, p. 66 ff.
[3] *Ib.* p. 81.

and dynamical teleology.[1] Whereas in statical teleology the processes of life are judged to be purposive in virtue of a given machine-like order or form underlying them, in dynamical teleology it is in virtue of their possession of a peculiar autonomy; and dynamical teleology leads, as Driesch thinks, to some form of vitalism. We suppose L. J. Henderson, who is a mechanist, might then be also named a statical teleologist; for, while on the whole persuaded that organization (the central issue between the mechanism and vitalism of to-day) is capable of explanation—though not as yet explained—in physico-chemical terms, he is also persuaded that the teleological concept of organization, if to be found also in sociology and in the meteorological cycle, is a necessary biological category, and that a mechanistic physiology is at fault in not recognizing this.[2] But, though he thus believes with Driesch in teleology as an 'irreducible peculiarity' of vital phenomena, he is not a dynamical teleologist in the neo-vitalist sense. He might allow that organisms, like machines, are inert embodiments of purposiveness; he would not allow that they are actuated by purposiveness.

(*d*) The anti-mechanists also fall into two main groups. In the first are the neo-vitalists, of whom Driesch is the most prominent representative. They contend that biological processes are not properly explicable as physico-chemical processes within the living matter of the organism, but that some non-physical principle (like Driesch's entelechy or unifying causality) impresses itself upon those processes, to suspend, regulate, or control the physical and chemical reactions. With such a principle at work, the outcome of events, experimentally considered at least, is no longer determinate and unequivocal. Bergson's *élan vital* is such another non-perceptual determiner. Now, as Bergson realizes,[3] the contention of neo-vitalism is relevant and weighty on the critical side, but on its positive side is beset with difficulties. Even granted the existence of the mysterious non-mechanical semi-psychical entity postulated in the theory, it is impossible to say where and how it works in the biological processes. In recent constructions, no doubt, there is none of the crudity ridiculed by Molière in the older vitalism when he declared the cause of sleep to be the 'dormitive virtue' (which reminds one of the Johnsonian legend that the noise of wheels was once attributed by the learned doctor to the strepituosity of circumrotatory motion). All the same the conception of neo-vitalism remains mystical in quality, and biological science is reluctant to entertain it. An entity such as Driesch formulates, which is neither an energy nor a material substance but an agent *sui generis*, non-spatial, albeit acting into space, non-material, but logically belonging to nature, may have a strange fascination for the metaphysician, but will hardly retain a place for itself in the world of scientific explanation. We are assured, moreover, that the second law of thermo-dynamics, which entelechy is said to be capable of suspending, will hold even in the obscure cases in morphology on which Driesch founds his theory.[4] We are also assured that the non-physical something which is supposed to intervene in physical and chemical processes is invariably dependent upon the existence of physical and chemical conditions, yet it is not explained what part these conditions play in bringing about the actual results.[1] Vitalism sets itself a hard task indeed in seeking to steer between the Scylla and Charybdis of the mechanical and metaphysical explanations.[2]

(3) *Biologism.*—(*a*) Even as a scientific hypothesis neo-vitalism appears already on the way to occupy an intermediate position. The issue now seems to lie between some kind of mechanism and a form of teleological theory even more anti-mechanistic than neo-vitalism. For want of a better name, the theory may be called 'biologism.' It is the biological as distinguished from the mechanical theory of life. It is vitalistic in a sense, for it regards it as impossible to conceive distinctively biological phenomena in physical and chemical terms. For it the autonomy of life is more than a statical conception involving a teleological and non-mechanical relationship between mechanical things and processes. The autonomy of life is a dynamical conception, involving a dynamical teleology. But it is the living organism itself, and not some directive force within it, as in properly vitalistic theory, that is dominant in organic activity. The organism exists as such, and its structure and activities are the expression of its existence.

(*b*) Here, as is claimed by J. S. Haldane,[3] a protagonist of the biological theory of life, we have a good working hypothesis, necessary to biologists, and capable of overcoming the failures of the physico-chemical conception. Biology, he urges, is something very different from physico-chemistry applied to life. Its phenomena differ, not merely in complexity but also in kind, from physico-chemical phenomena. Although physico-chemistry has much to teach us concerning the origin and destiny of the material and energy in the body, it fails to throw light upon the apparently teleological ordering of that material and energy. The inadequacy of the physico-chemical explanation appears when we enter into the deeper problems of the organism's activity, not to say fundamental problems, such as reproduction and heredity. Animal heat, respiration, circulation—to take these examples from physiology—all contain teleological (*i.e.* physiological) elements that do not yield to physico-chemical analysis. Life is a unity of structure, environment, and activity, and is not resolvable into mechanism. Separate a living part from its environment, or suspend its activity, and you alter it completely. What therefore matter and energy are to physics, or the atom to chemistry, the living organism is to biology.

(*c*) Haldane is further of opinion that, inconsistent with each other as are the biological and ordinary physico-chemical theories of life (so that personally he would as soon go back to the mythology of his Saxon forefathers as to the mechanistic physiology), a common meeting-ground between biology and physico-chemistry will yet be discovered. That will mean, however, not a reduction of the organic to the inorganic, but the inclusion of the inorganic within the domain of biology.[4] In such an opinion the contrast between the principles of mechanism and biologism is sharply revealed, but with it we seem to be carried beyond the universe of discourse of natural science.

(*d*) It appears to us that in their bearing upon scientific explanation the differences between the mechanist or statical teleologist and the biologist or dynamical teleologist (if we may wrest Driesch's terms to our own use) is not so very radical after all. It is significant that Henderson accepts the mechanistic hypothesis as *upon the whole* most consistent with the evidence,[5] and that Haldane advocates the biological hypothesis on account of the unsatisfactoriness of the *ordinary* mechanistic (*i.e.* physico-chemical) explanation.[6] They both accept the principle of organic autonomy, and are good Aristotelians (as indeed Driesch is also), and possibly they would unite upon the formula: 'Not mechanism *or* vitalism, but mechanism *and* teleology.' This is a thesis admirably supported

[1] *The History and Theory of Vitalism*, p. 5; cf. also *The Science and Philosophy of the Organism* (*Gifford Lectures*), Edinburgh, 1908, ii. 135 f.

[2] *Philosophical Review*, vol. xxvii. no. 6 [1918], p. 575 f.

[3] *Creative Evolution*, p. 44, note.

[4] L. J. Henderson, in *Philosophical Review*, xxvii. no. 6, p. 574.

[1] J. S. Haldane, *The New Physiology*, London, 1919, p. 137.

[2] Cf. R. Eucken, *Main Currents of Modern Thought*, Eng. tr., London, 1912, p. 181.

[3] *The New Physiology*, p. 48; cf. also *Mechanism, Life, and Personality*, London, 1913, *Organism and Environment*, New Haven, London and Oxford, 1917, *Life and Finite Individuality* (Two Symposia), London, 1918.

[4] *The New Physiology*, p. 19; *Mechanism, Life, and Personality*, p. 100.

[5] *Philosophical Review*, vol. xxvii. no. 6, p. 576.

[6] *The New Physiology*, p. 49.

by R. F. Alfred Hoernlé,[1] who would make the particular point that in biology teleology not only is compatible with mechanism but is 'logically dominant' over it. Teleological terms are required, he says, not as substitutes for physico-chemical terms but to express the dominancy of the structures and processes of life, which—as he goes on to say—cannot be reduced to exclusively physico-chemical terms without disregard of the difference, on which Bergson insists so strikingly, between the living and the dead.

(*e*) In an intimate and eloquent discussion of mechanism and vitalism J. Arthur Thomson[2] makes it abundantly clear that biologism is at present no more than a descriptive or methodological theory. It distinguishes itself from mechanism in demanding ultra-mechanical categories, but what these categories should be is not as yet determinate. He himself describes the organism in Bergsonian language as 'a historic being which has traded with time, and has enregistered within itself past experiences and experiments, and which has ever its conative bow bent towards the future.'[3] Hesitating to interpolate with Driesch and the positive vitalists a new agency or directive activity, he is content to say that the organism reveals new aspects of reality, transcending theoretically mechanical formulation.

3. Psychology.—(1) *Body and mind.*—(*a*) If the teleological standpoint is required in the scientific explanation of the world of organic nature, it is also required in respect of the world of mind or consciousness. The world of mind is the native sphere of purposive activity, and only a very abstract view of it can dispense with teleological categories. According to W. R. Sorley's[4] analysis, the contrast between a purely mechanical and a purposive system lies in this, that, although purpose is consistent with the law of causation and the principle of the conservation of energy, yet as the result of a purpose or mental idea there is a liberation of energy passing from the potential to the kinetic form, and the same purpose may also control, non-mechanically, the direction of the movement. Therefore it is not to account completely for the activity of a purposive system to describe it in merely mechanistic terms. When this position is challenged (as it is in psychology as well as in biology), as not fitting into the mechanistic hypothesis, the discussion passes inevitably into the speculative sphere.

(*b*) In psychology the mechanistic position founds upon the Cartesian law of psycho-physical parallelism, which represents the relation between brain-processes and psychical changes as one not of interaction but of concomitance, and it usually takes the form of the parallelistic hypothesis known as conscious automatism or psychical epiphenomenalism (*Begleiterscheinung*), in which inner or conscious states are accounted for as collateral products of the physical phenomena. On such principles as are embodied in this form of psycho-physical parallelism, the appearance of purpose or ideal direction is an illusion, and the consciousness of purpose either belongs to a different order or level of reality or is simply a result or effect, however vague, shadowy, impalpable, of the neural organization. On the first alternative, every neurosis has its psychosis, but they cannot affect each other. On the second alternative, every neurosis has its psychosis, but the neurosis cannot react even a very little upon the psychosis. Either, then, the mechanical theory does not apply to consciousness or the principle of the conservation of energy breaks down. The mechanist must either give up his case or overthrow the foundations of his faith. If this line of argument laid down by J. Ward[5] be valid, then we are free to turn from the mechanistic hypothesis to one that allows full value to the teleological appearance of conscious life, say, the animistic theory which has so long persisted in human thought and for which W. McDougall[6] has made out so strong a case in recent times, or the double-aspect theory with which the name of C. Lloyd Morgan[7] may be associated, and which J. Arthur Thomson favours as in line with his biological contention, largely based on a study of behaviour, that the organism is a psycho-physical unity.[8]

(2) *Psychologism.*—(*a*) But the working scientist need not commit himself to any speculative position on the problem of the relation between what we

[1] *Philosophical Review*, vol. xxvii. no. 6, p. 629 ff.
[2] *The System of Animate Nature*, vol. i. lect. v.
[3] *Ib.* i. 160.
[4] *Proceedings of the Aristotelian Society*, 33rd session, 1911–12, p. 216 ff.
[5] *Naturalism and Agnosticism*, vol. ii. pt. iii.
[6] *Body and Mind*, London, 1911.
[7] *Scientia*, xviii. [1915] 1–15.
[8] *The System of Animate Nature*, lect. vii., esp. p. 247 ff.

call body and what we call mind. If he is of opinion that psychology is more than physiology, as biology is more than physico-chemistry, he can at least affirm a descriptive or methodological 'psychologism,' transcending merely biological concepts and claiming teleological categories of its own, exclusive and irreducible. A merely physiological psychology, avers J. S. Haldane, is as inadequate as a mechanical physiology. A conscious organism, which reacts not only in space but also in time, and in its temporal reactions joins itself at once to the actual past and the potential future, shows itself to be more than a mere organism, such as we commonly regard a plant as being. The relation to its environment, which is established through perception and volition, is no mere external relation, as in the case of a mere organism. There is a real connexion between the external world and the internal organic world. The environment is 'teleologically determined' by our organic needs, and but for this 'teleological determinism' the world of our conscious experience would lack unity and coherence. To disregard therefore the psychological aspect of living things, especially human beings, and to describe their behaviour in other than psychological terms is to deal unduly in abstractions.[1]

(*b*) If we may extend a remark of J. Arthur Thomson,[2] in which this idea of the autonomy both of biology and of psychology is summed up, there is not one science of nature but several. There is the physical order of nature—the inorganic world—where mechanism is dominant (always on the assumption, as W. R. Sorley[3] reminds us, that qualitative differences are really reducible to quantitative differences of molecular and infra-molecular structure). There is the vital order of nature —the world of organisms—where mechanism is in logical subordination to teleology; and there is the psychical order of nature—the world of mind—where purpose is dominant. In biology the primacy of the biological standpoint, and in psychology the primacy of the psychological standpoint, is to be maintained.

(3) *Discontinuity.*—It may be thought that discontinuity of the categories makes against a unified theory of nature, such as mechanism offers. But a unified theory of nature does not require, says Hoernlé, 'the reduction of all universals to one kind, or the restriction of all variables to one type of values,' but may be achieved by 'the correlation of different types or groups or levels of phenomena.'[4] It is such a correlation, or cumulative integration, that is here supported. Nor need exception to it be taken in the name of ultimate or metaphysical unity. The categories of mechanism, life, and mind, which are fundamental hypotheses of natural science, are, in the wider view of philosophy, only provisional. It is possible, as J. S. Haldane has hinted, that the principle of continuity may yet be amply vindicated even in the scientific order of nature, and that without surrender to the mechanistic hypothesis. From his own standpoint of philosophical idealism he can say that the categories are the forms which the riches of the spiritual world assume in their progress towards the truly real.[5]

4. Sociology.—(1) *Two functions of psychology.* —A. E. Taylor[6] speaks of two functions of psychology. The first, which is not its proper function but which it exercises 'pending the majority of cerebral physiology,' is to set forth mental processes as mechanical uniformities of sequence. The other function is to treat of purposive activities and adjustments, and thereby to afford a suitable terminology for the sociological sciences, and in particular ethics and history. Apart from

[1] *Mechanism, Life, and Personality*, p. 111 ff.
[2] *Introd. to Science*, London, 1911, p. 163; cf. also *HJ* ix. [1911], x. [1912].
[3] *Moral Values and the Idea of God* (*Gifford Lectures*), Cambridge, 1918, p. 407.
[4] *Philosophical Review*, vol. xxvii. no. 6, p. 641.
[5] *The New Physiology*, p. 156.
[6] *Elements of Metaphysics*, London, 1903, p. 306.

the teleological symbols supplied by psychology, ethical appreciation and historical interpretation would be impossible. With this remark let us pass to the consideration of the teleological method in ethics and history.

(2) *Ethics.*—The teleological standpoint has its place in ethical theory, just as teleological symbolism necessarily enters into the appreciation of conduct. Among the possible divisions of ethical theories a fundamental one is into the teleological and the formal or jural. In the first case the moral standard is represented by the idea of good or value, in the second by that of duty or right. The teleological theory, which is found in Greek philosophy, takes the form either of hedonism or, as F. Paulsen,[1] borrowing an Aristotelian term, phrases it, of 'energism.' With Aristotle as with Plato the ethical end or ideal was the good personally realized in social relations as the actualization or full fruition of human powers and capacities. In modern ethical theory both the hedonistic and energistic forms of the teleological method have been revived. The formal or jural method is older than the other, as attaching itself to the legalistic stage of religion. Through Judaism it entered into theological ethics, and it received classical exposition at the hands of Kant, the fundamental idea of whose ethics is the original mental principle of the good will. As against a Kantian formalism and in favour of the teleological standpoint in ethical theory, it has often been urged that norms and motives of action are not abstract and transcendental principles but, as psychology and history teach us, generalized rules of the will which grow out of individual and social experience, and their value consists not in defining but in their power of promoting the ethical end.[2]

(3) *History.*—(*a*) The teleological principle has also been applied to the interpretation of the process of history. As we have already noticed, a teleological view of history took shape under the influence of Christianity, receiving various expression in Augustine and Thomas Aquinas. But it was not until Lessing and Herder, or rather not until Hegel, that history was reflectively and intimately treated in the light of the Aristotelian principles of continuity and development.

(*b*) We may distinguish in this connexion three types of historical theory. J. S. Mill recognized the principle of continuity, but in his 'inverse deductive' method he applied to historical development the atomizing, mechanizing principles of Democritus and Descartes, treating history as a kind of social dynamics, human motives and actions as causes and effects, and the course of events as a rigorously determined sequence. Against this view it may be maintained that the hypothesis of mechanical causation is irrelevant in the sphere of history and of sociology in general, as in the sphere of psychology in its most characteristic aspect. Psychical events are not duly appreciated by means of subpersonal categories. A similar criticism is applicable to Herbert Spencer's theory of history. Although Spencer, here following Comte, applies the idea of organic or super-organic evolution to the interpretation of the historical process, he never really breaks with the conviction—'fixed probably in his mind,' says J. T. Merz, 'through his engineering education'[3]—that change and progress in society, as in nature and mind, are explicable on mechanical principles.

(*c*) The second type of historical theory is represented by Hegel himself, for whom the course of events is a continuity, not of mechanical causation but of evolutionary development. It is still a rigidly determined movement, but it is teleologically conceived, the end dominating the process. 'As the germ carries within itself the whole nature of the tree, the flavour and the form of the fruits, so the first vestiges of mind virtually contain the whole history.'[4] The history of society is for Hegel the necessary evolution of the immanent Idea, and the process is fixed in all its stages. Through human interests and actions the final purpose of history is carried out, but the purpose itself—such is the absolute cunning of reason—is beyond and external to human interests and actions.[5]

1 *Introd. to Philosophy*, Eng. tr., London, 1895, p. 421.
2 Cf. G. Galloway, *The Principles of Religious Development*, London, 1909, p. 235 ff.
3 *Hist. of European Thought*, iv. 519, note.
4 *Philosophie der Geschichte*, ed. 1848, p. 21, quoted by Galloway, p. 5.
5 Cf. J. Ward, *Realm of Ends*, p. 149.

(*d*) It may be objected to this organic view that, in so generalizing the conception of historical development, it does not bring out its true nature as a process of interaction between conscious and self-conscious minds. Nor does it appear to offer a true rationale of human progress. A better explanation of the historical process, in our judgment, is implied in the words of G. Galloway, who, following Siebeck, says: 'Progress is the spiritual vocation of humanity: it is a task which it sets to itself, not an inherent necessity of its constitution. The . . . ideal is freely pursued, and what ought to be is never that which perforce must be.'[1] In other words, the organic view is to be replaced by the historical or spiritual view, in which the freedom of human personality is more clearly acknowledged.[2]

(*e*) The fuller justification of such a position must lie in the metaphysical sphere. It may be here observed that the third type of historical theory might be distinguished from the others as teleological indeterminism. In it development is acknowledged to be epigenetic or, in Wundt's phrase, creatively synthetic, whereas in the teleological and mechanical determinisms above named development is the necessary effect, as it were, of an attraction from before or an impulsion from behind, of a *vis a fronte* or a *vis a tergo*.

(*f*) It may be also observed that teleological indeterminism in the theory of historical science naturally leads in metaphysics to a form of spiritual pluralism (*q.v.*), that teleological determinism makes a ready alliance with pantheism, and that mechanical determinism is at home in a naturalistic or positivistic setting. Yet it is not without significance that in J. S. Mill a survival of the deistic tendency of thought is to be found. For it may be not unjustly said that deism, as a dogmatic or theological position, with its shallow rationalizing of religion and its mechanical conception of the relation of God to the world, largely promoted what J. Royce calls the 'mechanistic dogma' of our time. An 'absentee God' may be done without, so long as the mechanism of the universe keeps going. At any rate naturalism, deism, pantheism, and pluralism will meet us as we pass from the world of scientific explanation into that of philosophical and religious interpretation.

C. Teleology in spiritual interpretation.—**1. Universal teleology.**—As we view the world in its totality and seek to discover its meaning, we pass from empirical description and scientific or logical explanation to spiritual, *i.e.* philosophical and religious, interpretation. Here we are face to face with the metaphysical aspect of teleology, which is the aspect it has chiefly presented in history. The need of a philosophical interpretation of the world has always been more or less consciously realized, and in recent years there has been a renewal of interest in the deeper problems of nature, mind, and spirit. Philosophy and religion alike welcome the tendency among natural scientists to make incursions into what science has for long regarded as the 'foreign field' of metaphysics—a tendency begotten of the increasing recognition that no more than materialism does naturalism speak the last word on the perennial metaphysical problems. This has been largely due to 'the liberating influence of biology,'[3] and is marked among biologists. We have already noticed the idealistic position of J. S. Haldane, and Driesch has advanced beyond a conceptual phenomenalism, having even formulated a critical metaphysic which leans to theism.[4] The new and wider scientific outlook is well reflected in the significant postscript to T. C. Chamberlin's discussion of the geogonic, geological, and biological processes in his remarkable book, *The Origin of the Earth*:[5]

'It is our personal view that what we conveniently regard as merely material is at the same time spiritual, that what we try to reduce to the mechanistic is at the same time volitional; but whether this be so or not, the emergence of what we call the living from the inorganic and the emergence of what we call the psychic from the physiologic, were at once the transcendent and the transcendental features of the earth's evolution.'

1 *Realm of Ends*, p. 43.
2 Cf. W. James, *The Will to Believe*, New York and London, 1897, p. 245.
3 Pringle-Pattison, *The Idea of God*, p. 66.
4 *The Hist. and Theory of Vitalism*, pt. ii., esp. p. 232 ff.
5 Chicago and London, 1916.

2. Teleology and naturalism.—(*a*) It is the essence of naturalism to construe the phenomena of life, mind, and society in terms of the mechanical and non-teleological conceptions which serve in physical science. But we are persuaded that thus to reduce the world to a mechanism is to fail to account for large tracts of experience. Mechanism is an undeniably excellent methodical principle, but is inadequate as an ontological dogma. Moreover, with the mechanistic dogma teleology cannot live, *i.e.* teleology as philosophical interpretation. It has ever been the contention of teleologists from Aristotle onwards that meaning and purpose underlie all material and mechanical processes, that mind or spirit is ideally prior to matter and more fundamental to reality. Naturalism, it may be said, ignores the distinction implied in Lotze's remark that 'the machinery which produces the image of a phenomenon is not identical with the meaning of this image.'[1]

(*b*) The counter-contention of spiritual philosophy is to be justified on epistemological grounds, as by J. Ward in *Naturalism and Agnosticism.* Ward insists boldly with Kant that the intellect makes or fashions, though it does not create, nature. He shows that the fundamental principles of knowledge, unity, causality, and regularity have entered anthropomorphically into our conception of nature, and that nature itself as one and uniform is teleological, being found conformable to human intelligence and amenable to human ends. The result is that unity of nature and man in one rational and coherent scheme of things, that confronting of human reason by universal reason, in which idealism or spiritualism has always consisted. It is the fault of naturalism, as Pringle-Pattison expresses it, that it prematurely closes the record, that it substantiates the antecedents in abstraction from their consequents.

'There is no system,' as he says, 'no whole of being, no real fact at all, till the external gathers itself up, as it were, into internality, and existence sums itself up in the conscious soul.'[2]

3. The essence of teleological interpretation.—Teleological interpretation is then confessedly anthropomorphic, or, as F. C. S. Schiller would say, humanistic. It rests upon the general epistemological principle of analogy, and is itself a particular instance of it. According to the teleologist, the worlds of nature and history are to be interpreted after the analogy of the purposeful life of which man is conscious in himself. Since Hume and Kant, at any rate, the analogical character of the teleological principle has been widely recognized. We saw it in Lotze, who believed none the less that the category of end or purpose afforded a definite clue to the nature of ultimate reality. We may see it in Bergson, who, however, regards the category of end or purpose as applicable only to the lower scientific order of reality. Yet, as H. Höffding[3] points out, Bergson himself actually employs the principle of analogy along with that of intuition. With him intuition is only the first step towards the interpretation of reality. As mechanism proceeds by analogy in taking the organism to be a machine, and finalism in making it respond to a preconceived plan, so is it not to go by analogy to understand life as an *élan*, a thrust, an effort? But in this instance, it must be allowed, the analogy is drawn not as in finalism from the intelligent self-conscious life, but from the spontaneous and semi-conscious psychical life. While there is force in this criticism of Bergson's position, it does not follow that Bergson's philosophy of life is thereby discredited. All metaphysic, as Leibniz said, is founded on analogy.

[1] *Kleine Schriften*, iii. 229, quoted by Merz, iii. 549.
[2] *The Idea of God*, p. 215; cf. also p. 332.
[3] *Modern Philosophers*, Eng. tr., London, 1915, p. 290 ff. (see ref. at p. 292 to *Den menneskelige Tanke*, French ed., pp. 318–327).

Apart from the analogy of human experience, no kind of knowledge would be possible, and it is entirely reasonable to proceed by way of that analogy to the consideration of the truly and ultimately real. But it may be urged, as against Bergson, that the analogy of purposeful self-conscious activity—so central a feature in human experience—offers a better clue to the nature of the absolute experience than does any analogy based on experience which is subpersonal. In any case what is claimed here is that teleology is a valid principle of interpretation, and that divine purpose may be recognized as a true cosmic principle. We shall see that, if divine purpose is actually so recognized, the *analogia hominis* must not be pressed in detail. The category of purpose or end, viewed from the side of the Absolute, requires to be delicately handled.

4. Pragmatic teleology. — Pragmatism (*q.v.*) claims to be different from other philosophies in respect of the clearness of its consciousness that teleology is no more than a methodological postulate. It is astounded at the misunderstanding revealed in the recent criticism[1] that it assumes a teleological constitution of the universe guaranteeing in mediæval fashion satisfaction to human desires and needs—an assumption out of keeping, the critic adds, with the spiritual pluralism or radical empiricism which pragmatism generally professes. In reply F. C. S. Schiller[2] insists that, while the pragmatist makes use of the teleological principle, it is not for him an *a priori* truth that the universe is going to prove good and to be found favourable to his desires. His is a heuristic teleology. He assumes commensurability between the supreme reality and human faculty, and then acts upon the assumption in hope. In contrast to this methodological optimism, one recalls the attitude of Bertrand Russell,[3] who repudiates the 'will to believe' as an argument, and can only face the universe with 'unyielding despair.' For, according to his naturalistic view, the universe is blind to good and evil and indifferent to human interests. Perhaps, as C. A. Richardson[4] suggests, it is the preoccupation of logical pluralism with the objective side of experience that leads it to look upon the notion of teleology with doubt and suspicion. But more likely the attitude arises out of a personal conviction or resolution of character.

5. Teleology in personal idealism.—(*a*) Where personal idealism means spiritual pluralism of a theistic type, the concept of purpose applied to the interpretation of the universe yields a conclusion that satisfies. Consider first how thoroughgoing an application of this concept is embodied in personal idealism. It conceives reality, as in the monadisms of Leibniz and Lotze, as consisting of a plurality of experiencing subjects or spiritual centres of experience. In this it builds upon the analogy in respect of purposiveness between human persons and the lower forms of organic life, and upon the conjecture that even inorganic matter is composed of purposive individuals. Like organic species arrested in their evolution, or apparently so, these exhibit the minimum of spontaneity and the maximum of habit, according to the idea expressed by J. Ward, 'Routine presupposes antecedent living purpose.'[5] The essential nature of the monads or spiritual individuals is affirmed to be their self-activity, involving self-determination (conscious, subconscious, or unconscious) in

[1] J. M. Warbeke, in *Journal of Philosophy, Psychology and Scientific Methods*, xvi. [1919] 207, 'A Medieval Aspect of Pragmatism.'
[2] *Ib.* xvi. 548, 'Methodological Teleology.'
[3] *Philosophical Essays*, London, 1910, p. 60 ff.
[4] *Spiritual Pluralism*, Cambridge, 1919, p. 17.
[5] *Proceedings of the Aristotelian Society*, 33rd session, 1911–12, p. 260; cf. also C. A. Richardson, *Spiritual Pluralism*, p. 53.

reference to ends. Thus spirit and spontaneity, which naturalism banishes from the world, are restored on this panpsychist hypothesis throughout the whole vast range of experience. But that coherent experience may be made possible, a sympathetic *rapport* or responsive sympathy is, as with Lotze, postulated among the monads.

(*b*) With this the theory of personal idealism advances from its pluralistic base to its final theistic position, in which the world-ground is also teleologically conceived. Sympathetic *rapport* implies unity in the plurality, and unity implies a unifying principle, and the unifying principle is best stated not in the abstract terms characteristic of absolutist systems but in terms of that conative unity, that striving after the realization of ends, which is given at once in the most simple and the most complex individual experience; and in terms, moreover, of conscious and self-conscious activity, according to the teleological principle of the interpretation of the lower by the higher. Further, if we describe the world-ground as an ultimate self-conscious will, we are not to think of it, as in absolute idealism, as a purely immanent principle. Though God gives unity or system to the plurality of monads, He is not Himself the unity in which they subsist. There is a principle of distinction in a self-conscious mind, in virtue of which it belongs to itself and does not merely enter into other selves. So it is that G. Galloway,[1] *e.g.*, presses to a theistic conclusion.

(*c*) The map of reality consists, according to this theistic argument, of simple monads interacting within a common medium or environment, which is grounded in a transcendent self-conscious will. It is claimed that the theory offers a better key to the understanding of unity and individuality than absolute idealism or natural realism can supply. It is a brave attempt at any rate (and this is our particular point) to justify the teleological view of the universe on metaphysical grounds. Whether it yields too much to the voluntaristic psychology we do not pretend to judge; but we appreciate its consistency with the theism of the moral and religious consciousness, in which the teleological character of the world is felt.

'At the heart of religion and morality,' says Siebeck, 'is the feeling that the existence and development of the world is not an indifferent matter, but is designed to realise a highest Good.'[2]

When therefore ethical theism, with its religious conception of God as the absolutely good, is set beside the metaphysical theism of the pluralistic approach to reality, it seems possible to state a conclusion in terms such as these. (1) In the language of philosophy: though individual existences and personal spirits have a being for themselves and are variously endowed with spontaneity, the development of experience remains in the control of the world-ground. (2) In the language of theology: though the actions of the creature are not absolutely foreordained or predestinated but manifest spontaneity and freedom in various degrees, they fall within the providential government of God. (3) In the language both of philosophy and of theology, and in Galloway's concluding words, if the world have its ground in a self-conscious and ethical will, which comprehends and sustains all the individual centres of experience, faith in a providential order of things is sufficiently justified.[3]

6. Teleology of deism.—(*a*) While it may be said from the humanist side that the development of the universe is towards the goal of spiritual personality, it is difficult to conceive of the world-process *sub specie æternitatis.* The deistic conception of it, however, is an easy target for criticism. Its view of the world has been described as 'heterotelic.' The world is regarded as a sphere of divine purpose, but divine purpose is as it were imposed upon it from without. There is an inherent dualism in this, as J. S. Mill realized.

(*b*) In the traditional form of the 'argument from design,' where the setting is deistic, the divine Artificer fashioned the world to its present form out of an already given matter; or else, as in the ecclesiastical doctrine, the matter was first created out of nothing by divine power, then shaped by divine wisdom and beneficence. But this initial dissociation of matter and form is inconceivable, and has been 'as much a bugbear as a chimæra.'[1] The idea of external adaptation should be replaced by that of internal or immanent purpose. God is not beyond or even alongside His world, says a truer theism; He is within it as immanent life, will, intelligence.

(*c*) In the sphere of history, as in the sphere of nature, the deistic teleology is also superficial and inadequate. Its language, if not inappropriate in the world of concrete relationships in which religion lives and moves, can hardly be literally applied in philosophy. It looks upon God as a moral governor who imposes His laws upon man after the fashion of an earthly potentate. But, says a truer theism again, the divine laws are not externally imposed, but are immanent in man's heart and conscience; and the divine providence is not exercised *ab extra*, but is an immanent righteousness working in and through free human agency.

(*d*) May we not say that the end or purpose of God in nature and history is His self-manifestation or self-communication to personal self-conscious individuals capable of a spiritual response to Him whereby His own life receives enrichment? But, even in so saying, we speak in the manner of men in terms of time rather than eternity.

7. The purgation of purpose.—(*a*) With the deepening of its philosophical interpretation, the teleology of theism loses undoubtedly much of its traditional and popular meaning, but a substantial meaning may remain. The finite element of contrivance, with external adaptation of means to end, may rightly fall away from the idea of purpose as applied to the nature of the infinite experience. No part of the world is then in danger of being handed over, as virtually in deistic theology, to mechanical necessity; and the inorganic becomes essentially related or adapted to the organic, and both inorganic and organic to the whole cosmic process. It is the strength of idealistic interpretation that it can thus dispense in the cosmic reference with the 'theistic Demiurge'[2] and associate itself with what has been called an 'autotelic' view of the world-process. When purpose is no longer thought of as superinduced in creation and providence upon particular events of the world, but is intimately applied to the world in its totality, we learn to appreciate Kant's ideal of nature as a complete teleological system, in which for the intuitive or perceptive understanding the distinction of means and end is transcended, and the whole appears as the unity of its members and the members as the differentiation of the whole.[3]

(*b*) If the notions of contrivance and external adaptation are to be dismissed as unduly anthropomorphic, is the notion of a preconceived plan to be retained, or is the so-called plan but the nature or process of the whole? It would be easier for the personal idealist or theistic pluralist to retain the notion than for the absolutist. It was the

1 *Philosophy of Religion*, Edinburgh, 1914, pp. 402–456.
2 *Ueber Freiheit, Entwicklung, und Vorsehung*, 1911, p. 45 (quoted by Galloway, p. 439)
3 Galloway, pp. 447–449.

1 Ward, *Realm of Ends*, p. 70.
2 Bosanquet, *Principle of Individuality and Value*, p. 133.
3 Cf. Pringle-Pattison, *Idea of God*, p. 328.

conviction that God cannot be regarded, except by the logical imagination, as devising schemes and selecting methods that led Spinoza, from his standpoint of abstract monism or singularism, to repudiate the principle of human analogy altogether and to deny of God the faculties of intellect and will. These, as being exercised in the outcarrying of finite plans and purposes, could not be predicated of the eternal Being. There is danger as well as truth in such a position, but what we are here concerned to say is that Spinoza's views are not incompatible with the essential idea of teleology. He denounces externalism and anthropocentrism, but none the less he looks upon the world as a significant whole, necessitated indeed, but necessitated by the divine nature itself, which is the nature of the whole.

'It is the idea,' says Pringle-Pattison, 'of the divine necessity as a self-affirmed life, and not as a blind force acting within the universe like a fate which it undergoes, that constitutes the differentia between a theistic and a non-theistic doctrine.' [1]

(*c*) In support of Spinoza's objection to the notion of a pre-existent cosmic plan, it is pointed out that the conception of purpose therein involved is even inapplicable to human action of the highest kind, such as moral conduct or artistic production. We may therefore grant it to A. D. Lindsay,[2] a sympathetic interpreter of Bergson, that, if the world is a purposive system, it possesses a unity or individuality in time as well as in space. Apparently such a consideration lies behind Bergson's rejection of radical finalism—such as Leibniz's—as being only an inverted mechanism, as implying that things and beings realize a programme previously arranged ('*Tout est donné*'). To postulate the totality of the real as thus complete in the beginning is to make time (*q.v.*) of no account. If time *does* nothing, it *is* nothing. Yet, according to Bergson, time—not abstract spatialized time but concrete time or real duration (*la durée*) —is the very substance of our world, and there is no stuff more substantial or more resistant.

(*d*) The force of what Bergson here essentially contends for is acknowledged by idealistic thinkers. If the course of the world is preformed and predetermined—'the dull rattling off of a chain that was forged innumerable ages ago'[3] — there is indeed not much to choose between naturalism and idealism. In this connexion it is significant that naturalism and idealism, like fatalism and predestinarianism, often meet and, like righteousness and peace, kiss each other. It is also significant that the crusade of spiritual pluralism, in its various forms, against the absolutist systems is for the redemption of the spiritual values sold by them—'treacherously sold,' says F. C. S. Schiller[4] —into the bondage of naturalism. If then we abandon radical finalism with its illusion of preformation and predeterminism, shall we say that 'the history of the universe is the history of a great adventure'? So C. F. D'Arcy[5] puts it, in sympathy with the Bergsonian view.

(*e*) Where idealism differs from Bergsonism, if not from Bergson himself, is in holding that the adventure is not in the experience of the absolute but in the experience or from the standpoint of the finite subject. Moreover, for a theistic idealism there are bounds to the scope of the adventure. The theistic universe is fundamentally ethical. It is the very heart and core of theistic faith that an eternal purpose of good is working itself out in the world. In terms of modern Christian theology, the world is the scene of the progressive realization of the Kingdom of God.

(*f*) It is but to state the complementary side of this faith to affirm that the world must possess value and real existence for the divine experience, and that into the divine experience the time-process must enter somehow. The purpose which God possesses in Himself is independent of time, which is not as in Bergsonism an ultimate reality, yet it is somehow connected with the time-process in which it is being realized. How time is retained and yet transcended in God we do not know, nor can we. Yet we are not without a clue. In mystical contemplation and in artistic enjoyment the sense of time, as we are told, may almost vanish from the consciousness; and it is claimed that the life of the philosopher or artist bears in this respect some kind of analogy to the divine life. It is at least suggestive of the idea for which Pringle-Pattison contends, that purposive activity is the concrete reality and time only the abstract form.[1] If this be so, then Bosanquet's criticism of teleology, in the sense of 'aiming at the unfulfilled,' is so far met. Such a teleology, he says, gives undue importance to time and to the last term of a time-sequence.[2] But, says Pringle-Pattison:

'The last term is only important because in it is most fully revealed the nature of the principle which is present throughout. It is precisely this linkage of the first term with the last and, to that extent, the transcendence of the mere time-sequence in the conception of an eternal reality, that seems to me to be expressed by the profound Aristotelian idea of τέλος or End.' [3]

(*g*) The question may be raised here whether the purpose that may be attributed to the infinite ground of the universe is to be regarded as conscious or unconscious. On this question Bergson would appear to range himself in the succession of Schopenhauer (*q.v.*) and von Hartmann,[4] with this difference that for them the gates of the future are closed. Undoubtedly the *via media* of unconscious purpose avoids the difficulty of explaining how one self-consciousness may exist within another, the finite within the infinite, but it possesses inherent difficulties of its own. It has to account for inorganic arrangement and process, and for the transition from the unconscious to the conscious and self-conscious, nor can it explain the reason why the vital impetus should tend in one direction rather than another.

'If,' as W. R. Sorley says, summing up an illuminating discussion, 'purpose be admitted as necessary for the interpretation of organisms, and if organisms are held to have arisen out of inorganic material, then there is good reason to postulate that the process which led to organic and purposive life was itself animated by purpose,' not individual nor merely racial purpose, but universal purpose acting, moreover, not 'after the fashion of impulse' but 'in the manner of mind or consciousness.' [5]

This theistic postulate of universal conscious purpose is to be justified in face of the facts of dysteleology,[6] yet it appears a more reasonable postulate than that of unconscious purpose, and more hospitable too of human experience in the realms of fact and value.

8. Teleology and value.—The category of end or purpose, when purged of its finite incidents of preconceived plan and external adaptation of means to end, tends to pass into the category of worth or value (*q.v.*). In the teleological view of the universe the end, which is the nature of the whole, is an ethical end worthy of being purposed, *i.e.* worthy, so to speak, of enlisting the desire

1 *Idea of God*, p. 340.
2 *Proceedings of the Aristotelian Society*, 33rd session, 1911–12, p. 241.
3 W. James, *Principles of Psychology*, 2 vols., London, 1890, i. 453, quoted by Pringle-Pattison, p. 367.
4 *Humanism*², London, 1912, p. xxv.
5 *God and Freedom in Human Experience* (*Donnellan Lectures*), London, 1915, p. 217.

1 Pringle-Pattison, p. 358.
2 *Principle of Individuality and Value*, p. 135 ff.
3 P. 332.
4 See art. PESSIMISM AND OPTIMISM.
5 *Moral Values and the Idea of God*, p. 426 f.
6 Cf. Haeckel, *The Evolution of Man*⁵, 2 vols., Eng. tr., London, 1905, i. 86–88.

and effort of the Absolute. And may we not attribute desire and effort—conative activity—to God? May we not say that in the Infinite Experience conation and its correlative satisfaction are to be found, that, as Bosanquet[1] strikingly puts it, 'the contradiction of a conation co-existing with fruition must somehow be realized'? It seems to us that we must say this if the world is to be regarded as truly a 'vale of soul-making,' in which Providence rules and not fate, the concurrence of the living God and not the eternal decree, and in which spiritual values are created and realized. It is our belief that God is thus present and active in the process of the world, and that the true image of Him is not the pre-existent Creator of the deistic theology, nor the static timeless Absolute of acosmic pantheism, but the eternal Redeemer of the religious consciousness.

LITERATURE.—The literature of which the writer has made most use is mentioned for the most part in the footnotes. For the historical discussion of the subject histories of philosophy may be consulted. For the general history of philosophy, J. E. Erdmann (Eng. tr., 3 vols., London, 1890–91), F. Ueberweg[8 and 9] (4 vols., Berlin, 1898–1903), W. Windelband (Eng. tr., New York and London, 1893), A. K. Rogers[2] (London, 1907), A. B. D. Alexander[2] (Glasgow, 1908), C. C. J. Webb (London, 1915). L. J. Henderson, *Order of Nature*, Cambridge, U.S.A., and London, 1917, contains a useful sketch of the subject from the scientific standpoint. For ancient philosophy, E. Zeller (5 vols., Leipzig, 1876–1909), T. Gomperz (Eng. tr., 4 vols., London, 1901–12), W. Windelband (Eng. tr., London, 1900), R. Adamson (Edinburgh, 1908); also the works of E. Caird, J. Adam, and J. Burnet already mentioned. For modern philosophy, H. Höffding (Eng. tr., 2 vols., London, 1900), *Modern Philosophers* (Eng. tr., do. 1915), R. Adamson (2 vols., Edinburgh, 1903, esp. vol. i.), J. T. Merz—for nineteenth century—(esp. vols. 3, 4, Edinburgh, 1912–14), B. Pünjer, *Hist. of the Christian Philosophy of Religion* (vol. i., Eng. tr., Edinburgh, 1887); A. Caldecott, *The Philosophy of Religion*—for England and America—(London, 1901). For the systematic discussion works on metaphysics, philosophy of religion, and philosophy of science may be consulted: in addition to the works already mentioned, J. Johnstone, *The Philosophy of Biology*, Cambridge, 1914; *The Philosophical Review*, vol. xxvii. no. 6 [1918] (a series of articles on 'Mechanism and Vitalism'); *Mind*, new ser., no. 113 [1920] ('The Categories of Biological Science,' by F. H. A. Marshall); R. Otto, *Naturalism and Religion*, Eng. tr., London, 1907; J. Watson, *The Interpretation of Religious Experience* (*Gifford Lectures*), 2 vols., Glasgow, 1912 (historical and constructive); J. Lindsay, *A Philosophical System of Theistic Idealism*, Edinburgh, 1917; O. Pfleiderer, *Philosophy and Development of Religion* (*Gifford Lectures*), 2 vols., do. 1894; P. Janet, *Final Causes*, Eng. tr.[2], do. 1883; A. Trendelenburg, *Logische Untersuchungen*[2], Leipzig, 1862, II. 1 ff.; C. Sigwart, *Kleine Schriften*[2], 2 vols., Freiburg, 1889, 'Der Kampf gegen den Zweck,' ii. 24–67 (a useful essay); W. Wundt, *Logik*[3], 3 vols., Stuttgart, 1906–08; P. N. Cossmann, *Elemente der empirischen Teleologie*, do. 1899; L. T. Hobhouse, *Development and Purpose*, London, 1913; V. F. Storr, *Development and Divine Purpose*, do. 1906. The 'argument from design' is sympathetically discussed from a theistic standpoint in the last-named work, also by J. Martineau, *A Study of Religion*, 2 vols., Oxford, 1900; A. C. Fraser, *Philosophy of Theism*[2] (*Gifford Lectures*), Edinburgh, 1899; C. C. J. Webb, *Problems in the Relations of God and Man*, London, 1911; A. J. Balfour, *Theism and Humanism* (*Gifford Lectures*), do. 1915. See also J. M. Baldwin, *DPhP*, iii. B. 2. 1, for a full bibliography. See also the artt. END, EPISTEMOLOGY, THEISM, THEODICY, VALUE.

WILLIAM FULTON.

TELEPATHY. — Telepathy, 'feeling from afar,' is a term coined by F. W. H. Myers, on the foundation of the Society for Psychical Research in 1882, to express the apparently supernormal transmission of information from mind to mind in 'thought-transference' experiments and the like, just as 'telæsthesia' was suggested to cover the alleged facts of clairvoyance and clairaudience. It was defined as 'communication between one mind and another otherwise than through the known channels of the senses.' As thus defined, the notion was in the first place not free from vagueness. For, as a certain amount of hyperæsthesia of the known senses was admitted to occur under exceptional conditions, and this could be so extended as to amount to miracle, while it yet in a way explained away miracle, it was not clear how hyperæsthesia was related to 'telepathy.' Secondly, the definition was essentially negative, a declaration of ignorance, which suggested no agency or adequate cause for the phenomena it described. Now this was neither satisfactory nor a very strong or stable position logically. Even if the difficulty about the limits of hyperæsthesia is not raised, and if it is admitted that the possibilities of communication through the senses may be taken as fairly completely explored, we are impelled to develop such a definition in one of two directions. We may imagine some unknown sort of vibration, radiation, or 'brain-wave,' as a physical explanation of the phenomena alleged, undeterred by the facts that no positive support has yet been found for any such agency, and that, unlike physical forces, it would appear to be indifferent to distance; or else we may conceive telepathy as essentially psychic in its nature, and shall then tend to exalt it into a fundamental 'law' of spiritual being, as Myers himself subsequently inclined to do. But, so conceived, it is manifestly a challenge to further exploration of the spiritual world of which it claims to be a law; and yet it proves rather a double-edged weapon for believers in a spiritual world. It enables them indeed to hold that every mind, incarnate or discarnate, may in principle communicate directly with any other by telepathy; but it seems to formulate this possibility so broadly as to render it almost impossible for a discarnate mind to authenticate itself by communicating information. For any verifiable information must normally be, or have been, known to incarnate minds; and, if any living mind can 'tap' any other, and if knowledge can 'leak' subconsciously from any mind to any other, and still more if we entertain the somewhat fanciful but not unsupported hypothesis that all knowledge may be pooled in a vast 'cosmic reservoir' before it bubbles up in individual minds, the telepathic hypothesis can evidently be used to discredit nearly all the *prima facie* evidence in favour of 'spirit-communication.' Accordingly the opponents of this belief have made great play with it, even while holding also that the evidence for telepathy is itself insufficient to establish it as a *vera causa*.[1] This objection the believers endeavour to meet in various ways. They point out rightly that, if telepathy is a fundamental psychic law, it cannot be restricted in its operations to living minds. They argue, however, that unrestricted telepathy between incarnate minds, and such alone, is antecedently improbable, and quite unsubstantiated. Lastly, they try to develop methods of experimentation which avoid this objection, because the information communicated, though verifiable *ex post facto*, can be shown never to have been, as a whole, in the possession of any living mind. Hence the importance of 'cross-correspondences' between the information received through several channels and dovetailing into a coherent message; by this method some striking successes have been recorded, though different minds will long continue to vary widely in the estimation of their weight. Again, certain sorts of prediction may baffle explanation by telepathy. At present, however, no agreement, either about the nature of telepathy or about the degree to which it may be taken as a fact in nature, can be said to exist. More evidence is still required, and, until it is obtained, opinions will be determined not so much by the evidence itself as by the bias with which it is regarded.

The existing evidence is usually classified under the heads (*a*) *experimental* and (*b*) *spontaneous*. The former includes the evidence of hypnotization at a distance, recorded especially by Gibert and

[1] *Proceedings of the Aristotelian Society*, 33rd session, 1911–12, p. 251.

[1] Cf. art. PSYCHICAL RESEARCH.

Pierre Janet, and experiments at close quarters, though without contact between the 'percipient' and the 'agent,' in guessing such things as cards and numbers, in reproducing diagrams and figures, etc. The transition to the 'spontaneous' evidence is mediated by a few rare cases in which the experimental projection of a phantasm is attested, on the strength of which it becomes possible to conceive the ordinary 'ghost' as an apparition telepathically projected by the dying or the dead. In all these cases the transfer of information has an emotional interest which is generally lacking in experiments of the first class, and this may conceivably account for their apparent capacity to override the obstacle of distance, which conspicuously differentiates them from the former. Still it should be remembered that to ascribe these phenomena to telepathy is a hypothesis which is possible only if telepathy is established independently by experimental evidence. Accordingly it is on this that the real stress falls. Now, as regards this evidence, it may be said in general that its character is very similar to that for other supernormal phenomena. Much of it is bad, some respectable, none beyond cavil. Its quality is not better than that of the best evidence for some of the most extreme phenomena, such as 'materializations.' It is liable, moreover, to the same or similar sources of error, fraud (in the shape of codes, collusion, and mendacity), malobservation, lapses of attention, errors of memory, coincidence. The ultimate reason for these defects is that there plainly does not exist as yet any real experimental control of the phenomena and their conditions, so that the evidence cannot be accumulated at will, crucial experiments cannot be made, and the pragmatic test cannot be used to *apply* the doctrine of the direct intercommunication of minds and to distinguish the real from the alleged phenomena. As, however, this sort of situation occurs commonly enough in the beginnings of a science and sometimes lasts for centuries, it is no disproof of the reality of what is now provisionally called 'telepathy'; it may well be dispersed by pertinacious and concerted investigation, and in any case the matter should not be left in its present ambiguity.

LITERATURE.—This is largely the same as given in artt. PSYCHICAL RESEARCH and SPIRITISM. There may be mentioned in addition E. Boirac, *La Psychologie inconnue*², Paris, 1912, and *L'Avenir des sciences psychiques*, do. 1917, Eng. tr., *Our Hidden Forces* and *The Psychology of the Future*, New York and London, 1918; the art. by F. C. Hansen and A. Lehmann in *Philosophische Studien*, xi. [1895] pt. 4, 'Ueber unwillkürliches Flüstern'; E. Parish, *Hallucinations and Illusions*, London and New York, 1897; J. E. Coover, *Experiments in Psychical Research at Leland Stanford Junior University*, Stanford University, Cal., U.S.A., 1917; L. T. Troland, *A Technique for the Experimental Study of Telepathy and other Alleged Clairvoyant Processes*, 1917. All but the first of these attack the historical evidence, with some success, while the last two confess also (almost) complete failure in repeating the card- and number-guessing experiments of the Society for Psychical Research.

F. C. S. SCHILLER.

TELUGU-SPEAKING PEOPLES. — See DRAVIDIANS.

TEMPERAMENT. — The doctrine of the temperaments is at once one of the earliest and one of the most persistent and popular efforts to classify the diversities of mental character in relation to bodily characteristics. It has always been recognized that there are broad differences of type in mind, and that some of these differences are inborn, and, practically at least, unmodified throughout life. It was natural that these should be looked for mainly in the feelings and emotions, which appear both more dependent upon the bodily constitution and less under individual control than either cognition or will. The temperament is accordingly a permanent disposition to certain forms or degrees of feeling, so far as such disposition is dependent on the inherited organic constitution. The number of temperaments has been variously given as two, three, four, six, eight, and even much larger numbers, but on the whole the classic 'four' has held the field down to our own day, as if it corresponded in some mysterious way to some ultimate differences in mind or body, or both.

This number was derived originally from the four elements of Empedocles, fire, earth, water, and air, and the four qualities, warm and cold, dry and moist; on these in turn was formed Hippocrates' theory of the four cardinal humours of the body—blood, corresponding to air, warm and moist; phlegm to water, cold and moist; yellow bile to fire, warm and dry; and black bile to earth, cold and dry. From these came through Galen the names of the main temperaments, *sanguine*, *phlegmatic*, *choleric*, and *melancholic*. Occasionally physiologists have suggested other terms for the phlegmatic and the melancholic, as 'lymphatic' and 'nervous,' lymph and nerve being at least known constituents of the body;[1] but the names as well as the number of the old four have kept their ground. For the Greeks the temperament meant a mixture or union of the four elements, qualities, or humours; where this contained a certain ideal proportion of each, there was bodily and mental health; where an excessive degree of one or more, or an excessive defect, there was distemper or disease. There should therefore have been only one ideal temperament, and a large variety of *in*temperaments,[2] but actually the four temperaments were regarded as falling within the limits of health and as implying only a slight predominance of one or other of the four qualities. With the progress of physiology, the physical basis of the temperaments underwent a series of changes in the conception of the theorists; first the mixture was sought in the blood itself, as conveying nutriment to all the tissues of the body—*e.g.*, the proportion of fibrin to fluid in the blood, the width of the vessels, the porousness of their walls and of those of the tissues; then stress was laid on the tissues of the body themselves, and especially the nervous tissue, its strength and its excitability (Haller); and finally on the more delicate qualities of the nerves as shown in intensity, and in rate, persistence, etc., of impression and of reaction. Here we are probably nearest to the truth, since it is with the nervous system that mental qualities and degrees are most directly correlated, but it must be admitted that we have no really scientific knowledge as yet of the precise relation of one to the other.

The problem may be approached from another side by considering the actual characterization or description of the four temperaments, the psychical qualities which each reveals; these are inferred of course from the behaviour, more especially the emotional expressions and the reactions of the will upon impressions; and here also there has been a constant tendency to simplify by seeking the main features of the temperaments in two pairs of mutually opposed characters, such as receptivity and spontaneity; change and persistence; feeling and action; pleasure and pain, etc. The most satisfactory of these psychological accounts is that of Wundt, based on the strength or weakness, and on the quick or slow rate of change in feeling and in mental life generally.[3] Strong and quick is the choleric temperament; strong and slow, the melancholic; weak and quick, the sanguine; weak and slow, the phlegmatic.

1 Henle, *Anthropolog. Vorträge*, i. 108.
2 Volkmann, *Lehrbuch der Psychologie*⁴, i. 207 f.
3 Wundt, *Grundzüge der physiologischen Psychologie*⁵, iii. 637.

As E. B. Titchener has put it, 'the man who thinks quickly and feels strongly, is choleric, the man who thinks quickly and feels weakly, sanguine. The phlegmatic thinks slowly and feels weakly, the melancholic thinks slowly and feels deeply.'[1]

The classification does not adequately explain, however, the fact that the feelings of the sanguine are predominantly cheerful or pleasant, those of the melancholic predominantly painful or gloomy; and Höffding has suggested another pair of temperaments, or another division—'the bright and the dark temperament'—in order to explain 'the tendency to one or other of the two great opposites of the life of feeling, which gives colour and direction to the whole disposition.'

'This opposition is more fundamental than that upon which the other four temperaments are based, for it has its root in the fundamental conditions for the preservation of the individual organism.'[2]

More recently an interesting attempt to analyse the dominant characteristics by experimental methods has been given by Narziss Ach;[3] he finds that it is mainly on the strength or weakness of the 'determination,' along with the persistence or rapid falling away of the determining force, that the feelings, the associations, and generally the whole mental life depend; accordingly he makes these characters the basis of his five temperaments —for he adds a fifth, the *reflective* (*besonnene*) temperament.

Whatever the ultimate characters may be, mental or physical, they must be such as exercise a decisive influence on the whole life, inner and outer, of the individual. The facts that the pure temperament is rare; that it makes, as Volkmann says, 'an almost uncanny impression,' when it does appear; that most of us are of 'mixed' temperament (however illogical such mixture may be); that the old terms have lost all meaning, and that the scientific analysis is still to seek—these facts, which have led many psychologists to drop the doctrine of the temperaments altogether, do not dispose of the existence of broad and deep differences of mental type, mainly in the spheres of feeling and action, for which *some* names, and a scientific analysis, must be found.

The organism, through the afferent nerves, sends from its every part a stream of influence to the brain; to the functions of every tissue there correspond impressions and feelings which may or may not reach or effect separate consciousness, but which produce a mass-effect in the cœnæsthesia, or organic sensibility, and in the general feeling-tone which corresponds to it. This is the basis of the self-feeling: it is the inner or subjective aspect of the temperament. There is, as Henle says, a *tonus*, or degree of tension, in every nerve, even when the muscles which it contracts or the sense-organs from which it is impressed are 'at rest'; it differs in degree in different individuals; for each individual it varies from time to time, under varying conditions of health, fatigue, etc., but there is a relatively constant value for each below which it does not fall, so long as the nerves have life. Where the tension is high, response of feeling and action will be energetic and rapid; where it is weak, or low, response will be feeble and slow. The *tonus* is the physiological fact corresponding to the mass-feeling—vague and indefinite as it necessarily is —out of which the different moods of the individual, and his emotions, his passions, down to the simplest feelings of sensory pleasure and 'unpleasure,' emerge like waves on the sea. Like all feelings, the temperamental feeling is both an index of bodily condition and a cause of bodily expression and action; like all feelings, it influences alike the intensity, the quality, and the course of thought. Hence the detailed descriptions of character which we find in the older and even in some of the later writers on temperament are not without interest.

[1] *An Outline of Psychology*, p. 233.
[2] *Outlines of Psychology*, Eng. tr., p. 350.
[3] *Ueber den Willensakt und das Temperament*, Leipzig, 1910, p. 312 ff.

Johannes Müller,[1] who regards the *phlegmatic* as the highest type—the ideal temperament—finds that in such a man, with a well-developed intelligence, his phlegm enables him to accomplish results impossible to others, even with their livelier feelings and desires; easily retaining control of himself, he cannot be induced to acts 'of which he would repent on the morrow'; he can calculate in all security the chances of the success of what he undertakes; in danger, at the decisive moment, he is master of himself, wherever it is not a question of sudden decision and energy; 'he feels his ills little, and bears them patiently, nor is he much moved by those of others'; speed and quickness of choice often give others an advantage over him; but, 'when he has time before him, he arrives quietly at the goal, while others, heaping mistakes upon mistakes, are lost in endless side-issues.' On the other hand, Müller finds that the species of phlegm characterized by laziness, apathy, insensibility, irresolution, ennui, slowness of intellect, and the like, is not the true type, but a pathological form. The *choleric* has a remarkable power of action, both in energy and in persistence, under the influence of passion; his passions inflame at the least obstacle; his pride, his jealousy, his desire of vengeance, his thirst for domination, know no bounds, as long as his passion moves him. He reflects little, acts without hesitation, on the spur of the moment, because he is convinced that he is right, and above all because such is his will. He rarely turns aside from error, but follows the course of his passion to his own ruin and that of others. With the *sanguine*, pleasure is the dominant tendency, along with great excitability, and a short duration of any mood. Sympathetic and friendly to others, but without persistence or constancy; quick to anger, but equally quick to regret; prodigal of promises, but equally ready to forget them; credulous and confident, he loves to make plans, which he soon lays aside; indulgent to the faults of others, he claims the same indulgence for his own; easy to appease, frank, open, amiable, sociable, incapable of interested calculation. With the *melancholic*, sadness is the prevailing tendency; his excitability is equal to that of the sanguine, but disagreeable sensations are both more frequent and more durable than those of pleasure. The sufferings of others call out his sympathy to a high degree; for himself he is fearful, undecided, distrustful; a trifle wounds and offends him; the slightest obstacle discourages him, and renders him incapable of reasoning to overcome it; his thoughts are full of melancholy, and his sufferings appear to him beyond all consolation.

In their *Psychology in the Schoolroom*[2] T. F. G. Dexter and A. H. Garlick venture to describe, on behalf of teachers—for whom it is necessary to know their pupils' temperaments—not only the mental but also the external physical appearance of the types. The *sanguine*, lively, excitable, quickly but not deeply roused, with feeling generally uppermost in his character, has the circulatory and respiratory systems well developed, has red hair, blue eyes, skin fair, and face animated. The *choleric*, self-reliant and confident, with will uppermost, has the muscular system well developed, hair and eyes dark, complexion sometimes sallow, face impassive. The *phlegmatic* or lymphatic, mind heavy and torpid, sometimes nearly stupid, patient, self-reliant, and slow, has the abdomen large, face round and expressionless, lips thick, body generally disinclined to exertion. Finally the sentimental (i.e. *melancholic*), with great love of poetry, music, and nature, and marked indifference to the practical affairs of life, has the head large, eyes bright and expressive, figure slender and delicate, movements quick.

It may be doubted whether teachers would be well advised to guide their treatment by such physical characters as these, when noted in their pupils. Nor has the attempt been very successful to look in the different temperaments for predisposition to certain diseases of the body. It is, however, antecedently probable, and appears to be confirmed by experience, that different temperaments are liable to different forms of insanity; at least it is true that in insanity the differences of temperament are as clearly marked as in health.

As in drunkenness one man is 'talkative and boastful,' another 'maudlin,' another 'tetchy and violent,' another 'melancholy and silent'; so 'the lunatic of sanguine temperament . . . is puffed up and vain, his dreams are of marble halls and flattering voices; the choleric patient suspects everywhere the plots of his enemies, and hears voices insulting him or urging him to deeds of violence; and whilst his hallucinations are more often auditory than visual, the contrary is the case with the

[1] *Handbuch der Physiologie des Menschen*, French tr.[2], ii. 557.
[2] London, 1905, p. 343.

melancholic, and especially, as the name implies, with religious "visionaries."'[1]

It is especially in the melancholic, nervous, or, as it is called in extreme cases, the 'neurotic' temperament that the tendency to insanity is marked. T. S. Clouston gives a striking description of the modern phase of this temperament.

'The man of this temperament is in body small, shapely, tending towards a dark complexion, thin skin, with delicate features, a well-shaped head, a quick, bright, restless eye; in figure small and wiry, nervous, highly strung and sensitive, feeling pain keenly and tolerating it badly, subject to dyspepsia and insomnia. His muscles are incessantly active. He is quick in mind and body, imaginative, keen, sensitive, ever alert, fine in the grain, subtle, fond of intellectual work, not always resolute in decision because he sees there are two sides to every question, often artistic in feeling, ambitious, and with an ill-concealed contempt for fools. When run down, this man is "ill to do with." When he grows old he gets thin, dyspeptic, irritable, and often neuralgic. The diseases he is specially subject to are nervous and mental.'[2]

In religious psychology also the temperaments are of considerable importance, owing to the great suggestibility of some (the sanguine and melancholic) as compared with others, the greater excitability of the sanguine and choleric, the brooding tendency of the melancholic or nervous, the insusceptibility of the phlegmatic, and the excessive self-centring of the sanguine and choleric.[3]

The relative permanence of the temperament in the individual is not inconsistent with some gradual change over long periods of time, although there is no doubt that the temperament is that part of our mental and physical endowment which requires greatest effort or most violent and prolonged change of circumstances to modify. It has been thought that broadly the different stages of individual development and of racial evolution are marked by differences of temperament. Childhood is sanguine, youth sentimental or nervous, mature age choleric, and old age phlegmatic. The temperaments of primitive races are less obvious, but they seem to move from the phlegmatic and choleric (Negroes, Malayans) to the melancholic and sanguine (Mongolian, Caucasian); in Europe we have the sanguine Frenchman, the choleric Spaniard or Italian, the phlegmatic Teuton, and the nervous Briton. Women on the whole are sanguine or nervous, men choleric or phlegmatic.[4] These are of course mere rough general impressions. It has also been remarked that there has been a change of fashion in temperaments, or in what has been regarded as the ideal temperament: at one time the sanguine, it became the dark and melancholic (in the days of Byron), later the phlegmatic or indifferent, to-day perhaps the choleric—the man of energy.[5] Character in the highest sense of the word is something very different from temperament; the latter has to do with the form and manner, the quantity and degree of mental life, character with its quality, the intellectual, moral, and æsthetic values which that life recognizes and pursues; temperament gives the foundation on which character must build—it sets the problems which the training and the making of character have to solve; whatever we may think therefore of the popular classification of the four temperaments, the individual differences themselves on which it is based—differences of sensitiveness to impressions and to feelings, of strength and quickness of reaction, of energy and endurance—are of the utmost importance. It is to such differences and their measurement that the modern individual psychology is directing its attention; and from it we may hope in time to obtain a scientific account of temperament.

LITERATURE.—I. Kant, *Anthropologie in pragmatischer Hinsicht*[3], ed. J. H. von Kirchmann, Leipzig, 1880, p. 206; L. George, *Lehrbuch der Psychologie*, Berlin, 1854; J. Müller, *Handbuch der Physiologie des Menschen*, Coblenz, 1838–40, French tr.[2] A. J. L. Jourdan, Paris, 1851, ii.; H. Royer-Collard, 'Des Tempéraments considérés dans leurs rapports avec la santé,' *Mém. Acad. Roy. de Médecine*, do. 1843; W. Volkmann (von Volkmar), *Lehrbuch der Psychologie*[4], ed. C. S. Cornelius, 2 vols., Cöthen, 1894–95; R. H. Lotze, *Medicinische Psychologie*, new ed., Göttingen, 1896, *Mikrokosmus*, Eng. tr. E. Hamilton and E. E. C. Jones, 2 vols., Edinburgh, 1885–86; G. Rümelin, 'Ueber die Temperamente,' *Deutsche Rundschau*, lxiv. [1890] 397–412; J. Henle, *Anthropologische Vorträge*, Brunswick, 1876–80, i. 101, 'Von den Temperamenten'; Theobald Ziegler, *Das Gefühl*[2], Stuttgart, 1893; G. T. Ladd, *Outlines of Physiological Psychology*[5], London, 1896; E. B. Titchener, *An Outline of Psychology*, New York, 1897; W. Wundt, *Grundzüge der physiologischen Psychologie*[5], Leipzig, 1902–03, iii. 637; H. Höffding, *Outlines of Psychology*, tr. Mary E. Lowndes, London, 1893, p. 348 ff.; W. McDougall, *An Introd. to Social Psychology*[7], do. 1913 p. 116 ff.

J. LEWIS MCINTYRE.

TEMPERANCE.—There is much difference of opinion among writers on moral theology as to the true relationship between the three virtues of sobriety, moderation, and temperance. Each has had its claims to be the archetypal virtue, which includes the others, advocated by representative writers; but there seem to be very strong reasons why temperance should be regarded as the inclusive virtue, the chief being that it has held a place from early times among the 'cardinal' or principal virtues. From the first, Plato seems to accept this grouping of virtues as based upon a current classification, and it passes through Aristotle and Stoics into Christian thought. The definition of temperance given by Cicero may be accepted as typical:

'Temperantia est rationis in libidinem, atque in alios non rectos impetus animi, firma et moderata dominatio. Ejus partes sunt, continentia, clementia, modestia.'[1]

Plato shows a tendency to identify 'temperance' with 'continence'; in *Rep.* iv. 430 E he defines *σωφροσύνη* as follows:

κόσμος πού τις ἡ σωφροσύνη ἐστὶ καὶ ἡδονῶν τινῶν καὶ ἐπιθυμιῶν ἐγκράτεια.

Aristotle, however, defines the word as *μεσότης περὶ ἡδόνας* and distinguishes it from *ἐγκράτεια*. The temperate man (*σώφρων*), he says, does not feel the pressure of inordinate desires; the continent (*ἐγκρατής*) feels it, but holds desire in restraint.[2] So Cicero: 'Continentia est, per quam cupiditas consilii gubernatione regitur.'[3] In the NT the word *σωφροσύνη* occurs only in 1 Ti 2^{15} (*σώφρων* in 1 Ti 3^{2}, Tit 1^{8} $2^{2.5}$). *ἐγκράτεια* occurs in Ac 24^{25}, Gal 5^{23}, 2 P 1^{6}; *ἐγκρατεύομαι* in 1 Co 7^{9} 9^{25}; *ἐγκρατής* in Tit 1^{8}.

The general idea of temperance or moderation as an element in all virtue is peculiarly Greek, and it re-appears in Christianity.

'Temperance,' says Aquinas, 'is a cardinal virtue because that *moderation* which is common to all the virtues is peculiarly praiseworthy in the case of temperance.'[4]

This has been pointed out elsewhere.[5] It is perhaps most in accordance with modern ways of thinking to take as a basis the fact of personality and to consider the Christian as standing in a threefold relationship—to God, to his neighbour, and to himself. According to Augustine, there is a virtue corresponding to each of these relationships, as is implied in Tit 2^{12}, *ἵνα . . . σωφρόνως καὶ δικαίως καὶ εὐσεβῶς ζήσωμεν*.[6] Temperance is the form which

1 E. Parish, *Hallucinations and Illusions*, London, 1897, p. 188, quoting Paul Radestock, *Schlaf und Traum*, Leipzig, 1879, p. 209.
2 *The Hygiene of Mind*, London, 1906, p. 66 f.
3 See G. A. Coe, *The Spiritual Life: Studies in the Science of Religion*, New York, 1903; and E. D. Starbuck, *The Psychology of Religion*[2], London, 1901.
4 See L. George, *Lehrbuch der Psychologie*, p. 136 ff., and Dexter and Garlick, *op. cit.*
5 Volkmann[4], i. 211.

1 *De Invent.* ii. 53. 164. 2 *Eth. Nic.* vii. 2. 3 *Loc. cit.*
4 *Summa*, II. ii. qu. cxli. art. 7, concl.; cf. Aug. *de Beata Vita*, 32: 'Modestia utique dicta est a modo, et a temperie temperantia. Ubi autem modus est atque temperies, nec plus est quidquam nec minus.'
5 See art. MODERATION.
6 Bern. *Serm. 2 in temp. Res.* 11, alludes to this passage: 'Haec enim tria sunt conversationis nostrae maxime necessaria: quoniam primum debemus nobis, secundum proximo, tertium Deo.'

true self-love, duty to self, necessarily takes. It is the spirit of discipline, or rather the spirit of love consecrating itself—body, soul, and spirit—to God.

The function of temperance 'consists in restraining and moderating the desires wherewith we yearn for those things which are apt to turn us away from God's laws.'[1]

Hence the virtue of temperance consists in the moderate and regulated use of those pleasures of sense, especially of touch and taste, which are most apt to draw the soul away from God, and to overthrow the supremacy of the rational faculty in man.[2] Temperance implies the control of appetite at those points where its demand is most importunate and difficult to resist. While 'moderation' (*modestia*) means self-control in matters of less difficulty, 'temperance' is concerned with the instincts and passions which in average human nature are the strongest and the least easy to restrain.

The following points seem to be worthy of special note.

1. The aim of the 'temperate' man is *positive*, not negative. He aims not merely at the subjugation of his lower nature, but at the cultivation of moral and spiritual power. Temperance is the virtue of the man of high ideals who strives to win a 'sovereign self-mastery.' It implies 'no monotonous restraint, but an ordered use of every gift.'[3] The temperate man faces life and uses its gifts and blessings in the temper of an athlete training for a contest (1 Co $9^{25f.}$) or of a soldier engaged in a campaign (2 Ti $2^{3ff.}$). He exercises self-control 'not only in cutting off superfluities but in allowing himself necessaries'[4]—watchful against any form of self-indulgence that may bring him under the power of the world or of his lower nature (1 Co 6^{12}). He is not hindered or overpowered by circumstances, but controls them; he makes them subservient to his spiritual progress; he passes through them upwards and onwards to God.

So Augustine describes temperance as 'that action whereby the soul with the aid of God extricates itself from the love of lower (created) beauty, and wings its way to true stability and firm security in God.'[5]

2. Temperance holds a very prominent place in the earliest Christian teaching (cf. Ac 24^{25}). In the *Acts of Thecla* the substance of St. Paul's teaching is described as λόγος θεοῦ περὶ ἐγκρατείας καὶ ἀναστάσεως. In the early Christian usage of the word ἐγκράτεια was probably identified with sexual purity, and was gradually extended to include any form of world-renunciation and mortification of the body.[6] The words ἐγκράτεια, ἐγκρατεύεσθαι occur frequently in Hermas, but already the tendency is to connote by them the temper of self-control or temperance in general.[7] It includes control of appetite in the sphere of sex, food, and drink; but also the temper of moderation in expenditure, of sobriety in judgment and self-esteem, of self-restraint in matters of speech, etc. There follows a list of virtues in respect of which δεῖ μὴ ἐγκρατεύεσθαι. According to Hermas, ἐγκράτεια is in fact an archetypal and inclusive virtue. It is coupled with ἁπλότης in *Vis.* ii. 3.[8] It has a saving virtue. The 'first commandment' is ἵνα φυλάξῃς τὴν πίστιν καὶ τὸν φόβον καὶ τὴν ἐγκράτειαν.[9] Self-restraint is a fundamental duty because it is directly involved in that conflict between flesh and spirit which is the condition of our mortality and the occasion of moral victory or defeat. So Augustine asks:

'Cui peccato cohibendo non habemus necessariam continentiam, ne committatur? . . . Universaliter ergo continentia nobis opus est ut declinemus a malo.'[1]

3. Temperance or self-control forms part of 'the fruit of the Spirit' (Gal 5^{22}). 'Walk in the spirit and ye shall not fulfil the lust of the flesh.' As a gift or endowment of the Spirit it was supremely manifested in our Lord.

'Where,' asks Bernard, 'is temperance to be found if not in the life of Christ? Those alone are temperate who strive to imitate *His* life, . . . whose life is the mirror of temperance.'[2]

It is of self-control that Augustine is speaking when he exclaims, 'Da quod jubes et jube quod vis.'[3] The presence of the Spirit in man gives him liberty—the true freedom which consists not in following the impulses of the lower nature, but in fulfilling the will of God. Accordingly in Eph 5^{18} St. Paul seems to imply that the one infallible safeguard of temperance is the realization of the presence and action of the Holy Spirit in the soul.

4. The sin of intemperance is wrongly limited to one particular form of excess.[4] It may include want of restraint in work, in recreation, in intellectual speculation, in the pursuit of wealth or power, in the use of the faculty of speech. On this last point much stress is laid by some Christian moralists.[5] The fact is that the habit of loose, unrestrained speech paves the way for grave lapses from truth, purity, or good faith. It 'defiles the man' (Mt 15^{11}). It hinders or weakens that power of controlling 'the whole body' (Ja 3^{2}) which is essential to Christian perfection. St. James implies that the 'sovereign sway of the Christian conscience' must be exercised even in what seems a small sphere, and thence gradually extended to the whole field of human nature till man becomes 'Deo solo dominante liberrimus.'[6]

LITERATURE.—Augustine, *de Mor. Eccl.*, *de Continentia*, etc.; Ambrose, *de Off. Min.* i. 43; Aquinas, *Summa*, II. ii. qu. cxli.–cxliv.; J. Taylor, *Holy Living and Holy Dying*, London, 1847, ch. 2, § 2, *Sermons*, do. 1848, no. xvi. ('The House of Feasting,' pt. 2); B. F. Westcott, *Lessons from Work*, do. 1901, p. 269 ff.; H. Rashdall, *The Theory of Good and Evil*, Oxford, 1907, bk. i. ch. vii. § 4; Stopford Brooke, *The Kingship of Love*, London, 1903, serm. x.

R. L. OTTLEY.

TEMPLES.—A temple, in the original sense of the Latin word *templum*, meant a rectangular place marked out by the augur for the purpose of his observations, which were taken within a rectangular tent. An extended sense gave it the meaning of a consecrated place or building, of rectangular shape, 'inaugurated' by an augur. In this sense it was applied to the house of a god, though, strictly speaking, this meaning belonged to the *ædes*. In its primitive sense *templum* corresponds to the Gr. τέμενος, a place marked off as sacred to a god, in which a ναός, or house of the god, might be erected. As we shall see, an enclosed consecrated space often precedes an actual temple in our sense of the word, viz. the house of a god, a structure containing his image, and sometimes an altar, though not infrequently the altar stands outside the god's house (as in Greece) but within the sacred place, in the open air, as it did before any house for the god was erected. As images became more decorative and costly, it was natural to provide a house for them, though this might be done for a quite primitive image or even a fetish.[7] Less often, however, the chamber or house of the god contained no image; it was merely a place where he might invisibly dwell or which he might visit

[1] Aug. *de Mor. Eccl.* 35.
[2] Aquinas, *Summa*, II. ii. qu. cxli. art. 2.
[3] Westcott, *Lessons from Work*, p. 271.
[4] Bern. *de Consid.* i. 8.
[5] *De Mus.* vi. 15. 50.
[6] Cf. A. Harnack, *Expansion of Christianity*, Eng. tr., London, 1904, i. 111.
[7] See, *e.g.*, the list of things ἀφ' ὧν δεῖ τὸν δοῦλον τοῦ θεοῦ ἐγκρατεύεσθαι in *Mand.* viii.
[8] Cf. iii. 8, 'From faith is produced self-control; from self-control simplicity,' etc.
[9] *Mand.* vi. 1.

[1] *De Contin.* i. 17.
[2] *In Cant.* 22. 11.
[3] *Conf.* x. 29.
[4] For temperance in drinking see artt. ALCOHOL, DRUNKENNESS.
[5] See, *e.g.*, Aug. *de Contin.* ii. 3; Ambrose, *de Off.* i. 2 and 3; Butler, *Serm.* 4.
[6] Aug. *de Mor. Eccl.* xxi.
[7] Cf. the African fetish-hut.

from time to time.[1] Where a god has his image in such a place, those of other divinities may also stand there or in subsidiary chambers connected with it. In the popular sense of the word, 'temple,' while it is connected with worship, is not usually a place within which the people worship. The priests alone enter it; the laity may worship only within the precincts, if even there. Temples vary from the simplest and smallest buildings, as they mostly were at first, to the most elaborate and vast structures.

In studying the origin of temples, no single source for all can be found, as this differs in different regions. Nomads could have no temples, though they might have tribal sacred places, or sacred tents carried in their wanderings. With the advent of a more fixed mode of life and permanent dwellings, a similar dwelling for the deity became necessary, as is seen in 2 S 7^{2}. A variety of primitive temples is known, and it could have been only in the course of a long period of time that the more elaborate buildings came into existence, while, generally speaking, the intermediate stages are not always discoverable.

1. Origin of temples. — (*a*) *Sacred places.* — Among savages, and probably also among most groups of primitive men,[2] most of the rites of worship are carried on in the open air, sometimes because no images of divinities exist, or, where they do, they are not always enclosed within walls, and sometimes because spirits are regarded as connected with natural objects. Sacrifices are simply laid on sacred stones, or cast into the waters, or into the fire, or hung upon trees.[3] Worship takes place in the open air among many of the lowest tribes (Veddas, Australians, Mūṇḍās and other Dravidian tribes, Melanesians, Sakai, and Jakun), as well as among tribes at a higher level (some American Indians, Lapps, Buriats, etc.). This is often the result of a nomadic life, yet even nomads carry sacred images with them[4] or have a tent for these or for other sacred things.[5] Such open places for worship tend to become sacred and to be preserved inviolate for cult purposes, and there images are set up.

Examples of this are found among the Sakai, Jakun, Mūṇḍas, Fjort, and Indians of California.[6]

This is obviously necessary where a sacred tree or stone stands in such a place. Sometimes sacred places are associated with the traditional appearances of spirits, gods, or ancestors, and must therefore be holy for all time. The mere fact that a religious gathering takes place in a certain spot once is enough to give it sanctity, and the gathering becomes recurrent there. Such sacred places will usually be marked by images or symbols, or by boundary-stones forming an enclosure.[7] Single graves, often with a structure over them, and places of sepulture also become recognized places of cult.

The same preference for open-air worship in a recognized sacred place is found among the Chinese—*e.g.*, in the cult of the Altar of Heaven, which dates back to early times when the *genius loci* was worshipped at an altar under a tree.[8] The practice is also found in the primitive cult of the Indo-European races, as a result of their conceptions of deity, not dissimilar from those of savages. The sacred stone, the sacred tree or grove, the sacred spring, were places of cult and usually

1 Cf. the shrine or chapel of the god on the summit of the Babylonian *ziqqurat*, and the Jewish Temple.

2 But see § 1 (*c*) below.

3 For American Indian instances see J. R. Swanton, in *HAI* ii. 405.

4 C. Hose and W. McDougall, *The Pagan Tribes of Borneo*, London, 1912, ii. 186.

5 See § 1 (*e*) below, and cf. the Hebrew 'tent of meeting.'

6 W. W. Skeat and C. O. Blagden, *Pagan Races of the Malay Peninsula*, London, 1906, ii. 197; *ERE* iii. 144^{a}, viii. 362^{b}, ix. 2^{a}, 281^{b}.

7 Hose-McDougall, ii. 7, 15; artt. LAPPS, § 7, LANDMARKS AND BOUNDARIES, § 3 (*a*), (*d*).

8 See art. ALTAR (Chinese).

possessed an altar. The limits of the τέμενος were marked by boundary-stones, and within these stood an altar and a stone or post in which the deity resided. In early Indian worship there were no temples nor indeed permanent sacred places for cult—probably a result of earlier nomadic conditions prevailing after the people had become settled—and to some extent this is the case even now when temples have existed for centuries. So in early Rome there were holy places but no temples; and in ancient Persian religion there were neither images nor temples.[1] The custom and method of building temples were borrowed by the Romans first from the Etruscans and then from the Greeks. Teutons and Celts also worshipped first in the open air, and in their case the earlier cult is especially associated with the sacred tree or grove, though a spirit or god might be worshipped also on a mountain top, in a cave, or at a spring.[2] For the Gauls the evidence of Lucan is interesting in the passage where he describes a sacred grove near Massilia. The grove was tabu to the people; even the priest feared to walk there at midday or midnight, lest he should meet its sacred guardian. The trees were stained with sacrificial blood, but there were also altars, and the images of the gods were misshapen trunks of trees. The marvels of the grove are of a mythical kind.[3]

While sacred groves were general over the Celtic area, temples had begun to be built in both Cisalpine and Transalpine Gaul. The Boii had a temple in which were stored the spoils of war, and the Isubri (Isombri) had a similar temple.[4] Plutarch speaks of the temple where the Arverni hung Cæsar's sword, and Diodorus of 'temples and sacred places.'[5] The temple of the Namnite (Samnite) women, unroofed and re-roofed in a day, must have been a simple building.[6] In Gallo-Roman times elaborate temples were built after Roman models, as well as smaller shrines at sacred springs.[7]

Similar sacred groves existed among the Teutons, as many passages of Tacitus show.[8] 'What we figure to ourselves as a built and walled house, resolves itself, the farther back we go, into a holy place untouched by human hand, embowered and shut in by self-grown trees.'[9]

The use of the sacred grove continued during many centuries. But in these groves simple temples also stood, and are referred to by Tacitus, while sagas and later ecclesiastical writings speak of them, and the latter show that, when they were destroyed, a Christian church was often built on the site.[10]

The Latin names used for these are *fanum*, *casula*, and *templum*. The first was probably a mere hut in which stood the sacred image; the others were more elaborate buildings, whether of wood or of stone.[11]

The grove is thus a primitive holy place, which may have as an accessary a small structure for the image which later becomes a more elaborate temple. This worship in groves, which might become the seat of a temple, is also found among lower races.

The village shrine among the Dravidian tribes of India is an example. Under a sacred tree or grove stands a heap of stones or a mound; this may be replaced by a mud platform or a mud hut with a thatched roof, or by a small building of masonry with a domed roof and platform. These form an abode for the deity and are thus a primitive kind of temple.[12]

The early Semitic sanctuary was a sacred place associated with a theophany or with the continued presence of a spirit or divinity. This might be at a tree, a stone, on a hill, or in a cave.

These holy places were sacred territory enclosed by boundary stones or walls, with altar and *ashērāh*, or sacred pole. The 'high place,' or *bāmāh*, as its name denotes, was on a height, and in the enclosed space or court there were the altar, the *ashērāh*, and the *maṣṣēbhāh* ([*q.v.*] the abode of the divinity), while connected with these were 'houses,' probably of the priests, which sometimes contained images (2 K 17^{29}), though these were also enclosed in tents (2 K 23^{7}, Ezk 16^{16}).[13] These houses or tents represent a primitive temple within the *bāmāh*, and, though no clear traces of actual temples have been met with in excavations, these may have been the origin of actual Canaanite temples such as those at El Berith and Gaza (Jg $9^{46f.}$

1 Herod. i. 131; J. H. Moulton, *Early Zoroastrianism* (*HL*), London, 1913, pp. 53, 225, 391.

2 Cf. J. Grimm, *Teutonic Mythology*, tr. J. S. Stallybrass, London, 1882–88, iv. 1309.

3 Lucan, *Pharsalia*, iii. 399 f.

4 Livy, xxiii. 24; Polybius, ii. 32.

5 Plut. *Cæsar*, 26; Diod. Sic. v. 27.

6 Strabo, IV. iv. 6.

7 See art. CELTS, § XIV. 1.

8 *Germ.* 9, 39 f., *Ann.* ii. 12, iv. 73.

9 Grimm, i. 69; cf. art. OLD PRUSSIANS, § 4 (*c*).

10 Tac. *Ann.* i. 51, *Germ.* 40; Grimm, i. 80 ff.; B. Thorpe, *Northern Mythology*, London, 1851–52, i. 260; G. Vigfusson and F. Y. Powell, *Corpus Poeticum Boreale*, Oxford, 1883, i. 403.

11 Thorpe, i. 212; Grimm, i. 292.

12 W. Crooke, *The N.W. Provinces of India*, London, 1897, pp. 236, 244 f., 249, *Natives of N. India*, do. 1907, p. 236; artt. DRAVIDIANS (N. India), § 27, BENGAL, § 9, ORAONS, § 7; cf. E. B. Tylor, ii. 223 f.

13 A tent was used as a sanctuary in the temple of Beltis at Harran, and elsewhere (D. A. Chwolsohn, *Die Ssabier und der Ssabismus*, St. Petersburg, 1856, ii. 33), and by the Carthaginians as a portable shrine (Diod. Sic. xx. 65).

16[29]), probably consisting of an outer hall and an inner sanctuary for the image. The tents referred to resemble that provided for the Ark by David (2 S 6[17]), though it had previously been kept in some kind of building (1 S 3[3. 15]; cf. 2 S 7[6f.]), just as there were family or tribal houses of a god (Jg 17[5] 18[18. 30f.]). Remains of simple Phœnician temples suggest Egyptian influence; they are little more than a *cella*, rectangular, but open in front.[1]

Examples of 'high places' among other races are found among the Aleuts and Bhils,[2] while they existed also in primitive Greek religion, and indeed wherever a cult was carried on on hilltops.

(*b*) *Shrines at graves.*—The grave as a sacred place may be another point of departure for the temple, when it is associated with a structure—though it be no more than an enclosing wooden fence with shrubs, as among the Tami of New Guinea[3]—where a cult is carried on. Sometimes an altar is placed over a grave, as with the Mayans and possibly the Nicaraguans,[4] and by the Chinese for the half-yearly sacrifice to the spirits of the dead.[5] Sometimes a series of memorial stones is erected, not always, however, over a grave, like the menhirs and dolmen-like structures of the Khāsis,[6] the stone circles with a rectangular niche in their circumference found in Algeria, the rectangular, elliptical, or circular groups of stones in Syria,[7] and the stone circles in Britain, varying in size and elaboration up to that at Stonehenge.[8]

These circles, long regarded without evidence as 'Druidical temples,' were probably connected with a cult of the dead in pre-Celtic times, and so were a kind of temple, like the Fijian *nanga* presently to be referred to. Some have regarded such a circle as that of Stonehenge as a temple dedicated to the sun or other heavenly bodies.[9]

Akin to these are the sacred stone enclosures, or *nanga*, of the Fiji islanders, now existing only as ruins.

These formerly presented the form of a rough parallelogram enclosed by flat upright stones, divided into three compartments by cross walls called respectively the little, great, and sacred *nanga*, the last enclosing the sacred *kava* bowl. Trees stood round the enclosure, and outside, beyond the sacred *nanga*, was the *vale tambu* ('sacred house'), a bell-roofed hut. Here the foreskins of youths circumcised on behalf of a sick parent were offered to ancestral gods with prayers for the patient's recovery. In the *nanga* 'the ancestral spirits are to be found by their worshippers, and thither offerings are taken on all occasions when their aid is to be invoked,' and here firstfruits are presented to them. They were also used in the elaborate initiation ceremonies, the object of which was the introduction of the candidates to the ancestral spirits.[10]

Where large chambered tombs exist, as they do in many parts of the world, they have been used for worship of the dead, either at the time of the burial or at stated intervals thereafter. To this extent, therefore, they form temples, and sometimes they contain a conventional image of the dead like the human figures roughly sculptured on the walls of rock-hewn tombs in France.[11] The structures built over graves may be no more than large huts, of logs and thatch, like those built over the graves of kings and chiefs among the Banyoro and Baganda, but these are regarded as temples, with priests and attendants, where the spirits of the dead are consulted.[12]

In Fiji certain temples of a primitive kind are associated with graves and with the cult of the *kalouyalo*, or ancestor-gods.[13] Not unlike these are the huts of reed and grass built over the graves of chiefs in pre-historic Egypt, where offerings were made. They gave place to mud houses, and these again to structures of stone. Of the latter the *maṣṭaba* had a chamber for the statue of the deceased and a tablet for offerings. Funerary chapels were part of the tomb-structure, but, where pyramids were built, this chapel or temple was erected outside the pyramid, and in it gifts and offerings were made. Sometimes they developed into large temples, which, like the smaller funerary chapels, had lands attached to them for their maintenance.[1]

1 For the more elaborate Canaanite temples see art. ARCHITECTURE (Phœnician); and Lucian, *de Dea Syria*, 31.
2 See artt. ALEUTS, § 5, BHILS, § 3.
3 G. Bamler, in R. Neuhauss, *Deutsch Neu-Guinea*, Berlin, 1911, iii. 518.
4 *NR* ii. 799, iv. 61 f.
5 *ERE* i. 338[a].
6 P. R. Gurdon, *The Khasis*, London, 1907, p. 144 f.; cf. art. MUNDAS, § 4.
7 T. E. Peet, *Rough Stone Monuments and their Builders*, London, 1912, pp. 94, 116.
8 *ERE* iii. 301[b], iv. 408.
9 Cf. artt. STONES.
10 B. Thomson, *The Fijians*, London, 1908, p. 147 ff.; L. Fison, *JAI* xiv. [1885] 14 ff.
11 E. A. Parkyn, *An Introd. to the Study of Prehistoric Art*, London, 1915, p. 158 f.
12 J. Roscoe, *The Baganda*, London, 1911, p. 109 f.; *ERE* ii. 357[b].
13 *ERE* vi. 15[b].

(*c*) *Caves and temples.*—Caves occasionally served as scenes of a cult, and by their shape and enclosed space may have suggested the structural temple. The caverns of mid-Magdalenian times, which contained elaborate paintings of animals or even of human figures, have been regarded as the scene of religious or magical rites, but of this there is no direct evidence.[2] Where cave-dwellers used part of the cave as a shrine for an image or fetish, it might easily through conservatism still be regarded as the dwelling of a god, when men no longer used it for a dwelling. It might become a temple or be associated with a temple built above it. Caves used for burial purposes would doubtless also acquire a sacred character and be used for commemorative rites.

Thus some of the Canaanite 'high places' are associated with caves, which may have been abodes of the living or burial-places, and which, it has been conjectured, were used for oracular purposes or regarded as sanctuaries of a god.[3] Natural or artificial grottoes also constituted the earliest Phœnician temples.[4] An example of gods incarnate in animal shape inhabiting a cavern which served as a temple occurs in Fiji in the case of the gods Ndengei and Ratu-Mai-Mbulu, to whom prayers and offerings were made there.[5] Names of divinities worshipped in caves among the ancient Berbers are known, as well as the caves themselves with inscriptions to them. Sacrifices were probably offered in front of the entrance; within the cave niches contained sacred objects.[6] Rock temples are known in early Egypt and in N. Arabia, but they are most elaborate in India and Ceylon, where they are both hewn out of solid rock and sculptured in caverns. Some originated in Buddhist times, and many still exist as examples of striking architectural skill—*e.g.*, at Elephanta and Ellora.[7] Their prototypes are caves used as shrines and for the cult of Hindu gods in N. India.[8] Among the Caribs two caves were the places where sun and moon emerged and fertilized the earth. They were places of pilgrimage, were adorned with paintings, and contained images. Spirits were supposed to guard them.[9]

Another reason for caves becoming associated with worship is the belief that men first came out of them from their subterranean home. Examples of this are found in ancient Peru and other parts of America.[10]

Caves may also be the depositories of sacred or cult objects or of images of gods, and thus serve a purpose to which temples are also put.

The Arunta *ertnatulunga* is a rock crevice and sacred store-house containing *churinga* and their indwelling spirits. They are visited ceremonially and are highly sacred.[11] The Veddas keep their sacred arrows in caves to prevent them from being contaminated, especially by women.[12] The Hopi use clefts in the rock in which to place the *bahos*, or prayer-sticks, in honour of their deities, and the Coras and Huichols deposit ceremonial arrows and images in sacred caves.[13] The Ostyaks keep their images or stones representing the gods in sanctuaries in the hills guarded by a shaman.[14]

1 *A Guide to the Egyptian Collections in the British Museum*, London, 1909, p. 165 f.; *ERE* iv. 463.
2 S. Reinach, 'L'Art et la magie,' *L'Anthropologie*, xiv. [1903] 257; H. F. Osborne, *The Men of the Old Stone Age*[2], London, 1916, p. 423.
3 See the reff. in *ERE* iii. 178, vi. 681[b].
4 W. R. Smith, p. 180.
5 B. Thomson, p. 114; T. Williams and J. Calvert, *Fiji and the Fijians*, London, 1858, i. 217 f.; cf. *ERE* vi. 14[b], 15[b].
6 *ERE* ii. 507[b].
7 J. Fergusson, *The Rock-cut Temples of India*, London, 1864; see also artt. AJANTA, CAVES, ELEPHANTA.
8 *ERE* v. 10[a].
9 J. G. Müller, *Gesch. der amerikanischen Urreligionen*, Basel, 1855, p. 220.
10 *Ib.* p. 312.
11 Spencer-Gillen[a], p. 133, Spencer-Gillen[b], p. 267.
12 C. G. Seligmann, 'The Vedda Cult of the Dead,' *Transactions of the Third International Congress for the History of Religion*, Oxford, 1908, i. 66.
13 *ERE* vi. 786[b], 829[a]; C. Lumholtz, *Unknown Mexico*, London, 1903, ii. 27, 160.
14 J. Abercromby, *The Pre- and Proto-Historic Finns*, London, 1898, i. 162; *ERE* ix. 577[a].

(*d*) *The village-house, men's house, etc., as temple.*—In many regions where separate temples are unknown, the men's house, council-house, village-house, or the *kiva*, to some extent serves the purpose of a temple among its many other uses, and corresponds to the *prytaneum* of the Greeks and the *curia* of the Romans.

Religious dances or sacred dramatic plays are held in the 'village-house' among the Aleuts or in the 'assembly-house' of the Californian tribes, which may consist of a circular dome-shaped structure or a mere brushwood enclosure.[1] To the latter corresponds the bough *wurley* used in the fire-ceremony of the Warramunga tribe, in which certain men maintain for hours a continuous singing to the accompaniment of beating boomerangs.[2] Among many American Indian tribes, especially in the south-west, religious rites are associated with a 'sacred house,' as with the Hupa, which does not differ in construction from other houses in the village. Here sacred dances take place, and traditions are connected with it.[3] With the Pueblo tribes the *kiva* serves at once as sacred council-house, medicine-lodge, and temple of the members of a mystery society. In some districts *kivas* of ancient date are circular; more generally they are square and often below the surface of the ground. The pre-historic *kivas* of Colorado and Utah are of similar type. Women might not enter the *kiva* except to give food to husband or sons. *Kivas* are often very large, but the well openings are small, and entrance is gained by a ladder up to the roof, whence by another ladder descent is made to the interior from a hole in the roof. The walls are often decorated with symbolic paintings and are surrounded by a bench. At one end is an altar on which the symbolic objects of the society are placed, and before it is a dry sand 'painting,' representing gods and forces of nature.[4] Corresponding to these are the sacred lodges and club-houses of Melanesia and Papua, which are generally the nearest approach to temples in those regions. Examples are found in the 'sacred houses' of the Solomon Islands;[5] in the *toreu* of New Britain, etc.—a sacred enclosure with a large room where the dresses and masks were prepared and members of the society met, whence the spirit-personators of the ceremonies emerged, and which no woman or uninitiated male might approach;[6] in the *marawot* of the Bismarck Archipelago, a similar construction to the *toreu*, but with a special part containing images and visited by the *tena*, or magician, alone;[7] and in the house used in the *asa*-cult at Astrolabe Bay, where an ancestor-cult is practised.[8] The structure consisted mainly of wood and thatch. The 'men's house' in the same regions has often a sacred significance, and contains skulls and heads, effigies of the dead, and symbols associated with ancestor-worship, and sometimes masks, drums, and flutes connected with the mysteries and concealed from the uninitiated. These houses are often used for the worship of ancestors.[9]

(*e*) *The house-shrine as temple.*—Still another aspect of the primitive temple, sometimes suggesting a point of departure for more exclusive temple structures, is the hut or house a corner of which is set apart as a place or shrine for an image or sacred objects. This custom is well-nigh universal, and only a few examples need be noted.

Among the Banyankole in each hut is a special place for fetishes, consisting of a mound of earth a foot high, beaten hard, with grass laid upon it.[10] With Gold Coast tribes the *suhman* containing a spirit has an honoured place in a corner of the hut, where offerings are made to it, or, as with the Yoruba, the house-god Olarosa, represented in human form, is set up at the door, and huts have a recess in the wall for the fetish.[11] Here and there in Melanesia and Papua images of ancestors are kept in houses, or, as in certain islands off the western end of New Guinea, in a separate room of the house in which miniature wooden houses are placed for the souls to reside in. Offerings are made to them. In the chief's house are shrines for the souls of all who have died in the community. 'Such a house might almost be described as a temple of the dead.'[12] Among the Klemantans images are kept in the huts, or, as also with the Kayans, stand before them.[1] The Votiaks set their *vorsud*, or clan-god, on a shelf in the out-house.[2] In higher religions the household shrine is well known. Most Buddhist houses have their shelf with an image of Gautama. Shintōists treasure objects of private cult on a house-altar. In ancient Egypt each house had its domestic shrine, usually a recess or a cupboard with the figure of a household god.

In certain regions the temple seems to have arisen out of the private sanctuary of the king. In Mycenæ houses, especially the king's palace, had chapels as part of the structure, and the palace later became the temple. With the Phœnicians the temple was at first an annexe of the palace, like Solomon's temple at Jerusalem. Where a cult of the hearth-divinities, with libations thrown into the fire, existed—*e.g.*, in Roman houses—the house itself was a temple with the hearth as altar.

2. Actual temples in the lower culture.—We have seen that, while in many savage religions actual temples are unknown, many approaches to temples exist. Yet even savages are not devoid of temples of a primitive kind, for it was natural to suppose that, as the worshipper had a house, the god or spirit also should have one, either as the permanent shelter of his image or as the place whither he might resort and be approached by men in worship.

(*a*) The most primitive temples are probably those found in Africa, both Negro and Bantu. While frequently the 'place of praying' is a mere clearing under the tree in the village courtyard,[3] thus conforming to what was found in early Indo-European worship, sometimes an actual hut is provided for a god, not differing much from the ordinary hut.

On the Lower Niger the temples contain images standing on mud platforms, and the *ju-ju* house in the bush is secret to all but the priests, and contains images, while the walls are decorated with plates.[4] Similar temples exist among the Ewe, and that of the rain-god is painted with the colours of the rainbow.[5] The celebrated serpent-temple at Whydah was merely a circular hut, thatched with grass—a privilege allowed only to shrines and temples—standing in an oblong enclosure. In it the sacred snakes were kept.[6] In Dahomey temples are circular huts, so low that a man must bend double to enter one. Images stand in them on a platform of clay, before which are earthen pots and vessels smeared with blood, eggs, and oil. Some temples are elaborately decorated, and they as well as sacred groves are distinguished by calico streamers fluttering from poles or trees.[7] Among the Yoruba—*e.g.*, at Benin—the *ju-ju* temple consisted of a space of ground 150 yards by 60, surrounded by a high wall, and covered with short grass. At one end a long shed extended across the breadth, and under it stood the altar, made of three steps the whole length of the shed. This was slightly raised in the centre, and on it stood ivory tusks on bronze heads. In the centre of the enclosure were a kind of candelabra with hooks, and a well for the reception of the bodies of victims.[8] Among the Baganda temples resembled the king's house. They were conical structures with an elaborate reed thatch coming nearly to the ground, and supported on posts, with hide curtains for the doorway. They had also a sort of pinnacle composed of layers of reeds bound together and fastened to the top of the roof. The floor was strewn with a carpet of scented grass, dried, and cut to uniform length. These temples took some time to build, and their structure was frequently renewed. Some had also a court surrounding them, and in the case of the more important gods only the priests and mediums could enter it. In others the temple attendants had their huts in the court. Temples without courtyards could be approached and even entered by the people. The temple of the god of war was surrounded on three sides by a thick forest sacred to him. Each temple had its priests and mediums who lived in huts near by, where their vestments, worn on entering the temple, were kept. Young girls tended the sacred fire always burning in the temples, save in those which might not be entered by a woman. The larger temples had estates attached to them for their upkeep. Temples of gods had no images, for images were unknown, but they had a dais on which the invisible deity was supposed to sit, or on which his relics were kept. Sacred drums were stored in certain temples. Fetishes had also temples with priests and mediums, and there were special temples for the king's jaw-bone and umbilical cord,

1 *ERE* i. 305ᵃ, iii. 143ᵇ, 144ᵇ.
2 Spencer-Gillenᵇ, p. 382 f.
3 *ERE* vi. 880ᵇ.
4 F. S. Dellenbaugh, *North Americans of Yesterday*, New York and London, 1901, p. 233 f.; F. W. Hodge, in *HAI* i. 710; cf. *ERE* i. 336ᵃ, 822ᵃ.
5 F. Ratzel, *The History of Mankind*, tr. A. J. Butler, London, 1896–98, i. 325.
6 G. Brown, *Melanesians and Polynesians*, London, 1910, p. 60 f.
7 *Ib.* p. 72 ff.
8 *ERE* ix. 348 f.
9 R. Parkinson, *Inter. AE* xiii. [1900] 35, 42 f.; M. J. Erdweg, *Mittheilungen der anthropologischen Gesellschaft in Wien*, xxxii. [1902] 292 f.; H. Zahn, in Neuhauss, iii. 291, 308; cf. *ERE* ix. 341, 349, 351, 354.
10 J. Roscoe, *The Northern Bantu*, Cambridge, 1915, p. 133.
11 H. Ling Roth, *Great Benin*, Halifax, 1903, pp. 166, 171; cf. *ERE* ix. 278ᵇ, 280ᵃ.
12 R. H. Codrington, *The Melanesians*, Oxford, 1891, pp. 139, 173 ff.; J. G. Frazer, *The Belief in Immortality*, London, 1913, i. 315 f.

1 Hose-McDougall, ii. 7, 19.
2 Abercromby, i. 164.
3 C. W. Hobley, *Ethnology of the A-Kamba and other East African Tribes*, Cambridge, 1910, p. 86; cf. *ERE* ii. 358ᵃ.
4 A. G. Leonard, *The Lower Niger and its Tribes*, London, 1906, p. 465.
5 A. B. Ellis, *The Ewe-speaking Peoples of the Slave Coast of W. Africa*, London, 1890, p. 49.
6 *Ib.* p. 57.
7 *Ib.* p. 80.
8 Ling Roth, p. 150.

and others for his ghost.[1] Similar temples for divinities and for the royal jaw-bone existed among the Busoga, Banyoro, etc., but with these and the Baganda the creator-god had no temple.[2]

(*b*) In Melanesia temples are not common, but in the Admiralty Islands wooden, thatched huts of a beehive shape, with carved door-posts representing male and female figures, serve as temples. The doorway is closed by a hurdle. Skulls of pigs and turtles are attached to the rafters, as well as balls of human hair. A mystery was always made about the principal temple, which contained images, and was sometimes open, sometimes closed.[3] In Fiji each village had one or more temples (*bure*), built on a mound faced with stone rubble-work. The roof was high-pitched, with a projecting ridge-pole, and the height of the structure was twice its breadth. Each *bure* had two doors and a fire-place, and contained images, jars, boxes, mats, etc. From the roof hung a long piece of bark cloth reaching to the floor at one of the corner-posts, and marking the holy place which none but the priest approached to be inspired by the god, who descended by this cloth. The dead were sometimes buried in the *bure*, but the building was only used for worship on special occasions and often became ruinous in the interval. It served also as a council-house and chiefs' club-house. *Bures* were also erected in memory of the dead, and had an altar for offerings.[4] In the district of Tumleo, New Guinea, *paraks*, or temples, built of wood and standing on piles, are found. They consist of two storeys and have high gables, and are approached by ladders with hand-rails carved in the form of crocodiles and ape-like figures. Nothing but drums and flutes is found in the *paraks*, and these, played by men, signify the presence of the spirits, for whose worship the temples exist. A certain degree of mystery attaches to the *paraks*; no woman or child may enter them or loiter in their vicinity.[5]

(*c*) In certain parts of Polynesia—Society and Sandwich Islands—the temples, or *maræ*, were enclosures open to the sky and they were of three classes: national, local, and domestic.

The national temples, called *tabu-tabu-a-tea*, perhaps because of their wide-spread sacredness, were depositories of the chief images and the places where great festivals were held. Each of them was composed of several *maræ*, some with inner courts for the images, altars, and sacred dormitories for the chief divinities, all enclosed by stone walls on two sides. In front was a fence, and at the back a pyramidal structure often of large size, with images and altars before it. At Atchura this structure was 270 ft. long, 94 broad, and 70 high. Steps led to the top, which had a surface area of 180 by 6 ft. Within the enclosure were the priests' houses, and trees grew both within and around it, forming a dark grove. Offerings were placed in the *maræ*. Men alone usually took part in the festivals, but on the completion of the year women and children also attended, but were not allowed to enter the sacred enclosure. Local *maræ* were those belonging to the different districts; the domestic *maræ* were for the family gods. In both of these, as well as in the royal *maræ*, the dead were deposited, and were there under the guardianship of the gods.[6] In other districts —*e.g.*, Samoa—temples resembled the beehive thatched huts, or, again, the village house where the chiefs met served as a temple. In some cases groves as well as temples were used as places of sacrifice.[7]

(*d*) Among the coast Veddas temple structures exist. One is 12 ft. by 10, roofed, and facing eastwards, with the roof carried forward beyond the front wall and door. Outside this structure are a long pole, a well, and a tree with a platform, and just outside the door stands an altar. The interior is decorated with cloths and branches on the occasion of a ceremonial dance, and ceremonial garments are kept within it. Some of the village Veddas have temples of bark or of mud resembling their own huts. In these the shaman dances, and symbols of the spirits are kept.[1]

(*e*) With the Todas, worshippers of the sacred buffalo, the dairy forms the temple or sacred place, with its ceremonial vessels and other things, which are preserved there; and precautions are taken to prevent their contamination by the touch or look of unauthorized persons. Relics of heroes are also stored in them. These temple-dairies have usually two rooms, and are of the same form as the native huts.[2]

(*f*) As an example of various stages in the evolution of temples from simple to highly elaborate, over a large area, we may cite those known in N. and S. America. Most of the lower tribes, and some of the more advanced (Hurons, Iroquois[3]), had no temples. But usually there were sacred spots or shrines where ceremonies were performed, sacrifices offered, and images set up.[4]

Among the Hopi such places were called *pahoki*, 'prayer-house,' and often had nothing to mark them but prayer-sticks —sticks with feathers attached. Others were denoted by circles of stones—*e.g.*, the sun shrine with an opening to the direction of sunrise at the summer solstice—by a single stone, or by some natural mark on a rock.[5] To these correspond the sites on which are erected bowers or lodges for the public performances of mystery societies in other tribes, often containing an altar with sacred objects.[6] More elaborate shrines also exist among the Hopis and will be described later. In S. America corresponding to such shrines is the secret spot where the *botuto*, or sacred trumpet, of the Orinoco tribes is kept, so that women and children may not see it. With other tribes the insignia of a *piai* are tabu and are kept in a special shed or hut, which is also used as a place where he may be consulted. It is called a 'spirit-house' and is tabu.[7] Here also may be mentioned the special 'medicine-lodge' of many tribes, erected for the performances of the shaman, corresponding to that found among the Ural-Altaic tribes of N. Asia.[8]

With other tribes—*e.g.*, the Omaha—the sacred structure consisted of three sacred tents, or *tipis*, which were carried from place to place, like the Hebrew 'tent of meeting.' They consisted of poles tied together at the top, arranged in a circle, and covered with bison skins. They sheltered the three sacred objects—the sacred pole, the sacred buffalo-cow skin, and the sacred bag.[9] The household tent as a shrine containing an altar is also sporadically found—*e.g.*, among the Siksika, with whom each tent has an altar, a mere hole in the ground, in which sweet gum is burned.[10]

With the Apaches, Sioux, and others, sacred caves took the place of temples, where religious rites (tabu to women) were performed, or which were used as resorts for prayer.[11] In Florida the Apallachians had a cave-temple on the sun-mountain, Olaimi, 200 ft. long, and containing an altar and images. Images also stood at the entrance, which faced eastwards, so that the earliest beams of the sun fell upon it.[12] More elaborate still was a cave-temple of the Wiyataos, which had been used to celebrate rites by the followers of a culture-hero Wixipecocha, but was later turned into a structure with galleries, halls, and apartments. Into it the priests descended to perform sacrifices and ceremonies hid from the vulgar eye.[13]

Among the Chibchas the temples, each of which was dedicated to a god, were mere huts with clay walls, containing small stools on which idols were set. The floor was covered with grass, and mats hung on the walls. Those of greater importance had the distinction of having their chief posts set on the body of a sacrificed slave. Small shrines also existed

1 Roscoe, *The Baganda*, pp. 271 ff., 292 ff., 303, 308. Cf. artt. Head, § 5 (*f*), Mouth, § I.

2 Roscoe, *The Northern Bantu*, pp. 90, 131, 227, 246.

3 *JAI* vi. [1877] 414.

4 C. Wilkes, *Narrative of the United States Exploring Expedition during 1838–42*, London, 1852, ii. 53 f.; Williams, pp. 191, 223; B. Seeman, *Viti: an Account of a Government Mission to the Vitian or Fijian Islands*, Cambridge, 1862, p. 391.

5 R. Parkinson, p. 33 f.; Erdweg, pp. 295 f., 377.

6 W. Ellis, *Polynesian Researches*², London, 1832, i. 339 ff., 405; cf. Ratzel, i. 325.

7 G. Turner, *Samoa, a Hundred Years Ago and Long Before*, London, 1884, pp. 19, 152, 289.

1 C. G. and B. Z. Seligmann, *The Veddas*, Cambridge, 1911, pp. 168, 235.

2 W. H. R. Rivers, *The Todas*, London, 1906, pp. 56 ff., 422, 428.

3 See *ERE* i. 335ᵇ.

4 See § I above.

5 J. W. Fewkes, in *HAI* ii. 558ᵇ.

6 G. A. Dorsey, in *HAI* i. 227 f.

7 *30 RBEW* [1915], p. 137; T. Whiffen, *The North-West Amazons: Notes of some Months spent among Cannibal Tribes*, London, 1915, p. 212.

8 See, *e.g.*, artt. Navaho, Ojibwa, Shamanism.

9 Dellenbaugh, pp. 204, 208; J. O. Dorsey, *13 RBEW* [1896], p. 274.

10 W. Hough, in *HAI* i. 46.

11 J. G. Bourke, *FL* ii. [1891] 426; Fewkes, in *HAI* ii. 559; Müller, p. 69; *ERE* vi. 829ᵃ.

12 Müller, p. 69.

13 *NR* ii. 211; for other cave-temples see Müller, p. 184.

throughout this region, on hills or by lakes.[1] Among some Californian tribes structural temples, or *vanquechs*, in honour of the god Chinigchinich, consisted of an oval enclosure, four or five yards in circumference, with interior divisions formed by branches, stakes of wood, and mats, and containing a hurdle supporting an image.[2] The temples of the Natchez, one in each village, which stood on mounds, were huts about 30 ft. square and of a somewhat elaborate structure. They contained the sacred fire as well as a division in which sacred objects were kept. On a platform rested the remains of the 'sun-chiefs,' with sacred images, and in an innermost sanctuary was the holy image of the sun-god or hero. This temple was the object of great reverence.[3] Such sun-temples existed over a wide region in Florida, Arkansas, and Virginia, and were no more than large wigwams with thick mud walls and a dome-shaped roof with figures of eagles. Images stood in them, and women were excluded from them.[4] No more elaborate were the temples described by travellers among Virginian tribes, in the Mississippi region, among the Fox Indians, or in S. America with the Tupinambas.[5] Among the Huichols are temples (*tokpia*), 'god-houses,' and sacred caves, though the difference between the first two is not clear. The temples are larger than but otherwise resemble the houses, which are circular, stone-built, and roofed with thatch, and which possess a low entrance to the east. The roof is supported by upright beams. In the centre is a fireplace—a circular basin of clay. Niches in the interior walls contain ceremonial objects, and each of them is devoted to a god, and in charge of an officer of the temple. Flowers are offered with prayer in these niches. In front of the temple is a square open space for the 'god-houses,' in which the officers live who watch the temple. They are rectangular, of stone and mud, with a thatched gable-roof. The interior contains symbolic objects to please the gods. The people meet in the temples for shamanistic ceremonies. Chairs are placed for the deities invisibly present. Images are kept in sacred caves in the mountains, sometimes set in miniature temples there.[6] In the Pueblo region the more elaborate shrines were of the nature of temples. They consisted of sealed stone enclosures, sometimes with symbols painted on them, and they contained images and symbolic representations of supernatural beings. Among the Hopi the shrine of the earth-goddess is a sealed chamber in which is her image, seated. Every November at the 'new fire' ceremony a slab is removed, and offerings are placed in the shrine, while every four years the image is carried in procession. In all Pueblo shrines are placed permanent objects (images, stones, carved slabs, etc.) and temporary objects (prayer-meal, pollen, sticks, bowls of water, clay images).[7]

The council-house, men's house, the *kiva*, etc., as serving *inter alia* all the purposes of a temple, have been already referred to.[8] In the case of a *kiva*, or lodge of a mystery society, this is particularly marked. None but priests or the initiated may enter the sacred place; in it are made the sacred objects used in the ritual; and here prayers are said, smoke offerings presented, and other ceremonies—*e.g.*, purificatory rites—are carried on.

The rude stone structures just described form a primitive aspect of the more elaborate stone temples of barbaric peoples in N. and S. America. It was also natural that, where wooden temples existed, they should be replaced by temples of stone, as soon as more elaborate architectural methods were attained. Intermediate stages between these simple structures and the massive and elaborate temples—the ruins of which still command respect—are seldom met with, but Peter Martyr describes one in Hayti, and Schoolcraft another at Cayambe—a circle of sunburnt bricks 48 ft. in diameter and 13½ ft. high, with a small door, open to the sky.[9] Probably many of the Peruvian temples were of such a simple character, and even the great temple of the sun at Cuzco, comprising many buildings and apartments, though it was richly adorned with gold plates, cornices, and studs, and was provided with gardens and fields, had no great architectural character—mere squares and parallelograms of one storey, roofless or thatched.[10] Previous to the Inca rule, the temple was strictly a lofty altar with a chapel for the image. Under the Incas the chapel increased in size, encircling the altar, and was made elaborate by the addition of other buildings.[1] Certain remains of temples in Peru, however, show a greater architectural complexity than those described by early Spanish travellers.

The Mexican temples, *teocalli*, 'abode of the gods,' may be described as gigantic altars on which stood chapels for the images. There were many temples in each city, varying much in dignity.

The larger *teocalli* had a great outer court capable of holding a crowd of people. Within this space stood priests' houses, oratories, and chapels for lesser gods. There arose from it a pyramidal structure of earth faced with brick or stone, rising in stages, three to nine in number, each with a platform, to a height of 80 to 100 feet. Stairways, differently arranged, rose from the base to each platform, and thence to the top. Sometimes the stairway rose directly from base to summit up one of the faces of the pyramid; or it ascended at one of the angles to the first platform, at another angle to the second, and so to the top, in order that a religious procession in ascending might make a circuit of the structure. The platforms had palisades on which were stuck the heads of human victims. On the summit stood a tower or chapel, or sometimes two, containing the image of the god or gods to whom the temple was dedicated. In front of them stood the great stone of sacrifice and altars on which perpetual fire burned. The great procession of priests at the numerous religious services was visible to all who directed their eyes to the *teocalli*, as it made the ascent.[2]

The practice of placing temples on pyramidal structures is also found among the Mayans and throughout the whole area of Central America, but here the buildings were of a more ambitious kind, with elaborate architecture and sculpture.[3]

The mounds of the Mississippi region were thought to be of Mexican or Mayan origin, but it is now accepted that they were the work of Indian tribes—Cherokees, Shawnees, Delawares, Choctaws. Nor is it proved that every mound was crowned by a temple or altar. 'Whether these were sacred enclosures, sacrificial and temple mounds, are questions to be settled, if possible, by investigation and legitimate deductions.' Houses were built on some of the mounds, but occasionally travellers speak of a temple on a mound. In such a case the mound was of no great height, and the temple was a simple structure like that of the Natchez.[4]

3. Miniature temples.—Among many African tribes there is a custom of making a small hut for the spirits, about 2 ft. high. This stands in the village or outside, and offerings are made at it. It is supposed to contain 'an uncanny something,' and is a kind of temple of the dead, whose spirits are supposed to visit it.

In Uganda the hut is a veritable sanctuary, with a sort of altar for offerings.[5] In New Guinea some of the tribes set up little houses in the forest for the use of ancestral spirits, or place these within inner rooms of their own dwellings; others place the skull of the dead man in such a hut in the forest.[6] Similar miniature structures for ancestral ghosts are found in Indo-China and among the Gilyaks.[7]

4. Temples in the higher culture.—In higher civilizations the temple usually has a prominent place in religious life, and is architecturally of great importance. But here also it was evolved from simple structures, though these as well as the intermediate stages cannot always be traced in archæological sequence or from historical evidence. The series of articles on ARCHITECTURE deal with the structure of such temples in the greater religions, and it is unnecessary here to do more than offer a few general remarks.

(*a*) The great temples of ancient Egypt were preceded in pre-historic times by a simple structure of dried mud or a hut of wicker-work, not differing much from human dwellings and probably

1 T. A. Joyce, *South American Archæology*, London, 1912, pp. 33, 37.
2 *NR* i. 405.
3 Dellenbaugh, p. 207; *ERE* ix. 190b.
4 Ratzel, ii. 154.
5 Müller, pp. 69, 280; John Smith, *Virginia*, in *Hakluytus Posthumus or Purchas his Pilgrimes* (Hakluyt Soc. Ex. Ser.), Glasgow, 1905–07, xviii. 450 f.
6 Lumholtz, *Unknown Mexico*, ii. 27 ff., 148 f., 160 ff.
7 J. W. Fewkes, in *HAI* ii. 559.
8 § 1 (*d*) above.
9 Müller, p. 184; H. R. Schoolcraft, *Information respecting the History, Condition, etc., of the Indian Tribes of the United States*, Philadelphia, 1853–57, v. 94.
10 Garcilasso de la Vega, in Purchas, xvii. 340 f.; Schoolcraft, v. 89.

1 A. Réville, *The Native Religions of Mexico and Peru* (*HL*), London, 1884, p. 215.
2 Joseph Acosta, in Purchas, xv. 319 ff.; Réville, p. 47; *NR* ii. 577, iii. 430; see art. ALTAR (American), § 2.
3 See art. ARCHITECTURE (American), § 5; *NR* iv. *passim*.
4 *12 RBEW* [1894], pp. 17 f., 604, 609, 652, 660, 671.
5 Hobley, *Ethnology of the A-Kamba*, p. 85; A. Le Roy, *La Religion des primitifs*, Paris, 1909, p. 288; A. Werner, *The Natives of British Central Africa*, London, 1906, p. 47; artt. NYANJAS, § 2 (*c*), BANTU AND S. AFRICA, vol. ii. pp. 357a, 359a.
6 Frazer, *The Belief in Immortality*, i. 315 f.; *ERE* ix. 350a.
7 *ERE* vii. 231a, vi. 226a.

resembling African native temples. The hut was sometimes square, sometimes domed, and stood on a platform of earth to save it from inundation. Within it was the image of the god, and the only opening for light was the doorway or portico, with a mast at each side. In front was a court fenced with a palisade.

The hut gave place to a stone building, but, when additional rooms were built round the central 'house of the god,' and when the whole structure of the temple, with its spacious sphinx-guarded approach, pylons, courts for the worshippers, pillared halls for processions of priests, etc., was elaborated, the dark central chamber of the god, accessible to the higher priesthood only, remained as a constant factor, and contained the divine image or the sacred animal. The door was solemnly sealed with papyrus and clay at night, and as solemnly opened in the morning, before the day's ceremonial began. Thus what had once been the temple itself was now the inner sanctuary of a wide-spread temple, with all its multifarious buildings and chambers for purposes connected with the cult. The height of the Egyptian temple diminished from front to back.[1]

(*b*) The great temples of Babylon had probably originated in a structure of simple kind, oblong in shape, with a recess for an image. Excavations show that the great temples stood in a court with a vestibule, flanked by chambers.

The temple building consisted of a long outer hall, opening into a smaller one with the holy place, or *parakhu*, where stood the image of the divinity and an altar. The holy place was open to the priests alone, or to a worshipper accompanied by a priest for special religious purposes. An altar stood in the court and perhaps in the outer hall also. The names of temples are many, and some of them show their great sanctity, others are suggestive of height—'the house of the shining mountain,' 'the lofty house.' This points to the high tower-like structure, the *ziqqurat*, which stood beyond the important temples, or towered within the sacred enclosure where stood many temples dedicated to various gods, as well as the houses of priests—a grouping of religious buildings found in the larger cities. The *ziqqurat* was a storeyed tower or pyramid, consisting of a series of diminishing and superimposed cubes. These varied in number, and symbolized the mythical mountain of the world. Where it consisted of seven storeys, these represented the planetary zones, or the seven zones of the earth. Each storey was approached by an inclined pathway or a flight of steps, either directly up the face or diagonally across it, until the top, which formed a broad platform, was reached. On the platform stood a chamber for the god, containing a couch and throne, and perhaps an image. As with the Mexican *teocalli*, processions winding up the tower could be plainly seen below, and, while the Egyptian temple in its grandest development was spread over a large area, the Babylonian, as far as the *ziqqurat* was concerned, aimed at reaching a lofty elevation, and represented in miniature the structure of the universe. It seems to have been regarded also as the grave of the god to whom it was dedicated, and persons of importance were sometimes buried round it.[2]

Both Egyptian and Babylonian temples were endowed with lands which yielded large revenues. Hence, outside their religious purpose, they had great influence on the economic life of the nation. In the Babylonian temple area also, as the priests were administrators of the law, there were courts of justice, chambers where national archives were stored, and even banks.

(*c*) The Greek temple was preceded by the τέμενος, the open sacred place with its ἄγαλμα of the deity, altar, and other *sacra*. In the Ægean religion the sacred cave served as a temple where the Mother-goddess was worshipped, as in the double cave (upper and lower) of Dicte in Crete, where a rich store of cult objects has been found in recent years.[3] Palaces had their domestic chapel or shrine, plain and of small size, with a ledge at one end for images and sacred objects. The ruler was a priest-king, and in one instance, that of the palace of Knossos, 'the Place of the Double Axe' (λάβρυς), the whole building has the character of a temple.[4] Free-standing shrines or temples

[1] G. Maspero, *L'Archéologie égyptienne*, Paris, 1887, pp. 65 f., 106 f., *The Dawn of Civilization*, tr. M. L. McClure, London, 1894, p. 119; W. Max Müller, *Egyptian Mythology* (=*The Mythology of All Races*, xii.), Boston, U.S.A., 1918, p. 187 f.

[2] Maspero, *Dawn of Civilization*, p. 427; Herod. i. 181 f.; M. Jastrow, *Aspects of Religious Belief and Practice in Babylonia and Assyria*, New York and London, 1911, lect. v.

[3] C. H. and H. B. Hawes, *Crete the Forerunner of Greece*, London and New York, 1909, p. 112.

[4] *ERE* i. 146[a].

also existed, like that discovered at Gournia, a small enclosure 12 ft. square, in the heart of the town, in which were found many images and cult objects.[1] With the perfecting of the divine image, a house to shelter it became necessary, and the earliest type was no more than a rectangular oblong *cella*, or σηκός. To this was soon added an additional chamber, with open front and a couple of columns supporting an architrave, the corners of which rested on flattened columns attached to the ends of the side walls. These columns were at first of wood; the earliest stone columns date from the 6th cent. B.C. Throughout the whole period of Greek religion the rectangular *cella* remained as the central part of all Greek temples, though it was sometimes prolonged back and front with additional chambers, or surrounded by single or double rows of columns, while these were sometimes also introduced within the *cella*. Vitruvius, indeed, classifies temples according to the arrangement of the columns in relation to the *cella*.[2] The temples of the gods faced eastwards, and opposite the entrance stood the image of the god. The *cella* also contained an altar or altars, votive offerings, and treasure, the last being also stored in the chamber behind the *cella*. The temples were never large; they were merely houses for the image, and hence were often kept closed. They were decorated with sculpture and painting both within and without. The temple stood within a τέμενος, where the great altar was placed, and where the worship was carried on.[3]

(*d*) The Roman *templum*, as already shown, was originally a rectangular space of ground marked off by the augur, in which a tent was pitched for augural purposes, like the 'medicine-hut' of the shaman. Strictly speaking, the house of a god was the *ædes*, but the word *templum* was now applied to such a structure, inaugurated by the augurs, and usually of larger and more complicated structure than the *ædes*. In the earliest times divine dwellings were unknown. The grove, the cave, the hearth, were the earlier sacred places, or the *sacellum*, a small place consecrated to a god, enclosed by a fence or wall, but roofless, with an altar and possibly an image. The Romans, in erecting houses for the gods, were influenced by the Etruscans and the Greeks. The Etruscan temples were of wood, oblong, with one or more chambers and an open portico. The Roman temple had also a central *cella*, but of much greater breadth than the Greek, this feature being probably a result of Etruscan influence. The structure of temples, whether simple or elaborate, was generally determined by Greek architecture, though there were differences in detail—*e.g.*, the absence of columns at the back. Circular temples were also built; these had become common in Greece from the 4th cent. B.C., though it is not impossible that the form may be copied from the early Italian house.

Before building a temple, a space of ground was *liberatus et effatus* by the augurs, and consecrated by the *pontifex*. When the building was erected, it was dedicated to a god. In some instances, however, a building might be consecrated to religious use without the preliminary augural ceremony. Such buildings were *sacra*, or *ædes sacra*, like the temple of Vesta.[4] Outside the temple stood the altar, and within burned the sacred fire. In the temples were stored votive offerings, gifts, treasure of all lands, as well as the images of the gods.

(*e*) During the Vedic period in India, as has been seen, there were no temples. No trace of temples in the pre-Buddhist period is known, but, if any existed, they must have been of wood, as they still are in Burma, the use of stone in

[1] Hawes, p. 101.

[2] Vitruvius, *de Architectura*, iii. 2.

[3] For plans and details, architectural and structural, see art. ARCHITECTURE (Greek), and cf. art. ALTAR (Greek).

[4] For architectural details see art. ARCHITECTURE (Roman), and cf. art. ROMAN RELIGION, § IV.

architecture not having been introduced until Aśoka's reign, as a result of contact with the West. Religious edifices are certainly known for the first time in Buddhism. The primitive sacred object in Buddhism was not an image, but a relic. This at first was not set in a temple, but enclosed in a *stūpa*, or *tope* (Sinhalese *dāgaba*)—an elongated hemispherical structure standing on a base, the exterior often richly carved or ornamented, and crowned with a square capital and the *chhattra*, or umbrella. Many *stūpas* contained no relic, but were erected as commemorative objects. A path fenced by a railing surrounded the *stūpa*, for circumambulation. The *stūpa* was decorated with flags, streamers, and flowers; and it was the chief religious edifice of early Buddhism.[1] Another religious edifice was the *chaitya*, a name applied to any religious monument—*e.g.*, a *stūpa* with relics—but also restricted to a building corresponding to a temple or church, the '*chaitya* hall,' with pillared aisles and an apse containing a *stūpa* and an altar.

The earliest known structural building of this type—*e.g.*, at Ter, Haidarābād—consists of an apsidal chamber with high barrel-vaulted roof. In front is a square hall, or *mandapa*—perhaps a later addition, lower in height, with a flat roof supported by pillars. The façade above the roof of the hall has a niche containing now a Hindu image, which was probably at one time a window. Within the apse stood a *dāgaba*, now replaced by a Vaiṣṇava image. *Chaityas* of this type must have been common in India. Buddhism made use of rock excavations at an early time for *chaitya* halls, which sometimes had aisles.[2]

A third structure was the *vihāra*—a hall where the monks assembled, with cells at the sides for sleeping. The *vihāras* were later used as temples and became the centre of monastic buildings grouped around them. They usually stood beside *chaityas*, though they came to be furnished with chapels in which religious services could be performed as well as in the *chaitya*.

During ten centuries from Aśoka's time onwards cave *chaitya* halls and *vihāras* were excavated all over India.

In early examples at Bihār the *chaitya* halls are merely oblong chambers, sometimes with a cell or apse at the farther end for the *dāgaba* with its relic. Others are more elaborate. The façade of the cave represents the exterior of a wooden *chaitya* in all its details. The interior is apsidal. Pillars are cut in the sides, and in the apse is the *dāgaba*, which now has the image of Buddha in front of it. Some of these caves are highly elaborate in their carving both within and without, and are also pillared structures with aisles. The cave *vihāras* have a central pillared hall with cells at the sides for monks. Beyond the hall are one or more inner sanctuaries for images of Buddha. These are later additions. Here again the architecture and adornment varies from simple to highly elaborate. The earliest free-standing *vihāras* were probably simple halls with cells attached, and were sometimes of a storeyed pyramidal form, each successive storey decreasing in size, and giving a series of pillared halls one above the other, with cells for the monks on the terraces. This architectural structure supplied a form for all the later temples of southern Hinduism.[3] Attached to great monasteries, as at Peshawār, was a court, or *vihāra*, with cells for images, and beyond that, opening from it, a circular or square court surrounded by similar cells, and with a *stūpa* in the centre. These belong to the period of Mahāyāna Buddhism.

One of the earliest known temples, or *chaityas*, is at Bodh Gayā, in front of the Bo-tree of Buddha's enlightenment. Frequently restored, it was probably erected in the 6th cent., and is 160 ft. high by 60 ft. wide. It is rectangular with an elongated pyramidal form of nine storeys, each with exterior niches for images, and the interior *cella* contained originally an image of Buddha. Such a nine-storeyed tower-temple is unique in India, but is found frequently north of the Himālaya.[4]

Hindu temples doubtless owe much in their inception to Buddhism, and are of great variety in structure, size, and ornamentation. But there are two principal groups, one in Southern India of the so-called Dravidian style, and one in Northern India, each of which shows great uniformity in general plan. In S. India the structure consists of the temple proper, or *vīmana*, 'the vehicle of the gods'—a square building with a pyramidal roof which may have one or several storeys, like the storeyed *vihāra* of Buddhism. In this is the square cell containing the chief image of the god, and lit only from the doorway. Between the wall of the inner cell and the outer wall is the procession path, or *pradakśina*. Pillared porches or halls called *mantapams* (Skr. *mandapa*) precede the entrance, and are usually larger than the *vīmana*. *Vīmana* and *mantapam* stand in a walled enclosure with gate-pyramids, or *gopurams*, corresponding to the Egyptian pylons and often very imposing. Within the enclosure stand a pillared hall, priests' dwellings, tanks, and other structures. These temples are devoted to the Vaiṣṇava and Śaiva cults, and are not otherwise distinguishable apart from the sculptures and images. The earliest examples of the *vīmana* show its derivation from the Buddhist apsidal *chaitya* hall. The apse for the relic-shrine has become a cell for an image and is entered by a door. In another early example the circular apse has given place to a cell with altar and image, surmounted by a tower, and the hall in front, distinct from the cell, is pillared. Cell and pillared nave or *mantapam* are reproduced in all Jain and Hindu temples of later date, together with the storeyed tower. The enormous size and elaborate architectural and sculptural design of these buildings make them still marvellous rivals of the cathedrals of Europe. Some, besides the original enclosure with its gate-pyramids, have a second or even third exterior enclosure, with *gopurams*, shrines, porches, cells, etc. The *vīmana* in itself corresponds to the ordinary Hindu village temple, and in some examples has either been such a temple or is little more imposing than one of these. Sometimes two *vīmanas* dedicated to different divinities stand within the central enclosure. In S. India the largest group or congeries of temple buildings is at Śrīrangam. There are seven enclosures, leading gradually to the central shrine, and the three surrounding the central enclosure are crowded with temples, porches, halls, etc., while in each wall there are two or three *gopurams* of great height. 'The idea is that each investing square of walls . . . shall conduct the worshipper by regular gradations to a central holy of holies.'[1] While the temples of this kind are of comparatively late date, others of earlier date, but presenting the same general features, have been carved out of the solid rock and excavated internally, so that they are monolithic temples. The chief examples are the raths (*ratha*=*vīmana*) at Mamallapuram and the beautiful *kailāsa* at Ellora.[2]

The Northern temples (Fergusson's 'Indo-Aryan style')—*e.g.*, in Orissa—are characterized by a pyramidal curvilinear tower on a polygonal base in which is the central shrine, often quite small. The interior plan is square, and in the Orissan examples there are no pillars, or these are found only in modern additions. In front is a square porch with pyramidal roof, and sometimes in front of this again additional porches. The enclosing wall is always insignificant, if it is present at all, and has no *gopurams*. Other shrines are always subordinate to the towering temple proper with its porch. Even the more elaborate temples preserve these essential features—*e.g.*, the Kandarya Mahadeva, or temple of Śiva, at Khajurāho.

In all Hindu temples the inner cell or shrine with its image is the central feature round which all the other parts are grouped, and to which, however elaborate, they are all subordinate. The cell is cubical, of small dimensions, unornamented,

1 See art. STŪPA. 2 See art. CHAITYA.
3 J. Fergusson, *Hist. of Indian and Eastern Architecture*, i. 171.
4 *Ib.* i. 77 f.

1 M. Monier-Williams, *Brāhmanism and Hindūism*[4], London, 1891, p. 448; Fergusson, i. 368.
2 See art. ELLORA, vol. v. p. 270a.

and unlit save by the doorway, and is too sacred to be entered by any but the priests. The exterior building surrounding the cell is of the most elaborate workmanship, often of a kind which offers little clue to the method of producing it. In some districts enormous numbers of temples exist, ancient and modern, and at Benares, the sacred city, there are 1500, though none are older than the 18th century.

(*f*) In Nepāl the *stūpas* do not contain relics. Some are of flattened hemispherical shape with a square capital, 'umbrella,' and lofty finial or spire, like those in Tibet and China, and stand on a plinth on which are built shrines of the five Dhyanibuddhas. Others are lower and flatter; and others again stand on a structure with successive roofs. Buddhism in Nepāl is mingled with Saivism, and the characteristic temple is a square structure of several decreasing storeys divided by sloping roofs. Some are mounted on a pyramidal-stepped platform. These buildings are of wood and stone.[1]

(*g*) In Burma the *stūpa* (*tsedi*) is bell-shaped and stands on a series of platforms, and is crowned with a conical finial. The temples are of square form with projecting porches. In the thickness of the walls are narrow corridors with niches in which are images. A series of storeys arranged pyramidally and crowned with a slender steeple forms the roof. Ancient Buddhist temples in Siam have a rectangular outer enclosing wall, within which is the *bot*, also rectangular, with a porch. The interior is divided by pillars into a nave and single or double side aisles. Within are the high altar and image of Buddha. Behind the *bot* stands a *stūpa*, or *phra*. *Vihāras*, or *vihāns*, and *kamburiens* are buildings similar to the *bot*, but smaller, where the laity come to pray or hear sermons. The *bot* is accessible only to the priests. The *mondob* is a rectangular building enclosing a huge image of Buddha. One enclosure sometimes contains several of these structures, erected from time to time by devout Buddhists.[2]

(*h*) The earliest Chinese religion had no temples, and apparently the general use of these is due to Buddhism. With few exceptions the temples of the three religions, Confucianism, Buddhism, and Taoism, are mainly of one type, though they differ in size. The religion to which each is dedicated can be discovered only from their interior decorations and the images which they enshrine.

Buddhist temples are enclosed by a wall with an ornamental gateway. The temple has a series of porches or halls, opening from each other. Two of these form antechapels to the main structure with its altar and images of the three Buddhas, facing the entrance, and stalls for the monks. Before the images stands the table for offerings, with lamps and flower-vases. Beyond this another hall contains a *dāgaba*, and a final one enshrines the image of Kwan-yin. Within the enclosure are the various buildings for monks, pagodas, drum-tower, bell-tower, and other structures. The roof has the characteristic form of all Chinese buildings, concave, with projecting eaves, but more elaborately decorated than in secular buildings. Confucian temples are of the same general plan, the central 'Hall of Great Perfection' containing the tablets of Confucius, his disciples, and the twelve sages. Tables for offerings stand before these. Taoist temples contain the images of the Three Precious Ones, in imitation of the three images of Buddhist temples.

(*i*) In Japan, as in China, the earlier worship was in a consecrated enclosure open to the sky. Tradition assigns the first temples to a period near the beginning of the Christian era. Shintō temples are not large and conform in structure to the architecture of an age when tools were few and primitive. The quality of the wood used in the structure is of more importance than ornamentation and carving, whereas the carvings on Buddhist temples are highly elaborate, and have much gilding, lacquer-work, and painting. The oldest Shintō temples and many of the smaller ones are thatched. The type is similar to that of China, showing that Chinese influences prevailed.

The temple area, at least in the case of the greater temples, has several enclosures, with fences and gateways preceded by flights of steps. The grouping of the various structures differs according to the nature of the ground, usually on a slope, giving the chief eminence to the main shrine. Shintō temples, but rarely Buddhist, are preceded by the characteristic *tori-wi*, of two wooden uprights with cross-bars, the upper one projecting and curving upwards at the ends; they correspond to the gateways of *stūpas* and temples in India, like that of the *tope* at Sanchi, and to similar structures in religious architecture elsewhere.[1] The temple consists of two or three halls, one an oratory or prayer-hall for worshippers, an intervening hall, and the sanctuary open only to the priests. Shintō temples have no images, a mirror usually constituting the symbol of deity. Some temples are dedicated to more than one divinity. An altar stands in the shrine. The lay-worshipper, entering the prayer-hall, pulls a rope attached to a gong and so announces his presence to the deity before beginning his devotions. Within the temple enclosure, as in China, the grounds often being laid out artistically, stand a pagoda, drum-tower, belfry, stage for religious dances, library, votive-offering hall, store-houses, kitchen, priests' rooms, etc. This general description applies to both Shintō and Buddhist temples, though the latter are generally more gorgeous and imposing, and contain images, lights, votive offerings, lotus-flowers of silver-gilt, while the priestly ritual is elaborate. They are usually built of wood, with gilding and porcelain casing, and metal work; the roofs are of tiles.

(*j*) In Tibet the Buddhist monasteries are the chief architectural structures, occupying large areas and containing a square for assemblies, in which stands the temple.

This is a stone rectangular building, on the top of which is a pavilion with a roof of Chinese type. The interior is divided into a nave and side aisles by pillars, which are painted in yellow and red. The three great Buddhist images with their altar stand at one end. Other images stand along the side walls. There are no windows, and the interior, which is richly coloured or decorated with frescoes and hung with banners, is lit by lamps. Seats for the various officials and Lāmaist congregation are arranged according to a definite order. The temple is approached by a flight of steps and a gateway guarded by demoniac figures. In the vestibule are images of the kings of the four quarters, and also prayer-wheels. These, in larger temples, are placed in detached chapels, in which are images of lower divinities. Occasionally, as at Gyan-tse, a temple is built in stepped terraces, like a *vimana*, crowned by a drum-like structure, on which are a square and a *chhattra* canopy. Shrines to the different Buddhas occupy the various storeys.[2] The great 'cathedral' at Lhasa faces eastward, and is three-storeyed, the roof being of gold. The approach is through a pillared hall, adorned with pictures. Beyond this is an antecourt, leading to a pillared hall, shaped like a basilica and divided into aisles by a series of colonnades. It is lit from above, as there are no side windows. On the side walls are chapels. Lattice-work separates the cross aisles from the longer aisles, and on the west the sacred place is approached by a staircase. This is in form of a square, with six side chapels, three on each side. An altar stands in the centre, and on the west is a recess with an image of Buddha. Here too are the seats of the Dalai and Tashi Lāmas, and of abbots and lesser officials, as well as images, relics, prayer-wheels, etc.[3]

(*k*) The Hebrews had different kinds of sanctuaries before the Temple was built at Jerusalem. The 'tent of meeting' referred to in E was pitched outside the camp in the wilderness. There Moses communed with God, who appeared in a pillar of cloud (Ex $33^{7\text{ff.}}$, Nu $11^{24\text{f.}}$ 12^{5} 14^{10}). It is not described, and was obviously of a simple character. Its one guardian was Joshua, who 'departed not out of the tent' (Ex 33^{11}). The tent may have contained the sacred Ark, a kind of abode of deity, as Nu 7^{89} shows (cf. 2 S 15^{25}), though tent and Ark are never mentioned together. Such portable sanctuaries were used by the Semites, either in nomadic or in more settled times, in the latter case certainly in connexion with war, when the images were carried with the army. The Hebrew 'tent' was used for sacred divination like the Semitic portable sanctuary, and it may be compared with the sacred tents of the Omaha.[4] The Tabernacle, elaborately

[1] Fergusson, i. 277 f.; H. A. Oldfield, *Sketches from Nipal*, 2 vols., London, 1880.
[2] L. Fournereau, *Le Siam ancien, archéologie, épigraphie, géographie* (*AMG* xvii., xxxi.), Paris, 1896–1908; Spiers, in Fergusson, ii. 404 ff.

[1] See art. Door, § 2, vol. iv. p. 849a.
[2] L. A. Waddell, *The Buddhism of Tibet*, London, 1895, p. 287 ff.; Fergusson, i. 290 f.
[3] Waddell, p. 300; see also his *Lhasa and its Mysteries*, London, 1905, p. 361 ff.
[4] See § 2 (*f*) above.

described by P, and containing the Ark, was probably never more than an ideal priestly construction projected upon the past. The Ark was later kept in a 'house' or temple at Shiloh (1 S 1[9] 3[3. 15]), which may have been destroyed by the Philistines, who carried off the Ark. On its recovery, it was kept from time to time in private houses, and possibly in a tent (2 S 7[6]), as it was so kept later by David at Jerusalem (2 S 6[17]; cf. 11[11]). Tents were also used after the settlement in Canaan on the 'high places' (2 K 23[7], Ezk 16[16], 'sewn high places').

What the 'house' at Shiloh was like we have no means of knowing, but probably it was not elaborate. Micah's image and other religious objects were kept in an apartment of his house (Jg 17[5] 18[18]). When captured by the Danites, these were placed in a sanctuary at Laish. At Nob there was a sanctuary with its priesthood, containing an ephod and a table of holy bread (1 S 21).

Tent and high place were succeeded by the Temple built by Solomon. It stood within a great court as one of a series of buildings, including the palace, and was thus dominated by the latter, to some extent, though it was itself the chief building. It had its own 'court of the temple,' surrounded by a wall of stone and cedar.

The Temple was an oblong structure of stone, faced by a porch, in front of which stood two bronze pillars called Jachin and Boaz, like those in front of other Semitic temples. The structure, exclusive of the porch, which was of equal breadth with the Temple, was 60 cubits long, 20 broad, and 30 high. It was divided by a partition with doors into a Holy Place (*hēkāl*) and an Oracle, or Most Holy Place (*debīr*)—a square dark chamber 20 cubits in each direction, leaving a space of 10 cubits above it. The interior walls were lined with cedar, carved, and ornamented with gold, and the floor was of cypress. Between the walls of the structure and an outer wall, running round the sides and back to the height of 20 cubits, were three storeys of rooms for treasure and Temple ornaments. In the Temple wall, above these, there were latticed windows. The Oracle, or Most Holy Place, the *adytum*, was the dwelling of Jahweh, and contained the Ark with the cherubim. In the Holy Place stood the altar of shewbread, the altar of incense,[1] and ten candlesticks, five on each side. Outside the porch, which faced east, was the altar of burnt-offering, and near it a brazen sea supported by metal oxen, as well as ten smaller lavers on wheels. The people gathered for worship in the court, though it is called 'the priests' court.' The Holy Place was for the priests alone—a suggestive difference, appearing now for the first time.[2]

Thus the main features of the Temple were common with those of Syrian and Phœnician temples of the period—porch, outer chamber, and *adytum*—though some have suggested Egyptian influences in its construction.[3]

Ezekiel's ideal Temple has the same division of inner and outer sanctuaries and porch, but there are two courts, an inner one for the priests, an outer for the laity; and the sacred building was to be entirely dissociated from all secular buildings, and was also to be shut out from Jerusalem by the lands of the Zadokites.[4]

Zerubbabel's Temple of the restoration period had an outer court with walls and gates, and an inner court in which stood the altar of unhewn stones, and perhaps a laver. Into the inner court the laity appear to have had access for a time at least. The Temple itself had a Holy of Holies, but was unique among temples in possessing no representation or symbol of deity, the Ark having been lost. The presence of deity, however, was marked by the ritual of the Day of Atonement. The Holy of Holies was separated from the Holy Place by a curtain, and this chamber contained the table of shewbread, altar of incense, and the seven-branched candlestick. The Holy Place was entered by a curtain.

Herod's Temple, built about 20 B.C., was on a larger scale than any of its predecessors, but the general plan was the same.

[1] 1 K 7[48], perhaps a later addition to the text.
[2] 1 K 6 f., 2 Ch 3 f.
[3] Lucian, *de Dea Syria*, 31, describes the temple at Hierapolis, with its court, altar, pillars, *pronaos*, and *cellæ*. It faced eastwards.
[4] Ezk 48[8ff.].

A large outer court—'the court of the Gentiles'—was surrounded by porticoes or cloisters with marble pillars, built against the enclosing battlemented wall. Within the area, on a raised platform, was a second court surrounded by a terrace and an enclosing wall with nine gates, and with chambers and porticoes on its inner side. Within this none but Jews might enter. A wall across the breadth of this inner court divided it into two parts, the smaller of which was 'the court of the women.' The other part was open to male worshippers, and within its area stood the temple building, surrounded by a breastwork of stone enclosing the court of the priests. Within this court priests only could enter, except when a layman offered a sacrifice which required his presence. The Temple within this inner area was preceded by a lofty porch and gateway. This gave access to the *hēkāl*, or Holy Place, across the great door of which hung a curtain, and this again to the *debīr*, the Holy of Holies, across the entrance to which hung two curtains. Above these was an upper storey, and a side building of three storeys surrounded the Temple on three sides. In the *hēkāl*, which was open only to the priests, stood the table of shewbread, altar of incense, and seven-branched candlestick. The *debīr* was empty and quite dark, and was entered by the high-priest alone on the Day of Atonement. In front of the porch outside stood the altar of burnt-offering and the laver. The building was of white marble, and the eastern front and part of the walls were covered with gold.[1] The *debīr* was 20 cubits square; the *hēkāl* 40 cubits long, 20 broad, and 40 high. The porch was 100 cubits high, 100 broad, and 20 in depth, and extended on both sides beyond the Temple, with its side buildings, by some 15 cubits. Herod had raised many pagan temples throughout his dominions, and he erected this for the Jews in his capital partly as a matter of policy.

5. Conclusion.—A general survey of temples shows that the essential part is the *cella*, or chamber, for the image of the god, and that, whatever additions are made by way of increasing the splendour of the temple or as adjuncts to it, this remains constant, and is indeed its most important feature. It is the holy place, and is seldom if ever entered save by the priests. The temple at Eleusis forms an exception, for apparently there all was open to the worshippers. But generally worship takes place in the temple area or within the hall preceding the *cella*, which is very often dark and unlit by windows. The Jewish synagogue, the Muhammadan mosque, and the Christian church are not strictly temples, for they are not houses enclosing a divine image, but places of public prayer. Yet even in the mosque the recess, or *mihrāb*, indicating the direction of the *ka'bah*, towards which the worshipper prays, has a certain parallel to the *cella* with its image which the worshipper also faces. The great mosque at Mecca also contains the *ka'bah* with the sacred black stone, and the *ka'bah* is an old but reconstructed sanctuary within the mosque. In the Christian church the chancel and the sanctuary with the altar are not ordinarily open to the laity assembled in the nave, but yet they approach the altar at the Holy Communion.

Certain temples are national holy places, like the Pantheon at Rome, the *ka'bah* at Mecca, and similar great temples in important centres. Pilgrimages are often made to temples, and temples form asylums whither criminals flee for safety. Frequently there is much symbolism connected with the temple, and attention is paid to the direction in which it faces, most temples facing the east or the place of the rising sun. Very often in connexion with one great temple there will be a series of lesser shrines for other divinities, all forming a group of sacred buildings within the area. The area is usually enclosed by a wall with gates, which are often most elaborate, and avenues, while pillars and poles stand about it, and it is often decorated with flags and streamers. It is interesting also to notice how frequently with the change of a religion the old sacred places are retained, and successive buildings occupy the old site, or the same temple serves for new deities.

LITERATURE.—W. J. Anderson and R. P. Spiers, *The Architecture of Greece and Rome*[2], London, 1907; Daremberg-Saglio, *s.v.* 'Temple'; J. Fergusson, *Hist. of Architecture in all Countries*[3], ed. R. P. Spiers, 5 vols., London, 1891–93, *Hist. of Indian and Eastern Architecture*, ed. J. Burgess and

[1] Jos. *BJ* v. v., *Ant.* xv. xi.; Mishnāh, tr. *Middoth*.

R. P. Spiers, 2 vols., do. 1910, *The Temples and other Buildings in the Haram Area at Jerusalem*, do. 1878; G. R. M. Maindron, *L'Art indien*, Paris, 1898; Pauly-Wissowa, *s.v.* 'Tempel'; G. Perrot and C. Chipiez, *Hist. de l'art dans l'antiquité*, 9 vols., Paris, 1882–1911; O. Schrader, *Reallexicon der indogerman. Altertumskunde*, Strassburg, 1901, *s.v.* 'Tempel.'

J. A. MACCULLOCH.

TEN ARTICLES.—See CONFESSIONS, vol. iii. p. 851.

TEN COMMANDMENTS.—See DECALOGUE.

TENDAI.—See PHILOSOPHY (Japanese).

TERAPHIM.—See IMAGES AND IDOLS (Hebrew).

TEUTONIC RELIGION.—I. *INTRODUCTORY.*—**1. Position of the Teutonic peoples.**—We have no detailed information (and indeed little historic evidence of any kind) relating to the Teutonic peoples before the time of Julius Cæsar (58 B.C.). For the first one and a half centuries A.D., however, a comparatively large amount of evidence is obtainable. During this time the area occupied extended from the Rhine to the basin of the Vistula. From the Roman empire it was separated by the rivers Rhine and Danube and by a fortified line connecting these two rivers. On the east and south-east the boundaries of the Teutonic area cannot be determined with any precision—the plain of Hungary was occupied largely by Sarmatian peoples, but it seems probable that the Teutonic peoples extended into the basin of the river Dneister. In the north they undoubtedly occupied the kingdom of Denmark and considerable portions of the Scandinavian peninsula.

From the 3rd to the 6th cent. the Teutonic peoples extended their dominions considerably to the south-east, south, and west. The Goths conquered a large portion of S. Russia, and from about 260 to 270 the Romans had to give up to them their territory of Dacia (north of the Lower Danube); moreover, about the same time the Alamanni occupied the Black Forest region. During the 4th cent. bands of warriors, in ever-increasing numbers, began to enter the Roman service, and towards the close of the century a large section of the Goths was admitted *en bloc* within the Roman territories in the Balkan Peninsula. Between 406 and 486 all the western territories of the empire were conquered by the Teutonic peoples, of which the most important were: (1) Visigoths, who occupied S. France and Spain after 412; (2) Ostrogoths, who occupied Italy, 489–553; (3) Vandals, who crossed the Rhine in 406, and in 429 passed over into Africa, which they held for over 100 years; (4) Burgundians, who crossed the Rhine shortly after the Vandals and in 443 occupied S.E. France; (5) Alamanni, who went into Alsace and Switzerland about the same time; (6) Bavarians, who occupied the Alpine regions farther east probably about the same date; (7) Franks, who conquered and occupied successively one part after another of Gaul from 428 onwards, becoming supreme by their victory over the Visigoths in 507; (8) Langobardi, who, after occupying for some time the province of Austria and the Alpine regions to the south, passed into Italy about 568 and brought the greater part of the peninsula under their dominion; (9) English, who conquered and occupied most of the southern half of Britain from about the middle of the 5th cent. onwards.

Before the end of the 8th cent. a new series of movements began among the Northern peoples, an activity almost entirely maritime and lasting throughout the 9th and 10th centuries; this period was commonly known as the Viking Age. While it lasted, large numbers of piratical adventurers settled on the coasts of the Scottish islands, of Ireland, of the Netherlands, and of N. France. The last named, occupied by the vikings under the leadership of Hrólfr, son of Rögnvald, officer of Harold the Fair-haired, king of Norway, became after 911 the earldom of Normandy. From 866 onwards a large part of England too came under Scandinavian rule, though this domination was only temporary. In 870, however, those Norwegian chieftains who were unwilling to accept the sovereignty of Harold the Fair-haired began permanently to settle in Iceland, and more than 100 years later, in 985, Greenland was colonized from Iceland. Contemporaneous with these events were similar movements across the Baltic, which probably emanated mainly from Sweden. The establishment of the Russian kingdom (traditional date 859) was due to such bands of adventurers. In the East we hear of raids by parties of Scandinavians as far as the Caspian.

2. The conversion of the Teutonic peoples.—As conversion was in general due to direct contact with the Romans, we find those Teutonic peoples first converted who were settled within the territories of the empire. Before the middle of the 4th cent. the conversion of the Goths by Wulfilas to the Arian form of the Christian religion had begun and was practically complete within a generation. From them this religion must have spread very rapidly to the Gepidæ in E. Hungary and to other neighbouring peoples, since the Vandals appear to have been converted before the great movement to the West began. The Rugii in the province of Austria, the Langobardi, and some of the Burgundians also adopted the Arian form of Christianity, while the Franks before the close of the 5th cent. and the English in the 7th were converted to Catholicism. It was due largely to the efforts of Irish and English missionaries that between the 6th and 8th centuries the remaining peoples on the Continent (except the Danes), viz. Alamanni, Bavarians, Old Saxons, and Frisians, were converted. In the 8th cent. after great difficulty Charlemagne enforced the adoption of Christianity throughout the territory of the Old Saxons who had been conquered by him. Among the Danes and the Swedes missionary enterprises met with some temporary success, especially in the 9th cent. during the time of the missionary bishop Ansgar (826 to his death in 865). But Christianity was not permanently established in Denmark till after the defeat of Harold Gormsson by Otto II. in 973. In Norway Hákon I. (934–960) and his successors Harald II. and his brothers (960–975) were Christians, but the country was very little affected till the time of Olaf Tryggvason (995–1000), to whom conversion was really due. Many of the Scandinavians settled in the British Isles were converted before the close of the 9th cent., and these countries had become entirely Christian in the course of the 10th century. Some of the early settlers of Iceland had been converted to Christianity in the British Isles, but it was abandoned by their descendants and not established in the island till 1000. The traditional date of the establishment of Christianity in Sweden was 1008, but it was only towards the close of the 11th cent. that the heathen religion was entirely abolished. The adoption of Christianity by the Russians dates from 988.

3. Authorities.—(1) The little information which we possess relating to the religion of the Teutonic peoples during the period before their invasion of Roman territories in the 5th cent. is derived from the writings of Cæsar, Strabo, and Tacitus—especially from Tacitus' *Germania*, written in the 1st century. Some little evidence is also furnished by Roman inscriptions. Still less information is to be obtained from the period during which the Teutonic peoples living on the Continent were converted, though a few scattered notices are preserved in the writings of Ammianus Marcellinus (late 4th cent.), of Jordanes (*c.* 550), and especially of Procopius (about the same date). In the 8th and 9th centuries a little evidence is to be derived from laws and capitularies in which heathen practices are prohibited, and survivals of heathen practices are occasionally noticed in writings of a much later date. The authorities until the 6th cent. are entirely Greek and Latin, in the 7th Latin alone, and with the exception of Jordanes, a monk of Gothic family, we have no records of Teutonic nationality.

As to actual beliefs we learn very little. The only myth which has come down to us is of Langobardic origin and connected obviously with an attempt to explain the name of that people. It occurs for the first time in the *Origo gentis Langobardarum*, an anonymous work dating probably from the 7th century. There are also two German metrical charms from Merseburg which deal with mythological subjects (10th cent. MSS). Beyond this we have scarcely more than a few names, particularly those of the days of the week, which are translations from Latin and date probably from the 4th century.

(2) *English.*—In England most of the evidence available, which is but little, is contained in the writings of Bede († 735), who in the *Chronicle* attached to the *de Ratione Temporum* has left an account of the calendar used by the English in heathen times. A few references to their religion before conversion are preserved also in the *Ecclesiastical History*. No Anglo-Saxon poems have come down to us in a purely heathen form, but a certain amount of information relating to heathen practices and beliefs may be obtained from *Beowulf* and also from certain shorter poems, especially from charms. We may also learn something of the mythological conceptions of the English from glossaries, letters, and other writings.

(3) *Danes and Swedes.*—Certain foreign Latin works throw light on the religion of the Danes and Swedes. Particular mention may be made (for the Swedes) of the *Life of St. Ansgar* written by his disciple Rimbertus, and of the work of Adam of Bremen, who in the 4th book of his *History of the Church of Hamburg* gives an important description of the sanctuary at Upsala. Later Danish historians add considerably to our knowledge both of religion and of mythology for Danes and Swedes. In particular we have the *Danish History* of Saxo Grammaticus (*c.* 1200), much of the information in which is obtained from Icelandic sources. He himself acknowledges this in his reference to the men of Thule:

'Their stores, which are stocked with attestations of historical events, I have examined somewhat closely, and have woven together no small portion of the present work by following their narrative.'[1]

Some important evidence from earlier times is also to be obtained from inscriptions and sculptured monuments of the heathen period.

(4) *Norway and Iceland.*—(*a*) For the religion of Norway and Iceland far more abundant information is available from the Icelandic sagas, the evidence of which varies greatly in value. First in importance are the *Íslendinga Sögur* ('Stories of the People of Iceland'), anonymous works written chiefly in the 13th cent., though a few may be slightly older. These are based on oral sagas—stories preserved by oral tradition in a more or less fixed form of words—from the latter part of the 10th and early 11th centuries. Among these special mention may be made of *Eyrbyggja Saga*, which in its early chapters gives an account of the religious practices of a certain Thórólfr of Mostr, who emigrated to Iceland *c.* 884 to escape from Harold the Fair-haired. Much information relating to religion is also given in *Egils Saga, Njáls Saga, Víga-Glúms Saga*. These sagas tell us not only of the religion of Iceland itself, but also of the homeland Norway both before and after the settlement. For throughout the period covered by the *Íslendinga Sögur* (till *c.* 1030) it was customary for Icelanders to visit the home country, and consequently the scene of the sagas is often laid in Norway.

Next in order to these come the *Stories of the Kings of Norway*, contained in the important collection known as the *Heimskringla* by Snorri Sturlason († 1241). As an authority for the period of Harold the Fair-haired, he is not inferior to the writers of the *Íslendinga Sögur*, but his account of earlier periods, contained in the first saga, *Ynglinga Saga*, is legendary. The longer sagas of *Olaf Tryggvason* and of *St. Olaf*, in the *Flateyjarbók* and in the *Fornmanna Sögur*, offer a large amount of additional information, which in general is of a more legendary character than Snorri's sagas of the same kings, but all these sagas deal primarily with Norway. Much information too about religious practices and beliefs is contained in various stories of ancient time—the *Fornaldar Sögur*—which, like the *Íslendinga Sögur*, are for the most part anonymous, but of which the authority is much inferior to that of the latter. In part they are derived from earlier poems, some of which are inserted in the text. But there is no doubt that much fiction is embodied in these stories. The most important are *Hervarar Saga ok Heidhreks Konungs* and *Gautreks Saga*.

(*b*) For Norse mythology the chief sources of information are the poems commonly known as the Older Edda, the MSS of which date only from the 13th century. The poems themselves, on the other hand, are for the most part considerably older, most of those on mythological subjects dating probably from the 10th cent. and even in some cases from the 9th, and belonging consequently to the heathen period. The poems which give us most information are *Völuspá, Vafthrúthnismál*, and *Grímnismál*. The first deals with the cosmogony and fate of the gods. The second is in the form of a dialogue on mythological lore between Othin and the giant Vafthrúthnir. The third is a monologue by the disguised Othin, who gradually reveals himself by his mythological knowledge. Next in order of importance are *Lokasenna*, another dialogue poem in which Loki attacks various gods and goddesses with scandalous charges; *Skírnismál*, which tells of the wooing of Gerthr for the god Freyr; *Hymiskvitha* and *Thrymskvitha*, descriptions of the adventures of the god Thor; *Vegtamskvitha* ('Balder's Dreams'), a dialogue between Thor and a ferryman supposed to be Othin; *Alvíssmál*, a dialogue between Thor and a dwarf; *Hyndluljóth*, a dialogue between the goddess Freyja and a giantess Hyndla. Much mythology is also contained in the philosophical poem *Hávamál*, and incidentally in some of the heroic poems in the same collection.

In addition to the Edda poems there have been preserved the so-called 'skaldic' poems dating from the 9th and 10th centuries by known authors. The earliest of these (early 9th cent.) are fragments of poetry by Bragi Boddason, some of which are preserved, and which we know come from *Ragnarsdrápa*. To the late 9th cent. belong the *Ynglingatál* and *Haustlöng* by Thjóthólfr of Hvín, a genealogical poem describing the ancestors of the Norwegian royal family. To the same century belongs the poet, Thórbjörn Hornklofi. The *Eiríksmál*, an incomplete poem whose authorship is unknown, describes the death of Eric Blood-axe shortly after 954.

There are also extant two poems by Eyvindr Skaldaspillir, the *Hákonarmál* recounting the death of Hákon I. in 960, a copy of the *Eiríksmál*, and the *Háleygjatál*, a genealogical poem dealing with the ancestors of the earls of Lathir, and modelled on *Ynglingatál*. References to mythology are also contained in many other poems.

It is to be noted that our knowledge of mythology comes almost entirely from Icelandic sources, for even the Norwegian poems—including the poems of the Edda, many of which were doubtless composed in Norway—are preserved only in Icelandic MSS. The chief reason for this phenomenon is doubtless to be found in the peculiar faculty for oral tradition developed in Iceland during the 11th cent. or slightly earlier, for which it would be difficult to find a parallel in Europe, except in Ireland. The unusual conditions under which Iceland was converted afford another reason, for there Christianity was not forced from above, as in countries with monarchical government. Indeed in Iceland there existed no strong central power which could effectively stamp out the observances and eradicate the remembrance of the old faith. The traditions of the heathen age survived the hostility of the Church in the 11th cent. and formed evidently a leading source of literary and antiquarian interest to subsequent generations.

A systematic account of Norse mythology is given in Snorri's Edda (commonly called the Prose Edda), the first part of which, *Gylfaginning* ('the Befooling of Gylfi'), is entirely devoted to the subject. Much mythology too is also introduced incidentally into the second part, *Skáldskaparmál* ('the Language of Poetry'). The chief authorities used by Snorri here are the poems of the Edda (*Völuspá, Vafthrúthnismál*, and *Grímnismál*). He makes use also of some lost poems and also no doubt of oral tradition.

Another account, which, however, has very little in common with the Edda, is given by the same author in the opening chapters of *Ynglinga Saga*. In it the gods are represented as having lived on earth as the rulers of the Swedes in ancient times—an account in which the euhemeristic element is prominent. A certain amount of mythological information also is afforded by the *Fornaldar Sögur*.

(*c*) The chief authority for the ethics of heathen times is the Edda poem called *Hávamál*, which, properly speaking, appears to be a composite work, made up of five different poems. In substance it may be compared with Hesiod's *Works and Days* or with the early Egyptian *Wisdom of Ptah-hetep*.[1] Such maxims occur in several other Edda poems, particularly in *Fáfnismál* and *Sigrdrífumál*. They are also common in the earliest Anglo-Saxon poems, though these do not often contain distinctively heathen precepts. The ethical standards of heathen times are no doubt faithfully portrayed in early Norse poetry and in sagas relating to the same period. With certain reservations the same may be said of *Beowulf* and other Anglo-Saxon poems.

4. Difficulties.—One of the greatest difficulties which the student of Teutonic mythology has to face is the question of how far the mythology and religious practices found in Iceland alone or in Iceland and Norway were shared also by the Danes and Swedes or by the Teutonic peoples in general. Indeed so little evidence is available, except for Iceland and Norway, that neither positive nor negative conclusions can be drawn with any confidence. Thus we have no information except from Norwegian-Icelandic sources of some of the more important deities, such as Freyja and Heimdallr; yet are we justified in assuming that these deities were unknown except in Norway and Iceland? One is forced to hesitate; for occasionally evidence is forthcoming for characters or conceptions which one might justifiably have assumed to be the creation of Norse literature. Othin's horse, Sleipnir—to quote one instance—is

[1] Tr. O. Elton, p. 5.

[1] Tr. by E. A. W. Budge ('Egyptian Library').

represented as having eight legs in Norse mythology, and we find a clear representation of such a horse on an engraved monument at Tjängvide, Götland.[1] The riding *valkyrjur* too (one of the most picturesque conceptions of Norse mythology) might well have been regarded as the creation of Norwegian poetry, had we not met with the same conception on a Swedish inscription at Rök; indeed with great probability it may be traced also in an Anglo-Saxon charm.

Another difficulty which confronts the student is that at first sight there appears to be an irreconcilable discrepancy between the account of Norse mythology given by Snorri and the references to religious beliefs and observances recorded in the *Íslendinga Sögur*. The former represents Othin as the chief and most important god of the Norse pantheon; and the early poems of the Edda and of the skalds agree with this representation. The *Íslendinga Sögur*, on the other hand, scarcely records a single instance of worship of Othin. In them Thor is by far the most prominent deity, and after him Freyr. It is only in the *Fornaldar Sögur* and in the other sagas relating to the legendary period[2] that we find Othin prominent. The explanation of this fact is probably that the worship of Othin and that of Thor belong to different classes of the population; the former was the god of the royal families and of their military followers, while the latter was the god of the free population in general. Kingship never existed in Iceland, and very few settlers appear to have been of royal blood, and consequently the god of this class of society, though still celebrated in poetry, does not seem to have received any actual worship.

Lastly, one characteristic of Norse mythology may doubtless be accounted for by the fact that so much of our information is drawn from Iceland. In peculiar contrast to the mythologies of other peoples, the Norse deities are not associated with particular localities, and herein no student can fail to contrast Norse and Greek mythologies. Freyr indeed is traditionally associated with Upsala, and there are indications which connect Gifjón with Sjaelland; but these instances are rare. The homes of the gods mentioned in the Edda poems—Breithablik, the home of Balder, Himinbjörg, the home of Heimdallr, etc.—seem to be purely mythical. Some evidence is to be found in place-names, however, that various deities were connected with localities in Norway, Sweden, and Iceland as well as with districts in other Teutonic lands. The reason for this comparative absence of local association is obviously to be found in the fact that by their emigration the colonists were cut off from the ancient sanctuaries of their race.

II. *GODS, SPIRITS, AND MYTHICAL BEINGS.*—Since Norse literature offers an abundance of material for the study of its mythology and religion, it seems almost necessary to make it the basis of any description of Teutonic mythology and religion. In the following account under each heading an attempt will be made to show also how far the testimony available for the mythology of the other Teutonic peoples is corroborative or discordant. In the first place, it is convenient to distinguish between (1) beings essentially mythical and (2) beings or phenomena in themselves natural but treated mythologically.

i. BEINGS ESSENTIALLY MYTHICAL.—This class consists of the following: (1) *aesir* (sing. *áss*) and *vanir*, (2) *jötnar* (sing. *jötunn*), (3) *dvergar* (sing. *dvergr*), (4) *álfar* (sing. *álfr*), (5) *nornir* (sing. *norn*), (6) *valkyrjur* (sing. *valkyrja*), (7) *fylgjur* (sing. *fylgja*), (8) *landvaettir*, (9) such impersonal conceptions as Yggdrasil's ash.

[1] Cf. Du Chaillu, *The Viking Age*, i. 58.
[2] Cf. *Ynglinga Saga*.

1. Aesir and vanir.—(*a*) *Norse.*—It is a peculiar characteristic of Norse mythology that it possesses two classes of gods. To the *aesir* belong Othin, his sons Thor, Balder, Vali, Vitharr,[1] his brothers Vili and Ve,[2] and others. To the *vanir* belong Njörthr and his children Freyr and Freyja. Possibly also to the same class belongs Heimdallr, for, though this is not altogether proved by *Thrymskvitha*, 14, yet the fact that he is often associated with Freyja, apparently as her guardian, points in this direction.[3]

The story of the relationship of the two sets of gods is told most fully in *Ynglinga Saga*, 4. There had been a war between them, which was eventually settled by an exchange of hostages. Njörthr and his children were given as hostages to the *aesir*, and Hoenir accompanied by Mímir was sent as a pledge to the *vanir*. This story, in part at least, is known to early poetry. In *Völuspá*, 24, it is suggested that the *vanir* were successful, while in *Vafthrúthnismál*, 39, we are told that Njörthr had been given as a hostage to the *aesir*, and that he would return home to the *vanir* at the '*Ragnar Rök*.'

Apart from the *vanir* the divine mythology is confined to the *aesir*, in which term all the gods collectively are included. With them there are goddesses, known comprehensively as *ásynjur*, the chief of whom is Frigg, wife of Othin. Often Freyja of the *vanir* is included with this group.[4]

Besides the *aesir* and the *vanir*, we find two deities who belong to neither class and who indeed are never brought into connexion with the Norse pantheon, viz. Thorgerthr Hölgabruthr and her sister Irpa. Their worship was very prominent in Norway during the last years of the heathen age, especially under Earl Hákon of Lathir, who ruled Norway from 975 to 995 and who was specially devoted to their cult. Of myths connected with them we have no mention in Norse literature except what is apparently a confused reminiscence in *Skáldskaparmál*, 45. Their story is told only by Saxo,[5] who says that Thora (Thorgerthr) is the daughter of Cuse (*i.e.* Gusi), king of the Lapps, and wife of Helgi, the eponymous hero of Halogaland. It is generally believed that these deities hail from the north of Norway, and their character is Finnish (Lappish) rather than Norse.

Under the lordship of Othin the gods form an organized community, which is evidently modelled after the fashion of the ancient Scandinavian community. They have a council of twelve, whose duty it is to keep up the sacrifices, to deliberate on the government of the country, and to judge between man and man.[6] Councils of this type are found in many early Scandinavian countries, and there can be little doubt that in heathen times they had religious as well as judicial functions. In *Grímnismál* the gods are said to meet daily at Yggdrasil's ash. From the same poem we learn that each of the gods had a home of his own, the names of which are apparently mythical and generally adapted to the character of the god, Breithablik for Balder, Alfheimr granted as a tooth gift (*at tannfé*) to Freyr, etc. The most frequently mentioned is Othin's home of Valhöll ('the hall of the slain'), where he, together with the valkyries, entertains hosts of slain warriors, who pass their days in combat and their nights in feasting. In *Gylfaginning*, 23, some verses are quoted indicating that Njörthr loves living by the sea-shore, while his wife Skathi, daughter of Thjazi, a *jötunn*, prefers to dwell in her father's home, the mountains. Wherefore a compact is made by which they divide their time between the two places—Njörthr's home is called here

[1] Cf. *Gylfaginning*, 30, 51; *Grímnismál*, 17.
[2] Cf. *Gylfaginning*, 6.
[3] Heimdallr's father is not mentioned, but he is said to be the son of nine mothers, whose names are enumerated in the closing stanzas of *Hyndluljóth*.
[4] See art. GOD (Teutonic).
[5] Tr. O. Elton, p. 87 ff.
[6] Cf. *Gylf.* 20.

Nóatún. The association of Freyr with Upsala does not belong to this category.

Besides their individual homes, the gods collectively are said to inhabit Asgarthr. Their meeting-place is called Ytha-völlr.[1] In *Gautreks Saga*, 7, the hero Starkathr is represented as attending a conference of them held in a forest clearing. The significance of this (together with Yggdrasil's ash and the fact that *völlr* originally meant 'wood') is seen below, § IV.

A totally different account of the gods is given by Snorri, curiously enough, in the early chapters of *Ynglinga Saga*. Here they are represented as men who had once lived on the earth and come to Sweden from S.E. Europe. Othin is represented as dying and being succeeded in the leadership of the gods by Njörthr, whose reign was marked by prosperity and peace. The latter on his death was succeeded by his son Freyr, whose reign was of the same character. Freyr was succeeded by his sister Freyja, and she in turn by Freyr's sons, grandsons, etc., who are no longer represented as gods.[2] This story is no doubt of euhemeristic origin, but the association of Freyr with Upsala is ancient and traditional. In Saxo he is represented as instituting the Upsala sacrifices and is said to be the ancestor of certain Swedish warriors. *Ynglinga Saga* itself is largely based on an early poem *Ynglingatál*, which traces the ancestry of the ancient Norwegian royal family through the Swedes to Freyr, who is no doubt to be identified with Fricco of Adam of Bremen's account.[3]

There are many stories relating the appearances of the gods to men. These occur most frequently in the *Fornaldar Sögur*, and the deity most mentioned is Othin.[4]

(*b*) *Danish and Swedish.*—On examining non-Norse sources, we find a number of the Norse gods mentioned by Saxo, including Woden (Othin), Thor, Freyr, Frigg, and Oller (Ullr), as well as Balder and Hoder (Höthr), who, however, are by him represented as demi-god and human being respectively. It is not always clear how far Saxo draws from Icelandic sources, but there can be little doubt that these deities were known to him from Danish tradition. Freyr is constantly associated with Upsala and Sweden, and Saxo is also the only authority who gives the story of Oller (Ullr).[5] With Saxo the home of the gods is sometimes called Byzantium, which apparently is used to translate Asgarthr.

With regard to Swedish beliefs, we have important earlier evidence in Adam of Bremen's description of the sanctuary at Upsala. This contained the images of three gods, Thor, Woden (*i.e.* Othin), and a deity Fricco, who is in all probability to be identified with Freyr. No stories of the gods are, however, recorded from Sweden. In much earlier times we have a short account of the religion of the people of Thule (*i.e.* Scandinavia) written by Procopius.[6] The only deity specially mentioned by him is Ares, and it is not clear whether by this name we are to understand Othin or Tyr. An early trace of worship of Freyr may be preserved in the name Prove(n)—the god among the Wagri of N.E. Holstein.[7]

(*c*) *English.*—For the mythology of the heathen English we have little or no information except that to be obtained from names. The A.S. word *os*, corresponding to the O.N. *áss*, occurs as the name of one of the letters of the Runic alphabet (though here apparently its meaning is forgotten).[8] It also is to be found very frequently in personal names, as in Oswald, and the plural form occurs only in the genitive *esa* in an A.S. charm.[9] The form *van-* does not occur, except rarely in personal names—*e.g.*, Wanraed—unless this is possibly the origin of the prefix *wan-* in *wanseoc* ('epileptic'), in which case we might compare *elf-adl* in Saxon *Leechdoms*,[1] ii. 344. 20.

Othin's name also is preserved—A. S. Woden—as the ancestor of all the royal families except that of Essex, which traced its genealogy to a certain Seaxneat. His name is also preserved in 'Wednesday' (as a translation of 'Mercurius'). Thunor (O.N. Thorr) is known only from 'Thursday' (where his name is used to translate 'Juppiter') and from certain place-names, *e.g.*, Thunresleah and Thunresfeld.[2]

The name of Fri (*i.e.* Frigg) is preserved only in 'Friday' (as translation of 'Venus'), and Ti (Tiig) (O.N. Tyr) occurs in glossaries as translation of 'Mars,' and, like *os*, is the name of one of the letters of the Runic alphabet. His name is preserved also in 'Tuesday.' In Bede's account of the heathen English calendar two months (corresponding to March and April) are said to derive their names from goddesses called Rheda (Href?) and Eostre (Eastre). The existence of these deities has been doubted by some modern writers. We also find a reference, in a charm which appears to be a mixture of Christian and heathen beliefs, to Erce ('Mother of Earth'), with which we may compare Semnes Mate (Lettish).

Lastly, mention may be made of Ing, the name of one of the letters in the Runic alphabet. In the verses dealing with Ing he is said to have been seen first among the East Danes, but afterwards he went east over the sea, his car speeding after him.

(*d*) *German.*—With regard to German mythology, a fragment relating to gods is preserved in one of the Merseburg charms, in which we are told that Wodan and 'Phol' were riding to the forest when the pastern joint of the latter's horse was dislocated. Various deities tried by their incantations to put it right. The names mentioned are Frija and her sister Volla,[3] and Sinthgund and her sister Sunna. The only other myth recorded occurs in certain Langobardic writings and is rather striking.

'The two tribes of Vandals and Langobardi (then called Winniles) appealed to the gods for victory in their war with each other. The Vandals approached Woden, who replied: "Whatsoever I shall first look upon when the sun rises, to them will I give victory." The Winniles appealed to Frija, wife of Woden, who gave counsel that at sunrise the women of the Winniles should come with their husbands and let down their hair about their faces, like beards. And when Woden saw the Winniles women, he said: "Who are these Longbeards?" And Frija replied: "As thou hast given them a name give them also victory." And he gave them victory.'[4]

Apart from these references, the gods are known from the names of the week: Donar (O.N. Thorr; A.S. Thunor) throughout the German area; Fria (Frigg, Fri) at least in the greater part of German area; Wodan (Othin, Woden) only in the north-west and in Holland; Tiu (Ti, Tir) only in the south-west. Occasional references to the gods are also found in lives of missionary saints. Thus the worship of Wodan among the Alamanni is mentioned in Jona's *Life of Columbanus*, while in other cases German deities are no doubt intended by old names such as Juppiter. In a formula used after baptism and commonly supposed to have come from the region of the Old Saxons (though the language is rather peculiar) the convert is required to abjure Wodan and Thunor and Saxnot together with other monsters (*Unholden*) associated with them. This Saxnot is doubtless to be identified with the name that stands at the head of the genealogy of Essex. Lastly, in Alcuin's *Life of St. Willibrord* we hear of a god called Fosite. He was worshipped on a certain island, called after him and identified

1 *Gylf.* 24.
2 Cf. Saxo, tr. O. Elton, p. 228, 'sons of Frey.'
3 Cf. *Hist. of the Church of Hamburg*, iv. 26.
4 *Völsunga Saga*, ch. 11; *ib.* ch. 17; *Viga-Glúms Saga*, 26; cf. *Fornmanna Sögur*, xi. 134.
5 See art. God (Teutonic).
6 *Gothic War*, ii. 15.
7 Cf. Helmoldus, *Chron. Slavorum*, 153. 70. 84.
8 Cf. *Runenlied*, str. 10, C. W. M. Grein, *Bibliothek der angelsächs. Poesie*, ed. R. P. Wülcher, Leipzig, 1881–98, i.
9 *Ib.* p. 318.

1 Ed. T. O. Cockayne, *Leechdoms, Wortcunning and Starcraft of Early England*, 3 vols., London, 1864–66.
2 Cf. Thundersleigh in Essex and Thundersfield in Surrey.
3 Cf. 'Fulla' of Norse mythology.
4 *Origo gentis Langobardarum.*

by Adam of Bremen with Halogaland.[1] Grimm and others have identified this deity with Forsete, the son of Balder,[2] but discrepancies in the spelling of the two names offer difficulty.

In Gothic no names of deities have been preserved, unless we place in this category the name of the Runic letter Enguz (A.S. Ing). The word *ansis*, however (O.N. *aesir*), is mentioned by Jordanes in a curiously interesting connexion. He states that the Goths called their chiefs to whose good fortune they thought they owed their victory, 'non puros homines sed semideos id est anses.'[3] In earlier times Tacitus,[4] though unfortunately he seldom mentions Teutonic gods by their native names, twice mentions Mars and Mercurius among the deities of the Germans, and in the *Germania* specially mentions Mercurius as the deity most worshipped by them. There can be no doubt that the deities meant are the later Ziu and Wodan (N. Tir and Othin). In ch. 9 too he mentions Hercules and in *Annals*, ii. 12, a grove sacred to him. It is not so easy to ascertain the identity of this deity. Some modern writers believe Donar (O.N. Thorr; A.S. Thunor) to be intended; others think the reference is to a tribal deity.[5] In the same chapter Tacitus states that some of the Suevi worship with the symbol of a ship. Here again we are left in doubt as to the identity of the deity. Perhaps we may include the 'templum Tamfanæ' mentioned in *Annals*, i. 51, and 'lucum quem Baduhennae vocant' in iv. 73, if these be the names of deities. In *Germ.* 43 he speaks of a grove in which Castor and Pollux are worshipped under the name of deities. The fullest account, however, of a Teutonic deity is that of Nerthus,[6] who was worshipped by certain maritime peoples including the English, and whose sanctuary was situated on an island, the position of which is not clearly stated by Tacitus but is probably to be placed in the S.W. Baltic. It is to be observed that the name Nerthus is identical with the O.N. Njörthr, and, in spite of the difference in sex, we need scarcely doubt their original identity. Rites similar to those which Tacitus describes in connexion with Nerthus are associated with Freyr, son of Njörthr.

Apart from Tacitus, practically the only references to Teutonic deities occur in inscriptions upon altars raised by soldiers in the Roman service. Besides Mars, these inscriptions sometimes record a deity Nehalennia with the prow of a ship, and this may point to the identification with the Isis of Tacitus. In the introduction to *Germ.* 2 Tacitus states that in their ancient poems the Germans trace the origin of their race to a god called Tuisto ('son of earth'). His son was Mannus (? 'man'), and he again had three sons from whom three groups of peoples were named and descended—the Ingaevones (or Inguaeones), Ermi[n]ones, Istaevones. These group-names are mentioned also by Pliny the Elder, and a genealogy of the kind classifying Teutonic and other peoples is found in Merovingian times. We have no trace elsewhere of any god or hero called Istio, but there is some slight evidence for an Irmen. The name Ingaevones (or Inguaeones) is undoubtedly to be connected with A.S. Ing, who is associated in tradition with the Danes and with the titles Inguina Eodor and Frea Inguina, used in *Beowulf* of the king of the Danes. It is further to be noticed that in Norse the god Freyr and his descendants sometimes bear the title Yngvi, the full title of the god being Yngvi-Freyr or Ingunar-Freyr. His descendants—the ancient kings of Sweden—are known collectively as Ynglingar. It will be seen that there is some discrepancy between Norse and English tradition, the former connecting the name with Sweden, the latter with Denmark. Whatever may be the explanation of this, the association of the word with Freyr, the son of Njörthr, seems to point to some connexion with the worship of Nerthus—a conclusion which is confirmed by the fact that Tacitus, with whom Pliny is substantially in agreement, describes the Ingaevones as 'proximi oceano.'

2. Jötnar.—(*a*) *Norse.*—Giants or monsters play an important part in the stories of Norse mythology. When viewed collectively, they are called *jötnar* or *thursar*. Sometimes also we hear of the *hrimthursar* ('frost-giants') and *bergrisar* ('cliff-giants'). Most often, however, they appear singly, and the corresponding feminine form of the word *jötunn* is *gygr*. Unlike the *aesir*, they do not appear to form an organized community as a whole, though sometimes individual *jötnar* (like Thrymr, 'Lord of the Thursar') seem to have communities under their dominion. The home of the giants is known as Jötunheimar, lying, according to early story, far to the north-east, remote from Asgarthr, the home of the *aesir*. The general characteristics of the giants were huge form and superhuman strength.

The story of Skrymnir[1] tells dramatically how huge and strong a giant was conceived to be in Norse literature. For the god Thor took refuge one night in the thumb of one of his gloves, and, when he attempted to kill the giant with a blow of his hammer, Skrymnir only asked whether a leaf had fluttered down into his face.

Although the giants may have had monster shapes, it seems clear that sometimes the giantesses were deemed very beautiful, as in the case of Gerthr, to whose radiant beauty Freyr lost his heart.

It is necessary to distinguish between anthropomorphic and theriomorphic giants, though it is difficult to draw a definite line between them; *e.g.*, Loki has theriomorphic children. Many of the former class are mentioned in myth, the best known being Thrymr, Hymir, Hrungnir, Geirröthr, and Thjazi, all of whom fight with Thor, and are slain by him.

Sometimes the *jötnar* are on friendly terms with the *aesir*: Hyrrokin, a giantess, attended Balder's funeral, and it was through an appeal to her strength that the funeral ship was able to be launched. Further, we find a number of marriages between gods and giants; Njörthr married Skathi, the daughter of Thjazi.[2] Freyr married Gerthr, daughter of Gymir; and even Thor, despite his general hostility, had a son Magni by a giantess Jarn-Saxa. This giantess, with others, including the daughter of Geirröthr, appears as the mother of Heimdallr in *Hyndluljóth*, but this part of the poem (the short *Völuspá*) is commonly believed to be a late composition. The giants too are often represented as wanting to marry *ásynjur*; Thjazi carries off Ithunn, and Freyja was sued for by Thrymr. It may here be mentioned that anthropomorphic giants often had the power to assume the form of animals. In the incident referred to above Thjazi assumes the form of an eagle, and in *Vafthrúthnismál*, 37, the wind-demon Hraesvelgr is described as a *jötunn* in the shape of an eagle.

Although the giants are presumably gifted with tremendous physical strength, they are not always lacking in intelligence, for we have the incident of Othin's visit to the giant Vafthrúthnir in order to learn of his store of wisdom.

The chief theriomorphic *jötnar* are the Mithgarthsormr, or Jörmundgandr, and the Fenrisulfr, both of whom together with Hel are said to be the offspring of Loki and the giantess Angrbotha ('she who bodes distress'). Mithgarthsormr is represented in *Gylfaginning*, 34, as a kind of vast sea-serpent stretching round the earth. In *Hymiskvitha*, 23, Thor goes fishing and catches it on his hook. Fenrisulfr is a wolf which the gods succeed after great difficulty in fettering, though not until he has bitten off Tyr's hand, which has been placed in his mouth as a pledge of the good faith of the gods.[3] At the end of the world he will burst his bonds and attack the gods in conjunction with Mithgarthsormr, Loki, Surtr (a fire-demon), and other monsters. Although usually found in the company of the *aesir*, it would seem that Loki belonged to the *jötnar*. Here also we should perhaps mention Ægir, also called Hlér, a sea being, who is on friendly terms with the gods and visits them.[4] From *Fornaldar Sögur*, ii. 17, it seems clear that he was the son of Fornjotr, and in *Hymiskvitha*, 1, 2, he is described as a *berg-búi* ('cliff-dweller'), an epithet which is elsewhere synonymous with *jötunn*. His wife is called Ran,

[1] Cf. Adam of Bremen, *De Situ Daniae*.
[2] Cf. *Gylf.* 32. [3] Ch. 13.
[4] *Ann.* xiii. 57; *Germ.* 9.
[5] For Irmen cf. below, IV. (*f*) (ii.).
[6] *Germ.* 40.

[1] Cf. *Gylf.* 45.
[2] According to *Háleygjatál*, she was later also the wife of Othin.
[3] Cf. *Gylf.* 34.
[4] Cf. *Lokasenna* (prose introduction); *Bragaroethur*, 55.

and is said to have a net in which she catches all who perish in the sea. There is a suggestion too from the story in *Frithjófs Saga*, 6, that a man fearing death by drowning would do well to carry gold on his person in order to be received well in the halls of Ran.[1]

Apart from mythological works monsters are not infrequently mentioned both in the *Íslendinga Sögur* and in sagas of the kings, as well as in the *Fornaldar Sögur*, though they are more usually called *tröll* than *jötnar*.

As examples we may refer to the two demons (male and female) at Sand Haugar in the north of Iceland encountered by Grettir;[2] the female demon who ate eleven merchants in a rest house in the Norwegian mountains;[3] and the monster Brusi and his mother in the form of a black cat encountered by Ormr Stórolfsson in the *Saga of Olaf Tryggvason*.

In those *Fornaldar Sögur* which deal with the north of Norway, viz. *Ketil Saga Haengs* and *Grims Saga Lothinkinna*, monsters are frequently mentioned. It may be noticed that Thorgerthr Hölgabrúthr once appears among them,[4] and Saxo's *Danish History* abounds with such stories. Tales like these recall Procopius's remark: 'The rest of the inhabitants of Thule . . . worship many gods and demons in heaven and in air and in sea and certain other daemonias which are said to be in the waters of springs and rivers.'

A spring was the home of Mímir. His story is given in *Ynglinga Saga*, 4, where the *aesir* send him with Hoenir as pledges to the *vanir*, who cut off his head and return it to the *aesir*. Othin then smears the head with worts to preserve it and keeps it for divining purposes. In *Völuspá*, 45, Othin is said to converse with Mímir's head. We are told further[5] that under one of the roots of Yggdrasil's ash is Mímisbrunnr ('Mímir's spring'), in which are hidden cunning and wisdom. Othin came to the brook asking a drink and was refused until he left his eye as a pledge. This he granted, and in *Völuspá*, 28, the sybil says: 'Mímir drinks mead every morning from the pledge of Othin.'

A reference to a Miming is made by Saxo[6] in his story of Balder and Höthr. Here Miming is called the 'silvarum satyrus,' and is said to have in his possession a sword and magic bracelets, the former of which alone of all swords will prevail against the charmed life of Balder. At the beginning of *Thithreks Saga* too Mímir is the name of the smith, teacher of both Sigfrit and Velint. It is to be noted also that Miming was the name of Weland's famous sword in the poem of *Waldhere*.

Perhaps originally Mímir was famed for his wisdom, but later tradition laid stress on his skill in smith's work. His name is preserved in modern Swedish folk-lore—Mímis-sjö and Mímis-ä ('sea of Mímir' and 'river of Mímir'), both of which preserve his connexion with water. His name is also mentioned in the mediæval German poem *Biterölf* as 'Mîme the old.'

(*b*) *Anglo-Saxon.*—The A.S. forms corresponding to the Norse *jötunn* and *thurs* are *eoten* and *thyrs*, and both terms are applied in *Beowulf* to the monster Grendel, who with his mother dwells under a pool in the fens and makes attacks on the hall of the Danish king whose knights he devours. As far as we can gather, these beings are anthropomorphic. The story of Beowulf's encounters is clearly to be connected with those of Grettir and of Ormr Stórolfsson and presumably has its origin in a folk-tale. In A.S. literature ancient weapons are sometimes described as being made by the giants.[7] In the *Gnomic Verses*, which form the introduction to the Abingdon text of the *Anglo-Saxon Chronicle*, the *thyrs* is said to have his home in the fens.

1 For Ymir, the primeval giant out of whose flesh the world was made, see art. COSMOGONY AND COSMOLOGY (Teutonic).
2 *Grettis Saga*, ch. 65.
3 *Saga of Olaf the Holy* (*Heimskringla*), 151.
4 *Ketil Saga Haengs*, 5.
5 *Gylf.* 15 (drawn from *Völuspá*, 29).
6 P. 85.
7 '*Eald sweord eotenisc*' (*Beowulf*, l. 1558). The same expression is used for buildings of the past: 'Visible from afar are the (cities) skilfully built by the giants.'

(*c*) *German.*—There is no doubt that these monsters were known also in Germany, where we find for them the words *duris* (i.e. *thurs*) and *risi*. No stories dating from very early times happen to have been preserved, but mediæval German poetry and legend abound with references to such beings.[1]

3. Dvergar.—(*a*) *Norse.*—*Dvergar* is the name given collectively to the dwarfs in Old Norse literature, and to many of them are assigned individual names in *Völuspá*, 15 ff., where also their creation is mentioned. In *Gylfaginning*, 14, Snorri tells us that they first received life as maggots in the flesh of Ymir, but were endowed with intelligence by the gods, and given human shape. The *dvergar* were said to live either down in the earth or more frequently in stones (rocks), in front of which they were sometimes seen in the evening.

Svegdir one evening at sunset saw a dwarf sitting under a stone, and, when the dwarf called him to go into the stone, he assented, whereupon it shut behind him and naught has been heard of him since.[2]

It is perhaps to their connexion with rocks that the word for echo—*dvergmál* ('dwarf-speech')—owes its origin. In Norse literature they were renowned particularly for their skill in metal-work, and many were the wonderful things fashioned by their hands—so much so that a compound word has been formed to denote great skill, viz. *dverg-hagr*.[3]

On most occasions the dwarfs appear in human form, though small, but in *Reginsmál* Andvari lives in a water-fall in the shape of a pike and is caught in that form by Loki, who borrows Ran's net for the purpose. It is from him that Loki gets the gold required to ransom himself and his companions, Othin and Hoenir, from Hraethmarr, and this incident afterwards plays an important part in the *Völsunga Saga*. After this episode Andvari withdraws into the stone and curses all who shall possess the gold.

Possibly, too, 'Mimingus, sylvarum satyrus' mentioned by Saxo is associated with dwarfs, and possibly this Miming is identical with Völundr or Weland, the most famous of all smiths.

(*b*) The word corresponding to O.N. *dvergr* is to be found in all languages of the Teutonic peoples extant—O.H.G. *twerg*, A.S. *dweorh*. In A.S. literature we find a charm against a dwarf. Dwarfs also figure in German folk-lore. Thus in the *Seyfriedslied* the treasure which the hero won again after killing the dragon belonged in reality to some dwarfs, sons of Nybling.

4. Álfar.—For these see art. DEMONS AND SPIRITS (Teutonic), vol. iv. p. 633.

5. Nornir.—For these see art. DOOM, DOOM MYTHS (Teutonic).

6. Valkyrjur.—(*a*) *Norse.*—Valkyries, or 'choosers of the slain,' were supernatural maidens sent by Othin to determine the course of battles and to choose warriors for Valhöll. They are also known as *valmeyjar*, *skjoldmeyjar*, and *óskmeyjar*, and in *Völuspá*, 31—if the phrase is not an interpolation—they are called *nönnur herjans*. By the Edda poems, *Grímnismál*, 36, and *Völuspá*, 31, we are given certain information about them, and of the former poem Snorri has made use in *Gylf.* 36. In *Grímnismál* our attention is drawn mainly to one aspect of the valkyries—their duties in Valhöll; for Othin is represented in the poem as crying to his maidens to bear him the ale as they do to the *einherjar*, when they are feasting in the evening in the hall. Here we have the names of thirteen valkyries given.

Snorri inserts this stanza from *Grímnismál* in his elaborate account of Valhöll in *Gylf.* 38, expanding it in prose and adding that Othin sends these maidens to battle. He specially mentions

1 Cf. art. DEMONS AND SPIRITS (Teutonic), vol. iv. p. 634.
2 *Ynglinga Saga*, 15; also *Hervarar Saga*, 2.
3 See art. DEMONS AND SPIRITS (Teutonic), vol. iv. p. 633b.

Guthr, Rosta, and Skuld, the youngest norn, as undertaking this work. It is this function of the valkyries that the poet of *Völuspá* deals with in str. 31 of the poem. He gives us a picture of a band of valkyries, six in number and named, equipped and ready to ride into battle. From other references in Norse literature we learn that they were seen riding through the air and over the sea ('*lopt ok lög*'), white and shining with their helmets, shields, and spears—a splendid company of maiden warriors.[1]

With the valkyries may perhaps be compared the Slavic conception of the *vila*, who was thought to ride a seven-year-old stag and bridle him with snakes. The characteristic, attributed to her by the Slavs, of discharging fatal darts at men while in the air is especially interesting when compared with a similar reference in an A.S. charm.[2]

Other valkyries, who became the wives and lovers of heroes, and are represented as human in origin, although included by Othin among his battle-maidens, are mentioned below.[3] From a story in Saxo[4] we hear of maidens called 'nymphæ sylvestres,' who seem to be valkyries.

Hotherus (O.N. Höthr), the enemy of Balder, was hunting in a wood when he came to a lodge where he was greeted by certain wood-maidens. They told him that it was their lot to determine the fortunes of war and that often they secretly assisted their friends in battle, and gained for them the victory.

Since the valkyries were so closely bound up with the fate of warriors and the issue of battles, it is clear that they cannot be entirely dissociated from the norns. The close relationship between the two conceptions is clearly seen in the poem given in *Njáls Saga*, 156.

There in the accompanying prose account a certain Darruthr saw women riding twelve together to a bower, and, looking within, he saw that they had set up a loom of which 'men's heads served for weights, men's entrails for the weft and warp, a sword for the *skeith*, and an arrow for the *hrsell*.' They sang at their work and in their song seemed to describe themselves as valkyries, and finally they rode away, six to the south and six to the north.

Moreover, in *Gylf.* 36 Skuld, the 'youngest norn,' is included among the valkyries. In contrast with the norns, however, the valkyries are in Norse mythology associated chiefly with Othin, whose messengers they are, though in one passage quoted from Saxo they seem to assist Hother, who is an enemy of the gods.

(*b*) *Anglo-Saxon.*—In A.S. literature we find on several occasions the word *waelcyrge* (O.N. *valkyrjur*). In glossaries[5] it is glossed 'Erinys,' 'Bellona,' 'Tisiphone.' In Wulfstan's *Sermo ad Anglos* the *waelcyrge* are classed together with other undesirable people, and in a charm mention is made of certain women who ride over the land and array their forces. They hurl darts at human beings, who are thereupon seized with sudden pain. The word *waelcyrge* is not mentioned in the latter example, but there can be little doubt that the lines refer to them.

(*c*) *German.*—In German the word does not occur, though the idea does in the Merseburg charm, where they are called *idisi*. They are represented as fastening bonds, holding back the host, and tugging at the fetters.

7. Fylgjur.—For these see art. SOUL (Teutonic).

8. Landvaettir.—Just as the *fylgja* presided over the individual, so the *landvaettir* presided over the country as its tutelary spirits. A certain number of references are to be found to them in Norse literature, not the least interesting being the heathen law mentioned in the *Landnámabók*, iv. 7, which ordered that figure-heads of ships were to be removed on approaching the island, lest they should frighten the *landvaettir* with their 'yawning heads and gaping snouts.' In *Egils Saga*, 57, Egill turns a curse against the *landvaettir* of Norway in order to force them to drive away King Eric and Queen Gunnhildr, from whom he was fleeing. Sometimes *landvaettir* seemed to favour certain individuals, as was the case with Björn, the he-goat whom they accompanied to the assembly, while his brothers were accompanied by them when hunting and fishing.[1]

The *landvaettir* seem not always to be very clearly distinguished from the *fylgjur* of individuals; *e.g.*, in the *Saga of Olaf Tryggvason* (*Heimskringla*), 36, it seems to be suggested that the *landvaettir* of Iceland seen by the wizard are connected in some way with the great chiefs of the land. The word *vaettr* (pl. *vaettir*) is identical with A.S. *wiht*, 'creature,' etc., although the latter has not the specialized meaning of Old Norse. For the idea itself we may refer to the *genius loci* of the Romans.

9. Yggdrasil's ash. — Our information for Yggdrasil's ash is mainly derived from *Völuspá*, 19, 20, 27, and *Grímnismál*, 29–35. References also occur in *Fjölsvinnsmál*, 13–18. From *Völuspá* we learn that the ash Yggdrasil stands ever green over the well of Urthr ('Fate'), and from it falls dew into the vales beneath. Under this tree dwell the three norns. In *Grímnismál* not only do we learn that the *aesir* go daily to the judgment-seat under the ash, but we are given many details about its appearance.

It has three roots stretching in three directions. Hel dwells under one, the frost-giants under a second, and under the third the children of men. Its branches are the home of an eagle, a hawk, and a squirrel Ratatöskr, who bears messages to Nithhöggr dwelling below. Four harts gnaw the topmost branches, and many are the serpents which lie under its boughs.

In *Gylf.* 15f. Snorri adds that in the spring of Fate dwell two swans, from whom are sprung all birds of that race, and also from the branches of the ash drops dew called 'honey-dew,' on which bees feed. The ash is sometimes called Yggdrasil, Askr Yggdrasils. Laeráthr, Mjotvithr, and Mímameithr seem to be names for the same tree. In both *Grímnismál* and *Fjölsvinnsmál* we have indications that the ash is being gradually destroyed; a hart bites it from above, it rots in its side, and Nithhöggr gnaws it from beneath. And, according to *Völuspá*, 47f., when the last days come, it will shiver and groan. The golden foliaged Glasir which stands by 'Sigtyr's halls'[2] is perhaps to be identified with it. One other striking passage must be mentioned—*Hávamál*, 138, in which Othin is described as hanging on that tree of which no one knows from whose roots it proceeds.

A similar conception to that of a world-tree is certainly to be found among other Teutonic peoples—*e.g.*, among the Old Saxons, who worshipped the Irmensul. Several features in Adam of Bremen's description of the tree beside the temple of Upsala also recall Yggdrasil's ash.[3]

ii. NATURAL THINGS VIEWED MYTHOLOGICALLY.—**1. Day and night.**—From references in *Vafthrúthnismál*, 13, 25, Night, the daughter of Nörr, is depicted as driving across the sky her chariot and horse Hrímfaxi, from whose bit falls the spume which makes the dew in the valleys. Of Day we are only told that he is born of Dellingr. In *Gylf.* 10 Snorri gives further genealogical details.[4] In *Alvíssmál*, 30, is given a list of names by which Night is known among the *jötnar*, elves, and gods. In the document *Hversu Noregr Bygthist* we find a genealogy traced back to Swan the Red, son of Dagr, son of Dellingr, and of Sól, daughter of Mundilfari. For the personification of Night and Day, we may compare

1 *Helgakvitha Hjörvarthssonar*, 28, and *Hákonarmál*, *pass.*; cf. art. DEMONS AND SPIRITS (Teutonic), vol. iv. p. 633a.
2 Cf. below, § II. i. 6 (*b*).
3 Cf. below, § II. ii. 9. For the valkyries as swan-maidens see art. SWAN-MAIDENS.
4 P. 84.
5 Cotton MS, Vitellius A 15.

1 Cf. *Landnámabók*, iv. 12.
2 Cf. *Skáldskaparmál*, 36.
3 Cf. schol. 134 to Adam of Bremen.
4 See art. SUN, MOON, AND STARS (Teutonic and Balto-Slavic).

Greek mythology, especially the allusions to the chariots of the Sun and the Moon.[1]

2. Sun and moon.—For these see art. SUN, MOON, AND STARS (Teutonic and Balto-Slavic).

3. Rainbow.—To the old Norse people the rainbow was the bridge built by the gods to span the space between earth and heaven. Bifröst or Ásbru was its name, and it was triple-hued. Though it is made with cunning and of great strength, Snorri tells[2] that the day will come when it shall be broken. This bridge is referred to as Bifröst in the Older Edda, though it is not explicitly identified with the rainbow. In *Gylf.* 27 Heimdallr is named as guarding it against the frost and cliff giants.[3]

4. Winds and seasons.—In *Vafthrúthnismál*, 27, 37, references are made to the winds and seasons. The winds, according to the poet, arise from beneath the wings of the giant Hraesvelgr, who sits at the end of heaven in the likeness of an eagle. In *Vafth.* 27 Vindsvalr is said to be the father of Winter and Svasudhr of Summer. In *Gylf.* 18 f. Snorri gives further details, explaining that the difference between Summer and Winter is to be accounted for by the difference of parentage, for each has inherited the disposition of his father.

5. Thor.—In the preceding paragraphs we have been dealing with mythological conceptions which are scarcely distinguished from the natural bodies or phenomena which have given rise to them. There can be no doubt, however, that other mythological conceptions originated from similar phenomena in early times, though their identity with these was subsequently forgotten. Thus the name of the god Thor is identical with the word for 'thunder' preserved in English and German. The identity was practically forgotten in Norse owing largely to the fact that the word had gone out of use, but it is clearly preserved in Adam of Bremen's account of the Upsala sanctuary, where he speaks of Thor, 'qui tonitrus et fulmina . . . gubernat.'[4] We may refer also to the 'malleos joviales' which were carried off by the Danish prince Magnus on one of his raids among the Swedish islands, and which, according to Saxo,[5] had been venerated as symbols of thunder.

In English and German the name of the god is not distinguished, and consequently with the small evidence at our disposal it is not always clear which of the two was meant. The thunder-god (especially personifications of thunder) is of course wide-spread among the people of Europe. It is sufficient here to refer to the Taranis of the Celts (whose name appears to be identical with that of the Scandinavian Thorr), Juppiter Tonans of the Romans, Zeus Keraunios of the Greeks.

6. Othin.—Many writers hold that Othin originated in a personification of the wind. This view is largely bound up with the association of the god with the raging host, the antiquity of which is not very clear. The name Woden itself, which seems originally to have meant 'inspired or frenzied,' hardly furnishes a parallel to the case of Thor.

7. Jötnar.—It has been supposed by many writers that not only gods but also *jötnar* largely owe their origin to personification of natural phenomena. The *hrímthursar* ('frost-giants') indeed, of whom we often hear collectively, can hardly be of other origin. The friendly *jötunn* Aegir is very closely associated with the sea, for which his name is often used in poetry. There is some reason also for suspecting that Thrymr, the *jötunn* who steals Thor's hammer, may originally have been a counterpart of Thor, a rival thunder-god. It has been proposed by some that the *eoten* Grendel in *Beowulf* arose from a personification of storm-floods, but this explanation is open to the objection that the story is clearly based on an early folk-tale, the original locality of which has not yet been determined. If the *jötnar* in general had been derived from the personification of natural phenomena, one would expect to find an obvious meaning for their names, as in the case of Thor and perhaps of Thrymr, but as a matter of fact the etymology of the majority of their names is quite obscure.

According to another view, which has obtained more currency in recent times, the *jötnar* largely represent the communities of a more primitive race or civilization. This view also can be justified in some cases by the records. The giant Hrungnir fights against Thor with a hone, which may perhaps represent a stone hammer, and the word *berg-búi* ('cliff-dweller') points in the same direction. In some stories, as in the case of Grendel, the *jötnar* have cannibal propensities, and for this practice there is thought to be evidence in the way human bones are found mixed with those of animals in some caves. We may note also that the name Heithr is sometimes applied to witches of 'Finnish' (Lappish) origin, while in *Hyndluljóth* Heithr is said to be the daughter of the *jötunn* Hrungnir.

Occasionally also the word *jötunn* is applied in some MSS to persons also described as *Finnar*, as in the case of Swasi, father-in-law of Harold the Fair-haired. In the genealogies given in a document *Hversu Noregr Bygthist* some connexion is hinted at between *Finn* and *jötunn*. With the evidence at our disposal we are not yet in a position to determine their origin. It has been suggested also that the *dvergar* may be derived from communities of more primitive inhabitants.

8. Nornir.—The *nornir* bear so close a resemblance to the *völur*[1] ('wise women'), not infrequently mentioned in the sagas, that there can be little doubt that they are at least partly derived from them. Sometimes indeed the words *norn* and *völva* are used interchangeably.

9. Valkyrjur.—It is not unlikely that the *valkyrjur* have a similar origin. Sometimes the name is applied to human beings endowed with supernatural powers, as, *e.g.*, to Svava, the heroine of *Helgakvitha Hjörvarthssonar*, and to Sigrun in *Helgakvitha Hunding-bana II.*, and to Sigrdrifa, a valkyrie who was punished by Othin for not carrying out his commands. And, as most authorities identify her with Brynhildr, the term is applied to the latter also. This conception of human valkyries is not confined to the North. For, in Wulfstan's *Sermo ad Anglos*, *waelcyrgean* are mentioned beside *wiccean*, among a list of bad characters, from which the country is said to be suffering.[2] It is more difficult, however, to explain how the conception arose. We hear of fighting women more than once in Saxo, and the human *skjáldmeyjar* in the *Atlakvitha* point perhaps in the same direction.

10. Kings.—Among other human beings we may notice especially kings who were credited with supernatural powers both during their lives and after death. Two of the legendary kings of Sweden, Dómaldi and Olaf Trételgja, are said to have been put to death owing to bad harvests for which they were held responsible.[3] This belief lasted down to late times, since Gustavus Vasa is

[1] *E.g.*, Homeric *Hymns*, xxxi. 15 f., xxxii. 9 f., and, in particular, *Od.* xxiii. 244 ff. Cf. also 2 K 23[11].
[2] *Gylf.* 13.
[3] For reference to the rainbow in other mythologies we may compare *PC*[3] i. 298.
[4] iv. 26.
[5] *Gesta Danorum*, ed. A. Holder, Strassburg, 1886, p. 421.

[1] See art. DEMONS AND SPIRITS (Teutonic), vol. iv. p. 632[a].
[2] Cf. II. i. 6 (*b*).
[3] *Ynglinga Saga*, 18.

said to have complained that the Swedes blamed him for bad weather. Nor was it peculiar to the North. According to Ammianus Marcellinus, xxviii. 5. 14, it was customary among the Burgundians to depose their kings in time of famine as well as after military disaster.

11. The dead.—Norse literature shows by constant reference that to the dead were attributed supernatural powers. Among those most commonly referred to is that of bringing prosperity and abundant harvest.

In *Ynglinga Saga*, 12, the god Freyr is said to die, but his death is not announced to his subjects the Swedes. His dead body was preserved that prosperity might abound in the land. A similar story is told about Halfdan the Black, for his body after death was cut in four pieces, which were buried in different parts of the kingdom, so that all sections of the land might have plenteous years.[1] A similar belief underlies the story of Olaf Geirstatha-alf,[2] and that of Guthmundr,[3] who after death was thought by his people to be a god, and was therefore worshipped. Yet another example is to be found in *Landnámabók*, i. 14, where Thórólfr Smjörr is mentioned as being worshipped after death. A curious instance of worship of the dead occurs in *Kristni Saga*, 2, where the missionary Thorvaldr is taken by a heathen Kodran to see a stone in which the ancestor (*ár-madhr* or *spá-madhr*) of the latter is said to have dwelt for a long time. Kodran averred that, when the missionary had sprinkled the stone with holy water, his ancestor had come out and complained that the water had scalded his little children.

12. Yggdrasil's ash.—This is a very complex conception, as may be seen from the variety of phenomena attached to it.[4] The descriptions indeed are hard to visualize and are apparently inconsistent. Sometimes the ash seems to spread out over the whole world; sometimes again it is represented as a definite locality to which the gods ride or walk to hold their court. If the tree called Laéráthr in *Grímnismál*, 25 f., is to be identified with the ash, as seems probable, it must be regarded as standing very near to Othin's hall. Now it was, and indeed still is, the custom for country houses in the North, especially in Sweden, to have standing by them a tree known as *vårdträd* ('protecting tree'), on which the welfare of the house is supposed to depend. Such trees were doubtless regarded as especially sacred in heathen times, and it is not unreasonable to suppose that the original conception of Yggdrasil's ash may have been that of a *vårdträd* of the divine community. In *Völuspá* the reference to the ash seems to point to a tree on which the destiny of the gods depends rather than to an all-comprehending world-tree. That its origin is to be found in actual trees is rendered probable by the Irmensul, which likewise was all-comprehending ('universalis columna . . . quasi sustinens omnia'),[5] for this was a real tree, or rather a tree-trunk, in spite of the property assigned to it. Further, the adjuncts mentioned in *Grímnismál* and *Gylfaginning*—the harts, snakes, etc.—link it with grove sanctuaries. We may refer particularly to those of the Lithuanians and Prussians, especially to the sacred one at Romove. It was forbidden to injure any birds or animals in such groves. The description indeed of the sacred oak at Romove furnishes an interesting parallel to Yggdrasil's ash from real life. In the North itself we can find parallels for all the features involved; *e.g.*, snakes seem to have disappeared from the Northern sanctuaries before the date of our records, yet a very interesting analogy in some respects is furnished by the description of the sacred tree at Upsala in scholium 134 to Adam of Bremen's *History*.

iii. COSMOLOGY.—See art. COSMOGONY AND COSMOLOGY (Teutonic).

iv. ESCHATOLOGY.—See art. STATE OF THE DEAD (Teutonic).

D. E. MARTIN CLARKE.

[1] *Ynglinga Saga*, 9.
[2] *Flateyjarbók*, ii. ch. vi.
[3] Cf. the mythical *Hervarar Saga*, 1.
[4] Cf. accounts in *Grímnismál* and the Prose Edda.
[5] Rudolph of Fulda, *MGH Inscript.* ii. 676.

III. *WORSHIP.*—The Teutonic festivals are treated separately under the heading FESTIVALS AND FASTS (Teutonic). There are also separate articles on SACRIFICE (Teutonic) and HUMAN SACRIFICE (Teutonic). The various superstitions are covered under the headings DIVINATION (Teutonic), MAGIC (Teutonic), and ORDEAL (Teutonic). It remains in this section to speak of prophecy and the priesthood.

1. Prophecy.—According to Tacitus, *Hist.* iv. 61, numbers of women among the Germani were considered to possess the gift of prophecy 'in consequence of which many were revered as goddesses,' though he denies elsewhere[1] that the veneration paid to them was so great as this. One of the chief of these prophetic women was known as Veleda, a prophetess of the Bructueri, who ruled over considerable territory. To increase the honour in which she was held, she lived at the top of a high tower, and questions and oracular responses were conveyed between her and the public by a near relative 'like a messenger who had converse with the gods.'[2] The name Veleda, strictly speaking, does not appear to be a proper name but a Gaulish word for 'prophetess.'[3] We may here mention the story of the older Drusus, who in his last campaign was met on the banks of the Elbe by a woman taller than human who prophesied to him the manner of his death even as it afterwards came about.[4] According to Strabo,[5] the Cymbri had prophetesses who practised divination with slaughtered prisoners.[6]

2. Priesthood.—(*a*) *Priest.*—(i.) In Norway, and especially in Iceland, the duties of the priest were performed by the political leader of the people. During the colonization of Iceland the more important of the chiefs who went out from Norway built their own temples, not infrequently of the wood of which their temples had been made in Norway.

Thus we read in *Eyrbyggja Saga*, 4, that Thórólfr of Mostr built a temple to Thor of such wood. To this temple all the men in his own district had to pay a tax called 'temple-toll'; but the chief himself paid for the upkeep of the building and performed all the necessary duties in connexion with the temple and the temple services, while at the same time exercising judicial authority over the people of the neighbourhood. Again in *Hrafnkel's Saga Freysgótha*, 2, we are told that Hrafnkel raised a great temple in Athalból, where he 'made offerings to Freyr of the half of all the best things that he had.' Hrafnkel settled the whole of the valley and gave land to people on condition that he should be regarded as their chief and exercise the authority of priest over them.[7]

The priest was called *góthi*, and his office *gothorth*. In each *gothorth* was a consecrated place set apart for the *thing* (gathering of the people). Small settlers who were not of sufficient substance and authority to build temples of their own joined one or other of the *gothorth* so as to have the benefit of the temple services and the temporal protection of the *góthi*. So inseparable was the political function from that of the priest in Iceland that the *gothorth* formed the starting-point for the foundation of the constitution of Iceland. The title of *góthi* continued in existence after the adoption of Christianity, although now it had lost all religious significance and meant no more than magistrate (*lögsögumathr*). It is interesting to observe that the *gothorth* was a hereditary office and could even be bought and sold like any other property.[8]

This combination of priestly with secular authority existed also no doubt in Norway, whence the original priests of Iceland came, though—and here is a difference from Iceland—the power of the

[1] *Germ.* 9.
[2] *Hist.* iv. 65.
[3] Cf. Gael. *fíle.*
[4] Suetonius, *Claud.* 1.
[5] VII. iv. 3.
[6] See art. DIVINATION (Teutonic), vol. iv. p. 827.
[7] Cf. also *Egils Saga*, 86, 89; *Eyrbyggja Saga*, 15.
[8] Cf. *Vatnsdaela Saga*, 41 f.; *Bandamanna Saga*, 3.

local chiefs in Norway was subordinate to that of kings. The word *góthi* is occasionally applied to local chiefs—*e.g.*, to Thorhaddr the Old, who was *hof-góthi* at Maeren in Trondhjem [1]—and on several occasions we hear of priests in Iceland who had formerly possessed temples in Norway. The *Saga of Hákon the Good* (*Heimskringla*), 16, gives an account of a great sacrificial feast at Hlathir of which Earl Sigurthr sustained the whole cost himself; and from the *Saga of Olaf Tryggvason* (*Heimskringla*), 75, we learn that it had been the custom of Olaf's predecessors to offer sacrifice in Trondhjem. In poetry we sometimes meet with such expressions as *vörthr véstalls* ('guardian of the altar') applied to kings of the past. In all cases, here as in Iceland, it is clear that no exclusively priestly class existed, and that priestly duties were in all cases combined with temporal power.

For Denmark very little evidence is available. On three Runic inscriptions found in Fyn, and dating approximately from the 9th cent., the word *kuthi* (i.e. *góthi*) is found in combination with some proper name to form a compound word. Hróulfr and Ali are said to have been *nuRakuthi* (*Nora-góthi*) and *sauluakutha* (*Sölva-góthi*) respectively. It has been suggested that Nori and Sölvi are the names of men; but it seems at least equally probable that they are place-names.[2] If this is so, Hróulfr and Ali may have been local chieftains, like those on the west coast of Norway. It is significant that Saxo, who frequently refers to the laws and customs of heathen times, makes no references to a priestly class in Denmark.

For Sweden the evidence is more abundant. Adam of Bremen states in connexion with the great temple at Upsala:

'Assigned to all the gods they have priests to present the sacrifices of the people.'[3]

It does not necessarily follow perhaps from this statement that the duties of these persons were of an exclusively priestly nature. Elsewhere the evidence seems rather to point to a union in Sweden, like that in Norway and Iceland, of priestly duties with secular authority.

Thus we read in *Ynglinga Saga*, 47, that a famine which arose in the days of the legendary king Olaf Trételgja was attributed by the people to the king's remissness in offering sacrifices; and even towards the end of the 11th cent. we read in *Hervarar Saga, ad fin.*, of one Blótsveinn ('sacrificing-Sveinn') obtaining the throne in virtue of his promise to offer sacrifice on behalf of the people, which he actually carried out. Rimbertus[4] describes the formal deification of the Swedish king Ericus; and it will be remembered that the native dynasty, the Ynglingar, traced their descent from the god Freyr.

Thus, while the evidence is perhaps less direct and convincing for Sweden than for Norway, it seems on the whole to indicate a close union from the earliest times between secular and religious power.

(ii.) Except in Tacitus references to priests among the Teutonic peoples are of rare occurrence. In later times we read in the *History* of Ammianus Mercellinus[5] that the priests of the Burgundians were presided over by a chief priest who held his office for life. Jordanes[6] states that the priests of the Goths were of noble extraction.

(iii.) We learn from Bede[7] that the priests of the ancient English were forbidden to bear arms and to ride except on mares. Heathen priests are also referred to,[8] perhaps the most interesting instance being that of Coifi.

Eddius,[9] in his description of the shipwreck of Wilfrid off the Sussex coast, refers to the 'princeps sacerdotum idolatriae' standing before the country-people on a high mound and by his magic arts seeming to cast fetters on the hands of the people of God.

[1] Cf. *Landn.* iv. 6.
[2] Cf. L. F. A. Wimmer, *Die Runenschrift*, German tr. by F. Holthausen, Berlin, 1887, pp. 341 ff., 359 ff.
[3] iv. 27.
[4] *Vita Anscharii*, 26.
[5] xxviii. 5. 14.
[6] *De Rebus Geticis*, ch. 5.
[7] *HE* ii. 13.
[8] *Ib.* ii. 6, and elsewhere.
[9] Ch. 13.

(iv.) Among the Teutonic peoples of the Continent in ancient times the priest seems to have combined to a great extent spiritual with temporal powers. According to Tacitus, his duties were threefold: (1) the consultation of omens on public occasions, together with divination, the casting of lots, and the observation of the sacred horses;[1] (2) duties in connexion with the tribal assembly such as the proclamation of silence at the opening of the meeting, and the administration of punishment at the assembly and in time of war;[2] (3) the guardianship of the sacred groves, symbols, and other holy objects,[3] which they also carried with the host to battle.[4] They no doubt had duties also in connexion with the public sacrifices. Indeed it may be said that their functions as a whole were essentially of a public character. There is little or no trace of any mystical relationship existing between the priest and the god, or of any peculiarly spiritual qualification in the priest such as we find noted, *e.g.*, in the case of prophetesses like Veleda, or in the account of the Druids given by Diodorus Siculus.[5]

(*b*) *Priestess.*—(i.) In Iceland the word *gythja* ('priestess') occasionally occurs,[6] and seems to be applied to women belonging to the ruling families of Iceland (*i.e.* those who held *gothorth*).

In *Kristni Saga*, 2, we are told of a woman Frithgerthr who was 'in the temple offering sacrifices' while Thorvaldr was preaching the Christian faith hard by. The term *gythja*, however, is not applied to her, and it is possible that she was only acting as deputy for her husband, who was absent at the *althingi* ('general assembly'). Mention is made in *Vápnfirthinga Saga*, 10, of a woman called Steinvör, who is described as a *hof-gythja* ('temple-priestess') and who owned a *höfuth-hof* ('public temple') and claimed temple-toll. When she wished to enforce the civil authority of the *gothorth*, she was obliged to apply to her kinsman Brodd-Helgi for help. But that she was conscious of her full religious responsibilities seems to be borne out by the amusing account given in *Kristni Saga*, 5, of a 'flyting' between Thangbrandr the priest and one Steinvör, the mother of the poet Ref, who is without doubt to be identified with the *hof-gythja* of *Vápnfirthinga Saga*. Here we are told that, after she had preached heathenism to Thangbrandr at some length, she made the startling announcement that 'Thor challenged Christ to fight in single combat; but he dared not fight against Thor!'

Beyond this, references to priestesses in the old Scandinavian countries seem to point to persons of a different character, though these references are not very satisfactory.

In *Sturlaugs Saga Starfsama*, 18, we are told of 60 *hof-gythjar* in a temple, which, however, was Finnish. Again in *Ynglinga Saga*, 4, we are told that the goddess Freyja was a *blót-gythja* ('sacrificial priestess'), and that after Freyr's death she kept up the temple and sacrifices at Upsala.

Here also we may mention the story of Gunnarr Helmingr, who is related in ch. 278 of the *Saga of Olaf Tryggvason* (*Flateyjarbók*) to have personated the god Freyr after destroying his idol. Freyr's image was kept in a temple in Sweden, and his shrine is said to have been attended to by a young and beautiful woman who was known as his wife, and with whom he used to make an annual progress through the land, driven in a chariot. This person is not actually called a priestess (*gythja*), but at all events she apparently had charge of the sanctuary and interpreted the answers of the god. We may here compare the account of Freyja, who in *Ynglinga Saga*, 13, is said to have upheld the sacrifices at Upsala after the death of Freyr.

(ii.) We have no definite evidence for the existence of priestesses in the strict sense of the term among the other Teutonic peoples. Tacitus speaks of 'numbers of women of prophetic power,'[7] but these recall the *völur* rather than the priestesses of the North. The former existence of a priestess may, however, perhaps be inferred from the account of the sacred grove of the Nahanarvali, which is said[8] to have been under the charge of a priest 'muliebri ornatu.'

IV. *TEMPLES AND SANCTUARIES.*—(*a*) *Iceland.*—(i.) In Iceland the temples formed centres of jurisdiction, one belonging to each of the 39

[1] In the last duty he was accompanied by the king; cf. *Germ.* 10.
[2] *Ib.* 7. 11.
[3] *Ib.* 40, 43.
[4] *Ib.* 7.
[5] *Bibl. Hist.* v. 31.
[6] E.g., *Landn.* iii. 4, iv. 10.
[7] *Hist.* iv. 61, 65.
[8] *Germ.* 43.

gothorth. One of the fullest descriptions of such temples which we possess occurs in *Eyrbyggja Saga*, 4.

Here we are told that Thórólfr of Mostr set up a great temple to Thor by Thor's river. There was a door in the wall near one end. Inside stood the high-seat pillars containing the pegs which were called *reginnaglar* ('holy pegs'). On one of these pillars the image of Thor was carved.

'The interior of this temple was a very holy place. At the end of the temple farthest from the door there was an annexe like the choir of a church at the present time, and there in the midst of the floor stood a *stalli* which served as an altar, and thereon lay a jointless ring weighing twenty ounces on which all oaths are said to have been sworn. The priest wore this ring upon his arm at all assemblies. On the *stalli* stood also the sacrificial bowl wherein was a *hleitteinn* which served as a sprinkler, wherewith was sprinkled the blood from the bowl which was called *hlaut*. That was the blood which was shed by such creatures as were sacrificed to the gods. In the annexe round about the *stalli* were the gods ranged. To this temple all men had to pay tribute, and they were under an obligation to accompany the temple priests on all such journeys as *thing-men* now take with their chiefs, and the *góthi* kept up the temple at his own cost so that it should not fall out of repair, and in it he upheld the sacrificial feasts.'

Some additional details are furnished by the descriptions of the temple at Kjalarnes in *Kjalnesinga Saga*, 2, 4.

This temple was 60 ft. in breadth, and, like the one built by Ingimundr in Vatnsdaela,[1] 100 ft. in length. Thor was the god most honoured in this temple. The inner sanctuary was circular like the hull of a ship. Thor stood in the midst of it, and other gods on both sides. In front of them stood a *stalli* made with great skill and covered with iron. On it there was a fire which was never allowed to die down. They called it the 'consecrated fire.' On that *stalli* there lay also a great 'ring' of silver. The temple priest wore it on his arm at all assemblies. Men took their oaths on it in all law-suits. On that altar there lay also a great bowl of copper into which was poured the blood which came from the cattle which were sacrificed to Thor or from the men. This blood they called *hlaut*, and (the bowl they called) *hlaut-bolli*. Men and cattle were sprinkled with the *hlaut*, but the cattle which were sacrificed there were used for entertaining the company when sacrificial feasts were held. And the men who were sacrificed were sunk in the pool which was outside by the door, and which was called *blótkilda* ('sacrificial spring'). The temple was surrounded by a wooden fence too high to climb, and both the temple and the fence contained doors that locked. Finally we are told that the beams of the temple were very excellent.[2]

Thorhaddr the Old, like many another, took the temple-mould and the high-seat pillars from his Norwegian temple and used them for his temple in Iceland.[3] We are also told that Jörundr *góthi* raised a temple in Svertingsstathir.[4] Numerous other instances might be cited.

In *Kristni Saga*, 2, heathen sacrifices are mentioned as being offered in a temple at Hvamm. In *Hrafnkels Saga Freysgótha*, 3, we are told that Hrafnkel raised a great temple to Freyr in Athalból. This temple stood on a rock above a deep pool in the river and contained images of the gods which had some kind of robes or ornaments upon them. A temple dedicated to Freyr is also mentioned in *Víga Glúms Saga*, 5, as being 'on the south of the river at Hripkelsstathir.'[5] In ch. 24 of the same saga we read that there were three temples on Eyjafirthr. In ch. 25 we have an interesting confirmation of the accounts of the oath-ring mentioned above. In the temple in Diupadale on Eyjafirthr 'whoever took the temple-oath took in his hand the silver ring which was reddened in the blood of the cattle sacrificed and which weighed fully three ounces.' Possibly the ring of Tomar (Thunor) which was carried off from Dublin by King Charles Malachy II. in 994 was one of the sacred rings upon which oaths were sworn.[6] Here we may compare the *Anglo-Saxon Chronicle*,[7] where the oath-ring is represented as the most binding form of engagement known to the Danes.

(ii.) Not only the temple itself, but also the land round about, was regarded as sanctuary.

Thus in *Eyrbyggja Saga*, 4, we are told that Thórólfr of Mostr held as sacred a hill in the precincts of his temple on Thorsnes. Here the *thing* of the men of the Western Firths was held. No one was allowed to turn his eyes thither unwashed, and no blood was to be shed there. Thórólfr's sons preserved the sanctuary inviolate as long as they could; and, when it had been defiled with bloodshed by the Kjallekings,[8] the place was declared unhallowed and the *thing* removed to another part of the promontory, where the *dómhringr* is still pointed out to travellers—'That was one of the holiest of places.'

A curious tradition of sanctity is found in *Landnámabók*, ii. 16.

Authr the Deep-Minded was a Christian. 'She was accustomed to say her prayers at Cross-hills. She had crosses raised there, for she was baptized and a good Christian. Members of her family afterwards showed great reverence for that hill. A *hörgr* was made there when they began to offer sacrifices. They believed that they would pass into the hill when they died.'

(*b*) *Norway*.—(i.) From *Eyrbyggja Saga*, 3, we learn that, before Thórólfr of Mostr left Norway for Iceland, he had charge of Thor's temple on the island of Mostr, and was a great friend of Thor. The framework of this temple was transferred bodily to Iceland. Another island is mentioned in the *Saga of Olaf Tryggvason*[1] as containing a large temple dedicated to Thor. Guthbrandr of the Dales also possessed a temple dedicated to Thor.[2] His predecessor was a great friend of Earl Hákon of Hlathir. They had a temple in common in Guthbrandsdale, which contained figures of Thor and of Hákon's patron goddesses, Thorgerthr and Irpa. Thorgerthr is described as being as tall as a full-grown man and having a hood on her head. Thor was seated in his car, and all were adorned with clothes or ornaments and had gold rings on their arms. This temple and Earl Hákon's temple at Hlathir are said to have been the two chief temples in Norway.[3] When Earl Hákon first took possession of Norway, 'he commanded throughout his whole kingdom that the temples should be maintained,'[4] and later, when the emissaries of the emperor Otto had overthrown the temples of S. Norway, Earl Hákon caused them to be rebuilt and the heathen sacrifices to be re-established.[5]

Some interesting details of one of his temples (in Arkadale) are given in *Faereyinga Saga*, 23.

It stood in the midst of a wood and was surrounded by a paling and adorned with gold and silver, while the roof was lighted with several glass windows. Inside near the door was a figure of Thorgerthr Hölgabrúthr, beautifully adorned. The same story occurs in the *Saga of Olaf Tryggvason* (*Flateyjarbók*), 326, where we are told that Olaf stripped Thorgerthr of all her 'gold and silver and fine clothes' and dragged the idol at his horse's tail, finally beating it to pieces with a club and burning it along with the image of Freyr.

Olaf Tryggvason systematically destroyed Hákon's temples and despoiled the idols. He took from the door of the temple at Hlathir the large gold ring that Hákon had had made, and burnt the image of Thor which it contained.[6] In his missionary expedition to Inner Trondhjem he despoiled the temple at Maer, which contained many idols fixed on *stallar*, in the midst of whom sat Thor, 'an image of great size, all adorned with gold and silver.'[7] A curious and interesting account of a temple and image dedicated to Balder in the district of Sogn is mentioned in the *Saga of Frithjóf the Bold*.[8] It has been the custom to cast doubt on this evidence, but the details are not obviously fictitious, and it is difficult to imagine why they should have been invented. The account is at least as reliable as that of *Kjalnesinga Saga*,[9] which is usually accepted as probable.

(ii.) The word *hof* ('temple') frequently occurs in association with the word *hörgr*.[10] What exactly the *hörgr* was we do not know. From *Hyndluljóth*, 10, the *hörgr* seems to have been made of stones:

'He made me a *hörgr* built of stones. Now, this heap of stones is turned to glass.'

But in *Grímnismál*, 16, Njörthr is said to rule over *hótimbruthum hörgi* ('high-timbered *hörgrs*').

[1] Cf. *Vatnsdaela Saga*, 15.
[2] Here we may compare the story given in *Landn.* v. 12 of Ketilbjörn, who was so rich that he ordered his sons to make a cross-beam of silver in the temple which they were building on Mossfell. His sons, however, did not carry out his orders.
[3] Cf. *Landn.* iv. 6.
[4] *Ib.* v. 3.
[5] Cf. also 9, 19.
[6] Cf. *Annals of the Four Masters, sub an.* 994. *Sub an.* 876.
[8] Cf. *ib.* 9, 10.

[1] *Flateyjarbók*, 243.
[2] Cf. *Saga of Olaf the Holy* (*Heimskringla*), 118.
[3] Cf. *Njáls Saga*, 87, 88.
[4] Cf. *Saga of Olaf Tryggvason* (*Flateyjarbók*), 61.
[5] *Ib.* 87; cf. also 313–315.
[6] *Saga of Olaf Tryggvason* (*Flateyjarbók*), 248.
[7] *Ib.* 268.
[8] Ch. 1 and *passim*.
[9] Ch. 2, 4.
[10] Cf., e.g., *Helgakvitha Hjörvarthssonar*, 4.

The phrase '*hörgr* and *hof* high-timbered' occurs also in *Völuspá*, 7. It has been suggested that the word 'high-timbered' is merely conventional and that the *hörgr* was a stone structure as opposed to the wooden temples so common in Norway and Iceland. In *Örvar Odds Saga*, 29, we are told that Oddr 'burnt a *hof* and broke a *hörgr*'; but in the preceding verse both *hof* and *hörgr* are spoken of as being 'burnt.' *Hof* and *hörgr* are spoken of as burnt in ch. 165 of the *Saga of Olaf Tryggvason* (*Fornmanna Sögur*). But in ch. 141 of the same saga we are told that the king commanded '*hof* and *hörgr* to be broken and burnt.' The *hörgr* is frequently mentioned in connexion with women.

Thus in *Gylf.* 14 the goddesses are said to inhabit 'a *hörgr* which was a very fair house. It was called Vingólf.' In *Hervarar Saga*, 1, Starkathr is said to have carried off Alfhildr as she was in the act of reddening the *hörgr* by night after the great *dísarblót*. After the death of Authr the Christian, her relatives made a *hörgr* on the hill where she had set up her crosses.

The word is still traditionally connected with high places in popular speech. Thus, when the land lies deep in snow, the Icelanders say that 'only the highest *hörgar* jut out.' And in the Norwegian patois a dome-shaped mountain is called a *horg*. Perhaps the word is a survival of an older form of religion when places of worship were more primitive than the carefully constructed *hof*. It is obviously connected ultimately with the O.H.G. *haruc*.

(iii.) It will be seen that there are certain obvious discrepancies in regard to the use of the term *hörgr*. It appears in some cases to have been a cairn, but in others a building capable of habitation. Sometimes it is made of stone, in other cases perhaps of wood. The difficulty is increased by the fact that the word is obviously identical with the early German word *haruc*, which is used to gloss the words *nemus*, *lucus*, while the corresponding A.S. *hearg* is also perhaps used for 'grove.' Such sacred woods or groves were probably common in early times, since many place-names are compounded with the word *lundr* ('sacred grove'). Moreover, the usual name for the place of assembly in the North is *thingvöllr*, which must originally have meant 'wood of the assembly,' *völlr* being cognate with O.S. *weald* and O.H.G. *wald* ('forest').

The legendary sanctuary at Glasisvellir[1] was probably connected with a holy grove, and is no doubt identical with Glasir, the name of the tree by Valhöll, Othin's dwelling-place, mentioned in *Skáldskaparmál*, 34. It is in a forest clearing that the gods meet to decide the fate of Starkathr.[2] According to a mythological poem,[3] the gods meet every day to dispense justice under Yggdrasil's ash. Perhaps we may also instance Tomar's wood,[4] which was situated near Dublin. It has been suggested that this means 'grove of Thor.'

It is noteworthy that the two great assembly places, Frosta and Gaula, are both on peninsulas. Sacred islands may also have been known, as can perhaps be inferred from the recurrence of such names as Njardhrey, Vé-ey, Thorsey, and possibly Halogaland.

(*c*) *Sweden*.—(i.) The great temple of the Swedes was at Upsala.

'The Swedes have a most magnificent temple which is called Ubsola [Upsala] not far distant from the city of Sictona [Sigtuna]. In this temple, which is fitted [?] entirely with gold, they worship the statues of three gods. Thor, the most powerful of them, has his seat in the midst of the couch [?], while Wodan and Fricco occupy places on either side of him. . . . Wodan they represent as armed, just as our people represent Mars, while Thor with his sceptre seems to copy Jupiter.'[5]

'That temple is surrounded by a golden chain which hangs over the roof [?] of the building, and the gleam of which is visible to visitors at a distance; for the shrine itself stands on level ground with hills round it like a theatre.'[6]

(ii.) In the (contemporary) scholium 134 we have an interesting account of a holy grove which stood

[1] Cf. the *Tháttr af Nornagesti*, 1; *Hervarar Saga*, 1.
[2] Cf. *Gautreks Saga*, 7. [3] *Grímnismál*, 30.
[4] Mentioned in the *War of the Gaethil with the Gaill*, 113.
[5] Adam of Bremen, iv. 26. [6] *Ib.* scholium 135.

beside the temple, and which contained an evergreen tree of great sanctity.

'Near that temple there is a very large tree stretching out its branches afar and always green both in winter and summer. No one knows what kind of tree it is. There also is a spring in which it is the practice of the heathen to do sacrifice by sinking a living man in it. If he does not reappear, the prayers of the people will be fulfilled.'

The description of Yggdrasil's ash, which is said to overshadow Asgarthr,[1] is no doubt derived from the Upsala evergreen, as the description of the home of the gods is surely derived from some Northern sanctuary, in all probability the identical sanctuary at Upsala.[2]

There are many other references to this sanctuary in both Norse and Danish authorities, and it was in fact the most famous one in the North. In *Ynglinga Saga*, 12, and in Saxo, iii. 90, its establishment is attributed to the god Freyr, who in the former is represented as having lived and died at Upsala. This is no doubt also the scene of the story of Gunnar Helmingr, although in this story the place is not actually mentioned.

In *Jómsvíkinga Saga*, 12, we are told of a temple in Götland which contained 100 gods and also temple treasure and temple servants to offer the sacrifices, but, apart from the great temple at Upsala, we know little of the heathen temples of Sweden.

(*d*) *Denmark*.—No records of Danish temples appear to have been preserved. The chief sanctuary of the Danes was at Leire. This was no doubt a sanctuary of great antiquity. It is the home of the famous kings of the 6th cent., Hróarr and Hrólfr Kraki (the Hrothgar and Hrothwulf of *Beowulf*). In *Ynglinga Saga*, 5, it is said to have been the home of the goddess Gifjón and her husband Skjöldr, the eponymous ancestor of the Skjöldungar (A.S. Scyldingas), the Danish royal family. Like Upsala, the locality is remarkable for its barrows, some of which date from the earliest times.

The existence of ancient sanctuaries in the old Danish kingdom is also implied by some of the place-names; *e.g.*, Lundr, the name of the old ecclesiastical capital in Skåney, meant originally a 'sacred grove.' Cf. also Véborg (mod. Víborg; 'sanctuary town') and Helganes ('holy promontory') in Jutland; Óthinsé or Óthinsvé ('Othin's Sanctuary') on the island of Fyen, and Hlésey, besides many other Danish (and Norwegian and Swedish) place-names.

(*e*) *England*.—In England the worship of idols and the existence of heathen temples were well known to Bede. In A.D. 601 Pope Gregory sent a letter to the abbot Mellitus urging that, while he is to destroy the idols in England, he is to leave the heathen temples standing that they may be consecrated for purposes of Christian worship. He says expressly, 'It is their custom to slay many oxen in sacrifice to devils.'[3] The East Anglian king Redwald, who had been converted to Christianity on a visit to Kent, is said to have had in the same temple an altar for Christian worship and an *arula* at which to offer victims to devils;[4] and his son Earconberct is said to have been the first of the English kings who commanded the idols throughout his country to be destroyed.[5] When the Northumbrian Council decided to adopt Christianity, the high priest of the heathen, Coefi, rode to the sanctuary of Gudmanum on the Derwent, cast a spear into it, and commanded his companions to destroy and set fire to it with all its precincts.[6] References of a historical character to sanctuaries in this country are rare, however. But such place-names as Thunresleah, which must originally have

[1] *Gylf.* 15. [2] Cf. also *Skáldskaparmál*, 34.
[3] *HE* i. 30. [4] *Ib.* ii. 15.
[5] *Ib.* iii. 8. [6] *Ib.* ii. 13.

meant 'grove of thunder,' perhaps indicate the existence of groves sacred to the thunder-god among the ancient English, and there are other reminiscences of heathen worship no doubt preserved in such place-names as Thunresfeld and Wednesbury.

In *Beowulf*, 175, we hear of offerings made *aet haergtrafum*, which perhaps means 'shrines' covered with canopies. The word *haerg*, identical with Norse *hörgr*, is of frequent occurrence standing alone, and is used to translate various Latin terms such as *fanum*[1] and *idolum*. There are other passages in which the word seems to mean a 'grove,' as in German, and it is not uncommon in place-names—*e.g.*, Harrow. A number of other words which appear in Christian usage were presumably applied at first to heathen sanctuaries—e.g., *weofod* ('altar').[2]

(*f*) *The Continent*.—(i.) References to temples on the Continent are rare. In the 6th cent. a Frankish temple was destroyed by Radegund, wife of Chlotar. Gregory of Tours describes a temple at Cologne which contained figures of the gods and in which sacrificial feasts were held. The Frisians seem to have had temples, but the notices are not always clear.

(ii.) The word *fanum*, by which these sanctuaries are usually denoted, is also used of the Irmensul, which, according to Thietmar of Merseburg,[3] was an immense wooden shaft or pillar worshipped by the Old Saxons in a place called Eresburg. According to the *Vita S. Alex.* 3, this pillar was 'set up aloft in the open.' In their own language they call it 'Irmensul, quod latine dicitur universalis columna, quasi sustinens omnia.' It was cut down in the year 772 by Charlemagne, who spent three days destroying the sanctuary and carried off much gold and silver.

Among the heathen practices of the Old Saxons condemned in the *Indiculus Superstitionum* and elsewhere we hear of sanctuaries connected with woods, of springs connected with sacrifices, and of various places which are venerated as holy.

The chief sanctuary of the Frisians was that of 'Fosite's Land.' According to Alcuin's *Vita S. Willibrordi*, 10, it took its name from the god Fosite.

'For *fana* of this god were "constructed" (*constructa*) on it.' This place was held so sacred by the country folk that no one dared to touch the cattle or anything else that fed there. He also mentions a sacred spring on the island.[4]

Adam of Bremen[5] identifies this land with the island of Heilgiland (Halogaland). In the *Vita S. Bonifatii*, 23, we read of a sacred oak of gigantic size, the *robor Jovis*, which was cut down by the saint amid the clamorous protests of the heathen.

There is no doubt that sacred trees and groves were of frequent occurrence among all the Teutonic peoples of the Continent. In the *Translatio S. Alexandri*, 3, we are told that the Saxons worshipped trees and streams. Claudian speaks of 'groves grim with ancient religious rites and oaks resembling barbaric divinity.'[6]

The O.H.G. word *haruc*, like the O.N. *hörgr* and A.S. *hearg*, presents some difficulty, being used sometimes to gloss *nemus, lucus*, sometimes *fanum, delubrum*. It has been suggested by Mogk that the lack of clear distinction between the terms for the natural and the artificially constructed sanctuary is due to the utilization of old sanctuaries as sites for later temples.

(iii.) References to Teutonic temples in earlier times, in the works of Tacitus, are rare and doubtful. In *Ann.* i. 51 it is stated that Germanicus razed to the ground the temple which they called the temple of Tamfana and which was most frequented by those tribes. Again, in *Germ.* 40 mention is made of the *templum* of Nerthus, but it is not unlikely that the word is used loosely for 'sanctuary'—'the holy grove on an island in the ocean,' the home of the goddess Nerthus, who visits the nations in a consecrated car covered with a garment.

'One priest alone is permitted to touch it. He is able to perceive when the goddess is present in her sanctuary and accompanies her with the utmost reverence as she is drawn along by cows. It is a season of rejoicing, and festivity reigns wherever she deigns to go and be received. They do not undertake hostilities or take up arms; every weapon is put away; peace and quiet are then only known and welcomed, until the goddess, weary of human intercourse, is at length restored by the same priest to her temple. Afterwards the car, the garments, and, if you are willing to believe it, the deity herself, are cleansed in a secret lake. This rite is performed by slaves who are instantly swallowed up by its waters.'

The indications given by Tacitus are too vague to enable the site of this sanctuary to be fixed with any certainty, but it is not impossible that it was the Danish sanctuary of Leire. In that case Nerthus may have lived on as Gifjón. Her name, however, is identical with that of the Norse god Njörthr.

According to *Germ.* 9, 'the Germani deem it to be inconsistent with the majesty of the gods to confine them within walls or to represent them after any similitude of a human face; they dedicate groves and woods and call by the names of gods that invisible thing which they see only with the eye of faith.'[1]

Sacred groves are mentioned by Tacitus in several other places. Arminius's forces assemble in a wood sacred to Hercules.[2] Civilis brings his army together in a sacred wood.[3] According to *Germ.* 43, the Nahanarvali had a grove of ancient sanctity. It was in these groves that they kept the sacred symbols.[4] Here also were reared the sacred white horses which were never allowed to do work for mankind, but were employed to draw the sacred cars, when their neighing was carefully observed by the priest and king of the state.

According to *ib.* 39, the Semnones had a wood of immemorial antiquity and holiness. Here on certain occasions there met embassies from all the kindred peoples (the various branches of the Suevi) to celebrate their barbaric rites by the slaying of a man. The grove was held in reverence, and no one was allowed to enter unless he was bound with chains to signify his own humility and the power of the grove.

LITERATURE.—J. Grimm, *Deutsche Mythologie*[4], 3 vols., Berlin, 1876 (Eng. tr., *Teutonic Mythology*, London, 1880–88); E. Mogk, 'Deutsche Mythologie,' in H. P. Paul, *Grundriss der germanischen Philologie*[2], iii. 230–406, Strassburg, 1900; E. H. Meyer, *German. Mythologie*, Berlin, 1891; P. D. Chantepie de la Saussaye, *Religion of the Teutons*, Eng. tr., Boston, U.S.A., 1902; P. Herrmann, *Deutsche Mythologie in gemeinverständl. Darstellung*, Leipzig, 1906, *Nordische Mythologie*, do. 1903; K. Helm, *Altgerman. Religionsgeschichte*, Heidelberg, 1913, i.; H. M. Chadwick, *The Cult of Othin*, London, 1899, *The Origin of the English Nation*, Cambridge, 1907, esp. chs. ix.–xi.; W. A. Craigie, *The Religion of Ancient Scandinavia*, London, 1906; E. E. Kellett, *The Religion of our Northern Ancestors*, do. 1914; B. S. Phillpotts, *The Cambridge Medieval History*, ii., 'The Rise of the Saracens and the Foundation of the Western Empire,' London, 1913, ch. xv. (*C*) 'Germanic Heathenism'; J. Brand, *The Popular Antiquities of Great Britain*, ed. H. Ellis, revised and enlarged by W. C. Hazlitt, London, 1905; Tylor, *PC*[4], do. 1903; P. B. du Chaillu, *The Viking Age*, 2 vols., do. 1889; F. Kauffmann, *Deutsche Altertumskunde*, Munich, 1913; O. Montelius, in *Sveriges Historia*[2], vol. i., etc., Stockholm, 1903 (Ger. tr., Leipzig, 1906). For further information on the subject see B. S. Phillpotts, bibliography to ch. xv. (*C*) in *Cambridge Medieval Hist.* ii. 786–790.

For material on burial customs and archæology in general see *EBr*[11], *s.vv.* 'Germany' and 'Scandinavian Civilisation,' with the bibliographies appended.

Convenient edd. of most Norse works, both prose and poetry, are published by Sigurthur Kristjánsson, Reykjavík. An English ed. of all the early poetry with trr. is contained also in the *Corpus Poeticum Boreale*, by G. Vigfússon and F. York Powell, 2 vols., Oxford, 1883 (scarce). There are also several German and Scandinavian critical edd. of the Edda poems and of many

1 *E.g.*, in the passages quoted above from Bede, *HE* ii. 13.
2 Cf. also *hūsl*, an old pagan word for sacrifice, etc.
3 *Chron.* ii. 1.
4 Cf. also *Vita S. Liudgerii*, i. 19.
5 iv. 3.
6 *Cons. Stil.* i. 288.

1 Cf. also *ib.* 7, and *Ann.* i. 61.
2 *Ann.* ii. 12.
3 *Hist.* iv. 14.
4 See art. IMAGES AND IDOLS (Teutonic and Slavic).

of the sagas. The following list of the English translations may be found useful: *The Elder or Poetic Edda*, pt. i., 'The Mythological Poems,' tr. Olive Bray, printed for the Viking Club, London, 1908; *The Prose Edda*, tr. A. G. Brodeur, New York, 1916; *Laxdaela Saga*, tr. M. C. Press^2 ('The Temple Classics'), London, 1906; *Eyrbyggja Saga*, tr. W. Morris and E. Magnússon ('The Saga Library,' ii.), do. 1892; *Gísla Saga Súrssónar*, tr. G. W. Dasent, Edinburgh, 1866; *Kormaks Saga*, tr. W. G. Collingwood and Jón Stefánsson, Ulverston, 1902; *Víga-Glúms Saga*, tr. E. Head, London, 1866; the *Heimskringla*, containing *Ynglinga Saga, The Saga of Hákon the Good, The Saga of Olaf Tryggvason, St. Olaf's Saga*, etc., tr. W. Morris and E. Magnússon ('The Saga Library,' iii.–vi.), London, 1893–1905; *The Saga of Olaf Tryggvason*, tr. J. Sephton ('The Northern Library,' i.), do. 1895 (different from the *Saga of Olaf Tryggvason* contained in the *Heimskringla*); *Íslands Landnámabók* ('The Book of the Settlement of Iceland'), tr. T. Ellwood, Kendal, 1898; *Story of Egil Skallagrímsson*, tr. W. C. Green, London, 1893; *Grettis Saga* ('The Story of Grettir the Strong'), tr. E. Magnússon and W. Morris, new ed., do. 1900; also tr. A. Hight in the 'Everyman's Library,' do. 1914; *Brennu Njáls Saga* ('The Story of Burnt Njál'), tr. G. W. Dasent, Edinburgh, 1861 (also in 'Everyman's Library'); *Hrafnkels Saga Freysgótha*, tr. J. Coles in *Summer Travelling in Iceland*, London, 1882 (contains also *Bandamanna Saga* and the *Thórthar Hraethu Saga*); *Howard the Halt* (containing also *The Banded Men*, and *Hen Thorir*), tr. W. Morris and E. Magnússon ('The Saga Library,' i.), do. 1891; *Völsunga Saga*, tr. W. Morris and E. Magnússon, London and Felling-on-Tyne, 1870; *Three Northern Love Stories* (containing the *Saga of Frithjóf the Bold, Víglund the Fair, Gunnlaugs Saga Ormstungu, Hethinn and Högni*, etc.), tr. E. Magnússon and W. Morris, London, 1875. A list of English trr. of other sagas will be found in Craigie, *Icelandic Sagas*, ch. 7, p. 110; *Beowulf*, ed. W. J. Sedgefield^2, Manchester, 1913; also by A. J. Wyatt and R. W. Chambers, Cambridge, 1914, etc.; *Beowulf* has been translated by J. R. Clarke Hall, C. B. Tinker, F. J. Child, etc.; Bede, *Historia Ecclesiastica*, ed. C. Plummer, 2 vols., Oxford, 1896, tr. A. M. Sellar, London, 1907, tr. V. D. Scudder ('Everyman's Library'), do. 1910.

The most important German texts, chiefly charms, will be found in W. Braune, *Althochdeutsches Lesebuch*^{3}, Halle, 1888; and in M. Heyne, *Kleinere Altniederdeutsche Denkmäler*^{2}, Paderborn, 1877; Saxo Grammaticus, *Danish History*, bks. i.–ix., tr. O. Elton, London, 1894; Jordanes, *The Origin and Deeds of the Goths*, tr. C. Mierow^2, Princeton, U.S.A., 1915; Strabo, *Geography*, tr. H. C. Hamilton and W. Falconer, 3 vols., London, 1854–57; Tacitus, *Annals* and *Histories*, esp. the *Germany*, tr. by many and various scholars (*e.g.*, A. J. Church and W. J. Brodribb), London, 1877; Cæsar, *Commentaries on the Gallic War*, tr. T. Rice Holmes, do. 1908.

N. KERSHAW.

THAGS.—A secret organization of robber-stranglers called Thags existed for centuries in India, but it was put down by Lord William Bentinck's Government in the second quarter of the 19th century. Their history is full of incident and varied interest; here the religious and ethical aspects of the subject must be dominant.

1. Introduction.—The word *thag*, usually written *thug*, comes from a Sanskrit root *sthaga* meaning 'conceal,' which in the modern vernaculars becomes *thag* and means 'deceive.' The earliest reference to Thags comes from the middle of the 12th cent., and the first historical information about them from the end of the 13th cent.; but clear and full knowledge did not become available until the time when the organization was put down, about 1830. At that time there were thousands of Thags, well organized and extremely successful. They were all men of intelligence and capacity, most of them Hindus of good caste or respectable Muhammadans. Religion controlled their operations down to the last detail. How far back the fully organized confederacy reaches we cannot tell; but scattered fragments of information make it probable that in all essentials the conspiracy had been the same for several centuries.

2. Description.—Thags were ostensibly most respectable men, engaged in business, farming, or something else equally harmless. Their method was to start out in bands of from ten to two hundred in the month of October. They usually posed as merchants, but on occasion adopted other disguises, especially the dress and marks of ascetics. They possessed a secret vocabulary and a number of secret signs, which could be used without danger in the presence of outsiders. They travelled along or near the great roads used by merchants and money-porters, discovered which individuals or companies carried valuable goods or large amounts of gold and silver, and then with much skill and cunning contrived to win their confidence. They would then travel with them, it might be for days or even weeks, until time, place, and all else were favourable to their purpose, when, at a signal, they suddenly set upon the unsuspecting party, strangled them all in a few minutes, buried their bodies, distributed the booty, and decamped. They used a cloth in strangling their victims. Similar methods were practised on the rivers. One of the most extraordinary features of their history is the almost unbroken immunity which they enjoyed: it was only very rarely that a Thag was caught and punished for his crimes.

Thags believed their profession to be a religious duty, and all that they did was done under the sanction of religion. They were fully convinced that the goddess Kālī, the wife of Śiva, called also Durgā and Bhawānī, had commanded them to strangle and to rob, and had laid down all the rules which they followed in the course of their operations. Many Brāhmans were Thags; and, when there was a Brāhman member in a gang, he conducted the ceremonies. The neophyte, whether the son of a Thag or a new accession, was initiated in an impressive religious ceremony, and took a dread oath of absolute fidelity to the brotherhood. Before starting on the season's operations each gang met in a suitable place, and took part in a solemn act of worship. As soon as possible after every successful operation another religious ceremony was carried out. Once in seven days at least the goddess was worshipped, and on the greater occasions animals were sacrificed in her honour. They would not start on a journey, admit a new member, or decide upon an act of murder, unless the goddess granted them favourable omens. In every ceremony she was worshipped, and to her their prayers were offered. No image was used; but the pickaxe for digging the graves of their victims, solemnly consecrated, stood for the goddess, and was believed to be filled with her power and inspired by her to guide them. In every ceremony the offerings of *gur* (*i.e.* coarse sugar) and water were made to the pickaxe; over it every oath was taken; and at all times it was regarded with extreme reverence, confidence, and fear. On every occasion when *gur* and water were offered to the pickaxe, every fully qualified Thag also ate of the *gur* and drank of the water. At the close of each period of operations a percentage of the gains was solemnly presented to the goddess in one of her temples.

Among the rules which guided the Thags perhaps the most noticeable was the law that they must never strangle a woman.

3. Sources of the system.—The religious and political conditions of mediæval India provided the soil and the seed from which this extraordinary organization grew. The following facts require to be realized.

(*a*) In all parts of India to-day there exist criminal tribes,[1] *i.e.* tribes whose regular caste-occupation is some form of crime. In each case there is a belief that some divinity has imposed on the tribe the particular type of crime which it practises and has also laid down the rules under which it is followed. It is therefore the duty of every member of the tribe to make the practice of the crime his regular occupation, and to obey all the religious rules which are laid down for his guidance in it. So long as he does so, he regards himself as a religious man. A percentage of the gains is regularly dedicated to the god or goddess who gave the tribe its criminal profession. A few of these tribes profess Muhammadanism, and dedicate their gains to some *pir* (Muhammadan saint); but they are probably old criminal tribes which have undergone a shallow conversion to Muhammadanism. Criminal tribes are primitive people of very low social standing.

(*b*) All the chief forms of Hindu theology declare that the Supreme is exalted far above the petty distinctions of human

[1] J. N. Farquhar, *Modern Religious Movements in India*, New York, 1915, p. 424.

morality. The idea is to make Him truly absolute, to sever Him in the most decisive way, not only from the earthly and the sensual, but from all human conditions as well. Thus, from the very fact that in Himself He is completely separated from both good and evil, it becomes possible to acknowledge that He is indifferent to them and is equally the cause of both. Hence to suggest that God should bid men do what we call wrong seems to the Hindu to be not only quite natural but also inevitable.

(*c*) The Śākta sect of Hinduism, which worships the wife of Śiva, called Durgā, Kālī, Bhawānī, or simply 'the goddess' (Devī), and possesses a philosophical theology, falls into two sub-sects—the Right-hand and the Left-hand. The Left-hand sect has a cult which contains several extraordinary features. Only one need be mentioned here, viz. that for many centuries not only animal but also human sacrifice was offered. In 1835 the British Government prohibited human sacrifice, but until then it was common in the chief shrines of the goddess in North and Central India. According to the ritual law, only males can be sacrificed to her.

(*d*) In the worship of the goddess in the homes of the people, pots, pieces of metal, and diagrams are more often used than images; and both images and symbols, when duly consecrated, are believed to be filled with the presence and power of the goddess.

(*e*) In modern India there are many groups of ignorant Muhammadans who take part in Hindu worship. They not only join in the great festivals, but also visit Hindu temples and make offerings to the gods, in order to secure immunity from disease and to obtain other boons. Muhammadans of a low type thus readily adopt elements of the Hindu cult.

These facts enable one to realize that, in mediæval India, there might readily appear a community organized on the basis of the worship of the goddess and the practice of murder and robbery. At first it would differ but little, if at all, from an ordinary criminal tribe; and the first Thags would be ignorant Hindus who had been worshippers of the goddess before they formed the society to strangle and rob unwary travellers. To pass from participation in human sacrifice before the altar of the goddess to the search for victims for her on the high roads would be no violent change. Nor would even the thoughtful Hindu be shocked by the doctrine that the goddess had ordered the programme of murder. Hindu theology provides a substantial basis for the idea. Further, the fundamental document on which the worship of the Devī rests[1] is full of blood and horror. The story in that document of her struggle with a demon named Raktabīja and her final triumph over him was made by Thags the starting-point of the tale in which she commands the original Thags to strangle men.[2] The ritual law that only males should be sacrificed to her is clearly the source of the rule that Thags must not kill women. It would also seem quite natural to devotees of the goddess to use the pickaxe as a symbol instead of an image, and they would instinctively believe that the power and the will of the goddess were present in it.

Nor need we wonder that Muhammadans, in order to become Thags, were willing to participate in Hindu worship, since so many are to-day accustomed to supplement Muslim rites with the cult of Hindu divinities.

(*f*) India has usually been ruled, not by one Imperial Government, but by a multitude of petty states, each of which sought only to secure peace and order within its own narrow territory, and cared little or nothing for what happened outside. Nor has the individual Indian ever felt it to be his duty to go out of his way to secure the well-being of the Indian people as a whole. If, therefore, some of the subjects of one of these small states pursued a certain type of crime outside the limits of the state and brought back large gains, whereof they gave considerable percentages to the Government, on the one hand, and to the temples, on the other, both Government and people were usually only too willing to acquiesce in the arrangement, and to do all that was possible to protect the men who brought them so much prosperity.

These and similar facts account for the almost universal immunity which the Thags enjoyed. They were found all over India, were closely bound to one another by oath and interest, and were usually only too well able to take prompt vengeance on any who molested the brotherhood.

[1] *I.e.* the Chaṇḍī episode in the *Mārkaṇḍeya Purāṇa*.
[2] Sleeman, *Ramaseeana*, p. 127.

Thus only an Imperial Government using wide powers could successfully grapple with them.

4. The rise and fall of Thagī.—It seems clear that the Thag conspiracy was originally a Hindu organization, as we have already suggested, and that it came into being before the Muhammadan conquest of North India (1193–1293). In his *Śrīkaṇṭhacharita* the Hindu poet Maṅkha or Maṅkaka (fl. *c.* A.D. 1150) compares the thievish spring to a Thag.[1] Clearly by his time the community was already well known.

If the community was very successful, it would soon attract indigent Hindus of high caste, and there would be plenty of poor Brāhmans who would be eager to enter. It seems probable that, after the Muhammadan conquest, during one of the many periods when anarchy was wide-spread, the stranglers found unusual opportunities for their depredations, and waxed so rapidly rich that many Muhammadans became Thags and readily acquiesced in the established cult of the goddess. The great success and the wonderful immunity from punishment which the movement enjoyed would be to them clear proof of its divine origin. There is conclusive evidence that Muhammadan Thags looked back with great veneration to Nizām al-Dīn Awliyā, a famous Muslim saint, who lived at Delhi in the first quarter of the 14th cent., and that they regarded him as one of the founders of the system.[2] This fits in perfectly with our theory that, at some time after the conquest, numerous Muhammadans joined the community. It is probable that the event occurred about A.D. 1300. The story that Muhammadan Thags were all descended from seven famous tribes[3] may also have a historical root.

The confederacy lived and flourished for many centuries, and was still extremely prosperous at the moment when it had the ill fortune to attract the attention of the British Government in India. In 1829 special officers were appointed to investigate the system, and a serious campaign was started for the destruction of the whole organization. Within seven years the work was done. The success of this great effort is mainly due to the devotion and genius of Captain, later Major-General, Sir W. H. Sleeman.

5. Religious and ethical character of the Thags.—Those Europeans who had extended intercourse with Thags, during the period when the British Government were endeavouring to put the system down, gave very vivid descriptions of the kind of men they were.

(*a*) Every Thag was fully convinced that the goddess had created the system, and that she invariably saved Thags from punishment or disaster, so long as they obeyed the rules she had laid down for their operations. They were also immovably convinced that the consecrated pickaxe was so filled with the presence of the goddess as to be able to guide the Thags in their wanderings and to bring dire disaster on every one who disobeyed.[4]

(*b*) No Thag ever showed the slightest compunctions of conscience for his crimes. Sleeman writes:

'A Thug considers the persons murdered precisely in the light of victims offered up to the Goddess; and he remembers them, as a Priest of Jupiter remembered the oxen, and a Priest of Saturn the children sacrificed upon their altars. He meditates his murders without any misgivings, he perpetrates them without any emotions of pity, and he remembers them without any feelings of remorse. They trouble not his dreams, nor does their recollection ever cause him inquietude in darkness, in solitude, or in the hour of death.'[5]

Never did the strength of religious faith or the extraordinary domination which religion exercises over man's moral nature find clearer illustration.

LITERATURE.—W. H. Sleeman, *Ramaseeana, or a Vocabulary of the Language used by the Thugs, with an Appendix*

[1] Garbe, *Beiträge*, p. 187.
[2] W. H. Sleeman, *Rambles and Recollections of an Indian Official*, rev. and annot. ed. by V. A. Smith, London, 1915, p. 491.
[3] Sleeman, *Ramaseeana*, p. 11.
[4] *Ib.* p. 9.
[5] *Ib.* p. 71.

descriptive of the Fraternity, etc., Calcutta, 1836; *Report on the Depredations committed by the Thug Gangs*, do. 1840; Meadows Taylor, *Confessions of a Thug* (a novel), London, 1839, new ed., do. 1916; J. Hutton, *Popular Account of the Thugs and Dacoits*, do. 1857; *EBr*[11], *s.v.* 'Thugs'; R. Garbe, *Beiträge zu ind. Kulturgeschichte*, Berlin, 1903.

J. N. FARQUHAR.

THALES.—See IONIC PHILOSOPHY.

THĀNESAR. — Thānesar (Skr. *sthāṇvīśvara*, *sthāṇu*, a local name of Śiva, *īśvara*, 'lord'; also *sthāṇeśvara*, *sthāṇa*, 'shrine,' and *īśvara*) is a sacred town in the Karnāl District of the Panjāb, lat. 29° 59′ N.; long. 76° 50′ E., on the banks of the river Sarasvatī (*q.v.*). The Chinese pilgrim, Hiuen-Tsiang, describes it under the name of Sa-t'a-ni-shi-fa-lo, as the centre of the Hindu Holy Land (Dharmakshetra, Kurukshetra) and gives the local legends.[1] It has been identified with the Ostobalasara or Batangkaisara of Ptolemy.[2] In A.D. 1014 it was sacked by Maḥmūd of Ghaznī.[3] The most famous shrine was that dedicated to Chakrasvāmi, Viṣṇu, 'lord of the discus.' The statue is said to have been taken to Ghaznī to be broken up and trodden under foot. It was finally desecrated by Aurangzīb. Enormous crowds of pilgrims visit the place to bathe at eclipses of the sun.

LITERATURE.—A. Cunningham, *Archæological Survey of India Report*, ii. [Simla, 1871] 212 ff.; *IGI* xxiii. 305.

W. CROOKE.

THANK-OFFERING.—See SACRIFICE.

THEATRE.—See DRAMA.

THEFT.—See CRIMES AND PUNISHMENTS.

THEISM.—**1. Definition.**—The word 'theism' (Fr. *théisme*, Germ. *Theismus*) is a purely modern formation, implying a non-existent Greek θεισμός and an equally non-existent verb θείζω (on the analogy of μηδίζω, φιλιππίζω, and the like). As there is a certain vagueness about the meaning of the word in current English, it is necessary to begin this article with a convention as to the sense in which 'theism' will be employed in what follows. The word will be used throughout as a name for a philosophical theory as distinct from a practical religious faith. Perhaps the faith and the theory are never absolutely disjoined, but they are at least logically distinguishable. It may be doubted whether any man wholly untouched by the spirit of adoration and wholly devoid of love to God has ever been a genuine theist in philosophy, and again whether one can be in earnest with a philosophical belief in God without being led on to regulate his life by that belief. But it is at least possible to practise love of God and trust in God without making any conscious attempt to find a speculative explanation of the world. There are many who, in George Tyrrell's phrase, share the faith of Simon Peter without concerning themselves about his theology. The present article will be exclusively concerned with the philosophical conception of God as the ultimate ground of things. Current usage seems to require a further distinction. It seems necessary to discriminate theism not only from atheism (*q.v.*), the denial that God exists, and scepticism or agnosticism (*q.v.*), the refusal to answer any question about the ultimate ground of things, but also from deism (*q.v.*), which, in its way, also treats God as an ultimate ground. We shall probably not depart far from the implications of current language if we agree to define theism as the doctrine that the ultimate ground of things is a single supreme reality which is the source of everything other than itself and has the characters of being (*a*) intrinsically complete or perfect and (*b*), as a consequence, an adequate object of unqualified adoration or worship. Belief in a ground of things which is not intrinsically complete and perfect, and consequently no adequate object of adoration, but at best of respect and admiration, would at the present day probably be described by every one as deism rather than as theism. Thus the suggested definition in fact coincides with the famous formula of St. Anselm, that God is *id quo maius cogitari non potest*, 'the being than which none greater can be thought.'[1]

[1] S. Beal, *Si-yu-ki*, London, 1884, i. 183 ff.

[2] J. W. McCrindle, *Ancient India as described by Ptolemy*, Calcutta, 1885, p. 128.

[3] H. M. Elliot, *Hist. of India*, London, 1867–77, ii. 452 ff.

It is evident that theism, thus understood, is incompatible with polytheism (*q.v.*) and also with any doctrine, theological or metaphysical, which asserts a plurality of independent and equally ultimate 'reals,' whether in the form of a dualism between God, the good principle, and an immaterial evil principle (Zoroastrianism, Manichaeism [*qq.v.*]), or between God and matter, or in that of an ultimate plurality of unoriginated 'souls' or 'persons,' or in any other shape. All such doctrines involve the denial that there is any object which answers to the definition *id quo maius cogitari non potest*. For this reason the various modern theories of a finite or limited deity are inconsistent with strict theism. For a deity limited by restrictions arising outside his own nature is manifestly not the source of all reality other than himself, and thus not God in the sense in which we are using that word. And, if the 'limitations' are asserted to be self-limitations, due to the nature of God Himself (as in the philosophy of Hastings Rashdall), we have to face a dilemma. Either the presence of these limitations in the deity is a defect, and the deity is therefore not God in our sense at all, or their presence is not a defect, and there is then no sense in calling them restrictions or limitations, as it is their absence which would, in this case, be the defect.

It is mainly on the ground of alleged difficulties in the notion of the divine Omnipotence that these theories are recommended. But the difficulties seem due to misunderstanding. Omnipotence means only power to do whatever is consistent with God's own perfection. It is no real limitation of the divine power to hold, as most theologians and philosophers have done, that God cannot do what is in itself absurd—*e.g.*, cannot make a false proposition true, or make virtue vice, or annihilate Himself. The old Stoic boast that the sage is in one respect more powerful than God, because he can put an end to his existence if he grows tired of it, is a mere false paradox.

It is, perhaps, more important to be clear on the point that theism, as defined, is equally inconsistent with the type of philosophic monism called by James Ward 'singularism'—the theory that there is only one existent, the Absolute, and that this single existent is the true subject of all significant propositions. If we mean by God a being from whom all else that exists derives its being and who can be worshipped, then the belief in God necessarily implies belief in the real existence of beings who can worship God. To say that God is the source of existence implies that God is not all that exists. From a theistic point of view it is, no doubt, proper to call God, the being from whom all others are derived, the Absolute or unconditioned being, but only on the condition that the Absolute is not equated with all that really exists. The underived source of existence may, in virtue of its unique intrinsic completeness or perfection, be called the *ens realissimum*, but the very use of such a phrase implies that there are other *entia realia*.

It will probably be readily admitted that the ἓν καὶ πᾶν doctrine of Spinoza cannot be reasonably called theism, nor have the most distinguished representatives of singularism in

[1] *Proslogion*, ch. 2.

our own times shown any desire to claim the name of theists. It should be recognized that the popular language about a purely 'immanent God,' as opposed to the 'transcendent God' of orthodox Christian theology, is equally incompatible with genuine theism, inasmuch as it conflicts with the recognition of a real distinction between the supreme source of existence and the dependent existents. It is just this distinction which is vital in a theistic philosophy, and, for this reason, it may be taken as a fair test of the theism of a philosophy whether its way of conceiving the relation of its God to the world is compatible with a real recognition of the divine transcendence.

2. Philosophy and theism.—If we look at the history of European philosophy, it may be said that in the main the general trend of philosophic thought, even independently of the influence of positive religions, has been theistic, at least from the time of Plato to our own day. Even the agnosticism of Herbert Spencer, when all the qualifications with which it is enunciated by its author are taken fully into account, has a recognizable theistic tendency and might be said, apart from its blunders about dynamics, to be little more than a very crude reproduction of the 'negative theology' which is really one-half of the orthodox Christian doctrine of God. As will be shown directly, this tendency to theism is a direct consequence of the permanent influence of Plato on all subsequent developments in philosophy. Apart from materialism (*q.v.*), which has never produced a philosopher of the first rank, the main antitheistic influence in modern European philosophy has been that of Spinoza (*q.v.*), which has steadily affected metaphysical thought, perhaps even more outside than within the professionally philosophical schools, from the time of Jacobi and Lessing down to the end of the 19th century. This is partly accounted for by the powerful attraction exercised by the naturalistic strain in Spinoza's doctrine on the devotees of physical science, partly by the tendency of many of the most prominent 19th cent. representatives of the Hegelian line of thought to interpret Hegel (*q.v.*) in a Spinozistic sense.

Whether the Spinozistic interpretation of Hegel is the true one might admit of question, and it has been rejected by such eminent Hegelian students as Hutchison Stirling and J. M. E. McTaggart, in the one case for a definitely theistic interpretation, in the other for a version which has more affinity with the monadism of Leibniz (*q.v.*) than with Spinoza's singularism. But in the main Hegel has become known, at least in the English-speaking world, through the work of philosophers with strong Spinozistic prepossessions, with the consequence that the influence of Hegelian ways of thinking has been definitely hostile to theism. Even among professedly Christian theologians allegiance to Hegel in philosophy has usually led to an extreme 'immanence' doctrine of God which at least compromised the theistic position.

More ephemeral has been the influence excited in the last half of the 19th cent. by the pessimistic atheism of Schopenhauer (*q.v.*), and in the last twenty or twenty-five years by the brilliant, if incoherent, anti-Christian polemics of Nietzsche (*q.v.*). Both the pessimism of Schopenhauer and the antitheism of Nietzsche are, however, too little reasoned and too obviously matters of personal temperament to be regarded as of permanent philosophical importance. The influence of Hegel, also, and still more that of Spinoza, would seem to be for the present a spent force. In the present state of philosophy the most formidable rival to theism as an explanation of the world appears to be the thoroughgoing rationalist pluralism of the 'new realism,' represented at its best by the writings of Bertrand Russell and G. E. Moore. Of this doctrine, as well as of the supposed objection to theism arising from the evolutionist's alleged vision of Nature as 'red in tooth and claw,' something is said below (§ 17).

3. Plato. — The importance of Plato as the creator of philosophical theology makes it necessary to begin any serious account of theism as a philosophical theory with a clear statement of the Platonic position, so far as that position was expressed by Plato in his writings. To call Plato the creator of philosophic theology does not, of course, mean that the belief in God is an invention of Plato. As has often been remarked, the general trend of the best Greek thought on the problems of human conduct and destiny—as represented, *e.g.*, by such poets as Aeschylus and Euripides—is in the direction of a vague monotheism. And it cannot be seriously doubted that an earnest practical faith in God was characteristic of Pythagoras and of Socrates. Even the most unreasonable scepticism about the historical good faith of Plato's accounts of his master cannot obscure the fact that Socrates gave up the whole of his mature life to the execution of a mission to which he believed himself to have been called by God and died as a martyr to his calling. But this, so far as we know, was a matter of personal religious conviction rather than of speculative theory. Even Plato himself does not attempt a formal philosophical statement and justification of the belief in God until we come to the *magnum opus* of his old age, the *Laws*. In his best known earlier writings—*e.g.*, the *Republic*—great stress is laid upon the importance for the formation of moral character of an ethically adequate conception of the divine nature. God must be thought of as perfectly good, and current religion must be purged of everything which suggests that there is anything unethical in His character or that His dealings with men have any other purpose than their true good. It is just because God is perfectly good that (*Republic*, *Theaetetus*) the end of life may be said to be to 'become like God.' God fashioned the world and made it the best possible world because it would be unworthy of His goodness to make it otherwise (*Timaeus*). True piety is to be a 'fellow-worker' with God (*Euthyphro*). We are God's sheep and He is our shepherd (*Politicus*). The souls of the righteous are in the hand of God, and when they depart from us it is to be with Him (*Phaedo*). But this is, of course, the language of religion, not of science, and we are made to understand the difference by the simple fact that nearly all that is said of God, outside the *Laws*, beyond the one emphatic statement about His perfect goodness, is conveyed in 'myths,' *i.e.* in imaginative stories, as to which we are cautioned that we cannot undertake to pronounce on their strict truth. Nor is any attempt made to *prove* either the existence or the perfect goodness of God. In particular the story of creation in the *Timaeus* is, as we are explicitly warned, not to be taken as scientific truth, but as a tale which is the most probable that can be told about matters which lie outside the region within which scientific knowledge is possible. If we did not possess the *Laws*, it would be legitimate, as in fact it is not, to doubt whether Plato did not agree with Kant that reasoned scientific knowledge of God is impossible, though on grounds which are not identical with Kant's. In the tenth book of the *Laws*, however,[1] we have a formal proof of God's existence, wholly devoid of any features of mythical colouring, which is expressly declared to be conclusive. The argument, the main principle of which had been already anticipated in the *Phaedrus*,[2] is as follows. The most universal characteristic of things is motion and change. Now, motions are of two kinds, (*a*) impressed, and (*b*) original or spontaneous. Or, to use Plato's own phraseology, there are motions which are able only to move something else (impressed or communicated movements), and there are motions which 'move themselves as well as other things.' And native or spontaneous movement is logically prior to impressed or communicated movement. We cannot

[1] 887 A–899 E. [2] *Phaedrus*, 245 C–E.

regard all movements as impressed or communicated without falling into an impossible logical *regressus in indefinitum*. Further, 'motion which moves itself' is precisely what we mean when we talk of ψυχή, 'soul.' 'Soul' is simply a shorter name for the κίνησις ἑαυτὴν κινεῖν δυναμένη. It is just when we see a thing manifestly capable of internally initiated movement or change that we feel bound to say that the thing in question is 'animated' or has a 'soul.' It follows, then, that souls and their various 'motions' (judgment, volition, hope, desire, and the like) are prior to bodies and their motions or changes. All bodily processes are derivative from and dependent on 'motions' of the soul, and it is just for this reason that Plato explicitly denies the doctrine, often imputed to him by the uncritical, that 'matter' can be the principle of evil. Further, good souls, in the degree of their goodness, are sources of orderly and beneficent motions; evil souls, of disorderly and evil motions. Now, the great recurrent motions which science discovers in the universe (the periodic motions of the heavenly bodies) are all regular and orderly and belong to the class of the 'good' motions. Hence they must be due to good souls. (It had been carefully laid down in an earlier passage that all apparent irregularities and anomalies in these motions are only apparent and disappear as our science becomes more adequate.) If, then, we define God as a perfectly good soul, we may say that, since the great motions of the universe are all perfectly orderly, they must be caused by God. God, however, cannot be the only soul, or 'movement that moves itself.' For, though the *magnalia naturae* exhibit perfect regularity, there are also irregular and destructive motions, such as those, *e.g.*, of disease or those due to a wicked will; and these are just as actual as facts as anything else. Thus the facts of the universe bear witness to the existence of souls which are not wholly good. There must be at least one 'bad' soul, which is not God, and there may, of course, be as many more as are required to account for the observed facts. The transcendence of God is thus safeguarded.

Plato's language about the 'bad' souls has been misunderstood both in ancient and in modern times. Plutarch[1] thought that he had discovered in Plato's words the doctrine of an ultimate dualism between a good and an evil world-soul. This view did not find favour with the Platonists of antiquity, but has been revived in modern times by Zeller, from the weight of whose name it has obtained a wholly undeserved consideration. Plato says nothing about an evil principle, in the *Laws* or anywhere else. What he does say[2] is merely that all motions cannot be due to a single soul; there must be at least two, the 'beneficent' and 'that which has power to effect the contrary results.' The whole context suggests that the bad souls of which he is thinking are chiefly those of passionate and ignorant men, which, of course, are numerous. It should further be noted that, in the passage of the *Laws* containing the theistic argument, Plato speaks throughout in the plural of 'gods,' giving the soul which moves the sun as an example of his meaning. This is, however, a mere consequence of the fact that the legislation of the *Laws* is designed for an ordinary Greek community. It is assumed that the State religion of the colony will recognize 'gods many,' and Plato's object is to substitute the heavenly bodies, or rather the souls which move them, as types of regularity and beneficence, for the morally frail and passionate anthropomorphic deities of actual Greek cults. Of Plato's personal conviction of the unity of God there can be no real doubt. The unity of God, 'the best soul,' follows in fact, as we may see from the *Timaeus*, from the unity of the universe. The universe is one and is a rational system; therefore it is the product of one intelligence.[3] That a Greek writing for Greeks should allow himself to speak of θεοί explains itself; what is really significant is that Plato speaks so frequently, and just when he wishes to be most impressive, of θεός.[4]

From the goodness of God, since God is a soul (ψυχή), it follows that everything in the world is governed by a wise and beneficent Providence, and that God's dealings with man are perfectly and inexorably just. Thus the tenth book of the *Laws* definitely creates 'natural theology' as a branch of philosophy for the first time and indicates once for all its main doctrines—the existence and goodness of God, the reality of God's providential government of the universe, the immortality of the soul, and the correspondence between man's destiny and his works. These doctrines together make up what was known as 'natural' or 'philosophical' theology, as distinct from both 'poetic' theology—the stories told of the gods by the poets—and 'civil' theology, which consists in knowledge of the cultus prescribed by the State.[1]

The question whether Plato's theology amounts to a complete theism is not without its difficulties. On the one hand, there is no doubt that, as Burnet has said,[2] Plato regarded his doctrine of God as the central thing in his whole system. It is precisely the activity of God, the perfectly good soul, that connects the world of 'becoming,' *i.e.* 'Nature,' the world of all that we call empirical existence, with the system of εἴδη. The reason why there is a world of 'things' at all is just that God, the perfectly good soul, exists and is eternally active. The perfectly good soul, of course, has a perfect knowledge of 'the Good,' and its activity consists in reproduction or 'imitation' of the Good. Thus all existents other than God owe the very fact of their existence to God, as they owe it also to Him that they are what they are. Still it does not appear that the Platonic God is *all* that later theists have meant by the Supreme. He is an existent, though a perfect one, and beyond all existents there is the system of 'form' or 'numbers.' This is the pattern (παράδειγμα) after which God makes heaven and earth and all that is in them, and is thus something metaphysically prior to God Himself. If we understand by theism the doctrine that God is the sole unconditioned source not only of existents but also of real possibilities, we shall have to say that it is only in Neo-Platonism that Greek philosophy succeeds in being fully theistic.

A word or two may be said about the argument by which Plato establishes the existence of God. It contains in itself the germs of more than one of the 'proofs of the being of God' which have become traditional. Its presuppositions are two: (1) the universal validity of the principle of causality, and (2) the regularity of the cosmical motions—the 'reign of law' in the physical world. From the principle of causality, taken together with the assumption that there cannot be an infinite regress in the causal series, comes the conclusion that there must be an original cause (or causes) of all movements, which is 'self-moving'—*i.e.* a 'soul' or 'souls'—and from the regularity of the cosmic motions and the systematic interconnexion between them it follows that the ultimate 'mover' is the perfectly good soul. Thus Plato's reasoning combines in one argument the principle of the cosmological argument from the 'contingency of the world' to the existence of a First Cause and that of the argument from design, which is not degraded by Plato, as it has often been by modern apologists, into an argument from the alleged adaptation of the world to our individual convenience. As understood by Plato, the

[1] *De animae procreat. in Timaeo*, 1014 E.
[2] *Laws*, 896 E. [3] *Timaeus*, 30 D–31 B.
[4] In *Ep.* 13 he writes to Dionysius II. that he will distinguish letters of real importance from those which he is obliged to write as a matter of formal politeness by mentioning θεός and not θεοί in the opening sentences.

[1] The distinction in this form became fixed in consequence of the fact that it was adopted by the Roman encyclopaedist M. Terentius Varro and taken over from him by St. Augustine in the *de Civitate Dei*. The theology of the philosophers was called 'natural,' not, of course, with any thought of a contrast with 'revealed' truth, but because it was held to be scientific and true, unlike mythology, which the poets were believed to have invented, and the cultus of the State, which, as Hobbes puts it, 'is not philosophy but law.'
[2] *Greek Philosophy*, pt. i., *Thales to Plato*, London, 1914, p. 335.

argument from design is simply the argument from the intelligibility of the world of actual facts and events to intelligence in the cause which produces and sustains it.[1] Plato's argument is thus an *argumentum a posteriori*, in the correct scholastic, not in the inaccurate Kantian, sense of the phrase *a posteriori*; *i.e.*, it is an argument from the character of a known effect to the character of its cause. That there is a world of mutable things, and that, as scientific insight advances, the processes in this world of mutability are more and more found to exhibit conformity to intelligible laws, are assumed as empirically known truths, and without these empirical premisses the demonstration would not work. There is no hint in Plato of the line of thought which at a later date crystallized into the one genuinely *a priori* argument for the existence of God, the ontological proof, which, if valid, establishes its conclusion without any empirical premiss whatsoever.

4. Aristotle.—Aristotle's doctrine of God, though better known to the modern world than Plato's, is simply the Platonic doctrine rather more precisely expressed and shorn of its ethical and practical applications. With Aristotle, as with Plato, the doctrine of God is absolutely central, and the argument is once more based upon the assumption of the causal principle. Like Plato, Aristotle contends that communicated or impressed motion presupposes original or spontaneous motion, and like Plato he regards ψυχή as the one source of spontaneous movement. But here he is led to make a further refinement. The 'motions of the soul' arise from ὄρεξις, 'appetition,' and appetition is always appetition of something apprehended as good (ὀρεγόμεθα διότι δοκεῖ). This apprehension of an object as good is an exercise of νοῦς, an act of immediate intelligent apprehension. The apprehension is not itself a movement, though it gives rise to motions both of the soul and of the body. We must not then be content to trace back all motions to their origin in the 'movement which can move itself,' but behind even this we must look for an 'unmoved mover,' an unchanging initiator of all change. Otherwise we shall simply fall into an indefinite regress, and an indefinite regress in the order of efficient causes is unthinkable (the principle of the argument from the 'contingency of the world'). The unity of the supreme First Mover once more follows from the unity of the physical world. The whole physical world is a scene of 'becoming,' in which the potentialities latent in things are developed into actuality by the agency of efficient causes which are already themselves developed actualities. Behind every process of development lies the agency of such already developed actualities, and thus, just because there really is something and not nothing, there must be some actual agents which have never developed at all, but have been eternally and immutably active. From Aristotle's point of view, all processes of development depend upon the eternally regular and uninterrupted movements of the heavenly bodies. Hence there must be as many 'unmoved movers' as there are independent astronomical movements. Further, astronomical movements form a hierarchy. Each of the 50 odd concentric 'spheres' which Aristotle postulates to account for the apparent movements of the heavenly bodies has its own proper revolution and its own 'unmoved mover.' But there is one sphere which, without being enclosed by any other, encloses all the rest, and, according to the Aristotelian astronomy (which disagrees on this point wholly from Plato), communicates its movement to all the spheres it contains. This is the sphere of the fixed stars, which rotates uniformly on its axis in the period of 24 hours. The 'unmoved mover' of this sphere is consequently God. As that which He moves is one, and its movement is eternal, continuous, and regular, God is also one, eternal, immutable, the First Mover upon whom all motion in the universe depends.[1] So far Aristotle's doctrine is, in substance, that of Plato in the *Laws*, except that Aristotle has dogmatically committed himself to a particular astronomical theory, that of Eudoxus, which, for sound scientific reasons, did not commend itself to Plato. In his conception of the nature of the First Mover Aristotle departs more widely both from Plato and from true theism. God, as Aristotle describes Him, is not a ψυχή, but a νοῦς. And he infers from his doctrine that the First Mover must be unmoved the conclusion that the divine mind, unlike our minds, because it is unmoving, must eternally think one and the self-same object. Further, this object must be adequate to occupy the divine mind through eternity. It follows that the object of God's unbroken Sabbath of contemplation is God Himself. 'He thinks Himself and His thinking is a thinking of thinking (νόησις νοήσεως).'[2] In fact, though without the presence of God there could be no motion in the universe, God is supposed to be wholly unaware of the existence of the universe which He moves. He moves it by being an object of appetition to it, and thus it is aware of Him, but He is no more aware of it than the various objects of our human appetitions need be aware of us and our desire for them. The world's desire after God is precisely and exactly the 'desire of the moth for the star.' This conception, due apparently to Aristotle's own temperamental indifference to the practical life, of course strikes out of philosophical theology the doctrine of Providence and of the righteousness of God's dealings with man. In fact, since Aristotle held that 'goodness of character' is a different thing from 'goodness of intellect,' he is quite consistent when at the end of his *Ethics* he expressly denies that goodness of character or moral goodness is predicable of God.[3] God, in fact, becomes in Aristotle what Aristotle himself would have liked to be, if the conditions of human life would allow it—a mere 'magnified and non-natural' scientific thinker. In respect of this evacuation of all ethical content from the idea of God, Aristotle may fairly be said to be the founder of philosophical deism, as Plato was the founder of philosophical theism. It is clear that to Aristotle and his disciple Eudemus, who identifies the speculative life with the contemplation and worship of God,[4] the First Mover was an object of genuine worship and reverence, though the worship of such a being could have no real connexion with active good works; but a non-ethical deity, who knows nothing of humanity's needs and aspirations, can never become the centre of an enduring religion. Hence it is not surprising that, while Platonism continued throughout later antiquity to be the creed of educated religious men, Aristotelianism was reduced to simple naturalism within half a century of Aristotle's death by the third head of the school, Strato of Lampsacus.[5]

5. Epicureans.—The deism of the Epicureans is of no significance for natural theology. For all practical purposes the school were, what their opponents called them, pure atheists, since it was

[1] The notion of an unconscious intelligence or reason as the ground of things is excluded by Plato's doctrine that νοῦς can only exist in a ψυχή (*Sophistes*, 249 A, *Philebus*, 30 C, *Timaeus*, 30 B).

[1] See for all this in particular *Metaphysics*, 1072*a* 19–1073*b* 17, *Physics*, 258*b* 10 ff.

[2] *Metaphysics*, 1074*b* 33.

[3] *Ethica Nicomachea*, 1178*b* 7–23.

[4] τὸν θεὸν θεραπεύειν καὶ θεωρεῖν (*Ethica Eudemea*, 1249*b* 20).

[5] Cicero, *Academ.* ii. 38, *de Natura Deorum*, i. 35; Plutarch, *adv. Colotem*, p. 1115.

one of their principal tenets that the gods not merely take no interest in the doings of men but play no part in cosmology; the world has been formed and continues to exist *opera sine divom.* The only use made by Epicurus of gods is a trivial one; their existence accounts for the phantasms of superhuman beings which are seen in dreams.

6. Stoics.—In Stoicism, on the other hand, natural theology of a kind plays a prominent part, though the original Stoic doctrine can hardly be called theistic. The theology of Zeno, Cleanthes, and Chrysippus is a materialistic doctrine of immanence. The substance of all that exists is a single body; in fact, the universe is a 'fire.' The cosmic fire is intelligent, and it is this fire that is God. This doctrine, borrowed by the founders of Stoicism from Heraclitus, but put forward with a conscious opposition, which Heraclitus would not have understood, to the immaterialism of Plato and Aristotle, is the nearest counterpart that ancient thought has to show to the Spinozist conception of the one substance with its plurality of disparate but 'parallel' attributes. But with the Stoics it is not, as with Spinoza, thought, but extension, that is the 'Aaron's rod that swallows all the rest' of the attributes.

As to the details of the doctrine. God and the world, though really one, are logically distinguished. At one time in the history of the universe the 'fire,' or God, exists alone in its purity and contains within itself all the σπερματικοὶ λόγοι, or constitutive ratios, of everything. There follows a process of evolution, identified by the Stoics with the 'downward path,' or ὁδὸς κάτω, of Heraclitus, in which the σπερματικοὶ λόγοι of all things are unfolded and a world of diversified existents produced. There is a second and antithetical process, regarded as identical with the Heraclitan ὁδὸς ἄνω, or 'upward path,' and ending in an ἐκπύρωσις, or general conflagration; the plurality of diverse existents is once more converted into the original fire, and God is left once more as the only existent. The whole double process of evolution followed by involution constitutes a 'great year,' and the life of the universe is made up of an endless succession of such 'great years,' each repeating the events of the preceding without variation (a fancy which we know from a fragment of Eudemus preserved by Simplicius in his commentary on the *Physics* of Aristotle[1] to go back to the early Pythagoreans, and which has been revived in our own time by Nietzsche as the doctrine of 'eternal recurrence'). The details of the process of evolution belong to the Stoic physics and do not concern us here. In accord with this doctrine, God is sometimes declared to be the same as the κόσμος, or universe, sometimes distinguished from it. 'They use the word κόσμος in three senses, to mean (1) God Himself . . . who is, of course, imperishable and unoriginate, the artificer of the world-order, who resumes into Himself and again begets out of Himself the whole of being in accord with certain cycles of time; (2) the world-order formed by the heavenly bodies, (3) the composite of these two.'[2] Hence the full definition of God was that God is πῦρ τεχνικόν, ὁδῷ βαδίζον ἐπὶ γένεσιν κόσμου, ἐμπεριειληφὸς πάντας τοὺς σπερματικοὺς λόγους, καθ' οὓς ἕκαστα καθ' εἱμαρμένην γίνεται, 'a fire of craft [or 'art'] proceeding in order to the generation of a world, containing in itself all the constitutive ratios in accord wherewith all things come to be in the order of destiny.'[3] Strictly speaking, this doctrine, which equates God with the κόσμος, is not theism at all, since it denies that there are any real existents other than God. But religiously the founders of Stoicism, as we see from the well-known *Hymn* of Cleanthes, were fervent worshippers of God. It was characteristic of the school from the first that they insisted strongly on the moral side of theism. Like the Platonists, they were vigorous asserters of Providence and used the doctrine to justify even such things as astrology, prophetic dreams, oracles, and divination. Providence was, however, regarded as identical with absolute predestination, and scientifically explained by the rigid mechanical concatenation of all events in a single causal system. Hence, as may be seen from the controversial essay of Plutarch on *The Contradictions in Stoicism* (περὶ στωικῶν ἐναντιωμάτων), the devices by which the Stoic philosophers tried to conciliate their optimistic belief in the providential order with their materialistic monism were often really fatal to the ascription of moral goodness to God.

In the writings of the Stoics of the Roman period, from whom the ideas of the school have become familiar to the modern world, the materialistic and fatalistic side of the doctrine is less prominent. They often seem to be teaching a simple spiritual theism. It must be remembered that all these writers are later than, and were greatly influenced by, Posidonius of Apamea (first half of 1st cent. B.C.), who gravely modified the original doctrine of Zeno and Chrysippus by contaminating it with Platonism, as his contemporary, Antiochus of Ascalon, tried unsuccessfully to introduce Stoicism into the Academy. It is precisely those among the later Stoics, such as Seneca, who can be shown to depend most completely on Posidonius in whom the monism and materialism of Stoicism is least apparent. To understand the real tendencies of the system, it is important to study it as it was before Posidonius had Platonized it. For this purpose the anti-Stoic essays of Plutarch and the account of Stoic doctrine given in the life of Zeno by Diogenes Laertius are particularly valuable. Indispensable for special students is H. von Arnim's collection of the complete fragments of the Stoics of the pre-Roman period, *Stoicorum Veterum Fragmenta*, 3 vols., Leipzig, 1904–05.

The one really original contribution made by Stoicism to natural theology is the appeal to 'innate ideas' and the *consensus gentium* as an argument for the existence of God. The doctrine of innate ideas (κοιναὶ ἔννοιαι, *notitiae communes*) is a consequence of the Aristotelian criticism of Plato. According to the theory of method expounded more specially in the *Phaedo* and the central books of the *Republic*, the work of science begins with the provisional assumption of a theory (ὑπόθεσις) to account for a group of observed facts. If the observed facts (τὰ φαινόμενα) agree with the results of deduction from the ὑπόθεσις, the 'appearances' are said to be 'saved' by the theory, and it is so far vindicated. It may still, however, be called in question, and in that case will have to be defended by being deduced from some more ultimate premisses which the impugner himself admits. It thus becomes a task for dialectic (or, as we should say, metaphysics), the highest science of all, to make a critical examination of the provisional assumptions (the unproved postulates) of all the other sciences and to discover the real unquestionable presuppositions of all knowledge. Aristotle insisted, as against this view, that the special postulates of each science must be self-evident when once they have been formulated. For the Stoics this doctrine, that every science depends upon self-evident universal premisses, created a difficulty, as in their theory of knowledge they were, unlike Aristotle, extreme sensationalists, regarding particular sense-perceptions as the foundation of all knowledge. They were accordingly obliged to provide some criticism or test by which those universal propositions which are valid generalizations from sensation may be discriminated from those which are not. An obvious test suggested itself. Generalizations which are made only by certain special groups of men or by particular individuals may fairly be supposed to be due to temperamental, educational, national, or racial bias; those which appear to be made without exception by all men, no matter how widely they differ in temperament, education, national traditions, social institutions, may be presumed to be formed spontaneously, and therefore naturally, *i.e.* as a consequence of the intrinsic character of mind. It is thus reasonable to regard these generalizations as true and thus to take the *consensus gentium* as the best guarantee for the truth of a belief. The Stoic κοιναὶ ἔννοιαι, 'common' notions, are thus innate in the very sense in which Descartes afterwards used the word. It is not meant that we come into the world with them already in our possession, but that the formation of them is due to the normal development of intelligence independently of any kind of bias. As the most obvious examples of such common notions the Stoics instanced the beliefs, which they held to be common to all mankind, 'that there are gods and that they care for us.'[1] All this passed, mainly through Cicero, into the natural theology of the 17th century. This explains why modern natural theologians have often been anxious to prove the universal diffusion

[1] Diels, p. 732, 26 = Diels, *Fragmente der Vorsokratiker*[3], Berlin, 1912, ii. 355, 8.

[2] Diogenes Laertius, vii. 70, 137.

[3] Aetius, *Placita*, i. 7, 33 (Diels, *Doxographi Graeci*, Berlin, 1879, p. 305). The same definition was given of φύσις, 'nature.' Cf. Cicero, *de Deor. Nat.* ii. 57: 'Zeno igitur ita naturam definit, ut eam dicat ignem esse artificiosum, ad gignendum progredientem via.'

[1] Diog. Laert. vii. 36, 52.

of the belief in God and why their critics have often laid great stress on travellers' reports which have been supposed to indicate the existence of 'atheistic' savages. The Stoics themselves, in appealing to universal agreement, did not, of course, mean to deny the sporadic appearance of individual atheists. This could be accounted for as the consequence of individual prejudices due to improper education and 'unnatural' institutions. What was supposed to be demonstrated was merely that belief in God and Providence is too widely diffused to be regarded as anything but a spontaneous and 'natural' conviction. The position taken up by some modern apologists who deny that there has ever been a single convinced and sincere atheist is an exaggeration of the Stoic doctrine.[1] It may be added that the degradation of the argument from design or 'intentional causality' into the crude form which it assumes in so much of our popular apologetics is mainly due to the extravagant exaltation of man by the Stoic philosophy. With Plato and Aristotle teleology means simply that the world of historical existents and processes is so ordered that it realizes an end which has absolute intrinsic worth.[2] It is to the Stoics that we owe the coarsening of the thought into the assertion that man and man's convenience and comfort are the intrinsic and absolute good which is the end realized by the cosmic processes. Thus they maintained that plants and animals exist only to furnish man with food and raiment convenient for him, or even with agreeable luxuries.

Porphyry[3] quotes from Chrysippus the statement that 'the gods made us for ourselves and one another, but animals for us, the horse to help us in war and the dog in hunting, leopards, bears, and lions, to practise ourselves in valour upon. The pig was made for nothing but to be sacrificed, and God mixed soul with its flesh like a seasoning to make it readily digestible for us. Shell fish of all kinds and birds he contrived that we might have no lack of soups and *entrées*.'[4] According to Plutarch,[5] Chrysippus carried things so far that he asserted in his work περὶ φύσεως that God made bugs to prevent us from sleeping too long and mice to teach us to take proper care of our cupboards.

7. Neo-Platonism.—In any account of the popular theism of antiquity prominence would have to be given to the utterances of the later Platonizing Roman Stoics, such as Seneca, and to the earnest defence of the ethical side of theism by writers like Plutarch and his contemporary Maximus of Tyre. Plutarch's philosophical essays which deal with the theistic problem are specially interesting, as his determination to treat Providence and the moral government of the world by God as serious matters leads him into sharp and acute criticism not only of the perfunctory deism of Epicurus but also of the Stoic pantheistic necessitarianism (especially in the essay περὶ στωικῶν ἐναντιωμάτων, which aims at showing that the materialism, pantheism, and determinism of Zeno and Chrysippus are inconsistent with their moral optimism and professed belief in an ethical Providence). Interesting, however, as this theological literature is to the historian of Platonism, it cannot be said to add anything of value to philosophical theism. The Neo-Platonist school, founded in Rome by Plotinus (*c.* A.D. 205–270), worked out for the first time a thoroughgoing metaphysical theism which provided the philosophical basis for the Christian theism of the whole Middle Ages. For the purposes of the present article it will be most convenient to reproduce the main features of this doctrine as it is presented by the great systematizer of the school, Proclus (A.D. 410–485), in his στοιχείωσις θεολογική, *Rudiments of Platonic Theology*.[1] In what follows nothing will be quoted from Proclus which does not form part of the teaching of the whole Neo-Platonic school from Plotinus onwards.

In Plato's own theology, or at least in the statement of it which he gives in his writings, as we have seen, God is not quite all that the Christian theist has usually meant by God. God is the supremely good 'soul' and the source, it appears, of all existents other than Himself. But we are not positively told what is the relation of God to the supreme principles of the Platonic system, the forms (εἴδη, ἰδέαι) or numbers, and in the mythical picture-language of the *Timaeus* these forms (or numbers) are certainly represented as superior to God; they are the pre-existing model or pattern which God contemplates in fashioning the world of finite existents, or, as Plato calls it, the world of 'becoming.' There is no warrant anywhere in Plato for the psychologizing interpretation, often put on his language since the time of Philo of Alexandria, which makes the forms into thoughts of the divine mind. This means in modern language that, though God is regarded as the source of actuality, He is not unambiguously held to be also the source of all real possibility. In Neo-Platonism the further step is taken. God is thought of as the absolute *prius* of everything, and the world of existents as dependent on Him not only for its actuality but also for all its possibilities. God is no longer regarded as a soul or even as a mind, but is simply identified at once with the Good which is described in *Republic*, bk. vi., as the source of 'being and knowledge,' though itself 'on the other side of' both being and knowledge, and with the One which, according to Aristotle, Plato regarded as the οὐσία, or formal element, in the forms themselves and as the same thing as the Good.[2] The One thus becomes in Neo-Platonism a transcendent God of whom nothing can in strictness be predicated. It must not even be said to be good, since it is identical with goodness, not a subject to which goodness can be ascribed as an attribute. Nor must it be said to be or exist; it is not a being or existent, but the transcendent source of all being, and is therefore regularly said to be ὑπερούσιον, 'super-essential,' or 'super-substantial.'[3] God, thus conceived as the transcendent and ineffable source both of actuality and of real possibility (of existences and of 'essences'), is connected with the actual world by the Neo-Platonic theory of causality. The theory is commonly known as that of 'emanation,' but the metaphor of emanation is with Plotinus and Proclus only a metaphor, and the

[1] For a classic statement of the general Stoic view of the place of God in the scheme of things see, besides the famous *Hymn* of Cleanthes preserved in Stobaeus, *Ecl.* i. 1, 12, p. 25, 3 (critical text in von Arnim, *Stoicorum Veterum Fragmenta*, i. 121 f., also J. Adam, *Texts to illustrate a Course of Elementary Lectures on Greek Philosophy after Aristotle*, London and New York, 1902, p. 54 f., and A. C. Pearson, *The Fragments of Zeno and Cleanthes*, Cambridge, 1891), the eloquent conclusion of [Aristotle] *de Mundo*, 397, b 9 ff. The latter gives the Posidonian version and betrays Academic influence by ending with a direct quotation from the 'admirable Plato' of *Laws*, 715 E–716 A. Cicero's expositions of Stoic theology, based mainly on Posidonius, are too well known to require special mention.

[2] It is significant, as Burnet has remarked, that the very word 'teleology,' as its form shows, is derived not directly from τέλος but from the adjective τέλειος, 'whole,' 'complete.'

[3] *De Abstinentia*, iii. 20.

[4] Cf. Cicero, *de Nat. Deor.* ii. 37: 'Scite enim Chrysippus, ut clypei causa involucrum, vaginam autem gladii, sic praeter mundum cetera omnia aliorum causa esse generata: ut eas fruges atque fructus quos terra gignit, animantium causa; animantes autem, hominum. . . . Ipse autem homo ortus est ad mundum contemplandum et imitandum.'

[5] *De Stoicorum repugnantiis*, 1044 C.

[1] There is no good critical edition of this important work. The least defective is that in F. Creuzer's *Initia philosophiae ac theologiae*, 3 vols., Frankfort, 1820–22.

[2] *Metaphys.* A 987*b* 20: ὡς μὲν οὖν ὕλην τὸ μέγα καὶ τὸ μικρὸν εἶναι ἀρχὰς, ὡς δ' οὐσίαν τὸ ἕν. A 988*a* 14: ἔτι δὲ τὴν τοῦ εὖ καὶ τοῦ κακῶς αἰτίαν, τοῖς στοιχείοις ἀπέδωκεν ἑκατέροις ἑκατέραν.

[3] Here we have the origin of the mystical 'negative way' in theology, and of the familiar scholastic doctrine that nothing whatever can be predicated univocally of God and of any creature, as well as of the proposition *Deus est suum esse*; *i.e.* in God the distinction between existence and *essentia*, valid for every other existent, ceases to have any meaning. It is from this last thought that the famous ontological argument for the being of God was destined to take its origin.

theory requires to be explained a little more fully, as it was not only influential throughout the Middle Ages but is tacitly presupposed in the famous attempt of Descartes to establish the existence of God in the *Third Meditation*. Causality, as understood by the Neo-Platonists, does not necessarily imply antecedence in time and is always a relation between substantival terms, not between events. The relation is dyadic and subsists between a producer (τὸ παράγον) and something which the activity of the producer calls into being (τὸ παραγόμενον). The cause of anything is the ground not merely of the existence of that thing but of its being what it is and having the character it has (the cause of its *essentia* as well as of its actuality). Causality is a relation of 'participation' (μέθεξις) or 'likeness'; *i.e.*, the effect (τὸ παραγόμενον), since it derives the fact that it is and its whole quality from its cause (τὸ παράγον), is like its cause, exhibits the same character but in a less perfect form.[1]

The Neo-Platonist theology is strictly creationist, not in the popular sense of regarding the world as having been made at a definite date in the past (all the Neo-Platonists held strongly that Plato, like Aristotle, meant to teach the 'eternity of the world'), but in the philosophical sense of maintaining the causal dependence of everything in the world upon God and upon God alone. What 'really is' and what 'becomes' form a hierarchy of manifestations of the excellences contained 'eminently' in the One, each member of the hierarchy, according as it is at a farther remove from God, exhibiting these excellences in a less perfect way. Proclus adds the further point that the causal activity of the higher principles extends farther down in the scale of being than that of those below them.[2] The One, or God, as we have seen, is 'above being' and is absolutely simple, not because it is void of character, but just because all perfections are completely and perfectly united and interpenetrant in it.[3] The reason why the One creates at all is that the One *is* goodness, and goodness is, of its very nature, active. It must 'overflow.'[4] That which is immediately produced by the 'overflowing' is νοῦς, 'intelligence' or 'understanding.' Or rather, since the fundamental inferiority of produced to producer shows itself at this stage in the form of a dualism, it is νοῦς together with the objects it contemplates, τὰ νοητά, the connected system of scientific concepts. The two are inseparable, for the νοητά 'have no subsistence outside the understanding'; they are not a realm of 'things-in-themselves,' for which Neo-Platonism has no room. As mind or understanding is an imperfect image or mirroring of the divine One, so soul is a further image or mirroring of mind. And mind and soul together make up for the Neo-Platonist the whole system of ὄντα, real things. Bodies, the natural world as disclosed through the senses, are images of soul and are properly not ὄντα but γιγνόμενα; they 'are' not, they 'become'—*i.e.*, they are 'appearances,' though we must remember that they really do appear and are the appearances or shows of souls, which are real ὄντα. Below these real shadows of real things, just as God was placed above the real things themselves, stands that 'shadow of a shade,' πρώτη ὕλη, bare 'stuff,' which neither is nor appears, and, as a mere potentiality of something better than itself, may properly be called μὴ ὄν.[5]

Besides being causally dependent on God, the series of ὄντα and γιγνόμενα is further connected with the One by ἐπιστροφή, 'inversion' or 'reflexion.' The effect not merely proceeds from its cause, but is inverted or reflected back into its cause. This is, in fact, a consequence of the identification of the First Cause with the universal Good. For the good of anything is that to union with which the thing in question aspires, and the universal Good is therefore, according to the old definition of Eudoxus, that οὗ πάντα ἐφίεται, 'that which all things go for.' As all things have their source in God, so all things find their end or completion in Him. In souls and minds this process of inversion takes place, as Proclus puts it, γνωστικῶς, as a γνῶσις, or knowing. It is in turning back on their source in contemplation that they come by self-knowledge, and are thus inverted into themselves as well as into it. The soul gets to know itself in learning to know νοῦς, and νοῦς learns its own true nature in contemplation of the One; in both cases self-knowledge is got by reaching out of one's self towards the higher.[1] Thus the transcendence of God, though it is so complete that we may not even predicate 'being' of Him, in no way interferes with the truth that the whole world 'lives and has its being' in God and has no origin or support but God.[2] The monotheism of this philosophy of religion is, of course, no more affected by the belief of the Neo-Platonists in an elaborate hierarchy of superhuman beings whom they call θεοί than the monotheism of Christians by the belief in the various orders of the angelic hierarchy, or that of Milton by his application of the appellation 'gods' to the fallen angels in *Paradise Lost*.

It should be particularly observed that the Neo-Platonic school, by definitely making the One its God and teaching that the One is 'beyond being,' is committed to theism as against pantheism. The world is in the One, but, precisely because the effect is only an imperfect mirroring of its cause, it would not be true to say in the same sense that the One is in the world. The relation between God and the world is that of one-sided dependence. God, or the One, produces νοῦς, ψυχή, and bodies; they do not produce the One. In fact, in the mythology elaborated by Proclus the ἐγκόσμιοι θεοί occupy the lowest rank among the orders of beings to whom he gives the name 'god,' thus corresponding to some of the middle ranks of the mediaeval hierarchy of angels.[3]

8. Anselm.—As is well known, when the Christian Church began to feel the need of a philosophical foundation for its theology, it sought that foundation primarily in Neo-Platonism. The Neo-Platonic influence was exerted in three main ways—through the Cappadocian Fathers, who, without incurring the condemnation which was passed on the speculations of Origen, incorporated much of Origen's Platonism in their system, through the prominent part played in the development of Christian theology by St. Augustine and Boethius, and through the authority enjoyed by the writings of the supposed Dionysius the Areopagite, a superficially Christianized version of the theological and angelological speculations of Proclus. The Neo-Platonic conception of God thus became part and parcel of orthodox Christian thought. It is this conception that St. Anselm assumes in his famous attempt to prove the existence of God by an argument which, in one form or another, has been a centre of philosophical controversy from the date of its first becoming generally known to our own day—the so-called 'ontological proof' of the existence of God. St. Anselm's own formulation of his argument will be found in chs. 2–3 of the little tract, written before he had been called from his monastery at Bec, to which he gave originally the name *Fides quaerens intellectum* and afterwards that of *Proslogion seu Alloquium de Dei existentia*. The object of the reasoning is to show that the existence of God is in fact an immediately evident truth. Uncertainty about God's existence is possible only so long as we are unaware of the true meaning of the word *Deus*. The argument, as given by Anselm, runs thus. By 'God' we

1 The technical phrase of Proclus is that the characters which exist καθ' ὕπαρξιν—*i.e.* so as to be properly predicable of it—in the effect exist κατ' αἰτίαν in its cause. The scholastic way of putting the matter is to say that what exists *formaliter*—as constituting the *forma* or *essentia*—in the effect exists *eminenter* or *eminentiore modo*, 'in a more excellent manner,' in its cause. It is in virtue of this doctrine that the philosophical theology of Neo-Platonism and orthodox Christianity acquires a positive side. Though we may not predicate of God any 'perfection' (*i.e.* positive attribute) of a creature, yet, since all creatures are produced solely by God, we may say that their perfections are in God 'in a more excellent manner.' Hence, though we are forbidden to predicate anything univocally of God and a creature, we are permitted to reason *per analogiam* from beauty, wisdom, power, goodness in the creatures to the presence of super-excellent beauty, power, wisdom, goodness in the Creator.

2 This is intended to justify in particular the view that 'bare matter,' though it cannot be regarded as produced by mind or soul, is still created by the One, and so to get rid of the dualism of God and matter.

3 So the schoolmen maintain, on the same ground, that each attribute of God, power, wisdom, and the rest, *is* God.

4 As the Christian mystics say, 'love *cannot* be idle.'

5 The Neo-Platonist 'matter' is thus identical with that of Aristotle, but it is important that it is regarded as the remotest production of the One, not, as with Aristotle, as a principle independent of and coaeval with God.

1 Bodies are incapable of 'inversion into self,' and they are not inverted into their immediate cause, soul, γνωστικῶς.

2 When Kingsley in *Hypatia* makes his Neo-Platonic philosopher misquote St. Paul as saying that it is God who 'lives and has His being' in us, he is going wrong from mere ignorance of the doctrine he is criticizing.

3 For the sources of the preceding paragraphs see Proclus, *Institutio theologica*, props. 1–6 (unity and plurality), 7–14 (causation, the good), 15–20 ('inversion'), 21, 23, 24, 31–47.

mean 'that than which nothing greater can be conceived.' It seems that a doubt may be felt about the existence of anything answering to this definition, since Scripture tells us that the fool has said in his heart (*i.e.* has thought) that there is no God. Anselm, in reply to such a 'fool,' argues as follows. Even the fool who doubts or denies the existence of 'that than which nothing greater can be thought' must understand what this phrase means before he can doubt or deny that there is such a thing.[1] Thus it is certain that God, as defined, is *in intellectu*—a phrase which means simply that the words 'that than which nothing greater can be thought' have a definite meaning. But, if God were only *in intellectu* (*i.e.*, if there were no object answering to the definition), we could think of something greater than God, for we could at least conceive that such a being was not merely thinkable but real.[2] Thus the argument is that, if 'that than which nothing greater can be conceived' exists only *in intellectu*, 'that than which nothing greater can be conceived' is not 'something than which nothing greater can be conceived,' and this is a formal contradiction *in terminis*. It follows therefore[3] that God cannot be conceived as non-existent and therefore that God cannot be conceived not to exist. How then can it be true that the fool 'has said in his heart' that God does not exist? Only in the sense that the fool attaches no sense or a mistaken sense to the word 'God.'[4] These few lines contain the whole of the famous 'proof'; the rest of the pamphlet is really taken up with the identification of 'that than which nothing greater can be conceived' with the universal Good.

Before going any farther, it may be well to make one or two reflexions on the general character of the argument as given by its originator. This is the more necessary as Anselm's reasoning is not quite identical with that of Descartes, who gives his own ontological proof in his *Fifth Meditation*, and it is principally from Kant's criticism of Descartes' argument that the ontological proof is known to modern students of philosophy. It will be noted that Anselm expressly presupposes the Neo-Platonic conception of God; it is the One of Plotinus and Proclus of which he undertakes to prove the reality. We should also observe that Anselm for the first time attempts a proof which is *a priori* in the proper sense of the phrase. The existence of the world is not one of the premisses of his reasoning, whereas with the Neo-Platonists the reality of the many is the starting-point of all argument. Again, it is no valid retort to Anselm to urge that his proof depends upon a definition and on nothing else, but nothing can be proved simply from a definition, since all definitions are merely conventions about the meaning of a sign. Anselm is not, of course, concerned to deny the truth of this account of definitions or to maintain that men are not free to attach any meaning they please to the sign *Deus*. The real question is whether among all our concepts there is just one, the concept of 'an x such that nothing greater than x can be conceived,' which implies *as part of its meaning* the actual existence of the corresponding object. It seems to the writer of this article that Anselm is at least right in maintaining that, if we can frame the concept 'thing than which no greater can be conceived,' we are bound to think of the object thus conceived as actual. To admit that what we are necessitated to think may be false is fatal to all philosophy and all science, and no exception can be taken to Anselm's argument on the ground that it excludes such an ultimate agnosticism. The really difficult question is rather whether there is any such concept as 'thing than which no greater can be conceived.'[5] The problem is not whether, granting that Anselm's definition of God has a meaning, the actual existence of God is included in that meaning, but whether the words given as the definition have a meaning at all or are not rather an 'unmeaning noise,' like the words, *e.g.*, 'line so crooked that none crookeder can be conceived' or 'rational fraction so small that none smaller can be conceived.' This is the difficulty which we shall find arising in connexion with every version of the ontological argument which has been given by metaphysicians. Whatever we may think on this point, it is plain that a proof of the Anselmian type is not what is ordinarily meant in logic by proof or demonstration. Its real object is not to deduce the existence of God from any more ultimate or certain premisses, but to find a definition of God such that, when the definition is substituted for the *definiendum*, the proposition 'There is one and only one God' is seen to be self-evident. The real function of the argument is, like that of an Aristotelian 'induction,' not to demonstrate something, but to 'point something out.'

[1] 'Certe idem ipse insipiens, cum audit hoc ipsum quod dico . . . intelligit quod audit, et quod intelligit in intellectu ejus est, etiamsi non intelligat illud esse' (*Proslogion*, ch. 2).

[2] 'Convincitur ergo etiam insipiens esse vel in intellectu aliquid, quo nihil maius cogitari potest; quia hoc cum audit, intelligit; et quidquid intelligitur, in intellectu est. Et certe id, quo maius cogitari nequit, non potest esse in intellectu solo. Si enim vel in solo intellectu est, potest cogitari esse et in re: quod maius est' (*ib.* ch. 2).

[3] 'Sic ergo vere est aliquid quo maius cogitari non potest ut nec cogitari possit non esse: et hoc es tu, Domine Deus noster' (ch. 3).

[4] 'Nemo intelligens id quod Deus est, potest cogitare quia Deus non est; licet haec verba dicat in corde, aut sine ulla, aut cum aliqua extranea significatione' (ch. 4).

[5] Hobbes and others raised this question very pertinently when they replied to Descartes' argument from our possession of an 'idea of God' that we possess no 'idea' of God.

Anselm's argument was at once subjected to severe criticism by his contemporary Gaunilo of Marmoutiers, in his 'Apology for the Fool' (*Liber pro Insipiente*), a tract which more than sustains comparison for real acumen with the better-known criticisms of the *Critique of Pure Reason*. Gaunilo remarks that it is one of the premisses of the Anselmian argument that *id quo nihil maius cogitari potest* exists at least in the *intellectus* even of the atheistic fool. It is assumed that God exists *in intellectu*, and the only point discussed is whether He exists also *in re*. But what is meant by this statement? It may mean only that the fool understands the meaning of the statement 'God exists.' But we understand the meaning of many propositions which we know to be false. Hence the existence of God is not proved by simply urging that we know what the theist means when he says that God exists. To make the argument valid, it ought to be shown that the fool cannot understand what the theist means without also seeing that his assertion is true, and Gaunilo denies that Anselm has established this point. Arguing, not as an empiricist, but from Neo-Platonic premisses common to himself with Anselm, he urges that in point of fact we have no positive adequate concept of God;[1] and it adds nothing to our information to be told that God is greater than all the things of which we have positive concepts.[2]

So far Gaunilo (who has been oddly mistaken by some modern critics for an empiricist) is simply playing off the negative or agnostic side of the theology common to himself with Anselm against the positive, and it is significant of his real purpose, which is that of a mystic rather than of an empiricist, that he quietly replaces Anselm's definition of God as 'that than which nothing greater can be conceived' by the very different phrase 'that which is greater than all which can be conceived.' He then continues as follows. Even if I admit, what is itself questionable, that I understand the meaning of the phrase 'something which is greater than all which can be conceived,' Anselm's argument cannot force me to admit that there really is such a thing. All that the argument proves is that it would be inconsistent to admit that there is such a thing and at the same time to deny its reality, since, if it is not real, it is not greater than things which are conceived and are real. But the 'fool' is not really convicted of this inconsistency, since all that he admits is, at the outside, that he understands the sense of the words 'something greater than all that can be conceived.' To make Anselm's argument cogent, some proof ought to be supplied that this something actually exists. If this proof is once forthcoming, Anselm's further demonstration that the something in question is all that God is

[1] 'Neque enim rem ipsam quae Deus est, novi' (*Pro Insipiente*, § 3).

[2] 'Nec prorsus aliter adhuc et in intellectu meo constat illud haberi, cum audio intelligoque dicentem esse aliquid maius omnibus quae valeant cogitari' (*ib.* § 4).

held to be will be valid. It is to illustrate this second point that Gaunilo introduces the reference to the famous lost island by which he is principally remembered. If this lost island were described to me as wealthier and better than any inhabited land, I should readily understand the meaning of the words, and the lost island would be 'in my understanding' in the same sense in which God may be said to be in the understanding of the fool. But it would be idle to say that the island must also really exist somewhere in the ocean because it would otherwise not be, as by definition it is, richer than all habitable lands. Finally he contends that it is not, as Anselm had assumed, a *proprium* of God that He can only be thought of as existing. It is true, no doubt, that we who know that God exists cannot think the proposition 'There is no God' true, but neither can we think any other proposition to be false which we know to be true; *e.g.*, I cannot think it true that I do not exist at this moment, because I know it to be true that I do exist. There may be a sense in which it is possible to think of my own non-existence, but, if there is, it is equally possible, in the same sense, to think of the non-existence of God, even though we know that God does exist.[1] This last point, of course, anticipates Hume's criticism that whatever we can think of as existing we can equally think of as not existing, and if sustained is fatal to every argument of the ontological type.

Anselm's reply to his critic is contained in the short *Liber Apologeticus contra Gaunilonem respondentem pro Insipiente.* He points out, naturally enough, that Gaunilo's substitution of the phrase 'that which is greater than everything which can be conceived' for 'that than which nothing greater can be conceived' alters the character of the argument, and that Gaunilo's reasoning about the lost island is not a real parallel to his own proof, which, as he insists, is applicable only in the case of the concept 'that than which nothing greater can be conceived.' What he does not prove, but merely asserts, is that this phrase really has a definite meaning and is not a nonsensical or insignificant sound. On this point he is content to say that even the 'fool' must conceive the meaning of the words before he can deny that they stand for a reality.

It is very difficult to follow Anselm here. If his reasoning is sound, it will prove not only the real existence of God but also the existence (in the logician's sense) of nothing, round squares, equilateral right-angled triangles, fabulous monsters, the greatest of all integers, since it is beyond a doubt that the propositions 'There is no such thing as a round square,' 'There are no fabulous monsters,' 'There is no integer which is the greatest of all integers,' etc., are true; and it may then be argued that, since they are true, round squares, etc., must exist in the *intellectus* of the person who asserts the propositions. What Anselm is assuming is, as he himself says, that a proposition cannot be understood unless its 'parts' are severally understood. From this he infers that, if 'there is no such thing as *x*' is a significant proposition, *x* must be a significant term. The assumption is plainly not justified, since my ground for asserting the proposition may be precisely that *x* has no intelligible meaning. The state of the case, then, seems to be that Anselm's argument certainly proves that, if 'that than which nothing greater can be conceived' (or 'that which cannot be conceived as not existing') exists *in intellectu*, it also exists *in re*. But the question whether it exists *in intellectu* remains undecided.

9. Thomas Aquinas.—The history of the subsequent fortunes of Anselm's theistic argument is a highly interesting one. In the 13th cent., the golden age of scholastic philosophy, it was widely known and discussed by all the leading thinkers. In the main the mediaeval philosophers seem to have been disposed to accept it until it was rejected as a sophism by St. Thomas, whose great authority has ever since discredited it. The principal 13th cent. texts relative to the subject have been edited with an acute commentary by the Benedictine Augustin Daniels.[1] It is a singular fact that, though all the teachers of the second half of the 13th cent. seem to have felt themselves obliged to make their attitude to Anselm's argument clear, no theologian of the 12th cent. appears to have taken any account of it. The most probable explanation of this silence seems to be that of Daniels, that the circulation of the *Proslogion* was slow and the work unknown to theologians in general until well on into the 13th century. It is certainly not true, as is sometimes said, that acceptance of the argument was confined to the Oxford Franciscans. Of the fifteen scholastics whose writings are examined by Daniels, three (one of whom is Albert the Great) express no opinion on the validity of the proof, ten (including Alexander of Hales, Bonaventura, and Scotus) accept it, only two (Richard of Middleton and St. Thomas) reject it. These facts seem of themselves to show that the discredit into which the ontological argument fell —it will be remembered that, when Descartes revived it in the 17th cent., critics were quick to remind him that he was laying himself open to at least the suspicion of heterodoxy—was due almost entirely to the general recognition of the weight of St. Thomas's criticisms. They are, in fact, so formidable that they still repay the closest attention and are, in the present writer's opinion, altogether on a much higher philosophical level than the better-known polemic of the *Critique of Pure Reason.* The general position of Thomas is precisely what we should expect from a philosopher whose thought has been moulded partly by Neo-Platonism and partly by Aristotelianism. He holds that the existence of God can be, and has been, sufficiently proved *a posteriori*, by reasoning from the works of God to their Author, and consequently he accepts as valid both the argument from the necessity of an unmoved First Mover (the Aristotelian argument) and the argument from design, in the wide sense of an argument from final or intentional causality (the Platonic argument from order and intelligibility in the world to an intelligent Creator). But he rejects altogether and on principle the attempt to demonstrate the existence of God *a priori* (from a mere consideration of the content of the concept of God).

The most important of the relevant passages in the works of Thomas are *Summa contra Gentiles*, i. 10, 11, and *Summa Theologica*, I. qu. ii. art. 1, both dealing formally with the question whether the proposition 'God exists' is self-evident. His own view on this question is that the proposition is self-evident if the *essentia* of God is once adequately known, but, since we in this life do not behold the *essentia* of God, His existence is not self-evident to our understanding. It is not immediately evident to us that there is anything 'than which a greater cannot be conceived,' or that 'God cannot be thought not to exist'; on this point St. Thomas is in complete agreement with Gaunilo. Anselm's argument, in fact, is a sophism arising from failure to distinguish between that which is *notum per se simpliciter* and that which is *quoad nos notum*, evident to us. 'For *simpliciter* it is self-evident that God exists, since what God is is his *esse*' ('cum hoc ipsum quod Deus est sit suum esse'; *i.e.*, God's *essentia* or 'what' and His existence are identical). 'But because we cannot conceive what God is, it remains unknown relatively to us.'[2] Anselm's reasoning is fallacious because (*a*) not all even of those who admit the existence of God are aware that God is 'that than which nothing greater can be conceived'; and (*b*), even if every one were aware of this, it would not follow that God exists otherwise than *in intellectu*; *i.e.*, all that would be proved is that we can think of such an object without absurdity. So Thomas asserts against Anselm that there is no logical absurdity in supposing the non-existence of God.[3] The same considerations are urged in much the same language in the article of the *Summa Theologica* already referred to. Thomas's own view is[4] that the existence of God can be demonstrated *a posteriori*, by reasoning

[1] 'Cogitare autem me non esse, quamdiu esse certissime scio, nescio utrum possim; sed si possum, cur non et quidquid aliud eadem certitudine scio? Si autem non possum, non erit jam istud proprium Deo' (*ib.* § 7).

[1] *Quellenbeitr. und Untersuch. zur Gesch. der Gottesbeweise im 13 Jahrh. mit bes. Berücks. des Arguments im Proslogion des heil. Anselm*, Münster, 1909.

[2] *Contra Gent.* i. 11.

[3] *Ib.*

[4] I. qu. ii. art. 2.

from effect to cause. He relies on five such *a posteriori* arguments,[1] which are (1) the argument from the fact of motion to the First Mover; (2) the parallel argument from causal agency to a First efficient Cause; (3) the argument from possibility and necessity, known more commonly as the argument from the contingency of the world;[2] (4) the argument from the scale of 'degrees of reality,' by which we infer from the existence of greater and lesser goods the existence of a perfect good which is the cause of all lesser degrees of goodness (in virtue of the specifically Neo-Platonic theory of causality already explained); (5) the argument *ex gubernatione rerum*, *i.e.* from final or intentional causality. (Even the processes of inanimate nature are ordered or adapted to the realization of an end or good; this adaptation presupposes an intelligent intention, and, since inanimate things have no intelligence of their own, a supermundane intelligence.) St. Thomas's arguments are thus all of one type. They are all appeals to the principle of causality taken in combination with the denial of the possibility of an infinite regress. Both the appeal to the principle of causality and the refusal to admit the infinite regress are direct inheritances from the Platonic-Aristotelian philosophy. The former is invalidated if the soundness of the Kantian criticism of speculative theology be admitted; the latter requires reconsideration in the light of what may be called the 'logical realism' of Bertrand Russell and the 'new' realists. Scotus, in the *Scriptum Oxoniense*,[3] restates the Anselmian argument with a modification which seems obviously meant to meet the fundamental point in Gaunilo's criticism and anticipates a line of thought afterwards developed by Leibniz. God is defined as 'quo cogitato sine contradictione maius cogitari non potest sine contradictione,' 'that which can be thought without a contradiction but than which nothing greater can be thought without a contradiction.' The important modification is the addition to the definition of the first *sine contradictione*. As Scotus says, 'in cuius cogitatione includitur contradictio illud dicitur non cogitabile.' It thus becomes a preliminary to the ontological proof to show that God can be 'thought without contradiction'; *i.e.*, that we really have a concept of God, or that the word 'God,' or the phrase employed as by definition equivalent to the word, is not an unmeaning noise. When this condition is fulfilled, Scotus holds, the Anselmian inference from the *esse in intellectu* of the *summum cogitabile sine contradictione* to its *esse in re* is valid.

10. Descartes.—Descartes' theism, like that of his mediaeval predecessors, is predominantly of the Neo-Platonic type, and is intimately connected with the assumption, which underlies the reasoning of the *Meditations*, that the principle of causality, in the very form which had been given to it by Proclus, is evident by the natural light of the understanding. The extent to which the thought of Descartes is in fundamentals Platonic is probably not adequately realized by most of his readers. Even the most original feature of his philosophy, the thoroughgoing reduction of natural science to mechanics, is really a reversion from mediaeval Aristotelianism to the standpoint of the early Academy, and the metaphysics of the *Meditations* is thoroughly Neo-Platonic. We quite misconceive Descartes' meaning if we regard the presence of God in his system as an excrescence due to the necessity of artificially bringing together again the artificially sundered worlds of body and mind. Even from the point of view of a merely mechanical interpretation of the world, Descartes is, of course, much more true to the analogies on which mechanical interpretations are founded in assuming the direction of the mechanism by God than those modern half-philosophers who attribute to the cosmic machine an inherent power of directing and repairing itself. He has not forgotten, as the modern materialist tends to do, that behind the most complicated and perfect machinery there is always intelligence which is not that of the machine to start it, to direct its workings, and to repair it. But, beyond this, Descartes has reasons for asserting the existence of God which are wholly independent of his reversion to the mathematical and mechanical standpoint in physics and would have been equally strong if he had adopted any other type of physical doctrine. The theism of Descartes is, in fact, dictated by two considerations—his unqualified acceptance of the principle of causality and his adherence to the conception of the 'Perfect Being' as the only adequate object of the understanding, and therefore the 'natural good' of rational beings (the 'ben dell' intelletto,' to use Dante's phrase). He is a theist, not because he holds the mechanical view of nature, but for the same more ultimate reason which leads him to hold that view, that he is, like the whole Platonic succession, a rationalist and consequently regards the knowledge of the 'Supreme Being' as the culmination of science.[1] The actual proofs of theism offered by Descartes are two. In the third *Meditation* we have the *a posteriori* proof in the special form of an argument from our possession of an idea of God to the existence of God as the cause of the idea. This is, of course, strictly on Neo-Platonic lines. In the fifth *Meditation* the *a posteriori* proof is confirmed by an *a priori* proof which turns out to be, in principle, a restatement of the Anselmian argument with a modification which is by no means an obvious improvement.

The well-known argument of the third *Meditation* runs thus. I have an 'idea' of the 'Perfect' or 'Infinite' Being. My possession of this idea, like any other fact, demands a causal explanation. The explanation cannot be that I am myself the Perfect and Infinite Being and that the idea is derived from my immediate awareness of myself, because I am aware of myself as, in many ways, defective and limited. It is not derived from acquaintance with other persons or things, which are all no less limited and finite than myself; and it has not been obtained by an imaginative combination of the various perfections I have observed separately in different finite things, for internal simplicity is itself one of the perfections which I think of as constituting the 'Infinite Being.' Nor again is 'infinite' a merely negative expression. (If it were, it might, of course, be objected that, when I say 'infinite,' there is no definite concept corresponding to the word.) For in the order of logic the infinite is prior to the finite. If I had not already an intelligible concept of infinity, I could not even be aware of my own finiteness. There is thus only one possible cause of my possession of the idea of the Infinite Being. It must be the effect of a really existing Infinite Being, who possesses *eminenter* or *formaliter* all the perfection which my idea of the Infinite Being contains objectively, *i.e.* by way of representation. God therefore exists, and my idea of God may be said to be the mark which the Creator has stamped on His creature. It may be added that, to argue the point even more generally, I who have this idea could not exist if the object of the idea did not also exist. For, since time is no more than a sequence of moments, each independent of all the rest, conservation, continuance in existence, is logically equivalent to fresh creation at every moment, and it is certain that I have no power to create myself. (This is proved by urging that it is easier to bestow new excellences on what already exists than to create. If then I cannot bestow infinite wisdom or power on myself, as I know I cannot, *a fortiori* I am not my own creator.) If it is urged that my parents are my creators, and their parents in turn their creators, we fall into the infinite regress. Thus the mere fact of the existence of any finite thing is proof of the existence of the Infinite Being; *i.e.*, if anything whose existence requires an external cause exists (and the Cartesian *cogito* assures me of the existence of at least one such thing), there exists also a Supreme Being whose existence requires no external cause (another form of the argument called by St. Thomas the argument from possibility and necessity).

The argument from my possession of an idea of God is Descartes' own substantial contribution to the philosophy of theism. It must be carefully distinguished from the old Stoic appeal to the *consensus gentium*. Descartes' critics were not really hitting a blot in his reasoning when they said that savages and atheists do not possess this idea. Against such objections Descartes' own explanation, that he only meant that, given the knowledge of myself from which he starts, reflective analysis is sufficient to lead to the concept of an Infinite Being, is a sufficient rejoinder. He seems to be equally right in his contention that the concept of an Infinitely Perfect Being is logically implied in my recognition of my own finitude, just as T. H. Green maintains that the recognition of a morally 'better' implies the conception of a 'best.' The real point of weakness in the argument, so far as the present writer can see, lies elsewhere. Descartes is clearly right in maintaining that the concept of a Being who combines all perfections or excellences in the absolute internal simplicity of his own nature is not formed by a process of synthesis; it is clearly obtained by

[1] I. qu. ii. art. 3.

[2] The argument is that whatever is merely possible or contingent exists at some times but not at others. Hence, if all things are merely possible or contingent, there must have been a time when nothing existed at all. But (in virtue of the principle of causality), if there had ever been a moment when there was nothing at all, nothing could ever have come to be. Hence the fact that there is something now proves that there must be 'something in things' which is *necessary*, *i.e.* incapable of not existing. And the argument from the impossibility of an indefinite regress is then invoked to show that there must be *one* ultimate necessary being.

[3] See the relevant passages in Daniels, pp. 105–107.

[1] 'Perfecta scientia,' as St. Hilary puts it, 'Deum scire.'

the process of 'passing to the limit,' of which mathematical reasoning furnishes so many examples. But we are not really authorized to infer from our ability to conceive the limit of a series or of a sum of terms that a given series has a limit or a given sum a limiting value. Whether a series or a sum has a limiting value or not has to be discovered by examination in each special case; it is notorious that mathematicians down to a very recent date have been repeatedly led into fallacies by the assumption that limits exist where, in point of fact, they do not. Thus, when we have conceded to Descartes that there is an idea of the Infinitely Perfect Being and that this idea is presupposed in our own judgment that we and other things are finite, it does not follow of itself that the series of existents, arranged in ascending order of perfection (assuming such an arrangement to be possible), must have an actual upper limit. This is the very point which ought to be proved, and has not been proved. Descartes himself was presumably led to ignore the difficulty by the laxness with which he employs the word idea to cover alike memory-images, concepts, and judgments. When once he has allowed himself to call a judgment an idea, it is easy for him to think that he has bridged over the chasm between the concept of God and the judgment that God exists. The whole argument, it will be observed, is based on the combination of the Neo-Platonic doctrine of causality with the doctrine of representative perception. According to the latter doctrine, the direct and immediate object of apprehension, both in sense-perception and in thought, is never an extra-mental reality, but always itself mental or 'in the mind.' When this theory is combined with the view that everything that becomes has a cause and that all causality is imperfect mirroring, we get at once the proposition of Descartes that the cause of any idea must contain eminently or formally at least as much perfection as the idea contains objectively. 'Eminently' here answers to the κατ' αἰτίαν of Proclus, 'formally' to his καθ' ὕπαρξιν, 'objectively' to his κατὰ μέθεξιν.

The *a priori* or ontological argument of the fifth *Meditation* runs as follows. By 'God' I mean a being who has all perfections. But existence is a perfection. Therefore the being who has all perfections has existence; *i.e.* God exists. Or, in other words, just as I see when I analyse the idea of a [rectilinear] triangle that it includes the property of having the sum of the internal angles equal to π, so, when I analyse the idea of God, I find that it includes existence. God therefore exists and exists necessarily. (Thus Descartes seems to assume that there is just one existential proposition, and only one which is, in Kant's sense of the term, analytical, viz. the proposition 'God exists.') The objection that St. Thomas (now the recognized chief authority in all questions of theology) had rejected the Anselmian argument leads Descartes, in his *Reply* to the *First Objections*, to insist vehemently that his own proof is not that of Anselm, but differs on a vital point. The force of his own reasoning depends entirely on the fact that existence is already contained in the concept of God. Anselm[1] had said nothing about this, and that was why St. Thomas was reasonably dissatisfied with his argument; *i.e.*, the all-important point is that, according to Descartes, the proposition 'God exists' is analytic; Anselm had left it an open question whether it might not be synthetic. Historically this modification of the ontological proof is important, since Kant (who appears not to have known the writings of St. Anselm) makes it the main object of his attack on the proof to show that the proposition 'God exists' is synthetic. It is precisely because the proposition is synthetic, though the conditions which make the affirmation of an *a priori* synthetic proposition legitimate are, in this case, not fulfilled, that we can, according to Kant, have no speculative certainty of the existence of God. If Descartes should be right in regarding 'God exists' as an analytic proposition, Kant's antitheological polemic would become a mere *ignoratio elenchi*.

The further peculiarity of the Cartesian argument on which Kant fastens, that it improperly treats existence as a predicate or attribute, is not really of much importance. Whether all propositions can without violence to their meaning be represented as asserting (or denying) a predicate of a subject is an important question for formal logic, but seems to have no relevance to theology. If there is no predicate in the proposition 'God exists,' it must be held, on the same ground, that there is no predicate in such a proposition as 'Joseph dreams' or 'Esau hunts' or 'The rich man died.' *Per contra*, if dreaming, hunting, and dying are predicates in these propositions (as Kant, who professed to regard logic as a science created perfect by Aristotle, ought to hold, and presumably did hold), existence is a predicate in every proposition of the form 'x exists.' The only question it is relevant to raise about the Cartesian argument is the question whether in the special case of the *ens summe perfectum* existence (whether existence be regarded as a predicate or not) can be asserted to be part of the meaning of a concept.

Whether there is really so much difference as Descartes maintains between his own argument and Anselm's may be doubted. Certainly the definition from which Anselm starts (God is *id quo maius cogitari non potest*) does not specify existence as part of the meaning of the concept. But, since Anselm tries to show that admission of the definition is logically tantamount to admitting that 'God cannot be thought not to be,' the difference between him and Descartes seems to be that Anselm tries to prove the point which Descartes is content to assume without more ado. It is hard to believe, as Descartes does, that St. Thomas, who denied that God is *notum per se quoad nos*, and gave a very sensible reason for his denial, would have regarded the Cartesian version of the proof as anything more than a glaring *petitio principii*.

11. Spinoza.—With Spinoza's attempt to give a pantheistic turn to the Neo-Platonic and Cartesian lines of thought it is not necessary to concern ourselves further than to remark that the whole of the First Part of the *Ethics* is logically no better than one long *petitio*. The first, third, and sixth of the definitions already contain the two assumptions, that God = *substantia* = *causa sui* and that *causa sui* (which is defined as 'that whereof the nature cannot be conceived but as existing') exists. Where the whole doctrine has thus been taken for granted by arbitrary definition, it is really superfluous to add anything in the way of 'proof,' even if the 'proofs' themselves were more free than they are from formal logical fallacy. What Spinoza wholly evades considering is the question, which is really fundamental, whether the definition of *causa sui* is more than a 'meaningless noise.'

One particularly glaring example of Spinoza's singular carelessness about his initial definitions may be noted. He has taken from Neo-Platonism the first and most fundamental notion of his system, that of *causa sui* (τὸ αὐθυπόστατον of Proclus). Now, by calling a thing αὐθυπόστατον, the Neo-Platonists meant exactly what they said, that it 'causes' or 'produces' itself (προάγει ἑαυτό). Hence they confined the name αὐθυπόστατα to minds and souls and expressly maintained that the One, or God, having no cause, being unproduced, is not αὐθυπόστατον;[1] *i.e.*, they understood *causa sui* in a positive sense. Theologians had done the same thing; as Arnauld said in his comments on Descartes' *Meditations*,[2] no theologian would admit that God is *a se positive tanquam a causa*, but at most that God may be said to be *a se* in a purely negative sense —*i.e.*, in the sense that He is not an effect of anything else. Spinozism succeeds in appearing to satisfy our demand for an object of religious adoration only by a constant equivocation. It defines *causa sui* (= τὸ αὐθυπόστατον) in the positive Neo-Platonic sense as *id cuius essentia involvit existentiam* (τὸ τοῦ εἶναι ἑαυτῷ παρακτικόν) and then asserts of it all that Neo-Platonism had asserted of the uncaused One. To put the point rather differently, it defines God as 'that whereof the *essentia* implies existence' and transfers to God, so defined, what theologians have asserted of a God in whom the distinction between *existentia* and *essentia* is unmeaning. Spinoza commits the paralogism in set terms in the first sentence of the *Ethics*: 'Per causam sui intelligo id cuius essentia *involvit* existentiam, sive id cuius natura non potest concipi nisi existens.'

12. Locke.—Locke's proof of theism,[3] which he regards as having an evidence 'equal to mathematical certainty,' though in some ways perfunctory, is in its general character of the Neo-Platonic type. He does not refer to the *a priori* or ontological argument, and refuses to pronounce any opinion on Descartes' own special argument from our possession of an idea of God except to remark that 'It is an ill way of establishing this truth and silencing atheists to lay the whole stress of so important a point as this upon that sole foundation.' (As the context shows, Locke thinks that it would be a true and relevant criticism of Descartes to say that some men have no idea, and others false ideas, of God.) It is not quite clear whether Locke regards the certainty of theism as equal to the certainty with which we know actually perceived facts or the fact of our own existence. He says that we have more certainty of it 'than of anything our senses have not immediately discovered to us,' and again that 'we more certainly know that there is a God, than that there is anything else without us.' This certainty looks as if Locke held (as Descartes did not) that the existence of God is less certain than our own, and

1 The name of Anselm occurs neither in the *Objections* nor in Descartes' *Reply*. Apparently both he and his critic knew the Anselmian argument only at second hand, through Thomas. Descartes' point, to be strictly accurate, is that his own argument turns wholly on the contention that concepts in general contain only the 'possible existence' of a corresponding object, but the concept of God 'contains the necessary existence' of God.

1 Proclus, *Instit. theol.*, prop. 40: ἀνάγκη ἄρα τὸ αὐθυπόστατον εἶναι μετὰ τὸ πρῶτον.

2 *Objectiones Quartae*, § 'de Deo.'

3 *Essay*, bk. iv. ch. 10, 'Of our Knowledge of the Existence of a God.'

possibly less certain than that of the objects of actual and present sense-perception. But it is also possible that he only means that our certainty in the last two cases is immediate, but in the first depends on an ability, not found in all men, to follow the steps of a deduction. He may not intend to suggest that, to the man who can perform the deduction, its conclusion is inferior in certainty to any immediate cognition, 'intuitive' or 'sensitive.'

Locke's own proof is the usual *a posteriori* one based on the principle of causality and the empirical proposition (guaranteed by the *cogito*) that something (viz. myself) exists. It is also assumed, as usual, that a cause must contain more reality or perfection than any of its effects, as the Neo-Platonists had taught. The argument then becomes this: I exist; therefore I must have a cause; this cause cannot be 'bare nothing'; therefore it is a positive something. Since 'bare nothing' cannot be the cause of anything, therefore the cause of my own existence and that of all other existents must be eternal. (The impossibility of the endless regress and the 'contingency of the world' are not mentioned, but are of course tacitly presupposed.) An effect must derive all its properties from its cause. Therefore the 'eternal cause' must be the most powerful of things. (It is assumed that the cause has not only as much 'reality' as the effects, but more, and further that there can be only one 'eternal cause'—a point which Locke is hardly entitled by his own metaphysics to assume.) There is intelligence in myself, the effect, and therefore there is intelligence (of a higher degree) in the cause. The 'eternal cause' is thus 'most knowing' as well as 'most powerful.' From this Locke thinks it follows that this cause is what we mean by God; whether we use the name or not is a mere matter of vocabulary. 'There is an eternal, most powerful, and most knowing Being; which whether any one will please to call God, it matters not.' The rest of the chapter is given to an argument in proof of the immateriality of the eternal cause. The goodness of this cause Locke presumably held, as any Platonist might, to be inseparable from its wisdom. He does not seem to reflect that he has given no reason for supposing either the power or the intelligence of the 'eternal cause' to be perfect. His argument is thus only the familiar one from causality very badly stated and with most of its real premisses left unexpressed.

13. Leibniz.—Leibniz's treatment of the subject is far more adequate. In his system, at least as represented in his best known works, the proposition 'God exists' holds a unique position. It is a 'truth of fact,' and therefore, like all 'truths of fact,' synthetic. But it is the only truth of fact which is capable of demonstration. In general, only 'truths of reason,' analytic propositions, admit of formal demonstration, because the demonstration of a proposition is nothing but its analysis into simpler propositions which are seen on inspection to be identities. This is why the 'principle of contradiction' (*A* is not non-*A*) is regarded by Leibniz as the supreme principle of all truths of reason. Truths of fact (which all assert actual existence) do not fall under the principle of contradiction, but under that of sufficient reason, and thus, with the one exception of the proposition that God exists, they are not analysable into identities and cannot be formally demonstrated. The anomalous character of the proposition 'God exists' vanishes, however, when we discover from the papers published by Couturat[1] that Leibniz's real view was that all truths are analytic, the only difference between 'truths of reason' and 'truths of fact' being that the former can be resolved into identities by a finite number of steps of analysis, the latter require (like the extraction of the square root of an integer which is not a perfect square) an infinite number of intermediate steps.[2] It follows that God, being omniscient, knows all truths of fact *a priori* (*i.e.* sees them to be identities), just as Leibniz says more than once that God sees 'from eternity' in the 'notion' of Peter that Peter will repent of his denial, and in the 'notion' of Judas that Judas will die impenitent, and that the distinction between the necessary truths of reason and the contingent truths of fact means nothing to him. *Quoad nos* truths of fact are, in general, contingent merely because we cannot perform an infinite analysis. The peculiarity of the one truth of fact which is necessary *quoad nos*, 'God exists,' is merely that this proposition does not require for its proof *a priori* an infinite series of resolutions. In being capable of resolution into identities by a finite number of steps it resembles the truths of reason.

Consequently Leibniz is bound to hold that the Anselmian argument *a priori* from the meaning of the concept of God to the real existence of God is in principle valid. Since he also held that all propositions without exception are predicative, he naturally adopts the form of the argument used by Descartes, viz. that the predicate of the proposition 'God exists' is already implicitly contained in the subject. Descartes' proof is valid, but incomplete. To make it complete it is only necessary to show that the concept of God is a genuine concept, *i.e.* that it contains no contradiction, *i.e.* does not attempt to unite incompatible constituents.[1] Leibniz thinks that this can be shown by the consideration that the 'most perfect' or 'most real' being means the being of whom no simple positive predicate can be denied. (Any being of whom a positive simple predicate could be denied would be without the excellence or perfection for which that predicate stands.) Now, all complex predicates can be resolved into simple ones, and Leibniz holds that all *positive* simple predicates are compossible in a single subject just because they are all positive. If any two predicates are incompossible, one of them must deny what the other affirms. But no simple predicate denies anything. Consequently all simple predicates can 'inhere' in a single subject. This proves that 'the most real' being is possible. And Descartes has proved in the fifth *Meditation* that, 'if the most real being is possible, it is also actual.' Hence the 'ontological' proof, when completed by the preliminary proof that the most real being is possible, is a valid demonstration.[2] There is an obvious weakness in the argument. Leibniz assumes that, if we have one proposition, '*A* is *B*,' where *B* is a 'simple' predicate, and a second, '*A* is *C*,' and the two are incompatible, the proposition '*A* is *C*' must be capable of resolution into simpler propositions, of which one is '*A* is not *B*.' It ought to follow that, since the propositions '*A* is red' and '*A* is green' are incompatible, if 'red' is a simple quality, 'green' is a complex. But, in point of fact, green is as much a simple positive 'perfection' as red. This seems sufficient reason for regarding Leibniz's proof that the *ens realissimum* is possible as a failure. A more promising line of thought is suggested by the short memoir of 1701, *De la Demonstration Cartésienne de l'existence de Dieu du R. P. Lami*, where Leibniz is content to argue that the *ens a se* must exist because, if there were no *ens a se*, there would be no real possibilities—a position since made familiar by Lotze's adoption of it. It is worth noting that in the chapter of the *Nouveaux Essais* where Leibniz is commenting on the corresponding chapter of Locke's *Essay* he feels himself, as standing outside the Roman Church, free to say expressly that St. Thomas was wrong in rejecting Anselm's proof and to commend Descartes for rehabilitating it.

Leibniz naturally agrees with Locke that there are several ways of proving the existence of God and that none of the proofs should be neglected. He himself expressly recognizes three proofs besides the ontological.[3] These are (*a*) the cosmological argument from the actual existence of the world to the existence of God as its cause (the standing Platonic-Aristotelian proof); (*b*) the argument from 'eternal truths'—truths which involve no reference to time or particular temporal existents in time, and would still be true if the world of temporal existents had never existed—to the 'eternal' intellect of God as their source; (*c*) the argument from 'pre-established harmony.' This is a special version of the teleological argument from the order and purpose revealed in the world to an ordering and designing intellect as its source. Any remarks which the present writer desires to make upon these *a posteriori* theistic arguments will more naturally find their place in a later paragraph. But it should be mentioned that the use of the argument from design introduces a curious contradiction into Leibniz's peculiar metaphysic. From his view that all propositions are predications and that all true propositions can be analysed into identities it follows at once that, as he constantly asserts, every real existent (every monad) is the ground of all its attributes. Since existence itself, on this view, is a predicate or attribute, the world of existing monads ought to be its own ground, and there should be no need of any external cause to account for the order found in it. Accordingly we find

[1] *Opuscules et fragments inédits de Leibniz*, Paris, 1903, p. 518 ff.

[2] *Ib.* p. 518: 'Semper igitur praedicatum seu consequens inest subiecto seu antecedenti et in hoc ipso consistit natura veritatis in universum'; p. 519: the law of sufficient reason itself is a consequence of this, for 'alioqui veritas daretur, quae non posset probari a priori, seu quae non resolveretur in identicas, quod est contra naturam veritatis quae (semper) vel expresse vel implicite identica est'; p. 376: 'omnes propositiones existentiales sunt verae quidem, sed non necessariae, nam non possunt demonstrari nisi infinitis adhibitis.'

[1] Cf. what has been said above about the attitude of Scotus, by whom Leibniz may very possibly have been influenced.

[2] *Nouveaux Essais*, iv. 10, § 7: *Meditationes de Cognitione, Veritate et Ideis.*

[3] See the discussion of them in B. Russell, *A Critical Exposition of the Philosophy of Leibniz*, ch. ix.

Leibniz himself at times explaining why the actual world, rather than any other equally possible world, exists, by ascribing to the various possible worlds an 'appetence of existence' (*existuritio*) proportionate to their degree of internal harmony, and saying that the most orderly of them is actual just because its *existuritio* is a maximum,[1] but elsewhere, especially in more popular writings, treating existence as something which is conferred on the most orderly and harmonious of the possible worlds by God in virtue of His 'choice of the best.' Unless one is prepared, as the present writer after long study is not, to accuse Leibniz of insincerity, it seems impossible not to recognize here a fundamental inconsistency between his personal religious convictions and the logical requirements of his metaphysical system. If all true propositions are identities, philosophy must be atheistic.[2]

14. **Hume.**—The most important philosophical treatment of the theistic problem between Leibniz and Kant is unmistakably that of Hume in his *Dialogues concerning Natural Religion* (written apparently before 1751, though not published until 1779, three years after the author's death). In judging this work it must be borne in mind that it makes no pretence to expound the theology of the author. It is strictly what it purports to be, a conversation between a supporter of philosophic 'natural theology,' Cleanthes, a violent fideist, Demea, intended as a representative of orthodoxy, and a sceptic, Philo. The responsibility for the positions maintained by the three speakers rests entirely with themselves. Hume abstains from indicating his own sympathies except in the final sentence, where he suggests that the 'opinions' (he is careful not to say 'the arguments') of the 'natural theologian' Cleanthes probably come nearer to the truth than those of Philo, and those of Philo than those of Demea.[3] Hume's real position in natural theology, as in philosophy in general, seems to have been that of a consistent Academic. Genuine scepticism is a rare thing and liable to be misunderstood. So Hume's general philosophy has commonly been mistaken, as by T. H. Green, Huxley, and others, for a shallow sensationalistic phenomenalism. In reality he is neither a sensationalist nor a phenomenalist. He holds that there are insuperable difficulties in the Cartesian rationalism, and that, on the other hand, sensationalism leads to the conclusion that science is an impossibility. Being unable to accept either Cartesianism or sensationalism, and knowing of no third choice in philosophy, he adopts the sceptical attitude of ἐποχή, 'suspense of judgment.' There can be no question of seriously regarding principles presupposed in all science as false; at the same time Hume confesses himself unable to justify these principles. His real attitude towards theism seems to have been the same. It is probably true, and, as the letter to Elliot shows, Hume is very unwilling to believe that his leaning towards it rests on nothing more solid than emotional bias, but the alleged proofs of theism are open to criticisms which Hume does not know how to refute, and there are 'appearances' which it is hard to reconcile with the theistic 'hypothesis.' We have not, as it is to be wished we had, convincing proof of its truth, though Hume lets us see that personally he inclines to accept it. His attitude is neither that of a zealous 'infidel' nor that of a 'phenomenalist' and anti-theist. Neither the Hume of contemporary High Churchmen like Johnson and Wesley nor the Hume of Huxley's biography is the Hume of historical fact.[1]

[1] Cf. Couturat, *La Logique de Leibniz*, Paris, 1901, pp. 224–226, with the passages cited there.

[2] For a useful conspectus of all the more important utterances of Leibniz on the existence of God known before the publication of Couturat's volume of *Opuscules* see Russell, *Crit. Expos. of the Philosophy of Leibniz*, pp. 284–291, and, for a 'smashing,' but by no means final, attack on all the four arguments, ch. ix. of the same work.

[3] That this remark is made in good faith seems clear from Hume's letter to Gilbert Elliot of March 10th, 1751, where he speaks of Cleanthes as the 'hero' of the dialogue and asks his friend for any suggestions which will 'strengthen that side of the dialogue,' protesting against the ascription to himself of 'any propensity to the other side,' by which he plainly means the side of Philo. No one could suspect him of 'propensity' to the side of the 'mystic' Demea.

In form the *Dialogues*, like some of Plato's greatest works, are reported conversation. An unnamed narrator informs his friend Hermippus of the discussions between Cleanthes, Philo, and Demea. The narrator, it should be observed, is a theist.

'What truth so obvious, so certain, as the BEING of a God? . . . What truth so important as this, which is the ground of all our hopes, the surest foundation of morality, the firmest support of society, and the only principle which ought never to be a moment absent from our thoughts and meditations? But in treating of this obvious and important truth; what obscure questions occur, concerning the NATURE of that divine being; his attributes, his decrees, his plan of providence?'

There is no sign of irony in this utterance, and its seriousness is all the more probable that Hume proceeds to dwell on the intellectual difference between the characters of the dialogue, assigning an 'accurate philosophical turn' to Cleanthes the theist, 'careless scepticism' to Philo, and 'rigid inflexible orthodoxy' to Demea.[2] His obvious intention is to predispose the reader to find in Cleanthes the hero of the work. It is with the same object that, until the discussion is near its end, Demea, the zealot for unreasoning faith, is made to regard Philo as an ally against Cleanthes.[3] The intimate correspondence between what Cleanthes says about the impossibility of seriously acquiescing in complete philosophical scepticism and Hume's own utterances to the same effect in the *Treatise of Human Nature* further helps to indicate that we are not to take Philo's estimate of the theistic arguments as meant to be that of his creator. His function is not to refute Cleanthes, but to call attention to the difficulties and weak points in his exposition.[4] The precise position at the opening of the discussion is this. Cleanthes affirms the existence of a 'cause' of the universe and, reasoning by analogy from the products of art to those of nature, holds that this cause is a mind resembling our own. He denies the doctrine of the Neo-Platonists and Christian theologians that God is absolutely simple and therefore unknowable in His *essentia* to us, on the ground that this amounts to atheism. Philo and Demea are agreed in opposing him, though for different reasons—Demea because he accepts the negative theology, Philo on the ground that, as we have no experience of 'world-making,' we are not entitled to say that the order in the world presupposes a world-building intelligence. Cleanthes has rested his case on the old Platonic argument from 'orderly motion,' but has admitted that the argument is one from analogy. Philo replies that there is no sufficient basis for an analogical argument. He further appeals to the difficulties of the 'infinite regress.' If matter and mind must be effects of a cause, why must not that cause have a more ultimate cause, and so on *ad indefinitum*? Cleanthes declines to consider the problem: 'You ask me what is the cause of this cause? I know not; I care not; that concerns not me. I have found a Deity; and here I stop my enquiry. Let those go farther, who are wiser or more enterprising.' Philo not unnaturally replies: 'I pretend to be neither; and for that very reason, I should never perhaps have attempted to go so far; especially when I am sensible, that I must at last be contented to sit down with the same answer.'[5] Philo, it must be remembered, calls himself a theist, though he professes to regard the nature of God as totally unknown. The point at issue between him and Cleanthes is that Cleanthes maintains that the 'First Cause' is not only a mind but also 'a mind like the human,' and that the teleological argument is an 'experimental proof' of this. These two points are what Philo disputes and Demea regards as 'anthropomorphist' heresy. Philo, in fact, wishes, like Kant, to maintain that speculative theism is dependent upon the validity of the '*a priori* proof.' If we rely solely on the argument from

[1] That Hume was personally an orthodox Christian is, to be sure, unlikely, but there is no reason to suppose that he was much further removed from orthodoxy than more than one of the prominent 18th cent. latitudinarian bishops or Scottish 'moderates,' and in his philosophy he never commits himself to any view not compatible with the completest orthodoxy, as orthodoxy was understood in his day. Huxley's anti-clericalism is quite incompatible with Humianism.

[2] There is a certain want of definiteness about the position ascribed to Demea. He is spoken of as a 'mystic' and a depreciator of the powers of reason; on the other hand, he is the champion of the 'simple and sublime argument *a priori*'—an odd attitude for an irrationalist. Hume does not seem to have distinguished between negative theology, the creation of philosophic rationalists, and the scepticism of despair which arises from sheer distrust of reason. Philo's 'scepticism' is quite another thing, a mere declaration that, 'as at present advised,' he has not sufficient material for a definitive conclusion.

[3] Demea is, in fact, so little of a real theologian that he is unaware that it is actually unorthodox to maintain that the existence of God is known only 'by revelation.' Perhaps, like Hume himself, according to Johnson, 'he had never read the New Testament with attention,' and he almost certainly did not know that his position had been formally condemned by the Fifth Lateran Council.

[4] Huxley's exploitation of Philo for an antitheistic purpose rests on the false assumption that it is he who is the real 'hero of the dialogue.'

[5] Hume, *Philosophical Works*, ed. T. H. Green and T. H. Grose, London, 1874–75, ii. 410.

effect to cause, the known effect is not perfect and we are not entitled to infer that its author is free either from intellectual or from moral deficiencies, or even that 'several deities' may not combine to construct a world as many men co-operate to build a house or a ship. 'A man, who follows your hypothesis, is able, perhaps, to assert, or conjecture, that the universe, sometime, arose from something like design: but beyond that position he cannot ascertain one single circumstance, and is left afterwards to fix every point of his theology, by the utmost licence of fancy and hypothesis.'[1] The God of Cleanthes is, in fact, a 'finite deity,' and a finite deity is as bad as none at all. And, if reasoning by analogy be in place at all, analogy suggests that we should look on the material world as an animal of which God is, as with the Stoics, the soul, and thus we shall be led to affirm the eternity of the world (contrary to the position of Cleanthes, who has tacitly assumed that the thing to be accounted for is its origin). Or, again, if the world is more like an animal or vegetable than a watch or loom, why should we not infer that worlds are propagated rather than made? A comet may be the 'egg' of a solar system. Demea, of course, comments on the absence of any data for such 'wild' theories. But this is exactly the point on which Philo wishes to insist; 'we have no data to establish any system of cosmogony.' He insists, none the less, that such analogies as we have suggest that intelligence itself is caused by physical generation. Generation, itself an unintelligent process, is explained to be a 'principle of order in nature,' and 'we see every day the latter [intelligence] arise from the former [generation], never the former from the latter.' (It is, of course, obvious that Cleanthes is here making two very questionable assumptions—that the 'rational soul' is generated like the body, and that, because an oak or a spider is not rational, the growth of the one and the instinctive behaviour of the other are not guided by intelligence at all. 'Experience' does nothing to assure us of these negations.) Philo finally reaches the climax of his polemic against the *a posteriori* argument when he urges that the 'unguided' motions of material particles may give rise to 'an uniformity of appearance,' and thus 'account for all the appearing wisdom and contrivance' in nature. (As before, he makes the wholly illegitimate assumption that we know from experience that this has really happened. 'This we know to be the case with the universe at present. . . . May we not hope for such a position, or rather be assured of it, from the eternal revolutions of unguided matter?' Of course, experience does not warrant the statement that there is or ever has been 'unguided matter.') He had himself repudiated the notion that chance has any place in a scientific theory, but he ends by suggesting that the only reason why there is order in the world is that 'it happens' so.[2] Cleanthes reasonably retorts that the degree of harmonious adaptation in the known part of the universe to the needs of an intelligent civilization goes far beyond what Philo undertakes to account for—such order as is necessary 'for the subsistence of the species.' But Philo has made the main point for which he was concerned, that the *a posteriori* argument, taken by itself, is not adequate to establish the existence of the all-perfect or 'most real' being. Accordingly the dialogue now proceeds to consider the *a priori* argument by which the existence of the *ens realissimum* is to be established from an analysis of its own nature. The exposition of this argument is given to Demea, the spokesman of traditional theology, and the objections against it are put into the mouth of Cleanthes, the upholder of the argument from design, as well as into that of Philo. We now find Cleanthes and Philo allied against Demea, as we have hitherto had Demea and Philo combining against Cleanthes. The particular argument regarded as conclusive by Demea is one which ought more properly to be called *a posteriori*. It is, in fact, as he words it, a combination of two of the forms of the *a posteriori* argument admitted by St. Thomas—the argument from the fact of motion to a First Mover and the argument from the possible to the necessary. Since the indefinite regress is illegitimate, in arguing from effects to causes, we must come to a First Cause, and, when we ask why the 'succession of causes' should be what it is and not a different series, we are forced to answer that the First Cause is a 'necessarily-existent Being, who carries the *REASON* of his existence in himself; and who cannot be supposed not to exist without an express contradiction.'[3] (This last clause thus gets in the point of the ontological proof under cover of the argument from causality; this may be the justification for calling Demea's reasoning *a priori*. Or Hume may possibly mean that his argument is based simply on the general principle of causality and not on the special character of the effect under consideration, the actual universe.) Cleanthes urges against the proof the five following considerations. (1) No fact can be demonstrated *a priori*. 'Whatever we conceive as existent we can also conceive as non-existent. There is no being, therefore, whose non-existence implies a contradiction. Consequently, there is no being whose existence is demonstrable.' This agrees with Thomas's verdict on Anselm except for the fact that Hume disregards the fine distinction between what is evident *in se* and what is evident *quoad nos*. (2) We cannot know that 'the Deity' is a 'necessarily-existent Being' 'while our faculties remain the same as at present,' and therefore 'the words *necessary existence* have no meaning' to us. Here there seems to be a direct contradiction between Cleanthes and St. Thomas. But on looking more closely we see that Cleanthes is merely repeating his former objection in fresh words. By a 'necessary existence' he means one that cannot be thought of as not existing, and St. Thomas also admits that 'our faculties' do not allow us to perceive that God's existence 'flows from His essence.' St. Thomas's argument only went to show that there is a being who exists always. This contention Cleanthes does not refute, but merely denies without giving a reason; 'nor can the mind ever lie under a necessity of supposing any object to remain always in being.' (3) If there must be a 'necessary being,' or a being which cannot be thought not to exist, why may not 'the material universe' itself be this necessary being? 'For aught we can determine, it may contain some qualities which, were they known, would make its non-existence appear as great a contradiction as that twice two is five.'[1] (4) How can there be a first cause of an 'eternal succession of objects'? (5) In such a 'succession of objects' each may be said to be caused by something that preceded it, but there is no sense in asking for a cause of the whole chain. Demea adds that possibly the 'whole economy of the universe' is 'conducted by a necessity,' undiscoverable to us, which he compares with the arithmetical rule that the sum of the digits of any multiple of 9 is divisible by 9.[2] These reflexions really suggest more than they actually contain. Consideration (4), if thought out, raises the question whether the 'infinite regress' is really an impossibility, and consideration (5) is at least a hint of the more modern doctrine of ultimate pluralism that the universe may consist of a multitude of independent but inter-related constituents. Demea's remark deserves less consideration. It amounts manifestly to the suggestion that the 'material universe' itself may be the 'necessary' being whose existence follows from its 'essence,' and is inconsistent with the objection already urged against the ontological proof, that there is no existent which may not be conceived not to exist.

The discussion now turns to the moral character of the First Cause. Philo and Demea agree in arbitrarily assuming the pessimistic view of the general misery of creation and in particular of man. The case is argued by Philo with an abundance of rhetoric and manifest want of logic which of themselves suggest that Hume is treating him with some irony. That Cleanthes declares that he feels little of this misery himself and hopes that pessimists are not very common is a further indication that it is he who is the spokesman of Hume's own conviction, so far as any of the characters can be said to be so. Demea, of course, means only to infer from the pessimistic estimate of life that the true good of man is not to be found on this side of the grave, and is driven out of the company by disgust when Philo goes on to argue at great length, and with still more obvious begging of the question than before, that all the indications show that the cause or causes of the cosmic order are either incompetent, evil, or indifferent to morality. (It is almost incredible, again, that Hume was not aware that the whole of Philo's eloquence depends on the tacit assumption that nothing is good but pleasure. He merely revives the old Epicurean argument against Providence in its crudest form, and it is no surprise to an intelligent reader when he informs Cleanthes, after Demea's departure, that his real object has been merely to protest against the abuse of the topic of benevolent design by popular preachers. It is not quite so easy to believe him sincere in his assertion that, in spite of all that he has hitherto said, he thinks the evidence of rational design in nature overpowering and regards doubt about the existence of a 'Supreme Intelligence' as 'pertinacious obstinacy.') Philo's final conclusion is that the controversy between theists and atheists is at bottom verbal. The order and design in the world prove that its cause (he quietly abandons his own former objection to the demand for such a cause) bears an analogy, though, no doubt, a remote one, to the human mind. If theists would remember the remoteness and atheists the reality of the analogy, there would be nothing left to dispute. But he objects *in toto* to all 'religion' which goes beyond the intellectual admission of this one proposition (and thus is plainly meant to be insincere in his assertion that his 'philosophical scepticism' is 'the most essential step,' in an educated man, 'towards being a sound, believing Christian'). Deism—bare intellectual affirmation of the existence of an intelligent First Cause which exercises no influence whatever on the practical conduct of life—is manifestly what Philo really means to recommend. (His attack on 'religion' is little more than a denunciation of the 'horrors of the Inquisition' and contains a logical contradiction to which his creator must have been alive. He maintains, on the one hand, that 'religious motives' are so weak, by comparison with others, that 'religion' is impotent to influence conduct for the better, and, on the other, that it is so strong that all the worst evil in life is due to 'priests' who play on the fanaticism of the vulgar for their own interested purposes. It is hard not to believe that Hume is treating his puppet with intentional malice, just as he is treating Demea with malice when he represents him as welcoming Philo's description of the hopeless wretchedness of existence without any suspicion of its drift, though, as an educated man, he must have known what conclusions Lucretius had drawn from the same premisses.) Cleanthes, it is to be noted, listens to this assault on religion almost in silence and leaves Philo with the last word. It is to be supposed that he does not assent, though he may not see his way to 'dissolve the ἀπορία.'

15. Kant.—Much more closely knit is the assault on the whole of natural theology in Kant's *Critique of Pure Reason*. It should be remembered that Kant had not always been a disbeliever in the

[1] *Philosophical Works*, p. 414. [2] *Ib.* p. 428. [3] *Ib.* p. 432.

[1] *Philosophical Works*, p. 432. [2] *Ib.* p. 434.

possibility of demonstrating theism. In his thesis for his degree,[1] which aims at showing the irreducibility of the principle of sufficient reason to the logical principle of contradiction, he offers a proof, based on the former principle, that 'there is a being whose existence is antecedent to the possibility of itself and of all things, which being must therefore be said to exist with an absolute necessity.'[2] This is, in principle, the contention most fully developed later by Lotze.

As Kant states it, the argument runs thus. 'Possibility' means the absence of contradiction (*non repugnantia*) between the constituents of a 'complex notion.' The 'constituents' are thus presupposed as the 'matter' of the 'complex notion.' Thus a 'possibility' with no presuppositions, a 'possibility' when nothing whatever has been given as actual, is meaningless. It follows 'that nothing can be conceived as possible unless that which is real in every possible notion exists, and, indeed, exists with absolute necessity (since, if you leave this [reality] out of account, nothing whatever would be possible, *i.e.*, everything would be impossible). Further, he urges, this 'necessary reality' must be a single being. The argument for this is that, if we suppose 'the reals, which are, so to say, the matter of all possible concepts, to be found distributed among many existents' (*i.e.*, if we suppose a plurality of ultimate 'reals'), each 'real' will have limitations, *i.e.* 'privations,' negative characters. But negative characters have not, like positive 'realities,' an 'absolute necessity.' The supposed 'reals' will therefore all contain an element of contingency. The being which exists with absolute necessity must therefore be without any limitations and therefore infinite. (Like Leibniz's God, it must be the subject of every proposition affirming a positive 'perfection.') If there were more than one such infinite being, the very plurality would re-introduce contingency. 'Thus God, and one only God, is given as the absolutely necessary principle of all possibility.' Kant thus, by deducing the existence of God from the principle of sufficient reason, is already anticipating the doctrine of the *Critique* that all existential propositions are synthetic without exception. Descartes' ontological argument is pronounced to be invalid, precisely because it attempts to deduce the 'existence' of God from His 'essence' (thus treating an existential proposition as analytic), whereas, in the proof given by Kant, the 'possibility' of God is itself made to depend on His 'existence.'

Kant returns to the subject in his short essay on *The only Possible Proof of the Being of God.*[3] The proof offered is substantially that of his thesis of 1755, divested of scholastic terminology. Existence is not a predicate or determination of a subject, but the absolute positing of the subject itself; *e.g.*, when I am fully acquainted with the whole story of Julius Caesar and know every predicate of the hero of the story, it is still an intelligible question whether this Julius Caesar is a 'real' man or only the hero of a fiction, and by calling him a 'real' man I do not add an $(n+1)^{\text{th}}$ predicate to the n predicates which I have already asserted about him in telling the story. The difference between a 'real' and a merely possible thing lies not in what is posited in each case, but in the way in which it is posited. If I think of a thing first as possible and then as real, the same complex of predicates and relations is posited in both cases; but in the first case this complex is posited hypothetically (a complex of propositions are true about the thing if it exists), in the second case absolutely—*i.e.* categorically. I cannot think of anything as possible unless its predicates are all compatible with one another; *e.g.*, I cannot think of a triangle with four sides as possible, but I can think of a triangle with a right angle as possible. 'Both the triangle and the right angle are the data or material element in this possibility; the agreement of the first with the second in respect to the law of contradiction is the formal element of the possibility.' Since the material element (the data) as well as the formal is required to constitute a possibility, 'the internal possibility of all things presupposes some existence' (*irgend ein Dasein*), and 'it is wholly impossible that absolutely nothing should exist.' (In more modern language this means that the difference between the logically possible and impossible depends on the compossibility of some predicates and the incompossibility of others; thus, that there may be so much as the difference between what is logically impossible and what is possible, there must be predicates, and predicates are predicates of something. Hence there must be something, to be the subject of predicates if the very word 'possible' is to have a meaning.) Thus we get back to the starting-point of the proof of 1755. Possibility logically presupposes actual existence as its foundation. Therefore there is something actual, the elimination of which would destroy all 'internal possibility'; *i.e.* there is 'an unconditionally necessary being.' Kant then proceeds, as in 1755, to prove that the necessary being is one, simple, immutable, and eternal, and, as that which contains the data of all possibilities, is, in fact, the *ens realissimum.* From these attributes it is inferred that 'the necessary being is a spirit (*Geist*),' and this completes the proof that God exists.

It still remains for Kant to show that his form of the argument 'from the possible to the necessary' is the only valid theistic proof. The Cartesian proof of the fifth *Meditation* is set aside on the ground that it treats existence as a predicate. The familiar argument from the contingency of the world (the world is an effect, therefore it has a cause which is itself uncaused and therefore 'necessary') is unsatisfactory. Kant allows in this essay, as he does not in the *Critique*, that the inference to an uncaused First Cause may be valid. It is not so clear that 'this independent thing is unconditionally necessary,' *i.e.* that it cannot even be thought not to exist, since the demonstration of this turns on the principle of sufficient reason, which is not admitted by all philosophers. But, even if the point be conceded for the sake of argument, it is not proved that the absolutely necessary being is what we mean by God, *i.e.* is utterly perfect and utterly One. To establish this point (that 'the necessary being=the perfect being') we require to prove that, 'if X is perfect, X necessarily exists,' and this is just the ontological argument, with its treatment of existence as one predicate among others, over again (a point on which Kant expatiates more fully in the *Critique*). The teleological or, as Kant calls it, the physico-theological proof here, as in the *Critique*, comes off better. Like Hume's Philo (in one of his moods), Kant is convinced that there is such evident system, adaptation, and benevolence in nature that its author must be thought of as One, wise, and good. But, though the argument deserves to be enforced in the interests of practical piety, it is not enough to prove perfect wisdom or benevolence in the Creator, and thus not enough to prove that He is all we mean by God. The same criticism will meet us again in the *Critique*.

The argument for the dependence of the world on a 'necessarily existing being' recurs again, in a slightly different form, in a third 'precritical' work—Kant's inaugural lecture as professor on 'The Form and Principles of the Sensible and Intelligible World.'[1] As in the two works already considered, Kant assumes the Leibnizian conception of the universe as a complex of simple substances or monads. His object is to show that such a complex must depend for its existence and character upon a supreme and 'necessary' extramundane 'substance,' which is God. The theistic argument is more specially contained in §§ 17–22, and runs as follows. The principles of interrelation between a plurality of substances cannot have their complete ground in the existence of these substances. Each substance is indebted for its mere subsistence only to its cause (if it has a cause). But the relation of effect to cause is not *commercium* (reciprocal interaction), but *dependentia* (one-sided dependence), and what we have to account for is the *commercium* of the substances which make up the universe. Not all these substances can be 'necessary,' because, if they were, they would be absolutely without dependence on each other; there would be no *commercium* between them, and they would not form a world at all. The world, or 'totality

1 *Principiorum Primorum cognitionis metaphysicae nova dilucidatio*, Königsberg, 1755 (*Werke*, ed. G. Hartenstein, Leipzig, 1838–39, i. 367–400).
2 *Ib.* § ii. prop. 7.
3 *Der einzig mögliche Beweisgrund zu einer Demonstration des Daseins Gottes*, Königsberg, 1763 (*Werke*, ii. 109–205).

1 *De mundi sensibilis atque intelligibilis forma et principiis*, Riga, 1770 (*Werke*, ii. 395–425).

of substances,' is, therefore, a 'totality of contingents'; and 'the world, in virtue of its essence, consists of mere contingents. Moreover, no necessary substance is connected with the world (*mundus*) at all, unless as cause with effect, and therefore not as a part with a whole, since the parts of one and the same whole are connected by reciprocal dependence, a relation which does not affect a necessary being. The cause of the world, then, is an extra-mundane being and not a "soul of the world."' And the necessary being which is the extra-mundane cause of the world is one and not many. For the effects of different 'necessary beings' would stand in no relations of reciprocal dependence, since their assumed causes are not reciprocally inter-related. Hence the unity of the substances composing the world in a single system is a consequence of the dependence of them all on one being, and it follows that this one being is not a mere 'architect of the universe' (*i.e.* δημιουργός), but its Creator. Incidentally also the argument removes the ambiguity which had haunted Leibniz's account of the 'pre-established harmony' to God. It definitely makes the harmony itself dependent on God.[1]

Thus down to 1770 Kant shows no doubt of the possibility of demonstrating theism. The argument on which he relies in all the essays examined is one and the same—the Neo-Platonic argument *a posteriori*—and rests on the assumption that the world as given is an object for which we are bound by the principle of causality to seek an explanation.[2] The proof, as with the Neo-Platonists, aims at establishing the existence of the One—the single, internally simple and perfect, extra-mundane source of all the existents which together make up the κόσμος. The peculiarity of Kant's special version of it is that, to escape the criticisms which had been directed against Descartes, he sets himself to deduce the existence of a 'being which cannot be thought not to exist,' not from the logical concept of *ens realissimum*, but from the consideration that, in the universe itself, some combinations of predicates of the same thing and some combinations of relations between the same things are possible, and others not. The existence of an actual extra-mundane being once established as a pre-condition of the difference in intra-mundane things between what is possible and what is impossible, the internal unity, simplicity, and perfection of the necessary being are then deduced as consequences of its necessary existence. If this line of argument is not fallacious—*i.e.* if it really proves that something 'exists of necessity'—it clearly has the double merit of being free from the objection to the ontological proof, and of being equally untouched by the considerations urged by Philo and Demea in Hume against the *a posteriori* proof. If the principle on which Kant relies—that the possible presupposes the actual—is sound, his argument seems to be a complete speculative demonstration of the 'being of God' reduced to its most succinct expression. Why, then, did Kant, in his later 'critical' years, pronounce the question whether God exists to be transcendent—*i.e.* outside the legitimate limits of speculative investigation—and all 'proofs of the existence of God,' including that for which he had himself formerly claimed 'geometrical certainty,' mere fallacies?

In dealing with Kant's drastic assault on speculative natural theology in the *Critique of Pure Reason*, we may perhaps distinguish two questions which Kant himself naturally treated as one. It is one question whether Kant has proved that the demonstration of theism is impossible on the assumption that the special doctrine of his *Critique* as to the limits of human knowledge is true, but quite another question whether that doctrine *is* true, and consequently whether Kant has proved the fallaciousness of natural theology unconditionally. The first of these two questions no doubt permits of only one answer. Kant is clearly right when he asserts that all existential propositions are synthetic, at any rate (to repeat the distinction of St. Thomas to which Kant himself pays no regard) *quoad nos*. And it follows at once from this single consideration that, if, as the *Critique* maintains, the synthesis in a synthetical proposition must always in the end be effected by an application of formal 'categories of the understanding' to a material supplied in sensation or sensuous imagination, no synthetical proposition (and, by consequence, no existential proposition) can be affirmed of a subject which is purely 'intelligible,' a νοητόν. And Kant expressly makes this a main point in his criticism of the ontological proof. Unfortunately, however, this doctrine, if carried out to its full logical consequences, would lead to a result which Kant would have been the first to reject. For it follows that there can be no such sciences as pure arithmetic and pure geometry. The subjects about which synthetical propositions are asserted in these sciences are one and all *Objekte des reinen Denkens* no less than the *ens necessarium* or the *ens realissimum* of speculative theology. No element whatever supplied by sense enters into the mathematician's concept of a circle, a parabola, an integer, or a real number. Kant overlooks this all-important point because he assumes throughout his whole reasoning that, before I can demonstrate a proposition in geometry, I must draw the figure, and similarly that, before I can say what the sum of two integers is, I must count the units of which he supposes the integers to consist. The erroneous character of this view has been sufficiently demonstrated by the subsequent history of mathematical science, but ought to have been clear to Kant himself. Even if all geometry, as he tacitly assumes, were metrical geometry, he ought to have seen that Descartes' invention of co-ordinates had already made the drawing of figures in principle superfluous in geometrical science. His conception of arithmetic is even more superficial—in fact, on a level with Aristotle's. As Couturat has correctly observed, Kant's examples are all drawn from the demonstration of singular propositions (such as $7+5=12$). If he had asked himself how any general truth in the theory of numbers is proved (how, *e.g.*, we prove Fermat's theorem), he would have seen at once the inadequacy of his own theories. Indeed, mere consideration of a singular proposition which does not relate to integers (*e.g.*, the proposition $2{\cdot}5+3{\cdot}\dot{6}=6{\cdot}1\dot{6}$) might have taught him that arithmetic is not the same thing as counting, and even suggested to him that an integer is not a 'collection of units.'

With the discrediting of Kant's 'Transcendental Aesthetic' and the section of the 'Transcendental Dialectic' containing the famous antinomies, which may now be fairly regarded as a *fait accompli*, our task becomes the comparatively simple one of considering whether natural theology does or does not involve (as Kant alleges that it does) an illegitimate use of the principles of pure logic. From Kant's point of view, to be sure, it does. But this is just because Kant assumes that the only legitimate use of logical principles is their employment to order a material given by sense. If the doctrine of his 'Aesthetic' is rejected, and with it that part of the 'Dialectic' in which he absurdly tries to show that the mathematical doctrine of infinite series leads to antinomies,[1] it is no longer obvious that what Kant calls a transcendent employment of the principles of logic—*i.e.* their employment independently of application to 'the manifold' of sense—need be illegitimate. In fact, it is not clear that the whole of the general theory of arithmetic is not just such an employment of logical principles as 'constitutive of a *Denkobjekte*.' (It is certainly so if, as is probably the case, the series of natural integers can be defined wholly in terms of the primitive indefinables of logic.) One Kantian paralogism, in particular, may be noticed here, as it plays a prominent part in the assault on the theistic arguments. Kant complains that all the arguments for the 'necessary being' based on the causal principle depend on employing this principle, which is a mere rule for ordering the appearances of the sensible world, and has no meaning apart from these appearances, as a means of transcending the world of sense.[2] It might be a sufficient retort that the one form of causality with which we are intimately acquainted is our own volitional activity. In this activity, which is at once efficient and intentional causality, what are connected as cause and effect are not an earlier and a later event in the 'world of sensible appearances,' but the self, which does not belong to that 'world' at all, and an event

[1] 'Commercium itaque omnium substantiarum universi est externe stabilitum per causam omnium communem' (*ib.* p. 22).

[2] Philo, in Hume, it will be remembered, had at least suggested that this need not be the case; the material world may be its own explanation.

[1] On the absurdity of all this see, in particular, the crushing exposure of Couturat, *De l'Infini mathématique*, Paris, 1896, bk. iv. ch. 4.

[2] *Kritik der reinen Vernunft*[2], Riga, 1787, p. 637.

which does belong to it. Kant could not deny the causal relation between the rational self and events in the *Sinnenwelt* without ruining the foundations of his own ethics, but the admission of such causality ought to debar him from attacking natural theology on the ground that it 'uses the principle of causality as a means to transcend the world of the senses.' He only escapes open self-contradiction by his monstrous theory, which is not likely to find a defender at the present day, that the self with which we are acquainted is not the real self at all, but a phenomenal self apprehended by an inner sense. From the point of view of logic, the criticism is equivalent to a refusal to admit the validity of any logical inference from the terms of a series to a limit which is not itself a term of the series. It is not in itself any more absurd to hold that examination of the things and events of the *Sinnenwelt* in the light of the causal principle reveals their dependence on something which does not belong to that world than it is to hold that a series of which every term is a rational fraction can be shown to have a limit which is not a rational fraction. (This is, *e.g.*, the case when we represent a surd 'square root' as a recurrent continued fraction. Each of the 'convergents' is a rational fraction, but the limit of the series is not.) The general argument is thus invalid. No *a priori* reason can be given why the causal principle should not enable us to transcend the world of sense, and the only real question which remains is whether the particular arguments of theists will stand scrutiny on their merits. There is no general logical presumption against them of the kind Kant imagines.

We are thus brought to the consideration of the force of Kant's attack on natural theology taken by itself and apart from its connexion with a general theory of the nature of scientific knowledge which is certainly erroneous. We may therefore confine ourselves to the sections of the *Critique of Pure Reason* which profess to make a complete enumeration of the possible proofs of the existence of God and to convict each of the 'proofs' of fallacy, together with the 'Critique of all Speculative Theology,' in which Kant sums up his results.[1] The general line of argument is as follows. The scientific interpretation of facts consists in regarding any given actual condition of things as conditioned and asking for the antecedent facts which condition it. When they have been found, science once more requires an interpretation of them on the same lines, and so on *in indefinitum*. Every set of facts has thus to be regarded by the scientific intellect as conditioned by an antecedent state of things which has, in its turn, to be discovered. The scientific 'explanation' of the world is thus a task which, from its nature, can never be completed. Behind every set of conditions, however remote, at which we may arrive there is always a body of still more remote conditions to be discovered. (The conditions, in every case, like the facts they condition, are facts and processes of the *Sinnenwelt*.) The unending regress from conditioned to conditions, however, naturally suggests the thought that the process of explanation would be completed if we could find something ultimate, itself unconditioned but the condition of everything else. Thus we arrive at the notion of a being which 'exists necessarily' and contains in itself the explanation of everything else, the one and only being which is not contingent (*i.e.* a consequence of something other than itself). Next, it occurs to us that, if there is such a 'necessarily existing' being, it must, as the condition of everything else, contain in itself all that is truly real or positive; what is real in all limited and finite things must come to them from it. Thus we identify the *ens necessarium* with the *ens realissimum* ('*dasjenige was alle Realität enthält*'). Finally, since we ourselves, who are among the things dependent on this being, are intelligent moral persons, we 'personify' this being, and thus we arrive at the conception of God as the Supreme Being and source of the world. But the whole process has no scientific worth. The inference to the existence of a 'necessary being' is invalid because it employs the causal principle, which is really only a rule for the interconnexion of sensible events, as a means of connecting the sensible with the intelligible (a general criticism which has already been considered in the last paragraph); we have no positive conception whatever of the character of this necessary being (supposing it to exist), and the attempt to find one by identifying it with the 'most real being' will not stand examination, since it is logically possible that there might be a plurality of 'necessary' beings, each imperfect and finite (one may illustrate by the theory that 'ultimate reality' is a 'society' of unoriginate 'persons' without any Creator); and the attempt to prove the existence of a single 'most real being' directly is a pure sophism. The conclusion then is that, though speculation may suggest to us the possibility that God (conceived after the fashion of the Neo-Platonic 'One') is the source of the world, it can do no more. It cannot even prove that the possibility is more than 'logical'; *i.e.*, speculation may convince us that there is no internal contradiction in the notion of such a being; it cannot show that God is a 'real' possibility—*i.e.*, that there is no incompatibility between the existence of God and the actual facts of the world of experience, if we knew them all instead of being aware of a mere fragment of them. The whole value of speculative theism is to suggest this mere possibility, to warn us that we are not speculatively justified in regarding the sensible world as underived, but must keep an open mind. If, however, apart from all speculative philosophy, there are *practical* grounds for believing in God—*i.e.*, if the reality of absolute moral obligation can only be made intelligible by appeal to our dependence on God—then, for practical purposes, the open possibility is converted into a moral certainty. Kant means, as he explains,[1] that, in shaping the conduct of our lives, *il faut parier*. We must act either on the assumption that moral obligation is absolute or on the assumption that it is not; there is no third course. But all moral obligation, as is shown at length in the *Grundlegung zur Metaphysik der Sitten*,[2] is absolute, and there is no fact more certain than this. Without God as ruler of the world, however, the system of absolute obligations would be a logically flawless construction ('*in der Idee der Vernunft ganz richtig*'), but would have no 'reality of application to ourselves, *i.e.* would be without motives.'[3] A virtuous man is thus necessitated to a firm rational belief in theism, but that which makes the necessity is not the demonstrative force of the theistic arguments (which in fact is zero), but the virtuous man's immediate conviction of the absoluteness of moral obligations. This is what Kant meant when he described himself as abolishing knowledge to make room for faith.[4] If our unfavourable judgment on the 'Transcendental Aesthetic' is justified, we plainly cannot concede to Kant that all speculative theism must be baseless. The theistic arguments must be scrutinized on their merits, not condemned *en bloc* like the generals at Arginusae. With his usual love for formal schematism Kant urges that there can be three and only three ways of trying to prove the existence of the Supreme. We may attempt to

[1] *Kritik der reinen Vernunft*², pp. 611–670.

[1] *Kritik der reinen Vernunft*², p. 615. [2] Riga, 1788.
[3] *Kritik der reinen Vernunft*², p. 617.
[4] He must not be understood in a pragmatist sense. He did not mean that the existence of God is a speculation which a man may accept or decline 'at his own risk,' may adopt 'because up to the present it works,' or because inferences can be drawn from it which gratify the believer. The faith of which he speaks has its foundation in the conviction that the law of duty is absolute, and this proposition is admitted by the good man not as an 'hypothesis accepted at his own risk to see whether it works,' or because he chooses to accept it, but because, being a good man, he sees it to be true and certain.

prove the existence of the 'most real being' entirely *a priori* (*i.e.* without the use of any 'truth of fact' as a premiss) by arguing that existence is included in its very nature—the ontological proof; we may, departing from the strictly *a priori* method, employ the single truth of fact, 'something exists,' as one of our premisses, and then argue to the conclusion that a 'necessary being' exists—the cosmological proof; we may include among our premisses specific assertions about the character of the 'something that exists'; *i.e.*, we may argue from the marks of intelligent and benevolent design in the actual world to intelligence and benevolence in its source—the physico-theological proof. Each of these proofs is now to be shown unsatisfactory. The first is a pure verbal sophism and the second no better, and, as proofs of the existence of God, both the second and third have to be eked out by a silent combination with the first.

The refutation of the 'ontological' proof is one of the best-known passages of the *Critique of Pure Reason*. Kant speaks of the argument as the 'ontological (or Cartesian) proof.' He examines it only in the form in which it has been revived by Descartes, and was apparently not acquainted with its earlier history. His objection, put briefly, is simply this, that the proposition 'God exists' can only be got out of the concept of 'God' if existence has already been included in that concept. If I define God as a 'really existing *X*,' of course I can make the true proposition, 'If there is such a being as the God thus defined, then that being exists.' But I am not entitled to assert that there is such a being, and consequently not entitled to assert the consequent of the foregoing hypothetical proposition ('God exists') categorically. In fact existence is not a real predicate. The concept 'a hundred dollars' has precisely the same content whether the hundred dollars actually exist in my pocket or not. 'Our concept of an object may contain what and as much as you please, still we must go outside it to impart existence to the object.'[1] Hence the ontological proof is not really a proof of anything. 'The Idea of a Supreme Being is in many respects a most useful Idea, but just because it is merely an Idea it is wholly incapable of extending our knowledge of what exists by means of itself alone.'[2] Since Hegel undertook to rehabilitate the argument, it has been fashionable to retort on Kant that, though it may be true that the real existence of a sum of a hundred dollars cannot be inferred from analysis of the corresponding concept, the case is wholly altered when we come to deal with the unique and exalted concept of the Supreme Being. The present writer does not feel that Hegel's witticisms on this point are any answer to Kant's criticism. Kant is certainly right in saying that mere success in defining a concept without contradiction does not in general warrant our asserting that the concept has an 'extension.' The logical investigations which have issued in the creation of the modern 'exact' or 'symbolic' logic of Frege, Peano, and Russell have made this point even clearer than it could have been to the first readers of the *Critique*. If it is immediately evident that there is a member of the unit-class of which 'supreme being' is the class-name, there is neither room nor need for proof. If this is not immediately evident, proof is wanted. In general it cannot be inferred from the definition of a class that the class has members. If the class 'supreme being' or 'most real being' is an exception, we require proof that it is an exception to the rule, and neither Hegel nor any one else has ever offered anything in the way of proof. Thus, as against Descartes, Kant's argument is, in the present writer's opinion, decisive. Nor does he see that the original Anselmian proof fares any better. It is not directly touched by Kant's denial that existence is a predicate, since Anselm does not rest his case on the assertion that existence is a predicate. But Kant's counter-argument can equally be stated without raising this question. Whether existence is a predicate or not, it is equally true that we are not entitled to infer from the hypothetical proposition, 'If there is a God, that God is an existent,' the categorical proposition, 'God is an existent'; and this is what Anselm tries to do. He is really committed, as every defender of the ontological line of argument must be, to the attempt to prove that it is irrational to suppose that there might have existed nothing at all. In point of fact most of those who have tried to turn the edge of Kant's criticism have not attempted so desperate a task. They have consciously or unconsciously assumed as a premiss the proposition that something exists, and have been content to argue that, since something exists, God exists also. In doing this they tacitly admit the truth of the contention of Kant and St. Thomas that no purely *a priori* proof of theism is possible.

Kant's attack on the cosmological proof is more elaborate and, in the present writer's opinion, less successful. The rejection of the ontological proof does not depend in the least on the acceptance of the peculiar theory of knowledge expounded in the *Critique*. The proof had been rightly treated as a sophism in all the precritical essays in which Kant deals with the foundations of natural theology. The case of the cosmological argument is different; Kant's own precritical proof, based on the need for an actual ground of real possibility, was itself a form of the cosmological proof, and is thus among the inferences now rejected as illegitimate. We may therefore expect to find that the rejection of this type of argument does depend on the special critical theory of the limits of human knowledge, and is thus only valid on the hypothesis that the doctrines of the *Critique* are accepted. The typical form of the proof as stated in the *Critique* for examination is this: (*a*) If anything exists, an absolutely necessary being exists; but at least one thing (viz. myself) exists; *ergo* an absolutely necessary being exists; (*b*) a necessary being must be completely determined by its concept; the only concept which thus completely determines an object is the concept of the *ens realissimum*; *ergo* the concept of the *ens realissimum* is the only one by means of which a necessary being can be thought; *i.e.*, a Supreme Being necessarily exists. The argument thus consists of two stages: first, the proof that, because at least one thing exists, a necessary being exists, and, second, the proof that a necessary being can only be the Supreme Being.

Kant denounces this cosmological argument with special vehemence, as was only natural in one who had until his late middle age built on it with perfect confidence and then come to distrust it. His tone in criticizing it is not unlike that of a rather unscrupulous attorney determined to secure a verdict against the accused party by fair means or foul. He begins by a charge of general fraudulence. The cosmological proof professes to appeal to experience, but it is really only the old discredited ontological argument dishonestly disguised. For it only uses the appeal to experience to establish the result: 'There is *a* being which exists necessarily.' When we ask what this being is, we are referred back to the *ens realissimum* as the only thing which meets the requirements of the case. Therefore 'it is only the ontological proof from mere concepts which contains the force of the demonstration and the alleged experience is wholly superfluous.'[1]

The complaint is surely unfair. The objection to the ontological argument did not lie in the concept of the *ens realissimum*, but merely in the absence of an existential premiss. If, then, the new argument supplies the missing existential premiss, it is no objection to it to say that the necessary being of which it speaks turns out to be the *ens realissimum*. The only legitimate objection would be that the argument does not actually supply such an existential premiss as is really needed. This is what Kant next proceeds to urge.[2] He complains that it ought to be shown that the necessary being is the *ens realissimum*. To prove this, we require to establish two propositions, of which one is the simple converse of the other: (*a*) every necessary being is an *ens realissimum*, (*b*) every *ens realissimum* is a necessary being. But this second proposition is 'determined merely by *a priori* concepts,' and therefore 'the mere concept of the most real being' must be the ground for ascribing to it necessary existence. Thus we commit the fallacy of the ontological proof, the establishment of a proposition by mere analysis of concepts. This criticism seems wholly *verfehlt*. The real objection to the ontological proof was that it aimed at proving an existential proposition by mere analysis of concepts. There can be no logical objection to the attempt to prove by such analysis the hypothetical proposition, 'If anything is an (or the) *ens realissimum*, it is *ens necessarium*,' or the simple converse, 'If anything is *ens necessarium*, it is also *ens realissimum*.' Both these propositions are implications, not assertions of existence; the existential import is brought into the cosmological argument entirely by the preceding proof, or attempted proof, that, if anything exists (as we know to be the case), a necessary being exists. Kant is entitled to contend that this has not been proved; he is entitled to contend that the equivalence of *ens necessarium* and *ens realissimum* has not been made out. He is not entitled to treat the fact that the equivalence is an equivalence of concepts as proof of this second charge. Up to this point he is merely following the recommendation to give a dog a bad name and trust to its hanging him. We now come to the really relevant part of his onslaught. This consists of the following allegations: (1) the inference from the contingent to its cause has a meaning only in the sensible world, but the principle of causality is used in this proof to transcend the sensible world; (2) the argument from the impossibility of an infinite series of causes in the sensible world to a first cause is illegitimate; (3) the very notion of necessity presupposes conditions upon which the necessity in question depends, and it is therefore impermissible to cut short the regress from proximate to more ultimate conditions by the really empty concept of an unconditioned necessity; (4) the proof confuses the mere logical possibility of a concept (absence of internal contradiction) with its transcendental possibility, which 'requires a principle establishing the possibility of performing such a synthesis,' but this latter can only be established 'in the field of possible experiences.' All these objections are valid only on the hypothesis that the Kantian theories about the limits of scientific knowledge are true, and it has already been contended that this hypothesis (involving, as it does, the acceptance of the 'Transcendental Aesthetic' and the consequent recognition of the antinomies of the 'Transcendental Dialectic' as inevitable) is certainly false. In particular, it may be replied to (1) that all use of the principle of causality involves transcending the sensible world; consistent phenomenalism, as the work of such writers as Mach, Pearson, Avenarius, abundantly shows, is bound to eliminate

[1] *Kritik der reinen Vernunft*², p. 629. [2] *Ib.*

[1] *Kritik der reinen Vernunft*², p. 635. [2] *Ib.* p. 636.

the category of causality from science; to (2) that the 'cosmological argument' is not an argument from the impossibility of an infinite series of events at all. In fact it has been often maintained by thinkers who, like Aristotle, deny that the series of events has a first term, or, like St. Thomas, hold that it can only be known by revelation whether the series has a first term or not. The real bearing of the argument cannot be seen at all, so long as we think of causality, as Kant does throughout the *Critique*, as a mere rule of uniform connexion between earlier and later events. Its real foundation is in the conception of efficient causality (activity or agency). The point of the argument is that, if there is not a First Mover or First Agent (or 'movers' or 'agents' in the plural, as the case may be), the whole history of the world is a mere accident. Things are what they are because there 'happen to be' such and such agents, and the reason why there are just these agents and no others is that there 'happen to be' (or 'to have been') certain others by which the set first mentioned have been produced, and so on *in indefinitum*. This means that there might just as well have been no world at all, or one quite different from that which there is. An ultimate pluralistic realism, no doubt, might maintain this thesis, and we shall have to face it in the sequel. But it is an *ignoratio elenchi* to defend it by assuming phenomenalism *plus* an erroneous theory of the mathematical meaning of infinite series. The phenomenalism is further in flat contradiction with the presuppositions of Kantian ethics, for which it is indispensable that every human self shall be a 'first cause' of its own morally and legally imputable acts. If 'first cause' really means nothing intelligible, Kant's practical philosophy is no better than an idle sporting with insignificant words. One must add that the full force of the cosmological argument is only seen when it is combined with the argument from intentional causality. If the historical world-process has a meaning of any kind, whether its meaning lies in the direction of events towards an end or result or in their internal, quasi-aesthetic harmony, the explanation of it cannot, in the end, be merely that the constituents of the universe happen to be what they are. An ultimate pluralism must, to be consistent, deny that there is any meaning at all in the world-process. But, again, the Kantian phenomenalism affords no valid reason for entertaining this view. As to the last point, it does depend on the special principles of the critical philosophy, and, in particular, on the theory that an appeal to the senses lies at the root of all valid synthetic propositions. As has already been remarked, this theory is sufficiently disposed of by the simple consideration that every proposition in the theory of numbers is synthetic in Kant's sense of the word. In the present writer's opinion, then, Kant's attack on the cosmological argument (which he himself clearly regards as the central feature of his general assault on speculative theism) is a complete failure. He proves neither that the argument from the fact of existence to the existence of a 'necessary being' is fallacious nor that there is any sophism in the reasoning by which he himself had formerly established the equivalence of the 'necessary being' with the perfect or 'most real' being. This does not, of itself, prove that the cosmological argument is valid, but it does prove, if the remarks just made are in principle sound, that Kant's objections to the argument are unfounded. Even the complaint that we have no positive conception of either 'necessary' or 'most real' being only amounts to the true assertion that we do not know what it would be like to be God—a proposition which no reasonable theist, least of all an orthodox Christian theologian, need be concerned to deny. For the matter of that, I do not know what it would be like to be my cat, but that is surely an insufficient reason for denying the existence of my cat's mind.

Kant's treatment of the argument from intentional causality —the physico-theological proof, as he calls it—may be summarized more briefly. This argument, which he reduces to the argument from design, he regards with great respect as the most ancient, most obvious, and soundest of all. He assumes it as an undoubted fact that nature, so far as we know it, exhibits all the marks of intelligent purpose, and admits that it is correct to argue from such marks to a designing intelligence. It does not occur to him to explain away the appearances of order and purpose as merely apparent or as the results of anything in the nature of a struggle for existence. He is content to call attention to the limitations imposed on the argument by the imperfection of our knowledge of nature. It is only a part of nature with which we are acquainted, and any inference from the orderliness and purposiveness of that part to thoroughgoing order and purpose in nature everywhere has at best a degree of probability which falls short of certainty. We cannot therefore be sure even of the unity of the designing intelligence, since we do not know that, if all the empirical facts were before us, they would show absolute singleness of design. Even if we knew all the empirical facts, and knew that they all showed perfect unity of purpose, we could only infer that the intelligence which designed the natural order was very wise, very good, very powerful. We could not argue from any knowledge of empirical facts to infinite wisdom, etc. In particular, we only detect intelligence in the arrangement of the 'stuff' of the world, and thus, even if we knew all the facts, we could not use them as a proof of the existence of the Supreme Being, but at most as a proof of the existence of a demiurge or 'architect of the universe.' Thus, if a theologian appears to demonstrate the existence of God by the appeal to design in nature, it is only because he is illegitimately supplementing his reasoning by a concealed appeal to the ontological argument. In these criticisms, in which Kant is manifestly justified, he is, of course, urging considerations with which Hume had already made Philo confront Cleanthes. It is abundantly manifest that no empirical reasoning can establish the existence of a Supreme Being. Kant's final result, stated with his usual love for pedantic formal distinctions, is given in the section of the *Critique* which bears the special title 'Critique of all Theology based on Speculative Principles of Reason.' Theology, we are told, may be based on revelation or on mere reason. Rational theology, again, may think of its object (God) either as *ens realissimum* without further specification or with a further determination as the Supreme Intelligence. The first is transcendental theology, and its supporters may be called deists; the second is natural theology and is the doctrine of the theist. Natural theology, once more, may conceive God as the source of the order that actually exists (the natural order) or as the source of an order that ought to exist (moral order). It is only consideration of the latter that really gives us a right to postulate the existence of a Supreme Being; speculative theology, which attempts to establish the existence of God as required to explain the order of nature, is, as we have seen, condemned to failure, because it seeks to prove the reality of a being which cannot be an object of possible experience. Its value is simply that it shows us that there is no logical impossibility inherent in the notion of a Supreme Being. Thus it forbids us to assert that we know that there is no God, or that, if there is, He is not an intelligent being or is imperfect and limited like ourselves (it saves us from dogmatic atheism, deism, and anthropomorphism), and thus leaves us free to maintain the existence of a supreme spiritual principle, if the moral order proves to be unintelligible apart from the postulate that such a principle exists. For the present it may suffice to make two observations on this. The denial that God is an object of possible experience depends, of course, on taking a specific view of what is meant by experience. If it is indispensable to an experience that it should have an object into which sense-data enter as constituents (and this is what Kant always assumes), manifestly God cannot be experienced. But it may be observed that it is no ground of objection to speculative theology in particular to say that it claims to give us knowledge about a being which is not an object of 'possible experience' in this sense. The same thing is equally true of arithmetic or any other part of pure mathematics. The integers, *e.g.*, are not objects of experience in this sense; still less would it be possible to maintain that, when one utters the well-known proposition, 'Every integer can be represented as the sum of four squares, of which—except in the case of the integer 0—one at least is not 0,' one is not transcending possible experience. It would be quite impossible to verify the proposition by examining its validity for each successive integer (since there is an infinite number of them). Wherever I make a statement about a class with an infinity of members, I am dealing with an object which is not, in Kant's sense of the words, an 'object of a possible experience.' His doctrine reposes on the theory of his 'Aesthetic' that, in the case of arithmetical propositions, I can justify such an assertion by counting. But, though I could, *e.g.*, prove the proposition quoted to hold good for a few cases by actual counting, I manifestly cannot verify it or any other general proposition of the science by this method of appealing to intuition. Again, we may fairly ask why experience should be assumed to be concerned only with objects which fall under the 'forms of intuition.' Why are the saint's moments of vision to be from the outset excluded from experience? If they are included, the statement that God is not an object of possible experience at once becomes questionable. It is a standing defect of the *Critique* that the concept of experience itself has never been subjected by Kant to careful and searching criticism. The second observation which naturally suggests itself is that the sharp opposition between speculation and practice might prove on a closer examination to be misleading. All that Kant can claim to have shown, even if every one of his charges against natural theology could be sustained, is that the facts of physical nature do not warrant the theistic hypothesis. But it is surely as much part of the task of a speculative philosophy to explain the facts of the moral as it is to explain the facts of the physical order. The absoluteness of moral obligations is a fact of the moral order, and, if this fact is only intelligible from the theistic standpoint, then it may fairly be said that speculative philosophy is committed to theism. This was, indeed, Kant's own conviction, and his hard and fast severance between speculation and practice does less than justice to the view he intends to maintain. It gives rise to the misleading suggestion that he regards theism as a doctrine which is doubtfully true but had better be taught to the proletariat with a view to keeping them out of mischief and making them conveniently submissive to their 'betters.' This was not in the least what Kant meant, but his unfortunate verbal distinction between theory and practice is what gave colour to the jest of Heine that after abolishing God in the first *Critique* Kant revived Him in the second in the interest of his old butler's morals, as well as to the strange view of Bernard Bosanquet[1] that Kant's theism is an 'unessential survival.'

It would be wholly unjust to Kant to confine our attention to the destructive side of his treatment of philosophic theism; even more important is his positive teaching, which will be found most fully expressed in the *Kritik der praktischen Vernunft*.[2] If Kant's object was to destroy the

[1] *Essays and Addresses*, London, 1889, p. 129.
[2] Riga, 1788 (*Werke*, v. 116-153).

old speculative natural theology, it is even more his purpose to replace it by a positive moral theology, and it is probably true to say that it is primarily due to his influence that in our own time it is mainly upon the moral argument that popular theistic philosophy continues to base itself. As the Kantian moral theology has often been very imperfectly understood by its critics, it is necessary to state Kant's real position rather carefully, in order to put in the clearest light the differences between Kant and those who hold that the existence of God remains after all a 'pious opinion,' suggested but not established by the facts of the moral life, or those who hold that it is a doctrine recommended mainly by its comforting character. To appreciate the strength of Kant's position, it is necessary to understand that theism is not in any sense an arbitrary hypothesis tacked on to a system of ethics, or, as Bosanquet calls it, a 'survival' of belated superstition, but a logically necessary part of 'practical' philosophy. The argument starts from premisses which are taken as once for all established in the *Grundlegung zur Metaphysik der Sitten* and the *Analytic of Practical Reason.*[1] These premisses are as follows. The object which all moral action has in view is the realization of the highest or complete good. The complete good means a state of things in which the reasonable will finds full and complete satisfaction. Such a state of things implies two constituents: virtue (a right state of the will itself), and happiness (by which Kant means, as he says, a condition of things in complete accord with the rational will, *i.e.* the successful domination of rational will in the universe). If only the first constituent were real, *i.e.*, if the will of every rational being were morally wholly good, this would not of itself be enough to satisfy the demands of the rational will itself. We should not think a universe satisfactory or rational if it consisted of beings of perfect morality whose volitions were always defeated and disappointed by the course of things. The only condition of things which would satisfy our rational demand for the triumph of the virtuous will would be one in which every rational being should be happy (*i.e.* should find his volition effective), in proportion to the moral goodness of his will. The highest good—the object of the moral will—is thus a union of virtue with happiness, but a union in which the inner virtue of the agent is the condition and cause of his happiness.[2] So the highest good means a condition of existence in which a rational being is (*a*) deserving of happiness, deserving that his 'will be done, as in heaven so in earth,'[3] and (*b*) has the happiness which he deserves as a consequence of his deserving it. (More briefly, the highest good is that the actual order of things should be a moral order.) But—and here comes in the antinomy which Kant thinks indispensable in a *Critique*—the principle, as distinguished from the object, of the virtuous will is always to act from reverence for the unconditional obligatoriness of the moral law, without any consideration of the results of our conduct. We must, as moral beings, will the highest good, yet we must also, as moral beings, will to do right for its own sake, without even asking the question whether our right actions will result in bringing about this good or not. We cannot escape from this antinomy, as Kant holds we can from those of speculative reason, by dismissing it as illusory. For we are under absolute obligation to be virtuous, and we cannot be really virtuous without desiring the highest good, nor yet can we be really virtuous if we allow this desire to affect our will to do right because it is right, regardless of consequences. Thus, if morality is to be more than an empty dream, the union of virtue and happiness must be realized, though we must not set ourselves to realize it by treating virtuous action as a means to it. The realization of the union must be brought about for us, not by us. Now, experience shows abundantly that in the empirically known system of nature there is no dependence of happiness on virtue. The most virtuous man is not regularly the man whose will is actually done 'in earth,' nor the man whose will is done the man whose volitions are morally purest. The union must therefore be effected for us by a supreme power, not our own, in the 'intelligible world' which disposes the course of events so that, if we could see the whole infinite series at once, we should see that every man is happy in proportion to the degree in which he deserves to be happy. Further, since morality demands not merely that the virtuous shall be happy but that the happiness shall be a consequence of their virtue, we could not regard the union of virtue and happiness as effected by a mere blind 'natural tendency' in things. The virtuous man's virtue must be the motive of the disposing power to make him happy—*i.e.*, this disposing power must be thought of as an intelligent and absolutely holy *will*. Thus it becomes a postulate of morality that there is an absolutely wise and holy Supreme Being. We have already seen that the speculative use of reason in finding an explanation for natural events themselves suggested the hypothesis that there is a Supreme Being, though all our attempts to demonstrate the truth of this hypothesis proved to rest on fallacy. The consideration of the presuppositions of morality now shows us that, unless there is to be a hopeless conflict between our conception of the highest good and the first principle of duty, such a Supreme Being must really exist and, what is more, must be spiritual. Practical reason then does not introduce us to any new idea; if it did, there might be an insoluble conflict between its suggestions and the results of speculative criticism. It only gives us the right to affirm as a reality what speculative reason itself unavoidably suggests as a possibility, the complete dependence of the world on a Supreme Being, and enables us to determine the character of that Being so far as to say that it combines perfect wisdom, holiness, and power. Beyond this moral theology cannot go. It tells us what God must be if the world is to have moral order, and it tells us nothing more. Kant pushes this consideration so far that he is not content to say with the Neo-Platonists and scholastics that we do not know God *secundum essentiam suam.* Recurring to his view that an object of possible experience must have sensuous constituents (must be given in intuition), he in effect denies that we have any experience of God at all. 'Mystics' profess to experience the divine, but for that very reason Kant sets them down summarily as 'fanatics' who must not be allowed a hearing.

[1] That the *Critique of Practical Reason* should be divided, like the *Critique of Pure Reason*, into an 'Analytic' and a 'Dialectic'—of course there can be no 'Aesthetic' in this case—and that the 'Dialectic' must have its antinomy is a pure piece of pedantic formalism which Kant would have done well to dispense with.

[2] The words of this statement are not precisely those of Kant, but have been chosen to express as briefly and untechnically as possible the substance of his thought. It should be carefully observed that the central thought is not egoistic. Kant's point is that the 'ideal spectator,' apart from any consideration of his own happiness, would judge unfavourably of a world in which the will of the truly virtuous man was constantly thwarted by the 'force of circumstances.' My own happiness, as he is careful to state, only comes into the consideration in so far as I am one among the many rational and responsible beings in the universe. Nor is happiness understood in a merely hedonistic way. It is the condition in which things happen 'according to our will'—*i.e.* in which the rational will is really effectual.

[3] In fact, though Kant would have been horrified by so 'fanatical' a phrase, he is at bottom quite agreed with 'Dionysius' that 'deification' (θέωσις) is the ultimate goal of the moral life.

The value of Kant's moral argument for theism seems quite independent of our judgment of the critical philosophy as a whole. The phenomenalism which is the weakest point of the system only affects Kant's unfavourable estimate of specific religious experience. It might, indeed, be said with an appearance of plausibility that God as the source of the subordination of nature to the moral order is only brought in to solve a difficulty which Kant has created for himself by the abstract formalism of his ethics. No Kantian doctrine has come in for more unsparing reprobation than the famous theory that the moral worth of an act depends upon its being done from mere reverence for universal law as such, and is destroyed if any desire for a specific result influences the agent's motives. But, apart from this untenable theory, it may be said, there is really no antithesis between the supreme object of virtuous willing and its true principle; the realization of the good is at once object and principle. And thus the problem which, according to Kant, is solved for us by the existence of God is not a real problem at all. Yet such criticism surely misses the mark. The problem Kant has in mind still remains when the pure formalism of his own conception of the good will has been dismissed. One and the same conviction of the absoluteness of moral values, the right of δικαιοσύνη to control the world, compels us to pronounce the world evil and our own moral striving a vain show if the highest good is not realized or realizable, and also forbids us to aim directly at the realization of this highest good by doing moral evil that good may come out of it or leaving the right undone because the consequences of doing right are judged by us to be, in a certain case, bad. It is certain that good often comes out of moral evil, and that moral integrity itself often demands action which leads to bad results which would not have followed if the agent had been less virtuous.[1] Thus, quite independently of any special Kantian theses in ethics, we are confronted by the dilemma: either the order of things, rightly understood (the intelligible world), is a moral order and realizes the highest good or the highest good is not realized and all moral effort is senseless and foredoomed to failure, in which case the conviction of the absolute value of the good, on which morality is based, is a mere illusion. If this be so, the argument from the reality of absolute moral values to the all-wise, all-holy, and all-powerful Supreme Being, in the present writer's judgment, holds, exactly on the lines on which Kant has conducted it. It is precisely the same argument, divested of its incidental trappings of Kantian 'critical' phraseology, which Solovyof compresses into a sentence when he writes:

> 'The unconditional principle of morality, logically involved in religious experience, contains the complete good (or the right relation of all to everything) not merely as a demand or an idea, but as an actual power that can fulfil this demand and create the perfect moral order or Kingdom of God in which the absolute significance of every being is realized.'[2]

16. Lotze.—This article cannot undertake to follow the history of the treatment of theism in philosophy beyond Kant with any detail. To do so would require a substantial volume, and it does not seem to the present writer that anything which is new in principle has been added to the arguments for or against theism since Kant's development of the moral proof in the *Critique of Practical Reason*. An exception, however, may be made for Lotze, more particularly on the ground that he has done so much, in the face of Kant's critical repudiation of his own earlier position, to vindicate the speculative argument upon which Kant himself relied until advanced middle age.[1]

[1] See the entertaining illustrations of this point in V. Solovyof, *The Justification of the Good*, Eng. tr., London, 1918, pt. iii. ch. 6.

[2] *Ib.* p. 180. The whole of Solovyof's book is worth reading as a corrective to Kant's thesis that philosophical theology is exhausted by the one proposition that God exists.

It may seem strange to describe Lotze as reasserting the particular version of the cosmological argument which finds in God the necessary actual ground of possibilities, in view of the fact that Lotze himself, in the chapter on the 'Proofs of the Existence of God' in the *Grundzüge der Religionsphilosophie*, professes to have disposed of the cosmological proof in one or two paragraphs of not very profound criticism. Yet an analysis of his own argument will show that, though it is not quite identical with any former statement of the cosmological proof, it really follows the general lines of Kant's pre-critical argument for the 'being which exists with an absolute necessity.' The starting-point of Lotze's train of thought was historically determined for him by the necessity of taking up a definite attitude towards the philosophy of Herbart, and to a lesser degree of Hegel; this special concern with the problems raised in the metaphysics of Herbart further accounts for the very marked influence of Leibniz.[2]

Lotze starts with the fact of incessant change or becoming as the most obvious characteristic of the empirical world. The great problem of the metaphysician is to give an intelligible account of the pre-conditions of this universal fact of change.[3] We can neither dismiss change or becoming as a mere illusion (since, even if you deny all change in the objective world, the illusion itself has to be regarded as a process of change in the inner states of the existents which we call minds or souls) nor resolve the history of the universe into a process of absolute becoming, a wholly lawless succession of disconnected states. This would be fatal to the possibility of all knowledge whatever. Change or becoming, then, is real, and it is always grounded change. This is shown by our success in formulating laws of natural processes. If we find that A is regularly, though not always, followed by B, we must suppose that there is a reason in the state of things in which A was present why A should be replaced by B rather than by P or Q, and, if on special occasions A (which is commonly followed by B) is followed by P, there must again be a reason why it is, on these occasions, followed not by the usual B but by the unusual P. At the stage of reflexion reached in natural science we attempt to do justice to this demand for an intelligible interpretation of change by the view that the world is made up of a plurality of different 'things' ($A, B, C \ldots$), each exhibiting a succession of 'states' ($a_1, a_2, a_3 \ldots b_1, b_2, b_3 \ldots c_1, c_2, c_3 \ldots$). We then say that the changes of state of the various things are interconnected by laws according to which a definite change of 'state' in one thing (*e.g.*, the occurrence of a state a in A) gives rise to the corresponding change in another (the occurrence of a state b in B). This interpretation of the facts, Lotze urges, cannot be final. If the universe were really a collection of independent existents, or 'things,' how could the occurrence of a change of state in one of these existents be conditioned by changes of state in the rest? The very fact that, *e.g.*, A only exhibits the change from state a_1 to state a_2 on the condition that certain definite changes occur in a number of other 'things'—in a word, the 'interconnexion of things in obedience to determinate laws'—shows that the universe is not an ultimate plurality. We are bound to think of it as *one* being of which what we commonly call the various 'things' are partial expressions or activities. We must amend the statement that the changes of state in a plurality of things are related according to definite formulae into the statement that the one and only real 'thing' has a determinate nature or character of its own which it maintains unimpaired. It is this self-maintenance of the 'living whole'—M, as Lotze symbolically calls it—that requires that the change of which we speak as occurring in the thing A should be compensated in a definite way by connected changes, which we are accustomed to refer to the other things $B, C \ldots$. Strictly speaking, then, every change in any element of M is correlated with changes in all the rest. But some of these changes may be minimal and so escape our notice. Hence we are able for our human purposes to formulate laws which connect a definite change in one element with definite changes in a finite number of others, B, C, D, and treat all the rest of the elements as a remainder R, which is irrelevant. The world, then, is not a plurality but a unity-in-plurality. How the unity is effected is more than we can ever expect to know. We may say, 'The unity is the plurality,' but we must remember that the 'is' here is a copula of which the concrete modality

[1] Lotze's treatment of the subject is to be found partly in his *Metaphysik*, latest ed. Leipzig, 1912, Eng. tr.[2], 2 vols., Oxford, 1887; see particularly bk. i. chs. 6–7, with which may be compared the more condensed *Grundzüge der Metaphysik*, Leipzig, 1883, Eng. tr., *Outlines of Metaphysics*, Boston, U.S.A., 1886, particularly the chapter 'Of Causes and Effects' (Eng. tr., pp. 57–73), partly in the *Grundzüge der Religionsphilosophie*[3], Leipzig, 1894. A longer and more popularly written exposition is given in *Mikrokosmus*[5], 3 vols., do. 1896–1909, Eng. tr.[4], Edinburgh, 1894, bk. ix., 'The Unity of Things.' Only the general outline of Lotze's doctrine can be dealt with here.

[2] It must be remembered that Lotze was necessarily unacquainted with Leibniz's most important papers, which were mostly unpublished until after Lotze had arrived at his own fundamental doctrines; hence his version of the earlier philosopher's thought is not to be implicitly trusted.

[3] This was precisely the problem which had specially occupied Herbart and the Herbartians.

is not fully known to us. But it is important to be quite clear on one point of the first importance. The one 'living whole' *M* is not properly described as 'subject to universal laws.' If we think of the world as composed of things subject to general laws, it is quite impossible to give any ultimately intelligible account of the relation between the things and the laws. The absolute *prius* is not a complex of laws, but the concrete *M* and its individual acts of self-expression and self-maintenance. Since we are part of the contents of *M*, we can compare facts with facts, recognize likeness and differences, and so come to formulate general propositions. We can even carry this so far as, when we have formed the notions of 'class' and 'member of a class,' to think of *M*, the real world itself, as one member of a class of worlds, and to speculate on the possibility that there might be others—'possible' worlds, as Leibniz said. Then we may be led, as Leibniz was, into the insoluble problem why just this world *M*, and not a different one *N*, is real. But this whole way of thinking of possibilities as metaphysically anterior to reality, or of the hypothetical propositions we call laws as anterior to the individual facts we call the actualized cases of these laws, rests on illusion. Metaphysically speaking, it is the actual nature of *M* that accounts for our existence and our possession of the mental capacities which we exercise in framing laws and hypotheses. If *M* were other than it is, its elements would be different, and, if we were among these elements, our views as to what alternatives are possible would be different also. It is a radical error in philosophy to confound logical with metaphysical priority.[1]

How *M* can be the ἓν καὶ πολλά required by the theory we cannot say in detail. But we can see, at any rate, that *M* cannot be material. The only thing with which we are acquainted which, even imperfectly, discharges for a part of reality the functions which *M* must discharge for the totality is the soul which at once has or owns a multiplicity of states or activities and would have no life without them, and is yet aware of its own unity and its distinction from each and all of these states and activities. We are thus driven to think of *M* in terms of spirit. It must be akin to the soul, but must, at the same time, have all the differences from our souls which result from the consideration that it has nothing outside it, is wholly unique, and can meet with no resistance. We are thus led to think of *M* as an infinite spiritual and, Lotze adds, personal being, all-wise (because its knowledge has not to develop under difficulties and from point to point, like our own), almighty (because it is the absolute *prius*, anterior to all 'law' as well as to all fact), and, above all, all-good (Lotze weakens his case on this point by a half-hearted tendency to take a hedonist view of good, and so to reduce perfect goodness to mere 'benevolence'; a Platonist would have no difficulty, since the all-wise must have complete knowledge of the good, and to know the good is to act it out). *M* is also 'out of space' and 'eternal,' since geometrical and temporal relations are, and are what they are, as a consequence of *M*'s existing and being what it is. Thus the conception of *M* with which we began as 'the one real being' passes into the conception of the almighty and eternal God, and the close of our historical retrospect brings us back very close to the position of Neo-Platonism again. It calls for remark that, though Lotze's initial account of *M*, taken by itself, would suggest a pantheistic or immanence theory, the doctrine, as fully worked out, is definitely theistic. Lotze is careful to guard himself, even when he says that *M is* the world, by adding that 'is' here has a unique sense which it has in no other judgment, and is consequently not the 'is' which occurs in an ordinary identity. Later on we find that each soul, being aware of its own unity, is a real individual distinct from God and from every other soul, though it is from the creating and sustaining activity of God that the soul derives this character. And mere inanimate things are held to be a superfluous hypothesis. There are, according to Lotze, only the one living God and His acts. Some of these acts are souls with a real spiritual individuality of their own. In this way, while avoiding the customary theistic language about the transcendence of God, Lotze secures the same result by maintaining not that God is immanent in the world, but that the world is 'immanent in God.' The limitation of real individuality to souls naturally reminds us of the Neo-Platonic view that souls hold the lowest place in the system of ὄντα, bodies being not ὄντα but γιγνόμενα, 'what becomes,' or εἰκόνες τῶν ὄντων, 'images of ὄντα.' The resemblance with Neo-Platonism is even more marked when Lotze uses his view of *M* as the metaphysical *prius* of universal laws or eternal truths as a ground for urging that life, truth, and goodness are not, as the Aristotelian phrase has it, 'naturally prior' to God; God is Himself the concrete Life, Truth, and Good.

17. Logical pluralism.—The foregoing statement of the theistic argument as presented by Lotze provides an opportunity for considering the type of ultimate pluralism of which we have spoken as the most serious philosophical alternative to theism. This type of view is best represented in contemporary English philosophy by the writings of G. E. Moore and Bertrand Russell, though, as neither of these authors has ever directly attempted the construction of a metaphysical system, we must be content to indicate the general view to which their studies in logic, ethics, and the philosophy of the exact sciences seem to point. A pluralism of the type in question would take issue with Lotze over the validity of the ground on which he maintains the existence of such a being as *M*. It would insist on precisely that form of 'dualism' which Lotze assumes to be unthinkable —the 'dualism' of actual existence and hypothetical universal laws. It would be maintained that what we actually find the 'world' to consist of is a plurality of existing things standing in a complicated network of relations of all kinds with one another. These relations, it would be further said, cannot all be reduced, as Lotze assumes, to reciprocal causal inter-connexions. Causal connexion is only one of the many types of relation; there are others, such, *e.g.*, as the mere 'togetherness' or 'compresence' which language represents by the word 'and,' the 'disjunction' symbolized by 'or else,' and so forth, in which causality is not a component at all. Relations are all 'universals,' and no relation is an 'existent,' while 'existents' are all individual. We have to accept it as an ultimate fact which permits of no explanation that specific individual existents stand in certain definite relations to other specific individual existents. To ask why this is so is to ask a question quite as illegitimate as that which Lotze ascribes to the purely mechanical philosophers whom he ridicules for asking 'how being is made.' More particularly, the special problem which leads Lotze to frame the concept of *M*—the problem how a change of 'state' is brought about, how one thing can exhibit a succession of different states or first have a relation to a second thing and then lose it—would be declared illegitimate. According to the view which has been most elaborately developed by Bertrand Russell,[1] the proposition that at a certain moment A changes its state from a_1 to a_2, or changes its relation to B from R_1 to R_2, if expressed accurately, only means that the whole duration of A's existence can be resolved into two mutually exclusive classes of moments. In any moment of the one class A has the state a_1, or stands to B in the relation R_1; at any moment of the other class A has the state a_2, or stands to B in the relation R_2. And, further, every moment of the one class a_1 comes before any moment of the other class a_2. There is no moment in the whole conjoint class $a_1 + a_2$ at which A has both states or both relations, and no moment at which it has neither. Thus, strictly speaking, there is no such process as that which Lotze calls change, and we live, in fact, 'in a changeless world.' Fully thought out, this view leads to the position, adopted of recent years by Russell, that all existents really exist only at a mathematical instant. What we commonly call one and the same thing or one and the same mind is an infinite succession of different things or minds which we mistakenly regard as one, because the thing or mind which exists at a moment m_2 separated by a minute interval from a preceding moment m_1 is very much like its predecessor. Thus Lotze's argument is invalidated by denying the reality of the facts it is employed to make intelligible. As there are no changes, in the sense in which Lotze understands the word, there is no ground to assert the existence of *M* to account for them. All arguments for the reality of a 'being which necessarily exists' are thus invalidated; and it is, further, at least highly doubtful whether we can even form the thought of

[1] It will be clear from these last sentences why the present writer regards Lotze's argument for the unity-in-multitude of *M* as in principle identical with Kant's pre-critical argument for a 'necessary existent' as the foundation of real possibility.

[1] In *The Principles of Mathematics*, Cambridge, 1903. The later work of Russell and Whitehead, *Principia Mathematica*, Cambridge, 1910 and subsequent years, does not assume this metaphysic.

a 'being which cannot be conceived not to exist.' Causality, as commonly understood by metaphysicians, likewise disappears. The causal principle reduces to the modest proposition that an observed frequent sequence of an event of the class β on an event of the class a affords ground for the judgment that in cases not previously observed an event of class β is likely to have been preceded by an event of class a. How likely this conclusion is is then a mere problem in the mathematical theory of probability. Whether all events have causes or not remains an open question, and must always remain so. It is clear that such a theory leaves no room for theism in philosophy. If it is really the last word of metaphysics, belief in God loses all rational foundation, though it is, to be sure, still possible that the belief may 'happen' to be true. It must further be admitted that the theory has its strong points. It is by no means obvious that a philosopher is entitled to assume as axiomatic such a conviction about the thoroughgoing interconnexion of all events as Lotze makes the basis of his argument. In what sense or to what degree the 'world' is a unity is a question to which philosophy must find the answer. The interconnexion might conceivably be very much looser than Lotze is willing to admit. And it seems clear that the mathematical analysis by which the particular puzzle about change is eliminated is, *as far as it goes*, entirely justified.[1] Nor yet can it be denied that the very modest statement to which the principle of causality is reduced is all that is required at any rate for the purposes of natural science.

It still, however, remains a question whether we could possibly be content with a logical pluralism of the kind just described as the final answer to our intellectual demand for a rational explanation of the world. For the purposes of the present article it must be enough to call attention to a few of the considerations which suggest that such a theory can only be provisional. One may fairly doubt whether it can really be called an explanation or interpretation at all. The system of interrelated existents with which it presents us as the solution of a perennial intellectual problem seems to be simply the problem itself stated in an unusually abstract way. And it ought to be clear that, when it has been granted to the full that the special problem about the meaning of change has been eliminated, there is a more fundamental problem which the theory has simply left out of account. However true it may be that 'we live in a changeless world'—*i.e.*, that there never is a 'moment' in which anything is 'passing from one state to another'[2]—Lotze's main contention, that the analysis of the universe into relations and existents, which are the terms of the relations, rests on the uncriticized assumption that the successive steps of the logical construction by which we try to make things intelligible correspond exactly to the steps of the real process by which 'being,' so to say, constructs itself, has been left unanswered. Logical pluralism, no less than the 'panologism' of Hegel, simply assumes that the logically prior and the metaphysically prior are identical. The only difference is that the logic of Hegel is so much inferior as logic. To put the point in the simplest possible way, we cannot avoid raising the question why, out of the infinity of relations open to the study of the logician, some and only some are actualized—have existents as their terms. Logical pluralism has no answer to this inevitable question except that 'it happens to be so.' And this is really no answer at all. It amounts to saying not merely that the world might have been wholly different from what it is, but that there might equally well be no actual existents whatsoever. The theory fails to satisfy us for the same sort of reason as that which prevents the ontological proof from producing conviction. Just as that argument assumes that 'there must be something,' so the theory we are now considering assumes that 'there might just as well be nothing.' Now, we cannot prove that there must be something, nor can we prove that there might have been nothing; we have to start from the fact that there is something and that this something has a definite character. Hence, to the present writer, Lotze seems right in contending that it is the character of this something that accounts for the range of logical possibilities itself being what it is, and Kant in arguing that there is an actual ground presupposed by the very distinction between the possible and the impossible. In fact the logical pluralists themselves seem to admit as much when they rightly insist that the so-called laws of thought are laws not of thinking but of things. It is therefore by a rightful exigence of the intellect itself that we are driven to conceive of the structure of the world as explicable only by the metaphysically 'first' character of the 'necessary being'; and, when once we have taken this step, it is not hard to show that the 'necessary being' must have the character of the *ens realissimum*. It must be its own justification, its own *raison d'être*. If so much be granted, it follows at once that, though we can form no adequate positive concept of such a Supreme Being, the least inadequate way in which to think of it is in terms of the highest values known to us—*i.e.* by analogy with the human spirit at its best. How inadequate such an analogy is has always been patent. Even of the human spirit at its best we can only form very inadequate notions from what we see of its actual achievements, and our notion of the Supreme Reality which is the source of our estimates of worth, as of all other possibilities, must needs be doubly imperfect when it has to be framed in so unsatisfactory a way. But we can at least say that such a being must be all that we mean when we think of perfection in ourselves, and infinitely more. If we are not satisfied with theories which, under a disguise, offer us the unexplained detail of the world as its own explanation, it is only in the thought of the detail as throughout conditioned by the living Good that the intellect itself can finally acquiesce. Of course we cannot expect to know in particular how each constituent of this detail is consequent on the character of the Good —why, *e.g.*, it is 'best' for us in particular to be living on the particular planet on which we do live, rather than any other; why there should be just the number of members of our planetary system there are; why the range of colours we can perceive should be neither more nor less extended than it is; and the like. But the conviction that all this detail is as it is 'because it is best' gives an adequate reason why it is what it is, even though we may be quite unable to see why it is best.[1] And it is only the thought of the dependence of the world on the absolute Good which, by removing the artificial severance between the realm of fact and the realm of values, can achieve

[1] The question is *how* far does it go? Is an 'instant' more than a mathematical 'limit'? The 'Theory of Relativity' becomes important at this point (consult A. N. Whitehead, *Enquiry into the Principles of Natural Knowledge*, Cambridge, 1919).

[2] Yet it is surely true, as maintained, *e.g.*, by Whitehead, that 'passage' is just the fundamental fact about Nature, however we choose to analyse it. 'Nature' is, as Plato called it, a γιγνόμενον.

[1] It would be a superficial objection to say that 'because it is worst' would be also an answer to our question. Good (no one has done more to insist on the point than Moore) means something definite and positive. So 'best' has a meaning, but 'worst' has none, any more than 'so crooked that nothing can be crookeder' has.

the solution of the supreme intellectual problem, the reconciliation of science with life.

These considerations suggest certain further reflexions on the limitations of logical pluralism. The whole theory has manifestly been thought out in the exclusive interest of pure mathematics and the application of mathematics in the natural sciences, and for that purpose it works admirably. But there is more in heaven and earth than these sciences take into account. Even within their limits it remains to be seen whether the theory as it stands will really do all that a philosophy of the sciences should. The fundamental difficulty is that it is a consequence of the theory that, as has already been said, the establishment of scientific laws by induction comes to be simply a problem in the theory of probabilities. But the theory of probabilities, taken by itself, seems to give us no ground whatever for attributing to the conclusion of an inductive generalization any finite probability, however small.[1] Science would thus seem to be impossible in principle unless some as yet undiscovered premiss for induction, which is not included in the theory of probabilities, can be unearthed; and it remains to be seen whether such a premiss, if discovered, is consistent with the rest of the theory. Again, the replacing of the individual existents of popular common sense and ordinary science by infinite series of momentary individuals seems an absolutely necessary consequence of the initial assumption of the theory, and, so far as the things of the external world as conceived by common sense, or the constituents of the physical order as conceived by the physicist, are concerned, there might be no difficulty about it.[2] But it is quite another question whether the substitution does not destroy the whole significance of the moral realm, the system of intelligent spirits. It is not merely that it creates a difficulty in psychology, though surely it does create such a difficulty. The immediate witness of consciousness to our identity as subjects of experience is a real fact which no logical theory about the constitution of the world has a right to ignore. It may be that 'the mind thinks not always,' that there are intervals in which each of us is wholly unconscious, though such evidence as we have does not seem favourable to the supposition; but, at least when we are conscious, every conscious act fills an actual interval and yet has its absolutely unitary character. A 'duration,' though a brief one, is necessary to think the simplest proposition, and much more to draw the easiest inference. Yet the thinking of the proposition or the making of the inference is a unitary act only intelligible as the act of a unitary intelligence. It is nonsensical to say that, when I think 'God is,' this thought, as a mental event, is really made up of an infinity of momentary 'mental states' of similar but numerically different minds, or that the 'I' which resolves on a given act and the 'I' which carries out the resolve are each an infinity of different 'I's' with a further infinity of still different 'I's' between them. Only the elementary blunder in analysis of resolving activity into mere succession can account for the promulgation of such a view. It is a still more serious matter that the doctrine is wholly incompatible with the fundamental prerequisites of ethics. This point is capable of being developed in great detail and from more than one side, but in principle it should be enough to say that the denial of permanent personality is fatal to the conception of personality as having moral worth. If we analyse any act upon which a moral judgment would normally be passed into an infinity of momentary phases, no moral predicate can be ascribed to any one of these stages. The moral judgment for approval or condemnation has no meaning if it be applied to any such single stage; to be significant, it must be passed on the whole act, considered as one, and as an expression in act of the inner will of a subject who is one and the same from its first inception in thought to its completion. Similarly the notion of duty loses all its meaning with the relegation of permanent selfhood to the realm of illusion. That an act is my duty in the present situation means that it is something not yet done, but which ought to be done and to be done by me. But if 'I' only exist at a mathematical *punctum temporis*, the proposition that I ought now to do a certain act has no longer an intelligible significance. A merely momentary 'I' can do nothing and can be nothing except just what it is; 'ought' is a category which has no application to it. It is no mere accident that Russell should have dropped significant hints in his latest writings of conversion to the view that moral judgments are only 'subjective,' mere expressions of fundamentally irrational moods. The real outcome of a logical pluralism, put forward as the ultimate truth about what is, is not even that standing dualism of what is and what ought to be of which Lotze complains; it is rather the pronouncement that categories of value (there can be no reason to confine the conclusion to specifically ethical values) are one and all devoid of any real application. For those who cannot accept this result, Kant's moral argument for theism seems to the present writer unanswerable. For it is only if the Good is also the supreme principle of all existence that it becomes possible to understand how what is and what ought to be can form one 'world,' and from the recognition of the Good as the Supreme Being theism follows directly. This seems to be illustrated by the present state of philosophical opinion in our own country. Throughout the thirty years or so, from the seventies of the last century onward, in which Hegelianism, interpreted with a marked Spinozistic bias, was the dominant philosophy in academic circles, there was a natural tendency to make it almost the test of a man's philosophical capacity that his attitude towards the problems raised by the religious life should be an emotional pantheism; atheism was in discredit as indicative (as indeed it is) of lack of interest in or understanding of the whole realm of personal values; theism as a supposed mark of want of logical thoroughness. In the present generation the issues seem to be clearing. Philosophers are certainly tending, though not without exception, to range themselves into two camps. Those to whom the business of philosophy seems to consist mainly, if not exclusively, in providing a logical basis and a methodology for exact science appear to be identifying themselves with the doctrine of logical pluralism and taking up a definitely atheistic attitude which involves the denial of the objectivity of judgments of value; those, on the other hand, who are convinced that the business of philosophy is to make life, as well as science, intelligible, and consequently find themselves obliged to maintain the validity of these categories of worth apart from which life would have no significance, are, in the main, declared theists.

18. Objections to theism.—It may be desirable to add some brief observations on certain types of objections which are often quite sincerely raised against a theistic interpretation of the world. In principle none of these difficulties are novel; most of them find their expression in Hume and may be traced back far behind Hume to the literature of

[1] See the acute discussion by C. D. Broad, in *Mind*, new ser., cviii. 389–404, and the criticisms of P. E. B. Jourdain, *Mind*, new ser., cx. 162–180. Jourdain's criticisms do not seem to the present writer to affect the soundness of Broad's contentions.

[2] But the philosophical interpreters of the 'Theory of Relativity' would have something to say on this point.

the ancient world. Popularly these objections are often called 'scientific,' though their only connexion with modern natural science is that its discoveries enable some of them to be stated in a more impressive way. For the most part they are all summed up in the antitheological assertion of Lucretius that the existing world is too bad to have been created or to be administered by a divine intelligence, 'tanta stat praedita culpa.' Thus it is urged that the suffering of the animal creation is too great, the cost of the 'struggle for existence' too painful, for us to ascribe a world like that we know to a benevolent Creator. Or, again, it is said that an almighty Creator might have made the human race, in particular, such that it would not be exposed as it is to suffering, to constant struggle with its environment, to the consequences of its own mistakes and wrongdoing. It is then inferred that, if there is a superhuman intelligence behind nature, that intelligence is either deficient in wisdom or wanting in goodness. Now, obviously, criticisms of this kind rest upon premisses which may be fairly called in question. One might reasonably doubt whether the pessimistic interpretation of the facts which sees misery predominant everywhere in animal and human life has any real warrant. To an unbiased observer an animal does not seem normally to give signs that it finds its existence miserable, and it is notable that suicide is not common among men, and, unless the stories of the scorpions which kill themselves when surrounded by fire are true, apparently as good as non-existent among the lower animals. The misuse of the metaphorical phrase which describes the process by which species are selected for survival as a 'struggle' is too glaring to need more than a word of comment. If competition plays a prominent part in the economy of the animal and vegetable kingdoms, as it does in the economy of commerce, it no more follows that the life of every animal, or most animals (and ? vegetables), is one of wretchedness than it follows that all or most business men are hopelessly miserable.[1] Still, of course, it may be said that there is, at any rate, some suffering in the world and that perfect goodness would have permitted none at all. Such an argument, however, tacitly assumes that perfect goodness can have only one end, a hedonistic one, and thus permits of the answer that whatever the end which perfect goodness conjoined with omnipotence would propose to itself—and we clearly are not in a position to say what that end would be—it is at least unreasonable to suppose that it can be the mere promotion of agreeable feeling, an end which even we ourselves regard as a low one. If we could know the purpose of creation, it might well be that we should see that it is entirely good and at the same time could not be attained without the presence of an element of hedonic evil in things. Similarly, with respect to the objection based on the view that it would be 'better' that human beings should have been placed in a world where there were no unfriendly or intractable environment to master, and should have been *ab initio* infallible and impeccable, it is obvious that it loses its force if we decline to assume (1) the hedonistic identification of good with pleasure, and (2) the proposition that the good of the human race must be the sole or at least the principal design of God. If God's aim in dealing with us is to educate us into noble character—a much worthier aim than that of making us comfortable—it may well be that such an end could not be obtained except by the discipline of struggle with our surroundings, with our own mistakes and our own misdeeds. Nor have we the right to assume that the human race must necessarily be the sole or even the chief object of the divine care; we do know, unless ethics is a delusion, that a human soul is a thing of absolute worth; that it is of higher worth than everything else which God has created is more than we can know. Indeed there is a rival objection which proceeds on the opposite assumption. We are asked to think of the enormous spaces revealed to us by astronomy and the number and bulk of the heavenly bodies, and then to reflect on the absurdity of supposing that the fate of the inhabitants of one petty planet can count for anything in the scheme of the universe. Yet it is clear that here, too, the antitheist is reasoning (if it can be called reasoning) upon a false assumption. He is assuming that we know that the absolute worth of a member of the universe is estimated by its bulk and duration. Man must be of little value in the scheme of things because his body is tiny and its lifetime short. Plainly we have no right to make serious objections to the theist's belief in God's care for man on such flimsy grounds. If we do not know that man is the thing of highest worth in the creation, neither do we know that he is not. The one thing which a theist can affirm is that the absolute worth of moral personality must be respected in a system which is the work of God. 'Justorum animae in manu Dei sunt'; that is all we can say, but surely it suffices. If the Good is the principle of actuality, that means that we can say that a thing has come to be because it was better that it should be than that it should not; it is where and when it is because this is better than that it should be otherwhere and otherwhen; that befalls it which does befall it because it is best that it should befall—*i.e.*, God is alike Creator, Providence, and Judge of His creatures. Of course, if we had no grounds at all for our theistic conviction, difficulties like those mentioned might forbid us to entertain it as a mere 'extra' belief. But, if it is true, as has been urged in this article, that speculation and practice alike point to the eternal nature of God as the object in which both find their completion, we have a double exigence of the practical and the speculative reason on the side of theism, and in the presence of such an exigence we are justified in applying Newman's remark that 'a thousand difficulties do not amount to one doubt.' One might add that there is a third exigence—the specifically religious. It would be perhaps a more serious objection to theism than any we have yet considered to urge that our whole procedure in looking for a First Cause is vitiated by one obvious fallacy. The world, it might be said, even if it has attained its present structure as the result of processes which are in the last resort reducible to mere redistributions of unintelligent primary constituents, directed by no mind and having no end, still must, of course, have a perfectly determinate structure, and, as we ourselves happen to be included in that structure, of course we inevitably discover adaptations in our environment to our special needs, and are led to fancy that such adaptations are evidence of the direction of the world by an intelligence which aims at supplying our needs. But the real fact is simply that it is not the world that has been adapted to us, but we who have learned and are learning to adapt ourselves to the world. If we did not so adapt ourselves, we should not be here, and, if a time ever comes when our capacity for such 'adjustment' of our 'inner relations' to the 'outer relations' is exhausted, we shall cease to be here. If the actual course of events had been different, all the reactions which we now call good, because they further adaptation, might have hindered it, and those which now hinder it might

[1] And is it possible, in the present state of knowledge, to regard 'competition' as playing anything like the part Darwin assigned to it in determining the fate of 'varieties'?

have furthered it. If in such a state of things there had been reflecting beings at all, they, judging from their standpoint, would have called good all that we think evil, and evil all that we think good. They would have inferred benevolent divine activity from the existence of conditions which we should regard as indicating the control of nature by malignant 'diabolical' intelligences; and their inferences would have just as much foundation as ours. These considerations, it might be said, are a *reductio ad absurdum* not merely of all attempts to reason from 'Nature up to Nature's God,' but of the moral argument itself, since they show after all that standards of valuation are and must be in the end purely subjective. Since the human race exists, and so long as it continues to maintain itself, there must, of course, be no irresoluble discord between human estimates of value and the actual conditions of existence. But, as the illustration shows, we have no right whatever to argue from this simple and obvious fact to the dependence of existence on an absolute 'Good.' In fact, any of the races which have 'gone under' in the struggle for existence would be equally justified in asserting that existence depends on the absolute 'Evil.' Here, as it seems to the present writer, we are confronted by the real ultimate difficulty for theism. If there is, after all, no realm of absolute values, a line of thought which is throughout determined by the conviction that the realm of facts and the realm of values cannot be separated must manifestly be futile. It is just the recurrent fear that the 'realm of values' may turn out to be a fiction of our imagination that is, in speculation, the last enemy to be overcome. How is it to be met? The answer, it may be suggested, is the old one, given in the memorable utterance of Pascal: 'Tu ne me chercherais pas si tu ne me possédais. Ne t'inquiète donc pas.'[1] The sentences may be applied to ultimate doubt about the reality of every kind of human value. Is a man tempted to doubt whether there really is any absolute and certain truth, whether all our 'truths' may not be mere 'human' or even 'personal' points of view, βροτῶν δόξαι αἷς οὐκ ἔνι πίστις ἀληθής? Let him bethink himself that it is only because he is not unacquainted with truths that he can frame the notion of the absolutely true, and only because he has framed the notion that he can raise his doubt. So it is only because we are all along secretly aware that there are things which we ought unconditionally to do that the question whether any given accepted obligation is really unconditional can so much as be put. If we knew no beauty, we could not even ask ourselves whether our judgments about beauty rest on illusion. In like manner it is only because the absolutely Good and utterly Adorable has not left Himself without a witness in our hearts that we feel the need of an object to worship and are driven on from the worship of trees, or streams, or animals, or mighty men, or anthropomorphic deities, towards an object in which our adoration can at last find rest because that on which it is directed is adequate to sustain it. Prayer and adoration need no more justification than the questioning attitude towards things which leads to science, or the impulse to make things of beauty which leads to art, or the desire to do right which leads to morality. It is not for nothing that man, as the Greeks said, is the only animal who has a god. If we look at the matter from this point of view, we may fairly say that the Stoic appeal to the *consensus gentium*, though no formal demonstration, still contains a thought which goes to the very root of things. There are, of course, individual men who do not feel the impulse to seek for Him whom they may worship with a *rationabile obsequium*, as there are men with no sense of humour, or men to whom music means nothing, or men who cannot be made to see that the difference between right and wrong is anything more than the difference between what society will allow them to do and what it will not let them do without making them uncomfortable. The existence of such individuals is about as important in any one of these cases as in any other. Nor does the number of such men without a religion seem to be on the increase. In our own day the only effect of persuading men that the Most High is a dream appears to be that they transfer their worship to the demonstrably not most high; we get such quaint aberrations as the Comtist worship of 'humanity,' or the elevation of Marxian Socialism into a faith. The one real question is not what certain individuals are unable to feel the necessity of searching for, but what those who do seek find, *sed quid invenientibus?* The lives of the 'saints' are the real answer of theism to the last insistent perplexities of the doubter who lurks in each of us. Others, without the theist's faith, have often led noble lives; they have fought a good fight with the untowardness of a world which they have believed in their hearts to be stupid or malignant; yet the most clear-sighted among them, like Huxley, have confessed that mortal heroism is a losing game, a battle with the cosmic forces. Such heroes, after all, do but apply to the universe the saying of the Emperor Marcus about base men: 'The finest revenge is not to become like them'; they have revenged themselves on the world. What they lack—and one does not see how the lack is to be made good—is the secret of spiritual joy which belongs to those who are assured that it is the Good which is supreme in heaven and in earth. It would be tempting to develop this argument farther, from a slightly different point of view—that of love. To love, no less than to worship, it may be said, is an ultimate human need. At least, if a man does not feel the imperativeness of the need, we should probably say there was something 'inhuman' about him. And love too, like worship, seeks its adequate object — that which, without any yielding to illusion, a man can love with all his heart and mind and strength. Love, with no limitations, if it is clear-sighted, for us at least must be an *amor ascendens*, and, as it has its source in good (for real love is always for what is good, not for what is evil, in its object), so, unless it can at last rest in the supreme Good, which is good altogether, it must remain unsatisfied. But we cannot here pursue the point farther. Only one thing more will be said in conclusion, and that for the believer in 'science' who scruples at admitting the reality of the Good. Why do we believe in science at all? Why do we, as we must if we have this belief, refuse to entertain the possibility that the 'progress of science' is only bringing us nearer to a point at which the whole construction would be found to culminate in manifest and hopeless contradictions? As a mere logical possibility there seems to be nothing absurd about the suggestion. If we dismiss it, as we do, it is because we believe that knowledge is good, and because in our hearts, whatever we may say with our lips, we believe that the Good is real. Therefore, little as we know of the facts of the world, we work on in confidence that, however drastically the discovery of new facts may compel us to modify our statements of truth and to supersede as provisional results we once thought established for ever, no new fact of the infinity which might be discovered in an endless 'progress' will ever show that 'science' has been a secular nightmare of the race.

[1] *Pensées*, vii. 555 (ed. Brunschvicg, Paris, 1905).

LITERATURE.—Besides works mentioned in the text, the following may be recommended out of an enormous literature (it is, of course, impossible to make any attempt to ensure completeness, and only recent works have been named): S. Alexander, *Space, Time and Deity* (Gifford Lects.), 2 vols., London, 1920; A. J. Balfour, *The Foundations of Belief*[8], do. 1901; B. Bolzano, *Wissenschaftslehre*, vol. i. (1837; reprinted Leipzig, 1914); B. Bosanquet, *The Principle of Individuality and Value* (Gifford Lects.), London, 1912, *The Value and Destiny of the Individual* (Gifford Lects.), do. 1913; F. H. Bradley, *Appearance and Reality*, 2nd ed. revised, do. 1908, *Essays on Truth and Reality*, Oxford, 1914; R. Flint, *Theism*[5], Edinburgh, 1885, *Agnosticism*, do. 1903; A. Campbell Fraser, *Philosophy of Theism*[2] (Gifford Lects.), 1899; E. Gibson, *Le Thomisme*, Strasbourg, 1920; P. Hinneberg, *Die Kultur der Gegenwart*, pt. i. div. 5, *Allgemeine Gesch. der Philosophie*[2], Leipzig, 1913, esp. pts. B 2, 'Die patristische Philosophie,' by C. Bäumker, and B 4, 'Die christliche Philosophie des Mittelalters,' by C. Bäumker; F. von Hügel, *Eternal Life*, Edinburgh, 1912; W. R. Inge, *The Philosophy of Plotinus* (Gifford Lects.), 2 vols., London, 1918; H. H. Joachim, *A Study of the Ethics of Spinoza*, Oxford, 1901; J. M. E. McTaggart, *Some Dogmas of Religion*, London, 1906; J. T. Merz, *Hist. of European Thought in the Nineteenth Century*, 4 vols., Edinburgh, 1896–1914, *A Fragment on the Human Mind*, do. 1919; A. S. Pringle-Pattison, *The Idea of God* (Gifford Lects.), Oxford, 1917; B. Russell, *Critical Exposition of the Philosophy of Leibniz*, Cambridge, 1900, *The Principles of Mathematics*, i., 1903, *Philosophical Essays*, London, 1910, *The Problems of Philosophy*, do. n.d. [1912], *Our Knowledge of the External World*, Chicago and London, 1914; J. Royce, *The World and the Individual* (Gifford Lects.), 2 vols., London and New York, 1900–01; J. Royce, J. Le Conte, G. H. Howison, S. E. Mezes, *The Conception of God*, do. 1897; A. D. Sertillanges, *S. Thomas d'Aquin* (in 'Les Grandes Philosophes' ser.), 2 vols., Paris, 1910; W. R. Sorley, *Moral Values and the Idea of God* (Gifford Lects.), Cambridge, 1918; W. Temple, *Mens Creatrix*, London, 1917; B. Varisco, *I Massimi Problemi*, Milan, 1910, Eng. tr., *The Great Problems*, London, 1914, *Conosci te Stesso*, Milan, 1912, Eng. tr., *Know Thyself*, London, 1915; J. Ward, *Naturalism and Agnosticism* (Gifford Lects.), 2 vols., Edinburgh, 1899, *The Realm of Ends, Pluralism and Theism* (Gifford Lects.), Cambridge, 1911; C. C. J. Webb, *Studies in the Hist. of Natural Theology*, Oxford, 1915, *God and Personality* (Gifford Lects.), London, 1918, *Divine Personality and Human Life* (Gifford Lects.), do. 1920; T. Whittaker, *The Neo-Platonists*[2], Cambridge, 1918.

A. E. TAYLOR.

THEOCRACY.—The term 'theocracy' was coined by Josephus,[1] upon the analogy of 'aristocracy' and 'democracy,' to denote a certain kind of national polity. Any tribe or state that claims to be governed by a god or gods may be called a 'theocracy.' History has many different types; *e.g.*, the theocratic idea underlies Brāhmanism, Islām, the papacy, and the theory of 'kingship by divine right.' Yet there is probably no historical instance of a 'pure' theocracy. Just as the British constitution to-day, while predominantly democratic, has monarchic elements, so of old time the Hebrew commonwealth, for example, while predominantly theocratic, had democratic elements. Different polities are distinguishable historically, not because a single principle exhausts them, but because some one principle is dominant within them. The idea of government by God was the dominant one in Israelite polity. In this way it was unique, as Josephus claimed, among the polities of his time. It is the leading instance of theocracy for all times. It is the only one discussed here.

Theocracy came to Israel by survival. The earliest form of human society, so far as anthropology has yet discovered, was the clan or kindred-group. This appears to have been world-wide. In religion it was 'henotheistic,' a particular god belonging to a particular clan. He was part of it, as much a part as any human member. His relation to it was too many-sided to be summed up in any one word. In some ways a tribe's god was like a father, in some like a captain, in some like a king, and so on. But, as monarchy developed among the Semitic races, the relation of the god to the tribe came to be chiefly like that of a king. So, among them as well as elsewhere, there arose the early 'henotheistic' type of theocracy. Its best-known examples are Biblical: Chemosh ruled Moab, Milcom ruled Ammon, Jahweh ruled Israel, and so on. Sooner or later, however, this kind of theocracy perished in every settled land except one. The gods of such tribes as Edom and Moab passed away, with the tribal independence, before the attack of Assyria, or Babylon, or Persia. In other lands polytheism supervened on henotheism. There the gods slowly became rather an appendage of the state than its rulers. But in Israel the idea of the sole rule of a single God survived all the vicissitudes of history. It survived by development. Its history is the history of the way in which Hebrew thought about Jahweh's rule evolved to meet the varying challenge of national need. To set this out fully would be to write the whole story of Israel. Here a narrower question is in place: the idea of government by Jahweh being constant in Israel, how did the idea of its *method* evolve?

The study of the method of any kind of polity turns largely on the nature of its organs, for almost all civilized governments rule through organs. This is peculiarly so with theocracies, since it is only in legend that gods speak directly to their peoples. Josephus himself, in the very passage where he coins the word 'theocracy,' speaks, not of Jahweh, but of Moses, as 'our law-giver.' In Israel, as elsewhere, the organs of theocratic government were long associated with sacred shrines. Horeb, Shiloh, and Bethel are instances.[1] The shrine, so to speak, gave the organ authenticity. When doubt or dispute arose about Jahweh's Law, appeal would be made to the guardians of some great shrine.[2] These came to form a priestly class. At the great shrines, too, there soon began to be books of Jahweh's *tōrōth*;[3] here as well there were the few men who could write and read books. Traditionally, at least, the original Law had been given, and its first edicts written, at the shrine of Horeb or Sinai.[4] In later times, no doubt, when a Hebrew visited a shrine to learn Jahweh's will, its authorized exponent, the priest, would not only read the appropriate law, but explain it. Sometimes, again, he would need to extend an old principle to meet a new 'case.' So, little by little, the 'Law of Jahweh' would insensibly grow. For early Israel three things were indissoluble—Jahweh's shrine, Jahweh's book, Jahweh's priest. The three together formed the normal organ of theocracy.

The history of pre-monarchic Israel, however, has traces of two other theocratic organs—the so-called 'judge' and the 'prophet.' Of these a distinctive phrase is used: 'the spirit of the Lord came upon' so-and-so.[5] The phrase has variants,[6] but this is its usual form. It is the earliest explanation of the method of theocracy.[7] There are some hints that the 'judge' was usually connected with a sacred spot.[8] If so, this theocratic organ also cohered with the shrine. There was perhaps a similar connexion at first between the shrine and 'prophesying.'[9] Before the days of Samuel the

1 *C. Apion.* ii. 16.

1 The 'Ark of God' was originally a kind of movable shrine.

2 Cf. Ex 21^{6} and parallels; 1 S 2^{25} $7^{15ff.}$.

3 Cf. Jos 24^{26}, Dt $31^{9.\,24ff.}$, 1 S 10^{26}.

4 Ex $34^{4.\,12}$.

5 *E.g.*, Jg 11^{29}, Nu 24^{2}, 1 S 10^{10}.

6 Cf. esp. Jg 6^{34}.

7 It is possible that historical study will at length speak of three organs here instead of two, distinguishing the 'judge' from the warrior-'saviour.' For it has been implied above that to judge, in the ordinary sense of the word (cf. 1 S 8^{1-5}), was a function of the priest in Israel; and this was not confined to priests (*e.g.*, Jg $4^{4ff.}$, 1 S 4^{18} 7^{6}). Such 'judges' were thought of as organs of the 'spirit of Jahweh' (cf. Nu $11^{17ff.}$). One who had 'saved Israel' (cf. Jg 3^{31} 6^{14} etc.) was also such an organ. Not infrequently a 'saviour' became a judge as well, and later Hebrew writers, used to the constant union of the captain and the judge in the king, treated it as constant in the leaders of early times too (*e.g.*, Jg 2^{16} D $3^{9f.}$ D). Yet there seem to have been judges who were neither priests nor 'saviours' (Jg 10^{3} 12^{8-15}; cf. 1 S $7^{16f.}$ 8^{1}). To 'save Israel,' to judge, to serve at a shrine, were distinct theocratic functions, though two of them might unite in a single man.

8 Jg 4^{5} 8^{27}, 1 S 2^{25} $7^{15ff.}$.

9 Cf. 1 S $3^{20f.}$ 9^{19}.

Hebrew 'prophet' was probably hardly more than the wandering saint of other Eastern faiths[1]—a man who lived a separate and so a 'holy' life. In all lands these have frequented shrines, for, even where they have no 'official' connexion with the ritual, temples offer the best opportunities for the alms by which they live. The first band of 'prophets' named in the Hebrew records appears as 'coming down from the high place.'[2] Primitive thought does not readily isolate the different organs of a god's activity.

Scholars differ about the degree in which the religion of pre-monarchic Israel surpassed other tribal faiths, but all allow that within the period of the monarchy Hebraism became unique. In that period all the theocratic organs named above persisted, but in persisting changed. Every other Hebrew shrine was eclipsed by the Temple in Jerusalem, and at length disappeared. So, too, the Temple became at last the depository of the one recognized book of Jahweh's Law.[3] In Jerusalem, again, the priesthood of Israel ultimately concentrated. At crises in the history of the Southern Kingdom the high-priest sometimes played a decisive part,[4] and there is evidence that the Temple had a succession of priest-preachers who surpassed all contemporary priesthoods in the loftiness of their teaching and the purity of their lives.[5] Their permanent memorial is the book of Deuteronomy. It was only at the close of the monarchy that they became utterly corrupt—a fate that also befell the 'sons of the prophets'—and even then Jahweh's great witness, Jeremiah, was born a priest. Of the three other theocratic functions found in the times before the kings, two—leadership in war and judgment in peace—which had previously often united in a single person[6] now permanently blent in the king. While, of course, there were inferior captains and subordinate judges, he was both supreme captain and supreme judge. And he was effectively both. A king, unlike the earlier 'saviour,' held permanent office, and, unlike the earlier judge, had power to enforce his decisions. And he was king by the will of God. He was Jahweh's 'son,' as having His mind and acting under His guidance.[7] He was 'the Lord's anointed.' At times even a wicked king fell back upon Jahweh's help at the pinch of his people's need.[8] It is true that one king after another 'did that which was evil in the sight of the Lord,' and so repudiated the righteous God of Israel, but the ideal of a king who, like David, did the will of Jahweh remained a part of the hope of Israel. Ideally the Hebrew monarchy was theocratic.

The chief glory of monarchic Israel, however, was its prophets. They were different indeed from all other 'prophets'! With them the connexion of theocracy with shrines, maintained by the kings,[9] began to loosen. At times, again, the prophet must perforce denounce the priest. Yet the prophets, more than any else, were the true organs of theocracy. 'Thus saith the Lord' was their watchword. They spoke under the impulse of the Spirit. In a sense they kept God alive. It is true that, from the time of Elijah, Israel began to refuse their guidance, that at last the Northern Kingdom rejected it altogether, and that even in Judah they became the leaders only of a 'remnant.' But it was just this 'remnant' that meant so much for the future of the world. Israel is unique among theocracies because of its prophets.

The Exile was a signal proof of their greatness, for no other ancient people survived exile. 'To be carried captive' destroyed, as it was meant to destroy, nations and their gods together. Even in exile, however, Israel believed in the rule of its God. Of this creed the unknown prophet now called 'Deutero-Isaiah' was preacher *par excellence*. The Hebrew of the Return re-crossed the desert under the definite conviction that his God was leading him, as He had led Abraham.[1] In consequence a decisive change in the Hebrew idea of theocracy became complete. From Isaiah onwards the primitive notion that there were as many gods as there were nations had been gradually making way for the belief that there was but one God, and He the master of all nations. Only so could Jahweh save Jerusalem from Sennacherib, or redeem Judah from Babylon. Monotheism now entirely supplanted henotheism. While Israel was still Jahweh's 'peculiar treasure,' His theocracy was no longer limited to Canaan, but swayed the world.

Yet the immediate sequel was disappointing. 'Judaism'—to use the name appropriate after the Return—set out to be a pure theocracy. It rebuilt the old shrine; it gathered the ancient books; at length it made the ancient priesthood paramount. Yet it gradually became a splendid failure. The line of prophets dwindled away. The Jews looked in vain for kings like David. At last no priest dared, in the Lord's name, to add to His Law. And it seemed clear, besides, that the Lord did not rule the world. Theocracies tend to become hierarchies, and hierarchies tend to stagnate. Israel was now a hierarchy, and it looked as though Jahweh would sink to the level of the gods who had done great things in the past, but who did nothing in the present. The Jewish theocracy threatened to 'fossilize.'

Yet it escaped this fate. As the Psalms of the period show, there were always Jews who practised the creed that their God was still alive, and they knew that His time would come. The book of Daniel bears the same witness in a different way. It is the first apocalypse, and all apocalypses are theocratic. So, again, in its own way, is the book of Esther. The distinctive note of this epoch is not really its consummated ritual or its completed law, but its unextinguished hope. Israel believed that the future, as the past, was its God's and its own. There would be a perfect theocracy yet! The Kingdom of God would come!

There were two leading opinions about the way of its coming, readily separable in thought, though not always separated in fact. The one opinion found its aptest expression in the apocalypses. Broadly speaking, these expected a kingdom based on force, in which the Jew would rule all other nations—a kingdom won and maintained by a superhuman organ of God. This opinion laid hold of the external form of the old theocracy, kingship. It had an element of truth in it, for the NT has an apocalypse. In the interval before the perfect kingdom comes Christ does 'over-rule' all things and men, and this is a theocratic idea. Yet the other opinion is final for Christianity. Its earlier exponents were some of the later Psalmists; it lived in the quiet circles that 'waited for the consolation of Israel'; its perfect preacher was Jesus. He accepted the phrase 'the Kingdom of God,' and so looked for a theocracy, but He gave the phrase His own exposition and laid down the true method of the Kingdom's coming. It has been seen above that from the first a man who was the organ of

[1] *E.g.*, 1 S 10.
[2] 1 S 10^{5}.
[3] 2 K 22^{8} ('the' book).
[4] 2 K 11, 22.
[5] Cf. G. A. Smith, *Jerusalem*, London, 1908, ii. 111 f.
[6] See footnote 7 on p. 287.
[7] Cf. 2 S 7^{14}. The idea of a Divine monarch with an earthly vicegerent was quite common in the Semitic world (W. Robertson Smith, *Religion of the Semites*, lect. ii.).
[8] *E.g.*, 1 K 20^{13}.
[9] 2 S 6, 1 K $12^{26ff.}$.

[1] Cf. Ezr 8^{22}.

Jahweh was thought of as 'filled with' His Spirit. This was why and how he knew God's will. More than once it had been discerned, even by OT thinkers, that a perfect theocracy, therefore, could come only if all its citizens, and not a few only, had the Spirit of Jahweh.[1] This idea is really central in Jesus' teaching, though He was able to teach it only as men were able to bear it. With the Acts of the Apostles it became explicitly the master principle of Christianity. At the same time there began the evolution of the Christian doctrine of the personality of the Holy Ghost. There can be a perfect theocracy only when every man acts always under the guidance of the Spirit of God. Here is the culmination of Biblical theocratic doctrine. Yet here also is its euthanasia. For this kind of 'theocracy' does not satisfy the definition given above. It is not a 'theory of national polity.' The Christian doctrine of the Holy Spirit is naturally individual, and as naturally universal, but it is not naturally national.[2] Again, the term 'polity' implies government and its coercions, and one of the marks of the Spirit's sway just is that it is incoercive. Yet the husk of Israel's theocratic idea held a kernel of 'eternal' value. The last human society will be a Kingdom of God.

LITERATURE.—For Josephus's use of the term 'theocracy' see *HDB*, *s.v.*, vol. v. [1904] p. 337 (V. H. Stanton); for the facts about the general Semitic notion of theocracy see W. Robertson Smith, *The Religion of the Semites*, London, 1894, lect. ii., and *The Prophets of Israel*, do. 1897, lect. ii.; for the development of the idea in Israel and in the apocalyptic literature see the standard authorities on the religion of Israel, the theology of the OT, and the extra-canonical Jewish books; the corresponding authorities on the NT discuss the relation of the idea of the Kingdom of God to the earlier theocratic doctrine. Separate treatment of the subject is unusual.

C. RYDER SMITH.

THEODICY.—1. The term.—Theodicy (Germ. *Theodizee*, adapted from Fr. *théodicée*, which is compounded of Gr. θεός, 'God' + δίκη, 'justice') means literally the (or a) justification or vindication of God. Leibniz appears to have been the first to use the word in its distinctive sense. In a letter written in 1697 he spoke of employing it as the title of an intended work,[3] and in 1710 the work duly appeared. The complete title was, 'Essais de Théodicée sur la bonté de Dieu, la liberté de l'homme, et l'origine du mal.' Since Leibniz's time the word 'theodicy' has been in common use.

2. The concept.—In modern usage the scope of the term is vague and ill-defined. Sometimes it is employed, as by P. Janet and G. Séailles,[4] as equivalent to natural theology or philosophy of religion. For those writers theodicy comprises the general problem of religion, though it is also understood by them in a more particular sense, as comprising only the central problems of the nature of God and the relation of God to the world. In either of these senses it may escape the charge of being a theory put forward 'to save the situation.'[5] But in the usual sense it does not so readily escape such a charge. For as a rule the use of the term is more in keeping with its literal meaning, and theodicy is understood as the (or a) vindication of the divine providence or government in view of the existence of evil. The 'theodicean' assumes the validity of the theistic conception of God as powerful, wise, and good, and on this basis seeks to defend the divine administration: he would

'assert Eternal Providence,
And justify the ways of God to men.'[1]

3. Origin of the concept.—The need of such a defence and vindication is not felt in primitive religion under polydæmonism, with its animistic or spiritistic view of nature, because under polydæmonism the world is subject to a multitude of spirits both good and evil, who limit each other and are themselves limited by the natural order. Nor is the need felt even at the polytheistic stage of religious belief, with its multitude or hierarchy of gods as distinguished from spirits or godlings, because at this stage thought, if no longer naive and instinctive, is still uncritical, and the gods are conceived as being subject to fate or necessity or as governing a world already given and never properly under their control. At the monotheistic stage of religion, however, where thought is become critical and reflective, the problem of theodicy arises and calls for a solution. Sometimes, as in Persian religion, a dualism in the divine nature is postulated, and the world represented as the scene of a grand conflict between the principles of good and evil, in which good is destined to final triumph; and obviously a dualistic philosophy of religion, if it could be otherwise satisfying, would ease the problem. Under a monistic philosophy of religion, again, the tendency is actually to get rid of the problem, by minimizing evil or even by reducing evil to illusion. This tendency is observable in the cosmic and acosmic pantheisms of Stoicism and Brāhmanism respectively. Only in a philosophy of religion in which God is recognized as wholly good, and evil as truly evil, is the problem of theodicy felt in all its insistence. *Si deus bonus, unde malum?* Christianity, theistically interpreted, supplies such a philosophy, and in the course of Christian history the problem of theodicy received distinctive treatment in the ecclesiastical doctrine of the Fall. Whatever may be said as to the form of that doctrine, it stands for a principle which should be acknowledged in theistic interpretations of the world, namely the principle of human freedom and responsibility. It is not without significance that the classical theodicy or theistic apologia of Leibniz bears in its title not only 'the goodness of God' and 'the origin of evil,' but also 'the freedom of man.'

4. Leibniz's Théodicée.[2]—(*a*) In the problems of theodicy Leibniz had been interested since his boyhood, and he claims to have given more attention to them than most.[3] There are many references to them, certainly, in his correspondence during the last decades of the 17th cent. with Pellisson, Bossuet, and others; and the *Essais* itself also bears ample witness to his long-continued interest in them. It should be remarked, however, that the *Essais* is not, properly speaking, a systematic presentation of the questions involved in theodicy. It is, in Leibniz's own word, a 'tissu'[4] of what he had said and written in the course of the theological and philosophical discussions, centred in Pierre Bayle's works and especially his *Dictionnaire historique et critique*, which he carried on with Sophia Charlotte, queen of Prussia. From a letter of Leibniz's written to Sir Thomas Burnett in 1710 it appears that the *Essais* was compiled at the request of his friends and as a memorial to the deceased queen.[5] The book was extraordinarily popular, and apparently the author finds satisfaction in recording that it was welcomed

1 *E.g.*, Nu 11[29], Jer 31[34], Jl 2[28].
2 Except in the sense that every true nation, being an organic part of mankind and set to minister to the whole, is meant to be 'filled with the Spirit' for this office.
3 Cf. J. T. Merz, *Leibniz*, Edinburgh, 1884, p. 101.
4 *A Hist. of the Problems of Philosophy*, Eng. tr., 2 vols., London, 1902, vol. ii. pt. iv.
5 Cf. Plato, *Republic*, 380 A; and A. S. Pringle-Pattison, *The Idea of God*, p. 400.

1 Milton, *Paradise Lost*, bk. i. l. 25 f.
2 See also art. PESSIMISM AND OPTIMISM.
3 *Die philosophischen Schriften von Gottfried Wilhelm Leibniz*, ed. C. J. Gerhardt, 7 vols., Berlin, 1875-90, vi. 43.
4 *Ib.* vi. 11.
5 *Ib.* p. 10. Sophia Charlotte died in 1705; a common but erroneous impression is that the *Théodicée* was compiled during her lifetime.

by Catholics as well as Lutherans and Evangelicals.[1] No doubt the *Essais* served its purpose well in an age of theological rationalism, and helped to stem the tide of scepticism which was now beginning to threaten the foundations of religion itself.[2] But Leibniz's theistic apologia does not commend itself so readily in our time.

(*b*) It will be sufficient for the purposes of this article to indicate a few salient points in Leibniz's theodicy, for the sake of illustrating the difference between the older and the newer theism in apologetic method and outlook.

(1) *God.*—Unlike most recent exponents of a theistic philosophy of religion, Leibniz was of the belief that the being or existence of God could be demonstrated by purely logical or rational processes. Though he recognized, he did not make much use of, the ontological proof, and the proof, so peculiarly his own, from the 'pre-established harmony' is bound up very closely with his monadology; but the cosmological or ætiological proof and the proof from the eternal truths are both characteristic of his theology or religious philosophy and independent of his ontological scheme. In accordance with the principle of the cosmological or ætiological proof, Leibniz starts from the world of finite existents as contingent and infers an Existent which is not contingent but metaphysically necessary. There must be a sufficient reason or cause, he says, for the existence of the whole collection of contingent things which composes the world, and it is to be found in the Substance which carries with it the reason or cause of its own existence, and which is consequently necessary and eternal; and that Substance can only be God.[3] It may be objected to this argument that it is logically fallacious, as containing more in the conclusion than is contained in the premiss: as the premiss is contingent, so must also be the conclusion.[4] As for the proof from the eternal truths—*i.e.* truths which involve no reference to time or to the world of existents in time—it is largely dependent upon Leibniz's notion of possibility. For Leibniz, as not for Spinoza, the possible was wider than the actual, essence than existence; and he argues that, if the eternal or metaphysically necessary truths are real, and founded on something existent, that existent something must be the metaphysically necessary Being of God, in whom essence involves existence, and to be possible is to be actual. Without God not only would there be nothing existent, but there would be nothing possible.[5] Against this proof, as handled by Leibniz, it may be urged that it is inconsistent in one who regards the possible as wider than the actual, the essential than the existent, to regard truth as dependent upon existence; and that in any case we cannot on the premisses reach a necessary Being separate from the existent and actual world. In all such arguments indeed, as B. Russell points out, there is difficulty in avoiding Spinozism.[6]

(2) *The world.*—In presenting what may be named his teleological optimism Leibniz still moves on the high plane of metaphysical notions and *a priori* verbal proof, nor condescends to the lower empirical world, to which Bayle would bring him down. Founding upon the principle of sufficient reason and the idea of divine perfection, he holds that this is the best of all possible worlds; for, were a better world than this world possible, God would have chosen it. God is absolutely powerful, wise, and good; and His goodness moved Him to create and produce all possible good, His wisdom led Him by a moral necessity to the choice of the best, His power enabled Him to execute His great design.[7] It is curious to reflect that the Leibnizian optimism may be associated with the most diverse ethical valuations of life, optimistic, pessimistic, melioristic; which gives point to Schopenhauer's objection that, even if this is the best possible world, it does not prove that it is a world good enough to have been actualized.[8] An objection, this, on philosophical grounds, thus meeting Leibniz on his own plane, but it is on empirical grounds that the Leibnizian optimism has been most frequently challenged, from Voltaire's *Candide* down to the present. Nor could Leibniz himself ignore the empirical aspect of the problem of theodicy.

(3) *Evil.*—Accordingly—apart from his metaphysical theory of evil as necessary limitation appertaining to finite existence and the source of both moral and physical evil—we find him emphasizing the instrumental theory, according to which evil, especially physical evil, is to be interpreted as an instrument or means of good. In advocating this theory he sought to counter Bayle's contention that the strength of Manichæism was due to its conformity with an empirical rather than *a priori* conception of the world. Even from the empirical standpoint, Leibniz would reply, physical evil may be reasonably accounted for by the theory of instrumental value; and, as for moral evil, it could not be prevented by God without the subversion of the freedom of self-determination which belongs to spiritual beings and makes morality possible. By other empirical arguments also Leibniz supports his doctrine of optimism, but enough has been said to show that, while his theodicy is forced to recognize the standpoint of experience, it rests primarily—like his theistic proofs—on metaphysical considerations.

(*c*) The difference between Leibniz's theodicy and the modern attitude in theodicy may now be briefly stated. Leibniz approached the problem of evil with a God whose existence had already been proved, as also His character of absolute perfection in power, wisdom, and goodness; and it was therefore an altogether reasonable presupposition on Leibniz's part that this world as being the creation of such a God was the best possible. No matter what exception might be taken to the case as presented, the case itself was excellent. But nowadays, with the spirit of pessimism abroad in society, and the spirit too—not unakin—of anti-religious agnosticism, the problem of evil has become more acute, and one has learned to sympathize with W. James and others in their impatience with Leibniz's optimism and the complacency of his attitude towards, *e.g.*, a dogma like eternal punishment. The 'charmingly written *Théodicée*' is even described by W. James as a piece of 'superficiality incarnate'; as a 'cold literary exercise, whose cheerful substance even hell-fire does not warm.'[1] Such strictures are too severe, but let them be a reminder of the difference in spirit between the old and the new approach to the problem of evil. It would be quite untrue to say of modern exponents of theism that they compose theodicies 'with their heads buried in monstrous wigs.'[2] The modern theist is conscious of the failure of rationalistic or purely speculative theology to establish its claims, and of the necessity of fundamentally empirical methods in theology if scientific results are to be gained, and he therefore examines the world of experience in face of evil as an empirical problem, with the view of testing the reasonableness of the theistic faith in God as just, holy, and loving. And he is led to recognize that the observed facts of nature and history do not afford an unexceptionable argument for the goodness of God, and that after all the most solid ground of belief in the divine goodness lies in the needs and claims of the religious consciousness.[3] No doubt there would be a *circulus in arguendo* involved here if such considerations were put forward as a solution of the problem of evil.[4] On the one hand, it is by the faith of religion that God is affirmed to be perfectly good, despite the evil to be found in the world of His creation and governance. On the other hand, religious faith is based on the power of religion as a solvent, or at least a partial solvent, of the problem of evil: in religion men seek refuge from the various evils that assail, from without and from within—which shows that a non-rationalistic theism could not offer a real solution of the problem of evil. Nor does it profess to do so.

5. Theodicy and philosophical reflexion.—It is not necessary that this article should enter into a comprehensive discussion of the problem of theodicy from the side of philosophical explanation. This will be found in the art. GOOD AND EVIL, where it is affirmed with most students of the subject that 'every proposed solution either

1 *Die philosophischen Schriften von Gottfried Wilhelm Leibniz*, p. 12, note.
2 Cf. R. Flint, *Agnosticism* (*Croall Lecture*), Edinburgh, 1903, p. 115.
3 *Théodicée*, 7 (Gerhardt, vi. 106 f.).
4 Cf. B. Russell, *A Critical Exposition of the Philosophy of Leibniz*, Cambridge, 1900, p. 175.
5 *Théodicée*, 184 (Gerhardt, vi. 226 f.); cf. also *Philosophische Abhandlungen*, ix. 45 (Gerhardt, vi. 614).
6 *A Critical Exposition of the Philosophy of Leibniz*, pp. 181, 186.
7 *Théodicée*, 8 (Gerhardt, vi. 107), 116 (Gerhardt, vi. 167), 228 (Gerhardt, vi. 253 f.).
8 Cf. H. Höffding, *A Hist. of Modern Philosophy*, Eng. tr., 2 vols., London, 1900, i. 364.

1 *Pragmatism*, New York and London, pp. 23, 27.
2 *The Will to Believe*, New York and London, p. 43.
3 Cf., *e.g.*, G. Galloway, *The Philosophy of Religion*, p 440.
4 Cf. G. T. Ladd, *The Philosophy of Religion*, ii. 147.

leaves the old question '—*si deus bonus, unde malum?*—' unanswered or raises new ones.' None the less we should like to express our sympathy with a type of solution—partial as it must be—which is on the lines of Leibniz's theology, but which goes beyond Leibniz in its recognition of human freedom as real, in the sense of implying self-limitation on God's part. Self-limitation does not mean finitude, nor freedom unqualified indeterminism. Such a solution is not only consistent with the moral and religious consciousness, but alleviates also the burden of the mystery of evil; and it lends itself to attractive exposition in the speculative sphere, as in the humanistic or personalistic idealisms which arouse so much interest at present. Yet it still leaves God, as indeed must every theodicy, ultimately responsible for both physical and moral evil. At the same time the recognition of the instrumental worth of evil somewhat relieves the weight of the divine responsibility. Take it first in connexion with the problem of physical evil. Pain and suffering are no doubt largely retributive and to be accounted for as the wages of individual and racial sin. But retribution is not an end in itself, and the positive rather than the negative purpose of physical evil is being more and more emphasized. Through pain, hardship, and loss moral energy may be stimulated and character moulded and shaped to finer issues. In this aspect of it suffering may be twice blessed, blessing those who suffer and those brought into contact with them. Take it also in connexion with the problem of moral evil. Here again the instrumental theory applies, and evil may be regarded as for education and discipline. In fact many theists regard moral evil or sin as having been always under the divine control, and interpret it as necessary like physical evil to human development. It is the discord without which there could be no harmony, the shade without which there could be no light. Through sin man learns his weakness, and his need of strength from on high. Through sin, and its direful effects in society, he learns the meaning of brotherly service and the measure of the sacrificial love of God.[1] Christianity looks for the time when man's moral education shall be brought to completion, and his suffering and sin have served their purpose. Yet, when all is said, the problem of evil remains.

6. Theodicy and the religious consciousness.—The discussion of the problem of evil on empirical grounds, and in particular of the instrumental theory of value, leads us to a consideration of the religious solution. There is a philosophical theodicy, and there is a religious theodicy. In the first, evil is explained—or an attempt is made to explain it—in the light of the divine goodness; in the second, evil is not explained, nor is there any attempt to explain it—it is simply to be overcome. As Eucken has remarked, 'religion does not so much explain as presuppose evil';[2] and, as P. T. Forsyth so well insists, a religious theodicy is not 'an answer to a riddle but a victory in a battle.'[3] In a religious theodicy it is not man who justifies God's ways, but God who justifies His own ways, and that not by accounting for the world's evil, but by saving men from it. While this is said, religion can no more than philosophy escape the problem of evil. For the individual believer in God and His goodness the problem receives a practical solution through the victory of his faith: he estimates life no more by hedonistic standards, but discovers the Supreme Good in moral and spiritual union with God. From the universal point of view the religious solution of the problem may be stated broadly in terms of the teleological idea. The end or purpose revealed in the universe is the creation of free ethical personalities capable of personal intercourse with God and of reflecting as in a flawless mirror the divine image and likeness.[1] To that purpose the presence of evil is subservient, and there are traces of it even in animate nature, which we have too often regarded as merely a field of struggle and carnage.

'There is a legitimate scientific sense,' says J. Arthur Thomson, 'in which it may be said that Man is part of the system of Nature and the crown of its evolution; and it is assuredly of some significance that he can find in Animate Nature far-reaching correspondences to his ideals of the True, the Beautiful, and the Good.'[2]

We might therefore be content to state our theodicy in the following terms, which give due regard to the fact—made clear in modern science—that our world is still in the making, and which also illustrate the newer empirical as distinguished from the older rationalistic way of approach to the problem of evil, as well as the pragmatic tendency in modern theology and religious philosophy:

'While this world is far from being as yet the best possible world, nevertheless in view of its general constitution it may be regarded as the best possible *kind* of world in which to have man begin his development, and . . . the evils which exist in the world furnish no good reason for abandoning belief in a God who is both good enough and great enough to meet every real religious need.'[3]

LITERATURE.—References to the problems of theodicy may be found in works on the history and philosophy of religion, dogmatic theology, and general philosophy. See in particular the literature mentioned in the artt. GOOD AND EVIL, PESSIMISM AND OPTIMISM. Useful discussions will also be found in the following works, selected chiefly from recent philosophical and theological literature: O. Pfleiderer, *The Philosophy of Religion*², Eng. tr., 4 vols., London, 1886–88, esp. iv. 1–45; G. T. Ladd, *The Philosophy of Religion*, 2 vols., do. 1906; G. Galloway, *The Philosophy of Religion*, Edinburgh, 1914; J. Müller, *The Christian Doctrine of Sin*, Eng. tr., 2 vols., do. 1877, 1885; H. Siebeck, *Lehrbuch der Religionsphilosophie*, Freiburg i. B., 1893; J. Kremer, *Das Problem der Theodizee in der Philosophie und Literatur des 18 Jahrhunderts*, Berlin, 1909; O. Lempp, *Das Problem der Theodizee in der Philosophie und Literatur des 18 Jahrhunderts*, Leipzig, 1910; J. Martineau, *A Study of Religion*², 2 vols., Oxford, 1899; J. R. Illingworth, in *Lux Mundi*¹⁵, London, 1904; C. F. D'Arcy, *God and Freedom in Human Experience*, do. 1915; B. H. Streeter and others, in *God and the Struggle for Existence*, do. 1919; J. Arthur Thomson, *The System of Animate Nature*, 2 vols., do. 1920; D. S. Cairns, *The Reasonableness of the Christian Faith*, do. 1918; A. S. Pringle-Pattison, *The Idea of God* (*Gifford Lectures*), Oxford, 1917; W. R. Sorley, *Moral Values and the Idea of God*, Cambridge, 1918; C. C. J. Webb, *God and Personality*, London, 1918; J. Caird, *The Fundamental Ideas of Christianity*, 2 vols., Glasgow, 1899; H. G. Wells, *God the Invisible King*, London, 1917; W. S. Urquhart, *Pantheism and the Value of Life*, do. 1919; D. C. Macintosh, *Theology as an Empirical Science*, do. 1919; P. T. Forsyth, *The Justification of God*, do. 1916; R. Eucken, *The Truth of Religion*, Eng. tr., do. 1911.

WILLIAM FULTON.

THEODORE OF MOPSUESTIA.

—See ADOPTIANISM, ANTIOCHENE THEOLOGY.

THEOGNIS.

—Theognis is the name attached to a collection of some 1389 erotic, convivial, reflective, and hortatory elegiac verses whose chief interest for this article is that they are the fullest extant repertory of Greek ethical commonplace in the half-century preceding Plato and the tragedians. The collection begins with invocations to Apollo, Artemis, and the Muses, and a dedication to a young friend Cyrnus, to whom many of the quatrains and couplets are addressed, and whose name may be meant by the seal that perhaps marks their genuineness.[4] But many verses lack this certification. Some are addressed to other

[1] Cf. W. Adams Brown, *Christian Theology in Outline*, Edinburgh, 1907, p. 209.
[2] *The Truth of Religion*, p. 500.
[3] P. T. Forsyth, *The Justification of God*, p. 220.

[1] It is here that, in a more extended treatment, the 'theodicean' aspect of the doctrine of immortality might be considered.
[2] *The System of Animate Nature*, lect. xx. f.
[3] D. C. Macintosh, *Theology as an Empirical Science*, London, 1919, p. 217.
[4] Line 19.

friends, including a Simonides who may be the poet.[1] After the first 100 lines there is little sequence or coherence of ideas. There are many repetitions, and some of the verses occur in the fragments of Solon, Phocylides, Tyrtæus, and Mimnermus. These considerations, and the fact that quotations in Plato[2] and in a passage attributed by Stobæus[3] to Xenophon are susceptible of various interpretations, raise many problems about the composition of the poem, if it is in any sense a unity, and have given rise to an extensive German literature of hypothesis most conveniently surveyed in E. Harrison's *Studies in Theognis*.[4] Harrison argues plausibly, if not always quite convincingly, that the poems as they stand form a connected sequence. His book concludes with an excellent chapter on the life and times of Theognis. He was a noble of Nisæan Megara, who apparently at one time was also a citizen of Hyblæan Megara in Sicily. He spoke of the terror of the Medes,[5] and is therefore conjectured to have lived to see the invasion of Xerxes. He lived in a time of social and political revolution at Megara, vaguely known to us from three references in Aristotle's *Politics*[6] and from one passage in Plutarch.[7] His temper was embittered by the temporary triumph of the popular party,[8] the loss of his property,[9] and the exile,[10] which was perhaps the cause of the travels in Eubœa, Sparta, and Sicily to which he refers.[11] To these experiences we may trace his pessimism,[12] his cynicism,[13] his harping on the hardships of poverty that constrains a man to deeds to which his will does not consent,[14] his complaint that money makes the man and that mercenary marriages corrupt the breed of men,[15] his emphasis on the virtue of faith[16] or loyalty to caste, club, and mates[17] in times of trial, and his frequent use of 'good' and other ethical terms in the political or social sense.[18]

Too much has been made of this last idea by Theognis's translator J. H. Frere,[19] by Nietzsche, whose own philosophy is largely based upon it, and by Grote, who, however, admits that the ethical meanings are not absolutely unknown.[20] Theognis is merely the chief example, the conveniently quotable *locus classicus*, so to speak, for a natural human tendency. We still speak of the better classes as they did in Aristotle's time,[21] and Homer characterizes menial tasks as the services that the worse sort perform for the good.[22] We cannot infer that the ethical idea was lacking.[23] We can only say that before Plato it was easier to confound pure or absolute ethics with prudential, conventional, tribal, caste, or political morality than it has been since. Much the same may be said of the naive inconsistency between Theognis's general commendations of truth, justice, good faith, and kindliness, and his passionate prayers for vengeance,[24] his (perhaps ironical) counsel to set your heel on the empty-headed demos,[1] to be all things to all men,[2] to adapt yourself to your environment with the protective resemblance of the polyp which takes the hue of the rock to which it is clinging,[3] and to flatter and cajole your enemy well till you have him in your power and then take your revenge.[4] The last precept appears almost as nakedly in one of the noblest Greek poets, Pindar.[5] Plato first laid it down that the good man will not wrong even his enemy, and Plato did not apply the principle to international politics in the Tolstoyan way. Lastly, the erotic verses of Theognis—most of them, to be sure, in a separable and perhaps spurious part of the collection,[6] dealing with themes repugnant to modern feeling — seem to us incompatible with the conception of him as a moralist and still more with the use of his elegies as a school-book. They were indeed, on the hypotheses of R. Reitzenstein,[7] mainly banquet songs. But, however that may be, Theognis's own use of the verb 'admonish'[8] classes them in some sort with the literature of prudential precepts and moral admonition known by the name of ὑποθῆκαι.[9] And no less a moralist in his own esteem than Isocrates recommends the study and excerpting of them as entirely edifying. At any rate, whether in excerpts for school use or otherwise, they were, like Solon and Hesiod, learned by heart by educated Greeks of the 5th cent., and so provide many texts for amplification in Pindar and the Greek drama, and for discussion in Greek philosophy.[10] An exhaustive dissertation on this subject would be of interest, but would require the nicest discrimination. Harrison[11] collects the parallels in Pindar and Bacchylides, some of them perhaps overstrained. It is not easy to determine how many of the resemblances in tragedy are conscious reminiscences. The chorus in Sophocles, *Œd. Col.* 1226 ff., is clearly an expansion of the melancholy lines 425 ff.:

'Not to be born into life were the best for us, creepers on earth's face,
Never to look on the sun's burning and pitiless rays;
Happiest lot of the living is theirs who come quickest to Hell Gate
Laid out quiet and stark, wrapped in a mantle of earth.'[12]

Jebb on *Antigone*, 622, quotes Theognis, 403, as one of the anticipations of the untraced 'quem Juppiter vult perdere dementat prius.' *Antigone*, 297, echoes Theognis, 221, in the sentiment that the man who thinks that he alone is wise is himself void of wisdom. Soph. frag. 356 repeats the commonplace that health is best and justice fairest of things;[13] frag. 525 the humorous fancy that even Zeus cannot please all, whether he rains or holds up.[14] But these are only conspicuous examples of an indeterminate list. When Euripides praises the man who is as true to absent as to present friends,[15] we cannot be certain whether he is or is not paraphrasing Theog. 93–95, and the same holds of the coincidence between *Phœnissæ*, 438–440, and Theog. 717 f. in the sentiment that

1 469, 667.
2 *Meno*, 95 D ff.
3 *Flor.* lxxxviii. 14.
4 Cambridge, 1902.
5 764.
6 1302 B, 1304 B, 1300 A.
7 *Quæst. Græc.* 18.
8 53 ff., 1013–1016.
9 346, 1200, 667 ff.
10 219, 332.
11 783.
12 165–169, 425–429.
13 129 f., 161–164, 209, 275, 299, 360, 375, 615, 621, 653, 857–861, 1135 ff.
14 391, 155, 175, 267, 384, 620, 649, 667 ff., and *passim*.
15 190; cf. H. Spencer, *The Principles of Ethics*, 2 vols., London, 1892–93, § 233.
16 πιστός, 77, with Plato, *Laws*, 630; cf. 80, 88, 121, 209, 283, 416, 529, 861, 1137, and *passim*.
17 ἑταῖρος, 79, 91, 95, 97, 98, 113, 115, 411, 416, 643, 851, 1169 (the abstract καχεταιρίης).
18 28, 32, 43, 57. For ἀρετή (often in the Elizabethan sense of 'virtue') cf. 129, 147–150 (ethical?), 402, 654, 699. In 865 and 1003 it is courage in battle. For σώφρων, 'sober,' politically, intellectually, or morally, cf. 379, 431, 437, 454, 483, 497, 665, 701, 754, 1138, and Shorey in *AJPh* xiii. [1892] 361.
19 Reprinted in the vol. containing Hesiod, Callimachus, and Theognis, in Bohn's Classical Library, London, 1856.
20 *A Hist. of Greece*, new ed., London, 1888, ch. 9, *in fin.*
21 *Pol.* 1282.
22 *Od.* xv. 324.
23 Cf. 11, 147–149, 315 ff., 465.
24 337–340, 344, 348, 362, 872.

1 847.
2 63, 213.
3 215–219, a passage much bespoken and imitated. Cf. A. C. Pearson, *The Fragments of Sophocles*, London, 1917, frag. 307. L. Schmidt, *Die Ethik der alten Griechen*, Berlin, 1882, ii. 224, takes it of the traveller who is to do at Rome as the Romans do. Ion, frag. 36, Plutarch, and Pseudo-Phocylides, 47, reprobate the sentiment.
4 363; see J. Girard, *Le Sentiment religieux en Grèce d'Homère à Eschyle*[3], Paris, 1887, p. 157; Schmidt, ii. 312.
5 *Pyth.* ii. 84.
6 1230–1389.
7 *Epigram und Skolion*, Giessen, 1893.
8 ὑποθήσομαι, 27, 1007, 1049.
9 See Isoc. *ad Nic.* 43 f.
10 Antisthenes is said to have written a commentary in five books (Diog. Laert. vi. 16).
11 P. 314.
12 Cf. R. C. Jebb, on Bacchyl. v. 160, in *Bacchylides, the Poems and Fragments*, Cambridge, 1905; and P. Decharme, *Euripide: l'esprit de son théâtre*, Paris, 1893, p. 119 ff.
13 Theog. 255.
14 *Ib.* 24 and 801.
15 *Supp.* 867, *Hippol.* 1001.

wealth is all-powerful. Plato's saying[1] that a spirit of reverence (αἰδώς) is a better inheritance than great riches is, the present writer thinks, a distinct reference to Theog. 409. Isocrates, i. 19, equals Theog. 72, and i. 29, Theog. 105.

Among the chief commonplaces of Greek ethics expressed by Theognis[2] are man's dependence on the gods,[3] and his ignorance of what the future has in store,[4] his duties to the suppliant and the guest,[5] and to parents,[6] the doctrine of the mean,[7] of nothing too much,[8] of κόρος and ὕβρις,[9] the late punishment of the wicked,[10] the dangers of slander[11] and of light oaths,[12] the admonition that all true gains are costly,[13] that ill-gotten gains do not abide,[14] that the lust for wealth is insatiate,[15] and that the boastful word (ἔπος μέγα)[16] or the forsworn forecast[17] provokes the gods and invites nemesis, the complaint that shame and reverence are exiled from a degenerate world,[18] and that men value nothing but wealth.[19] Other commonplaces, whether of ethics or of criticism of life, are the immortality of song,[20] the praise of patience,[21] the Anacreontic, Epicurean, or Horatian 'Carpe diem,' evil communications,[22] 'in vino veritas,'[23] there is no perfect man,[24] the ingratitude of children,[25] the foible of censoriousness and self-praise,[26] and the generalized metaphor of the 'counterfeit' man.[27] His convivial and social precepts, his slight anticipations of later motives of satire,[28] and his somewhat cynical, political,[29] or worldly wisdom[30] do not further concern us here. Lines 823 and 1181 are in apparent contradiction on the justification of tyrannicide. Theognis apparently does not mention the confounding of the innocent with the guilty, or the jealousy of the gods except as involved in the nemesis that attaches to the too confident oath.[31]

As an aristocrat he, like Pindar, emphasized nature against teaching.[32] No teacher can put sense into a man,[33] or make a bad man good. Plato[34] finds a contradiction between this and the admonition to associate only with the good because from them you will learn good only. But it is Theognis's belief that it is easier to corrupt the good than to reform the bad. In lines 155–159 there is a suggestion of the noblest thought of mature Greek ethics, the idea that the mutability of fortune and our common frailty impose the duty of leniency and compassion upon all men.[35]

Especially interesting are Theognis's direct appeals and protests to Zeus. He complains that the prosperity of the wicked casts doubt upon the moral government of the world.[36] This, however, is rather a development of the motive of Menelaus's speech in the *Iliad*[37] than the startlingly new thought which Croiset finds in it.[38] Theognis's protest against the visitation of the sins of the fathers upon the children, which results from the late punishment of the wicked,[1] invites illustration both from the OT and from later ethical literature.[2]

[1] *Laws*, 729 B.
[2] See Schmidt, i. 10; A. and M. Croiset, *Hist. de la litt. grecque*, Paris, 1887–99, ii. 148 f.
[3] 134, 165, 171, 687. [4] 585, 1075–1078. [5] 143 f.
[6] 131, 821; cf. Hesiod, *Works and Days*, 185 f.
[7] 220, 331, 335, 559 f. [8] 219, 335, 401.
[9] 151, 153, 603–606, 693. [10] 203. [11] 324.
[12] 399; cf. 1195.
[13] 463 f., 1027 f.; cf. Hesiod, *Works and Days*, 286 ff.
[14] 198–202; cf. 329. [15] 227, 596, 1158. [16] 159.
[17] 559, 'il ne faut jurer de rien'; cf. Archil. frag. 76; Soph. *Antig.* 388 f.; Pindar, *Ol.* xiii. 83.
[18] 291; cf. 86, 635, 647.
[19] 523 f., 621, 1116 ff., 699 ff. [20] 237 ff.
[21] 320, 355, 445, 555, 591, 637, 1029.
[22] 31, 305; cf. Schmidt, i. 272. [23] 99.
[24] 799, 902. [25] 275–278. [26] 611.
[27] 117, 119, 965; cf. Plato, *Laws*, 916 D.
[28] 295, 453, 595, 1215.
[29] 43, 233, 283 ff., 331, 367 ff., 341, 603, 671 (the ship of state), 793, 805, 833, 845, 947.
[30] 303 f., 423, 575, 903 ff., 963. [31] 660.
[32] Schmidt, i. 160; Shorey, *TAPA*, 1910, p. 188.
[33] 430 (ἐνθέμεν), 435 (ἔνθετον); cf. Arist. *Eth.* x. 9. 3; Plato, *Rep.* 518 C (ἐντιθέναι).
[34] *Meno*, 95 C ff.
[35] Cf. Soph. *Œd. Col.* 565–569; Isoc. i. 29.
[36] 373 ff., 743 ff. [37] xiii. 631.
[38] Cf. also Hesiod, *Works and Days*, 270 ff.; and Archil. frag. 84 (6).

LITERATURE.—The fullest recension of the text is in the latest ed. of T. Bergk's *Poetæ Elegiaci*, Leipzig, 1915. The edd. of Immanuel Bekker (Leipzig, 1815) and F. G. Welcker (Frankfort, 1826) and the critical literature of the subject are discussed in Harrison's book referred to above. Cf. also T. Hudson Williams, *The Elegies of Theognis*, London, 1910.

PAUL SHOREY.

THEOKRASIA.—See GREEK RELIGION, vol. vi. p. 421 f.

THEOLOGY.—1. Definition.—Theology may be briefly defined as the science which deals, according to scientific method, with the facts and phenomena of religion and culminates in a comprehensive synthesis or philosophy of religion, which seeks to set forth in a systematic way all that can be known regarding the objective grounds of religious belief.

According to its etymological meaning, the word 'theology' denotes 'discourse or doctrine concerning God.' In this sense it was used among the Greeks to describe the work of poets like Homer and Hesiod when they wrote of the gods and their doings, and that of philosophers like Plato and Aristotle when they speculated regarding the supreme reality or ultimate ground of all things. In early Christian literature the distinctive appellation of 'theologian' is applied to the author of the Apocalypse, probably because he maintained the divinity of the λόγος, asserting the identity of the λόγος that became flesh in Christ with God (Θεός). In this sense the term is applied to orthodox Greek Fathers like Athanasius and Gregory Nazianzen, who distinguished themselves in defending the personality and divinity of the λόγος. But doctrine concerning God—His being and attributes—is only one branch or department of theology, as that is now commonly understood. Man's knowledge of God is part of the content of that matter of human experience which is termed 'religion,' and which includes other content also, referring to the world of nature and of man, to sin and death, to salvation and immortal life. And, as science in general deals with some definite department of human experience, it is more in accordance with the proper conception of science to regard theology as that branch of science which deals with the department of human experience known as religion, from which experience man's knowledge of God and divine things is obtained. Theology is the science which, by right use of reason, in accordance with proper scientific method, correlates, systematizes, and organizes the matter of human religious experience in such a way as to reach a unified body of coherent doctrine, fitted to satisfy the mind's demand for truth and to furnish guidance for the practical life.

As the science of religion it deals not merely with the subjective contents of the religious consciousness, or the opinions, emotions, and actions of men in the religious sphere, but also with the objective grounds of religion and the ultimate truth or reality which underlies and explains the religious experience of mankind. It is not merely the science of religions dealing with the various historical religions which have developed among men (though that is a part of it), but the science of religion regarded as an important department of human experience, which claims to be no mere subjective delusion, but to have a real and rational foundation in objective reality or fact.

2. Theology and religion.—As theology is the science of religion, religion precedes and is wider

[1] 731 ff.; cf. 203–208.
[2] Cf. Jer 31[29f.]; Spencer, *Principles of Ethics*, § 140; Schmidt, i. 71 ff.

than theology and furnishes it with the matter with which it deals. In all departments of human life and activity experience, in which feeling, intuition, and volition are the predominant factors and reason or intellection is as yet implicit, precedes theory or science, which seeks to exhibit and make explicit the reason, thought, or principles of truth and reality underlying and accounting for the experience. Thus the use of numbers in the relations and activities of the practical life precedes the science of mathematics; the practical use of speech precedes the science of language; the use of reasoning in practice precedes the science of logic; and the sailing of the seas in ships precedes the science of navigation. So too the experience and use of religion as a practical factor in life's activities precedes the science of religion, or theology. And, as men may attain considerable efficiency and success in various departments of life without having rationalized or reduced their experience to system and exhibited its underlying principles, so men may live a truly religious life and have a rich and full religious experience without having attained to any very clear or coherent system of theology. But, while a man may be religious without being a theologian, religious experience is necessary to enable a man to be a competent theologian; and the fuller and richer his religious experience has been, the more likely is he to prove a trustworthy and satisfactory theologian.

Schleiermacher was so impressed with the importance of the part played by feeling or emotion in religion that he gave it not merely the predominant but the exclusive place. Over against the long prevailing definition of religion as consisting in 'knowing and doing homage to God,' he defined religious piety as in its essence consisting neither in knowledge nor in action but in a determination of the feeling. The root of all religion he held to be man's feeling of absolute dependence on some power or powers other than himself. But this dictum, while it emphasizes the important truth as to the large part played by feeling in religion, if strictly taken, is one-sided and exaggerated, in that it ignores the part played by the cognitive faculty in forming some conception, more or less definite, of the power or powers on which we depend, and the part played by the will in choosing and adopting means for getting into harmony with that Supreme Power or Being, which are elements characteristic of all religion.

In theology, as distinct from religion, the cognitive faculty, or reason, is predominant. It succeeds religion, and seeks by a right use of reason on the matter of experience furnished by religion to evolve out of it a system of connected and coherent truth to which the term 'science' can be properly applied.

3. **Theology and science.**—The aim of science in any of its departments is to apply reason, with its powers of analysis and generalization and its laws of inference, induction, and deduction, to the data of experience in that department in such a way as to discover the laws or principles underlying and relating the given facts and phenomena and to unify the entire content of experience in that department into a coherent systematic whole or body of truth such as may be described as knowledge of reality. Inasmuch as theology seeks to do this as regards the data of human experience in the realm or department of religion, it is rightly described as a branch of science. The instrument which the scientist makes use of in ascertaining, analysing, and systematizing the facts or data of experience in the department selected for scientific investigation is the reason with its powers and laws of perception, conception, evidence, inference, etc. And reason is the instrument made use of by the scientific theologian in investigating the facts and phenomena of religious experience and building up a science of theology not less than is the case in other departments of science. Lack of clearness as to the place and function of reason in theology is apt to lead to confusion and disagreement as to what theology is and what are its aim and scope. Thus in some quarters it is maintained that theology differs from other sciences inasmuch as the matter with which religion is concerned is given to us by revelation and not by reason as in the other sciences. But this contrast between reason and revelation as sources of knowledge is unsound. Reason is not the source from which, in any case, we get the matter which we build up into science, but merely the instrument by means of which we grasp, analyse, classify, co-ordinate, and systematize that matter which is given to us by revelation from without in experience. This is as true of other sciences as it is of theology. As a matter of fact, the material which we build up by use of reason into the natural sciences, as they are called, such as mechanics, chemistry, biology, etc., is given to us by revelation from without in experience not less than the matter which we seek to build up by use of reason into a systematic scientific theology. The latter is just as much matter of experience, which the reason must seek to apprehend and co-ordinate into a coherent whole of knowledge of the truth, as is the former. The knowledge got by using reason to grasp, co-ordinate, and systematize the given matter of experience is of the same kind in both cases. In both cases it rests ultimately on a foundation of faith—faith in the reliability of our faculties of knowledge (perception, cognition, inference, etc.) and on the ultimate reasonableness or cognizability of all that is given to us in experience. We go on using our powers of perception, cognition, inference, etc., in reference to what is given to us from without in experience, never doubting that the knowledge thus reached is real knowledge or knowledge of truth and reality, even though we may know and realize that our knowledge in any department of experience is incomplete and leaves room for progress. Thus the physicist may realize that he does not know the ultimate nature of matter, the mathematician may be puzzled to explain what space and time are, and the biologist may feel that he does not know what, at bottom, life and consciousness are.

But the fact that there remain unsolved questions of an ultimate kind, in regard to the data of experience in various departments, does not nullify or render valueless the results of scientific investigation and systematization in those departments. It merely shows that our knowledge of what is revealed to us in experience is as yet incomplete, and that an adequate synthesis of knowledge or metaphysic of being has not yet been reached by us, not that such a metaphysic is unattainable. So too with the data of religious experience. It is the function of theology as a branch of science to collect, examine, analyse, compare, classify, co-ordinate, and systematize all that is revealed to us in this department of experience, so as to reach a whole of scientific knowledge in this sphere, as in other departments of experience and knowledge. We must use our reason as far as it will go in synthesizing or giving us rational knowledge of what is given in experience. And, if there are problems of an ultimate kind in this science, as in other sciences, which still remain obscure or inadequately solved, this does not invalidate the knowledge reached by the application of sound scientific method to the data of experience, nor deprive it of the right to be regarded as science or knowledge of truth. It merely shows that our science in this sphere is incomplete and spurs us on to reach out towards a more comprehensive synthesis of all our knowledge in an adequate metaphysic or philosophy of being.

4. Theology and philosophy.—It is here that the science of religion passes over into the philosophy of religion, that highest form of knowledge which is the consummation aimed at by theology. Science in all its departments is limited and incomplete as knowledge of reality. It leaves unsolved ultimate questions as to the nature and relations of matter and mind or spirit, space and time, life and consciousness. It is the function of philosophy, as the ultimate form of knowledge, to grapple with these ultimate problems and seek a satisfactory solution of them. And it is along the lines of moral and religious experience, and the data furnished thereby, that light on such ultimate problems may most hopefully be looked for.

Kant, in his *Critique of Pure Reason*, began a movement in philosophy which has had far-reaching influence on modern theology as well as on philosophy. His contention is that in unifying the given matter of perceptive experience into an ordered and coherent world-knowledge the mind or reason of the percipient subject makes use of forms of perception and cognition which are subjective (*i.e.* belonging to the nature or constitution of the knowing mind), not objective (*i.e.* belonging to the object or reality as it is in itself apart from its being known or cognized). Kant thus concluded that the world of which we have definite knowledge, through grasping and unifying the given matter of experience by means of the subjective forms of perception and cognition, is but a phenomenal world or a world as it appears to a conscious subject endowed with powers of perception or cognition like man, not a noumenal world or thing-in-itself existing exactly thus apart from being perceived or known. Thus exact scientific knowledge, according to Kant, is limited to knowledge of the phenomenal world and cannot reach to ultimate reality. The use of those very forms of perception and cognition which give definiteness to our knowledge makes it knowledge of the phenomenal as contrasted with the ultimately real or thing-in-itself. All scientific or theoretic knowledge is thus knowledge of the phenomenal only. If there be a noumenal world of reality, and if it be in any way accessible to us, this must be in some other way than that of rational knowledge. Kant maintains that access to a noumenal world of reality is gained by us, not through the pure reason but through the practical reason or moral consciousness, by means of which we may and do reach a kind of faith-knowledge of God, freedom, and immortality, which, though not rational theoretic knowledge, such as we have in science, is yet of value for the moral and religious life. This demarcation of the limits of valid, rational, scientific or theoretic knowledge, and differentiation from it of the kind of knowledge got through moral and religious experience or through supernatural historic revelation is characteristic of many theological writers since Kant. The argument of the *Critique of Pure Reason* is supposed to be conclusive against the possibility of our ever reaching any rational metaphysic or valid theoretic knowledge of ultimate reality. Huxley and Spencer pressed Kant's conclusion into the service of their doctrine that God or ultimate reality is and must remain unknown and unknowable by man, and that therefore a science of theology is impossible. Hamilton and Mansel endeavoured to reconcile the agnostic conclusions of Kant in regard to a rational metaphysic with the acceptance of traditional Christian doctrine as grounded on revelation, not on reason. The Ritschlian school accept Kant's conclusions as to the impossibility of a rational, theoretically valid, knowledge of God or ultimate reality, and so rule out all natural or rational theology as incompetent; but, while eliminating all metaphysic from Christian theology as untenable, they seek to retain in large measure the traditional Christian theology as grounded on a divine historic revelation culminating in Christ, of which Scripture is the record. As with Kant, they seek to find a grounding for this in the immediate deliverances of the moral and religious consciousness, which furnishes them with a basis for 'value-judgments' where valid theoretic knowledge fails. This sharp differentiation between the kind of knowledge got by making use of reason, our cognitive faculty, in grasping, analysing, and systematizing the data of perceptive experience in the sphere, say, of physics or chemistry and the kind of knowledge got by using reason in the same way—call it practical reason or what you will—in grasping, co-ordinating, and systematizing the data of moral and religious experience is arbitrary and unconvincing. The world of reality revealed to us in experience—whether the ordinary perceptive experience which grounds our common knowledge or the moral and religious experience which grounds our religious knowledge—is one whole, and our knowledge of it, however acquired, should be capable of being synthesized as one coherent whole. The attempt of the Kantians and Ritschlians to rule out all metaphysic and natural theology as going beyond the proper limits of the reason, and yet to build up a theology of value-judgments founded on the needs of the moral consciousness or practical reason or on the data of a historic divine revelation, is not satisfying to the inquiring mind that seeks for unity and coherence and consistency in its knowledge. Theology, as the philosophy of religion, is to be looked upon, not as the rival or opponent of rational science, but rather as its copestone and completion.

True theology can never come into conflict with true science. For it includes all the data and verified results of true science among its material or postulates. It seeks to co-ordinate or synthesize all our knowledge into a comprehensive and coherent whole of truth or knowledge of reality, based upon the data of human experience regarded as a whole, tested, analysed, co-ordinated, and systematized by sound scientific methods.

5. Reason and intuition.—Akin to the distinction which Kantians draw between the theoretic reason, which gives us definite knowledge of a phenomenal world, and the practical reason, which gives us vague knowledge of noumenal reality, is the distinction which more recent philosophers such as Henri Bergson draw between reason, or intellect, and instinct, or intuition, as sources of knowledge. Intuition, it is alleged, brings us more immediately into touch with the living flowing stream of reality, of which as individual persons we form a part, and enables us to adapt ourselves thereto more surely and satisfactorily than reason or intellect, whose forms of thought and processes of inference are adapted to matter that is fixed or static rather than to the ever-changing creative flux of actual reality or real time. But this contrast or antithesis between intuition and intellect, like that between faith and reason, is unsound. The intuitions of a rational being are just an implicit form of reason. And it is better in every way for a rational being such as man that what is implicit in consciousness should be made explicit and fitted into the comprehensive synthesis of rational cognition, which alone deserves the name of knowledge. The only supreme authority and court of appeal for rational conscious beings is reason based on an ultimate ineradicable faith in the reasonableness of our experience, which is the underlying assumption of all science, including theology. To subject reason to intuition or instinct as instrument of knowledge is to incur moral and intellectual bankruptcy which is unworthy of a rational being such as man. It is to take a step downwards towards the brutal condition, not upwards towards the goal of true personality.

For conscious rational beings the only reality which has or can have any meaning is reality which is or may be apprehended by rational consciousness. In the case of reality of which we are, or suppose ourselves to be, dimly aware in subconscious apprehension or intuition, it is assumed that to a more perfect or adequate consciousness this would evidence itself as real. Reality for us means reality apprehended or apprehensible by a conscious being. To affirm an unknown reality may mean simply that we are dimly aware of the existence of some power or force which we have not yet been able to adjust to our incomplete synthesis or scheme of knowledge. But to affirm a reality which is, and which must ever remain, inaccessible to every conscious apprehension is to affirm a contradiction in terms or to use words without meaning.

Practical reason, faith, intuition or instinct, to which some would point as the proper guides in theology rather than what they call the pure or theoretic reason, are all forms of conscious apprehension which enable us to build up the data of experience into some more or less coherent whole of knowledge. The data to be unified and synthesized in a science of systematic theology are not indeed given to us by reason from within, but by revelation from without. Reason, however, is our only proper instrument for the apprehending, co-ordinating, and systematizing of these data.

6. Theology and the Bible.—Some theologians conceive of the task of theology as that of setting forth in coherent systematic form the content of that revelation concerning God, the world, and man of which the Bible is the inspired record. But, while this points to a very important department of theology, it is too narrow a view to take of the scope and function of theology as a whole. There are other materials or data for theological construction besides those furnished by the Bible, which cannot be overlooked or ignored by the scientific theologian who takes a wide and comprehensive view of his subject. The revelation of ultimate reality given in the natural world around us with its varied facts and phenomena, which it is the function of natural science to investigate, furnishes material which the theologian must interpret and construe. So too the course of general human history, which it is the function of historical science to present and elucidate in the light of general principles or laws, affords data of experience which are of value for theological construction. And the moral consciousness of mankind generally, the investigation of which is the special task of the science of ethics, furnishes important material to the scientific theologian to help in the upbuilding of a system of theology. But the revelation given in the history and religious experience of Israel as a nation and of the outstanding personalities among that people, culminating in the fact of Christ and the foundation of the Christian Church, is of such supreme importance and unique significance in the religious sphere that it is customary and convenient to distinguish between the general revelation to mankind as a whole in nature and history and conscience, which is treated of under the heading of natural theology, and the special historic revelation culminating in Christ, which is treated of under the heading of specifically Christian theology, and which may be regarded not as something entirely different from natural theology, but rather as its crown and completion.

7. Classification of theological sciences or disciplines; theological encyclopædia.—Having such a vast and varied material to deal with, theological science has many branches or disciplines with aims and methods differing according to the material dealt with and the purpose kept in view. To elucidate and classify these various disciplines is the function of what is known as theological encyclopædia, which itself constitutes a branch of theological study.

Religion as an object of investigation has two aspects: (*a*) a historical aspect, under which it is to be regarded as a historical phenomenon appearing under various forms among various peoples with characteristics which furnish ample material for historical inquiry and investigation; and (*b*) a normative aspect, under which it appears as a present inner power of life making claim to truth and to the right to regulate individual and social life. This twofold aspect of religion furnishes us with guidance for classifying the branches of theology, which is the science of religion, into two main divisions: (*a*) the *historical or phenomenological* branches, including all those sciences which deal with religion on its phenomenological side as an actual appearance in history; and (*b*) the *normative or constructive* branches, including those sciences which deal with religion as a present-day reality and power, claiming to be truth by which the practical life of man should be moulded and regulated. The distinction already referred to between natural theology and specifically Christian theology furnishes ground for suitable further subdivision of the material falling to be dealt with under these two main divisions, thus affording a basis for a convenient classification of theological disciplines or branches of study.

(*a*) The investigation of religion in its phenomenological aspect may be conveniently subdivided into (i.) a general branch dealing with the phenomenology of the ethnic religions other than Christian that have appeared in history, which will include (1) history of religions, with a descriptive account of the distinctive features and characteristics of religious beliefs as they have appeared in history, (2) comparative study of religion, and (3) psychology of religion in so far as historical investigation can throw light on that; and (ii.) a special branch dealing with the phenomenology of the Christian religion. This will embrace, under the general heading of Biblical science, (4) linguistics, or a study of the Bible languages and the principles of interpretation and exegesis; (5) Biblical introduction, or investigation into text, date, authorship, and historical setting of the various books of the Bible; (6) Biblical history and antiquities, and (7) Biblical theology, which aims at setting forth by means of impartial exegesis the ideas as to God, man, and the world and their relations set forth in the different Biblical writings; and, under the general heading of ecclesiastical history, (8) Church history, or the history of the spread of the Church, (9) history of doctrine, and (10) symbolic, or the history of the different creeds and confessions in which Christian doctrine has been embodied.

(*b*) The investigation of religion in its normative and constructive aspect may be subdivided into (iii.) a general branch dealing with the presentation, defence, and application of the truths of natural religion, including (11) the apologetic of religion generally, (12) natural theology, (13) philosophic ethic; (iv.) a special branch dealing with the presentation, defence, and application of the truth of Christianity as the highest and final form of religion; this embraces (14) the apologetic of the Christian religion; systematic theology, which includes (15) Christian dogmatic, and (16) Christian ethic; and practical theology, which includes (17) homiletic, (18) liturgic, (19) catechetic, or paideutic, (20) pastoral theology, (21) ecclesiastical polity, and (22) evangelistic theology, or the theory of missions; (v.) the final synthesis of the truths reached in the various theological disciplines, historic and theoretic or normative, which is the aim of (23) the philosophy of religion, in which theology reaches its consummation.

8. Method in theology.—The method to be made use of in dealing with the data of theological science in its various branches will vary with the matter dealt with and the purpose or end in view.

In the historical or phenomenological branches of theology the end in view is simply the ascertainment and accurate presentation of historic fact, and the methods to be made use of are those which are appropriate to historical inquiry in general.

(1) Thus in setting forth the *history of religions* the investigator must make himself acquainted as widely as possible, by observation and inquiry, with the features and characteristics of extant religions as they now appear and are practised among men. He must further acquaint himself with the historic origin and development of these religions by the study of such books, monuments, and other records of the past as are available. Careful observation and industrious inquiry and research are thus the methods most needful for success in this department of theological science.

(2) In the *comparative study of religion* the investigator must use the material furnished by the history of religions, and seek by analysis, comparison, and spiritual insight to show the relations of the various religions to one another and their grading as manifestations of the common spirit of religion. This calls for more of speculative thought and philosophic reflexion, as regards method, than the previous discipline.

(3) In *psychology of religion* the investigator must discuss the origin and form of religion generally from the psychological point of view, and seek to show what part the various mental faculties and capacities—intelligence, feeling, desire, will, imagination, etc.—have in religious experience, and how they enter into and manifest themselves in religions. The methods appropriate to scientific psychology—observation, reflexion, induction, and deduction—have proper application in this discipline.

(4) *Biblical linguistics*, which is the study of the languages in which the Bible was originally written, is just a branch of philology, and the methods of philological study and inquiry have here their proper application. Hermeneutics and exegetics, which deal with the interpretation of the text of Scripture, may be brought in under linguistics.

(5) In *Biblical introduction* the methods of the lower or textual criticism and of the higher or historical criticism have a proper place. Textual criticism investigates the various manuscripts of the Bible that have come down to us and the various readings in the texts of these manuscripts, and seeks by rational principles to get as nearly as possible at the true original text. Historical criticism investigates the evidences of compositeness in different books of the Bible and seeks with the help of tradition and of a knowledge of contemporary history to gain reliable knowledge as to the composition, date, authorship, and historical setting or circumstances of the various books of the Bible, and to estimate their place and function as elements in a progressive revelation.

(6) *Biblical history* deals with the history of the Jewish people and the rise of the Christian Church as recorded in the Bible, while Biblical antiquities has to do with the archæology, chronology, and geography of the Bible.

(7) *Biblical theology* (including Biblical psychology) aims at unfolding and presenting in a clear and orderly form the doctrinal conceptions or ideas presented by the various writers of the OT and NT. It is the crown and completion of Biblical science, and, for those who accept the Bible as the inspired record of a divine revelation, it is of supreme importance for furnishing material towards the upbuilding of a comprehensive, normative, systematic theology. But of itself it is a purely historic discipline, aiming at the accurate presentation of historic fact and recorded thought in an impartial objective way, without meantime taking into account the bearing of that on permanent normative religious truth. The methods to be used in Biblical theology are those of sound philology and impartial scientific exegesis or interpretation, so as to make sure that the ideas or doctrines set forth are those of the various Bible writers themselves, unmodified by any subjective theological bias of the interpreter. The work of adjusting the scheme of thought faithfully gathered from the Scriptures by sound impartial exegesis to a comprehensive scheme of normative systematic theology is the important task of the Christian systematic theologian.

(8) *Church history*, or the history of the spread of Christianity, aims at recounting accurately the gradual enlargement of the area known as Christendom, the conflict of Christianity with anti-Christian forces, and the growth of the Church's constitution and cultus, showing how the polity and worship of the Christian Church developed as time went on, and how divisions over questions of constitution and government and cultus arose among Christians.

(9) The *history of doctrine* describes the dogma, or body of doctrine, accepted by the Christian Church, and traces its development along the centuries.

(10) *Symbolic* gives a more detailed attention to the various 'symbols'—creeds or confessions—that have been formulated from time to time in the Church's history than can be given in a general history of doctrine. These are obviously purely historical disciplines, aiming at the ascertainment and accurate presentation of historic facts, for the achievement of which the proper methods to be used are the methods of impartial historical research and inquiry.

(11) The *apologetic of religion* in general has as its function to inquire into the nature and essence of religion generally and to establish the truth of the religious view of the world over against all irreligious, antitheistic, or agnostic views. It aims at discussing and exhibiting (α) the nature and essence of religion in general; (β) the nature and validity of religious belief and the relation of the knowledge got thereby to the knowledge of natural objects gained through perception and rational cognition; (γ) the truth and reality of what is postulated and affirmed in religious belief, as against atheism, materialism, agnosticism, and other forms of unbelief; (δ) the rational proofs for the existence of God or the ways in which the human mind by valid process rises to the apprehension of supreme personal Spirit as the ultimate reality, from reflective contemplation of the changing natural world and its phenomena, of the course of human history, and of the facts of the moral consciousness; (ε) the evidence contained in the general revelation given to all men for the immortality of the soul and a future state.

(12) Closely associated with the general apologetic of religion is that systematic presentation of the truths underlying natural religion to which the name of *natural theology* is usually given. Its aim is to set forth in a methodical orderly way all that may be known concerning God and the world and man, and their mutual relations, from that general revelation which is given in nature, mind, and history. It is the dogmatic of natural religion, as philosophic theism is its apologetic.

(13) Akin to natural theology is *philosophic ethic*, whose aim is to ground a science of practical conduct on the immediate deliverances of the moral consciousness and the knowledge of God and duty derivable therefrom. The ethic of Kant, associated with what he described as a 'religion within the limits of pure reason,' may be taken as illustrative of the aims and methods of philosophic ethic, defective though it may be as a presentation of the results of such ethic, even as his 'religion within the limits of pure reason' is defective as a presentation of the truths of natural theology. In this region of natural theology and philosophic ethic the aim is to reach not merely historic but permanent normative truth, in which the mind of the rational thinker can find rest and by which practical conduct can be regulated. The methods by which alone, if at all, such results can be reached are those of speculative thought and philosophic reflexion on the data of moral and religious experience—not merely of our own personal experience, but of the experience of mankind generally as far as that can be ascertained, analysed, and used as the basis of rational inference, induction, and deduction. A great accession to the material or data of experience, on which a comprehensive and satisfactory philosophical theology and ethic may be grounded, is given us when we take into account the special revelation, culminating in the fact of Christ, of which the Bible is the record. Apart from this, indeed, the data on which natural theology and philosophic ethic seek to build are so incomplete that the probable conclusions reached are lacking in fullness of content and convincing power. The new data of experience furnished by this special revelation not only add cogency to the probable conclusions reached by philosophic theism and ethic, but also bring a greater fullness of content to constructive normative theology, by which it is enriched and made more satisfying to the mind and heart of man.

(14) *Christian apologetic* has as its function to indicate the nature and essence of the Christian religion, grounded on the historic revelation of which the Bible is the record, and to set forth in order the evidences of its truth. It deals with such questions as these: (α) the idea of revelation, its spheres and modes, and the manner of its apprehension; (β) the idea of inspiration and its results; (γ) the trustworthiness of the Bible as a reliable record of fact and experience; (δ) the evidences of a progressive revelation of divine things given in the Bible and the significance of the fact of Christ as consummating and completing that revelation; (ε) the evidences of the truth of the gospel proclaimed by Christ and its fitness to meet human need and to bring salvation and satisfaction to mankind. Christian apologetic clears and prepares the way for

(15) *Christian dogmatic*, which aims at setting forth in accurate and systematic manner, and in such a way as to show its consistency with all our other knowledge of truth, the intellectual content of the Christian life as that becomes our inward possession on the ground of divine revelation through the receptivity of faith. It presupposes and includes the conclusions reached by philosophic reflexion in the sphere of theism and natural theology, and gives added cogency and convincing power to them and greater richness and fullness of content to our knowledge of God the supreme reality, as not only intelligent personal Spirit but holy loving Father. It is usually subdivided into (α) theology proper, or the doctrine of God involving an exposition and justification of the Christian conception of God as triune, which was the prominent feature of Greek Christian theology in the 4th cent. when various forms of unitarianism (Monarchianism, Sabellianism, Arianism) were combated by Athanasius and the Cappadocian Fathers; (β) Christology, or the doctrine of the Person of Christ, to which the attention of the Church was particularly directed after the Council of Nicæa (A.D. 325) by the theories propounded by Apollinaris, Nestorius, and Eutyches, which were condemned at the Councils of Constantinople (A.D. 381), Ephesus (A.D. 431), and Chalcedon (A.D. 451); (γ) pneumatology, or the doctrine of the Holy Spirit, to which attention was first prominently given by the Church when the views of Macedonius were condemned by the Council of Constantinople; (δ) anthropology, or the Christian doctrine of man; (ε) hamartiology, or the doctrine of sin, which first came to the front in the controversy between Augustine and Pelagius in the 5th cent.; (ζ) soteriology, or the Christian doctrine of salvation, which, through Augustine and Pelagius, became an important feature in Western theology, receiving fresh development at the hands of Anselm, Bernard of Clairvaux, and Thomas Aquinas, who devoted attention to the redemptive work of Christ and its application to sinful men, and engaging prominently the thoughts of theologians in the Reformation period when the doctrines of justification by faith and reconciliation with God came into prominence; (η) ecclesiology, or the doctrine of the Church and the sacraments, which first received prominence in the early Church at the hands of Cyprian of Carthage (A.D. 250), was further developed by Augustine (in his *City of God*) and Thomas Aquinas (in his *Summa Theologiæ*), and received much attention from Lutheran and Calvinistic theologians at the Reformation and from Ritschl and Anglican High Churchmen in modern times; and (θ) eschatology, or the doctrine of the last things, which has occupied a foremost place in recent theological discussion.

(16) *Christian ethic* has as its aim to set forth the content of the Christian life as it works itself out in disposition and action on the ground of the self-activity that is rooted in Christian faith. It looks upon the Christian life from the view-point of man and his duty, while dogmatic looks upon it rather from the view-point of God and His will. Both deal with the same subject-matter, viz. God and man and their relations to one another, but under different aspects or from different view-points, so that, while they belong together to systematic theology, they are most conveniently treated as separate or distinct branches of that science. Christian ethic presupposes the conclusions of philosophic ethic, just as Christian dogmatic presupposes those of natural theology. But it adds new fullness and richness of content and new power to philosophic ethic through the new data of moral and religious experience, centred in the fact of Christ, which it contributes. The first attempts to formulate Christian ethic in separation from Christian dogmatic were made by Lambert Daneau, a French Protestant, in 1557, and G. Calixtus, a Lutheran, in his *Epitome Theologiæ moralis* in 1634. Since the time of Schleiermacher this separate treatment of Christian ethic as a branch of theology has been generally followed in Germany, Britain, and America; and numerous works on Christian ethic have appeared in which

the relevant material is dealt with under different divisions. A convenient division followed in the main by Martensen and other writers is (i.) general introduction, dealing with (α) the definition and scope of Christian ethic, its relation to other disciplines, and its place in a classification of ethical systems; (β) fundamental conceptions of the science—end, norm, and motive; (γ) postulates of the science, theological, anthropological, cosmical, and eschatological; (δ) the source of our knowledge of the Christian moral ideal, the content of that ideal, and the means of its realization; (ii.) individual ethic, dealing with the origin and progress of the Christian life in the individual soul and its manifestation in the virtues and graces of the Christian character; (iii.) social ethic, dealing with the realization of the Christian ideal in the various spheres of society—the family, the Church, the State or nation.

Practical Christian theology in its various departments treats of the Christian religion from the point of view of its power to expand and to build up Christian life in the Church. It includes those disciplines that are concerned with the application of Christian theology in the practical sphere. It is art rather than science.

(17) *Homiletic* deals with the art of sermon-making.

(18) *Liturgic* deals with worship and its forms.

(19) *Catechetic*, or paideutic, deals with the religious instruction of the young.

(20) *Pastoral theology* deals with the duties of the pastoral office.

(21) *Ecclesiastical polity* deals with Church government, law, and procedure.

(22) *Evangelistic theology*, or theory of missions, deals with the best methods of propagating the Christian religion at home and among heathen peoples abroad.

The methods appropriate for use in the upbuilding of a scientific normative Christian systematic theology, into which the content of Biblical theology as a historical discipline is taken up and adjusted, are in part the methods commonly made use of by science in general—analysis, classification, inference, induction, deduction, etc.—but partly also the less easily applied methods of philosophic reflexion and speculative thought, by means of which the philosopher must seek to bring unity and consistency into his entire knowledge of the real. The God revealed in the Bible and through Christ and Christian experience — the triune God of Christian revelation—must be related and harmonized through rational thought with the God of the theistic proofs and natural theology, if our theology is to be at once Christian and philosophic.

(23) *Philosophy of religion*, which is the highest stage or form of theology, has for its data the results reached as truth by the use of scientific method in the previously mentioned theological disciplines; and its aim is to combine these elements of truth in a comprehensive synthesis of knowledge, such as will exhibit the relations of the various aspects or parts of truth and their harmonious cohesion in an organic whole of truth or reality. Its special function is to harmonize the results reached by reflective thought along the line of philosophic theism and natural theology with the results reached through believing appropriation of the Christian revelation.

If reason is indeed the means whereby we apprehend and know truth and reality, then we should not rest satisfied until what we accept as true or real is shown to commend itself to our reason as reasonable, and so 'worthy of all acceptation.' We must therefore strive to make our theology rational or reasonable, if it is to be the expression of truth. If, again, the Christian revelation concerning God and the world and man and their relations be true, as Christians believe it is, then the Christian philosopher must strive to make his philosophy and metaphysic religious and so adequate to embrace and express the truth of religious, and specifically of Christian, experience. Only when theology becomes rational and philosophy becomes religious can there be hope of such a union between the two as will yield a satisfactory philosophy of religion which will also be the most adequate and satisfactory metaphysic of being. To reach such a philosophy of religion is the worthy aspiration of the Christian speculative theologian who, while not ignoring the importance of faith alike in science, theology, and philosophy, strives to secure that the faith on which he rests shall be a reasonable faith.

LITERATURE.—i. *Theological Encyclopædia*: A. Hyperius, *De ratione Studii Theologici*, Basel, 1556; S. Mursinna, *Primæ Lineæ Encyclopædiæ Theologicæ*, Halle, 1764; F. E. D. Schleiermacher, *Kurze Darstellung des theologischen Studiums*, Berlin, 1811; K. R. Hagenbach, *Encyklopädie und Methodologie der theologischen Wissenschaften*[12], Leipzig, 1880, Eng. tr., New York, 1884; J. F. Räbiger, *Theologik oder Encyklopädie der Theologie*, do. 1880, Eng. tr., 2 vols., Edinburgh, 1884–85; R. Rothe, *Theologische Encyclopädie*, Wittenberg, 1880; K. F. G. Heinrici, *Theologische Encyklopädie*, Freiburg, 1893; James Drummond, *An Introd. to the Study of Theology*, London, 1884; Alfred Cave, *An Introd. to Theology*[2], do. 1896; E. O. Davies, *Theological Encyclopædia*, do. 1905.

ii. *History of religion.*—F. B. Jevons, *Introd. to the Hist. of Religion*[3], London, 1904; C. P. Tiele, *Outlines of the Hist. of Religion*[6], Eng. tr., do. 1896; G. F. Moore, *Hist. of Religions*, i., Edinburgh, 1914.

iii. *Comparative study of religion.*—Tiele, *Elements of the Science of Religion* (*Gifford Lectures*), 2 vols., Edinburgh, 1897–99; L. H. Jordan, *Comparative Religion*, Edinburgh, 1905; P. D. Chantepie de la Saussaye, *Manual of the Science of Religion*, Eng. tr., London, 1892; F. Max Müller, *Anthropological Religion* (*Gifford Lectures*, 3rd ser.), do. 1892; A. Kuenen, *National Religions and Universal Religions* (*HL*), do. 1882; J. Estlin Carpenter, *Comparative Religion*, do. 1913.

iv. *Psychology of religion.*—S. Baring Gould, *Origin and Development of Religious Belief*, 2 vols., London, 1869–70; R. Alliott, *Psychology and Theology*, do. 1855; W. James, *The Varieties of Religious Experience* (*Gifford Lectures*), do. 1902; Newman Smyth, *The Religious Feeling*, New York and London, n.d.

v. *Linguistics.*—(*a*) Hebrew: A. B. Davidson, *An Introductory Hebrew Grammar*[16], Edinburgh, 1900, *Hebrew Syntax*, do. 1894; S. G. Green, *Handbook to OT Hebrew*, London, 1901; M. Adler, *Student's Hebrew Grammar*, do. 1900; S. R. Driver, *Treatise on the Use of the Tenses in Hebrew*[3], Oxford, 1892; W. Gesenius, *Hebrew and English Lexicon of the OT*, ed. F. Brown, S. R. Driver, and C. A. Briggs, do. 1906.

(*b*) Greek: G. B. Winer, *A Treatise on the Grammar of NT Greek*[9], tr. W. F. Moulton, Edinburgh, 1882, *Grammatik des NT Sprachidioms*[8], ed. P. W. Schmiedel, 2 vols., Göttingen, 1894–98; F. W. Blass, *Grammar of NT Greek*[2], Eng. tr., London, 1905; NT Greek Lexicons by C. L. W. Grimm, J. H. Thayer, and H. Cremer; J. H. Moulton and G. Milligan, *The Vocabulary of the Greek NT*, London, 1914– ; R. C. Trench, *Synonyms of the NT*[8], do. 1876.

vi. *Biblical introduction.*—(*a*) OT: Driver, *An Introd. to the Lit. of the OT*[8], Edinburgh, 1909; C. H. Cornill, *Introd. to the Canonical Books of the OT*, London, 1907; J. E. McFadyen, *Introd. to the OT*, Edinburgh, 1905.

(*b*) NT: J. Moffatt, *An Introd. to the Lit. of the NT*[3], Edinburgh, 1911; A. S. Peake, *A Critical Introd. to the NT*, London, 1909; G. Salmon, *A Hist. Introd. to the Study of the Books of the NT*[4], do. 1889; B. Weiss, *A Manual of Introd. to the NT*, Eng. tr., do. 1896.

vii. *Biblical history.*—H. P. Smith, *Old Testament History*, Edinburgh, 1903; A. C. McGiffert, *A Hist. of Christianity in the Apostolic Age*, do. 1897.

viii. *Biblical archæology.* — Driver, *Modern Research as illustrating the Bible*, London, 1909; F. Delitzsch, *Babel and Bible*, Eng. tr., do. 1903; H. V. Hilprecht, *Explorations in Bible Lands during the 19th Century*, Edinburgh, 1903; C. H. W. Johns, *Ancient Assyria*, Cambridge, 1912; E. König, *The Bible and Babylon*, Eng. tr., London, 1905; A. H. Sayce, *The Religions of Ancient Egypt and Babylonia* (*Gifford Lectures*), Edinburgh, 1902; E. Schrader, *Die Keilinschriften und das AT*[3], Berlin, 1903.

ix. *Biblical criticism.*—(*a*) Textual: C. E. Hammond, *Outlines of Textual Criticism applied to the NT*[6], Oxford, 1902; E. Nestle, *Introd. to the Textual Criticism of the Greek NT*[2], Eng. tr., London, 1901; F. G. Kenyon, *Handbook to the Textual Criticism of the NT*[2], do. 1912.

(*b*) Historical: S. R. Driver and A. F. Kirkpatrick, *The Higher Criticism*[2], London, 1912; T. K. Cheyne, *Founders of OT Criticism*, do. 1893; McFadyen, *OT Criticism and the*

Christian Church, do. 1903; W. Robertson Smith, *The OT in the Jewish Church*[2], do. 1902.

x. *Biblical theology.*—(*a*) OT: G. F. Oehler, *Theology of the OT*, Eng. tr., 2 vols., Edinburgh, 1874–75; H. Schultz, *OT Theology*, Eng. tr., 2 vols., do. 1892; Davidson, *The Theology of the OT*, do. 1904; C. F. Burney, *Outlines of OT Theology*, London, 1899; W. H. Bennett, *The Theology of the OT*, do. 1896.

(*b*) NT: G. B. Stevens, *Theology of the NT*, New York, 1899; B. Weiss, *Lehrbuch der bibl. Theologie des NT*, Berlin, 1868, Eng. tr., 2 vols., Edinburgh, 1882–83; W. Beyschlag, *NT Theologie*[2], Berlin, 1896, Eng. tr., Edinburgh, 1896; Moffatt, *The Theology of the Gospels*, London, 1912.

xi. *Church history.*—J. K. L. Gieseler, *Lehrbuch der Kirchengesch.*, 5 vols., Bonn, 1828–57, Eng. tr., Edinburgh, 1853–65; J. A. W. Neander, *Allgemeine Gesch. der christl. Relig. und Kirche*, 11 vols., Hamburg, 1825–53, Eng. tr., London, 1850–58; G. P. Fisher, *Hist. of the Christian Church*, New York, 1888; P. Schaff, *Hist. of the Christian Church*, new ed., 12 vols., Edinburgh, 1883–93; H. C. Sheldon, *Hist. of the Christian Church*, 5 vols., New York, 1894.

xii. *History of doctrine.*—Hagenbach, *A Hist. of Christian Doctrines*[5], Eng. tr., 3 vols., Edinburgh, 1880–81; A. Harnack, *Hist. of Dogma*[3], 7 vols., Eng. tr., London, 1894–99; Sheldon, *Hist. of Christian Doctrine*, 2 vols., New York, 1886; G. P. Fisher, *Hist. of Christian Doctrine*, Edinburgh, 1902; W. G. T. Shedd, *Dogmatic Theology*, 3 vols., Edinburgh and New York, 1889–94; I. A. Dorner, *A System of Christian Doctrine*, Eng. tr., 4 vols., Edinburgh, 1880–82; J. Orr, *Sidelights on Christian Doctrine*, London, 1909; R. Seeberg, *Lehrbuch der Dogmengesch.*, Leipzig, 1908; F. Loofs, *Leitfaden zum Studium der Dogmengesch.*[4], Halle, 1906; H. B. Workman, *Christian Thought to the Reformation*, London, 1911; A. C. McGiffert, *Protestant Thought before Kant*, do. 1911; C. E. Moore, *An Outline of the Hist. of Christian Thought since Kant*, do. 1912.

xiii. *Symbolic.*—P. Marheineke, *Christliche Symbolik*, 3 vols., Heidelberg, 1810–13; Winer, *Comparative View of the Doctrines and Confessions of the Various Communities of Christendom*, Eng. tr., Edinburgh, 1873; J. A. Möhler, *Symbolik*[10], Mainz, 1889; Schaff, *A Hist. of the Creeds of Christendom*, 3 vols., London, 1877; K. J. von Hefele, *Conciliengesch.*, 10 vols., Freiburg, 1855–90, Eng. tr., Edinburgh, 1871–96; W. A. Curtis, *A Hist. of Creeds and Confessions of Faith*, Edinburgh, 1911.

xiv. *Apologetic.*—(*a*) General: A. Campbell Fraser, *Philosophy of Theism*[2] (*Gifford Lectures*), Edinburgh, 1899; R. Flint, *Theism*[2], do. 1878, *Antitheistic Theories*, do. 1879; G. P. Fisher, *The Grounds of Theistic and Christian Belief*[2], London, 1902; J. Iverach, *Theism*, do. 1900; J. Ward, *Naturalism and Agnosticism*[2], 2 vols., do. 1903; B. P. Bowne, *Studies in Theism*, New York, 1880; J. Martineau, *A Study of Religion*, 2 vols., London, 1888.

(*b*) Christian: Butler, *Analogy*, London, 1736; A. B. Bruce, *Apologetics*, Edinburgh, 1892; H. Schultz, *Outlines of Christian Apologetics*, New York, 1905; J. Wendland, *Miracles and Christianity*, Eng. tr., London, 1911; A. C. Headlam, *The Miracles of the NT*, London, 1914.

xv. *Dogmatic.*—(*a*) Natural theology: Plato, Aristotle, Origen, John Scotus Erigena, Augustine, Anselm, Aquinas, Descartes, Spinoza, Leibniz, Kant, Fichte, Schelling, Hegel, Paley, Chalmers, A. B. Bruce, A. J. Balfour.

(*b*) Christian dogmatic: (1) Earlier Alexandrian: Clement, Origen, Athanasius, Cyril of Jerusalem, Gregory of Nyssa; (2) Antiochene: Theodore of Mopsuestia, Theodoret, Chrysostom; (3) Later Alexandrian: Cyril of Alexandria, John of Damascus; (4) Latin: Tertullian, Cyprian, Augustine, Gregory the Great; (5) Middle Ages: Isidore, Peter Lombard, Anselm, Aquinas, Bernard of Clairvaux, Albertus Magnus, William of Occam; (6) Reformation: Luther, Melanchthon, Calvin, Zwingli, Knox; (7) Counter-Reformation: Bellarmine, Petavius, Moehler, Hunter, Rosmini, Gioberti; (8) Puritan: Baxter, Owen, Thomas Goodwin, John Goodwin, John Lightfoot; (9) Arminian: Arminius, Limborch, Grotius, John Wesley, Richard Watson, W. B. Pope; (10) Calvinistic: Jonathan Edwards, C. Hodge, A. A. Hodge, W. G. T. Shedd; (11) Modern German: Schleiermacher, Ritschl, Herrmann, Kaftan, Reischle, Harnack, Haering, Pfleiderer, Lipsius, Biedermann, Dorner, Frank, Martensen, Luthardt; (12) British and American: R. W. Dale, J. Denney, J. Orr, J. Candlish, H. R. Mackintosh, W. N. Clarke, W. Adams Brown, T. B. Strong, H. C. G. Moule.

xvi. *Christian ethic.*—Newman Smyth, *Christian Ethics*[3], Edinburgh and New York, 1893; R. L. Ottley, *Christian Ethics*, London, 1889; A. B. D. Alexander, *Christianity and Ethics*, do. 1914; H. L. Martensen, *Den Christelige Ethik*, 3 vols., Copenhagen, 1871–78, Eng. tr., London, 1893; Dorner, *System der christl. Sittenlehre*, Berlin, 1885, Eng. tr., London, 1887; T. von Haering, *Das christl. Leben* (*Ethik*)[2], Stuttgart, 1907, Eng. tr., London, 1909; J. Gottschick, *Ethik*, Tübingen, 1907.

xvii. *Practical theology.* — W. Gladden, *The Christian Pastor and the Working Church*, New York, 1898; A. V. G. Allen, *Christian Institutions*, do. 1897; J. J. van Oosterzee, *Practical Theology*, Eng. tr., London, 1878; A. Vinet, *Homilétique*, Paris, 1853, Eng. tr., Edinburgh, 1853, often republished; Christian Palmer, *Evangelische Pastoraltheologie*, Stuttgart, 1860; P. Fairbairn, *Pastoral Theology*, Edinburgh, 1875; Shedd, *Homiletics and Pastoral Theology*, New York, 1876.

xviii. *Philosophy of religion.*—O. Pfleiderer, *The Philosophy of Religion on the Basis of its History*, Eng. tr., 4 vols., London, 1886–88; B. Pünjer, *Hist. of the Christian Philosophy of Religion*, Eng. tr., Edinburgh, 1887; Hegel, *Vorlesungen über die Philosophie der Religion*, 2 vols., Berlin, 1832, Eng. tr., 3 vols., London, 1895; K. C. F. Krause, *Zur Religionsphilosophie und speculativen Theologie*, Leipzig, 1893, *Die absolute Religionsphilosophie*, 2 vols., 1835; H. Lotze, *Grundzüge der Religionsphilosophie*[3], Leipzig, 1882, Eng. tr., London, 1892; G. Teichmüller, *Religionsphilosophie*, Breslau, 1886; J. D. Morrell, *Philosophy of Religion*, London and New York, 1849; J. Caird, *Introd. to the Philosophy of Religion*[2], do. 1889; E. Caird, *The Evolution of Religion*, 2 vols., Glasgow, 1893; G. S. Morris, *Philosophy and Christianity*, New York, 1883; G. Galloway, *Studies in the Philosophy of Religion*, Edinburgh, 1904; J. Lindsay, *A Philosophical System of Theistic Idealism*, do. 1917; A. M. Fairbairn, *The Philosophy of the Christian Religion*[2], London, 1902.

D. S. ADAM.

THEOSOPHICAL SOCIETY.—I. Definition and scope.—Every great religion has two parts, an inner and an outer, a spirit and a body, 'the knowledge of God,' which 'is Eternal Life,' and its dogmas, rites, and ceremonies. The inner part, 'the wisdom of God in a mystery,' spoken of by St. Paul as known to 'the perfect,' is that which has, since the 3rd cent., been known in the West as 'theosophy'; in the East it has been known for ages under its Sanskrit equivalent, *Brahma-vidyā*, 'God-wisdom,' 'God-knowledge,' or 'God-science.' Such theosophy, or mysticism, the direct knowledge of God by man, belongs equally to all great religions, as their sustaining life, and may be possessed by any individual, even outside any religious organization. The Brahmavadins, 'knowers of God,' in Hinduism; the Gnostics, the 'knowers,' who, Origen declared, were necessary to the very existence of the Christian Church; the *shaikh* in Islāmic Ṣūfism—these are typical theosophists from the standpoint of the modern Theosophical Society. No man is truly a theosophist who has not direct knowledge of God, but he may win this through any religion or by his own unaided efforts.

Theosophy, in the modern as in the ancient world, proclaims the possibility of such knowledge, as the inevitable result of the immanence of God. Man is essentially a spiritual being, his self, or spirit, being an emanation from the Universal Self, or Universal Spirit, God, as a ray is an emanation from the sun. Hence, to know himself, his deepest self, is to know God; he can sink in consciousness into the depths of his own being, beyond the body, the passions, the emotions, the mind, the reason; these are all his, but they are not he; he can pass beyond them all, and realize himself as separate from them, the pure 'I,' pure being. This is the universal experience of those who, successfully, seek the Kingdom of Heaven within, and it is followed by the recognition that this Universal Being into which the self opens transcends all the beings in which it is manifested, and is alike in all. Out of this experience, repeated for every one who becomes a knower of God, or theosophist, are built the two fundamental truths of theosophy: the immanence and transcendence of God, and the solidarity, or brotherhood, of all living beings. The realization of the first truth, man's identity of nature with God, as a fact in consciousness, and the subsequent realization of the second, his identity of nature with all around him, by a blending of his self with their self, a conscious dwelling in their forms as in his own—these sum up theosophy in its fullest and deepest sense. The man who has thus reached self-realization in God and in all beings is a theosophist; those who deliberately aim at such self-realization are also generally called theosophists.

The word 'theosophy' has further, historically, a second meaning: it denotes a body of truths, or facts, concerning God, man, and the universe; and these may conveniently be classified under three heads: religion, philosophy, and science.

On these truths is based its system of ethics, rational, inspiring, and compelling. In considering this body of truths we are not studying a system invented and published in modern days; we have to do with what has aptly been termed the Wisdom-Tradition, handed down in all civilized countries, ancient and modern, by a long succession of prophets, teachers, and writers. It may be traced in the *Upaniṣads*, *Purāṇas*, and epics of the Hindus, and in the six systems (*darśanas*) of Hindu philosophy; it underlies many of the Chinese systems, especially Taoism, and is seen in such books as *The Classic of Purity* and in the writings of Lao-tse; it is found in Egypt, as in *The Book of the Dead* and the papyri from which its religion has been re-constructed; it appears in the fragmentary records of Assyria and Chaldæa; in the *Gāthas* and other scriptures of the Pārsīs; in the Hebrew Scriptures as expounded by the Ḳabbālā and the Talmud; in the Christian, as treated by the early Fathers of the Church, and by such Gnostic writers as Valentinus, Basilides, and a host of others; in Pythagoras and Plato, with the Pythagorean, Platonic, and Neo-Platonic schools, with Plotinus, Iamblichus, and the theurgists; it is taken up from these by the doctors of Islām and the Ṣūfī mystics; appears in the Rosicrucian students of alchemy and astrology, in Rosenkreutz, Paracelsus, Bruno, Eckhartshausen, Boehme, Eckhart, Vaughan, Bacon, More, Fludd—all these and scores of others have assimilated and handed on the Wisdom-Tradition; it has lent its symbols to masonry, and hidden some of its mysteries in masonic ceremonies; it peeps out of Scandinavian and Celtic folk-lore, out of the Hawaiian legends and Maori traditions, the unburied temples of the Mayas and Quiches, the magic of the Zuñis and other N. American Indian tribes. Its revival and its systematization into a coherent and inter-related body of doctrines, separated from non-essential and irrelevant teachings—this is modern, and is the work of the Theosophical Society, a modern association. But the doctrines themselves are scattered everywhere, through all times, in all places.

The test to be applied to a religious doctrine which claims to be theosophical is catholicity. 'Semper, ubique, et ab omnibus'—such is the test. For all religions come from a single source, the Divine Wisdom, and have as founders divinely inspired men—men who have climbed up the ladder of evolution till they have reached perfection in humanity, and have entered on the superhuman evolution. Such men we call 'masters,' and we regard them as the guides and directors of the evolution of humanity; the similarities in doctrines and ethics, pointed out by comparative mythology and comparative religion, we regard as due to the fact that all the founders of religions are members of the one lodge of masters, possess the same knowledge, and are guided by the same principles.

The universal—*i.e.* theosophical—doctrines of religion are: the unity of God; the manifestation of God as a Trinity for the building of a universe; the existence of graded orders of intelligences, a vast hierarchy of beings, forming the inhabitants, visible and invisible, of a universe, or a solar system. The doctrine of reincarnation, taught in every religion, though in some temporarily overlaid, belongs to the domain of philosophy rather than to that of religion; the immortality, or rather the eternity, of the spirit belongs also to philosophy more than to religion, when dealt with intellectually; the law of action and reaction—*karma*—falls under science, as do the constitution of a solar system and of man.

2. Religious teachings.—(*a*) *The unity of God*, the universal one Existence which is the source of all existences actual and potential, the super-life and super-consciousness in which all lives and consciousnesses inhere, eternal beneath the transitory, changeless beneath the fleeting, unsupported but the support of all, all-embracing, all-containing, the One without a second—this is the central teaching of theosophy as of all religions, the first universal truth of religion.

(*b*) *The Trinity of the manifested God* is the second great and universal truth of religion, and therefore of theosophy. Theosophy speaks of the manifested God as the Logos, borrowing the term from Plato, Philo, and the Fourth Gospel.

'Coming forth from the depths of the One Existence, from the One beyond all thought and all speech, a Logos, by imposing on Himself a limit, circumscribing voluntarily the range of His own Being, becomes the Manifested God, and tracing the limiting sphere of His activity, thus outlines the area of His universe. Within that area the universe is born, is evolved, and dies; it lives, it moves, it has its being in Him; its matter is His breath; its forces and energies are currents of His life; He is immanent in every atom; all-pervading; all-sustaining; all-evolving; He is its source and its end, its cause and its object, its centre and circumference; it is built on Him as its sure foundation, it breathes in Him as its encircling space; He is in everything, and everything in Him. Thus have the Sages of the Ancient Wisdom taught us of the beginning of the manifested worlds. From the same source we learn of the Self-unfolding of the Logos into a threefold form; the First Logos, the Root of all Being, the *Will* which outbreathes and inbreathes the worlds; from Him the Second Logos, manifesting the two aspects of life and form, the primal duality, making the two poles of nature between which the web of the universe is to be woven—life-form, spirit-matter, positive-negative, active-receptive, Father-Mother of the Worlds—the *Wisdom*, or Pure Reason, "mightily and sweetly ordering all things," sustaining the universe; the Third Logos, the Universal Active or Creative *Mind*, that in which all archetypically exists, the source of beings, the fount of fashioning energies, the treasure-house in which are stored up all the archetypal forms which are to be brought forth and elaborated in matter during the evolution of the universe, the fruits of past universes, brought over as seeds for the present.'[1]

(*c*) *The hierarchy of beings* is the third truth universally accepted: the 'seven spirits before the throne of God'; the primary emanations of the Supreme Trinity; the ranks of secondary Logoi, who rule congeries of solar systems, down to the Logos of a single solar system. In such a system the vast hosts of spiritual intelligences (the *devas*, archangels, and angels of religions), the grades of spirits encased in human bodies, the sub-human intelligences and those not yet even awakened to intelligence—all these, with the solar Logos at their head, form the ladder of lives, and evolve within the system. The sub-human intelligences include all nature-spirits, the gnomes, fairies, etc., who play so great a part in folk-lore, the living though limited intelligences who make all nature a living responsive organism instead of a soulless mechanism, whom little children sometimes see, and who are visible to the ordinary seer.

(*d*) The fourth truth in theosophy is that of *universal brotherhood*, the inevitable deduction from the preceding; since there is but one life in all forms, all forms must be inter-related, linked together, and, however unequal they may be in development, they none the less make one huge family, are 'of one blood.' The universal brotherhood of theosophy differs from the political conception of 'equality,' the foundation of modern democracy, in that it postulates identity of origin and of potentiality, but recognizes varying degrees of development, the latter yielding the hierarchy of beings, or ladder of lives. In this freemasonry resembles it, with its broad division of mankind into the enlightened and the profane, and the subdivisions of the enlightened into degrees and graded officers, uniting the essential equality with a hierarchical order and due subordination. In this both theosophy and freemasonry are in harmony with nature, increasing power going hand-in-hand with increasing knowledge and increasing

[1] A. Besant, *The Ancient Wisdom*.

responsibility. Wisdom, supported by strength and made manifest in beauty, rules in a true brotherhood, as in nature.

It is interesting to note that these four primary religious truths of theosophy, of universal religion, are but the intellectual formulation—for the instruction of the people—of the two primary spiritual truths directly contacted by the knower of God, the gnostic, the theosophist. The first three are religious dogmas, expressing intellectually the first spiritual truth; the fourth is the expression in the outer life of the second spiritual truth. The spiritual truths can be *known* only by individual self-realization; they may be intellectually taught and believed as the fundamental dogmas of universal religion, theosophy. A dogma is the intellectual presentment of a truth known by the spirit, and believed on external authority.

3. Philosophical teachings. — Philosophically, theosophy is idealistic; consciousness is primary, the one indubitable fact, which can neither be strengthened nor weakened by argument. 'I am' is the testimony of consciousness to itself, and naught can disprove its witness, since every disproof, every argument, must be addressed to that same consciousness, and imply its existence. To the All-Self, matter is but the limitations imposed by Himself on His thoughts; to us, evolving in a universe which is the manifestation of our Logos, matter is His thought, limitations imposed on us by His thought and activity—limitations which we cannot transcend until we can realize ourselves in Him. Human thought, though feeble and undeveloped, is of the same nature as divine thought, and increases its power over matter with its increasing growth; thought is the one creative and moulding power, and, as evolving man realizes this, and so clarifies his lower nature that this aspect of the self can work through it, he becomes the master of that lower nature and of his surroundings, the creator and controller of his destiny. By thought, mastering the science of physical nature, he bends it to his will and utilizes it; by thought, mastering the science of the emotions, he builds virtues and destroys vices; by thought, mastering the science of mind, he subdues its turbulent energies into orderly obedience; by thought, directing will and controlling activity, he brings all things, within and without, into subjection to the self, 'the inner ruler, immortal.' Only by such fit rule and due subjection can man attain perfect health of body, emotions, and mind, and reach the highest good. Hence many of the practical theosophical teachings deal with this power and control of thought.

The eternity of spirit—more loosely spoken of as the immortality of the soul—is an integral part of theosophical philosophy. It is an inevitable deduction from the identity of nature of the human and the universal Self; 'unborn, undying, perpetual,' it is eternal as God Himself. The continuity of consciousness is equally inevitable, since the self is conscious and continuous, and in the self must consequently abide all its experiences, of which a successive survey is memory. The extent to which these memories are carried on by the material sheaths, or bodies, of the self—*i.e.* the survival of the individual and the person—will be better considered under the constitution of man.

The method of the unfolding of this continuous and conscious self in the human kingdom is by reincarnation. Reincarnation is, in fact, the only doctrine of immortality that philosophy can look at, as Hume said.[1] It means that the self, having unfolded to the human stage, appropriates matter from the three worlds (see below) and builds it into bodies, suitable for life in those worlds, beginning in the stage of barbarism, as a savage of a low type. During earth-life he gathers experiences, pleasant and painful; after death he meets the results of these experiences—the lower in the intermediate world, where he suffers in the appropriate body of matter belonging to that world, and the higher in the heavenly world, where he enjoys in the appropriate body of matter belonging to that world, and converts all these experiences into mental and moral capacities. When all are thus converted, he returns to earth-life, bringing with him these capacities wrought out of experiences, into new bodies built to express and utilize them. In these he goes through a similar cycle, gathering, suffering, transmuting, and so on and on; each birth brings the fruitage of the preceding lives to start the new pilgrimage, and this is the inborn character and temperament mental, moral, physical. Step by step he climbs the ladder, working under inflexible and inviolable laws, until he reaches the stature of the perfect man; he passes through all the classes of the school of life until he has mastered all that this world has to teach, and is *asekha*—he who has no more to learn. He is then a man, beyond birth and death, 'fitted for immortality,' ready for work in the larger life.

[1] In his Essay 'Of the Immortality of the Soul.'

4. Scientific teachings.—Theosophy differs from modern science in the fact that it includes under 'science' investigations into superphysical worlds. Its methods are the same: investigation by observation of objective phenomena, reasoning on observations, framing of hypotheses, discovery of invariable sequences (*i.e.* of natural laws), repeated experiments to verify deductions, and formulation of results. It uses the senses for observation, but the senses intensified — supersenses, in fact—responding to vibrations of matter finer than that which affects the physical senses.

As with modern science, so with theosophical—'occult science,' it is usually called—there is a body of accepted facts, laid down by recognized experts and largely reverified by later experiments, and a fringe of modern discoveries, constantly added to, revised, and modified. The accepted facts have been established by generations of occult experts, and their existence is often referred to in the scriptures of various religions; the more accessible of these are being constantly reverified by occult students to-day, but the larger cosmological facts are beyond our reach. Any discoveries made by students are subject to revision and modification, as observations are repeated and the instruments of observation are improved.

(*a*) *The constitution of the universe.*—The broad outline of this comes from the seers of the past, and is largely confirmed in the scriptures. It appears reasonable to us, and is congruous with the observations which we are able to make. The laws of analogy and recapitulation confirm it, for we see its outlines repeated in miniature within our own range of observation, and we see sequences rapidly repeated in miniature which the seers have described as occurring in a universe—as the æonian evolution of the kingdoms of nature is mimicked in the growth of the embryo in the womb. A universe consists of seven kinds of matter, or planes, of which the densest is called physical or solid; the next finer, astral, or watery; the next, mental or fiery; the next, spiritual or airy; the next, superspiritual or ethereal; and the two finest, divine. What are called solar systems are all on the physical plane of the universe, and a solar system repeats within itself the seven kinds or states of matter, these subdivisions of the vast cosmic plane forming its planes, or worlds.

Within a solar system these subdivisions can be mostly studied by less developed seers, and we are in a field of research open to the occult student of our own day. We find in relation to our own earth: 'physical matter,' all formed by aggregations of similar physical atoms, similar except that some are positive, some negative; these aggregations are grouped into solids, liquids, gases, and three kinds of ethers; 'astral matter,' formed by aggregations of astral atoms, differing from physical atoms in shape, and grouped into states corresponding to the physical; 'mental matter,' formed by aggregations of mental atoms, again distinguishable by their form, and again grouped as before; the 'spiritual' and 'superspiritual worlds' are formed on the same plan, each having its own type of atom and its own corresponding states of aggregation. Of the 'divine worlds' we cannot directly speak.

(*b*) *The constitution of man* is analogous to that of the solar system, and hence the possibility of knowledge concerning it. As said, he is a fragment of the Universal Self, and he is clothed in the matter of his system. In the divine world dwells his true self, the monad, and his consciousness appropriates matter from each of the five worlds below in order that he may know and conquer them; as the continuing 'I,' he uses matter from the superspiritual, spiritual, and the finer regions of the mental world; this is the 'spiritual body' of which St. Paul speaks; it grows and evolves through the whole cycle of reincarnation, and beyond, but is not changed or lost in birth or death; probably St. Paul refers to this when he speaks of our 'house not made with hands, eternal in the heavens,' which he says 'we have.' It is this spirit in the spiritual body which is the reincarnating Ego, or individual, though the term is often used to indicate only the consciousness working in the finer mental matter, in what is termed 'the causal body,' a subdivision of the spiritual taken separately. When the reincarnating Ego takes a new birth, he appropriates some of the coarser matter of the mental world for his 'mental body,' some of the matter of the astral world for his 'astral body,' some of the matter of the physical world for his 'physical body'; his consciousness, in thinking, uses mental matter; in desiring or sensating, uses astral matter; in acting in the physical world, uses physical matter; these are 'the three worlds' in which his evolution goes on, and in which he is affected by birth and death, and is a personality, or person, *i.e.* the individual, as limited in expression by grosser matter; the mental body is closely related to the brain, though not dependent on it, save for activity in the physical world; the astral body is mainly correlated with the cerebro-spinal and sympathetic ganglia and nerves, and the glands; the three bodies interpenetrate each other, mutually acting and reacting throughout waking life. In sleep consciousness withdraws from the physical body, clothed still in its astral and mental garments, living then in the astral world, and sometimes, on its return, impressing on the physical brain some of its experiences in vivid and coherent 'dreams'; it keeps in magnetic touch with its physical body. In death this magnetic touch is broken off, and the consciousness dwells for a while in the astral world, called often 'the intermediate world,' in relation to those who have passed away from earth. After a while the astral body dies, and the man passes in the mental body into the mental world, or heaven, where he abides for a period extending to many centuries, the length depending chiefly on the richness of his intellectual, emotional, and artistic past life on earth. When he has assimilated all the experiences of this nature accumulated on earth, the mental body disintegrates, the consciousness withdraws to the spiritual body with all it has gathered to enrich the Ego. Then the Ego builds a set of new bodies for a new pilgrimage in the three worlds, and returns to them by birth. Thus the evolution of man is carried on in three worlds, brooded over by the spirit—himself—the spirit garnering the results and unfolding thereby; he is an inhabitant of the three during waking life; of two during sleep and for a period after death; of one during his heavenly life. The lowest, the physical body, is at present the most perfectly organized, and therefore the most capable of receiving impressions from without and transmitting them to the consciousness. The astral body is rapidly becoming organized, and its proper senses are developing, so that it is receiving and transmitting many impressions from the astral world, though generally with a lack of sharpness and accuracy; these include the phenomena of second-sight, premonitions, warnings, visions, perception of phantasms of the living and the dead, etc.—the phenomena to which modern psychology is paying so much attention. An increasing number of people are 'sensitive,' or 'psychic,' and are using the supersenses, *i.e.* the senses of the astral body, more or less consciously. The mental body is becoming well organized in educated people, but more in relation to its organ, the brain, than as an independent vehicle of consciousness, active in its own world. Consciousness, in the mental body, is in-turned rather than outward-turned. The occultist, having by the practice of special methods—meditation, concentration, etc.—artificially forced the evolution of the astral and mental bodies beyond the normal, is, as regards these, many centuries ahead of his time; he uses the supersenses for life in the astral and mental worlds in his waking consciousness, and thus carries on his investigations in them as the physical scientist does in the physical world. The dying of the three bodies, and the building of new ones for each successive life-period, is the cause of the loss of memory of past lives; that memory is in the reincarnating Ego, and is shared by the consciousness when animating the lower bodies only if, in those bodies, the man has realized himself as one with the higher.

(*c*) *The law of action and reaction* is universal, and exists in the worlds of emotion, thought, and spirit as much as in the physical world. Hence a man can build his character as scientifically as he can build up his body, and disregard of the mental and moral laws is as destructive of mental and moral health as disregard of physical laws is destructive of physical health. The study and utilizing of the laws, summed up as *karma*, forms an important part of theosophical work.

(*d*) *Evolution.*—The monad gradually unfolds his powers by coming into touch with matter and appropriating portions of it; he thus passes through the mineral, vegetable, and animal kingdoms, until in a highly developed animal the intelligence reaches the human stage; thenceforward reincarnation under *karma* is his means of unfolding. Humanity, on our globe, takes on a fresh type—more delicately organized as to the nervous system—that of a root-race, when a considerable number of reincarnating Egos are ready to develop a higher quality of consciousness. The third, or Lemurian, race, was the first to assume the really human type in the middle period of its evolution—the previous types being embryonic; the surviving remnants of the Lemurian are the negroes and the many negroid peoples scattered over the world. The fourth, or Atlantean, race with its seven sub-races—of which the Toltec, Akkadian, Turanian, and Mongolian peoples are typical—is still the most numerous. The fifth, or Āryan, race has already five sub-races—the Āryans of India, the Mediterranean Āryans (Arabs, the later higher-class Egyptians, etc.), the Iranians, Celts, and Teutons—and has yet to develop two more. These varying types afford to the reincarnating Egos the necessary varieties for their evolution, each Ego taking birth in the races and sub-races as often as is necessary for the unfolding of the qualities characteristic of each.

(*e*) *Human perfection.*—By repeated reincarnations under inviolable law, each man reaping exactly as he has sown, man reaches his temporary goal—human perfection. At the present stage of evolution it is possible for him to reach this goal in advance of the evolutionary term, which will last yet for many millions of years. By strenuous exertions and noble and unselfish living, he may attract the attention of the spiritual guardians of mankind, who will teach him how to quicken his evolution, so that he may enter on 'the path of holiness,' pass through its five initiations—or stages of widening consciousness—and become a 'master,' the last of the five initiations opening the gateway of superhuman evolution. He may then pass into other worlds, or enter the ranks of the guardians of this world, as he wills. From the hierarchy of these guardians have come the founders of world-religions, the lesser prophets and teachers being their disciples.

5. The ethics of theosophy.—These are not definitely formulated into any code, but consist of the highest and purest teachings of the world's noblest saints, prophets, and founders of religions. All that is sweetest and most lofty in the world's Bibles, all that is most inspiring and ennobling in the writings of its philosophers and moralists, forms the ethics of theosophy. As man lives by the highest ethic he can grasp, he becomes capable of appreciating ethic yet sublimer; the theosophist strives to live by the spirit of Christ rather than by any legal code, and, cultivating love, he hopes to be enlightened by the lords of love. Broadly speaking, that which works with the Divine Will in evolution is right; that which works against it is wrong; and the best examples of that Will are found in such divine men as the Buddha and the Christ. These the theosophist looks up to as examples, and strives to reproduce their likeness in himself.

6. The Theosophical Society.—This association was founded on 17th Nov. 1875, in New York City, U.S.A., by Helena Petrovna Blavatsky and Henry Steele Olcott. The former was a Russian noblewoman, of extraordinary psychic endowments, and these had been trained and cultivated to the highest point by her 'master,' an Eastern occultist; she gave up social rank, wealth, and family to seek him in Tibet, and spent some years with him near Shigatze, after which, returning to the world, she gave the rest of her life to carrying out his directions. In America she met, at the famous Eddy farmhouse, a man who had won high distinction during the Civil War, Colonel Henry Steele Olcott, and he became her pupil. She endeavoured first to collaborate with the American spiritualists, but, failing in this, she, with Olcott, founded the Theosophical Society; she became its corresponding secretary, an office which she held for many years, and he its president; its organization is due to him and he remained president until his death in 1907, when the present writer was elected as his successor.

The unit of organization is a lodge, of not less than seven members; when a number of lodges, not less than seven, exist in any territory, they may group themselves into a section, or national society, which is self-governing, within the wide limits of the general constitution. The central ruling body consists of president, vice-president, treasurer, recording secretary, a general council consisting of the general secretaries, each elected by his own national society, with not less than five additional councillors, chosen by the general secretaries. It meets once a year and deals only with matters affecting the whole Society; but it may not meddle with the business of the sections, unless there be a transgression of the general constitution. The annual report of 1917 showed 19 national societies, 1074 lodges, with 28,673 active members. Round each lodge are gathered a considerable number of sympathizers and helpers, but these are not entered on the rolls. The headquarters of the Society were first in New York; in 1879 the founders left America for India, and fixed the headquarters in Bombay; in December 1882 they moved to Adyar, a suburb of Madras, and there the headquarters have since remained. The Theosophical Society owns there an estate of 266 acres, with several fine buildings, and a library which is known all over the world of scholarship as possessing the finest existing collection of *Upaniṣads*, as well as some unique Sanskrit MSS.

While the Society exists for the purpose of spreading the ideas formulated above, it does not impose belief in them on its members, who, providing they accept the principle of universal brotherhood, are absolutely free to think as they will. Admission to membership is obtained on recommendation of two Fellows of the Society, and the acceptance of the following objects:

'To form a nucleus of the Universal Brotherhood of Humanity, without distinction of race, creed, sex, caste or colour.

To encourage the study of comparative religion, philosophy, and science.

To investigate the unexplained laws of Nature and the powers latent in man.'

The following, written many years ago by the present president, states the general position of the Theosophical Society:

'The Theosophical Society is composed of students, belonging to any religion in the world or to none, who are united by their approval of the above objects, by their wish to remove religious antagonisms, and to draw together men of good will, whatsoever their religious opinions, and by their desire to study religious truths and to share the results of their studies with others. Their bond of union is not the profession of a common belief, but a common search and aspiration for Truth. They hold that Truth should be sought by study, by reflexion, by purity of life, by devotion to high ideals, and they regard Truth as a prize to be striven for, not as a dogma to be imposed by authority. They consider that belief should be the result of individual study or intuition and not its antecedent, and should rest on knowledge, not on assertion. They extend tolerance to all, even to the intolerant, not as a privilege they bestow, but as a duty they perform, and they seek to remove ignorance, not to punish it. They see every religion as an expression of the DIVINE WISDOM, and prefer its study to its condemnation, and its practice to proselytism. Peace is their watchword as Truth is their aim.

Theosophy is the body of truths which forms the basis of all religions, and which cannot be claimed as the exclusive possession of any. It offers a philosophy which renders life intelligible, and which demonstrates the justice and the love which guide evolution. It puts death in its rightful place as a recurring incident in an endless life, opening the gateway of a fuller and more radiant existence. It restores to the world the Science of the Spirit, teaching man to know the Spirit as himself, and the mind and body as his servants. It illuminates the Scriptures and doctrines of religions by unveiling their hidden meanings, and thus justifying them at the bar of intelligence, as they are ever justified in the eyes of intuition.

Members of the Theosophical Society study these truths, and Theosophists endeavour to live them. Every one willing to study, to be tolerant, to aim high, and to work perseveringly, is welcomed as a member, and it rests with the member to become a true Theosophist.'[1]

There have been some offshoots from the Theosophical Society which have become independent of the central organization, but which spread the same truths. There are two international societies, with headquarters in America, and some scattered independent bodies in Germany and Austria.

LITERATURE.—i. *TEACHINGS OF THEOSOPHY.*—C. W. Leadbeater, *An Outline of Theosophy*, London, 1902; Lilian Edgar, *Elements of Theosophy*, do., 1903; Ethel Mallet, *First Steps in Theosophy*, do. 1905; Annie Besant, *Popular Lectures on Theosophy*, do. 1910, *The Ancient Wisdom*, do. 1897, *Seven Principles of Man*, do. 1892, *Re-incarnation*[4], do. 1905, *Death and After*, do. 1893, *Karma*, do. 1895, *Man and his Bodies*[2], do. 1900; C. W. Leadbeater, *The Astral Plane*, do. 1895, *The Devachanic Plane*, do. 1898; H. P. Blavatsky, *The Key to Theosophy*, do. 1893, *The Secret Doctrine*, 2 vols., do. 1888; A. P. Sinnett, *Esoteric Buddhism*, do. 1883, *The Growth of the Soul*, do. 1896.

ii. *ON WORLD RELIGION AND THE WISDOM-TRADITION.*—G. R. S. Mead, *Fragments of a Faith Forgotten*, London, 1900, *Orpheus*, do. 1908, *Thrice-Greatest Hermes*, do. 1906; C. W. Leadbeater, *The Christian Creed*[2], do. 1904; Annie Besant, *Four Great Religions*, do. 1897, *The Religious Problem in India*, do. 1902, *Esoteric Christianity*, do. 1901, *Popular Lectures on Buddhism*, do. 1907; Isabel Cooper-Oakley, *Traces of a Hidden Tradition in Masonry and Mediæval Mysticism*, do. 1900.

iii. *ETHICAL.*—Annie Besant, *In the Outer Court*, London, 1895, *The Path of Discipleship*, do. 1896; H. P. Blavatsky, *The Voice of the Silence*, do. 1899; Mabel Collins, *Light on the Path*[3], do. 1896; Annie Besant, *Bhagavaḍ Gītā*, trans., do. 1899, *Studies in the Bhagavaḍ-Gītā by a Dreamer*, do. 1894, *The Doctrine of the Heart*, do. 1899, *The Wisdom of the Upanishats*, do. 1906, *Dharma*, do. 1899.

iv. *SCIENTIFIC AND OCCULT.*—Annie Besant and C. W. Leadbeater, *Occult Chemistry*, London, 1909, *Thought Forms*, do. 1905; C. W. Leadbeater, *Man Visible and Invisible*, New York, 1903, *Clairvoyance*, London, 1899, *Dreams*[2], do. 1903; Annie Besant, *Introduction to Yoga*, do. 1913, *The Building of the Kosmos*, do. 1894, *The Evolution of Life and Form*, do. 1899, *Some Problems of Life*, do. 1900, *Thought-Power, its Control and Culture*, do. 1901; Bhagavān Dās, *The Science of the Emotions*, London and Benares, 1900, *The Science of Peace*, do. 1904, *The Science of Social Organisation*, Benares, 1910.

A. BESANT.

[1] *Theosophy*, p. 91.

THEOSOPHY.—Theosophy has characteristics which relate it closely to religion, and somewhat more remotely to philosophy. It also attempts to determine man's place in the universe and to solve the riddles of life and of death. Like religion, it aims at guaranteeing to its followers a more favourable destiny by showing them the way of healing and salvation. Like philosophy, it proposes to have recourse only to the resources which nature, on the one hand, and the human intellect on the other, place at its disposal, and it is by knowledge that it saves men. But the knowledge which it obtains is not grounded on the observation of facts which are within the reach of ordinary intelligences; it is intuitive, dependent on the exceptional clear-sightedness of men on a superior level, and communicated by them to their disciples. There is then a theosophical knowledge, just as there is a religious and a philosophical knowledge. Besides, it may well be that the content is throughout materially the same. Such a concept, *e.g.*, as that of the immortality of the soul may be found in all three. By what distinctive marks then can we recognize that a doctrine is theosophical? Now we know that there is a criterion which makes it possible for us, without risk of error, to distinguish between what is philosophical and what is religious. If a doctrine has been established by means of observation, induction and deduction, it is philosophical; it is religious if there has been concerned in its origination an intuition operating under the influence of feeling and imagination; it is only at subsequent stages that the ordinary processes of the human intellect intervene. Theosophy also begins with affirmations having an intuitive basis, and its constructions may have great emotional and imaginative significance. Having once secured this foundation, it may proceed, like theology, to construct, in accordance with the demands of reason, a system of satisfying coherence. The difference between theosophy and religion lies neither in their ideas nor in their method. It is in the attitude which the religious man, on the one hand, and the theosophist, on the other, assume towards the objects presented. The one hopes to work, by fear, reverence, and adoration, upon the will of powerful beings for his own advantage; the other depends upon himself, upon the immediate efficacy of his own knowledge and action; religion is humble, whereas theosophy is proud.[1]

This self-reliance the theosophist has in common

[1] It is to be noticed, however, that, though the suggestion of pride is justifiable in connexion with the esoteric tendencies, the prevailing intellectualism, and calm acceptance of grades of religious capacity noticeable in modern theosophical teaching, yet there is also an element of humility frequently to be found in the modern theosophical attitude. There is a constant reference to teachers or adepts, and it is urged that their teaching should be accepted with implicit faith. The general efficacy of knowledge in obtaining the desired results may indeed be exaggerated and become an incentive to pride, but the individual thinker is not encouraged to depend merely on his own knowledge or even on the knowledge of his contemporaries. He, and they also, must look backwards with reverence to the past and accept the teachings which have been handed down from remote ages and are rediscoverable for men of the present age when the more modern excrescences upon religious systems have been removed.

with the magician. Both—the one more consciously than the other—admit the existence in the universe of hidden forces, for the control of which knowledge of them is sufficient. Both also show individualistic tendencies. They detach themselves from the religious community and break through the tradition officially recognized around them. But we may notice at least this difference between the magician and the theosophist: the one aims at using his power in an external way—he desires to control nature for the advantage or the disadvantage of his fellows; the other is a contemplative, who acts but little except on himself and for his own sake.[1] The theosophical spirit has left a very deep mark upon Indian thought. It is possible to trace its influence from its origin to our own day. India would be for the investigator a remarkable field for study if the chronological sequence of ideas and systems were not enveloped in a darkness which up to the present time has not been penetrated. It is impossible for us to date the most important of the texts from which we derive our information. Many of them are much later than the period when the theories which they set forth were formulated. Under such circumstances it becomes exceedingly difficult to settle the debit and credit side of the account of each school. Perhaps, however, one result may be considered to be now established: there has been in India a continuity of theosophical tendency. The systems interlace with and influence one another. The intuition on which their authors pride themselves consists in perceiving afresh the 'truths' which a kind of heredity has tended to fix in the Indian mentality. The task of the great philosophical schools has to a large extent been that of systematizing the ideas already worked out in the *Upaniṣads*. Buddhism would be unintelligible if the way had not been prepared for it, if not in these very schools, at least in antecedent groups bearing a very strong resemblance to them. And the reformers who have appeared in India in such large numbers since the Middle Ages have drunk at the same source. If, then, we cannot yet dream of giving a strictly historical presentation of theosophical speculations, it is at least not impossible to discern the order in which the principal systems have appeared. We shall follow (1) the development of this thought in circles which are, if not, strictly speaking, Brāhmanic, at least closely related to Brāhmanism (the *Upaniṣads* and the Vedānta, the Sāṅkhya, and the Yoga); (2) the transformation of theosophy into religion (into Jainism and Buddhism); (3) its incursions into popular religions of long standing, with which it has associated itself, not without a certain sacrifice of its own character and significance; and finally

[1 This statement should, however, be slightly modified when applied to modern theosophy in India. On the one hand, this shows an affinity to magic, in that it is greatly interested in the details of existence upon planes other than the physical, and so takes up a slightly materialistic attitude to those existences which are ostensibly non-material. The inhabitants of the astral and mental planes might for practical purposes be described as materializations of spiritual entities. Again, a distinct claim is put forward by theosophy to the discovery and use of hitherto unknown laws of nature, and the power which is thus put into the hands of the expert occultist who is also a theosophist is not altogether different from the power claimed by the magician. But, on the other hand, it must be frankly acknowledged that the modern theosophist in India does not, like some magicians, separate himself from the community to such an extent as to desire to use his powers for merely selfish purposes. Further, the ends at which he aims are ultimately of a spiritual rather than of a materialistic character, and in this he shows his superiority over the Christian Scientist in respect of the excessive attention paid by the latter to the claims of bodily health. It is thus undoubtedly true that the modern theosophist is a contemplative, to the extent that he places the spiritual far above the material, but he is perhaps less inclined than his forefathers in India to be interested merely in his own concerns, and he is more inclined to use for social purposes the powers which contemplation and thought-concentration have secured for him.]

(4) we shall see how modern theosophy in India is dominated by ancient philosophical tradition.

1. The Brāhmanic theosophy.—(1) *The beginnings.*—The two tendencies which characterize Hindu thought throughout its course appear early in Brāhmanic circles. The one is the spirit of tradition: the rites and formulas do not show the expected results unless they are repeated just in the way in which the 'fathers' instituted them at the beginning. Not only will every innovation and every addition be avoided, but an even more necessary requirement is that the sacred acts shall be performed only by those who are in possession of liturgical knowledge, viz. by the Brāhmans. The *dharma*, *i.e.* the rule, which derives its authority simply from its antiquity, thus gradually extends its domination over men's minds. It becomes systematized in one of the six *darśaṇas*, the *Pūrvā Mīmāṃsā*. Anxious care in observing traditional forms has created the power of the priesthood. The fathers of families have been deprived of their religious importance to the advantage of the Brāhmans. The gulf between sacred and profane makes itself more and more evident.

Contrariwise, it is the spirit of novelty which manifests itself in the other tendency. During all the Vedic period the treasury of hymns and rites is taking form and being constantly enriched. If the gods have at first made use of these, it is not the gods who have revealed the knowledge of them. The *ṛṣis* have 'seen' and have communicated their visions to men.[1] The gods would have preferred to have the exclusive proprietorship.

Signs of this double tendency are to be found even in the same texts. We may be sure that, in circles as yet differing slightly from one another, tradition and originality existed side by side without offence. Why should they have entered into conflict? Did not both of them find their point of departure in the same hymns? Most of the Vedic deities can scarcely be distinguished from the forces and elements in which they reveal their power. They have almost no characterization, and they represent vaguely the divine which permeates the objects and phenomena of nature. Out of this naturalism, frequently rude in character, there easily emerge the pantheistic conceptions which were so soon to dominate Indian theosophy. Besides, do not ritualists and innovators alike make knowledge the essential condition of religious efficacy? Are not both of them Brāhmans, *i.e.* the heirs of the magicians who were charged at the beginning with the protection of the sacred rite from the pernicious influence of evil spirits? Finally—and most important of all—do not both believe that there is in every being and in every sacred act a mysterious energy which establishes harmony and co-ordination between man and the universe? And are they not now on the earth, like the 'fathers' of ancient times and the gods in the heavens, the depositaries and the agents of this mysterious force, creator of order and of life? When there is the thought of turning the secret power of the sacrifice to the benefit of the individual, with a view to assuring him of happiness beyond the grave and guaranteeing him against a second death which would be final, there are here the essential elements of theosophic doctrine—desire for deliverance from suffering and death, hope to succeed by personal effort, confidence in the saving efficacy of knowledge.

(2) *The ancient Upaniṣads.* — Theosophical thought, which is to be found in germ in the hymns and in the *Brāhmaṇas*, obtains form and consistency in the *Upaniṣads* (*q.v.*). Certainly the authors of those old treatises were far from

[1] See art. INSPIRATION (Hindu).

having broken their connexion with the traditional cult. But they love to give the sacred actions a symbolic interpretation which will relieve them of their mechanical and formal character. A still more significant thing is that they manifest a well-marked esoteric tendency: usually a long time is spent in appealing to the master before he consents to reveal the supreme truth, and the disciple is under obligation not to transmit it himself except to a particularly dear and well-qualified person. The method of discovery is always intuition; thought proceeds by abrupt illuminations. Moving impetuously and boldly, it puts assertions side by side with one another without concerning itself about their contradictoriness. It does not demonstrate; it is content to illustrate by beautiful metaphors and arresting similes.

In an as yet vague form the idea of the essential unity of the universe was implicitly contained in the Brāhmanic theory of sacrifice. There is now posited the existence of a Being in which all that is finds its reality. This Being is called *Brahman*, the name of the energy which manifests itself in the sacred action. It is also designated the *ātman*, *i.e.* the self or the soul of all that lives.

'Let one worship *Brahman*, knowing that he is the reality. Let one worship the *ātman*. The *ātman* has for body the life; for form, the light; for essence space. It can take all forms according to its inclination. . . . It permeates all the world. . . . It is the essence of life; it is the essence of myself.'[1]

Thus the theme is stated which the *Upaniṣads* go on to develop and repeat without intermission.

This Being is one and absolute. He has no determinations. One can say nothing of him except that he is. No definition is possible. We may at least try to name him, so convinced are we still that we know the Being of which we know the name. He is 'that,' *tat*. He is 'No, no,' for we deny every quality, which would serve only to limit him. He is the reality—the reality of realities, *satya satyasya*. Beyond the reach of all comparisons, he is bliss, a negative bliss, and, in consequence, absolute. He is without a second. He is my *ātman*, the reality of *me*. There is an identity between the *ātman* which I am and *Brahman*. 'I am *Brahman*.' 'Thou, thou art that.' The universal soul and the individual soul are one.

The world also is real. It derives its reality from *Brahman*, the only reality. A parallel between the psychical and the cosmical is founded upon the unity between the individual soul and the world soul. The cosmos and the ψυχή are the two aspects of the same reality, and the parallel elements which constitute them sustain themselves upon each other.

Finally, *Brahman* is the reality not only of the individual and of phenomenal existence, but also of transcendental existence. For there are two forms of *Brahman*, the one corporeal, the other incorporeal; the one mortal, the other immortal; the one mobile, the other immobile; the one manifested (*sat*), the other transcendent (*tyat*).[2]

In its individualized form the soul could not have the bliss which is the exclusive prerogative of the Absolute Being. The limited Ego is in contact with the non-Ego, and is unhappy while experiencing the alternations of pleasure and of pain, the impermanence and the vanity of finite things. In truth, 'he who is another than himself is suffering.' This misery is born of individuality and lasts equally long. The active self, the *jīva*, is involved, through its activity, in a series of existences of which each one is determined as to its quality by the quality of the existence which has preceded it. 'According as a man acts, according as he conducts himself, so is he reborn.'[3] 'Through good work a man is reborn in a good state, through evil work in an evil state,'[4] and so on, indefinitely. If the life is evil, it is because the man in his ignorance believes himself a person and says, 'I am such and such a one, this thing belongs to me.' This error and the activities which result from it entangle him in the meshes of a life which ever begins anew. Thus the wise man yearns after repose in the Absolute, in the bosom of a Being in whom alone are permanence and truth. How shall a man succeed in quenching individuality, which is the cause of all suffering? It is not by means of action, since action on the contrary is a source of individual life. Even asceticism has only the value of a propædeutic: it tends towards salvation, but it does not save. One way only is open to the soul desirous of deliverance, and that is knowledge. Knowledge is necessary, not now of rites and their meaning, but of *Brahman* himself. And since knowledge of *Brahman* means realization of the identity of the self and the Being who alone exists, one must be able to say to this Being: 'Thou, thou art the *ātman* of all that exists. That which thou art, I am that. . . . Thou art the Reality.' This saving knowledge can be reached only through inner vision. The individual suppressing his senses destroys all contact with the outer world and finds *Brahman* in himself. 'The eye would not flash forth to meet him, nor word, nor sense, nor works, nor ascetic practices. But if the mind is calm, if the heart is pure, then one contemplates the indivisible *Brahman*. One cannot know him except in the heart.'[1] If the Absolute cannot be grasped, one may at least approach him by intense meditation directed towards the symbols of him, and very especially by meditation upon the mystic syllable *Om*, for 'in truth this syllable is *Brahman*; in truth it is the supreme existence; it is the best fulcrum of existence; it is the ultimate ground.'[2] United with *Brahman*, the individual self has no more a distinct consciousness. 'It is when there are two existences that one hears, sees, and knows the other, but when for any one everything has become his own proper self, how could there be anything which he could see, hear, and understand?'[3] Moreover, absorbed in the Being who is altogether happiness, he shares in this infinite bliss.

(3) *The Vedānta.*—Of the six philosophical schools which claim connexion with Brāhmanism—more exactly, of the six schools which Brāhmanism has claimed as its own and which it has annexed—three only have given assistance to the elaboration of theosophical doctrine. They are the Sāṅkhya, the Yoga, and the Vedānta (*qq.v.*). The last school is the only one of the three which devotes itself to an explicit continuation of the ancient *Upaniṣads*. We shall therefore begin with it, although, very probably, it did not attain its full development until after the two others.

The name Vedānta does not designate a single homogeneous school. There is a strictly monistic Vedānta: reality pertains to *Brahman* alone; all outside of him is nothing but appearance (*advaita*); this is the thesis of Śaṅkara,[4] at the beginning of the 9th century. Other Vedāntins profess a modified monism—the Viśiṣṭâdvaita of Rāmānuja (*q.v.*; 11th century). Others finally abandon monism altogether, not in the sense that they put mind and matter over against each other, but because they allow an essential difference between the individual self and the universal self; these last attach themselves to Mādhva (*q.v.*; 12th century). But, however great their differences, the three teachers all invoke the authority of Bādarāyaṇa, the reputed author of the *Vedānta-Sūtras*, and all three have written on this older teaching a commentary which is the fundamental text of their respective schools.

Rāmānuja has more right than Śaṅkara to claim to continue the teaching of the *Sūtras*. But Śaṅkara more than the two others, more even than Bādarāyaṇa, is in the line of succession to the *Upaniṣads*. While Rāmānuja and Mādhva are explicitly theistic and teach that God, the author of all grace, saves those who give to Him the worship of love and faith, Śaṅkara attributes to God (Īśvara) an apparent existence only, and an accessory rôle in the genesis of salvation. Consequently the history of theosophical doctrines in India is directly concerned with Him alone.

The first *sūtra* of Bādarāyaṇa thus states the object of the Vedānta: 'Now comes the study of *Brahman*.' To know *Brahman*, it is not enough to open the eyes and the ears and search for Being in the world which surrounds us. Between the Ego and the non-Ego there is an irreducible opposition: the senses and the understanding which perceive and appreciate the non-Ego either transfer to the object the qualities of the subject or transfer to the subject that which they believe they know of the object. In either case external cognition is vitiated by error; the true name of this pretended knowledge is 'nescience' (*avidyā*). Outside of us the senses and the understanding give us only the cognition of the phenomena of 'becoming.' Now Being, in reality, does not 'become'; it is. If it were 'becoming,' it would not 'be'; for it is impossible to see how that which is not could come to be. All becoming is only an appearance, an illusion.

This Being, the only reality, retains in the Vedānta the name of *Brahman*. This is the absolute *Brahman*, without determination, or, as the Vedāntins say, without quality; beyond time and space and causation, for time, space, and causation belong to the world of appearance, of *avidyā*. 'Being is one; all plurality results from false knowledge.' As it is impossible for me to doubt the reality of myself—I could not express this

[1] *Śatapatha Brāhmaṇa*, x. vi. 3. 1 ff.
[2] *Bṛh. Ār. Up.* ii. iii. 1.
[3] *Ib.* iv. iv. 1.
[4] *Ib.* iii. ii. 13.

[1] *Muṇḍ. Up.* iii. i. 8 f.
[2] *Kāṭha Up.* i. ii. 15–17.
[3] *Bṛh. Ār. Up.* iv. v. 15.
[4] See art. Śaṅkarāchārya.

doubt except in affirming my existence—'I am *Brahman*,' provided that 'I' am denuded of every quality and of all contingency, of everything which constitutes my individuality. In this way I am *Brahman* entire, for *Brahman*, being absolute, could not have parts.

Nescience is not only a relation between the subject knowing and the object known; it is also the relation which emerges between the absolute *Brahman* and the world of names and forms. To this cosmic power, more particularly, the name *māyā* is given. *Māyā* (*q.v.*) signifies the alteration which takes place in *Brahman* and in the self as both pass from the category of the Absolute into those of time, space, and cause—an illusory alteration, which affects the ultimate Being and the self only in appearance. *Māyā* modifies on the one hand *Brahman* and thus creates the world; but it modifies also in the same way the Ego and creates the individual Egos. By the existence of *māyā* the unqualified *Brahman* becomes the qualified *Brahman*, the effect-*Brahman*, the lower *Brahman*. Śaṅkara gives to this *Brahman* also the name of God, Īśvara; but this God, His attributes, and the world which the lower *Brahman* creates, preserves, and destroys, do not exist save in virtue of nescience; all is phenomenal, illusory. From the point of view of true knowledge, there is neither cause nor effect; neither Īśvara nor world; neither agent nor act; but only Being unchangeable, indeterminate. Under the influence of *māyā*, the *ātman* becomes a *jīva*. The *jīva* becomes individualized through everything which serves it as a substratum, or *upādhi*—the body, the senses, the power of action, and the faculties of knowledge. But the attributes of the *jīva* have no more reality than those of Īśvara. Truly speaking, the self is not a product; it is incorporeal, spiritual, immutable, infinite, one.

For practical purposes and provisionally, both the world and the individual exist. To both of them even Śaṅkara pays considerable attention. Both are subjects and objects of action. Their destiny is determined by *karma*. 'An act cannot be annulled; this is the universal law; or, at least it cannot be annulled except through working out the result.' Action produces life, and life produces action. The self which acts will be reborn for action, and, again, for rebirth. The chain of causes and effects has not had a beginning. How could it have an end? Fortunately, cause and effect, act and result, are the work of nescience. And what nescience has produced, knowledge will destroy. 'As long as nescience has not been abolished, the individuality of the self is not abolished, and the individual soul continues to be the sphere of good and evil.' The individual can, by a knowledge of *Brahman*, escape from *karma* and the misery of a limited life. If he has discovered how he may attain this by a severe spiritual discipline, he can, through concentrating his thought upon himself and by a kind of spontaneous effort, reach the 'perfect vision,' *i.e.*, he can perceive the *ātman* in himself and thus have an intuition of his identity with the supreme *Brahman*. This vision destroys in him the remnants of personality and dissipates the mirage of the empirical world. He is saved. He is *Brahman*, and in consequence he is, in an absolute sense, being, thought, and bliss.

(4) *The Sāṅkhya.* — The Sāṅkhya (*q.v.*) is of ancient origin, for its influence upon primitive Buddhism cannot well be disputed. The main pronouncements of the school are, however, of later date, and several centuries subsequent to the birth of Buddha. Fortunately there are other works—*e.g.*, the *Mahābhārata* and some ancient Buddhistic writings—which mark out the path of development from the *Upaniṣads* to the classical form of the Sāṅkhya. As we now have it, the Sāṅkhya, realistic and atheistical, is Brāhmanical. It has no difficulty in including the Veda among the standards of knowledge. It may be that, originating outside of Brāhmanism, it was at a later date recognized by the latter, and has paid for this advantage by an adhesion, more or less nominal, to the authority of revelation. Nevertheless, as we find in works undoubtedly orthodox the antecedents of several essential doctrines of this system, it is more probable that it has originated from the same circles as those in which the ancient *Upaniṣads* were elaborated. Its genesis can be best explained if it is regarded as a product of reaction against the radical idealism which is implicit in the *Upaniṣads* and develops in the Vedānta.

The Sāṅkhya posits the absolute reality of the empirical world. If it is said that the world of things is the theatre of a perpetual becoming and that it is impossible to predicate being of that which is impermanent, its answer is that a thing is not real only at the moment when it manifests itself; it has also a subtle state, in which it exists potentially in its cause. For the effect is already to be found in its entirety in the cause: 'The effect and its cause are one.' To affirm the reality of things when they are in the subtle state is to assert that they are already substantial. The ordinary man is unable to see them in their causes because his senses are too gross. If, by ecstasy or as a reward of exceptional merit, he intensifies his power of vision, he will perceive the subtle as easily as the gross.

Whether subtle or gross, the world is essentially composite and changing. Now every complex thing implies a simple Being for the sake of whom it is formed; everything that changes changes only for the sake of an immutable Being. Thus, over against a substance composite and changing, the Sāṅkhya philosophy posits a simple and stable substance; with the *prakṛti*, which is the sphere of becoming, it contrasts the *puruṣa*, which is Being. Everything that acts or is acted upon, everything that changes and lives, the object known, the act and the organs of knowledge, all depend upon *prakṛti*. This includes ψυχή as well as φύσις, since, in the living being, the ψυχή must nourish itself like the φύσις, in order to sustain life and growth.

The change which emerges in the physical and psychical universe is a regular evolution, taking the form of a determination, a growing complexity, an increasing materiality. In its creative aspect evolution brings the gross out of the subtle. At the dissolution of the world the gross resolves itself into the subtle. The Sāṅkhya, which has minutely described the successive phases of the evolutionary processes, posits 24 principles (*tattvas*) which are arranged in order, from the *prakṛti*, the common foundation of all phenomenal existence, to the gross elements and their combinations. It is because the *prakṛti* is not simple that it has been able thus to produce all the things of the physical and mental world. It is threefold. It is composed of three factors, themselves substantial, which are called *guṇas*. These are *sattva*, *rajas*, and *tamas*, goodness, passion, and darkness. It is by their presence in infinitely varying quantities that things affect men differently.

The 18 *tattvas* which in the evolution emerge between *prakṛti* at the one end and the gross elements at the other unite to form the 'characteristic body,' the *linga śarīra*. The *linga śarīra* is subtle and is to the gross body as the cause is to the effect; it explains the differences, both physical and psychical, which distinguish individuals from one another. Whilst the gross body is destroyed by death, the *linga śarīra* passes from birth to birth and constitutes the identity of the individual in the series of its existences. In every life it becomes richer or poorer according to all that a man thinks, does, or resolves. It is like capital which bears as interest the quality of succeeding existence. The characteristics of the *puruṣa*, or the soul, are directly the converse of those of *prakṛti*. The *puruṣa* is simple, immutable, inactive, unproductive, without *guṇas*. It is also multiple. Because all the souls have not the same kind of knowledge, and because some are free and others are still bound, it follows of necessity that there is an infinity of souls. But the *puruṣa* is in itself independent of all individualization to such an extent that we can always speak of it in the singular. The *puruṣa* is light and understanding; it is light without even having anything to illumine; it thinks without even having any object of knowledge.

Being and becoming, both infinite, are not placed simply over against each other. There is a relation established between them which explains creation, knowledge, and salvation. The neighbourhood of the *puruṣa* in fact causes in the *prakṛti* an excitation which leads in it to the formation of a subtle body in connexion with each *puruṣa*. But the subtle body is only the substratum of the conscious life. That emerges in virtue of the immediate presence of the soul. It is the form in which is expressed the relation between the *puruṣa* and *prakṛti*. Now this relation involves suffering for the soul. It is real, but it is not inherent in the soul. Because it is real, deliverance is necessary; because it is not inherent, deliverance is possible.

Both the *puruṣa* and the *prakṛti* have to submit to certain consequences of the relation in which they are bound. When illuminated by the *puruṣa*, the modifications which take place in the ψυχή of the individual become conscious. These again are reflected upon the soul, which thus becomes subject to all the interplay of the affections. It is in this roundabout way that the soul arrives at a knowledge of itself. For, though it is the subject of all knowledge, the *puruṣa* cannot know itself directly. This knowledge becomes possible through a reflexion coming from the mirror provided by the internal organ. The *puruṣa*, full of light but inactive, and the *prakṛti*, active but unconscious, stand to each other in the relation of the paralytic to the blind. Their association is discovered to be beneficial for both. In the service of the *puruṣa*, the *prakṛti* is creative, and this creation has no other end than to make knowledge possible for the soul—which knowledge necessarily eventuates in salvation.

A slow and elaborate process is necessary to break the bond and suppress suffering. This is the main intention—not to destroy actual suffering, which on other grounds would be impossible, but to make it abortive in its germ or in the persistent dispositions stored in subtle form in the internal organ. A slow internal struggle brings a man from the natural state—*i.e.* the morbid state—to absolute healing. Works and asceticism may prepare the ground, but it is knowledge which is truly efficacious. By means of study, self-contemplation, and meditation, we may arrive at an assertion of the truth: 'I am not; nothing is mine; this is not me.' One thus gets a direct perception of the distinction between the Ego and the *prakṛti*. To establish this distinction is to destroy the bond and to see the *puruṣa* in its absolute purity. Henceforth the soul has no other substratum than itself; there is no further association with the subtle body, no reflexion cast by it; the soul is healed.

The *prakṛti* also derives advantage from a deliverance which, in effect, suppresses suffering for it, inasmuch as suffering is not felt except for so long as the *prakṛti* is illumined by the soul. As it would not be creative except in relation to the soul and its salvation, it ceases to be active and returns to the original equilibrium of the *guṇas*. Moreover, this healing has no value except for the liberated soul. 'Since, notwithstanding the infinity of time, there are still souls not liberated, there will be such to all eternity.'[1]

(5) *The Yoga.*—It might be asked if in the history of Indian theosophy the place of the Yoga (*q.v.*) is truly next to the Vedānta and the Sāṅkhya, if its affinities are not in an altogether different direction and with the group of systems which, though they adopted many theosophical ideas, are obviously theistic and devotional in tendency. Does it not make a place for God, for that Īśvara who is a 'soul apart,' a unique Being, eternal, all-powerful, all-good, all-knowing, exposed to no suffering, to no desire or change? Does not this God show an infinitely benevolent activity on behalf of men desirous of salvation? Does He not vouchsafe spiritual vision to His elect? Does not the *yogī*, to obtain salvation, surrender himself to God with that feeling of complete abandonment which is called *praṇidhāna*? Finally, is not salvation obtained by means of a discipline in which the strictly intellectual processes have little place? What have the recognized means for purifying the body and delivering the soul from the organ of thought to do with the pursuit of *jñāna*, the knowledge which brings salvation?

It is easy to answer these objections. First of all we may remark that the rôle attributed to Īśvara in the scheme of salvation is really secondary. After the preliminary process is gone through, there is no further intervention of divine assistance to second the efforts of the *yogī*, and everything happens as if he had only his own powers to rely upon. Further, the supreme end is not, by any means, as in theistic religions, eternal life in God or near God; what is desired is the absolute isolation of the individual soul. It follows that, probably, when the Yoga came to be systematized, Īśvara was merely a survival of a period when practices of asceticism and sorcery were associated with Śiva, a god whose vigorous personality might seem incompatible with an exclusively human conception of salvation. In fine, Īśvara was no more an inconvenient intrusion in the Brāhmanical Yoga than in the monistic Vedānta; it is even possible that his presence was indirectly the sign of the penetration of the Yoga by the theosophical spirit.

The Yoga, desirous of specially emphasizing the practical conditions of meditation and saving ecstasy, would naturally disregard study and reflexion, since neither of them was of service in securing the marvellous powers for which the *yogī* was ambitious. But, as in Brāhmanizing itself it had adopted very nearly in its entirety the doctrine of the Sāṅkhya, there was really no need to indicate the acquisition of knowledge as among the demands imposed by the need for salvation. This acquisition could have been considered as implicitly prescribed from beginning to end. In any case it is interesting to point out that in an *Upaniṣad* greatly influenced by Yoga ideas, the *Maitri Upaniṣad*, the examination of reflexion had a place among the members of Yoga. Perhaps we have in this a proof drawn from a period before the Yoga became entirely allied to the Sāṅkhya.

In other characteristics the Yoga shows itself faithful to the theosophical spirit. It rests upon very ancient beliefs closely related to magic. The remarkable manifestations of patience, will-power, and intelligence reveal the presence of supernatural faculties and imply in their possessors a new acquisition of energy. Besides, the accomplishment of salvation depends entirely upon personal effort. There is no possible doubt that the Yoga belongs legitimately to the same spiritual family as the Sāṅkhya and the Vedānta.

[1] *Sāṅkhya Sūtras*, i. 158.

Properly speaking, the Yoga is the act by which the senses and the understanding are held in restraint; turned resolutely in one single direction, the mind acquires greater force and certain new faculties. The processes regarded as efficacious had already been employed for a long time when Patañjali formulated his theory of them. If, as is probable, the author of the *Yoga Sūtras* is the same as the illustrious grammarian of the same name, then this spiritual discipline was systematized in the 2nd cent. B.C. But, in the influence which from the beginning it exerted upon Buddhism, we have proof that it goes much farther back. The proper object of the Yoga, as supplied with doctrines by the Sāṅkhya, is, as the first of the *Sūtras* says, 'the suppression of the modifications of the thinking principle,' *i.e.* of the understanding. Freed from all *chitta*, the *puruṣa* regains its own nature. We are not concerned, as in the Vedānta, with recognizing by an effort of thought the identity of the Ego and the universal self; nor with distinguishing, as in the Sāṅkhya, the self from that which is not the self; the aim is to bring about the integration of the soul, in which consists her salvation.

The *yogī* pupil has difficult conditions to fulfil. A long and painful process of preparation is imposed upon him, so that he may triumph over all the obstacles inherent in the feebleness of man. It is in the first phase of this process that devotion and the practice of mortification have their parts to play. Whenever this propædeutic has fulfilled its functions, the adept may proceed to exercises which lead to the suppression of the intellectual functions and the detachment of the soul. According to the authoritative scheme, the programme of this gymnastic is divided into eight members. Five of these rubrics aim at the bringing of the body under control. They comprise interdictions and injunctions, prescriptions relative to the positions to be taken in meditation, and others which have for their aim the control of breathing, and, finally, the procedure which has to be followed in restraining the senses and destroying communications between the mind and the external world. There is special insistence upon the regulation of the breath, on the ground that individual life and thought are bound up with respiration, and that to control the one is to dominate the other. When, finally, the body has been purified, it becomes possible to exercise control on thought; three kinds of exercises lead it progressively towards unification, the destruction of individuality, and isolation.

Another method, more violent and more complicated, is founded upon a most bizarre kind of physiology. Through modifying and even stopping the circulation of the vital spirits in the channels of the body, the *yogī* succeeds in suppressing the natural functions of the understanding and in exalting the power of action and of vision. Strange phenomena accompany the last phases of this spiritual process: colours appear which are invisible to the ordinary man; sounds are heard; the *yogī* sinks into a 'mystic slumber.' Sometimes also the strain of so much effort ends in madness. The texts expatiate at great length on the manifold advantages which Yoga brings to its disciples. First of all there are benefits of an entirely mundane character: health, youth, and beauty. Especially there is obtained a 'sovereign power' which enables those who possess it to realize immediately all that they desire, to make themselves at will exceedingly small or big, light or heavy; to control the elements; to guide the will or sentiments of another; to change the nature of substances, to distribute their personality amongst several different bodies, etc. But for the *yogī* the spiritual results have more value. In seven stages the soul obtains liberation, first of all from the external world, then from the hindrances which come to it through its association with the organs of the intelligence and the will. Liberated from the world of results, the soul rejoices in pure tranquillity; dissociated from the internal organs, it tastes the ineffable delights of ecstasy, and reaches without any distraction the state of integration (*kaivalya*) in which is its salvation.

Before leaving Brāhmanic theosophy, we may point out that in more than one characteristic it is very closely connected with Western occultism (*q.v.*). Our theosophists have, like the Vedāntists, a marked tendency towards monism; their anthropology has borrowed much from the Sāṅkhya philosophy; they authorize exercises which are not without analogy to those prescribed by the Yoga.

2. Theosophy as the germ of new religions.—In

Brāhmanism the theosophical doctrines are placed alongside of the old tradition, and religious society remains confined to the old framework. When theosophy is transformed into a religion, the conditions are altogether altered. Henceforth a man becomes a member of a community, not because of his birth, but because of his adherence to a certain belief; the idea and the group are co-extensive. Moreover, theosophy ceases to be a mere intellectual doctrine; it takes entire possession of the individual, and aims at maintaining among its adherents the unity of discipline and of life.

Two religions have sprung from the movement of thought which we find permeating the old *Upaniṣads*, viz. Jainism and Buddhism. Seeing that they are born in the same spiritual environment, it is not strange that they should have many characteristics in common. Their doctrines, their legends, their rules of life, have an unmistakable air of family relationship. The worship itself, in its outer forms, is so similar in various particulars that from the outside one might easily confuse the two systems; witness only the tale of Aśvaghosa in which one finds King Kaniṣka worshipping a Jain *stūpa* under the impression that it is Buddhistic. Jainism and Buddhism are both products of the process of crystallization which was a feature of the period of the ancient *Upaniṣads*. Besides Brāhmans practising strict observance of rites and a solitary asceticism, India has been familiar with what one might call wandering cenobitism. The teachers, accompanied by their disciples, go from place to place, not settling down anywhere except during the months of the rainy season. These *parivrājakas*, in the course of instructing their pupils, discuss the most diverse subjects. The groups are not closed. Round about a knot of faithful disciples there gathers a numerous body of adherents and friends. If Jainism and Buddhism have been able to transform themselves into Churches, the reason is that they have understood better than some other *saṅghas* how to attach the laity by solid bonds and to organize the community by fixed rules. There is now no doubt that Jainism is prior to Buddhism. Buddhists themselves do not hesitate to admit the fact. But Jain writings are certainly posterior—and very much so—to those of Buddhism. It may well be that, if there has been borrowing, the Jains have been the debtors. If we begin with them, it is not in order to lay stress on the relative dates, but rather because, on the whole, the Jainist Church has remained more faithful to the theosophical tradition of the *Upaniṣads*.

(1) *Jainism*.—Jainism (*q.v.*) has all the characteristics of a theosophical religion. It puts at the centre of its teaching the doctrine of *karma* (*q.v.*), and shows itself chiefly interested in human destiny. It aims at delivering men from the misery of the *saṁsāra*. It demands that the individual should be the instrument of his own regeneration. It searches for the saving truth beyond phenomena and sensible perception, and, as a consequence, asserts the authority of persons endowed with exceptional faculties of vision and knowledge. It places itself outside the Brāhmanic tradition. Nothing more is heard of Īśvara. Jainism is a 'human' doctrine. Śaṅkara sees in this a reason for its condemnation. Because it opposes to Vedic tradition a new rule, this theologian accuses it of not being 'revealed.' And yet Jainism also makes it a duty for its disciples to have faith in the words of an omniscient master, who made known the way of emancipation, who has triumphed over the world of death, and who, because of this, has received the surname of Jina ('the Victorious').

Perhaps because the Jains appeal to omniscient teachers, they have promulgated a theory of knowledge which forbids any absolute affirmation or denial. Every proposition has a relative value only (*anekāntavāda*); a thing is not thus; in a way it is this; I can say that a thing is not, that it is, and that it is not, that it 'cannot be spoken of,' etc., only if it is understood that these predicates are true merely relatively and under certain reservations (*syādvāda*). As far as one can conjecture from the examples which illustrate the various dialectic 'refractions' (*bhanga*), the aim of the *syādvāda* is to show that nothing can be known except in relation to the totality of the universe, where birth, duration, and death rule together, and that, relatively to this indeterminate universe, things are themselves indeterminate. 'Everything is indeterminate by the very fact of its existence.' [1] The aim of this doctrine was to destroy at one and the same time the monistic dogmatism of the Vedānta and the negations of the sceptical schools.

Everything in the universe comes under one or other of the five categories of substances (*dravya*): soul (better, life), space, merit, non-merit, and material molecules. Souls (*jīva*) and molecules (*pudgala*) are infinitely numerous; space, merit, and non-merit are single. Merit (*dharma*) has the effect of furthering the progress of the soul; non-merit (*adharma*) leaves it stationary. The progress of the soul is the consequence of its *karma*.

In fact, the soul is by its nature limited and active. As limited, it has the dimensions of the body, which serves as its substratum; it is lessened and increased along with the body. As active, it receives in virtue of its *karma* an influx of material molecules, which, according to their quality, are black, blue, grey, yellow, rose-colour, and white, and which affect the *jīva* by giving it various colours. This influx of karmic matter is the bond which links the soul to the *saṁsāra*. The individual who aspires to salvation has the task of purifying his soul. By asceticism he eliminates the *pudgala* which stain it. By draining off the acquired *karma*, asceticism is the essential factor in *nirjarā*, or the burning up of the effects of *karma*. Thus one of the characteristics of Jainism is the extreme importance which it assigns to *tapas*. It is not sufficient to annul the past; it is also necessary to prevent the formation of new *karma*. And this desirable result is produced by discipline, by *saṁvara*. In its two principal forms it prevents the entrance of the karmic *pudgala* into the *jīva*; the two forms are control (*gupti*) and good behaviour (*samiti*). By *gupti* the soul represses the activity of the body, of speech, and of the mind; by *samiti* it so behaves as not to injure or offend any one. Reflexion and meditation are also efficacious means of discipline and of defence against the pernicious influx. Right vision (*i.e.* right faith), right knowledge, and right conduct complete the way of deliverance. And, just as an elixir does not heal any one except him who knows it, has faith in it, and applies it properly, so the Three Jewels cannot produce deliverance unless they are united.

Henceforth, liberated from the *saṁsāra*, the zealous Jain is a *siddha*, a perfected being. He is disburdened of all karmic matter. He is without colour. His soul, lightened of every hindrance—like a flame which rises by its own strength—begins its course upwards towards the higher regions of the universe. There he enjoys a happy and eternal existence. *Mokṣa* has the effect of rendering the *jīvas* detached and free.

(2) *Buddhism*.—Buddhism also is a theosophy which has expanded into a religion. If the 'high priest' of Ceylon can give his approval to the catechism drawn up by Colonel Olcott, and, still more, if the communities of Ceylon, Burma, Japan, and Mongolia give their adhesion to the fourteen articles in which the same writer gathers together the fundamental beliefs of Buddhism, the reason lies in the unmistakable affinity between the tendencies of present-day Buddhism and those of Western theosophical societies. But we have no need of external proof to enable us to assert the fundamentally theosophical character of the teaching of Gautama Buddha.

'As the ocean has only one savour, the savour of water, so the doctrines which I teach and the rule which I establish have only one savour, that of salvation.' [2] Buddha wishes to save men, not from sin, but from suffering and death.

He summons all men to salvation. 'The gate of immortality is open for all beings. Let him who has ears come, hear the Word and believe.' [3]

He rejects the authority and traditional knowledge of the Brāhmans. 'In a line of blind men who attach themselves to one another, the first does not see, the man in the middle does not see, the last does not see. Such are the discourses of the Brāhmans. Their faith is without foundations.' [4]

He makes salvation a personal matter for each individual. 'Be your own lamps; be your own refuge. Do not search outside yourselves for a lamp or a refuge.' [5] 'You must yourselves make the necessary effort. A Buddha is only a counsellor.' [6]

Finally, the framework of the building erected by Buddha

[1] *Sarvadarśana Sutras*, p. 29. [2] *Chullavagga*, IX. i. 4.
[3] *Majjhima Nikāya*, i. 170. [4] *Ib.* ii. 169 ff.
[5] *Dīgha Nikāya*, ii. 101 (=*Mahāparinibbānasutta*, ch. ii.).
[6] *Dhammapada*, v. 276.

is constructed almost entirely from materials borrowed from the Brāhmanical schools, nurtured in the teaching of the *Upaniṣads*.

The method of salvation which Buddha preaches to men includes rules of life and truths of an intellectual character. But since it is well understood that his teaching has but one savour, there is no hint that men should practise virtue because it is virtue, or search for knowledge because of the practical or intellectual satisfaction which knowledge brings. Morality and learning, in intention at least, are looked at only from the narrow point of view of salvation. Thence come the limits within which they move. In fact, Buddha did not wish to teach either morality or science, but only a therapeutic of the will and a therapeutic of the intelligence. When once a man is healed from moral evil and from error, he may work onwards towards salvation.

(*a*) *Therapeutic of the conduct.*—Only a soul purified by moral discipline can receive with profit the teaching of the Law. The most formidable enemy of salvation is the desire for sensual enjoyment. Sensuality figures in all the lists of depravities, infections, obstacles, and hindrances. It is against sensuality that men have chiefly to struggle. Hence the imperious necessity of exercising constant control over the senses. Of all the virtues vigilance is most characteristic of Buddhistic moral teaching.

(*b*) *Therapeutic of the intellect.*—Knowledge is not less necessary than good conduct. Like good conduct, it has chiefly a negative value. In theosophies closely connected with Brāhmanism knowledge is a working out of deliverance in a positive manner, because upon the topics of God, the world, the soul, and human destiny there is a body of knowledge directly efficacious for salvation. But the point of view of Buddha and his earlier disciples is quite different. That which they want is to deliver the mind from unfavourable thoughts which may hinder the individual or at least lead him in a false way. It can be understood how different are the conditions under which the spiritual struggle presents itself according as one admits or denies the existence of eternal and immutable beings, whether immanent or transcendent or both. Buddha's aim was to show that in the succession of phenomena no cause was revealed which was not itself phenomenal, and to deduce from this proposition the consequences affecting the moral life of the individual. The earliest Buddhism neither knew nor wished to recognize anything other than phenomena. Phenomena, both physical and psychical, constitute *dharma*. In us and outside of us we reach nothing but *dharma*, not because of our mental incapacity, but because neither in us nor outside of us is there anything but *dharma*. The constituents of *dharma* are not hung, as it were, upon a substance of which they are the momentary phases; they are themselves the whole reality. Primitive Buddhism is thus at the opposite pole from the Vedānta, which abstracts from phenomena and regards Absolute Being as the only reality.

Whether subjective or objective, phenomena are incessantly changing, and things are involved in a perpetual flux. Phenomena are just those states of individuals and objects of which the essential characteristic is complexity. Now only the simple and homogeneous can be permanent. The human individual is an assemblage of five kinds of aggregates, and this composite is modified from moment to moment. What is called the individual (*pudgala*) is a series, more or less lengthy, of the phases of composites continually altering. The movement of aggregates, or of combinations of aggregates, does not take place by chance, or without any system. One cause determines the condition of every new combination, and this cause is the quality of the antecedent combination. With conscious individuals, who alone are interested in the theory of salvation, the causal combination is an agent, and his action produces results of two kinds; it manifests itself externally as the immediate cause of phenomena, and internally as a modification of the doer himself of the action. *Karma* may be defined as the reaction of the act upon the subject. This reaction takes place generally at 'the dissolution of the body after death,' in such a way that the binding force of one individual life reappears in another individual life. As Buddhism has discarded every hypothesis not connected with visible forms of existence, it does not posit a subtle body as the vehicle of *karma*, or an Iśvara as the controller of resultants. Even at a distance *karma* is a force which works mechanically. Moreover, it fulfils in Buddhism the function of explaining the congenital differences which are found among men, and of awakening in the hearts of the faithful adherents the feeling of their moral responsibility.

Karma is far from being a doctrine specifically Buddhistic. The same cannot be said of the two sets of rules the discovery of which transformed the potential into the actual *buddha*: the Four Noble Truths and the Twelve Causes. These Buddhism has always claimed as its own. The Truths are suffering, its cause, its suppression, and the way which leads to suppression. 'What is impermanent, that is suffering.'[1] 'The craving for existence and for the cessation of existence are the causes of suffering.'[1] 'The suppression of suffering consists in the destruction of the craving by the complete suppression of desire.'[2] We arrive at suppression by following the Noble Eightfold Path—right knowledge, right willing, right speech, etc. The ultimate significance of the Twelve Causes is to explain suffering without having recourse to any principle except those recognized by Buddhism, viz. the aggregates, *karma*, and the Noble Truths. Through one causal link after another, the life of suffering is connected with its deepest source, viz. ignorance. In this way there is excluded the notion of a soul which would be essentially and incurably suffering. There is eliminated also the interference of a God who imposes the suffering upon His creatures; if the misery came from outside, it would not be in the power of man to put an end to it. It does not belong to the Ego as a permanent substance, and, since the older theosophy had shown that man cannot find God except in and through the Ego, Buddhism, in denying the *ātman*, is compelled also to deny *Brahman*, the original and immanent cause of the universe.

[1] *Saṁyutta Nikāya*, iv. 26.

If Buddhism is a theosophy, it is much more a religion. Religion aims at satisfying much more varied needs than does an essentially intellectual doctrine. Religion is a manner of living, and not only a manner of thinking. The necessities of life and of controversy soon compelled Buddhism to extend considerably the range of its practical and dogmatic teaching.

In ethics Buddhism was far from confining itself to the limits imposed by the demands of salvation. In seeking to give the greatest possible effectiveness to its moral pronouncements, Buddhism does not take the trouble to co-ordinate systematically the lessons which circumstances suggest. When it addresses itself to the laity—as frequently happens—it disregards the special conditions of the strictly religious life, and its precepts obtain a universal significance. The exclusive interests of personal salvation are then so far from its thought that the virtues which it enjoins have a social and human value—compassion, charity, humility. Similarly there is an expansion of doctrine. Questions kept in reserve at the beginning soon had to be investigated, and the reason for this was that facility might be obtained for discussing them with rival schools. Ontological and epistemological topics soon became the order of the day. It was inevitable that, even within the limits of Buddhism, some divergent solutions would be proposed. Hence the appearance of sects in which tendencies showed themselves which had hitherto remained latent: the realistic schools of the Sarvāstivādins, the idealistic schools of the Yogāchāras, the nihilist schools of the Mādhyamikas.

The later disciples of Buddha deliberately abandon the prudent agnosticism of their Master. Their speculations are concerned with the transcendental world (*lokottara*). Even the fundamental unity of the universe is affirmed (doctrine of the *tathatā*). It is noteworthy also that Buddha himself, who from the earliest times had been regarded as the perfect example of humanity, comes to represent, in the theory of the Threefold Body, at one and the same time, phenomenal existence, non-sensible existence, and absolute existence—the body of creation, the body of bliss, and the body of the Law.

But, even when considerably amplified, conduct and knowledge are not given more than a negative importance as regards salvation. Upon the soil cleared by them the problem is now to construct the properly religious life. On what plan will this building be erected? It will be no matter of astonishment that, being at once theosophical and religious, Buddhism has conceived a double ideal of life and has proposed two different methods. To become *arhats* and accomplish their own salvation was the aim of the *sthaviras* of the ancient Church; they are the adherents of the Lesser Vehicle. Those of the Greater Vehicle

[1] *Mahāvagga*, I. vi. 20. [2] *Ib.* I. vi. 21.

aspire to become *bodhisattvas* and believe in religious solidarity.[1] It was enough for the first to transform a sinner into a saint; the others have more ambition; they desire that the sinner, following in the footsteps of Buddha, should become a saviour. It can easily be understood that the way of the *arhat* and the career of the *bodhisattva* separated themselves perceptibly from one another.

(α) *The way to arhatship.*—Conversion makes of the Buddhist a new man. He 'enters into the current.' By an energetic and long-continued struggle he destroys in himself the adverse principles. Two roads to the goal now open up before him. The one is through a series of spiritual exercises. Meditation and intense concentration secure in him serviceable tranquillity (*śamatha*). No more of attachment, no more of desires; the very residues of desire are destroyed. The results of the liberation of the heart are clear vision (*vipaśyanā*) and wisdom (*prajñā*). The other way is that of enfranchisement (*vimokṣa*). The path to the awakening is by ecstatic contemplation (*dhyāna*). From ecstasy to ecstasy the monk rises in eight stages (the *samāpatti*) to a state of being which is neither thought nor the absence of thought. It is the suppression of voluptuous ideas, of discursive ideas, of joy, of breathing—the abolition of the world of forms by that of space, and of the world of space by that of knowledge; of the world of knowledge by that of the non-existence of things, and of the last by that in which there are neither ideas nor the absence of ideas. Arrived at this already very elevated stage, the *arya* enters into possession of superior powers (the six *abhijñā*). But it is necessary to go even higher. A ninth and last *samāpatti* leads to the 'dissolution of all conscious perception,' to 'the awakening,' to *sambodhi.* When one has taken the way of wisdom or of enfranchisement, one becomes an *arhat* (*q.v.*), a saint. The *arhat* has done 'that which he had to do.' When his *karma* is drained off, he will be extinguished without his last thought or his last aggregate giving rise to a further thought or a further combination.

(β) *The way to Buddhaship.*—As the ideal is higher, the method is more complicated. The career of the *bodhisattva* (*q.v.*) demands a long preparation and solemn pledges. There must emerge in the man the 'thought of illumination' (*bodhichitta*), that he should take the vow to do everything to arrive at the goal (*praṇidhāna*); that by an act of will he should 'assign' to the advantage of another his actions and the fruit of his actions (*pariṇāmanā*). Then commences the struggle properly so called. In order to obtain illumination, the *bodhisattva* must provide himself with a double equipment, merit and knowledge. The programme which has to be followed includes acts of worship, rules of conduct, and the practice of meditation. The object is to acquire successively the ten perfections (*pāramīta*), each corresponding to a spiritual world (a *bhūmi*). At the end of this long ascent the *bodhisattva* obtains finally the illumination which makes him a *buddha, i.e.* a liberator of creatures, an ultra-phenomenal being still sojourning for a time in the phenomenal world.

For *arhat* and *bodhisattva* the eventuality is the same—*nirvāṇa* (*q.v.*), extinction. What does it matter that neither Buddha nor his authorized disciples have said what *nirvāṇa* is? If one knows that it is the abolition of suffering and death, of relative and individual existence, that is enough to make it an infinitely desirable state. If Buddha has gained control over natures of the most diverse qualities, it is just because he has left them the liberty of imagining a *nirvāṇa* conformable to their needs and their aspirations.

Let us take a look backwards. We may agree that Buddhism has certainly characteristic marks of a theosophical system. It regards ignorance as the source of all the evil of living, and knowledge as the panacea of suffering. It seeks to deliver its adherents from the fear of death. It endeavours to upset the Brāhmanical methods of salvation. It denies that texts or doctrines have any direct value for salvation, and it affirms the value of 'vision,' of intuition arrived at by internal concentration and ecstatic meditation. It demands that every man should be the architect of his own salvation, and, even though it multiplies the 'saviours,' it no less emphasizes for the individual the necessity of personal effort. It teaches that knowledge is power, and that spiritual excellence manifests itself outwardly in extraordinary faculties. It breaks through the traditional framework and urges the individual to work without procrastination towards his regeneration and so to arrange matters that this labour shall fill his whole life.

[1] See artt. HĪNAYĀNA, MAHĀYĀNA.

3. Introduction of theosophy into sectarian religions.—Brāhmanism in its different aspects was only one of the forms of the religious life; in every period there was also the popular current, powerful, infinitely varied, and mobile. Just as in the sacerdotal tradition minutely elaborated rites occupy the principal place, gods and demons are central in the popular religion, and the worship which is given to them, mixed throughout as it is with superstitions and gross practices, answers more fully to the idea which is generally held of devotion and of piety. These two religious contents have not existed side by side without exerting an influence upon each other. We have here to do only with the influence exerted by the theosophy of Brāhmanism. This influence is only a particular illustration of the growing preponderance which the sacerdotal caste obtained in all the moral life of India, and of which the Buddhistic writings themselves give unmistakable evidence. Nothing is more natural than this primacy. The Brāhmanical families had at their disposal two powerful forces, tradition and cohesion. In a society which was crumbling to its foundations they formed a solid group, cemented by community of interest and of ambitions and reinforced by the habits of knowledge and of virtue. Popular forms of worship, legal and social rules, and secular poetry no doubt flourished to a large extent outside of Brāhmanical circles; but the influence of the latter has none the less succeeded in filtering through at every point. Just as Sanskrit, the scholastic idiom of the Brāhmans, invaded the epic and the drama, the popular style, and the literature of business, so the Brāhmans made themselves the theologians of the sectarian religions. They applied to them the methods of their systematizing temperament. They also introduced into them their conceptions of being, of the world, and of destiny, hesitating less to popularize these conceptions since Buddhism had already deprived them of their esoteric character.

We have in the *Mahābhārata* (*q.v.*) excellent evidence of the appropriation by Brāhmanism of materials which were without doubt independent. This document is all the more significant because it shows clear traces of successive accretions, and because its slow elaboration was carried through during the many centuries when the Brāhmans were gradually establishing their spiritual domination. We may regard the poem as completed, in the form in which we know it, at the time when neo-Brāhmanism was triumphant, *i.e.* in the 4th or 5th cent. A.D. And this voluminous encyclopædia of the traditional knowledge of the Hindus is something more than a witness; it was also one of the agents, perhaps the most effective of all, in the expansion of Brāhmanism in India. Before, during, and after the composition of the great epic, a mass of writings emerge to illuminate or supplement its evidence—sectarian *Upaniṣads, Dharmaśāstras* (as the first of which we may regard that which bears the name of Manu), *Purāṇas,* books written in prose or in verse by the numerous reformers of Hinduism or under their influence. Unfortunately the investigation of this rich literature has not yet been completed.

By gaining entrance into works definitely popular, the ideas whose development we have hitherto followed in the texts of a school or in the monastic literature began to exert a powerful influence upon the general thought of India; and nothing proves more effectively the plasticity of religious thought than the faithfulness with which conceptions originally monistic and antitheistic persist, almost unchanged, in sects permeated with the most ardent devotion.

As in the ancient theosophy, the soul is haunted by the thought of death: 'Every being is in fear of death.'[1] 'Some men in their fear of death have died of fear.'[2] 'The world is under the attack of Mṛtyu. How dost thou not think of it?' 'Do to-day that which you will have to do to-morrow: do this morning what you will have to do to-night. Death does not trouble itself with what one has done or with what one has not done. It seizes a man as a wolf carries off a lamb.'[3] There is not a moment to lose: 'the days pass away; life wears to an end. Rouse yourself and run.'[4]

The new religious conceptions bring home to men the necessity and the way of salvation: 'Let a man search for a remedy through the suppression of suffering and let him apply it without murmuring. Then he will be free from misery.'[5] It is the individual life which is full of suffering and death; it is necessary to get deliverance from it: 'Death has two syllables, for it is *mama*, everything that I consider as my own. *Brahman* has three syllables, *na mama*, for in it nothing is mine.'[6] There is always the same hate of the body and its fugitive pleasures: 'Let one becoming an ascetic, abandon this stinking body, full of filth and urine, subject to old age and disappointment, the abode of maladies, burnt by passions and perishable.'[7] 'All the joys which arise from contact with the world are a source of suffering; they begin: they end; the wise man does not find in them any pleasure.'[8]

How is man to be saved? The means of salvation have become more numerous and more varied. There is nothing more interesting than to mark the persistence of the ancient ideas and the traditional formulas. The new has not destroyed the old. Salvation is the result of an effort entirely personal. 'Strengthening your soul by your soul, vanquish the enemy who reclothes the forms of desire, and who is difficult to strike.'[9] 'The *yogī* is he who finds within himself his happiness, within himself his pleasure, within himself his light.'[10] 'Let a man establish the self by the self and suffer not the self to be overwhelmed, for no man has any other friend than himself, or any other enemy than himself.'[11] Salvation is still the result of knowledge, a knowledge which is acquired by concentration of thought and meditation: 'Knowledge is the best vessel (for traversing the sea of the *saṁsāra*).'[12] To know *Brahman* is to obtain peace 'which has as its final result *nirvāṇa*';[13] it is oneself to become *Brahman*.

As may be seen from the last passages, it is the solution of the Vedānta which obtains most favour of all those proposed by the Brāhmanical schools. Recourse is had readily to the Sāṅkhya when one wishes to analyze the universe and the soul, or to the Yoga for teaching as to the practice of concentration and ecstasy; but the theory of *mokṣa* remains essentially monistic and pantheistic. As far as the evidence gathered from the great epic is concerned, the doctrine which is adhered to is not the radical monism of Śaṅkara (which was indeed later than the centuries during which the *Mahābhārata* was finally redacted), but the monism of the *Upaniṣads* and of Bādarāyaṇa: the world of names and forms is real, but it is *Brahman* who is the reality of its reality. The *Bhagavad-Gītā* does not leave any doubt on this point:

'Others offering me the sacrifice of knowledge, give to me worship as to a being at once universal and individual, who, under various forms, extends himself in every direction.'[14] 'The knowledge of goodness is that through which is seen in all beings the one imperishable Being, a whole in every particular being.'[15] 'One portion of me has entered into the world of living beings, as the soul of the individual, the imperishable portion.'[16] 'The knowledge by which thou wilt perceive all beings without exception in thyself and then in me, will for ever give thee a refuge from error.'[17] 'In the Brāhman, in the ox and the elephant, in the dog and also in the eater of the flesh of the dog, the wise man sees only one and the same being.'[18] 'He who sees me in everything and everything in me, is never far from me, and I am never far from him.'[19]

God is immanent in all beings, but He is not confused with them; He is the principle of life which animates them, the principle of all spirituality.

Finally, He is not only immanent; He is also transcendent. Things are in Him, but He is not in them. The world of phenomena does not exhaust His nature. He has an inferior nature which reveals itself in names and forms, and a superior nature which is also a living soul. He is distinguished from the immortal and imperishable *Brahman* of which He is the foundation, just as He is the foundation of eternal law and perfect blessedness. Thus, without going beyond the limits of the *Bhagavad-Gītā*, we can see theism substituting itself for the original pantheism, and a personal God taking the place of *Brahman*. The evolution completes itself in the modified monism of Rāmānuja, and the spiritualistic dualism of Mādhva. The worship of the *guru*, which is so persistent a characteristic of the modern sects, has its source in the same conceptions. God, who is the essential excellence in all beings and in all the categories of being, specially manifests His adorable nature in the persons who behold and who reveal the truth.

When, in a passage from the *Bhagavad-Gītā* which has just been quoted, the god alludes to the 'others,' who offer the sacrifice of knowledge, he puts them over against those who render the worship of love. At once pantheistic and theistic, the poem places on the same level the two methods of salvation—knowledge and *bhakti*. The explanation is that in Hindu thought nothing which has once been acquired is ever altogether eliminated. Tradition and novelty, animism and ritualism, naturalism and theosophy, scholasticism and mysticism—in short, the most contrary ideas—live together in the same minds and in the same writings. In theory the *advaita* may be professed, but in fact the *dvaita*, and even a plurality of co-eternal principles, is affirmed. It is, as it were, tacitly understood that an affirmation has value in itself, and that it is not annulled by adjacent affirmation. In his everyday life Śaṅkara was a Vaiṣṇava—we could hardly imagine this in reading his commentary on the *Vedānta Sūtras*. These men duplicate themselves with wonderful ease. So it is vain to attempt to apply to the *Bhagavad-Gītā* the critical processes devised for Western works. In separating the disparate elements and the successive layers, we should succeed only in ruining the unmistakable artistic beauty of the poem. Works much later than the *Bhagavad-Gītā* exhibit a character equally composite. Theosophic conceptions and formulas are mingled with effusions of an ardent and humble piety. One marks this characteristic in many writings attributed to the founders and poets of the reforming sects, Kabīr, Tulsī Dās, Chaitanya, etc. The most recent representatives of an enlightened Vedānta, Ramakṛṣṇa and Vivēkānanda, also unite the *bhakti-mārga* with a phraseology which has become traditional since the period of the older *Upaniṣads*. There has been formed in India as it were a stock of words, ideas, and illustrations which belongs to every one and from which every one has the right to draw and is in the habit of drawing. One example will be sufficient to show how heavy a weight this theosophy of the past lays upon a thought which in other respects shows itself to be original and independent.

Nānak (*q.v.*), the founder of Sikhism, and his successors connect themselves with the religion of *bhakti*. They teach that a man is saved by the fervent worship of God, or by the worship of the *gurus*, the interpreters of God, and of the Book, the perpetual incarnation of the *gurus*. But the God of the Sikhs is like the *Brahman* of the *Upaniṣads*, and frequently borrows His name from the latter. In His own proper nature He is *nirguṇa*, without attributes; when He creates the world by means of *māyā*, He is also immanent in the phenomenal world and becomes *sarvaguṇa*, endowed with all qualities. In order to be saved, one must discover God in the heart; through self-concentration the mind eliminates all duality. To know God is to make oneself identical with God. God unites with Himself the man who knows Him, and this man is not reborn. As regards this life, salvation wins for him who is assured of it unbounded happiness, and death has no more terrors for him.

1 *Mahābhārata*, iii. 2. 40.
2 *Ib.* iii. 101. 15.
3 *Ib.* xii. 283. 9 ff.
4 *Ib.* xii. 329. 8.
5 *Ib.* iii. 219. 28.
6 *Ib.* xiv. 51. 29.
7 *Laws of Manu*, vi. 76 f.
8 *Bhagavad-Gītā*, v. 22.
9 *Ib.* iii. 43.
10 *Ib.* v. 24.
11 *Ib.* vi. 5.
12 *Mahābh.* xii. 291. 44.
13 *Bhag.-Gītā*, ii. 70 ff.
14 *Ib.* ix. 15.
15 *Ib.* xviii. 20.
16 *Ib.* xv. 7.
17 *Ib.* iv. 35.
18 *Ib.* v. 18.
19 *Ib.* vi. 30.

The great Vaiṣṇavite and Saivite sects are, quite as much as Sikhism, impregnated with theosophy. Their appearance is in itself evidence of an individualism in revolt against the excessive pressure of a religious tradition. Those who assert the authority of the Vedas are ridiculed. The framework in which the divine is placed is broken; no great importance is any longer attached to the name which the gods bear—Śiva or Viṣṇu, the label is different, but it is always the same god. The human framework is also broken; the religious value of caste is denied, and all men are called to salvation. The distinction between the sacred and the profane is abolished. Generally the first concern of the reformers is to put Sanskrit on one side in favour of an exclusive use of the popular language.

'The whole world for me,' says Nānak, 'is a sacred enclosure. Whoever loves the truth is pure.' 'All food and drink which come from God are pure.'[1]

The mechanical and the excessively ritualistic elements in the old religion are removed. Religion tends to become more human, more closely connected with ordinary life; the *Bhagavad-Gītā* has already expressed something approaching a sentiment of human solidarity, then an idea new in India. Moreover, religious tolerance becomes almost universal. Royal inscriptions prove that Brāhmanism, Jainism, Buddhism, Śaivism, and Vaiṣṇavism have their representatives in the same families, and the sovereigns extend their favours to all the communities. Is it not clear that religion has become an affair of the individual, and that the son is not in this respect bound to follow the example of his father?

Unfortunately the sects which were originally the boldest very soon fall into the old errors, or, rather, a new tradition, also altogether tyrannical, is established in place of the ancient tradition; or, still more frequently, the older safeguards are restored and most weighty concessions are made to the prevailing ideas. The popular language takes on, in its turn, a sacred character. Caste and restrictions about food recover all their influence. One returns to the old formalism and to the grosser superstitions; and the work of reform, to which men constantly address themselves, has always to be done over again.

Their admission into the popular religions was not a clear gain for theosophical ideas. They remain in the outer courts, in an altogether subordinate position. In the *Bhagavad-Gītā* everything that is merely a heritage from the past, a survival, is theosophical. The elements which are truly living and fruitful are of an entirely different origin. The religious emotion and the fervour of feeling which spring up in hearts full of adoration do not come from the *Upaniṣads* or their derivatives. Far from celebrating the triumph of theosophic ideas in India, the sectarian writings rather indicate their failure, since they make salvation depend on the love and grace of a personal and transcendent God.

4. [Theosophy and ancient Indian philosophy.—In dealing with the introduction of theosophy into sectarian religions we have been tracing what might be described as a waning of the influence of theosophy. In the *Gītā* and in the sectarian writings theosophical elements are largely overlaid by materials gathered from other sources. But the last few decades have witnessed a remarkable revival of theosophical teaching. This is to a great extent connected with an incursion of influences from the West and especially with the teachings of Madame Blavatsky and Mrs. Besant. The authority of Madame Blavatsky has been largely discredited, but Mrs. Besant is still a living force and her followers are numerous. Indeed India can claim a larger number of theosophists than any other country in the world. The latest available report (1917) shows 385 Indian lodges, with a total of 7344 members, among whom are some outstanding personalities. Their literary activity is great, at least in quantity, and the flow of publications from the headquarters at Adyar, near Madras, is unceasing and influential. The implicit influence of theosophical ideas is even more important than that which is explicitly allowed, and theosophical literature is frequently to be found in the hands of thinking men who would disclaim any connexion with a theosophical society. The popularity of theosophy is not, however, always due to purely theosophical causes.

Theosophy in India glories in having no creed, and thus claims to appeal to men of all creeds and to interpret for them the hidden values of their respective religions. But, though it is without a creed, theosophy has a threefold aim which is stated by Mrs. Besant, as follows:

(1) 'To form a nucleus of the Universal Brotherhood of Humanity . . . ; (2) to encourage the study of comparative religion, philosophy, and science; (3) to investigate the unexplained laws of Nature and the powers latent in man.'[1]

The popularity of theosophy at the present time in India is largely due to a judicious combination of those three aims. Unless we give a very wide interpretation to the term, the two first are not particularly theosophical, but they are universally acceptable, and they thus strengthen the appeal of the third—the only properly theosophical enterprise. The first aim affords an opportunity for an easy transition from religious to political activity and a reinforcement of the former through the popularity of the latter. The second sets itself in seemingly attractive opposition to the harsh judgments of certain apologists for particular religions, and appeals to that specious liberality of mind which finds expression in the oft-repeated assertion that one religion is as good as another. It calls forth the retrospective tendency which seems to be inherent in all theosophy and thus enables theosophy to serve itself as the heir of the ages. Emphasis is laid upon the idea of a hidden tradition which is traced through the magic of mediæval Europe, through the lore of the Knights Templar and the mystics, through Freemasonry and the speculations of alchemists and astrologers, until the ultimate source is postulated in the Great White Brotherhood, a vague and indefinite society which Madame Blavatsky alleges to have existed from time immemorial in the mountains of Tibet and to have delegated one of their number to act as her Master during a period of many years. This mystic brotherhood is believed still to have operative power and to have charge not only of the education and development of the human race, but also of cosmic evolution. Their doctrines embody the truths which are said to be at the basis of all religions, but, on investigating the matter more closely, we find that they are in a very special manner the fundamental principles of Indian thought. Theosophy thus gives a universal importance to Indian philosophical speculation and in so doing inevitably enhances its popularity in India. It levies contributions from all the more important Indian systems, taking from the *Upaniṣads* the doctrine of a fundamental unknowable and characterless Unity, and the identity of the human and the divine; from the Sāṅkhya the idea that spiritual advancement consists in a gradual detachment from the processes of the phenomenal world; from Buddhism the idea of *karma* and transmigration; and from Yoga the conception of various occult methods by which freedom of thought and

[1] Cf. M. A. Macauliffe, *The Sikh Religion*, i. 243; cf. i. 43.

[1] *Theosophy* ('People's Books'), London, n.d. [1912], p. 89.

spirit may be won. Further, by an application of its ideas of graded being and of development extended over many generations, it is able to allow a moderate amount of justification even to the grosser forms of the popular religions, and thus carry farther the process of infusing theosophical ideas into the cults of the people which, as pointed out, had but moderate success in earlier centuries.

As in Indian philosophy generally, so in theosophy the ultimate Being is an unknown and unknowable ground of all things, acquiring character as a Logos with the triple functions of will, wisdom, and activity. This differentiates itself into the human monads, having a similar triplicity. The human monad descends through various grades of being until it reaches the causal body, which has also a slightly lower mental aspect, uniting it with the grades of being of which even an ordinary man may be aware, and forming the basis of personality as we know it. The mental body has as its appropriate sphere the heavenly world, but the soul as it proceeds downwards enters also the astral world or the world of emotion and desire, and finally reaches the physical world. Over and over again there is incarnation reaching downwards ultimately to the physical world, and in each incarnation new experiences are obtained, leading, if rightly used, to the development of the soul. The supreme aim of the soul is to rise upwards to its original source, and the degree of ascent will be proportionate to the use it has made of the experiences of each incarnation. The working of the law of *karma* is inexorable. A man will receive the fruit of the deeds done in the body, and according to his good or his evil will be the duration of the period spent on each plane before another incarnation takes place. The aim of the whole process is to get rid of the separating sheaths of personality and reach absorption in the Absolute.

Theosophy is thus definitely committed to the doctrine of reincarnation and transmigration, with, on the one hand, its plausible explanation of the inequalities of human life, its stern insistence on moral consequences, its distant prospect of negative salvation, and, on the other hand, its ethical weakness arising out of its tendency to fatalism and encouragement of procrastination, and its lonely outlook as it traces the succeeding phases of individual development and promises reunion with those we love only in a 'togetherness' of absorption in which the definite character which was the object of our love altogether disappears.

The doctrines of theosophy claim a scientific basis in experience, but this experience is found to be very different from the experience of the ordinary man. It is dependent on the development of our latent powers, by the use of which we may acquire that knowledge which is already possessed by the masters of the human race, the adepts or initiates, and which may give to us a wonderful penetration into the hitherto undiscovered laws of nature. It is at this point that theosophy differentiates itself most completely from philosophy. Once make the initial assumption that the operation of these powers is possible and that the latent faculties can be exercised, and all is easy. We may attain a wonderful amount of detailed knowledge about the lower at least of the super-physical planes. We may discover, *e.g.*, that even during physical life the astral body projects a few inches beyond our physical body, and that it is shaped like an egg; also that various astral bodies are formed by the vibrations of thought and desire, the vibrations of unselfish affection producing bodies of pale rose colour, intellectual effort resulting in yellow bodies, devotional feeling in blue, etc. We may discover also facts on a higher ethical level—*e.g.*, that our prayers produce beings functioning as guardian angels and that our thoughts eventuate in actual astral existences, fulfilling the purposes into which our vague wishes would have been transformed, had opportunity waited upon our desires. In short, with an almost total disregard of the law of parsimony and of the rule against the multiplication of entities, we may explain many of the mysteries of our present life and many of the hitherto unexplained problems of nature by simply transferring the difficulty to a higher plane and 'discovering' beings personally responsible for what previously appeared to be a mysterious occurrence. It is at least doubtful whether modern theosophy in India distinguishes sufficiently between subjective imagination and the controlling power of objective facts, and this considerably lessens the force of the rebuke which it administers to our materialism, diminishes the value of its insistence upon the power of thought and prayer, and weakens its encouragement to explore farther than has yet been done the phenomena of spiritualism and telepathy as well as the more weighty experiences of the mystics of all ages.]

Conclusion.—The history of theosophical ideas, far more than that of religious ideas, allows us to establish the spiritual unity and continuity of India. Moreover, we have here an excellent field of observation for any one who wishes to know the meaning of theosophy, its principles, its aspirations, its method, and its influence upon life. With the idea that Indian theosophy is typical of this form of thought, we shall rapidly pass in review its principal characteristics.

(*a*) The most obvious quality is its concentration on the self, which not only occupies the first place in its scheme of thought, but also concerns itself with the Ego as if it were the only existence—as if everything else existed only for it and in reference to it. This theosophical individualism is both proud and exclusive. The vulgar intelligences, concerned with superstitions and traditional practices, are despised, and with jealous care the precious truth is guarded for a small number of the elect. 'There is nothing in common between popular religion and knowledge.'[1] As if to show clearly the existence of a double current in religious thought, a verse in the *Mahābhārata*[2] says that the gods, women, and the worlds have only one divinity, one *guru* only, but that the Brāhmans have two, Agni and Brahman, the god of sacrifice and the Being without a second.

(*b*) It is always flattering to belong to a privileged group; esotericism was an attractive element in theosophy. And there were others. Those who were terrified by threatening death and mysterious destiny, those who were shocked by the spectacle of physical and social injustice, found in the doctrine of *karma*, *saṁsāra*, and *mokṣa* just the solution fitted to give them moral serenity and courage to live. All the theosophical systems teach some way of salvation; they deliver their followers from the painful prospect of a second death, from an interminable series of lives poisoned by the expectation of death.

(*c*) Another advantage: truth is not arrived at slowly and patiently by study and reflexion; it is grasped by sudden internal vision. Once the premisses have been given by intuition, a rigorous dialectic can construct a system whose scientific appearance has an element of attractiveness for persistently intellectualistic minds eager to 'know.'

(*d*) The intuitive method is not only rapid and apparently trustworthy; it is also very fruitful.

1 Śaṅkara, *passim*; cf., e.g., *Comm. on the Vedānta-Sūtras*, p. 820.

2 *Mahābh.*, i. 95. 7.

It reveals that which neither analysis nor induction could discover—the supersensible world. Theosophy thus gives satisfaction to the mystical needs in human nature. Then, when one knows that the sensible world is only an insignificant part of being, and that, side by side with the very limited realm of knowledge, there is an infinite transcendental world, one resigns oneself easily to the most glaring logical impossibilities.

(*e*) Finally, the laws of material nature are not valid except for material bodies. Theosophy has been also a discipline of sublimation and dematerialization. Marvellous perceptions and an indefinite enhancement of intellectual and active powers are also privileges which India has always held in the highest esteem.

If now we ask what theosophy in fact did for individual and social life in India, we shall see that it has had some results which are excellent and others which are harmful. On more than one occasion it has vindicated the rights of the individual and struggled against authorities altogether dependent upon tradition. Theoretically at least, it has placed itself outside of social distinctions. It has made salvation a personal affair of the individual. It has opened the eyes of men to the foolishness of their futile occupations and the vanity of sensual pleasures and temporal possessions. It has taught them to seek for happiness in the contemplative life and in peace of heart. But it has also taught contempt of the ordinary life and of finite existence. It has ignored the possibility of progress in human affairs. It has been a school of pessimism. Its followers have searched for the absolute and the whole, when life can give only the relative and the partial. They have thought it possible to arrive by a leap at truth, when in fact nothing has really been secured by this intuitive method and everything has to be begun over again. It has lowered the dignity of virtue by making it a means and not an end. In condemning action and individualizing salvation, it has shown itself dangerously anti-social. Frequently, it is true, these bitter fruits have not been produced, for it has, on occasion, neglected its fundamental principles. Buddhism, *e.g.*, has preached the highest virtues without making them the instruments of salvation. This is intelligible, for in Buddhism, side by side with theosophy, there is a large dose of humanity.

LITERATURE.—A. Barth, *Quarante Ans d'indianisme*, 4 vols., Paris, 1914–18; A. C. Lyall, *Asiatic Studies*[2], 2 vols., London, 1907; E. W. Hopkins, *The Religions of India*, do. 1896; M. Monier-Williams, *Brāhmanism and Hindūism*[4], do. 1891; P. Deussen, *Allgemeine Geschichte der Philosophie*, Leipzig, 1894–1908, i.–iii.; P. Oltramare, *L'Histoire des idées théosophiques dans l'Inde*, Paris, 1906, i., *La Théosophie brahmanique*.

H. Oldenberg, *Vorwissenschaftliche Wissenschaft; die Weltanschauung der Brāhmana-Texte*, 1919; P. Deussen, *Sechzig Upanishad's des Veda*[2], Leipzig, 1905; A. E. Gough, *The Philosophy of the Upanishads and Ancient Indian Metaphysics*, London, 1882; P. Deussen, *Das System des Vedânta*[2], Leipzig, 1906; R. Garbe, *Die Sāṃkhya-Philosophie*, do. 1894, *Sāṃkhya und Yoga* (*GIAP*), Strassburg, 1896; L. Suali, *Introduzione allo Studio della Filosofia indiana*, 1913; B. Faddagon, *The Vaiśesika-System*, 1918; H. Oldenberg, *Die Lehre der Upanishaden und die Anfänge des Buddhismus*, 1915.

Mrs. Sinclair Stevenson, *The Heart of Jainism*, London, 1915.

H. Kern, *Hist. du bouddhisme dans l'Inde*, tr. G. Huet, 2 vols., Paris, 1901, *Manual of Indian Buddhism* (*GIAP*), Strassburg, 1896; H. Oldenberg, *Buddha*, Eng. tr., London, 1882; L. de la Vallée Poussin, *Bouddhisme*, Paris, 1909; T. Suzuki, *Outlines of Mahāyāna Buddhism*, London, 1907.

E. W. Hopkins, *The Great Epic of India*, New York, 1901; R. Garbe, *Die Bhagavadgîtâ*, Leipzig, 1905; P. Deussen, *Vier philosophische Texte des Mahābhāratam*, do. 1906; F. Otto Schrader, *Introduction to the Pāncarātra*, 1916; M. A. Macauliffe, *The Sikh Religion*, 6 vols., Oxford, 1909; R. Schmidt, *Fakire und Fakirtum im alten und modernen Indien*, Berlin, 1908; J. C. Oman, *The Mystics, Ascetics, and Saints of India*, London, 1905, *The Brahmans, Theists and Muslims of India*, do. 1907.

PAUL OLTRAMARE.

[Additions in brackets by W. S. URQUHART.]

THERAPEUTÆ.—The Therapeutæ[1] were a radical offshoot of the movement in pre-Christian Judaism which threw up an order like the Essenes (*q.v.*); but, unlike the Essenes, they were purely an Egyptian phenomenon, a religious confraternity, or θίασος, residing in the neighbourhood of Alexandria, and particularly on the low hills to the south of Lake Mareotis, leading the life of studious recluses and organized on semi-monastic lines. Outside Egypt, indeed outside this district, they are never heard of. They were a local development.

1. Source of information.—The only authority for the subject is a short treatise *de Vita Contemplativa* (περὶ βίου θεωρητικοῦ ἢ ἱκετῶν [ἀρετῶν], or, better, Φίλωνος ἱκέται ἢ περὶ ἀρετῶν τδδ'), included in the works of Philo. It is first quoted by Eusebius.[2] The rise of the monastic movement in the Church drew his attention, and evidently the attention of others, to a tractate which offered striking precedents and parallels for the cœnobitic discipline of Christians, and the general opinion came to be that the Therapeutæ were really Christian monks. This anachronism can be traced from Eusebius and Epiphanius onwards; it flourished right down to the beginning of the 18th cent., when the French scholar, B. de Montfaucon, published his *Livre de Philon de la vie contemplative, etc., traduit sur l'original grec, avec observations, où l'on fait voir que les Thérapeutes dont il parle étoient Chrestiens* (Paris, 1709). So completely had the Therapeutæ been identified with the origin of Christian monachism that even by the 6th cent. *vita therapeutica* had become the Latin equivalent of ἀσκήτικος βίος.

This unhistorical interpretation did one service; it preserved the Philonic treatise. But it was responsible for vehement discussion between Protestants and Roman Catholics—discussion which was so prejudiced that it threw next to no light upon the Therapeutæ (except, of course, to disprove the Eusebian ecclesiastical contention); it was also responsible for an avenging scepticism in the 19th century. To suppose,[3] on the evidence of Eusebius and Jerome,[4] that Philo re-visited Rome *c.* A.D. 44, was impressed or converted by St. Peter, and returned to join this ascetic community of St. Mark's Christian converts near Alexandria, was to expose the *de Vita Contemplativa* to unjust suspicion in a more critical age. The naive theory provoked an equally naive scepticism. It is not creditable, but it is hardly surprising, to find that in the 19th cent. the Therapeutæ were almost blotted out of existence. Some Jewish scholars, especially Graetz,[5] seemed as anxious to disavow any connexion with the poor Therapeutæ as Roman Catholics were to dub them monks; they attempted to rid Judaism of these recluses by relegating them to the 3rd cent. A.D. as Christian monks, the treatise being assigned to some Encratitic, semi-heretical source. Other writers[6] also dated the *de Vita Contemplativa* in that period, although they more prudently regarded it as a Jewish sketch of some ideal, ascetic community. It was reserved for P. E. Lucius[7] to twist the stray threads of this scepticism into a stout denial that the Therapeutæ had ever existed except in the imagination of a Christian *c.* A.D. 300, who ingeniously used Philo's name and authority to create a monastic community in the first half of the 1st cent. A.D. This aberration of criticism carried away many writers great and small. French and English scholarship, however, came to the rescue, in L. Massebieau's study,[8] Renan's decisive judgment,[9] and F. C. Conybeare's work.[10] P. Wendland reinforced the defence,[11] and the historical authenticity of the

[1] See *ERE* viii. 782[b]. [2] *HE* ii. 17, ii. 18. 7.

[3] As the *de Vit. Con.* was indubitably Philo's, the only logical way of explaining this panegyric on Christian monks was to make Philo himself a Christian when he wrote it.

[4] *de Vir. Ill.* 8. [5] *GVI*[2] iii. [1863] 463 f.

[6] *E.g.*, M. Nicolas, *RThPh*, 3rd ser., vi. [1868] 25–52, and A. Kuenen, *The Religion of Israel*, Eng. tr., London, 1874–75, iii. 217–223.

[7] *Die Therapeuten und ihre Stellung in der Geschichte der Askese: eine kritische Untersuchung der Schrift: De vita contemplativa*, Strassburg, 1879.

[8] 'Le Traité de la vie contemplative et la question des Thérapeutes,' *RHR* xvi. [1887] 170–198.

[9] *Journal des Savants*, 1892, pp. 83–93, as already, *ib.* 1874, p. 798 f.

[10] *Philo about the Contemplative Life, or the Fourth Book of the Treatise concerning Virtues: critically edited, with a Defence of its Genuineness*, Oxford, 1895.

[11] *Die Therapeuten und die philonische Schrift von beschaulichen Leben: ein Beitrag zur Gesch. des hellenistischen Judenthums*, Leipzig, 1896.

treatise was finally vindicated. Whether it was composed by Philo or by some contemporary Jew is another and a subordinate question. The important point is that the treatise is a pre-Christian or non-Christian description of actual recluses in the Judaism of Egypt about the end of the 1st cent. B.C. or the opening of the 1st cent. A.D. Conybeare's edition is the standard authority on the Greek text. His translation[1] is followed in this article. Both he and Massebieau have made out a good case for the hypothesis that the *de Vita Contemplativa* originally was a sequel to the lost Philonic account of the Essenes in the ἀπολογία ὑπὲρ Ἰουδαίων, from which Eusebius drew his information. But their interpretation of details in the account of the Therapeutæ is sometimes open to serious criticism.

2. Characteristics.—According to Philo, the Therapeutæ are part of a movement which is known outside Egypt[2]—the more or less organized semi-philosophical, semi-religious retreat from cities and a corrupting civilization to the simple life of retirement. Though the movement is not confined to the environs of Alexandria, it is there that the Therapeutæ are most numerous.[3]

They are Jewish recluses who reside in simple huts, at a short and suitable distance from one another (*i.e.*, they resembled the cœnobites of Pachomius in a later day, instead of being hermits and anchorites). Each hut has a sacred chamber (μυστήριον or μοναστήριον σεμνεῖον), reserved for their sacred books (the Law, the Prophets, the Psalms, and other writings, οἷς ἐπιστήμη καὶ εὐσέβεια συναύξονται καὶ τελειοῦνται, 'by means of which religion and sound knowledge grow together into a perfect whole'). After praying at dawn, they devote the day to meditation upon the Scriptures; these include writings or commentaries (συγγράμματα) 'drawn up by the ancient founders of their sect,' by which Philo probably means the literature current under the names of men like Enoch and Abraham, whom he regarded as the primeval ascetics and recluses, the ideal progenitors of the Therapeutic movement. The method of study is allegorical interpretation (τὴν πάτριον φιλοσοφίαν ἀλληγοροῦντες), and one outcome of it is the composition of sacred hymns. Prayers at sunset close the day. Such is the life in each hut.[4] On the seventh day the various members meet for common worship; they arrange themselves according to age, sitting on the ground with 'the right hand between the chest and the chin, but the left tucked down along the flank.' The senior recluse then delivers an address, to which all listen in silence, merely nodding assent. A partition, ten or twelve feet high, separates the men from the women, so that the latter can hear the speaker without being seen by the male recluses.

The seventh day[5] is their day for relaxation. On the other days no one eats before sunset, and some go fasting almost entirely for three or even six days, in their contemplative raptures. But all use oil (as a physical refreshment, unlike the Essenes[6]), and on the seventh day all 'propitiate the mistresses hunger and thirst, which nature has set over mortal creatures'; the diet is simply water and cheap bread, flavoured with salt, and occasionally supplemented by hyssop. None[7] of your drunken Greek symposia! Philo anticipates Lucian in his scorn of these rowdy gatherings.

Once every seven weeks[8] they assemble for their supreme festival, 'which the number fifty has had assigned to it,'[9] robed in white and with looks of serious joy. At a given sign from one of their leaders they arrange themselves in ranks, raising eyes and hands to heaven ('their hands, because they are pure from unjust gains, being stained by no pretence of money-making') and praying for a blessing on the festival. Then the senior members recline, in order of seniority, upon their cheap, rough couches; on the left side of the room the women also recline. The younger novices wait upon the older members, for the Therapeutæ (like the Essenes)[1] decline to be served by slaves; 'they deem any possession of servants whatever to be contrary to nature,' which makes all alike free at birth. It is not a banquet of luxuries; no wine, only cold water, heated for those who are delicate; no meat—for the Therapeutæ are vegetarians, living on nothing but bread and salt, with hyssop for the more delicate palates, the hyssop being added 'out of reverence for the holy table of offering in the sacred vestibule of the temple,'[2] to signify that the Therapeutæ are too humble to emulate the unleavened bread reserved for the priests. But, before this Spartan meal is eaten, a quiet address or allegorical exposition of Scripture is delivered by the president. The rest listen in breathless silence; but, if the speaker does not make his meaning clear, they are allowed to indicate their perplexity by a slight movement of the head and a right-hand finger. When he is considered to have spoken long enough, all clap their hands three times. A hymn then follows, sometimes composed in honour of God by the singer (cf. 1 Co 14^{26}), 'either a new one which he has made himself, or some old one of the poets that were long ago.' Each member has to sing a hymn in rotation, while the rest join in the chorus. Only after this religious service of an address and praise—nothing is said of prayer[3]—does the banquet proceed.

The final act of the festival[4] is the famous παννυχίς, or all-night celebration of a sacred singing dance,[5] by men and women in two choruses, each headed by a chosen leader. Each of the choirs, the male and the female, begins by singing and dancing apart, partly in unison, partly in antiphonal measures of various metres, 'as if it were a Bacchic festival in which they had drunk deep of the divine love.' Then both unite to imitate the choral (Ex $15^{1.\ 20\text{-}21}$) songs of Moses and Miriam[6] at the Red Sea, sung as thanks εἰς τὸν σωτῆρα θεὸν (cf. Rev 15^{3}). It is a thrilling performance, this choric dance and exulting symphony; 'but the end and aim' of it all 'is holiness' (the exodus symbolizing, of course, the mystical release of the soul from material bondage). Instead of being drowsy after this all-night ecstasy, the Therapeutæ are more wide-awake in the morning than they were at the beginning of their vigil; they turn to the East, 'and, so soon as they espy the sun rising, they stretch out aloft their hands to heaven and fall to praying[7] 'for a fair day, and for truth and for clear judgment to see with.' Then they separate to resume the ordinary day's contemplation in their separate cells.

Such, says Philo, is the method of life practised by these true 'citizens of heaven and of the universe.' The term 'citizens' is deliberately chosen. They abjure cities, he means, but none the less, indeed all the more on that account, these recluses belong to a higher polity.

3. Religious significance.—A complete renunciation of the world, resembling that demanded by Jesus in Lk 18^{29}, lay at the foundation of the Therapeutic society. What they abjured was money rather than matter. In the austerity of their zeal they voluntarily handed over their property to others,[8] since absorption in money-making and the cares of life not only took up too much time and thought but also fostered injustice. Having divested themselves of their possessions, 'they flee without turning back, having abandoned brethren, children, wives, parents, all the throng of their kindred, all their friendships with companions, yea, their countries in which they were born and bred.'[9] Philo describes this with a wistful enthusiasm, as he had described the renunciation of Enoch[10] and of Abraham.[11] But he is careful to explain why they prefer solitude to cities. It is only because intercourse with the unsympathetic world would injure them, 'not from any harsh and deliberate hatred of mankind'—a disclaimer[12]

[1] In *JQR* vii. [1895] 755–769.

[2] Philo is trying not only, as he does elsewhere, to show that the recluse tendency is Greek as well as Jewish, but to link the Therapeutæ to the wide-spread phenomenon of *cultores dei* (*deorum*), as their name of 'devotees' (θεραπευταί) permitted. In this way he seeks to interpret them to his readers, just as he had already (*de Vit. Con.* 1-2) contrasted them with the inferior 'philosophers' of Greece on the one hand, and with the silly Egyptian worshippers of animals on the other. His attempt to explain θεραπευταί as possibly meaning 'healers' of the soul is equally unhistorical. So far as it is not the official title of the community, it means what it meant in the case of the Essenes, whom Philo himself had called θεραπευταὶ θεοῦ. The variant title ἱκέται meant 'suppliants.'

[3] *De Vit. Con.* 3.

[4] So constant is their sense of God's presence that even in their dreams they have visions of nothing but the divine ἀρετῶν καὶ δυνάμεων, while many men talk in their sleep of what they have been studying.

[5] *De Vit. Con.* 4.

[6] Cf. *ERE* v. 398^{a}.

[7] *De Vit. Con.* 5–7.

[8] *Ib.* 8.

[9] This seems to have been a festival, partly modelled on the five weeks or pentecostal type (for here as elsewhere the Therapeutæ show distinct affinities with Palestine) but celebrated seven times a year, at the expiry of every 49 (7 × 7) days. On the resemblances between this periodical festival and the Feast of Weeks in the book of Jubilees see A. Epstein in *REJ* xxii. [1891] 14 f., 20 f., as well as on the similar institution among the Abyssinian Jews (Falasha).

[1] *ERE* v. 396^{b}.

[2] *De Vit. Con.* 9.

[3] Is this omission accidental? Or was prayer regarded as a part of private devotion (cf. *ERE* x. 191^{b})?

[4] *De Vit. Con.* 10.

[5] A trait of popular religious worship in Egypt (cf. *ERE* v. 238^{a}; and, generally, x. 359^{a}).

[6] Miriam, in some quarters of early mystical literature, is the counterpart of Isis, and she plays an important rôle in Gnostic speculations, as Reitzenstein points out (*Poimandres*, Leipzig, 1904, p. 136 n.). Her popularity among the Therapeutæ is probably another Egyptian touch.

[7] Lightfoot (*Saint Paul's Epistles to the Colossians and to Philemon*[7], London, 1884, pp. 85, 372) took this to mean sun-worship; but the Therapeutæ did not practise sun-worship any more than the Essenes did (see *ERE* v. 398^{a}, note 4).

[8] Unlike the Essenes, and the primitive Christians (Ac 2^{45}), with whom Eusebius (*HE* ii. 17) would fain connect them on this account, the Therapeutæ did not pool their funds for the benefit of the community.

[9] *De Vit. Con.* 2.

[10] *De Præm. et Poen.* 3.

[11] *De Abrah.* 3.

[12] He had made the same disclaimer of misanthropy in speaking of Abraham (*de Abrah.* 4).

of the *odium humani generis* for which Jews were blamed by the outside world. Philo always protested against the people who withdrew into seclusion, simply because they lacked public spirit. He also anticipated the criticism which might be passed on the Therapeutæ, that they acted from a morbid misanthropy. Hence his defence and admiration of them. The Therapeutæ, in fact, realize for Philo what he had always dreamt of, a small (only a small) number or θίασος of spiritual athletes, acting from the highest of motives, carrying out a counsel of perfection, and capable of making the supreme renunciation in order to attain the highest vision of God and truth.[1] To them he applies his favourite Platonic metaphor of the wealth with eyes (*i.e.* the mystic rapture of the soul enriched with the vision of truth); no wonder, when they possess this inward treasure, that they abandon their blind wealth (τὸν τυφλὸν πλοῦτον)[2] to blind worldlings! For their renunciation does not empty life. It is not a mere negation; it is the soul surrendering to a higher passion for God (ὑπ' ἔρωτος ἁρπασθέντες οὐρανίου), which enriches life past dreams of avarice. The Therapeutæ are recluses and students, but their spirit is an ecstatic yearning for the positive vision of Truth. 'It is as easy to close the eyes of the mind, as those of the body,' Bishop Butler wrote;[3] it is still more easy, Philo felt, to let the eyes of the mind be closed by luxury and money-making, and he applauds the Therapeutæ for sacrificing their great possessions and position in order to keep the higher vision unimpaired.

Another feature of the Therapeutæ which goes to Philo's heart is that their allegorical interpretation of the OT does not render them indifferent to the actual rites and institutions of Judaism. He disliked the ultra-spiritualists[4] who evaporated the historical element in religion, and dropped all adherence to the forms of their faith. But he delighted in people like the Therapeutæ who, *e.g.*, attached, as he did, in his own enthusiasm, a high mystical sense to the number 'seven,' and yet not only kept the seventh day strictly but also celebrated a special festival after every 49 days, out of their reverence for that perfect number and its multiple (7×7). This appeared to him to be a healthy form of mysticism. The Therapeutæ appealed to Philo more than the Essenes did, because they were on old Jewish lines, adherents of the Mosaic law, respectful to the Temple at Jerusalem, and capable of attaining the heights of contemplative ecstasy without abandoning the lowly duties prescribed by the Torah.

A third feature which evidently pleased the gentle Philo was their freedom from angry controversy and flashy rhetoric. With his eye not only upon the quarrels of Greek sages at their symposia but also upon the rabbinic disputants at Jerusalem, he tells of the unostentatious style practised by the Therapeutic speakers, of the rapt attention shown by the audience, and of the respectful demeanour of the gathering—exalting the very virtues which Paul recommended to the showy, noisy Christians at Corinth (cf. 1 Co 14[23f.]). Philo loves them for their quiet demeanour. The Therapeutæ never wasted their time over rabbinic exegesis of the letter of Scripture. They gazed placidly through that, as through a glass, into the mystical significance which held them spellbound. Their wisdom was pure and peaceable; it combined plain living and high thinking, and the sages never lost their tempers.

All this, added to their philosophic aspirations

1 Cf., e.g., *de Mut. Nom.* 4.
2 *De Vit. Con.* 2.
3 *Sermons* (ed. W. E. Gladstone, Oxford, 1896), x. § 13.
4 Cf. *ERE* i. 310b.

and their distaste for luxury, moved Philo to write his panegyric. He professes that it is nothing but the bare truth. Certainly it is not a Defoe-like work of fiction. At the same time, his enthusiasm probably leads him to idealize the Therapeutæ; a disproportionate amount of space is surrendered to a scornful criticism of the Greek symposia, in which Plato as well as Xenophon is censured; and he forgets to explain how the Therapeutæ lived, if they did no work and held no property. Did they depend, like Buddhists, on charity? It is one of the questions which Philo forgets to answer. The main outline of the sketch, however, has all the marks of accuracy. Though he was not a member of the community, it was so near to Alexandria that he could easily have heard of its life and even visited it. His admiration may have heightened the colours, but it did not invent the content, of his delineation. The tone of his account resembles that in which Izaak Walton, in his biography of George Herbert, speaks of the little settlement of recluses at Little Gidden, under the spiritual guidance of Nicholas Ferrar.

The Therapeutæ were organized on lines resembling the later *lauras* of monasticism in Egypt, *i.e.* in a group or encampment of separate residences, with a common hall for special gatherings; they lived in huts, set close enough for fellowship and for mutual protection against an attack of robbers (which was a common experience of such communities). Plainly, they acted in self-defence when occasion required. The differences between them and the Essenes are patent. The Therapeutæ confined themselves to a life of contemplation; they were a small community of men and women who had been well-born and wealthy,[1] and who lived in a Chartreuse-like retreat; they were not religious communists, and they had no interest in prophecy (their dreams being not of the future but of the celestial order); they fasted, as the Essenes did not, and their relation to women was quite different. Both the Therapeutæ and the Essenes were 'holiness' movements, but the former displayed some unique features, especially the combination of individual contemplation with a periodical outburst of emotional fervour in the common song and dance.

Nothing is known of their history. They are one of the local, transient phenomena of the age that baffle modern curiosity. A single ray of light falls on this tiny community, at the bridge between B.C. and A.D., but we do not know who founded them or what became of them. Philo's description was never followed up by any subsequent writer. Gibbon[2] thought it 'probable that they changed their name, preserved their manners, adopted some new articles of faith, and gradually became the fathers of the Egyptian Ascetics.' This is guess-work, however. A community which was recruited like the Therapeutæ could not survive like the Essenes; so much is clear; and Therapeutism probably was an ephemeral product, an anticipation rather than an ancestor of the later Christian monasticism in Egypt. Abraham E. Harkawy, the Petrograd scholar, in his edition of Kirkisānī, the 10th cent. Karaite savant,[3] points out that Kirkisānī includes among the Jewish sects one called the Margārites, to whom the 'Alexandrine' belonged; this sect practised allegorical interpretation, as a rule abjured laughing, and were called Margārites, or 'cave-folk.' Harkawy identifies the 'Alexandrine' with Philo, and the Margārites with the Therapeutæ, as a branch of the Essenes—a view shared by Bacher,[4] but doubted by Poznański.[5] It seems an interesting, if vague, recollection of the Therapeutæ, lingering in the Judaism which had surrendered its interest in these recluses to the Christian Church.

4. Compositions.—The Therapeutæ were not only ascetics but also students; yet no trace of their literature has survived. (*a*) The λόγος, or hymn, coloured by Jewish Hellenism, which is discussed by A. Dieterich,[6] has been sometimes assigned to them. But it shows euhemeristic syncretism; there is nothing specifically Therapeutic about its language or ideas, and, although it does refer to the rescue of Israel from the Red Sea, this is too general to serve as an identification-mark for the choric song of the Therapeutæ (see above). The Therapeutæ are less analogous to the circle of this hymn than an anticipation of the Encratites (*q.v.*) in their aversion to marriage and their avoidance of wine and animal food.

1 ἀνθρώποις εὐγενέσι καὶ ἀστείοις (*de Vit. Con.* 9).
2 *Decline and Fall of the Roman Empire*, ch. xv. note 163.
3 *Memoirs of the Oriental Section of the Archæological Society at St. Petersburg*, viii. [1894] 247–319.
4 *JQR* vii. 703.
5 *REJ* l. [1905] 19–23.
6 *Abraxas*, Leipzig, 1891, pp. 138 f., 145 f.

(*b*) Nor is the book of Wisdom distinctively Therapeutic, as some[1] thought.

The emphasis on ὅσιος and on ὁσιότης, rather than on the more outward εὐσέβεια, certainly suggests that Wisdom emanated from some inner circle or set of Jewish pietists, but there are no indications that point decisively to the Therapeutæ, not even the casual use of θεραπεύειν in $10^{9.16}$. $3^{13f.}$ is not in praise of celibacy, and, even if it were, the tendency to exalt celibacy in the later Judaism was not confined to the ascetic cohabitation of the sexes among the Therapeutæ.[2] 4^{7-9} simply echoes the common reflexion that life is measured by its content of wisdom, not by length of years; it has nothing particularly to do with the Therapeutic regulation[3] that seniority was reckoned by the years spent within the society. The allusion in 7^{28}–8^{2} to the wise man being wedded to Wisdom (τὸν σοφίᾳ συνοικοῦντα . . . ταύτην ἐφίλησα καὶ . . . ἐζήτησα νύμφην ἀγαγέσθαι ἐμαυτῷ) resembles the description of the nun-like recluses in the *de Vita Contemplativa*, 8 (for the most part 'aged virgins, that have preserved intact their chastity . . . because of their zeal and longing for Wisdom; with whom they were anxious to live,' in order to bring forth not mortal children but 'the immortal progeny which the God-enamoured soul is alone able to bring forth of itself').[4] But this metaphorical description applies in the one case to men, in the other to women, and it is too general and common (cf., *e.g.*, Sir 15^{2}, Pr 2^{17}) to be confined to the Therapeutæ; in *de Vita Contemplativa*, 8, Philo is speaking as he speaks elsewhere.[5] Finally, the Therapeutic custom of offering prayer at sunrise (see above) was not peculiar to them among the Jews, so that Wis 16^{28} ('one should be before the sun in giving thanks to thee, and one should plead with thee at the dawning of light') need not be a glimpse of these recluses—the less so, that nothing is said about their eastward position by the writer of Wisdom, who is simply moralizing about the story of the manna.

5. Origin.—In view of the various Oriental and Hellenistic influences which were playing upon the later Judaism towards the close of the 1st cent. B.C., a phenomenon like the existence of the Therapeutæ, with their celibacy, their aversion to social life, their absorption in a divine θεραπεία, and their mystical speculations, all carried out 'in accordance with the most holy counsels of the prophet Moses,'[6] is not altogether surprising.

'The societies of the Essenes and the Therapeutæ . . . belong, just as the mediæval and modern Hassidic asceticisms belong, to Judaism quite as much as do any of its more normal institutions.'[7]

It is still less surprising to find such a gild or monastic settlement in Egypt. The soil of Egyptian popular religion was full of 'monastic germs'; there were men and women recluses in the Serapeum at Memphis, whose θεράπευσις embraced both study and mystical dreams; the very name of θεραπευταί was connected with the worship of Isis,[8] which also had its mystic raptures, combined with an emphasis on asceticism and celibacy; the climate itself, and the gaunt deserts, stretching away from the cities and townships, invited those who had recluse tendencies. It was in Egypt that the monastic movement of the Church first developed its varied and most distinctive forms three centuries later, and the development was no more surprising upon the basis of primitive Christianity than that of the Therapeutæ or of the Essenes upon the basis of orthodox Mosaism. One of the most suggestive parallels to the Therapeutic discipline is to be found in the contemporary account of the Egyptian philosopher-priests which is given by Chaeremon, the Egyptian ἱερογραμματεύς. It is quoted by Porphyry,[9] and some sentences deserve to be quoted here for the light they throw upon 'monastic' lines of development in pre-Christian Egypt.

'They chose sanctuaries (ἱερά) as the place in which to study philosophy, since to dwell with the statues of the gods was in harmony with their utter longing for vision (τῆς θεωρίας). Besides, this gave them security, owing to the reverence felt for the gods, since all men honoured these philosophers as if they were sacred creatures. They also lived in solitude, only mixing with other people at the sacred assemblies and festivals. . . . Having renounced every other employment and all human toils (πόνους ἀνθρωπίνους), they gave up the whole of their existence to the contemplation and vision of things divine . . . for to be in constant association with divine knowledge and inspiration delivers men from all lust (πλεονεξίας), subdues the passions, and rouses life to intelligence (σύνεσιν). They were also studious to be frugal in food and clothing. . . . Their hands were always inside their garments. . . . When they were not engaged in purification, they ate bread cut up along with hyssop, as they declared hyssop was extremely potent in purifying bread. . . . They trained themselves to endure hunger and thirst and scanty food through all their life. . . . The day they spent in the worship of the gods (εἰς θεραπείαν τῶν θεῶν), singing hymns to them three or four times, at dawn and at eventide.'

The origin of the Therapeutæ lay in Jewish Hellenism, as that was specially affected by its Egyptian environment. Nothing more is required to explain the ascetic and mystical habits of these recluses beside Lake Mareotis. But it would be uncritical to dismiss this problem without some reference to the question which has repeatedly been asked: Do not several traits of the Therapeutic discipline recall Buddhistic monasticism—*e.g.*, the combination of a cœnobitic life with study and devout contemplation, and the vegetarianism? The latter is one of the marks which sharply distinguish the Therapeutæ from the Essenes, who were not vegetarians. But there is at least one feature of the Essenes themselves which is analogous to Indian practices,[1] and it is open to conjecture whether some Buddhistic influence had not penetrated Egyptian Hellenism by the 1st cent. B.C., as it is sometimes held to have penetrated the later Gnosticism.[2]

Robertson Smith,[3] after observing that 'in Egypt, the doctrine that the highest degree of holiness can only be attained by abstinence from all animal food, was the result of the political fusion of a number of local cults in one national religion, with a national priesthood that represented imperial ideas,' added that 'later developments of Semitic asceticism almost certainly stood under foreign influences, among which Buddhism seems to have had a larger and earlier share than it has been usual to admit.'

The Therapeutic avoidance of animal food need not, of course, be Buddhistic; the practice of the Orphic societies in Egypt or of the Neo-Pythagoreanism which affected the Essenes in other ways[4] may account for it as well as for the stress on hymns,[5] the παννυχίς, and some other features. Indeed, so far as our scanty data go, with regard to the Therapeutæ or the Essenes, the evidence does not appear to warrant any hypothesis of direct Buddhistic influence, although the Orientalism which had filtered into Jewish Hellenism, even in Egypt, by the 1st cent. B.C. may have contained some elements of Buddhistic religious tendency. The trade connexions between Alexandria and India, and the intercourse of both countries ever since the 3rd cent. B.C., make it quite possible to suppose that Indian merchants reached Egypt by the 1st cent. B.C. Rohde points this out in another connexion, detailing the Indian and Buddhistic elements in Greek fiction.[6] But the interaction

[1] *E.g.*, Ewald, *The Hist. of Israel*^{2}, Eng. tr., London, 1880, v. 377, and A. Gfrörer, *Krit. Gesch. des Urchristenthums*, Stuttgart, 1831, ii. 280 f.

[2] *ERE* i. 179; K. Lake, *The Earlier Epistles of St. Paul*, London, 1911, p. 188 f.

[3] *De Vit. Con.* 8: 'For they do not regard as elders those who can count their years and are merely aged, but, on the contrary, account these to be still mere infants, in case they have been late in embracing the vocation.'

[4] This is the Philo who had written so extraordinarily about Tamar (*Quod Deus immut.* 29).

[5] *E.g.*, in *Cherubim*, 13 f.

[6] *De Vit. Con.* 8.

[7] I. Abrahams, *Studies in Pharisaism and the Gospels*, Cambridge, 1917, p. 121.

[8] See the Cyzicus inscription, *e.g.*, quoted by A. Mordtmann, in *RA* xxxvii. [1879] 258 f.

[9] *De Abstin.* iv. 6–8.

[1] Cf. *ERE* v. 398^{b}, note 5.

[2] Cf. *ib.* ii. 432, vi. 234.

[3] *Rel. of the Semites*^{2}, London, 1894, p. 302 f.

[4] *ERE* v. 401^{a}.

[5] This again distinguishes them from the Essenes. C. A. Bugge, in his recent study of the Essenes (*ZNTW* xiv. [1913] 167 f.), argues that the Palestinian Essenes must have cultivated song and music like the Egyptian Therapeutæ; but there is no 'must' about the matter. Had hymns been a prominent feature of the Essenic cultus, they would have been mentioned by Philo or Josephus.

[6] *Der griech. Roman und seine Vorläufer*^{2}, Leipzig, 1900, p. 581 f.

was not marked.[1] A trait like the presence of the 'nuns' is almost sufficient by itself to justify disagreement with the verdict of Mansel:

'The Therapeutæ . . . appear to have sprung from an union of the Alexandrian Judaism with the precepts and modes of life of the Buddhist devotees, . . . in their ascetic life, in their mortification of the body and their devotion to pure contemplation, we may trace at least a sufficient affinity to the Indian mystics to indicate a common origin.'[2]

On the other hand, even after allowing for the Neo-Pythagorean and Orphic environment, as well as for the fact that certain phenomena of this recluse life spring up independently on any soil at the touch of organized monasticism,[3] we may leave open the possibility that the Therapeutæ and perhaps the Essenes more or less unconsciously developed features which owed their original suggestion to Buddhistic sources. One of the main reasons for hesitating to admit even this possibility is the fact that Buddhistic influence on Gnosticism, two centuries later, appears to be almost unrecognizable, although Gnosticism might be expected to show distinct affinities with this line of Indian religious practice and speculation.

LITERATURE.—Besides what has been noted in the course of the article, the following may be chronicled as among the few significant contributions which the interminable discussions of the subject have thrown up: the notes of H. de Valois (Valesius), the great 17th cent. editor of Eusebius; Thomas Browne, *Dissertatio de Therapeutis Philonis adversus Hen. Valesium*, London, 1695 (Therapeutæ=converts of St. Mark, who afterwards became the monks described by Palladius); two critical letters by J. Bouhier (*Lettres pour et contre, sur la fameuse question, si les solitaires appelés thérapeutes dont a parlé Philon le Juif, étoient chrétiens*, Paris, 1712), which Conybeare calls 'the best commentary on the *de Vita Contemplativa* ever written'; A. F. Gfrörer, *Krit. Gesch. des Urchristenthums*, Stuttgart, 1831, vol. i. pt. 2, pp. 280-299; and A. Neander, *General Hist. of the Christian Religion and Church*, Eng. tr., London, 1850-58, i. 81-85.

None of the older dictionary or encyclopædia articles deserves mention. The main help has been given by critics of Philo—*e.g.*, H. P. Delaunay, *RA* xxii. [1870-71] 268 f., xxvi. [1873] 12 ff., and in *Moines et sibylles dans l'antiquité judéo-grecque*[2], Paris, 1874, pp. 10-57; B. Tideman, *ThT* v. [1871] 177-188; A. Edersheim, *DCB* iv. 368-371; L. Cohn, *JQR* v. [1893] 38-42; J. Drummond, *ib.* viii. [1896] 155-172 (reviewing Conybeare's ed.); and E. Schürer, *GJV*[4], iii. 687-691 (still reluctant to give up his scepticism); or by writers like E. Renan, *Hist. du peuple d'Israël*, Paris, 1887-95, v. 366-380; O. Zöckler, *Askese und Mönchthum*, Frankfort, 1897, i. 128 f.; E. Zeller, *Die Philosophie der Griechen*[4], Leipzig, 1876-1903, III. ii. 377 f.; M. Friedländer, *Die religiösen Bewegungen innerhalb des Judenthums im Zeitalter Jesu*, Berlin, 1905, pp. 197 f., 265 f.; W. Bousset, *Die Religion des Judentums im NT Zeitalter*[2], do. 1906, p. 536 f.; E. Bréhier, *Les Idées philosophiques et religieuses de Philon d'Alexandrie*, Paris, 1908, pp. 321-324; W. M. Flinders Petrie, *Personal Religion in Egypt before Christianity*, London, 1909, p. 63 f.; O. Pfleiderer, *Primitive Christianity*, Eng. tr., 1906-11, iii. 1-8, 18 f.; and H. Leclercq, *DACL* ii. 3063-3075.

JAMES MOFFATT.

THERIANTHROPISM.—See LYCANTHROPY.

THEUDAS.—See MESSIAHS (PSEUDO).

THEURGY. — Theurgy ($\theta\epsilon\nu\rho\gamma\iota\alpha$) — the direct working of God—is closely connected with certain systems of mysticism and theosophy. The word itself is not often used by those who claim that supernatural effects are produced through them by divine action; they more often ascribe the miraculous effects to good 'spirits,' whom God uses for His purposes, and they call this system of divine working 'magic,' frequently 'white magic,' as distinguished from 'black magic,' which is supposed to be the work of diabolical spirits. Vaughan has given a good definition of it. He says:

'I would use the term theurgic to characterize the mysticism which claims supernatural powers generally,—works marvels, not like the black art, by help from beneath, but as white magic, by the virtue of talisman or cross, demi-god, angel, or saint. Thus theurgic mysticism is not content, like the theopathetic, with either feeling or proselytising; nor, like the theosophic, with knowing; but it must open for itself a converse with the world of spirits, and win as its prerogative the power of miracle. This broad use of the word makes prominent the fact that a common principle of devotional enchantment lies at the root of all the pretences, both of heathen and of Christian miraclemongers. The celestial hierarchy of Dionysius and the benign dæmons of Proclus, the powers invoked by Pagan or by Christian theurgy, by Platonist, by Cabbalist, or by saint, alike reward the successful aspirant with supernatural endowments; and so far Apollonius of Tyana and Peter of Alcantara, Asclepigenia and St. Theresa, must occupy as religious magicians the same province. The error is in either case the same—a divine efficacy is attributed to rites and formulas, sprinklings or fumigations, relics or incantations, of mortal manufacture.'[1]

Some form of belief in theurgy is at least as old as history and literature. Homer's heroes are constantly raised beyond themselves and perform deeds which seem to be done through them by the Olympian divinities who come to their aid. Oriental as well as Grecian mythology everywhere assumes theurgic powers. The eclectic Gnostics, who drew upon many popular religions and sacred books as the sources of their divine *gnosis*, also believed and taught that great divine powers became available to those who were initiated and who thus received something of the fullness—the Pleroma—of the Godhead.

The Neo-Platonists, especially in their later periods, gave new impetus to theurgy and were unwittingly the transmitters of it into Christian circles. Plotinus, the founder of the movement, was a metaphysician of high rank and a noble mystic whose influence on Christian mysticism can hardly be overestimated, but he was not interested in occult knowledge or in theurgic phenomena. His Syrian successors, however, Porphyry and Iamblichus, were concerned with the problem of discovering and applying divine powers or energies in the sphere of human action. Iamblichus, who strongly reveals Gnostic influences, turns the ideas and hypostases of Plotinus into divinities, *i.e.* personified beings, and he holds that these 'intelligences' work wonders in the macrocosm outside and in the microcosm within man. These divine powers come into the soul of the mystic on high occasions, possess it, and enable it to do works beyond human capacity. There are, according to Iamblichus, hierarchal orders of these divine powers in varying ranks, and it belongs to mystical wisdom to know how to invoke the higher and more benign powers and to gain their theurgic assistance. This theurgic system is set forth in Iamblichus' treatise *de Mysteriis*. Proclus, the last important name among the Neo-Platonists, was a much greater philosopher than Iamblichus, but he also expounded a system of theurgy and encouraged belief in hierarchal powers, arranged in triadic orders, who work divinely and mysteriously through those who are raised into union with these higher powers.

Through the Gnostics, through the Neo-Platonists, especially through the Christian Neo-Platonist who wrote under the pseudonym Dionysius the Areopagite, and above all through contact with the pagan world and its wide-spread belief in magic, the Christian Church unconsciously absorbed a multiform faith in theurgy. Angels of many orders, saints who have been glorified, the Virgin Mary and her divine Son, can and do work wonders, it is believed, for faithful worshippers. Water and bread and wine and other elements of nature are by miraculous divine grace transformed into spiritual substances, become, in fact, the real divine presence, and supply to the recipient supernatural powers, which *work* mightily within the soul. Many Roman Catholic saints and many 14th and 15th cent. mystics believed themselves possessed of special theurgic powers. Stigmata of nail-prints were believed to be divinely produced in the hands and feet of Francis of Assisi and of Catharine of Siena. Others had the power to 'levitate' them-

[1] See G. Faber's cautious survey and verdict in his *Buddhistische und Neutestamentliche Erzählungen*, Leipzig, 1913, pp. 10-29.
[2] *Gnostic Heresies*, London, 1875, p. 31 f.
[3] *ERE* x. 729 f.

[1] *Hours with the Mystics*, i. 36.

selves and to soar above the earth in moments of possession. Others had the miraculous gift of shedding tears in extraordinary measure or of emitting fragrant odours from their body in periods of ecstasy, while still others underwent profound physical transformations or radiated light like a self-luminous body. The entire field of theurgic phenomena is thus intimately bound up with the psychology of hysteria and auto-suggestion. Automatism of many types is now scientifically recognized. It seems to the 'subject,' when parts of his own body perform functions without his conscious volition, as though some foreign person had entered and possessed him and were using his hands or his feet or his lips. Where the results are beneficent and constructive, it seems natural to believe that divine power has come to his assistance and is working a miraculous work through him, so that theurgy appears, to persons of this type, to rest upon facts of experience.

An immense revival of theurgy came in with the rise of humanism and during the period when science was emerging from the stage of superstition and pseudo-science. This revival was due, in large measure, to the influence of Neo-Platonism and of the Jewish Ḳabbālā, both of which the early humanists studied with zeal and enthusiasm. Pico della Mirandola (1463–94) gave great prominence to the symbolical, mystical, theurgical Ḳabbālā, and he also glorified the writings of the Neo-Platonists. W. R. Inge quotes the following passage from Pico's *Apology* which illustrates the mental attitude of the first humanists:

'One of the chief charges against me is that I am a magician. Have I not myself distinguished two kinds of magic? One, which the Greeks call γοητεία, depends entirely on alliance with evil spirits, and deserves to be regarded with horror, and to be punished; the other is magic in the proper sense of the word. The former subjects man to the evil spirits, the latter makes them serve him. The former is neither an art nor a science; the latter embraces the deepest mysteries, and the knowledge of the whole of Nature with her powers. While it connects and combines the forces scattered by God through the whole world, it does not so much work miracles as come to the help of working nature. Its researches into the sympathies of things enable it to bring to light hidden marvels from the secret treasure-houses of the world, just as if it created them itself. As the countryman trains the vine upon the elm, so the magician marries the earthly objects to heavenly bodies. His art is beneficial and Godlike, for it brings men to wonder at the works of God, than which nothing conduces more to true religion.'[1]

Reuchlin (1455–1522) carried the study of the Ḳabbālā and of Neo-Platonism still farther and laid the basis for the theurgy and magic which swarm in the writings of Cornelius Agrippa of Nettesheim, Paracelsus, Valentine Weigel, and, in a distinctly less degree, Jacob Boehme. All these theosophically-minded thinkers believed that it was possible to come into possession of direct divine wisdom or light and thereby to discover the secret of the universe and to use the secret in marvellous theurgic ways. Reuchlin expressed this view, in 1517, in a passage which is translated in the appendix to the *Three Books of Occult Philosophy by Henry Cornelius Agrippa.*[2] He says:

'God, out of love to his people, has revealed the hidden mysteries to some of them, and these can find in the dead letters the living spirit. For Scripture consists of single letters, visible signs, which stand in a certain connection with the angels as celestial and spiritual emanations from God. By the pronunciation of the one, the others also are affected; but with a true Cabalist, who penetrates the whole connection of the earthly with the heavenly, these signs, rightly placed in connection with each other, are a way of putting him into immediate union with the spirits, who through that are bound to satisfy his wishes.'

A still better account of the theurgic operations which are believed to work through those who catch the divine secret and find the light is given in the words of 'J. F.,' who translated Agrippa's *Occult Philosophy* into English in 1651. The passage is in the 'Preface to the Judicious Reader,' and is as follows:

[1] *Christian Mysticism*, p. 269, footnote 2.
[2] Ed. W. F. Whitehead, Chicago and London, 1898, p. 251.

'This is true and sublime Occult Philosophy. To understand the mysterious influences of the intellectual world upon the celestial, and of both upon the terrestrial; and to know how to dispose and fit ourselves so as to be capable of receiving the superior operations of these worlds, whereby we may be enabled to operate wonderful things by a natural power—to discover the secret counsels of men, to increase riches, to overcome enemies, to procure the favour of men, to expel diseases, to preserve health, to prolong life, to renew youth, to foretell future events, to see and know things done many miles off, and such like as these. These things may seem incredible, yet read but the ensuing treatise and thou shalt see the possibility confirmed both by reason and example.'

Once more in modern times there has appeared a recrudescence of theurgy in spiritualistic and theosophical circles. The element of fact in it now, as of old in the days of humanism and of Neo-Platonism, is due to the automatisms, *i.e.* to subliminal action, emerging without the subject of the action being conscious that it is initiated by him. It seems to be done through him and not by him and thus is attributed to God, or to spirits who 'possess' him.

LITERATURE.—Jules Simon, *Hist. de l'école d'Alexandrie*, 2 vols., Paris, 1844–45; E. Vacherot, *Hist. critique de l'école d'Alexandrie*, 3 vols., do. 1846–51; *Theurgia: or, The Egyptian Mysteries, by Iamblicos*, tr. Alexander Wilder, London, 1912; J. Reuchlin, *De Verbo Mirifico*, Basel, 1494, *De Arte Cabbalistica*, Hagenau, 1517; Agrippa of Nettesheim, *De Incertitudine et Vanitate omnium Scientiarum et Artium*, tr. J. F., London, 1651; Franz Hartmann, *Life and Teachings of Paracelsus*, do. 1896; R. A. Vaughan, *Hours with the Mystics*, 2 vols., do. 1860; W. R. Inge, *Christian Mysticism*, do. 1899; R. M. Jones, *Spiritual Reformers in the 16th and 17th Centuries*, do. 1914, esp. chapters on Weigel and Boehme.

R. M. JONES.

THIRTY-NINE ARTICLES.—See CONFESSIONS.

THOMISM.—**1. Name.**—Broadly speaking, Thomism is the name given to the system of philosophy and theology founded by St. Thomas Aquinas (*q.v.*). Strictly speaking, it is the name given to a group of opinions taught by St. Thomas and held by what is known as the Thomistic school, which is mainly but not exclusively composed of Dominicans.

2. Historical survey.—The foundation of Thomism is incontestably due to the personal influence of St. Thomas Aquinas. It should not, however, be forgotten that Albert the Great did much to prepare the way for the birth of the new system, so that the names of both master and pupil will ever remain inseparable in the great work. Although there were many points of contact between the minds of Albert and Thomas, the genius of the one was entirely different from that of the other. The mind of Thomas was more critical than Albert's. The latter does not possess his subject quite perfectly; there is a lack of precision in details and a certain want of synthesis necessary to unify his knowledge. On the contrary, Thomas possesses his matter perfectly; above all, he has a power for order; his precision is nicer and his analysis finer; his vision is more penetrating and more embracing; and his power of analysis is on equal footing with his power of synthesis. Albert revealed to his age an intellectual world unknown to it; Thomas with the débris of the intellectual world of the ancients created a new one. Both aimed at incorporating Aristotle into Christian philosophy and theology. Albert's endeavour has the merit of initiative, but it remained incomplete and only provisional; Thomas with a magician's hand forwarded the work and produced a masterpiece which he embellished with a finish undreamed of by Albert.

Before the time of St. Thomas several attempts had been made to synthesize the sum of human knowledge, but nothing of any great value had been the result. The work of reformation undertaken by St. Thomas was so vast and complicated that it is not surprising that he was at first a little hesitating and diffident; but, as he advanced in years and learning, his vision became clearer, and at the age of thirty he took up a position that, with regard to most things, was definite and final. Being perfectly familiar with all the problems discussed by philosophy and theology, and having carefully weighed the value of the respective solutions and examined the systematic points of view already attempted, he saw that a perfect system necessarily demanded the unification of the whole of knowledge. This perfect ordering of the whole of knowledge which he bequeathed to the world was due to his sublime metaphysical sense. It is because St. Thomas surpassed the host of thinkers of his time as metaphysician that he produced a unique work.

In philosophy he is the first to proclaim the autonomy of reason; and he has produced his philosophic works without once having recourse to an authority other than experience and reason to establish his conclusions and defend them. Starting from the 'sensible' world as from a secure basis, St. Thomas passes to the region of the absolute, to the highest and purest intellectualism. In theology he proclaims the autonomy of revelation. At the outset he maintains the impossibility of a real conflict between the natural and supernatural orders which have the same source of truth, viz. God. Thus he synthesizes natural and supernatural, nature and grace, faith and reason. To assimilate his thought it is necessary to understand, above all, the functioning of his general synthesis, and especially of his metaphysics, which rules the whole economy of his work. Eclecticism has no meaning with regard to Thomistic doctrines; their value and strength reside essentially in the marvel of their unity and solidarity.

3. Progress of Thomism. — The Dominican order gradually took up the teaching of St. Thomas, but not without opposition; some of its members were still imbued with the doctrines of Augustinism, and these could not be converted to a new system in a day.

Robert Kilwarby, archbishop of Canterbury and a Dominican, condemned St. Thomas's theory of the unity of substantial form, on 18th March 1277. A few years later, however, the English Dominicans were among the most resolute defenders of this doctrine. In Germany Ulrich Engelbert de Strasbourg († 1277) inclined towards Augustinism and the Neo-Platonism of the Arabs. Eckhart († 1327) was much inclined towards Neo-Platonism. Thierry († towards 1315) was an Augustinist strongly influenced by Avicenna: the latter never hesitated to combat the doctrine of St. Thomas.

In France the great adversary of the new system was Durand de Saint-Pourçain. In Italy Umbertus Guidi was punished by the Dominican Provincial Chapter of Arezzo in 1315 for attacking St. Thomas; and the General Chapter of Puy (1344) cautioned Thomas of Naples for opposition to St. Thomas. Many chapters of the Dominican order encouraged and promoted Thomistic doctrines. Worthy of mention are the General Chapters of Paris (1286), of Saragossa (1309), of Metz (1313), of Castres (1329), of Brive (1346). So great indeed was the attachment of the Dominicans to the *Summa Theologica* that the celebrated Spaniard Arnauld de Villeneuve († 1311) wrote a work against the Dominicans in 1304 (*Gladius jugulans Thomistas*), in which he accuses the Dominicans of preferring the study of the *Summa* to that of the Bible. Two centuries later Erasmus formulated the same reproach.[1]

4. Introduction of St. Thomas's writings as text-books in schools.—At the end of the 13th cent. the Bible was the principal text, and the *Sentences* of Peter the Lombard was the theological text *par excellence*. The Dominicans introduced the reading of the *Sentences* 'in via Thomae,' *i.e.* according to the thought of St. Thomas. Other schools following this example taught the *Sentences* 'in via Alberti,' 'in via Durandi,' 'in via Scoti,' etc. Not until the end of the 15th cent. did the Dominicans substitute entirely the *Summa* for the *Sentences*.

[1] *Opera Omnia*, Leyden, 1703–06, iii. 515.

5. Thomistic polemics.—The fights sustained by the Dominican order during the end of the Middle Ages in defence of their school were (1) to make a good stand against Augustinism, and (2) to defend certain doctrines special to Thomism.

(*a*) *General.*—In favour of Augustinism a great reaction was made by the Friars Minor in a work composed by William de la Mare. The Oxford Dominicans replied in a work known as the *Corruptorium.* A further work, *Correctorium Corruptorii*, was published by two Oxford Dominicans, William de Makelsfeld and Richard Knapwell. At the end of the 13th cent. another general defence of Thomism was written by Robert de Bologne, *Apologeticum pro St. Thoma.* Last of all a great work (unfinished) was written by a celebrated Thomist, Hervé Noël de Nedellec, master at the university of Paris and master-general of the Dominicans, *Defensa doctrinæ Sti. Thomæ Hervœus Natalis.*

Other important works written towards the end of the Middle Ages are *Defensiones theologiæ divi Thomæ Aquinatis*[1] by John Capreolus († 1444), who was called the 'princeps Thomistarum,' and *Clypeus Thomistarum contra modernos et Scotistas*[2] by Pierre Niger († 1481). Diego de Deza († 1523), the illustrious protector of Christopher Columbus, wrote two polemical works in favour of Thomism, of which the more important is: *Novarum defensionum doctrinæ Angelici Doctoris beati Thomæ de Aquinas super quatuor libros Sententiarum quæstiones profundissimæ et utilissimæ* (Seville, 1517).

(*b*) *Special.* —(1) St. Thomas formulated the theory of the unity of the human person by making the intellectual soul the only *form* of the human composite. Against the Averroism (taught at Paris) which held the unicity of intellect for the human species, and against Augustinism, which held the plurality of forms, several treatises were written by Thomists—*e.g.*, by Pierre de Tarantaise, Gilles de Lessines, William de Makelsfeld, Thomas de Sutton, Jean de Faënza, etc.

The General Council of Vienne defined the Thomistic doctrine on this matter, which was further confirmed by the 5th Council of Lateran (1515), and by Pope Pius IX. in a letter to the archbishop of Cologne (15th June 1857).

(2) The question of the nature of religious poverty and its practice by Christ and the apostles was hotly discussed between the Dominicans and the Friars Minor. The discussion became so disastrous that Pope John XXII. condemned as erroneous and heretical the doctrine that Christ and the apostles did not possess anything, or did not perform acts of proprietorship, viz. buying and selling; etc. (12th Nov. 1323, *Cum inter nonnullos*).

(3) There was another theological combat between the Dominicans and the Minors with regard to the blood of Christ shed during the Passion. The Minors said that it ceased to be united to the divinity of Christ, the Dominicans that the union did not cease. Eventually Pope Pius II. forbade both parties to discuss the question further.[3]

(4) The Dominicans strenuously fought against the nominalism[4] of the 14th cent. of which Durand de Saint-Pourçain and William Ockham were the leaders.

[1] New ed., 7 vols., ed. C. Paban and T. Pègues, Tours, 1900–08.
[2] Venice, 1481.
[3] All the literature of this quarrel is to be found in a MS in the Bibliothèque of Paris (*Cat.* 12390, fol. 1–78; also cf. Benedict XIV., *de Servorum Dei Beatificatione et beatorum Canonizatione*, bk. ii. ch. 30).
[4] See art. REALISM AND NOMINALISM.

(5) The Averroism against which Albert the Great and St. Thomas fought was renewed again at the beginning of the 16th cent. in Italy. Thomas de Vio, called Cajetan, published a commentary on the *de Anima* of Aristotle (Florence, 1509). A few years later the Council of Lateran (19th Dec. 1513) condemned the teaching of Averroism on the point, and further exacted that professors of philosophy should solve contrary arguments, which Cajetan held only theologians could do.

(6) In the 14th cent. disputes concerning the Immaculate Conception arose. St. Thomas undoubtedly leaves the question unsolved, but he was at great pains to show that the Blessed Virgin was not excluded from the redemption. St. Thomas says that the precise moment of sanctification is unknown; he therefore never propounded the question whether Mary was sanctified at the very instant of conception. He believed it better to be silent on this point, although, had he followed his personal inclination, he had without doubt concluded in the affirmative, as his first declaration witnesses in *IV. Sent.* I. dist. xliv. qu. 1, art. 3, ad 3. But his superior theological sense did not let him, in presence of the silence of tradition and the negative position of many theologians, and in particular the reserved attitude of the Church. The endeavour to drag St. Thomas to the negative or positive side is to force his meaning, since he voluntarily abstained from either.

6. Renascence of Thomism.—In the 14th and 15th centuries there was an intellectual decadence in philosophy and theology. Thomism could not altogether abstract itself from the influence of the time. However, even in the 15th cent. there was notable vitality among Thomists like John Capreolus, St. Antoninus of Florence, and Jean de Torquemada. At the end of the 15th cent. the intellectual life of Thomism received new vigour, which manifested itself in the 16th cent. and continued for two centuries afterwards. In 1551 the General Chapter of Salamanca ordered the text of St. Thomas's writings to be used as text-books in all its schools. Hence at this time the great commentaries began to be written. Cajetan wrote from 1507 to 1522; Conrad Köllin on the *Prima secundæ* (Cologne, 1512); François de Vittoria (whose commentaries remained in MSS) and Barthélemy de Medina from 1577 to 1578; Banez from 1584 to 1594; Sylvester Ferrariensis on the *Summa contra Gentiles* (Venice, 1534). The humanist movement of the 16th cent. had a great influence on certain Thomists. François de Vittoria took the lead; of his disciples the most famous was Melchior Cano († 1560), whose work, *de Locis theologicis*, is a tribute to the humanist movement by its purity and beauty of style. Two new doctrines issued from the humanist state of thought: Ambrose Catharin († 1553) put forward new theories on predestination and grace; and Barthélemy de Medina formulated probabilism. Thomists combated the former doctrine; whilst in answer to the desire of Pope Alexander VII. they combated strongly probabilist doctrines.

7. Thomism and the Council of Trent.—Thomists held an important part in this council. The Thomistic school had grave interests at stake on account of the dogmatic question regarding the doctrine of justification. Of the five members of the commission instituted by Paul III. to study this question three were Dominicans, of whom Barthélemy Spina, master of the Sacred Palace, was the most active. The decree on justification was not drawn up without the help of St. Thomas. The text of the decree as regards the mode of preparation for justification[1] is taken in its every detail from the *Summa*, III. qu. lxxxv. art. 5. The decree numbers six acts preparatory to justification. They are the same in nature, number, and order as in the *Summa* (*loc. cit.*). Also, in the following chapter of the decree the causes of justification are exactly those given by St. Thomas in the *Summa*, I. ii. qu. cxii. art. 4, and II. ii. qu. xxiv. art. 3.

[1] Sess. vi. ch. vi.

The official catechism (published by the council), in which the doctrine of the Catholic Church is contained and which was compiled for the use of the clergy, was drawn up by three Thomists—Leonard de Marinis (archbishop of Lanciano), Gilles Foscarari (bishop of Modena), and François Foreiro (theologian to the king of Portugal).

As soon as the Council of Trent was finished, Pope Pius V. on 11th April 1567 proclaimed St. Thomas a doctor of the Church.

8. Thomism and Molinism.—See art. MOLINISM; also see below § 12.

9. Thomism and Jansenism.—In his posthumous work *Augustinus* (Louvain, 1640) Jansenius strove to prove that the new theology, especially that of Molina and Suarez, was against the doctrine of St. Augustine and contrary to the doctrine authorized by the Catholic Church.[1] The *Augustinus* aroused much opposition among the Jesuits. After an examination of the book, the Dominicans found that it militated not only against Molinism, but also against Thomism. Two Dominicans wrote against Jansenius—Alexander Sébille (*de Augustini et SS. Patrum de libero arbitrio interpres thomisticus adversus Cornelii Jansenii doctrinam*, Mayence, 1652), and Bernard Guyard (*Discrimina inter doctrinam Thomisticam et Jansenianam*, Paris, 1655).

10. Thomism and probabilism.—The theory of probabilism (*q.v.*) was unfolded by Barthélemy de Medina, a Dominican, in his *Expositio in Primam Secundæ D. Thomæ* (Salamanca, 1577). The Jesuits generally adopted this new theory. But, since the ease with which any opinion could be made probable, provided the contradictory was probable, led to grave abuses, Alexander VII. asked the Dominicans to combat strongly the probabilist doctrines. This they did, and from that time no Dominican theologian has written in favour of probabilism.

11. Neo-Thomism and the revival of Scholasticism.—At the beginning of the 19th cent. Scholasticism (*q.v.*) began to revive, and there followed a revival of Thomism. The encyclical *Æterni Patris* of Pope Leo XIII. (4th Aug. 1879) set up St. Thomas Aquinas as the great model and master of Catholic philosophy and theology. From that time all schools have studied the works of the master and have endeavoured to make his thought their own. The endeavour to keep in touch with the progress of modern science, and to show that the fundamentals of Thomism are in perfect accord with the latest discoveries of science, was set on foot, not, as is sometimes supposed, by the Institut Supérieur de Philosophie of Louvain University, but by the Thomist Sanseverino, one of the most learned and vigorous promoters of the movement. This is evidenced by his work, *Philosophia Christiana cum antiqua et nova comparata*. This great movement has been fostered and developed by the Institut Supérieur de Philosophie, founded by Cardinal Mercier at Louvain. Certain *Revues* are now published in which the teachings of Neo-Thomism and Neo-Scholasticism are consistently set forth. The *Revue Thomiste* and the *Revue néo-scolastique de Philosophie* are worthy of mention.

12. Essence of Thomism.—Thomism is above all a system of philosophy and theology. Now a

[1] See art. JANSENISM.

system necessarily implies harmony and solidarity among the doctrines of which the system is built up. In proportion as a system lacks unity, so much is it less of a system. Many philosophers and theologians have endeavoured to give systems of knowledge to the world, but on examination it is found that they lack the first essential of a system, viz. solidarity of thought in every department. If certain principles are laid down in metaphysics, no doctrine in any department of applied metaphysics (as, *e.g.*, in psychology, cosmology, natural theology, ethics, etc.) should be at variance with those principles. Moreover, if a system claims to be a system of the *whole* of knowledge, both of that attained by human reason and of that attained by revelation, then no doctrine formulated by natural reason should be at variance with the doctrines formulated by faith; and conversely. It is evident that, if there be a system of this nature, it is eminently constructive or synthetic. Every stone in the structure must be in its proper place, and, if the building is to stand firm, there must be some grand unifying principle or foundation upon which it is built up. Now, just as in any architectural building there cannot be several foundations, but only one ultimate foundation, so in Thomism there is one fundamental principle unifying the system and imparting harmony and solidarity to every department which it embraces.

13. The fundamental principle of Thomism.—An examination of the various departments of Thomist metaphysics, of applied metaphysics, and of the whole realm of Thomist theology will show that the fundamental doctrines of each department are applications to various matters of a great principle inculcated by Aristotle in his metaphysics. It is the principle of the real distinction between *act* and *potentiality*. One has not far to seek in order to understand what is meant by 'act' and by 'potentiality.' 'Act' means perfection; 'potentiality' means absence of perfection. A thing in the state of potentiality is in an imperfect state, and is therefore capable of receiving what it lacks, viz. some perfection or an act (as it is termed in scholastic language), whereby it ceases to be in a state of potentiality and is brought to a state of having some perfection. There are, as is evident, many kinds of states of potentiality and many kinds of corresponding states of act, but it is not necessary to enter into a discussion of them, since the doctrine underlying them all is one and the same. Furthermore, it is clear that the state of potentiality must be really distinct from the state of act; for, if this be not true, then 'to run' and 'to be able to run,' 'to know' and 'to be able to know,' 'to be hot' and 'to be able to be hot,' are one and the same, which is absurd. Hence there must be a real (extra-mental) distinction between the two states. This principle, then, may be formulated thus: *Between the state of potentiality and the state of act there is a real distinction.* Further, the first unfolding of this principle necessarily implies that that which is in a state of potentiality cannot cease to be in that state unless it be 'moved' from that state by something which is in the state of act; *e.g.*, cold water has the potentiality to become hot, but it is impossible for cold water to become hot unless it be 'moved' from that state by something that actually possesses heat. It will be seen that this conclusion is an immediate inference of the real distinction between potentiality and act. Hence the principle in a more explicit way may be formulated thus: *Potentiality, which is really distinct from act, can never become act unless it be reduced to act by something which is in act.*

This is the fundamental principle of the entire Thomist system; established at the outset in metaphysics, it is applied without exception to the fundamental doctrines in every department of Thomist philosophy and theology. Whoever draws a single conclusion which is in any way at variance with this principle, although he may hold all other doctrines of the Thomist system, ceases *ipso facto* to be a Thomist.

14. The application of the principle.—(*a*) *In metaphysics.*—The Thomist doctrine of real distinction between essence and existence in created things, wherein essence is conceived as a potentiality and existence as an act, is an application of the principle; likewise the real distinction between substance and its accidents, wherein substance is conceived as in potentiality to the accidents which are its acts or perfections; likewise the doctrine concerning the nature of dimensive quantity, the essence of which is not that it actually extends the parts of a corporeal substance in place, *i.e.* in triple dimension, but that it distributes the parts of that substance within the substance itself (which internal parts are only potentially distributed in triple dimension by dimensive quantity), and that it has the capability or potentiality of *actually* extending those parts in place according to triple dimension. Upon this doctrine of the nature of dimensive quantity is founded the doctrine of the real presence of the whole body of Christ in a small consecrated Host; also the doctrine of the virgin birth of Christ, of His passing into a room, the doors being shut, etc. Likewise the important doctrine of cause and effect, or the principle of causality, is an application of the aforesaid fundamental principle. An analysis of 'that which begins to be (effect) must have a reason (cause) for its inception' shows the underlying great principle.

(*b*) *In psychology.*—The doctrine of the unity of the human composite, viz. that the intellectual soul is the substantial form of the body, and that it is the only form, is an application of the same principle. The 'prime matter,' a pure potentiality, which is informed by the intellectual soul (or act) receives from this act all that makes it body, and human body, and living. Through the same principle it follows that the faculties of intellect and will are really distinct from the substance of the soul, because they are the acts or perfections of the soul, which in regard to them is a potentiality. As a consequence it also follows not only that every faculty is really distinct from its object as potentiality to act, but also that, in regard to it *as object*, every faculty is passive, not active. Hence the important doctrine that the human intellect is a passive, not active, power or faculty, in that it receives, and does not make, its object of thought *as object*.

Further (and this is most important from the point of view of Thomism *versus* Molinism), the human will, which is the faculty of choice, must ultimately be moved to the very act of choosing by something which is in act; and the reason is that, before the act of choosing (given everything necessary for this action save this action itself), the will is in a state of potentiality and must therefore be 'moved' by something outside it to the state of perfection which is 'choosing.' Only God, the *actus purus*, can move the will to the very act of choosing; if aught else did this, the will *ipso facto* would cease to be free. This is the Thomistic doctrine of physical premotion, which is a rigorous application of the aforesaid fundamental principle.

(*c*) *In cosmology.*—In this department of applied metaphysics the fundamental question concerns the precise nature of body, as body. Applying the aforesaid principle, Thomism concludes that body, as body, is a composite of two principles, one of which is substantial form and the other prime matter. Prime matter is a pure potentiality of which the substantial form is the act; and between the two, as a consequence, there is a real distinction.

(*d*) *In natural theology.*—The classic proof for the existence of God, viz. from the existence of motion in the world, is nothing more than a rigorous application of the same principle. Motion is here taken in its widest sense, embracing not only local motion but every kind of 'passing from potentiality to act.'[1]

(*e*) *In ethics.*—All the doctrines concerning habits and their formation, of the passions, of virtues and vices, of laws, etc., have their mainstay in the same fundamental principle.

(*f*) *In theology.*—For the existence of God see above (*d*). It is only necessary to run through the *Summa* to see that the same principle is fundamental in the doctrines concerning revelation and concerning inspiration (in which is implied the doctrine of cause and effect, and in particular of instrumental causality). By an understanding of the same great principle it is concluded that God alone is pure act with no admixture of potentiality whatsoever, whilst everything created contains both potentiality and act. It is further concluded not only that God's essence is identically the same as His existence, but that His intellect and His will, His attributes of unity, goodness, truth, His knowledge and love are likewise identically the same as His essence. The same grand principle underlies the whole of the doctrine concerning the mystery of the trinity of persons in God. A further application is to be found in the treatise on the angels, whose existence is really distinct from their essence, whose minds and wills are really distinct from their substance, etc. Thus through the whole of the *Summa* one finds the same principle applied. It will be necessary to take only two more cases in order to show the solidarity of Thomistic doctrines. According to St. Thomas, the sacraments are the instrumental causes of grace; they are not mere channels through which grace is infused into the soul; they are real, physical, instrumental causes which produce or infuse grace into the soul. The soul in regard to the sacramental grace that informs it is a potentiality (*potentia obedientialis*), and grace is the act.

The final instance we shall take to illustrate the application of the fundamental principle of Thomism concerns the doctrine of actual grace. Just as in the natural order it was concluded that the human will is physically premoved by God to the act of choice,[2] so in the supernatural order an actual grace is nothing more than a physical premotion in that order. Hence the Thomists speak of 'gratia efficax ab intrinseco,' a grace intrinsically or of its very nature efficacious, and not of grace, intrinsically indifferent, to be made efficacious by consent of the will to accept, or to remain inefficacious by refusal of the will to accept. Thus Thomism, by a relentless logic, applies the great principle to the doctrine of actual grace. To the mind of St. Thomas, in spite of the apparent difficulties, this doctrine is the only logical conclusion. For Thomism the theory of Molina or Suarez bristles with more difficulties in that the theory subverts the doctrines of God as the Prime Mover of all things, of causality, and of the great metaphysical principle: *Potentiality, which is really distinct from act, can never become act unless it be reduced to act by something which is in act.* In short, for the sake of a difficulty in applied metaphysics (*i.e.* the freedom of the will under God's physical premotion), Molina and Suarez gainsay a principle already established in metaphysics, just as he who, on account of some difficulty in mixed mathematics, gainsays a principle of pure mathematics.

[1] Cf. *Summa*, I. qu. ii. art. 3, *Prima via*.
[2] See above (*b*).

Any conclusion other than the one drawn above wrecks a system of the whole of knowledge in the mind of the Thomist. It is owing to the perfect consistency of application of the grand fundamental principle aforesaid to every department of knowledge that Thomas bequeathed to the world a sublime system remarkable for its perfect unity, harmony, and solidarity of thought.

LITERATURE.—For the history of Thomism generally: *Dictionnaire d'Apologétique*, *s.v.* 'Frères Prêcheurs, Leur doctrine' (P. Mandonnet); *CE*, *s.v.* 'Thomism.' For the progress of Thomism: *Acta capitulorum generalium ordinis Prædicatorum*, Rome, 1893–1904, ed. B. M. Reichert, ii. 196–391 (of the Dominican order).

For Thomistic polemics: Mandonnet, 'Premiers Travaux de polémique thomiste,' in *Revue des Sciences philosophiques et théologiques*, vii. [1913] 46 ff.

Concerning the nature of religious poverty: A. G. Little, *The Grey Friars in Oxford*, Oxford, 1892, p. 320; Felice di Tocco, *La questione della poverta nel secolo xiv.*, Naples.

Concerning the blood of Christ during the Passion: MS in the Bibliothèque de Paris, *Cat.* 12390, fol. 1–78; Benedict XIV., *de Servorum Dei Beatificatione et beatorum Canonizatione*, bk. ii. ch. 30, in *Opera*, Venice, 1788.

For Thomism *versus* Nominalism of 14th cent.: C. Jourdain, *La Philosophie de S. Thomas d'Aquin*, Paris, 1858, ii. 216; K. Werner, *Die nominalisirende Psychologie der Scholastik des späteren Mittelalters*, Vienna, 1882.

For Thomism and the Immaculate Conception: *IV. Sententiarum*, I. dist. xlii. qu. 1, art. 3, ad 3; N. del Prado, *Santo Tomas y la Immaculada Vergan*, Salamanca, 1909; F. Morgott, *La Doctrine sur la vierge Marie, ou Mariologie de saint Thomas d'Aquin*, Paris, 1881, p. 139 ff.

For Thomism and the Council of Trent: A. Reginaldus, *Dissertatio de Catechismi Romani auctoritate*, Toulouse, 1648, Naples, 1765; A. Theiner, *Acta genuina SS. œcumenici Concilii Tridentini*, 2 vols., Agram, 1874.

For Thomism and Jansenism: Le R. P. Guillermin, 'De la grace suffisante,' *Revue Thomiste*, ix.–xi. [1901–03].

For the revival of Thomism: G. Sanseverino, *Philosophia Christiana cum antiqua et nova comparata*, 5 vols., Naples, 1862; *Revue Thomiste* and *Revue néo-Scolastique de Philosophie*, *passim*.

For Thomism *versus* Molinism: literature under art. MOLINISM.

For the essence of Thomism: Thomas Aquinas, *Summa Theologica* and *Summa contra Gentiles*; N. del Prado, *de Veritate fundamentali philosophiæ christianæ*, Fribourg (Switzerland), 1889, new ed., 1911, *de Gratia et libero arbitrio*, 3 vols., do. 1907; artt. AQUINAS and MOLINISM.

ÆLRED WHITACRE.

THRACE (Θρῄκη, Θρᾴκη).—Thrace was the name given in classical times to the mountainous region lying north of Greece proper. The inhabitants (Θρήϊκες, Θρέϊκες, Θρᾷκες) were a barbarous people, having no close affinities to the Greeks in language, culture, or originally in religion. In the last field, however, their influence on their more civilized neighbours was considerable, beginning early and continuing fairly late. In particular, they appear to have been partly responsible for the remarkable change in the spirit of Greek religion which took place about the beginning of the classical epoch or shortly before it. This change must not be thought of as something revolutionary, akin, *e.g.*, to the conversion of most of N. Europe from Roman Catholicism to Protestantism at the Reformation; for the large majority, probably if not certainly, religious beliefs and practices changed little if at all; it was rather the introduction of a new element, which rendered possible the holding by many Greeks of ideas either unknown to their fathers or existing among them in a very undeveloped form, and largely forgotten when first we hear anything definite about the Greek race.

1. Origin and history of the Thracians.—The Thracian invasion of the country which they occupied in historical times is part of a wider movement from the north into the hilly region of the Balkans and the countries west and east of that district (Bosnia and Herzegovina on the one side, the Caucasus and Armenia on the other). The invaders were of Indo-European stock, probably originally from the Carpathians. Driven perhaps by the pressure of Slovak tribes from the region of the Vistula, or possibly from sheer restlessness or desire for fresh territory, they occupied the country in successive waves. The Phrygians (*q.v.*) and tribes most closely related to them, together with the Armenians, occupied the Asiatic district for the most part; the Thracians seized chiefly upon the European sector. That Thracian and Phrygian were related stocks was already recognized in antiquity,[1] and modern philology, together with arguments drawn from their religious and social organization, inclines us to believe that this is substantially correct. Throughout Greek history the Thracians, or the majority of them, remained politically independent, protected both by their great courage and by the difficult nature of their country; Rome, after much trouble, succeeded in subduing them, the ferocious Dacians finally yielding to Trajan. They remained, however, an intractable people, little influenced by the civilization of their rulers. Finally, about A.D. 400, their ancient priestly tribe, the Bessoi, were converted to Christianity. Some 200 years later a Slovak invasion swept over the country, and from that time begins the history of what ultimately became the Balkan peoples.

2. **Ethnology.**—The Thracian races fall, broadly speaking, into two groups—a northern and a southern. The latter, inhabiting the region of the Haimos and Strymon, included, besides the Bessoi already mentioned, the Bisaltai, Thynoi, Bithynoi, Sakai, Dioi, Odrysai, and other tribes; the former or Getic group consisted of a smaller number of peoples, individually more important than the tribes just mentioned. Besides the powerful Getai themselves, we must count among them the still more formidable Dacians (Δᾶκοι, Δᾶκαι, Δῖοι), who are often confused with them, and the Agathyrsoi, whose name seems to indicate that they were held in no great esteem by their Scythian neighbours (the first two syllables are probably to be connected with Zend *agha*, 'bad'), and who appear from Herodotos[2] to have practised the very primitive custom of group-marriage. On the whole, the northern group shows certain cultural affinities with the Germanic tribes, the southern with the Orientals, especially, as already mentioned, with the Phrygians.

3. **Language.**—As the Thracians seem to have had no knowledge of writing, the few inscriptions we have from Thrace are late and never in the native tongue. There remain, however, a number of glosses, some 36 of which we may take as genuine Thracian words; about 25 names of plants given as Thracian by Dioscorides; and a considerable number of proper names, both of persons (including deities) and of places. From these it appears that their tongue was Indo-Germanic, of the E. European group, having as its nearest ancient congeners Phrygian and Armenian. Traces appear of two distinct linguistic stocks, the result presumably of the blending of two races; and this we may consider along with the fact reported by Herodotos[3] that the cult practised by their chieftains differed from that of the common people.

4. **Material culture.**—It has been pointed out[4] that Homer does not consider the Thracian culture as an inferior one. In the *Iliad* the Thracians are for the most part the allies of the Trojans; Priam's treasury includes a cup of their giving;[5] the son of Antenor was brought up in Thrace and married there;[6] Rhesos comes to Priam's aid with a strong Thracian contingent.[7] On the other hand, some of them at least trade with the Greeks.[8] No hint is given that they are in any sense savages; in particular, the followers of Rhesos encamp in a soldierly manner.[9] But there is no need to suppose, as Helbig does, that the Thracians of that day, under Phœnician or other foreign influence, were enjoying a short period of 'hothouse' culture which brought them for a time to higher levels than they ever afterwards attained. The true explanation seems to be that Homer knows nothing of the later division between Greek and barbarian, and that the Greeks of his day were not a highly civilized people themselves. A race which lived under the rule of feudal barons, practised the blood-feud, allowed wer-gelt, occasionally mutilated or otherwise ill-treated a dead foe, was not quite free from the custom of human sacrifice, and buried its dead much in the fashion of the historical Thracians,[10] besides keeping up the old custom of bride-price and having only very rudimentary manufactures and handicrafts, was not much superior to the Thracians of historical times. The difference was that the Greeks developed with marvellous rapidity in the next 300 years or so, while the Thracians remained backward.[11]

Passing to classical authors of the later periods, we find our chief account of Thrace in Herodotos.[12] His whole attitude towards the Thracians, while not unfriendly,[1] is clearly that of civilized man describing interesting barbarians; and this is certainly justified. They are, he tells us, a numerous race, of little political importance owing to their lack of unity; their culture is on the whole uniform. They despise agriculture, counting it more honourable to be idle and to live by plunder. They have, however, some arts, as they can weave very good cloth of hemp fibre.[2] To this we may add, what sundry later authors tell us, that they showed skill in making various tools and weapons of iron.[3] They were accustomed to dye their hair and tatu their skin. They were, in some cases at least, polygynous; that they lived under father-right, not mother-right, is clear from the facts that they paid bride-price and that marital jealousy was strongly developed, though the chastity of an unmarried girl was quite disregarded—*i.e.*, their women were apparently thought of chiefly as valuable property, belonging to their fathers so long as they were unmarried—hence the light view taken of their immoralities, for any children that they might bear out of wedlock would also belong to their own family—but afterwards belonging to their husbands, who had paid for the exclusive use of them. When we add that as a race they were cattle-breeders and especially famous for their horses from very early times,[4] it is clear that we shall not be far wrong in comparing them to some one of the principal Basuto peoples, such as the Amazulu, before the latter attained unity of government under T'Chaka. Physically, however, they were at the other end of the colour-scale, being fair-skinned and yellow-haired.

Finally, four points should be noted as giving the clue to many features in their religion. According to the practically unanimous voice of antiquity, (1) the Thracians were desperately brave, having little fear of death; (2) they were excitable, and, in particular, had a bad name for unrestrained indulgence in sexual passion; (3) they were heavy drinkers; and (4) they were intensely fond of music, performing well on both flute and lyre. In addition, their country was a mountainous one, in which caves were no rarity.

5. **Religion.**—We may take as our starting-point the famous passage of Herodotos, v. 7: 'They worship only the following gods, Ares, Dionysos, and Artemis; but their kings . . . reverence Hermes above all other gods, swear by him alone, and say that they are descended from Hermes.' We must in the first place remember that the names in the above passage are not to be taken too literally. Whereas a modern writer, if he said that a particular race worshipped Buddha, would mean exactly what he said, and the Hebrew prophet[5] who speaks of the name of his God as being 'great among the Gentiles' means his words to be startlingly paradoxical, a Greek always assumes that the gods of all nations are much the same as his own and never scruples to talk of the Egyptian cult of Hermes or the Roman worship of Hera, meaning thereby Thoth and Juno. We shall see that, taken as it stands, Herodotos' statement is true of one deity only.

(*a*) *Ares.*—That Ares is a Thracian deity is a fairly wide-spread opinion. As far back as Homer[6] we find Thrace mentioned as the home of the war-god, and later writers echo Homer.[7] Ares has, moreover, certain non-Greek features; his cult is wholly without any of those higher forms which distinguish, *e.g.*, Apollo or Athene and remains throughout that of a war-god pure and simple. Homer's whole attitude towards him is one of dislike; he supports the Trojans throughout; and in his ritual we find one feature paralleled in Thrace[8] hard to parallel in purely Greek cult—the dog-sacrifice to him under the name of Enyalios at Sparta.[9]

At the same time it must be confessed that none

[1] οἱ Φρύγες Θρᾳκῶν ἄποικοί εἰσι (Strabo, x. 471).
[2] iv. 104. [3] v. 7.
[4] W. Helbig, *Das Homer. Epos*, Leipzig, 1884, p. 9.
[5] xxiv. 234; we are not told who made the cup.
[6] xi. 222 ff. [7] x. 434. [8] ix. 71 f.
[9] x. 471. [10] See below § 5 (*h*).
[11] The present writer holds the view of Andrew Lang, van Leeuwen, and other scholars that the Homeric poems are substantially the work of one man, and he would put their date about the 10th cent. B.C. For the Homeric customs above mentioned see *Il.* ix. 632, xxii. 371, xxiii. 175 (the poet clearly disapproves strongly of the sacrifice), and xxiii. *passim*, *Od.* xv. 224, 272 ff., xx. 355, and many other passages. Elaborate manufactures or works of art are regularly the work of gods (as *Il.* xviii. 468 ff.) or imported (as *Od.* iv. 615). Simple weaving and the like are done at home, as *Od.* ii. 94. Cf. the account of Thracian arts above.
[12] Chiefly v. 2–8. References to other passages of Herod are cited in the notes. For fuller authorities see Tomaschek, *Die alten Thraker*, i. 111 ff.

[1] Between Greeks as a whole and Thracians as a whole no bitterness seems to have existed. The references to Thracians as bloodthirsty savages are mostly in comparatively late authors—*e.g.*, Hor. *Od.* I. xxvii. 2. The writer is of opinion that the detestable conduct of certain Thracian mercenaries in the Peloponnesian War (Thuc. vii. 29) may have had something to do with this, while later their savage battles against the Romans prejudiced the latter against them.
[2] Herod. iv. 74, vii. 75.
[3] References in Tomaschek, i. 119.
[4] Cf. Hom. *Il.* x. 436. [5] Mal 1[11].
[6] *Il.* xiii. 301 and elsewhere.
[7] *E.g.*, Verg. *Æn.* iii. 35.
[8] *Vita Euripidis*, i. (vi.) ταύτην δὲ (τὴν κύνα) Θρᾷκες, ὡς ἔθος θύσαντες ἔφαγον.
[9] Plut. *Quæst. Rom.* 290*d*; Paus. III. xiv. 9; Arnob. *adv. Nat.* iv. 25. Such a sacrifice, however, is not wholly unknown elsewhere in Greece.

of the above features are conclusive against his Greek origin. Among a people brave enough, but not fond of war for its own sake, the war-god might well remain 'functional'—too important to be altogether neglected, too unpopular to develop. Among the traditional friends of Troy are also Apollo, Artemis, and at times Zeus himself; not much can be made from a single feature of an obscure ritual;[1] and the references to Thrace need mean no more than that the Thracians, being warlike, had a popular cult of a war-god. And we must remember that the cult of Ares is very old in Athens and Boiotia, and that his name is not only plausibly derived from an Aryan root, which in itself proves nothing, but has a characteristically Greek formation.[2]

We conclude therefore, on the whole, that the Thracians did not originate the Greek cult of Ares, but had from very early times a war-god of their own, about whose ritual we must be content to remain ignorant. It is worth mentioning that Herodotos seems to speak of him as an oracular god in one rather obscure passage.[3]

(*b*) *Dionysos.*—The case of Dionysos is very different, and there is little serious doubt that here Herodotos and the numerous later authors who speak of this god as Thracian are literally correct.[4] The chief arguments in favour of this statement are as follows:

(i.) *Philological.*—The first two syllables of the name are apparently to be connected with the Thracian tribe-name Dioi. Further, a Phrygian inscription gives us the formula *με διως κε ζεμελω*, which almost certainly means 'By heaven and earth.' We thus have a god with a name of which the first part has close Thraco-Phrygian affinities, while the rest is certainly not Greek, whose mother is apparently the earth-goddess of the Thraco-Phrygian stock.[5]

(ii.) *Traditional.*—Strabo definitely calls the cult of Dionysos Thraco-Phrygian.[6] When first we hear of the god at all, it is in connexion with the Edonian king Lykurgos;[7] and his cult is called Thracian far more persistently than that of Ares by authors of all ages. Moreover, all tradition is agreed that he is not genuine Greek. It is true that the usual birth-legend (not the 'Orphic' story; see below) makes him a Theban; but even there he is disowned by his kin and has to win his way into prominence against the vehement opposition of Pentheus;[8] while many similar tales indicate that his cult had to force an entrance into Greece. It is true that many, if not all, of these are misinterpreted ritual tales; but that they were persistently misinterpreted in the same way, as stories of persecution, strongly suggests that a folk-memory of real opposition lies behind the interpretation if not the stories themselves.

(iii.) *Facts of cult.*—On the one hand, very early Greek agricultural festivals either are not Dionysiac, like the Attic Thesmophoria, or present Dionysos as an obvious intruder, like the Anthesteria. On the other hand, the Thraco-Phrygian region is the home of all manner of orgiastic nature-cults,[9] and one detail of the worship of Dionysos which we have good reason to suppose primitive, viz. the oracle, is Thracian and hardly Greek at all.[10] He seems always to have been a wine-god as well as a god of nature in general, and a wine-god we find him in Thrace, which was a wine-growing country very early.[1] Further, he is connected in cult with Sabazios, who is probably Phrygian.

From Thrace, then, his cult spread through Greece some time, probably not very long, before the dawn of Greek history. In Homer he is apparently a foreign god, little known and not much regarded; of the five mentions of him two[2] are certainly interpolations, one[3] is unimportant, the others come in the story of Lykurgos. When we come to the Homeric hymns, however, he is a well-known and important deity, and all later literature is full of references to him. It would appear then that somewhere after the downfall of the Homeric (Achaian) culture, and during the period of reconstruction, of which very little is known, his worship crossed the border and was carried, it is no longer possible to say exactly how, or by whom,[4] to all parts of Greece, meeting with considerable opposition, but finally establishing itself as part of the state religion and becoming largely civilized in the process, though recrudescences of its original barbarism, such as the well-known one in Italy,[5] were always possible.

No detailed description of the cult of Dionysos in Thrace has come down to us from antiquity; but it is not difficult to frame one from various scattered notices,[6] from the wilder and more savage features of his Grecian cult, from the traces of the ancient worship still to be found in N. Greece, and from what we know of similar rites elsewhere.

We learn, firstly, that the most prominent feature of the ritual was a wild orgiastic ceremony held normally, if not always, at night. In this the worshippers worked themselves up into a state of frenzy by dancing and shouting (hence the numerous names of the god, such as Euhios, Iakchos, and perhaps Bakchos,[7] which are derivable from ejaculations or from words meaning 'shout' or 'cry'), to the accompaniment of savage music. They were dressed in the skins of wild animals—we hear especially of fawn- and fox-pelts (*νεβρίδες, βασσάραι*)—and carried the thyrsos, a spear-like implement covered with the sacred ivy, or the narthex (fennel-wand). It is obvious that for an excitable people, not highly civilized, and susceptible to strong sexual emotion, and therefore to nervous emotion of all kinds, including religious enthusiasm,[8] the violent exercise under the stimulating surroundings of their mountainous country in the clear night air would of itself produce an abnormal condition; and this seems to have been further encouraged by the free use of wine and perhaps other artificial stimulants. The result was, at least in many cases, and particularly among their women, a condition of frenzy, involving anæsthesia, abnormal strength and endurance, and other such symptoms, followed by fainting and exhaustion. The natural explanation, to any one at that stage of culture, was that the worshippers were possessed by their god (*ἔνθεοι, κάτοχοι*); and therefore we find them called by his name (*βάκχοι, βάκχαι*). That Dionysos himself was present was

[1] The odd ritual of Ares Γυναικοθοίνας (Paus. VIII. xlviii. 4, 5) may point to Amazonianism, which is not Greek. But this is exceedingly doubtful.

[2] The forms Ἀρήϊος (Hom. Ionic) and *ἀρεύιοι* (Alkaios) indicate a stem in *-ειυ-*; cf. *πρεσβήϊον* and *πρέσβυς*. The root is akin to Skr. *ras*, 'roar.' See C. A. M. Fennell in *ClR* xiii. [1899] 306.

[3] vii. 76, *ἐν τούτοισι τοῖσι ἀνδράσι* Ἄρεός *ἐστι χρηστήριον*. The context is corrupt, and it is uncertain who are referred to, quite possibly not Thracians at all.

[4] The counter-theory, that he is a Cretan deity, is supported by J. E. Harrison (*Prolegomena*[2], ch. viii.). The arguments for it reduce to (*a*) the fact that a cult of a god of this type did exist in Crete from very early times and remained so powerful that Zeus himself was absorbed by it; (*b*) certain very primitive features of Cretan Dionysiac ritual. But, in view of the overwhelming arguments in favour of Thrace, these phenomena are of little weight. The former is common to many localities; the latter is naturally explained by supposing that the worship of Dionysos, once it was imported, found favour in Crete because it was so like the native worship, and so was but little modified.

[5] *CGS* v. 94. The attempts to make Semele a thunder-cloud or the like are too absurd to deserve more than passing mention. The syllables *-νυσο-* are unintelligible, but possibly connected with the holy mountain Nysa, which is variously located but apparently Thracian in Homer.

[6] x. 471; cf. Plut. *Alex.* 2.

[7] Hom. *Il.* vi. 130 ff.

[8] The best known form of the legend is that given in Euripides, *Bacchæ*. Even in this the final birth of Dionysos, from the thigh of Zeus, does not take place in Thebes.

[9] Cf. art. PHRYGIANS.

[10] See Eur. *Hec.* 1267; Arist. *ap.* Macrob. *Sat.* I. xviii. 1.

[1] Hom. *Il.* ix. 72; Arist. *loc. cit.*

[2] *Il.* xiv. 325, and *Od.* xi. 325.

[3] *Od.* xxiv. 74.

[4] It was an age of wandering prophets (see Rohde, *Psyche*[4], ii. 63 ff.). The favourable reception of the women may have had a good deal to do with it also.

[5] Liv. xxxix. 8 ff.

[6] To save a multitude of quotations, we refer the reader for detailed authorities to the authors cited in the Literature at the end of this article.

[7] The root is perhaps Ϝαχ- (Curtius), in both names, Iakchos being ϜιϜακχος. Euhios is derived from the well-known cry εὐοῖ.

[8] The present writer holds religious and sexual emotion to be essentially the same; see, *e.g.*, W. James, *Varieties of Religious Experience*, London, and New York, 1902, *passim*. The frequency of 'conversions' and the like during adolescence and the regular employment by mystics of all nationalities of erotic metaphors are among the facts supporting this view.

a commonplace, familiar to us from many literary and artistic representations of the rites, from Euripides to Titian and Keats;[1] the skins in which the worshippers dressed were those of animal *avatars* of the god; and the culmination of the rite was the tearing in pieces and devouring of one of these animals.

It is far from impossible that in some cases the victim was a man or a child. That the Getai practised a form of human sacrifice we know;[2] Themistokles sacrificed three captives to Dionysos ὠμηστής;[3] the legends of Pentheus, etc., point the same way; and in the modified Dionysiac ritual of Tenedos[4] the cow whose calf is to be the victim is tended like a woman, and the calf when born has buskins put on it before being killed.

We have so far a quite normal ritual of a vegetation deity, of the kind familiar from the *Golden Bough*.[5] The god visits his worshippers in early spring (the time of most of the festivals),[6] is welcomed by them, and is joined to them by a sort of primitive sacrament. Of the death or expulsion of the worn-out god, later in the year, we do not hear so much, but there are traces of it. In the legend of Lykurgos already referred to the king pursues the god into the sea—the throwing of the vegetation-spirit into water is a very common rite; there was a strong tradition that he had died, and was buried at Delphi;[7] and there is also a legend of his descent into Hades to fetch up Semele.[8] We are therefore, in view of these facts and on the analogy of all similar ritual elsewhere, justified in supposing that his death was part of the ceremonial of his cult; and this belief is strengthened by the curious relic of Dionysiac worship found in Thrace by R. M. Dawkins,[9] in which the death of one of the characters in the mummers' play is a prominent feature. Closely allied with this went the ceremony representing his birth and cradling in the λίκνον, or winnowing-fan. The last detail, however, marking him definitely as a corn-god, is Greek rather than Thracian.[10]

In the ritual of Dionysos the forms of the god change bewilderingly. We have reason to suppose him to have been conceived as bull, goat, kid, sheep, serpent, stag, and even pig,[11] for all these animals, besides the fox and perhaps others, were sacred to him, and, as he is at times said to have taken the forms of some of them, notably bull and serpent, we may conjecture that he was more or less identified with the others as well. But in iconography he is always human, and he had human *avatars*, as might be expected from the human sacrifices.

(*c*) *Divine kings; Lykurgos, Pentheus, Rhesos, Orpheus.*—Several of the legends seem to indicate that in Thrace, as elsewhere, there existed kings of the type familiar from the investigations of J. G. Frazer—*i.e.* incarnations of the local god, who ended by being sacrificed, possibly devoured. As the Greeks probably never had had this sort of king—certainly had forgotten it—they naturally misunderstood the legends. Thus none of the

[1] *Bacchæ*; *Endymion*; the 'Bacchus and Ariadne' in the National Gallery.

[2] See below, § (*g*).

[3] Plut. *Them.* 13.

[4] See Ælian, *Nat. Anim.* xii. 34. The Thracian ritual seems to have been toned down almost into a normal sacrifice.

[5] See for full references the index vol. to *GB*[3], *s.v.* 'Dionysus.'

[6] For a few examples see art. FESTIVALS AND FASTS (Greek), *ad fin.*

[7] See Plut. *de Is. et Os.* 365*a*.

[8] *GB*[3], pt. vii., *The Spirits of the Corn and of the Wild*, London, 1912, i. 15.

[9] Described in his art. 'Archæology in Greece (1906–1907),' in *JHS* xxvii. [1906] 284 ff.

[10] Hence Dionysos' title λικνίτης (Plut. *loc. cit.*); cf. Serv. on Verg. *Georg.* i. 166.

[11] A selection of the relevant passages will be found in *CGS* v. 303 f.

above mythological figures exactly correspond to the Frazerian type. Lykurgos persecutes Dionysos; but the form which his persecution takes is a pursuit (probably originally ritual) of the god and his attendants and the flogging of them with the βουπλήξ, by which is possibly meant, not an ox-goad, but a whip of bull's hide, a fertilizing *februum* like the hide thongs of the Roman Luperci. He is not torn in pieces by the god's followers, but in one way or another (the legend varies in detail) is punished, by blindness or otherwise, and imprisoned in a cave.[1] Pentheus opposes the Bakchai and is torn in pieces by them. Orpheus is a royal priest of Dionysos and is torn in pieces by the Mainades—an act for which late mythologizers assign sundry fanciful reasons.[2] Rhesos is a vague figure, but it has been urged that his name may be connected with *rex* (Gothic *raiks*) and the royal Thracian name Rhescuporis. After his death he appears—the exact sense and reading are matters of dispute—to be represented by the author of the play bearing his name as becoming an oracular deity or semi-deity (ἀνθρωποδαίμων) of somewhat Dionysiac type.[3] Add to all this the facts that the Getic priest-king was called 'god'[4] and that we get as a royal name of frequent occurrence the word Kotys, which is a by-form of Kotyto, and it becomes at least plausible that the cult of Dionysos and other gods of the same kind in Thrace had at its head in early times[5] a priest-king who was the incarnation of the deity and ended by being violently put to death to make way for a fresh incarnation.

(*d*) *Orphism.*—Of the persons mentioned in the last section one is of such importance as to deserve separate treatment, viz. Orpheus. Concerning this priest-king the tradition of antiquity is fairly constant. He is a more or less historical figure;[6] he existed some time before the Trojan War;[7] he was a Thracian,[8] son of King Oiagros and a Muse, usually Kalliope, sometimes Polymnia. He was a priest of Dionysos, founder of Dionysiac mysteries, public and private, and originator of the Orphic βίος, *i.e.* way of life.[9] He was also a seer, a magician, a 'theologian' in the Greek sense of the word,[10] a marvellous musician. His home, when exactly localized, is generally said by our earlier authorities to have been Mt. Pangaion, the site of an ancient and famous Dionysiac shrine, while later writers locate him on the coast of Thrace, near the mouth of the Hebros. After various adventures, the most notable of which was the descent into Hades, familiar in later literature from Vergil's handling of it in the *Georgics*, he was

[1] See Soph. *Ant.* 955 ff., and Jebb, *ad loc.*

[2] For examples see Serv. on Verg. *Georg.* iv. 519.

[3] See Rohde, i. 161, who rather too confidently assumes Rhesos to have been a faded god. W. Leaf (*JHS* xxxv. [1915] 1 ff.) goes too far in the opposite direction. On the whole the present writer is of opinion that Rhesos may really have been a half-forgotten king of some Thracian tribe, who after his death was supposed to give oracles. The ancient evidence is to be found in *Il.* x.; [Eur.] *Rhes.* 955 ff.; Polyæn. vi. 53.

[4] Strabo, vii. 298.

[5] Presumably not in historical times, as one can hardly suppose that none of our authors would have mentioned it in that case.

[6] For an isolated expression of doubt see Cic. *de Nat. Deor.* i. 38 (108), 'Orpheum poetam docet Aristoteles nunquam fuisse,' which from the context is almost certainly a denial of Orpheus' existence. But Aristotle may merely have meant to deny his authorship of the 'Orphic' poems.

[7] Contemporary with the Argonauts, according to most versions of their story—*e.g.*, Pind. *Pyth.* iv. 176, and Apollonios Rhodios.

[8] 'Thracius Orpheus' (Ver. *Ec.* iv. 55) is his stock epithet.

[9] βίος is perhaps the nearest Greek equivalent of 'sect' or 'persuasion' and greatly resembles the NT use of ὁδός (Ac 9[2]). It signifies a form of life depending on certain religious or philosophical principles and is applied especially to the Orphic and Pythagorean bodies.

[10] *I.e.*, not a writer on the theoretical basis of religion in general, or of any particular religion, but one who describes the nature, relationships, etc., of deities. In this sense Hesiod, *e.g.*, is a 'theologian' (θεολόγος).

torn in pieces by a band of women, possessed by real or pretended Dionysiac frenzy.[1]

From what is said above it is clear that all this may have some historic foundation—*i.e.*, that the legends regarding him go back to some real happenings in connexion with the ritual of Dionysos. The death of an Orpheus, and consequently his descent into Hades, and presumably also his resurrection in a new incarnation, may have taken place, not once but many times.[2] But tradition crystallized all these forgotten personalities into one picturesque figure, the founder and Messiah of a religion of mystical other-worldliness.

The chief tenets, so far as we can reconstruct them, are as follows.[3] At the end of a long succession of deities[4] comes Dionysos-Zagreus, the son of Zeus and Persephone.[5] This god, while an infant, was beguiled by the Titans, who gave him a mirror and other toys and then tore him in pieces and devoured him, all but his heart, which was saved by Athene. The god was re-created by his father, who swallowed the heart and re-bore the child; the Titans were destroyed by the thunderbolt, and from their ashes sprang man. Man is therefore a creature of mixed origin, containing a divine principle (Dionysos) and an evil one (the Titans). The main object of his existence is to get rid of the latter element—a task which cannot be completed in one lifetime. To further it, however, it is necessary to live in strict ritual purity, avoiding the use of meat, wearing white garments, shunning the polluting presence of corpses and of women in child-birth,[6] and practising chastity,[7] all these being observances well known in ancient ritual and not peculiar to Orphism. In addition, it seems that the higher class of Orphics practised a more or less definite ethical code.[8] Side by side with all this went, as might be expected, a lower, popular form, in which a sort of begging friars drove a thriving trade in indulgences, so to call them, 'persuading not only individuals but cities,' says Plato,[9] 'that their sins can be purged with sacrifices and pleasant merry-makings'; *i.e.*, performing quasi-magical rites, effective *ex opere operato*, quite independently of the moral condition of the person concerned, at prices proportioned to the wealth or superstition of their clients.

To return to the higher forms of Orphism. After a life spent in moral and ceremonial purity the soul of the Orphic believer was rewarded in Hades, apparently for 1000 years,[10] or ten times the supposed maximum length of a human life, while those who had sinned, but not beyond remedy, were punished for the same period. After this came reincarnation, not necessarily in human form. Next came another period in Hades, and so on, the process being known apparently as the κύκλος, or cycle of reincarnations.[1] Release from this could be obtained by a series of good lives on both sides of the grave—for apparently each world was the heaven or purgatory of the other. After a triple good life on either side—three on earth and three in Hades—the soul had purged itself from the stain of 'original sin' and was free to enter a permanent paradise, with no more prospect of reincarnation, and in the enjoyment of divine or heroic[2] rank.

This theology, and much besides, was embodied in a large literature, attributed either to Orpheus himself or to his pupil Mousaios,[3] the oldest parts of which probably date from the 6th cent. B.C., while the latest representatives, the *Hymns* and Orphic *Argonautica*, are about 1000 years later.[4] Of this the greater part has perished, and especially the earliest and most valuable part; and we have of undoubted and fairly early Orphic origin only one set of documents, the so-called Petelia Tablets, gold plates found in Orphic graves in S. Italy. It appears from these that a pious Orphic was in the habit of burying with his dead friend directions for his conduct in Hades, to aid him to secure final bliss, since no doubt it was charitable to suppose that the life just completed was the last of the series of good lives required to qualify for escape from the circle.[5]

The tablets present the following picture of Hades. The soul, apparently after long and thirsty wanderings, travels along a road flanked on either side by springs. Avoiding the left-hand spring,[6] it addresses the guardians of the right-hand one, declares itself to be of divine race, and begs for a draught of 'the cold water which floweth forth from the lake of Memory.' The request is granted, and the soul is hailed as having 'endured that which aforetime it had never endured.' It addresses Persephone and the other deities of the under world and is admitted into their society.

The poem to which all these tablets go back is of unknown authorship and date, but it is evident that it or something like it stands behind the passages of Pindar and Plato already cited and also behind much that is to be found in other authors, mostly late. The connecting link is to be found in Pythagoreanism, which, it would seem, found Orphism already established in S. Italy, and incorporated much of its teaching. This results in a confusion between the two systems so complete that it is practically hopeless, with our imperfect documents, to say definitely with regard to any eschatological passage that it is purely Orphic or purely Pythagorean. Through the Pythagorean exiles who reached Greece proper after the dispersion of their communities in Magna Græcia the higher forms of the doctrine became known to Plato, in whom consequently we find side by side strong Orphic-Pythagorean influence and hearty contempt for Orphic charlatanism. Not dissimilar is the attitude of Aristophanes, who, on the one

1 For full authorities, and variants of the myth, see Gruppe. We give a few of the leading references: priest and founder of mysteries: Eur. *Hipp.* 952 ff.; Aristoph. *Ran.* 1032; Herod. ii. 81; Plut. *Quæst. Con.* ii. 635*e*; seer: Plat. *Prot.* 316D; magician: Eur. *Alc.* 966 (973), *Cycl.* 639; musician: Pind. *loc. cit.*, and Verg. *loc. cit.*

2 Cf. Proclus, *in Plat. Remp.* 398: Ὀρφεὺς ἅτε τῶν Διονύσου τελετῶν ἡγεμὼν γενόμενος τὰ ὅμοια παθεῖν λέγεται τῷ σφετέρῳ θεῷ.

3 The details varied (see Rohde, ii. 115 ff.; Gruppe, col. 1121 ff.). The Orphic writings being largely lost, much has to be patched together from various sources, many of them obscure.

4 The theogony does not differ from the Hesiodic in essentials; the chief departures are the insertion of the World-egg laid by Night and of two vague deities, Phanes and Erikapaios.

5 *I.e.* sky-god and earth-mother. Persephone = Zemelo = the Semele of the Theban myth. The source of the name Zagreus is doubtful.

6 See esp. Eur. Κρῆτες, frag. 475*a* Dindorf, and *Hipp.* 952.

7 See *Hipp.* 1002. Hippolytos is apparently represented as the ideal Orphist.

8 For reference to this see *Hipp.* 992 ff., and Pind. *Ol.* ii. 76.

9 Condensed from Plat. *Rep.* ii. 364 E.

10 This is the figure given by Plat. *Rep.* x. 615 A, B; cf. Verg. *Æn.* vi. 748; of these the former is probably Orphic-Pythagorean, the latter contains the Orphic-sounding phrase *rotam uoluere*. For other Platonic myths containing similar eschatology see J. A. Stewart, *The Myths of Plato*, London, 1905; cf. A. Dieterich, *Nekyia*[2], p. 84 ff. In Pind. frag. 98 (110) the soul spends only eight years in Hades (*i.e.* an *oktaeteris*; cf. art. CALENDAR [Greek], § 3) before its final earthly life, after which it attains heroic rank.

1 The word is found in the Petelia Tablets and elsewhere in Orphic literature. This account of Orphic eschatology is put together largely from Pind. *Ol.* ii. and frag. 98–110. In the latter we take the disputable words ποινὰν παλαιοῦ πένθεος as meaning 'atonement for her (Persephone's) ancient grief' (at the murder of Zagreus).

2 The tablets have ἄλλοισι μεθ' ἡρώεσσιν ἀνάξεις and also ὀλβιὲ καὶ μακαριστέ, θεὸς δ' ἔσῃ ἀντὶ βροτοῖο. The confusion is natural enough in a religion which has much to say of the beatified dead (ἥρωες) and also claims divine ancestry for all men. Ordinarily, a Greek sharply differentiated between a god, who did not die at all, and a hero, who had been an ordinary man but continued to live in some way after bodily death.

3 Plat. *Rep.* ii. 363 C, 364 E, and commentators.

4 Onomakritos edits and interpolates Musaios in the time of Hipparchos, son of Peisistratos, Herod. vii. 6; Orphic writings falsely called pre-Homeric, Herod. ii. 81.

5 Text and tr. by G. Murray in J. E. Harrison, *Proleg.*[2], appendix.

6 Probably Lethe, of which a soul drinks before reincarnation. The finally purified soul has no need to forget.

hand, parodies private mysteries of the Orphic type in the *Clouds* and, on the other, draws in the *Frogs* on the same type of ideas for his half-serious picture of the other world.

Another problem which we cannot solve with any great exactness is the amount of non-Thracian thought which goes to the making of Orphism as we know it. The very name of the founder is in doubt, for, while to some it appears a Thracian name,[1] others point to the occurrence of Greek cognates[2] as indicating it to be Greek. As to the doctrines, it is unreasonable to suppose that the Thracians produced so elaborate and quasi-philosophical a system of reincarnation; this is rather the result of Greek reflexion on Thracian Dionysiac material. Thrace, on the other hand, is the likeliest claimant for the grotesque myth on which the whole system rests; but here again we do not know how much was contributed by obscure superstitions from backward corners of the Greek world. The asceticism we may not unfairly call Thracian, though the details of it are not definitely non-Hellenic.

Exactly what form the Orphic religion took, in its externals, and how long it remained a potent force, cannot be very precisely determined, still less what proportion of the Greek peoples was seriously affected by it. With regard to the first point, however, it would appear that Orphism had but little organization. There was, and could be, no Orphic state anywhere, and, though there was no doubt a considerable number of Orphic congregations (*θίασοι*), there was no central authority to connect them, nor have we any right to suppose that they were identical with each other in doctrine and practice. It was as if there existed a form of Freemasonry in which each lodge was a law unto itself, and there was no very definite common ritual and no recognized means of communication between the various lodges. Also, though many of the greatest individual minds, notably Pythagoras and Plato, and probably Socrates also, were at one time or another affected by the cult, we have no evidence that it was a particularly numerous body. Pythagoreanism, which seems to have been much more organized and had decided political leanings, was still the faith of a minority, as is seen by its helplessness when popular feeling in Italy turned against it; Orphism, being non-political and probably still more the religion of the few, was not persecuted. As to the length of its existence, we have seen that Orphic documents were still being written in the 4th cent. A.D., but, like other productions of that epoch, they show unmistakable traces of syncretism, and of Orphism we have little or nothing outside of literature. Therefore, on the whole, we are disposed to attach less importance than Dieterich does to the undeniable coincidences between Orphic imagery, *e.g.*, and that of certain Gnostic and Christian writings; we would look for the source of that imagery, and the many common points of ritual and belief in Christian and non-Christian cults, to the numerous Hellenized Oriental faiths rather than to Orphism proper, holding that the language which once was chiefly, if not peculiarly, Orphic had become common property,[3] while Orphism itself had become very unimportant. This, however, cannot be considered as settled beyond reasonable doubt.

[1] See Tomaschek, ii. 52.

[2] Orphe, given as a Laconian name in Serv. on Verg. *Buc.* viii. 29; the Bœotian name Ὀρφώνδας; ὀρφός, the name of a fish in Æl. *Nat. Anim.* xii. 1; and the root of the adj. ὀρφναιός.

[3] Thus the 'cold water' of the formula above quoted is found again on Osirian tombs (G. Kaibel, *IG Siciliæ et Italiæ*, Berlin, 1890, nos. 1488, 1705, etc.), and on at least one which is traditionally Greek in its wording, *ib.* no. 1342; finally appearing as the Christian *refrigerium*; cf. the 'water of life' of the NT.

We may now consider briefly the moral value of the Dionysiac and Orphic cults. That they were immoral in the obvious sense is not likely. It is true that Livy,[1] *e.g.*, makes out Dionysiac orgies to have been horrible riots of lust and violence; but he is speaking of a late form of the worship, far from its native place, and has all the Roman prejudice against any secret conventicle—the same prejudice which later gave rise to the same tales about the early meetings of the Christians. But in a broader sense we may say that all such cults were immoral, for they were untrue to Hellenism, replacing its clear envisagement of the facts of life with a misty other-worldliness, sure to lead to intellectual decay, however brilliant the first flowerings of its mysticism might be in such a mind as that of Plato. Not till the nonage of the ancient world did such doctrines really become prevalent; and the overthrow of the Pythagorean communities, primarily political, may be thought of as also an unconscious revolt against a force traitorous to Greek civilization.[2]

(*e*) *Artemis.*—Here we need have no doubt that Herodotos is not to be taken too literally. All we have any reason to believe—since of a Thracian origin of the cult of Artemis properly so called we have not the faintest trace—is that some great nature-goddess was worshipped in that country. We can give at least two names of such deities. Kotyto, or Kotys, though generally spoken of as Phrygian, was also Edonian.[3] Another deity, who was to some extent naturalized in Greece in fairly early times,[4] was Bendis, whose cult is mentioned together with that of Kotyto by Strabo.[5] Of the details of her worship we know but little; the torch-race mentioned by Plato[6] fits well enough with any deity equated with the torch-bearing Artemis, but is by no means peculiar to her; and of the native worship of her we hear chiefly that it was noisy.[7] Probably enough there were a score of such female personifications of the fertility of nature, worshipped with orgiastic rites not unlike those of Dionysos himself, possibly in connexion with him.[8]

(*f*) *Hermes.*—With regard to Herodotos' statement that the Thracian kings especially venerate Hermes, we are not aware that any very convincing explanation has been offered, but, in view of the facts mentioned in the next paragraph, we suggest that he means Hermes Chthonios and identifies with him some one of the deities after the pattern of Zalmoxis.

(*g*) *Zalmoxis.*[9]—Our chief authority for this deity is again Herodotos, who informs us[10] that the

[1] xxxix. 10, and elsewhere in his description of the Bacchanalian affair.

[2] The above account of the origin and progress of Orphism, while in our opinion the correct one, has been controverted by R. Eisler (*Weltenmantel und Himmelszelt*, Munich, 1910, ch. v.). He endeavours to prove that its origin is due to Asiatic, particularly Persian, influences, and this theory is accepted by some later writers (*e.g.*, Mrs. A. Strong, *Apotheosis and After Life*, London, 1915, p. 274). We hold that, with all deference to Eisler's great learning and industry, his arguments are wholly insufficient for the Orphism of the times of Pythagoras or of Plato, whatever light they may throw on the mongrel system which at the beginning of the Christian era went by that name.

[3] Æsch. Ἠδωνοί, frag. 55 Dindorf: σεμνὰ Κότυς ἐν Ἠδωνοῖς; cf. the common royal name Kotys.

[4] 419 B.C., see Plat. *Rep.* i. 237 A ff.; cf. schol. *ad loc.* and commentators.

[5] *Loc. cit.*

[6] *Loc. cit.*

[7] βαρβαρικὸς κλύδων, Procl. in *Tim.* 26*e*.

[8] Or in conjunction with some of the other Dionysiac deities, such as Sabazios (Thraco-Phrygian).

[9] Also called Gebeleïzis (Herod. *loc. cit.*). The name is generally written Ζάλμοξις, but with one exception the MSS of Herodotos give Σάλμοξις. As σ and ζ are often confused in Thracian, both forms may be correct.

[10] IV. xciv f. Part of this passage, xciv. 4, runs: οὗτοι οἱ αὐτοὶ Θρήϊκες καὶ πρὸς βροντήν τε καὶ ἀστραπὴν τοξεύοντες ἄνω πρὸς τὸν οὐρανὸν ἀπειλεῦσι τῷ θεῷ, οὐδένα ἄλλον θεὸν νομίζοντες εἶναι εἰ μὴ τὸν σφέτερον. This has been oddly misunderstood,

Getai worshipped him, and so exclusively that they regarded no one else as a true god, even the heavens themselves. What his nature was we can gather in part from the rationalistic story told of him, that he was a slave of Pythagoras, who, returning home, taught a variant of his master's philosophy, insisting especially on the immortality awaiting the faithful. To prove this, he disappeared for a time, hiding in an underground room; after three years he returned, and so made every one believe that he had been in Hades and was come again. It is noteworthy that the same story is told of Pythagoras himself,[1] and it smacks strongly of the tales, Greek and other, of superhuman persons who live in caves or under mountains and thence return occasionally or in some way intervene in human affairs.[2] With this story we must join the decided suspicion of Herodotos himself[3] that Zalmoxis is a local divinity, not a mortal at all, and the statement of Strabo[4] that he was worshipped in an ἀντρῶδες χωρίον in Mt. Kogaionon. He is clearly, like Dionysos himself, a god belonging to the under world, but not excluded from the surface of the earth, on which, we may perhaps suppose from the myth, he was thought to appear every year, as Dionysos frequently did every second.[5] As an infernal deity, he received a curious sacrifice, if sacrifice is the proper term to apply to what seems to have been rather a sort of fantastic messenger service. Once every four years the Getai chose a man by lot, whom they tossed in the air and caught on spear-points. If he died, he was deemed to have become immortal;[6] if not, the god had rejected him, and he was disgraced. Before being tossed, he was charged with the messages of the people to the deity—a curious form of the idea, found among many races, that the dying can take to the dead the mandates of the living.[7]

(*h*) *Other religious practices.*—Besides the cult of definite gods, we have a few facts relative to the general religious attitude of the Thracians. In particular, we have Herodotos'[8] description of a funeral ceremony, which sounds oddly like Homer's account of the funeral of Patroklos. The corpse, if of an important man, lies in state three days, during which mourning and sacrificial feasts go on; finally there comes the actual funeral, when the body is buried or burned, a mound raised, and games of various kinds, the principal one being a single combat, are celebrated. This was the usual rite, and it indicates at any rate high honour paid to the dead.[9] The duel especially may reasonably be thought to be a form of blood-sacrifice. This, in some of the wilder tribes, was no mere form; beyond Krestone, we are told, lived a race which practised *sati*; the favourite wife, chosen, it would seem, after careful examination of the claims of the whole *harîm* by the surviving relatives, was sacrificed by her next-of-kin at the tomb and then buried with her husband.[1] The Trausoi again made a death a subject of rejoicing, and mourned at a birth.[2] We see, then, that the whole of Thracian religion was permeated by the idea of the vast importance of the future life.

(*i*) *Summary: general characteristics of Thracian religion.*—We find in Thrace a religion of a barbarous kind, but by no means incapable of development into something higher and more spiritual. The chief marks of barbarism, besides the revolting character of some of the rites, were (*a*) the largely magical character of much of the ceremonial, unconnected with anything either ethical or spiritual, and tending rather to excite than to elevate; and (*b*) the materialistic conception of the future life. Gods such as Zalmoxis live underground, occasionally intervening for the bodily good of their worshippers[3] and rewarding the faithful departed with drunken feasts; or so one gathers from the rationalizing story of Zalmoxis already quoted, in which he is represented as feasting the Thracians, and the taunt of Plato that the inferior sort of Orphics considered eternal drunkenness the highest possible felicity.[4] This is not to say that Thracian religion was always of a sensual character. It is noteworthy that the northern races, or some of them, had a reputation not only for courage but also for virtue and even for superhuman powers.

Thus the Getai are the 'bravest and most righteous' of the Thracians; the holy Hyperboreans live somewhere near the Thracian region; in and near the neighbouring Scythian country are the sacred and ascetic Argippaioi, the just Issedones, and the Neuroi, who are all magicians, besides the Sauromatai, who are of Amazonian stock; while the glorified shade of Achilles haunts various localities of the Black Sea region.[5]

A great part at least of this persistent attribution of saintly or magical distinction to the northern districts may well have for its justification the natural complement of the strong sexuality of those races—asceticism, which, as we have already seen, was a strong feature of Orphism. Another reason no doubt is simply the fact that many of these peoples were distant and unknown.[6] Yet another is, quite likely, the existence, not of whole nations, but of castes, which were priestly. We have already seen that the Bessoi certainly, and other tribes probably, had divine kings, and this often enough, as in Egypt, means the domination of a sacerdotal clan or caste.

To sum up, therefore, Thrace had, so far as we can learn from the observations of its nearest civilized neighbours in classical times, a religion predominantly chthonian, other-worldly, orgiastic, gloomy, often cruel and barbaric, but not unspiritual—a sharp contrast with the brightness of the characteristic Greek cult of the Olympian deities.

LITERATURE.—(i.) *Ethnology, etc., of Thrace*: J. A. Tomaschek, *Die alten Thraker*, pt. i., 'Übersicht der Stämme,' *SBAW* cxxviii. [1893] pt. ii., 'Die Sprachreste,' *SBAW* cxxx. [1893].

as if τῷ θεῷ meant 'their god,' which would involve a contradiction in terms: 'They threaten the god they believe in because they don't believe in him.' The correct translation is of course 'Heaven' or 'Zeus'; cf. lxxix. 1 f.: ἐπεθύμησε Διονύσῳ Βακχείῳ τελεσθῆναι . . . ὁ θεὸς (Zeus, not Dionysos) ἐνέσκηψε βέλος, and many other passages in which ὁ θεὸς means 'sky' or 'heavenly bodies.'

1 Hermippos, *ap.* Diog. Laert. viii. 41. This story is perhaps imitated from the one in Herodotos, which probably is an invention of the Greeks of the Pontos.

2 Examples in Rohde, i 111 ff.

3 iv. 96.

4 vii. 298.

5 His festivals were regularly trieteric, *i.e.* in alternate years, by the Greek (inclusive) method of counting. Did this originate in a custom of shifting the cultivation every other year, vouched for by Horace, *Od.* iii. 24, 'nec cultura placet longior annua,' as occurring among the Getai? Among a people backward in agriculture the practice may well have varied, the period of cultivation lasting for one, two, or three years in different districts according to the richness of the soil. The author owes this suggestion to Farnell.

6 iv. 93: Γέτας τοὺς ἀθανατίζοντας (this becomes their stock epithet); v. 3.

7 The idea is particularly common in modern Greek ballads.

8 v. 8.

9 The exact interpretation given to these facts depends upon the view taken of the origin of ἀγῶνες in general. The present writer holds that they do not originate in funeral ceremonies, or connote divine or quasi-divine honours, though they are often associated with both. The duel, however, is, like the Etruscan gladiatorial shows, definitely a sacrificial rite in this case.

1 v. 5.

2 v. 4; cf. Eur. Κρεσφόντης, frag. 452 Dind.

3 Plato (*Charm.* 156 D) mentions 'physicians of Zalmoxis' and appears playfully to interpret ἀπαθανατίζειν as referring to their skill. They were probably a sort of shamans or medicine-men, who may, like their Siberian confrères, have combined medicine and prophecy.

4 *Rep.* ii. 363 D.

5 See Herod. iv. 13, 32–36, 23, 26, 105, 110 f., 55; cf. Lykophron, *Alex.* 186 ff.

6 Cf. the piety of the Homeric Ethiopians (*Il.* i. 423).

The former deals chiefly with history and ethnology, the latter with linguistics.

(ii.) *Thracian cults*; L. R. Farnell, *CGS*, Oxford, 1896-1909, v. (Ares, Dionysos); J. E. Harrison, *Prolegomena to the Study of Greek Religion*[2], Cambridge, 1908 (Dionysos; also Orphism); see also the articles 'Bendis,' 'Dionysos,' 'Kotys,' in Roscher.

(iii.) *Orphism and related cults*: see esp. E. Rohde, *Psyche*[4], 2 vols., Tübingen, 1907; A. Dieterich, *Nekyia*[2], Leipzig, 1913; O. Gruppe, art. 'Orpheus' in Roscher; E. Abel, *Orphica*, Leipzig and Prague, 1885 (texts).

Further references to ancient and modern authorities will be found in the above works.

H. J. Rose.

THRESHOLD.—See DOOR.

THUGS.—See THAGS.

THUNDER.—See PRODIGIES AND PORTENTS, STORM, STORM-GODS.

TIBET.—The Tibetans are entitled to be regarded as one of the most 'religious' peoples in the world, if by 'religion' is understood not only 'the belief in spiritual beings,'[1] but also the *binding* influence of that belief, as formulated by their Church, for the better regulation of their worldly actions in everyday life, and for procuring for them by pious observance of the inculcated maxims the satisfying hope of a higher position in the life after death. Not only is the proportion of the population in Tibet which devotes its life to religion greater than that in any other country, being at least about one to eight of the population[2]—monks, nuns, non-celibate priests, and neophytes—but the life of the laity is also dominated and pervaded by their religion to an exceptional extent.

1. Climatic environments.—The peculiarities in the climate and physical character of Tibet, and its topographical position, between the two great civilizations on either side, the Indian and the Chinese, from both of which it has derived the elements of its composite form of Buddhism, explain to a considerable extent the peculiarities of its religion. The vast awe-inspiring solitudes with the rigorous nature of the climate have impressed themselves visibly on the religion of the country. And Nature has contributed, by the massive physical barriers she has erected against access to that land, to maintain to the present day the isolation of that country from the rest of the world, and thus to preserve the more ancient and archaic forms of religion and superstitions.

Perched on the summit of the great plateau of Central Asia, and stretching across over twenty-two degrees of longitude, in the palæarctic region, from the Himālayas to the Kuen-lun mountains and Western China, it includes the loftiest table-land on the surface of the earth. Although generally called a plateau, it is in fact covered with innumerable hills and mountains, cut up by ravines, the stretches of level land being relatively few and far apart. The general elevation of the permanently inhabited tract seldom falls below 11,000 feet above sea-level, while a very great extent of the country exceeds 16,000 feet, which is about the limit there of perpetual snow. Its highest border lies along the Himālayas, rising in mountains, the highest on the globe, from which its surface slopes gradually eastwards into China—a feature explained by the fact that in not very remote geological times the land of Tibet formed part of the bottom of the China Sea of the Pacific; and the writer has picked up fossil shells on the Tibetan side of the Himālayas which were of the same species as those he obtained from similar strata-formations on the outskirts of Peking. This also explains why the Mongolic racial elements and the Chinese forms of civilization predominate in Tibet, and why China has maintained for so long its suzerainty there.

[1] E. B. Tylor, *PC*[3] i. 424.

[2] The census of the population hitherto taken was that by the Chinese in 1737, which gave the proportion of the Lāmas as one to three of the total population. At the present day about one to eight appears to be near the mark, in accordance with the present writer's own observations and those of W. W. Rockhill.

Geographically, it is usual to divide Tibet latitudinally into North (Chang) and South (Kham), the North-land comprising all the Northern and Central and much of Western Tibet, and the South comprising South and South-Eastern Tibet. This division is also generally followed by the Tibetans themselves, though they erect Central and South-Western Tibet (U-Tsang), with their twin centres of Lāmaism, at Lhāsa and Tāshilhunpo, into a separate, and for them the chief, division of their country, which they call Bod (pronounced Pöt). The former division they call sTod-Bod (pronounced Tö-Pöt), or 'Upper Bod,' which is the origin of our modern name 'Tibet,' derived from the phonetic spelling of mediæval European travellers to whom only this northern division was accessible, and latterly applied by Europeans to the whole of Bod, though wrongly so. This is also the source of the Chinese name for the country of T'u-Fan, or 'the land of the *T'u* barbarians of the West.'

The northern division, or Chang, through its extreme altitude, has a terrible climate and is uninhabited for the greater part of the year, being mostly used as summer-grazing grounds by nomad shepherds and traversed by miners and occasional caravans of merchants at that season. It consists of a series of parallel mountain-ranges running east and west, with muddy valleys intervening. In these depressions lie a great number of lake-basins, many of which have no outlet, so that their water is salt, and some of their shores are white with borax crystals. It is an altogether treeless region, interspersed with grassy tracts used for summer pasturage. On the other hand, Central and more especially South-Eastern Tibet, which are of considerably lower elevation, are traversed by the Brahmaputra, and upper reaches of the Irrawady, Mekong, Salween, and Yangtse rivers and their tributaries are for a considerable part wooded, enjoy a less rigorous climate, and are the seat of most of the settled population. But the total population of the whole country is probably not more than 3,500,000[1]—*i.e.* a little less than the entire population of Scotland. Snow falls more or less, even at Lhāsa, in every month of the year.

2. Popular religion.—Living in such a rigorous climate and isolated amidst such severe surroundings, the Tibetan builds his daily fears and hopes on his religion, and, despite its inveterate devil-worship, it is not without its elevating and inspiring influence. The current of Buddhism which runs through its tangled paganism has brought to the Tibetan most of the little civilization which he possesses, and has raised him correspondingly in the scale of humanity, lifting him above a life of semi-barbarism by setting before him higher hopes and aims, by giving milder meanings to his demonist mythology, by discountenancing sacrifice of animal lives, and by inculcating universal charity and tenderness to all living things. Their Buddhism, unlike that of the Burmese, is not, however, an educational factor in secular teaching or in the mysteries of their religion; for the Lāmas, while living on the laity by their ministrations as priests, restrict their learning to themselves, like the Brāhmans and most priestly orders of old, and they contemptuously call the laity 'the dark (ignorant) people' (*mi-nag-pa*) and 'the worldly ones' (*hjig-rten-pa*), though they condescendingly

[1] This is the estimate of W. W. Rockhill (*Land of the Lāmas*, p. 296), and it generally agrees with that of the present writer.

also call them 'the givers of alms' (*sbyinbdag*), at the same time making it understood that it is the donors who benefit most by the exercise of this charity. And certainly the last epithet is well deserved, for the Tibetans, the most priest-ridden people in the world, are among the most lavish in their religious gifts.

Notwithstanding the large amount of non-Buddhist elements in Lāmaism, derived from the pre-Buddhist shamanism of the Bon-cult,[1] it is surprising to find how deeply the everyday life and notions of the laity are leavened by the Buddhist spirit. The doctrine of metempsychosis and its *karma* and the potency of acquired merit by good deeds enters into the ordinary habits and speech of the people to a remarkable extent. Their proverbs, folk-lore, songs, and lay dramas are full of it; and they explain human as well as animal friendships on this principle. Even practices which are clearly dishonest and sinful are at times justified on the same principle, or rather by its abuse. Thus the more sordid Tibetan reconciles cheating to his conscience by naively convincing himself that the person whom he now attempts to defraud had previously swindled him 'in a former existence,' and that justice demands retribution. Congenital defects, even such as blindness, dumbness, and lameness, and also accidents are viewed as retributions due to the individual having in a previous life abused or sinned with the particular limb or organ now affected. Indeed this is the orthodox dogma of Buddha's own teaching and forms the basis of the *Jātakas*, or tales of the previous births of Buddha, which are diffused by itinerant or friar Lāmas, and greatly impress the people; a few of the better-known *Jātakas* in manuscript copy or in block-printed booklets form, with the manuals of ritual and divination, the chief books of those Tibetan laity who are able to read; and they also form the subject of the chief dramas enacted by the laity.

This wide-spread belief in metempsychosis also influences the people in the treatment of their cattle and other dumb animals. They treat these exceptionally humanely, and life is seldom wantonly taken. The taking of animal life unnecessarily, even for food, is largely prohibited, and, although in such a cold climate animal food is an essential staple of diet, the professional butchers are stigmatized as sinners and are the most despised of all classes in the country. Yet human prisoners are at times cruelly tortured and mutilated, possibly in some measure after the example set by the Chinese, and possibly in some measure as a deterrent from crime among a rather lawless people. But nearly every crime, even the most heinous, the murdering of a Lāma, may be condoned by a fixed scale of fines; and, when the fine is not forthcoming, the punishment is inflicted, and the prisoner, if not actually killed, is set free, mutilated or maimed (as there are no prisons), to serve as a public warning to other evil-doers. Many of the maimed and blind beggars who swarm around Lhāsa are criminals punished in this way.

The tolerant spirit of Buddhism has, however, stamped more or less distinctly the national character, the mildness of which contrasts strongly with the rough and semi-barbarous exterior of the people. Testimony to this trait is afforded by the experiences of all intimate observers of the people in their own country, as recorded by the present writer and others. Huc, writing of the lay regent of Lhāsa, describes him as a man whose 'large features, mild and remarkably pallid, breathed a truly royal majesty,' while 'his dark eyes, shaded by long lashes, were intelligent and gentle.'[2]

[1] See below, § 3.
[2] *Travels in Tartary, Thibet, and China*[2], Eng. tr., ii. 168.

Similarly Rockhill and others have described many of the headmen and leading Lāmas with whom they came into intimate contact.[1] The spirit of consideration for others expresses itself in many grateful acts of genuine politeness and kindness. Tibetans usually present a stirrup-cup of wine to the departing visitor or traveller, bidding him God-speed and adding, 'May we be able to present you with another as welcome on your return.' The seller of an article other than eatables usually gives his blessing to the buyer in terms such as these: 'May good come upon you,' 'May you live long,' 'May no sickness happen,' 'May you grow rich,' to which the buyer replies with 'Thanks'—'*Thug-rje-chhe*,' literally 'Great mercy,' which recalls the French *merci* tendered on similar occasions.

The personal names of both boys and girls are largely borrowed from mystical Buddhism—*e.g.*, Dor-je-tshe-ring, 'the thunder-bolt of long life,' Dolma (spelt *sgRol-ma*, the Tibetan translation of the Sanskrit name Tārā, the Indian goddess of mercy); and the influence of this religious habit is also seen in the names of various places.

The common oaths or plights of asseveration are mainly Buddhist in character. The oath most commonly used by merchants and the laity as an asseveration in ordinary conversation is, 'By the Powerful Saint' (Śākyamuni, *i.e.* Buddha), or 'By the three Holiest Ones'—the Buddhist Trinity.

The non-Buddhist features and practices of the Tibetan religion, however, are also conspicuous, and reflect their pre-Buddhist cult, the shamanistic Bon. The physical environment of their life, in their rigorous climate where they see Nature in her roughest mood, in pitiless fury of storms and cold, terrorizing the brave as well as the timid, has impelled them to worship the more obvious forces of Nature as malignant demons which seem to wreck their fields and flocks, and vex them with disease and disaster. Their inveterate craving for material protection against those malignant gods and demons, as they thought them to be, has caused them to pin their faith on the efficacy of charms and amulets, which cherished objects are seen everywhere dangling from the dress of every man, woman, and child, not even excepting the Lāmas themselves. These charms, as we have seen,[2] are mostly sentences of Sanskrit texts borrowed from mystical Indian Buddhism, and they are supplemented by bodily and other relics of holy Lāmas, such as bits of their dress, crumbs dropped by them, nail-parings, etc.; and by these charms the Tibetans believe that they muzzle or bind or banish the devils.

A more cheerful and graceful side to their worship is seen in their popular practice of planting the tall inscribed 'prayer-flags,' which picturesquely flutter in the breeze around every village, and in the strings of inscribed flaglets which flaunt from house-tops, bridges, sacred trees, and passes, and from other places believed to be specially infested by malignant spirits or sprites.

As the people live in an atmosphere of the marvellous, no story is too absurd for them to credit, if only it is told by Lāmas. They are ever on the outlook for omens, and the everyday affairs of life are governed by a superstitious regard for lucky and unlucky days and the influences of unpropitious planetary portents. Although special divinations are sought from professed astrologer Lāmas in the more serious events in life—in birth, marriage, sickness, and death, and often in sowing, reaping, building, etc.—each layman determines for himself the auguries for the more trivial matters

[1] See, *e.g.*, the description by the present writer of the regent of Tibet (*Lhasa and its Mysteries*, p. 401 f.).
[2] See art. CHARMS AND AMULETS (Tibetan).

of his ordinary business, for travelling, buying and selling, mending, etc.[1] And yet we are apt to forget that Confucius and Cicero—to mention only these instances—believed in astrological auguries.

Pilgrimages to sacred shrines are very popular,[2] and little is thought of the hardships and expenses of long journeys for this purpose. Every opportunity is seized to visit celebrated shrines and to circumambulate the numerous holy buildings and sacred spots.

Prayers ever hang upon the lips of the people in the intervals of their work and even during their work. But the prayers are addressed chiefly to devils, threatening them with punishment through the saints and deified Buddhas, or imploring them for freedom or release from their inflictions;[3] or they are plain, naive requests for aid in obtaining the good things of this life. At all spare times, day and night, the people ply their prayer-wheels (*q.v.*), and tell their beads and mutter especially the mystic Sanskrit six-syllabled spell, *Oṁ ma-ṇi pad-me Hūṁ!*, '*Oṁ!* the jewel in the lotus *Hūṁ*,'[4] the sentence which, they are led to believe, gains them their goal, the glorious heaven of eternal bliss, the paradise of the fabulous Buddha of Boundless Light (Amitābha) or 'the Boundless Life' (Amitāyus [*q.v.*]). Yet with all their strivings the Tibetans seem never to obtain real peace of mind in religious matters.

3. Bon or pre-Buddhist religion.—The aboriginal pre-Buddhist religion of Tibet is called by the people *Bon* (pronounced *Pön*); and those who profess it are called *Bon-pa*, *i.e.* 'the Bons.' The meaning of the word is unknown. It is essentially a shamanist, devil-charming, necromantic cult with devil-dancing, allied to the Taoism of China, and, like the latter, has become largely intermixed with Buddhist externals. But it still retains its essentially demonist character. It was actively suppressed and its establishments were destroyed by the Tibetan rulers on their conversion to Buddhism from the 7th cent. A.D. onwards, at the instigation of the Lāmas, as it indulged freely in animal and human sacrifices; and it is still strictly forbidden by the Lāmaist hierarchy which holds the temporal rule in Central and Western Tibet. But it is still largely and openly professed over the greater part of Eastern and South-Eastern Tibet, the most populous part of the country, which for many centuries has been under Chinese rule and outside the domination of the Grand Lāmas. Indeed it was an appeal by the people of these provinces to China to protect them and their Bon religion that induced the Chinese to administer these provinces on behalf of the Bons. This unsuspected fact of the wide prevalence of the Bon religion there was brought to light by W. W. Rockhill in his extensive travels in these provinces,[5] where he found it to be much more popular and prevalent than Lāmaism. It was especially popular among the settled agricultural people, whilst the nomads, whose business led them into the territory of the Grand Lāmas, were more attached to Lāmaism. So numerous were its adherents that Rockhill estimated that about two-thirds of the population of Tibet were Bons. In Central and Western Tibet, where the repressive policy of the Lāmas prevents the profession of the Bon cult, it is rare to meet with any Bon priest. The present writer has met only a few itinerant priests who were clandestinely performing their demonist rites for villages in remote places; they were wholly illiterate and uncouth-looking men, exceptionally dirty, with long shaggy hair, and bedecked with little tufts of wool and tiny flags; and they indulged in devil-dancing antics and incoherent chants.

[1] See art. DIVINATION (Buddhist).
[2] See art. PILGRIMAGE (Buddhist), 5 (*d*).
[3] See art. PRAYER (Tibetan). [4] See art. JEWEL (Buddhist).
[5] *Diary of a Journey through Mongolia and Tibet*, pp. 68, 86 f.

In Eastern Tibet, however, where they are free to practise their cult, the Bon priests live in large flourishing monasteries, which they call *gom-pas*, like the Lāmaist establishments; and they have many images of gods and saints and demons generally resembling in appearance those of Lāmaism, but bearing different names. Their chief god they call gShen-rabs Mi-bo, who is reputed to be a deified priest analogous to the Lāmaist Padma Sambhava. They have bulky printed and MS books of ritual, which Rockhill found to consist of a Sanskritic jargon for the most part interspersed with other meaningless words. The present writer observed that the words in some of their MSS, which are written in the Tibetan script, were the Lāmaist Sanskritic words spelt backwards: the lotus-jewel formula of the Lāmas[1] was spelt 'Muh-em-pad-ni-mo,' thus, while attesting their borrowing from Lāmaism, emphasizing their anti-Lāmaist character. The *swastika* also, which they use extensively, is invariably figured with its ends or 'feet' turned in the reverse direction to that of the *swastika* proper (the feet of the latter turn to the right in the direction of the sun's course), and thus indicate the Bon cult to be of a lunar character, which is evident not only from the bloody sacrifices, but also from the predominance of the dragon-worship therein.

A significant glimpse into the original character of the Bon cult is obtained from the Chinese annals of the 5th and 6th centuries A.D. (*i.e.* before the introduction of Buddhism into Tibet), where the rites of the Tibetans are described:

> 'The officers (Tibetan) are assembled once every year for the lesser oath of fealty. They sacrifice sheep, dogs, and monkeys, first breaking their legs, and then killing them afterwards, exposing the intestines and cutting them into pieces. The sorcerers having been summoned, they call on the gods of heaven and earth, of the mountains and rivers, of the sun, moon, stars and planets, saying: "Should your hearts become changed, and your thoughts disloyal, the gods will see clearly and make you like these sheep and dogs." Every three years there is a grand ceremony, during which all are assembled *in the middle of the night* on a raised altar, on which are spread savoury meats. *The victims sacrificed are men*, horses, oxen, and asses, and prayers are offered up in this form: "Do you all with one heart and united strength cherish our native country. The god of heaven and the spirit of the earth will both know your thoughts, and if you break this oath, they will cause your bodies to be cut into pieces like unto these victims."'[2]

Even in the Buddhist period, in the 8th cent. A.D., similar bloody rites were celebrated by the professing Buddhist king of Tibet in concluding a treaty with the Chinese.[3]

The attire of the Bon priest in his special celebrations[4] is a coat of mail armour, from the shoulders of which project small flags, and a high-crowned hat bordered by effigies of human skulls and ornamented by flags and tufts of wool; a sword and shield are in the hands to fight the demons. (The black-hatted devil-dancers are of the Bon sect.) On ordinary occasions they wear a red robe, and occasionally have human skulls embroidered on their dress. Their hair is worn shaggy, and not tonsured like the Lāmas. They offer on their altars wool and yak hair, and images of men and animals made of dough, presumably, as shown by the present writer, instead of the sacrificed animal of the primitive cult.

Whilst the present-day Bon religion has acquired many of the externals of Lāmaism, many of the elements of the old Bon religion have been incorporated into the latter, just as so many of the pagan rites of Roman and Celtic heathendom have

[1] See art. JEWEL (Buddhist), § 7.
[2] S. W. Bushell, 'Early History of Tibet from Chinese Sources,' in *JRAS*, 1880, p. 441.
[3] Cf. L. A. Waddell, 'Ancient Historical Edicts at Lhāsa,' in *JRAS*, 1909, p. 941.
[4] See the figure in L. A. Waddell, *Buddhism of Tibet*, p. 30.

been incorporated into the later Christianity. The reformed Lāmaist Church of the Yellow-hat sect employ many rites which are transparently Bon, such as the necromantic expelling of the death-demon and the demons of sickness, and much of their divination-ritual. The unreformed Red-hat sects practise the old Bon rites to a much greater extent, including the erection of masts attached to dogs' and sheep's skulls, to 'bar the door' to the earth- and sky-demons.[1]

4. Lāmaism and its sects and rites.—The various aspects of Lāmaism and its sects and rites have already been described in previous articles.[2]

LITERATURE.—S. W. Bushell, 'The Early History of Tibet from Chinese Sources,' in *JRAS*, 1880, p. 435 ff.; A. Grünwedel, *Mythologie des Buddhismus in Tibet und der Mongolei*, Leipzig, 1900; E. R. Huc, *Travels in Tartary, Thibet, and China, 1844–46*, Eng. tr., 2 vols., London, 1851–52; C. F. Köppen, *Die lamaische Hierarchie und Kirche*, Berlin, 1859; C. R. Markham, *Narrative of the Mission of George Bogle to Tibet*², London, 1879; W. W. Rockhill, *The Land of the Lāmas*, do. 1891, 'Tibet from Chinese Sources,' in *JRAS*, 1891, pp. 1–291, *Diary of a Journey through Mongolia and Tibet in 1891 and 1892*, Washington (Smithsonian Inst.), 1894, *Notes on the Ethnology of Tibet*, do. 1895; E. Schlagintweit, *Buddhism in Tibet*, Leipzig, 1863; L. A. Waddell, *The Buddhism of Tibet*, London, 1895, *Lhasa and its Mysteries*, do. 1905, 'Buddha's Diadem,' in *Ostasiatische Zeitschrift*, i. [1912–13] 133–168, 'Dhāraṇī Cult in Buddhism,' *ib.* ii. [1913–14] 155–195, 'Dhāraṇīs translated from Tibetan,' in *IA* xliii. [1914] 37–95.

L. A. WADDELL.

TIME.—1. Introductory.—Temporal characteristics are among the most fundamental in the objects of our experience, and therefore cannot be defined. We must start by admitting that we can in certain cases judge that one experienced event is later than another, in the same immediate way as we can judge that one seen object is to the right of another. A good example of the immediate judgment in question is when we hear a tune and judge that of two notes, both of which come in our specious present, one precedes the other. Another direct judgment about earlier and later is made in genuine memory. On these relations of before and after which we immediately recognize in certain objects of our experience all further knowledge of time is built.

It must be noticed that the relation, as given in experience, connects what we may call protensive events, *i.e.* events that have some duration, and not momentary events or moments. We are not directly aware of events without duration, still less of moments of empty time, and therefore are not directly aware of the relations between such objects. Momentary events, moments of time, and the relations which order them in a series are all known only after a long process of reflexion, abstraction, and intellectual construction. This does not necessarily imply that they do not exist in nature, still less that they are subjective and arbitrary; all that is meant at present is that they are not the objects of direct awareness. Again we must notice that the relations of before, after, and simultaneous with, as given in experience, are not mutually exclusive. Protensive events may very well overlap, and therefore we must recognize that the most general relation between them is that of partial precedence or consequence. Of course, when we become familiar with the conception of momentary events and see how convenient it is, we tend to define partial precedence in terms of them and their relation of total precedence. But the opposite direction must be followed if we want to start with the experienced facts and trace the logical development from them of the scientific notion of time. We must take the experienced relation of partial precedence as fundamental and define momentary events, moments, and the relation of total precedence in terms of partial precedence and events of finite duration.

That such a course is possible is shown by the fact that it has recently been followed to a satisfactory conclusion by Norbert Wiener in the *Transactions of the Cambridge Philosophical Society*, and by A. N. Whitehead in his *Principles of Natural Knowledge*. We may compare the duration of experienced events with the extension of visible and tangible objects, and the relation of partial precedence with the partial overlapping of two extended objects in the field of vision. The problem of defining momentary events, moments, and the serial relation of before and after in terms of protensive events and partial precedence is closely comparable to that of defining material points, geometrical points, and the relations of before and after on a straight line in terms of extended objects and their partial overlapping. The problem for time is, however, easier than that for space, because in the former we have only to deal with a relation that generates a one-dimensional series, whilst with the latter the experienced facts force us to define a three-dimensional manifold.

2. Time and space.—The analogy between time and space has long been recognized; and it will be useful to consider at this point just how far it goes and where it is supposed to break down. Let us consider the likenesses and the alleged differences.

(*a*) *Likenesses.*—(1) Most objects of immediate experience possess a kind of magnitude called extensity, and such objects stand in certain immediately recognizable relations to other objects of the same sense experienced along with themselves. Also the parts of any one such object have relations of this kind to each other. Similarly the objects of our experience have another kind of magnitude called protensity or duration. Such objects have to others of the same kind the relation of partial (or, in special cases, total) precedence, and this relation can be recognized immediately. Likewise the parts of a single specious present can be seen to have this relation to each other.

(2) The relations in each case have magnitude. Just as one object in the field of view can be more to the right of another than a third, so one event in the field of memory or in the specious present can precede another event by a longer interval than some third one.

(3) In each region there is the same close and peculiar connexion between the kind of magnitude possessed by the terms and the kind possessed by the relations. It is possible to say that the interval between two events A and B is as long as the duration of some event C, just as it is possible to say that the distance between two sticks laid in the same straight line is the same as the length of some third stick.

(4) It is commonly believed that, when the analysis is made into moments and momentary events, all the events in the history of the world fall into their places in a single series of moments. So too it is supposed that, when the analysis is made into material and geometrical points, all the points in the world take their places in a single three-dimensional series of geometrical points.[1]

(*b*) *Alleged differences.*—(1) It is commonly held that all events have temporal relations to each other, but that psychical events have no spatial relations. This is denied by a small number of philosophers, notably by Samuel Alexander.

[1] *Buddhism of Tibet*, p. 484 f.

[2] See artt. ABBOT (Tibetan); ATĪṢA; BHUTĀN, BUDDHISM IN; CELIBACY (Tibetan); CHARMS AND AMULETS (Tibetan); CHORTEN; DEATH AND DISPOSAL OF THE DEAD (Tibetan); DEMONS AND SPIRITS (Tibetan); DIVINATION (Buddhist); FESTIVALS AND FASTS (Tibetan); IMAGES AND IDOLS (Tibetan); INCARNATION (Tibetan); INITIATION (Tibetan); JEWEL (Buddhist); LĀMAISM; LOTUS (Indian); PADMASAṂBHAVA; PRAYER (Tibetan).

[1] We shall consider later what the Theory of Relativity has to say as to the impossibility of separating time and space and as to the notion of one single time-series.

Without questioning the possibility of correlating psychical events with positions in space, we must hold that this alleged difference is a genuine one. If in introspection we do contemplate our states of mind in the same sense as in perception we contemplate other objects, it seems clear that our states of mind show no trace of being extended or standing in spatial relations, but do have duration and stand in temporal ones. Alexander would, however, deny that we can contemplate our states of mind. If this be so, it would of course be quite possible that we should fail to become aware of the spatial characteristics of our mental states, even though they possess them; but of course we have no right to pass from this merely negative position to the conclusion that they actually do possess them. Alexander's positive reasons are bound up with a large and complex metaphysical theory into which we cannot here enter. In any case the present difference is merely an external one, and would not affect the essential similarity of space and time.

(2) A much more important point is that time is said essentially to involve the distinction between past, present, and future as well as that between before and after. Now nothing in space obviously corresponds to these distinctions in time.

(3) Closely connected with this alleged difference are a number of rather vague statements often made—*e.g.*, that parts of space co-exist, but that only the present moment exists.

These two supposed differences between space and time may be treated together. They rest largely on confusions into which it is very natural to fall. The distinction between past, present, and future is not one which, like that between before and after, lies wholly in the experienced objects, but is one that rests on the relations between experienced objects and the states of mind in which they are experienced. To begin with, the distinction between present and not-present at any rate may be usefully compared with that between here and elsewhere in space. Here means near my body; elsewhere means distant from my body. If we want an analogy to the distinction between past and future, we can find one in the distinction between things before and things behind our body. It is true, however, that this analogy is incomplete, and that for an important reason, though one extraneous to the nature of time. The reason is that our practical and cognitive relations towards the future are different from those towards the past. We know a part of the past at any rate directly by memory, but we know the future only indirectly by probable inference. There is no analogy to this in space; our knowledge of what is behind our body is of the same kind and of the same degree of certainty as our knowledge of what is in front of it. But we may imagine that a distinction like that between past and future would have arisen for space also, if we had been able to see straight in front of us but had never been able to turn our heads or our bodies round.

The distinction is sometimes drawn that the past is fixed and unalterable, while the future depends, in part at any rate, on our volitions. In what sense is this true?

Without involving ourselves in controversies about free will and determination, we may at least assume that the laws of logic apply to propositions about the future. Hence any proposition asserting the occurrence of any future event must be true or false, and cannot be both. In that sense the future is as determinate as the past. But two points have to be noticed. (i.) However much I may know about the laws of nature, I cannot make probable inferences from the future to the past, because I am not directly acquainted with the future, but I can make probable inferences from the past to the future; *i.e.*, although every possible proposition about the future is even now determinately true or false, I may be able to judge now, from my knowledge of the past and present and of the laws of nature, that some propositions about future events are much more likely to be true than others. (It must of course be remembered in this connexion that a proposition that is actually false may be much more likely to be true on my present information than one that is actually true.) (ii.) I know with regard to certain classes of events that such events never occur unless preceded by a desire for their occurrence, and that such desires are generally followed by the occurrence of the corresponding events. But the existence of a desire for x does not increase the probability that x *has* happened. If it did we might be said to affect the past in exactly the same sense in which we are said to affect the future. Thus the assertion that we can affect the future but not the past seems to come down to this: (*a*) that propositions about the future can be inferred to be highly probable from a knowledge of the past and present, but not conversely, because of our lack of direct acquaintance with the future; and (*b*) that the general laws connecting a desire for x with the occurrence of x always contain x as a consequent and never as an antecedent.

3. Relation of time to logic.—This brings us to the very important question of the relation of time to logic. If we say of any event e that it is present, this proposition will generally be false, and will be true only at one moment. It seems, then, as if the truth of the proposition altered with time. Any other proposition asserting the occurrence of an event—*e.g.*, Queen Anne is dead—seems to be equally at the mercy of time. Then again there seem to be other propositions that are totally independent of time—*e.g.*, $2\times2=4$. These are sometimes called eternal truths; they always state relations between universals, and all our *a priori* knowledge is of such propositions. Lastly, there are propositions which essentially involve time, but claim to apply to any time; *e.g.*, whenever it rains and I am out without my umbrella, I get wet. Thus, on the face of it, there seem to be three kinds of propositions as regards relation to time: (1) eternal truths, which are independent of time because they deal with the timeless relations of timeless objects; (2) hypotheticals asserting temporal relations between classes of events—these contain an essential reference to time, but not to any particular time; (3) propositions which assert the occurrence of particular events, and which *seem* to be true at certain times and false at all others, though this is not really so.

There are two points to notice about the last class of propositions. (*a*) All propositions about events essentially contain a reference to time, and all propositions about particular events essentially contain a reference to the particular time at which the event happens. This reference is not always made explicit; but, until this has been done, we cannot say that the verbal form stands for any definite proposition. (*b*) We have to distinguish between the time at which a judgment is made and the time involved in the proposition that is judged. When the latter is not made explicit in the verbal expression of the judgment, it is a convention of language to assume that the time in the proposition is intended to be that at which the judgment is asserted. Thus, if I say 'It is raining,' this verbal expression, since it clearly intends to refer to a particular event, is incomplete and stands for no definite proposition; for it says nothing about the time at which it rains. It therefore seems to be sometimes true and sometimes false. But, as actually asserted, the words would be taken to express my judgment of the proposition, 'It is raining at the time at which I say "It is raining."' And this proposition is timelessly true or false, subject to a further correction which we shall add in a moment. In fact, whenever we are told that a proposition is sometimes true and sometimes false, we know that we are dealing with an incomplete statement about an event, and that the real state of affairs is that a propositional function of the form 'e happens at t' gives true propositions for some values of t and false propositions for other values. But the propositions themselves are timelessly true or false.

It is important to notice that in practice there is always the possibility of any verbal statement about events, no matter how carefully put, being sometimes true and sometimes false. We are not directly aware of moments of time, and so can date events only by other events. And the persons who read or hear our verbal expressions may know only by some description the event which we use for purposes of dating. Now we can never be certain theoretically that only one unique event answers to any description however complicated, and often there is real ambiguity in practice. Take, *e.g.*, the amended expression offered above: 'It is raining at the time at which I say "It is raining."' To any reader of this article the expression remains ambiguous, because he knows the event that is used for dating only by the very ambiguous description, 'The writer's statement of the words "It is raining"'—a description which applies to dozens of different events. In practice the difficulty is solved in conversation by the fact that all the manifold circumstances under which the particular conversation takes place go into the description and make it practically unambiguous. In writing, the difficulty is solved practically by using as the origin of dates some event, such as the birth of Christ, whose full description is so complicated that it is almost certain that only one event answers to it. But the theoretical difficulty remains, and so we are tempted to say that any proposition about events is sometimes true and sometimes false. But the proper thing to say is that any verbal expression referring to events, no matter how carefully put, always runs a theoretical risk of ambiguity—*i.e.*, it might with equal propriety make one reader think of one proposition which is true, and another of another proposition which is false.

We can now apply these general results to the special case of events being sometimes future, and then present, and finally past. The statement '*e* is present' is essentially incomplete and ambiguous, for, as we loosely say, it is sometimes true and sometimes false. The first thing, then, is to fill in the special time involved in the proposition. We then get '*e* is present at *t*,' where *t* is some definite moment fixed by some system of dating from a well-known and presumably unique event. What does this statement mean? Assuming that there are such things as moments, it means that *e* is at the moment *t* in an analogous way to that in which an object is at a position in space. The statement '*e* is present at *t*' may be compared with the statement 'Mr. Asquith is present at the meeting,' which means that his body is in the place where the meeting is held. In all complete statements of the form '*e* is at *t*' we must understand the word 'is' as standing for a timeless copula, and distinguish it from the 'is' of the present tense, which is contrasted with 'was' and 'will be.' Let us denote the 'is' of the present tense by 'is now.' Then the statement '*e* is now present' is an incomplete statement which is interpreted in use to mean '*e* is at (or occupies) the same moment as my assertion that it is now present'; '*e* is now past'='*e* was present'='*e* is at a moment earlier than my assertion that *e* is now past.' Similarly, '*e* will be present'='*e* is now future'='*e* is at a moment subsequent to my statement that *e* is now future.' The laws of logic are of course concerned with the timeless copula, and they presuppose that statements containing tenses are reduced in the way suggested above.

4. Past, present, and future.—We see, then, that the real source of the distinction between past, present, and future, and of the difference here between time and space, is that our judgments as well as the events judged about are in time, whilst our judgments about things in space are not in any obvious sense in space. These three distinctions correspond to the three possible temporal relations between our judgments and the events which our judgments are about. These distinctions are important, and they have been enshrined in language because they are correlated with important epistemological and psychological differences. Some states of mind are essentially contemporary with their objects—*e.g.*, the immediate awareness of visual sense-data when I open my eyes.[1] Other states are essentially later than their objects—*e.g.*, memories. If we exclude the possibility of prophecy, we may state the important epistemological proposition that all states of mind which give us an immediate knowledge of existents are either contemporary with, or later than, their objects.

It is important to notice that these statements are not merely analytic. There is a psychical difference between memories and awarenesses of contemporary sense-data which is open to introspection (though, of course, there may be marginal cases where the difference falls below the threshold of distinguishability), so that the statement that the former succeed and the latter are contemporary with their objects is a synthetic proposition.

We must, moreover, take into account the facts described in psychology as the specious present. In the first place, we must say that, if an object be known directly by a state of mind which succeeds it by more than a certain short time *t*, which seems to be fairly constant for a given individual, the state counts introspectively as a memory, and the object is judged to be past. If the period between the object and the direct awareness of it be not greater than *t*, the awareness does not count for introspection as a memory, and the object is judged to be present. To say, then, that an object has been present and is now past means that (*a*) it is (timelessly) the object of an immediate awareness which succeeds it by less than *t*, and (*b*) that my statement 'It is now past' succeeds it by more than *t*. We have still, however, to consider what is meant by the presentness of a state of mind. This seems to mean that, if a state of mind be the object of an act of introspection which succeeds it by less than a certain short period, the state presents a certain peculiar characteristic which it does not present to any later act of introspection.

We can now deal with such statements as that only the present exists, or that the present is a mere transition from one infinite non-existent to another. These phrases are mere rhetoric rooted in confusions. It is perfectly true, of course, that the whole history of the world is not a complex of co-existing parts (in the sense of parts existing at the same time), as a table is. But this does not mean that it is not a whole, or that one part of it exists any less than any other part. To say that *x* no longer exists, or does not yet exist, simply means that it occupies a moment before or after my statement about it. At another moment I may make another statement of the same verbal form about *x*, and, since this no longer stands for the same proposition, it may no longer be true (*i.e.* no longer stand for a true proposition). But this involves no change in *x* itself. That *x* exists at a certain moment simply means that *x* occupies that moment, and this is timelessly true. Similarly, the fact that this moment has a certain temporal relation to any definite assertion that I may make about *x* is timelessly a fact. That it has different and incompatible temporal relations to various assertions of the same verbal form made by me is also timelessly true, and is not merely compatible with but also a necessary consequence of *x*'s existence at its own moment. An event must continue to *be*, if it is to continue to stand in relations; the battle of Hastings continues to precede the battle of Waterloo, and therefore both these events must eternally be at their own respective moments. That both have ceased to be present merely means that they precede any assertion that I or my contemporaries can make about them; that both were once present merely means that both are contemporary with some assertions made about them.

[1] It is better for the present not to call these states of mind either perceptions or sensations, because the object of a perception is generally supposed to be a physical object or its state, and this may exist millions of years before the perception—*e.g.*, the perception of a distant star. Similarly, to call these states of mind sensations would lead to misunderstandings, owing to the ambiguities of that word and the widely held belief that sensations do not have objects.

The fallacy which we have to avoid is that of confusing two different senses of co-existence. In one sense the parts of any related whole co-exist; in another only those events that occupy the same moment of time co-exist. It is clear that the whole course of history does not co-exist in the second sense, and it is thought that this prevents it from co-existing in the first. Yet this is necessarily false, since it is admitted that events do have and continue to have temporal relations, and therefore they must form a related whole all of whose parts have being. The confusion is increased by the belief that past, present, and future are essential characteristics of objects in time in the same way as before and after are, instead of being analysable into the temporal relations of states of mind and their objects.[1]

When it is once recognized that the whole course of events is in a certain sense a *totum simul*, it becomes easy to see the answer to the famous theological problem: How can God's foreknowledge of men's actions be compatible with the freedom of men's wills? The answer is as follows. Whether men's wills be free or not, every man's future actions are as completely determinate as his past ones; this is a mere consequence of the laws of logic. If indeterminism be true, then no amount of knowledge about events previous to a moment *t*, and about the general laws of nature or the particular habits of a man, will enable us or even God to infer with certainty what the man's volition at *t* actually is, although it is eternally perfectly determinate. These two statements are clearly quite compatible. Finally, in spite of the fact that God cannot *infer* the man's volition at *t*, He may at any and every moment be directly aware of it in precisely the same way as we are aware directly (and not merely inferentially) of certain events through memories which are themselves later events. The facts that at a certain moment t_1 God can have a state of mind whose immediate object is the volition of a man at some later moment t_2, and that no amount of knowledge of events before t_2 would enable Him to *infer* the volition at t_2, are perfectly compatible; and they cease to be even paradoxical when we compare the case of memory and note that there is no essential difference between past, present, and future.[2]

5. Reality of time.—A great many philosophers have been concerned to deny the reality of time. Their arguments fall into two groups: (1) those that depend on the supposed infinity and continuity of time, and are therefore equally applicable to space; and (2) those that depend on the supposed peculiarities of time—*e.g.*, on the distinction of past, present, and future. Before considering the arguments in detail, it will be useful to make some quite general reflexions.

(i.) It is a matter of direct inspection that the immediate objects of some of our states of mind have temporal characteristics. It is as certain that one note in a heard melody is after another in the same specious present and that each has some duration as that some objects in my field of view are red or square and to the right or left of each other. It is then quite certain that *some* objects in the world have temporal characteristics, viz. the immediate objects of some states of mind. Now it is also certain that these objects exist at least as long as I am aware of them, for, in such cases, I am obviously not aware of *nothing*. Hence there cannot be anything self-contradictory in the temporal characteristics found in these objects, for otherwise we should have to admit the existence of objects with incompatible characteristics. Hence there is no obvious reason why temporal characteristics should not also apply to what is not the immediate object of any state of mind. It follows, then, that criticism cannot reasonably be directed against temporal characteristics as such, but only against the descriptions that we give of the temporal characteristics of experienced objects, and the conclusions that we draw from them or the constructions that we base on them. And arguments that refer to the infinity and continuity of time are really directed against a construction based on what we conceive to be the essential characteristics of the time element which is undoubtedly present in the objects that we experience; for we are not directly aware of infinite duration or of the continuity—in the mathematical sense—of time. If we suppose that such criticisms are successful, the conclusion ought not to be either that reality has no temporal characteristics (for it is quite certain that at least some parts of it have), or that time, as an inference or construction extending the temporal characteristics of experienced objects to others, is unreal (for this goes much too far). The only justifiable conclusion would be that one particular way of describing and extending the temporal characteristics of experienced objects is unsatisfactory, and that it behoves us to look for a better one. This point has not commonly been grasped by philosophers who claimed to disprove the reality of time.

(ii.) It is thus obviously of importance to be clear as to what is the particular view of time that is attacked by special arguments. The important distinction for us to make is this: it is possible to hold (*a*) that there is a series of moments of time, and that events occupy some of them but are distinct from them, and have temporal relations to each other in virtue of those which subsist between the moments that they occupy; or (*b*) that there are no such things as moments distinct from events, but that events really do have direct temporal relations to each other; or (*c*) that there are no moments, and that even events only *appear* to have temporal relations to each other. It is clearly possible to deny (*a*) without denying (*b*). To do this can hardly be called denying the reality of time; it should rather be called denying the absolute theory of time in favour of the relative theory. It is only philosophers who deny both (*a*) and (*b*) and support (*c*) who can strictly be said to deny the reality of time. It is quite possible, however, that some arguments might be equally fatal to (*a*) and to (*b*).

It will be well at this point to say what we can about the controversy between absolutists and relativists. The absolute theory strictly means that temporal relations between events are regarded as compounded out of two relations—(1) that of an event to the moment of time which it occupies, and (2) the relation of before and after between moments of time. The relative theory holds that there are no moments, but that temporal relations hold directly between events. Its most important philosophical upholder is Leibniz, though he goes a good way farther in the direction of (*c*); it is also held, with a good deal of misunderstanding and confusion, by many modern physicists of a philosophical bent. We may say that the relative theory stands at one remove, and the absolute theory at two removes, from what we find in the objects of immediate experience. Here we find, as we have seen, events of finite duration and relations of partial precedence. The relative theory replaces these objects by series of momentary events of no duration, and the relations by those of total precedence and simultaneity. The absolute theory takes the farther step of introducing a new set of entities, viz. moments which have no duration and stand in relations of total precedence but never of simultaneity, and a new relation, viz. that between a momentary event and the moment which it occupies.

Neither theory has been very accurately stated by most of its supporters; *e.g.*, Newton, the chief upholder of the absolute theory, was mainly concerned with the measurement of time and the desire for a constant rate-measurer. But the two theories, when thought out, may be reduced to what has been stated above. We may say at once that we know of no way of deciding conclusively between the two. But, although moments and momentary states *may* exist, we now know that all their

[1] The point can perhaps be made clearer by reflecting that a tune has a pattern in time in exactly the same sense as a wallpaper has a pattern in space.

[2] We can, of course, remember much that we could not infer.

work can be done by certain logical functions of nothing but events of finite duration and their relations of partial precedence. Hence both theories may be said to sin by assuming entities which are not necessary to science and cannot be either directly or indirectly verified (viz. momentary events in the relative theory, and moments in the absolute theory), and the absolute theory is the worse sinner of the two. As certain logical functions of what actually exists (viz. certain classes of classes of events), moments do exist; but whether there also exists anything having the same logical relations but of the type of individuals and not of that of classes of classes it seems totally impossible to determine. It is, however, often convenient to continue to speak in terms of moments, and this is harmless for the reasons given above.

We can now deal with the special arguments against time.

(1) Those based on its supposed infinity commonly confuse infinity with endlessness. They generally proceed on the assumption that what is meant by the infinity of time is that it has neither a first nor a last moment. But this would be perfectly compatible with the whole course of time lasting for no more than a second. The fractions between 0 and 1, arranged in order of magnitude, have neither a first nor a last term, and yet the interval between any two of them is less than unity. But all attempts to prove that time or the series of events must have an end fail. So do attempts to prove that they cannot have ends. The most celebrated argument on both sides of this question is contained in Kant's first antinomy. His argument against the endlessness of time, interpreted as charitably as possible, comes to the statement that, because there are definite points in the time-series—in particular, the point which we have reached when we read Kant's argument—therefore the series must have a definite beginning point. Otherwise, Kant says, the series of events could never have reached the definite point which it admittedly has reached. The argument is, of course, a complete *non-sequitur*, for it practically amounts to saying that a series cannot have *any* definite term unless it has *end* points. And this is sufficiently refuted by considering that the number +2 is perfectly definite, although the series of numbers with signs has neither a first nor a last term.

Arguments to prove that time or the series of events in time cannot have a beginning are perhaps more plausible. It is difficult for us psychologically to imagine a first event or a first moment, because all the events that we can remember have been preceded by others. Also there are special difficulties connected with causation in the notion of a first event, which do not apply to a first moment or to a last event. A first event is one which no event precedes, though there may of course be moments that precede a first event. Now, the only plausible general proposition about causation seems to be that, if the whole universe were completely quiescent for a finite time, it could not begin to change.[1] This means that, if the universe be in the same state at any two moments t_1 and t_2 and at all moments between them, it will be in the same state at all moments later than t_1. Now, to say that a change happens at t_1 means that, if the state of the universe at t_1 be s_1, and if it also be s_1 at any later moment t_2, then there is a moment between t_1 and t_2 at which its state is different from s_1. It follows from this definition that to say that a first event happens at t involves that the universe has been in the same state for a finite time before t. And this is contrary to our proposition about causation. If, then, we accept this proposition as an *a priori* truth, there cannot be a first event, though there might be a first event in certain isolated parts of the universe (*e.g.*, the creation of the world) provided that there had never been a first event in other parts (*e.g.*, in the mind of God). But, of course, there remains the doubt whether our axiom about causation be not a mere prejudice masquerading as an *a priori* law.

It must be carefully noted that, if there be a first event, there need not be a first moment of time, and that, if there be a first moment of time, there need not be a first event. Again, if there be a first moment of time and no first event, either there might be no moment, except the first, that was not occupied by an event, or there might be a duration unoccupied by events. These consequences follow from the continuity of time, and have often been overlooked by philosophers ignorant of the mathematical theory of continuity.

Leibniz based his main argument against the absolute theory of time on the fact that, if it were true, there might be a period, finite or infinite, before any event happened. This period must be definite; and yet, the moments of time having no intrinsic difference, there is no reason why it should be ended or limited by one moment rather than another. If, on the other hand, we avoid this by assuming that there is an event at every moment of time, there is no reason for assuming *both* events and moments, for the series of events will suffice.

This argument is a sound one against assuming that there *are* moments, though it certainly cannot disprove that there may be moments. If there were moments, they would doubtless have intrinsic differences, though we could not discover them; we must further recognize some ultimate facts, and one of these might be that the course of events is preceded by such and such a duration of empty time.

We may sum up our conclusions as follows. Arguments to disprove the reality of time from its infinity and continuity either confine themselves to criticizing infinity and continuity as such or introduce considerations about causality. Arguments of the first kind would be equally fatal to *any* infinite or continuous series, and therefore prove too much, for they would destroy the series of real numbers. And we now know that all such arguments do rest on confusions and on an insufficient analysis of the notions of infinity and continuity. There is therefore no reason why the series of moments at any rate should not be either (*a*) endless or (*b*) of infinite length. The second set of arguments can apply only to events and not to the supposed series of moments, because causation is concerned with events and not with empty time. We saw that, if a certain plausible axiom about change be true, there cannot be a first event. This would not, however, prove that the whole series of events has lasted for an infinite time, though the present writer knows of no objection to such a possibility. There is no more objection to the series of events being endless than to any other series being endless—*i.e.*, there is none at all. The result is that all danger of a valid antinomy against time vanishes. (i.) Whether the axiom about change be true or not, it is equally possible that the series of moments shall be (*a*) endless or terminated, and (*b*) of finite or of infinite length. (ii.) If the axiom about change be true, the series of events cannot have a beginning, but may (*a*) have an end or not, and (*b*) be of finite or of infinite length.

(2) Arguments against the reality of time which turn on the distinction of past, present, and future may be dealt with shortly. One argument asserts that the past and the future do not exist, and that the present is a mere point without duration. It is then supposed that what occupies no finite duration cannot be real, and this disposes of the present. An argument of this kind is used

[1] The universe here must be taken to include God, if there be one.

by Leibniz against absolute time, though it would presumably apply to events just as well. It is met, of course, by the consideration that past, present, and future are all always equally real, and that these characteristics do not belong to events as such, but in virtue of the temporal relations between them and certain psychical events.

A somewhat different argument against the reality of time has been produced by J. M. E. McTaggart.[1] His argument is that every event is past, present, and future; and that the attempt to avoid the incompatibility of these predicates by saying that the event has been future, is present, and will be past involves a vicious circle or a vicious infinite regress. The answer is that, whenever we consider any definite statement about the pastness, presentness, or futurity of an event, we can see that there is no contradiction. Take a definite statement by McTaggart that Queen Anne's death is now past and has been present and future. Suppose we interpret this to mean that Queen Anne's death is not the direct object of any awareness (even a memory) which is contemporary with McTaggart's statement, but that it is contemporary with some states of mind (*e.g.*, Lord Bolingbroke's) which precede McTaggart's statement; and that it is later than some thoughts about it (*e.g.*, William III.'s), which also precede the statement. Then those three propositions seem to be timelessly true, perfectly compatible, and to contain all that is meant in the assertion by McTaggart that Queen Anne's death is past and has been present and future.

We may conclude, then, that no satisfactory proof has been offered even that absolute time is unreal, still less that the series of events and their direct temporal relations are unreal.

6. Measurement of duration.—It seems to have been the question of a rate-measurer that led Newton to the theory of absolute time. Newton considers a number of periodic events which are roughly isochronous, and compares their rough isochronism with 'absolute time, which flows uniformly.' It is an unfortunate way of introducing absolute time. In the first place, it is of no practical use to any one. Whether absolute time flows uniformly or not, we can only observe events and must use them, or processes based on them, as our rate-measurers. Again, the statement that absolute time flows uniformly is thoroughly obscure. Time cannot be said to flow, for this seems to imply that time changes; and this would make time consist of a series of events in time. Nor is it at all clear what Newton meant by uniformity in this connexion. Presumably the meaning must be that the moments of time form a series like the real numbers. What we really want to know is whether we can find any periodic process such that the time that elapses between corresponding stages in each repetition is the same. But no essential reference to absolute time is involved here. We must beware of confusing the two statements: (1) there are definite intervals of a certain determinate duration, and this duration is independent of our methods of measurement; and (2) there are absolute moments of time, and the interval between any two of these has a definite magnitude. The latter implies the former, but not conversely. The real problem is: Granted that there is a definite interval between pairs of events, how are we to measure it?

There is a special difficulty in measuring intervals of time between events which is not nearly so much felt in measuring the distance between things. This difficulty is in the temporal analogue to superposition. We may carry a rod about with us in space, and we may have fairly good reasons to believe that it has not altered in length. The corresponding procedure in time-measurement is to find some process which can be started and stopped at any moment and can be assumed to have the same period whenever it is repeated. Such processes may be called isochronous. But, even when an isochronous process has been secured, it cannot be used to measure time in the same direct way in which a rod can be used to measure length. A rod will not as a rule fit an exact number of times into what we want to measure; it is therefore divided into a number of equal parts. Similarly we want an isochronous process that can be divided into equal subdivisions which can be easily recognized; *i.e.*, we want a process which itself consists of a number of similar processes which all occupy equal times. Now, it is not nearly so easy to be sure that a process takes the same time whenever it is repeated as to be sure that a rod keeps the same length wherever we use it; and it is much less easy to divide a process into parts that occupy equal times than to divide a rod into parts that have equal lengths. The recognizable divisions in a process of change are largely fixed for us, while divisions on a rod can be fixed by us with marks without affecting the rod as a whole.

Nevertheless the assumptions that have to be made, and the peculiar mixture of observation and convention that is involved, are the same in principle for the measurement of time and of space. The fact is that we can make immediate comparisons both of length and of time with a certain amount of accuracy. We believe that these judgments are the more accurate the nearer the objects to be compared are in time and space, and the more similar the circumstances under which each is inspected. Trusting to these immediate judgments, we see reason to believe that both the lengths of rods and the time taken by processes may vary when the rods are moved or the processes repeated. But we believe that the variation always depends on the fact that change of position in space or time involves change in the relations of the rod or the process to pieces of matter, and that mere changes of position in absolute time and space—if such could be—make no difference. We have learned by experience what are the most important factors that determine change of length or of period, and we can allow for them. It is found that the periods of recurrent processes are, on the whole, more largely affected by changes in the surroundings than are the lengths of such bodies as steel rods.

Our method of determining an ideal rate-measurer is somewhat as follows. We begin with some process which is sensibly isochronous—*e.g.*, the swing of a pendulum, or the time taken for a complete rotation of the earth on its axis. We can judge of this isochronism with a certain amount of accuracy by direct comparison in memory, just as we can compare lengths by looking at them. We can go farther than this. Just as we are greatly helped in our comparison of lengths by putting the objects to be compared side by side, so we can use expedients to help our judgments of the isochronism of processes. If we start two pendulums together and their periods be not exactly the same, the divergence will become more and more marked the longer they swing. If no divergence be noted after many swings, we may conclude that each swing of one takes the same time as the corresponding swing of the other. This does not prove that the successive swings of either are isochronous; for the period of each may be varying according to the same law. But, if we also find that the period of one of these processes synchronizes with the corresponding period of some other

[1] 'The Unreality of Time,' *Mind*, new ser., xvii. [1908] 457–474.

sensibly isochronous process which is physically very different, it becomes very improbable that there should be any law by which the successive periods of two such very different processes alter in precisely the same way. We are therefore justified in concluding *tentatively* that the successive periods of these sensibly isochronous processes are actually isochronous.

The next step is to state all the laws of nature which involve time on the assumption that equal intervals of time are measured by complete periods of such processes. We find, *e.g.*, that, if it be supposed that the successive rotations of the earth on its axis are isochronous, the laws of motion can be very simply stated and are very nearly verified by all the mechanical phenomena that we can observe. So far we are entirely in the region of what can be experienced or rendered very probable from what we experience. But now a conventional element enters. We shall probably find that, when time is measured by an actual physical process and when our laws have been stated in terms of time so measured, a closer investigation shows that there are slight divergences from the laws which cannot be accounted for by mere experimental errors. The last stage in the determination of the equality of times now begins. We argue that the suggested laws are so simple and so nearly true that the most reasonable plan is not to keep the same time-measures and complicate the laws, but to suppose that the laws are rigidly true but the time-measurer not perfectly accurate; *i.e.*, that successive periods of this physical process are not perfectly isochronous. We therefore erect the laws into principles, define equality of times by them, and apply the necessary corrections to our old time-measurer. There is nothing particularly arbitrary about this. We believed, to begin with, as the result of direct judgments assisted by the use of such expedients as have been described above, that a certain periodic process is isochronous. We admitted, however, that deviations from isochronism so small as to escape the notice of any direct method are possible. We then stated our laws in terms of time as measured by this process, and found them to be simple and very nearly true; but, if they are to retain their simple form and become quite true, a small correction must be made in the assumed isochronism of the process. This contradicts nothing that we have deduced from our experience; for we admitted all along the possibility of errors too small for direct detection. The procedure has the least trace of arbitrariness if, as is often the case, we can see the physical cause of the lack of complete isochronism in our time-measurer and can fully explain this lack in accordance with the laws which we have erected into principles. This has happened, *e.g.*, with the earth as a time-measurer, where we can explain its small defect from isochronism, when once we have to assume it, by the frictional effect of the tides acting according to the laws of mechanics. Even when no physical cause can be detected for the presumed lack of isochronism, it is always possible to suggest a hypothetical one. But, in so far as this has to be done, our procedure does become more arbitrary; and a point may be reached where a full explanation of all the phenomena demands a real change in the form of the laws with or without a change in the time-measurer. This has happened in recent years to the laws of motion, mainly through investigations on the movements of small electrically charged particles with a velocity comparable to that of light.

7. Theory of Relativity.—The next point to be considered is the criterion of beforeness, afterness, and simultaneity among events which are not the objects of any one experience. We have seen that in favourable cases we can immediately judge that one event that we experience is after another that we experience. Other people can make similar judgments about events in their experience. But we cannot directly judge of the temporal relations of events which we do not directly experience. Matters are on exactly the same footing with spatial relations. I may be immediately aware that one object in my field of view is to the right of another in the same field, and another man may be able to make similar judgments about his visual sense-data. But it remains to be seen what is meant by saying that an object which *A* experiences is at the right of one which *B* experiences; or again what is meant by the statement that of two objects which no one experiences—*e.g.*, two atoms—one is to the right of the other. What is wanted is to be able to date events in a time-series which is neutral as between *A*'s experience and *B*'s, and shall contain events that do not fall into the direct experience of any one. In this problem we must carefully distinguish between two questions which are liable to be confused: (1) How do we come to understand the nature of the relations in the neutral time-series?, (2) How do we know with regard to any two definite events, e_1 and e_2, whether e_1 is before or after or simultaneous with e_2?

The answer to the first question is that the relations in the neutral series are regarded as having the same logical properties as those which we directly experience, or at any rate as being capable of definition in terms of the logical properties of these relations. Possibly a temporal relation as experienced by *A* has a sensuous particularity different from that possessed by one experienced by *B*; just as it is impossible to say whether the quality of what *A* sees and that of what *B* sees are precisely the same when they say that they perceive the same colour, and no available test can detect any discordance between their experiences. But, of course, the sensuous particularity is what is shed when we consider a neutral time-series, and only the logical properties of the relations (*e.g.*, transitivity, asymmetry, etc.) are important.

The distinction between the space and time of each man's experience and a neutral space and time runs parallel with the distinction between the immediate objects of each man's experience and neutral (or, as we call them, physical) objects. However we suppose physical objects to be constituted, and whatever we suppose to be the relation between our minds and them, it must be assumed that physical objects are in the neutral space, and that their changes take place in the neutral time and make themselves known to us by correlated changes in the immediate objects of our experience.

It is not necessary here to consider how a number of people, $M_1 \ldots M_n$, come to agree that certain events, $e_1 \ldots e_n$, in their respective sense-data are all correlated with the same physical event. But it is necessary to notice that they will find, first of all in the case of sound, that, if their physical laws are to give at all a simple and complete account of what they may expect to hear under given circumstances, they must assume that the sounds heard by various people, and all correlated by them with a single physical event, are not in general contemporary with each other. The greatest accuracy and simplicity is introduced into the laws of sound by supposing that the hearing of the sounds by the various people takes place at times dependent on the positions of their bodies in physical space and on the spatio-temporal position of the single physical event correlated with all these sounds. This example brings out three very important points. (1) The determination of the temporal relations between events in the minds or in the immediate objects of the minds of different people can be accomplished only when these events have been correlated in some definite way with supposed neutral physical events; (2) the temporal relations then assigned are such as to make the laws telling us what sensations to expect in given circumstances as simple and accurate as possible; (3) it follows from these considerations that the determination of a neutral time-series and of the positions of physical objects in a neutral space must proceed *pari passu*.

Suppose, *e.g.*, that we say that the velocity of sound is v centimetres per second: (1) we want to connect all the known facts about the sounds which people hear under circumstances that can be directly experienced; (2) we want to do this compatibly with the assumptions which have already been made as to what heard sounds are to be classed together as connected with one physical event; and (3) we want our laws which sum up the known facts and anticipate experience to be as simple as is compatible with accuracy. We find that these ends can best be accomplished by supposing that *A*'s hearing of s_a and *B*'s hearing of s_b (s_a and s_b being both correlated with the single physical event *S*) take place at times $t+\frac{x_a}{v}$ and $t+\frac{x_b}{v}$ respectively, where t is the date of *S* in the neutral time-series, and x_a and x_b are the respective distances between the place where *S* happens in physical space and *A*'s and *B*'s bodies as physical objects. We must remember that the correlation of several sounds heard by different people with a single physical event and the assignment of positions in neutral space to physical events are themselves carried out on the same general principles as the dating of events in neutral time and as the measurement of duration already described; *i.e.*, we start with instinctive judgments of rough accuracy, and then proceed to a more accurate determination of our terms, guided by the general motive of maximizing the accuracy and simplicity of scientific laws.

As we have seen, sound is the first and most obvious case where it is necessary to assume different dates for different members of a group of sense-data which are all correlated with a single physical event. The more accurate researches of science necessitate a similar process for dealing with the sense-data of sight, and so the notion of a velocity of light is introduced. These velocities, once determined, furnish a criterion of before and after among physical events, and, through them, for events in different minds.

Let us denote any moment at *A* by the symbol $^{a}t_r$, and an event which happens at the point *A* at the moment $^{a}t_r$ by $^{a}e_r$. Let us use the same notation for events and moments at *B*. Then we can say: An event $^{a}e_r$ precedes an event $^{b}e_s$ if a disturbance leaving *A* at $^{a}t_r$ reaches *B* not later than $^{b}t_s$. Now it is found that we have no reason to believe that any disturbance travels faster than light. It can be shown that, if the above be our sole criterion for before and after between events at different places, there will be pairs of such events of which we have no reason to say that one is either before, after, or contemporary with the other.

To see this, consider the following case. Let $^{a}e_1$ happen at *A* at $^{a}t_1$. A signal which leaves *A* at $^{a}t_1$ cannot reach *B* *before* a certain moment $^{b}t_2$. Again, a signal that reaches *A* at $^{a}t_1$ cannot have left *B* *after* a certain moment $^{b}t_0$. On our criterion, therefore, $^{a}t_1$ is before any moment that is after $^{b}t_2$ and is after any moment that is before $^{b}t_0$. But how are events at *B* which happen between $^{b}t_0$ and $^{b}t_2$ related in time to the event $^{a}e_1$? Take an event $^{b}e_x$ such that $^{b}t_x$ is between $^{b}t_0$ and $^{b}t_2$. You cannot say that it is before $^{a}t_1$; for a disturbance leaving *B* at $^{b}t_x$ would reach *A* later than $^{a}t_1$. But you also cannot say that $^{a}t_1$ is before it; for a disturbance leaving *A* at $^{a}t_1$ would reach *B* later than $^{b}t_x$ (viz. at $^{b}t_2$). Hence on our criterion we can neither say that $^{b}e_x$ is before $^{a}e_1$ nor that $^{a}e_1$ is before $^{b}e_x$. Moreover, there is an infinite number of events at *B* of the form $^{b}e_x$ where x is between 0 and 2. Thus we cannot cut the knot by saying that, since they are neither before nor after $^{a}e_1$, they are contemporary with it. For they are not contemporary with each other. Thus one and only one of the class of events $^{b}e_x$ can be taken to be contemporary with $^{a}e_1$, and the rest, so far as our criterion goes, must be held to be neither before, after, nor simultaneous with $^{a}e_1$. We are thus compelled to recognize that we may have no means of deciding whether a pair of events at different places in physical space are contemporary or not in physical time.

We can, if we like, accept this result, and build up our physics on the assumption that physical time really is non-connexive; *i.e.*, that, though all events have temporal relations to some events, none have temporal relations to all events. This has recently been done very fully and ably by A. A. Robb.[1] Or we may take the more usual course of assuming that physical time really is connexive, but that in certain cases all criteria fail to determine the actual temporal relations which subsist between events in different places. We then must simply make a convention (to return to our example) that one particular event of the class of events at *B*, whose temporal relations to $^{a}e_1$ are left doubtful by our criteria, is contemporary with $^{a}e_1$, and that whatever precedes this one precedes $^{a}e_1$ and whatever follows it follows $^{a}e_1$. It is customary to assume that the event at *B* which comes midway between $^{b}e_0$ and $^{b}e_2$ is contemporary with $^{a}e_1$; but it must be noticed that this is a mere convention, though doubtless the most reasonable one to make. (On our notation this event would naturally be $^{b}e_1$.)

We must notice further that, for this convention to be determinate at all, we must assume that we know that the time-measurer at *B* goes at the same rate as that at *A*, and that both go uniformly. Now, if the time-measurers cannot be moved about, their synchronism can be determined only by sending signals from one to the other—*e.g.*, light-signals. And, even if they can be moved about, our only test for the continuance of their synchronism, when they have been moved apart and are no longer in view together, is by light-signals. On the other hand, the question whether our tests for synchronism by light-signals are genuine tests (*i.e.* involve synchronism in physical time) depends on whether the velocity of light relative to the system containing the time-measurers is constant in time and the same in all directions. And this last point cannot be determined *until* the time-measurers in two places have been synchronized; for it is obvious that to measure a velocity we need to know the time in two places. We see, then, that the possibility of synchronizing time-measurers and the uniformity of the velocity of light stand and fall together, and that neither can be proved independently of the other. If we allow that the velocity of light relative to the system is constant and uniform in all directions, our tests for synchronism and uniformity in our time-measurers are valid; if we allow that the criteria ensure physical synchronism, the physical velocity of light (as distinct from its *numerical* measure on our convention) will be constant and uniform. But neither question is or ever will be capable of independent settlement; and therefore we simply have to make a convention that the meaning to be attached to synchronism in different places is agreement with the tests based on light-signals, and another convention that distances shall be so measured that the measure of the velocity of light relative to the system is independent of time and of direction.

Suppose now that the people on a system *S* determine their spatio-temporal co-ordinates in this way, and that the people on another system S^1, moving with uniform translational velocity relative to *S*, determine their spatio-temporal co-ordinates similarly. Let them arrange, as they can do, that the time-measurers at the origin of each go at the same rate; and further let them arrange their units so that the velocity of light as measured by each from experiments with sources and mirrors fixed in their own system shall have the same numerical measure. Then (*a*) it can be proved that each will find the same numerical measure for the velocity of light, even though the sources and mirrors be in uniform motion relative

[1] *A Theory of Time and Space.*

to the two systems. (*b*) It is possible to find equations connecting the spatio-temporal co-ordinates which the people on S give to any momentary event which they observe with those which the people on S^1 give to the same event. These are the celebrated transformations of the Theory of Relativity. They are, as we should expect, perfectly reciprocal, since the relative motion of S and S^1 is a perfectly mutual phenomenon. But (*c*) they lead to certain rather startling results. (1) Lengths along and at right angles to the direction of relative motion which are judged to be equal by the people on one system will be judged to be unequal by those on the other. The ratio depends on the relative velocity and on the value of the velocity of light which is common to the two systems.[1] (2) Events in different places which are judged to be contemporary by the people on one system will be judged to occur at different times by those on the other system, and the difference of time will depend on the distance apart parallel to the direction of relative motion.

Although the observers on the two systems thus differ, they cannot criticize each other. Each has pursued precisely the same plan in setting out his co-ordinates and synchronizing his time-measurers. And it would be quite futile for one to claim that his results are the right ones because his system is at rest and the other is in motion. For the relative motion is completely reciprocal, and neither absolute motion nor any consequence of it can be observed. Lastly, it is equally futile for one to say that he is at rest 'relative to the ether,' while the other is in motion; for we know that no experiment whatever has been able to demonstrate motion 'relative to the ether,' and this motion may fairly be dismissed as a fiction. The upshot of the matter is that there is nothing to choose between their respective judgments, and that all the laws of nature can be stated as truly and will have precisely the same form, no matter which of an infinite number of systems in uniform translational motion be taken as the basis for spatio-temporal co-ordinates. This result, with the mathematical consequences that flow from it, is known as the Theory of Relativity. Its philosophical importance is that it enables us to see the tacit assumptions that are made when we talk of events at different places being contemporary; and the fact that measurement of distance is entangled with time, since the distance between two objects at any time involves a decision as to what is meant by the same time in two different places. Though it no more completely refutes the possibility of absolute space and time than does any other argument (for after all it only deals with our numerical measures and leaves it open whether one system of time-measurers is physically uniform and synchronous and one system of space-measures directly represents distances in physical space), yet it helps to render the notions of absolute space and time still more spectral and remote from all possible experience than before. For it enables us to see that there are a certain indeterminateness and conventionality even in the measurement of the distance between physical objects and of the lapse between events; and that therefore what we can know is even at a farther remove than we had thought from the points of absolute space and the moments of absolute time.

The Theory of Relativity sketched above was first fully stated by Einstein in his classical paper, 'Über das Relativitätsprinzip und die aus demselben gezogenen Folgerungen,' which appeared in the *Jahrbuch der Radioaktivität und Elektronik* for 1907. This may be called the restricted Theory of Relativity. It may be briefly characterized as consisting of an experimental fact and a philosophical principle suggested by a great number of facts. The philosophical principle is that, since we can never observe absolute time, space, or motion, even if there be such things, the laws of physical phenomena as learned from experiment and observation must retain the same *form* for acts of observers in uniform motion relative to each other. This persistence of form (or *covariance*, as it is technically called) in the differential equations that express the laws of nature does not in general imply that the actual *magnitudes* measured by two observers in uniform relative motion will be the same.

E.g., an observer moving with his instruments relative to an electrically charged body will detect magnetic as well as electrical forces, whilst one who is at rest with his instruments relative to this body will observe only electrical forces. But the differential equations connecting the effects noted by one observer with each other and with his x, y, z, and t co-ordinates will be precisely the same as those connecting the effects noted by the other observer with each other and with *his* x, y, z, and t co-ordinates.

This principle by itself, however, would be of little use, since it does not enable us to say what connexion exists between the co-ordinates of the two observers. But, if there be some physical magnitude, which is not merely covariant but also *invariant* as between different observers in uniform relative motion, the transformations connecting the two sets of co-ordinates can be found. Now the velocity of light *in vacuo* is found to fulfil this condition; its actual numerical value is found to be the same by all observers. The mathematical consequences of this fact lead to Einstein's set of equations connecting the x, y, z, t co-ordinates of one observer with those of another who is moving relative to the first. The precise significance of Einstein's principle of the 'Constancy of Light Velocity' has been indicated above, and shown to be connected with the way in which we are forced to lay out a system of co-ordinates and to define simultaneity between events in different places.

Einstein's restricted theory has gained many triumphs. It explains at once what is known as Fresnel's dragging-coefficient for light passing through matter that moves relative to the observer. It also accounts for the change of mass with velocity which is observed when small particles move with speed comparable to that of light. The principle necessitates slight changes in the previously accepted form of some of the laws of nature. Maxwell's equations and the equation of continuity in hydrodynamics do indeed at once and without modification fulfil the condition of covariance. But the laws of mechanics, as they stand, are not in accord with the principle and need modifications which only become practically important in dealing with the motion of matter with velocities comparable to that of light.

Considerable philosophic importance, in connexion with the nature of time, attaches to the work of Minkowski.

On the ordinary Newtonian mechanics the form of the laws of nature is unchanged if the three spatial axes be twisted in space about their origin as a rigid body. Now Minkowski showed that the Lorentz-Einstein transformation is equivalent to a twist of the same nature performed on a set of *four* mutually rectangular axes in a four-dimensional space. Three of these axes are the ordinary spatial ones, the fourth is the time axis multipled by c, the velocity of light, and ι, the root of -1. So far the theory must be regarded as a merely elegant mathematical device, since the fourth axis is imaginary in the mathematical sense, and the angle of solution is also imaginary. But, if we do not assume that the geometry of the four-dimensional 'space-time' is Euclidean, a much more important meaning can be attached to Minkowski's interpretation of the relativity transformations. If we suppose the geometry of 'space-time' to be hyperbolic (*i.e.* the geometry of Lobatchewski), the relativity transformation corresponds to twisting a set of four real axes as a rigid body through a real angle about the origin. The axes are now x, y, z, and ct, and c simply depends on the different units that we use in measuring time and space; so that really we are dealing with a four-dimensional

[1] This is the famous Lorentz-Fitzgerald contraction.

manifold in which space and time are homogeneous with each other, but whose geometry is not Euclidean but Lobatchewskian.

The work of philosophical mathematicians since Minkowski's death has consisted largely in developing the notion that the ultimate data in the world are events in space-time, *i.e.* events extended both in space and in time. The content of a specious present forms an example of such data. Space and time as used in the sciences only emerge at the end as elaborate mathematical constructions built on the immediately perceptible relations between extended events.

The best exposition of this point of view is contained in A. N. Whitehead's *Principles of Natural Knowledge*, which begins with a severe criticism of the concepts of classical physics and proceeds to elaborate the notions of space, time, and matter from the crude data of sense and their immediately given spatio-temporal relations. It seems hardly possible to doubt that this is the right path for further research, but it demands a combination of philosophical and mathematical abilities of so high an order that few can tread it successfully. Alexander in his *Gifford Lectures* at Glasgow has developed the notion of space-time with great fullness from the purely philosophic side, but, at the time of writing, his lectures have not appeared in print, and it is impossible to give a fair account of his views from the short synopses which are alone available.

It remains to say a few words about the generalized Theory of Relativity. So far we have only considered observers in *uniform* relative motion and have laid down a principle of relativity for them. Einstein has occupied himself in the last few years in removing this restriction and thus bringing gravitation, which fell outside the older theory, into the scope of the Theory of Relativity.

A particle is said to be under the action of no force if it move uniformly in a straight line. But the question whether it moves in a straight line and whether it moves uniformly is clearly relative to our spatial axes and to our measure of time. If, *e.g.*, a particle moves uniformly in a straight line relative to the rectangular axes x and y, it will not do so relative to axes which rotate about the origin in the xy plane. Accordingly, relative to one set of axes it will be said to be under the action of no force, whilst relative to the second set it will be said to be under the forces needed to produce the observed accelerations. Now the 'forces' introduced by these mere changes of our axes of reference are in one respect very much like the force of gravitation. They, like it, affect all forms of matter indifferently and depend only on the mass, not on the special nature of the matter. On the other hand, a genuine gravitational field cannot be altogether transformed away by a suitable change of axes, as a purely geometrical field can be. For any one particle this can be done by choosing axes fixed in the particle, but relative to these axes the other particles in the field will still be accelerated. Now it seems clear that a mere change of axes could not make any difference to the form of the laws of nature, and thus, if gravitation were capable of being transformed away merely by a suitable change of axes, the principle of relativity would assert that the presence of a gravitational field makes no difference to the form of the laws of nature. For the reason mentioned above the principle of relativity cannot be taken in this unrestricted sense. It may, however, be taken to assert that the form of the law of nature is unaltered in a gravitational field up to a certain (as yet undetermined) order of differential coefficients.

It is now necessary to see the bearing of these results on the constitution of the 'space-time' of nature.

It has been proved by Riemann that the metrical geometry of any space is completely determined when the 'linear element,' *i.e.* the interval between any pair of infinitely near points, is expressed as a known function of the differentials of the coordinates. Thus a three-dimensional Euclidean space is completely defined by the equation

$$ds^2 = dx^2 + dy^2 + dz^2$$

for the linear element. Now the metrical properties of four-dimensional space-time will be completely determined when ds^2 (the interval of any pair of adjacent points in it) is expressed as a known function of dx^2, dy^2, dz^2, dt^2, $dxdy$, $dxdz$, $dxdt$, . . . etc. In space-time, therefore, the ten coefficients of dx^2, dy^2 . . . must be known in order to determine ds^2. In general these coefficients will be functions of x, y, z, t; they are denoted by the letters g_{xx}, g_{yy}, g_{xy}, etc. Any transformation of axes corresponds to a change in these g's and therefore to a change in the form of the linear element. It follows that, as regards forces introduced simply by changes of axis, it is a matter of perfect indifference whether we say (a) that the geometry of space-time is such and such and that such and such forces are acting, or (b) that the geometry of space-time is such as to produce the appearance of these forces. The g's can be regarded either (a) as completely determining the forces on a given assumption about the geometry of space-time; or (b) as determining the metrical properties of space-time itself. The extended Theory of Relativity prefers to take the second view of them and to drop all reference to forces; on the first view the g's are of the nature of potentials. Now, in theory, any function whatever might be chosen for the g's. But, in fact, all parts of nature are subject to gravitation. This means that the choice of g's is not absolutely unrestricted, but that in every permissible system of axes for describing nature the g's will be subject to a set of differential equations connecting them with each other and with the x, y, z, and t of that system. These equations then express the law of gravitation and at the same time express it as a fundamental property of space-time.

It is extremely difficult to render Einstein's theory intelligible without mathematics, and the mathematics needed is somewhat formidable. It is hoped, however, that the above slight sketch may illustrate that extreme entanglement of time with space and with matter which undoubtedly occurs in our crude sense-data and is now seen to persist even in the most refined speculations of mathematical physics. It may perhaps be added that Einstein's generalized theory, as distinct from the special philosophic interpretations which may be put on it, is not a mere idle speculation, but has already explained the anomalies in the perihelion of Mercury, and has correctly foretold the amount of deviation in a ray of light due to its passing near a heavy body like the sun.

8. Historically important speculations about time.—Our knowledge of time as of space owes more to the labours of mathematicians and physicists than to those of professed philosophers. The sharp distinction between time and what changes, and between space and what moves in it and is extended, is largely due to the development, first of mechanics, and latterly of electrodynamics.

To the Greeks we owe much less with regard to time than with regard to most matters of philosophic or scientific speculation. This may perhaps be ascribed to the late development of dynamics; the Greek approach to the problems of time was mainly by way of astronomy. Of course, Zeno's celebrated arguments have an important bearing on change and continuity, and, whatever may have been the real intention of their author, they remained the best discussion on these subjects so closely related to time until the final treatment of infinity and continuity by Dedekind and Cantor in the latter part of the 19th century. Time plays an important part in the *Timæus* of Plato; and, although his treatment cannot be called satisfactory, it has the merit of distinguishing time from what is in time.

Plato says that God wished the created world to resemble the intelligible one as far as possible. Now, it was not possible for it to be eternal, and the nearest analogue to eternity which He could provide was to make 'a moving image of eternity.' This is time, and it is closely connected with the motions of the heavens; eternity 'rests in unity,' but the image 'has a motion according to number.' Before the heavens were created, there were no days, years, etc.; but, when God created the heavens, He created these divisions of time also. Time was thus created *with* the heavens, and, if one were to be dissolved, so would the other be. But Plato does not appear to identify time with the motion of the heavens, though it is difficult to see what he supposes it to be in itself. According to Plato, past and future are created species of time which we wrongly transfer to the eternal essence; strictly 'was' and 'will be' are to be asserted only of generation in time, for they are motions. The analogy of the moving image to the eternal is that the created heavens have been, are, and will be in all time. This view has something in common with that of Spinoza, who makes things as they really are for *ratio* timeless, but holds that this timelessness cannot be grasped by *imagination*, which represents it confusedly as duration through endless time.

Aristotle defines time as 'the number of motions relative to before and after.' Number here appears to mean what is numbered. The now is borne along with the movable as a point may be regarded as moving and making up a line. So in a sense there is only one now, though in another sense there are many nows. This is obviously a very unsatisfactory metaphor, and there seems no reason to think that Aristotle was really clear as to the distinction between time and motion.

The Schoolmen in the main adopted Aristotle's views, though with certain modifications. St. Thomas Aquinas, in the tract *de Instantibus*, discusses time and change with some fullness. He draws a distinction between the time in which angels perform their acts and that in which men and matter operate. The time of angels is discrete, that of men continuous; the difference arises from the fact that continuity is essentially connected with matter, while angels are separated substances. An instant for an angel is the time occupied by a single act; it may thus correspond to a long period in our time. This may be compared with Royce's views about the varying lengths of the specious present in various beings.

In modern philosophy the men who have most concerned themselves with time are Leibniz and Kant. Leibniz argued strongly for the relative view of time in his letters to Clarke, who represented Newton and the absolute theory. His arguments turn mainly on the identity of indiscernibles and the principle of sufficient reason. Leibniz carefully distinguished duration from the relation of before and after, and he compared duration to the extension of matter. Leibniz's view is that time is a system of possible positions of possible events related by before, after, and simultaneous with. He holds that all possible worlds must be in time, though, of course, the particular temporal relations of the actual world are contingent. To make Leibniz's theory coherent, it would be necessary to be much clearer than he is as to the relation between the time-series of each monad and the time-series of the universe. He attempted to explain the relation between successive states of the same monad by saying that the earlier ones have the quality of being desires for the later ones. As an attempt to replace relations by qualities this clearly fails, since 'desire for' anything is clearly a disguised relation. And as an attempt to *define* before and after it also fails; for it is clearly a synthetic proposition that desire for *X* precedes *X*. Then again it seems essential to Leibniz's doctrine of the reflexion by one monad of the states of another that we should have some account of the temporal relations between corresponding states in different monads. The state of a monad at a given moment in its own time-series is presumably the reflexion of the *contemporary* states of other monads; but we are not told what is meant by a time-series common to the monads, nor is it clear that this would be consistent with Leibniz's dislike of relations.

The absolute theory of time has never had much philosophic support; there can be little doubt that Leibniz had the better of Clarke. Perhaps the best arguments for absolute time and space are to be found in Bertrand Russell's *Principles of Mathematics*. They do not seem to the present writer to be conclusive, and their author has latterly taken a much more relativistic view.

Locke, Berkeley, and Hume insisted that the notion of time comes from the succession of our ideas. But they never made it clear how their temporal relations are connected with the time that is used in physics. Berkeley and Hume in particular fail to give any reasonable account of the distinction that we certainly make between the temporal order of our ideas and the temporal order of the objects which we claim to know by them. It is a great merit of Kant to have seized on the importance of this point in his 'analogies of experience,' though the distinction will certainly not bear the superstructure which he built on it. He attempted to prove that the distinction involves the permanence of substance (which he seems to identify with the chemical law of the conservation of mass) and the law of causation among experienced objects. But his arguments are entirely inconclusive even to prove that, in order to make the distinction, we must *believe* in these principles; much less to prove, what the transcendental method always tends to confuse with this, that the principles are true.

Time plays perhaps more, and more important, parts in Kant's philosophy than in any other.

(1) In the *Æsthetic* he tries to prove that it is a form of intuition, the form appropriate to the internal sense. This seems to mean that, just as we can only perceive physical objects as being in space, though there is no reason to think that things-in-themselves are spatial, so we can only perceive ourselves and our mental states in introspection as being in time, though there is no reason to think that we really are in time. This certainly seems to raise the special difficulty that, unless we know ourselves as we are and not merely as we appear, we cannot know what our forms of intuition are, but only what they appear to be, whilst Kant's argument certainly assumes that we know what they are. (2) In the *Dialectic*, as we have seen, Kant has an antinomy about time. This apparently would, if valid, overthrow not merely absolute time but also the temporal character of events and the temporal relations between them. We have already seen how grave are the difficulties in the way of any such conclusion, and how entirely powerless Kant's arguments are to prove it. (3) In the *Analytic* time plays an important part in the difficult doctrine of the schematism of the categories. The position seems to be that the categories as pure conceptions of the understanding cannot be applied immediately to the manifold given in sense, even after that has been synthesized by imagination. They have to be mediated through time; thus the category of ground and consequent, which is purely logical, can be applied to the world of sensible experience only after it has been schematized into the temporal form of cause and effect. The whole argument here is confused and weak to a remarkable degree; the principle appears to be that the manifold of sense is provided with temporal characteristics by intuition; that these remain and are elaborated by the syntheses of imagination; and that then the categories can be applied if they be first schematized so that they and the synthesized manifold share the temporal characteristic in common. (4) Kant's critical solution of his own antinomy is that the infinity involved in time is not an actual infinite, as it would have to be if time applied to things-in-themselves, but is only the power that we have of always synthesizing farther than we have yet gone in constructing a temporal series. To this Lotze makes the very pertinent criticism that it surely depends on the nature of things-in-themselves whether we shall be indefinitely supplied with material to synthesize.

The modern development of our knowledge about time is due mainly to two sets of people: (1) philosophical mathematicians, like Dedekind and Cantor, who have given a satisfactory analysis of infinity and continuity, and thus finally refuted all antinomies based on these; (2) mathematical physicists who have been led by their studies in the optics of moving systems to elaborate the Theory of Relativity. The pioneer in this work is Lorentz; the theory itself was first formulated by Einstein; and the mathematical and philosophical consequences have been drawn and elaborated by Einstein, Minkowski, Robb, Whitehead, and others.

It is also necessary to mention among recent philosophers Bergson, in whose works time, nominally at any rate, plays an important part. Bergson holds that the attempt to treat time as similar to space is a perverse one philosophically; it may work very well in dealing with dead matter, but it shows its falsity in biology, psychology, and philosophy. He also falls foul of the mathematical theory of the *continuum* as applied to time; he admits that it is internally consistent, but denies that it describes what anybody really means by change and motion. Bergson's arguments seem to rest partly on a comparison between change as a sense-datum (*e.g.*, the peculiar characteristic of what we see when we look at the second hand of a watch as distinct from the hour hand) and physical change, and partly on the erroneous view that a whole of related states cannot be a change unless each of its terms be a change. Again, in some of his remarks about memory he seems to suppose that, because a memory-act is a later awareness of an earlier event, the earlier event and the later awareness must somehow be contemporary. Finally, he seems to think that the ordinary view of time is refuted by the facts, of which he is strongly convinced, that no two total states of mind at different times can be exactly alike, that there are not, strictly speaking, distinct elements which can recur as parts of different mental states, and that no amount of knowledge about earlier states will enable us to foretell later ones completely. But Bergson's most characteristic doctrines belong to the subject of change rather than to that of time.

LITERATURE.—(*a*) *Historical.* — Plato, *Timæus*; Aristotle, *Physics*; St. Thomas Aquinas, *de Instantibus.* (*b*) *Absolute and relative theories.*—Leibniz, *Letters to Dr. Samuel Clarke*, London, 1917; Bertrand Russell, *The Principles of Mathematics*, Cambridge, 1903, i. (*c*) *Reality of time.*—Leibniz; Kant, *Critique of Pure Reason*; F. H. Bradley, *Appearance and Reality*, 2nd ed. revised, London, 1902; J. Ellis McTaggart, 'The Unreality of Time,' *Mind*, new ser., xvii. [1908] no. 68, p. 437 ff.; H. Bergson, *Time and Free-will*, Eng. tr., London, 1910, and *Matter and Memory*, Eng. tr., do. 1911. (*d*) *Measurement of time and Theory of Relativity.*—H. Poincaré, *Science et méthode*, Paris, 1908, and *La Valeur de la science*, do. 1908; H. A. Lorentz, *The Theory of Electrons*, London, 1909; H. Minkowski, *Raum und Zeit*, Leipzig, 1909; L. Silberstein, *The Theory of Relativity*, London, 1914; C. D. Broad, *Perception, Physics, and Reality*, Cambridge, 1914; A. A. Robb, *A Theory of Time and Space*, London, 1911; A. S. Eddington, *Report on the Relativity Theory of Gravitation*, do. 1918. (*e*) *Physical time as a construction.*—B. Russell, *Our Knowledge of the External World*, London, 1914; A. N. Whitehead, *Principles of Natural Knowledge*, Cambridge, 1919.

C. D. BROAD.

TINNEH.—See DÉNÉS.

TIPITAKA.—See LITERATURE (Buddhist), vol. viii. p. 85[b].

TIRUPATI. — Tirupati, vulg. Tripetty (Tel. Tirupati, *tiru*, Skr. *śrī*, 'venerable,' *pati*, 'lord'), a town in Chittoor District, Madras (lat. 13° 38′ N., long. 79° 24′ E.), is a famous place of pilgrimage, situated on the Tirumalai or sacred hill, usually known to Europeans as Upper Tirupati, in contrast to the lower town at its base. The whole area is considered sacred, and up to 1870 had never been visited by Europeans. Mark Wilks states that he was on duty for eighteen months in the neighbourhood, and, though he frequently climbed the adjoining hills, he could never catch even a distant view of the pagoda.[1] The belief that much crime was committed without detection in the holy town led to the issue of an order by Government that it should be thrown open to the District officials. This at first produced considerable local opposition; but European visits now cause little sensation. The sanctity of this hill-range rests on the legend that it forms part of the sacred mountain Meru. The range has seven principal peaks, each of which is sacred and has a name and legend of its own. One of the peaks, known as Śeshāchalam, 'serpent hill,' takes its name from the belief that it was torn from Meru by Ādi Śesha, the primordial snake, who contended in a trial of strength with the wind-god, Vāyu. Vāyu raised so great a tempest that the peak was blown away and fell to earth in its present position. Near this peak the great temple stands. Little can be seen of it, and no European has been allowed to enter it. It is a building of little architectural beauty or importance, but the cultus of the deity is interesting as an example of the amalgamation of local non-Aryan beliefs with orthodox worship. Within a small chamber lighted by lamps is the idol, a stone image of Viṣṇu, seven feet in height. It represents the god as Chaturbhuja, 'four-armed,' one of the right hands holding the discus (*chakra*), one of the left the conch-shell (*sankha*), the second right hand pointing to the earth to draw attention to the miraculous origin of the holy hill, while the remaining left hand grasps a lotus. The deity possesses 1008 titles, the most common of which are Śrīnivāsa, 'dwelling with Śrī or Lakṣmī,' goddess of prosperity, and Venkaṭachalapati, the title of the sacred hill, which has been adopted into Sanskrit from the Tamil *ven*, 'white,' *kadam*, 'hill slope,' thus showing that the deity was adopted into Brāhmanism from a Dravidian cult. By visitors from the Deccan and N. India he is generally known as Bālāji, which, according to Monier-Williams,[1] is the name of a human incarnation of Viṣṇu or Kṛṣṇa of whom little is known, save that he was remarkable for many extraordinary qualities, and that he lived in the neighbourhood of the sacred hill. Hence visitors to the shrine generally invoke him by the title of Govinda, 'cow-keeper,' one of the names of Kṛṣṇa. It is remarkable, however, that, according to common belief, the image worshipped was originally one of Śiva. The transformation of the Śaiva cult to that of Viṣṇu is traditionally ascribed to the reformer Rāmānujāchārya (born *c.* A.D. 1017). It is said that he procured a conch-shell and discus of gold, which he placed before the image and closed the temple doors. When the shrine was opened next day, it was found that these emblems of Viṣṇu were grasped in the hands of the image, and therefore it was really Viṣṇu. The tangled hair (*jaṭa*), the cobras carved upon the body, and various other peculiarities indicate that it was intended to represent Śiva, and the priests, who are Dīkshita Brāhmans, admit that they belong to the Śaiva sect. The god is provided with a consort, Padmāvatī, said to be the incarnation of a mortal woman, and the offerings are believed to have been originally collected to provide for the marriage of the pair. In an ante-room there is a brass vessel with a bag hanging in it, into which money and jewels are placed. On the other side are two gongs, one of which, when struck, utters the name Govinda, the other Nārāyaṇa—both titles of the god. Many pious persons observe the custom of collecting in their homes monthly contributions which are placed in a money-box and finally offered at the shrine.[2] The anthropomorphism of the cult is shown in the belief that the deity annually announces to certain persons that he needs shoes, which they make and present.[3] Various rites indicate the non-Aryan character of the worship. Thus a feast called *Gangājātra*, 'Ganges festival,' is held in the early spring, when a figure is made of clay or straw, before which animals are sacrificed—a custom quite opposed to true Vaiṣṇava beliefs. Even Brāhmans, who will not attend personally, send victims. When the sacrifices are over, the image is burned, and much rude merriment follows. Some votaries carry on their heads a structure made of bamboo, resembling a car, adorned with coloured paper, and supported by iron nails that

1 *Hist. Sketches of the South of India*[2], Madras, 1869, i. 246 n.

1 *Brāhmanism and Hindūism*[4], London, 1891, p. 267 f.

2 E. Thurston, *Ethnographic Notes in S. India*, Madras, 1906, p. 352.

3 Thurston, *Castes and Tribes of S. India*, iv. 310 f.

often pierce the flesh of the bearer, who submits cheerfully to the torture. At the *Gangammā* festival held at the temple 'language truly filthy and obscene' is used to the goddess herself.[1] The explanation of this custom is obscure.

'Abusive language is believed in certain circumstances to bring good luck to the person against whom it is directed.'[2]

On this theory the obscenity may possibly be regarded as a form of mimetic magic intended to repel the powers of evil from the deity, and thus advance her powers of promoting fertility.[3]

Again, on the road leading up to the temple 'small stones heaped up in the form of a hearth, and knots tied in the leaves of the young date palms may be seen. These are the work of virgins who accompany the parties of pilgrims. The knots are tied in order to ensure the tying of the *tāli* string on their necks [at marriage], and the heaping up of stones is done with a view to ensuring the birth of children to them. If the girls revisit the hill after marriage and the birth of children, they untie the knot on a leaf, and disarrange one of the hearths. Men cause their names to be cut on rocks by the wayside, or on the stones with which the path leading to the temple is paved, in the belief that good luck will result if their name is trodden on.'[4]

The hope of recovery from sickness and the desire for male offspring are the chief causes of vows being made to the god. The vow need not be performed immediately on receipt of the blessing. Death merely transfers the obligation to the heir, and it is said that the god is never defrauded. A common offering by women is the hair of their heads, which is shorn off by barbers, more than half the women who visit the temple returning with their heads clean shaven. J. A. Dubois[5] describes a custom of binding the idol in chains of silver, apparently with the object of preventing him from leaving the temple. The same writer[6] speaks of the custom of women who desire children passing a night in the temple. He also alleges that at the festival, when the image is taken in procession, the Brāhmans select the most beautiful women as wives of the god; they are branded with a hot iron, and, after serving for some years, are dismissed with a certificate of good conduct which ensures that, as they wander through the country, their wants will be abundantly supplied.[7] By other accounts, when such a woman becomes too old to please the deity, the priests make a mark on her breast, the emblem of the god, and give her a patent certifying that she acted for a certain number of years as one of his wives, that he is now tired of her and recommends her to the charity of the public. H. A. Stuart, however, denies that any dancing-girls attend the god; but he admits that the state of morality among priests and pilgrims has deteriorated, even celibate Bairāgīs and priests taking their paramours with them up the sacred hill. In the Deccan it is very common for a woman to make a vow that, if she is relieved from sickness or other trouble, she will shave her head to the god at Tirupati. After being shaved, she walks thrice round the temple, worships the image, pays a fee to have lighted camphor waved round the idol, receives a pinch of the sugar offered to the god, distributes food to the poor and to the monkeys which swarm round the temple, offers charity, and returns home.[8] The tonsure of children is also performed at the temple.[9]

LITERATURE.—This art. is mainly based on an excellent account of the place by A. F. Cox, *Manual of the N. Arcot District*, Madras, 1881, p. 146 ff., supplemented by later information supplied by its writer. In addition to the authorities quoted, see J. B. Tavernier, *Travels in India*, tr. from ed. of 1676 and ed. V. Ball, London, 1889, ii. 243. For various references to the worship of the god among the people of S. India see also E. Thurston, *Castes and Tribes of S. India*, Madras, 1909, i. 195, 335, 389, ii. 43 f., 112 ff., iii. 42, 461, iv. 310, 326 f.

W. CROOKE.

1 *Madras Government Museum Bulletin*, Madras, 1901, iii. 267 f.
2 J. G. Frazer, *Pausanias*, London, 1898, ii. 492.
3 *GB*³, pt. i., *The Magic Art*, London, 1911, ii. 100.
4 Thurston, *Ethnographic Notes*, p. 351.
5 *Hindu Manners, Customs, and Ceremonies*³, tr. H. K. Beauchamp, Oxford, 1906, p. 591.
6 P. 593 f.
7 P. 601 f.; cf. Thurston, *Castes and Tribes*, ii. 117; N. Manucci, *Storia do Mogor*, Eng. tr., London, 1907–08, iii. 143 f.
8 *BG* xxii. [1884] 64.
9 J. E. Padfield, *The Hindu at Home*, Madras, 1896, p. 97 f.

TITANS.—The Titans, like the Giants (*q.v.*), are potencies belonging to an early pre-Olympian stage of Greek mythology. The two tend to be confused by late authors, but in origin they are distinct. The Titans are distinguished from Giants by the following well-marked characteristics: (1) they are gods (θεοί), and as such immortal, whereas the Giants are mortal; Τιτῆνες θεοί, 'Titans, gods,' is a fixed formulary in Hesiod's *Theogony*; (2) they are sky-potencies (Οὐρανίωνες)[1] as contrasted with the Giants, who are earth-born (γηγενεῖς); Titans and Giants alike are to Hesiod the offspring of Earth and Heaven, but the Titans tend skywards, the Giants with their snake-tails earthwards. To Shakespeare Titan is the sun.

'And Titan, tirèd in the mid-day heat,
With burning eye did hotly overlook them.'[2]

To Pausanias[3] Titan, according to the local legend of Titane, is 'brother to the sun,' and Pausanias himself held that Titan 'was great at marking seasons of the year.' Empedocles holds a less specialized and perhaps juster view; he places side by side

'Gaia and billowy ocean and air with its moisture,
And *Æther, the Titan*, embracing the All in a circle.'[4]

The Titan Phaethon is the sun and sun's charioteer; the Titaness Phoebe is the moon; the Titans Atlas and Prometheus are the sky-pillars supporting Ouranos. The Titans are an integral part of that primeval cosmogony of earth and sky, ousted in Greece by the anthropomorphic Olympians, but remembered as part of their Indo-European heritage by the Northern Muses who came to Helicon and taught their lore to Hesiod.

The etymology of Gigas, 'giant,' is uncertain; that of Titan is happily secure, and it throws a flood of light on the function of these sky-potencies of older date and explains in a flash the two Titan myths—(*a*) the Titanomachia, (*b*) the rending of Zagreus, which, but for this etymology, must have remained obscure. Three glosses of Hesychius make it certain that *Titan* means simply 'king.' They are as follows: τιτῆναι· βασιλίδες (the word glossed is from a lost play of Æschylus); τιήνη (for τιτήνη)· ἡ βασίλισσα, and τίταξ· ἔντιμος. ἢ δυνάστης. ὁ δὲ βασιλεύς. Titan is king, 'honoured one,' but —and here is the interesting point, or rather series of vitally interconnected points—he is the king of the old order, the king-god or divine king, and as such he is a sky-potency, for one main function of the old king-god was to order the goings of the heavenly bodies and generally to control the weather. Here we have that odd blending of physical phenomena with human and social potencies which lies at the back of most gods and certainly of Zeus himself.

The Titanomachia is at once clear. For on the physical point of view it is, as described in Hesiod,[5] just a half-humanized thunder-storm, Zeus, the new sky- and thunder-god, fighting the old sky-potencies; from the theological point of view it is the new anthropomorphism against the old religion of the king-god or medicine-man who controls the weather. The Olympian religion naturally regarded these old Titan kings as criminals, rebels against high heaven, condemned to Tartarus for their sin of ὕβρις; they are the counterpart of the arch-Titan Prometheus.

1 *Il.* v. 898. 2 *Venus and Adonis*, 177. 3 II. xi. 5.
4 H. Diels, *Die Fragmente der Vorsokratiker*, Berlin, 1903, p. 38
5 *Theog.* 665 ff.

The second Titan myth, the rending of Zagreus, is less transparent, but in the light of the Titan kings even more illuminating, for we catch the king in his earliest stage of all, when he was tribal elder or medicine-man, not yet fully developed into kingship. The Titans, according to a version of the story as early as Onomakritos,[1] lure away the infant Zagreus, dismember, and (in some versions) cook and eat him. The story is an initiation myth based on the familiar initiation ritual of the mock death and resurrection of the initiate. The initiators are the elders or dynasts of the tribe, the embryo-kings.[2] The Titans as old-world kings are well in place; as a form of giant they are absurd. The name Zagreus takes us to Crete, and in Crete we find the Titans in a connexion that again points to initiation mysteries. The Cretans, according to Diodorus,[3] said that in the time of the Kouretes those who were called Titans ruled over the region of Cnossos, where were shown the foundations of the house of Rhea and a sacred cypress-grove of hoary antiquity. These Titans again must have been the old king-medicine-men, contemporary with the Kouretes and, like them, initiators into the 'men's house' of the Mother Rhea.[4] On a red-figured *hydria* in the British Museum[5] Zagreus is depicted as actually devoured by the Titans, and these Titans wear the characteristic dress of Thracian chieftains. We may safely infer that the Titan myth of the rending of Zagreus was known from Thrace to Crete, and we may suggest that it arose in that early stratum of 'satem'-speaking population known to the later Greeks as 'Pelasgian' — a stratum specially addicted to the mystery-cults of the son of Semele.

LITERATURE.—M. Mayer, *Die Giganten and Titanen*, Berlin, 1887. For the Titans as Ouraniones, J. E. Harrison, *Themis*, Cambridge, 1912, pp. 453-460. The right etymology of Titan from the root *ti*, 'honour,' was first seen by L. Preller, *Gr. Mythologie*⁴, Leipzig, 1894, p. 44. Its meaning as 'king' was made clear by F. Solmsen, in *Indogermanische Forschungen*, xxx. [1912] 35. The full significance of the 'king' meaning in relation to the mystery-rite of the *omophagia*, as practised in Crete and by Thracian chieftains, was established by A. B. Cook, *Zeus*, Cambridge, 1914, i. 655 ff., in relation to his republication of the British Museum vase in pl. xxxvi. The previous literature of the subject will be found in Cook's notes. On p. 655, note 2, he rightly points out that the present writer's former derivation (*Prolegomena to the Study of Greek Religion*², Cambridge, 1908, p. 493, and *Themis*, p. 15) of the word 'Titan' from Τίτᾰνος, 'white-clay man,' is erroneous. As initiators the Titans probably were daubed with white clay, but the name is not derived from the disguise.

J. E. HARRISON.

TITHES.—1. Origin and purpose.—Tithes are connected, on the one hand, religiously, with offerings of firstfruits (*q.v.*); on the other hand, politically, with tribute and taxation. While taxation often took the form of a tenth, the amount might vary, less or more, though the name 'tenth' (*decima*, δεκάτη) was retained. Voluntary offerings to a deity soon became customary, and even necessary, especially where kings began to impose taxation and tribute, and where a god was now thought to be a divine monarch. To keep up his sanctuary was as much an obligation as to keep up the royal person and court. An early example shows this. The people of Tyre paid tithes to Melcarth as king of the city, and the Carthaginians similarly sent their tithes to Tyre.[6] W. R. Smith[7] shows that in this case the tithe was as much political as religious. The voluntary offering necessarily became tribute also, as the ritual of a sanctuary became more elaborate, the sanctuary itself more splendid, and the attendant priests more numerous. Why a tithe or tenth should have been fixed on so generally is not clear, but probably it is connected with primitive views about numbers, or with methods of counting—*e.g.*, by fingers and toes.[1]

In Babylon, whether the tithe was native or borrowed, its use is found in the time of Nebuchadrezzar II. Earlier evidence is so far lacking, and there is no trace of it in the Assyrian period. It was a due paid to the temple of a god from the land, and was paid by all, including the king, who assigned to temples founded by him an annual amount from cultivated lands and from the treasury. Numerous tablets concern tithes, and show that the people were taxed for support of the temple. Tithe was of the nature of a fixed charge on the land and even became negotiable. Such tablets may be regarded as of the nature of a receipt for payment of tithe, which was generally paid in kind—corn, oil, sesame, dates, flour, oxen, sheep, and asses—though this might be commuted for a money payment. One man sometimes paid it collectively for a group of men, and possibly this signifies a systematic collection of tithe in one district by an authorized person.[2] At the same time Babylonian kings had a tithe of all imports, as had also Persian satraps.[3] In S. Arabia tithes were used for the erection of sacred monuments.[4] Cyrus, on the advice of Crœsus, caused his soldiers to devote a tenth of their booty to Zeus.[5] The tithe as a tax on land was well known in Greece and Rome, and the payment of a tithe to temples on special occasions was not uncommon. Pausanias gives many instances of this—*e.g.*, a tenth of war-booty being set aside to make an image or a vessel for a temple.

In Egypt there was apparently greater freedom. Temples were usually provided with lands for their upkeep, but the gods expected to receive a share of the produce of fields, vineyards, orchards, and fish-ponds. The kings in time of war dedicated a tenth of their booty to the temples, as well as of tribute levied on vassal states and of prisoners who were made slaves of the conqueror.[6]

Zoroastrian literature refers to the fourth rank of men—traders, artizans, market dealers, etc.—who should pay a tithe to the high priests and to the king.[7] Chinese sacred literature mentions a tenth of the produce of 'the fields' being annually levied; whether as a religious tribute or not is not clear.[8]

The *Confucian Analects*[9] tell how 'the Duke Gae enquired of Yew Jŏ, saying, "The year is one of scarcity, and the returns for expenditure are not sufficient. What is to be done?"' He desired to take two tenths, instead of the usual statutory single tithe, from the allotments cultivated in common, against which Yew Jŏ protested.[10]

2. Tithe in the Old Testament.—Among the Hebrews the relation of tithes to firstfruits[11] is complicated, and opinions differ as to whether they were distinct or not. Firstfruits would naturally vary in quantity. Tithe expresses more or less a fixed proportion. Perhaps the tithe represents firstfruits made systematic, or different names may have been favoured at different times and in different localities. The tithe is called 'an heave offering' in Nu 18^{24}, but the two are apparently separate in Dt $12^{6ff.}$. In the later legislation firstfruits and tithes appear to be distinguished.

The tithe, which is not mentioned in the Book of the Covenant, appears first in the Northern

1 Paus. VIII. xxxvii. 3.
2 See art. KOURETES AND KORYBANTES.
3 v. 66.
4 See artt. MOUNTAIN-MOTHER and KOURETES AND KORYBANTES.
5 E. 246.
6 Diod. Sic. xx. 14.
7 *Religion of the Semites*², p. 246.

1 See art. NUMBERS (Introductory).
2 C. H. W. Johns, *Babylonian and Assyrian Laws, Contracts, and Letters*, pp. xi, 205 f.; M. Jastrow, *The Religion of Babylonia and Assyria*, Boston, U.S.A., 1898, p. 668; G. Maspero, *The Dawn of Civilization*, tr. M. L. McClure, London, 1894, p. 678.
3 Aristotle, *Œcon.* 1345*b*, 1352*b*.
4 W. R. Smith, p. 247.
5 Herod. i. 89.
6 Maspero, p. 126.
7 *Rivāyats* (*SBE* xxxvii. [1892] 425; cf. p. 443).
8 *Shi King*, vi. 7 (*SBE* iii.² [1899] 370 f.).
9 Bk. xii. ch. ix. §§ 1-4.
10 J. Legge, *The Chinese Classics*, Hongkong, 1861-72, i. 119.
11 See art. FIRSTFRUITS (Hebrew).

Kingdom in the time of Jeroboam II. as the material given for a feast at the sanctuary (Am 5^{11}; cf. 4^{4}), though the feast was one for the rich at the expense of the poor. Here it appears as a fixed tribute. In Gn 28^{22} (E) Jacob promises a tenth of all to God—perhaps a reflexion of later custom, though not necessarily so—and Melchizedec receives a tenth of all (14^{20}). In 1 S $8^{15.\ 17}$ tithe is paid to the king, and perhaps he devoted this to the upkeep of some sanctuaries. The tithe in the Deuteronomic Code is not a forced tribute. The tithe of corn, wine, and oil, with the heave offering, free-will offering, and firstlings of herd and flock, are to be brought to the sanctuary and eaten there as a feast with servants and Levite (Dt $12^{6f.\ 17f.}$). Here the connexion with firstlings suggests that the tithe was the firstfruits of produce, or perhaps included these. This was a private feast at the sanctuary, and may have been a reform due to the fact that the ruling classes, as in Am 5^{11}, secured the best for themselves. It was not a direct due for the priesthood or for public religious services. If, however, the distance to the central sanctuary was too great for the offering to be taken there, it might be commuted for money, and this would furnish the material for the feast at the sanctuary as before (Dt $14^{22ff.}$). Every third year the tithe was to be laid aside to furnish a feast or feasts at home for the Levite, stranger, fatherless, and widow (14^{28} $26^{12f.}$).

Does the tithe here referred to form the equivalent of the firstfruits, the ritual of which, as perhaps forming part of the tithe, is detailed in Dt $26^{1f.}$? Probably they are ultimately the same, including an offering of part as firstfruits, and a feast for Levite and stranger, just as in 18^{4} firstfruits are to be given to the priests. If so, the words in 26^{11}, 'Thou shalt rejoice in all the good which the Lord thy God hath given unto thee, and unto thine house, thou, and the Levite, and the stranger,' would refer to the feast and be equivalent to the feast on tithe of $14^{22f.}$, while the earlier part of ch. 26 would refer to the offering of part as a firstfruits offering.[1]

Is the third year's tithe additional to the tithe given each year, or is it a special form of treating tithe in the third year? Here again opinions differ, but most regard it as a diverting of the usual tithe for the benefit of the local priesthood, who would be deprived of the tithes through the new custom of feasting at the central sanctuary. Others regard it as a second tithe, and this is supported by the LXX, which reads for 'the year of tithing' 'the second tithe,' τὸ δεύτερον ἐπιδέκατον. But two tithes in every third year would mean a large amount, and it is unlikely that such demands would be made, or, if made, carried out.

In the Priestly Code tithe assumes the form of a fixed due. A tithe of the produce of the land, of fruit, and of the herd and flocks (*i.e.* of their yearly increase) is 'holy unto the Lord.' If commuted for money, one-fifth part of the value is to be added (Lv $27^{30f.}$). This is probably the tithe of produce referred to in Nu $18^{23f.}$, which was to be given to the Levites, they in turn giving a tenth of it to the storehouse for the support of the priests (cf. Neh $10^{37f.}$), who received now also firstfruits of corn, oil, and wine (Nu 18^{12}). The tithe of cattle and sheep in Lv 27^{32}, which is to be 'holy unto the Lord,' may represent the firstlings used at the Deuteronomic tithe-feast, but claimed later by the priests (Nu $18^{15ff.}$) as apart from the Levites, but it is not referred to in Neh 10^{37}, where the tithe is described (cf. 12^{44} $13^{5.\ 12}$), and may be a later addition. It is, however, mentioned as paid to the priests in To 1^{6}, by Philo,[1] and in the *Book of Jubilees* (32^{15}). Rabbinic authorities regard it as furnishing, along with a second tithe of produce (Lv 27^{30})—additional, therefore, to the tithe of produce in Nu 18^{21}—a feast for the tither and guests at Jerusalem, as ordained in Dt $14^{22f.}$ The purpose of the Priestly Code was probably to abrogate the law of the tithe in Deuteronomy, but later harmonizers did not take this view and spoke of two tithes, and even three, the third-year tithe of Deuteronomy being regarded as an additional one.[2] The law of P is reflected in Hezekiah's legislation, which ordered that firstfruits and tithes of produce, sheep, and oxen should be brought for the priests and Levites (2 Ch 31^{4}); hence, if the tithe of animals is in addition to the original law of Lv $27^{30f.}$, it may have come into force after Nehemiah's time.

In Neh $10^{34ff.}$ firstfruits and firstlings and firstfruits of dough were for the priests, and tithes of produce for the Levites—the latter collected by the Levites under the supervision of a priest, and a tithe of the tithe being given to the priests (cf. 12^{44}). The tithe, however, was not always paid to the Levites, as Nehemiah discovered, and they had to cultivate their own land. At Nehemiah's remonstrance it was paid ($13^{10ff.}$). At a later time the priests themselves collected the tithe,[3] and the subsequent history of the Levites in connexion with it is obscure, while they no longer shared in the tithe, either from the time of Ezra[4] or from that of John Hyrcanus.

The Pharisees, as well as the regulations of the Talmud, considered minutely the things to be tithed (Lk 11^{42}), the former even paying tithes of garden herbs—mint, anise, cumin.

Under the Rabbinic system of three tithes referred to above, the first was collected yearly; the second was due in the first, second, fourth, and fifth years; the third in the third and sixth years. Two were thus taken every year, except in the seventh year, when the land lay fallow. The poor's tithe suggested tithing of earnings, all of which was given to them. Extravagant claims were made for the virtue of tithe; *e.g.*, through it Israelites escape the twelve months' punishment in hell which is the lot of the wicked.[5]

In Ezekiel's proposed legislation, which marks the transition to P, the first of all the firstfruits of everything is reserved for the support of the priests. There is besides a tax paid to the prince for the support of ritual and feasts out of wheat, oil, and flocks ($44^{30f.}$ $45^{13f.}$; cf. 20^{40}). No mention is made of tithes, nor are the payments to be made to the priests as in P.

3. Early and mediæval Church usage.—In the Christian Church the need of supporting the clergy, who were early withdrawn from secular business, was recognized, but the system of tithe was not generally resorted to for several centuries. Once it did become general, tithe was regarded, on the analogy of its use in the Jewish Church, as *de jure divino*, and supported by such passages as Mt 10^{10}, Lk 10^{7}, 1 Co $9^{7ff.}$—an argument which Selden was the first to show groundless, in his work on the subject. Until the 4th cent. little is heard of it, and some writers regard the matter from a totally different point of view from that which was later adopted. Irenæus, referring to tithes in the Jewish system, says characteristically that Christians, as 'those who have received liberty, set aside all their possessions for the Lord's purposes, bestowing joyfully and freely not the less valuable portions of their property.'[6] Origen

[1] Cf. S. R. Driver, *Deuteronomy* (*ICC*), Edinburgh, 1895, *in loc.* The passage in Dt 18^{4} assigning firstfruits of corn, wine, and oil, and of wool to the Levites is out of harmony with the other Deuteronomic legislation, if firstfruits and tithe were one and the same.

[1] Philo, *de Præmiis Sacerd.* § 2, *de Carit.*, § 10.
[2] Jos. *Ant.* IV. iv. 3 f., viii. 22; cf. IX. xiii. 3; To 1^{7}.
[3] Jos. *Ant.* XX. viii. 8, ix. 2, *Vita*, 12, 15.
[4] So the Talmud, *Yebhāmôth*, 86; Ḥûllîn, 131; *Kethūbhôth*, 26.
[5] *JE* xii. 151*b*.
[6] *Adv. Hær.* IV. xviii. 2.

regards tithes as something to be far exceeded in Christian giving,[1] and Epiphanius says that tithe is no more binding than circumcision.[2] Augustine regards the tithe as something due by Christians to God, though he and others are prompted also by the finer ideal of freedom in all Christian giving. It was inevitable, however, that, as the Church spread far and wide, circumstances should make it necessary to fall back upon rule, based upon legal provision, and the old standard of a tenth was set up, and the Christian priest was compared in this matter to the Jewish priest and Levite. Ambrose and many other Fathers accordingly maintain that tithes should be given, but their views were not generally accepted in the Eastern Church. Even in the West there is evidence that 'this species of ecclesiastical property was acquired not only by degrees, but with considerable opposition.'[3] The moral duty of paying tithe was now generally taught, but, even after it was made a matter of law, tithe was paid reluctantly and irregularly. In A.D. 585 the Council of Mâcon ordained its payment, while priests were to use it in helping the poor and in redeeming captives. He who refused to pay it was to be excommunicated. Other councils enjoined it, but it was not until the time of Charlemagne that it became matter of law. In one of his capitularies he ordained it to be paid to churches and clergy. Preachers had already exhorted strenuously towards its payment as tending to Christian perfection, and doubtless it was now more generally rendered. At the same time it has to be remembered that, apart from ecclesiastical law, under Roman law colonists had to pay a tenth to the State as rent from the *ager publicus*. This had already in large measure fallen into the hands of the Church. While the ecclesiastical tithe was usually paid to the bishop, who apportioned it, Charlemagne's capitulary regulates its division into three parts—for the bishop and clergy, for the poor, and for the support of church fabrics. In later times tithe was often appropriated to particular churches and to monastic foundations. Once the payment of tithe became a matter of legal due, excommunication or temporal penalties were decreed against those who refused to pay it. Meanwhile abuses had risen in connexion with the appropriation of tithe. Sometimes, instead of appropriating it to a church, monastery, or diocesan treasury, a proprietor would appropriate it to his own uses or even sell it. It had also become common for ecclesiastics to grant tithes to laymen as an award for service or in recognition of their protection. These were now regarded as evils, and it was set forth as a legal maxim that all tithes are of ecclesiastical origin. Where they had been appropriated by laymen, they were withheld from the Church only by robbery or by feudal grant (*decimæ infeudatæ*). No layman could possess tithes without risking his salvation. Hence the Third Lateran Council of 1179 forbade detention of tithes by laymen as well as transference of them to other laymen. The Council also declared that any one who violated this decree endangered his soul, and would be deprived of Christian sepulture. As a result of this, many tithes were restored to ecclesiastical use. Towards the 13th cent. tithe was also extended from the fruits of the earth, or predial tithes, to all kinds of profit and wages. It was divided by the canonists into (1) predial—derived from the fruits of the ground; (2) mixed—of things nourished of the soil, or those due partly to its productiveness, partly to human skill and labour; (3) personal—from the profits of trade and merchandise. But generally the second division is included in the first. Ecclesiastical law in the Middle Ages laid down precise rules regarding what was tithable and what was not, those who were exempt, the sale or transference of tithe to laymen (a custom which gradually came into use), the superiority of tithe to State taxes, and the like.

[1] *In Num.* hom. xi. [2] *Hær.* 50.
[3] H. Hallam, *View of the State of Europe during the Middle Ages*[11], London, 1855, ii. 145.

4. English law and practice.—In England legislation on the subject seems to date from the latter part of the 8th century. Pope Adrian in A.D. 785 enjoined payment of tithe on the Anglo-Saxon Church. This was confirmed in later ecclesiastical councils and synods, sometimes by royal orders. The idea that the civil grant of tithe dates from an alleged charter of Ethelwulf (A.D. 855) is now abandoned; and in any case it appears to grant a tenth of the land, not of produce.[1] In King Edgar's reign failure to pay tithe was made legally punishable (A.D. 950). Towards this time the growth of parish churches was attended by their endowment with part of the tithe paid by the landowner, who was usually the founder of the church, to the diocesan or monastic treasury. In course of time, and with the extension of the parochial system, it became a matter of legal presumption that the local tithe was the property of the rector. In many places rectories with their tithes were the property of monastic establishments, a vicar being appointed to perform the duties of the charge. The Reformation brought about great changes, and, where the rectorial tithes belonged to monasteries, at their dissolution the tithes became the property of the crown. They were now frequently granted to lay impropriators, thus being completely dissociated from their original purpose. The rectorial tithe was the 'greater' tithe, and such tithe or part of tithe as was paid to vicars was the 'smaller.' The greater tithes were generally predial; the smaller were mixed and personal. These distinctions were practically wiped out by the Tithe Commutation Act of 1836, although long before that date commutation of tithe paid in kind for a money payment had been general. By the Act of 1836, tithe, with a few exceptions, was now commuted for a fixed rent-charge, based on a seven years' average of the price of corn—wheat, barley, and oats—the amount being that which formed the legal tithe at the date of the Act. With the difference in values since 1836, the result has not been for the benefit of the recipient of tithe. Further legislation has modified details in procedure. The Tithe Act of 1918 amends the Acts, 1836 to 1891, and orders that the sum payable under these Acts in respect of tithe rent-charge on or before 1st Jan. 1926 shall be the sum payable, as ascertained by the septennial average prices under the Corn Returns Act, 1882, in January 1918. Tithe rent-charge is thus fixed up to 1st Jan. 1926, at £109, 3s. 11d. But the Board of Agriculture and Fisheries shall, after 25th Dec. 1925 and in succeeding years, compute in the same manner as for this septennial average the average price of corn for the preceding *fifteen* years. The sum payable as tithe rent-charge after 1st Jan. 1926 shall be ascertained on this fifteen years' computation.

5. Teinds in Scots law.—In Scotland tithes are known as teinds, and are almost entirely predial, including *decimæ mixtæ*, and only in exceptional cases personal. They were divided into parsonage and vicarage teinds, the former being leviable from grain (wheat, oats, and barley), the latter from natural grass or bog-hay, certain vegetables, butter, cheese, calves, lambs, herring, etc. Where an incumbent was appointed by the patron, he

[1] Hallam, ii. 263.

received the whole teind. In other or 'patrimonial' parishes the teind belonged to the bishop, or to a religious house, and the vicar who served the parish received stipend out of the teinds, sometimes a small part of the vicarage teinds. When teinds first began as such in Scotland is not known with certainty, but they are frequently mentioned in charters of the 12th cent., as well as in writs of that period to enforce their payment. Canons of provincial councils in the pre-Reformation period regulate this payment and appropriation. Many abuses arose regarding teinds, and the decrees of the Lateran Council were often ignored. Certain ecclesiastical lands (*i.e.* lands which were the property of monastic orders) were granted freedom from payment of tithe by papal privileges. When such lands were feued to laymen, this exemption also passed to them. In view of the coming Reformation, ecclesiastics frequently made grants to landowners, called titulars, conferring heritable rights to teinds by feu or by long lease. At the Reformation church lands passed into the hands of laymen by grant from the crown or otherwise, but payment of teind still continued, though the stipends of ministers were entirely at the will of proprietors and were of the scantiest amount. In 1537 the General Assembly petitioned the Privy Council to make permanent provision for the maintenance of ministers. The Council thereupon decreed that one-third of all ecclesiastical revenues should be divided between ministers and the crown. On the rent-rolls being made up, this sum was found to amount to over £6000. But, as a result of imperfect returns, remission, and refusal of payments, much less than half of this sum was available. In 1567 Parliament, under the scheme known as the 'assumption of thirds,' ordered that 'the haill thrids of the haill benefices of this realme' be paid now and for all time coming to ministers until 'the Kirk come to the full possession of their patrimonie, quhilk is the teindes.' This third was never paid in full, but the system remained in force until 1633. While Parliament thus recognized the right of the Kirk to teinds—a proprietary right fully enjoyed by the pre-Reformation clergy—that right was nullified, and teinds had been 'evicted from their former owners, diverted from their former use, and acquired and dealt with by the crown and nobles as their own property.'[1] An Act of 1617 appointed a commission authorized to augment stipends out of teinds, and a number of stipends were so treated. In 1627, as a result of Charles I.'s intention to receive surrenders of alienated church lands and teinds, and of the opposition which this roused, a commission was appointed to deal with the subject and to make provision for churches. Submissions were made to the king by those who had benefited by grants of teinds or were interested in them, and as a result he issued his 'decreets-arbitral,' which were confirmed by Act of Parliament in 1633, and commissioners were appointed to deal with the whole matter. Teinds were to be valued at 'the fifth part of the constant rent which each land payeth in stock and teind where the same are valued jointly,' or, if valued apart, the commissioners were to declare their value. Titulars of teinds were to sell them to heritors at nine years' purchase, but only so far as not already devoted locally to the minister of the parish. The valuation thus made fixed the amount of teind for all time coming, and the minister's stipend was to be paid out of the commuted teinds as a permanent endowment, with a further possible augmentation. Stipend thus forms a paramount claim upon teind. These decrees were confirmed by Act of the Scots

[1] J. M. Duncan, *The Parochial Ecclesiastical Law of Scotland*[3], p. 230.

Parliament in 1633, and still continue to regulate the right to teinds and the payment of stipends of ministers of the Established Church. The whole matter of teinds was vested in commissioners, but was transferred under the Union of 1707 and subsequent Acts to the Lords of Council and Session, acting as a Court of Commission of Teinds. This Court of Teinds deals with all matters regarding teinds, and in particular hears all claims for augmentation of stipend out of the unexhausted or free teinds, where such exist in the possession of the proprietors after payment of stipend. Such claims can be preferred only twenty years after a previous claim has been upheld.[1]

In valuing teinds under the Act of 1633, the valuation was made either in grain or in money. Where stipend is payable according to value of grain, it is valued according to fiars prices of the county, as determined by a local court who strike the value for the crop and year.

LITERATURE.—J. M. Duncan, *The Parochial Ecclesiastical Law of Scotland*[3], ed. C. N. Johnston, Edinburgh, 1903; *Green's Encyclopædia of the Law of Scotland*, new ed., ed. J. Chisholm, do. 1909–14; C. H. W. Johns, *Babylonian and Assyrian Laws, Contracts, and Letters*, do. 1904; H. Lansdell, *The Sacred Tenth*, 2 vols., London, 1906; A. S. Peake, art. 'Tithe' in *HDB*; G. F. Moore, art. 'Tithes' in *EBi*; R. J. Phillimore, *Ecclesiastical Law of the Church of England*[2], ed. W. G. F. Phillimore and C. F. Jemmett, 2 vols., London, 1895; J. Selden, *The History of Tithes*, do. 1618; W. R. Smith *The Religion of the Semites*[2], do. 1894, pp. 244 ff., 458 ff.; John Spencer, *De Legibus Hebræorum ritualibus, et earum rationibus*, Cambridge, 1685.

J. A. MACCULLOCH.

TITHES (Greek).—It is difficult to separate tithes (δεκάτη) and firstfruits (ἀπαρχή), since the tithe is only a special form of firstfruit. Many nations and tribes, if not nearly all, have had the custom of setting apart a portion of their goods for the gods; and when, as was sometimes the case, the king or chief was a sort of god, he took his share by compulsion. It seems to have been a wide-spread belief that some sacrifice was due to the local spirits whenever men broke new ground, built a settlement, or bridged a river; and it was certainly common in very early times to leave a portion of the new land to the possession of the old divinity. Perhaps for the same reason portions of the fruits of the earth were left, or otherwise given to the gods. It is not likely that this portion was always the same fraction of the whole; but the tenth was found to be a convenient fraction early and in many nations, among them the Jews. No doubt the decimal numeration had something to do with this choice.[2] In Greece a few traces are known of the early custom just mentioned—*e.g.*, the sacred groves of Artemis, with game that no men might kill except in a sacred hunt.[3]

The Pelasgians are said by Stephanus to have offered the tithe, which in later days they dedicated at Delphi;[4] and Herodotus[5] tells how the Hyperboreans used to send their annual tithe to Delos. The tithe is not mentioned in Homer; and the earliest records come with the inscriptions, although legendary tithing is spoken of earlier. When Agamemnon conquered Mycenæ, he is said to have dedicated a tenth to the gods.[6] An epic poem, the *Europia*, two lines of which are quoted by Clement of Alexandria,[7] mentions the dedication of tithes at Delphi. The Liparians, on conquering the Etruscans, dedicated a tithe of the spoils at Delphi.[8] After the Persian invasion the Greeks took an oath to tithe all those cities which

[1] *Green's Encyclopædia of the Law of Scotland*, ed. J. Chisholm, xii. 103 f.; Duncan, p. 313 f.

[2] δεκατεύω = 'I count.'

[3] Philostr. *Imag.* i. 28, *Heroicus*, 286 = 665; Xen. *Anab.* v. 3. 9; *IG Sept.*, Berlin, 1892–1908, iii. 1. 654 (2nd cent. after Christ); cf. the ἱερὸν κυνηγέσιον mentioned in Demosth. *c. Aristogeitona*, A, Introd.

[4] Stephanus, *s.v.* 'Αβορίγενες; Dionysius, i. 18. 49.

[5] iii. 33.

[6] Diod. xi. 65.

[7] *Strom.* i. 349 (Sylburg).

[8] Diod. v. 9.

had sided with the enemy.[1] Tithes of that great struggle are also mentioned as being upon the Athenian Acropolis.[2] A helmet exists that was part of a war-tithe, dedicated by Hiero probably from the spoils of Cumæ.[3] Tithes of spoils are recorded also from the battle of the Eurymedon.[4] Tithe is a certain restoration in the inscription that records how the Cnidians built their θησαυρός at Delphi.[5] Statues on the Sacred Way at Branchidæ bear the inscription of tithe.[6] Two colossal figures were purchased with the tithe of Platæa;[7] the Clitorians also dedicated another as a 'tithe from many cities.'[8] A bronze Apollo in the Pythium at Athens belongs to the 4th cent.;[9] and an archaic bronze figure of the 'Apollo' type bears the word 'tithe.'[10] Even the private person speaks with pride of the tithes that he offered to Athene, to the amount of more than half a talent.[11] Most of the dedications of arms and spoils are without the distinctive word; but the war-tithe is recorded from the following places: Apollonia,[12] Athens,[13] Bœotia,[14] Branchidæ,[15] Crete,[16] Mantinea,[17] Megara,[18] Sparta,[19] Thessaly;[20] at Delphi by Athenians,[21] Caphyes,[22] Cnidians,[23] Liparians,[24] Spartans,[25] and Tarentines;[26] at Olympia by Clitorians,[27] Eleans,[28] Messenians,[29] Spartans,[30] Thurians.[31]

Other tithes are mentioned in Anaphe,[32] Arcadia,[33] Argolis,[34] Athens,[35] Bœotia,[36] Calabria,[37] Calymna,[38] Crete,[39] Cyrene,[40] Delos,[41] Delphi, Didymi[42] and Epidaurus[43] in Argolis, Halicarnassus,[44] Ithaca,[45] Megara,[46] Naxos,[47] Pæstum,[48] Paros,[49] Rhodes,[50] Samos,[51] Thera,[52] Siphnos.[53] They are dedicated by men or women, or by groups of persons, to Apollo, Artemis, Athene, Demeter, Heracles, Zeus. The articles tithed are all kinds of produce, corn and the fruits of the earth, hunting, fish, gotten minerals, or the profits of trade and industry. Thus we find the Siphnians tithing the output of their mines,[54] the Corcyreans their fish,[55] the Samian merchants their profits.[56] Before the Persian invasion the farmer offers a tithe of his farm;[57] other early dedications of tithes are made by fullers[58] and shipwrights.[59]

1 Herod. vii. 132: δεκατεῦσαι. 2 Dem. *Timocr.* 741.
3 *CIG*, 16; *IGA*, 510. 4 Diod. xi. 62.
5 Paus. x. 11. 5; *BCH* xxii. 592.
6 C. T. Newton, *Hist. of Discoveries at Halicarnassus, Cnidus, and Branchidæ*, London, 1862–63, inscr. vol., no. 66.
7 Herod. ix. 81; Paus. v. 23. 1, x. 13. 5.
8 Paus. v. 23. 6. 9 *CIA* ii. 1154, 1204.
10 *American Journal of Archæology*, new ser., ii. [1898] 50.
11 Lys. *Polystr.* 686. 12 Paus. v. 22. 3.
13 *CIA* i. 334; Paus. i. 28. 2.
14 *IGA*, 191; *Amer. Journ. Arch.*, new ser., ii. 250.
15 Newton, p. 777.
16 *Monumenti Antichi*, iii. [1891] 402 ff.
17 *IGA*, 100; H. Collitz, *Sammlung der griech. Dialekt-inschriften*, Göttingen, 1884–1905, i. 1198.
18 *IG Sept.* i. 37. 19 Paus. iii. 18. 7. 20 *IG Sept.* (*Thera*).
21 Paus. ix. 13. 9. 22 *BCH* xviii. 177. 23 *Ib.* xxii. 592.
24 *Diod.* v. 9. 25 Xen. *Anab.* v. 3. 4; Plut. *Ages.* 9.
26 Paus. x. 13. 10. 27 *Ib.* v. 23. 7. 28 *Ib.* vi. 24. 4.
29 *Die Inschriften von Olympia*, Berlin, 1896, p. 259.
30 Paus. v. 10. 4. 31 *IGA*, 548.
32 *IG Insularum Maris Ægii*, Berlin, 1895–1908, iii. 257 f.
33 Collitz, i. 1198.
34 *Ib.* iii. 3407; *CIG*, 1172; *IG Peloponnesi et Insularum Vicinarum*, Berlin, 1902, i. 580, 977.
35 *CIA* i. 210. 36 *IG Sept.* i. 1739[16], *IGA*, 191, etc.
37 *IG Siciliæ et Italiæ*, Berlin, 1890, p. 643.
38 L. Ross, *Inscr. Græcæ ined.*, Naples, 1834–35, iii. 298.
39 *CIG*, 2556.
40 Collitz, iii. 4839, 4840; *CIG*, 5133; *Mittheilungen des deutschen archäol. Instituts*, xxiii. [1898] 22.
41 *BCH* xxvii. 65, xxx. 214.
42 Collitz, iii. 3407. 43 *Ib.* iii. 3335. 44 *CIG*, 2660.
45 *IG Sept.* iii. 1. 654. 46 Paus. i. 42. 5. 47 *IGA*, 408.
48 *Ib.* 542.
49 *Mittheil. des deutsch. arch. Inst.* xvii. [1902] 196.
50 *IG Insularum Maris Ægii*, i. 817*a* 3.
51 *Herod.* iv. 152. 52 *Ib.* iii. 57.
53 *IG Insularum Maris Ægii*, iii. 431.
54 Herod. iii. 57; Paus. x. 11. 2.
55 Paus. x. 9. 3, v. 29. 9. 56 Herod. iv. 152.
57 *CIA* iv. Suppl. 1. 373[121], p. 182.
58 *Ib.* iv. 373 f., p. 42. 59 *Ib.* iv. 1. 373[234], p. 198.

We also read of a butcher,[1] a courtesan,[2] and others who speak generally of a tithe of their work.[3] Sometimes friends or relatives offer the tithe for another.[4] Some of the female statues of the Acropolis were tithes.[5] See also art. FIRST-FRUITS (Greek).

LITERATURE. — Daremberg-Saglio, *s.v.* 'Dekate'; Pauly-Wissowa, *s.vv.* ἀπαρχαί, δεκάτη; H. Lansdell, *The Sacred Tenth*, 2 vols., London, 1906; W. H. D. Rouse, *Greek Votive Offerings*, Cambridge, 1902, ch. ii. and index; J. Selden, *The Hist. of Tithes*, London, 1618; W. R. Smith, *The Religion of the Semites*², do. 1894, pp. 244 ff., 458 ff.

W. H. D. ROUSE.

TLINGIT.—The Tlingit, who occupied the coast of Alaska from Portland Canal to Copper River, were organized into two main phratries and one subsidiary phratral group, and the phratries were subdivided into clans. The character of their country and their manners and customs were almost the same as those of the Haida (*q.v.*), though the northern towns had not adopted the elaborately carved poles so characteristic of the latter, and their potlatches were conducted in a somewhat different manner.

1. Cosmological beliefs.—The outlines of Tlingit belief were like those of the Haida and indeed of the other tribes of the North Pacific coast, but in details there were considerable divergences. Like the Haida, they believed that the earth was flat and the sky a solid vault hung above it like an inverted cup and tenanted by various supernatural beings. The stars were supposed to be towns and their light the reflexion of the sea. The sun and moon were also occupied by special beings, and more regard was paid to the sun than by the Haida. Shooting stars were supposed to be live coals thrown down by departed spirits, and the northern lights were those spirits at play. Under the earth was an old woman called Old-woman-under-the-earth, who supported a great post, on which the solid land rested. According to one story, she was the sister of four brothers, who were favourite heroes of Tlingit mythology, and who in early days travelled all over the world killing harmful animals, putting things in order, and establishing customs for future generations. One of these brothers, Kashkatlk, was a powerful shaman who succeeded where his brothers had failed, and was frequently called upon to restore them to life, while another, Hlkayak, was always getting them into trouble by his impetuous and trifling character. He was suspected of an amour with his own sister, and, when his brothers discovered that their suspicions were well founded, they drove him away, and he became the wielder of the thunder. His sister, overcome with shame, went down into the earth at a place where the extinct crater of Mt. Edgecombe now is, near Sitka, and became Old-woman-under-the-earth. The remaining brothers and their mother were turned into rocks while trying to cross the Stikine River, and they may be seen there at the present day. According to the version of this story told at Wrangell, the sister was also turned into rock at that place and Old-woman-under-the-earth was an entirely different person. Old-woman-under-the-earth liked to receive food and prayers from human beings, and she was especially fond of girls because they made the fires on earth which warmed her. When she did not get enough attention from mankind, she became angry and moved her pole, causing an earthquake. Others said that the earthquake was caused by her anger at some persons who were teasing her, and Veni-

1 *IGA* 543. 2 Herod. ii. 135; cf. *BCH* xv. 113.
3 *KAT* 172, *BCH* vi. 192[53].
4 *CIA* i. 349; Collitz, iii. 3448; *IG Insularum Maris Ægii*, ii. 258.
5 *E.g.*, the pillar base 150 in Acrop. Museum; cf. *CIA* iv. 1. 373[202. 216].

aminoff[1] was told that it was because Raven was angry with mankind and was trying to drive her away in order that the earth might fall into the sea. Though Hlkayak was said to cause thunder, it was more often ascribed, as in the case of the Haida, to a huge bird; the flapping of its wings produced the thunder and the opening of its eyes the lightning; it lived principally on whales, which it carried up into the mountains, and their bones were often found there. Still another story relates that several brothers became wizards in order to rescue their sister from a giant slug which had dragged her up on the side of a steep cliff, and, having learned to fly, afterwards became thunder beings. When a peal of thunder was heard, people shook themselves and jumped into the air, crying, 'Take all my sickness from me.'

2. Supernatural beings.—Except in the general way common to all American tribes, we do not hear much of sky-beings. The 'above-people' of the Haida were said to have been first heard of through the Tlingit, however, and the conception of Tāxēt's house also originated with them, although they did not recognize any special being of that name.

The four brothers have been referred to as the originators of culture and customs, but they by no means supplant Raven, whose personality, functions, and attributes were the same here as on the Queen Charlotte Islands.[2] It is ethnographically important to note that he began his career on the Nass River, and, according to some accounts, returned to its head as his final home.

In connexion with Raven we have the nearest approach to a supreme deity that the Tlingit seem to have possessed, for the heaven-god of the Haida appears to be entirely wanting among them. This personage was called Raven-at-the-head-of-Nass (Nasshakiyehl), and it was from him that Raven obtained the sun, moon, stars, and eulachon to distribute all over the world. Some of the more thoughtful Indians at the present day elevate this being to a position far above that which he occupied aboriginally, but there is no doubt that he always had a real existence. He was called in some stories 'the king of birds,' and Raven was therefore subordinate to him. Up to the present time, however, no account of him has been obtained in the northern Tlingit towns—a fact which may indicate that Tsimshian and Haida influence has been instrumental in creating him.

Although held in considerable regard, killer-whales did not receive a tithe as much attention as among the Haida, nor do they appear to have been associated with points and reefs. Land-otters, however, and the land-otter men (*kushtaka*)—the Tlingit equivalent of the *gagihit*—played a great part in Tlingit mythology and in the rites of shamans, and were viewed with even greater terror. We also find a counterpart of the Haida Property-woman called Tlenahidak, and a counterpart of Master-carpenter. The increased importance of hunting is shown by the conception of Mountain-dweller, who lived far back among the mountains and had a house always abundantly stocked with game. Mountains generally were called upon for a fair wind. Other patron-deities were undoubtedly believed in, but the tendency in this direction does not appear to have been as strong as among the Haida. Another belief peculiar to the Tlingit was in a race of seal-men. When one of these was seen, they poured a bucket of fresh water into the ocean. The grizzly bears and mountain-sheep, which are wanting in the Queen Charlotte Islands, were naturally held in greater regard than there, and, when bears were killed, their skins were hung up and adorned with eagle-down and red paint, being addressed meanwhile with soothing words. If this were not done, it was feared that the bear's relatives would be angry and would kill the hunter. Favourite among Tlingit myths was that of a hunter named Kats, who was captured by a female grizzly bear that killed her bear-husband in order to marry him. His children by her were a famous race of bears known as 'Kats's children.' They destroyed many people and committed great depredations, but were at last killed, and in later times figures of them served as heraldic crests in many of the most prominent families. There were also special tabus regarding mountain-sheep and the handling of their skins.

People obtained good luck by grasping at the sun's disk and pretending to put it upon anything that they desired to be lucky. Like the Haida, the Tlingit gave food to any thing or any being that they wished to help them, and called to it, mentioning their wants. Everything was believed to have a spirit connected with it—there was one in every trail that a person followed and in everything that he did.

3. The dead.—The regions of the dead are said to have been three—one below and two above the plane of earth. The first was the country of the killer-whales, and was for those who had been drowned, and the third, or highest, was for those who had died by violence, corresponding to the Tāxēt's house of the Haida. The approach to this place was through a hole reached by a single log, and this was guarded by a person who admitted only such as had perished in the prescribed manner. The trail thither was infested by grizzly bears and other animals. All other persons passed after death to the lower sky-country Sagi-kawu-ani ('souls' home'), which corresponded closely to the Giettlgai of the Haida. The person who was to go thither found himself on a trail, and, following it, came to a fork. One of the two paths had been much trodden upon, while the other was very faint. The former came out on the bank of a river, beyond which were the houses of the departed, but, however loudly the new-comer shouted to the other souls to carry him across, they paid no attention until by chance he yawned, when they exclaimed that a soul had arrived, ferried him over, and gave him food. This river was said to be formed by the tears which women shed over the departed, and therefore it was not good to weep much until one's friend had crossed the river. A story recorded by Krause[1] adds the important fact that only the souls of those who had friends among the spirits got to the other side, the remainder being forced to wander about miserably, and also that the river itself was as green and bitter as gall. The souls were dependent for their food on what their friends put into the fire for them, and all had to do their own work except those for whom slaves had been killed. Cremation, which was well-nigh universal among the Tlingit, was accounted for by the belief that only those whose bodies were burned could go near the fire in the spirit-world, the others being forced to shiver near the doors of the houses. According to Veniaminoff,[2] the path of those whose friends wept much was muddy and watery, but for those whose friends wept less it was smooth and even. A world for wicked persons was sometimes spoken of, called Yehlkiwakawo ('Raven's home'), and would seem to be in the place where Raven lived, but it is possible that the belief was due to missionary influence.

4. Rebirth.—As among the Haida, belief in rebirth was general—so much so that it is said

[1] *Ap.* A. Krause, *Die Tlinkit-Indianer*, p. 268 f.
[2] See *ERE* vi. 473.

[1] P. 280.
[2] *Ap.* Krause, p. 282.

that a poor person would wish to die in hope of being reborn in a higher position in life. If a pregnant woman dreamed of some dead relative, it was believed that her child would contain his soul, and in consequence the child was given the relative's name. A belief in four rebirths followed by annihilation has also been recorded, but this was perhaps a distorted rendering of the Haida idea of reincarnation.[1]

5. Shamanism.—Shamanism reached its highest development among the Tlingit, and nowhere on the coast were shamans of such exalted social rank, so well thought of, or so powerful. When performing, the Tlingit shaman was dressed much like his Haida counterpart, but he also assumed a wooden mask, and, besides being possessed by one principal spirit, he was, if not possessed, at least accompanied, by several subordinate ones. The latter were represented on the masks by small figures round the eyes, jaws, ears, etc., of the principal figure, and were supposed to strengthen the corresponding features of the shaman. Still other spirits had charge of his rattle. With each of the masks went a certain number of songs. One of the most popular spirits was the wood-worm, which enabled the shaman's mind to pierce through anything just as the wood-worm cuts through wood. In addition to his other neck ornaments, the shaman sometimes had a bird's head tied in front. He had an assistant, who took charge of his paraphernalia, beat time for him, and told the other people what to do. This assistant was generally the man who was to succeed to his office. According to Veniaminoff,[2] the successor was a son or sister's son, but for a son to succeed to his father's position seems to have been the exception. The right to certain spirits might be inherited, and in saying that this seldom happened Krause has gone decidedly too far.[3]

Not infrequently the spirit came to a novitiate shaman on the death of his predecessor, but often he was compelled to stay as long as two weeks in the mountains and woods before it showed itself. When it finally made its appearance, it usually sent him the land-otter, the tongue of which he wrenched out, catching the blood on a little bundle of sticks. Krause[4] says that the shaman killed this land-otter by exclaiming 'Oh!' four times very loudly, each time in a different tone of voice. He also notes that none of the sticks in his bundle were retained except those on which the blood had fallen. As the shaman drew out the tongue, he exclaimed, 'May I be skilful in my new calling,' 'May I be able to charm and dance well,' etc. The tongue was afterwards concealed in the bundle, which was then kept in an out-of-the-way place, for, if an uninitiated person were to come upon it, he would lose his reason. The skin he removed carefully and preserved as a visible mark of his calling, but he buried the flesh in the earth. The part played by land-otters in shamanism and in mythology generally inspired the Tlingit with such respect and dread that, before the coming of the Russians, they would not shoot one of them.

If a person could not otherwise succeed in becoming a shaman, he might go at night to the grave of some dead shaman and take from the body a tooth or the end of one of the little fingers, and place it in his mouth. A shaman who did not observe certain regulations carefully might be killed by his own spirits, and, on the other hand, he could throw them into one who did not believe in him and destroy him.

The great exhibitions or performances of the shamans were undertaken only during the new or full moon. Shamans then called upon their spirits to bring good fortune and health to their town and people. From the morning of the day before that appointed until the following morning none of the relatives of the shaman who were to assist him might eat or drink. They cleansed themselves internally by drinking water and introducing a feather into the throat to bring on vomiting. At sunset all entered the appointed house, which had been thoroughly cleansed and provided with new floor-planks. Then the shaman came out from behind a screen and began to run round the fire, his friends singing all the time, until the spirit came to him.

Veniaminoff[1] divides the spirits that spoke through shamans into spirits from above, land-spirits, and water-spirits. The first were the souls from the above-country already referred to. The land-spirits appeared in the form of land-animals, but were said to be the spirits of those who had died a natural death and who had their dwellings in the distant north. The water-spirits appeared in the forms of sea-animals, and were in fact the spirits of those animals. According to Krause,[2] every Tlingit, whether shaman or not, had his own protecting spirit, but this belief does not seem to have assumed the importance which it bears among the inland Indians.

6. Witchcraft.—As shamanism had reached its highest development with the Tlingit, so also had witchcraft, which might almost be described as a diseased shamanism. A wizard accomplished his object by obtaining some portion of the person or clothing of the victim and laying it by an unburned body, among the ashes of a burned body, or on the body of a dog. When a person was suspected of being a wizard, his hands were bound behind his back and he was imprisoned in an empty hut without food and with nothing to drink but sea-water. There he was kept until he confessed, lost his reason, or died, unless his friends were powerful enough to liberate him. The person who confessed to having bewitched any one was forced to wade out into the sea with the medicine or compound which had caused the illness and to scatter it upon the water, accompanying his actions with certain formulæ. Instead of being imprisoned, a suspected wizard was sometimes bound hand and foot and exposed on the beach for the rising tide to cover him. Sometimes he was dealt with in a still more summary manner. Among other accomplishments, wizards and witches were universally believed to possess the power of flight.

7. Charms, etc.—The principal families and many in humbler circumstances kept charms to bring wealth and good fortune. They believed in all sorts of signs, which they extracted from, or rather read into, natural phenomena, and they thought that natural phenomena would be affected by the breaking of this or that tabu. After a person had died, his body was carried through a temporary hole in the side of the house, and a dog, dead or alive, was thrown out after it, either that the spirits might follow it out of the house or that the dead man might be protected in his journey to the spirit world.

LITERATURE.—The monumental work of A. Krause, *Die Tlinkit-Indianer*, Jena, 1885, is the authority on the subject. Most of the important mythological material contained in I. Veniaminoff and other early writers has been gathered into it. See also J. R. Swanton, 'Social Condition, Beliefs, and Linguistic Relationship of the Tlingit Indians,' in *26 RBEW* [1908], p. 391 ff., and 'Tlingit Myths and Texts,' *Bull. 39 BE* [1909]; F. Boas, report v. 'On the North-Western Tribes of Canada,' in *Report of the British Association for the Advancement of Science*, 1889, p. 801 ff.

JOHN R. SWANTON.

TOAD.—See ANIMALS.

[1] See art. HAIDA, § 17. [2] *Ap.* Krause, p. 284. [3] P. 286. [4] P. 285.

[1] *Ap.* Krause, p. 291. [2] P. 292.

TODAS.—The Todas are a small community, about 700 in number, living on the undulating plateau, about 7000 ft. above sea-level, of the Nilgiri hills in Southern India. They are a purely pastoral people who eschew all other occupations. They are provided with the products of agriculture by the Badagas, a Canarese tribe who also live on the plateau, while the Kotas, allied to the jungle peoples of Southern India, furnish their metal-work and pottery. Except for these commercial relations, the Todas form a wholly separate community and have few other relations with the Badagas or Kotas. With the Kurumbas, a jungle tribe living on the slopes of the Nilgiris, the Todas have even less frequent relations, and these arise chiefly out of the Toda belief that the Kurumbas are sorcerers.

1. Social organization.—The people are divided into two sections called the Tartharol and the Teivaliol, each of which is strictly endogamous, though irregular unions are allowed between men and women of the two. Each section is divided into a number of exogamous clans. Each clan owns a number of villages, or *mad* (commonly called *mand*), and takes its name from the *etudmad*, or chief of these villages. The villages are small settlements, sometimes consisting of only one or two houses with a dairy and buffalo-pen. They are scattered over the hills, but most of the villages of a clan are near one another. Each clan is divided into two divisions called *kudr*, 'horn,' which should properly be, and usually are, only two in number. These divisions are of importance only in ceremonial. Another division of the clan is the *polm*, by which the sharing of communal expenses, such as those incurred in the repair or rebuilding of the chief dairies of the clan, is regulated. The Todas recognize the existence of the family, or *kudupel*, as a social unit, and this often corresponds with the *polm*. One clan, the Melgarsol, has an exceptional position in that, though belonging to the Tartharol, it shares many duties and privileges with the Teivaliol.

Descent is always patrilineal. A man belongs to the clan of his father. The effect of fatherhood is not determined by marriage, however, but by a ceremony of giving a bow and arrow which takes place at the seventh month of pregnancy. This ceremony is not performed at every pregnancy, but a person is regarded as the child of the man who was the last to perform this ceremony with his or her mother.

The Todas practise polyandry, nearly always of the fraternal type.[1] Formerly this practice was possible in a pure form owing to the existence of female infanticide. Though girls are probably sometimes killed at birth, the practice is now less frequent. There is still a considerable excess of men, but polyandry is often combined with polygyny, producing a state which may be regarded as a variety of group marriage.[2] In addition to orthodox marriage there is a regular system of unions in which a woman has connubial relations with one or more men called *mokhthodvaiol*. This kind of union may take place between a Tarthar man and a Teivali woman or *vice versa*, thus differing from marriage proper, which is confined to members of one section. The orthodox marriage is between cross-cousins, and this institution is reflected in the nomenclature of relationship which in several respects resembles that of the Tamils. The cross-cousin is classified with the spouse, the mother's brother with the father-in-law, and the father's sister with the mother-in-law. Betrothal in infancy is customary, and this practice is probably responsible for a custom of transferring wives from one man to another which has now become very frequent. The custom seems to have been originally one by means of which a widower could obtain a wife in a community where, through the practice of infant betrothal, every woman is already bespoken, but it has now become a process set in action whenever one man desires the wife of another.

The people are governed by a council of five called the *naim*, one of the members of which should properly be a Badaga. This council is chiefly engaged in settling disputes arising out of the transference of wives. It is also the business of the *naim* to arrange when ceremonies shall be performed, especially those of the more important dairies. There is a headman called *monegar*, but he is chiefly concerned with the payment of the assessment to the Government, and the institution is almost certainly recent. On the other hand, the headship of the clan is certainly an old institution. Its functions are not especially important, and this also holds good of the headship of the *kudr* and *polm*.

2. Religion.—The Todas believe in certain superior beings who may be regarded as gods, and speak of them as 1600 or 1800 in number, but these are the customary Toda expressions for an indefinitely large number. The two most important are Ön and Teikirzi. Ön is a male deity who presides over Amnodr, the world of the dead. He is believed to have created the Todas and their buffaloes and to have been himself a dairyman. More important in the minds of the people is Teikirzi, a female deity, who is believed to have lived on the Nilgiris and ruled the people. Most of the Toda social and ceremonial laws are ascribed to her ordinance. These two deities are not especially connected with hills, but nearly all the others seem to be hill-deities, each being associated with a special hill-top. Two are river-gods, associated with the two chief rivers of the district.

The ritual of the Toda religion is concerned almost exclusively with the buffaloes and the treatment of their milk. The dairies are the temples; the dairymen are the priests; and various incidents in the lives of the buffaloes, such as their movements from one grazing ground to another, the first milking, and the giving of salt, have become the occasion of ceremonial which has a religious character. This ritual stands in a definite relation to the gods, for these beings are mentioned in the formulas of the dairy ritual, the general character of which indicates that they must be regarded as prayers. The names used for the deities in these prayers differ from those used in ordinary speech, and form part of a series of expressions called *kwarzam*, in which special names of deities, buffaloes, dairy utensils, and other objects are uttered, preceded by the word *idith*, said to mean 'for the sake of.' The dairies and the buffalo-herds form a somewhat complicated organization, especially among the Tartharol. Every village has a number of buffaloes devoid of any element of sanctity, and their milk is churned in a dairy, also devoid of sanctity, with no special ritual. Most of the buffaloes, however, belong to herds with special names with varying degrees of sanctity, and in correspondence with these there are great differences in the elaborateness of the ritual with which the milk is treated and in the ceremonial regulations of the lives of the dairy-priests. This complicated system is confined to the buffaloes of the Tartharol, the Teivaliol having only one variety of sacred buffalo, but the most sacred kinds of dairy of the Tartharol must be tended either by Teivali men or by men of the Melgars clan, which occupies an intermediate position between the two main sections.

[1] *ERE* viii. 427. [2] *Ib.*

The lowest grade of Tarthar dairy is called *tarvali*. Its ritual is comparatively simple and is confined to the evening milking and churning. When the dairyman enters the dairy, he bows down and touches the threshold with his forehead, touches certain dairy vessels ceremonially, lights the lamp, and utters a prayer before beginning to churn. After churning he holds the churning-stick to his forehead, uttering the sacred syllable 'Oñ.' He also repeats the prayer of the dairy after milking.

The dairy next in order of sanctity differs in the possession of a bell (*mani*). The dairyman is not allowed to put his food on the ground; both curd and milk are put on the bell with the utterance of the sacred syllable; and the chief milk-vessel is beaten three times with the bark of the sacred *tudr* tree (*Meliosma pungens* and *Wightii*), the same syllable being uttered. The dairymen of this grade are allowed to sleep in the ordinary hut only on certain days of the week. Ordinary people are not allowed to drink the milk of buffaloes tended at this dairy.

Certain villages have dairies with special features of ritual, but the next kind of dairy in order of sanctity which occurs in every Tarthar clan, except the Melgarsol, is the *wursuli*, the dairyman of which must be taken either from the Teivaliol or from the Melgars clan. The restrictions on his conduct are more numerous and the ritual of milking and churning is more complex, special features being that he wears his cloak in a particular way, and that the proceedings of both morning and evening have an equally ceremonial character. In many dairies of this rank there are two rooms, the inner of which contains the more sacred dairy vessels. The dairyman, or *wursol*, is allowed to sleep in the village and have intercourse with women only on two nights of the week.

All these dairies are situated at the villages where the people live, though they may be at some distance from the dwelling-houses. The highest kind of dairy, called the *ti*, on the other hand, is situated far from the villages. Each herd has several dairies, all of which are remote from the dwelling-places of the people. The dairyman, called *palol*, must be of the Teivaliol, and his attendant, the *kaltmokh*, must come either from the Teivaliol or from the Melgars clan. The *palol* is not allowed to visit a village or have intercourse with any persons other than dairymen of his own rank, his *kaltmokh*, and men of the Melgars clan who are privileged to visit the *ti* dairy and drink buttermilk. Intercourse with women is entirely forbidden except on one occasion after the *palol* has held office for eighteen years. The ritual of the *ti* is far more complex than that of any village dairy. In this dairy the vessels are more numerous and have special names different from those of the less sacred forms of dairy. The more sacred vessels, viz. those which come directly into contact with the milk of the buffaloes, are always kept in an inner room, together with the bell or bells, and are not allowed to come into contact with the vessels which, being used to contain the products of the churning, are regarded as less sacred. The details of milking and churning are more elaborate and more strictly regulated than in the village dairies, and the prayers are longer and more frequently repeated.

The proceedings when the buffaloes move from one grazing ground to another have a definitely ceremonial character. This is especially elaborate in the case of the *ti* dairies. The more sacred vessels are carried by the *palol*, while the others are taken by the *kaltmokh*, assisted by a man of Melgars, who leads the way. There are elaborate ceremonies of purification of the dairy which is about to be occupied, and a special prayer for the welfare of the buffaloes is offered before going to rest. On the following day there is a ceremony in which the *kaltmokh* takes a leading part. His head and body are rubbed with a mixture of milk and clarified butter, and he is given a ball of a special kind of food larger than he can possibly eat, the remainder of which he has to leave on the spot where the ceremony has taken place. An invocation is uttered that evils of many kinds may afflict the boy, and this is followed by another invocation that these evils may be averted. At some dairies milk and butter are rubbed on certain stones.

Before entering upon office every dairyman undergoes certain ceremonies which may be regarded as a kind of ordination. These increase in complexity with the increasing sanctity of the dairy, but the chief feature common to all is a process of purification by drinking and washing with the water of a stream which is used only for ceremonial purposes. The ceremony is named either after this process or after the act of lighting a lamp, this being the first duty of the newly ordained dairyman. An important part of the ceremony is the use of certain leaves to rub the body and as drinking vessels. The ordinary dairyman uses the leaves of a bramble for this purpose, while the *wursol* and *palol* use the leaves and bark of the sacred *tudr* tree. Another feature is the use of the special kind of cloth which is worn by the *palol*. A fragment only is used by the lower grades, while the *wursol* and *palol* assume a complete garment of this material. The village dairyman of the lower grades touches the various vessels of the dairy, beginning with the less sacred, as the final stage of his ordination, while the *wursol* and the dairymen of certain other villages touch a buried vessel, called *mu*, specially disinterred for the occasion. The ordination of the *palol* is preceded by a qualifying ceremony in which after certain purifying rites the candidate in a state of nudity receives food from an old woman. Though the woman must be past the age of child-bearing, the original object of the rite is probably to test whether the candidates are likely to submit successfully to the abstinence which is incumbent upon the holder of the office of *palol*. In the ordination ceremony proper of the *ti* dairy the rites of purification last for a whole week, and in the later stages of the ceremonial the candidate drinks water from the sacred *tudr* leaves three, seven, and nine times seven times. The *palol* touches a bar of the opening into the pen in which the sacred buffaloes are enclosed at night as the final act with which he enters into office.

An important ceremony of another kind is named after the buttermilk, called *pep*, which is put into the milking-vessel before milking is commenced. A vessel called *mu* is kept buried in the buffalo-pen of the chief village of each clan, and, if this has been tampered with, or if a dairy has been defiled or the bell of the dairy has been taken to a funeral, a new vessel has to be procured and consecrated, the ceremony, however, being called the consecration of the buttermilk. The chief feature of the ceremony is the sanctification of the new vessel with the earth of a buffalo-pen taken from the footprints of one of the buffaloes.

Another ceremony is performed about the fifteenth day after the birth of a calf to one of the sacred buffaloes, and still another when salt is given to the buffaloes. There seems to be little doubt that the great ritual development of the business of the dairy is connected with a belief in the sanctity of the milk of the sacred buffaloes. At the present time the buffaloes themselves are not regarded with any special veneration, and it would seem as if this had been transferred to certain cattle-bells called *mani*, so old that their tongues have been lost, and to the vessels which come directly into contact with the milk of the buffaloes, while another specially sacred object is the vessel, called *mu*, which is buried in the buffalo-pen of the chief village of each clan (see above).

3. Sacrifice and offerings.—An important ceremony is one in which a male buffalo-calf is killed and its flesh eaten, this being the only occasion on which a Toda should eat the flesh of a buffalo. At the *ti* dairy the ceremony, which may be regarded as sacrificial, takes place three times a year; at the other dairies it should probably be annual, but now takes place more frequently. After a prayer in which the calf is asked to appear to certain deities, and after it has been stroked with leaves of *tudr*, the animal is killed by being struck with a log of the *tudr* tree, the bark and leaves of which are prominent in the dairy ritual. The right fore-limb is of especial importance, being placed near the middle of the fire at which the flesh is roasted and eaten together with the pelvis, feet, and head by the dairyman.

There is an annual ceremony in which a fire is lighted by the *palol* at the foot of certain hills, the summits of which are believed to be occupied by gods. Clauses are added to the ordinary prayer asking that fruit may ripen and honey abound.

The ceremonies which have been described are performed regularly, and their occasions arise chiefly out of the necessary events of the pastoral life, the last described standing alone in its reference to vegetation and means of subsistence other than those provided by the buffaloes. The ceremonies now to be described are more occasional and depend on the commission of some act which has offended the gods and thus brought illness or some other misfortune upon the offender. In these cases the central feature of the ceremony is an offering to the gods of either a buffalo or a buffalo-calf, a piece of the cloth worn by the more sacred dairymen, or a ring.

The simplest kind of offering, often made when some mistake has occurred inadvertently in a ceremony, is to undertake not to kill or part with a buffalo, but allow it to die a natural death. In this case there is little ceremony, the donor simply stating that he is giving the buffalo to the gods while he salutes an elder. A more ceremonial offering of a buffalo-calf is made if a misfortune is ascribed to some serious offence against the dairy, such as stealing milk or its products, quarrelling in the dairy, or going to it in an impure state. In this case the calf is given by the offender to the people of the other *kudr* of his clan. All members of the *kudr* of the offender have to leave the village for a month, at the end of which, after purification with fasting, the calf is driven across certain ceremonial stones to be received by members of the other *kudr*. For minor offences a piece of cloth or a ring is offered with similar rites, the offering passing in every case from the *kudr* of the offender to the people of the other *kudr* of the clan. In all cases prayers are offered, which include in some cases supplications for the health of the people and their buffaloes.

4. Divination.—The offerings just described are made as the result of the finding of diviners called *teuol*, or god-men. The decisions are given when the *teuol* are in a state of frenzy and in a language which is said to be Malayalam. It is believed that they are the utterances of some of the gods. The diviners are often consulted at funerals, usually to discover the cause of death or illness either of men or of buffaloes, or the cause of any harm which has happened to a dairy or its contents. In the case of illness they usually find either that the patient has committed some offence against the dairy or that he is the victim of the sorcery of the Kurumbas.

5. Birth and childhood ceremonies.—Two ceremonies are performed during pregnancy; in the first the wrists of the woman are burnt while she is undergoing seclusion, while the second ceremony is that already mentioned in which the presentation of a bow and arrow determines the fatherhood of the child. Various ceremonies occur at the end of a period of seclusion which follows childbirth. Until a child is three months old no one but the mother is allowed to see its face, and at that age a ceremony is performed in which the face is uncovered and the child is allowed to look at the sun. Ceremonies are also performed when the name is given, when the ears are pierced, and when a lock of hair is cut, the last ceremony only taking place on the day after the second funeral (see below) of a Tarthar man.

6. Death.—The funeral ceremonies are very elaborate and take place on two different occasions often separated by many months. At the first ceremony the body is cremated on a pyre, the orthodox position being face downwards. Several rites are performed before cremation, among them being one in which a cloth is given by a near relative of the deceased to men who have married into the family, the cloth being then placed on the corpse by the wives of these men. In the case of a man the cremation is preceded by a ceremony in which earth is thrown three times into a buffalo-pen by the Teivali dairyman at a Tarthar funeral and by the relatives if the dead man is one of the Teivaliol. In most Tarthar clans the body is placed before cremation in a special three-roomed dairy. Buffaloes are killed, varying in number in different clans. In each case the right hand of the dead man is made to clasp one of the horns, and lamentations are uttered in which each person addresses the dead buffalo by the same term of relationship as he would use to the deceased. Immediately before the body is burned, it is swung three times over the fire upon a representation of a bier. When the body is consumed, a piece of the skull is recovered from the ashes and kept, wrapped with some of the hair in a cloak, for the second funeral ceremony. In the interval these relics are kept in a special village, where they are saluted by any Todas who visit the place. Formerly the body was smoke-dried, after it had been eviscerated, if the cremation ceremony was delayed.

At the second funeral ceremony the earth-throwing rite is repeated. At a Tarthar funeral a ceremony is performed in which the relics are sprinkled with the blood of a buffalo mixed with the bark of the *tudr* tree. This is done by a Teivali man, wearing the cloak in which the remains have been wrapped, after which he touches the remains with a bow and arrow. Buffaloes are killed, as at the first ceremony, and the men dance with a tall pole obtained from Malabar. During the following night the final ceremony takes place, in which the relics together with a number of other objects are burned within a stone-circle. The ashes are interred at an opening in the circle, and the grave is covered with a stone. A bell is then rung and a new pot broken on the stone, after which all go away without turning back to look at the resting-place of the ashes.

The dead are believed to go to a place called Amnodr in the west and below the earth. The god Ön presides over this world of the dead, where the people live much the same kind of life as on earth. The dead travel to Amnodr by a definite route, which differs in some respects for Tartharol and Teivaliol. In each case the dead perform acts on the way by which they lose their love of the earth and regain the vigour of health. They have also to cross a bridge of thread, running the risk of falling into a river full of leeches. Those Todas who have offended against the dairy or have been selfish and jealous are thus delayed in their journey to Amnodr. One of the Tarthar clans, that of Taradr, has an Amnodr, distinct from the rest, at Perithi in the Wainad, where there are still some Toda settlements.

7. Sacred days and numbers.—Many Toda ceremonies must be performed on definite days of the week, and this is probably connected with an institution in which each clan has one or more days on which a large number of activities are forbidden. Thus, on the *madnol*, or village day, neither dairymen nor women are allowed to leave the village, and nothing may be sold or taken away. There are various restrictions on conduct, and funeral and other ceremonies may not be held. Among the Tartharol there are similar restrictions on days sacred to each kind of dairy, so that in a village which has dairies of several different kinds few days of the week are left for the performance of the ordinary activities of life.

Sacred numbers are very prominent in the ritual, three and seven being the most important. Many ritual acts are performed three times, a threefold rite being usually associated in the dairy ceremonial with the utterance of the sacred syllable 'Oñ.' This number is also prominent in the funeral rites, especially in connexion with the ceremonial throwing of earth and the swinging of the body over the pyre before it is burned. The sevenfold performance of ceremonial acts only occurs in the dairy ritual and is especially prominent in the ordination ceremonies. Several of the most ancient lamps of the dairy are said to have had seven cavities or seven wicks.

8. Sorcery.—Two kinds of sorcery are practised, in one of which an incantation is uttered over some hair, preferably that of the person it is designed to injure. This is then hidden in the thatch of the proposed victim's hut. In the other form the sorcerer uses a bone or lime, which is then buried near the village of the proposed victim. In each case the incantation resembles the ordinary form of prayer, but with less explicit reference to the gods. It consists mainly of an enumeration of the misfortunes which it is hoped may fall upon the victim. The trouble is removed or averted by a corresponding formula as the result of negotiations with the sorcerer to whom the misfortune has been ascribed by one of the diviners.

There are many points of similarity between the ceremonial of the Todas and that of the Hindus, the sanctity of the milk-providing animal being an important feature common to both. There is reason to believe that the two main sections of the Todas differ in origin, and it is probable that the Teivaliol represent the earlier settlers and that they mixed with an indigenous people who practised interment of the dead preceded by some kind of mummification. The Tartharol seem to be later comers, who either brought the practice of cremation or accentuated its importance. The complexity of the dairy ritual is probably due to their influence, and they seem to have adopted the practice, so frequent in India, of employing the earlier settlers as their priests.

A point of especial interest is the relation of the Todas to the stone-circles and other megalithic structures on the Nilgiri hills. The people at present take little interest in these monuments, and this is intelligible if they were erected by the older stratum of the population represented by the Teivaliol, whose beliefs have been put into the background by the greater influence of the purely pastoral Tartharol. Stones of various kinds enter into the ritual of the dairy. The burial of the ashes at the entrance to a stone-circle at the end of the second funeral and the ritual throwing of earth into the buffalo-pen at both funeral rites suggest that the body was once interred in a buffalo-pen, and this is perhaps confirmed by the burial of the dairy-vessel called *mu* in a pen and by the sanctification of this vessel with earth taken from this spot. These features of ritual point to the circular pens as part of the culture of the older people, and in this connexion it is noteworthy that the most ancient dairies are circular and afford characteristic examples of the round house with conical roof. It may also be noted that these dairies are surrounded by stone walls, in one case by two such walls.

LITERATURE.—H. Harkness, *A Description of a Singular Aboriginal Race inhabiting the Summit of the Neilgherry Hills*, London, 1832; W. E. Marshall, *A Phrenologist among the Todas*, do. 1873; W. J. Breeks, *An Account of the Primitive Tribes and Monuments of the Nilagiris*, do. 1873; W. H. R. Rivers, *The Todas*, do. 1906.
W. H. R. RIVERS.

TOHUNGANS.—See POLYNESIA.

TOKEN.

TOKEN.—In its broadest sense a token is any portable object serving as a sign or proof of authenticity or credit, by which the issuer guarantees that the claim indicated by the token will be satisfied on its presentation in the proper quarter. In numismatics it signifies a coin-like piece of metal or other material representing money of much more than its intrinsic value, for which money the issuer undertakes to redeem the token when presented; it is also loosely applied to tickets admitting to certain privileges, such as the holy communion, or serving instead of letters of recommendation or other forms of credential.

1. Antiquity. — Many vague statements have been made as to the use of tokens or *tesseræ* (*symbola, synthemata*) for identifying persons who had been initiated into mysteries, but nothing of the kind has been identified. *Tesseræ* were largely used in Roman times for giving admission to shows or entitling to share in the distribution of grain (*tesseræ frumentariæ*), and some of these bear Christian symbols (one is extant in ivory bearing an anchor, two fishes and ΑΩ). No Christian *tesseræ hospitalitatis* (memorials of hospitality for which a return might be claimed when they were presented) have been identified as extant. *Tesseræ* were also used as credentials, serving instead of *litteræ commendatitiæ* or *commendatoriæ*.[1] Such *tesseræ* would have been used when persons were sent to confessors in prison to minister to them. *Tesseræ* may also have been used to identify the faithful when they desired admission to religious gatherings. Such use is *a priori* possible and probable, but it is important to remember that nothing of the kind, so far as is known, has survived from antiquity bearing a specially Christian character. Even among pagan *tesseræ*, those relating to religious bodies are rare. A certain number are extant bearing the names of the *magistri* and other dignitaries of the *sodalitates* who made distributions at festivals, such as the *magistri Minervales*; there are also *tesseræ* inscribed 'Sacr(a) Lani(vina) iuven(alia),' which were used at the festival of the college of Iuvenes at Lanuvium.

As regards Byzantine times, a certain number of *tesseræ* of churches, convents, confraternities, and other pious institutions have been described; they may have served, as in the West, for the distribution of alms and also for the control of various payments due to the personnel of churches and religious bodies. Such are, *e.g.*, an anonymous bronze *tessera* with the busts of the Virgin and St. Demetrius, and another with God the Father (inscr. ἅγιος ἅγιος ἅγιος) and a bunch of grapes on the reverse, which, it has been suggested, may have been used for the remuneration of cantors. The pieces used for charitable distributions are inscribed (in Greek) with such texts as 'He that hath pity upon the poor lendeth unto the Lord,' 'Blessed are the merciful, for they shall obtain mercy.'

2. Méreaux of the Roman Catholic Church.—The token, or *jeton de présence*, issued to the clergy in collegiate churches as a record of their presence at mass, at the canonical hours, and at other offices, in order that they might claim the statutory payment for their services, was most commonly known as a *méreau*. The Latin word *merellus* (*merallus, maralus*, etc.) is of uncertain derivation. Other names met with are: *plomb* (*plonc, plommet, plumbus*, etc.), even when made of other metal than lead (*plommez de cuyvre* at Aire in 1527), *enseigne, signum, marque, manuel, palot* (*pallotus*), *moneta capituli, simbolum*, etc. Many of these terms, signifying merely distribution-token, on the presentation of which a share in funds or privileges could be claimed, were not confined to the tokens of religious bodies, but extended to all kinds of corporations. It is uncertain when *méreaux capitulaires* were first introduced; the mention in a charter of the cathedral church of Tours (1216) of a *distributio nummorum matutinalium* does not necessarily refer to such *méreaux* as distinct from ordinary coins, and the *méreaux* which are mentioned in charters of 1167 and 1173 are passes, or *tesseræ* of identification,

[1] Cf. the phrase of Tertullian, *de Præscript.* xx.: 'dum est illis [*i.e.* ecclesiis] communicatio pacis, et appellatio fraternitatis, et contesseratio hospitalitatis.'

without any special connexion with religion. The earliest undoubted documentary reference to their use in churches seems to date from 1375, when Charles V. granted to the canons of the collegiate church of Langeac (Haute Loire) the right of having struck at the Royal Mint of St. Pourçain *merelli* for distribution to clerks and canons present at offices; they were to be of copper, lead, or tin, and to be carefully distinguished by their types, which are specified, from coin of the realm. None of these seems to have been identified. Next in date comes a reference in 1401. In a clause of his will Charles VI. ruled that the distributor of the Sainte Chapelle 'ne baille les méreaux jusqu'à la fin des heures de Notre Dame.' In a letter of 18th July 1401 he announces his intention of carrying out during his lifetime the new system outlined in his will; no one of the clergy who misbehaved or absented himself was to receive *méreaux*. A 15th cent. statute ordered that on every Saturday all the canons, chaplains, and clerks of the Sainte Chapelle should attend in the pay-room and bring their *méreaux* to show what each had earned. But there are extant church-*méreaux* which by their style must be earlier than the documents referred to, and the substitution of these for the custom of paying in actual money at the time, or for pricking in, or for tallies, may date from early in the 13th century. In 1557 the canons of Mâcon claimed that they had had for 'more than three or four centuries' the right of distribution of leaden *jetons* for the payment of choristers and other priests serving in the church; what foundation their claim possessed is not known. Nearly all the examples known come from France or the Low Countries, where *méreaux* were also used by abbeys, convents, hospitals, infirmaries, parish churches, and confraternities. The popular English term 'abbey token' for what are really reckoning-counters must not be taken to prove the existence of the custom in England; there is no evidence for such use in this country.[1]

Such tokens were cashed from time to time by the receivers of the various funds on which they were issued; sometimes they could be exchanged by the cellarer for victuals; and they often had a modified circulation. As long as this did not extend outside, so as to encroach on the currency of the realm, no objection was raised to any body issuing such *méreaux*. But, when it was the custom, as it was at Saint-Amé (Douai) or at Arras (where *méreaux* were used inscribed 'merellus mandati pauperum'), for the clergy to give away such tokens, entitling to portions of victuals, as alms to the poor, it is easy to see how the circulation might extend outside. In 1577 the Cour des Monnaies had to forbid the use of *méreaux* issued by the chapter of Autun except for distributions to the clergy; they had got into circulation in the town. In the case of certain pieces, especially of places in the Low Countries, it is matter of dispute whether they are really church-*méreaux* or base coins, of which the circulation was enforced by local authorities; such are the lead *deniers* of the Abbesses of Maubeuge, which circulated throughout Hainault until they were forbidden in 1541, the copper *deniers* of Notre Dame de Termonde, the 'yellow-money' of the chapter of Notre Dame de Cambrai. The rare *méreaux* of Carthusian foundations, such as the Certosa at Pavia or St. Mary Magdalen at Louvain, were used not for the remuneration of the clergy, but for alms-giving. A similar subsidiary use of *méreaux* is illustrated by the custom at Lembeke (near Eecloo, E. Flanders), where *méreaux* were used for the distribution of alms under the foundation of G. Kerremans (1717); tokens of the value of two *patards* were given to each of the poor who attended at catechism in preparation for communion, and of one *patard* to children who were zealous in preparation for their first communion.

[1] See, however, § 6 below.

The metal of which church-*méreaux* are made is usually lead, copper, or brass; the ruder specimens in the baser metal may be cast in moulds, but a large proportion are struck from engraved dies. The slate moulds used for casting the *méreaux* of the parish church of St. Julien at Ath, mentioned in letters-patent of 1478, are still in existence. Non-metallic substances such as leather or paper could also be used, but specimens in such material, if they survive, are very rare; a find made in demolishing a wall of the cathedral of Limoges seems to indicate that *méreaux* of leather were used there.

A few typical inscriptions and types found on *méreaux* may be mentioned. The St. Omer pieces are inscribed 'Mo(neta) Ecc(lesiae) Santi Audomari,' with the arms of the chapter, and 'Presentibus dabitur'; those of St. Martin des Champs read 'Distributio pro beneficiatis.' The series of the Ste. Chapelle dating from after 1448 reads 'Capella Reg(u)alis Palacii Parisiensis.' An ordinance of that year shows that those used for prebendaries and cantor bore a long cross with the crown of thorns on it, those for chaplains and clerks had a royal crown; other kinds then in use were ordered to be withdrawn: such were pieces marked with a cross, lance-head, and nail, representing relics in the chapel. Some series bear the names of the various offices for which they were used, as *matines*, *prime*, *tierse*, *missa*, *sexte*, *nonne*, *vespres*, *comp(lies)*. Dates do not appear before the 16th century. The value in money which the pieces represent is frequently expressed as 'VI . D . T' ('six deniers tournois'). A series mentioned in the archives of St. Pierre d'Aire (Artois), and described by Rouyer,[1] may be given as typical.

There were (*a*) *plombs des matines* or *deniers Marchant*, worth one *denier Parisis*, distributed daily after matins, and paid from the fund known as *du Marchant*; these occur from 1484 to 1637; (*b*) *plombs de la Croix* or *de la procession du vendredi* and the *plombs Lambert* or *du trésorier*; these represent particular foundations, and were of different values, given to canons, cantor, or other clergy; they are not mentioned after the 17th cent.; (*c*) *plombs obituaires*, i.e. *monetæ anniversariorum*, given to those who assisted at anniversary obituary services; (*d*) *plombs des heures canoniales*, instituted 20th June 1571, distributed to each canon present at the canonical hours; (*e*) *plombs des revêtus*, distributed in the 17th and 18th centuries at the masses said at the high altar to the canons who assisted the celebrant as deacons or sub-deacons; (*f*) *plombs des jours capitulaires*, for ordinary meetings of chapter, from 1571 onwards; (*g*) *plombs des chapitres spirituels*, from 1758, for chapters dealing specially with matters of cult; (*h*) *plombs des vicaires*, poor priests or clerks employed by canons to take their more arduous duties, as early as 1465; (*i*) *plombs de la confrérie de Notre Dame Panetière*, or *plombs du Salve*, from about 1520 down to 1790, for offices of the confraternity.

Some specimens of the *moneta anniversariorum* have survived; one belonging to St. Pierre d'Aire has on the obverse a death's head, on the reverse a bone and a key in saltire between three stars. Another inscribed 'Moneta anniversariorum' has a crowned *A* between two lilies; on the other side 'Requiescant in pace,' the mark of value 'XII.,' and three lilies. Yet another is inscribed 'Obit solenel' and dated 1585; and there is a pair of *méreaux* inscribed 'Orate Deum pro vivis' and 'Orate Deum pro defuntis' respectively.

A subsidiary use of tokens, more or less corresponding to the use as communion passes,[2] has at times prevailed in the Roman Catholic Church. There is a tradition that Cardinal Pole in Queen Mary's time made use of such tokens in order to distinguish those who conformed from those who did not. Communion certificates in the shape of tokens or tickets were given to those going to communion at St. Andrew's, Glasgow, from 1840

[1] *Rev. num. fr.* xiv. [1849] 363 ff.
[2] Described in § 3 below.

to 1850. At certain churches in Rome communicants at Easter receive them after they have been present.

3. Tokens of the Reformed Church. — The earliest mention of *méreaux* (*marreaux*, *marrons*, *marcqs*) in the Reformed Church abroad is in the registers of the Geneva Council; on 30th Jan. 1560 Calvin advised their introduction, but there is no evidence that they were actually used at Geneva before 1605. On the other hand, the French Protestants immediately adopted Calvin's suggestion, and there are tokens of the Walloon Church at Amsterdam as early as 1586. These tokens (which in the first Helvetic Confession are called *tesseræ*) were used for quite a different purpose from that of the *méreaux* of the Roman Catholic Church; they were certificates, issued to all persons considered after examination to be satisfactory in regard to religious knowledge and moral character, admitting them to partake of the sacrament of the Lord's Supper. In 1584, *e.g.*, Mme. Duplessis-Mornay and all her household were refused tokens for communion at Montauban because she dressed her hair in the court fashion instead of wearing the Huguenot hood. Extant specimens of these French Reformed Church tokens seem to be not earlier than the 17th cent.; they bear appropriate types, such as a chalice, or a shepherd feeding his flock, and the initials of the names of the churches, and sometimes dates; such inscriptions as 'Ne crains rien, petit troupeau' also occur. Copper *méreaux* with an angel-shepherd, and the inscription 'In unum conducam reliquum Israel, Mich. 2,' or 'Christ est le pain de vie,' of good 17th cent. workmanship, were probably made for Protestants in Paris. Another similar piece reads 'Christ habite en nos cœurs par foy,' and bears a flaming heart transfixed by two arrows.

The first French church to employ this kind of *méreaux* was at Nîmes (before 1562). Except at Sedan and Troyes (where it was introduced in 1564), none of the Reformed churches of the East is known to have used it. It was especially popular in Poitou, no fewer than 45 churches in that district being represented. Such pieces are commonest from 1740 to 1840, and are often very rude, being the handiwork of the elders themselves. The material is usually lead, tin, or a mixture, and they are most commonly cast (five moulds are extant), though some are struck. The French Reformed church at Erlangen in Bavaria began to use *méreaux* in 1689, and the same mould has remained in use down to present times.

In England the books of St. Saviour's Church, Southwark, show that communion tokens were used as early as 1559. It was the custom at Southwark to collect Church dues by 'selling the communion'; thus, in 1596, 2000 tokens were sold at 2½d. each; and a similar practice prevailed at St. Peter Mancroft, Norwich. At Durham and elsewhere in the 17th cent. it was the custom to take Easter reckonings of such people as partook of the holy communion, and account with them and deliver and receive tokens. The names of communicants were written down, and they received tokens which at the time of the administration of the sacrament were demanded again, so that it might be known who had paid their Easter offerings and who had failed to do so. The use of tokens in Presbyterian churches in England was derived from Scotland towards the end of the 17th cent., but the earliest actually bearing a date is of 1724 (Etal). Tokens are known of the Established Church of Scotland, the Independent Presbyterian party, the Reformed Presbyterian Church, or Cameronians, the English Presbyterian Church, the Associate Secession Congregation, the Relief Church, the General Associate Congregation, the United Associate Congregation, the United Presbyterian Church, and the Free Church of Scotland. Printed cards have now, as in Scotland, generally ousted metallic tokens.

But it was in Scotland that the sacramental token was most generally used. By the law of the Church of Scotland, no one was permitted to come to the Lord's Supper unless he or she had been provided with a communion token, which was issued after examination had shown the would-be communicant to be of good character and properly instructed. The tokens were sometimes kept as certificates of character, serving the same purpose as ancient *tesseræ*. The Scottish tokens were at first probably written or stamped cards; such 'tickets' were in use as early as 2nd May 1560 at St. Andrews, and continued often to be used after metal tokens were introduced; the word 'ticket' is frequently used indifferently of either. Written tickets were used as late as 1656. The date of the introduction of metal tokens has not been determined. The use of them has continued in both the Presbyterian Churches and in the Scottish Episcopal Church down to the present day, although in the larger towns they have been almost entirely superseded by printed cards. Recently established denominations, such as the United Free Church and the Free Presbyterian Church, appear to use only the latter. The metallic tokens are most often made of lead, tin, or a mixture, but brass, iron, copper, and even leather (the last only at the Secession congregation at Ceres, 1743) have been employed; the Crown Court Chapel, London, and the Presbyterian Church at Charleston used silver tokens, and for the first Reformed Presbyterian Church of New York they were made of ivory. They are generally cast in stone moulds, but are sometimes struck from dies. The oldest extant dated piece is of 1648, but a dated one of 1588 is recorded (Glasgow). At first they were distinguished merely by the initials of the parish (and this occurs as late as 1866); later came the initials of the minister, with 'M.' prefixed. Incuse numerals sometimes indicate the table to which a communicant was admitted when the number was very large. Religious symbols (heart, burning bush, vine, lily, chalice and bread) appear towards the end of the 17th century. The Covenanters' conventicle tokens bear simple texts, such as 'Holiness to the Lord,' without indication of parish or date; and texts are common from the beginning of the 19th century. The cross, which is common on Episcopalian tokens, also occurs on some of Presbyterian origin. In some large towns we find the burgh arms and the initials of the deans of gild. Views of churches first appear in the 18th century.

From Scotland the Presbyterians naturally carried the usage, not only to England, but to other countries such as Ireland, where the oldest dated token known to have been struck is that of the Old Presbyterian Congregation of Larne, of the year 1700. Stamps and moulds for many of these Irish tokens are illustrated by G. R. and D. Buick.[1]

4. Monnaies des innocens et des fous. — A curious phase of Church life is illustrated by satirical 'coins' issued by the bishops and other dignitaries (including archbishops, cardinals, and even popes) who were elected by the clergy at the ecclesiastical saturnalia known as the *fêtes des innocens* or *fêtes des fous*. Such festivals flourished, according to documentary evidence, from the 13th to the 17th cent., especially at Amiens, but also at other places such as Chartres, Reims, Laon,

[1] See reference under Literature.

Senlis, St. Quentin, Roye, Péronne—chiefly therefore in the north of France, but also as far south as Besançon. These dignitaries issued tokens struck in lead, bearing such inscriptions as 'Joha. Fournier eps. S. Aug. 1560,' 'Moneta nova Adriani Stultorum Pap(e),' 'Moneta epi(scopi) innocen(tium),' as well as texts such as 'Homo non in solo pane vivi(t),' 'Iudica Domine nocentes me,' 'Stultorum infinitus est numerus.' The types are sometimes saints, as on Jean Fournier's piece just mentioned, which was struck by the Augustinians at Amiens and bears St. Augustine. Rebuses are also in common use. Most of these pieces come from Amiens, and bear dates from 1499 to 1583. The custom of issuing tokens on these occasions also prevailed at Thérouanne, Lille, and perhaps Aire, but in those places no attempt was made at humour, and the types are religious or allegorical.

5. The boy-bishops.—The boy-bishops who were elected at certain churches in England on St. Nicholas' Day and held office for a week are also supposed to have issued leaden coins. The extant specimens, which seem all to come from Bury St. Edmunds, all bear a head of St. Nicholas or a mitre and are modelled more or less on the groats and pence of the 15th century. They are usually inscribed with an invocation to St. Nicholas on the obverse; on the other side we find inscriptions such as 'Ave rex gentis,' 'Ave rex gentis Anglor. Mile,' 'Ecce nova facies quia, Ecce reges Angelor(um).' The words 'Ave rex gentis Anglorum miles Regis angelorum' are the beginning of an anthem for the Feast of St. Edmund. The constant association of these pieces with St. Nicholas suggests that they were issued by the boy-bishops. On the other hand, it has been argued that they were used for the same purpose as the *méreaux* or *jetons de présence* described in § 2. It would, it is true, be strange if such a method of distribution were confined in this country to a single chapel (that of the Hospital of St. Nicholas) in St. Edmundsbury; but this argument cuts both ways. Another Bury piece inscribed 'Siglum Gilde Sci. Nicho(lai)' round the bust of the saint on the obverse, and on the reverse 'Congregacio Duooe' round the letters 'S T N,' appears to be connected with the Gild of the Translation of St. Nicholas; but from the published description it may perhaps be a seal and not a token.

6. Church tokens of the Near East.—The right of coinage by sacerdotal authorities has always existed in the Levant and is revived in periods of stress. During the Russo-Turkish War the churches and convents and the Jewish communities of Constantinople issued much token-money for small change. After the Peace of San Stefano the Turkish authorities called in from the provinces all the metallic token-money issued in the first half of the 19th cent., but the custom still persists. Silver, copper, and lead were issued for the metallic tokens, but many of these issues took the form of small cardboard tickets of different colours. Typical examples are the silver 'obol of St. Irene' (from Smyrna), the copper of St. George's (from Smyrna), dated 1775, and the cardboard pieces of the churches of Maronia (20, 10, and 5 paras, 1894), of St. George at Apolloniada (Apollonia ad Rhyndacum, 10 and 5 paras), of St. Michael at Goulion near Apollonia (10 and 5 paras, 'legal tender inside the church'), of St. John the Divine at Yeronda (Didyma, 5 paras); while the Sefarite synagogue, the synagogue of Akrida, and other Jewish communities are represented by both copper and cardboard.

LITERATURE.—(1) *Antiquity.*—F. X. Kraus, *RE* ii. [1886], *s.v.* 'Tesseræ'; G. Schlumberger, 'Monum. num. et sphrag. du moyen âge byz.,' *RA*, new ser., xl. [1880] 193–212, and 'Méreaux, tessères et jetons byz.,' *Revue numism. franc.* III. xiii. [1895] 91–96; M. Rostovtsew and M. Prou, *Catalogue des plombs de l'antiquité, du Moyen Age et des temps modernes*, Paris, 1900.

(2) *Roman Catholic Church.*—The literature is very scattered. Besides the index to the *Revue numism. franc. s.v.* 'Méreaux,' see esp. J. Rouyer, 'Notes pour servir à l'étude des méreaux,' *Rev. num. fr.* xiv. [1849] 356–377, 446–464; 'Méreaux de la Sainte Chapelle,' *ib.*, new ser., vii. [1862] 481–497; J. de Fontenay, *Manuel de l'amateur de jetons*, Paris, 1854; A. Forgeais, *Collection de plombs historiés trouvés dans la Seine*, do. 1862–65, 3rd ser., 'Variétés numismatiques'; A. Chassaing, 'Méreaux de la collégiale de Langeac,' *Rev. num. fr.* III. iii. [1885] 179–182.

(3) *Reformed Churches.*—J. de Pétigny, 'Méreaux des églises calvinistes,' *Rev. num. fr.* xix. [1854] 67–80; E. Delorme, 'Le Méreau dans les églises réformées de France,' *Bull. Soc. Hist. Prot.* xxxviii. [1888] 204–213, 316–325, 371–381, 483–492; H. Gelin, *Le Méreau dans les églises réf. de France*, Saint-Maxent, 1891; J. Rouyer, 'Méreaux de cuivre frappés à Paris . . . pour l'usage des protestants,' *Rev. num. fr.* III. xi. [1893] 385–405; T. Burns, *Old Scottish Communion Plate*, Edinburgh, 1892; E. F. Herdman, *Sacramental Tokens of the Presbyterian Churches in England*, Morpeth, 1901; G. R. and D. Buick, 'On a Small Collection of Presbyterian Communion Tokens,' in *Ulster Journal of Archæology*, ix. [1903] 17–30; A. J. S. Brook, 'Communion Tokens of the Established Church of Scotland,' *Proc. Soc. Ant. Scot.* xli. [1906–07] 453–604.

(4) *Monnaies des innocens.*—J. R.[igollot], *Monnaies inconnues des Evêques des Innocens, des Fous, etc.*, Paris, 1837; A. Danicourt, 'Enseignes et médailles . . . trouvées en Picardie,' *Rev. num. fr.* III. v. [1887] 49–67; A. Demailly, 'Inventaire d'une sér. inéd. de monn. des Evêques des Innocents, etc.,' *Mém. Soc. Ant. de Picardie*, xxxvi. [1908] 1–170.

(5) *Boy-bishops.*—D. H. Haigh, 'Leaden Tokens,' *Numism. Chronicle*, vi. [1843] 83–90; C. Roach Smith, 'Pilgrims' Signs and Leaden Tokens,' *Journ. Brit. Archæol. Assoc.* i. [1846] 200–212.

(6) *Near East.*—A. Sorlin-Dorigny, 'Droit de monnayage des communités non-musulmanes,' *Rev. num. fr.* III. i. [1883] 216–223.

G. F. HILL.

TOLERATION.—1. The policy.—The word 'toleration' in its legal, ecclesiastical, and doctrinal application has a peculiarly limited signification. It connotes a refraining from prohibition and persecution. Nevertheless it suggests a latent disapproval, and it usually refers to a condition in which the freedom which it permits is both limited and conditional. Toleration is not equivalent to religious liberty, and it falls far short of religious equality. It assumes the existence of an authority which might have been coercive, but which for reasons of its own is not pushed to extremes. It implies a voluntary inaction, a politic leniency. The motives that induce a policy of toleration are various, such as mere weakness and inability to enforce prohibitory measures, lazy indifference, the desire to secure conciliation by concessions, the wisdom to perceive that 'force is no remedy,' the intellectual breadth and humility that shrink from a claim to infallibility, the charity that endures the objectionable, respect for the right of private judgment.

However lamentable the fact may be, it should not surprise us that greater intolerance has been found in Christian nations than among any other peoples. Polytheism allows of an indefinitely enlarging pantheon. Its theology admits the existence of separate national gods among the various nations. But monotheism not only denies the existence of any such divinities; it regards the homage offered to them as a derogation from the worship due to the true God. Christianity, therefore, as well as the Judaism on which it is based, is necessarily intellectually intolerant. The same idea applies to Muhammadanism, which is always an intolerant religion as regards doctrine, even when it is not actively persecuting alien faiths. Then both Christianity and Muhammadanism claim to be universal religions; they are essentially aggressive; and the positive missionary work which this fact implies easily passes over into overt acts for the repression of idolatry and polytheism, contrary as they are to the genuine Christian temper. Add to this the fact that moral earnestness, at its best mounting to enthusiasm, in extreme cases degenerating into fanaticism, urges the devotees of a missionary religion towards a militancy which the hereditary adherents of non-aggressive religions have less inducement to adopt. When paganism is not tolerant, this is generally due to resentment against those who have attacked it, unless political motives are the real grounds of action. The persecution of Elijah and the adherents of Jahweh by Jezebel was occasioned by the prophet's vehement opposition to the introduction of the rites of the Phœnician Baal into Israel. The persecution of the Jews by Antiochus Epiphanes was due to their refusal to admit Hellenizing practices into their national life.

2. Indian toleration.—It has been asserted that Hinduism is the most tolerant of religions. This may be true as regards others than Hindus, because, being entirely racial and hereditary, it cannot proselytize. Judaism is also racial and hereditary, but not exclusively so, because it can admit proselytes. Hinduism has no opening for such. Accordingly, it must tolerate alien faiths, unless, like Tibetan Buddhism, it forbids immigration. Aśoka, the Constantine of Buddhism in India (3rd cent. B.C.), had monuments of his legislation cut in stone expressing his liberal treatment of religion as follows:

'The king, beloved of the god, honours every form of religious faith, but considers no gift or honour so much as the increase of the substance of religion, whereof this is the root—to reverence one's own faith and never revile that of others.'

The Muhammadan invasion put an end to tolerance in India by introducing cruel persecution of Hinduism with a wholesale destruction of the temples; but this was intermittent, the incursions of Turks, etc., taking the form of raids, from the 11th till the 17th cent., when the Mughal empire was established in Delhi. Akbar, the most famous of the Mughal emperors, aimed at combining all the inhabitants of his religion in his own eclectic theism. He held disputations in his palace every Friday when Brāhmans, Buddhists, and Parsis expounded their views as freely as Muhammadans.

3. Greek toleration.—The toleration of the Greeks for great varieties of religious beliefs may be attributed to their intellectual breadth, but also to the syncretism which admitted a plurality of divinities into its pantheon. Accordingly, as Adam remarks,

'There was comparatively little persecution for religious beliefs in Greek antiquity. Religious institutions and ceremonies were carefully guarded; but in respect of dogma the limits of toleration were very wide. We may infer from a remark of the Platonic Socrates that the Athenians in general cared little what a man believed, so long as he did not attempt to proselytise.'[1]

The Orphic believers, who, as the same authority states, were 'analogous to modern dissenters,' were tolerated since they showed no sign of abstaining from the religious services which the city ordained. The Pythagoreans, on the other hand, were attacked because they used their religious organization for political ends.[2] The death of Socrates appears to have been due mainly to animosity against the philosopher on account of his friendship with proscribed leaders of the aristocratic party. He was seventy years old at the time, and his daring teaching had long been tolerated without any interference on the part of the authorities.

4. Roman toleration.—It was a principle of Roman state policy to allow conquered nations to continue the practice of their indigenous religious rites ('Cujus regio ejus religio'). The old Latin cults were not propagandist, and they admitted of alien rites for alien peoples. Nevertheless difficulties arose, imposing limits on this easy tolerance in several ways: (1) by provincials coming to Italy and even to Rome with a claim to bring their own religions with them; (2) by missionaries of these alien faiths propagating them and by Roman citizens adopting them; (3) by the enforcement of the new state worship of the emperor throughout the empire; (4) by the dread of dangerous magic and the suspicion of immoral and cruel proceedings among the adherents of the foreign cults; (5) by a notion that public calamities might have been caused by neglect of the worship of the old divinities ('atheism').

[1] J. Adam, *The Religious Teachers of Greece* (*Gifford Lectures*), Edinburgh, 1908, p. 7; cf. J. E. Harrison, *Prolegomena to the Study of Greek Religion*, Cambridge, 1903.

[2] See Adam, p. 355.

But there were differences. The Twelve Tables had forbidden the introduction of new gods into Rome. Nevertheless for commercial reasons the Jews had a dispensation granted them to practise their religion in various parts of the empire, including the imperial city. But they were supposed to be confined to their own quarters in each locality—the ghetto. They spread their ideas, however, especially among women of the upper classes—in particular in Rome and Damascus, where it became the fashion to 'Sabbatize.' At first the Christians obtained tolerance on account of their Jewish origin, and it was not till their separation from the Jews became marked that they were interfered with by the authorities; nor was that the case at once even then. The Acts of the Apostles shows us Christians protected by Roman magistrates and police when attacked by Jewish mobs. By the time of Nero, however, in Rome the distinction between the two communities had become evident, and then the Christians were no longer sheltered by the licence for Jews. Christianity was not a *religio licita*. It is true that many unlicensed cults were winked at, in particular the religions of Syria and Egypt—the worship of Mithra, the Dea Mater, Serapis, etc. This was due to their great popularity. Christianity was not popular; it was too stern on the vices of paganism. W. M. Ramsay has shown reason for thinking that the tolerance of the Flavian emperors did not secure the protection of the Christians from local outbreaks. Nevertheless, on the whole, previous to the great Decian persecution the authorities were not disposed to initiate active measures against them. When Pliny wrote to Trajan expressing his perplexity at the Christianity of Bithynia and the consequent desertion of the pagan altars, the emperor replied ordering him (1) not to seek out the Christians, (2) to discourage informers, but (3) to punish convicted persons who had been brought before him for judgment. This rescript has been described by some as a persecuting order and by others as a decree for the easing of the case of the persecuted Christians. In fact it was both. Evidently Trajan was opposed to active persecution and favoured a policy of leniency; but his clear pronouncement requiring the punishment of definitely convicted Christians left no alternative but sentence of death for such people. This was the first formal order to that effect. Previously Christianity was implicitly illegal; henceforth it was to be explicitly illegal. In this respect the rescript was a limitation on the Roman policy of toleration. The persecution which had been carried on with exceptional ferocity at Lyons and Vienne under the gentle Marcus Aurelius was stayed by his worthless son Commodus owing to the intercession of his concubine Marcia, who appears to have been a Christian catechumen. This act of toleration cannot be raised to the level of state policy. It was purely personal in its origin, and it emanated from an unprincipled character.

When the emperor Valerian was captured by the Persians, the persecution which he had instigated was brought to an end by his son Gallienus, who issued a rescript in A.D. 260. It has not been preserved. But Eusebius[1] quotes a letter from this emperor to the bishops of Egypt written in the following year, in which he gives directions in accordance with his rescript. He there states that he has issued an order throughout all the world encouraging all to come out of their religious retreats and ordering that no one may molest them. Eusebius adds that there is another ordinance addressed to other bishops in

[1] *HE* vii. 13.

which the emperor grants them permission to recover their cemeteries in which they worshipped (τόποι θρησκευσιμοί). Gallienus's rescript has been claimed as the first Roman edict of toleration; but Uhlhorn and Harnack have shown that our knowledge of it does not indicate that Christianity was now made a *religio licita*. Two things only are ordered: the Christians are not to be molested; their property is to be restored. Since the churches had registered themselves as burial clubs and mutual benefit societies (*collegia fratrum, collegia tenuiorum*), it was in their social relations and with regard to their possession of property that Gallienus was now protecting their rights. Nevertheless, although Christianity was still illegal, in point of fact, since it was not to be molested, this was a policy of toleration. It cannot be justified on grounds of consistency; but practical politics are often guilty of inconsistency and prove themselves all the more humane for their freedom from legal pedantry. In the line that Gallienus was taking we see the exact opposite to his father's calculating measures of repression, devised with the deliberate, but now hopeless, design of stamping out Christianity. Gallienus's mild policy by no means gave to the Christians the legal rights which could assure them against future persecution. They enjoyed in consequence a whole generation of immunity from attack; but all along this was in a condition of unstable equilibrium, since nothing had been done to settle it on a sound legal basis. We might compare the situation to that of the Stuart 'Indulgences.' Christianity was not yet a *religio licita*.

Legalized toleration did not appear till after the last and greatest persecution. It was then seen in two stages. The first of these was spasmodic, insincere, and illogical, but still definite and effective. Galerius, the fierce instigator of the persecution which bears the name of the senior emperor Diocletian, who had been his reluctant associate in it, seized with death-bed terrors, issued the most extraordinary decree ever conceived by a Roman emperor (April, 311). Galerius first takes credit to himself for endeavouring to bring the Christians back to the ancient laws and discipline of the Romans, and, after a jibe at their divisions, for which he suggests he has supplied a wholesome corrective, he gives orders that his subjects may again be Christians ('ut denuo sint Christiani') and hold their assemblies, 'provided they do nothing contrary to the discipline.' Galerius concludes with the remarkable sentence, 'and for this indulgence the Christians will make the prayers of loyal subjects to their god.'

Toleration was not yet the settled policy of the empire. Where it was practised, it was too much subject to the caprice of the individual ruler. Maxentius at Rome was openly anti-Christian and Maximin Daza elaborated subtle devices for the destruction of Christianity; even later, during part of his period of government, Licinius favoured the pagans to the detriment of the Christians. The final stage was reached in the Edict of Milan. That magnificent Magna Charta of religious liberty issued from a meeting of Constantine with Licinius at Milan towards the end of the year 312, after the defeat of Maxentius. Maximin's evasion of the order of toleration granted by Galerius was the occasion which gave rise to it, but the new edict was much more statesmanlike than its curious predecessor, resting on a broader basis, breathing a nobler spirit, and establishing a surer policy. It was issued throughout the whole empire in the year 313. The Edict of Milan is the work of the great emperor Constantine, who induced his colleague Licinius to join him in it. There can be no doubt that Constantine was thoroughly convinced by the enlightened principles that it contains. His colleague's assent must be ascribed to political necessity, and subsequent events showed that Licinius was by no means loyal to it except under compulsion. Unfortunately the original rescript has been lost, but Licinius's edition of it, sent out a few months later, has been preserved, both the original Latin by Lactantius,[1] and a Greek translation, slightly differing verbally, by Eusebius.[2] The toleration granted is absolute and unconditional. It is expressly applied to the Christians, for whose benefit it clearly shows that it was primarily intended. But it also includes devotees of all other religions. This went far beyond the spirit of the ancient world, and indeed only occasionally and in the teaching of exceptional and rare minds has such toleration reappeared until quite modern times, when it has been seen in Cavour's dictum of 'a free Church in a free State.'

Constantine did not live up to his own principle. No sooner did he adopt Christianity than he began to patronize it, and his patronage soon took the form of interference and control. The Christian emperors were rarely more tolerant than the Church of their day; and, as this Church was stern in the denunciation of heresy and schism, too often the imperial government stepped in to give effect to the ecclesiastical sentence. Sometimes it went farther, the emperor taking sides and enforcing his own will, if for orthodoxy against the heretics, if in favour of heresy, as in the support of Arianism by Constantius and later by Valens, against the Catholics. Later emperors interfered in the Christological controversies with the Nestorians and the Monophysites. The iconoclastic emperors were regarded as persecutors of the Church when they took strong measures to put down image-worship. Therefore, while Christianity is not only tolerated but legalized as the religion of the State, the policy of toleration so brilliantly anticipated by Constantine is now buried out of sight, like an untimely birth. The tables are turned, and paganism, ceasing to persecute, comes to be itself persecuted. First magical rites are prohibited as dangerous to the State and the citizens; then the worship of the old gods is prohibited and their altars and temples are demolished. Theodosius II. is the most conspicuous figure in this anti-pagan crusade. On the other hand, it is to be noted that the Christian emperors never went the lengths in murderous violence to which the persecuting pagan emperors had gone. There was nothing approaching the devastating Decian and Valerian persecutions. On the rare occasions when the death penalty was inflicted this was nearly always for magic and sorcery, not as the suppression of a false doctrine but for the extirpation of a dangerous practice. The persecution of paganism naturally led its champions to preach toleration. Libanius argued for the principle of absolute toleration. The pagan reaction under Julian was based on a profession of tolerance, but the emperor was not entirely true to his profession.[3]

5. Early Christian toleration.—The early Christian Fathers advocated toleration, not merely in self-defence, but on principle. Tertullian was most emphatic in asserting this principle:

'Humani juris et naturalis potestatis est unicuique quod putaverit colere, nec alii obest aut prodest alterius religio. Sed nec religionis est cogere religionem, quae sponte suscipi debeat, non vi: cum et hostiae ab animo libenti expostulentur.'[4]

Lactantius maintained the inherent wickedness of persecution.[5] The bigotry which appeared among the Fathers of the 4th cent. was not allowed to prevail without protest. Athanasius advocated a conciliatory attitude for winning heretics back to the faith. While Augustine denounced heretics and schismatics—especially Pelagians and Donatists—Hilary of Poitiers was a thoroughgoing advocate of toleration. Ambrose condemned the persecution of the Priscillianists, and Martin of Tours denounced it as an atrocious crime because it went so far as killing. The Fathers were slow to sanction the death penalty for heretics; Augustine, while advocating milder measures of persecution, was opposed to this extremity.

6. Mediæval toleration.—During the early part of the Middle Ages persecution was comparatively rare, even in the case of sorcery, which, it was thought, could be counteracted by the more potent

[1] *De Morte Pers.* 48. [2] *HE* x. 5.
[3] Cf. art. PERSECUTION (Early Church).
[4] *Ad Scapulam*, 2. [5] See *Div. Inst.* v. 20.

influence of the rites of the Church. But with the rise of the Inquisition in the 13th cent. a greater rigour of ecclesiastical discipline crushed out the spirit of tolerance.

7. Toleration in the Renaissance and the Reformation.—The irreligious and pagan habits that accompanied the Renaissance issued in an easy indifference which favoured an unprincipled tolerance. But the intellectuality and breadth of view that it engendered went farther and gave rise to a reasoned doctrine of toleration. Sir Thomas More, while sanctioning persecution, admitted the abstract excellence of the opposite course. Montaigne's scepticism and liberal idea of life made for tolerance. On higher grounds Erasmus laboured incessantly for the same end, combining inimitable wit with immense learning, exposing the folly as much as the wickedness of ignorant, narrow-minded persecution. The duty of absolute toleration was insisted on by Castellio, a Frenchman, who had been a friend of Calvin when the Reformer was a professor at Basel. Denouncing the execution of Servetus, he argued that, if the end of Christianity be the diffusion of a spirit of beneficence, persecution must be its extreme antithesis, and that, if persecution can be the essential element of a religion, that religion must be a curse to mankind.

Most of the Reformers were not advocates of universal toleration; but Zwingli regarded error as not inherently blameworthy and held that it should be tolerated. He went farther and showed a comprehensive appreciation of human excellency apart from religious differences.

Lælius Socinus was a pronounced advocate of religious liberty, and a clear assertion of the principle is put forth in the Socinian Catechism of Rakow. The German Anabaptists and the Dutch Arminians also advocated this principle.

8. The German settlement. — The Peace of Augsburg (1555) was arranged between the Roman Catholics and the Lutherans; it excluded the Reformed Church, both Zwinglian and Calvinistic, as well as all the minor sects. Further, this arrangement left it to the princes of the several states to decide which of the two permissible types of religion should be adopted and imposed on their subjects. Disagreements between the two parties concerned and the exclusion of the Reformed Churches led to the Thirty Years' War. This was concluded with the Peace of Westphalia (24th Oct. 1648), to which there were three parties —the Roman Catholics, the Lutherans, and the Reformers. It made provision for none of the minor sects. The princes were allowed to pass from one of the three religions to the other and to require their selected religion to be imposed on their subjects to the exclusion of all other religions, or to admit other religions, as they saw fit. This right was called the *jus reformandi*. It implied a limited and optional toleration.

Subsequently two influences arose to widen the conception of religious liberty: (1) pietism, which, as both non-dogmatic and charitable, tended towards universal toleration; and (2) the effect of the school of natural law. Pufendorf maintained that no one could be compelled to embrace a given religion and held it to be a fatal necessity that dissensions should exist within the Church. Christian Thomasius, the typical illuminist, bases the principle of religious liberty on his fundamental conception of law. He distinguishes morality from law, on the ground that law is coercive while morality cannot be coerced. Much more is this the case with religion. The difference between the spheres of the prince and the clergy is that it is the duty of the prince to coerce and the duty of the clergy to teach. The clergy should fight heresy with instruction, not by appealing to the secular arm. While urging these principles in all his works, Thomasius devotes three treatises especially to the exposition of them, viz. the two 'Programmata,' *Programma de tolerantia dissidentium in controversiis religionis* (1693) and *Programma varia testimonia Martini Lutheri de tolerantia dissidentium in religione complectens* (1697), and the more popular work in the vernacular entitled *Das Recht evangelischer Fürsten in theologischen Streitigkeiten* (1696). In these works he maintains that all dissidents are to be tolerated so long as they do not disturb the public peace. Frederick William I. of Prussia used the *jus reformandi* in favour of allowing Roman Catholics to live in his Protestant state, and his son Frederick the Great adopted a policy of toleration for all religions with the cynical idea that, since they arose only from the ignorance of the people, they were equivalent in the region of dogma and to be distinguished only by their greater or less ethical import. Thus, since morality is independent of articles of faith, absolute religious liberty should be conceded. In a rescript of 15th June 1740 he says: 'All religions are equal and good so long as those who profess them are upright people.' There was a temporary reaction under Frederick William II., after which the right of religious liberty spread first through Prussia and then through the other German states, although the territorial state recognition of the three favoured religions remained—a policy of general toleration, but not of religious equality.

9. England and America.—In the 16th cent., under the Tudors, the extreme Puritan party, which had shared with other Protestants in the persecutions of Roman Catholic times, did not obtain religious liberty. But the principle of toleration was maintained by the Baptists and the Congregationalists, although there were some limits to the applications of it. The early Congregationalists would exclude from its privileges both Unitarians and Roman Catholics, the latter as themselves a persecuting party and a danger to Protestant liberty. But John Robinson, a large-minded man of liberal views, drew up a covenant for the Pilgrim Fathers who sailed in the 'Mayflower' and founded New England. The first instrument of this covenant conferred equal civil and religious rights on every member of any commonwealth. A little later the colony of Maryland, founded by a charter from Charles I., granted toleration to Roman Catholics as well as to Protestants. Its first law runs as follows: 'No person professing to believe in Jesus Christ shall be in any way molested or discountenanced for his or her religion, or in the free exercise thereof.'

The Pilgrim Fathers, who had claimed liberty at home, have been blamed for the inconsistency of intolerance in their own colony when they were settled in America. The defence is that the exclusive theocracy that they established implied that they regarded themselves as a Church rather than as a State, and as such would refuse membership to unfit persons in accordance with a fundamental Congregational principle. But they have often been unfairly accused of narrowness through a confusion of two different positions—that of the early settlers in New England who had come from John Robinson's church in Holland and were the real Congregationalist immigrants, and that of the Puritans who settled later in Massachusetts. The latter were Presbyterians who had never adopted the principles of religious freedom. It was not until the separation from England that complete equality in religion was established in the United States.

10. The English problem.—In the 17th cent. neither the bulk of the Presbyterians nor the Episcopal party as a whole had any idea of toleration. Under the early Stuarts Laud and the High Church, having the upper hand, persecuted the Presbyterians. Under the Long Parliament the Presbyterians tried to force the Covenant on the whole nation. Cromwell took a wider view and ordered his 'triers' not to molest Protestant godly men who preached the gospel, whatever their ecclesiastical principles might be, and he gave the Jews a legal footing in England.

At this time the Baptists, the Congregationalists (then known as Independents), and the Quakers maintained the principle of religious liberty—the last-named body basing it on their doctrine of the inner light, which excluded all ecclesiastical and official interference with the individual soul. The protest of the five Independents at the Westminster Assembly (1643), which was mainly Presbyterian in composition, maintained the right of religious liberty.

Later, on the Presbyterian side, Richard Baxter laboured for large measures of comprehension, and John Goodwin, generally regarded as a Congregationalist, but described by Rufini as 'a Puritan *sui generis*—a rationalist Puritan,' maintained that every religion, sect, or schism should be tolerated so long as there was no attempt to interfere with the security of the State. Milton, claimed by both Presbyterians and Congregationalists, but not wholly committed to either party, in triumphantly vindicating the freedom of the press, pleaded eloquently for religious toleration. In the *Areopagitica* he showed that persecution was both unnecessary for the preservation of truth and a hindrance to the discovery of truth. He would tolerate all Protestants, including Socinians, Arminians, and Anabaptists, but not Roman Catholics. On the Anglican Church side the more liberal-minded writers were in favour of toleration and comprehension. Chillingworth affirms that Protestants are inexcusable if they do violence to the consciences of others. He holds it to be a great sin to force on other people our own interpretations of Scripture, arguing that this was the cause of all the schisms and discords of Christianity. John Hales took a similar line in his tractate *Schism and Schismaticks* (1636). Jeremy Taylor, in his famous *Liberty of Prophesying* (1646), was contending for freedom of speech against the tyranny of the Covenant under the Long Parliament.

The reaction at the Restoration and the passing of the Act of Uniformity (1662), followed by the Conventicle, Five Mile, and Test Acts, narrowed the State Church position and imposed great disabilities on Nonconformists; these were to some extent relieved a little later by James II.'s Indulgences, but at the expense of the rights of Parliament. Legal toleration did not appear till the Revolution. In the Declaration of Breda Charles II. promised to respect tender consciences; but, when well established on the throne, he had not the moral courage to stand to his word.

William III. obtained his invitation to England mainly as the champion of religious liberty. His aim was to bring about an agreement between the Church of England and Protestant Dissenters. While in his own country, he had been profoundly affected by the ideas of the Dutch Arminians. In England his most trusted adviser, Bishop Burnet, had adumbrated the policy which the king afterwards adopted in a *Modest and Free Conference between a Conformist and a Nonconformist* (1663). William first aimed at comprehension in 'A Bill for Uniting their Majesties' Protestant Subjects.' The failure of this measure to pass in the House of Commons necessitated another line of action.

II. The Act of Toleration.—The Act of Toleration, which was passed in the year 1689, gave relief to Nonconformists from their chief disabilities; but it did not grant complete religious liberty; much less did it establish religious equality in the eyes of the law. It exempted Nonconformists from the pains and penalties of the Act of Uniformity, the Conventicle Act, and the Five Mile Act; at the same time it required people who desired to avail themselves of its privileges to take the oaths of allegiance and supremacy and make a statutory declaration against Romish superstitions, and it ordered Nonconformist ministers to subscribe to the Articles of the Church of England with the exception of three—those referring to the traditions of the Church, to the homilies, and to the consecration of bishops and priests, a fourth exception, that of the article on infant baptism, being allowed for Baptist ministers. Further, it enacted that every Nonconformist place of worship should be certified by a bishop, an archdeacon, or a justice of the peace. Quakers were allowed to make a solemn declaration instead of taking the oaths and were required to declare their belief in the Trinity and in the inspiration of the Bible. Neither Roman Catholics nor Unitarians were included in the concessions allowed by this Act, and even orthodox Nonconformity was still illegal, the persecuting laws remaining on the statute-books, and only the exaction of their penalties being forbidden. While this measure was logically inconsistent, it was practically serviceable as far as it went. It secured a considerable amount of toleration.

The same year (1689) saw Locke's first *Letter Concerning Toleration* published anonymously in Holland in Latin. It was translated into English immediately. A second and longer letter, and a third longer still, followed in reply to answering letters. Yet a fourth letter completes the series in Locke's work; this is not finished. The collection has become a literary classic on the subject of toleration. Locke bases his argument on the ground that the rightful sphere of the State is wholly confined to externals and does not extend to religion, which is internal. He holds that not only the doctrines and 'articles of faith,' but also 'the outward form and rites of worship,' are out of the province of the civil magistrate. Such a position goes beyond toleration. Logically it involves disestablishment, because, if the State is not competent to deal with religious matters at all, it follows that it should not patronize or support a favoured religion any more than persecute a religion of which it disapproves. With regard to persecution, Locke holds that it is anti-Christian, since love of our fellow-men is of the essence of Christianity, and it cannot be maintained that persecutors are actuated by love to their victims in the cruelties which they perpetrate. But, while on these principles Locke would tolerate Jews as well as all Protestant sects, his toleration does not extend to Roman Catholics or atheists. With regard to the former, though he does not name them in his argument on the subject, he says:

> 'That church can have no right to be tolerated by the magistrate, which is constituted upon such a bottom, that all those who enter into it, do thereby, *ipso facto*, deliver themselves up to the protection and service of another prince.'[1]

He would also exclude persons who hold views subversive of society and atheists, who, he considers, are to be included in that category.[2] Thus he regards both these parties as obnoxious to the State and to be excluded from toleration on political grounds, not for their religious views. Locke carries his idea of toleration beyond the political sphere to the ecclesiastical, arguing for liberty of thought within the Churches themselves. He writes:

> 'What think you of St. Athanasius's Creed? Is the sense of that so obvious and exposed to every one who seeks it; which so many learned men have explained so different ways, and which yet a great many profess they cannot understand? Or is it necessary to your or my salvation, that you or I should believe and pronounce all those damned who do not believe that creed, *i.e.* every proposition in it? which I fear would extend to not a few of the church of England; unless we can think that people believe, *i.e.* assent to the truth of propositions they do not at all understand. If ever you were acquainted with a country parish, you must needs have a strange opinion of them, if you think all the ploughmen and milkmaids at church understood all the propositions in Athanasius's Creed; it is more, truly, than I should be apt to think of any one of them; and yet I cannot hence believe myself authorized to judge or pronounce them all damned: it is too bold an intrenching on the prerogative of the Almighty; to their own Master they stand or fall.'[3]

Under Queen Anne the toleration that had been obtained by the accession of William and Mary was threatened by the Schism Act, which made it illegal under heavy penalties for any one to keep a

[1] *Works*, new ed., London, 1823, vi. 46. [2] *Ib.* p. 47.
[3] *Ib.* p. 410 f.

private school or teach in a seminary unless he signed a declaration of conformity to the liturgy of the Church of England and obtained a bishop's licence to teach on production of a certificate that he had taken the communion according to the rites of the Church of England during the preceding year. The queen's death stayed the execution of this drastic measure, and it was repealed in the reign of her successor, George I. From this time onwards toleration with regard to religious views and practices was firmly established; but its limitations were still numerous. It was the minimum of concession to those who had previously been the victims of persecution. Active persecution was no longer allowed. But the negative policy of exclusion and prohibition left galling grievances long unrelieved. Toleration is far from religious equality. The very practice of it involves an exalted position of power enjoyed by the people who tolerate as opposed to an inferior position in which the tolerated are living. It is not inconsistent with the monopoly of privileges by the one class and the refusal of them to the other. If those privileges are rights of citizenship, toleration is even possible side by side with serious injustice. The tolerated may be denied political power, the parliamentary and municipal franchise, the opportunity of election as members of Parliament or of corporations, access to public schools, colleges and universities, whether as pupils or as teachers, and a host of other national rights and privileges. So it was that under the Georges, and even throughout much of the 19th cent., Nonconformists, Roman Catholics, Unitarians, Jews, and others suffered from various forms of exclusion. The abolition of the Corporation and Test Acts, Catholic Emancipation, the admission of Jews to Parliament, the permission to dispense with the member's oath extracted in order to meet the case of Mr. Bradlaugh, the throwing open of the universities to Nonconformists, the enlarged foundation of grammar schools, and the extension of popular education generally, irrespective of ecclesiastical distinctions, were all steps beyond mere toleration towards the goal of religious equality—a goal which in several directions its advocates have not yet completely attained.

12. Toleration in France.—The fight for religious liberty which was waged principally in Germany, Switzerland, Holland, and England during the 16th and 17th centuries passed on to France in the 18th century. The Edict of Nantes (1598) had conceded toleration for Protestants; the revocation of that Edict (1685) restored and aggravated persecuting intolerance. Bayle established the intellectual basis of toleration in his *Dictionnaire* and in a work entitled *Commentaire philosophique sur ces paroles de Jésus-Christ: Contrain-les d'entrer*—a refutation of the misuse of a text popular with persecutors from the time of Augustine. He holds it to be immoral to compel men to profess religion in which they do not believe, and also irrational, because it discourages the discovery of truth. No one, he maintains, has a right to claim such complete possession of truth as not to need to compare his ideas with those of other men. Montesquieu, in *De l'Esprit des lois* (1748), argues for religious liberty and exposes the futility of coercion. Rousseau, in his *Contrat social*,[1] affirms the complete liberty of individual beliefs; nevertheless, holding that intolerance is inherent in Christian dogma, he would abolish this and establish a civil profession of faith in truths indispensable to a well-organized social life, including that of the existence of God. But it was Voltaire who by his scathing sarcasm did more than any other man in France during the 18th cent. to put an end to persecution and secure tolerance for the Protestants. The ideas of these champions of religious liberty powerfully moulded the course of the French Revolution in regard to religion and the universal toleration that has since prevailed in France.

13. The present situation.—A policy of toleration now obtains throughout Western Europe, North America, the British, French, and Italian colonies, and India, where it is a safeguard of peace and good order under British rule. It is established in Japan and practically observed throughout the provinces of China. It is also practised generally throughout S. America. Eastern Europe and Western Asia are still excluded from its privileges. The exclusiveness of Tibet is national rather than religious in character. Thus it is apparent that the policy of toleration has been adopted throughout the greater part of the civilized world.

Apart from the liberalizing of legislation, great progress has been made by means of Modernism in Roman Catholic countries and by the general spread of Christian charity, culture, knowledge of history, scientific methods of criticism, and the study of comparative religion, by the softening of manners, by scepticism, and by religious indifference, all tending to cool the ardour of the persecuting spirit and so to establish toleration. The champions of liberty now resent the use of the term as representing a gracious concession on the part of the privileged and claim to go far beyond it in their demand for the abolition of all theological and ecclesiastical privileges and the establishment of absolute religious equality.

Cf. also artt. PERSECUTION.

LITERATURE.—The literature of toleration is immense. A few of the more important works are Tertullian, *ad Scapulam*; Lactantius, *Divinæ Institutiones*; Vincentius, *Epistolæ*, 93, 17; Marsilius of Padua, *Defensor Pacis*, 13th cent.; Faustus Socinus, *Opera*, 2 vols., Irenopolis, 1656; Milton, *Areopagitica*, London, 1644; John Goodwin, *Plea for Liberty of Conscience*, 1644; Locke, *Epistola de Tolerantia*, Gouda, 1689, Eng. tr., London, 1689; P. Bayle, *Commentaire philosophique sur ces paroles de Jésus-Christ: Contrain-les d'entrer*, 2 vols., Cantorbery, 1686, *Supplement du Commentaire*, etc., Hamburg, 1688; S. Pufendorf, *De habitu religionis Christianae ad vitam civilem*, Bremen, 1687, Eng. tr., London, 1698; C. Thomasius, *Disputatio an haeresis sit crimen*, 1697; Rousseau, *Contrat Social*, Paris, 1762; F. M. de Voltaire, *Traité sur la tolérance*, do. 1763, etc.; J. S. Mill, *On Liberty*, London, 1859; Jules Simon, *La Liberté de conscience*[5], Paris, 1872; J. C. Bluntschli, *Gesch. des Rechtes der religiösen Bekenntnissfreiheit*, Elberfeld, 1867; P. Schaff, *The Progress of Religious Freedom as shewn in the Hist. of Toleration Acts*, New York, 1889; H. Fürstenau, *Das Grundrecht der Religionsfreiheit nach seiner geschichtl. Entwicklung und heutigen Geltung in Deutschland*, Leipzig, 1891; M. Creighton, *Persecution and Tolerance*, London, 1895; Wallace St. John, *The Contest for Liberty of Conscience in England*, Chicago, 1900; L. Dubois, *Bayle et la tolérance*, Paris, 1902; L. Robert, *Voltaire et l'intolérance religieuse*, do. 1904; Luigi Luzzatti, *La Libertà di Conscienza e di Scienza*, 1909, French tr., Paris, 1911; G. Bonet-Maury, *Hist. de la liberté de conscience en France (1598–1905)*[2], do. 1909; W. E. H. Lecky, *Hist. of the Rise and Influence of the Spirit of Rationalism in Europe*, auth. ed., London, 1910; A. A. Seaton, *The Theory of Toleration under the later Stuarts*, Cambridge, 1911; H. F. Russell Smith, *The Theory of Religious Liberty in the Reigns of Charles II. and James II.*, do. 1911; Lord Acton, *Hist. of Freedom and other Essays*, London, 1907; Francesco Rufini, *Religious Liberty*, Eng. tr., do. 1912; J. B. Bury, *A Hist. of Freedom of Thought* (Home University Library), do. 1913.

W. F. ADENEY.

TOLERATION (Muhammadan). — Muslim toleration may be considered under two distinct aspects, with respect to (i.) the faithful themselves, and (ii.) non-Muslims.

(i.) Within the circle of the Muslim Church the basis for toleration is found in the saying traditionally attributed to Muḥammad: '*Ikhtilāfu ummatī raḥmat*^{un},' 'Difference of opinion in my community is a (manifestation of divine) mercy.' In accordance with this principle, it has been possible for the four schools (*madhhab*) of theologians and legists into which the Sunnīs are divided, viz. Ḥanafī, Mālikī, Shāfiʿī, and Ḥanbalī, to exist side by side, and for each of them to permit difference of opinion even in its own midst. There has been

[1] Bk. iv. ch. 8.

abundance of controversy between these schools, but instances of open violence have been rare.[1] A similar basis for toleration was found in the traditional saying of the Prophet: 'My community will become divided into 73 sects,' and rendered possible the ample sectarian development in the Muhammadan world. Instances have occurred from time to time of the persecution of one sect by another,[2] but a more characteristic feature of the Muslim Church has been the freedom allowed to the exposition of religious doctrine, and the common sentiment of princes and people has generally condemned intolerance on the part of professed theologians.[3]

(ii.) The recognition of rival religious systems, as possessing a divine revelation, gave to Islām from the outset a theological basis for the toleration of non-Muslims. Judaism and Christianity are represented in the Qur'ān as forms of the primitive faith given to man and taught by a series of prophets from Adam onwards:

'Men were of one religion only; then they disagreed with one another.'[4] 'Mankind was but one people; then God raised up prophets to announce glad tidings and to warn, and He sent down with them the Book with the truth, that it might decide the disputes of men.'[5]

But Jewish and Christian teachers had corrupted the purity of this primitive faith, which Muḥammad as 'the seal of the prophets'[6] came to proclaim anew.

This recognition of a common God is put forward in the Qur'ān as the basis for friendly relations with the followers of rival creeds, in the following verses:

'Say to those who have been given the Book and to the ignorant, Do ye accept Islam? Then, if they accept Islam, are they guided aright; but if they turn away, then thy duty is only preaching.'[7] 'Those who have inherited the Book after them [*i.e.* the Jews and the Christians] are in perplexity of doubt concerning it. For this cause summon thou [them to the faith], and walk uprightly therein as thou hast been bidden, and follow not their desires; and say, In whatsoever Books God hath sent down do I believe; I am commanded to decide justly between you; God is your Lord and our Lord; we have our works and you have your works; between us and you let there be no strife; God will make us all one, and to Him shall we return.'[8] 'Dispute ye not, save in kindliest sort, with the people of the Book; save with such of them as have dealt wrongly [with you], and say ye, "We believe in what has been sent down to us and hath been sent down to you. Our God and your God is one, and to Him are we self-surrendered."'[9]

Muslim theologians have found a sanction for the toleration of religions other than Judaism and Christianity in passages such as the following:

'To every people have We appointed observances which they observe; therefore let them not dispute the matter with thee, but summon them to thy Lord: Verily thou art guided aright: But if they debate with thee, then say: God best knoweth what ye do.'[10] 'If any one of those who join gods with God ask an asylum of thee, grant him an asylum in order that he may hear the word of God; then let him reach his place of safety.'[11] 'They who had joined other gods with God say, "Had He pleased, neither we nor our forefathers had worshipped aught but Him, nor had we, apart from Him, declared anything unlawful." Thus acted they who were before them. Yet is the duty of the apostles other than plain-spoken preaching?'[12]

The clearest injunction of toleration is in the verse, 'Let there be no compulsion in religion,'[13] and forcible conversion is condemned in the words:

'But if thy Lord had pleased, verily all who are in the world would have believed together. Wilt thou then compel men to become believers? No soul can believe but by the permission of God.'[14]

In harmony with the injunctions of the Qur'ān is Muḥammad's letter to the bishops, priests, and monks of Najrān promising them the protection of God and His apostle for their churches, their religious services and monastic institutions, and freedom from disturbance or any interference with their rights, so long as they remained faithful to their obligations.[1] He permitted the Jews in Medīna to practise their own faith, until their implacable hostility led to their expulsion from the city, and he gave instructions to Mu'ādh b. Jabal, whom he sent on a mission to Yaman in 10 A.H., that he was not to compel any Jew to abandon his religion.[2]

The teaching of the Qur'ān and the practice of the Prophet thus served as a clear basis for toleration of the Christian and Jewish faiths. As mention is made of the Sabians in the Qur'ān,[3] they also were considered to have received some divine revelation and therefore to be entitled to toleration; it is possible that the Harranians (*q.v.*) and Mandæans (*q.v.*) claimed to be Sabians in order to enjoy the same toleration.[4] Their practice of heathen rites naturally gave offence to orthodox Muslim feeling, and the khalīfah al-Qāhir (932–934) is said to have consulted the jurist Abū Sa'īd al-Istakhrī as to whether the Sabians should continue to be tolerated or not, and was told that, as they were neither Jews nor Christians, but worshipped the planets, they ought to be exterminated; however, the khalīfah allowed the Sabians to buy themselves off and disregarded the decision of this pious theologian.[5] About forty years later his successor, Ṭā'i'li-amrillāh, promulgated a fresh edict of toleration in favour of the Sabians, guaranteeing to them protection for themselves, their wives, and property, and free access to their temples and places of prayer, and the undisturbed performance of the rites of their religion.[6] Their last temple was not destroyed until 1230, and then by the heathen Mongols.[7]

Political expediency, and the desire of the jurists of the 2nd cent. of the Hijra to make the religious law tally with the accepted practice, prompted the extension of a similar toleration to such faiths as were not mentioned in the Qur'ān, but were found to have adherents in the rapidly growing Muhammadan empire; *e.g.*, when Arab rule was extended into Persia, it was averred that Muḥammad had given directions that the Zoroastrians were to be treated exactly like the Ahl al-kitāb ('people of the Book').[8]

The Zoroastrians appear to have been but little disturbed in the exercise of their cult up to the period of the fall of the 'Abbāsid dynasty.[9] There is even an account of a Muhammadan general (in the reign of Mu'taṣim, 833–842) who ordered an *imām* and a *mu'adhdhin* to be flogged because they had destroyed a fire-temple in Sughd and built a mosque in its place.[10] In the 10th cent., three centuries after the conquest of Persia, fire-temples were to be found in almost every province.[11]

Even the Manichæans (*q.v.*), though not entitled to toleration according to Muhammadan law, survived as a separate sect until the end of the 10th cent.; in the reign of Ma'mūn, Yazdānbakht, the leader of the sect, held a public disputation with the Muslim theologians in Baghdād.[12]

The severe condemnation of idolatry in the Qur'ān[13] seems to have made any toleration of idol-worshippers impossible for a Muslim ruler, but already in the reign of Hārūn Muslim law had granted the privilege of paying *jizyah* to idolaters—worshippers of idols, fire, and stones—and thus gave them a place among the tolerated cults.[14] The khalīfah 'Uthmān, in dealing with the heathen Berbers, followed the precedent of 'Umar in regard to the Zoroastrians, and allowed them to pay *jizyah*.[15] In India the Brāhmans appear to have paid *jizyah* from the earliest days of Arab domination,[16] and to have been allowed to retain their faith undisturbed, but the building of new temples was held to be illegal.[17] Though during the later Muhammadan conquests there was a considerable destruction of Hindu temples, the settled Muhammadan governments appear often to have respected the state endowments granted by the former Hindu rulers to religious foundations, as was done in the case of the temple of Brahmanābād in the province of Sind, where Muhammadan rule was first established in India. At a much later date, in the 16th cent., the Muhammadan government of Bengal is said to have raised the large sum of £100,000 a year by licensing the worship of Jagannāth in Orissa,[18] and even Ḥaidar 'Alī and Tīpū Sulṭān, usually so notorious for their

1 See *RHR* xxxvii. [1898] 178 f.
2 See art. PERSECUTION (Muhammadan).
3 C. Snouck Hurgronje, 'Le Droit musulman,' *RHR* xxxvii. 174–184; I. Goldziher, *Die Ẓâhiriten*, Leipzig, 1884, p. 94 ff., *Vorlesungen über den Islam*, Heidelberg, 1910, pp. 51–53, 183–185.
4 x. 20. 5 ii. 209. 6 xxxiii. 40. 7 iii. 19. 8 xlii. 13–14. 9 xxix. 45. 10 xxii. 66–67. 11 ix. 6. 12 xvi. 37. 13 ii. 257.
14 x. 99, 100; cf. xvi. 84, xxiv. 53, xlii. 47, and lxiv. 12.

1 Cætani, *Annali dell' Islām*, ii. 351.
2 Balādhurī, *Futūḥ al Buldān*, p. 71.
3 ii. 59, v. 73.
4 Al-Nadīm, *Kitāb al-Fihrist*, ed. G. Flügel, Leipzig, 1871–72, i. 320.
5 Al-Nawawī, *Biographical Dictionary*, ed. F. Wüstenfeld, Göttingen, 1842–47, p. 725.
6 Chwolsohn, *Die Ssabier und der Ssabismus*, ii. 537 f.
7 *Ib.* i. 232. 8 Balādhurī, pp. 71 (*fin.*), 79, 80.
9 D. Menant, 'Les Zoroastriens de Perse,' *RMM* iii. [1907] 212.
10 Chwolsohn, i. 287.
11 Mas'ūdī, *Les Prairies d'Or*, Paris, 1861–77, iv. 86; see art. GABARS.
12 Al-Nadīm, p. 338.
13 iv. 115–120, xxi. 98–100, lxvi. 9, etc.
14 Abū Yūsuf, *Kitāb al-Kharāj*, p. 73.
15 Balādhurī, p. 80, lines 16–17.
16 Elliot, *The Hist. of India*, i. 176, 476.
17 *Ib.* iii. 380.
18 W. W. Hunter, *A Statistical Account of Bengal*, xviii. [London, 1877] p. 190.

intolerance towards their Hindu subjects, made grants of money to the monastery of Śringēri, one of the most famous shrines in S. India.[1] The same tradition survives in present Muhammadan states in India, such as Ḥaidarābād and Bahāwalpūr, which still assign revenues for the support of Hindu temples.[2]

Even in such a barbarous country as Baluchistān the Hindus enjoyed religious toleration in consideration of their payment of *jizyah*. 'They were free from persecution and molestation; in any dispute with the tribesmen they could appeal to their protector or the headman for a fair hearing and a fair settlement; the honour of their women was respected; their religion was tolerated; no one tampered with their customs.'[3]

The non-Muslim living under a Muhammadan government was styled a *dhimmī* (lit. 'one with whom a compact has been made'), and the conditions under which he lived were supposed to be regulated by the agreements made with the Muslim conquerors as they extended their dominion over various cities and districts. As an example of such an agreement, the conditions may be quoted that are said to have been drawn up when Jerusalem came under Muslim rule in A.D. 638:

'In the name of God, the Merciful, the Compassionate! This is the security which 'Umar, the servant of God, the commander of the faithful, grants to the people of Aelia. He grants to all, whether sick or sound, security for their lives, their possessions, their churches and their crosses, and for all that concerns their religion. Their churches shall not be changed into dwelling-places, nor destroyed, neither shall they nor their appurtenances be in any way diminished, nor the crosses of the inhabitants nor aught of their possessions, nor shall any constraint be put upon them in the matter of their faith, nor shall any one of them be harmed.'[4]

The theory was that the *dhimmī*, in return for tribute paid and in consideration of good behaviour, received protection from the Muslim government and immunity for life, property, and religion. Tradition attributed to the Prophet a warning against the disregard of this compact: 'Whoever wrongs one with whom a compact has been made [*i.e.* a *dhimmī*] and lays on him a burden beyond his strength, I shall be his accuser.'[5] 'Whoever torments the *dhimmīs*, torments me.'[6] A similar consideration for them was shown by the khalīfah 'Umar, who in his testament enjoined on his successor: 'I commend to your care the *dhimmīs* of the Apostle of God; see that the agreement with them is kept, and that they be defended against their enemies, and that no burden be laid upon them beyond their strength.'[7] Similarly, 'Alī, when he appointed Muḥammad b. Abī Bakr governor of Egypt in 36 A.H., bade him do justice to the *dhimmīs*.[8] In a like spirit, the Turkish code ordains that the *dhimmīs* are not to be disturbed in the exercise of their religion.[9]

The actual practice appears to have varied according to local conditions and the character of the local government; and by the 2nd cent. of the Hijra, when some codification was made of the law relating to the *dhimmīs*, more harsh and intolerant regulations had come into force than those of earlier times. But in the first century of Arab rule the various Christian churches enjoyed a toleration and a freedom of religious life such as had been unknown for generations under the Byzantine government. We have the contemporary testimony of the Nestorian patriarch, Īshō'yabh III. (A.D. 650–660), who, writing to the primate of Persia, says:

'The Arabs, to whom God at this time had given the empire of the world, behold, they are among you, as ye know well; and yet they attack not the Christian faith, but, on the contrary, they favour our religion, do honour to our priests and the saints of the Lord, and confer benefits on churches and monasteries.'[1]

Indeed, the Church to which this ecclesiastic belonged exhibited a remarkable expansion under Muhammadan rule; missionaries were sent from Persia to China and India, both of which were raised to the dignity of metropolitan sees in the 8th cent.; about the same period the Nestorians gained a footing in Egypt, and later spread the Christian faith right across Asia, and by the 11th cent. had gained many converts from among the Tatars.[2] But by the 2nd cent. of the Muhammadan era the condition of the Christians had become less tolerable. The victorious armies that established Arab rule over Syria and Persia appear to have been little swayed by religious considerations, and under the rule of the Umayyads the Christian and other non-Muslim religious communities seem to have been little regarded except as sources of revenue; but under the 'Abbāsids a change in the attitude of the government made itself felt. The orthodox reaction which supported this dynasty and the union of the spiritual and temporal power which characterized it tended to make the administration of the existing laws more oppressive. In the course of the long struggle with the Byzantine empire the khalīfahs had had occasion to distrust the loyalty of their Christian subjects, and the treachery of the emperor Nikephoros was not improbably one of the reasons for the harsher treatment initiated by Hārūn al-Rashīd (786–809), who ordered the Christians to wear a distinctive dress and give up to Muslims the government posts which they held. But the prescriptions of the jurists and theologians[3] were often more intolerant than the actual practice of the government, and it would be rash to assume that the treatment meted out to the non-Muslim population corresponded exactly with the principles which they laid down. Hārūn's great jurist, Abū Yūsuf,[4] leaves no alternative to the Arabs of the Riddah (*i.e.* the Defection, after the death of the Prophet) or to the idolatrous Arabs, except death or the acceptance of Islām, but Cætani[5] has proved that the early conquerors had no power to enforce such a principle, and historical facts do not show that any such alternative was actually imposed on the heathen Arabs.

But protests against cruelty towards the *dhimmīs* are not wanting in the works of Muslim legists themselves; *e.g.*, Abū Yūsuf[6] claims for the *dhimmīs* gentle treatment; they are not to be beaten when called upon to pay *jizyah*, or to be made to stand in the sun, or to be tormented in any way; and he makes an earnest appeal to his patron, Hārūn, on their behalf:

'It is incumbent on the commander of the faithful (may God grant thee his aid!) that thou deal gently with those that have a covenant with thy Prophet and thy cousin, Muḥammad (the peace and blessing of God be upon him!), and that thou take care that they be not wronged or ill-treated and that no burden be laid upon them beyond their strength, and that no part of their belongings be taken from them beyond what they are in duty bound to pay, for it is related of the Apostle of God (the peace and blessing of God be upon him!) that he said, Whosoever wrongs one with whom a compact has been made [*i.e.* a *dhimmī*] or imposes a burden on him beyond his strength, I shall be his accuser on the day of judgment.'[7]

Ibn Qāsim al-Ghazzī († 1512) maintains that the majority of Muslim jurists hold that the *dhimmī* must be treated with kindness and consideration and not with contempt, when he comes to pay the

1 *Annual Report of the Mysore Archæological Department for the Year 1916*, Bangalore, 1917, pp. 73–75.
2 M. A. Macauliffe, *The Sikh Religion*, Oxford, 1909, v. 246; *Punjab States Gazetteers*, vol. xxxviA. [Lahore, 1908] p. 183.
3 *Census of India, 1911*, vol. iv. [Calcutta, 1913], *Baluchistan*, pt. i. p. 175.
4 Ṭabarī, i. 2405.
5 Balādhurī, p. 162; Yaḥyā b. Ādam, *Kitāb al-kharāj*, Leyden, 1896, p. 54, *ad fin.*
6 Al-Makīn, *Historia Saracenica*, Leyden, 1625, p. 11.
7 Abū Yūsuf, p. 71.
8 Ṭabarī, i. 3247, line 1; cf. his instructions to Ma'qil b. Qays, i. 3430, line 14.
9 M. d'Ohsson, *Tableau général de l'empire othoman*, Paris, 1820, iii. 44.

1 J. S. Assemani, *Bibliotheca Orientalis*, Rome, 1719–28, vol. iii., pt. i., p. 131.
2 J. Labourt, *De Timotheo I. Nestorianorum Patriarcha*, Paris, 1904, p. 37 ff.
3 See art. PERSECUTION (Muhammadan).
4 P. 73, *ad fin.*
5 ii. 829, v. 337 f. 6 P. 70. 7 P. 71.

jizyah.[1] Commenting on this passage nearly two centuries later, al-Birmāwī († 1694) enters a protest against such fanatical glosses on *Qur'ān*, ix. 29, as are referred to in art. PERSECUTION, and holds that the phrase 'being humbled' implies only conformity to the regulations of Islām in regard to the *dhimmīs*, and that these words give no justification for the rough treatment sometimes inflicted on a *dhimmī* when he paid *jizyah*—*e.g.*, that he should be made to stand with bent head and back before the collector of the tax, who should slap his face and pull his beard—for (as he rightly says) there is no evidence that the Prophet or any one of the khalīfahs acted in such a manner.[2]

A powerful influence in the direction of toleration in a period when feeling was acerbated against the Christians, and when the disorder in Muhammadan administration made their position more precarious and exposed them to the tyranny of local officials, was the extension of the religious orders, especially that of the Qādiriyyah, and the popularizing of that mystical presentation of religious thought in which devout Muslims found consolation after the devastations of the Mongol conquests. 'Abd al-Qādir al-Jīlānī († 1166), the founder of the order referred to, emphasized the virtues of charity and meekness, and his attitude and that of his followers towards the Christians was kindly and sympathetic.[3] The tendency of Persian mysticism was opposed to any emphasizing of religious differences, and the teaching of the poets who wrote under the influence of this mystical movement often made for tolerance; a well-known example is the story of Abraham in Sa'dī's *Būstān*,[4] in which the patriarch is rebuked by God for refusing his charity to an aged fire-worshipper on the ground of his infidelity. But in the present article attention may rather be drawn to instances of toleration in contrast to the fanatical usage of legislation; *e.g.*, though the so-styled Pact of 'Umar[5] forbade the building of new churches, there was considerable variation of opinion among the Muslim legists themselves on this question, from the more liberal Ḥanafī doctrine, which declared that, though it was unlawful to build churches and synagogues in Muslim territory, those already existing could be repaired if they had been destroyed or had fallen into decay, while in villages where the tokens of Islām were not apparent new churches and synagogues might be built, to the intolerant Ḥanbalī ruling that they might neither be erected nor be restored when damaged or ruined. Some legists held that the privileges varied according to treaty rights: in towns taken by force no new houses of prayer might be erected by *dhimmīs*, but, if a special treaty had been made, the building of new churches and synagogues was allowed. But, like so many of the lucubrations of Muslim legists, these prescriptions bore but little relation to actual facts. Schoolmen might agree that the *dhimmīs* could build no houses of prayer in a city of Muslim foundation, but the civil authority permitted the Copts to erect churches in the new capital of Cairo. The fact that 'Umar b. 'Abd al-'Azīz (717–720) ordered the destruction of all recently constructed churches, and that more than a century later the fanatical al-Mutawakkil (847–861) had to repeat the same order, shows how little the prohibition of the building of new churches was put into force; and both Christian and Muhammadan historians record numerous instances of the erection of new churches, some of them buildings of great magnificence.[1] Al-Muqtadir (908–932) even gave orders himself for the rebuilding of some churches at Ramlah in Palestine, which had been destroyed by Muhammadans during a riot.[2]

Muslim law made death the punishment for apostasy (*q.v.*), and the convert to Islām was not allowed to return to his former faith, but instances are not unknown of a more tolerant view vindicating freedom of conscience in such cases.

Even the mad Ḥākim (996–1020), whose persecutions caused many Jews and Christians to abandon their faith, ordered the churches that had been destroyed to be rebuilt, and the property settled on the churches that had been taken from the Christians to be restored to them, and allowed the unwilling converts to return to their old faith.[3] It is stated by more than one Muhammadan writer that Moses Maimonides under the fanatical rule of the Almohads in Spain feigned conversion to Islām, but fled to Egypt and there openly declared himself to be a Jew; that towards the end of his life a Muslim jurisconsult from Spain denounced him for his apostasy and demanded that the extreme penalty of the law should be inflicted on him for this offence; but the case was quashed by al-Qāḍī al-Fāḍil 'Abd al-Raḥīm b. 'Alī (one of the most famous of Muslim judges and prime minister of Saladin), who authoritatively declared that a man who had been converted to Islām by force could not rightly be considered to be a Muslim.[4] Jewish writers, jealous for the honour of their great co-religionist, have disputed the accuracy of this story, though the first who narrates it, Ibn al-Qiftī, was himself a contemporary of Maimonides;[5] but in reference to Muhammadan toleration it is of interest to note that the decision of al-Qāḍī al-Fāḍil is reported without contradiction or condemnation. In the same spirit, when Ghāzān, ilkhān of Persia (1295–1304), discovered that the Buddhist monks who had become Muhammadans at the beginning of his reign (when their temples had been destroyed) only made a pretence of being converted, he granted permission to all those who so wished to return to Tibet, where among their Buddhist fellow-countrymen they would be free once more to follow their own faith. J. B. Tavernier[6] tells a similar story of some Jews of Ispahan who were so grievously persecuted by the governor 'that either by force or cunning he caused them to turn Mahometans; but the king (Shāh 'Abbās II. [1642–1667]), understanding that only power and fear had constrained them to turn, suffer'd them to resume their own religion and to live in quiet.' The Yazīdīs who were forced to accept Islām under the oppressive rule of Badr Khān Beg in 1844, were permitted by an imperial firman to return to their own creed three years later.[7]

The practice of Muhammadan governments seems, generally, to have been to leave to each separate protected community the management of its internal affairs, and to permit the religious leaders to administer the laws as to marriage, inheritance, etc., in accordance with the ordinances of the particular faith as accepted by the persons concerned, in some instances in criminal cases also,[8] though, according to Abū Ḥanīfah, there was no obligation resting on the Muhammadan government to recognize the decisions of such a judge or on the *dhimmīs* to conform to them.[9] But, if an appeal was made to the Muslim judge, he would decide the case on the basis of the Qur'ān and Muslim law, and some jurists held that the State could even insist on the application of Muslim law in cases of inheritance in which the public treasury would thereby derive more benefit than if the special law of the *dhimmīs* concerned

1 *Fatḥ al-Qarīb*, ed. L. W. C. van den Berg, Leyden, 1894, p. 625 f.
2 *Ḥāshiya 'alā sharḥ Ibn Qāsim al-Ghazzī*, Cairo, 1879, p. 326.
3 T. W. Arnold, *The Preaching of Islam*[2], p. 329.
4 ii. 37–54, ed. C. H. Graf, Vienna, 1858, p. 142 f.
5 See art. PERSECUTION (Muhammadan), vol. ix. p. 767.

1 For examples see Arnold, *The Preaching of Islam*[2], pp. 66–68.
2 Eutychius, *Annales*, ed. L. Cheikho, Paris, 1906–09, ii. 82.
3 Ibn Khallikān, *Biographical Dictionary*, tr. MacGuckin de Slane, Paris, 1843–71, iii. 451.
4 Ibn al-Qiftī, *Ta'rīkh al-Ḥukamā'*, ed. J. Lippert, Leipzig, 1903, p. 318, line 5, p. 319, lines 16–19; Abu'l-Faraj, *Ta'rīkh Mukhtaṣar al-Duwal*, Beirut, 1890, p. 417 f.; Ibn Abī Uṣaybi'ah, *'Uyūn al-anbā' fī ṭabaqāt al-aṭibbā'*, ed. A. Müller, Königsberg, 1884, ii. 117.
5 See A. Berliner, 'Zur Ehrenrettung des Maimonides,' in *Moses ben Maimon: sein Leben, seine Werke und sein Einfluss. Zur Erinnerung an den siebenhundertsten Todestag des Maimonides*, Leipzig, 1914, ii. 103 ff.
6 *Six Voyages through Tartary into Persia and the East Indies*, Eng. tr., London, 1677, p. 160.
7 G. P. Badger, *The Nestorians and their Rituals*, London, 1852, i. 133 f.
8 Arnold[2], p. 146.
9 Mawardī, *Constitutiones Politicæ*, ed. M. Enger, Bonn, 1853, p. 108 f.

were applied.[1] It is recorded of Khayr b. Nu'aym, a judge in Egypt about the middle of the 8th cent., that, after hearing the cases of the Muslims inside the mosque, he would sit on the steps outside the gate in the afternoon and hear the cases of the Christians and Jews, testing the value of the evidence of the witnesses by inquiring into their credibility among their co-religionists.[2]

An important testimony to the toleration of Muslim rule is the fact that persecuted Christian and other sects took refuge in Muhammadan lands, to enjoy there the undisturbed exercise of their several cults. When the Byzantine emperor, Leo, in 714, instituted a persecution against the Montanists and the Jews, forcibly compelling them to submit to baptism, while some burnt themselves alive rather than suffer the loss of religious freedom, others fled for safety into the neighbouring Arab territory.[3] The persecuted Spanish Jews at the end of the 15th cent. took refuge in Turkey in enormous numbers.[4] The Calvinists of Hungary and Transylvania and the Unitarians of the latter country long preferred to submit to the Turks rather than fall into the hands of the fanatical house of Hapsburg;[5] and the Protestants of Silesia in the 17th cent. looked with longing eyes towards Turkey and would gladly have purchased religious freedom at the price of submission to Muslim rule.[6] The Cossacks, who belonged to the sect of the Old Believers and were persecuted by the Russian State Church in 1736, found in the dominions of the sultan the toleration which their Christian brethren denied them.[7]

Of toleration in the Muhammadan world generally it may be said that it was more operative in the earlier centuries of the Hijra than in the days of the decline of the khalifate or the unhappy period of the Mongol conquests or in modern times when the pressure of Christian Powers exasperated Muslim feeling. The civil government has as a rule been more tolerant than the clergy, and the regulations of jurists have seldom been put into force with all their rigour; though practice has varied with time and place, the persecutions[8] that have occurred have been excited by some special and local circumstances rather than inspired by a settled principle of intolerance. The judgment of A. de Gobineau is on the whole justified by the facts of history:

'Si l'on sépare la doctrine religieuse de la nécessité politique qui souvent a parlé et agi en son nom, il n'est pas de religion plus tolérante, on pourrait presque dire plus indifférente sur la foi des hommes, que l'Islam. Cette disposition organique est si forte qu'en dehors des cas où la raison d'Etat mise en jeu a porté les gouvernements musulmans à se faire arme de tout pour tendre à l'unité de foi, la tolérance la plus complète a été la règle fournie par le dogme. . . . Qu'on ne s'arrête pas aux violences, aux cruautés commises dans une occasion ou dans une autre. Si on y regarde de près, on ne tardera pas à y découvrir des causes toutes politiques ou toutes de passion humaine et de tempérament chez le souverain ou dans les populations. Le fait religieux n'y est invoqué que comme prétexte et, en réalité, il reste en dehors.'[9]

To this sober conclusion of the historian may be added the eloquent outburst of one of the Spanish Muhammadans who was driven out of his native country on the occasion of the last expulsion of the Moriscoes in 1610:

'Did our victorious ancestors ever once attempt to extirpate Christianity out of Spain, when it was in their power? Did they not suffer your forefathers to enjoy the free use of their rites at the same time that they wore their chains? Is not the absolute injunction of our Prophet, that whatsoever nation is conquered by Musalman steel, should, upon the payment of a moderate annual tribute, be permitted to persevere in their own pristine persuasion, how absurd soever, or to embrace whatever belief they themselves best approved of? If there may have been some examples of forced conversions, they are so rare as scarce to deserve mentioning, and only attempted by men who had not the fear of God, and the Prophet, before their eyes, and who, in so doing, have acted directly and diametrically contrary to the holy precepts and ordinances of Islam which cannot, without sacrilege, be violated by any who would be held worthy of the honourable epithet of Musalman. . . . You can never produce, among us, any bloodthirsty, formal tribunal, on account of different persuasions in points of faith, that anywise approaches your execrable Inquisition. Our arms, it is true, are ever open to receive all who are disposed to embrace our religion; but we are not allowed by our sacred Alcoran to tyrannize over consciences. Our proselytes have all imaginable encouragement, and have no sooner professed God's Unity and His Apostle's mission but they become one of us, without reserve; taking to wife our daughters, and being employed in posts of trust, honour and profit; we contenting ourselves with only obliging them to wear our habit, and to seem true believers in outward appearance, without ever offering to examine their consciences, provided they do not openly revile or profane our religion: if they do that, we indeed punish them as they deserve; since their conversion was voluntarily, and was not by compulsion.'[1]

LITERATURE.—Balādhurī, *Futūḥ al-Buldān*, ed. M. J. de Goeje, Leyden, 1866; Ṭabarī, *Annals*, ed. M. J. de Goeje and others, do. 1879–1901; Abū Yūsuf Ya'qūb b. Ibrāhīm, *Kitāb al-Kharāj*, Cairo, 1302 A.H.; Michael the Elder, *Chronique de Michel le Syrien*, ed. J. B. Chabot, 4 vols., Paris, 1899–1901; L. Cætani, *Annali dell' Islām*, Milan, 1905–14; H. A. Gibbons, *The Foundation of the Ottoman Empire*, Oxford, 1916, pp. 73–81; A. de la Jonquière, *Hist. de l'Empire Ottoman*, new ed., 2 vols., Paris, 1914; H. M. Elliot, *The Hist. of India, as told by its own Historians*, 8 vols., London, 1872–77; D. Chwolsohn, *Die Ssabier und der Ssabismus*, St. Petersburg, 1856; George Campbell, *Handy Book on the Eastern Question*, London, 1876, ch. ii.–iv.; Sidney Whitman, *Turkish Memories*, do. 1914, ch. xii.; T. W. Arnold, *The Preaching of Islam*[2], 1913; Cherāgh 'Alī, *The Proposed Political, Legal and Social Reforms in the Ottoman Empire and other Mohammadan States*, Bombay, 1883; J. Denais, 'Le Fanatisme en Turquie,' *La Nouvelle Revue*, cvii. [1897]; Aḥmad Riza, *Tolérance musulmane*, Paris, 1897; Ahmad Zakī Beg, 'Al-muslimūna wa'l-dhimmiyūna wa'l-mu'āhidūna,' *Al-Muqtabas*, iv. [Cairo, 1908] 251 ff.; Muḥammad b. Muṣṭafā b. al-Jazā'irī, *Al-iqāmat al-barahīn al-'iẓām 'alā nafy al-ta 'aṣṣub al-dīnī fi'l-islām*, Algiers, 1319 A.H. (A.D. 1902); L. Cheikho, 'Uhūd nabiyyi 'l-islām wa'l-khulafā'i 'l-rāshidīn li 'l-naṣārā,' *Al-Mashriq*, xii. [Beirut, 1909] 609 ff., 674 ff.; Muḥammad Shiblī Nu'mānī, *Huqūq al-dhimmiyyīna*, Amritsar, 1911; Carra de Vaux, *La Doctrine de l'Islam*, Paris, 1909, p. 152 ff.; F. Giese, *Die Toleranz des Islam*, Weimar, 1915. T. W. ARNOLD.

TOLSTÓY.— I. Early life and manhood.—Lev Nikoláevich Tolstóy (1828–1910), novelist, social reformer, and religious mystic, was born on 28th Aug. (O.S.), 1828, at Yásnaya Polyána ('Bright Glade'), the home of the family, in the government of Tula, about 130 miles south of Moscow. Lev was the youngest of four sons. His mother having died when he was three, and his father five or six years later, the boy went in 1840 to the university town of Kazán in eastern Russia, where he lived under the charge of an aunt, whom he held in grateful remembrance. After two years' study he left the university without a degree. The blame is usually laid upon the professors, but some portion of it must be attributed to Tolstóy's own dissipated and irregular life. Returning to his estate, he interested himself in the life of his peasants, with the disappointing results recorded some years later in his *A Morning of a Landed Proprietor* (1856). He admits that he did not really know their life, and that he was aiming at their betterment only from the outside. It was, however, the beginning of that interest in 'the people' which led him at last to throw in his lot with the peasants and the poor. In 1851, to escape from the idle dissipation of his class, he fled to the Caucasus, where he wrote his earliest works—*Childhood*, *A Morning of a Landed Proprietor*, and *The Incursion*—and planned *The Cossacks*, sold ten years later to pay a gambling debt.

Childhood (1852), *Boyhood* (1854), and *Youth*

1 *REJ* xxix. [1894] 209–211.

2 Al-Kindī, *Kitāb al-Quḍāh*, ed. R. Guest, London, 1912, p. 351.

3 Michael the Elder, ii. 489–490; Theophanes, *Chronographia* (*PG* cviii. 810, 812).

4 La Jonquière, *Hist. de l'empire ottoman*, new ed., ii. 501.

5 *Ib.* i. 266; J. Scheffler, *Türcken-Schrifft*, 1664, § 45 f.; T. Gasztowtt, *La Pologne et l'Islam*, Paris, 1907, p. 51.

6 Scheffler, § 48.

7 La Jonquière, ii. 482.

8 See art. PERSECUTION (Muhammadan).

9 *Les Religions et les philosophies dans l'Asie centrale*, Paris, 1865, p. 24 f.

1 J. Morgan, *Mahometism Explained*, London, 1723–25, ii. 297 f., 345.

(1856) form an autobiographical fragment, thinly disguised under fictitious names. Here, as elsewhere, Tolstóy doubles himself, to bring out the dual nature, the natural and the spiritual man of which he was always conscious in himself. Irténev represents the lower nature, his friend Nekhlyúdov the higher. The latter reappears in the *Landed Proprietor* and in *Resurrection*, just as in *War and Peace* Pierre Bezúkhi, and in *Anna Karénin* Konstantín Levín, are Tolstóy himself in that struggle between flesh and spirit which ended only with life. There is truth in Leo Wiener's statement that even the Christ of his religious writings is still the image of the author, and that 'it is Christ-Tolstóy that becomes the final and lasting stage of his spiritual evolution.'[1] This autobiographical fragment reveals Tolstóy as an awkward child, morbidly sensitive to his appearance; a boy, confessing frankly every shade of evil in his heart, such as the rise of sexual feeling; and a youth 'in search of an ideal,' whose one faith was in the possibility of virtuous perfectibility. Beyond this, his creed, though retaining the forms of the Orthodox Church, had become dust, ready to crumble at a touch. Yet we see the beginnings of many things which appear and reappear in his writings to the end—a shame of being rich while others want, a deep hatred of injustice, and the clear poetic vision of Nature and her loveliness.

The Cossacks (1863) represents Tolstóy's revulsion from the artificial and vicious life of cities and his class. The natives had their vices, but they sinned naturally and frankly, and thus escaped the deeper corruption of hidden immorality. In contrast with their bold outdoor life, Tolstóy saw himself (the Olénin of the story) as a degenerate weakling.

Joining the army in 1851, Tolstóy commanded a battery at Sevastopol; and in his three sketches —*Sevastopol in December, 1854, Sevastopol in May, 1855, Sevastopol in August, 1855*—we find the seeds of thought that were to fructify in his *War and Peace*, and many an indignant denunciation of the violence by which nations are governed. The conviction of the sheer wickedness and brutality of war sank deep into his soul and grew with the years. The sketches probably saved his life; by the emperor's orders the young man was removed to a place of safety. On the fall of Sevastopol in 1855 he was sent with dispatches to St. Petersburg, and his career as a soldier came to an end.

Of this period, and up to his marriage in 1862, Tolstóy could never afterwards think without shame. Between 1857 and 1861 he travelled in Germany, France, Italy, Switzerland, England, and Belgium, to study their educational methods, wrote many books on education, and started schools for peasant children on his estate. Yet alongside this generous interest in 'the people' the tides of the passions of the natural man never ceased to flow. His own words in his *My Confession*[2] frankly reveal this moral duality:

> 'I cannot recall those years without dread, loathing, and anguish of heart. I killed people in war and challenged to duels to kill; I lost money at cards, wasting the labour of the peasants; I punished them, fornicated, and cheated. Lying, stealing, acts of lust of every description, drunkenness, violence, murder—there was not a crime which I did not commit, and for all that I was praised, and my contemporaries have regarded me as a comparatively moral man. Thus I lived for ten years.'

On 23rd Sept. 1862 Tolstóy married Sófiya, second daughter of a Dr. Behrs of Moscow, who bore him thirteen children, several of whom died in infancy. Fifteen years of unbroken domestic happiness followed. Tolstóy was busy with his schools, his works on education, the management of his estate, and, above all, the writing of his greatest novels, *War and Peace* (1864-69) and *Anna Karénin* (1873-77), in which appear all the problems round which his mind never ceased to work—war, the peasants, the land and the serfs, education, the universal duty of manual labour, and, at the root of all, religion and the ethical duties flowing therefrom. Then suddenly, to the dismay of the literary world, Tolstóy cast aside the art in which he was acknowledged the greatest living master, and devoted the remainder of his life to moral and religious tales for peasants and children, and an examination of the Gospels, the Creed, and the foundations of violence on which he believed the entire system of civil government rested. His literary ambitions had been treason to the deepest convictions of his soul. The literary caste set up to teach what they did not know, and for the sake of his family he had shared their delusions:

> 'The new conditions of my happy family life completely drew me away from all search for the general meaning of life. All my life during that time was centred in my family, my wife, my children, and, therefore, in cares for the increase of the means of existence. The striving after perfection, which before had given way to the striving after perfection in general, after progress, now gave way simply to the striving after making it as comfortable as possible for me and my family. Thus another fifteen years passed.'[1]

The struggle to break away from this treason to the higher life led to great family unhappiness, and ultimately to his mysterious and tragic end.

2. Ethical and religious ideas.—Tolstóy's principal works after his 'conversion' are *My Confession* (1879-82), *Critique of Dogmatic Theology* (1880-82), *The Four Gospels Harmonized and Translated* (3 vols., 1880-82), *My Religion* (1884), *What shall we do then?* (1884-86), *Moral and Religious Tales, The Kingdom of God is within you* (1893), *What is Art?* (1897), and *Resurrection* (1899), his last great novel, in which he sums up his indictment of Church and State and the entire structure of society. It is from this vast mass of literature that we must now attempt to deduce the religious and ethical convictions into which, with endless vacillations, Tolstóy finally settled.

(1) Tolstóy's fundamental conviction is that the one purpose of life is to know God by bringing all relations of humanity into harmony with His will. In reply to the decree of the Holy Synod which excommunicated him in 1901 he states his creed:

> 'I believe in God, whom I understand as Spirit, as Love, as the beginning of everything. I believe that He is in me and I in Him. I believe that God's will is most clearly and comprehensibly expressed in the teaching of the man Christ, whom to understand as God and pray to I consider the greatest blasphemy. I believe that the greatest true good of man is the fulfilment of God's will, but His will is this, that men should love one another and in consequence of this should treat others as they wish that others should treat them, as, indeed, it says in the Gospel that in this is all the law and the prophets. I believe that the meaning of the life of every man is, therefore, only in the augmentation of love in himself; that this augmentation of love leads the individual man in this life to a greater and ever greater good, and gives after death a greater good, the greater the love is in man, and at the same time more than anything else contributes to the establishment of the kingdom of God in the world, that is, of an order of life with which the now existing discord, deception, and violence will give way to free agreement, truth, and brotherly love of men among themselves. I believe that there is but one means for success in love, and that is prayer, not public prayer in temples, which is directly forbidden by Christ (Matt. vi. 5-13), but such as Christ has given us an example of,—solitary prayer, which consists in the establishment and strengthening in our consciousness of the meaning of our life and our independence of everything except God's will.'[2]

(2) Tolstóy warns us that, when he calls God 'Father' and speaks of His 'will,' he is not to be understood as meaning that God is a personal being. He admits that, when he prays, he is inconsistent with his doctrine of the impersonality of God: it is a necessity forced on him by the fact that he himself is a person. The doctrine of the Trinity is blasphemy. Metaphysical speculations conceal God; nothing reveals Him but love in its

[1] *Lev N. Tolstóy: an Analysis of his Life and Works* (*Complete Works of Count Tolstóy*, tr. and ed. L. Wiener, xxiv. 293).
[2] Ch. ii. (*Works*, xiii. 8 f.).

[1] *My Confession*, ch. iii. (*Works*, xiii. 16).
[2] *Answer to the Decree of the Synod* (*Works*, xxiii. 235 f.).

application to human life. The fundamental idea of *The Kingdom of God is within you* is that God is, in every man, the revelation of life and the power by which man lives and acts upon the world. Whatever approves itself to the God within has divine sanction and right. Since God thus acts naturally through man, miracles are impossible.

(3) Tolstóy's conception of Christ passed through many fluctuations. In the Crimea he dreamed of a new Christianity 'purged of dogma and mysticism,' giving happiness here on earth. At his brother Nikoláy's funeral he projected 'a Life of Christ as a Materialist.' After reading a German work on the Gospels he inclined to agree with the author that Christ never existed. In the end, while admitting His existence, he denied indignantly His divinity. 'To recognise Christ as God is to renounce God.'[1] On the theory of His divinity the Temptation becomes absurd—'God is tempted by God Himself.' The miraculous Birth is an invention to cover His mother's shame. The Resurrection is 'a trite, contemptible invention,' contrary to reason and needing the invention of other miracles to support it. He is 'the living Christ' only in the sense in which all men live on in the spirits of those who come after them. Jesus is grouped with other great religious teachers of the world, such as Confucius, Buddha, Lao-tse. These views are asserted with a peculiar earnestness: 'I am standing with one foot in the grave, and I have no need to feign.' The truth is that Tolstóy had almost a personal interest in thus emphasizing the human side of Christ: he found in it those elements of wavering of which he was conscious in himself. The Temptation, the shrinking of His soul at the visit of the Greeks, the agony in the Garden, the cry 'My God, my God' on the Cross, seemed to bring Him nearer to his own weaknesses and vacillations. There was even a moment, he held, when Christ resolved to use violence against violence and advised His followers to sell their garments and buy swords; and it was only in the Garden that He was able to overcome the terrible temptation by prayer.

(4) Tolstóy's attitude to Scripture settled down into acceptance of nothing that did not commend itself to the God within himself. The OT is non-essential to Christianity. The Church doctrine of the infallibility of Scripture—myths, miracles, contradictions, immoral stories, and all—only commits the soul to untruth. Yet he admired the OT stories and the Gospel parables as the highest form of art, taught them to the peasant children in his schools, and advocated that cheap unabridged copies be given them, not one word omitted:

> 'The book of the childhood of the race will always be the best book of the childhood of each man. . . . There is no book like the Bible to open up a new world to the pupil and to make him without knowledge love knowledge.'[2]

After giving elaborate interpretations of the Four Gospels, he warns his readers against all interpretations: let each man read for himself in the spirit of a little child. To get nearer the original meaning he learned Greek; and he used his new-found instrument in the most uncritical and arbitrary way. The Four Gospels were the heart of the Bible; the Sermon on the Mount was the heart of the Gospels; and a few sayings of Christ formed the heart of the Sermon. Whatever in Scripture did not harmonize with these few sayings and Tolstóy's vast 'private interpretation' of them was set aside without scruple as no part of the true original teaching; and, as one has said, if he cleared away superstitions of the Church, he created others of his own.

[1] *Three Letters on Reason, Faith, and Prayer* (*Works*, xxiii. 472).

[2] *The School at Yásnaya Polyána* (*Works*, iv. 308, 310).

(5) In substance, Tolstóy reduces Christianity to five commandments of Christ in the Sermon on the Mount:

(*a*) *Thou shalt not be angry* (Mt 5[21-26]).—He takes this prohibition absolutely, omitting 'without a cause.' It forbids, not killing merely, but the anger from which violence flows. In his own experience he found that contempt was the root of anger; and, since contempt was possible only to inferiors, he strove to divest himself of the worldly possessions, standing, and privileges which gave him a false sense of superiority over those who were sons of the one Father. If it be said that Christ in this passage speaks of the penalty of judgment and fire for this sin, Tolstóy replies that He never prescribed this penalty, the mention of which only indicates the severity of His condemnation of it. In his discussion of Mt 23 he does not seem to recognize that Christ's indignation against the Pharisees must be a breach of His own law against anger, if understood in the absolute sense.

(*b*) *Thou shalt not commit adultery* (Mt 5[27-32]).—Tolstóy interprets the words in v.[32], 'saving for the cause of fornication,' as meaning that the husband by divorcing his wife 'causes her also (as well as himself) to commit adultery.' His views pass through several stages and are influenced by his own early lapses. For the first fifteen years of his married life his ideal for woman was the duty of motherhood. He disapproved of celibacy and held that monogamy is 'the natural law of humanity.' The close of *What shall we do then?* is an impassioned appeal to women to fulfil 'the highest act of life,' the duty of maternity. *Domestic Happiness* (1859), however, warns against basing the happiness of marriage on the romantic fever of the senses called love, from which motherhood is the true escape. This view persists through *War and Peace* and *Anna Karénin*. In the latter a young and beautiful woman, married to a man much older than herself, turns to feed her starved heart to an illicit passion; and the suicide in which she ends is, in the author's intention, far less the punishment of her infidelity to her husband than of her unfaithfulness to her lover and their child—the burning out through jealousy of her lover's affection, and her unworthiness of her own maternity. The *Kreutzer Sonata* (1889) marks the extreme development of his views—a sordid story of the murder of a guilty wife and the acquittal of the husband on the ground that he had merely defended his honour. The title implies that in Tolstóy's view Beethoven's music irritates and hypnotizes soul and sense into crime. His final position is given in his *Epilogue to the Kreutzer Sonata* (1890), written to defend himself against many attacks. In substance, he demands an absolute chastity, whether in the married or in the unmarried life. The teaching of the gospel is 'in the first place that a married man must not be divorced from his wife, in order to take another, and that he must live with the one with whom he has come together (Matt. v. 31–32; xix. 8); in the second place, that for man in general, both married and unmarried man, it is sinful to look upon woman as an object of enjoyment (Matt. v. 28–29), and, in the third place, that for an unmarried man it is better not to marry at all, that is to be absolutely chaste (Matt. xix. 10–12).'[1] He admits, however, that this absolute chastity is not a precept, but an ideal, to which the race is meant to approximate. To the objection that this ideal would annihilate the race he replies coolly, Why not? Both Church and science foretell an end of the world; why should it not come through the increase of virtue?

(*c*) *Thou shalt not swear* (Mt 5[33-37]).—This means much more than mere simplicity and truth of speech: 'Yea, yea; nay, nay.' Christ forbids us to bind ourselves by an oath to any human power or authority. To do so is to abjure the freedom of conscience, which is the divine within us, and to make ourselves the slaves of a human will which may be the enemy of the will of God. It is the deliberate renunciation of Christianity. In short, this command of Christ strikes at the root of all military power, since all armies rest on an oath of allegiance to some human authority; and this plain command the Church explains away, knowing that, if it were obeyed, the entire structure of society, and its own institution as part of it, would fall to the ground.

(*d*) *Resist not evil* (Mt 5[38-42] 7[2-5] etc.).—This doctrine of non-resistance dominates all the rest of Tolstóy's teaching. It was the first command of Christ which he understood, and it opened the meaning of all the others. Physical force, being an outrage on the freedom of conscience, which is the Kingdom of God within the soul, must never be applied to make any man do what he does not wish to do. Compulsory military service, the whole system of civil and criminal law and government, parliaments, courts, judges, police, jails, taxation, even the payment of debts—all stand condemned as unchristian. Property must be abolished, since it rests on force; it is not merely theft, but murder, because human life is the price paid for it. He prophesied the bankruptcy of the present system of violence; and, were he alive, it is conceivable that he would point to the Great War and the horrors of Bolshevism as the fulfilment of his prophecy. Non-resistance is the only way to destroy violence. 'As fire does not put out fire, so evil does not put out evil.' Given a non-resisting community, 'no enemies—neither Germans, nor Turks, nor savages—would kill or torture such people.' His fanatical and uncompromising Russian mind admitted no limits to this doctrine. If he saw a madman attack a child or a horde of savages fall on his own wife and children, this command of Christ forbade him

[1] *Works*, xviii. 430.

absolutely to protect them by force. The worst that can happen by not resisting is death, whereas to resist is to 'act contrary to the law of Christ, which is worse than death.' We need not hesitate to say that this carries the doctrine to the point of insanity. The natural instinct of a normal conscience is to protect the weak and the defenceless from a drunkard or a madman.

(*e*) *Wage no war* (Mt $5^{43-45.48}$, Lk $6^{32f.}$).—The five commandments of Christ form five widening circles: (1) the individual heart—harbour no anger; (2) man and woman, the family—avoid carnal lust; (3) private worldly relations with others—bind the conscience by no oath or promise; (4) relations to the State—resist no evil by force; (5) the human race—regard no nation as your enemy: 'If they make war on you, submit, do good, and wage no war.' It is absurd to say that Christ, who forbade anger to the individual, now allows anger, and murder which is the fruit of anger, to communities and nations.

From the Sevastopol sketches, on through *War and Peace*, *The Kingdom of God is within you*, and innumerable pamphlets, etc., Tolstóy never ceased to strip war of its 'glory' and to hold up its naked falsity, cruelty, and bestiality. Under all its fine names its true purpose is murder. Three causes are named: '(1) the unequal distribution of property, that is, the robbing of one class of people by another, (2) the existence of a military class, that is, of people educated and destined for murder, and (3) the false, for the most part consciously deceptive, religious teaching, in which the young generations are forcibly educated.'[1] Patriotism is the chief war-criminal—a sentiment fostered by pageants which hypnotize the people into 'loyalty,' by alliances with or against other nations, based on an unreal love and a created hate. There is no such thing as a good patriotism, the aim of all patriotism being that of 'Deutschland über Alles,' to exalt our own nation over others, by violence if need be. It is this sentiment that puts into the hands of rulers a diabolic weapon, making possible military conscription and all the cruelties, atrocities, and bestialization of invasions and battlefields. The one remedy is the substitution for love of country of love for man as man, and the refusal of individuals to submit to military service, be the consequences what they may. Tolstóy had a profound distrust of peace congresses and courts of arbitration, because 'the decision of the court of arbitration against the military violence of the states will be executed by means of military violence.'[2]

(6) Following out his doctrine of human freedom, Tolstóy attacked all current forms of education as the forcible ruin of life and ethics. The schools on his estate were based on absolute freedom. The children came when they pleased, sat where they liked, were at liberty to speak, had no home lessons to torture them. Yet the order and attention were perfect. The teaching included walks in the fields, explanations of natural sights and sounds, history, folk-tales, stories and parables from the Bible, by far the finest instrument of education. Tolstóy wrote a series of tales, which had a great success in Russian schools; but he held that it is the peasant children who can teach us to write, not we them: they are nearer the original harmony of beauty, truth, and goodness than men, whose education has been a system of destroying that harmony. His views are summed up thus:

'I am convinced that the school ought not to interfere in that part of the education which belongs to the family; that the school has no right and ought not to reward and punish; that the best police and administration of a school consist in giving full liberty to the pupils to study and settle their disputes as they know best.'[3]

He opposed 'popular education' because it was not popular, but compulsory, based on violence, and hated by both parents and children, who forgot its artificial results as quickly as they could.

'Schools which are established from above and by force are not a shepherd for the flock, but a flock for the shepherd.'[4]

From infant school to university the system was arbitrary, mechanical, and out of relation to life and its needs. To compel all child-natures to pass through a standardized system, without freedom of choice, is torture. In fine, education has become an elaborate system of demoralizing child-nature, which is good, in the interests of the world and its evils. At an early age it severs the natural bond of parent and child, and of the great mother, Nature herself, and it does so in a way which fosters lying, hypocrisy, and vice, and destroys individuality.

(7) In *What is Art?* Tolstóy sweeps aside with contempt all theories of mere æsthetics and 'art for art's sake,' and reduces the criteria of art to the following: (1) art must spring from a genuine feeling in the artist; (2) this feeling must have the power of infecting others with the same emotion; (3) it must have the power of uniting men by this infection of a common hope, joy, love, or whatever it be: if it separates men, it is not art. The more widely it unifies men, the more worthy is it of the name. 'Upper class art,' dependent on an artificial training, springs from no living infectious emotion in the artist, who has to write, paint, etc., to please his rich patrons, who lead idle, artificial, and parasitic lives. Such art grows ever narrower in its appeal, and its patrons ever prouder of its exclusiveness, whereas 'great works of art are only great because they are accessible and comprehensible to every one,' like the story of Joseph and the parables of Christ. Whole generations of artists, singers, poets, players, artisans, workmen, are practically serfs for the production of false exclusive art—an art which is simply the expression of the pride, sensuality, and weariness of life of the men and women who pay them.

All good art, being universal, depends on universal emotions which unify men by infection. What these are is revealed by 'the religious perception' that all human good is contained in 'the fraternal life of all men, our love-union among ourselves.'

Hence 'the Christian art of our time can be and is of two kinds: (1) art transmitting feelings flowing from a religious perception of man's position in the world in relation to God and to his neighbour—religious art in the limited meaning of the term; and (2) art transmitting the simplest feelings of common life, but such, always, as are accessible to all men in the whole world—the art of common life—the art of a people—universal art. Only these two kinds of art can be considered good art in our time.'[1]

The name of art is denied to emotions which divide men, as patriotism, or religious sectarianism, or the honour given for wealth, education, rank, or profession. The theory has met with much ridicule; but, making allowance for some exaggeration in Tolstóy's dislike of the conventional forms in which every art seeks expression, we may agree with Kropotkin that *What is Art?* is a much-needed protest against the over-artificiality into which modern art has drifted.

(8) Tolstóy's doctrine of the future life may be described as a kind of pantheistic immortality. His novels overflow with studies of death and the process of dying. The higher ranks meet death with reluctance and complaining, the poor with cheerfulness and faith. Of Natálya, the old stewardess in the home of his childhood, he says: 'She executed the best and highest act of this life,—she died without regrets or fear.'[2] During the period of his 'conversion' thoughts of suicide became so strong that he had to hide a rope that hung in his dressing-room and could not trust himself to go out hunting with a gun. There was no meaning in life, no end to which it moved. He was saved from suicide by the discovery that the end was God, God in whom he lived, and moved, and was. The fear of death is a 'superstition' due to the fact that men live in a mere fragment of their own nature and of the world, and this the lower fragment of their carnal and personal being, instead of their rational consciousness in its relation to the sum of things, which is God. Life is given to be a ministry of life to the world, and

[1] *Who is to Blame?*, Letter on the Transvaal War (*Works* xxiii. 458).
[2] *Concerning the Congress of Peace* (*Works*, xxiii. 440).
[3] *The School at Yásnaya Polyána* (*Works*, iv. 237).
[4] *On Popular Education* (*Works*, iv. 15).

[1] *What is Art?*, ch. xvi., tr. Aylmer Maude, London, 1905 (of this tr. Tolstóy in a Preface says: 'I request all who are interested in my views on art only to judge of them by the work in its present shape.' The tr. is from the original MS, and is free from the mutilations of the Russian censor).
[2] *Childhood*, ch. xxviii. (*Works*, i. 136).

it lasts just so long as this ministry is being fulfilled. To cast it away in suicide when it becomes unpleasant to us is sinful, partly because just then is probably the time when this ministration truly begins. Moreover, it is in this life of universal ministry that man finds the only true immortality. Personal immortality is impossible, because true life is the deliberate sacrifice of all personal ends. Resurrection and reincarnation would be nothing better than a return to the carnal and personal relations which are spiritual death. Life is an ever onward movement of reason and love, and the only real death is to arrest the movement at any given point. Live onward beyond the old self, and life becomes a living part of the growing good of the world. This is the life eternal and the only true immortality for man.

3. The last phase.—The life of the great Russian ended in a mysterious tragedy of conscience. For many years his life consisted of a struggle to bring his practice into harmony with his principles by escaping from his class, his wealth, his family. In *My Religion*, written in his fifty-sixth year, he lays down five conditions of human happiness: (1) a life that does not break the link with Nature —the open sky, sunlight, fresh air, soil, plants, animals; (2) work, physical labour, giving appetite and sleep; (3) family life; (4) a free and living intercourse with all the various classes of mankind; (5) health, and a natural and painless death. These conditions are open most widely to the peasant, and grow narrower the higher you rise in the privileged classes, the Tsar, *e.g.*, holding intercourse with none but a few of his jailers. Hence Tolstóy's later years were one long effort to transform himself into a peasant; and the asceticism which formed part of his strangely complex nature finally struck out the third condition, the family life. He transferred to his wife the responsibility of managing his estates, and, although he continued to live in the family mansion, it was, as far as possible, as a poor man working with his hands. It was a compromise which gave no peace of conscience. More than once he left his home intending never to return, but family affection always drew him back. The family friction which resulted is portrayed in the form of fiction in *Walk in the Light, while ye have Light* (1888). One's sympathies are not entirely on the husband's side; the countess had much cause for complaining that the burden of the children, the estates, and the publication of his books was transferred to her shoulders. In spite of a true affection between them, they drifted apart.

Tolstóy's actual departure from his home came about through the question of the copyright of his works. From 1882–83 the countess, to counterbalance her husband's neglect of the estates, became the publisher of his writings; and in 1894 she deposited in a public museum for safety large quantities of his manuscripts, producing evidence afterwards that they were given her by Tolstóy. This was done, evidently, to protect herself from a deliberate attempt by one of his disciples, V. G. Tchertkóf, to deprive her of them and of all control of their publication. In 1891 Tolstóy, having convinced himself that to make money by his moral and religious writings was sinful, made public announcement that any one was free to publish his works written from 1881 to the time of his death. About the same time he gave Tchertkóf the right of first publication, in Russian and in English, of his future writings. Although this was almost equivalent to copyright, Tchertkóf was not satisfied with it, and set about a long series of intrigues to induce Tolstóy to make a will in his own favour, and without the knowledge of the countess, on the ground that only through him would his works be published in accordance with his publicly expressed wishes. An unhappy aspect of the affair is that his youngest daughter, Alexandra, was in the intrigue against her mother. After many tentative wills had been drawn up and signed, a final one was made on 22nd July 1910, bequeathing all his productions and the manuscripts themselves into the full possession of his daughter Alexandra. An 'explanatory note' stated his wish that 'all papers extant at the time of his death shall be handed to V. G. Tchertkóf, that he may examine such documents and publish what he may consider suitable.' This will was signed on the stump of a tree near Tchertkóf's house, after a long series of unscrupulous intrigues, and when the old man of eighty-two was fast breaking up in both body and mind. At 5 o'clock on the morning of 28th Oct. 1910 he left his home for ever, accompanied by his daughter Alexandra and his disciple Dr. Makovítsky. His son Ilyá, in his *Reminiscences*[1] of his father, traces his flight to the intolerable moral torture of the dilemma of confessing all to his wife or of repudiating the will. He started with no object but to hide himself somewhere, anywhere. He went first to see his sister Mary, a nun of the Shamárdino convent, and expressed to her his intention of taking a peasant's cottage and living near her; but his daughter, fearing that her mother should discover his whereabouts, carried him off secretly, with the intention of securing a passport and leaving Russia. The old man, however, was nearing his end. At Astápovo he had to be removed to the house of the stationmaster, where he lingered on till the morning of Sunday, 7th Nov. 1910 (20th, N.S.). Tchertkóf, professing to guard him from intrusion, refused to allow the countess—who had learned where he was only through a message from a newspaper office—to see her dying husband until he was in the article of death and past the power of recognizing her.

Thus passed away in darkness the greatest of modern Russians. Nevertheless, he had attained moral and spiritual unity as nearly as was possible to a nature so vast and turbulent. The common idea that his life is broken into two distinct parts is a mistake. His 'conversion' is simply the emerging into clear consciousness of those ideals of truth and right towards which we see him striving even in the midst of his most dissolute life. His fixed idea was God, and, in spite of all appearances, the effort to make God all and in all gave to his life a great and solemn unity. He was like a wild tumultuous river with the fall of the mountains behind it, thwarted by rocks, gorges, precipices, but never ceasing to turn and twist and foam around and over every obstacle in its thirst for the sea.

LITERATURE.—*The Complete Works of Count Tolstóy*, tr. and ed. Leo Wiener, with an *Analysis of his Life and Works*, 24 vols., London and Boston, U.S.A., 1904-05 (vol. xxiv. contains an extensive bibliography in English, German, and French up to date of publication); Aylmer Maude, *Life of Tolstoy*, vol. i., *The First Fifty Years*, London, 1908, vol. ii., *The Later Years*, do. 1910, abridged ed., *Leo Tolstoy*, do. 1918, *Tolstoy and his Problems*, London and New York, 1901; C. E. Turner, *Count Tolstoi as Novelist and Thinker*, London, 1888; C. A. Behrs, *Recollections of Count Leo Tolstoy*, Eng. tr., do. 1893; Paul Birukoff, *Leo Tolstoy: His Life and Work* (autobiographical memoirs, letters, and biographical material, compiled by Paul Birukoff and revised by Leo Tolstoy), Eng. tr., do. 1906; P. A. Sergyeenko, *How Count Tolstoy lives and works*, Eng. tr., do. 1899; *Reminiscences of Tolstoy*, by his son, Count Ilyá Tolstoy, Eng. tr., do. 1914; E. M. de Vogüé, *Le Roman russe*, Paris, 1886, Eng. tr., do. 1913, *Le Tolstoïsme et l'anarchie*, do. 1900; G. H. Perris, *Leo Tolstoy, the Grand Mujik, A Study in Personal Evolution*, London, 1898; C. T. H. Wright, in *EBr*[11], *s.v.*; M. Arnold, *Essays in Criticism*, 2nd ser., London and New York, 1888; G. Brandes, *Impressions of Russia*, Eng. tr., London, 1889; P. Kropotkin, *Russian Literature: Ideals and Realities*, do. 1905; W. E. Henley, *Views and Reviews*, do. 1890; F. Grierson, *Modern Mysticism*, London, New York, Toronto, 1914; C. Sarolea, *Europe's Debt to Russia*, London, 1916; *Review of Reviews Annual, 1906: Tales and Talks of Tolstoy*, ed. W. T. Stead.

J. S. CARROLL.

TOLTECS.

1. Origins.—The beginnings of the Toltec peoples are enveloped in the fogs of mythology. Their origin is rather mysteriously attributed to the acts of a certain hero-god, Quetzalcoatl ('a twin'), compounded of two words *quetzalli*, a plume of green feathers, and *coatl*, a serpent, in other words, a plumed-serpent (-god). Some wild speculations and pious conjectures have identified him with St. Thomas, and others with the Messiah. Another mysterious hero-god (personage) who has been closely linked with Quetzalcoatl was Votan, the reputed founder of the civilization of the Mayas, for a time a contemporary and rival people with the Toltecs.

In the pre-Toltec period of history in Mexico and Central America the Nahua and the Maya were the two leading civilizations. Quetzalcoatl, the plumed-serpent divinity, was the creator of man,[2] the founder of the new order of things among the Nahua peoples. Like the Maya peoples of Yucatan and Central America, the Nahuas did not confine

[1] *Reminiscences of Tolstoy*, Eng. tr., London, 1914.
[2] Bancroft, *NR* iii. 272, 275.

their colonies or activities to any one area of territory, though their main settlement was on the plateau of Mexico. In the 6th and 7th centuries the Toltec Chichimec tribes, representing the Nahua power, migrated from Central America and settled down on the Mexican plateau, in proximity to the wonderful lakes of that region.[1] Of the Nahua tribes who made their homes in this region the Toltecs were one of the prominent sections, the beginnings of whose separate and independent existence cannot be sharply depicted.

2. History.—At the opening of historic times the Toltecs were in possession of Anáhuac (a section of the plateau of Mexico) and outlying territory. While the civilization was old, the name Toltec was new, possibly derived from Tollan or Tulan, the original capital of the empire. The boundary lines of the Toltec sovereignty cannot be fixed, though it probably did not exceed that of the Aztec domain of later times. It is thought to have extended so far west as to have covered Michoacan, which was never conquered by the Aztecs, and stretched eastward to the Gulf of Mexico, including also the Totonac territory of Vera Cruz. The many tribes and peoples of which the Toltec empire was composed cannot be identified by name with any of the later nations found in Anáhuac. Outside the so-called Toltec empire, the peoples, particularly in the north, were regarded as barbarians and were popularly known as Chichimecs.

From the 7th to the 12th cent. the Toltec empire was in the main ruled by a confederacy which resembled the alliance of a later time between Mexico, Tezcuco, and Tlacopan with capitals at Culhuacan, Otompan, and Tollan respectively. Each capital in its turn became the dominant force in the confederacy. Tollan on the river Quetzalatl is reputed to have reached the highest point in culture, splendour, and fame. It is now represented by the little village of Tula, about 30 miles north-west of the city of Mexico. Culhuacan was the only one of the three capitals of the confederacy to survive by name the bloody revolution by which the empire was finally overthrown, and to maintain anything of her earlier greatness. The confusion and often contradiction between the numerous reports and records and manuscripts of the native and Spanish writers lays a heavy burden upon a historian; but Bancroft and Nadaillac are apparently faithful to the best evidence available in those writers. Let us make a survey of the history and constitution of the Toltec empire, so called, during its five centuries of domination in the central plateau of Mexico, based on the representations of Bancroft and Nadaillac.[2]

The pre-eminent personage in the beginnings of this new agglomeration of tribes and peoples was Hueman the prophet. It was through his line that a powerful priesthood ruled the destinies of the Toltec empire from its inception to its downfall. The government was in reality a theocratic republic, in which each leader directed his own tribe both in war and in peace, but all were more or less subservient to their spiritual leader in all matters of national import. Seven years after the arrival of these peoples in Tollan the heads of families and chiefs met in assembly and decided to change their form of government, and establish a monarchy, in order to consolidate their strength against any possible future challenge to their rights as a people. On the advice of Hueman, the chiefs sent an embassy to the reigning king of the Chichimecs to ask for a son or other relative to be crowned king over the Toltecs, accompanied by a specific requirement of agreement on the part of the Chichimec king that the Toltecs should ever be a free and independent people, owing no allegiance whatever to the Chichimecs, although the two powers would enter into an alliance for mutual defence and aid. The Chichimec king was only too ready to seize such an opportunity, and sent back with the embassy his second son with the required guarantees, to be crowned first king of the Toltecs at Tollan under the royal name of Chalchiuh Tlatonac, 'shining precious stone.' This young king, by his splendid bearing, fine character, intelligence, and amiability, immediately won the admiration and affection of the people. His coronation and accession to the throne took place about the first quarter of the 8th cent., between 710 and 720.[1] Immediately after his accession the young king and his counsellors laid down a law that the time limit of a king should be 52 years, at the end of which he should abdicate in favour of his oldest son, to whom he might, however, act as adviser. If the king should die before the time limit had been reached, the unexpired term should be filled by magistrates elected by the people. The next task of the king was to find a wife to provide an heir to the throne, so that the dynasty might be perpetuated. The amiable young king left this choice entirely to his subjects—at least so the records say—to their joyful satisfaction. Their choice fell upon the daughter of Acapichtzin, who himself had been a candidate for the throne when it was proposed to found a kingdom. Two Nahua documents give a rival story of the beginnings of the monarchy, but the main features are not so widely different.[2]

Chalchiuh Tlatonac, the first Toltec king, died at the end of 52 years and was buried in the chief temple, about A.D. 771. His son and successor was Ixtlilcuechahuac. He had a peaceful and prosperous reign. The signal event of his rule, and near its conclusion, was a meeting of all the wise men under the direction of the old prophet Hueman. This assembly collected all the Toltec ancient and modern documents, and after a prolonged conference and careful investigation, compiled the *Teoamoxtli*, 'book of God.' On its pages they inscribed the Nahua annals from the creation down; also their religious rites, their governmental system, laws, and social customs; their methods of agriculture; their arts and sciences, and especially astrology; their methods of computing time and interpreting their writings. To these wealthy pages was added a chapter on the forecast of the future events of the kingdom, including the disaster through which it was crushed and destroyed.

The third king, Huetzin, succeeded to the throne about 823. The fourth king, Totepeuh, sometimes given as the second king of Culhuacan, came to his father's throne at the end of 52 years; and handed it down at the same time limit to his son Nacaxoc, the fifth king at Tollan, who was succeeded by Nauhyotl, or Mitl. This sixth reign stretched over 59 years. During all these six reigns there was great advance made in building new cities, beautifying old cities, erecting new temples, one of especial magnificence at Quauhnahuac and another at Tollan rivalling even the Temple of the Sun at Teotihuacan, a city which surpassed Tollan in extent and beauty. These more than 300 years saw the Toltec empire well and prosperously established over a large territory and many peoples.

Looking back at some of the details of those reigns, we gather a few significant facts. The annals of Culhuacan mention Totepeuh (the fourth Toltec king) as the second king of that city. He waged several successful wars, notably in the province of Huitznahuac, where he found, conquered, and married a princess Chimalman, who bore him an heir named Ceacatl Quetzalcoatl. This notable scion of the royal family succeeded in establishing certain laws of succession which prevailed down to the end of the empire; but the most far-reaching act was the conclusion of an alliance between the crowns of Culhuacan, Otompan, and Tollan. Each king was to be independent in his own domain; but in affairs of general interest the three rulers were to constitute a council, in which the king of Culhuacan was to rank first, with a title almost equivalent to emperor. Otompan took the second rank and Tollan the third. The date of the formation of this confederacy or empire was about A.D. 856.

After Quetzalcoatl had ruled in Culhuacan about ten years, he met obstinate opposition to his authority from his enemies. He was a radical reformer whose ideas ran counter to those of the reigning pontiffs. He modified much of the religious ritual and abolished human sacrifices. These sacrifices had had a first place from pre-Toltec times at Teotihuacan, and more or less general acceptance in Culhuacan and Tollan. He absolutely prohibited them in the temples of Tollan, and so stirred up the enmity of the powerful priesthood of Otompan and Culhuacan. The nobility of Tollan also, who resented the curbing of their religious liberties, became jealous of their brothers of equal rank among other peoples of the empire. Nevertheless, Tollan became the metropolis of the confederacy. In the magnificence of her palaces and temples, in the skill and fame of her artists, if not in her population, Tollan surpassed all her rivals on the plateau. This was too much for the other centres, and active aggressive opposition, political,

[1] *NR* v. ch. iii.
[2] *Pre-historic America*, Eng. tr., new ed., London, 1895.

[1] *NR* v. 244 ff. [2] *Ib.* v. 248–250.

magical, and religious, raised its weapons of warning. Quetzalcoatl's aversion to the shedding of blood is said to have caused the abandonment of his throne, against the ardent wishes of his more warlike friends, and his crossing over to the eastern part of the plateau of Huitzilapan in 895. His successor in Tollan, Nacaxoc, known under several other names, was the fifth king of the Toltecs.

The reign of Nauhyotl, or Mitl, the sixth king of Tollan, was marked with great prosperity and peace. His entire energy and strength were devoted to the promotion of the glory of his city, where he re-affirmed and carried out the reforms of his predecessor. Cholula, a rival sacred city, really stirred him to vigorous action, in building greater temples and more attractive shrines to prevent pilgrimages from Tollan to the rival city. He also built superb temples in other provinces to the south outside the boundaries of Anáhuac.

Nauhyotl, or Mitl, at his death, was succeeded by his queen, Xiuhtlaltzin, who reigned four years. She showed wonderful wisdom and skill in her direction of public affairs, and her death was greatly lamented by her subjects. Her son and successor was Matloccoatl, whose reign covered 949 to 973; he was succeeded by Tlilcoatzin, who ruled from 973 to 994, and who was followed by Tecpancaltzin. The records of this period are almost a blank, except that in Culhuacan Quetzallacxoyatl was succeeded in 953 by Chalchiuh Tlatonac (II.) and the latter in 985 by Totepeuh, the second king of that name.

We now approach the period when the Toltec empire was descending the slopes of ruin. The annals of this period are scarlet with the sanguinary struggles between the powerful tribes and bands from the north and north-west and the civil and religious authorities of the empire. The extensive records of the period of the downfall of the Toltec empire are confusion worse confounded. They abound with tales of marvel and mystery, as if intending to throw dust into the eyes of the reader.

Spanish writers still speak of Tollan as the empire, but Nahua documents find in that city the 'occurrences which caused the destruction of the Toltec power.' Whether this is the truth or not, it seems that a battle was fought between the king of Culhuacan and the king of Tollan, and, while this contest was going on outside the city, a party of invaders was admitted into Tollan. Civil strife followed in the streets between three rival sects, until the city itself was nearly in ruins. The three allied powers fought each other, and later there came a period of famine and pestilence in the land. These events occurred between 1040 and 1047.

Defence was so weakened, the reins of government so loosened, that dependencies took advantage of their opportunity to renounce Toltec authority and declare their independence.

The other Toltec cities of power, Culhuacan, Otompan, and Tezcuco, seem to have gone down before Tollan. Invaders from the north and north-west, from the powerful Chichimec tribes and Nahua peoples, fell upon the weakened Toltecs without mercy and took possession of all their cities and territory. The cities of the confederacy were plundered and burned except Culhuacan, whose king seems to have made a 'delivering' alliance, about A.D. 1060.

The Toltec power was overthrown. The last years of its struggle for existence are inextricably mixed. Plots, intrigues, battles, invasions, assassinations, blot the escutcheon of the once noble kings of the Toltec empire. Many of the nobility of the Toltecs are said to have migrated before the storm burst. They went to foreign provinces with their families, their treasures, and their other movable wealth. But the Toltec peoples of the humbler classes remained in Anáhuac. Some of them are said to have maintained a national existence for a time in Culhuacan, and possibly in Cholula. But they finally became the subjects of the invaders, whose language and customs were probably identical with their own. Even the sanguinary records do not warrant us in believing that the Toltecs as reported were reduced to merely a few thousands in number. The Toltec collapse was the fall of an empire, not the annihilation of a nation. The succeeding period was a struggle to secure the authority which fell from the hands of the Toltec rulers.

3. Physical features and culture.—The Toltecs, we are told,[1] were tall, well built, with clear yellow complexions; their eyes were black, their teeth white, their hair black and glossy, their lips thick, their noses aquiline, and their foreheads receding. They had thin beards, and little hair on their bodies. Their mouths made an agreeable impression, but their facial expression was severe. They were brave, cruel, and vengeful, and their religious rites were sanguinary.

They were intelligent, eager to learn, and are said to have been the first [in Mexico] to construct roads and aqueducts; they used the ordinary metals except iron, cut precious stones, built houses of stone laid up in lime mortars; knew how to spin, weave, and dye cloth; and built mounds similar to those found so plentifully in the Mississippi valley.[2] Their cities were marvels of construction, beauty, and durability. Their temples were ornate with sculptured bas-reliefs and hieroglyphics, cut in porphyry, basalt, and obsidian.

Their commerce was important and pioneering. Their products were exhibited yearly at fairs, spread before the public in the cities of Tollan and Cholula. Though they seemed not to have used iron, they did work in gold, silver, copper, tin, and lead. They were skilled in making fine jewellery, in which precious stones, such as emeralds, turquoises, and amethysts, were mounted. Cholula was famous for its pottery in the form of vases, utensils for the house, idols for the temples, and ornaments for the people.

The weapons used by the Toltecs were slings, bows and arrows, spears, and darts pointed with silex, obsidian, porphyry, copper, or bone. The warriors wore padded cotton armour, practically impenetrable to arrows or javelins, and so heavy that a warrior once fallen could not always get up again. Their round shields of light flexible bamboo were decorated with feathers and covered with cloth or the skins of animals which they had killed in hunting. The shields of the chiefs were decorated with plaques of gold as a mark of their rank.

4. Human sacrifice. — Prisoners of war were often sacrificed to their gods. Funeral ceremonies were also accompanied by the burning of women upon the funeral pile of their husbands; this the women joyfully accepted because it opened to them the door into the first celestial sphere, where they could follow their husbands and thus avoid Mictlan, a gloomy and solitary abode.

5. Religion.—The religious system of the Toltecs is a chaos of ceremonies and ritual, so entangled with the pre-Toltec era and modified in the subsequent Chichimec-Aztec period that little definite and specific can be affirmed beyond those items already mentioned above in § 2. Even the many extracts from native and Spanish writers given by Bancroft and Nadaillac convey merely a hazy idea of the so-called religious systems of the Nahua nations of which the Toltecs were a part. Their multitudinous polytheism only adds to the confusion and attests that religion, mysticism, and mythology were such a conglomerate of everyday life that even the alleged documents of native writers could not disentangle them.

6. Calendar and hieroglyphic language.—The so-called Mexican calendar, found on a block of porphyry uncovered in the old city of Mexico in 1790, probably supplies us with the Aztec astronomical cycle. The Mexicans kept a solar year, and a lunar year only for religious holidays; the latter was divided into periods of thirteen days, corresponding to the phases of the moon.[3] The Toltecs (and Mayas) had a month of twenty days, apparently based on the normal number of a man's fingers and toes.[4] The key to the ancient hieroglyphic language of the peoples of Mexico and Central America, as found on their great monuments at Palenque and Copan and other remarkable ruins, is practically lost.[5] A few signs are known, but, until a sure key is established, we shall have to rely mainly on the native sources, as reported to and by Spanish writers, for any information regarding the hieroglyphic era of the pre-Aztec, and even of the Aztec, peoples.

Even the most comprehensive works on the Toltecs are inadequate and insufficient in method to clear up the problems that native and Spanish authors pour out on the table of the modern student of ancient Mexico.

1 Nadaillac, p. 275 f. 2 *NR* i. 24. 3 Nadaillac, p. 306.
4 See art. CALENDAR (Mexican and Mayan).
5 *NR* ii. 119.

LITERATURE.—(1) *Maya material*: F. S. Clavigero, *The Hist. of Mexico*, Eng. tr., London, 1787; E. K. Kingsborough, *Antiquities of Mexico*, do. 1830–48; C. E. Brasseur de Bourbourg, *Manuscrit Troano*, Paris, 1869–70; *Codex Cortesianus*, Madrid, 1892; J. J. Hoil, *Book of Chilam of Chumayel*, Philadelphia, 1913; E. H. Thompson, 'The Home of a Forgotten Race: the Mysterious Chicheu Itza in Yucatan Mexico,' *National Geographic Magazine*, xxv. [1914] 585–648, 'Aztec Calendar,' *ib.* p. 689; J. Zimmerman, '"Hewers of Stone": Ruins of Mitla, Mexico,' *ib.* xxi. [1910] 1002–1019; A. C. Galloway, 'An Interesting Visit to the Ancient Pyramids of San Juan Teotihuacan,' *ib.* pp. 1041–1049; W. F. Sands, 'Mysterious Temples of the Jungle,' *ib.* xxiv. [1913] 325–338; S. G. Morley, 'Excavations at Quirigua, Guatemala,' *ib.* pp. 339–361; Cyrus Thomas, 'Aids to the Study of the Maya Codices,' *6 RBEW*, 1888, pp. 253–271.

(2) *Codices, Aztec and earlier*: E. T. Hamy, *Codex Telleriano-Remensis*, Paris, 1899; E. Seler, *Codex Fejérváry-Mayer*, Berlin and London, 1901–02, *Codex Vaticanus*, no. 3773, do. 1902–03, *Codex Borgia, eine altmexikanische Bilderschrift*, Berlin, 1904–09.

(3) *Studies of early Mexico*: H. H. Bancroft, *Works*, San Francisco, 1882–90, vols. i.–v., *Native Races*; J. F. A. du P. Nadaillac, *Pre-historic America*, London and New York, 1885.

(4) *Popular reading*: L. Biart, *The Aztecs: their Hist., Manners and Customs*, tr. from French, Chicago, 1886; T. S. Denison, *The Primitive Aryans of America*, do. 1909.

I. M. PRICE.

TOMB.—See DEATH AND DISPOSAL OF THE DEAD.

TONGANS.—**1. Introduction.**—Tonga—or at least the Tonga of this article—is the name of a group of islands in the Western Pacific, lying to the north of New Zealand, the east of New Caledonia, and the south of Fiji and Samoa. It is sometimes known as the Friendly Isles, the name given it by Captain Cook. The Tongans who inhabit this group are a tiny nation of the Polynesian race. Although few in number—about 20,000 only—their nationality is clearly marked, and they can easily be distinguished from their neighbours the Fijians and Samoans. Typical Tongans are tall, large-limbed, of a light coffee colour, with upright forehead and straight hair; but a little acquaintance with them shows that there has been an admixture with a race that was short and had receding foreheads. This agrees with their traditions, which state that, when the Tongans came to the group, some five or six centuries ago, it was already occupied by an aboriginal race. Traces of these have been found in one of the volcanic islands, but the vestiges have not been scientifically examined. Still it is clear that the Tongans, and Polynesians generally, have emigrated from a distance; and the most probable theory is that of Fornander, that they came from the head of the Persian Gulf.

Old navigators used to speak of the Tongans as 'the most splendid savages in existence,' and they were certainly the terror of the neighbouring groups, all of which are said to have been once conquered by them. They acknowledge themselves to be mentally inferior to the European; but it cannot be said that they come very far behind; and occasionally students at Tubou College have achieved results that could be equalled only by the best pupils in English schools. A fair measure of the size of their brains may surely be found in their language, which contains, it is estimated, at least 10,000 words in use. The verbs have about 20 voices, and the pronouns are developed to such an amazing extent that there are more than 100 ways of saying 'our,' against two in English, 'our' and 'our own.' As the adjectives, too, have many degrees of comparison, and there are more than two articles, shades of meaning can be produced to an almost infinite extent. That the Bible translates well into a language like this is not surprising; but geometrical treatises, and such works as Milton's *Paradise Lost*, can also be well rendered.

Physically, then, and mentally, the Tongans stand high; and it comes as a surprise that their spiritual development, as represented by their old religion, was low. Their pantheon was a medley, and their theology unredeemed by any gleams of philosophy as in the religion of India.

2. The gods of Tonga may be divided into three classes.

(1) In common with other parts of Polynesia, their great gods comprise the two groups of the Tangaloa and the Maui (pronounced Mow-y: Mow as in *now*). The *Tangaloa* were the earlier group, and consisted of Tangaloa 'Eiki ('Lord Tangaloa,' or 'Tangaloa the Elder'), Tangaloa Tufunga ('Tangaloa the Smith, Carpenter, or Artificer,' who made axes and built canoes), and Tangaloa 'Atulongolongo ('Tangaloa the Sender-forth-of-sound'). The *Maui* group consisted of five persons: Maui Motu'a ('Old Maui,' or 'Maui the Father'), Maui Loa ('Maui the Tall'), Maui Buku ('Maui the Short'), and Maui 'Atalanga ('Maui the Vigorous Planter'). This last had a son called Maui Kijikiji (pronounced Kitsikitsi: 'Maui the Violent, the Mischievous'), who was, of course, the grandson of Maui Motu'a.

There were, however, older gods than any of these. One was called Tama-bo'uli-ala-mafoa ('Son-of-the-Darkness-that-can-have-a-dawn'). Some accounts represent him as the original deity. Another of the primitive gods was 'Eitu-matubu'a ('Eitu-of-the-olden-time'). He is spoken of as the father of the Tongan people. Another of these gods was Hikule'o, the Tongan Satan. *Hikule'o* means 'the echo,' and there is no doubt that this was the original signification of the name; but as it *might* mean 'Watching Tail,' the legend grew up that the tail of this deity was so long that when he, the god, went about, the tail kept watch at home. But even now the Tongans, when they hear an echo, say it is Hikule'o walking in the woods; and the other explanation was evidently an afterthought.

These with others were the original gods of Tonga. By and by a division of departments took place. To the Tangaloa was assigned the Sky (or Heaven); to the Maui group the Under World; and to Hikule'o the World and Bulotu (Hades). But in order to keep Hikule'o in his place, as he was a god that delighted in mischief, a cord was attached to him, one end of which was held by Tangaloa in the sky, and the other by a Maui in the under world, to prevent his leaving Bulotu to damage the world. This division was effected by an older god than any, namely, Taufulifonua ('Frequent-Upsetter-of-the-land'), who also assigned the sea to Hemoana, and the woods and dry land generally to Lube (the Dove). Hemoana's name is sometimes pronounced Heimoana, and the present writer *believes* that Tongavalevale spoke of him as Hea-Moana, though he is unable to speak positively on that point. *Hea-Moana* would signify 'Hea-of-the-deep-sea'; *Hemoana* would be simply 'the Deep Sea' = Oceanus. His shrine was the banded sea-snake. These were the Olympian gods of Tonga; but, with the exception of Hikule'o, they were rarely worshipped, and few if any temples were erected in their honour. The exception is due to the fact that Hikule'o was a mischievous god, and must therefore be propitiated.

(2) The second class of gods were an inferior race, who had their shrines in animals, birds, fishes, trees, whales' teeth, clubs, and even stones. Yet these were the gods worshipped by the people, and their temples were to be found in every village. Here are a few of them: Tu'i 'Ahau ('King of the town of 'Ahau'), whose shrine was a volcanic stone of peculiar shape; Tu'i Lalotonga ('King of Rarotonga,' or perhaps of the world below Tonga), whose shrine was the dragon-fly; Taliai Tubou (the god of the reigning dynasty while yet heathen),

whose shrine was a shark [Mariner renders *Taliai Tubou* by 'Wait there, Tubou,' which is certainly incorrect; Taliai Tubou was probably the name of a king]; Bulotu Katoa (the Pleroma of the Spirit World, who presided over hurricanes, and agriculture), whose shrine, we think, was a tree at Kolonga [Mariner mentions several the present writer has never heard of: Tubou Toutai ('Tubou the Mariner'; Tubou is the familiar designation of the king, and one of his family is usually called Tubou Toutai); Hala'evalu ('Eight Ways'; also the name of a chief); 'Alo'alo ('the Fanner'), the god of wind and weather, rain, harvest, and vegetation; Tu'i Bulotu ('King of the Spirit World')]. Other gods resided in the turtle, the cuttle-fish, the kingfisher, etc. Fonokitangata's shrine was a war-club. These were, so to speak, the private gods of the people, and the shrine of each was tabu to its worshippers. Thus the people of Te'ekiu were forbidden to eat the octopus, that being the shrine of their god. In the neighbouring villages, however, it would be freely eaten. In Nomuka one particular family were thus debarred from eating turtle, while the rest of the town were free to partake of that delicacy.

(3) In addition to these there were a number of supernatural beings whose position in the Tongan pantheon is not clear. They were looked upon as gods, and the term expressive of highest deity was applied to them; but they were never worshipped, nor were temples built to them. On the contrary, they were looked upon with contempt, and their follies freely portrayed and laughed at. It is curious to see these ascriptions of high divinity and expressions of contempt standing side by side. Is it that these were the gods of the inferior race which the Tongans found in the group when they landed?

Take an instance or two. Jiji and Faiga'a were two goddesses in this class, who had set their affections on a Tongan of great masculine beauty called Bajikole. He, tired of their attentions, plaited two large baskets of cocoa-nut leaves, put one goddess in each, and, shouldering them like a Chinaman, conveyed them into the bush, and hung them on the branch of a tree, and left them there for two years, until the baskets rotted, and they fell to the ground. They made another attempt on his affections, and he finally got rid of them by inveigling them into his fish traps, and leaving them at the bottom of the sea, where they lay until Tangaloa took pity on them, and sent a god to release them. Take another instance. In this case also it was two goddesses, who set out to meet a mortal lover. While waiting for him, they took off their heads to dress their hair. Suddenly his footsteps were heard, and they put their heads on again; but in the hurry one of them put hers on hind before; and when she attempted to move, her face went one way and her legs another. It is extremely puzzling to meet with tales like these, referring to those to whom the titles of highest deity are given: and yet, after all, they do but recall the vagaries of the Olympian deities as described by Homer, when

'Unextinguished laughter shook the skies.'

On the subject of ancestor-worship, Mariner speaks positively (vol. ii. p. 97): 'That there are other Hotooas or gods, viz. the souls of all deceased nobles and mataboofes.' The present writer was disposed to agree with him at first, especially as it was a custom of the people to go to the cemeteries to pray, even after a sacrifice had been presented at the temple. But further inquiry has convinced him that they did so because they fancied themselves nearer the spirit-world in such places. Intelligent chiefs like Valu, who were acquainted with heathenism, are equally positive in the other direction, and deny that they looked upon the spirits of deceased chiefs as gods. We think the truth lies between the two statements, and that Mariner himself gives us a key to the solution of the question. In vol. i. p. 376, he speaks of Feenow as being frequently inspired by the spirit of Mumui (a late king of Tonga). Now we can readily understand that in such circumstances Feenow would pray to Mumui, and others would join him; so that in time Mumui would be looked upon as a god. This would account for such gods as Tu'i Lalotonga, Tu'i 'Ahau, Taliai Tubou, and others. All the inquiries of the present writer negative the assertion that the spirits of chiefs as a general thing became gods. We may then look upon the gods of the first class as primitive, brought by the Tongans from their original home, and the third class as the gods of the aboriginals whom they conquered. The second class contained also some primitive gods, but was recruited largely from the spirits of ancestors—*i.e.* the spirits of certain deceased chiefs by whom kings and notable personages fancied themselves to have been possessed.

The other point the present writer made special inquiries about was whether the Tongans worshipped the clubs, whales' teeth, animals, trees, stones, etc., before which they placed their offerings, or the god who was supposed to be temporarily residing in them. The answer was decisive. The clubs, trees, etc., were simply the *vaka*, the god itself was spiritual. *Vaka* signifies a 'mode of conveyance,' usually a canoe, but also a carriage, or anything by which one is conveyed from place to place.

Probably we may see here a development of their spiritual ideas. The oldest class—Tangaloa, Maui, Hemoana — were undoubtedly corporeal. Their bodies performed all the functions of human bodies, and they were inflamed with human passions. But the Tongans had long ceased to pray to them, and scarcely any vestiges of their worship remained when the missionaries came. The third class of gods, too, were corporeal, but there are no signs of worship being paid them at any time. These two classes existed side by side; but long before the introduction of Christianity both had been discarded as objects of worship, which was paid only to the second class. In other words, the Tongans had worked out a theology, which had, at any rate, this noble feature in it, that God was a spirit, and they that worship Him must worship Him in spirit.

The general Tongan term for supernatural beings is *fa'ahikehe*. This is often shortened into *fa'ahi*, and when the adjective *lahi* ('great') is added—*fa'ahi lahi*—the idea conveyed is that of full deity. *Fa'ahi* signifies properly 'a party,' 'a side' (as in cricket); or it may be short for *fa'ahinga*='kind,' 'class,' 'race,' 'species,' 'genus.' *Kehe*='other' (ἕτερος, not ἄλλος), so *fa'ahikehe* is 'different folk,' 'other kind of people.' The usual word for 'God' is *'Otua*. Mariner spells it *Hotooa*, but there is no *h* in it. The inverted comma represents a guttural, a half *k*, which is one of the difficulties of the language. It is not readily recognized by the European ear, and is mostly neglected by foreigners, while being as intractable as the Ayin in Hebrew. The present writer has failed to find any derivation for *'Otua*, or meaning other than 'God,' and believes it to be a primitive Polynesian word. In some parts of the Pacific it appears as *Atua*.

The other great word is *'Eiki*='Lord,' which is used as in English for both earthly and heavenly lords. Hence it is not so high a term as *'Otua*. Indeed it seems sometimes to mean only 'supernatural.' Thus a corpse is called *ha me'a faka'eiki*, which apparently signifies 'a thing belonging to the spirit world.' Probably Mariner was thinking of this when he said (vol. ii. p. 130): 'The human soul after its separation from the body is termed *hotooa*, *i.e.* a god or spirit.' He is certainly wrong in that statement. It is clear that *'eiki* was not the original form of the word, which the laws of the language point out to have been *ikeiki*.

We must not pass over the fact that the members of one of the dynasties of kings were regarded as gods. This was the earliest line of kings, and their title was *Tu'i Tonga* ('King of Tonga'). They were certainly looked upon as in some sense divine beings; and instances are on record of prayers being offered to them. Words applied only to the gods were used in addressing them; such as *'Ēi*, already referred to, *ha'ele*, and *'afio*, used of the movements of deity. The face of the Tu'i Tonga was termed the 'sky,' and to him, as the representative of the gods, were presented the 'first-fruits.' This ceremony, called the *'inaji*, or 'portion,' is described by Mariner (vol. ii. p. 196). When a Tu'i Tonga died, he was said to be 'missing' (*hala*), and he was buried in a *ziqqurat*, or pyramid of steps. This was called a *langi*, or 'heaven'; and many of them remain in tolerable preservation, and excite the wonder of the visitor by the huge size of many of the stones, some of which measure over 20 ft. in length.

Many, probably most, of the names of the Tu'i Tonga have been preserved, and their history curiously reminds us of the story of the Carlovingians and Merovingians in France. One of the Tu'i Tonga, called Takalaua, was murdered, and his son and successor Kau'ulufonuafekai, from weariness or fear, devolved the duties of government on his younger brother, reserving to himself the honours and emoluments of the office. His brother assumed the title of Tu'i Ha'a Takalaua ('King of the Takalauans'), and soon got all the power into his hands, the Tu'i Tonga becoming a *roi fainéant*. After a few generations, however, the Tu'i Ha'a Takalaua became effete, and the government was handed over to another branch, called the Tu'i Kanokubolu ('King of Kanokubolu,' the town in which he lived). This is the title of the present dynasty. Representatives of the other two lines, however, still exist, but the titles are not used. The representative, however, of the Tu'i Tonga holds even now a quasi-sacred position, and is still addressed as the gods used to be; and words sacred to deity are used for all his movements.

Mariner mentions another semi-divine person called the Veachi (vol. ii. p. 80). This part of his narrative is very perplexing, as neither Veeson nor Thomas nor any of the modern chiefs knows anything about him.

The word used all over Polynesia for 'religion,' 'worship,' 'prayer,' etc., is *lotu*. Fortunately this has a meaning in Tongan, and signifies 'a seeking for something that is hard to find.' Thus when famine prevails, the people *lotu kai, i.e.* go all over the land looking for food. It is also used for the restlessness of a caged animal seeking an outlet, and for the cry of an animal for its mate or companions. This is not the only word common to Polynesia which finds its meaning in Tongan. *Tabu* (or *taboo*), now of world-wide use, signifies in Tongan that something which might be opened is closed. These and other considerations lead one to think that the Tongan language comes nearer than most of the dialects to the original Polynesian tongue.

3. **The religious rites** of the Tongans were few. There was nothing in their religion corresponding to our idea of worship. If they wanted something—rain, fair winds, good crops, successful fishery—or if they wished to prevent some calamity—such as sickness, death, hurricanes, war—they would seek the favour of a god, would offer sacrifice and pray. But to come into his temple, to worship, to sing his praises, to dwell upon his attributes—this was a foreign idea altogether. Hence there was very little in the Tongan religion to cultivate the conscience, or to control the passions, or to elevate the thoughts. Mariner thinks otherwise, and we would gladly believe his favourable report of the Tongan character. But all our information—and much of it goes back to Mariner's time—contradicts his statements. He even contradicts himself. The Feenow he speaks so highly of was a monster of iniquity; and there is no doubt that for centuries theft, murder, lust, treachery, and almost everything in the catalogue of evil, have been rife in Tonga. No man's life or property, and no woman's honour, was safe for a day.

They never went to their gods empty-handed; a piece of kava root for making the native drink was a *sine qua non*. Baskets of food, too, were usually brought in addition, and presented to the god or his priest. One of the party would then state the object of their visit, and implore the deity to grant their request, or use his influence with the gods of Bulotu in their favour. Sometimes the priest would remain silent; at other times he would object that their gifts were too small. If he spoke at all, he spoke as the god, being supposed to be 'possessed' by the god at the moment. John Thomas says (Farmer's *Tonga*, 128): 'Often there was another person present, the friend of the god, who acted as mediator, and addressed the priest on behalf of the offerers.' Hingano, a chief lady of great age, described to the present writer how she and others would take baskets of food to the door of Taliai Tubou's temple in Nuku'alofa, and, bowing down, would implore the god's favour. Shortly a white (*sic*) foot would be protruded from beneath a curtain, which they would kiss and then retire.

If their object was to deprecate a calamity, as in a case of sickness, the rite assumed a darker hue. Fingers were cut off, wrapped in banana leaves, and presented; or children were strangled, and their bodies brought as a sacrifice. When prayers were offered to Fonokitangata, the sacrifice was always an adult. Generally a man obnoxious to the community was hunted down and killed, and his body brought in a basket and laid before the priest; but Mariner speaks of a chief of rank being killed in one instance. The offerers, clothed in old and dirty mats, and wearing necklaces of chestnut leaves, would squat on the ground at a distance, and weep and beat their breasts, while the priest, holding in his hand a war club, the shrine of the god, would listen to their prayers with his eyes fixed upon the club or upon the ground. Sometimes he would reply in his ordinary voice, but more often in unnatural tones, as if some one were speaking in him; and frequently he would begin to shake as if in a fit, and to roll about and foam at the mouth. Any words he might utter whilst in this condition were eagerly caught up as the direct utterances of the god. After a while the shaking would cease, and the priest, striking the ground with the club, would announce that the god had departed. Mariner (vol. i. p. 160) has a good description of this kind of possession; and he evidently thought that the phenomena were not altogether voluntary, but that a real possession of some kind took place—a belief which was shared by some of the earlier missionaries.

4. The Tongans believed in **the immortality of the soul.** Mariner, Veeson, and Thomas are agreed on this point.

Veeson says (Farmer's *Tonga*, p. 131): 'One day they were conversing about a person that was lately dead, and said, "He goes to the island through the sky." "How can he be," said I, "in that place, when he is dead, and his body here? Did you not bury him some moons ago?" But all they answered was, "But he is still alive." And one took hold of my hand, and, squeezing it, said, "This will die, but the life that is within you will never die"—with his other hand pointing to my heart.'

Mariner and Veeson, too, agree in stating that this immortality is enjoyed only by the upper classes: the souls of the Tu'as, or common people, die with their bodies. This, no doubt, was the belief of the upper classes, who looked down upon the Tu'as as little better than animals; but it is no evidence of the belief of the Tu'as themselves. Thomas says more truly: 'Of the faith of the common people there was no certainty.'

The 'island' referred to was called Bulotu, and 'through the sky' meant 'over the horizon.' Bulotu is, the present writer thinks, a primitive Polynesian word, and is the name for Paradise in all the dialects. It was situated west or north-west of Tonga, and could be reached by sea. At least the ballads speak of canoes touching there; but how the disembodied spirits got there is not stated. Mariner tells us (vol. ii. p. 101) that Bulotu was believed by the Tongans to be a large island, stocked with all kinds of useful and ornamental plants in a state of high perfection, and that when these were plucked others would immediately occupy their place. The whole atmosphere was filled with a most delightful fragrance; there were also beautiful birds of all kinds, and abundance of hogs—all of which were immortal unless killed to provide food for the gods. At the moment a bird or a hog was killed, another living bird or hog came into existence. Further on he gives another account of Bulotu brought by a canoe which touched there:

'The crew landed, and proceeded to pluck some breadfruit; but to their unspeakable astonishment, they could no more lay hold of it than if it was a shadow. They walked through the trunks of trees, and passed through the substance of the houses without feeling any resistance. They at length saw some of the gods, who passed through the substance of their bodies as if there was nothing there.' The gods were supposed to have no canoes, not requiring them; 'for if they wished to be anywhere, there they are the moment the wish is felt.'

Now, is this again a development? For the ballads, which date from a time long antecedent to the visit of Mariner, give a very different description. According to them, everything in Bulotu was material. Its entrance was guarded by a woman with eight tongues. There was a large canoe for the gods to voyage in, which was called Langotangata ('the human-rollered'), because it was dragged down to the sea on living rollers, each being a human being. The same trees grew as on earth: cocoa-nuts, breadfruit, yams, etc.; and provision was made for the favourite pastimes of chiefs. There were eminences for netting wood-pigeons, reefs for shark-catching, *'ulua* to be fished, and gigantic clams to be dived for. Ovens of food were cooked as on earth, and kava was prepared and drunk. The houses had solid posts, and the roofs were constructed in the usual way. One of the halls in Bulotu was panelled with the pupils of men's eyes 'which sparkled and flashed.' The women had a hall lined with mirrors—a veritable crystal palace. There was a *Vaiola*, or Fountain of Life, whose waters were so potent that a child plunged into it grew up to manhood in a few days. There was also a *Vai-lolofafanga*, or Fountain of Perfumery, and other delights of women (see 'Voyage of Faimalie,' *Tubou College Magazine*, vol. iii. p. 39).

5. Cosmogony.—The earliest chapters of the Tongan genesis ran somewhat as follows:

Some seaweed and slime clung together, and were carried away by the sea, and washed up on the island of Totai in Bulotu. By and by there grew up between them a large metallic stone called Tou'iafutuna ('Pregnant-how-long-ago!'). Suddenly it began to shake, and sent out a sound like thunder; and, splitting, there sprang out a male and a female twin. The male was called Biki ('Sticky') and the female Kele ('Slimy'). Again the huge stone rolled about as if there was an earthquake, and other twins sprang out: the male called Atungaki (?), and the female Maimoa'alongona ('Vagaries-of-sound'). Again the stone groaned, and twins sprang out, called 'Land-turtle' and 'Sea-turtle.' Again the stone sounded and earthquaked, and twins sprang forth, Hemoana (the Sea-snake), and Lube (the Dove).

They grew up and married, *i.e.* the first pair and the second and the third. The eldest child of Biki and Kele was a son, Taufulifonua ('Frequent-overturner-of-the-land'[1]). The next was a girl called Havea-lolofonua (Havea-of-the-underworld'). The second pair had a girl called Vele Lahi, and the third pair a girl called Vele Ji'i. (*Vele* signifies 'longing' or 'desire'; *Vele Lahi*='Desire the Elder,' *Vele Ji'i*='Desire the Younger'). Sticky and Slimy created a new land called Tonga Mama'o ('Distant Tonga'), and put on it Taufulifonua and Havea-lolofonua.

[The next incident is unprintable, but is a realistic setting of the words, 'And they were both naked, the man and his wife, and were not ashamed.' They were ignorant even of the sexual function, which they discovered only by accident. The result was a boy called Hikule'o ('the Echo,' the Tongan Satan: see above).]

Then Havea said to Vele Lahi and Vele Ji'i, 'Come and marry your brothers as I have done, for there is no man for you.' They did so, and Vele Lahi gave birth to the Tangaloas, and Vele Ji'i to the Maui family. Then Taufulifonua divided the heaven and earth as stated above.

In process of time the Tangaloas ordered Tangaloa 'Atulongolongo to go down and see in what condition the world was. So he entered into the Kiu (? 'Sea-lark'), and went down, and flew in all directions, but could not see any land, only shallows. Then went he up to heaven and reported to the Tangaloas that there was no land, only something that looked like shallows. Said the heavenly chief, 'Wait seven nights, and then go again and see': so Tangaloa 'Atulongolongo remained seven days in the sky, and then went down to look at the shallows. The bottom was evidently coming up, and he reported to heaven, 'It looks like a reef.' He said also, 'I can find nothing to stand on and rest.' So they said, 'Go to Tangaloa the Smith, and let him throw down the dust of the pumice he sharpens his axes with.' So Tangaloa Tufunga did so, and threw down the dust of his grindstone, and produced the island of 'Eua. On this being reported, Tangaloa was sent down to stand there and watch. By and by a bit of the shallows would become dry, and ultimately a large land grew up, which consisted, however, only of sand. Tangaloa reported, 'My land is large, but nothing will grow on it.' Then said Lord Tangaloa, 'Take this seed, and set it in the land you have discovered.' It was a *fue* (convolvulus). So he set it, and it overspread the land. Then said he, 'There is vegetation enough, but no people: and Lord Tangaloa and the other heavenly chiefs replied, 'Go and split the root of the *fue*.' He did so, and it rotted and produced a grub. So he reported to the sky, 'A great thing is lying in the *fue* I split.' They ordered him to cut it in two, and to call the head Kohai ('Who is it?') and the tail Koau ('It is I'). He did so, and both parts became men: as did also a little piece that had adhered to his beak. This was called Momo ('Little Bit'): and he with the other two were the first men.

Now at that time Maui the Elder ordered his family to go on board a canoe, and fish up lands. There were four Maui in the canoe: Maui Loa, Maui Buku, and Maui 'Atalanga with his son Maui Kijikiji; and they took their mother Vele with them. She was the maker of mats and fine robes. They called at Manuka, a part of Samoa that was already above the waters. And Maui Kijikiji, leaping ashore, went to get a fish-hook. Meeting the chief's wife, he ravished her; and she, taking kindly to him, revealed her husband's secret, that the magic fish-hook, which would bring up lands, was not a bright and glittering one, but an old and rusty hook, stuck in the reeding. So they got the hook, and, having tried it successfully near Samoa, sailed on boldly, and pulled up Tonga and many other groups of islands. When they came to 'Eua, and saw the three men, they asked whether they had any women; and on their replying 'No,' they went and fetched three, so that they might have one each.

At that time the sky was very low, and an ironwood tree that stood in Tonga reached quite up to heaven. So 'Eitu-Matubu'a was wont to climb down, and visit the earth; and, cohabiting with a woman in one of the islands, had a child by her called 'Aho'eitu. When he grew to man's estate, he asked who and where his father was; and was directed by his mother to climb up the ironwood tree, and seek him in the sky. He finds him, is recognized, and sent to play with his brothers, who become jealous, and finally kill and eat him. 'Eitu, finding this out, makes them vomit into a large tub, and covers the *disjecta membra* with the leaves of the tree of life (*Nonu*). By and by the fragments cohere, and ultimately 'Aho'eitu is found sitting up alive. His brothers are punished by being turned out of heaven, and have to serve 'Aho'eitu on earth, who becomes the first Tu'i Tonga, superseding the children of the 'grub.' The Maui afterwards pushed the sky higher up, as it is at present.

Now the Maui dwelt in the under world, but one of them, Maui 'Atalanga, said to his brethren, 'Have you any objection to my living on the earth, if I visit you from time to time?' And they said, 'No.' So 'Atalanga went up to the earth, taking his young son Kijikiji with him. He lived in Vava'u, and married a mortal wife. Now Maui 'Atalanga did not plant in Vava'u; for he was a mighty planter, and there was not land enough; so he had his plantation in the under world. He kept this, however, a secret from his son Kijikiji, for he was such a mischief. But Maui Kijikiji tracked his father by his footsteps, and, seeing him lift a bush and descend into the earth, waited a while and followed him. Many tricks did he play, until one day his father sent him to Maui the Elder to get a fire-stick. Kijikiji kept quenching the fire and going back for more. At last old Maui told him to take the whole log. This was of enormous size, but the young Maui took it up with ease. Old Maui, who had not recognized his grandson, perceiving that he was a superhuman being, challenged him to wrestle—with the result that the elder Maui was thrown and left for dead. 'Atalanga, hearing of it, strikes his son with his spade and kills him. On going, however, to see how his father was faring, he finds the old man alive, and rather pleased than not with his defeat by his grandson, and angry with his son for having killed him. They apply, however, the leaves of the tree of life, and Maui Kijikiji revives. His next exploit is to carry some fire from the under world to earth, in spite of the efforts of his father to prevent him. They then devote themselves to fighting with and destroying the monstrous animals that infested the world—a huge rat, a gigantic bird called the Moa, a lizard, and some carnivorous trees, etc. Maui 'Atalanga is at last devoured by a huge dog that lived in a magic cave which opened and closed automatically; and his son, after killing the dog, died of grief for his father, etc.

LITERATURE.—The principal authorities on the state of Tonga in early times are these: William Mariner, *An Account of the Natives of the Tonga Islands*[2], London, 1818; G. Veeson, *Authentic Narrative of Four Years' Residence in Tongatabu*, do. 1810; S. S. Farmer, *Tonga and the Friendly Islands*, do. 1855. [Mariner's is a most valuable work. He gives evidence

[1] *Tau* is sometimes intensive. This would then mean 'complete-overturner.'

of being possessed of no common ability, and of an excellent memory; and, if the present writer has ventured to differ from him, it is for the following reasons: (1) the shortness of Mariner's stay—only 4 years; (2) his obvious want of acquaintance with the niceties of the language; (3) the considerable time that elapsed between his leaving Tonga and the writing down of his reminiscences; (4) the fact that the present writer's acquaintance with Tonga extends over a period of 40 years; (5) that most of his information was taken down from the lips of the 'Last of the Bards,' a once heathen chief called Tongavalevale, who was the repository of their folk-lore and ballads; (6) that he has had access to the unpublished journals of the Rev. John Thomas, Wesleyan minister, who went to Tonga in 1826, and was the first missionary to make a lengthened stay.]

J. EGAN MOULTON.

TONGKING.—Ethnographically Tongking is divided into two parts: South Tongking, the special domain of the Annamese race, and North Tongking, bounded on the north by the Annamo-Chinese frontier, on the east by the sea, on the west by the range where the waters separate into the Red and Black Rivers (Song-Koi and Song-Bo), and on the south by a line bisecting the provinces of Kwang-Yen, Bac-Giang, Thai-Nguyen, Tuyen-Kwang, and Yen-Bay. This Upper Tongking has an area of 54,700 square kilometres, and a population of 374,528, belonging to 26 different ethnic groups. There are no Annamese or Chinese except officials and merchants; the country is peopled chiefly by Tai, Man, or Yao, Pa-Teng, Meo, Lolo, Muong, and a very small number of representatives of far more ancient ethnic groups, such as the La-tchi (La-ti) and the Keu-Lao.

I. *TAI.*—The Tai element, most important in point of numbers (239,179 individuals—about 60 per cent of the total population), is divided into numerous sub-groups, the most important being the Thô (146,000), who are found round Cao-Bang, the Nung (66,000), and the Black Tai (14,500). The Tai have a strong admixture of Chinese and Annamese and are thus closely related to the Siamese and Laotians.

1. Physical characteristics.—The Tai are strong and of a lively disposition, careless, fond of pleasure and play, and extraordinarily indolent. This race seems to be on the decrease; there are few births, and infant mortality is very high. They are not absolutely averse to mixed marriages: their daughters may marry Chinese or Annamese if they choose, and their sons take wives from any variety of the race whatever, even from the Man; these mixed marriages produce a stronger and more provident race than the pure Tai.

The Tai live in the plains and low valleys by preference. Their houses are, as a rule, built on piles, the ground-floor being reserved for live-stock and poultry, the upper storey for the inhabitants. The Nang and several other tribes dress like the Chinese; the rest of the Tai follow the Annamese fashion, but wear much brighter colours—indigo blue is almost universal—and far more ornamentation. Rice is the staple food. The Tai also use beans, sweet potatoes, and gourds; pork is their most usual meat, chickens and ducks being reserved for feast-days; they also eat fish. Tea is their chief beverage, though they sometimes drink too much wine or spirit made from fermented grain. The use of tea and betel is practically universal among them; opium is confined to the rich.

The Tai are essentially farmers. They cultivate rice, maize, buck-wheat, beans, peas, sweet potatoes, and sesamum. Industry and commerce are practically non-existent owing to the indolence of the race. They can, however, distil alcohol, weave cloths, make rich embroidery, and do fine basket-work. The Thô even spin a little silk.

2. Religion.—On their original animism the Tai have superimposed a confused mixture of Taoist, Buddhist, and Confucian ideas, derived from the Chinese and Annamese. A few priests or lettered men have a vague knowledge of the cosmic system of the *di-kinh.*

They believe that the primordial principle of nature gave birth to the male and female principles, from which issued everything and everybody. The male principle is the sun, the sky, the intellectual soul of men; the female is the dark earth, the moon, the vital and sensual soul of beings. Man has three subtle souls, or *hôn*, which emanate from the male principle, and seven or nine (according as the sex is male or female) vegetative souls, or *viá*. At death these *viá* return to the earth whence they came, while the *hôn* go to the infernal regions. Here we see the influence of the Buddhist doctrine of the transmigration of souls and their purification by punishment. After undergoing the punishments which they have merited, they may approach the throne of the emperor of Jade, the supreme Taoist idol.

The great majority of the people, a most superstitious race, confine themselves to the worship of the evil spirits which infest the air and lie in wait for man even in the most insignificant actions of his life. These are combated by means of forethought and offerings, and especially by the help of more powerful good spirits which are rendered propitious by devoted worship. Among the good spirits the genius of the hearth and the tutelary deity of the village are held in highest honour; of the evil spirits, which have different names in the various Tai groups, the most dreaded are the spirits of people who have died a violent death and the chicken-spirits that insinuate themselves into people, especially women, and give them the evil eye. Of course the Tai believe in white and black magic, spells, lots, and philtres.

Their priests are chiefly sorcerers, who earn their living by offering sacrifices to the spirits, exorcizing the sick, and warding off all the evils invoked against man. They also choose the material with which to build villages or houses, the propitious day for beginning any work, etc. Among the Tai they are nearly all connected with an official cult, but there are independent sorcerers and sorceresses.

The only temples that the Tai possess are small rustic pagodas, nearly all dedicated to the tutelary genius of the locality.

Their religious festivals are borrowed from the Annamese; but among certain tribes, particularly the White and Black Tai, there are some festivals which seem peculiar to the race. (1) *Kin lao mao* ('drink,' 'alcohol,' 'drunk') takes place in September. All the inhabitants of the village meet in one of their houses for a banquet, which is followed after sunset by music and singing. The feast lasts three days, during which no one may enter or leave the village. (2) *King pang* ('to eat bread') takes place in January. It is characterized by round dances to the accompaniment of chants. Among the White Tai it is the women who dance, among the Black Tai the men. (3) *Kin tien* ('to eat coined money') takes place in December in honour of the dead. It lasts three days, with banquets, dancing, and singing. Both men and women take part.

Ancestor-worship exists among the Tai, but only a more or less slavish imitation of Annamese ritualism. It is practised chiefly among the Thô, who preserve the names of their ancestors to the fourth generation, make offerings at prescribed times, and train their children to honour the dead as the protectors of the hearth. Only those who have died a natural death have a place on the family altar; those who have died a violent death, out of doors, have only a small outside altar, usually built in the garden.[1]

3. Myths and legends.—Among all the Tai is found the tradition of a universal deluge, from which the god of the earth saved only a brother and a sister—a poor but pious couple—who shut themselves at his command inside a hollow pumpkin, with some rice for provision. After the subsidence of the waters the present-day races were born from the union of this couple.

4. Medicine.—The Tai regard nearly every illness as the work of evil spirits, and the best medicine is the sorcerer; the more enlightened members of the race sometimes admit that there are natural ailments, which they treat with simples and mineral products borrowed from the Chinese pharmacopœia.

[1] It should be noticed that the Tai know nothing of the property called *hu'ö'ng hoa* in Annam—an inalienable part of the patrimony reserved to meet the expense of the cult of the dead and the upkeep of the tombs. As a rule after a few months, at most after four years, the Tai have nothing more to do with the tombs.

5. **Marriage.** — Although the manners of the Tai are not so free and easy as those of the Laotians, youths and maidens meet freely to sing and play—which often leads to sexual relations; all that Tai morality requires is that there be no tangible proofs of these relations, and hence recourse is had to abortive measures or the suppression of children.

The father is the unquestioned head of the family, yet it is only among the highly Annamitized Tai that he chooses a mate for his child; among the Tai of the right bank of the Red River the young people make their own choice. The proposal is made by a go-between; the young man pays a dowry, and the engagement is settled after a sorcerer has compared the genealogical forecasts of the couple, in order to see whether any supernatural influence opposes their union. The engagement is generally long—from three months to three years—and is rather expensive for the *fiancé*, who is expected to give a great number of presents. The engaged couple are bound to observe the strictest reserve; they are not allowed to take any notice of each other until the wedding-day, while they have complete liberty in their relations with the other young people of both sexes. The marriage-ceremony itself is borrowed from the Annamese.

The outstanding characteristic of marriage among the Tai—with the exception of the Thô in the west, the Nung, and the Thô-Ti—is the quaint custom of separating husband and wife after the celebration of their union: among some tribes the wife spends a fortnight with her parents and a fortnight with her husband; among others she cannot go to her husband except when invited. This state of affairs comes to an end with the appearance of pregnancy, or, in cases of sterility, at the end of the fourth year of married life, when the wife takes her place at the family hearth. As the separated husband and wife retain complete liberty of behaviour outside with people of their own age, Tai morality suffers some strange drawbacks from this custom. The Tai youths marry usually between twenty-three and twenty-five, the girls between sixteen and eighteen.

The Thô of the west and several other tribes practise marriage by adoption and marriage by contract also. A poor young man can enter a rich family without paying the usual dowry, on condition that he takes his father-in-law's name, and lives with and works for his father-in-law. Should he wish later to live apart with his wife, he is liable to pay an indemnity to his father-in-law. A young man can also marry without paying a dowry and without changing his name, by undertaking a contract to serve his wife in her father's house for a stated number of years—from four to seven. If he dies before the contract has expired, his widow is responsible for his debt. These two forms of marriage, which are not held in high esteem, entail no long engagements and no costly wedding-feasts.

Polygamy is allowed by the Tai, but seldom practised; the number of wives is usually limited to two, only the first having honour and authority at the hearth, the other being practically her servant. Among the White Tai, however, the daughter of a chief has the rights of first wife, no matter when she is married. The Tai woman, though she enjoys a life of perfect freedom in her youth, becomes after marriage a sort of beast-of-burden; all the hard work in the fields and in the house falls on her. She has no real individuality till she becomes a mother. Divorce is rare; by right only the husband can seek it; in actual life it is the wife who applies for it. Repudiation is still more rare and is nearly always due to sterility.

6. **Birth.**—The house of the mother is forbidden to strangers during and for a certain time after confinement. If they did enter, they might themselves be contaminated and bring harm to the child. The confinement is made known to those outside by a branch of shaddock and a piece of coal among the Thô of the west, by a piece of wood, a knife, and a green branch among the Thô of the east, fastened to the ladder of the house. The first visitors to enter the house of the mother have to pass over a burning brand or a pail of water, into which red-hot iron is plunged. The Tai woman is delivered nearly always in a standing position, holding on to ropes with her hands. The eastern Thô alone light a brazier on the camp-bed whither she is afterwards carried. The placenta is secretly buried by the midwife. The birth is announced with libations to the ancestors by the head of the family. A propitious day is chosen for putting the child in the sack that does duty as swaddling. The choice of a name is surrounded with the same superstitious fears as are found among the Annamese, and the same unpleasant designations are chosen.

7. **Death and disposal of the dead.**—The Tai originally practised cremation and still do so for certain chiefs. As a rule they have now adopted burial. Funeral honours are paid only to men over 18 years of age and to married women. The rites are imitations of those of the Annamese. The medicine-man determines the position of the coffin and the situation of the grave. The deceased is dressed in his best clothes and a pair of new sandals, and is put into a coffin containing about 10 kilogrammes of ashes. On the bier are placed some duck-feathers to help him to ford the rivers of the other world, and a pencil and paper for him to make his wishes known. On the day of burial—usually the third after death—the corpse is placed on a paper catafalque and taken to the cemetery with great ceremony. The one idea at this juncture is to prevent the dead from returning to torment the survivors at home and at the same time to protect him from evil spirits. It is for this purpose that the medicine-man is employed; he brandishes his sword at intervals round the coffin and the mourners, who strew the road with gold and silver paper in order to tempt the evil spirits to stop and gather it up. The coffin is then put into the grave under the protection of the medicine-man's sword; food is placed on the tomb, near which the catafalque is burned—a house for the dead in the other world. Among the Chong-Kia Tai, when the coffin has to cross a river, the children stretch a piece of cloth from side to side for the souls of the dead, to keep them from wandering. Commemorative rites are not observed regularly by the Tai, except where they are very much under Annamese influence.

8. **Tabu.**—There seems to be only one kind of tabu among the Tai, viz. the entering or leaving a village during a local festival. Strangers are warned to turn back by notices placed outside the village.

II. *MAN.*—This Chinese name, which means 'barbarous,' 'rude,' is applied in Tongking to the ethnic group of the 'children of Pan-Hù or Phien-Hù,' who claim to be descended from the union of the dog Pan-Hù with the daughter of the emperor of China, whose inveterate enemy had been vanquished by Pan-Hù. The Man, or Yao, probably inhabit the high parts forming the basin of the Li-Kiang in the north, and are about 50,651 in number in N. Tongking and much more numerous in the west than in the east. Their various groups have been classified in six great families issuing, they say, from the six sons of Pan-Hù: the Man Côc, or 'horned Man'; the Man Tiên, or *sapèque*

Man; the Man Lan-Tien, or 'indigo-tinted Man'; the Man Quân Trăng, or 'blue-trousered Man'; the Man Quân Côc, or 'short-trousered Man'; and the Man Cao-Lan, or 'great rainbow Man.' The Man Côc, most numerous and most important, live in the highest parts of the country; lower down are the Man Tiên; the Lan-Tien hardly ever are found at a greater altitude than 300 metres; the others follow by various stages to the borders of the deltic plains; as a rule, they all find life in the valleys uncongenial.

1. **Physical characteristics.**—The Man are not so tall as the Tai, but are more robust, more intelligent, and much more active. As they have no rice, their staple food is maize, vegetables, and yams. They eat meat sparingly, chiefly pork, rarely buffalo or ox, never the dog—for this is the totem of their race. They do not chew betel, but both men and women smoke tobacco and the rich consume opium.

Their houses are built sometimes on the ground, sometimes on piles, and sometimes half-and-half. A random group of these houses forms a village, and the village is scarcely ever surrounded by a wall. The Man borrow their style of dress from either the Chinese or the Annamese according to their locality. The women's garments are embroidered on the skirts, facings, neck, and sleeves with bright red and blue designs so intricate and elaborate that it takes three years to embroider one costume. Their hair-dressing is also elaborate, and is nearly always finished off with a large turban having coloured edging and embroidery.

The Man are essentially agriculturists; but they are also good blacksmiths, and can make the trinkets that their women use, and also paper from bamboo-fibre. They are good fishers and hunters.

2. **Religion.**—Their beliefs are like those of the Tai, but even more confused—a few vague notions from the three great religions of China; but the mass of the people are animists, though not quite so superstitious as the Tai. Ancestor-worship is held in great honour among them. They have the same flood legend as the Tai. The Man have only a few pagodas dedicated to the tutelary deity of the village. They are nearly always built against a fruit-tree. They have medicine-men who present offerings, exorcize spirits, and work cures. The reputation of these sorcerers varies with the Man Côc according to whether they have or have not received complete initiation to the third degree. Among the other tribes initiation generally comprises only one degree. The Man worship consists in sacrifices, songs, and dances. They observe the Chinese feasts with varying regularity. They have also two curious local feasts celebrated with great pomp, especially by the Man Côc. The one takes place every three years in certain tribes, every five years in others, and commemorates the rescue of the Man race when—so long ago as to be in the region of hypothesis—it was shipwrecked in sight of the Chinese coast on its way from an island in the east. The second feast, called 'the great fast,' comprises five days of extraordinary pomp, and occurs only once in ninety years. We have no data of any value on its origin or symbolic meaning.

3. **Medicine.**—Their medicine comes from the Chinese, but the Man would not believe in the efficacy of any medicine that was not accompanied by incantations and exorcisms.

4. **Metamorphism.**—The Man believe that their neighbours, the Mao, have a third cutting of teeth in their old age, and after death escape from their graves and reappear as tigers.

5. **Marriage.**—The Man do not attach much importance to virginity. When a child is born before marriage, it is suppressed without a thought of the law which demands a fine for such an offence. Violence is also punished by a fine. The young people themselves, and not their parents, arrange their marriages. The young man makes his choice, then tells his parents, who send a go-between to make proposals to the parents of the girl. After examining the genealogical forecasts, the go-between may, at a second visit, discuss the amount of the dowry and the presents to be offered by the suitor. The engagement is concluded when the young man himself brings all or some of the presents. All intercourse between the engaged couple is stopped until the wedding-day, which is signalized by the customary banquets; the couple drink a cup of rice-wine together and prostrate themselves before the ancestral altar. They live together after the marriage-ceremony. The daughter-in-law must scrupulously avoid touching her husband's parents, though she serves her father-in-law at table.

The Man are also familiar with marriage by adoption and contract. Among the Man Cao-Lan the newly-married couple do not live together until two or three months after the marriage-ceremony. Among the Man Quân Trăng the marriage is preceded by a term of three years spent by the young man in his future father-in-law's house, the girl being usually about thirteen or fourteen at this time. The youth may marry her at the beginning of the three years on condition that he indemnifies his father-in-law for the three years' service which he owes. If pregnancy occurs during this term, the parties are bound to each other; if the youth changes his mind before the end of the term, he can leave without paying or receiving anything; if he is dismissed, he can claim an indemnity for the service rendered. After marriage the couple serve seven years in the paternal home of the husband.

Polygamy is practised among the Man; the number of wives is usually restricted to two, the first alone having authority in the house. The Man Quân Trăng allow polygamy only in exceptional cases. The material status of woman is high among the Man, the men doing all the heavy work; her legal status is different: she is the property of her husband, who can give her away and repudiate her. She, on the other hand, is not allowed to leave him. In cases of adultery the husband has the right to send his wife back to her parents and reclaim the dowry that he paid for her; if he keeps her, he can claim damages.

6. **Birth.**—From the third month of pregnancy sexual relations cease, and the woman abstains from fat, green vegetables, and garlic. She is not allowed to sew or embroider except outside her house. The Man Lan-Tien believe that, if a pregnant woman were the first to cross a new bridge, it would fall; that the touch of such a woman spoils rice and alcohol; the Man Quân Trăng, on the other hand, keep her away from these things for her own sake, in case they should cause miscarriage. The birth is announced to outsiders by a bunch of grass hung on the door among the Man Côc, by threads stretched across the door among the Quân Trăng; no announcement is made among the Lan-Tien. The Man woman is delivered sitting on a little stool. No fire is put under the bed after delivery. The placenta is taken far away and hidden in a hole in a tree or rock; it is buried under the mother's bed among the Man Lan-Tien; if eaten by an animal, it would bring misfortune on the child. Children born out of wedlock among the Quân Trăng belong to the mother; but the father, if known, is liable to pay a fine and give two months' service free in the house of the mother's parents to repay them for the loss of work caused by the birth. They practise adoption freely and thus receive into their families many Annamese children as their own.

7. **Death and disposal of the dead.**—The Man Côc used to burn their dead, and this custom survives west of the basin of the Red River. The Lan-Tien nearest the delta buried only those over fifty; the Quân Trăng buried all the heads of families. The burial rites are copied from the

Annamese. The Man Côc do not make 'the white silk soul' or catafalque; a sorcerer of the second degree exorcizes the tree from which the coffin is to be made so that the tree-spirit may not come to torment the dead.

III. *PA-TENG.* — The Pa-Teng, about 200 in number, live near the Man on the heights separating the Red River and the Clear River (Song-Ka). They are often classed with the Man, but are really separate linguistically. Their beliefs and customs are practically those of the Man.

IV. *MEO.* — The Meo, or 'cats,' numbering 21,471, are found in Cao-Bang, Bao-Lac, Lao-Kay, and Coc-Len as well as in the provinces of Thai-Nguyen and Yen-Bay. They claim to have come originally from the Chinese provinces of Yun-Nan, Kwei-Chu, and Tse-Chuen. Their last invasion into Tongking, in 1860, was very violent.

1. **Physical characteristics.**—The Meo are little and squat, very vigorous on their short legs, brave, hardy, and independent; they can be very abstemious, but are inclined to eat and drink heavily. Maize is their staple food; they eat very little meat, and drink a great deal of alcohol, but tobacco is not used and betel is unknown among them. Their rustic huts, of *pisé* or mud, are dirty to repulsiveness.

2. **Religion.** — Their traditional beliefs are borrowed from China and are very unprecise and wavering. They dread evil spirits—among others, the souls of beheaded people and of the unburied dead. A vague form of ancestor-worship is practised; it amounts to a few prayers and offerings of food, which are quickly consumed by the survivors. They are familiar with the flood-legend of the couple saved in the hollow pumpkin. Their priests are sorcerers.

3. **Marriage.**—Paternal authority is not strong. The young people make their own choice of mates, and marriage is accomplished through a go-between. In some districts the suitor has both to pay a dowry and to serve his future parents-in-law for two years before marriage. The Meo marry freely with other ethnic groups. Marriages are always accompanied by dances, songs, and games; if the bridegroom cannot afford the expense, he may leave it for his father-in-law to bear, on condition that he and his wife give so many years' work in payment. Marriage by capture is also found: the youth may carry off the girl who has been denied him, and he atones for his offence by paying a heavy dowry. Polygamy is allowed, but is not practised except when the first wife has no children. In adultery the husband has the right to kill the culprits, but as a rule he is content with repudiating his wife and taking back the dowry.

4. **Birth.**—There is nothing to mark the house on the occasion of a birth; the mother is delivered sitting and remains indoors for 33 days. The placenta is buried in front of the house, if the child is a boy; under the fire-place, if it is a girl.

5. **Death and disposal of the dead.**—The Meo bury their dead. The watch by the corpse consists of three days' feasting and dancing; the children of the deceased invite him to join in the banquets, and even slip a piece of food between his teeth. By the side of the corpse, which is dressed in new clothes and fixed in an upright position to a wall of the hut, a dead dog, killed for the purpose, is placed. The two are bound together by a strip of paper going from the dog's mouth to the dead man's wrist. The dog's duty is to guide his master in the other world. The coffin and the body are taken to the grave separately; the body is carried on a litter and is followed by the sorcerer, the family, and some friends, while guns are fired to frighten the evil spirits. When the grave is filled in, the litter is broken over it, some food (which must be renewed for several days) is placed on the tomb, and the funeral-procession returns to a banquet at the deceased's house.

V. *LOLO.*—The Lolo, a people almost certainly originating in the Brahmaputra valley, are about 2300 in number in Tongking and live chiefly in the region of Bao-Lac.

1. **Physical characteristics.**—Of medium height, muscular and well built, with fine regular features and a copper complexion, they recall to the Western mind the Bohemians of Europe. They are luxurious and indolent, marrying only among themselves; but their race is degenerating through the use of opium. Their chief foods are rice, maize, vegetables, and gourds, meat being reserved for festivals. They make alcohol from fermented maize. They use no betel and very little tobacco, but indulge in opium to excess.

Their houses are built on piles in the rich villages; in poor villages they are wretched huts placed on the ground. In dress the Lolo resemble the Chinese or the Thô according to locality, but their garments (those of the women in particular) are shorter and much more elaborately embroidered. The Lolo are great agriculturists and hunt and fish a little.

2. **Religion.**— Their beliefs and psychical life vary according as their villages are next a Tai, Man, or Meo clan. Their chief cult appears to be that of evil spirits, and they countenance ancestor-worship, theoretically. They also have the story of the flood and the survival of their ancestors in a pumpkin.

3. **Marriage.** — Marriage, which takes place during the night, comprises no religious ceremonies, but simply banquets and dances. After marriage the wife lives only two or three nights with her husband, and then returns to her parents until pregnancy privileges her to take her place in her husband's home. Marriage by capture is practised, the captor paying a double dowry. Adultery is punished by the death of both offenders. Polygamy exists only in theory.

4. **Birth.**—The rites connected with birth have no peculiarities among the Lolo. Adoption is of frequent occurrence, either by free consent or as the result of a bargain, and is the occasion of great festivities.

5. **Death and disposal of the dead.**—Burial takes place, without ceremony and in presence of relatives only, three days after death. For nine days in the case of a man, eight for a woman, and six for a child, the family keep a fire burning on the tomb, and after that take no more trouble. Certain tribes exhume the dead, after one or three years, with great pomp, and put the head or all the bones into a little wooden box, which is then placed on a neighbouring rock, where the survivors can see it while at work. Their ancestor-worship is very crude. The place of the tablet is often taken by a representation of the dead made from an orchis stem and little bits of paper, placed against a partition or between the wall and the roof of the hut.

6. **Tabu.**—Women after puberty are forbidden to eat pork, chicken, duck, or dog, and must not even cook their food in dishes which have been used for preparing these foods; hence the necessity of two fire-places and two utensils in a Lolo house.

VI. *MUONG OR MON.* — The Muong or Mon are an ethnic group centring in the province of Hoa-Binh. They are of uncertain origin, but appear to be closely connected with the Annamese, whom they resemble strongly in physical type, dress, and customs. Their religion is a development of the popular animism of the Annamese.

It should be noted that in one thing they are very different from the Annamese: among the Muong the relations between the sexes before marriage are very free. Whenever a girl becomes pregnant, her family and that of her seducer are made to pay a fine to the village. As among the Annamese, the blood-test is applied when the father of a child denies his paternity. Marriage is celebrated according to the Annamese rites. Accouchement takes place on a camp-bed under which the usual fire is kept burning, and the house is marked to outsiders, after the delivery, in the same way as among the Annamese. The placenta is buried underneath the house itself. The dead are buried in accordance with the Annamese rites. The corpse is placed in a coffin made from a hollow tree-trunk and set up in front of one of the doors of the hut. Outside, and facing it, there stands on a bamboo tripod a basket containing a little dog killed for the purpose, some rice, alcohol, and incense-sticks. A special cord binds the tripod to the coffin. After the coffin has been let down and the grave filled in, a wide-mouthed jar is emptied near the stone which marks the position of the dead man's head; and, if rain-water comes and fills this jar again, it shows that the grave has been well chosen and it brings a thousand blessings to the survivors. The bodies of the *quan-lang* (village chiefs) are kept, it appears, for three years before burial in front of the ancestral altar; a long bamboo tube leading from the hermetically-sealed coffin right up beyond the roof of the hut preserves the hut from mephitic vapours.

VII. *KEU-LAO.*—The Keu-Lao, of whose origin and customs we know next to nothing, form an ethnic group of seven families in the neighbourhood of Dong-Vâu.

VIII. *LA-TCHI.* — The La-tchi or La-ti are about twenty in number and live in the village of Chi Ka, near the upper valley of the Song-Chay. Though resembling the Annamese of the delta in physical type, they claim to be aboriginals. They are very little known and seem to live like the Meo. Their characteristic trait is their abstention from pork, the diet *par excellence* of the Far East, because, they say, their orphaned ancestors were fed by a sow.

LITERATURE.—E. Lunet de Lajonquière, *Ethnographie du Tonkin septentrional . . .*, Paris, 1906; A. Bonifacy, 'Contes populaires des Mans du Tonkin,' in *Bull. de l'École fr. d'Ext.-Or.* ii. [1902] 268–279, 'Étude sur les langues parlées par les populations de la Haute-Rivière Claire,' *ib.* v. [1905] 306–327; A. Chéon, 'Notes sur les Muong de la province de Sontay,' *ib.* v. 328–367; E. Diguet, *Etude de la langue Taï*, Hanoï, 1895, *Les Montagnards du Tonkin*, Paris, 1908.

ANTOINE CABATON.

TONGUE. — **1. Physiology.** — The essential organ of taste is 'the mucous membrane which covers the tongue, especially its back part, and the hinder part of the palate.'[1] Here are found certain cells, arranged in groups which are known as 'taste-buds' and are connected with two cranial nerves. Sensations of taste are intermingled with accompanying sensations of touch, and often of smell.[2]

'There appear to be distinct terminal organs for bitter tastes, for sweet tastes, for acid tastes, for salt tastes, and possibly for other tastes, all differing from the terminal organs for tactile sensations, and from the structures, whatever they may be, which are concerned in general sensibility.'[3]

Modern knowledge of the physiology of taste began (1665) with Malpighi (1628–94), who employed the newly invented microscope.[4] The sense of taste was grouped by Aristotle under that of touch, both operating only through immediate contact.[5] Pliny notes that the human palate also possesses the sense of taste, and he gives many details about the variety in the tongues of animals.[6] An Anglo-Saxon leech-book, in prescribing 'for men in whom the string under the tongue is badly swollen,' says that 'through the string first every disorder cometh on the man.'[7] But the chief significance of the tongue for primitive thought is obviously in regard to the faculty of speech, to which it contributes, together with the throat and lips, in the modulation of the voice. That vibration of the vocal cords which is called 'voice' is modified by the varying shape of the resonant chamber formed by the mouth. The tongue, however, is not indispensable to speech; Huxley refers to a case in which conversation remained quite intelligible though the tongue had been completely amputated.

1 T. H. Huxley, *Lessons in Elementary Physiology*, new ed., London, 1900, p. 354.
2 G. F. Stout, *A Manual of Psychology*², London, 1904, p. 195.
3 M. Foster, *A Text-book of Physiology*⁶, pt. iv., London, 1900, p. 1519.
4 M. Foster, *Lectures on the Hist. of Physiology*, Cambridge, 1901, pp. 94, 100.
5 *De Anima*, bk. ii. ch. 10.
6 *HN* xi. 37.
7 J. F. Payne, *English Medicine in Anglo-Saxon Times*, Oxford, 1904, p. 153.

2. Localization of psychical function.—This characteristic of primitive thought concerning the physical organs[1] is frequently illustrated by primitive practices in regard to the tongue. Since the nervous system and the minuter structures of the tissues were unknown to the ancients, the tongue was thought to possess an *inherent* faculty of speech, as something residing in it, so that the faculty or its special qualities could be transferred by acquisition or assimilation of the tongues of specially gifted animals or men.

Thus, among the Tlingits of Alaska, the chief of the spirits sends the candidate for shamanism 'a river-otter, in the tongue of which animal is supposed to be hid the whole power and secret of shamánism. . . . If, however, the spirits will not visit the would-be shamán, or give him any opportunity to get the otter-tongue as described above, the neophyte visits the tomb of a dead shamán, and keeps an awful vigil over night, holding in his living mouth a finger of the dead man or one of his teeth; this constrains the spirits very powerfully to send the necessary otter.'[2] 'In Bohemia the tongue of a male snake, if cut from the living animal on St. George's Eve and placed under a person's tongue, will confer the gift of eloquence.'[3] 'A North American Indian thought that brandy must be a decoction of hearts and tongues, "because," said he, "after drinking it I fear nothing, and I talk wonderfully."'[4] In S.E. Australia 'one of the Wakelbura was observed to take the tongue out of a certain grey-and-white lizard called Bungah, and give it to his little son, a child of about thirteen months old, and gave as a reason for doing so that after eating the tongue his child would soon be able to talk.'[5] 'When a child is late in learning to speak, the Turks of Central Asia will give it the tongues of certain birds to eat.'[6] The converse is illustrated by the belief that the saliva of a queen touching the tongue of a bird gave it human speech.[7] Among the Nubians, 'before the tongue of any animal is eaten, the tip is cut off; on human analogy they believe that "here is the seat of curses and ill-wishes."'[8] It is a common custom of hunters to cut out the tongues of animals that they have killed. Perhaps 'the removal of the tongues is sometimes a precaution to prevent the ghosts of the creatures from telling their sad fate to their sympathising comrades, the living animals of the same sort, who would naturally be frightened, and so keep out of the hunter's way.'[9] The cannibal practice of eating the tongue of a slain enemy is partly based on the idea that the localized qualities are in this way acquired.[10]

3. Ordeals.—The idea of the localization of psychical function and its ethical qualities underlies different forms of the tongue-ordeal.

Lady Anne Blunt records an interesting case of this in connexion with a dispute as to the parentage of a child: 'The matter, as all such matters are in the desert, was referred to arbitration, and the mother's assertion was put to the test by a live coal being placed upon her tongue.'[11] Here the original thought seems to have been that the truth would be elicited when the inherent falsehood of the tongue was, if necessary, burnt out. Similarly, in case of theft among certain W. African tribes, use is made of a needle which the operator 'thrusts through the tongue of each member of the household in succession, to discover the thief, it being believed that it will fail to pierce the tongue of the person who committed the theft.'[12]

Reference to the tongue-ordeal among E. African natives was recently made in the British House of Commons: 'A native chief was investigating a case of cattle theft in the presence of

1 See art. BODY, vol. ii. p. 755 ff.
2 *NR* iii. 147, quoted by H. Spencer, *Descriptive Sociology*, London, 1873–1910, i. 266 n.
3 *GB*³, pt. v., *Spirits of the Corn and of the Wild*, ii. 270.
4 *Ib.* p. 147.
5 Howitt, p. 402.
6 *GB*³, pt. v., *Spirits of the Corn and of the Wild*, ii. 147.
7 *LP* i. 97.
8 E. Crawley, *The Mystic Rose*, London, 1902, p. 111. The thrusting out of the tongue in derision or contempt (Is 57⁴; Livy, vii. 10; Cicero, *de Oratore*, ii. 66 [266]) may be in origin a concentrated curse.
9 *GB*³, pt. v., *Spirits of the Corn and of the Wild*, ii. 269 f., where numerous examples and parallels will be found.
10 J. Robinsohn, *Die Psychologie der Naturvölker*, Leipzig, 1896, pp. 64, 67.
11 *A Pilgrimage to Nejd*², London, 1881, i. 10.
12 A. B. Ellis, *The Tshi-Speaking Peoples of the Gold Coast*, London, 1887, p. 201.

the District Commissioner, Mr. Dundas. The chief called on the accused, one of his people, to go through the native form of ordeal by fire, by licking a hot knife. Mr. Dundas did not prohibit this procedure, but took care that the knife was not sufficiently heated to burn the tongue of the accused.'[1] An ordeal of a different kind is undergone by the medicine-man in certain tribes of Central Australia. The tongue is mysteriously mutilated, and 'remains throughout life perforated in the centre with a hole large enough to admit the little finger.'[2] But this may rather be an example of the frequent practice of mutilating an organ before its special use in order that it may be used with impunity (cf. circumcision, etc., at puberty).

4. Religious usages.—The tongue is not often named as a separate offering in the rites of sacrifice.

The Homeric Greeks concluded a feast by casting the tongues of the victims upon the fire, over which they poured the drink-offering.[3] 'According to some accounts, the tongues of the victims were assigned by the Greeks to Hermes, as the god of speech, or to his human representatives, the heralds.'[4] The Yakut made a special sacrifice, for a sick man's recovery, of tongue, heart, and liver, consuming the rest of the meat themselves.[5] In the horse-sacrifice of the shamanists of N. Asia the tongue of the sacrificed animal is torn out (in order to make its spirit dumb under the shaman's control?).[6]

Honey was placed on the tongue of one who was being initiated into Mithraism, as was the custom with newly-born infants;[7] we may compare with this the ceremonial tasting of milk and honey by those being baptized into the Christian faith.[8] In this connexion may be noticed the miracle of healing ascribed to Martin of Tours, wrought by anointing the tongue of a dumb girl with oil after exorcism.[9] The wide-spread rule of silence (*q.v.*) during particular religious ceremonies falls beyond the scope of this article, but the idea of the localization of function probably underlies the Indian usage recorded by Devendranath Tagore:

'On another elephant sat the Rajaguru (religious preceptor of the Raja) dressed in the ascetic's brick-coloured robe, and silent. He had his tongue encased in wood, lest he should speak.'[10]

5. Penalties.—In the light of these illustrations of the fundamental idea of localized function (or 'diffused consciousness'), we may better understand certain barbarous mutilations widely practised by way of penalty or revenge. These have often survived into times relatively more civilized than those of their origin, when the idea that first prompted them has been lost, viz. the idea of penalizing the guilty organ in which the original evil resides.

The Laws of Ḥammurabi enacted that in certain cases an adopted son denying his new parents was to have his tongue cut out.[11] According to 2 Mac., when the seven brethren were being tortured, the king 'commanded to cut out the tongue of him that had been their spokesman' (7⁴). Judas Maccabæus, 'cutting out the tongue of the impious Nicanor, said that he would give it by pieces to the birds' (15³³). Maximus and two other opponents of Monotheletism were dragged from Rome to Constantinople, where their tongues and right hands were cut off, before they were driven into exile.[12] Blasphemy for the fifth time was punished by excision of the tongue, according to a law (1347) of Philip of Valois (1293–1350).[13] Evagrius writes of the heretic Nestorius: 'I learn from one who wrote an account of his demise, that when his tongue had been eaten through with worms, he departed to the greater and everlasting judgment which awaited him.'[14] The instinct which doubtless created this legend worked also in Fulvia's savage action, when she thrust her needle through the tongue of her dead enemy, Cicero.[1] 'The Clarendon Papers, quoted by Southey, state that at Henley-on-Thames, as late as 1646, it was ordered that a woman's tongue should be nailed to a tree, for complaining of the tax levied by Parliament.'[2]

6. 'Figurative' usages.—The selected evidence already given will prepare us to recognize a deeper meaning in many phrases of ancient literature which the modern mind is apt to dismiss as simply figurative and poetical. The Biblical usages will sufficiently illustrate this. The quality of 'a backbiting tongue' is as inherent as that of 'an angry countenance' (Pr 25^{23}); a lying tongue hates those that it wounds (26^{28}); the tongue devises wickedness, like a sharp razor (Ps 52^{2}); Job asks more literally than most readers suppose, 'Is there injustice on my tongue?' (6^{30}). The Servant of Jahweh declares that his Master has given to him the disciple's tongue, that he may know how to help the weary by his words (Is 50^{4}). In the Messianic future the tongue of the stammerers will be prompt to speak plainly (32^{4}), the tongue of the enemies of Israel will consume away in their mouth (Zec 14^{12}). The tongue is not named in the well-known narrative of Isaiah's call (Is 6), but the cleansing of his lips by the live coal illustrates the principle of the localization of psychical function. So in the NT, when the tongue is said to defile the whole body, and to be a restless evil, full of deadly poison (Ja $3^{6.\,8}$), there is a hidden intensity of meaning derived from primitive thought. The importance of this is seen in regard to such a phenomenon as the 'gift of tongues,'[3] which implies that the local and quasi-independent organ has been taken possession of by the Spirit of God. This is more difficult for the modern mind to conceive sympathetically than it was for the ancient, largely because we have lost touch with the idea of the localization of psychical function and ethical attributes, and have replaced it by that of the cerebral centralization of consciousness.

LITERATURE.—J. G. Frazer, *GB*³, pt. v., *Spirits of the Corn and of the Wild*, London, 1912, ii. 269 f. (where a number of primitive practices in regard to the tongue are collected in a long footnote); J. B. Mayor, *The Epistle of James*³, do. 1910, pp. 219–221, discusses the ethical aspects of the use and abuse of the tongue. See also H. Wheeler Robinson, art. 'Tongue' in *DAC*.

H. WHEELER ROBINSON.

TONGUES.—See CHARISMATA.

TONSURE.

—Tonsure is the shaving or cutting of the hair after a particular fashion as a sign of reception into the clerical order and to the privileges pertaining thereto. As a rite it is preparatory to the reception of holy orders, and is administered by the bishop or by a mitred abbot or by certain privileged priests in whom its administration has been vested by the pope. At first it was part of the ceremony of ordination, but was separated from it towards the end of the 7th century. The origin of the tonsure is obscure, but from passages in the Fathers it is clear that long hair in men was considered effeminate or worse, and this was particularly true in the case of monks. Epiphanius censures some Mesopotamian monks for their long hair against the rule of the Church, and Jerome is particularly indignant at the custom.[4] A monk's hair had thus to be cut short, though not shaven, as this was the custom with the priests of Isis.[5] The earliest tonsure was probably no more than a close cutting of the hair of the entire head, though this may have become a shaving of the whole head after the manner of

1 As reported in the *Manchester Guardian* of 6th May 1914.

2 Spencer-Gillen^a, pp. 523–525, with accompanying photograph. A Hebrew name for an enchanter is 'a master of the tongue' (Ec 10¹¹).

3 *Od.* iii. 333–341.

4 *GB*³, pt. v., *Spirits of the Corn and of the Wild*, ii. 270, where references will be found.

5 F. B. Jevons, *An Introd. to the Hist. of Religion*², London, 1902, p. 146.

6 W. Radloff, *Aus Sibirien*², Leipzig, 1893, ii. 26.

7 F. Cumont, *Les Mystères de Mithra*³, Brussels, 1913, p. 162.

8 *ERE* ii. 386ᵇ.

9 Sulpicius Severus, *Dial.* iii. 2; cf. Mk 7³³⁻³⁵.

10 *The Autobiography of Maharashi Devendranath Tagore*, Eng. tr., London, 1914, p. 131.

11 C. H. W. Johns, *The Oldest Code of Laws in the World*, Edinburgh, 1903, p. 42, § 192; cf. S. A. Cook, *The Laws of Moses and the Code of Ḥammurabi*, London, 1903, p. 134.

12 W. F. Adeney, *The Greek and Eastern Churches*, Edinburgh, 1908, p. 130.

13 Fernand Nicolaÿ, *Hist. des croyances, superstitions, mœurs, usages et coutumes (selon le plan du Décalogue)*, Paris, 1902, i. 380 (numerous other examples given).

14 *HE* i. 7.

1 C. Merivale, *Hist. of the Romans under the Empire*, new ed., London, 1904, iii. 206.

2 Edward Eggleston, *The Beginners of a Nation*, London, 1897, p. 67.

3 See art. CHARISMATA, vol. iii. p. 370.

4 Epiph. *Hær.* lxxx.; Jerome, *Ep.* xxii. 'ad Eustoch.,' § 28.

5 Herod. ii. 36; Martial, xii. 29.

the Nazirites and those under a vow (Nu 6^{18}, Ac 21^{24}).[1] It may also have been adopted by monks as a symbol of a penitential life, since penitents had their hair shorn. This is the Eastern form of tonsure, or that of St. Paul. Bede tells how Theodore of Tarsus, before being consecrated by Pope Vitalian in A.D. 668, waited four months for his hair to grow, that it might be shorn into the shape of a crown (the second or Western form of tonsure, or St. Peter's), 'for he had the tonsure of St. Paul the apostle, after the manner of the Eastern people.'[2] The Petrine tonsure consists in leaving only a circlet of hair round a shaven crown, this symbolizing the crown of thorns or the crown of Christ's royal priesthood. It had displaced the Pauline form in the West, and is first mentioned by Gregory of Tours (6th cent.), and was worn by Pope Gregory the Great (A.D. 590–604), who sent Augustine to England.[3] It is ordered in the 41st canon of the Council of Toledo (A.D. 633)—that 'all clerics must shave the whole front part of the head, and leave behind only a circular crown' of hair on the lower part. While tonsure arose as a monastic custom, it was soon adopted by all clergy, probably before the end of the 6th cent., and the Quinisext Council of 692 appoints it for such lesser orders as readers and singers.

A third form, that of St. John—or of St. James, as its upholders claimed—seems to have been peculiar to the Celtic Church, and occasioned great controversy with the missionaries from Rome, who were astonished to find it in use in Britain, and vigorously combated its use. Nevertheless it continued to be used long after the Synod of Whitby (A.D. 664), which decided against it. What precisely its nature was is uncertain. The Irish Druids are known to have used a tonsure, perhaps denoting servitude to the gods, as it was customary for a warrior to vow his hair to a divinity if victory were granted him.[4] The Druidic tonsure seems to have consisted in cutting all the hair on the anterior part of the head from ear to ear, except a small patch at the forehead.[5] This was looked upon as the tonsure of Simon Magus, regarded as the archdruid or Magus. It has been thought that the Celtic Christian tonsure resembled this and was retained through national feelings. But there was apparently some difference, possibly slight, and it is hardly likely that, while other Druidic observances were banned, this would be retained. Two views are held regarding the Celtic Christian tonsure. (1) It left the hair long at the back, the upper part of the front being shaved so as to leave a band of hair round the forehead from ear to ear.[6] This view was first mooted by Thomas Innes, who says:

> 'The tonsure of the Scots was not fully round and did not reach the hindermost part of the head, and therefore resembled a crescent or semi-circle.'[7]

(2) All the front of the head was shaved, to a line from ear to ear, behind which the hair was grown.[1] Each of these forms has strong supporters, but the former is probably confirmed by Ceolfrid's account of his discussion with Adamnan, who wore the Celtic tonsure, and to whom he said:

> 'You who think you are advancing to the crown of life which has no end, why do you wear on your head the representation of a crown which has an end, as Simon Magus did? His tonsure resembled a crown in front but on closer inspection was seen to be imperfect.'[2]

The adherents of the Petrine tonsure generally ascribed the origin of the Celtic to Simon Magus, by way of contempt, or, for the same reason, to the swine-herd of King Loigaire MacNeill.[3] At an earlier time St. Patrick, who was tonsured after the then prevailing Roman manner, viz. the whole head shorn, tried to induce its adoption, but apparently in vain.[4] According to Bede, the community at Iona and the others subject to it accepted the Petrine tonsure about A.D. 716, but other Britons did not conform then.[5] The Celtic tonsure, carried by emigrant Britons to Armorica, was known there in the 9th century.

The Latin form of tonsure with regulars leaves often no more than a circlet of hair; with seculars it is smaller. According to the Synod of Placentia (A.D. 1388), it was to be of the breadth of three fingers. Once the tonsure has been received, it must always be retained.

LITERATURE.—Besides the works cited, see E. Martène, *de Antiquis Ecclesiae Ritibus*, Venice, 1783; artt. 'Tonsur' in *PRE*[3], and in H. J. Wetzer and B. Welte, *Kirchenlexicon*[2], Freiburg i. Br., 1882–1901.

J. A. MACCULLOCH.

TONSURE (Buddhist).—There is no mention of tonsure, and no regulation as to the method to be adopted in wearing or not wearing the hair, in the 227 original rules of the Buddhist order of mendicants. But in the *Khandhakas*, or collection of subsidiary and supplemental rules, completed at the end of the first century after the Buddha's death, we find the following paragraphs:

> 1. 'You are not, O Bhikkhus, to wear long hair. Whosoever does so, shall be guilty of a minor breach of the regulations [*i.e.* of a *dukkaṭa*]. I allow you, O Bhikkhus, hair that is two months old, or two inches long.'
> 2. 'You are not, O Bhikkhus, to smooth the hair with a comb, or with a snake's hood [*i.e.* with an ivory instrument so shaped], or with the hand held in that shape, or with pomade, or with hair-oil.' . . .
> 3. 'I allow you, O Bhikkhus, the use of razors, of a hone to sharpen the razors on, of powder prepared with Sipāṭika-gum to prevent them rusting, of a sheath to hold them in, and of all the apparatus of a barber.' . . .
> 4. 'You are not, O Bhikkhus, to have the hair of your heads or on your face cut by barbers, nor to let it grow long.' . . .
> 5. 'You are not, O Bhikkhus, to have your hair cut off with a knife.'[6]

We should not draw, from the fact of these paragraphs being found among the subsidiary rules, any conclusion that they belong to a later time than the original rules. The subsidiary rules refer quite often to what were evidently older customs in the order, and only legalize and give authority to practices already followed, though not mentioned in the older rules. But we should notice in the first place that there is no mention of scissors. The reason of this is curious; scissors had not then been invented. This is confirmed by an exception to rule 5 above. If a *bhikkhu* had a sore on the head, and the hair round it could not be removed by a razor, then a knife might be used.[7] In this case no doubt, if scissors had been

[1] And also as a mark of servitude to God, since Roman and Greek slaves had their heads shaven.
[2] Bede, *HE* iv. 1.
[3] Greg. *Vitæ Patrum*, xvii.; Joannes Diac. *S. Gregorii Magni Vita*, in *PL* lxxv. 230.
[4] Adamnan, *Life of St. Columba*, ed. W. Reeves ('Historians of Scotland'), Edinburgh, 1874, p. 237; J. H. Todd, *St. Patrick: his Life and Mission*, Dublin, 1864, p. 455; P. W. Joyce, *A Social Hist. of Ancient Ireland*, London, 1903, i. 234; J. Rhys, *The Origin and Growth of Religion as illustrated by Celtic Heathendom* (*HL*), London, 1888, p. 213, *Celtic Britain*[4], do. 1908, p. 73 f.
[5] L. Gougaud, *Les Chrétientés celtiques*, Paris, 1911, p. 198, quoting *MS Cotton, Otho E*, xii. fol. 112[b].
[6] J. Dowden, 'An Examination of Original Documents on the Question of the Form of the Celtic Tonsure,' *Proceedings of the Society of Antiquaries of Scotland*, xxx. [1895–96] 325 ff.; John Smith, 'de Tonsura Clericorum,' Appendix to Bede, *HE* (*PL* xcv. 327 f.).
[7] *Civil and Eccles. Hist. of Scotland, A.D. 80–818* (Spalding Club Publications, xx.), Aberdeen, 1853.

[1] Reeves, *Introd.* p. cxiv; Todd, p. 487; Bede, v. 21.
[2] The tonsure here referred to was a mere segment with a half circlet of hair in front and the hair worn full behind.
[3] Bede, v. 21; Rhys, *Celtic Britain*[4], p. 74; Gougaud, p. 197.
[4] A. W. Haddan and W. Stubbs, *Councils and Ecclesiastical Documents relating to Great Britain and Ireland*, Oxford, 1869–78, ii. 292, 328.
[5] Bede, v. 22.
[6] *Vinaya*, ii. 107, 134, tr. in *Vinaya Texts*, iii. 69 f., 138 f.
[7] The word *satthaka* (*Vin.* ii. 115) has been rendered 'scissors' by Sten Konow, *JPTS*, 1909, p. 55. But this cannot be right. See Buddhaghoṣa as quoted in *Vinaya Texts*, iii. 90.

then known in the Ganges valley, their use would have been allowed, at least as an alternative.[1]

The members of the order, we see, were to be shaven, not only on the face, but all over the head; and the shaving had to be performed, not by a barber, but by fellow-members. Why was this the rule? Undoubtedly because this was the custom previously followed by the *religieux* belonging to the other orders that we know to have been older than the Buddha's time. It was only natural that men who had devoted themselves to the higher life, and whose main duty was the learning by heart and the repetition of texts dealing with the higher life as they conceived it, should have thought it becoming to themselves to avoid, not only the use of fashionable clothing, but also the elaborate hair-dressing then habitually used by men of the world. The medallions carved in bas-relief on the stone railings round the Bharhut tope may serve as illustrations of these turban-like arrangements, in which strips of brocaded cloth are intertwined with the hair (left long), the faces being clean shaven.[2] Though the sculptures are later in date, earlier texts confirm the general style by descriptions ambiguous without the help of such illustrations.

There is one passage in a very early text, about the same age as the five paragraphs, which confirms the suggestion that those paragraphs probably give us the earliest customs as to shaving followed in the order. That is *Dīgha*, i. 90, in the *Ambaṭṭha Suttanta*, where a Brāhman, reviling the adherents of the new movement, and in fact referring to the Buddha himself, calls them 'shavelings, sham friars, the off-scouring of our kinsman's heels.'[3] It is clear that, in the view of the compilers of this passage, the members of the order had their heads shaven. Another such passage is preserved in the popular anthology called *Dhammapada*, 264, which says: 'Not by his shaven crown is one a *samaṇa*' (a member of any order of *religieux*, a 'religious'), if he be irreligious. It should be noticed that the technical word used is not *bhikkhu* (a member of the Buddhist order), but *samaṇa*, which included non-Buddhist orders also.

In the much later legend of the Great Renunciation—it is at least about seven centuries later than the event which it purports to relate—we are told that the first act of the future Buddha after he had 'gone forth' was:

'Taking his sword in his right hand, and holding the plaited tresses of his hair, and its twisted decoration with his left, he cut them off. So his hair became two inches long, and lay close to his scalp curling from the right, and so it remained his life-long; and his beard the same.'[4]

Now the oldest representations of the Buddha that we possess—the so-called Græco-Buddhist bas-reliefs and statues—are an endeavour to reproduce the coiffure thus described. This story, therefore, as to the imperfect form of the tonsure habitually followed by the Buddha himself, must have been credited, incredible as it seems to us, at the date of those sculptures, not only in the Ganges valley, but also beyond the present frontiers of India, in the extreme north-west. In the second place, the inventors of the story ascribe to the Buddha the belief that every *religieux*—not only Buddhists, for there were none then—should have the hair cut quite short. In other words, they claim a pre-Buddhist origin for the custom followed in the Buddhist order. Perhaps the whole episode is merely invented as a popular explanation of the odd rule as to two inches in the first of the five paragraphs quoted above.

1 *Vinaya*, ii. 134, tr. *Vinaya Texts*, iii. 139.
2 See figs. 21 and 22 in Rhys Davids, *Buddhist India*, pp. 94–97.
3 The whole episode is translated in Rhys Davids, *Dialogues of the Buddha*, i. 112 ff.
4 *Jātaka-nidāna*, p. 64 (vol. i. of the *Jātaka*, ed. Fausböll).

At the present time the *bhikkhus* in Burma, Siam, and Ceylon hold theoretically to the two-inch rule, but in practice never appear in public without the head and face clean shaven. The numerous sects of Buddhists in Tibet and Mongolia, China, and Japan have long ago forgotten, if they ever knew, the ancient rule. But we have no exact particulars as to when and where they have enacted and carried out any newer rules of their own.

LITERATURE.—*Vinaya Piṭaka*, ed. H. Oldenberg, 5 vols., London, 1879–83; T. W. Rhys Davids and H. Oldenberg, *Vinaya Texts*, 3 vols., Oxford, 1880–85 (*SBE* xiii., xvii., xx.); Rhys Davids, *Buddhist India* ('Story of the Nations' ser.), London, 1903, *Dialogues of the Buddha*, 2 vols., Oxford, 1899–1910 (*SBB* ii., iii.); *The Jātaka, with its Commentary*, ed. V. Fausböll, tr. Rhys Davids, London, 1877–97, i.

T. W. RHYS DAVIDS.

TONSURE (Chinese).—**1. Confucian.**—Confucianism, being a system of ethics, has no priests or monks. The tonsure is therefore unknown in it.

2. Buddhist.—(*a*) *Monks.*—The Buddhist tonsure was brought into China by monks from India. The whole head is shaved once a month or oftener. With boys brought up in monasteries, being either dedicated by their parents to a religious life or bought by the monks for that purpose, the tonsure takes place early, but with others the age is often eighteen or twenty. At the reception of a novice the liturgy directs that the introducer of the candidate shall ask the chapter assembled that the tonsure may be granted. This acceded to, the vows are taken.[1] A rite which is apparently a constant sequel of the tonsure consists of the branding of the head with from three to eighteen small circular spots.[2] A mutilation of one or more fingers is also sometimes undergone. An explanation of the Buddhist tonsure given by some of the Chinese is that it indicates the 'desire to put away . . . everything of the world, so that the monk does not claim as his own even his hair.'[3]

(*b*) *Nuns.*—Aspirants are received at the age of ten into the nunnery, and their novitiate continues till they are sixteen. During these years only the front part of the head is shaved, but all the hair is shaved when they become nuns. A woman desiring to become a nun must obtain the consent of parents, husband, or guardians.

'One of these must act as sponsor to her at the time of initiation and must hand the razor to be employed in shaving her head to the Prioress who is to perform the ceremony.'[4]

3. Taoist.—(*a*) *Monks.*—Taoist monks shave all about the crown, but the rest of the hair is allowed to grow long and is gathered together into a top-knot fastened by a wooden article like the back of a tortoise.[5] In some cases all the hair is allowed to grow.[6]

(*b*) *Nuns.*—Taoist nuns do not shave their heads, but have their hair done up on the top of their heads.[7]

4. Dislike of the tonsure.—Though Buddhism has benefited largely in the past from the favour of emperors, the tonsure has often been very obnoxious to the governing classes in China, who doubtless took it as the outward sign of the celibate priesthood, which severs its connexion with the family, entirely against Chinese ideas of the paramount importance of domestic life. Memorialists inveigh strongly against it. The following are instances:

In A.D. 624, in a memorial to the emperor requesting the suppression of Buddhism, it was stated that it caused people to

1 L. Wieger, *Buddhisme chinois*, Ho Kân Fu, 1910, i. 151.
2 S. Couling, *Encyclopædia Sinica*, Shanghai, 1817, *s.v.* 'Tonsure'; *The Chinese Recorder*, Shanghai, ix. [1878] 181 ff.
3 J. Doolittle, *Social Life of the Chinese*, London, 1866, ii. 241.
4 *Woman's Work in China*, vii. [1883] 27 ff.
5 W. Milne, in *The Chinese Repository*, xiii. [1844] 25.
6 Doolittle, ii. 243.
7 J. H. Gray, *China*, London, 1878, i. 104.

'shave their heads and abandon their ruler and their parents.'[1] The memorialist says again: 'Before the Western Tsin Dynasty [A.D. 256–317] reigned, the ruling dynasties enacted stringent laws by which the people of the Middle Kingdom were prevented from shaving the head at pleasure.'[2]

In A.D. 995 an edict threatened severe punishment to those who were 'shaved surreptitiously' without first obtaining permission of their district prefect to become monks or nuns.[3]

In A.D. 1408 it was decreed that, 'if any person surreptitiously took the tonsure to become a monk,' he should be punished with a term of hard labour, and after that become a husbandman.[4]

The determination of the Chinese Government to keep the tonsure as well as the age of receiving it under their control is seen in other enactments. Taoists are also mentioned in some of these cases.[5] Eight blows was the punishment under the Manchu dynasty to Buddhist or Taoist who in the one case took the tonsure and in the other did up his hair on his own account.[6] At the same time monks were not allowed to go about without the tonsure, and pupils adopted by the Buddhist clergy had to be tonsured. Those in monasteries without the tonsure had to return to secular life, being neither monks nor laymen.[7] This was the case also in A.D. 1458 for those who had been tonsured after twenty, but the culprits were to be banished for life;[8] and in A.D. 1537 it was decreed that not only those who privately shaved their heads, but also their parents, neighbours, and helpers,[9] were to be punished.

5. Ridicule of the tonsure.—The tonsure of the Buddhist lends itself to the derision of the Chinese, who are very susceptible to anything that opens a way to mockery or banter. One term applied to the Buddhist monk is 'bald-headed ass,' another is 'bald-headed thief.'[10] As a further example of the way in which the shorn and shaven priest is despised may be instanced the curious custom of shaving the head of a young boy in order that the evil spirits may think that he is of no consequence—in fact worthless to the parents—and thus pass him by uninjured. The boy is then called 'Buddhist priest.' The present writer saw an instance of this in the case of a neighbour's son in Canton.[11]

6. The Manchu tonsure.—A species of tonsure was practised by every male except monks in China under the Manchu rule of the country. The hair is now allowed to grow, instead of the greater part of it being shaved off.

7. Tonsure of children.—Young children's heads are also shaved to a large extent. The first shaving of an infant's head, when a month old, often has a religious character, being done before an idol or the ancestral tablets.[12]

LITERATURE.—See the works referred to in the footnotes.

J. DYER BALL.

TONSURE (Hindu).—*Chūḍā*, 'tonsure,' is the name of an ancient rite in India, also called *chūḍākaraṇam* or *chūḍākarma*, *chaulam*, which is performed on boys, sometimes on girls also, and derives its name from the tuft of hair left on the top of the boy's head (*chūḍā*). According to the ancient rule, this rite is to be performed when the boy is three years old, or, in the lower castes, in his fifth or seventh year. The boy is dressed in new clothes, and placed on his mother's lap. A barber cuts his hair with a razor, while sacred verses from the Veda are recited. The hair is thrown on a heap of cow-dung, and afterwards dug into the ground (see Hillebrandt, *Rituallitteratur*, Strassburg, 1897). It is interesting to note that this rite, as pointed out in Gerini's monograph on the tonsure rite in Siam, has spread into Siam, together with other Brāhmanical institutions. In India it has been invested with some legal importance, the Sanskrit lawbooks stating that a boy on whom the ceremony of tonsure has been performed in the family of his birth is no longer capable of being affiliated to another person (see Jolly, *Tagore Law Lectures*, Calcutta, 1885). The tonsure rite is carefully kept by many castes of the present day, though the time of its performance varies. Thus the Kanoj Brāhmans of Poona perform the rite when a boy is from six months to two years old; the Lingayats, after a year; the Vanis, at any time from six months to five years. Sometimes the child is taken to the village temple for the ceremony, or after its performance (see the *Bombay Gazetteer*, *passim*; Rai Bahadur L. B. Nath, *Hinduism*, Meerut, 1899). The tonsure rite is supposed to belong to the common heirloom of Indo-European nations, because similar rites and superstitions occur in the Avesta of the Zoroastrians, and, particularly, among some Slavic nations, such as the Servians and Bohemians.

LITERATURE.—J. Kirste, 'Indogermanische Gebräuche beim Haarschneiden,' *Analecta Graeciensia*, Graz, 1893; Potanski, *Die Ceremonie der Haarschur bei den Slaven und Germanen*, Cracow, 1896.

J. JOLLY.

TOPHET.—Although the OT references to Tophet, the scene of the Moloch sacrifices in the Valley of Hinnom, leave no doubt as to its great importance in the popular religion of Judah in the period before the reformation under Josiah, the place itself is mentioned only in the following places: 2 K 23^{10}, Is 30^{33}, Jer $7^{31f.}$ $19^{6.11.12-13}$. The similar word in Job 17^{6} is clearly not to be understood in this connexion. The original pronunciation of the word, which is transliterated in the LXX Τάφεθ or Θαφέθ, is unknown, the Masoretic pronunciation in this case, as in others, being due to the substitution of the vowels of בֹּשֶׁת, 'shame.' Moreover, the etymology of the word is quite uncertain, and it cannot be determined whether the final *t* is radical or is merely the feminine ending. In Is 30^{33} indeed the form is תָּפְתֶּה, which, if the text could be trusted, would be evidence of the former alternative, unless the word should be understood as having a double feminine ending such as יְשׁוּעָתָה (Ps 3^{3}). But against this supposition is the fact that the word is construed as masculine in its immediate context. In any case, since, with the exception of Is 30^{33}, it always has the definite article or is capable of being so pointed, it is evident that it is not strictly a proper name. We may reasonably infer that there were several *tophets*, although we know only of the one which was situated in the Valley of Hinnom.

Robertson Smith,[1] arguing from the fact that 'at the time when the word תפת first appears in Hebrew, the chief foreign influence in Judæan religion was that of Damascus (2 K 16),' sought to connect the word with the Aramaic *tfaya*, which means a 'stand or tripod set upon a fire . . . of which we might, according to known analogies, have a variant *tfāth*. The corresponding Hebrew word is אַשְׁפֹּת (for *shfāth*), which means an ashpit or dunghill, but primarily must have denoted the fireplace.' But this explanation of the word by an Aramaic etymology takes for granted that the cult practised at the *tophet*, or at any rate the precise ritual of the cult, was a comparatively new-fangled thing in the 7th cent. B.C., and there are grave difficulties in such an assumption. Even if Ahaz did bring from Damascus a new contrivance for burning the children's bodies, why should it have kept in Hebrew its Aramaic name, when the Hebrew language itself possessed the same word with the ordinary dialectic difference? When the same king introduced in Jerusalem the innova-

1 J. J. M. de Groot, *Sectarianism and Religious Persecution in China*, Amsterdam, 1903, p. 37.
2 *Ib.* p. 39.
3 *Ib.* p. 73 f.
4 *Ib.* p. 83.
5 *Ib.* pp. 97, 114.
6 *Ib.* p. 100; also see p. 80.
7 *Ib.* p. 114.
8 *Ib.* p. 85.
9 *Ib.* p. 88.
10 E. J. Dukes, *Every-day Life in China*, London, 1885, p. 183, and see also Chinese-English dictionaries.
11 Also see Gray, i. 112, note 1.
12 Doolittle, i. 122 f.

1 *The Religion of the Semites*2, p. 377.

tion of a great stone altar, it was called by the Hebrew word for 'altar,' not the Aramaic. Moreover, it is extremely improbable that such a practice as the sacrifice of the first-born should have been suddenly introduced into Jerusalem as late as the 8th cent. B.C. When it is considered how hard debased superstitions have died in our own country—if indeed they are dead—we can understand the survival or even the recrudescence in Palestine of aboriginal superstitions, but not the adoption of so terrible a rite as human sacrifice by a people who had reached an altogether higher level of religion. The OT is unintelligible unless it is recognized that the population of Palestine in the days of the kings of Judah and Israel was not so homogeneous as later writers imagined it to have been, and that the true-born Israelites were in a minority. In a fusion of races there is, no doubt, a tendency for the higher to be drawn down to the level of the lower. When a man of fairly good intelligence, but not possessed of any strong religious convictions, marries a thoroughly superstitious woman, it is the wife's superstition rather than the husband's intellect that will be the dominant factor in the household. And that the sacrifice of the first-born was a deeply-rooted Canaanite cult is proved not only by the excavations at Gezer,[1] but also by more than one passage in the OT. It is most significant that the E document of the Pentateuch represents God as commanding Abraham to sacrifice Isaac (Gn 22^{2}), and that the same document in its legislation (Ex $22^{29f.}$) puts the first-born of men and cattle on exactly the same level, not requiring the redemption of the former as is ordered in Ex 34^{20} (J). And that a law allowing, if not requiring, the sacrifice of the first-born was at one time issued in Jahweh's name is evident not only from Ezk $20^{25f.}$, but also from Jeremiah's protest (7^{31}; cf. 19^{5}) that Jahweh had never commanded or contemplated any such cult. Although Ahaz is the first king of Judah of whom it is definitely stated that he sacrificed his first-born, it would be unsafe to conclude that he was the first who actually did so; for what had been done by earlier kings unheeded may well have called forth a vehement protest in the days of Isaiah. Certainly, if the stories of David recorded in the books of Samuel are based on a sound tradition, and are not merely what later prophets of the non-reforming party thought David must have done, there would be no difficulty in supposing that even David had presided over the Moloch cult at the *tophet* in the Valley of Hinnom. On the other hand, it must not be forgotten that, as the story of the Rechabites proves, certain strata of the population remained till a late period aloof from and uncontaminated by the Canaanite elements, and it is doubtless these non-Canaanite elements that we ought to credit with the attempts made from time to time to abolish the worst of the pre-Israelite superstitions which threatened to swamp the religion of Jahweh. There is no reason to question the statements in the book of Kings that reforms were attempted in the days of Asa and of Jehoshaphat.

While it is not improbable that the method of burning the bodies at the *tophet* in the Valley of Hinnom was the same as that adopted elsewhere,[1] it is by no means clear that either the cult itself or its ritual came from Damascus. It must not be overlooked that the *tophet*, or at any rate the place of the *tophet*, is called in Jer 19^{5} 32^{35} 'the high places of the Baal.' The point of Jer 7^{32} is that in the massacres which may be expected corpses not slain in sacrifice will be buried at the *tophet*—proof of the impotence of the *tophet* sacrifices to avert the divine wrath.

Robertson Smith, in discussing the meaning of Is 30^{33}, writes as follows:

> 'It appears that Tophet means a pyre, such as is prepared for a king. But the Hebrews themselves did not burn their dead, unless in very exceptional cases, and burial was equally the rule among their Phœnician neighbours, as is plain from researches in their cemeteries, and apparently among all the Semites. Thus, when the prophet describes the deep and wide pyre "prepared for the king," he does not draw his figure from ordinary life, nor is it conceivable that he is thinking of the human sacrifices in the valley of Hinnom, a reference which would bring an utterly discordant strain into the imagery. What he does refer to is a rite well known to Semitic religion, which was practised at Tarsus down to the time of Dio Chrysostom, and the memory of which survives in the Greek legend of Heracles-Melcarth, in the story of Sardanapalus, and in the myth of Queen Dido.'[2]

But surely at a time when sacrifices were being offered to Moloch, *i.e.* the king, at the *tophet*, a statement that a *tophet* has been prepared for a king must have suggested the ritual of the Valley of Hinnom; the prophet declares with grim Hebrew irony that a *tophet* has indeed been prepared for a king, only in this case the king will be the victim and not the recipient of the sacrifice.

How long *tophets* remained in Palestine it is impossible to say. It is asserted (2 K 23^{10}) that the one in the Valley of Hinnom was defiled by Josiah; but this statement occurs in a passage which appears to be secondary, and, even if Josiah tried to put a stop to the cult, there may have been a recrudescence of it after his death; and beyond the limits of his diminutive kingdom it probably continued considerably later. It is difficult to see why Jeremiah should have published his denunciation of the *tophet* in the fourth year of Jehoiakim, if it had been abolished once for all in the eighteenth year of Josiah. And if, as seems probable, Deuteronomy is to be dated in the 6th cent. B.C., it is evident that as late as that time it was still necessary, at least in some parts of Palestine, to protest against the sacrifice of children (Dt 18^{10}). Moreover, the prophecy in Is 30, though based on a genuine utterance of Isaiah, bears many evidences of having been modified at a later date, and, if Asshur here, as in $11^{11.\,16}$ and $19^{23ff.}$ (cf. Ezr 6^{22}), means the Seleucid empire, the king referred to in the present form of the passage may be Antiochus Epiphanes. It is certainly not impossible that in some outlying districts of Palestine, such as Ammon, Moab, or Edom, the cult associated with the *tophets* held its own down to the 2nd cent. B.C.

LITERATURE.—S. D. F. Salmond, art. 'Tophet, Topheth,' in *HDB*; W. Robertson Smith, *The Religion of the Semites*², London, 1894.

R. H. KENNETT.

TÔRĀH.—See LAW.

TORCH (Greek and Roman).—In common with other races, the Greeks and Romans held many festivals at night, when torchlight was a practical

[1] That the skeletons found at Gezer belonged to children who had been sacrificed appears more natural than the explanation adopted by J. G. Frazer (*GB*³, pt. iv., *Adonis, Attis, Osiris*, London, 1914, i. 108 f.), nor is the greater age of some of the children whose skeletons were found in Tell Ta'annek conclusive proof to the contrary. It is evident that the redemption of the first-born must have been a not uncommon custom before it was required by law (Ex 34). Parents would endeavour to save their children by substituting some other victim, and, if all went well afterwards, would assume that the god had been satisfied. In time of great distress, however, it would be imagined that the god had not been contented with the substitute and demanded his real due. See art. REDEMPTION.

[1] 'The human holocaust is not burned on an altar, but on a pyre or fire-pit constructed for the occasion. This appears both in the myths of Dido and Heracles and in actual usage. At Tarsus a very fair pyre is erected yearly for the burning of Heracles; in the Carthaginian sacrifice of boys the victims fall into a pit of flame, and in the Harranian ox-sacrifice the victim is fastened to a grating placed over a vault filled with burning fuel: finally, Isaiah's Tophet is a broad and deep excavation filled with wood exactly like the fiery trench in which, according to Arabic tradition, the victims of 'Amr b. Hind and the martyrs of Nejrān found their end' (Robertson Smith², p. 376 f.).

[2] P. 372 f.

necessity, and need have no particular religious significance. But the torch was also important in various ceremonies where its presence was not merely utilitarian; and in many cases where it may have been originally used for merely practical purposes it acquired a sacred or symbolic meaning. In agricultural festivals, *e.g.*, the use of fire is a well-known rite, although its precise significance may be doubted. Mannhardt and Frazer have collected a large number of customs which illustrate fire-ritual as a means of promoting the growth of crops and animals.[1] The underlying idea may sometimes be a belief that earthly fire represents the sun; and torches, carried over the fields, may be the means, by sympathetic magic, of 'making sunshine.' It is more probable, however, that the fertility which the use of fire is believed to cause is to be explained by its purifying power.

In Greek myth and ritual the torch is specially connected with Demeter. According to the Homeric hymn, the goddess, after the rape of Persephone, rushed wildly in search of her daughter with lighted torches in her hands. The hymn deals with the Eleusinian mysteries, and it is probable that the actual rites observed by the initiated were attributed to the example of the goddess. The Eleusinia[2] included a 'torch-day' (*lampadum dies*), when the *μύσται* roamed along the shore with torches. They supposed themselves to be imitating the wanderings of Demeter; but the original meaning of the rite was doubtless to purify the land and ward off pestilence from the crops. In the same way the early Eleusinians seem to have purified their children by making them pass over the fire, as the myth of Demophon, in the same hymn, appears to indicate.[3] The most solemn ceremonies at Eleusis took place at night, when the hall of the mysteries (*μυστικὸς δόμος*) was lit by torches. One of the chief officials was called the 'torch-bearer' (*δᾳδοῦχος*), and a priest bearing the same title took part in another festival (the Lenæa), and assisted at a rite of purification or atonement of sin.[4] Juvenal[5] speaks of the torch as the special emblem of the Eleusinian priest.

The torch is an attribute of various Greek deities besides Demeter. Persephone has the same emblem as her mother. In literature and art we find the torch regularly associated with Hecate, perhaps as a moon-goddess.[6] Artemis is also commonly represented with a torch in literature[7] and in art from the 4th cent. B.C. Here the torch may be the symbol of a moon-goddess; but Farnell,[8] who holds that Artemis was originally an earth-goddess, thinks that it belongs to her as a deity of vegetation. The torches which in art are a frequent attribute of the Mænads are perhaps best explained by reference to their nocturnal festivals. Finally, Ares sometimes carries a torch, an appropriate emblem for the god of war.[9]

In Greek custom the most conspicuous example of the use of torches is in the torch-race (*λαμπαδηφορία*, *λαμπαδηδρομία*, or, most often, simply *λαμπάς*). This competition is best known as Athenian; but it is also recorded for other Greek states, and Alexander included it in most of the festivals which he established in various cities. In Athens the torch-race was a feature of various festivals, in honour of Prometheus, Athene (in the Panathenæa), Hephæstus, Pan, Bendis, Hermes, and Theseus. It was even held in the festival of the dead (*ἐπιτάφια*). The date of its institution is unknown, but it was first held in honour of Prometheus, the fire-bringer, at whose altar the competitors lit their torches. As regards the festival of Pan, we know that the race was instituted after the battle of Marathon. At the Bendidea it was run on horseback, and was a novelty in the time of Socrates; elsewhere the race was on foot. The competitors were apparently chosen from the several Attic tribes. The torch was passed from one member of a team to another, at fixed intervals along the course, and the victory rested with the team whose lighted torch first reached the goal—an altar on which fire was kindled with the torch. This procedure gave rise to the famous simile of Lucretius ('et, quasi cursores, vitaï lampada tradunt'), the idea of which is found in Plato.[1] An equally famous line in Æschylus[2] also refers to the race, although the exact point is doubtful.

Æschylus might possibly have meant that all the runners in the winning team have an equal share in the victory, the last no less than the first; but more probably he refers to the fact that the winning torch was handed in by the last to receive it. This man would be first in relation to the rival teams, but last in relation to his own.

The Greeks themselves explained the torch-race as a commemoration of the gift of fire by Prometheus;[3] but the original motive must have been something more than a mere commemoration. The essential feature seems to lie in the transference of fire from one altar to another at the greatest possible speed. It is probable, therefore, that the underlying idea is the need of carrying fire from a pure source to take the place of a polluted fire. At Athens all fires were extinguished before the race began (at least in the Promethea), and were rekindled from the new fire. A belief in the pollution of fire is shown in the Argive custom of extinguishing fire after a death, and rekindling it from another source *ὡς μεμιασμένον*.[4] Similarly the fires at Platæa were defiled by the presence of barbarians, and new fire was brought from the sacred hearth of Delphi. The attraction of such a rite to the cults of Prometheus and Hephæstus needs no explanation. Athene, too, might well have adopted a torch-race, as being the patron of handicrafts and metal-working, for which fire was a necessity; but more probably she claimed the torch-race as the supreme head of the city. The race seems less appropriate to the other gods, with the possible exception of Pan. The theory that he was a sun-god cannot be accepted; but fire certainly played a part in his ritual, and an ever-burning lamp was maintained in his cave under the Acropolis. Most probably, however, the Athenians instituted the race in his honour to commemorate his appearance to the runner Philippides after the battle of Marathon. Once established, the race became popular, and was attached to other festivals without any special religious fitness.

The Romans had no torch-race, and the torch was less prominent in their ritual than in Greek religion. But the same ideas can be traced in Italy as appear in Greek fire-rites, although it is not always possible to distinguish the indigenous from the borrowed element; *e.g.*, the festival of Diana at Aricia (Nemi) no doubt belongs to a primitive Italian stratum, but it is impossible to say how far Greek influence may have modified its

1 W. Mannhardt, *Der Baumkultus der Germanen und ihrer Nachbarstämme*, Berlin, 1875, p. 497 f.; J. G. Frazer, *GB*², London, 1900, iii. 313, and *GB*³, pt. vii., *Balder the Beautiful*, do. 1913, vol. i. ch. v.

2 See art. MYSTERIES (Greek, Phrygian, etc.), § 1 (*a*).

3 See E. Rohde, *Psyche*, Freiburg i. Br., 1894, p. 29; F. B. Jevons, *An Introd. to the Hist. of Religion*, London, 1896, p. 365 f.; T. W. Allen and E. E. Sikes, *The Homeric Hymns*, do. 1904, p. 9 f.

4 Suidas, p. 1404: *Διὸς κῴδιον*; L. R. Farnell, *CGS*, Oxford, 1896–1909, iii. 161 f.

5 xv. 140.

6 Roscher, p. 1888 f.; but see also *CGS* ii. 509 f.

7 First in Soph. *Œd. Tyr.* 206.

8 *CGS* iii. 459.

9 Cf. Soph. *Œd. Tyr.* 27.

1 Lucr. ii. 78; Plato, *Laws*, vi. 776.

2 *Agam.* 314: *νικᾷ δ' ὁ πρῶτος καὶ τελευταῖος δραμών.*

3 Hyginus, *Astron.* ii. 15; *Anth. Pal.* vi. 100.

4 Plut. *Quæst. Græc.* 24.

details. In this festival women whose prayers before child-birth the goddess favourably heard bore lighted torches to her shrine. It is difficult to say whether this custom is a survival of a purificatory rite (Diana representing a forest deity or the goddess of agriculture) or whether the torch is only a symbol of the moon-goddess, who was the natural patron of women in child-birth.

In Greek and Roman private life the torch was an important feature in marriage, as the bridal procession took place at night or towards evening. As early as Homer[1] there is mention of this torch-light procession. It was the duty of the bride's mother to light the nuptial torch.[2] In Italy the bride was also escorted to her new home by torch-light, under the protection of Juno Domiduca or Iterduca. Hence the god of love, both in Greece and in Rome, is often represented with a torch—an idea no doubt assisted by the common conception of love as a 'fire.'

The torch had also funereal associations to the Romans, being used to light the pile on which the corpse was burned. Those who applied the torch averted their faces.[3] The 'two torches' (of marriage and death) are mentioned by Propertius[4] and Ovid.[5]

LITERATURE.—The λαμπαδηφορία has been frequently discussed—*e.g.*, by A. Mommsen, *Heortologie*, Leipzig, 1864, p. 282; P. Foucart, in *Revue de Phil.* xxiii. [1899] 112; N. Wecklein, in *Hermes*, vii. [1872] 437; Daremberg-Saglio, *s.v.* 'Lampadēdromia'; J. R. S. Sterret, in *AJPh* xxii. [1901] 393.

E. E. SIKES.

TORRES STRAITS.—See NEW GUINEA.

TORT.—See DELICT.

TORTOISE.—See ANIMALS.

TORTURE.—*Quæstio*, said Baldus de Periglis, an interpreter of that word of dire significance in Roman law, 'is a certain kind of inquisition made for the purpose of tearing out the truth ('eruendae veritatis') by torments and bodily pain.' Few institutions have more signally failed even to afford rational excuse for their evil existence as a method of extracting evidence. Starting from a deep instinct of violence, it consistently made manifest its inherent viciousness, which no fundamentally good intention could redeem and no humane afterthought of qualification and exception could withhold from pernicious and cruel consequences. Unlike the ordeal (*q.v.*), which was in some measure an appeal to a fairly equal chance, torture was without even the negative virtue of offering a percentage of probabilities of right and truth in its results. It is difficult to think of any principle which could make it really assist in evoking truth from reluctant witnesses or reliable confession from accused persons. The one point of affinity to ordeal was the resort to torture when there was a deficiency of direct legal evidence. Its basis in injustice is shown not only in its penalizing the innocent and unconvicted, but in the fact that its applicability was long confined in both Greece and Rome to slaves—significant of its palpable unfitness for freemen. It never was universal, though in ancient use among Assyrians, Egyptians, Medes, and Japanese; it does not appear in the early laws of Chinese, Hindus, or Jews. There is no mention of it in the OT record. The metaphoric heaping of coals of fire on the head probably refers to torture, as appears from a Muhammadan penalty of a live coal laid on a lascivious palm. From a remote age torture prevailed in Greece for slaves, and, although freemen were generally exempt, the exemption was overborne in cases of conspiracy and murder. Slaves in Athens were subject to torture in causes civil as well as criminal. At times the actions were determined by balancing the testimonies of the slaves of the opposing litigants put under the pressure of the wheel, the ladder, the rack, or the burning tile. Grecian practice has not transmitted any code; that was reserved for Roman law, which unfortunately hardened into permanence the crude tradition of force which it shared with Greece.

[1] *Il.* xviii. 492.
[2] Eur. *Iph. in Aul.* 732, *Phœn.* 344, *Med.* 1027.
[3] Virg. *Æn.* vi. 224. [4] iv. (v.) 11, 46. [5] *Her.* xxi. 172.

In this exposition we are not dealing with torture as a method of punishment, to which some speculations give an earlier place than belongs to the torture of witnesses or accused persons. It is as a process for obtaining testimony or confession, chiefly in causes criminal, that torture has historically played its most unreasoned and baneful part. In the Roman Republic it had wide currency in spite of sharply defined restrictions which instructively exhibit the efforts, too tardily made and not thoroughgoing enough, to modify and restrain an institution for which abolition was the only remedy. And yet credit must be given to the insight and humanity of some of the distinctions made. The exemption of freemen gave way under imperial impulses when lese-majesty was imputed. The general safeguard that there must be vehement presumptions of guilt before resort to the torture was clear enough in theory, but was widely ignored in practice. Most curious fact of all perhaps is the frankness of the authorities grouped in the *Digest* on the primary desirability of doing without torture, on the frailty and peril of the method as an engine for ascertaining facts, on the delusive character of confessions induced by modes which were tests not of truthfulness but of physical endurance, and on the danger to third parties from the allegations wrung from men willing to say anything to save themselves. Evidence of slaves under torture was declared inadmissible against their masters, but there were exceptions of some intricacy. The apostle Paul (Ac 22[24ff.]) pleaded with success his right as a Roman freeman as a protection from examination under the scourge. Mainly used only in causes criminal, the institution made good its footing in some civil causes also. Exemptions of minors, patricians, priests, and pregnant women were inapplicable when charges of treason were made. The direction of Antoninus Pius that torture was not to be used to secure betrayal of alleged accomplices was as wise as it was humane, but the very object of getting at other culprits came ultimately to be a main occasion of its employment. The provisions of the *Digest*[1] and the *Code*[2] systematize several contradictory doctrines 'de quaestionibus' illustrative of a considerable development. The emperors were not long in discovering what Dante was to illustrate by extreme examples, that treason was the worst of crimes. This was the creed too of Anglo-Saxon as well as of later feudal criminal law, and it encouraged violent processes of detection. In Rome the kind of torture with widest currency was that of the *equuleus*, or rack, which passed on as perhaps the worst legacy of Roman law to mediæval Europe.

The abolition of the barbarian ordeal by the Lateran Council of 1215 left a vacuum which was partly filled by a still worse expedient—the Roman method of 'tearing out the truth.' Under the Salic law ordeal and torture had co-existed, but the latter for slaves only, the provisions obviously echoing Roman practice. The Ripuarian code apparently countenanced ordeal alone. The renaissance of Roman law explains the return of torture after some measure of abeyance. In

[1] xlviii. 18. [2] ix. 41.

France and Italy it seems to have re-established itself during the 13th century. Continental charters cited by Du Cange[1] gave exemption from torture. Its French name, *gehenne*, was fit enough. There were many modes—the *brodequin*, the *estrapade*, the *chevalet*—all used in the *question préparatoire*, preliminarily in the trial, and in the definitive *question préalable* after conviction to disclose accomplices. In England, though without place in the common law, it was practised as an abuse notably in the anarchy under King Stephen and in King John's processes of extracting treasure from the Jews. The *peine forte et dure*, however, or torture by pressure of weights to compel a prisoner to put himself 'upon the country' or verdict of a jury, appears about 1300. Under Edward II. in 1311 papal inquisitors in the trial of the Templars applied torture admittedly never legally countenanced in England before. Though long without regular sanction in the courts for crime, the practice of torture crept in with what may be called council government under the Tudors. As always, secret courts favoured secret methods, and torture loved the darkness. With Shakespeare and other Elizabethan dramatists 'rack' and 'strappado' were household words. Coke might excommunicate the institution from the common law, but Coke and Bacon alike countenanced it in practice when the scent of treason was strong.

In Scotland the law and practice appear to have nearly paralleled the state of things in England. Isolated examples of torture, such as that given by way of punishment to the murderer of James I., may have been preceded, as one annalist asserts, by judicial torture at his trial. So late as 1542 the point of law was established that a confession procured by torture was null. George Buchanan, in spite of the risks that he himself had run from the Inquisition, recognizes without censure the obtaining of proofs by torture. The deplorable inhumanities resulting from the witchcraft craze, nurtured in Scotland by the sapience of the demonologist James VI., and absolutely paralleled by the like frenzy in England and France, were a distressing combination of the mischiefs of torture with a recrudescence of the ordeal. The victims were often old, miserable, and insane; the pitiful and pitiless mania, however, was not merely a British but equally a European crime; its creed on the Continent was of one context with that in Britain; everywhere the witch-finders used the same methods of pain. It was the last stage of a sort of common law of torture, although the variety of local usage shows a wide range of divergence in detail. In the Covenant time a last outburst of persecuting zeal revived the decadent engine of violence. A dubious tradition traces the thumbikins in Scotland to a Russian origin.[2] Museums of torture such as those of Nuremberg, The Hague, and the Tower of London—competitions in horror as they are—unite in a kind of commonplace of malignancy. Authorities on torture in like manner dwell with the same tedious insistence on the *indicia*, or preliminary evidences needed to justify torture, and on the conditions of its infliction. The *Summa Angelica*, a great cyclopedia of instruction to confessors, enjoins the interrogation to judges in confession whether they had put people to torture without sufficient *indicia*, which was very rightly classified as a deadly sin. Now and again a tractate of law and practice of torture, such as that of Paulus Grillandus, breaks away from its companions in the great folio vol. xi. of Zilettus (1584) by its superior realism. Grillandus distinguishes with grim precision the five degrees of torture: now a mere threat, now a suspension on the rack for the space only of an Ave Maria or a Paternoster, now a graver suspension for the space of a Miserere, now for a period which might reach into hours, and, last degree of all, where the victim's limbs, weighted down, were jerked and twisted till the agony was greater than the amputation of the hand. It is marvellous how men endured such torments, but that they did so is attested by occasional observations by the judges or assessors of court who wrote the treatises. Grillandus, *e.g.*, drawing upon his experience at Pisa and at Rome, registers the wonderful case of a most cunning thief whose absolute impassiveness was ascribed to certain words that he whispered when the torture was applied until a slip of paper was found bearing as a charm the Scriptural text (well known for its use in amulets) 'Jesus autem transiens.' Finally, however, with the charm removed altogether, this stout malefactor defied the torture again by his whispered invocation so that it was necessary to abandon the torture. And still greater cases, the commentator concludes, were seen at Milan and Rome when certain words touching the milk of the Virgin enabled the victim to go through the torment as if he slept. This particular variety of charm was reported to be no less effective as a counter-charm, but Grillandus shows no faith in its potency as an aid to the prosecutor.

An unfortunate feature of torture was its adoption by the inquisitorial courts of the Church for the investigation of charges of blasphemy, heresy, and the like. Was persecution not, like the Inquisition itself, a confusion of a secular with a sacred function, in which the analogy of treason to an earthly potentate carried priests of religion to extremes not compatible with the conception of a majesty which, though wounded, was divine? Whatever of error lurked in the concept itself, the tribunal which was its executive of vindication added to the wrong in principle by a series of false directions of the practice in prosecution. It surely was a blunder worse than a crime to adopt methods which doubly branded with public odium courts which were designed by processes of barbarism to repress the freedom of the human mind. The fact that already by the middle of the 13th cent. papal dispensations to churchmen were needed for irregularities in the use of torture casts a lurid light on the procedure. No safeguard of institutions is so sound as publicity—the liberty of moderate criticism, the freedom of defence, and the avoidance of the abuses which wait upon invisible dungeons and courts. Secrecy inevitably means tyranny and obscurantism. The refusal of counsel for the accused was a fundamental and far-reaching error in a 'court of inquisition into heretical depravity,' which by its very object tended to unite the zeal and interest of both prosecutor and judge against the heretic. The double sanction of royal and ecclesiastical authority sometimes enabled the machinery against heresy to be used for political rather than spiritual ends. The most notorious persecution of the 16th cent. was in the Netherlands, and torture was the keynote of its procedure. The Renaissance had not wholly escaped the persecutions which rose to their evil eminence during the transition period in which the swaying boundary-line came to a stand between Lutheran reform and Roman orthodoxy. In 1532 the Constitutions of Charles V. codified for Germany a system which incorporated torture among the fundamentals of procedure. His establishment of the Inquisition in 1550 inaugurated a period of atrocities perhaps worse than any other in human history. Philip II. of Spain found in the Duke of Alva a spirit of

1 *Glossarium Mediæ et Infimæ Latinitatis*, new ed., Niort, 1883–87, vi., *s.v.* 'Quæstio.'

2 Maclaurin, *Arguments and Decisions*, preface, p. xxxvii.

merciless executive in the Netherlands, scarcely less jealous of public liberty than of private creeds, and Alva's *horrenda gloria* of death penalties earned for him not only his downfall but also the execration ever since attached to his name. Out of that fierce time aptly came its strange definitive and callous expression in a contemporary book, the *Praxis Rerum Criminalium* of Josse de Damhoudère, a councillor under both Charles and Philip in the Netherlands, published in French and Latin in 1554 and repeatedly afterwards, remarkable among other things for its matter-of-course attitude to torture, which makes only too intelligible the excesses of practice under the most illustrious and excellent Alva, whose honour and sagacity a preface in some editions incidentally extols. Woodcuts queerly illustrate the varieties of crime, while seven whole chapters on torture make transparent the vices of a system the radical barbarity of which, despite its antiquity of sanction expounded by generations of civilian glossators and jurists, all its touches of humanity—and there were some—were hopeless to redeem. Damhoudère harrows the modern soul perhaps most by his passionless exposition as of a principle doubtless imperfect, yet itself of the nature of things. Leading modes indicated are by the rope (*i.e.* the rack), by water forced through the mouth, by oil internally administered, by burning pitch or lime, by hunger, cold, or the thumbscrew, by mice or parasites that gnawed the flesh, or by fire intensified by basting the body with oil—these were only a few of at least fourteen species of torments. What wonder that Damhoudère after this enumeration should consider that torture often could most happily (*felicissime*) be applied by scourging alone? Two pictures complete the impression, one showing a victim girt and twisted with ropes and swung stretched out with weights at his feet, the other an idyllic group of the doctors, knights, priests, old men, children, and prospective mothers, who were benignly excusable from torture.

It was a law from which no conceivable evolution could eliminate the initial anomalies (1) of punishing an accused by torture before he was found guilty or a witness before he was proved a perjurer; or (2) of torturing an accused after conviction when torture was no part of the sentence, and when the judge's function was ended and the process was no part of the trial. These were dilemmas from which no escape was ever devised, and they gave effectual leverage to criticism when—late in the day, it must be owned—the opposition developed energy enough to make abolition of torture a direct object of humane propaganda. Illustrious opinions against torture were many; those in its favour were perhaps less illustrious. Augustine, Ulpian, Quintilian, and Montaigne could be cited on one side, and Demosthenes, Aristotle, Bodin, and Pothier on the other. But the lawyers were indifferent, and their neutrality and acquiescence gave the practice a long lease of life. Roman tradition persisted little shaken in Europe till Beccaria and Voltaire threw a new intensity into attack on abuses, and the objection to torture passed from being a mere dissent into a positive and earnest movement to repeal what was at once a futility and a cruel injustice. From the middle of the 18th cent. until the beginning of the 19th the Continental countries by degrees followed the example of repeal set by Great Britain. Torture had died out in England by the middle of the 17th cent.; it was abolished for Scotland by statute in 1708. Its extinction on the Continent has been assigned in Prussia to 1740, in Portugal to 1776, in Sweden to 1786, in France to 1789, in Russia to 1801. But in the last-named country it is said that so late as 1906-07 political prisoners underwent grievous treatment in a 'museum of torture' comprising brutalities in which 'scorching of the feet at the fire' was among the least revolting. In the Far East the persistence of the evil has been still greater. In China the usage has long held, and presumably still holds, place as a fundamental law. But in Japan it was abolished in 1876. Suspicion, however, obtains that in Oriental lands, despite reforms and prohibitions, illegitimate torture is still secretly carried on. One main fact in Europe is perhaps that, while the lawyers 2000 years ago already saw the fallacy and futility of torture, seventeen centuries had passed before its abolition was taken firmly in hand. The many generations of clerical jurists and judges did no better than the laymen, accepting the institution and 'passing by on the other side,' if indeed the ecclesiastical tribunals were not the worst offenders. The divorce of the judges from all legislative function has much to answer for in checking the critical initiative of amendment sometimes induced by judicial experience. Abolition at last came neither from the logic of the law nor from the impulse of the Church, but from the impassioned zeal of humanitarian philosophy.

LITERATURE.—**H. C. Lea**, *Superstition and Force*[4], Philadelphia, 1892, pp. 428–590; **F. Helbing**, *Die Tortur*, 2 vols., Berlin, 1902; **James Williams**, art. 'Torture' in *EBr*[11]; **F. Zilettus**, *Tractatus Universi Juris*, Venice, 1584–86, vol. xi., pt. i., pp. 241–306, including treatises *de Tortura* by Jacobus de Arena, Guido de Suzaria, Franciscus Casonus, Baldus de Periglis, Paulus Grillandus, and others; **J. de Damhoudère**, *Praxis Rerum Criminalium*, new ed., Antwerp, 1570, chs. 35–41; **Antonius Matthæus**, *De Criminibus*[2], Amsterdam, 1661; **W. Lithgow**, *The Totall Discourse of the Rare Adventures . . . of 19 yeares Travayles from Scotland to . . . Europe, Asia, and Africa*, London, 1632, new ed., Glasgow, 1906, pp. 400–410; **F. Heinemann**, *Der Richter und die Rechtspflege in der deutschen Vergangenheit* (vol. iv. of *Monographien zur deutschen Kulturgeschichte*, ed. Georg Steinhausen), Leipzig, 1900, pp. 44–69 (with numerous reproductions of old plates); **Sir G. Mackenzie**, *The Laws and Customs of Scotland in Matters Criminal*[2], Edinburgh, 1699; **John Maclaurin** (Lord Dreghorn), *Arguments and Decisions in . . . Cases before the High Court of Justiciary*, Edinburgh, 1774, preface, citing Lord Royston's MS Notes on Sir G. Mackenzie (now owned by writer of this article); *Summa Angelica de casibus conscientiae correcta secundum exemplar ipsius Reverendi Patris Fratris Angeli de Clauasio*, Rothomagi, 1513, *s.vv.* 'Interrogationes,' 'Tortura,' folios clxxxvii., cccxlvi. verso; **R. D. Melville**, 'The Use and Forms of Judicial Torture in England and Scotland,' in *Scottish Hist. Review*, ii. [1905] 225 ff.; **Daines Barrington**, *Observations on the More Ancient Statutes*[3], London, 1769; **D. Jardine**, *A Reading on the Use of Torture in the Criminal Law of England*, do. 1837; **R. S. Gundry**, 'Judicial Torture in China,' in *Fortnightly Review*, new ser., xlvii. [1890] 404 ff.; **F. Pollock** and **F. W. Maitland**, *Hist. of English Law*, 2 vols., Cambridge, 1895; **Montaigne**, *Essais*, bk. ii. ch. 5 (no. lxv.); **Montesquieu**, *Esprit des lois*, bk. vi. ch. 17; **C. Beccaria**, *Trattato dei Delitti e delle Pene*, Monaco, 1764, numerous translations, commentary by Voltaire, various editions; **Z. B. van Espen**, *Jus Ecclesiasticum*, Louvain, 1778, ii. 330; **W. E. H. Lecky**, *Hist. of the Rise and Influence of the Spirit of Rationalism in Europe*, auth. ed., London, 1910, i. 330; **H. Hallam**, *View of the State of Europe during the Middle Ages*, ch. viii. pt. 3; **H. T. Buckle**, *Introd. to the Hist. of Civilization in England*, new and rev. ed., with notes, etc., by J. M. Robertson, London, 1904, ch. xviii., p. 716 f.; **T. B. Macaulay**, *Hist. of England from the Accession of James II.*, chs. ii. and xiii.; **Gregor Alexinsky**, *Modern Russia*, tr. B. Miall, London, 1913.

G. NEILSON.

TOTEMISM.—I. Introductory.—The word 'totem' is derived from *ototeman*, which in the Ojibwa and cognate Algonquian dialects means 'his brother-sister kin.' Its grammatical stem *ote*, meaning the consanguine kinship between uterine brothers and sisters, the group of persons recognized as by birth or adoption collectively related together as uterine brothers and sisters who cannot intermarry, is never used alone.[1] The word was introduced into the English language by J. Long[2] in the form of *totam*. This he wrongly defined as the favourite spirit which each of the savages (Chippewa or Ojibwa) believes watches over him, adding:

[1] J. N. B. Hewitt, in *HAI* ii. 787.

[2] *Voyages and Travels of an Indian Interpreter and Trader*, London, 1791.

'This *totam* they conceive assumes the shape of some beast or other, and therefore they never kill, hunt, or eat the animal whose form they think this *totam* bears.'[1]

The first to give an account, accurate as far as it goes, of totemism on the American continent was Peter Jones, himself an Ojibwa chief, but an ordained Wesleyan Methodist minister and missionary to his tribe. He wrote the *History of the Ojebway Indians*, published without a date in London after his death, which took place in 1856. He says:

'Their belief concerning their divisions into tribes is that many years ago the Great Spirit gave his red children their *toodaims*, or tribes, in order that they might never forget that they were all related to each other, and that in time of distress or war they were bound to help each other. When an Indian in travelling meets with a strange band of Indians, all he has to do is to seek for those bearing the same emblem as his tribe; and having made it known that he belongs to their toodaim, he is sure to be treated as a relative. Formerly it was considered unlawful for parties of the same tribe to intermarry, but of late years this custom is not observed. . . . Each tribe is distinguished by certain animals or things, as for instance the Ojebway nations have the following toodaims: the Eagle, Reindeer, Otter, Bear, Buffalo, Beaver, Catfish, Pike, Birch-bark, White Oak-tree, Bear's Liver, etc. etc. The Mohawk nation have only three divisions or tribes—the Turtle, the Bear, and the Wolf.'[2]

What Jones calls a tribe is now usually called a clan or gens, meaning a group, not necessarily localized, of persons regarded as united by a bond of kinship real or fictitious, extended beyond the family properly so called to a brotherhood bearing the same name and including strangers who have been formally adopted into it. This brotherhood or clan may, and frequently does, extend also beyond the boundaries of the local body called by Jones a nation, but now usually known as a tribe.

In the meantime Sir George Grey, then governor of S. Australia, in the account of his travels in W. Australia, drew attention to the similarity between the Australian *kobong* and the American totem, describing the *kobong* at some length and giving genealogical lists to illustrate the mode of descent.[3] A series of articles in the *Fortnightly Review*[4] on 'The Worship of Animals and Plants' by J. F. McLennan was suggested, at all events in part, by Grey's observations. It was this series of articles, with McLennan's important but erroneous speculations, which finally brought the subject of totemism before the scientific public in Britain. Among others whose attention they attracted were Lord Avebury (then Sir John Lubbock) and W. Robertson Smith. It was especially the use made of totemism by the latter in the speculations embodied in his important work, *The Religion of the Semites*, that started the controversies incessantly waged on the subject from that day to this.

2. Definition; plan of the article.—Totemism as exemplified in N. America and Australia, where it has been found in the fullest development, is a form of society distinguished by the following characteristics: (1) it is composed of clans or bands of men each united among themselves by kinship real or fictitious, a kinship frequently extending beyond the limits of the local tribe; (2) the clan is distinguished by the name of some species of animal or plant, or more rarely of some other natural phenomenon, such as the sun, rain, etc.; (3) the species or object which gives its name to the clan is conceived as related to the clan, and to every member of it, in some mystic way, often genetically; and in this case every individual specimen of the object, where it is an animal or plant, is regarded as belonging to the clan; (4) such species or object is usually the subject of a religious or quasi-religious emotion, and every individual specimen is the subject of tabus or prohibitions: subject to certain limitations, ceremonial or in self-defence, it may not be injured or killed, or (where eatable) eaten; (5) moreover, as in all societies organized on the basis of kinship, the members of the clan are entitled to mutual defence, protection, and resentment of injuries. They may not marry or have sexual intercourse within the clan.

These characteristics are general, but they vary to some extent not merely from area to area, but from tribe to tribe. After detailing a few typical examples, it will be necessary to mention others where totemism seems to be decadent, and then to consider whether it has ever prevailed among peoples where it is not now to be found, and lastly to inquire into its origin. Various influences tending to modify, submerge, or destroy it will be indicated from time to time in the course of the article.

3. Typical examples.—(*a*) *America.*—Somewhat fuller accounts than that of Peter Jones are now available concerning the totemism of the Ojibwas. They were divided into about 40 exogamous totemic clans, of which those of the Crane, Catfish, Loon, Bear, Marten, and Wolf were the principal, and the first five appear to have been the original. The other clans are said to have been formed by the segmentation of these. Nearly all the clans are named from animals of either land or water. Members of a totem-clan were held to be closely related to all other persons of the same totem, even though belonging to different tribes.[1] We have no information whether the Ojibwa clans regarded themselves as having descended from the totems whose names they bore; but the clans of some other Algonquian tribes claim such descent. Thus, among the Delawares or Lenape the Tortoise, Turkey, and Wolf clans (the three chief clans of the tribe),[2] among the Sauks the Fox, Eagle, Bear, Beaver, Fish, Antelope, and Raccoon clans,[3] among the Menomini the Bear, Golden Eagle, Wolf, and other clans,[4] and among the Ottawas the Carp clan,[5] are specified as tracing their lineage to the animals after which they are named; and in the last-mentioned tribe the Bear clan ascribed its origin to a bear's paw without explaining the precise nature of the relationship. However this may be, the Ojibwa Bear clan was held to resemble the bear, its totem, in disposition. The members were surly and pugnacious, the acknowledged war-chiefs and fighting men of the community; the war-pipe and war-club were committed to their custody. The Crane clan took its name (Bus-in-as-see, 'Echo-maker') from the loud, clear, ringing cry of the crane; members of the clan were thought to possess naturally a loud ringing voice, and they were the acknowledged orators of the tribe.[6] We are not informed whether in their personal appearance, dress, or ornaments the Ojibwa totem-clans were ordinarily in the habit of imitating the totem-animals, as some other tribes do. The Abenaki, also an Algonquian tribe, painted their totems on their arms, breasts, and legs.[7] An Ojibwa sometimes had the figure tatued on him, or carried some

[1] P. 87. [2] P. 138.
[3] *Journals of Two Expeditions of Discovery in N.W. and W. Australia*, London, 1841, ii. 225 ff., 391.
[4] New ser., v. [1869] 407 ff., 562 ff., vi. [1870] 194 ff.

[1] J. G. Frazer, *Totemism and Exogamy*, iii. 46 ff., citing various authorities.
[2] *Ib.* p. 40, quoting J. Heckewelder, *Trans. Hist. and Lit. Com. Amer. Phil. Soc.* i. [1819] 246 f.
[3] Mary A. Owen, *Folk-Lore of the Musquakie Indians*, London, 1904, p. 8.
[4] W. J. Hoffman, *14 RBEW* [1896], pt. i. pp. 39–41, 43.
[5] Frazer, iii. 55–67, citing *Lettres édifiantes et curieuses*, new ed., Paris, 1781, pp. 168–172.
[6] *Ib.* p. 55, citing W. W. Warren, *Coll. Minnesota Hist. Soc.* v. [1885] 43 ff.
[7] Hoffman, p. 65 n., quoting J. A. Maurault, *Hist. des Abenakis*, Quebec, 1866, p. 23.

other token by which his totem might be known.[1] Unfortunately our reports are chiefly confined to the social aspects of the Ojibwa organization, so that we have little or no information as to the religious outlook. Religion is inextricably mingled with other aspects of savage life; hence we may be sure that it reacted upon social and political life. Among their neighbours, the Sauks or Musquakies, dances in honour of the totems were held. At these dances—a religious exercise—those who took part were covered with masks and dresses to resemble the totemic animals, so dreadful that the women were seriously frightened, and the old masks were therefore destroyed and milder ones substituted.[2] Special ceremonies were performed by the Bear clan of the Ottawas to soothe a bear when they killed it, including an offering to the dead animal of its own flesh. When a member of that clan or of the Carp clan died, he was buried, whereas by command of the totem a member of the Great Hare clan was cremated—at least, whenever he died at a distance from home.[3] Among the Menomini a member of the Bear clan who, when hunting, met a bear would apologize and ask forgiveness before killing it; and no member of the clan could eat of the meat (though members of other clans might do so) except the hunter himself, who was permitted to eat of the paws and head, the bones of the head being carefully preserved in a place of honour in the wigwam as a relic of the totem-animal to which due reverence must be paid.[4] The Ojibwa reckoned descent and kinship through the father only; but there is some evidence that they formerly reckoned through the mother only—a change possibly accelerated by white, and particularly missionary, influence. Such a change is known to have occurred elsewhere.[5]

The Iroquois, a confederacy of six tribes in what is now the state of New York, on the other hand, were matrilineal. They were organized in totemic clans, of which all of them possessed three—the Bear, Wolf, and Turtle—some of them eight. There is some reason to think that the larger numbers were derived by segmentation from the three original clans, though it is possible that, in some of the cases at all events, the number of the three clans may have been augmented by the adoption of captives from other tribes, who formed separate clans. The clans were exogamic, but in the eight-clan tribes they were formed into two phratries. The members of the clans were not allowed to marry indiscriminately into any other clan; they could marry only into a clan of the opposite phratry, the phratry thus becoming the exogamic unit in place of the clan. On the social side of Iroquoian totemism we have fairly full information. The members of a clan were united for mutual defence and the resentment of injuries; and the phratries, where the tribe was organized in phratries, had certain important functions at the death of a chief and the election of his successor.[6] On the religious aspect, however, our information is sadly deficient. There is one account by a chance traveller, in which the Iroquois were stated to believe in their descent from the turtle (or tortoise), the bear, and the wolf—their three chief totems;[7] and among their

[1] Frazer, p. 59, quoting Edwin James, *Narrative of the Captivity and Adventures of John Tanner*, London, 1830.
[2] M. A. Owen, p. 51 f. [3] Frazer, iii. 67, 66. [4] Hoffman, p. 65.
[5] E. S. Hartland, *Mem. Amer. Anth. Assoc.*, iv. [1917] 48; cf. Frazer, iii. 58; cf. also the derivation of 'totem' at the beginning of this article.
[6] L. H. Morgan, *Ancient Society*, London, 1877, pp. 70–98, *League of the Ho-dé-no-sau-ne, or Iroquois*, new ed., New York, 1904, i. 74–120; H. Hale, *The Iroquois Book of Rites*, Philadelphia, 1883, pp. 48–75. These are all summarized by Frazer, iii. 7 ff.
[7] Frazer, iii. 18, citing T. Dwight, *Travels in New England and New York*, London, 1823.

myths one has been preserved by a scientific inquirer relating how the turtle became a man and the progenitor of the Turtle clan.[1] But neither L. H. Morgan nor Horatio Hale, to whom we are indebted for nearly all that we know of the organization of the Iroquois, has told us anything concerning the intimate relations between the totem and its clan, or the aspect in which the totem was regarded by the clan, or the members by one another.

The Iroquois, however, had one custom common to a number of N. American tribes. Each clan had a stock of personal names appropriated to it only, which other clans of the same tribe were not permitted to use, so that, if a person's name was known, it was possible to say to what clan he belonged. To such a length was this custom carried by some tribes that, when the clan organization began to decay, a child could be assigned to another clan than that into which by hereditary descent he was born, by the simple process of giving him one of the personal names belonging to the latter clan—at all events if the clan recognized the child and thereby confirmed the choice.[2] The clans of some of the N. American tribes performed ceremonies for the control of their totems for the common good of the tribe. This was the practice, *e.g.*, among the Omaha.[3] But its utmost development is found in the southwest of the United States among the various tribes of Pueblo Indians.[4]

(*b*) *Australia*.—In Australia totemism has been crossed, and among some tribes superseded, for exogamic purposes by a system of marriage-classes.[5] The consequent variation in the social arrangements of the different tribes has introduced a confusing factor into the totemic organization. Among those tribes whose organization has been least affected is the Dieri, inhabiting part of the Lake Eyre basin in S. Australia. They possess a number of clans of which the names of 27 are known. Their totems belong chiefly to the animal world; but the list includes some vegetable totems and such objects as rain and red ochre. It seems to be common to all the tribes in the Lake Eyre basin, though it is not ascertained whether all the totems are recognized by every tribe. Each tribe, like some of the Iroquois tribes, is divided into two moieties, or phratries, some of the clans belonging to one phratry and the rest to the other. These phratries are called by the Dieri Kararu and Matteri respectively; and, as among the Iroquois, not only the clan but also the phratry is exogamous. A Kararu man must marry a Matteri woman, and conversely a Matteri woman a Kararu man; but within the limits of the opposite phratry the mate may belong to any clan. Both the clan and the phratry descend in the female line, the children in all cases taking those of the mother.[6] The Dieri clans do not claim their totemic animals or plants as ancestors. More than one legend accounts for them.

According to one story, the totems (*murdus*, properly *madas*) came out in an unfinished condition from the earth in the midst of Lake Perigundi and lay on the sandhills around the lake until the warmth of the sun strengthened and raised them up as human beings, whereupon they separated in all directions. Hence the *madas* (totemic clans) are now scattered all over the country. According to another story, a malignant *mura-mura*, or supernatural being, was killed by the people for his misdeeds, but came to life again. He followed footprints, and, finding the people busy fishing, opened his mouth and swallowed water, fish, and men. Some escaped, running off in all directions, and to every one as they ran he gave a *mada*. In proof of the story, rocks are pointed out which are said to be the body of the *mura-mura* in question, and his teeth.[7]

If we may trust one account, the Dieri do not regard the animal or plant which is their totem as sacred, but will kill or eat it.[8] It is not, however, certain that we can rely on this statement. Its author, for a long time a mounted constable in the district, and hence brought much into contact with

[1] *2 RBEW* [1883], pt. ii. p. 77.
[2] Morgan, *Ancient Soc.*, p. 78; Hartland, pp. 35, 40. See, on the organization of Iroquoian clans, *Amer. Anthrop.* xix. [1917] 392 ff.; also Frazer, iii. 13, 42.
[3] *3 RBEW* [1884], pp. 238, 240 f., 248; cf. p. 227.
[4] See below, § 4. [5] See below, § 4 (*b*).
[6] Howitt, p. 90 ff. [7] *Ib.* pp. 476, 779–781.
[8] *JAI* xxiv. [1895] 168.

the natives, was, we know, mistaken in other matters with respect to them. In general throughout Australia the clansmen regard their own totem with reverence.

Thus, in the Wakelbura tribe we are expressly told that the totem-animal is spoken of as 'father.' 'For example, a man of the *Binnung-urra* (Frilled-lizard totem) holds that reptile as sacred, and he not only would not kill it, but would protect it by preventing another person doing so in his presence. Similarly a man of the Screech-owl totem would call it "father," and likewise hold it sacred and protect it. . . . A man who was lax as to his totem was not thought well of, and was never allowed to take any important part in the ceremonies.'[1] In the tongue of the Wotjobaluk *yauerin*, 'flesh,' is used for totem, indicating the close relationship of the totem and the totem-clan.[2] Grey, writing of the tribes of W. Australia, reports that 'each family [clan] adopts some animal or vegetable as their crest or sign, or *kobong*, as they call it,' and that 'a certain mysterious connection exists between a family and its *kobong*, so that a member of the family will never kill an animal of the species to which his *kobong* belongs, should he find it asleep; indeed he always kills it reluctantly, and never without affording it a chance to escape. This arises from the family belief that some one individual of the species is their nearest friend, to kill whom would be a great crime. Similarly a native who has a vegetable for his *kobong* may not gather it under certain circumstances and at a particular period of the year.'[3] So far is this belief in a connexion between the totem-clan and its *kobong* carried that in the Wakelbura tribe, 'when a man could not get satisfaction for an injurious action by another, he has been known to kill that beast, bird, or reptile which that man called "father," and thus obtain revenge, and perhaps cause the other to do the same, if he knew of it.'[4] Such is the influence of belief that the killing of a man's totem has been known to hasten his death.

An interesting development of totemism in Australia is the assignment of a number of sub-totems to each totem. Thus in the Wotjobaluk tribe the Deaf Adder totem has for sub-totems the Native Cat, Black Swan, Tiger-Snake, Sulphur-crested Cockatoo, Crow, and Dingo; and the other totems have similar lists.[5] Where, according to the peculiar exogamic regulations, the phratries developed into marriage-classes, the sub-totems were attached to the latter. Ultimately the result was to divide the universe between the various classes and sub-classes—a result expressed in diagrammatic form in accordance with the points of the compass by the Wotjobaluk, who buried their dead orientated to agree with the diagram thus obtained.[6] What the reason was for assigning these sub-totems to the different totems and classes has not been ascertained; to us it seems arbitrary. At any rate the Australian native extended the regard for his totem to the sub-totems comprehended in the totem-clan or class to which he belonged.

A man of the Buandik tribe, we are told, 'does not kill or use for food any of the animals of the same sub-division with himself, excepting when hunger compels; and then they express sorrow for having to eat their *warigong* (friends) or *tumang* (their flesh). When using the last word they touch their breasts to indicate the close relationship, meaning almost a part of themselves.'[7]

Another custom developed extensively in Australia, but (as already intimated) not unknown among the Sioux in N. America, and elsewhere, is that of the performance of ceremonies by a totem-clan for the purpose of exercising control over the totem—*e.g.*, for multiplying its numbers, especially where it was edible, or for ensuring its capture, or, where it was injurious, for driving it away. The *intichiuma* ceremonies of the Arunta have by the investigations of Spencer and Gillen become the best known; they are perhaps the most elaborate, but by no means the only, ceremonies of the kind. The Dieri and other tribes perform such ceremonies, though it is not clear in all cases that the performers are confined to members of the totem-clan. From the analogy of cases both in Australia and in the islands of Torres Straits we may probably assume that they are. Whether these ceremonies should be called religious or magical is a question of terminology, though it seems certain that the performers are under the influence of emotional excitement such as we usually connect with religious rites.

Little is known about the relations of the clansmen in Australia among themselves. From vague references by Howitt and others it would seem that they enjoyed mutual defence and responsibility. But offences were brought before a tribal council, by whose decision blood-revenge was pursued in a quasi-legal manner and, if resisted, ultimately involved the whole tribe in the blood-feud.

(*c*) *Africa*.—Another area in which totemism has been found is that large portion of Africa which is occupied by the Negro and Bantu races. Of the totemism of some of these peoples, particularly of the Negroes, our information is fragmentary. Concerning the Tshi-speaking Negroes of the Gold Coast we have on the whole most information. They are divided into totemic clans, or 'families,' of which the principal are twelve in number, viz. Leopard, Buffalo, Dog, Parrot, Plantain, Corn-stalk, Servant, Red-Earth, Palm-oil-Grove, Abadzi, and Dumina or Dwimina. The meaning of the names of the last two clans is uncertain. The last is probably a local variant of the name of the Nsonna, or Bush-Cat, clan; and, according to some accounts, Abadzi, which may mean 'cannibal,' is another name of the Ntwa, or Dog, clan. About certain of the clans little or nothing beyond the name is known, and questions of identity arise on some of them. These difficulties are incidental to traditional lore where we are dependent upon natives who are not familiar with all the clans about which inquiries are made. To the Leopard clan the leopard is sacred, though members of it are reported now to abstain from the flesh of all the *felidæ*. No member may kill a leopard; if he were to do so by accident, he would exclaim, 'I have killed my brother,' and would put palm-oil on the wounds. If he sees a dead leopard, he must scatter shreds of white cloth upon it and anoint the muzzle with palm-oil, as a sign of respect and sorrow. If a dead leopard is brought into the town, the members of the clan smear themselves with chalk (a sign of mourning) and bury the body. If on a journey a member of the clan were to meet a leopard, he would turn back. The Buffalo, Bush-Cat, Dog, and Parrot clans abstain from eating the totem-animal. The Bush-Cat clan, it is said, abstain from killing not only a bush-cat, but also a crow, under penalty of sores on their bodies. Formerly, if they found a crow or a bush-cat dead, they would bury it, and with the crow a piece of white cloth, with the bush-cat a piece of speckled cloth. The traditional accounts which have reached us of the origin of these clans do not generally claim genetic descent from the totem.

One account states that 'people originally came from the earth, sky, sea, mountains, and the animals, etc., that came with them are their totems'; *e.g.*, the Parrot clan came with the parrots on their loads; the Dog clan came from a river with a broom and with a dog carrying fire.

Other clans, fewer in numbers and conjectured to be of more recent origin, claim that they are descended from an actual animal which possessed the power of assuming human shape at will. In the case of two such clans tales belonging to the Swan Maiden type are told to account for them. The totem-animal is revered. It is addressed as 'grandfather,' a title of respect used in addressing the kings of Ashanti. It is supposed to help the clansmen in various ways; and restraint is said to be placed upon it in order to compel it to grant the wishes of the tribe. There are no marks or dresses distinguishing the clans; but, when a member of

1 Howitt, p. 147 f.
2 *Ib.* p. 241.
3 *Journals*, ii. 228.
4 Howitt, p. 148.
5 *Ib.* p. 121.
6 *Ib.* p. 453 f.
7 L. Fison and A. W. Howitt, *Kamilaroi and Kurnai*, Melbourne, 1880, p. 168 f., quoting a correspondent; cf. E. M. Curr, *The Australian Race*, do. 1886–87, iii. 460.

the Leopard clan dies, the mourners (clansmen) make spots on their bodies with red, white, and black clay to represent a leopard, and scratch the figure of a leopard on the wall of the house and on the coffin. The Nsonna clan in the like case put white clay or white cloth round their necks, because the crow which the clan respects has a white band round its neck. The clan is always matrilineal and exogamous; and it has a common burial-place. There is said to be a belief that at death a clansman becomes or transmigrates into an individual of the totemic species, and, further, every clansman's life is bound up with one such individual, so that, if it dies, he will also die.[1]

The Bantu have for the most part advanced from maternal to paternal descent, though among some tribes we find an intermediate stage. This has not been without its effect upon their totemism, which in several ways varies from the pattern of true matrilineal totemism. The Bechuana, who occupy the centre of S. Africa, are divided into a number of independent 'tribes' generally called by totemic names and having totemic practices and beliefs. In many cases, however, these 'tribes' are not true totemic clans. Since the wife always goes to reside with her husband, the result of the change to paternal descent is to collect the members of the clan together, instead of distributing them as in a matrilineal people, and hence the clan tends to become identified with the geographical and political tribe. Every Bechuana tribe is ruled by a chief, whose totem is recognized as that of the tribe. The political conditions were such that before the European occupation of the country members of a tribe who were discontented with their chief used to desert him and go to a neighbouring rival, with whom they were sure of a welcome. Thus a powerful chief was liable to be reduced to weakness, and perhaps conquered by a neighbour, if his rule was unpopular. It followed that a tribe frequently comprehended members of many totemic clans. But they all accepted the chief's totem, and in time became indistinguishable from the true clansmen, though we do not read of any formal adoption into the clan or of any blood-covenant. The chief is always addressed by the name of the totem, as 'O Crocodile!' 'O Lion!' The Bechuana word for 'totem' is *siboko*, which has led Van Gennep to propose the name 'sibokism' to distinguish the S. African variety of totemism. The chief's totem is held sacred, and the animal, plant, or other object is regarded with fear and reverence.

Thus the Banoku, 'they of the porcupine,' are reported to 'sing,' *i.e.* 'feast, worship or revere' that animal. 'When they see any one maltreat that animal, they afflict themselves, grieve, collect with religious care the quills, if it has been killed, spit upon them and rub their eyebrows with them, saying: "They have slain our brother, our master, one of ours, him whom we sing." They fear that they will die if they eat the flesh of one.' Yet they doctor a new-born child with it, mixed with the juice of certain plants.[2] The Bakuena, 'they of the crocodile,' call the animal their father; 'they celebrate it in their festivals, they swear by it, and make an incision in the ears of their cattle, by which they distinguish them from others.' They call it 'one of them, their master, their father.' Similar practices are recorded of other clans. 'No one dares eat the flesh or clothe himself with the skin of the animal the name of which he bears. If this animal is hurtful, as the lion, for instance, it may not be killed without great apologies being made to it and its pardon being asked. Purification is necessary after the commission of such a sacrilege.' The Bataung, 'they of the lion,' 'carefully abstain from touching his flesh as other people do; for how could one think of eating his ancestor?' Nor does even the chief dare to wear, like other chiefs, a lion's skin by way of royal mantle.[3]

[1] A. B. Ellis, *The Tshi-speaking Peoples of the Gold Coast*, London, 1887, p. 206; J. M. Sarbah, *Fanti Customary Laws*, do. 1897, p. 4; *JAI* xxxvi. [1906] 178 ff.

[2] T. Arbousset and F. Daumas, *Narrative of an Exploratory Tour to the N.E. of the Colony of the Cape of Good Hope*, tr. J. C. Brown, Cape Town, 1846, p. 176.

[3] *Ib.* p. 213 f.; E. Casalis, *The Basutos*, London, 1861, p. 211.

But totemism is decadent among the Bechuana, and has been so for a period which probably dates from before the coming of the European,[1] due partly to the change to paternal lineage, partly to the political conditions, and partly to the keeping of herds of cattle, a custom that seems to have been adopted from the Hottentots.

America, Australia, and Africa are the three chief areas in which totemism has been found widely spread and fully developed. It will be perceived that each of them has its own type, though variations in detail are found in individual tribes and peoples. The remaining areas are India and Melanesia.

(*d*) *India.*—In India totemism is found only among the non-Aryan tribes, and chiefly among the Dravidians. Of these we may take the Orāons on the plateau of Chotā Nāgpur in Bengal as representing the type. Though they have to a great extent emerged from the hunting and pastoral stages of culture, totemism 'still forms the fundamental feature of their social organization in so far as kinship, marriage, and relations of the sexes are concerned.' They are divided into a number of exogamous clans distinguished by names supplied by 'the fauna and flora of their past and present habitats'; and to these, 'with the acquisition of a knowledge of agriculture and the use of metals, a few new totem names have been since added.' The animal and vegetable names amount in number to 62. There are also (probably of more recent origin) two mineral totems, those of Iron and Salt; two which may be called place-totems, viz. Bāudh, an embanked reservoir of water, and Jūbbi, a marsh or surface-spring; and two which belong to a class known elsewhere, called 'split-totems' as involving tabus of a portion only of an animal or vegetable, and frequently known by the name of that portion. Among the Orāons these split-totems are Anvir (rice-soup) and Kispōttā (pig's entrails). Sexual union within the totem-clan is reckoned incestuous, though at the present day, if a marriage takes place in which the rule is infringed wittingly or unwittingly, the offending pair, after paying a fine and giving a feast to the clansmen by analogy with the usual caste practice in India, are formally re-admitted to the tribe and their union is thus legalized. The remaining ordinary totemic tabus are observed. 'An Orāon must abstain from eating or otherwise using, domesticating, killing, destroying, maiming, hurting or injuring' his totem. A wife, in addition to the tabus of her own clan, is required to observe those of her husband's while she actually resides in his village. Men of the clan whose totem is any kind of tree may not go under the shade of the tree or use its produce in any shape. But some modifications have been introduced where the totem is an indispensable article of diet or household use.

Thus members of the Paddy clan abstain only from eating the thin scum on the surface of rice-soup when left standing in a cool place; members of the Salt clan abstain only from taking raw salt, the tabu not extending to food or drink in which salt is an ingredient or flavour; members of the Iron clan abstain only from touching iron with their lips or tongue; members of the Pig clan are forbidden only to eat the head of the pig; members of the Bārā clan, of which the *Ficus Indica* is the totem, may eat the fruit whole, but not by dividing it in two.

On the other hand, the tabus of some clans have been extended to objects having a real or fancied resemblance to the totem or bearing the same or a similar name.

Thus members of the Tiger clan not only have to observe various tabus in reference to the tiger and to the wolf, but also must abstain from eating the squirrel's flesh, since the squirrel is striped like the tiger, and they may not marry in the month of Māgh (December–January) because the name Māgh rhymes with *bāgh*, the Hindi word for 'tiger.'

[1] W. C. Willoughby, *JAI* xxxv. [1905] 298.

In this case the foreign word *bāgh* points to a late and highly artificial origin for such a tabu, which is obviously due to the timidity of superstition. Other additional tabus have been suggested to be due to the fusion of clans, just as some 'split-totems' may have arisen from the opposite process of the division of clans.

'The general attitude of an Orāon to his clan-totem is that of a man to his equal—to his friend and ally,' though some periodical practices seem to indicate a more religious regard—at any rate for its effigy. But totemism is now in decay, as it is over the rest of India. An unintentional breach of a tabu is no longer believed to entail any serious consequences, though looked upon with social disapproval. There is no difference between the clans in personal dress or adornment, nor is a man supposed to partake of the qualities of the totem. There are very few traditions of the origin of totem-names. Such as there are do not reveal any belief in the descent of the clan from the totem, but rather in some other relation between the totem and the human ancestor of the clan. The Orāons are patrilineal.[1]

(*e*) *Melanesia*.—In Melanesia (including New Guinea and the islands of Torres Straits) there is a tendency to associate with the principal totem of a clan a number of subordinate totems which have been called 'secondary,' 'subsidiary,' or 'linked' totems. The western islands of Torres Straits have for many years been the scene of successful missionary enterprise. Under this influence the totemism which formerly existed among the people has almost disappeared. But twenty years ago the members of the Cambridge Anthropological Expedition, who spent some time on the islands, were able to recover very definite evidence of its existence. The population was divided into a number of exogamous totemic clans. As a rule each clan had subsidiary totems in addition to its chief totem. 'In some cases two or more clans might have the same chief totem, while differing in their subsidiary totems'—which looks like the fission of an original clan. Members of a clan were distinguished by wearing an emblem of the totem, or more rarely bearing it in cicatrices or keloids on the flesh. Personal belongings also, it is said, were adorned with a representation of the owner's totem. Descent was reckoned in the male line; but adoption seems to have been practised. In conformity with patrilineal reckoning there was a tendency to a geographical distribution of the clans. This, however, was apt to result in quarrelling; and the missionaries had accordingly succeeded in inducing the people, at all events of one of the islands, to abandon the localization of the clans.

'The solidarity of the totem-clan was a marked feature in the social life of the people, and it took precedence of all other considerations; not only so, but there was an intimate relationship between all members of the same totem [-clan] irrespective of the island or locality to which they might belong and even warfare did not affect the friendship of totem-brethren. Any man who visited another island would be looked after and entertained as a matter of course by the residents who belonged to the same totem as himself.'[2]

The clans were grouped in two classes or phratries. On the island of Mabuiag these two phratries were respectively known as 'the children or people of the Great Totem' and 'the children or people of the Little Totem.' The former comprised the Crocodile, Cassowary, Snake, and Dog clans (all land animals); the latter the Dugong, Shovel-nosed Skate, Shark, Ray, and Green Turtle clans (all water animals). On this island there is no sufficient evidence that the phratries regulated marriage during recent times; but there is reason to think that they were exogamous on some other of the islands. Members of a clan might not kill or eat the totem; but this did not apply to the Dugong and Turtle clans, for both dugong and turtle were important articles of food on the islands, which are somewhat barren. Members of the clan, however, were not allowed to eat of the first dugong or turtle caught, but might partake of those subsequently caught. They performed ceremonies to entice the animals to the island and ensure a good season. They could, on the other hand, by magical rites with the contrary intention, prevent them from coming. A mystical relation was held to subsist between the totem and the clan. He was said to be 'all same as relation, he belong same family.' The Cassowary, Crocodile, Snake, Shark, and Hammer-headed Shark clans were reputed to be truculent and to like fighting. The peaceable clans were the Shovel-nosed Skate, Ray, and Sucker-fish; while the Dog clan was sometimes peaceable and at other times quarrelsome—all like the totem-animal. Certain of the clans, possibly all, had formulæ which they repeated in going into a fight, and which were either magical or in the nature of invocations to the totem. The prayer is in some stages of civilization near akin to the spell.[1]

4. Decadence of totemism.—The foregoing examples will sufficiently indicate the chief characteristics of totemism in the five great areas in which it has been found. It is apparent that in each area totemism was by no means a new phenomenon. It arises in a low condition of savagery and is connected in its typical forms with matrilineal descent. But, even before contact with Europeans, it had begun to assume forms very divergent from what we understand by normal totemism, leading in some cases to degeneration and disintegration.

(*a*) *America*.—Among the divergences found in N. America those of the coast-dwellers of the north-west are the most remarkable. The Tlingit, inhabiting S. Alaska, are divided into two exogamous phratries or classes, called after the raven and the wolf respectively;[2] and these two phratries are again divided into a number of totemic clans. The members of a clan are believed to be related to one another more closely than to those of other clans even of the same phratry. They reckon descent through the mother and as a consequence are not gathered at one place, but distributed as social groups and not geographical. Yet each clan usually derived its origin (and most of them, at the present day, their names) from some village or camp which it once occupied. They seem, however, to have had alternative names (if F. Boas's account is correct) derived from the animal, or one of the animals, which they claimed as a badge. In point of fact the emblems or representations on the north-western coast, generally called totems, are rather badges or crests. The clans of each phratry, indeed, all use the totem of the phratry; they also use a number of other badges, some of which are the special property of the clan, or of some sub-clan, and are guarded with much jealousy. They carve and paint the badge on the so-called totem-poles erected in front of the dwelling-house, or on a grave. These poles are, however, less frequently erected by the Tlingit than by some of their neighbours. The badge is also exhibited on many other articles of property, worn as a mask or hat used as a disguise at dances, potlatches, and funeral ceremonies, and painted

[1] S. Chandra Roy, *The Orāons of Chōtā Nāgpur*, Rānchī, 1915, p. 324 ff.; cf. Frazer, ii. 284 ff., and the authorities there referred to.

[2] A. C. Haddon and W. H. R. Rivers in *Reports of the Cambridge Anthrop. Exped. to Torres Straits*, Cambridge, 1901–08, v. 161.

[1] Haddon and Rivers, *ib.* v. 153–186.

[2] J. R. Swanton, *26 RBEW* [1908], p. 407, suggests that these two phratries may have had a racial origin.

on the faces of the clansmen. It is not now held that the clan or phratry is descended from the totem or animal represented, though it may be suspected that in former times this was believed. At present stories are told by the clan or sub-clan claiming a badge of its acquisition by an ancestor through an adventure with the animal in question, such animal being often conceived as of superhuman power.

As Frazer points out, many of 'these tales have the true totemic ring about them; they point clearly to the former identification of the clanspeople with their totems, which is only another way of saying that the present people are supposed to be descended from the totemic animals.'[1]

To this it may be added that, according to Boas's report, 'the animal and a member of its clan are considered relations. Thus the wolf gens will pray to the wolves, "We are your relations; pray don't hurt us!" But notwithstanding this fact they will hunt wolves without hesitation.'[2]

The truth is that the more or less permanent settlement of all the tribes along the coast—at least from the Tlingit to the Kwakiutl—in villages, and their increasing civilization, have led to the division of the population into ranks or castes and to a continually higher value being set on the crests or badges as marks of rank and wealth, and as symbols, if not guarantees, of descent from a distinguished ancestor. This has resulted in an accumulation of crests, some clans or sub-clans obtaining a larger number than others; and some of the crests were used by more than one clan.

'The great majority of Tlingit personal names referred to some animal, especially that animal whose emblem was particularly valued by the clan to which the bearer belonged.'[3]

Of these names many seem to have been peculiar to one or other of the clans. The solidarity ordinarily subsisting between members of a clan is found, among the Tlingit, rather between the members of a phratry.

'According to the unwritten Tlingit law it was incumbent upon everyone belonging to a phratry to house and feed any other member of that phratry who should visit him, no matter from how great a distance he might come'; and it was a mark of good manners, therefore of high caste, not to abuse such hospitality.[4]

Any serious collision at a potlatch arising out of the rivalry of opposing parties of dancers was averted or stayed by the host's people, who rushed between them bearing the emblem of their phratry or making the call of the animal whose name was that of the phratry. When a man died, the funeral ceremonies were conducted by the opposite phratry, who were afterwards entertained at a mourning feast by the relatives of the deceased. On the whole it may be conjectured that the two phratries represent original totem-clans, out of which the existing clans or groups, whether social or local, have developed. There was also reckoned among the Tlingit population a small group at Sanya, called the Nexádi ('People of Nex,' a creek in the neighbourhood), who stood outside both phratries and might marry into both. They bore the Eagle crest or badge and had personal names having reference to the eagle. They were doubtless a small intrusive population, which Swanton, the latest investigator of the Tlingit, suggests as perhaps of Athapascan derivation.[5]

Coming down from north to south along the coast and islands of Alaska and British Columbia, we find a similar organization, differing however in detail, among the various peoples, with an increasing emphasis laid on rank and the possession of crests, until we reach the Kwakiutl. The Kwakiutl proper (or Southern Kwakiutl, as they are often called to distinguish them from the Heiltsuk, their northern congeners) are organized in 'tribes,' which in turn are subdivided into exogamic groups distinguished not, as a rule, by totemic names but by the collective form of the name claimed as that of an ancestor, by geographical names, or by 'names of honour.' The evidence seems to show that they are neither definitely patrilineal nor matrilineal in descent, but in a state of transition, since a child may belong to any 'clan' or exogamic group to which one of its ancestors belonged at the arbitrary discretion of its parents. Each exogamic group, like the ordinary clan of several of the tribes east of the Rocky Mountains, had a number of personal names appropriated to it; and to assign a child to such a group it was enough to give it one of these names. In this way it appears to have become *ipso facto* a member of the group; it might even belong to more than one at the same time. What was more important in Kwakiutl society was the possession of crests and the privileges that they carried. These were obtained in three several ways: (1) they might be inherited by direct patrilineal descent from an ancestor who acquired them through an adventure in the course of which he obtained the protection and guidance of a *manitu*, or spiritual helper, for himself and his descendants; direct inheritance of this kind, however, was comparatively rare; (2) more usually they were obtained by marriage; the payment of a bride-price secured not only the bride, but also the right of membership in her 'clan' or exogamous group, the crest and privileges of the bride's father, and a good deal of other property; (3) the third method was to obtain them by killing the owner, as in the case of the position and privileges of the King of the Wood of Nemi. The privileges include not only the use of the crest but also the right to the membership of certain societies and the ownership and exclusive right to practise certain dances connected with the ceremonials of the societies. They are, however, not acquired for the benefit of the son-in-law in the case of marriage, but for his successor, whoever he may be. Seeing, moreover, that the number of noblemen is fixed, and there is only one person at a time who personates the ancestor and has his rank and privileges, the person entitled must wait for a vacancy before he can be admitted to them. He may wait in vain; for before a vacancy occurs the owner may change his mind, or even after the person entitled has obtained the privileges he may devest them and confer them upon some other successor.

This is manifestly not totemism, for the societies operate only during the winter, when they dominate the social organization to the exclusion of the kinship and local groups. It may have been influenced by true totemic conceptions, from which it may even have sprung. But its cause must be sought in the increasing power of wealth, the consequent development of rank, and the desire for display.[1]

The transformation that thus seems to have overtaken totemism among the Kwakiutl is in process also among the Pueblo tribes of New Mexico and Arizona. Here the cause is different. In these tribes, originally organized in totemic clans and phratries with matrilineal descent, the struggle for existence in an arid country has evolved a sense of dependence upon the supernatural powers and a religious ritual and elaborate ceremonies, partly religious and partly magical, for the production of rain and maize. At first these ceremonies appear to have been performed by the appropriate clans, as we have found in other areas. In some cases they are so still, as among the Zuñi, but aided and superintended by the priests of the various deities. In other cases,

[1] iii. 273 f.
[2] *Report of 59th Meeting of British Assoc. 1889*, p. 819.
[3] Swanton, *26 RBEW*, p. 421. [4] *Ib.* p. 427.
[5] *26 RBEW*, pp. 396–449; Boas, *Rep. Brit. Assoc. 1889*, p. 819 ff.

[1] Boas, *Rep. U.S. National Museum, 1895*, Washington, 1897, pp. 334, 338, 340, 342, 358.

as among the Hopi, the Snake clan has been superseded for this purpose by an 'order' or society, the members of which were probably at the beginning recruited exclusively from the clan. The rule is now somewhat less strict, embracing others besides members of the clan, though the members of the society are limited.[1] In fact the latest inquiries appear to show that the societies or fraternities have broken away and become quite independent of the clan organization.[2]

(*b*) *Australia.*—Turning to Australia, we find that among the Central tribes the totemic clans have been carried far towards their complete conversion into societies performing magico-religious rites, the object of which is the multiplication of the totemic animal or plant. The Warramunga hold that the totem-clans originated each from a single ancestor, half-beast, or half-plant, from whose body emanated a number of spirit-children; and the descendants of the clan are all animated by these spirit-children. The ceremonies are here performed by the clan in a definite order, representing in dramatic fashion the traditional history of the clan. The Warramunga and the tribes to the north of them are definitely patrilineal with exogamic clans; but the members of the clan in every generation are believed to be continual reincarnations of deceased ancestors. The Arunta, on the other hand, have ceased to regulate their marriages by totemic exogamy and now regulate them solely by class-divisions consisting of the pristine moieties of the tribe, which have been doubly subdivided, so that they are now eight in number. There are various places in the territory of the tribe which are totemic centres believed to be haunted by the spirit-children of the original ancestors. One of these spirit-children is held to have entered the body of every pregnant woman, according to the totemic centre near or at which she first felt herself pregnant. In this way the 'clan' of the child is ascertained, and in no case does it depend upon that of the father or mother. The resulting group passing under a totemic name is clearly no true clan.

'There is no such thing as the members of one totem [-group] being bound together in such a way that they must combine to fight on behalf of a member of the totem [-group] to which they belong.'

Inasmuch as every death is supposed to be due to witchcraft, revenge has to be taken by somebody. Normally this duty would fall on the clansmen of the deceased. But among the Arunta it would seem to be the members of the local group who undertake it.

'In fact,' say Spencer and Gillen, summing up the subject, 'it is perfectly easy to spend a considerable time amongst the Arunta tribe without even being aware that each individual has a totemic name'; but the fact of his belonging to one or other of the divisions governing marriage is soon apparent.

These groups thus passing under totemic names perform under the direction of their respective headmen from time to time, as the headman concerned decides, the ceremonies known as *intichiuma*. These ceremonies are not, like those of the Warramunga, the property of the entire group, but each of them belongs to a specific individual, who alone has the right of performing it or of requesting others to do so. One consequence of this is that they are not performed in a definite series: they are fragments and may be given in any arbitrary order. They have ceased to be a representation of the traditional history of the group; they have become mere magical rites. Further, in the tribes both south and north of the Central group, consisting of the Arunta and their immediate neighbours, a man is forbidden to kill, injure, or eat his totem. In some of the tribes, though patrilineal, the prohibition also applies more or less absolutely to the totem of the clansman's mother—probably a relic of an older matrilineal condition. Among the Arunta, however, there is no such prohibition. Indeed the members of a totem-group are expected to eat of the totem during the ceremonies; and they have liberty to do so at other times, though only sparingly. The conclusion from these and other facts is irresistible that the Central tribes of Australia are finding their way out of normal totemism, and that of these tribes the Arunta and their immediate neighbours to the north (the Kaitish, Unmatjera, and others) are the farthest advanced on the road. Their totemic organization is not merely decadent; it is obsolescent. Such remains of it as persist are preserved only as societies held together for the performance of certain magical or religious rites and as the carriers of certain religious traditions, but no longer as organic social groups.[1]

But decadent totemism often takes another course in its transformation. In most totemic communities it is customary to assemble the growing youths for the purpose of what are generally called the puberty ceremonies. By means of these ceremonies the youths of the tribe are taken from their mothers' care and out of the society of women and children, are submitted to tests of courage and endurance, educated in sexual matters and in the customs and traditions of the tribe, and fitted henceforth to take their part in the life of the tribe as adult and fully admitted members. Such initiation rites are prominent all over Australia. Among the Central tribes they have been developed beyond all others. They have been made very severe, not to say cruel; they have been elaborated into four distinct stages and protracted through years, though not of course continuous during that period. Their performance is everywhere one of the important occasions on which the tribe comes together. The members are summoned by special messengers with traditional formalities. But the actual performance of the greater part of them is secret, in the sense that no one is allowed to witness or take part in it who has not previously been in a similar manner initiated.

(*c*) *Africa.*—There is evidence of the existence of totemism in W. Africa from Senegambia southward in almost all the populations. In many places, however, where it is decadent or obsolete it is replaced by secret societies which dominate or supplement the nominal government. Thus at Old Calabar there is a very powerful society known as Egbo, divided into numerous grades. The king is the head. It has in a rough and ready way the whole administration of the law in its hands.[2] Farther south, in the cataract region of the Lower Congo, is a secret society known as Nkimba. According to the latest researches, it is entered about the age of puberty. The candidates are chosen by the *nganga*, or medicine-man. The ceremonies take place in the forest, where the camp is jealously guarded from all intrusion. There the candidates remain for a period variously stated as from one or two months to five or six years. They are painted white, and a narcotic is administered. They are subjected to a number of tests, such as the imposition of a new name and an oath of secrecy, and to flagellation. They are circumcised, if not already in that condition. They are taught a new language, and it is believed

[1] The various minutely detailed accounts of the Pueblo Indians and their ceremonies have been admirably summarized by Frazer, iii. 195 ff.

[2] A. L. Kroeber, 'Zuñi Kin and Clan,' *Anthrop. Papers of the Am. Mus. Nat. Hist.*, xviii. [New York, 1917] 145 n., 150 ff.; J. W. Fewkes, *19 RBEW* [1900], pt. ii. p. 965.

[1] Spencer-Gillen[a], pp. 34, 112–127, 167–211, 467–473; Spencer-Gillen[b], pp. 143–225.

[2] H. Webster, *Primitive Secret Societies*, New York, 1908, p. 115 ff.; *Journ. African Soc.*, iv. [1905] 306. Cf. art. SECRET SOCIETIES (African).

by the women and other non-initiated that they are put to death and brought to life again. They are instructed in the religious beliefs and moral rules to which they must in future conform. Various prohibitions are enforced during and after their retirement. If approved for the purpose, they may become fetish-priests or medicine-men; otherwise they become simply adult men, ready to take part in public life. This is obviously little more than the puberty rites of ordinary totemic peoples; but there is reason to think that the Nkimba tends to become more magical in its purview. Those who have passed through it have acquired a character in some degree sacred and mysterious; a special tie is established between them; they regard one another as brethren and render mutual aid. Another society called Ndembo, often confounded with the Nkimba, exists on the Congo. A Ndembo is not held periodically, but one is established whenever the elders of the village direct. It appears to have a specially sexual aim; men and women are admitted, and sexual licence is said to be encouraged in the camp; and to such a length is the comedy of death and resurrection carried that, on returning after the conclusion of the ceremonies, those who have been subjected to them pretend to have lost all remembrance of their previous life, act in the most foolish manner, and are only gradually recalled to ordinary sense and behaviour. The object of the Ndembo appears moreover to be more specialized, more decidedly magical, than that of the Nkimba.[1] It seems probable that all these secret societies have been developed from, or at least deeply influenced by, the initiatory rites of totemic tribes.

The Herero of S.W. Africa, who have been massacred and almost entirely destroyed by the Germans, offer a peculiarly difficult problem, not yet entirely solved. They were divided into clans called *eanda* (plur. *omaanda*) reckoning descent exclusively through the mother. A tradition of their origin is related, deriving it from a pair who emerged from the trunk of an *omborombonga* tree in the far North, whose children were all daughters fructified by contact in some way or other with various objects of the external world. These objects became the totems of their descendants. Among them may be enumerated the sun, rain, the tree, the marmot, the koodoo, the chameleon, besides others the significance of whose names is disputed. The members of an *eanda* called themselves brothers-in-law (not brothers) of the totem. The blood-feud attached to the *eanda*, which moreover, formerly at least, was exogamic. Side by side with the *eanda* stands another organization, apparently of more recent origin, the *oruzo* (plur. *otuzo*). The *oruzo* descends exclusively in the paternal line. It is also totemic; and among the totems appear the chameleon, the sun, the koodoo, rag, necklace of beads. The members of an *oruzo* are distinguished by the mode of dressing their hair, by their food-tabus, and by special sacrificial regulations. The colour and shape of the horns of the cattle which an *oruzo* possesses also differ from those of every other *oruzo*. The institution of the *oruzo* is attributed to the medicine-men; and there can be little doubt that it is specially a religious organization for the maintenance of the sacred fire of the family and the worship of ancestors. All cattle belong to the *oruzo*, for the Herero are a pastoral people, and their wealth consisted of cattle until the Germans deprived them of their stock. The cattle never descended to or through females, at all events if there was a male descendant to inherit them. The food tabus of the Herero are probably not all totemic. The Herero have no

[1] E. de Jonghe, *Les Sociétés secrètes au Bas-Congo*, Brussels, 1907, p. 15 ff.

totemic badges or signs.[1] The totemism prevalent among them is thus widely divergent from the common type. Its twofold organization is manifestly the result of a conflict between matrilineal and patrilineal institutions. How that conflict originated is obscure; but it is obviously not unconnected with the growth of ancestor-worship and the introduction of herds of cattle among a hunting and perhaps rudely agricultural people, and the consequent changes of mode of life and social arrangements. The country which they now inhabit is steppe, almost desert, and quite unsuitable for agriculture. After the rains there is for a time abundant pasture, which at other seasons must be sought in the deep and sheltered dales with which the land is intersected. The change to a pastoral life may be surmised to have occurred when or shortly before they penetrated to their present possessions, not probably more than five or six centuries ago. The consequent development of their institutions is even yet incomplete.

At the other extremity of the area occupied by the Bantu are found the Baganda, the most highly civilized of the race. They were governed by kings probably descended from a Hamitic stock which conquered the country several centuries ago.

'The Baganda are divided into a large number of totemic clans, the members of which observe the two fundamental canons of normal totemism, since they abstain both from injuring their totem and from marrying a woman of the same clan.' Each clan has a principal and a secondary totem, and takes its name from the former. 'Both totems are sacred to members of the clan, who may neither kill nor destroy them. Other people, however, may kill or destroy them for a reasonable purpose, without hurting the feelings of members of the clan.'[2]

The Baganda trace their lineage in the male line; but a woman's children were taught in infancy to respect her totems and to avoid them. When they grew up, they adopted their father's totems and ceased to regard those of their mother. Yet they were forbidden to marry into their mother's clan. For these and other reasons it seems clear that descent had originally been reckoned in the maternal line, and that, as in the case of the Herero, though on different lines, the transition had been recently and incompletely effected.[3] Like the clans of certain N. American tribes, each clan had special names appropriated to its children; hence the clan to which a man belonged was recognized by his name.[4] The king had a large harem. His children, however, took the totem of their mother; and it was naturally deemed an honour for a clan to give a king to the realm by means of the union of one of its female members with the king. From this honour certain clans were excluded for reasons which are now unknown. To obviate this some of the excluded clans joined more favoured clans, so that their daughters might marry the king and have children who might be in the succession to the throne. Another reason for the union of clans was to better the position of a despised clan. Clans so associated obtained the right to use the totem of the more honourable clan; yet they were so little regarded as relations by the members of the latter that intermarriage between members of the two clans was not forbidden. The Lung-fish clan (the largest of all) also was in an exceptional position in that its members were not subject to the rule of exogamy.[5] The totems are usually some species of animal. A few species of trees and other vegetables are found as totems, besides beads and other articles of human manu-

[1] F. Meyer, *Wirtschaft und Recht der Herero*, Berlin, 1905, p. 25 ff.; E. Dannert, *Zum Rechte der Herero*, do. 1906, p. 11 ff.; Frazer, ii. 356; [S. African] *Folklore Journal*, i. [Capetown, 1879] 37 ff., ii. [1880] 61; *Report on the Natives of S.W. Africa and their Treatment by Germany*, London, 1918, p. 37.

[2] Frazer, ii. 472 f.

[3] Hartland, *Mem. Amer. Anthrop. Assoc.*, iv. 18.

[4] J. Roscoe, *The Baganda*, London, 1911, p. 135.

[5] *Ib.* pp. 187, 137, 148, 134.

facture; and 'split-totems' and other anomalous totems (as a tailless or a spotted cow, and rain-water from roofs) are not unknown.[1] Notwithstanding the existence of a system of law and administration of justice, the sense of clan-solidarity remained strong. The blood-covenant was practised and was considered more binding than common oaths.[2] Murder was rare; but cases of murder and manslaughter, when they occurred, were taken up by the clan. The clan of a murdered man might accept and share a fine, instead of insisting on the punishment of death; and, on the other hand, the clan of the wrong-doer contributed to the payment. 'When a member of a clan wished to buy a wife, it was the duty of all the other members to help him to do so'; when a person got into debt, or was fined, the clan combined to assist him to pay the debt or fine.[3] Thus the totemism of the Baganda, while preserving many, if not most, of the essential features normally present, departs widely from more typical totemism. The religious aspect, though not quite absent, has fallen into the background before polytheism and the cult of the dead. The kingship and the organization of the kingdom have been imposed by a non-Bantu conquering people, which brought a military class, imperfectly assimilated by the bulk of the people when the English occupation took place. This people probably introduced domestic animals, some of which have become totems; and its influence is perhaps also to be traced in the 'split-totems.' Secondary totems are met with elsewhere, as we have seen.

Totemism is decadent also among the tribes of the Congo. It there manifests itself chiefly in tabus, though totemic tabus are only a few of the tabus observed. Among the Bangala of the Upper Congo the totem-animal may not be killed or eaten. A woman after marriage observes her husband's totem as well as her own. A child born to them takes the totems of both parents, until a council of both families determines which totem it is to take permanently—usually the father's. The Bangala are patrilineal.[4]

(*d*) *India.*—In continental India the decadence of totemism has been caused chiefly by the spread of Hinduism, and with it the extension of the caste system. The origin of caste has not yet been entirely cleared up. Within the Hindu system it is largely, if not mainly, occupational. As applied to the Dravidian and other races of the peninsula, it is transforming, or has transformed, independent tribes into castes; and by means of legends, some of them doubtless consciously forged to manufacture claims, these tribes have succeeded in gaining reluctant and often strongly contested admission as castes into the Hindu social hierarchy. The Reddi or Kāpu, the largest caste in the Madras Presidency, are probably descended from a Dravidian tribe which in the early centuries of our era was powerful in India. They are now a great caste of cultivators, farmers, and squireens in the Telugu country and rank next to the Brāhmans in Hindu society there. They are divided into a number of sections, for whose names fanciful etymologies have been found, and for some of them legends have been invented. One of these sections, the Panta Kāpus, are again severed into two endogamous divisions. But they are said also to have true totemic septs, of which the following are examples:

(1) Magili (*Pandanus fascicularis*): the women of this sept do not, like those of other castes, adorn themselves with the flower-bracts; and a man of the sept 'has been known to refuse to purchase some bamboo mats, because they were tied with the fibre of this tree'; (2) Ippi (*Bassia longifolia*): this tree and its products must not be touched by members of the sept; (3) Mancham (cot): members of this sept avoid sleeping on cots; (4) Arigala (*Paspalum scrobiculatum*): members of this sept do not use this grain as food; (5) Chintaginjalu (tamarind seeds): these seeds may not be used or touched by members of the sept; (6) Puccha (water-melon): the fruit may not be eaten by members of the sept.

Moreover, the names of various exogamous Kāpu septs are suggestive of totemism, such as the Cow, Grain, Buffalo, Sheep, Fowl, Goat, Elephant, as well as various plant-names, though others, such as Cart, Army, Hut, Harrow, Woman's Skirt, Plough, are more doubtful.[1]

This is not an uncommon type of caste. It suggests that the caste in question is a transformed tribe, and that the divisions of the caste originate from totemic clans, many of which retain their totemic names and some of their tabus, though other subdivisions have forgotten them or originated in a different manner. The Khangārs are a low caste of village watchmen and field-labourers in the Central Provinces, almost certainly of non-Aryan origin. They are divided into numerous exogamous septs, all of which are said to be totemic. 'The members of the sept usually show veneration to the object from which the sept takes its name.' Thus the Barha sept is named from *barāh*, 'pig,' this sept worshipping the pig; the Chirai from *chiriya*, 'bird,' this sept revering sparrows; the Ghurgotia from *ghora*, 'horse,' towards which the members practise certain observances; the Kasgotia from *kāusa*, 'bell-metal,' which is tabued by the sept; the San from *san*, 'hemp,' pieces of which are placed by members of the sept near their family god. The Hanumān sept is so called from the monkey-god, and the Viṣṇu sept from Viṣṇu, the god worshipped by it.[2]

In the United Provinces there are also many tribes and castes, probably of Dravidian origin, among whom totemism is traceable. Such are the Agariya of Mirzāpur, who have seven septs, all exogamous and apparently of totemic origin: the Markām named from the tortoise, which the members will not kill or eat; the Goirār from a certain tree which they will not cut; the Paraswān from a tree (*Butea frondosa*) which they will not cut and whose leaves they will not use for platters; the Sanwān from hemp (*san*), which they will not sow or use; the Baragwār from a tree (*Ficus Indica*) which they will not cut or climb and from the leaves of which they will not eat; the Banjhakwār, said to be named from *beng*, 'frog,' which the members of the sept will not kill or eat; and the Gidhlē, the members of which will not kill or even throw a stone at a vulture (*gidh*). The Agariya are patrilineal; and they have been deeply influenced in other ways by Hinduism. Indeed they call themselves Hindus in religion, though they worship none of the regular Hindu deities. There are, however, traces of a previous matrilineal condition. They practise tatuing, and many of the marks inscribed on their bodies are probably totemic in origin, 'but the real meaning has now been forgotten, and they are at present little more than charms to resist disease and other misfortunes, and for the purpose of mere ornament.'[3] The social and political conditions of India are such that almost the only possible relics of totemism consist in the names of the septs and the prohibitions of marriage within the clan and of eating, killing, or using the totem. Hindu influence leads to the ascription of descent to human beings rather than to animals or plants, concerning which tales are told to account for the totemic name and observances. The organization of the tribe or caste by means of a council and the police regulations render unnecessary the union of members for mutual protection. Hence, and owing to the universal tendency of caste to subdivision, the sense of solidarity is greatly weakened and is daily decreasing in force.[4]

[1] Roscoe, p. 133 ff.
[2] *Ib.* p. 268.
[3] *Ib.* pp. 20, 266, 268, 12.
[4] *JRAI* xl. [1910] 365.

[1] E. Thurston, *Castes and Tribes of S. India*, Madras, 1909, iii. 222 ff.
[2] R. V. Russell, *The Tribes and Castes of the Central Provinces of India*, London, 1916, iii. 439.
[3] W. Crooke, *Tribes and Castes of the N.W. Provinces and Oudh*, Calcutta, 1896, i. 1 ff.
[4] See H. H. Risley, *The People of India*[2], ed. W. Crooke, London, 1915, pp. 95–109, for a general consideration of the evidence; and, for the evidence itself, also his *Tribes and Castes of Bengal*, 2 vols., Calcutta, 1891–92, *passim*; Crooke,

(*e*) *Melanesia*.—There are signs that totemism was developing in the islands of Torres Straits into an anthropomorphic cult. Traditions are found of culture-heroes associated with various clans. Of these Sigai and Maiau on the island of Yam appeared first in the likeness of a hammer-headed shark and a crocodile respectively. For each of them a shrine was erected, the essential feature of which was a turtle-shell model representing either a hammer-headed shark or a crocodile; under each of these was a stone in which the spirit, the so-called *augud* ('totem'), resided.

Uninitiated persons were not allowed to visit these shrines, 'nor did they know what they contained: they were aware of Sigai and Maiau, but they did not know that the former was a hammer-headed shark and the latter a crocodile; this mystery was too sacred to be imparted to uninitiates. When the heroes were addressed it was always by their human names, and not by their animal or totem names.'[1]

Each was associated in his animal form with one of the two phratries or groups of totem-clans. Warriors before going to battle prayed to them. Totem-dances were celebrated and songs were sung, which were believed to have an effect upon the weather, by the shark-men and crocodile-men, dancing separately and wearing feathers coloured white or black according to the party to which they belonged. On Mabuiag and Muralug the hero was Kwoiam, a warrior-hero, who himself was called an *augud*. In the Muralug group of islands he was regarded as the 'big *augud*' and 'the *augud* of every one in the island.'

He is said to have made and worn 'two crescentic objects of turtle-shell, which blazed with light when he wore them at night-time, and he nourished them with the savour of cooked fish. These objects were termed *augud*; . . . and they became the insignia of the two phratries into which the old totem-clans of Mabuiag were grouped.'[2]

'When attacking an enemy the warriors formed into two columns, each of which was led by a head-man who wore the Kwoiam emblems.'[3]

Like Sigai and Maiau, he possessed a sacred shrine. It was situated on the island of Pulu; there his crescentic emblems were kept, and thence they were taken with certain ceremonies to be borne before the appropriate phratry in war.[4]

A similar evolution has been observed in Fiji.

'The people of the interior of the island [of Viti Levu] form a number of independent communities which may probably be regarded as tribes, and each of these has a number of divisions and subdivisions, which in the relatively high development of Fijian society have departed widely from the character of the septs into which a totemic community is usually divided. The animals from which descent is traced, and whose flesh is prohibited as food, are usually associated with the larger groups which seem to correspond to tribes, though the divisions of the tribe often have sacred animals or plants peculiar to themselves in addition to those which are *tabu* to them as members of the tribe.'[5]

Rivers goes on to give examples.

The tabued animal of the people of Cawanisa is an aquatic creature called the *dravidravi*, from which they believe themselves descended; and none of the divisions have restrictions peculiar to themselves. The sacred animal of the Nadrau or Navuta people is the *qiliyago*; some of its divisions have restrictions peculiar to themselves, the Wailevu division eating neither the dog nor a fish called *dabea*, the Kaivuci respecting the snake. Other animals were held sacred in other parts of the island, the people believing in descent sometimes from the tabu animal of the tribe, sometimes from that of the smaller group. Marriage is regulated by kinship alone, and there is no evidence at present of totemic exogamy. It is manifest that this kind of totemism is widely divergent from what is usually reckoned normal totemism. Nor is this to be wondered at, seeing how far Fijian civilization has progressed. Yet it presents 'the three characteristic features of the institution: belief in descent from the totem, prohibition of the totem as an article of food, and the connection of the totem with a definite unit of the social organization.' Rivers discovered evidence among these hill-tribes 'that the sacred animals had become gods, which had, however, retained their animal form definitely.' Certain rules of conduct given to the Nadrau people by the bird *qiliyago* showed an early stage in the evolution of a god from the totem-animal. In the Rewa district in the low country things had gone a step farther. 'Here each village had a deity called *tevoro*, with a name which usually showed no sign of an animal origin, but in many cases these deities had the power of turning into animals, and in such case the people of the village in question were not allowed to eat the animal.' Thus the people of Lasakau, a division of Bau, had a *tevoro* who turned into a bird called *sese*. 'The bird could not be eaten, and here, as in the hills, it was clear that the restriction extended to the whole people and was not limited to either of the two divisions of which the Lasakau people are composed.'[1]

These are not the only cases which he mentions; but they are probably enough to render the evolution plain.

It is almost unnecessary to remark that totemism may decay, especially where it comes under European influence, by simple neglect.

Thus the Winnebago, a Siouan tribe of N. America, tracing their descent from animals who were transformed into human beings and became ancestors of the various clans, treat the totem-animal in no way differently from other animals, hunting it and eating it if edible. Descent is patrilineal, and a child used always to take a name of his father's clan; but this is falling into desuetude. The reckoning of descent has become irregular; and the sacred bundle of the clan occasionally now passes out of clan-possession.[2]

Again, the Diegueno of California were all formerly totemic. Descent is paternal. Clan exogamy is still observed by many of the clans, but not by all. Some, like the Blue Wild-Cat clan, regard the totem-animal as brother. But many of the clan-names have ceased to be totemic, and the clans have become, or are becoming, mere local groups. The clan-name is frequently taken as a personal or family surname under modern conditions.[3]

Such cases may be found elsewhere than in America.

5. Traces of totemism among non-totemic peoples.—Over a large area of the globe, embracing Europe, the greater part of Asia, S. America, and Polynesia, the north of Africa, and the extreme north of N. America, inhabited by the Eskimo, totemism is now unknown. But among many of the peoples of these regions certain beliefs and practices have been reported which seem to bear traces of a former prevalence.

(*a*) *Polynesia*.—Rivers' discoveries, just referred to, in Melanesia find their analogies in Tonga and Tikopia.

In the former he learned that 'each family had its *otua* [a Polynesian word, usually written *atua*, meaning "god" or "ancestor"], some of which were animals and some stones, while a man might also be an *otua*. Examples of animal *otua* were the octopus, the flying fox, and the pigeon. . . . An animal was never eaten by those whose *otua* it was, and I was told,' he says, 'that there was definite belief in descent from the animal.' Similarly on the island of Tikopia he found a number of animals called *atua*. 'Some of these animal *atua* belong to the whole community and may be eaten by no one on the island; others belong to one or other of the four sections into which the people are divided.' Thus the octopus is the *atua* of the Kavika; but it is forbidden as food not only to them but also to the whole people. The Taumako may not eat the sea-eel or a bird called *rupe*—prohibitions limited to this division of the people. The Fangalele may not catch an *one* fish. The Tafua may not eat the fresh-water eel, the flying fox, or the turtle, the two latter 'being also prohibited as food to the whole community, though regarded as especially sacred to the Tafua.' There was also evidence that the Kavika were believed to be descended from the octopus, the Taumako from the eel, the Tafua from the flying fox; and it was believed that one man of this division became after death a fresh-water eel, while two men of the Fangalele became, the one an *one* fish, the other a *moko* bird. There are also plant and vegetable *atua*, to which corresponding restrictions attached.[4]

Thus there is reason to think that totemism had at one time existed and had left traces attributable to no other cause. Elsewhere in Polynesia there are relics more or less distinct of the same conditions.

(*b*) *Egypt*. — We are naturally reminded of Egypt. The origin and early development of Egyptian religion are obscure. What we find is that in the earliest period known to us by the

Tribes and Castes of N.W. Provinces and Oudh, passim; and the other works referred to in Crooke's notes to Risley's observations. Cf. also Crooke's observations in *PR*[2] ii. 148–159.

1 A. C. Haddon, in *Anthropological Essays presented to E. B. Tylor*, Oxford, 1907, p. 185.

2 *Ib.* p. 184. 3 *Ib.*

4 *Reports Camb. Anthrop. Exped.* v. 373 ff., 367 ff., 80; Frazer, ii. 18–24.

5 W. H. R. Rivers, *Man*, viii. [1908] 134.

1 *Man*, viii. 134 f.; *JRAI* xxxix. [1909] 158.

2 *Amer. Anthrop.*, new ser., xii. [1910] 212, 214.

3 *Univ. of California Publications*, xiv. [1918] 167 ff.

4 *JRAI* xxxix. 156 ff.

monuments each nome or district had its own peculiar object of adoration in some animal, which was regarded with indifference or, in consequence of local quarrels, with hostility in the adjacent nomes. Moreover (in spite of changes during the country's long history, in spite of the evolution into higher polytheism and of the syncretism which gradually won its way, at all events among the educated classes), the same attitude towards these animals prevailed to the end. One nome venerated the ibis, one the crocodile, one the cat, one the gnat, one the ram, one the *oxyrhynchus* fish, and so on. Some of these are domesticated animals; in the earliest period, however, domesticated animals do not appear. The monarchy seems to have been introduced by a people which invaded Egypt and conquered the aborigines. The invaders carried the standard of a falcon, from the name of which (*heru*) that of Horus, later regarded as the last of the gods who reigned over Egypt, is derived. When the objects of adoration took human form, becoming anthropomorphic gods, these were identified with various animals, and are represented on the monuments with the heads of the appropriate animals. The animals remained sacred, as their numerous mummies attest; and various legends were told to account for their relation to the respective gods. At Bubastis, where the cat was venerated, the goddess Bast had her seat; Ombos, where the crocodile was honoured, was the sacred town of the crocodile-headed god, Sebak; the ram-headed god, Khnūm or Ammon-Rā, was worshipped at Thebes, and there precisely was the place where the sheep was revered. As a result of the unification of the country under the kings, syncretism in theology spread, and the various gods tended to be identified with one another and with the animals honoured in the different towns. At length the myth and worship of the culture-hero, Osiris, prevailed throughout the land; and his myth included a story of how the various gods fled, 'disguised in brutish forms,' from the rage of his enemy Typhon. In short, all sorts of devices are adopted to account for the local gods and animals venerated in the different cities and districts and to unify the religion. These devices were probably known to, or at least accepted by, the educated classes only. All the other classes remained attached to their local deities.[1] The evidence points to the prevalence at one time in the valley of the Nile of a form of totemism, which possibly included various trees and other vegetables (for these, though less prominent than animals, are not unknown in Egyptian religion), and which by a series of steps was slowly merged and elevated into a polytheistic worship tending ever in the minds of the educated more and more to monotheism.[2]

Of the original social organization, however, we know little beyond the fact that it was matrilineal. The woman was mistress of the house; the husband on marriage was received as a guest or went to reside with her. Those men who could afford it kept harems, the members of which were under the governance of the chief wife. It is a probable conjecture from the available information that society was constituted of clans, in later ages directly or indirectly giving birth to trading and other gilds. The custom of the husband going to reside with his wife secured the local concentration of the clan and facilitated the conversion of the clan-settlement into the nome and the dominance of a single animal-totem in each nome.

1 A. Lang, *Myth, Ritual and Religion*, ii. ch. xv.; E. Naville, *RHR* lii. [1905] 357 ff.; *RHR* li. [1905] 238; A. Wiedemann, *Religion of the Ancient Egyptians*, Eng. tr., London, 1897, chs. vii.–viii.

2 A. H. Sayce, *The Religions of Ancient Egypt and Babylonia*, Edinburgh, 1902, p. 116.

All this was doubtless the result of the agricultural occupations of the people. What were the relations of the members of the clan to one another or to the totem we are not informed.

(*c*) *Greece.*—Scientific controversy has raged over the question whether remains of totemism are discoverable in ancient Greece. Salomon Reinach, Toutain, and Van Gennep have been the protagonists. Andrew Lang pointed out the various remains of animal-worship among the Greek peoples — in Thessaly the Myrmidons claiming descent from the ant and revering ants; in the Troad and the islands the mice sacred to Apollo Smintheus and a tribe referred to by an oracle as mice; the adoration of the wolf at Delphi and Athens and of the sheep on Samos; the descent of Tennes, the hero of Tenedos, from a swan; the invocation of Hecate as a dog and the sacrifice to her of a dog;[1] the Artemis of Arcadia, identified with Callisto, a nymph who is fabled to have been metamorphosed into a she-bear, from which the Arcadians claimed descent; the similar tale of the Brauronian Artemis in Attica, served by girls called bears, dancing with the gait of bears and probably in archaic times wearing bear-skins; and a hundred other such myths, rituals, and metamorphoses.[2] Nor has he been alone in discerning that such cases pointed to a primitive totemism, outgrown and misconstrued before the dawn of authentic history. The social organization of Athens has also been examined. The γένος and φρατρία have been pronounced parallel in all essentials with the organization of the Australian totemic clan and phratry.[3] There are good reasons for suspecting that originally matrilineal descent was the rule, of which vestiges subsisted down to historical times.[4] Though this view has been challenged,[5] and it is undoubted that agnatic descent prevailed in historical times, the suspicion is not without solid foundation. Probably the pre-historic population of the period called the Mycenæan age was matrilineal and was conquered by a patrilineal military people from the north, who formed the dominant classes in the Homeric age, and under whom Greek society was transformed and reorganized. On the whole we are justified in accepting with L. R. Farnell the theory that various remarkable cults—the Arcadian worship of Zeus Lycæus and of Artemis Calliste, the Attic worship of Zeus Polieus, and perhaps some others—can be explained only by a survival of what is in effect totemism.[6] But, if so, then other cults and myths of which the connecting links have been lost may with the more likelihood be assigned to the same origin.

(*d*) *Ireland.*—Over the rest of Europe the traces of totemism are still more uncertain. They will be found, as in Greece, if at all, on the side of belief and practice which may be called quasi-religious rather than in social observances such as marriage restrictions; for under the dominance of Christianity and the social ideas, Hebrew and Roman, carried with it society has been shaped for two millenniums. In Connemara and the islands off the west coast of Ireland persons bearing the name of Conneely, who are descended from the clan Conneely, an old family of Iar-Connaught, claim 'that they have seal's blood in them, and that is why they are such good swimmers.'

A story is told of some members of the clan who at a distant period were changed into seals. Since then, it is said, no Conneely can kill a seal without afterwards having bad luck.

1 *Myth, Ritual and Religion*, i. 277. 2 *Ib.* ii. 211.

3 A. W. Howitt and L. Fison, *JAI* xiv. [1885] 142 ff.

4 Hartland, *Primitive Paternity*, London, 1909, i. 265, ii. 18.

5 L. R. Farnell, *ARW* vii. [1904] 70; H. J. Rose, *FL* xxii. [1911] 277 ff.

6 *CGS*, Oxford, 1896–1901, i. 41, 58, 91, ii. 434, 441 (cf. iv. 116, v. 106; and J. E. Harrison, *Themis*, Cambridge, 1912, *passim*, esp. ch. v.).

Seals are said to be regarded with profound veneration. They are called Conneelys, and are said to be the souls of departed friends. We are told that 'in some places the story has its believers who would no more kill a seal, or eat of a slaughtered one, than they would of a human Conneely.'[1]

Both in Ireland and in the Scottish isles are stories and customs which point to an extinct totemism as the best explanation; and the same explanation has been offered, with more or less probability, of various beliefs and practices in Wales and England as well as in other European countries.[2]

(*e*) *W. China.*—In W. China among the Lolos, an aboriginal mountain people of Szechwan, there is something more than traces of totemism.

Their 'surnames always signify the name of a tree or animal or both tree and animal,' and 'these are considered as the ancestors of the family bearing the name. This name is often archaic. Thus the surname Bu-luh-beh is explained as follows:—Bu-luh is said to be an ancient name for the citron, which is now known as *sa-lu*. The common way of asking a person what his surname is, is to inquire "What is it you don't touch?" and a person of the surname just mentioned would reply "We do not touch the *sa-lu* or citron." People cannot eat or touch in any way the plant or animal, or both, which enters into their surname. The plant or animal is not, however, worshipped in any way.

People of the same surname may marry if there is no obvious relationship. There are, however, groups of two or three surnames amongst whom intermarriage is forbidden; and no explanation of this is given. There are also groups of two or three surnames who are called comrades, and intermarriage amongst them is favoured.'[3]

The Chinese themselves are on a higher plane of civilization, and totemism is unknown. But from sundry prohibitions its existence has been suspected. Among some other peoples of S.W. Asia and various islands of the Indian Archipelago totemism has been either found or suspected. In Madagascar and in the Polynesian islands a number of superstitions have been ascribed with more or less probability to an original totemism no longer forming part of the social organization.

(*f*) *American.*—In Central and S. America also customs and beliefs have been interpreted as traces of totemism. Thus in Peru, where the various clans were localized, each clan worshipped its ancestor, and the tendency seems to have been for such objects of worship to assume the form of an animal, vegetable, or some other natural phenomenon. Each clan, moreover, had a distinctive dress. But our information is too imperfect to permit of a definite opinion on the subject.[4] The Bororo of Brazil claim to be araras (a bird with a red plumage) and believe a neighbouring tribe, the Trumai, to be water-animals, while a certain cannibal tribe is descended from the jaguar.[5] In N. America it was usual for a young man at adolescence, or a man who wished to acquire special powers, to go out into the woods and fast for days in order to acquire a guardian spirit, which usually took the form of an animal. It was revealed to him in a vision in which his austerities culminated; and when it took the form of some animal, a portion or symbol of that animal became his fetish or medicine. Thereafter he obeyed the restrictions and prohibitions believed to have been communicated to him by the vision. There was a tendency among some tribes, particularly in the north-west, for the guardian spirit (*súlia* or *manitu*) to be inherited by his descendants. And some writers have seen in this the origin of totemism.[6] A variety of the practice in Central and S. America is known under the name of nagualism (Quiche *naual*, 'the knowing one' or 'sorcerer'), in which some natural object, commonly an animal, is believed to have a parallel relation with a human being, so that for weal or woe their fates are mutually dependent. The *nagual* is sometimes chosen by divination for an infant at birth, but more often obtained, like a *manitu*, by fasting and prayer.[1] It seems that the *nagual* is a purely personal acquisition and is not inherited like the *súlia*. It should, however, be pointed out that neither the belief of the Bororo nor the *manitu* or *nagual* of other tribes has the marks of true totemism. It has no relation to a clan, nor is it in any way related to the social organization: where the *manitu* descends, it is only to the children or remoter issue of the original possessor, and in such case the descent has only taken place under the influence of patrilineal kinship.

(*g*) *Australia.*—In Australia among the Kurnai and some other tribes of the south-east the two sexes have animals respectively regarded as their protectors, with whom the life of individual members of the sex is supposed to be bound up. Fights between the sexes on behalf of their sex-totems often occurred, as a means, or a preliminary, to marriages.[2] Here again, and for the same reason as in nagualism and the other American beliefs just referred to, the sex-totems are, whatever their origin, entirely unconnected with true totemism.

6. Origin.—The origin of totemism has been the subject of much discussion and speculation among anthropologists. It is only necessary here to refer to a few of the hypotheses offered. That which is identified with the name of Hill-Tout has already been incidentally dealt with. Though accepted by some American anthropologists, it has not generally found favour on either side of the Atlantic. Frazer, having previously adopted the theory that the totemic clan was in its primitive form and purpose a society for the multiplication by magical ceremonies of the totem-animal or vegetable, and so for ensuring a continuance of provision for the food and prosperity of the community, so far as the totem-animals and vegetables were edible or otherwise available for use,[3] has relinquished that hypothesis. Instead, in his latest conjecture he is now inclined to the opinion, suggested by observation on the part of Spencer and Gillen of the peoples of Central Australia, and on the part of Rivers of the Melanesians, that totemism originated in a primitive explanation of conception and childbirth. The latter people hold that their mothers were impregnated by the entrance into their wombs of spirit-animals or spirit-fruits, and that they themselves are severally nothing but the particular animal or fruit which effected a lodgment in the mother and in due time was born into the world as a human being. Hence they partake of the character of the animal or fruit in question and refuse to eat all such animals and fruits. The supposition is that these beliefs become in particular cases hereditary and result in the evolution of clans derived respectively from ancestors who originated from the animals or fruits.[4] Such a theory, however, encounters the same difficulties as the theory which ascribes the origin of totemism to the *manitu* become hereditary.

Earlier than either of these theories Frazer had suggested 'that the key to totemism might be found in the theory of the

[1] *FLJ* ii. [1884] 259; *FLR* iv. [1881] 104; C. R. Browne, *Proc. Roy. Irish Academy*, 3rd ser., v. [1899] 262; *JAI* ii. [1873] 448 f.; G. L. Gomme, *Archæol. Rev.* iii. [1889] 219.

[2] G. L. Gomme, *loc. cit.*; N. W. Thomas, *FL* xi. [1900] 227 ff.; *RHR* xxxviii. [1898] 295; S. Reinach, *Cults, Myths and Religions*, Eng. tr. i. 1.

[3] *JAI* xxxiii. [1903] 105.

[4] E. J. Payne, *Hist. of the New World called America*, Oxford, 1892–99, i. 400, 403 n., 462, 463; *Man*, xiii. [1913] 116.

[5] K. von den Steinen, *Unter den Naturvölkern Zentral-Brasiliens*, Berlin, 1894, p. 352.

[6] C. Hill-Tout, *Trans. Roy. Soc. Canada*, 2nd ser., ix. [1903] 61; and *JAI* xxxiv. [1904] 326 ff.

[1] O. Stoll, *Die Ethnologie der Indianerstämme von Guatemala* (Suppl. to *AE* i.), Leyden, 1889, p. 57; D. G. Brinton, *The Myths of the New World*³, Philadelphia, 1896, p. 122, and *Nagualism*, do. 1894, p. 59; D. D. Granada, *Reseña Histórico-descriptiva de antiguas y modernas Supersticiones del Rio de la Plata*, Monte Video, 1896, p. 591.

[2] Howitt, p. 148.

[3] *Fortnightly Rev.*, new ser., lxv. [1899] 647 ff., 835 ff.

[4] Frazer, iv. 57 ff.

external soul, that is, in the belief that living people may deposit their souls for safe keeping outside of themselves in some secure place, where the precious deposit will be less exposed to the risks and vicissitudes of life than while it remained in the body of its owner.'[1] This hypothesis, though founded on a widely spread practice and belief, has not, he frankly admits, been confirmed by further research, inasmuch as 'the evidence which connects this theory of external human souls in animal bodies with totemism appears to be insufficient to justify us in regarding it as the source of the whole institution.'[2]

Andrew Lang, towards the close of his life, was led to emphasize the social aspect of totemism. He advocated a theory similar to that first propounded by Herbert Spencer, and adopted by the German scholar, J. Pikler,[3] that the origin is to be sought in names. According to this theory, bands of men, having been given names from outside, either by way of distinction or as nicknames, accepted these names and came to fancy that they themselves were in a mystical connexion with them, or rather with the things signified by the names, and then the course of social organization, from one cause or another, led first to the preference for wives of another band having a different name, and subsequently to a positive prohibition to marry a woman of the same band and necessarily having the same name—in other words, to clan-exogamy.[4] The influence of names, and the inveterate tendency to regard a name as a real objective existence belonging to and having a mystical connexion with the person or thing signified by it, are practically universal in the lower culture. But why these names were appropriated and accepted by the various bands is left unexplained. Lang apparently agrees with Frazer that the institution of exogamy is distinct from totemism, and that totemism as a matter of fact preceded exogamy.[5] It certainly is a usual, but not quite invariable, accompaniment of it. Lang indeed offers explanations of the origin of exogamy, but it cannot be said that his speculations are more satisfactory than those of previous inquirers.

A. C. Haddon some time ago hazarded a suggestion of the 'possible origin of one aspect of totemism.' It is that there were numerous small human groups in favourable areas, each occupying a restricted range in which a certain animal or plant or group of animals or plants might be specially abundant, and that they consequently utilized these as a food-supply and for other purposes, the superfluity of which could be bartered for the superfluities of other groups.

Thus 'the group that lived mainly on crabs and occasionally traded in crabs might well be spoken of as "the crab-men" by all the groups with whom they came in direct or indirect contact. The same would hold good for the group that dealt in clams or in turtle, and reciprocally there might be sago-men, bamboo-men, and so forth. It is obvious that the men who persistently collected or hunted a particular group of animals would understand the habits of those animals better than other people, and a personal regard for these animals would naturally arise. Thus from the very beginning there would be a distinct relationship between a group of individuals and a group of animals or plants, a relationship that primitively was based, not on even the most elementary of psychic concepts, but on the most deeply seated and urgent of human claims, hunger.'

Here Haddon agrees with Lang that the name of the group was probably imposed from without and adopted by the group thus named. Once accepted, the name and the regard for the animal, or whatever was the object signified by the name, would result in a mystical connexion being held to exist between the object and the human group, which might issue in the object being tabued instead of used as originally, and, on the other hand, in magic being worked to secure a continuous supply of the object. As part of the tabu, or incident to it, exogamy, originating in a preference for women of contiguous groups, might be developed.[1]

E. Durkheim, envisaging chiefly the Australian evidence, considers totemism as a religious institution. According to him, it is the religion of a sort of anonymous and impersonal force manifested in various animals, men, and emblems, none of which possesses it entire, but all of which participate in it. It is the god adored in all totemic cults; but it is an impersonal god without name or history, immanent in the world, diffused in an innumerable multitude of things. It is, in short, *mana* (*q.v.*) or *orenda*. It is not, however, represented under its abstract form, but is conceived as a species of animal or vegetable—in a word, under a sensible form—each group of men taking for ensign the animal or vegetable diffused most plentifully in the neighbourhood of the place where the group was accustomed to assemble. The totem is really only the material form under which this immaterial substance, this energy diffused through all sorts of heterogeneous beings (which is the sole object of the cult), is represented to the imagination. It is the symbol not only of the impersonal totemic principle or god, but also of the definite society, the clan, of which it is the totem. It is the standard, the emblem, by which each clan distinguishes itself from the others, the visible sign of its personality, the mark borne by every one that makes part of the clan, whether men, beasts, or anything else. All are sacred in varying degrees; but most sacred of all—more even than the totem-animal or other object itself—is the artificial standard or emblem of the clan. Since all who communicate in the same totemic principle are sacred, the totem is the source of the moral life of the clan, and all are morally bound to one another, with definite duties towards one another of help, vendetta, and so forth. The totem is thus not only a material but a moral force, which may easily transform itself into a divinity properly so called. Totemism therefore is bound up with the organization of society. It is practically assumed as the earliest form of religion and of society everywhere.[2] In the striking work of which the main thesis is here imperfectly summarized Durkheim elaborates this thesis with infinite pains and abundance of illustrations. But everything rests on the assumption of primitive universality, which no attempt is made to prove. Large spaces of the world, however, remain in which totemism has never yet been found. More or less probable traces of it may, indeed, be discerned in these areas; or they may hereafter be discovered. Meanwhile Durkheim's theory remains a brilliant conjecture, and nothing more.

In its insistence on an attitude towards nature and on a psychology different from that of civilized mankind it avoids the rock on which most of the hypotheses heretofore considered have split. This was also emphatically laid down, as the condition of success in solving the question of the origin of totemism, by E. Reuterskiöld, a Swedish scholar, in an article which appeared almost contemporaneously with Durkheim's work. This article is an extension of part of a previous essay by the same author published in 1908. He urges that totemism is connected with an impersonal conception of life. A group of men are allied with a group of animals. There is nothing personal, nothing individual, in their union. It is an association peculiar to the primitive mode of thought, which does not compare one thing with another: if it finds likeness between them, it identifies them. For primitive man the individual is nothing; the group or the species is

[1] Frazer, p. 52. [2] *Ib.* p. 55.
[3] *Der Ursprung des Totemismus*, Berlin, 1900.
[4] Lang, *The Secret of the Totem*, chs. vi. and vii.
[5] iv. 9.

[1] A. C. Haddon, Presidential Address to Anthropology Section, *Report of 72nd Meeting of Brit. Assoc.*, 1902, p. 745 ff.
[2] *Les Formes élémentaires de la vie religieuse*, Paris, 1912, pp. 269, 294, 334, etc.

everything. Man did not picture himself as lord of creation. He did not sever himself in thought from other living creatures; he was only a part of a great community. He felt himself closely united with a kind of animal living in his neighbourhood and coming in touch with him. It was no accident that he associated himself with one or other species. Totemism has its various sides—religious, magical, and social. These were in the origin undistinguished from one another. The distinction between them came later, with the development of individualism and analysis.[1]

In this way Reuterskiöld would explain the origin of totemism. Without saying that he has completely solved the question, the opinion may be expressed that he has realized the conditions of primitive life and thought sufficiently to define at all events some of the conditions to be fulfilled and so lead to a solution. In endeavouring to explain the attitude towards nature of the tribes of Central Brazil Von den Steinen not only says that they draw no strict line of demarcation between man and brute; he uses the emphatic expression that, to understand it, 'we must think the boundary completely away.' There is thus no impediment to their assimilating themselves to one or another animal. Indeed, the Bororo declare, as we have seen, that they are red araras, not that they will become araras after death, nor that they were araras in a previous existence, but that they are araras here and now. From this attitude of mind we can see how it follows that in their stories human modes of life and thought are attributed to the lower animals, and indeed, as frequently in savage tales, it is often impossible to say whether the actors are human or brute; it follows also that marriages between the former and the latter are in the tales contemplated without aversion or are even regarded as natural, and that interchanges of shape are quite ordinary incidents. It is no question of naming. Totemism is founded on something deeper than that. It assumes a community of nature between men and other creatures; and the existence of the individual is ignored, except as a small and subordinate part of a group, thought of as a whole. It was part of the organization of society which is bound up with the general concept of the world indicated above—a concept by no means confined to totemic peoples, but not always issuing in the same type of organization. How or why particular totems were chosen is a difficult question, but, however interesting, relatively unimportant.

In strict acceptation of the term totemism is not a religion. The respect of the clan for its totem arises out of the attitude of mind just explained. The relation of the clan to its totem assumes a mystical aspect and generates an intense feeling of kinship. This frequently is expressed in the belief that they are descended from the totem-species. As civilization evolves, this belief becomes modified into the shape of a story of the adventure of a human ancestor with the totem-species. Although regarded with reverence and looked to for help, the totem is never, where totemism is not decadent, prayed to as a god or a person with powers which we call supernatural. In fact, in that stage of culture totemism usually co-exists with the cult of the dead and often with the worship of other spirits and gods accurately so called.

Its connexion with the social organization, on the other hand, is very intimate. Probably beginning in a more or less inchoate recognition of kinship, it develops the clan-feeling and the clan-organization and by means of clan-exogamy binds the whole tribe together. Whether exogamy actually precedes totemism in point of time or not, there can be no doubt that the interaction of the two strengthens and develops it, until exogamy is seen as an essential element of totemism in its full force. When, in the course of evolving civilization, totemism begins to decay, exogamy may and often does continue to exist independently. And the cases are numerous where the clan-system and exogamy have arisen and existed for long periods without any other element of totemism, so far as we know. So various are the forms of totemism that it has been maintained with plausibility that they are due to a fortuitous concurrence of causes which has united elements originally diverse but tending to converge into a system on the whole marvellously similar wherever it obtains, just as the disintegration, and in many cases the dissolution, of the system have historically been due to a concurrence or a sequence of causes of the opposite kind.

LITERATURE.—The most comprehensive account of totemism is J. G. Frazer, *Totemism and Exogamy*, 4 vols., London, 1910. It is indispensable to every student of the subject, and it includes a reprint of his early work, *Totemism*, Edinburgh, 1887, and of his subsequent artt. in *The Fortnightly Review*, new ser., lxv. [1899] 647 ff., 835 ff., and lxxviii. [1905] 162 ff., 452 ff. Other important works are Andrew Lang, *Social Origins*, London, 1903, *The Secret of the Totem*, do. 1905, and his earlier work, *Myth, Ritual and Religion*, 2 vols., do. 1887; W. Robertson Smith, *The Religion of the Semites*², Edinburgh, 1894; F. B. Jevons, *An Introd. to the Hist. of Religion*, London, 1896; four artt. by L. Marillier, on 'La Place du totémisme dans l'évolution religieuse,' in *RHR* xxxvi. [1897] and xxxvii. [1898]; Salomon Reinach, *Cultes, Mythes et Religions*, vols. i. and ii., Paris, 1905–08, Eng. tr., London, 1912, *Orpheus*, Paris, 1909; J. Toutain, 'L'Hist. des religions et le totémisme,' in *RHR* lvii. [1908], and A. van Gennep's reply in *RHR* lviii. [1908]; A. A. Goldenweiser, 'Totemism, an Analytical Study,' in *JAFL* xxiii. [1911], with replies by R. H. Lowie in *American Anthropologist*, new ser., xiii. [1911], by A. Lang, *ib.* xiv. [1912], by W. D. Wallis, *ib.* xv. [1913], and the consequent discussions, including an art. by A. A. Goldenweiser, in *ib.* xx. [1918]. Articles bearing on totemism will be found in various volumes of *ASoc*, 1897–1907. Works in German are numerous, but of less importance. The remaining literature in English will be found in the usual anthropological periodicals and other works published in England and America, many of which have been referred to in the text. Other important works have been indicated in the course of the article. E. SIDNEY HARTLAND.

TRACTARIANISM.—See OXFORD MOVEMENT.

TRADE.—See COMMERCE.

TRADE UNIONS.—A trade union has been defined as 'a continuous association of wage-earners for the purpose of maintaining or improving the conditions of their employment.'[1] This definition would not be regarded as an adequate account of the objects of a trade union by many labour leaders of the present time, but it may stand with the proviso that there are large questions of politics and industrial reconstruction which under modern conditions have a direct or indirect bearing upon the 'improvement of conditions.' The underlying basis of the movement is the power of combination, and the progressive realization of this power by the masses of the workers in various countries has gone far to revolutionize the face of civilization. Labour is no longer a suppliant pleading for justice, but a strong man armed, presenting demands which he has the power to enforce. How will that power be used? The time seems appropriate for a consideration of the ethical aspects of the trade union movement.

1. Historical.—Trade unionism, like parliamentary government, is the child of the passionate instinct of the British people for civic freedom. It has been transplanted to the colonies, adopted by the working people of every nation in Europe, carried

[1] *ARW* xv. [1912] 12 ff. The author's previous work, to which reference is made, is entitled *Till frågan om uppkomsten af sakramentala måltider med särskild hänsyn till Totemismen*, Upsala, 1908.

[1] Sidney and Beatrice Webb, *History of Trade Unionism*, p. 1.

across the Atlantic to America. It pervades the whole world of intelligent white labour, but England was its cradle.

Attempts have been made to trace its descent from the craft gilds (*q.v.*) of the Middle Ages, but those institutions are to be regarded as associations of masters rather than of men, and there is little or no evidence of the existence of permanent associations of wage-earners before the 18th century. It was then that the differentiation between employer and employed became more and more marked until a great gulf was finally set between them by the transformation of industry effected by the introduction of machinery and the institution of the modern factory system of production on a large scale. The trade union movement was a direct response to the change of conditions.

In the early part of the 18th cent. continuous associations of wage-earners generally took the form of friendly societies, with sick and funeral funds attached; but, as the century wore on, and the effects of the industrial revolution, in divorcing the worker from the instruments of production and degrading his position, became more apparent, they inevitably assumed a different character. The meetings of the clubs afforded opportunities for talk about questions of wages and conditions of labour, and we find Adam Smith writing:

'People of the same trade seldom meet together, even for merriment and discussion, but the conversation ends in a conspiracy against the public, or in some contrivance to raise prices.'[1]

This was what the early trade unions appeared to be to the governing classes of those days—'a conspiracy against the public'—and they were only taking the same view as had been taken by the governing classes long before. Combinations of workmen were held to constitute a danger to the State, and from early times a series of statutes had been directed against them. The earliest of these appears to have been the statute 33 Edw. I. c. 1 (1305).

It stamped as conspirators 'all who do confeder or bind themselves by oath, covenant or other alliance, as relates or extends to combinations or conspiracies of workmen or other persons to obtain an advance of, or fix the rate of, wages, or to lessen or alter the hours or duration of the time of working, or to decrease the quantity of work, or to regulate or control the mode of carrying on any manufacture, trade, or business, or the management thereof.'

From this it may be seen that labour questions, including the limitation of output, were much the same in the first part of the 14th cent. as they are to-day. The statute goes on to declare 'combinations or conspiracies of masters, manufacturers, or other persons' to be equally illegal; they too were regarded as constituting a danger to the State; and the principle that all combinations, whether of masters or of men, should be suppressed in the interest of the public may be said to underlie most of our earlier industrial legislation. But, as time went on, the tendency was for the laws against labour to be rigidly enforced, while those in its favour were very laxly administered or allowed to fall into oblivion.

The Act of Edward I. was followed by a series of others of the same nature. In the 18th cent. they became more and more frequent with the rise of the new associations. At least fifteen were enacted in the reign of George III. before the year 1800. That year marks an epoch. The whole of the existing Combination Acts were consolidated in a new law which made all associations of workmen (and of employers) illegal, and membership of such an association a criminal offence (39 and 40 Geo. III. c. 106).

The position of the workers now was that, while no attempt was made to extend already existing State regulations as to wages, hours, and conditions of employment so as to apply them to the altered circumstances of the times—and many of them had become practically inoperative—they were debarred by statute from what seemed the only chance of escape, association for mutual protection. But, in spite of this, associations were formed, some of which, as the direct result of this repressive legislation, took the form of secret societies with strange oaths and revolutionary rites, and the next twenty-five years were full of trouble and discontent. Eventually by the Acts 5 Geo. IV. c. 95 (1824) and 6 Geo. IV. c. 129 (1825) the Combination Laws were repealed and association for the purpose of regulating wages or hours of labour was expressly legalized.

The position of the trade unions was now secure. Some forty-five were discovered in 1824 to have managed to maintain a precarious existence in spite of the Combination Laws, but, when the laws were repealed, trade unions sprang into life all over the country. The next few years were a period of great industrial activity, and the work of organization was taken in hand in earnest. It was also a time of great political activity, and soon after the passing of the Reform Act of 1832 we find that the unions had already accumulated members and funds sufficient to make them a distinct power in politics. They threw themselves heartily into the movement initiated by Robert Owen—the membership of his 'Grand National Consolidated Trades Union' in 1834 has been estimated at half a million—but on the whole stood aloof from the Chartist movement which played such an important part in the history of the working classes between 1837 and 1848. Between 1850 and 1860 trade unionism made rapid strides on the old lines, and then there was a marked increase of political interest with the Reform Bill of 1867 as its centre.

The Trade Union Act of 1871 marked another stage. Though the repeal of the Combination Laws had left the workers free to combine, all combinations 'in restraint of trade' were still illegal. The funds of any such society therefore did not enjoy the protection of the law, but were at the mercy of any official who had access to them. As a matter of fact the trust had been very seldom abused, but the position was unsatisfactory, and the Act remedied it, and also strengthened the position of the unions in other respects. In 1875 a further Act recognized employers and workmen (they were no longer called master and servant) as equal parties to a civil contract, and 'peaceful picketing' during a strike was expressly permitted. Thus 'collective bargaining, with all its necessary accompaniments, was after fifty years of legislative struggle finally recognized by the law of the land.'[1]

Ten years later the movement entered upon a new phase. The leading spirits were no longer content to proceed steadily upon the old lines, and John Burns and Tom Mann became the apostles of a more militant and aggressive creed. A 'new unionism' came into existence which was inspired by the doctrines of socialism (*q.v.*). Its spirit was manifested in the labour unrest of 1889–90. This has been in its turn outpaced by the still newer unionism of the 20th cent., which is syndicalist instead of socialist and regards the general strike as its weapon. But, at all events up to the outbreak of the war in 1914, the great bulk of trade unionists seem to have been content, as Joseph Clayton has said,

'to proceed steadily on the old lines—distrusting revolutionary sentiments, favouring the return to Parliament of their officers, of whose abilities and honesty they are well aware, believing that by collective bargaining they can achieve a more comfortable life for themselves and their families and that

[1] *Wealth of Nations*, bk. i. ch. 10.

[1] Webb, *History of Trade Unionism*, p. 275.

legislation of a social character is also needed to improve their position.'[1]
Beyond the outbreak of the war we do not propose to go.

The total number of trade unions in existence at the end of 1913 is given in the *Labour Year Book* as 1135 with a membership of just under four millions—more than double what they had been ten years before.

2. Moral and economic justification of trade unionism.—No one would be likely to deny that trade unions are a necessary feature of modern industrial life, and most people would admit that they are on the whole a salutary feature. Our forefathers may have been sincere in their belief that the State could not afford to allow such associations to exist, that they constituted a real danger to the public; but in those days there was little knowledge of the conditions under which the 'lower classes' lived and little sympathy with the workers themselves. Moreover, the existing order was taken for granted. It was recognized that there were evils which called for alleviation, but the ideas of the most sympathetic did not get farther than palliation; prevention was beyond their scope. Such attempts as were made in early times to regulate industry by legal enactments were crude; and, when the great crisis of the 18th cent. arrived and there was the most urgent need of strong and intelligent control, there was no one who saw the meaning and implications of the change. The industrial revolution went its way unfettered; the old industrial order was swept away and chaos supervened; whole classes of workers became involved in a condition of unparalleled servitude, poverty, and degradation. But the governing classes failed to realize that, if there was a possible element of danger in the existence of combinations of workers, the existence of such a state of things was a far greater danger and in addition an intolerable disgrace to any civilized country. From the fetters riveted upon us in those evil days we as a nation have been for a century endeavouring with infinite struggles and effort to set ourselves free. The conscience of the public was at last aroused, but long before it was aroused the workers had learnt to help themselves; the State at last awoke to some sort of a sense of its responsibilities, but the driving power which lay behind the various enactments was the power of the associations of workers. This is the first and broadest ground of justification of unionism. It has laid the foundations of a new industrial order, and those foundations were laid in the power of two far-reaching ideas—the realization of the power of combination and the conception of the organization of labour.

Another debt which the country owes to trade unionism is the emancipation of large sections of its population from the cold and selfish individualism of past days. It is a debt which is not generally realized and seldom acknowledged; but no one who knows anything of the actual working of trade unions, or is brought much into contact with their members, can fail to see how strong the bonds of fellowship are, how clearly the members realize their dependence upon one another, how ready they are to bear one another's burdens if occasion arises. Trade unionism is full of paradoxes, and none of them is more striking than that action which appears to be hard and selfish is found sometimes upon investigation to be based upon the most unselfish motives, or that practices which intelligent workers themselves admit to be unjustifiable in theory are invested with a strong moral sanction as the only means for the protection of the weak.

[1] *Trade Unions*, London, 1913, p. 27.

On these two broad general grounds—that it has pointed the way to the establishment of a new industrial order, and that it has recalled us to a sense of a forgotten side of our social order—it may be said that the trade union movement has abundantly justified itself. We shall now proceed to consider some of the special manifestations of its activity which have been at different times the subject of criticism.

(*a*) *Strikes.*—The strike (*q.v.*) has always been the trade unionist's most effective weapon. He can do much to protect himself by the method of mutual insurance or collective bargaining, but the strike gives him the power of bringing pressure to bear if he desires to enforce an agreement or to secure an improvement in wages or conditions of labour. The question whether it is a fair weapon is therefore fundamental. At present the right to strike has been practically acknowledged by the law, but the concession has only been gradual. At first all strikes were regarded as conspiracies and illegal; then there came a stage at which the right to strike was tacitly acknowledged, but the courts condemned them on the ground of assumed 'malicious intent'; next attempts were made to discriminate between different kinds of motive; and now the tendency seems to be to uphold the right to strike as such.

The relation between employer and employed has been regarded in law since 1875 as a civil contract between two theoretically free and equal individuals. It is in some cases a contract of very short duration, but it does not differ in nature from longer contracts. A weekly-wage-earner is in this respect in the same position as a highly placed salaried official. He therefore has the right to terminate his contract when he pleases, so long as he does not contravene its terms. But the essence of a strike is that it is the simultaneous termination of many contracts, and it derives its power from the fact that it is inconvenient or even harmful to the employer, and generally meant to be so. Now no one would deny that any worker where wages are inadequate or conditions intolerable has the right to say to an employer, 'I will not work for you for such wages or under such conditions.' Nor will it be denied that many of the workers have a right to say this simultaneously as a joint protest. Finally, it is hard to see how they would be wrong in endeavouring to persuade others to do the same. If these three points are conceded, the right to strike is established in principle.

The strike then, regarded as a protest, is a lawful weapon, but the days are long past when strikes were simply protests. To-day in the majority of cases they are used as weapons of offence. Even as such they are doubtless often justifiable, but weapons of offence are used to threaten or to inflict injury: that is what they are for; and, if it is conceded that the use of such weapons is allowable in industrial warfare, there would seem to be need of some controlling power to see that they are used fairly. A strike may be simply an instrument of tyranny and oppression.

Moreover, the whole question has assumed a new aspect in recent years as the result of closer association between different classes of workers and the enormous increase of power which the strike has derived from their simultaneous action. A strike on a large scale is no longer a mere matter between employers and employed: the whole nation may be affected. An unpleasant feature of some recent strikes has been the frank admission by their promoters that it was their deliberate intention to cause such general inconvenience and even injury as would force a settlement in their favour, simply to put an end to them. Such action is narrow and selfish and is condemned by public opinion. In no civilized country can any one body of men be allowed to hold the nation to ransom at their pleasure. The State is greater than any of its component parts, and is morally bound to take measures to protect the nation as a whole from exploitation by any section of it.

The question of picketing is closely connected with that of strikes. A strike really is a device to starve an employer out; its efficacy depends upon the completeness with which his supplies of labour can be cut off. It is therefore of the first importance to the strikers to see that no one else takes their place, and that none of the workers continue their work. Hence an elaborate system of sentries and pickets. There is nothing to be urged against 'peaceful persuasion,' but it is obvious that, at a time when strong emotions are aroused, such a practice needs careful watching if the persuasion is not to be allowed to degenerate into intimidation or even violence.

The Act of 1875 rendered liable to a fine or imprisonment 'every person who, with a view to compel any other person to abstain from doing or to do any act which such other person has a legal right to do or abstain from doing, wrongfully and without legal authority *watches or besets* the house or other place where such other person resides or works'; but declared that attending at or near the house or place 'in order merely to obtain or communicate information' shall not be deemed watching or besetting.

(*b*) *The limitation of output.*—There are some things about trade unionism which will never be understood unless they are regarded as projected against a background of injustice and petty tyranny. The deliberate limitation of output is one of them. It has been, and is still, the practice of some unions not to allow their members to do more than a given amount of work in a given time. A bricklayer, *e.g.*, may not lay more than a given number of bricks in a day. This practice is unjustifiable from the economic point of view, because the object of industry is production and the worker who systematically produces less or worse work than he might is not true to his trade. It is also morally unjustifiable because every one is bound in honour to accomplish to the best of his ability the task which he has taken in hand. And intelligent labour is ready to admit this. On what grounds then is it defended? On the ground that it is the only protection that can be devised for the weak against the lowering of the rate of wages by an unscrupulous employer. It was found that an employer who had already agreed to a certain piece-rate, on finding that the best of his men were earning wages which seemed to him in his short-sightedness preposterous, went back upon his word and proceeded to cut the rate, with the result that the slow or weak among the workers were no longer able to earn the weekly wage which he himself had considered as fair when he fixed the original piece-rate. Labour, in order to remove any such excuse for a lowering of wages, resolved that no member of the trade, whatever his strength or speed, should be allowed to outpace the rest. The best workers were called upon to make a sacrifice, but it was made readily and it rested upon altruistic motives. It is an anomaly, and it is injurious to industry. As the progressive organization of industry proceeds, the need of it will probably disappear. Meanwhile it remains, not without a touch of pathos, as an indication of the dislocation which has invested in the eyes of the workers a practice which they would not really defend with the sanction of self-sacrifice.

(*c*) '*Ca' canny.*'—The policy of limitation of output is sometimes adopted upon less defensible grounds. We do not refer to those cases in which a man does less than he might, or as little as he can contrive, out of personal resentment towards an employer or as a protest against a system which he believes to be unjust. Such cases are not uncommon, but it is doubtful whether any union would deliberately support them with its formal sanction. But many unionists believe that there is only a certain amount of work to be done, and that there will not be enough to go round if the standard of production per man is too high. This 'lump-of-labour' doctrine of the worker is the complement of the old 'wages-fund' theory of the capitalists of the 19th cent., who believed that there was only a certain sum available for wages, and that, if one set of workmen got more, it meant that of necessity another set would get less. Both were equally fallacious. There is neither a fixed amount of work nor a fixed sum available for wages; both are elastic. The way to increased wages lies through increased production, for it is out of the value of the product that wages, like salaries and the cost of raw materials, are paid. To limit production is to lessen the fund out of which wages are paid. There is also a belief that, if the best workmen are allowed to force the pace, the result will be a subtle reduction of the standard of earnings of the average worker—a 'bell-wether' is regarded as an abomination—and the best protection against this danger (which is a real one) is held to be a sort of standardization of output comparable to the standardization of hours and wages in which the workers have found protection and safety. But it seems indisputable that, if the best workers in a trade are circumscribed and shackled, the whole trade must be the worse for it, workers included.

(*d*) It is difficult to estimate the truth of the charges of tyranny, intimidation, and violence which have often been brought against the trade unions. There have doubtless been many cases of such things in the industrial history of the last 150 years. Violence has been used against employers; intimidation and violence have been used against other workers who failed to come into line. What we want to know, and what is very difficult to find out, is to what extent, if at all, the unions have condoned such action. We should be safe, however, in asserting that violence forms no part of the trade union programme, and we may go further and say that with the growth of trade unionism there has been a distinct improvement in the conduct of strikes. Violence and bloodshed are certainly less common now than they were.

(*e*) It has been said that the organization of labour on modern lines is an idea which we owe to the trade unions. Has this organization in some cases been carried too far? Employers often complain that they find themselves fettered and obstructed by trade union regulations which seem to them to be merely meticulous and vexatious. There is probably some truth in this. Trade unionism, on its defensive side, has surrounded itself with an elaborate system of bulwarks against every conceivable possibility of an attack. These regulations are not arbitrary; the initiated know that they are applications in detail of some principle which the workers regard as important. They are born of mistrust, and they will not disappear until employers and employed learn to understand one another better and feel that they are co-partners in the same enterprise. But it should be realized that industry cannot work in chains.

Trade unions are 'an inevitable product of modern economic life.' They are now almost universally recognized, and the recognition is based upon the fact that the conditions of labour are now group conditions and that the worker who forms a simple unit of a large group is powerless to bargain successfully with an employer. The employer occupies a superior strategic position, and the worker's only hope is in association. It is undeniable that, where large associations of industrial units are formed, there is a danger of tyrannous action, and the larger the association, the greater the danger; but it is equally undeniable that the circumstances of the time seem to call for such associations, and the danger should be confronted. The advantages to be gained are great, and the danger can be met with the assistance of the legislature and the law-courts.

LITERATURE.—Sidney and Beatrice Webb, *Hist. of Trade Unionism*, London, 1902, *Industrial Democracy*, do. 1911; H. H. Schloesser, *Trade Unionism*, do. 1913; A. and M. P. Marshall, *Economics of Industry*, do. 1881; G. Howell, *Trade Unionism New and Old*, do. 1907; C. M. Lloyd, *Trade Unionism*, do. 1915; C. Watney and J. A. Little, *Industrial Warfare*, do. 1912.

L. V. LESTER-GARLAND.

TRADITION.—The word 'tradition' means, etymologically, 'handing over.' The conception of tradition, therefore, implies (*a*) a 'deposit' which is handed over, and (*b*) 'depositaries,' *i.e.* persons who are in possession of the deposit, and are commissioned to preserve it and transmit it to successors. Most religious systems claim to bear within themselves a deposit, consisting of ceremonial, myth, dogma, or ethic, or of some of these elements, revealed by some ultimate divine or quasi-divine authority, and meant to be handed down to posterity by a succession of duly qualified trustees. This article discusses the part which the principle of tradition has played in the history of Christianity.

1. Christ and Jewish tradition.—There is not much uncertainty regarding the attitude of the Founder of Christianity towards the Jewish tradition which He found already in existence. He was Himself a member of the Jewish Church, and disclaimed any idea of being a rebel against it: 'Think not that I came to destroy the law or the prophets: I came not to destroy, but to fulfil' (Mt 5^{17}). It would be generally agreed that His object was, not to abolish the traditional Mosaic deposit or to annihilate the depositary society—the 'congregation of the Lord,' the 'Israel of God'—but rather to develop and expand the then existing Jewish Ecclesia into the 'Kingdom of God' and to reform and purify the deposit by blending it with the gospel, or 'good news,' of a glorious age to come. In regard to the reform of the deposit, He insisted primarily upon its re-moralization. The classical passage for this is, of course, the famous saying about Corban (Mt 15^{1-20}, Mk 7^{9-23}), with the affirmation, which follows, that it is not the things which go into a man, but those which come out of the man, that defile the man. This may appear, at first sight, to challenge in principle the whole conception of the ceremonial deposit and brusquely to deny any spiritual value to outward observances. It certainly claims an infinitely higher place for ethical values as compared with ceremonial precepts; it might be taken, further, to imply that the sole seat of religious authority for a pious Jew lay in the written Word, the *Tôrāh*, and that the oral tradition of the Rabbis was comparatively worthless. An even stronger implication as to the transitory nature of the Rabbinical tradition is contained in the saying about the 'new wine' and the 'old wine-skins' (Mk $2^{21f.}$, Mt $9^{16f.}$), though it is to be noted that Luke (5^{39}) appends a saying which may seem to point in the other direction—'The old (wine) is better.'

It may perhaps be said also that, to a certain extent, Christ demanded the re-intellectualization of the deposit. The authority of tradition is subordinated, not merely to that of the moral law embodied in the written Word, but to that of common sense. This is illustrated by His various sayings on the subject of the Sabbath. The impression which we gain from a review of the teaching of Christ, as recorded in the Synoptic Gospels, is that His attitude towards the Rabbinical tradition was simultaneously both reverential and critical, both conservative and progressive. There are two other pieces of evidence which should be considered in this connexion. Opinions differ as to the amount of historical value which should be assigned to the Fourth Gospel; but it is to be presumed that the exceedingly hostile attitude assumed by the Johannine Christ towards 'the Jews' is at least based upon genuine reminiscences of one side of the teaching of Jesus; and the declaration that the worship of the future was to be conducted neither on Mount Gerizim nor at Jerusalem, but throughout the whole earth, 'in spirit and in truth,' represents an attitude as anti-Rabbinical as it is possible to conceive. On the other hand, sayings recorded by 'Matthew,' the specifically Jewish evangelist, seem to represent Jesus as a whole-hearted supporter of tradition, though a severe critic of the moral shortcomings of its depositaries. 'Not one iota or one vowel-point shall pass away from the law until all be fulfilled' (Mt 5^{18}) is a passage in which the characteristic Jewish doctrine of the eternity of the *Tôrāh* seems to be proclaimed; He adds that, unless the zeal of His converts for the literal observance of the Law exceeds even that of the scribes and Pharisees, they cannot hope to enter into the Messianic Kingdom (5^{20}). The official, as distinct from the personal, authority of the Rabbis appears to be affirmed in the saying, 'The scribes and the Pharisees sit on Moses' seat: all things therefore whatsoever they bid you, these do and observe: but do not ye after their works,' etc. ($23^{2f.}$). Another saying in the same chapter contains the warning that Christ's insistence upon the supreme importance of moral conduct is not meant to imply any contempt for ceremonial minutiæ, in their proper place: 'Ye tithe mint and anise and cummin, and have left undone the weightier matters of the law, judgement, and mercy, and faith: but these ye ought to have done, and not to have left the other undone' (v.^{23}). On the other hand, it is fair to remember that the denunciations of the hypocrisy and quibbling casuistry of the Rabbis recorded by St. Matthew equal in intensity and bitterness the Johannine Christ's most vehement invectives against 'the Jews.' It seems probable that the Rabbinizing utterances in the First Gospel represent ironical sayings of Christ, which the first evangelist has misunderstood and taken literally, in accordance with his Judaistic presuppositions.

We may sum up this section of our inquiry by observing (*a*) that, in the view of the Founder of Christianity, the Jewish Church was in any case destined to be expanded and transformed into the 'Kingdom of God,' and that His attitude towards Jewish tradition must, therefore, have been of an interim and provisional nature, which will not necessarily give us the clue to His attitude towards the whole principle of tradition, as such, in religion; (*b*) that, for the time being, He had no desire to deny the value or divine origin of the main body of the Jewish deposit; it seems that His invectives against the *de facto* depositaries had reference rather to their personal shortcomings than to the official authority which they claimed; (*c*) that He insisted upon the subordination of the existing oral tradition to the authority of Scripture, the moral law, and common sense; and (*d*) that He was a deadly foe to that tendency towards the hypertrophy of ceremonialism, and the evanescence of moral and intellectual content, which is familiar to the historical student as the weakness to which traditional religions are peculiarly liable.

2. Christ and Christian tradition. — We now approach a question on which opinions are, and have been for many centuries, acutely divided. It seems clear that Christ did not, on any showing, contemplate the eternal permanence of the Jewish tradition; but did He Himself mean to found a new one? Did He design to promulgate a new deposit, a body of dogmatic and ethical truth revealed by Himself for the first time? Did He mean to found a society as the guardian of this deposit and its authorized expounder? Did He institute a class of depositaries within the society, empowered to decide as to its true contents in cases of dispute? Or did He mean to make a complete breach, in theory and principle, with the great religions of the ancient world as they had historically grown up, and to propagate, not so much an organized religion as a philosophical point of view or a mode of emotional feeling? In other words—Is Christianity to be regarded as the perfect traditional religion, the crown and flower of that whole process of traditional evolution which may be traced down the centuries, possessing a deposit of immutable truth and authentic, life-giving sacraments, and preserved by a majestic, supernatural society, a Kingdom which is in this world, yet not of it? Or was Christianity, as designed by its Founder, meant to involve a complete break with the past, and an entirely fresh start upon non-dogmatic, non-sacramental, non-ecclesiastical lines?

3. The 'Catholic' view of tradition.—It is a well-known fact that at the present day three-quarters of Christendom would return an unhesitating affirmative to the question, Did Christ intend to be the Founder of a traditional religion? We may refer to this great majority of Christians as the 'Catholic' part of Christendom—not with the object of begging any controversial questions, but merely in order to have a convenient label for denoting that system of faith and practice which is, in its general outlines, common to the 'pre-Reformation' Churches—*i.e.* to the Roman, Eastern Orthodox, Coptic, Abyssinian, Armenian, Syrian Jacobite, Chaldæan, and Malabarese communions —and which was inherited by them from the ancient undivided Church of the Græco-Roman Empire, of which they are fragments. The 'Catholic' view of tradition maintains that the deposit of faith (*depositum fidei*) was partly taken over by Christ from the existing Jewish Church and partly revealed by Him to His apostles and other hearers during His earthly life and especially during the 'great forty days,' which, according to St. Luke (Ac 1[3]), intervened between His resurrection and ascension, and during which He spoke of 'the things pertaining to the Kingdom of God.' He thus committed to them—either by stamping with His own approval certain already existing Jewish beliefs or by Himself revealing fresh truth for the first time—in germ and essence the great doctrines of the orthodox faith and the system of sacraments which He instituted for the salvation of mankind. He told His adherents that they were to consider themselves as being the true Israel, *His* Ecclesia, which, in some sense, He would build upon Peter as a foundation (Mt 16[18]). With this divinely-founded society He promises to be present all the days, even unto the consummation of the age (28[20]), and to it He promises to send the Paraclete, who would guide its members into all truth (Jn 16[13]). These promises are interpreted by 'Catholics' as guaranteeing the 'infallibility' of the Church in the interpretation and definition of the authentic contents of the deposit. It is, further, believed that within the Church the special task of preserving (and, when need should arise, of defining) the deposit was committed by Christ to the twelve apostles and to their successors, the bishops.

According to this view, therefore, all that Christ instituted was (1) a deposit (no doubt embodied at first in a way of life, rather than in an exactly formulated creed, and expressed, so far as it was verbally expressed at all, in pictorial rather than logical or metaphysical terms), and (2) a depositary class, consisting of the twelve men whom He had designated, in apocalyptic language, as the satraps of the future Kingdom. It would be hardly correct to speak of Him as having instituted the depositary body, the Church, inasmuch as this was conceived of as being, not a new society, but the only orthodox remnant of the old Jewish Church. But in these rudimentary beginnings the possibility of a magnificent development was given. The living force of the Christian tradition spontaneously generated the same complex mechanism for its own preservation and perpetuation as may be seen, endeavouring to struggle into existence, in the fields of Zoroastrianism and Buddhism. The first element in this apparatus to appear was the canon of Scripture. At first the only Scriptures which the Christian Church possessed were those of the Jewish Church, or, rather, of the Jewish Church as it existed outside Palestine. The Bible recognized in most parts of the earliest Christian Church was the Septuagint Old Testament, containing the books now called Apocrypha; so that, from the first, the oral tradition, vested in living depositaries (the apostles and their successors), was, to a certain extent, controlled by the existence of written documents, believed to embody some at least of the main constituents of the deposit. The Marcionite controversy of the 2nd cent. compelled the Church to form a collection of apostolic writings for the purpose of demonstrating the identity of the deposit, as she maintained it, with that committed by Christ to the original depositaries, and refuting the Gnostic claim to possess a secret tradition other than, and opposed to, the ecclesiastical tradition. This apostolic collection became canonized as 'the New Testament' of equal authority and inspiration with the original Scriptures, the 'Old Testament' of the Jewish Church.[1] In the 2nd cent., too, we observe the first beginnings of the baptismal creeds, brief formulæ whose threefold structure was derived from the threefold invocation of the Father, Son, and Holy Ghost in the solemn words of baptism, and intended to summarize the essentials of the orthodox faith in a form which could be committed to memory by persons of the weakest intellectual capacity.[2] The canon of Scripture and the baptismal creeds were thus the two great contributions of the 2nd cent. to the organization whereby the Catholic deposit was perpetuated and safeguarded against any essential change of content. The last great development of apparatus for safeguarding the authenticity of the deposit is to be found in the institution of ecumenical councils—the characteristic invention of the 4th century.[3] In the 2nd and 3rd centuries it had been possible for Hippolytus, Irenæus, and Tertullian to appeal to the unbroken succession of the bishops and to point to their unanimous consent as a proof of the authenticity of the ecclesiastical tradition, as against the alleged secret traditions of the various Gnostic sects. But towards the end of the period of persecution it came to be realized that the bishops themselves, the chief depositaries of the faith, might disagree as to its content; and these disagreements could only be resolved, in Christianity as in Buddhism, by the expedient of summoning a council representing, in theory or in fact, the complete body of chief depositaries, *i.e.* the total episcopate of the world. The object of a council was not so much to discover fresh truth as to determine what, as a matter of fact, was the doctrine which had been believed in the Church from the beginning. Hence, though each bishop

[1] See art. BIBLE IN THE CHURCH, I. 1 f.
[2] See art. CONFESSIONS, 8.
[3] See art. COUNCILS (Christian: Early, to A.D. 870).

had, in theory, the right to put before the council that version of the faith which he had received from his predecessors and which had been handed down to his local church from its first founder, the greatest weight was naturally attached to the testimony of the great 'apostolic sees.' Complete unanimity in the acceptance of one particular version of the faith would, of course, have stamped it in the minds of Catholic Christians as unquestionably authentic and apostolic; but, if complete unanimity had been possible of attainment, it would probably have been unnecessary to summon councils. The principle was, therefore, arrived at that an overwhelming majority of the depositaries, especially if it included the occupants of one or more of the great apostolic sees, had the same authority as the whole body. This principle is expressed by St. Vincent of Lerins when he says, or implies, that the consensus of 'paene omnes' is as good as that of 'omnes [sacerdotes].'[1] Hence it follows that a small minority of the depositaries, contumaciously refusing to submit to the authority of the majority, necessarily becomes schismatic. Another famous expression of the right of a majority among the depositaries to decide what is the true version of the deposit is to be found in St. Augustine's celebrated aphorism: 'Securus iudicat orbis terrarum, bonos non esse, qui se diuidunt ab orbe terrarum in quacumque parte terrarum.'[2]

It is true that most of the so-called ecumenical councils were not actually representative of the total episcopate of the world. They became ecumenical in virtue of their acceptance, immediate or gradual, by the majority of bishops. We are here concerned solely with theory, and need not go into the question as to how far theological controversies during the first thousand years of Christianity were merely the reflexion of political, national, or racial antagonisms. It is sufficient to note that each of the great decisive doctrinal formulations of the conciliar period was followed by a split between the majority, which accepted, and the minority, which rejected, it. Thus, after Nicæa and Constantinople, a separate, 'non-juring,' Arian Church came into existence among the Goths and other northern barbarians; after Ephesus a 'non-juring' Nestorian Church[3] was constituted in Syria and Persia; after Chalcedon the Monophysite Church,[4] which still includes most of the Christians of Egypt and Armenia, split off from the rest of Christendom. But, whilst shedding, so to speak, these dissentient bodies round its periphery, the 'great Church,' the Church of the majority of the depositaries, the Church of the Græco-Roman Empire, the 'Melkite' or 'Imperial' Church, as it was derisively called by the Eastern schismatics, held together round the imperial throne and the great apostolic see of Rome, maintaining its majestic unity unbroken, with the brief exceptions of the Zenonian and Photian schisms, for a thousand years. In the 'Great' or 'Melkite' Church, as it stood on the eve of the Great Schism of 1054, the fourfold structure of traditionalism, towards which the Buddhist and Zoroastrian faiths had been dimly groping their way, had come into full, explicit, and conscious existence, in the most imposing and magnificent form which has ever existed upon earth. The Church, the hierarchy, the canon of Scripture, and the ecumenical councils are all there, each fulfilling its harmonious part in the task of preserving, elucidating, and defining the apostolic deposit.

4. The Reformation and tradition. — The Reformation (*q.v.*) was, in essence and in its earlier stages, a revolt not so much against the authority of the deposit or of its Founder as against that of the existing depositary class in Western Europe—a revolt occasioned by the corruption and exactions of the pope and the hierarchy. In the first fervour of indignation against the vices of the clergy it seemed necessary to deny the whole principle of a body of men divinely commissioned to safeguard the Christian revelation. The mental outlook and *Weltanschauung* of the earlier Reformers was just as scholastic as that of the mediæval theologians, and demanded, just as imperiously, a clear-cut body of dogmatic theology as an essential element in religion. Hence, only those elements in the deposit were discarded the rejection of which followed immediately from the rejection of the hierarchy; and a new basis of authority had to be found for the Christian tradition. This basis was found in 'the Bible, and the Bible only.' We have seen that, for Catholic Christians, the structure of the orthodox faith was raised upon two pillars—the oral tradition of the Church and the Scriptures. The logical effect of the Reformation was to knock away the first of these pillars, leaving the second standing; and so adamantine was (and is) the cohesion and solidarity of orthodox Christianity that for three hundred years it was able to remain practically intact throughout Protestant Europe, balanced upon the solitary surviving pillar. The last hundred years have witnessed the gradual erosion of this pillar, through the continual dropping of the rains of Biblical criticism, and the consequent collapse in those regions of the superincumbent structure. This result, however, could not then have been foreseen. The great orthodox Protestant theologians of the 16th and 17th centuries only designed to modify the Catholic theory of authority in the following sense:

> 'We quite agree with the Catholic in holding that there *is* a changeless deposit of eternal truth, and that this was imparted by Christ our Lord to the apostles as depositaries, during His earthly life and the "great forty days"; but we deny that the functions of the apostles as depositaries were meant to be transmitted, or were transmitted, by them to any successors. Their functions as guardians of the truth were purely temporary, and ended at their deaths. They were, however, divinely inspired to write the New Testament, in which, together with the Old Testament, the deposit is fully and sufficiently contained. Thenceforward, the sole authority for the content of revealed truth was and is to be found in the written Word of God; and councils and synods have no authority other than that which may attach to the piety and learning of their members.'

It would, perhaps, be unfair to assert that this doctrine of the Bible, isolated and abstracted from the life of the teaching Church, as the sole fount of religious truth, necessarily presupposes the mechanical theories of 'verbal inspiration' which prevailed during the era of Protestant scholasticism, though it certainly did much to encourage them. Two difficulties, however, at once made themselves felt: (1) 'If the authority of the Church is practically *nil*, how do we know what "the Bible" is, *i.e.* what books ought to be included in the canon and what not? Because, hitherto, it has only been on the authority of the Church that we have believed in the canonicity and inspiration of these particular books.' (2) 'As some parts of the Bible are admittedly written in an obscure style, how are the unlearned to decide what the true meaning is?' The former difficulty, which the Catholic theologians of the counter-Reformation were not slow in pressing upon their opponents, at once raised the question of the canonicity of the Apocrypha, books which were uncongenial to the Reformers because of the passage (2 Mac 12[43-45]) commending prayers for the dead. A similar difficulty was created for many Protestant Christians by the *prima facie* incompatibility of the Epistle of St. James with Lutheran solifidianism—a fact which caused Luther to describe it as an 'epistle of straw.' The second was emphasized by the fissiparous tendencies which immediately began to manifest themselves in reformed Christendom, converting it into a chaos of sects, which ranged from the high scholastic orthodoxies of Luther and Calvin down to the Arianism of Socinus and the crazy extravagances of the Münster Anabaptists. The patent contradiction between the Protestant theory of the simplicity and obviousness of the meaning of Scripture and the infinite diversity of opinions held by those who professed to accept it as the sole authority for the outlines of the Christian deposit was satirized in the celebrated couplet of Werenfels of Basel:

> 'Hic liber est in quo quaerit sua dogmata quisque
> Invenit et pariter dogmata quisque sua.'

[1] *Commonitorium*, iii. 6.
[2] *C. Epist. Parmen.* III. iv. 24.
[3] See art. NESTORIANISM.
[4] See art. MONOPHYSITISM.

To the former of these objections the Reformers replied by taking the short Palestinian canon of the OT, as now held by the Jewish Church, on the ground that (as Jerome had urged) the Jews must surely themselves know what their own Scriptures were (thus abandoning the primitive Christian tradition which had taken over the longer, Septuagintal canon from the Hellenistic Jew) and by affirming that, so far as the NT Scriptures were concerned, their authority was manifest on the face of them, in virtue of the sublimity and elevation of their style and doctrines. This reply obviously settled nothing as to the disputed case of the Epistle of St. James, inasmuch as the question at issue between Luther and his opponents on the subject of this book was precisely this—Were its doctrines to be called 'sublime' or pernicious? To the second question, also, no very satisfactory reply was ever given. In logic the orthodox Protestant divines were compelled to maintain, and did in fact maintain, that the whole system of Nicene and Chalcedonian doctrine could be deduced with unerring certainty from the text of the NT, given a prayerful and reverent spirit on the part of its readers. But the 'subordinationistic' passages in St. Paul's Epistles (cf. 1 Co 11^3 15^{28} etc.) and those in which the Logos and the Spirit are apparently identified (cf. Ro $8^{9f.}$, 2 Co 3^{17}), together with the patent fact that Socinus and his followers regarded themselves as 'prayerful' and 'reverent,' must have made the orthodox Protestants doubt in their inmost hearts whether the matter really was as simple as this; and hence they sometimes show signs of being, unwillingly, driven back upon the conception of a teaching Church as the authorized interpreter of Holy Writ.[1] The Thirty-Nine Articles characteristically take up a position which may be interpreted as consistent either with the Catholic view of tradition and Scripture as joint authorities for the truth of the deposit or with the Protestant conception of the book of the Scriptures as the sole authority, independent of any living exponent.

So we are told that 'Holy Scripture containeth all things necessary to salvation,'[2] that the three creeds are apparently only to be believed 'because they may be proved by most certain warrants of Holy Scripture,'[3] that 'General Councils may err, and sometime have erred,' and that 'things ordained by them as necessary to salvation have neither strength nor authority, unless it may be declared that they be taken out of Holy Scripture.'[4] On the other hand, 'the Church . . . hath authority in controversies of faith' and is 'a witness and a keeper of Holy Writ.'[5]

So far as a coherent conception of the relations of tradition to Scripture can be wrought out from these statements, it has been attained by Hooker, whose *Ecclesiastical Polity* appears to be based on the now antiquated assumption that the Chalcedonian theology can be deduced from the text of the NT as directly and irresistibly as the movements of the heavenly bodies can be deduced from a set of astronomical tables. A characteristic and explicit expression of the thoroughgoing Catholic view within the Anglican Communion is to be found in Thorndike's declaration that an indispensable mark of the true Church is 'the preaching of that word and that ministering of the sacraments which the *tradition* of the whole Church confineth the sense of the Scriptures to intend.'[6]

It is well known that the new Protestantism of the Continent would go much farther than the old in its attack upon the Catholic tradition, and that it would in fact dispute not merely the authority of the depositaries, but that of the deposit and the Founder Himself. Its contentions may be summed up under two headings, (1) philosophical and (2) historical. (1) *Philosophical.*—Starting from Kant's denial of the validity of the categories of the theoretical understanding within the noumenal sphere, Ritschl (*q.v.*) and his followers would deny the possibility of a deposit of intellectual truth altogether. Owing to the creaturely limitations of man's understanding, intercourse with God is a matter of emotional feeling and right conduct, not of strictly intellectual apprehension. (2) *Historical.*—It is admitted that the essence of the Catholic deposit and of the traditional conception of Christianity can be traced back from the ecumenical councils, through the sub-apostolic writers, into the NT itself; and the modern liberal Protestant finds no difficulty in allowing their natural sense to such passages as 2 Th 2^{15}: 'Stand fast, and hold the *traditions* (τὰς παραδόσεις) which ye were taught, whether by word, or by letter of ours'; 3^6: 'Withdraw yourselves from every brother that walketh disorderly, and not after the *tradition* which they received of us'; and notably to the Pauline, or deutero-Pauline, injunction, τὴν παραθήκην φύλαξον (1 Ti 6^{20}), in which 'the deposit' is expressly mentioned.

It would now be conceded that St. Paul regarded Christianity as a dogmatic, sacramental deposit, of which the 'apostles' were, in a general sense, the depositaries. But it is contended that in this respect there is an absolute gulf between the teaching of Jesus and that of Paul; that Jesus regarded Himself merely as a teacher of ethics, or as the prophet of a new eschatological enthusiasm; that the movement which He initiated was of a purely emotional kind, though fraught with an *Interimsethik* valid only for the very brief period of time which, in His view, remained before the collapse of the existing world-order and the inauguration of the New Kingdom; and that, as Jesus believed in the imminence of this catastrophe, He could have had no idea of promulgating a deposit or constituting a depositary class. On this view it is Paul himself who was the real founder of Catholic Christianity. It was he who transformed the vague and formless apocalyptic enthusiasm of the first Christian generation into a mystery-cult, with wonder-working sacraments; it was he who taught Christendom to identify the Prophet of Nazareth with the Logos of Platonic and Stoic metaphysic, thereby laying the foundations upon which later ages were to build the elaborate structure of Trinitarian and Christological dogma; it was he or his immediate successors who taught primitive Christians to regard themselves as members of a mystic international brotherhood, the new Ecclesia or Congregation of God, thereby institutionalizing Christianity as a Church and a hierarchy. It is obvious that this view, if it can be historically sustained, destroys the whole traditional conception of Christianity by severing the connexion between the deposit, as it stands, and its alleged founder. The history of Christianity then becomes exactly analogous to the history of Mazdæism and of Buddhism. It is the history of the gradual overlaying of the teachings of the founder by dogmatic, sacramental, mystical, and hierarchical integuments derived from other religions: 'Catholicism' is to authentic Christianity what Lāmaism is to primitive Buddhism. The classical expression of this view is still, perhaps, Harnack's great *History of Dogma*, in which the majestic pageant of Church history is exhibited as a gradual working out of that 'acute secularization' of Christianity initiated by the well-meaning, though mistaken, desire of St. Paul to commend the new religious movement to persons who had grown up in the atmosphere of the Hellenic and Anatolian mystery-religions. It follows from this view that the whole of the 'Catholic' deposit, including the great central doctrines of the Trinity, Incarnation, and Atonement, must be discarded, and not merely those comparatively peripheral portions of it which were dropped by the great 16th cent. Reformers; so dogma as an essential element in Christianity will disappear entirely, and institutionalism will be reduced to the minimum consistent with the practical efficiency of religion. Despite the many conscious or unconscious attempts that have been made to becloud the issue, this question, Is the Catholic deposit *in toto* substantially what was promulgated by Christ, or is it a vast mass of Græco-Roman accretion which has nothing whatever to do with His authentic teaching?, is the primary and crucial question that lies before the religious thought of Europe at present, and will probably have to be answered decisively, in one sense or the other, before one hundred years are over.

5. Recent developments.—Within the sphere of traditional Christianity three additional developments deserve brief mention. These are all, it may be observed, confined to the Western or Latin Church, as in the East the era of petrifaction, which set in with the death of St. John of Damascus and precludes the possibility of development, still holds sway. (1) The first of these is analogous to what may be noticed in the case of Lāmaism, viz. the tendency to concentrate the functions of the depositary class in the hands of a single chief depositary or supreme pontiff. So, within the Roman Church, the pope was declared by the Vatican Council of 1870 to be endowed, when performing his office of supreme pastor and teacher of Christians, with the same infallibility (*q.v.*) as that which Catholic traditionalism attributes to the Church; and this belief is concisely

[1] Cf. the affirmation of the *Confession of Würtemberg*: 'Credimus et confitemur quod . . . haec ecclesia habeat jus judicandi de omnibus doctrinis,' quoted by E. C. S. Gibson, *The Thirty-Nine Articles*, London, 1896, p. 513.
[2] Art. 6. [3] Art. 8. [4] Art. 21. [5] Art. 20.
[6] *Theological Works*, 10 vols., Oxford, 1844–56, iv. 895.

summed up in the 'I am tradition' of Pius IX.—a remark in which an unfriendly critic might discern a recrudescence of the old priest-king idea. (2) The second development is the tendency, analogous to what we see in Judaism, with its attempts to form 'a hedge around the Law,' to protect the real deposit by surrounding it with a kind of secondary deposit as with an armour. In Judaism this protective armour or integument was supplied by the *dicta* of the Rabbis. In Latin Catholicism the opinions of theologians have, in practice, come to assume the same position. Outside the central nucleus of the deposit, consisting of doctrines which are strictly *de fide*, there is a fringe, or penumbra, of 'pious opinions' which are *proxima fidei*, based, not upon the decrees of ecumenical councils, but upon the *consensus theologorum*. To deny these opinions is not indeed heretical, but may be censured as 'temerarious' or 'offensive to pious ears.' In practice the distinction between the dogmas of the primary deposit and the pious opinions of the secondary does not appear to be very clear; and even local traditions regarding the authenticity and sanctity of particular holy places and objects, which in principle are merely a matter of ordinary human evidence, are sometimes treated with as much respect—and criticism of them is as much resented—as though they belonged to the inner nucleus of the deposit of faith. (3) The third development represents a reaction against the former two, and is popularly called 'Modernism.' In its extreme French and Italian forms, Modernism (*q.v.*) is logically identical with the extreme Ritschlian Protestantism sketched above. It denies that Christ meant to promulgate a deposit, or would have had any authority to do so if He had so meant; and regards Him rather as a religious genius, not exempt from the errors and limitations of His age and country, who merely gave the first impulse to a wave of emotional feeling, which has reverberated down the centuries and is still affecting myriads of human souls. This view is, of course, entirely destructive of Catholic traditionalism as described above. In England, Germany, and America, however, the Modernist movement has taken a more moderate form; and, within the Anglican Church, the corresponding movement has raised a very interesting problem—that of the relation between the spiritual contents of the deposit, which the Anglican Modernist would not deny that Christ promulgated, and the conceptual forms borrowed by the early Fathers and councils from Greek metaphysic to contain it. Whilst the Anglo-Catholic would maintain that the Church was divinely inspired to choose the right conceptual forms, and that these, having received ecumenical sanction, cannot be discarded by the individual believer, the Anglo-Modernist regards the forms as having no more than a purely human authority, and as capable from time to time of variation or even of supersession.[1] The question of the depositary class does not seem to have been directly raised in these discussions, but it is probable that the Anglo-Modernist would regard the whole Church or Christian people, and not any specialized class within it, as being the depositary.

LITERATURE.—J. L. Jacobi, *Die kirchl. Lehre von der Tradition und heiligen Schrift*, Berlin, 1847; H. J. Holtzmann, *Kanon und Tradition*, Ludwigsburg, 1859, art. 'Tradition' in *RGG*; A. Tanner, *Über das kathol. Tradit. und protest. Schriftprincip*, Lucerne, 1862; A. W. Dieckhoff, *Schrift und Tradition*, Rostock, 1870; P. Tschackert, art. 'Tradition' in *PRE*³ xx. 8–13; Otto Ritschl, *Dogmengesch. des Protestantismus*, i. 'Biblicismus und Traditionalismus in der altprotestant. Theologie,' Leipzig, 1908; A. M. Fairbairn, *Catholicism: Roman and Anglican*², London, 1899; A. Sabatier, *The Religions of Authority and the Religion of the Spirit*, Eng. tr., do. 1904; W. Sanday and N. P. Williams, *Form and Content in the Christian Tradition*, do. 1916. The Roman Catholic point of view may be studied in J. B. Franzelin, *De divina traditione et scriptura*², Rome, 1875; L. de San, *De divina traditione et scriptura*², Bruges, 1903; J. V. Bainvel, *De Magisterio vivo et Traditione*, Paris, 1905.

N. P. WILLIAMS.

[1] Cf. W. Sanday and N. P. Williams, *Form and Content in the Christian Tradition*, for an exhaustive comparison and contrast of these two points of view.

TRAGEDY.—See DRAMA.

TRAINING (Religious).—Religion is an attitude towards God. It expresses itself in acts of appreciation of values by individuals and groups. These actions are rooted in the basal instincts. They may be few and irregular; they may be gross expressions of wild passion; or they may be refined and well-disciplined reactions of the whole personality in the presence of eternal values. The differences are determined chiefly by training the inner life to react consistently to higher ideals and motives, and by training conduct to habitual and adequate expression of appreciation.

There is a broad sense in which religious training is a feature of all forms of religion, from primitive animism with favourite incantations up to the cultured forms of ritual, all transmitted to successive generations by imitation and other educative processes. But this article deals only with the specific types of religious training now practised or proposed in the English-speaking world.

By religious training is meant a systematic effort to preserve, improve, propagate, and transmit religious life, by methods commonly used in education, such as imitation, instruction, discipline, and inspirational and ideal-forming agencies, in correlation with other means of promoting religion. It goes even farther in some minds; and not without justification the claim is made that educational training, no matter how secular or technical, is not complete or adequately motivated unless in its aim and spirit it leads up into that social purpose which is the chief part of religion (Herbart, Coe).

1. Background.—The types of religious training which now prevail have arisen by connected development (1) out of a long and diversified history of maladjustment between childhood and the Christian Church, (2) out of numerous artificial theologies and individualistic theories of religion, and (3) out of an utter lack, until recently, of any psychology of religion or of childhood.

(1) The historical background of religious training may be found (*a*) in the stereotyped forms of worship and religious expression handed down to successive generations through church and family life; (*b*) in the catechism and confirmation class, where formal drill and authoritative doctrine and precept have long produced educational results of some importance in religious life. (*c*) A nearer background exists in the modern Sunday schools, first with their memorized Bible lessons, and since 1870 with their uniform lessons taught by rather feeble hortatory methods.

(2) The theoretical background is found in an individualistic theology. The corner-stones of this theology were the natural sinfulness of every man, the impending judgment of punishment therefor, and the miraculous atonement of Jesus Christ, which made possible the repentance and pardon of the individual sinner. The supernatural factor was magnified; the human ways and means were subordinated, and the ethical discrepancies passed unnoticed. The process was conceived as judicial on the basis of a retributive penology now discarded in the best judicial practice. The instruction given was not regarded primarily as educative, but rather as dogmatic, evangelistic, and hortatory. No important significance was attached to the teachings of Jesus about the growth of the spiritual

life or the conditions of the ground into which the seed shall fall.

The social gospel lately found to be so conspicuous in the teaching and life of Jesus was unknown. For lack of it the process of salvation was essentially self-regarding, which is doubtless the main reason why Christianity has been so long and slow in making its way in the world. When the era of modern missions dawned, three significant things happened. (*a*) The individual gospel was proclaimed from social and really Christian motives, and the result was good so far as it went, but incommensurate with the effort expended. (*b*) Actual conditions in mission fields and the emergence of social ideals at home forced an expansion of missionary aims so as to include social service—a gospel which was not always well correlated with the other. (*c*) As soon as this social gospel had time to reveal its character and possibilities, results became overwhelming; and the missionary prayer is no longer for the opening of doors, as it was a half-century ago, but for teachers, doctors, nurses, farmers, and skilled workmen, by hundreds, to carry a full-orbed Christian civilization into all the lands whose Macedonian calls are coming unsolicited.

(3) Until the last quarter of the 19th cent. psychology was a thing remote from religion. It had not then as now stressed the unity of the self, as against a number of more or less independent 'faculties' bearing little relation to religion. Nor had child psychology made known the extent to which the mind is at first rudimentary, and subject to the continuous and slow changes which the long human infancy makes possible.

Psychology and social and educational science have found no place in the theory of religion until the last generation, and even yet there are those in every religious body who shudder at the thought of applying scientific methods to the propagation of religion. But it is out of these diverse conditions ancient and modern that a theory and practice of religious education is now rapidly taking shape.

2. Theory and aim.—There is a type of religious education which perpetuates the theoretical background of intellectualism and individualism. Its propositions are arranged in logical order, and not in the order in which they arise in human experience. They are held to be authoritative, and are taught in dogmatic form. Under this theory the service which education renders to religion is to make these formulæ known, and here the service ends.

Under the other type the service rendered by education to religion is much broader. The knowledge to be imparted is not dogmatic but inspirational; not an end, but a means to spiritual values; not generalized and abstract, but presented concretely and made illuminating to the pupil's present life. This type of religious training includes habits of worship, attitudes towards the natural world, ideals of life, deeds of service, the relations sustained to the smaller and larger groups of one's fellow-men, and, in fact, every form of useful expression which can be given to inner spiritual life.

(1) The theory on which any adequate plan for religious training is based includes the following fundamental ideas as to the development of religion. (*a*) The presence of the religious life is felt not only in worship and in the conventional forms of religious expression, but especially in character and in social purpose, which subordinates all interests to the supreme values of life. (*b*) The religious life is a continuous growth, not a thing produced artificially, or judicially instituted at the moment of a passing experience. (*c*) This growth involves not a special organ or faculty, but the whole personality. It involves even the group of persons, and it tends to realize in them their oneness with the larger whole of society and of the world in God. (*d*) Finally, the growth of the religious life is normal, vigorous, and healthy, in proportion as its true nature is understood, as favourable conditions for its growth are provided, and as consistent work and painstaking devotion are given to its cultivation.[1]

(2) The following educational facts and principles are also involved in the theory of religious training. (*a*) The subject of an educative process is a person with all his inherited equipment of race instincts and family traits, as well as his undeveloped mental, moral, and religious powers. It is the business of education, not to eradicate or supplant any of these, but to develop and cultivate them, and subordinate them to the highest ends. (*b*) Education is more than instruction. It not only builds up many and rich concepts, which shall serve as a basis for judgment and action by a member of society; but it also takes measures to establish desirable habits, and to create ideals of commanding dignity and emotional power. (*c*) Education uses concrete materials for this purpose. It selects for its use those human experiences best fitted in character and grade to accomplish the particular purpose in view. The treasures of the race have become very rich in such material, so that the selection and preparation of it is a task demanding the skill of educational experts.

(3) The thing that is aimed at in religious education is (*a*) to put one as early and as completely as possible in possession of that rich treasure of experience which has come down from the past, and has been gathered from the ends of the earth, especially those parts of it which are richest in their meanings for a man's life in the world with other people and as a worker with God. (*b*) A further aim is to turn the full force of that experience, in the form of socialized ideals and purposes, as a motive power upon conduct and upon the ordering of the programme of life. This is an individual aim, but it is far more. It enlists churches, homes, and communities in this motivation of conduct for the well-being of society at large. (*c*) It is believed that the instruction to be gathered from the parable of the soils (Mk 4^{2-20}) is a lesson of education, in which the minds mellowed by long processes of nurture are those which respond quickly and whole-heartedly to the evangel. Such nurture would seem therefore to be the most direct and effective way of co-operating with the Spirit of God for the evangelization of the world.

3. Content.—Since religion and its promotion are understood to be, to some extent at least, an enterprise in education, it is necessary to choose for such instruction that material which will be most fruitful religiously. Rather vague ideas prevail on this subject, due to lack of critical analysis of the values to be sought, and to incomplete knowledge of how to produce and conserve those values.

The educational reformers of a century ago established the principle of gradation of material—*i.e.*, that the ability of children to understand and master material changes as they grow older. The material must therefore be chosen with reference to this changing ability; *e.g.*, the incident of a boy robbing a bird's nest can be understood and remembered by a five-year-old child, but the moral interpretation of the same incident is better suited for a mind several years older.

The fallacy of catechetical instruction is partly a pedagogical one. It consists in presenting adult abstractions to children—in offering strong meat instead of milk to babes. A similar

[1] George A. Coe, *A Social Theory of Religious Education*, New York, 1917.

fallacy has vitiated much of the Bible teaching in Sunday schools where 'uniform' lessons have been chosen for young and old alike. If the children had a story which they could understand and remember on one Sunday, they must feed on Prophets and Epistles for several weeks before they might expect another children's lesson. Of course adaptations by editors and teachers could do something to overcome the discrepancy in grading, but it is only making the best of a bad case. It is wholly unnecessary for religious instruction to be subjected to these hindrances, now that the principles of grading are understood and have been applied to the materials used in religious training.

There is also a religious fallacy in catechetical instruction, appealing as it does exclusively to the intellect with logical propositions dogmatically conceived and expressed. The emotional and social aspects of the child's religious life are the first to be required for the development of ideals and the motivation of conduct. The intellectual formulations satisfy better the mature religious needs of adults, and the different needs of children should be provided for.

In selecting and grading the materials for religious education there are a number of considerations to be provided for.

(1) The language of religion must be acquired. As in any field of human experience, the language and the thought develop together. Some terms are advanced and technical, but many are elementary. The history and practice of religion, the reading of the Bible, and the social environment offered by a religious community can make familiar to children, nurtured in such an atmosphere, all the elementary concepts of religion, and the words and phrases which express those concepts. They can make known a few of the landmarks of religious history, at least by their names and by some characteristic incidents associated with those names.

A properly graded curriculum therefore provides for young children a selection of simple Bible incidents on subjects within their experience, or a like class of subjects taken from biography, literature, and life. For this purpose one may choose stories about children, animals, natural objects, and the things familiar to childhood, especially those which contain some of the language and forms of religion, but none of the generalizations and abstract principles in which religious teaching is so often couched.

(2) The child inherits certain capacities for a moral and religious life. But each individual must shape his concepts of that life from the examples of other experiences seen and heard by him. His education consists in becoming acquainted with these selected experiences of others, in reading meaning into them, and in shaping his own habits, judgments, and ideals, with reference to the experiences so set before him. This formation of concepts represents a later stage of religious development than the language stage mentioned above, but the later mingles with the earlier stage, and they move forward together. A class of more meaningful experiences is chosen for this purpose, such as the parables of Jesus, tales of moral heroism, events in which service and sacrifice are exemplified, the revealings of motives and of character and of loyalty to persons and to ideals, and the superiority of moral and spiritual values over those values which are chiefly carnal and commercial.

It is therefore the business of religious education to bring into the life of youth an abundance of human incidents rich in moral and religious meaning; to present these experiences with sufficient detail and pedagogical skill to assure them an atmosphere, an emotional vitality, and some permanence; and to give definite guidance to each youth in the construction of his own habits, judgments, and ideals, out of the concrete materials furnished to him. The selection of material for this purpose out of the Bible or from other sources is the most responsible and difficult task of religious education. It is also the point at which failure has been most complete in nearly every curriculum thus far proposed for religious training.

(3) While it belongs to the province of science and general education to develop in youth a conception of the causal connectedness of the world and of its unity, consistency, and organization under natural law, it is a well-known fact that this is not generally done. Such reflexions arise more frequently in connexion with religion than elsewhere, and it is proper that religious education should provide in place of discarded cosmologies a better instruction, which can serve the common people as a credible philosophy of nature. Nothing can do more to disintegrate religious faith and moral integrity than lack of a believable philosophy of the world. Such a philosophy is entirely within the mental compass of enlightened youths; and they have a right to it as a support for their faith and as a part of their education. Indeed they will have it. The only uncertainty is as to how good or how poor a philosophy they shall work out for themselves if wise help is withheld from them.

For the few but important lessons on this subject the creation stories and a few other portions of Scripture will serve as occasion for wise and modern instruction. A few of the great chapters in the history of science are required. These need to be correlated, not only with the names of discoveries and inventors, but with the forward movements in the world's life, and the human values which they have enhanced.

(4) A task of religious education still more important is the interpretation to young minds of the world of human life. We live and act in a world of purpose and meaning, as well as in a world of natural law and causal connexion. It is out of this purposive life that real values arise; and it is with those values that religion is concerned. There is no gain for religion in knowledge of the Scripture, or of the facts of nature, and no benefit in formal covenants and ordinances, unless in the human heart there is an ideal which throws over all these things an emotional glow that enriches them with meaning and value. It is doubtless the same thing that is spoken of as the Spirit of God in the human heart taking the things of Christ and showing them to us.

Religious teachers generally try to do this. Most expository Bible teaching is so intended. So also is the preaching. But the efforts are desultory, and the results are not cumulative. A need is felt for a programme or a definite policy, based on a sound philosophy and on educational principles, to give continuity and cumulative effect to the propagation of religion. It can hardly be claimed that such a programme has yet been proposed, although efforts have been made in that direction, and in some cases with gratifying results.

The choice and arrangement of material awaits a fuller agreement upon Christian ideals and the fundamental philosophy of religion. In this task the interpretation of the world of human life is the chief factor. What is called the social gospel has already gone far to supplement and modify the individualism of the former day. But 'a theology for the social gospel,' as Walter Rauschenbusch calls his book,[1] has not yet formulated itself in popular thinking. In the light of such a theology and philosophy, there is required a re-defining of the virtues and of the unifying principle by which those virtues are correlated in the good man. The new sense of the structural character of society, the place and function of the individual within the structure, and the interactions between the structure and its members must have much weight in determining what the content of a religious education curriculum ought to be, and what educational aims and values ought to be conspicuous in that material.

(5) The great issues over which men and nations have struggled in the world's forward movement need to be made known to young people, and

[1] New York, 1918.

their meanings interpreted. Such issues were drawn in OT times by the prophets against royal and ecclesiastical dignitaries. Jesus defined an issue between the Pharisees and the new religion of the inner life. Every forward step, every reform, every moral and spiritual achievement from that day to this, can be of great service to those whose motives and ideals are forming. They are needed as a background for the tasks and problems of to-day, as a guide in defining present and future issues, and as an inspiration to loyalty in trying situations. Here will appear biographies of men and women who have caught visions of an improved world and have helped to realize those visions. Here also belong the rise and fall of institutions in response to the changing needs of the world. Out of such rich and varied sources are being selected the graded and sifted materials for a curriculum of religious training.

4. Method and organization.—While the history of pedagogy has been progressive, and general education has profited by every improvement, religious training has been slow to take up improved methods. Memoriter catechetical teaching is still common. Hortatory and semi-expository teaching of the Bible is quite general in church schools, the aim being evangelistic and not primarily educative.

There is a marked tendency to reconstruct, not only the curriculum in ways already indicated, but also the method and organization. In method these changes consist in a larger use of direct narrative in connexion with concrete story material used in the lower grades; the immediate oral reproduction by pupils of the narrative so presented;[1] the increased use of pictorial and graphic representation, and the tendency to substitute for the leaflet, pamphlet, or bare Bible specially prepared text-books of a more permanent and attractive character.

But the most important tendency is towards things to be done, as an expression in real life of the moral and religious impulses, as they awaken in childhood and youth. Daily conduct, positions taken on moral questions before associates, missionary work, community betterment, neighbourly and charitable work, and worthy social activities in general, offer a welcome field for religious training in this growing aspect. Out of such activities arise deeper and truer thinking and finer emotional responses than any didactic method can produce.

Modern forms of church organization provide for a department of religious training in the local church. This department is free to adopt methods in harmony with improved educational and religious ideas, and to introduce a curriculum something like that outlined above. Only in those local churches where the broad full meaning of religious education has been discussed and appreciated has the reconstruction taken place. But the number of these churches is increasing; they are profiting by experience; and their results are watched and reported.

In several American communions, notably the Protestant Episcopal, the Congregational, and the Presbyterian, important steps have been taken to reconstruct the denominational machinery on educational lines. Numerous officials are employed to propagate the principles and ideals of religious training in the local churches, and to aid in the installation of better systems. These methods are especially successful in missionary fields, (1) because there the need is more obvious, and (2) because these fields are not bound by tradition to antiquated methods as many of the churches are.

While the prospect for the future of religious education is best in the direction of denominational organization, there is also a distinct movement on foot for community organization disregarding ecclesiastical divisions, or at least bringing them

[1] W. J. Mutch, *Graded Bible Stories*, Ripon, Wis., 1914.

into co-operation.[1] This plan calls for a local board and a superintendent, who shall inaugurate a school system parallel to the other system or systems in the same community. Less time would be required for the religious than for the general and vocational schools; yet the effectiveness of it cannot be estimated by the time spent. In addition to the direct values of such training the material of general education is re-interpreted and given new meaning and dignity from the spiritual aspect. Teachers who have training in the principles of education, as well as personal fitness and inspiring leadership, soon make apparent the large possibilities of religious training, both in its own field and in its effects on the whole structure of society.

In Britain and in some other European countries the schools supported at public expense are expected to furnish some instruction of a religious nature. Recognition is made of denominational preferences, and teachers are assigned to groups with this in mind. In France religious instruction is entirely excluded from all public and private schools of general education, and the members of religious orders are disqualified as teachers. This of course does not prevent the teaching of religion in the churches. In the United States of America religion is excluded by the laws of the States from the public schools; but entire freedom is given for this instruction under church or community supervision. In some States the pupils are released for one session each week from required attendance at a public school on condition of spending that time under approved religious instruction, proportionate credit being given if such work is satisfactorily done.

In general it may be said that the ideals and content of religious education have been reconstructed in accordance with modern ideas. The realization of the better ideals has been achieved in a limited degree, and every year marks distinct gains. But the progress is retarded (1) by conservative traditions among earnest religious people, who have not seen the spiritual values in a religious life conceived developmentally and socially; (2) by inadequate conceptions of and facilities for training in religious activity and self-expression, and (3) by lack of united and trained leadership in the re-organization of religious education in local communities. It seems to be the task of Christian colleges to raise up a generation of men and women who have the religious and educational ideals and the ability and enthusiasm to organize them into the life of our time.

A good central organization for the study of religious education, for the comparison of results, and for the promotion of this large interest in the life and thought of the world exists in the Religious Education Association (Henry F. Cope, Secretary, 1440 East 57th Street, Chicago, Ill.). It was founded in 1903 by representatives of all religious faiths. It has held important annual conventions, mostly in American cities. These conventions have done much to shape thought, guide effort, and stimulate experiment. The volumes of the bi-monthly magazine of the Association entitled *Religious Education* furnish much material in the history and discussion of this subject.

Other related articles in this Encyclopædia may be referred to as follows: EDUCATION (Moral), CHRISTIANITY, CHURCH, CONFIRMATION, CATECHISMS, BIBLE, SUNDAY SCHOOL.

LITERATURE.—H. F. Cope, *Religious Education in the Church*, New York, 1917; B. S. Winchester, *Religious Education and Democracy*, do. 1917; W. W. Smith, *Religious Education*, Milwaukee, 1909; W. S. Athearn, *The Church School*, Boston, 1914; G. A. Coe, *Education in Religion and Morals*, New York and London, 1904, *The Psychology of Religion*, Chicago and London, 1917; E. S. Ames, *The Psychology of Religious Experience*, London and Boston, 1910.

WILLIAM JAMES MUTCH.

TRANCE.—See HYSTERIA, DHYANA, YOGA.

TRANSCENDENCE.—See IMMANENCE.

[1] W. S. Athearn, *Religious Education and American Democracy*, Boston and Chicago, 1917.

TRANSCENDENTALISM. — The term 'transcendental' plays an important part in Kant's *Critique of the Pure Reason*—'transcendental æsthetic,' 'transcendental analytic,' etc.—and through the influence of the critical philosophy the term has become familiar in modern thinking and even in popular literature. Kant did not originate the term; but he gave it new vigour and a new orientation.

1. Pre-Kantian transcendentalism.—(1) *Use of the term in scholastic logic.*—Before Kant's time 'transcendental' and 'transcendent' were familiar terms in the scholastic logic and were practically equivalent in meaning, although he sharply distinguished between them. To the scholastic logicians these terms were used of those most general notions that could not be subsumed under the ten Aristotelian categories. They rose beyond or transcended them. Spinoza uses 'transcendental' in this sense of the most general notions and gives his view of how psychologically they originate.[1] Strictly speaking, these *transcendentalia* or *transcendentia* belonged to a realm above ordinary categorical logical thinking and as such were beyond the province of logic proper. Various enumerations of these transcendental notions are given. Albertus Magnus gives *ens*, *unum*, *bonum*, and *verum*; and very generally these, along with *res* and *aliquid*, make up the list of the six *transcendentalia*. Their interrelations are stated and various subtleties regarding them introduced by different schoolmen. *Ens* was as a rule regarded as super-transcendental, the rest being passions or modifications of being (*passiones entis*). This category in scholastic philosophy was pretty much what the 'Absolute' is in modern philosophy.[2]

(2) *Use of the term in theology.*—To the schoolmen, however, logic was only the handmaiden of theology, and so we find these terms more or less always moving into the area of theological speculation. These transcendental notions had their reality in the mind of God, who is transcendent *par excellence.* The passage in Augustine[3] where he posits the transcendental ideas in the divine mind became classical and is quoted by all the great mediævalists. It is historically the fusion of Greek thought with Christian experience. Plato speaks of the good (τὸ ἀγαθόν) as transcending being (ἐπέκεινα τῆς οὐσίας),[4] and Plotinus uses the phrase often.[5] Transcendent is simply the Latin equivalent of ἐπέκεινα, 'beyond.' At times this tendency became extreme, as in the case of Erigena and the mystics who speak of God as above all predicates—*ὑπεραληθής, ὑπέρσοφος, ὑπεραιώνιος*, 'above truth,' 'above wisdom,' 'above eternity.'

Transcendentalism in theology, then, means the position that God's knowledge and character are perfect, absolute as distinct from man's knowledge, which is imperfect, and from man's virtue, which is immature; as such it is part of the very essence of theology and the unmovable conviction of religion. But it may become falsified through over-emphasis and dangerous through over-refinement of subtlety. Ordinary living religious experience speaks of the divine in plain speech, ascribing to God organs, actions, passions, movement, change, purposes, and this is done without any feeling of incongruity—even when the divine spirituality is clearly recognized. Transcendentalism becomes over-subtle when it objects to this, and it is usually when religious experience is at a low ebb and beset by foes that this form of transcendentalism gains a hearing. Even in the OT, as Schultz points out,[1] we have the beginning of reflective transcendentalism. It is more evident in the Septuagint translation and in the post-Biblical Jewish literature, and it operates dominantly in Philo until God becomes the Great Unknowable. In the history of Christian theology we find the superimposition of this metaphysical and mystical transcendentalism on the direct religious thought of the NT. Edwin Hatch, in his famous Hibbert Lectures,[2] maintains that the great creeds of Christendom buried religion under this metaphysic; and in his zeal he has overstated the case; for transcendentalism in the sense of God's absoluteness is an integral part of religion and of theology, but, when it makes this a mode of throwing discredit on man's knowledge and of undermining man's notions of right and wrong, when it empties God of feeling, purpose, and initiation, then it becomes false and dangerous.

It is better to deal here with the special forms of transcendentalism in this sense, before discussing the Kantian and post-Kantian usage of the term, as these forms of thinking have their roots in a soil different from that which is specifically and dominantly under the influence of Kant.

2. Extra-Kantian transcendentalism. — Transcendentalism in the theological and philosophical sphere means, in a general way, the recognition of God as exalted in thought and character above man and sensible objects. It is thus contrasted with phenomenalism, naturalism, and materialism, and, one may say, also agnosticism, for, although the agnostic may grant the existence of such a Being, the concession is of no value either for knowledge or for morality. In this sense every religious view of the world is transcendental. When, however, we ask what the relation between man's knowledge and virtue and God's is, the real problem of transcendentalism emerges, and, according to the answer given, thinkers fall into different classes, which for purposes of clearness may be distinguished as follows.

(1) *Extreme transcendentalism.*—Those who hold that God is utterly incomprehensible to us, and that knowledge and virtue in Him are quite different, not only in quantity but also in quality, from what we mean by these terms, are extreme transcendentalists in the sphere of ontology. Modern examples are Hamilton and Mansel, who, borrowing a Kantian distinction, maintained that our predicated knowledge of God is regulative not speculative truth, that it was given, not to satisfy the reason, but to guide the practice of man, not to tell us what God is in His absolute nature, but what He wills us to think of Him in our present conditioned state. This phase of transcendentalism arose as a protest against what Hamilton calls 'the scheme of pantheistic omniscience so prevalent among the sequacious thinkers of the day.'[3] Speculative theologians have always had leanings towards this mode of reasoning regarding the divine, and its influence can be traced in theology from the days of Origen. While the ordinary religious consciousness speaks of God as wise and good, and cannot help so doing, yet these terms in reality do not apply to Him, and are to be understood anthropopathically. He has deigned

[1] *Ethics*, pt. ii. prop. xl. schol. 1.

[2] For the scholastic logical usage consult C. von Prantl, *Gesch. der Logik im Abendlande*, Leipzig, 1855–70, iii. 245 ff.; J. Veitch, *Institutes of Logic*, Edinburgh, 1889, p. 175; Sir W. Hamilton, *Lectures on Metaphysics and Logic*, Edinburgh, 1860, iii. 198; also Reid, *Works*[2] (ed. Hamilton), do. 1849, p. 687 f.; R. Eucken, *Gesch. der philosoph. Terminologie*, Leipzig, 1879.

[3] *De Diversis Quæstionibus*, i. 46.

[4] *Rep.* 509 B.

[5] *E.g.*, *Enneades*, v. i. 6, where God is described as ἐπέκεινα ἁπάντων, 'beyond all things.'

[1] *OT Theology*, Eng. tr., Edinburgh, 1892, ii. 114.

[2] *The Influence of Greek Ideas and Usages upon the Church*, ed. A. M. Fairbairn, London, 1890, ch. ix.

[3] *Discussions on Philosophy and Literature*, etc., London, 1852, pp. 1–37, quoted by H. L. Mansel, *The Limits of Religious Thought*[4], p. 191.

to accommodate this revelation to our limited intelligence, but it is, after all, only an accommodation (συγκατάβασις), and the true method of theology is to strip away all these predicates and to proceed *via negationis*. The danger here is obvious, viz. forgetting of the truth that man is made in the image of God, and forgetting that thinkers are apt to cut apart God and man, and thereby religion and reason alike become unreal and untrustworthy. Under this impulse religious men fall back on an authority which has no basis in our rational or moral nature, or on some occult faculty apart from reason; and others, strictly adhering to the working of the understanding, leave the transcendental sphere of Being alone. Outside the small circle illuminated by the understanding there may be Something, but to us it is unknown and unknowable. Agnosticism as regards ultimate reality is the result of this attitude.

(2) *Religious transcendentalism.*—Others, again, maintain also God's transcendental character, but they hold that man's knowledge is accurate as far as it goes, that in quality, though not in quantity, it is the same as God's, and that morality in man can not be different in essence from what it is in the divine, that the pathway of true knowledge and moral progress leads to God. God's revelation is certainly an accommodation, but this accommodation itself is an education of man by God, progressing from less to more and conserving in its more perfect stages continuity with the earlier, and besides the process is self-correcting. J. B. Mozley[1] gives a very fair view of this position as regards the OT. God dealt with men as they were, but in such a way as to lead them onwards and upwards. Man makes God in his own image, but it is because God first made man in His image. Augustine, who often speaks of God as incomprehensible—as indeed every religious mind must do, so that Hamilton has no difficulty in compiling a catena of such passages from various writers—yet maintains that our intellectual and moral strivings are but a returning to the Source whence intelligence and goodness spring. The human mind and heart participate in transcendent knowledge and goodness, and the aim of theology is to ascend by this road to God; only to man the grace of the Holy Spirit is necessary to initiate and guide this quest. The method here is not so much that of negation as of eminence (*via eminentiœ*), and it differs from pure philosophical or epistemological transcendentalism both in its insistence on the need of grace and in its proper valuation of other aspects of experience besides the pure intellect. It is this that 'Rabbi' Duncan has in view when he defines transcendentalism as 'the denial of that which renders man's knowledge an inferior kind of knowledge';[2] and it is in this sense that F. D. Maurice is a transcendentalist when in somewhat exaggerated fashion he fathers on Mansel's theory such frightful consequences.

(3) *Epistemological transcendentalism.*—Distinct from this again is what one may call pure epistemological transcendentalism, according to which the highest knowledge in man becomes identical with, and indistinguishable from, the divine knowledge. Thus Boethius:

> 'Sense judges figure clothed in material substance. Imagination figures alone without matter. Thought transcends this again, and by its contemplation of universals considers the type itself which is contained in the individual. The eye of intelligence is yet more exalted, for overpassing the sphere of the universal it will behold absolute form itself by the pure force of the mind's vision.'[3]

[1] *Ruling Ideas in Early Ages*, London, 1877.
[2] *Colloquia Peripatetica*[3], ed. W. Knight, Edinburgh, 1871, p. 111.
[3] *Consolation of Philosophy*, tr. H. R. James, London, 1897, p. 189.

From the plane of intelligence, according to Boethius, all the contradictions of the ordinary experience are reconcilable. Thus to God they harmonize, and to us as far as we look at them from this point of view. No one can fail to notice the similarity between this and the method of modern absolutist transcendentalism, with its solving of contradictions and its transcendental intuition. This school speaks in such a way as to lead the ordinary reader to suppose that the individual can attain by knowledge to the divine point of view—a claim which it is extremely difficult to distinguish from omniscience.

(4) *Moralistic and mystical transcendentalism.*—The term, however, may be applied, and often is applied, to those who are keenly conscious of the limitations of the human mind, and impatient and sceptical regarding its slow ratiocinative processes, but who hold that man's moral nature or his feelings or intuitions can give immediate access to the divine. Typical thinkers of this school are Pascal, Schleiermacher, and Ritschl. They lay stress on the supremacy of the heart—'The heart makes the theologian'—or on the value of feelings or intuitions; and a strong current to-day draws many along the pathway of the subconscious towards God. Thus we have schools of moralistic and mystical transcendentality. They disparage reason and logic, and find refuge in the alogical departments of the soul. The so-called New England transcendentalism[1] combines both mysticism and moralism with a large element of vague eclecticism, but it may, for purposes of classification, be included here.

3. Kantian transcendentalism.—To appreciate modern transcendentalism both in its philosophical and in its more popular application, we must briefly review Kant's view of knowledge.

(1) *The factors in knowledge.*—To Kant knowledge—mathematics and the physical sciences—involved two factors, one due to the activity of the mind, the other due to sense-data. He did not doubt the fact of knowledge itself, nor did he concern himself with its psychological origin. He found in knowledge a synthesis of these two elements. Nothing could form the subject-matter of knowledge but what came from sense-data, but then sense-experience itself was a chaos without the principles supplied by the understanding and the activity of the mind; even perception itself required space and time—mental forms. To him God, the world, and the soul could not become the objects of scientific knowledge and therefore they were transcendent; *i.e.*, they were outside the limits of possible knowledge. There can be no doubt that Kant had a horror of those who spoke familiarly of God, as if He were an object of sense-perception, and that his real anxiety to mark clearly the boundaries of possible knowledge was largely due to fear of intrusion from this quarter. He thus distinguishes clearly between 'immanent principles which apply solely within the limits of possible experience' and transcendent principles 'which are intended to reach beyond these limits.'[2]

Kant did not deny the reality of God, or of the soul, or the ultimate essence of matter, but he did strongly insist that the pure reason got into hopeless difficulties when it tried to apply the principles valid in the sphere of phenomena to these extra-phenomenal entities. To him we owe the very prevalent modern view that science has its own domain—it includes all knowledge, though not all reality—and religion and morality have their domain; that the marches between them should be clearly defined; and that there should be no raids, excursions, or alarums from one side or the other.

(2) *Transcendental principles.* — Having thus excluded transcendent realities from the domain of the understanding, because we can have no scientific knowledge of them, he shows that in knowledge itself there were principles like causality—the categories, in short—which were not due to sense-data. Those principles are transcendental (as distinct from transcendent), which means both that they are not due to sense and that they can be shown to constitute knowledge. Without sense-data they are empty, but sense without them is blind.

Transcendental to Kant then means constitutive

[1] See § 4 (1) below.
[2] *Kritik der reinen Vernunft*, ed. G. Hartenstein, Leipzig, 1853, iii. 245.

of valid knowledge, and a transcendental inquiry, such as his own critical method, 'concerns itself, not so much with objects, but with the way in which we know objects in so far as this may be possible *a priori*.'[1] What reality in itself may be is not the aim of the critical philosophy to determine, but to find out that element in knowledge which makes it valid and to guard knowledge against the admission of anything which cannot be scientifically known. Kant is not concerned with ontology but with epistemology, and the two to him are not identical. Kant thus sharply distinguishes between transcendent and transcendental. He uses the former term in a disparaging sense, while the latter means constitutive of knowledge—what makes knowledge possible.

'The term *transcendental*,' says R. Adamson, 'probably has, for English ears, an unpleasant ring, and will suggest metaphysical efforts to transcend experience. It must be understood, however, that *transcendental* method is simply the patient and rigorous analysis of experience itself. For any question or theorem which might pass beyond possible experience, Kant reserved the term *transcendent*; and the distinction, if not the mode of expressing it, is accepted by all his successors. Neither in Kant nor in Fichte is there anything in the slightest degree resembling what is commonly called metaphysics.'[2]

David Masson[3] traces through all history two tendencies in regard to the origin of knowledge—one fathering all knowledge on sense-experience (this may be called empiricism), the other maintaining that 'there are elements in knowledge, the origin or reason of which transcends or lies beyond the horizon of historical conditions.' Historically it is the conflict of these two that we find in the controversy between Locke and Leibniz or between Mill and Hamilton. The transcendental position is summed up in the famous phrase: 'Nihil est in intellectu quod non prius fuerit in sensu—nisi ipse intellectus.' There is no doubt that Kant is a transcendentalist in this sense, yet for him transcendental meant something different. He is not interested in innate ideas or intuitions. He is dealing with knowledge as it exists, not as it grows, and he finds in it what sense alone does not explain, but rather what explains sense, unifying forms or principles, supplied by the mind itself, which give receptivity to sense-data and combine them together into adequate knowledge. Ultimately the formal unity of the mind itself is involved in knowledge. Thus he might agree even with the physiological psychologist in his analysis of knowledge and yet maintain the necessity of the unity of the mind.

(3) *Pure and practical reason.*—Although Kant maintained that God, the world, and the soul as noumenal realities could not be objects of knowledge or constitutive of knowledge—that they were not transcendental in his strict sense of the term—yet he allowed that they were present in knowledge regulatively. The mind was constrained to aim at unity, and this striving was due to the regulative influence of these ideas of the reason. It is this part of his system that he himself calls transcendental or critical idealism. As ideas in the mind they were transcendental, though only regulatively so; yet in themselves as realities they are transcendent as far as knowledge goes—they are beyond the bounds of knowledge. Sometimes indeed he speaks of the reality of the material world as the 'transcendental object,' where we might expect him, if he were strict in his own use of terms, to use transcendent. And he speaks of it in such a way as to suggest a *substratum* which is the outward cause of our perceptions, but for the understanding it is simply x, an unknown quantity. His transcendental object is the limit which our understanding can reach in dealing with phenomena from the side of the receptivity of mind, just as 'the transcendental unity of apperception' is the limit on the side of the mind's synthesizing activity. Neither of these is noumena for the understanding, for it knows nothing of noumena.[1] If one were to regard this only as Kantianism, the first review of the *Kritik*—that of Christian Garve of Breslau, in the *Göttingische Gelehrte Anzeigen* of 19th Jan. 1782—might have force:

'This work . . . is a system of the higher or transcendental idealism—an idealism which embraces both mind and matter, transforms the world and ourselves into ideas, and represents the objective world as derived from appearances which the understanding combines in the interdependent whole of experience. . . . The cause of these ideas is to us unknown and unknowable.'[2]

But what pure reason cannot attain to, practical reason can. Morality needs transcendent realities as postulates, and, because the sphere of morality is to Kant more real than, or as real as, the sphere of knowledge, this postulation is necessary and valid. The transcendent of knowledge becomes the transcendental of morality. God, the world, the soul, freedom, and immortality become real here. We cannot prove their existence, it is true, by cognitive methods, but they are imperatively demanded by the facts of the moral life, of which facts he had no doubt.

4. Post-Kantian transcendentalism. — Kant's system was profound in its effects, different thinkers adopting those parts of it which served their turn, so that the complexion of their transcendentalism is determined by their point of contact with his view. His influence touched the English-speaking world at first largely through the works of Coleridge, Carlyle, and Emerson.

(1) *The teaching of Coleridge, Carlyle, and Emerson.*—Coleridge's philosophical function 'may be defined by saying that through him was transmitted an opportune suffusion of Kant and Schelling into England as of light softened through a stained-glass medium, and that into this suffusion he also resumed whatever of Anglo-Platonism had been floating long neglected in the works of old English Divines.'[3] Thus the distinction between the 'reason' and the 'understanding' became familiar, and 'transcendental philosophy' acclimatized in English speech. The reason could overcome the impotence of the understanding and get hold of unseen realities.

'As the elder Romans distinguished their northern provinces into Cis-Alpine and Trans-Alpine, so may we divide all the objects of human knowledge into those on this side, and those on the other side of the spontaneous consciousness; *citra et trans conscientiam communem*. The latter is exclusively the domain of pure philosophy, which is therefore properly entitled *transcendental*, in order to discriminate it at once, both from mere reflection and *re*-presentation on the one hand, and on the other from those flights of lawless speculation which, abandoned by *all* distinct consciousness, because transgressing the bounds and purposes of our intellectual faculties, are justly condemned, as *transcendent*.'[4]

It is clear that Coleridge has no interest in accurately reproducing Kant. To him transcendentalism is just emphasis on the spiritual side of man's nature, and this is the meaning also to Carlyle:

'The grand unparalleled peculiarity of Teufelsdröckh is, that with all this Descendentalism, he combines a Transcendentalism, no less superlative; whereby if on the one hand he degrade man below most animals, except those jacketed Gouda Cows, he, on the other, exalts him beyond the visible Heavens, almost to an equality with the Gods.'[5]

Under the influence of Coleridge and Carlyle, and the general romantic movement of the time,

[1] *Kritik der reinen Vernunft*, iii. 49.
[2] *Fichte* (Blackwood's Philosophical Classics), Edinburgh, 1881 p. 112, note.
[3] *Recent British Philosophy*, Edinburgh, 1865.

[1] See J. P. Mahaffy and J. H. Bernard's ed. of Kant's *Kritik*, London, 1889, ch. xiv., and also his *Prolegomena to any Future Metaphysic*, ed. J. P. Mahaffy, London, 1872, Appendix B.
[2] Quoted by W. Wallace, *Kant* (Blackwood's Philosophical Classics), Edinburgh, 1882, p. 60.
[3] Masson, *Recent British Philosophy*, p. 54.
[4] S. T. Coleridge, *Biographia Literaria*, London, 1817, vol. i. ch. 10 (Everyman's Library ed., do. 1906, p. 129).
[5] *Sartor Resartus*, bk. i. ch. 10.

transcendentalism came to mean the recognition of supersensible realities, and the spiritual nature of man—that man was more than 'an omnivorous biped that wears breeches.' A passage from Coleridge shows the influence of this attitude in the sphere of interpretation:

'The intelligible forms of ancient poets,
The fair humanities of old religion,
The power, the beauty, and the majesty
That had their haunt in dale, or piny mountain,
Or forest, by slow stream, or pebbly spring,
Or chasms, and watery depths; all these have vanished;
They live no longer in the faith of reason.
But still the heart doth need a language.'[1]

The faith in 'the light that never was on sea or land,' 'the vision and the faculty divine,' the fight against a crude interpretation of man's spirit as ultimately matter, and the protest against literalism in all its forms, characterize transcendentalism at this stage; and this is still the sense of the word in extra-philosophical literature. In New England Emerson and others, rebelling against an orthodoxy that tended to make men wholly sinful and corrupt and the will of man necessarily in bondage, and impatient of dogmas derived from a revelation confined to one book, initiated a movement that got the name 'transcendentalism' more in derision than in honour, but the term was accepted, and the claim made that all the best in the world's thought was here included. Carlyle, who, in spite of his sympathy with Emerson, saw in this movement an extravagant disregard of facts and an enthusiastic eclecticism, warned Emerson against the dangers ahead:

'You seem to me in danger of dividing yourselves from the Fact of the Universe, in which alone ugly as it is can I find any anchorage.'[2]

James Martineau—himself a transcendentalist in the Carlylean sense, whose intellectual history is a pilgrimage from the bondage of empiricism—does not take Emerson seriously. No doubt New England transcendentalism became extravagant, welcoming the ravings of the Swedenborgian and of the unregulated mystic as possible revelations, yet it never became a system, and its airy optimism is explicable and defensible as a protest and a reaction; yet to its influence is largely due the fact that to many, if not to most, in our day transcendentalism means hopeless and unwarranted idealism — unworkable dreaming. It was not patient enough to be lasting, and, with all its boasted catholicity and insight, it was blind to the facts that gave the old orthodoxy its seriousness and its power of rejuvenescence. On the other hand, it was a refreshing and liberalizing movement.

(2) *Science and transcendentalism.*—Kant's influence was felt in a very different quarter—among those whose interests were devoted to science. Thus Lange, the historian of materialism, interpreting Kant, as he thought, confines man's knowledge of reality to the results of science, but contends for a world above this created by our moral and spiritual needs—an unsubstantial world of ideals, a transcendentalism which is like a painted cloud; and this attitude has more or less existed since, differing according to the amount of reality the individual thinker gives to this beautiful but airy realm. It is found in the historian Buckle, and has been well described as a 'consolatory private transcendentalism.'[3] Herbert Spencer's magnanimous handing over of the Unknowable to religion is an example of this 'private transcendentalism.' It is due to a one-sided exploitation of Kant without regard to Kant's moral certainty. To Kant the moral nature of man planted man in an intelligible real world, although knowledge left him only in the phenomenal, with just a glimmer of the noumenal breaking through, but this transcendentalism which, as in Lange's case, pretends to be its lawful heir finds the phenomenal the real, and the transcendental the vague and the shadowy.

[1] *The Piccolomini*, act ii. sc. iv. l. 123 ff.
[2] *Correspondence of Carlyle and Emerson*, London, 1883, ii. 11.
[3] Masson, p. 249.

Others more alive to the reality of religion have sought to place this transcendentalism side by side with scientific results, while conscious all the time of the hostility between the two. Thus W. H. Mallock[1] attempts to hold by the results of science and yet to allow the demands of religion validity; and this attitude was prevalent in the past century.

In psychology the theory of psycho-physical parallelism exhibits the same tendency—a species of eirenicon between phenomenalism and transcendentalism. The results of science are accepted; its principles are unquestioned; and then these same facts are explained as if nothing but psychical data were involved. It is a truce born of perplexity—a compact that real issues will not be raised on either side. It is not difficult to see how closely related to Kant these tendencies are, for it may not unfairly be said that he himself adopted without questioning the results of science and also the deliverances of a spiritual philosophy due to religion and held them both without consistently uniting them.

Paulsen, one of Kant's most faithful modern disciples, contends that science will never give up its claim to explain everything mechanically; yet metaphysics must give to this realm of science an idealistic interpretation. One may be the most rigid materialist at one moment, and yet be wholly transcendentalist as a philosopher at another. The scientist will never admit any supernatural agent, and the only way of peace is to admit his claim; yet somehow to transform all into spiritual reality is the task of the philosopher. It is because of this felt dualism that transcendentalism in its pure form as absolutism claims for itself to be the true heir and rightful corrector and interpreter of Kant.

(3) *Absolute transcendentalism.* — 'Transcendentalism' in modern philosophy is used of that world-view known at times as absolutism, objective idealism, neo-Hegelianism, or rationalism. The term 'transcendentalism' traces this system historically to Kant's theory of knowledge. As we saw above,[2] 'transcendental' to Kant meant at least two things. (*a*) Those principles in knowledge which in the nature of the case did not originate in sense-experience are transcendental. In this sense of the term Kantianism allied itself with that tendency in British thought which recognized *a priori* or original data both in knowledge and in morality—what may be generically named intuitionalism. Leibniz's famous revision of the empirical formula may be taken as the watchword of this school: 'Nihil est in intellectu quod non prius fuerit in sensu *nisi ipse intellectus.*' The controversy between Hume and Reid, between Mill and Hamilton, is one between psychological empiricism and psychological transcendentalism, just as the controversy between hedonism and intuitionism is a phase of the same in the sphere of ethics. This was the outstanding question in British philosophy for many a day. Masson in his *Recent British Philosophy* gives a readable account of the state of matters in his time, and 'transcendentalism' is used by him of those systems which recognize in the mind more than sense-data. Spencer considers it one of the merits of evolution that it supplied a means of reconciliation between these opposing views. According to him, what was native to the individual was the residuary deposit of racial experience. Thus evolution reconciled empiricism and transcen-

[1] *Religion as a Credible Doctrine*, London, 1902.
[2] See § 3.

dentalism. (*b*) But 'transcendental' meant to Kant constitutive of knowledge—those principles which, though not due to experience, yet made experience itself coherent, above all, the unity of the self. All the content of knowledge came from experience, but the active self made knowledge. Besides, reason had as regulative principles the ideas of the self, the world, and God, and in its practical working reason got into touch with these realities. It was this side of Kant's teaching that issued in transcendentalism, as it came to be understood in English-speaking countries in the first half of the 19th century. Hamilton welcomed the Kantian system chiefly because he found it in harmony with the limits of our knowledge as propounded by himself, but others welcomed it because in their view it taught that man by his reason was more than a mere creature of the senses. Thus Carlyle, in his paper on Novalis,[1] points out that German transcendentalism denies the absolute existence of matter, that it makes space and time forms of the understanding; therefore to God 'Time and Space are not laws of His being but only of ours,' and so He is omnipresent and eternal; and 'the black Spectre, Atheism . . . melts into nothingness.' Again the transcendentalists recognize a higher faculty than understanding, viz. reason. Thus the invisible world is brought near us, and we feel in every thought that in God 'we live, and move, and have our being.' It was in this way that transcendentalism also at first became known in America.[2]

The transcendental unity of the self which Kant understood of the individual knower, and which by theoretical reason gave him no substantial subject or soul, was raised by Kant's successors in Germany to the level of a universal principle and an active subject, and thus knowledge was made adequate to grasp all reality. Reality now became subject and object, and epistemology became ontology. The transcendent of Kant vanished completely; it became immanent in knowledge. Fichte laid stress on the creative activity of the self in such a way that the object, the world, was called into being by the subject. Schelling, whose views changed considerably from one stage in his history to another, regarded the Absolute as the background of subject and object alike, but itself a *neutrum* of indifference, and he made intellectual intuition the eye by which intelligence grasped this whole. Hegel tried to do equal justice to both subject and object: 'the real is the rational,' and 'the rational is the real,' and Absolute Spirit is the whole, which becomes conscious of itself through a dialectical process. For some time this mode of thinking, through its novelty and obscurity, was unintelligible and obnoxious to English thinkers,[3] but, when it did take a hold in Britain, it was with such force that it conquered the philosophical chairs in our universities with few exceptions, and exercised an orthodox tyranny against which it was difficult to contend. To Hamilton,[4] who viewed with extreme repugnance the philosophy of the Absolute, must be attributed the revival of philosophical speculation in Britain, and his pupils were able to understand the German philosophy which then was an enigma and a puzzle to others who in Britain interested themselves in speculation.

[1] *Miscellaneous Essays* (People's Edition), London, 1872, ii. 183 ff. The essay was originally published in the *Foreign Review* [no. 7] in 1829.

[2] See J. Veitch, *Memoir of Sir William Hamilton*, Edinburgh, 1869, p. 421 ff.

[3] See J. H. Stirling, *The Secret of Hegel*, 2 vols., Edinburgh, 1865, Preface.

[4] See his 'Philosophy of the Unconditioned' (*Discussions on Philosophy and Literature*, pp. 1 ff., 605) where he ascribes the theory of Schelling and Hegel to Cardinal de Cusa—a sufficient indication of the value he placed on it.

(4) *Modern developments.*—Ferrier's *Institutes of Metaphysic*[1] was perhaps the first systematic exposition of transcendentalism in our tongue, although others had by that time acquainted themselves at first hand with its varied expositions in Germany—some repelled by it (*e.g.*, John Cairns),[2] others enthusiastic in their advocacy (*e.g.*, Hutchison Stirling, whose *Secret of Hegel* was an elaborate attempt to make Hegel intelligible to English-speaking students). It was, however, through the teaching and writings of Thomas Hill Green (*q.v.*) that transcendentalism became a philosophical force in Britain. Evolutionism, while it attempted to reconcile the older empiricism and transcendentalism, did so from below, by trying to relate man's knowledge and man's morality with animal life and animal activity in general, but the new transcendentalism, while acknowledging that in one sense man is a part of nature, yet explained knowledge and morality from above. Knowledge, according to this view, is explicable as the reproduction in man of the eternal self-consciousness of God, and morality is the realization of the immanent Eternal. The following passage from William James describes the spread of this movement in Britain:

> 'For many years adherents of this way of thought have deeply interested the British public by their writings. Almost more important than their writings is the fact that they have occupied philosophical chairs in almost every university in the kingdom. . . . It follows from their position of academic authority, were it from nothing else, that idealism exercises an influence not easily measured upon the youth of the nation—upon those, that is, who from the educational opportunities they enjoy may naturally be expected to become the leaders of the nation's thought and practice. . . . Carlyle introduced it, bringing it as far as Chelsea. Then Jowett and Thomas Hill Green, and William Wallace and Lewis Nettleship, and Arnold Toynbee and David Ritchie—to mention only those teachers whose voices are now silent—guided the waters into those upper reaches known locally as the Isis. John and Edward Caird brought them up to the Clyde, Hutchison Stirling up the Firth of Forth. They have passed up the Mersey and up the Severn and Dee and Don. They pollute the bay of St. Andrews and swell the waters of the Cam and have somehow crept overland into Birmingham. The stream of German idealism has been diffused over the academical world of Great Britain. The disaster is universal.'[3]

'Transcendentalism' came to be used of this new movement, although the term was not a favourite one with the idealists themselves. It was used by Henry Sidgwick[4] especially of the teaching of Green; by A. J. Balfour,[5] who contributes a chapter of criticism, and who even then could say:

> 'In English-speaking countries it is within the narrow circle of professed philosophers, perhaps the dominant mood of thought; while without that circle it is not so much objected to as totally ignored.'[6]

William James used it of all objective idealists, however these may differ among themselves, while Caldwell uses it of Bosanquet's teaching in his *Gifford Lectures*, which he describes as 'the last striking output of British transcendentalism or absolutism.'[7]

(5) *Neo-Hegelianism and Christianity.*—What gave this philosophy its vogue, to begin with at any rate, in Britain was undoubtedly the fact that to many minds it appeared as a *defensor fidei.* It seemed to supply an answer to materialism and empiricism on the one hand, and a vague scepticism and agnosticism on the other. It could be preached, and was preached often, by men who adopted the familiar phrases of sacrosanct religious thinking which were associated in the public mind with Christian values, and thus it came to be regarded

[1] Edinburgh, 1854.

[2] See A. R. MacEwen, *Life and Letters of John Cairns*, London, 1895, pp. 160–163.

[3] *A Pluralistic Universe* (*HL*), London, 1909, p. 53 f.

[4] *Outlines of the Hist. of Ethics*[2], London, 1888.

[5] *The Foundations of Belief*[2], London, 1895.

[6] *Ib.* p. 137.

[7] *Pragmatism and Idealism*, p. 14.

as a type of Christian philosophy. Hutchison Stirling found in Hegelianism a new version of Calvinism. Green used it to demolish the traditional English sensationalism and hedonism, and amidst the scepticism which prevailed regarding the historical elements of Christianity used it to rear a Christianity of ideas and ideals, from which dualism we are still suffering—witness the controversies concerning the historic Jesus and the eternal Christ. John Caird, afraid of the inroads of Spencerian and Manselian scepticism and Huxley's agnosticism, found in Hegel's teaching an ark of refuge and a citadel of defence. It was thus a movement of deliverance, of reform, and of religion. Not a few of its most zealous advocates were men destined for theology who found here a more congenial home. But, as time went on and this system began to be developed, the difficulties, tendencies, and obscurities inherent in it, as well as the dangers, revealed themselves. Just as in Germany Hegel's system allied itself at first with orthodox theology and then, in the hands of Strauss and Feuerbach, swung back to practical atheism and materialism, so also in our own country time has made it plain that this system is no guarantee of Christian faith or morals. Green [1] speaks with philosophic sorrow of those who find in poetry and religion the satisfaction for their ideals and aspirations, though they harbour scientific views which contradict these. He is sorry because such people do not proceed to frame or adopt a coherent philosophical system; forgetting that what gave transcendentalism its interest and vitality among the educated was not its speculative scheme—that was always a puzzle more or less—but the idea that this philosophy conserved spiritual values, and that what is fast loosening its hold on this class to-day is the feeling, rightly or wrongly entertained, that these interests are being betrayed or disregarded in the interests of the coherence of the system itself. To begin with, it is widely felt that transcendentalism speaks too confidently of its own power to present a perfectly explicable view of the world—to exhibit all reality in thought categories. Its manner is apt to strike the observer as being haughty and supercilious, and its language would lead one to think that a claim to something like omniscience is arrogated—a claim so contrary to our broken experience as human beings, and so opposed to that humility which serious thinkers have always regarded as the fitting attitude for all searchers of truth.

(6) *Faith and knowledge.*—No one has done more among our professional philosophers to abate this soaring gnosticism than Campbell Fraser, with his insistence on the function of faith as lying at the very basis of knowledge itself, as accompanying and regulating its advance all along its operations. Reality is richer than thought, nor is it possible to factorize reality into thought terms. The limits of human knowledge are obvious even in the most daring schemes of rationalism, and philosophy has again to face the problem of the relation between faith and reason.

Again, it is felt that transcendentalism does not do justice to the reality of the external world. To it the external world is only an object for a subject, and the tendency of all idealistic schemes is to lapse into solipsism. This solipsism may be of the human individual or of the One Supreme Subject, but in essence it is the same. Sidgwick suggested the term 'mentalism' [2] as a more adequate description of this tendency. Whatever term we use, the tendency itself is undeniable, and

[1] *Prolegomena to Ethics*, Oxford, 1883, p. 2.

[2] The term 'mentalism' or 'immaterialism' is also used by James S. Ferrier.

the reaction is seen in the movement known as neo-realism,[1] but the tendency is acutely felt by reasonable idealists, as, *e.g.*, by A. S. Pringle-Pattison;[2] yet one wonders if his own view of creation is not just a residuum of this old leaven of mentalism which he cannot purge out of his system. He has no difficulty in regard to the creation of souls, which, if it means anything, means something new, but he cannot admit the creation of matter. Yet, if God existed in His fullness before any person now living existed—if such an assumption is tolerable—why should creation as applied to matter be considered incredible? It is futile to try to explain matter as thought-elements, either in the mind of man or in the mind of God. When a philosopher arrives at such a view, it is surely the sane course for him to examine his reasoning again.

(7) *The problem of personality.*—The personality of man in this system, as we see from its modern developments, becomes insecure, or, if that danger is avoided, it is at the price of God's personality that man's is safeguarded. Thus there are those who, like Bosanquet, lay stress on the Supreme Personality or Individuality, and tend to make men but aspects of this Being's life. Others lay stress on man and make God the totality of men—a college or community of spirits, eternal *a parte ante* as well as *a parte post*. To conceive of God as a perfect personality, above and apart from men and the world, and yet originating and sustaining both, seems an absurdity to this scheme of thinking.

> 'History is the biography of the Absolute; science the natural history of the Absolute; philosophy the self-consciousness of the Absolute, recalling and arranging its past being in unconsciousness, and discovering thereby the laws of its own thought.'[3]

The outcome is seen in a book like Bradley's *Appearance and Reality*, in which the Absolute is everything—God, men, nature, spirits good and evil—and yet somehow it is all that in the bliss of an absolutely consistent whole. Personal idealism, pragmatism, and, above all, theism, will never take such a theory seriously.

5. The task of philosophy.—The modern world is alive to the fact that the intellect alone is not man, and that reality is not to be construed solely by its means. Emphasis is now laid on the will and the emotions as well, with the result that the moral life—the sphere of ideals—is given its own place. When this is recognized, then it becomes clear that reality is not a perfection which the mind has to mirror, but an ideal which has to be achieved. Nothing is more deadening and more untrue than to think of reality from man's point of view as a perfect 'is'; for the moral life at any rate reality is in ideals—'the best is yet to be.' Thus only can man's freedom be saved from the cloudland of illusion, and thus only can evil and sin—the root of all our intellectual as well as of all our moral problems—be faced as our moral nature imperatively calls on us to face them. Our duty in regard to these, unless our whole nature be itself a delusion, is not so much to explain them as to abolish them. To tell us that 'this very presence of ill in the temporal order is the condition of the perfection of the eternal order' [4] is to treat man's moral nature with insincerity. Transcendentalism has no eschatology, because to it the Absolute—*i.e.* all that is—is already perfect and cannot be more so, and yet a philosophy or a religion without an eschatology offers nothing to man's needs, imposes a veto on man's passion for reformation, and does away with

[1] See art. REALISM.

[2] *The Idea of God* (*Gifford Lectures*), Oxford, 1917, ch. x.

[3] Cairns, in *Life*, by MacEwen, p. 163.

[4] J. Royce, *The World and the Individual* (*Gifford Lectures*), New York and London, 1900–01, ii. 385.

his felt need of redemption. These are some of the difficulties that most modern thinking men feel in regard to modern transcendentalism, and the recognition of them has led to a very general revolt against it in recent years from within the philosophic world itself. Pragmatism, neo-realism, neo-Kantianism, personal idealism, are but some of the phases of this revolt. It cannot be said that these views, any or all of them, are free from difficulties; and at the present moment it is impossible to say what the future may have in store for philosophy. The best we can wish for it is that it free itself from the tyranny of phrases and become intelligible and interesting; that it may have the humility to attempt to solve real problems that perplex men; that it be freed from its disdain regarding men's abiding convictions; that it abstain from any language which would throw doubt on the great ideals and values of life; and that it realize the necessity of satisfying the heart as well as the head. God, nature, man—these are the realities. Transcendentalism tends to forget the second, and to make the first and third coequal; pragmatism forgets the first, and naturalism the first and third. The task of philosophy is concerning these three, and transcendentalism is valuable when the claims of naturalism become exorbitant; but it must not, without becoming false, succumb either to humanism on the one hand or to pantheism on the other.

LITERATURE.—The *OED* gives an idea of the variety of meaning attached to the word 'transcendental,' and R. Eisler, *Wörterbuch der philosoph. Begriffe*[3], 3 vols., Berlin, 1910, gives the philosophical usage. For the pre-Kantian logical usage and the mediæval theological usage the Histories of Philosophy and of Theology must be consulted. For New England transcendentalism see art. EMERSON. Joseph Cook, *Transcendentalism*, Boston, U.S.A., 1877, is a vigorous popular criticism of Emersonianism in the interests of orthodoxy. The literature under artt. COLERIDGE and CARLYLE is instructive for the early influence of German transcendentalism in a popular form in Britain.

A short account of the history of British transcendentalism, or absolutism, is given by Robert Mackintosh, *Hegel and Hegelianism*, Edinburgh, 1903, chs. vi. and vii. O. Pfleiderer, *Religionsphilosophie auf geschichtl. Grundlage*, Berlin, 1878, and *Development of Theology*, Eng. tr., London, 1890, gives the history of post-Kantian idealism from a theological point of view. J. H. Stirling, T. H. Green, John Caird, Edward Caird, J. Watson, H. Jones, W. Wallace, J. Royce, J. Macbride Sterrett, G. S. Morris give a version of Hegelian transcendentalism of a religious character. F. H. Bradley, *Appearance and Reality*[2], London, 1902, is mainly negative. For the revolt against transcendentalism in Germany see H. Vaihinger, *Die Philosophie des Als Ob*, Berlin, 1911. French philosophy since Cousin and Renouvier, down to Bergson, has been more or less generally anti-rationalistic and personalistic. James Seth, *English Philosophers and Schools of Philosophy*, London, 1912, is instructive for English thinking; an older book by D. Masson (quoted above) deals with Mill and Hamilton—the conflict between transcendentalism and intuitionism. The works of A. Campbell Fraser, Henry Sidgwick, and A. J. Balfour lay stress on primitive convictions and are in spirit against Hegelian gnosticism. See the literature under artt. NEO-KANTIANISM, REALISM, and PRAGMATISM. William Caldwell, *Pragmatism and Idealism*, London, 1913, gives ample information as to anti-rationalistic literature in Britain, Germany, France, and America.

D. MACKENZIE.

TRANSFORMATION.—See METAMORPHOSIS.

TRANSMIGRATION.

TRANSMIGRATION (Introductory and Primitive).—Reincarnation is the passage of the soul from one body to another, usually of the same species, among higher races often with ethical implications, the lot of the soul on earth being determined by its behaviour in a former life. Transmigration, metempsychosis, and other terms are often used in an almost identical sense, but also in a vaguer way, implying at times that the soul itself assumes an animal form, sometimes permanently, sometimes only as a prelude to another reincarnation or to final destruction or absorption. Somewhat different is the creed which may be termed 'alternation of existences'; it involves the belief that man is double, a counterpart in another world corresponding to the earthly body or embodied soul in this world and taking the place of the latter when its turn comes to quit this world. Separate existence, reincarnation, annihilation, and transmigration are the possibilities that present themselves to the primitive mind when it inquires into the fate of the soul. We cannot say why one belief rather than another has been adopted in any specific instance; but it is clear that the resemblance of children to parents (or other relatives) has played some part, especially in W. Africa. The complex of beliefs is therefore to some extent a semi-scientific creed, taking the place of a biological account of heredity, and based on reasoning that we can follow. It seems equally certain that the widespread belief in transformation (or change of bodily form) during life must have had its effect on eschatological doctrine; and here the creed goes back to what must be some of the most archaic elements of human speculation. Those two factors are, however, at times to some extent combined, when a rise or fall in the scale of existence is put down to the merit or demerit of previous births. Both in reincarnation and in transmigration doctrines the life or lives that succeed the human life on earth are sometimes regarded as limited in duration, sometimes as indefinitely prolonged; where some accident interferes with the due course of reincarnation, the lot of the soul may be a kind of third state, neither reincarnation nor annihilation (or absorption), but separate existence (as an evil spirit).

Many widely distributed customs appear to be connected with the belief in reincarnation. Thus, in Africa and America children are buried by the wayside, near the mother, under the eaves, or in other situations that would in the eyes of the natives facilitate reincarnation; in parts of Central Australia and in Africa people are buried in the place of their birth.[1] But it must be recalled that, generally speaking, the common feeling that it is well to be buried with one's own people implies no more than the view that this is necessary to ensure the solidarity of the family in the future life. The custom of killing the first-born[2] has been explained for some areas by the belief that this child is, in special measure, an embodiment of the father or grandfather; and the abdication of a king, as in Tahiti, in favour of an infant son has been put down to the same cause. The belief in transmigration again in certain areas has led to the sacrosanctity of certain species, and the totemism (*q.v.*) of some regions, such as S. Africa and Oceania, has been referred to this origin.

[1] See art. DEATH AND DISPOSAL OF THE DEAD (Introductory and Primitive), § VII. 3 (*e*).

[2] See art. FIRST-BORN (Introductory and Primitive), § 3.

A well-developed scheme of reincarnation or transmigration, if we except the anomalous case of the Central Australian tribes, as to whose real belief there is some doubt, is generally found only among peoples who either have attained a certain stage of culture, as in India, or have almost certainly been in contact with or influenced by a higher culture, as among W. African tribes. The W. African tribes among which a reincarnation creed has been recorded in more or less detail are the Mandingo, Ewe, Edo, and Ibo. The belief is also known among the Yoruba, who lie geographically between the Ewe and the Edo; but details of their ideas on the subject are lacking.

1. West Africa.—(*a*) *Mandingo.*—As regards the Mandingo, we have only a summarized account of their beliefs,[1] which differs widely from another account from a portion of the area;[2] a summarized account is always liable to mislead, and, in view of the large divergences recorded in other areas in the transmigration and reincarnation beliefs, it is prudent to await further details from the French territories before classifying the belief as aberrant.

According to Delafosse, every living being and every natural phenomenon depends for its nature on a *niama*, 'dynamic spirit'; the word *nia* is applied to a genius, *niama* to a spirit, which may be that of a genius, a human being, a sacred object, an animal, a rock, etc. The *niama* of a dead man can reside where it likes—in the corpse, in the hut, in a sacred object, or in the body of a living being whose *niama* it absorbs. Certain magicians attribute their powers to the possession of the *niama* of a genius or of a dead man. The *niama* of a man for whom the due rites have not been performed may reincarnate itself in a solitary animal, or in a human being, who goes mad. It is therefore clear that, though the *niama* may be reincarnated, it is by no means invariably the case, and, where reincarnation takes place, it differs in kind from the reincarnation in which the more easterly tribes believe (see below). Side by side with the *niama* we have the *dia*, or breath of life, which passes at death into another being; it is not the object of any cult; it is found only in living beings and passes only into another being of the same species, save on the rare occasions when it animates the body of a totem. This belief is, in form, on all fours with those of other Negro tribes; but it is hardly possible to speak of reincarnation, which implies some degree of identity, some measure of personality.

According to Monteil, the Khassonke believe that *dya* is soul, force, or shadow, while *ni* means breath; if this is correct, the meanings are just the reverse of what they are in the foregoing account of Mandingo beliefs, and it seems clear either that we are in the presence of a far-going disintegration of creed or that, as has probably happened farther east, the belief has come from without and has been worked up by each tribe in its own fashion. In any case it seems improper to give a generalized account of the beliefs of a mass of tribes if such varied views have to be regarded as identical.

(*b*) *Ewe.*—According to the Ewe belief, every man has two souls—a *luwo agbedo*, or life-soul, and a *luwo kuto*, or death-soul; the former is visible when a man casts a short shadow, the latter when he casts a long shadow. The death-soul accompanies a man into the grave and then goes to the land of the dead; the life-soul leaves the body at death and goes sighing mournfully and seeking for a resting-place; each man has also a breath-soul. That the shadow-soul is more than a shadow is clear from the fact that sleep is attributed to the absence of the shadow-soul, waking to its return, and dreams to its activity outside the body.

The land of the dead appears to be the same as Amedzowe, the place of man's origin—a land not on earth, but in heaven, where everything corresponds more or less closely to the things of this life. In Amedzowe are yams, corn, cotton, bush, and all that surrounds a man in this life, not, however, in bodily form, but spiritually, so to speak; and the human inhabitants of Amedzowe live and thrive on these things in their spiritual form. Life in Amedzowe, however, is more than a duplication of this world; for, when a child dies soon after birth, a priest may declare that it was a great king in Amedzowe and has died in order to return to the scene of its former glories. Conversely, the things of this world may influence the course of events in Amedzowe; if a man remains too long away from the other world, he will fall ill, for the dwellers there prepare to break down his hut; and, to save him, his associates in this world must each bring a blade of grass and lay it on the roof of his house, as a symbol of the re-roofing of his spiritual house. In Amedzowe a man has a spiritual aunt (*tasi*) and other relatives; from her he must obtain permission to leave the world of spirits and come to the world of men.[1] Some of those who come to this world are so dearly loved by their spiritual relatives that they have to give a promise, called *gbetsi*, to return after a short time; these are the children who die young; this promise has been personified and is regarded as in some measure an evil genius, for it incites men who break it to evil deeds and especially to suicide or to acts that will bring about a violent death. Generally speaking, the lot of a man in this life and his abilities are determined by the fate announced to him by his *tasi*; but here, as elsewhere, there is a fundamental contradiction in the creed of the Ewe, for, as will be seen below, the *aklama*, or genius, is also held responsible for a man's lot in this life.

Side by side with this curiously untheological creed we find the belief that Mawu, the supreme god, is a dweller in Amedzowe and is the king who sits in judgment on the departing soul before it takes up its abode in this world. Not only so, but we find also the view that the lot of man, or at least his term of life, is determined, if not by Mawu, at any rate by Mawu's intercession with Death, whom he begs to spare one of his earthly children. If, as appears to be the case, the Ewe beliefs are the result of syncretism, there can be no doubt as to which are the older elements in their creed; for the god of death, Ogiuwu, is found also among the Edo, from whom they were separated by the Yoruba influx, and whose views as to reincarnation at the present day come much closer to those of the Ibo, their neighbours on the east.

There is, however, another side to the Ewe beliefs; this is the *aklama*, *kla*, or, in the language of the neighbouring Twi, *okra*; it is often identified with the *luwo*, but an older and more correct conception seems to be that it is a genius or tutelary spirit. Another authority says that *kra* is the collective name for *ṅunu*, all the spiritual beings that surround a man, whether they be evil or good, human or demonic. Westermann connects the word *aklama* with Efik *akaṅa*, a promise to return to the other world. If this derivation is correct, the conception of *aklama* as a tutelary spirit has arisen in the same way as that of its counterpart, *gbetsi*, by the personification of a promise, but Efik is a member of a different group of languages and topographically remote; the derivation must therefore be received with caution; it is none the less possible that both words are derived from the same root or form, especially if it should be the case that the reincarnation idea has been introduced from without or fostered in its growth by foreign influence.

Every man has a *kla*, or, perhaps, properly speaking, one or more, for the *aklama* figurines worshipped by a man are often in duplicate, male and female, in any case with only a single arm, as an indication of the identity of *aklama* and human being. Children sometimes carry an *aklama*

[1] Delafosse, *Haut-Sénégal-Niger*, iii. 165.
[2] C. Monteil, *Les Khassonké*, p. 142.

[1] It is perhaps not without significance that the *tasi* is the father's sister; for the Ewe are matrilineal, or at most in a transition stage; and we can hardly suppose that the father's sister has normally such influence in the family; the belief in question therefore either must be young or, more probably, has come to them from without.

figurine on their backs, and, in the case of twins, each carries the figurine of the other; it is not without importance that these twin figurines are found in areas, such as Sierra Leone, where the reincarnation belief is not found, at any rate at the present day. One name for these figurines is *ame we luwo*, 'the soul of a man'—a phrase which makes clear the present deeply-rooted confusion between *luwo* and *aklama*. The *aklama* lives in Mawuwe, probably the same as Amedzowe, till Mawu gives it permission to enter a man, which it does before birth; the child to which it is assigned is known in advance, however; for the priest can interrogate the *aklama* as to the future lot of the unborn child. In some places the *kla* receives offerings annually, probably on the birthday of the child, for the *kla* is named from the day of the birth and is also known as the younger brother of Mawu. The *aklama* seeks only the welfare of his ward, so long as the latter fulfils his obligations; otherwise he may punish him with disease, madness, or other ills, or, more properly, may allow him to fall a victim to them. The obligations just mentioned include abstention from certain foods, generally, or for a period, or on certain days. In some unexplained way the *aklama* is associated with a man by virtue of his being made by Mawu out of certain earth; for, when a thief has a thievish son, it is said that Mawu formed both of the same earth, and hence their *aklama* are alike. A man comes to the world with his character formed once for all, and it seems in reality to be that of his *aklama*; a man's nature (*dzogbe*) is said to leave him at death, and, though it is believed to be conditioned by his *aklama*, it seems difficult to distinguish them.

So far as we have gone, there has been some confusion between *aklama*, *dzogbe*, and *luwo*; after death this confusion is increased. The images of the *aklama* are broken in pieces or thrown away, for their owner needs them no longer. The *aklama* seems now, like the *luwo*, to be termed *ṅoli* ('ghost' or 'spirit') and is questioned a few days after death to find out who was responsible for his death. The final destination of the *ṅoli* is Tsie or Agume, the place under the earth, the road to which passes through a river; Kutiame is the ferryman, and his fee is twelve cowries. Another account says that the dead man meets Liagbe at the entrance of a town, and she questions him as to his deeds in this life; she has a great wound, which he must lick; and, though this is a detail on which we have no other information, it seems highly probable that Liagbe should be identified with the spiritual aunt (*tasi*).

Native beliefs are rarely so clear and unambiguous as a written account commonly assumes them to be; but it is impossible to study the foregoing summary without feeling that syncretism must be reckoned with as a possible explanation. A knowledge of the beliefs of the peoples to the east of the Ewe can only strengthen the probability of this explanation; for here too we find diverse ideas combined, and some of them agree so closely with the Ewe creed that any possibility of separate origin must be rejected; at the same time, the general balance of the elements of the creed is so different, and the terminology so different (except where the creeds agree, as noted above), that we can hardly accept the theory of a common origin of the whole complex as the explanation of the points of agreement, which are not relatively numerous.

(*c*) *Edo*.—The Ewe language is closely akin to the Edo and forms a member of the group of languages named from the best known member, which is spoken in Benin city and the neighbourhood. It is somewhat surprising that as regards the subject of this article the terminology differs *in toto* from that of the Ewe, as is made clear by the following table:

	Ewe	Edo	Ibo
Genius . .	*aklama*, *kla*	*ehi*, *ekosi*, *ima*	*či*, *eṛi*; cf. *ikeṅga*.[1]
Shadow (soul)	*luwo*	*agogo*	*onyinyo*, *ndò*.
Breath . .	*gbogbo*	*eti*	*ṅdò*, *ume*, *uzu*.
Spirit . .		*orio* (?)	*mwo*.
Ghost . .	*ṅoli*		cf. *akalagoli*.[2]
Ward . .			(*ṅw*)*ago*.
Other world .	Amedzowe	Elimi	Owamwo, Okwa.
Promise .	*gbetsi*		*akaṅa*; cf. *ikeṅga*.

Broadly speaking, *ehi* corresponds to our idea of soul, for the *agogo* is said to disappear on the day that a man's body is put into the grave; in the Kukuruku country there are traces of belief in a breath-soul (*eti*), which does not, however, correspond to the *dya*, for *eti* is said to be the breath of *ehi*, which dies in Elimi before it comes to this world. Osa (god) is said to take a man's *eti* to Elimi, where it turns into a man with a body (*i.e. ehi*). Two *ehi* are usually distinguished, *ehinehi* (*ehinowa*) and *ehinoha*, sometimes identified with *ekosi*, sometimes with *ehogai*, the *ehi* of a childless person. Some say that *ehinowa* is in Elimi, while *ehinoha* is on the back of a man's neck; others say that *ehinoha* is a man's shadow in Elimi, or that *ehinowa* is on the top of a man's head; the latter statement was qualified by the addition that there was another *ehi* in Elimi. Some say that *ehinowa* comes to earth when a man dies, thus reproducing the idea of alternation already found among the Ewe, others that *ehinoha* lives in Elimi and comes to earth as *ehinehi* when a man dies. It is also said that *ehinowa* goes at death to Elimi and returns for sacrifices and offerings; in Elimi this *ehi* may lay claim to a woman for whom his earthly counterpart paid bride-price without being able to secure her as a wife. Some say that *ehinowa* is sent by Osa to animate a child already conceived, others that it brings a child to a man, others again that it 'does things for a man,' *i.e.* is his genius. *Ehinoha's* functions are equally a matter of opinion; it is on the back of a man's neck, or is the servant of *ehinowa* and takes sacrifice to him in Elimi, or lives in Elimi and comes to earth when its ward dies, or is a man's shadow in Elimi, where *ehinowa* is also, or corresponds to *eṛe*—a man's enemies (perhaps, rather, evil spirits), to whom he sacrifices on the road.

We reach a somewhat different cycle of ideas when we find *ehinoha* regarded as a 'bush soul,' injury to which means sickness for the human being. It is also said to be the 'king of the bush' and to be richer than *ehinowa*; when it receives a sacrifice, it is satisfied and turns its back. The prevailing view is undoubtedly that *ehi* brings a child from Elimi but is not identical with it; some say that the dead go to Elimi and are reborn seven times in the same or another family, alternately as male and female. Though there is some confusion between the *ehi*, they seem to be clearly distinguished from the man himself; they are real genii, but so far bound up with their human counterpart that his health is sometimes regarded as dependent on the state of the bush *ehi*. On the whole, the *ehinoha* is a bad genius that leads a man astray, spoils things, and, so far as the identity of man and *ehi* is accepted, refuses to remain in this world. The word *ehi* is found in Kukuruku in the form *ezi*, with which may be compared the Ibo *eṛi*,[3] *eṣi*.

(*d*) *Ibo*.—Among the Ibo, who number several millions, there is much diversity of view; but only a small percentage of the tribes have been adequately investigated; the following summary relates to the Awka and Asaba districts. West of the Niger the belief is that an entity known as *či*, sometimes identified with *eṛi*, sends the new human being into the world; the reincarnated person and the reincarnation are known respectively as *ago* and *ṅwago*. The *či* is normally a dead person, but in some areas may be the father or mother of the child. East of the Niger the *či* is in the main, like *ikeṅga*, a personal protective deity, with only slight traces of a connexion with the reincarnation belief; there is no explicit statement that the *či* sends a child into the world. The *ikeṅga* may perhaps be equated with the Ewe *gbetsi*, especially if, as seems probable, it is etymologically connected with Efik *akaṅa*, the promise to return to the other world. The Ibo are quite clear in their belief that a person is reincarnated, normally in his (or her) own family, at any rate if he has been buried with his fathers; children of tender years will assure the inquirer with the utmost solemnity

1 A personal protective spirit. 2 Evil spirit.
3 ṛ represents a breathed r.

that they are their deceased grandfathers or grandmothers; and the identity of the ancestor is determined by divination. A child that speaks before it opens its eyes is said to be relating what it saw in Owamwo and is at once exposed in the *ajoifia*; it is also asserted that a man who has been unlucky in one existence may decide, on opening his eyes for the first time in a new life, that it is the same world in which he was unhappy before, and resolve to give up the struggle, whereupon the new-born child dies on the spot.

The relation between *či* and *ago*, west of the Niger, may be compared with that of godchild and godparent; the relation sets up a bar to marriage, and a man may not even marry into the *umunna* (sept) of his *či*; two people who have the same *či* may not marry, nor yet may their children, though apparently a man may marry the fellow *ṅwago* of his sister. There is a saying that the child who is one's *ago* (*ṅwago*) should have been the child of a man's own loins; both must be of the same quarter; if the *či* has no heir of his own, the *ago* inherits the property. Curiously enough, the *onye bi owe*, the reincarnated person, who is sent into the world by the (living) *či*, and who ought by analogy to stand to the child in a closer relation than the *či*, is in point of fact regarded as a comparative stranger; he may come from another *ebo* (quarter) or from a different tribe altogether, and his ritual prohibitions do not concern the child, who has to observe those of his *či*.

There are traces of the view that *či* and *ṅwago* form two links in a continuous chain, at any rate where the *či* is not a living person, the *ṅwago* of one generation being the *či* of the next; and this affords a satisfactory explanation of the views as to prohibitions. At the same time, it must be remembered that the *či* is properly a personal protective deity, in fact a personal *alose*, and that the facts are, in other directions, best accounted for on this hypothesis; it must not, however, be forgotten that east of the Niger an *alose* may be the *či*, or, according to another account, may itself be reincarnated. East of the Niger also we sometimes find the view that the *ago* goes to the next world with a dead man, while the *oglisi* pegs that represent it are thrown away; so that here the *ago* is regarded as the *či*; it is, at any rate for a time, to some extent represented by the *ndičie*, or ancestral figurines. Curiously enough, the *umunna* (sept) claims to have a collective *ago*, just as it has a collective *ndičie*, though in the nature of things an *ago* which sends to this world a corporation, not individual human beings, is unthinkable.

West of the Niger there is a good deal of confusion between *či* and *eṛi*, which is properly a genius, and may perhaps originally have been a breath-soul (cf. Kukuruku *eti*, 'breath').[1] If this is the case, *eṛi* is now none the less distinct from the man, for ceremonies are performed to bring it to the house, and in many cases it is identified with *či*. Perhaps two streams of belief flowing together, one placing *či* in Owamwo, the other locating *eṛi* in this world, have coalesced, so that ideas associated with *či* came to be attached to *eṛi*, and *vice versa*.

It has been pointed out that the words *akaña* and *ikeñga* are in all probability connected etymologically; it is by no means unlikely that *kla* and *aklama* are from the same root; for *la* and *na* may well be alternative forms of a suffix, and the transition from *kala* to *kla* is a well-established phonetic change in W. Africa. There is some reason for supposing that the original idea is that of a promise, though in Ewe the term *gbetsi* is now used in that sense, while *aklama* has become a genius; but further research is needed in other areas before any definite pronouncement can be made. It is tempting to connect the root *ka* with the Egyptian *ka*, which was a double of the man and believed to be after death, with the mummy, a denizen of the tomb;[1] but, though there are clear traces of mummification in W. Africa, probably due to Egyptian influence, and though nothing is more probable than that Egyptian ideas in traversing the continent would have undergone fundamental changes, there is no positive evidence to connect any of the beliefs mentioned above with any article of the Egyptian creed.[2] The possibility of Egyptian influence must, however, be kept in mind, for Egyptologists appear to accept the evidence produced by L. Frobenius[3] as to Egyptian influence in the present Yoruba area in the 6th cent. B.C. That the terms of the Yoruba language show no connexion with those cited above is of no importance, for there can be little doubt that the Yoruba tribe has come down from the north and may not have been in occupation of the area in question, if indeed it existed, at the period in question.

2. South Africa.—In many parts of S. Africa, and sporadically in other parts of Africa, there is a belief that the dead are transformed into certain species of animals, or at any rate that they assume this form to appear to the survivors; it has been maintained, not quite convincingly, that some Bantu tribes[4] suppose themselves to be transformed at death into their totems. This belief is, however, definitely reported from the west coast, among the Siena and the Twi, as well as in the north-east of the Congo Free State. Among the Zulu the transformation is supposed to be into a species of serpent.

3. Madagascar.—In Madagascar the belief in transformation is also found, though here doubtless of Indonesian origin; and we see a different lot in the future state assigned to various social grades; this is of course a common feature of eschatological doctrine not connected with the theory of moral retribution.

4. Central Australia.—According to Spencer and Gillen, the tribes of Central Australia believe that children are reincarnations of their ancestors (totem) and are continually reborn;[5] but the testimony of Strehlow, a witness well acquainted with the language of the Arunta tribe, directly contradicts this;[6] for he maintains that the native belief is that the soul of every man goes at death to the Isle of the Dead, there to be annihilated by a flash of lightning; in certain cases it is believed that a totem-ancestor is himself reborn, but after this reincarnation he does not return.

[1] The following forms may be compared:

Edo	Sobo	Kukuruku	Ibo
ehi, eti	*eṛi*	*ezi*	*eṛi.*

Cf. also the undoubtedly related words for 'ear':

eho	*eṛo*	*ezo*	*nti* (=*eti*).

[1] See art. DEATH AND DISPOSAL OF THE DEAD (Egyptian).

[2] In modern Egyptian folklore the *quarina*, equated by Seligman with the *ka*, is held to be the spiritual counterpart of a man, which has nothing to do with his immortal soul; it plays the part of a good or bad angel. It is of course possible that this resemblance to present-day W. African beliefs is due to convergence; we can hardly assume that both are simple replicas of ancient Egyptian beliefs, nor yet that the course of development has been identical; but there is at least a *prima facie* case for inquiry.

[3] *Und Afrika Sprach*, Berlin, 1912.

[4] See art. BANTU AND S. AFRICA, § 3 f.

[5] Spencer-Gillen[a], pp. 123, 127; Spencer-Gillen[b], pp. 145, 174.

[6] *Globus*, xci. [1907] 285, xcii. [1907] 123; see also literature below.

Strehlow's account of Aranda (Arunta) belief is as follows:

The totem-ancestors dropped some of their *churinga*, which were transformed into trees, rocks, etc., from which proceed *ratapa*; these are completely formed boys and girls of reddish colour and have both body and soul; they are invisible to ordinary mortals. When a woman passes a spot (*kuanakala*) where the transformed body of an ancestor is, and where consequently the *ratapa* associated with that ancestor dwell, one of the latter, when it recognizes a suitable (*i.e.* of the correct clan) woman, enters her body and causes various symptoms. The child belongs to the totem of the ancestor associated with the spot.

There is a second method by which an ancestor impregnates a woman, but this does not seem to imply any kind of reincarnation, though the ancestor is called in both cases the *iningukua* of the child. The ancestor is said to come out of the earth and throw a small bull-roarer (*namatuna*) at a suitable woman, in whose body it takes human form.

Both kinds of impregnation are said to be equally frequent, and the difference is recognized in the face of the child, which is narrow in the first, broad in the second kind.

An *iningukua* can also, very rarely, enter a woman's body in person; and a child thus originated has light hair; in such a case the soul goes at death like other souls to the Isle of the Dead, and is annihilated by a flash of lightning. There is therefore no question of repeated reincarnations, and only in the third case can we really speak of an Aranda belief in the doctrine, so far as can be seen from Strehlow's narrative.

This account agrees with much of what is reported by Spencer and Gillen;[1] though these authors speak of reincarnation of ancestors, they really mean an incarnation of spirit-children left behind by the totem-ancestors. And even among the Aranda we hear of the totem-ancestors[2] living in water-holes.

Perhaps it is most probable that large local variations of belief account best for the differences between Strehlow and the English authors. In this connexion the account of R. H. Mathews[3] is of interest, though it must be remembered that he is probably relying on information derived from others. Some of the Chingali believe in repeated reincarnations of ancestors, and a change of sex occurs each time;[4] others say that women are not reincarnated and consequently deny at any rate the change of sex; the northern Chingali deny the reincarnation creed altogether and come very near the doctrine set forth by Strehlow for the Aranda.

5. Other areas.—The totemism of Indonesia[5] and Oceania[6] has been traced both by Wilken and by Rivers to the belief that the sacrosanct animal species is the residence of ancestral souls. Transmigration theories are also found sporadically in New Guinea (*q.v.*) and N. and S. America. The Bororo Indians of Brazil believe that they become *arara* birds after death and in dreams; other tribes say they pass into other birds. The *arara* is kept as a pet and mourned at death, though the wild bird may be killed for its feathers; yet the Bororo say, 'We are *arara*.' According to von den Steinen, the earliest form of the belief was that the native said, 'I have a bird,' not 'I am a bird,' which flies at night and which remains as the natural form of the person when a magician or other evil-disposed being hinders his return to human form (*i.e.* causes his death). But it is only in parts of Australia and W. Africa that these forms of eschatological creed are an element of real importance.

LITERATURE.—J. G. Frazer, *GB*³, xii., *Bibliography and General Index*, *s.v.*; *RHR* xxxvii. [1898] 385; N. W. Thomas, *Anthropological Report on the Edo-Speaking Peoples of Nigeria*, 2 pts., London, 1910, *Anthropological Report on the Ibo-Speaking Peoples of Nigeria*, 6 pts., do. 1912–14; K. von den Steinen, *Unter den Naturvölkern Zentral-Brasiliens*, Berlin, 1894, pp. 353, 512; B. Hagen, *Unter den Papuas*, Wiesbaden, 1899, p. 225; A. van Gennep, *Tabou et totémisme à Madagascar*, Paris, 1904; *Baessler-Archiv*, ii. [1911] 73; M. Delafosse, *Haut-Sénégal-Niger*, Paris, 1912; C. Monteil, *Les Khassonké*, do. 1915; C. Strehlow, 'Die Aranda- und Loritja-Stämme in Zentral-Australien,' in *Veröff. städt. Völker-Museum Frankfurt a. M.*, 1908 ff., I. ii. [1908] 51 ff., etc.

N. W. THOMAS.

1 Spencer-Gillen^b, pp. 156 f., 161.
2 Spencer-Gillen^a, p. 445.
3 *Proc. Roy. Geog. Soc. Queensland*, xxii. [1907] 75 f.
4 Cf. Spencer-Gillen^b, p. 148.
5 See art. INDONESIANS.
6 See artt. AUSTRALASIA, MELANESIANS.

TRANSMIGRATION (Buddhist).—Theoretically Buddhism teaches neither the existence of the soul nor its transmigration, but insists on the revolution, or 'stream' (*saṁsāra*), of existences. In its practical influence on the popular mind, however, this doctrine amounted to much the same as any other doctrine of transmigration. It amalgamated everywhere with the animistic conception of the soul, whether human or other; it inspired the people with the feeling of a certain continuity of life-relationships through various existences; it impressed the popular mind with a degree of fatalism—the belief that every event in one's life was the result of past deeds. The doctrine, when formulated, contained more or less sensuous descriptions of the better lives in the heavens, besides horrifying details of purgatorial existences; and these aspects of the teaching resulted in the growth of a respectable volume of visionary literature during the course of the history of the religion in various countries.[1] Thus, in spite of the higher doctrine of the ideal Buddhist perfection in *nirvāṇa*, and in spite of the psychological and metaphysical formulations of the teaching of *karma* and *chitta*, the Buddhist conception of transmigration may be treated in the same category as other doctrines of the same kind.

According to the regular teaching, the *saṁsāra* consists in an indefinite revolution of renewed existences produced and prolonged according to the qualities of the *karma* (*q.v.*), which is the matrix as well as the *vis a tergo* of the enduring existences. It is said repeatedly:

'No beginning is known of the eternal revolution (*saṁsāra*) of the beings, streaming and flowing to and fro [in the ocean of births and deaths], being covered by ignorance (*avijjā*) and fettered in thirst (*taṇhā*).'[2]

In this vast ocean of renewed births there are innumerable streams of existences, conditioned by their respective deeds and retributions, flowing uninterruptedly not only in the continuity of the individual being but also in the solidarity of a group of existences. Now the groups of existences are classified into five *gatis* ('courses,' 'modes of life')—the heavenly life, the human life, the animal life, the ghostly life, and the purgatorial (or hellish) life; or into six, by adding the *asura* (or furious spirits).[3] Another classification is that of the *bhava* ('being') or *loka* ('realm,' the cosmic installation of beings) into three—the formless heavens, the heavens with forms, and the material worlds with desires and greed.[4] In this connexion it is to be noted that the Buddhist doctrine of transmigration emphasized the affinity and solidarity of the *karma* and all its consequences within a group of existences, whether a specific world in the cosmic system, the local division of the abode, or the class division in social life; in short, any and every link, material, physical, moral, emotional, intellectual, or social, is the cause and a manifestation of the solidarity of existence due to the common *karma*. The principle of the solid-

1 In *Saṁyutta-nikāya*, ii. 254–262, Mahā-Moggallāna, the great disciple of Buddha, well versed in supernormal attainments, narrates to his fellow-monk Lakkhana his visions of beings tortured and purified in the purgatories and the causes of their sufferings. Thence we have a long series of similar narratives, for which see, *e.g.*, the opening of the *Mahāvastu* (ed. E. Sénart, Paris, 1882–97, i.), or B. Nanjio, *A Catalogue of the Chinese Translation of the Buddhist Tripiṭaka*, Oxford, 1883, nos. 561, 677, 679, 706, etc.
2 *Saṁyutta-nikāya*, ii. 178 f., etc.
3 See art. COSMOGONY AND COSMOLOGY (Buddhist), esp. §§ 5–8
4 The five or six circles are graphically represented in the *bhavachakra* (the cycle of existence), for which see art. AJANTA, on the *Nidāna* (vol. i. p. 258^b).

arity is the *karma*, and its manifestation is the *bhava* or *dhātu*, the latter of which means the characteristics (common to the beings within a group), the specific circle of existence, community, common destiny.

How the different *dhātus* are produced; what are the reciprocal actions and reactions of the psychical factors and environmental factors in the process of the development of *karma*; what are the conditions of the individual *karma* being attracted to and incorporated into the common *dhātu*—these and associated questions gave rise to varied speculations in the Buddhist schools, the whole forming a web of subtle argument and grotesque fancy, in which are mingled Buddhist cosmology, psychology, ethics, and sociology. This is a subject which awaits further investigation.[1]

The practical effects of the Buddhist doctrine of *saṁsāra* were a deepening and broadening of the feeling of the continuity of life. Though often vulgarized through its amalgamation with animistic beliefs, the effect of the doctrine was to extend affection and attachment in human relationships to the former and coming lives, even to animal and plant life, which was held to be continuous and closely associated with human life, and to elaborate those sentiments through the belief in deeper causes, remoter connexions, and wider aspects of being than those of the present life.

This point can be illustrated from the folk-lore and literature of every Buddhist people, and one of the flowers of romantic literature—the Japanese literature of the 11th cent.—is dominated by this sentiment of continuity. There the delicate yet strong tie of human affection was associated with the idea of its continuity through lives beyond death, as well as with the idea of nature as inspired by physical surroundings and their changes. Unfortunately both W. G. Aston and Karl Florenz, in their histories of Japanese literature, hardly touch this point.

Another point in the effect of the teaching of *saṁsāra* is the belief in the occasional appearance of persons who can remember their former lives. In fact, it seems that Buddha himself regarded this faculty as one of his supernormal attainments (*iddhi*) and one of the criteria of saintliness. Everywhere in Buddhist literature we find mention of the three special faculties (*tevijjā*)—the divine vision, the divine hearing, and the clear recalling of one's former lives (*pubbenivāsa*). This belief gave rise to a rich literature of *Jātaka* (*q.v.*) and the allied literature of *Nidāna* and *Avadāna*, which aimed at supplying that belief with concrete illustrations and impressing believers with the close association of the lives of Buddha and Buddhist saints with those of all other beings, besides inculcating morals by the stories. Thus it was no wonder that some persons claimed to have the same faculty, whether by chance or as a result of training. The folk-lore and legends of Buddhist countries are full of instances, and a noteworthy point in them is that many of those endowed persons are children, whose remembrance of their own former lives is mostly said to lose its vividness as they grow older.[2]

LITERATURE.—See artt. COSMOGONY AND COSMOLOGY (Buddhist), JĀTAKA, KARMA, and the literature cited there.

M. ANESAKI.

TRANSMIGRATION (Celtic).—**I.** There are two passages which clearly assert the belief in metempsychosis among the ancient Celts. Cæsar (*de Bell. Gall.* vi. 14) tells us that the principal point in the teaching of the druids is that the soul does not perish, but, after death, passes from one body into another. Diodorus completes the evidence of Cæsar and states it precisely:

'Among the Galatæ [Gauls or Germans] the doctrine of Pythagoras prevails, namely, that the souls of men are immortal and after a fixed number of years begin to live again, the soul entering into a second body' (v. 28).

But is Diodorus giving the teaching of Pythagoras or that of the Celts? If the former, it would be wise to attach only a relative importance to the precision of his words; if the latter, it must be admitted that, according to the belief of the Celts, the passage of the soul into another body does not follow immediately upon death, and that, while the soul awaits its reincarnation, it continues to live, though under conditions which are not those of the life on earth. This interpretation would make it possible to reconcile the passages in Cæsar and Diodorus with the evidence of ancient writers who have transmitted Celtic conceptions regarding the future life in which the idea of metempsychosis does not occur.

Diodorus goes on to say:

'Therefore, during the funerals of the dead, they throw into the funeral pyre letters written to the dead relatives in the expectation that the dead will read them.'

It seems, therefore, that the man whose body was burned acted as a messenger between the living and the ancestors whom he was about to meet again in the other world. It is the idea of the immortality of the soul and of another world that is emphasized by the Latin writers.

Valerius Maximus (II. vi. 10) tells that there was an ancient custom among the Gauls of lending each other sums which were repayable in the lower world, so firmly were they persuaded of the immortality of the soul. Pomponius Mela (iii. 2), after stating that, according to the druids, the soul is eternal and that there is a second life among the *manes*, adds that they burn and bury along with the dead things which are useful to the living, and that, formerly, they postponed the settlement of business affairs and debts until the time when debtors and creditors would meet in the lower world; there were even people who voluntarily cast themselves into the funeral pyre of their kindred in the expectation that they would rejoin them in the new life. The idea of a new life after death and before reincarnation was thus one of the most cherished and deep-seated beliefs of the ancient Celts. As to where that new life was spent, Valerius Maximus and Pomponius Mela employ the ordinary terms of Roman mythology for the other world (*inferos, manes*); but Lucan is not content with that superficial assimilation:

'You assure us, Druids, that it is not the silent dwellings of Erebus nor the pale kingdoms of Dis who inhabits the depths, at which the souls arrive; the same breath directs their members in another world ['orbe alio'], and, if your songs declare what can be known, death is in the heart of a long life' (*Pharsalia*, i. 449–456).

There has been an endeavour to fix the meaning of 'orbe alio.' In the Latin of the time of Lucan it can mean only 'another region of the earth' and not 'another celestial globe' (see S. Reinach, *RCel* xxii. [1901] 454).

The commentaries on the few and vague Greek and Latin texts which bear upon the ancient Celtic belief in metempsychosis do not lead to any further precision. In particular, we cannot determine whether the teaching of the Celts was borrowed from the Pythagorean school. Such was, however, a tradition of antiquity. The passage from Diodorus quoted above lacks clearness, but as early as the beginning of the 1st cent. B.C. Alexander Polyhistor (frag. 138 [*FHG* iii. 239]) wrote that Pythagoras had the Gauls (Γαλάτας) as disciples. Timagenes (*ap.* Ammianus Marcellinus, xv. 9) seems to connect the organization of the druidic corporations with Pythagoras with regard to the doctrine of the immortality of the soul. Valerius Maximus (II. vi.) declares that he would consider the belief in the immortality of the soul a foolish thing if it were not for the fact that the belief of the Gauls on that matter agreed with that of Pythagoras. But the Celtic doctrine, though showing analogies with the Pythagorean doctrine, was not identical with it: it did not distinguish between the fate of the wicked and

[1] Cf. *Saṁyutta-nikāya*, ii. 140–177, and artt. ABHIDHARMA KOŚA VYĀKHYĀ, COSMOGONY AND COSMOLOGY (Buddhist).

[2] See Lafcadio Hearn, *Gleanings in Buddha-Fields*, Boston and New York, 1897, ch. x.; H. Fielding, *The Soul of a People*, London, 1898, pp. 324–343.

that of the just; the other life is neither a punishment nor a recompense, and, in fact, the idea of justice is entirely absent from the Celtic conception.

2. We have another source of information in the legends preserved by Irish epics, which tell of historical personages and seem for the most part to be anterior to Christianity.

In the middle of the 6th cent. of our era St. Finnen met at Mag Bile (Moville, Co. Down) a warrior named Túan Mac Cairill, who lived all alone in his den; at first he would not allow the saint and his disciples to enter his dwelling, but he ended by making them welcome and showing them hospitality. They refused to accept anything from him, however, until he had told them of his adventures, which were by no means ordinary. Túan Mac Cairill had come from Spain to Ireland 312 years after the Flood along with the first inhabitants, Partholon, the son of Sera, and 24 couples. When the number of immigrants had increased to 5000, an epidemic destroyed them one after another, until only one survived to tell the tale, that one being Túan Mac Cairill. For 22 years he was the only inhabitant in Ireland; then Nemed, son of Agnoman, who also came from Spain, landed on the island, after a storm, with four men and four women. On his arrival Túan went into hiding; he fasted for three days, and, having lain down to sleep one night, he awoke in the morning in the form of a stag. He led the herds of deer in Ireland until the extinction of the race of Nemed. Then he became a boar, and remained in that shape as long as the men of Semion, son of Stariat, from whom the Firbolg are descended, were in possession of Ireland. He next became a vulture during the reign of Beothach, son of Iarbonel, an ancestor of the Tuatha Dé Danann; and, once more, a fish, when the sons of Milé conquered Ireland. One day he was caught by a fisherman, brought to the wife of king Cairell, cooked, and eaten by her. At the end of the usual period he was born again as an infant and was called Mac Cairill, *i.e.* son of Cairell. Up to his second birth as a man Túan had lived 320 years: 100 as a man, 80 as a stag, 20 as a boar, 100 as a vulture, and 20 as a fish.

Certain details of this metempsychosis should be noticed: in all his successive shapes Túan preserved the consciousness and recollection of his previous existences, and his human intelligence persisted during his lives in the bodies of animals; his metamorphosis took place only when he had reached the extreme limits of old age and decrepitude; it occurred only in the neighbourhood of the house in which he lived during his first life as a man; and, finally, his change of body took place only after a fast of three days.

There is another Irish legend dealing with metempsychosis, though in a less varied and definite manner than that of Túan—the history of Mongán, son of Fiachna.

One day Mongán had a discussion with his *fili*, Forgoll, as to where king Fothad Airgdech, who was slain by the Fian Caoilte, had fallen. It was agreed that if, in the space of three days, Mongán failed to prove that Fothad had fallen at the river Larne in Ulster, and not at Duffry in Leinster, as Forgoll maintained, his goods and his person should become the property of the *fili*. Mongán's wife broke into lamentations which increased as the time went on, but Mongán waited calmly in the firm belief that a witness would come from a distant country to attest the truth of his statement; for Mongán heard the steps of the mysterious traveller from afar. On the third day, at nightfall, a warrior appeared, who, when brought into the presence of Forgoll, pointed out the exact spot where Fothad had been buried, and even gave the inscription on his tomb. While narrating the death of Fothad, the warrior called Mongán as witness to the truth of his story, and named him by the name of Fionn. The warrior was Caoilte, and Mongán was thus a reincarnation of Fionn, living about three centuries after him. The legend gives us no information about the incarnations of Fionn between the end of his first life and his reincarnation in Mongán, but probably they were similar to those of Túan Mac Cairill.

Other Irish legends allude to cases of metamorphosis, but they do not seem to take place at the end of a life. There are also epic stories presenting beings which have had a second birth, but those beings belong to the world of fairies and have no bearing upon the study of human metempsychosis.

3. The Welsh romances also contain numerous examples of metamorphosis. Perhaps there are traces of metempsychosis in the romance of Taliesin, in which he tells in verse of all the places where he has been since the beginning of the world, and in the poem entitled *Kat Goddeu* ('Battle of Goddeu'), in which the poet enumerates all the shapes which he has taken: sword, star, book, eagle, ship, serpent, etc. But the story of Taliesin is preserved only in MSS of the 17th cent., and the ancient poems attributed to the celebrated bard of the 6th cent. cannot be earlier than the 12th. It is difficult to disentangle the real archaic elements contained in them.

To sum up: it is practically only in the texts of the writers of antiquity that definite evidence is found of a Celtic belief in metempsychosis: among the Irish, metempsychosis is an exceptional phenomenon, a kind of privilege enjoyed by heroes; what we find among the Welsh is a literary tradition rather than the traces of an ancient belief. Whatever may be the ingenuity of modern scholars, it cannot on this subject make up for the lack of documentary evidence.

LITERATURE.—H. d'Arbois de Jubainville, *Le Cycle mythologique irlandais et la mythologie celtique* (*Cours de littérature celtique*, ii.), Paris, 1884; *The Voyage of Bran, son of Febal*, ed. K. Meyer, 'With an Essay upon the Irish Vision of the happy Otherworld and the Celtic Doctrine of Rebirth,' by A. Nutt, London, 1895–97.

G. DOTTIN.

TRANSMIGRATION (Egyptian).—There are three different ideas which refer to changes of personality: (1) the union with a god, (2) the transmigration of the soul into an animal for a life-time, (3) the voluntary metamorphosis of the person temporarily into another form for his own benefit.

(1) The *divine union* is often stated in the *Book of the Dead*, as 'I am Ra' or 'I am Thoth'; this was the person entering into such union with the god that he had all the compelling power and safety of the god. Even in the earliest inscriptions, on the cylinders before the 1st dynasty, the dead is *sen*, or brother, to a god; or *sensen*, allied, associated, in touch, or united, with a god.

(2) The question of *transmigration* has been disputed. The Greek authors refer to it as an undoubted belief; but there seems to be no Egyptian text which refers to the idea. Two scenes have been supposed to indicate it; these are judgment scenes (Seti I. sarcophagus and tomb of Rameses III.)[1] showing a pig being driven from the judgment. Yet, as referring to justified men, it cannot be the soul driven away as a pig. In most judgment scenes there is present the devouring monster, a blend of hippopotamus and crocodile, waiting to devour the guilty; but no such monster appears where the pig is, and so it seems likely that the pig is the flesh-eating animal, driven away so as to be quite apart from the justified king. The Greek testimony is so strong that it seems unlikely to have all been derived from the metamorphoses. As all the authors are post-Persian, it is possible that the idea really did blend with Egyptian belief during the Persian occupation, when other Indian ideas came into Egypt, such as asceticism. Transmigration is plainly stated in the *Korē Kosmou*, of the Persian period, probably about 500 B.C.[2] After this it is natural that the Greek writers, Herodotus, Plato, Theophrastus, Plutarch, and others, should ascribe the belief to the Egyptians of their times, unconscious that it was a new importation.[3]

(3) The belief in *metamorphosis* (*q.v.*) was general, as a magic process. The earliest Egyptian tale turns on a wax model being transformed into a living crocodile. The *Book of the Dead* has a series of magic chapters (76–89) to give power to the dead person to be transformed into 'whatever form he pleases,' into a golden hawk, a divine hawk, a god, a lily, the god Ptah, a phœnix, a heron, a swallow,

[1] I. Rosellini, *Monumenti del Culto*, lxvi., Pisa, 1834; J. G. Wilkinson, *The Manners and Customs of the Ancient Egyptians*, new ed., London, 1878, iii. 467.

[2] W. M. Flinders Petrie, *Personal Religion in Egypt before Christianity*, London and New York, 1909, pp. 43, 47.

[3] See passages quoted in Wilkinson, iii. 462–464.

an earth-worm, or a crocodile; and lastly the power of being united to its own body. The following examples are parts of chs. 86, 89, and all of 88:

'I am the Swallow; I am the Swallow. I am the Scorpion-bird (or white bird), the daughter of Rā. . . . And that which I went in order to ascertain, I am come to tell. Come, let me enter and report my mission. And I, entering, and ascertaining who cometh forth through that gate of the Inviolate one, I purify myself at that great stream, where my ills are made to cease, and that which is wrong in me is pardoned, and the spots which were on my body upon earth are effaced. . . . Here am I, and I come that I may overthrow mine adversaries upon earth, though my dead body be buried' (86). 'For I am the Crocodile god in all his terrors. I am the Crocodile god in the form of man. I am he who carrieth off with violence. I am the almighty Fish in Kamurit. I am the Lord to whom one bendeth down in Sechem' (88). 'Oh, thou who bringest; oh, thou runner who dwellest in thy Keep, thou great god; grant that my soul may come to me from whatsoever place wherein it abideth. . . . Let my soul (*ba*) be caught and the spirit (*khu*) which is with it, wheresoever it abideth. Track out among the things in heaven and upon earth that soul of mine, wherever it abideth . . .' (89).

LITERATURE.—J. H. Breasted, *Development of Religion and Thought in Ancient Egypt*, London, 1912, p. 277, and works quoted above.

W. M. FLINDERS PETRIE.

TRANSMIGRATION (Greek and Roman).—I. *GREEK*.—The notion of transmigration (παλιγγενεσία),[1] *i.e.* the passage after death of the human or animal soul from the mortal body to a new incarnation in another body of the same or another species, necessarily rests upon a belief that the soul itself is immortal, or at any rate more lasting than the body. Pherecydes,[2] who was born about 600 B.C. and is reputed to have been the teacher of Pythagoras[3]—which does not necessarily mean more than that he was earlier in time—is said to have been the first to introduce the doctrine. On the other hand, Herodotus[4] declared that it was the invention of the Egyptians and was derived from them by those Greeks who adopted it, and whose names, though he knew them, he declined to mention. It has been recognized that this is an allusion, at least in part, to Empedocles; for Herodotus would have had no scruple in giving the names of Pherecydes and Pythagoras, who were already dead. It is, however, impossible to accept Herodotus' account, because (1) the best authorities are inclined to doubt whether the Egyptians ever held the doctrine in question,[5] and (2) the Greek evidence indicates that the belief, if not indigenous, goes back to a remote past. Moreover, the notion that Pythagoras was influenced by Indian modes of thought with which he became acquainted in Ionia or elsewhere[6] is altogether unconvincing. The truth seems to be that a belief in the transmigration of human souls into other bodies after death was a relic inherited from the primitive or savage ancestors of the European peoples. It is expressly attributed to the Gauls,[7] and less explicitly to the Thracians and Scythians.[8] In fact it must have developed independently in many parts of the world,[9] without direct transmission from place to place, especially in connexion with the idea that the limited supply of souls necessitates the reappearance of the same soul in various earthly bodies. Thus in popular tales the change of a man into a beast involves the assumption that, though the body is different, the soul remains the same; *e.g.*, in the metamorphosis of Odysseus' companions into swine their intelligence remained unaffected.[10] Not that this popular tradition ever became widely effective: except for

1 Serv. on *Æn.* iii. 68.
2 Suid. *s.v.*
3 Diog. Laert. i. 118, viii. 40.
4 ii. 123.
5 How and Wells, *A Commentary on Herodotus*, London, 1912, *ad loc.*; cf. art. TRANSMIGRATION (Egyptian).
6 T. Gomperz, *Greek Thinkers*, Eng. tr., London, 1901, i. 127.
7 Cæs. *de Bell Gall.* vi. 14; Diod. v. 28.
8 Pomp. Mela, ii. 18.
9 *PC* ii. 2 ff.
10 Hom. *Od.* x. 240 and the schol.

one not very clear example,[1] stone inscriptions show no trace of a belief in transmigration, while Euripides refers to a second incarnation as an actual impossibility, whose realization might have been welcome as a divine instrument of discrimination between the good and the bad.[2] But, although there is nothing to show that the belief struck deep, or was cherished outside certain particular circles, it was brought into prominence by the religious upheaval which undoubtedly took place in the 6th cent. and became associated with the worship of Dionysus and the Orphic cults. Thus the notion that the soul is imprisoned in the body as in a dungeon is attributed by Plato and his commentators to the Orphic mystics.[3] Two famous passages in Pindar presuppose the doctrine of transmigration. In one of these Persephone sends the souls back to earth in the ninth year when they have been purified from their ancient sorrow;[4] and in the other those who have thrice made their abode on either side of death are destined at last to reach the islands of the blest.[5] It seems more likely that Pindar derived this doctrine from the Orphic mysteries than indirectly through the Pythagoreans.[6] The prevalence of this mystical belief and its religious potency are illustrated with remarkable clearness in certain inscriptions on golden tablets found in S. Italy, near Rome, and in Crete, which are chiefly attributed to the 4th or 5th centuries B.C. and published as an Appendix to J. E. Harrison's *Prolegomena to the Study of Greek Religion*, Cambridge, 1903, p. 660 ff. One of these contains some words which form part of the appeal of the purified soul: 'I have flown out of the sorrowful weary Wheel; I have passed with eager feet to the Circle desired.' This refers to the mystical Wheel of Fortune which in its revolutions symbolizes the cycle of successive lives necessary to be traversed by the harassed soul before its final release. This specific cycle of progress, as well as the more general conception of a κύκλος in human affairs, is traditionally attributed to the Orphic-Pythagorean sphere of thought.[7] In the Orphic hymns[8] this has so far developed as to include a statement that an exact reproduction of the movements characteristic of the present world-era may be expected when the revolving wheel comes round to the same point again; but it is not easy to reconcile this with the opportunity which, as we have seen, is given to particular souls to obtain their release.[9] Aristotle's reference to the Orphic poems as an authority for the opinion that the soul enters the body from outside in the process of respiration accords well enough with the doctrine now under discussion.[10] Further, the Orphic prohibition of a diet of animal flesh, evidenced by Euripides and Aristophanes,[11] points in the same direction.

In popular estimation[12] transmigration is particularly associated with the name of **Pythagoras.** Much of what has been established as belonging to the Orphics, the imprisonment of the soul in the body as a retribution for past ill-deeds, the undeviating recurrence of the cycle of existence,[13] the prospect offered of ultimate escape after purification,[14] and the abstinence from a flesh diet—limited, however, by the reservation that it did not apply to the flesh of such animals as are

1 *Epigr.* ed. G. Kaibel, Berlin, 1878, p. 304.
2 *Herc. Fur.* 653 ff.
3 *Phæd.* 62 B, *Cratyl.* 400 C.
4 Frag. 96 Schr.
5 *Ol.* ii. 68.
6 E. Zeller, *Pre-Socratic Philosophy*, Eng. tr., London, 1881, i. 71; but see schol. on v. 104.
7 See a note by the present writer on Soph. frag. 871.
8 Frag. 225.
9 Frag. 226.
10 *De Anim.* I. v. 410*b* 28.
11 *Hipp.* 951; *Ran.* 1032.
12 Cf. Shakespeare, *Merchant of Venice*, IV. i. 131, *Twelfth Night*, IV. ii. 54.
13 Diog. Laert. viii. 14; Zeller, i. 474, note 2.
14 E. Rohde, *Psyche*[5], Tübingen, 1910, p. 165, note 2.

offered in sacrifice to the Olympian gods[1]—is established for the Pythagoreans by not less convincing testimony. It would seem, therefore, that, when founding his brotherhood, Pythagoras appropriated much that was characteristic of contemporary religious asceticism. Nevertheless the reincarnation of souls in various bodily shapes is so closely associated with the person of Pythagoras that he must be held to have inculcated it with peculiar vigour. There is a good deal of legendary matter relating to him, most of which can be traced to the authority of Heraclides Ponticus.[2]

To this source we owe the famous story that it was permitted to Pythagoras to retain the memory of his previous incarnations, and that he established his credibility on the occasion of a visit to the Heræum at Argos by identifying as his own, before seeing the inscription, the shield of Euphorbus, son of Panthus, which he was bearing when slain by Menelaus before the walls of Troy.[3] Heraclides was also responsible for the statement that Pythagoras claimed to have lived as Æthalides, the son of Hermes and herald of the Argonauts, before he became Euphorbus, that as Æthalides he obtained from his father Hermes the offer of any gift he might choose save immortality, and that thus he received the privilege of remembering his previous fortune while on the earth and in Hades. After Euphorbus died, he became Hermotimus and subsequently Pyrrhus, the Delian fisherman, before his final re-birth as Pythagoras.[4] Further, Pythagoras declared that after the lapse of every 207 years his soul returned to the light of the sun.[5] Accordingly, if the birth of Pythagoras is placed in 572, the date of Euphorbus will be 1193 and of Æthalides 1400.

There is, however, much better evidence than these fables that Pythagoras seriously taught the doctrine in the almost contemporary verses of Xenophanes:[6] they say that once, as he was passing by, he pitied a dog that was being beaten and exclaimed: 'Beat him no more; for his soul is my friend's, as I recognized when I heard his voice.' It was therefore his belief that the same soul could dwell in a beast as in a man, and that there is a universal kinship between all living things.[7] He did not hesitate to ascribe reasonable souls to animals, holding that the activity of their reason was impeded by the unsuitability for its exercise of their physical organs.[8] Aristotle describes the possibility of any soul taken at random passing into any body as a Pythagorean fable.[9] The punishment of souls for their misdeeds by successive incarnations in corporeal dungeons was a theme developed by the Pythagoreans in a manner hardly to be separated from the Orphic,[10] and the results of their joint influence are to be found in the Platonic myths.

Empedocles in his poem entitled 'Purifications' (καθαρμοί) took over the doctrine of transmigration from the Orphic-Pythagorean school without making any attempt to combine it with his philosophical system. Indeed it is difficult to see how it was possible for him to advocate the immortality of the soul consistently with his doctrine that the vitality of the soul is the result of an aggregation of corporeal substances. Thought and consciousness are concentrated in the blood which envelops the heart.[11] Aristotle's assertion that, according to Empedocles, the soul is compacted from all the elements[12] is generally discredited as a misconception; and his further remark in the same passage that each of the elements is soul is equally misleading. But, even if the materialism

1 Iambl. *Vit. Pyth.* 85; Aristoxenus, *ap.* Diog. Laert. viii. 20, makes the prohibition apply only to the ram and the plough-ox.
2 Pauly-Wissowa, viii. 476.
3 Hor. *Od.* I. xxviii. 10; Ov. *Met.* xv. 160 ff.; schol. Hom. *Il.* xvii. 28.
4 Diog. Laert. viii. 4, 5; schol. Ap. Rhod. i. 645; schol. Soph. *El.* 62.
5 Diog. Laert. 14.
6 B 7 Diels.
7 Porph. *Vit. Pyth.* 19.
8 Aët. *Plac.* v. xx. 4 (H. Diels, *Doxographi Græci*, Berlin, 1879, p. 432, 15).
9 *De Anim.* i. 3. 407*b* 22.
10 For an attempt to distinguish Pythagoreanism from Orphism see F. M. Cornford, *From Religion to Philosophy*, London, 1912, p. 198 ff.
11 B 105 Diels.
12 *De Anim.* i. 2. 404*b* 11.

of Empedocles is somewhat less explicit than is sometimes represented, logical justification is still to seek for his pronouncement concerning the punishment of guilty souls in a purgatory lasting for 30,000 years[1] and his personal experience of the wretchedness of the wandering spirit which is harassed by its weary passage through air and sea and earth: 'Ere now have I been a youth and a maiden, a bush and a dumb fish in the sea.'[2] A discrimination of the degrees of transgression is involved in the assignment of the less base souls to the higher forms of animal or plant life: these inhabit the bodies of lions among beasts or appear as bay trees in the world of vegetation.[3] The best of them become prophets, bards, physicians, and chieftains, and at last return as divine beings to the company of the gods.[4] As a consequence of this doctrine Empedocles, like the Pythagoreans, prohibited the eating of flesh and the slaughter of animals, which he stigmatized as the shedding of kindred blood, the murder of a son by his father or of a father by his son.[5]

In several of his dialogues, particularly in the *Phædo*, *Phædrus*, *Republic*, and *Timæus*, **Plato** associates the doctrines of the immortality and pre-existence of the soul with its transmigration. The variations to be found in his descriptions are not of serious moment and do not admit of being discussed in detail.

According to the *Phædo*,[6] those who in this life have failed to emancipate themselves from the burden of the corporeal element cannot rise to the purer element above, but, being dragged down into the visible world, haunt burial grounds as ghostly apparitions until they are again imprisoned in another body. Of these the sensual become asses or similar animals, the violent and unjust wolves or kites, but those who, though lacking the philosophic impulse to virtue, have lived an ordinary respectable life may become bees or ants, or even men who in their next incarnation prove themselves just and moderate. Only those who have devoted themselves in this life to philosophy are entirely exempt from any further incarnation and pass to the pure ethereal homes destined for them in the upper world.[7] In the *Phædrus*[8] the souls of the dead are punished or otherwise treated according to the measure of their human actions for 1000 years, until the period of reincarnation arrives, when they are allowed a limited area of choice, so that it often happens that the soul of a man comes into life as a beast, and that of a beast which had formerly been human again enters into the body of a man. A much more elaborate account is given in the myth of Er the son of Armenius, how a great variety of choice comprising the lives of every animal and of men in every condition is offered to the allottees whose time for reincarnation has arrived. The order of choice is determined by ballot, but even the soul which drew the last lot had plenty of opportunities for selection left. The narrator of the myth was a witness of the choices made by some of the famous heroes of antiquity; how Orpheus chose to be a swan, Thamyras a nightingale, Ajax a lion, Agamemnon an eagle, and Thersites a monkey, while Odysseus, who drew the last lot, wearied of his former ambition, was delighted to find still available for him the life of an ordinary man free from all anxiety.[9] In the *Timæus*[10] the creator fashions as many souls as there are stars, and distributes one to each star, in order that later, after a period of contemplation, they may be embodied in human form. If during the time of probation the soul lived well, he would return to his ethereal habitation; but, if he failed, he would suffer a new incarnation as a woman; and, if his wickedness continued, he would sink down among the beasts until his corporeal taints had been thoroughly purged away. In the same dialogue Plato explains the evolution of birds and other animals as arising from the deterioration of human souls. Birds, with their feathers taking the place of hair, are developed from men who are harmless but light-minded. The four-footed beasts of the earth were originally men who had never given themselves up to the study of philosophy, since they no longer heeded the revolutions in the head, but followed the impulses of those parts of the soul which are situated in the breast.[11]

Critics have not been entirely agreed as to how far Plato was a serious believer in transmigration,[12] some holding that the entire description was purely a play of fancy, and others that, though he may have credited the successive incarnations

1 B 115, 6 Diels.
2 B 117 Diels.
3 B 127 Diels.
4 B 146, 147 Diels.
5 B 136, 137 Diels.
6 81 E.
7 *Ib.* 114 C.
8 249 B.
9 *Republic*, 617 D–620 D.
10 41 D.
11 *Ib.* 91 E.
12 See the authorities quoted by J. Adam in his note on *Rep.* 618 A.

of human souls, he cannot have extended his belief to their passage into animal shapes. It should of course be noticed that all these descriptions, if not actually parts of a myth, have a mythical colouring, and must be read subject to the warning given by the Platonic Socrates in the *Phædo* :[1]

'No sensible man will affirm that these matters took place exactly in the way that I have described. But to hold that either this or something like it is the truth in regard to our souls and their habitations, appears to me, *now that the soul has been shown to be immortal*, to be no unreasonable or unworthy venture.'

So long as this limitation is borne in mind, there is no valid reason for mistrusting Plato's sincerity.

Transmigration does not cohere with the Stoic doctrine of the soul's nature; but there are some grounds for thinking that **Posidonius** held the pre-existence and immortality of the soul in the limited sense in which it was possible for a Stoic to affirm them consistently with a belief in the ἐκπύρωσις.[2] It was, moreover, natural that a Stoic should speak of a periodic reincarnation[3] as a consequence of the dogma that every conflagration introduces a new era in which the experience of the past will be exactly repeated. But that either Posidonius or any of the Stoics believed in a series of successive incarnations within the limits of the current world-period is, notwithstanding the isolated statements of certain of the doxographical sources,[4] open to very grave doubt.[5]

According to **Plotinus**, the future destiny of the soul depends on the use it has made of its several functions and capacities during each particular incarnation. Hence we should constantly strive upward, not yielding to the images of sense or carnal cravings.

Thus he who has exercised his human capacities again becomes a man, but those who have lived by sensation alone become animals. If, without yielding to active passion, they have remained immersed in sluggish perversity, they may even become plants.[6] There is always retribution for an ill-spent life: the bad master becomes a slave, the abuser of wealth a poor man; the man who has murdered his mother becomes a woman and is murdered by a son.[7] On the other hand, those souls which are pure and have lost their attraction to the corporeal will cease to be dependent upon body. So detached, they will pass to the region of being and the divinity, which cannot be apprehended by a human vision as if it were akin to the corporeal.[8]

II. *ROMAN*.—There is no evidence among the Romans of an indigenous belief in transmigration, but several of their poets acknowledged the influence of Greek speculation, and of Plato and Pythagoras in particular. Horace mentions[9] the 'Pythagorean dreams' of Ennius, who thought that his soul had once inhabited the body of Homer and earlier that of a peacock.[10] Vergil, in a famous passage,[11] takes more serious notice of Pythagoreanism, when he describes the purification of souls in the under world, and their return to human bodies after the completion of the cycle of 1000 years. Ovid[12] introduces Pythagoras himself making an eloquent appeal against the slaughter of animal life, based upon the identity of the soul-substance which permeates our bodies and theirs.

LITERATURE.—The best sources of information are the works of E. Rohde, T. Gomperz, and E. Zeller mentioned above. For Pythagoras see art. PYTHAGORAS; also A. E. Chaignet, *Pythagore et la philosophie pythagoricienne*, 2 vols., Paris, 1873; and for Plato J. A. Stewart, *Myths of Plato*, Oxford, 1905; and E. S. Thompson's ed. of Plato, *Meno*, London, 1901, pp. 286-297.

A. C. PEARSON.

TRANSMIGRATION (Indian).—The doctrine of the transmigration of souls is in India the presumption which underlies not only Buddhism and Jainism, but also the philosophical systems of the Brāhmans and the whole of Hinduism. In the ancient Vedic period it had as yet no existence. At that time the Indian peoples were still filled with a keen delight in life, and the righteous man looked forward to eternal continuance of existence after death. They believed that good men ascended to heaven to the companionship of the gods, and there led a painless existence, free from all earthly imperfections—a happy life, which was usually depicted as an enjoyment of sensual pleasures, but was yet occasionally conceived in a higher spiritual sense. The necessary consequence of this belief was the view (very rarely expressed in the Veda) that the souls of the wicked sank down into the abyss of hell. This naive representation of the soul's fate after death experienced a real change when, suddenly and without any transitional stages that we can perceive, the Indian people was seized by the oppressive belief in transmigration, which holds it captive to the present day. The conviction that every individual enters again after death upon a new existence, in which he gathers the fruit of merit earlier acquired, and has to endure the consequences of sins previously committed, meets us for the first time in a work belonging to the second period of Indian literature, the *Śatapatha Brāhmaṇa*, 'the Brāhmaṇa of the hundred ways.' Since then this thought has been regarded in India as a doctrine that needs no proof, which only the adherents of a crude materialism could doubt. It is a significant fact—to which H. Oldenberg first drew attention—that belief in transmigration at its very first appearance in the literature assumed the form of the harassing thought of a continual recurrence of death. How this belief, which lies at the root of Indian pessimism, could take the place apparently immediately of the innocent joy in life which greets us in the ancient times in the hymns of the Rigveda is an interesting question, but one that can be answered with only a certain measure of probability. Certainly the Indian doctrine of transmigration is not to be derived from one definite source alone; there are undoubtedly several streams of thought, which hardly admit of being definitely traced, but which were distinct in their origin. In order to ascertain the main source, we must have recourse to general folk-lore.

Among peoples in a low stage of civilization in very many parts of the earth there is found the belief that the souls of men after death pass into the trunks of trees or the bodies of animals, but especially into the bodies of birds, reptiles, and insects. Hence a choice is open to us between the following alternatives. We must suppose either that the Aryans of India, when they came into closer contact with the rude aboriginal inhabitants of the Indian peninsula, received from them the idea of the continued existence of men in animals and trees, and appropriated it to themselves; or that this conception had maintained its hold upon the lower strata of the Aryan people themselves from savage times, and then in an age adapted to constructive speculation thoughtful men had set themselves to develop from it the theory of transmigration. The second of these two possibilities is the more probable. Whatever view, however, may be accepted as correct, under any circumstances the primitive belief—whether it be that of the Indian aboriginal tribes or that of the lower strata of the Aryan people—gave merely the first impulse to the formation of the doctrine of transmigration; for no primitive people possesses more than the conception of the immediate prolongation of human existence in animals and trees. Among

[1] 114 D.
[2] A. Schmekel, *Die Philosophie der mittleren Stoa*, Berlin, 1892, pp. 250-255.
[3] M. Ant. xi. 1.
[4] Diels, *Doxographi Græci*, pp. 175, 571. 19, 587. 19, 614. 13.
[5] Rohde, ii. 325 n.
[6] *Enn.* iii. 4. 2.
[7] *Ib.* iii. 2. 13.
[8] *Ib.* iv. 3. 24.
[9] *Epist.* II. i. 51.
[10] Pers. vi. 10.
[11] *Æn.* vi. 748.
[12] *Met.* xv. 98-142, 153-258.

the Aryans of India the theory, as it meets us for the first time in the literature, appears already fully formed in the shape of belief in a permanently continued but ever-changing existence. And the different forms under which the individual lives are in their rank, and the measure of happiness or misery which they experience is regarded as dependent on moral conduct. At the basis of the Indian conception of transmigration lies the immovable conviction that there is no unmerited happiness and no unmerited misery, that each man shapes his own fortune down to the smallest details. This conviction has given to the Indian people a power to endure suffering which has often enough excited the wonder of foreign observers.

Since the Indian recognized that no explanation of the apportionment of happiness and misery, of joy and sorrow, by the moral state of the individual was to be found in the present life, he concluded that man's fate is determined by his good and evil deeds in a former existence. A moral qualification, therefore, according to this view, attaches to the soul; and this corresponds exactly to the sum of its good and evil deeds, and demands reward or punishment in the next existence, if not in the present.

Granted, then, that we endure in the present life the consequences of our own behaviour in the past, the conditions must have been precisely the same in the previous existence; the joy and sorrow that we experienced therein were again the consequences of our own actions in a preceding life, and so on without end. For that part of the individual, therefore, which was involved in the cycle of existences no beginning could be assigned. It was thus that quite early in India the theory of the endless pre-existence of the soul was developed; and the doctrine of the soul's eternal duration in the future was inferred according to the law that that which is without beginning is also endless, and in accordance with the ancient popular view of the permanence of personal existence in heaven. The belief in the eternity of soul was followed by belief in the eternal existence of the universe.

Life for the ease-loving Indian was overshadowed by the belief in transmigration. The thought of wandering perpetually through the bodies of men, animals, and plants, of being compelled in each existence to experience more pain than joy, and perpetually to renew the pangs of death, occasionally also to sojourn for a time in hell—this thought must have been dreadful for the Indian. Nor would he be sufficiently compensated by the prospect of being able to gain heaven by his merit, and to raise himself to divine honours. For with the very ascent to divine honours no more than a transitory success has been gained. Even the gods, according to the transmigration theory, are involved in the cycle of existence, the *saṁsāra*, and must again descend to lower forms of life when their time comes round, that is, when the power of former merit is exhausted through the enjoyment of divine position and honours. The popular gods, therefore, have ceased to be eternal and omnipotent beings, as they were in Vedic times.

According to this view, therefore, the wheel of existence rolls on without rest or intermission, and hurries living creatures perpetually to renewed suffering and renewed death. Naturally, then, the question must have been raised whether there is no deliverance, no release, from this constantly renewed existence upon earth.

The hypothesis that once in the course of time the previous deeds of a living being may meet with their complete reward or punishment, and that, therefore, the basis for a re-birth may and will disappear, was not made in India. According to the Indian view, when a living being dies there always remains a remnant of merit and guilt still unrewarded and unpunished, from which is derived the germ of a new existence. Even sacrifice and deeds of piety or asceticism cannot deliver from the necessity of renewed birth and death. In the *Śatapatha Brāhmaṇa* it is said that the powers of death which pursue men from one existence to another may be appeased by sacrificial offerings, and that by such offerings release may be obtained from the return of death. This thought, however, is soon abandoned, and is supplanted by the conviction that no sacrifices can do more than secure temporary happiness in higher forms of existence.

Since, then, in India it had become the supreme aim of spiritual endeavour to find this release, the issue could not fail to be the conviction that success had been attained; not by the way which had been previously followed and which no longer afforded inward satisfaction, but by the way of *knowledge*, which, in fact, might be trodden only by a few. In the knowledge of the essential nature of things, which is veiled from ordinary sight, was found the means of deliverance from the pressure of worldly existence. This saving 'knowledge' removes 'ignorance,' *i.e.* the empirical view of the universe which is natural to man, but is mistaken and perverted. With ignorance disappears also desire, which fetters man to existence, and is the cause of all action; as, on the other hand, successful resistance to the desires of the senses promotes the entrance of knowledge. Saving knowledge has the power—to use the technical Indian expression—of 'consuming the seed of works,' and so making impossible for all future time a continuance of migration.

The entire course of thought as hitherto developed is already contained in substance in the ancient *Upaniṣads* (*q.v.*). For them saving knowledge consists in the recognition of the sole existence of the Brahman, the soul of the universe, of the illusory nature of the phenomenal world, and especially of the identity of the individual soul, the *ātman*, with the Brahman. In what way the saving knowledge is conceived in Buddhism, in the religion of the Jains, and in the philosophical systems of the Brāhmans (Sāṅkhya, Yoga, Mīmāṁsā, Vedānta, Vaiśeṣika, Nyāya), must be ascertained from the respective articles. Cf. also art. MOKṢA.

LITERATURE.—Leopold von Schroeder, *Indiens Literatur und Cultur*, Leipzig, 1887; A. Barth, *Religions of India*[3], London, 1891; E. W. Hopkins, *Religions of India*, London, 1896; P. Deussen, *Philosophie der Upanishads*, Leipzig, 1899, Eng. tr., Edinburgh, 1906; A. E. Gough, *Philosophy of the Upanishads*[2], London, 1891; H. Haigh, *Leading Ideas of Hinduism*, London, 1903.

R. GARBE.

TRANSMIGRATION (Jewish).—Metempsychosis, or the migration of the soul (Heb. *gilgūl*, 'rotation' or 'cycle'), is a doctrine which forms part of a system of esoteric mysticism tolerated rather than approved or furthered by Judaism. Its beginnings are difficult to trace. Whether they were Egyptian or Indian—probably through Gnostic or Manichæan intermediaries—this doctrine, no doubt, had to accommodate itself to other Jewish conceptions before it could be assimilated and adopted, and it had to undergo such a profound modification as to give to Jewish metempsychosis a character of its own.

The belief in the migration of the soul presupposes the existence of the soul; and a whole esoteric system about the creation of the soul, and the conception of sin and redemption, are the fundamental principles upon which such a doctrine must rest. The relation between spirit and matter, soul and body, must be determined, as must the question of pre-existence as well as that of the finality of soul and body. An attempt will here be made to do justice to these problems, however succinctly. The questions of punishment and reward, of God's justice and mercy, are also involved. It must be borne in mind that any theory, if it was to be accepted by Jews, had to be subjected to a process of close adaptation to the fundamental principles of Judaism, and must not run counter to the Law. Now, if migration of the soul is to be accepted as a part of philosophic speculation concerning sin and redemption, it has to formulate its theory in accordance with Judaism.

1. Creation of souls.—God is the creator of everything; therefore souls are His creation. But does God continue His act of creation? Does He continually create souls as soon as any human being is on the point of being born? The answer of the believer in metempsychosis is that He does not. His creation came to an end with the close of the sixth day. At the beginning the souls were created. The power of God is thus limited to what He had done on that occasion. Before creating Adam, God had finished the creation of all the souls of man, but, His work of creation being overtaken by the end of the sixth day, He did not continue it, and produced only those evil spirits which hover between the pure divine soul and the earthly matter (the *mazzîqîm*; see art. MAGIC [Jewish]).

A distinct line of demarcation is not drawn, however, and, as will be seen, a soul can assume the form of a demoniacal spirit. The souls created, then, are of a limited number, as the creation was only a limited act, and had to come to an end at a definite period of time. These souls are God's creation, not any emanation from God. This very essential point should be remembered, for it separates Jewish metempsychosis widely from Buddhist. The souls at the end of the migration are not absorbed into a kind of divine pantheistic fluid; they are conceived as having an individual existence; they live separately and fully conscious of their individuality; they dwell in the heavenly halls or in Paradise in rapt contemplation of the divine glory; thither they are allowed to return at the end of their peregrination through the lower world. The souls of the born and the unborn, of those who have already been in the sublunar world and of those who have not yet been in that world, are dwelling together in the heavenly halls, or in the treasury of God (Dt 32[34]). No clear distinction is made between these two categories of souls. It is all so vague in this world of theosophic speculations, and contradictions are not seldom found; schools of thought have sometimes blended their teaching without any successful attempt at harmonizing contradictory views. All that comes is readily accepted, so long as it is not diametrically opposed and so long as it comes as an ancient mystical tradition. Thus the pre-existence of all human souls affects the Messianic eschatology. The soul of the pre-existing Messiah is fully conscious of its own individual pre-eminence in this world. Though a spirit, the Messiah dwells among the other souls, and He is fully aware of the tribulations of the people of Israel; He weeps over their sufferings and anxiously asks the angel who is in His company when the time will arrive for His revelation (M. Gaster, *Chron. of Jerahmeel*, London, 1899, xx. 9). Moses in his ascent to heaven sees the souls of the great and pious, of those who have lived upon earth, and of those who are to come to life hereafter—among others David and Aqiba (*ib.*). This view is found also in the book of Enoch and in other Apocalypses, though the theory of migration is not there clearly connected with it.

The one definite outcome is that no new souls are created for each child that is born, the number of souls being limited. Everything created has a specific purport. Even the angels have not been created without purpose. They are God's messengers; they carry out His wishes and commands in the heavens above and on the earth beneath; above all, they are created for the purpose of singing to their Master and of praising Him in angelic choirs. Such, then, is the purpose of the entire creation. The angelic action is typical of the human man, the highest and most perfect creature after the angels. He must by his action approach the divine, and his whole life must be a long-sustained hymn of praise to God. But man, made of the dust of the earth, cannot rise to such perfection unless the divine soul lifts him up and unless the divine Law guides him steadily upwards towards heaven. His life is a constant struggle between the grossly material inclinations inherent in his earthly nature and the high spiritual promptings of his divine soul. According to the way in which he inclines, his soul will become more or less contaminated by the contact with matter; it will lose more and more of its spiritual lustre and purity. For man has absolute free will; he is master over his own actions. This is an axiom; otherwise the whole principle of reward and punishment has to be abandoned. And yet, with that naive inconsistency so characteristic of this mystic philosophy, predestination is not excluded. Nothing happens which has not been pre-ordained, yet no attempt is made to bridge this gulf.

2. Incarnation of souls.—The souls have been created for a specific use; they must enter human bodies; but the choice is not left to them, either of the bodies to be selected or of the time of entry and the time and manner of exit. As soon as a woman conceives (see art. BIRTH [Jewish]), an angel appears before God with the sperm, and God decrees the future life of the yet unborn babe. Its whole life is thereby determined—whether it will be rich or poor, high-stationed or lowly, wise or foolish, long-lived or short-lived, good or bad, pious or wicked; even its future helpmeet is proclaimed in heaven to the joy and satisfaction of the heavenly hosts. In order to obviate too glaring a contradiction in a later version of this legend of the 'Creation of the Child' (see Gaster, *Jerahmeel*, ix. 19 f.), the moral qualifications of the future man and woman have been omitted. The soul, which is very reluctant to give up its heavenly abode and enter the human body, especially if the shell is that of a wicked one, is forcibly seized by the angel and carried through the bliss of heaven and the agony of hell, to see the reward for good actions and the punishment for evil deeds. Although the soul forgets it all with entry into this world, yet a dim recollection remains, a subconscious image, which is the guiding principle in elementary recognition of good and evil. Every man has within himself a standard of right and wrong given to his soul in its premundane existence. Another version (*Zôhār*, ii. 96*b* ff.) describes the incarnation of the soul in the following manner:

> God created all the souls from the beginning, in the very form in which they would afterwards appear in this world. He beheld them and saw that some of them would be wicked. At the time when the soul is to descend, the Lord calls it and says, 'Go to such and such a place.' The soul replies, 'Let me remain here and not be defiled in that other world.' The Lord answers, 'From the beginning thou hast been created for the purpose of getting into this world.' Then the soul submits, and descends against its will. The Law which helps the soul says to it, 'See how the Lord had mercy on you. He has given you His precious pearl (the Law) to help you in this world, so that ye may return pure.' But, if laden with sin, the soul must obtain purification so as not to be delivered to Gehinnom; for two rows of angels and demons are waiting for the soul; the good to lead to Eden and the evil spirits to Gehinnom; and to be saved from punishment the soul migrates from body to body.

3. Life of the soul on earth; migration; defeat of evil spirits.—Now the soul begins its course upon earth. It must endeavour to obtain the absolute mastery over the body and not to become its slave. In the first entry the soul is absolutely pure and without blemish. It is not met by the obstacle of 'original sin.' The principle upheld throughout is that 'each man dieth by his own sin' (Ezk 18[26]). But the weakness inherent in matter soon makes itself felt, and, moreover, there are the temptations placed in its way through the envy and spite of the evil spirits (*mazzîqîm*), who, though they partake of some spiritual character, are imperfect compared with the pure soul, and are anxious to drag it down to their own level.

A still greater cause lies at the root of this attempt of the evil spirits to lead the pure soul away—a desire to frustrate by the means of sin and transgression the divine plan of creation. God has created the world and man in it for His glory. Through trial and trouble man must win the crown of eternal bliss. The finite number of souls forms part of this divine plan. A term is thereby set for man's spiritualization, for an infinite number of souls might make that end impossible of being reached. But, as there is a limited number, it is obvious that the desired consummation would set in as soon as the last soul had passed through the human body, or, rather, had entered the last human body. For then all the souls created would have fulfilled their mission upon earth, and all the human beings through whom they had passed would have reached the highest degree of moral development of which they were capable, so that the progress of mankind and of the world would have attained its ultimate goal, or, to put it in the words of the mystics, the Kingdom of Heaven upon earth would then be established, the time reached for the advent of the Messiah. Already in the Talmud the saying is found, 'The son of David will not come before all the souls in bodies will come to an end.' The power of the evil spirits would then be entirely broken, and only good would reign in the world. The spirits, therefore, try to entice the soul and defile it by all manner of temptation and sin. The result is that the contaminated soul must be kept out of the heavenly bliss, and the divine plan is effectively checked. Like a 'shell' (*qᵉlîfāh*), the evil spirits surround the soul, making the material covering still more impenetrable to light and truth, as they are clinging close to the body like an additional covering. In the later development of this system the evil spirit 'cleaves' to the body of the person whose soul is to be obstructed, and the spirit is then called *dibbūq*. It has entered into a more intimate connexion with the body, and is no longer an outer covering, or *qᵉlîfāh*, originating from the 'other camp,' the *siṭrā aḥarāh*.

But the demons strive in vain to impede the steady development and unfolding of God's plan. They may delay its speedy consummation; they cannot indefinitely frustrate it. The soul which has been contaminated can be purified again; the sin committed can be atoned for, and even here the means is given to the soul to achieve its own purification. The soul retains its own consciousness and is sensible to its own failings; it realizes the bitterness of punishment and the tragedy of not being allowed to ascend on high and stand again before God in its pristine purity. For it flits about the world as a disembodied spirit, hovering between heaven and earth, and waiting for the chance of atonement or punishment. This comes to it by being re-embodied, and thus the soul migrates from one being to another. It is not made clear, however, whether the soul in this new incarnation remembers its former existence or whether it realizes it when it is leaving this second body, and continues its migration until all the blemish has been eliminated. This transmigration is thus the means of defeating the work of the evil spirits, of hastening the emptying of the divine treasury of unborn souls, and of bringing about the close of the cycle and the advent of the Messiah.

4. The justice of God.—(*a*) *Theories of rewards and punishments.*—The migration of souls is made to serve another and still higher and more direct purpose, the justice of God. The grave problem which has haunted every form of faith has been: how to reconcile the happiness of the sinner and the trials and sufferings of the pious and good with the justice of God. Every religion has endeavoured to form a theodicy. Most of them have relegated the solution of this problem to the life after death, finding the answer in rewards and punishments to be meted out in another world filled with bliss and unutterable torments. Such teaching presupposed the eternity of the soul, and in some form or another a combination of soul and body if the latter is to suffer the torment of hell, unless it was supposed that the souls would continue an individual conscious existence capable of enduring torments as well as rejoicing in heavenly bliss. This is, however, not the place to follow further this extremely complicated problem. It was, after all, a subtle way out of the difficulty, and it was not quite free from a possible reproach of selfishness. The goodness of the soul or the purity of life obtained for that individual soul alone happiness and bliss. No one else was directly benefited by it, except perhaps that such a good and pious man served as an example to others. But the world in general apparently had nothing from him, and his virtuous life led nowhere except to his own exaltation. Not so with the belief in the migration of the soul. Here, upon earth, in the sight of all, the sinner—whosoever he might be—had to expiate his sins. Here he had to suffer for the wrong committed, and here obtain, as it were, the pass for the heavenly regions. By this slow purification and reunion with the other purified souls, moreover, a cycle was completed, at the end of which the Messianic period would begin. By his actions the whole world would benefit, and the general progress and welfare of mankind would be hastened and consummated.

Thus the soul of Adam, because he had sinned, had to begin a period of migration through other bodies and thus pass through David, who, by the sin which he had committed with the wife of Uriah, impeded the complete purification of Adam's soul. But, by its final entry into the last descendant, the Messiah would also bring about the desired result meant by the divine plan when Adam, the first man, was created.

The soul of Abel passed into Moses, or, according to another theory, the soul of Adam passed into Moses, who sinned at the rock, and then into David, who sinned with Uriah's wife, and, finally, into the Messiah, thus linking the first with the last.

There are, as it were, successive incarnations of the same pre-existing soul, and for their sakes the world has been created. There cannot be any doubt that these views are extremely old. Simon Magus raises the claim of former existences, his soul passing through many bodies before it reaches that known as Simon. The Samaritan doctrine of the *taheb* teaches the same doctrine of a pre-existing soul which was given to Adam, but which, through successive 'incarnations' in Seth, Noah, and Abraham, reached Moses, for whom it was originally formed and for whose sake the world had been created. The element which is absent here is that of migration for the purpose of purification. The latter gives to 'migration of souls' a peculiar character. Not only is the world perfected thereby (*tiqqūn*), but the sinner expiates his sin in this world in the new existence in which his soul reappears. It may enter the body of a pious man, and by his good deeds he will cleanse the dross still adhering to the soul and facilitate its ascent on high. If the pious suffer, it is only and solely for sins committed in a previous existence, and thus suffering is not a punishment for sins now committed, but a 'purgatory' for evil deeds of a former life. The explanation of the prosperous sinner is not quite so clear. Here use had been made of the other doctrine of punishment and reward after death. The sinner benefits from the good deeds that he had performed in a previous existence. He prospers now, so that *all* his reward is eaten up by him in this world, and nothing but punishment and tortures is reserved for him in the life after death. This presupposes that the soul of the wicked is beyond 'redemption' in this world, and is sent to Gehinnom for punishment. This seems to be the view taken by 'the Saba' in the *Zôhār* in the passage quoted above (§ 2). The cycle of the soul is thus broken. It is not made quite clear how it is to be completed; but it seems that, according to some, a soul which has just sunk to this lowest level of contamination, instead of being sent to Gehinnom, becomes an evil spirit in this world, which is anxious to enter living bodies for torment or for that punishment which starts from the lowest rung of the ladder and is to lead up to the highest without recourse to punishments in 'hell.' Such a soul becomes a *dibbūq*. To exorcize it, to free it from this temporary existence as quickly as possible, and thus hasten the new cycle of evolution, is a meritorious deed, a real *tiqqūn*, an 'improvement' and perfection.

No attempt is made to reconcile these two separate systems of punishment and reward; they are often mentioned side by side in the *Zôhār* and other kabbalistic treatises. In the Targum to Ec 8[5] the suffering of the pious and the happiness of the wicked have already been explained in a somewhat similar manner, inasmuch as the pious suffer for small sins in order to enter afterwards directly into heaven, and the sinner enjoys the fruit of some good deeds here, so that hereafter he is to go straight to torment and punishment.

(*b*) *Kabbalistic theory.*—The kabbalist, however, adds and superimposes the new theory of suffering and happiness, not for sins and good deeds performed in the person's lifetime, but for sins done during previous existences. The punishment was expected to fit the crime. Thus, if a man had sinned by his eyes, he would be reborn blind or suffering with his eyes, and, similarly, every other part of the body would then be affected by the sin committed through that part in the previous existence. Moral sins would have to be expiated in a similar manner; for, according to some of the oldest and most accredited teachers, transmigration is not limited to that from one human body to another human body. The soul of the wicked passes also into animal bodies corresponding with the character of the sin. In later schools the transmigration has been extended also to plants, stones, and metals. As an example of the former it may be stated that the soul of an adulterer passes into the body of a female stork, for it is believed that the storks punish adultery with death.[1] Thus an explanation was found for the prohibition of mixing various kinds of seeds and the cross-breeding of animals, for they disturbed the normal laws of nature and caused great suffering to the souls of such mixed products. Similarly, the peculiar command of marrying the deceased brother's wife (*yibbūm*) has its reason and justification in this doctrine of migration. The soul of the childless man cannot return to its source, for the soul has remained barren and is cut short in its earthly career before it has been able to pass through all the stages of purification. Hence the reason why the child born was to be called 'in the name' of the deceased, though it does not follow that it must bear the same name. In fact, the child of Ruth, which was a 'restorer of souls' to Naomi, did not bear the name of Ruth's dead husband. The new-born babe would receive the soul of the dead and continue his earthly life.

5. Number of migrations.—There is a difference of opinion as to how many times a soul would migrate before it had run its entire course. The majority of kabbalists incline to the opinion that no soul migrates through more than three bodies. The real course is that in which the soul has performed the whole of the 613 commandments of the Law, by which alone perfection is attained. For the shortcomings in one existence the soul is punished in the next, and then also performs some good deeds. Others think that the soul passes through a greater number of changes. It is held that the fate of the soul of the sinner is decided after three migrations, at the end of which a thoroughly wicked soul becomes an evil spirit—a demon—while that of the pious may be reincarnated times without number. In this case the ascent of the soul from the lower to the higher degree of purity and perfection is asserted.

6. Various other theories; purposes of metempsychosis.—It is held that builders of the Tower of Babel were divided into three categories, which were punished in accordance with the degree of wickedness of which they were guilty. The first lost the unity of language, and were dispersed upon the face of the earth. The second—a more daring category—were changed into all kinds of animals, and their souls were sent into animal bodies. The third—the thoroughly wicked section—were changed into demons. The change of the body of Nebuchadrezzar into a wild animal, as told by Daniel (Dn 4[33]), lent further countenance to the possibility of a human soul dwelling in an animal body. The rules for slaughtering special animals and for the blessing by which the cutting is accompanied rest upon the same principle of thereby possibly saving a penitent soul from dwelling too long in the body of an animal. It is liberated by a religious act which assists it in its further migration. All this forms part of the *tiqqūn*, the improvement and perfection of the world, the preparation for the Messianic rule. The covenant before Mt. Sinai was made by God with *all* the souls which He had created: 'Neither with you only do I make this covenant and this oath; but with him that standeth here with us this day before the Lord our God, and also with him that is *not here with us* this day' (Dt 29[14f.]), for He did not speak only to those who were there, but also to those who were not there on that day, in their material form, *i.e.* in human bodies.

By this migration of good souls to good men and contaminated souls to sinners and evil-doers a certain affinity of souls was established, which led to the identification of such souls in the various stages. As mentioned before, the soul of Abel or of Adam was that of Moses, and the souls of the ten brothers of Joseph became the souls of the ten martyrs whom the legend described as contemporaries. In fact, this tendency of recognizing the older souls in more recent bodies developed in the later schools of kabbalistic speculations established by Luria, Vital Calabrese, and others into a regular system. Lists have been drawn up and books have been compiled (*Sēpher hag-Gilgūlīm*, Frankfort, 1684), in which the reincarnations of the good and evil men of the past have been duly recorded. Such spiritual genealogies—if we may use such a term—have found their way even into bibliographical and historical compilations. In

[1] The Heb. name for stork is *ḥăsîdhāh*, which, by a popular etymology, may be explained to mean 'the chaste' or 'the pious.'

addition to the complete reincarnation, there came the newer doctrine of impregnation (*'ibbûr*). The soul of a good man is sometimes not strong enough to fight successfully the temptations of the world, and another soul is temporarily grafted upon that which he already possesses, so that it is made almost unassailable. The older teaching runs that the spiritual forces of man are regularly heightened on Sabbath eve by the temporary addition of a new soul, which departs with the close of the Sabbath. In the same manner a soul is grafted temporarily on to the pious man. The object of all this is to hasten the perfection of the world and the advent of the Messiah. By means of migration the soul has fulfilled the object of its creation—to pass through man and to lift man higher and to bring him nearer the divine. This doctrine, being a justification of God's ways with men, is, at the same time, a source of comfort to the pious, and a source of terror to the sinner. It reconciles man to suffering and trials, and at the same time explains the hidden meaning of many a law and ceremony which seem obscure. It is a vindication of the divine character of the Law, for its ultimate result is to be the rule of heaven upon earth.

7. Date and origin.—This doctrine of migration is nowhere to be found systematically developed. Wherever it occurs, it is tacitly assumed as well known, and no explanation is given in detail. It has, therefore, been pieced together and reconstructed by the present writer mostly from the Zoharistic literature, viz. the *Zôhār*, the *Zôhār Ḥādāsh*, and the *Tiqqūnîm*, which represents a more or less homogeneous view on migration, whenever it is referred to. While these are by far the most complete writings, they are by no means the oldest. This brings us to the question of the date and probable origin of this doctrine among the Jews.

All the beginnings of esoteric teachings are lost in the mist of antiquity, and, when such doctrines finally see the light of day, they have, as a rule, a long history behind them. It is, therefore, a fallacy to date the origin of metempsychosis among the Jews from the time when it becomes known publicly in the 9th or 10th century. The masters of the occult science never doubted its Jewish character or its old origin. Was it not part of that heavenly mystery handed down from Adam on through all the great men of the past? With great ingenuity they endeavoured to find proofs for it in the Scriptures by means of an exegesis which was fantastic in the extreme. A few examples will suffice. They are taken at random from the *Zôhār*, and they are found in large numbers in Manasseh ben Israel, *Nishmat Ḥayîm*, bk. iv. chs. 8–10.

'Till thou return unto the ground' (Gn 3[19]) is interpreted to mean that the body alone returns to the ground; the spirit, however, is reborn.

'Naked shall I return thither' (Job 1[21]) is interpreted literally as meaning 'to the womb,' *i.e.* being reborn.

'The word which he commanded to a thousand generations' (Ps 105[8]) is interpreted to mean that it refers to the same soul passing through innumerable generations, for God's command had been given once to all the souls, and these souls are reincarnated over and over again.

'One generation goeth, and another generation cometh' (Ec 1[4]). The fact that the passing away of the generation is mentioned first is a proof that this must have existed before; otherwise it ought to read 'one generation cometh and another generation goeth.'

'Which are already dead more than the living which are yet alive' (Ec 4[2]) is interpreted to mean that the living are still uncertain as to the future fate of the migration of their souls.

A proof of 'impregnation,' or the addition of a soul, is also deduced from the following verses: 'Ye shall therefore separate between the clean beast and the unclean,' etc. (Lv 20[25]), meaning that a clean soul shall be added, not an unclean. 'Shall flocks and herds be slain for them, to suffice them?' etc. (Nu 11[22]), is taken to mean the addition of souls. 'O God, the God of the spirits of all flesh,' etc. (Nu 16[22]), means also those that are added to strengthen them 'should one man sin' whose soul proved too weak, as it had no support. 'Doeth good to his own soul' (Pr 11[17]) means that a man attaches another soul to himself.

The letters of the name of Ad(a)m have been taken as the initials for *A*dam, *D*avid, *M*oses, and *M*essias; hence it was proved that the soul of Adam passed through all these. The letters of the name M(o)sh(e)h (Moses) are the initials of *M*oses, *S*eth, and *H*abel (Abel); hence the soul of Abel passed through Seth to Moses. The numerical value of the letters of the names of the ten tribes corresponds to the numerical value of the names of the reputed ten sages who suffered martyrdom. These examples could easily be multiplied from later kabbalistic literature, but they all follow the same line of argument. There cannot, however, be the slightest doubt that the doctrine of metempsychosis was borrowed from other religious systems, and is not Jewish at all. It will remain an open question whether the denial of the resurrection of the dead attributed by Josephus (*Ant.* XVIII. i. 4 [16]) to the Sadducees implies denial also of reward and punishment, or whether it extended only to the life beyond the grave, and that they believed in the reward and punishment in this world. His allegation that they believed that the soul died with the body is too strange to be accurate. The vindication of God's justice would most easily be found if it means that the soul migrates from one body to another, as they did not deny the divine origin of the soul. Whatever the remoter origin of it may be, it cannot be gainsaid that the atmosphere of Palestine was saturated with mystical and esoteric teachings of every kind, one among them being that of metempsychosis. The Gnostics and Manichæans held fast to it; Neo-Platonism did not deny its possibility, and thus almost insensibly it crept into Judaism. The Palestinian Targumim show traces of it, inasmuch as in some places they speak of a second death (so Dt 33[6]), which can only mean at least a life twice repeated upon earth; this is possible only if the soul migrates from one body to another (so also Baḥya, *ad loc.*; cf. also Targum to Is 22[14]). Saadya Gaon (†942) in the 10th cent. inveighs against such tenets, held, as he says, by a certain Karaite sect, although it was probably rather a mystical heterodox section of Rabbanite Jews who believed also in the migration of souls. A few centuries later Abraham Bedaresi (1280), a rationalist philosopher, in his letter to R. Solomon ben Adreth, no. 8, protested against this doctrine; but they were the only opponents, for the wave of mysticism was rising steadily with the narrowing of the political outlook and the change of social conditions. With the appearance of the *Zôhār* the older kabbalistic literature was pushed into the background, and many an ancient mystical treatise was forgotten, unless it became embedded in the *Zôhār*—*e.g.*, the treatise by 'the Saba,' 'the venerable' (*i.e.* Rab. Hamnuna), in the form of a commentary on the Biblical section '*Mishpāṭîm*,' Ex 22, which is found now in the *Zôhār* Ex 94[a]–114[a]. In older writings, *Qānā* and *Bāhîr*, and in those of Naḥmanides (1263), R. Solomon ben Adreth (*c.* 1300), and Isaac of Akko (*c.* 1330), faint traces of this doctrine can be detected. They show that in these mystic schools echoes of the older theory of metempsychosis had been heard and recorded. Whenever referred to, it is always an ancient tradition. Since the 13th cent. the *Zôhār* has swayed the mind of the larger section of a Jewry despondent and broken by ruthless persecution.

The dark Middle Ages began for the Jews when they came to an end for the other nations in Europe. The writings of Rekanati (14th cent.)

and Baḥya (14th cent.) prepared the way for the development.

Palestine—in a lesser degree the adjoining Babylon—seems to have been throughout the centre of mystical speculations. Thither Naḥmanides had gone, and a great school flourished in Akko for some centuries from the 12th onwards. The flow of the Spanish emigrants at the end of the 16th cent. was also towards Palestine. In Safed there arose the school of Luria (1534–72; commonly known by the initials of his name Ari=*R*abbi *I*saac *A*shkenazi), Vital Calabrese, Cordovero, Poppers, and others. Among other doctrines, they developed, in the writings *Kavvānôth*, *'Ēṣ Ḥayîm*, etc., much further the tenets of metempsychosis as a punishment for the wicked and an exalted reincarnation for the pious. The *tiqqūn*, or improvement of the world by delivering souls from the chain of migration, became one of the prominent features of this school, which led to that of the Hasidim. Remarkable legends of such deliverance are henceforth told. Every pious and great kabbalist performed them, none, however, so effectively as the master Luria himself. The history of the deliverance of such a soul in Safed is one of the most vivid autobiographies of a 'wandering soul' (first published in the *'Ēmeq ham-Melekh* of Nāphtali Herz, Amsterdam, 1648). The belief that certain persons are the *gilgūl* of other persons who had lived before them is still strongly held by those to whom the *Zôhār* is an inspired book and the teaching of divine revelation. This belief strengthens in them the concept of God's righteousness, and the conviction that, if the time were hastened for all the created souls to pass through the human body, the advent of the Messiah and the Kingdom of God upon earth would be hastened.

LITERATURE.—The books mentioned in the course of this attempt at a synthetical exposition of the doctrine of metempsychosis—the first of its kind—form the only literature that can profitably be mentioned. Manasseh ben Israel, *Nishmat Ḥayîm*, bk. iv., treats it apologetically. A. Franck, *La Kabbale*³, Paris, 1892; A. Jellinek, *Beitr. zur Gesch. der Kabbala*, Leipzig, 1851–52; D. H. Joël, *Sohar*, Leipzig, 1849, have incidentally, of course, referred briefly also to this apparently unimportant section of kabbalistic Zoharistic speculation. See also literature to art. ḲABBĀLĀ.

M. GASTER.

TRANSMIGRATION (Teutonic).—It is clear that the doctrine of metempsychosis was held by the early Teutonic peoples, though the amount of evidence is limited and for the most part dates from a time when heathen beliefs, if not forgotten, were at least misunderstood. Such evidence as exists is chiefly derived from Scandinavian records. The only reference in early poetry is to be found in *Sigurðarkviþa hinn skamma*, 45, where Hogni refuses to hold Brynhild back from self-destruction:

> 'Let no man stay her from the long journey, and may she never be born again (*aptrborin*).'

More striking evidence for the belief is furnished by the prose passages contained in *Helgakviþa Hjorvarðssonar* and *Helgakviþa Hundingsbana*, ii. At the end of the former it is said that Helgi and Sváva, the hero and heroine, were born again (*endrborin*); in the latter we are told that the heroine Sigrún was Sváva reincarnate, and later that both she and her husband Helgi Hundingsbani were born again as Kára and Helgi Haddingjaskati. A reference is given to *Káraljóð*, a poem now unfortunately lost, which dealt with the adventures of these persons. Moreover, in the *Gautreks Saga*, c. vii., Starkaðr is reviled as an *endrborinn jotunn*, a 'giant' reincarnate; his grandfather Starkaðr is said to have been a *jotunn* (c. iii.).

With the introduction of Christianity metempsychosis came at last to be regarded as 'an old wives' tale.' For a time it still survived among the half-heathen population: to his horror St. Olaf found himself regarded as the reincarnation of a legendary king, one Olafr Geirstaðarálfr (*Flateyjarbók*, ii. 135).

It is not to be overlooked that in all these cases the men—though not the women—bear the same names in each incarnation. As among certain primitive peoples of the present day, the name is regarded as something more than a mere label; it is intimately connected with the soul of its possessor, so that a child inheriting the name of a dead person necessarily inherits the soul as well. An interesting reference to this belief may be cited from *Flateyjarbók*, i. 255: Thorsteinn Uxafót, a follower of Olafr Tryggvason, is visited in a dream by the ghost of a man called Brynjarr; it bestows a treasure on him and asks in return that one of Thorsteinn's children should be baptized under the name Brynjarr, since it desires a Christian reincarnation for its heathen soul.

In the *Islendinga Sogur* there are no actual references to metempsychosis, though the practice of naming children after lately deceased kinsmen (*Njals Saga*, ch. 89, *Eyrbyggja Saga*, ch. 12, *Laxdæla Saga*, chs. 36, 56) points to the existence of some such belief. But the passage in *Sturlunga Saga*, ix. 42—*þótte þeim nu Kolbeinn aptr kominn ok endrborinn*—is no true instance of this kind, since Thorgils Boðvarsson, referred to here, was born in 1226, nineteen years before the death of Kolbeinn Arnorsson, of whom he seemed to be the reincarnation. To the present day, however, it is believed in Norway and Iceland that, if a ghost appears to a pregnant woman in her sleep, it is seeking a namesake (*gaar efter Navnet*); and accordingly the child is baptized with the name of the dead person (cf. K. Maurer, *Zeitschrift des Vereins für Volkskunde*, v. 99). Sophus Bugge, moreover, states that he had heard *reise upp atte* ('raise up again') used in the west part of Telemarken with reference to the naming of a child after a dead person (*Home of the Eddic Poems*, London, 1899, p. 333).

Among the other Teutonic peoples the evidence for anything in the nature of metempsychosis is very meagre. An Anglo-Saxon charm (T. O. Cockayne, *Leechdoms, Wortcunning, and Starcraft of Early England*, London, 1864–66, iii. 66 ff.; C. W. M. Grein, *Bibliothek der angelsächs. Poesie*, Göttingen, 1857–65, i. 326 ff.) advises a woman who cannot bring forth a child to step thrice over the grave of a dead man, using an incantation for the safe delivery of her offspring. It is a question much in need of investigation whether the same idea can be traced in certain usages said to be practised in connexion with burial-places of the heathen age in various parts of Northern Europe.

It may be mentioned in conclusion that Appian (*Hist. Rom.* iv., 'de Rebus Gallicis,' 3) describes the Germans who followed Ariovistus as 'scorning death because of their hope of rebirth' (θανάτου καταφρονηταὶ δι' ἐλπίδα ἀναβιώσεως). In view of what is said of the Gauls by Diodorus, v. 28, and Lucan, *Pharsalia*, i. 454 ff. (with the scholia), it is not unlikely that the reference here is to a belief in metempsychosis, though one cannot deny the possibility that Appian's statement may be due to a misunderstanding of the Valhalla doctrine.

LITERATURE.—G. Storm, *Arkiv för Nordisk Filologi*, ix., new ser., v. [1892] 199–222; K. Maurer, *Zeitschr. des Vereins für Volkskunde*, v. [1895] 98 ff.; P. Herrmann, *Nordische Mythologie*, Leipzig, 1903, pp. 35–37; O. L. Jiriczek, 'Seelenglauben und Namengebung,' in *Mitt. der Schles. Gesellsch. für Volkskunde*, i. 3 [Breslau, 1895] 30–35.

BRUCE DICKINS.

TRANSUBSTANTIATION.—See EUCHARIST.

TRAPPISTS.—Trappists is the popular name for the Reformed Cistercians, or Cistercians of the Strict Observance, now the chief division of the order.

The art. MONASTICISM[1] outlines the successive reforms named after Benedict, Cluny, Cîteaux. By 1600 the Cistercians themselves had yielded to the spirit of luxury, despite the restoration in Spain promoted by Martino de Vargas. Though Richelieu and Mazarin furthered many attempts to recall them to the letter of their vows, and though their centralized constitution might have facilitated this, a general reform was refused. Here and there a few abbeys did return to the ideals of St. Stephen Harding, the Jansenist reform of St. Cyr and of Port Royal being well known. Armand-Jean le Bouthillier de Rancé (1626–1700), abbot *in commendam* of La Trappe from the age of ten, abandoned court life in 1662 and entered one of the reformed abbeys as a novice. Two years later, having again professed, he came to take charge of his own inaccessible Norman abbey. Finding that the few monks had not shared his experience and would not share his ideals, he pensioned them off and colonized the place from other reformed abbeys. The community improved on the original austerities, taking only one vegetarian meal daily, abstaining from literature and from speech except for urgent purposes. The ideals were published by de Rancé in his *Traité de la sainteté et des devoirs de la vie monastique* (1683), and in his posthumous *Règlemens généraux de l'abbaye de la Trappe* (1701); but only a single community of nuns and two Italian monasteries adopted them. For a century they were unimportant, though other Reformed Cistercians undertook missions to Africa which had some temporary success.

The French Revolution broke up the home; the abbey was suppressed, and the premises were converted into a foundry for cannon. This was the real birth of the order. In 1791 Dom Augustine de Lestrange, master of the novices, took a score of monks to Val Sainte, Switzerland, imposing a rule stricter than ever; postulants flocked in; colonies were sent to many lands; a congregation was formed, and Dom Augustine was appointed father abbot. When the Trappists were hunted to Poland, Germany, and Italy, their zeal only increased. A nunnery was formed at Stapehill near Wimborne; a party of monks that wandered through Pennsylvania, Kentucky, Missouri, and Illinois returned to France on the fall of Napoleon, occupying La Trappe and Belle Fontaine; presently five priories were established in France, and a great college at Soligni. Before his death in 1827 Dom Augustine saw abbeys grow up in Belgium and Italy, besides two more in France. One was founded at Coalville in Leicestershire and named after the great Bernard. The cowl of his friend Alberic was taken in 1848 by an expedition from La Meilleraye in Brittany, which settled in Kentucky at an abbey named Gethsemane. Mount Melleray in Ireland sent another colony to Dubuque in Iowa, and both establishments thrive, though all the fathers are aliens. A second Irish abbey arose at Roscrea in Co. Tipperary.

Outward disasters again intensified the spiritual life. La Trappe was destroyed by fire in Aug. 1871; 1450 fathers and brothers were again expelled from France in 1880; but the austere ideals were embraced by nearly all Cistercians outside Austria-Hungary. After two constitutional changes they were formally recognized in 1892 as the Order of Reformed Cistercians, with an abbot-general at Rome; and this success was crowned six years later by the purchase of the original premises of Cîteaux. In 1903 they were expelled from France in common with most other congregations; two communities went to Nova Scotia and New Brunswick, one to Oregon, one to Brazil; two tiny groups have taken refuge near Kingsbridge and Salisbury. Belle Fontaine has endeavoured to uphold the agricultural ideals of St. Benedict, especially by its Canadian offshoots at La Trappe, where the Ottawa joins the St. Lawrence, at Lake St. John, and in Manitoba. No establishment in England offers even to its co-religionists any educational, medical, or philanthropic service. Settlements in Japan, China, Syria, Asia Minor, Algeria, Belgian Congo, and Natal have undertaken mission work, but no impartial observer has anything to say as to results. The finest Protestant tribute is that an abbey is 'an asylum for the poor and helpless, the shipwrecked, the conscience-stricken, and the broken-hearted.'[1]

Attached to each of the 71 monasteries and annexes is a body of brothers who do the rougher field work; in all there are about 2000 of these, and 1600 professed fathers. Twenty-one priories contain 2000 nuns and lay sisters. Three Italian monasteries still follow the rule of de Rancé as once used at La Trappe, but do not belong to the Reformed Cistercians; they have only 50 members.

LITERATURE.—A. Félibien, *Description de l'Abbaye de la Trappe*, Paris, 1671; P. de Maupeou, *Vie du Père A. J. Le Bouthillier de Rancé*², 2 vols., do. 1709; J. Marsollier, *Vie de dom Armand Jean le Bouthillier de Rancé, abbé de la Trappe*, 2 vols., do. 1703; P. Hélyot and M. Bullot, *Hist. des ordres monastiques religieux et militaires*, do. 1860 (orig. ed. 1714–19), vol. vi. ch. i.; *Dictionnaire des ordres religieux*, ed. M. L. Badiche, 4 vols., do. 1858–59 (forming ser. i. vols. xx.–xxiii. of J. P. Migne, *Encyclopédie théologique*, do. 1844–66); F. Pfannenschmidt, *Illustrierte Gesch. der Trappisten*, Paderborn, 1873; *Use of the Cistercian Nuns of the Strict Observance of Our Lady of La Trappe*, London [1886]; J. L. Allen, in *Century Magazine*, new ser., xiv. [1888] 483–496; M. Hartry, *Triumphalia Chronologica Monasterii S. Crucis in Hibernia*, ed. D. Murphy, Dublin, 1891; Hyacinthe de Charencey, *Cartulaire de l'abbaye de Notre-Dame de la Trappe*, Paris, 1891; *Us de l'ordre des cisterciens réformés précédé de la règle de S. Benoît et des constitutions*, Westmalle, 1895; C. F. R. de Montalembert, *The Monks of the West*, Eng. tr., 6 vols., London, 1896; *Abrégé de l'histoire de l'ordre de Cîteaux par un moine de Thymadeuc*, St. Brieuc, 1897; *Odyssée monastique Dom A. Lestrange et les Trappistes pendant la Révolution*, Imprimerie de la Grande Trappe, 1898; *Les Trappistes au Japon* [Hongkong, 1899]; *L'abbaye de Notre-Dame du Lac et l'ordre de Cîteaux au Canada et dans les Etats-Unis*, Montreal, 1907; Max Heimbucher, *Die Orden und Kongregationen der kathol. Kirche*², 3 vols., Paderborn, 1907–08; Wetzer-Welte², *s.v.*; *PRE*³, *s.v.*

W. T. WHITLEY.

[1] Vol. viii. p. 792 f.

[1] J. L. Allen, *Century Magazine*, new ser., xiv. 484.

TRAVANCORE.—Travancore (Malayālam Tiruvitānkūr, 'place where the goddess of prosperity resides'), a native state in the extreme south-west of the Indian peninsula, takes its name from Tiruvankod, 30 miles south of the capital, Trivandrum.

'It has been truly remarked that "it will be difficult to name another land which, within so narrow limits, combines so many, so varied, and such precious natural blessings."'[2]

1. History.—Travancore is said to have formed part of the ancient kingdom of Kerala. During the 11th cent. A.D. it was conquered by the Cholās; in the 13th cent. it was invaded by the Pāndyās of Madura. The present kingdom was founded in the first half of the 18th cent. by Mārtānda Varma, and in 1795 it became a protected state under the British Government. Since then it has enjoyed prosperity under a well-regulated government, and it has been conspicuous for the maintenance of order, religious toleration, and encouragement of education.

2. Area and population.—The area of the state is 7593 sq. miles, and the total population at the census of 1911 was 3,428,975, of whom 93·8% are rural and 6·2% urban. The density of the population is high: 452 per sq. mile for the whole area, and 686 if mountains, lakes, and forests are ex-

[2] *IGI* xxiv. 2 f.

cluded. The people are of the usual S. Indian Dravidian type, and they preserve many characteristic usages, in particular the matriarchal forms of the household and system of marriage.

'Among the Marumakkatāyom [Malayālam *maru*, 'next,' 'other,' *makkal*, 'children,' *tāyam*, 'portion'] Hindus the family is matriarchal, *i.e.*, traces its descent from a common ancestress. The Tarwād [Malayālam *taravātu*, *tara*, 'village,' *pātu*, 'place'], as the family is called, consists of brothers and sisters and the descendants of the latter along the female line. The eldest male member, called the Kāranavan ['originator'], manages the Tarwād. In such a system the wives and children of the male members have no place. It may happen, however, that a Kāranavan may be allowed to bring in his wife and children to live in the Tarwād, but this is not necessary, nor have they any legal status in the family. The male members who are married usually visit their wives in the houses of the latter. When, however, under modern conditions, they feel able and inclined to support themselves, living apart from the Tarwād, they settle with their wives in houses of their own. In this way the putting up of separate homesteads receives a stimulus. But the Tarwād, as such, is split up only when a partition takes place with the consent of all the members. Among Makkatāyom Hindus the joint family does not generally continue single after the lifetime of the parent, especially the male parent. At the death of the father the sons divide and go and live in separate houses with their wives and children, the mother residing with one of the sons in the original household. The unmarried sons, if any, usually live with the mother. In regard to the Nampūtiri Brāhmaṇs, however, the eldest son alone marries, the other sons living with him in the family.'[1]

The chief castes are the Nāyar ([*q.v.*] honorific plural of Nāyan; Skr. *nāyaka*, 'leader') numbering 592,655, best known on account of their peculiar marriage customs.[2] The Īzhuvans or Illavans, who take their name from Īzham, the Malayālam name for Ceylon, are immigrants from that island, cultivate coco-nut and palmyra palms, make the drink known as toddy (Skr. *tāla*, 'the palmyra tree'), and distil country spirits; they number 546,265. The Pulayans (*pula*, 'pollution'), numbering 185,314, are agricultural labourers. The Channān or Shānān (Tamil *shāru*, 'toddy') cultivate the palmyra palm and make coarse sugar. Brāhmans number 55,643; among them the most remarkable are the Nambūrī, Nambūtirī, or Nambūdrī (Malayālam *nambu*, 'the Veda'; *othu*, 'to teach'; *tiri*, Skr. *śri*, 'holy'), who aim at following the original Vedic rites and practise elaborate rules of purification, while they allow the younger sons of the family to enter into polyandrous relations with Nāyar women.

3. Religion.—Classified by religion, the population consists of: Hindus, 2,282,617, 66·57%; Christians, 903,868, 26·36%; Muhammadans, 226,617, 6·61%; animists, 15,617, ·46%; Jews, Buddhists, and Jains, 100.

(*a*) *Hindus*.—Of the triad, Brahmā, Viṣṇu, Śiva, the cult of Viṣṇu is most popular; in the form of Ananta Padmanābha ('the endless, from whose navel springs the lotus') he is the patron deity of the state, with a famous temple at the capital Trivandrum, which is visited by crowds of pilgrims. Among the minor deities the following are the chief: Vighneśvara ('obstacle Lord'), the Gaṇeśa or Gaṇapati of other parts of India; Subhramaṇya, Skanda, Kārttikeya, or Velāyudha, like Gaṇeśa a son of Śiva, the guardian who protects the helpless and punishes the wicked—a cult special to the Tamil and Malayālam peoples; Śāsta ('ruler'), Aiyappan or Aiyanār ('honourable father'), the most popular minor deity, chief of the ghosts (*bhūta*), who rides over the land mounted on a horse or elephant, sword in hand, to disperse all obnoxious spirits. Besides these the lower classes worship a host of godlings or minor spirits, male and female, the females attendants of the goddess Bhadrakālī, the males classed as followers of Śiva.

[1] *Census of India, 1911*, vol. xxiii. pt. i. p. 41.

[2] H. H. Risley, *The People of India*[2], London, 1915, p. 206 ff.; L. K. Anantha Krishna Iyer, *The Cochin Tribes and Castes*, London, 1912–13, ii. 22 ff.; V. Nagam Aiya, *Travancore State Manual*, ii. 352 ff.; E. Thurston, *Castes and Tribes of S. India*, Madras, 1909, v. 307 ff.; E. Westermarck, *The Hist. of Human Marriage*, London, 1891, pp. 116 f., 452 f.

(*b*) *Christians*.—These show a notable increase, from 498,542 in 1881 to 903,868 in 1911. The Hindu compiler of the *Travancore Census Report* for 1911 writes:

'It may be remarked here that the degeneration of the socio-economic institution of caste that showed itself in the sequestration and neglect of the labouring classes, the indifference of lay and ecclesiastical Hindu bodies in the matter of the preservation of their faith as a living force in the intellectual and moral life of the people, the atmosphere of unsuspecting toleration one breathes on all sides, the great sympathy and help accorded by the rulers of the State, the status which the religion itself enjoys, and last but not least, the self-sacrificing zeal and devotion of the missionaries as a class and of the pioneers in particular—all these gave vigour to the work and assured the results. While natural increase has been unsteady and irregular, propagandist activity has been such as to make it difficult to reduce to definite proportions the augmentation which it succeeds in bringing about—so rapid and great it has been.'[1]

The following are the details of the Christian population: Syro-Roman, 293,407; Syrian Jacobite, 202,059; Roman Catholic, 173,724; Congregationalist, 81,573; Reformed Syrian, 74,866; Anglican, 56,251; Salvationist, 16,794. The Church Missionary Society commenced work in 1816, the London Missionary Society in 1806, the Salvation Army in 1891.

(*c*) *Muslims*.—Muhammadan missionaries are said to have visited Malabar as early as A.D. 710, and the story of the conversion of the last of the Perumāls suggests that traders from Arabia arrived as early as the 8th cent. A.D.[2] In more recent times, under the rule of Haidar 'Alī and Tīpū Sultān of Mysore (A.D. 1761–99), compulsory proselytism added large numbers to the faith. The present Muhammadans are either indigenous, immigrants from the Coromandel Coast, or recent settlers from Arabia, Sindh, Gujarāt, Kachh, or Bombay, who came for purposes of trade. The first differ little from the Hindu population except in matters of belief. Those who were converted by the Musalmān kings of Mysore are known as Moplah (Malayālam Māppila, probably 'great child,' an honorary title conferred on converts), or Jonaka, Shonaga, a corruption of Yavana, 'Greek.' The Moplahs are notorious fanatics, and in several cases bodies of them have fiercely resisted British troops. The Mettan are descendants of old Musalmān merchants and of their converts. The Tulukkan (Skr. Turashka, 'Turk') belong to the immigrant class.

(*d*) *Animists*.—Animism prevails widely among the hill tribes. Spirits (*chāvu*, *chāvar*, 'death,' 'the dead') are invoked by those afflicted with disease or suffering from starvation, a long string of the names of ancestors being recited. These spirits are of two kinds: (1) those who have met with a violent death from wild animals; (2) those who have died before the age of seven. They are propitiated by animal sacrifice and oblations of spirituous liquor on a platform erected for the purpose. The forest spirits must be propitiated before a tree is cut, and special patches of the forest are left uncut because they are supposed to be inhabited by some spirit. The hill people also worship godlings who possess neither priests nor temples, the oldest member of the family offering sacrifices and oblations to trees in which they are believed to dwell. Totemism has not been recognized among the hill tribes, but they respect the cow and will not kill the elephant, the vehicle and manifestation of Śāsta. In November–December, the harvest season, they worship their weapons and tools, bows, arrows, sickles, and knives.

LITERATURE.—N. Subrahmanya Aiyar, *Census of India, 1901*, vol. xxvi., *Travancore*, Trivandrum, 1903, *Census of India, 1911*, vol. xxiii., do. 1912; V. Nagam Aiya, *Travancore State Manual*, 3 vols., do. 1906; G. Oppert, *Original Inhabitants*

[1] *Census of India, 1911*, vol. xxiii. pt. i. p. 195.

[2] *Ib.* p. 104 ff.

of Bhāratavarṣa or India, London, 1893; S. Mateer, *Native Life in Travancore*, do. 1883, *The Land of Charity*, do. 1871.

W. CROOKE.

TREASON.—See CRIMES AND PUNISHMENTS.

TREATIES.—1. Their place in international law and ethics.—The history of treaties, as formal agreements between nations, ratified by the respective governments, throws some light on the development of international ethics; and the formulæ and ceremonies connected with the sanctions employed at various times, to give validity to the pacts, are of interest to the historian of religion. Throughout the whole of antiquity the gods presided over all treaty-making, and the oath was a predominant factor; the transition from ancient to modern times is marked by a steady decline of this religious element. For the present purpose the juristic aspect of treaties may be ignored. But it is necessary to define their general position in regard to law. They belong to the sphere of what is known as 'international law'; but the rules known as international law 'lie on the extreme frontier of law,'[1] and it is only more convenient, not necessarily more correct, to treat them as a branch of law rather than of morals. The difficulty of regarding them as properly a branch of law lies in the fact that there is no fixed authority (unless it be a universal League of Nations) that can lay down and enforce these rules as between nations, and the rules are liable to be broken with impunity by any nation that has the power and the will to defy them. No pact between two nations can bind a third which was not a consenting party. But treaties, which are one of the most important means by which 'international law' is laid down, are valuable as a record of the development of morality, for the very reason that they 'express national opinion in a peculiarly deliberate and solemn manner.'[2] The history of treaties accordingly illustrates the growing sense of nations —which, by a legal fiction or a bold metaphor, are moral persons[3]—for morality in international relations. It also illustrates the constant struggle to discover some means of enforcing the observance of pacts.

'Upon a scrupulous fidelity in the observation of Treaties, not merely in their letter but in their spirit, obviously depends, under God, the peace of the world. *Pacta sunt servanda* is the pervading maxim of International, as it was of Roman Law.'[4]

In the earliest times of which we have record this fidelity was reinforced by religious ceremonies, calling of the gods to witness, with oaths and imprecations.[5] In modern times these religious appeals, as also the giving of pledges, hostages, and the like, have generally fallen into desuetude except in the case of treaties with savages, and the observance of treaties has been left to the conscience of the parties; but, as this could no more be relied upon than when it required to be fortified by oaths, one of the chief objects of treaties in modern times has been the establishment of a balance of power in one form or other, so as to make the violation of them a risky undertaking. Finally, the impossibility of obtaining permanent equilibrium between groups of nations has raised the question of a universal League of Nations, which, in the form which it has assumed in the Treaty of Versailles of 1919, may be regarded as the highest development that the treaty has so far reached, since, by creating a determinate authority capable of enforcing the rules, it seeks to merge international law and (so far as law can make men moral) international morality in one. Previously to this treaty, little had been done in this direction beyond the general recognition that promises and signatures are futile, and that the only security lies in 'the establishment of a just and stable order.'[1] But how to ensure that the wrongdoer who, feeling himself strong enough, wantonly violates his word and destroys the peace of the world or breaks the laws of war shall be punished has seemed an insoluble problem, since his very act implies an assurance of impunity. W. G. F. Phillimore suggested[2] that each state that is a party to a treaty should contract with each and every other state that is a party, that, in the event of war between it and any other state that is a party to the treaty, it will observe towards the state with which it is at war all the agreed rules of the laws of war; and, if the rules are violated, then any other state party to the treaty may consider it an offence against itself that the law has been violated, such violation being considered an indirect injury, by reason of the lowering of the standard of conduct. The weak point of this arrangement is that interference on the side of law and order is merely permissive; it requires to be made imperative, and its scope extended so as to cover the maintenance of the peace of nations, and not merely the observance of the laws of war.

It is generally agreed that 'international morality—if not international law—calls upon every State to use every means at its disposal, without giving offence—for example, friendly suggestion, moral suasion—to prevent the outbreak of war, or, when it has begun, to help the contending parties to compose their differences. A war between two nations directly or indirectly concerns all nations, members as they are of the international community. There is not and there cannot be any principle of law, of ethics or of religion, prohibiting peaceful States from doing their utmost to bring about a cessation of carnage and devastation.'[3]

The League of Nations converts this negative into a positive injunction to interpose, and removes the offence from the most forcible methods of doing so. For art. 16 of the Covenant of the League declares that any resort to war in breach of its covenants by a member of the League is an act of war against all other members, which is to be met by a complete severance of relations of every kind, personal, financial, and commercial, with the offender, supported by the necessary military force. The provisions of this article may even be extended to cover the case of a state which is not a member of the League and refuses, in the case of a dispute, to adopt the obligations of membership. It is obvious that even this machinery will not suffice to suppress the ambitions of a state that feels itself strong enough to defy the greater part of the world; but it is equally obvious that such a state will be less ready to take the plunge than it would be if no such machinery existed.

Although the experience of the Great War of 1914–18 dashed the high hopes which were entertained as a result of The Hague Conferences of 1899 and 1907, it is unreasonable to regard those proceedings as a mere 'misprint in the world's history.' They were attended by the representatives of nations so numerous and so important that it was possible to say that in the result of their deliberations 'we have what may be regarded as the common judgment of mankind expressed in the most solemn manner in which an international engagement between nations is capable of expression' on such vital questions as the desirability of substituting arbitration for war.[4] For the first time, too, an international court was established

[1] W. E. Hall, *Treatise of International Law*[4], Oxford, 1895, p. 17.
[2] *Ib.* p. 9.
[3] De Garden, *Hist. générale des traités de paix*, vol. i. p. ii.
[4] R. J. Phillimore, *Commentaries upon International Law*, ii. 56.
[5] See artt. OATH.

[1] W. G. F. Phillimore, *Three Centuries of Treaties of Peace*, p. 146.
[2] *Ib.* p. 167.
[3] Coleman Phillipson, *Termination of War*, p. 75.
[4] Choate, *The Two Hague Conferences*, p. 34.

to give effect to the principle agreed upon by the conference. Now it is true that this solemn judgment was abrogated by the wanton action of a single one among the signatories, and the whole fabric of international relations tottered. But the foundation remains, to which The Hague Conferences contributed certain elements of solidity, if only by producing unanimity among a greater number of nations than had ever before been parties to a treaty. Such unanimity was secured again among an even greater number, and, when a fresh start was made in 1919, the problem of securing adequate sanction for the engagements between the nations by means of a League of Nations was attacked with the more insight and chance of success, because it was known wherein the old conferences had failed.

Among the chief reasons for the failure of treaties to preserve the peace are the misconception of their object as the termination of war merely, and not also the establishment of permanent peace, and the lack of elasticity in their terms. If they are drawn merely to settle the questions outstanding at the time, without care being taken not to sow the seeds of fresh conflict by imposing harsh conditions, restraining progress and liberty and ignoring the claims of the peoples concerned, they do little more than temporarily suppress forces which break out with the greater violence at the first opportunity. For the same reason, they should not be so rigidly drawn as to prevent reconsideration in the light of new conditions, and should include the necessary machinery for such reconsideration.[1]

2. Historical development: antiquity.—(*a*) The earliest treaties of which we have any detailed record relate to the two cities of Lagash and Umma, on either side of the Shatt-el-Hai in Babylonia.[2]

Entemena, patesi of Lagash (about 2850 B.C.), records an arbitration of earlier date in the time of Mesilim, king of Akkad. The actual patesis of Lagash and Umma are not named; the dispute is settled by the gods; the god Enlil presides over the conference and invites the parties to make the treaty; the boundary is fixed at his command by Ningirsu, god of Lagash, and by the city-god of Umma; even Mesilim acts only at the command of his goddess Kadi. This is obviously an extreme instance of the religious sanction; the parties are supposed to live and move and have their being entirely in their local gods.

A second treaty between the same two cities was made about 2900 B.C. by Eannatum, patesi and king of Lagash, and Enakalli, patesi of Umma. A great boundary-ditch was dug, and the plain of Gu-edin, which was in dispute, was restored to Ningirsu, god of Lagash. Shrines to Enlil, Ningirsu, and other gods were erected along the new frontier beside the pillars of delimitation, and it was doubtless at the altars of these shrines that the parties took oaths in ratifying the treaty: 'On the men of Umma have I, Eannatum, cast the great net of Enlil. I have sworn the oath, and the men of Umma have sworn the oath to Eannatum.' He invokes the vengeance of Enlil on the men of Umma if they 'alter this word.' He also invokes other gods, to whom he has made suitable offerings, to enforce the treaty.

In the third treaty, the terms of which were imposed on Umma by Entemena of Lagash (about 2850 B.C.), we have a similar imprecation: 'If the men of Umma ever violate the boundary-ditch of Ningirsu or that of Nina, in order to lay violent hands on the territory of Lagash . . . then may Enlil destroy them, and may Ningirsu cast over them his net, and set his hand and foot upon them.' The imprecations recall those which are invoked on the violators of Babylonian boundary-stones; naturally the same means were employed to secure the validity of legal engagements of all kinds.

(*b*) The famous treaty between Rameses II. and Khetasar (Hattusil), prince of the Hittites (*c.* 1300 B.C.), is recorded in three copies, of which two are hieroglyphic, at Karnak and in the Ramesseum, while the third is the Hittite-Babylonian version, or rather fragments of two copies thereof, from Boghaz Keui.[3] Two Hittite envoys brought the text of the treaty written on silver tablets, the design of which is described:

On one side 'a figure in the likeness of Setekh, embracing the likeness of the great chief of the Kheta, surrounded by the words: "The seal of Setekh, the ruler of the heavens; the seal of the treaty which Khetasar . . . made." That which is within the frame of the design is the seal of Setekh, the ruler of the heavens. That which is on its other side is a figure in the likeness of the goddess of Kheta, embracing the figure of the princess of Kheta, surrounded by the following words: "The seal of the Sun-god of the city of Arinna, the lord of the land; the seal of Petkhep, the princess of the land of Kheta, the daughter of the land of Kezweden, the priestess (?) of Ernen, the mistress of the land, the votaress of the goddess." That which is within the frame of the design is the seal of the Sun-god of Arinna, the lord of every land.'

Thus the treaty is reinforced by being placed under the seals of the gods themselves. In addition we find the following invocations, corresponding to similar paragraphs usually attached to other documents which were intended to be permanently valid:

'As for the words of this contract . . . a thousand gods, male gods and female gods, of those of the land of Kheta, together with a thousand gods, male gods and female gods of those of the land of Egypt, they are with me as witnesses to these words: "the Sun-god, lord of the heavens," and various other gods, including those "of the mountains and the rivers of the lands of Kheta and of Egypt, of the heavens, the earth, the great sea, the winds, and the clouds."' These are invoked to desolate the house, the land, and the subjects of the violator of the treaty, and, as for him who keeps it, to preserve his health, and his life, together with his issue, his land, and his subjects.

(*c*) The covenants recorded in the OT are for the most part between single persons; but certain forms and ceremonies were doubtless common to such covenants and international treaties. Such were the setting up of a pillar and a heap of stones as witness, the invocation of the God of Abraham and the God of Nahor, Jacob's oath 'by the fear of his father Isaac,' and the sacrifice and eating of bread in the mountain, in the covenant between Jacob and Laban (Gn 31^{44-54}). The treaty between Isaac and Abimelech (Gn $26^{28ff.}$) is similarly accompanied by feasting and oath-taking. In Joshua's peace with the people of Gibeon the princes of the congregation swore by the Lord God of Israel (Jos $9^{15.19}$). The ceremony of cutting an animal in twain and passing between the halves was used by the Hebrews in covenants between God and man (Gn $15^{7ff.}$, Jer $34^{18ff.}$),[1] as by other nations in connexion with purification and oath-taking; but the derivation of the phrase כרת ברית from this division of a victim is doubtful, to 'cut a covenant' being rather parallel to ὅρκια τάμνειν and *fœdus ferire* or *percutere* or *icere*;[2] whether these phrases refer to the cutting down of the victim, however, seems uncertain.

(*d*) The writers of antiquity give details of a number of more or less picturesque ceremonies accompanying oath-taking in treaties between less civilized nations. Of these the most important is the blood-covenant.[3]

The Scythians mixed wine with their own blood in a bowl, dipped their weapons into it, took oaths and uttered imprecations, and finally pledged each other in the mixture.[4] The Arabians made the incision with a sharp stone, smeared the blood on seven stones, and invoked Orotalt (Dionysos) and Alilat (Urania).[5] The *locus classicus* is Tac. *Ann.* xii. 47 (the Armenians suck each other's blood): 'id foedus arcanum habetur, quasi mutuo cruore sacratum.' It was also in later days a Saracen custom, and it was a reproach to Isaac Angelus that he conformed to it in making peace with that nation.[6] Other ceremonies are collected by Dumont.[7] In China the

[1] Graham Bower, in *Grotius Soc. Papers*, iii.

[2] L. W. King, *Hist. of Sumer and Akkad*, London, 1910, pp. 101 ff., 126 ff., 164 ff.

[3] R. von Scala, *Die Staatsverträge*, i. no. 13; *Mitt. der deutsch. Orient-Gesellschaft zu Berlin*, no. 35, p. 13 ff.; J. H. Breasted, *Ancient Records of Egypt*, Chicago, 1905-07, iii. [1906] 373-391; S. Langdon and A. H. Gardiner, *Journal of Egyptian Archæology*, vi. [1920] 179-205. The passage quoted is from the Egyptian version, in which the Egyptian scribe has turned the Hittite sun-goddess into a male deity.

[1] E. J. Pilcher, in *PSBA* xl. [1918] 8-14.

[2] E. McClure, *ib.* p. 41.

[3] See art. BROTHERHOOD (Artificial).

[4] Herod. iv. 70.

[5] Herod. iii. 8; cf. i. 74: Medes and Lydians.

[6] Nicetas Choniata, *de Isaacio Angelo*, ii. 5 (536); *PG* cxxxix. 775.

[7] *Corps universel diplomatique*, vol. i. p. xxxiv ff.

blood-covenant was also in use, and treaties were confirmed by oaths and imprecations and accompanied by the sacrifice of an ox. In a treaty of 544 B.C. the formula is: 'May the gods of the hills and the rivers, the spirits of former emperors and dukes, and the ancestors of our seven tribes and twelve States watch over its fulfilment. If any one prove unfaithful may the all-seeing gods smite him, so that his people shall forsake him, his life be lost, and his posterity cut off.'[1]

(*e*) Coming to the Western nations, we find that the international relations depicted in the Homeric poems, though primitive, include the making of truces, with oaths, for the burning of the dead;[2] oaths, invocation of the gods, imprecation on the treaty-breaker, with sacrifice and feasting, also accompany a treaty between Greeks and Trojans.[3] In the historical period in Greece we find certain primitive survivals, as when Aristeides administered the oath to the Greeks and took it himself on behalf of the Athenians, throwing pieces of hot iron (μύδροι) into the sea. But as a rule the oaths are the ordinary ones (νόμιμοι ὅρκοι) in the name of the chief gods (ὅρκιοι); or, as in the alliance between Athens, Argos, Mantineia, and Elis (420 B.C.), the instruction is that each party should swear its most binding national oath over perfect victims (τὸν ἐπιχώριον ὅρκον τὸν μέγιστον κατὰ ἱερῶν τελείων). The tendency is to increase the number of gods invoked, in the futile hope of increasing the force of the oath.

In a treaty between Carthage and Philip V.[4] in 216 B.C. the following deities are invoked: Zeus, Hera, Apollo, the Genius (δαίμων) of the Carthaginians, Heracles and Iolaos, Ares, Triton, Poseidon, the gods of the army (θεοὶ οἱ συστρατευόμενοι), the Sun, Moon, and Earth, the rivers, harbours, and waters, all the gods who rule Carthage, all the gods who rule Macedon and the rest of Greece, all the gods who preside over the campaign (οἱ κατὰ στρατείαν). The Magnesians in allying themselves with Smyrna (mid. 3rd cent. B.C.)[5] swear by Zeus, Earth, Sun, Ares, Athene Areia, Artemis Tauropolos, the Sipylene Mother, Apollo ὁ ἐν Πάνδοις, all the other gods and goddesses, and the Good Fortune of King Seleucus. The Smyrnæans substitute Aphrodite Stratonikis for Apollo and omit the Good Fortune of the king.

The inscriptions frequently omit the instructions as to the gods in whose names the oaths are to be taken, prescribing merely the nature of the undertaking, as:

'I will fight for the Bottiæans who enter into the pact, and will keep the alliance with them faithfully and without guile, showing all zeal according to the pact; and I will bear no ill-will because of what has happened in the past.'[6]

Formulæ of imprecation frequently accompany the oath; in the simplest form (as in the alliance between Athens and Corcyra in 375 B.C.)[7] it is: 'If I keep the oath, may much good befall me, but if not, the contrary'; but destruction is sometimes invoked on the perjurer and all his house.[8] The inscriptions give some information as to the machinery for administering the oath.[9] The more distinguished the oath-taker, the more solemn was the oath. Frequently the oath was taken *en masse*; thus in the peace with Selymbria (408 B.C.)[10] the Athenian generals, trierarchs, hoplites, and 'any one else who was there' took the oath for Athens, while the whole people of the Selymbrians swore on the other side. Provision was sometimes made to keep the consciences of the parties alive by a periodical renewal of the oath—*e.g.*, at each Olympiad (Eretria and Histiæa)[11] or every year (Athens and Dionysius I.).[12]

The gradual moralization of international relations in the Greek world is well illustrated by the treaties of *asylia*, which have for their object to do away with the rough-and-ready methods of reprisals between individuals or states.[1] The most famous instance is the treaty between Œantheia and Chaleion (5th cent.), restricting seizures to the open sea, imposing fines for breach of the regulations, and prescribing the proper tribunals for trying cases.[2] The Greek attitude to the ethics of treaties does not differ from that of other nations; practice also, as usual, fails to conform to precept, and there is the customary laying of the blame for breach of oath on the other party.

Archidamos before Platæa calls the gods and heroes of the Platæans to witness that it was they and not the Lacedæmonians who first broke their oath.[3] The Athenians took the trouble to record a breach of faith by the Lacedæmonians on the stone on the Acropolis which bore the text of the broken treaty.[4] Again, the Athenians and Ceians inscribed on a stone the names of certain people of Iulis who had broken faith and been condemned to death; these people, however, returning to Ceos, tore up the stone; and, finally, the Athenians again provided for the restoration of the stone with the names of the offenders (363 B.C.).[5]

(*f*) Roman usage shows, as might be expected from the Roman legal genius, a more highly organized conception of international relations. The whole procedure of making treaties was laid down, and carried out by a definite body of officials, the college of *fetiales*, whose function was[6] to be the guardians of good faith in international relations.[7] This religious body represented the Roman people in all public international acts, such as making war and peace. Their origin was early, and was attributed to one or other of the kings; in fact neighbouring communities, such as the Latins and Samnites, had analogous magistrates, so that the institution must have been Italic in origin. The derivation of their name is uncertain. There were twenty in the college, one from each *curia* of the two primitive tribes, Ramnes and Titienses, men of good family, in early days at least of course non-plebeians. Their head was known as the *magister fetialium*. A fetial mission for contracting a peace consisted of at least two, the *pater patratus* and the *verbenarius*. The procedure was as follows, supposing that the peace was to be made outside Rome.

The *verbenarius* inquired whether he and the *pater patratus* were to make peace; if so, he asked leave to take the *verbenæ* (*herba pura*, or *sagmina*), *i.e.* a piece of turf from the soil of the Capitol, which rendered the persons of the mission inviolable (we may compare the legal fiction by which the site of an embassy is now considered to be the territory of the nation it represents). The fetials also carried with them sacred vessels, the sceptre of Jupiter Feretrius, and a flint knife (representing Jupiter Lapis, a primitive touch) from his temple. The *pater patratus* wore priest's clothing, not of linen, and a woollen fillet on his head. The *verbenarius* selected him from his colleagues by touching his head with the *sagmina*. They proceeded to the place selected, and, in presence of the generals and armies, and the fetials of the enemy, the terms of peace were read, and the *pater patratus* swore to them on the sceptre of Jupiter Feretrius, calling to witness Jupiter, Mars, Quirinus, and all present. He then slew a pig[8] with the flint knife, invoking death on the Roman people if they should break the peace. Then he threw away the stone (a detail recalling the throwing away of the axe in the Attic Buphonia) saying: 'If I wittingly violate my oath, may all others prosper, while Jupiter casts me out, even as I cast away this stone.'

The scene of the swine-sacrifice by fetials is represented on Roman coins of the time of Augustus commemorating the ancient treaty between Rome and the Gabines, and an analogous sacrifice by warriors, evidently engaged in making a treaty of some kind, is a common type on other Roman coins, as well as on those of the Italic revolt

1 C. Phillipson, *Internat. Law and Custom of Anc. Greece and Rome*, i. 387 f., who adds that 'amongst the uncivilized races of to-day the formal oath, imprecation, and sacrifice—sometimes of human victims—are the invariable accompaniments of the conclusion of treaties.'
2 *E.g.*, *Il.* vii. 375 f., 408 f.
3 *Ib.* iii. 103 f., 268–301, iv. 156 f.
4 Polyb. vii. 9.
5 Michel, *Recueil d'inscr. grec.* 19.
6 *IG* i. 52; *c.* 422 B.C.
7 Hicks and Hill, *Greek Hist. Inscr.* no. 106.
8 Michel, *loc. cit.*
9 See Lécrivain in Daremberg-Saglio, *s.v.* 'Fœdus.'
10 See Hicks-Hill, no. 77.
11 Michel, 7.
12 Hicks-Hill, no. 112, if the restoration is correct.

1 See Lécrivain in Daremberg-Saglio, *s.v.* 'Fœdus,' p. 1204.
2 Von Scala, i. no. 58.
3 Thuc. ii. 74.
4 *Ib.* v. 56. 3.
5 Hicks-Hill, no. 118.
6 Varro, *de Ling. Lat.* v. 15 (86).
7 See A. Weiss in Daremberg-Saglio, and E. Samter in Pauly-Wissowa, *s.v.*; Phillipson, *Int. Law and Custom of Anc. Gr. and Rome*, ii. ch. xxvi.
8 Cf. Virg. *Æn.* viii. 641.

against Rome in 91–88 B.C.[1] When Livy[2] describes a similar ceremonial among the Carthaginians, substituting a lamb for a pig, he is perhaps only attributing Roman customs to them; Polybius[3] is careful to distinguish, saying that the Carthaginians swear by their own gods, while the Romans perform the ceremony evidently regarded as peculiar to themselves. After the ceremony the fetials signed the text and brought it to Rome, and the whole college pledged itself to secure that it should be duly observed. It is hardly too much to say that the account given of the functions of the fetials reveals as highly organized a system, and as dignified a conception of the legal essence of the treaty, as has ever been realized. But it is a mistake to suppose that this organization is the expression of a high ethical standard.[4]

3. Middle Ages and modern times.—(*a*) The *Pax Romana* makes records of treaties during the empire scanty.[5] The swearing of oaths lingers on into the modern period.

In the treaty between Justinian and Chosroes (A.D. 561) the 12th article contains the invocation of God and the prayer that God may be compassionate to him who keeps the peace and may fight on his side, but that he may be the adversary of the deceitful man who seeks to overthrow the pact. The oath taken in the treaty of Andelot between Guntram, king of Burgundy, and Childebert, king of Austrasia (A.D. 587), is 'by the name of Almighty God and the indivisible Trinity, and all things divine, and the awful Day of Judgment.' In 842 Louis II. of Germany and Charles II. of France swear 'per Domini Dei amorem et Christiani Populi et nostram communem conservationem.' A treaty made in the 12th cent. by the city of Spalato[6] contains an imprecation: 'in the name of the Triune God, of the 118 Fathers, the 12 Apostles and all the Saints.' The oath is sometimes taken over relics, but most commonly over the Holy Gospels; *e.g.*, in the peace between Pope Alexander III. and the Emperor Frederick I. (1177) the representatives swear: 'Iuramus in manibus vestris super haec sancta Dei Evangelia quod pacem . . . bona fide servabimus, et absque fraude. Sic Deus nos adiuvet, et haec Sancta Dei Evangelia.'

The formula 'jurer en son âme,' 'jurare in animam suam,' appears frequently in treaties between England and France or the Low Countries.

Excommunication was the logical sequel to violation of a treaty-oath (as specified, *e.g.*, in the truce for the renewal of the Treuga Domini at the Council of Narbonne, 1054). Gradually the oath fades away into the promise.

In the treaty of commerce between Henry VII. and Philip, Duke of Burgundy (1495), the commissioners, in a declaration 'to all faithful Christians . . . Eternal Greeting in the Lord,' *bona fide* promise and oblige themselves, on the pledge and obligation of all their goods present and to come, to procure the observance of the treaty; these obligations are to be delivered to the deputies of each side in the church of the Virgin Mary at Calais. The king's undertaking to ratify the agreements made by his commissioners is given '*bona fide* and on the word of a King,' and the duke promises '*bona fide* and on the word of a Prince.' In the treaty of 1604 between Philip III. of Spain and James I. of England the gradual obsolescence of the oath is markedly visible in the clause: 'They shall make a like promise on the word of a King and Prince, and even swear on the Holy Gospels, if they are thereto required by the other party.'

The most modern example of an oath is said to be that taken in the cathedral of Soleure in the alliance between France and Switzerland in 1777. Thus finally disappeared that element which was, 'in a certain sense, the underlying basis of the whole body of the ancient laws of nations.'[7]

It was not uncommon for a party to a treaty to obtain absolution from his oath.

Thus Maximilian I., a few months before the League of Cambrai (1508), had made a treaty with Venice; one of the articles of the League summoned him by a papal brief to the aid of the Church and gave him reasons for breaking his oath. The pope dispensed François I. from his oath taken in the Treaty of Madrid (1526) and Henri II. from his oath at Vaucelles (1550).

A second clause was sometimes inserted, intended to prevent any party from seeking, or accepting the offer of, dispensation from his oath (*e.g.*, in the cession of the Spanish crown to Charles III. in 1703).[1] But, since release from this second obligation could obviously be obtained in the same way as from the first, it was as futile as an attempt to prevent the repeal of a law by inserting a clause imposing a death-penalty on any one who should propose such repeal. Modern treaty-custom recognizes the vanity of all such artificial supports to good faith.

The most sweeping and perhaps most futile example of absolution from a treaty-oath is provided by the bull of Pope Innocent X. describing numerous articles in the Peace of Westphalia (1648) as 'null, vain, invalid, iniquitous, unjust, condemned, reprobated, frivolous, void of force and effect,' and dispensing anybody who pleased from his oath taken thereto.[2] The explanation of this outburst lies in the fact that this treaty was 'the first fundamental pact of Europe which struck at the root of the foreign temporal authority of the Pope.'[3]

The king in recent treaties merely engages and pronounces upon his royal word that he will sincerely and faithfully perform and observe the terms of the contract.[4] Finally, the parties to the Treaty of Versailles (1919) merely 'agree' to the covenant of the League of Nations and the closing formula is simply: 'In Faith Whereof the abovenamed Plentipotentiaries have signed the present Treaty.'

(*b*) Religious formulæ are also used to a considerable degree as introductory clauses from mediæval times onwards, but in this feature treaties merely fall into line with all important documents. The commonest introductory formulæ are 'In the name of the Most Holy and Undivided Trinity' (*e.g.*, in the treaty between Charles the Simple and Henry I. of Germany, 926, or in the Treaty of Vienna, 9 June 1815) and 'In the name of our Lord Jesus Christ.' A more florid style is naturally observable in the treaty between Frederick II. and Abu-Zakaria-Yahia, king of the Saracens of Tunisia, in 1231.

'In nomine Dei misericordis, miseratoris. Incipimus cum laude Dei maximi et, invocatione illius prelaudata, petimus prosperitatem. Laus Deo, scienti abscondita, futura, extantia, qui est eternus, post finem omnis viventis.'

The importance of the religious sanction made it long a moot point whether nations of different religions could make valid treaties with each other (a point, however, which Grotius decided in the modern sense), or, again, whether it was obligatory on all Christian nations to be leagued together against the infidel. In modern times it is recognized that treaties are governed by natural law alone, and the religious element, either in the content or in the phraseology of treaties, has naturally become much less discernible—to such a degree that the profession of Christian principles in the Holy Alliance (26th Sept. 1815) between Austria, Prussia, and Russia makes a deep and justifiable impression of insincerity.

In this remarkable alliance (the real object of which was anti-revolutionary) the contracting parties 'solemnly declare that the present Act has no other object than to publish in the face of the whole world their fixed resolution, both in the administration of their respective States and in their political relations with every other Government, to take for their sole guide the precepts of the Holy Religion, namely the precepts of Justice, Christian Charity and Peace, which . . . must have an immediate influence on the Councils of Princes and guide all their steps as being the only means of consolidating human institutions and remedying their imperfections.'

It is significant that the pope was not invited to join this alliance, and that Britain was prevented

1 H. A. Grueber, *Coins of the Roman Republic in the British Museum*, London, 1910, ii. 56, 98, 332, etc.
2 xxi. 45.
3 iii. 25.
4 J. S. Reid, in *JRS* vi. [1916] 172.
5 For treaties before Charlemagne see Barbeyrac's *Supplément* to Dumont's *Corps universel diplomatique*, from Charlemagne onwards Dumont's work itself, and for the modern period the various collections, especially Martens'.
6 Dumont, i. 88.
7 Phillipson, *Int. Law and Custom of Anc. Gr. and Rome*, i. 389.

1 J. J. Schmauss, *Corpus Juris Gentium*, Leipzig, 1730, ii. 1165.
2 Phillipson, *Termination of War*, p. 208.
3 R. J. Phillimore, *Comm.* ii. 58.
4 Oakes and Mowat, *Great European Treaties*, p. 4.

from doing so 'by the forms of the British constitution.'[1]

(*c*) Apart from professions of this sort, the actual protection of the religious freedom of peoples involved in a settlement by treaty has often formed the subject of special articles.[2]

An early and remarkable instance is in the treaty between Justinian and Chosroes, in A.D. 561, in which a special article provided that Christians in Persia should enjoy freedom of worship, and on their own part should not attempt to make proselytes among the Magi. In modern times the Treaty of Westphalia marked an advance in religious toleration. The Treaty of Paris in 1763, recognizing the conquest of Canada, made special provision for liberty to the new Roman Catholic subjects of the king of Britain to follow their own religious worship. The Treaty of Oliva in 1660 (between Poland and Sweden) protected the co-religionists of either power in the territory of the other. In 1867, when Russia ceded Alaska to the United States, it was provided that the civilized inhabitants should not be interfered with in their religion. And in 1913, by the Treaty of Constantinople, Muslims resident in Bulgarian territory were guaranteed the enjoyment of religious liberty, and the name of the sultan as khalif was to continue to be pronounced in their public prayers. 'It is incumbent on the acquiring sovereign to allow to the inhabitants of the annexed territory the free exercise of their religion when it is not incompatible with good order and the fundamental dictates of morality. The obligation is not, of course, a legal one, but its sanction is rooted more deeply than that of positive enactments.'[3]

Hence the necessity of actual stipulations, such as those enumerated, is not usually felt.

(*d*) Of more importance, as indicating moral progress, than professions relating to religious principles, or even than provisions for religious freedom, is the degree of solicitude shown by the contracting parties for the general interests of the people. W. G. F. Phillimore[4] remarks that, except in the matter of religious toleration, the Treaty of Westphalia paid scant regard to the interests of the people. From 1648 to the recognition of American independence in 1783 the chief consideration in treaties is paid, as in older days, to the rights and interests of sovereigns and reigning families. In the next period, down to 1859, there is increased recognition of the rights of states. Still, by the General Act of the Congress of Vienna, *e.g.*, states and populations were trafficked in, with absolute disregard of the peoples concerned, who might as well have been slaves or cattle.

Since 1859 'little regard is paid to the supposed rights and interests of individual sovereigns or reigning families, and a new principle has arisen, viz. the rights of nationalities.'[5]

4. Conclusion.—Certain moral considerations which arise in connexion with treaty-making and treaty-breaking may be stated, though no solution is necessarily offered of the questions involved.

(*a*) The construing of treaties is a matter of equity. They are covenants *bonæ fidei*, and are not therefore to be technically construed.

'Discrimen actuum bonae fidei et stricti juris, quatenus ex jure est Romano, ad jus gentium non pertinet.'[6] The principle of the *Digest*, 'voluntatem potius quam verba spectari placuit,' applies with especial force.[7] 'There is no place for the refinements of the courts in the rough jurisprudence of nations.'[8]

In antiquity a famous instance of the breach of this principle was the murder of Hippias by Paches.[9] The classical example in modern writers, however, is the action of the French who, having destroyed the fortifications of Dunkirk in accordance with the Treaty of Utrecht, proceeded to construct a still stronger place at Mardick, a few miles away. The principle by which a provision may be 'extended' so as to include a case to which the same reason applies as applied to the case originally envisaged, or may be 'restricted,' so that an ally excludes the application of a provision to a case obviously improper (as when, having promised to aid an ally in all its wars, it is asked to join in an unjust war)—this principle of extensive or restrictive interpretation assists contracting parties in adhering to the spirit rather than the letter of the treaty.[1]

1 Oakes-Mowat, p. 34.
2 W. G. F. Phillimore, *Three Centuries*, pp. 55 f., 145; Phillipson, *Termination of War*, p. 309.
3 Phillipson, *loc. cit.*
4 *Three Centuries*, p. 14.
5 *Ib.* Doubts are already being expressed as to the permanent value of this principle; cf. Sir A. W. Ward, *Securities of Peace*, p. 9.
6 Grotius, *de Jure Belli ac Pacis*, ii. 16. 11; see R. J. Phillimore, *Comm.* ii. 79.
7 L. 16. 219.
8 Hall[4], p. 356.
9 Thuc. iii. 34.

(*b*) Since governments are representatives of justice, morality, and religion, it is assumed[2] that a treaty containing an engagement to do or allow that which is contrary to morality or justice is invalid. 'Pacta, quae turpem causam continent, non sunt observanda.'[3] Since a large number of treaties are forcibly imposed on a conquered by a conquering state, it is obvious that this principle provides innumerable opportunities for dispute and repudiation, under the next heading.

(*c*) How far is a treaty invalidated by the employment of force on the part of one of the parties? To this it is generally agreed to answer that there is no force in the plea that one of the parties consented through fear, or in face of superior force, such as would invalidate a private contract, since such treaties are only a way of terminating war, which is entirely determined by force. 'No inequality of advantage, no lesion, can invalidate a Treaty.'[4] But it is equally clearly held that treachery or duress exerted against the representative of a state amply justifies the repudiation of a treaty. The classical instance is Napoleon's extortion of terms from Ferdinand VII. at Bayonne.

(*d*) Fraud is also clearly held to invalidate a treaty, for then there is no real freedom of consent on the part of the deceived party.[5] The distinction is sometimes a little delicate between positive fraud and *suppressio veri*.

In the negotiations for the Webster-Ashburton Treaty (1842) Webster suppressed a map which was favourable to the British cause. The map could have been found, as Greville admitted, if the British authorities had caused proper search to be made, and Lord Ashburton agrees that he had no legal cause for complaint.[6] Yet it is to such cases as this that the remark of Hall[7] may be applied: 'It is recognized that there is an international morality distinct from law, violation of which gives no formal ground of complaint, however odious the action of the ill-doer may be.'

(*e*) The question of how far a party can liberate itself from obligations has been brought into special prominence by Germany's repudiation of its pledge to Belgium in 1914. To the doctrine that 'necessity, when real and *bona fide*, overrides the obligation of the promise' R. J. Phillimore[8] replies:

'It is manifest that the State, like the Individual, which takes advantage of every change of affairs to disengage itself from the obligations of a solemn covenant, weakens the foundations of that good faith on which the peace of the world depends.'

So too Hall:[9]

'Modern writers, it would seem, are more struck by the impossibility of looking at international contracts as perpetually binding, than by the necessity of insisting upon that good faith between States without which the world has only before it the alternatives of armed suspense or open war, and they too often lay down canons of such perilous looseness, that if their doctrine is to be accepted, an unscrupulous State need never be in want of a plausible excuse for repudiating an inconvenient obligation.'

Pedants such as those on whom Frederick the Great relied to justify his acts are to be found in all ages and countries. The Conference of London (1871) made the declaration:

'It is an essential principle of the law of nations that no Power can liberate itself from the engagements of a treaty, or modify the stipulations thereof, unless with the consent of the contracting Powers by means of an amicable arrangement.'

This declaration, which was signed by all the

1 R. J. Phillimore, *Comm.* ii. 96 f.
2 *Ib.* ii. 64 and 111.
3 *Dig.* II. xiv. 27. 4.
4 R. J. Phillimore, *Comm.* ii. 63; cf. Phillipson, *Termination of War*, p. 162.
5 Hall[4], p. 342.
6 Crandall, *Treaties, their Making and Enforcement*, p. 14.
7 P. 15.
8 *Comm.* ii. 100.
9 P. 366.

leading Powers of Europe, was provoked by Russia's attempt to evade its obligations under the Treaty of Paris of 1856, on the ground that lapse of time had changed the conditions. Although no specific declaration to the same effect appears to be included in the covenant of the League of Nations or in the treaty with Germany, the case seems to be covered by article 16, which provides for the prevention or punishment of breaches of covenant in general.

(*f*) How far does honour demand the intervention of one of the guarantors, in the case of a collective guarantee, when agreement is not reached between all parties?[1] Bluntschli holds that each guarantor is bound to act separately in such a case. Lord Derby (in connexion with the Luxemburg Convention of 1867) held that honour (but not legal obligation) compelled each guarantor, in concert with the others, to maintain the engagements; but that, if concerted action was not obtainable, then a guarantor would have the right, but not necessarily the legal obligation, to act. It is obvious that this difficulty could be avoided by care in drafting, and that, unless Bluntschli's view be accepted, the collective guarantee is not likely to be very valuable until we have reached a higher code of international honour than prevails at the present time. The covenant of the League of Nations meets the case by making joint intervention obligatory on all its members.

LITERATURE. — *ANTIQUITY*. — J. Dumont, *Corps universel diplomatique du droit des gens*, Paris, 1726–31, vol. i. p. xxxiv ff.; A. E. Egger, *Etudes hist. sur les traités publics chez les Grecs et chez les Romains*², Paris, 1866; Daremberg-Saglio, ii. 2 [1896], *s.vv.* 'Fetiales' (A. Weiss) and 'Fœdus' (C. Lécrivain and G. Humbert); R. von Scala, *Die Staatsverträge des Altertums*, Leipzig, 1898, i.; C. Michel, *Recueil d'inscriptions grecques*, Paris, 1896–1900; W. Dittenberger, *Sylloge Inscriptionum Græcarum*², Leipzig, 1898–1901 (³1915–); E. L. Hicks and G. F. Hill, *Manual of Greek Historical Inscriptions*, rev. ed., Oxford, 1901; E. Samter, art. 'Fetiales' in Pauly-Wissowa, vi. [1909]; C. Phillipson, *The International Law and Custom of Ancient Greece and Rome*, 2 vols., London, 1911.

MEDIÆVAL AND MODERN TIMES. — Besides the general treatises on international law from Grotius onward: T. Rymer, *Fœdera*, 20 vols., London, 1704–32; *A General Collection of Treatys, Declarations of War, Manifestos, and of Public Papers relating to Peace and War*, 4 vols., do. 1732; Dumont, *Corps universel diplomatique*, 8 vols., with *Supplément* by J. Barbeyrac and J. Rousset, 5 vols., Amsterdam, 1739; G. F. de Martens, *Recueil des traités . . . des puissances et états de l'Europe depuis 1761*², 8 vols., Göttingen, 1817–1835, with the continuations; G. de Garden, *Hist. générale des traités de paix*, 15 vols., Paris, 1848–87; R. J. Phillimore, *Commentaries upon International Law*, London, 1854–61, vol. ii., chs. vi.–ix.; L. de Mas-Latrie, *Traités de paix et de commerce . . . des chrétiens avec les Arabes de l'Afrique septentrionale au moyen âge*, Paris, 1865; S. B. Crandall, *Treaties, their Making and Enforcement*, New York, 1904; C. Phillipson, *Termination of War and Treaties of Peace*, London, 1916; W. G. F. Phillimore, *Three Centuries of Treaties of Peace and their Teaching*, do. 1917; A. Oakes and R. B. Mowat, *Great European Treaties of the Nineteenth Century*, Oxford, 1918; Graham Bower, *Treaties of Peace* (Grotius Soc. Papers, iii. [1918]); Sir A. W. Ward, *Securities of Peace*, London, 1919.

THE HAGUE CONFERENCES.—J. H. Choate, *The Two Hague Conferences*, London, 1913; F. W. Holls, *The Peace Conference at The Hague*², do. 1915; P. Zorn, *Die beiden Haager Friedens-Konferenzen von 1899 und 1907*, Stuttgart, 1915; J. B. Scott, *The Hague Conventions and Declarations of 1899 and 1907*², London, 1916.

G. F. HILL.

TREES AND PLANTS.—I. Introductory.—

All plants are sacred. This principle of the followers of Zoroaster lies at the root of all plant-lore, all tree-cults. All plants possess the gifts of immortality and health.[2] The subject enters into every form of religion, and its ramifications are traceable in different aspects and degrees from the tree of life to the May-pole. It rests on the earliest conceptions of the unity of life in nature, in the sense of communion and fellowship with the divine centre and source of life. The oak of Mamre, the ash Yggdrasil, the *ashērāh*, the oak of Dodona, the *Ficus ruminalis*, the Bodhi-trees, the pine-cones, and the seven-branched candlestick, even the modern Christmas-tree with its lights and its fruit and its fillets, are instances of the vast area in folk-lore, tradition, and social custom which has been influenced by early reverence for the sacred tree.

[1] Hall, p. 360.

[2] *RGG* ii. 506.

The sacred tree is thus deeply rooted in the primitive religious ideas of the human race. The spring, the rock, the tree are all visible manifestations of the divine spirit. They are found associated in the most ancient sanctuaries as different symbols of life; and this life, in earth or water or tree, is one with human life. The same divine spirit lives and works in all and manifests itself in each and all. The secret of religion is the recognition of this life as divine; its duty is the obligation of fellowship and worship which comes of this recognition.

In the earliest stage the sacred tree is more than a symbol. It is instinct with divine life, aglow with divine light. It is at once the tree of life and the tree of the knowledge of good and evil. This animistic stage is traceable in folk-lore and myth, in traditional survivals in later ritual, and in savage cults in more recent and even modern times. In the history of religious development it lies behind the historic era. The burning bush, living and aglow with the divine voice, gives a conception of this earliest stage.

In the second stage the sacred tree is planted in holy ground. It is representative of the deity. It is the dwelling-place of the deity. The priest-king is its champion, and is himself the embodiment or incarnation of the god.[1] It is as priest-king at Mamre that Abraham arms his trained servants and leads them against the kings of the earth. It is an archaic survival in an archaic fragment (Gn $14^{13f.}$). The champion of the tree-god must be loyal to the cult. A new sanctuary must be consecrated by the planting of the sacred tree, though not always of the same tree. The oak-Zeus of Dodona adopted under certain conditions the white poplar and the plane. Abraham, the champion of the oak or terebinth of Mamre, planted a grove, *i.e.* a tamarisk, at Beersheba. Agamemnon, as guardian of a sacred tree, and himself enjoying the divine title ἄναξ ἀνδρῶν and worshipped as a chthonian Zeus in Laconia, planted a plane-tree at Delphi and another at Caphyæ in Arcadia.[2] These plantings are examples of the second, or representative, stage of tree-worship.

The third is the symbolic stage. The 'grove,' or *ashērāh*, the common adjunct of the Canaanite shrine, is the most familiar example of this stage. It was a wooden pillar, representative like the living tree of the deity, 'the token of the deity's presence or a magnet for attracting it.'[3] There are traces of it in the sanctuaries at Samaria (2 K 13^6), at Bethel (23^{15}), and even in the Temple at Jerusalem (23^6).

The differentiation of the one deity into the 'gods many and lords many' of local and national cults led to the iconic representation of the tree-god. The stump takes human shape. The Hermæ, wooden or stone pillars swelling towards the top, were crowned with the head of Hermes. The rude figure of Priapus as protector of gardens was of a similar character. The *caduceus* of Hermes, a wand with a triple shoot, may refer also to his origin as a tree-god.[4] Silvanus is represented in a similar form, with his sacred pine and also with the *caduceus* as a symbol. And in this connexion the statement of Pausanias

[1] A. B. Cook, *ClR* xvii. [1903] 277.

[2] *Ib.*

[3] L. R. Farnell, *ERE* vi. 397^b.

[4] O. Seyffert, *A Dict. of Classical Antiquities*, ed. H. Nettleship and J. E. Sandys, London, 1904, pp. 285 f., 515; Mrs. Philpot, *The Sacred Tree*, do. 1897, p. 76.

and Pliny is significant, that in ancient times the images of the gods were made of wood.[1] And with the differentiation of the deity into the gods of the nations there came the differentiation of the tree into the trees sacred to the several gods. The oak was specially sacred to Zeus. The *Ficus ruminalis* of the Palatine was originally the sacred tree of Rome, though Juppiter was associated with the oak on the Capitoline Hill.[2] The cult, in early times as wide as the world, was narrowed when no sanctuary could be dedicated to Apollo which was unfavourable to the growth of his sacred laurel.[3]

Primitive worship was essentially an act of fellowship and communion with the deity. The vestment of the worshipper was the sheep-skin or the goat-skin specially sacred to the deity worshipped, as the white robe of righteousness is the symbolic vestment of the Christian worshipper. This is generally traceable in theriomorphic cults, as in the Lupercalia. But it is traceable also in tree-worship. The victor in the Olympic games was treated as the human representative of the tree-god. He was decked with olive and crowned with a helmet filleted and crested with the twig of the sacred tree.[4] The English Jack-in-the-Green of the old May-day sports and the Kentish Holly-boy and Ivy-girl of the Shrove-tide revels[5] are reminiscences of this worship.

Sacrament and worship are closely linked together. In the archaic tradition of Abraham (Gn 14[18]) Melchizedek, king of Salem, brought forth bread and wine; and he was 'priest of the most high God' (El Elyon). Sacramental communion with the deity is the essence of the mysteries, and the mysteries belong to the primitive stages of religion: 'I fasted; I drank the kykeon; I took from the basket.' This was the touching of the *sacra*, the sacramental core of the mysteries of Eleusis. They were rites sacred to Demeter the Earth-Mother.[6] She is the Mountain-Mother (*q.v.*), the mother of the gods, represented with her pillar-shrine, the pillar of her sacred tree. She may be compared not only with Isis, but with Hathor and her sacred sycamore. Hathor nourished the wandering souls in the cemeteries of Egypt with food and drink. The Cretan Demeter in her mysteries nourished her mystics in life. The mysteries of Dionysus belong to the same cycle of ideas. Dionysus combined in himself the rites of the beer-god Sabazios of Thrace and of the mystery-god Zagreus of Crete.[7] The *haoma* of the Persians, the *soma* of the Hindus, the *ambrosia* of the Olympian gods, were all means of sacramental communion, a partaking of the tree of life.[8]

The sacred tree, instinct with the divine life, is vocal with the word and the will of the deity. A prominent feature of the Zeus-cult of Dodona was its oracle. 'And the giving of oracles was a chthonian prerogative.'[9] David is to consult the oracle of the mulberry-trees before he attacks the Philistines (2 S 5[24]). God called unto Moses from the midst of the bush in Horeb (Ex 3[1-4]). The sacred tree is alight with the wisdom of God. To partake of the acorns of Zeus was to acquire wisdom and knowledge.[10] The burning bush points to the symbolic meaning of the seven-branched candlestick in the Temple. It is a budding and blossoming almond (Ex 37[17-24]). The imagery of the rod out of the stem of Jesse, and the Branch growing out of his roots, the setting of the sevenfold gift of wisdom, is another illustration of the same truth (Is 11[1-3]; cf. LXX). And this again illuminates the meaning of the tree of the knowledge of good and evil (Gn 2[17]). It is the oracle of the God of righteousness, as the seven lamps are 'the eyes of the Lord . . . beholding the evil and the good' (Ps 15[3]; cf. Zec 4[10], 2 Ch 16[9]). The tree of knowledge is the oracle of religious and moral wisdom.

1 Philpot, p. 32.
2 *Ib.* p. 28.
3 *Ib.* p. 36.
4 *ClR* xvii. 274 f.
5 See art. SHROVE-TIDE.
6 J. E. Harrison, *The Religion of Ancient Greece*, London, 1905, p. 48.
7 *Ib.* p. 53.
8 Philpot, pp. 122–127.
9 *ClR* xvii. 179.
10 Philpot, p. 36.

2. The animistic stage in tree-worship.—The tracing of this stage in its original simplicity is almost as elusive as animism itself. In prehistoric times it was already being absorbed in higher religious conceptions and revelations, in the higher physical and religious and ethical development of the human race. Jahweh 'finally triumphed over the *bᵉʿālîm*, not by avoiding them, or by destroying them, but by absorbing them.'[1] This is the principle in all religious development. The burning bush was not merely the oracle of Horeb; it was the dwelling-place of Jahweh (Dt 33[16]). The fable of the trees and the bramble king was spoken 'by the plain [oak or terebinth] of the pillar that was in Shechem' (Jg 9[6-21]). It is a survival of ancient religious conceptions, an apologue or parable familiar in early tree-worship. The story of the thistle and the cedar is another (2 K 14[9]).[2]

'Tree-worship pure and simple, where the tree is in all respects treated as a god, is attested for Arabia . . . in the case of the sacred date-palm at Nejrān. It was adored at an annual feast, when it was all hung with fine clothes and women's ornaments.'[3]

The sacred *erica* in the temple of Isis at Byblos was said to have grown round the body of Osiris. It was a stump wrapped in a linen cloth and anointed with myrrh. It represented the dead god. It is suggested that this explains the mystery of the draping of the *ashērāh* (2 K 23[7]).[4] There are similar survivals in Greek ritual. Incense was burned and the tree was decked with fillets and honoured with burnt offerings. Mrs. Philpot gives[5] an illustration of a fruit-tree dressed as Dionysus—another example of draping as part of this early ritual. Cook in his exhaustive monograph on the cult of the oak-Zeus[6] has traced it through all the earliest sanctuaries of the Mediterranean area, especially in Dodona and Crete, and has given his conclusion as follows:

'Zeus was at each of these cult-centres conceived as a triple divinity (sky-god+water-god+earth-god) dwelling in a sacred oak and served by a priestly-king, who was regarded as an incarnation of Zeus himself and whose duty it was to maintain the sun's heat by magical means.'[7]

The Minotaur, the Ægean horns of consecration, and the axe[8] are also features in this ancient ritual.

This survey of the primitive cult is a key to the early worship of the sacred tree, not only in Celtic folk-lore and Gaulish sculpture, but in the survivals of pagan worship. E. Clodd gives a study of the 'primitive pagans' of S. Nigeria which sums up the animistic conception of tree-worship.

'A recent traveller among the "primitive pagans" of Southern Nigeria reports this speech from a native: "Yes, we say, this is our life—the big tree. When any of us dies his spirit does not go to another country, but into the big tree; and this is why we will not have it cut. When a man is sick, or a woman wants a child, we sacrifice to the big tree, and unless Oso'wo wants the sick man, our request is granted. Oso'wo lives in the sky, and is the Big God. When any of us dies away from this place, his spirit returns to the big tree."'[9]

Among the Hamitic tribes the crude animism has developed into a sort of polytheism with one highest god, Wāq.[10] He is the big god of the big tree of Nigeria.

1 *ERE* ii. 291b.
2 W. Robertson Smith, *Religion of the Semites*, Edinburgh, 1889, p. 126.
3 *Ib.* p. 169.
4 *Ib.* p. 175 n.
5 P. 31.
6 *ClR* xvii. 174 ff., 268 ff., 403 ff.; xviii. [1904] 75 ff., 325 ff., 360 ff.
7 *Ib.* xvii. 403.
8 *Ib.* xviii. 85.
9 *Animism*, London, 1905, p. 74.
10 *ERE* i. 56b.

The tree-cult of the aboriginal Africans is to-day largely associated with ancestor-worship. Trees planted round the graves of their ancestors acquire a sacred character. The great tree on the verandah of a dead man's home becomes the shrine of his spirit. And it is held that the highly-developed tree-cult of the Hereros is a direct off-shoot of ancestor-worship. One tree is hailed with the words: 'Holy art thou, our ancestor.'[1] The facts must be accepted, but the inference may be questioned. The polytheism and the ancestor-worship are both to be traced to the more primitive forms of animism represented in Ægean evidence as the cult of the Great Spirit or the oak-Zeus. They are both due to the principle of differentiation in the development of religious conceptions.

'Anthropomorphism is in some cases preceded by theriomorphism, but theriomorphism is never generated out of anthropomorphism.'[2]

All life in primitive ages is one, and in its movement inspires fear, not only the fear of God, but the 'fear' of Isaac (Gn 31^{42}). It is Jacob who 'sware by the fear of his father Isaac' (31^{53}). And Jacob by his wrestling attained the title of Israel (32^{28}). Abraham was the priest-king of Mamre, Melchizedek the priest-king of Salem. At Olympia and probably at Dodona the challenge of the priestly king gave rise to a regular athletic contest.[3] Minos as priest-king of Cnossus had a reign of limited duration. He was king for a period of nine years, when he withdrew to the Idæan cave to hold converse with Zeus.[4] Theseus, by his victory over Minos under the guise of Taurus, succeeded to the sun-king's rights as champion of the oak-Zeus.[5] Is it not evident that, behind and prior to the hero-worship of Theseus and the veneration for Israel, there is the ritual and there are the *sacra* of the deity, whether Zeus or El Elyon or Jahweh, the Great Spirit of primitive animism?

3. The sacred plantation.—The planting of the sacred tree or grove is a farther step in the development of tree-worship. The primitive priest-king does it as champion of the tree-spirit, under the conscious guidance of God. Eden is the most familiar example of a sacred plantation (Gn $2^{8f.}$). The practice of primitive religion colours the language and imagery of poet and prophet (cf. Nu $24^{5f.}$, Ps 104^{16}, Is 61^{3}). The riddle and parable of Ezekiel has new meaning when read in the light of early ritual:

'A great eagle . . . came unto Lebanon, and took the highest branch of the cedar: He cropped off the top of his young twigs, and carried it into a land of traffick; he set it in a city of merchants. He took also of the seed of the land . . .; he placed it by great waters, and set it as a willow tree. And it grew, and became a spreading vine of low stature' (Ezk 17^{3-6}; cf. vv.$^{22-24}$).

In Ægean art the living tree is represented sometimes singly, sometimes in groups of three, or in groves. It is at times close to an altar, or even growing from it; in one case the goddess sits under it. The palm-tree, the fig, and the cypress are most frequent; but the pine, the plane, and the vine also appear.[6] It may even spring from the *bucrania*, or 'horns of consecration,' which themselves represent the sacred bull, the theriomorphic representation of the oak-Zeus.

At Athens the original cult was that of the oak:

'Nondum laurus erat; longoque decentia crine
Tempora cingebat de qualibet arbore Phoebus.'[7]

There are in the Caryatides, or nut-maidens, traces of a nut-grove, the nuts themselves being known as the acorns of Zeus. Later, after this first stage of substitution, 'Zeus took over the olive.'[8] These ἀθῆναι, or nurses of Zeus, gave their name to the city, and later to the goddess whose cult overshadowed that of Zeus on the Acropolis.[1] In the Academy at Athens there were twelve sacred olives in the precinct of Athene.[2] Demeter had her sacred oaks, and the boy who pronounced the Eleusinian formula at Athenian weddings, ἔφυγον κακόν, ηὗρον ἄμεινον, was wreathed with oak and thorn.[3] There was a grove planted for Demeter at Dotium by the Pelasgians before they migrated from Thessaly to Cnidus. And Ovid, telling the story of the judgment on Erysichthon, speaks of the tree of Demeter as an oak, adorned with fillets and tablets by the people.[4]

These plantings are wide-spread, and traceable to the earliest sites. Hercules planted two oaks at Heraclea Pontica in Bithynia.[5] Æneas planted a huge oak-tree, lopped and decked as a trophy, on the tomb of Mezentius the Etruscan. The crown of golden oak-leaves from Vulci implies that the Etruscan kings were representatives or champions of the oak-Zeus. The tree planted by Æneas was itself identified with the king: 'manibusque meis Mezentius hic est.'[6] The identification of tree, god, and king is general. Romulus and Remus were worshipped in the Comitium under a sapling planted from the *Ficus ruminalis* on the Palatine. The Bodhi-tree of Anurādhapura, long the capital of Ceylon, is over 2000 years old. It was planted by Tissa—a branch of the original Bodhi-tree, at Gayā in India.[7] The sanctuary of 'Uzzā at Naḥla near Mecca consisted of three trees[8]—another link with the wide-spread cult of a triple tree-god, as sky-god, water-god, and earth-god in one.

The chain of evidence is unbroken from East to West; the triple-headed gods of Gaul, sitting cross-legged on their throne as in India, point to closer contact with the neolithic age than even Greece and Syria. The sacred flint of the temple of Jupiter Feretrius on the Capitoline Hill at Rome, the 'antiquum Jovis signum,' the home of Jupiter Lapis, has been regarded as an unhafted neolithic celt, preserved among the aborigines of Latium from an immemorial past.[9]

The sacred tree, the sacred plantation, was the seat of authority, the seat of judgment. The Romans met for council 'in aesculeto.' The senate of the Galatian Celts met at a place called Δρυνέμετος, doubtless sacred to their national cult: κελτοὶ σέβουσι μὲν Δὶα, ἄγαλμα δὲ Διὸς κελτικὸν ὑψηλή δρῦς.[10] Deborah the prophetess 'dwelt under the palm tree of Deborah, . . . and the children of Israel came up to her for judgment' (Jg 4^{5}; cf. 1 S 22^{6}, Jg 6^{11}). In 458 B.C. the Roman envoys were sent to complain that the Æqui had broken a treaty concluded in 459. They were bidden to make their complaint to a huge oak on Mount Algidas under the shadow of whose branches the Æquian commander had his quarters.[11] The *prætorium* under the sacred oak is certainly a primitive trait.[12]

A sacred rowan-tree in Ireland derived its origin from the rowan of Dubhros, the Black Forest, in Co. Sligo.

The tree had grown from a quicken-berry dropped by the Tuatha Dé Danann, who had brought it from the Land of Promise. It was guarded by a giant named Searbhan, who could only be slain by three blows from his own club, and had a single broad fiery eye in the middle of his black forehead. He was overcome by Diarmait, the culture-hero of Irish folk-lore.[13] He

1 *ERE* i. 164b. 2 *Ib.* i. 573a.
3 Cf. Ovid, *Met.* i. 446. 4 *Od.* xix. 179; Strabo, 476.
5 Cook, *ClR* xvii. 411.
6 *ERE* i. 142–144; cf. Cook, *ClR* xvii. 407.
7 Ov. *Met.* i. 450 f.; cf. Cook, *ClR* xviii. 84: Drymas, Ægeus, Codrus.
8 Cook, *ClR* xviii. 86.

1 Cook, *ClR* xviii. 86. 2 *ERE* i. 59a.
3 *ClR* xviii. 84.
4 *Ib.* p. 76; Ov. *Met.* viii. 738 ff. 5 *Ib.* p. 79.
6 Verg. *Æn.* xi. 5–16; *ClR* xviii. 362.
7 *ERE* i. 599b. 8 *Ib.* i. 660b.
9 *ClR* xviii. 365.
10 Max. Tyr., *Dissert.* viii. 8; cf. *ClR* xviii. 79, 369.
11 Livy, iii. 25. 12 *ClR* xviii. 365.
13 Rhys, *Celtic Heathendom*2, p. 355 ff.

dwelt in a hut among the branches and was so great a magician that he could not be killed by fire, water, or weapons of war.

Here again there is the sacred tree, the fierce-eyed guardian, triply inviolate, the challenge, and the contest so frequently met with in the legends of the sacred grove. And in Danu (the Welsh Don), the goddess-mother of the Tuatha Dé Danann, is there not a link with the Demeter of Greek myth, and in the name itself an echo of the Δάν (acc. Δᾶν) of the oak-Zeus, and of Jana, Diana, Artemis on the slope of the Aventine? She is the earth-goddess, the Dea Dia of the Romans, the Dan of the Dorian Greeks: *οἱ γὰρ Δωριεῖς τὴν γὴν δᾶν λέγουσι καὶ δίαν.*[1]

4. The sacred stump.—The Lion Gate at Mycenæ is one of the earliest aniconic representations of the worship of the sacred tree. The pillar of which the lions are the supporters tapers downwards like the ancient Herm.[2] The subject has been very fully treated in art. POLES AND POSTS; but some further links may be noted.

The pillar-shrine of Cnossus with its sacred doves is recognized by Cook as a 'conventionalised but still aniconic form of a triple tree-Zeus.'[3] The Lydian cult of Zeus *ἀσκραῖος* was connected with the oak. A coin of Halicarnassus represents him 'as a bearded god crowned with rays and standing between two oak-trees, on each of which is a bird.'[4] In the same city there was a cult of Aphrodite *ἀσκραία*. This cult gave its name to the city of Aphrodisias.

The coins of this city 'show the leafless trunk of a tree with three branches. Sometimes the three branches rise separately from an enclosure of trellis-work. Sometimes they spring from a single trunk, on either side of which is a naked man wearing a Phrygian cap: the one on the left wields a double-axe; the one on the right kneels or runs away, turning his back upon the tree [a feature still preserved in folk-lore]. Sometimes . . . the tree is flanked by two lighted altars.'[5]

The priest of the Cappadocian cult of Bellona at Rome is represented with a branch in one hand and the two-headed axe in the other—a further link with the oak-cult of Crete.[6]

Amid the early rites of Etruria and the *sacra* of Rome there are further associations with this cult. Hermes is represented in a fragment of Aristophanes as *τρικέφαλος*; so also is Janus on a coin of Hadrian.[7] Janus is also represented with a spear; and his title Quirinus is understood in reference to the oak-god. The Sabine *curis*, the oaken spear, the Quirites, the men of the oaken spear, are thus related to Janus Quirinus or Jupiter Quirinus.[8] The spear is a variation of the sacred stump. The tree-god is often represented by a post, sceptre, or spear.

The *trixylon* associated with Juno Sororia and Janus Curiatius is a symbol of this triple Janus. It consisted of two vertical beams and a cross-bar, the rude form of a cross. The 'yoke' under which the conquered were forced to march was of three staves or spears, and is also traced to the cult of Janus Quirinus. The door-posts (*januæ*) were sacred to him, as the threshold was to the Earth-Mother.[9]

The sprinkling of the blood on the door-posts in Hebrew ritual (Ex 12^7, Ezk 45^{19}) and the shaking of the threshold in the vision of Isaiah (Is 6^4 RV) are examples of the same cycle of ideas—the sacredness of the posts and the threshold as tokens of the Deity.

The *caduceus* is another variation of the sacred rod. It consisted of a triple shoot, the central shoot forming the handle, the two side shoots being folded back into a double knot. The elder lends itself to this by its opposite shoots, and the tree is tabu in the folk-lore of the West. It is not lucky to burn it. Judas hanged himself from an elder-bush. The *lituus* of the augur is another variation of the sacred rod. So also the mysterious twisted rods used in what is probably a funeral procession in the decoration of Etruscan tombs at Norchia and Tarquinii.[1] In the fresco at Tarquinii, while most of the figures have the twisted rod, 'the symbol of the Etruscan Hades,' one of the leading figures has the *lituus*, and prominent among these is the hammer borne aloft, 'a frequent emblem of supernatural power.'[2] The figure of the god with the hammer is frequently met with on Celtic monuments.[3] The Y cross with its mystic Pythagorean meaning has also some ancient link with these Etruscan rods.[4] A hazel-twig of this shape is in use as the divining-rod for tracing water.

The Etruscan *lucumones*, or kings, were representatives of Jupiter. Their crown was of golden oak-leaves, with acorns, gems, and fillets. They acted as vice-gerents of the oak-god. Their golden *bulla* was the symbol of the sun-god—another link with the oak-Zeus. They used a sceptre with an eagle, and were preceded by the lictor bearing the axe with the bundle of rods. Cook suggests that these may be a conventional substitute for the trees of the tree-god.[5] These were all part of the royal insignia of the ancient king. Is it not possible to trace the origin of the English regalia to the same source?

In the Inventory of 1649 are enumerated the 'large staff with a dove on the top, formerly thought to be all gold, but upon trial . . . found to be the lower part wood within and silver-gilt without'; the 'small staff with a fleure de luce on the top . . . found to be iron within and silver-gilt without'; 'one staff of black and white ivory with a dove on the top'; and the two sceptres, one with the cross, and one with the dove.[6]

These are all symbols of authority, such as are found in the *sacra* of the ancient races of Europe. The sceptre with the cross, the wooden rod with the dove, the rod with the 'fleure de luce' may be compared with the tau-cross, the blossoming stump, and the dove-pillars of the Etruscan and Ægean cults. The rods laid up before the Lord in the tent, 'one for each father's house' (Nu 17^2 RV), 'twelve rods,' and the budding of Aaron's rod (v.[8]) point to similar associations on Semitic soil. And the cross with its *spolia opima* was the most honoured sign of Jupiter Feretrius at Rome. The *feretrum*, from which he took his name, was the lopped trunk of the ancient oak, venerated by the shepherds of old, forming a wooden cross to which votive armour was attached.[7] The cross in the folk-lore of Rome was a sign of the primitive oak-cult—a token of the presence of the oak-king, a shrine for the offering of the trophy of right to the oak-god.[8] Was Pilate altogether unconscious of this when he said: 'What I have written I have written' (Jn 19^{22})? And was St. Paul too in his 'foolishness of preaching,' and in his witness to the power of the Cross and of Christ crucified, unconscious of the other tradition of the power of the cross, when he wrote:

'Unto the Jews a stumblingblock, and unto the Greeks foolishness; But unto them which are called, both Jews and Greeks, Christ the power of God, and the wisdom of God' (1 Co $1^{23f.}$)?

5. Trees many and gods many.—The sacred tree signified universally in primitive ages the presence of the deity. The one tree with its nursery-grove was the shrine of the one God. But east and west, in hill or in valley, in north aspect or in south, the tree varied.[9] And, as the tree varied in species, the god varied in name. Then the tree and the god of the clan grew to be the tree and the god of

1 *Etymologicon Magnum*, ed. F. Sylburg, Leipzig, 1816, p. 60. 8; *ClR* xvii. 177.
2 Seyffert, pp. 50, 285.
3 *ClR* xvii. 407.
4 *Ib.* 416.
5 *Ib.*
6 Seyffert, p. 96.
7 *ClR* xviii. 367, n. 19.
8 *Ib.* pp. 369, 373.
9 *Ib.* p. 369.

1 G. Dennis, *The Cities and Cemeteries of Etruria*, London, 1848, i. 253.
2 *Ib.* pp. 310–312.
3 G. Grupp, *Kultur der alten Kelten und Germanen*, Munich, 1905, p. 154 f.
4 Dennis, i. 253.
5 *ClR* xviii. 361 f.
6 W. H. Stacpoole, *The Coronation Regalia*, London, 1911, p. 33.
7 *ClR* xviii. 364 f.
8 Verg. *Æn.* x. 423, xi. 15 f.
9 Verg. *Georg.* ii. 109–113.

the district, and in turn the tree and god of the nation. The parable of the bramble king (Jg $9^{8ff.}$) is true to fact. The olive, the fig, the vine had established their fame and their rule; they would not submit to another; the bramble had ambition to rival even the cedar of Lebanon.

Trees many led on to gods many.[1] The oak-Zeus at Athens took over the olive. Apollo remained true to his sacred laurel. This development is most marked in Greek art and Roman verse:

> 'Populus Alcidae gratissima, vitis Iaccho,
> Formosae myrtus Veneri, sua laurea Phoebo.'[2]

The Semitic nations stand apart from this tendency to assign a particular tree to a particular god,[3] whether from reaction to monotheism or from adherence to the primitive conception of the oneness of the divine spirit. They had sacred trees in great number, but they were all sacred to one god localized in village, clan, or nation. In India each Buddha had his own tree, and Gautama himself, after having passed through 43 incarnations as a tree-spirit, eventually found wisdom under the sacred tree of Brahmā, the *pipal*-tree, or *Ficus religiosa*.[4]

This triumph of the gods over the nations and the consequent interlacing of the tree-cults, sometimes by expansion, sometimes by absorption, resulted in certain cases in the distinction between tree-gods and tree-demons. As the *jinn* or *genii* of the Arabs were gods out of touch with men, outlaws, dehumanized, 'abominations of Moab and Ammon,' so the wood-demons of the German forest or the Polynesian islanders were the foes and the dread of their conquerors—or their neighbours. And in the controversy between the supporters of ancestor-worship and the supporters of animism based on the presence in nature of the divine spirit this wide-spread belief in wood-demons and unlucky trees is in favour of the latter. In an age when 'every valley had its king,'[5] and every hill its shrine and its sacred tree, as in these islands in Celtic times, and when feuds were frequent between clan and clan, the jealousy of the clan would separate between god and god, and between tree and tree, and people the forest-clad hills with every form of terror and danger. The only bond of safety was in the nation's god and in the king as the champion of his rights. All around was danger and death: 'for I the Lord thy God am a jealous God' (Ex 20^5; cf. 2 Co 11^2). This is the language of religion, not the language of ancestor-worship; and it may be traced in tree-worship and demon-lore from earliest times.

A blasted or stricken oak might be the messenger of misfortune:

> 'De coelo tactas memini praedicere quercus.'[6]

The Abors in Assam regarded the rubber-tree as the abode of two malignant spirits; another haunted the plantain and stinging-nettle.[7] The satyrs and devils of the OT, the *jinn* of the Arabian stories, the centaurs and cyclops, fauns and dryads of Greek and Latin mythology, the wood-maidens, wild-men, and elves, the wild-women of the Tyrol, and the green-ladies of Neufchâtel, in their different degrees of mischief or maliciousness, were haunting terrors of the old world.[8] The Neraides of Macedonian folk-lore are tree-spirits. It is not well to lie down in the shade of a tree, for it is there that the tree-demons appear. At this day the country-folk avoid especially the plane, the poplar, and the fig-tree, for these are favourite haunts of fairies.[9]

1 Verg. *Georg.* ii. 116 f. 2 Verg. *Ecl.* vii. 61 f.
3 Philpot, p. 39. 4 *Ib.* p. 14.
5 C. I. Elton, *Origins of English History*^{2}, London, 1890, p. 238.
6 Verg. *Ecl.* i. 17. 7 *ERE* i. 33^a.
8 Philpot, p. 52 ff.
9 G. F. Abbott, *Macedonian Folklore*, Cambridge, 1903, p. 244.

In Ireland ghosts and apparitions haunt isolated thorn-bushes.[1] To call up the Tolcarne troll near Newlyn, an incantation was necessary, and three dried leaves must be held in the hand, 'one of the ash, one of the oak, and one of the thorn.'[2]

> 'Sing Oak, and Ash, and Thorn, good Sirs,
> (All of a Midsummer morn)!
> England shall bide till Judgment Tide,
> By Oak, and Ash, and Thorn!'[3]

The creation myth of the Tanganarin natives in Australia holds that Punjil fashioned man out of the bark of a tree. Another tree was tabu, and haunted by a bat; the tabu was broken; the tree was violated; the bat flew away, and death came into the world.[4] Daphne is the name both of the laurel and of the spirit within it. The *numen* of a palm-tree is not called Tamar, but Ba'al Tamar. The former conception is Indo-European, the latter Semitic.

> 'The Indo-European could never free himself from the identification of his gods with nature. . . . The Semite, on the other hand, was accustomed from the earliest times to distinguish between the object and its *ba'al*.'[5]

Among the nymphs were Philyra, the linden, Rhœa, the pomegranate, Helike, the willow, and Daphne, the laurel. Mrs. Philpot notes:

> 'In later times an attempt was made in some cases [*e.g.*, Daphne in Laurum, Lotis in Lotum, Dryope in Arborem][6] to explain the connection by metamorphosis . . . but it is extremely probable that this was an inversion of the primitive nexus.'[7]

The classic passages for the oak of Dodona are Hom. *Od.* xiv. 327 f., xix. 296 f. In Hom. *Il.* xvi. 233 f. the oracle is mentioned; Vergil refers to it in *Georg.* ii. 15 f. The oak was also sacred to Ceres;[8] before harvest worship must be rendered to her, and the worshipper must be crowned with a wreath of oak.[9] The willow is associated with Hera at Samos, and with Artemis at Sparta. Artemis was the goddess of the nut-tree and the cedar in Arcadia, of the laurel and the myrtle in Laconia.[10] The laurel is sacred to Apollo; the priest-king Anius is guardian of the tree and the shrine.[11] The olive is specially connected with the cult of Athene at Athens. The pine is associated with Pan and Silvanus, the cedar with the Accadian deity Ea, the sycamore with the Egyptian goddess Nuit (Hathor). The cypress was sacred among the Persians, and in the West, together with the poplar, it belongs to the chthonian deities. The vine and the ivy were closely connected with the rites of Dionysus.[12] The ash and the elm appear in Scandinavian mythology as the first man (Ask) and the first woman (Embla), and the ash Yggdrasil is connected with the court of the gods.[13]

Celtic folk-lore has many points of contact with the ancient oak-cult of the Mediterranean area, with variations due to local developments under northern conditions. The δρύτομος of Dodona, the αἰγειροτόμοι, or poplar-fellers, at Athens, the κισσοτόμοι at Phlius,[14] have their representative in the tree-felling god Esus on the Paris monument.[15] The ancient axe-ritual of Dodona, Crete, and Etruria appears in the sculptures of Sucellos and other deities in Celtic lands.[16] On the Trier monument the deity is felling an oak-tree on which are three cranes. The Tarvos trigaranus, the bull, before the oak-tree, with two cranes on the back and one between the horns, is another variation of the Paris altar.[17]

1 W. Y. Evans Wentz, *The Fairy-Faith in Celtic Countries*, Oxford, 1911, p. 70.
2 *Ib.* p. 176.
3 Rudyard Kipling, *Puck of Pook's Hill*, London, 1906, p. 32.
4 *ERE* i. 34, 36^a, ii. 36^b, 45^b. 5 *Ib.* p. 285.
6 Ovid, *Met.* i. 452, ix. 345, 350–393.
7 P. 59 f. 8 Ovid, *Met.* viii. 741–743.
9 Verg. *Georg.* i. 347–350. 10 Philpot, p. 29.
11 Verg. *Æn.* iii. 79–82. 12 Philpot, *passim*.
13 *Chambers's Encycl.* new ed., Edinburgh, 1888, *s.v.* 'Ash.'
14 Paus. II. xiii. 3. 15 Grupp, p. 153.
16 *Ib.* pp. 154–156. 17 *Ib.* p. 165.

The cult of Cernunnus supplies another link. He is represented in the Cluny Museum with stag's horns, the ring on each horn referring to the sun.[1] In the silver bowl from Gundestrap in Denmark he is cross-legged, Buddha-like, with stag's horns, and on his right a stag and a bull.[2] In a wax tablet at Pesth he is called Jupiter Cernenus; on a Rheims monument he is with a stag and an ox, and at Saintes with several *bucrania*. The presence of the sun-wheel in Paris, and the bull-masks at Saintes, point to his original identity with the Zeus of Crete. In one case he is represented with a chain.[3] His name is almost certainly connected with the horns. In folk-lore he probably survives in Windsor Forest as Herne the Hunter, who walks

> 'round about an oak, with great ragg'd horns;
> And there he blasts the trees, and takes the cattle,
> And makes milch-kine yield blood, and shakes a chain
> In a most hideous and dreadful manner.'[4]

It is not unlikely that the Horn-dancers of Abbots Bromley in Staffordshire commemorate some early pagan rite connected with the oak-cult of Zeus Cernunnus. Bagot's Park is a celebrated oak-forest. The village-games in old times took place round the Beggar's Oak. Though now held early in September, in Robert Plot's time (1641–96) they took place about Christmas. The dancers wore stag-horns (reindeer, kept in the church). It is noteworthy that the Pesth tablet of Jupiter Cernenus has also an echo in a modern dance—a horned figure among the mummers of Mohacs on the Danube.

The oak also entered into the ritual of invoking Zeus as a rain-god. On the Lycæan mountain of Arcadia was a shrine sacred to Zeus, in which was a spring to which the priest went in time of drought. He touched the water with a sprig of oak, when a vapour would rise and spread in fruitful showers over the land. In Brittany the fountain of Barantin in the Forest of Brécilien served the same purpose. Water was thrown on a slab near the spring, and rain would then fall in abundance, accompanied by thunder and lightning. The well was near the fabled shrine of Merlin, one of the Celtic types of the sun-hero, and it was overshadowed by a mighty tree. Rhys suggests that the spring, the tomb, the slab, and the tree 'all belonged to the Celtic Zeus.' There is a similar story connected with the Snowdonian tarn Dulyn, the Black Lake, where the slab was called the Red Altar.[5] There is also in the moorlands of Staffordshire, near Ipstones, a strong spring overshadowed with oak and mountain-ash long known as the Thundering Well. The name alone remains, but it may be grouped among the sites sacred to the Celtic Zeus as rain-god. Within the last few years a Celtic chambered tomb has been discovered within a short distance of the well.

The ash is also among the sacred trees of Ireland. In the parish of Borrisokane, Co. Tipperary, there was in 1833 a huge ash called the Big 'Bell' tree.[6] The name is derived from the word 'Billa,' which occurs in Magbile, 'the plain of the old tree,' the present Moville.[7] This name has been connected by Windisch with *bile* or 'Beli,' king of Hades, the consort of Danu. This Beli represents Cronos in his darker character as Death, and suggests that the Big 'Bell' trees of Irish folk-lore were ash-trees sacred to the Celtic Cronos.[8] The ash was also sacred to the Celtic Silvanus: 'Silvane sacra semicluse fraxino.' He presided over woodlands, clearings, and gardens.[9]

1 Grupp, p. 164. 2 *Ib.* p. 288. 3 *Ib.* p. 164.
4 Shakespeare, *The Merry Wives of Windsor*, IV. iv. 29.
5 Rhys, *Celtic Heathendom*², p. 183 ff.
6 W. G. Wood-Martin, *Traces of the Elder Faiths of Ireland*, London, 1902, vol. ii. pp. 155–160.
7 *The Martyrology of Gorman*, ed. Whitley Stokes (Henry Bradshaw Soc. Publications, ix.), London, 1895, p. 319.
8 Rhys, *Celtic Heathendom*, p. 678. 9 *Ib.* p. 65.

The white-thorn has also its sacred associations. It is unlucky to cut it down. A 'lone thorn' is regarded with special veneration. Christianity took over its sanctity. The Crown of Thorns was said to have been made of white-thorn. An old thorn near Tinahely, Co. Wicklow, is still called 'Skeagh Padrig,' or 'Patrick's book.' In Britain 'the holy thorn' of Glastonbury has similar venerable associations. The hazel appears in Irish romance as the tree of knowledge. The yew among the Druids was a symbol of immortality.[1] Celtic folk-lore has many other traditions of tree-worship. The first man sprang from an alder, the first woman from a mountain-ash. The berries of the rowan are a charm against all disease. There are also trees which were inauguration trees. One, an old sycamore in Coollemoneen in the parish of Killadown, is called 'the honey-tree.' A tree in the parish of Kilmactaign is called 'the fern-tree,' *i.e.* the alder.

6. Tree-offerings and tree-rites.—The cult of the sacred tree had its offerings and its rites. There are even survivals of the offering of the highest sacrifices. The natives of the Vindhyan uplands of India until lately offered human sacrifices to trees.[2] In the animistic worship of the Ainus the worship is vocal.[3] At the close of the bear-festival the head of the bear is set up on a pole, called 'the pole for sending away,' and the skulls of the other animals which are hung up with it are called 'divine preservers' and are at times worshipped.[4] This is a link with the *bucrania* which form so integral a part in the sacrificial tokens of Aryan worship. Plutarch states that Theseus on his return from Crete put in at Delos, and instituted a dance in imitation of the mazes of the labyrinth.

> 'He danced it round the altar Keraton which was built entirely of the left-side horns of beasts.'[5]

This was known as the 'crane dance,' and is certainly in some way associated with the cult of the Celtic tree-god Sucellos or Esus with his three cranes, and with the Tarvos trigaranus of the Paris monument.[6] A note in Langhorne's Plutarch states that the crane commonly flies in the figure of a circle, which together with the *swastika*, or conventional labyrinth sign, is symbolic of the sun-cult. The dance round the May-pole and the Jack-in-the-Green festivities within our own memory in May Fair, London, are survivals of the same rites.

The griffins in Assyria and in Asia, in their attitude of devotion,[7] have their counterpart in the vision of the Temple in Ezekiel:

> 'And it was made with cherubims and palm trees, so that a palm tree was between a cherub and a cherub' (41¹⁸).

In a Mexican MS the tree breaks into two branches in the shape of a tau-cross, each branch with three blossoms; the tree is surmounted by a parrot, and is supported by two men, standing, each with his right hand raised in the attitude of devotion.[8]

Trees were hung with votive offerings. In India the sacred banyan-tree is represented with six elephants in the act of worship.[9] In Egypt it is the sycamore with jars and fruit, and the worshipper before it has the right hand raised.[10] Elsewhere it is a tree sacred to Artemis, hung with the weapons of the chase.[11] Wreaths were worn and garlands were carried in various Greek rites; and this use of wreaths points to some analogy with tree-worship in the two pillars before the Temple at Jerusalem.[12] Robertson Smith gives a coin from Paphos with similar detached pillars before a temple, each surmounted above the cornice by a dove as in the rude pillar-shrine of Crete. Whether

1 Grupp, p. 145. 2 *ERE* i. 35ᵇ. 3 *Ib.* p. 248ᵇ.
4 *Ib.* p. 250ᵇ.
5 Plut. *Lives*, tr. J. and W. Langhorne, new ed., London, 1823, i. 55.
6 Grupp, p. 165. 7 Philpot, p. 6. 8 *Ib.* p. 17, fig. 9.
9 *Ib.* p. 42. 10 *Ib.* p. 44. 11 *Ib.* p. 45.
12 W. R. Smith, p. 469.

they were candlesticks or not, they were wreathed in pomegranates.[1] On the eastern gateway of the Buddhist tope at Sānchi the sacred tree is represented with worshippers. It divides into two main branches, like that in Mexico, and there are two smaller trees, one on either side. The central tree is being wreathed in garlands.[2] The Bodhi-tree of Kanakamuni breaks into three branches and is also hung with festoons.[3] This custom still survives in the West. Rhys has collected recent evidence from Glamorganshire of holy wells overshadowed by thorn or other trees, on which rags were fastened.[4] And the present writer some thirty years ago saw a bush hung with red rags in one of the islands of Aran off Galway. It is one of the last relics of the cult of the sacred tree, like the practice of 'touching wood' to avert a change of 'luck,' still in use in this country.

The tree is also a trophy of victory. As late as the 4th cent. of the Christian era a pear-tree at Auxerre was hung with trophies of the chase and venerated as a god.[5] The 'Stock-im-Eisen' in the centre of Vienna is the stump of a sacred larch, now studded and bound in iron, the last remains of trophies with which it was originally hung. The Irmensul had a similar origin.[6] Romulus celebrated his victory over the Cæninenses by his institution of the *spolia opima* in honour of Jupiter Feretrius:

> 'He cut down a great oak that grew in the camp, and hewed it into the figure of a trophy: to this he fastened Acron's whole suit of armour, disposed in its proper form. Then he put on his own robes, and wearing a crown of laurel on his head, his hair gracefully flowing, he took the trophy erect upon his right shoulder, and so marched on, singing the song of victory before his troops. . . . This procession was the origin and mould of future triumphs.'[7]

The 6th cent. Gallican poet Venantius Fortunatus, author of the *Vexilla regis*, who lived when the honour of the sacred tree was still more familiar to the Gauls than the shame of the Cross, lifts up the old faith in his great hymn of the Passion:

> 'Pange lingua gloriosi proelium certaminis
> Et super crucis tropaeo dic triumphum nobilem,
> Qualiter redemptor orbis immolatus vicerit.
>
> Crux fidelis inter omnes arbor una nobilis
> Nulla tamen silva profert fronde, flore, germine:
> Dulce lignum dulci clavo dulce pondus sustinens.'[8]

7. The tree of life.—The sacred tree was the source and the sustenance of life. Worship, sacrament, and mystic charm are closely linked together. The *soma*-plant, the Iranian *haoma*, is the sacred food of the gods in Asia, and corresponds to the *ambrosia* of the Greek world.[9] The Vedic *amṛta* or *soma* had in it the principle of life and was withheld from ordinary men: it was, however, to be taken by the initiated.[10]

In Sparta, in early times, the dead were laid upon palm branches and leaves of the olive. In the forest land of northern Europe hollowed oaks were used in the burial of the dead.[11] The practice among the Oddfellows of each member dropping a sprig of sweet herbs on the coffin in the grave is a survival of the same early rites. In Abyssinia the branches and twigs of the ghost-tree are used by the pagan Kunamas as a protection against sorcery and as charms and amulets at childbirth and death.[12] In Babylonia the idea is more strictly defined. The god Nin-gish-zida is 'master of the tree of life.'[13] In time of drought the priest of the Lycæan Zeus let down an oak-branch to the surface of the water.[1] Codrus, when he devoted his life to his country, dressed as a woodman. Cook notes:

> 'If the last of the Athenian kings on so solemn an occasion appeared as an oak-cutter armed with an axe, we may be sure that this was no mere disguise but the ancient ritual costume of an oak-king.'[2]

The cult of the sacred tree embraces the highest rites in life and in death. The rite of tree-marriage in India in its surviving forms is mainly conventional.[3] The idea of reincarnation may in some cases explain it, but the rites seem to point to other and more primitive ideas. The Agariā, a Dravidian tribe of Chotā Nāgpur, have a special regard for the *sāl*-tree, which is used at their marriages.[4] The *bali*, or totem, system prohibited marriage between those who have the same totem. Among the Marathas the *devaks*, or marriage-guardians, though they no longer form a bar to the union of two worshippers of one *devak*, still have some share in the marriage-rite.

> 'The *devak* is usually some common tree such as the bel, fig, banyan, or the sami. In its commonest form it is the leaves of five trees, of which one, as the original *devak* of the section, is held specially sacred. It is worshipped chiefly at the time of marriage.'[5]

It has already been suggested that in primitive ages every valley, as Elton says, had its own king. Each king would be the champion and priest of the sacred tree, and this tree as indwelt by the divine spirit would be sacramentally united in all rites of initiation or other social *sacra* with the tribe or clan. The five leaves represent a pentapolis, or group of five states, one or other, as in ancient Rome,[6] choosing the common priest-king of the five, preference therefore being given to the leaf which represented his sacred tree. Similar customs banning all marriage within a totem-clan have been observed among the Bantu tribes of S. Africa. The mushroom totem of the Awemba is an example of a vegetable totem.[7]

Again, it would appear that the root-idea in the animistic cult of the sacred tree is religion rather than totemism or ancestor-worship; these are perhaps only relics of the primitive age—results of anthropomorphic development and differentiation, degenerate conceptions of the earlier animistic principle of the unity of the divine spirit of life.

The mistletoe-bough in the Christmas feast and 'kissing under the mistletoe' are relics not only of the oak-cult of the Druids, but of its connexion with primitive marriage-rites. This cult rests on the authority of Pliny,[8] and the special virtues ascribed to mistletoe are also referred to by him. Cook has some valuable notes on the mistletoe, which give support to Frazer's conjecture 'that the sun's fire was regarded as an emanation of the mistletoe.'[9] Cook bases his argument on the cult of Ἴξιος Ἀπόλλων at Ixiæ in Rhodes, a town named after the mistletoe. The cult is not definitely referred to in connexion with the oak, but 'it is probable, because the Rhodians regarded the oak as the sun-god's tree.' In the story of the punishment of Ixion there is, he suggests, another link between the mistletoe and the sun-cult. Ixion was the father of Peirithoüs, whose constant associate was Dryas.

> 'The relationship thus established between Ἰξίων the mistletoe and Δρύας the oak is scarcely fortuitous.'

A scholium on Euripides, *Phœn.* 1185, reads:

> 'Zeus in his anger bound Ixion to a winged wheel and sent it spinning through the air. . . . Others say that Zeus hurled him into Tartarus. Others again, that the wheel was made of fire.'

This flaming spin-wheel has been commonly understood as the sun-god. Cook concludes:

[1] Cf. 2 Ch 4[12f].
[2] Philpot, p. 15, fig. 8.
[3] *Ib.* p. 41, fig. 19.
[4] Rhys, *Celtic Folk-Lore*, Oxford, 1901, i. 354 ff.
[5] Philpot, p. 20.
[6] Baedeker, *Oesterreich*[22], Leipzig, 1890, p. 17; *ERE* ii. 45[a].
[7] Plut. ed. Langhorne, i. 98.
[8] H. A. Daniel, *Thesaurus Hymnologicus*, Halle, 1841–55, i. 163.
[9] *ERE* ii. 13[b].
[10] Philpot, p. 125 f.
[11] *ERE* ii. 18[a].
[12] *Ib.* i. 56.
[13] *Ib.* ii. 295[b].

[1] *ClR* xviii. 88; Paus. VIII. xxxviii. 3.
[2] *ClR* xviii. 84.
[3] *ERE* viii. 431.
[4] *Ib.* i. 180; cf. i. 233.
[5] *Ib.* ii. 338[b].
[6] Plut. ed. Langhorne, i. 182.
[7] *ERE* ii. 352 f.
[8] *HN* xvi. 44; *ERE* iii. 295[b].
[9] *GB*[2] iii. 455; *ClR* xvii. 420.

'It has not, however, been hitherto observed though indeed the fact is obvious, that Ἰξίων is derived from ἰξός and that the mistletoe was on Greek soil thus intimately associated with the sun-god.'[1]

An old Staffordshire custom of keeping the mistletoe-bough throughout the year and then burning it in the fire under the Christmas pudding probably rests on some tradition of the perpetuation of the sacred fire. The mistletoe represented during the winter the 'sap of the oak,'[2] and this formal burning of it, like the feeding of the sacred fire of Vesta from the oak-grove of the Palatine slopes, expresses the principle of life. It has not been customary to use mistletoe in the decoration of churches at Christmas; but W. Stukeley[3] reports a curious custom from York:

'On the Eve of Christmas Day they carry mistletoe to the high Altar of the Cathedral and proclaim a public and universal liberty, pardon, and freedom to all sorts of inferior and even wicked people at the gates of the city, towards the four quarters of Heaven.'[4]

There was in Plutarch's time a shrine of Fortuna Viscata on the Capitol at Rome. This may be the Fortuna Primigenia near the temple of Jupiter, where stood the oak of Jupiter Feretrius.

The *rota Fortunæ* survived till lately at Douai, when about midsummer 'a large wheel called the *roue de fortune* was carried in procession before a wicker-work giant known as *le grand Gayant*, and other figures called *les enfants de Gayant*. These wicker giants were certainly the Druid divinities, whose colossal images of wicker-work are described by Cæsar':[5] 'Alii immani magnitudine simulacra habent; quorum contexta viminibus membra vivis hominibus complent: quibus succensis, circumventi flamma exanimantur homines.'[6]

The mistletoe-bough and the various customs connected with it are all survivals of the solar cult, and, with the wreaths, axes, spears, cranes, and doves, point to the true meaning of the worship of the sacred tree. The mistletoe-bough is made the type of the Golden Bough:

'Quale solet silvis brumali frigore viscum
Fronde virere novâ, quod non sua seminat arbos,
Et croceo fetu teretes circumdare truncos:
Talis erat species auri frondentis opaca
Ilice.'[7]

The yew was also regarded as a symbol of immortality.[8] The name *eburos*, mid-Irish *ibhar* (*Taxus*),[9] enters into place-names and clan-names —*e.g.*, Eburacum (York), Eburodunum (Yverdon), Eburones. The last-named is an instance of a tribe or clan taking its name from a tree-deity.

There was a yew in Belach Mughna in the west of Leinster—'a great sacred tree, and its top was as broad as the whole plain. Thrice a year did it bear fruit: it remained hidden from the time of the Deluge until the night on which Conn of the Hundred Battles was born, and then it was made manifest. Thirty cubits was the girth of that tree, and its height was three hundred cubits. However, Ninine the poet felled that tree.'[10]

Cell-eo in the *Martyrology of Gorman* is the 'church of yews.' And there is an ancient hallowed site in Staffordshire, with only the memory left of its All Saints' dedication, the New Year festival of the Celts, which is now marked by the Hanchurch Yews. The churchyard yew is an ancient symbol of the tree of life.

In the story of Eden the command went forth: 'Of every tree of the garden thou mayest freely eat: But of the tree of the knowledge of good and evil, thou shalt not eat of it: for in the day that thou eatest thereof thou shalt surely die' (Gn 2$^{16f.}$).

No ban is put on the tree of life till the command is broken. Was the tree hidden like the yew of Mughna? Could it be found only by those initiated and instructed, as in the quest of the Golden Bough? It stood in the midst of the garden:

'Latet arbore opaca
Aureus et foliis et lento vimine ramus,
Junoni infernae dictus sacer: hunc tegit omnis
Lucus, et obscuris claudunt convallibus umbrae.'[1]

Was it so shut in and shadowed that it could not be found? Is there anything parallel in the imagery to that of the Cretan labyrinth?

It has been suggested that in an earlier version of the Eden story there was but one tree, the tree of life, and it is to be noted that in Gn 3^{3} the tree with its forbidden fruit is described as being 'in the midst of the garden,' as is the tree of life in 2^{9}. And in most of the myths of paradise there is the conception of the one tree.

The Norse Yggdrasil in its complexity is the central tree of the universe: 'The chief and most holy seat of the gods is by the ash Yggdrasil. There the gods meet in council every day. It is the greatest and best of all trees, its branches spread over all the world and reach above heaven.'[2]

The garden reached by the Chinese king in quest of the glories of paradise had 'a wondrous tree in its midst, and a fountain of immortality, from which four rivers, flowing to the four corners of the earth, took their rise.'[3] The central tree with its fruit in the old willow pattern dish is a familiar illustration:

'The Chinese temple, there it stands
And there's the tree of many lands'—

in other words, the universe-tree of China.

Hercules, in the garden of the Hesperides, 'conquered the protecting dragon and secured the golden sun-fruits from the central tree.'[4] The garden of Indra contained five wonderful trees, the chief of which was the *paridjata*, 'the flower of which preserved its freshness throughout the year, contained in itself every scent and flavour, and gave happiness to whoever demanded it. It was, moreover, a test of virtue, losing its splendour in the hands of the sinful, and preserving it for him who followed duty.'[5]

It was but a step in the development of myth to differentiate between the tree of life and the tree of knowledge; and it was a step in the revelation of truth. The tree of life has the promise of immortality and bliss.

The sacred books of the Parsis state that 'the original human pair, Maschia and Maschiana, sprang from a tree in Heden, a delightful spot where grew homa or haoma, the marvellous tree of life whose fruit imparted vigour and immortality. The woman at the instance of Ahriman, the spirit of evil, in the guise of a serpent, gave her husband fruit to eat and so led to their ruin.'[6]

The story of Eden ends in ruin, but it is ruin which has the promise of regeneration (Gn 3^{15}). There is the way of the tree of life, and Christian mysticism found it in the way of the holy Cross. The drama of religion closes with the vision of the holy city, New Jerusalem, and the throne of God and of the Lamb:

'In the midst of the street of it, and on either side of the river, was there the tree of life, which bare twelve manner of fruits, and yielded her fruit every month: and the leaves of the tree were for the healing of the nations' (Rev 22^{2}).

Ethics and religion have each their part in keeping 'the way of the tree of life' (Gn 3^{24}); they are the supporters of the wheeling sword, the whirling flaming circle of the solar disk, the most sacred symbol of the Sun of Righteousness.

8. The tree of knowledge.—The oracle is an integral part of tree-worship.

Joshua at Shechem 'took a great stone, and set it up there under an oak, that was by the sanctuary of the Lord. And Joshua said unto all the people, Behold, this stone shall be a witness unto us; for it hath heard all the words of the Lord which he spake unto us' (Jos 24$^{26f.}$).

It was a witness to the oracle at Shechem. The 'plain of Meonenim' is the 'terebinth of the diviners (Jg 9^{37}). In Africa the trees planted round the ancestral graves were tended by women whose oracles were listened to in times of crisis.[7] Tree-divination was practised by the Ainus.[8] The oracular virtue of the oak of Dodona was assigned to the depths of its root.[9] The oracle was

1 *ClR* xvii. 420. 2 *ERE* iii. 295^{b}.
3 *Medallic History of Carausius*, London, 1757–59, ii. 163 f.
4 J. Brand, *Observations on Popular Antiquities*, ed. H. Ellis and J. O. Halliwell, new ed., London, 1848, i. 525.
5 *ClR* xvii. 421. 6 *De Bell. Gall.* vi. 16.
7 Verg. *Æn.* vi. 205–209. 8 Grupp, p. 145.
9 H. Pedersen, *Vergleich. Grammatik der kelt. Sprachen*, Göttingen, 1909–11, i. 365.
10 Whitley Stokes, *The Martyrology of Œngus the Culdee* (H. Bradshaw Soc. Publications, xxix.), London, 1905, p. 259.

1 Verg. *Æn.* vi. 136–139.
2 *The Prose Eddas*, tr. G. W. Dasent, Stockholm, 1842, *ap.* Philpot, pp. 113–115.
3 *Ib.* p. 134.
4 Hesiod, *Theog.* 215 ff.; Philpot, p. 136.
5 Philpot, p. 129. 6 *Ib.* p. 130.
7 *ERE* i. 164^{a}. 8 *Ib.* i. 248^{b}.
9 Philpot, p. 94.

chthonian. The witch of Endor raised spirits from the earth (1 S 28[13]).

'Altior ac penitus terrae defigitur arbos;
Aesculus in primis: quae quantum vertice ad auras
Aethereas, tantum radice in tartara tendit.'[1]

At Delphi the sacred laurel of Apollo grew in the cleft of the rock.[2] The chthonian rock-altars on the Areopagus at Athens are carpeted in spring-time with asphodel. Did this suggest the phrase, κατ' ἀσφοδελὸν λειμῶνα, in Hom. *Od.* xi. 539, xxiv. 13? Both passages are assigned to the very latest or Athenian stratum of the Odyssey.

The rustling in the mulberry-trees (2 S 5[24]) has its counterpart in the story of Æacus. He consulted an oak, a sapling from Dodona:

'Tu mihi da cives: et inania moenia reple.
Intremuit, ramisque sonum sine flamine motis
Alta dedit quercus.'[3]

The sacred cedar of the Chaldæans was not only the tree of life but 'the revealer of the oracles of earth and heaven.' The name of Ea, the god of wisdom, was supposed to be written on its core.[4]

The hazel appears in Irish romance as the tree of knowledge. The mystical fountain known as Connla's Well was overshadowed by nine mystical hazel-trees. The nuts were of the richest crimson colour and teemed with the knowledge of all that was choicest in literature and art. The nuts fell into the spring, where they were eaten by the salmon which frequented the spring. Therefore the salmon was the wisest of all things. In the story of Kulhwch, in the *Mabinogion*, the salmon of Llyn Llyw is stated to have been the first animal created, and its memory to surpass that of the eagle, the owl, the stag, and the blackbird. The source of its wisdom was the many-melodied hazel of knowledge.[5] The culture-god of the Celtic world has been identified with Mercury, and with the Gaulish deity Ogmios, the god of eloquence and wisdom. His name in Welsh survived in the word *ofydd*, one skilled or versed in anything. In Ireland he appears as Ogma, one of the ancient Goidelic group of the Tuatha Dé Danann. He was in a special sense the diviner or discloser among the gods.[6] The divining-rod is the surviving relic of the tree-oracle, and the hazel is the favourite tree from which it is cut. In France it was the custom to cut it on Wednesday, Mercury's day. This also points to the association of the hazel with the Gaulish Mercury. He was known also as the god 'qui vias et semitas commentus est,' and the custom of beating the bounds with a hazel-switch is another link with ancient rites.

Irish literature represents crimson nuts as forming the food of the gods.[7] The crimson berries of the mountain-ash explain its sanctity. It has been suggested that it is the original counsel-tree of the Northern races.[8] In Ireland the mountain-ash and the birch are still held sacred, and in Staffordshire in the 17th cent. Plot states that it was held dangerous to do wanton damage to the tree.[9] It is still, under the name 'wicky,' a favourite tree in the country districts. Evelyn[10] states that it was held in such veneration in Wales that it was found in every churchyard. It is still found in old burial-grounds in Yorkshire. In Derbyshire a little cross made of the witch-wiggin is held as a protection against witchcraft. The rites observed in cutting it belong to the earliest ages of tree-worship. It was to be cut on St. Helen's Day. It must be cut stealthily from a tree never seen before, and carried home by any way save that by which the wood-cutter had gone

[1] Verg. *Georg.* ii. 290–292. [2] Philpot, p. 98.
[3] Ovid, *Met.* vii. 628–630. [4] Philpot, p. 131.
[5] Rhys, *Celtic Heathendom*[2], pp. 554–556.
[6] *Ib.* p. 5 ff. [7] *Ib.* p. 356.
[8] J. Holden MacMichael, *Antiquary*, xlii. [1906] 369.
[9] *Ib.* p. 370. [10] *Ib.* p. 371.

on his secret and sacred quest.[1] As the care-tree it has been taken over by the Church in the rhyme:

'Care Sunday, care away,
Palm Sunday, and Easter Day.'

Care Sunday is Passion Sunday, the Sunday before Palm Sunday.[2]

The holly is the Irish *cuilenn*, the Welsh *celynen*, the O.E. *holegn*; it is not a variant of 'holy.' The persistence of its red berries in winter and its Christmas associations give it a high place among the trees of the north. It enters into place-names in Ireland, as in Druimm Cuilinn, now Drumcullen, barony of English, King's County. More noticeable is its occurrence as a personal name, Macc Cuilinn, bishop of Lusk.[3] The effigy of the Holly-boy in the Kentish Shrovetide revels may be regarded as a substitute for the oak with its ancient religious association. At the close of the revels it was burned.[4] The Christmas burning of the Yule-log is another link in the same chain, as the burning of the mistletoe-bough is the evidence of the continuity of the sacred fire.

The Christmas blossoming of the Glastonbury thorn and the Christmas-tree (of late introduction in England), with its lights and flowers and fruits, have been associated with the 'strange blossoming power of nature connected with St. Andrew's Day' (30th Nov.). These were transferred in the Middle Ages to the Christmas festival.[5]

'Christmas-Eve was given to the memory of Adam and Eve, and this led to the Paradise-plays which formed a prelude to the Nativity-plays. The Cross of Christ was held in ancient legend to have been made of "a tree which had sprung from a slip of the Tree of Knowledge." In the Paradise-play this tree was brought in laden with apples and decked with ribbons.'[6]

The lights form an integral part of the earlier ideas of this tree-ritual.

In old Icelandic legend there is the story of a mountain-ash at Mödhrufell which on Christmas Eve was covered with lights that the strongest gale could not extinguish. These lights were its blossoms. In French legend, Perceval comes across a tree illuminated with a thousand candles; and in another story Durmals le Galois twice saw a magnificent tree covered with lights from top to bottom.[7]

In Icelandic folk-lore lights are seen in the rowan-tree, and in Celtic folk-lore the scarlet berries of the rowan-tree are the source of wisdom. Is there not here a link between the light of wisdom and the bright fruit belonging to the tree of knowledge? The flamens wore the scarlet tuft in their caps.[8]

'Simonides tells us that it was not a white sail which Ægeus gave, but a scarlet one, dyed with the juice of the flower of a very flourishing holm-oak, and that this was to be the signal that all was well.'[9]

The story of Ægeus and Theseus has its parallel in the sign of the 'scarlet thread' at Jericho (Jos 2[18]).

The rod of Aaron was the rod of the priesthood, and the priest's lips were to keep knowledge (Mal 2[7]).

At the return from Captivity 'the Tirshatha said unto them, that they should not eat of the most holy things, till there stood up a priest with Urim and with Thummim' (Ezr 2[63]). The breastplate of judgment contained these sacred lots (Ex 28[30]). The sacred oracles are in the charge of the priest: 'for he is the messenger of the Lord of hosts' (Mal 2[7]).

The rod was the token of this authority; and the rod of Aaron was a rod of almond. The Hebrew word for 'almond' is *shāḳēdh*, connected with the root 'to watch.' It is the tree of watchfulness, the tree of light. Jeremiah of the priests of Anathoth, in the opening of his prophecies, sees the vision of an almond-rod. It is the token of the watchfulness of God:

[1] Macmichael, *Antiquary*, xlii. 422.
[2] *Ib.* p. 426.
[3] *Martyrology of Œngus*, pp. 382, 431; cf. 202 f.
[4] Brand, i. 68. [5] Philpot, p. 167.
[6] *Ib.* p. 169. [7] *Ib.* p. 171 f.
[8] Plut. ed. Langhorne, i. 189 n.
[9] *Ib.* p. 51; cf. *EBi*, col. 4316.

'Then said the Lord unto me, Thou hast well seen: for I will hasten my word to perform it' (Jer 1[12]).

And in the open vision of death it would seem that the blossoming of the almond-tree symbolizes the light of the presence of God (Ec 12[5]), the light of wisdom and knowledge: 'Because the preacher was wise, he still taught the people knowledge' (12[9]).

The early cult of the sacred tree among the Jews left its mark in the Temple of Jerusalem. Robertson Smith notes that, as the two pillars Jachin and Boaz, so also the golden candlestick had associations with this ancient cult.[1] The pillars were wreathed with pomegranates; the candlestick was a budding and blossoming almond. If the former witness to the tree of life, the latter witnesses to the tree of knowledge.

Light was the first of the gifts of life; and it is in the light alone that religion can fulfil the duties of life. A Babylonian seal figured by Mrs. Philpot shows the sacred tree with seven branches, three on the right and four on the left, with a fruiting branch drooping on either side. On the right is a figure sitting with outstretched hand, the head crowned with the horns of a bull; on the left is another figure sitting, without the bull-mask, but with a snake behind it.[2] It recalls in some points the story of Eden; but it is also a link in the development of the seven-branched candlestick of the Temple.

The sacred twig, the sacred fire, the priest-king who is guardian and champion of both, and who is also the representative of the majesty of the sun, each and all witness 'at sundry times and in divers manners' to the religious fellowship and communion which man enjoys with the divine spirit. Silent adoration is called for in the presence of the tree of life. The tree of the knowledge of good and evil is vocal in the light of divine wisdom:

'And I turned to see the voice that spake with me. And being turned, I saw seven golden candlesticks; And in the midst of the seven candlesticks one like unto the Son of man . . . and his voice as the sound of many waters' (Rev 1[12-15]).

This voice is the voice of divine wisdom, vocal at Dodona and Cnossus and Delphi, vocal in the burning bush, and vocal to-day in 'the spirit of wisdom and understanding, the spirit of counsel and ghostly strength, the spirit of knowledge and true godliness . . . and the spirit of God's holy fear.'[3] And this fruit of the Holy Spirit is the fruit of the sacred tree:

'And there shall come forth a rod out of the stem of Jesse, and a Branch shall grow out of his roots: And the spirit of the Lord shall rest upon him' (Is 11[1f.]).

It is true to-day, as in the earliest ages of animistic religion, that 'the fear of the Lord is the beginning of wisdom' (Ps 111[10]).

LITERATURE.—The authorities are quoted in the footnotes.

THOMAS BARNS.

TREE OF KNOWLEDGE, TREE OF LIFE.—See TREES AND PLANTS.

TRIADS.—See TRIMŪRTI, TRINITY.

TRIMŪRTI.

—Though the *Rigveda* does not contain the conception of a supreme spirit manifested in three forms (*trimūrti*), which is the Hindu doctrine of the Trinity, it contains elements which have contributed to form that belief. In the first place, Agni as the god of fire has three forms: he is the sun in the sky, lightning in the aerial waters, and fire on earth. On this idea is based much of the mysticism of the Vedic period, and it is reflected in the ritual by the threefold character of the sacrificial fire. Secondly, in prayers such as 'May Sūrya protect us from the sky, Vāta from the air, Agni from the earthly regions,'[1] appears a tendency to reduce all the gods to manifestations of three chief deities, each representative of one of the three divisions, sky, air, and earth. Yāska[2] tells us that his predecessors in Vedic interpretation held that all the gods could be reduced to three, Agni, Vāyu or Indra, and Sūrya, though he himself does not adopt this view. A further step towards the amalgamation of the gods is seen in the *Maitrāyaṇī Saṃhitā*,[3] which holds that Agni, Vāyu, and Sūrya are all sons of Prajāpati, the creator god.

The further development of the doctrine occurs only in the later *Upaniṣads* as the outcome of the adoption of the principle of the absolute (*brahman* or *ātman*). In the *Taittirīya Āraṇyaka*[4] or *Mahānārāyaṇa Upaniṣad* the highest self (*param-ātman*) is identified with Brahman (by which Brahmā is probably meant), Śiva, Hari, and Indra; the identification with Hari is probably a later interpolation, as it spoils the metre, but it is doubtless an old change in the text. In the *Maitrāyaṇī Upaniṣad*[5] Brahmā, Rudra, and Viṣṇu appear as forms (*tanavaḥ*) of the absolute, which itself is incorporeal, and again[6] are declared to correspond respectively with the *rajas*, *tamas*, and *sattva* aspects of the absolute. The same triad is found in other texts such as the *Prāṇāgnihotra*, *Brahma*, *Nṛsiṃhottaratāpanīya* and *Rāmottaratāpanīya Upaniṣads*.

The comparative lateness and esoteric character of the doctrine are shown by the almost total absence of the conception from the epics, where it appears definitely only in the statement of the *Mahābhārata*:[7]

'In the form of Brahmā he creates; his human form [*i.e.* Viṣṇu] preserves; in his form as Rudra will he destroy; these are the three states of Prajāpati.'

This is the classical form of the doctrine which is repeated in the *Harivaṃśa*, in Kālidāsa's *Kumārasambhava*, and not rarely in the later literature. The personality of the trinity is varied slightly according to sectarian preferences: thus in the Śaiva view[8] the absolute, which is Śiva, is manifested as Brahmā, Viṣṇu, and Bhava, the last a personal form of Śiva; the Nimbārkas and other sects[9] identify Kṛṣṇa with the absolute, distinguishing him from Viṣṇu as one of the trinity. There is some uncertainty whether the formation of the definite idea of a trinity was preceded by the conception of Viṣṇu and Śiva as merged in a unity, attested by the term Harihara, which appears first in the *Harivaṃśa*; this view, however, is rendered probable by the fact that the epic appears to have identified Viṣṇu and Śiva as equals before it combined Brahmā with them as their peer. A characteristically late idea recognizes a trinity of the Śaktis, or personifications of the power of the three gods: Vāch or Sarasvatī as that of Brahmā; Śrī, Lakṣmī, or Rādhā as that of Viṣṇu; and Umā, Durgā, or Kālī as that of Śiva. For this there is no Vedic parallel, though in the *āprī* hymns of the *Rigveda* a triad of sacrificial goddesses is found in Sarasvatī, Iḍā, and Bhāratī.

Serving as it does to reconcile rival monotheisms with one another and with the philosophic doctrine of the absolute, the theory of the Trimūrti presents no such close similarity to the Christian doctrine of the Trinity as to render derivation from Christian influences either necessary or probable, though chronologically the existence of such influence is

1 P. 467 f. 2 P. 130.
3 *Book of Common Prayer*, Order of Confirmation; cf. Is 11[2f.] LXX.

1 x. clviii. 1. 2 *Nirukta*, vii. 5. 3 IV. xii. 2.
4 x. xiii. 12; cf. P. Deussen, *Sechzig Upanishad's des Veda*, Leipzig, 1905, p. 252, n. 2.
5 iv. 5, 6. 6 v. 2.
7 III. cclxxii. 46—an interpolation, according to E. W. Hopkins, *Great Epic of India*, New York, 1902, p. 184.
8 *Liṅga Purāṇa*, I. xviii. 12.
9 R. G. Bhandarkar, *Vaiṣṇavism, Śaivism, and Minor Religious Systems* (=*GIAP* iii. 6), Strassburg, 1913, p. 79.

quite possible. It is, however, conceivable that the idea developed under the influence of Mahāyāna Buddhism, which possesses the notable triads of Buddha, Dhyāni-buddha, and Dhyāni-bodhisattva on the one hand, and of the Dharma-, Nirmāṇa-, and Sambhoga-kāyas of a Buddha on the other. The Buddhist art of Gandhāra, followed by that of Tibet, China, and Japan, is prone to depict groups of three deities, Buddhas, or *bodhisattvas*, and it is to this influence that we may assign the existence of such sculptures as that from the cave of Elephanta, Bombay, which presents the three gods in one statue, and affords the inspiration for the *ekā mūrtis trayo devāḥ* of the *Matsya Purāṇa*,[1] a passage often wrongly interpreted to mean 'One God and three persons.'

LITERATURE.—J. Muir, *Original Sanskrit Texts*, iv.², London, 1873; A. A. Macdonell, *Vedic Mythology* (=*GIAP* iii. 1), Strassburg, 1897; A. Barth, *The Religions of India*, Eng. tr., London, 1882; E. W. Hopkins, *Religions of India*, do. 1896; A. B. Keith, *Indian Mythology* (=*Mythology of All Races*, vi.), Boston, 1917; A. Grünwedel, *Buddhist Art in India*, Eng. tr., London, 1901; L. de la Vallée Poussin, *JRAS*, 1906, pp. 943–977; N. Söderblom, in *Transactions of the Third Internat. Cong. for the History of Religions*, ii. [Oxford, 1908] 391–410.

A. BERRIEDALE KEITH.

TRINITARIANISM. — See TRINITY, RELIGIOUS ORDERS (Christian).

TRINITY.—1. The term and concept. — (*a*) The term 'Trinity' (from Lat. *trinitas*) appears to have been first used by Tertullian,[2] while the corresponding Greek term 'Triad' (*τριάς*) appears to have been first used by Theophilus the Christian apologist,[3] an older contemporary of Tertullian. In Tertullian, as in the subsequent usage, the term designates the Christian doctrine of God as Father, Son, and Spirit.

(*b*) Although the notion of a divine Triad or Trinity is characteristic of the Christian religion, it is by no means peculiar to it. In Indian religion, *e.g.*, we meet with the trinitarian group of Brahmā, Śiva, and Viṣṇu; and in Egyptian religion with the trinitarian group of Osiris, Isis, and Horus, constituting a divine family, like the Father, Mother, and Son in mediæval Christian pictures. Nor is it only in historical religions that we find God viewed as a Trinity. One recalls in particular the Neo-Platonic view of the Supreme or Ultimate Reality, which was suggested by Plato in the *Timæus*; *e.g.*, in the philosophy of Plotinus the primary or original Realities (*ἀρχικαὶ ὑποστάσεις*)[4] are triadically represented as the Good or (in numerical symbol) the One, the Intelligence or the One-Many, and the World-Soul or the One and Many. The religious Trinity associated, if somewhat loosely, with Comte's philosophy might also be cited here: the cultus of humanity as the Great Being, of space as the Great Medium, and of the earth as the Great Fetish.

(*c*) What lends a special character to the Christian doctrine of the Trinity is its close association with the distinctive Christian view of divine incarnation. In other religions and religious philosophies we meet with the idea of divine incarnation, but it may be claimed that nowhere is the union of God and man so concrete and definite, and so universal in its import, as in the Christian religion. As Augustine said,[5] if in the books of the Platonists it was to be found that 'in the beginning was the Word,'[1] it was not found there that 'the Word became flesh and dwelt among us.'[2] It is the very central truth of Christianity that God was historically manifest in Christ, and that He is still revealed in the world as the indwelling Spirit of the Church or community of Christ's founding. This Christian faith in the incarnation of the divine Word (*λόγος*, *sermo*, *ratio*) in the man Christ Jesus, with whom the believer is united through the fellowship of the Holy Spirit, constitutes the distinctive basis of the Christian doctrine of the Trinity.

2. The development of the doctrine.—The limits of this article preclude any attempt to trace in detail the development of the Trinitarian idea from its beginnings in the Bible to its final formulation in the orthodox creeds. In various articles of this Encyclopædia this ground is traversed, such as the comprehensive art. GOD; the artt. on particular developments of ancient Christian thought like the Alexandrian, Antiochene, and Cappadocian Theologies; the artt. on individual Christian theologians like Athanasius and Augustine; the artt. on heretical phases of Christological and Trinitarian belief like Adoptianism, Arianism, Monophysitism, Nestorianism. It will be convenient, however, to take here a general conspectus of the development in question.

(*a*) The *Old Testament* could hardly be expected to furnish the doctrine of the Trinity, if belief in the Trinity is grounded (as stated above) upon belief in the incarnation of God in Christ and upon the experience of spiritual redemption and renewal through Christ. It is exegesis of a mischievous, if pious, sort that would discover the doctrine in the plural form, 'Elohim,' of the Deity's name, in the recorded appearance of three angels to Abraham, or even in the *ter sanctus* of the prophecies of Isaiah. It may be allowed, however, that the OT ideas of the Word of God and the Wisdom of God are adumbrations of the doctrine, as recognizing the truth of a various self-revealing activity in the one God.

(*b*) In the *New Testament* we do not find the doctrine of the Trinity in anything like its developed form, not even in the Pauline and Johannine theology, although ample witness is borne to the religious experience from which the doctrine springs. None the less Christ is acknowledged as the eternal Son of God and the supreme revelation of the Father, and the quickening Spirit of life is acknowledged to be derived 'from on high.'[3] And so, when the early Christians would describe their conception of God, all the three elements—God, Christ, and the Spirit—enter into the description, and the one God is found to be revealed in a threefold way. This is seen in the baptismal formula,[4] 'In the name of the Father, and of the Son, and of the Holy Ghost,' which at least reflects the usage of the apostolic Church, and in which the members of the Trinity are already all three associated together. It is also to be seen in the familiar words of St. Paul,[5] 'The grace of the Lord Jesus Christ, and the love of God, and the communion of the Holy Ghost.' This last has been called, and justly so, the great Trinitarian text of the NT, as being one of the few NT passages, and the earliest of them, in which the three elements of the Trinity are set alongside of each other in a single sentence. If the passage contains no formulated expression of the Trinity, it is yet of great significance as showing that, less than thirty years after the death of Christ, His name and the name of the Holy Spirit could be employed in conjunction with the name of God Himself. Truly, if the doctrine of the Trinity appeared

[1] J. N. Farquhar, *Religious Literature of India*, Oxford, 1920, p. 149.

[2] 'Custodiatur *οἰκονομίας* sacramentum, quae unitatem in trinitatem disponit' (*adv. Praxean*, 2).

[3] *τῆς τριάδος, τοῦ θεοῦ καὶ τοῦ λόγου αὐτοῦ καὶ τῆς σοφίας αὐτοῦ* (ii. 15). But perhaps the earliest appearance of the term is in Clem. *Excerpt. ex Theod.* § 80; cf. A. Harnack, *Hist. of Dogma*, Eng. tr., 7 vols., London, 1894–99, ii. 209 n.

[4] *Enn.* v. 1, cited by C. C. J. Webb, *God and Personality* (*Gifford Lectures*), London, 1918, p. 43.

[5] *Conf.* vii. 9; cf. C. C. J. Webb, *Problems in the Relations of God and Man*, London, 1911, p. 236.

[1] Jn 1¹. [2] Jn 1¹⁴. [3] Lk 24⁴⁹. [4] Mt 28¹⁹. [5] 2 Co 13¹⁴.

somewhat late in theology, it must have lived very early in devotion.

(c) The story of the Trinity in *ecclesiastical history* is the story of the transition from the Trinity of experience, in which God is self-revealed as the Father or Creator and Legislator, the Son or Redeemer, and the Spirit or Sanctifier, to the Trinity of dogma, in which the threefold self-disclosure of God is but the reflexion, as it were, of a threefold distinction within the divine Nature itself. With the transition from the Trinity of experience to the Trinity of dogma the theological statement tends to lose touch with the gracious figure of the historical Christ. In the Nicæno-Constantinopolitan Creed, in which the Eastern development of the doctrine of the Trinity culminated, the dogma still retains its connexion with its positive ground and basis in the incarnate life of Christ; but in the Athanasian Creed, which represents the form which the dogma finally assumed in the West, it appears to have lost the connexion altogether, and to move entirely in the transcendent realm.

Five stages in the dogmatic development may be distinguished.[1] (1) The formal identification of the pre-existent Christ (of the Pauline and Johannine theology) with the Logos of Greek philosophy. In the NT the identification is in the practical rather than speculative interest, but in Justin Martyr and the apologists it may be regarded as the first step in the logical process whereby the historical figure of Jesus Christ was caught up into the purely speculative sphere. (2) The doctrine of the eternal generation of the Logos or Son (hitherto regarded primarily as the cosmological principle of revelation and not therefore co-eternal with God). This doctrine, due to Origen, which may be expressed in other words as the eternal Fatherhood of God, entered into the Athanasian theology. Formulated in the interests of the divinity of Christ, it conserved also—as against Sabellian views—the distinction between the Father and the Son. On the other hand, the subordinationism it implied and acknowledged, while countering dyotheistic and tritheistic tendencies, lent support to the Arian conception of the Son as a creature, especially after the Origenist theory of eternal creation (which enabled Origen himself to regard the Son as still primarily a cosmological principle) had been abandoned. (3) The doctrine of the consubstantiality of the Son with the Father. This was affirmed against Arianism at Nicæa, where the concept—if not as yet the actual term—*homoousios* (ὁμοούσιος) as applied to the eternal Son was amply vindicated. As Athanasius taught, in jealous regard for the divineness of the Christian incarnation and redemption, there was an absolute likeness between the Father and the Son, and also a co-inherence or mutual immanence (περιχώρησις, *circumincessio*) of their Persons.[2] (4) The doctrine of eternal distinctions within the divine Nature, according to the formula of 'three Hypostases in one Ousia or Substance' (τρεῖς ὑποστάσεις, μία οὐσία). To the Cappadocian theologians (Basil, Gregory of Nazianzus, Gregory of Nyssa) we owe the final settlement, for which this formula stands, of the dogmatic terminology. In distinguishing between *hypostasis* and *ousia*, the former denoting a real principle of distinction within the divine Nature and the latter the divine Substance or Nature (φύσις) itself,[3] they sought to lift the orthodox doctrine out of the Sabellian modalism which recognized no distinction in reality between the Father and the Son, so impairing the significance of the historical Christ, and at the same time to vindicate it against the opposite error of heathen polytheism (tritheism), of which it was so often accused. Moreover, the Cappadocians gave to the third member of the Trinity, the Holy Spirit, the definite place and character which He now possesses in the Eastern orthodoxy, as being also a Hypostasis in the Godhead, consubstantial with the Father, and proceeding from the Father through the Son. (5) The doctrine of the double procession from the Father and the Son (the *filioque* clause, added to the Nicæno-Constantinopolitan Creed on canonically indefensible grounds[1]) —a doctrine which represents the difference between Western orthodoxy and Eastern (with its view of procession as from the Father alone, the unitary source of deity[2]); which was conceived, in the interests of the divine unity, as counteractive of the subordinationism contained in the Eastern formulas; and which under Augustine's influence found its way into the Athanasian Creed. Curiously enough, the Athanasian Creed (so called) thus differs theologically from the Nicæno-Constantinopolitan Creed in its original Eastern form on a point on which Athanasius's own sympathies would have lain with the Eastern symbol. The Greek (Athanasian) theology found the divine unity in the Father, the one fountain-head of deity, so leaving room for the conception of the Son and the Spirit as subordinate to the Father. The Roman (Augustinian) theology found the divine unity in the divine Nature or Substance, with the result that, as the distinctions between the three Hypostases or Persons became weakened under the doctrine of the co-inherence, so attractive to the non-metaphysical Westerns,[3] there remained no proper foothold—so to speak—for the doctrine of subordination.

3. The statement of the doctrine.—(*a*) The ecclesiastical doctrine whose stages of development have been indicated may be briefly stated as follows, and the form of statement would commend itself as a whole alike to the Western or Roman Catholic and the Protestant Church. For, although the doctrine of the Trinity was the subject of much discussion, dogmatic and speculative, in the Middle Ages and at the Protestant Reformation, and has been since, it has been formulated all along on the lines of the Nicæno-Constantinopolitan and Athanasian Creeds. Both Roman Catholics and Protestants—generally speaking—yield formal adherence to these symbols, and the old orthodoxy remains still the new.

(*b*) There are then (as the statement may run) three Persons (Hypostases) or real distinctions in the unity of the divine Nature or Substance, which is Love. The Persons are co-equal, inasmuch as in each of them the divine Nature is one and undivided, and by each the collective divine attributes are shared. As a 'person' in Trinitarian usage is more than a mere aspect of being, being a real ground of experience and function, each divine Person, while less than a separate individuality, possesses His own hypostatic character or characteristic property (ἰδιώτης). The hypostatic characters of the Persons may be viewed from an internal and an external standpoint, *i.e.* with reference to the inner constitution of the Godhead or to the Godhead as related to the cosmos or world of manifestation. Viewed *ab intra*, the hypostatic character of the Father is ingeneration (ἀγεννησία), of the Son filiation, of the Spirit procession; wherefore, 'the Father is of none, neither begotten nor proceeding; the Son is

[1] Cf. W. Adams Brown, *Christian Theology in Outline*, Edinburgh, 1907, p. 142.
[2] Cf. Jn 17^{21}.
[3] See, further, art. TRITHEISM, 3.

[1] Cf. T. B. Strong, *A Manual of Theology*[2], London, 1903, p. 168 ff.
[2] μία πηγὴ θεότητος.
[3] Strong, p. 170.

eternally begotten of the Father; the Holy Ghost eternally proceeding from the Father and the Son.'[1] Viewed *ab extra* (for Love functions externally as well as internally, is centrifugal as well as centripetal[2]), the hypostatic character of the Father is made manifest in creation, whereby a world is provided for beings who should be capable of experiencing fellowship with the divine Love; the hypostatic character of the Son in redemption, whereby the alienating power of sin is overcome; and the hypostatic character of the Spirit in sanctification, whereby human nature is quickened and renewed and shaped to the divine likeness. Yet, while this is said, as there is no separation in the unity of the Godhead, so the one God is manifested in the threefold work of creation, redemption, and sanctification; moreover, each of the Persons as sharing the divine attributes is active in the threefold work, if with varying stress of function. Verily the doctrine of the Trinity *exit in mysterium*.

(*c*) It should, perhaps, be emphasized that the Trinitarian statement is never tritheistic, in the sense of affirming three separate self-conscious and self-determining individualities in the Godhead. When it is affirmed that there are three Persons in one God, the word 'person' is used archaically, and not in the modern sense of a centre or core of personality. It was a word employed by Tertullian[3] as on the whole the best word by which to convey the idea of an inner principle of distinction or individuation (ὑπόστασις); and it was a good enough word when it bore a vaguer and more flexible meaning than it bears nowadays in Western Europe. To say that there are three separate personalities in the Godhead would be polytheism. To say that there are three eternal principles of distinction or modes of subsistence in the Godhead is not polytheism—although in the speculative construction of the Trinity it might lead, and has sometimes led, to a theoretical pluralism or polytheism.

4. The speculative construction of the doctrine.—(*a*) Although the Christian Church soon came to look upon the Trinity as an incomprehensible mystery of revelation, which reason might not probe, her theologians have not refrained whether in ancient or in modern times from speculation upon the doctrine. In mediæval times, indeed, the doctrine of the Trinity was 'the high school of logic and dialectic.'[4] Then, as before and since, recourse was often made to the principle of analogy, in order to throw light upon the mysterious notion of tri-personality in the Godhead. It is a principle that has received classical treatment at the hands of Augustine, who employed in particular the analogies of the human self-consciousness and the relationship of love. It is not pretended, however, that by such analogies the doctrine of the Trinity may be rationalized. And, clearly, such analogies fail on one side or the other to satisfy the conception of 'three Persons in one Nature.' On the one hand, the psychological analogy of the self-consciousness does justice to the unity of the Nature, but not to the distinction of the Persons. This is as true, it has been remarked,[5] of Dorner's construction founding upon Hegel's 'being in itself, being for itself, being in and for itself,' as of Augustine's 'memory, understanding, and will'[6] (in each of which he found the whole rational nature expressed), or, as we might add, of his

[1] *Westminster Confession*, ii. 3.
[2] Cf. S. A. McDowall, *Evolution and the Doctrine of the Trinity*, Cambridge, 1918, p. 53 f.
[3] *Adv. Praxean*, 11 f.
[4] Harnack, *Hist. of Dogma*, vi. 183.
[5] T. Haering, *The Christian Faith*, Eng. tr., 2 vols., London, 1913, ii. 918.
[6] *Memoria, intelligentia, voluntas*; cf. *de Trin.* ix.–xv.

'mind, self-knowledge, and self-love.'[1] On the other hand, the social analogy of love does justice, more or less, to the distinction of the Persons, but not to the unity of the Nature. In this case the three elements of the analogy are the loving subject, the loved object, and the mutual love which unites them. The subject and the object possess, to be sure, more than sufficient independence for the purpose in view, but it is difficult to see how the love which unites may be accepted as a distinct person, even in the vaguest sense of that term. The application of the psychological analogy may be regarded as an attempt to satisfy the *theoretical* interest attaching to the traditional dogma for which the Logos-conception stands, namely, the explanation of the relations between God and the world. On the assumption that the human individual is a microcosm, bearing traces of the divine Personality upon him, it would seek to make more intelligible the unity in diversity, or more precisely the unity in triplicity, affirmed in the orthodox view of the Godhead. Again, the construction of the Trinity which is founded upon the social analogy may be regarded as an attempt to satisfy the *practical* interest attaching to the traditional dogma, namely, the vindication of the truly divine character of the Person and Work of Jesus Christ. On the assumption that the love-created social unit is the real microcosm, it would make more intelligible the triplicity in unity which is also affirmed in the orthodox view of the Godhead. Perhaps the social analogy has been the more influential of the two. It certainly offers a picture of the inner constitution of the Godhead that corresponds to the Christian Gospel: 'The love of the Eternal Father is for ever satisfied in the Eternal Son; the Father and the Son are for ever bound together in the Holy Spirit, who is the bond of the Divine Love.'[2]

(*b*) In modern constructions of the doctrine of the Trinity there is a tendency to make much of the microcosm of human personality as carrying traces of macrocosmic Reality. God is to be interpreted, it is said, according to the teleological principle of the highest, and human personality is the highest thing we know. The result is that, as C. C. J. Webb[3] has indicated, we hear a good deal nowadays, even in non-Unitarian Christianity, of 'the Personality *of* God,' whereas the historical doctrine is that of 'Personality *in* God.' This raises the question whether the future of Christianity lies in its associating itself with the modern philosophical movement of personalism or in the renewal of its old alliance with Platonism. Into such a question we may not enter, but we would cite a recent instance of a discussion of the Trinity in which human personality figures as the key to the mystery of the Godhead. It is S. A. McDowall's[4] contention that there is more than analogy between human and divine personality, there is also identity in their nature. The Trinity within us is more than suggestive of the truth that in God personality is also triune. If we might borrow the language of Julian of Norwich,[5] the 'made Trinity' actually points to 'the unmade blessed Trinity.' If the Godhead be a Personality, it must indeed be a unity, but the unity—like the unity of human personality—is composed of three persons, which, although not self-existent but completely interpenetrating, are differentiated from each other by the stress of their individual functioning.[6] Personality, whether in God or in

[1] *Mens, notitia, amor*; cf. *de Civ. Dei*, xi. 26.
[2] Strong, p. 166.
[3] See *God and Personality*, lect. iii.
[4] Pp. 62 f., 95.
[5] Cf. W. R. Inge, *Personal Idealism and Mysticism*, London, 1907, p. 28.
[6] McDowall, p. 108.

man, could not really exist if it did not thus involve an internal manifold.[1] For the elaboration of these positions reference must be made to the book itself. The discussion is cited here only as illustrating a recent tendency in the application, in Trinitarian speculations, of the principle of analogy.

5. Economic and essential trinity.—(*a*) The transition from the Trinity of experience to the Trinity of dogma is describable in other terms as the transition from the economic or dispensational Trinity (*τρόπος ἀποκαλύψεως*) to the essential, immanent, or ontological Trinity (*τρόπος ὑπάρξεως*). At first the Christian faith was not Trinitarian in the strictly ontological reference. It was not so in the apostolic and sub-apostolic ages, as reflected in the NT and other early Christian writings. Nor was it so even in the age of the Christian apologists. And even Tertullian, who founded the nomenclature of the orthodox doctrine, knew as little of an ontological Trinity as did the apologists; his is still the economic or relative conception of the Johannine and Pauline theology. So Harnack holds,[2] and he says further[3] that the whole history of Christological and Trinitarian dogma from Athanasius to Augustine is the history of the displacement of the Logos-conception by that of the Son, of the substitution of the immanent and absolute Trinity for the economic and relative. In any case the orthodox doctrine in its developed form is a Trinity of essence rather than of manifestation, as having to do in the first instance with the subjective rather than the objective Being of God. And, just because these two meanings of the Trinity—the theoretical and the practical, as they might also be described—are being sharply distinguished in modern Christian thought, it might be well if the term 'Trinity' were employed to designate the Trinity of revelation (or the doctrine of the threefold self-manifestation of God), and the term 'Triunity' (cf. Germ. *Dreieinigkeit*) adopted as the designation of the essential Trinity (or the doctrine of the tri-personal nature of God).[4]

(*b*) It should be observed that there is no real cleavage or antithesis between the doctrines of the economic and the essential Trinity, and naturally so. The Triunity represents the effort to think out the Trinity, and so to afford it a reasonable basis. The first Christians had with St. Paul a saving experience of the grace of the Lord Jesus Christ, and of the love of God, and of the communion of the Holy Ghost;[5] and the theologians of the ancient Church sought to set forth the Christian experience in logical terms of reason. In the effort they were led, inevitably, to effect an alliance between the gospel of their salvation and the speculative philosophy, and more especially the Platonism, in which they had been trained, while, in making room for the Christian gospel within the world—not altogether hospitable—of the Greek philosophy, they found themselves translating their empirical knowledge of God—the God and Father of the Lord Jesus Christ—into a doctrine of diversity or multiplicity, as distinguished from merely abstract unity, within the divine Nature itself. In other words, in thinking out the Trinity they arrived at the Triunity. None the less the greatest and most influential of the Christian Fathers, Origen, Athanasius, Basil and the Gregories, Augustine, all acknowledged that, for all the light thrown upon it in the Biblical revelation, the divine Nature remained for them a mystery transcending reason.[6]

[1] McDowall, p. 218.
[2] *Hist. of Dogma*, ii. 209, 260. [3] *Ib.* iii. 8.
[4] Cf. W. N. Clarke, *An Outline of Christian Theology*, Edinburgh, 1898, p. 161.
[5] Cf. 2 Co 13^{14}.
[6] Cf. J. R. Illingworth, *The Doctrine of the Trinity*, London, 1907, ch. vi.

(*c*) It is claimed, however, especially by Catholic thinkers, that, logical mystery as the Trinity undoubtedly is, it not only conserves the spiritual values of the Gospel, but may be said to enshrine or encasket them. The Athanasian Creed, *e.g.*, is declared to be in effect a sublime and magnificent hymn of the Christian faith, having a power all its own to stir and uplift the souls of believers with the greatness and mystery of the divine redemption in Jesus Christ. That being so, it may be allowed that there is justice in the contention that acceptance of the Triunity does not commit one to the adoption of obsolete modes of thought, but only to acceptance of the authoritative Christian tradition which the terms of the Greek philosophy served to symbolize, and with whose continued vitality they have become invested.[1]

(*d*) But in consequence of a wide-spread failure, especially within the Protestant Church, to appreciate the symbolism in which the traditional Christian convictions are embodied, and to recognize in the doctrine of the Three in One any more than a sacred mysterious formula, modern Christian theology is thrown back more and more upon the historical revelation in Jesus Christ and the inward experience of Christian believers as the practical ground and basis of Trinitarian doctrine, being less concerned with what God is in Himself than with what He has shown Himself to be—less concerned with the Trinity of essence than with the Trinity of manifestation. It is part of the modern empirical movement in theology, chiefly associated with the names of Schleiermacher and Ritschl. When thus employed practically, as interpretative of Christian experience, rather than theoretically, as a doctrine of reality beyond and even apart from experience, the Trinity may be regarded as summarizing the different ways in which the knowledge of God may be held. (1) He may be thought of as the self-disclosed God and, as such, known to men as the ultimate and absolute Being, whose ways are past finding out. (2) He may be thought of as the self-disclosing God and, as such, known to men in nature and history and, above all, in the character and purposes of Jesus Christ. (3) He may be thought of as the self-imparting or self-communicating God and, as such, known to men as indwelling power. God revealed, God revealing, God abiding—in these three ways God makes Himself known, and they correspond to the elements of the Father, the Son, and the Holy Spirit in the Trinitarian formula. If then, theoretically, the Trinity is 'the affirmation of a full rich life in God as distinct from all abstract and barren conceptions of his Being,' it is, practically, 'the affirmation that the true nature of God must be learned from his historic revelation in Christ, and from the experience which Christ creates.'[2]

(*e*) Doubtless such a statement is liable to the charge of Sabellianism (modalistic Monarchianism), but it may readily be defended against such a charge. In Sabellianism the divine nature is an abstract undifferentiated unity known only in three successive modes or manifestations, none of which is complete or permanent; they are but names,[3] and may not be translated into fundamental factors in the divine experience. Here the elements of the Trinity are acknowledged to be rooted eternally in unseen reality, so that God is always the Father, the Son, and the Spirit, although known through the threefold self-manifestation or not known at all.

(*f*) In the system of Christian theology the

[1] Cf. Illingworth, p. 238. [2] Adams Brown, p. 162.
[3] Epiphanius, *Hær.* lxii.: ὡς εἶναι ἐν μιᾷ ὑποστάσει τρεῖς ὀνομασίας; cf. J. Tixeront, *Hist. des dogmes dans l'antiquité chrétienne*, 3 vols., Paris, 1909–12, i. 349, 483 f.

doctrine of the Trinity does not usually fit well into the general doctrine of God, and often bears the character of a doctrine apart. There is much to be said for Schleiermacher's view—in his case reflecting, it may be, a Sabellian attitude—that the Trinity falls to be discussed at the end of the dogmatic system. One could not properly speak, he urged, of the Father, the Son, and the Spirit until one had expounded the Christian faith regarding the Son and the Spirit. None the less, it is quite possible vitally to relate the Trinity, conceived scripturally as a Trinity of manifestation, to the general Christian conception of God.[1] (1) There is no difficulty with the doctrine of the Father, who in the new formula as in the old is God in all His fullness of being and life; from which fullness the Son and the Spirit subtract nothing. (2) The doctrine of the Son is not without difficulty in this connexion. The old formula rested on the assumption that the divinity of Christ (the Christian conviction of which was the experiential ground of the doctrine of the Son) was to be discovered in the metaphysical constitution of His person, and accordingly by the way of analysis, whereas the new formula founds upon the principle that the secrets of personality do not yield themselves to 'searching' but to observation, and that accordingly the divinity of Christ is to be traced and recognized, if anywhere, in the unfoldings of His character and life. Moreover, the old formula also implied that there existed a fundamental difference of nature between God and man, so that the incarnation of the divine Word was nothing if not a stupendous miracle. The new formula, under the ruling modern conception of divine immanence, would imply that the divine-human Christ may be reached along the lines of God's normal working in His world. God is to be conceived as always present and active in the world, manifesting Himself continuously in nature and history, yet manifesting Himself supremely and fully only in the Person and Work of Jesus Christ. In Jesus Christ we have at once true man arising out of humanity and true God coming forth from the Godhead. In other words, Jesus Christ is the perfect expression of the divine Nature in terms of human character and life. With such a new criterion of divinity, and such a new conception of the relationship between the divine and the human, an assured place may be found — it is claimed—for the doctrine of the Son in the modern doctrine of God. (3) The doctrine of the Spirit may also be seen to be fulfilled in the new doctrine of God towards which modern Christian thought appears to be advancing. For the Spirit is but the immanent God Himself, working more freely in the souls of men as righteousness and power because of the new channels of influence He has opened up for Himself through Jesus Christ. In short, God Himself (ὅλος θεὸς) is the Father revealed; God Himself is in Christ revealing; God Himself is the Holy Spirit abiding. The form of the ancient dogmatic conception may be changed, but the substance of it remains. Still as of old we know God in His threefold relationship to men, and in each relationship we have very God Himself. Wherefore we may still unite in ascribing glory to the Father, and to the Son, and to the Holy Spirit, as it was in the beginning, is now, and ever shall be, world without end.

LITERATURE.—See the histories of Christian doctrine by A. Harnack, F. Loofs, R. Seeberg, J. Tixeront, G. P. Fisher, J. F. Bethune-Baker; also works on dogmatic theology, such as the classical expositions of John of Damascus, Thomas Aquinas, and John Calvin; and, among modern expositions, those of F. Schleiermacher, A. E. Biedermann, M. Kähler, F. H. R. Frank, H. Martensen, I. A. Dorner, R. Rothe, F. A. B. Nitzsch, J. Kaftan, T Häring, T. B. Strong, C. Hodge, W. Adams Brown, W. N. Clarke. Among special discussions see Augustine, *De Trinitate*; D. Waterland, *The Importance of the Doctrine of the Holy Trinity* (*Works*, Oxford, 1856, vol. iii.); F. C. Baur, *Die christliche Lehre von der Dreieinigkeit und Menschwerdung Gottes in ihrer geschichtl. Entw.*, 3 vols., Tübingen, 1841–43; G. Krüger, *Das Dogma von der Dreieinigkeit und Gottmenschheit*, do. 1905; F. Schleiermacher, *Über den Gegensatz zwischen der sabellianischen und der athanasianischen Vorstellung von der Trinität* (*Werke*, Berlin, 1835–64, i. 2); J. R. Illingworth, *The Doctrine of the Trinity*, London, 1907; W. Adams Brown, *The Trinity and Modern Thought*, New York, 1907. See also relevant matter in recent works like H. M. Gwatkin, *Studies of Arianism*, Cambridge, 1882; R. C. Moberly, *Atonement and Personality*, London, 1901; R. L. Ottley, *The Doctrine of the Incarnation*, 2 vols., London, 1896; H. R. Mackintosh, *The Person of Jesus Christ*, Edinburgh, 1912. In *HDB*, *DCG*, and *DAC* there are elaborate articles, with bibliographical notes, on the Scriptural and early Church doctrine of the Trinity. See also the literature under art. GOD.

W. FULTON.

[1] Cf. W. N. Clarke, *The Christian Doctrine of God*, Edinburgh, 1909.

TRITHEISM.—1. Definition.—Tritheism (Gr. τρεῖς, 'three,' and θεός, 'God') is the belief in three Gods. As such, it is a form of polytheism, defined as the belief in many Gods or in more Gods than one.

2. Christianity and tritheism.—So far as the present writer is aware, no historical religion may properly be called tritheistic. Where divine triads or trinities are found, they are not distinguished from other divinities as true or real gods from idols. (1) On the other hand, the charge of being tritheistic has often been preferred against the Christian religion, as presented in the doctrine of the Trinity. (2) The Christian Church has, however, expressly dissociated itself from Trinitarian views tending to tritheism. (3) Moreover, liability to the charge of tritheism is regarded as sufficiently damaging also to speculative constructions of the Trinity. In what follows the writer would expound these three statements one by one.

3. The charge of tritheism.—(*a*) The accusation of being tritheistic, which has often been made against Christianity, is in a sense justified. For undoubtedly the doctrine of the Trinity has been, and is still, conceived among simple uneducated Christians in a naively tritheistic way. Sometimes also a naive tritheism is found even in theological statement, as when in so-called transactional theories the Atonement is represented as the result of a bargain between the first and second Persons of the Trinity.

(*b*) But the Christian religion, like other historical religions, must be judged by the affirmations of its best and most representative minds, and not by the crudities of the uninstructed or the aridities of theological pedantry. It is affirmed by the representative minds of Christianity that the accusation of tritheism is unjustified, being largely founded upon misunderstanding of the theological terms in which the Trinity is formulated. They would insist that there is a world of difference between the formula, 'There are three Gods,' or even the formula, 'There are three distinct or separate individuals in the class known as God,' and the formula in which the orthodox doctrine may be summarized, 'There are three Persons in one God.' In fact the Trinity is declared to be at bottom an assertion of the divine unity. If in the light of the Christian revelation we are led to affirm three eternal distinctions in the Godhead, we must still hold fast to the old faith of Israel's prophets and say, 'These three are one.' Admittedly, however, there are ambiguities and associations to mislead in the Trinitarian terminology. In particular, the ambiguity of the word 'person' is allowed to be a source of much misunderstanding. To set forth the true theological meaning of this word should be enough, it would be added, to vindicate the doctrine of the Trinity against a charge so obnoxious as that of tritheism. We are reminded in this connexion of how the early Christian thinkers abhorred the suggestion even that in affirming the Trinity they were reinstating heathen polytheism.

It should be remembered[1] that there was no word 'person' in the vocabulary of the Greek-speaking theologians, who shaped the doctrine of the Trinity to the authoritative form it assumed in the Nicæno-Constantinopolitan Creed. 'Person' (Lat. *persona*, 'an actor's mask'), as it appears in the Athanasian Creed, was intended to represent the Greek *ὑπόστασις*. Now 'hypostasis' ('sediment' or 'dregs,' lit. 'standing under or below') was used about the beginning of the Christian era to signify a real concrete existence or actuality in contradistinction to a mere appearance having nothing solid or permanent underlying it, such as a comet in comparison with a rainbow. Through Origen's influence it came to be employed in the theological terminology as the designation of a member of the Trinity, as in the Cappadocian formula, 'Three Hypostases in one Nature or Substance' (*φύσις, οὐσία*).[2] 'Hypostasis' then stood for a real independence—a real principle of individuation or distinction—*within* the Being of God, and ceased to be regarded, as in the Stoic use, as theologically equivalent to *οὐσία* or *φύσις*. It may be that the term 'hypostasis' as applied to the members of the divine Trinity suggested an independence or individuality of too complete a sort, as though the Father, Son, and Spirit were as separate in the class God as Peter, James, and John in the class named man;[3] but this suggestion was corrected, at least for speculative minds, by the Logos-Christology deriving from St. John and St. Paul, in which the idea of immanent distinctions in the unity of the Godhead received recognition. On the other hand, the tritheistic suggestion was in a sense accentuated for the Latin-speaking theologians by the selection, due probably to Tertullian,[4] of the word 'person' as the translation of *ὑπόστασις*. Though *persona*, as its original meaning might show, implied only a temporary and superficial kind of individuality (an implication more definitely conveyed by *πρόσωπον*, lit. 'face,' by which *persona* was often rendered in the later Greek theology), it implied also the dignity and worth of a rational nature. A 'person' in the early centuries of the Latin Church was an individual viewed in a legal aspect (the word often meant a litigant or a party to a contract as well as a player) as the subject of rights and duties, if not as yet in the philosophical sense of a self-conscious and self-determining Ego—a sense which has attached itself to the word in modern times. Yet even the ancient legal and relative associations of 'person' would impart ambiguity to its theological use, especially in popular thought, and the ambiguity would tend to increase in European usage as the word approximated more and more to the modern philosophical sense of personality. So it is not surprising that there has been a strong tendency to tritheism in Western theology, especially among the people; and that non-Christian thinkers, notably Jewish and Muhammadan, have so often viewed the doctrine of tri-personality in God as virtual or veiled tritheism.

4. Tritheism as a heresy of dogma.—(*a*) Although aberrations from the orthodox doctrine were in the East towards a modalistic Monarchianism (Sabellianism) rather than tritheism, it was in the East—among the Greek-speaking theologians—that a form of tritheism actually arose to meet with the condemnation of orthodoxy. The movement in question illustrates the reaction of Christological discussion and controversy upon the doctrine of the Trinity. Christology lay in the heart of the Trinitarian dogma, and the development of Christology naturally led to a revision of the dogmatic terms.

(*b*) As a definite phase in the history of Christian thought tritheism appeared *c*. A.D. 550 in Monophysite circles, being associated chiefly with the names of John Askusnages and John Philopon. The latter, an Alexandrian philosopher and a distinguished Aristotelian, of whose work entitled *Διαιτητής* important fragments have been preserved in the writings of John of Damascus,[5] appears to have been the most influential of the school. As a Monophysite John Philopon was opposed to the Chalcedonian description of the Person of Christ as consisting of 'one person in two natures' (*ἓν πρόσωπον* or *μία ὑπόστασις ἐν δύο φύσεσιν*), and contended that Christ's was a single nature compounded of the divine and the human. That is to say, in Christology *φύσις* or *οὐσία* and *ὑπόστασις* were to be viewed as synonymous terms.

(*c*) When this Christological position is applied to the doctrine of the Trinity, the question is at once raised as to whether the orthodox formula of three Hypostases in one Substance can be maintained. If one *οὐσία*, is there not but one *ὑπόστασις*; if three *ὑποστάσεις*, are there not three *οὐσίαι*? The affirmative to the first question leads to a form of Unitarianism, the affirmative to the second to a form of tritheism.

(*d*) John Philopon started from the consideration of the three *ὑποστάσεις* and reached, accordingly, a tritheistic conclusion as to the divine *οὐσία* or *φύσις*: *ἔστω τρεῖς φύσεις λέγειν ἡμᾶς ἐπὶ τῆς ἁγίας τριάδος.*[1] So he and his followers were named by their opponents 'tritheists' (*τριθεῖται*), although we are told[2] that they would not actually have confessed themselves as believers in three Gods. If theirs was a theoretical, it was not also a practical, tritheism, like the Trinitarian notions of the transactional theorists mentioned above (which amply justified the protest of the earlier Unitarians). It appears, however, that John Philopon admitted the notion of a common Nature (*οὐσία κοινή*), if holding it in what might have been named later a nominalist sense; but Damian[3] (578–605), the Monophysite patriarch of Constantinople, held so pronouncedly realistic a view of the one Substance, at the same time apparently regarding the three Persons as true reals or separate individualities, that, like Peter the Lombard in a later day, he was accused of teaching a Quaternity rather than a Trinity, and his followers were labelled 'tetradites' (*τετραδῖται*). The tritheists were definitely opposed in the name of the orthodox dogma by John of Damascus, who in seeking to emphasize as against them the unity of the Godhead gave—as Augustine did—a modalistic flavour to his theological exposition.[4]

5. Tritheism as an error of speculation.—It has been remarked[5] that in the tritheistic movement (so called) and the counter-movements it evoked we may find the roots of the mediæval controversy between nominalism and realism. The remark is illustrated by the case of Roscellin, the best-known representative of the older nominalism. According to Roscellin, universals were not reals, but merely subjective conceptions (*flatus vocis*).[6] And, if this principle holds of the Nature or Substance of God, then the Persons of the Trinitarian formula must be regarded as distinct self-consciousnesses, and the unity of the Godhead as but a nominal and generic unity. Thus on philosophical principles Roscellin reached a theoretical tritheism, which, however, at Anselm's instance, was condemned at Soissons in 1092.[7] And over and over again, from the beginnings of Christian theology down to the present, speculative constructions of the doctrine of the Trinity have had to encounter—sometimes in the irony of things—the damning charge of being tritheistic. In the ancient Church, as Callistus accused Hippolytus of dyotheism, so Dionysius—maintaining the Roman tradition of unspeculative adherence to the

[1] See the recent discussion of Trinitarian terminology in C. C. J. Webb, *God and Personality* (*Gifford Lectures*), London, 1918, esp. lect. ii.

[2] Cf. Greg. Naz. *Or.* xxxix. 11 f.

[3] Greg. Nyss. ii. 188, and other writers quoted by R. Seeberg, *Lehrbuch der Dogmengeschichte*, Erlangen and Leipzig, 1895, § 21, d.

[4] *Adv. Praxean*, 11 f.

[5] *De Hær.* 83.

[1] Leontius, *de Sectis*, actio v. c. 6, quoted by J. Tixeront, *Hist. des dogmes dans l'antiquité chrétienne*, 3 vols., Paris, 1909–12, iii. 196; cf. also Photius, *Biblioth.* codd. 21, 24, 75; John of Ephesus, *Hist. Eccl.* v. 1–12.

[2] Timothy, *de Receptione Hæreticorum* (*PG* lxxxvi. 1, col. 61).

[3] *Ib.* col. 60.

[4] In *de Fide orthodoxa*. For summary discussions of Tritheism as a heresy of dogma reference may be made to the artt. 'Johannes Askusnages,' 'Johannes Philoponus,' in *PRE*[3] ix. and the art. 'Tritheistischer Streit' in *PRE*[3] xx.

[5] A. Harnack, *Hist. of Dogma*, Eng. tr., 7 vols., London, 1894–99, iv. 126 n.

[6] Cf. Anselm, *de Fid. trin.* 2 f., *Ep.* ii. 35, 41.

[7] Roscellin and the nominalists were dubbed by Anselm *dialectice hæretici* (*de Fid. trin.* 2); cf. F. Loofs, *Leitfaden zum Studium der Dogmengeschichte*[3], Halle, 1893, § 60, 4.

unity of the Godhead—preferred the accusation of tritheism against Origen's teaching.[1] Yet Origen's doctrine of the eternal generation of the Logos or Son entered into the orthodox formulas, and a follower of Origen, Gregory Thaumaturgus, mightily championed the unity of the Godhead against the polytheists (tritheists).[2] Again, in the mediæval Church even Abelard was suspected of tritheism, and yet it was Abelard's aim and endeavour to mediate between the extremes of a tritheism like Roscellin's and pure modalism, and his sympathies lay with modalism rather than tritheism.[3] Once again, if it is not invidious to select so modern an instance, W. Adams Brown comments as follows on W. N. Clarke's constructive presentation of the essential Trinity:

'It is hard to see how these "centres of conscious life and activity" can be distinguished from separate personalities.'[4]

And yet W. N. Clarke[5] so emphasizes the Trinity of manifestation, as distinguished from the Trinity of essence, as to be far away indeed from tritheism. It all illustrates the fact that, while the doctrine of the Trinity, as set forth in the Nicæno-Constantinopolitan and Athanasian Creeds, will have no traffic with tritheism, it is difficult in the theological exposition of the dogma to steer a safe course between tritheism and a Sabellian modalism (in which the Father, Son, and Spirit are merely three modes or aspects of the one God)—which serves to give point to Augustine's famous remark that the alternative to the affirmation of the three Persons is silence: 'dictum est tres personae, non ut illud diceretur, sed ne taceretur.'[6]

LITERATURE.—See art. TRINITY. W. FULTON.

TRUST.—In the wide sense of confidence in a supernatural Power on which man feels himself dependent, trust enters as an element into practically all religions from the lowest up to the highest. Savages rely on their fetish to bring them success in the chase, and other peoples on their national god to give them victory in war. But such trust possesses no ethical quality and need not further detain us. Only when the superior and supernatural Power is conceived in more or less ethical fashion can a trust emerge that has ethical and religious value. Religious trust, in the only sense worth considering, is confidence in and reliance upon the eternal Power on which we hang, as one that is working towards a worthy end and guiding the course of events in wisdom and goodness. It is the trust that comes to expression in Ps 36[5ff.]:

'Thy lovingkindness, O Lord, is in the heavens; thy faithfulness reacheth unto the skies. Thy righteousness is like the mountains of God. . . . And the children of men take refuge under the shadow of thy wings.'

Were the facts of life uniformly of a kind to render the moral purpose and control of God obvious and unmistakable, the exercise of trust would make no particular demand on our energies. Since, however, they are far from being so, the world not seldom seeming to ride roughshod over man and his values, trust always carries with it the idea of a triumph over difficulties. In the Epistle to the Hebrews it is presented in the light of an act of heroism: 'He endured, as seeing him who is invisible' (11[27]).

Trust of this kind is not of course to be looked for in the religion of primitive races or in religions that are merely national. Nor does it emerge with any distinctness in the pantheistic religions of India. The Indian conception of the world-order as governed by the principles of *karma* and *saṁsāra* (transmigration) is not at bottom ethical, and the corresponding piety consists not in submission to that order as something good, but in the desire to escape from it, and in the exercises through which the goal of absorption in Brahman is attained. Bhāgavatism, it is true, acknowledges a single God who is personal and gracious; and in its conception of *bhakti*, or devotional faith, as the way of deliverance from the wheel of birth and rebirth, resignation appears, if not as a constituent, at least as a fruit.[1] But *bhakti* is far less ethical trust than a mystical 'abiding' in the 'Adorable,' and the piety of Bhāgavatism as mirrored in the *Bhāgavad-Gīta*, intense though it is, is for the most part of the usual Indian type.

In the religion of the Greek dramatists, of Plato, and of the later Stoics, trust holds an assured though not a prominent place. Sophocles expresses the conviction that, however things may seem to us in our short-sightedness, if we could only see the purposes of the gods in their totality, we should know them to be good, and that 'nothing to which the gods lead man is base.' Of the just man Plato declares:

'Even when he is in poverty or sickness, or any other seeming misfortune, all things will in the end work together for good to him in life and in death: for the gods have a care for any one whose desire is to become just and to be like God, as far as man can attain the divine likeness, by the pursuit of virtue.'[2]

Even more striking are the words of Epictetus: 'Do with me what thou wilt: my will is thy will: I appeal not against thy judgments.'[3] In the *Epinomis*, a dialogue wrongly ascribed to Plato, it is said: 'Pray to the gods with trust.'[4] And of Socrates Xenophon says that he must have believed in the gods, since he trusted them: πιστεύων δὲ θεοῖς πῶς οὐκ εἶναι θεοὺς ἐνόμιζεν.[5]

But, though in the higher Greek religion trust had a firm basis provided for it and secured a certain amount of recognition, its full significance was far from being realized. Nowhere do we find it put forward as a central element in piety or a spring of strength and goodness. It was in the Hebrew prophets and their spiritual successors that it first really came into its own. Everywhere in the Bible we are met by utterances of fervent and steadfast trust in God. And its religious importance is clearly recognized. Isaiah sees in it the only source of safety: 'If ye will not trust, ye shall not be established' (7[9]). Jeremiah speaks to the same effect: 'Cursed is the man who trusts in man and makes flesh his arm, and whose heart turns aside from Jahweh. . . . Blessed is the man who trusts in Jahweh and whose confidence Jahweh is' (17[5.7]). To trust in Jahweh and do good is presented in Ps 37 as the sum of religion. In the NT the idea of trust, deepened by a new feeling for God's care for the individual, occupies a position of still greater prominence. Outside the Synoptic Gospels, however, it is to a large extent merged in the idea of faith (*q.v.*). It is faith in the sense of belief that is established as the condition of salvation. This change of emphasis—as we shall see, it amounts to nothing more—is intelligible when we remember that the gospel was preached as, in the first place at least, a message to be received. None the less it created for the Church a serious problem and one that had to wait long for a satisfactory solution. The problem has to do with the mutual relations of faith and trust. By St. Paul,[6] and also in the Epistle to the Hebrews, faith

1 Cf. Harnack, iii. 90, 93. 2 *Ib.* iii. 101 f.
3 *Ib.* vi. 182.
4 *Christian Theology in Outline*, Edinburgh, 1907, p. 152.
5 In his *Outline of Christian Theology*, Edinburgh, 1898, and more especially in his *Christian Doctrine of God*, do. 1909.
6 *De Trin.* v. 9.

1 See art. BHAKTI-MĀRGA.
2 *Rep.* x. 613 (tr. B. Jowett, *Dialogues of Plato*[3], Oxford, 1892, iii. 329).
3 Quoted from A. Schenkl, *Epicteti Dissertationes*, Leipzig, 1894, p. 158, by L. R. Farnell, *The Evolution of Religion*, London, 1905, p. 205.
4 πιστεύσας τοῖς θεοῖς εὔχου, quoted by W. H. P. Hatch, *The Pauline Idea of Faith* (*Harvard Theological Studies*, iii.), Cambridge, Mass., 1917, p. 69.
5 *Memorabilia*, I. i. 5. 6 *E.g.*, Ro 4.

is conceived in a way that makes the two practically identical. But what if its object is thought of as a doctrine which must first be assented to before trust can enter? In that case faith, while including trust, will contain in addition a purely intellectual element, either intellectual submission, if the doctrine is authoritatively given, or intellectual insight, if it is the product of a rational process. Adopting the first alternative, the older Protestant theologians in their analysis of faith established *notitia* and *assensus* as the necessary preliminaries to *fiducia*. The vice of this solution is that it destroys the independence of faith—in other words, of religion—by binding it to an act external to it and without moral quality. The faith described by Paul as trust in God is presented as at bottom subjection to the Church or the Bible as the guarantor of religious truth. And its independence is equally subverted if, adopting the second alternative, we regard it as receiving its object from philosophical reflexion. The true solution of the problem lies in the recognition that in faith itself there is a cognitive element, and that its object is given not in the form of a doctrine, but in the form of an ideal value. Face to face with the great values that are supremely embodied in the life and cross of Jesus and that are summed up in the conception of a kingdom of the good, we affirm them on the ground of their worth as the manifestation of the eternal Power that works at the heart of things, the eternal Reality on which the universe no less than our human life is founded. Faith is nothing else than just this feeling for the ideal and, above all, the moral values and this affirmation of their cosmic significance. So interpreted, it is one and the same thing with trust in God, for what is trust in God but trust in the good as the central might on which we and the whole universe hang? If there is a difference, it is that in the idea of faith the emphasis falls on the cognitive aspect, and in the idea of trust on the volitional.

LITERATURE.—See the works referred to in the footnotes and those given in art. FAITH (Christian). W. MORGAN.

TRUSTS.—See ECONOMICS.

TRUTH.—See ERROR AND TRUTH.

TSHI-SPEAKING TRIBES.—See NEGROES AND W. AFRICA.

TSIMSHIAN.—The Tsimshian belong to the northern group of coast Indians, but differ markedly from the Haida and Tlingit (*qq.v.*) in language. Their social organization is also somewhat divergent, since instead of two phratries they have four —Eagle, Wolf, Kanhada, and Gyispawaduweda— each embracing many small local groups or clans. There are three chief Tsimshian divisions: the Tsimshian proper, living on the lower Skeena River and the coast to the south, the Niska of Nass River, and the Kitksan of the upper Skeena. The last does not border on the coast and is intermediate between the coast tribes proper and the true interior tribes of Athapascan lineage. Most of the information that we possess regarding Tsimshian religion is from the Niska, but there seems to have been little difference between their beliefs and those of the other divisions.

1. Cosmological beliefs.—The earth was believed to be flat and circular. It was supported by a man named Amala ('smoke hole'), who lay on his back and held upon his chest a spoon made of the horn of the mountain-goat. This was filled with grease, and in it stood a pole, on which the earth rested. When he became tired, he lifted the pole, and the earth shook. The pole, with the earth on it, was turning round in the bowl of the spoon, the grease in which served to make it revolve easily. Sun, moon, and stars belonged to the sky and did not turn with the earth. This reference to the turning of the earth seems to point to White influence, but the association of grease with the being under the earth is paralleled by something related of the Haida Atlas, Sacred-one-standing-and-moving, and is probably genuinely aboriginal.

2. Supernatural beings. — The supernatural beings, so far as we are acquainted with them, were much the same as those among the Haida (*q.v.*). They had a supreme heaven-god called Laha ('on the air'), a perfect counterpart of the Haida Power-of-the-shining-heavens. From the information regarding him gathered by Boas, however, it seems that he approached much nearer to the monotheistic idea of a supreme being.

'Heaven is the great deity who has a number of mediators called Neqno'q. . . . Heaven rules the destinies of mankind; Heaven taught man to distinguish between good and bad, and gave the religious laws and institutions. Heaven is gratified by the mere existence of man. He is worshipped by offerings and prayer, the smoke rising from fires being especially agreeable to him. Murderers, adulterers, and those who behave foolishly, talking to no purpose, and making noise at night, are especially hateful to him. He loves those who take pity upon the poor, who do not try to become rich by selling at high prices what others want. His messengers, particularly sun and moon, must be treated with respect. Men make themselves agreeable to the deity by cleanliness. Therefore, they must bathe and wash their whole bodies before praying. For the same reason they take a vomitive when they wish to please the deity well. They fast and abstain from touching their wives if they desire their prayers to be successful. They offer everything that is considered valuable—eagle-down, red paint, red cedar bark, good elk-skin lines, etc. The offering is burnt.'[1]

The ethics of this, especially in the matter of acquiring wealth, seems so different from the aboriginal code found elsewhere that it is probable that the native informant's statements were tinged with missionary teaching, and that Heaven, or Laha, was elevated to a position above that which he occupied in earlier days. There can be no doubt, however, as to the existence of a sky-god 'first among equals.'

The Tsimshian prayed less often to their heaven-god than to the minor deities, or 'mediators,' whom they generally asked for food and fair weather. Sometimes they prayed to the supernatural beings collectively. The most important 'mediators' are stated to have been the sun and moon, spirits appearing in the shape of lightning strokes, and animals. The Raven, also called Skämsem, was believed in and had the same functions and general character as among the Tlingit and Haida. They also believed in the sea grizzly bear, or Hagulâk, which may have been originally a Haida conception, since his home was called Helahaidek ('near the Haida country'). In his house he had four kettles called Lukewarm, Warm, Hot, and Boiling. The killer-whales seem to have been his servants, since they were known as 'Hagulâk's men.' There was also a one-legged man similar to the Master-hopper of the Haida.[2]

Besides praying to the deities, a person could force them to grant his desires by rigid fasting. He had to abstain from food and from seeing his wife for seven days, lying in bed motionless all that time. Then he might rise, wash himself, comb the right side of his head, and paint the right side of his face, after which he might look at his wife. A less rigid form of fasting extended over four days only. To make the ceremony very successful, the man's wife must join him, but, if the wife should be untrue to her husband, the effect of the fasting would be destroyed. Whatever twins wished was believed to be fulfilled, and they were appealed to especially to control the

[1] Boas, in *Rep. of Brit. Association for Advancement of Science*, 1889, p. 845 f.
[2] See art. HAIDA, § 19.

weather and bring eulachon and salmon. Numbers of tabus governed hunting and fishing, particularly the fishing of eulachon, which run into the Nass River in great numbers and are, or were, a principal source of wealth to the people. The first of these fish to be caught were roasted on a peculiarly-shaped frame made of elder-berry wood and with special ceremonies, the man who handled it praying meanwhile for an abundance of fish.

3. The dead.—The principal world of the dead was reached by following a trail and crossing a river. According to one story, a man who fainted and passed to the spirit-world was saved by a perforated stone hung round his neck as an amulet, which thwarted the endeavours of four shamans to remove his heart. Whether those who had died by violence or drowning went to regions distinct from the others is not recorded. At least at the mortuary feasts food was put into the fire for the dead.

4. Shamanism.—Nothing is known of Tsimshian shamans which would in any way distinguish them from those of the Tlingit and Haida, except that their bodies, like those of the common people, were cremated.

5. Witchcraft.—The wizard cast his spell by putting some article taken from the victim into a box containing portions of a human body. Strings were fastened inside this box, and, if the wizard wished his victim to die slowly, he fastened the object some distance above the body, but, if he desired him to perish at once, he cut the string, thereby precipitating the object upon the body. Afterwards he had to go round the house in which the person whom he had killed by witchcraft was lying, and later he had to walk round his grave and rub himself, pretending to cry all the time. Unless he observed these rules, he would himself perish. If it was believed that a person had been killed by witchcraft, the Tsimshian would take out his heart and lay a red-hot stone against it, wishing at the same time that the wizard might die. If the heart burst, it was expected that their wish would be fulfilled; if not, it was a sign that their suspicions were unfounded.

LITERATURE.—Nearly all the available Tsimshian material is contained in F. Boas, report v. 'On the North-Western Tribes of Canada,' in *Report of the British Association for the Advancement of Science*, 1889, p. 801 ff., report vi. *ib.* 1890, p. 562 ff., report x. *ib.* 1895, p. 523 ff., in *Bull. 27 BE* [1902], and in *31 RBEW* [1909-1910].

JOHN R. SWANTON.

TUKĀRĀM.—In Tukārām there culminates an important section of the *bhakti* school[1] and his verses have all the authority of a 'Veda' for most of the twenty million Marāṭhī-speaking people of one of India's noblest races, among whom are to be found some of the greatest Indian reformers of the day. Both for his poetic genius and for his unique place in the people's heart he is happily described as 'the Robert Burns of India' who marks 'the era of the efflorescence of Mahārāshtra's people.'[2]

1. Sources.—(*a*) *Biographical.*—Two serious difficulties confront the modern biographer of Tukārām. (1) All the Marāṭhī *Lives* of Tukārām are drawn almost exclusively from a single authority, the poet-saint Mahīpati (1715–90), whose accounts in the *Bhakti Vyāya* (chs. xlviii.–li.) and the *Bhakti Līlāmṛita* (chs. xxv.–xl.) were written in 1762 and 1774 respectively, more than a century after Tukārām's end in 1650, 'long enough for legends to grow.' (2) We have 'no authentic and properly sifted account of his life,' but only 'a mass of legends and traditions that have gathered round Tukārām'[3] and show a distinct 'tendency towards deification.'[4] Yet we have 'at least some facts of historical accuracy to start with,'[5] and Mahīpati's 'detailed legends . . . seem to be in every way as deserving of being critically worked out as those of the early Christian martyrs to which they often bear a strong resemblance.'[6]

A few sources earlier than Mahīpati have been indicated recently by V. L. Bhawe. Besides (1) Tukārām's autobiographical poems (see below) and (2) the *abhaṅgs* of Rāmēshwar Bhaṭṭ, the leading disciple of Tukārām,[1] there are (3) a brief life of Tukārām by his grandson, Gōpāl Buwa, (4) the autobiography of Bahinābāī, another disciple of Tukārām who dictated her own life-story, giving the names of some of Tukārām's contemporaries who figure prominently both in Mahīpati and in Tukārām's own poems,[2] and (5) a source a century earlier than Mahīpati, a work written by one named Krishnadās Bairāgī on Keśav Chaitanya Sampradāya, which gives the important '*guru*-succession' of Tukārām and helps us to settle important dates in his life, this work being quoted by name and its facts given by one Niranjan.[3] Some would add a sixth source earlier than Mahīpati, in Narahari Mālu, author of *Bhaktikathāmṛita*, but he must be pronounced utterly untrustworthy, though he is followed by a few Marāṭhā authors.[4]

The investigation concerning biographical material has gone far enough to conclude with safety that, despite much unsifted tradition, 'miracle and wonder-working,' Mahīpati's account has a solid substratum of historical accuracy. Moreover, he uses his sources with discrimination, rejecting what he discovers to be unreliable.[5]

(*b*) *Autobiographical.*—The true text of Tukārām's writings has not yet been critically ascertained, and between the several collections there is a wide difference as to the number of poems included, ranging from 4621 in the edition generally accepted[6] to 8841 in one[7] described by R. G. Bhandarkar as 'uncritically made.'[8] Even the former is based on MSS admitted to have been 'corrected,' 'further corrected,' and 'arranged.' The problem remained in abeyance for fifty years until Bhawe in 1919–20 edited and published the first two instalments, numbering about 1300 poems, of what he claims is 'Tukārām's Original Gāthā,' written by one of Tukārām's fourteen disciples, one Santājī the Oilman whose MS[9] bears a date in one place three years earlier than Tukārām's death. All that can be said at present is that scholars are patiently investigating the problem of a critical text of Tukārām's writings. His verses were probably all extempore and were taken down by at least one or two of his immediate disciples. It is almost certain that every collection contains poems which are not really his, and we are also quite unable to fix their chronological order—a serious disadvantage. They are practically our only source of information regarding his teaching.

2. Life.—Penetrating 'a wilderness of surmise and guess,' we are safe in deciding that Tukārām was born the same year as John Milton, in 1608, though later research may push the date farther back. From at least seven generations Tukārām inherited a devotion to the god Viṭhobā of Paṇḍharpūr.[10] It is first as a Śūdra grain-seller in his own native Dēhū, eighteen miles north-west of Poona, that Tukārām comes before us. His father Bōlhōbā, having married off his three sons with lavish outlay, sought to hand over his business to the eldest, whose predilection, however, for an unworldly life led to this responsibility falling on Tukārām at the early age of thirteen. The first four or five years appear to have been prosperous, but they were followed by a succession of disasters in business and home, so that young Tukārām's capital disappeared. Many stories are told illustrating his honesty, simple-mindedness, and spiritual devotion, Viṭhobā being represented as his unfailing helper on all occasions. All these stories probably have a solid basis of fact.

A great famine in 1629, during which his elder wife[11] died crying for bread, was the last in a succession of sorrows which led him to give up all business and worldly attachment. Sitting on the river bank with his younger brother Kānhōbā, he threw into the stream his half of the business papers and handed over the remainder to Kānhōbā, while he dedicated himself wholly to Viṭhobā.

The spirit of poetry came to him in a dream, commanding him to complete the unfinished task

1 See artt. BHAKTI-MARGA, MYSTICISM (Hindu).
2 D. Mackichan, *The Indian Interpreter*, vii. [1912] 165, 173.
3 W. B. Patwardhan, *The Indian Interpreter*, vii. 19.
4 *Poems of Tukārām, Indū Prakāsh*, ed. Bombay, 1869, p. 2.
5 Patwardhan, *The Indian Interpreter*, viii. [1913] 11.
6 L. J. Sedgwick, *JRASBo*, no. lxv. vol. xxiii. [1910] p. 127 f.

1 See *Bhaktilīlāmrit*, ch. 40. 209.
2 V. L. Bhawe, *Mahārāshtra Sāraswat*, Poona, 1919, pp. 193, 242 f.
3 *Ib.* p. 190, note 1. 4 *Ib.* p. 391. 5 *Ib.* p. 374.
6 *Indū Prakāsh*, Bombay, 1869, now out of print.
7 By Tukārām Tāṭyā, Bombay, 1889.
8 *Vaiṣṇavism, Śaivism and Minor Religious Systems*, in the *Encyclopædia of Indo-Aryan Research*, Strassburg, 1915, p. 94.
9 Bhawe, *Tukārām's Original Gāthā*, vols. i.–ii., Thana, Bombay, 1919–20.
10 See art. PAṆḌHARPŪR.
11 His wife Rakhmābāī being 'constitutionally asthmatic,' he had married another, Jijābāī or Āvalī, daughter of a well-to-do Poona merchant.

of his great predecessor Nāmdēv, *bhakta* and poet. In another dream he received his all-important *gurū-mantra* — *Rām-Krishna-Hari*, the secret mystic formula which finally initiated him as a Hindu teacher. This was at the hands of one Bābājī Chaitanya of the line of Rāghav Chaitanya and Keśav Chaitanya—a possible indication that Tukārām had some connexion with the Chaitanya sect of the Vaiṣṇavites. A series of events setting forth his dealings with Brāhmans constitutes the most important part of his life-narrative.

One such story provides an interesting Hindu parallel to the Quaker doctrine of the sacramental significance of every meal. A Chinchwād Brāhman, Chintāmanī Dev, had invited Tukārām to dine with him, and, the Śūdra's plate having been laid the usual distance from the Brāhman's, Tukārām made the strange request that two more be laid, one for his own god and another for Gaṇpati, worshipped by his host, his explanation in an autobiographical poem being: 'If you enjoy a meal in faith, God sits down to dine with you.' Another event, one of the most critical in his life, demonstrates Tukārām's reverence for Brāhmans, even at the height of his renown. Rāmēshwar Bhaṭṭ, a Brāhman scholar jealous of the Śūdra's fame, had not only moved the public authorities against him but had personally enjoined silence upon him. 'But what of the poems already written?', asked their docile author. 'Throw them into the river,' was the cruel reply, and into the river the whole bundle went, covered with a stone. It was Tukārām's darkest hour, but, to the astonishment of all, several days later the sheets were seen floating on the river and were taken out unharmed. Rāmēshwar's deep repentance followed, the poet replying in gentle verse: 'If your mind is pure your enemies will be your friends.' And it was true enough in this case, for Rāmēshwar became his lifelong disciple.

Of the many incidents illustrating Tukārām's religious views one is of a Vedāntist Brāhman who persisted in reading to this Vaiṣṇavite *bhakta* a pantheistic treatise to which Tukārām agreed to listen only on condition that he might be covered with a blanket. When the blanket was lifted after an hour's reading, Tukārām was found seated with his fingers in his ears, his defence being that he could not listen to the Advaita doctrine that God and His worshippers were the same.

The miraculous is found interwoven throughout Tukārām's life-story. His birth is viewed as an incarnation. He performs many miracles to help the poor. Viṭhobā miraculously intervenes at every point to vindicate and deliver his faithful devotee. In this legendary material is to be included, unquestionably, the account of Tukārām's 'ascension' on which Mahīpati has expended all his powers, giving rise to the popular Hindu belief[1] that Tukārām was carried away to Vaikuṇṭha (the Hindu heaven) in the car of Viṣṇu. The probability is, as suggested by P. R. Bhandarkar, that 'he met his death by drowning,' in the holy river of his own village, in 1650, whether by what is called *jalasamādhī*, or prearranged drowning, as in the case of some other Indian *sādhus*, or whether 'the constant expectation of God's coming to fetch him away produced an illusion, and in obeying a fancied call from the opposite bank he ran into the river and was drowned, it is very difficult to say.'[2] The various traditions concerning Tukārām's influence after death must also be regarded as legendary.

3. Autobiography.—Though there is as yet no critical edition of Tukārām's *abhaṅgs*[3] in existence, his autobiographical poems are generally accepted, and his self-revelations give the impression of being sincere and genuine. Of his kindness and unselfish service for others, on which Mahīpati dwells so often, he himself tells us nothing, his autobiographical verses being wholly concerned with the personal and spiritual side of things. 'It is his own religious life that occupies his soul.'[4] The *abhaṅgs* classified as 'autobiography' in the English translations of the poems by J. N. Fraser and K. B. Marāṭhē[5] number over 500, and there are many hundreds more given up to confession, invocation, and aspiration. He tells us but little of his life in the world, though he often dwells on his guilt and misery. The poems of self-accusation, about 300, reveal a sense of sin whose depth is rare in Hindu literature, though his relation to God is personal and pantheistic by turns.

'Fallen of fallen, thrice fallen am I' (343). 'I am a great fallen sinner. . . . My heart is witness to me that I am not redeemed' (126). This conviction of sin is often closely associated with extreme mental depression: 'False is "mine," false is "thine." False is Tukā, false is his faith. He speaks falsehood to the false' (2345). Sorrow, resulting from the death of parents, favourite wife, and eldest son, and from business failures, clearly led him to his self-dedication: 'It is well, O God, that I became a bankrupt, and was crushed by the famine; this is how I repented and turned to thee' (113). And his dedication was complete: 'Rank, race, colour, creed and caste—all are gone' (2790).

Patwardhan has made a 'tentative' effort to depict Tukārām's long inward struggle.[1] That this earnest pilgrim reached some worthy goal would appear from the poems, about 80 in number, under the heading 'Triumphant Happiness' in Fraser and Marāṭhē.

'I have found a sea of love, an inexhaustible flood. I have opened a treasure of spiritual knowledge; it diffuses the lustre of a million suns arisen in thy worshippers' souls' (573).

This, however, is by no means his habitual mood, which is rather one of despising his self-complacency. He has a passionate desire to help and serve those around, and, though he is far too often censorious, sometimes to the point of coarseness, yet he has something to say of constructive worth to his age and people. And it is chiefly as a preacher that he views himself. Though he lays no emphasis on Vedic lore, he has nevertheless a message invested with authority.

'These are not my words: I am a hired servant of Viṭhobā' (1420). Earnest and sincere preachers are badly needed, for there are impostors who eat and drink and who do even worse: 'Their desires are set on shawls and pots and money.' 'Matted hair and ashes are a scandal when the mind has no patience and forbearance' (1199). 'Such people sink themselves and destroy the ship of salvation,' but a true preacher 'rescues others by the sweet perfume of his words.'

4. Experience of bhakti.—To fathom Tukārām's deepest secret we need to explore his experience of *bhakti*, the 'clinging affection of the heart' for a personal God, though the god in Tukārām's case was a village-idol, surrounded by Puranic gross mythology and superstitious animism. The idol he worshipped was even one 'standing for both' Kṛṣṇa and Śiva,[2] but whether Tukārām recognized this plurality of gods at Pandharpūr we cannot say. In this unpromising soil Tukārām's *bhakti* grows, with pantheism and idolatry as twin-stems on the same tree. And, though his *bhakti* is too often a mere emotion, fugitive and fleeting, with more of longing than of satisfaction, it is yet free from those sensual extravagances that have degraded some forms of Indian *bhakti*. In Tukārām we probably see Indian *bhakti* at its best.

If it be asked in what Tukārām's *bhakti* experience consisted, the answer might be given in the words of the *Nārada-bhakti-sūtra*: 'surrendering all actions to God and feeling the greatest misery in forgetting God.'

'Tukā has his home in the Inconceivable' (1578). 'Wheresoever I go, thou art my companion: thou takest me by the hand and guidest me. As I walk along, I lean on thee' (2149).[3] 'No particular time is necessary,' says Tukārām, 'for the contemplation of God, it should be done always.'[4] And again: 'God is ours, certainly ours, and is the soul of all souls. God is near, certainly near, outside and inside.'[5]

His deep sense of sin offered a serious obstacle to the quest of his soul.

[1] See L. R. Pāngārkar, *Śrī Tukārām Caritra*, Poona, 1920, pp. 495–512.
[2] *Two Masters: Jesus and Tukārām*, Bombay, 1903, p. 11.
[3] An *abhaṅg* is an Indian metre, somewhat irregular, words rhyming at certain intervals.
[4] J. N. Farquhar, *Religious Literature of India*, London, 1920, p. 300.
[5] *The Poems of Tukārām*, 3 vols., Madras, 1909–15; the references by simple figures below are to this useful work.

[1] See *Fergusson College Magazine*, vol. i. no. 3 [1910], pp. 4–16.
[2] See J. N. Farquhar, *Religious Literature of India*, p. 301.
[3] See also a poetic rendering in N. Macnicol, *Psalms of Marāṭhā Saints*, Calcutta, 1919, p. 71.
[4] Narayan G. Chandāvarkar, *Speeches and Writings*, Bombay, 1911, p. 527.
[5] Bhandarkar's tr., *Vaiṣṇavism*, p. 95.

'The Endless is beyond, and between him and me there are the lofty mountains of desire and anger. I am not able to ascend them, nor do I find any pass.'[1] 'I know my faults, but I cannot control my mind . . . I am a slave of the senses' (1369).

Did 'any pass' over the 'mountains' ever appear on his horizon? He would appear to have had glimpses of one.

'I know not how to cleanse me of sin, so I have seized thy feet. . . . If thou dost take a thing in hand, what is impossible?' (2035). 'Thou hast saved many a humble, many a guilty, many a sinful man. Tukā dwells at thy feet; preserve him, O God' (248). 'What prayer can I put up? . . . Up till now, I felt sure that some of my service had been accepted. Now nothing but the struggle is left me: I see no sign of assurance in him who stands hand on hip' = Viṭhobā (3010). 'Though I made myself ceremonially pure, some impurity would still cling to me' (2968).

Inward purity thus becomes the prime necessity.

'What I delight in is purity of heart' (2632). 'What you need is a clean heart and a spirit at peace' (2309). 'Blessed are the pious, for their heart is pure. . . . Their hearts are filled with devoted love' (894).

The urgent question therefore comes to be: How shall this purity be realized? Ceremonies are unavailing, as are also pilgrimages.[2] Tukārām has full confidence that God can fulfil His child's desire, and to the crucial question how the divine blessing is obtained the answer comes repeatedly: 'It is *bhāva*' (812).

'My single-minded *bhāva* has put an end to pilgrimage to and fro' (2773). 'God comes quickly and stands where he finds *bhāva*' (3671). ''Tis *bhāva* that moves us and is fitly called the means of salvation' (2597). 'Without *bhakti* and *bhāva* everything else is useless trouble.'[3] 'Lay reasoning or learning aside in a bundle, for here *bhāva* is the one great criterion.'[4]

What is *bhāva*? His modern interpreters are not always clear. Bhandarkar says that it is 'faith, love, or the pure heart,'[5] and also that it has different meanings in different contexts.[6] Sometimes *bhāva* is that heart-religion which is guarantee of the vision of God without conscious effort, a parallel being found in the *Śvetāśvatara Upaniṣad* reference to 'those who by the heart know the Supreme Spirit who dwells within.'[7]

Bhakti, therefore, as experienced by Tukārām, seems to have concerned itself chiefly with realizing a change of heart. 'The great precept of religion is to hear God in the heart' (812). And, with a change of heart, he longs for some assurance of the change:

'Whether I am indeed God's child, truly accepted by him, how am I to know? How shall I know of a surety that my heart is purer, my mind less tainted with anger? For if love be not in my heart how has my heart been changed?' 'Fortunate, indeed, are those persons in whose heart dwells forgiveness.'[8]

Three lines of solution appeared to Tukārām: concentrated personal meditation on God and His saints, persistent self-examination that shall root out self-esteem, and such utter self-abandonment to God that no voice shall be desired but His.[9] Deep humility, simple faith in the divine protection, and complete abandonment of self to God comprise another triple secret of *bhakti*.[10] Tukārām had travelled a long rough road in quest of peace. *Yoga* he had found unavailing, as well as *mantras*, austerities, and the five fires. On the summit of *bhakti* he found three graces whose fragrance reaches us in his pages: pity, pardon, peace.

'He who gives to God simple-hearted devotion . . . within his soul there dwell pity, pardon, peace.'[11] 'There is no Saviour of the needy save God alone: in Him are pity, pardon, peace.'[12] 'Where pity, pardon, peace abide there God dwells. Thither He runs and makes His home . . ., and where these graces have free play He tarries.'[13]

[1] Bhandarkar's tr., *Vaiṣṇavism*, p. 96.
[2] *Ib.* p. 95. [3] *Ib.* p. 95.
[4] Bhandarkar's tr., *Marāṭhī Writings*, Bombay, 1919, p. 223.
[5] *Vaiṣṇavism*, p. 109.
[6] *Marāṭhī Writings*, p. 187.
[7] *Ib.* p. 187 f.
[8] Bhandarkar's tr., *Vaiṣṇavism*, p. 97.
[9] Bhandarkar, *Vaiṣṇavism*, pp. 40, 54, *Marāṭhī Writings*, pp. 315–321.
[10] *Ib.* p. 431 f. [11] *Ib.* p. 436.
[12] *Ib.* p. 581. [13] *Ib.* p. 535 f.

5. Teaching.—Tukārām is never systematic in his psychology, his theology, or his theodicy. He oscillates between a Dvaitist and an Advaitist view of God and the world, leaning now to a pantheistic scheme of things, now to a distinctly Providential, and he does not harmonize them. He says little or nothing of cosmogony, and, according to him, God realizes Himself in the devotion of His worshippers. Likewise, faith is essential to their realization of Him: 'It is our faith that makes thee a god' (1785), he says boldly to his Viṭhobā. On the other hand, God makes Himself accessible to man's feeble apprehension by means of visibility, the idol thus becoming a proof of divine condescension: 'He has embodied himself in forms to suit our pleasure' (1753). Man is a child of God. Indeed, the figure of childhood is pressed sometimes so far as to sacrifice reverence and dignity, the same applying to Tukārām's view of God as Mother, though in the latter he finds a solution of many perplexities. All this deals with man's 'natural' state, but separation has entered, sin being viewed variously. It is sometimes a mere breaking of caste rules, sometimes a breach of morality, and again, and very often, it is *mīpaṇa*, a word often on his lips and perhaps best rendered by 'self-centredness,' though this is inadequate. We have seen how deep was his sense of sin and what means of salvation were disclosed to him. Brāhmanical or mystic intuition and verbal theology were deprecated as much as austerities. Men should waste no time in argument, but throw themselves at God's feet. Specific hindrances to salvation are found in the above *mīpaṇa*, in indulgence of desire, fear of ridicule, learning, and disputation. What the religious life meant to him we have already seen. Mere renunciation leads to nothing, and indeed everything is worthless save a personal experience of religion. Tukārām's 'good man' must possess humility, peaceableness, kindness, truthfulness, contentment, and simplicity.

He is mostly despondent of his fellow-men: 'I am sick of mankind' (994), and for relief he turns to 'the saints,' about whom he has hundreds of verses, setting forth their calling, character, and service to mankind. At the other end of the scale of creation animals call forth his real sympathy. Whether he held to *ahiṁsā* is not quite clear. Reincarnation he accepts (972), but he is not sure whether to prefer mortal rebirth, for the power of God's name could break his *karma*. Conscious communion on earth was far preferable to being merged in the unconsciousness of Brahman.

Patwardhan has shown that Tukārām's 'doctrine of *bhakti*' comprised a conception of the Divine Motherhood which gave Tukārām a God of love and tenderness, a sense of human insufficiency which led to conflict between faith and 'the flesh,' devotion thus being frustrated by human frailties, and a defective view of life 'that was at best one-sided. His end was individual, the peace and solace and beatific rest of his own restless soul. . . . Tukārām was a pessimist in regard to this world. . . . The *bhakti* of the future ought to be broader based, fuller veined, and larger souled.'[1] A defect sometimes pointed out is that the claim of human need 'is a rare mood and very seldom expressed in his poems'[2] and that 'there are but few traces of the passion of winning others.'[3] It is a 'defect,' however, very largely repaired by his self-forgetting service as set forth in the pages of Mahīpati.

6. Relation to Hinduism.—Tukārām acquiesced in the greater part of the conventional Hinduism of his day while himself living on a loftier plane. Often therefore he speaks with two voices. Temple ceremonies he does not condemn, but his heart aspires to something higher. About Viṭhobā, however, there is no kind of ambiguity, for, as an incarnation of Kṛṣṇa or Viṣṇu, Viṭhobā was the bigger half of Tukārām's spiritual life,

[1] *Indian Interpreter*, vii. 19–30.
[2] N. Macnicol, *Psalms of Marāṭhā Saints*, p. 31 f.
[3] Farquhar, *Religious Literature of India*, p. 300.

though again faith was always the channel. Inwardly he experienced the living God, though outwardly it was an idol he worshipped.

'There is scarcely a theological or philosophical system to be found in his writings, but so far as philosophical thinking may be traced, he tends to be a monist.'[1] 'Tukārām was thus a devotee only of Viṭhobā of Pāṇḍharpūr and a monotheist in this sense. Though he worshipped the idol at the place, still he had always before his mind's eye the great Lord of the universe.'[2]

In some verses indeed he holds that the stone idol was a mere stone, neither embodying nor symbolizing the divine. The inconsistency of such a position he appears to have realized, but he does not solve it. Hence the millions in the Deccan who follow him in idolatrous practices and the thousands who share his theistic aspirations have both much to support them. Hence too a theistic society like the Prarthanā Samāj[3] so recently as 20th June 1920 failed to pass a resolution that 'any member who performs a domestic or any other ceremony with idolatrous rites or worships any idols while performing such rites will *ipso facto* cease to be a member of the Bombay Prarthanā Samāj.'[4]

A similar ambiguity exists in his references to caste and holy places. Caste was accepted by Tukārām as an institution of the Hindu world, and he did not carry to its logical conclusion his conviction that God does not consider a man's caste, all His worshippers being equally dear to Him (2077). In personal inward religion Tukārām was democratic enough, but he was too much of the 'mild Hindu' to fight the battle of religious rights and privileges.

Tukārām was in no sense a 'reformer,' as the word is commonly understood: he was a sage with lofty principles in a degenerate time, a sage who for lack of courage, conviction, or inspiration allowed his protests to lapse after he had uttered them.

7. Influence.—Tukārām has quite a unique place in the inner life of his own people. Besides the Vārkarīs, a pilgrim sect devoted to him, every member of which visits Paṇḍharpūr not only at the two annual festivals but on other *ēkādaśīs*, or 'monthly-elevenths,' named *vārīs*, and whose preachings of equality and disregard of caste have been 'a valuable counterpoise to Brāhman domineering,'[5] there are some fifteen million Deccan peasants of all castes and creeds who sing his verses in the fields by day and in companies around some flickering lamp at night. His poems form a substantial part of the hymn-book of the Prarthanā Samāj (*q.v.*) of Western India, now in its ninth edition and containing 500 of his *abhaṅgs*. His terms 'Viṭhobā, Pāṇḍuraṅg' etc., being unacceptable to *ēkēśwarīs* (monotheists), the simple term 'God' has been substituted.[6] That Tukārām has exercised a great nationalizing and democratizing influence among the people of the only Indian nation that has ever ruled over any considerable portion of India can hardly be doubted. His moralizing force cannot be said to have been so great, in view of idolatrous conditions in the Deccan to-day. But the Viṭhobā of Tukārām still inspires a phenomenal type of devotion in his devotees. From as far distant as Madras, women have been known to make at Viṭhobā's shrine the hair-offering called *vēṇīdān* (*vēṇī*='braid,' *dān*='gift') by having their heads shaved as do Brāhman women at Gaya, and all Paṇḍharpūr pilgrims have such an affection for their god that no *darshan* is complete without the pilgrim's head touching Viṭhobā's feet. No fewer than 140,000 people take this *darshan* at a single festival, at the rate of 12,000 daily. Some of them accomplish the journey by prostrating their form at every step in honour of Viṭhobā, some thus rolling along for more than 40 miles;[1] one case is known of a man rolling like a log from Nāgpur, hundreds of miles away, at the rate of two miles a day, the journey taking two years.[2] Tukārām's moving verse has done not a little to inspire this tragic devotion in men and women alike.

All attempts to classify Tukārām have failed. He was neither an orthodox Hindu nor a Hindu Protestant. He lived according to the rules of a gigantic religious system with much of which he disagreed while enjoying an inward experience transcending the system, for spiritual intercourse with God and His 'saints' was the sum and substance of Tukārām's religion. He belongs therefore to none of the stereotyped forms, and, to be understood and appreciated at his proper worth, he must be approached without any kind of dogmatic prejudice, whether Hindu or Christian. Those who have no definite creed and who follow no organized system find in him a kindred spirit. He cannot be classed as a mystic, for he had no extraordinary visions, and he followed Hindu rules of living. We may regard him as a devoted theist living his own inward life amid idolatrous surroundings.

'You can find much in Tukārām's poetry that runs parallel with the teachings of Christ save its principles and spirit. These latter, eclectics easily read into his words, and when they cannot do so they put them there. Tukārām was one of the greatest saints of India, and as such he has influenced and is still influencing the devotional trend of his own people. In the case of us Christians he is one of the most powerful of sidelights. Only a few weeks ago he threw me into the very arms of my Lord.'[3]

At the close of an examination into 'The Alleged Indebtedness of Indian Theism to Christianity' the conclusion is reached:

'Certainly either Tukārām was actually in contact with Christian teaching, which is by no means improbable, or he was a remarkable instance of a *mens naturaliter Christiana*.'[4]

Of these two alternatives we incline to the second, as there has been no evidence adduced as yet pointing to Tukārām ever having been 'in contact with Christian teaching,' and, while he has much kinship with the NT writers, none of the fundamental doctrines of the Christian Church, with the possible exception of faith, can be traced in his pages.[5] The kinship is indeed so close that a knowledge of his poems, at least in their English translation, should be regarded as an indispensable preparation for missionary work among his people. That nearly three centuries ago Tukārām should have proclaimed so clearly the inefficacy of all merely external rites and should have insisted so constantly on inward experience as the one essential of true religion offers to the Christian evangelist a most useful point of contact with the people of India.

LITERATURE.—This has been indicated in the footnotes. For a fuller treatment of the subject see J. N. Fraser and J. F. Edwards, *Life and Teaching of Tukārām*, Madras, in the press.

J. F. EDWARDS.

TULASĪ-DĀSA.—1. Life.—Little is certainly known about the life of Tulasī-Dāsa (commonly pronounced 'Tulsī Dās'), the greatest poet of mediæval Northern India, beyond two or three dates and a few accidental particulars mentioned in his writings.

A life of the poet is said to have been written by his friend and companion, Vēṇī-mādhava Dāsa. It is referred to by Śiva

1 Farquhar, p. 300.
2 Bhandarkar, *Vaiṣṇavism*, p. 95.
3 See art. PRARTHANĀ SAMĀJ.
4 *Subōdh Patrikā*, 27th June 1920, with *Dhyānodaya* comments, 1st July 1920.
5 *BG* xx. [1884] 471–473.
6 Bhandarkar, *Marāṭhī Writings*, pp. 506–513.

1 *BG* xx. [1884] 470.
2 J. Murray Mitchell, *IA* xi. [1882] 155.
3 N. V. Tilak, in an unpublished paper.
4 N. Macnicol, *Indian Theism*, London, 1915, p. 279.
5 See J. Murray Mitchell, *JRASBo* iii. [1849] for the opposite view.

Siṁha, who wrote in the latter half of the 19th cent., but no copy of it is now known to exist. We have two personal documents relating to the poet—a deed of arbitration, and an entire book of the *Rāmacharita-mānasa*, both in his own handwriting.

There are numerous traditions concerning him, some of which may be accepted with considerable confidence. He is said to have been born at Rājāpur, in the present United Provinces of Bāndā, about A.D. 1532, and to have been a Sarwariā Brāhmaṇa of the Parāśara *gōtra*.[1] His father's name was Ātmārāma, and his mother's Hulasī, his own name being Rāma Bōlā. In one of his verses[2] he tells us that he was abandoned by his parents immediately after his birth, and with great probability it is assumed from this that he was one of those unfortunate children known as *abhuktamūla*, born under the beginning of the currency of the asterism Mūla. Such a child is said to be destined to destroy its father, and the only remedy is to abandon it on its birth, or, at best, so to arrange that its parents shall not look upon its face during the first eight years of its existence. He was picked up by a wandering Sādhu, who, in token of the sacred leaf used in the ceremony of purification of the infant, renamed him Tulasī-Dāsa ('Servant of the *tulasī*-plant'), and by this name he was henceforth known. With this Sādhu, who was probably also his *guru*, or spiritual preceptor, Narahari-Dāsa, he wandered all over Northern India. From his *guru* he learnt the story of Rāma,[3] but owing to his ignorance (? of Sanskrit)[4] he could not at first grasp its importance. At length, after frequent hearings, he learnt it so far as his intelligence would allow, and then determined to write it in the vernacular for his own benefit and for that of others similarly situated. When he grew up, he lived as a householder, and married a girl named Ratnāvalī, the daughter of one Dīnabandhu Pāṭhaka, by whom he had a son named Tāraka, who died at an early age. He was devoted to his wife and could not bear to be separated from her. She was a firm Vaiṣṇava, and on one occasion, when she had gone on a visit to her people, she reproached him for following her and for not showing equal affection to Rāma. Struck with remorse, Tulasī at once left her and took to an ascetic life. He is said to have seen her only once again in after years, and then not to have recognized her. With his head-quarters at first in Ayōdhyā and subsequently in Benares, he made long journeys over Northern India preaching the gospel of Rāma. At first he met with considerable opposition, but his holy life and his attractive personality conquered all obstacles, and, even in Benares, the head-quarters of Śiva-worship, he won universal respect. His fame as a poet spread far and wide and gained him many friends and followers, the most famous of whom were Rājā Māna-siṁha (Mān Singh) of Ambēr († 1614) and the celebrated 'Abdu 'r-Raḥīm Ḫānḫāna (1556–1627). A wealthy landowner of Benares named Ṭōḍar Mall (who is to be distinguished from Akbar's finance minister of the same name) was one of his closest friends, and a touching poem which Tulasī-Dāsa wrote on his death has survived among his most cherished verses. After Ṭōḍar Mall's death his heirs quarrelled as to the disposal of the property, and referred the matter to Tulasī-Dāsa as arbitrator. The deed of arbitration in his handwriting is still in existence and is dated Sambat 1669 (=A.D. 1612).

[1] No fewer than four places claim the honour of being his birthplace. The claim of Rājāpur is that best established. His caste has been a subject of dispute. According to some authorities, he was a Kānyakubja Brāhmaṇa.

[2] *Vinaya-pattrikā*, 227, 2.

[3] *Rām.* i. 30.

[4] He was never a good Sanskrit scholar, and some of his few verses in that language contain grammatical blunders.

Bubonic plague appeared in India in 1616, and lasted for eight years. The poet seems to have been attacked by it, for one of his minor works, the *Hanumān Bāhuka*, describes his sufferings from some such disease. After temporary relief he had a relapse and died in Benares in A.D. 1623.[1]

2. Works.—More than twenty formal works, besides numerous short poems, have been attributed to Tulasī-Dāsa, but some of these are certainly apocryphal, and others are of doubtful authenticity. The most generally accepted list mentions twelve, viz. six minor and six major. The minor works are the following: (1) *Rāma-lalā-Nahachhū*, (2) *Vairāgya-saṁdīpinī*, (3) *Barawai Rāmāyaṇa*, (4) *Jānakī-maṅgala*, (5) *Pārvatī-maṅgala*, (6) *Rāmājñā*. The six major works are (7) *Kṛṣṇagītāvalī*, (8) *Vinaya-pattrikā*, (9) *Gītāvalī*, (10) *Kavittāvalī*, (11) *Dōhāvalī*, and (12) *Rāmacharita-mānasa*.

Tulasī-Dāsa was a Smārta Vaiṣṇava; *i.e.*, while a worshipper of Rāmachandra, he also adhered to the tradition (*smṛti*) of ordinary Hinduism and followed the general religious customs of his caste. This involved, among other things, the worship of the god Śiva and the practice of eating his meals apart. In both respects he differed from the more thorough Vairāgī Vaiṣṇavas, who had abandoned tradition, and who worshipped only Viṣṇu in one or other of his incarnations and ate in company. During his stay in Ayōdhyā he associated with these Vairāgī Vaiṣṇavas and there composed the first three cantos of the *Rāmacharita-mānasa*. Subsequently, being unable to agree with them on points of discipline, he migrated to Benares and there completed the poem.

His devotion to Rāmachandra as an incarnation of the Supreme is illustrated by the above list of works. With two exceptions (nos. 5 and 7) they all deal directly or indirectly with that deity. No. 7 is a collection of hymns in praise of Kṛṣṇa, another incarnation of Viṣṇu. No. 5 is a short poem describing Śiva's marriage with Pārvatī, a subject also treated at some length as an episode in the *Rāmacharita-mānasa*. As already stated, Tulasī-Dāsa paid special reverence to Śiva as a great and kindly god, although by no means on a level with Rāmachandra. It was Śiva who, out of love for the world, communicated Rāma's history to Pārvatī and thereby made it known to mortals.

A brief notice of each of the works named above will suffice.

(1) *Rāma-lalā-Nahachhū*.—The genuineness of this is disputed. It is a short poem describing the 'nail-paring' ceremony at the investiture of Rāmachandra with the sacred caste-thread. This ceremony is a village rite still kept up on such occasions and at weddings in Oudh and Bihār, and the whole poem is in rural style and in rural metre.

(2) *Vairāgya-saṁdīpinī* ('Kindling of Quietism') describes the true nature of holiness. It advocates *vairāgya* (absence of passion), and the description of the perfect peace resulting from absolute self-surrender to the Deity is not without poetic beauty.[2]

(3) The *Barawai Rāmāyaṇa* is a summary of the history of Rāmachandra in the Barawai metre. It is very short and, as we have it, probably incomplete. It is rejected by some authorities.

(4) *Jānakī-maṅgala* and (5) *Pārvatī-maṅgala*.—These are two short works celebrating the marriages of Sītā to Rāmachandra and of Pārvatī to Śiva respectively. The authenticity of both is doubtful. In no. 4 the order of events differs from that given by the poet in his more important works. The

[1] See G. A. Grierson, *Proceedings ASBe*, 1898, p. 147 ff.

[2] The whole has been translated by G. A. Grierson in *IA* xxii. [1893] 198 ff.

Pārvatī-maṅgala is dated Sambat 1643 (=A.D. 1586).

(6) *Rāmājñā.*—This is a collection of verses to be used as omens previous to undertaking a journey or other important task. The contents are in the main a history of Rāmachandra in seven chapters, each of seven septads of verses, or 343 in all. The omen is found by selecting a verse by lot—a kind of *sortes Virgilianæ*. It is dated Sambat 1655 (=A.D. 1598).

(7) The *Kṛṣṇagītāvalī*, the first of the major works, has been already referred to. As its subject demanded, Tulasī-Dāsa wrote it, not in his customary Awadhī, but in the Braj Bhākhā dialect. It is one of the least read of the poet's works, but well repays perusal, as it contains many beautiful passages. He has entirely avoided debasing religion by that association with eroticism which spoils so much of the literature devoted to Kṛṣṇa.

(8) The *Vinaya-pattrikā* ('Petition') is one of the most important works of the poet, in which his most intimate feelings towards the Deity and that Deity's relations to the human soul are displayed with a freedom from reticence and poetic fervour that have rarely been equalled.

An interesting legend accounts for its origin. Tulasī, harassed and terrified by persecution, writes this petition to Rāmachandra—the loving, almighty, God—appealing for His protection. The whole forms a series of prayers, addressed, one by one, to the various minor gods as door-keepers and courtiers of the Supreme, and then, in an outburst of passionate entreaty and self-humiliation, to the Deity Himself. The final verse tells how, as in the case of an earthly monarch, the petition was granted under Rāma's own signature.

The *Vinaya-pattrikā* is one of the most admired works of the poet, but the difficulties of its language have discouraged many readers. The intense fervour of the writer often carries him into an extremity of passion, bursting forth in an elliptical style very different from the limpid beauty of his narrative poems. Again, the very form of the poem militates against its easy comprehension. It is a petition to a sovereign, expressed in a courtly vocabulary full of high-flown words and phrases. These belong to the nature of the case and are here most appropriate, but they do not tend to make the poem comprehensible to any one who is not a Sanskrit scholar. In spite of these surface defects, this admirable work deserves the closest study from any one who would become acquainted with the religious history of India. We have here a man whose influence for good over generations of Indians cannot be exaggerated, laying bare the inmost recesses of his heart, and openly proclaiming that at which other writers with the same experiences have only dared to hint. It is a book of confessions, but the confessions of a pure and faithful soul.

(9) In the *Gītāvalī* Tulasī-Dāsa appears in a new character, that of a *māgadha*, or panegyrist. It is a book of songs intended to increase in his readers their love for a tender, loving God. Again, as elsewhere, the love which he teaches is that of a child to his father. For the songs he has used the Braj Bhākhā dialect as the traditional vehicle of expression, and the dominant tone is not, as in the *Vinaya-pattrikā*, passion, but sweetness and charm. In this way he gives the whole history of Rāmachandra in a delightful style, quite different from that of his formal epic. There is no verse in the book which is not a complete little picture, and most attractive of all are those in the first book, in which he tells of the baby life of his hero and his brothers. It is a true gospel of the infant Rāma.

(10) Different again is the *Kavittāvalī*. Here the poet, in the character of a *vandin*, or bard, tells of the glory of Rāma, so as to encourage the faithful with a picture of the Deity's power. The language is Awadhī mixed with Braj Bhākhā. No work of Tulasī-Dāsa shows his extraordinary mastery of vocabulary so well as this. His subject is heroic, and, without having needless recourse to Sanskrit, he writes in a heroic style. In the battle scenes the words themselves by their very sound echo the clash of arms and the cries of the combatants, and, in the description of the burning of Lankā, the crackling of the flames. The narrative closes with the sixth book. The seventh, which is nearly half of the whole, consists of a number of short poems in the *kavitta* metre written at different times and here collected by their author. They have no direct connexion with the preceding books, and, being full of personal allusions, form a valuable source of information as to the poet's times and experiences. It is here that we learn about his birth and parentage and about the persecutions to which he was subjected, and from one verse we gather that the date of the compilation was somewhere between A.D. 1612 and 1614. A supplement, in the same metre, is the *Hanumān Bāhuka*, already referred to, in which he tells how he was attacked by plague.

(11) *Dōhāvalī.*—The title means a collection of verses in the *dōhā* metre, and it is by no means certain what is meant by it. There is a work of this name (see below), but some authorities maintain that the list alludes to a poem called the *Rām Satsaī* ('Seven hundred verses [also in this metre] in Praise of Rāma'). Many good scholars consider that this was written, not by the poet, but by another author of the same name. It is a rather tasteless production, but, if genuine, is not without importance, as the fifth chapter gives in great detail what purports to be the poet's doctrine regarding works as opposed to faith.[1] The difficulty in the way of accepting the work now called the *Dōhāvalī* as that referred to in the list is that it is largely composed of verses already occurring in the *Rāmacharita-mānasa*, the *Rāmājñā*, and the *Rām Satsaī* itself. Out of a total of 572 verses no fewer than 258 have been so identified, and there are quite possibly more. If genuine, there must have been a nucleus of original verses to which subsequent admirers have added others, so as to compile a kind of anthology of the poet's best *dōhās*. This is the present writer's opinion, and, if it is correct, the final recension must have been sufficiently long after the composition of the *Rām Satsaī* for the latter to have become recognized as the work of our poet.

(12) The *Rāmacharita-mānasa* ('Lake of the Gestes of Rāma') is commonly called the *Tulasī-kṛta Rāmāyaṇa*. This epic, the poet's greatest achievement, and also, in point of time, probably his first, was begun in A.D. 1574, when its author was about 43 years of age, and upon it his fame chiefly rests. It has been described as the Bible of ninety millions of people, and is certainly more familiar to every Hindu of Northern India than our Bible is to the average English peasant. There is not a Hindu of Hindōstān proper, whether prince or cottar, who does not know its most famous verses and whose common talk is not coloured by it. Its similes have entered even into the language of Indian Muslims, some of whose most ordinary idioms, though they know it not, made their first appearance in this work.[2]

The life of Rāmachandra, considered as an incarnation of the Supreme, is here dealt with in a formal epic. The subject is the same as that of the celebrated Sanskrit *Rāmāyaṇa* of Vālmīki, but the epic of Tulasī-Dāsa is in no way a transla-

[1] Tr. G. A. Grierson in *IA* xxii. [1893] 229 ff.

[2] See G. A. Grierson, 'Tulasī Dāsa, Poet and Religious Reformer,' *JRAS*, 1903, p. 447. Much of what follows is condensed from this paper.

tion of that work. We have an independent story, built on the same foundation, but differing from it in the treatment of episodes and in important details.[1] The author himself states that he has taken his account from many different sources, and it has been shown that the principal of these, besides Vālmīki's work, were the *Adhyātmā Rāmāyaṇa* (a section of the *Brahmāṇḍa Purāṇa*), the *Bhuśuṇḍī Rāmāyaṇa*, the *Vasiṣṭha Saṁhitā*, and the *Prasanna-rāghava* attributed to Jayadēva.[2]

As illustrating the estimation in which this poem is held in India, the following very popular legend may be quoted. Rāmachandra denoted his approval of Vālmīki's epic by appending his signature to a copy of it. Thereupon the monkey-god Hanumān, with his nails, wrote another *Rāmāyaṇa* upon a rock, and took it to Rāma. The latter approved of it also, but said that, as he had already signed Vālmīki's copy, he could not sign another; he had better show it to that poet. He did so, and, as Vālmīki saw that it would eclipse his own work, by a stratagem he induced Hanumān to fling it into the sea. Hanumān, in complying, prophesied that in a future age he would himself inspire a Brāhmaṇa named Tulasī, who would recite his (Hanumān's) poem in the tongue of the common people and destroy the fame of Vālmīki's epic.

There can be no doubt that its reputation is well deserved. The *Rāmacharita-mānasa* is one of the great epics. It has its prolixities and its episodes that jar upon European tastes, but, even so, no one can read it without being impressed by its high poetic merit. The various characters are vividly and consistently described, and live and move with all the dignity of a heroic age. The style is most admirably varied. There is the infinite pathos of the passage describing Rāma's farewell to his mother; the rugged, harsh language telling of the horrors of the battlefield; when occasion requires it, a sententious, aphoristic method of dealing with narrative, teeming with similes drawn, not from the traditions of the schools, but from nature herself; and, suffusing all, a life-giving atmosphere of the purest poetry. To us its weakest side is that which, to a Hindu, is its strongest—the character of its hero. To the poet, Rāmachandra is necessarily, as God manifest on earth, a perfect character. Even when the old story shows him performing unknightly deeds, Tulasī must call them virtues and plead that the end justifies the means. Or, again, the foulest treachery, such as that of Vibhīṣaṇa towards his brothers, is extolled because the traitor is accepted and rewarded by the hero.[3] But this is one of the obligations of the story and of the author's view of the divinity of Rāma. The human characters are to our ideas far more sympathetic. There are the impetuous and loving Lakṣmaṇa; Sītā, the ideal of an Indian wife and mother; Bharata, constant and tender, the model of the true *bhakta*; and Rāvaṇa—the Satan of the epic—destined to failure, and fighting with all his demon force against his fate.

One of the most striking features of the poem is the writer's capacity for seeing things. More than any other literature, Indian poetry has its stock similes—the lotus, the water-lily, the bee, the moon, and so on. Even the best Sanskrit poems often give the impression of being largely the work of the closet, not of the open air. Tulasī-Dāsa employed the same old similes—he would not have been Indian if he had avoided them—but thousands of others are his own. Little expressions—the turn of a sentence or an apt

[1] *E.g.*, the account of the great battle outside Laṅkā is quite different.

[2] See L. P. Tessitori, *Il 'Rāmacaritamānasa e il Rāmāyaṇa*, reprinted from *Giornale della Società Asiatica Italiana*, xxiv. [1911] (reviewed by G. A. Grierson, in *JRAS*, 1912, p. 794 ff.), and Sītā Rām, in *JRAS*, 1914, p. 419 ff.

[3] The authors of the *Hindī Navaratna* (pp. 88, 289) point out that, with one exception, none of the numerous Hindī poets who told the tale of Rāma ever thought of condemning Vibhīṣaṇa's conduct. The exception is Kēśava-dāsa, a court poet who lived amid knightly surroundings. He also has the courage to condemn Rāma's treatment of Sītā.

epithet—show how he had seen and studied the world for himself.

It would be a great mistake to look upon him merely as an ascetic. He was a man that had lived. He had been a householder—a word of much meaning to an Indian—and had known the pleasures of a wedded life, the joy of clasping an infant son to his bosom, and the sorrow of losing that son ere he had attained his prime. He appealed not to scholars, but to his countrymen as a whole, the people whom he knew. He had mixed with them, begged from them, prayed with them, shared their pleasures and their yearnings, and, on the other hand, had contracted intimate friendships with the greatest men of the emperor's court. All this we find reflected in the pages of his writings.[1]

His works have suffered the fate which has befallen those of other famous Indian authors. Imitators have written poems which they have passed off as his, and numerous *kṣēpakas*, or apocryphal additions, have been inserted in his epic. He has suffered too from the attentions of commentators without end, most of whom have wasted energy in discovering hidden meanings in the simplest passages, while they discreetly avoid the real difficulties. Finally, his epic has actually been translated into Sanskrit, and there are critics who have maintained that the translation is the original, and that the *Rāmacharita-mānasa* is nothing but a barefaced theft of another's poetry.[2]

3. Religious ideas.—The religious ideas of the poet are of great importance in the history of India. Seventh in descent of teacher and pupil from the great Rāmānanda (*q.v.*), he was a thorough Vaiṣṇava and follower of the *Bhakti-Mārga* (*q.v.*). He taught that there is but one Supreme Being, and that man is by nature sinful and unworthy of salvation. Nevertheless the Supreme, in His infinite mercy, became incarnate in the person of Rāmachandra to relieve the world from sin. Rāma has returned to heaven, where, besides being the ineffable Supreme, he is still Rāma, and where, in consequence, we have now a God who is not only infinitely merciful, but who knows by actual experience how great are man's infirmities and temptations, and who, though Himself incapable of sin, is ever ready to extend His help to the sinful being who calls upon Him. On all this follows, as a corollary, the doctrine of the universal brotherhood of man, and the duty which man owes to his neighbour. His definition of sin is that which is contrary to the will of Rāma, and it is only by acknowledging this, and by abandoning himself to utter loving faith in Rāma's power to save him from its thraldom, that a man can escape from the weary round of perpetual transmigration. The doctrine of the fatherhood of God and of the necessity of *bhakti*, or devotional faith, had long been known. In Northern India Rāmānanda had been its great exponent, and Tulasī-Dāsa put forward no novelty. His claim for consideration is that his teaching was successful. His own pure life and the magic of his poetry have done for the *Bhakti-Mārga* what the eloquence of hundreds of other teachers failed to do. The fact that he was a Smārta Vaiṣṇava must not be forgotten. He belonged to no sect, and founded no sect, but was just an ordinary Hindu, accepting all the Hindu mythological machinery. While worshipping Rāma as the Supreme, he paid adoration to Śiva and the other gods. His attitude to them was much the same as that of the official teaching of one branch of the Christian Church: to Rāma alone he offered λατρεία, to the others δουλεία, to Śiva ὑπερδουλεία.

A few words must be devoted to the poet's use of the word *māyā*. Occasionally he refers to it in terms that can only be interpreted as meaning the influence which hides Bráhma from the soul—the *māyā* of the Śiva-worshipping Vēdāntins, to whose doctrines he was strongly opposed. But all his

[1] Cf. *JRAS*, 1903, p. 452.

[2] See G. A. Grierson, in *JRAS*, 1913, p. 133 ff.

uses of the word in this sense are merely cases of similes and the like, and in no way form part of his real teaching. We may attribute this use of the word to his own association with the worship of Śiva. Elsewhere he employs the word in two different senses: in one it means merely 'magic,' and is the evil force used by demons in their combat with Rāma's army; in the other it represents a combination of the Gnostic demiurge and the Christian 'Tempter';[1] it is a personality, a female, subordinate to the Supreme, and, to a certain extent, His agent. In the latter capacity she sets the whole world dancing, yet she herself is set a-dancing, like an actress on the stage, by a movement of the Lord's eyebrows. She sullies every one, even the gods, with her temptations; and the Deity sometimes sends her forth specially to tempt some pious person who begins to show overweening pride.[2] As the world, the flesh, and the Devil in one, she leads mankind to sin, but, if a man has true *bhakti*, he is surely armoured against her, and she cannot approach him.[3]

Above all, Tulasī-Dāsa taught that the Supreme is a personality. While not denying the existence of the *Nirguṇaṁ Bráhma* of the *Upaniṣads*—a being totally devoid of all qualities, of whom the only thing that can be said is 'he is not this or that'—he maintained that the idea of such a being was beyond the comprehension of the human mind, and that the only God whom it was possible to adore was the personal (*saguṇa*) manifestation of the impersonal (*nirguṇa*).[4]

The practical result of the general adoption of Tulasī's religious attitude has been of the greatest importance to Northern India. In the poet's own time the masses of Hindōstān had two alternative religions open to them. One was the crude polytheism of the worship of village godlings, the other was the Kṛṣṇa-cult. The first still exists, but controlled and thrust into the background by Tulasī's faith. What the Kṛṣṇa-cult becomes among the uncultivated masses the religious fate of Bengal has shown. It inevitably tends to become a sex-worship, and its text-books teem with the most passionate, most licentious descriptions of the love adventures of Kṛṣṇa among the herdmaidens. All else is lost, and there gradually develop the unnameable horrors of a Śākta-cult. Upper India has been saved from this by Tulasī-Dāsa.

LITERATURE.—G. A. Grierson, 'Notes on Tul'si Das,' *IA* xxii. [1893] 89, 122, 197, 225, 253 (this is the only complete account in English of the poet's life and works; a few errors in it have been corrected in the preceding pages), 'Tulasī Dāsa, Poet and Religious Reformer,' *JRAS*, 1903, p. 447 ff.; Gaṇēśa-vihārī Miśra, Śyāma-vihārī Miśra, and Śukadēva-vihārī Miśra, *Hindī-Navaratna*, Allahabad, 1910 (an account in Hindī of the nine great writers in that language); cf. the same authors' *Miśrabandhu-vinōda*, Khaṇḍwā, 1913, p. 304 ff. (a general history of Hindī literature in the same language).

Numerous edd. of all the poet's works have been published in India, but few of them possess critical value. Two excellent edd. of the *Rāmacharita-mānasa* have been published, viz. that issued in 1889 by the Khaḍga-vilāsa Press in Bānkipur and that issued in 1903 by the Kāśī Nāgarī-prachāriṇī Sabhā of Benares. Both are critically edited and have elaborate introductions dealing with the poet's life and writings. For those not familiar with the language the writer can recommend a good ed., with a line-for-line Hindī commentary and much general information concerning the poet, by Rāmēśvara Bhaṭṭa, Nirṇaya-sāgara Press, Bombay, 1904. The same editor has issued from the Indian Press, Allahabad, 1913, a similar ed. of the *Vinaya-pattrikā*, which can be recommended to students. It is believed that it is intended to issue all the poet's works in this series.

A good, if somewhat literal, Eng. tr. of the *Rāmacharita-mānasa* has been made by F. S. Growse (1st ed., Allahabad, 1880-81). It has been several times reprinted in India.

G. A. GRIERSON.

[1] For a full account see *Rām.* vii. dō. 70 ff., Benares edition.
[2] *E.g.*, the divine saint Nārada (*Rām.* i. dō. 128 ff., Ben. ed.).
[3] *Rām.* vii. ch. 116, Ben. ed.
[4] See *Rām.* vii. dō. 13 and following *chhand.*

TUNGUS.—1. Area, distribution, number, and history.—The name Tungus is usually derived from the word Tung-hung ('Eastern barbarians'), by which these people were known to the ancient Chinese. They call themselves Avankil (sing. Avanki) or Donki. The Tungusic tribes are the most widely distributed of all the native tribes of Siberia; they live in small groups all over Siberia as far west as the river Taz, as far east as the island of Sakhalin, as far north as the Arctic shore, and as far south as the middle of Manchuria. In spite of this distribution, the language and social anthropology of these tribes are the least known of all the Siberian peoples, the Samoyed, Turkic and Mongolic tribes, and Koryak and Chukchi, even the Gilyak and the Ainu, having had more space given to them in anthropological literature than the Tungus. As a reason for this may be cited the fact that the Tungus usually live in the interior of the continent, in places difficult of access and, with the exception of the Lamut, far away from the coast. The total number of Tungus belonging to the various tribes was 76,504 in 1897, while in 1911 there were only 75,204.

The Tungusic tribes are usually divided into Northern Tungusic and Southern Tungusic. Of these the Northern Tungusic group comprises: (1) Samogir, (2) Nigidal, (3) Olchi, (4) Oroki, (5) Manegu, (6) Tungus proper (including Lamut and Orochon). The Southern Tungusic group comprises: (1) Manchu, (2) Daur, (3) Solon, (4) Gold, (5) Orochi.

The Northern Tungus are at the stage of reindeer culture like the Magdalenian man in Europe, though at the same time they know the use of iron, which they brought from their more southern home. They belong to the Neo-Siberian group. The Southern Tungus are horse nomads, cattle-breeders, and fishermen, and in some places also agriculturists, and in the towns artisans. The Siberian Tungus emigrated from Manchuria partly in the seventh and partly in the thirteenth century after the Mongolic conquest, but their armies had probably invaded Siberia frequently even in the pre-Christian era. The first Tungus subdued by the Russian authorities in Mangazei in 1603 were the Tungus of the lower Tunguska. In 1615 a large Tungus force was defeated by the Russians on the Yenisei, and about 1623 all the Tungus of Central Siberia were forced to pay taxes. The Tungus of the Amur country, together with their territory, were made subject to Russia about fifty years ago.

Although the Northern Tungus live now under a very primitive culture, their pedigree goes as far back as that of the Turkic people, and they therefore present a case of degeneration under the influence of environment. Nowhere is this more clearly shown than in their folk-tales, which in comparison with the really primitive tales of the Samoyed are rather sophisticated. The old Chinese chroniclers used to comment on their two powerful neighbours as barbarians of inferior culture, *i.e.* their north-western neighbours in the pre-Christian era, the Turks of the present day, and their north-eastern, the Tungus. But, as both of them appear under a variety of tribal and dynastic names, it is difficult sometimes to know which of these peoples are of Tungus and which of Turkic race. They are more easily classified by their customs and characteristics, while the Mongols, whose name, used in a broad sense, is applied to both these races, seem to have no characteristic cultural features and are probably a mixture of the two races influenced by their steppe environment more than the Turks and Tungus, and brought to prominence through Jenghiz Khan's (himself a Mongol) conquest.

There are several peoples mentioned by the Chinese who can with some probability be considered to be of Tungus race. Such are (1) the Sushen, who lived north of the Liao-Tung peninsula and paid tribute in arrows and arrowheads to the emperors of the Shang dynasty (1766–1154 B.C.); (2) the Sienpi, who occupied an important strategic position in the Korea and north of China before the Great Wall was constructed (221–209 B.C.); these were the peoples who helped to cause the movement of the Hiung-nung westward, who in their turn pushed the Yue-chi (Turks) to Djungaria; in the 2nd cent. A.D. one branch of the Sienpi, the Jwen-Jwen (Zhu-Zhu) rose to power, but they are not heard of after the 6th cent., when the Tu-Kiu (Turks) emancipated themselves from the Jwen-Jwen yoke; (3) the Tlu, who in the 3rd cent. A.D. lived in the forest between the Upper Temen and Yalu rivers; (4) the Moho (Uki), who in the 7th cent. A.D. inhabited the valley of Sungari and who were the founders of the state of Puhai; (5) the Khitans, who in 925 overthrew this dynasty and founded the Liao (Iron) dynasty; (6) the Niu-chi (Yu-chi), who in their turn overthrew the Liao dynasty in A.D. 1125 and lived in the Shan-Alin uplands; their dynasty was called Kiu (Golden); Jenghiz Khan subdued them in 1234, but in the 14th cent. the Niu-chi reasserted themselves and founded the Manchu dynasty, which in 1644 occupied the throne of China after the Ming dynasty and reigned till 1912.

There are certain characteristics and customs common to most of those peoples as well as the modern Tungus. One is the extensive use of the bow and arrows with iron or stone blades. The arrows are of definite type and adaptable for the use of poison. The arrows and skins are also used for the payment of taxes. Other characteristics are the use of richly-adorned aprons, by both sexes, the braiding of the hair into two plaits, also by both sexes, the breeding of pigs, and the exposing of the dead by placing them on high platforms. These habits are not associated with the Turks and were probably imposed on the Chinese by the Tungus. Thus Marco Polo calls the Chinese empire by the tribal Tungus name Khitai (Cathai), and the Russians call it that even now.

2. Linguistics.—Since the time of Castrén the Tungusic tongues have been classed with the Ural-Altaic group, and, as they have not been sufficiently well known, even modern linguists like Tucker call them 'uncultivated,' while the fact is that, although the language of the Tungus (with the exception of the Manchu and Dauri) has not reached the stage of being written language, in grammatical forms, especially in verbal forms, we see a greater variety of simplifications than in many Aryan languages. The Manchu writing is in a modified form of Uiguric, the old Turkic character based again on the Soghdian.

The linguistic division, based on the results of the most recent researches, is into four groups: (1) the well-defined Manchu group, including Sibo, (2) the Gold group, including Olcha, Orochi, and Orok, (3) Tungus proper, including Lamut, Managir, Solon, and Daur, (4) Sanagir and Negda (on the lower Amur). The extent of this group is problematical, as it is possible that it can be united with group (3).[1]

The Northern Tungus dialects are preserved in a purer form than the Southern, which have come under Mongolic and Chinese influence, yet these differences are not very important, and we can use linguistics as the surest means of tracing the existence of Tungusic tribes in any given region. In many places the Tungus use another language as well as their own.

As in language, so also in social anthropology and shamanistic religion, we can see a certain connexion between all the Tungusic tribes. But the preservation of their own language is not necessarily an indication of the preservation of their physical type.

3. Physical type.—As has been said, there has been contact between the Chinese, the Mongols, and the Tungus-Manchu since the 11th cent. B.C. and probably earlier, but it was based chiefly on conquest and on intermarriage among members of the royal families. Migrations *en masse* did not begin, as far as is known, till the 7th cent. and during the time of Jenghiz Khan. It is probable that the Koreans are a Chinese-Tungus mixture and that the Tungus have played a greater rôle than is known in the formation of the modern Japanese nation.

Deniker places the Tungus among the Northern Mongolians, whom he defines as people with oval or round faces and prominent cheek-bones, who inhabit Manchuria, Korea, Northern China, and Mongolia. He places the Kalmuk alongside of the Manchu and the Northern Tungus hunters. Maak, Schrenck, and Mainoff point out the difference in physical type between the Northern and the Southern Tungus. This is also supported by the present writer. Broadly speaking, the difference consists in this, that the Southern type approaches the so-called Mongol type (almost high stature, round and low-headed), while the Northern type approaches the type of the Eastern Palæo-Siberians (low stature, intermediate or long-headed, and average or high-headed). While the mixture of the Southern Tungus with other neighbouring tribes has been going on for so long that it is very difficult to make any record of it, and the Manchu type practically disappeared among the population of north-east China, the Northern Tungus, especially those isolated in the Arctic region, are comparatively unmixed, or in any case it is easy to trace their mixture. This is especially true in the case of the Tungus between the Lena and the Yenisei, who live in thoroughly Tungus or Tungus-Yakut land, while the Tungus between the Lena and the Okhotsk Sea live scattered among the Palæo-Siberians (Koryak, Chukchi, and Yukaghir). The latter were the secondary object of study of the Jesup Expedition of the U.S.A. some ten years ago, while the Tungus between the Yenisei and the Lena were studied by the Oxford-Philadelphian Expedition in 1914–15. The only racial admixture that has to be considered in the case of the Arctic Tungus between the Yenisei and the Lena is with the Yakut.

With the help of the genealogical method in dealing with the social anthropology of the North-Western Tungus (in North Central Siberia) it is possible to distinguish the following grades of Tungus metisation.

(A) The *Tungus*, whose genealogical table, as far back as could be recorded, does not show any foreign admixture; (B) the *Tungus-Yakut*, who call themselves Tungus, and are such linguistically and socially, but who have begun in the last two generations to intermarry with the Yakut; (C) the *Dolgan*, who were Tungus, but who for a long time have intermarried with the Yakut and have created socially, physically, and linguistically a new type; they consider themselves to be a separate nation, their language approaches more nearly to the Yakut, and in physique they look more like the Tungus; (D) the *Tungusized Yakut*, who live in the western part of the Yakutsk territory, and the eastern part of the Turukhansk country, all on the Tungus land; the other Yakut call them Tungus (Tongus); they are in a minority among the Tungus.

The Tungus-Yakut approach in their stature, and head and facial forms, to the Yakut (*q.v.*), who, on the whole, are of a more Mongolic type than the Northern Tungus, while the Dolgan, though they stand further from the pure Tungus than the Tungus-Yakut do, are yet in all these three aspects more like the Tungus than like the Yakut, or, we might say, they return to the physical type of the Tungus.

4. Technique. — Most of the Siberian Tungus are at the stage of reindeer-culture, though they differ from such *pur sang* reindeer-breeders as the Lapps or the Eskimo in that their technique is not so highly specialized and their carvings and drawings on reindeer-bone or mammoth-ivory are not so perfect; very few of them have any knowledge of making half-underground huts, most of them still having fur tents similar in structure to those in their original southern home. In spite of centuries spent in a land where there are no horses, or only the small Siberian ponies which are used for driving but not for riding, they still preserve their old habits of horse-riding, exchanging the horse for the reindeer. In mythology and religion also their southern origin is apparent from time to time. Thus on the grave of a deceased shaman must be placed driftwood figures of a goat, a horse, or a dromedary—animals which have not been known to them for many generations.

The Tungus who do not live in the tundra as reindeer-breeders, but inhabit the steppes and the forest, are mostly hunters, and occasionally horse- and cattle-breeders. Only in the Amur and Baikal region do we find stationary groups.

Among the Northern Tungus iron is much more used than among the Samoyed. Until quite

[1] This table is the result of a verbal communication from W. Kotwicz, the Tungusic scholar of Petrograd University.

recently tatuing was common among the Tungus of the Yenisei, charcoal alone being used as colouring matter, and no bright colours.

One of the most characteristic features of the original Tungus costume is the beautifully decorated apron, which has in some places degenerated into a small covering for the sexual organs. Birch-bark is not so much in use as among the Ostyak, but the typical Tungus canoes are made of birch-bark sewn into shape. The Tungus ornaments are typical of a migratory people. They have no permanent style—we do not see on them either the conventionalized zoological-anatomical figures of the Samoyed or the rich ornamental designs of plant form so often met with among the neighbouring tribe of Yakut. Yet in their mode of life the Tungus exhibit more neatness, more cleanliness, and more reserve than any other tribe of Northern Asia, and probably this was the reason for the classic name that Castrén gave them, however few he saw. He called them 'the gentry of the Siberian aborigines.'

5. Sociology. — The original Tungus social division was into clans, named after the clan-ancestor or the river on whose banks they dwelt. At the present time the remnants of the clans are grouped together into local groups, with local river and other names. This arrangement was forced upon them by the Russian Government, but their internal organization and government, as far as it goes, rests with their council of elders and a prince, elected for three years and re-elected as many times as they wish. Langa, a Hukachar prince, and a great shaman of the Llimpiisk Tungus of the Yenisei tundra, has been prince for twenty-five years.

Married people are always known as the 'father of So-and-so,' 'the mother of So-and-so,' even if the Russian Christian name is used—*e.g.*, Ivan's father.

(*a*) *Marriage.*—Marriage restrictions are very numerous. Not only are blood-relations and clan-relations debarred from marrying, but two brothers of one family may not marry two sisters of another family. The exchange of children in marriage is not allowed, except among the Pankagir Tungus. The terminology connected with relationship by marriage is regulated by the age-classes. Thus *kynniv* would be the name used by the husband for the father, elder brother, and other male relatives of his wife, and *anikynniv* for her elder female relatives, while for his wife's younger male relatives he would use the term *kutetiv*, and for her younger female relatives *kukim*. There is a special relationship, called *kalliv*, between two men who have married sisters. The reindeer which plays a part in the marriage ceremony, *i.e.* on which the bride rides to the bridegroom's home, is called Havakin (from the god Havaki) among the Yenisei Tungus and Savakin among the Tungus of the Okhotsk region. This reindeer is never used for any work, and is never searched for if he gets lost. When he grows ill or old, he is killed, but not eaten. He might be called the reindeer of the bride's individual spirit. The most important feature of the match-making is the settlement of the *kalym* (wife-price).

(*b*) *Birth.*—At childbirth the woman is considered unclean, and is obliged to go away from the tent for confinement. After three or four days she returns from her seclusion and is purified by jumping three times through the fire. Hickisch[1] says that the placenta is eaten. Among the Tungus of the Yenisei-Lena region the placenta is usually hung on a tree or a pole in a skin bag. On the whole, a Tungus woman gives birth to her child very easily. If, however, there are any complications, the Tungus and also the Yakut woman is placed in a kneeling posture, with her hands tied to the tent poles, and subjected to a forcible massage with a log of wood by the woman who attends her. To help his wife, the Tungus husband cuts down a tree and drives a wooden wedge into it. If this has no effect, a shaman is summoned.

[1] *Die Tungusen*, p. 84.

(*c*) *Burial.*—All the belongings of the dead man are placed near his body. The classical way of burying a man was to sew a reindeer skin round the body and put it in a coffin standing on four high poles or on a high platform,[1] while a woman was buried on the ground and covered over with trees. Among the sea and river tribes the dead were often buried in small canoes. Now the Russian mode of burial in the ground prevails, except where the ground is frozen. The *chum* (tent) where the death occurred is promptly removed to another place. On leaving the place where a dead person had been buried, his relatives used, in olden times, to let fly two or three arrows towards him.

(*d*) *Initiation of a shaman.*—A young shaman (*haman*), who has shown signs of devotion, wisdom, and nervous sensibility, is prepared for his office by an old shaman, who teaches him the secrets of the shaman's assistant spirits. After a year or more of frequent intercourse with the young shaman, the old shaman gives him the shaman's coat and drum. The shaman's chief spirits are: *etigr*, in the form of a long serpent, who has power over epidemics, sickness, and all manner of diseases; *iiniany*, in human form, with eagle's wings, on which he carries the shaman from place to place, who also protects animals from diseases; *arkunga*, a prophet-spirit; and lesser spirits such as *khaniny*, *miryada*, *torunga*.

The shaman's coat (*hamahek*) must be made of wild reindeer hide. His cap (*haarken*) is an iron circlet with representations of wild reindeer antlers. His boots are called *haman unta kupuri*, and his belt *angayaptun*. Hanging from the lower edge of his coat he has a fringe of reindeer- or fox-skin, called *chiurukta*. A fringe at the back, longer than the others and with a bell at the end, is called *irginde*. Projecting from his shoulders are the 'iron elk antlers of the shaman' (*arkalan*). On the *gilde* (iron circles attached near the antlers at the back) hang pieces of iron (*budilar*), which are the shaman's arrows against *hargi* (malicious spirits). In the middle of the back of the shaman's coat are hung representations of the sun and moon. These are considered the most important features of his costume, and the sun is often sewn on a piece of skin taken from the head of a bear. *Gagk*, the swan, is on the back, and *ukang*, the diver, on the front of the coat. *Gieli*, a fish (*taimen*) frequently met with, is also represented there, and so too are *kandi*, 'the shaman's *dakali*' (small birds). On his apron (*haman haalme*) there are also representations of the sun and moon, and the shaman's staff (*haman tyevim*) has a human face (of an ancestor) and bear's feet. Sometimes a human face is found on the sun which is hung on the skin from the bear's head. All these accessaries suggest ancestor-man-bear-worship, as also do the traditions. All the objects used by the shaman have their special names; the shaman's cap, *e.g.*, is designated by a different word from that used for an ordinary cap, and, if a common term is used, the word *haman* is prefixed. The shaman's drum is oval in shape, and the drumstick, *giho*, is long and narrow, with jingles.

6. Gods and spirits.—Animism is highly developed in the Tungus religion. The spirits living everywhere in nature have to be propitiated. They are more or less independent of the highest god, Havaki. The mischievous spirits in folk-tales are called *chiulugdy* and *gamondo*. Both these creatures use a special 'bad language,' which occurs in the tales and is understood by the shamans. The malevolent spirits are called *hargi*. The chief *hargi* lives in the virgin forest (*taiga*) of the north. He has enormous eyes placed outside his face and a flat nose, and the black hair on his head and face is like the *taiga* after a storm. He can assume the form of an enormous bear, a wolf, or a bison. The Tungus of the Nerchinsk

[1] The name given to this old form of coffin is *buni mongin*.

and Yakutsk districts call the *hargi* spirits *buni*; to the *buni* of the water they give the name *garan*, and to the *buni* of the earth that of *dorokdi*. The stronger the influence of Christianity, the worse becomes the character of the *buni*. Then there are other spirits, the spirit-owners of flies, of various animals, and even of thieves, *shuro*.

The chief god, Havaki, is anthropomorphic, but is connected with the sun. Sometimes the sun with the face of a man in it is supposed to represent him. Among the Tungus of the present generation the conception of the highest god is very vague, though the conception of spirits living everywhere in nature has still a strong hold on them all, Christian and non-Christian.

7. Sacrifices. — Private sacrifices of food are offered without any special preparations, but the sacrifices to the spirits connected with fertility are more important and must therefore be performed in the presence of a shaman, who knows the method of procedure. Thus the spirit-owner of wild reindeer is propitiated by an offering of the head of a mountain-sheep. The chief abode of this spirit, according to the Yenisei Tungus, is on the rock Hulgadzyakit, between the Upper Kureika and Lake Chirinda. The spirit-owner of lake-fish inhabits a place near Mount Umtupkan, to the east of Lake Chirinda, and at the beginning of the fishing season ceremonies are held to propitiate him. To ensure success in trapping, the Tungus will use in the construction of the traps at least one piece of wood which has been used by a shaman during his shamanistic performances. But the *turu*, or stick, which is the 'tree on which the shaman climbs to the sky,' is never used for this purpose, being too sacred. It is too *hooma*—a word used to express an idea similar to that of Melanesian *mana*.

8. Animal worship.—The veneration of the bear is especially highly developed. When a bear is killed and brought home, a ceremony called *kuk* is held. The heart and liver of the bear are cut into pieces, cooked, and divided among those present (exclusively males). Each person, before eating his piece, bows before the bear and assures him that it was the Russians who killed him, and not the Avankil (Tungus). Another remnant of a ceremonial bear-dance is *ikandzyedzyem* ('we are singing'). The bones of the bear must be placed just as they are in a bag, and hung on a tree. If one bone is lost, the spirit of the bear will hold the hunter responsible for it.

The eagle is also treated with great veneration, and it is expressly forbidden to kill him. For both these animals the Tungus use that adjective which they also use in speaking of heroes, *i.e.* *hooma*.

To all other animals which are not especially venerated the Tungus always behave, as they say, 'carefully,' lest the animal should become extinct. When a slit is made in the ear of the reindeer for purposes of identification, the hair that is cut off must not be thrown away, but must be hung on a tree or put in some safe place. The head and feet of the wild reindeer must not be thrown away; a special platform is sometimes erected for their reception, while the teeth of the wild reindeer are kept as *tygak* (amulets). There is a fox custom which drives the procurers of fox-skins to despair. After the fox has been trapped, his muzzle is cut off and carefully preserved. The skin may then be used, but the meat must be placed safely on a platform.

LITERATURE. — Jakinth Bichurin, *Information concerning Peoples living in Central Asia in Ancient Days*, Petrograd, 1851; M. A. Castrén, *Nordische Reisen und Forschungen*, do. 1849–62, vol. ix. 'Grundzüge einer tungusischen Sprachlehre,' *Ethnologische Vorlesungen*, do. 1857, vol. iv.; M. A. Czaplicka, *Aboriginal Siberia*, Oxford, 1914, *My Siberian Year*, London, 1916; M. A. Czaplicka and H. U. Hall, *Report of the Expedition to the Yenisei* (in the press); J. Deniker, *The Races of Man*[11], London, 1910; G. E. and M. E. Grum-Grzymailo, *A Description of Travels in W. China* (Russ.), Petrograd, 1896–99; C. Hickisch, *Die Tungusen*, do. 1879; F. Hirth, *The Ancient History of China*, Leipzig, 1908; H. H. Howorth, *Hist. of the Mongols*, London, 1876–88; D. L. Jochelson-Brodsky, *The Anthropological Types of the Women of the Extreme North-East of Siberia*, Moscow, 1908; A. H. Keane, *Man, Past and Present* (rewritten by A. Hingston Quiggin and A. C. Haddon), Cambridge, 1920; R. Maak, *A Journey to the Amur in 1855* (Russ.), Petrograd, 1859; I. I. Mainoff, *A Contribution to the Study of the Tungus of the Yakut Territory* (Russ.), Irkutsk, 1898; S. Patkanoff, 'Essay on the Geography and Statistics of the Tungusic Tribes of Siberia,' *Bull. Imp. Russ. Geog. Soc.* [Petrograd, 1906]; L. Schrenk, *Die Völker des Amurlandes*, Petrograd, 1891; J. Talko-Hryncewicz, *Materyaly do Ethnologji i Antropolojii Ludów Azji Środkowej* (Pol.), Cracow, 1910; C. E. Ujfalvy, *Les Aryens au nord et au sud de l'Hindou-Kouch*, Paris, 1896.

M. A. CZAPLICKA.

TUNIS. — See AFRICA, BERBERS AND N. AFRICA.

TUPI-GUARANI.—See BRAZIL.

TURKS.—I. *ETHNOLOGY*.—**1. Origin of the name.**—The terms 'Turk,' 'Turkish,' and 'Turkic' are used in two different senses: to designate either those peoples belonging to the Turkic linguistic family or those peoples from Asia who appear from time to time in military history under leaders of Turkic speech. With the advance of ethnological knowledge, the former use is being abandoned for the wider term 'Turanian,' and the latter practice is falling into disuse. The name 'Turan' is much wider than the term 'Turk' and in any case is not synonymous with it. It must be noted that, while we hear of the Turks under that name in S. Russia even in the 1st cent. A.D., they only established themselves in Turkestan ('Land of the Turks'), the country named after them, in the 4th cent. A.D. Before that the country was known as Iran or Iranistan ('Land of the Iranians'), and stretched farther west into the present Iran. Thus one must be careful not to confuse the archæology of Turkestan relating to the Iranian period with that which can be ascribed to the Turks.

The earliest information about the Turks, to be found in the Chinese annals from 2356 B.C. onwards, alludes to them under the name of Hiung-nung, or slaves of the Hiung, while the name Tu-Kiu, or Turks, becomes prominent in the 6th cent. A.D. only when a prince of the Assena dynasty, Tiumen, rose to power. But we hear of the name Turk in connexion with the Turkish invaders of Europe in the pre-Christian era. Pomponius Mela in the 1st cent. A.D. calls them Turcae and says that they live near the Budini, and Pliny the Elder in the same century uses the name Tyrcae of a people in the neighbourhood of the Don. Though the various Turkic invaders of Eastern and Western Europe were chiefly known by the names of their leaders (Kipchak, Nogai, Seljuk, Osmanli), the name Turk as a generic term for the whole race is that most frequently used up to the present day. The Turks themselves with the exception of some Anatolian Turks call themselves by a dynastic or clan name.

2. Origin of the race.—The Chinese annals refer to the Hiung-nung as their north-western barbarian neighbours, and make a distinction between them and their north-eastern neighbours, the Tung-hung, afterwards the Tungus. The third Central Asiatic race, the Mongols, do not seem to have so long a pedigree, and it is possible that they form a branch of the Tungus or the Turks, or are a combination of both left behind and isolated on the steppes. This may be so, if we assume that the Turks and Tungus are two independent races which entered into the composition of the sub-races of Japan, China, and Tibet. The analysis of the fundamental types of both these races shows striking differences, but in comparison with the North and South Asiatic type they may both be called Mongoloid. Even assuming that the Tungus and Turks, as well as the Mongols, are the closest descendants of the original *homo Asiaticus*, yet, when they first appear in history, the two races differ widely in language, physical type, and culture. If the remains of bronze culture in the Upper Yenisei valley with burial masks, some of which are prominently Aryan in character, can be definitely ascribed to the early Turks, who knows whether their Mongoloid type was not after all an acquired character due to their mixture with the Mongoloids?

So much for the anthropological evidence as to the origin of the Turks. Not less important from the point of view of the folklorist is the origin of the race as explained by tradition. Perhaps the most wide-spread is the legend (found also among the Mongols) of a she-wolf, or white she-wolf, who found and reared an abandoned boy, subsequently the founder of the Turkish race. This she-wolf, Ak-biuri, saved the little boy from the bad god Erlik and brought him to Altun-dagh ('Golden Mountains') to an Altun-kii ('Golden Cave'). Two days later the boy began to call her mother, and six days later he began to call her father. De Guignes suggests that this is merely a version of the Roman tradition brought back by the Huns after they returned from their invasion of Europe.[1] But as a matter of fact the story might have travelled in the opposite direction, or the origin might have been independent, for the Chinese describe the shields of the Turks as having representations of a wolf before the approximate date of the Roman story. Then almost as widely spread is the legend of their first ancestor being the eldest son of Japheth, son of Noah. It is hard to ascertain whether the legend relating to still another ancestor, the son of the virgin-widow, Alanqua, has also a Biblical background.

3. **Cradle of the race.** — There are several hypotheses as to the geographical position of the original home of the Turks. H. H. Howorth seeks it in the southern parts of the Altai (Altun-dagh). Richthofen considers the region of the Amur, Lena, and Selenga their problematic original home. Parker suggests not the Altai Golden Mountains but some other mountains of the same name in the present Chinese province of Kin-Shan.

Recent archæological discoveries in the Altai-Sayan region as well as study of the aborigines of the forest regions of these mountains support Howorth's theory.[2] While it is still difficult to know with certainty to whom to attribute the bronze remains of the Minusinsk, called by the Russians by the vague name of 'Chud' remains (*Chujoi*, 'stranger'), there is no reason not to suppose that the country was inhabited always by the Turks, who were influenced in their bronze culture by some Iranian people from Central Asia, though also by the Chinese. The investigation of the bronze culture in the region of Kuban (N. Caucasus) will probably throw light on this question, if the Kuban culture is found to be more similar to the Minusinsk than to the other bronze stations in E. Russia—*e.g.*, the Ural (Perm). However, the fact that the customs and implements of the pre-bronze era (neolithic and late palæolithic) persist through the bronze period (probably 8th–3rd cent. B.C.) and the iron age and to some extent even till to-day points to the conclusion that the bulk of the population there remained the same, *i.e.* Turkish. The implements referred to are those used in the preparation of food and for agriculture.

The popular explanation that the bronze culture of Minusinsk is the work of a peaceful agricultural people of a higher type than the Turks, afterwards destroyed by the invasion of iron culture nomad people, who were, as no one now doubts, Turks, is not based on historical facts. We do not hear of the destruction of an empire at the stage of bronze culture in the Chinese annals—a fact worth noting—though mention of less significant movements at the beginning of the iron age from Central Asia towards the north-west is fairly frequent. If we assume that the pre-bronze and bronze age inhabitants of the Altai were of Turkic stock and in danger of invasion from the south-east or west, there is no reason why they themselves should not develop warlike industries which the so-called iron age remains represent. The bronze industry survives for some time during the next period, but the arrowheads, spears, daggers, and stirrups are produced in greater quantities than non-military bronze objects. The example of the Great War has shown us how easy it is to divert industrial power from one channel to another.

Most of the graves of the iron age in the Altai-Sayan district are communal, called by the Turks *chaa-tas* (the Russians call them *kurgans*), and are probably war graves. The inscriptions to be found on some of the burial stones all date from the iron age.[1] Those on the Southern Yenisei are earlier (about the 6th and 7th cent. A.D.) than those south of Lake Baikal along the Orkhon. The language of these inscriptions is one of the old Turkish dialects, the Uigur, belonging to a people politically very prominent to whom are attributed the remnants of Karakorum as their capital. Thus the earliest cultural remains of the Turkish race are nearer to Western than Eastern Asia, and the Turks at this early stage of their history, even if we take only the iron age, were living on a higher level of civilization compared with their near neighbours than they do now. It would seem that their subsequent mixture with invaders coming from the East has lowered their standard of culture, though in their subsequent history they several times developed local civilizations, notably under the Timurids in Turkestan and under the Ottomans in Byzantium.

But of course the attribution of cultural remains of the bronze and iron ages to the Turks does not carry them very far back, considering the antiquity of Chinese history. The first mention of the Turks here appears in 2356 B.C., while the bronze remnants of Minusinsk may be dated about 700–300 B.C. This was the time when unknown bronze flourished in the Volga-Kama-Ural district and in Scandinavia around the Baltic, when Greek settlers round the Black Sea and in Scythia were producing wonderful local art, when in Persia Darius and Xerxes were encouraging the development of local civilization which was in turn overturned by Alexander, who set up Hellenistic polities in its place. But Minusinsk was in neither of these circles, and its resemblance to Scythian culture is counterbalanced by its similarity to the Chinese. Then the second culture, that of the iron age, coincides with the rule of the Arabs over the Sasanid Persians and with the empire of the Khazars on the Lower Volga.

The attribution of both bronze and iron periods on the Yenisei to the Turkish race does not necessarily decide the question of the place whence

[1] J. de Guignes, *Hist. générale des Huns*, 4 vols. in 5, London, 1756–58, vol. i. pt. ii. bk. i.

[2] A. V. Adrianoff, *Travels to the Altai and beyond the Sayan Mountains in 1881*, Omsk, 1888, *Sketches of the Minusinsk Country*, Tomsk, 1904; J. R. Aspelin, 'Sur l'âge de bronze altai-ouralien,' *Compte-rendu Congrès international d'Archéologie à Stockholm*, 1874, i. 562; N. N. Kosmin, 'Chern,' *Sibirskiya Zapiski*, no. 3 [1916], pp. 95–112, 'Tuba,' *ib.* no. 4 [1918], pp. 23–49; O. Montelius, 'Orienten och Europa,' *Antiq. Tidskrift*, xiii., Stockholm, 1864; A. M. Tallgrèn, *Collection Zaoussailov au Musée historique de Finlande*, i. Helsingfors, 1916; *Collection Tovostine des antiquités préhistoriques de Minusinsk conservées chez le Dr. Karl Hedman à Vasa, Chapitres d'Archéologie sibirienne, Soc. Finlandaise d'Archéologie*, Helsingfors, 1917.

[1] P. M. Melioranski, 'Decipherment of the old Turkic Inscription on a Stone found in the Aittam-Oi in the Village of Kenkolsk in the Aulieata District,' *Mem. E. Sect. I.R.Arch.S.*, 1899, xi. 1–4, pp. 271–273; O. Donner, 'Sur l'origine de l'alphabet turc du Nord de l'Asie,' *Journ. Soc. fin.-ougr.* xiv. [1896] 1; V. Thomsen, 'Inscriptions de l'Orkhon déchiffrées,' i. 1894, *Mém. Soc. fin.-ougr.*, 1894, v. 54, 1896, i. 224.

they sprang. All we know now of the inhabitants of the Iish (Russ. Chern) or Black Forest of the Altai points to this, however, that their present character and customs are results of their environment and are similar to the customs and character of the earliest inhabitants of those regions. The original Turks were not steppe nomads living by warfare and constantly changing their camping places, but cattle-breeders and agriculturists devoted to their fields and forests and knowing the system of slave labour, while so advanced politically as to form confederations. Perhaps the most important proof of the origin of the Turks in the Altai region is the resemblance of the art found in the old picture writings in the region to the art of the most primitive and typical Turks of the present day, whether in the form of cattle brands or rock drawings. Further, the burial customs of these people seem to have been unchanged by time and are now practised as in the place of their origin. There must have been in all ages Turkic tribes living on the outskirts of the empires whose mode of life was more nomadic and who consequently mixed to a greater extent with other nomads. Those tribes were, however, not the true Turks as described in the Orkhon inscriptions, but Kazaks, who correspond to the Russian Cossacks, or frontier half-military guards.

The hypothesis of the Altaian origin of the Turks is in opposition to the theory launched some 50 years ago by Castrén and since uncritically accepted by some Finnish and Russian ethnologists (Otto Donner, Klementz), that the Samoyed originated in the Altai and Sayan Mountains and migrated from there to the north. If, further, the Samoyed are identified with the Finns, as they are by some people, the Finns, who in modern times developed the high culture of the Scandinavians, become the ancestors of the bronze age people of Minusinsk.

The linguistic authority of Castrén seemed sufficient to make people accept his theory without investigation, but his whole hypothesis was based on the supposition of the historian Fischer in the 18th cent. that the inhospitable region of the Arctic could not be the home of the Samoyed on account of its frigid character and poverty. The only support was of a linguistic character, that at the time of Castrén some Tatar clans in S. Siberia (the Kamashints) could speak Samoyed. Moreover, this theory holds that many other Tatars, of Uriankhai and Minusinsk, like the Koibal, Soyon, Beltir, and Karagass, are Turkicized Samoyed, one branch of which was pushed by the advance of the Turks towards the north. Such is Castrén's theory.

That the Samoyed might have originated further south than they are now is possible, but they must have always been fairly far north. All their present culture, which can be called 'reindeer' culture, shows that they are under the influence of a period of Arctic environment too long to trace their origin. The few linguistic observations of the Samoyed tongue in S. Siberia only prove that some of the clans of the Samoyed migrated from the north further south. Neither in physical type nor in customs do either of these doubtful Samoyed resemble the real Samoyed. While an uninterrupted chain of ethnological and, above all, archæological evidence, as well as Chinese and Arab historical mentions, ties the Turks to the Black Forest of the Altai mountains, from which they spread at an early date over the Sayan and Orkhon, no archæological remains can be ascribed to the Samoyed, and no ethnological evidence supports the theory of Castrén.

The relationship between the Samoyed and Finnic races is still an open question, but in any case historical and archæological evidence of early Finnish culture does not go further east than the Ural (Perm). By dismissing, therefore, the Samoyed-Altaian theory, one dismisses also the claim of the Finns to an Altai-Sayan cradle. Possibly further archæological discoveries may reveal still earlier Turkic inscriptions than those of the Yenisei, but they can only be found more to the south, since the inscriptions to the east of the Yenisei, *i.e.* the Orkhon, are one or more hundred years later. The relation between the Minusinsk bronze antiquities and the archæological remains of the steppes of the Black Sea attributed to the Scythians has been recently studied carefully, and a close resemblance was found.[1] Minusinsk was taken in this respect as a centre from which this culture spread towards the Black Sea.

[1] E. H. Minns, *Scythians and Greeks*, Cambridge, 1913, p. 261.

This is important as throwing light on the puzzle of the origin of the Scythians, though no one can doubt now the kinship, if not identity, of the Eastern Scythians and the Turks. If the cradle of the Turks is to be sought in the forest of the Altai with its environment which encourages a sedentary and agricultural mode of life—and the steppes and valleys between the Altai and Baikal are full of evidences of the sedentary culture of this people—it is still true that in comparison with the old Chinese, the Turks, especially their eastern branches, must be considered barbarians. Besides, there never has been a uniform culture spread over the various Turkic nations, nor did they ever live in a mass undivided by foreign races. This is why it is difficult to be certain whether some of the clans mentioned first by the Chinese and then by the Arab writers can be considered Turks. It is much easier to make this distinction among the contemporary Turks, even though they appear also under various names of Tatar, Tuba, or Osmanli.

A few words must be said about the name 'Tatar.' R. G. Latham[1] points out that the less we use the term Tatar or Tartar, the sounder will be our ethnology. He also calls attention to the mistake of coupling the Manchu and their dynasty with the Tatars. One of the earliest mentions of the word 'Tatars' is found in the old Turkish inscriptions of the Orkhon ascribed to Bilge-Khan.[2] About this time (8th cent.) the 'Otuz-Tatar' ('Thirty Tatar') lived to the east and south-east of Baikal and were dependent on the Turkish confederacy. Chinese history does not mention them till the 9th century. According to N. A. Aristoff,[3] the Otuz-Tatars were originally Turks, while the Mongolian scholar Bichurin is inclined to call them Mongols. In the same inscription on the Orkhon is a mention of the 'Tokuz-Tatars' ('Nine Tatars').

The term 'Tatar' is closely connected with the term 'Tatan.'[4] The people living in the present Khalka from the 9th cent. were called Tatan. They were divided into many *aimán*, or unions of clans. The strongest of these were the Mongol, Taigut, Kere, and Tatar.[5] These were divided into clans, but all of them used the tribal name of Tatan. The Mongols successfully fought the Niuchi (Tungus) in the middle of the 12th cent., and towards the end of this century the Mongol ruler, Temujin, was elected head of all the Tatans and a great part of China under the name of Jenghiz Khan. The house of the Mongol-Tatan reigned from 1206 to 1638. The Mongol *aimán* of the Tatan confederacy subdued the Tatar *aimán* before they started on their European conquest, but it is doubtful whether all the Tatan accepted the name of this one *aimán*. On the contrary, the name Mongol came into greater prominence than that of Tatan or Tatar through Jenghiz Khan. It is probable, however, that some of the Jenghiz Khan hordes were known to their neighbours as Tatan. When Carpini came as an envoy from the pope to the Khan Kuyuk, he may have made a mistake between Tatan and Tatar, so in the 13th cent. all the geographers named the land between the Caspian and the Chinese Seas Great Tartary. It is perhaps because the Chinese historians often called Tatan 'Tata' (a mistake now corrected by them) that many Asiatic scholars, such as H. J.

[1] *Descriptive Ethnology*, 2 vols., London, 1859, i. 265.
[2] P. M. Melioranski, 'On the Orkhon and Yenisei Monuments with Inscriptions,' *Journ. Min. Educ.*, St. Petersburg, 1898, p. 882.
[3] 'Notes on the Ethnic Composition of the Turkic Tribes and Nations' (Russ.), *Liv. An. Times*, 1896, iii.–iv. p. 295.
[4] J. Bichurin, *Notes on Mongolia* (Russ.), St. Petersburg, 1828.
[5] *Ib.* i. 129, 221–227.

von Klaproth,[1] confuse the two names Tatan and Tatar.

The first people to call all Mongols Tatars were probably the Russians, and they gave this name also to the tribes who had settled along the Volga, and who seem not even to have been Tatan but various Turks brought within the Mongol-Tatar army, who after the death of Jenghiz Khan were pleased to regain their independence. At the present day Tatars, whether on the Volga, in the Crimea, the Caucasus, or Siberia, represent a fairly pure strain of Turks. Among the problematic Turks may be placed the Scythians, Parthians (though their descendants, the Turkomans, are among the most representative Turks now), Yue-chi (whose descendants, the Rajputs, are certainly a non-Turkic people), and Ye-tha, or Ephthalites, called also White Huns (these seem to have been different in type and habits from the Huns who migrated westward). All these peoples are variously ascribed to the Tungus or Turks; some others, as the original Bulgars and Avars, are sometimes counted as Turks, sometimes as Finns; and the Nogai, Kipchak, and Usbeg are regarded as either Mongols or Turks. The Dungans are placed between the Chinese and Turks, and the Horsak (Sokra and Horpsa) are the Buddhist Turks of Tibet. Finally, the Usuni (Wusun) are attributed by some to the Turks and by some to 'Aryans' of Central Asia. Some other peoples are without doubt Turks, as the Hiung-nu, Khakas, Kirgis, Uigur, Tukiu (Assena), Seljuk, Khazar, etc.

II. *DIVISION OF THE MODERN TURKS.*—The distribution of the Turks is so wide and their geographical environment so varied that it is difficult to speak of the Turkish type from an ethnological standpoint. Politically, too, what is called Turkish is often only Muhammadan and quite different in nationality. We find that in the pre-war Turkish empire of Asia Minor, N. Africa, and S.E. Europe there were far fewer Turks in an ethnological sense than there were in the pre-war Russian empire.

i. THE SIBERIAN TURKS.—**1. Yakut.**—See art. YAKUT.

2. Siberian 'Tatars.'—According to religion, the Siberian Tatars can be divided into two groups: Muhammadans and shamanists. The Muhammadans are: (1) the Tobolsk Tatars, in the Tobolsk government, (2) the Barabine (Baraba) Tatars, in the Kainsk district, (3) the Chulim Tatars, in Mariinsk district, (4) the Tomsk-Kuznietsk Tatars, in the Kuznietsk and Barnaulsk districts. The shamanists are: (5) the 'Chern,' or Black Forest Tatars, in the Biisk district, (6) Teleut and Telengit, in Biisk and Kuznietsk districts, (7) Kumandints, in Kuznietsk and Biisk districts, (8) Shorts and Lebedints, in Kuznietsk district, (9) Kyzyl and Kamashints, in Achinsk district, (10) Koibal, Sagai, and Kachints, in Minusinsk district, (11) Karagass, in the forest of Nijne-Udinsk district. The total number of Siberian Tatars in 1911 was about 250,000.

The Tatars of the Tomsk government speak their native Turkic language, and only 30 per cent of them know Russian as well. In the Yeniseisk government only 12 per cent know Russian. The Teleut of the Kuznietsk district are perhaps the most Russified, while the Telengit along the Bia and the Katun are all baptized, and partly Russified, partly Mongolized. The following natives seem to be mixed with the Yenisei-Ostiak and Samoyed, or, as some think, are Tatarized Samoyed: the Kumandints, Shorts, Lebedints, Kyzyl, Kamashints, Koibal, Kachints, and Karagass. The most genuine Turks are those 'Tatars' who inhabit the region of the Altai forests—the 'Chern' Tatars.

ii. CENTRAL ASIATIC TURKS.—The Central Asiatic Turks, all of whom are Muhammadans, can be divided according to their mode of life into (*a*) steppe nomads, and (*b*) village- or town-dwellers. The steppe nomads are: (1) the Kirgis or Kazak, (2) the Kara-Kirgis, (3) the Kara-Kalpak, (4) part of the Turkomans, (5) part of the Usbegs. The village- and town-dwellers are: (6) Sarts, (7) Taranchi, (8) most of the Usbegs (with the Kipchak), (9) most of the Turkomans.

1. Kirgis-Kazak and Kara-Kirgis. — The Kirgis-Kazak live in the northern and eastern part of the Aral-Caspian basin, and in the Orenburg steppes, so they are lowlanders. The Kara-Kirgis live on the slopes of Pamir, Altai, and Tian-Shan. They are mountaineers. There are, however, other Kirgis, to whom this name may be applied historically and ethnologically, who lived from the 6th cent. A.D. in the Yenisei valley and migrated to Semirechie, forced forward by the advances of the Russians in the 18th century. They are often identified with the 'Khakas' (Castrén, Klementz, Kasmin, Radloff), and the inscriptions found in the valley of S. Yenisei are attributed to them. The Kirgis-Kazak call themselves Kazak, *kaz* meaning 'goose,' *zag* meaning 'crow,' *i.e.* the steppe birds, the free birds of the steppe. The Russians call them Kirgis-Kazak to distinguish them from their own Cossacks (Kazak). The Kirgis-Kazak derive themselves from the Usbeg, and they derive the Kara-Kirgis from dogs. But the Kara-Kirgis call themselves brothers of the Kirgis-Kazak, and in fact are probably one of their branches. Out of 4·7 millions of these Kazak only about 400,000 are Kara-Kirgis.

The Kirgis-Kazak were divided into three groups, called *orda*—the southern, or great *orda*, 'Ulu-dschus,' the little *orda*, 'Kishi-dschus,' to the west, towards European Russia, and the middle *orda*, 'Orta-dschus,' in the typical steppe country. But, when they began to mix with one another and to increase in numbers, they divided into clans, and each clan had its own *tamga*, or clan symbol, with which the horses and dromedaries were marked. The heads of the clans were called Sultans, while the nobility was called Tiuri or Ak-suek, 'White Bones.' They trace their ancestry from Jenghiz Khan, notwithstanding that the latter was a Mongol. All the other people were called Kara-Suek, 'Black Bones.' Lately, however, marriage prohibitions between these castes have been withdrawn, and the social division is based on material considerations.

The felt hut of the Kirgis is called *yurta*, and a group of *yurta* is called *aul*. Herds of sheep, horses, and dromedaries are their chief form of property. In sharp contrast to their lightly-built houses are their graves, especially among the Turkestan and Semirechie Kirgis. They look like small towers and are made of bricks and clay. The subjugation of the Kirgis by the Russians began in 1734 and took more than 90 years—even during the Great War some groups of Kirgis considered themselves independent.

2. Kara-Kalpak.—The Kara-Kalpak, or 'Black Caps,' are akin to the Kirgis-Kazak, and live in Turkestan, especially in the Syr-Daria district, where they form half of the population. They number about 134,000 (1911). They seem to be taller than the other Kirgis, and lead half-sedentary lives, part of them being agriculturists. Some 20,000 of them live in Khiva.

3. Sarts.—The Sarts (1,847,000 in 1911) were originally a mixture of the original Iranian inhabitants, the Tajik, with their Turanian conquerors,

[1] *Mémoires relatifs à l'Asie sur les Tatares*, 3 vols., London, 1826-28.

the Usbeg. They busy themselves with commerce, but occasionally take to agriculture and cotton-plant growing, in which they are not as successful as the Tajiks, though they know the use of the *arika*, irrigation canals. All the Sarts speak Turkish, and are Muhammadans (Sunnite); they have many followers of the Ṣūfi order. In physical type they approach nearer to the Iranians.

4. Taranchi.—The Taranchi are very like the Sarts. They also live in winter in villages, *kishlak*, and their summer houses are called *sakla*. They migrated to Russian Turkestan from Kulja at the same time as the Dungan after Kulja passed to China. They number about 83,000 (1911) and live in the Semirechie country, in the Ili basin, and partly in the Transcaspian country. They are agriculturists, especially busying themselves with vegetable gardens, but prefer commerce. They are Muhammadans, but their women do not cover their faces as the Sart women do.

Besides the Taranchi there are various Turkish tribes on the Eastern slopes of the Tian-Shan, in Kashgar, Yarkand, and Khotan, who are the supposed descendants of the Uigur. Their language is sometimes called Turki, and is possibly one of the oldest types of Turkish. They form the most easterly branch of the Central Asiatic Turks, and probably remained behind when the first westward movements began. They ruled in Kashgaria from the 10th to the 12th century. Though in time they became Muhammadans, early Nestorian teaching has left its traces; they still use the Syriac alphabet and possess a book of the 11th cent. in this writing, called *Kudatku Billik*. They are a 'free self-governing people.' Some of them have been to Mecca (800 miles to the Siberian Railway, then through Odessa to Jedda). They consider Stamboul their religious and political capital. The Turks and generally the Muhammadans in Asia are more prosperous than the Buddhists, though the Buddhists are protected by the Chinese Government.

The Kirei of N.W. Mongolia are supposed to have come from the source of the Amur. In the 11th and 12th centuries the Kirei were an important power, and were probably of Nestorian creed. Whether the mythical Prester John (a Christian priest who reigned in some Christian Asiatic kingdom) was their king it is difficult to say. They are not heard of for a long period after the time of Jenghiz Khan. They now differ from the Buddhist Mongols in being Muhammadans. They live on the banks of the Upper or Black Irtish and the greater part of the Western Altai pastures and the Jungaria plains as far as Lake Zaisan. They train hawks, falcons, and golden eagles for hunting such game as gazelles, foxes, and even wolves. Like the Kazak, they claim Jenghiz Khan (a Mongol) as their ancestor.

5. Usbeg.—The Usbeg (about 600,000 in 1911; including Kipchak, about 660,000) form the majority of the inhabitants of the Samarkand district and parts of Ferghana and Syr-Daria districts. In Bokhara and Khiva they are the ruling people, like the Osmanli in Turkey. Their name is probably derived from Usbeg Khan of the Golden Horde (1312–40); in the 16th cent. they founded in Turkestan the Khanates of Khiva and Bokhara. They are a mixture of three elements: Turks, Iranians, and Mongols. The Turkish element is probably predominant, though in the case of the Usbeg of Khiva it is the Iranian type that predominates. Since the Usbeg exchanged their nomad life for a sedentary one, their customary law, *adat*, has lost ground, and is being replaced by written law, *sharī-at*. Father-right is very strong, but the position of women is on the whole better than among the Sarts and Tajiks. Though the Usbeg now imitate the Sarts in making huts covered with clay, and live in small villages encircled by walls like fortresses, here and there the old felt *yurta* is still found.

6. Turkomans of Transcaspia.—The Turkomans live to the number of about 600,000 in the Transcaspian territory and also partly in Persia, Khiva, and Bokhara. Until the Russian occupation of Merv they were nomad horse-breeders. Although some of them were subject to Persia, their boast has been that 'not one Persian could cross their frontier without a string round his neck.' In 1881 the Russians destroyed their power by capturing their principal fortress, Geok-Tepe, and their slave trade has been suppressed. They now live in clay or raw brick houses, and, in some places, in Russian wooden houses. They are Muhammadans, but follow the unwritten customary law. The clan division is still strong, and all migrations are made in clan groups. Endogamy is enforced. As the male population is abundant, the *kalym* for the wife is very high, and in some places the unmarried men form 27 per cent of the population. On the whole they seem to be a democratic people.

The chief clans of the Turkomans are: (*a*) the Chaudors (Chaudur), in the north-west part of Ust-Urt and the Kara-boghar Gulf; near (*b*) the Yomuts or Yamuds, extending from Khiva across the Ust-Urt and along the shore of the Caspian to Persia; (*c*) the Goklans or Goklens, settled in the Persian province of Astarabad; they are said to be the most civilized and friendly of all the Turkomans; (*d*) the Tekkes (Taka), who were the most important tribe when the Russians conquered Transcaspia; they are first heard of in the peninsula of Mangishlak, but were driven out by the Kalmuks in 1718 and subsequently occupied the Akhal and Merv oases; the Russians inflicted a crushing defeat on them at Geok-Tepe in 1881; (*e*) the Sakars inhabit the left bank of the Oxus near Charjui; (*f*) the Sarik (Saruk) are found in the neighbourhood of Panjdeh and Yulatan; (*g*) the Salor (Salore), an old and important tribe, suffered much in the course of fights with the Tekkes, and in 1857 migrated to Zarabad in Persian territory near the Hari-rud; (*h*) the Ersazis (Ersars) are now found chiefly near Khoja Salih; they were once a very important tribe on the upper Oxus.

The Central Asiatic territories, which belong to Russia, have a total population of from five to six millions, of which at least from four to five millions are Turks. Eastern or Chinese Turkestan has a population of about two millions, excluding Kulja and Jungaria. Jungaria has about 600,000 and Kulja 150,000, the overwhelming majority in all these three provinces being Turks. Besides the Turks of the north we find some Mongols, and in the east and south Tibetans.

iii. THE VOLGA 'TATARS.'—The Volga Tatars are those Turks who have been settled on the Lower Volga since the Hunnic invasions, and, since their hold has been strengthened by frequent invasions, they are partly mixed with the Mongols, the Finns, and, since the 13th cent., the Russians. After the break up of Jenghiz Khan's empire they belonged to the great *orda* of Kipchak (Kipchak being mainly a political and not a racial term). After the fall of the Kipchak the Khanates of Kazan and Astrakhan continued to exist. The Khanate of Kazan was conquered by Russia in 1552, the Khanate of Astrakhan in 1557.

1. Kazan Tatars.—The Kazan Tatars number more than a million, and their centre is in the government of Kazan, though they extend on both banks of the Volga as far as the government of Saratov.

2. Astrakhan Tatars.—The Astrakhan Tatars, to the number of some 50,000, live at the mouth of the Volga. Some of the Volga Tatars, such as the Cheremiss, Chuvash, and other middle Volga tribes, and the Bashkir, are supposed to be of Finno-Ugrian origin, but they are now Turks in speech and Muhammadans in creed and social life. Muhammadanism was introduced among the Volga Turks in the 10th century.

3. The Bashkir.—The government of Orenburg

is a great district for the Mordvins and the Bashkir. The latter are also found in Ufa, Perm, Samara, and Vyatka governments. Latham[1] says that the Bashkir are as entirely Turks in language and features as are the Kirgis. They are shepherds, herdsmen, but above all bee-masters. After the battle of 1552, when the power of the Tatars of the Volga was broken, the Bashkir submitted themselves to Russia, against whom they have not ceased to rebel. Their number is about 392,000.

4. Teptyar.—A typical mixture of races, something like that of the Chulim Tatars of Siberia, where it is difficult to define which racial element predominates, are the Teptyar. When the Khanate of Kazan fell, a mixed population of Turks, Cheremiss, Votiak, Chuvash, and Mordvins fled to the east of Ural; out of these has arisen a population which the other Turkish tribes call Teptyar; they are partly shamanist, partly Muhammadan.

iv. THE PONTUS OR CRIMEAN AND NOGAI TATARS.—The Khanate of the Crimea, originally Nogai (a political division of Tatars similar to the Kipchak who came there in the 13th cent.), was by the middle of the 16th cent. more or less Osmanli politically. In 1778 they became independent, but in 1784 became subject to Russia. They are known as excellent agriculturists and growers of grapes and tobacco.

The hill tribes of the Crimea who migrated there before the Nogai in the 11th or 12th cent. from Asia Minor, and are probably a branch of the Seljuk, are shepherds. The culture of the Crimean Tatars is more like that of Kazan and Astrakhan Tatars than like that of the Osmanli. Their total number is about 300,000. The same Nogai Tatars are to be found in Lithuania and Rumania to the number of 5000. They are now mostly Christian, and mixed with the local population.

Another branch of the Nogai occupied the country between the Tobol and the Yaik rivers at the beginning of the 17th century. They were transplanted by Peter the Great to the banks of the Kuma and Kuban, but a small group remained behind at the mouth of the Volga and are called Kundur Tatars.

The Nogai are very Mongol in physiognomy. Some people attribute to them the tumuli of the Orenburg government.

v. WESTERN TURKS.—**1. Turks of the Caucasus.**—The Turks of the Caucasus—properly speaking, the Azarbaijan Tatars—are the inhabitants of the province of which Tabriz is the capital. They number about two millions. They seem to be Turks speaking a Yagatai dialect, who invaded Persia during the Seljuk period (11th cent.). They are also called Iliyet, *i.e.* tribes or clans. Each clan has its own *ilkhani*, appointed by the Shah.

Some of these clans are: (*a*) the Kajara, near Astrabad; the present dynasty of Persian Shahs comes from this tribe; (*b*) the Ayshars of Azarbaijan province (a group of these immigrated to Anatolia and live now in Anti-Tawins); (*c*) the Shekakis; (*d*) the Karakoyunlu; (*e*) the Karagazli; (*f*) the Bahalu; (*g*) the Inamlu; (*h*) the Kashkai, who probably arrived at Herat before the Persians.

Azarbaijan Tatars are mixed with the Persians; other Turks of the Caucasus, living in the mountains along the upper parts of the rivers Cheghem, Baksan, and Kuban, are mixed with the natives of the Caucasus and are physically of local type.

2. Turks of Anatolia.—(*a*) *Osmanli and Seljuk.*—The term Osmanli or Ottoman, used in a strict sense, means 'descendant of Osman,' a chief who gathered round him a nation at the end of the 13th and beginning of the 14th century. Recent researches have proved[2] that the Osmanli Turks (who until the revival of nationalism in Eastern Europe never called themselves Turks, but always Osmanli) are a tribe of Turks who lived in Persia for a considerable time before they moved to Asia Minor. It was probably as refugees before the advance of the army of Jenghiz Khan that they appeared in the 13th cent. and with the permission of the Seljuks of Konia settled on the Asiatic remnants of the Byzantine empire. As the Osmanli have no written history before the capture of Constantinople, all that we know about their early history is founded on tradition. Their clan is supposed to be descended from Khorasan, but we know more about Ertogul, who was the father of Osman. Osman owned only the small territory of Sugur, and it is not certain (Gibbons) that he and his people were Muhammadans, like the Seljuks, until he married into a Muhammadan family. It was the political unrest in E. Europe that helped the descendants of Osman to conquer all the Balkan Peninsula and Byzantium. The invasion of Asia Minor by Timur at the beginning of the 15th cent. stopped but for a very short time the successes of the Osmanli in Europe. If we consider that the Osmanli were originally only a small clan, and that the Seljuk and other Turks looked down upon them and did not join with them, we must conclude that the bulk of the Osmanli nation was recruited from some race other than the Turkish. Recently the name Osmanli became the term applied to all the subjects of the pre-war Turkish empire.

Many of the Turks of the old Byzantium who belonged to the Osmanli empire were not Osmanli in the strict sense. Thus the supposed remnants of the Seljuks of the 11th cent. are called Koniots. It is interesting to note that Byzantine authors mention a Turkish colony which settled in Macedonia on the river Vardar in the 9th century.

(*b*) *Turkomans.*—The Turkomans of Anatolia are spread all over Anatolia, but are specially numerous in the central part and in E. Taurus. They are more Mongolian in type than the Osmanli or Seljuk. They are nomads, but not to the same extent as the Yuruks. Their summer residences (*yaila*) are close to their winter houses (*kishla*). Some of them are Shī'ahs, others Sunnites. They seem to have been first heard of in Anatolia in the 12th cent. and are mentioned by the historians Nicetas and Anna Comnena as 'Turcomans.'[1] They were opposing both Seljuk and Ottoman rule and probably migrated from C. Asia under their own political régime.

(*c*) *Yuruks.*—The Yuruks live chiefly in the mountains, but also in the plains from Smyrna to the E. Taurus. They are typical nomads.

Old ethnologists sometimes mistook the religious communities of the Muhammadan sects for distinct Turkish nations—*e.g.*, the Kizil-Bash (*q.v.*), or Red Heads, living in the Angora region of Asia Minor, Persia, Afghanistan, and the Caucasus.

III. *RELIGION.*—We shall deal only with the religion of the Turks before they accepted Muhammadanism; it has persisted up till now among some Turks of Central Asia and Siberia. There is evidence (the Buddhist writings in Uigur character) that some of the Central Asiatic Turks were followers of Buddha about the 8th century. Still more has been heard about Christian Nestorian influences. In fact, there is a permanent sign of these in the form of Uigur written characters modelled probably on the Soghdian. The Arabs captured Samarkand in 706, but Muhammadanism in Central Asia was introduced later, and to some extent it is still spreading. The original religion of the Turks is a shamanism of

[1] *Ethnology*, i. 378.

[2] H. A. Gibbons, *The Foundation of the Ottoman Empire*, London, 1916.

[1] W. M. Ramsay, *The Intermixture of Races in Asia Minor*, London, 1917.

the Southern type, *i.e.* with a well-marked dualism. Their shamanistic ceremonies and mythology are more highly developed than those among any other shamanistic people. It is this religion that can be called genuinely Turkish.

1. Gods and spirits.—The highest good god is Yulgen, while the symbol of evil is Erlik, who lives in the darkness. Another higher being is Kudai, who is a sort of medium between men and the highest beings. The spirit owner of the hearth is called Bel, and was so called by the Turks who were responsible for the old Yenisei inscriptions; several names of the gods appear in them. Then there are seventeen high rulers ruling over various parts of the Turkish lands. The Altai ruler is called Altai-Khan, and lives in the source of the river Katun. Yulgen himself is so good-natured that, when he wants to punish men for failing to give him sacrifice, he asks Erlik to do it. Yulgen is very often identified with the idea of the sky, Tengri, or with light, Yaryk. The sky is generally the home of all good spirits. Ara-neme or Tengri Yulgen lives in the seventh sky. He has a mother, three sons, and twelve daughters. His eldest son is the god of thunder and rain, and his third son, Timur-Khan, is the god of war. One of his peculiarities is that an arrow passed through his throat and since then he stutters. Kun, the sun, is of female sex, while the moon, Ai-ada, is a husband of the sun. All the mountains, forests, lakes, and rivers have their spirit owners, *eelu,* whose functions are not quite clear. They seem rather benevolent if propitiated. The same cannot be said about the spirit assistants of Erlik, called *kara-neme,* who, even if propitiated, may be found harmful. They are known also under the names of *kuremes, asa, rozyr.* Images of gods and spirits are made of various materials and are called *tyns* or *kurmes.*

The chief office of the shaman is to use his sacred drum (*tiungiur*) and keep off by its sound the malevolent spirits. The shamans themselves are in some tribes of two types, some to ward off the bad powers (black shamans) and some to propitiate the good powers (white shamans, who are very often not professional but merely heads of the families).

The goddess of birth is held in great regard; her name among the Altai Turks is Umai, among the Siberian Tatars and the Yakut, Ayisit.

2. The soul.—The Turks of the Altaian Black Mountains (Chern) consider the soul of a man to be composed of several parts or of several independent souls. Each of these performs a special function—*e.g.*, the *tyn,* from *tynip,* 'I breathe.' One can hear the *tyn's* sound when it leaves the body. *Tyn* and another soul, the *suzy,* are man's vitality. The *suzy* (from *su,* 'water,' and *uzak,* 'long,' *i.e.* 'long-lived') can leave the body for a while, but, if it is absent too long, the *tyn* perishes. The *kut* is another kind of vitality (*kutup,* 'I vanish'). Its absence causes disease. The *tula* is a soul implying wisdom which differentiates man from animals, who do not possess it. The *sur* is a man's shadow (*surmet,* 'picture'). After a man's death the *sur* continues to dwell in the house for about forty days, but it keeps its independent existence even when it goes to another place; this soul, and one called the *sune* (*su nep,* 'I advise'), seem to survive man and are ultimately reincarnated.[1]

3. Ceremonies.—Sacrifice to the sky is one of the most persistent ceremonies found among the old and modern Turks. It is called *tigir* (*tayi* among the Minusinsk Turks) and is performed every third summer. No women are allowed to assist at the ceremony, which is held on the top of a mountain in a sacred birch spinney. The old fire (*ulug ot*) is made, and after many incantations a new fire is lighted from the old one. It is protected by the shamans lest it should go out, which would mean a catastrophe for the tribe. A he-goat or a ram is sacrificed, but no blood must be shed and no cry heard from the sacrificial animal.

During the sacrifice to Yulgen among the Altaians similiar precautions are taken, and the whole fore-quarters of a horse are boiled on the 'old fire,' while the hind-quarters are boiled on the new fire. During both ceremonies each head of a family attaches a thread of flax to the sacred birches—that is the path for their wishes to go to the high being—and eagle feathers attached to the threads carry them farther up. The meat boiled on the old fire is then taken round in the direction of the sun and burnt on the same fire. If the smoke goes up in a straight line, the sacrifice is accepted. Then only a feast is held, and the choicest meat is offered to the *kam* shaman, or medicine-man. Among the Kirgiz he is called *baksa* if belonging to the same clan, or *duana* if belonging to another clan. The meat prepared on the new fire is consumed, while remnants of the feast together with the implements used are burnt again on the old fire.

The birch plays a very important rôle in all Turkic ceremonies, and, whether the Turks live in steppes or tundras, birches are either brought from the forest regions or are symbolized by driftwood poles. This as well as veneration of forest animals and birds (and not steppe or tundra animals) seems to point again to the forest origin of the race.

The summer sacrifice to Yulgen (called also Bai-Yulgen) lasts for two or more days, and it is usually on the second day that the shamanistic performances are held. The *kam* is preparing for a journey to the various spirits and gods living in the skies above. He ceremonially feels various spirits represented on his drum. While the company eats the offered meat, the *kam* sings:

> 'Accept this, O Kaira Khan!
> Master of the drum with six horns
> Draw near with the sound of the bell!
> When I cry "Chokk!" make obeisance,
> When I cry "Me!" accept this!'

Then he offers a garment to Yulgen with a song:

> 'Gifts that no horse can carry—
> Alas! Alas! Alas!
> Gifts that no man can lift—
> Alas! Alas! Alas!
> Garments with triple collar
> Turn them thrice before thine eyes,
> Let them be a cover for the steed,
> Alas! Alas! Alas!
> Prince Yulgen, full of gladness,
> Alas! Alas! Alas!'

Then only the shaman summons all the spirit assistants represented on the drum to enter it. He sings and then is silent for a while, and a noise of various birds and animals, whom he is imitating, is heard. Then he begins to beat his drum and to dance round the people, touching them occasionally with his drum or drumstick. The fire is extinct, the shaman's voice becomes weaker, and the sound of the crackling of the birch in the middle of the room indicates that the shaman has fled to the skies. Sometimes the *kam* gives an account of what he sees while he travels, sometimes only after coming back. In the sixth sky he encounters the moon, in the seventh the sun, and from the highest sky he can reach—only a few *kams* reach the ninth sky—he prays to Yulgen:

> 'Lord, to whom three stairways lead,
> Bai-Yulgen, possessor of three flocks,
> The blue vault which has appeared,
> The blue sky that shows itself,
> The blue cloud that whirls along,

[1] V. L. Wierbicki, *The Natives of the Altai,* Tomsk, 1893, pp. 73–78.

The blue sky so hard to reach,
Land a year's journey distant from water,
Father Yulgen thrice exalted,
Shunned by the edge of the moon's axe,
Thou who usest the hoof of the horse;
O Yulgen, thou hast created all men
Who are stirring round about us.
Thou, Yulgen, hast bestowed all cattle upon us,
Let us not fall into sorrow!
Grant that we may withstand the evil one!
Let us not behold Kermes,
Deliver us not into his hands.'[1]

LITERATURE.—See the authorities quoted in footnotes and also: *Asiatic Russia*, ed. Emigration Committee (Russ.), St. Petersburg, 1914; V. V. Barthold, 'New Investigations of the Orkhon Inscriptions' (Russ.), *Journ. Min. Educ.*, do. 1902, pp. 231–325; L. Cahun, *Introd. à l'histoire de l'Asie*, Paris, 1896; M. A. Castrén, *Ethnologische Vorlesungen*, pt. iv. of *Nordische Reisen und Forschungen*, St. Petersburg, 1857; E. Chavannes, 'Documents sur les Tou-Kiue (Turcs) occidentaux,' *Coll. Doc. Orkhon Exp.* vi., do. 1903; M. A. Czaplicka, *The Turks of Central Asia*, Oxford, 1918; V. Giuffrida-Ruggeri, *Prime linee di un 'Antropologia Sistematica Dell' Asia*, Florence, 1919; H. H. Howorth, *Hist. of the Mongols*, London, 1876–88, also Review of M. A. Czaplicka's *Turks of Central Asia*, in *Nature*, London, 13th Nov. 1919; D. A. Klementz, *Antiquities of the Minusinsk Museum* (Russ.), Tomsk, 1886; B. Laufer, Review of M. A. Czaplicka's *Turks of Central Asia*, in *Amer. Anthrop.*, New York, April–June, 1919; R. Martin, *L'Age du bronze au musée de Minoussinsk*, Stockholm, 1893; W. W. Radloff, *Ethnological Survey of the Turkic Tribes of Southern Siberia and Jungaria* (Russ.), Tomsk, 1887, also *Aus Sibirien*, Leipzig, 1884; Rashid al-Din Tadib, *Hist. des Mongols de la Djami el-Tevaikh*, in *E. J. W. Gibb Memorial*, London, 1899; E. D. Ross and F. H. Skrine, *The Heart of Asia*, do. 1899; C. E. Ujfalvy de Mezö-Kövesd, *Les Aryens au nord et au sud de l'Hindou-Kouch*, Paris, 1896; H. Vambéry, *Das Türkenvolk in seinen ethnologischen und ethnographischen Beziehungen*, Leipzig, 1885.

M. A. CZAPLICKA.

TURKESTAN.—See TURKS, MONGOLS.

TUSCARORA INDIANS.—See IROQUOIS.

TUSHES AND OTHER PAGAN TRIBES OF THE CAUCASUS.—The Caucasus presents, as is well known, one of the most remarkable ethnological and linguistic regions in the world.[2] The reason is not far to seek: this narrow neck of land between the Black Sea and the Caspian has formed for centuries a bridge between S.E. Europe and Asia Minor. Armenians and Iranians (Tāts) press up from the south; Slavs and Tatars descend from the north; at least one Iranian people, the Ossetes,[3] has forced its way into the very centre of the region. In the midst of these intruders are the Caucasians proper, guarded by the mountain-system of the Caucasus.

The religious history of the Caucasian peoples is analogous to their political and ethnological records; only linguistically and (for the most part) racially have they maintained their independence. Of their ancient paganism but one fragment of any value has been preserved. Regarding the 'Albani,' who occupied the eastern portion of the country between the Terek and the Kura,[4] Strabo writes thus:

'The gods they worship are the Sun, Juppiter, and the Moon, but the Moon above the rest. She has a temple near Iberia. The priest is a person who, next to the king, receives the highest honours. He has the government of the sacred land, which is extensive and populous, and authority over the sacred attendants, many of whom are divinely inspired and prophesy. Whoever of these persons, being violently possessed, wanders alone in the woods, is seized by the priest, who, having bound him with sacred fetters, maintains him sumptuously during that year. Afterward he is brought forth at the sacrifice performed in honour of the goddess, is anointed with fragrant ointment, and is sacrificed together with other victims. The sacrifice is performed in the following manner. A person, having in his hand a sacred lance with which it is the custom to sacrifice human victims, advances from the crowd and pierces the heart through the side, which he does from experience in this office. When the man has fallen, certain prognostications are indicated by the manner of the fall, and these are publicly declared. The body is carried away to a certain spot, and then they all trample upon it, performing this action as a mode of purification of themselves.

The Albanians pay the greatest respect to old age, which is not confined to their parents, but is extended to old persons in general. It is regarded as impious to show any concern for the dead or to mention their names. Their money is buried with them; hence they live in poverty, having no patrimony.'[1]

He also states,[2] on the somewhat dubious authority of Megasthenes, that the Caucasians practised coition in public and ate the corpses of their dead relatives.

The religious history of the Caucasus is as varied as its other records. Central Caucasia was not converted to Christianity until the 4th cent., and the gospel first penetrated E. Transcaucasia after the defeat of Khusrau (Chosroës) I. by Justinian in the middle of the 6th century. Mazdaism, on the other hand, was introduced into E. Caucasia in the Arsacid period (186–265), and in E. Transcaucasia it had superseded Christianity by the time of the rise of Islām in 646. In consequence many Caucasian peoples possessed a religion which was an undigested mass of primitive paganism, Mazdaism, Christianity, and Muhammadanism. Among certain tribes, notably the closely kindred and geographically contiguous Tushes, Pshavs, and Khevsurs, this state of affairs still obtains, as was also the case among the Dadianic Svanetians until their nominal conversion (or, rather, reconversion) to Christianity in 1865.

So far as present conditions are concerned, the religions professed by the Caucasian peoples are as follows:

(1) Georgians (Karthvelians): Lazes, Ajars, Yengiloi, Kabardinians, and Cherkess, Muhammadan (the two latter relatively recent converts from Christianity); Tushes, Pshavs, Khevsurs, Svanetians, and Abkhases, pagan (or semi-pagan); Mingrelians, Imeretians, Gurians, and Grusinians, Georgian Christians.[3]

(2) Eastern Caucasians (Chechens, Avars, Kazikumyks, Kyrins, etc.), Muhammadans.

(3) Turko-Tatars (Kumyks, Kirgis, Kakmyks, etc.), Muhammadans or Lamaists.

(4) Iranians: Tāts, Muhammadans; Ossetes, semi-Christians or semi-Muhammadans, with numerous pagan survivals.

(5) Armenians, Christians.

The present article is restricted to the pagan or semi-pagan peoples of the Caucasus, especially the Khevsurs, with whose religion that of the Pshavs and Tushes is practically identical.[4] These peoples possess an interest greater than their numbers seem to warrant. Like so many Oriental religious systems, such as Manichæism (*q.v.*) and the religions of the Mandæans, Nusairis, Kizil Bash, Yezidis (*qq.v.*), etc., they present a syncretism analogous to late classical developments or to the Græco-Egyptian system.[5]

I. Tushes, Pshavs, and Khevsurs.—The Tushes, Pshavs, and Khevsurs are three small, contiguous tribes of Karthvelian stock, numbering, in 1912, 6600, 11,000, and 7700 respectively;[6] and their religious systems are so similar that they need not be discussed separately.

(*a*) *Sanctuaries.*—The *khati*, or place of prayer and sacrifice,[7] is synonymous with the community

1 M. A. Czaplicka, *Aboriginal Siberia*, London, 1914, pp. 298–303.

2 The best ethnological maps of this region are by N. von Seidlitz, in *Petermanns Mitteilungen*, xxvi. [1880] Taf. 15; R. von Erckert, *Der Kaukasus und seine Völker*, Leipzig, 1887; *Dorožnaya karta kavkazkago kraya*, Tiflis, 1903; *Ethnografičeskaya karta kavkazkago kraya*, Tiflis, 1909 (cf. the review by A. Dirr, in *Petermanns Mitteilungen*, lvii. [1911] pt. 2, p. 94 f.); and, for the Karthvelian region only, by H. Schuchardt, in *Petermanns Mitteilungen*, xliii. [1897] Taf. 6. For the Tushes, Pshavs, and Khevsurs see also the special map by G. Radde, in *Izvěstiya kavkazkago otděla imp. russ. geograf. obščestva*, xi. [1880]. For an ethnographic map in the 1st cent. B.C., see J. de Morgan, *Mission scientifique au Caucase*, ii. pl. xiv., and for the distribution of the various tribes according to the classical authors, see the map by B. Latyshev, in his *Scythica et Caucasica*, ii.

3 See art. OSSETIC RELIGION.

4 De Morgan, ii. 191–196.

1 XI. iv. 7 f. (=p. 503 C). 2 XV. i. 56 (=p. 710 C).

3 Cf. W. F. Adeney, *The Greek and Eastern Churches*, London, 1908, pp. 344–348.

4 For the Ossetes see art. OSSETIC RELIGION.

5 See artt. ATTIS, CYBELE, GRÆCO-EGYPTIAN RELIGION, etc.

6 A. Dirr, in *Petermanns Mitteilungen*, lviii. [1912] pt. 1, p. 138.

7 The word *khati* properly means 'idol,' 'image'; it is also used to denote an 'angel,' or personification of heaven or nature, possibly as being an 'image' of the Supreme God (cf. Merzbacher, *Aus den Hochregionen des Kaukasus*, ii. 75, 90 f.).

itself; and so completely has *khati* lost its primary meaning of 'image' that prayer is made to it quite as earnestly as to its divinity, the *batoni-khati* ('image-lord'). The *khati* usually stands on a hill, in a grove of trees (planes, oaks, etc.) which are considered holy, which no axe may touch, and beneath which no wild animal may be killed. The sanctuary always consists of more than one building, surrounded by a rude stone wall. A small chapel, artlessly constructed of irregular slabs, contains the 'image,' the *drosha* (banner of the clan, borne in battle, and regarded with awe),[1] and the costly silver vessels from which the sacred beer, brewed in the *khati*, is drunk, etc. Near the *khati*, but within a hedge of its own, is a small, dark building to house the brewing apparatus, drinking-cups, and the like; and close by, under the shade of a great tree decked with rags, etc., is an altar, about 1½ m. high, which is adorned with humble offerings, while over it is a bowl with an aspergillum, and behind it frequently stands a stone idol. By the altar is a stone-paved pit into which the blood of the sacrificial victim flows through a quadrangular opening; and feet and bones of sheep, kine, etc., bear witness to the zeal of the worshippers. Near this usually stands another altar-shaped column resting on a square base; and on it are piled horns of wild animals, brought as offerings to the sanctuary. A special hut is erected for brewing the beer, which only the proper servants of the *khati* may prepare; and *darbasi*-dwellings and assembly-places are provided for the ministers of the shrine. The sacred vessels (mostly of silver and often bearing Christian symbols) are jealously guarded against profanation or theft; and at high festivals the worshippers drink from them the sacred beer.[2]

As the terrestrial home of the celestial *khati*, the *khati*, in its aspect of place of prayer and sacrifice, serves as means of communication between heaven and earth, so that in each crisis of life it is visited for prayer to the divinity dwelling there. While almost every village has its own *khati*, three, all dedicated to St. George (see below [*d*]), possess special sanctity—those in the villages of Gudani and Khakhmati, and the *khati* of Karatis-Jvari in Likoki. The two former are the oldest in Khevsuria, and all three enjoy large estates.

The *khati* of Gudani is called 'leader of God's hosts' and contains the chief *drosha* of the Khevsurs. It possesses great power against theft (hence it is invoked when a raid is to be undertaken) and against disease, insanity, and sterility. The *khati* Sameba-Zrolis-Zferi, in the village of Ukan-Khalo, is the special patron of hunters and thieves, and has peculiar power over the clouds. The *khati* of Karatis-Jvari is particularly potent against all evil spirits, which appear in the form of hedgehogs, swine, etc.; and his sacrifice, in case of misfortune, is a goat, which, it should be noted, is offered only to evil spirits. In the village of Atabe is a *khati* dedicated to St. Kvirik, lord of the mainland, whom all angels obey, and who has his throne next to God.

(*b*) *Priests.*—Some uncertainty prevails concerning the various orders of the priesthood. The lowest rank is that of the *shulta*, of whom each *khati* has three, chosen annually from the community by the *khuzi* and the *dekanossi*. The *shulta's* duties are to guard the property of the sanctuary, to supervise and assist the agricultural work on the land belonging to the *khati*, and to see the harvest safely garnered. Like the other ministers of the *khati*, they must lead a blameless life, and for several weeks before each feast intercourse with women is forbidden. They may not enter the *darbasi*, this privilege being reserved for the higher functionaries.

The next in ascending rank are the *dasturi*, chosen by the *khuzi* from the community, either for a definite period or for an individual feast. Their name is of Persian origin (Pahlavi-Pers. *dastūr*), but in the Iranian priesthood the *dastūrs* occupy the highest rank.[1] The duties of the Khevsur *dasturi* are to receive the barley from the *shulta*, prepare the firewood, obtain the wild hops (cultivated hops may not be used), and brew the sacred beer. During this process they must be barefooted, bareheaded, and ungirdled, may not leave the sanctuary, and are forbidden to speak.[2] At the festivals they must prepare and serve the food of the *khuzi* and *dekanossi*, and perform a like service for the attendant worshippers. When the *khuzi* slays the sacrificial offering (*svaraki*), the *dasturi* and *dekanossi* hold its feet, and they sprinkle the sacrificiant and his family with its blood. During four weeks previous to a feast the *dasturi* must refrain from conjugal relations and may not go near a *boseli* (menstruation-hut). While the *shulta* are all equal in rank, there are various degrees among the *dasturi* according to the periods for which they are chosen; and, together with the *shulta*, they administer the finances of the *khati*.

The real priest of the *khati* is the *khuzi*, who is chosen, not by the community, but by the soothsayer (*kadagi*) or seeress (*mkitkhavi*). A future *khuzi* is usually a man of standing, favourably known for shrewdness and eloquence; and the sign by which he is elected is normally illness of himself or of one of his relatives (failure to recover from such illness, however, means that he has been rejected by the *khati*). Once chosen, the *khuzi* cannot be removed against his will; he is deemed holy, and no one dares insult him by word or deed. On the other hand, a man selected by *kadagi* or *mkitkhavi* cannot refuse to accept the dignity of *khuzi*, under penalty of divine anger. The *khuzi's* duties are the performance of religious rites (some of which, in much distorted form, are of Christian origin, as shown by their invocation of the Trinity) and the offering of prayers, which—for material blessings alone—are addressed to the *batoni-khati* (as the mediator of the divine will) rather than to the supreme deity. The *khuzi* also slaughters the *svaraki* by cutting its throat, and he and the *dekanossi* receive its skin and half of its flesh. He performs marriages, conducts festivals for the dead, blesses the people at the great feasts, and foretells the outcome of illness by placing the cap and girdle of the afflicted person under his pillow and dreaming over them.[3] He is likewise the guardian of the sacred *drosha*, before which the people kneel when it is shown them on high festivals; and at such times he solemnly curses any who may possibly prove traitors, holding high a bowl of beer and pouring it on the ground with the words, 'So may the house, the family, the fortune of the faithless be emptied!' Like the *dasturi*, he must observe the utmost purity before festivals, even an erotic dream sufficing to defile him.

The *khuzi* is assisted by several *dekanossi*, likewise chosen by the *kadagi* or *mkitkhavi*, and bound by the same rules as govern him. With the *dasturi* they hold the sacrificial victim while he cuts its throat; with him (or for him, if he is prevented from taking part in the festival) they repeat the prayers and bless the people; and they light the candles in the *khati*.[4]

[1] Cf. art. BANNERS.

[2] The emphasis laid on the sacred beer may be a reminiscence of the Indo-Iranian *soma-haoma* rite (see artt. HAOMA, SOMA), despite the wide-spread custom of drinking intoxicants in connexion with sacred ceremonies (see *ERE* v. 79).

[1] See art. PRIEST, PRIESTHOOD (Iranian).

[2] The prohibition of speech (cf. also below, p. 487) looks very like a survival of Zoroastrianism (see *SBE* v. [1880] 109, 290–292, xviii. [1882] 135, xxiv. [1885] 283 f.); but, on the other hand, to go barefoot and ungirdled are heinous sins in Mazdaism (*SBE* v. 106 f., 287).

[3] Cf. art. INCUBATION, of which this dreaming is really a form.

[4] The *khuzi*, *dekanossi*, *dasturi*, and *shulta* roughly correspond respectively to the fourfold hierarchy of bishop, priest,

A somewhat problematical figure in the hierarchy[1] is the *khevis-beri* ('valley-elder'). It seems, on the whole, that he was originally the political or administrative head of the valley, and as such was the bearer of the *drosha* and the leader of the army. In this manner he naturally became protector of the *khati*, and so developed by degrees into a religious leader, particularly as his older political importance steadily diminished. Traces of this, however, yet remain. He is still the one who uplifts the *drosha* at certain feasts; and, unlike the *khuzi*, *dekanossi*, *dasturi*, and *shulta*, he inherits his dignity; and it is only in the case of extinction of a family in which the office of *khevis-beri* is hereditary that he is chosen by the *khuzi*. He is the faithful transmitter of ancient ritual; but his precise relation to the *khuzi* is uncertain.

(*c*) *Sorcerers.*—Among the Khevsurs sorcerers and priests co-operate. The *kadagi* is chosen at New Year by *khuzi* and *dekanossi*. Usually he is neurotic, and he delivers his messages in the characteristic manner of shamans.[2] He is the mouthpiece of the *khati* and is consulted in all important events of life, especially in cases of illness, when he designates the particular offering necessary to propitiate the deity whose anger has caused the affliction. In certain *khatis*, as in Khakhabo, the *kadagi* even has the right to carry the *drosha*. The female counterpart of the *kadagi* is the *mkitkhavi*, who is often a hysteriac. Despite the restrictions imposed on all other Khevsur women, the *mkitkhavi* holds rank equal to that of the *kadagi*. The *mkitkhavis* divine by means of water, grains of corn, etc.; and, if they declare that the cause of an illness is a deity's desire to obtain the person afflicted, the latter is clad in white, and a vow is taken that his hair shall be uncut for three years, etc.

There is another class of sorceresses, the *mesulta*—women and girls who sustain a peculiarly close relation to the supernatural world. To approach the spirits of the departed, the *mesulta* lies upon the ground, grows pale, and falls into deep slumber, often broken by a gentle murmuring, which is regarded as converse with the dead. Since, however, too much speech regarding the other world is dangerous, the *mesulta*, on awakening, uses language which is intentionally obscure. If a child falls ill before reaching the age of two years, the *mesulta* is consulted. She tells from what departed spirit the illness comes; and the child's name is changed to that of the deceased in question (in similar illness of an older child the aid of the *kadagi*, not the *mesulta*, is sought).

(*d*) *Deities.*—Reminiscences of Christianity are so numerous that it is not always easy to say exactly what is essentially the religion of the Khevsurs and kindred tribes. The supreme deity is Morigi, creator and omnipotent, who dwells in the seventh heaven and is the god of the living, whereas Christ is the divinity of the dead.[3] The Trinity, occasionally invoked in prayers, is regarded as three angels; the Blessed Virgin receives honour as one of the chief angels; and SS. Peter and Paul are the angels of wealth and abundance. Morigi leaves the actual administration of the world to his delegates, the *khatis*, each of whom has his special function and is aided by two messengers (*esauls*), one good and the other evil, through whom the *khati* rewards or punishes mankind. The *esauls* united form the heavenly host (*lashkari*; Arab. *laškar*, 'army'), to which the 'sisters' of the *khati* also belong. A special shrine is erected to these 'sisters' in the *khati* of Khakhmati, and there three maidens from Kajeti (the land of the demons) dwell—Ashe, Simen, and Samdsimari—who are represented as children and who, when sent by the *khati*, cause the children of the guilty to fall ill.[1]

The principal deity, for all practical purposes, is the patron saint of the Caucasian region, St. George of Cappadocia, from whom the land of Georgia is popularly supposed to have received its name.[2] The majority of churches in Georgia are dedicated to him, as are the three chief *khatis* of the Khevsurs—Gudani, Khakhmati, and Karatis-Jvari. He not only causes the herds to multiply, but he heals animals and men and protects his worshippers in time of peril. He is, furthermore, a storm-god and solar deity, and his throne is on a lofty mountain,[3] whence he sends upon the fields of the wicked the hail which his servants, the *divs* (Av. *daēva*, 'demon'), bring from the sea at his bidding. To avert his wrath, no work is done in the fields on Mondays, Fridays, and Saturdays from June till harvest, special watchers being appointed to see that this tabu is not violated. Chapels are erected in his honour on hill-tops, to which pilgrimage is made annually; and at Khakhmati sacrifices are made to his dog, a wind-demon, for having once protected the Khevsur herds against a band of devils.

(*e*) *Festivals.*—The chief Khevsur festivals fall about Easter, Ascension Day, and New Year's Day. The most important is celebrated in the *khati* of Gudani, beginning on Good Friday and lasting four days; but in memory of our Saviour's thirst (Jn 19^{28}) bread and salt alone are eaten, and only a little beer may be drunk. Twelve weeks later the great national festival, said to commemorate the liberation of the land from foreign invasion, is celebrated at the *khatis* of Khakhmati and Karatis-Jvari, and also throughout Pshavia and Tushetia. At these festivals the number of sacrificial victims is very large, from 500 to 600 sheep and 20 to 40 cattle being offered at Khakhmati alone, and the quota of each family being at least five sheep. The priests receive the skin and half of the flesh, which is salted to keep, the remainder being cooked by the *dasturi* and eaten by the assembly, together with bread and abundant beer. This beer is solemnly blessed by *khuzi* and *dekanossi*, after which the *dasturi* presents it first in the sacred silver vessels to these priests and then to the laity;[4] but it is consumed so generously that the festival frequently degenerates into a drunken revel. Women are not admitted to the feasts and may not pass beyond a certain line in the *khati*,[5] where they receive their share of beer and viands. Near a *khati* on a hill in the village of Arkhoti is a special *nishi* (place where a saint has performed a miracle) for children, and to this are brought loaves baked expressly for them.

deacon, and subdeacon of the Orthodox, Roman, and Anglican Churches, and this may indeed be their origin; it is less likely that they are reminiscences of the *zarathushtrotema*, *andarzpat*, *ratu*, and *mobed* of Zoroastrianism (for whom see art. PRIEST, PRIESTHOOD [Iranian]).

1 Cf. the divergent opinions cited by Merzbacher, ii. 85.

2 See art. SHAMANISM.

3 The seven heavens represent Jewish Talmudic tradition (see *JE* i. 591, vi. 298); for Morigi as god of the living cf. Mt 22^{32}; and the concept of Christ as god of the dead is probably borrowed from the doctrine of His descent into Hades (1 P 3^{19}).

1 This explains the function of the *mesulta* in healing infants.

2 Stemmer, in Wetzer and Welte, *Kirchenlexikon*², Freiburg, 1882–1901, v. 330; cf. also *AS*, April, iii. 101 ff. In reality, however, 'Georgia' is probably derived from Pers. Gurj(istān), the name of the land in question (Adeney, p. 344, note).

3 Cf. the mystic awe associated with the mountains Kasbek in Ossetia (Merzbacher, i. 848–853) and Elburz, the latter being called Orfi Itub ('Abode of the Blest') by the Abkhases, Ashka Makhua ('Mountain of the Gods') or Nash Hamakho ('Holy Height') by the Cherkess, and Jinn Pādišāh ('Lord of Spirits') by the Turkish-speaking tribes (*ib.* i. 599–601); its name is derived from the Persian Albūrz (Av. Hara Berezaiti), itself a famous abode of *dīvs* (cf. *ERE* viii. 507a).

4 Apparently a reminiscence of celebration of the Eucharist.

5 Probably reminiscent of the narthex of early Christian churches.

(*f*) *Status of women.*—Until a daughter-in-law has entered the household, a Khevsur woman's life is one of toil. She not only aids her husband in working in the fields and tending the cattle, but must also mow and thresh, bring wood and water, cook food, make clothing, etc. When her son brings home his bride, however, the mother-in-law becomes the administrative head of the house, and nothing may be done without her approval.

(*g*) *Marriage and divorce.*—Betrothal frequently takes place while the future bride and groom are still children; and in such a case the boy's father is obliged, until the girl reaches maturity, to send annual presents to the bride's father, while at New Year a brother or sister of the groom takes to the bride a 'luck-loaf' (*bedis-kveri*), which she is bound to eat. The marriages are always arranged by a female marriage-broker, who takes some small present from the parents of the groom to the father of the bride. After betrothal the girl may seek no other alliance, and theft of her by another man entails severe consequences on him and her, besides being a deep disgrace to the intended groom and his family. Marriage between persons even remotely akin is strictly forbidden, with the result that, since all the inhabitants of a village belong to a single family, men and women of the same community very seldom wed.

On the marriage day the father of the groom sends to the bride's father, by two men of standing, two sheep, one of which is killed at the *khati*, the other in the bride's house. The girl's mother bakes two large festival loaves (*kada*), and all the maidens of the village escort the bride, with her parents and kinsfolk, to the end of the village, where one of the *kadas* is eaten. The bride's escort now return home, while the bride, with some of her more distant relatives, follows the two men sent by the groom's father, all but the girl being mounted on horseback. During this journey the second *kada* is eaten, and when she reaches the village which is to be her future home the bride is met by all its inhabitants, the distance which they come to greet her being proportionate to the respect shown her. Arrived at the groom's house, the bride is entertained in a separate room by the women of the family, while her escort are feasted. Meanwhile the groom hides till summoned by the feasters; and he then receives the place of honour, but may share in neither banquet, song, nor dance, being permitted to drink only a single glass of brandy. The women likewise are debarred from the men's feast and dance, this being probably a Muhammadan survival, since no such restriction exists among the Christian Karthvelians. This revelry usually lasts three days, during which the groom may not come near his bride; and bride, groom, and escort then return to her home, where a similar feast is given. The groom now goes back to his own village, where he remains an entire year, forbidden to visit even the village of the bride, the only exception being when the groom has no parents, in which case his bride remains with him from the first to manage his household. When the year has expired, the groom sends his nearest kinsmen to fetch the bride, who is again escorted by some of her own relatives. The *dekanossi* and *khevis-beri* are now summoned, and the former sews together the garments of the bridal pair in token of their union, while the girl's mother prepares the nuptial bed, to which she leads the wedded pair. After the first three nights, the groom no longer shares this bed, but seeks his bride only by stealth; and it is not until the birth of their first child that the pair live together openly. The conjugal act involves ritual defilement for three days.

Despite the absence of outward manifestations of affection, and notwithstanding the life of toil imposed upon the married woman, she occupies a position of great respect. Except for very rare instances, she guards her fidelity to her husband with extreme care; and if convicted of adultery, she takes her life. Her symbol of wifehood is her kerchief (*mandili*); and if she throws this between two men who are fighting, they must at once desist from their quarrel.

The older form of wedding among these tribes was marriage by capture, which is still frequent, usually with the connivance of the girl. This is regarded as an insult to the kinsmen of the man to whom she was betrothed, and the robber's relatives must pay them a fine of 16-30 cows and make rich presents to the girl's father. In addition to this, the brothers and cousins of the girl insult the robber by 'jumping on the roof' (*banse shekhtoma*) of his house until he slaughters a sheep and gives them a young ox and a copper kettle. If, however, the girl is carried off against her will, a deadly feud arises between the kinsmen of the robber and those of the intended bride and groom, often resulting in destruction of property and life, while the girl seeks an opportunity to escape to her chosen husband.

Polygamy is permitted, but is rare unless the wife is sickly, ages prematurely, or bears only girls; but if a second wife is taken, the husband must give five cows to the family of the first.

The bride brings a dowry with her, but the groom has no claim upon it, whereas the wife has the right to make herself a new dress annually at her husband's expense. The property of husband and wife is kept separate, and neither may be the other's heir. Sons alone may inherit; if the marriage is childless, or only girls are born, the village is the heir.

Divorce is rare, for, even if a wife is thus dismissed for laziness, barrenness, or sickliness, her husband must pay her 16 cows for the marriage and one cow for her work during each year of wedded life except the first and the last. A divorced wife may marry again, and is still entitled to a new dress each year at her first husband's expense. On the other hand, any children of the first marriage belong to their father; and though a temporary exception is made in the case of an unweaned infant, this child also goes to its father as soon as it is grown. A man is deeply disgraced if his wife leaves him; and in such a case she must promise never to marry another man, a violation of this pledge formerly involving the death both of the woman and of her second husband.

Under no circumstances may a man ill-treat his wife—a rule which is enforced by the entire community. Since the family (*ojakhi*) is strictly subordinated to the community (*tamoba*), so that ostracism involves entire forfeiture of communal protection, rights to communal pasturage, etc., the ruling of the *tamoba* is one of much effect in all departments of life in the individual household.

(*h*) *Death and disposal of the dead.*—Death being believed to defile the house, the moribund are carried into the open air, and there breathe their last, surrounded by the members of their household. Since the corpse is deemed a source of uncleanness, its preparation for its final resting-place is the duty of young, unmarried persons (lads for males, and girls for females) called *narevebi* ('defiled'),[1] who shear the head of the corpse (if it be male), clothe it in a shroud of white and red,[2] and dig for it a long, narrow, shallow, stone-lined grave, in which it is laid uncoffined.[3] Contact with *narevebi* entails defilement; and they may not enter their own homes until (after five or six days) they have taken repeated cleansing baths. For a year the kinsmen of the deceased let their beards grow, wear old clothes turned inside out (thus hiding the usual adornments of dress), and carry no weapons. The departed (unless a child, who is unwept) is formally bewailed, the men lamenting silently, the women aloud; and one of the latter recites or sings laudations of the deceased, the others joining in the refrain. A funeral feast is prepared and blessed by the *khuzi*, who also recites an ancient prayer containing reminiscences of the Old and New Testaments.

The corpse is borne to the grave by the *narevebi*, while the kinsmen and other male residents of the community stand weeping softly at the boundary of the village. Of the family only the widow accompanies the body to its final resting-place, and she leads the dead man's completely caparisoned horse,

[1] Cf. the Iranian *nasā-sālārs* (see *ERE* iv. 503 f.).

[2] For minor variations see Merzbacher, ii. 97, note 3.

[3] In certain regions wooden coffins are coming into use.

which bears his clothes and weapons, as well as food and drink for his journey to the other world. Arrived at the grave, she strikes the horse thrice, saying, 'Serve thy master in the future life as faithfully as thou hast served him here below.'[1] The widow is escorted by wailing women, eulogizing the departed, and when the corpse is laid in the ground, one of them falls into ecstasy, describing the arrival of the soul in the abode of the blest. At most only a few loaves are buried with the corpse, or, in the case of a child, some apples or the like. The horse is given to the nearest or dearest kinsman (usually the maternal uncle), and is carefully tended throughout its life. It may carry neither man nor burden, and to sell it is to disgrace its late owner, who still needs it to ride before his departed kinsmen in the other world. If, however, certain specified conditions permit its sale, the purchaser pays only half its actual value, and the seller must provide a substitute; for it is, in reality, the property of the dead.

While burial is now practised by the Caucasian tribes under consideration, the older form of disposal of the dead was to lay them in small house-like structures above ground. The characteristic form of this corpse-house is thus described by M. Kovalevsky:[2]

They are, 'as a rule, situated on the summit of hills. In shape they are like a prolonged quadrangle; they are constructed of stones put together without cement, and have two entrances, one on the southern and one on the northern side.' Within, 'on both sides of a passageway which is left free, stone ledges at a certain level from the earth are to be seen with the mummified bodies of the deceased either sitting or lying on them. Different objects, belonging to everyday life, but no armour, are found in these burial places, where the wind freely enters and birds are likely to come.'[3]

Immediately after the return from the grave, an ox is killed; and the relatives and *narevebi* thrice take a piece of its roasted liver into their mouths and spit it out, this being called 'the re-opening of the mouth' (*sapiris khsno*), since, until this rite is performed, they are denied both meat and milk. Meanwhile the other mourners are entertained with bread and cheese; and on the following day the flesh of the roasted ox is eaten by the relatives and the *narevebi*.

The 'keeping of silence' (*piris abshera*)[4] is likewise a noteworthy mourning rite. On the day of burial the nearest relatives of the deceased choose two men and one woman from his kinsfolk and shut them in a room where a fire is burning. After partaking of a large milk-loaf, they may not utter a word until the '*khuzi* of souls' comes at evening and blesses the loaf, which they turn about themselves thrice. They then go silently home, and each lays a piece of wood at the window of the dead man's house, after which speech is permitted, and they may share the general meal.

A second festival in honour of the deceased is held a few days after his burial; and at this time there is a horse-race[5] in which the victor receives the weapons, etc., of the departed, although they are not actually given him until a year has elapsed. Throughout this year the soul of the dead is supposed to visit his earthly home and to protect it, so that on the second Saturday of Great Lent a special meal (*sulta-kreba*, 'assembly of souls') is prepared for him. Various gifts are laid near loaves of bread placed on the ground, and these become the property of any one who hits them with arrow or bullet; the men then visit the *khati* to drink beer brewed at the expense of the community, while the women, gathered in the house of mourning, lament the dead and drink to the repose of his soul.

1 Formerly the horse was doubtless sacrificed at the grave.

2 *Archæological Review*, i. [1888] 321.

3 This form of superterrene disposal of the dead, to which the Avesta distinctly refers (*Vend.* v. 10; cf., further, D. Menant, *Les Parsis*, Paris, 1898, pp. 183 f., 213 f.), is fairly wide-spread, being found not only among Tushes, Pshavs, and Khevsurs, but also in Ossetia (Merzbacher, i. 690, 815–818), Seistan (G. P. Tate, *Seistan*, Calcutta, 1910–12, p. 276), Baluchistan (*IGI* vi. 283), and the Hindu-Kush (G. S. Robertson, *The Kâfirs of the Hindu-Kush*, London, 1896, p. 641 ff.). A highly developed form is probably to be seen in the so-called 'Tomb of Cyrus' (for a description of which see A. V. W. Jackson, *Persia Past and Present*, New York, 1906, pp. 280–293). A somewhat similar idea is found in the rock-tombs of the Achæmenian kings, the entrances to which imitate the portals of a palace; and these have analogues in Asia Minor (R. Leonhard, *Paphlagonia*, Berlin, 1915, pp. 242–287) and in Judæa (*JE* iii. 436 f., vii. 145 f.). In the light of his further studies, the present writer believes that his note on ancient Persian burial rites (*ERE* iv. 505) requires considerable revision; and the connexion between this superterrene disposal and primitive Persian and Caucasian dolmen-burial (J. de Morgan, *Mission scientifique en Perse*, Paris, 1894–1905, iv. 15–58, and *Mission scientifique au Caucase*, i. 41–82), cliff-burial or rock-burial (for examples at Pandrān, in Baluchistan, see *IA* xxxii. [1903] 342 f.), and the Zoroastrian *dakhmas* (*ERE* iv. 504) also requires consideration.

4 Cf. above, p. 484b, note 2.

5 The Ossetes have a similar custom (Merzbacher, i. 819).

The great memorial feast (*tzel taveri*) is held at the expiry of the year. The mourners now cut their hair and beards, don new clothing, and feast so bountifully that excessive potations frequently lead to confusion and quarrels. This feast may also be given by a bachelor or childless widower in his lifetime for the weal of his soul in the future world; but he may not partake of it himself, although, as he hides from the feasters, he may listen to their laudations of him, thus playing the *rôle* of the dead and securing the benefits of the other world which his lack of posterity would otherwise deny him.

(*i*) *Heaven and hell.*—Heaven is a huge fortress, many storeys in height, reaching to the sky. It is illumined by the sun, and on its edge is a great spring, from which the blest drink joyfully.[1] The righteous are graded according to merit as regards the storeys in which they dwell, and each Sunday they receive from God their celestial food, the very sight of which assuages their hunger. Hell, on the contrary, is a dark,[2] square abode to which devils take the damned. Between this world and the next is a perilous bridge, at whose farther end the judges of the dead are seated.[3] Sinners fall into a shoreless river of tar, where they swim in eternal agony, tormented by terrible thirst, while special sins have special punishments, liars and slanderers, *e.g.*, having boiling water poured over them.

(*j*) *Miscellaneous.*—The blood-feud (*q.v.*) flourishes among the Khevsurs, but presents no noteworthy features, although it may be observed that the maternal uncle is especially prominent, either as the avenger of the murdered or as the first to be attacked by the avengers of the slain. Only compensation may be claimed for the murder of women and children; and for non-fatal injuries to men a regular tariff of much minuteness is in force, even murder itself being commutable by a *wergeld*.[4]

In a case of mere suspicion the accused may clear himself by a solemn oath, taken in the *khati* at night. Here an interesting survival of Iranianism is seen in the fact that, while taking oath, the accused holds a live cat, which is deemed the most unclean of all animals,[5] and prays that the corpse of the real murderer, and the corpses of all who might have proved his innocence, but failed to do so, may be followed by a cat in the future world. Or, after food has been placed on the grave of the murdered, one of the latter's kinsmen draws a drop of blood from an ear of the accused and of his kinsmen, cursing the suspected person, if he be guilty, to be the servant of his victim in the life to come. After this both parties share the food, and reconciliation is complete.[6] If, after condemnation, the guilty man refuses to pay the fine imposed upon him, the creditor may demand such payment from some third person whom he chooses without the knowledge of that person. This man, called *mzevali*, may transfer the debt to a fourth, doubling the amount; and the fourth to a fifth, again doubling the sum, and so on, until the debt, enormously enlarged, finally devolves again on the original debtor, who must pay the whole. No one may refuse to be a *mzevali* under penalty of having erected, near his house, a stone image smeared with human excrement, and with a cat or dog[7] hung on a stick thrust into it, the whole being accompanied by a curse. Such disgrace results in ostra-

1 Evidently a reminiscence of Rev 22[1].

2 This idea is probably Iranian in origin (cf. *Arta Viraf*, ed. and tr. M. Haug and E. W. West, Bombay, 1872, chs. xviii., liv., and *SBE* v. 114, xviii. 57, 75).

3 This may be either Iranian or Muhammadan (see *ERE* ii. 852).

4 For details see Merzbacher, ii. 50–56.

5 See *SBE* xviii. 419.

6 For details see Merzbacher, ii. 56–58.

7 Probably Muhammadan in origin, since Islām, unlike Zoroastrianism, abhors the dog (*ERE* i. 512; T. P. Hughes, *DI*2, London, 1896, p. 91a).

cism of the *mzevali*, who can avert it only by paying the amount demanded, killing a sheep, and sharing it with his opponent and with invited witnesses, after which 'the souls are set free.'

2. Svanetians. — The Svanetians, numbering about 16,500 in 1912, are the modern representatives of the Soanes or Suani of Strabo and Pliny.[1] Their religion is by no means so interesting as that of the Khevsurs, etc., and primitive elements are far less prominent.[2] From Iranianism they retained a sort of prayer to the sun and moon; from Christianity a form of anointing a child by its mother in lieu of baptism, and a veneration for Christ, the Virgin, and St. George; from Judaism a reverence for Elijah; and they still abstain from work on the three Sabbaths—Friday of the Muhammadans, Saturday of the Jews, and Sunday of the Christians. They practise the strictest endogamy, only residents of the same village being permitted to wed—possibly (though by no means certainly) an Iranian survival.[3] Superfluous female children were formerly smothered as soon as born. Burial might take place only in clear weather, rain (in view of the great precipitation) being regarded as ill-omened; and food was laid on the grave for the soul's journey to the other world.

3. Importance of Caucasian religion. — The rather scanty fragments of paganism found in the Caucasus are of more interest than appears on the surface. The Karthvelian stock seems to have had its original home much farther to the south in Asia Minor and to have been driven steadily northward by the invaders who established their empires in Mesopotamia.[4] Thus they found an abode in eastern Cappadocia, Pontus, Armenia, and the Caucasus; but under pressure of Armenians from the west, and of Iranians from the south,[5] they had reached, by the time of Strabo,[6] a territory extending from the lower course of the Kelkid Irmak to that of the Kura, and thence to Lenkoran on the Caspian, the northern boundary being the Caucasus range. The Karthvelian group thus represents the descendants of the ancient Colchidians, Soanes, Iberi, and Albani,[7] the latter corresponding to the Khevsurs, Pshavs, Tushes, and kindred tribes.

If this theory is correct, from the modern paganism of these three Karthvelian tribes we may infer the general character of the religion of a once considerable part of eastern Asia Minor. But perhaps we may go a step farther. We then have a knowledge that in Asia Minor there were at least three zones of religion: one represented by an orgiastic nature-cult, shown by the worship of Cybele and Attis (*qq.v.*) in the west and north; the second exemplified by the developed polytheism of the Hittites (*q.v.*) in the centre and south; and the third characterized by a primitive type of religion, mixed with shamanism, in the east. The enthusiasm of the orgy appealed to the decaying faiths of Greece and Rome; the polytheism, with a high degree of civilization, yielded only slowly to its foes; but the primitive savagery, with a low grade of civilization, was driven by invaders of higher type to the recesses of the Caucasus, where it still lingers, commingled with reminiscences and influences of the nobler religions of Zoroastrianism, Christianity, and Muhammadanism.

LITERATURE.—The principal literature on the paganism of the Caucasian tribes (chiefly in Russian) has been summarized by G. Merzbacher, *Aus den Hochregionen des Kaukasus*, 2 vols., Leipzig, 1901 (esp. ch. xiii. for the Svanetians, and ch. xxvii. for the Khevsurs, Pshavs, and Tushes). Nothing of importance on this subject has appeared since; of earlier literature not specified by Merzbacher, mention may be made of M. Kovalevsky, 'Om dyrkan af förfädren hos de kaukasiska folken,' in *Ymer*, 1888, pp. 111–122. For the scanty classical accounts of the Caucasus and its inhabitants see B. Latyshev, *Scythica et Caucasica e veteribus scriptoribus Græcis et Latinis*, 2 vols., Petrograd, 1893–1906. For ethnology and ancient history see esp. E. Chantre, *Recherches anthropologiques dans le Caucase*, 4 vols., Paris, 1885–87; J. de Morgan, *Mission scientifique au Caucase*, 2 vols., do. 1890; S. Zaborowski, 'Le Caucase et les Caucasiens,' in *Revue anthropologique*, xxiv. [1914] 121–133.

LOUIS H. GRAY.

[1] Strabo, XI. ii. 19 (=p. 499 C); Pliny, *HN* vi. 4; see especially de Morgan, ii. 182 f., 188 f.

[2] For a summary see Merzbacher, i. 372–375, and for a description of a Svanetian funeral see *ib.* pp. 447–450. A like statement holds good for the Abkhases, who numbered about 60,000 in 1912 (see especially Žanašvili, in *Izvěstiya kavkazkago otděla imp. russ. geograf. obščestva*, xvi. [1894] 1–64).

[3] Cf. *ERE* viii. 456–458.

[4] For an outline of this history see de Morgan, i. 27 f., 197, ii. 121–129, 274–280.

[5] See de Morgan, ii. pl. xi. ('Les Colonies aryennes dans le Caucase et l'Arménie'), for the course of these migrations. His suggestion (ii. 276; cf. i. 22, ii. 105 f.) that the Karthvelian group corresponds to the ancient Vannic is scarcely supported by what little we know of Vannic religion (see art. ARMENIA [Vannic]). It is equally doubtful whether the Hittites (*q.v.*) can be regarded as akin to the modern non-Aryan Caucasians, despite his arguments (i. 23, 26, 197, ii. 64).

[6] De Morgan, ii. pl. xiv. ('Carte ethnographique du Caucase au 1er siècle de notre ère').

[7] See above, p. 483.

TUTELARY GODS AND SPIRITS.

TUTELARY GODS AND SPIRITS.—The conception of a tutelary guardian genius or guiding spirit believed to protect and watch over certain persons and objects appears to arise as soon as the powers of observation and generalization are sufficiently developed to bring about a systematized scheme by which natural phenomena come to be divided into classes and assigned to particular departmental deities and spirits. In some cases high gods are associated with special functions—*e.g.*, in Mexico, where Tlaloc is regarded as the god of rain and water, and therefore has the special office of fertilizing the earth.[1] But more frequently it is the numerous spirits by which primitive man supposes himself to be surrounded that become the patrons or guardians of individual men. Any extraordinary event that demands the help of an intervening agent provides the impetus to penetrate more deeply into the nature of the supernatural powers and to establish a more intimate alliance with them. Thus, to the primitive mind, the constant motion of water is controlled not by natural law but by some supernatural agency resident within the stream. At first it appears simply as a mystic impersonal force, but, as the mind becomes capable of more definite ideas, the conception of a spiritual being having personality is evolved.

The Trojans, *e.g.*, originally regarded a sacred river as containing *mana* (*q.v.*), and, in consequence, they sacrificed a bull to the stream by throwing the animal into the water whole and entire. 'In later times, when they had reached the animistic stage, an altar was erected by the side of the river on which a bull was offered, the belief being that the spirit in the water came out and consumed the essence of the sacrifice.'[2]

As soon as the notion of a local spirit allied to a natural object is developed, the desire to seek the aid of the supernatural being speedily follows. The Iroquois at their festivals thank the good spirits and every object that ministers to their wants for the assistance rendered by them.[3] In process of time a tutelary guardian genius is assigned to every individual, whose special function it is to guide, protect, and warn the man under his care. This guardian spirit may be acquired in various ways and take different forms. It may reveal itself at birth, or may await the 'crisis' reached at puberty. It may be the spirit of some ancestor or great chief or mighty magician; or it may belong to a deity whose dwelling is not with men. From these spirits the personal name and even the nature of an individual are frequently received, and to them man naturally looks for guidance and protection.

[1] H. H. Bancroft, *NR* iii. 324.

[2] E. O. James, *Primitive Ritual and Belief*, London, 1917, p. 226.

[3] E. B. Tylor, *PC*³, ii. 205.

1. Forms of guardian spirits.—(*a*) *Placenta.*—

Among the Kooboos, a primitive tribe of Sumatra, the navel-string and afterbirth 'are the good spirits, a sort of guardian angels of the man who came into the world with them and who lives on earth; they are said to guard him from all evil. Hence it is that the Kooboo always thinks of his navel-string and afterbirth before he goes to sleep or to work, or undertakes a journey.'[1] If he were not to think of them, he would deprive himself of their care. The Battas, another tribe of Sumatra, believe that each man, in addition to his external soul, has 'two invisible guardian spirits (his *kaka* and *agi*) whose help he invokes in great danger; one is the seed by which he was begotten, the other is the afterbirth, and these he calls respectively his elder and his younger brother.'[2]

Among the northern tribes of Central Australia the navel-string is frequently cut off with a stone knife and, with the afterbirth, hidden in a hole in the ground or some other concealed spot, the belief being that, were it not preserved, the child would die, since it is thought to contain its spirit.[3] Here we find the germ of the belief which, in its more developed form, attributes to the placenta, etc., the function of a tutelary genius.

In Iceland it is an ancient belief that 'the child's guardian spirit or a part of its soul has its seat in the chorion or fœtal membrane, which usually forms part of the afterbirth, but is known as the caul when the child happens to be born with it. Hence the chorion was itself known as the *fylgia* or guardian spirit. It might not be thrown away under the open sky, lest demons should get hold of it and work the child harm thereby.' If it were buried under the threshold where the mother stepped over it when she rose from bed, the child in after life had a guardian spirit in the shape of a bear, eagle, wolf, ox, or boar.[4]

(*b*) *Animals.*—Not infrequently a man's guardian spirit is thought to manifest itself under the form of an animal.

Among the Ibans or Sea Dayaks of Borneo the *ngarong*, or spirit-helper, after having in a dream appeared in human form, makes himself known in the likeness of an animal. 'On the day after such a dream the Iban wanders through the jungle looking for signs by which he may recognize his "Nyarong," and if an animal behaves in a manner at all unusual, if a startled deer stops a moment to gaze at him before bounding away, if a gibbon gambols about persistently in the trees near him, if he comes upon a bright quartz-crystal or a strangely contorted root or creeper, that animal or object is for him full of a mysterious significance and is the abode of his "Nyarong."'[5] It does not, however, follow that every Iban has a *ngarong*. Many a young man goes out to sleep on the grave of some distinguished person or in some wild and lonely spot and lives for some days on a very restricted diet, hoping that a *ngarong* will come to him in his dreams, but only one in 50 or 100 men is fortunate enough to have his wish gratified. When the *ngarong* takes on an animal form, all individuals of that species become objects of special regard to the Iban, and he will not, of course, kill or eat any such animal. Even if the *ngarong* changes its form, he will continue to respect the species in which it first appeared. The cult may spread through the whole family, the children and grandchildren being under an obligation to respect the animal-form to which the *ngarong* belongs.

Among the Omaha Indians an animal as a guardian spirit is assigned to every man at puberty, and so close is the bond uniting them that the man is supposed to acquire the qualities of the creature that is his guardian. If, in the vision which determines his tutelary genius, he sees an eagle, he will have a keen and piercing foresight; if, on the other hand, it is a bear that appears to him, he will be slow and clumsy and therefore likely to be killed in battle.[6] This belief, that a man acquires the nature of the animal that is his guardian, has led the Thompson Indians of British Columbia to perform a mimic battle before setting out on the warpath, in which each man portrays on his body and imitates the sounds of his guardian animal.[7] Similarly in W. Africa, when a man is initiated into a secret society, the animal that he sees in his dream during his 'magic sleep' becomes his guardian spirit or patron.[8]

In Central America nagualism[9] is one of the ancient forms of worship which still flourish. It 'consists in choosing an animal as the tutelary divinity of a child, whose existence will be so closely connected with it, that the life of one depends on that of the other.' The animal is selected in one of three ways—(1) by priestly divination; (2) by the father and friends drawing animal figures on the floor of a hut at the mother's confinement, the figure that remains at the moment of delivery being the guardian; (3) by noticing the bird or beast first seen by the watchers after the confinement.[10] Sometimes a child's *nagual* is discovered by means of a calendar, in which all the names, places, and provinces of beasts, birds, fish, stars, etc., are recorded. Some of these horoscopes have a wheel painted on them; others portray a lake surrounded by the *naguals* in the form of various animals.[1] This method—employing astrological calculations based on a written document—is obviously a later development of nagualism.

[1] *GB*³, pt. vii., *Balder the Beautiful*, London, 1913, ii. 162, n. 2.
[2] *Ib.* p. 223 f., n. 2. [3] Spencer-Gillen^b, p. 607 f.
[4] *GB*³, pt. i., *The Magic Art*, London, 1911, i. 199 f.
[5] C. Hose and W. McDougall, 'The Relations between Man and Animals in Sarawak,' *JAI* xxxi. [1901] 200. For the spelling see Hose-McDougall, *The Pagan Tribes of Borneo*, ii. 109, n. 2.
[6] *GB*³, pt. v., *Spirits of the Corn and of the Wild*, London, 1912, ii. 207.
[7] J. Teit, *The Thompson Indians of Brit. Columbia* (*Memoir Amer. Museum Nat. Hist., The Jesup N. Pacific Exped.*, vol. i. pt. iv.), New York, 1900, p. 356.
[8] *GB*³, pt. vii., *Balder the Beautiful*, ii. 256 f.
[9] See art. ANIMALS, § 28. [10] *NR* iii. 458.

Among the Algonquins of N. America the tutelary genius is known as a *manitu*, or supernatural being, associated with streams, cataracts, rocks, mountains, and forests. In nearly every case it manifests itself under the form of a beast, bird, or reptile of uncanny appearance, although occasionally it assumes human proportions. At the age of puberty youths are made to retire to a solitary place to undergo a period of fasting. The first thing that appears in a dream to the novice is regarded as his guardian spirit, to whom he looks in after life for guidance and protection. The man destined to be a warrior will have a vision of an eagle or a bear, a serpent will appear to the future medicine-man, a wolf to the hunter. To complete the bond, a portion of the guardian is worn about the person, which is regarded rather as an embodiment than as a representative of a supernatural power. It therefore seems that the guardian spirit is only one of a large class of spirits to which the common name of *manitu* is given.[2] The same belief is found among the Iroquois and Hurons, the genii being called *okies* or *otkons* instead of *manitu*.

2. Functions of guardian spirits. — (*a*) *The relation of guardian spirits to totems.*—Among some of the Algonquin tribes a man's guardian is identical with his clan totem, but, since the former belongs solely to an individual, while the latter is the inherited possession of every member of the clan, the tutelary genius cannot be explained in terms of totemism.[3] The similarity between the clan totem and the guardian spirit has led several anthropologists to derive the one from the other.[4] On this hypothesis the clan totem is simply the guardian spirit of an ancestor, who acquired it for himself in a dream at puberty, and through his influence and credit succeeded in transmitting it by inheritance to his descendants, who form a clan, and regard as their totem the animal in which the tutelary genius manifested itself.

Thus, in the case of the Iban, Hose and McDougall think that 'it seems difficult to deny the name "individual totem" to the species' comprehended under the name of *Ngarong*. Similarly when 'all the members of a man's family and all his descendants, and, if he be a chief, all the members of the community over which he rules, come to share in the benefits conferred by his *Ngarong*, and in the feeling of respect for it and in the performance of rites in honour of the species of animal in one individual of which it is supposed to reside. In such cases the species approaches very closely the clan-totem in some of its varieties.'[5] Unfortunately, however, for this theory, on the authors' own evidence there are no signs of clan totemism in Borneo.[6]

For support of this view of the origin of totemism (*q.v.*) its advocates are driven to various American theories such as those of F. Boas, who thinks that the totems of the Indians of British Columbia have been developed from the personal *manitu*; and of Alice C. Fletcher, who is led to a similar conclusion by a study of the totems of the Omaha tribe. In this connexion, however, it should be remembered that, while it is perfectly true that guardian spirits are occasionally inherited among certain N. American tribes, and not acquired for each individual separately,[7] and therefore in process of time may become the totems of the clans, yet, since inherited guardian spirits are usually regarded as less powerful than those acquired by individuals,[8] they are hardly likely to be taken over as the protectors of the clan. Moreover, there is no evidence forthcoming that a totemic

[1] D. G. Brinton, 'Nagualism,' *Proc. Amer. Phil. Soc.*, vol. xxxiii. no. 144 [Philadelphia, 1894], pp. 25, 32.
[2] J. G. Frazer, *Totemism and Exogamy*, London, 1910, iii. 373 f.
[3] Tylor, 'Note on the Haida Totem-Post,' *Man*, ii. [1902] 2 ff.
[4] E. S. Hartland, *FL* xi. [1900] 68; A. C. Haddon, *Report of 72nd Meeting of Brit. Assoc.*, 1902, p. 742; W. H. R. Rivers, 'Totemism in Polynesia and Melanesia,' *JRAI* xxxix. [1909] 176 ff.; C. Hose and W. McDougall, *The Pagan Tribes of Borneo*, London, 1912, ii. 109; F. Boas, 'The Kwakiutl Indians,' *Report U.S. Nat. Mus.*, 1895, p. 336; H. Hubert and M. Mauss, 'Esquisse d'une théorie générale de la magie,' *ASoc* vii. [1904] 32 ff.
[5] ii. 109. [6] ii. 99.
[7] Teit, *Thompson Indians*, p. 320 ff.
[8] Teit, *The Shuswap*, Leyden and New York, 1909, p. 605.

clan has actually grown up in this way either in America or elsewhere. Where the original conditions are supposed to be typically manifested—*e.g.*, in the Banks Islands[1]—no trace remains of the existence of clan totemism, except perhaps in a few very doubtful survivals in secret societies. Again, we must not lose sight of the fact that in America and the Pacific, as compared with Australia, we are dealing with a relatively advanced, not to say degenerate, form of totemism,[2] and that this 'American theory,' as we may call it, of the origin of the institution rests entirely upon a few cases derived from the N. American Indians. In Australia, where the custom is seen in a much more primitive form, there is no evidence of guardian spirits becoming clan totems, while in Africa examples are also wanting. We therefore conclude that the theory which seeks the origin of totemism in the personal guardian spirits of individuals is devoid of proof, at any rate in the present state of our knowledge.

(*b*) *Guardian spirits of houses and villages.*—In most of the W. African tribes there is a class of ancestral spirits called 'the well disposed ones,' whose function is to protect and benefit their particular village or family, acting in conjunction with the village or family fetish. It is supposed that the spirit of a man lingers about a house some time after his death, and, although it is able to injure the children and others by embracing them, it performs the office of a guardian to the family by keeping off evil spirits.[3]

The Kenyahs recognize a minor deity called Bali Atap, who 'protects the house against sickness and attack, and is called upon in cases of madness to expel the evil spirit possessing the patient. A rude wooden image of him stands beside the gangway leading to the house from the river's brink; it holds a spear in the right hand, a shield in the left; it carries about its neck a fringed collar made of knotted strips of rattan; the head of each room ties on one such strip, making on it a knot for each member of his roomhold.' Another god, Bali Utong, brings prosperity to the house.[4]

'In Tonquin every village chooses its guardian spirit, often in the form of an animal, as a dog, tiger, cat, or serpent,' although occasionally a human being is selected.[5] The Khonds have tutelary deities of house, village, groves, etc., which survive in the later Hinduism. The *Rigveda* recognizes Vāstoshpati, the 'lord of the house,' to whom the law[6] orders oblations to be made. This Vedic divinity is associated by W. Windisch with Vesta and Hestia, and compared to the Celtic *vassus, vassallus*, originally 'house-man,' and thus associated with the 'king of the house-men.'[7] In Hinduism, however, a female deity, Jara, is assigned to the guardianship of the house. Although she is represented as a demoniac power, she is friendly towards her votaries, provided that she is worshipped with incense, food, flowers, and so forth.

The Ainus have a fetish called Inao, invested with life, whose function is to look after the health and general wellbeing of the family. His special dwelling-place is in the north-east corner of the hut, at the back of the family heirlooms. Occasionally, in times of trouble, he is brought out from his corner, stuck in the hearth, and there prayed to by the head of the family. He is supposed to have been sent down from heaven to be the husband of the goddess of fire, and to help her to attend to the wants of men, and therefore he is called 'the ancestral governor of the house.'[8]

3. Offerings to guardian spirits.—Since guardian spirits exercise such a powerful influence over the lives and destinies of men, it is not surprising that they are frequently the recipients of offerings to appease their wrath or secure their favour and beneficence.

The Thai of Indo-China, *e.g.*, offer firstfruits of rice at harvest to the guardian spirit of the family before the household partake of the new crop. Besides the firstfruits at harvest, 'the guardian spirit receives some of the parched grain in spring' at the time when the first thunder of the season is heard. 'When all is ready, the rice is served up together with fish, which have been caught for the purpose, on a table set in a corner which is sacred to the guardian spirit. A priest drones out a long invitation to the spirit to come and feast with his children; then the family sits down to the table and consumes the offerings. At the close of the banquet the daughter-in-law of the deceased ancestor [*i.e.* the guardian] hangs up a basket containing rice and fish for his use in the corner, after which she closes the shrine for another year.'[1] The same people believe that large animals of the forest — wild oxen, buffaloes, rhinoceroses, elephants, etc.—have their guardian spirits, and, in consequence, the prudent hunter is careful to exorcize the invisible guardians so that they may not harm him when he eats the flesh of the animals killed in the chase. Spirits are also supposed to guard the clearings to which the deer come by night to drink, and the hunter must sacrifice a fowl to them from time to time in order to secure his prey.[2] A similar custom prevails among the Indian tribes about Green Bay, Lake Michigan. Every creature is regarded as having a particular guardian spirit, and therefore, when a young girl seized a mouse to eat it, her father first fondled it tenderly to appease the *genie* who has charge of mice, in order that his daughter might not suffer from her meal.[3]

Among the Ewe-speaking natives of Togoland (W. Africa), before the new yams are eaten, 'every house-father takes a raw piece of yam and goes with it to his loom (*agbati*) and prays: "May the Artificers take this yam and eat! When they practise their art, may it prosper!" Again he takes a raw yam and goes with it under the house-door and prays: "O my guardian spirit (*aklama*) and all ye gods who pay heed to this house, come and eat yams! When I also eat of them, may I remain healthy and nowhere feel pain. May my housemates all remain healthy!" After he has invoked their protection on his family, he takes a cooked yam, crumbles it on a stone, and mixes it with red oil. With this mixture he goes again to his loom and prays as before.' Again he crumbles a cooked yam and prays first at the entrance of the homestead, then under the house-door: 'He of my guardian gods and he of the watchers of the house who likes not yams mixed with oil, let him come and take the white yam from my hand and eat!'[4]

Among the Kayans of Borneo and several of the African tribes it is customary at sowing a rice-field to reserve a certain portion at the entrance for the guardian spirits, who at harvest are invited to come and take their share. It is supposed that they will content themselves with eating the grain in their private preserves and not poach on the crops destined for the use of man.[5]

'In the Tenimber and Timor-laut Islands, East Indies, the first-fruits of the paddy, along with live fowls and pigs, are offered to the *matmate*,' or spirits of ancestors, 'which are worshipped as guardian spirits or household gods.'[6] The Yorubas of the Slave Coast sacrifice fowls to their guardian spirit (*olori*), which is supposed to dwell in the head, by mixing some of the blood of the animal with palm-oil and rubbing it on the forehead.[7] The *tindalo* in Florida, one of the Solomon Islands, are also approached by sacrifice on certain occasions—*e.g.*, before a planting, a voyage, or a fight.[8] The N. American Indians offer dogs and horses to the 'medicine bag,' to which they look for safety and protection through life.[9]

Among some of the Algonquin tribes, when a man's guardian spirit is identical with his clan totem, should he be compelled to kill the sacrosanct animal, due apology would be paid to it before destroying it, certain portions of the flesh being preserved as an offering to the *man'ido* (guardian).[10] Herein again lies an important distinction between a tutelary genius and a totem, even when the two are inseparable. The former is regarded as so intimately associated with an individual that prayers and sacrifices may with impunity be offered to it, but the latter is more closely concerned with the food group or clan and therefore is seldom the recipient of offerings from individuals. Apart from the evidence of Carl Strehlow, that the hymn which is sung at the *intichiuma* of the kangaroo describes the offering of a morsel of kangaroo fat to make the fat of the kangaroos increase,[11] the act of oblation can hardly be said to form a part of the totemic rites in Australia—the home of the most elementary form of totemism.[12] We therefore conclude that tutelary gods and spirits have arisen out of animistic and theistic conceptions rather than from ideas connected with totemism, although it is undoubtedly

1 *JRAI* xxxix. 176 ff.
2 A. Lang, *Method in the Study of Totemism*, Glasgow, 1911.
3 Mary H. Kingsley, *West African Studies*², London, 1901, p. 112.
4 Hose-McDougall, *Pagan Tribes*, ii. 13 f.
5 *GB*³, pt. i., *The Magic Art*, i. 401 f.
6 *Laws of Manu*, iii. 89 (*SBE* xxv. [1886] 91).
7 'Vassus und Vassallus' in *Berichte über die Verhandlungen der königl. sächs. Gesell. (philol.-histor. Classe)* ii. [1892] 174.
8 J. Batchelor, *The Ainu and their Folk-lore*, London, 1901, p. 97.

1 *GB*³, pt. v., *Spirits of the Corn and of the Wild*, ii. 121 f.
2 A. Bourlet, 'Les Thay,' *Anthropos*, ii. [1907] 619.
3 *Relations des Jésuites*, 1672, p. 38, quoted by Frazer, *Totemism and Exogamy*, iii. 133 f.
4 *GB*³, pt. v., *Spirits of the Corn and of the Wild*, ii. 60 f.
5 *Ib.* i. 233 f. 6 *Ib.* ii. 123.
7 A. B. Ellis, *The Yoruba-speaking Peoples of the Slave Coast*, London, 1894, p. 125 f.
8 R. H. Codrington, *The Melanesians*, Oxford, 1891, p. 132.
9 Frazer, *Totemism and Exogamy*, iii. 391, 400.
10 W. J. Hoffman, 'The Menomini Indians,' *14 RBEW* [1896], pt. i. p. 64 ff.
11 *ZE* iii. [1871] 12, verse 7.
12 Cf. art. Sacrifice (Introductory and Primitive).

true that in America the doctrine of the clan totem has developed side by side with that of the guardian spirit conceived as an animal. Elsewhere, however, the patron spirit is much more closely allied to animism and theism. Wherever animistic conceptions prevail, there the notion of a tutelary genius will be found in some form or other. As spirits give place to gods, the spiritual guide and protector of individual men has his place in the pantheon, till in the Christian Church the doctrine of a guardian angel watching over, succouring, and defending the faithful on earth is raised to a higher and more spiritual level. 'Are they not all ministering spirits, sent forth to do service for the sake of them that shall inherit salvation?' (He 1[14]). This is the function of the guardian angels in the NT; they are to lead men safely to the kingdom of heaven by helping them to attain salvation.

It is not the Biblical conception that angels are the personification of nature powers, or merely the means of securing the favour and help of supernatural beings. They are consistently represented as a body of created spiritual beings intermediate between God and man (Ps 8[5]), whose function it is to act as messengers to mankind or attendants upon God's throne (Dn 7[9f.], Ps 91[11] 103[20], Is 6, Gn 16, Jg 13, Lk 1[11. 26]). Jerome thinks that every individual, whether baptized or not, has from his birth an angel commissioned to guard him,[1] while Chrysostom[2] and Basil hold that only the baptized enjoy the privileges of having a tutelary angel. Thomas Aquinas teaches that only the lowest orders of angels are sent to men, and therefore they alone are guardians.[3] No doubt the Biblical account of the ministry of angels was inherited from the world-wide doctrine of tutelary gods and spirits, and to an extent influenced by it, but at the same time it is evident that the line of development has been on a higher and more spiritual level.

LITERATURE.—The authorities are quoted in the footnotes.

E. O. JAMES.

TUTIORISM.—See RIGORISM, PROBABILISM.

TWINS.—The birth of twins in the human species is an event so unusual that it has almost everywhere drawn popular attention and evoked expressions of emotion, varying from extreme terror through the whole gamut of fear, repugnance, suspicion, anxiety, perplexity, hope, and joy. The first impulse seems to be to regard twins as unnatural and monstrous, and therefore as portending evil. The unfortunate babes and their mother have been looked upon as guilty of a serious crime—a crime calculated to call down the vengeance of the higher powers. Accordingly they must be at once put to death, and the offence repudiated and cleared from the land. Or their birth has been taken to be a message from the divinity conveying a warning of impending evil, only to be thrust aside by their immediate slaughter or by a variety of superstitious observances, intended by abstinence and humiliation to avert the threatened calamity.

1. Tabu of twins: its mitigation, ceremonies, and superstitions.—Among the peoples by whom this view of the birth of twins has been taken are those of Australia, the East Indian Archipelago, nearly the whole of Africa, the greater part of the aboriginal population of America, the population of the north-east of Asia, the non-Aryan tribes of India, and the backward classes and populations of Europe. In ancient times similar beliefs are reported of the Assyrians and Babylonians, the

[1] *Comm. in Matt.* 18[10] (bk. ii. § 139).
[2] *In Ep. ad Coloss.* hom. iii.
[3] *Summa Theol.* I. qu. cxiii. art. 4.

Aryan population of India, and the Egyptians. Where the superstition has the fullest power both mother and children are at once put to death.

A typical illustration of this proceeding is found among the Negro population of the Niger Delta. Even when the mother is allowed to live, she becomes an outcast and must pass the rest of her days in the forest. If she ventures near a town or village, any paths that she may use will be defiled and unfit for the inhabitants. 'She must not drink from the same spring or water-supply as her own people; she must not touch anything belonging to them. The consequence is that the mothers of twins simply die from hunger and exposure, or they take their own lives.' A slave-woman is the professional killer of twins. She takes each child by the feet and the neck and breaks its back across her knees. 'The bodies are then placed in an earthen pot and taken into a dense part of the bush and there left to be devoured by wild animals and insects. In some parts of this district the children are not killed, but simply thrown into the bush to be devoured.' It is no wonder that 'May you become the mother of twins!' is reckoned a frightful curse, and quarrelling women do not need to utter it in words: it is sufficient to hold up the fist, raising the index and middle finger in a V form, and the gesture is understood.[1]

The Negro peoples of W. Africa are very severe against the offence of giving birth to twins.

Among the Ibo such an event defiles the whole quarter, the inhabitants of which 'are obliged to throw away all the half-burnt firewood, the food cooked and the water brought in the previous night—everything, in a word, in the shape of nourishment, solid or liquid.'[2]

Mitigation of the law has, however, taken place. The mother is not always put to death or driven into the forest to die of hunger and exposure. At Arebo in Benin, if her husband be a man of wealth, he may redeem her with another victim.[3] More generally there are provided 'twin-towns'—cities of refuge, to which these unfortunate women may escape, or to which they can go when expelled from their own homes. There they must reside for a time to undergo purification. The period is stated by Mrs. D. Amaury Talbot,[4] speaking of the Ibibios, near the mouth of the Cross River, to be twelve moons. This, we may be sure, is the least penance that can be imposed on them.

Leonard writes that 'the women, looked on as unclean for the rest of their lives, are obliged to reside in villages, which are known as Twin-towns, or the habitations of defiled women, appointed for that particular purpose. From this time forth the husband, whether he be head of the house or not, is obliged to maintain a wife who has been so defiled; although at the same time he is strictly forbidden to cohabit or to have any dealings with her, being, as he is in every religious and personal sense, human and spiritual, divorced from her. But in spite of the fact that to him, as well as to all the members of his or her community, the woman is unclean and therefore tabu, the penalty of death being inflicted on both in the event of their breaking the law in this direction, she is allowed to form connections, but on no account to marry with strangers, or men belonging to outside communities, and the offspring resulting from such intercourse becomes, as a matter of course, the property of her husband, or the head of the house. . . . But in the event of the defiled woman herself bearing twins again, these must be destroyed unknown to any one. For, if known, the probabilities are that the death of the mother would be demanded by the household and the community as well. Or if not killed, she would be driven into the bush and left to die, although, if discovered by a stranger, he is at liberty to claim her as his own property,—that is at least if he feels inclined to run the risk of a venture so truly provocative of offence.'[5]

In Ibani, westward of the Ibibio country, the mother was, and perhaps is still, quarantined in an out-of-the-way hut for sixteen days, after which she went through a ceremony of purification by the priests. The father, or head of the house, was required to offer certain sacrifices. The threatened evils were thus averted, and the purified mother was then received back into the family circle.[6] Among the Ibibios, however, if the mother die in childbirth of twins, she may not be carried to burial by the ordinary door of the hut or along the ordinary paths of the village; she is borne through a hole broken for the purpose in the wall of the hut and along a path specially cut through the bush.[7]

[1] *JAI* xxix. [1899] 57; C. Partridge, *Cross River Natives*, London, 1905, p. 38; *Journ. Afr. Soc.* vii. [1908] 66.
[2] A. G. Leonard, *The Lower Niger and its Tribes*, London, 1906, p. 461.
[3] *ZVRW* xxx. [1913] 95, citing W. Bosman, *Nauwkeurige Beschryving van de Guinese Goud-Tand-en Slave-Kust*, Amsterdam, 1709, ii. 335; cf. M. H. Kingsley, *West African Studies*, London, 1899, p. 455.
[4] *Woman's Mysteries of a Primitive People*, London, 1915, p. 24.
[5] P. 460.
[6] *Ib.* p. 459.
[7] Mrs. Amaury Talbot, p. 215.

The lot of the children in Nigeria and adjacent countries has also been mitigated, to the extent that one only of them is now in most places put to death.

The Bassari of Togoland, *e.g.*, preserve the boy if the twins are of different sexes, or the stronger of the two if of the same sex, and bury the other alive in a big pot. A fowl is offered and cut in two. Half of it is buried with the condemned twin as a reminder to the latter of its close relationship with the surviving twin, so that the spirit of the buried child may not avenge itself on the survivor. Subsequently-born twins are both buried alive. Women who have borne twins, though apparently not driven away, are not allowed to take part in the agricultural labour (a woman's special work) of sowing and harvest, until the dead twin has reappeared as a subsequent child.[1]

A similar modification of the children's fate is found among the Bantu tribes. On the Lower Congo one of the twins is often neglected and starved to death. The reason given for this is that the mother does not like the extra trouble involved in caring for the two; but it is doubtful whether this is a sufficient explanation. When a twin dies, or is thus starved, it is buried at cross-roads, like a suicide or a man struck by lightning. A piece of wood is carved into an image of a child and put with the live twin, that the latter may not be lonely; and if the second child die, the image is buried with it.[2] The custom of giving the survivor a wooden figure in place of the twin that dies is also found among the Negro Yorubas and other W. African tribes, both Negroes and Bantu. It is said to keep the survivor from pining for the deceased, and to give the spirit of the deceased a habitation.[3] This arises from the special sympathy alleged to exist between twins, of which we shall find illustrations elsewhere.

Twins are regarded by the Kafirs of the south-west as scarcely human, and their mother is taunted with the disgrace. Yet, until Chaka stopped the custom, a twin was specially sought out, as being fearless and wild, to lead an attacking army in war. Among the Zulus twins are not counted in the number of children. One of the twins is always killed, remaining of course nameless. Nor is the survivor given a name until he is about sixteen years old, but before he is circumcised. If the survivor die, he is not allowed to be mourned, for fear of angering the *amatongo* (the ancestral spirits). If both twins are hidden, and so preserved, it is deemed they are united by sympathy as one flesh; and, if one die afterwards, he must not be mourned, lest the other should suffer.[4] To the Basukuma, or Bagwi, south of Lake Victoria Nyanza, the birth of twins is a great calamity, foretelling as it does a prolonged drought and great suffering among men and cattle. Consequently, when other means fail to produce rain, twins, if they can be found, are put to death.[5]

In British E. Africa the Akikuyu and the Akamba also regard the birth of twins as very unlucky; and the babes are, or perhaps one of them is, killed and thrown into the bush. Among the Akikuyu, however, the ban is limited to a first parturition; in such a case the twins are believed to prevent their mother from bearing again. But, among both the Akikuyu and their ethnically allied neighbours the Akamba, the birth of twins to a cow is deemed still more disastrous. Accordingly the calves are, or at least one of them is, always slaughtered, and among the Akamba the cow also, while the Akikuyu content themselves with putting a necklace of cowries, doubtless by way of amulet, round her neck. What is no doubt a modern alleviation permits one of the twin children to be given to a family of a different clan, becoming thus the child of that family, all relationship with its natural parents being severed. Another alternative among the Akamba, as likewise among the Nilotic Negro Dinkas, prescribes the substitution of goats for the sacrifice of the babes.[6]

The neighbouring Nandi, a Nilotic Negro tribe, look upon the birth of twins as an inauspicious event, and the mother is unclean for the rest of her life. Doubtless in earlier days she was put to death or expelled from the community. Even now her life must be a burden to her. 'She is given her own cow, and may not touch the milk or blood of any other animal. She may enter nobody's house until she has sprinkled a calabashful of water on the ground; and she may never cross the threshold of a cattle kraal again.' Special names, as is often the case, are given to the children.[7] The El Konyi, a branch of the Nandi, in the Elgon district, have rendered her lot a little less intolerable. But even there she is shut up for a while in the hut, and elaborate purificatory ceremonies must be performed with a medicine-man's assistance before she is released. Even if a cow produce twin calves, ceremonies are performed, and they are redeemed with the slaughter of a sheep.[1]

In both N. and S. America the custom of putting twins, or at least one of them, to death seems to have been universal.

The aborigines of the northern part of the upper basin of the River Amazons allege a curious reason for their dislike of twins. To give birth to twins is to descend to the level of the beasts—a thing to be avoided at all costs. The unfortunate mother therefore will leave the second child (or, if of different sexes, the girl) in the lonely spot in the bush whither she has, in accordance with custom, retired alone to be delivered.[2] The Salivas on the Orinoco call the mother nicknames, saying she is a rodent. Their objections, however, seem to go deeper than this; for the Saliva husband believes that the second twin is the offspring of adultery. A chief has in fact been known to give one of his wives a whipping in public for having dared to bring forth twins, and to threaten the others with similar consequences if they did the same.[3] From a pastoral letter by the archbishop of Lima in the year 1649, quoted by von Tschudi, it appears that the Peruvians of that date offered twins and children born feet first to some *huaca*, or supernatural being, and preserved their bodies or buried them in their houses.[4] Other records show that the birth of twins was regarded as unnatural and unlucky and demanding sacrifices and ceremonies lasting many days.[5] The North-Eastern Maidu of California who inhabited the foothills and western slopes of the sierra regarded the birth of twins as an exceptionally bad omen. The mother, it is said, was often killed and the newly-born children were either buried alive with her body or burned.[6] Among the Seri of the Californian Gulf 'triplets are deemed evil monsters and their production a capital crime.'[7]

In Australia the usual reason assigned for killing one or both twins is the economic reason that the mother has not enough milk for them, and moreover cannot rear them and also get her food. This is of a piece with the prevalent custom of infanticide, even of a single child, when the mother already has one dependent upon her. But among some tribes at least it does not appear to be the only reason.

Among the Euahlayi the husband suspects his wife of infidelity. Among the Arunta, where twins are reported as of extremely rare occurrence, they are attributed to two spirit-individuals entering the mother's body at one and the same time. By the northern tribes they are destroyed as something uncanny.[8]

On the island of Nias twins are universally disliked and dreaded.

In the province of West Nias it is believed that they will grow up evil doers; if a boy and girl, they are specially evil, the one will become a murderer and the other a poisoner. Formerly the younger used to be hung on a tree in a sack, there miserably to perish. The Dutch government and missionaries, it seems, have put an end to this cruelty. But the natives are still shy even of the parents. The father gets a priest to make a magical image of a board roughly cut in human shape, which is put up in the house as an amulet to prevent a second such misfortune. Until it is ready, the parents dare not speak to any other persons, lest they make them sick and give them jaundice; nor will their neighbours of the same *kampong* enter the house where the birth has taken place until the image is put up. At Lolowua in East Nias both children are thrust alive into a sack, taken far from the *kampong* and hung up in the bush, together with the after-birth. The house in which they have been born is avoided by other women, lest they incur the same misfortune. At Lahewa in North Nias the birth of twins is feared because it is held that, if they are allowed to live, some other members of the family must die. It is thus a matter of self-defence to put them to death. Their birth is moreover a sign of evil, such as failure of harvest, fire, epidemics, cattle-disease, and the like, threatening the whole *kampong*.[9]

---

1 *Globus*, lxxxi. [1902] 190.

2 J. H. Weeks, *FL* xix. [1908] 421, 423.

3 A. B. Ellis, *The Yoruba-speaking Peoples*, London, 1894, p. 80; M. H. Kingsley, *Travels in W. Africa*, do. 1897, p. 473; R. H. Nassau, *Fetichism in W. Africa*, do. 1904, pp. 206, 270.

4 Dudley Kidd, *Savage Childhood*, London, 1906, p. 45 ff.

5 J. F. Cunningham, *Uganda and its Peoples*, London, 1905, p. 305.

6 C. W. Hobley, *JRAI* xl. [1910] 435; W. S. and K. Routledge, *With a Prehistoric People*, London, 1910, p. 149; C. Dundas, *JRAI* xliii. [1913] 519, xlv. [1915] 301; C. W. Hobley, *The Ethnology of the A-Kamba*, Cambridge, 1910, p. 61; A. H. Post, *Studien zur Entwicklungsgeschichte des Familienrechts*, Oldenburg, 1890, p. 334.

7 A. C. Hollis, *The Nandi, their Language and Folklore*, Oxford, 1909, p. 68.

1 K. R. Dundas, *JRAI* xliii. 67.

2 T. W. Whiffen, *FL* xxiv. [1913] 45, *The North-West Amazons*, London, 1915, pp. 120, 150.

3 W. E. Roth, *30 RBEW* [1915], pp. 320, 325, quoting J. Gumilla, *Hist. Nat. . . . del Rio Orinoco*, Barcelona, 1791, i. 189.

4 J. J. von Tschudi, *Peruvian Antiquities*, Eng. tr., New York, 1853, p. 176.

5 *Globus*, xc. [1906] 305, citing *Documentos ineditos del Archivo de Indias*; cf. J. G. Frazer, *GB*³, pt. i., *The Magic Art*, London, 1911, i. 266.

6 R. B. Dixon, *Bull. Am. Mus. Nat. Hist.* xvii. [1905] 230.

7 W J McGee, *17 RBEW* [1898], pt. i. p. 281.

8 J. Dawson, *Australian Aborigines*, Melbourne, 1881, p. 39; J. G. Frazer, *Totemism and Exogamy*, London, 1910, i. 549; K. L. Parker, *The Euahlayi Tribe*, do. 1905, p. 51 f.; Spencer-Gillen[a], *passim*, Spencer-Gillen[b], p. 609; C. Strehlow, *Die Aranda- und Loritja-Stämme in Zentral Australien*, Frankfort-on-Main, 1907–11, i. 14.

9 J. P. Kleiweg de Zwaan, *Die Heilkunde der Niasser*, The Hague, 1913, p. 177.

Among the Kayan of Borneo, the motive alleged for exposing one of the twins in the jungle is to preserve the life of the other; for it is believed that a sympathetic bond exists between twins 'which renders each of them liable to all the ills and misfortunes that befall the other.'[1]

In Madagascar also twins were put to death.

Among the Antambahoaka the excuse for this treatment was that they would in any case die, or if not they would go mad or would sooner or later attempt the life of their parents. In the province of Imerina it was apparently the custom formerly to kill the twins. More recently, though this custom was abandoned, the parents were required to hand one of them over to a relative; and, if a woman belonging to the royal family gave birth to twins, both they and the mother were sent away and lost their rank.[2]

Exposure or murder by violence is in fact a common fate of one or both twins—a fate they share with other children deemed unlucky, such as misshapen babes or, as in Madagascar, those born on certain days which are subject to tabu.[3] Gradually, however, this untoward fate has, among many peoples, been lightened. The twins are still regarded as uncanny or even dangerous, but ceremonies are performed to ward off the evil.

The Ewe of Togoland, W. African Negroes, hold them to be fetish-children: in that capacity they must not be put to death, but they will not live long; they will die and go back to the fetish. Meanwhile, as a mark of distinction they wear special beads; and their parents set up in the corner of the house a fetish of a pair of buffalo-horns and in some districts a carved wooden doll or puppet. If any of their kin fall sick, presents are brought to the twins or to the fetish, and the twins propitiate the fetish. In the former German administrative district of Anecho the birth of twins is the occasion for a feast of eggs and beans boiled with the leaves of certain shrubs to all women who have already borne twins—a feast repeated every year afterwards. In the same district the twin-fetish is also invoked at a funeral feast on setting up two posts with a dog's skull bound upon them as a 'medicine.' At Great Be in the district of Lome-land, on the day when twins are born, an old woman who has herself borne twins comes and leads the father and mother out of the door, the one to the right, the other to the left in reverse directions round the house and then back into the house, in order that the twins may not die. Four months later the twins are taken, preceded by two young people playing on the flute, to the so-called twin-market, where some women who have already borne twins are found offering goods for sale (though this is not a regular market); and an old woman formally buys a few things for the twins. The object of this ceremony is to be able to say that the twins have been to market, for, until this is accomplished, the mother cannot leave the house. On their return they receive their names, and the father prepares the name-giving feast for the relatives, and also for those women of the village who have borne twins. Sometimes an unborn child is promised as wife to a man conditionally on its proving a girl. If one of the twins be a girl thus betrothed before her birth, the wooer performs a curious ceremony. On the day of the birth, after the circumambulation of the hut by the parents, he performs the same march seven times with some grass in his mouth, a hat of palm-bast, and leaves on his arm. Many spectators witness this ceremony by which he ratifies the compact and expresses his intention of marrying the girl. But he must take care not to laugh, otherwise he will go out of his mind. It is deemed more favourable that both children should be of the same sex. It is said that, if one of the twins die, the survivor carries about for the rest of his life a small wooden figure as a memento of his dead twin.[4] In another district, among the Konkomba, it is reported that a wedding gives occasion for no feast, except when a twin marries; then a great feast takes place, because twins are fetish-children.[5] The various peoples of Togoland, indeed, attach much importance to the birth of twins. Among the Ho, a tribe of Ewe, when twins, a boy and girl, are born, neither of the parents may eat or speak until an elaborate series of purificatory ceremonies, accompanied by feasting and the drinking of palm-wine, has been performed over them by others who are also parents of twins and who are paid for the rites. If these customs were omitted, the twins would become cripples. To the twins and their parents the flesh of hussar-apes and rats is forbidden. If any one shoot a hussar-ape, the parents of twins are expected to beat him with a stick.[6] The exact relation between the hussar-ape and twins is difficult to determine. It has been claimed that the hussar-ape and the long-tailed monkey (*Meerkatze*, a species of *cercopithecus*) are 'individual totems' of twins, and that twins may never kill or eat the latter, whereas they may kill, but may not eat, the former. Twins while asleep are said to go in the shape of these animals into the fields to eat maize; and if one such creature be killed, the corresponding twin will die. When the parents cultivate land, they sow a patch with maize for the special behoof of the twins thus changed, that they may be able to eat the grain; and the patch in question is never harvested. When one of the twins dies, a long-tailed monkey is sought in the forest and called by the name of the deceased child into a calabash, which is closed as if it were within and brought home to be honoured.[1] These are not exactly totemic superstitions; but they disclose a belief in the identity of, or at least an intimate personal connexion between, twins and these apes, such as we shall find in British Columbia between twins and salmon.

The Akoviewe, another Ewe tribe, have somewhat similar superstitions. The father of twins is forbidden to eat the flesh of hussar-apes; nor may he eat the remains of fruits eaten by these creatures. When the midwife sees that twins are about to be born, she relinquishes her place as soon as one is born lest she be afflicted with consumption, or at least a cough which will last the rest of her life. Certain vegetables and fruits are laid in the water wherewith the mother and children are bathed. A special feast with drinking of palm-wine is provided for the people of the surrounding villages. No presents must be made to one of the twins only, but both must be treated alike.[2] Among another tribe, the Kpenoe, neither parent must leave the house until the twin-customs have been performed. These consist, as among the Akoviewe, in the drinking of palm-wine, which is provided for all who give the twins cowries, and in a feast for all who come together from the outlying villages. The parents of twins already born come together to perform the customs and to dance, and the twins are carried on the neck that every one may see that the customs are carried out for them. These customs are very expensive. Twins must be clad alike so long as they are children.[3] They must eat yams a month earlier than other people, otherwise they will die.[4]

Notwithstanding the practices and beliefs just mentioned, the Ewe are said to look upon twins with favour.

For the Ho the birth of twins is a very great joy; it is regarded as better than riches. Among the Fo, another tribe of Ewe, such births are frequent. The children are regarded as children of Ohoho, a supernatural being with whom indeed they seem to be identified. Not only twins, but three children at a birth are favoured. A prayer for twins and triplets is even offered on certain occasions. The last-born is looked upon as the highest in rank. Special names are appropriated to children thus born. Special customs even in eating are prescribed to the mother. A woman who has borne twins wears round the neck a chain or string of beads as evidence of the honourable fact. Whatever the relation of Ohoho to the twins, he receives a cult, and in case of their danger or serious illness sacrifices are offered. A bank of clay is made just outside the entrance of the hut, where the cult is performed. If one of the twins is a girl, and she dies before the other, a wooden figure is made and stuck beside the clay-bank, to prevent the death of the boy—a custom disregarded if the boy happens to die first.[5]

It must be obvious, from these elaborate regulations, that, if the Ewe and their immediate neighbours favour the birth of twins and triplets, their joy is not without trembling. Such births are not in the order of nature; they are uncanny, equivocal; and, though they may be a blessing, if the proper precautions be not strictly observed they may be quite the reverse. Twins are credited with special connexions with the spirit-world: they are fetish-children; they are more or less identified with a supernatural being, or with certain of the lower animals whose shape they have power to take. Another observer in fact says that every unusual or remarkable event places the Ewe in an extraordinary situation with regard to his divinities, so that he must seek by special performances to re-enter into harmony with the upper world; consequently the birth of twins, as one such event, is not a joyous fact, but an evil omen.

The parents, he says, are kept in the hut for twenty-five days or longer, that they may not look on the heavens before the twin-customs have been carried out, else either in parents or in the children an unnatural change would take place: they would become like iron bars—possibly by the act of the lightning-god, whose badge or emblem is an iron bar. The account he gives of the customs is not identical in all particulars with those already mentioned; but their effect appears to be the same, and he notes that the details vary from district to district.[6]

1 C. Hose and W. McDougall, *The Pagan Tribes of Borneo*, London, 1912, ii. 156.

2 A. van Gennep, *Tabou et totémisme à Madagascar*, Paris, 1904, p. 176; Rendel Harris, *Cult of the Heavenly Twins*, p. 23.

3 See artt. Abandonment and Exposure.

4 *ZVRW* xxvi. [1911] 24, 46, 96, 100, 127.

5 *Ib.* xxvii. [1912] 92.

6 J. Spieth, *Die Ewe-Stämme*, Berlin, 1906, p. 202 ff.

1 *Anthropos*, vi. [1911] 457, vii. [1912] 91.

2 Spieth, p. 616. 3 *Ib.* p. 694. 4 *Ib.* p. 708.

5 *Anthropos*, vii. 89–92; Spieth, p. 308; *Globus*, xcvii. [1910] 247.

6 C. Spiers, *ARW* xv. [1912] 163. The same view of joy with trembling and anxiety seems to result from what we are told

Turning from the Negroes to the Bantu, we find that the ambiguous position of twins is well exemplified by the Thonga.

Among them the customs vary, as among the Ewe, in different districts. Formerly one at least of twins was put to death. In some places this custom continues; elsewhere their advent is a cause of rejoicing, and women even wish for twins and beg from the happy mothers a portion of the fat wherewith they smeared their bodies, in the hope by the same means to obtain a similar result. Yet in some groups (tribes or 'clans') which do not put twins to death their birth is considered a special defilement. The mother is at once removed from the hut, which is burnt together with its contents. She is placed in a shelter behind the village. All the women assemble and start out in all directions to draw water in old calabashes from all the wells and pools of the neighbourhood. As they go, they sing an invocation to the rain, and on returning they throw the water over the mother and babes, who are further purified by the medicine-man with a drug which he has prepared. The details of their purification vary to some extent; but, until it is accomplished, no one in the village is allowed to eat, and the following day work in the fields is forbidden, for it would prevent the fall of rain. The mother in her shelter outside the village is allowed no communication with the other inhabitants, except possibly one girl who helps her in nursing the twins. To remove the defilement, she must pass it on, like that of a widow, by means of incomplete sexual intercourse, to four men successively. The first three of these victims at least will die in consequence. After each sexual act the medicine-man prepares a vapour-bath for her. When all four acts are accomplished, she returns to her parents' house, and there entertains a lover whose relations with her result in another child. She thus completes her purification, and her husband fetches her home. But in some places she is not admitted through the doorway: she crawls through a hole made in the back of the wall; and the husband is subjected to certain rites. The twins themselves are treated in many respects differently from ordinary children. Usual ceremonies are omitted; they are weaned earlier; and there is a general antipathy to them. Special precautions to protect them and their mother are also taken on the occasion of a ceremonial mourning visit.[1]

On the other side of S. Africa, in what was German territory, the Herero consider the birth of twins as 'the greatest and most fortunate event which can happen to a mortal Omuherero.'

Both father and children are specially privileged. Yet the parents are immediately placed under a tabu; they may not speak or be spoken to, nor have any contact or intercourse with any one except those who wait on them, who are known, as well as the children and their parents, by the epithet of 'twins' (*epaha*); they are ejected from the village; all clothes and ornaments are taken off them; and they receive in exchange a few old worthless skins. Messengers call together the whole 'tribe,' and every one must appear with all his cattle, else he will be bewitched and die. The father goes to meet his guests and is received, as if he were an enemy, with all sorts of missiles, while the women raise a terrible lamentation. This, however, is only ceremonial. He with the other *epaha* meets them at the village, where each of the visitors brings him an offering, and, if male, is 'consecrated' in return by him, if female, by the mother. A hut is then built for the parents, and an ox is slaughtered, which all the people must taste, beginning with the parents, and a small piece of the meat is held to the toes of both twins. The remaining meat is taken to the parents' newly-built hut, of which they then take possession. During the following days the father goes in procession round the village, visiting two or three houses each day. At every house the ceremonies are repeated: the offerings are made to him, the 'consecration' by him, the slaughter of an ox, the cooking and ritual tasting of its flesh are repeated, and the remainder is carried to his house. When he has finished the circuit of his own village, he commences that of the neighbouring villages. If the meat becomes too plentiful, he asks for living cattle instead of slaughtered, and adds them to his own herd. No one will dare to refuse him. Every father of twins has the right to represent the chief of the village, when the latter is absent, in his priestly functions. A twin boy also possesses all the priestly privileges: for him there is no meat, no milk forbidden, and nobody would dare to curse him. When the chief of the village dies, he inherits the priestly dignity associated with the chieftainship.[2]

It would seem, therefore, that the tabu encircles the twins and their parents not as accursed but as sacred; the curse rests on the community, and the offerings made to the father and the 'consecration' he bestows are intended to avert it and restore and redintegrate the ordinary life.

The Baganda regarded twins as due to the direct intervention of Mukasa, the god of Lake Victoria Nyanza, who was said to show his esteem for certain women in this manner; and great care and numbers of tabus were necessary to retain his favour. The position was evidently one of great delicacy; for any mistake on the part of the parents, or any sickness that befell the twins, was looked upon as the result of the god's anger, which might extend to the whole clan. The word 'twins' might not be mentioned until the rites were at an end. The persons of the parents were sacred. They wore a distinctive dress, and no one might touch them. The mother could not go out of doors by day without covering her head. No one was allowed to enter the house except the husband and wife, and a few relatives. The men and the women were required to enter through a separate opening cut for each sex in the back of the house. The doorway was blocked up. The nails and hair of both parents were not cut until the ceremonies had all been completed, save that at one point in the rites the father's hair was shaved in a particular fashion. The ceremonies were lengthy. They included the beating of special drums, a round of visits to the father's and mother's parents and to the members of both clans, at which there were feasts and dancing, a curious rite referred to below, and a final ceremonial dance by women. The father during the ceremonies wears on his ankles a number of small bells, to give notice of his coming and prevent molestation. He is privileged to enter any one's garden and take what produce he pleases to feast his guests. In fact, being under the god's protection, he may do almost anything he likes. When the ceremonies are completed, his tabu is not yet over. For this he must wait until he has taken part in the next war. He must then take the bundle of hair and nails of which he has been shorn in his purification and cram it into the mouth, or tie it round the neck, of the first enemy he kills. It is only after this that he ceases to wear a distinctive dress and returns to ordinary life. The twins themselves remain sacred all their lives. A special ceremony was performed when a twin went to war for the first time and killed a man. If twins died in infancy, their deaths were announced with a euphemism and they were embalmed, placed in a new cooking pot, and buried in waste land. Women avoided their graves lest the ghost should enter them and be born again of them. There was no mourning for them, but, if the ceremonies were incomplete, they were continued as though they were still alive.[1] The neighbours of the Baganda, the Bahima or Banyankole, possess a Twin totem-clan. Yet among them, even in the Twin clan, twins are the subject of tabu. They must not, however, be spoken of disparagingly, lest an ancestral ghost overhear and be angry.[2]

It is needless to detail the ceremonies to which the birth of twins gives occasion among other Bantu peoples. Though differing among the various tribes, they are all founded upon the feeling that the birth is an uncanny event, often expressly ascribed to divine intervention. Fortunate it may be for the parents; to the community in general it is a source of peril and ill omen, which must be bought off by gifts and ceremonies; and, until those ceremonies are completed, the twins and their parents are as a rule secluded from intercourse with the world. Sometimes, but rarely, as among the Bushongo of the Upper Congo, the birth of twins is frankly welcomed as a very happy occurrence.[3] Even where general rejoicing takes place, it is a joy with trembling. The tabu is enforced; and special rites must be performed to restore the normal relations of the people.

Among the Masai, a Hamitic tribe of E. Africa, the birth of twins, which is not very rare, causes the greatest pleasure, especially if both be boys.

To mark their parents' pride, a thong of leather adorned with cowries is hung round the neck of each; and, while the elder is retained by the mother, the younger is often nursed by one of her fellow-wives. No tabu and no ceremonies are reported.[4]

It may be noted here that, wherever the birth of twins, as among the Masai, is stated to be comparatively frequent, they are received with more or less favour.

The Lattuka, a Nilotic Negro tribe of the Sudan, among whom twins are rare, while apparently not regarding them per-

of other Negro peoples (L. Desplagnes, *Le Plateau central nigérien*, Paris, 1907, p. 233; *Journ. Afr. Soc.* ix. [1910] 179, x. [1911] 31, xvi. [1917] 43; *ZVRW* xxx. 95; Leonard, *Lower Niger*, p. 462; *L'Anthropologie*, xiv. [1903] 90).

[1] H. A. Junod, *The Life of a South African Tribe*, Neuchâtel, 1912–13, ii. 394–400; cf. also his *Les Ba-ronga*, do. 1898, p. 412 ff., and *Rev. d'Ethnographie et de Sociologie*, i. [1910] 149, 167.

[2] E. Dannert, [South African] *Folk-Lore Journal*, ii. [Cape Town, 1880] 104 ff., also his *Zum Rechte der Herero*, Berlin, 1906, p. 20; F. Meyer, *Wirtschaft und Recht der Herero*, do. 1905, p. 61.

[1] J. Roscoe, *The Baganda*, London, 1911, pp. 64 ff., 81, 124, 358, *JAI* xxxii. [1902] 32–35, 49, 53, 60, *Man*, x. [1910] 42 f.; cf. Frazer, *GB*[3], pt. ii., *Taboo and the Perils of the Soul*, London, 1911, p. 384, *Totemism and Exogamy*, ii. 482.

[2] J. Roscoe, *The Northern Bantu*, Cambridge, 1915, p. 117, *JRAI* xxxvii. [1907] 100, 107.

[3] E. Torday and T. A. Joyce, *Notes ethnographiques sur les Bushongo*, Brussels, 1911, pp. 112, 57, 56.

[4] M. Merker, *Die Masai*, Berlin, 1904, p. 51.

sonally with disfavour, hold that they threaten misfortune to their father. If he went hunting buffaloes, he would be killed or wounded; and, if he wounded an antelope, it would escape him. He therefore takes precautions by not leaving the village until the spell is broken by another woman bearing twins, or his wife another child.[1]

In India and adjacent countries twins are generally held to be inauspicious, though there are differences in this respect. All the peoples, however, seem to be agreed that the birth of twins of different sexes is serious. It is held that their connexion in the womb has been too close: it has been sinful, amounting to prenatal incest.[2]

Among the inhabitants of the Siamese Malay States, while twins (a rare occurrence there) are considered lucky, it is otherwise with triplets: they are accursed.[3] In any case, it is considered by the Kurmi and Kawar of the Central Provinces that the sympathy between twins is dangerously close, and various rites are adopted to break their connexion, else, if misfortune or death happens to the one, the other also will suffer or die.[4] The Tang Khul Nagas of Assam are divided in opinion. Some villages welcome twins; others object to having among them a woman who gives birth to more than one child at a time, looking (like some of the S. American tribes) upon her as a lower animal. At Ukhrul, if both are boys, their father is regarded as a descendant of some cannibal line like the tigers, and he ought to be carefully watched. It is interesting to note that the villages where they are welcomed connect them with fruitfulness of the crops.[5]

On the island of Celebes it is held by the Macassars and Buginese that one of twins is often a crocodile. The same curious belief is found in Java, where it is said that on such occasions a double offering is brought to the crocodile for his 'humanity'; and at Windesi, New Guinea, a story is told of a woman who gave birth to twins, one of them an iguana.[6] The Balinese, at least among the highest castes, call twins of different sexes 'betrothed'—a practice which Wilken traces to an origin from a time when no forbidden degrees were yet in existence, and when such twins at marriageable age used to be made to marry one another.[7] The idea, persisting into a later stage, might account for the imputations of prenatal incest just referred to. In some of the Moluccas twins are not regarded with favour. In these they are often attributed to superfetation; and in the Babar Archipelago one of them is sent to another village—in earlier days death was probably its doom.[8] In other islands, on the contrary, they are desired, and are looked upon as the gift of the sky-god or male principle,[9] though they are even then in some islands handed over to kinsmen to be brought up.[10] In the Aaru Archipelago, where they are much desired, they are looked upon as an omen of a good tripang and pearl harvest.[11] The Melanesian peoples of Eastern New Guinea regard twins with disfavour; among the Southern Massim the mother was formerly permitted to put one to death, while among the Northern Massim she is ridiculed as a pig.[12] Their kinsmen of the Banks Islands, on the other hand, favour them; but, if boy and girl, they are regarded as man and wife. Rivers thinks that in former days such twins were probably killed—an opinion supported by the practice and belief of the natives of the Duke of York Islands and New Britain.[13] On the whole, in the neighbouring Solomon Islands twins are liked; in Florida Island only there is said to be a suspicion of double paternity; while in Lepers' Island they are conjectured to be the gift of a certain supernatural being named Tagaro.[14] It may be further mentioned, to illustrate the opposite opinions that may be held by even the same race, that

1 *Emin Pasha in Central Africa*, London, 1888, p. 237. Speaking generally, the Nilotic Negroes rejoice with trembling.

2 Ancient India: authorities collected by Rendel Harris, *Boanerges*, p. 183 ff.; cf. *ARW* v. [1902] 271, 273. Kashmir: *Census of India*, 1911, xx. 145. Panjab: *ib.* xiv. 302. Baluchistan: *ib.* iv. 87. Central Provinces and Berar: *ib.* x. 158; R. V. Russell, *The Tribes and Castes of the Cent. Prov. of India*, London, 1916, iv. 73. Todas: W. H. R. Rivers, *The Todas*, London, 1906, p. 480. Cochin: L. K. Anantha Krishna, *The Cochin Tribes and Castes*, Madras, 1909–12, i. 272. Nāga Tribes of Manipur: T. C. Hodson, *The Nāga Tribes of Manipur*, London, 1911, p. 133 f. Khasis: P. R. T. Gurdon, *The Khasis*, do. 1907, p. 127.

3 N. Annandale and H. C. Robinson, *Fasciculi Malayenses*, London, 1903–04, ii. 64.

4 R. V. Russell, iii. 396, iv. 73.

5 *Census of India, 1911*, iii. [*Assam*] pt. i. p. 77; cf. *FL* xxi. [1910] 311.

6 G. A. Wilken, *De verspreide Geschriften*, The Hague, 1912, iii. 86 n., iv. 147; cf. *GB*[3], pt. v., *Spirits of the Corn and of the Wild*, London, 1912, ii. 212.

7 Wilken, i. 459.

8 J. G. F. Riedel, *De sluik- en kroesharige rassen tusschen Selebes en Papua*, The Hague, 1886, pp. 74, 176, 355.

9 *Ib.* pp. 136, 238, 264, 392, 450.

10 *Ib.* pp. 136, 355.

11 *Ib.* p. 264.

12 C. G. Seligmann, *The Melanesians of Brit. New Guinea*, Cambridge, 1910, pp. 488, 705.

13 W. H. R. Rivers, *The Hist. of Melanesian Society*, Cambridge, 1914, i. 145; *JAI* xviii. [1889] 292; Rendel Harris, *Boanerges*, p. 174. Cf. the Balinese.

14 R. H. Codrington, *The Melanesians*, Oxford, 1891, p. 230.

in New Ireland, since to bespell a woman might cause her to bear twins, it is to be inferred that they were not there desired.[1] On the Micronesian island of Yap, an outlier of the Pelew Archipelago, one of twins was given to a relative, else they would both die—an obvious attempt, as in the Moluccas and the Central Provinces of India, to break the connexion between them.[2] The Igorots of the Philippine Islands assign a different reason for the same custom: it is to avert the evil omen of their birth.[3] The Ainus allege that one of them would die.[4]

To the Gilyaks of the island of Sakhalin twins are a source of disquiet, if not of fear. Such births are said to be relatively common, and usually either both boys or both girls. One of the pair is believed to be offspring of the Mountain-man, a supernatural being haunting mountain and forest, with whom the people are careful to keep on good terms. This child ought to be returned to his formidable parent as soon as possible; but, since there is no means of identifying him with certainty, both twins must be treated alike. In consequence of this origin, twins after death are not cremated as other corpses are, for fear that the Mountain-man will punish all who take part in the funeral by loss of their eyesight. Even the parents have by the birth become related to the Mountain-man and must be buried also. Twins are believed to be endowed with superhuman powers, and are, so long as they live, regarded with terror. But those who die early are chiefly feared, for, having returned to the supernatural world before they had time to become accustomed to men and to feel themselves as their likes, they have special power to harm them. Their family therefore place a small model of a Gilyak *yurte* either inside or outside the dwelling and put into it a carved wooden figure representing the deceased. To this figure they bring offerings every day of portions of their own food; and the practice is continued for three generations. At last the great-grandchildren take the figure from the dwelling to a neighbouring mountain with great ceremony and there leave it, and with it a final offering of food. Then for the first time the community feels safe in neglecting any further observances. On account of this fear of twins, women and girls are strictly forbidden to listen to tales of twins, nor may women even accept gifts of small household furniture from acquaintances who have given birth to twins, lest the misfortune of twins should in either case be communicated, though this liability does not attach so seriously to gifts of objects of metal. The names of twins once bestowed are retained; no other children are allowed to have the same; nor does a twin ever take the name of a deceased elder of the family, according to the usual custom.[5]

The ancient Assyrians held the birth of twins to be a calamity, except in the royal family.[6] Modern Syrians, on the contrary, if the evidence of refugees at Boston may be trusted, regard it as bringing good luck.[7] According to modern Egyptians about Karnak, one of twins may be a wild cat, whose soul goes out at night on the prowl, when the owner is asleep.[8] To the Bulgarians twins are a misfortune, to avert which the mothers of bride and bridegroom at the wedding simultaneously drink brandy.[9] Even in the north-east of Scotland twins are so far regarded as unlucky that one of them, even though married, will be childless.[10]

On the American continent also twins were regarded as mysterious.

The Shuswap, who occupy part of the Fraser River and Columbia River basins in British Columbia, expressly hold them to be 'great mystery.' Though the mother's husband is deemed to be their real father, the black bear generally, but sometimes the grisly bear, or the deer, is believed to have influenced their birth. Whichever animal it was, it appeared to the mother in dreams and became the *manitu*, or spirit-protector, of the children throughout their lives. They are deemed lucky on this account; but it does not prevent their tabu. At their birth their parents shift camp to the woods, even in midwinter; and they are not allowed near other people for four years. During this time the father or, if he dies, the mother washes and scours them every day with fir-branches—a common method of cleansing from pollution.[11] The southerly neighbours of the Shuswap, the Ntlakapamux of the lower Fraser River and Thompson River basins, say that the mother is usually apprised beforehand by the repeated appearance of the grisly bear in her dreams. The children are accordingly treated differently from other children, and are called 'grisly-bear-children' or 'hairy feet.' The grisly bear is their *manitu*. Their parents are under tabus like those of the Shuswap. Special ceremonies are performed at their birth, and they are during the first four years washed like Shuswap twins. It was held that a birth (especially of twins) immediately changes the weather.[12] Farther inland the Déné treat the bear when caught

1 P. G. Peekel, *Religion und Zauberei auf dem mittl. Neu-Mecklenburg*, Münster, 1910, p. 127.

2 *Globus*, xci. [1907] 142.

3 F. H. Sawyer, *Inhabitants of the Philippines*, London, 1900, p. 258.

4 A. H. Post, *Studien zur Entwicklungsgesch. des Familienrechts*, p. 335.

5 B. Pilsudski, *Anthropos*, v. [1910] 760.

6 *RHR* lxv. [1912] 407, reviewing C. Fossey, *Présages assyriens*; *ARW* v. 272.

7 *JAFL* xvi. [1903] 136.

8 *ARW* xvi. [1913] 629.

9 *ZVRW* xxxi. [1913] 247.

10 *FL* xxv. [1914] 349.

11 *Jesup N. Pacific Exped. Publications*, New York and Leyden, 1900 ff., ii. 586, 589; cf. *Rep. Brit. Ass.*, 1890, p. 644.

12 *Jesup N. Pac. Exped.* i. [1900] 310, 374.

with the greatest consideration and respect, and propitiate it. Among their observances neither a dog nor a menstruating woman nor the father of twins, as long as both twins are alive, is allowed to touch it. The reason is that these are all legally impure, and it is feared that the fellows of the victim will be so irritated by unclean contact that they will henceforth stubbornly avoid the traps or snares of those guilty of such a slight. The father of twins is required to offer gifts to the community 'to wash out his shame.'[1] The Nez Percés in the north-west of the United States, on the other hand, welcome twins as lucky both to the family and to themselves.[2]

The Nutka of Vancouver Island and the Kwakiutl, who inhabit the northern end of the island and the opposite shore of the mainland, connect twins with salmon. The former, though not exactly identifying them with salmon, believe them to be in some way related to them. Hence the parents, whose banishment from the village extends only to two years, among their various tabus and rites, must avoid fresh food, particularly salmon. Wooden images and masks representing birds and fish are exhibited round the hut and near the adjacent river by way of invitation to birds and fish to visit the twins and be friendly to them; the father moreover sings certain songs with the same intention. It is believed that the salmon accordingly throng to see them, and the birth of twins is an omen of a good salmon year. If the omen be not fulfilled, it is a presage of their early death.[3] The Kwakiutl regard twins as having in their previous existence been actually salmon. They therefore warn them against going near the water, lest they be retransformed into salmon. A stricter tabu than those of the tribes mentioned above rests on the parents; for they must separate for sixteen months and each pretend to be married to a log, with which they lie down every night. During this period they are required to perform certain ceremonies and conform to certain observances. Among others the father may not catch salmon, the mother may not dig clams, else both salmon and clams will disappear; and the parents may not borrow canoes or paddles, or their owners would have twins. The birth of twins causes permanent backache to the parents; to avert this each parent procures for intercourse with the other a person of the opposite sex, who will, it is believed, be attacked by the backache instead. On the other hand, young women who desire to bear children squat and lean over the pit above which twins have been born. At the death of a twin no one is allowed to wail for him; and among the observances the surviving twin is washed in the water used to wash the corpse.[4] Traces of a similar belief to that of the Kwakiutl are found among the Skqomic, a Salishan tribe farther south, with reference to another kind of fish called *tsai anūk*; and, as everywhere else in British Columbia, the parents are subject to a strict tabu and purification.[5] In Mexico the Tlaxcalans call twins snakes; and they are believed able to cure bites of serpents and other animals, as well as pain or inflammation of the tendons, especially of the feet and ankles. Triplets will be kings.[6] It is believed by the Yuchi, formerly of Georgia and Alabama, that twins and deformed or abnormal children are sent by 'the supernatural beings to be guides to the people,' and they are accordingly taken great care of.[7] There is some evidence that among the Cheyenne twins were a subject of tabu.[8]

2. Origin, parentage.—Many peoples entertain the belief that a human father can beget only one child at a time. This has led to the suspicion, as among the Saliva of the Orinoco and the Euahlayi of New South Wales already noted, that the second child is due to the mother's infidelity. The same belief is attributed to the Chibchas and to the Hottentots.[9] It is held also by the peoples of the Warri District of Nigeria.[10] It was formerly entertained in Europe. The father had the right of deciding on the birth of a child whether it should be brought up or destroyed; and, if he had any suspicion as to his wife's loyalty, the child was often put to death. On this ground definitely it was held excusable to expose or put to death twins and triplets. A number of mediæval legends among the Germans and other Teutonic peoples are elaborations of this theme.[11] The belief in superfetation is almost a necessary corollary to the belief that the twins are due to two fathers. Hence also the second-born child is commonly held to be the elder or higher in rank, as among the Negroes.

But there is another, and perhaps older, view, more widely held, that they are the result of divine impregnation.

In W. Africa we have seen that they are called 'fetish-children.' To the Fo of Togoland they are the children of Ohoho. The Efiks of Calabar, the Ikwes of the Upper Cross River, and the Ibibio pronounce one of them to be the offspring of an evil spirit.[1] So the Warundi of E. Africa attribute them to an 'incubus,' and regard their birth as a favour, which the jealous spirit is likely to recall, or to take the mother or her husband in payment for it. To obviate this, the important event is celebrated by a variety of ceremonies, including songs, dances, and gifts to the parents (nominally oblations for the spirit), which have a way of disappearing as by enchantment. Two entirely black sheep are bought for the twins; they must preserve and care for them as long as they live. The sheep in turn are said to be the children's guardians, the receptacle and symbol of their spirits, their fetish.[2] In Indonesia likewise the birth of twins is ascribed to a demon. One of them, according to belief in the island of Nias, is due to superfetation caused by such a being, as is also the birth of an albino. Other causes are recognized in the eastern province of the island, as roughness or anger on the mother's part towards her parents or sister, continued cohabitation during pregnancy, or the eating of a double fruit. To the last we shall recur. Like the Warundi, the North Niasese fear that some other members of the family will die if the twins are allowed to live; and they are therefore put to death. They are also held to be an omen of various kinds of calamity.[3] The Bakaua of New Guinea think that 'evil spirits have had a hand in the game,' wherefore one of the twins is killed.[4] According to the Bontoc Igorot of Luzon, one of the twins is the offspring of an *anito* (ghost of the dead). The quieter one, therefore, or the larger, is put in a pot and buried alive.[5] The Buck of Demerara also regard twins as the offspring of an evil spirit named Pernowhari.[6] In Essequibo a British commissioner reports that a native medicine-man not many years ago ascribed an outbreak of sickness to one of twins who had just been born. He said it was the child of a *kenaima*, a wizard or person of supernatural powers, because 'a woman could not naturally produce two children at a birth'; and the unfortunate child at his instigation was burnt alive.[7] The Melanesians of Lepers' Island hold that twins may be the gift of a spirit called Tagaro; in Florida Island there is a suspicion of the mother's infidelity to her husband, but it is generally accepted that she has trespassed on the sacred place of a ghost 'whose power lies that way.'[8] In the Moluccas twins are attributed to the sky-god, Upulero, probably as father.[9] This belief may be compared with that of the Thonga tribes of S.E. Africa, who call twins 'children of heaven' and in this capacity ascribe to them special powers; and the mother is called Tilo, 'heaven.'[10] The ancient Peruvians held that one of twins was the son of the lightning, to which they prayed as the lord and creator of rain, and the earthly parents were made to undergo divers tabus and ceremonies. There is some evidence that they offered the twins, probably to the lightning; at any rate, if they died young, the bodies were enclosed in pots and kept in the dwelling-house as sacred things.[11]

As among the Gilyaks one of twins is taken to be the offspring of the Mountain-man, so their neighbours the Ainus of Sakhalin believe one of them to be that of a supernatural being, on the ground that one man can beget only one child at a time. This is a perpetual shame to the mother; and there is reason for believing that one is destroyed at birth, as indeed the oldest account expressly affirms. At all events the Ainus state that only one survives, and that one of human paternity. It is also said that, like the Japanese, they hold that, when twins are born, the younger is bold, strong, and lucky, while nothing distinguishes the elder from ordinary men. They, however, seek by means of sacrifice, prayer, and talismans to prevent such births. They avoid women who have given birth to twins; but, contrary to the Gilyaks, they hold that nothing is so likely to convey the infection as objects of metal.[12] Farther

1 *Anthropos*, v. [1910] 129, 975.
2 H. J. Spinden, *Mem. Amer. Anthr. Assoc.*, vol. ii. pt. iii. [1908] p. 246.
3 *Rep. Brit. Assoc.*, 1890, p. 591 f.
4 *Ib.* 1889, p. 847; *ib.* 1890, pp. 610, 614; *ib.* 1896, pp. 574, 577; *Jesup N. Pac. Exped.* iii. [1905] 322, 375; cf. *31 RBEW* [1916], p. 887 (a Bellabella tale).
5 *Rep. Brit. Assoc.*, 1900, pp. 481, 523 f.
6 F. Starr, *Notes upon the Ethnog. of S. Mexico*, Davenport, Iowa, 1900, p. 22.
7 F. G. Speck, *Ethnol. of the Yuchi Indians*, Philadelphia, 1909, p. 110.
8 *JAFL* xxi. [1908] 315.
9 *ARW* v. 272.
10 *JAI* xxviii. [1899] 107.
11 Jacob Grimm, *Deutsche Rechtsalterthümer*, Göttingen, 1854, p. 456; J. and W. K. Grimm, *Deutsche Sagen*, Berlin, 1818, ii. 30, 233, 291.

1 Partridge, pp. 38, 257 f.; Mrs. Amaury Talbot, p. 23; *Anthropos*, vii. 89.
2 J. M. M. Van der Burgt, *Un grand Peuple de l'Afrique équatoriale*, Bois-le-Duc, 1904, p. 71 f.
3 E. Modigliani, *Un Viaggio a Nías*, Milan, 1890, p. 555; De Zwaan, p. 178.
4 R. Neuhauss, *Deutsch Neu-Guinea*, Berlin, 1911, iii. 400.
5 A. E. Jenks, *The Bontoc Igorot*, Manila, 1905, p. 60.
6 *FL* xv. [1904] 343, citing *Demerara Daily Chronicle*, of 27th Jan. 1904.
7 Rendel Harris, *Cult of the Heavenly Twins*, p. 5, quoting the report.
8 Codrington, p. 230.
9 Riedel, pp. 136, 238, 264, 392, 450.
10 Junod, *Life of a S. African Tribe*, ii. 294, *Les Ba-ronga*, p. 412.
11 *GB*³, pt. i., *Magic Art*, i. 266 f., citing the Jesuit J. de Arriaga; von Tschudi, p. 176 f.; *Globus*, xc. [1906] 305. Cf. *Essays and Studies presented to William Ridgeway*, Cambridge, 1913, p. 369 f.
12 *Anthropos*, v. 770; Rendel Harris, *Boanerges*, p. 161.

north, on the mainland of Asia, the Kamchatkan tribes ascribe twins to 'the wolf in the forest.' The birth of twins is consequently not only a misfortune but also a sin (intensified if both are girls); every one promptly runs out of the house, leaving the mother and children alone. To prevent such an event, the Itälmens (one of the tribes) set up a figure of a wolf, made of grass, pretending that it is the husband of the young women, and renewing it year by year.[1]

The somewhat indefinite ascription by the various tribes of the north-western coasts of N. America to grisly bears and other land animals, or to salmon or other fish, indicates rather a belief that twins are a reincarnation of such creatures than that they are directly generated by them upon the mother, though these beliefs are by no means far apart.

The Lillooet considered that the twins were the real offspring of the grisly bear; but some held that he 'acted through' the husband. Twins were by many said to be 'grisly bears in human form,' and, when a twin died, his soul went back to the grisly bears and became one of them. When a twin died, his body was deposited in a fir-tree far from graves and human habitations, and the grisly bear was supposed to take it away.[2]

The belief in reincarnation is very wide-spread; it has been discussed by the present writer in his *Primitive Paternity*.[3]

The Semang, a Negrito tribe of Perak, hold that certain birds are the souls of human beings; they are born as children in consequence of being eaten by women; and, when a woman eats a soul-bird with its egg, the result is twins.[4]

Pregnancy caused by various kinds of food is a wide-spread superstition discussed in *Primitive Paternity*, ch. ii. Twins are attributed by many peoples to the eating of double fruits and similar things.

The belief on the island of Nias has already been referred to. It is shared in the E. Indies by the Malay populations of Sumatra, the Tagalas of the Philippines, and the Malagasy; in S. America by the Arawaks and the aborigines of Paraguay; in W. Africa by the Ibibio, in Europe by the Germans, the Magyars, and the French of Poitou.[5] There is even a trace of it in England around Malvern, where it is said that nuts are a presage of the number of children to be born in the year, and 'double nuts presage a considerable number of twins.'[6] Among the Zulus, it is said, other objects in pairs are not eaten, nor are two articles at once received from the hand of another, lest the birth of twins result.[7] The Euahlayi, an Australian tribe, think that babies hang on trees ready to enter into any passing woman; and twins are attributed, as among the Arunta, mentioned above, to two baby-spirits hanging on one branch and dropping on the same woman. But it seems that the woman's husband is reluctant to acknowledge more than one of them.[8] This points to the superstition of double paternity discussed above. On Mabuiag, in Torres Straits, twins are ascribed to the act of a magician, or to the mother when pregnant touching or breaking a parasitic plant.[9] Among the Maidu of California it was thought that, if the father wore two caps at the time of conception, twins would be produced.[10] In some of the Molucca Islands the same result was caused by the mother lying on her back at the time of conception.[11]

3. Powers.—Twins are believed to possess extraordinary powers.

An account is given in a Chinese narrative dating from the 14th cent. of a magician who procured the fœtus from a woman pregnant of twins to use it for the purpose of divining; and it is remarked that special 'spiritual power' was attributed to the fœtus of twins.[12] Among the Iroquois twins are believed able to foretell future events and perform other remarkable things; but they are said to lose the power if a menstruating woman prepares their food.[13] So the Golahs of Liberia hold that twins have the privilege of learning things by means of dreams. They are thus able to see and identify bush-goats in which, according to native belief, human beings are reincarnated. They lose the privilege, however, if they eat of animals which they have so identified, for they would be eating men.[1] This power appears to extend into adult life. Twins among the Igarra of S. Nigeria are able to prognosticate with regard to the offspring of a pregnant woman, but only while children. They are ascribed to good spirits and looked upon with favour as among some other peoples. The younger of the two is regarded as the elder; but both must be treated exactly alike: any favouritism will lead to the death of one of them. They cannot be poisoned, for no poison will have any evil effect on them.[2] The Thonga about Delagoa Bay, who regard twins with hostility, utilize a twin girl, when the caterpillars of a beetle called *nunu* swarm in December or January, to lead the procession of women who have been employed in collecting the insects from the bean-stalks to throw them into a neighbouring lake with a spell to get rid of the plague.[3] On the occasion of the cattle-plague at Dobischwald, in Austrian Silesia, a bonfire is made to drive the cattle through; and twin brothers are necessary to fell the tree of which the fire is made.[4] The Polish peasant, as a spell against 'the pest' (probably the cattle-plague), causes a furrow to be drawn around his field by a pair of twin oxen led by twin brothers.[5] Twins are credited in Lower Nubia and Egypt with the power of shape-shifting, to the extent at least of becoming cats at night and stealing milk and food and eating chickens. This can be prevented only if the father, immediately after their birth, puts them in a cold oven for a short time.[6] The Hausa suppose twins to have a special power of picking up scorpions without injury.[7] The belief of the Tlaxcalans of Mexico in the curative powers of twins has been mentioned above. The Kwakiutl also attribute to them powers of curing disease. The British Columbian and other tribes of the north-west attribute to twins a variety of extraordinary powers. They influence, or at least prognosticate, success in hunting, and the plentiful supply of salmon and other fish, though among some tribes they may not themselves catch salmon. On the other hand, they are exposed to danger of various kinds and must be carefully protected by ceremonies and otherwise.[8] Among the Negroes of the Sherbro in the colony of Sierra Leone there is a practice of resorting to twins for dealing with various complaints, most usually by women. 'Twin-houses,' or *sabo*, each consisting of a small rude framework covered with a thatch of grass, form a sort of shrine. Upon a wooden grid beneath the thatch is spread a white cloth, on which are put lumps of concretion from an ant-hill; and a white streamer floats from a rough pole in front of the structure. This little shrine is set up *ad hoc*, and is served by two persons who are of twin birth, but not necessarily of the same mother. Under their direction and to their profit, the two twin-houses are erected and a ceremonial dance is arranged. A fowl is then sacrificed and the patient is washed all over by these two priests of the *sabo* in medicine provided by them.[9]

The powers of twins are sometimes extended to their parents.

To cure a sprain, the mother of twins is in Ceylon made to trample the limb every evening for a couple of days.[10] Among the Brahuis of Baluchistan, to cure the tertian fever, a twin is called on to knot a blue thread five or seven times, and this is hung round the patient's neck and is believed to drive the fever away.[11] In Maryland it is asserted that the mother of twins has power to drive whooping-cough from a child by giving it a piece of bread and butter.[12] Among the Baganda a ceremony apparently intended to communicate fertility to the plantains is performed by the father and mother, and an effigy of each child is made, partly consisting of a plantain-flower.[13] Among the Basoga, on the north-east of Lake Victoria Nyanza, the birth of twins is a joyous event, though both the twins and their parents are subjected to tabu and ceremonies to render them innocuous. In the north-western district the persons of both father and mother are sacred; the former goes on a round of visits, and is believed to carry blessing wherever he goes. In the central district the children are held to be of divine origin. Their mother must sow her seed before any woman of her clan. The twins must be brought to the field of any clanswoman who is about to sow; and the sowing is performed in their presence.[14] The Bateso, a Nilotic tribe bordering on Lake Kyoga, welcome the birth of twins, though they and their mother are secluded, as among the

[1] *GB*[3], pt. vi., *The Scapegoat*, London, 1913, p. 178, pt. v., *Spirits of the Corn and of the Wild*, ii. 173 n.; Rendel Harris, *Boanerges*, p. 163, both citing G. W. Steller, *Beschreibung von dem Lande Kamtschatka*, Frankfort and Leipzig, 1774.

[2] J. Teit, *Jesup N. Pac. Exped.* ii. 263; cf. iii. 375.

[3] London, 1909, vol. i. ch. 3.

[4] W. W. Skeat and C. O. Blagden, *Pagan Races of the Malay Peninsula*, London, 1906, ii. 4, 215 f.

[5] Rendel Harris, *Boanerges*, pp. 129, 168, 401; *JAI* xxii. [1893] 209; W. E. Roth, *30 RBEW* [1915], pp. 320, 325; Mrs. Amaury Talbot, p. 23; Hartland, *Primitive Paternity*, i. 37, citing various authors.

[6] Mrs. E. M. Leather, *The Folk-lore of Herefordshire*, London, 1912, p. 256.

[7] D. Kidd, *Savage Childhood*, p. 48.

[8] Parker, p. 50.

[9] *Rep. of Cambridge Anthrop. Exped. to Torres Straits*, v. [1904] 198.

[10] *Bull. Amer. Mus. Nat. Hist.* xvii. [1905] 230.

[11] Riedel, p. 74.

[12] J. J. M. de Groot, *The Religious System of China*, Leyden, 1892–1910, vi. 1340.

[13] F. W. Waugh, *Iroquois Foods*, Ottawa, 1916, p. 59.

[1] *Anthropos*, vi. 1038.

[2] Leonard, p. 462.

[3] Junod, *Life of a S. African Tribe*, ii. 401.

[4] *GB*[3], pt. vii., *Balder the Beautiful*, London, 1913, i. 278.

[5] W. J. Thomas and F. Znaniecki, *The Polish Peasant*, Chicago, 1915, i. 215.

[6] *Man*, x. 26.

[7] A. J. N. Tremearne, *Hausa Superstitions and Customs*, London, 1913, p. 94.

[8] *Brit. Assoc. Rep.*, 1889, p. 847, 1890, pp. 574, 591, 614, 644, 1900, p. 481; *Jesup N. Pac. Exped.* ii. [1908] 586, 620, iii. [1905] 322.

[9] T. J. Alldridge, *The Sherbro and its Hinterland*, London, 1901, p. 149.

[10] *IA* xxxiii. [1904] 57.

[11] D. Bray, *The Life-history of a Brahui*, London, 1913, p. 106.

[12] *JAFL* xii. [1899] 273.

[13] Roscoe, *Baganda*, p. 67 f., *JAI* xxxii. 33.

[14] Roscoe, *Northern Bantu*, pp. 217, 219, 235.

Basoga, while the father pays visits to members of his own and his wife's clans, communicating the blessing of increase wherever he is received.[1]

In fact, it is chiefly in the control of the weather and the promotion of fertility—two results closely connected with one another—that the powers possessed by twins are generally held to lie.

Power over the elements, especially over rain and snow, is almost universally attributed to them by the natives of British Columbia. The Shuswap hold that, if a twin bathe in a lake or stream, it will rain.[2] The Tsimshian think that whatever twins wish for is fulfilled—among other things the weather. Therefore they pray to wind and rain, 'Calm down, breath of the twins!'[3] Among the Kwakiutl by swinging a ceremonial rattle they can cure disease and procure favourable winds and weather.[4] Nutka twins produce rain by painting their faces black and then washing them, or by merely shaking their heads.[5] In the Central Provinces of India one of twins will prevent injuries to crops from excessive rainfall or hailstorm by painting his right buttock black and the left any other colour and standing in the direction of the wind; at harvest-time husbandmen (apparently not necessarily twins) adopt this course for the abatement of a gale.[6] In S. Africa twins are said to be able to foretell the weather by their feelings; this seems to be a relic of a belief in control of the weather, control having faded into prediction.[7] A little farther north, the Bathonga, in case of drought, employ a ceremony to cause rain. The women, stripped or covered at most with a grass petticoat, go in procession led by a mother of twins to the grave of twins, or of an abortion, buried in a dry place, and pour water on it, or dig up the remains and bury them again in the mud near the water.[8] Among the Wanyamwesi of what was German E. Africa a twin about to cross a river, stream, or lake, or in a storm on a lake over which he is sailing, fills his mouth with water and spurts it out, saying, 'I am a twin.' The object of this ceremony is to prevent harm befalling him or his companions.[9] At Upoto on the Upper Congo, where rain is usually abundant, a twin is called in to make excessive rain cease. He puts some rain-saturated earth on the fire, and calls upon the rain to cease and the earth to dry up. Here twins also are credited with occult power which enables them by blessing or cursing to cause the success or failure of a hunting or fishing expedition.[10] In Gabun, French Congo, the images of twins, preserved after ceremonies performed over them, are apparently held to ensure the continued fertility of their mothers.[11] From a consideration of the traditional disappearance of Romulus, the first of the legendary kings of Rome, who, it will be remembered, was one of twins, J. G. Frazer has made the ingenious conjecture that the ancient Romans 'shared the widespread superstition that twins have power over the weather in general and over rain and wind in particular.'[12] The superhuman powers of Gilyak twins and the posthumous cult of such as die have already been referred to.

4. Cult of divine twins.—So far, abundant reason has been given for the conclusion that twins, being out of the ordinary course of nature, are held by many peoples to be children of extraordinary powers, or of portentous and even dangerous birth, and consequently that they, or at least one of them, must be at once exposed or put to death, and, where this practice is abandoned or has not arisen, they and their mother (frequently their father also) must be surrounded with tabus; and they are invoked for various purposes, chiefly for rain and fertility. Rendel Harris, who has investigated the subject, has in a series of works established the existence, from a remote antiquity, in Mediterranean countries of a cult of divine twins, some indications of which are also found elsewhere. The twins of Greek legend, Castor and Polydeuces (called by the Romans Pollux), have of course long been known, and other twins of less renown have been recognized. But the wide range of the cult, and the number of cases in which twins have been worshipped, had not previously been understood. Castor and Polydeuces with their sister Helen were traditionally the children of Leda, born, in some versions, out of an egg. Tyndareus, king of Sparta, the husband of Leda, though regarded by Homer as their father, was credited in some accounts with the paternity of Castor only, the other two being the children of Zeus. It has been mentioned above that this belief in a divided paternity of a multiple birth is not unusual among the lower races; it is therefore one of the marks of the archaic origin of the cult of Castor and Pollux. The former, being the son of a mortal father, was himself mortal. Pollux, however, obtained from Zeus the boon of sharing his immortality with his brother and living with him alternately a day under the earth and a day with the gods. Their legend attributed to them a number of adventures; and they were worshipped as θεοὶ σωτῆρες, protectors of travellers by water, and thence of travellers in general, the guardians of hospitality and of oaths, and were represented as riding on magnificent white steeds. As twins they were connected with the sky, with thunder and storms; hence probably not only their patronage of travellers by sea, but also their character as Dioscuri, sons of Zeus, and their reputation as divine spearmen. By virtue of their descent from Tyndareus, they were special patrons of the kings of Sparta.[1] Other twins were also known in Greece—Herakles and Iphikles, Amphion and Zethus, and others male and female. Rendel Harris has also made out a good case for the existence of twin-sanctuaries in the peninsula and adjacent islands, leading to the inference that the twin superstition in Greece was not different from that found in other quarters of the globe.

The worship of the Dioscuri early passed to Italy, where it is attested on the coins of Magna Græcia and the mirrors of the Etruscans. It became firmly established at Rome after the well-known didymophany at the battle of Lake Regillus.[2] But from the very beginnings of the city the twin superstition seems to have been accepted. The tale of Romulus and Remus is conclusive on the point. They built Rome, as Amphion and Zethus built Thebes, one brother slew the other—neither of these incidents is by any means strange in legends of twins—and the surviving twin disappeared in a thunderstorm, doubtless another way of expressing his relation to the sky and the storm-cloud.

The Aśvins, perhaps originally divine horses before they became charioteers, are well-known figures in the *Rigveda*. They are rain-makers, probably connected with the lightning—certainly with the sky; they grant fertility to men as well as to the earth, and they aid the sailor and the traveller. In Asia Minor and Palestine the cult of the Twins appears from a very ancient date. Esau and Jacob and other twins found in the Hebrew Scriptures are personages whose pristine form and attributes it is no longer possible to recover from the attrition of time and the erasive energies successfully wielded by generations of pious editors. Traces, however, of the twin-cult linger in the names of various places, like Ibn Alraq, near Jaffa, which has been identified with a place called in the book of Joshua Bne Baraq, 'sons of lightning'; and the account in the second book of Maccabees of the defeat by Judas Maccabæus of Timotheus almost certainly contains a Dioscuric tradition. Barca in N. Africa, a colony of Cyrene, seems to be connected with lightning; and the *silphium* plant, which was sacred to the Twins, is the emblem of Cyrene upon its coins. The Pharos at Alexandria was dedicated to the saviour-gods. There is reason for suspecting legends, and perhaps the cult, of divine twins among both the Phœnicians and the Arabs.

1 Roscoe, *Northern Bantu*, p. 265.
2 *Jesup N. Pac. Exped.* ii. 587; cf. *Brit. Assoc. Rep.*, 1890, p. 644, 1900, p. 481.
3 *Brit Assoc. Rep.*, 1889, p. 847; *31 RBEW*, p. 545.
4 *Brit. Assoc. Rep.*, 1890, p. 614.
5 *Ib.* p. 592.
6 *IA* xxviii. [1899] 111.
7 D. Kidd, *Savage Childhood*, p. 47.
8 H. A. Junod, *Rev. d'Ethnog. et de Soc.* i. 141, *Life of a S. Afr. Tribe*, ii. 296, 334, *Les Ba-ronga*, pp. 412, 416.
9 *GB*³, pt. i., *The Magic Art*, i. 268 f.
10 Rendel Harris, *Boanerges*, p. 85.
11 R. H. Nassau, *Fetichism in W. Africa*, pp. 309, 314.
12 *GB*³, pt. i., *The Magic Art*, ii. 183.

1 *GB*³, pt. i., *The Magic Art*, i. 48 f.
2 L. Preller, *Römische Mythologie*³, Berlin, 1881–83, ii. 300.

Farther north it is quite clear that Edessa was from ancient times a seat of the Twin-cult. The Twins were there known as Monim and Aziz. When Christianity superseded the old paganism, Jesus Christ and the apostle Thomas took their place. The Syriac *Acts of Thomas* shows that Thomas, or Judas Thomas, as he is called, was regarded as the twin of Christ. With his Lord's assistance he performs in the legend a number of deeds which are beyond doubt Dioscuric. Among the apostles James and John seem also to have been regarded as twins: whence probably their *sobriquet* Boanerges, 'sons of thunder.' In various countries of Europe there are vestiges of Dioscuric cult in historical writers like Tacitus and in popular tales. A pagan altar has been found at Notre Dame, Paris, with a dedication by the boatmen of the Seine to certain Celtic divinities, and among them the Heavenly Twins. The ancient gods all over Europe and the Christian East have been succeeded by saints who perform similar functions and are often called by similar names. Many of these are in pairs or triads, and some of them are explicitly reputed to be twins or triplets, not merely in Christian profession and martyrdom, but by birth. They have frequently assonant names, or names which are variants of one another, according to a wide-spread custom of calling twins by names specifically given to twins, or names which are echoes of each other. A few of these may be mentioned from Rendel Harris's list.

Such are Speusippus, Eleosippus and Meleosippus, martyrs, of Langres, whose cult spread westwards from Cappadocia; Florus and Laurus, builders (in Russia, patron saints of horses) and martyrs; Protasius and Gervasius, martyrs, whose relics Ambrose opportunely found at Milan for the confusion of the Arians; Cosmas and Damian, physicians and martyrs, whose cult seems to have been known from the Euphrates to Kent. Others might easily be enumerated.

The electrical phenomenon sometimes appearing on the masts and yards of vessels during a storm in the Mediterranean was anciently held to be a manifestation of Castor and Pollux; and it was a good omen when the light was double.[1] This same phenomenon is now credited to St. Elmo, a patron saint of sailors, whose name occurs in a variety of forms, and of whom nothing whatever is known. Rendel Harris has shown reason for believing that in some of its forms the name is connected with Remus, who with Romulus was commemorated at San Remo on the coast of Italy. Romulus and Remus preceded Castor and Pollux in the veneration of the Romans. They were exposed, according to the legend, in a rude boat on the Tiber; and from floating on the river they probably made their way, like other figures of the Twins, to sea as the patrons and protectors of seamen and voyagers.

Several pairs of mythical twins are found on the western continent. Of these the best known are the twins of Iroquoian tradition, Ioskeha and Tawiscara.

According to their legend, a woman named Ataensic fell down through a rift in the sky upon the primeval waters, for there was no land as yet. By the advice of the turtle the animals dived, brought up soil, put it on the turtle's back, and so formed the earth to receive the falling heroine, who was pregnant and promptly gave birth to a daughter. The daughter became in her turn pregnant of two boys, Ioskeha and Tawiscara. The latter was evil of nature: he refused to be born in the natural manner, and, breaking his way out through his mother's side or armpit, ended her life with his own birth. The brothers grew up. Ioskeha went about providing the earth, until that time arid, with water. But the evil twin attempted to foil him by creating a gigantic frog to swallow all the water. A quarrel ensued, as in the case of Romulus and Remus and other twins in the Old World. Ioskeha, using the horns of a deer, vanquished Tawiscara, whose weapon was only a branch of the wild rose, and drove him away to the extreme west, his blood gushing from him at every step and turning into flint as it fell. The victor then established his lodge in the far east, opened a cave in the earth and brought forth all kinds of land animals, formed men, instructed them in the art of making fire and in the growing of maize; and it is he who imparts fertility to the soil.[1] Ioskeha is therefore the culture-hero and divine helper of the Huron-Iroquois; and the deeds and combat of the Heavenly Twins are the foundation of their mythology.

[1] Pliny, *HN* ii. 37.

Without pausing to consider any other N. American twins, we may turn to Peru.

From before the times of the Incas the Peruvians seem to have worshipped as creator a god whose name has come down to us as Ataguju, conjectured by Brinton to be properly Atachuchu, 'lord of the twins.' From him proceeded the man Guamansuri, who seduced the sister of certain Guachamines, 'rayless ones' or 'darklings.' She proved pregnant and produced two eggs, but died in putting them into the world. From these eggs emerged two brothers, Apocatequil and Piguerao, names which have also suffered some deformation. Apocatequil was the more powerful. By touching his mother's corpse, he brought her back to life; he slew the Guachamines, who had destroyed his father; he released the race of Indians from the soil by turning it up with a golden spade. The thunder and lightning were due to him; thunderbolts were his children. Stones held to be thunderbolts protected from lightning, gave fertility to the fields, and were esteemed as love-charms. 'In memory of these brothers, twins in Peru were deemed always sacred to the lightning; and when a woman or even a llama brought them forth, a fast was held and sacrifices offered to the two pristine brothers, with a chant commencing *A chuchu cachiqui*, "O Thou who causest twins," words mistaken by the Spaniards for the name of a deity.'[2]

The Bakaïri, a Carib tribe in the northern part of the Amazon basin, have a legend of twins who were culture-heroes.

The Bakaïri were then few and oppressed by the jaguars, who are indistinctly imagined with traits of both the lower animals and humanity. Their mother, captive to the jaguars, became pregnant by sucking two finger-bones of Bakaïri killed by the jaguars. She died before giving birth to her children; and they were cut from her body by the Cæsarian operation. The boys, who are called Keri and Kame, were fostered by the jaguar, their mother's captor. They had not yet human form, but manipulated one another to complete it. They then avenged their mother's death on their foster-father. With the help of the vultures they procured the sun and moon. They stole fire from the fox (*canis vetulus*). From the Ochobi water-snake they obtained water and made the rivers. From various animals they got hammocks, sleep, stones to build houses, arrows, tobacco, manioc, and cotton. They invented flutes and dancing. They made various tribes of men; and Keri is honoured as the ancestor of the Bakaïri. They quarrelled, but made the dispute up again. Finally they disappeared, nobody knows whither.[3]

There are other mythical twins in S. America, but the subject need not be pursued.[4] In New Zealand, Melanesia, and Micronesia there are moreover legends of two brothers, or a band of brethren, who appear to be culture-heroes, though the opposition of beneficent and malicious or of wise and stupid brethren is also developed; but they are not specifically described as twins.

If we inquire into the origin of the cult, it seems clear that the Dioscuri, as the sons of Zeus, were regarded as divinities of light. It has been long ago pointed out that their appearances are represented as taking place in the middle of the summer about the first full moon after the solstice.[5] So also there can be little doubt that the Aśvins in India were divinities of the dawn and possibly the evening twilight. From divinities of light they would naturally pass to wield, or personify, the lightning (Zeus's weapon) and the storm. They came to be looked upon as protectors from the violence of the elements, and thence of voyagers on river or sea, and, by extension of the idea, of travellers generally. Their powers would gradually grow until they covered a still larger area of human life. The same connexion with light and lightning is to be traced on the American

[1] The original authority is *Jesuit Relations*, x. *Hurons* [1636], Cleveland, U.S.A., 1896, p. 125. D. G. Brinton, *Myths of the New World*, New York, 1868, p. 169, *American Hero-Myths*, Philadelphia, 1882, p. 53, amplifies the story from other sources.

[2] Brinton, *Myths of the New World*, p. 152; J. G. Müller, *Gesch. der amerikan. Urreligionen*[2], Basel, 1867, p. 327.

[3] K. von den Steinen, *Unter den Naturvölkern Zentral-Brasiliens*, Berlin, 1894, p. 372 ff.

[4] Rendel Harris, *Boanerges*, p. 155; P. Ehrenreich, *Die Mythen und Legenden der südamerikanischen Urvölker*, Berlin, 1905, p. 44.

[5] Preller[3], ii. 302.

continent, where they further tended to become culture-heroes. But this does not account for their duality, except in so far as they may be held to represent the morning and evening, the dawn and the disappearance of light. It is perhaps due to an innate tendency in the human mind to repeat, to echo, to balance, or to contrast. This psychological quality constantly exhibits itself in every department—in philosophy, theology, mythology, literature, art, ethics. It is responsible for the dualism of the great religions, for the frequent reduplication of incident in a fairy-tale, for the symmetrical grouping of figures in a work of art, and for dramatic nemesis. In the domain of mythology and religion, whether pagan or Christian, it has doubtless been emphasized by the mystery attaching to the comparatively infrequent phenomenon of human twins. The beneficent and maleficent sides of their tabu are expressed in the opposition of characters and frequently in the double pedigree.[1]

5. Afterbirth as twin.—The Baganda hold a curious belief that the afterbirth, or the navel-string (there is a variation as to this between the two accounts given by Roscoe, to whom we are indebted for the information), is the twin or double of the child to whom it belongs.

The afterbirth was enclosed in a broken cooking-pot, covered with leaves and placed at the root of a plantain-tree—if a boy, at the root of a plantain from which beer was made; if a girl, at the root of a plantain used as a vegetable. We are told that 'the afterbirth was called the second child, and was believed to have a spirit, which became at once a ghost.' On account of this ghost the plantain was guarded, to prevent any one not belonging to the clan from partaking of the beer made from it, or of the food cooked from it; else the beer or the food, by being consumed, would be lost to the clan, and the child would then die in order to follow the ghost of its twin. To obviate this catastrophe, the grandfather ate the food and drank the beer, so retaining the ghost of the afterbirth in the clan. More elaborate was the care taken of the king's umbilical cord, to which the ghost of the afterbirth attached, and which was always spoken of as if it were the afterbirth itself: hence probably the confusion between afterbirth and cord. A special officer, called the *kimbugwe*, who was second only to the *katikiro*, or prime minister, was appointed to the charge of it. He occupied an enclosure next to the king's, in which was a temple built for the 'twin.' Once a month at new moon he carried the 'twin,' wrapped as it always was in bark-cloth, into the presence of the king, who took it out of its wrappings, inspected it, and returned it to the *kimbugwe*. He then exposed it in the doorway of the temple for the moon to shine upon it, anointed it with butter, wrapped it up again, and restored it to its place in the temple. When the king died, the *kimbugwe* made way for a new *kimbugwe* to take charge of the new king's 'twin'; but it still remained his duty to care for the old king's 'twin,' and to provide for the upkeep of its temple and enclosure. In due time the dead king's jaw-bone, to which the king's own ghost was believed to adhere, would be added to his 'twin' and kept at the temple, where he would continue to be venerated.[2] Even the jaw-bone and umbilical cord of the god Kibuka were preserved in his temple on an island of Lake Victoria Nyanza; and they are now in the Ethnological Museum at Cambridge.[3]

To the south of Uganda and west of the great lake, in Kiziba, formerly in German territory, similar customs and beliefs prevail.

The afterbirth, we are told, is considered as a kind of human being, and on the birth of twins the children are spoken of as four, instead of two, each afterbirth being looked upon as a child.[4]

In ancient Egypt also there seem to be traces of the same idea.

Monuments of the earlier dynasties show an object which has been identified as the king's afterbirth carried upon a standard in procession, together with the usual symbolical standards of animals. Its use continued to the end of the Egyptian kingdom, though its shape was gradually conventionalized. The goddess represented as presiding at the birth of Queen Hatshepsut wears on her head an object remarkably like the reliquary containing the navel-string of Kibuka; and in other representations the same goddess wears a vase-like object which may be intended for such a reliquary. Though there are not many texts referring to the afterbirth or navel-string, importance—not to say sanctity—does seem to have been attached to 'the umbilical cord of Osiris.' Horus is described as rescuing it from Seth and depositing it 'in its place in Herakleopolis,' or, as the Egyptians called the city, 'House-of-the-Child-of-the-King.' It has also been suggested that the object carried on his head by the moon-god Khons (and perhaps Khons himself) was evolved from the Pharaoh's afterbirth. There was some relation in Uganda between the moon and the royal 'twin.'[1]

In this connexion the common Hamitic strain in the ancestry of the royal houses both of Egypt and of Uganda will be remembered. At present, however, the interpretation of the Egyptian evidence has hardly got beyond the conjectural stage.

LITERATURE.—The only writer who has made a special study of the subject is J. Rendel Harris, whose three volumes, *The Dioscuri in the Christian Legends*, London, 1903, *The Cult of the Heavenly Twins*, Cambridge, 1906, and *Boanerges*, do. 1913, are indispensable. The principal sources of information apart from these are to be found in works dealing with the customs or the myths of various peoples, as indicated in the references above.

E. SIDNEY HARTLAND.

[1] See art. DOUBLES.

[2] Roscoe, *Baganda*, pp. 52, 54, 235, 110; *JAI* xxxii. 33, 45, 63, 76.

[3] Roscoe, *Baganda*, p. 303; *GB*[3], pt. iv., *Adonis, Attis, Osiris*, London, 1914, ii. 197; A. M. Blackman, *Journ. Egyp. Archæology*, iii. [1916] 199.

[4] H. Rehse, *Kiziba, Land und Leute*, Stuttgart, 1910, p. 117.

[1] C. G. Seligmann and M. A. Murray, *Man*, xi. [1911] 165; Blackman, pp. 199, 235.

TYPOLOGY.

1. Definition and scope.—Typology is the science, or rather, only too often, the curious art, of discovering and expounding in the records of persons and events in the OT prophetical adumbrations of the Person of Christ or of the doctrine and practice of the Christian Church. It is thus a branch of that method of interpreting Scripture which is sometimes called 'spiritual' and sometimes 'mystical,' as opposed to the literal or grammatical interpretation. Origen, as is well known, spoke of several subdivisions of this 'spiritual' method, and highly favoured it. It was not his invention. Already both pagan and Jewish writers had found in it an admirable expedient for extracting edification from passages in their sacred books which seemed to be trivial, perplexing, or even of doubtful moral worth, if taken at their face value. It flourished particularly at Alexandria, and was much used by Philo. The practice of allegorizing the OT Scriptures became so popular, and the defining line between allegorizing and typology in the strict sense is so uncertain, that it is necessary at the outset to refer to the former; both branches of this mystical interpretation, as used by Christian writers, aimed at elucidating the latent principles of Christianity in the OT, but, if a definition between them is demanded, it is supplied by Herbert Marsh (bishop of Peterborough, 1819–39) in these terms:

'According to one mode [*i.e.* typology] facts and circumstances . . . have been applied to other facts and circumstances, of which they have been described as representative. According to the other mode [*i.e.* allegorizing] these facts and circumstances have been described as mere emblems'; or, again, 'An allegory is a fictitious narrative, a type is something real.'[2]

This last sentence requires some modification: allegorizing may accept the historical truth of the narrative treated, but does not depend upon it; typology, the bishop holds, demands its historical truth. Van Mildert brings us nearer to the true test when he says:

'It is, indeed, essential to a Type, in the Scriptural acceptation of the term, that there should be competent evidence of the Divine *intention* in the correspondence between it and the Antitype.'[3]

Again, Westcott says:

'A type presupposes a purpose in history wrought out from age to age. An allegory rests finally in the imagination, though the thoughts which it expresses may be justified by the harmonies which connect the many elements of life.'[4]

Any account, however, of the history of typology must take into consideration the fact that this

[2] *Lectures on the Criticism and Interpretation of the Bible*, Cambridge, new ed., 1838, lect. v. pp. 350, 354.

[3] *An Inquiry into the General Principles of Scripture-Interpretation (BL)*, Oxford, 1815, p. 239. But see A. B. Davidson, *Old Testament Prophecy*, p. 236 f. for a criticism of this view.

[4] *The Epistle to the Hebrews*[3], London, 1903, p. 202.

distinction between type and allegory was not at all times recognized, and there must always be room for difference of opinion as to how far the interpretation offered of any passage 'rests finally in the imagination.' One characteristic feature of the history of typology is the divergence of opinion as to the limits of justifiable exposition of types.

The fundamental principle at the heart of this method of interpretation is that of the continuity of revelation and the divine unity of Scripture. In days when the historical sense and the recognition of progressive revelation were still inchoate it was the natural way of evidencing this unity of revelation. It is the product of the ages when history was regarded as a series of catastrophic events rather than as the unfolding of an age-long process, and it was therefore of immense value as a means of showing that history is not a mere series of accidental events, but the accomplishment of a divine purpose. Thus, though typology, as a branch of serious theological study, is now generally discredited and practically obsolete, surviving only for devotional and homiletic purposes, it is not deserving of the scorn to which not only its outworn usefulness but also the arbitrariness and fancifulness of some of its former champions expose it. In any case the place it holds in the NT itself deserves careful study. It is proposed in this article to discuss (1) the extent and character of typological references in the NT, (2) the general history of typology in later times, and (3) its strength and weakness as a method of interpretation.

2. In the New Testament.—From the first it was an integral and essential feature of the gospel of Jesus Christ to establish and maintain an unbroken connexion with the old covenant. Jesus was aware that His teaching was such as to precipitate a cleavage with the traditions of the Jews. He therefore emphasized the essential unity: 'I am not come to destroy but to fulfil.' In the synagogue at Nazareth He expounded Is 61 as a scripture that day fulfilled in the ears of His hearers. He saw in John Baptist the fulfilment of the 'Elijah' prophecy. After His resurrection He expounded to His disciples 'in all the scriptures the things concerning Himself.' He taught that they 'testified to' Himself. Further, He illustrated His message from OT parallels, as when He referred to Elijah at Zarephath, and Elisha and Naaman (Lk 4^{25-27}). On two occasions He is recorded to have referred in particular terms to events of the old covenant, viz. the sign of the prophet Jonah, and the lifting up of the brazen serpent. At these we must look more closely.

Concerning the sign of the prophet Jonah, Matthew ($12^{39f.}$) interprets the sign as Jonah's confinement in the belly of the whale foreshadowing Christ's burial and rising. Luke ($11^{29f.}$) omits this application (though Plummer[1] contends that it is implied in δοθήσεται). Matthew and Luke agree in giving the application that the contrast between the penitence of the Ninevites and the impenitence of the Jews at the preaching of a greater than Jonah is the warning sign. We have to inquire therefore whether Mt 12^{40} is an interpolation by the evangelist, and also whether Jonah can be justly regarded as a type. The story is now generally accepted as an allegory of the experiences of Israel, and as such is typical of Christ, in so far as the whole history of Israel is prophetic, but, regarded as a personal history, the story of Jonah corresponds so little with the ministry of our Lord in principle, and offers so many difficulties in detail, that the suggestion worked out by Sanday,[2] that Mt 12^{40} is not a saying of Jesus, is very attractive.

With regard to the reference to the brazen serpent, apart from the difficulty of treating the discourses in the Fourth Gospel as the actual words of Jesus, the case is clearer. But the treatment is markedly on broad lines of principle and suggestiveness rather than detailed and exhaustive. The incident referred to was already regarded as mysteriously embodying a spiritual principle (Wis $16^{6f.}$), especially as it apparently contravened a divine law.[3] Jesus intimates that that principle will be revealed in His own ministry, and the terms in which He speaks of it are such as to express that principle in the broadest possible way, for the lifting up of the Son of Man is a conception not exhausted by reference to the manner of Christ's death. In a very similar way Jesus spoke of His Body in terms of the Temple, because the Temple 'as the seat of God's presence among His people'[1] exhibited a principle to be more perfectly fulfilled by the Body of Christ.

[1] A. Plummer, *St. Luke* (*ICC*)[4], Edinburgh, 1901, p. 306.
[2] *Inspiration*[3] (*BL*), London, 1896, lect. viii., note A, p. 432.
[3] Justin, *Dial.* xciv.

Our Lord's example in this matter of reference to the OT Scriptures may be summed up as a full recognition that the principles of truth enshrined in the OT were to receive in Himself a fuller and clearer explication, and that therefore the OT Scriptures are full of teaching concerning Him; His practice therefore encourages us to search the Scriptures for the revelation of such principles, but it may be questioned if we can derive from His teaching any justification for the exploitation of formal resemblances or for indulgence in the fascination of elaborate working out of details.

Throughout the NT the same reverence for the dignity and true spiritual value of the OT is marked. Even in those books which show the clearest leanings towards mystical interpretation, in instances where the correspondence seems most far-fetched (*e.g.*, Mt $2^{15.23}$), or the argument most alien to our modern ways of thought (*e.g.*, Gal 3^{16} or 1 Co 10^4), the respect for the old covenant as a real revelation and the loftiness of purpose sharply distinguish the writers of the NT from even their immediate followers. Nothing in the NT can be compared with the puerilities of such a work as the *Epistle of Barnabas*, which degrades the old covenant to 'a mere riddle of which Christianity is the answer,'[2] and which solemnly sees in Abraham's 318 men a foreshadowing of the Cross of Jesus, because the Greek numerals are T I H ![3] Even in the Epistle to the Hebrews—a work clearly influenced by Alexandrian methods of thought—the OT is never merely allegorized, and the restrained treatment of the figure of Melchizedek and of the Tabernacle ritual in that book affords a marked contrast to the fanciful elaboration with which both have been treated by later writers. A recognition of typological methods of thought is essential for a true understanding of the NT.

The extent of possible typological references is remarkably small.

Patrick Fairbairn[4] gives the following list. But he has to confess that even this would be regarded by some as too long a list.

Persons: Adam, Melchizedek, Sarah and Hagar, Ishmael and Isaac, and by implication Abraham, Moses, David, Solomon, Jonah, Zerubbabel, and Joshua.

Events: the preservation of Noah, the Passover, the Exodus, the passage of the Red Sea, the giving of manna, the veiling of Moses' face, the water flowing from the smitten rock, the serpent in the wilderness, and some other events (see 1 Co 10), besides the Tabernacle with its furniture and services.

At any rate it is important to note that all these references occur quite naturally and that nowhere is there any sign of a studied exploration of the OT for possible types.

3. History of typology. — This may for convenience be divided into three groups rather than periods, though each group corresponds roughly to a period in the history of the Church.

(*a*) The first is that of the apologetic use of types to prove as against Jewish or pagan objector the antiquity of the Christian faith or to refute heretics. The very purpose of the apologists exposed them to fancifulness. Whereas the author of the Epistle to the Hebrews would show his readers that what they valued in the old covenant was but a shadow preparing the world for better and enduring things to come, Justin had to show that what the Jew

[1] B. F. Westcott, *The Gospel according to St. John*, London, 1882, on Jn 2^{19}.
[2] Westcott, *A General Survey of the History of the Canon of the NT*[6], London, 1889, p. 46.
[3] Gn 17^{23}; *Ep. Barn.* ix. 8.
[4] *The Typology of Scripture*, 2 vols., Edinburgh, 1845–47, [6]1880, i. 40.

objected to in the Christian gospel lay hidden in the Jewish Scriptures. We can understand how he came to hold that the outstretched arms of Moses at Rephidim prefigured the cross of Christ, or even how the bells on the high priest's garment were a mystical foreshadowing of the apostolate.[1] Against heretics the aim was partly to refute the very fanciful interpretations of those false teachers who, as Hippolytus puts it, 'by seducing those ignorant of the holy Scriptures into such like fancies make fools of them.'[2] The Catholics met such errors, not by a rejection of typical or allegorical interpretations, but by the application of a canon of truth or tradition, which limited typological exploration to the treatment of narratives in the canonical books and to the illumination of truths revealed in Scripture — a limitation not always observed in later times. When we come to Origen, we find him using and extolling the allegorical method because so he could reply to Celsus's objection to some passages in the OT. Herein he simply took over the already long-established method of dealing with difficulties in Homer. His intellectual greatness saved him from the extreme rashness of his predecessor Clement, though he adopted his recognition of a manifold sense of Scripture (viz., on the one hand, the literal or grammatical; and, on the other, the allegorical, anagogical, and tropical). It must be remembered that, though Jerome accuses Origen of allegorizing to such an extent that 'historitatis auferat veritatem,' Origen recommended the retention of the literal sense where it was profitable, but the literal often failed to edify (*πολλαχοῦ γὰρ ἐλέγχεται, ἀδύνατον ὄν τὸ σωματικόν*),[3] and then the superiority of the spiritual over the carnal was made manifest, and again that Origen did not regard his interpretations in the least as 'resting finally in the imagination,' for he says:

> *καὶ δῆλον, ὅτι Μωσῆς ἑώρα τῷ νοὶ τὴν ἀλήθειαν τοῦ νόμου, καὶ τὰς κατὰ ἀναγωγὴν ἀλληγορίας τῶν ἀναγεγραμμένων παρ' αὐτῷ ἱστωριῶν.*[4]

(*b*) The school of Alexandria, inheriting this tradition from so great a master, carried the discovery of mystical significance in the Scriptures to excess, finding in the method a vast field of opportunity for the edificatory use of the Bible. The school of Antioch resisted this use; Theodore of Mopsuestia entirely rejects allegorical interpretations. Time showed both how attractive and how dangerous the practice was. Arnobius points out how well the method meets the need of pagan writers, but calls attention to the fact that in the lack of any sound rule of interpretation anything can be proved from the Scriptures.[5] Tyconius Afer endeavoured to establish rules for the proper surveying of the 'forest' of Scripture, and to systematize what he calls the 'reduplicationes' of the Bible. Being a Donatist, he fell under the condemnation of Augustine, who speaks slightingly of his work.[6] Augustine's own rule is thus summarized:

> 'Iste omnino modus est, ut quicquid in sermone divino neque ad morum honestatem neque ad fidei veritatem proprie referri potest, figuratam esse cognoscas.'[7]

On the whole the Latin writers were more restrained than the Greek, more tenacious of historicity, and therefore more inclined to typical interpretation proper than to what is merely allegorical; yet Jerome, for all his criticism of Origen's methods, is himself fairly free in dealing with Scripture. As time went on, the ignorance of the original Hebrew that fell upon the Church removed one of the surest restraints against unprofitable fancifulness.

1 *Dial.* xlii. xc.
2 *Ref. omn. hær.* v. 3.
3 *De Princ.* iv. 20.
4 *In Evang. Ioann.* vi. 2.
5 *Adv. gentes*, v. 32 ff.
6 In *de Doctrina Christiana*, iii. 30 (42).
7 *Ib.* iii. 10 (14).

(*c*) The third group or period is that in which typology took its place in constructive theology, and begins with the Schoolmen. Their task was to prove that the Christian faith is rational and to reconcile it with the doctrines of the current Aristotelianism. In the first stage of Scholasticism reason was subjected to faith. The example of the Fathers in admitting a threefold sense of Scripture was generally followed. Erigena indeed speaks of an 'infinite sense,' and was led by his mysticism to use the allegorizing method freely; the Scriptures to him were as a peacock's feather, every particle glittering with divers colours. Rabanus Maurus admits a fourfold sense. Others went farther, acknowledging a sevenfold or even an eightfold sense. In the later stages of Scholasticism, particularly after the rise of the theory of the twofold nature of truth, and the spread of mysticism, some schools practically scorned the literal interpretation of Scripture on the ground that 'litera occidit, spiritus vivificat,' and 'carried this often to such an extreme, as to leave scarcely a trace of the simple meaning.'[1] It must be acknowledged that some, like Hugo of St. Victor and St. Thomas Aquinas, tried to restrain such indulgence.[2]

The combined influences of the Revival of Learning and the establishment of the Bible as the sole *regula fidei* brought about in the writings of the Reformers a very much sounder attitude. Both Luther and Calvin are remarkable for the sanity and critical acumen of their commentaries. Reaction from Scholastic fancies and a new reverence for the plain teaching of Scripture produced this result; but soon the demand for popular expositions of Scripture (and perhaps the dearth of really scholarly teachers) brought typology into great favour, and it became a definite branch of hermeneutics. In this connexion the name of Coceeius of Leyden in the 17th cent. is prominent, although he adopted no definite system, and seems to have been content with a formal resemblance to justify typological interpretations. Others, however, did endeavour to systematize the method.

Salomon Glassius published at Jena in 1623–36 a work in five books called *Philologia Sacra*, of which one part is devoted to the study and classification of types. His work was incorporated in English in Benjamin Keach, *Tropologia: a Key to Open Scripture Metaphors and Types*, London, 1681, and is referred to as a principal authority by T. H. Horne, *An Introd. to the Critical Study and Knowledge of the Holy Scriptures*, the first ed. of which (in 3 vols.) appeared in 1818–21, the tenth and last being issued (in 5 vols.) in 1856. Glassius divides types into two main classes—'innate,' or those specifically asserted to be such in Scripture, and 'inferred.' These are further subdivided, the first into those which Scripture 'expresse ostendit' or 'tacite insinuat,' the second into those which are 'oblati' or 'contorti.' The last are to be rejected. He adds nine canons for classifying or recognizing types. The canons are not particularly helpful, but they afford the author the (to him) valuable opportunity of refuting Bellarmine's recognition of a type of the Mass in the story of Melchizedek—a recognition, of course, far older than Bellarmine. The fact reveals one reason why the Protestant theologians were anxious to find clear rules to govern typology. Other popular works on the subject were Thomas Taylor, *Moses and Aaron, or the Types of the OT opened*, London, 1653; Samuel Mather, *OT Types Explained and Improved*, do. 1673, rewritten by Catherine Fry and published in 2 vols. in 1834 under the title *Gospel of the Old Testament* (regarded by some as the fullest exposition of the subject); and K. Vitringa, *Observationes Sacrae*, 3 vols., Franeker, 1689–1708.

The last named deplores the rise of rationalism, and certainly the rationalistic and unimaginative temper of the 18th cent. was inimical to the practice of typology. Something of the 18th cent. methods of thought affects Marsh's *Lectures on the Criticism and Interpretation of the Bible*, and here we find a quite definite rule as to the scope of typology laid down. He will admit no types except those which Glassius had called innate. He defends this

1 T. A. Liebner, *Hugo von S. Victor*, Leipzig, 1832, quoted by K. R. Hagenbach, *A Hist. of Christian Doctrine*, Eng. tr., Edinburgh, 1880–81, ii. 171.

2 'Pro fundamento tenenda veritas historiae' (*Summa*, I. qu. cii. art. 1).

position with much good sense and learning, though it is really a confession of weakness and inability to discover the principles which govern the practice of the NT writers.

At the beginning of the 19th cent. the subject attracted attention. It was much affected in circles influenced by the Evangelical Revival. Typology engaged the eloquence and learning of the Bampton lecturers in 1814 (Van Mildert) and 1824 (J. J. Conybeare), and of the Hulsean in 1826 (Temple Chevallier), besides giving rise to a good deal of other literature. But the spread of scientific criticism and the study of ancient religions, and before long of comparative religion, were destined to strike a death-blow to typology as a recognized branch of hermeneutics.

The religion of the Jews was for a time regarded as beneath the notice of the student of religion, and, when it came into its own again, a much broader view of the relation between the old and new covenants held the field. Thus De Wette wrote that the entire OT is a great type of Him who was to come, and that Christianity lay in Judaism as leaves and fruit lie in the seed.[1] Again, Clausen finds the foundation of the connexion between the 'deeper apprehension and the immediate sense' in the law of general harmony by which all individuals, in the natural as well as in the spiritual world, form one great organic system.[2] The impress of the modes of natural science upon this utterance did not recommend it to those whose conception of the supernatural and providential alienated them from the rising naturalism, but the effects of modern methods of scientific study are already apparent in Fairbairn's *Typology*, since the publication of which no standard work on typology has appeared. It survives now principally in devotional works or in the expositions of those to whom the results of Biblical criticism are still unwelcome. Sometimes it is pursued with dignity and real spiritual value (as in the works of Andrew Jukes), but sometimes with a distressing puerility or even offensiveness. It must be acknowledged that, on the other hand, modern writers of the critical school have unduly ignored the importance of typology—an attitude to which that of Edwin A. Abbott offers a brilliant exception. In his view the NT, and particularly the Fourth Gospel, is full of typical suggestions. In this way, believing the author to record what he took to be facts, but with a definite spiritual intention, he reconciles the rejection of the historicity of the narrative with the retention of its spiritual import. In a word, he allegorizes the records, while acknowledging that the author believed that he was recording facts, but facts with a typical significance.

This view is of importance in two respects. First, it reminds us of the fact that the symbolic significance of things and words held a far greater place in the thought of ancient times than it does with us, who have learned to form abstract conceptions and to search for exact definitions. *E.g.*, the NT writers can speak of the 'blood of Christ' without explanation, in a manner that perplexes us. In the second place, it is based on a fundamental principle of sound interpretation, viz. the endeavour to discover what the original author of any document meant to convey. When we read of Melchizedek, or the ritual of the Tabernacle, or of David, it is not enough to ask what those passages may suggest to us; we must first ask what they suggested to the original readers. If the principles of truth which they then suggested be one with the principles more clearly seen in the fuller revelation in Christ, then the imperfect revelation may be regarded as typical of the fuller yet to come, because so mankind was being prepared for the clearer light. Now, David's career is so presented in the OT as to subordinate the imperfections of his character to those qualities which suggested the ideal of a perfect Shepherd-King; the ritual of the Tabernacle was such as to awaken a sense of sin which the sacrifices could never satisfy, and the figure of Melchizedek held up to men (even if the story be simply legendary) a dim conception of a Priest-King greater than Abraham or the priesthood of Aaron's line. Inasmuch as such dimly seen ideals are the result of God's spirit working in the human spirit, we can justly speak of a divine intention in these records, and, without disregarding the human element or ignoring the original meaning, we see in them the gradual unfolding of a divine purpose, much as we can see in the lonely flowering of the first snowdrop an earnest of the summer glory of the garden.

4. The strength and weakness of typology.—The passing of typology need not cause alarm. Just as the discovery of the law of evolution necessitates a broader sweep of investigation on the part of those who to-day put forward the argument from design, but has not invalidated that argument, so our conception of the oneness of revelation is to-day based on a broader view of the OT, but is not therefore the less true or the less deeply founded. Typology not only bred fancifulness and, what was worse, quarrelsomeness among the theologians, but it tended to reduce revelation to the character of a jig-saw puzzle, for, at least in many interpretations, the types are scattered haphazard through the OT, and are quite unrecognizable as such until the antitype is revealed. Any one who has studied the works of art which typology has inspired will remember the chaotic confusion of the typical series as compared with the order of the antitypical. To-day we recognize the guiding hand of God in history as the typologists could not, and so see a deeper and truer continuity of revelation. But that in its day this system of expounding the mystical relation between the OT and the NT had a marked educational value can be seen from the widely popular *Biblia pauperum*, illuminated MSS of which exist as early as the 13th cent., and from a development of it, *Speculum humanæ salvationis*, of which over 200 MSS survive. The invention of printing made these works still more widely popular. The same fact is evidenced by works of art ranging from the frescoes in the catacombs, through mosaics such as those in Santa Maria Maggiore in Rome[1] or San Marco in Venice, down to the magnificent series of windows in King's College, Cambridge. Indeed this connexion of typology with Christian art suggests the very close association of typology with æsthetics. That love of mystery which is almost universal has in reality an æsthetic aspect; for some it is satisfied in the dramatic ritual of the Mass, and for those who repudiated this conception of worship it has been satisfied by the exploration of the mystical sense of the OT, somewhat as the Qur'ān supplied decorative motifs in Moorish art. This seems likely to give a permanent vitality to devotional typology, especially since the revival of popular mysticism. A word of caution may be offered. The history of typology shows how easily devotion may degenerate into fancifulness and unprofitable exercise of ingenuity. Only the most chastened of saints and the most self-restrained of scholars are immune from this danger; typology has always flourished in times of ignorance and

[1] Quoted from an article in J. C. H. Bähr, *Symbolik des Mosaischen Cultus*, Heidelberg, 1837, i. 16.

[2] *Hermeneutik des NT*, Leipzig, 1841, p. 335.

[1] On these cf. J. P. Richter and A. C. Taylor, *The Golden Age of Classical Christian Art*, London, 1904, a work full of references to early typology.

decay of learning, but its suggestions are not without value and helpfulness if they are received gratefully, much as one might derive illuminating thoughts from the contemplation of a sacred picture, rather than as revelations possessing dogmatic authority.

LITERATURE.—In addition to authorities referred to in the text: E. W. Hengstenberg, *Christology of the OT*[2], Eng. tr., 4 vols., Edinburgh, 1856–63; F. A. G. Tholuck, *Das Alte Testament im Neuen Testament*[5], Gotha, 1861; Edward Riehm, *Messianic Prophecy*[2], tr. L. A. Muirhead, Edinburgh, 1891; R. F. Horton, *Revelation and the Bible*, London, 1892; R. L. Ottley, *Aspects of the OT (BL)*, do. 1897; A. B. Davidson, *Old Testament Prophecy*, Edinburgh, 1903, chs. xii.–xiv.; C. A. Briggs, *General Introduction to the Study of Holy Scripture*, do. 1899.

Typological works.—E. F. Willis, *The Worship of the Old Covenant, considered more especially in Relation to that of the New*, Oxford, 1880; Andrew Jukes, *The Types of Genesis*[3], London, 1875, *The Law of the Offerings in Leviticus i.–vii.*[3], do. 1854; see also Holy Bible, ed. C. I. Scofield, Oxford, 1909.

J. R. DARBYSHIRE.

U

UDĀSĪS.—The Udāsīs are the principal religious order of the Sikhs (*q.v.*). Also known as Nānak-putrā, 'sons of Nānak,' the founder of Sikhism, they are probably the oldest of the Sikh orders, but ascribe their foundation to Srī Chand, Nānak's elder son. The term *udāsī* is derived from Sanskrit *udās*, 'sad,' and means 'sorrow' or 'sadness.' The Udāsīs were separated from the active or militant Sikhs by the third *gurū* of that sect, Amar Dās, but he did not excommunicate them, as is sometimes stated. This separation is also ascribed to Arjan, the fifth of the Sikh *gurūs*. Whoever effected it, the severance marks the cleavage in the Sikh sect which definitely ranged it against the Muslim Mughal power, leaving the Udāsī order still in touch with orthodox Hinduism. Nevertheless the tenets of the order, deeply coloured as they are with Hindu asceticism, did not prevent its finding many followers among the descendants and disciples of the Sikh *gurūs*. Thus the sixth *gurū*, Hargovind, is said to have allowed Srī Chand to adopt Gurdittā, his eldest son, into the order by making him his direct disciple—a statement not free from chronological difficulties.

The Udāsī order was at an early period divided into four chapters (*dhuān*, lit. 'fires'). Their founders were Bābā Hasan or Hasna, Phūl, Gondā, and Al-mast—all four said to be disciples of Gurdittā. Of these founders the first bears a Muhammadan name (Hasan) and the last a purely Arabic title, *al-mast* denoting one drunk with love or devotion. Al-mast Sāhib, or 'the holy ecstatic,' is now represented at Nainī Tāl and Jagannāth, places far from the Panjāb and Sikh-dom alike. Gondā Sāhib is revered at Shikārpur in Sind, as well as at a shrine near Amritsar in the Panjāb, while the other two possess shrines in the Panjāb hills only. This distribution points to efforts made by the earlier *gurūs* to spread Sikhism, or at least a quietist type of it, over India generally. The followers of these four chapters constitute the senior assembly (*barā akhārā*) of the order, its junior, or *chhoṭā akhārā*, having been founded later by Pherū, a disciple of Har Rāi, the seventh Sikh *gurū*. In theory all Udāsīs are celibate, but those who are so in practice are styled Nangā (or 'naked') Udāsīs. Sir Edward Maclagan, however, gives a different explanation of the term Nangā.

He describes their usual dress as red in colour, but 'a large section of them go entirely naked, except for the waistcloth, and rub ashes over their bodies. These, like the naked sections of other orders, are known as Nange; they pay special reverence to the ashes with which they smear their bodies, and which are said to protect them equally from either extreme of temperature. Their most binding oath is on a ball of ashes.'[1]

As smearing the body with ashes symbolizes also death to mundane things, the Nangā Udāsīs are probably strict celibates, and hence the Nange are correctly so described. Another chapter of the order, sometimes said to be one of the four *dhuān*, is called the Bhagat Bhagwān, or 'devoted to God' (Bhagwān). Its tradition connects it with Hinduism, for, it is said, a Sannyāsī, by name Bhagatgir, once visited the shrine (*derā*) of Bābā Nānak, the founder of Sikhism, when on his way to Hinglāj, a great place of Hindu pilgrimage in Baluchistān. Nānak's grandson, Dharm Chand, poured food into Bhagatgir's bowl, but failed to fill it. The addition, however, of a pinch of *karāh prasād*, or sanctified meal, blessed with the words, *Srī wāh gurū*, 'All hail to the *gurū*,' caused the bowl to be filled forthwith. This miracle converted Bhagatgir. It was confirmed when the goddess Hinglāj appeared to him and his companions as they kept their vigil before Nānak's shrine and thus fulfilled the object of their pilgrimage. Bhagatgir and his followers became disciples of Dharm Chand, assuming the title of Bhagat Bhagwān. The principal *akhārā*, or meeting-place, of the chapter is at the Bibiksar tank at Amritsar, but it also has subordinate *akhārās* at Barelī and other places in Hindustan and claims no fewer than 370 *gaddīs*, or monastic foundations, in eastern India. The Bhagat Bhagwāns wear the matted hair (*jaṭṭa*) of the Sannyāsī, with a chain round the waist, and smear their bodies with ashes. But in their beliefs they accept Nānak's precepts and follow his rules as to eating and the like.

Yet another chapter is the Sangat Sāhib, which is admittedly not one of the four *dhuān*. Gurū Har Rāī had a cook, named Pherū, whom he taught, investing him with a black girdle and cap, and sending him as a commissary to the southern Panjāb—his native country—and towards the Indus, with a mission to collect the dues paid by the Sikhs to the *gurūs*. When Gurū Govind Singh abolished this system and destroyed the *masands*, or commissaries, whose oppression had caused grave discontent, Pherū made no resistance, though no one dared arrest him, and waited on the *gurū*. Impressed by his righteousness, the *gurū* gave him half his *pagrī*, or turban, in token that he was admitted to a share in his *gurū's* authority, and promised that his following should prosper. The *gurū* further bestowed on him the title of Sangat Sāhib, 'holy companion,' and sent him back to the scenes of his former activities, where he increased the number of his followers. In or before 1896 the Sangat Sāhib, as the chapter is called, established a peripatetic *akhārā*. One of its most noted disciples, an ascetic named Santokh Dās, worked many miracles. The Sangat Sāhibīās, or adherents of the chapter, are numerous and influential in the south and west of the Panjāb, but, as their traditions show, they are not completely under the control of the Sikhs or the regular Udāsīs. Another tradition assigns

[1] *Census of India, 1891*, vol. xix., *Punjab and Feudatories*, p. 152.

the foundation of the chapter to a follower of the famous Sultān Sakhī Sarwar, who was converted by Gurū Govind Singh, and it undoubtedly comprises many who used to affect the cult of that saint and perhaps still combine with it their acceptance of Sikh doctrine. The chapter, however, possesses the Brahmbhūt *akhārā* at Amritsar and an institution at Lahore, so it is distinctly affiliated to orthodox Sikhism, and in the great Sikh State of Patiāla, where it is called the Bakhshīsh Sangat Sāhib, it pays special reverence to the *Ādi Granṭh*, or original *Granṭh* ('Book') of Bābā Nānak, and has an *akhārā* of its own, distinct from those of the four *dhuān*. Lastly must be mentioned the Rāmdās Udāsīs, a sub-order ascribed to another Gurdittā (who was a grandson of one of Bābā Nānak's converts) and established by one of the later *gurūs* in a monastery at Rāmdās, where the sub-order possesses a fine temple, at some distance from Amritsar. Each subdivision of the Udāsīs has its own organization for collecting and administering funds. Each is presided over by a head abbot (*srī mahant*), to whom the ordinary *mahants*, or monks, are subordinated.

The Udāsīs generally are recruited from all Hindu castes and will take food from any Hindu. Sometimes, but not invariably, or even usually, congregated in monasteries, they are generally found wandering to and from such sacred Sikh places as Amritsar, Dera Nānak, and Kartārpur in the Panjāb, but they are also said to be numerous in the Mālwa to the south of it, and at Benares. The principal seats, however, lie in the central Panjāb and in the District of Rohtak, where Sikhism is by no means dominant. Their usages are not uniform. Some wear long hair like Sikhs, others matted hair like Sannyāsīs, and others again cut the hair. Some affect the *tilak*, or caste-mark, others avoid it. The dead are often cremated in the Hindu way, but apparently are sometimes buried. When a body is burnt, a *samādh*, or mausoleum, is erected to some Udāsīs, but this privilege must be confined to those of special sanctity or *mahants*. While the majority are ascetics, some frankly engage in secular callings. Maclagan gives the following picture of their relations with the Panjāb villagers:

'In Ludhiāna the Udāsīs are described as mostly Jāṭs by origin, the *chelā* or disciple and successor being usually chosen from this tribe, and are found to be in possession of the *dharmsālās* in Hindu villages, where they distribute food to such as come for it and read the *Granṭhs* both of Bābā Nānak and of Gurū Gobind Singh, although they do not attach much importance to the latter. The head of the college is called a *mahant* and the disciples *chelās*. They live in Sikh as well as in Hindu villages, and it is probably on this account they do not quite neglect Gurū Gobind Singh. They rarely marry; and if they do so, generally lose all influence, for the *dharmsālā* soon becomes a private residence closed to strangers. But in some few families, such as that of Jaspāl Bāngar, which keeps a large *langar* or almshouse going, it has always been the custom to marry, the endowments being large enough to support the family and maintain the institution; but the eldest son does not in this case succeed as a matter of course. A *chelā* is chosen by the *mahant*, or by the family. If a *mahant* whose predecessors have not married should do so, he would lose all his weight with the people. The great shrine at Dera Bābā Nānak, in the Gurdāspur District, is in the custody of a community of Udāsī *Sādhs*, whose *mahant* used to be appointed with the consent of the Bedīs. Another shrine at the same place known as Tāhlī Sāhib, from a large *tahlī* or shīsham tree[1] which grew close to it, was founded by Srī Chand, and is also looked after by *mahants* of the Udāsī order.'[2]

Thus the Udāsīs display all the normal features of an Indian religious order—a lofty ideal, readily abandoned in practice, professed adherence to a reformed faith, tempered by judicious compromise with the established system, and the inevitable evolution from an ascetic celibate order into a hereditary caste. In the last phase of the Sikh régime the Nānakputras had sunk to employment as escorts to caravans, their sacred character as 'sons of Nānak' ensuring them against attack.

[1] *Dalbergia sissoo*.

[2] *Census of India, 1891*, xix., *Punjab and Feudatories*, p. 153.

LITERATURE. — E. D. Maclagan, *Census of India, 1891*, xix. and xxi., *Punjab and Feudatories*, Calcutta, 1892.

H. A. ROSE.

UDYĀNA.—See SWĀT.

UGRA, UGRIAN OSTIAKS.—See OSTYAKS.

UGRO-FINNS.—See FINNO-UGRIANS.

ŪKHARS.—See RŪKHARS.

ULTRAMONTANISM.—Ultramontanism is the term applied, often in a hostile or critical spirit, to the tendency to centralize in the papacy the doctrinal teaching and government of the Catholic Church. More vaguely still it is applied in general to extreme Roman Catholicism, to the tendency to emphasize all that separates Catholics from other Christians or from other men. Often enough it is used, quite inappropriately, as a mere nickname for ordinary Catholics who are conscious of their obligations as members of a universal Church. Thus the Catholic parties in the German and Belgian Parliaments have been called Ultramontane, though they would certainly not admit that they take their politics from Rome.

Historically the word 'ultramontanus' was in occasional use in Central Europe from the 11th cent. onwards in a merely geographical sense, just as 'citra-montanus' was used in Italy, to describe a man who lived south of the Alps. It does not seem to have been commonly used with any theological significance till the 17th cent., when it was applied to those who opposed the prevailing Gallican tendencies in France. The counter-reformation in general, and especially the pontificate of Sixtus V. at the close of the previous century, had done much to organize the central administration of the Church, while, on the other hand, the growing power and self-consciousness of the French monarchy tended to insist upon, and to express more definitely as principles, Gallican practices which might be traced back to the 13th century. It is in opposition to Gallicanism (*q.v.*) that Ultramontanism has its most definite meaning, and Fénelon, the Jesuits, and others who opposed the ecclesiastical policy of Louis XIV. and the Four Articles of 1682, were, in a sense, the first Ultramontanes. In the 18th cent., when the influence of religion was at its lowest, Gallican principles kept a strong hold on the French Church, but they found their most complete expression in the writings of the German Febronius and in the policy of Joseph II. The Ultramontanism which opposed Gallicanism and Josephism was little more than the assertion of the universal character of the Church, which both these systems tended to obscure, and an effort, far from successful till the 19th cent., to assert the right of the Church to live her own religious life without the constant interference of the State.

Formal Gallicanism, with its Four Articles, may be said to have been destroyed in France by the Revolution. The fall of the *ancien régime* liberated the Church; numbers of the more Gallican clergy were discredited by joining the Constitutional Church; and Catholicism was purified and revivified by suffering and persecution. No more striking manifestation of papal power had yet been seen than the act which, in accordance with the Concordat, practically deprived thirty-seven bishops of their sees. The Concordat was thus an Ultramontane act, and, though Napoleon added to it the Gallican *articles organiques* and, when he quarrelled with the pope, tried to make the Four Articles the law of the State, nothing could restore the old pre-

Revolution Gallican system. The spirit, however, survived and inspired both the statesmen of the restored monarchy and many of the more old-fashioned clergy, yet the Restoration was also the period in which the Ultramontane movement of the 19th cent. received its most powerful expression in the writings of Joseph de Maistre, de Bonald, and Lamennais. These men realized that the Revolution had destroyed the old foundations on which men had rested their habits of thought and action, and that a fresh start had to be made. De Maistre knew that the revolutionary spirit was still abroad, stronger perhaps than ever, and his *Du Pape* (1819) is an appeal as much to practical utility as to principle. It is only the Christian Church which has in it the strength to overcome 'the Revolution'; and without an infallible papacy the Church is, like the States-General, reducing the monarchy to a shadow and therefore slipping back into revolution. He was disappointed with the immediate effect of his book, but his rigid, authoritative mind had great influence on the Ultramontanes of the middle of the century. A man of far greater intellectual power than de Maistre, the Vicomte de Bonald emphasized the weakness of the individual man in finding out for himself the essential principles of thought and conduct. What a contrast between the disagreement of philosophers and the agreement of practical men about practical matters! The individual reason rightly, therefore, falls back for support on the convictions of society and on tradition. This 'traditionalism' Lamennais combined with the Ultramontanism of Joseph de Maistre. Lamennais's passionate temper always made him push a thing to its extreme limit, and he turned de Bonald's trust in tradition into a universal test of truth. The voice of the pope was for him the expression of this 'universal consent.' In his first stage he combined legitimacy with Ultramontanism; in his second he appealed to the people and tried to make democracy the exclusive ally of the Church. The *Avenir*, which Lamennais and his friends edited in 1831, was probably the most brilliant expression of the earlier stage of 19th cent. Ultramontanism. The enemy which the *Avenir* fought was the Gallican tradition of State control over the Church which had been reinforced by the revolutionary doctrines of State-absolutism. The aim was liberty—liberty of conscience, of association, of education, of the press. Devotion to Rome was the great instrument of liberty, for the papacy represented the universal aspect of the Church and was independent of the different governments. It provided also an element of fervour and historic sentiment at a time when Europe, under the influence of the Romantic movement, was casting off the 18th cent. and all its works and recapturing the power of religious enthusiasm. The exclusive form in which Lamennais's ideas were expressed ultimately set Rome itself against him, but the movement continued under wiser men, Lacordaire, Montalembert, de Ravignan, and others. They succeeded in all but destroying the old Gallican spirit and in putting a new life into the French Church. In the Revolution of 1848 the Church, which had been so unpopular in 1830, exercised a powerful influence.

The defeat of Gallicanism, however, brought out a division in the Ultramontane ranks which the struggle had concealed. The Falloux Law, which was passed under the Second Republic and which broke down the old State monopoly of education, led to the first open breach. On one side Montalembert, Falloux, and Dupanloup were prepared to make concessions to the State in order to secure an invaluable piece of legislation, and because they shared in the ideas of their time so far as these were not definitely opposed to Catholic principle. On the other side were a number of Catholics whose policy became characteristically identified with a newspaper, the party of the *Univers*. Louis Veuillot, the editor of the paper, may without much exaggeration be called the leader of the party; he was certainly its noisiest and most popular mouthpiece. The aim of this school went much farther than merely to acquire for the Church the control of her own religious life. They wished to secure for her the predominance which in an ideal world the spiritual would have over the temporal, and which in fact the Church did partly enjoy in the Middle Ages. Such an aim was incompatible with the ideas and practices prevailing among a people who were far from being mediæval in faith, but Veuillot and his party were prepared to fight for it by bitter antagonism to free-thinkers, by opposition often bitter enough to those, even should they be bishops, whom they considered lukewarm Catholics, and by making the most of the support of the State, if it should happen to be on their side, even when that State was the autocratic Second Empire. The archbishop of Paris himself, Sibour, brought out the difference between the two schools in a letter to Montalembert (1853):

'When twenty-five years ago,' he said in substance, 'we boldly professed ourselves "Ultramontanes," the Ultramontane school was then a school of liberty. We defended the independence of the spiritual power against the encroachments of the temporal power, but we respected the Constitutions of the Church and of the State. The Pope was not the whole Church nor the Emperor the whole State. On the one side there were bishops and councils with a real authority, on the other aristocratic and democratic elements with their rights. No doubt there are times of crisis when both the Pope and the civil government may override all rules. The old Ultramontanes admitted this, but they did not turn the exception into a rule. The new Ultramontanes have pushed everything to extremes and accepting to the full the idea of power they have argued extravagantly against all liberties whether in Church or State.'[1]

Another French bishop could write that the fanaticism of the *Univers* had done more harm to religion than that of Voltaire. It is indeed difficult at first to understand Veuillot's popularity among French Catholics. He seems the most perfect representative of that 'insolent and aggressive faction' which never tired of calumniating their brethren in the faith and of trying to force their private opinions on the Church. For men not of the faith, whom he considered its enemies, for free-thinkers, for 'the race of Cain,' he had no pity. He had never any hesitation in distinguishing between the wheat and the tares. Yet the *Univers* was read in nearly every *cure* in France, and Veuillot appealed far more than Montalembert to most French Catholics. To begin with, he was intensely democratic. Himself a man of the people, he was always thinking of the people. It was his passionate desire to protect the simple from the aggressive irreligion of the bourgeois free-thinker, while his fondness for the extreme point of view in controversy, his scorn of moderate opinions, and his intolerable abuse of the military metaphor in matters of religion were more in sympathy with French character than the constitutionalism of the Montalembert school.

It must be added that the extreme character of French Ultramontanism under the Second Empire is partly to be accounted for by the reactionary policy adopted by Pius IX. when he returned from the exile to which he had been driven in spite of his liberal reforms. To the world at large the most complete expression of this reactionary policy was the Syllabus of 1864. More sympathy would be felt now than in optimistic mid-Victorian days for a document which declared that the world had gone astray by the neglect of God and of Catholic principles. At the time, however, what appeared

[1] Cf. Lecanuet, *Montalembert*, iii. 104.

to be a declaration of war against 'modern civilization' was taken as an official confirmation of all the excesses of the *Univers.*

'Ultramontanism' is a word much used in German politics and religious controversy of this period, but so heavy was the hand of the Erastian State in the first half of the 19th cent. that the word meant no more than the natural claim of German Catholics to manage their own spiritual affairs. Josephism survived longer in Germany than Gallicanism in France, and it was reinforced first by the current German philosophy of State-absolutism and later by the growth of conscious German nationalism. There was an important Catholic revival in the twenties and thirties, closely connected with the Romantic movement, but it had little effect on religious politics. The first struggle for liberty and the first victory occurred not in any of the Catholic states but in Protestant Prussia. The imprisonment in 1837 of the aged archbishop of Cologne and the support given him by Pope Gregory XVI. led to a popular movement in his favour and a general protest against the action of the Government. When Frederick William IV. came to the throne in 1840, he inaugurated a new policy and Prussia, by the freedom which she allowed the Catholics, became a model for other German states. The Revolution of 1848 extended this liberty to different parts of the country, but it was followed by a reaction, especially in S.W. Germany. Two schools began to be distinguishable in the fifties. One was that of Mainz, led by Bishop Ketteler, with the *Katholik* as its organ, devoted mainly to practical work and social problems, but in close union with Rome and therefore soon to be called Ultramontane. Closely connected with it was the more learned group of Würzburg, where Denzinger, Hettinger, and Hergenröther were teaching. The rival school was that of Munich in alliance with the Bavarian Government and the University. Its leading spirit was Döllinger, and it was interested mainly in the philosophical and historical aspects of theology and was very jealous of any Roman interference with German science. The education of the clergy came to be a subject of much controversy, for in Germany seminary and university training had long gone on side by side. A number of the bishops distrusted the theological teaching and the atmosphere of the universities, while Döllinger and the Munich school suspected intensely the training given by the Jesuits in the German College in Rome, were contemptuous of Roman theology, fought against the revival of Scholasticism, and dreaded the spread of Jesuit influence in and through the German seminaries. In time they came to see in the power of the State a means of checking this 'Romanization,' and Döllinger, who had fought for the Church against Josephism and been called an Ultramontane in 1848, now began to appeal to the State against Ultramontanism. Yet among the German Ultramontanes there was little of the extravagance of the *Univers.* No doubt, as controversy grew more bitter, there were violent language and personal attack on both sides, and the air had to be cleared in Germany, as elsewhere, by the Vatican Council.

In Italy the more extreme Ultramontanism was represented by the *Civiltà Cattolica*, a review published in Rome under the editorship of Carlo Curci and a small number of Jesuits who were a curiously independent body and often quite out of sympathy with their more moderate brethren across the Alps and even in Italy. The *Civiltà* was notorious for its support of the *Univers*, for its extreme papal doctrines, and for its personal attacks on more liberal though equally devoted Catholics.

There was an echo of these continental battles even in England in the controversy which was aroused by the reviews edited by Acton and his friends, first the *Rambler* and then the *Home and Foreign Review.* These reflected, though in a more moderate form, the views of Döllinger and the Munich school. On the other side the lead was taken by William George Ward and the *Dublin Review.* Neither side disputed the authority of strict definitions of dogma; but the controversy turned on the amount of respect due to the general guidance of Rome. Acton claimed absolute liberty outside dogmatic definitions, while Ward looked to the papacy for positive direction. A loyal Catholic, he maintained, should accept not only the defined teaching but the 'doctrinal intimations' of Rome.[1]

Underneath these controversies of the sixties we seem to see two tendencies at work. The more liberal Catholics wished, in various degrees, to keep in touch with the times, to make the best of the learning, the thought, the science, the political conceptions of the age. With some this might and did lead to a real contempt for traditional Catholic practices and methods. The Ultramontanes, on the other hand, felt the danger which lay in excessive sympathy with the 'spirit of the age.'

'The "Rambler" . . . appeared to Mr. Ward to worship the modern ideal, both in ethics and in politics, with an unreserve which was quite inconsistent logically with the principles of Christianity.'[2]

Ward had no hope in the movement led by Döllinger. To him contemporary thought was moving away from Christianity, and the one essential thing was to react against it, to preserve the purity of the faith and of Catholic ideals. Push this point of view farther, much farther than Ward ever pushed it, and you come to Veuillot's extravagances with his conflict between the 'race of Abel' and the 'race of Cain.' Now the papacy under Pius IX. undoubtedly took the Ultramontane side, and the liberals found themselves more or less in opposition to the tendencies prevailing in Rome, while the Ultramontanes were anxious to make these tendencies prevail everywhere and, in opposition to the nationalism of the day and the attacks on the temporal power, to magnify the authority of Rome in the government and teaching of the Church. Veuillot, *e.g.*, looked forward to the time when papal bulls would take the place of all conciliar deliberation. Thus it is that the question of the doctrinal authority of the pope was raised and that the Syllabus led to the Vatican decree of infallibility. Yet there is a certain unreality about the controversies which raged round the Council in 1869 and 1870, for the number of those who actually disbelieved in papal infallibility was small indeed. The papal Definition of the Immaculate Conception in 1854 had been accepted universally. What most of the opposition feared was the added governmental authority which they conceived the decree would give to the pope, the increase which it would produce in all those centralizing and autocratic tendencies which they dreaded.

'I am much more concerned,' said Montalembert, 'about the government of the Church than about the definition of Papal Infallibility.'[3]

It is obvious too that the opposition of Dupanloup and the 'Inopportunists' was due to the fear that the Definition would lead to conflict with the State and would emphasize the differences between the Church and modern society. The language of the more extreme Ultramontanes in speaking of the pope as 'inspired,' or in such mad phrases as 'when the Pope thinks, it is God who meditates

[1] W. Ward, *W. G. Ward and the Catholic Revival*, p. 146.
[2] *Ib.* p. 139.
[3] Lecanuet, iii. 456.

in him,' must have contributed not a little to make the 'liberals' fear that the Definition might mean the triumph in the Church of the more extreme faction.

The Definition came, after months of discussion, in a form more moderate than even such Ultramontanes as Ward had originally expected. It had the effect of making a clearer distinction between the doctrinal and the administrative functions of the papacy. It is no longer possible for an Ultramontane to claim that every utterance of the pope on matters of faith is protected by God from error. Papal infallibility is defined and in so far limited, and the conditions laid down in the Definition have seldom, if ever, been satisfied by the papal doctrinal pronouncements of the last forty years.

Ultramontanism became, therefore, a vaguer term after 1870. The party of the *Univers* continued, indeed, to exist and to carry on its controversial methods in support of the temporal power of the pope or of the royalist movement in France. It saw in a political *coup d'état* the only defence against the attack which from 1879 onwards the Republican party directed against Catholic education, the religious orders, and other forms of Catholic life. Louis Veuillot died in 1883, but the *Univers* remained the most popular of Catholic newspapers until its place was partly taken by Paul de Cassagnac's Bonapartist *L'Autorité*. It seems absurd, however, to call this party Ultramontane, seeing that at least during the pontificate of Leo XIII. its aims were opposed to those of the papacy. The pope was anxious to reconcile the Catholics with their governments both in France and in Germany. In Germany he succeeded in bringing the *Kulturkampf* to a close, though at the cost of putting pressure in 1886 on the so-called Ultramontanes of the Centre party, in order to secure their support for Bismarck's seven years' army estimates, whilst in France his policy of urging the French Catholics to accept the Republic met with much opposition from the royalists.

In a sense, however, the term 'Ultramontanism' may be rightly applied to the administrative centralization which is a mark of papal policy since the middle of last century. The enthusiasm felt so widely among Catholics for Pius IX., the great prestige of Leo XIII., a conscious reaction against disruptive national movements, the mere improvement in the means of communication—these are some of the causes which explain such a centralization. It was a particular feature of the pontificate of Pius X. and of the measures which he took against 'Modernism.' It has certainly helped to protect the unity and the tradition of the Church in the midst of growing hostility or at least indifferentism, and often enough Rome has proved more broad-minded than the local ecclesiastics. Thus two of the greatest bishops of the second half of the century, Ketteler and Manning, were appointed by the direct action of the papacy. Many Catholics would, however, welcome a reaction in the direction of the constitutional traditions of the Church, especially in such matters as the election of bishops and their synodal meetings.

LITERATURE.—It is difficult to give a bibliography on so general a subject. For the Gallican controversy see art. GALLICANISM; for 19th cent. Ultramontanism, F. Nielsen, *History of the Papacy in the XIXth Century*, Eng. tr., 2 vols., London, 1906. An excellent study of the question is to be found in Wilfrid Ward, *William George Ward and the Catholic Revival*, do. 1893; E. Lecanuet, *Montalembert d'après son journal et sa correspondance*, 3 vols., Paris, 1895–1902, contains the best account of the controversy with Veuillot. For a defence of Veuillot on general grounds cf. Jules Lemaître, *Les Contemporains*, do. 1888–98, vi. For the Catholic controversies in Germany cf. G. Goyau, *L'Allemagne religieuse : le Catholicisme*, 4 vols., do. 1905–09. For the Vatican Council see art. COUNCILS (Christian : Modern); for the measures taken by Pius X. against the Modernists see art. MODERNISM.

F. F. URQUHART.

'UMAR AL-KHAYYĀM

'UMAR AL-KHAYYĀM.—Although much has been written by European biographers concerning the celebrated astronomer and poet of Nīshāpūr, 'Umar ibn Ibrāhīm al-Khayyām or al-Khayyāmī, generally known in Persia as 'Umar Khayyām, the greater part consists of legends derived from late and untrustworthy sources, while the facts of his life and character remain singularly obscure, notwithstanding that since 1897 one contemporary and several early notices have become available. Khayyām or Khayyāmī is a family name, and does not indicate that either 'Umar or his father was a tent-maker by trade. The dates of his birth and death are uncertain. Probably he was born between A.D. 1025 and 1050, and the evidence of his contemporary, Niẓāmī 'Arūḍī, shows that his death took place after 1115 and some years before 1135, and that he was buried at Nīshāpūr in the Ḥīra cemetery;[1] the date A.D. 1123 given by some authorities may well be correct. On chronological grounds alone, the story of his friendship at Nīshāpūr with two school-fellows who afterwards rose to eminence—Niẓāmu 'l-Mulk, the great vizier of the Seljūq sultans Alp Arslān and Malikshāh, and Ḥasan al-Ṣabbāḥ, chief of the so-called 'Assassins'—is extremely improbable; and, though it occurs in the history of the Mongols by Rashīdu'ddīn († A.D. 1318), it must be regarded as a fiction.[2] 'Umar received the education of a scholar, including literature, natural science, theology, philosophy, and medicine. We possess two treatises on algebra and geometry from his pen;[3] of seven other works on scientific and metaphysical subjects only the titles have been preserved.[4] Adopting astronomy as a profession, he was chosen in A.D. 1074 to take part in, and apparently to preside over, a commission of astronomers appointed by Niẓāmu 'l-Mulk and Sultan Malikshāh for the purpose of reforming the calendar.[5] Their labours resulted in the institution of the Jalālī era, named after the honorary title (Jalālu'ddīn) of Sultan Malikshāh, and in the publication of the astronomical tables known as *Zīj-i Malikshāhī*, which were edited by 'Umar Khayyām.[6] Like most mediæval astronomers, 'Umar practised astrology, and two of his predictions are recorded by Niẓāmī 'Arūḍī,[7] who observes that 'Umar had no great belief in such prognostications. During the period of disturbance following the death of Malikshāh (A.D. 1092) he seems to have left Nīshāpūr. He was at Balkh in A.D. 1112–13, and at Merv two years later.[8] Possibly it was at this time that he made the pilgrimage to Mecca, 'not from piety but from motives of prudence, and, when he reached Baghdād on his homeward journey, refused to meet the learned scientists of that city who were eager to become acquainted with him.'[9]

Besides a few Arabic poems, 'Umar wrote a number of Persian quatrains (*rubā'iyyāt*). That he was regarded as a writer of occasional verse rather than as a poet appears from the fact that his name is not mentioned at all in the oldest extant work containing biographies of Persian poets, the *Lubābu 'l-Albāb* of 'Aufī (*c.* A.D. 1220),

1 *Chahār Maqāla*, tr. E. G. Browne in *JRAS*, 1899, p. 806 f.
2 E. G. Browne, 'Yet more Light on 'Umar-i Khayyām,' in *JRAS*, 1899, p. 409 ff., *Literary History of Persia*, ii. 190 ff.
3 F. Woepcke, *L'Algèbre d'Omar Alkhayyámí*, Paris, 1851, *Catalogue of the Oriental MSS in the Leyden Univ. Library*, Leyden, 1851–73, iii. 40.
4 E. D. Ross, 'The Life and Times of 'Umar Khayyám,' biog. introd. in Methuen's ed. of Edward Fitzgerald's version of the *Ruba'iyyat*, with a commentary by H. M. Batson, London, 1900, p. 73 ff.
5 Ibnu'l-Athīr, *Kāmil*, ed. C. J. Tornberg, Leyden, 1868–74, x. 67.
6 Ḥājjī Khalīfa, *Lexicon Bibliographicum*, ed. G. Flügel, London, 1835–58, iii. 570.
7 *JRAS*, 1899, p. 806 ff.
8 *Ib.* p. 806 f.
9 Ibnu'l-Qifṭī, *Ta'rīkhu 'l-Ḥukamā'*, ed. J. Lippert, Leipzig, 1903, p. 244.

and only incidentally by Daulatshāh (end of the 15th cent.); moreover, the author of the *Chahār Maqāla*, who treats of poetry and astrology in separate sections, places 'Umar among the astrologers and makes no reference to his poems. The most ancient MS, preserved in the Bodleian Library and dated A.D. 1461, contains 158 *rubā'īs*; a facsimile of this text has been published by E. Heron-Allen.[1] In later MSS and editions the number of quatrains is very much larger. The question as to their authenticity was first raised in 1897, when Valentin Schukovski published in Russian in *al-Muẓaffarīyé* (a *Festschrift* in honour of Baron Victor Rosen) his famous article entitled "'Umar Khayyám and the "Wandering" Quatrains.'[2] Here Schukovski shows that 82 quatrains ascribed to 'Umar are to be found in the works of other Persian poets. Since the publication of his article the number of 'wandering quatrains' has risen to 101, representing 46 different poets[3]—a total which would be enormously increased if the entire field of Persian poetry were explored in a systematic manner, and if account were taken of anonymous quatrains, either written as variations on those which already formed part of the collection or added to it for no better reason than that, 'Umar being specially and pre-eminently a quatrain-writer, it was natural to ascribe to him any favourite *rubā'ī* of which the authorship was unknown. Even in the oldest and presumably least adulterated MS the proportion of 'wandering quatrains' already discovered and assigned to their proper authors is about 12 per cent. Of the remainder many are likely to be genuine, but we have no means of identifying the original 'Umarian nucleus or determining its size. The whole collection must be viewed, not as the work of an individual, but as an anthology reflecting various aspects of Persian spiritual and intellectual life and covering a period of six centuries.

It follows that the character of 'Umar Khayyām cannot be read in the *Rubā'iyyāt* attributed to him, which give expression to diverse and often radically inconsistent modes of thought. Two notices, however, cited by Schukovski from writers of the 13th cent. throw some light on the matter.[4] The first, by Ibnu'l-Qifṭī (see reference above), describes 'Umar as a man who tried to conceal his want of religion and shrank from uttering his real opinions. Concerning his poetry, Ibnu'l-Qifṭī remarks that it is widely circulated and reveals an irreligious spirit to those who look below the surface, although its literal sense is sometimes in accord with the teaching of the Ṣūfīs.[5] He then quotes four Arabic verses, of which the following is a translation:

> 'If my soul is content with a livelihood sufficient for my needs, which is gained by the labour of my hands and arms,
> I am safe from all changes and accidents, and care not whether Time threatens me or flatters my hopes.
> Have not the revolving heavens determined to reduce all happiness to misfortune?
> Therefore, O my soul, abide patiently in thy sleeping-place: its towers will not topple down until its foundations have collapsed.'

Najmu'ddīn Dāya († A.D. 1256), author of a mystical treatise entitled *Mirṣādu'l-'Ibād*, reckons 'Umar among those unhappy philosophers and materialists who have gone astray from the truth, and quotes two sceptical quatrains[6] as evidence of his 'utter shamelessness and corruption.' This passage is important because it shows that an ardent Ṣūfī of the 13th cent. looked upon 'Umar as an enemy to mysticism; and, inasmuch as the *rubā'īs* quoted are probably authentic, we cannot but agree with his judgment so far. The charge of materialism, when brought by Ṣūfīs and theologians against scientists and philosophers, carries no weight: 'Umar is as unlikely to have been a materialist as he is likely to have been a free-thinker and pessimist. It should be noted, further, that the name Khayyām occurs in twelve quatrains, and constitutes at least a presumption in favour of their authenticity, and that these, together with the two quoted by Najmu'ddīn Dāya, exhibit the principal elements of the *Rubā'iyyāt*, viz. hedonism, philosophical contempt for the *profanum vulgus*, attacks on the orthodox, lamentations for the cruelty of fate, meditations on the incompatibility of a supreme intelligence with the sufferings of life and on the nothingness of man, hope of divine mercy, and a certain morality which recognizes the duty of doing good to others. 'But the Ṣūfī mysticism seems to be excluded, although the poet often makes use of Ṣūfistic terms.'[1]

LITERATURE.—Besides the literature given in the footnotes: E. G. Browne, *A Literary History of Persia*, London, 1906, ii. 246–259; R. A. Nicholson, Introd. to the ed. of Fitzgerald's version of the *Rubā'iyyāt*, do. 1909; J. B. Nicolas, *Les Quatrains de Khèyam*, Persian text and French tr., Paris, 1867.

REYNOLD A. NICHOLSON.

UNCLEAN.—See HOLINESS, TABU.

UNCTION (Christian).—As a religious rite, and apart from social usages, unction was taken by the Christian Church immediately from the Jews, though for some purposes it was borrowed by the Jews from other nations. In the OT unction was used in the 'consecration' of priests, kings, prophets, and places.[2]

1. In connexion with the complete rite of baptism.—This use of unction was almost universal from very early times up to the Reformation.

(*a*) *The New Testament*.—It is disputed whether the apostles used unction in the rite of Christian initiation. In 2 Co 1$^{21f.}$, 1 Jn 2$^{20.27}$, all Christians are said to have been anointed. This is undoubtedly metaphorical, but it perhaps points to the actual use of oil in the apostolic age before or after baptism, at least in some places; as it was then certainly in use for other purposes,[3] the metaphor would in that case be more apposite. On the other hand, in Acts, where two accounts are given,[4] in which in addition to the baptism proper the laying on of hands is described, unction is not mentioned. Tertullian certainly thought that the apostles used it in connexion with baptism, for he traces it back to the 'primitive discipline' of the OT.[5] It is possible that it was used in the apostolic age in some places, but not in others, and it is noticeable that laying on of hands and anointing are not for this purpose joined together in the NT, though they were both there used for other purposes.[6] Or it is possible that the custom of anointing at baptism arose in sub-apostolic times, being due to a literal interpretation of the NT metaphor.[7]

(*b*) *The subsequent ages*.—After NT times or at least from the middle of the 2nd cent. onwards unction was used, sometimes preceding, sometimes following, immersion, or both before and after. But it is necessary to note that, originally and for many centuries, immersion and its complement, which in the West from the 5th cent. onwards has been known as 'confirmation,' were as a normal

[1] London, 1898.
[2] A full abstract by E. D. Ross appeared in *JRAS*, 1898, p. 349 ff.
[3] A. Christensen, *Recherches sur les Rubā'iyāt de 'Omar Ḫayyām*, Heidelberg, 1905, p. 30.
[4] *JRAS*, 1898, pp. 354 ff., 361 ff.
[5] See art. ṢŪFĪS.
[6] Nos. 126 and 508 in *The Quatrains of Omar Khayyám*, ed. and tr. E. H. Whinfield, London, 1902.

[1] Christensen, p. 35 f.
[2] See §§ 4, 5, 6 below.
[3] See § 2 below.
[4] Ac 8$^{14ff.}$ 19$^{2ff.}$.
[5] *De Bapt.* 7.
[6] Cf. Mk 5^{23} 6$^{5.13}$ 7^{32} 8$^{23.25}$, Ac 28^{8} etc.
[7] See, on the one side, F. H. Chase, *Confirmation in the Apostolic Age*, London, 1909, p. 59; on the other, H. J. Lawlor, art. CONFIRMATION, vol. iv. p. 2^{a}.

rule a single rite; and it is immaterial to consider whether any particular anointing belongs to the one part or to the other.

We get no light on the subject in the scanty literature of the first three quarters of the 2nd cent.; but it is to be remarked that unction is not mentioned in the *Didache*, though it gives the words of baptizing into the threefold Name.[1] Towards the end of the century Tertullian tells us that unction was administered after the immersion, as a long-standing custom;[2] Irenæus says that the Gnostic Marcosians used it in the parody of Christian baptism;[3] and early in the 3rd cent. Hippolytus says that the Naassenes (or Ophites) used it.[4] Theophilus of Antioch also mentions unction as being the reason of the name 'Christian,'[5] and thus implies his belief that the custom was apostolic.

Irenæus and Hippolytus, in the works mentioned, do not actually say that the Catholics used unction, though we may infer this from the fact that the Gnostics were clearly copyists in their baptismal rites; but the matter is now set at rest by the fact that the 'so-called *Egyptian Church Order*' in all its versions has unction, in this case before as well as after immersion (though the fragmentary Latin version, which appears to be the oldest, is wanting in the description of the rite before immersion). R. H. Connolly has shown that this Church Order, at least in the main, dates back to Hippolytus himself.[6]

Later in the 3rd cent. the custom of anointing at baptism is attested by Cyprian[7] and Origen;[8] but it was not used by the Novatians.[9] There are frequent references to unction in connexion with baptism in the Church Orders and in the Fathers from the 4th cent. onwards; there was usually an anointing before immersion and either one or two anointings after: if two, then the presbyter administered the former, the bishop the latter. But a peculiar custom prevailed in the early Syrian Church. There we find only one anointing, and that before immersion, so that in this Church the 'confirmation' took place before the rite at the font, instead of after it, as everywhere else and as in the NT.

The evidence for this custom is now full and complete;[10] it continued till the 5th or 6th century. Probably Severus (patriarch of Antioch, A.D. 512–519) introduced the post-baptismal unction among the West Syrians (Monophysites), and the catholicos Ishū'yahbh III. (A.D. 647–658) among the East Syrians (Nestorians). The only known exception is in a commentary ascribed to Ephraim,[11] where an unction after immersion is mentioned. But this work is probably not Ephraim's. These commentaries are a catena of notes on the OT, many by Jacob of Edessa, some headed 'Of Ephraim,' though the heading is often doubtful, and the extracts may be paraphrases rather than quotations. If at any point they are not in accord with attested sayings of Ephraim (as is the case here), we may safely conclude that they are not his.

The ordinary custom, then, from the time of Hippolytus, was to have an anointing before, and at least one after, immersion; in that case ordinary olive oil was generally used before immersion and chrism or unguent (μύρον) after, the latter being oil mixed with balsam, spices, etc. But there are several exceptions. In Theodoret[12] 'chrism of μύρον' is used before immersion; in the Armenian and East Syrian rites oil is used throughout.

(*c*) *At the effeta.*—This was a ceremony in the West (called in Spain *effetatio*) which took place several days before baptism, and was named from the Aramaic *Ephphatha* ('Be opened'), the ears and nose being touched. For this ceremony oil was originally used, as we see in John the Roman Deacon's *Epistle to Senarius*[1] and in the works of Ildephonsus, bishop of Toledo.[2] Afterwards, as in the *Gelasian Sacramentary*[3] and in later pontificals, saliva was used instead.

In several authorities, such as Ambrose,[4] the *Bobbio Missal*,[5] the *Stowe Missal*,[6] Alcuin,[7] and Amalarius of Metz,[8] neither saliva nor oil is explicitly mentioned at the effeta itself; but in the *Gregorian Sacramentary*[9] and the *Gelasian*, and often elsewhere, the effeta takes place just before the anointing of shoulders and breast. It is quite possible that this anointing may be the unction which takes place just before immersion, put into an earlier position.

(*d*) *In consecrating the font.*—In both East and West oil or chrism or both were often poured in the form of a cross into the water at the consecration of the font. This we find in Ildephonsus[10] in Spain; at Rome in the *Ordo Romanus Septimus*;[11] in Gaul in the *Missale Gallicanum Vetus*,[12] also in the *Bobbio Missal*[13] and the *Missale Gothicum*;[14] and in most Western pontificals. It is also common in the East. It is mentioned in the writer who poses as Dionysius the Areopagite;[15] and is found in the Greek rite of baptism,[16] and the Armenian,[17] the Coptic, West Syrian, Maronite, and (in some MSS) the East Syrian.[18]

(*e*) *During the catechumenate.*—There are a few traces of an earlier unction than that of the effeta mentioned above. Augustine, speaking of our Lord's anointing the blind man with the clay in Jn 9[6], says that Jesus 'perhaps made him a catechumen.'[19] This may refer to a custom of unction at the reception of candidates into the catechumenate. In Spain Isidore of Seville speaks of catechumens being anointed before they became 'competentes,' *i.e.* accepted candidates for baptism.[20] The Roman Synod held A.D. 402 speaks of their being anointed at the third scrutiny.[21] But the phrase 'oil of catechumens' usually means the oil administered just before immersion, as opposed to the chrism administered after. In the later Western authorities three oils are distinguished: (1) 'holy oil,' to sign the 'heathen child' on the breast and between the shoulders before immersion;[22] (2) 'holy chrism,' after immersion; (3) 'sick man's oil.'[23]

(*f*) *Consecration of the chrism.*—In the West the chrism was ordinarily hallowed by the diocesan bishop, in the East by the patriarch, on Maundy

1 § 7 (c. A.D. 120?). The view of J. Armitage Robinson, that the *Didache* only represents a piece of false antiquarianism, and does not give us a true picture of Christian life, is perhaps not very probable (*JThSt* xiii. [1912] 339 ff.; and *Barnabas, Hermas, and the Didache* [Donnellan Lectures], London, 1920, Appendix A).
2 *De Bapt.* 6–8; cf. *de Res. Carn.* 8, *adv. Marc.* i. 14.
3 *Hær.* I. xxi. 3 f.
4 *Ref.* v. 2.
5 *Ad Autol.* i. 12 (c. A.D. 180).
6 *The So-called Egyptian Church Order and Derived Documents* (*TS* viii. 4), Cambridge, 1916.
7 *Ep.* lxx. [lxix.] 2.
8 *In Lev.* hom. vi. § 5, *in Rom.* hom. v. § 8; but we have these in the Latin translation only.
9 Theodoret, *Hær. Fab. Compend.* iii. 5 (5th cent.).
10 For the evidence see art. CONFIRMATION, and R. H. Connolly, *The Liturgical Homilies of Narsai* (*TS* viii. 1), Cambridge, 1909, p. xlii ff.
11 *In Joel* 2[24]. Lawlor (*loc. cit.*) suggests that the word '*midhé*' ('baptized') here means 'baptizandi.' But in view of Syriac usage this is impossible.
12 *In Cant.* i. 2.

1 § 4 (c. A.D. 500).
2 *De Cogn. Bapt.* i. 27 f. (7th cent.).
3 Ed. H. A. Wilson, Oxford, 1894, p. 114.
4 *De Myst.* i. [3].
5 J. M. Neale and G. Forbes, *Ancient Liturgy of the Gallican Church*, Burntisland, 1855–67, p. 269.
6 F. E. Warren, *The Liturgy and Ritual of the Celtic Church*, Oxford, 1881, p. 210.
7 *Ep.* xc. (8th cent.).
8 *De Eccl. Off.* i. 23 (9th cent.).
9 Ed. H. A. Wilson (Henry Bradshaw Soc., xlix.), London, 1915, p. 54.
10 *De Cogn. Bapt.* 109.
11 § 10 (in J. Mabillon and M. Germain, *Museum Italicum*, Paris, 1687–89, ii.).
12 Mabillon and Germain, i. 324.
13 Neale and Forbes, p. 268.
14 Ed. H. M. Bannister (H. Bradshaw Soc., lii.), London, 1917, i. 77.
15 *De Hier. Eccl.* ii. 7 (μύρον).
16 F. C. Conybeare, *Rituale Armenorum*, Oxford, 1905, p. 403.
17 *Ib.* p. 95; H. Denzinger, *Ritus Orientalium*, Würzburg, 1863, i. 387, 394.
18 Denzinger, i. 207, 276, 346, 373.
19 *In Johan.* tract. xliv. § 2.
20 *De Eccl. Off.* ii. 21.
21 Can. 8.
22 See § 1 (*c*) above.
23 Ælfric, *Ep.* ii. (c. A.D. 1000), in H. Soames, *The Anglo-Saxon Church*[3], London, 1844, Suppl. p. 12 f.

Thursday; so, in the West, in the *Gregorian*[1] and *Gelasian*[2] *Sacramentaries*. Leo the Great implies that the same custom existed in Egypt in the 5th century.[3] Proterius, bishop of Alexandria, was murdered on that day, and Leo says that 'the hallowing of the chrism has failed.' But in the East Syrian and Malabar rite, where ordinary oil is used instead of chrism, it is consecrated by the presbyter at the time of baptism;[4] a little of the 'holy oil' said to be descended from St. John is added.[5] There were elsewhere some exceptions. At the first Council of Toledo (A.D. 400) permission was given to consecrate chrism at any time.[6] In Gaul it was perhaps consecrated on Palm Sunday.[7] Formerly the Armenians sometimes allowed diocesan bishops to consecrate the oil,[8] but this is now confined to the catholicos.

The rule that bishops alone may hallow the chrism is laid down in the West at the first Council of Toledo,[9] by Pope Innocent I.,[10] at the second[11] and third[12] Councils of Carthage, at that of Hippo,[13] by Augustine,[14] at the Council of Vaison in Gaul,[15] and at the second Council of Seville,[16] by Amalarius of Metz,[17] and by Thomas Aquinas;[18] also in Egypt, early in the 4th cent., by Didymus of Alexandria.[19] But in time of persecution in 'Africa' presbyters were allowed to consecrate the chrism, as John the Deacon tells us.[20] In the West the oil, as opposed to the chrism, was ordinarily consecrated at the time of the service by the officiant, whoever he might be.

(*g*) *Meaning of the unction.* — Originally the anointing was considered to be the consecration of the Christian to the royal priesthood.[21]

So Tertullian compares the baptismal unction to the anointing of the Aaronic priests.[22] The same idea is found in the 3rd cent. in the *Older Didascalia*;[23] and (emphatically) in the derived *Apostolic Constitutions*.[24] Jerome, apparently alluding to unction, and using the word 'baptism' in its widest sense, says that 'the priesthood of the laymen is baptism.'[25] The idea of consecration to the priesthood is also found in Augustine,[26] Ambrose,[27] John the Deacon,[28] Isidore of Seville,[29] Alcuin,[30] and his disciple Rabanus Maurus,[31] and became a commonplace. The consecration was specially connected, by John the Deacon, Alcuin, and many others, with the anointing of the head immediately after immersion.

A special significance was attached to the post-baptismal unction[32] in places where the laying on of the hand was dying out, or was less emphasized, and even in Egypt, where that ceremony was long retained. The gift of the Spirit, elsewhere associated with the imposition of the hand, was then ascribed to the unction.

This is the case with Sarapion of Thmuis in Egypt,[33] Ambrose (probably),[34] and even Pope Innocent I.[35] The North Italian author of the *de Sacramentis* says that at the signing (with chrism) the bishop (*sacerdos*) invokes the Holy Ghost in His sevenfold gifts.[36] Even Augustine[37] and Pacian of Barcelona[38] speak in the same sense. In the East, where the imposition of the hand in confirmation died out early, we should expect the same thing; and Cyril of Jerusalem[39] says that the object of the *μύρον* is to convey the Holy Ghost. Narsai (an East Syrian) apparently calls the unction 'the drug of the Spirit,' and certainly says that the Spirit is given by it.[1]

In the developed Eastern rites we sometimes find the association of the gift of the Spirit with the chrismation; explicitly in the Coptic rite in the prayer at the unction after immersion,[2] and in the Ethiopic.[3] Other Eastern rites are confused on this point, but, as immersion and confirmation are never separated in them, they are not particularly careful to ascribe a special significance to one or other part of the service.

(*h*) *Unction at the reception of heretics.*—This is in reality part of the question which we are now considering. For, as all agreed that the Holy Spirit could not be given outside the Church, even in the great controversy between Cyprian and Pope Stephen as to heretical baptism in the 3rd cent., the ceremony used when heretics were converted and admitted to the Church had normally as its object the reception of the Holy Ghost. It was the custom in the West and in 'Africa,' and originally (it seems) in at least some parts of the East, to receive heretics by the imposition of the hand. But in places where the latter ceremony was less emphasized they were received by unction.

This was the case in Didymus of Alexandria,[4] at the councils of Orange on the Rhone[5] and of Epaon in Burgundy,[6] and at the Trullan Council of Constantinople.[7] Basil also directs the reception of heretics by unction,[8] and Gregory the Great says that this was the custom in the East.[9] Theodoret says that the Novatians were anointed on reception, because they did not use unction in baptism.[10]

2. Unction of the sick.—The early history of this subject has too often been considered, by writers of all schools of thought, merely from the point of view of post-Reformation controversies. It is more profitable to put these, in the first instance, on one side, and to deal with the purely historical question of the use by the Early Church of unction for sick people, whatever was the purpose of such unction. In the opinion of the present writer, it will be found that the evidence for unction of the sick is very much the same, as regards time, as that for unction in connexion with baptism, the only difference being that, while for the latter the evidence of the 2nd cent. is stronger than that of the 1st, for the former the case is reversed, and the evidence for unction of the sick, which is strong in the apostolic age, is less so in the age which followed it. It will be found, it is believed, that the commonly expressed opinion on this subject will have to be reconsidered.[11]

(*a*) *The New Testament.*—Unction of the sick is mentioned as having been used during our Lord's ministry: in Mk 6^{13} the Twelve 'anointed with oil many that were sick, and healed them.' In the subsequent period it is commended by St. James;[12] the sick man is to call for 'the presbyters of the church,' who are to pray over him, 'having anointed him with oil in the name of the Lord,' and this 'prayer of faith' is both for bodily healing and for forgiveness of sins. We read also of our Lord anointing with saliva[13] in performing cures; and of the figurative anointing of the eyes with eye-salve in the Apocalypse.[14] The 'oil and wine' used by the Good Samaritan had no religious significance,[15] though they have received a spiritual interpretation. The passage in St. James is referred to by Origen[16] and Chrysostom.[17] The

1 Ed. Wilson, p. 49.
2 Ed. Wilson, p. 69 ff.
3 *Ep.* clvi. 5.
4 Denzinger, i. 372; G. B. Howard, *The Christians of St. Thomas and their Liturgies*, Oxford, 1864, p. 38.
5 A. J. Maclean and W. H. Browne, *The Catholicos of the East and his People*, London, 1892, pp. 247, 269.
6 Can. 20.
7 L. Duchesne, *Christian Worship*³, Eng. tr., London, 1903, p. 320.
8 Denzinger, i. 55.
9 Can. 20.
10 *Ep. ad Decent.* 3.
11 Can. 3 (A.D. 387 or 390).
12 Can. 36 (A.D. 397).
13 Can. 24 (A.D. 393).
14 *De Bapt. c. Donat.* v. 28.
15 Can. 3 (A.D. 442).
16 Can. 7 (A.D. 619).
17 *De Eccl. Off.* i. 27.
18 *Summ. Theol.* III. qu. lxxii. art. 3.
19 *De Trin.* ii. 15.
20 *Ep. ad Senar.* 7.
21 1 P $2^{5.9}$, Rev 1^6 5^{10} 20^6.
22 *De Bapt.* 7.
23 F. X. Funk, *Didascalia et Constitutiones Apostolorum*, Paderborn, 1905, i. 210.
24 iii. 16 (*c.* A.D. 375).
25 *Adv. Lucif.* 4.
26 *De Civ. Dei*, xx. 10.
27 *De Myst.* vi. [30].
28 *Ep. ad Senar.* 6.
29 *De Eccl. Off.* ii. 25.
30 *Ep.* xc.
31 *De Inst. Cler.* i. 30 (9th cent.).
32 Or, in the early Syrian Church, to the unction before immersion.
33 *Sacramentary*, § 16 (*c.* A.D. 350).
34 *De Myst.* vii. [42].
35 *Ep. ad Decent.*
36 iii. 2 [8] (*c.* A.D. 400?).
37 *Serm.* 227 (Benedictine ed.).
38 *Serm. de bapt.* 6 (4th cent.).
39 *Cat.* xxi. [*Myst.* iii.] 3 (A.D. 348).

1 Connolly, *Lit. Hom. of Narsai*, pp. 43, 45.
2 Denzinger, i. 209.
3 *Ib.* p. 230.
4 *De Trin.* ii. 15.
5 Can. 1 (A.D. 441).
6 Can. 16 (A.D. 517).
7 Can. 95 (A.D. 692).
8 *Ep. canonica prima*, clxxxviii. 1 (4th cent.).
9 *Ep.* xi. 67, ad Quiricum (6th cent.).
10 See § 1 (*b*) above.
11 See § 2 (*b*) below.
12 Ja $5^{14f.}$.
13 Mk 7^{33} 8^{23}, Jn $9^{6.11}$.
14 3^{18}.
15 Lk 10^{34}.
16 *In Lev.* hom. ii. § 4.
17 *De Sacerd.* iii. 6 [§ 196].

latter implies that the unction of the sick was still practised in his day: he is speaking of the power of the priest to forgive sins.

(*b*) *2nd and 3rd centuries.*—The first known reference to the unction of the sick after St. James applies to the reign of the emperor Septimus Severus (A.D. 193–211), or more probably to a time before his accession. Tertullian says[1] that the Christian Proculus Torpacion had once (*aliquando*) healed 'Severus, the father of Antoninus' [Caracalla] by anointing. If unction was used for the healing of a sick heathen, *a fortiori* it would be used for Christians. It might be held that this was a purely medical use of unction. But any possible doubt on this head has been taken away by the investigations of R. H. Connolly with regard to the *Egyptian Church Order* (already referred to).[2]

In the Latin as well as in the Ethiopic version of this Church Order there is a form given for the blessing of the oil for the sick, offered apparently by the laity.[3] This form we may with confidence assign, with the great bulk of this work, to Hippolytus of Portus, and therefore we have evidence of unction of the sick at Rome early in the 3rd century. The form states that the unction is for the healing of the body, but nothing is said of spiritual blessing. This new evidence shows that we must correct the statement of the committee of the Lambeth Conference of 1908, that 'there is no clear proof of the use of unction for the sick in the Christian Church until the fourth century'[4]—a statement which has been frequently repeated.

(*c*) *From the 4th cent. onwards.*—In the 4th cent. we have a series of Church Orders which show that unction of the sick was a common practice. In the *Testament of Our Lord*[5] a form is given for blessing oil and water for healing; this prayer is independent of the Hippolytean form, and much fuller; it incidentally refers to spiritual benefits. The oil would be for application, the water for drinking. The *Apostolic Constitutions* give a form[6] for consecrating oil and water by the bishop, or in his absence by the presbyter; this refers to healing, but incidentally also to demons and other spiritual ills. This form is not found in the epitome (of the eighth book of *Apost. Const.*) known as the *Constitutions through Hippolytus.*[7] In the *Canons of Hippolytus*[8] oil for the sick and firstfruits are blessed; no form is given, but 'Gloria Patri' is added. In the *Sacramentary of Sarapion*[9] oil and bread and water for the sick are blessed, doubtless by the bishop, as the book contains only the portions of the services said by him.

The form contains the words 'Let every Satanic energy . . . depart from . . . these thy servants,' and it has been suggested that this shows that the oil was consecrated at the time of use.[10] Elsewhere in this work there occurs, after the anaphora, a 'prayer concerning the oils and waters that are offered' [by the laity]. In both these prayers bodily healing is primarily asked for, then spiritual blessings, and protection against demons and the like. A form for consecrating oil for the sick is found also in G. Horner's *Statutes of the Apostles.*[11]

In the above works the people seem to have brought the oil (and water and bread) for the sick to be blessed by the bishop or presbyter, and then to have applied it themselves, in spite of Ja 5^{14}. At the same time they also brought firstfruits to be blessed.

We have a good deal of other evidence of the use of unction for the sick, the earliest referring to Egypt.

Palladius, bishop of Helenopolis, in his *Historia Lausiaca*, describes how the monks of that country in the 4th cent. used oil for the sick—Benjamin of Nitria,[1] Macarius of Alexandria,[2] and John of Lycopolis.[3] The first of these monks healed the sick by touch of the hand or by oil consecrated by himself. Sozomen also tells us how the monks of Egypt in that century anointed a paralytic with oil and healed him;[4] and Rufinus makes a similar statement.[5] On the other hand, Athanasius mentions only imposition of the hand in healing the sick; the Catholics would not allow an Arian to lay a hand on a sick man's head.[6] Thus unction and laying on of the hand were alternatives, and we see the same thing in the NT: Mk 5^{23} 6^{5} 7^{32} $8^{23.\,25}$ [Mk] 16^{18}, Mt 9^{18}, Lk 4^{40} 13^{13}, Ac $9^{12.\,17}$ 28^{8}—all of our Lord and the disciples.

In the 4th cent. Chrysostom says that the sick were healed with oil from the church lamp,[7] and this was afterwards a common practice.[8]

In the 5th cent. Pope Innocent I., asked if the sick might be anointed with chrism (*sanctum oleum chrismatis*), and if bishops might anoint, answers in the affirmative; the oil blessed by the bishop may be applied by any Christian if necessary, but it cannot be applied to penitents, because it is of the nature of a sacrament.[9]

Some eighty or more years later Cæsarius, bishop of Arles († 542), says in one of his sermons: 'Whenever any sickness comes, let the sick man receive the body and blood of Christ and then anoint his body,' and the promise made by St. James will be fulfilled.[10] And in another sermon he says that it is better than magic uses to go to the Church and receive the body and blood of Christ, and faithfully and copiously to anoint (*perungerent*) oneself and one's own with blessed oil, and to receive not only healing of the body, but also remission of sins, as James the apostle says.[11]

Here then, in the beginning of the 6th cent., it is contemplated that the sick man should ordinarily anoint himself, though the oil has previously been consecrated.

From the 6th cent. onwards we read of the 'oil of the cross' in healing. This was oil touched by a relic of the true cross, and was considered to be especially efficacious.[12]

Among the Easterns we find the use of oil for the sick to be almost universal.

(*d*) *Armenians* in practice anoint only sick priests, not deacons or lay people.

The *Instruction in the Christian Faith*, by Chosrov, says that the unction is for the healing of the body and the forgiveness of lighter sins; the apostles sometimes laid hands on the sick, and sometimes anointed; unction is not essential, but prayer is, and, if necessary, this sacrament may be administered without the anointing of oil.[13]

The earliest mention among the Armenians of unction as a preparation for death is *c.* A.D. 800; and no rite for the anointing of the sick is found in any ancient euchologion or *mashtotz.*[14] The old Armenian office for the visitation of the sick consists of prayers and communion.[15] Denzinger mentions an Armenian custom of anointing the faithful (not only the sick) on Maundy Thursday with butter (not oil), blessed by the bishop.[16]

(*e*) *East Syrians* (*Nestorians*).—In the *Ṭakhsā*, or Missal, it is directed that the holy oil of baptism is not to be used for consecrating churches or for anointing the sick;[17] for unction of the sick

1 *Ad Scap.* 4.
2 See § 1 (*b*) above.
3 Connolly, *So-called Egyp. Church Order*, p. 176; E. Hauler, *Didascaliæ apostol. fragmenta Veronensia Latina*, Leipzig, 1900, i. 108.
4 *Report*, London, 1908, p. 138. For a possible reference to oil, water, and bread for the sick in Clement of Alexandria (*Excerpta*, 82) see F. E. Brightman in *JThSt* i. [1900] 261.
5 i. 24 f. (*c.* A.D. 350).
6 viii. 29 (*c.* A.D. 375).
7 Given by Funk, ii. 72 ff.
8 Can. iii. (4th cent.?); ed. H. Achelis, *Die Canones Hippolyti* (*TU* vi. 4), Leipzig, 1891, § 28 f.
9 § 17 (*c.* A.D. 350).
10 J. Wordsworth, *Bishop Sarapion's Prayer Book*, London, 1899, p. 77*n*.
11 London, 1904, pp. 162–178. This is in a long interpolation, and the date is not certain.

1 *The Lausiac Hist. of Palladius*, ed. C. Butler (*TS* vi. 1, 2), Cambridge, 1898–1904, § 12 (ii. 35 f.).
2 § 18 (ii. 47 ff.).
3 § 35 (ii. 100 ff.).
4 *HE* vi. 20, 29.
5 *Ib.* ii. 4. F. E. Brightman gives other instances in *JThSt* i. [1900] 260.
6 *Encycl. Ep.* 5.
7 *In Matt.* hom. xxxii. § 6.
8 See § 2 (*f*) below; several other instances are given by W. E. Scudamore in *DCA* ii. 1454 f.
9 *Ep. ad Decent.* 8 (A.D. 416). The authenticity of this letter has been questioned, but without much probability. As late as the beginning of the 8th cent. Bede, in his *Exposition of the Epistle of St. James*, says, on Innocent's authority, that laymen may anoint themselves.
10 *Serm.* 265, § 3, col. 437, in the appendix to vol. v. of the Benedictine ed. of Augustine (also *PL* xxxix. 2238).
11 *Serm.* 279, § 5, Ben. ed., col. 465 (also *PL* xxxix. 2273).
12 For this and similar oils see *DCA* ii. 1453.
13 T. E. Dowling, *The Armenian Church*, London, 1910, p. 135 f.
14 *Ib.*
15 It is given in F. C. Conybeare, *Rituale Armenorum*, p. 114 ff.
16 i. 190.
17 Syriac text (Urmi, 1890), p. 147. This part has not been translated into English.

a single collect is appointed, and is to be said by the priest when he blesses the oil.[1] In this Church *ḥnānā* (lit. 'mercy'), dust from the tombs of the martyrs, is mixed with oil and water and applied to the sick person.[2] In the ordination of presbyters prayer is offered that 'they may lay their hands on the sick and they may be healed.'[3]

(*f*) *The Copts* have an office of the 'holy oil' which they call 'the lamp' (φανός);[4] imposition of hands is included in it, and seven presbyters officiate. The Greek Orthodox also have a direction to anoint the sick with 'the holy oil from the lamp.'[5]

(*g*) *The West Syrians* (*Jacobites*) also have an office for blessing 'the oil of catechumens, which is also the oil of the sick.'[6]

(*h*) *The Orthodox.*—Here seven priests, if they can be had, administer the oil. The Russian *Longer Catechism* says[7] that unction with oil is a sacrament, in which, while the body is anointed with oil, God's grace is invoked on the sick to heal him of spiritual and bodily infirmities; and it then quotes Mk 6^{13}, Ja $5^{14f.}$.

(*i*) *Unction of the sick in England.*—Theodore, archbishop of Canterbury, in his *Capitulare* (A.D. 680), says that Greeks allowed presbyters, if necessary, to make the exorcized oil and chrism for the sick, but Romans confined the consecration of it to the bishop.[8] The *Excerptiones* of Egbert, archbishop of York (A.D. 732–766),[9] say that the sick are to be anointed with oil hallowed by bishops (*sacerdotibus*), and that the presbyter is to have the eucharist always ready, that the sick may not die without communion.[10] King Edgar's *Canons* (A.D. 960) order every priest to have unction for the sick.[11]

Ælfric's[12] *Canons* (*c.* A.D. 1000) direct the priest to 'have hallowed oil apart for children [*i.e.* for confirmation], and apart for sick men, and always to anoint the sick in bed. Some sick men are fearful, so that they will not consent to be anointed' [they feared that unction would kill them]. If a man is anointed and recovers, and then once more falls sick, he can again receive unction; it is not an ordination, but in it is healing and forgiveness.[13]

The form of blessing the oil is given in the *Pontifical of Egbert*, archbishop of York.

It prays that it may be to every one who touches it for protection of mind and body, for the driving away of all pains and all infirmities, and every sickness of body; and refers to the anointing of priests, kings, prophets, and martyrs.[14]

The form in the present *Roman Pontifical* is nearly the same.

In the later instances we see the restriction of the administration of the oil to a priest. This led to the practice of extreme unction, and then unction was made to precede the last communion. The anointing of the sick was retained in the First Prayer-Book of Edward VI. (1549), and was on the forehead, and explicitly for the healing of both soul and body. It was omitted in the Second Prayer-Book (1552), but restored by the Non-jurors.

3. Extreme unction.—When the anointing of

1 Syriac text (Urmi, 1890), p. 98.
2 The directions are given in Denzinger, ii. 517 f.
3 *Ib.* ii. 236.
4 *Ib.* ii. 484.
5 J. Goar, *Euchologion*, Paris, 1647, p. 436 (2nd ed. Venice, 1730); see also § 2 (*c*) above.
6 Given in Denzinger, ii. 551. We may contrast the direction among the East Syrians given in § 2 (*e*) above.
7 R. W. Blackmore, *The Doctrine of the Russian Church*, Aberdeen, 1845, pp. 97, 239.
8 § 35; E. Martène, *De Antiquis Ecclesiæ Ritibus*², Antwerp, 1736–38, I. vii. 3, § 7; L. d'Achery, *Spicilegium*, Paris, 1723, i. 487. For Bede see § 2 (*c*) above.
9 But they are probably later than Egbert; see *DCB* ii. 51ᵇ.
10 D. Wilkins, *Concilia Magnæ Britanniæ et Hiberniæ*, London, 1737, i. 103.
11 W. Maskell, *Monumenta Ritualia Ecclesiæ Anglicanæ*, London, 1846–47, i. p. ccxxiv.
12 There was an archbishop of Canterbury, and one of York of this name, nearly contemporary, and a homilist who was perhaps different from both.
13 Maskell, i. pp. ccxxv, ccxxxiii.
14 *The Pontifical of Egbert*, ed. W. Greenwell (Surtees Society), Durham, 1853, p. 120.

the sick came to be looked upon principally as a preparation for death, it received this name, which properly means 'the last of the unctions' but was popularly understood to mean unction administered to those *in extremis*; it was no longer, unless in exceptional cases, for the healing of the body, but was for spiritual benefit only. The name is not found before the end of the 12th cent.; it appears first in Peter Lombard;[1] after that it became common. But the idea itself is found in the 10th cent., in Ælfric.[2]

We find frequent directions on the subject in the Middle Ages. The Synod of Exeter under Bishop Quivil (held in 1267) says that extreme unction is for the healing of the body and for forgiveness of sins; it is not the least venerable of the sacraments, and no money is to be exacted for it; the clergy are not to absent themselves from their parishes except of necessity, lest any die without confession, viaticum, and extreme unction; some ignorant persons refuse to receive this last-mentioned rite, and the clergy are to preach about it.[3] The Synod of Worcester under Bishop Woodloke (held *c.* 1308) has the same directions, except about the money.[4] And in Scotland we find similar rules in the 13th century. Every sick person over 14 years of age in danger of death should receive extreme unction, and no fee is to be charged. It may be repeated if necessary, and no restriction is laid down on this point.[5]

Aquinas deals at length with extreme unction in the supplement to his *Summa Theologica*, written between 1265 and 1271. He says[6] that it is a sacrament because it avails for the remission of sins, whereas the oil of catechumens [administered before baptism] does not do so. This sacrament was instituted by Christ Himself, though He promulgated it through the apostles; some, however, think that He left it to the apostles to institute.[7] Olive oil is the convenient 'matter,' as in Ja $5^{14f.}$, and it is to be first consecrated by the bishop, as in all other unctions.[8] Extreme unction must have a 'form,' as all other sacraments of the new law have; this form is a prayer, as in St. James, but the intention of the minister is expressed in the words 'By this holy unction,' etc.[9] Aquinas proceeds to deal with the theological significance of the rite. It avails for the remission of sins, as St. James says, and also for the healing of the body, just as immersion in baptism cleanses the soul through the cleansing of the body.[10] It does not impress 'character,' like ordination or confirmation, seeing that it may be repeated.[11] Aquinas then deals with the minister of extreme unction. It cannot be conferred by a layman, like baptism, as it is not so necessary, nor yet by deacons, for St. James speaks of 'presbyters'; but the administration is not confined to bishops alone.[12] With regard to the recipients of extreme unction, Aquinas remarks that it is not for those who are in health, nor for all the sick, but only for those who are near death. It is the last remedy which the Church can confer. It is not for madmen, unless in lucid intervals, nor for young children, as it is a remedy for actual sin, not for the relics of original sin, unless indeed these are strengthened in some way by actual sin. Only certain portions of the body, not the whole, are to be anointed, the mutilated being anointed on that part which is nearest to the lost limb.[13] Further, extreme unction can be repeated without injury, but not in the same illness.[14] Elsewhere Aquinas says that by it men are prepared for worthy communion [*i.e.* the viaticum]; it is inferior to baptism and the eucharist, and is not of necessity, but is for progress in the Christian life.[15]

Maskell[16] gives the rite of extreme unction from the *Sarum Manual* (his copy is dated 1543):

After a prayer referring to Ja $5^{14f.}$ and asking for restoration to health ('saluti pristinæ restituere'), the priest anoints the eyes, ears, lips, nostrils, hands (the laity on the palms, the priests on the outside, as they had already been anointed on the palms at ordination),[17] the feet, and the back, or in the case

1 *Sent.* IV. ii. 1.
2 See § 2 (*i*) above.
3 Cap. 6; Wilkins, *Conc.* ii. 134 f.
4 Wilkins, ii. 294 f.
5 *Ecclesiæ Scoticanæ Statuta*, ed. J. Robertson (Bannatyne Club), Edinburgh, 1866, ii. 34, 58.
6 Qu. xxix., art. 1.
7 Art. 3.
8 Art. 4–6.
9 Art. 7–9; see below for the 'form.'
10 Qu. xxx., art. 1 f.
11 Art. 3.
12 Qu. xxxi.
13 Qu. xxxii.
14 Qu. xxxiii.
15 III. qu. lxv., art. 3.
16 *Monumenta*, i. 83. The *Rituale Romanum* has almost the same directions (ed. G. Catalani, Padua, 1760, i. 332 ff.).
17 See § 4 below.

of a female the front. At each anointing he prays for forgiveness in these words: 'By this unction and His most tender mercy, may the Lord forgive thee whatsoever thou hast done amiss through sight' (hearing, etc.). A psalm is said between each anointing, and after the unctions a blessing is given, referring to purification of mind and body. Then follows a prayer which has special reference to the sick man's approaching death, but this is not in the Bangor MS quoted in Maskell's note, and seems to be later than the rest. The sick man is then communicated if he is capable of retaining what he swallows; otherwise he is assured that spiritual communion suffices, and the well-known words are quoted: 'Tantum crede et manducasti.'[1] In the *Pontifical of Magdalen College*, probably of Hereford or Canterbury and of the 12th cent., the first prayer mentioned above ends differently; here there is only one unction, in which the references to the various senses are combined.[2] In this *Pontifical* two different prayers follow the blessing, referring to the forgiveness of sins.

Only one priest is mentioned in the *Sarum Manual* as administering unction, but Walter Raynold, archbishop of Canterbury (1313–37), speaks of *sacerdotes* in the plural; and W. Lyndwood glosses this by saying 'two at least, except in case of necessity.'[3] Raynold says that all over fourteen years of age should receive extreme unction;[4] and also that it can be repeated only if a year has elapsed.[5]

The oil was consecrated on Maundy Thursday;[6] and this was the case also at Rome.[7] By a constitution of J. Peckham, archbishop of Canterbury (1278–94), any unused oil was burnt.[8]

The Council of Trent says that extreme unction was instituted by our Lord as a sacrament of the NT, outlined (*insinuatum*) by St. Mark, and commended to the faithful and promulgated by St. James. The 'matter' is oil blessed by a bishop, for the unction represents the grace of the Holy Spirit, and the 'form' is 'By this unction,' etc.[9] The effect is primarily forgiveness and strengthening of the soul, and occasionally restoration of bodily health; the ministers are bishops and presbyters. Extreme unction is to be used for those who appear to be dying; if they recover and then again fall ill, it may be repeated.[10] See also art. EXTREME UNCTION.[11]

4. Unction at ordination.—The idea of anointing at ordination is consecration to God and endowment with His gifts. The custom is derived from the OT, where kings, high priests, priests, and prophets are anointed.

In Ex 29^{7}, Lv 8^{12}, Moses anoints Aaron, whose anointing is also mentioned in Ps 133^{2}, Sir 45^{15}. In Ex 28^{41} 29^{21} 30^{30}, Lv 8^{30} 10^{7}, Aaron's sons are anointed as priests; in Lv 21^{10}, Nu 35^{25}, high priests in general receive unction. In 1 K $19^{15f.}$ Hazael, Jehu, and Elisha are anointed. The unction of prophets in Ps 105^{15}, Is 61^{1}, is perhaps metaphorical. The anointing was with olive oil and spices in Ex $30^{23ff.}$.

The same conception is found in the name 'the Christ,' 'the Messiah' ('the Anointed One'), as in Lk 4^{18}, which quotes Is 61^{1}, in Ac $4^{26f.}$, which quotes Ps 2^{2}, in Ac 10^{38}, and in He 1^{9}, which quotes Ps 45^{7}; cf. also Dn 9^{24}.

But, while in Eastern ordinals we frequently read of anointing in a metaphorical sense, the actual unction at ordination was confined to the West.

(*a*) At the consecration—or, as it was originally called, the ordination—of a bishop unction is not so ancient as the laying on of the hand, or as the custom of putting the book of the gospels on the elect's head. But it is found at Rome in the 5th century.

Leo the Great says: 'Now there is a nobler rank of Levites [deacons], there are elders [presbyters] of greater dignity, and priests [bishops] of holier anointing ['sacratior est unctio sacerdotum'].'[1] Elsewhere he says that 'it is not the prerogative of earthly origin which obtains the unction, but the condescension of divine grace which creates the bishop,'[2] and that 'the unction of the Holy Spirit consecrates priests.'[3] It is just possible, but not likely, that the unction here is only metaphorical.

In the 6th cent. Gregory the Great refers to this unction of the bishop;[4] and it is found also in Gaul, but not in 'Africa,' and perhaps not in Spain.[5] In *Egbert's Pontifical*, of the 8th cent., both head and hands were anointed;[6] and this was the case at Rome also.[7] In England the bishop's head was twice anointed, first with chrism mixed with oil, then (just before the unction of the hands) with chrism only; on each occasion was said:

'May thy head be anointed and hallowed with celestial blessing in the pontifical order, through the unction of holy chrism and oil and our blessing, in the name of the Father and of the Son and of the Holy Ghost, Amen.'[8]

(*b*) Unction at the ordination of a presbyter was not the custom of the earlier Roman Church, as Pope Nicholas I. explicitly states in 864.[9] It is not in the *Leonine Sacramentary* nor in some MSS of the *Gregorian*;[10] but it became general in the West after the 9th cent., and was introduced at Rome. Amalarius of Metz († 837) says that in Gaul the presbyter's hands were anointed at ordination by the bishop.[11] In *Egbert's Pontifical* the presbyter's head was also anointed,[12] but this seems soon to have been dropped.

(*c*) Unction of the hands at the ordination of deacons seems to have been a peculiarity of the Celtic and Anglo-Saxon rites; it is mentioned in Gildas's *Epistle*[13] (*c.* A.D. 560) and in *Egbert's Pontifical*.[14]

In all these cases the unction of the hands was on the palms.[15]

5. Unction at the coronation of kings.—The idea of this unction was the same as that of the unction at ordination. It is taken from the OT.

In 1 S 9^{16} 10^{1} 16^{13} Samuel anoints Saul and David; in 2 S 2^{4} men of Judah anoint David (so metaphorically Ps 89^{20}); in 1 K $1^{34.39}$ Zadok and Nathan anoint Solomon, Zadok applying the oil; in 1 K $19^{15f.}$ Elijah anoints Hazael and Jehu; in 2 K 11^{12} 'they made [Joash] king and anointed him.' Hence comes the phrase 'the Lord's Anointed' in 1 S 16^{6} and elsewhere, also in La 4^{20}, and even of Cyrus in Is 45^{1}; and in Jotham's parable, Jg 9^{8}, the trees 'anoint a king over them.'

This unction is first mentioned as a Christian custom in the Acts of the sixth Council of Toledo[16] (A.D. 638). The Visigoth kings in Spain were anointed at their inauguration. We read of unction at that of King Wamba in 672.[17] And in

1 'Only believe, and thou hast eaten.' The saying is from Augustine, *in Johann.* tract. xxv. 12 (on Jn $6^{28f.}$), 'crede et manducasti'; but he is not speaking specially of spiritual communion.

2 Ed. H. A. Wilson (H. Bradshaw Soc., xxxix.), London, 1910, p. 190.

3 *Provinciale seu Constitutiones Angliæ*, Oxford, 1679, bk. i. tit. 6, 'Cum magna reverentia.'

4 *Ib.*

5 *Ib.*, tit. 7.

6 *Ib.*, tit. 6, 'Cum sacris.'

7 E. G. C. F. Atchley, *Ordo Romanus Primus* (Library of Liturgiology and Ecclesiology), London, 1905, p. 97.

8 Maskell, i. p. ccxl.

9 Ct. Aquinas above.

10 *Canones et Decreta*, sess. xiv., 'de Sacr. Poen. et Extr. Unct.,' 1–3.

11 The subject of unction of the sick is treated very fully by F. W. Puller (*The Anointing of the Sick*, London, 1904), but the present writer had not the advantage of having seen that book before compiling this article. Puller gives at length the evidence of which only an outline is here attempted. He is specially concerned to refute the later teaching about Extreme Unction and to advocate what he argues to be a more primitive use. His argument is greatly strengthened by R. H. Connolly's investigations as to the 'so-called *Egyptian Church Order*'; see § 1 (*c*) above.

1 *Serm.* lix. 7 (*de Pass. Dom.* viii.).

2 *Ib.* iii. 1 (on the anniversary of his consecration).

3 *Ib.* iv. 1.

4 *In I. Reg.* ch. 10, quoted by J. Morinus, *Commentarius de sacris Ecclesiæ Ordinationibus*, Paris, 1655, IV. vi. 2. § 2.

5 Morinus, § 1.

6 Ed. Greenwell, p. 3; Martène, vol. ii. col. 101.

7 Morinus, § 2.

8 Maskell, iii. 263, 269.

9 E. Hatch, in *DCA* ii. 1514b.

10 Ed. H. A. Wilson, p. 6. This also applies to the consecration of bishops (Wilson, p. 5).

11 *De Eccl. Off.* ii. 13.

12 Ed. Greenwell, p. 24.

13 § 106; see art. ORDINATION (Christian), vol. ix. p. 543b.

14 Ed. Greenwell, p. 21; Martène, vol. ii. col. 100; see also cols. 110, 179.

15 See § 3 above.

16 J. D. Mansi, *Sacrorum Conciliorum nova et amplissima Collectio*, Florence and Venice, 1758–98, x. 659–674. On the whole subject of the inauguration of kings see R. M. Woolley, *Coronation Rites*, Cambridge, 1915. The 'cornu illud de quo reges unguebantur' of the *Pilgrimage of 'Etheria'* ('Silvia') refers, not to Christian practice, but to a supposed relic of OT times (Duchesne, *Christian Worship*^{3}, p. 510).

17 Woolley, pp. 33, 120.

France Pippin, father of Charlemagne, was anointed in 750.[1] But in these cases there is no mention of crowning, and the anointing was the central feature of the rite.[2] On the other hand, the emperors who were crowned for many centuries at Constantinople—for no emperor was crowned at Rome before Charlemagne — appear not to have been anointed before the 9th cent. (when Basil the Macedonian [867–886] is thought to have received unction),[3] or, as some believe, not before the 12th or 13th cent.;[4] in the latter case the earlier references are metaphorical only. In the Greek rite of coronation as fully developed, and hence in the Russian rite which is derived from it, unction is a prominent feature.[5] It is uncertain if Charlemagne was anointed *as Roman emperor*.[6] It will thus be seen that unction at the inauguration of kings is earlier than at that of emperors. Both England and France claimed to have a miraculous chrism sent down from heaven for the purpose.[7]

The Abyssinians have the custom of unction at the coronation of the Negus; it is probable that this is not derived from European practice, but is directly deduced from Holy Scripture.[8]

The coronation service for an English king found in *Egbert's Pontifical* is the most ancient of those extant; it is printed by Martène[9] and Maskell,[10] and the latter gives in his notes a collation of the same service in the *Leofric Missal*. In Egbert the king is anointed once only, on the head, one of the bishops ('unus ex pontificibus') saying the prayer, and the others anointing him. There is here no coronation of a queen-consort, though we find one later (with unction), in the 10th century.[11] There was more than one recension of Egbert's office; that called the *Liber Regalis*, which probably dates from the time of Edward II., remained almost unchanged till the coronation of James II.[12] In the service in the *Sarum Pontifical* given by Maskell[13] the king's hands, head, breast, shoulder-blades, and elbows ('ambae compages brachiorum') are anointed.[14] The custom of anointing has been retained in England ever since the Reformation, at the coronation of a king, of a queen-regnant, and of a queen-consort. Notices of unction at the coronation of James I. and his queen, of Charles I., Charles II., James II., William and Mary, and Victoria may be found in *Hierurgia Anglicana*.[15] At the coronation of George V. the king was anointed thrice in the form of a cross (four Knights of the Garter holding over him a rich pall of silk or cloth of gold): first on the crown of the head, then on the breast, then on the palms of both hands.[16] Charles I. was anointed first on the palms of the hands, then (after a prayer) on the breast, then between the shoulders, then 'on the boughs of both arms,' then on the crown of the head;[17] this followed the more ancient custom. The English coronation rite is the only remaining office in Christendom where the full rites of the anointing and all the details of solemn investiture are still extant.[18] The chrism was, before the coronation, consecrated by the Dean of Westminster if a bishop, otherwise by the Archbishop of Canterbury; but in the case of William and Mary the oil was blessed in the coronation service itself; this addition to the latter was dropped from the time of Anne.[1]

In France Napoleon I. was anointed on head and hands at his coronation; and his consort Josephine likewise.[2]

In Scotland unction was first allowed at a king's inauguration in 1329.[3] After the Reformation there were four Scottish coronations: James VI. was crowned in 1567, when one year old; his consort, Anne of Denmark, was crowned in 1590; Charles I. was crowned as King of Scotland in 1633, Charles II. in 1651; at the first three coronations unction was used, but not at the last.[4]

On the continent of Europe we find anointing retained at coronations in the reformed rite at Prague in 1619, in Prussia in 1701, in Denmark from 1559 to 1840, in Sweden from 1675 till our own day, and in Norway in modern times.[5]

6. Unction at the consecration of churches, etc.—This also is taken from the OT.

Jacob anointed the stone in Gn 28^{18}, and S. R. Driver remarks that this was a very common idea among primitive peoples.[6] The tabernacle was anointed in Ex 30^{26} 40^{9}, Lv 8^{10}, Nu 7^{1}. In Is 57^{6} we read of the pouring of a drink-offering to the 'smooth stones of the valley.'

From an early date churches and altars were consecrated with chrism.

We read of this in Gaul at the councils of Agde or Agatha[7] and Epaon,[8] in the *Canons* of Egbert of York,[9] in his *Pontifical*,[10] in Isidore of Seville,[11] Rabanus Maurus († A.D. 815), the disciple of Alcuin,[12] and Walafrid Strabo († A.D. 849).[13] In the *Sarum Pontifical*[14] twelve places in the church and the altar are anointed with chrism; holy water is also used. But neither oil nor chrism was used in reconciling a desecrated church.[15]

We find the same custom in the East. In pseudo-Dionysius the Areopagite (*c.* A.D. 500?) the altar is consecrated with unguent (μύρῳ).[16] The West Syrians (Jacobites) use chrism in consecrating altars,[17] as also do the Greeks.[18] From the 8th cent. we read of the Armenians consecrating churches with unguent,[19] even in the case of the rededication of a desecrated church.[20] Among the East Syrians (Nestorians) the consecration of a church is called *syāmīdhā* ('laying on of the hand') and is of two kinds, with and without oil; the former is for new or rebuilt churches, or for rededicating a church which has been desecrated owing to some very grave cause, and must be performed by a bishop; the latter is intended for use after minor accidents or breaches of the ecclesiastical law, and may be performed by priests commissioned by the bishop. In the former each wall and the altar and the outer lintel of the sanctuary door towards the nave are signed with the oil in the form of a cross.[21]

In the *Sarum Manual* of 1543 bells also are dedicated with oil and chrism,[22] and, at a much earlier date, in *Egbert's Pontifical*.[23] Similarly the Armenians dedicate with chrism the semantron—a wooden board struck by a mallet, and much used by Eastern Christians to call the people to church.[24] The Armenians also solemnly dedicate a cross, even for private use, with unguent.[25] In *Dunstan's Pontifical* the chalice is anointed when it is dedicated.[26]

1 Woolley, p. 34. 2 *Ib.* p. 167. 3 *Ib.* p. 179.
4 F. E. Brightman, in *JThSt* ii. [1901] 383 ff.
5 Woolley, pp. 25, 29, 177.
6 See the discussion in Woolley, pp. 40, 169.
7 *Ib.* pp. 73, 103. 8 *Ib.* pp. 30, 180. 9 ii. 10, ord. 1.
10 iii. 74. It may also be seen in the Surtees Soc. (ed. W. Greenwell), p. 101. Some think that it is later than Egbert.
11 Woolley, p. 65. 12 *Ib.* p. 69.
13 iii. 3. In his notes Maskell refers to earlier authorities also.
14 *Ib.* pp. 19, 22.
15 New ed. revised by V. Staley, London, 1902–04, ii. 118, 121–124, 283 f.
16 D. Macleane, *The Great Solemnity of the Coronation*², London, 1911, p. 30. In this work the full office is given with elaborate notes.
17 *Ib.* p. 328. 18 *Ib.* p. 314.

1 Woolley, pp. 80, 86. 2 *Ib.* p. 107.
3 *Ib.* p. 137. 4 *Ib.* pp. 80, 138 f.
5 *Ib.* pp. 143–156.
6 *The Book of Genesis* (Westminster Com.), London, 1904, p. 267.
7 Can. 14 (A.D. 506). 8 Can. 26 (A.D. 517).
9 Can. 51 (A.D. 732–766). 10 Martène, ii. 13, ord. 2.
11 *Ad Leudef.* 10. 12 *De Inst. Cler.* ii. 45.
13 *De Reb. Eccl.* 9. 14 Maskell, i. 163, 185 ff.
15 *Ib.* iii. 308 ff. 16 *Hier. Eccl.* iv. 12.
17 E. Renaudot, *Liturgiarum Orientalium Collectio*², Frankfort-on-Main, 1847, ii. 57.
18 Goar, *Euchologion*, pp. 837 f., 842.
19 Conybeare, *Rit. Arm.* p. 6. 20 *Ib.* p. 33.
21 A. J. Maclean and W. H. Browne, *The Catholicos of the East*, p. 303 f.
22 Maskell, i. 158 f. 23 Ed. Greenwell, p. 118.
24 Conybeare, p. 39; see also Maclean-Browne, pp. 210, 213, 251.
25 Conybeare, pp. 46, 51.
26 Martène, ii. 13, ord. 4. For further details as to unction at the consecration of churches and altars see art. CONSECRATION.

In England the Caroline divines used oil in consecrating churches. The Puritans objected that 'they shew us that the church, by the bishop's anointing some stones thereof with oil, and sprinkling others with water, and using from the Roman pontifical some more prayers, some more ceremonies upon it, becomes a ground more holy.'[1]

7. Unction of a dead body.—From the first the Christians prepared the body for burial either by embalming or with spices and unguents (μύρα);[2] this was in contrast to the Roman custom of cremation. References to the Christian usages in this respect are found in Tertullian,[3] Clement of Alexandria,[4] Minucius Felix[5] (early 3rd cent.?), and in the *Acta* of Tarachus, a martyr in the Diocletian persecution (A.D. 304).[6]

As an ecclesiastical act we find it, in the East, in pseudo-Dionysius the Areopagite; the hierarch [bishop] and the rest salute the dead body, and the hierarch pours oil on the departed, just as before baptism the candidates are anointed with the oil of the sacred chrism.[7] In Goar's *Euchologion* we read of a corpse being anointed just before burial with oil from church lamps, or of a cinder from the thurible being placed on it.[8] This custom is also found in the books of the East Syrians (Nestorians) and of the Armenians, where clergy anoint the departed, the Armenians calling it a sacrament;[9] but in practice, while in the case of a departed dignitary the East Syrians retain the solemn final kiss of peace, they do not appear to use unction.[10] The office used by the Armenians for the purpose may be seen in Denzinger.[11] In the West, Theodore, archbishop of Canterbury, says that dead monks were carried to church and anointed on the breast with chrism before the mass.[12]

LITERATURE.—This is given in the footnotes.

A. J. MACLEAN.

UNDER WORLD.—1. Origin of the belief.—The wide-spread conception of an under world in religion and myth is generally, though not invariably, associated with the dead. An under world of the dead is not the only conception of their dwelling-place: spirits may lurk about the place of burial or linger among the abodes of the living; they may dwell in distant regions or islands, or they may ascend to a place in the sky. These conceptions may be held simultaneously, especially where differences of rank or ideas of retribution suggest separate places for different classes of souls. They are also connected, especially in the lower culture, with the idea that man has several souls which after death separate and abide in different localities. They may also result from the mingling of different tribal or racial beliefs.[13] We do not know what ideas the earliest men had regarding the dead, or how soon the belief in a spirit or soul, apart from the body, was entertained. But, while it must have been obvious that death had brought about some difference between the dead and the living, it is doubtful if the dead were ever regarded as absolutely extinct and cut off from all life and action. The wide-spread and early custom of burial, the practice of placing articles by the corpse, and the feeding of the dead at the grave, all suggest the contrary. It is not improbable, therefore, that the dead man was regarded as passing some kind of existence in the grave. The grave was his house, and it was this idea perhaps that led to the custom of making very elaborate tombs for the dead, of which the chambered barrow forms an example. That the dead lived on in the grave, while their return among the living was feared, is also suggested by the belief that they could come from it in the body—in which we find the root of the vampire belief[1]—and by the customs of heaping a mound of earth or placing heavy stones on the grave, and binding the dead with cords.[2] Many folk-traditions represent the dead as coming in the body from the grave,[3] and the idea of their still living in the grave or barrow is seen clearly in early Scandinavian tradition. Thus the grave was in itself a small under world. This was more emphasized where several persons were buried in one tumulus or grave, or where the separate graves of members of one family or clan lay side by side. The grave or graves as a subterranean dwelling-place easily passed over into the conception of a hollow region under the earth, an under world where the dead lived. At whatever time the conception of the soul, spirit, or shade arose, it did not alter this belief. The spirit might come and go from the grave or inhabit with other shades the larger under world.

The formation of a belief in an under world was also aided by observed phenomena. The sun seemed to rise out of the earth or sea in the east and to sink into these again in the west. What then more natural than to suppose that during the night it passed through some underground region, to emerge again in the morning? This under world (sometimes thought of as beneath the sea into which the sun seems to sink) through which the sun passed was then associated with the abode of the dead, and in many descriptions of the latter we are expressly told that, when it is night here, it is day there, and *vice versa*. Hence, too, the entrance to the abode of the dead is not always near at hand, but far off, usually towards the sunset, and their dwelling-place is reached only after a long and perilous journey.

Yet for many races the under world was not visited by the sun. Being under the earth, it was a dark and gloomy place, and this was accentuated by the fact that those who inhabited it were shades or shadows. Here, too, we may see another conception leading to the idea of another world. The eyes of the dead were closed; they were in darkness. Their shades were faint replicas of living beings, seen only in dreams and darkness. Where could such have their abode? The grave was a dark, hollow place, and men knew also that caves leading into the interior of earth grew darker as the entrance was farther left behind. There must then be a dark, hollow place within the earth, fit abode for those now shut off from light.

Thus the under world may be a shadowy, undesirable place, or, again, it may be a reflexion of the upper world, now light, now dark, as the sun visits or leaves it.

2. The under world in ancient religions.—It is surprising that cultured races in the past hardly abandoned the belief in a gloomy under world. The Babylonians called this region Aralu, and it was conceived as a vast underground dwelling, as 'the land without return,' the dark abode of all the shades of the dead, with its entrance in the west, the region of sunset. The sombre goddess Eresh-Kigal and the terrible god Nergal ruled over it. Seven walls, pierced by as many gates,

1 *Hierurgia Anglicana*, new ed., ii. 237.
2 Lk 23[56].
3 *Apol.* 42, *de Idol.* 11; and, for embalming, *de Res. Carn.* 27.
4 *Pæd.* ii. 8 [62].
5 *Octavius*, 12.
6 § 7; T. Ruinart, *Acta primorum martyrum*[2], ed. R. Massuet, Amsterdam, 1713, p. 436.
7 *Hier. Eccl.* vii. 8.
8 P. 538.
9 Denzinger, i. 190.
10 Maclean-Browne, p. 287.
11 ii. 523 f.
12 *Capitulare*, § 115 (A.D. 668); see also d'Achery, i. 490.
13 On these varying conceptions see artt. BLEST, ABODE OF THE; STATE OF THE DEAD.

1 See art. VAMPIRE.
2 For many examples see J. G. Frazer, 'On Certain Burial Customs as illustrative of the Primitive Theory of the Soul,' *JAI* xv. [1886] 64–104.
3 J. A. MacCulloch, *CF*, p. 102 f.

surrounded this place of terror, where 'dust lay thick on door and bolt,' where the shades dwelt with dust for their food, in darkness and gloom, among terrible evil spirits and demons. All these ideas are vividly set forth in the story of the descent of Ištar to Hades. How far other conceptions of a better region or of retribution were held by the Babylonians need not be discussed here. Gloomy as was the fate of the dead in Aralu, there was a worse fate, viz. where burial rites had not been performed and the spirit had to wander, consumed by gnawing hunger and feeding on offal.[1]

The older Hebrew conception was not dissimilar, and the strong desire to be buried in the family grave or by the side of relatives suggests that Sheol or Hades, like the under world elsewhere, was 'originally conceived as a combination of the graves of the clan or nation.'[2] The shades (*rĕphāim*) dwelt in the under world, outside the rule of Jahweh, distinguished from each other according to their state on earth, but in a region of darkness, dust, and silence. The state of the shades in Sheol is seen from such passages as Ps 115^{17}, Job 7^{9} $10^{21f.}$, Is $14^{9f.}$, Ezk $32^{17f.}$. While the later belief was generally different from this, it still kept the idea of an under world, but now generally as an intermediate state of the dead, waiting for the day of judgment in different compartments of it, better or worse, for the righteous or the wicked. Sometimes it was a place of torment for the wicked at death, or it or a subterranean Gehenna became the place of torment after the judgment.[3]

An under world does not appear consistently in Egyptian beliefs regarding the dead, their state and locality, which were of a conflicting nature. In the earliest period, and indeed all through the later periods, the soul was associated with the body in its sepulchre, leaving it and returning to it. An under world is spoken of here and there, probably connected with the grave. But many other regions—on earth's surface or in heaven—were open to the dead. In the Osirian religion the blissful abode was in heaven or elsewhere, and it was sometimes regarded as lying in a deep hole under the earth.[4] The theology of the religion of Rā pictured the soul traversing the other world in the bark of the sun by night, passing through guarded gates into twelve successive regions, peopled by gods, demons, and the dead. These regions were either underground or in what corresponded to an under world—the valley through which the sun passed behind the Mountain of Sunset until it reappeared in the east. This was the Duat, or Tuat, the hidden part of the world.[5]

According to O. Schrader, the primitive Indo-European conception of the realms of the dead was that the ancestral spirits dwelt in the earth. They made no distinction between this region of the dead and the tomb.[6] In Vedic times in India, probably as a result of the newer custom of cremation, Yama's kingdom, to which the spirits of the fathers went (the *pitṛs*), was a heavenly one, but it is probable that it had formerly been a subterranean region.[1] The Vedic hells as well as those of Brāhmanic and later Hindu belief are abysses of the under world;[2] yet even in the earlier (Vedic) period we hear of the fathers being in the earth, and in the age of the epics Yama's realm is in the south, beneath the earth.[3]

The Greeks preserved the idea of an under world of the dead, Hades, the hidden place, intact for a long period. See art. UNDER WORLD (Greek).

The Roman under world, Dis, was the abode of the *manes*, and this belief was connected with the earlier one, that the soul rested with the body in the tomb. In the Comitium at Rome the *lapis manalis* covered an opening which was supposed to lead to the underground abode of the shades, whence they came up to be fed on the days when the stone was removed. Other approaches to the under world were known—*e.g.*, the cave of Avernus at Naples. But to the Romans the under world was never such a definitely expressed object of belief as it was to the Greeks.

The Scandinavian and Teutonic under world, Hel, the hollow place, was perhaps an extension of the hollow barrow or tumulus in which the dead were supposed to live feasting and occupying themselves with the good of their kindred. Though later conceived as a gloomy place of punishment, this description applies more properly to Niflhel, lower than Hel. All men at first went to Hel,[4] which, in the Elder Edda, is hardly a place of gloom. As described in *Balder's Doom*, a road leads through the under world by grassy plains to the mighty hall of Hel (*i.e.* the goddess who rules over Hel). Walls are decked with shields, and beer stands ready on tables.[5] The myths seem to prove that Mimir's fountain of immortal mead and his grove, and Urd's fountain, were in the under world.[6]

Similarly in the old mythology of the Finns and of the Esthonians the region of the dead is an under world. By the Finns it was called Tuonela, and, possibly through Christian influences, it had come to be regarded as a place of punishment. The Esthonians called their under world Porgu, and it was supposed to be reached through a cave.[7]

The old native religion of Japan, Shinto, regarded the dead as still living in the tomb, but the Japanese also had a belief in a dark and repulsive under world called Yomi ('darkness') and Ne no kuni ('the root country'), with divinities of death and plague. Though not specifically said to be the region of the dead, it would appear to have been, as the name Yomi is used for the state of the dead or the grave, while the place itself, regarded as a region of corruption, suggests the decay of the tomb. Yomi was later identified with the Buddhist hell.[8]

3. The under world in the lower culture.—Among the lower races opinions as to the locality in which the dead exist are as various as in the beliefs of the higher races, but the conception of an under world frequently occurs, and its nature and conditions are described with great detail.

1 A. Jeremias, *The Babylonian Conception of Heaven and Hell*, tr. J. Hutchison, London, 1902; M. Jastrow, *The Religion of Babylonia and Assyria*, Boston, U.S.A., 1898, p. 563 ff., *Aspects of Religious Belief and Practice in Babylonia and Assyria*, New York, 1911, ch. vi.; art. BABYLONIANS AND ASSYRIANS, § 4.
2 R. H. Charles, *EBi*, col. 1339.
3 See art. ESCHATOLOGY, § 10; R. H. Charles, 'Eschatology' in *EBi*, *Critical Hist. of the Doctrine of a Future Life in Israel, in Judaism, in Christianity*, London, 1899.
4 W. Max. Müller, *Egyptian Mythology* (=*Mythology of all Races*, xii.), Boston, U.S.A., 1918, p. 176.
5 A. Erman, *A Handbook of Egyptian Religion*, Eng. tr., London, 1907, p. 109 f.; A. Wiedemann, *The Realms of the Egyptian Dead*, tr. J. Hutchison, do. 1901; E. A. T. Wallis Budge, *The Gods of the Egyptians*, do. 1904, i. 170.
6 *ERE* ii. 30 f.; A. Bergaigne, *La Religion védique*, Paris, 1878–83, i. 77 f.

1 E. Hardy, *Indische Religionsgeschichte*, Leipzig, 1898, p. 23.
2 See *Rigveda*, vii. 104.
3 A. Berriedale Keith, *Indian Mythology* (=*Mythology of all Races*, vi.), Boston, 1917, pp. 101, 159.
4 *Fáfnismál*, x. 39.
5 G. Vigfusson and F. Y. Powell, *Corpus Poeticum Boreale*, Oxford, 1883, i. 182.
6 See art. BLEST, ABODE OF THE (Teutonic).
7 A. von Schiefner, *Kalewala*, Helsingfors, 1852, Rune 15; W. F. Kirby, *The Hero of Esthonia*, London, 1895, i. 100, 124.
8 W. G. Aston, *Shinto*, London, 1905, pp. 106, 181, 187; B. H. Chamberlain, *Ko-ji-ki*, Yokohama, 1883 (*TASJ* x., Suppl.), p. 36; art. BLEST, ABODE OF THE (Japanese), § 1.

Such an under world, sometimes situated beneath the sea, is known to some of the tribes of New Guinea, sometimes as a place resembling this world, sometimes much superior to it, while, as with the Waga-Waga, it is said that, when it is night here, it is day there, and *vice versa*, suggesting that it is visited by the sun during our night.[1] A region under the sea, called Tsiabiloum, is the place of spirits, according to the New Caledonians—a delightful place, far more fertile than earth, where sickness, death, toil, and darkness are unknown.[2] In many parts of Melanesia the other world is above ground, often on a distant island, but in the eastern group of islands it is below the earth and is called Panoi and other names. It is a peaceful place and on the whole resembles the upper world. But, according to some, the spirits die there, and then revive in another Panoi, situated below the first.[3]

Generally in Polynesia, while a superior heavenly region was reserved for men of rank or for those slain in battle, there was an under world for all the other spirits of the dead, called Po, or Sa-le-fee, or other names. This region was mainly regarded as a gloomy, undesirable place, though sometimes, as in Raratonga, it was pleasant and bright.[4]

In N. America the Eskimo have a belief in various regions for different people, but among the different tribes the under world constantly appears, now as a better, now as a worse place.[5] The American Indian tribes are far from uniform in their beliefs; the under world of the dead is found mainly among the tribes of the south-west, but sporadically elsewhere. It is reached after a long journey, and is generally a pleasant region, and also the place whence the first men emerged on earth's surface.[6] Occasionally, as with the Tlingit, the underworld abode is one of several, and it is to it that drowned persons go.[7] Similar distinctions, according to rank or manner of death, occurred with the Mexicans, whose under world, Mictlan, was a gloomy place, reserved for those who did not go to one of the other regions. This resembled the dismal under world of the Peruvians, the place allotted to the bulk of the people. An under world of the dead is less frequently met with among the S. American tribes—*e.g.*, the Matacos, the Muyscas, and the Patagonians, who thought that vast underground caverns contained the souls of the dead. None of these were unpleasant places.[8]

Among African tribes, both Bantu and Negro, the belief in an under world is very common. This country of the dead is usually reached through a cave or hole in the ground, or through a pool or lake. Especially with the Bantu it is a region much like the earth, with villages, forests, rivers, etc., but among some Negro tribes it is less desirable, as some of their sayings suggest.[1] Stories of descent by the living to this underground region are widely spread over Africa.

[1] A. Goudswaard, *De Papoewa's van de Geelvinksbaai*, Schiedam, 1863, p. 77; J. L. D. van der Roest, *Tijdschrift voor Indische Taal- Land- en Volkenkunde*, xl. [1898] 164 f. (Papuans of Windessi); R. E. Guise, *JRAI* xxviii. [1899] 216 (Hood Peninsula); M. J. Erdweg, *Mittheilungen der anthropologischen Gesellschaft in Wien*, xxxii. [1902] 297 (Tumleo); G. Bamler, in R. Neuhauss, *Deutsch Neu-Guinea*, Berlin, 1911, iii. 514 f. (Tami); C. Keysser, in Neuhauss, iii. 149 (Kai); S. Lehner, in Neuhauss, iii. 472 f. (Bukaua); C. G. Seligmann, *The Melanesians of British New Guinea*, Cambridge, 1910, p. 655 f.

[2] R. P. Lambert, *Mœurs et superstitions des Néo-Calédoniens*, Nouméa, 1900, p. 13 f.

[3] R. H. Codrington, *The Melanesians*, Oxford, 1891, pp. 273, 275 f.

[4] See, for further details, artt. BLEST, ABODE OF THE (Primitive and Savage), § 3; POLYNESIA, § 9.

[5] F. Boas, *6 RBEW* [1888], p. 588 (Central Eskimo); E. W. Nelson, *18 RBEW* [1899], pt. i. p. 423 (Eskimo of Bering Strait).

[6] *11 RBEW* [1894], pp. 68 (Sia), 512 (Mandan), 517 (Hidatsa); *17 RBEW* [1898], pt. i. p. 292 f. (Seri); *NR* iii. 528 (Navaho); H. B. Alexander, *American Mythology* (=*Mythology of all Races*, x.), Boston, 1916, pp. 147, 274.

[7] *26 RBEW* [1908], p. 460 ff.

[8] I. A. Baldrich, *Las Camareas Virgenes*, Buenos Ayres, 1890, p. 12; T. Falkner, *A Description of Patagonia*, Hereford, 1774, p. 142 f.

4. The under world in Christian belief.—Through both Jewish and pagan influences the locality of the souls of the dead in Christian belief was placed beneath the earth, either as an intermediate state, with part of it as a paradise region (Irenæus, Tertullian), or, more generally, a place of punishment. This belief is illustrated from theological writings, legends, poems (*e.g.*, Dante's *Inferno*), and art. It has now ceased to be a vital part of Christian belief.

5. The under world as fairyland.—In the art. FAIRY it is shown how frequently the abode of the fairies, dwarfs, and such like beings is underground, and various theories for this folk-belief are discussed—*e.g.*, that which regards fairies as spirits of the dead.

6. Divinities of the under world.—The divinity who reigns over the under world is frequently a personification of that region itself, and this is more particularly the case where, *e.g.*, Earth and Under-earth are conceived as personified in one being. The earth-goddess is also the ruler of souls (*e.g.*, Demeter or Persephone), with the under-earth people, the Δημήτριοι or ὑποχθόνιοι, as her subjects.[2]

LITERATURE.—This is referred to in the footnotes. See also artt. STATE OF THE DEAD, DESCENT TO HADES (Ethnic).

J. A. MACCULLOCH.

UNDER WORLD (Greek).

UNDER WORLD (Greek).—The Greek conception of the under world is the product of a long process of evolution. The following strata can be clearly determined.

1. An under world which is strictly local, and in which the attributes of the dead are purely physical.—This conception is well expressed in a vase in the Central Museum at Athens. This archaic vase is of the type known as 'prothesis,' a class of vase used in funeral ceremonies and decorated with funeral subjects. Two mourners stand lamenting, one on either side of a grave, erect on which is a 'prothesis' vase. Within the grave itself is represented what the mourners believed the grave to contain: (*a*) the *eidola*, little winged figures of the dead, and (*b*) a great snake. The under world was to the vase-painter strictly local; it was the grave itself. The little winged *eidola*, shrunken men, represent the individual dead, strengthless and vain; the great snake represents the collective might of the dead, the δαίμων of life and reincarnation, the immortality of the γένος or tribe. This δαίμων in human form was the tribal hero, in later monarchical days the king, like the ancestor of the Athenians, envisaged as half-man, half-snake. He was essentially a local power, and to him the fertility of the local earth was due; his temple was his tomb. This belief in the snake-hero was essentially the faith of a settled people of agriculturists to whom the local earth with its perennial crops was all-important—a people who practised field-magic. With the heroic age, its shiftings of peoples, its conquests and migrations, the conception of the under world, dependent like all other religious conceptions on social developments, was bound to change. This brings us to the next development or stratum.

2. An under world remote, non-local, Pan-Hellenic—in a word, the Homeric or heroic under world.—In *Odyssey*, xi., the so-called *Nekuia*, we have a description of an under world which, though its kernel is undoubtedly local, *i.e.* Bœotian, has become in virtue of many accretions Pan-

[1] See artt. BLEST, ABODE OF THE (Primitive and Savage), § 5; BANTU AND S. AFRICA, § 4; NEGROES AND W. AFRICA, § 3; Alice Werner, *African Mythology* (=*Mythology of all Races*, vii.), Boston, ch. iv. f.

[2] See art. EARTH, EARTH-GODS, § 7 f.

Hellenic. This under world is no longer a local grave, but a vast remote kingdom of the dead, separated from the living world by the stream of Okeanos, but in confused fashion accessible by a trench dug in the earth. The old conception partly lives on. This under world of Homer reflects of course the Homeric social structure. We have the great mass of the people represented by the 'strengthless heads of the dead,' who 'sweep shadow-like around,' and with whom Odysseus holds no converse; and we have the souls of great particular heroes, who, after drinking of the black blood, can hold converse with the living. Instead of the collective δαίμων, the snake, we have individual aristocratic heroes who emerge in truly heroic fashion. The function of these splendid Homeric dead is not to fertilize the earth for their successors, but to live on themselves after their kind, though in more shadowy fashion. They are no longer either physical or local; they are functionless—no longer perennial, but merely immortal and quite non-moral.

To the literary *Nekuia* of Homer must be added the great fresco of Polygnotus, the Nekuia painted by him in the Lesche at Delphi of which Pausanias has given us a detailed account.[1] The Nekuia of Polygnotus is, if we may trust Pausanias, based not on the *Odyssey* but on another Bœotian epic now lost, the *Minyad*. In it stress is laid on a new element just dawning in the *Nekuia* of the *Odyssey*, and this brings us to our third stratum.

3. An under world which is moralized, containing new elements—retribution and purification.—These two elements appear very clearly in a black-figured amphora at Munich.[2] To the right is Sisyphos rolling up his stone, to the left the Danaids are filling their bottomless cask. Sisyphos stands for retribution, the Danaids mark the transition to purification.

In the *Nekuia* of Homer Odysseus, after he has had speech of various heroes whom he has known in the upper world, sees as in a vision, but does not speak with, Minos the judge of Hades, Orion the mighty hunter, and the great criminals Tityos, Tantalos, Sisyphos. Of these figures the two first are marked by one great characteristic: they are doing in Hades what they did in the upper world. Minos, who judged Crete, is judging in Hades; Orion is still hunting wild beasts. But the three 'criminals' have been usually supposed to be, not carrying on their normal pursuits, but being 'tormented.' S. Reinach has brilliantly and conclusively shown that the three 'criminals' also are depicted as carrying on their earthly activities; it is only a later moralizing age that supposes them 'tormented.' We will take only one instance—Sisyphos rolling his stone. Sisyphos is the ancient king of Corinth, and, like all other ancient kings, a δαίμων of weather and sky powers. He controls the sun; in a sense he is the sun. It is his business to roll the ball of the sun, the huge stone, up the steeps of heaven, whence eternally it rolls down again. The senseless punishment becomes intelligible as a periodic function eternally incumbent. Hades is peopled with the δαίμων powers of an elder world; it is the dower-house of antique religion.

The Danaids are analogous figures; but about them have grown up accretions more complex; they stand not only for retribution but also for purification, and they are ultimately connected with the mystery-cult of Orpheus. Primarily, however, they are quite simple figures; they are the daughters of the old Danaos, king of Argos. He makes the weather, and they make the rain; they are well-nymphs, projections of ancient rain-making ceremonials; they carry water in order that water may well forth from sky and earth. They are

[1] x. 28–31. [2] Jahn Cat. 153.

depicted as on the vase pouring water in a *pithos*-well, the bottom pierced to communicate with and fertilize the earth. But their labour is ceaseless, *i.e.* periodic, year by year. But, when their nature as rain-makers is forgotten, the ceaseless labour is thought of as a punishment, a retribution; they are 'condemned to carry water in leaky vessels'; they, the fertility-bringers, are doomed to endless, barren toil. What was their crime? But for Pausanias,[1] we could never have guessed. He saw in the Nekuia at Delphi figures represented as carrying water in broken vessels, and he explains them as 'of the number of those who held the Eleusinian mysteries to be of no account.' They are the uninitiated, never purified in the upper world; they ceaselessly seek purification in the world below. Thus the well-nymphs, with their simple physical function as perennial fertilizers, have been moralized by a later and mystical theology.

In the Hades of Homer there are no water-carriers, no uninitiated, for Homer knows nothing of the mysteries. His theology has reached the retribution, but not the purification, stage. But from Homer onwards, as has recently been shown by Gilbert Murray, the conceptions of bliss and torment are in ancient literature, and we may add in ancient art, 'always connected with the mysteries,' whether Orphic or Eleusinian. The mental pictures of Heaven and Hell which were current in ancient times and are still to a certain extent traditional among us are based on the actual ritual of the mysteries. The scenery and arrangements, so to speak, of the other world are, in the first instance, projections of the initiation-ceremonies. Such is the purgatorial water-carrying of the uninitiated Danaids.

LITERATURE.—J. E. Harrison, *Prolegomena to the Study of Greek Religion*, Cambridge, 1903, ch. xi. 'Orphic Eschatology,' *Themis*, do. 1912, pp. 517–531; S. Reinach, 'Sisyphe aux enfers et quelques autres damnés,' in *RA* i. [1903] 154–200; A. Dieterich, *Nekyia: Beiträge zur Erklärung der neuentdeckten Petrus-apokalypse*, Leipzig, 1893; L. Radermacher, *Das Jenseits im Mythos der Hellenen*, Bonn, 1903; Gilbert Murray, 'The Conception of Another Life,' *Edinburgh Review*, Jan. 1915.

JANE E. HARRISON.

UNEMPLOYMENT.—See EMPLOYMENT.

UNIATS.—See SYRIAN CHRISTIANS.

UNIFORMITY.—See LAW (Natural), ORDER.

UNITARIANISM.—Unitarianism, an English term derived from the Latin *unitarius* (first used of a legalized religion in 1600[2]), is applied to a mode of religious thought and organization founded on the conception of the single personality of the Deity in contrast to the orthodox doctrine of His triune nature. The corresponding term 'Trinitarian' was first used in the modern sense by Servetus in 1546. The adjective 'Unitarian' has sometimes been employed beyond the limits of Christianity—*e.g.*, in connexion with Muhammadanism; this article deals only with the development of modern Unitarianism on Christian lines. The place of the corresponding doctrine in the NT and the early Church must be studied in the usual authorities on historical theology.

1. Beginnings on the Continent.—The general movement of humanism at the opening of the 16th cent. led to a variety of speculation which was largely stimulated by the publication of the Greek text of the NT by Erasmus (1516). His omission of the famous Trinitarian verse, 1 Jn 5[7], and his aversion to the scholastic type of disputations produced a marked effect on many minds. The earliest literary trace of anti-Trinitarian tendencies is usually found in a treatise of Martin Cellarius

[1] x. xxxi. 11. [2] See § 4 below.

(1499–1564), pupil of Reuchlin, and at first a follower and friend of Luther. In 1527 he published at Strassburg a work entitled *de Operibus Dei*, in which he used the term *deus* of Christ in the same sense in which Christians also might be called *dei* as 'sons of the Highest.' The first treatise of Servetus (1511–53), *de Trinitatis Erroribus*, followed in 1531. The minds of the young were on the alert. Teachers, theologians, lawyers, physicians, mathematicians, men of letters and science, were all astir. They travelled and discussed, and new views were carried far and wide. In Naples a young Spaniard, John Valdes, became the centre of a religious group of noble ladies for the study of the Scriptures till his death in 1541; and in 1539 Melanchthon found it necessary to warn the Venetian senate of the existence of widespread Servetianism in N. Italy. Out of this circle comes Bernard Ochino (1487–1565) of Siena, who passes slowly through Switzerland to London, serves as one of the pastors of the Strangers' Church (1550–53) till it is broken up by Queen Mary, takes shelter again in Zürich, and finally migrates to Poland in 1559, and joins the anti-Trinitarian party. There Catherine Vogel, a jeweller's wife, had been burned at the age of 80 in 1539 at Cracow for believing in 'the existence of one God, creator of all the visible and the invisible world, who could not be conceived by the human intellect.'[1] An anti-Trinitarian movement showed itself at the second synod of the Reformed Church in 1556, and in 1558 secured a leader in the person of a Piedmontese physician, George Blandrata. Dutch Anabaptists started various heretical movements, and David Joris of Delft (1501–56) declared in his *Wonder-book* (1542) that there is but 'one God, sole and indivisible, and that it is contrary to the operation of God throughout creation to admit a God in three persons.' Thousands of Protestants from Germany, Alsace, and the Low Countries, migrated to England in the reign of Henry VIII., and the Strangers' Church under Edward VI. contained also Frenchmen, Walloons, Italians, and Spaniards.

2. Beginnings in England.—English thought was not unaffected. In the 15th cent. Reginald Peacock, bishop of Chichester, had opened the way by his two treatises, the *Repressor of overmuch Blaming of the Clergy*[2] and the *Book of Faith*,[3] to the discussion of the relative values of Scripture, tradition, and reason as grounds of faith, and had pleaded for freedom of investigation. Lollard and Anabaptist diverged in different directions from orthodoxy along independent lines. On 28th Dec. 1548 a priest named John Assheton abjured before Cranmer the 'damnable heresies' that 'the Holy Ghost is not God, but only a certain power of the Father,' and that 'Jesus Christ, that was conceived of the Virgin Mary, was a holy prophet . . . but was not the true and living God.' In the following April a commission was appointed to search out all Anabaptists, heretics, or contemners of the Common Prayer. A number of London tradesmen were brought before this body in May. The opinions which they recanted included the statements 'that there was no Trinity of persons; that Christ was only a holy prophet and not at all God; that all we had by Christ was that he taught us the way to heaven.'[4] Occasional executions took place, such as that of the surgeon George van Parris, of Mainz, in 1551 for saying that God the Father was the only God, and Christ was not very God. The Eastern counties, being in constant communication with Holland, supplied most of the victims, down to Bartholomew Legate, of Essex, who declared Christ a 'mere man,' but 'born free from sin,' and who was the last sufferer by Smithfield fires (1612), and Edward Wightman, who was burned a month later at Lichfield, charged with ten various heresies as incongruous as those of Ebion, Valentinus, Arius, and Manes.[1] One foreign teacher, Giacomo Aconzio (Latinized as Acontius, born at Trent about 1520), held his own through the troubled times. Engineer and theologian, philosopher and lawyer, mathematician and poet, he came to England in 1559, and received a post at Elizabeth's court, which he managed to retain even when Bishop Grindal excommunicated him two years later for advocating tolerance to Anabapists. In his *Stratagemata Satanæ*[2] he drew a distinction between articles of faith necessary to salvation and beliefs derived from them which might be matters of dispute. Adhering to Scripture, he declared the Father to be 'the only true God'; affirmed the moral, not the essential, filiation of Jesus Christ; and asserted the subordination of the Holy Spirit to the Father. But the time was not yet come for his full influence in England.

3. Types of speculation.—Three types of speculation were thus in the European field by the middle of the 16th century. (1) That of Servetus was founded on the 'dispositio' of Irenæus and the 'economy' of Tertullian;[3] the Trinity was a Trinity of manifestations or modes of operation; when God is all in all (1 Co 15²⁸), 'the Economy of the Trinity will cease.'[4] His theology was Christocentric: 'There is no other person of God but Christ . . . the entire Godhead of the Father is in him.'[5] (2) Many of the Anabaptists were Arians. (3) A humanitarian view of Jesus, recognizing a miraculous birth, was beginning to claim attention. The last of these succeeded in establishing itself in the east of Europe before English Unitarians began to move.

4. The Socinian development.—When Blandrata reached Poland in 1558, he found that there were already some anti-Trinitarians in the Protestant synod. Seven years later they were excluded, and they consequently formed a small group which refused to call itself by any other name than Christian, though other titles (such as the Minor Church) were sometimes applied to it. In 1579 the settlement of Faustus Socinus in their midst led to the establishment of a new theological type to be long known in Western Europe as Socinianism (*q.v.*).

Socinus (1539–1604) belonged to a distinguished Italian family, the Sozini, in Siena. His uncle Lelius Socinus (1525–62) had evaded the Inquisition by flight to Switzerland in 1547. He became the friend of Calvin and Melanchthon; he visited England; he travelled to Poland. He did not escape controversy and suspicion; he would not deny the doctrine of the Trinity, but he would accept it only in the words of Scripture. Faustus Socinus was of a more aggressive temper. At twenty-three years of age he published his *Explicatio primæ partis primi capitis Evangelii Johannis*,[6] in which he ascribed to Christ only an official and not an essential deity. A long series of works followed, and in 1578 he accepted an invitation from Blandrata, then in the service of Prince John Sigismund of Transylvania, and went to Kolozsvár. Blandrata had invoked his aid against Francis Dávid, who rejected all forms of

[1] Wallace, *Antitrinitarian Biography*, ii. 139, quoting Polish historians.
[2] Ed. C. Babington (Rolls series, xix. 1, 2), London, 1860.
[3] Ed. J. L. Morison, Glasgow, 1909.
[4] Gilbert Burnet, *Hist. of the Reformation of the Church of England*, London, 1679–81, bk. i., new ed., Oxford, 1829, ii. 229.

[1] Anti-Trinitarian opinions were developed in the first Baptist Church founded in London in 1613, by Thomas Helwys. See W. H. Burgess, *John Smith, the Se-Baptist*, London, 1911.
[2] Basel, 1565.
[3] *De Trin. Error.* p. 48.
[4] *Ib.* p. 82.
[5] *Ib.* p. 112 f.
[6] Rakow, 1662.

cultus addressed to Christ.[1] Socinus pleaded for the *adoratio Christi* as obligatory on all Christians, and urged that the *invocatio Christi* should not be forbidden. In 1579 he settled in Poland, where the rest of his life was spent. The members of the Minor Church were converted to his views, which found expression in the *Racovian Catechism* issued in Polish in 1605, a year after his death.[2] A Latin edition followed in 1609. The Polish adherents of Socinus failed, however, to hold their ground. Deprived of their right to office, their leaders were powerless. Roman Catholic reaction triumphed. Their college at Rakow was suppressed, and finally in 1660 they were offered the option of conformity or exile. Some went to Germany and Holland; some carried their worship to Transylvania, and maintained a slender separate existence till 1793. But the influence of Socinus was perpetuated in the massive volumes of the *Bibliotheca fratrum Polonorum quos Unitarios vocant*, published at Amsterdam (1665-69). His theology rested on a rigid view of the authority of Scripture.[3] The modern methods of historical criticism were of course unknown. Philosophy raised no difficulties about the supernatural, but reason started objections from the side of the multiplication-table.

'The essence of God is one,' says the *Racovian Catechism*, 'not in kind but in number. Wherefore it cannot in any way contain a plurality of persons, since a person is nothing else than an individual intelligent essence. Wherever then there exist three numerical persons, there must necessarily in like manner be reckoned three individual essences, for in the same sense in which it is affirmed that there is one numerical essence, it must be held that there is one numerical person.'[4]

But Socinus admitted the application of the term 'God' to Christ in an inferior sense (Jn $10^{34f.}$), and argued from Jn 3^{13} that after his baptism Christ had been conveyed to heaven, where he had beheld his Father, and heard from him the things which he was afterwards sent back to earth to teach. Raised again to heaven after his resurrection, he was made the head of all creation, with divine authority over the world, and in that sense God. He was thus no 'mere man,' and deserved divine honour. Modern Unitarianism has departed widely from this Christology. Apart from the necessarianism of Priestley, it is nearer to Socinus in its view of human nature, which he treated (against the Calvinists) as endowed with free will, and capable of virtue and religion. But the Polish Unitarians did not regard it as intrinsically immortal. A future life would be a gift direct from God, its conditions being made known by Christ. For those who did not fulfil them there was no hell, only extinction.

Unitarianism acquired ecclesiastical status also in the adjoining province of Transylvania. In 1563 Blandrata was invited by Queen Isabella to the court of her son Prince John Sigismund. At Kolozsvár (Klausenburg) he was brought into contact with Francis Dávid, who had been sent by his Roman Catholic teachers to Wittenberg. There Dávid had passed into Lutheranism, but afterwards, dissatisfied with its doctrine of the sacraments, he joined the Calvinists. His distinction led to his appointment (1564) as bishop of the Hungarian churches in Transylvania. Under Blandrata's influence he began to doubt the separate personality of the Holy Spirit, and became involved in discussions with the Calvinist leader, Peter Melius. In these debates Melius is said to have first used the word *Unitarius*. Dávid was strong enough to carry large numbers of clergy and laity with him. In 1568 a royal edict was issued, granting entire freedom of conscience and speech, and giving legal recognition to 'the Four Religions,' Roman Catholicism, Lutheranism, Calvinism (or Reformed), and 'the Klausenburg Confession.' More than 400 preachers with their churches, and many professors in colleges and schools, ranged themselves under Dávid's supervisorship. Dávid, however, soon advanced another step, and questioned the propriety of prayer to Christ. Blandrata's attempt to influence him through Faustus Socinus (1578) did not convince him, and in the following year, under a Roman Catholic prince, Dávid was tried for innovation in doctrine and sentenced to imprisonment. Five months later (Nov. 1579) he died in the castle of Deva in his seventieth year.

The name *Unitarius* first appeared in an authoritative document in a decree of the Synod of Lécsfalva in 1600. It was formally adopted by the Church in 1638. For two centuries after Dávid's death the community was in frequent danger from political and religious vicissitudes. Their churches were transferred to Calvinists or to Roman Catholics; they were deprived of their schools; they were debarred from public office. A statute of 1791, however, confirmed their position as one of 'the Four Religions,' and they have since enjoyed ecclesiastical peace.[1] They have now about 140 churches, chiefly among the Szeklers of Transylvania, with a few in Hungary, including a vigorous modern foundation in Buda-Pesth. Till 1919 their bishop sat in the Hungarian House of Peers. At Kolozsvár they have a university, and they have devoted great attention to education. No doctrinal subscription is imposed upon their ministers, and under the influence of progressive change, and contact with Unitarian teaching in England and America, the Socinian Christology has been abandoned. The official hymn-book of 1865 made no provision for the worship of Christ.

5. Growth of Unitarianism in England.—The teaching of Socinus gradually made its way into England. The Latin version of the *Racovian Catechism* was sent to England with a dedication to James I.; it was formally burned in 1614. Two Socinian works appear in the first two catalogues of the Bodleian Library (1620-35), but a considerable number may be traced in the catalogue by Thomas Hyde in 1674. Bishop Barlow, himself once librarian, in *Directions for the Choice of Books in the Study of Divinity* (originally drawn up in 1650 and expanded after 1673), named numerous others in connexion with a syllabus of the principal questions at issue between Socinians and other Reformed communions.[2] Theology was deeply concerned with the claims of the Roman Catholics on the one hand and the controversies of the Puritans on the other, and from the days of Richard Hooker (1553-1600) a series of writers discussed the respective authority of the Church, the Scriptures, and reason. Doubtless revelation was necessary, but Scripture was its medium. If it was the teacher of theology, what was theology, asked Hooker, but the science of divine things? and 'what science,' he went on to ask, 'can be attained unto without the help of natural discourse and reason'?[3] The Arminian revolt against Calvinism tended in the same direction, and 'the ever memorable' John Hales (1584-1656), when he

[1] See below.

[2] The town of Rakow, founded in 1569, was the ecclesiastical base, with a school and university (1602).

[3] His treatise *de Auctoritate S. Scripturæ*, written in 1570, was first published at Seville, and claimed by a Jesuit Lopez as his own. Commended in 1728 in a charge by Bishop Smallbrooke, it was translated into English by Edward Combe in 1731.

[4] Eng. tr. by Thomas Rees, London, 1818, § iii. ch. i. p. 33.

[1] Cf. Michael Lombard Szentabrahámi, *Summa Universæ Theologiæ Christianæ secundum Unitarios*, Klausenburg, 1787. The above was written before the great majority of Unitarian Churches passed under Rumanian rule by the Peace of 1919.

[2] *The Genuine Remains of Dr. Thomas Barlow, late Bishop of Lincoln*, London, 1693.

[3] *Laws of Ecclesiastical Polity*, bk. iii. ch. viii. 11, ed. Keble, Oxford, 1836, i. 473.

left the Synod of Dort after hearing Episcopius expound Jn 3^{16}, 'bid John Calvin good-night.'[1] A stream of protest flowed on against the attempt to define the mysteries of the Godhead beyond the terms of Scripture. It had been the plea of Acontius in the *Stratagemata Satanæ*; and William Chillingworth (1602–44) owned him as his teacher of the mischief of creeds which led to the 'persecuting, burning, cursing, damning of men for not subscribing to the words of men as the words of God.'[2] Chillingworth was indebted for acquaintance with Socinian literature to Lord Falkland. He had seen some volumes in the rooms of Hugh Cressy of Merton College, Oxford, who 'claimed to have been the first to bring in Socinus's books.' Cressy afterwards became a Benedictine monk; Falkland was designated by John Aubrey 'the first Socinian in England.' Other and wider influences were at work. Lord Herbert of Cherbury (1583–1648) in his *de Veritate*[3] analysed the whole faculties of the mind, and discovered among its *notitiæ communes*, innate, of divine origin, and indisputable, certain 'common notions' of religion in five articles. These he exemplified historically twenty years later in the *de Religione Gentilium* (completed in 1645), one of the earliest treatises in comparative theology. The great authority of Grotius (1583–1645) gave special weight to his exposition of Christianity in the *de Veritate Religionis Christianæ*.[4] He discourses of the attributes of God, but is silent about His triune nature. He proves that there was such a person as Jesus, that he rose from the grave and was worshipped after his death. He vindicates his character as Messiah, but never mentions the Incarnation. His *Annotationes* on the NT were equally free from traditional dogma. It was not surprising that Stephen Nye, the author of the *Brief History of the Unitarians also called Socinians*,[5] should affirm that he 'interpreted the whole according to the mind of the Socinians.' Under such influences diversity of opinion was recognized as inevitable. Writers so different as Hales, Jeremy Taylor,[6] and Milton[7] declare in almost the same words that heresy is not a matter of the understanding; the faithful pursuit of reason did not make a heretic; the mischief lay in the influences that perverted the will. Chillingworth thought it possible to reduce all Christians to unity of communion by showing that diversity of opinion was no bar to it. That all Christians should think alike was an impossibility; it remained for them to be 'taught to set a higher value upon those high points of faith and obedience wherein they agree than upon those points of less moment wherein they differ.'[8] Such writers did not adopt the theology of Socinus, but they were in agreement with him in his plea for Scriptural statements rather than dogmatic creeds. 'Vitals in religion,' said Benjamin Whichcote (1609–83), the leader of the Cambridge Platonists, 'are few.'[9]

Meanwhile an occasional English traveller like Paul Best (1590–1657) had visited Poland and returned infected. Milton noticed in the *Areopagitica*[10] the 'stay'd men' sent by 'the grave and frugal Transilvanian' to learn the 'theologic arts' of England. The danger of Socinianism was spreading. The Convocations of Canterbury and York agreed in June 1640 to prohibit the import, printing, or circulation of Socinian books; no minister should preach their doctrines; laymen who embraced their opinions should be excommunicated.[1] A series of angry writers denounced them with shrill abuse. Parliament made the denial of the Trinity a capital crime (1648), but an English translation of the *Racovian Catechism* was published in 1652 at Amsterdam, followed by *A Twofold Scripture Catechism* from the pen of John Biddle in 1654. These works led the Council of State to order John Owen, whom Cromwell had made Dean of Christ Church and Vice-Chancellor of the university of Oxford, to prepare a reply. His *Vindiciæ Evangelicæ* appeared in 1655.

'Do not *look* upon these things,' he wrote with heat,[2] 'as *things afar* off wherein you are *little concerned*; the *evill* is at the *doore*; there *is* not a *Citty*, a *Towne*, scarce a *Village* in *England*, wherein some of this poyson is not poured forth.'

6. Influence of Biddle and Locke.—John Biddle (1616–62) has often been called the father of English Unitarianism. Sprung from the family of a Gloucestershire yeoman, he came up to Oxford in 1634, and graduated M.A. in 1641. The Gloucester magistrates appointed him shortly after to the mastership of the free school in the parish of St. Mary de Crypt. There his Biblical studies led him independently to doubt the doctrine of the Trinity, the particular difficulty being the deity of the Holy Ghost. Imprisonment in Gloucester and at Westminster did not prevent him from publishing his views, which became more and more opposed to the prevailing orthodoxy. Released in 1652, he founded for the first time gatherings for the exposition of the Scriptures on anti-Trinitarian lines, and these developed into regular meetings for worship. Biddle's catechism shows distinct Socinian influence in the views that Christ as man was taken up into heaven to be instructed for his prophetical office, that God's love was universal, and that Christ died to reconcile man to God, not God to man. But Biddle did not adopt the Socinian practice of prayer to Christ. In spite of imprisonment and exile in the Scilly Islands (1654–58) he gathered followers in increasing numbers. They were sometimes called Biddelians, sometimes Socinians, but they are said to have preferred the name Unitarian to all others.[3]

The death of Biddle in 1662 and the Act of Uniformity checked the movement as an organization for worship, but it continued as a mode of thought. The constant plea for a return from the creeds to the Scriptures led Milton finally into an Arian Christology. Thomas Firmin (1632–97), a wealthy and generous mercer, who had been the friend of Biddle and also had close relations with Archbishop Tillotson (1630–94), promoted the circulation of literature. The *Brief History of the Unitarians, also called Socinians*, was published at his request in 1687. The Toleration Act of 1689 excluded those who denied the Trinity on the one side, and Roman Catholics on the other. But an active controversy broke out the following year, which resulted in the production of a long series of Unitarian tracts (1691–1705) largely financed by Firmin, in which the chief ecclesiastical disputants, John Wallis and William Sherlock,[4] were cleverly played off against each other, and the argument was enforced on grounds of Scripture and early patristic testimony. The Unitarian influence was so strong that Parliament found it necessary (1698)

[1] Letter of Anthony Farindon (17th Sept. 1657) prefixed to the *Golden Remains*, London, 1659.
[2] *The Religion of Protestants*, Oxford, 1638, iv. § 16, referring to Acontius, vii.
[3] Paris, 1624, London, 1633.
[4] Leyden, 1627. [5] London, 1687.
[6] In the *Liberty of Prophesying*, London, 1646; ed. 1817, sect. ii. p. 32.
[7] In his last tract, *Of True Religion, Heresy, Schism, Toleration*, London, 1673, p. 6.
[8] *Religion of Protestants*, iv. § 40, p. 209 f.
[9] *Moral and Religious Axioms*, ed. Salter, London, 1753.
[10] London, 1644.

[1] Canons iv. and v. [2] 69.
[3] The name has been found by Alex. Gordon in a controversy between Henry Hedworth and William Penn in 1672. The pamphlets are preserved in the Friends' Library at Devonshire House, Bishopsgate, London, E.C.
[4] Cf. John Barling, *A Review of Trinitarianism*, London, 1847, p. 71; John Hunt, *Religious Thought in England*, 3 vols., do. 1870–73, ii. 201 ff.

to threaten the profession of the obnoxious heresy with cumulative penalties amounting to the loss of all civil rights, and three years' imprisonment. But in the meantime a new and powerful influence had entered the field. In 1695 John Locke (1632–1704) had published his treatise on *The Reasonableness of Christianity*.

Locke's *Letters concerning Toleration* [1] and his *Essay concerning Human Understanding* [2] had already placed him at the head of contemporary English thinkers. It was a lamentable sign of the heated temper of the time that the inquiry into the essential nature of Christianity was published anonymously. Locke did what Grotius and Hobbes (in the *Leviathan* [3]) had done before him. He went back to the Gospels and the first preachers of the new faith, and found that their message consisted in the proclamation of Jesus as the Messiah, the proof of this character resting on his fulfilment of prophecy and his miracles, especially the Resurrection. He had indeed already confided to his journal in 1681 the pregnant remark that the miracles were to be judged by the doctrine, and not the doctrine by the miracles. But he could still say in 1703 that the Scripture had God for its authority and truth without any mixture of error for its matter. This did not, however, prevent him from recognizing the occasional character of the apostolic letters; and in the paraphrases of the Epistles of St. Paul [4] (published after his death), by treating their teaching as relative to the age and persons for whom it was designed, he really laid the foundation of the historical method. His whole theory of knowledge, however, and his polemic against innate ideas, led him to fall back on the conception of revelation, and to find in Scripture an ultimate authority for religious truth. Meanwhile the violence of some of the Trinitarian controversialists drove many minds along the paths already trodden by Milton and Sir Isaac Newton in the direction of some form of Arianism. William Whiston (1672–1752), who had succeeded Newton at Cambridge as Lucasian professor in 1703, was deprived for this heresy in 1710; and it was in the background of the treatise of Samuel Clarke (1675–1729) on *The Scripture Doctrine of the Trinity*, [5] though he objected to the ancient Arian statement, 'there was [a time] when there was no Son.'

The formularies of the Church of England prevented anything like general change within its ranks. But Protestant Dissent was not organized on the basis of dogmatic creeds. The English Presbyterians under the leadership of Richard Baxter (1615–91) had ardently desired comprehension in the Establishment, but they had as ardently repudiated what they called 'human impositions.' Driven out of the Anglican Church, and unable to create a Presbyterian polity, they found themselves side by side with the Congregationalists in 1689. When they took out licences for places of worship, their trustees avoided doctrinal tests, though they themselves were mainly Calvinistic. They often devoted their chapels to 'the worship of God by Protestant Dissenters.' Sometimes the Presbyterians were named, sometimes the Independents, sometimes both conjointly. They reserved to themselves, in the language of Timothy Jollie of Sheffield (1659–1714), 'liberty to reform according to Scripture rule in doctrine, discipline and worship.' [6] The way was thus open to gradual theological modification. The process was slow, and its operation unequal in different places. Pastors and people did not always move together. The transition through varying types of Arianism naturally took place at varying rates; *e.g.*, Nathaniel Lardner (1684–1768), after resting in Clarke's Arianism, finally abandoned it in his *Letter* on the Logos.[1] The result was that at the beginning of the 19th cent. nearly 200 chapels were occupied by Unitarians, whose principles were unfavourable to sectarian activity. When the Manchester Academy (now Manchester College, Oxford) was opened in 1786, its first principal, Thomas Barnes, who dedicated it 'to Truth, to Liberty, and to Religion,' was himself an Arian. His colleague, Ralph Harrison, became a Unitarian. True to the practice of their forefathers, the founders refrained from imposing any tests on either tutors or students. The Presbyterian Board, established in 1689, governs the Presbyterian College at Carmarthen—the continuator of a series of academies, the first of which was founded on the same basis by Samuel Jones, sometime fellow of Jesus College, Oxford, one of the 2000 ejected ministers of 1662.

7. The work of Priestley and Belsham.—The process of theologic change was promoted from another side. Joseph Priestley (1733–1804), bred among the Independents, threw off the Calvinistic theology of his youth, and, after resting a little while in Arianism, reached in 1768, while minister at Leeds, a simple humanitarian view of the person of Jesus. His scientific studies had already gained him the fellowship of the Royal Society (1766), and his *Appeal to the Serious and Candid Professors of Christianity* [2] carried his name in 30,000 copies all over England. His industry, his wide range of knowledge, his clearness of thought and style, his fearless utterance, his untiring earnestness, his elevation of purpose and purity of life, his simple piety, secured for his theological and philosophical teaching a dominant position in Unitarian thought. At Doddridge's Academy at Daventry he had studied Hartley's *Observations on Man*, [3] and adopted a materialist view of human nature. But this in no way impaired the religion which he learned from the Gospels. The teachings of Jesus, guaranteed by his miracles and triumphantly established by his resurrection, supplied him with a positive ground for faith; and the identification of the God of revelation with the Sole Cause of all phenomena, including every form of human activity, created a type of religious sentiment which long pervaded Unitarian devotion. In his *Doctrine of Philosophical Necessity Illustrated* [4] he affirmed that his doctrine should produce 'the deepest humility, the most entire resignation to the will of God, and the most unreserved confidence in his goodness and providential care.' [5] Among the Yorkshire acquaintances of Priestley was Theophilus Lindsey (1723–1808), vicar of Catterick on the Tees. A movement had been started by a small group of the clergy of the Establishment for the relaxation of the terms of subscription. The failure of a petition to Parliament led Lindsey to resign his living (1773) and make his way to London. There in 1774 he opened an auction-room in Essex Street, Strand, as a Unitarian chapel, and thus 'first organized Unitarian Dissent as a working force in the religious life of England.' [6] He used the Anglican liturgy adapted to 'the worship of the Father only.'

The London movement was reinforced in 1789 by the appointment of Thomas Belsham (1750–

[1] London, 1689–92. [2] London, 1690.
[3] London, 1651.
[4] *A Paraphrase and Notes on the Epistles of St. Paul to the Galatians, Corinthians, Romans, and Ephesians*, London, 1709.
[5] London, 1712.
[6] *Pastoral Care Exemplified* (funeral sermon for his father), London, 1704, p. 28.

[1] *A Letter writ in the Year 1730, concerning the Question whether the Logos supplied the Place of a Human Soul in the Person of Jesus Christ*, London, 1759.
[2] London, 1770. [3] London, 1749.
[4] London, 1777. [5] § ix.
[6] J. H. Allen, *Hist. of Unitarians*, etc., p. 152.

1829), once like Priestley an Independent, to a theological tutorship in a college at Hackney. A scholar of no small attainments, he wielded a vigorous pen, and took a leading share in promoting the development of denominational activity. This was opened in 1791 by the foundation of the 'Unitarian Society for promoting Christian knowledge and the Practice of Virtue by the Distribution of Books.' Lindsey, Priestley, and Belsham were its leaders. The preamble and rules, drawn up by Belsham, contained the first public profession of belief in the proper unity of God, and of the simple humanity of Jesus Christ, in opposition both to the Trinitarian doctrine of three Persons in the Deity and to the Arian hypothesis of a created Maker and Preserver of the world. The love of civil and religious liberty prompted a petition the next year (1792) for the abolition of the penal laws affecting religion, to which Charles James Fox lent his aid, and this was accomplished in 1813 (so far as Unitarians were concerned) by the repeal, through the efforts of William Smith (1756–1835), M.P. for Norwich, grandfather of Florence Nightingale, of the clauses of the Toleration Act which rendered the profession of Unitarianism illegal. Meanwhile local Unitarian associations had been founded, and a denominational literature was springing up. Chapels long closed were reopened; new congregations were assisted; a Unitarian Fund was started; and missionaries were sent out to various parts of the kingdom. Endowed by the Act of 1813 with civil rights, the Unitarians proceeded to form an association for protecting them (1819); and finally in 1825 a number of separate organizations were amalgamated in the British and Foreign Unitarian Association. This body was created to promote the principles of Unitarian Christianity. But its founders refrained from imposing any definition of them on its adherents. In the spirit of the English Presbyterians of a century and a half before, they left each member free to interpret them for himself.

The type of Unitarianism then prevailing was largely shaped by the writings of Priestley and Belsham. There were still Arians of different degrees (designated as 'high' and 'low') among both ministers and congregations. But the emphasis of controversy fell more and more clearly on the humanity of Jesus, and the proof of this lay in the Scriptures. The doctrine of their plenary inspiration was indeed denied. Criticism had already distinguished different documents in Genesis. The narratives of the birth of Jesus were inconsistent with each other, and one or both might be rejected. But both the OT and the NT contained 'authentic records of facts and of divine interpositions,' and Charles Wellbeloved, principal of Manchester College, York, could write in 1823:

> 'Convince us that any tenet is authorised by the Bible, from that moment we receive it. Prove any doctrine to be a doctrine of Christ, emanating from that wisdom which was from above, and we take it for our own, and no power on earth shall wrest it from us.'[1]

On this basis Jesus was presented as 'a man constituted in all respects like other men, subject to the same infirmities, the same ignorance, prejudices and frailties,'[2] who was chosen by God to introduce a new moral dispensation into the world. For this end the Holy Spirit was communicated to him at his baptism. He was instructed in the nature of his mission and invested with voluntary miraculous powers during his sojourn in the wilderness, and, thus equipped as the Messiah, was sent forth to reveal to all mankind without distinction the great doctrine of a future life in which men should be rewarded

[1] *Three Letters to Archdeacon Wrangham*², London, 1823, p. 51.

[2] Belsham, *A Calm Inquiry into the Scripture Doctrine concerning the Person of Christ*, London, 1811, p. 447.

according to their works. Of this the supreme proof was found in the Resurrection, to which his death on the cross as a martyr to the truth was a necessary preliminary; and he was destined to reappear to raise the dead and to judge the world. From this scheme all theories of atonement and satisfaction disappeared. Priestley with his usual frankness had admitted that a necessitarian 'cannot accuse himself of having done wrong in the ultimate sense of the words.'[1] But, though this type of Unitarianism was deficient in the sense of sin and produced a curious reluctance to recognize the existence of a 'soul,' its teachers lived habitually at a high moral tension, demanding a constant conformity of the will of man to the will of God. Associated with the emphatic assertion of the Father's wisdom and beneficence, such views naturally anticipated the final victory of good. Thomas Southwood Smith (1788–1861) in his *Illustrations of the Divine Government*[2]—a book warmly admired by Byron, Moore, Wordsworth, and Crabbe—powerfully impressed on Unitarian thought the doctrine of universal restoration, which had already found utterance in one of Cromwell's chaplains, and gained various champions (Hartley among them) in the 18th century.[3]

8. Legal difficulties.—The modifications of belief which had brought many of the occupants of chapels erected by Presbyterians and Independents to Unitarian theology at last aroused the attention of those who remained orthodox. Besides a number of meeting-houses, the Unitarians were in possession of two important trusts—Lady Hewley's Charity in York (1704), and Dr. Williams's Trust in London (1716). A suit was instituted against Lady Hewley's trustees in 1830. Legal proceedings were slow and costly, and on 23rd Dec. 1833 judgment was finally given against them. One of the trustees was the minister of St. Saviourgate Chapel (which Lady Hewley had habitually attended), Charles Wellbeloved. It was at once seen that the whole tenure of the chapels was endangered. A long period of litigation followed, but the Law Lords finally confirmed the first decision in 1842. Meanwhile numbers of suits were threatened for the recovery of the buildings, burial-grounds, and endowments which had descended in undisputed succession through generations of pastors and laity. Between Lady Hewley's pastor, John Hotham, and Charles Wellbeloved there had been but one ministry, that of Newcome Cappe (1755–1800); the three pastorates covered 144 years. In the presence of such continuity of tenure the claim of the existing occupants was irresistible, and in 1844 the Dissenters' Chapels Act, introduced by the Government, gave the needed relief. Without naming either Presbyterians or Unitarians, it secured to such Dissenting congregations as had no creeds or tests the right to change their opinions as they saw fit in the lapse of time.[4] The chapels subsequently built by Unitarians, and the funds raised for the support of their ministers, have been almost invariably founded on the principle known as 'open trust.' The consciousness of this historic evolution supplies the key to the conflict of tendencies in modern Unitarianism between the impulse to theological denominationalism and the desire to realize on however small a scale the 'Catholic communion' which had been the ideal of the English Presbyterians who followed Baxter.

9. Martineau and the modern school.—The most potent personal influence in the latter direction was that of James Martineau (1805–1900) (*q.v.*).

[1] *Illustrations of Philosophical Necessity*, 1777, § xi. (*Works*, ed. Rutt, iii. 518).

[2] Glasgow, 1816.

[3] See art. UNIVERSALISM.

[4] Cf. the speech of W. E. Gladstone, on the second reading, *Parliamentary Debates on the Dissenters' Chapels Bill*, London, 1844, p. 165.

In his first work, *The Rationale of Religious Inquiry*,[1] he abandoned the position of the older Unitarianism, which would have accepted the doctrines of the Trinity, the Atonement, and everlasting torments, if they could be found in the Scriptures. 'No seeming inspiration,' he affirmed, 'can establish anything contrary to reason.'[2] Three years later in the famous Liverpool controversy (1839), in the midst of incisive criticisms of the evangelical scheme of salvation, he laid the foundations of a new view of revelation no longer as a communication of truth, certified by miracles, but as an appeal to the conscience and affections—and a fresh interpretation of the moral life on the basis of free will instead of necessity. Meanwhile he was reading Strauss, and soon reached the conclusion that belief in miracles was not essential to Christianity. The Messianic function of Jesus was thus undermined. Wellbeloved had already insisted on the contemporary significance of many of the prophecies supposed to refer to Christ. When the miracles were disowned, the second guarantee of the supernatural character of Jesus fell away: the followers of Locke found themselves deprived of their 'reasonable' Christianity, and the faith of Christ seemed to become only a superior kind of natural religion. Martineau meanwhile pursued a double line of study. In a group of articles in the *Westminster Review* he expounded the Tübingen reconstruction of the origins of Christianity on its critical side, while on the philosophical he vindicated the communion of the human spirit with the Divine, and presented Jesus as the expression, within the limits of our nature, of the righteousness and love of God. Revelation was thus transformed from supernatural instruction into the realization of more exalted character; its medium was not a written word, but a higher personality. To establish the principles of spiritual theism and find a place in man's soul for that 'dwelling in God and God in him' which Priestley had described as the highest type of personal devotion was the aim of a long series of brilliant articles in the *Prospective* and *National Reviews*, which culminated in two great treatises, *Types of Ethical Theory*[3] and *A Study of Religion*.[4] By these works, as well as by his sermons and occasional *Addresses*, he exercised an influence which went far beyond his own denomination, so that Gladstone described him as 'the greatest of living [English] thinkers.'[5]

Other writers were not inactive beside him. The saintly John James Tayler (1797–1869), in his *Retrospect of the Religious Life of England*,[6] delineated with singular breadth of view and literary charm the significance of contrasted principles of authority and freedom; and from his pen came the first formal discussion of the Johannine question in England in his *Attempt to ascertain the Character of the Fourth Gospel*.[7] A long series of scholars had pleaded for the revision both of the text and of the translation of the NT; and, by the advice of the veteran John Kenrick, George Vance Smith was invited to join the company of the Revisers (1870). In James Drummond (1835–1918) Unitarianism possessed a theologian of the older school of learning, whose works on *The Jewish Messiah* (1877), *Philo Judæus* (1888), *Inquiry into the Character and Authorship of the Fourth Gospel* (1903), and *Studies in Christian Doctrine* (1908) maintained the tradition of devout scholarship. John Relly Beard (1800–76) led the way to modern dictionaries of the Bible by his *People's Dictionary of the Bible*,[1] and made other valuable contributions to theological literature. Cultivated laymen, also, such as Edgar Taylor, Samuel Sharpe, and H. A. Bright, rendered no small services to the Unitarian cause. Most influential of all, perhaps, in its protest against prevailing supernaturalism was *The Creed of Christendom*[2] by William Rathbone Greg. Francis William Newman and Frances Power Cobbe found many readers; and the writings of Ralph Waldo Emerson and Theodore Parker, together with the studies of Max Müller, opened the way to religion beyond the bounds of Christianity. The Hibbert Trustees, who sought to promote the spread of Christianity in 'its simplest and most intelligible form,' were the first to inaugurate in 1878 a series of lectures on the history of religions, and Manchester College included that subject in its theological course as early as 1875. The discourses of Martineau, J. Hamilton Thom, and Charles Beard provided varied illustration of the preacher's power; and the sermons and hymns of Stopford Brooke, after his withdrawal from the Church of England in 1880, presented, with a rich glow of poetic beauty, the main features of religion as understood by Unitarians.

10. Church organizations.—While English Unitarians have been active in education and philanthropy (witness their domestic missions in important urban centres, established on unsectarian principles after the visit of Joseph Tuckerman of Boston, Mass., in 1833), they have not attempted to secure large numerical increase. New chapels have been built, but denominational zeal has never been active. Congregational independence has been sturdily maintained. In 1882 a National Conference was organized, which has now 365 congregations in the United Kingdom on its roll, but they have no common name. Proposals for united action on Presbyterian lines were made by Martineau in 1888, but the demand for congregational autonomy defeated them. The individualism fostered by the constant plea for liberty is unfavourable to the growth of corporate church-life. Generous funds have been raised in aid of ministers' incomes and insurance, and the Conference has found it necessary to lay down educational qualifications for access to these benefits, and has thus constituted an accredited class of religious teachers. Unitarianism has thriven actively in some districts of Wales, but it has little hold in Scotland. The oldest of its congregations north of the Tweed was founded at Edinburgh in 1776. In Ireland Thomas Emlyn was prosecuted at Dublin in 1703 for denying the deity of Christ. Ulster Presbyterianism witnessed a movement against subscription which culminated in 1726 in the formation of a separate Presbytery of Antrim on a non-subscription basis. Many of the ministers passed through Arianism to Unitarianism, and in 1830 the Remonstrant Synod of Ulster was formed. At the same time, largely through the zeal of Martineau, then assistant pastor in Dublin, an Irish Unitarian Christian Society, embracing both individuals and congregations, was established in Dublin, which was merged (1835) in an Association of Irish Non-subscribing Presbyterians and other Free Christians, including the Presbytery of Antrim, the Synod of Munster, and the Remonstrant Synod of Ulster. Finally, in 1910 the Antrim Presbytery and the Ulster Synod united for purposes of church government under the name of the Non-subscribing Presbyterian Church of Ireland.

11. Unitarianism in America.—Unitarianism in America sprang out of the Congregational order

[1] London, 1836. [2] *Rationale*, p. 127.
[3] 2 vols., Oxford, 1885. [4] 2 vols., Oxford, 1888.
[5] J. E. Carpenter, *James Martineau, Theologian and Teacher*, London, 1905, p. 413.
[6] London, 1845, new ed. by J. Martineau, do. 1876.
[7] London, 1867.

[1] 2 vols., London, 1847–48.
[2] London, 1851, 8th ed., 2 vols., 1883.

of the New England churches. Their theology was Calvinistic, but the 17th cent. foundations were based upon religious covenants instead of dogmatic creeds. Thus the First Church in Boston affirmed:

> 'We . . . do hereby solemnly and religiously promise and bind ourselves to walk in all our ways according to the rule of the Gospel, and in all sincere conformity to [Christ's] holy ordinances, and in mutual love and respect to each other, so near as God shall give us grace.'[1]

The way was thus open, as in English Dissent in the 18th cent., to gradual theologic change. The literature of the Trinitarian controversy passed across the Atlantic, and the leaven of discussion in the works of Sherlock and South, Clarke and Whiston, supplemented by the writings of the Unitarian Emlyn, began to produce its effect. A slow movement towards Arianism and Arminianism set in, invigorated by reaction against the 'great awakening' under Jonathan Edwards (1735) and the early preaching of George Whitefield (1740). Jonathan Mayhew (1720–66) and Charles Chauncy (1705–57), pastors in Boston, led the way towards a more liberal faith. Under the ministry of James Freeman (1759–1835) the congregation of King's Chapel purged their Anglican liturgy of all references to the Trinity (1785). By this act, says the historian of the chapel, the first Episcopal church in New England became the first Unitarian church in the New World. The writings of Priestley and Lindsey were freely circulated, and at the end of the century the doctrine against which they protested had been rejected by all the Boston ministers but one. The name Unitarian was indeed rarely attached to the churches, but the mode of thought and worship prevailed more and more widely. It was found all the way from Portland (Maine) to Charleston (S. Carolina).

In 1803 William Ellery Channing (1780–1842) came to Boston and began the ministry which so powerfully influenced Unitarian thought. In reaction against a still powerful Calvinism, with its doctrines of human depravity, the wrath of God, and the atoning sacrifice of Christ, he proclaimed 'one sublime idea,' which he defined as 'the greatness of the soul, its divinity, its union with God by spiritual likeness, its receptivity of his Spirit, its self-forming power, its destination to ineffable glory, its immortality.'[2] This was the real challenge to New England orthodoxy; it operated with no less force in dispelling the materialism of Priestley and giving a fresh impulse of spiritual life to Unitarianism on both sides of the ocean. With this exalted view of man's true being, Channing declared himself surer that his rational nature was from God than that any book is the expression of His will; and reason and conscience were thus enthroned in the ultimate seat of judgment. Neither philosopher nor scholar in the technical sense, he exercised by his religious genius and the force of his ethical appeal a far-reaching influence both in the United States and in Europe. 'Always young for liberty,' he protested against every form of sectarian narrowness. He cheerfully took the name Unitarian because unwearied efforts were made to raise against it a popular cry, and he never was in any sense a Trinitarian. But he believed in Christ's pre-existence; he accepted his miracles. He would not, however, exclude from his fellowship the stoutest humanitarian, though he might repudiate the miracles altogether. For such a mind denominational aggressiveness was impossible, and this spirit was infused into the leaders of the movement which culminated in the foundation of the Divinity School of Harvard University in

[1] Allen, p. 171.

[2] J. W. Chadwick, *William Ellery Channing*, Boston, 1903, p. 246, quoting without date 'one of the letters of his later life.'

1816, when the Unitarian controversy was at its height.

> 'It being understood,' said the constitution, 'that every encouragement be given to the serious, impartial, and unbiassed investigation of Christian truth; and that no assent to the peculiarities of any denomination be required either of the Students, or Professors, or Instructors.'

The movement of which Channing was the most distinguished representative soon demanded some kind of organization. Literature must be circulated, congregations assisted, and churches built. In 1825, on the same day on which English Unitarians formed their association,[1] the American Unitarian Association was constituted. A noble line of eminent scholars, theologians, historians, jurists, poets, statesmen, accepted its principles and gave dignity to its profession of faith. It was not long, however, before new forces appeared on the field. The study of German philosophy produced a school of New England transcendentalism. Ralph Waldo Emerson (1803–82) (*q.v.*) resigned the pulpit of the Second Church in Boston on the question of the observance of the Lord's Supper, and six years later his famous 'Address to the Harvard Divinity School' (1838) signalized the breach of the new thought with the older views of revelation and miracle. Theodore Parker (1810–60) emphasized the same theme in a much criticized sermon on 'The Transient and Permanent in Christianity' (1841), followed by his widely read 'Discourse of Matters pertaining to Religion' (1842). A new type of Christianity without miracle was thus presented, emphasizing the divine immanence in nature, and holding up the religion of Jesus—the love of God and the service of man—as the 'absolute religion.' Unitarianism fell into the snare from which Channing would fain have saved it, and developed an orthodoxy of its own. When Henry Whitney Bellows of New York proposed to organize the churches (1865) in a National Conference, and its members adopted the declaration that they were 'disciples of the Lord Jesus Christ,' a group of bolder spirits formed a 'Free Religious Association,' where Emerson's name appeared first on the list. In 1894, however, the Conference repudiated all authoritative tests, and simply accepted 'the religion of Jesus, holding, in accordance with his teaching, that practical religion is summed up in love to God and love to man.'[2] The developments of criticism, science, and philosophy, the study of comparative religion, the desire for the widest possible fellowship, and the growing demands of philanthropy, have all contributed to broaden the outlook in every direction, and in 1900 the 'International Council of Unitarian and other Liberal Religious Thinkers and Workers' was formed in Boston. It has since held large and successful gatherings in London, Amsterdam, Geneva, Boston, Berlin (1910), Paris (1913), and Boston (1920), assembling a wide representation of different nationalities and faiths.

As in England, so also in America, Unitarianism has been an important influence in religious thought. It represents a mode of approach to the great problems of human life and destiny in which it is closely allied with the time-spirit. Its looseness of denominational organization makes its advance over so vast an area slow and hesitating, but its churches steadily increase, and in 1918 the list (including Canada) comprised 490 societies. The Divinity School at Harvard University gradually broadened out under the administration of Charles W. Eliot (1869–1909) into a school of scientific theology and independent research. The Meadville Theological School (Pennsylvania), founded in 1844, and the Unitarian Theological

[1] See § 7.

[2] George Willis Cooke, 'Unitarianism in the United States,' *EBr*[11] xxvii. 596.

School at Berkeley (California), founded in 1904, have remained more definitely within Unitarian lines.

12. World-wide influence.—(*a*) *The Colonies and India.*—The British Dominions, Canada, Australia, New Zealand, Africa, all have Unitarian churches. English and American Unitarians are also in close touch with the Theistic churches of India, and with Unitarian work in Japan, and receive students from the Far East into their theological colleges, besides sending out representative ministers to preach and lecture.

(*b*) *Germany.* — Continental thought has been affected by the same general influences which produced the Unitarian movement in England and America. The writings of the English Deists of the 18th cent. helped to foster German rationalism, and the critical study of the Scriptures led to the abandonment of doctrines of mechanical inspiration and Biblical authority. Belief in miracles was partly undermined by the influences of science and philosophy; and the *Leben Jesu*[1] of D. F. Strauss, together with the investigations of F. C. Baur into the development of the early Church, opened new paths for the historical treatment of the origins of Christianity. The results reached by Baur were modified by the subsequent researches of some of his own pupils, but a powerful school of thought, led by teachers such as H. Holtzmann (Strassburg), C. Holsten (Heidelberg), Carl von Weizsäcker (Tübingen), A. E. Biedermann (Zürich), R. A. Lipsius (Jena), O. Pfleiderer (Berlin), reached a position which was substantially Unitarian, though it did not employ the name or lead to withdrawal from the State Church. In 1863 a liberal union was founded under the title of the 'Protestantenverein,' which gave practical expression to this mode of thought. It still exists, though in a state of somewhat diminished activity. Recent theological liberalism has tended to take one of two directions. Under the influence of Albrecht Ritschl (*q.v.*) of Göttingen, a higher value has been ascribed to the person of Jesus, quite apart from external miracle, than was usual among the older 'liberal' theologians. Among the leaders in this direction are A. Harnack, W. Herrmann (Marburg), and H. H. Wendt (Jena). On the other hand, the study of Christianity in connexion with the religions of the empire has led younger scholars to emphasize its relations with contemporary phenomena; and along these lines the late professors W. Wrede, J. Weiss, and W. Bousset, and the brilliant group led by H. Gunkel, E. Troeltsch, C. Clemen, H. Weinel, W. Heitmüller, and H. Lietzmann have all been working. The valuable translation and commentary issued under the general editorship of Johannes Weiss,[2] and the long series of *Religionsgeschichtliche Volksbücher*, represent the general attitude of liberal theology on the problems of primitive Christianity.

(*c*) *France.*—A similar movement of thought, though more limited in range, may be traced in France, since the appearance of Renan's *Vie de Jésus*,[3] within the Reformed Church, represented especially by A. Coquerel (*fils*), Albert and Jean Réville, and a distinguished group of scholars and preachers. When the 'Séparation' took place in 1905, the Reformed Church split into two bodies, the 'National Union of Evangelical Reformed Churches' retaining a Confession of 1872, and the liberal group designating itself the 'National Union of Reformed Churches,' which is powerfully represented in the Theological Faculty of Paris, and exercises the greater influence both in the pulpit and in the press. Liberal Lutherans like Maurice Goguel and Eugène Ehrhardt share the same general view.

(*d*) *Switzerland.*—Swiss Protestantism has been affected in like manner. The abolition of formal tests of orthodoxy by the Genevan Church opened the way for a type of Christianity essentially Unitarian; and in German Switzerland the theologians of Basel and Zürich have made important contributions to both Biblical and dogmatic studies on similar lines. Practical interest in social questions is now to some extent withdrawing attention from the critical and historical inquiries of the older liberalism, and even leading to a partial reaction towards the language and ideas of orthodoxy.

(*e*) *Holland.*—A similar tendency shows itself in Holland. In the second half of the 19th cent. the Dutch Reformed Church, the Remonstrants, the Mennonites, and the Lutherans were all affected by the philosophical and scientific modes of thought which generate Unitarian theology. Scholars like J. H. Scholten, A. Kuenen, and C. P. Tiele educated successive generations of students in the newer methods of critical investigation. Many of the younger ministers of the present day, however, without returning to orthodoxy, are more inclined to recognize spiritual values in some of the old doctrines of the Church, and, while they claim to be 'liberals,' are at the same time unwilling to be classed as 'modern.' Their view of human nature is not optimistic. The natural man must be regenerated by the Spirit of Christ; for this generation there is no other way.

(*f*) *Other countries.* — In Italy a little group, assisted by various university professors, is conducting a monthly periodical, *La Riforma Italiana*, on Unitarian lines with the names of Mazzini and Channing blazoned upon its cover. There are Unitarian congregations in Denmark, Sweden, and Norway. The veteran poet Matthias Jochumssen in Iceland († 1920) espoused the same cause, and communicated his enthusiasm to his countrymen in the United States. Even among the educated negroes of Lagos on the W. African coast religious thought has produced spontaneously an active movement in the same direction.

LITERATURE. — R. Wallace, *Antitrinitarian Biography*, 3 vols., London, 1850; J. J. Tayler, *Retrospect of the Religious Life of England*², ed. James Martineau, do. 1876; G. Bonet-Maury, *Des Origines du Christianisme unitaire chez les Anglais*, Paris, 1881, tr. E. P. Hall, *Early Sources of English Unitarianism*, London, 1884; A. Gordon, *Heads of English Unitarian History*, London, 1895, and *EBr*¹¹, *s.v.* 'Unitarianism'; J. H. Allen, 'The Unitarians,' in *A Hist. of the Unitarians and Universalists in the United States*, New York, 1894, pp. 1-246; S. A. Eliot, *Heralds of a Liberal Faith*, 3 vols., Boston, U.S.A., 1910; biographies of Martineau, Channing, and Theodore Parker.

J. E. CARPENTER.

UNITED BRETHREN.

—See MORAVIANS.

UNITED EVANGELICAL CHURCH.

—See LUTHERANISM.

UNITED FREE CHURCH.

—See PRESBYTERIANISM.

UNITED METHODIST FREE CHURCH.

—See METHODISM.

UNITED PRESBYTERIAN CHURCH.

—See PRESBYTERIANISM.

UNITED PROVINCES OF AGRA AND OUDH.

—These provinces, in which Oudh, a separate jurisdiction since its annexation in 1856, was included in 1877, were up to 1902 known as the North-West Provinces. The change of title was mainly due to confusion with that of the

[1] 3 vols., Tübingen, 1835.

[2] *Die Schriften des Neuen Testaments*, 2 vols., Göttingen, 1906.

[3] Paris, 1863.

North-West Frontier Province, which was formed out of some Districts of the Panjāb. The joint jurisdictions of Agra and Oudh extend between N. lat. 23° 52′ and 31° 18′, E. long. 77° 3′ and 84° 39′, with a total area of 107,267 sq. miles and a population in 1911 of 47,182,000. The Provinces contain a hilly and submontane tract to the north-west; Bundelkhand, a part of the Central Indian plateau to the south; while the central and more important region constitutes the W. and Central Indo-Gangetic Plain, the basin watered by the rivers Ganges and Jumnā (*qq.v.*). The Districts between these two main rivers until they join at Allāhābād (*q.v.*) are known as the Duāb, 'land of the two waters.'

1. History.—The United Provinces form one of the best-known historical regions of India. The aboriginal population, wrongly classed as Dravidian (*q.v.*) by Risley, was probably of the Mon-Khmer stock. These 'pre-Aryans' have left traces in stone implements in the hills and plains, cup-marks on boulders in the northern hills, and cave paintings in the Kaimūr range to the south. At some unknown date, possibly about 1000 B.C., the so-called 'Aryans' who had been settled for a considerable period in the E. Panjāb[1] seem to have moved gradually eastward, and the *Mahābhārata* and the *Rāmāyaṇa* epics describe the fortunes of two bodies of Kṣatriyas, one to the west with their capital at Hastinapur (*q.v.*), the other at Ayodhya, the modern Ajodhya in the Faizābād District. One wave of invaders or colonists seems in the early period to have moved along the base of the Himālaya into Magadha or Bihār; the other occupied Madhyadeśa, the 'Middle Land,' or the Duāb and its surrounding Districts.[2] For the earliest period there is no settled history till the time of Gautama Buddha (*c.* 407–487 B.C.). The next fixed date is that of Chandragupta Maurya (321–297 B.C.), the Sandrocottus of classical writers, who rose to power after the invasion of Alexander the Great. His grandson was the famous Aśoka (*q.v.*), three of whose pillar edicts have been found in the Provinces. We know little of the Kushān or Śaka invaders who entered India about the middle of the 2nd cent. B.C. The Gupta dynasty rose to power from about A.D. 320 until 450, when the first Hun invasion took place. This is remarkable because many of the Rājput (*q.v.*) houses sprang from its chiefs. In 1018 Maḥmūd of Ghaznī, the first Muhammadan invader, raided the Provinces, and under the early Muhammadan kings Delhi was the capital, being succeeded by Agra early in the 16th century. Bābur defeated the Afghān king Ibrahīm in 1526 and founded the Mughal empire, which with its capital at Agra or Delhi, under Humāyūn, Akbar, Shāhjahān, and Aurangzīb, lasted till the death of the last in 1707. Then commenced a period of anarchy until by treaty with Asafu-d-daula, Nawāb of Oudh, most of the eastern portion passed into the hands of the British. This was followed by further large cessions as the result of the Marāṭha war in 1803. In 1833 the Provinces were separated from Bengal and placed in charge of a lieutenant-governor. Since that time the only serious disturbance of order occurred in the Mutiny of 1857.

2. Ethnology.—The population is of a mixed type, made up of the pre-historic Mon-Khmer stratum leavened by successive entries of foreigners: Aryans, Scythians, Huns, Musalmāns. In the E. Gangetic Plain there is considerable congestion, the density of population rising to 706 per sq. mile. The people occupy 106,020 villages and 435 towns (of which 24 rank as cities), the most important in order of population being Lucknow, Benares, Agra, Cawnpur, Bareilly, Meerut. Muhammadans favour a town life much more than Hindus; out of 1000 of each faith only 72 Hindus as compared with 269 Musalmāns are urban. This concentration in towns is one cause of the progress of Islām.

3. Religion.—Hindus (85·04 %) are much in excess of Muhammadans (14·77 %) or Christians (·38 %), but now Hindus are slowly decreasing, and there is an increase in Muhammadans and Christians. The progress of Islām is not to any great extent the result of direct propaganda, but is due largely to social conditions. Muhammadans are more prolific; they live more in towns and under less insanitary conditions than Hindus; their diet is more varied and liberal, and they are less addicted to the use of drugs like the preparations of hemp; they marry later and allow widows to remarry, while high-caste Hindus prohibit widow-marriage. On the other hand, their women suffer in health from seclusion (*parda*), and, being confined to the house, they are more liable to attacks of plague.[1]

(*a*) *Brāhmanic Hinduism.*—What has been termed Brāhmanic Hinduism is the creed of the better classes, while the lower castes are largely animistic. It is impossible to draw the line between these forms of belief, which in all grades of society converge and intermingle. Orthodox Hinduism is regulated by a body of Brāhmans numbering 4¾ millions, many of whom enjoy a high reputation for sanctity, act as domestic priests, or study theology, philosophy, and ethics at sacred places like Benares. Those of a lower grade act as guides at places of pilgrimage, cast horoscopes, and practise various kinds of magic. The majority, however, exercise no religious functions, and make their living by agriculture or domestic service, or take employment in the army or the police. Some of the most sacred places of Hindu pilgrimage are found in these Provinces: Hardwār, shared by Śaivas and Vaiṣṇavas; Mathurā, devoted to the cult of Kṛṣṇa; Prayāg or Allāhābād, the sacred junction of the Ganges and Jumnā.[2]

(*b*) *The development of monotheism.*—An important development in recent times is the tendency to adopt a form of monotheism.

To quote R. Burn, 'the general result of my enquiries is that the great majority of Hindus have a firm belief in one Supreme God, called Bhagwān, Parameshwar, Ishwar, or Narain. Mr. Bailie made some enquiries[3] which showed that this involved a clear idea of a single personal God; but I am inclined to think that this is not limited to the more intelligent, but is distinctly characteristic of Hindus as a whole. . . . There has been much discussion as to whether this monotheistic idea has been a natural result of contact with Islām or Christianity. As pointed out above, however, the idea of a single personal God was not unknown to Hindus long before they came into touch with adherents of these two religions, and I am inclined to think . . . that the tendency of Hinduism, with all its eclecticism and elasticity, is to develop more on the lines of indigenous beliefs, than on an entirely new direction copied more or less from some foreign religion.'[4]

'The Hindu who is a Saiva or a Vaishṇava has no real place for Parameshwar in his religious ideas, and would probably explain his presence by saying he was Śiva or Vishṇu. According to the Purānic philosophy, Parameshwar is the universal spirit when manifested as a personal god, who, according as he is dominated by activity (*rajas*), goodness (*saitva*), is separated from the divine personalities, Brahmā, Śiva and Vishṇu. This, however, is merely stated to explain his relation to them; for it is a recondite theory which does not trouble the ordinary Parameshwar worshipper. To him Parameshwar is the supreme personal God, who made the world, is pleased by good and displeased by evil deeds, but is too much exalted to trouble much about mundane affairs. If the Hindu is not professedly a Saiva or a Vaishṇava, he will look on Śiva and Vishṇu as on the whole

[1] See artt. DELHĪ, vol. iv. p. 543, PANJĀB, vol. ix. p. 605.
[2] Manu, *Laws*, ii. 21.

[1] *Census of India, 1911*, vol. xv., *United Provinces and Oudh*, pt. i. p. 108 ff.
[2] See art. PILGRIMAGE (Indian), § 7.
[3] *Census of India, 1891*, vol. xvi., *N.-W. Provinces and Oudh*, pt. i. p. 197.
[4] *Ib.* p. 73 f.

subordinate to him, though much more valuable helpers in times of trouble. Still, nebulous as his idea of Parameshwar may be, it makes him at bottom a monotheist. But it is to some extent wrong to say that he "worships" Parameshwar. He may or may not repeat his name in the morning, and occasionally he has the *Sat Nārāyaṇ Kathā* recited in his honour; but this is all. It is a waste of time to importune a god with prayer and sacrifice when his attitude is one of suave aloofness; and the Hindu reserves his attentions for the minor gods and godlings.'[1]

(*c*) *Islām*.—The local distribution of Muhammadanism is dictated partly by historical, partly by economic causes.

'The Muhammadan is found chiefly where Muhammadans held sway in the past: in Meerut and Rohilkhand Divisions, the "Home Counties" of the Moghul Empire, in Agra, Farrukhābād, Jaunpur and Oudh, all centres of Muhammadan States or provinces. In Cawnpore, Allāhābād and other districts with large cities, his tendency to urban life is sufficient to explain his numerical strength; this is also a factor which affects his presence in such historically Muhammadan centres as Agra, Meerut, Lucknow, Fyzābād, and Bareilly.'[2]

(*d*) *Jainism*.—Jains, numbering 75,427 in 1911, show a tendency to decrease. The city mercantile class, deficient in virility owing to their sedentary habits, produce small families, and, as E. A. H. Blunt reports, the country Jain shows little enthusiasm for or knowledge of his religion.

'The truth seems to be that whatever theoretical differences may exist between Jainism and Hinduism, yet the followers of the same creeds in the same community do not differ very greatly in their practice. The bar to their intermarriage is no more insuperable than between Roman Catholics and Protestants. . . . Men of to-day think less about religion because the stress of modern conditions leaves them less time for other than mundane affairs. The active pursuit of religion, which means the active performance of ritual, is postponed to old age; the official or professional man takes to religion when he retires.'[3]

It is natural also that, when a Jain girl is married into a Hindu family, she rapidly succumbs to the influence of the more popular faith. Jainism being reticent and unenterprising, she naturally adopts religious usages which enjoy more prestige and which are regulated by Brāhmans, whom Jains themselves employ for their domestic rites.

(*e*) *Sikhism and other faiths*.—Sikhs, numbering 15,186, are foreigners, mostly sepoys or policemen. Parsis, Jews, and Brāhmans are also foreigners and possess little influence, while Buddhists, representatives of a faith once dominant, now number only 780, and are mainly confined to the Tibetan frontier, with a few Nepalese, Chinese artizans, Magh cooks, and other smaller groups.

The Ārya Samāj is chiefly confined to the upper and educated classes, and seems as yet to have made little impression on the peasantry.[4]

(*f*) *Christianity*.—Christians show a remarkable increase. The propaganda began with the visit of a Roman Catholic priest to Agra in 1578. It became active through the work of Henry Martyn at Cawnpur in 1810. In 1811 the Baptist Missionary Society, and in 1813 the Church Missionary Society, entered the field. Christians, including those in the Native States, numbering 58,518 in 1891 and 102,955 in 1901, increased to 179,694 in 1911.

'The new convert, may be, is no better than his predecessors; but a new generation, the children of the first generation of converts, is growing up. If the missionaries could and can get little out of that first generation, the second generation is in their hands from their earliest years. The children of the converts, born in Christianity, are very different to their parents; their grandchildren will be better still. It is this which provides the other side to the black picture so often drawn of the inefficiency of Christian conversion. And this generation is now beginning to make its influence felt. The Hindu fellows of these converts have now to acknowledge not only that they are in many ways better off than themselves, but that they are better men. And this has undoubtedly contributed to the better esteem in which Christians are regarded. . . . A convert, no doubt, is still outcasted, but he is now regarded as a member of a fresh caste, and Hindus bear with his idiosyncrasies as they do with those of any other caste.'[1]

LITERATURE.—R. Burn, *Census of India, 1901*, vol. xvi., *N.W. Provinces and Oudh*, 3 pts.; E. A. H. Blunt, *Census of India, 1911*, vol. xv., *United Provinces of Agra and Oudh*, 2 pts.; W. Crooke, *The N.-W. Provinces of India: their History, Ethnology, and Administration*, London, 1897, *The Tribes and Castes of the N.-W. Provinces and Oudh*, 4 vols., Calcutta, 1896; V. A. Smith, *The Early Hist. of India*[3], Oxford, 1914; A. A. Führer, *The Monumental Antiquities and Inscriptions in the N.-W. Provinces and Oudh*, Allāhābād, 1891; H. M. Elliot and J. Dowson, *The Hist. of India, as told by its own Historians*, 8 vols., London, 1867–77; *IGI* xxiv. [1908] 132 ff.

W. CROOKE.

1 *Census of India, 1911*, vol. xv. pt. i. p. 126 f.
2 *Ib.* p. 107.
3 *Ib.* p. 112.
4 See *ERE* ii. 57 ff.; *Census of India, 1911*, vol. xv. pt. i. p. 132 ff.

UNITY.—See CHURCH.

UNIVERSALISM.—**I. Uses of the term.**—The word 'universalism' has been used in at least three distinct senses. (*a*) It is convenient to take first in order the use of the word which is in fact the most modern. It designates the setting aside of the belief that a nation or a race is privileged to enjoy the special protection and favour of God, or of a deity whom it recognizes as peculiarly its own; and contemplates all nations and races as standing, actually or potentially, in one and the same relation to one and the same God. Universalism in this sense has become current largely owing to the influence of F. C. Baur; its opposite is particularism. In the OT the view of the special relation of a deity to a people is expressed in such passages as Jg 11[24], when Jephthah says to the Amorite: 'Wilt not thou possess that which Chemosh thy god giveth thee to possess? So whomsoever the Lord our God hath dispossessed from before us, them will we possess.' The steps by which this particularism yielded to the larger thought, first of Jahweh's rule over all peoples as God above all gods, and next as being the only God, whose sway is universal, but who has chosen Israel as His special care, are sufficiently familiar. There are within the pages of the OT occasional indications of a desire to extend to other nations the Messianic hope and the kingdom of God.[2] In the NT we are familiar with the distinction between the universalism of St. Paul and of the Lucan writings,[3] in contrast with the exclusiveness of the Jew and the Judæo-Christian, who, if they did not entirely disapprove the proffer of the gospel to the Gentiles, yet wished to make conditions and impose practices which St. Paul strongly repudiates. In the NT the larger view seems to win its way from the announcement of a salvation which, beginning from Israel, shall be unto all peoples, to the Apocalyptic vision of the 'great multitude which no man could number, out of every nation, and of all tribes and peoples and tongues,'[4] and of a New Jerusalem whose gates are never shut.

(*b*) The second use of the term 'universalism' has to do with the theological question of the extent of the benefit wrought by the atoning death of Christ, and with the relation of the Calvinian doctrines of election and predestination (*qq.v.*) to the expressed purpose of the gospel, that all men might be saved. The Arminians had maintained, as the second of their five points, 'that Jesus Christ by His death and sufferings made an atonement for the sins of all mankind in general, and of every individual in particular,' but they went on to say that none could be partakers of this benefit but those possessing a true faith, which can belong only to those who are regenerated by the operation of the Holy Ghost. This was condemned as error by the Synod of Dort (1618). There were many, however, who desired to mitigate the lan-

1 *Census of India, 1911*, vol. xv. pt. i. p. 145.
2 See, *e.g.*, Is 19[23-25].
3 *E.g.*, Gal 3[28], Col 3[11], Ac 10[35] 17[24-28].
4 Rev 7[9].

guage of absolute predestination and particular redemption. Among these were John Cameron, professor in the Protestant seminary of Saumur (1618–22), and his pupil, Moyse Amyraut, professor of theology at Saumur (1633). The aim of both was to vindicate for the Deity a larger and more real benevolence and goodwill to mankind than was contemplated in the Canons of Dort. They postulated a general will to save all men, but, in order to be effective, this required to be reinforced by the exercise of a particular will. The merits of Christ's passion and death were in themselves sufficient, but not efficient for all men. In other words, though the impetration is universal, the application is individual: the general will is not a will *decreti* but *præcepti*, and it may be wholly resisted by mankind in bondage to sin. The universality of salvation is conditioned; the promise is *sub conditione fidei*. A similar distinction is made between objective grace, an offer of pardon to all, and subjective grace, which is the application to the individual by the particular will of God. The special action of grace is variously described: sometimes it seems identical with 'effectual calling'; in other connexions it is that which brings a man to the knowledge of the truth, and, acting through the intellect upon the heart, brings about conversion.[1] The doctrine of this school is known as 'hypothetical universalism.' Its promulgation led to some persecution of Amyraut in France, to the withdrawal by the Swiss Reformed Churches of their students from the seminary at Saumur, and the elevation of that of Sedan in its place as the centre of French Protestant orthodoxy. Amyraut and his friend Paul Testard were summoned to appear before synods of the Reformed Church of France at Alençon (1637) and Charenton (1644–45); they were acquitted on all charges of heresy, but this acquittal was strongly reprobated by the rigid Calvinists of the Reformed Church. It was, however, approved and defended by the learned Jean Daillé (Dallæus) (1594–1670), pastor of Charenton, who published in 1655 *Apologia pro duabus Synodis Nationalibus*. The position of the High Calvinists was defended by Friedrich Spanheim (1600–49), professor at Leyden, in his *Disputatio de gratia universali* (1644), followed by *Exercitationes* (1646).

The controversy spread to England, where John Davenant (1576–1641), bishop of Salisbury, who had attended the Synod of Dort, was engaged in finding a 'middle way' between the Remonstrants and the Supralapsarians, and did this with a special reference to the *Gallicana Controversia*, in his *Dissertationes duæ de Morte Christi et de Prædestinatione*, published at Cambridge in 1650. John Owen had already denounced the 'error' of universal redemption and those 'who try to go a middle way between the Churches of France and the Arminians,' especially in his anonymous work *Salus Electorum Sanguis Jesu* (1648). The term 'universalist' was applied to the advocates of universal redemption perhaps first by Obadiah Howe, whose work, *The Universalist Examined and Convicted*, appeared in 1648. The controversy engaged the ready pen of Richard Baxter, then at Kidderminster, who thus alludes to his early work upon it:

'Another Manuscript that lyeth by me, is a Disputation for some *Universality of Redemption*, which hath lain by me near Twenty years unfinished . . . partly because at last came out after *Amyraldus* and *Davenant's Dissertations*, a treatise of *Dallæus*, which contained the same things, but especially the same Testimonies of concordant Writers which I had prepared to produce.'[2]

This work, entitled *Universal Redemption of Mankind by the Lord Jesus Christ*, was published in 1694 by Joseph Reid, who had been Baxter's assistant and had transcribed his MS in the year 1657.

It is to be remembered that throughout this period the doctrine of 'general redemption' was being taught by the early English Baptists, known as General Baptists from their opposition to the doctrine of particular election. Of these the first was Thomas Helwys (1550?–1616?), who had been the chief supporter of John Smith's little congregation in Amsterdam, and had been baptized by him, and who returned to England after Smith's death in 1612. He set forth the doctrine of general redemption in a document of a few pages printed in 1611 and entitled *A Short and Plaine Proof by the Word and Workes of God . . . that all men are redeemed by Christ*. He was the founder of congregations in London and the home counties.

(*c*) Universalism in the third sense denotes the doctrine held by persons and churches called 'Universalist.' With some minor differences, all such agree in the belief in the final salvation of all mankind. The opponents of this doctrine are designated by its adherents as partialists or limitarians.

The assertion and defence of this doctrine are based mainly on the language of the NT, as, *e.g.*: 'All that the Father giveth me shall come to me; . . . and this is the Father's will which hath sent me, that of all which he hath given me I should lose nothing' (Jn $6^{37.\ 39}$). 'And I, if I be lifted up from the earth, will draw all men unto me' (12^{32}). 'As in Adam all die, even so in Christ shall all be made alive' (1 Co 15^{22}). 'God was in Christ, reconciling the world unto himself' (2 Co 5^{19}). 'That . . . he might gather together in one all things in Christ, both which are in heaven, and which are on earth' (Eph 1^{10}). 'God our Saviour; who will have all men to be saved . . . for there is one God' (1 Ti $2^{3.\ 4.\ 5}$). 'For the grace of God hath appeared, bringing salvation to all men' (Tit 2^{11}). 'The Lord is . . . not willing that any should perish, but that all should come to repentance' (2 P 3^{9}). 'And he is the propitiation for our sins: and not for ours only, but also for the sins of the whole world' (1 Jn 2^{2}). 'Death and hell were cast into the lake of fire' (Rev 20^{14}).

In scriptural argument the Universalist contention has mainly turned on the following points:

(1) The purpose of God: see Ac 3^{21}, ἀποκατάστασις πάντων, where the recovery of a primal condition, once forfeited, is certainly indicated; the end is to be as the beginning.

(2) The means and sanction of such recovery by the office and work of Christ. 'Therefore as by the offence of one judgment came upon all men to condemnation; even so by the righteousness of one the free gift came upon all men unto justification of life' (Ro 5^{18}). 'That he by the grace of God should taste death for every man' (He 2^{9}).

(3) The nature of the ultimate salvation. 'Then cometh the end, when he shall have delivered up the kingdom to God, even the Father; when he shall have put down all rule and all authority and power. For he must reign, till he hath put all enemies under his feet. The last enemy that shall be destroyed is death. For he hath put all things under his feet. But when he saith all things are put under him, it is manifest that he is excepted, which did put all things under him. And when all things shall be subdued unto him, then shall the Son also himself be subject unto him that put all things under him, that God may be all in all' (1 Co 15^{24-28}). The consummation is reached by the divine indwelling in every human soul.

2. Universalism in Patristic literature.—When the expectation of a speedy coming of the end and a Messianic reign of a thousand years on earth died away in Christian circles, attention was directed to the idea of a world-process, involving an evolution of a spiritual realm, supplanting the material universe, which Gnosticism in its various forms had made familiar. Christian Platonism set itself to combine the promises of the gospel with the more spiritual elements of Greek philosophy. When the Christian philosophers of Alexandria undertook to set forth a true gnosis, as against the several false ones, they had to exhibit salvation on the scale not of the individual, but of the cosmos.[1]

In the view of Clement of Alexandria († A.D. 220) God's purifying discipline of man extends beyond this life.

[1] See art. AMYRALDISM.

[2] *Reliquiæ Baxterianæ*, London, 1696, bk. i. pt. i. p. 123.

[1] See art. ALEXANDRIAN THEOLOGY.

Death is the means whereby the soul is made more immediately subject to redeeming influences, and through correction and repentance may rise to various stages of spiritual development, the highest of which is eternal communion with infinite goodness, love, and truth. This is the completion of that likeness of God wherein man was made at the beginning.

Origen († A.D. 254) extended the notion of the discipline of souls much farther both in scope and in detail. His mind was at once more laborious and more speculative than Clement's.

He conceived a chain of existences in which the human life of this world is but a link. Souls arrive from an infinite past, in which their experience and their discipline have been carried on with the most varied results, to exercise here their privilege of free will, to rise or to sink according as they have accepted or resisted the spiritual influences that are perpetually striving for their redemption. Into future æons beyond this life Origen carries the divine work of leading souls towards the goal of all sentient being, which is attained in likeness to God, for in the end God will be all in all. Fallen angels and demons will be rescued to share with mankind the ultimate salvation. It is to be noted that, when Origenism was anathematized as heresy, under Justinian (A.D. 541–543), it was not his view of the universality of salvation that was condemned, but then, as afterwards, his doctrine of the pre-existence of souls and of the final salvability of devils.

Gregory of Nyssa († A.D. 394) moves towards the same result from his central conviction as to the ultimate annihilation of all evil. For he says:

'If God will be in all existing things, evil, plainly, will not then be among them.'[1] 'The resurrection is nothing else than the reconstitution of our nature in its original form.'[2] Nothing that had its origin from God will fall out of His kingdom. When all the evil that is intermingled with things that are is melted out by cleansing fire, everything that originated from God will become such as it was from the beginning, before the evil entered into it.

The same view was taken by Didymus of Alexandria († A.D. 395), who explicitly endorsed Origen's opinion on the conversion of devils.

Among the later Fathers of the Church in the East it suffices to mention Theodore of Mopsuestia († A.D. 428), an opponent of Origenism, who maintained that sin and its penalty were both agents in the moral purposes of God as conducive both to self-knowledge and to repentance, and thus effective for the restoration of the wicked.

The current of Alexandrian thought came again to the surface in the 9th cent. in the mind of John Scotus Erigena († A.D. 877), in the form of a pantheistic theodicy. He predicts, at the conclusion of a complicated and somewhat inconsistent scheme, the absorption of all into the divine; wickedness, death, and misery are all transformed into goodness, life, and blessedness; and the *consummatio mundi* is that God is all in all.[3]

In the period immediately preceding the Reformation some form of belief in universal salvation is found in connexion with very various forms of doctrine and life; *e.g.*, this belief is seen in combination with the Antinomianism of the Brethren of the Free Spirit (*q.v.*), and the fanatical asceticism of the Albanensian Cathari.[4]

3. Universalism in Germany.—A certain prevalence of Universalism among the German Anabaptists has been attributed to the influence of Hans Denk, scholar and mystic (1495–1527), but his extant writings do not show that he gave it any prominence in his teaching. That the Anabaptists were largely credited with such opinion is evident from cap. xvii. of the *Augsburg Confession* (1530), where there is formal condemnation of the Anabaptists 'who believe that there will be an end of the punishments of the damned and the devils.'

At the end of the 17th cent. and the beginning of the 18th controversy was very rife on three points—the eternity of punishment, the millennium, and the restitution of all things. A number of the publications of this time, especially on the last-named topic, are embodied in a great work published in three volumes folio at Frankfort in

[1] *De Anim. et Resurr.* [2] *Ib.*
[3] *De Divisione Naturæ*, v. 30. [4] See art. ALBIGENSES.

1701–10, entitled Μυστήριον ἀποκαταστάσεως πάντων, *oder das Geheimniss der Wiederbringung aller Dinge*, compiled by Johann Wilhelm Petersen (1649–1727). Petersen had been professor at Rostock and a prominent divine of the Lutheran Church. He was deposed from office in 1692, because of his having embraced Universalist opinions, to which he had been converted by his wife, Johanna Eleanora von Merlau. She had been influenced in this direction before her marriage by the writings of the English mystic, Jane Lead, whose opinions were widely circulated in Germany by her disciples, who constituted the Philadelphian Society.[1] Petersen was a very voluminous writer, and both he and his wife contributed largely to the contents of the great compilation.

For many years after the appearance of Petersen's work a great number of writings, for and against the doctrine of restoration, were published. On the orthodox side appears the great name of Johann Lorenz von Mosheim (1694–1755). On the other side the most remarkable publication, in permanence and popularity, was the little work entitled *The Everlasting Gospel*, which, having run through many editions in Germany from 1700 to 1745, was destined to achieve wide influence in America. It professed to be written by Paul Siegvolk, but it is known that the author's real name was Georg Klein-Nicolai, for which Paul Siegvolk is a transparent disguise, effected with the aid of German, Latin, and Greek.

Such subjects as eternal punishment were from this time open to latitudinarian treatment in Germany, but it remained for F. D. E. Schleiermacher (1768–1834) to give to his contemporaries and successors a definite direction towards Universalism. Among systematic theologians the one who has most closely followed Schleiermacher (*q.v.*) in his eschatology is the Zürich professor, Alexander Schweizer (1808–88).[2]

4. Universalism in England.—It has been inferred, from a mandate of Simon Langham, archbishop of Canterbury, dated 5th Nov. 1368,[3] that doctrines of universal salvation, extending even to the salvability of devils, were current at that time in England. A number of opinions are condemned as erroneous, extending from the possible salvation of Saracens, Jews, and pagans to beliefs such as, *e.g.*, 'it is not possible that one should be damned for original sin without actual sin,' and that the nature of demons may not be essentially irreparable. This mandate is addressed to the Chancellor of the University of Oxford, and it is surely more probable that it intends to deal with the possible re-appearance of Origenistic speculation in academic disputations than with any popular advocacy of such views.

The 42nd of the English Articles of 1553 has for its title 'That all men shall not be saved at the length,' and it runs:

'They also are worthy of condemnation who endeavour at this time to restore the dangerous opinion, that all men, be they never so ungodly, shall at length be saved, when they have suffered paines for their sins a certain time appointed by God's justice.'

It is generally admitted that this condemnation is directed against Anabaptist opinions promulgated by foreign refugees who had then recently come to England in large numbers and been permitted to establish churches. Such doctrine is not attributed to the English Lollards, save probably in one document, viz. *The Protestation of the Clergy of the Lower House within the Province of Canterbury, with Declaration of the Faults and Abuses which heretofore have and now be within the same, worthy*

[1] See art. PHILADELPHIANS.
[2] H. R. Mackintosh, 'Studies in Christian Eschatology,' in *Exp*, 8th ser., viii. [1914] 128 ff.
[3] D. Wilkins, *Concilia Magnæ Britanniæ et Hiberniæ*, London, 1737, iii. 75.

special Reformation (1536), where, under no. 4, we read:

'That if there be a place where they [souls departed] be punished, God is not yet born, nor He that shall redeem the world.'

Here, obviously, not a doctrine of temporary punishment, but one of no punishment at all, is condemned. The return of foreign Protestants to their own countries on the accession of Queen Mary (1553) probably accounts for the withdrawal of the Articles 40, 41, and 42.

It would have been strange if, in the general outburst of the most diverse religious opinions from 1640 onwards, the maintenance of universal salvation had not found a place. It is warmly advocated in a little anonymous book entitled:

'Divine Light, manifesting the love of God unto the whole world: with the True Church.

Wherein the holy Spirit of Truth manifesteth the Glory of God in Christ, exalting Christ, a spiritual Christ, and All-saving Jesus; shewing that Christ is a sure Foundation, and chief Corner-Stone for all Spirituall building, unto the raising up lively hopes for all People to proceed in Beleeving the greate Mercies and loving-kindnesses of our God in Christ, in whom God hath redeemed us his saints, and *All*; having wrought all things for us, and all in Christ, wherein wee are made perfect.

Sent forth by the Minister of the Lord Jesus, whom He hath appointed his servant for the Good of All:

In bringing Glad Tidings of Good Things unto the whole Creation. Esai 52. 7. 13.

. . . .

The Lord will worke for the manifestation of his Truth in this his due time. Printed in the year 1646.'

The author does not deny that the elect are found in every age, but they are those who are chosen to proclaim to the world general redemption and the holy covenant. It is evident that the work attracted much attention, for in *A Testimony to the Truth of Jesus Christ as also against the Errours, Heresies and Blasphemies of the Time and the Toleration of them, Inscribed by the ministers of Christ within the Province of London, December 14, 1647*, we find that the 'errours against God's eternal decree of Election and Reprobation' are taken verbatim from the *Divine Light*. Under date 4th Feb. 1646 the Lords and Commons put forth an order for a day of public humiliation 'for the growth and spreading of Errors, Heresies and Blasphemies,' and among the 'errors' enumerated are two, referred to *Divine Light*:

'(*a*) "That God's eternal election is of all men, one as well as another"; (*b*) "that all shall be saved at last, both men and devils, and that they that deny it are the great Antichrist; that true faith is to believe it; and that though this Faith of general redemption were but in three persons only in the world, it should be sufficient to save all the rest of the Creation."'[1]

In the so-called Draconic Ordinance, passed by Parliament in 1648, while deniers of the Trinity are threatened with death, those who maintain that all men shall be saved are declared liable to imprisonment.

Another vigorous little tract, of six pages, written by Henry Horn and published in 1653, deserves mention in connexion with the *Divine Light*, viz. *The Light of God spreading itself in all the dark Corners of the Earth; with glad Tydings to all People, with a Restauration of all Things, and the Lyon's Power overthrown.*

At this time three men were itinerating in the country, preaching Universalism, and gathering small bodies of adherents. They often preached in churches, but more frequently challenged the clergy in public disputation after the manner of the 'gifted brethren' of the army. These were William Erbury (1604–54), Gerrard Winstanley († 1652), and Richard Coppin († 1659). The last-named was frequently imprisoned; his works largely consist of accounts of debates with his clerical opponents and his judges. One of his chief contentions is that there may be redemption from hell, and in support of this he argues that, in Biblical language, 'everlasting' does not mean 'endless.'

[1] *Hell broke loose*, London, 1646, p. 5.

The latter point is elaborated at length by Samuel Richardson, a Baptist, in his work entitled *Of the Torments of Hell: The Foundation and Pillars thereof discovered, searched, shaken and removed, with infallible Proofs, that there is not to be a Punishment after this Life, for any to endure, that shall never end*, printed in 1658, and reprinted in *The Phœnix*, ii. [1708]. In this little work the author carries himself beyond the end proposed, and convinces himself of the ultimate salvation of all men.

In 1661 appeared an anonymous treatise entitled *A Letter of Resolution concerning Origen and the Chief of his Opinions*, reprinted in *The Phœnix*, i. [1707]. The author was George Rust, who in 1667 became bishop of Dromore. His statement of Origen's opinions is not mere exposition, but reveals the author as more than favourable to the notion of universal restitution.

A classic of Universalist literature was being produced at this period by Jeremiah White (1629–1707), Fellow of Trinity College, Cambridge, and chaplain to the Protector. The book was not printed until 1712, and did not then bear the author's name. The title is *The Restoration of all Things, or a Vindication of the Goodness and Grace of God, to be manifested at last in the Recovery of his whole Creation out of their Fall. Rev xiv. 6.* White approaches his subject from the predestinarian side; his style is forcible, simple, and dignified, reminding the reader of the Cambridge Platonists.

Isaac Barrow (1630–77) had already approached the subject from the Arminian side in his sermons, nos. 39–42, 'The Doctrine of Universal Redemption Asserted and Explained.'[1]

Thomas Burnet (1635?–1715), Master of the Charterhouse, towards the end of his life, wrote a Latin treatise, *de Statu Mortuorum et Resurgentium*, which he circulated in MS among his friends, strictly enjoining that it was not to be printed. After his death, however, it appeared in print (1727), and subsequently in an English translation (1733). The author is perhaps not very clear as to the processes and stages by which the soul after death arrives at the general resurrection and the last judgment, but he is unmistakably opposed to the doctrine of endless punishment. He maintains, however, that this doctrine should not be publicly discredited, but used as a deterrent from sin in popular teaching.

Archbishop Tillotson (1630–94) held that the Biblical language as to future punishment is to be regarded as a divine threatening of wrath to come, which in God's mercy may not be literally realized.

The views of George Cheyne (1671–1743) inclined towards Universalism.

Popular preaching of Universalist doctrine had a brief success in London under the vigorous advocacy of James Relly (1720–78). He had been a convert of Whitefield's, and was for some time a preacher among his adherents, but he espoused the doctrine of a 'finished salvation' in Christ, maintaining that all sin and all suffering for sin had been accomplished and ended in the passion of Christ, and that mankind has therefore expiated all offence in the person of Christ, its corporate head. The only offence for which man is still accountable consists in the disbelief or the ignoring of this fact. Relly made a convert of John Murray, who in 1770 carried his doctrine to America.

Elhanan Winchester (1751–97) came from America in 1787, and in the following year published *The Universal Restoration Exhibited in Four Dialogues*. He gathered a large congrega-

[1] *Works*, London, 1830–31, iii.

tion in Parliament Court, London, and was succeeded there, on his return to America in 1794, by William Vidler (1758–1816), who had been a Baptist minister at Battle, and, on embracing Universalism in 1792, had been expelled, with his congregation, from the Kent and Sussex Association of Baptist Churches. Vidler was not successful in maintaining a large congregation in London, but did great service to the cause he advocated by establishing in 1797 a periodical entitled *The Universalist's Miscellany*, which in 1802 became *The Universal Theological Magazine*. This continued from 1797 to the end of 1805, and was succeeded by *The Monthly Repository* (1806–37), a valuable record of men and movements on the liberal side of the old dissent.

Universalism, apart from any attempt at the organization of a Church, found an advocate in Sir George Stonhouse († 1793), a Syriac scholar of eminence, who had spent much time in the examination of Syriac MSS in Continental libraries. At Oxford he had been a member of the little band of Methodists over whom John Wesley presided, nicknamed the Holy Club, and had maintained, against his fellow-members, the doctrine of universal restitution. In later life he resided at East Brent, Somerset, and was much interested in a society formed in the neighbouring parish of Burnham and called the Burnham Society, 'to study philosophy and polemic divinity and debate on the difference of religious opinions, in brotherly love.' The minutes of the society record discussions on the pre-existence of souls and universal restitution.[1] Stonhouse published (anonymously at Bristol in 1761) *Universal Restitution a Scripture Doctrine*, and two subsequent volumes on the same subject in 1768 and 1773.

Another independent study is *The Restitution of All Things: An Essay on the Important Purpose of the Universal Redeemer's Destination* (1785), by James Brown, chaplain of the British garrison at Savannah in the Province of Georgia. The author is apparently quite unaware of any efforts or any books of purport similar to his own.

At the close of the 18th cent. Universalism began to spread among English Unitarians. John Prior Estlin, of Bristol (1747–1817), published *Discourses on Universal Restitution* (1813), directed principally against the doctrine of the final annihilation of the wicked. A more generally interesting treatment of the subject was put forth by T. Southwood Smith (1788–1861), in his *Illustrations of the Divine Government* (1816).

David Thom (1793–1862), minister of the Scotch Church, Rodney Street, Liverpool, having been licensed by the Presbytery of Glasgow, was in 1825 censured and suspended by that Presbytery upon charges of heresy, which, however, lay entirely within the sphere of Calvinistic doctrine. His adherents formed an independent congregation, which soon became known as Berean Universalists, for Thom now espoused the doctrine of a 'finished salvation,' analogous to that of Relly, and constructed on a distinctly Calvinistic basis. His works consisted of laborious and often paradoxical interpretations of Scripture, but in 1850 he republished Jeremiah White's *Restoration of All Things* with a historical preface. The same year marked the appearance of a magazine, *The Universalist*, edited by Richard Roe, to which Thom became a constant contributor, his efforts being largely devoted to restraining the Unitarian tendencies of contemporary Universalism, especially in the United States.[2]

Universalism has, at a later time, been approached from various sides by writers within the Church of England, notably F. W. Farrar,[1] Andrew Jukes,[2] and Alfred Gurney.[3]

5. Universalism in Scotland.—As early as 1755 certain small congregations in the Merse (Berwickshire) which had been associated with the Reformed Presbytery (a branch from the Cameronian side of the Scottish Covenanters) united in declaring their belief in 'the boundless love of God and the universal mediation of Christ.' Feeling the need of a pastor, they solemnly set aside three young men considered fit for the office, and, after a day of consecration and prayer, determined by lot which of the three should be recognized as their pastor. The lot fell upon James Purves (1734–95). This was in 1769; and, as they desired to have direct recourse to the Scriptures of the prophets and apostles as the source of true knowledge, ecclesiastical and civil, Purves was directed to apply himself to the study of the original tongues, and for this purpose went to the University of Glasgow. In 1776, many families of the original body having settled in Edinburgh, he was appointed pastor over them, but did not relinquish his relation with the societies in the Merse. Purves having publicly advocated Universalist views, his congregation in 1792 adopted the title of Universal Dissenters. Later, in 1813, it became generally known as Unitarian. In 1812 T. Southwood Smith became minister of the congregation, the charge having been vacant since the death of Purves. During the period of his ministry he studied medicine, and, having graduated M.D. in 1816, became subsequently well known as a pioneer of sanitary reform. The congregation is now represented by St. Mark's Chapel, opened in 1835.[4]

Neil Douglas (1750–1823), who in 1809 seceded from the Relief Church, established Universalist congregations in Greenock and Glasgow, and preached in many other places. His successor, William Worrall († 1828), continued his work, and congregations were established in Glasgow, Greenock, Johnstone, Paisley, Ayr, and Falkirk, which united in an annual conference. He published three volumes of a periodical entitled *The Gospel Communicator*. Probably a survival of his activity is to be seen in the Universalist Church of Stenhousemuir, Larbert, the only congregation in the United Kingdom still bearing the title Universalist.

James Morison (1816–93) founded the Evangelical Union in 1843 on the basis of three universals: universal love of God, universal atonement of Christ, universal work of the Holy Ghost. Declaring that the sacrifice of Christ was for all men everywhere, Morison stops short of universal salvation; the obstacle, in his view, is not, as in Amyraldism, the lack of special grace in the individual, but 'unbelief, the only obstacle to salvation which the death of Christ has not removed.'[5]

6. Universalism in America.—The progress of Universalism in America has found a competent and judicious historian in Richard Eddy; hence its main lines may be readily traced and succinctly stated.

The first advocates of universal salvation were probably the German Baptists, called Dunkers or Tunkers,[6] who were settled in Germantown, Pa., as early as 1719, and there established a church. They brought or imported Universalist books from Germany, and among them was *The Everlasting Gospel*, attributed to Paul Siegvolk (see above). The translation and printing of this, which may

[1] Extracts, etc., were printed in 1798.
[2] D. Thom, *Sermons with Memoir*, London, 1863.

[1] *Eternal Hope*, London, 1878.
[2] *The Second Death and the Restitution of All Things*[12], London, 1887.
[3] *Our Catholic Inheritance in the Larger Hope*, London, 1888.
[4] *MS Register of Minutes, St. Mark's Chapel, Edinburgh; and Historical Account*, printed in 1908.
[5] W. Adamson, *Life of the Rev. Dr. James Morison*, London, 1898, p. 127.
[6] See art. SECTS (Christian).

be regarded as the primary document of American Universalism, is probably due to the influence of G. de Benneville, who, after having suffered persecution for preaching Universalism in France and Germany, settled in Pennsylvania in 1741. The title runs thus:

'The Everlasting Gospel, commanded to be preached by Jesus Christ, Judge of the Living and Dead, unto all creatures, Mark xvi. 15. concerning the Eternal Redemption found out by him, whereby Devil, Sin, Hell and Death, shall at last be abolished, and the whole Creation restored to its primitive Purity; being a testimony against the present Anti-christian World. Written in German by Paul Siegvolk, and translated into English by John S[echla]. Germantown: Printed by Christopher Sower, MDCCLIII.'

There is abundant evidence that in the latter half of the 18th cent. Universalism was spreading widely in the Episcopal, Congregational, and Presbyterian Churches. Controversy was roused especially by the anonymous publications of Charles Chauncy, of Boston (1705–87), *e.g.*, *Salvation for all Men* (1782). But the organization of societies on a basis distinctly Universalist is due to John Murray (1741–1815), who, deserted on account of his Rellyan views by his former friends in Whitefield's Connexion, and broken by domestic afflictions, had determined to seek refuge and obscurity in the New World. The ship that bore him and was making for New York was driven by a storm into shoal water off the coast of New Jersey. It became necessary to land part of the cargo, and of this Murray was left in charge. Wandering on shore, he came to a settlement called Good Luck, and met with its founder, an aged man named Thomas Potter, who, in addition to his farm buildings, had built a meeting-house, and confidently expected that the Lord would send him a preacher. He hailed Murray as the heaven-sent messenger of the gospel, and constrained him to preach. An inscription on a granite boulder now marks the spot where Potter and Murray met, and records that on 30th Sept. 1770 Murray first preached in America. For some time after this Murray itinerated as a preacher among orthodox Baptists, until in 1774 he settled at Gloucester, Mass., with a congregation many of whom had been already influenced by the teaching of Relly. Here in 1779 some of these joined with Murray in a church covenant; this marks the earliest form of organization among American Universalists.

Murray's later ministerial life was spent in Boston, but at this time a new centre of Universalist activity was formed in Philadelphia by the labours of Elhanan Winchester. Winchester's followers, who were at first known as Universal Baptists, joined the adherents of Murray in organizing 'The First Independent Church of Christ commonly called Universalists.' A convention, held in Philadelphia in 1790, drew up Articles of Faith and a plan of church government. The third of these Articles runs:

'We believe that there is One Mediator between God and man, the man Christ Jesus, in whom dwelleth all the fullness of the Godhead bodily; who, by giving himself a ransom for all, hath redeemed them to God by his blood; and who, by the merit of his death and the efficacy of his Spirit, will finally restore the whole human race to happiness.'

Murray and his adherents adopted these Articles in 1791, and subsequently altered them in a Rellyan direction. But the personal friendship of Murray and Winchester could not avert divergence between their followers; for, while Murray advocated a 'free and finished justification' obtained at once by the expiatory suffering of Christ, and summed up in the words 'no future punishment,' the adherents of Winchester suspected a perilous tendency to Antinomianism in these views, and Winchester's own teaching included an elaborate eschatology involving a millennial reign of Christ with the saints on earth, their ascent into the heavenly places, the conversion of this world into a lake of fire for the age-long punishment of devils and wicked men, and the ultimate purification and elevation of both to final sanctification.

Another view which would appear to be more definitely Antinomian in tendency than Murray's was propounded by Caleb Rich of Warwick, Mass. (1750–1821), and attained a certain local ascendancy. According to this, as at the creation the soul was inserted into the mortal frame, so now with each individual soul; it remains untainted by the deeds and desires of the flesh, and at the dissolution of its material envelope rises again to God in its original purity.[1]

Notwithstanding these divergencies, it is remarkable that in Aug. 1803 the Convention of Universalist Churches of New England, held at Winchester, N.H., in which 38 societies were represented, agreed upon a Profession of Faith which is still the standard of American Universalism. This, known as the Winchester Profession, is as follows:

'Article i.—We believe that the Holy Scriptures of the Old and New Testaments contain a revelation of the character of God and of the duty, interest, and final destination of mankind.

Article ii.—We believe that there is one God, whose nature is Love, revealed in one Lord Jesus Christ, by one Holy Spirit of Grace, who will finally restore the whole family of mankind to holiness and happiness.

Article iii.—We believe that holiness and true happiness are inseparably connected, and that believers ought to be careful to maintain order and practise good works; for these things are good and profitable unto men.'

The general consensus marked by the Winchester Profession prepared the way for a new departure, and for the commanding influence of a new leader in the person of Hosea Ballou (1771–1852). He published in 1805 *A Treatise on Atonement* (subsequently much revised). This little work severed Universalism from its origins in Calvinism, and lifted it from controversy to a level of affirmation and construction. It sought to build up a theology on the one postulate of God's universal and everlasting love. Ballou finds the reality of atonement not in the appeasing of God's wrath and the reconciliation of God to man, but in the reconciliation of man to God.

'To believe in any other Atonement than the putting off of the old man, with his deeds, and the putting on of the new man, which after God is created in righteousness and true holiness, is carnal-mindedness and is death.'[2]

While he emphasizes God's dealings with man in the way of moral discipline and retributive justice in the present life, and insists on the continuity of the divine judgment of the individual from day to day, he anticipates that death will in some way so quicken the powers of the soul and enlighten all spiritual faculties that nothing that can be called penal lies before it in a future state. Though he did not lay stress upon the doctrine of no future punishment, his implicit adherence to it had certain definite consequences. Ballou rejected the deity of Christ, and thus espoused Unitarianism some years before it became dominant in the Congregational churches of Boston. But the Unitarians were strongly opposed to Ballou's views as to death and the future life, and Channing went so far as to say that Ballou ascribed 'the power to death of changing and purifying the mind,' thus 'burying moral evil in the grave.' Another consequence was what is known as the 'Restorationist Controversy,' which proceeded intermittently from 1817 until 1831, and led to an actual division in the Universalist body. It began with a friendly controversy between Hosea Ballou and Edward Turner, published in a periodical called *The Gospel Visitant*. Ballou took the side of no future punishment, but declared that at that time he was not absolutely convinced on the subject.

1 Cf. with this the view attributed to Helen Burns, *i.e.* Maria Brontë, by her sister, Charlotte Brontë, in *Jane Eyre*, ch. vi.

2 *A Treatise on Atonement*[14], Boston, 1902, p. 123.

In 1822 a further stage was reached, in which Jacob Wood, who wrote under the name 'Restorationist,' gave evidence of the difference of opinion which at this time prevailed in the Universalist body, and of the incompatibility of the two doctrines—viz. that 'of universal salvation at the commencement of a future state' and that 'of the final restoration of all men by Jesus Christ,' adding:

'The doctrine which admits all characters alike to heaven at death, is subversive of a just distinction between virtue and vice.'

This diversity of opinion led to an actual schism. In 1831 a number of Universalist churches formed the Massachusetts Association of Universal Restorationists, which continued for ten years. The great majority, including many who had a doctrinal affinity with the Restorationists, strongly disapproved of the secession. The seceders, while adopting the Winchester Profession, altered, in 1833, the first clause of Art. iii. so as to read:

'We believe in a retribution beyond death, and in the necessity of faith and repentance.'

The 'no future punishment' creed disappeared in 1878 as the motto of Universalism, when the Universalist ministers of Boston and its vicinity approved a declaration of faith, in which these words occur:

'We believe that repentance and salvation are not limited to this life . . . Salvation, . . . whether effected here or in the future life, is salvation by Christ, and gives no warrant to the imputation to us of the "death and glory" theory.'

Art. ix. runs:

'Whatever differences in regard to the future may exist among us, none of us believe that the horizon of eternity will be relatively either largely or for a long time overcast by the clouds of sin and punishment, and in coming into the enjoyment of salvation, whensoever that may be, all the elements of penitence, forgiveness, and regeneration are involved. Justice and mercy will then be seen to be entirely at one, and God be all in all.'

Already for many years the objections to Universalism from the side of the Unitarians had been disappearing, as the views here stated were gaining ground among Universalists. The Universalists, combining a liberal faith with an evangelical fervour, appealed to many whom the drier light of Unitarianism did not reach, and without any formal alliance the two denominations have been constantly associated in social efforts and religious sympathy.

In 1903 a centennial meeting, held at Winchester, N.H., re-affirmed the Profession in its original form. In 1899 the following 'conditions of fellowship' had been appended to Art. iii. in a general convention held at Boston:

'The acceptance of the essential principles of the Universalist Faith, to wit: (1) The universal fatherhood of God; (2) the spiritual authority and leadership of His son, Jesus Christ; (3) the trustworthiness of the Bible as containing a revelation from God; (4) the certainty of just retribution for sin; (5) the final harmony of all souls with God.'

The latest statistics of the Universalist Church in America record the names of over 600 recognized ministers, and a still larger number of parishes and meeting-places; seven in Canada, some of which have fellowship with Universalist conventions in the United States. There are numerous women's missionary societies and mission circles; a regular mission is maintained in Japan, and a congregation has been formed in Cuba. There are also eight colleges, theological schools, and academies.[1]

LITERATURE.—Hosea Ballou, *The Ancient Hist. of Universalism*, Boston, U.S.A., 1829, new ed., 1885; T. Whittemore, *The Modern Hist. of Universalism*, do. 1830, 2nd ed. vol. i. (all published), do. 1860; Richard Eddy, *Hist. of Universalism* (American Church History Series, x.), New York, 1894, *Universalism in America*, 2 vols., Boston, 1884–86 (with a bibliography); T. Allin, *Universalism Asserted*[8], London, 1899; Lives of Murray, Ballou, etc.

JAMES EDWIN ODGERS.

[1] *Universalist Register and Year Book, 1918.*

UNIVERSALITY.—I. **Definition.**—The universal is defined by Aristotle as 'whatever may naturally be predicated of many things,'[1] or 'that is called universal which naturally belongs to more than one thing.'[2] The important word in these definitions is 'naturally.' It is explained by the following:

'I call that universal which belongs to the subject, distributively, essentially, and as it is what it is';[3] in scholastic terms, 'which is true *de omni, per se*, and *quatenus ipsum*.'

By *de omni* Aristotle means 'in every case and always.' *De omni* is merely the enumerative or collective universal. *Per se* and *quatenus ipsum* explain the 'naturally.' There are four senses of *per se*: (1) when the predicate is part of the definition of the subject, (2) when the subject is part of the definition of the predicate, (3) that which is not predicated of any other subject, (4) when the subject itself is the cause of the predicate. Aristotle says the expressions *per se* and *quatenus ipsum* are the same, but he seems to have in view *per se* in the first and the second sense only; for he has just said that whatever is universal is inherent in things necessarily, and subsequently he says that everything is inherent in either of those ways or according to accident, but accidents are not necessary.[4] This is what Aristotle means by universal in the strict sense—the primary universal, the universal as it occurs in mathematics, as when we say that triangles have their internal angles equal to two right angles, or that two contradictory predicates, 'straight' or 'curved,' imply the notion line.

Grote and Prantl reduce the third and fourth senses to the first. Grote says of the third:

'The predicate must not be extra-essential to the subject, nor attached to it as an adjunct from without, simply concomitant or accidental.'

Of the fourth sense he says:

'The like distinction holds in regard to events: some are accidentally concomitant sequences, which may or may not be realized (*e.g.*, a flash of lightning occurring when a man is on his journey); in others, the conjunction is necessary or causal (as when an animal dies under the sacrificial knife).'[5]

The same identifications are made by Prantl:

The latter explains the third sense of *per se* thus: 'what is enunciated not in predicative manner as property, but as individual substance, remains identical with itself in the multiplicity of possible predicates.'[6]

Prantl expressly identifies the fourth sense of *per se* with the first. The third and fourth are both regarded as resting upon the activity of the creative concept and its necessary causality.

The meaning of Aristotle seems to be this. In certain cases attributes are essentially conditioned by the nature of the subject in which they are found, but we do not see this. The predicates may not after all be true *de omni*. Similarly with regard to events. The nature of the living thing may essentially condition the effect of the wound, but after all it may not. Such wounds may not be always fatal. We cannot, therefore, make such universals the basis of a demonstrative science. We do not see the primary universals or the necessity which belongs to such universals.

This interpretation of Aristotle, common to Prantl and Grote, is in accordance with the scholastic treatment of demonstration, especially the *demonstratio potissima*. The property of risibility as flowing from the definition of man as a rational animal is an illustration of the third sense of *per se*. Risibility was supposed to belong to man essentially. This is certainly not evident in itself and has led to an extremely different interpretation of Aristotle, put forward by Saint-

[1] *De Interp.* vii. [2] *Met.* (vi.) vii. 13 (1038b).
[3] *Anal. Post.* i. 4.
[4] *Ib.* i. 4, 6; cf. H. Aldrich, *Artis Logicæ Rudimenta*[4], ed. H. L. Mansel, Oxford, 1862, Appendix K.
[5] George Grote, *Aristotle*, London, 1872, i. 312.
[6] Prantl, *Gesch. der Logik im Abendlande*, i. 122.

Hilaire and Mansel. With regard to the third sense of *per se*, both interpret it as referring to the existence of the substance. Saint-Hilaire says:

'The individual substance is never necessary; and, moreover, it is for itself alone, and is never in a subject other than itself.'

As to the fourth sense he says:

'No more does it carry in itself a character of necessity; thus in the example chosen by Aristotle, there is no necessity that the man die by strangulation; for there is a crowd of other totally different causes of death.'[1]

This would restrict the universal and the necessity it involves to the first two senses of the words *per se*. In this restriction Mansel agrees with Saint-Hilaire, and puts forward a theory of the demonstrative syllogism which limits it to the demonstrations of mathematics.

2. The two universals.—The truth is that Aristotle has two universals—the primary universal, where subject and predicate are co-extensive and convertible, which is characterized by necessity, and another universal in which this is not the case. In one passage he says:

'By universal, here, I mean that which is not convertible with its subject.'[2]

His object is to show that such a universal, unless it issues in a primary universal, is valueless for science. The universal in the strict sense belongs to mathematical science and other deductive sciences; the other universal belongs to the uniformities of co-existence and sequence which experimental science investigates. Locke, Dugald Stewart, and Mansel have regarded deductive science, especially mathematics, as involving an essentially distinct logical procedure from that of the inductive sciences. J. S. Mill seeks to reduce mathematics to the inductive level. Mediæval thought and Platonism tend to enlarge the scope of demonstration. The teaching of Aristotle is the same as that of Locke, Stewart, and Mansel.

It is this distinction of the two universals which some later logicians seem to have in view. Petrus Hispanus distinguishes between predicable and universal. Predicable is affirmed of many things, but universal exists in many things.[3] Others make the distinction turn upon whether in the proposition we tell of the subject *quid sit* or *quale sit*—what it is or what are its attributes or characters. According to this, that only is a universal which is predicated of inferior classes; but a predicable which is also predicated of co-ordinate classes would not be a universal. There are thus five predicables, but only two universals—genus and species.[4]

3. The problem of universals.—The above doctrine of universals considers the universal as its nature is affected by the precise relation in which the predicate can stand to the subject in a proposition; and the distinction of universals which it sets up affects the consideration of universals taken in their widest sense. The most difficult problem relating to universals—a problem still unsettled—is that concerning their existence. Do they exist only in the mind? If outside the mind, where? Are they mere names?

4. Plato and Aristotle.—

'Two things,' says Aristotle, 'may be fairly ascribed to Socrates—inductive arguments and universal definition, both of which are concerned with the starting-point of science. But Socrates did not make the universals or the definitions exist apart; his successors, however, gave them separate existence, and this was the kind of thing they called Ideas.'[5]

1 J. Barthélemy Saint-Hilaire, *Logique d'Aristote traduite en Français*, Paris, 1839–44, iii. 24.
2 *Anal. Post.* ii. 17.
3 Petrus Hispanus, *Summulæ logicales*, tract. ii.; cf. R. Sanderson, *Logicæ Artis Compendium*, Oxford, 1707, bk. i. ch. ii.
4 Burgersdyk, quoted by Mansel in Aldrich, *Artis Logicæ Rudimenta*, p. 24.
5 *Metaphysica*, 1078b 28, tr. W. D. Ross, Oxford, 1908.

'They at the same time treat the Ideas as universal substances, and again as separable and individual. That this is not possible has been shown before. The reason why those who say the Ideas are universal combined those two views in one, is that they did not make the Ideas substances identical with sensible things. They thought that the sensible particulars were in a state of flux and none of them remained, but that the universal was apart from these and different. And Socrates gave the impulse to this theory, as we said before, by means of his definitions, but he did not *separate* them from the particulars; and in this he thought rightly, in not separating them.'[1]

These remarks of Aristotle are aimed at the Platonic theory of Ideas—the theory as expounded in the earlier dialogues. Whether in the later dialogues the Platonic theory undergoes a change we shall consider below. Aristotle knows of no such change. Plato's theory as conceived by Aristotle is as follows:

Plato supposed that there existed, besides the individual things of sense, which are continually changing and passing away, another kind of beings, apart from matter and movement, which he termed Forms or Ideas, by participation in which each individual and sensible thing is made to be what it is. These Ideas are eternal and self-subsistent. Material things participate in them, and are copies of the Ideas, which in themselves exist in an intelligible region apart from the world. When we, on perceiving sensible things, form general concepts, we, according to Plato, revive by reminiscence the recollection of the Ideas, with which we were familiar in a previous state. What we term a general concept is the Idea in its subjective existence as an intelligible form in our intellect. Archer Butler[2] and others have distinguished the Platonic Idea from the general concepts of the understanding; but this separation is rejected by Bonitz and Zeller.[3]

Whatever may be thought of this theory, it is remarkable that the most essential objections to it have been brought forward by Plato himself in the *Parmenides*.

'Perhaps,' says Jowett, 'there is no passage in Plato showing greater metaphysical power than that in which he assails his own theory of Ideas. The arguments are nearly, if not quite, those of Aristotle.'[4]

The difficulties—how without division or multiplication the Ideas can participate in the many, or the many in the Ideas; the necessity of a still higher universal to unite the Idea itself with its corresponding phenomena; the so-called third-man argument; most serious of all, the uselessness of Ideas for knowledge, arising from their disconnexion with our minds and with phenomena—are here set forth.

'The perplexities,' says Jowett, 'which surround the one and many in the sphere of the Ideas are also alluded to in the Philebus, and no answer is given to them. Nor have they ever been answered by any one else who separates the phenomenal from the real.'[5]

This statement may be allowed to stand, but the question arises: Did Plato separate the phenomenal and the real, or did he unite them? The answer is: He did both. 'Separation' is a category of the spatial and temporal. The Idea is spaceless and timeless,[6] yet it does not exist in total aloofness from phenomena. It is in this way that we answer the difficulties which have been raised in this connexion, and which have led to the theory of a 'later Platonism.' There is in reality no essential change. The force of these objections—perhaps derived from the Megaric school, perhaps pressed home by Aristotle—was no doubt felt by him. But what happened in this case is what in such cases always happens. The old point of view is retained and an effort is made to show that it answers the new questions. In this respect there is a striking parallel between the later philosophy of Plato and that of Fichte. Originally, in Fichte, the Ego projects from itself a purely phenomenal world. Schelling showed

1 *Metaphysica*, 1086a 32.
2 *Lectures on the Hist. of Ancient Philosophy*2, p. 370 f.
3 *Plato and the Older Academy*, Eng. tr., London, 1876, p. 241, note 42.
4 *The Dialogues of Plato*3, tr. B. Jowett, Oxford, 1892, iv. 5 (Introd. to *Parmenides*).
5 *Ib.* p. 7.
6 *The Parmenides of Plato*, ed. T. Maguire, Dublin, 1878, p. xxvi.

that the world in its turn produces the Ego, and thus 'turned over a leaf' in the history of philosophy. The Absolute is in the world, therefore, as well as in the Ego. Fichte in his later philosophy seeks to show that his Absolute—the Ego, pure Being—is the active living power in phenomena. In the *Philebus*, *Sophist*, and *Timæus* Plato does the same. The Idea is spaceless and timeless, but nevertheless one with mind and life and power in the phenomenal world.

It is just in this that the change wrought in the philosophical standpoint by Aristotle consists. He denies the transcendent existence of the Idea or universal, and places it in the composite world of matter and form. The world thereby ceases to be merely phenomenal. Matter itself becomes something positive. It is no longer a mere negativity. The centre of gravity has passed from the ideal to the real world. Both Plato's and Aristotle's doctrines have been called realism. Both affirm the reality of the Idea or Form; but in Plato it is a reality above the world, in Aristotle in the world. Aristotle rejects the detached existence of the universal. He holds that the subjective concept is related to the objective reality, but in place of the transcendent existence of the Ideas, in contradistinction to individual objects, he regards the Essence or Form as immanent in the things. The precise nature of this immanence, in Aristotle, has been a matter of dispute. According to Hamilton,[1] he has been viewed as 'a Realist, a Conceptualist, and a Nominalist, in the strictest sense.' The questions at issue are formulated by Porphyry thus: whether genera and species do really exist in nature, or in mere conceptions only; whether, if existing, they are bodies or incorporeal; whether they are inherent in the objects of sense or disjoined from them.[2] Even though Aristotle brought down the Idea from its super-celestial sphere and embodied it in things, it still has an existence in the Divine Being, the Form of Forms. If the Divine Mind be one with things, *i.e.*, if Aristotle be interpreted pantheistically, we have still the questions as to the nature of this union—the unity and multiplicity of the Idea. If the Divine Mind be different from things—*i.e.*, if he be interpreted theistically—the Idea has a transcendent existence, if not in itself, still in the Divine Mind where the unification of the Idea lies; and what is the nature of it is the subject of the great controversy between nominalism and realism in the Middle Ages. The difficulty consists in this: that, if the universal is merely something repeated over and over again, in individuals, then genera and species fall asunder into merely resembling individuals, essential community of nature is denied; but, if such repetition be rejected, and the universal be considered as some one thing throughout the individuals, then the plurality becomes merely phenomenal and illusive. Extreme representatives of realism, like William of Champeaux, held that the universal exists for itself as a universal in individual things, and were thus led into pantheism.[3]

5. Moderate realism.—In the moderate realism of St. Thomas Aquinas we have a fusion of Aristotelian and Platonic realism. St. Augustine had already interpreted Plato's Ideas as the thoughts which God had of things before He created them. St. Thomas Aquinas admits the existence of the universal or the Form in a threefold sense, *ante rem*, *in re*, and *post rem*.[4] The universal *ante rem* corresponds to the Platonic Ideas, understood as archetypal ideas in the mind of God—the patterns

[1] Reid's *Works*, ed. Hamilton, p. 405, note 1.
[2] Porphyry, *Introd.* ch. i.
[3] Prantl, ii. 130.
[4] *Ib.* iii. 110 ff.

in the Divine Intellect after which all things were made. With regard to the universal *in re* or *a parte rei*, the universal nature does not exist as the same in the individuals as it exists in them objectively. It is only alike in them. We, in our consideration of it, regard it as a unity or community of nature, as one and the same in all. The universal nature exists as a universal, in the human intellect, by virtue of its power of recognizing the common nature. This is the universal *post res*. But, if the universal, as universal, exists thus only in the act of recognition in the mind, we seem to be impaled on the difficulty of Parmenides, which he put to the youthful Socrates, and which is briefly this: What then is this common nature which is known by the mind? Moderate realism answers this question by its doctrine that universals are fundamentally in things. 'Universalia sunt formaliter in mente fundamentaliter in rebus ipsis.'

> 'To the universal nature thus fundamentally taken, it does not essentially belong, to be one or many, in the intellect or out of the intellect, in individuals or outside them, communicable to a number or incommunicable.'[1]

If we ponder on this universal, we shall not find it so very different from the timeless and spaceless Idea of the *Philebus* and *Sophistes*. At any rate, it approaches the conception by which Plato sought to allay the difficulties and doubts he himself raised in the *Parmenides*.

6. The Scotist formalism.—It was almost inevitable that this doctrine, placing at the roots of things an Essence or Form in itself subject to no individualizing conditions, should beget a new form of realism. This is precisely what did happen. Duns Scotus distinguishes carefully between the unity of an individual and the unity of a universal nature. The last he conceives almost as certain modern logicians conceive the unity of a variable in a propositional function. The universal appears in the particular individual things, but it is apprehended as universal by the understanding. In itself it is neither particular nor universal, but just what it is. It is something antecedent to universality and particularity, but, as antecedent in itself, indifferent to either.[2] This is what distinguishes the realism of Duns Scotus from the earlier realism of Bernard of Chartres or William of Champeaux, that universals are not apprehended as *actu* such in objective reality.[3] This would be to reduce them to individual unities; or, rather, numerically the same nature would pervade the individuals. In the system of Duns Scotus a primitive universal unity — matter — is progressively pluralized and individualized by form, almost as a single throb of Bergson's *élan vital* is broken into its manifold reverberations in nature. Each throb, however, is in Scotus a system of unities; and it is evident that these universals, if they are neither to be pluralized in the individuals nor consolidated into a single being in a real universal, must be conceived as passing over into the individuals, and yet as each retaining its own unity in them. This is the view that underlies the doctrine of formalism elaborated in the Scotist school. Universality is thus conceived as in the things, not by a distinction of reason, as moderate realism would hold, not by a *distinctio realis*, as extreme realism would hold, but by a formal distinction, which still allowed it to be identified with the series of individual things.

7. The realism of Francis de Mayronis.—It is obvious that such a view approaches very close to

[1] Thomas Marie Zigliara, *Summa Philosophica*, 3 vols., Paris, 1884, i. 317.
[2] Prantl, iii. 208.
[3] Stöckl, *Gesch. der Philosophie des Mittelalters*, ii. 802; cf Couturat's *variable* (*Encycl. of the Philos. Sciences*, i. 148 f.).

the doctrine which regards the universal as such as existing in things, and, if we regard this universal as numerically one with the universal as contemplated by the Divine Mind, we are in danger of being led back to a pantheism such as was actually held by Bernard of Chartres. If now we are to escape such pantheistic conclusions, there is one, and only one, way of escape within the same general point of view: it is to give the universal a self-existence, as Plato did, independent of the Divine or any mind. This step was taken by the greatest of the disciples of Scotus—Francis de Mayronis. Relations are divided by Mayronis into *relationes secundum esse* and *relationes secundum dici.* The former are between things which in their entire being fall under the category of relation; the latter are between things which, taken by themselves, are absolute, but are understood with reference to something else and remain entitatively distinct from the relation into which they enter.[1] This corresponds to what has been recently called the monistic and the monadistic view of relations. To Mayronis, however, it is a classification of relations, not of theories about relation. Such relations are moreover real, not mere *relationes rationis,* and have a being distinct from the existence of the things between which they exist. The relation between the subject and object of knowledge is so distinct from its terms that it exists separately—from which it follows that ideas are veritable entities.[2] Universals in themselves therefore exist neither in the soul nor in things. They are not a something as against another something; but they are something as against nothing or as against a mere mode or manner of being. They are eternal in the negative sense of being timeless. They are not necessary, nor are they contingent. They have an intelligible being from themselves essentially distinct from God. With Duns Scotus, Mayronis distinguishes between *esse essentiæ* and *esse existentiæ.* It is the latter *esse* that comes from God. To the same kind of being—*esse essentiæ*—belongs the *primum principium complexum, i.e.* the principle of contradiction, which he regards as a hypothetical copulative proposition.[3] In all this we may see in Francis de Mayronis a mediæval 'new realist.'

8. Nominalism.—The realism of the Scotists tends towards pantheism or else to the setting up of uncreated entities independent of the Divine Mind. The only other course is to identify completely the universal with individual things, *i.e.* to give up the universal as such, to recognize only individual things—the doctrine of nominalism. It has been sometimes questioned whether mediæval nominalism is really nominalism and not rather conceptualism. With regard to the early nominalism, it is hard to put any other interpretation on the opinion attributed to Roscellinus by Anselm, that universals are *flatus vocis.* His pupil Abelard is supposed to have approached more nearly to the conceptualist standpoint. But what is cited in support of this points really the other way. Abelard bases his view on that definition of the universal which is given by Aristotle and quoted at the beginning of this article, and which is based on the proposition. What Abelard seems to mean is that the universality arises from the universal statements we are able to make, and not from anything intrinsic in the thing. This metaphysical denial implicitly carries with it the rejection of conceptualism. And the same implicit rejection must be attributed to Occam, although

[1] Stöckl, ii. 869.

[2] Rousselot, *Etudes sur la Philosophie dans le moyen âge,* iii. 71; Hauréau, *De la Philosophie scolastique,* ii. 392.

[3] Prantl, iii. 285-287.

Hamilton says that 'the later Nominalists, of the school of Occam, were really Conceptualists.'[1] Occam's doctrine is called 'terminism.' The *conceptus* is *id quod terminat actum intelligendi.* This is not something that exists *subjectively* in the mind, but something that exists *objectively.* The universality is not therefore something in the mind, but is the result of the act of the mind by which it gives signification to the term. It is in accordance with this that he claims for understanding an intuitive knowledge of objects of sense, rejects *species sensibilis* and *species intelligibilis,* merges the *intellectus possibilis* in the *intellectus agens.*[2]

9. Modern philosophy; the psychological problem.—All the problems of modern philosophy have been set to it by mediæval philosophy. The problem of the universals is no exception. The schools of Aquinas, Scotus, and Occam present to modern philosophy a problem which had to be solved psychologically. What constitutes the community of nature between general thoughts within us and things outside us? We have seen that, metaphysically, philosophy has been driven in Occam to give up the belief in a common nature in things.

(1) *Hobbes.*—In modern philosophy we find the psychological consequence in Hobbes. The idea of a common nature in thoughts is given up. Thoughts are as individual as things. 'There is nothing,' says Hobbes, 'universal but names.'[3]

(2) *Locke.*—To Locke, on the other hand, all knowledge consists in the perception of the agreement or disagreement of ideas. Names can be general only if they stand for general ideas. Locke has been termed a nominalist. It has even been stated that he could be interpreted as a realist. But, if conceptualism means finding the universal in the idea, then Locke is what he has been generally considered, a conceptualist.

According to Locke, 'the mind makes the particular ideas received from particular objects to become general . . . by considering them as they are in the mind, such appearances, separate from all other existences, and the circumstances of real existence, as time, place, or any other concomitant ideas. This is called abstraction, whereby ideas taken from particular beings become general representations of all of the same kind, and their names general names, applicable to whatever exists conformable to such abstract ideas.'[4] 'General ideas are fictions and contrivances of the mind, that carry difficulty with them, and do not so easily offer themselves as we are apt to imagine. For example, does it not require some pains and skill to form the general idea of a triangle (which is yet none of the most abstract, comprehensive, and difficult), for it must be neither oblique nor rectangle, neither equilateral, equicrural nor scalenon; but all and none of these at once? In effect, it is something imperfect, that cannot exist; an idea wherein some parts of several different and inconsistent ideas are put together.'[5]

(3) *Berkeley.*—This doctrine Berkeley, the protagonist of modern nominalism, attacked in the Introduction to *The Principles of Human Knowledge.*

'Whether others have this wonderful faculty of abstracting their ideas, they best can tell. For myself I find indeed I have a faculty of imagining, or representing to myself, the idea of those particular things I have perceived, and of variously compounding and dividing them. I can imagine a man with two heads; or the upper parts of a man joined to the body of a horse. I can consider the hand, the eye, the nose, each by itself abstracted or separated from the rest of the body. But then whatever hand or eye I imagine, it must have some particular shape and colour. Likewise the idea of a man that I frame to myself, must be either of a white, or a black, or a tawny, a straight, or a crooked, a tall, or a low, or a middle-sized man. I cannot by any effort of thought conceive the abstract idea above described. And it is equally impossible for me to form the abstract idea of motion distinct from the body moving, and which is neither swift nor slow, curvilinear nor rectilinear; and the like may be said of all other abstract

[1] Reid's *Works*[8], p. 406, note 2.

[2] Stöckl, ii. 988, 992. 3.

[3] Hobbes, *Human Nature,* London, 1650, ch. v. § 6 (*English Works,* ed. Sir W. Molesworth, London, 1839-45, iv. 22).

[4] *Essay concerning Human Understanding,* London, 1690, bk. ii. ch. xi. § 9.

[5] Bk. iv. ch. vii. § 9.

general ideas whatsoever. To be plain, I own myself able to abstract in one sense, as when I consider some particular parts or qualities separated from others, with which, though they are united in some object, yet it is possible they may really exist without them. But I deny that I can abstract from one another, or conceive separately, those qualities which it is impossible should exist so separated; or that I can frame a general notion, by abstracting from particulars in the manner aforesaid—which last are the two proper acceptations of *abstraction.*'[1]

Berkeley explains precisely what he means by universality:

'It is, I know, a point much insisted on, that all knowledge and demonstration are about universal notions, to which I fully agree. But then it does not appear to me that those notions are formed by abstraction in the manner premised—*universality*, so far as I can comprehend, not consisting in the absolute, positive nature or conception of anything, but in the relation it bears to the particulars signified or represented by it; by virtue whereof it is that things, names, or notions, being in their own nature *particular*, are rendered universal.'[2]

In the edition of 1734 he says:

'And here it must be acknowledged that a man may *consider* a figure merely as triangular; without attending to the particular qualities of the angles or relations of the sides. *So far he may abstract.* But this will never prove that he can frame an abstract, general, inconsistent *idea* of a triangle. In like manner we may consider Peter so far forth as man, or so far forth as animal, without framing the forementioned abstract idea, either of man or of animal; inasmuch as all that is perceived is not considered.'[3]

(4) *Hume.*—Berkeley's doctrine on this subject was pronounced by Hume to be 'one of the greatest and most valuable discoveries that have been made of late years in the republic of letters,' and he believes that he himself adopts it; but Hume's view was essentially different. Berkeley had said that all general *names* signify indifferently a great number of particular ideas.'[4] Hume attributes to him the opinion 'that all general ideas are nothing but particular ones, annexed to a certain term, which gives them a more extensive signification, and makes them recall upon occasion other individuals, which are similar to them.'[5] This is Hume's own doctrine. He holds that the idea before the mind is always some particular idea. Abstract ideas are in themselves individual, but, when we have found a resemblance among several objects, we apply the same name to all. The name, being applied to other individuals, different in some respects from the idea we have first on hearing it, does not revive the idea of all these individuals, but the custom of applying the name to them and a readiness to survey any of them, which produces any other individual one for which we have occasion. It is clear that Hume differs from Berkeley in this, that he does not recognize, as Berkeley did, the power the mind has of regarding the individual idea as representing and standing for the class to which it belongs. In Hume the idea is particular, and only possesses the power in association with the name of calling up other particular ideas. The nominalist doctrine, as it appears in Berkeley and Hume respectively, determines the counter-conceptualist doctrines of Reid and Brown.

(5) *Reid.*—Reid contends that Berkeley unwillingly or unwarily grants all that is necessary to support abstract and general conceptions:

'If a man may consider a figure merely as triangular, he must have some conception of this object of his consideration; for no man can consider a thing which he does not conceive. He has a conception, therefore, of a triangular figure, merely as such. I know no more that is meant by an abstract general conception of a triangle.' 'He who considers Peter so far forth as man, or so far forth as animal, must conceive the meaning of those abstract general words *man* and *animal*, and he who conceives the meaning of them has an abstract general conception.'[6]

(6) *Brown.*—According to Brown, the feeling of resemblance in certain respects is the true general notion, or general idea, as it has been less properly called, which the corresponding general term expresses.[1] Brown holds that between the perception of two or more objects and the invention and employment of the general term there must rise in the mind an intervening general notion of resemblance, the feeling or notion of the resemblance being immediately subsequent to the perception. It is the omission of this stage of the process that constitutes in his view the error of the nominalists. Thus, as Reid regards the power of considering a figure merely as triangular, or Peter merely as man, as a proof of having the abstract and general conception, so Brown regards the circumstance of felt resemblance between two or more objects as the general notion of such objects. Brown has been criticized by Hamilton, but J. S. Mill in his *Logic* has been influenced by Brown's view.[2]

(7) *James Mill.*—James Mill held that a general idea is that of a combination of individuals belonging to the class. The word 'man' calls up the ideas of an indefinite number of individuals. The name 'man' is the name of every individual and of the whole combination.[3] This confounds general and collective terms. 'Tree' does not mean a wood.

(8) *Hamilton.*—According to Sir W. Hamilton, the opposing parties are really at one. The whole controversy arises from not distinguishing the images of sense and the unpicturable notions of intelligence. The solution depends on the distinction expressed in German by the terms *Begriff* and *Anschauung.* The images of the imagination, which were what Berkeley and the nominalists meant by ideas, are individual.[4]

If it were only this distinction that was wanting, the controversy would have ended long ago. Not to mention the schoolmen, the distinction was present to Berkeley himself.[5] The really important question is, What is the relation between thought proper or pure intellection and imagination? Is the image always necessary to the realization of the concept? Hamilton held that it was:

'The concept *horse*, I say, cannot, if it remain a concept, that is a universal attribution, be represented in imagination; but, except it be represented in imagination, it cannot be applied to any object, and, except it be so applied, it cannot be realised in thought at all.'[6]

This is what Hamilton termed the 'relativity of concepts.'

(9) *J. S. Mill.*—When this view of the relativity of the concept to the image is adopted, there is but little difference between the conceptualism of Hamilton and the nominalism of J. S. Mill.

According to Mill, 'We have only complex ideas of objects in the concrete: but we are able to attend exclusively to certain parts of the concrete idea: and by that exclusive attention, we enable those parts to determine exclusively the course of our thoughts as subsequently called up by association; and are in a condition to carry on a train of meditation or reasoning relating to those parts only, exactly as if we were able to conceive them separately from the rest.'[7]

The distinction between Hamilton's view and Mill's thus reduces itself to that of 'a potential universality as against an universal potentiality,' but in neither writer is there an attempt to account for or to show the necessity of the relativity of the concept, or, what is the same thing, the power of a partial consideration of an idea to lead out beyond it.

(10) *Mansel.*—A different view of the relation

1 Berkeley, *Works*[2], ed. Fraser, i. 242.
2 *Ib.* i. 247. 3 *Ib.* i. 249. 4 *Ib.* p. 250.
5 *Treatise of Human Nature*, ed. Green and Grose, i. 325.
6 *Works*[8], p. 408.

1 *Lectures on the Philosophy of the Human Mind*[19], Edinburgh, 1856, p. 296.
2 Hamilton, *Lectures on Metaphysics*, ii. 303 ff.; J. S. Mill, *System of Logic*, bk. i. ch. v. § 3, bk. ii. ch. ii. § 3 note; cf. W. S. Jevons, *Pure Logic*, London, 1864, pp. 133–135.
3 James Mill, *Analysis of the Phenomena of the Human Mind*, new ed., London, 1869, i. 268.
4 *Ib.* ii. 296 ff.
5 Berkeley, *Works*[2], ed. Fraser, ii. 325.
6 Hamilton, *Lectures on Logic*, i. 135.
7 Mill, *An Examination of Sir William Hamilton's Philosophy*[4], London, 1872, p. 393.

between the concept and the image is taken by Mansel:

'I see lying on the table before me a number of shillings of the same coinage. Examined severally, the image and superscription of each is undistinguishable from that of its fellow; but in viewing them side by side, *space* is a necessary condition of my perception; and the difference of locality is sufficient to make them distinct, though similar, individuals. The same is the case with any representative image whether in a mirror, in a painting, or in the imagination waking or dreaming. It can only be depicted as occupying a certain place; and thus as an individual, and the representation of an individual. It is true I cannot say it represents this particular coin rather than that; and consequently it may be considered as the representative of all, successively but not simultaneously. To find a representative which shall embrace all at once, I must divest it of the condition of occupying space. . . . If we substitute Time for Space the same remarks will be equally applicable to the objects of our internal consciousness.'[1]

Mansel seems thus to have thought that the concept embraces all objects under it, simultaneously. But, if this were so, it would be a collective, not a general, concept. In the case selected—the shillings—the image may be regarded as identical with the concept, and this image and concept are alike indifferently representative of any shilling. As Hamilton says:

'The whole generality [of concepts] consists in this—that though we must realise them in thought under some singular of the class, we may do it under any.'[2]

(11) *Problem of the synthetic power of the concept; Hegel and Lotze.*—This, however, raises the important question of what is meant by 'realising under.' Mansel's doctrine is that the concept, to become universal, must be divested of all present relation to the image. The latter is only called in to verify its possibility. The existence of such imageless thought has been the subject of important investigation by H. J. Watt and others of the Würzburg school.[3] Without entering into the psychological inquiry, it may be pointed out that there must be some element in the concept by which it relates itself to the image and some element in the image by which it corresponds to the concept. Many are inclined to find this element in tendency or will, as that which gives vitality and meaning to the concept. It would be nearer the truth to say that will is will, and tendency is tendency, only through the concept. We have already remarked that Hamilton did not attempt to explain the relativity of the concept. It is nevertheless the underlying problem of his 'law of the conditioned' and 'conditions of the thinkable systematized.' It may be said to be the fundamental principle of Hegel's *Logic*. And it is precisely this feature of the concept as a sort of intussuscipient principle that Lotze has in view when he says:

'Of the true universal, on the other hand, which contains the rule for the entire formation of its species, it may rather be said that its content is always precisely as rich, the sum of its marks precisely as great, as that of its species themselves; only that the universal concept, the genus, contains a number of marks in a merely indefinite and even universal form; these are represented in the species by definite values or particular characterisations, and finally in the singular concept all indefiniteness vanishes, and each universal mark of the genus is replaced by one fully determined in quantity, individuality, and relation to others.'[4]

In the last chapter of the *Posterior Analytics* Aristotle asserts the existence of a faculty—the organ of primary truths, the basis of demonstrative science—by means of which reason can pierce the objects of sense and penetrate to the universal and the cause. The whole of mediæval philosophy assumes such a power. Aquinas, Scotus, Occam, all alike imply it. Modern philosophy uniformly rejects it. Empiricism expressly denies it. Idealism denies any real essences distinct from thought.

1 *Prolegomena Logica*², p. 16 f.
2 *Lectures on Logic*, i. 129.
3 See F. Aveling, *On the Consciousness of the Universal and the Individual.*
4 Lotze, *Logic*², Eng. tr. ed. B. Bosanquet, Oxford, 1888, i. 52.

But, if intellect and its laws are in correlation with, and form an organic unity with, space, if the inner essences of things and the forces which control them determine, and are determined by, spatial relations,[1] it will follow that the formulæ of physical and chemical text-books are no mere descriptive statement, no mere analytical elaboration of working concepts, but that these concepts are, as Hegel, Hamilton, and Lotze by implication describe them, concepts of entities and forms of energy which really exist, move, and are moved.

LITERATURE.—Plato, *Opera omnia*⁴, 10 vols., ed. G. Stallbaum, Gotha, 1858–60; T. Gomperz, *Greek Thinkers*, tr. L. Magnus and G. G. Berry, London, 1901–12, ii., iii.; W. Archer Butler, *Lectures on the Hist. of Ancient Philosophy*², ed. W. H. Thompson, 2 vols., do. 1874; T. Maguire, *An Essay on the Platonic Idea*, do. 1866; Aristotle, *Organon, Metaphysica, De Anima*; John I. Beare, *Greek Theories of Elementary Cognition*, Oxford, 1906; X. Rousselot, *Etudes sur la Philosophie dans le moyen âge*, 3 vols., Paris, 1840–42; B. Hauréau, *De la Philosophie scolastique*, 3 vols., do. 1850; A. Stöckl, *Gesch. der Philosophie des Mittelalters*, 3 vols., Mainz, 1864–66; C. Prantl, *Gesch. der Logik im Abendlande*, 4 vols., Leipzig, 1855–70; Locke, *Essay concerning Human Understanding*, ed. A. C. Fraser, 2 vols., Oxford, 1894; Berkeley, *Works*, ed. A. C. Fraser, 4 vols., do. 1871, ²1901; Hume, *A Treatise of Human Nature*, ed. T. H. Green and T. H. Grose, 2 vols., new impression, London, 1909; Reid, *Works*⁸, ed. Sir W. Hamilton, Edinburgh, 1880; W. Hamilton, *Lectures on Metaphysics and Logic*, 4 vols., do. 1859; H. L. Mansel, *Prolegomena Logica*², Oxford, 1860; Antonio Aliotta, *The Idealistic Reaction against Science*, tr. Agnes McCaskill, London, 1914; Francis Aveling, *On the Consciousness of the Universal and the Individual*, do. 1912.

GEORGE J. STOKES.

UNIVERSE. — See COSMOGONY AND COSMOLOGY, ESCHATOLOGY, NATURE.

UNPARDONABLE SIN.—See SIN (Christian).

UPANIṢADS.

UPANIṢADS.—The Sanskrit treatises or dialogues known as the *Upaniṣads* are the expression of the philosophical speculation of Indian sages and teachers during many centuries. The period of their fullest fruition, when with most originality and insight Hindu thinkers proposed to themselves and to the circle of their pupils solutions of the world's greatest mysteries, both mental and spiritual, is supposed to have been from the 8th to the 6th cent. before our era. The *terminus a quo* is the age of the *Brāhmaṇas*; for the *Upaniṣad* literature appears as tertiary strata after the early Vedic poetry and the prose treatises of the *Brāhmaṇas* with their minute ritual and ceremonial observances. The strata perpetually overlap, and the limits suggested are to be understood only in a broad and general sense. There can be little doubt, moreover, that substantially the earliest *Upaniṣads* antedate the rise and extension of Buddhism in the 5th and following centuries. Buddhist teaching appears in the most important respects to be dependent on doctrines and premisses already formulated and expounded in the older *Upaniṣad* literature. There are many, however, and perhaps insuperable difficulties in the way of drawing up a precise genealogical scheme of doctrinal and literary development in India or for its sacred books. In their present form neither the Buddhist nor the more ancient *Upaniṣad* treatises are free from the contamination of later elements. For the majority of the *Upaniṣads* no such early origin can be claimed, although all or practically all give more or less definite expression to ancient speculative thought. Many that pass under the name are of comparatively recent date, originating in the early centuries of the Christian era. Some also are to be referred to an altogether later time.

1. Title and date.—With regard to the meaning and implication of the title *Upaniṣad* itself there is little or no doubt. It is derived from the

1 See artt. SPACE, POWER.

Sanskrit root *sad*, 'to sit down,' 'to be seated,' with the prefixed prepositions *upa* and *ni*. Originally therefore it implied the sitting down at the feet of the teacher, the attitude of the pupil who respectfully listens to his master's words. In ordinary usage, however, the word is employed to express the doctrine itself which the teacher inculcates, and, finally, mystical or secret doctrine in general. It is in this sense that the *Upaniṣad* teaching is the *Vedānta*, the end (*anta*) and aim of the Veda, the substance and sum of all true wisdom; and in practice, and in all the Brāhmanical literature, the word is thus confined to the highest and most abstract teaching or knowledge, the speculative doctrines which are regarded as within the province of *śruti*, divine revelation. Its use as a title of the treatises in which the doctrines are conveyed may be compared to the Greek εὐαγγέλιον, or the English 'Gospel.'

The native Indian equivalent of *upaniṣad* is *rahasyam*, 'secret,' 'hidden.' The latter term apparently always connotes the idea of secrecy or concealment of a text or doctrine, the knowledge of which should be communicated only to those who are accounted worthy. Thus in one passage it is enjoined that the father shall teach the doctrine to his eldest son, 'but to no one else, whoever he may be.'[1] This conception of a secret or esoteric knowledge has always determined the treatment by the Hindus of their sacred writings, and in many of the sects is maintained to this day as an inviolable principle of their religion.[2]

The number of these treatises is very considerable. A late collection cites more than 100 names. And, if all works, early or late, that inculcate mystical teaching or propound special theories or doctrines concerning the unseen are to be regarded as having just claim to the title *Upaniṣad*, there would seem to be no reason why such treatises should not be indefinitely multiplied at the present time. The total number, according to Barth,[3] 'amounts to nearly 250,' including an 'Allah' *Upaniṣad*, assigned to the time of Akbar. Most of the later *Upaniṣads* are sectarian in character, and with more or less fidelity expound *Upaniṣad* doctrine from the point of view of the popular religions, exalting Viṣṇu or Śiva, or endeavouring to promote the discipline and teaching of the Yoga, or with other limited aim. Many are attached more especially to the *Atharvaveda*, and of these the majority are of comparatively late origin. The treatises quoted or referred to by Śaṅkara in the 9th cent. in his commentaries on the sacred texts are usually and no doubt correctly supposed to be the oldest. They all, however, contain earlier and later material, strata of thought or language which have been worked up and welded together, and have all undergone modification and interpolation at the hands of later teachers and revisers. These older works are few in number, and together with some of the earlier Atharvan treatises may be regarded as forming the *Upaniṣad* group of the sacred writings in the more restricted sense of the term.[4]

2. Authorship.—Of the authors of these treatises nothing is known with certainty. Many names of teachers or authorities have been preserved, and in some instances the documents themselves contain lists or genealogical tables of descent, which trace the origin of their doctrine and confirm its authority by appeal to ancient divine sanction. It is probable that for a considerable period the teaching was entirely oral, within the care and custody of the schools of learning. The names recorded, so far as they are genuine, are those of the heads of the several schools. Within these schools the doctrines taught were regarded as a sacred and secret trust. On this subject most of the older treatises contain strict and similar injunctions. In the more ancient *Upaniṣads* also the instruction is generally conveyed in the form of dialogue, the teacher replying to the questions or answering the doubts of his disciples, who seek from him an exposition of the highest knowledge or a solution of the problems and mysteries of this life and of the future after death; sometimes also, in Socratic fashion, the teacher is himself the questioner. Essentially therefore the dialogues represent and give expression to the unsatisfied longings of the human mind and heart.

3. Classification.—It is usual to classify these older treatises in three or four groups, which may be distinguished not only by the character and fullness or otherwise of their teaching, but by the style and diction which they employ, and the more or less archaic nature of their composition. It is not possible, however, to go beyond a provisional and general statement or to have much confidence in details of arrangement which may find expression in a definite scheme of chronology. As a whole the *Upaniṣad* literature is later than the *Āraṇyakas* (*q.v.*) and earlier than the condensation of philosophical rule and precept into mnemonic *Sūtras*. The internal dependence and succession set forth below is substantially that of Deussen, to whose work all students of Indian literature and philosophy are greatly indebted. On broad lines and in substance the arrangement may be accepted, at least provisionally. With our present knowledge broad and tentative conclusions only are justified. Earlier and later elements in thought and style and composition are not always separable, or capable of being assigned to their right position in the history of the texts. Some treatises, notably perhaps the *Śvetāśvatara*, which in its extant form and on general grounds is placed comparatively late in the chronological order, contain archaic elements, on which have been imposed later doctrines until the various strands of thought are almost inextricably interwoven, and the teaching presented is with difficulty reduced to self-consistency.

(1) The oldest group consists of six treatises, written in prose of an archaic style. At the head of the group are the *Bṛhadāraṇyaka* and the *Chhāndogya Upaniṣads*, which are acknowledged to be the most complete and authoritative exponents of *Upaniṣad* doctrine. The other members of the group, in the order named, are the *Taittirīya*, *Aitareya*, *Kauṣītaki*, and *Kena*. The last-named is composed partly in verse, and as regards its teaching also seems chronologically to approximate to the second group.

(2) In the second group the composition is almost entirely metrical. The oldest and most independent member of the group is the *Kaṭha* or *Kāṭhaka Upaniṣad*. There follow the *Īśā*, *Śvetāśvatara*, *Muṇḍaka*, and *Mahānārāyaṇa*. The authors of the *Īśā* and *Śvetāśvatara* are said to be directly indebted to the *Kāṭhaka* both in doctrine and in expression; and a similar mutual relation is maintained between the last three treatises on the list. In all these the leading principles of the *Upaniṣad* teaching, which in the earlier group appear to be in a formative stage and open to discussion, are apparently regarded as established doctrines.

(3) In the treatises of the third group there has been a return again to prose, but the prose is of a type distinct from that of the earlier *Upaniṣads*, and approximates to the style of the classical Sanskrit. The group consists of three members only, *Praśna*, *Maitrāyaṇīya*, and *Māṇḍūkya*. The inference with regard to their later origin is hardly disputable, and is

---

[1] *Chhānd.* III. xi. 5; cf. *Maitr.* vi. 29: 'this most mysterious secret shall be imparted to none who is not a son or a pupil, and who has not yet attained tranquillity.'

[2] Cf. Pr 23[9], Mt 7[6]; Deussen, *Philosophy of the Upanishads*, Eng. tr., p. 10 f., who points out that in Greek philosophy the same thought recurs of a doctrine too sacred or difficult of apprehension to be allowed to become the property of all.

[3] *Religions of India*[3], Eng. tr., p. 65 f.

[4] The eleven *Upaniṣads* known to Śaṅkara, substantially at least in the form in which they are now extant, have been translated by Max Müller in *SBE*, vols. i. and xv. These are the *Chhāndogya*, *Kena*, *Aitareya*, *Kauṣītaki*, *Īśā* (or *Vājasaneyī*), *Kaṭha*, *Muṇḍaka*, *Taittirīya*, *Bṛhadāraṇyaka*, *Śvetāśvatara*, and *Praśna*. Renderings of these and others are available in all the principal languages of Europe and India. It is of course probable that Śaṅkara was acquainted with other treatises of *Upaniṣad* character, some of which may be among those which have been preserved; but, if so, they are now known under different names. The Sanskrit texts are published in many series, and also separately; see the 'Literature' at the end of this article.

sustained by the character of the teaching which they present.[1] Two at least of these, *Praśna* and *Māṇḍūkya*, together with the *Muṇḍaka* in group (2), are attributed to the *Atharvaveda*.

(4) By far the larger number of the *Upaniṣad* treatises are sectarian in character, or belong to the *Atharvaveda* or the systems and schools of the principal sects. For the most part they are written in prose, more rarely in verse, or in prose and verse intermingled. Their doctrine or teaching varies with the sect to which they belong. They apply *Upaniṣad* principles to sectarian ends, and to establish the religious doctrines of their several creeds. The most interesting perhaps and important are those attached to the Yoga philosophy. With not a little force they urge and maintain the fundamental doctrines of the Yoga faith. Many, but not all, of the *Upaniṣads* of this group are accessible in modern renderings. Thirty or more are usually enumerated as the oldest and most instructive: *Ātmabodha*, *Nārāyaṇa*, *Mahā* (Vaiṣṇavite); *Atharvaśiras*, *Kaivalya* (Śaivite); *Brahmavidyā*, *Jābāla*, *Āruṇeya*, *Sannyāsa*, *Yogatattva* (Yoga, or Sannyāsa), etc.

4. Translation and interpretation.—The difficulties of translation and interpretation of these treatises are considerable. Like the other scriptures of the Veda, the texts have certainly been preserved in the Śākhās with fidelity and accuracy from ancient times. Previous, however, to a final determination of form and limits they were evidently treated with much freedom, being revised, re-edited, interpolated, or abridged, and in general made to conform to later or individual standards of orthodoxy and belief. A considerable number of them were made accessible for the first time in a Western rendering at the beginning of the 19th cent. by Anquetil du Perron, who worked from a Persian translation in the year 1656 of a collection of 50 *Upaniṣads* known as *Oupnek'hat*.[2] The text itself is the strangest medley of Latin and Persian, with Sanskrit words transliterated or adopted, almost unintelligible without a key. As is well known, Schopenhauer (*q.v.*) regarded the publication as epoch-making in the history of Western philosophy and made it the basis of his own system.[3] Thirty years later Rāmmohun Roy, the great Indian reformer and founder of the Brāhma Samāj (*q.v.*), published English translations of several treatises. He was followed in English, French, or German by H. T. Colebrooke, E. B. Cowell, P. Regnaud, O. Böhtlingk, A. Weber, and others. The most important and satisfactory renderings are those by Max Müller in *SBE*, and by Deussen in his *Sechzig Upanishad's*. The latter contains introductions to the several treatises which are of great value.

5. Contents and analysis.—A brief analysis of the older and doctrinally the more significant treatises will enable a fair conception to be formed of their general scope and character. Often the *Upaniṣads* are not easy to analyse on account of the desultory nature of their style and contents. The abrupt changes of subject, the absence of any logical method or arrangement, the universal employment of metaphor are constant stumbling-blocks in the way of classification or orderly analysis. The entire treatment is suggestive rather of intimate oral instruction than of methodical exposition. There is little development of thought, nor is any attempt made to set forth a progressive and complete exposition of the truth as the authors conceive it. The most important writings are the *Bṛhadāraṇyaka* and the *Chhāndogya*.

[1] For a full statement of the reasons for the order adopted, and the mutual dependence of the several treatises, see Deussen, p. 22 ff.

[2] *Oupnek'hat* (*id est, Secretum tegendum*), originally published in 1801–02 in 2 vols. Each vol. contains an Introduction: *Monitum ad Lectorem*, followed by a *Dissertatio*, and a prefatory note on the Persian text on which the translation is based. The Latin rendering is succeeded by lengthy *Emendationes et Annotationes*, *Animadvertenda*, and *Supplementum*; and at the close of vol. ii. an explanation is given of the technical Sanskrit terms used in the text. See also Deussen, *Sechzig Upanishad's*, p. 830 ff.

[3] See Max Müller, in *SBE* i. p. lviii ff., who gives an example of du Perron's style from his rendering of the *Chhāndogya Upaniṣad*.

(*a*) The *Bṛhadāraṇyaka Upaniṣad* is the most interesting, as it is the richest in content, of all the *Upaniṣads*, and presents the most systematic exposition of doctrine. It is attached to the Vājasaneyin school of the *Yajurveda*, and in its present form is appended to and forms part of the *Śatapatha Brāhmaṇa*, of which, according to the Mādhyandina śākhā, it forms the last of the fourteen *kāṇḍas*, or collections, into which the *Brāhmaṇa* is divided. In the Kāñva śākhā, or school, it is the seventeenth book. The *Upaniṣad* in its existing form is composite, and not the work of one author. It comprises six *adhyāyas*, or chapters, of which the last two are of later date and adopt a different theological and philosophical standpoint, especially, as it seems, with regard to the doctrine of transmigration. The first four *adhyāyas* are Vedāntic, and of these the earlier two exhibit the philosophic doctrine of the *ātman*, which is represented as superseding and transcending the polytheistic worship of the gods. The third and fourth chapters may be regarded as the kernel of the treatise, in which is recorded the final teaching of the *Upaniṣads* in its essential and most characteristic form. In reply to questions addressed to him Yājñavalkya with elaborate detail and subtlety expounds the metaphysical doctrine of *Brahman* or the *ātman*. If the name represents a real individuality, and is not merely a title under whose shelter many convergent thoughts and reasonings have found expression, Yājñavalkya may claim a place with the greatest thinkers of the world or of any age.

The earlier chapters of the first *adhyāya* are to a large extent occupied with symbols and fanciful plays upon words. *Mṛtyu*, or death, is at the beginning of things, and produces successively the elements, speech (*vāch*), the Vedas, sacrifice, etc. The whole is explained as intended to promote the worship of Virāj. The third chapter is the *Udgītha Brāhmaṇa*, representing under the form of a contest of the *devas* and *asuras* in song (*udgītha*) the antagonism of good and evil. The *asuras* defeat all the senses in turn, but are themselves overcome by the agency of *prāṇa*, or the breath, and victory remains with the *devas*. The passage is too long to quote, but is a good example of the allegorizing method of the *Upaniṣads*. In the fourth and following chapters various cosmological theories and processes, more or less fanciful, are set forth, concluding with the fundamental assertion of the unity of the self (*ātman*) with the triad *nāma*, *rūpa*, *karma*, or name, form, and work, as examples of which are given *vāch* (speech), *chakshus* (the eye), and *ātman*, *i.e.* the bodily or lower self. 'Thus that being a triad is one, that self (*ātman*); being one, it is that triad (*i.e.* the *ātman*); therefore is it immortal, guarded (covered) by the true. *Prāṇa* (breath) is the immortal, *nāmarūpa* (name and form) are the true; by these is the breath guarded.'

Following upon the teaching of the first *adhyāya*, the second expounds the true *vidyā*, the higher knowledge or doctrine of the *ātman*, with which the last paragraph of the first *adhyāya* seems to form a link. The first chapter, which is found in substance also in *Kauṣ.* iv., is remarkable in that it represents a Brāhman as seeking enlightenment from a ruler of Kṣatriya race, Ajātaśatru of Benares (Kāśī), who refutes his erroneous conceptions of the *Brahman* and makes known to him the real truth concerning the nature of the *ātman*. This representation of the dependence of a Brāhman upon Kṣatriya instruction is usually understood, and probably rightly, to be indicative of an early condition of Indian society, in which the Brāhmans did not hold the practical monopoly of all knowledge which was theirs in later times; they were equalled or surpassed by members of the warrior caste. The discussion makes free use of metaphor and simile, and many passages present difficulties of interpretation. In the first chapter Gārgya Bālāki, a Brāhman, proposes a series of definitions or identifications of the *Brahman*, which are in turn shown to be defective. Its true nature is then explained under the figure of profound slumber (*suṣupti*); the sleeper is at rest, unconscious, no longer subject to any external disturbance or influence. 'From that *ātman* all *prāṇas* (senses), all worlds, all *devas*, all creatures proceed. The secret (*upaniṣad*) therefore is "the true of the true" (*satyasya satyam*, or "the reality of the reality," *i.e.* the most essential reality). The *prāṇas* are the true, of them he (the *ātman* or *Brahman*) is the true.' . . . 'The forms of *Brahman* are two, material and immaterial, mortal and immortal, the lasting and the transient, being and other-being (*sat* and *tyad*, this and that, the real and the unreal). . . . Further, with regard to the *ātman* this is the material, which is distinct from the breath and the ether within the body (*ātman*); this is the mortal, the permanent, the *sat*. Of this material, this mortal, this permanent, this *sat*, the essence is the eye, for it is the essence of the *sat*. Breath, however, and the ether within the body are immaterial; this is the immortal, the impermanent, the *tyad*; of this immaterial, this immortal, this impermanent, this *tyad*, the essence is the *puruṣa* (person) in the right eye; for it is the essence of the *tyad*. . . . Accordingly its significance (*ādeśa*, instruction, rule) is expressed by *neti neti* (not so, not so); for beyond this, that you say it is not so (*iti na*), there is nothing further. Its name however is "the reality of reality" (*satyasya satyam*); that is the senses (*prāṇās*) are the real, and it is their real.'[1]

The fourth chapter expounds the doctrine of the true *Brahman*, the all-comprehending and universal Self, in the form of an instruction given by Yājñavalkya, as he is about to abandon the world for the life of a recluse, to his wife Maitreyī. The narrative is repeated with unimportant variations in IV. v., and seems there to be more in place.[2]

'"If, sir, this whole earth, full of wealth, were mine, should I thereby be immortal?" "No, no," Yājñavalkya replied, "as the life of the rich would be thy life. There is no hope of immortality by wealth." And Maitreyī said: "What is the worth to me of that whereby I do not become immortal? What my lord knoweth declare to me." . . . And Yājñavalkya said: "Not indeed for the love of husband is the husband dear; but for the love of the self (*ātman*) the husband is dear. Not indeed for the love of wife is the wife dear; but for the love of the self (*ātman*) the wife is dear."'

The same formula is then repeated for sons, wealth, cattle, the Brāhman and Kṣatriya castes, the worlds, gods (*devas*), Vedas, creatures.

'Not indeed for the love of all is all dear; but for the love of the self (*ātman*) is all dear. The self indeed is to be seen, to be heard, to be perceived, to be heeded, O Maitreyī. When the self indeed has been seen, heard, perceived, known, then all this is known.

Who knows the Brāhman caste other than in the *ātman* (self) him the Brāhman caste rejects; who knows the Kṣatriya caste other than in the *ātman* him the Kṣatriya caste rejects; who knows the worlds other than in the *ātman* him the worlds reject; who knows the gods other than in the *ātman* him the gods reject; who knows the Vedas other than in the *ātman* him the Vedas reject; who knows the creatures other than in the *ātman* him the creatures reject; who knows everything other than in the *ātman* him everything rejects. This Brāhman and Kṣatriya caste, these worlds and gods, these Vedas, all these creatures, this all, it is the self (*ātman*).'

'As the sea is the meeting-place of all waters, of all contacts the skin, of all tastes the tongue, of all scents the nose, of all forms the eye, of all sounds the ear, of all thoughts the mind (*manas*), of all sciences the intellect, of all actions the hands . . . the feet of all movements, speech of all the Vedas; as a lump of salt has no within or without but consists entirely of taste, so indeed that *ātman* has no within or without but consists entirely of knowledge; having arisen from these creatures (elements), into them it again vanishes; after death there is no consciousness.'

'For where there is as it were duality there one sees the other, smells the other, tastes the other, greets the other, hears the other, perceives the other, touches the other, knows the other, but where the self (*ātman*) alone is all this, how should he see another, smell another, taste another, greet another, hear another, perceive another, touch another, know another? How should he know him whereby all this is known? He, the *ātman*, is "not so, not so" (*neti neti*); incomprehensible for he is not comprehended, indestructible for he is not destroyed, unattached for he does not attach himself; unfettered, he is not pained nor suffers harm. How then should one know the Knower?'

After a fifth chapter, in which the doctrine of *Brahman* is set forth and elaborated under the symbol of honey (*madhu*), the *adhyāya* concludes by reciting the stem or genealogical tree (*vaṁśa*), giving in succession the names of the teachers by whom the doctrine has been transmitted, leading up to *Brahman* and Svayambhū the self-existent.

Apart from the divine or mythological origin to which the succession is traced it is impossible either to affirm or to disprove the correctness of the names given in these lists. It is sufficiently probable that the fame and names of the masters of the schools would be preserved within the schools themselves, and not likely that the lists are entirely due to imagination or invention. The presence of the records here would seem to indicate that the two *adhyāyas* once formed a separate whole, which has been more or less interpolated, and incorporated with other parts into a single treatise. A similar list, coincident with this for two-thirds of its length, is found at the close of the fourth *adhyāya*, and a different and shorter genealogical stem at the end of the *Upaniṣad*. There are variations also in the two recensions of the text.

The Yājñavalkya books, *adhyāyas* III. and IV., begin with his acceptance of a challenge by King Janaka, which none of the other Brāhmans venture to take up. In nine chapters questions on abstract and metaphysical problems touching the life after death and the nature of the self are put to him by his rivals, and by his successful dealing with these he vindicates his claim to be the wisest of all. The ninth chapter concludes with a renewed challenge on the part of Yājñavalkya to meet any questions put to him, but no one ventures to assume the rôle of questioner. The book is in general introductory, asserting the authority and predominance of the great teacher, who is to expound the ultimate truth in the dialogue of the succeeding *adhyāya*.

In the first chapter of the book King Janaka Vaideha repeats various definitions of *Brahman* that have been given to him, as speech (*vāch*), breath (*prāṇa*), sight or the eye (*chakshu*), hearing (*śrotra*), mind or will (*manas*), the heart (*hṛdaya*). Yājñavalkya has no difficulty in proving that these are imperfect explanations, useful approximations to the truth, but not the truth itself. In the second and following chapters Yājñavalkya assumes the part of instructor, still under the control, from which it is difficult or impossible to escape, of simile and metaphor. *Brahman* is the *puruṣa* in the eye, mysterious, and to be described only in negatives (*neti neti*, 'not so, not so'). The self is the true and only light, within the heart, self-illuminating and himself the light of all.

'Then is a father not a father, a mother not a mother, the worlds not worlds, the gods not gods, the Vedas not Vedas. Then a thief is not a thief . . . a mendicant not a mendicant, a hermit not a hermit; unvexed by good, unvexed by evil, he has then overpassed all the sorrows of the heart.

Though he then sees not, yet is he seeing, though he sees not; for there is no interruption of seeing for the Seer, because he is imperishable; but there is no second, no other, distinct from him, that he could see.'[1]

A similar assertion is made with regard to the senses of smell, taste, speech, hearing, thought, sensation or touch, knowledge; all designed to show that the affirmations and predicates of ordinary life are meaningless when applied to the *ātman*:

'Where there is as it were another, then would one see the other, smell the other, taste the other, address the other, hear the other, think the other, feel the other, know the other. A solitary ocean is the Seer, without a second (*advaita*); that is the Brahma-world, O King.'[2]

The fourth chapter further illustrates and explains the nature of the *ātman*, the fifth is the instruction to Maitreyī, as in II. iv., and the sixth and last chapter of the *adhyāya* gives the *vaṁśa*.

The fifth *adhyāya* opens with an invocation, asserting the twofold nature of the *Brahman*, and quotes an old authority for the saying that *Brahman* is space (*kha*, 'ether'), 'the ancient air-filled space.' There follows the well-known parable of Prajāpati and his disciples:

'The three (races of) Prajāpati's sons, gods, men, and *asuras*, lived as students with their father Prajāpati. Their period of studentship finished, the gods said: "Be pleased to tell us, sir." He said to them this syllable *Da*. "Have you understood?" he said. "We have understood," they said, "you bade us subdue ourselves (*dāmyata*)." "Yes," he said, "you have understood."

Then the men said to him: "Be pleased to tell us, sir." He said to them this same syllable *Da*. "Have you understood?" he said. "We have understood," they said, "you bade us be generous (*datta*)." "Yes," he said, "you have understood."

Then the *asuras* said to him: "Be pleased to tell us, sir." He said to them this same syllable *Da*. "Have you understood?" he said. "We have understood," they said, "you bade us be merciful (*dayadhvam*)." "Yes," he said, "you have understood."

This same divine voice, the thunder, repeats *Da Da Da*, that is, Subdue yourselves, Be generous, Be merciful. Therefore should these three be enjoined, self-restraint, generosity, mercy.'

The further chapters of the book relate for the most part to types or similes of *Brahman*, which are explained as more or less adequate representations of the truth. The most interesting is the exposition of the significance of the four feet (*pada*) of the *gāyatrī*, the sacred invocation or 'Magnificat' of the Brāhmans.[3] Each foot has a special meaning. The fourth (*turīya*) is the bright foot (*darśatam padam*), and symbolizes the bright or shining one, the sun or the *puruṣa* in the sun. The last chapter is an invocation of Āditya, or the sun, repeated in *Vājas. Up.* xv.–xviii.

[1] *Bṛhad.* II. iii.; cf. III. ix. 26, IV. ii. 4, iv. 22, v. 15. It is difficult, perhaps impossible, to find English equivalents for the Sanskrit terms which are employed. The 'lasting' and 'transient' are from the point of view, as it were, of human appreciation, as the hills are lasting and a spiritual vision is fleeting or transient. Max Müller renders by 'solid' and 'fluid'; Deussen has 'das Stehende und das Gehende.' The negative doctrine of *neti neti* is the extreme refinement of *Upaniṣad* teaching with regard to the nature of the higher *Brahman*.

[2] Cf. also *Chhānd. Up.* VI. xiii., VII. xxiv.

[1] *Bṛhad.* IV. iii. 22 f. [2] *Ib.* 31 f.

[3] *Rigveda*, III. lxii. 10, v. lxxxii. 1; cf. VI. iii. 6.

The sixth and final *adhyāya* is *khila*, additional or supplementary.[1] It supplies little new information or teaching, and is in parts even more highly metaphorical and difficult. The usual genealogy or list of successive teachers follows, and Yājñavalkya's authority is claimed for some at least of the instruction offered.

(*b*) It is hardly necessary or worth while to follow through in similar detail the *Chhāndogya*, which shares importance with the *Bṛhadāranyaka* as the most ancient written source of *Upaniṣad* doctrine. It is attached to the *Sāmaveda*, and is divided into eight chapters, or *prapāṭhakas*, not all of which are parts of the original treatise. There has been combination, adaptation, and insertion; but no data are available for determining the changes that have been made or for restoring the primitive form. The additions or interpolations are probably more numerous than the losses.

The treatise is highly charged with symbolism. Meditation on the sacred syllable *Om* is enjoined, which is the essence (*rasa*) of all things, and is the *udgītha*, on which in its successive forms as *prāṇa*, *vāch*, etc., the *devas* meditate in their rivalry with the *asuras*.[2] *Om* is the immortal imperishable sound (*svara*), and is identified with *prāṇa*, *praṇava*, or the *udgītha*, to the syllables of which a symbolical interpretation is given.

(*c*) The *Kaṭha* or *Kāṭhaka Upaniṣad* is placed by Deussen at the head of his second class, the ancient metrical *Upaniṣads*. It belongs to the literature of the Black *Yajurveda*, of which the Kathas formed a well-known school; and it is perhaps the best-known of the *Upaniṣads*, having been rendered into English by Rāmmohun Roy in the early part of the 19th century. Since that date many editions and translations have been published. Its historical and literary affinities are not easy to determine. Deussen finds evidence of direct dependence of the *Īśā* and *Śvetāśvatara Upaniṣads* upon the *Kāṭhaka*; and that the *Śvetāśvatara* has exercised an indirect and less powerful influence upon the two other members of the group, the *Muṇḍaka* and *Mahānārāyaṇa*. The general classification may be accepted, but the details of interrelationship are still very obscure.

The text of the *Upaniṣad* consists of two *adhyāyas* or six *vallīs*, the first three of which contain the story of Nachiketas and the three gifts which he obtained from Death, the all-knower. The fourth *vallī* is a further exposition by Death of the mystery of the *Brahman*, and a polemic against pluralism. In the fifth and sixth *vallīs* the *ātman* or *Brahman* is described under various figures or metaphors, the one Self and lord, all-comprehending, self-existent, the eternal thinker. They who discern the Self within are wise and secure to themselves eternal happiness and peace. The legend of Nachiketas is found also in the *Brāhmaṇa* of the Black *Yajurveda*,[3] and is there explanatory of a well-known religious rite. To judge from analogy, the myth was probably invented to account for the existence of a rite which bore this name, the original circumstances or foundation of which had been forgotten.

Nachiketas is the son of Vājaśravasa, a religious householder, who at the call of religion is represented as making the voluntary surrender of all his worldly possessions (*sannyāsa*) in order to provide for his spiritual interests. The name perhaps signifies 'unnoticed,' 'unobserved,' and was designed, as in many other instances, to secure that the child should be inconspicuous, and 'unobserved' by the watchful powers of evil. Vājaśravasa distributes all his goods in alms, and Nachiketas, knowing that the *sannyāsa* of the father involves the giving away of the son also, is anxious to learn his fate. His father replies that he will give him to Yama, signifying thereby that filial relations and claims have thenceforward no meaning for him, as being dead to the world. Nachiketas takes the answer literally, and goes off to the house of Yama, where he stays for three days, and in the absence of the master of the house is left without entertainment. Yama on his return is annoyed that a Brāhman guest has been thus inhospitably treated, and offers him in compensation three gifts, which he is to choose for himself. There is no difficulty with regard to the first two gifts. They are granted in full and without hesitation. For the first Nachiketas asks that the anger or indifference of his father may be overcome, and that he may be moved to kindness and consideration towards himself. The second request is for an explanation of the fire-sacrifice, the ritual of which Yama expounds, and promises that it shall henceforth bear his name, the Nachiketas rite; a knowledge of the three Nachiketas fires and rightful performance of the sacrifice will ensure for the sacrificer heaven and abiding peace. The difficulty arises with the third boon:

'When a man is dead, there is a doubt—some say He is, others He is not. This I would fain know, taught by thee. This is the third gift that I choose.'

'Hereon even the gods of old have been in doubt. Hard to understand and recondite is this subject. Choose another boon, Nachiketas; do not urge me, excuse me this.'

'True that the gods have hereon been in doubt, and thou thyself, O Death, hast acknowledged it to be hard to understand. But no teacher may be found so capable as thou; no other boon is comparable to this.'

'Choose long-lived sons and grandsons, cattle in plenty, elephants, gold, and horses; choose rich possessions on the soil, and life for thyself as many years as thou wilt.

If there is a boon equivalent in thine eyes, choose it—wealth and long life. Be lord over the wide earth, Nachiketas; I grant thee consummation of all desires.

Whatever desires are difficult to realize here below, ask according to thy will—noble maidens with their chariots and music, not to be won by men, I give them thee for service. Ask me not, Nachiketas, concerning death.'

'What profit has a man of these things, O Death, evanescent as they are, that impair the vigour of all the senses? A full life-time even is brief. Keep your chariots, dance and song.

Man's happiness consists not in wealth. Shall we grasp wealth, whensoe'er we see thee? Our life is but as long as thou dost ordain. This boon, however, alone do I choose.

Who that has had foretaste of that which perishes not nor changes, mortal and fettered here to earth, would find pleasure in a long life, when he has given due thought to beauty and indulgence and pleasure?

That, O Death, on which doubt rules here below, declare to us what will be in the great Hereafter. No other boon does Nachiketas choose than that which unlocks this mystery.'[1]

Yama is under the necessity of yielding; and he begins by congratulating Nachiketas on his preference for knowledge rather than wealth or pleasure. But it is not an easy way:

'Though anxiously sought it is not to be gained when taught by common men, and without a teacher access thereto there is none—so small that it eludes the grasp of the mind.

Reasoning will not find the way, but taught by another it is easily learnt. It is thine now; a true seeker art thou; an inquirer such as thou is to be desired.'[2]

The exposition then begins with the identification of the sacred syllable *Om* (*q.v.*) with the *Brahman*. It is one of the most commonly chosen metaphors of the *Upaniṣad* writers:

'This syllable is *Brahman*, this syllable is the Supreme; he who knows this syllable, whatever he wishes is his.'[3]

The text then sets forth in metaphysical terms the nature of the transcendent Seer (the *ātman*) and the conditions under which he may be known.

'The Seer is not born, and does not die; he has no origin and no descent. Unborn, eternal, abiding is that Ancient One. He dies not, when the body dies.

If the slayer thinks that he slays, if the slain thinks himself slain, they both are in error; there is no slayer, and no slain.

Smaller than the small, greater than the great, the Self is concealed here in the heart of the creature. Free from desire and from grief, his senses subdued,[4] a man sees the majesty of the *ātman*.

Sitting he moves far; lying he goes everywhere. That god of joy and not-joy who save myself has power to know?

Bodiless in the bodies, changeless in the changing, the wise man discerns the *ātman*, great, all-pervading, and is saved from sorrow.

Not by dissertation nor by wisdom nor by much sacred lore is that *ātman* to be gained; only by him whom he chooses is he to be gained; to him the *ātman* discovers his own being.

He who has not desisted from evil, who is restless, ill-content, whose mind is not at ease, even by knowledge cannot gain him.

Him to whom Brāhman and Kṣatriya are alike indifferent,[5] and death would be diminution,[6] who could really find?'[7]

In the third *vallī* the Self, the highest *Brahman*, is the charioteer sitting in the chariot (the body), *buddhi* (intellect) guides the car, *manas* (mind or will) is the reins, the senses are the horses, the objects of sense the road on which they run:

---

1 Cf. *Chhānd. Up.* v. i. f.; *Kauṣ. Up.* II. iii., III. iii.; *Praśna Up.* II. iii.

2 Cf. *Bṛhad. Up.* I. iii. 1 ff.

3 III. i. 8; see *SBE* xv. p. xxi ff.; Deussen, p. 262 f.

1 I. i. 20 ff.

2 I. ii. 8 ff.

3 *Kaṭha*, I. ii. 16.

4 *Dhātuprasādāt*, Deussen, *gestillten Sinnendrangs*; cf. *Taitt. Ār.* x. x. 1; *Śvet. Up.* III. xx. The variant reading *dhātu:prasādāt* is followed by Max Müller, 'by the grace of the Creator' (*SBE* xv. 11; Deussen, *Sechzig Upan.* p. 274 f.).

5 *Odana*, as food merely for the body; cf. *Ep. Phil.* iii. 8.

6 *Upasechanam*, a diluent, relaxation of power, and therefore inconceivable.

7 *Kaṭh.* I. ii. 18–25.

'He who has understanding, is self-controlled and ever pure, he reaches that realm whence there is no rebirth.

He who guides his car with understanding, wisely handles the reins (*manas*), he wins through to the goal of his journey; there where is the highest place of Viṣṇu.

Higher than the senses are material things, higher than material things is the mind, higher than the mind is the intellect, higher than the intellect is the great Self (*ātman*).

Higher than the great Self is the undiscerned (*avyaktam*), higher than the undiscerned is the *puruṣa*, higher than the *puruṣa* there is nothing; that is the goal, the highest way.

In all creatures it lies hidden, the *ātman*, invisible, discerned only by the keenest intellect. The touchstone of the finest is the fine.'[1]

Nachiketas therefore obtains his boon:

'He who has perceived that which is beyond hearing or touch or sight, undecaying, without taste or smell, eternal, without beginning or end, higher than the great, unchanging, he is delivered from the jaws of death.'[2]

The remainder of the *Upaniṣad* presents variations of the same theme and is of interest not only for the reiteration and emphasis of central doctrines, but also for the picturesque metaphors which it employs to set them forth. The inadequacy of these and of all metaphors is acknowledged, but they are aids to the mind in its attempts to comprehend the incomprehensible. He is *prāṇa* (breath), *agni* (fire), the *puruṣa* in the midst of the body, lord of the past and the future. In reality the *Brahman* is undifferentiated. 'He goes from death to death who sees difference here.' Through almost the whole of the fourth *vallī* there runs the refrain, 'This is that,' reality is one and indivisible.

The *Kāṭhaka Upaniṣad* gives a stronger impression of unity and of singleness of design and thought than most of these treatises. There is little to suggest diversity of authorship or revision and alteration of the text. It is probable that changes of this nature have taken place, but they have been on a comparatively small scale. The recurrence of the name of Nachiketas at the close of the first and second *adhyāyas*, with the assurance of salvation to those who possess the knowledge of the mystery of the *ātman*, expounded to him by Death, has been supposed to indicate the union into one of two treatises, originally distinct. The inference is hardly justified by the context and the form under which the name appears. It is perhaps more probable that the verse in which it occurs at the end of the *Upaniṣad* is an insertion.

(*d*) One of the most difficult of the *Upaniṣad* treatises both in form and in interpretation is the *Śvetāśvatara*. In the introduction to his translation of the *Upaniṣad*[3] Max Müller expresses this view, and further in a few lines controverts the idea that the name ('the white mule') implies Christian authorship or participation. Not only is the language abrupt, entangled, and defiant of the rules of grammar, but the thought seems repeatedly to lose itself and to represent not one but many phases of doctrine and belief. Not the less perhaps on this account it is of very great interest. Among the more important *Upaniṣads* this treatise is the leading exponent and representative of Sāṅkhyan doctrine, and it is in the *Śvetāśvatara* that the earliest use of the name Sāṅkhya with a technical connotation appears to occur. To reconstruct its history with any certainty—a writing doubly palimpsest, as it has been termed—is probably impossible. It is a medley of thought and teaching in which almost every phase of Hindu philosophical speculation seems to struggle for expression. Nothing is known of the Śākhā of the *Śvetāśvatara*, the school within which the scripture was guarded, studied, and taught. Together with the *Kāṭhaka*, *Taittirīya*, and others it was recognized as belonging to the Black *Yajurveda*.

It is probably right to regard the original basis or nucleus of the *Upaniṣad* as Vedāntic. It was known to the author of the *Vedānta Sūtras*, and

[1] *Kaṭh.* iii. 8-12. [2] *Ib.* iii. 15. [3] *SBE* xv. p. xxxii.

Saṅkara wrote a commentary upon it. The relation of the individual and the universal Self is asserted and discussed from an entirely Vedāntic point of view. On this basis, however, were superimposed theistic and sectarian statements of belief and doctrine, which introduced freely the dogmas of the sects, and even the names of sectarian divinities. Sāṅkhya and Yoga conceptions also, intermingled and reiterated, and in some parts predominant, contribute to form a whole which, as it appears in the extant literature, is probably the result of some centuries of discussion and revision in the schools. The *Upaniṣad* therefore does not readily lend itself to explication and analysis. Its moods change too rapidly to be fixed and indexed. The text also is in many instances corrupt, and out of various readings, which seem to be more or less conjectural, it is sometimes only possible to select that which appears to give a tolerable sense.

The treatise begins with an interrogation and a challenge: What is the cause, the ultimate principle and groundwork, of all? and the answer is *Brahman*. Whence is our birth, our life, our sustenance, and at whose bidding do the joys and sorrows come that we endure? Speculative replies are dismissed as incredible, as that time, nature, necessity, etc., either alone or in combination, should be the final cause. The individual Self is then depicted, the divine essential force (*devātmaśakti*), revealing itself as self or soul through and under the veil of its qualities (*guṇa*), figuratively described as a wheel with many spokes, etc.; by the practice of meditation and self-discipline (*dhyānayoga*) the seers learnt to know this hidden force. Verse 7 supplies the Vedāntic interpretation: in the highest *Brahman* the triad (of the user, the used, and the governor, *bhoktṛi*, *bhogya*, *preritṛi*, *i.e.* the Self, the universe, and God) become one;[1] nothing further remains to be known, everything has been declared under triple form, and this is *Brahman*. The following verses of the chapter are descriptive of the Self under various figures or illustrations; self-knowledge is to be obtained by meditation on the sacred syllable *Om*.

The first seven verses of the second *adhyāya* are a hymn in praise of Savitṛ, made up for the most part of 'tags' from the *Vājasaneyin* and *Taittirīya Saṁhitās*. The rest of the chapter is written in the spirit of the Yoga, adoration of the god who is above and behind all phenomena.

The opening of the third *adhyāya* again is sectarian; Rudra is creator, sustainer, lord of all. The (impersonal) *Brahman* is higher than all, and those who know the great *puruṣa*, shining as the sun beyond the darkness, are immortal. The *puruṣa* is the incarnate Self (*ātman*).

'Without hands or feet he grasps and moves, eyeless he sees, earless he hears. He knows what can be known, but none knows him; him they name *puruṣa*, the first, the great. Smaller than the small, greater than the great, he dwells as the *ātman* in the heart of the creature. Passionless, by the grace of the creator one sees him unmoved (*akratum*, lit. 'without will,' Deussen, *willensfreien*), the great lord. I know him, the unaging Ancient, the self of all, all-pervading, omnipresent; for him rebirth is stayed, whom the seers proclaimed immortal.'[2]

The fourth *adhyāya* exalts the sun-god, whose functions and attributes are figuratively expounded and interpreted in a Vedāntic sense. Peace and immortality are the possession of him who knows the god, Śiva, the eternal, creator of all, dwelling in the heart of man:

'Of him there is no image whose name is Great Majesty. His form is not visible, none ever sees him with the eye. They who with heart and mind know him thus dwelling in the heart become immortal.'[3]

The section ends with a brief prayer to Rudra.

The fifth *adhyāya* contains teaching on the two themes of knowledge and ignorance, of the means of deliverance from the latter, and of the *Brahman* as transcending all. He manifests himself in various ways, 'migrating through his own works,' and is seen now in this and now in that shape, incarnate under many forms. In the sixth and last *adhyāya* neither nature nor time is the source of all, but *Brahman* alone. He is the beginning and cause of all, the one god, hidden in all beings, without parts or attributes, immortal, the lord, protector and ruler of the universe. This is the supreme mystery in the Vedānta, not to be communicated to one who is unworthy.

6. History of doctrine.—It would seem, therefore, that the characteristic central doctrine of the *Upaniṣads*, the doctrine of *Brahman* or the *ātman*, was at first developed and systematized within Kṣatriya circles and at the courts of kings. This combination of royal functions with the mood of a philosopher or a poet was not unfamiliar to Oriental experience. The Brāhman, on the other hand, occupied himself almost exclusively with

[1] Cf. I. 12. [2] III. xix ff. [3] IV. xix f.

the ritual and the securing of his class ascendancy; and only later adopted a doctrine of the universe which had been formulated by others, but which harmonized with his modes of thought, and lent itself readily to his schemes for the establishment of his own predominance on the basis of secret or superior knowledge. These references to a Kṣatriya monopoly of the highest knowledge, imparted by kings to Brāhmans at their request, have been preserved and handed down within the Brāhman literary schools, and it seems improbable that such statements would have been allowed to pass if they had not been in accord with the facts. Probably also the doctrine and several duties of the *āśramas* (*q.v.*), whether widely practised or not, afforded an opening and facilities for the assimilation of the new knowledge. In later times the position was reversed, and with the establishment of intellectual and class pre-eminence the Brāhmans confirmed their claim to a monopoly of the supreme wisdom; and this was conceded to them the more readily as the other castes became more and more immersed in political intrigue or business enterprise. In the issue, by perseverance and the skilful use of opportunity, the Brāhmans secured the first place in knowledge as in honour, and were regarded as the depositories of the secrets of wisdom and right instruction.

7. Essential doctrine.—This highest and most treasured teaching, for which divine authority was claimed, was formulated as the cardinal doctrine of the *Upaniṣad* literature, an idealistic monism, which consisted essentially in the assertion that all is one, 'one only without a second,' and as a necessary corollary that the material universe as it manifests itself to and is approached through the bodily faculties is unreal (*māyā*). Only *Brahman*, the unknown Self (*ātman*), is in possession of a real existence. *Brahman*, moreover, is an abstract impersonal neuter, not an individual or masculine. The attribute of personality, as all other attributes, is denied to him, and he or 'it' can only be defined, if such may be called definition, by negatives (*neti neti*). The human self, the self of the living being (*ātman* or *jīvātman*), is subject to delusion only so far as it imagines itself to be an individual, distinct from all other selves. In reality it is itself the supreme Self (*ātman*), identical with *Brahman*; there are not two or many selves; but *Brahman* and every so-called individual self are one and the same. There is no 'difference,' in the realm of true understanding and insight. 'One only without a second' (*ekādvitīyam*) expresses the ultimate thought and the fundamental postulate of the speculation of the *Upaniṣads*; or, as the doctrine has been formulated by Deussen and others in the form of an equation which summarizes *Upaniṣad* teaching in this respect,

Brahman=*ātman*.

The formula is not of course due to or used by the authors of the *Upaniṣads* themselves.

8. Secondary teaching. — This idealistic and monistic doctrine of the sole reality of *Brahman* underlies all the teaching of the *Upaniṣads*. Although not peculiar to the Indian literature, it is there developed in its most complete form and carried to its utmost logical conclusion. A considerable portion, however, of these treatises expounds what is generally known as the doctrine of the lower *Brahman*, a compromise or concession to the view which the ordinary man takes of the universe as stable, for all practical purposes permanent, conditioning his daily life, limiting and satisfying his outlook upon reality. This teaching was avowedly for those, and for those only, who were incapable of comprehending the higher knowledge, whose mind worked within the limitations imposed by the faculties of the body. For these there was constructed or traditionally maintained a cosmology or doctrine of the universe, in which *Brahman* appears as the creator of a real world, which is then informed, sustained, and its working ensured by his universal and vitalizing presence. In this sense *Brahman* is immanent in the universe, which has no existence apart from him, and will ultimately be resolved or cease to be, returning into the source from which it came. *Brahman* therefore in the cosmological theory of the *Upaniṣads*, which is throughout secondary and does not contain or convey the secret of the highest knowledge, becomes individualized, endowed with properties and capacities, and an apparent or provisional reality is allowed to the universe and to the souls therein. The human *ātman* or *jīvātman* possesses a measure of freedom and individuality of its own, it thinks and determines, and of its own free and enlightened will promotes its return to the *paramātman*, the supreme soul whence it was derived. Thus far therefore the *Upaniṣads* may be said to contain the germs at least of a real theism. It is for the most part in the later treatises and especially in the *Śvetāśvatara* that these doctrines are set forth. They were not, however, developed on theistic lines, and it is probable that they represent speculation or belief which was in its origin entirely independent of the severe idealism of the *ātman* doctrine, tentatively harmonized with the latter and subordinated to it in the *Upaniṣad* teaching. All things would ultimately return to their primitive source, and their impermanent and unreal character would be made manifest. Thus the higher doctrine or faith was conserved under the forms and as the ultimate truth of the lower.

9. Psychology.—To the same secondary teaching belongs the psychological doctrine of the *Upaniṣads*, so far as these treatises may be said to present a consistent or coherent doctrine concerning the human soul. It is evident that this teaching also is derived from external sources, originally independent, and only artificially and with difficulty accommodated to the fundamental presupposition of *Upaniṣad* thought. Where all souls are one, and there is no difference, there is no room and no need for a psychology. On the lower plane of teaching, however, souls created by or emanating from *Brahman* are in a certain sense distinct and individual, although this impression or conviction of distinctness is ultimately due to *māyā* and to *māyā* alone. Some provision therefore must be made for their return, their final and universal reunion with *Brahman*, if a permanent duality was to be avoided. The last alternative as a solution of the mystery of the soul's nature and existence did in fact find expression in some of the *Upaniṣads* in premonitions and intimations of the later doctrine of the Sāṅkhya, which is avowedly dualistic. In general, however, the psychological teaching expounds two independent themes or subjects—the states of the soul, and the means or methods of its return. No definite connexion is made between these, or any relation suggested. They are due to different systems of thought, and no attempt apparently is made or regarded as necessary to co-ordinate them. The latter doctrine, including especially that of the two paths, is closely related to the wider doctrine of predestination.

The four conditions or states of the soul are: (1) the waking state; (2) dream-sleep, in which the soul remains conscious and active in its dreams; (3) dreamless slumber, *suṣupti*, *suṣupta*, in which the soul is passive, and unconscious of its environment; (4) *turīya*, *turya*, *chaturtha*, the 'fourth' state, which is more or less artificial, and is unknown to the older *Upaniṣads*. It was perhaps invented to secure or complete the correspondence with the four *āśramas*, the *turīya* being the sublime but undefinable state to which the *sannyāsin* had attained. The three earlier states received also mystical names: *vaiśvānara*, that which is common to all, the habitual mode or outlook of all men; *taijasa*, luminous, vigorous, intense; *prājña*, intelligent. Similar states or stages are familiar in the experience of European and other mystics.

(1) The waking state is the normal condition of the natural man, who without reflexion accepts the universe as he finds it, believing it to be real. The mystical title *vaiśvānara* is apparently intended to suggest that to the natural faculties of all such men the same physical universe presents itself.

(2) In dream-sleep the soul fashions its own world in the imagery of its dreams, 'the spirit serves as light for itself.'[1] To the dreamer the scenes and experiences through which he passes in his dreams appear real, and in this his dream-world no other has part. The illusion of duality, however, is still maintained; there is one who knows and another that is known. In other passages the spirit is represented as quitting the body during the dream-sleep and wandering hither and thither, returning sometimes only with difficulty to its accustomed home.

(3) In the third state all distinct consciousness of knowing subject and known object is superseded, the human spirit is one with the eternal Knower, the supreme intelligence, *prājña ātman*. In the teaching of the earlier *Upaniṣads* this is apparently the final state, the consummation of bliss in union with *Brahman*. 'When a man has fallen so sound asleep, and has so completely and perfectly been lulled to rest that he knows no dream-image, that is the Self, that is the immortal, the fearless, that is *Brahman*.'[2]

(4) The introduction of a fourth state appears to have been based upon a recognition of the transitory character of the *suṣupti*. The slumber is interrupted, and the spirit of the slumberer may then return to the waking state in which it is troubled and anxious, and the external visible universe is regarded as a real object of knowledge. 'When the three states named have ceased, and the spiritual subsists alone by itself, contrasted like a spectator with all existing things as a substance undifferentiated, set free from all existing things, this spiritual state is called the *turīya*.'[3] In this state the *ātman* has realized a permanent union with *Brahman*, which is not liable to interruption by any return to a lower condition; nor is it interfered with or destroyed by engaging for a time in any of the illusory activities of ordinary life. Worldly duties and employments do not affect the soul that is one with *Brahman*.[4]

10. Eschatology.—The Indian doctrine of the two paths, the *devayāna* and the *pitṛyāna*, the way of the gods and the way of the fathers, by one or the other of which the souls of the dead make their way from this world to a future abode of happiness or misery, presents easily recognized parallels to similar teaching in other faiths. That the theory was of independent origin in India admits of little doubt. Later it was elaborated and brought into close association with the kindred doctrine of transmigration and was then carried far by wandering Indian missionaries; and in this way it may not improbably have suggested or influenced the beliefs of other peoples, especially the Mithraic teaching concerning the ascent of the soul to the highest heaven. As early as the *Rigveda* reference is made to the *devayāna* as the path by which Agni bears the offerings to the gods, and on which the gods themselves descend to partake of the sacrifices. On the same road the faithful worshipper ascends through successive stages or 'stations' to the highest felicity in *Brahman*. The passages in the *Upaniṣads* which enumerate the 'stations' give no indication of the origin of the theory, nor attempt to explain its meaning or significance. The earliest is probably *Chhānd.* IV. xv. 5 f.:

'He (who knows this) . . . (after death) goes to light (*archis*, brightness, *i.e.* of the funeral fire), from light to day, from day to the light half of the moon, from the light half of the moon to the six months of the sun's northward movement, from the months to the year, from the year to the sun, from the sun to the moon, from the moon to the lightning. Thereupon an unearthly guide (*puruṣa*) conducts them to *Brahman*. This is the path of the Devas, the path of *Brahman*. They who proceed thereby do not return to the changing life of man.'[1]

The *pitṛyāna*, on the other hand, is the way of darkness, for ignorant and defiled souls, and progress is marked by analogous but contrary stations; *e.g.*, the dark half of the moon is substituted for the light half, etc. Those who travel on this road do not reach the year or the sun, but are detained in the moon till their *karma* is exhausted, after which they return to earth, and are again subject to rebirth:

'But those who in a village fulfil their religious duties and give alms (*i.e. gṛhasthas*) go to the smoke, from the smoke to the night, from the night to the dark half of the moon, from the dark half of the moon to the six months of the sun's southward movement. They do not attain to the year. From the months they go to the world of the fathers (*pitṛloka*), from the world of the fathers to the ether, from the ether to the moon. . . . Here they dwell as long as aught remains (*i.e.* of *karma* and its consequences), then return again by that way to the ether, from the ether to the wind (*vāyu*). Having become wind he (the *gṛhastha*) becomes smoke, having become smoke he becomes vapour, having become vapour he becomes cloud, having become cloud he descends in rain. These then are born as rice or corn, herbs or trees, sesamum or beans. . . . They who have lived a good life in this world will as a reward attain a good rebirth as a Brāhman, or a Kṣatriya, or a Vaiśya; but they who in this world have lived a shameful life will attain a shameful rebirth, as a dog or a pig or an out-caste (*chaṇḍāla*).'[2]

There is thus in the *Upaniṣads* tentative if somewhat indefinite teaching with regard to the fate of the soul at and after death. Two conceptions were apparently involved, which were in all probability originally independent and belonged to different orders of ideas. Neither of them was due in its inception to the thinkers of the *Upaniṣads*, but both were derived from external and preexisting sources. The thought of a return of the soul to the earth, to be embodied again in human or animal form, or even in the form of an insect or plant, is common to nearly all primitive peoples, and is undoubtedly of great antiquity. The distinct thought of a recompense of felicity or suffering in another world for the deeds done upon earth is neither universal nor so old. It has usually been accepted as an alternative to the earlier view of the soul's future destiny, superseding or displacing but not amalgamating with it. The contribution which the *Upaniṣad* thinkers made was in effect to combine these ideas by transferring the retribution from an unknown and future sphere to the known and visible present, and by asserting the precise equivalence of the recompense after death to the deeds, good or evil, of the earthly life. Thus all the elements of the Indian doctrines of *karma* and transmigration are found in the oldest *Upaniṣads*. They obtain here their final and fullest expression. No evidence or proof, however, is offered in support of these theories, nor is any reference given to previous history or development, which might explain or justify the statements made. They are supported, as is all the teaching of the *Upaniṣads*, by an appeal to the authority of eminent teachers of the past. It seems strange that no attempt should be made to fortify so important a doctrine as transmigration by reference to analogy, or to a wider and reasoned view of life as a whole. They are simply recorded as the definite and complete statement of the final destiny of the soul.

11. Summary.—Thus a very considerable part of this literature is occupied with doctrines that belong to the lower *Brahman*, and are avowedly inferior to the ultimate and supreme truth that *Brahman* is all in all. They are half-truths,

[1] *Bṛhad.* IV. iii. 9.

[2] *Chhānd.* VIII. xi. 1; cf. *Bṛhad.* IV. iii. 21 ff.

[3] *Sarvop.* 8; cf. *Māṇḍ.* vii.; *Maitr.* vi. 19, vii. 17.

[4] On the states of the soul see Deussen, p. 296 ff., and the references there given. Deussen regards the introduction of the fourth stage as due in part to the increasing prevalence of the Yoga doctrine, which involved the belief that by intense meditation, abstinence, and self-control the union of the human spirit with the one eternal spirit might be secured.

[1] *SBE* i. 68; cf. *Chhānd.* V. x. 1 ff., *Bṛhad.* VI. ii. 15 f., *Kauṣ.* I. ii. 3.

[2] *Chhānd.* V. x. 3 ff. (*SBE* i. 80 ff.); cf. Deussen, p. 334 ff. and references.

guiding and controlling the practical life of the universe, which lose interest and significance when the full truth is apprehended by the soul. 'He who knows' need not concern himself about any of these matters, whether of belief or practice. This doctrine, the doctrine of the *ātman*, alone is 'true' in the exact sense of the word. And the consciousness of this seems always to underlie the most precise exposition of doctrines, which in form at least conflict with it. *Brahman* alone is real; all else is *māyā*, illusion. This word appears first in its technical meaning in the *Śvetāśvatara Upaniṣad*, where so many conflicting trains of thought meet and find a home. Essentially, however, and apart from its late literary expression, the doctrine of the universe as shadowy and unreal is far older in India than the literary employment of the term *māyā* would suggest. It is presupposed in most of the teaching that concerns the material universe, and is more or less consciously accepted by all Indian sects at the present day. The man who knows this, that *Brahman* alone exists, is truly wise. He realizes the unreal elusive character of the things that are seen, and has apprehended the supreme truth that *Brahman* only *is*, and that he himself is *Brahman*.

12. Ethics.—The *Upaniṣads* also enforce ethical teaching, but in a desultory manner. There is a considerable element of moral and religious instruction, commending a practical life of sobriety and devotion in sincerity and love of the truth. It is undoubtedly this ethical content that has given to these treatises their unique position among the sacred books of the Hindus. Self-restraint, generosity, loving-kindness are cardinal virtues, the observance of which is incumbent upon all who seek deliverance from the entanglements of this world and final union with the Supreme. The aim and purpose for all and each is release from the *saṁsāra*, the perpetual round of rebirths, and return to the original and eternal source of all in God. Thus the ethical teaching of the *Upaniṣads* is essentially self-interested and individualistic; virtue is to be practised for the sake of personal and private advantage in the cessation of rebirth (*punarmṛityu*, repeated or reiterated death), when the soul reaches its final end in the one Supreme. The morality taught in these books is therefore negative rather than positive. It is a doctrine of abstinence from all that would hinder the severance of worldly bonds, rather than of positive delight in that which is good. The ideal of a devout life is that of the *sannyāsin*, the ascetic, who has renounced all, and is self-centred in profound and uninterrupted meditation. The doctrine thus expounded is that upon which Buddhism has drawn, in the Hīnayāna at least, for its ideal of the perfect monk, and is closely connected with the later Yoga, in which the teaching was systematized and carried to extremes of asceticism and self-torture. In its essential elements it is undoubtedly older in India than the period of the *Upaniṣads*, and gives expression to the austere quality which is native apparently to some forms of Indian religious life. The *Upaniṣads*, moreover, never lose their hold of idealism. To this all other teaching is subordinated. The veil of *māyā* is cast over all. And neither in ethics nor in theistic statement is there the same conviction or earnestness that is apparent in the exposition of the monistic doctrine of the *Brahman*.

LITERATURE.—i. *General.*—P. Deussen, *The Philosophy of the Upanishads*, Eng. tr., Edinburgh, 1906; H. Oldenberg, *Die Lehre der Upanishaden und die Anfänge des Buddhismus*, Göttingen, 1915; M. Bloomfield, *The Religion of the Veda (from Rig-Veda to Upanishads)*, New York and London, 1908, lect. vi.; R. W. Frazer, *Indian Thought, Past and Present*, London, 1915; M. Winternitz, *Gesch. der indischen Literatur*, pt. i., Leipzig, 1908, pp. 196–228; N. Macnicol, *Indian Theism*, Oxford, 1915; F. Max Müller, *Three Lectures on the Vedānta Philosophy*, London, 1894, *The Six Systems of Indian Philosophy*, do. 1899; L. D. Barnett, *Brahma-Knowledge, an Outline of the Philosophy of the Vedānta as set forth by the Upanishads and by Saṅkara*, do. 1907; A. S. Geden, *Studies in the Religions of the East*, do. 1913, pp. 255–301; A. Barth, *The Religions of India*[3], Eng. tr., do. 1891, ch. ii. pt. 2, 'Philosophic Speculations of the Upanishads'; A. E. Gough, *Philosophy of the Upanishads*, do. 1882; A. A. Macdonell, *A Hist. of Sanskrit Literature*, do. 1900, pp. 218–243, and literature, p. 442 f.; E. te Peerdt, *Die Grundworte des indischen Monismus aus den Upanishads des Veda*, Jena, 1914. See also artt. BRAHMAN, BRĀHMANISM, HINDUISM, NEGATION.

ii. *Translations*: F. Max Müller, *The Upanishads*, in 2 vols. (*SBE* i. and xv.), Oxford, 1879 and 1884; P. Deussen, *Sechzig Upanishad's des Veda*, Leipzig, 1897; A. H. Anquetil du Perron, *Oupnek'hat (id est Secretum tegendum)*, Latin tr. from Persian and Sanskrit, with dissertations, annotations, etc., 2 vols., Strassburg, 1801–02; F. Mischel, *Das Oupnek'hat*, German tr., Dresden, 1882; Rammohun Roy, *Translation of the Cena Upanishad, one of the chapters of the Sāma Veda*, according to the gloss of the celebrated Shankarāchārya, Calcutta, 1816, *Translations of the Ishopanishad, one of the chapters of the Yajur Veda*, do. 1816, also of the *Kuth.* and *Moonduk*, do. 1819; E. Roer, *The Brihad Aranyaka Upanishad*, with the commentary of Sankara Āchārya, the gloss of Ānanda Giri, Eng. tr. of text and of part of the commentary, do. 1848–74; *The Upanishads, the Taittiriya, Aitareya, Svetāśvatara, Iśa, Kena, Katha, Praśna, Munduka and Mandukya*, tr. from E. Roer, ed. with an Introd. by Manmatha Nath Dutt, do. 1907; O. Böhtlingk, *Bṛhadāranjakopanishad in der Mādhjaṁdina Recension*, St. Petersburg, 1889; S. Sitarama Sastri, *The Upanishads* (in Sanskrit and English) and Sankara's *Com.* (in English), Madras, 1898 ff.; Śriśa Chandra Vasu, *The Upanishads* (in Sanskrit and English), *with the commentary of Mādhavāchārya* (in English), Allahabad, 1909 ff.; *The Twelve Principal Upanishads*, Eng. tr., with notes from the com. of Sankarāchārya, and the gloss of Ānandagiri, published by Rajaram Tukaram Tatya, Bombay, 1906; *The Minor Upanishads*, with original text, introd., Eng. rendering and commentaries, printed and published by Swami Virajananda, Mayavati, 1913; K. Nārāyaṇasvāmi Aiyar, *Thirty Minor Upanishads*, Madras, 1914; L. D. Barnett, *Some Sayings from the Upanishads*, done into Eng. with notes, London, 1905; *Selections from the Upanishads*, translated into Eng. with notes from Sankara Āchārya and others, ed. J. Murdoch, Madras, 1895.

A. S. GEDEN.

URIM AND THUMMIM.—See DIVINATION (Jewish).

USURY.

USURY (Babylonian).—'Usury' is a wide term and commonly covers many transactions, distinct in their origin and purpose; and it is doubtful whether any custom existed in Babylonia which exactly anticipated any modern interpretation of the term. Interest on loans, rent of estates, wages, anything paid to any one for the use of anything the right to which is not thereby alienated, may be brought under the heading usury from one point of view or another. It would not, however, be accurate to regard this as a definition of usury for the purposes of this article, nor would it be advisable to limit the meaning to either the exaction of exorbitant interest or ruinous charge for accommodation. In fact it may be doubted whether the Babylonians contemplated any transaction with which they were acquainted as answering to anything we understand by usury.

We must remember that the foundation of economic affairs was, from the earliest times with which we are acquainted to the latest for which we have evidence from cuneiform sources, the farming of sheep and cattle or of agricultural produce. In consequence, the natural increase of flocks and herds being at least 200 per cent per annum, that of crops in the fertile soil of Mesopotamia at least 400 to 500 per cent, the rate of interest was excessively high according to our standard. But such returns, given security from loss by misfortune or disorder, must have led to a rapid increase of wealth. A fortunate possessor must soon have owned more than he could possibly protect. He was bound to employ others as shepherds or labourers merely to conserve his property. Unless he could command the services of slaves or subjects, he had to pay for such services. He might, and in Babylonia usually did, allot a portion of his flock to some shepherd to tend, demanding back after the pasturing and breeding season, his own again with a stipulated rate of increase, which we may loosely call usury. He might let out his farm or part of it to husbandmen, demanding a stipulated share of the crops, and leaving the rest as wages for the labour expended. Whether this constituted usury or not may depend on whether the amount demanded as return from the labourer bore a more or less reasonable relation to the average crop likely to be obtained. The reasonableness of the transaction depended upon many considerations which would be differently regarded then and now. In cases where a man's former prosperity had enabled him to realize his profits in the more stable form of money, he might lend that money as an accommodation to one who had less or even none, on the understanding that he was to receive again his own with usury, but where to draw the distinction between fair interest and usury must depend, not only on the custom of the country, but also on the yield it might reasonably be expected to produce when invested directly in agriculture or farming.

So long as the return for the accommodation which a creditor demanded kept well within the naturally expected profit to be made by the borrower, both were sharers in the benefits brought about by the accommodation. The abuses which might constitute usury arose by a demand for excessive return or by failure to accept responsibility and share in unexpected and unavoidable loss which fell on the borrower. It must early have occurred to the lender to demand security for his loan. By an early established custom the person of the debtor was held as security. This personal security extended over all the borrower's possessions. The debtor who failed to pay had to work off his debt somehow, and it was recognized as fair that the members of his family should be called upon to help him to discharge his debt. Thus he might assign any or all of his family—wife, children, or slaves—to work off his debt. This was to their advantage as much as to his, for they were thus secure of a living, though precluded from the profit of their labour, while, if he was bankrupt, he had no means of providing for them any more than for himself.

But the situation was full of possibilities of oppression, and the rich or prosperous man would soon have become master or partial owner of his poorer brethren indebted to him. So long as such a master treated his dependents fairly, and the land was secure from foreign conquest, a few rich men with a large industrious body of well-treated servants, certain of adequate maintenance, might well constitute a prosperous community. But the raids made in war, the spoliation of the rich man's capital, or the failure of a crop must have reduced the dependents to great misery. The tendency to accumulate wealth in the hands of a few avaricious men might work in the same direction through the tendency to strike hard bargains with labour. A benevolent or far-sighted ruler must early have seen that an overworked or underfed population would grow discontented and so be unreliable in case of invasion to maintain the security of the land against foreign aggression. Hence legislation was introduced to check the abuses which might lead to an undue exploitation of labour by capital.

The celebrated Code of Ḫammurabi, the best-known body of legislation dealing with the subject, which we must regard as the outcome of innumerable other attempts in the same direction, devotes a large part of its regulations to controlling the tendencies of the state of society to permit oppression by the exaction of unfair enforcement of the literal terms of what had been entered upon as a free contract. These regulations of the code are already dealt with in the art. LAW (Babylonian), vol. vii. p. 817 f., and may be briefly summarized here. When a debtor owed for rent or share of crops and was unable to pay by reason of the failure of the crops not due to his own negligence, he was allowed to postpone payment to the next year. It was not legal to insist on the payment of any debt in one special form of tender, though this was often specified in a contract. Produce was made legal tender in any case, thus obviating the difficulty of its realization in a land where money was scarce, and equalizing the variations of exchange. The right of a creditor to seize the person of the debtor or of his dependents, and hold him or them in servitude until the debt had been worked off, was an obvious opening for great abuse, but was modified by the Code. By its enactment that such service should not excuse ill-treatment and, in any case, should not extend beyond three years, it clearly eliminated much injustice. The text of the Code as treated in art. LAW (Babylonian) was not then complete; but a contemporary, or at least very early, copy from Nippur[1] gives one of the lost sections enacting that, if a man borrow grain or money from a merchant and has not grain or money sufficient to repay him, he shall give the merchant whatever he has in his power in place of the debt that he owes in the presence of the city elders, and the merchant may not decline to accept it. This was a far-reaching enactment, and may be suspected of aiming specially at indebtedness to foreigners, or at any rate to men not exactly neighbours. By far the larger number of debts of which we have any record were owed to the temples, which stood to the people in the relation of agricultural banks. Their advances were of the nature of loans to tide over scarcity at seed-time, or to meet the expense of harvest operations when the last year's produce had already become exhausted, though a fresh crop was now in sight. They were mostly for a short term without interest, interest being demanded only in the case of delay to repay at the fixed time. Many of these temples were large land-owners, and also owned numerous flocks or herds. They, like other great owners, often farmed on the *metayer* system, furnishing to their tenants seed, agricultural instruments, and working animals, while advancing wages in kind. The numerous records of temple transactions which have reached us, due to the recovery of large temple archives, may easily have distorted the picture that we are able to draw of social life at that period, but they must have dominated the general custom. The landlord on this system was bound by that custom and his own interest, as well as by humanity, to see that his debtor, who was his tenant, should not be oppressed at any period of the year by want, tending to paralyse his efforts for their mutual profit.

In spite of all such regulations it is evident

[1] See *AJSL*, April, 1915, p. 225.

that debt and the servitude to which it led were very common features of Babylonian society. It was further met by a general amnesty from debt, or *seisachtheia*, proclaimed by many a sovereign apparently to inaugurate his new reign, to secure popularity and encourage loyalty and thereby to achieve power to maintain his rule. The ability thus to remit debts doubtless lay in the power which the king had over temple revenues, as the temples were the chief holders of credit. Their responsibility to the citizens who sustained that credit was never lost sight of. They were called upon to redeem members of their city who became captives in war if these were without means to redeem themselves. The temples were stewards of their wealth for the god who watched over the welfare of his people. The loss to certain members of debts unpaid was a loss to the community at large who had furnished the source of their wealth, but, as this was the result of prosperous years, it might fairly be taxed to equalize over a term of years the incidental losses due to accident or bad seasons, to the 'hand of God,' or to enemy action. To grant such an amnesty, which seems to have involved a general release from debt and the restoration of liberty to prisoners and hostages for debt, was regarded as an 'establishment of equity' and was the prelude to fresh legislation. It is not completely clear that this amnesty touched private debts; it had in view rather debts to the temples, which were naturally in the power of the king. If private indebtedness was cancelled, it is difficult to see how injustice to the private creditor was avoided or what compensation he could have received for the forfeit of his capital and interest.

Most writers on the subject appear to have regarded the rates of interest charged for loans as exorbitant, but the high interest is associated in all periods with oriental custom and economic conditions. The multiplication of capitalists and the competition between them for investments have reduced the rate of interest under modern conditions to what we regard as fair, but any national scarcity of raw material or capital is bound to raise the rate again. Practically the risk involved determines the rate charged for a loan. Professional money-lenders were then more rare, and had to take greater risks. The profits which a borrower was able to secure by actual trading or farming were so high that accommodation for interest was less attractive to the lender unless the rate was high.

LITERATURE.—For the laws regarding usury see C. H. W. Johns, *The Oldest Code of Laws in the World*, Edinburgh, 1903, §§ 45–126; for the *metayer* system, *ib.* § 253. See also Johns, *Babylonian and Assyrian Laws, Contracts, and Letters*, do. 1904. For the financial position of the temples, C. H. W. Johns, *The Civilization of Babylonia and Assyria*, Philadelphia and London, 1915. For *seisachtheia*, M. Schorr, 'Eine babylonische Seisachthie aus dem Anfang der Kassitenzeit' (*SBAW*, 1915, pt. 4); S. Langdon, *PSBA*, 1914, p. 102.

C. H. W. JOHNS.

USURY (Christian).—**1. In the New Testament.**—The words of Jesus contain allusions to borrowing and lending, but, as we should expect of one who refused to be a judge and divider (Lk 12^{14}), there are no direct precepts to guide the Christian conscience. Mt 5^{42} and Lk $6^{34ff.}$ are but exhortations to an open-hearted charity. The Parable of the Talents (Mt 25^{14-30}) and the Parable of the Pounds (Lk 19^{11-27}) allude to banking and interest, but in casual phrases, not in the pith and marrow of the teaching. Borrowing itself would be frequent enough in that age and country, not so much of the commercial type,[1] but more of the loose and personal kind, as between friend and friend, kinsman and kinsman. The shiftless Oriental is a ready if somewhat conscienceless borrower, and the Syrian peasant who to-day loans out his earnings in petty usury doubtless had his like-minded ancestor in the changeless East.[1] The ethic of these personal borrowings was adequately covered by the general principles enunciated by Jesus; there was no call, nor was it His method, to deal with usury as an economic and commercial factor.

What mattered for the future centuries was that by His life and example even more than by His words the great Master had suggested a certain attitude towards this world's goods. Himself reared among the poor and needy, He lived the life of a travelling teacher without home or material possessions; to those who left house and kindred and lands for His sake He had promised everlasting life (Mt 19^{29}); and to the rich young ruler, morally perfect though he claimed to be, He had given the arresting command to sell all and give to the poor (Mt 19^{21}). Among the slaves and the folk of the lower orders who formed the majority of the early converts such teaching was treasured and, it may be, unduly emphasized; its potency appears in the communistic movement of Acts (4^{32}) and in the fact that from the beginning dear to the heart of the Christian society was the care of the poor. It is as but one phase of a general attitude to this world's goods that we must explain the Church's dislike of usury. In their simple, fraternal communities, with their pervasive atmosphere of kindly charity, the hard bargainer for gain was a chilling and unwelcome intruder, the personification of the spirit of the alien world without.

2. In the Fathers.—The early Fathers looked upon usury with severe disapproval. They may have been influenced in certain cases by the classical moralists, but the determining standard for them was the OT legislation and the general principles of the NT teaching, more especially a strained interpretation of Lk 6^{35}.

Tertullian,[2] Cyprian,[3] and Clement of Alexandria[4] accept as still binding on Christians the OT precepts (Ex 22^{25}, Dt 23^{19}, Ps 15^{5}, Ezk 18^{8}), the first-named regarding the prohibition of interest as only a preparation for the higher demand of the Gospel to forgo even the capital: 'Quo facilius assuefaceret hominem ipsi quoque foeneri perdendo cuius fructum didicisset amittere.' Apollonius ranks usury with games of chance.[5] Lactantius condemns it.[6] The Fathers of the 4th and 5th centuries write to the same effect, only with a rising vehemence that suggests that the evil was increasing in decadent times. To Chrysostom it is *σύνδεσμος ἀδικίας*,[7] to Ambrose it is *rapina*,[8] Augustine places it in the category of crime: 'Audent etiam foeneratores dicere, non habeo aliud unde vivam. Hoc mihi et latro diceret, deprehensus in fauce; hoc et effractor diceret . . . et leno . . . et maleficus.'[9] Basil[10] and Gregory of Nyssa[11] in homilies of like spirit denounce the usurers as a breed of vipers that gnaw the womb that bears them.

The standpoint of the Fathers, however, is not to be explained as a mere narrow reading of Scripture: it is the view of men whose Christian conscience abhorred the exploitation of the defenceless and unfortunate. The practice of usury is regarded throughout this period not as an economic but as a moral question. Borrowing was still largely for the urgent personal needs of poor men who were fit subjects not for exaction but for charity. It was the soulless miser—living safely and meanly, gloating over his gains ill-gotten by pitilessly farming the necessities of the needy—who sat for the portrait of the usurer and drew the fire of the preacher. The Christian conscience was finely sensitive to the obligation of charity. Wealth was the gift of God, and men were but stewards, *dispensatores* not *possessores*.

[1] See art. 'Interest,' in *DCG*.

[1] G. M. Mackie, *Bible Manners and Customs*, London, 1898, p. 84.
[2] *C. Marc.* iv. 17.
[3] *Test.* iii. 48.
[4] *Strom.* ii. 18.
[5] *Ap.* Eusebius, *HE* iii.
[6] *Div. Inst.* vi. 18.
[7] *Hom. lvii. in S. Matt.*
[8] *De Bono mortis*, xii.; cf. *de Tobia, passim.*
[9] *In Psalm.* cxxviii.
[10] *Hom. in Ps.* xiv.
[11] *Oratio c. Usurarios.*

'Understand then, ye rich, that ye are in duty bound to do service, having received more than ye yourselves need. . . . Be ashamed of holding fast what belongs to others. Imitate God's equity and none shall be poor.'

This note struck in *The Preaching of Peter* is typical. To a teacher like Ambrose rights of property were a creation of avarice; charity or almsgiving was an act of simple justice.[1] In all this the Church is moving in the realm of precept and ideal; law on the subject is not yet.

3. In the canons of the Councils.—Antagonism gradually hardened into prohibition,[2] as the Church developed in power after Constantine. At first she deals only with her own clerics, who, as guardians of ecclesiastical property, must have had practical difficulties and temptations. By the 17th canon of the Council of Nicæa deposition is prescribed for usurious clerics. In the statute of the Council of Elvira (305–306) ordering expulsion from the Church of any person 'si vero in ea iniquitate duraverit' the mention of laymen is doubtful, but by 345 we find the Council of Carthage declaring it reprehensible in laymen. This view is repeated by the Council of Aix-la-Chapelle (789), and by the 9th cent. ecclesiastical law becomes positive in extending the prohibition to the laity: bishops are to require all Christians to abstain from usury and to punish the recalcitrant.[3] Legislation threw its net ever wider as the evil increased, and the whole armoury of ecclesiastical pains and penalties was turned upon the offenders. Thus a canon of the 3rd Lateran Council (1179) ordained that 'manifest usurers shall not be admitted to communion, nor, if they die in their sin, receive Christian burial.' The 2nd Council of Lyons (1274) went farther, forbidding any community, corporation, or individual to permit the letting of houses to foreign usurers. Spiritual penalties are reinforced by civil: by another canon the wills of unrepentant usurers were declared invalid, thus bringing usury definitely within the jurisdiction of the ecclesiastical courts.[4] The Council of Vienne (1311) brought matters to a climax, declaring the civil law on usury as of no effect and branding as a heretic any one who pertinaciously held that usury was not sinful.

4. In the Middle Ages.—This growing stringency indicates the advance of a tide that could not be checked. 'Since in almost every place the crime of usury has become prevalent,' admits the canon of the 3rd Lateran. Significant is the concession made in favour of the Jews by the 4th Lateran: only grave and excessive usury is forbidden them. By the 11th cent. commerce was finding new channels; towns were arising, markets opening, and thus problems of trade became urgent. Churchmen themselves needed large sums for building and for Crusades. This activity in the money market called for readjustments and new methods. The Church had to reconsider her whole attitude to trade and economic practice. The old view that business was an evil, with its roots in covetousness, had to go. The interchange of goods by which men lived had to be accepted; only its methods must be jealously examined. Christian principles had to be applied in detail. Over against Roman law, as codified by Justinian and studied in the schools, Churchmen had to set forth their own rule and standards. This task fell to the Schoolmen, pre-eminent among whom stands Thomas Aquinas. Even as he formulates his judgments on usury he has to make concessions, and, once one gap is made in the hedge of restriction, other gaps appear as the centuries pass, until

[1] Cf. A. J. Carlyle, in *Property*, London, 1913, ch. v.
[2] Endemann, *Grundsätze der canonistischen Lehre*, § 2.
[3] Council of Meaux (845), can. 55.
[4] W. J. Ashley, *An Introd. to English Economic History and Theory*[9], i. 150.

it becomes a question whether there is a hedge at all.

The scholastics based their judgment on more than the OT and gospel precepts.[1] (*a*) They accepted the dictum of Aristotle,[2] made familiar to us from *The Merchant of Venice*, that barren metal does not breed. Money was regarded merely as a medium of exchange; the modern concept of capital had not been evolved. The fact was overlooked that the money borrowed could purchase, *e.g.*, a cow, and a cow does breed. (*b*) Roman law distinguished between consumptibles (*e.g.*, a loaf) and fungibles (*e.g.*, a house). In *mutuum* the thing borrowed was for consumption; its whole value lay in its first use; the use and the substance were inseparable; an adequate compensation was made when an equal quantity was returned. In this category money was ranked. When A borrowed money from B, his ownership over it was absolute; it was more than *possessio*, it was *dominium*; the process of exchange had the quality of a sale, and to sell an article and then charge for the use of it was unjust.

This, then, was the decision of the canonist conscience: in itself the loan of money did not justify a charge for its use. In those days of limited opportunity for investment it was doubtless often a gain to the lender to find a man willing to accept custody of the money, so long as it was returned intact. And the Schoolmen were ready to face the logic of facts and to make allowance for special cases. The custom sprang up of admitting compensation on various extrinsic grounds.[3]

(*a*) Bargains were not kept. A delay in payment might inflict serious loss. Was there to be no compensation? Certainly. So the lender was allowed to fix a fine to be paid if the bargain was not kept, the *pœna conventionalis*, and this fine was frequently as high as the amount of the original debt. This sum represented the difference between the creditor as he actually was and as he should have found himself had the bargain been kept—hence the name *interest*, 'that which is between.' As the civil law had allowed the defaulting debtor to be imprisoned or even to become a slave, this money payment was really a milder punishment.

(*b*) Suppose a man who had lent his money were compelled himself to borrow at a high rate of interest through the failure of the debtor to repay. For such a real expense capable of proof compensation was allowed by practically all Schoolmen —*damnum emergens*.

(*c*) By handing over money to another the lender deprived himself of the gain he might have made in various ways (*lucrum cessans*). Aquinas disapproved of this as a basis of claim, a future gain being regarded as too hypothetical. It was selling what did not exist and by a hundred chances might never exist. But this plea by the 15th cent. gained wide acceptance.

(*d*) Another extrinsic title which won its way to approval later than the others was that based on the risk—*e.g.*, in maritime ventures—that the sum borrowed would not be restored (*periculum sortis*).

(*e*) Once delay in payment (*titulus moræ*) was recognized as a reason for compensation, the practice easily sprang up of lending gratuitously for a short period and charging for delay beyond that period. This was but a step from the modern method of calculating interest.

It was not only by these strictly guarded avenues that money could pass for gain; the Middle Ages offered two other modes of investing money: (*a*) rent-charges, and (*b*) partnership.

(*a*) A squire drawing a fixed rent for a piece of land could transfer to another that right. Real productive property (*res frugifera*) was the indispensable basis for this contract; but the privilege was extended later to shops, toll-rights, etc., so that even the small trader and artisan could raise money to expand their business in this way.

(*b*) The stay-at-home merchant could entrust his goods to an agent—*e.g.*, the owner of a trading ship—and might bargain for a share of the profit of the venture. This partnership assumed many forms, the approval of the canonists requiring two conditions: (1) the investor remained the owner of his capital; and (2) he shared in the risk, thus earning a moral right to a share of the profits.

In view of all these gaps in the hedge, it is difficult to maintain that the ban on usury seriously hampered trade and commerce. Indeed, no school-made dictum would have been suffered

[1] *E.g.*, Thomas Aquinas, *Summa*, II. ii. qu. lxxviii.
[2] *Politics*, i. 3, § 23.
[3] Cf. Ashley, ii. 397 ff

long to impede forces so potent as the trading instinct in man and the international necessity of commerce. The masses during these centuries still lived largely by agriculture and the primitive crafts. Neither artisan nor farmer had a big margin of wealth to tide over ill-health or bad harvests or grievous taxation. In such conditions the petty usurer was a temptation and a snare, as he is to-day in similarly undeveloped communities—*e.g.*, India and Egypt. Moreover, interest calculated per month, as was the system then in vogue, resulted in exorbitant charges. As the zealous guardian of the poor and the distressed, the Church was probably wise to keep her ban on usury. Her policy was certainly a long step in advance of the pagan practice by which the debtor was suffered to fall to the status of a slave. After the inroads of the barbarians, moreover, there was a period of chaos; commerce was stagnant rather than seeking for new outlets. What wealth an impoverished society possessed was swallowed up in the necessities of life; only after her recovery would there be free wealth for development, and that found open channels in partnerships and rent-charges. When capital was thus scarce and lending the monopoly of a few, unlimited freedom to impose interest would have led to abuse and produced a social cancer in that unripe age. Further, the Church was not herself detached from the realities of the economic world. She was one of the largest holders of property and monies, and Churchmen, as stewards of that material wealth, were driven to find ways and means of investment. The lessons of their own practical difficulties were not lost on them, as in their experience of the *montes pietatis.*

The Franciscans, with their sensitiveness to the needs of the poor, instituted at Orvieto (1463), Perugia (1467), and elsewhere these philanthropic loan-funds with a view to giving small loans to the poor on the security of pledges. 'But,' writes Ashley, 'even with papal patronage and the promise of spiritual and temporal advantages to those who should subscribe towards so charitable a work, the managers of the *montes* found it necessary to make a small charge for the loan in order to cover working expenses.'[1]

A wordy warfare followed between the various orders, resulting in the notable judgment of the Lateran Council of 1515 by which the *montes* were allowed to levy moderate interest, provided their object was to cover working expenses and not to make a profit. Such a verdict could not fail to have far-reaching effect. The Church which had resisted usury in the interests of the poor was now compelled to allow moderate interest to an institution which existed on behalf of the poor. The Council itself apparently felt that the question had reached a new phase, and re-defined usury thus:

'This is the proper interpretation of usury, when gain is sought to be acquired from the use of a thing not in itself fruitful (such as a flock or a field), without labour, expense or risk on the part of the lender.'

The controversy on the triple contract in the 16th cent. also shows forces moving towards the admission of interest. A capitalist class was emerging—a process that was aided by the large profits made by traffic in Indulgences for which the Church herself was responsible. The powerful banking house of the Fuggers of Augsburg was behind John Eck who championed this method of investment at the University of Bologna in 1515, and John Major argued with cogency in its favour.[2]

Three different contracts with three different men were allowed: (1) a contract of partnership, (2) a contract of insurance against loss of capital, (3) a contract of insurance against fluctuation of profit. Could a merchant make all three contracts with one man? That meant that his capital was guaranteed, so was a fixed return. Was this usurious?

At Bologna there was no decision. Yet the

[1] Ashley, ii. 450.
[2] *In iv. Sententiarum*, dist. xv. qu. 49.

campaign taken up by Major and others might have achieved success but for the wave of reaction that came with the counter-reformation. Liberal opinion was swamped, and a reversion was made to a stricter standard by the bull *Detestabilis Avaritiæ* of Sixtus V. (1586), which revived the sternest condemnation of usury as 'detestable to God and man, as condemned by the sacred canons, and as contrary to Christian charity.'[1]

5. The Reformation and after.—The yoke of authority was broken by the Reformation and it was inevitable that in the freer atmosphere of Protestantism the binding strictures on usury should be cast off. Not that that process was unopposed. On the contrary, the removal of the Church's ban only showed how strong was the popular sentiment against the practice; witness Martin Luther's earlier deliverances on the subject.[2] These are not the scientific judgments of the theologian, but rather the utterance of a son of the people, feeling keenly that oppression at the hands of the nobles and rich city merchants which led to the peasants' rebellion; there was also in the case his Christian fury against the Jewish usurers' ensnaring of his fellow-believers.[3] His zeal for moral reform tended to swing him back to the strictest standard of the Fathers. He called on ministers to preach against usury (1540). In more reasoned mood, however, in cases where the participators are not poor, he allows rent-charges on real land and interest that compensates for actual loss (*damnum emergens* and *lucrum cessans*), provided the charge is moderate (four or five florins to the hundred).[4]

Melanchthon professes to accept the traditional, Scriptural prohibitions.[5] But a practical guiding consideration to his mind is whether the usury is so immoderate as to have a disintegrating effect on the commonwealth, a consideration forced upon him doubtless by his study of classical times:

'Societas civilis non potest esse perpetua cum non servatur aequalitas . . . Exhauritur ergo altera pars et non servatur aequalitas, sicut res ipsa ostendit ubi concessae fuerunt immoderatae usurae. . . .'[6]

He allows a payment 'supra sortem,' not only in cases of *damnum emergens* and *lucrum cessans* to those engaged in lucrative trade, but even where there is no *titulus moræ*, provided always the interest is moderate: 'Licet stipulari de eo quod interest etiam ante moram.'[7]

It was left to Calvin, however, to finally open the sluice, and that, too, without any such intention on his part. His standpoint is really the same as that of his contemporaries.[8] Only he wrote to Œcolampadius a guarded opinion, the substance of which was seized on and the reservations slurred over. The opinion expressed was not for everybody. He hesitated to make any concession, feeling, on the one hand, that to condemn usury altogether was to impose restrictions severer than the Lord Himself desired, and, on the other hand, that, if he yielded an inch, some would take an ell. And what he feared came to pass.

[1] The Catholic Church has been slow to give official sanction to usury. As late as 1745 the *Vix Pervenit* of Benedict XIV. follows canonist lines. Not till 1830 did the Holy Office allow, in a particular case, that interest could lawfully be taken for money lent to merchants who were in lucrative trade. Cf. J. M. Harty, 'Historical Evolution of the Catholic Teaching on Usury,' in *Irish Theol. Quarterly*, iv. [1910] 17.
[2] *Sermons*, 1519, 1524.
[3] *Letter against the Sabbathers*, 1543.
[4] G. Schmoller, *Zur Gesch. der nationalökonomischen Ansichten in Deutschland während der Reformationsperiode*, Tübingen, 1861, p. 110 f.
[5] 'Haec divina testimonia amplectamur et sciamus usuras vere displicere Deo' (*de Contractibus* [*Opera*, ed. H. E. Bindseil, Halle and Brunswick, 1843–60]).
[6] *Ib.* [7] *Ib.*
[8] *Comm. in Ps* 15[5]: 'Sciamus ergo contractus omnes quibus alter ex alterius damno lucrum inique captat quocunque tandem nomine vestiantur damnari'; cf. *Serm. in Dt. xxiii.*

Lk 6[35], the letter runs, has been badly twisted from its real sense; Jesus merely wished to correct the vicious custom of the world whereby men readily lent to the rich, who could pay back, and not to the poor. Dt 23[19] was political and not to bind us further than reason and equity allowed. The strictures in the Psalms and Prophets were applicable to the Hebrews: our circumstances are different. The Aristotelian argument, to which Ambrose and Chrysostom subscribed ('pecunia non parit pecuniam'), is of no great moment. It is a specious quibble. Interest proceeds from money as naturally as rent from a field or house. A money gain is allowed for the use of a house. So money can be made fruitful when land is purchased and yields a yearly revenue. The argument is clinched by an illustration. A rich man, A, well endowed with landed property and other income, is short of ready money. Another man, B, is not so rich, but has abundance of ready money. A asks B for a loan of money. B could easily buy land for himself or he could have the land bought with his money hypothecated to him till the debt was repaid. Suppose instead of that he contents himself with the interest, the fruit of the money, is that to be condemned when the harsher contract is reckoned fair? That would be nothing else than playing with God, a child's game.

While thus Calvin does not condemn all usury, he does not give it indiscriminate approval, nor will he countenance it as a trade. Finally, he lays down seven conditions, the important being that usury was not to be demanded of men in need or distress; poor brethren were to be considered; the welfare of the State was to be safeguarded; and the legal rate was not to be exceeded.[1]

A world eager for commercial freedom found it convenient to drop Calvin's qualifications, while his concessions were seized on as authority for a new standard. When the theologian had yielded the principle, the jurist was ready to rush in and establish the case at all points. Molinæus[2] demolished with meticulous detail the old arguments of the canonists. Though his book was placed on the Index, it was freely republished and circulated widely. More especially in the Netherlands, where Reformation principles were spreading and commerce was developing, the new views found open ears. Salmasius preached the cause in a series of brilliant volumes;[3] but practical needs were probably more eloquent than argument. In Germany early in the 16th cent. several State legislatures began to allow *Interesse*, when stipulated in advance, and in 1654 the imperial diet did likewise. In Italy, under the shadow of Roman Catholicism, discussion did not arise till late, but in the busy commercial towns, by allowing interest to be bargained for beforehand from an early period and exploring other avenues of ingenuity, the prohibition of usury was rendered ineffective. In France the power of the Church maintained the ban until the Revolution. Not till 1789 was the prohibition removed. Turgot's *Mémoire sur les prêts d'argent*, the classic vindication of usury in France, did not see the light till 1789.

6. Opinion in England.—Christianity arrived in the infancy of English civilization and stamped her character from the beginning on social and political developments. Accordingly, the attitude of mind shown towards usury in popular literature[4] and in early statutes is in harmony with the teaching of the Church. Indeed it would appear that not till the Jews arrived after the Conquest did the trade become a problem at all. The English people have always been healthily disposed towards commerce—indeed their very existence depends upon it—and they would be prompt to protest if the ban on usury were found restricting trade. What emerges is the opposite: a keen desire to grapple with and shackle the traffickers in usury. Complaints were often made that the ecclesiastical courts were not stringent enough.[5] Progressive civilians sought further powers to stamp out the evil—*e.g.*, in the ordinance framed

[1] *Johannis Calvini Epistolæ et Responsa*, ed. Beza, Geneva, 1575, p. 355.

[2] *Tractatus contractuum et usurarum redituumque pecunia constitutorum* (1546).

[3] *De Usuris* (1638), *de Modo Usurarum* (1639), *de Fœnere Trapezitico* (1640).

[4] *E.g.*, *Piers Plowman*, under 'Avarice.'

[5] W. Cunningham, *Christian Opinion on Usury*, p. 45.

by the London municipality in 1363.[1] The exact point of offence is defined in the revised statute (1390) which describes usury as 'a promise for certain without risk.' The wide-spread bitterness towards the Jew was one other illustration of the popular verdict against usury. The very exorbitance of the interest allowed—2d a week per £1, *i.e.* 43⅓ per cent—was enough to breed odium, and kings made rather a questionable use of these strangers. Feeling rose so high that the Jews were expelled in 1290, and in the following century (1376) the citizens of London called for the same measure against the Lombards, the agents of the grievous papal exactions, who had taken over the detested trade.

The way to change was prepared by the relaxations of the canonists themselves, but more by the fact that in the 15th cent. money transactions were altering in character. The borrowers were no longer poor men in need, nor barons suddenly confronted with some savage taxation or a levy for a crusade. Traders making good profits now needed money for developing business; they were willing and ready to pay for loans. And many began to find themselves in better times with a margin to invest: the phenomenon of capital was emerging. Still, when Henry VIII. in 1545, under the guise of limiting charges, really sanctioned interest at 10 per cent, he was probably in advance of public opinion. At any rate a wave of reaction followed, and the Act was repealed under Edward VI. Warm controversy marked the closing decades of the century. On the one side, divines who 'too much squinted towards Moses' preached a stricter standard than even the canonists and attacked rent-charges and partnerships.

The 'little more' of interest was likened to a sixth finger, a monstrosity; the usurers were as ivy on the oak, all-devouring. 'To what shall I liken this generation? They are like a butler's box; for as the counters at last come to the butler, so all the money cometh to the usurer.'[2]

There are indications of resentment of another kind caused by the arrival of a 'new rich' and the dispossession of old families by these 'ungracious pettie Brokers.'[3] Irresistible forces, however, drove the other way. 'But goode Lorde, how is the worlde changed,' writes Thomas Rogers, 'that which Infidels cannot abide, Gospellers allowe.'[4] The Reformation had broken the old spell of authority, and disciples of Calvin found ready listeners. Henry Bullinger and others spread abroad the newer view that usury was forbidden only so far as it was 'biting.' But, as Cunningham has it,

'The most important factor was the revolution in English commerce which occurred during the 16th century; for various circumstances had combined to bring about an entire recasting of the ordinary business system of the country. For one thing, the exclusive trading of the great gilds had suffered a series of severe blows and it was open to anyone to engage in commerce and win its rewards. The great improvements in the management of estates—as well as the planting of new industries—brought much wealth into the hands of many citizens all through the country. . . . For the first time in the history of England the circumstances were present which rendered the general formation of capital possible.'[5]

The Act of 1571 marks the victory of the liberal school. The rate was lowered to 8 per cent in 1624, but more significant was the fact that in that measure no attempt was now made to distinguish between usury and interest. The controversy smouldered on, but really for the time being the question had been settled by the advent of capital and the consequent changed conditions of commerce. The point at issue altered to the rate

[1] *Liber Albus*, tr. H. T. Riley, London, 1861.

[2] Henry Smith, *Works*, ed. Thomas Fuller, i. 99.

[3] Thomas Lodge, 'An Alarum against Usurers,' London, 1584 (*Complete Works*, Glasgow, 1883, i. 14).

[4] See W. Cunningham, *Growth of English Industry and Commerce*, vol. ii. sect. 189.

[5] *Ib.* sect. 190 (*b*).

of interest, for the limitation of which Thomas Culpepper, Josiah Child, and others pled. John Locke entered the lists with *Some Considerations of the Consequences of lowering the Interest and raising the Value of Money* (1691), but it was in another connexion that he made his most significant utterance, anticipating the next phase of the controversy: 'For it is labour indeed that puts the difference of value on everything.'[1] Jeremy Bentham's classic *Defence of Usury* also indicates a fundamental fact which makes this a perennial question, 'The children who have eaten their cake are the natural enemies of the children who have theirs.'[2]

The repeal of the usury laws in 1839 appeared to be 'the end of an auld sang.' But the freedom was abused. The usurer with his merciless exactions again came under control by the Money-Lenders Act of 1900, which requires the registration of their business names and addresses and allows the court, where the lender prosecutes for debt, to cancel the contract if the rates are excessive. Petty loan business, however, still survives.

7. The modern phase of the problem.—History repeats itself in the present phase of the controversy. Usury has come to mean exorbitant interest, but the legitimacy of interest is still debated. The early attacks on usury were motived by the Church's sympathy with the oppressed poor; the latest attack finds its strength in the plea that interest is an unjust tax on the labouring classes.

'But observe, my Lord,—and observe as a final and inevitable truth—that whether you lend your money to provide an invalided population with crutches, stretchers, hearses, or the railroad accommodation which is so often synonymous with the three, *the tax on the use* of these, which constitutes the shareholder's dividend, is a permanent burden upon them, exacted by avarice, and by no means an aid granted by benevolence.'[3]

Henry Smith said that the usurer was like a butler to whom all the counters returned. What offends the moralist to-day is that money is lent by those who have abundance and returns to them to increase that abundance, the increase being the unpaid dues of labour, which alone, the argument runs, produces wealth.

'It is not only that "every gate is barred with gold," but that year by year the burden of the past is becoming heavier on the present. Wealth passes down from father to son like a gathering snowball, at the same time as industry gets massed into larger and larger organizations, and the guidance and spirit of industry is taken more and more out of the hands of the worker and given to the capitalist.'[4]

By interest, then, the socialist claims, the rich are made richer and the poor poorer and the stability of the social organism is disturbed—the evil that Melanchthon had feared.

Is interest, then, an unjustifiable tax that could be eliminated? The experience of the Franciscans with their *montes pietatis* and Proudhon with his Exchange Bank[5] may well give pause. In spite of the strength of the socialist indictment, neither in theory nor in practice has the way out been demonstrated. The contention that labour alone creates value and that interest is the unpaid wage of the labourer and therefore wrong is not established unless it is reckoned that the service rendered by capital involves no sacrifice. The waiting or abstinence of the capitalist has not been swept out of court in spite of Lassalle's picture of the 'ascetic millionaires of Europe . . . like Indian penitents or pillar saints . . . holding a plate towards the people to collect the wages of their abstinence.'

'It is not true that the spinning of yarn in a factory after allowance has been made for the wear-and-tear of the machinery, is the product of the labour of the operatives. It is the product of their labour, together with that of the employer and subordinate managers, and of the capital employed; and that capital itself is the product of labour and waiting: and therefore the spinning is the product of labour of many kinds, and of waiting.'[1]

Could even a socialist community abolish interest and so give the labourer the full value of his labour? The difficulty lies in the fact that so many kinds of labour are not immediately productive. A vintage is harvested in 1920 and valued at hundreds of pounds. But in 1940 that value has increased enormously. Can labour be recompensed according to the value in 1940? It would be simple if the labourers could wait till 1940. But can they? Somebody must wait, and that is the plea for interest—the price of waiting. Interest has been defined as 'human impatience crystallized into a market rate . . . the premium that a man is willing to pay for this year's over next year's goods.'[2]

Only if all labour yielded products of immediate use could the community return to each man each year value for his whole labour. But in a progressive society effort must constantly be made for bettering conditions: expenditure must be put forth on schemes that can yield no immediate return. If the present generation is to hand on to the next finer means of transport and a nobler social equipment, can they do so without denying themselves a portion of the value of their labour? Is sacrifice not inherent in progress? A socialist state might possess itself of much capital, but that capital would not be inexhaustible. Some day the question would arise: where is the capital to come from for these improvements? How can a wage be paid to those engaged in these enterprises with deferred returns except by raising some contribution from other fields of labour? This could be done only by raising the price of other goods above the cost of their labour value, or by paying the labourers less than the value of their labour. Thus the socialist society has to impose a burden upon its citizens and deny them the full value of their labour just because of this fact that certain goods take time to mature; *i.e.* the element of waiting cannot be eliminated, and the price of that waiting must be paid.

'The complaint against interest is after all only a complaint that the great advantages of rapid progress cannot be had for nothing.'[3]

What practical policy can be suggested? It is admitted that laws directed against the usurer simply lead to more exorbitant charges to cover the risk of breaking the law. The most successful antidote is the co-operative bank, which meets the needs of those most subject to temporary distress, such as the artisan and the peasant farmer. The popular dislike of interest springs from the worker's resentment towards the idle rich. That privileged individuals should draw from a community enough for a life of idleness and luxury 'will always be regarded as a fundamental immorality.'[4] But, as Cassel goes on to point out, that really calls for a more equal distribution of the nation's wealth rather than tampering with the method of interest. Society must consider rather the methods by which superabundant wealth comes into a few idle hands—as the laws of inheritance, unearned increment, and all forms of monopoly. Meantime the concern of the Christian Church is not to dictate any particular economic method but to maintain a zealous watchfulness over all developments in behalf of her ideals of justice, charity, and brotherhood.

1 *Of Civil Government* (*Collected Works*, London, 1777, vol. ii. ch. v. § 40).
2 London, 1787, letter x.
3 John Ruskin, 'Usury,' *On the Old Road*, London, 1885, ii. 223 f.
4 W. Smart, pref. to Böhm-Bawerk.
5 C. Gide and C. Rist, *A Hist. of Economic Doctrines*, tr. R. Richards, p. 308 ff.

1 A. Marshall, *Principles of Economics*[6], London, 1910, p. 587.
2 Irving Fisher, *Elementary Principles of Economics*, p. 371.
3 G. Cassel, *The Nature and Necessity of Interest*, p. 179.
4 *Ib.* p. 182.

LITERATURE.—H. Leclercq, *Hist. des Conciles d'après les documents originaux par C. J. Hefele*, Paris, 1907 ff.; P. Schaff, *Hist. of the Creeds of Christendom*, 3 vols., London, 1877; Max Neumann, *Gesch. des Wuchers in Deutschland*, Halle, 1865; F. X. Funk, *Gesch. des kirchlichen Zinsverbotes*, Tübingen, 1877; K. Knies, *Politische Oekonomie*, Brunswick, 1853; W. Endemann, *Die nationalökonomischen Grundsätze der canonistischen Lehre*, Jena, 1863, *Studien in der romanisch-kanonistischen Wirthschafts- und Rechtslehre*, 2 vols., Berlin, 1874–83; Max Weber, *Zur Gesch. der Handelsgesellschaften im Mittelalter*, Stuttgart, 1889; W. Roscher, *Political Economy*, tr. J. J. Lalor, Chicago, 1878; W. Cunningham, *Christian Opinion on Usury*, London, 1884, *Growth of English Industry and Commerce*, Cambridge, 1882; W. J. Ashley, *An Introd. to English Economic History and Theory*^{9}, London, 1913; *Liber Albus*, compiled 1419 by J. Carpenter, tr. H. T. Riley, do. 1861; H. Bullinger, *The Decades*, 5 vols. in 4, Cambridge, 1849–52; J. Jewel, *Works*, ed. J. Ayre, do. 1850, iv. 1293; H. Smith, *Works*, ed. T. Fuller, Edinburgh, 1866, i.; C. Gide and C. Rist, *A Hist. of Economic Doctrines*, tr. R. Richards, London, 1915; E. von Böhm-Bawerk, *Capital and Interest*, tr. W. Smart, do. 1890; Irving Fisher, *Elementary Principles of Economics*, New York, 1918; A. Marshall, *Principles of Economics*^{6}, London, 1910; G. Cassel, *The Nature and Necessity of Interest*, do. 1903; G. O'Brien, *Mediæval Economic Teaching*, do. 1920.

JOHN DOW.

USURY (Hebrew).—**1. Terms.**—These do not throw much light on the moral and religious ideas connected with the subject.

לוה, 'borrow,' also means 'join,' and has been supposed to imply the dependence of the borrower on the lender, but it is more probable that there is no connexion between the two uses of the root. שׁאל, 'ask,' is also used in the sense of 'borrow,' and the *Hiph.* in that of 'lend.' עבט is used for 'borrow on pledge (or security),' and the *Hiph.* for 'lend on security'; חבל is similarly used. As the last two roots are also used in the sense of 'bind,' they have been supposed to imply the binding of the debtor to the creditor. Nouns from these roots are used for 'pledge' or 'security.' ערב is used for 'be surety,' 'give pledges,' etc. For 'lend at interest' we find נשׁא, נשׁה, and נשׁך; נֶשֶׁךְ='interest.' *Nmashakh* also means 'bite'; and *neshekh* is supposed to mean 'something bitten off,' or to refer to the injurious and ruthless behaviour of a creditor in exacting interest. The AV 'usury' for *neshekh* simply meant 'interest' when AV was translated, and the suggestion which it now makes of exorbitant interest is misleading; it is simply 'interest,' as far as the mere word is concerned, apart from the implications of any special context. Thus the obviously neutral word תַּרְבִּית, EV 'increase,' from רבה, 'to be great,' is often used as a parallel and synonym of *neshekh*; and the word is rendered in the LXX by τόκος, and in the Vulg. by *usura*, which are simply the ordinary words for 'interest.'

2. History.—Debt plays only a small part in the OT, partly, no doubt, because it was not an important factor in primitive times, though it became more so as Israel grew more civilized and life more complex. In an agricultural community the failure of the crops might lead to borrowing (Neh 5^{3}). A man might be involved in debt by becoming security for a friend (Pr 6^{1}). In later times taxation for a native government or for the payment of tribute to a foreign suzerain was a source of debt (Neh 5^{4}). As far as the OT is concerned, debt always seems to have originated from such causes; the OT has little or nothing to say about the spendthrift who got into debt through sloth or extravagance. Moreover, commercial borrowing, which is a source of profit to the borrower, though known at a very early period in Babylon—*e.g.*, in the time of Ḫammurabi—does not seem to have existed in ancient Israel. There is no certain and definite information as to the rate of interest. The clause Neh 5^{11}, 'Restore . . . the hundredth part of the money,' has been understood to mean that interest was at the rate of one per cent per month, 12 per cent per annum, and that creditors were to forgo their interest; but most recent authorities—*e.g.*, Batten, *ICC*—read *mashsha'th*, 'interest,' for *m^{e}'ath*, 'hundredth.' Twelve per cent would probably be too moderate, the interest being determined mainly by the urgent need of the borrower. The consequences of debt might be serious; loans were sometimes obtained on the security of land or houses, *i.e.* on mortgage; when the debtor could not pay, the creditor took the property. Where there was no such security, the debtor and his family might be sold as slaves (2 K 4$^{1-7}$, Neh 5$^{4f.}$).

3. Moral and religious significance.—Like other misfortunes, the distress which necessitates borrowing is sometimes regarded as judgment on sin (Dt 15^{6} 28$^{12.\ 44}$), and it is one of the characteristics of the wicked man that he borrows and does not repay (Ps 37^{21}). But usually the OT sympathizes with the debtor and seeks to help and protect him; his position is regarded as the result of unavoidable misfortune. It is the duty of the prosperous man to help his poor neighbour in distress by benevolent loans; it is not to be a pure matter of business (Dt 15$^{7-11}$, Ps 37^{26} 112^{5}, Pr 19^{17}). Necessaries are not to be pledged; thus the widow's ox, or her clothing, or a millstone are not to be taken in pledge (Dt 24$^{6.\ 17}$, Job 24^{3}); clothing when pledged must not be kept over night (Ex 22^{26} JE, Dt 24^{13}). In fact the OT does not regard with approval the practice of taking pledges (Job 22^{6} 24^{9}).

In view of the fact that the insolvent debtor and his family might be sold as slaves, Ex 21$^{2-11}$, which directs the emancipation of the Israelite slave at the end of the seventh year, was an attempt to give some measure of relief to the debtor. This attempt is carried to an extreme in Dt 15$^{1-6}$, which appoints a שְׁמִטָּה, EV 'release,' at the end of every seven years, when all debts were to be cancelled. The sequel shows what a large-hearted generosity the Deuteronomic writer demanded from his fellow-countryman: 'Beware that there be not a base thought in thine heart, saying, The seventh year, the year of release, is at hand; and thine eye be evil against thy poor brother, and thou give him nought' (15^{9}). There is, however, no evidence that the law was ever enforced; it is on the face of it impracticable. Indeed, the Deuteronomic writer himself seems conscious that he is only setting forth an ideal. This appears from 15^{4}. We may set aside the AV 'Save when there shall be no poor among you,' and adopt the RV 'Howbeit there shall be no poor with thee,' *i.e.* no one shall need to borrow, 'for Jahweh will surely bless thee . . . if only thou diligently hearken unto the voice of Jahweh thy God, to observe to do all this commandment.' As Driver says in his comment on this passage, there will be 'no occasion for the present law to come into operation, if only the nation so comports itself as to merit Jehovah's blessing.' On the other hand, if Israel disobeyed other commandments, so that there were poor, the nation was not likely to observe this particular ordinance; in either case, it would be a dead letter; so it seems to have been. Other authorities propose the less probable rendering, 'Howbeit there *should* be no poor in thee,' *i.e.* the nation should establish a social system which would make poverty impossible. The Priestly Law of jubile (Lv 25) has a similar object to the release. It provides that at the year of jubile all land shall go back to the family to which it originally belonged, and that an Israelite sold for a slave through poverty shall be treated as a hired servant and released. As the loss of the family inheritance or of personal freedom was often due to debt, this law would have mitigated the unhappy consequences of what we should call bankruptcy. Here again this law, like that of the release, was a dead letter. Nevertheless, these laws are evidence of the anxiety of the legislators that neither an individual nor a family should be permanently ruined by insolvency.

A persistent feature of OT teaching is the prohibition of interest as between Israelite and Israelite, although interest may lawfully be taken from a foreigner (Ex 22^{25} JE, Dt 23$^{19.\ 20}$, Lv 25$^{36.\ 37}$ H, Ps 15^{5}, Pr 28^{8}, Ezk 18$^{8-17}$ 22^{12}, Neh 5).

Interest would often be exorbitant, and indebtedness the occasion or pretext for fraudulent and unjust claims, successfully asserted through the corrupt administration of the law or by sheer violence. There can be no doubt that borrowing and its consequences contributed to the transference of the land from the yeoman farmers to comparatively few wealthy landlords against which the prophets protested. Doubtless the evils of the system largely arose from exorbitant interest, and from the rapacious and unscrupulous behaviour of creditors; but, as has already been pointed out, *neshekh*, EV 'usury,' is not usury in its modern sense of excessive interest, and we cannot give it that meaning in the OT passages in which it occurs; it means interest generally. It is true that Ex 22^{25} specially refers to the poor, but even there Benzinger and Nowack are probably wrong in holding that it means only excessive interest; and in later passages there is no ground for any such limitation. As we have said above, the writers had not commercial loans in view, and their teaching was not intended to apply to interest in that connexion. The objection to interest seems to rest on two main grounds: (1) that the prosperous man with a superfluity should help those in difficulties, suffering from want; if gifts were impossible or undesirable, at least there should be free loans; (2) as in modern times, it was constantly the interest that ruined the debtor, where he might have repaid the capital, so that the social evils which crushed the poor were largely associated with interest; the simplest and most effective remedy seemed to be to prohibit interest altogether. In other words, the principle involved is that wealthy men should see in the misfortunes of their fellows a claim for generous assistance and not an opportunity for adding to their wealth by exploiting the need of the unfortunate.

The prohibition of interest and the other provisions in favour of debtors, like many other humane provisions in the OT, apply only to Israelites; lending to foreigners is expressly allowed (Dt 23^{20}), and is spoken of as a privilege granted by God to the faithful Israelite (Dt 28^{12}). This is another example of the particularist attitude often found in the OT.

LITERATURE.—See sections on 'Debt' in *Heb. Arch.* of Ewald, Benzinger, and Nowack; the commentaries on the passages cited, especially Driver on Ex 22^{25} (*Cambridge Bible*, Cambridge, 1911) and Dt 15^{1-8} (*ICC*, Edinburgh, 1896); and the present writer's artt. 'Debt' and 'Usury' in *HDB*.

W. H. BENNETT.

USURY (Jewish).—**1. General views of Mishnāh and Talmud.**—In the Mishnāh and Talmud usury is indicated either by the Biblical word נֶשֶׁךְ or, as is more frequently the case, by the term רִבִּית. Both terms denote money, food, or any article which a man gives on loan to his fellow-man, on the condition that the latter repays something for the loan in addition to the original sum lent. The discrimination made in modern times between 'usury' and 'interest' is unknown to Jewish law. All 'increase,' whether large or small, is prohibited. Judaism has ever regarded the lending of money by one Jew to another Jew as merely a way of relieving the latter's temporary distress, an act of pure charity. The basic assumption is that the borrower is poor and wants money to satisfy his own personal wants. It is one of the 365 'negative' precepts of Judaism that a Jew may not lend on interest to another Jew. This prohibition is based on Lv 25^{37}, 'Thou shalt not give him thy money upon usury, nor lend him thy victuals for increase.' Another of the 365 'negative' precepts of Judaism is that a Jew may not borrow from another Jew on interest. This is derived from Dt 23^{19}, 'Thou shalt not lend upon usury to thy brother'—the peculiar 'Hiphil' form of the verb (תַּשִּׁיךְ) leading the Rabbis to infer that the prohibition is aimed in this case at the borrower.[1] Likewise the Judaism of Talmud and Mishnāh forbids any Jew to be an intermediary or agent or surety or witness in any usurious transaction between Jew and Jew. The Rabbis by a curious exegesis derived this prohibition from the redundancy of the phraseology in Ex 22^{25}, 'If thou lend money to any of my people that is poor by thee, thou shalt not be to him as an usurer, neither shalt thou lay upon him usury.' The mediæval Jewish codes lay it down that, in the case of a Jew who has become a convert to another religion, it is forbidden to a Jew to lend to, or borrow from, him on interest. Likewise it is forbidden to a Jew to lend to, or borrow from, a Karaite Jew on interest.

2. Different kinds of usury.—The Talmud and the mediæval Jewish codes enumerate several kinds of 'increase' (רִבִּית). These are (*a*) רִבִּית קְצוּצָה, *i.e.* 'fixed increase,' (*b*) אֲבַק רִבִּית, *i.e.* 'the mere dust of increase,' (*c*) מֶחֱזֵי כְּרִבִּית, *i.e.* 'the semblance of increase,' (*d*) רִבִּית דְּבָרִים, *i.e.* 'increase payable by some means other than money.' They all refer, of course, to dealings between Jew and Jew. The first of these denotes the ordinary transaction where interest in money is paid direct on a loan, in violation of the express command of Scripture. The second (often called 'Rabbinical increase' as distinguished from the first, which is frequently known as 'increase under the Mosaic Law') denotes interest paid in some indirect way connected with bargain and sale, or interest the amount of which was not stipulated nor mentioned at all when the loan was first transacted but which was paid more or less gratuitously by the borrower or taken voluntarily by the lender with the consent of the borrower. It also covers cases where interest was paid by the borrower on the mere anticipation of a loan. A rule of this kind would forbid, on the ground of usury, the sale of futures, made when the market-price has not yet been fixed. Thus the Talmud says:

'A man should not say to his neighbour "Give me a kor of wheat and I will return it at threshing-time" because the market-price of wheat might rise in the meantime and the lender would profit.'[2] Or, again, 'a lender may not lodge in the borrower's house free of charge nor may he rent anything from him at less than the standard rate.'[3]

The third of the four above-mentioned kinds of 'increase' refers to interest paid out of sheer gratitude for a past loan or as the motive for inducing a future one. *E.g.*, after repayment of a loan a borrower might send a gift to the lender on the mere grounds that the lender's money had been in his (the borrower's) hands. This is forbidden. Or, again, if A has received a loan from B, he should not greet B in the street (out of gratitude) unless he had been in the habit of doing so before. A borrower should not consent to be a tutor to the son of the lender, gratuitously, unless he had been this before receiving the loan. The fourth form of 'increase' is illustrated by the case of a Jew who, after receiving a loan from a friend, honoured the latter by allowing him to perform some religious duty in connexion with synagogue-worship or home-ritual.

It is astonishing to read what an emphasis the Talmudic Rabbis laid on all these sins of 'moral' usury. A loan from one Jew to another should be an act of kindness without the least expectation of profit. This, the OT view, was upheld by the Rabbis inexorably, in spite of changed times and conditions.

Turning again to the already-mentioned four species of 'increase,' we should say that (*a*) רִבִּית

[1] See T.B. *Bābhā Meṣi'a*, 61*a*.
[2] *Ib.* 75*a*.
[3] *Ib.* 64*a*.

קְצוּצָה, where charged, was recoverable at law, before the Jewish court ('Beth Din'). If the defendant refused, he was flogged by order of the court, until he consented to pay. The case of (*b*), אֲבַק רִבִּית, was different. This was not recoverable. But, if the lender desired 'to fulfil his duty in the sight of Heaven,' it was obligatory on him to return the interest to the borrower. In other words, it was an act of religion, not of law.

According to the mediæval Jewish codes, the prohibition against taking or giving interest was suspended in the two following cases:

(*a*) Acting Rabbis or teachers of the Law, in borrowing from, or lending to, one another articles of food such as grain, etc., were allowed a fixed interest up to 20 per cent. But such charges were not to be made with frequency lest they might thereby set an undesirable example to the laity. As Rabbis were not commercial men, such transactions were not to be regarded as usurious. It was merely one of the ways of Rabbis helping one another and helping themselves at the same time. It hence came under the heading of 'charity' rather than 'usury.' (*b*) Money left by bequest or gathered for the support of orphans or the poor, or for the upkeep of schools for religious instruction or for the building of a synagogue, might be lent out on interest. This relaxation was made inevitable by the fact that in most countries of mediæval Europe Jews were precluded by the prevailing laws from investing any funds in landed property, and, as all the usual avenues of commerce were closed to them, they felt complete justification in investing public funds on what was, in the strict sense, an undeniably usurious basis.

3. Usury as between Jew and Gentile.—According to Maimonides,[1] a Jew lending money to a Gentile is religiously bidden to charge interest. Maimonides regards this as one of the 'affirmative' precepts of Judaism, deriving it from Dt 23[20], which, according to him, should be translated 'unto a stranger thou *must* lend money on *interest*.' But this view of Maimonides has been severely criticized by the later Jewish legalists and codifiers, and has never found acceptance generally. The prevailing Jewish doctrine is simply that in all transactions between Jew and Gentile interest may be given and taken by both parties.

Commerce is unsectarian. Usurious transactions, as was natural, frequently involved both Jew and Gentile. Hence it was only to be expected that, where Gentile intervention took place in a loan between Jew and Jew (and *vice versa*, where Jewish intervention took place in a loan between Jew and Gentile), there should be a temptation on the part of a Jewish lender or borrower to find a loophole for taking or paying interest, and thus evading the Jewish prohibition of usury as between Jew and Jew. The mediæval Jewish codifiers were well aware of all these contingencies, and their enactments on many a nice point in this connexion are very searching. Here, *e.g.*, are a few specimens culled from the *Shūlḥān 'Ārûkh* of Qaro:[2]

'Suppose the money of a Jew is deposited in the hands of a non-Jew who went and lent it to another Jew on interest. If the non-Jew was responsible for the safety of the money then the Jew is allowed to receive the accruing interest. But if the non-Jew is not responsible for the safety of the money, then interest is prohibited.' 'Suppose the money of a non-Jew is deposited with a Jew. If the latter is responsible for its safety then he may not lend it to a Jew on interest. But if he assumed no responsibility for the money, then he is allowed by Jewish law to lend it to a Jew. But he must not do this because it might convey a wrong impression.' 'A Jew says to a non-Jew, Come and lend out my money for me on interest [to Jews] and I will pay you wages for your work. This is prohibited, because the money belongs to the Jew and his clerk has no responsibility. But if a non-Jewish money-lender asks his Jewish clerk to do the same, the latter is allowed by Jewish Law to do it. But, in fact he must not do it on account of the wrong impression which might be conveyed.' 'Suppose a Jew borrows from a non-Jew on interest, then it is forbidden for a fellow-Jew to be a surety unless the lender distinctly stipulated that in case of default of payment he would not make the first claim against the surety [who would then sue the borrower and thus infringe the prohibition of usury as between Jew and Jew].'

These are but a few instances out of a large number given in the *Shūlḥān 'Ārûkh*.

4. History underlying the Jewish laws concerning usury.—In OT times the Israelites were essentially an agricultural people with no genius for commerce. It was feared that usurious transactions between one Israelite and another might result in the alienation of one tribe's inheritance into the hands of another. This would mean an open violation of the law in Nu 36[7], 'So shall not the inheritance of the children of Israel remove from tribe to tribe; for every one of the children of Israel shall keep himself to the inheritance of the tribe of his fathers.' But usurious dealings between Israelite and non-Israelite were not looked upon as likely to lead to an infringement of this Mosaic Law. On the contrary, it was felt that any gain accruing to the Israelites from such transactions might be most usefully applied to the development and enrichment of the soil of the Holy Land. In later times, in the epoch of the Mishnāh and the Talmud up to the 5th cent. A.D., the Jews mostly dwelt in agricultural settlements in Babylonia, Palestine, and other parts of the world. The Talmudic legislators then found it necessary to enact the law of אֲבַק רִבִּית as mentioned above. Jewish farmers and agriculturists were to be financed by their co-religionists free of all interest. Such was the humanitarian spirit of brotherliness breathed by the Mosaic Law. Were usury permitted even in the slightest degree, debts would grow to such proportions that the creditors would eventually confiscate the entire property of the debtor, and the solidarity of the Jewish people would be utterly broken up. But no such enactments were applicable to the cases of usurious dealings between Jews and Gentiles. There was no love between these two branches of mankind; and, as the Gentile was allowed by law to charge the Jew exorbitant interest, the Jew had no alternative but to do likewise. In fact so hard did the lot of the Jew become through the oppressive measures of the Church that he felt himself justified in adopting no matter what expedients for protecting himself and defeating the foe. In Judaism the duty of self-preservation eclipses all other laws.

The year 1179, however, brought about a vital change. Pope Alexander III. in that year excommunicated all Christian usurers, so that henceforward Christians were debarred by canon law from taking usury. The Church decreed that all taking of interest was forbidden by Scripture as well as opposed to the laws of nature. It made no difference whether interest was low and reasonable, or high and extortionate. But, as canon law did not apply to Jews, the Church put no bar in the way of Jewish usurers; and kings soon found out how useful these Jews could be to the depleted exchequers of their realms. There are many instances in European history generally where wealth amassed by Jewish money-lenders fell into the hands of the king either during the life-time of its owner or after his death. There was a process of squeezing the Jew, sponge-like. Indeed, so indispensable did Jews become to the impoverished coffers of the State that many a mediæval monarch objected to their forced conversion to Christianity, because, once Christians, they would come within the net of canon law, and the annexation of their money would be forbidden. Thus, as Joseph Jacobs has shown, kings actually demanded to be compensated for every Jew converted to Christianity. In spite of the strongest protestations by the papal authority against usury in any form, the kings and princes of mediæval Europe were really the arch-usurers of their day. The rate of interest charged by the Jewish money-lenders was excessively high. But they were forced to this course by the pitiless rapacity of the governments as well as by the inhuman laws then in vogue which put the severest restrictions upon the Jews

[1] *Yad Hā-ḥăzāḳā*, 'Laws of Lending and Borrowing,' vi. 6.
[2] *Yōrĕh Dē'āh*, 'Laws of Usury,' 169.

in their efforts to earn an honest and reputable livelihood. The would-be Jewish trader was shackled. In England, Spain, and many other European countries he was absolutely forbidden by law to follow most of the trades and handicrafts which were open, without question, to all other citizens; and when, in rare instances, freedom was given, it was penalized and embittered by the imposition of special taxation. The Church left the Jews nothing to do except to deal in money or second-hand clothing.

But it would be erroneous to suppose that the usurers of the Middle Ages were confined solely to Jews. The increasing spread of commerce and commercial enterprises in those days made it imperative for governments to devise expedients for evading the canonical embargo upon usury. Italy was the first European country to start this evasion. Others soon followed—with the result that the competition between the Christian (chiefly Italian) and Jewish money-lenders in England became so keen as to render the Jews less indispensable than they formerly were to the English Exchequer. Their expulsion from England by Edward I. was the corollary of this fact.

5. The views of modern Judaism on usurers and usury.—The somewhat disproportionate tendency of Jews in recent times to follow the trade of money-lending may be set down as a piece of sheer atavism. Racial characteristics have a way of surviving long after the original causes which created them have disappeared. But it must be strongly emphasized that money-lending is considerably on the decrease among Jews of the 20th century. Commerce, handicraft, the professions of law, medicine, dentistry, literature, art and science generally—the young Jews of the present day are entering these callings in great numbers and with great gusto. Many of them are recruited from the ranks of the poorest parents. The trade of usury is looked upon with shame; and the usurer is stigmatized as a reproach to his people. In some Jewish communities to-day the money-lender is forbidden to have any voice in the affairs of the Synagogue and is socially tabued by the better classes among his co-religionists.

In fine, the attitude of modern Judaism towards usury practically coincides with the attitude of the Judaism of the OT, the Mishnāh, the Talmud, and the mediæval codes. The attitude of the OT is summarized in Ezk 18[13], '[He] hath given forth upon usury, and hath taken increase: shall he then live? he shall not live . . . his blood shall be upon him.' On this passage the comment of the Talmud is, 'The money-lender is compared to a murderer.'[1] The Mishnāh[2] includes the usurer among those who are disqualified from giving evidence in a court of law. The *Shulhān 'Ārûkh*—the code on which modern orthodox Judaism, whether as creed, law, or life, is based—says:

'When can usurers be considered as having returned from their evil ways and as being again admissible as witnesses in a court of law? When they have torn up all the documents on which the principal and interest due to them from clients are recorded, with the complete and final resolution that they will never again lend on interest, not even to non-Jews. They must also restore to their former clients all the interest they have ever taken from them. If they can no longer identify all their clients they must devote the money to communal purposes.'[3]

These voices of the past are still expressive of general Jewish opinion to-day.

LITERATURE.—In addition to the works mentioned in the footnotes, see Joseph Jacobs, *The Jews of Angevin England*, London, 1893; W. J. Ashley, *An Introd. to English Economic History and Theory*, do. 1888–93, vol. i.; I. Abrahams, *Jewish Life in the Middle Ages*, do. 1896; H. Graetz, *Hist. of the Jews*, Eng. tr., do. 1891, iii.; *JE*, art. 'Usury'; J. D. Eisenstein, *Ozār Dīnīm Oō-minhāgim*, New York, 1917, art. 'Ribbit.'

J. ABELSON.

1 T.B. *Bābhā Meṣī'a*, 61*b*.
2 *Sanhedrin*, iii. 3.
3 See *Ḥōshen Mishpāt*, xxxiv. 29.

UTILITARIANISM.

I. *INTRODUCTORY*.—The term 'Utilitarianism' is used for both an ethical theory and a practical movement. The practical movement will be dealt with under II. 3. ii. below. As an ethical theory it signifies that the ultimate end is and ought to be general happiness, and that those actions are right which bring the greatest happiness to the greatest number. In Mill's words: 'The creed which accepts as the foundation of morals, Utility, or the Greatest Happiness Principle, holds that actions are right in proportion as they tend to promote happiness, wrong as they tend to produce the reverse of happiness. By happiness is intended pleasure, and the absence of pain; by unhappiness, pain, and the privation of pleasure.'[1] Or, as Sidgwick says, 'By Utilitarianism is here meant the ethical theory,' first distinctly formulated by Bentham, 'that the conduct which, under any given circumstances is objectively right, is that which will produce the greatest amount of happiness on the whole; that is, taking into account all whose happiness is affected by the conduct.'[2] By happiness Sidgwick means pleasure and absence of pain; and pleasure he defines as 'feeling which the sentient individual at the time of feeling it implicitly or explicitly apprehends to be desirable;—desirable, that is, when considered merely as feeling.'[3]

For utilitarianism Sidgwick prefers 'some such name as Universalistic Hedonism.'[4] He says 'universalistic' in order to show that the utilitarian end is general, not individual, happiness. Cf. Mill: The utilitarian standard 'is not the agent's own greatest happiness, but the greatest amount of happiness altogether.'[5] Hedonism (*q.v.*) is a general term including all systems of ethics which regard pleasure as the end actually aimed at (psychological hedonism), or as the end that ought to be aimed at (ethical hedonism). We may say that strictly the latter is alone worthy of consideration, for psychological hedonism, if true, makes any system of ethics irrelevant. But the earlier utilitarians based their theory of general happiness on the psychological assumption that man always desires pleasure. 'Nature has placed mankind under the governance of two sovereign masters, *pain* and *pleasure*. It is for them alone to point out what we ought to do, as well as to determine what we shall do.'[6] Even J. S. Mill did not clearly distinguish between psychological and ethical hedonism.

The name 'utilitarian' (taken from 'utility' in the sense of pleasure and exemption from pain) was first used by Bentham in 1781. In 1802, writing to Dumont, he said: 'To be sure a new religion would be an odd sort of a thing without a name: accordingly there ought to be one for it—at least for the professors of it. Utilitarian (Angl.), Utilitairien (Gall.) would be the more *propre*.'[7]

In his earlier writings Bentham used the word 'utility' with great freedom. In later life he preferred to speak of 'felicity' or 'happiness' as pointing more clearly to the ideas of pleasure and absence of pain. 'Utilitarian' had been so little used by Bentham that J. S. Mill believed himself to be the first to apply it to those who accepted the greatest happiness principle. Mill tells us that he found the word in Galt's *Annals of the Parish*. It is there used to designate people who held certain revolutionary views current at the end of the preceding century. It was through Mill that 'utilitarian' and 'utilitarianism' became the generally accepted names for the party and the creed.

II. *HISTORICAL*.—Utilitarianism, both as an ethical theory and as a practical movement, is English. The idea of the greatest good for the greatest number is no doubt to be found in Greek philosophy, in the Stoic conception of the 'citizen-

1 *Utilitarianism*[13], London, 1897, p. 9 f.
2 *The Methods of Ethics*[7], IV. i. § 1, p. 411.
3 *Ib*. II. iii. § 1, p. 131.
4 *Ib*. IV. i. § 1, p. 411.
5 *Utilitarianism*[13], p. 16.
6 Bentham, *Principles of Morals and Legislation*, I. i. (*Works*, Edinburgh, 1859, i.).
7 *Works*, x. 92, 390.

ship of the world.' Leibniz, again, by establishing the general good or happiness as the end of law and of morality, is spoken of as the precursor of utilitarianism.[1] And the French materialists of the 18th cent., especially Helvétius, Montesquieu, and von Holbach, were to some extent occupied with the same ideas. But the movement to which the name is given is an English movement, and, while it demands fairly exhaustive treatment historically, the historical account may be confined to English writers.

1. We must begin with **Hobbes**. The theory of association, which played so large a part in the earlier utilitarian speculation, can be traced to him, although he never worked it out. His influence, which continued for two centuries, is best seen in the effect it produced upon those who opposed his theories. His conception of man as an unsocial and egoistic being with an insatiable desire for power, and his notion of morality as political obligation, had to be answered. And these answers were often the means of modifying the philosophical beliefs of his opponents, among whom were the utilitarians.

The answer to Hobbes made by the Cambridge Platonists does not concern us here. A contemporary of theirs, however, **Richard Cumberland**, foreshadowed utilitarianism in his *De Legibus Naturæ*, published in 1672. This work was lengthy and confused, and utilitarian principles were combined with others. Cumberland's object was to prove, as against Hobbes, that morality was natural, man being by nature social. He defined good as 'preservation,' following Hobbes here, but he included in preservation both perfection and happiness. Most stress was laid on the latter, and most practical use was made of it in the working out of the theory. Individual happiness, he held, must coincide with the good of all because of the Divine sanction: 'The greatest Benevolence of every rational Agent towards all, forms the happiest state of every, . . . and therefore the Common Good is the supreme Law.'[2]

A popular fallacy makes **Locke** (*Essay concerning Human Understanding*, 1690) the founder of English utilitarianism. Moral action was necessarily felicific to Locke, but this he held in common with other non-utilitarian moralists. He did not adopt the greatest happiness principle, and he did not work out the pleasure side of his theory. Empiricism, largely due to him, was, of course, of immense importance in the development of utilitarianism.

An answer in the 18th cent. to the unmitigated egoism of Hobbes came from the Moral Sense school. Their method was psychological rather than rationalistic, and took the form of a new account of human nature. Of this school **Hutcheson**, through his emphasis on benevolence, approached nearest to the position which utilitarianism was to take up, and from Hutcheson came the formula 'the greatest happiness for the greatest numbers' which, slightly changed, becomes so familiar in Bentham. Bentham states that he got this formula from Priestley. That was probably a mistake, as it does not occur in Priestley's works.[3] The exact formula used by Bentham, 'the greatest happiness of the greatest number,' is found in a translation (1767) of Beccaria's *Dei Delitti e delle Pene*. Whether it was suggested to him by Hutcheson is not known.

In 1731 there was published anonymously a small dissertation prefixed to Law's translation of King's *Origin of Evil*. It was entitled *Preliminary Dissertation: concerning the Fundamental Principle of Virtue or Morality*. The author was **John Gay**. This was the first definite statement of the utilitarian position. Brown, Tucker, and Paley are the logical successors of Gay. Their theories, so far as essentials are concerned, may be regarded as expansions of Gay's outline. In the *Dissertation* Gay treats first of the criterion of virtue, then of motive, and lastly of the theory of association, which was the psychological groundwork of his theory of ethics. The 'immediate criterion' of virtue Gay found in the will of God. But, as God must will the happiness of men, the latter is the 'criterion' of God's will. Happiness is defined as a 'sum of pleasures.' The motive of the moral agent is egoistic, for all desire is desire of pleasure. Gay is then faced with the fundamental difficulty which beset all the utilitarians, up to and including John Stuart Mill, of proving the coincidence of the pleasure of the individual and of society. For, if men were and could be actuated only by a desire for their own pleasure, it was manifest that the coincidence of the pleasure of the individual with general pleasure must be proved before the latter could become an object of desire. Gay met this difficulty with his theory of 'sanctions.' He enumerated four sanctions—the natural, the social, the legal, and the religious. He emphasized the last, for he realized that there is no sanction which can ensure the complete coincidence of the pleasure of society and the pleasure of the individual except the supernatural sanction. It is their emphasis on this sanction which constitutes Gay, Brown, Tucker, and Paley theological utilitarians, and which, starting as they did with the selfish theory of the moral motive, renders their system of utilitarianism alone consistent. In his discussion of the supernatural sanction Gay brings out clearly his theory of obligation, which became the accepted one. The moral imperative was not categorical but conditional, he held—conditional on the required action being a means to the happiness of the individual. Complete obligation to virtue could then come from God only, for He alone could make the coincidence between 'my happiness and general happiness' perfect.

> 'Thus those who either expressly exclude, or don't mention the will of God . . . must either allow that virtue is not in all cases *obligatory* . . . or they must say that the good of mankind is a sufficient obligation. But how can the good of mankind be any obligation to *me*, when perhaps in particular cases, such as laying down my life, or the like, it is contrary to my happiness?'[1]

The latter part of the *Dissertation* is given up to the discussion of psychology. The psychological basis for ethics Gay found in association. Through the law of association other things beyond the pleasure of the individual might be desired as proximate ends, though the ultimate end was pleasure. In this way altruistic desires might be developed. Gay held it unimportant that the ultimate motive was always egoistic. If a man helped another, his immediate motive being kindness, the fact that his ultimate object was to benefit himself was of no consequence.

It has seemed worth while to discuss Gay's treatise rather fully because, though it consisted of only 30 pages, was published anonymously, and attracted little notice at the time, it contained all the essentials of theological utilitarianism. In fact we find no important modification of Gay's utilitarianism made by any one until we come to John Stuart Mill.

In 1740 **David Hume** published his first treatise on Ethics, being book iii. of the *Treatise of Human Nature*. The *Inquiry concerning the Principles of Morals* was published in 1751. Hume's standpoint was very different in the two works. It is

[1] See H. Höffding, *A History of Modern Philosophy*, 2 vols., London, 1900, i. 368.
[2] *De Legibus Naturæ*, London, ch. 1.
[3] See W. R. Sorley, *A History of English Philosophy*, Cambridge, 1920, p. 220.

[1] *Dissertation*, p. xxi.

unnecessary to discuss the cause of this change; so far as concerns ethics, the *Inquiry* seems to represent his real position. In his analysis of the moral motive in this work Hume approaches modern utilitarianism. But he exercised no influence until the time of J. S. Mill. In the *Treatise* Hume makes the moral motive ultimately egoistic; his position is substantially that held by Gay, and afterwards found in Hartley, Brown, Tucker, Paley, Bentham, and James Mill; whereas in the *Inquiry* his account of human nature implies originally altruistic as well as egoistic tendencies. Disinterested benevolence is natural.

'Whatever contradiction may vulgarly be supposed between the *selfish* and *social* sentiments or dispositions, they are really no more opposite than selfish and ambitious, selfish and revengeful, selfish and vain.'[1]

Hume's treatment of the moral motive is more important than his treatment of the principle of utility. He accepted the latter, but he did not use it consistently in his analysis of the virtues.

Between Hume's two works there appeared *Observations on Man, his Frame, his Duty, and his Expectations* (1749) by the physician **David Hartley.** In this work Hartley elaborated the theory of the association of ideas in a way which greatly influenced the later associational school and especially James Mill.[2] Hartley was not a typical associationist-utilitarian. Much of his work was given up to theological discussions. He accepted the utility principle, but, like J. S. Mill, he held that there were qualitative differences in pleasures. In practice also he seems to have held that conduct should be guided by 'obedience to the Scripture precepts' rather than by consideration of consequences. He was probably the first to raise the difficulty of the hedonistic calculus.

'It is impossible,' he says, 'for the most sagacious and experienced persons to make any accurate estimate of the future consequences of particular actions, so as, . . . to determine justly, what action would contribute most to augment happiness and lessen misery.'[3]

2. Theological utilitarianism. — Just twenty years after Gay's *Dissertation* there appeared the *Essays on the Characteristics* (1751) by **John Brown.** In 1768 the first volumes of Tucker's *The Light of Nature Pursued* were published, and in 1785 came Paley's *Principles of Moral and Political Philosophy.* Brown, Tucker, and Paley, along with Gay, are the exponents of theological utilitarianism, the first definite form which utilitarianism took, and which in its time exercised an immense influence. A generation trained in Locke was not disposed to adopt the system of the Moral Sense school, but welcomed the rival system whose groundwork was a conception of consciousness as composed of separable atoms, sensations and ideas, aggregated into clusters.

The outline of theological utilitarianism was found in Gay's *Dissertation,* and neither Brown, Tucker, nor Paley added anything vital to it, though they amplified and popularized it. J. S. Mill says that Brown in his *Essays* on Shaftesbury's *Characteristics* produced an able argument for utilitarianism. It is to the second of the essays that Mill refers. Brown's argument was, in brief, that common sense pointed to conduciveness to happiness as being the essence of virtue. He argues that 'those very affections and actions, which, in the ordinary course of things, are approved as virtuous, do change their nature, and become vicious in the strictest sense, when they contradict this fundamental law, of the greatest public happiness.'[4]

[1] IX. ii. (*Essays Moral, Political, and Literary,* London, 1907, ii. 255).
[2] See art. ASSOCIATION.
[3] *Observations*[6], London, 1834, p. 504.
[4] '*On the Characteristics of the Earl of Shaftesbury*'[2]; *Essays,* II. iii. 134.

The ultimate end Brown gives as the 'voluntary production of the greatest happiness.'[1] The moral motive, he holds, is egoistic. 'The only reason or motive, by which individuals can possibly be induced to the practice of virtue, must be the feeling immediate, or the prospect of future private happiness.'[2] How can the end and the motive be reconciled? 'The lively and active belief of an all-seeing and all-powerful God' alone can do it, a God 'who will hereafter make them happy or miserable, according as they designedly promote or violate the happiness of their fellow-creatures.'[3] This is all entirely in line with Gay. Brown did not touch psychology. For that he definitely refers his readers to Gay.

Abraham Tucker was an extraordinarily prolix writer. There are seven volumes of *The Light of Nature Pursued.* The first four appeared under the name of 'Edward Search' in 1768; the last three were issued posthumously. Like Gay, Tucker turned his attention to psychology, and, like him, he held that ultimately men were egoists—though not in the sense of Hobbes. Altruistic tendencies were explained by contiguity and translation. Tucker was a convinced determinist. Free agency is to him no more than the dependency of actions upon volition.[4] The will follows the strongest motive. All this was thoroughly consistent with the Lockean groundwork and with the ordinary utilitarian theory of obligation. Two points remain to be stated. Tucker says that there are no qualitative distinctions in pleasure. This had been implicit in Gay and others. The second point has reference to the hedonistic calculus. Tucker argued, and Paley followed him here, that there must be general rules of expediency, and that these must be followed rather than any effort made to calculate the probable felicific consequences of any particular act. Tucker states many of the modern objections to the calculus.

'Our tastes,' he says, 'varying as much as our faces makes us very bad judges of one another's enjoyments. . . . Nor do we judge much better of our own pleasures, for want of being well aware of their aptness to cloy upon repetition and to change their relish perpetually according to our disposition of body or mind or the circumstances we happen to stand in.'[5]

In 1785 **William Paley** published his *Principles of Moral and Political Philosophy.* Paley received a complete philosophical system from his predecessors, and he acknowledged freely the debt he owed, in especial to Tucker's *Light of Nature Pursued.* But he applied and popularized their principles, and that so successfully that they are now associated almost exclusively with his name. His definition of virtue—'the doing good to mankind, in obedience to the will of God, and for the sake of everlasting happiness'[6]—lends itself easily to caricature. Though his views did not differ in any essential from those of the previous theological utilitarians, he emphasized more unpleasantly than any of his predecessors the selfishness of the moral motive, and the doctrine of rewards and punishments after death. He was consistent on obligation. 'We can be obliged,' he said, 'to nothing, but what we ourselves are to gain or lose something by.'[7] It is possible, however, to make too much of the weaknesses of theological utilitarianism as found in Paley, and to forget the sound sense of most of his teaching. In computing the consequences of actions he taught that we must consider what would ensue if all men acted as the individual was acting. '"Whatever is expedient, is right." But then it must be expedient on the whole, at the long run.'[8] The particular consequence of

[1] '*On the Characteristics of the Earl of Shaftesbury*'[2]; *Essays,* II. iii. 137.
[2] *Ib.* II. vi. 159.
[3] *Ib.* II. ix. 210.
[4] Cf. *Light of Nature Pursued,* I. xxiv.
[5] *Ib.* I. xxii. § 11.
[6] *Principles,* I. vii.
[7] *Ib.* II. ii.
[8] *Ib.* II. viii.

forgery is a damage of twenty or thirty pounds to the man who accepts the forged bill: the general consequence is the stoppage of paper-currency.[1] And he brushed aside the specious argument that an act done in secrecy brings no general ill consequences. 'Those who reason in this manner do not observe, that they are setting up a general rule, of all others the least to be endured: namely, that secrecy, whenever secrecy is practicable, will justify any action.'[2] Paley analysed the commonly accepted morality of his time to prove that considerations of utility underlay it, and he applied the utility criterion to pressing problems of the age. He exercised very considerable influence, and his *Principles* became the standard text-book at Cambridge.

3. Empirical utilitarianism and the philosophical radicals.—i. *Ethical theory of Bentham.*—**Jeremy Bentham** was born five years after Paley, but he lived until 1832, Paley having died twenty-seven years before. Paley went to Cambridge, and Cambridge became the centre of his form of utilitarianism. Bentham went to Oxford, but it was in London that he gathered disciples round him and founded his school. The *Introduction to the Principles of Morals and Legislation* was printed in 1780, but it was not published until 1789, four years after Paley's *Principles* had appeared, and only then through the insistence of Bentham's disciples, jealous of their master's fame.

Bentham made little mention of his indebtedness to his predecessors, but of Hume's *Treatise* and of the treatment of utility in it he said: 'For my own part, I well remember, no sooner had I read that part of the work which touches on this subject, than I felt as if scales had fallen from my eyes.'[3] Priestley also, according to his own account, influenced him. Apart from these acknowledgments, and those to French and Italian utilitarian writers, he states his ethical position as though it were original to himself. So far as his theory is concerned, the only originality lay in his treatment of the hedonistic calculus. At the same time utilitarianism will always be associated with the name of Bentham. There is no doubt that the hold it obtained on men's minds was largely due to his thorough application of the utility principle in the spheres of economics, jurisprudence, and politics, and to his gathering round him a devoted group of followers who applied, taught, and popularized his doctrines.

Bentham's ethical theory is found chiefly in three works—*A Fragment on Government* (1776); *The Principles of Morals and Legislation* (1789), where, however, the author's first concern is with jurisprudence rather than with ethics; and the *Deontology* published posthumously in 1834. J. S. Mill held that the *Deontology* had been considerably altered by John Bowring, who edited it. The crude egoism of Bentham's theory is more apparent in it than elsewhere, but there seems no reason to doubt that it substantially represents his views.

Bentham assumed dogmatically the hedonistic end, 'the greatest happiness of the greatest number.' His 18th cent. individualism led him to picture society as composed of a number of separate and largely antagonistic units. As J. S. Mill put it in his 'Essay on Bentham,' written at a time when he was emerging from the influence of Bentham:

> 'Bentham's idea of the world is that of a collection of persons pursuing each his separate interest or pleasure, and the prevention of whom from jostling one another more than is unavoidable, may be attempted by hopes and fears derived from three sources—the law, religion and public opinion.'[4]

[1] *Principles*, II. viii. [2] *Ib.* II. vii.
[3] *A Fragment on Government*, I. xxxvi. footnote.
[4] Mill, 'Essay on Bentham,' in *Dissertations and Discussions*, i. 362.

Bentham's point of view with regard to sanctions was somewhat different from that of the theological utilitarians. They used sanctions to prove the ultimate harmony of the interests of each with the interests of all. For this reason they laid stress on the religious sanction. Bentham's attitude was that of a political reformer rather than a theorist. He strove for reform of the constitution and of law —for a system of penalties which would make it the interest of the individual to act for the general good. He did not attack the problem of cases where no system of legal rewards and punishments could bring about this coincidence.

The list and number of sanctions differed in the three ethical works, but in the *Principles* Bentham mentioned four. They are practically the sanctions of Gay—the physical sanction, or the material consequences of actions such as 'disease produced by dissipation'; the political sanction, or legal penalties and rewards; the moral sanction, or public praise and blame; the religious sanction, or the effect of religious hopes and fears. The last was of little importance: 'As to such of the pleasures and pains belonging to the religious sanction, as regard a future life, of what kind these may be, we cannot know. These lie not open to our observation.'[1] Bentham's teaching on sanctions is summarized by himself in the following passage:

> 'It has been shown that the happiness of the individuals, of whom a community is composed, that is, their pleasures and their security, is the end and the sole end which the legislator ought to have in view: the sole standard, in conformity to which each individual ought, as far as depends upon the legislator, to be *made* to fashion his behaviour. But whether it be this or any thing else that is to be *done*, there is nothing by which a man can ultimately be *made* to do it, but either pain or pleasure. . . . There are four distinguishable sources from which pleasure and pain are in use to flow: considered separately, they may be termed the *physical*, the *political*, the *moral*, and the *religious*: and inasmuch as the pleasures and pains belonging to each of them are capable of giving a binding force to any law or rule of conduct, they may all of them be termed *sanctions*.' In a footnote he adds: 'Sanctio, in Latin, was used to signify the *act of binding*, and, by a common grammatical transition, *any thing which serves to bind a man*: to wit, to the observance of such or such a mode of conduct.'[2]

Bentham, driven by the determination to have some weapon with which to attack abuses consecrated by custom, elaborated the hedonistic calculus. The morality of an act, he said, was to be decided not by 'intuition,' but by a scientific calculation of the consequences of the act in terms of pleasure. In order that the calculation should be scientific certain things must be taken into account, viz. the intensity and duration of the pleasure, its certainty, its propinquity (Sidgwick points out that this has no *locus standi* unless it affects the certainty), its fecundity, or 'the chance it has of being followed by sensations of the same kind,' and its purity, or 'the chance it has of not being followed by sensations of the opposite kind.' The extent of the pleasure, or the number of people affected, should also be taken into account and the whole so balanced that the total quantity of pleasure attendant on an act should be known.

Quite consistently Bentham disallowed any difference in quality in pleasure: Other things being equal, pushpin is as good as poetry. 'Each to count for one and no one for more than one' was the principle according to which pleasure should be distributed.

ii. *The practical movement.*—Bentham used his greatest happiness principle for the reform of the constitution of law, especially criminal law. His political theory was in harmony with his psychology. Members of Parliament, he held, must be restrained, and constrained, to act for the general good; so he urged that government should be put into the hands of all, and advocated universal suffrage, voting by ballot, and annual parliaments.

[1] *Principles*, I. iii. § 10. [2] *Ib.* I. iii. §§ 1, 2.

In 1776 Bentham's first work, *A Fragment on Government*, was published anonymously. Towards the end of his life the *Catechism of Parliamentary Reform* appeared, and *The Constitutional Code* was published posthumously. Not only political theory but also jurisprudence received attention at his hands. 'He found the philosophy of law a chaos,' Mill said, 'and left it a science.'

Bentham attracted a band of disciples and founded a school. It is to the efforts of his disciples that we owe the publication of the bulk of his works, for Bentham seems to have been indifferent to the fate of his writings. Among all Bentham's followers James Mill had the greatest ability. He joined Bentham in 1802. From that time the philosophical radicals were a group of men with a definite ethical, political, and economic faith. J. S. Mill said of this creed

'It was not mere Benthamism but rather a combination of Bentham's point of view with that of the modern political economy and with the Hartleian metaphysics. Malthus' population principle was quite as much a banner and point of union among us as any opinion specifically belonging to Bentham.'[1]

Bentham and James Mill were contemporary rather than successive leaders of the school, as Leslie Stephen makes them out to be. Mill lived only four years after Bentham's death. A prominent part was also played by George Grote, the two Austins, and, last of all, J. S. Mill. In 1824 the *Westminster Review*, the organ of the school, was first published, and did much to spread its creed. Psychology was supplied by James Mill in his *Analysis of the Phenomena of the Human Mind*. Mill adopted the association psychology of Hartley, but discarded his cumbersome physiological theory. His theories of the self, the external world, and belief—largely Hume's position—were also accepted by the school. In economics the views of Ricardo and Malthus were adopted. As they held the theory of the iron law of wages, the only method of amelioration lay, they thought, in restraining the increase of population. Their general policy was one of laissez-faire, and this attitude was a contributory cause to their disappearance from politics. They returned some members to the first reformed parliament, but they were afterwards swallowed up by the Whigs.

iii. *John Stuart Mill.*—J. S. Mill spoke of his father as 'the last of the 18th century.' He himself was a transition thinker, and many of his inconsistencies are explained by his endeavour to reconcile hedonism and idealism—to reconcile Bentham and Coleridge, styled by him 'the two great seminal minds of England in this age.'

J. S. Mill gradually moved away from the position of Bentham and his father. In 1826 came what he called 'a crisis in my mental history,' when he fell under the influence of German idealism.

'I never, indeed, wavered in the conviction that happiness is the test of all rules of conduct, and the end of life. But I now thought that this end was only to be obtained by not making it the direct end. Those only are happy (I thought) who have their minds fixed on some object other than their own happiness; on the happiness of others, on the improvement of mankind, even on some art or pursuit, followed not as a means, but as itself an ideal end.'[2]

In 1835 Mill published in the *London Review* an answer to Adam Sedgwick's criticism of Paley. Under the influence very largely of Sedgwick and of W. Whewell the theological utilitarianism of Paley had lost its prestige in Cambridge. In his reply to Sedgwick Mill indicated what was his own theory of human nature—that man is originally altruistic. After his father's death he spoke out more plainly, and in 1838 there appeared in the *London and Westminster Review* his 'Essay on Bentham.' The substance of his criticism of

[1] *Autobiography*, new ed., London, 1908, p. 60.
[2] *Ib.* p. 81.

Bentham is that his reading of human nature was too narrow. He 'failed in deriving light from other minds.' Nor were his nature and circumstances such as to furnish him with a 'correct and complete picture of man's nature and circumstances.'[1] The influence of the idealism of Coleridge, Wordsworth, Carlyle, Sterling, and Maurice can be traced in the following paragraph:

'Man is never recognised by him as a being capable of pursuing spiritual perfection as an end; of desiring, for its own sake, the conformity of his own character to his standard of excellence, without hope of good or fear of evil from other source than his own inward consciousness. Even in the more limited form of Conscience, this great fact in human nature escapes him. Nothing is more curious than the absence of recognition in any of his writings of the existence of conscience, as a thing distinct from philanthropy, from affection for God or man, and from self-interest in this world or in the next.'[2]

In his small work *Utilitarianism* Mill united the two ends of pleasure and spiritual perfection by his theory of qualitative differences in pleasure, and conscience reappeared there as the internal sanction to be added to Bentham's external sanctions. In an essay published in the *Westminster Review* in 1852, entitled 'Dr. Whewell on Moral Philosophy,' Mill, probably under the influence of Mrs. Taylor, whom he had just married, reverted to the narrower and more orthodox utilitarianism which he held in early life. This essay of Mill's, however, was only one move in the controversy between himself and the leaders of the school of 'Paley reversed.' That school, led by Sedgwick and Whewell, after superseding Paley in Cambridge, found itself confronted with a new Benthamism—a Benthamism which in the hands of Mill maintained its hold on men's minds by means of a wider interpretation of human nature.

Mill's defence of utilitarianism which appeared in *Fraser's Magazine* in 1861, and was published in book form in 1863, was largely directed against the Cambridge school.

'I must again repeat,' he said, '. . . that the happiness which forms the utilitarian standard of what is right in conduct, is not the agent's own happiness, but that of all concerned. As between his own happiness and that of others, utilitarianism requires him to be as strictly impartial as a disinterested and benevolent spectator. In the golden rule of Jesus of Nazareth, we read the complete spirit of the ethics of utility. To do as one would be done by, and to love one's neighbour as oneself, constitute the ideal perfection of utilitarian morality.'[3]

As Sorley says, Mill claimed for utilitarianism that 'it is not selfish, because it regards the pleasures of all men as of equal moment; it is not sensual, because it recognizes the superior value of intellectual, artistic, and social pleasures as compared with those of the senses.'[4]

Mill separated himself most completely from his predecessors in teaching that pleasures differ not only quantitatively but qualitatively. 'It is quite compatible,' he said, 'with the principle of utility to recognize the fact, that some *kinds* of pleasure are more desirable and more valuable than others';[5] and again, in the oft-quoted words, 'It is better to be a human being dissatisfied than a pig satisfied; better to be Socrates dissatisfied than a fool satisfied'[6]—in all of which he really surrenders the utilitarian position and strikes a responsive note in the hearts of those who feel the inadequacy of a hedonistic ethic. For hedonism Bentham's position is the only consistent one: Quantity of pleasure being equal, pushpin is as good as poetry. If there are higher and lower pleasures—and common opinion would seem to agree with Mill here—some other standard than pleasure is set up. Pleasure is no longer the criterion. It would not, moreover, be correct to regard this as a passing phase in Mill's mental

[1] 'Essay on Bentham,' in *Dissertations and Discussions*, i. 350.
[2] *Ib.* p. 359.
[3] *Utilitarianism*[13], p. 24 f.
[4] W. R. Sorley, *A Hist. of English Philosophy*, p. 258.
[5] *Utilitarianism*[13], p. 11.
[6] *Ib.* p. 14.

development. In *Liberty* his mind was turning that way when he took for the motto of his third chapter von Humboldt's saying, 'the end of man is . . . the highest and most harmonious development of his powers to a complete and consistent whole.' His paragraph on qualitative differences in pleasure contrasts, however, with his statement a few pages earlier in the *Utilitarianism* as to the theory of life on which the utilitarian ethic was grounded—'namely, that pleasure, and freedom from pain, are the only things desirable as ends; and that all desirable things . . . are desirable either for the pleasure inherent in themselves, or as means to the promotion of pleasure and the prevention of pain.'[1]

Mill departed from Bentham also in his emphasis on the internal sanction of conscience, which he defined as 'a feeling in our own mind; a pain, more or less intense, attendant on violation of duty.'[2] That the growth of conscience was largely dependent on right education—on the attaching of the appropriate sanctions to acts—that psychologically it was to be explained by association, Mill held with Bentham. But he also held that the core of conscience was the 'social feelings of mankind; the desire to be in unity with our fellow creatures. . . . The social state is at once so natural, so necessary, and so habitual to man, that, except in some unusual circumstances or by an effort of voluntary abstraction, he never conceives himself otherwise than as a member of a body.'[3] Here he follows Hume and Hartley in attributing to man natural altruistic tendencies, in crediting him with 'sympathy,' as opposed to Bentham's theory of self-interest as the motive of action.

Mill's often criticized 'proof' of utilitarianism rested on the doctrine of psychological hedonism.

'The only proof capable of being given,' he said, 'that an object is visible, is that people actually see it. . . . In like manner, I apprehend, the sole evidence it is possible to produce that anything is desirable, is that people do actually desire it. . . . No reason can be given why the general happiness is desirable, except that each person, so far as he believes it to be attainable, desires his own happiness. This, however, being a fact, we have not only all the proof which the case admits of, but all which it is possible to require, that happiness is a good: that each person's happiness is a good to that person, and the general happiness, therefore, a good to the aggregate of all persons.'[4]

The word 'desirable' may mean 'what can be desired' or 'what ought to be desired.' If we interpret it in the former sense, Mill meant that it was psychologically possible to will 'general happiness.' It is more probable that he meant 'ought to be desired.' Sidgwick says:

'Mill must be understood to mean in saying that "the general happiness is *desirable*" that it is what each individual *ought* to desire. . . . But this proposition is not established by Mill's reasoning, even if we grant that what is actually desired may be legitimately inferred to be in this sense desirable'—and this passing from the is to the ought is surely by no means an obvious step. He continues: 'For an aggregate of actual desires, each directed towards a different part of the general happiness, does not constitute an actual desire for the general happiness, existing in any individual; and Mill would certainly not contend that a desire which does not exist in any individual can possibly exist in an aggregate of individuals.'[5]

Thus Mill's attempt to prove that general happiness is the ethical end failed.

His account of sympathy also, though important, is not always consistent. From his statement of psychological hedonism it appeared that man was originally a wholly selfish being actuated by desire for his own personal interest. In that case sympathy would be originally selfish. Mill never admitted that. At times he laid the greatest stress on man's social disposition. But if man is social, he is sympathetic by nature.

[1] *Utilitarianism*[13], p. 10. [2] *Ib.* p. 41.
[3] *Ib.* p. 46. [4] *Ib.* p. 52 f.
[5] H. Sidgwick, *The Methods of Ethics*[7], III. xiii. 388.

For fuller account of the Mills see art. MILL, JAMES AND JOHN STUART.

The most distinguished of Mill's younger associates was **Alexander Bain** of Aberdeen. Bain was a thoroughgoing utilitarian. His most important work, however, was done in psychology: *The Senses and the Intellect* was published in 1855 and *The Emotions and the Will* in 1859. For associationism he said the last word that can be said. The point of chief interest in his ethics is his treatment of disinterestedness. 'To obtain virtue in its highest purity, its noblest hue,' he said, 'we have to abstain from the mention of both punishment and reward.'[1] 'So far as I am able to judge of our disinterested impulses, they are wholly distinct from the attainment of pleasure and the avoidance of pain. They lead us, as I believe, to sacrifice pleasures, and incur pains, without any compensation.'[2] Sorley says of Bain: 'He had no illusions—except the great illusion that mind is a bundle of sensations tied together by laws of association.'[3] In the light of this metaphysical theory of the self—with slight variations the accepted theory of the utilitarians—it is easier to understand the utilitarian conception of an end which is a succession of pleasant feelings, 'a sum of pleasures,' and which left reason out of account.

4. Evolutional utilitarianism; Herbert Spencer and Leslie Stephen.—Spencer's ethical views are found chiefly in the first and last parts of the *Social Statics* and in *The Principles of Ethics.* The first part of the latter, *The Data of Ethics,* was published separately in 1879; the remainder of the *Principles* in 1892–93. The *Social Statics* was published in 1851, eight years before Darwin's *Origin of Species.* But even at that date the evolutionary hypothesis had taken hold of Spencer's mind—it was in the air. Then Darwin, by his investigations into the origin of species, by his researches into the variation of forms found in different natural surroundings, by his emphasis on the principle of natural selection as explaining these variations, gave a wide-spread currency to the evolutionary theory. Nor must the part which A. Russel Wallace played be forgotten. Darwin also saw, however, that natural selection alone would not explain evolved conduct, for the more evolved conduct is, the smaller a part does natural selection play, because civilized society protects the unfit and does not allow them to be exterminated. This difficulty was overcome by the—now largely discredited—hypothesis of the transmissibility of acquired characters. Evolution by natural selection—or, in his own phrase, 'survival of the fittest'—and by means of the transmission of acquired characters was for Spencer the explanatory and synthesizing principle of all knowledge.

Ethics, however, was Spencer's main interest. Everything else led up to this. For his ethics see art. SPENCER, HERBERT, 2 (5). Our concern here is with the relation of Spencer's ethical system to utilitarianism. We have to see why he himself called it 'rational utilitarianism' as opposed to the empirical utilitarianism of Mill, and why it is generally known as evolutional utilitarianism. Spencer's opposition was directed against the method of utilitarianism, not against its greatest happiness principle. He accepted pleasure as the good, though even here he was not consistent. 'Life is good or bad,' he said, 'according as it does, or does not, bring a surplus of agreeable feeling.' 'The good is universally the pleasurable.' Pleasure is the end and is 'as much a necessary form of moral intuition as space is a necessary

[1] A. Bain, *The Emotions and the Will*[3], London, 1880, p. 297.
[2] *Ib.* p. 295. [3] *Hist. of English Philosophy*, p. 262.

form of intellectual intuition.' But Spencer was an evolutionist as well as a utilitarian, and at other times we find the good defined as 'preservation of human society' or 'quantity of life measured in breadth as well as length.' It is true that he stated that conduct tending to preservation of life was good because life involved a 'surplus of agreeable feeling.' 'The implication . . . is that conduct should conduce to preservation of the individual, of the family, and of the society, only supposing that life brings more happiness than misery.'[1] This supposition is never proved. At times he emphasized progress and pictured an ideal society, rather than happiness, as the ethical end. At times the emphasis was on being, at other times on happiness or well-being.

It was the method, however, rather than the end of empirical utilitarianism that Spencer opposed. His object was to find 'for the principles of right and wrong in conduct at large, a scientific basis.' He criticized specifically the hedonistic calculus of Bentham, and emphasized the value of general rules (as indeed had been done by most utilitarians with the exception of Bentham) rather than particular decisions in individual cases. He wrote to Mill:

'The view for which I contend is that morality properly so-called—the science of right conduct—has for its object to determine *how* and *why* certain modes of conduct are detrimental, and certain other modes beneficial. These good and bad results cannot be accidental, but must be necessary consequences of the constitution of things; and I conceive it to be the business of moral science to deduce, from the laws of life and the conditions of existence, what kinds of action necessarily tend to produce happiness, and what kinds to produce unhappiness. Having done this, its deductions are to be recognized as laws of conduct; and are to be conformed to irrespective of a direct estimation of happiness or misery.'[2]

To get the premisses whence deductions could be made Spencer turned his attention to 'absolute ethics' as opposed to 'relative ethics'—absolute ethics being the ethics of an ideal society where conduct was perfectly adapted and produced pleasure unalloyed with pain. Spencer did not seem to appreciate the fact that, if such a society existed, the question of morality would not arise, for by hypothesis all conduct was perfectly adapted to social environment—there was no conflict of desires. From study of this ideal society Spencer considered it possible to deduce general rules as to what 'conduct must be detrimental and what conduct must be beneficial.' He had then to consider further how these general rules were applicable to existing society. By this method relative ethics would be derived from absolute ethics. The extraordinary artificiality of this is apparent. Spencer himself admitted that the method had not turned out to be so fruitful as he expected. The four principles which he found for the guidance of conduct cannot be said to be derived from absolute ethics. They were justice, negative beneficence, positive beneficence, and enlightened self-interest. Justice was non-interference.

'Every man has freedom to do all that he wills, provided he infringes not the equal freedom of any other man.'[3] This principle owed its origin to Spencer's pronounced individualism rather than to any study of absolute ethics. Negative beneficence required that each man must perfectly fulfil his own nature 'without giving unhappiness to other men in any direct or indirect way.'[4] Besides positive beneficence there was enlightened self-interest which demanded that, 'whilst duly regardful of the preceding limitations, each individual shall perform all those acts required to fill up the measure of his own private happiness.'[5]

Spencer's system is not held, at least in Spencer's form, by any thinker of the present day.

In 1882 Leslie Stephen published *The Science of Ethics*. In the preface he associated himself with the utilitarians in the words 'writers belonging to what I may call my own school, to Hume, Bentham, the Mills, G. H. Lewes, and Mr. Herbert Spencer.'[1] He did not follow Spencer in defining the good as length and breadth of life; he defined it as the 'health of the social organism.' 'Society may be regarded as an organism,' he said. This organism implied 'a social tissue, modified in various ways so as to form the organs adapted to various specific purposes.' The working of evolution could be seen in the social organism.

Leslie Stephen was opposed, like Spencer, to the hedonistic calculus. 'Life is not a series of detached acts,' he said, 'in each of which a man can calculate the sum of happiness or misery attainable by different causes.' Like Spencer he held that the evolved state was necessarily a happy one. The radical criticism of Stephen's theory, as of all evolutionary theories of ethics, is that he took what is, namely the trend of evolution, and identified it with the ideal, with what ought to be.

5. Rational utilitarianism; Henry Sidgwick.—E. Albee in his *History of English Utilitarianism*, published in 1902, spoke of Sidgwick's *Methods of Ethics* as 'the last authoritative utterance of traditional utilitarianism.' Though a utilitarian, Sidgwick differed in some ways from all his predecessors. He was 'a Utilitarian,' but 'on an Intuitional basis.'[2] He found in certain fundamental 'intuitions' the basis of his system, whereas the earlier utilitarians were opposed to all forms of intuitionism, though in J. S. Mill a new spirit of understanding and appreciation of the rival school had begun to show itself. Sidgwick, further, though an ethical hedonist, discarded psychological hedonism, which had formed part of the stock-in-trade of preceding utilitarian writers, including J. S. Mill.

Sidgwick's analysis of the nature of desire was very similar to Butler's. 'Our conscious active impulses,' he said, 'are so far from being always directed towards the attainment of pleasure or avoidance of pain for ourselves, that we can find everywhere in consciousness extra-regarding impulses, directed towards something that is not pleasure, nor relief from pain.'[3] He naturally discarded also the utilitarian theory that extra-regarding impulses were not primary but were due to 'association' and 'translation.'

'So far as we can observe the consciousness of children, the two elements, extra-regarding impulse and desire for pleasure, seem to coexist in the same manner as they do in mature life. In so far as there is any difference, it seems to be in the opposite direction; as the actions of children, being more instinctive and less reflective, are more prompted by extra-regarding impulse, and less by conscious aim at pleasure.'[4]

By ridding utilitarianism of psychological hedonism Sidgwick did good service. And he cleared the ground of the psychological difficulty as to how the individual can will the pleasure of others when it conflicts with his own pleasure. Only the form of the difficulty, however, was changed, not the reality; for, though Sidgwick saw the possibility, he found himself, at the end of his analysis, unable to see the reasonableness of gratifying a desire for the happiness of others when opposed to individual interest. The problem took the following shape for him. A fundamental moral intuition (at one time called a deduction from two intuitions and expressed differently at different times) directed a man to prefer his own lesser good to the greater good of another. This was the formal principle of benevolence (formal because the nature of the good was not yet known) which provided the 'proof' of utilitarianism. Sidgwick's further 'proof' that the nature of the good was pleasure

1 *Principles*, ch. iii. § 9 f.
2 *Autobiography*, ii. 88.
3 *Social Statics*, I. vi. § 1.
4 *Ib.* I. iii. § 2.
5 *Ib.* I. iii. § 2.

1 Preface, p. vii.
2 Preface to the 6th and subsequent editions of *The Methods of Ethics*.
3 *The Methods of Ethics*[7], I. iv. 52.
4 *Ib.* I. iv. 53.

amounted to little more than the acceptance of what purported to be the verdict of common sense. He arrived too rapidly at the conclusion that the good was desirable sentient life, and from that it was no great step to define it as pleasure.

Sidgwick found a second principle—the maxim of prudence, that 'one ought to aim at one's own good on the whole'—to be as fundamental as that of benevolence. This maxim, when one's own good or pleasure is emphasized rather than good 'on the whole,' brought confusion into Sidgwick's theory. He admitted that there were times when a choice had to be made between individual and general pleasure and when all mundane sanctions failed to reconcile them. To rationalize his system a harmony between universal and particular reason had to be shown. This harmony depended on the existence of a supernatural Being. Unable to accept the Christian faith and gaining no positive assurance from psychical research of an all-good and all-powerful Being, Sidgwick left his system with the dualism in it unresolved. For a further account of Sidgwick's ethics see art. SIDGWICK (HENRY).

6. Present-day utilitarianism.—Little has to be said about utilitarianism after the time of Henry Sidgwick. To-day it is not a theory of paramount importance in ethics. As J. S. Mackenzie says, it is still the dominant view among writers on economics, but it has ceased to have much hold on English ethical thought.[1] Two schools can be distinguished. One contains Sidgwick's disciples. E. E. Constance Jones, who may be taken as representative of this school, has under the title *Rational Hedonism* re-stated Sidgwick's position and met objections to it.[2] Another school, that of the rationalist utilitarians, has found a spokesman in J. M. Robertson. In his *Short History of Morals* Robertson calls Sidgwick's ethical logic inconclusive, 'leaving as it did that earnest thinker conscious of a need for a future state.'[3] There is, however, an unresolved antagonism in Robertson's own theory. For, while accepting the greatest happiness principle as the ethical end, he says, 'there can be no stronger "obligation" than that of following your own happiness as you see it.' The two ends, he thinks, would often be in harmony owing to the individual's natural altruistic tendencies, or to pressure exerted by society or the working of conscience. A man 'cannot, unless he is abnormally selfish, escape discomfort in knowing that he has practised injustice or failed in reciprocity.'[4] But what of the 'abnormally selfish' man? In Robertson's theory, no blame, in the ethical sense, attaches to him for his failure to act for the common good. He is what he is through no fault of his own. The criminal is the result of 'pathological conditions,' or a 'product of maleducation or stress of circumstances.' Free will is demolished and with it moral responsibility. 'For the critical utilitarian . . . the bad character remains bad, baseness remains baseness, the liar a liar, the thief a thief; and his task is simply to try to guard himself and society against each form of evil in the best way, as society guards against the madman, in whose case even the free-willer recognizes the physical causation.'[5] And what of the man, not necessarily abnormally selfish, who in spite of the discomfort of conscience, acts contrary to the interests of others, doing what appears to himself to be for his own pleasure? He is, on Robertson's principles, doing that which is his own strongest 'obligation'; nor does any blame

1 *Introduction to Social Philosophy*[2], Glasgow, 1895, p. 433.

2 E. E. Constance Jones, art. SIDGWICK (HENRY), vol. xi. p. 500, and artt. in *IJE* vi., and elsewhere.

3 J. M. Robertson, *A Short Hist. of Morals*, London, 1920, p. 447.

4 *Ib.* p. 362.

5 *Ib.* p. 449.

attach to his action, for by hypothesis he cannot act otherwise than he does—which does not seem to leave much room for either ethical theory or moral conduct.

III. *CRITICAL.*—**1. The utilitarian theory of duty.**—Utilitarianism failed signally in dealing with duty. It tended to 'identify duty with coercion; to change the "ought" if not into a physical "must," at least into the psychological "must" of fear of pain and hope of pleasure.'[1] This was the natural outcome of the psychological hedonism on which the ethical theory was based. Bentham said of pleasure and pain that it was for them alone not only 'to point out what we ought to do' but 'to determine what we shall do.'[2] On this basis he was consistent in adding in the *Deontology* that it was 'very idle to talk about duties,' and that 'ought is a word that ought to be banished from our vocabulary.'

According to psychological hedonism, all desire was desire for pleasure, and the strongest desire excited by the keenest pleasure moved to action. Bain said:

> 'Wherever two present sensations dictate opposite courses, there is an experiment upon the relative strength of the two. The resulting volition discloses the stronger, and is the ultimate canon of appeal.'[3]

On such a foundation as this no place is left for the concept of moral obligation.

But the consciousness of duty could not be ignored—the consciousness of something higher than and conflicting with inclination, in the light of which inclination 'ought' to be suppressed. Utilitarians accordingly dealt with the duty consciousness empirically by explaining its genesis and function. It owed its origin, they said, to sanctions external or internal; pleasures and pains so attached to acts that the individual forbore to follow his first inclination and to act for his own selfish interest, and acted for the interests of all. Now there is no doubt that an individual is brought to a consciousness of moral obligation and to a knowledge of particular duties through social influences. It is not here, but in its account of the ultimate nature of moral obligation, that the utilitarian explanation is inadequate.

Later utilitarianism, as represented by Sidgwick and his school, was not hampered by psychological hedonism. Sidgwick said:

> 'It seems then that the notion of "ought" or "moral obligation" . . . does not merely import (1) that there exists in the mind of the person judging a specific emotion . . . nor (2) that certain rules of conduct are supported by penalties which will follow on their violation. . . . What then, it may be asked, does it import? What definition can we give of "ought," "right," and other terms expressing the same fundamental notion? To this I should answer that the notion which these terms have in common is too elementary to admit of any formal definition.'[4]

Sidgwick thus refused to resolve the 'ought' into anything else. As we have seen in the account of the views of J. M. Robertson, rationalist utilitarianism has no place in its system for moral obligation. The 'ought,' as understood by the ordinary moral consciousness, is excluded from any determinist system. For this reason, it is not certain that on a thoroughgoing analysis of the system of Sidgwick and his school any logical place would be found for the concept of moral obligation.

2. Motive and intention.—The controversy as to whether the proper object of moral praise and blame is 'motive' ('spring of action') or 'intention' (the 'object of desire') is a historic one. 'An action done from duty,' Kant said, 'derives its moral worth, *not from the purpose* which is to be obtained by it, but from the maxim by which it

1 J. Dewey and J. H. Tufts, *Ethics*, London, 1909, p. 355.

2 Bentham, *Principles*, I. i.

3 *The Emotions and the Will*[3], London, 1880, p. 401.

4 *The Methods of Ethics*[7], I. iii. 31 f.

is determined.'[1] In opposition to this we have the utilitarian position. 'There is no such thing,' Bentham said, 'as any sort of motive that is in itself a bad one.'[2] And J. S. Mill: 'The morality of the action depends entirely upon the intention.'[3] 'Intention' Mill defined as 'what the agent wills to do,' as opposed to motive, 'the feeling which makes him will so to do.' It is important to note that Bentham and the Mills were entirely consistent in holding that moral quality did not lie in motive. On their own theory, that pleasure was the only motive, they could have come to no other conclusion.

'Let a man's motive be ill-will; call it even malice, envy, cruelty; it is still a kind of pleasure that is his motive: the pleasure he takes at the thought of the pain which he sees, or expects to see, his adversary undergo. Now even this wretched pleasure, taken by itself, is good.'[4]

The sharp line drawn by utilitarianism between motive and intention has had a considerable influence. It has tended to induce other moral theories which rested on a truer psychological basis to make a separation between motive and intention, attributing moral quality to one only. Secondly, it has tended to make morality external. With regard to the first point the truer attitude seems to be to regard motive and intention as distinguishable but not separable—as the affective and ideational sides of the same thing—and to hold that moral judgment belongs to the two taken together, to the whole moral act. Dewey's definition of motive and intention puts this well: 'Intention is the outcome foreseen and wanted; motive, this outcome *as* foreseen and wanted.'[5]

With regard to the second point, utilitarianism, finding moral quality to reside in consequences, though in 'attempted' consequences, made morality an external thing. According to Mill:

'The morality of the action depends entirely upon the intention—that is, upon what the agent *wills to do*. But the motive, that is, the feeling which makes him will so to do, when it makes no difference in the act, makes none in the morality: though it makes a great difference in our moral estimation of the agent, especially if it indicates a good or a bad habitual *disposition*—a bent of character from which useful, or from which hurtful actions are likely to arise.'[6]

The last part of this paragraph seems to point to character as the final object of moral judgment, and to make it a good in itself. This, however, is illusory. At the end of ch. iv. Mill states the position clearly in the following words:

'This state of the will [will to do right] is a means to good, not intrinsically a good; and does not contradict the doctrine that nothing is a good to human beings but in so far as it is either itself pleasurable, or a means of attaining pleasure or averting pain.'[7]

3. The hedonistic calculus.—J. M. Robertson says that the great task which faces moralists to-day is a system of 'applied ethics.'[8] Utilitarianism professes to supply a scientific calculus—the hedonistic calculus of Bentham—which renders this system of applied ethics possible.

Bentham summed up his schema of mensuration in the lines:

'*Intense, long, certain, speedy, fruitful,* pure—
Such marks in *pleasures* and in *pains* endure.
Such pleasures seek, if *private* be thy end:
If it be *public*, wide let them *extend*.
Such *pains* avoid, whichever be thy view:
If pains *must* come, let them *extend* to few.'[1]

While still adopting Bentham's calculus, most of his successors plead not for a fresh inquiry into every act but for rules founded on well-considered utility.

Is the utilitarian calculus *theoretically* possible? Some moralists, including J. S. Mackenzie, have denied that it is. The calculus implies that a quantitative judgment is applicable to pleasures, that a certain intensity can be balanced by a certain duration of pleasure. The difficulty about the calculus, however, is not theoretical but practical. There is no known unit of mensuration. Further, pleasure-pain values vary according to persons, times, and circumstances. Albee says that the one really fatal objection to the calculus in his opinion is that urged by Spencer in the *Social Statics* that 'there would necessarily be an important shifting of the scale of hedonic values with every stage of intellectual or moral progress (or decadence), whether on the part of the individual, the community, the nation, or the race.'[2] This practical difficulty, the lack of scientific precision, is intensified when we remember that the pleasure-pain consequences have to be estimated for all 'whose interests appear to be concerned.'[3] Who are these? Our own family? Our fellow-countrymen? The present generation? Or must we act so as to promote the welfare of future generations? J. S. Mill did not limit happiness to mankind. The good act is one by which happiness is 'to the greatest extent possible, secured to all mankind; and not to them only, but, so far as the nature of things admits, to the whole sentient creation.'[4] This widening of the scope of the calculus is in keeping with the modern conception of organic life as a whole. In practice, however, utilitarians have narrowed the scope of the calculus, which seems to point to its failure as a scientific rule.

4. Pleasure the ethical end.—Against those utilitarians who said that pleasure was the only thing which could be desired some critics of utilitarianism have held that pleasure cannot be the object of desire at all, and that, if not an object of desire, it cannot be the ethical end. It seems, however, truer to hold that pleasure may be desired, and further that pleasurable things may be, and often are, desired because they are pleasant. Nor should we, with Green, deny the possibility of a 'sum of pleasures' as the ethical end, for by this is meant no more than pleasure lasting as long as possible and as intense as possible.

The first criticism of pleasure as the ethical end that must be made is that it lacks the *quality of virtue* which the moral consciousness demands in the good and affords no explanation of the essence of the particular virtues. Huxley's statement, 'If it can be shown by observation or experiment that theft, murder, and adultery do not tend to diminish the happiness of society, then, in the absence of any but natural knowledge, they are not social immoralities,'[5] has simply to be denied.

J. S. Mill's admission of a qualitative difference in pleasures is really an admission that for moral conduct one must transcend pleasure as either the supreme standard or the supreme good. Further, as Green said, there must be permanence in the ethical end. Pleasure does not fulfil this requisite. 'And after all it does seem a pretty definite and

1 *Theory of Ethics*[6], tr. T. K. Abbott, London, 1909, p. 16.
2 *Principles*, ch. x. § 2.
3 *Utilitarianism*[13], p. 27, footnote.
4 Bentham, *Principles*, ch. x. § 2. x. footnote.
5 J. Dewey and J. H. Tufts, *Ethics*, p. 250.
6 *Utilitarianism*[13], p. 27, footnote.
7 *Ib.* p. 61. The controversy between the utilitarian and the intuitionist is perhaps the most far-reaching of ethical discussions, and Spencer's reconciliation is a false one, while Sidgwick's position is really a confession that both are true but irreconcilable—a dualism. James Martineau is the greatest modern exponent of intuitionalism, as against either utilitarianism or evolutionism, and there can be little doubt that in general men of high moral sense feel that 'because right is right to follow right were wisdom in the scorn of consequence.' As Mill agreed, it makes a great difference in our estimation of the person what motive he acts from, and our estimation of the person is the main factor in the case.
8 *Short Hist. of Morals*, p. 429.

1 Bentham, *Principles*, IV. § 2, footnote.
2 E. Albee, *A Hist. of English Utilitarianism*, London, 1902, p. 387 f.
3 Bentham, *Principles*, ch. iv. § 5.
4 *Utilitarianism*[13], p. 17.
5 *Nineteenth Century*, i. [May, 1877] 537.

important point to take, that transient pleasures have in them no element of progress, contribute nothing to the permanent interests which unify (or, in fact, constitute) a life.'[1] And it is too *simple*. Utilitarianism attracts by its simplicity, but it is simple because it fails to do justice to all the facts of life. Man's nature cannot be explained in terms of feeling only.

Again, pleasure lacks *motive efficiency*. Utilitarianism has dispensed with the categorical imperative, and in itself it has no driving power.

Is there no truth, then, in the theory that the good is pleasure? There is the truth that the good must be pleasant, otherwise it cannot be an object of desire. The nature of the good is not pleasure, and yet pleasure is a result and accompaniment of the good. 'Man's chief end is to glorify God,' but those who glorify God will experience pleasure in the highest degree. They 'enjoy Him for ever.' And the glorifying of God involves the promotion of the well-being of humanity, which is not inconsistent with the promotion of pleasure. Kant based his argument for immortality on the fact that reason demands the harmony of pleasure and virtue, and since they do not always or ever perfectly unite here they must on the ground of rational congruity be at one somewhere.

Utilitarianism as an ethical theory is weak, but as a principle of political action it is not without its working value.

LITERATURE.—In addition to the books referred to in the article, mention may be made of the following: W. L. Courtney, *Constructive Ethics*, new ed., London, 1895; C. Douglas, *John Stuart Mill*, Edinburgh, 1895, *The Ethics of John Stuart Mill*, do. 1897; T. H. Green, *Prolegomena to Ethics*[5], Oxford, 1906; C. B. Roylance Kent, *The English Radicals*, London, 1899; J. MacCunn, *Six Radical Thinkers*[2], do. 1910; H. R. Marshall, *Mind and Conduct*, New York, 1919; J. Martineau, *Types of Ethical Theory*[2], Oxford, 1886; A. Seth Pringle-Pattison, *The Philosophical Radicals*, Edinburgh and London, 1907; G. de Ruggiero, *Modern Philosophy*, London, 1921, pp. 242-246; J. Seth, *English Philosophers and Schools of Philosophy*, London and New York, 1912; W. R. Sorley, *Ethics of Naturalism*[2], London, 1904; Leslie Stephen, *The English Utilitarians*, do. 1900.

A. W. HASTINGS.

UTRAQUIST.—See HUSSITES.

V

VADAGALAIS.—See PRAPATTI-MARGA, SECTS (Hindu), § 4.

VAIRĀGĪ.—See BAIRĀGĪ.

VAIŚĀLI.—The ancient city of Vaiśāli (Viśālā of *Rāmāyaṇa*;[2] Pali Visāli; Chinese Fei-shê-li) was equally sacred to the Jains and the Buddhists long ago. It is now represented unquestionably by the village named Basāṛ or Basāṛh (not Besarh or Bēsārh, as in nearly all books), situated in the Hājīpur subdivision of the Muzaffarpur District of the Bihār and Orissa Province, in 25° 59′ N. and 85° 8′ E. The site of the city occupies a space about ten miles in circuit, which includes several villages besides Basāṛh and many ruined mounds. The most interesting group of remains, situated near the village of Bakhirā at the north-west corner of the site, probably stands outside the line of the city walls, which, so far as is known, appear to have been built of mud, not masonry. The largest and most prominent mound, evidently the site of the fortified palace or headquarters of the local ruler, stands in the south-east corner of the city area and is called Bisālgaṛh, 'the fort of Rājā Bisāl,' the eponymous hero of the place. The village of Basārh is on the south and south-west of that mound. The identity of Vaiśāli with the group of remains associated with the village of Basāṛh is conclusively proved by the survival of the ancient name with only slight modifications; by geographical bearings taken from Patna and other places; by topographical details as compared with the description recorded by Hiuen-Tsiang (Yuan-Chwang), the Chinese pilgrim in the 7th cent.; and by the finding on the spot of sealings of letters inscribed with the name Vesāli. The documents, which were addressed to officials and other residents, have totally disappeared. The sealings found number about 1000, of which two or three bear the name of the town. The collection ranges in date from about 200 B.C. to A.D. 500, and is of much interest for many reasons, but need not be further described here, as it gives no information concerning the history of religion.

[1] H. Barker, in *Mind*, 1904, p. 418.

[2] I. i. 47, st. 13 in Schlegel's text.

Although the site of Vaiśāli has been visited and described by three professional archæologists, Cunningham, Bloch, and Spooner, their explorations, owing to limitations of opportunity, have been extremely slight and superficial, so that in reality very little is known concerning the local remains of antiquity. The area of the city seems to offer tempting possibilities for future inquirers. No distinct local tradition of the ancient glories of the city has survived. The identity of the site has been completely forgotten by the people, and is known only to a few students of Indian antiquities. No pilgrims visit the ruins, and no considerable modern temple or shrine exists among them. Yet few places in India have stronger claims upon the veneration of both Jains and Buddhists. Vardhamāna Mahāvīra, commonly spoken of as the founder of the Jain Church, belonged to a noble family of Vaiśāli, where he was born and spent all his earlier life. After he had entered upon the ascetic career, he is said to have resided in his native town or the immediate neighbourhood for twelve rainy seasons, during which travelling was unlawful for persons of his profession. The Jain scriptures often mention Vaiśāli.[1] The archæologists have not sought for Jain remains on the site, and nothing in their reports would lead the reader to suppose that the Basāṛh area was the birthplace of Jainism, as it is known to moderns.

Brāhmanical tradition ignores Vaiśāli almost completely, and no remarkable event in the history of orthodox Hinduism seems to be connected with the locality, although in the 7th cent. the territory of which Vaiśāli was the capital contained several scores of Hindu temples, besides hundreds of Buddhist monasteries, mostly dilapidated and deserted. The Jain establishments at that time were still numerous, and remains of them must survive. Nobody has thought of even looking for them. Such attention as the site has received has been bestowed almost exclusively on efforts to trace Buddhist holy places described by Hiuen-

[1] The best account of the life of Mahāvīra is that in ch. iii. of Mrs. Sinclair Stevenson's *The Heart of Jainism*, which gives a summary of the conflicting legends of the various sects. See also H. Jacobi, *Jaina Sūtras*, pt. i. (*SBE* xxii.), and art. ĀJĪVIKAS.

Tsiang. The discovery of the sealings mentioned above was accidental in the first instance. The earlier Chinese pilgrim, Fa-Hian, who visited Vaiśāli at the beginning of the 5th cent., mentions only a few of the most notable sacred buildings which were then standing. His account implies that in his time the city was inhabited and that the holy places were maintained. The sealings establish beyond doubt the fact that during the reign of Chandragupta II. (*c.* A.D. 375–413), at the time when Fa-Hian was travelling, Vaiśāli was an important place, governed by a prince of the imperial Gupta family. It was in the province of Tīra or Tīrabhukti, the modern Tirhut. The decay of the city and the gradual desertion of the Buddhist institutions took place in the interval between A.D. 405 and 637, the approximate respective dates of the visits of Fa-Hian and Hiuen-Tsiang. The ruin of the city may be ascribed to the decline of the Gupta power and the troubles connected with the Hun invasions of the 5th and 6th centuries. Nothing is known concerning the local history between the days of Buddha, about 500 B.C., and the visit of Fa-Hian nine centuries later.

In the time of Buddha Vaiśāli was the capital of the Lichchhavis, a tribe, people, or nation who were regarded as a section of the Vṛji (Pali Vajji) nation. But Hiuen-Tsiang distinguishes the Vaiśāli territory from the Vṛji country to the north-east, roughly equivalent to the modern Darbhangā District. The origin and affinities of the Lichchhavis, who certainly were foreigners, afford much room for speculation. Spooner seems to suggest that they were domiciled Persians. The writer of this article believes that they were of Mongolian race, akin to the Tibetans and other Himalayan peoples. They had many peculiar customs, quite different from those of ordinary Hindus. Manu[1] treats them as Vrātya Kṣatriyas, who did not observe fully Hindu *dharma*. They lived under the government of an aristocratic oligarchy or senate, of which the president was called king. The legendary splendours of their capital are often mentioned in Buddhist books. The *Dulva*, or Tibetan *Vinaya*, thus describes them:

> 'There were three districts in Vaiśāli. In the first district were 7000 houses with golden towers; in the middle district were 14,000 houses with silver towers; and in the last district were 21,000 houses with copper towers: in these lived the upper, the middle, and the lower classes, according to their positions.'

The city was imagined as a kind of earthly paradise, beautified by splendid buildings and charming parks, in which countless birds made melody. The Lichchhavis were believed to have lived in a round of continuous festivities. The chiefs waged war with both Bimbisāra and Ajātaśatru, the kings of Magadha with whom Buddha had dealings. The city, according to an early tradition in the *Dulva*, was reckoned among the six great cities, the other five being Śrāvastī, Saketa, Champā, Varāṇasi (Benares), and Rājagṛha.

The political pre-eminence of Vaiśāli at an extremely ancient period is indicated by the strange story in the *Bhadda-Sāla Jātaka*.[2]

> We are told that the wife of Bandhula, commander-in-chief of the Śrāvastī kingdom, felt a longing incident to the condition of pregnancy, and insisted on her lord taking her to Vaiśāli, because, she said, 'I desire to go and bathe and drink the water of the tank in Vesāli City where the families of the kings get water for the ceremonial sprinkling.' Although it is impossible to explain the allusion fully, it is clear that the water from a particular tank at Vaiśāli was essential for the lawful consecration of 'the kings,' whoever they may have been. The Lichchhavis resisted Bandhula and were all killed.

Vaiśāli stood on the ancient royal road leading from Pāṭaliputra (Patna) to Nepāl, the line of which is marked by four Aśoka pillars and other notable ancient remains. The city thus was in direct communication with the imperial capital and with many places of high importance in the olden time. The distance from Patna is about 27 miles in a direction a little west of north. The Lichchhavis and their city disappear from view for about eight centuries from 500 B.C. to A.D. 300, when they reappear as the source from which Chandragupta I. (*q.v.*), the founder of the imperial Gupta dynasty, derived his power. That chief married a Lichchhavi princess, and his powerful son, Samudragupta (*c.* A.D. 330–375), habitually described himself as the 'son of the daughter of the Lichchhavi.' Probably the Lichchhavis of Vaiśāli had been subject to the suzerainty of the Kushans, had become independent when the Indo-Scythian dynasty waned, and then had made themselves masters of Pāṭaliputra. Their own city certainly held an honourable position in the reign of Samudragupta's successor, Chandragupta II. (*q.v.*). At a later date we hear of a Lichchhavi dynasty of Nepāl. The city then vanishes again from history. When Hiuen-Tsiang visited it about A.D. 637, it was almost deserted, and he had to lodge in a small monastery occupied by a few monks of the Lesser Vehicle. They showed him all the sites of the Buddhist holy places according to the notions they had adopted 1100 years after the events of Buddha's lifetime. Among the show-places was the site of the meeting of the Second Council.[1]

The group of remains near Bakhirā at the north-west corner of the city alone can be identified satisfactorily with objects described by Hiuen-Tsiang. It is impossible to doubt that the Aśoka lion-pillar still standing is that seen by him, or that the tank beside it is his 'monkey-tank.' If the locality should ever be explored properly at any future time, as the site of Taxila is being examined by Sir John Marshall, many interesting discoveries may be anticipated, and further identifications of monuments may be possible.

LITERATURE.—Vaiśāli is mentioned eight times in the Pali *Jātakas* (see Eng. tr. ed. E. B. Cowell, Cambridge, 1895–1913, Index vol., *s.v.*). Other Buddhist literature frequently refers to the town in connexion with the Second Council (see art. COUNCILS [Buddhist]), the residence of Buddha (*q.v.*), and the distribution of his relics (see art. RELICS [Eastern]). The accounts of the Chinese pilgrims **Fa-Hian** (ch. xxv.), and **Hiuen-Tsiang** (Yuan-Chwang) may be read in any of the trr. with variations. The statements of the Tibetan *Dulva* are tr. by **W. W. Rockhill**, *The Life of the Buddha*, London, 1884. The copious Jain literature about Mahāvīra is cited by **A. F. R. Hoernle**, annual address in *Proceedings ASB*, 1898, and **H. Jacobi**, *Jaina Sūtras*, pts. i. and ii. (*SBE* xxii. [1884], xlv. [1895]). See also **A. A. Guérinot**, *Essai de bibliographie Jaina*, Paris, 1906, and 'Notes de Bibliographie Jaina,' in *JA*, 1909, pp. 47–148. Ch. iii. ('The Life of Mahāvīra') in **Mrs. Sinclair Stevenson**, *The Heart of Jainism*, London, 1915, supplies particulars not available elsewhere.

The geographical position, topography, and ancient remains of the site are discussed in *IGI* vii. [1908] *s.v.* 'Basārh'; **A. Cunningham**, *Archæol. Survey of India Rep.*, i. [Simla, 1871], xvi. [Calcutta, 1883]; **T. Bloch**, *Ann. Rep. Archæol. Survey of India for 1903–04*, Calcutta, 1906, pp. 73–122, with survey map; **D. B. Spooner**, *ib. for 1913–14*, do. 1917, pp. 98–185; **V. A. Smith**, 'Vaiśāli,' *JRAS*, 1902, pp. 267–288; and **F. E. Pargiter**, *JASB*, vol. lxvi. pt. i. [1897], p. 89.

For the Lichchhavis (*al.* Nichchhavi, Litsabi) see **V. A. Smith**, 'Tibetan Affinities of the Lichchhavis,' *IA* xxxii. [1903] 233–236; and **S. C. Vidyabhusana**, 'The Licchavi Race of Ancient India,' *JASB* lxxx. [1902], no. 2; but the subject needs further investigation.

VINCENT A. SMITH.

VAIŚEṢIKA.

VAIŚEṢIKA.—The name of one of the six philosophical systems of the Brāhmans. Just as we are able to establish a close relationship between the two oldest systems, the Sāṅkhya and the Yoga, and between the third and fourth, the Mīmāṁsā and the Vedānta, a third pair is formed by the Vaiśeṣika philosophy in connexion with the Nyāya, the latest of the systems. Both the Vaiśeṣika and the Nyāya teach the origin of the universe from atoms (*aṇu*, *paramāṇu*, *kaṇa*), and

[1] *Laws*, x. 22. [2] No. 465 of Cambridge tr., vol. iv. p. 94.

[1] See art. COUNCILS (Buddhist).

therefore introduce an entirely new element into the world of Brāhman thought. Further, both systems have in common the precise definition and arrangement of logical ideas upon which their influence and fame depend. These common characteristics have led to a complete fusion of the two systems in the later philosophical literature of India, and to a failure to distinguish Vaiśeṣika and Nyāya doctrines on the part of earlier European students of Indian thought. Now, however, for a long time access to the original sources has enabled us to determine the originally distinctive character of the two systems. The Nyāya used to be regarded erroneously as the earlier, and it is only recently that the priority of the Vaiśeṣika has been recognized.

Its founder bears the name of Kaṇāda, Kaṇabhakṣa, or Kaṇabhuj. All three names have the same meaning, viz. 'devourer of atoms'; whence it follows that these titles must have been originally terms of mockery bestowed on account of the atomistic character of the Vaiśeṣika doctrines. Such harmless nicknames, which in course of time have become real names, are often met with in the Indian world of letters.

Kaṇāda is supposed to have composed his textbook, the *Vaiśeṣikasūtras*, between 200 and 400 A.D. In it he proposes to teach the true discernment of all that may be known, and for that purpose assumes six categories, which in his judgment comprehend all existing things. In discussing these categories and their subdivisions, he treats of the most diverse problems, especially in cosmology and psychology, so that a complete system of philosophy is built up upon his doctrine of the categories. The following are the categories: 1. substance (*dravya*); 2. quality (*guṇa*); 3. movement or action (*karman*); 4. association (*sāmānya*); 5. difference (*viśeṣa*); 6. inherence (*samavāya*).

To the category of substance are assigned: earth (*i.e.* all organic bodies and all inorganic substances with the exception of the remaining four elements), water, fire, air, ether, time, space, soul, and the organ of thought (*manas*). To begin with, it appears to us strange that time and space are included among substances. Kaṇāda's conception of substance, however, is wider than ours; he intends by it that which has qualities and movement, and is the immediate basis of phenomena. The difficult question as to the nature of time and space, to which Kant was the first to give a final answer, is discussed, strangely enough, only incidentally and occasionally, in the whole of Indian philosophy. In this respect the Sāṅkhya philosophy has made a distinct advance, in that it regards time and space as two qualities of the eternal matter regarded as a unity.

The exposition of the category of substance affords Kaṇāda the opportunity of setting forth his atomic doctrine, which is derived from Buddhist sources. This has been shown by W. Handt in his treatise on the Vaiśeṣika philosophy.[1] According to the doctrine of Kaṇāda, the atoms of earth, water, fire, and air are eternal and uncreated. Although they themselves have no extension, their heterogeneous nature is the cause of the extension and visibility of the combinations of atoms. How this is to be understood, and where the visibility of these combinations begins, on these points Kaṇāda himself—to judge from the silence of the *Vaiśeṣikasūtras*—does not seem to have propounded any definite views. Later teachers of the school set forth the theory that an aggregate of three atoms (*try-aṇuka*)—others say, of three double atoms (*dvy-aṇuka*)—possesses extension, and that it is visible in the shape of the dust mote (*trasareṇu*) dancing in the sunlight.

The whole of this doctrine is vigorously combated in the philosophical works of the Vedānta and Sāṅkhya, and indeed for reasons obvious on both sides. The adherents of these two systems assert that, if the individual atoms do not possess extension, the aggregate cannot be extended; for every quality of a product is determined by the similar quality of its material cause.

The cosmogony of the Vaiśeṣika system depends upon its theory of the atoms. It is also dominated by the wide-spread Indian conception, that periods of creation and destruction of the universe follow one another in regular order; and on each occasion the evolution and decay of the universe are effected in the same way and by the same causes. The following explanations are in conformity with the exposition of W. Handt,[1] only that they do not begin, as he does, with the dissolution of the universe, but with its development.

During the period of dissolution, by which, however, the three infinitely great and therefore eternal and unchanging substances, ether, space, and time, are unaffected, no combination of the four elements of gross matter takes place, nor any union between the numberless individual souls and the atoms. But the souls retain their merit and demerit in a latent condition in the shape of dispositions. When the retributive force of merit and demerit with all its inevitable consequences, which here also, just as in the other systems of Indian philosophy, is the power that urges the universe on its course, is again aroused, the period of dissolution comes at once to an end. The souls therefore unite afresh with the atoms; and by this means a movement is started in the atomic elements which marks the beginning of a new creation of the material universe. This movement first originates in the atoms of the air, giving rise to double atoms, and through them to the gross material air which rushes forth and fills space. Thereupon within the elements of air the atoms of water combine together, whence in the same way the great ocean of the universe is produced. Within this ocean again the earth atoms come together, and form after the rise of double and triple atoms the solid mass of the firm earth. Finally, the element of fire comes into being, its atoms also combining in the same way within the water. Its origin is effected within the water, which in a certain sense represents the guard that restrains the destructive force of the fiery element, in order that its destroying power may be prevented from interfering with the organic course of the evolution of the universe. After the material universe has thus come into being, empirical existence begins afresh for the souls. These unite with bodies in accordance with the consequences of their work, still unexhausted from the preceding world-cycle; and in a new series of existences heap up for themselves merit and guilt, and earn reward and punishment until the cycle comes to an end. In the Sāṅkhya philosophy no cause is assigned compelling the dissolution of the universe; but in the Vaiśeṣika the process of its dissolution is accounted for in a very remarkable way. By their continual wandering through numberless bodies the souls are so weakened and exhausted that they need a long period to recruit. Just as living creatures upon earth after the sufferings and toils of the day sink at night to sleep, and remain for a time unconscious and without experience of pleasure or pain, so a universal night spreads over the universe, wherein the individual souls may recover from the sufferings of the *saṃsāra*. It is evident that so remarkable an explanation was not possible in a system which,

[1] *Die atomistische Grundlage der Vaiśeshika-Philosophie nach den Quellen dargestellt*, Rostock, 1900.

[1] *Op. cit.* pp. 56–58.

like the Sāṅkhya, maintained that souls were destitute of qualities. Only a soul that actually experiences, wills, and knows could be thought of as in a condition of exhaustion. That, in fact, the Vaiśeṣika philosophy does conceive of souls as endowed with qualities of their own will be understood from a consideration of the second category.

The process of the dissolution of the universe goes on, then, in the following manner. The affections disappear which are evoked by the action of merit and demerit in the individual souls, and which form the bond between body, the senses, and the external world. The motive force therefore is restrained which maintains the cycle of existence. The bond is consequently broken which exists by the power of merit and demerit between the material atoms and individual souls. The four atomic elements are now dissolved in regular succession, the earth in water, the water in fire, the fire in air. The process of the dissolution of the atomic elements is effected in the reverse order to that of the formation of the material products from the atoms, affecting first the triple atoms, and after their destruction, when only double atoms remain, seizing in turn upon these, so that finally each of the four elements maintains its existence in the form of isolated atoms.

From this statement of the cosmology of the Vaiśeṣika system, which the original texts present in connexion with the category of substance, we turn to the category of *quality*. This category comprises the ideas of colour, taste, smell, touch (together with temperature), number, extension, individuality, connexion, separation, priority, posteriority, knowledge, joy, pain, desire, aversion, and will. This list Śaṅkaramiśra enlarges in his commentary on *Vaiśeṣikasūtra* I. i. 6, with seven other qualities, which, though included in the seventeen preceding, yet in his opinion deserve special mention. They are weight, fluidity, adhesiveness, sound (the characteristic quality of the ether, which is the medium of the undulations), after-effect (or self-reproduction, *saṃskāra*, manifesting itself in three ways, as continuance of movement in obedience to a given impulse, elasticity, and memory), finally, merit and demerit.

It will be seen that this enumeration comprises mental as well as material properties. This affords Kaṇāda an opportunity under the category of quality of developing his psychology. Contrary to the philosophical teaching of the Vedānta and Sāṅkhya, mental qualities according to the Vaiśeṣika system are attached directly to the soul, as has been indicated above, but only in the form of dispositions. For no psychological process is possible for the soul that finds itself in an isolated condition. It is only in consequence of the soul's union with the organ of thought (*manas*) that its faculties are capable of activity. Both souls and the organ of thought are eternal substances; but the soul is all-pervading, *i.e.* not bound down to time and space, while the organ of thought is an atom. The latter is the intermediary between the soul and the senses, since urged by the soul it betakes itself on each occasion to that sense through which the soul desires to perceive or to act (for the capacities of walking, speaking, etc., are, according to the Indian view, comprised under the idea of the senses; a distinction is therefore made between the senses of perception and action). Thus the organ of thought continues to move as long as it is actuated by a process of perception or a bodily activity. If it rests motionless in the soul, the union of the latter with the senses ends, and no perception or act or experience is possible.

Kaṇāda declares the organ of thought to be an atom, because in his view different perceptions or other psychological processes do not take place simultaneously, but always one after the other, though frequently in exceedingly swift succession. On account of its minute size as an atom the organ of thought can unite at any given instant only with a single sense, and can only convey the idea of a single object. If the organ of thought were omnipresent like the soul, or if the soul could enter into immediate relation with the objects of knowledge, all objects would be simultaneously perceived. As the organ of thought, on the one hand, imparts the quickening power to the soul, so, on the other, it acts as a kind of check by preventing the soul from exercising more than one function at the same time.

The subdivisions of the third and fourth categories, those of movement (or action) and association, are of little significance. Difference, the fifth category, on the contrary, holds an important place in the Vaiśeṣika system, inasmuch as by virtue of it the difference of the atoms renders possible the formation of the universe. The name, therefore, of the entire system, Vaiśeṣika, is derived from the word for difference (*viśeṣa*).

From the very beginning, the sixth category, inherence (or inseparability), the enunciation of which reflects great credit on the insight of Kaṇāda, attracted the attention of Sanskrit scholars. This conception is clearly distinguished from that of occasional or separable connexion, which is regarded as a subdivision of the category of quality. The relation expressed by inherence subsists, for example, between the whole and its parts, the genus and the species, the particular object and the general idea with which it is associated, between a thing and its properties, between movement and that which is moved.

Later teachers added to these six categories a seventh, *non-existence*. This conception is one which has proved very injurious not only to the development of logic, but also to philosophical speculation in the later works of all schools. Bearing in mind the negative tendency of all Indian thinking, we can readily understand how Indian philosophers were led to work out this idea with ever-increasing refinement. Of this the division of the category of non-existence into four subdivisions furnishes a ready proof. Instead of 'future existence' the Indian says 'prior non-existence'; 'posterior non-existence' for 'past existence.' The simple relation existing between two things that are not identical (to give the usual example, between a pot and a cloth) is described as 'mutual (or reciprocal) non-existence,' and the actual impossibility of a thing (as of the son of a barren woman) as 'absolute non-existence.'

LITERATURE.—F. Max Müller, *Six Systems of Indian Philosophy*, London, 1899, ch. ix.; M. Monier-Williams, *Indian Wisdom*[4], London, 1893; L. Suali, *Introduzione allo studio della filosofia Indiana*, Pavia, 1912; B. Faddegon, *The Vaiṣeṣika System*, Amsterdam, 1918; *Sarva-darśana-saṅgraha*, ch. x., tr. by Cowell and Gough[2], London, 1894; *Vaiśeṣika Aphorisms*, tr. by A. E. Gough, Benares, 1873.

R. GARBE.

VAIṢṆAVISM.—I. Introductory.—The term 'Vaiṣṇava' is applied to that Hindu sect the members of which worship in a special way Viṣṇu, as contrasted with the two other greater sects, the Śaiva, or worshippers of Śiva, and the Śākta, or worshippers of Śakti, the female personification of energy. Their worship is not to be confounded with the orthodox worship paid by the higher classes of Hindus to Viṣṇu as their individual patron deity (*ishṭa-devatā*). Like Śaivism, Vaiṣṇavism is a form of monotheism, the setting aside of the triune equality of Brahmā, Śiva, and Viṣṇu in favour of a single god.

No attempt has been made at the more recent enumerations to collect statistics of the numbers of these sects. Few of the rural classes follow any distinctive sect, and it has been found impossible to record the numbers of their adherents with any approach to precision.[1]

2. The development of the worship of Viṣṇu.—Since the Vedic period the development of the cult of Viṣṇu has undergone many modifications. Though he is an important deity in the mythology of the *Brāhmaṇas*, Viṣṇu occupies only a subordinate position in the *Rigveda*, his essential feature being that he takes three strides, interpreted by some authorities to mean the rising, culminating, and setting of the sun, but more probably meaning the course of the solar deity through the three divisions of the universe.[2] The later development of his personality has been fully investigated by R. G. Bhandarkar, who traces its stages as follows: in the 5th cent. B.C. a religious reform arose like that which gave origin to Buddhism and Jainism, but based on theistic principles; this soon assumed a sectarian type in the form of the Pāñcharātra or Bhāgavata religion;[3] this, again, was combined with the cult of Nārāyaṇa, 'the resting-place or goal of gods'; soon after the Christian era the Ābhīra tribe of shepherds contributed to it their tribal hero Kṛṣṇa; in the 8th cent. this faith, the predominant feature of which was *bhakti*, or love, came into contact with the doctrine of spiritual monism and world-illusion promulgated by Śankarāchārya (*q.v.*); the hostility to spiritual monism gathered to a head in the 11th cent., when Rāmānuja (*q.v.*) made strenuous efforts to displace it by the religion of *bhakti* in a re-invigorated form; he was followed in the north by Nimbārka, who advocated the cow-herd element and enjoined the cult of Rādhā, mistress of Kṛṣṇa; the same policy was continued in the 13th cent. by Madhva or Ānandatīrtha, who established the doctrine of pluralism and brought into prominence the name of Viṣṇu as supreme god; in the north Rāmānanda added the cult of Rāma, and his successor Rāmānuja that of Nārāyaṇa; Kabīr in the 15th cent. preached strict monotheism, the cult of Rāma, and condemned idolatry; Vallabha in the 16th cent. founded the erotic cult of Kṛṣṇa and Rādhā, and Chaitanya in Bengal that of the boy Kṛṣṇa and Rādhā, a corruption which led to the degradation of Vaiṣṇavism; in the Deccan Nāmdev and Tukārām discarded the worship of Kṛṣṇa-Rādhā, cultivated a more sober type of worship, disseminated their ideas not in Sanskrit but in the vernacular languages, preached pure love of God, and laid stress on personal purification of heart and morals as necessary to salvation.[4]

3. Viṣṇu and his incarnations.—Vaiṣṇavism has thus developed on several distinct lines according as the object of devotion, Viṣṇu, varies in his manifestations, incarnations, or 'descents' (*avatāra*). This theory tends towards syncretism, the absorption of the lower animal-gods or totems of the more primitive tribes into the Brāhmanical pantheon. The incarnations of Viṣṇu are sometimes enumerated as six, ten, or twenty in number; but the most important are those of Kṛṣṇa and Rāma.[5] The cult of Rāma goes back in the *Vāyu Purāṇa* to about the 5th cent. B.C.; in the *Rāmāyaṇa* of Vālmīki, which in its original form is based on pre-Buddhistic materials, while its kernel was probably composed before 500 B.C., and the more recent portion was probably not added till the 2nd cent. B.C. and later,[1] Rāma is depicted as a high-souled hero, and thus with his faithful wife Sītā he won the affections of the Indian people. But it was not till the 11th cent. of our era that his cult was fully developed. This cult is described in the *Viṣṇu Purāṇa*, which seems to go back to the Gupta period (A.D. 320-455).[2] The tenth book of the *Bhāgavata Purāṇa* has exercised a more powerful influence than any other work of its class, was translated into Hindī by Lallū Rām Kavī under the title of *Prema Sāgara*, 'The Ocean of Love,' and is now the most popular manual of the cult of Kṛṣṇa.[3] The cult of Vāsudeva-Kṛṣṇa seems to be mentioned by the Greek traveller Megasthenes; and, if it prevailed in the period of the first Maurya emperors, it must have originated long before that time, and probably owes its development to that stream of thought which began with the *Upaniṣads* and culminated in Buddhism and Jainism.[4] Kṛṣṇa seems to have been a local deity known as Gopāla, 'cow-herd,' or Govinda, probably a later form of Govid, 'finder of cows,' which was an epithet of Indra.[5] He was worshipped by the Ābhīra shepherds, who wandered with their flocks over the region from Mathurā to Dwārkā. With this pastoral deity, by a process of syncretism, was combined the cult of an ocean-god of the western sea localized at Dwārkā. How far this cult was influenced by Christianity, brought by nomad tribes like the Gurjaras from Central Asia, is still a question of controversy.[6] The imperfect combination of the cults of Mathurā and Dwārkā is shown by the vagueness and inconsistencies of the legends which were invented to account for the later Kṛṣṇa cult.

4. The subdivisions of the Vaiṣṇavas: influence of the creed: sacred places.—The subdivisions of the Vaiṣṇavas follow the teaching of the great missionaries, of whom an account has elsewhere been given.[7] The most important is that of the Śrī Vaiṣṇavas, founded by Rāmānuja, the followers of whom are more numerous in Southern than in Northern India. The second school is that of Madhva, or Ānandatīrtha, who preached the doctrine of duality (*dvaita*), in opposition to the non-duality of Śankarāchārya. The third follows the teaching of Rāmānanda, whose characteristics were that no distinction was made between the Brāhmans and the so-called 'untouchables,' and the use of the vernacular tongues as the medium of his teaching. The fourth is the Vallabhāchārya, whose worship of the *guru* has led to much scandal.[8]

Vaiṣṇavism is essentially monotheistic, while Śaivism is often ultimately pantheistic or, rather, is apt to relapse into pantheism, though it, too, is monotheistic.[9]

> 'Taken as a whole, one of the chief characteristics of the United Provinces population is a real and unaffected kindliness. Vaishnavism would certainly appeal to them, and if adopted, would tend to enhance the very quality which would cause its adoption.'[10]

It represents to a large extent the Buddhistic

---

1 *Census of India, 1901*, vol. i., *India*, pt. i. p. 362; *ib. 1911*, pt. i. p. 114 f.

2 A. A. Macdonell, *Vedic Mythology* (=*GIAP* III. i.), Strassburg, 1897, p. 37 f.

3 See art. BHAKTI-MĀRGA.

4 R. G. Bhandarkar, *Vaiṣṇavism, Śaivism and Minor Religious Systems* (=*GIAP* III. vi.), Strassburg, 1913, p. 100 ff.; see artt. HINDUISM, vol. vi. p. 702 f., BENGAL, vol. ii. p. 492 f., KABĪR, KABĪRPANTHĪS, vol. vii. p. 632 ff., Tukārām.

5 Bhandarkar, p. 41 f.; J. Dowson, *A Classical Dict. of Hindu Mythology and Religion*, London, 1879, p. 361.

1 A. A. Macdonell, *A Hist. of Sanskrit Literature*, London, 1900, p. 309.

2 V. A. Smith, *The Early Hist. of India*³, Oxford, 1914, p. 21 ff.; art. PURĀṆAS, vol. x. p. 452.

3 Macdonell, *Hist. Sanskrit Lit.*, p. 302; *Prema Sāgara*, tr. F. Pincott, London, 1907; F. S. Growse, *Mathurā*³, Allahabad, 1883, p. 52 f.

4 Bhandarkar, p. 9; J. W. McCrindle, *Ancient India as described by Megasthenes and Arrian*, Calcutta, 1877, p. 201; Growse, p. 279.

5 Bhandarkar, p. 35 ff.

6 *Ib.* p. 38; Growse, p. 67 ff.; J. Kennedy, 'The Child Krishna, Christianity, and the Gujars,' *JRAS*, October, 1907, p. 951 ff.; G. A. Grierson, 'Modern Hinduism and its Debt to the Nestorians,' with discussion, *ib.* April, 1907, pp. 311-335, 447-503.

7 Art. HINDUISM, vol. vi. p. 703 ff.

8 *Ib.* p. 705; see also artt. RĀMĀNUJA; MĀDHVAS, MADVĀCHĀRĪS; RĀMĀNANDĪS, RĀMĀWATS.

9 *Census of India, 1911*, xv., *United Provinces*, pt. i. p. 128 ff.

10 *Ib.* p. 130.

type of life and morals, in which regard for the sanctity of life (*ahiṃsa*), human and animal, is a predominant feature.[1] Tod records that the spread of Kṛṣṇa-worship among some of the Rājputs (who generally, being warriors, favoured the Śaiva cult) exercised an ameliorating influence on their life and manners.[2] On the other hand, Dubois expresses a less favourable view of the sect in S. India.

'The feeling of aversion which orthodox Brahmins entertain for Vishnavite Brahmins is shared by Hindus of all castes. A stigma of reproach appears to cling to them. It cannot be the the case, however, that the disfavour with which they are regarded is entirely due to their worship of Vishnu. I think it must be largely imputed to their excessive pride and arrogance, their extreme severity, and their supercilious manners; for though all Brahmins share these characteristics, it is generally acknowledged that the Vishnavites display them in an intensified form.'[3]

Again, the erotic tendency of some Vaiṣṇava literature, particularly in connexion with the cult of Kṛṣṇa and Rādhā, has aroused opposition among the more sober-minded Hindus, and it must be noted that the rival cult of Rāma is singularly free from excesses of this kind. Growse remarks on one set of their poems:

'If ever the language of the brothel was borrowed for temple use, it has been so here.'[4]

In Bengal the licentious habits of some orders are notorious.

'The Bairāgī and Bairāgan [male and female] Vaishnavas are of evil repute, their ranks being recruited by those who have no relatives, by widows, by individuals too idle and depraved to lead a steady working life, and by prostitutes. Vaishnavī or Boistubī, according to the vulgar pronunciation, has come to mean a courtezan.'[5]

In N. India the cult of Viṣṇu or Kṛṣṇa is specially observed at Mathurā (*q.v.*) and the adjoining towns of Brindāban and Gokul (*qq.v.*); Viṣṇu is worshipped at Purī as Jagannāth (*q.v.*); he has a famous shrine at Badarīnāth (*q.v.*); in Gujarat Kṛṣṇa is worshipped at Dwārkā; at Pandharpur in the Sholāpur District, the Deccan, Viṣṇu is worshipped as Viṭhobā; in the south his chief seats are Conjeeveram and Tirupatī. The Vallabhāchāryas have their chief temples at Gokul and at Nāthdwāra in the Mewār State of Rājputānā. Rāma-worship centres in the scenes described in the *Rāmāyaṇa*, Ayodhyā, Chitrakūt, and Nāsik.

LITERATURE.—Many of the authorities have been quoted in the article. The Vedic texts connected with Viṣṇu have been collected by **J. Muir**, *Original Sanskrit Texts*, London, 1858–72, iv.[2] [1873] 63 ff. The Vaiṣṇava sects are described by **H. H. Wilson**, *Essays and Lectures on the Religion of the Hindus*, London, 1861–62, i. 30 ff. On the connexion of Kṛṣṇa-worship and Christianity see **J. Kennedy**, 'The Child Krishna, Christianity, and the Gujars,' *JRAS*, October, 1907, p. 951 ff.; **G. A. Grierson**, 'Modern Hinduism and its Debt to the Nestorians,' *JRAS*, April, 1907, pp. 311–335, 447–503, with the discussion, and his art. BHAKTI-MĀRGA, vol. ii. p. 539 ff., and the note in *JRAS*, April, 1913, p. 144. On Vaiṣṇavas in general see *BG* ix. pt. i. [1901] 530 ff.; **E. W. Hopkins**, *The Religions of India*, Boston, 1895, and London, 1896, p. 388 ff.; **M. Monier-Williams**, *Brāhmanism and Hindūism*[4], London, 1891, p. 95 ff.; **W. Ward**, *View of the Hist., Literature, and Religion of the Hindoos*[2], Serampore, 1815, ii. 6 ff.

W. CROOKE.

VALENTINIANISM. — Valentinianism is a form of Gnostic teaching which originated with Valentinus, about the middle of the 2nd century. The term is a somewhat vague one, for Valentinus was generally regarded as the chief master of gnosis, and all the Gnostic schools were affected in some degree by his influence. His name was often attached to systems which had borrowed from him superficially, as well as to those which had grown directly out of his teaching.

[1] H. Kern, *Manual of Indian Buddhism* (=*GIAP* III. viii.), Strassburg, 1896, p. 68 ff.; V. A. Smith, *The Oxford History of India*, Oxford, 1919, p. 38 f.

[2] J. Tod, *Annals of Rajasthan*, Oxford, 1920, ii. 619.

[3] J. A. Dubois, *Hindu Manners, Customs, and Ceremonies*[3], Eng. tr., Oxford, 1906, p. 122.

[4] P. 215.

[5] J. Wise, *Notes on the Races, Castes and Trades of Eastern Bengal*, London, 1883, p. 161.

1. Life and writings of Valentinus.—Of the life of Valentinus only a few scattered notices have come down to us. He was born on the coast of Egypt, at the end of the 1st or the beginning of the 2nd cent., and was educated at Alexandria. For some time he worked in that city as a Christian teacher, but eventually migrated to Rome, where he lived during the period between the episcopates of Hyginus and Anicetus (A.D. 137–166). He must have come forward as a Gnostic teacher before his arrival in Rome, for Justin mentions him among the conspicuous heretics,[1] and appears to have discussed his theories in the *Syntagma*, written about A.D. 160. Epiphanius states that he first became the head of a sect in Cyprus, and that he broke with the Church because he was passed over in the election of a bishop. A personal grudge of this kind is, however, commonly imputed to famous heretics in the controversial writings, and there is no reason to doubt that Valentinus advanced towards his later position by a natural process of reflexion, which would be stimulated by the Gnostic atmosphere of the Alexandrian Church. It is more than probable that he never formally detached himself from orthodox Christianity.

Valentinus was the author of a number of writings which have now perished, with the exception of a few fragments. His works included hymns, homilies, epistles, and possibly a treatise entitled *Sophia*. A late tradition makes him the author of a Gospel, but of this there is no evidence. His adversaries themselves pay tribute to his eloquence and intellectual power, and their testimony is fully borne out by the meagre specimens of his own writing which have been preserved. His system as a whole is known to us only from hostile witnesses, whose acquaintance with it had been formed at second hand; but through this obscuring medium it is still possible to recognize in Valentinus the foremost of the Gnostics, and one of the most gifted and versatile minds of the early Church. He was at once a poet, a philosopher, and a great religious teacher. Out of the chaotic materials of Gnostic tradition he constructed a harmonious body of thought in which there are not a few elements of real speculative value.

2. Sources.—Of the patristic accounts of Valentinus the earliest was that of Justin, and an outline of it has possibly been preserved in Irenæus, *adv. Hær.* I. xi. 1–3. Hippolytus described the system in an early work which is now lost, but can be partially reproduced from pseudo-Tertullian, Philaster, and Epiphanius. Our remaining sources are Irenæus, Tertullian, and the *Philosophumena* of Hippolytus; but Tertullian is for the most part directly dependent on Irenæus. Hippolytus and Irenæus—the two cardinal authorities—are broadly in agreement, but their differences are sufficient to prove that they worked independently. Preference has often been given to the account of Hippolytus, which is shorter, clearer, and more symmetrical. But a number of indications make it almost certain that Irenæus is closer to original sources, although he has presented his material with little discrimination, and has confused the teaching of Valentinus himself with that of his disciples. The notices of the controversial writers are supplemented by the *Excerpts from Theodotus*, a selection of passages from an early Valentinian writer which is appended to the *Stromata* of Clement of Alexandria. The value of this source is much impaired by the difficulty of arranging the detached sentences in any intelligible order, and by the intrusion of comments which cannot with certainty be distinguished from the text. A curious problem arises from the similarities in thought, and occasionally in lan-

[1] *Trypho*, 35.

guage, between the *Excerpts* and the account in Irenæus. A direct connexion is not probable, but there is reason to believe that the writer quoted by Clement and the main authority consulted by Irenæus have made use of the same document. In addition to the sources enumerated, we have the *Fragments* of Valentinus himself, by which we are enabled in some degree to check and interpret the evidence of the patristic writers. A number of fragments have also been preserved from the works of later Valentinian teachers—notably the Letter of Ptolemæus to Flora, which is quoted at full length by Epiphanius,[1] and the extracts from the commentaries of Heracleon, which are given by Clement and Origen.

3. The system of Valentinus.—It is stated by Irenæus[2] that Valentinus adapted the principles of current Gnosticism to a doctrine of his own; and his system clearly betrays this dependence on earlier phases of the Gnostic movement. At Alexandria he can hardly have failed to come into personal contact with Basilides, and the influence of the older teacher is apparent in various details of his system (*e.g.*, the multiplication of æons, the doctrine of the passions as alien spirits invading the soul, the conception of the hebdomad as the sphere of the Demiurge). To Basilides, too, he may have owed the impulse to build a philosophical theory on the basis of Gnostic tradition. For the most part, however, he reverts from Basilides to the older Gnostic constructions. It seems to have been his purpose to form a comprehensive system which should gather up in itself the more valuable elements of all previous gnosis. To this we may attribute the complexity of detail which marks the system, and which has sometimes been set down to later elaboration. From this too we can best explain the remarkable diffusion of Valentinian gnosis. All the Gnostic sects were able to recognize in it their own characteristic tenets, brought into a larger context, and impregnated with a deeper meaning. As Valentinus borrowed from the earlier types of Gnosticism, so he adopted many suggestions from those Eastern religions which lay behind the whole Gnostic movement. The division of æons into groups of eight, ten, and twelve recalls the similar grouping of divinities in the Egyptian religion. The conception of the Pleroma as made up of thirty æons has its obvious counterpart in the thirty supreme gods of Zoroastrianism. Some of the details in the history of Sophia and the Soter appear to be taken directly from the Syrian and Phrygian myths of the mother-goddess rather than from their Gnostic analogies. But, while thus elaborating the mythological framework, Valentinus informs it, to a far greater extent than any of his predecessors, with a philosophical significance. Hippolytus may be right in his contention that the system is largely indebted to the Pythagorean theory of numbers; but the chief philosophical influence (as Hippolytus himself acknowledges) is undoubtedly that of Plato. Valentinus endeavours in his own fashion to work out the Platonic conception of an ideal world reflecting itself in the world of visible things. His doctrine of the soul as longing to be restored to the kingdom of light from which it has fallen is ultimately derived from Plato. The Gnostic mythology, as remoulded by him, partakes in some measure of the character of the Platonic myths. His æons are no longer separate divine beings but aspects of the nature and activity of God. They spring from one another not by a process of birth, but by one of emanation. The traditional episodes of the Gnostic history of redemption are more than half allegorized into inward experiences in the life of the soul. Gnosticism in the hands of Valentinus attempts to transform itself into a real philosophy, offering a solution of the metaphysical problems of the origin of evil, the relation of spirit to matter, the creation of the world, the nature and destiny of man.

[1] *Hær.* xxxiii. 3. [2] I. xi. 1.

With Valentinus the distinctively Christian element is much more pronounced than in earlier Gnosticism. He had begun his career as a Christian teacher, and perhaps never regarded himself as alienated from the Church. So far as can be ascertained, he instituted no peculiar rites or sacraments to mark out his following as a separate sect. All through his system we can trace the desire to bring his thought into as close relation as possible to the Christian teaching, and with this intention he makes a continual appeal to Scripture. In no recorded instance does he fall back on the esoteric writings which were favoured in Gnostic circles. His practice is rather to make use of the Scriptures acknowledged by the Church, OT and NT alike, and to read the esoteric meaning into them by a forced application of the allegorical method. But, while he thus appeals to Scripture in order to commend his teaching to orthodox Christians, he regards it as at best a secondary source of revelation. This is apparent as well from his highly subjective mode of interpretation as from his explicit statement:

'Many of the things written in the public books are found also written in the Church of God. . . . The law written in the heart is the people of the Beloved' (*i.e.* the spiritual race has come from God, and is itself an immediate source of divine knowledge).[1]

Not only does Valentinus accept the Christian Scriptures, but in his scheme of redemption he makes room for Christian believers as the 'psychical' class, intermediate between the 'pneumatic' and the 'hylic.' Earlier Gnosticism had allowed only for the higher class, predestined to life, and the lower, in which all spiritual potentialities were lacking. In the Valentinian system the third class is also capable of salvation, although in an inferior degree. This estimate of the 'psychic' natures was not due, as the Fathers complain, to arrogance and exclusiveness, but to a genuine solicitude for the mass of ordinary Christians. But the Christian affinities of the system are most clearly discernible in its central motive; for its various speculations all converge in a doctrine of redemption, in which the chief place is assigned to Jesus. The redemption is conceived, in the first instance, as the deliverance of the spiritual element from matter, but it was connected, at least in Valentinus's own teaching, with a pure and lofty ethic.

'The heart is cleansed by the expulsion of every evil spirit; . . . and when the only good Father visits it, it is sanctified, and gleams with light; and he who possesses such a heart is so blessed that "he shall see God."'[2]

It would be too much to say that with Valentinus Gnosticism joined hands with Christianity, but we may fairly credit him with a sincere endeavour to mediate between the two forms of teaching. He sought, on the one hand, to bring Gnosticism into closer sympathy with the Church and, on the other, to secure the Church's recognition of the elements of truth in Gnosticism.

The Valentinian system as described by the Fathers, whose evidence is consistent, in the main, with that of the *Fragments*, falls into two clearly marked divisions: (1) the events within the Pleroma, (2) the history of the creation and redemption. One difficulty, however, which has often been considered as of paramount importance, meets us at the outset. According to Irenæus, the æon who stands at the head of the Pleroma has a female consort, while Hippolytus, who is here supported by the *Fragments* and the *Exc. Theod.*, speaks of one supreme principle who is the

[1] *Frag.*, quoted in Clem. *Strom.* vi. 6.
[2] *Ib.*, in *Strom.* ii. 20.

source of all being. Irenæus himself admits that on this point there was difference of opinion among the Valentinian schools. The discrepancy is not, perhaps, so serious as might appear at first sight, especially when we remember that for Valentinus the æons tend to be little more than metaphysical abstractions. He apprehends the supreme principle as a unity, but as still containing within itself the possibility of distinction. This, indeed, is the presupposition of the whole system—that the original unity was capable from the first of a self-unfolding into the multiplicity of being.

The supreme æon, whether conceived as monad or as dyad, is moved by an inner necessity of love to impart his fullness, and by a process of emanation there arises the series of æons which constitutes the Pleroma. Bythos and Sige put forth Nous and Aletheia, from whom proceed the two pairs, Logos-Zoe and Anthropos-Ecclesia. These four pairs, or 'syzygies,' make up the ogdoad, which is complete in itself—a Pleroma within the Pleroma. The process of emanation is then continued by the two lower pairs of the ogdoad. Logos and Zoe project the five syzygies of the decad: Bythios-Mixis, Ageratos-Henosis, Autophues-Hedone, Akinetos-Syncrasis, Monogenes-Makaria. From Anthropos and Ecclesia proceed the six syzygies of the dodecad: Paracletos-Pistis, Patrikos-Elpis, Metrikos-Agape, Aeinous-Synesis, Ekklesiastikos-Makariotes, Theletos-Sophia. When the Pleroma is thus constituted, it is enclosed within itself by Horos (the boundary), which, according to Irenæus, is also interposed between Bythos and Sige and the remaining æons. The doctrine of the Pleroma is borrowed by Valentinus from older Gnosticism, but is modified in the light of metaphysical principles. Absolute Being goes forth from itself in the æons of the ogdoad, while in the decad and dodecad the powers immanent in these higher æons are drawn out and determined, first on the ontological, then on the more active, side. It will be noted that in these lower pairs the male is designated by an adjective, the female by a substantive—in keeping, apparently, with the Valentinian doctrine that the female contributes a vague substance, on which the male imposes form. The harmony of the Pleroma is broken by the presumption of Sophia, the youngest æon, who aspires, by one account, to comprehend the unknowable Father, by another, to create like the Father in virtue of her sole activity. She produces an abortion, but, on the prayer of the other members of the Pleroma, two new æons, Christos and the Holy Spirit, are put forth by Nous and Aletheia, and separate Sophia from her formless offspring. It falls out of the Pleroma, but is sought out by Christos and the Spirit, who endow it with form and then return. As a thank-offering for the restored harmony the thirty æons in fellowship put forth a new æon, Jesus.[1]

The second part of the system is concerned with the events outside of the Pleroma, after the departure of Christos from the lower Sophia (called in Irenæus by the Aramaic equivalent 'Achamoth'). Bereft of her helper, she is afflicted by the four passions of fear, grief, perplexity, and supplication; and Jesus, the common fruit of the Pleroma, is sent forth to be her consort and deliver her. Her passions are detached from her and become independent principles—the fear changing into psychic, the grief into hylic, the perplexity into demonic, substance, while the supplication takes the form of a path of repentance. (A simpler type of the myth derives the four material elements from the passions of Sophia.) The psychic sphere is called, as in Basilides, the hebdomad, and is presided over by the Demiurge, while below this sphere is the cosmos, and lowest of all the chaos of unformed matter. From the Demiurge proceed the souls of men, but he is controlled, unawares to himself, by his mother Sophia, and as a result of this twofold influence certain souls are spiritual, others psychic, the rest belonging wholly to the element of matter in which they are incarnated. For the redemption of human souls Jesus is produced by the immediate power of Sophia, and is born of Mary. It was assumed by all Valentinian schools that his body was non-material, and Valentinus compares it, in one of the extant *Fragments*, to water conveyed by a canal. As to the nature of his body, however, there was a divergence of views which led, as will presently be noted, to important consequences. The redemption accomplished by Jesus extends to all souls that are not hopelessly estranged from the higher world, but the pneumatic and psychic partake of it in different mode and measure. The former belong by their nature to the higher sphere, and require nothing for their deliverance but the moulding influence of gnosis imparted by Jesus. Their goal is an ascent into the Pleroma, where they are finally mated with angelic beings. Psychic souls attain to salvation by faith and good works, by which, with the aid of Jesus, they make up for their inherent deficiency; and the sphere to which they are raised is the heaven of the fallen Sophia. In each of the three worlds, therefore (the Pleroma, the lower heaven, the cosmos), a deliverance is necessary, and is effected in each case by a different redeemer. Sophia is saved by Christos, her offspring by Jesus, the fruit of the Pleroma, while Jesus, the son of Mary, redeems the souls of men. It may be inferred from several indications in the *Exc. Theod.* and the earlier account of Hippolytus that the three Saviours were sometimes conceived as aspects of a single redeeming power, and this may have been the original teaching of Valentinus.

[1] A variant account in Iren. I. xi. 1 (apparently supported by the *Exc. Theod.*) makes Sophia herself fall from the Pleroma, and give birth to Christos, along with a kind of shadow. Christos separates himself from his mother and returns to the Pleroma, and Sophia, left with the shadow, produces another son, the Demiurge.

From this brief survey of the system it is evident that Valentinus conserves, and even accentuates, the mythological traits of older Gnosticism, while seeking, as far as possible, to rationalize them. Instead of unmeaning names, the æons bear designations which imply intellectual or religious qualities. The several stages of the history are determined not by astral conceptions but by a speculative scheme, carefully thought out, though in many respects obscure. Valentinus, moreover, has made a deliberate attempt to overcome the dualism implicit in all Gnostic thought. The cause of Sophia's fall, and of the consequent origin of evil, is not so much a sin as a presumption, due to an impulse in itself good. Her fall takes place within the Pleroma, where she continues to abide. The Pleroma no longer stands in sharp opposition to the lower world but is linked up with it and is the ground of its existence. The Demiurge, though an inferior power, is imperfect rather than evil, and his work is capable of being transformed into something higher. The worlds without the Pleroma are copies of it on a lower plane, and at each descending stage its history is repeated. One of the most significant of the changes due to Valentinus is the addition of Horos to the Gnostic cosmogony. For the Oriental conception of two opposite realms of being he substitutes the Greek one of a limit, preserving all existences in their due place and order. To a Greek instinct we may likewise assign the pervading thought that the divine activity, at each stage of the cosmic process, impresses form on formless substance. But with all his effort Valentinus does not succeed in resolving the dualism which lay at the foundation of Gnostic theory. It is tacitly assumed that from the beginning there existed along with God a world of alien matter or not-being. This is capable, in varying degrees, of being moulded by the divine Artist, but in the end there is a residuum with which He can do nothing. The world of utter chaos is left over to the demons; the 'material' souls can look for no participation in the Redeemer's gift.

4. Underlying purpose of the system.—Valentinus is at once a philosopher and a religious teacher, and from this double point of view we must consider the underlying purpose of his system.

(1) On the one hand, he seeks to bring the abstract and inaccessible God into relation to the actual world. The Pleroma is the first outgoing of God from Himself, the manifestation of the Absolute in a sphere of being which is still, in some sense, one with Him. This process of self-unfolding is continued on an ever-descending scale until at last the divine principle is merged in the depths of matter. A hymn of Valentinus, preserved by Hippolytus, gives vivid expression to this normative idea.

'I behold all things suspended by spirit; I perceive all things borne on by spirit—flesh suspended from soul, soul upheld by air, air suspended from æther, and fruits produced from Bythos, and the child born from the womb.'

Matter, it is here implied, is linked with the cosmos, the cosmos with the lower heaven, this with the Pleroma, and this again with Bythos, from which absolute source all being has its birth. In another striking passage[1] Valentinus compares the world to an imperfect image of God, which is inscribed, however, with the name of Him whom it represents so as to authenticate it:

[1] Quoted in *Strom.* iv. 13.

'The form is not exactly to the life, but the name supplies what is wanting in the effigy; the invisibility of God co-operates with that which has been fashioned.'

Thus the whole universe is conceived as an infinite gradation of being, instinct, though ever more faintly, with the power which has called it forth. Valentinus, in other words, is struggling with the idea which had hovered before the minds of Greek thinkers ever since the days of Plato, and which finally received its classical form in Plotinus. His thought is disguised and hampered by the Gnostic imagery in which he clothes it, but from the philosophical point of view he may be classed as one of the chief precursors of Neo-Platonism.

(2) The philosophical interest is, however, subordinate. Valentinus was primarily a theologian, and it was in the effort to solve religious problems that he was led to the speculations on which he bases his system. The controversial writers, who are intent on exposing the absurdities of the heretical teaching, are chiefly occupied with these strange speculations; but they are far less prominent in the surviving utterances of the Valentinians themselves. The *Fragments* and the *Exc. Theod.* only touch on them incidentally. Heracleon, in the extracts from his commentaries which we possess, makes hardly any reference to the Pleroma, and the questions which he discusses are intrinsically as much Christian as Gnostic. His suggestions are considered seriously and sometimes accepted by Clement and Origen. The Valentinian theology, like that of the Church, has its centre in the problem of redemption, but this is approached from the metaphysical, instead of the ethical or mystical, side. Redemption, as understood by the Gnostic thinkers, is the deliverance of spirit from the material element in which it has become entangled. How is this fall of spirit out of its native sphere to be explained? No answer is possible except that some disaster has taken place in the spiritual world, and the Gnostic sets himself to discover its nature and origin. Not only so, but he is required to show how the primal error has been corrected. There can be no redemption for men on earth unless we have the assurance that order has been re-established in the upper world; the restoration, like the fall, must begin from above. Valentinus, therefore, sets out from the doctrine of the Pleroma, and the redemption achieved in heavenly places after Sophia, by her error, had destroyed the original harmony. But these speculations form only the background of the system. They supply a prologue in heaven, which is not to be mistaken for the real drama, although it provides the key by which it must be interpreted. Valentinus, like the orthodox teachers, is occupied all along with the redemption accomplished by Jesus, and differs from them chiefly in his endeavour to correlate it with a universal redemption. This involves him, however, in further differences, which affect his whole religious attitude. In spite of his desire to construe the universe as the harmonious unfolding of a single principle of being, he is compelled, like other Gnostic thinkers, to fall back on an ultimate dualism. The fall of spirit cannot be metaphysically explained unless it is assumed that from the beginning there existed something alien to God. This duality reveals itself in the world of men as well as in the cosmos generally. Souls differ from one another in kind, and are not capable of the same redemption. Valentinus makes a genuine effort to break through the exclusiveness to which all previous Gnostics had stood committed. At the risk of inconsistency he recognizes the intermediate class of 'psychical' men, and it is one of the chief objects of his system to find a place for them within the scope of the redeeming process. But in the end he is driven back on the traditional Gnostic doctrine that only the spiritual can be truly saved, and that their salvation is nothing else than the inherent prerogative of their nature.

'Ye are originally immortal, and children of eternal life, and ye would have death distributed to you, that ye might spend and lavish it, and that death may die in you and by you; for when ye dissolve the world, and are not yourselves dissolved, ye have dominion over creation and all corruption.'[1]

In this remarkable saying Valentinus appears to hint at a lofty doctrine of the obligation resting on 'spiritual' men in virtue of their privilege. They are placed in this world of death, or have voluntarily entered it, in order that they may co-operate with the higher powers, and that through them the dominion of death may at last be utterly destroyed. In the light of such a saying it is impossible to doubt the noble religious temper of the great Gnostic. The very doctrine which in other leaders of the movement had served to foster a spirit of egoism and of contempt for the inferior mass of men is transformed by him into a supreme motive for human service. Yet the conception of one class of men who are marked out as essentially different from others is none the less made prominent. These higher natures alone are destined to a true redemption, and for them the work of a redeemer is hardly necessary. Like others they acknowledge Jesus as their Saviour, but what they receive from him is little more than the apprehension of their own native excellence as the children of light. It is this failure on the part of its noblest representative to reconcile the Gnostic teaching with Christian ideas that stamps it most unmistakably as alien, in its fundamental character, to the gospel.

5. Subsequent history of Valentinianism.—The history of Valentinianism after the founder's death is very imperfectly known to us, but there is evidence that the sect extended itself rapidly, and found adherents in Italy, Gaul, N. Africa, Egypt, Syria, and Asia Minor. Tertullian describes it as in his time 'frequentissimum plane haereticorum collegium.' According to Hippolytus, it came to be divided at an early date into two schools—the Eastern, or Anatolic, and the Western, or Italic—and the fact of this division is confirmed by the *Exc. Theod.*, which purport to give the doctrines of 'the so-called Eastern Valentinianism.' The schism, we are told, was brought about by a difference of opinion as to the nature of the earthly body of Jesus. The Easterns maintained that he assumed a pneumatic body, while the Westerns taught that his body was psychical, the Spirit descending on him at his baptism in the likeness of a dove. Both of these views are represented in the *Exc. Theod.*, and from this it has been inferred that the division cannot have been so sharp as Hippolytus affirms, or that it must have followed some other line of cleavage. Clement, however, may have made his extracts from several writers, belonging to different schools, or Theodotus himself may have quoted from other Valentinians, with whom he was not in full agreement. Why the dispute should have turned on an issue that appears so secondary and artificial it is difficult to say. It may be that the Christological controversy which was to rend the Church a century later was anticipated in some fashion by the Gnostic thinkers. More probably the question as to the nature of the Redeemer's body served merely to focus some radical difference of view as to the scope and purpose of the redemption itself. At all events, it is significant that the sect was divided on a matter that concerned not the speculative construction, but the doctrine of the Person of Christ. We have here a strong confirmation of the view that Valentinianism was much more closely allied to

[1] *Strom.* iv. 13.

orthodox Christianity than the records of the Fathers might lead us to suppose. This conclusion is further borne out by the extant writings of the two leaders of the school who were next in influence to Valentinus himself, and both of whom appear to have been his personal disciples—Ptolemæus and Heracleon.

(*a*) *Ptolemæus.* — In his system as a whole Ptolemæus adhered closely to Valentinus — so much so that Irenæus has made little effort to discriminate his separate teaching. He added, we are told, new and more complicated details to the æonology, and thought of the æons as personal beings, not merely as modes and aspects of the divine nature. In his doctrine of redemption he laid peculiar emphasis on the relation of the work of Christ to that of the Demiurge. But besides the notices in the Fathers we possess the Letter of Ptolemæus to Flora—the one document of 2nd cent. gnosis which has come down to us complete. In writing to a Christian of whom he hoped to make a convert, Ptolemæus would no doubt present his views with studied moderation, but his Letter, however we regard it, must be taken as an authentic statement of Valentinian doctrine. It deals with the specific question of the validity of the Law, and distinguishes (1) a Law given by God Himself, (2) a Law proceeding from Moses, (3) a Law appended by the elders to this Mosaic code. In the Law given by God three elements are likewise distinguished: (1) spiritual precepts, which are of permanent value and were endorsed by Jesus; (2) commandments, which were only for a time and were abrogated by Jesus; (3) ordinances that must be interpreted in a typical or symbolic sense. The teaching of Jesus is accepted throughout as the one criterion of truth. Ptolemæus betrays his Gnostic presuppositions by identifying the God of the Law with the Demiurge, whom he conceives as an inferior and imperfect God, just rather than absolutely good. But the Letter is evidence that the Valentinians not only were interested in Christian problems but also could discuss them with a sober and critical judgment which we too often miss in the orthodox theologians.

(*b*) *Heracleon.* — The name of Heracleon is attached by Epiphanius to a fantastic mythological system, but this account of his teaching may confidently be set aside, in view of the considerable fragments which have been preserved from his own commentaries. It may be gathered from these that he accepted the Valentinian construction, but that he employed it chiefly as a background for understanding the redemptive work of Jesus. Like Valentinus, he recognizes three classes of men, and makes the salvation of the 'spiritual' consist in an inner enlightenment by means of gnosis. He appears to concede, however, that even the spiritual natures are capable of a fall. He holds, too, that after being saved themselves they must re-enter the world and help to redeem the 'psychic.' In his conception of the Person of Christ he adopts a strongly docetic position.

(*c*) *Marcus.*—If Ptolemæus and Heracleon stand for a Valentinianism which had much in common with orthodox Christianity, a different tendency is represented by Marcus, who flourished about the same time. For the doctrines of Marcus we have practically no other source than Irenæus, whose account of their superstitious and immoral character is perhaps coloured by prejudice. None the less it is evident that Marcus developed the ideas of Valentinus in a one-sided fashion and thereby distorted them. The characteristic feature of his system is number-symbolism. From the numerical values of divine names he seeks to discover the nature and order of the æons and the mode by which the world has come into being. The Valentinian theory of redemption is connected by Marcus with the ideas of contemporary magic and astrology. He formed a sect which seems to have stood quite outside of the Church, with institutions of its own and special baptismal rites, accompanied by exorcisms. From such a development as that of Marcus it was manifest that the Valentinian system, in anything like its original form, could not long maintain itself. In the hands of the master and his more enlightened disciples it was capable of serving a genuine philosophical and religious interest. But it had been evolved by an artificial process from the crude speculations of primitive Gnosticism, and reverted in course of time to the earlier type.

For several centuries Gnostic sects continued to arise which called themselves Valentinian, and which preserved the language and occasionally some of the ideas of Valentinus. The *Pistis Sophia* and the other Coptic writings may on this ground be assigned to the Valentinian school, although their connexion with it is otherwise remote. We hear of Valentinians in Italy about A.D. 360, and in Spain at the end of the 4th century. But these late survivals belong to the general history of the decline of Gnosticism, and the true Valentinian movement had exhausted itself within two or three generations of the founder's death.

LITERATURE.—The subject of Valentinianism is discussed in all the general works bearing on Gnosticism (*q.v.*). The *Fragments* of Valentinus were first collected in J. F. Grabe, *Spicilegium SS. Patrum*², 2 vols., Oxford, 1714, which is still valuable. They are reproduced, with commentary, in A. Hilgenfeld, *Ketzergesch. des Urchristentums*, Leipzig, 1884, in which the patristic accounts of the system are also fully discussed. One of the ablest of modern accounts of Valentinianism is that of E. de Faye, *Gnostiques et gnosticisme*, Paris, 1913, pp. 39–245. The relation of the *Exc. Theod.* to Irenæus is discussed by F. W. Dibelius, *ZNTW* ix. [1908], x. [1909] 230 ff. G. Heinrici, *Die Valentinianische Gnosis und die heilige Schrift*, Berlin, 1871, and R. A. Lipsius, art. 'Valentinus,' in Smith's *DCB* iv. 1076 ff., are still indispensable. The most useful work on later Valentinianism is A. E. Brooke, *The Fragments of Heracleon newly edited from the MSS*, Cambridge, 1891 (=*TS* i. 4).

E. F. SCOTT.

VALHALLA.—See BLEST, ABODE OF THE (Teutonic).

VALIDITY.—I. Introductory.—The notion of validity (from Lat. *validitas, validus, valere*, 'to be strong') is largely employed in modern post-Kantian thought, and receives a wide and various application. A comprehensive discussion of the notion is a desideratum, and would form a useful introduction to the philosophical and scientific disciplines, including philosophy of religion. In treating of it one must reckon with the fact that validity is a 'nebulous phrase'[1] in philosophical usage, so that it is difficult to invest it with a clear and unambiguous meaning. The terms with which it appears to be most frequently associated, with which indeed it is often identified, are those of truth and value. Thus the validity of a judgment has been described as its corrected value,[2] the validity of an argumentation or inference its truth-producing virtue,[3] or—as it might otherwise be expressed—its truth-conveying capacity. Lotze's valuable and suggestive treatment of the term[4] has done much to fix its use in philosophy; and it seems to the present writer that an examination of Lotze's discussion will serve to bring out the general nature and scope of validity. An examination, further, of the distinction between

[1] F. H. Bradley, *Appearance and Reality*², London, 1897, p. 376.

[2] L. T. Hobhouse, *The Theory of Knowledge*, London, 1896, p. 486.

[3] *DPhP* ii. 748.

[4] *Logic*², Eng. tr., 2 vols., Oxford, 1888.

origin and validity will illustrate the application of the notion.

2. The datum of thought.—With Lotze the discussion of validity belongs to the doctrine of thought, and the problem of validity arises first in connexion with the ideas or rudimentary concepts composing the material with which thought sets out upon its work of reflexion. The first operation of thought is to convert impressions (its ultimate antecedents) into ideas or meanings, so as to prepare 'logical building-stones'[1] for its subsequent structures. As a result of this operation each impression receives a certain objectivity or validity.

Thus 'green' or 'red,' *e.g.*, remains an object for consciousness as such after the cessation of the external stimulus which produces the impression. We no longer present it to ourselves 'as a condition which we undergo, but as a something which has its being and its meaning in itself, and which continues to be what it is and to mean what it means whether we are conscious of it or not.'[2]

Moreover, its validity or objectivity of meaning for ourselves is confirmed and tested in the experience of others.[3] But the validity or objectivity of an idea, meaning, or thought-content is not validity or objectivity in the sense of some kind of real existence independent of thought. Logical objectification, which converts subjective impressions into objective ideas, cannot give external reality, or reality beyond thought; so that no question of ontological as distinguished from logical validity is here raised. Indeed it is matter of indifference whether certain parts of the world of thought indicate something 'which has besides an independent reality outside the thinking minds, or whether all that it contains exists only in the thoughts of those who think it, but with equal validity for them all.'[4]

In his discussion of the Platonic world of ideas[5] Lotze offers a sharper representation of the nature of validity, describing it as an ultimate and underivable conception designative of reality apart from existence and occurrence. The reality of an idea or thought-content is similar to that which belongs to truths and laws; and, though wholly unlike the reality belonging to things or events, it is a form of reality which the mind cannot but acknowledge.

'We all feel certain in the moment in which we think any truth, that we have not created it for the first time but merely recognized it; it was valid before we thought about it and will continue so without regard to any existence of whatsoever kind, of things or of us.'[6]

The idea or thought-content is thus essentially eternal or timeless, being independent of its manifestations in the reality of existence or of its realization in the reality of thought (as occurrence or event). So Plato taught. It is true that Plato ascribes existence to the ideas or universal notions, but it is Lotze's contention that he does not thereby seek to hypostatize their eternal validity into an existence at all resembling the existence of things or events. Here the traditional interpretation of the Platonic doctrine is affirmed to be on wrong lines.[7] Plato's supercelestial world of ideas, without local habitation, and composed of pure intelligence, has no sort of affinity with what we ordinarily call the real world (and Plato may be said to indicate this in the very sublimity of the language in which he describes its wondrous landscape).[8] But the traditional interpretation, though false, is not without excuse. For in the Greek tongue there was no technical equivalent for validity or reality not inclusive of existence, and it was impossible for Plato to predicate reality of

[1] i. 13. [2] i. 14; cf. ii. 203. [3] i. 3.
[4] i. 16. [5] ii. 200–222. [6] ii. 212.
[7] But see J. Royce, *The World and the Individual* (*Gifford Lectures*), 2 vols., New York, 1901, i. 227.
[8] Cf. A. S. Pringle-Pattison, *The Idea of God in the Light of Recent Philosophy*[2] (*Gifford Lectures*), Oxford, 1920, p. 346.

the ideas without at the same time substantiating them, or subsuming them under the general denomination of substance, existence, or real being (τὸ ὄν, οὐσία). Even Aristotle was forced to attribute to the ideas a secondary sort of existence (δευτέρα οὐσία). From all which it should appear that validity may be regarded with Lotze as the designation in modern philosophy of reality apart from actual existence—yet predicable of the existent.

The doctrine of validity, as we may have gathered, grows in the course of Lotze's discussions, and attaches in its developed form to the product of thought, but our chief interest in it under this head is in relation to the datum of thought, or the object of thought as such; and the question may now be asked, Can we accept the test by which Lotze would recognize the validity of the idea or thought-content—the test or mark, as already noted, of being a self-identical object for all consciousness? The sameness of the presentation of the idea is declared to be the sufficient criterion of its validity. This is, at any rate, the consistent Lotzean doctrine, and it goes hand in hand with the notion that thought is equipped at the outset of its reflective task with a systematic body of ideas or concepts. But, just as this notion is vigorously assailed in recent logical theory, so also is the aforesaid criterion of validity. Validity belongs to an idea, it is urged, not because it is an identical object or content of thought for all consciousness (any subjective construction like the 'chimæra' or the 'centaur' might be made to acquire validity according to the Lotzean measure of it), but because it is a determining factor in controlling or directing the movement of experience. 'Validity always refers to rightfulness or adequacy of performance in an asserting of connection—not to the meaning as detached and contemplated.'[1] Or, as it is otherwise put, the meaning or idea as such possesses its validity in its 'dynamic' and not its 'static' reference.

3. The process of thought.—The problem of validity is here concerned with the relation of thought as a logical process or activity to thought as a product or issue. The distinction involved is depicted by Lotze, in a well-known metaphor, as the distinction between the winding ascent and the clear prospect.[2] According to Lotze, the thinking act or process is essentially subjective, and the formed product essentially objective. This he illustrates, on the one hand, from the variety of the paths leading to the summit and, on the other, from the sameness of the scene which eventually unfolds itself before the eyes of the wayfarers. But is it a purely formal or subjective validity that belongs to logical forms and laws? A purely formal validity, implying no kind of relation between the logical activity and real existences and events is—as we may well agree—inconceivable. No single logical operation could be carried through, even as a mere subjective process of thought, 'unless the object upon which it is exercised contained in itself some characteristic which invited or at least allowed it.'[3] As the tool must fit the hand, so it must also fit the thing.[4] The forms and laws of thought cannot be 'mere singularities of our mental organisation,' but must exhibit 'a constant and regular adaptation to reality.'[5] Or—to recur to the former metaphor—just as the ascent and the summit are comprised within the same geographical territory as the landscape which opens at length to the traveller's gaze, so there must be some sort of relationship between the logical operation and

[1] J. Dewey, in *Studies in Logical Theory*, Chicago, 1903, p. 75; see also footnote, p. 76.
[2] ii. 279. [3] ii. 253. [4] i. 8. [5] i. 9.

what takes place in the object-matter[1]—unless the sceptical contention holds that, for aught we know, the process of thought may not mediate a valid knowledge of reality at all.

But, while the subjective processes of thought are more than merely formal, they are not to be regarded as constitutive of the valid world. In forming conceptions, in classification, in judgment and inference, we do not go through processes which take place in things.

'The world of valid truth does not' in Lotze's view of it 'undergo a series of contortions and evolutions, paralleling in any way the successive steps and missteps, the succession of tentative trials, withdrawals, and retracings, which mark the course of our own thinking.'[2]

The activity of the various logical processes is not of a constitutive but of a strictly intermediate and instrumental value. The winding path is only a means to the attainment of the prospect, and must be left behind; the scaffolding[3]—to cite another well-known illustration—is only a means to the construction of the building, and must be taken down to allow the full view of the result. In each case, however, it is a necessary and indispensable means. This illustrates Lotze's contention that, despite the subjectivity of the thinking process, its results may still be objectively valid. Although the principle of reality is not discoverable in the process, it may still be present in the product. How this may be Lotze is hard put to it to show; but that it is so, that subjectivity does not necessarily imply invalidity, is one of his 'most invincible convictions.'[4]

The difficulties that beset Lotze in his endeavour to interpose between the scepticism that could not admit the validity of thought for reality and the idealism that in making thought determine reality seemed to find an ultimate identity between them were largely due to the externalism of his representation of the relation between the thought-process and the thought-product; and one sympathizes with the plea of the 'genetic logic' that the activity and the content of thought should be viewed more historically, from the standpoint of their generating conditions in the movement and readjustment of experience. 'It is no mere accident of language that "building" has a double sense—meaning at once the process and the finished product.'[5] The product of thought is simply the process carried on to its completion. There can be no possible divorce or separation between the formal and the material in thought. In the activity of thought we are not cast loose from dependence upon material conditions and circumstances. It is only when thinking is improperly regarded as a merely formal activity, having validity or meaning in abstraction from the actual content of experience, that the general problem arises of the validity of the thinking process.

4. The product of thought.—What now of the validity of the ideas which result from the reflective process, after the work of thought has been done upon them, and they have been harmonized and made coherent with the rest of experience? That it is a real validity we do not doubt, though Lotze's test of it—namely, sameness of presentation for all consciousness—remains unconvincing. But is it a real validity in more than a logical sense? Is it ontologically or metaphysically real? It must be freely admitted that on Lotzean principles the final product of thought belongs still to the sphere of ideas and falls short of the reality of existence. If the reality of existence is not found in the logical forms of the concept, judgment, or inference, no more is it to be found in the logical thoughts themselves.

Lotze's failure to bridge the gulf between the world of organized ideas and the reality of existence, so that 'no shade that wanders in that realm which is valid without existing, can take upon itself the body of actuality, and be,'[1] may be chiefly traced again to the externalism involved in his initial assumptions. For, in discovering the sole material for thought in the inner world of ideas, he makes a separation in the very beginning between thought and real existence. Thus it is the externalistic relation, not of the process of thought to the product, but of the datum of thought to reality, that is now in question. On Lotzean principles the realm of thought is, as it were, an inviolate continent that reality cannot invade, only surging and breaking upon its coast. Or, rather, reality is the inviolate continent, and thought is the surging sea. Accordingly, in the end thought must still be confined in its operations to the inner world of ideas, and the ideal remain separated from the real—although, as already noticed, Lotze himself clung resolutely, even in face of the principles of his logic, to his belief in the ontological reference in the subjective idea. But it is left to other faculties than thought—to perception, experience, intuition, feeling—to be the means of enabling the mind to establish contact with reality and attain objective truth.

From the 'genetic' standpoint in logic it is maintained that this twofold objective reference, in the beginning and the end of the work of reflexion, should be interpreted historically, 'as indicating a particular place of generation and a particular place of fulfilment in the drama of evolving experience.'[2] Again, from a standpoint of metaphysical idealism according to which the relation between thought and reality is organically conceived it is maintained that reality must be present in the beginning of the thinking process if it is to be reached at the end, and must cooperate with the activities of thought in the production of results.[3]

5. Origin and validity.—(*a*) *Introductory.*—A consideration of the question of origin and validity should throw further light upon the notion of validity. From the revolutionary standpoint of pragmatism it may be a 'musty old antithesis'[4] that is here involved, but the distinction between origin and validity is generally regarded as one of real importance in philosophy, and as worthy of fresh discussion in the light of the new emphasis upon development or evolutionary growth.[5] In the thought of D. G. Ritchie it was a distinction of cardinal significance, and it received a many-sided application at his hands.[6] R. R. Marett[7] offers a statement of the distinction in application to ethical theory. But his statement may readily be generalized; when generalized, it might run thus: origin represents the point of view from which judgments are explained by reference to their historical development, validity is the point of view from which they are explained by reference to their present worth and significance. There appears to be fairly general agreement among recent writers that, while the difference between the two points of view is not to be glossed over, there is a danger of falsifying judgments in abstracting from conditions of origin and development.

1 ii. 280.
2 Dewey, p. 77; Lotze, ii. 252-282, also ii. 283.
3 i. 9.
4 H. Jones, *The Philosophy of Lotze*, Glasgow, 1895, p. 80.
5 Dewey, p. 79.

1 Jones, p. 280. 2 Dewey, p. 84. 3 Jones, p. 334.
4 F. C. S. Schiller, *Studies in Humanism*², London, 1912, p. 244.
5 Cf. J. B. Baillie, 'Truth and History,' in *Mind*, new ser., vii. [1898] 506-522.
6 See *Philosophical Studies*, ed. R. Latta, London, 1905, *passim*; also *Darwin and Hegel*, London, 1893, Essay on 'Origin and Validity.'
7 In *Personal Idealism*, ed. H. Sturt, London, 1902, p. 224.

(*b*) *In logic.*—First consider the distinction between origin and validity as applied to logic, taking logic as designative of the whole philosophical discipline which has to do with the question of validity in knowledge. Here the problem of origin and validity is that of the relation between psychology and logic in respect of the treatment of thought. A clear distinction between the two disciplines used to be drawn in this respect. Psychology, it was said, describes the conditions under which thought originates as a psychical process; logic views thought apart from such conditions and in reference to the standard of truth and reality. In other words, psychology was held to be a purely descriptive science, and logic purely normative or regulative. To psychology fall questions of genesis and history; to logic questions of authority, worth, value.

'Logic is not concerned with the manner in which the elements utilized by thought come into existence, but with their value, when they have somehow or other come into existence, for the carrying out of intellectual operations.'[1]

But in the recent logical movement there is a strong tendency to supersede or dispose of this antithesis between origin and validity, or, as it is expressed less epistemologically, origin and value. It is said that judgment, with conception and inference, depends for its significance, for the measure of its validity, upon the stage of organization in which it begins; and, accordingly, the appraisement of the claim to validity should not be made in abstraction from the actual conditions and circumstances of origination.[2] Psychology should enter into logical evaluation.

None the less 'philosophical logic' abides by its essential position. While acknowledging the importance of genetic and historical considerations, it still affirms with Lotze that psychological analysis fails to reveal the complete significance of the operations of thought. The problem of validity or worth transcends the natural history of mental products. Indeed, as B. Bosanquet puts it, natural selection is not at all interested in natural history. 'It is being equal to the whole situation' (*i.e.* to the situation not of yesterday but of to-day) 'that is the criterion for logic as for morals.'[3]

(*c*) *In ethics and politics.*—From the above it would appear that in logic there is no irreconcilable difference between the 'genetic' and the 'philosophical' theorists, between the standpoints of origin and of validity; and one is prepared for a similar conclusion in ethics and politics. The tendency to dispose of the distinction between origin and validity certainly here exists, and again reflects the recent emphasis upon the genetic and historical. But, if the study of ethics and politics means only 'translating the present into terms of the past,'[4] then we need not be astonished at the prevalence in our time of ethical and political scepticism. To trace the ancient pedigree of an idea or institution is not, however, to explain it fully or really, much less to explain it away, and empty it of all ideal meaning. The line of ethical development, *e.g.*, may be traced from the lowest stage of customary morality to the recognition of the inherent goodness of the moral life,[5] without thereby necessarily affecting the question of the validity of the moral judgment. A pernicious custom or fantastic belief may be the antecedent and the partial cause of a moral rule now rightly regarded as binding. Sociological fact spells in philosophy neither validity nor invalidity.[1] On the other hand, it may be contended from the side of philosophy that but for the immanence of the ideal in the historical process there would be no ethical and political, *i.e.* no sociological development at all. The evolution of society is only properly interpreted in teleological as distinguished from mechanical terms—in terms of the *vis a fronte* rather than the *vis a tergo*. Validity is to be put before origin, intuition before evolution. But, while this is said, we are not compelled to recognize with the intuitionist or formalist in ethics, or with the 'natural rights' theorist in politics, the existence of any *a priori* norm independent of the life of society. To recognize such a norm or standard would indeed reduce to confusion the notion of moral or political personality. The categorical imperatives of intuitionism in ethics and of the theory of 'natural rights' in politics are not immediate self-evident data, but possess the mediate validity attaching to moral and political ideals which must be shown to be constitutive of ideal society.[2]

(*d*) *In religion.*—The distinction between origin and validity should be maintained also in religion, if at the same time the effort should be made, as in logic, ethics, and politics, to reconcile the two standpoints. Recent study in the history and psychology of religion has accentuated the tendency to neglect or confuse the distinction between the origin and the validity of religious ideas. Religion is traced in its historical development from its beginnings in the animism or spiritism of tribal religion,[3] through the polytheism of national religion, to the monotheism of universal or spiritual religion; and it is sometimes thought that the history of the evolution of religious belief is its sufficient explanation. Or, again, religion is investigated in its psychological origin and stated in terms of human need, emotional, cognitive, practical; and, again, it is sometimes thought that the psychological genesis of the religious experience is its sufficient explanation. But the question of validity is not superseded by the historical and psychological methods of study. Religion no more than morals or logic is to be handed over to the historian or the psychologist. Their explanations are provisional, their interpretations but working hypotheses. The last word on religion is not with the historian or psychologist as such, but with the metaphysical philosopher. And, even if the metaphysician can find no place for religion within the system of his thought, it does not follow that the idea of God is false and the religious consciousness an illusion.

If we are truly to interpret the historical religious development of mankind, must we not again postulate—as in the history of morals—the immanence and directing activity of the ideal? And, if we are truly to interpret the nature of religious experience, must we not postulate a reality corresponding to the object of faith? At every stage of religious culture the object of faith and worship is claimed to be trans-subjectively real. Inasmuch, however, as the reality of religion transcends the mundane order of experience, this ontological claim is incapable of scientific proof. But the cognitive element implied in religious faith should not on that account be ignored or its claim disallowed. Apart indeed from belief in the validity of the objective reference of religion the values of the religious experience can hardly

[1] Lotze, i. 34; cf. also i. 10, ii. 246 f., 251; also D. G. Ritchie, *Philosophical Studies*, pp. 134–171.
[2] Cf. Dewey, pp. 14 f., 62 f.
[3] B. Bosanquet, *Logic*², 2 vols., Oxford, 1911, ii. 273.
[4] Ritchie, p. 282.
[5] Cf., *e.g.*, L. T. Hobhouse, *Morals in Evolution*, 2 vols., London, 1906.

[1] See, further, on origin and validity in ethics, W. R. Sorley, *Moral Values and the Idea of God* (*Gifford Lectures*), Cambridge, 1918, pp. 54–72.
[2] Cf. R. Latta, in Ritchie, p. 41.
[3] For a pre-animistic or non-animistic theory of the origin of religion see R. R. Marett, *The Threshold of Religion*, London, 1909.

be maintained. 'Faith divorced from reality, like the flower severed from its roots in the earth, is doomed to wither and die.'[1]

Where the objective reference of religious faith is held to be a reality and no illusion, it must still be allowed to the standpoint of origin that it is impossible to make a rigid separation between psychological fact and logical meaning. Just as in secular and scientific knowledge a judgment having the appearance of immediate certainty is often found to involve subjective experience, so a palpable element of subjectivity enters often into the judgments of religion. *E.g.*, when the mystical visions of the mediæval saint shape themselves into direct and immediate revelations of the transcendent mysteries of Catholic dogma, we can hardly fail to detect the influence of the subjective or psychological factor in experience, especially if we have followed the course of the dogmatic development in Christendom.[2] A parallel might be cited in the claims of modern 'spiritualism,' whose communications from the dead — even granted that they have a real foundation—are sometimes quite obviously the product of a liberal Protestant eschatology.

Yet, when all allowance is made for subjectivity in religious experience, the consciousness of the Beyond—of the Beyond that is within—still remains, with the problem attaching to it of the validity of religious knowledge. While we have asserted that the ontological postulate implied in the religious consciousness is not scientifically verifiable, we do not thereby confess the invalidity or irrationality of the analogical mode of reasoning which religious philosophy has perforce to adopt in common with scientific theory, but of which it makes a more characteristic use. We must not here enter into a defence of the method of analogy in theistic argumentation, and in particular of the application to divine reality of the anthropomorphic ideas of personality, purpose, and value. It is a merit, to our mind, of the personalistic trend in recent philosophical thought that it finds the only possible clue to the interpretation of God and divine things in the analogy of human experience at its best and highest. But we may be permitted to observe that in the modern theistic use of the *analogia hominis*, which is reflective and critical, only a general agreement and correspondence, and not an identity, is affirmed between God and man in their personal aspects. Nor does it follow from the vindication of the analogical method in religious philosophy that any particular analogy is ultimately valid. Beyond the general logical or epistemological question, Is the method of analogy capable of conveying religious truth?, lies the ontological inquiry, Does the method of analogy actually convey it in such and such a case? Thus here, as in connexion with the process of thought in general, the problem of validity passes into the wider problem of truth.[3]

See also artt. ANALOGY, EPISTEMOLOGY, TELEOLOGY, VALUE.

LITERATURE.—References to the subject are to be found in general works on logic and metaphysics, also in works on the philosophies of science, history, and religion. The books of which the present writer has made the most use are cited in the footnotes. See also F. H. Bradley, *The Principles of Logic*, London, 1883; J. N. Keynes, *Studies and Exercises in Formal Logic*³, do. 1894; F. C. S. Schiller, *Formal Logic*, do. 1912; J. M. Baldwin, *Thoughts and Things; or, Genetic Logic*, 2 vols, do. 1906, 1908; C. Sigwart, *Logic*, Eng. tr., 2 vols., do. 1895; F. Paulsen, *Introd. to Philosophy*, Eng. tr., do. 1895; H. Sidgwick, *Philosophy: its Scope and Relations*, do. 1902; B. P. Bowne, *Theory of Thought and Knowledge*, New York, 1897; E. Troeltsch, *Psychologie und Erkenntnistheorie in der Religionswissenschaft*, Tübingen, 1905; L. T. Hobhouse, *Development and Purpose*, London, 1913; Carveth Read, *The Metaphysics of Nature*², do. 1908; F. H. Bradley, *Essays on Truth and Reality*, Oxford, 1914; B. P. Bowne, *Personalism*, Boston and New York, 1908; F. C. S. Schiller, *Humanism: Philosophical Essays*², London, 1912; R. R. Marett, *Psychology and Folk-Lore*, do. 1920; H. Höffding, *La Pensée humaine*, Fr. tr., Paris, 1911.

WILLIAM FULTON.

[1] G. Galloway, *The Principles of Religious Development*, London, 1909, p. 257.

[2] Cf., on St. Teresa, G. Galloway, *The Philosophy of Religion*, Edinburgh, 1914, p. 255.

[3] For a useful discussion of the principles of analogy, teleology, and value in religion see Galloway, *The Philosophy of Religion*, pp. 334-360.

VALLABHA, VALLABHĀCHĀRYA.—The strength of Hinduism lies in its manysidedness, its power of adapting itself to the various tendencies of human nature, both the good and the evil. Of this we have a conspicuous illustration in the numerous sects that arose in the course of the development of the Vaiṣṇava form of this religion.[1] Already in Śaivism (*q.v.*) the same desire to appeal to different sides of human nature had been manifested in the various aspects in which the character of the god Śiva had been presented—as the impersonation of the dissolving processes of nature as well as of its eternal reproductive power, as the typical ascetic and as the learned sage. But this variety in the characters ascribed to the god does not appear to have resulted in a corresponding variety of sects of the type that is seen in Vaiṣṇavism (*q.v.*). In Vaiṣṇavism, with its worship of a god who was believed to have manifested his sympathy with the world's suffering by frequent descents upon the earth (*avatār*), the masses of the people found the elements of a religion that seemed to bring God near to their faith and love. The personal element in religious life began to have fuller play, and with this the tendency to split into subdivisions or sects speedily revealed itself. Notwithstanding its rigid conservatism in religion regarded as a social institution, the Hindu mind has always shown a marvellous receptivity of new doctrine, provided the new teacher fulfils the Hindu idea of a religious leader and does not place himself in antagonism to the social system with which Hindu life is bound up. Of this type were Rāmānuja (*q.v.*) and Madhva (*q.v.*) of S. India, and the founders of the two earliest sects of Vaiṣṇavism, Vallabha in Upper and Western India, and Chaitanya (*q.v.*) in Bengal. The teaching of the former two was based on distinctive philosophic views as to the ultimate problem of the relation of the Supreme Spirit to the human spirit and to the material world; the latter two, while also holding their own distinctive doctrines in regard to the philosophical question, made devotion to Kṛṣṇa and his worship the real centre of their systems. The sects founded by these four teachers are the principal sects of Vaiṣṇavism. In addition to these many other minor sects came into existence such as the Rāmānandīs (*q.v.*), or Rāmāwats. Among the Vaiṣṇava sects are also included reforming movements such as that of Svāmī Nārāyaṇa, whose teaching was a protest against the revolting immoralities of the Vallabhāchāryans, while the theistic Kabīrpanthīs (*q.v.*) and the Sikh sect founded by Nānak (*q.v.*) find a place in the same list.

1. Life of Vallabha.—The Vallabhāchārya sect owes its foundation to Vallabha, who, together with his direct descendants who succeeded him in the headship of the community, was regarded as an incarnation of Kṛṣṇa or as embodying a portion of Kṛṣṇa's essence. The story of Vallabha's birth has come to us with many legendary accretions intended to enhance his authority as a religious teacher and to increase the reverence of his followers.

Vallabha was born about A.D. 1479. He was the second son of a Tailinga Brāhman named Lakṣmaṇa Bhaṭṭ, who along with his wife fled from Benares, where a violent dispute had taken

[1] See art. SECTS (Hindu).

place between Muhammadans and Sannyāśis. They found themselves in a wild spot called Champāraṇya, and here the child was born. The legend narrates how a palace of gold sprang up on the lonely spot where the child was born, how the gods showered down flowers, and how divine music filled the air. The parents, trusting in the promise of Kṛṣṇa that their child should be one of his incarnations, left their infant to the protection of the god. On their return journey, after peace had been restored at Benares, they again passed through the place where they had deserted the helpless infant. They found the child alive and well, playing in the midst of a flame of sacrificial fire. They brought him to Benares and gave him the name of Vallabha. When the child reached the age of six or seven, he was placed under the tuition of Nārāyaṇa Bhaṭṭ. The legend, which is written in Bṛjbhāṣā, goes on to describe the rapidity of his apprehension, which enabled him in the course of four months to master the four *Vedas*, the six *Śāstras* (schools of philosophy), and the eighteen *Purāṇas*. At the age of eleven he lost his father, and, bidding farewell to Gokul, a village on the left bank of the Jumnā, he started on a pilgrimage through India. At a certain town in the south of India he made a rich merchant of the place, named Damodardās, a convert to his doctrine. These two travelled thence to Vijayanagar, where the ancestors of Vallabha on his mother's side lived. At the court of Kṛṣṇa Dēva, the king of the place, Vallabha engaged in a religious disputation with the Śaivas. The king was so pleased that he bestowed on Vallabha rich presents of gold and silver, one portion of which he devoted to the manufacture of a handsome golden waist ornament for the image of the deity in a temple in the city, another to the discharge of debts incurred by his father, retaining only a fourth for his own use.

His success in disputation led to his being elected by the Vaiṣṇavas as their chief with the title of *āchārya*. From this dates the rise of his great influence. He continued his pilgrimage for nine years throughout different parts of India, accomplishing a journey of over 12,000 miles. Returning to Brindāban, he is said to have been honoured by a visit from the god Kṛṣṇa in person, who enjoined him to introduce the worship of Bāla Kṛṣṇa, the infant Kṛṣṇa, Kṛṣṇa in his adolescence, which subsequently became widely diffused under the name of Rudra Sāmpradaya.

Vallabhāchārya ultimately settled at Benares. Among the works which he produced there during this residence or during earlier visits to the city was a commentary on the *Bhāgavata-Purāṇa*. During his lifetime Vallabhāchārya is said to have made 84 devoted proselytes to his doctrine.

2. The Mahārājā Gosāinji. — Vallabhāchārya was succeeded in his *gādī*, *i.e.* his position as *āchārya*, by his son Viṭhalnāth, his eldest son having died soon after his father. This Viṭhalnāth, the second *guru* of the sect, proved an able successor. Like his father, he made long journeys, visiting the same places and in addition extending his travels to Dvārka, through Cutch, and to Mālva and Mevār. Turning southwards, he came to Paṇḍharpur, the seat of the worship of Viṭhoba among the Marāṭhās of the Deccan. He is said to have made 252 disciples. His proselytes came from many classes — Banias, Bhāṭṭias, Kunbīs, Sutārs, Lohārs; a few Brāhmans and Musalmāns were also among his adherents. All, though of various castes, enjoyed the privilege of eating together at the same table—a privilege that was soon rescinded.

Viṭhalnāth, who was known by the name Gosāinji, took up his residence at Gokul, the birthplace of Kṛṣṇa, and was frequently designated Gokul Gosāinji, a name adopted by his male descendants. After his death each of his seven sons established his own *gādi*. They dispersed themselves throughout India in order to diffuse their doctrines. Each claimed to be an incarnation of Kṛṣṇa and made numerous proselytes.

The fourth son, Gokalnāth, was the most celebrated of these propagators of the new doctrine. He infused vitality into the tenets of the community both by his teaching and by his writings, and his descendants have always claimed pre-eminence among the members of the sect. They keep themselves separate from the other communities, while these profess equal veneration for all. It was probably about this period of the dispersion of the sons of Viṭhalnāth that those religious heads first acquired the title of Mahārājā or Mahārājā Gosāinji. The descendants of these Mahārājās now number probably over 70, of whom about ten have their seats in Bombay and one or two at each of the following places: Surat, Ahmadabad, Nagar, Cutch, Porabandar, Amreli, Jodpur, Bundi, Koti. Only two or three of them have any knowledge of Sanskrit; the rest are grossly ignorant and indulge in the worst forms of luxurious living. They endeavour to live up to the title which has been given them in respect of costly apparel and dainty viands. They aspire to the acquisition of wealth and property, and, as their votaries are drawn very largely from the wealthier and more luxurious communities and are for the most part very scrupulous in the observance of religious custom, and as the Mahārājās, on the other hand, are not modest in their exactions, the opportunities of the latter for fulfilling their worldly ambitions are ample. At their various seats they possess temples with residences attached. There they celebrate daily their special worship in the presence of crowds of followers, men and women, and indulge in those licentious practices which have won for them, especially in later times, a shameful notoriety.

The process by which this development was reached is profoundly instructive to the student of Indian religion and is in strict analogy with the history of many other religious and spiritual movements.

3. Hedonistic tenets. — The Vallabhāchāryans have often been called the Epicureans of India, and the history of their cult can be traced through stages similar to those which marked the development of Epicurean morals. Epicurus started from a particular view of the constitution of the world. On it he based his conception of the *summum bonum* as ἀταραξία, freedom from anxiety and mental disturbance, but having no explicit association with grossness and sensuality of life. In the hands of his successors these features soon revealed themselves in the coarsest type of hedonism—a result which might have been anticipated from the hedonistic root of the founder's teaching. As of Epicurus, so of Vallabha it may be said that there is no reason to believe that he held the doctrine or sanctioned the practice which by a natural process evolved themselves in the teaching of his successors. His life was not unlike those of the other founders of religious sects in his time. His personal activity was that of a teacher of religion. He made long pilgrimages and gathered, through the influence acquired by his life and teaching, devoted disciples. But his teaching contained the hedonistic root from which all subsequent evils were to spring. He too started from a specific conception of the relation of the Supreme Spirit to the finite spirit. His philosophical tenets have been traced back to the teaching of Viṣṇu Svāmī, a commentator on the texts of the *Veda*; Vallabha taught that individual human spirits were like sparks from the Supreme Spirit and, though separate, identical in essence with it.

On this he based his view that asceticism was not the way by which man should commend himself to God. He maintained that God was not to be worshipped by fasting and self-mortification, that the individual soul was entitled to reverence as a portion of the Supreme Soul, and that the body which enshrined it should be fostered and not subjected to the austerities enjoined in ascetic systems. The 'way' which he advocated was summed up in the name *pushṭi-mārga*, the way of eating, drinking, and enjoyment.

It has been already indicated that the Vallabhāchārya cult attached itself to Kṛṣṇa, *avatār* of Viṣṇu, and especially to Kṛṣṇa in his adolescence, Bāla Kṛṣṇa, whose amorous sports with the *gopīs*, or cowherdesses, of Mathurā, the modern Mattrā, are the theme of the tenth book of the *Bhāgavata-Purāṇa*. This book was translated from Sanskrit into Bṛjbhāṣā under the name of *Premsāgar* ('Ocean of Love'). It was selected by Vallabhāchārya as the foundation of his system. The original purpose of the book was, it is held, to symbolize spiritual devotion under the figure of earthly love; but in its interpretation by succeeding Mahārājās of the sect, it was converted into a code of vicious immorality, not only sanctioning, but enjoining, the most hideous sensuality.

4. Cult of the guru.—The *Siddhānta Rahasya*, ascribed to Vallabhāchārya and claimed by him as a direct revelation from God, deals with themes of a different order. It contains the doctrine of the origin of sin and the mode of its expiation. It consists of only about a dozen lines in Sanskrit, in the course of which we find a characteristic suggestion as to the supreme importance of the *guru*, the Gosāinji, the mediator between God and the sinner:

'The offering which has (in the first instance) been enjoyed by its owner is not acceptable by the god of gods. Therefore, in the first instance, in all doings everything should be dedicated.'[1]

The dedication in the first instance, here referred to, is that which takes place when the offering is made to the *guru*, through whom it reaches Kṛṣṇa, of whom he is the manifestation. Of the terrible use made of this doctrine evidence is given below. Another writer of this school is even more explicit in his assertion of the lofty claims of the Gosāinji:

'Whoever holds his *guru* and Śri Thākurji [the god] to be different and distinct shall be born a *sichāna* [a kind of bird]. Whoever disobeys the orders of his *guru* shall go to Aśipatra and other dreadful hells and lose all religious merits.'[2]

Śri Gokalnāth, that fourth son of Viṭhalnāth above referred to, in his *Vachanāmṛt* ('Nectar of Precept'), in his exposition of the *pushṭi-mārga*, dwells with even more precision on the fate of those who disobey their preceptors:

'He who getting angry in his heart maligns his *guru* and utters harsh terms towards his *guru* becomes dumb, and after that he becomes a serpent. He is then born a creature of the region of the vegetable kingdom, and after that he is born a creature of the region of the dead. As he remembers Śri Bhagavān [god], in the same way he remembers and repeats in his mind the name of his *guru*.'[3]

Another of the books of the sect runs riot in its laudation of Śri Gosāinji or Viṭhalnāth, the second in this dynasty of *gurus*.

'He is possessed of all virtues; he is the very personification of the most excellent being [God]; he is all incarnations. He is himself the creator of the endless crores of worlds wherein his glory is diffused all over.'[4]

In the *Gurusevā*, another production in the same line, it is said:

'When Hari [God] is displeased with any one, the *guru* saves him [the sinner] from the effects of the god's displeasure. Therefore a Vaiṣṇava should serve his *guru* with his body and money. The principal *gurus* are Śri Āchāryaji and Śri Gosāinji and the whole family called the Vallabha family. The worship of the *guru* is to be performed in the same way as the worship of God.'[5]

This high claim made on behalf of the *guru* is not confined to this one sect. The attitude of many Hindus towards their chosen *gurus* is often marked by a similar reverence; the peculiarity of the claim made on behalf of these Vallabhāchārya *gurus* is that it is put forth on behalf of a family line, a kind of religious dynasty, not of a *guru* chosen in each case by the devotee, but of one who is set over him in virtue of the right of birth and natural succession. This is quite in keeping with the title borne by these Mahārājās and the worldly ambitions with which it was associated. It may also

[1] *Siddhānta Rahasya*, quoted in *Hist. of Sect of Mahārājās*, p. 80 f.
[2] Tract by Harirāya, quoted in *Hist. of Sect of Mahārājās*, p. 82.
[3] *Vachanāmṛt*, quoted in *Hist. of Sect of Mahārājās*, p. 82.
[4] Bṛjbhāṣā MS, entitled *Astākohar Tika*, quoted in *Hist. of Sect of Mahārājās*, p. 83.
[5] *Gurusevā*, quoted in *Hist. of Sect of Mahārājās*, p. 84.

be said to be the root of all the degeneracy and moral corruption that have made their name and the name of their sect so notorious.

5. Initiation rites.—In all Vaiṣṇava sects there is a special ceremony of initiation into the community accompanied by the repetition of a formula expressing reverence for either Kṛṣṇa or Rāma. In the Vallabhāchāryan sect this rite may be administered at the early age of three or four years. In some parts of India it is performed at a somewhat later age. A rosary or necklace, called *kaṇṭhi*, of 108 beads made of *tulsi*-wood is passed round the neck of the candidate for initiation, and he is taught the use of the eight-syllabled prayer: '*Śri Kṛshṇaḥ śaraṇam mama*,' 'The blessed Kṛṣṇa is my refuge.'[1]

There is a second initiation called *samarpaṇa*, or dedication, which, in the case of males, takes place in the eleventh or twelfth year, and, in the case of females, upon marriage or shortly before it. This rite is also called *Brahmasambandha* ('union with Brahma'). The formula repeated on this occasion begins with the eight-syllabled formula of the first initiation and continues thus:

'I who am suffering the infinite pain and torment produced by enduring for a thousand measured years separation from Kṛṣṇa do to the worshipped Kṛṣṇa dedicate my body, organs of sense, life, heart and other faculties, and wife, house, family, property with my own self; I am thy slave, O Kṛṣṇa.'

There is nothing in this formula that goes much beyond the expressions of devotion that one meets with in other forms of Hindu worship. In form it does not go beyond the '*tan, man*, and *dhan*' that enters so constantly into the expression of Hindu devotion. But the sense in which this dedication was enjoined and accepted by the Vallabhāchāryas is made clear in a commentary on Vallabha's *Siddhānta Rahasya*. The commentator, who was no other than the celebrated Gokalnāth, the grandson of Vallabha, the famous fourth son of the second *guru*, Viṭhalnath, thus expounds the formula:

'Therefore in the beginning, even before ourselves enjoying, wives, sons, etc. [*putrādi* includes daughters along with sons] should be made over because of the expression *sarva vastu* ['all things'] occurring in the text. After marriage, even before using her ourselves, the offering of her [the wife] should be made with a view to her becoming usable [by ourselves].'

6. Sensual practices.—In this conception we have the *fons et origo* of the gross sensuality that is bound up with the religious practices of this sect. The amorous deeds of the adolescent Kṛṣṇa, who is the object of its worship, were understood in their literal carnal sense, and union with Kṛṣṇa was sought through carnal union with the *guru*, or religious head, who claimed to be the incarnation of the god, through whom alone the god was accessible to the worshipper. It is only when one realizes the hold which this interpretation of the above-quoted formula of initiation took of the blind votaries of these *gurus* that one can conceive the possibility of the debauchery that has so long disgraced the religious exercises of this community, through so many generations. The husband who regards with complacence the desecration of the virtue of his wife, the father who consents to the violation of his daughter by these debauched pretenders to religious sanctity, is obsessed with the monstrous delusion that spiritual gain can come to him and his through the sensual indulgence of his spiritual guide. The male worshipper is himself eager to submit to any degradation that appears to do reverence to these high-priests of defilement. He drinks with avidity the water that has been wrung out of the wet garments of this filthy being, eats with relish the remnants of his meals, chews over again the *pān supāri* (leaf with betel-nut) which has been spat out of the mouth of this divine *guru*.

[1] Monier-Williams, *Brāhmanism and Hindūism*[4], p. 135 f.

The immorality of the temple-worship quickly spread itself into the whole life of the community. The *rās mandalī* (carnal love-meeting) became a well-known institution in many places. The purpose of these gatherings was to re-enact the scenes of the mythological story of Kṛṣṇa's amorous sporting with the *gopīs* by the waters and in the woods of Mathurā.

Doctrines and practices such as have been described were bound to call forth, sooner or later, protests from within the community itself. With the spread of education and other enlightening influences some of the better spirits awoke to shame and indignation. One of these was Karsandas Mulji, a resident of Bombay, who in 1856 raised his voice and in the columns of the *Satya Prakāsh* ('The Light of Truth'), a weekly paper, began to fulminate against the exactions and corrupt practices of the Vallabhāchāryan Mahārājās. The Mahārājās had at that time suffered a few set-backs to their pretensions. These furnished an opportunity to the dissatisfied in the community. The Mahārājās had begun an attack on the Brāhmans, of whose influence with the people they appear to have become jealous. Those of their own community who were eager to see abuses among themselves corrected undertook to assist the Mahārājās in their conflict with the Brāhmans on condition that they would reform their own practices. The Mahārājās, yielding to this pressure, agreed to accept the proposed reforms, which, among other things, demanded the cessation of the adulterous behaviour of the Mahārājās towards the women of their families, especially in the winter temple-service at four o'clock in the morning, and of the violation of the young girls of the community. The reformers aimed also at relief from the heavy money exactions which the Mahārājās knew so well how to levy by means of threats of their displeasure. To these and to some other demands of a minor character the alarmed Mahārājās gave an unwilling consent, stipulating that the agreement should not come into operation for a year. Further, the Mahārājās had been worsted in their attempt to secure exemption from appearance in courts of justice, their objection to appear in person being due to the idea that it would be a degradation to them to sit lower than a European. The High Court of Bombay refused to entertain their claim. When, during an action, a litigant proposed to subpœna the Mahārājās as witnesses, they closed their temples, and their followers, who could not take their meals without paying the morning adoration to the Mahārājās and the image, were kept without, fasting. These fasting followers were released from their unhappy plight only on their subscribing a bond which pledged them to obey the Mahārājās and to undertake in no circumstances to summon them to a court of justice. All this gave rise to a large amount of newspaper criticism, which tended to weaken the prestige of the Mahārājās.

In 1860 the Mahārājā of Surat came to Bombay and, by presiding at the distribution of prizes at the Gujarāti Girls' Schools, appeared to place himself on the side of social reform. Invited to a meeting at which the question of the remarriage of widows was to be discussed, the Mahārājā appeared among the opponents of the suggested reform and apparently got the worst of it in this public discussion. The editor of the *Satya Prakāsh* then challenged the Mahārājā to a discussion in the press. The Mahārājā ventilated his views through the columns of the *Svadharmavardhak* ('Promoter of our Religion'), a paper published under his patronage. The editor of the *Satya Prakāsh* replied in an article entitled 'The Primitive Religion of the Hindus and the Present Heterodox Opinions,' which set forth the heterodox character of the sect of the Mahārājās. In the course of this article he made certain allegations regarding the Mahārājās which became the subject of an action for libel. This article appeared in the year 1860. In the following May the Mahārājā filed an action for libel against the editor and the printer of the paper. The leading men of the Bhaṭṭia community, at the instigation of the Mahārājā, attempted to interfere with the course of justice by resolving that none of the caste, under pain of excommunication, should give evidence against the Mahārājā. This action on the part of the leaders of the community led to a charge being brought against them for conspiracy, on which they were found guilty and sentenced to heavy fines. The Mahārājā libel case came on for hearing on 26th Jan. 1862. This *cause célèbre* occupied the High Court during 24 sittings spread over a period of 40 days. Thirty witnesses were examined for the plaintiff and the same number for the defendant (Karsandas Mulji), some of the latter being men of learning and eminence in the community. The case excited the most profound interest among the different communities in the city. It led to a complete exposure of the lives and practices of the Vallabhāchāryan Mahārājās. The verdict was in favour of the defendant on the main issue of justification, with costs, and for the plaintiff on the defendant's plea of 'not guilty,' without costs. With respect to this part of the plea the Chief Justice took the view that a public writer could not make an attack on the character of an individual in his private capacity, although he might be depraved and an adulterer, and besides that the defendant was not justified, without previous knowledge of the plaintiff's misconduct, in publishing an attack on him, although the allegation subsequently turned out to be true. The Puisne Judge, on the other hand, held that the article was an attack not on the private character of the plaintiff, but on his character as a Mahārājā, or religious preceptor, and that the defendant was quite aware of the existing practices of the sect. The issue of the trial was a complete success for the defendant reformer, an important victory for the cause for which he stood, and a crushing exposure of licentiousness in the high places of religion.

Many who witnessed this trial more than fifty years ago must have hoped that the death-blow had been given to the prestige and to the licentious practices of the Vallabhāchāryan Mahārājās. But the astounding fact is that the Vallabhāchāryan Mahārājās still continue to flourish. About twenty years after the trial a Mahārājā of the sect was found guilty of complicity in a mail robbery and sentenced at Rajkot to a term of imprisonment. One might have expected that the entire Vallabhāchāryan community would have been shocked by this revelation of depravity in a religious leader. This aspect of the case seems to have affected them little. The sentence to imprisonment moved the community on other and quite different grounds. They were stricken with horror at the thought of the danger to the caste of their Mahārājā that was involved in his being condemned to eat the prison food. Leading merchants in Bombay organized a meeting at which it was resolved to petition the Government to relax the prison rules in favour of this sacred personage! Needless to say, their petition was unheeded. Probably in no other country than India would it have been possible for any system to survive such exposure.

This episode in the history of the Vallabhāchāryas has been narrated here for these reasons, that it led to the full disclosure of the real character of the teaching of this sect and of the width of the gulf which lies between morality and religion in the current conceptions of multitudes of the people of India, and that it also illustrates the powerlessness of public opinion, as it exists in India, to grapple with social customs that rest on religious sanctions having their roots deep down in the amorphous soil that is the product of ages of pantheistic thinking.

LITERATURE.—A clear statement of the place of the Vallabhāchāryans is contained in M. Monier-Williams, *Brāhmanism and Hindūism*[4], London, 1891. A very full history of the sect, with a detailed account of the Mahārājā libel case, will be found in a *Hist. of the Sect of Mahārājās or Vallabhāchāryas in W. India*, London, 1865. The chief authority of the sect is the *Bhāgavata-Purāṇa*, the tenth book of which, containing the history of Kṛṣṇa, was translated into Brjbhāṣā with the title *Premsāgar* ('Ocean of Love'). Among the books of the sect are the following: the *Bhagavat Tīkā Subodhini*, the *Siddhānta Rahasya*, both ascribed to Vallabha, the *Vachanāmṛt* ('Nectar of Precept'), ascribed to Śri Gokalnāth (a kind of commentary on the *Pushti-mārga*), *Gurusevā* ('Guru-Worship'), *Virchīta Bhakti Siddhānta Vivṛti* (a commentary by Gokalnāth on the above *Siddhānta Rahasya*, the work of his grandfather), the *Pushti Pravāha Maryādā Tika* by Hararāya, the *Viṭhalesha-ratnavivarana*, and numerous minor tracts in Sanskrit ascribed to the chief founders of the sect.

D. MACKICHAN.

VALUE.—1. The nature of value.—Value is one of the last of the great philosophic topics to have received recognition, and even now the *Encyclopædia Britannica* has an article only on economic value. Its discovery was probably the greatest philosophic achievement of the 19th cent., but opinions on the subject are not yet crystallized, and it is still one of the growing points of philosophy and one which seems likely to overshadow older issues. Reflexion at present commonly starts from the antithesis of 'fact' and 'value,' and the difference between the standpoints of 'description' and 'appreciation.' It is widely held that consciousness of value differs in kind from consciousness of fact. It is posterior to the latter, and represents a reaction upon fact. It is an attitude assumed towards fact, a weighing of fact in relation to an agent, and his feelings, desires, interests, purposes, needs, and acts; and it expresses his appreciation (approbation) or reprobation (depreciation) of it in this relation. It follows (1) that a certain subjectivity, or, better, a relation to personality, is inherent in all values; (2) that values arise out of the mind's practical attitude, when it reacts upon stimulation, and that for a purely theoretic or contemplative view no values would exist; (3) that values are something superadded upon the other qualities of objects by the mind, in order to express their relation to its purpose and acts, and do not inhere in objects *per se*. Indeed they seem to be even more subjective, variable, and personal than the 'secondary' qualities of objects, and hence are often called 'tertiary' qualities. Nevertheless they are also objectified and projected into objects, when these are regarded as valuable objectively and *per se*, or when the 'validity' of actual valuations and of existing values is called in question. Hence 'superpersonal' or 'over-individual,' and even 'eternal' and 'absolute,' values are recognized by many philosophers. Moreover, the genesis of values and their relations to the objects of desire to which they refer, to the value-feelings which accompany them, and the *valuation-processes* and value-judgments by which they are reached, instigate to a number of psychological inquiries, while their validity raises the deepest questions of epistemology, metaphysics, and religion. All the questions raised, moreover, are complex and contentious, and have had a history which it is not easy to unravel.

2. The history of the notion.—Historically the importance of the problem of value has been recognized very slowly, gradually, and grudgingly, and, moreover, its philosophic history is obscure, no early philosophy having made it central, or even expressly considered it. In the light of subsequent developments, however, we may trace its emergence to the Platonic doctrine (in *Republic*, vi.) of the Idea of Good. When Plato conceived the Good as the culmination of the Ideal world and as the principle which was to unify, systematize, and organize all the other 'forms,' he was really putting 'value' above 'being,' conceiving it as the supreme principle of explanation, and expressing the same thought as Lotze, when he declared that the beginning of metaphysics lies in ethics. For he was proposing to view all being teleologically, and to make its relation to a 'good' or end (an ethical notion) essential to its being. This was to affirm not only the objective validity of the 'tertiary' qualities, but also their supremacy over the others. Plato, however, did not himself develop this line of reflexion, nor succeed in inducing philosophers in general to investigate the problem of values. To the more naturalistic they seemed all too human to be attributed to ultimate reality. Spinoza's wholesale repudiation of their objectivity, at the end of bk. i. of his *Ethic*, is typical in this respect. The modern developments of the subject proceed from Kant, who, however, came upon it rather incidentally at the end of his philosophic career, and apprehended its significance very imperfectly. Kant's philosophizing had ended in the theoretic *impasse* that certain vitally essential beliefs (in God, freedom, and immortality) could not be scientifically justified. Yet they had to be presupposed, he believed, for purposes of action; *i.e.*, to carry on life it was necessary to act *as if* they were true. He devised therefore the notion of a practical postulate, which was to be practically imperative without being theoretically cogent, attaching it to the Moral Law of unconditional obligation, and endowing it with objects of 'faith,' which were to be carefully distinguished from objects of knowledge. He thus established (1) a dualism between faith and knowledge which had obvious interest for theology, and (2) a supremacy of the practical over the theoretic reason, which was more fruitful, because less naive, than Plato's. The latter result tended to raise 'values' above 'facts,' though the former at first masked this consequence, and it took subsequent philosophy a long time to overcome the Kantian dualism. Both, however, were prolific of further developments, divergent from the main line of post-Kantian speculation, which was too intellectualistic to notice that, just as the existence of fact must be conditioned for us by our knowledge, so our knowledge must in turn be conditioned by our interests and the prospective value of the objects of our cognitive endeavours. For a long time the investigation of value was carried on only in Germany, and even there progress was slow. The first (probably) to see that here was a new problem was F. E. Beneke (1797–1854), the only empirical psychologist among the German philosophers of his time, and hence a victim of Hegel's intolerance. Already in his *Grundlegung zur Physik der Sitten* (1821) he sees that, if the science of morals is practical, the notion of value lies at the root of it. He lays it down that the value which we attribute to a thing is determined by the pleasure which it has excited in us, and he makes the whole of ethics depend on feelings of value. In his *Grundlinien des natürlichen Systems der praktischen Philosophie* (1837–40) he makes it more explicit that valuations arise in the mind as reactions upon stimulations and depressions produced by the things of the external world, distinguishes between subjective and objective valuation (*Wertgebung*), and traces the growth of 'dispositions' to value and to desire. R. H. Lotze (1817–81) revived the Platonic idea that good ranks above being, wanting metaphysic to show that what *ought* to be conditions what *is* (*Metaphysik* of 1841), and that 'Nature is directed to the accomplishment of Good,'[1] and interpreted the 'ontological' proof of the existence of God as meaning that the totality of value cannot be utterly divorced from existence. In the endeavour to vindicate value he had the sympathy of his theological colleague at Göttingen, Albrecht Ritschl (1822–89), who agrees with him that the facts of concrete experience are the source of our general notions, and not, as Platonism has always held, pale reflexions of the latter. Hence personal experience is not deducible from metaphysics, but *vice versa*.[2] Ritschl, however, started rather from the Kantian dualism of faith and knowledge and tried to differentiate them still further. Faith he equipped with distinct objects, those of religion—an independent method, which it shared with ethics and æsthetics—distinct from that of metaphysics and science, and formulated in value-judgments, differ-

[1] *Microcosmus*⁴, Eng. tr., Edinburgh, 1894, i. 396.
[2] *Theologie und Metaphysik*, Bonn, 1881, pp. 32–40.

ent in kind from theoretical judgments, though equally capable of validity and certainty. It was therefore to misconstrue the essential meaning of religious affirmations to take them as expressions of theoretic insight rather than of moral trust. It is mainly to Ritschl that is due the current antithesis between value-judgments and judgments of fact, and the attempt to regard the sciences as different in kind according as they use the one or the other. Ritschl, however, recognized that this separation could not be really carried through. He observes:

'All continuous cognition of the things which excite sensation is not only accompanied but also guided by feeling' (pleasure-pain, as indicative of value for self, by way of enhancement or inhibition), and 'in so far as attention is necessary to attain the end of knowledge, will becomes the vehicle of the purpose of exact cognition; the proximate motive of will, however, is feeling, as expressing that a thing or an activity is worth desiring. . . . Value-judgments therefore are what determine all connected knowledge of the world, even when it is carried out in the most objective fashion. Attention during scientific observation . . . always declares that such knowledge has a value for him who exercises it.'[1]

This seems to render all theoretic judgments dependent on, and subordinate to, value-judgments; but Ritschl distinguishes between concomitant and independent value-judgments. In the sciences value-judgments accompany the theoretic, whereas 'independent value-judgments are all cognitions of moral ends or impediments thereto in so far as they excite moral pleasure or displeasure, or otherwise set the will in motion to appropriate goods or to ward off evils.' The religions also are composed of such independent value-judgments expressing man's attitude towards the world. From Ritschl's position it was easy to pass to that of W. Windelband (1848–1915), who, while sharply distinguishing between judgments and evaluations or judgments about judgments (*Beurteilungen*), emphasized that the latter are involved in every judgment in that it affirms or denies, approves or disapproves. Logic, therefore, becomes a science of values, a third normative science, along with ethics and æsthetics, and like them aims at the discovery of universally valid 'norms.' Philosophy becomes the critical study of the universally valid values; their recognition is its duty and its aim.[2] Windelband was followed by H. Rickert[3] and H. Münsterberg (1863–1916).[4] The Austrian schools of C. von Ehrenfels (1850–) and A. Meinong (1853–1920) devote themselves to the discussion of the objects and sorts of values, and their relation to desire and will, the laws of the valuation-process, and the accompanying feelings, and apply to all values the economic law of marginal utility. The rise of pessimism and the influence of Schopenhauer (1788–1860), by raising the question of the value of life as a whole, emphasized the importance of values. F. W. Nietzsche (1844–1900) effectively drew attention to the transformations of values, and set himself, before he went mad, to bring about a 'transvaluation' (*Umwertung*) of all the accepted values. Josiah Royce (1848–1917) acclimatized the distinction between appreciation and description in the English-speaking world with his *Spirit of Modern Philosophy* (1892), and since then there has been a good deal of (rather unsystematic) discussion of the problems of value, especially in America, though the intellectualistic bias of the dominant 'idealism' has been unfavourable to it. The pragmatists, however, were glad to recognize the presence of valuations in cognitive processes, as a proof of the fictitious nature of 'pure' thought and 'absolute' truth. They emphasize the human, purposive, and personal character of value, tend to regard all values as relative, primarily to the particular situation which is valued, and declare the existence and efficacy of values to be plain, empirical facts.

3. Sorts and criteria of value.—As the result of this historical development it is generally admitted that distinct species of value exist, though there is no agreement as to what they are. However, it is clear that several sciences have been specialized to study them. Thus (1) *economic* value has long been recognized as a fundamental notion of political economy, which, ever since Adam Smith, has divided it into value in use, *i.e.* the utility of objects for human purposes, or, as J. S. Mill said, their 'capacity to satisfy a desire or serve a purpose,' and value in exchange, *i.e.* their power to induce or compel people to pay (other valuables) for the use of them. The former is simply teleological value, which refers to the relation of means and end; the latter arises when an object is not only useful but also difficult to procure, and is the special concern of economics (*q.v.*).

(2) That *ethics* deals with values is also agreed, though there is much dispute as to what the specific ethical values are and how they are related.

(3) *Æsthetic* values are also beyond dispute.

(4) *Pleasure* must be regarded as a positive and *pain* (unpleasantness) as a negative value, since even the most ascetic do not really succeed in holding that pleasure is, or in denying that pain is, as such bad. The opposite doctrine, that all values are ultimately reducible to pleasure-pain, is commoner, but need not disturb the classification of values. For, even if the question whether objects are valuable because they give pleasure or give pleasure because they are desired (valued) were decided in favour of the former alternative, it would still be true that the other values are at least relatively independent. Consciousness of value does not directly imply consciousness of pleasure-pain, nor vary concomitantly with it; *e.g.*, in conscious wrongdoing an ethical value which is felt not as pleasant, but as painful, is nevertheless recognized. Similarly the æsthetic value of a work of art may be recognized, which is yet declared to give no pleasure and to leave the spectator 'cold.'

(5) It has been mentioned that, according to the school of Ritschl, the objects of the *religious* consciousness are really values, and affirmations about them are essentially value-judgments. And, though other theologians dissent from it, this view gets considerable support both from the psychology of religion, which interprets religious beliefs as expressions of spiritual needs, and from every theological admission that faith, as well as reason, is operative in the apprehension of religious truth.

(6) There are good reasons for recognizing the distinctiveness of *biological* or *survival*-values. For they are capable of objective scientific study, and cannot be simply represented, as Herbert Spencer thought, by the hedonic values. Pleasures are not always conducive to life, nor are all pains evil. The relations of survival to pleasure-pain are complex; so are its relations to the ethical values, as is vividly brought out by the ethics of pessimism. Moreover, the survival-values enter into all other values: the value of every being, belief, and institution is affected by its survival-value—between the limits of such a high degree of positive value as to compel universal assent and so high a negative value as to entail complete extinction and universal reprobation.

(7) Several schools of philosophy hold that logic is the science of *cognitive* values, and that truth is the positive, error the negative, value; and this

[1] *Die christliche Lehre von der Rechtfertigung und Versöhnung*[4], Bonn, 1895–1900, iii. 194 f., Eng. tr., Edinburgh, 1900, p. 204.
[2] *Präludien*, Freiburg i. Br., 1884.
[3] *Der Gegenstand der Erkenntnis*[2], Tübingen, 1904.
[4] *The Eternal Values*, Boston and London, 1908.

treatment is often implied also where it is not avowed. It would seem to be borne out by the far-reaching analogy between logic, ethics, and æsthetics as 'normative' sciences, and proved by the conformity of logic with the criteria generally used to distinguish values.

As criteria two primary oppositions appear to be used: (1) that between existence and value, the 'is' and the 'ought.' Even though there are in man natural tendencies to approve of what has succeeded in establishing itself, and to bring into being what is considered worthy of being—*i.e.* both to realize ideals and to idealize the actual—there remains a considerable discrepancy between the existent and the valuable. It cannot (ordinarily) be argued that, because a thing exists, it is valuable, or that, because it is valuable, it must exist. What is need not be what ought to be, nor need what ought to be exist. Hence the 'laws' of a science of values are not natural uniformities, but 'norms,' *i.e.* precepts or imperatives; they formulate not what actually does happen, but what ought to happen 'normally,' *i.e.* if the persons concerned recognize and submit to the order proper to the subject.

(2) Values appear to be positive and negative. As they express the attitude of a subject to an object, they indicate the acceptance or rejection, pursuit or avoidance, of the former, the attractiveness or repulsiveness of the latter. They occur therefore in couples of antithetical predicates, both admitting of degrees of intensity. Hence values may compensate, cancel, or neutralize each other, and the final value of an object may vary according to the balance between its positive and negative value, or become practically *nil.* A state of consciousness which is 'neutral,' and an object which is 'indifferent,' are cases of such zero values.

(3) All values are disputable. They involve a relation to a valuer whose valuation need not be correct, and need not be accepted. The allegation of a value, therefore, is not equivalent to its validity. All values are to be understood as primarily claims to value, which may be allowed, disallowed, or reversed, when other values are considered. In some cases such reversal is normal: thus, if *A* and *B* are enemies or have opposite interests, what is 'good' for *A* is normally 'bad' for *B*, and *vice versa.*

With the aid of these criteria the following kinds of value can now be enumerated. (1) *Hedonic* values are the pleasant (positive) and the unpleasant or painful (negative). (2) *Æsthetic* values are the beautiful (positive) and the ugly (negative); also the attractive-repulsive, the fitting-improper, the noble-vulgar, the elegant-coarse, and many others. (3) *Utility* values are the good (positive) and the bad (negative); also the useful-useless. These last, though they properly have reference to the relation of means and ends ('the good'), naturally pass over into ethics, when this science is conceived 'teleologically,' *i.e.* as the science of the final end or supreme good. (4) Other *ethical* values, relative to other conceptions of ethics, are marked by the oppositions of 'good' and 'evil,' 'right' and 'wrong,' 'ought' and 'ought not.' 'Good' and 'bad' seem sometimes to be used absolutely in ethics, but this usage hardly proves the existence of 'absolute' values. On closer inspection, the meaning is seen to be good or bad *for* the ethical end, however that is conceived. (5) *Religious* conceptions reveal their character as values by the frequency of such dualistic antitheses as God-devil, salvation-damnation, election-reprobation, holy-sinful, sacred-profane; also by the frequency with which religious arguments turn out to be postulates of faith. (6) *Logic* falls into line with the values 'true' and 'false,' 'truth' and 'error.' These also claim to be absolute; but whether what is believed true is so may be disputed, just as whether what is believed good, or right, or beautiful, or valuable, or conducive to survival actually has the value which it claims. Even what is felt as pleasant is not always conceded to be a 'true' pleasure, nor is every 'imaginary' pain said to be 'real.' This illustrates also a further confirmation of the whole doctrine, that the various value-predicates are freely transferable from one species of value to another.

4. Value and fact.—The recognition of logic as a science of values entails a radical revision of the antitheses between fact and value, existence and value, the 'theoretic' and the 'practical.' If all 'truths' are values, there can be no absolute separation of the practical, the sphere of values, from the theoretic, the sphere of facts. Facts, being the objects of truths, must all imply values, and it must be vain to search for any existence which is wholly free from valuations. Now this is precisely what history shows. (1) The search for 'true reality' in pure and unadulterated 'fact,' uncontaminated by any work of the mind, in an unconditional datum which has merely to be recognized, has always been vain. Only the moral to be drawn is not, as idealism supposes, that reality is the work of 'pure thought.' The thought which cannot be rooted out is a valuing thought, which is aiming at ends and selecting means, and accepting, rejecting, and variously manipulating the data presented to it in the whole process of 'recognizing' reality. Thus the absolute antithesis between fact and value collapses, because fact without value cannot be found. (2) The very fact that it is considered so desirable to find it proves that it is impossible to do so. For the importance attributed to the discovery of fact, and the eulogistic sense in which 'reality' is opposed to 'appearance' or 'illusion,' are, in fact, values. This comes out especially in doctrines about the 'degrees of reality,' which are plainly degrees of value, or about the distinction between 'reality' and 'existence.' (3) It is not psychologically possible to reach any 'fact,' except by a process permeated throughout by values, viz. a purposive endeavour to attain an end ('good') by a choice of the 'right' means, which implies selective attention, preferences for what seems valuable, and the influence of concomitant value-feelings and of a variety of prejudices and forms of bias. (4) Lastly, it seems a conclusive logical reason for holding that every 'fact' alleged must contain a latent value, that it claims not only to be 'true' but also implicitly to be better than any other judgment it was possible to make under the circumstances. Its maker was probably aware of this, and consciously preferred it to all alternatives that occurred to him; but, even where he did not think of any, they remain logically conceivable, and hence the actual judgment is only justifiable by its logical claim to be the best. Hence the value-relation and attitude can never be eradicated from even the merest and most stubborn 'fact.'

Nor, conversely, can a recognition of fact be wholly eliminated from knowledge. Pure value exists as little as pure fact. It would be pure fancy or sheer postulation, and neither fancies nor postulates are elaborated without regard to fact. They are made to be realized, and, when they are recognized as impossible, their value is destroyed or impaired. It is said to be 'no use' to postulate the impossible or to cherish utterly unrealizable ideals. This recognition of fact, however, is always relative to the existing state of knowledge, and may be modified as knowledge grows. Knowers are often conscious of this, and assume their facts for the purposes of an inquiry or a science, hypothetically and experimentally. Hence it is not to be supposed that what is taken as fact, and formally is 'fact,' must remain so. It may turn out to be only a methodologically convenient 'fiction.' In general it may be concluded that, since values inhere in all the 'facts' that are recognized as such, they are themselves facts, and that the antithesis between values and facts cannot be made absolute. Values are not simply fortuitous and gratuitous additions to facts, which are merely subjective and should be eliminated by strict science, but are essential to cognitive process and compatible with any sort and degree of objectivity. Facts too are always reactions—upon prior facts—and are generated by their evaluation; and, moreover, these prior facts may have been merely hypothetical constructs recommended by their prospective value.

5. Value and existence.—It would seem to follow from the relations between value and fact that values cannot be denied existence in any world that can exist for man, and this in several senses. (1) They are operative in and on human minds, and find expression in human acts and embodiment in human institutions; (2) they can occur in, and relatively to, any universe of diction, however fanciful; (3) hence also in ideals and fictions, both of which are sometimes said to be incapable of real existence, and cited as objections to the connexion of values with existence. But both must be so related to real existence as to be applicable to it and to conduce to its successful manipulation. Otherwise they become false ideals and futile fictions. Also an ideal which is recognized as impossible appears to lose *pro tanto* its obligatoriness and power of attraction. 'Ultra posse nemo obligatur.'

Whether it is possible to infer the existence of a valuable object from a recognition of its value alone is a question of great importance for religion. For the objects of the religious consciousness appear to be largely or wholly of this kind, and the religious 'proofs' of their existence to be ultimately such inferences. They are, moreover, stubbornly persisted in, in spite of the protests of common sense against their validity, and have an important function also in the other sciences, in which they are not recognized so openly, but masquerade as 'axioms' and '*a priori* truths.' In discussing then in its generality this inference from value to existence, we should remember that all values are initially claims, which may fail of validation; hence it will hardly seem valid to rest the reality of the valuable objects on what may be an unsound claim, viz. on the demand for them alone, unsupported and unconfirmed by experience. Logically they are to start with nothing but postulates. It may be legitimate to take them as methodological principles, but even then they must be regarded as hypotheses to be assumed experimentally, until they have adequately approved and verified themselves by their applications to the actual problems which they concern. For example, it may be legitimate to extract from the actual pursuit of ends and of happiness by men the methodological assumptions that all things are to be regarded as tending towards a supreme all-embracing end and towards universal happiness; but can it be maintained that *therefore* such an end is actually operative, or that perfect happiness (*i.e.* everlasting and unalloyed pleasure unaccompanied by pain) is possible? To justify such inferences two further assumptions would seem to be required, viz. that the whole of reality is conformable with human nature and bound to satisfy its demands. Now these assumptions, traditionally described as the axiom of the ultimate rationality of existence, are evidently themselves nothing but values for which existence is postulated, and, if they are to be admitted as axiomatic truths on their own assurance, it is difficult to see what limits can be set to the postulation of objects of desire. Even as it is, methodological postulates are given great, and perhaps undue, facilities in verifying themselves, because, so long as they work at all, their failures can always be ascribed to the imperfection of our knowledge, and so are not counted against them. Thus nothing short of total failure to predict the course of events need lead us to abandon the postulate of their 'causal connexion.' Hence the testing of a value-postulate always, in a sense, presupposes its truth—though not in any sense that makes this presupposition alone a sufficient reason for regarding it as absolutely true; still it is better to get a postulated value confirmed by experience than to accept the mere recognition of value as an adequate guarantee of its existence. What kinds and amounts of experimental confirmation are to be considered adequate to verify the existence of postulated objects of value will naturally depend on the specific subject-matter, and, as in addition the various values sought and got need not be in harmony with each other, and some may prefer one sort and others another, and as, moreover, the relevance of some of the values found to the existences to be proved may be called in question, opinions will probably long continue to differ on these matters.

6. Value and validity. — It follows from the above that the transition from value to validity is by no means a matter of course, though this is often assumed, both as regards ethical and as regards logical values. In both cases the motive is the difficulty of validating value-claims, which is a long, and indeed theoretically an unending, process. Hence the temptation to allege absolute and self-proving values which are independent of their working in experience. The absolute values alleged, however, are only formal claims, as comes out very clearly in Kant's account of the absolute value of personality and of the 'law' of duty. The declaration that every person should be treated as an end in himself is merely a recognition of the formal claim that every person makes to be so treated (even though he never is so treated, and apparently could not be, in the actual order of things), which may serve as a definition of personality; while the moral 'law,' that duty should be unconditionally fulfilled, is merely a paraphrase of the obligatoriness of the ought-value; in neither case is any light thrown on the questions how, concretely, any one should be treated, or what, concretely, his 'duties' are. Similarly every judgment formally claims to be true, absolutely and unconditionally, and, as it mentions no restrictions to its claim, it may be said to be so; but, as this is so, however false a judgment may turn out to be, it establishes no presumption in favour of its real truth. Thus it is quite possible, and indeed necessary, to inquire whether the values claimed are really possessed, and to question the validity of the values actually recognized. This indeed is one of the chief occupations of a critical philosophy. It means that the problem of value occurs also in the sphere of values; the antithesis of 'ought' and 'is,' which was supposed to differentiate value and fact, arises again over the value of values, when they are taken as facts for the purpose of assessing their value. The explanation perhaps is that error and failure are possible in all human operations, and hence also in the estimation of values. The values which are claimed are subject to revision and correction, and, if it is decided that they are, but ought not to be, they can be called either 'false' or 'wrong'; for it is intrinsically as legitimate to use the value-predicates of logic as those of ethics to describe their failure.

The difficulty of determining the precise connexion between value and validity is, however, largely due to the obscurity of the notion of validity itself. We are accustomed to regard validity at first as an absolute and (theoretically) unquestionable degree of value, and to illustrate it from the ideal validity of logic and of ethics. On examination, however, this sense of validity appears to be merely formal, and to be nugatory or null as a guarantee of real value. For in both these sciences the valid and the valuable fall apart. Neither is the valuable necessarily valid, nor is the valid necessarily valuable. Every moral order makes extensive use of inferior moral motives; every science uses probable but invalid reasonings. Whether the ideal validity is ever reached, or would be valuable if it were, seems more than doubtful. Hence it seems proper to reduce the meaning of validity to a high, or generally recognized and practically indisputable, degree of value, and to make value determine validity, and not validity value.

7. Value and valuation.—If value is conferred upon an object by a personal attitude towards it, it is clear that all objects can be valued by being included in a valuation-process. Many objects, however, are so variously valued according to circumstances, or are so rarely important enough to be valued at all, that they are conceived as neutral or indifferent *per se*. So it is only if an object is constantly valued in a particular way that its value adheres to it and it comes to seem intrinsically valuable. For it then emancipates itself from the personal valuation and makes its valuation look like a mere recognition of an already existing value. Values acquire objectivity in other ways also. Thus the personal reaction expressed in a value-judgment carries a formal claim to universality, since every one initially regards himself as the measure of all things, until he is instructed by the dissent of others. This claim therefore maintains itself only while it is not disputed, and should not be taken as more than methodological. By the comparison of value-judgments it appears that different persons value very differently; hence many value-judgments, being in dispute, are regarded as 'merely subjective.' About others many or all are found to agree, and these may thereby acquire every degree of 'objectivity.' Thus objects which have obtained social recognition as valuable come to rank as objective values. A value that has risen to be objective may then maintain itself without continuing to be valued, and even though, under the circumstances, its value may have been converted into the opposite. Thus, once a literary work is ranked as a 'classic,' its value remains uncontested, even though few care for it or even read it, except for examination purposes; and King Midas no doubt continued to think gold most valuable in spite of his inability to digest it. It cannot always be assumed therefore that, because a value is current and is recognized, it is fully functional, any more than that it is right.

There are then plenty of objective values, which any valuer encounters and has to recognize as given. But they may nevertheless all be conceived as products of valuation-processes, and as presupposing prior value-judgments. For when the valuation of an object has been repeated and has grown familiar, the conscious and reflective value-judgment becomes superfluous, and an immediate apprehension of value results, just as immediate perception supersedes judgment about familiar objects of cognition. In other cases, it is true, this process does not occur in the history of the individual, but it can then be traced in that of the race, whose achievements the individual inherits. An object may, *e.g.*, be apprehended as pleasant, beautiful, or right, without a judgment or process of valuation; but the immediacy of its value-claim is no bar to any inquiry into why it is so valued, how it has come to be so, and whether it ought to be so, and really is as beautiful, right, or pleasant as it seems to be. Hence the values which are psychically data, and psychologically immediate, may always be logically mediated and made objects of valuation-processes and explicit value-judgments. They then function as facts to be evaluated.

8. Transvaluations. — The process of reflective reconsideration of given values continually leads to changes in their status. Hence 'transvaluations' must be regarded as normal and entirely legitimate occurrences in every sphere of values, though they are not everywhere as socially prominent as in the annual changes of the fashions.

As Dewey says, 'All valuation is in some degree a revaluation. Nietzsche would probably not have made so much of a sensation, but he would have been within the limits of wisdom, if he confined himself to the assertion that all judgment, in the degree in which it is critically intelligent, is a transvaluation of prior values.'[1]

One sufficient reason for this is that, strictly speaking, it is not psychologically possible to repeat a valuation. The second time the valuation has lost its novelty, and the delight of discovery is gone; it is acquiring familiarity and beginning to breed contempt or indifference; or again it is growing easier, and the resistance to it is diminishing, as habituation renders it less repugnant. Moreover, valuations necessarily vary according to the changes in the organic needs which condition them. His tenth penny bun will neither taste as good nor be valued as highly by a hungry boy as his first. No doubt these changes in value are little noticed because many of them are slight, unimportant, and ephemeral; but they would anyhow be obscured by the general bias in favour of stability. Unless it is discounted, it will hardly be recognized that stable values are exceptions rather than the rule. They bulk large because they are attended to and selected. Their stability is always more or less a construction for methodological purposes, like the extraction of stable objects out of the flux of happenings. It is always to some extent a fiction, because it is never absolute, and because there are no eternal values, none that endure unchanged and untransformed by new valuations for ever, unless it be life itself —so long as that lasts. It may even become a dangerous illusion, if its character is not understood, and it is made an obstacle to salutary and necessary changes. In such changes the old values always condemn the new, and *vice versa*, often with tragic results. Transvaluations are the stuff out of which heroes and martyrs of 'reform' or 'loyalty' are made, at every step in human progress. The question of what is the right value is unanswerable for the time being, because it is precisely the question which is being fought out. But we can predict that such changes will always be opposed, for there is always a conservative and a progressive party with respect to any change. These party attitudes are essentially valuations, as any one can discover from himself, if he is openminded, and also distracted, enough to have a 'cross-bench mind' and to feel the force of both the opposite contentions. Nor are these the only conflicts which may lead to a change of values. Every society, and nearly every soul, is full of conflicts between opposing valuations, and any variation in their relative strengths may entail a change in values. The chief agency which blinds

[1] *Essays in Experimental Logic*, London, 1916, p. 386.

us to these transvaluations is the stability of words; for these change their form much less rapidly than their meaning.

9. Conclusions.—The above survey of the problems of value may be regarded as confirming most of the preliminary points noticed in § 1. The philosophic importance of the subject has been attested by the great variety and universal prevalence of values. The provisional definition of value as essentially a personal attitude, as a recognition of the supremacy of the category of personality, has maintained itself and proved a clue to the labyrinth of values. It also renders somewhat nugatory the psychological debates of the schools of Meinong and von Ehrenfels as to whether values are rooted in feeling, will, or desire. For a personal attitude is a concern of the whole man and not of psychological abstractions. If, however, it is thought necessary to pick one among such psychological phrases, it is probably best to say that value is a personal attitude, of welcome or the reverse, towards an object of interest. For few are likely to dispute that 'interests' are relative to personality. This relativity, however, is not to be regarded as importing any objectionable subjectivity into values, just because it proves to be the source also of their objectivity. For it turns out that all objects are pervaded by values and constituted for man by valuations, and hence their avowed values may just as rightfully belong to them as the values latent in their other qualities. Accordingly the opposition between value and fact breaks down. 'Facts' are themselves values, values established in the endeavour to analyse out the factor of givenness contained in experience, and presupposing purposive manipulation of apparent 'facts.' They are thus 'made' things, though they are not made out of nothing, but out of previously recognized facts which are subjected to criticism to determine what they 'really are.' Values are also acts in so far as they presuppose valuations, purposive manipulations of data, and judgments; also in that they have prospective reference to action, and are intended to guide it. Accordingly, the belief that values belong to the practical side of life is well founded, and even truer than it seemed; for in ultimate analysis logic also is a science of values. Its 'theoretic' values presuppose purposes, selections, choices, and judgments which are acts, and do not differ in kind from those which are openly 'practical.' It is clear also that the notion of value as something gratuitously superadded upon fact must be modified, if it is interpreted as meaning that values are something unreal, artificial, and optional. Reality in its fullness contains and exhibits values, and they are ejected from it only by an effort of abstraction, which is relative to certain restricted purposes, and is never quite successful. Values therefore are not to be regarded as gratuitous additions to reality, made out of the superfluity of human perversity, but as its highest qualities and the culminating points of its significance for us.

LITERATURE.—The literature is extensive but scattered, and often raises the questions about value only incidentally and in connexion with other problems. The historical part of it has been mentioned above in § 2; the modern is still largely contained in periodicals, in English especially in the *Journal of Philosophy and Psychology* (from 1915), in discussions conducted between W. M. Urban (vol. xiii. [1916] nos. 17, 25, xiv. [1917] 12, 26, xv. [1918] 15), J. Dewey (xii. [1915] 19, xv. 10), H. W. Schneider (xiv. 6, 26), R. B. Perry (xiv. 7), D. W. Fisher (xiv. 21), F. C. S. Schiller (xii. 25, xv. 19), W. R. Wells (xv. 18), etc. In *Mind* artt. by S. Alexander (new ser., i. [1892] 31 ff.), J. S. Mackenzie (iv. [1895] 425 ff.), O. C. Quick (xix. [1910] 218 ff.), may be mentioned. From the German literature on 'axiology,' A. Meinong, *Psychologisch-ethische Untersuchungen zur Werttheorie*, Graz, 1894, *Ueber Annahmen*, Leipzig, 1902; C. von Ehrenfels, *System der Werttheorie*, 2 vols., do. 1897–98; J. C. Kreibig, *Psychologische Grundlegung eines Systems der Werttheorie*, Vienna, 1902; G. Simmel, *Einleitung in die Moralwissenschaft*, 2 vols., Berlin, 1892–93, and *Philosophie des Geldes*, Leipzig, 1900; H. Maier, *Psychologie des emotionalen Denkens*, Tübingen, 1908, must be mentioned. In English W. M. Urban, *Valuation: its Nature and Laws*, London, 1909, is as yet the only work expressly and solely devoted to the theory of values, but the importance of the subject is being recognized in all quarters. Cf. B. Bosanquet's Gifford Lectures, *The Principle of Individuality and Value*, London, 1912, and *The Value and Destiny of the Individual*, do. 1913, for the absolutist attitude towards the subject; H. W. Stuart, in *Studies in Logical Theory*, by J. Dewey and others, Chicago, 1903, and in *Creative Intelligence*, New York, 1917; H. M. Kallen, 'Value and Existence in Philosophy, Art and Religion,' *ib.*; F. C. S. Schiller, *passim*, esp. in *Humanism*[2], London, 1912, chs. i., iii., and ix., for the pragmatist; also J. Ward, *Psychological Principles*, Cambridge, 1918, ch. xvi. § 2; and C. T. H. Walker, *The Construction of the World in Terms of Fact and Value*, Oxford, 1919.

F. C. S. SCHILLER.

VAMPIRE.—1. Introduction.—A vampire may be defined as (1) the spirit of a dead person, or (2) his corpse, re-animated by his own spirit or by a demon, returning to sap the life of the living, by depriving them of blood or of some essential organ, in order to augment its own vitality. This forms a particular aspect of the general belief that ghosts, or spirits sent by sorcerers, can annoy the living in various ways, or cause their sickness or death.[1] The vampire is often one who has died an untimely death, or whose after life is unhappy, or a dead sorcerer, wizard, or other obnoxious person. Blood being a well-known soul- or life-vehicle, it was supposed that ghosts (or vampires) were eager to obtain it, as is seen from the well-known example of the shades for whom Odysseus sacrificed sheep on his visit to Hades,[2] as well as from the custom of pouring blood upon graves. Tylor suggests that, when it was seen how certain persons grew thin and bloodless day after day, the easy explanation was that a nocturnal ghost or demon was sucking out their life.[3] Hence the vampire belief might originate. The superstition is also connected with the fear which is aroused by the dead, partly because they are often seeking or calling the living, and, in those aspects of it which concern the return of the revitalized corpse, it is an extension of what may have been a primitive conception, viz. that the dead have a life of their own in the grave, which was, in fact, often erected as a kind of house, more elaborate than the houses of the living. Many tales both from savage and from barbaric peoples show that the dead are still living in the tomb and can encounter any intruder upon it (as in Scandinavian belief), or come forth from it to talk and feast with the living or to cause them annoyance. It was also held that a malicious spirit might take possession of a corpse and vitalize it for sinister purposes. The boundary-line between life and death seems to have been but vaguely defined. To prevent the return of the dead, whether bodily or as a ghost, many precautions were in use—*e.g.*, enclosing the grave with a high fence, piling heavy stones upon it, diverting the course of a stream in order to bury in its bed and then permitting it to flow as before, binding the corpse securely (though this was done for other reasons also) or mutilating it.[4]

2. Range and examples of the vampire superstition.—While the most gruesome examples of this superstition (the vampire as a revitalized corpse) are to be met with among the Slavic peoples, in modern Greece, and in China, it is found in many other parts of the world and has been entertained in remote ages. It is not easily separated from

1 See, *e.g.*, *ERE* i. 540.

2 *Odyssey*, xi. 34 f.; H. C. Trumbull, *The Blood Covenant*[3], Philadelphia, 1898, p. 113 ff.; cf. art. BLOOD, § 7.

3 *PC*[3] ii. 191.

4 Numerous examples are given by J. G. Frazer, 'On Certain Burial Customs as illustrative of the Primitive Theory of the Soul,' *JAI* xv. [1886] 65; and in artt. DEATH AND DISPOSAL OF THE DEAD (Introductory), § XI., INDONESIANS, § 12; J. Déchelette, *Manuel d'archéologie*, Paris, 1908–10, i. 471; H. F. Osborn, *Men of the Old Stone Age*[2], London, 1916, p. 271.

other beliefs of a like kind. Not only the dead, whether in bodily or in ghostly form, prey upon the living, but demons also, who sometimes have originated from ghosts, suck the blood of the living or feed on corpses.

Beliefs of this kind regarding spirits of certain dead persons are found sporadically in Polynesia, Melanesia, Indonesia, in India, and among African and South American tribes. Among higher races traces of the idea of the dead feeding on the living are found among the ancient Babylonians and other Semites, and in Egypt regarding the *khu*. In ancient Scandinavia the idea that the dead were alive in their barrows gave rise to the belief that they might become unhallowed monsters of the vampire kind, as is seen from the *Grettis Saga*. Parallels occur in Saxon England and among the early Teutons and Celts. In modern Greece the vampire belief has prevailed for many centuries, but largely moulded by Slavic influences.[1] The Slavic superstition holds that various persons become vampires after death. The corpse is re-vitalized and thirsts for blood. Its ravages begin with relatives, then it attacks other victims, and these in turn become vampires. When the grave of a suspected vampire is opened, the corpse is found undecayed, the lips stained with blood. Its ravages occur by night: the grave must be re-entered by cock-crow, else the vampire must remain wherever he is, stiff and helpless. A great epidemic of vampire superstition occurred in Hungary in the 18th cent., which was investigated by a royal commission.[2] In China a vampire belief exists, and offers a curious parallel to that of the Slavs.[3]

3. Rites of riddance.—Among the Slavs, when a grave is opened and the corpse is found to be fresh, swollen with blood, and life-like, it is transfixed through the region of the heart with a stake of aspen or maple (Russia), blackthorn or hawthorn (Serbia), but this must be done with one blow, for two blows would restore it to life. A suspected corpse is also buried in this way. A vampire at Laibach in 1672 is said to have pulled out the stake and thrown it back.[4] A person who committed suicide was often buried at cross-roads, the body transfixed with a spear or stake, in Britain and elsewhere, in order that the ghost might not walk, but perhaps in earlier superstition lest it should become a vampire. This was forbidden in England by law in 1824.[5]

Sometimes also the head of the vampire was cut off.[6] The heads of murderers whose spirits the living feared were also cut off and destroyed, or set between the legs or beneath the body. Another effectual way was to burn the corpse to ashes, but care was taken to drive back into the fire every creature which might come from it—worms, snakes, beetles, birds, etc.—lest the vampire should have embodied itself in one of them, and so resume its foul work. This was done among the Slavs, and in Bulgaria a sorcerer armed with a saint's picture is supposed to drive the vampire into a bottle containing some of its foul food, and, when corked up, the bottle is thrown into the fire.[1] In Greece any corpse which is found not to have suffered dissolution, as well as any suspected of being a vampire, was, and even now still is, exhumed, cut to pieces, and burned, to prevent its further wandering as a *revenant*. Boiling water or oil was poured on the grave, and the heart was torn out of the body and dissolved in vinegar.[2] This is a reversion to the old pagan custom of cremation of the dead, and, in spite of Slavic influences, the Slavic method of staking the body is not in use.

In China suspected corpses were allowed to decay in the open air before burial, or, when buried, were often exhumed and burned. In the absence of the corpse from the grave, the coffin-lid was removed, thus letting in fresh air, which prevents the body from re-entering it. When the corpse was roaming about, rice, red peas, and pieces of iron were strewn round the grave; it could not pass these, and was found stiff and dead on the ground, and could then be burned.[3]

To guard against the attacks of vampires, various charms, amulets, sacred symbols, and magic herbs are commonly used in the various countries where the belief exists.

4. Love motive in the vampire belief.—Sometimes the vampire may have intercourse with the widow or other woman. This is part of a widespread belief that the dead or ghosts can have sexual union with the living, and, as far as revitalized corpses are concerned, this motive is found in the ancient Greek story of the girl Philinnion, who after her death was found with the youth Machates in her father's house as his lover, leaving him at dawn.[4] In such stories as this the vampire is linked to the ghostly *mahr*, or nightmare, in its erotic aspect on the one hand—the *mahr* comes into a room through the keyhole, as the vampire does—and to the mediæval *succuba* on the other, in so far as the latter, like other erotic demons, preys upon the vital powers of man, so destroying them.

The vampire-lover theme is also illustrated by the 'Dead Rider' cycle, as in Burger's *Lenore* or Scott's spirited version, *William and Helen*. Burger's poem is based on the folk-belief that a dead man appears to those dearly loved—lover, wife, or child—because they sorrow so much, or in order to draw them to the grave. The living person rides with him on horseback or follows him, ignorant that he is really dead. Usually they reach the churchyard. The corpse sinks into his house—the grave—and the living barely escapes being entombed, or sometimes dies at the grave. Of this there are Scandinavian, Icelandic, Albanian, Breton, Scots, and English versions, and it is even found among the Araucanians as a purely native tale.[5]

5. Vampire and wer-wolf.—Attention has been drawn elsewhere[6] to the connexion between the kindred superstitions of the vampire and the wer-animal. The main links are that the dead may become wer-wolves or other wer-animals and prey on the living,[7] and, as in Greece and among the

1 J. C. Lawson, *Modern Greek Folk-Lore and Ancient Greek Religion*, Cambridge, 1910, p. 361 ff.; Leo Allatius, *De quorundam Græcorum opinationibus*, Cologne, 1645, ch. 12 ff.

2 J. Máchal, *Slavic Mythology* (= *The Mythology of All Races*, iii.), Boston, 1918, p. 231 f.; A. Calmet, *Traité sur les apparitions des esprits et sur les vampires*, new ed. ii.

3 J. J. M. de Groot, *The Religious System of China*, Leyden, 1892–1910, v. 723 ff.

4 W. R. Ralston, *Russian Folk-Tales*, pp. 271, 324, *Songs of the Russian People*, p. 413.

5 H. J. Stephen, *New Commentaries on the Laws of England*6, London, 1868, iv. 152; R. Hunt, *Popular Romances of the West of England*, do. 1865, p. 253; Frazer, *JAI* xv. 66. Cf. *ERE* iv. 419b.

6 See reff. in Frazer, *JAI* xv. 66; Ralston, *Russian Folk-Tales*, p. 324; K. Helm, *Altgerman. Religionsgeschichte*, Heidelberg, 1913, p. 133; *ERE* iv. 433a.

1 Ralston, *Russian Folk-Tales*, pp. 314, 324; J. Curtin, *Tales of the Fairies and of the Ghost World*, London, 1895, p. 177; Tylor, *PC*3 ii. 193.

2 Lawson, pp. 371, 488, 502 f.; J. T. Bent, *The Cyclades*, London, 1885, p. 45.

3 De Groot, v. 725, 744, 749 f.

4 Phlegon, *Mirabilia*, 1; for vampires taking the form of men to deceive women cf. *ERE* i. 538b.

5 N. F. S. Grundtvig, *Danske Kæmpeviser*, Copenhagen, 1847, no. 90; J. Arnason, *Icelandic Legends*, tr. G. Powell and E. Magnusson, London, 1864–66, i. 173; A. Dozon, *Contes albanais*, Paris, 1881, p. 281; T. H. de La Villemarqué, *Barzaz-Breiz*4, do. 1846, i. 271 f.; Sir Walter Scott, *Minstrelsy of the Scottish Border*, London, 1839, p. 319 ('Clerk Saunders'); *County Folk-Lore (Suffolk)*, i., do. 1895, p. 81; A. H. Keane, *Man Past and Present*2, do. 1920, p. 410; cf. also H. H. Ploss and M. Bartels, *Das Weib*10, Berlin, 1913, i. 608.

6 In art. Lycanthropy, § 4.

7 Cf. also *ERE* v. 527b.

Slavs, that the man who was a wer-wolf in his lifetime becomes a vampire after death.

A further link of connexion is found in the fact that both vampires and wer-wolves are believed to cause storms, drought, famine, and cattle-plague; both are killed by an aspen stake; and the vampire is sometimes the offspring of a witch and a wer-wolf (or the devil).[1] While the wer-wolf is often a witch or wizard who has assumed animal form, both of these are often blood-suckers and eaters of human flesh, with all the perverted tastes of a vampire.[2]

The earth personified, occasionally as Cerberos, was sometimes supposed to be an eater of the dead.[3] Demoniac beings of the under world were also represented as eaters of the dead—Chimæra, Eurynomos, the Egyptian 'eater of hearts' or 'eater of the dead,' etc.[4]

6. The vampire in literature.—Such a superstition has naturally attracted some attention in literature. Byron has an effective passage referring to it in *The Giaour*. His prose work on the subject (unfinished) was completed by Polidori and dramatized by Charles Nodier. Hoffmann introduces it in one of the tales in *The Serapion Brethren*. It is also the subject of Théophile Gautier's *La Morte amoureuse*, and of a story in J. S. Le Fanu's *Green Tea*. But the whole superstition has received the most effective treatment, with the greatest verisimilitude, from Bram Stoker in his *Dracula*,[5] which embodies in a striking manner all that is believed on the subject in Transylvania.

LITERATURE.—R. Andree, *Ethnographische Parallelen und Vergleiche*, 2 vols., Stuttgart, 1878–89; A. Calmet, *Traité sur les apparitions des esprits et sur les vampires*, Paris, 1751, ii., Eng. tr., *The Phantom World*, London, 1850; W. Hertz, *Der Werwolf*, Stuttgart, 1862; S. Hock, *Die Vampyrsagen und ihre Verwertung in der deutschen Litteratur*, Berlin, 1900; O. von Hovorka and A. Kronfeld, *Vergleichende Volksmedizin*, do. 1908–09, ii. 890 ff.; F. Liebrecht, *Zur Volkskunde*, Heilbronn, 1879; W. Mannhardt, in *Zeitschrift für deutsche Mythologie und Sittenkunde*, iv. [1857] 259 f.; M. Ranft, *Tractat von dem Kauen und Schmatzen der Todten in Gräbern*, Leipzig, 1734; C. J. Simrock, *Handbuch der deutschen Mythologie*[4], Bonn, 1874; E. B. Tylor, *PC*[3], London, 1891; Dudley Wright, *Vampires and Vampirism*, do. 1914.

J. A. MACCULLOCH.

VANCOUVER ISLAND INDIANS.

—The Indians of Vancouver Island are not a homogeneous people, but belong to three clearly defined groups. The northern part of the island is occupied by tribes of Kwakiutl speech; they are closely related to tribes occupying the mainland of British Columbia to the east and for a considerable distance north of Vancouver Island. The south-eastern part of the island is occupied by Coast Salish tribes. These are but a comparatively small section of the widely spread Salish stock, who are distributed south into the United States as far as the lower Columbia Valley. The remainder of the island — roughly speaking, the southern two-thirds of the west coast—is inhabited by a group of tribes variously known as Nutka (from one of the best known tribes of the group) or Aht. These Indians are almost entirely confined to Vancouver Island; the extreme north-western part of Washington, however, in the neighbourhood of Cape Flattery, is occupied by the Makah Indians, an offshoot of the Nutka group. The Kwakiutl and Nutka tribes are quite clearly, if somewhat remotely, related in speech. The Salish languages may also prove to be related to Kwakiutl and Nutka, but only remotely so at best. These three groups of tribes exhibit numerous interinfluences, the dominant position, on the whole, being held by the Kwakiutl Indians of the north. In this article the religion of the Nutka Indians will be taken as the type for the aborigines of Vancouver Island. Data on the other tribes will be found in art. SALISH.

Beliefs and practices of a more or less definitely religious character enter so largely into almost every phase of Nutka life that it is not altogether easy to mark off religion as a separate subject for ethnologic treatment. For practical purposes the subject of Nutka religion may be considered as embracing the beliefs in supernatural beings of various sorts, prayer, the acquisition of 'power' either by means of amulets and the help of definite beings or by means of the performance of secret rituals of predominantly magical content, shamanism and witchcraft, beliefs in souls, tabus of various sorts and other beliefs of more or less clearly religious reference, and public rituals.

1. Supernatural beings.—It is very difficult to classify the various beings of a supernatural order that are recognized in Nutka belief. They range all the way from a Sky Being, who seems almost on the point of becoming comparable to our own conception of a Supreme Being, down to patrons or guardian spirits (*genii loci*) of specific objects, such as individual cedar trees or house-beams. The line between beings endowed with a more or less distinctive personality and mere amulets is strangely difficult to draw, as, midway between these two types, there are a considerable number of monsters whose only *raison d'être*, so far as humanity is concerned, is that some part of their body can be utilized for amuletic purposes. On the whole, the personality of the majority of Nutka supernatural beings cannot be said to be very firmly defined. As regards their relation to humanity, they might be classified as objects of prayer, beings capable of granting 'powers' of a great many different sorts, beings that are impersonated in rituals, generally in ritualistic dances, beings that figure in myths and family legends, and beings that are visibly represented, by those privileged to do so, as crests. This classification is not a mutually exclusive one, however, as many supernatural beings appear in more than one connexion.

Thus, the Wolf is important in ritual, legend, and crest representation, and is believed to grant 'powers' or 'medicines.' On the other hand, the Whale is important as a crest and mythological being, but does not figure in public ritual, while hunting powers and other gifts are bestowed by him in legends and by virtue of inheritance of such legendary gifts rather than directly in the actual present. Differing from the Whale is the Thunder-bird, in that he is not identified with an actual animal species, and that he is very frequently, perhaps most frequently of all beings, impersonated in ritual performances. Again, such a being as the Ahlmakoh, a kind of demonic wood-spirit, plays an important part in ritual and as an amulet-dispenser, but is never represented as a crest (his mask is used only in connexion with a ritual).

It is difficult in some cases to tell whether a particular type of being is conceived of as a single personality, like the more important gods and goddesses of the Greeks, or as embracing a class of numerous individuals, like our fairies. The latter is probably far more often the case, though true examples of individualized beings undoubtedly also occur. Sometimes the Indians themselves seem to waver between contradictory conceptions, as in the case of the Thunder-bird. He is generally, it seems, thought of as a distinct individuality (legend has it that there were originally four Thunder-bird brothers, but that three of them were destroyed by the Woodpecker), yet the tendency to localize his home on some particular mountain-peak and the necessarily different localizations current among the different tribes have led in the

1 Ralston, *Songs*, pp. 409, 411.

2 For examples see Mary H. Kingsley, *Travels in West Africa*, London, 1897, p. 490; *ERE* iii. 158b, vii. 237a, viii. 345b; cf. C. Hose and W. McDougall, *The Pagan Tribes of Borneo*, London, 1912, ii. 117, note 1; W. Crooke, *PR* ii. 263; Apul. *Metam.* i. 11 f.; cf. *ERE* viii. 288b; *NR* iii. 152; H. J. Bell, *Obeah*[2], London, 1893, p. 165 f. For other examples see *ERE* i. 212a.

3 Cf. Hecate as σαρκοφάγος, in the Orphic Hymns, like the stone sarcophagus.

4 Lucian, *Dial. Mort.*, xxx. 1, *Nekyom.*, 14; Paus. x. xxviii. 4; W. Max Müller, *Egyptian Mythology* (=*The Mythology of All Races*, xii.), Boston, 1918, p. 179; A. Dieterich, *Nekyia*, Leipzig, 1893, p. 49 ff. For other examples see *ERE* iii. 207. Cf. A. N. Didron, *Christian Iconography*, tr. M. Stokes, London, 1886, ii. 141.

5 London, 1897.

minds of some to the rationalizing conclusion that there is more than one Thunder-bird in existence.

In a class by himself is the Sky Chief, who enters hardly at all into the life of the natives except as an object of prayer. He is believed to dwell in the sky and to be, in a general way, the dispenser of life and happiness to mortals. He is not represented either pictorially or in rituals, and never, so far as known, occurs as a character in the mythology, not even as creator or transformer. So pale is his personality that one might be tempted to look for Christian influence, were it not for the obviously standardized form, and hence presumably great age, of the prayers addressed to him.

As in all Indian mythologies, a large number of animals are represented as human or semi-human characters in Nutka myths, many of them being endowed with supernatural powers. Few of these, however, can be considered as of interest in a purely religious connexion; the attitude of the Indian towards many of them is comparable to our own in reference to the fantastic characters of a romance or fairy-tale or even, not infrequently, to the purely human characters of a modern novel. The Raven, *e.g.*, while important in some of the more northern Pacific Coast tribes as a creator or transformer, plays the part in Nutka mythology purely of a greedy trickster or buffoon, comparable to the European Reynard the Fox. The belief that animals are descended from human-like beings of the mythological period finds its counterpart in the belief that animals to-day, when out of sight of people, divest themselves of their animal blankets and look, talk, and act like ordinary human beings. Most of the animals represented in the mythology and a large number not so represented are impersonated, by means of face paints, masks, and ceremonial regalia, in the dances of the Wolf ritual (a few of these dances are the Raven, the Woodpecker, the Sea-gull, the Wasp, the Halibut, the Octopus, and the Deer). Even in this connexion, however, it is doubtful if the animal beings themselves, as a whole, have further religious significance than that their representation has become associated with a ritual which is charged with the quality of religious emotion. The animal dances as such seem to be of interest largely as pantomimic performances. Among all these animal beings, however, there are at least some that have a degree of religious importance. 'Powers' may be obtained (or were legendarily obtained) from the Wolf, the Whale, the Hair-seal, the Sea-otter, the Shark, the Beaver, and others. Of particular importance among these is the Wolf. The Wolves are believed to form a supernatural community of their own, with four special fast runners of the chief and the Raven as news-teller. They are looked upon with great reverence—an attitude that finds its fullest expression in the Wolf ritual, founded, according to its origin legends, by the Wolves themselves.

In the mythology we also meet with a number of human-like figures that belong to the supernatural world without being identified with either animals or monsters. Here belongs the creator Kapkimiyis, who created the first man out of the thigh of the first already existent woman, made the island of Tsisha, the home of the Tsishaath tribe descended from them, and assigned them the various foods, animal and vegetable, that they and their descendants were to use. Kapkimiyis is evidently a purely local figure, and he is doubtless paralleled by local creators in the other Nutka tribes. Another important figure in the mythology is Kwatiyat, a sort of creator or, better, transformer, who experienced many curious adventures and did much to give the world its present shape. The rock-carvings in the interior of Vancouver Island are believed to be his work. He is still alive, but it is not known where he resides. With him is often associated his brother, who, like the Raven, is a trickster. Another transformer is known as Causing-everything-to-be-different. His work consisted chiefly in transforming various maleficent monsters into the relatively harmless animals that we know to-day.

We need no more than refer to a few of the host of powers with which the Nutka Indian peoples the land, the sea, and the air. The Heitlik, 'Wont-to-glide-to-the-ground,' is a snake-like, scaly being who darts out lightning with his red tongue. He is generally represented as gliding on the rocks, coiling up or down a tree, or coiled like a belt about the Thunder-bird. When seen, a bit of his tail should be lopped off and preserved as an amulet for success in whaling and other sea-mammal hunting. The Yaai are fairy-like folk that dwell on the summits of mountains. They wear feathers on their heads and are associated with fire and the *aurora borealis*. They are peculiarly elusive beings, frequently dissolving into foam. A supernatural bird, the Mikhtach, said to resemble a female mallard duck, is a potent source of luck in hunting. The Ahlmakoh, already referred to, is a kind of forest ogre, evidently related to the Nutlmis, or Fool-dancer, of the Kwakiutl; his nasal mucus is valued as an amulet for invulnerability. The Chiniath are brownie-like woods-folk who do all sorts of strange things, such as hunting for sea-cucumbers as though they were seals; they give power to those who are fortunate enough to see them. The Pokumis are wild and elusive beings, transformed from human beings that have become estranged from human ways or overcome by intense cold. The Pokumis are often represented in the pantomimic dances of the Wolf ritual. The Shishchikuhl is a large animal-like monster who lives inside a mountain and whose red hair is a powerful amulet for success in war. A two-headed being, the Totohtsaktso, reddish in colour and with a tail attached to each of his heads, is particularly virulent as 'medicine'; a small part of his body is a powerful amulet in both war and hunting. He is doubtless the Nutka equivalent of the Sisiutl so often represented in the art of the Kwakiutl Indians. The Tsatsokhta is an enormously strong being with red, shaggy hair and with his right foot large, his left extremely small. The earth of his tracks is a strength-giving 'medicine.' One of the most important of Nutka supernatural powers, in ritual and legend as in the acquirement of 'medicine,' is the Hena, a class of beings conventionally represented by, but not actually believed to be identical with, quartz crystals. They have the power of incredibly rapid flight and make a loud, whizzing noise. They have become closely associated in Nutka belief with the Wolf ritual, their characteristic sound being identified with the supernatural whistling that is believed to emanate from the wolves and that is imparted to the initiates of the ritual. It is therefore not surprising that the quartz-like Hena is held to be found also in the body of a wolf, of whom it forms a sort of subsidiary soul.

It is remarkable that the power emanating from most of the supernatural beings of the Nutka is intimately bound up with some amulet-like or fetish-like object, generally some part of his body that is, often with considerable violence, taken from him. The conception of a benevolent attitude towards the seeker after 'power' and of a spiritual guardianship over him—a conception that prevails among so many American Indian tribes—is, on the whole, signally absent here. It is present in some degree in the legendary accounts of ancestral experiences of the acquisition of power, yet even here the chief emphasis is always placed on the supernatural object acquired and handed down or on the privilege of ceremonially representing such an experience, not on the notion of a mystic relationship.

2. Prayer.—Prayer is often held to represent religious feeling at its purest, particularly when the prayer is individual and of unstandardized form. Among the Nutka Indians prayers are, so far as known, always of strictly standardized form. They are either sacred songs sung at a ritual by a group or by an individual in the presence of the community (such prayers, *e.g.*, are addressed to the Wolves of the Wolf ritual or in the rite of exorcism in the same ritual) or they are private, and indeed secret, spell-like formulæ addressed to the Sky Chief in the course of the important secret rituals referred to below. The feeling that animates the former class of prayers is perhaps more intensely emotional; it may be characterized as fear or awe glorified into exaltation. The latter class have more of a magical than purely religious connotation, and this in spite of the fact that they are addressed to the nearest approach that the Nutka have to a generalized Supreme Being. They are self-seeking in tone; more often than not they directly plead for a superiority in success at the expense of others.

Generally the secret ritual prayers are for some specific gift, as wealth, success in hunting or fishing, good luck in love, proficiency in the performance of a ritualistic act, or whatever else, good or evil, one may desire the fulfilment of. As a rule, however, the specific prayer is preceded by a more general *tichsimich*, or prayer for life.

A typical example of such a 'life prayer' is: 'Look down on me, O Chief, have pity on me. Cause me to be alive. Cause to be sent back whatever evil words may be said of me by any one. If at any time one prays in secret for my death, may I cause his curses to recoil on himself; may I cause him to swallow his own [evil words]. Cause me to be without affliction, O Chief. Grant me, O Chief, thy wealth [or whatever else one desires]. . . .'

While the private prayers of the Nutka are strictly standardized in form, the texts of the prayers seem to differ considerably according to the varying family traditions. Here, as throughout Nutka life, family exclusiveness in matters of privilege and secret lore is much in evidence.

3. Acquisition of power; secret rituals.—Like so many other primitive peoples, the Nutka feel the necessity of continuous supernatural assistance in the pursuit of the ends of life. The individual must, whenever possible, eke out his own powers by the support of some of the mysterious influences that surround him. Prayer can do much for him; the mere possession of an amulet or fetish or 'medicine' probably more; still more efficacious is a token resulting from an encounter with a supernatural being. The handling of all such tokens, as well as of all supernatural objects or animals not actually identifiable with specific beings, is regularly hedged about by various tabus. Generally fasting and a period of sexual continence are required, also absence from the home. A token may not be lightly rejected, if disaster is to be avoided. One must also know beforehand just how it is to be utilized, what one must do or say in order to secure the benefits of its supernatural influence. Frequently one must be careful to take only the right half. Frequently, also, it may not be taken into the house, but must be kept in a secret spot in the woods. Its power may be communicated by rubbing or other handling, or a small piece of it may be directly used as an amulet; thus a bit of it may be inserted in the cedar-bark wrapping of a sealing or whaling harpoon. Every Indian possesses a considerable number of 'medicines,' for various purposes and of different degrees of potency. Their possession is generally a secret to all but the immediate heirs of their acquirer or inheritor; certain 'life medicines' may even be kept entirely secret until the approach of death. It is interesting to note that the mere possession of secret or magical lore is itself 'good medicine.' As one parts with knowledge, his power of resistance to adverse influences is lessened.

It is not always possible to secure the special assistance derived from supernatural helpers or inherited fetishes. Hence the main reliance of the Nutka Indian for the success of his hunting, fishing, or other ventures is on the punctilious performance of certain private magical ceremonies that we have termed 'secret rituals.' There is an astonishing number and a bewildering variety of such rituals. Every family possesses, by secret inheritance, enough to guide it safely through life. Sometimes several versions of a magical ritual—one derived, say, from the paternal, the other from the maternal, tradition—are known by an individual, but they may never be combined or confused. The secret rituals are always performed in a hidden spot at a considerable distance from the house; for the more elaborate rituals the various families have prepared spots deep in the woods, often near pools or in caves. The rituals range in complexity from comparatively simple magical performances, prayers, and spell-pronouncements lasting but a single night to elaborate ceremonies extended over a month or more. The former are either abbreviated versions of more elaborate rituals or relate to the easier quests, such as salmon-trolling; the latter are concerned with the more hazardous or exacting pursuits, such as whaling, sea-lion hunting, or sealing. Each secret ritual is in effect a prayer and magical compulsion toward some desired end—success in trapping fish, spearing cod, harpooning sea-otter, whaling, acquiring wealth, gaining love, bewitching an enemy; even the satisfaction of such unusual desires as success in stealing or the learning of a raven's speech may be compassed by the performance of a magical ritual. The details of each ritual differ according to specific family tradition and the nature of the end sought. The constant features seem to be prayer, the pronouncement of spells, the observance of tabus, rubbing with 'medicines,' bathing and rubbing down with hemlock branches (until the skin peeled, in the practice of the hardier aspirants for success), the wearing of cedar-bark and feather regalia and the laying on of symbolic face-paints, and, most important of all, the performance of magical actions. In principle these actions are dominated by the philosophy of sympathetic magic and by the symbolic efficacy of imitation and the handling of effigies.

Thus, the aspirant for success in whaling may spend hours diving into a pool and coming up to the surface and blowing in imitation of a whale or, bent over the ground, in humping his back like that of the whale; or he may make out of twigs rude effigies of a whaling canoe, its occupants, harpoon and floats, and the hunted sea-mammal.

The magical practices not infrequently included bizarre or revolting features, such as rubbing with the skulls of one's ancestors or the use of a new-born babe that had been stolen, killed, and had its eyes gouged out (a symbolic representation of the whale that is blind to his pursuer and allows himself to be caught). Needless to say, these secret rituals have little or no purely social bearing. The magic ritualist may, however, be accompanied by a close relative, say a son or nephew—frequently, in the more elaborate types, by his wife. Not the least interesting thing about the secret rituals is their dependence for success on a proper calendric placing. The most auspicious season for their performance is the period between the winter and summer solstices, when the days are progressively longer; during a given month it is the days of the waxing moon that should be chosen. The symbolism of this is as obvious as it is world-wide. Indeed, there is every reason to believe that what little precision of solar and lunar observation the Nutka Indians attained was conditioned by the necessity of correctly delimiting the span of auspicious days.

4. Shamanism.—The Nutka shaman, or medicine-man, is such by virtue of supernatural power personally acquired by him or, at least theoretically, by right of inheritance from an ancestor who had himself (or herself) acquired such power. Properly speaking, the acquirement of shamanistic power[1] is on a par with the acquirement of any other type of supernatural power, as for hunting or fishing. In either case the possession of power may be due to the magic inhering in the performance of a secret ritual, to the acquirement of a supernatural token or amulet-like object ('medicine'), with or without the inter-

[1] See art. SHAMANISM.

position of a supernatural being, or to the inheriting of a family 'medicine.' What distinguishes the medicine-man is the function exercised by his power, the class of being from whom it is derived, and the manner of holding and exercising this power.

The main functions of the medicine-man are the location of disease, generally conceived of as a worm-like malefic object that has been lodged in the body of the sufferer by an ill-wisher, the detection, if required, of the causes of the disease, and its removal. The divining, in a trance-like state, of future or distant events and the supernatural causation of disease are also frequently within the province of the medicine-man, but need not be.

The supernatural beings and 'medicines' that bestow shamanistic power are rarely the same as those that give power for other purposes. There is a long list of eerie or unusual objects whose discovery and retention are believed to make a man a shaman—at least to a limited extent, for a really powerful shaman has generally a number of sources of supernatural guidance. The specific beings that grant shamanistic power belong to two classes, 'birds' and 'fish.' Certain birds—*e.g.*, ducks—certain land animals, and certain fish are believed to be powerful shamans themselves and to meet once a year in a doctoring contest. The leader of the 'birds' is a supernatural bird known as Khwini, or Khwili, who is said to belong to the Sky Chief; the leader of the 'fish' is a small eel-like marine fish. The former has the greatest shamanistic power of all. The shamanistic being (animal) bestows power not so much by way of a dream, as so commonly in aboriginal America, as by the amuletic virtue of his own body. This is in accord with the general materializing tendency that pervades Nutka religion.

The power of the 'medicine' amulet or being is, in the case of the Nutka shaman, exercised by virtue of its actual presence in his body. A shaman's supernatural power (*manitu* [*q.v.*]) is not a mystic influence that guides him, but resides in a concrete object that he is believed to keep inside his hand or chest. A powerful shaman may have half-a-dozen or more such 'medicines' in his chest, in supernaturally reduced form. These are never made visible to the laity except on special occasions, such as at a very severe illness or during the *tsayek* ritual, when the shaman may hold them up for inspection. The shamans are believed to have the power of causing their 'medicines' to fly through the air to any place or person desired. The wide-spread conception of the 'flying' or 'shooting' of disease-causing substances seems, by an easy transition, to have been transferred to the Nutka materializations of the *manitu* concept. The *modus operandi* of the Nutka shaman differs according to circumstances. The usual methods are: sucking of the part affected (actually or supposedly), manipulation after rubbing the fists against the hands, resuscitation by uttering certain syllables in a conventional manner, and the singing of specific medicine songs. These songs are often dreamed during the performance of a secret ritual for the attainment of shamanistic power.

5. Soul beliefs and supernatural phenomena.—The Nutka Indians say that the course of life is like the walking of a man on a straight line as thin as a hair. If he misses a single step, he drops down and dies. The soul or living essence of a human being is conceived of as a wee mannikin, a shadowy doublet, which can be held in the palm of a shaman. It may leave the body through the crown of the head, but may either return of its own accord or be brought back through the ministrations of a shaman. If it fails to return, it means that it has reached the land of disembodied spirits, that its possessor, in other words, is dead. It is then referred to by a term, *cheha*, which may be rendered 'ghost,' but which is more freely used to refer to any discarnate spirit and even to any eerie or highly unusual being, such as an elephant. The ghost is always thought of as evil, and great efforts are taken to rid of its malign influence a house in which a person has died.

Distinct from the soul is the *hlimaksti*, often translated 'heart.' This is not the anatomical heart, but the mind or 'soul' in its psychological, not theological, sense. It is the seat or principle of intelligence characteristic of human beings alone, and is generally localized in the heart or breast.

According to one legend, the creator Kapkimiyis made a vertical column of ten faces, stuck close together, and put it into the breast of the first man as his seat of intelligence. This is the *hlimaksti* of to-day. If all ten faces look in one direction, the man's will is strong; if five look one way, five the other, he is in a state of evenly-balanced hesitation. The first woman had no *hlimaksti* put inside of her; hence women are believed to be more flighty and less intelligent than men.

The life after death is supposed to be located in an under world, which is divided into a 'good' and a 'bad' section. In the 'good' quarter are little streams in which spring-salmon run and form the food of the ghostly inhabitants. The spring-salmon of the world of the living are believed to be sent up here by departed spirits. The occupants of the 'bad' quarter of the underground world eat lice. In the opinion of some Indians, the dead turn into wolves or owls. This belief does not necessarily exclude the other.

As among all primitive peoples, there is a vast number of beliefs current among the Nutka in regard to supernatural phenomena and relations. Only a very few of these need be touched upon here. An eclipse of the sun or moon is caused by a supernatural being known as Codfish-in-the-sky, who holds the luminary in his mouth. During an eclipse each of the Indians would rush off to perform a secret ritual for trolling fish. The magical concept at the basis of this practice is evident: the fish eventually trolled for was to bite just as the Codfish was biting the eclipsed sun or moon. Another very curious belief is referred to by the term 'going off to another place.' The Indians believe that at two unknown periods during the year a big tide comes in at night and shifts about everything in the village, houses and all. After a short time, during which it is difficult to keep awake, everything is shifted back to its proper place. Should one be lucky enough to keep awake during this periodic shift, and be engaged in a secret ritual, he is certain to prove successful in whatever he is praying for.

Perhaps the most interesting belief concerning the relation of human beings to the supernatural world is that which regards twins as salmon incarnations. So much is this taken as a matter of course that it is believed that a twin child involuntarily bursts into tears when it sees a salmon being treated cruelly. Both twin children and their father are subject to many onerous tabus, and the children are not expected to live long. The significant thing about twin fatherhood is that it makes of the father a mere instrument of the salmon-world. The appearance of twins is looked upon as a harbinger of an unusually big salmon run, and the father devotes all his energies during the fishing-season to the singing of songs, the performance of secret rituals, and the observance of tabus intended to propitiate the salmon and provide his fellow-villagers with a maximum catch. Should he disregard the injunctions of the salmon-world implied by the birth of twins, dire misfortune is certain to befall him.

6. Rituals.—Ceremonialism, both social and religious in character, is very prominent in Nutka life. It is somewhat arbitrary to divide ceremonies into the two classes, as, on the one hand, a religious quality (some sort of legendary or supernatural background) is rarely absent from even the most matter-of-fact or casual ceremony (say, a naming feast or invitation ceremony), while, on the other, every more properly religious ceremony, such as the elaborate and peculiarly sacred Wolf ritual, is given the setting of a secular *potlatch* (giving feast) and regularly contains numberless features that have a purely social, not religious, significance. The two major ceremonies of primarily religious connotation are the Wolf ritual (known by the natives as *tlokwana*) and a shamanistic performance termed *tsayek*. The former undoubtedly has a native Nutka nucleus, but has been much influenced by the winter feast of the Kwakiutl Indians. The latter ceremony is primarily at home among the more southern Nutka tribes; it is also found among the Coast Salish and Quileute (north-west coast of Washington).

The Wolf ritual differs considerably among the various Nutka tribes in its origin legend and in its ceremonial details. In essence it is a quasi-dramatic representation, at least in native theory, of certain legendary occurrences.

Just as a young man or woman, in the legendary past, is believed to have been carried away by the wolves to their supernatural home, to have been taught many religious dances and songs, and to have returned to his people with these immaterial gifts, so, in the ceremony of to-day, the novices, who are to be initiated into the ceremony, are represented as seized by wolves that break into the village and as carried off into the woods, there to be taught particular dances, which, after they are rescued by the villagers and exorcized, they perform among their own people in a state of religious frenzy. The dances vary greatly in character, but are largely pantomimic, referring either to animals, occupations, or supernatural beings. Many of them are inspired by a spirit of savage recklessness that may take the form of self-torture or ceremonial killing. The association of all those (novices and old initiates) who dance a particular dance into a 'secret society' is a very much more weakly developed concept than among the Kwakiutl. On the other hand, the individuals who are banded together throughout the ceremony as wolf-performers, by hereditary right, may be looked upon as constituting a true confraternity.

In a rather vague way the Wolf ritual may be interpreted as a kind of placating of the powerful supernatural beings that appear to us as wolves, but there can, in actual fact, be no talk of a definite function of the ceremony. It is a complex historical growth that serves as a traditional setting for the public expression of religious emotion (awe and exaltation) and for the satisfaction of certain artistic needs. Even the spirit of ribald humour finds expression in it. To a large extent, also, the purely religious and artistic motives are overlaid by the desire, so characteristic of West Coast culture, to enhance one's social prestige by display and a lavish expenditure of wealth. As usual with great tribal ceremonies, it undoubtedly means different things to different temperaments.

The *tsayek* ceremony is ostensibly undertaken, like so many other great tribal ceremonies among American Indians, for the cure of a sick person who has not profited by ordinary shamanistic treatment. The main feature of the ceremony is the singing of a peculiar type of songs, accompanied by beating of sticks and certain conventional gesticulations and jumps. Each Indian that takes part in the ceremony sings a number of such *tsayek* songs that have become his property by family inheritance. Novices who are to be initiated into the *tsayek* ceremony sing these songs for the first time. In the course of the ceremony another and more advanced type of initiation takes place—that of those who have had some supernatural shamanistic experience, or who have a hereditary shamanistic right, into the formal status, often theoretical rather than actual, of shaman. This part of the ceremony offers suggestive parallels to the well-known Midē′wiwin of the Ojibwa and other Algonquian tribes. Indeed, the two types of initiation, *tsayek* proper and shamanistic, may be looked upon as constituting a series of degrees not unlike the more intricately developed system of shamanistic degrees current among the Algonquian tribes.

LITERATURE.—The information in this art. is based on the author's MS notes. For further literature on Nutka religion see: F. Boas, 'The Nootka,' in *Sixth Report on the North-western Tribes of Canada, Report of the British Association for the Advancement of Science*, Leeds meeting, 1890, pp. 582–604, 'The Nootka' (religious ceremonials), in *The Social Organization and the Secret Societies of the Kwakiutl Indians* (*Report of the United States National Museum*, 1895), pp. 632–644; E. Sapir, 'Some Aspects of Nootka Language and Culture,' *American Anthropologist*, new ser. [1911], 15–28, 'A Girl's Puberty Ceremony among the Nootka Indians,' *Transactions of Royal Society of Canada*, 3rd ser., vol. vii. [1913] sect. ii. pp. 67–80; G. M. Sproat, *Scenes and Studies of Savage Life*, London, 1868; James G. Swan, *The Indians of Cape Flattery* (*Smithsonian Contributions to Knowledge*, vol. xvi. pt. viii. [Washington, 1870] pp. 1–106). For literature on Kwakiutl religion see: G. M. Dawson, 'Notes and Observations on the Kwakiootl People of the Northern Part of Vancouver Island and adjacent Coasts,' *Proceedings and Transactions of Royal Society of Canada*, vol. v. [1887] sect. ii. pp. 63–98; F. Boas, 'The Kwakiutl,' in *Sixth Report on the North-western Tribes of Canada, Report of the British Association for the Advancement of Science*, Leeds meeting, 1890, pp. 604–632, 'Notes on the Kwakiutl,' in *Eleventh Report on the North-western Tribes of Canada, Report of the British Association for the Advancement of Science*, Liverpool meeting, 1896, pp. 569–580, *The Social Organization and the Secret Societies of the Kwakiutl Indians*, pp. 311–737. For literature on Coast Salish religion see: F. Boas, 'The Lku′ñgEn,' *Report of the British Association for the Advancement of Science*, Leeds meeting, 1890, pp. 563–582, 'The Lku′ñgEn' (religious ceremonials), in *The Social Organization and the Secret Societies of the Kwakiutl Indians*, pp. 644–646; C. Hill-Tout, *British North America, I. The Far West, The Home of the Salish and Déné*, London, 1907, 'The Salish Tribes of the Coast and Lower Fraser Delta,' *Annual Archæological Report*, 1905, Appendix to Report of Minister of Education, Ontario, pp. 225–235, 'Report on the Ethnology of the Sīciatl of British Columbia, a Coast Division of the Salish Stock,' *JAI* xxxiv. [1904] 20–91, 'Ethnological Report on the StsEēlis and Sk·aúlits Tribes of the HalkōmēlEm Division of the Salish of British Columbia,' *ib.* pp. 311–376, 'Ethnological Studies of the mainland HalkōmēlEm, a Division of the Salish of British Columbia,' *Report of the British Association for the Advancement of Science*, Belfast meeting, 1902, pp. 355–449, 'Notes on the Sk·qō′mic of British Columbia, a Branch of the great Salish Stock of North America,' *Report of the British Association for the Advancement of Science*, Bradford meeting, 1900, pp. 472–549.

EDWARD SAPIR.

VANNIC RELIGION.—See ARMENIA.

VASUBANDHU.

VASUBANDHU.—Vasubandhu (*c.* A.D. 420–500), the second of three brothers of a Kauśika Brāhman family, was born at Puruṣapura (Peshawar) in Gandhāra (Kandahar), and is one of the most prominent figures in the history of Buddhism. His not less celebrated elder brother, Asanga, is well known as the first propounder of the Yogāchāra school of Buddhism, *i.e.* Buddhist idealism. Of the youngest brother, Viriñchivatsa, we know nothing.

1. Life.—There are three different traditions concerning Vasubandhu's life: (1) *The Life of Vasubandhu*, translated by Paramārtha into Chinese;[1] (2) *passim* in *Si-yu-ki* ('Records of the Western Countries') by Hiuen-Tsiang, (3) the Tibetan tradition in Tāranātha, etc. The general drift of them is as follows:

Vasubandhu, a contemporary of Vikramāditya (=Skandagupta, A.D. 455–480), and his son Bālāditya (*c.* 485–) took orders in the Sarvāstivāda (realism) school, having studied under Buddhamitra (Manoratha, according to Hiuen-Tsiang) the whole of the sacred books, *i.e.* the three collections (*Tripiṭaka*), of the school to which he belonged. Afterwards he studied the doctrines of the Sautrāntika (the school which accepts the *Sūtra* as its sole authority), thinking them more reasonable, in many points, than those of his own school, and he determined to formulate an eclectic system out of the two lines of doctrine along which his mental activity had been directed. In order to do so, it was indispensable for him first

[1] B. Nanjio, *Catalogue of the Chinese Translation of the Buddhist Tripiṭaka*, Oxford, 1883, no. 1463.

to acquire a thorough knowledge of the Sautrāntika doctrines. With this object he went to Kaśmīra (Kashmīr), the head-quarters of the study of the doctrine, carefully disguising himself and assuming a false name, lest the scholars of that country should be jealous and refuse to instruct him. There, for many years, under the guidance of Saṅghabhadra, he studied the doctrine, against which he would, however, frequently dispute, basing his objections on the teachings of the Sautrāntika itself. Skandila, the teacher of Saṅghabhadra, had his suspicions aroused by the extraordinary ability of the unknown student, and at last ascertained that he was none other than Vasubandhu, whereupon he advised him secretly to go back to his own land, lest some factious people should kill him. Vasubandhu therefore returned to his home, where he composed a poem of 600 verses called the *Abhidharmakōśa*,[1] a compendium of *Abhidharma-mahāvibhāṣā*,[2] and sent it to Kaśmīra. The king of Kaśmīra and the scholars were at first delighted with it, imagining that he was expounding and propagating their doctrine; but, on the advice of Skandila, who knew that the compendium was not quite favourable to their sect, the author was asked to write an explanation. So he expounded the verses in a prose commentary, with the addition of seven verses and one chapter on the non-Ego. These verses together with the commentary are called *Abhidharma-kōśa-śāstra*.[3] Vasubandhu afterwards travelled to Ayodhyā (Oudh) and was converted by his brother Asanga to the faith of the Mahāyāna, and composed many treatises in defence of his new creed, with commentaries on various Mahāyāna works. He died there (in Nepāl, according to Tibetan tradition) at eighty years of age.[4]

2. Works.—Vasubandhu's first literary undertaking seems to have been the composition of his *Paramārthasaptati* ('Seventy [Verses] on the First Principle'), in which he refuted and destroyed all the ground principles of the Sāṅkhya philosophy as put forth in the *Sāṅkhya-śāstra* by Vindhyavāsa, by whom Buddhamitra, Vasubandhu's teacher, had been defeated in an ecclesiastical dispute. This fact gave general satisfaction, and King Vikramāditya rewarded him with three lacs of gold.

Before turning to his Buddhist works, we may make a few additional remarks. First, it must be borne in mind that about the 2nd cent. B.C. Kātyāyanīputra founded the Sarvāstivāda school and composed the *Jñānaprasthāna* ('First Steps to Knowledge'), a simple catalogue *raisonnée* of the technical terms of his doctrine as contained in previously published 'six-branch-treatises' (*ṣaṭpāda-śāstra*). At the beginning of the 2nd cent. A.D. a very detailed commentary on this work, called *Abhidharma-mahāvibhāṣā* ('Thorough Discussion of the *Abhidharma*'), was composed by 500 *arhats* of Kaśmīra. In this work we have not only a detailed explanation of the text, but also a minute discussion of each topic, so that the commentary became immediately a mine of dogmatics and the sole authority for the sect, by whom it was widely studied in Kaśmīra. Hence its special name *Kaśmīra-vaibhāṣika* ('Vibhāṣā-follower of Kaśmīra'). This Sarvāstivāda doctrine is realistic and teaches a direct perception of external objects. Its rival doctrine is that of the Sautrāntika, which, though also realistic, asserts an indirect perception instead of a direct one. The two doctrines were the most influential in Hīnayānism. Vasubandhu, though originally a Sarvāstivādin, was a free-thinker, and did not blindly follow either his orthodox tenets or his lately adopted Sautrāntika ideas. Scholars designated his guiding principle 'a preference of reason,' and his eclecticism is shown in his celebrated work *Abhidharmakośa*, called by native scholars 'the ingenious treatise.'

It is divided into eight treasure-houses (*kośasthāna*):

(1) Elements } natural and supernatural in general.
(2) Power }
(3) Worlds—effect }
(4) Actions—cause } natural in special.
(5) Passions—auxiliary circumstances }
(6) Sages—effect }
(7) Sacred knowledge—cause } supernatural in special.
(8) Meditation—auxiliary circumstances }

In addition to the above eight sections, one section, called *Pudgala-viniśchaya* ('Exposition of Personality'), is devoted to the argument of the non-Ego. This he composed when invited by the Kaśmirean Vaibhāṣika to explain the object of his work. To the first chapter a dogmatical explanation of the word *Abhidharma* is prefixed. It says that *Abhidharma* means 'confronting the thing,' *i.e.* insight. The thing to be confronted is of two kinds. The one aimed at is *nirvāṇa*, or final beatitude; the other mediated by is the four verities, or immanent characters of things. This confronting of things, *i.e.* insight, is called pure. It is the final *Abhidharma*. This pure insight can be called into existence by preliminary insight and teaching; the former consists in innate, acquired, and exercised insight; the latter implies the use of many standard works of the sect indirectly conducive to the origination of pure insight. These preliminary elements are called the conventional *Abhidharma*. As Vasubandhu in his work sums up the essential contents of the *Abhidharma* literature of his predecessors, and as this literature is the main source of his treatise, his work is entitled *Abhidharmakośa* ('Repository of the *Abhidharma*'). In this way he set forth concisely all noumena and phenomena and the *rationale* of the non-Ego, derived chiefly from the sources of the Sarvāstivāda school, but some tenets were taken from the Sautrāntika school and sometimes he introduced his own views.

Although Vasubandhu sympathized in his work with the Sautrāntika and showed his preference for it as the more reasonable, he was by no means satisfied with these realistic speculations, in which he was immersed until he came to the second stage of his philosophical development. When converted to Mahāyānism, he adopted the subjective idealism of that school, which he completed and systematized in his not less celebrated epitomic composition *Vijñaptimātratā-triṃśaka* ('Thirty [Verses] on "Mere Idea"').[1] The philosophical school based on this treatise teaches that all phenomena, both material and non-material, originate in mind, which is divided according to its action into eight 'ideas' (*vijñānāni*), viz. (1–5) five ideas belonging to the five sense organs, (6) idea of mind (*mano-vijñāna*), (7) mind-idea (*mano-vijñāna*), or stained mind-idea (*kliṣṭa-mano-vijñāna*), (8) receptacle-idea (*ālaya-vijñāna*). The seeds (*bīja*) or possibilities of all phenomena are retained in the eighth idea, whence comes the so-called objective world, in consequence of which we are disturbed and rove about in painful efforts after peace. If we once fully understand that nothing else exists but mind, then the objective world ceases to exist for us, and those eight confused ideas are turned into eight kinds of enlightened wisdom (*jñāna*) by means of which we can unite in the *tathatā* ('thusness') which transcends speech and thought.

The *Abhidharmakośa* and *Vijñaptimātratā-triṃśaka* are the two most celebrated of Vasubandhu's twenty odd works, and represent the successive development of his philosophical views.

It seems that towards the end of his life he reached a quite different phase of belief. He composed 24 verses entitled *Longing for the Birth* (in Sukhāvatī, *i.e.* the Paradise of the West), being a summary of the *Aparimitāyus-sūtra*,[2] to which he subsequently added a commentary. These verses with the commentary, regarded as one work, are called the *Aparimitāyus-sūtrōpadeśa*.[3] From them we see that he believed in the Amitābha (*alias* Aparimitāyus) doctrine, *i.e.* the doctrine of salvation by the grace of the Author, while in the two former phases of Buddhism through which he had passed no such idea occurs, nor is the name of Amitābha even mentioned.

LITERATURE.—*Life of Vasubandhu*, tr. from the Chinese by W. Wassilieff, in his *Buddhismus*, Germ. tr., St. Petersburg, 1860, pp. 235–243, and by J. Takakusu, in *Tong-pao*, Leyden, 1904; Hiuen-Tsiang, *Si-yu-ki*, *passim*, French tr. by Stanislas Julien, *Mémoires sur les contrées occidentales*, 2 vols., Paris, 1857–58, Eng. tr. by S. Beal, *Buddhist Records of the Western World*, 2 vols., London, 1884; Tāranātha, *Geschichte des Buddhismus in Indien*, Germ. tr., ed. A. Schiefner, Leipzig, 1869 p. 118 ff.; J. Takakusu, 'A Study of Paramārtha's Life of Vasubandhu and the Date of Vasubandhu,' *JRAS*, Jan. 1905; Pu-kwang, *Ko-sha-lung-ki* (commentary on *Kośaśāstra*), i. 33.

U. WOGIHARA.

[1] Nanjio, no. 1270. [2] *Ib.* no. 1263.
[3] *Ib.* nos. 1267 and 1269.
[4] For a complete list of his Buddhist works see Nanjio, Appendix i. col. 371 f.; cf. J. Takakusu, 'A Study of Paramārtha's Life of Vasubandhu,' *JRAS*, Jan. 1905.

[1] Nanjio, no. 1215. [2] *Ib.* nos. 25, 26, 27, etc.
[3] *Ib.* no. 1204.

VEDAS.—See LITERATURE (Vedic and Classical Sanskrit), VEDIC RELIGION.

VEDĀNTA.—*Vedānta* in Sanskrit signifies the 'end or final aim of the Veda.' The word was employed at first to denote the older *Upaniṣads* (see art. UPANIṢADS), but generally serves as the name of the most wide-spread of the six philosophical systems of the Brāhmans (*i.e.* Sāṅkhya, Yoga, Mīmāṁsā, Vedānta, Vaiśeṣika, Nyāya). In the Vedānta the pantheistic doctrine of the Brahman, the All-One, is systematically developed, and placed on a philosophical foundation. The founder of the Vedānta, or rather the first teacher who made a formal presentation of it (in the *Vedāntasūtras* or *Brahmasūtras*) was Bādarāyaṇa.[1] Since, however, his treatise is set forth in the form of aphorisms—precisely like the *sūtras* or 'clues' of the other philosophical schools of India—which in themselves are completely unintelligible, it is impossible to gain a satisfactory knowledge of the system from his work alone. This is first supplied by the expositions of the numerous native commentators, of whom the most important was the renowned Vedāntist Śaṅkara, who lived *c.* A.D. 800. Besides expounding the *Brahmasūtras*, Śaṅkara composed a large number of commentaries on the *Upaniṣads*, and wrote several independent treatises on the Vedānta philosophy. It is reasonable to suppose that the conceptions of Śaṅkara agree in all essentials with the views set forth by Bādarāyaṇa. Nearly all educated Hindus in modern India, except in so far as they have embraced European ideas, are adherents of the Vedānta; and three-fourths of these accept Śaṅkara's interpretation of the *Brahmasūtras*, while the rest are divided among the varying explanations of the system offered by one or other of the remaining commentators.

The fundamental proposition of the Vedānta philosophy is in agreement with the doctrine of the ancient *Upaniṣads*, viz.: 'the ātman (*i.e.* our self or our soul) is identical with the Brahman, the All-Soul.' Since, then, the eternal and infinite Brahman, the power that works in everything, cannot consist of parts, or be subject to change (for everything that consists of parts, and is liable to change, is perishable), it follows that every one is essentially not a part or an emanation of the Brahman, but is Brahman entire and indivisible. Nothing real exists besides Brahman; 'there is one only, without a second.' Therefore in India the Vedānta doctrine in the form in which Śaṅkara has presented it is called the 'doctrine of non-duality.'

In opposition to the fundamental thought of the Vedānta, as thus set forth, is arrayed not only experience, which teaches the existence of a manifold variety of persons and things, but also the ceremonial law of the Veda; for the latter is based upon the belief in transmigration and retribution, and therefore takes for granted a multitude of individual souls. This twofold contradiction is refuted by the assertion that both experience and the ceremonial law of the Veda depend upon the 'ignorance' (*avidyā*) natural to every man, by which the soul is prevented from distinguishing itself from the body, the psychical organs and other controlling influences, and from recognizing that the empirical universe is an illusion (*māyā*). In truth, the entire world of phenomena is merely a delusion, comparable to a *fata morgana*, which disappears on closer examination; or like a dream-image, which seems real only to the sleeper, but vanishes in waking hours.

There is only one thing in the universe which is unaffected by this power of illusion—our self, the soul. This self admits of no proof, but it also stands in no need of proof, for it is in itself the basis of all argument, and therefore is already established antecedent to any possibility of proof. Similarly, also, it cannot be denied, for every one in denying it assumes and testifies to its existence. The self, moreover, cannot be anything distinct from Brahman, since Brahman alone exists. Everything that is asserted of the Brahman—pure, spiritual nature, omnipresence, eternity, etc.—holds good, therefore, of our soul. Here in our inner self we must look for knowledge. In himself alone, in the depths of his own being, can man find the solution of the riddle of the universe, and know the only true real.

Whence 'ignorance' arises, by which the true condition of things is hidden from us, the Vedānta philosophy does not inquire. It tells us only that ignorance is removed by 'knowledge' (*vidyā*), or 'universal perception' (*saṁyag-darśana*). If this universal perception has been attained, and t ereby the illusory nature of everything that is not soul, and the absolute identity of the soul with Brahman understood, the determining conditions for the earthly existence of the soul are removed. For this earthly existence is itself indeed only an illusory appearance. He who knows 'I am Brahman' has gained emancipation from the *saṁsāra*.

Since Śaṅkara recognizes the unconditional authority of the *Upaniṣads*, he is compelled to take account of their entire contents, which to a considerable extent are in opposition to the doctrine here set forth. He accomplishes this by setting up two systems side by side with one another—(1) the higher or esoteric knowledge (*parā vidyā*), which adopts the metaphysical standpoint, and proclaims the doctrine of the non-dualistic Brahman, as it has just been stated, to be the absolute truth; and (2) the lower or exoteric knowledge (*aparā vidyā*), which takes its stand at the popular empirical point of view, and offers a popularly religious explanation of the universe. While in the 'higher knowledge' the Brahman is free from all attributes and qualities (*nirguṇa*), in the 'lower knowledge' it appears endowed with the attributes of personality (*saguṇa*). It is owing to ignorance that these attributes are ascribed to the Brahman, for men who cannot rise to the height of the metaphysical standpoint need an object of worship. In the lower knowledge, therefore, the Brahman appears as a personal God, who creates and rules the universe, and rewards or punishes men according to their deeds. The universe also is looked upon as real, and the statements of the Upaniṣads with regard to the wandering of the soul through innumerable bodies hold good. The lower knowledge teaches that the soul is constrained by the psychical organs, the bodily senses, the vital principle, and the moral determination, that under such limitations it completes the cycle of metempsychosis, and that by believing worship it may attain to the lower personal Brahman. Union, however, with the lower Brahman, the Brahman of attributes, is merely an inferior temporary lot. Complete deliverance is attainable from the metaphysical point of view solely by the knowledge of the higher Brahman, the Brahman without attributes. Everything that is taught in the lower knowledge is worthless for him who has learnt to know himself as the eternal indivisible Brahman; for he understands that the lower Brahman is a product of ignorance, that qualities are attributed to it merely for the purposes of worship which do not really belong to it, and in the light of the supreme knowledge are seen to be an illusion. He who has attained to this knowledge is no

[1] For a remark regarding his date see art. MĪMĀṀSĀ.

longer led astray by the delusive appearance that surrounds him. In complete indifference towards the course of the world he awaits the end of his life, the continuance of which is explained on exactly the same principles as in the Sāṅkhya (see the art. SĀṄKHYA). At death the wise man is lost in Brahman.

Among the commentators who dissent from Śaṅkara's interpretation of the Vedānta, and who represent one or other of the philosophical and religious standpoints of various sects, the most renowned is Rāmānuja, who lived in the 11th cent. after Christ. Rāmānuja (*q.v.*) in his exposition of the system approximates to the lower exoteric knowledge of Śaṅkara, and as an adherent of the Pāncharātra doctrine introduces into Bādarāyaṇa's treatise views which are nearly related to the Christian standpoint, but are alien to the true Vedānta doctrine. In his view the individual souls are not identical with the supreme soul, *i.e.*, as he represents it, with God, but are separate and distinct as in the Sāṅkhya-Yoga. The cause of their earthly existence is not 'ignorance,' but unbelief; and deliverance is union with God, to be gained not by 'knowledge,' but by believing love (*bhakti*) towards God. In the history of the Vedānta philosophy, therefore, the same theistic tendency makes its appearance which may be observed under the form of the system of Yoga in the further development of the Sāṅkhya doctrine.

LITERATURE.—In his *Bibliography of the Indian Philosophical Systems* (Allahabad, 1859) F. E. Hall enumerates no fewer than 310 Sanskrit works on the Vedānta; and even in the most recent times no year passes without the appearance in all parts of India of numerous treatises on this philosophy written partly in Sanskrit and partly in the vernaculars. The best and most detailed presentation of the Vedānta doctrine as interpreted by Śaṅkara is to be found in P. Deussen's *System des Vedānta*, Leipzig, 1883; cf. also A. Barth, *Religions of India*³, London, 1891; F. Max Müller, *Six Systems of Indian Philosophy*, London, 1899, ch. iv., and *Vedānta Philosophy*, London, 1894; M. Monier-Williams, *Indian Wisdom*⁴, London, 1893; H. Haigh, *Leading Ideas of Hinduism*, London, 1903; P. Deussen, *Philosophie der Upanishads*, Leipzig, 1899, Eng. tr., Edinburgh, 1906; *Vedānta-Sūtras*, with commentaries of Śaṅkara and Rāmānuja, tr. by G. Thibaut in *SBE*, vols. xxxiv. xxxviii. xlviii.; P. Deussen, *Die Sūtras des Vedānta*, tr. Leipzig, 1887; *Sarvadarśana-saṅgraha*, tr. by Cowell and Gough, 2nd ed., London, 1894, ch. xvi.; M. Walleser, *Der ältere Vedānta*, Heidelberg, 1910.

R. GARBE.

VEDDAS.—1. Geographical distribution and mode of life.—The Veddas, the aboriginal inhabitants of Ceylon, are to be regarded as the island representatives of the short, long-headed, pre-Dravidian jungle tribes of India. Formerly they extended over the whole island (for there is no reason to doubt that the Yakkas of the *Mahāvamsa* were Veddas); now the few surviving relatively pure-blooded Veddas who do not practise agriculture are to be found in the park country of Uva, while communities carrying on a rough cultivation, whose members have more foreign blood in their veins, exist in the poorer part of the Eastern Province and that part of the North Central Province known as Tamankaduwa.

At the present day the Veddas may be divided into three classes, viz. forest, village, and coast Veddas, each showing certain characteristic social features. The forest Veddas, reduced in number to a few families in the wildest parts of the island, have alone kept up their old mode of life. Living on game, honey, yams, and fruit, they are still able to collect these in sufficient quantity not only to support life, but to leave a surplus to barter with the 'Moormen' on their annual visits or to take into the nearest Sinhalese village to exchange for iron, cloth, pots, and occasionally rice and coco-nuts. So long as this sort of life is possible, communities are necessarily small and the old mode of habitation in caves and rock shelters persists, but where the country is less wild the Sinhalese have killed down the game to such an extent—even where they have not settled—that the Veddas have been obliged to take to cultivation, and for this purpose they have organized themselves in villages and at the same time have commonly intermarried with the Sinhalese. It is in this way that the second class of Veddas, the village Veddas, have originated; indeed the process has been going on for hundreds of years, and there is evidence that centuries ago there were 'Vedda' communities—*i.e.* communities with enough Vedda blood to be called Veddas by their contemporaries—politically organized and having chiefs who were in constant relation with the Sinhalese court. This process of contact metamorphosis has had as its most striking result the complete loss of the original Vedda (non-Aryan) language, while the identity of the relationship systems of the Veddas and Sinhalese is presumably to be attributed to the same cause. The coast Veddas are Veddas settled in the coastal area of the Eastern Province who have intermarried with the local Tamils, whose physical type they have acquired and whose beliefs they largely share. In the following account the term 'Vedda' must be taken to mean forest Veddas, unless village Veddas are specifically mentioned.

The Veddas have never been metal workers, and, although they have no traditions concerning the use of stone implements, the quartz artefacts described by the cousins Sarasin and others must, at least provisionally, be attributed to them. The iron blades to their arrows, their axe-heads and irons for 'flint and steel' strike-a-lights, are the only metal tools they use. These arrow heads and axes were noted in the 17th cent. by Robert Knox, who mentions the silent trade for metal in exchange for flesh and honey practised by the wilder Veddas.

Apart from their skill as hunters the Veddas have but the bare beginnings of a few arts and crafts. They make no pottery except where they have learnt it from the Sinhalese. Personal ornaments scarcely exist, yet the rocks of some of the caves bear very rough drawings of men and animals and the skin bag in which honey is collected. They are drawn by women and were said to have no religious or other special significance. The Veddas have no musical instruments, but during their dances they frequently beat time with their hands on the abdomen; and C. S. Myers, who has examined phonograph records of their songs, considers that they are simpler in structure than any other native songs hitherto published, and indeed represent the very beginning of melody-building.

2. Social organization.—The Veddas have a clan organization with descent in the female line; the clans are exogamous, though this rule is not strictly adhered to. Two intermarrying clans, the Morane and Unapane, are considered superior to the others, with whom they should not intermarry. Monogamy is the rule and divorce is unknown, the correct marriage being the cross cousin, especially with the daughter of the mother's younger brother. A high standard of sexual morality is maintained in both the married and unmarried. There is close comradeship between a man and his wife's father; an unmarried man assists his mother's brother, his actual or potential father-in-law, in most activities, and this association continues after marriage. A man's *baena* (sister's son, daughter's husband) is always welcome to hospitality in cave or hut, when other relatives would not intrude. Though descent is in the female line, inheritance is in the male line. A Vedda has little personal property, his axe and bow and arrows being his most important possessions, but land, or, more strictly speaking, hunting and fishing rights, the tenancy of certain caves, as well as the right to the combs of the rock bee on definite tracts of land, descend from father to son, or are presented to a son-in-law on his marriage.

The Veddas have no regular chieftainship, but the eldest man of each small group exercises considerable authority, the importance of such men being enhanced by the Sinhalese and other officials, who naturally make a point of dealing with the most intelligent and authoritative member of a group.

3. Religion.—The basis of the Vedda religion is the cult of the dead, and the Vedda point of view can be best appreciated by considering the customs observed when a death takes place. When a man, woman, or child dies, the body is left in the cave or rock shelter in which death from sickness occurred. The body is not washed, dressed, or ornamented in any way, but is allowed to lie in the natural supine position and is covered over with leaves and branches. The cave is then deserted for some years, and, if any bones are left when the Veddas return, they are thrown into the jungle. When an attempt is made to discover the reason for the desertion of the place of death, the usual answer is to the effect that 'if we stayed we should be pelted with stones,' and some Veddas, including the least contaminated, definitely stated that it was the spirit, or *yaka* (fem. *yakini*, pl. *yaku*), of the dead man who would cause stones to rain on anybody staying near the corpse. Although fear of the dead (expressed by leaving the site of death) occurs among all the wilder Veddas, a few old men were by no means confident that all men on their death became *yaku*; no doubt the spirits of important and influential men survived, but whether this applied to quite ordinary individuals was more doubtful, and in one community there was a special ceremony the object of which was to settle this point.

Each Vedda community consists of a small number of families who, since cousin marriage prevails, are doubly related by blood and marriage; the *yaku* of the recently dead, called collectively the Nae Yaku, are supposed to stand towards the surviving members of the group in the light of friends and relatives who, if well treated, will continue to show loving kindness to their survivors, and only if neglected will show disgust and anger by withdrawing their assistance or even becoming actively hostile.[1] Hence it is generally considered necessary to present an offering to the newly dead, usually within a week or two after death, though a few Veddas stated that they would not hold a Nae Yaku ceremony until they specially required the help of the *yaku*, or until misfortune threatened or overtook them. Among most Veddas the offering must consist of cooked rice and coco-nut milk, the food that every Vedda esteems above all others; but betel-leaves and areca-nut are often added, and the oldest survivor of a small group of 'wild' Veddas said that this offering would in the old days have consisted of yams and water, if, as was often the case, coco-nuts and rice could not be obtained.

In each community there is one man, called *kapurale* or *dugganawa*, who has the power and knowledge requisite to call the *yaku*; and in the ceremony of presenting the offering called *Nae Yaku Natanawa* (literally, 'the dancing of the Nae Yaku') this man calls upon the *yaka* of the recently dead man to come and take the offering. The *kapurale* (who may conveniently be spoken of as the shaman) becomes possessed by the *yaka* of the dead man, who speaks through the mouth of the shaman in hoarse, guttural accents, saying that he approves of the offering, that he will assist his kinsfolk in hunting, and often stating the direction in which the next hunting party should go. Besides the shaman, one or more of the near relatives of the dead man may become possessed, but this, though common, is not invariable. The *yaka* leaves the shaman soon after he has promised his favour and success in hunting, the shaman always collapsing as the spirit goes. After the ceremony all the men, women, and children of the group who are present eat the offering, usually on the spot on which the invocation took place, though this is not absolutely necessary. It was clear that this eating of food which had been offered to the *yaku* was an act of communion, and an essential part of the ceremony which was thought to bring health and good fortune; for some communities even anointed the heads of their dogs with the milk of the offering, explaining that this was done because of their value.

Besides the *yaku* of the recently dead there are other important *yaku*, chief among whom are Kande Yaka and his brother Bilindi Yaka. Kande Yaka is the spirit of an ancestor, a mighty hunter in his day; he is invoked to give success in hunting, and during the ceremonial dance given in his honour a realistic pantomime of tracking and killing a deer is performed. Spirits of the dead were believed to go to Kande Yaka and become his attendants, and immediately after death it was necessary for a spirit to resort to Kande Yaka in order to obtain permission to accept offerings from his living relatives, and to obtain power from him to assist them in return for their offerings, or to cause them injury in the event of their bad behaviour. Thus Kande Yaka, who is of especial assistance in hunting, becomes lord of the dead. We have, however, little doubt that to the majority of Veddas Kande Yaka is especially the *yaka* who gives success in hunting, and that his relation to the dead does not leap to their minds on the mention of his name as does the idea of his helpfulness in hunting; for Kande Yaka was essentially a friendly and helpful *yaka*, who, unlike many other *yaku* usually beneficent, never sent sickness; in fact, Kande Yaka the spirit scarcely differs as patron of hunters from Kande Wanniya the mighty hunter, still living and showing kindness and helpfulness towards the people among whom he dwelt.

The Nae Yaku, Kande Yaka, Bilindi Yaka, and certain other *yaku* doubtless belong to the primitive Vedda culture, and to this day these are the important *yaku* among the wilder Veddas. But centuries of contact with Sinhalese and Tamils have led to the recognition of a number of Sinhalese and Tamil dæmons (or gods) as *yaku*. Thus, running roughly parallel with the three conditions of Veddas mentioned in § 1, three stages of development can be recognized in the Vedda religion: (1) the cult of the dead, including the cult of the spirits of recent ancestors, *i.e.* of the Nae Yaku and the *yaku* of certain Veddas who have been long dead and may well be regarded as heroes; the most important of these is Kande Yaka; (2) the cult of foreign spirits, who have become naturalized and have taken the friendly protective nature of the Vedda *yaku*; the cult of the *yaku* of a number of named 'Vedda chiefs' may be considered to belong to this stratum; one of these, Panikkia Yaka, is the canonized spirit of one Panikki Vedda, *i.e.* Panikki the Vedda, who is mentioned in a 16th cent. manuscript; this man, who seems to have been the chief of a group of mixed Vedda and Sinhalese blood, was in fairly intimate contact with the Sinhalese court; (3) the cult of foreign spirits who, though not generally regarded as such, have retained their foreign nature and are, in the main, terrible or even hostile. Another feature of this stratum of thought is the endowment of true Vedda *yaku*

[1] The benevolent nature of the Vedda *yaku* is very noticeable and contrasts with the malignant character of almost all Sinhalese *yaku*. The Sinhalese attitude towards the spirits of the dead generally is fear, while that of the Veddas may be called love; there is certainly a desire for, and belief in, the possibility of companionship and communion with the kindly dead on appropriate occasions.

with foreign attributes. The god Skanda, or Kanda Swami, as he is often called in Ceylon, is worshipped at Kataragam in the south of the island, chiefly by Tamils. There are no Veddas in this district now, but formerly the forests in the neighbourhood were inhabited by Veddas who were known as the Kovil Vanamai Veddas, *i.e.* 'Veddas of the temple precincts,' and they cannot but have been much influenced by the worship at the great temple. In the Eastern province the present writers met some Veddas who were known by the same name, and witnessed a dance performed seven days after the death of a member of the community. Here the *yaka* of the dead man was said to go to 'the Kataragam God' before joining Kande Yaka. Among most village Veddas Indigollae Yaka had taken the place of Kande Yaka; he gives good fortune in hunting and is invoked in the Nae Yaku ceremony. Gale Yaka was also important among village Veddas, but possibly in some localities this is only another name for Indigollae Yaka. Among the wilder Veddas Gale Yake was never mentioned, and Indigollae Yaka, if known at all, was looked upon as a foreign spirit attendant upon Kande Yaka.

The *kiriamma*, literally 'the grandmothers,' are the spirits of Vedda women; many are named and seem to be specially associated with rocks and hill-tops. From one aspect they have a malignant character, for, though they are said to love children, they often steal them and cause their death through sickness. Veddas gathering rock-honey will usually propitiate them by an offering of honey.

The worship of the *yaku* consists essentially of ceremonies during which the shaman or chief performer dances himself into an ecstasy—a condition, we have no doubt, of genuine dissociation of consciousness—during which he is thought to be possessed by the *yaka* whom he invokes. These dances are often pantomimic, and, though in different localities the ceremonial varies, especially as regards elaboration, the ritual of each dance is fixed by tradition. Various objects are proper to certain *yaku*, the most important being the *aude*, a ceremonial representation of an arrow, the blade from 8 to 16 inches long, hafted into a wooden handle considerably shorter than the blade. Ordinary arrows are also used in dances, while for some ceremonies an elaborate set of properties is required. It was noticed that, once an article was used in connexion with the *yaku*, it was not placed on the ground. The *kirikoraha*, literally 'milk bowl,' a vessel filled with the white juice squeezed from coco-nut meat, was a necessary part of the ceremonies in which Kande Yaka, Bilindi Yaka, or the Nae Yaku were invoked, and the main features of the dance centred round this bowl. No attempt is made here to describe any of these ceremonies;[1] it may, however, be mentioned that women never take part in the dances, though they are always present, and may become possessed by the *yaku*.

The method of invocation of the *yaku* is essentially the same in all Vedda ceremonies; an invocation is sung by the shaman and often by the onlookers, while the shaman slowly dances, usually round the offering that has been prepared for the *yaku*. Sometimes the invocations are quite appropriate and consist of straightforward appeals to the *yaka* for help, or recite the deeds and prowess of the *yaka* when he too was a man. But at other times the words seem singularly inappropriate; probably in many of these instances they are merely the remains of old Sinhalese charms that are not only displaced from their proper position and function, but have become so mangled in the process as to have become incomprehensible. As the verses are recited over and over again, the shaman dances more and more quickly, he unties his hair, which falls over his face as he throws his head forward, his voice becomes hoarse, his speech staccato, his movements spasmodic, and his eyes take on a fixed expression; he is then possessed by the *yaka*, and, although he does not lose consciousness completely and can co-ordinate his movements, he does not in his normal condition retain any precise recollection of what he has said and has only a general idea of the movements he has performed. When the shaman is in this condition, another member of the community always follows him, often with hands upon his waist, ready to support him if he should fall. This often happens, the shaman falling backwards apparently unconscious; the condition does not, however, last long, the performer suddenly regaining his feet and continuing to dance. Trembling and shivering—which certainly occurs—is said to mark the entry of the *yaka* into the shaman. When the *yaka* leaves the shaman, the latter always falls back exhausted. Partial collapse during the ceremony does not necessarily indicate the departure of the *yaka*.

The invocations by which the Veddas call upon the *yaku* fall into two main groups: the first, distinguished by their simple form, are straightforward requests to the spirits of the dead to provide game and yams, or to show their loving kindness by partaking of the food provided by their descendants; the second group, embracing a considerable range of beliefs, are all longer and more complicated and often contain references to events which happened before the spiritual beings to whom they are addressed attained their full power as *yaku*. In nearly all the invocations animals and articles of food are not mentioned by their usual name, but described by periphrases. Only the simplest invocations have been selected as examples; many are very complicated and undoubtedly show Sinhalese influence, while the Veddas themselves either give them meanings quite different from those of the texts or have lost the significance entirely and are content to intone sounds almost or quite meaningless to them. The two following invocations (nos. 1 and 2)[1] to the Nae Yaku are from a forest and a village community respectively:

(1) 'Salutation! Salutation! Part of (our) relatives! Multitude of relatives! Having called (you) at the (right) time (we) gave (you) white sambā (rice); (you) ate, (you) drank. Do not think any wrong (of us); we also eat (and) drink.'

(2) 'Our father who went to that world come to this world. Take the rice. Come quickly to place (for us) the sambar deer, to place the spotted deer. Take this betel leaf. Come very quickly. Come quickly my mother's people. Take the rice, take the rock honey, take the betel leaf. To place the sambar deer, to place the spotted deer, come very quickly.'

The next (no. 16) is an invocation to Kande Yaka, and the fourth (no. 24) is sung when collecting rock-honey:

(16) 'King of the Hills, who continues to go from hill to hill, cause rain. (He is) the Wanniyā of the Chief place of the hill, who causes to fall the hoofs of excellent sambar deer, from foot (print) to foot (print), from Rērannē Damanē (the grass plain of teals) to Kandē Damanē (the grass plain of the hill).'

(24) 'Lady New Goddess, (you) must show (me) a bee-hive to-day. Having chopped (it out) I will hide (it) and go.'

As already stated, possession by the *yaka* is to be considered as due to a dissociation of personality; the traditional movements, words, and music all tend to bring about a more or less automatic condition which seems to be more easily induced the longer the practitioner has been shamanizing Nor must the somewhat prolonged training of the shaman be forgotten. The present writers are convinced that there is no trickery about these ceremonies.

The shaman invoking a *yaka* holds or exhibits the special object (*e.g.*, the *aude*) proper to that *yaka*, and it seemed to be thought that the *yaka* first comes to this and then enters the body of the shaman. Each *yaka* has his traditional mode of behaviour. The shaman possessed by Kande Yaka goes through the pantomime of tracking and killing sambar deer; Bambura Yaka spears a wild boar and is wounded by it before he succeeds in killing it; Dola Yaka smokes out rock-bees' nests and collects the honey. These pantomimes are often extremely dramatic. The *yaku* examine the offerings set out for them, and, if favourable, express approval, some straightway prophesying

[1] See for these C. G. and B. Z. Seligman, *The Veddas.*

[1] The numbers preceding the invocations here given refer to those in ch. x. of the present writers' monograph, where all the invocations collected are printed and their meaning discussed.

good hunting (each in his own department); for, though Kande Yaka is patron of all food supplies, there are other *yaku* each of whom is separately invoked for help in getting yams, rock-honey, and tree-honey. The *yaku* have their methods of showing approval of the offerings; usually they scatter some of the food, sometimes they feed a favoured member of the community or place leaves dipped in the sacred food upon his chest, or, putting his arms on his shoulders, the shaman, gasping and quivering, delivers a message of good omen from the *yaku*. Sometimes a *yaka* asks why he has been called. Is it because any one is sick? And, if any one is brought forward, he will feed him or anoint him with sacred food which is thought to cure the sickness.

The manifest object of most ceremonies is to obtain food, but there is no suggestion that any of them are performed to increase the food supply, as are the *intichiuma* ceremonies of Australia. They are also performed to cure sickness, and it is in this connexion that the *Pata Yaku* ceremony may be mentioned. This ceremony is held for a pregnant woman, that she may have safe delivery. Masses of bast are used on all the various properties necessary for the *yaku*; hence the name, signifying 'bark *yaku*.' No reason could be given for any figure in the dance, nor was there any known tradition connected with it, as was the case with most other ceremonies. A noticeable feature of the dance was that it was necessary for the woman's father to take part in it and that he dropped an arrow on the ground several times and leapt over it. Certain Sinhalese demons known as the Pata Yaku personify disease, but these have no connexion with bast, and it is impossible to say why the Pata Yaku should have been taken over from the Sinhalese.

Apart from the tendency, already mentioned, of certain *yaku* to be associated with hill-tops, no definite locality is considered their home; on the other hand, they are certainly not thought of as being habitually in close proximity with the living. Magical practices play a very small part in the life of the Veddas; their charms we believe to have been taken over from the Sinhalese, and it certainly is no exaggeration to say that the Vedda conception of the supernatural is embodied in their *yaku* beliefs, to whose influence usual or unusual events are alike attributed. No creation traditions or myths referring to the natural features of the country could be discovered among the wilder groups of Veddas.

LITERATURE.—John Bailey, 'Wild Tribes of the Veddahs of Ceylon,' *TES*, new ser., ii. [1863]; E. Deschamps, *Au Pays des Veddas: Ceylan*, Paris, 1892; Robert Knox, *An Historical Relation of Ceylon*, London, 1681; H. Nevill, *Taprobanian*, Bombay, 1887, i.; H. Parker, *Ancient Ceylon*, London, 1909; L. Rutimeyer, 'Die Nilgalaweddas in Ceylon,' *Globus*, lxxxiii. [1903]; P. and F. Sarasin, *Die Weddas von Ceylon*, Wiesbaden, 1892; C. G. and Brenda Z. Seligman, *The Veddas*, Cambridge, 1911.

C. G. and B. Z. SELIGMAN.

VEDIC RELIGION.—DEFINITIONS.—With a view to avoiding confusion, it is advisable to define at the outset the sense in which each of the three terms 'religion,' 'mythology,' and 'magic' (witchcraft) is to be employed in the present article. Religion means, on the one hand, the body of beliefs entertained by men regarding the divine or supernatural powers, and, on the other, that sense of dependence on those powers which is expressed by word in the form of prayer and praise, or by act in the form of ritual and sacrifice. Mythology means the body of myths or stories which give an account of gods and heroes, describing their origin and surroundings, their deeds and activities. Mythology is thus included in, though not coextensive with, that aspect of religion which is concerned with belief. Magic means that body of practices which, instead of seeking to gain the goodwill of divine, beneficent powers by acts of worship, is largely directed against demoniac and hostile agencies, and aims at affecting the course of things directly, without the intervention of deities. Magic as such, being essentially different from religion and representing a more primitive stage of belief, is excluded from the scope of this article except where, as is sometimes the case, it is inextricably mixed up with religious ritual.

1. MEANING AND IMPORTANCE OF THE SUBJECT.

By the general term 'Vedic religion' is here understood the religion of the Vedic period of Indian literature, which extends from some time after the Aryan immigration into the north-west of India, that is, from at least as early as B.C. 1300, down to about B.C. 200.

Vedic religion is peculiarly important as a branch of study. It is not only the earliest body of religious beliefs preserved in a literary form, but it also represents a more primitive phase of thought than is recorded in any other literature. It can, moreover, be traced step by step through the various stages of its development. It is, finally, the source of the religion of the modern Hindus, which can thus be historically followed up to its origin throughout a period of well over 3000 years. As a natural result of its value to the investigator of religious thought in general, the study of Vedic religion gave birth, in the latter half of the 19th cent., to the sciences of Comparative Mythology and Comparative Religion.

2. STAGES OF VEDIC RELIGION.

Three main successive stages may be clearly distinguished in the religion which is recorded in three corresponding phases of Vedic literature, viz. in (*a*) the Vedas, (*b*) the Brāhmaṇas together with the Sūtras, (*c*) the Upaniṣads.

(*a*) The religion of the four **Vedas**, regarded as a whole, is concerned with the worship of gods largely representing personifications of the powers of nature; the propitiation of demoniac beings comes only to a limited extent within its sphere.

The oldest and most important of the four Vedas, the Rigveda, from which considerable portions of the others are borrowed, is a collection of metrical hymns containing a large mythological element. These hymns are mainly invocations of the gods meant to accompany the oblation of Soma juice and the fire sacrifice of melted butter. The polytheism of this Veda assumes in its latest hymns a pantheistic colouring. Only a very few of its hymns are connected with witchcraft.

The hymns of the Atharvaveda, on the other hand, consist largely of spells meant for magical application, while their religion is pronounced pantheism.

The contents of the two other Vedas are entirely sacrificial in purpose. The Sāmaveda is almost exclusively composed of verses borrowed from the Rigveda to be applied in the ritual of the Soma sacrifice. The Yajurveda consists of ritual formulas, largely in prose, which, not being directly addressed to the gods, are practically of a magical type. The religious phase which it represents is, in spirit, identical with that of the Brāhmaṇas.

(*b*) The **Brāhmaṇas** are discursive theological treatises in prose dealing with the Vedic ritual; while the Sūtras, text-books composed in a very concise style, largely condense and systematize the contents of the Brāhmaṇas or add new material on domestic and everyday observances. The main difference in the mythology of the Brāhmaṇas, as compared with the Rigveda, is their recognition of a father-god as chief of the deities; while the general character of their religious belief is explicit pantheism. As to cult, they represent a ritual system which, in complexity of detail, far surpasses anything the world has elsewhere known.

(*c*) Though generally forming a part of the Brāhmaṇas, as a continuation of their speculative side, the **Upaniṣads** really represent a new religion which is in virtual opposition to their ritual or practical side. This new, purely pantheistic religion is dominated by the doctrine of transmigration, a doctrine unknown to the Vedas, and only incipient in one of the Brāhmaṇas. A world-soul takes the place of the father-god of the Brāhmaṇas. Its nature is the main object of speculation; and the identity with it of the individual soul is the great fundamental doctrine of the Upaniṣads. The religious aim now is no longer the obtaining of earthly and heavenly happiness by sacrificing correctly to the gods, but the release, as a result of true knowledge, from re-birth by absorption in the world-soul.

3. Vedic Religious Beliefs.

The following account of Vedic beliefs, which are almost entirely mythological, starts from the statements of the Rigveda, to which the subsequent developments of the Vedic period are, if of sufficient importance, in each case added.

(*a*) Cosmogonic beliefs.—Judged by their fragmentary references to the origin of the world, the poets of the Rigveda usually regarded it as having been mechanically produced like a building, the material being wood, and heaven and earth being supported by posts. The agents in the construction are regularly either the gods in general or various individual gods.

The last book of the Rigveda, however, contains a few cosmogonic hymns which represent other views. One of these (x. 90), though among the latest of the period, preserves a very primitive belief. It accounts for the origin of the world from the body of a primeval giant, whom the gods sacrificed. His head became the sky, his navel the air, and his feet the earth; while from his various members the four castes were produced. This being, called Puruṣa, or man, and interpreted pantheistically in the hymn itself as 'all this, both what has become and what shall be,' reappears as the world-soul in the Atharvaveda and the Upaniṣads.

There are, again, two cosmogonic hymns of the Rigveda which explain the origin of the universe, philosophically rather than mythologically, as a kind of evolution of the existent (*sat*) from the non-existent (*asat*). In another hymn of the same type, the agency of a creator (*dhātā*) is, after the evolution of the ocean through heat (*tapas*), introduced to produce in succession sun and moon, heaven and earth, air and ether. There is also a hymn (x. 121) in which heaven and earth and the great waters are described as the creation of Hiraṇya-garbha, the golden germ, who is said to have arisen in the beginning, to be the one god above all gods, and is finally invoked as Prajāpati, lord of all created things. It is to be noted that in the cosmogonic hymns the waters are commonly thought of as coming into existence first. In the Atharvaveda the all-god appears as a creator under several new names, especially as Skambha, 'support'; also as Prāṇa, 'breath'; Kāma, 'desire,' and others.

The cosmogony of the Brāhmaṇas requires the agency of the creator Prajāpati, who is not, however, always the starting-point. Sometimes the waters come first: on them floats the golden germ (*hiraṇya-garbha*), from which arises the spirit that produces the universe. This contradiction is due to the theories of evolution and of creation being combined. One cosmogonic myth of the Brāhmaṇas describes how the submerged earth was raised by a boar. The latter in post-Vedic mythology developed into an *avatār* of Viṣṇu.

(*b*) Theogonic beliefs. — Heaven and earth are ordinarily regarded in the Rigveda as the parents of the gods in general. It is only very rarely that other gods are spoken of as parents of the rest; thus Dawn is once said to be the mother of the gods, and both Brahmaṇaspati and Soma are mentioned as their father. The cosmogonic hymns connect the origin of the gods chiefly with the element of water; but one of them describes the gods as born after the creation of the universe.

(*c*) Origin of man.—The Vedic beliefs regarding the origin of the human race were somewhat fluctuating; the ultimate source of man was, however, always thought to be divine. Agni, the god of fire, is at least once said to have begotten the race of men, and certain families of seers are regarded as independently descended through their founders from the gods. Usually, however, the human race is traced to a first man, either Manu or Yama, both of whom are sons of Vivasvat, a solar deity.

4. The Vedic Gods.

The Vedic Indian believed in the existence of a large number of supernatural beings, varying in character and power. They comprise two main groups: on the one hand, gods who are almost exclusively benevolent and receive worship; on the other hand, demons who are hostile and whose operations have to be counteracted by the help of the gods or by ritual expedients. The divine powers, again, may be classed as higher gods, whose power pervades the world and controls the great phenomena of nature; and as lesser divinities, whose activities are restricted to a limited sphere or are conducted on a smaller scale: for instance, tutelary deities and elves. The divine nature is further shared by men of days gone by: ancient heroes who are associated with the deeds of the gods, and ancestors who live with the gods and receive worship like them. Finally, at the bottom of the scale, we find many inanimate objects and implements which are deified, being invoked and worshipped like divine beings.

A. *The Higher Gods.*

The gods are usually stated in the Rigveda and Atharvaveda, as well as the Brāhmaṇas, to be thirty-three in number; but there are occasional deviations or inconsistencies in regard to this belief. Troops of deities, such as the storm-gods, are, of course, not regarded as included in this number. The thirty-three are, in the Rigveda, divided into three groups of eleven, distributed in earth, air, and heaven, the three divisions of the universe. These three groups, now containing eight, eleven, and twelve deities respectively, appear in the Brāhmaṇas under the name of Vasus, Rudras, and Adityas.

Gods originally mortal.—The gods, as has already been shown, were believed to have had a beginning. But they were not thought to have all come into being at the same time; for the Rigveda occasionally refers to earlier gods, and the Atharvaveda speaks of ten gods as having existed before the rest. Certain deities are, moreover, described as the offspring of others. The Atharvaveda and the Brāhmaṇas also expressly state that the gods were originally mortal, adding that they overcame death by the practice of austerity. The same thing is implied in the Rigveda, where the gods are said to have acquired immortality by drinking Soma or by receiving it as a gift from Agni and Savitṛ. In the post-Vedic view, the immortality of the gods was limited to a cosmic age.

Their physical attributes.—The gods of the Veda are anthropomorphic in appearance. The parts of their bodies, which are frequently mentioned, are in many cases, however, little more than figurative illustrations of the phenomena of nature represented by the deity. Thus the arms of the sun are nothing more than his rays; and the tongue and limbs of Agni merely denote his flames. Some of the gods appear equipped as warriors, especially Indra; others are described as priests, especially Agni and Bṛhaspati. All of them drive through the air in luminous cars, drawn chiefly by steeds, but sometimes by other animals.

Their food.—The favourite food of men is also that of the gods, consisting of milk, butter, grain, and the flesh of sheep, goats, and cattle. It is offered to them in the sacrifice; this is either conveyed to them in heaven by the god of fire, or they come in their cars to partake of it on the litter of grass prepared for their reception. Their favourite beverage is the exhilarating juice of the Soma plant.

Their abode.—The home of the gods is described as heaven, the third heaven, or the highest step of Viṣṇu (the zenith), where, cheered by draughts of Soma, they live a life of bliss.

Their attributes.—The most prominent characteristic of the Vedic gods is power; for they are constantly described as 'great' and 'mighty.' They regulate the order of nature and vanquish the great powers of evil. They hold sway over all creatures: no one can thwart their ordinances or live beyond the time they appoint; and the fulfilment of wishes is dependent on them. Their omniscience, which is restricted within narrow limits, is seldom referred to. It is an attribute which is emphasized in the case of Varuṇa only. The Vedic gods are benevolent beings who bestow prosperity on mankind, the only one in whom injurious traits appear being Rudra. They are, moreover, moral according to the standard of an early stage of civilization. They are described as 'true' and 'not deceitful,' being friends and protectors of the honest and righteous, but punishing sin and guilt. They are not, however, above employing craft against the hostile, and occasionally practise deceit even without the justification of a good end.

Since, in most cases, the Vedic gods have not yet become dissociated from the physical phenomena which they represent, their figures are indefinite in outline and deficient in individuality. Having many features, such as power, brilliance, benevolence and wisdom in common with others, each god exhibits very few distinctive attributes. This vagueness is further increased by the practice of invoking deities in pairs—a practice making both gods share characteristics properly belonging to one alone. When nearly every power can thus be attributed to every god, the identification of one deity with another becomes easy. There are, in fact, several such identifications in the Rigveda. The idea is even found in more than one late passage that various deities are but different forms of a single divine being. This idea, however, never developed into monotheism, for none of the regular sacrifices in the Vedic period were offered to a single god. Finally, in other late hymns of the Rigveda, we find the deities Aditi and Prajāpati identified not only with all the gods, but with nature as well. This brings us to the beginning of that pantheism which became characteristic of later Indian thought.

Henotheism.—The practice of invoking individual gods as the highest, frequent even in the older parts of the Rigveda, gave rise to Max Müller's theory of the 'henotheism' or 'kathenotheism' of that Veda, which he defines as 'the belief in individual gods alternately regarded as the highest,' the god addressed being for the moment treated as an independent and supreme deity, alone present to the mind. Criticism has, however, shown that we have here only to do with an exaggerated form of praise which does not amount to a distinct type of religious thought.

The Vedic gods may most conveniently be classified as deities of heaven, air, and earth, according to the threefold division suggested by the Rigveda itself.

1. CELESTIAL GODS.—The historically oldest among the gods of the sky, as going back to the Indo-European period and identical with the Greek Zeus, is **Dyaus**, Heaven. The personification here hardly went beyond the notion of paternity (Dyauṣ pitar = Ζεῦ πάτερ, Jūp-piter). Dyaus is generally coupled with Pṛthivī, Earth, when the two are celebrated as universal parents. He is once described as armed with a bolt, and, in another passage, as smiling through the clouds in allusion to the lightening sky.

Another and much more prominent deity of the sky is **Varuṇa**, the greatest of the Vedic gods beside Indra. He, too, dates from an earlier period, for in name he is probably identical with the Greek Οὐρανός, and in character he is allied to the Avestic Ahura Mazda. Varuṇa is the chief upholder of physical and moral order (*ṛta*). By his ordinance heaven and earth are held apart; he regulates the course of sun, moon, and stars; he causes the rivers to flow and the clouds to fertilize the earth with rain. Omniscient, he witnesses men's truth and falsehood. He is angry with sinners, whom he severely punishes, binding them with his fetters. But he is gracious to the penitent, releasing men not only from their own sins, but from those committed by their fathers. The prayer for forgiveness of guilt is characteristic of the Varuṇa hymns, which in general are the most exalted and ethical in the Veda. With the development of Prajāpati as creator and supreme god in the later Vedas, the importance of Varuṇa waned, till in the post-Vedic period he retained only the dominion of the waters as god of the sea.

Five gods represent various aspects of solar activity. The oldest of these, **Mitra**, the 'friend,' probably a personification of the sun's beneficent power, is an inheritance from the Indo-Iranian period, being identical with the Persian sun-god Mithra, whose cult became so widely diffused in the Roman empire during the 3rd and 4th centuries A.D. In the Rigveda he has almost entirely lost his individuality, and is hardly ever invoked except in association with Varuṇa.

Sūrya, etymologically allied to the Greek Ἥλιος is the most concrete of the solar deities, this being the regular name of the luminary. He is the husband of Dawn. His car, often referred to, is generally described as drawn by seven steeds. He is the soul of all that moves or is fixed, all creatures depending on him. He prolongs life, and drives away disease. His eye and his all-seeing power are often spoken of; and he is besought to declare men sinless to Mitra and Varuṇa.

Savitṛ, the 'stimulator,' represents the quickening activity of the sun. Bestowing immortality on the gods as well as length of life on man, he also conducts the spirits of the dead to where the righteous dwell. To him is addressed the most famous stanza of the Rigveda (iii. 62. 10), with which he was in ancient times invoked at the beginning of Vedic study, and which is still repeated by every orthodox Brāhman in his morning prayers. It is called the *Sāvitrī* from the deity, or the *Gāyatrī* from the metre:

> 'May we attain that excellent
> Glory of Savitṛ the god,
> That he may stimulate our thoughts.'

Pūṣan, the 'prosperer,' personifying probably the bountiful power of the sun, appears chiefly as a pastoral deity, who protects cattle and guides them with his goad. He is a guardian of paths; and, knowing the ways of heaven, he conducts the dead to the abode of the fathers.

Though occupying quite a subordinate position in the Rigveda, and less frequently invoked than the four gods just mentioned, Viṣṇu is historically the most important of the solar deities; for he has become one of the two great gods of modern Hinduism. His three strides, typifying doubtless the course of the sun through the three divisions of the universe, constitute the central feature in his mythology. His highest step is heaven, the abode of the gods. He is frequently said to have taken his three strides for the benefit of man. This general trait is illustrated by the Brāhmaṇa myth in which Viṣṇu assumes the form of a dwarf as an artifice to recover the earth, now in possession of demons, by taking his three strides. Viṣṇu's characteristic benevolence was in post-Vedic mythology further developed in the doctrine of his *avatārs* ('descents' to earth), or incarnations for the good of humanity.

Uṣas (cognate to Ἠώς and *Aurora*), goddess of dawn, the daughter of Dyaus, is the only female deity invoked with frequency in the Rigveda, and is the most graceful creation of the Vedic seers. Being a poetical rather than a religious figure, she did not, like the other gods, receive a share in the Soma offering.

The **Aśvins** ('lords of steeds'), twin gods of morning, sons of Dyaus, eternally young and handsome, are addressed in many hymns. They very frequently receive the epithet *nāsatya*, 'true.' Uṣas is born at the yoking of their car, on which their spouse Sūryā, daughter of the sun, accompanies them. They are characteristically succouring deities. Delivering from distress in general and from shipwreck in particular, they are also divine physicians. They have several traits in common with the two famous horsemen of Greek mythology, the Διόσκουροι, sons of Zeus and brothers of Helen. The origin of these twin deities is obscure; it is perhaps most likely that they represent either the twilight, half dark, half light, or the morning and evening star.

2. ATMOSPHERIC GODS.—**Indra** is the dominant deity in the aerial sphere. While Varuṇa is the great moral ruler, Indra is the mighty warrior. Indra is, indeed, the favourite and national god of the Vedic Indian. An indication of this is the fact that more than one-fourth of the Rigveda is devoted to his praise. He is a mythological creation of an earlier period; for Indra is a demon in the Avesta. Though he is more anthropomorphic than any other Vedic god, his original character is still tolerably clear. He is primarily the thunder-god, and his conquest of the demon Vṛtra is the central feature of the mythology which surrounds him. Henee *Vṛtra-han*, 'slayer of Vṛtra,' is his chief and specific epithet. Armed with his bolt (*vajra*), elated by copious draughts of Soma, and aided by the Maruts, or storm-gods, Indra engages in the fray. The fight is terrific; for heaven and earth tremble with fear as the conflict rages. The constant repetition of the combat corresponds to the perpetual renewal of the phenomena of the thunderstorm which underlie the myth. The result of the victory is the release of the waters for man and the recovery of the light of the sun. Indra thus became a god of battle whose aid is constantly invoked in conflicts with earthly foes. He is often described as the protector of the Aryan colour, and vanquisher of the black race. One of his commonest epithets is *śakra*, the 'mighty one' (which in the Pāli form of Sakka became his regular name in Buddhist literature). Certain immoral traits appear in Indra's character. He occasionally indulges in acts of capricious violence, such as slaying his father or shattering the car of Dawn. He is greatly addicted to Soma, which he drinks in enormous quantities to stimulate him in his warlike exploits. One entire hymn of the Rigveda (x. 119) consists of a monologue in which Indra, inebriated with Soma, boasts of his greatness and power. While Varuṇa, after the period of the Rigveda, gradually sank into obscurity, Indra in the Brāhmaṇas became the chief of the Indian heaven (*svarga*), and even maintained this position in the period of the Purāṇas, though, of course, subordinate to the trinity Brahmā-Viṣṇu-Śiva.

Three of the less important deities of the air are connected with lightning. **Trita**, a somewhat obscure god with the epithet *āptya*, 'watery,' mentioned only in detached verses of the Rigveda, seems to represent the 'third' (*tritas* = Greek τρίτος) form of fire. He goes back to the Indo-Iranian period, both his name and his epithet occurring in the Avesta. In the Rigveda he appears as a presser of Soma, who aids Indra in slaying Vṛtra and the three-headed demon Viśvarūpa, or performs the latter exploit himself. He kindles the celestial fire, and even appears as a form of fire. His home is hidden and remote. As almost identical in origin with Indra, he was ousted by the latter at an early period. In the Brāhmaṇas he appears as one of three sons of Agni, the other two being Ekata and Dvita. In the epic poetry Trita survives only as the name of a human seer.

Apāṃ napāt, 'son of waters,' also goes back to the Indo-Iranian period. Rarely mentioned in the Rigveda, he is described as clothed in lightning and shining without fuel in the waters. He thus represents the lightning form of fire as produced from the thundercloud.

Mātariśvan is referred to only in scattered verses of the Rigveda as a divine being who (like the Greek Prometheus) brought down the hidden fire from heaven to earth. He was originally, in all likelihood, conceived as an aerial form of Agni, with whom he is sometimes actually identified. His character then underwent a transformation; for in the later Vedas, the Brāhmaṇas, and the post-Vedic literature he appears as a wind-god.

It is somewhat remarkable that **Rudra**, the early form of the post-Vedic Śiva, who in the Rigveda occupies a very subordinate position, like that of Viṣṇu, should have risen to parallel pre-eminence with Viṣṇu in a later age. Rudra is usually described as armed with bow and arrows, but sometimes he appears with a thunderbolt and lightning shaft. He is fierce and destructive like a wild beast, being 'the ruddy boar of heaven.' The most striking feature of the hymns addressed to him is fear of his terrible shafts and deprecation of his wrath. For he slays men and cattle, and assails with disease. He is, indeed, the one malignant deity of the Vedas. His malevolence, however, unlike that of a demon, is not the only side of his character. For he is a healer as well as a destroyer, being even lauded as the greatest of physicians. Thus he is often besought not only to preserve from calamity, but to bestow welfare on man and beast. The euphemistic epithet **Śiva**, 'auspicious,' which begins to be applied to him in the Rigveda, grows more frequent in the later Vedas, till it finally becomes his regular name in post-Vedic mythology. With the increasing use of this epithet, the malevolence of Rudra becomes more pronounced in the later Vedas. The White Yajurveda, which adds various disgraceful attributes, furnishes the transition to the terrific and repulsive Śiva of Hindu mythology. The exact basis of Rudra is somewhat obscure; but the inference from the evidence of the Rigveda seems to be justified that he originally represented the destructive agency of the thunderstorm. His uncanny and baleful traits have, however, also been explained as starting from the conception of a deity of mountain and forest whence storm and disease attack man and beast.

The sons of Rudra and Pṛśni (the 'mottled' cloud-cow) are the **Maruts**, or storm-gods, also often called Rudras, a group of thrice seven or thrice sixty deities, the constant allies of Indra in his conflicts. They are described as like fires at their birth, and as 'born from the laughter of lightning.' They are young warriors, armed with spears and battle-axes, wearing helmets and decked with golden ornaments. Their headlong course is often graphically depicted. They ride on golden cars which gleam with lightning: with their fellies they rend the mountains and shatter the lordly trees of the forest. They share to some extent the destructive as well as the beneficent traits of their father Rudra. Their lightning-bolt slays men and kine. But they also bring healing remedies, apparently the rains with which they fertilize the earth.

The god of wind is not a prominent deity in the Rigveda. Under the more anthropomorphic form of **Vāyu** he is chiefly associated with Indra. As **Vāta** (the ordinary name of wind), he is described in a more concrete manner (often in connexion with the verb *vā*, 'to blow,' from which the word is derived), being coupled only with the less anthropomorphic god Parjanya.

A personification of the rain-cloud is **Parjanya**, son of Dyaus. He is not a prominent deity, being invoked in only three hymns of the Rigveda, which, however, describe his activity in the rainstorm very vividly. He quickens the earth with rain, causing abundant vegetation to spring up. He also bestows fertility on the animal world. He thus comes to be spoken of as 'our divine father.'

The waters, **Āpaḥ**, are praised as divine powers in four hymns of the Rigveda. They are celestial, abiding in the home of the gods. The aerial waters are the mothers of one of the forms of Agni, Apāṃ napāt, son of waters. But, as flowing in channels and having the sea for their goal, the waters are also terrestrial (cf. 3). They are young wives, mothers, goddesses who bestow boons and come to the sacrifice. They not only bear away defilement, but cleanse from moral guilt, the sins of violence, cursing, and lying. They also grant remedies, healing, long life, and immortality.

3. TERRESTRIAL DEITIES.—Rivers are not infrequently personified and invoked in the Rigveda. Thus the **Sindhu** (Indus) is celebrated as a goddess in one hymn, and the **Vipāś** (Biās) and **Sutudrī** (Sutlej), sister streams of the Panjāb, in another. The most important and oftenest lauded is, however, the **Sarasvatī**. Though the personification goes much further here than in the case of other streams, the connexion of the goddess with the river is never lost sight of in the Rigveda. In the Brāhmaṇas, Sarasvatī has become identified with the goddess of speech, and in Hindu mythology she appears further modified as the goddess of eloquence and wisdom, invoked as a Muse, and regarded as the wife of Brahmā.

Earth, or **Pṛthivī**, the broad, nearly always associated with Dyaus, is often spoken of as a mother. The personification is rudimentary, the attributes of the goddess being chiefly those of the physical earth.

By far the most important of the terrestrial deities is **Agni**, god of fire. Next to Indra, he is the most frequently invoked of the Vedic gods, being celebrated in about one-fifth of the hymns of the Rigveda. It is only natural that the personification of the sacrificial fire, the centre of the Vedic ritual, should engross the thoughts of the poets to such an extent. *Agni-s* (Lat. *igni-s*) being also the ordinary name for fire, the anthropomorphism has not proceeded far. The bodily parts of the god have an unmistakable connexion with the various aspects of the sacrificial fire. Thus Agni is called 'butter-backed,' 'butter-faced,' and 'butter-haired,' with reference to the oblation of *ghī* (*ghṛta*) cast on the flames. His teeth, jaws, and tongues are associated with the action of burning. Agni is borne on a brilliant car, drawn by two or more steeds, which he yokes to bring the gods, for he is the charioteer of the sacrifice.

Beyond his sacrificial activities, little is said about the deeds of Agni. It is otherwise mainly his various births, forms, and abodes that occupy the thoughts of the Vedic poets. Agni is usually called the son of Dyaus and Pṛthivī, sometimes also the offspring of Tvaṣṭṛ and the waters. But owing to the daily production of Agni from the two firesticks, they, too, are his parents. He is then a newborn infant, also called 'son of strength' because of the powerful friction required to kindle the flame. He wakes at dawn, for the fire is lit every morning. He is thus the youngest of the gods; but he is also old, having conducted the first sacrifice.

As not only terrestrial, but sprung from the aerial waters and having been brought from heaven, Agni is often spoken of as having a triple character. This threefold Agni is the earliest Indian trinity, probably the prototype not only of the later Rigvedic triad of Sun, Wind, Fire, connected with the three divisions of the universe, but also of the triad Sun, Indra, Fire, which, though not Rigvedic, is still ancient. There may be a historical connexion between this triad and the conception of the later Hindu trinity of Brahmā - Viṣṇu - Śiva. This triad of fires may, further, have suggested, and would explain, the division of a single sacrificial fire into the three which form an essential feature in the cult of the Brāhmaṇas.

As kindled in innumerable dwellings, Agni is also said to have many births. He assumes various divine forms and has many names; in him are comprehended all the gods, whom he surrounds as a felly the spokes. Though scattered in many places, he is one and the same king. It was probably from such speculations on the nature of Agni that an advance was made to the conception of a unity pervading the many manifestations of the divine which has been noted above (p. 603a).

As the deity most intimately associated with the everyday life of man, Agni is spoken of as an immortal who has taken up his abode among mortals in human dwellings, and is constantly called a 'guest' and 'lord of the house.' Being the conductor of the sacrifice as well as the summoner of the gods, he is very frequently described as a 'messenger,' who moves between heaven and earth. Agni is, however, most characteristically called a 'priest,' usually by the generic terms *ṛtvij* and *vipra*; or specifically 'domestic priest' (*purohita*), oftenest of all 'invoker' or 'chief priest' (*hotṛ*). He is, in fact, the great priest among the Vedic gods, as Indra is the great warrior. Agni is a mighty benefactor of his worshippers, whose enemies he consumes. The benefits which he confers are chiefly domestic welfare and general prosperity, while those which Indra grants are mostly the rewards of victory.

Agni is frequently spoken of in the Rigveda as a 'goblin-slayer,' a trait surviving from what is perhaps the oldest phase of the cult of fire as warding off the attack of evil spirits.

Since the Soma sacrifice forms, by the side of fire-worship, the other main feature in the ritual of the Rigveda, the personification of the juice of the Soma plant is naturally one of its most prominent deities. Judged by the number of hymns addressed to him, **Soma** is third in importance among the Vedic gods, coming next to Agni from this point of view. Since the plant and the juice are constantly before the eyes of the priests as they sing the praises of the god, the personification is vague. The imagination of the poets dwells chiefly on the processes of pressing and straining, which it overlays with chaotic imagery and mystical fancies of almost infinite variety.

As the most important of herbs, Soma is spoken of as 'lord of plants' or as their king, being also designated 'lord of the forest.' There are many references to Soma growing on the mountains. Heaven, however, is regarded as its true and original home; and the myth of its having been brought down to earth by an eagle (*śyena*) is often alluded to.

The mental stimulation produced by drinking Soma is expressed by one of the poets of the Rigveda with the words: 'We have drunk Soma, we have become immortal, we have entered into light, we have known the gods.' Its exhilarating power is, however, dwelt upon chiefly in connexion with Indra, whom it inspires in his mighty conflicts with the aerial demons. Soma thus came to be regarded as a divine drink, which bestowed immortality on the gods, being called *amṛta* (allied to Greek ἀμβροσία), the 'immortal' draught. Hence the god Soma places his worshipper in the imperishable world of eternal light and glory, making him immortal where Yama dwells. Healing power is similarly attributed to Soma. The juice is medicine for the ailing man, and the god heals the sick, making the blind to see and the lame to walk.

In some of the latest hymns of the Rigveda, Soma begins to be somewhat obscurely identified with the moon. In the Atharvaveda and the Yajurveda this identification is explicit in several passages. It is already a commonplace in the Brāhmaṇas, which explain the waning of the moon as due to the gods and fathers consuming the ambrosia of which it consists. One of the Upaniṣads, moreover, states that the moon is king Soma, the food of the gods, and is drunk up by them. In post-Vedic literature, finally, Soma is a regular name of the moon. This somewhat remarkable coalescence of Soma with the moon must have started from the exaggerated terms in which the poets of the Rigveda describe the celestial nature and brilliance of Soma. It was doubtless furthered by the imagery in which the poets of the Rigveda indulged. Thus Soma is spoken of as swelling in the waters (with which it was mixed), and Soma in the bowls is once even compared to the moon in the waters. Soma is often called *Indu*, or 'drop.' This word shared the fate of Soma, also becoming a regular name of the moon in the post-Vedic period.

Soma must already have been an important feature in both the mythology and the cult of the Indo-Iranian period; for the Avestan Haoma shows many points of agreement, in both directions, with the Soma of the Rigveda.

4. ABSTRACT DEITIES.—One result of the advance of thought, during the period of the Rigveda, from the concrete towards the abstract was the creation of abstract deities. Of the two classes which may be distinguished, the earlier and more numerous one seems to have started from epithets which were applicable to one or more older deities, but which came to acquire an independent value, as the want of a god exercising the particular activity in question began to be felt. When the type was once established, the creation of direct abstractions of this kind became possible. We have here names denoting either an agent (formed with the suffix *-tṛ* or *-tar*, the Lat. and Gr. *-tor*, *-ter*), such as Dhātṛ, 'creator,' or an attribute, such as Prajāpati, 'lord of creatures.' The *agent gods* are nearly all of rare occurrence, appearing for the most part in the latest book of the Rigveda. Thus Dhātṛ, an epithet of Indra and Viśvakarman, appears also as an independent deity who creates heaven and earth, sun and moon. In the post-Vedic period Dhātṛ has become one of the regular names of the creator and preserver of the world. Of rarer occurrence are **Vidhātṛ**, the 'disposer,' **Dhartṛ**, the 'supporter,' **Trātṛ**, the 'protector,' and **Netṛ**, the 'leader.' The only agent god mentioned with any frequency in the Rigveda is **Tvaṣṭṛ**, the 'fashioner' or 'artificer,' though no hymn is addressed to him. He is the most skilful of workmen, having among other things fashioned the bolt of Indra, and a new drinking-cup for the gods. He shapes the form of beings and presides over generation. He is a guardian of Soma, which is called the 'mead of Tvaṣṭṛ,' and Indra drinks it in his house. He is the father of Saraṇyū, wife of Vivasvat and mother of the primeval twins Yama and Yamī. The origin of this deity is obscure. He may in the beginning have represented the creative activity of the sun; having then, because of his name, become the centre of attraction for myths illustrative of creative skill, he finally came to fill the place of a divine artificer in the Vedic pantheon. Oldenberg thinks that Tvaṣṭṛ, the 'artificer,' was originally a direct abstraction of artistic skill. He regards the solar deity Savitṛ, the 'stimulator,' whose name is similarly formed, as from the outset an abstraction of this type.

There are a few other abstract deities whose names were originally epithets of older gods. They are of rare and late occurrence in the Rigveda, their appellations being mostly compound in form and representing the supreme god who was being evolved at the end of the Rigvedic period. The historically most important among these is **Prajāpati**, 'lord of creatures.' Originally an epithet of such gods as Savitṛ and Soma, the name is mentioned in a late verse of the last book of the Rigveda as that of a distinct deity in the character of a creator. Prajāpati is often in the Atharvaveda and the White Yajurveda, and regularly in the Brāhmaṇas, recognized as the chief and father of the gods. In the Sūtras he is identified with Brahmā, his successor in the post-Vedic age. Similarly, the epithet **Viśvakarman**, 'all-creating,' appears as the name of an independent deity, to whom two hymns of the last book of the Rigveda are addressed. In the Brāhmaṇas, Viśvakarman is expressly identified with the creator Prajāpati, while in post-Vedic mythology he appears, doubtless owing to the name, as the artificer of the gods (like Tvaṣṭṛ in the Rigveda). Hiraṇya-garbha, the 'golden germ,' once occurs in the Rigveda as the supreme god, described as the 'one lord of all that exists.' In the Yajurveda he is expressly identified with Prajāpati, and in the later literature his name appears chiefly as a designation of Brahmā. In one curious instance it is possible to watch the genesis of an abstract deity of this type. The refrain of a late hymn of the Rigveda refers to the unknown creator with the interrogative pronoun *ka*: 'What god should we with sacrifices worship?' This led to the word Ka being used, in the later Vedic literature, as an independent name of the supreme god. In the Atharvaveda **Rohita**, 'the red one' (whose female form is Rohiṇī), has become a distinct deity in the capacity of a creator, the name having originally been an epithet of the sun. The only abstract deity of this type occurring in the oldest as well as the latest parts of the Rigveda is Bṛhaspati, 'lord of the spell,' of whom **Brahmaṇaspati** is a frequent doublet. He has been regarded by Roth and other Vedic scholars as a direct personification of devotion (*brahma*). To the present writer it seems more likely that he is only an indirect deification of the sacrificial aspect of Agni, with whom he is often identified. As the companion and ally of Indra, Bṛhaspati has been drawn into the myth of the release of the cows, which he is frequently described as delivering from the demon Vala. His most prominent characteristic is, however, his priesthood. As the divine *brahmā* priest, he seems to have been the prototype of the god Brahmā, chief of the later Hindu trinity. The name Bṛhaspati itself survived in post-Vedic mythology as the designation of a sage, teacher of the gods and regent of the planet Jupiter.

The second and smaller class of abstract deities comprises personifications of abstract nouns. There are seven or eight of these occurring in the last book of the Rigveda. Two hymns are addressed to *Manyu*, 'wrath,' and one to *Śraddhā*, 'faith.' *Anumati*, 'favour' (of the gods), *Aramati*, 'devotion,' *Sūnṛtā*, 'bounty,' *Asunīti*, 'spirit-life,' and *Nirṛti*, 'decease,' occur in only a few isolated passages. These abstractions become commoner in the later Vedas. Thus *Kāma*, 'desire,' first appears in the Atharvaveda, where the arrows with which he pierces hearts are already referred to; he becomes in post-Vedic mythology the well-known flower-arrowed god of love. In the same Veda *Kāla*, 'time,' and *Skambha*, 'support,' are cosmogonic powers, while *Prāṇa*, 'breath,' and some other analogous abstractions are identified with Prajāpati. *Śrī*, as a personification of beauty or fortune, does not begin to appear till the Brāhmaṇa period.

A purely abstract deity, often incidentally celebrated throughout the Rigveda, is **Aditi**, 'liberation,' 'freedom' (literally 'un-binding': *a-diti*), whose main characteristic is the power of delivering from the bonds of physical suffering and moral guilt. She, however, occupies a unique position among the abstract deities owing to the peculiar way in which the personification seems to have come about. She is the mother of the small group of deities called Ādityas, often styled 'sons of Aditi.' This expression at first most probably meant nothing more than 'sons of liberation,' according to an idiom common in the Rigveda and elsewhere. The word was then personified, with the curious result that the mother is mythologically younger than some at least of her sons, who (*e.g.* Mitra) date from the Indo-Iranian period. The goddess Diti, mentioned only three times in the Rigveda, probably came into being as an antithesis to Aditi, with whom she is twice mentioned there and several times in the later Vedas. The Atharvaveda speaks of her sons, the **Daityas**, who in post-Vedic mythology are demons, enemies of the gods.

5. GODDESSES, in general, play an insignificant part in the Vedas, taking no share in the government of the world. The only one of importance is **Uṣas** (p. 604[a]). Next comes **Sarasvatī**, who, however, ranks with only the least prominent of the male deities. Very few others are celebrated in even as much as one entire hymn. Such are *Pṛthivī*, Earth (p. 605[a]); *Rātrī*, Night, the sister of Dawn, conceived not as dark, but bright with stars; *Araṇyānī*, goddess of the forest; and *Vāc*, goddess of speech. Others are only sporadically mentioned. Such are *Puraṃdhi* and *Dhiṣaṇā*, goddesses of plenty. Less often referred to are *Rākā* and *Sinīvālī*, spoken of as bountiful goddesses; in later Vedic texts they appear as the presiding deities of full and new moon respectively. *Kuhū* is also mentioned in these texts as a personification of the new moon. *Iḷā* is a sacrificial goddess, the personification of the oblation of milk and butter. With her is also mentioned *Mahī* or *Bhāratī*, another sacrificial deity. The wives of the great gods are still more insignificant, being mere names formed from those of their consorts, altogether lacking in individuality. Thus *Agnāyī*, *Indrāṇī*, *Varuṇānī* are the names of the spouses of Agni, Indra, and Varuṇa respectively. *Rudrāṇī*, as the wife of Rudra, first appears in the Sūtras. The 'wives of the gods' (*devānām patnīs*), occasionally mentioned as a group in the Rigveda, have a special place assigned to them, apart from the gods, in the cult of the Brāhmaṇas.

6. DUAL DIVINITIES. — A peculiar feature of Vedic religion is the invocation of pairs of deities whose names are combined as dual compounds. About a dozen such pairs are celebrated in entire hymns, and about half a dozen more in detached verses of the Rigveda. By far the largest number of hymns is addressed to the couple **Mitra-Varuṇa**, though the names most frequently compounded in the dual are Heaven and Earth (*dyāvāpṛthivī*). Most likely the latter pair, having been associated as universal parents from the Indo-European period onwards, furnished the analogy for this dual type. They are also often called the Two Worlds (*rodasī*) in the Rigveda.

7. GROUPS OF DEITIES.—Among the creations of Vedic mythology we also find a few more or less definite groups of deities, generally associated with some particular god. The Maruts who, as we have seen (p. 605[a]), attend on Indra, form the most numerous group. Under the name of Rudras, they are also occasionally associated with their father Rudra. The smaller group of the **Ādityas**, of whom Varuṇa is the chief, are constantly mentioned in company with their mother Aditi. Their number in the Rigveda is stated to be seven or, with the addition of *Mārtāṇḍa*, eight; while in the Brāhmaṇas and later it is regularly twelve. One passage of the Rigveda enumerates six of them: Mitra, Aryaman, Bhaga, Varuṇa, Dakṣa, Aṃśa; Sūrya was probably regarded as the seventh. A much less important group, without individual names or definite number in the Vedas, is that of the **Vasus**, whose leader is, in the Rigveda, generally Indra, but in later Vedic texts generally Agni. In the Brāhmaṇas their number is stated to be eight. There are, finally, the **Viśvedevās**, or all-gods, who are invoked in many hymns. It is an artificial sacrificial group, intended to include the whole pantheon, and thus to ensure the omission of no deity when all were meant to be invoked. But in spite of its name, this comprehensive group was, strange to say, sometimes conceived as a narrower one, associated with others like the Vasus and Ādityas.

B. *LESSER DIVINITIES.*

1. ELVES, GENII. — Besides the higher gods already described, a number of lesser divine powers are known to the Rigveda. The most prominent of these are the **Ṛbhus**, a deft-handed trio who by their marvellous skill acquired the rank of deities. Among their five main feats of dexterity, the greatest consisted in transforming the bowl of Tvaṣṭṛ into four shining cups. The bowl and the cups have been variously interpreted as the moon with its four phases or the year with its seasons. The Ṛbhus further exhibited their skill in renewing the youth of their parents, by whom Heaven and Earth seem to have been meant. The myth of the Ṛbhus having rested for twelve days in the house of the sun is probably an allusion to the intercalation of twelve days at the winter solstice, so as to bring the lunar year of 354 days into harmony with the solar year of nearly 366 days.

Occasional mention is made in the Rigveda of **an Apsaras** ('moving in the waters'), a celestial water-nymph, the spouse of a corresponding genius named **Gandharva.** Occasionally more Apsarases than one are spoken of. In the Atharvaveda and later, the Apsarases form a class, regularly associated with the Gandharvas; and though they are still connected with the waters and clouds, their sphere is here, as well as in the Yajurveda, extended to the earth, where they haunt the different varieties of fig-trees called Nyagrodha, Aśvattha, Udumbara, and Plakṣa, in which the music of their cymbals and lutes is heard. In the Brāhmaṇas they appear as nymphs of great beauty, devoted to song, dance, and play. Several individual names of Apsarases are mentioned in the later Vedas, but the only one occurring in the Rigveda is that of *Urvaśī*. In an obscure hymn (x. 95) she engages in a dialogue with her earthly spouse *Purūravas*, whom she has forsaken. The myth of their alliance is told more fully in one of the Brāhmaṇas. *Gandharva* is, in the Rigveda, a single being (like the Gandarewa of the Avesta), who dwells in the aerial sphere, guards the celestial Soma, and is (as in the Avesta) connected with the waters. In the later Vedas the Gandharvas form a class associated with the Apsarases in a stereotyped manner, and are brought into relation with marriage and with wedding ceremonies. In the post-Vedic period the Gandharvas have become celestial singers.

2. TUTELARY DEITIES.—There are a few divinities of the tutelary order, guardians watching over the welfare of house or field. One of these is *Vāstospati*, 'lord of the dwelling,' rarely mentioned in the Rigveda, where he is invoked to grant a favourable entry, to remove disease, and to bestow protection and prosperity. The Sūtras prescribe that Vāstoṣpati should be propitiated when a new house is to be occupied. *Kṣetrasya pati*, 'lord of the field,' is besought in the Rigveda to grant cattle and horses and to confer prosperity. The Sūtras state that he is to be worshipped when a field is ploughed. *Sītā*, the 'furrow,' is once invoked in the Rigveda to dispense crops and rich blessings. In a Sūtra she appears as the wife of Indra. Here, too, *Urvarā*, the 'arable field,' with her garland of threshing-floors, is supplicated to bestow welfare.

C. *HEROES.*

The heroes of the Rigveda are all ancient seers or priests. (1) The most important of them is **Manu or Manus** (which also means 'man'), the ancestor of the human race, styled 'our father' by the poets, who also speak of the sacrificers of their own day as 'the people of Manu.' Regarded as the son of Vivasvat, he bears the patronymic Vaivasvata from the Atharvaveda onwards. He is thus a doublet of Yama as progenitor of mankind. He is represented as the institutor of sacrifice. Soma is said to have been brought to him by the bird, and Indra is described as drinking the Soma of Manu to fortify him for the conflict with Vṛtra. In the Śatapatha Brāhmaṇa, Manu plays the part of Noah, being saved in a ship from a deluge, which has swept away all other creatures, by a fish (in post-Vedic mythology an *avatār* of Viṣṇu). Manu then became the ancestor of the human race through his daughter Iḷā, who was produced from his offerings. (2) **Atharvan** is frequently mentioned in the Rigveda as an ancient fire-priest, who practised devotion along with Father Manu. In the Atharvaveda he appears as a companion of the gods, being related to them and dwelling in heaven. The name is also found in the plural as that of a group of fathers. In the Atharvaveda, the Atharvans are described as destroying goblins with a magical herb. (3) **Dadhyañc**, son of Atharvan, is a sacrificer who kindled Agni in the days of old. A myth told about him is that the Aśvins gave him a horse's head, with which he proclaimed to them where the mead of Tvaṣṭṛ was to be found. Indra is also connected with this myth; for he is said to have discovered the horse's head, and with the bones of Dadhyañc to have slain ninety-nine Vṛtras. (4) **Atri** is one of the ancient seers most frequently mentioned in the Rigveda. The myth of his deliverance from a fiery chasm by the Aśvins is often referred to. He is also said to have found the sun when hidden by the demon Svarbhānu and to have placed it in the sky. The Atris are a family of seers to whom the authorship of the fifth book of the Rigveda is attributed. (5) **Kaṇva** is another ancient seer and sacrificer often spoken of in the Rigveda. He is said to have been befriended by Agni, Indra, and the Maruts; and to have been specially aided by the Aśvins, who restored his eyesight. Most of the hymns of the eighth book of the Rigveda are attributed to his descendants the Kaṇvas. (6) **Kutsa** is one of the very few Vedic heroes who exhibit warlike traits. He is chiefly connected with the Indra myth. Riding on the same car as Indra and acting as his charioteer, he is even invoked with Indra in the dual. He is especially associated with Indra in slaying the demon Śuṣṇa. When Kutsa was pressed by his foes, Indra tore off the wheel of the sun to aid him. Nevertheless Indra sometimes appears as hostile to Kutsa, delivering him into the hands of an enemy. Several hymns of the first and ninth books of the Rigveda are assigned by tradition to the seer Kutsa. (7) Much less frequently mentioned in the Rigveda is the seer **Kāvya Uśanā**, whose characteristic feature is wisdom. He, too, is associated with Indra. He is said to have fashioned for Indra the bolt for slaying Vṛtra; and once joins him and Kutsa in slaying the demon Śuṣṇa. (8) Some names, moreover, appear predominantly or exclusively in the plural as representing families or groups of ancient seers, who, if in some cases historical in origin, have become invested with mythological traits. A frequently mentioned group of this kind are the **Aṅgirases**, who are closely associated with Indra in the myth of the capture of the cows. They are described as seers who are the sons of the gods, and who by sacrifice obtained immortality as well as the friendship of Indra. They receive offerings of Soma, and are invoked like gods. When used in the singular, *aṅgiras* is nearly always an epithet of Agni, who is called the first seer Aṅgiras or the chief Aṅgiras. The word *aṅgiras* appears to be etymologically identical with the Greek ἄγγελος, 'messenger.' This points to the Aṅgirases originally having been regarded as messengers between heaven and earth, attendant on Agni. But if they were mythical in origin, they came to be regarded as an actual priestly family, the composition of the ninth book of the Rigveda being attributed to them. This is also indicated by the compound term Atharva-aṅgirasaḥ, 'the Atharvans and Aṅgirases,' a designation of the Atharvaveda which occurs in that Veda itself as well as later. (9) Another group of ancient priests are the **Bhṛgus**, chiefly connected with the myth of the communication of fire to men. The Indian Prometheus, Mātariśvan, brought the hidden Agni from heaven to the Bhṛgus, who established and diffused the sacrificial fire on earth. In two or three passages of the Rigveda they are referred to as if an actual tribe of bygone days. In the later Vedic literature, Bhṛgu is the eponymous hero of a tribe, and regarded as a son of Varuṇa. (10) A definite numerical group of ancient priests, but rarely referred to in the Rigveda, are the 'Seven Seers' (*sapta ṛṣayaḥ*). They are associated with the gods and called divine. Their number may have been suggested by the seven technical priests, of whom they would then represent the prototypes. In the Śatapatha Brāhmaṇa they are regarded as the seven stars in the constellation of the Great Bear, and are stated to have themselves been originally bears. This identification was doubtless brought about by the sameness of number in the two groups, aided by the similarity of sound between *ṛṣi*, 'seer,' and *ṛkṣa*, which in the Rigveda means both 'star' and 'bear.' (11) The above groups are all spoken of as 'fathers,' and nearly all of them, besides a few others, are mentioned as races of ancestors to whom worship is paid. Those thus characterized in the Rigveda are the Navagvas, Vairūpas, Aṅgirases, Atharvans, Bhṛgus, Vasiṣṭhas. The last four, whether mythical in origin or not, appear in the historical aspect of families to which the composition of the Atharvaveda and two books of the Rigveda was attributed.

D. *ANIMALS.*

Animals play a considerable part in the mythological and religious ideas of the Veda. (1) Among them the **horse** is prominent as drawing the cars of the gods. There are also mentioned in the Rigveda at least four individual steeds, probably all representing the sun, which are regarded as deities and objects of worship. The most notable of these is *Dadhikrā* or *Dadhikrāvan*, to whom four hymns are addressed. He is described as a swift and victorious steed, regularly invoked with Uṣas, occasionally with Agni, the Aśvins, Sūrya, and others. The divine horse *Tārkṣya*, addressed in one short hymn of the Rigveda, is a god-impelled mighty steed, a vanquisher of chariots, speeding to battle. In one or two later Vedic texts Tārkṣya is referred to as a bird; and in the epic and later literature he is identical with the swift bird Garuḍa, the vehicle of Viṣṇu. A third steed, several times mentioned, is *Paidva*, spoken of as white, a dragon-slayer, a conqueror invincible in battles, worthy to be invoked like the god Bhaga by men. Lastly, there is *Etaśa*, the swift steed who draws the bright form of the sun, but also contends in a race with Sūrya. (2) The **cow**, however, is the animal which occupies the most important position in Vedic mythology and religion. Cows, representing beams of light, draw the car of Dawn. Rain-clouds, especially in the Indra myth, are personified as cows; Pṛśni, the mother of the Maruts, being an individualization. The bountiful clouds are doubtless the prototypes of the many-coloured cows, mentioned in the Atharvaveda, which yield all desires in the heaven of the Blest, and which are the forerunners of the Cow of Plenty (*Kāmaduh*) of post-Vedic poetry. The animal herself is already regarded as sacred in the Rigveda; for one of the poets impresses on his hearers that she should not be killed, and she is frequently designated by the term *aghnyā*, 'not to be slain.' She is even addressed as a goddess; and the divinities Iḷā, Aditi, and Pṛthivī are sometimes conceived in the form of a cow. In the Atharvaveda the worship of the cow as a sacred animal is fully recognized. That the tendency to deification had already begun before the Aryans entered India is proved by the evidence of the Avesta, which shows that the sanctity of the cow is at least as old as the Indo-Iranian period. (3) In the Rigveda the **goat** is the animal that draws the car of Pūṣan. This is also the form of the divine being Aja Ekapād, 'the one-footed goat.' In the later Vedic literature we occasionally find the goat connected or identified with Agni. (4) The **ass** appears in Vedic mythology only as drawing the car of the Aśvins. (5) The **dog** is met with in the form of the two brindled hounds of Yama, chief of the dead. (6) The **boar** has, in the Yajurveda, a cosmogonic character, as the form assumed by the creator Prajāpati when he raised the earth out of the waters. From this conception the boar incarnation of Viṣṇu was developed in Hindu mythology. (7) The **tortoise** has, in the later Vedas, acquired a semi-divine position; for in the White Yajurveda he is spoken of as 'lord of waters,' and in the Atharvaveda he appears under the name of Kaśyapa, beside or as identical with Prajāpati, receiving the epithet *Svayambhū*, 'self-existent.' In the Śatapatha Brāhmaṇa, Prajāpati is said, when producing all creatures, to have changed himself into a tortoise. This transformation became, in Hindu mythology, the tortoise incarnation of Viṣṇu. (8) A **monkey** named Vṛṣākapi appears in an obscure myth told in a late hymn of the Rigveda as a favourite of Indra. (9) Another late hymn contains a panegyric of **frogs** as bestowing cows and long life. (10) The bird frequently figures in Vedic mythology, as the **eagle** (*śyena*) that brings the Soma to Indra. *Noxious animals* in Vedic mythology generally appear as demons or exhibit demoniac traits. (11) The **serpent** is here the most prominent. This is the form which the powerful demon Vṛtra, the foe of Indra, is thought to possess; for he is frequently designated as *ahi*, 'the snake.' The serpent, however, also shows a beneficent aspect in the divine being Ahi Budhnya, 'the dragon of the deep,' who is supposed to dwell in the fathomless depths of the aerial ocean. In the later Vedas, the serpents (*sarpāḥ*) are mentioned, along with the Gandharvas and others, as a class of semi-divine beings that dwell on earth, in air, and in heaven; and in the Sūtras, offerings to them are prescribed. In the Sūtras, we for the first time come across the Nāgas, human beings in appearance, but serpents in reality. In the Hindu period, serpent-worship is found all over India. Since there is no trace of it in the Rigveda, while it prevails widely among the non-Aryan tribes, the conclusion seems justified that, when the Aryans overspread India, the land of serpents, they found the cult diffused among the aborigines and borrowed it from them.

E. *DEIFIED INANIMATE OBJECTS.*

Besides the great phenomena of nature, various features of the earth's surface, as well as artificial objects, are treated as deities in the Vedas. This is a fetishistic worship of inanimate things chiefly regarded as useful to man.

1. *Mountains* are frequently addressed as divinities in the Rigveda, but only along with other natural objects, such as rivers and plants, or in association with gods. *Parvata*, 'mountain,' is even invoked with Indra in the form of a dual compound. Besides rivers and waters, already mentioned as terrestrial goddesses, *plants* (*oṣadhi*) are regarded as divine powers. One entire hymn of the Rigveda is devoted to their praise, chiefly with reference to their healing powers; the Atharvaveda refers to a medicinal plant as 'a goddess born on the goddess earth'; and the Black Yajurveda prescribes an animal sacrifice to plants for the obtaining of offspring. Large trees, called 'lords of the forest' (*vanaspati*), are also sometimes addressed as deities, mainly in association with waters and mountains.

2. Various *sacrificial implements* are deified. The most important is the *sacrificial post*. It is praised and invoked in a whole hymn of the Rigveda, in which posts set up by priests are described as gods. The *sacrificial litter* (*barhis*) is also deified, and the '*divine doors*,' by which the sacrificial enclosure is entered, are goddesses. The *pressing stones* (*grāvan*) are addressed as deities in three hymns of the Rigveda; spoken of here as immortal, unaging, more mighty than heaven, they are invoked to drive away demons and destruction. The *mortar and pestle* used in pounding the Soma plant are invoked in the Rigveda. In the Atharvaveda divine power of the highest order is ascribed to *ucchiṣṭa*, the 'remnant' of the sacrifice, as well as to various sacrificial ladles. The agricultural implements named *śuna* and *sīrā*, probably the ploughshare and the plough, are invoked in a few verses of the Rigveda, and, in the ritual, receive the offering of a cake.

3. *Weapons*, finally, are sometimes deified; armour, bow, quiver, arrows, and drum being invoked in one of the hymns of the Rigveda. The drum alone is also celebrated in an entire hymn of the Atharvaveda.

4. *Idols* seem not to have been known in the age of the Vedas; at all events they first begin to be referred to in the later additions to the Brāhmaṇas and in the Sūtras. One verse of the Rigveda, however, seems to allude to some image of Indra.

5. *Material objects* treated as symbols of deities are occasionally mentioned in the ritual literature. Thus the wheel (*cakra*) represents the sun in various ceremonies; and it appears in Hindu mythology as one of the weapons of the solar deity Viṣṇu. A piece of gold, sometimes in the form of a disk, also indicates the sun on certain ritual occasions. A symbol must have been used by the phallus worshippers (*śiśnádevāḥ*), who are mentioned with repugnance in the Rigveda. In the post-Vedic period the phallus or *liṅga* became typical of Śiva's generative power, and its worship is widely diffused in India at the present day.

5. Demons.

a. The demons which are often mentioned in the Vedas are of two kinds. The higher and more powerful class, the aerial foes of the gods, are generally called **Asuras** in the Atharvaveda and later. This word, however, rarely means 'demon' in the Rigveda, where it usually preserves the older sense of 'being of mysterious power,' and denotes a god (*ahura* in the Avesta). The earlier notion of the conflict between a single god and a single demon, as exemplified by Indra and Vṛtra in the Rigveda, gradually made way for that of the hostility of gods and demons as two opposing hosts. This is the regular view of the Brāhmaṇas. Here the Asuras, no less than the gods, are regarded as the offspring of Prajāpati; here, too, the Asuras often vanquish the gods at the outset, being finally worsted only by artifice.

In the Rigveda the terms *dāsa* and *dasyu*, properly the name of the dark aborigines overcome by the conquering Aryans, are frequently used also to designate aerial demons, adversaries of the gods. A group of demons are the **Paṇis** ('niggards'), primarily the foes of Indra, who with the aid of Saramā tracks and releases the cows hidden by them.

Of individual demons, by far the most frequently mentioned is **Vṛtra**, the 'encompasser,' the formidable opponent of Indra. His mother being called Dānu, he is also sometimes alluded to by the metronymic term *Dānava* (which later becomes the name of a class of demons). Another powerful demon is **Vala**, the personified cave of the cows, which he guards, and which are set free by Indra and his allies, notably the Aṅgirases. Other demon adversaries of Indra are **Arbuda**, described as a wily beast, whose cows Indra drove out; **Viśvarūpa**, son of Tvaṣṭṛ, a three-headed demon slain by both Trita and Indra, who seize his cows; and **Svarbhānu**, who eclipses the sun (his successor in Hindu mythology being Rāhu). There are several other individual demons, generally described as Dāsas, and slain by Indra in favour of protégés: such are Śuṣṇa, Śambara, Pipru, Namuci, Dhuni, and Cumuri, besides some half dozen others who were originally, in all likelihood, terrestrial foes.

b. The second or lower class of demons are terrestrial goblins, enemies of men, as Asuras are of gods. By far the most common generic name for them is **Rakṣas.** They are nearly always mentioned in connexion with some god who destroys them. The much less common term *yātu* or *yātudhāna* (primarily 'sorcerer') alternates with *rakṣas*, and perhaps denotes a species. Terrestrial demons appear in the shape of various animals or birds, having also the power to assume human forms in order to deceive. With human shape they often combine some monstrous deformity; they are even described as blue, yellow, or green in colour; they are male and female, have families, and are mortal. Greedy for flesh and blood, they attack men by entering into them, thus causing disease and madness. As they prowl about at night, and the sacrifice is the main object of their malignity, Agni is naturally the god oftenest opposed to them, and most frequently invoked to burn, ward off, or destroy them. An important group of goblins, scarcely alluded to in the Rigveda but often mentioned in the later Vedas, are the **Piśācas**, eaters of raw flesh or of corpses. Besides some other groups of goblins of lesser importance, there were included in Vedic belief many other hostile agencies, such as those of disease, which it was one of the main tasks of magic to counteract. Only a few among the groups of terrestrial spirits were thought to be, after the manner of elves, helpful to men, as in harvest work, or in battle by terrifying the foe.

6. Religious Practice.

a. The cult of the Vedic Indian has three aspects. It endeavours, in the first place, to win the favour of the gods, who are almost without exception benevolent. It further aims at warding off the hostility of the demons, who are malevolent, here having recourse to practices which for the most part are not of a religious, but of a magical character. Lastly, its attitude towards ancestors is a combination of its treatment of gods and of demons; for, while ancestors receive worship as divine beings, means are taken to prevent them from unduly prolonging their uncanny presence among the living.

b. The worship of the gods has two sides, finding expression either by word or by act. Praise of their greatness and power, or prayer for welfare and forgiveness of sin is addressed to them on the one hand; sacrifice consisting of food and drink is offered on the other. Prayer and praise, which include frequent invitations to the sacrifice, are largely metrical in form, entirely so in the Rigveda. **Prayer** in the Vedas is almost entirely of the ritual type, intended to accompany a ceremony, or at least to form part of a liturgy. In the creative age of the Rigveda new prayers were produced for ritual purposes; but in the age of the later Vedas, with the development of a system which foresaw almost every desire and prescribed the offering to ensure its fulfilment, prayer was nothing more than the mechanical application of ready-made formulas. It is doubtful whether, even in the earliest period, much room was left, owing to the highly ritual type of the worship, for independent prayer. The latter could hardly in any case have gone beyond the expression of a concrete desire addressed to a particular deity; it could certainly not have had the character of a communion of the worshipper with divine powers. Prayer was, however, by no means necessarily accompanied by a ceremonial act. Thus the hymns of the Rigveda addressed to Uṣas were recited without any attendant offerings; the same was the case, according to the ritual texts, with the prayers to Agni, Uṣas, and the Aśvins in the morning litany of the Soma sacrifice, as well as with the daily invocations muttered at the morning and evening twilight devotions.

As the hymns of the Rigveda, in addressing prayers to a god, aim at securing his goodwill, they are, in the first place and to a large extent, panegyrics which praise the greatness and power, the mysterious nature, and the exploits of the deity in question. The petition for the gifts hoped for, when the favour of the god has thus been won, is then briefly added. The benefits desired are almost entirely of a material, not of a moral, kind. They are mainly expressed by such general terms as treasures and blessings, protection and victory; when stated in detail they consist in long life and vigorous offspring, cattle and horses, cars and gold; or the punishment of enemies, niggards, and Brāhman-haters by their goods being taken away and bestowed on the pious. Rarely does the worshipper pray that his thoughts may be righteous, that he may refrain from doing what displeases the gods, that he may be reconciled to an offended deity, or delivered from the bonds of guilt; and his supplications lack the note of passionate appeal, deep aspiration, mental struggle, or humble submission to the divine will. As regards its efficacy, prayer was held to be scarcely less potent than sacrifice in gladdening and stimulating the gods. But a hymn had to be composed with faultless art, 'as a skilful workman constructs a car'; it had to be freed from imperfections 'as grain is winnowed with the flail.' Then it invigorated the god like draughts of Soma, stimulating him to new deeds; then it increased the mighty strength of Indra so that he slew the dragon. When prayer is thus thought, even in the Rigveda, to exercise the direct influence of a spell, magic is already beginning to encroach on the domain of religion. A similar tendency is observable in regard to the sacrifice which accompanied the prayers to the gods.

c. The general character of the Vedic **sacrifice** is essentially supplicatory, as it aims only at the obtaining of future benefits to be bestowed by the gods, and is not concerned with the past. What seem to be expiatory sacrifices are in reality of this order also, for they are accompanied by supplications that the guilt incurred should not be punished. Such expiatory sacrifices are of two kinds. They are either intended to mollify the wrath of a god aroused by the transgression of his divine will, being generally offered to Varuṇa, the guardian of moral order and punisher of sin; or they aim at removing guilt as a kind of impalpable substance much as if it were a disease, producing this result either by the aid of a god, especially Agni, or by means of fire, water, medicinal plants and spells, which are supposed to burn, wash, purge, or drive it away without the invocation of divine powers. This latter type belongs mainly to the sphere of the Atharvaveda, where magic supplants religious practice. Even a sacrifice made in fulfilment of a vow, after a god has granted a boon, is in reality only a supplicatory offering postponed, as when in the Atharvaveda Agni is promised an offering in the name of a lunatic, if the latter recovers his reason; or when, in the Brāhmaṇa story of Śunaḥśepa, the childless king vows, if a son is born to him, to sacrifice that son to Varuṇa. Thank-offerings in any true sense are unknown to the Vedic cult, the very verb 'to thank' not being found in the vocabulary of the language. An approach to the notion of a thank-offering is only to be found in a Sūtra passage, in which certain sacrifices are prescribed on a man regaining his health.

The conception of the effect of sacrifice which prevails in the Rigveda is that the offering wins the favour of a god and induces him to fulfil the accompanying prayer. The Soma offering satisfies, gladdens, strengthens the god, who loves the sacrificer and hates the niggard. The reward that follows is a voluntary act of the god, resulting from the benevolent attitude induced by the offering. It is not regarded as the repayment of a debt, though the sacrificer feels that the god cannot well help requiting him. While conscious of being in the presence of a mighty being, the sacrificer does not look on himself as infinitely far removed from the god, who is his old friend, and whose right hand he grasps. Even in the Rigveda, however, traces are already to be found of the notion that the sacrifice exercises compulsion not only over gods, but also over natural phenomena without requiring the co-operation of the gods. Here again we have the intrusion of magic into the domain of religion. In the ritual of the Brāhmaṇas we find that the latter has already been largely supplanted by the former.

d. The Vedic ceremonial was essentially based on the use of a **sacrificial fire**, 'the mouth of the gods,' into which the offerings were cast, and by which they were conveyed to the gods. Exceptionally only, fire was not the instrument of sacrifice. Thus the oblations to aquatic deities were cast into water, those to the dead were placed in small pits at the funeral sacrifice, while offerings to Rudra and demons were thrown into the air, hung on trees, buried, or disposed of in other ways. In the ritual there was beside the sacrificial fire a litter of grass (*barhis*), the soft seat on which the gods sat down to enjoy the offering. On this litter, according to the ritual texts, the oblations were deposited for a time, before being committed to the flames which conveyed them to heaven. Thus the gods were conceived as partaking of the sacrifice both on the litter and in their celestial abode. Agni is even invoked, in one and the same passage of the Rigveda, to bring the gods to the sacrifice and to take it to them in heaven (vii. 11. 5). This contradiction is doubtless to be explained by the survival of the litter in the ceremonial, from the time when offerings were presented on it alone. The burning of the litter at the end of the rite may perhaps originally have formed the transition to offering sacrifices in fire.

In the Vedic ceremonial, even of the earliest period, we have to distinguish between the simpler ritual of the single domestic fire and the more complicated and technical ritual conducted with the three fires, which are independent of the former, though they may originally have arisen by its division. The single domestic fire was maintained by every head of a family, who performed the rites connected with it himself. The three fires were set up only by men of position and wealth, becoming a centre round which the sacrificial activity of many Brāhmans and priests revolved. Certain regular rites, such as the daily morning and evening sacrifice or the new and full moon ceremonies, were performed in essentially the same manner with the three fires as with the one, the ritual of the latter, however, being simpler. But the domestic rites were conducted with the one only, while the Soma sacrifice could be carried on with the three only. The chief of the three fires, called Gārhapatya (doubtless representing the old domestic fire of the hearth), was the only one always maintained, the other two being taken from it for every sacrifice requiring their employment. It was used for the practical purposes of heating the vessels and preparing the offerings. The second, the Āhavanīya, situated to the east, was that in which the gods received their offerings. The third or Dakṣiṇa fire, placed in the south, the quarter specially connected with the souls of the dead and evil spirits, was used for offerings relating to those two classes of uncanny beings. About this fire and the pits dug around it, the ritual of the sacrifices to the manes chiefly moved.

When a fire was established for purposes of the cult, it was either produced by means of the fire-sticks (called *araṇīs*, and consisting of a lower slab of soft and a drill of hard wood) or fetched from certain places, as the house of a rich owner of herds or of a great sacrificer. At the four-monthly sacrifices offered at the beginning of the seasons and at the Soma sacrifice, a new fire was rubbed and united with the old Āhavanīya, doubtless with the intention of giving it new vigour.

e. With regard to the **material of the sacrifice,** the Vedic Indian, as a general principle, offered to the gods what was his own favourite food. It comprised the chief produce of the dairy and of agriculture: milk, in its various forms, and butter, together with the two principal kinds of grain, barley and rice (the latter, perhaps, not being used in the earliest period), cooked or baked in different ways. Among these, the products of the cow were unmistakably believed to have a more sacred and mystical import. In the cult of the dead, libations of water were characteristic. As beef and goats' flesh, less frequently mutton, were the principal kinds of meat eaten, cattle, goats, and sheep were the usual victims in the animal sacrifice, the he-goat, it would seem, being regularly offered on all lesser occasions. On the other hand, animals the flesh of which was either not eaten at all or only exceptionally eaten, such as the pig, dog, deer, as well as fish and birds, were not sacrificed to the gods. It is true that, in the rare and costly horse-sacrifice, an animal was offered the flesh of which was never a regular article of diet. This is, however, to be accounted for by the intrusion of magic into the domain of sacrifice; for the intention underlying the ceremony was to transfer the swift power (*vāja*) of the horse to the royal sacrificer. This sacrifice was, indeed, akin to a peculiar tendency in the sacrificial ceremonial, to offer to a god what corresponded to his special individuality. Thus to the goddesses Night and Morning was offered the milk of a black cow having a white calf. In the animal sacrifice, a victim was often chosen which agreed with the deity not only in sex, but in colour and other qualities. The starting-point of this practice was probably the notion that the eater acquires the qualities of the animal he eats, and that his strength is increased most by eating the flesh of the animal most like himself. Thus the mighty Indra, who is constantly called a bull in the Rigveda, commonly receives the sacrifice of a bull, as also of a buffalo, to which he is often compared. The sun-god Sūrya has a white he-goat offered to him.

The victim was killed by strangulation, and without bloodshed. With an evident desire of avoiding blood-guiltiness, it was addressed with such verses as 'Thou dost not die; no harm is done thee; thou goest to the gods by pleasant paths.' The ceremonial dealing with the disposal of the carcass was divided into two distinct sacrificial acts. In the first place, after an incision had been made, the caul (omentum) was extracted, being thereupon cooked and solemnly offered to the gods. This rite was concluded by the distribution of presents to priests and by purifications. The second act of the ceremonial consisted in cutting up the carcass into parts, certain sections of which were offered to the gods, while others were eaten by the priests. What remained was distributed among sacrificers, priests, and Brāhmans. A magical rather than a religious notion underlies the practice of men eating the remnants of the sacrifice of which the god has first partaken; for those remnants must have been regarded as of the nature of a medicine, which transfers to man the divine blessing connected with the sacrifice, or the particular power implied in the individual offering. The separate sacrifice of the caul was perhaps a relic of a time when that was the only portion of the victim which, owing to its agreeable odour, was presented as a burnt-offering to the gods. The blood of the victim was, in the Vedic ritual, not eaten, but was poured out as an offering to the Rakṣases or lower demons, who were regarded as fond of blood, and who similarly received the offal of the grain used in making baked offerings. Analogously, offerings made to beings thought to have an uncanny nature, such as Rudra or the souls of the dead, were not partaken of by the sacrificer. Thus a bull offered to Rudra might not be eaten or even brought into the village; and funeral cakes presented to the manes might only be smelt.

In connexion with the animal sacrifice, the interesting question as to whether the **human sacrifice** was known in the ritual of the Vedas suggests itself. The only certain trace of such a sacrifice is to be found in the important ceremony of building the brick fire-altar (called *agni-cayana*). Here it is prescribed that five victims—man, horse, ox, ram, he-goat—are to be sacrificed to different gods, and their five heads walled up in the lowest layer of the edifice. The object of this ceremony, which was a magical rite rather than an actual sacrifice, was to give stability to the altar. It is mentioned in the Śatapatha Brāhmaṇa as the custom of a not very remote past, for which other rites had been substituted. The human sacrifice (*puruṣa-medha*), which the ritual books describe in detail, was probably only an innovation invented to imitate the horse-sacrifice. But of any actual human sacrifice there is no certain trace in Vedic India. Neither the evidence of ancient stories, like that of Śunaḥśepa, nor the evidence of various Buddhist legends, is by any means conclusive.

Not only were food and drink presented to the gods to satisfy their hunger and thirst, but an intoxicant, of which the sacrificer also partook, was offered to them. This was the juice of the Soma plant, which was pressed, mixed with milk or other ingredients, and presented to the gods. Soma was certainly not the popular drink of the Vedic Indian, whose favourite intoxicant was called *surā*. How, then, is it to be accounted for that, in this case, he did not offer to the gods what he liked best himself? The explanation is that, having during the Indo-Iranian period been adopted in the cult instead of the earlier mead of the Indo-European age, it retained, by the force of tradition, its old-established position even in the Vedic cult.

Occasionally we find that objects which do not constitute food are sacrificed. Thus a man who desires the possession of deadly weapons sacrifices iron nails. Here again we see the intrusion of witchcraft; the sacrifice becoming a means of obtaining something analogous to the objects offered.

f. Priests.—Vedic India was already far removed from that primitive condition of things in which every man was his own priest, and did not require the services of persons possessing technical knowledge as intermediaries between him and the divine powers. On the contrary, it is certain that, even in the period of the Rigveda, there already existed a priestly class qualified by special knowledge and magical qualities to act for others in the difficult and dangerous intercourse of man with gods and spirits. There were, indeed, already a number of sacerdotal families, like the Vasiṣṭhas and Viśvāmitras, in which the art of praying and sacrificing correctly was practised as a hereditary calling, all of them employing the same cult, notably that of the Soma sacrifice, practically in the same way. There were no public priests; for there was no public worship of a national, tribal, or even congregational character. Vedic worship was of an essentially private type, sacrifice being performed on behalf of its individual institutor (*yajamāna*) by the priests who acted for him and whose prayers belonged to him. This, coupled with the fact that idols were not used, accounts for the absence of temples in Vedic India.

Two sacerdotal types have to be distinguished in the Vedic cult: the domestic priest (*purohita*), whose function it was to superintend the worship of his employer; and the officiating priest (*ṛtvij*), who had to play a certain prescribed part in an individual sacrifice.

The **Purohita** was generally in the service of kings only, though Brāhmans occasionally appeared in an analogous capacity in the houses of men of high position. That the employment of a Purohita in a royal household was considered essential is indicated by a Brāhmaṇa passage which states that the gods would not eat the food of a king who had no Purohita. The domestic priest was appointed by the king, and held his office for life, being often succeeded by his son. In the ceremony accompanying the appointment, the same verse was employed as when the bridegroom takes the hand of the bride in the wedding rite. The Purohita was, in fact, the king's right hand man, giving the directions for all the royal ceremonies and sacrifices. Even in the Rigveda the whole prosperity of the country is said to depend on the Purohita, 'the guardian of the realm,' and the Purohita Devāpi at the sacrifice employs a spell to procure rain on behalf of his royal master, while in the Atharvaveda another Purohita uses spells to secure victory in battle.

Of the sacrificial priests there were several, with definite functions and technical names, the chief being the Hotṛ or 'invoker,' the Udgātṛ or 'chanter,' the Adhvaryu or officiating 'sacrificer,' and the Brāhman or superintending priest; in the period of the Rigveda the Hotṛ was the most important, later the Brāhman became so. The Purohita was probably not any one of these, though he might be employed to perform the functions of one of them; in the earlier period he sometimes appears acting as Hotṛ, in the later as Brāhman. Thus in the Rigveda the Purohita Devāpi is chosen as a Hotṛ, and Agni is called both a Purohita and a Hotṛ.

The Rigveda contains a list of seven kinds of sacrificial priests, and this was probably the regular number, not only then but in the Indo-Iranian period. Seven priests still appear in various parts of the sacrificial ceremonial in later times, though, with the development of the ritual, additional ones were otherwise employed. The Avesta, which has eight sacrificial priests, probably added one to the original number. It is, in any case, a striking fact that the Zaotar, the leading priest who recites the Gāthās in the Iranian Haoma sacrifice, corresponds, in both name and function, to the Hotṛ who recites the verses of the Rigveda in the Vedic Soma sacrifice. The most important of these seven Vedic priests were the Hotṛ and the Adhvaryu. It was the duty of the former to recite the hymn which, in the chief libations of the Soma sacrifice, celebrated a particular god and invited him to drink Soma. When the hymns of the Rigveda were composed, their seers (*ṛṣis*) themselves doubtless played the part of the Hotṛ at the sacrifice; and that the latter was, in the earlier period, regarded as the leading priest is clear from his furnishing the type for Agni, the priest god. The Adhvaryu performed the practical part of the ceremonial, tending the fire and the litter, arranging and cleaning the utensils, pressing and offering the Soma. The remaining five acted as assistants to one or other of the two chief priests. The Agnīdh, or 'fire-kindler,' helped the Adhvaryu in tending the sacrificial fire. The Upavaktṛ or 'exhorter' (known also as Praśāstṛ, 'director,' and Maitrāvaruṇa, 'priest of Mitra and Varuṇa'), whose duty it was to give various orders to other priests, plays the part, in the animal sacrifice, of the only assistant, and in the Soma sacrifice, of one among the several assistants of the Hotṛ. The three other priests of the ancient list belong to the Soma ritual exclusively: the Potṛ, or 'purifier,' and the Neṣṭṛ, or 'leader,' became quite unimportant in the later Vedas, while the main function of the Brahman was to recite hymns addressed to Indra, in the same way as the Hotṛ, whose assistant he was. In the later ritual this priest came to be called Brāhmaṇācchaṃsin, while the old name, Brahman, acquired the technical sense of the priest who superintended the whole sacrifice, and whose duty it was to know the three Vedas.

g. Sacrifices.—The Vedic cult consisted of regularly recurrent or of occasional sacrifices. Our knowledge of the former is derived from the ritual literature, for there are only few and obscure traces of them in the hymns of the Rigveda, which is almost exclusively concerned with the Soma sacrifice. It is, however, probable that they were performed, at least in their main features, during the earliest Vedic period. These regular sacrifices are of three kinds, as connected with the course of the day, the month, and the year, being performed, respectively, twice a day, twice a month, and three times a year. Each of the first two kinds could be conducted, though without any difference in ceremonial form, either with the single domestic fire or with the three sacrificial fires. On the other hand, the annual sacrifices, which were celebrated at the commencement of the three seasons, required the greater ritual of the three fires. It was a general characteristic of all periodic sacrifices that they were never addressed to one single god.

The daily rites took place morning and evening. They consisted, on the one hand, of fire-offerings to the gods, and, on the other, of gifts of food presented to all beings. The latter comprised offerings placed on the threshold and elsewhere for the deities and spirits in and around the house; a libation to the souls of the dead in the southern quarter; food scattered for dogs and birds; and meat and drink given to needy human beings.

The monthly sacrifices, which were celebrated at new and full moon, consisted of cooked oblations or of cakes offered to the gods. Among the numerous deities receiving them, the most prominent was Indra.

The seasonal sacrifices were offered every four months, at the beginning of spring, of the rains, and of the cool weather. Throughout these the Maruts are the most prominent deities. In the ceremonial which inaugurates the rainy season, Karīra fruits are offered with a view to procuring rain and consequent plenty. Then also two figures of dough covered with wool, and intended to represent a ram and a ewe, are sacrificed in order to promote the increase of flocks. In these two offerings the influence of magical notions is clearly observable. With the seasonal celebration of the rains was combined a great expiatory sacrifice with which Varuṇa was specially associated.

In the ceremonial of the third or autumn sacrifice was included an offering to Rudra Tryambaka, intended to avert his attacks from the flocks and to conciliate his healing power. At a place where four roads meet, the abode of uncanny beings, a flat cake was deposited on or buried in a molehill, to indicate that it was presented to the mole as the animal of Rudra, who would thus refrain from injuring other animals. With this ceremonial was combined a great sacrifice to the dead, a kind of All Souls' festival.

We now turn to the extraordinary sacrifices, which are not limited to any fixed period. One of these is the independent form of the animal sacrifice. According to the ritual texts, it should take place annually; but the statements as to the time of year it should be performed are fluctuating and indefinite. Another form of the animal sacrifice is included in the Soma sacrifice.

Of all forms of cult the **Soma** sacrifice appears as the most important in Vedic literature. It was, however, probably not so important in actual life, as few could have possessed means sufficient for its performance. As compared with the recurrent sacrifices, it rather bore the character of an extraordinary act of liberality practised by the rich towards gods and priests. Though the time for its performance was not definitely fixed, later texts recommend the spring as the most suitable period. Soma was not offered to different gods according to circumstances, like a cooked oblation or an animal victim. On the contrary, it was offered, within the stereotyped scheme of the three pressings of Soma made at morning, noon, and evening, in honour of a prescribed series of gods intended to include all deities except perhaps Rudra. In this ceremonial the important gods were all addressed by name, the lesser ones being included in the comprehensive term Viśve devāḥ, or 'all-gods.' The Soma sacrifice, in fact, constituted a general carouse for gods as well as for priests. Indra was, however, the most important deity and the central figure of the whole ceremony; thus the Soma pressed at midday belonged to him alone in addition to his share of the morning and evening libation. The ceremonies of the Soma sacrifice were of a complex nature. Even the simplest and fundamental form of it, the Agniṣṭoma ('praise of Agni'), required the ministration of sixteen priests. This rite occupied only one day; other Soma sacrifices lasted for several days, up to twelve; while another class, called *sattras* or 'sessions,' sometimes extended to a year. These prolonged Soma sessions formed an unimportant exception to the rule that every sacrifice was performed for a single individual; for here a number of Brāhmans combined in such a way that each, while officiating as a priest in the usual manner, was accounted a sacrificer (*yajamāna*). The texts which deal with the Soma sacrifice furnish sufficient details for a complete picture of its ceremonies, which in the main were doubtless the same in the period of the Rigveda. Numbers of priests and lay spectators thronged the sacrificial ground, on which burned the three fires strewed around with sacrificial grass. Between the fires was the *vedi*, an oblong shallow excavation somewhat narrowed in the middle and covered with a litter of grass for the reception of the offerings to the gods. Scattered about were to be seen sheds, posts for tying up victims, the seats and fire-altars of the various priests, vessels containing water for various purposes, pressing implements, tubs, and bowls for Soma. Among them moved about the officiating priests and their assistants, in whose midst were to be seen the sacrificer (*yajamāna*) and his wife, emaciated by initiatory asceticism. The priests were engaged in preparing or offering the sacrificial cakes and the libations of milk; in sacrificing eleven he-goats to various gods; in pressing, purifying, mixing the Soma juice; in pouring it into or out of various vessels, presenting it to the gods, or drinking their share. All these operations were accompanied by the calls, recitations, chants of the priests as they carried out the details of the ritual, which were far too numerous to indicate here.

The Soma sacrifice was preceded by a protracted ceremony of initiation (*dīkṣā*), which was undergone by the sacrificer and his wife, and was followed by another of purification (*avabhṛtha*). Both of these ceremonies were probably known to the Rigveda. The Dīkṣā belongs to the ancient type of magical rites which were intended as a preparation for intercourse with gods and spirits by producing an ecstatic condition. It consisted in seclusion and various forms of asceticism (*tapas*) ending in physical exhaustion. Fasting was a chief element in the preparation for this as well as other rites. A preliminary bath was taken, as in the wedding ceremony, for the removal of injurious substances which would nullify the effects of the initiation. On the other hand, no bath might be taken during the course of the Soma sacrifice, for it would have been regarded as washing off the sanctity communicated by the Dīkṣā. As in the funeral and some other rites, the hair and beard were cut off and the nails pared, because they were considered impurities.

In the ceremony called *avabhṛtha* ('carrying down' to the water), with which the Soma sacrifice terminated, the black antelope skin and the sacred cord used by the sacrificer and his wife since the beginning of the Dīkṣā were thrown into the water along with the Soma shoots which had been pressed out and the sacrificial utensils which had been in contact with the Soma. Finally, the sacrificer and his wife, as well as the priests, descended into the water to wash off the supernatural powers which they had acquired, and on emerging put on fresh garments. The offerings and texts which accompanied the Avabhṛtha ceremony were chiefly addressed to Varuṇa, the god who delivers from guilt.

h. Rites of family life.—As the Vedic wedding ceremony had in its main features probably come down from the Indo-European period, it retained much that belongs to the domain of witchcraft rather than that of religion. Thus the act, on the part of the bridegroom, of taking the hand of the bride, was intended to place her in the power of her husband. The seven steps which the young couple took and the food which they ate together were meant to establish friendship and community. Future abundance and male offspring were aimed at when the bride, after being conducted to her husband's house, was placed on the hide of a red bull and took upon her lap the son of a woman who had borne only living male children. The worship of the gods, on the other hand, was somewhat in the background during this ceremony. It was chiefly concerned with Agni, the god most closely connected with domestic life. Thus the husband led his bride three times round the newly-kindled nuptial fire, which it was the duty of the couple to maintain henceforth throughout their lives as their domestic fire. The invocations addressed to the gods were mostly of the nature of benedictions. The long wedding hymn from the Rigveda was also recited. Various offerings, moreover, were made, especially one of parched grain strewn by the bride with hollowed hands.

After sunset the husband led his bride out of the house, and, as he pointed to the pole-star and the star Arundhatī, the young couple exhorted each other to be constant and undivided for ever. The wedding was followed by three nights of conjugal abstinence, meant doubtless to exhaust the patience and divert the attacks of hostile demons.

Similarly, in the rites performed both before and after birth for the welfare of children, the magical aspect predominated over the sacrificial. Thus a powdered drug was dusted into the nostrils of a pregnant woman to ensure the sex of her offspring being male; and unripe fruits of the Udumbara tree were attached to her in order to communicate to her child the exuberant maturity which that fig attains.

On the tenth day after birth, when the period of impurity was over, the ceremony of giving the child his name was performed. In the third year the rite of tonsure, accompanied by an oblation, took place. The boy's hair was cut and arranged so as to be worn in accordance with the custom of the family. The hair which was cut off was buried. A similar ceremony was performed when the beard of the youth at the age of sixteen was shaved.

But by far the most important rite connected with boyhood was that of initiation or 'introduction' (*upanayana*) to a religious teacher, which took place at the respective ages of eight, eleven, and twelve in the case of boys of the first three castes. Standing at the sacred fire, the preceptor invested the boy, whose head had been shaved, with a girdle, which he wound round his waist three times from left to right, at the same time pronouncing certain formulas. He then grasped the boy's hand and, placing his own on the pupil's heart, recited a verse indicating that he had assumed power over the boy's will. On this occasion the youth also received a garment, a staff, and a sacred cord to be worn over one shoulder and under the other arm. During the whole course of his subsequent apprenticeship, the religious pupil (*brahmacārin*) was required to practise chastity, to refrain from certain kinds of food, to tend his preceptor's fire with fuel, and to beg food in the village. But his chief duty was to study the Veda and to learn the famous Sāvitrī stanza from the Rigveda as an introduction to that study. By the rite of initiation, which was regarded as a spiritual birth, the pupil had become one of the 'twice-born,' qualified to eat the remnants of sacrificial offerings. Though this ceremony is not even alluded to in the Rigveda, it must have been known at that time, for it can be traced back to a still earlier age. The evidence of the Avesta shows that among the ancient Persians a youth of fifteen was received into the community of Zoroaster with a sacred cord; and among primitive peoples similar rites have been found all over the earth to symbolize reception into the community of men as an entry into a new life. This ancient rite was in India transformed into a spiritual ceremony which gave admission to the community of those qualified for the study of sacred knowledge.

The period of apprenticeship was terminated by the ceremony called *samāvartana*, or 'return,' the main element of which was a bath intended to indicate symbolically that the quality of religious studentship (*brahmacarya*) was washed off.

The funeral rites, finally, belong to the sphere of the domestic ritual; it will, however, be more convenient to deal with them later as part of the ceremonial relating to death and the future life.

i. Rites relating to public life.—Even in ceremonies which assumed a public character because connected with the person of the king, the sacrifice was still instituted by him as an individual; and though prayers for the country and the people might be incidental to it, there existed no form of sacrifice which was offered in the name of the tribe or the nation. In the royal ceremonial, magical practices were, as we found to be the case in the domestic ritual, more prominent than sacrificial acts. The first of these celebrations calling for description are the consecration (*abhiṣeka*) of the king and the royal inauguration (*rājasūya*). Neither of these is mentioned in the Rigveda, and they were probably developed in the later Vedic period; but the magical elements which they contain are most likely very old. Both these celebrations included Soma rites. In the consecration ceremony the king was seated on a chair covered with a tiger skin and made of the wood of the Udumbara, the tree which to the Indian was typical of plenty. A cup, also made of Udumbara wood, was filled with a fluid compounded of butter, honey, rain-water, and other ingredients. With this fluid the king was anointed or rather besprinkled. In the Rājasūya a similar besprinkling took place; but it was followed by a series of further rites intended to secure success of all kinds. These included a symbolical raid on a herd of cows; the discharge of arrows at feeble relatives of the king, who were plundered; and a game of dice in which a cow was the stake, and which was won by the king.

Another ceremonial, regarded as still more dignified and efficacious, was the Vājapeya ('draught of vigour'), a kind of Soma sacrifice, which might be performed not only by kings, but even by men of royal descent or of the Brāhman caste. Its most characteristic feature was a chariot race, evidently a magical rite intended to secure for the sacrificer the swift power embodied in the horse. It also included a rite called the 'ascent of the post' (*yūpārohaṇa*). A wheel made of wheaten flour, and symbolical of the sun, was placed on the top of a sacrificial post. Mounting by means of a ladder, the sacrificer grasped the wheel as he uttered the formula, 'We have reached the sun, ye gods.' On descending to the ground he seated himself on a wooden throne and was besprinkled as in the inauguration ceremony. This part of the Vājapeya rite aimed at the attainment of exalted position.

The splendour of royal ceremonial, however, culminated in the horse-sacrifice (*aśva-medha*). It was not a thank-offering, as might at first sight be inferred from the words of the Brāhmaṇa description of each king who performed it, 'He victoriously traversed the earth and offered the horse-sacrifice.' It was in reality a supplicatory sacrifice offered, after military successes, for the fulfilment of the king's highest wishes in the future. According to the ritual texts, this sacrifice is addressed to the gods in the aggregate, but with special reference to Prajāpati (an evidently late trait); but there are indications that it may originally have been addressed to Indra the Vṛtra-slayer, an obvious god to associate with a rite which is a glorification of military heroism. The horse itself represents swift vigour, a quality which the king aims at obtaining and increasing in himself by means of this sacrifice. The ceremony was begun by bathing the horse, when a four-eyed dog (that is, one with two spots above its eyes) was killed with a club by a man of low origin. The horse, having been consecrated, was allowed to roam about free for a year, guarded by a retinue of armed youths. During the interval the sacrificial ground was the scene of various offerings and rites, while stories were recited, chants sung, and lutes played. High and low, young and old, took a share in the pomp of the ceremonial. At length, when the year had come to an end, the horse was sacrificed during the course of a Soma offering of three days' duration. In the later Vedic ritual the horse is accompanied by a number of other victims; but in the Rigveda (two hymns of which are concerned with the horse-sacrifice) mention is made only of Pūṣan's he-goat, which announces the offering to the gods. Before the carcass was cut up, the chief consort of the king lay down beside the dead horse, while obscene conversations were carried on between the priests and the women of the royal household. Before the caul was offered, the priests propounded and solved riddles among themselves, as they had already done at a previous stage of the ceremonial. The whole rite concluded with a purifying bath at the end of the third day.

7. Death and Future Life.

A. *Beliefs.*—**a.** The soul, variously called *asu*, 'spirit,' *manas*, 'mind,' *ātman*, 'breath,' *prāṇa*, 'respiration,' was thought to be separable from the body during unconsciousness, and to continue its existence after the body had been destroyed by cremation or burial. But, though imperishable, it was not believed to prolong life as a mere spirit or shadow, but to retain its personal identity in a corporeal state; for the body, purified by the power of Agni and freed from all imperfections, shares in the existence of the other world. The doctrine of transmigration is not to be found in the Vedas; its beginnings are met with in the Brāhmaṇas, where the notion of repeated births and deaths in the next world appears; but it shows itself fully developed even in the oldest Upaniṣads, and must have been generally accepted by 600 B.C., since Buddha would not otherwise have received it into his system without question.

The spirit of the deceased proceeds upward through the air on the path trodden by the fathers (*pitara*) to the realm of eternal light. It is natural that Agni, who burns the corpse, should have been regarded as the conductor of the soul on its journey. Arrived in heaven, where he recovers his former body in a complete and glorified form, the departed meets the fathers who revel with Yama, and receives from the latter a resting-place. According to the Śatapatha Brāhmaṇa, the dead, on leaving this world, make their way between two fires, which burn the wicked but allow the good to pass. The latter proceed either by the path which leads to the fathers or by that which leads to the sun. The Upaniṣads also hold that there are two paths for the good: by the one, those who possess complete knowledge of the world-soul go to Brahmā; by the other, those whose knowledge is imperfect reach the world of heaven, whence, after the fruit of good works has been exhausted, they return to earth to be born again. On the other hand, those who are ignorant of the self go to the dark world of evil spirits, or are reborn on earth. To illustrate the mystery of the future life, the Kaṭha Upaniṣad tells the myth of Naciketas, who, on visiting the realm of death, is informed that those who have not enough merit for heaven and immortality fall again and again into the power of death and, entering upon the cycle of existence (*saṃsāra*), are born repeatedly with a body or as a stationary object; that he who controls himself reaches Viṣṇu's highest place; but that there is no hell for the unworthy.

b. Heaven.—The abode of the fathers and Yama is situated in the highest or third heaven, where is eternal light. It is also described as the highest point of the sun or the highest step of Viṣṇu. Here is a tree in the shade of which Yama drinks with the gods. In the Atharvaveda it is stated to be a fig-tree (*aśvattha*). Heaven is believed to be the reward of the righteous, of heroes who risk their lives in battle, of those who practise rigorous penance, and, above all, of those who bestow liberal sacrificial gifts. The Atharvaveda is full of references to the bliss in store for the latter.

The deceased, on entering heaven, see again father and mother, wives and children. Sickness is left behind; bodily imperfections or frailties are unknown; and old age cannot prevail. There are neither rich nor poor, neither oppressors nor oppressed. The life of the blest is passed among the gods, more especially in the presence of the two kings Yama and Varuṇa. Here the sound of the lute and of songs is heard; streams of Soma, *ghī*, milk, honey, and wine flow; and there is spirit-food and satiety. Bright, many-coloured cows, which yield all desires, are at hand. The life in heaven is thus one of indolent material bliss, devoted to sensual joys. In the Upaniṣads the life in the heaven of the gods, being followed by re-birth, is a lower and transient form of bliss; only those who know the truth reach the higher stage, the condition of changeless joy and unending peace which results from absorption in the world-soul.

c. The blest who dwell in the third heaven are called *pitṛs* or 'fathers.' By these are generally meant early ancestors who made the paths by which those who have recently died join them. Different races of them are distinguished (p. 608), the Aṅgirases being more especially associated with Yama. The fathers are also spoken of as lower, higher, and middle; as later and earlier; all being known to Agni, but a few only to their descendants. The fathers are fond of Soma, feasting with the gods and leading the same life as they do. Being immortal, they are even spoken of as gods. Great cosmical actions, like those of the gods, are sometimes attributed to them; thus they are said to have adorned the sky with stars, and to have placed darkness in the night and light in the day. As the burning of the corpse was in no sense a sacrifice, the corpse-devouring Agni was distinguished from the Agni who wafts the offering to the gods; and, similarly, the path of the fathers from that of the gods. The Śatapatha Brāhmaṇa goes further, discriminating between the heavenly world (*svarga loka*), that is, the world of the gods, and that of the fathers (*pitṛ-loka*). The fathers are prayed to like the gods, being entreated to hear and to protect their worshippers, and to refrain from punishing their descendants for any sin humanly committed against them. They are also besought to give riches, offspring, and long life to their sons; individual ancestors being sometimes invoked by name. Coming to the sacrifice on the same car as Indra and the other gods, they drink the pressed Soma as they sit on the litter of grass to the south (the quarter of the dead). They arrive in thousands and range themselves in order on the sacrificial ground. They receive oblations, which are, however, different from those offered to the gods.

d. The chief of the fathers is **Yama,** to whom three hymns of the Rigveda are addressed. He is only spoken of as a king who rules the dead, but it is implied that he is a god as well. He is, as is natural, specially associated with Agni, the conductor of the dead. Yama is the son of Vivasvat and of Saraṇyū, Tvaṣṭṛ's daughter. He was a mortal, who chose death and abandoned his body. Finding out the path for many, he passed to the other world, whither the ancient fathers have gone. Having been the first of mortals that died, he is called 'our father.' As a mythological creation, Yama goes back to the Indo-Iranian period, corresponding to Yima, son of Vīvahvant, in the Avesta. The most probable conclusion to be drawn from the available evidence seems to be that Yama represents the chief of the souls of the departed, as having been the first father of mankind and the first of those that died. This conclusion is supported by the fact that in the Avesta Yima is the ruler of an earthly paradise. It is, perhaps, also borne out by the appearance of Yama and his sister Yamī in the character of twins in a hymn of the Rigveda, where the very repudiation of their incest points to the existence of a belief in the descent of mankind from primeval twins. Some scholars have, however, identified Yama with various phenomena of nature, such as Agni, the sun, or the moon. In the Rigveda Yama's foot-fetter (*paḍbīśa*) is referred to as parallel to the bond of Varuṇa, and his messengers that seek the lives of men must have inspired feelings of dread. It is not till the Atharvaveda and the later mythology that Yama becomes more closely associated with the terrors of death, and assumes the character of a regular god of death; though even in the epic his domain is not limited to hell.

The owl and the pigeon occasionally appear as Yama's emissaries; but his regular messengers are two dogs, described as four-eyed, broad-nosed, brindled, brown, sons of Saramā. They guard the path to the other world or wander about among men, keeping watch on them; and they are besought to grant continued enjoyment of the light of the sun. Their functions seem to have been thought to consist partly in tracking out among men those who are to die, and partly in keeping guard on the path over those who are about to enter the realm of Yama. The conception of a watch-dog of the dead goes back to the Indo-Iranian period, as shown by the evidence of the Avesta, where a four-eyed hound is stated to keep guard at the head of the bridge which leads to the other world. If the epithet *śabalas* ('brindled') is identical with the Greek κέρβερος, the notion of a dog of death must go back even to the Indo-European age.

e. Hell.—As the virtuous, in the opinion of the Vedic seers, were rewarded in the future life, it is natural to suppose that they believed in some kind of abode for the wicked. The evidence of the Rigveda cannot, however, be said to go beyond showing that this was regarded as an underground darkness. But there can be no doubt that the belief in a regular hell exists in the Atharvaveda, which speaks of the house below, of black and lowest darkness, the abode of goblins and sorceresses, called *nāraka loka* as contrasted with *svarga loka*, the heavenly world of Yama. The torments suffered in this infernal region are also once described. It is not, however, till the period of the Brāhmaṇas that the notion of future punishment appears fully developed. Thus the Śatapatha Brāhmaṇa states that every one is born again after death and, being weighed in a balance, receives reward or punishment according to his deserts. Nothing is said in the Vedas of a final judgment or of a destruction and renovation of the world.

B. *THE CEREMONIAL*.—**a. Funeral rites.**—Cremation was the normal method of disposing of the dead in Vedic times. That burial was also practised to some extent is undoubted, though the ritual books have no rules regarding it, except in so far as the bones of the cremated are interred. The predilection of the Vedic theologians for the god of fire was most probably the reason for incineration having already become the almost universal practice among the Aryans in India. The beard and hair of the dead man were cut off and his nails trimmed; his body was anointed, decked with a garland, and dressed in a new garment, which he was intended to wear in the next world. The corpse was then carried or driven to the burning ground; a bundle of twigs was tied to it, in order to efface the footsteps and so prevent death from making its way back to the living. The dead man was then exhorted, with verses from a funeral hymn of the Rigveda, to go by the ancient paths, past the two dogs of Yama, to the fathers. The widow, who had mounted the pyre and lain down beside the corpse, was now called upon to rise and take the hand of her new spouse (her husband's brother). That the ceremonial excluded the burning of the widow is undoubted; but the ritual act which was required to recall her to life shows that her ascent of the pyre was symbolical of the actual immolation of bygone times. Indeed, it must be assumed that this ancient custom, though not sanctioned by the Vedic ritual, survived through the Vedic period in the families of military chiefs. Having by their example gradually spread to other classes, it became, in later times, a universal practice throughout India. If the deceased was a warrior, his bow was taken from his hand, an indication that at one time it was burned with him; if he was a sacrificer, his combustible utensils were placed with him on the pyre. Here we have a survival of the ancient custom of providing the dead with the chief articles of their property for use in the next life. At the same time as the corpse was burned, a cow and a he-goat were sacrificed. These animals, however, did not represent property, but were intended as a means of deflecting the consuming power of fire to them as substitutes for the corpse; and, by a fiction, Agni was supposed not to burn the dead man, but to send him 'done' to the fathers.

The mourners, on returning from the burning ground, bathed, changed their clothes, and refrained from looking round. On entering the house of the deceased, they touched purifying or auspicious objects such as water, fire, or cow-dung; and finally removed the sacrificial fire of the dead man by some aperture other than the door.

A death was followed by a period of impurity, varying from three days to ten, according to the degree of kinship. As the return of the soul was feared during this time, the surviving relatives took constant precautions to avoid infection. Thus only food which was bought or presented by others was eaten, evidently to guard against introducing anything tainted into the system.

Generally on the third day, what remained of the bones of the cremated man was collected, placed in an urn, and temporarily buried, to the accompaniment of the Rigvedic verse, 'Approach thy Mother Earth.' During this ceremony the deceased was no longer thought of as in the realm of Yama, but as actually present. This inconsistency is no doubt due to a primitive belief surviving beside the more recent conception of life in the heavenly world.

Last of all—according to the Brāhmaṇas, after the lapse of years—a burial mound was erected, the bones being exhumed for the purpose of removal to a suitable spot. During the following night music was performed, cymbals being beaten and the lute (*vīṇā*) played, the female mourners repeatedly going round the bones with their left hands towards them. On the following morning, the bones were taken to a place, out of sight of the village, where the ground was free from thorns but permeated with roots. A hole or furrow having been made, the bones were deposited and a mound of stone and earth was erected over them. Grain was scattered on the mound as food, while milk and water were poured into small pits dug around it, as drink for the deceased. When the mourners returned, various precautions were taken to prevent death from following the living; thus a stone or a clod was deposited as a boundary. The Rigveda refers, in a funeral hymn, to the erection of a stone to divide the living from the dead.

Though the Vedic Indian retained many primitive beliefs in the ceremonial concerned with the future life, he had advanced far beyond the terrors which inspire the funeral rites of the savage. The verses which he employed in that ceremonial, while combined with much petty ritual and betraying much zealous care for his own well-being, at the same time reflect trust in the gods, as guardians of the dead, and filial piety towards ancestors. If we find here no traces of deep feeling and genuine sorrow, this is largely due to the fact that the impersonal formulas contained in the ritual text-books are the only available evidence for this period.

b. Spirits.—The most striking contradiction in the Vedic view of the future life was the belief, though the Rigveda describes the deceased as conveyed direct to the fathers by the funeral fire, that the dead man did not join the fathers at once, but continued to lead a separate existence near the living for a year. The soul in this intermediate stage was distinguished by the name of *preta*, 'departed spirit,' as opposed to the ancestral spirits fully recognized as *pitara*, 'fathers.' During this transitional state it did not receive the regular monthly oblation to the manes of the sacrificer, but was honoured individually with separate offerings. At the end of the period it was received into the community of the fathers with a special ceremony which, strange to say, has nothing to do with that accompanying the final burial of the bones. Vedic literature has nothing to say about ghosts in any other sense than that of Pretas. There is, however, a passage in the Yajurveda stating that one who sheds the blood of a Brāhman will be excluded from the world of the fathers; and the evidence of early Buddhist texts may perhaps justify the inference that, even in the Vedic period, there was a belief in ghosts as spirits in the exceptional state of suffering torments on earth in punishment of guilt.

c. Ancestor-worship.—It remains only to sketch briefly the cult of the Vedas in so far as it was concerned with the dead. The regular sacrifice to ancestors, offered to father, grandfather, and great-grandfather, was celebrated every month at new moon. It was called *śrāddha* or 'offering given with faith' (*śraddhā*). For the purposes of this rite, a space was marked off in the south-east, the region which was sacred to the manes, and which the performers faced during the whole ceremony. Then the sacrificial fire was fetched and the food for the dead, consisting mainly of rice, but also of other offerings, prepared. Three small pits, a span long and four fingers broad and deep, having been dug and bestrewn with Darbha grass, an odd number of Brāhmans were seated, entertained, and received gifts. Libations to Soma associated with the fathers, and to Agni, conductor of the sacrifices to the dead, were also offered. A firebrand having been placed beside the pits to drive away demons who might have intruded themselves among the fathers, the latter were summoned to the offering and invoked to bestow wealth on their descendants. Jars of water were then set down beside the pits; the sacrificer took one with his left hand and, pouring water into the pits, mentioned the name of the ancestor to whom the offering was made. Grasping the sacrificial ladle also with his left hand, he placed one-third of the food in the form of a cake in each pit, invoking the fathers to partake of the offering. In conclusion, pieces of cloth were presented to the ancestors as clothing. The whole ceremony was interspersed with verses addressed to the fathers.

Our knowledge of this ceremonial is entirely derived from the ritual works of the Vedic period. There is nothing about it in the Rigveda, as it is not accompanied by hymns to the mighty gods with whom that Veda is concerned. Nevertheless, there can be little doubt that, in its essential features, it already existed in the earliest Vedic age; for its general character is extremely primitive: there is no trace of the souls of the dead abiding in heaven; the gifts offered to them are not sent up by the sacrificial fire, but are placed in the earth; and the spirit waits in or on the earth to be fed and clothed. The only details which probably do not go back to the times of the Rigveda are the offerings to Soma and Agni, as well as the presence of Brāhmans.

LITERATURE.—John Muir, *Original Sanskrit Texts*, 5 vols., especially vols. iv. and v. ('Vedic Cosmogony and Mythology'), London, 1873, 1884; A. Bergaigne, *La Religion védique*, 3 vols., Paris, 1878–1883; A. Barth, *The Religions of India*, Eng. tr., London, 1882; A. Hillebrandt, *Vedische Mythologie*, 3 vols., Breslau, 1891–1902, abridged ed., 1910; E. Hardy, *Die vedisch-brahmanische Periode*, Münster, 1893; E. W. Hopkins, *The Religions of India*, Boston, 1895, London, 1896; H. Oldenberg, *Die Religion des Veda*, Berlin, 1894, [2]1917; *Die Lehre der Upanishaden*, Göttingen, 1915; W. Caland, *Altindischer Ahnencult*, Leyden, 1893, *Die altindischen Todten- und Bestattungsgebräuche*, Amsterdam, 1896; W. Caland and V. Henry, *L'Agnistoma: description complète de la forme normale du sacrifice de Soma dans le culte védique*, 2 vols., Paris, 1906; A. Hillebrandt, *Ritual-Litteratur*, Strassburg, 1897; A. A. Macdonell, *Vedic Mythology* (=*GIAP* iii. 1a), do. 1897; E. Lehmann, 'Die Inder,' in Chantepie de la Saussaye, *Lehrbuch der Religionsgeschichte*, 2 vols., Tübingen, 1905; M. Bloomfield, *The Religion of the Veda*, New York and London, 1908; R. E. Hume, *The Thirteen Principal Upanishads*, Oxford, 1921.

A. A. MACDONELL.

VEGETARIANISM.—In this article an attempt is made to confine the discussion to those portions of the subject which ultimately have a practical bearing, even though the way may lie through the investigation of some rather complex ethical principles. The omission of all investigation into the history of vegetarianism is dictated not only by fidelity to this aim, but also by the consideration that in this particular subject no sound inferences as to modern problems can possibly be drawn from any records of the past. It is, *e.g.*, interesting to learn that the poet Ovid wrote in favour of a vegetable diet as being natural to primitive man. But what we want to know is how far his words were effective. They may have been, and yet no one has recorded the effect; or they may have been dictated at first by dismay at the sight of great excess in flesh food. They are anyhow by themselves no evidence of vegetarian practice; and, if they were, we should be unable to connect it securely with the gradual decline of Rome. In short, at all times the important question has been, not the practice of an exceptional minority, but that of the mass of the population—just the large complex fact which has never been recorded.

That omission leaves two principal aspects of the question to be considered: (*a*) the physiological argument, which is treated as of subordinate importance, owing to the evidence to be gathered from facts being still very incomplete; and (*b*) the ethical argument, including our duty to the lower animals, the bearing of the example of Christ, and the question how far a non-flesh diet is a help to the higher life.

1. The physiological argument.—In several treatises on vegetarianism much has been written on the physiological effects of a flesh or non-flesh diet, but very little of any value. The truth is that before any scientific conclusion can be arrived at—in other words, before any broad inference can be drawn from experiments—the question must be so far simplified that it becomes abstract: that is to say, experiments have to be conducted under conditions which do not obtain in ordinary life.

It is impossible to make sure that any two sets of experiments deal with the same data; *e.g.*, no one could ascertain how great in any given case has been the influence of mind upon the bodily tissues. Wonderful records are given of endurance exhibited by vegetarians on a spare diet of fruit, and of prolonged effort not only of brain but of muscle. But it is quite uncertain whether the spirit of the individuals in question has not affected the result so as to make it useless as a guide in cases where such spirit is wanting. Again, the more the problem is considered, the more formidable grows the question of time. Supposing, *i.e.*, that a fair number of individual lives have been under observation and in all cases the health has been well maintained on a vegetarian diet, it is still open to a sceptic to insist that an examination of the next generation, or perhaps the next two or three, is required before the experiment can be deemed conclusive or scientific. If any one is convinced that the children of vegetarians are born infirm—in other words, that the human stock loses vigour if abstinence from meat becomes general—it is ridiculous to urge in answer that facts yield anything like a scientific disproof of the contention. No experiments which can pretend to be exhaustive have yet been made, and there is very little likelihood of any such being undertaken. Supposing—what is not easy to suppose—that some hundreds of adults allowed themselves to be subjects of experiment, there is no guarantee that similar results would be gained from people who were victims of compulsion or involuntary abstainers, or from enthusiastic votaries of a new cult, or from men and women of different antecedents and different occupations. Thus the condition of a convert to a particular diet at the age of 40 is not a sure indication of what would be the effect of a similar diet on another man of the same age, still less on another of 20, or on a child of 10 years old, or on a woman of any age.

Moreover, the question is obscured by the varieties of diet comprised under the title 'vegetarian.' Large numbers of people abstain from meat, but not from fish; others from brown meat, not from chicken; others eat meat once a week; others eat eggs, but no meat or fish, and so on. Then there is the complex question of starchy foods and sugar. A sound opinion seems to be that the mischief caused by too much starch is quite as serious as that due to the uric acid found in meat. Add to all these uncertainties the startling differences in different constitutions, anyhow for a time, and the incredible skill and delicacy required before any chemical analysis can certify food-values with any precision, and it is indisputably clear that the physiological question concerning diet is not at present advanced beyond the stage where rough probability is the only guide to conduct. In other words, we must be prepared to find that in the absence of sure knowledge there has been and is and will be a proportionate amount of dogmatism.

It is further noteworthy that, in this country at any rate, inquirers are debarred from what would seem a promising source of information, viz. the medical profession. For not only has there always been and is still a reluctance on the part of medical men as a profession to undermine the importance and prestige of science by preaching the sanative power of unassisted nature, but it appears that till quite recently the preparation for the practice of medicine has not included any study of dietetic questions or of food-values. Thus in a matter of great complexity, which for our enlightenment requires bold but very careful experiment and the most scrupulous observation of results, little or nothing has been done which could give promise of a scientific induction. We are thrown back on amateur and haphazard experiments, and it may be said that such innovations on convention and tradition as have been effected have been introduced by outsiders and rather obstructed than favoured by medical opinion. To this professional attitude parallels from other professions could be easily adduced. Hence, when it is claimed for vegetarianism that the case in its favour is rooted in science and can be proved by experiment, no cautious student of the subject will yield a ready assent. The truth is that the strongest arguments for it are based on other considerations which are not, strictly speaking, scientific. That is to say, many individuals are convinced that their health has been permanently benefited by forgoing the eating of meat—nor has any one the right, scientifically speaking, to doubt the truth of their conviction—but, if the number of such were ten times what it is, it would still be illogical to argue that the residue of mankind would benefit to an equal degree. Among the complexities of the subject is the difficulty of ascertaining how far the experiment in any case has been fairly tried, at what age, after what antecedents, and, perhaps most important of all, with what degree of faith. For, along with other uncertainties, many individuals have experienced a varying amount of discomfort in the early stages of the new régime. Of those a considerable proportion, totally unable to face this or any discomfort, abandon the attempt and give themselves out as evidences of vegetarian failure—a testimony wholly worthless in reality, but quite sufficient to deter most of us from such an innovation in our habits. Equally fallacious are the indications afforded by the physique of foreigners, especially Orientals, though the crudest generalizations, based, if on anything at all, on nothing better than travellers' unverified gossip, frequently pass current as substantial evidence. Such facts, indeed, as have been accurately observed and reported can obviously give ground for nothing better than conjecture.

2. The ethical argument.—The appeal to human compassion in the matter of the treatment of animals, though logically cogent, has been made with very little success even in this country, where the sentiment of kindness towards animals is strongly developed, as compared with that of other European peoples. If man could prove that flesh-foods were indispensable to his existence, of course there would be nothing more to be said. Nor would it be denied that, if such food maintained him in rude health more certainly than any other, he is right to eat it. But humane vegetarians assert that neither of these contentions can be verified, that, on the contrary, so large a proportion of mankind has subsisted in vigour on fruits and herbs for many generations together that the plea of necessity breaks down in presence of admitted facts. If this be so, no defence is possible of the practice of taking the lives of animals. Moreover, as long as man accustoms himself to kill them for food, knowing or suspecting that he could live quite well if he spared them, his whole attitude towards them is vitiated by selfishness. Very few individuals can concern themselves seriously or for long together about the welfare of animals while they are conscious that society as a whole condones the slaughter of them for no other reason than that flesh foods are preferable, or that a certain amount of inconvenience would be caused by a change of diet. Till the ethical question is fairly faced, the general conscience is violated by the daily commission on the largest scale of an act which we uneasily suspect to be a crime. Further, unless there had been a conspiracy to hide the facts, the hideousness of the slaughter-house system would long ago have roused public sentiment to a pitch of fury; and even now, assuming what is very doubtful, that the butchering is as painless as possible, there remains against man's whole treatment of his helpless fellow-creatures the broad indictment that to rob millions of them of life unnecessarily is a kind of murder.

It is difficult to say what answers to the above arguments are made, as public opinion is too lax on the question and custom is too strong to have allowed the matter to be fairly discussed. The truth is, an enormous majority of people are too much under the yoke of custom to be awake to the moral appeal. Many would readily admit that they cannot meet it, nor are they at pains even to excuse themselves save on the plea of convenience. Meanwhile it would be difficult to measure the mischief caused to our social life by this particular form of heedlessness. Compared with foreigners, Britons are peculiarly sensitive to the claims of the animal kingdom. Such kindness as we show is based on religion, but is also the outcome of an inherited sentiment, powerful to-day, but, it must be admitted, of somewhat recent growth. If, then, both sentiment and religion are flouted by any particular custom, and little or no protest is raised against it, the very foundations of our moral principles are assailed by a deadly form of insincerity, all the more deadly for being largely unsuspected. Indeed, if these considerations are sound, we, as a society, are under the ban of Christ's denunciation of the Pharisees, who were guilty in proportion as they were blind.

But there must be plausible arguments for a practice so general as the slaying and eating of animals. Probably the most prevailing is the idea that it makes on the whole for health. The physiological aspect of the question must be dealt with separately. Here it is only necessary to observe that, granted the fact, there need be no dispute as to the principle asserted. It may be conceded that man is on so much higher a plane than animals that his welfare must take precedence of theirs in all cases where there is a direct conflict. But that there is such a conflict is exactly what the humanitarians deny. They maintain that the evidence of fruits, cereals, etc., being sufficient to support human life in full vigour is abundant; and their main argument is not that men should suffer in order to spare animals, but that, as long as there is reason to believe that animal flesh is no better (indeed is inferior) as food for man than fruits and vegetables, it cannot be right to kill animals and eat them.

To this it is replied that, if abstinence from meat became general, intolerable evils would result, such as the means of livelihood being taken from millions of workers, and the loss of skins which are needed for clothing and which are supplied at present from animals bred or preserved for food. There would be a prospect also of large industries being destroyed and thousands of workers being thrown out of employment.

One obvious answer to these misgivings is that they are based on the assumption that a vast revolution in diet could come about suddenly. There is of course no reason to assume anything of the kind, least of all in a country where conservative prejudice on this subject is adamantine. But that is not the kind of answer that touches the conscience. The truth is, the results of conduct in this case, as in many others, are far too uncertain to be worth arguing about. Nor would there be any need to forecast the future with the laborious precision which is often affected, if once it were made clear that obedience to divine law means obedience in spite of uncertainty as to results. The training of the Apostles was directed to this end throughout, that they should walk by faith and not by sight. But to limit obedience to occasions of utility is to destroy its faithfulness. Thus, if man recognizes the claims of animals to good treatment, it is futile to defend the slaughter of them because the results of the opposite line of conduct are not easy to foresee. This is the point at which religious considerations supplement ethical. If we believe that God has committed animals to us, we are bound to treat them kindly, even if the results were likely to be far more inconvenient than they possibly could be. Indeed, the experience of food shortage has taught us that all the difficulties supposed to be inherent in vegetarianism are faced without hesitation as soon as the situation is understood. In other words, professing followers of Christ ignore what is admittedly a divinely sanctioned claim, but recognize it as soon as ever 'provision for the flesh,' against which St. Paul (Ro 13^{14}) and our Lord (Mt 6^{25}) warn us, seems to be in question.

A more solid objection is advanced when it is urged that the Founder of our religion and the Pattern of our conduct did Himself habitually partake of animal food. How can humane-minded people take their stand on a divinely sanctioned law which the Son of God Himself disobeyed?

To face this objection fairly, it is necessary to point out that the oft-quoted parallel of Christ's silence concerning slavery is not at first sight applicable. Against slavery He did undoubtedly establish principles of charity between man and man which were certain, if followed, to overthrow the institution sooner or later. But it cannot be said that any teaching of His can be quoted which bears at all directly against the practice of slaying animals for food; and it is quite legitimate to argue that He had no such objection to the practice on humane grounds as He must have had against the practice of depriving a fellow-man of his liberty. Moreover, the question is not, 'Why did He refrain from denunciation?' so much as, 'Why did He participate in the practice?'

The explanation must take account of the main purpose which—as far as we can grasp it—the Saviour set before Himself in His work on earth. From no other point of view can the fragmentary character of Christ's ethical teaching be understood. But any adequate statement on such a theme would range far beyond the limits of this article. This much, however, may be said, that, in proportion as any interpretation of Christ's work falls short of the full doctrine of the NT as to His person, it will fail in explaining the gaps in the ethical teaching. In other words, if Jesus is regarded only as a divinely-gifted prophet, His life and teaching were not only abortive, but needlessly so. With slight precaution He could have escaped an early death and extended His teaching and the sublime example of His conduct for other fifty years. There is no way of meeting this criticism except by holding fast to the Christology of St. Paul and St. John. The task before the Lord was not to teach mankind, but to save them by His incarnation, death, resurrection, and the gift of the Holy Spirit from heaven. Now, while engaged on this task, He gave just enough time to evangelization to reveal what human life would be if men lived it in the full conviction and certainty of God's love and presence among them. The revelation was grievously misunderstood at the time and subsequently, owing to men's tendency to turn the gospel into a burden of moral law, more crushing than that of Moses because more spiritual and exacting. Therefore the teaching was in the main barren of precepts dealing with everyday conduct. The danger of literalism of interpretation was imminent, and we may conclude that, if Jesus had given us anything like a complete code of moral precepts, or even a full picture of a sinless life extended far into old age, our attention would have been diverted finally and completely from the difficult task of understanding His work of redemption to the far simpler but hopeless endeavour to live up to the level of His moral example—*i.e.*, to reject God's scheme of salvation owing to utter inability to rise up to its meaning. Hence the Saviour refrained from all attempt to guide His followers by rules, but gradually taught them—what they are still very slow to learn—that their lives were to be quickened by the Holy Spirit whose indwelling was to be to them their strength and inspiration for all time. In view of this prospect, we can understand why His ethical teaching was so suggestive but so paradoxical, so figurative, and incomplete. It was designed, not to save us from the trouble of thinking, but to turn our thoughts to the Comforter whom He promised to send.

But, in considering the moral example of Christ, we have to recognize the fact that He resolutely declined to gratify the expectation of the Jews that He should set before men a pattern of conduct to be imitated unintelligently. Not only the Pharisees but all mankind are ready to go through almost any unpleasantness if thereby they can escape the pain of recasting their ideas. From the beginning of His ministry, however, Christ set Himself sternly against this temper. His first word spoken in public (Mt 4^{17}) was an echo of the Baptist's injunction: 'Change your minds: for the Kingdom of the Heavens is come nigh.' Clearly the Lord intended that deep principles should be learned by men, and that, as they were learned, human conduct should change. Supposing, then, that He had set Himself in opposition, not specifically to a principle of conduct, but to a social custom the meaning of which was widely misunderstood, that would have been an attempt, foredoomed to failure, to improve human life without human co-operation; for it is certain that moral improvement cannot be achieved if we do not know what we are doing and why we are doing it.

Therefore Christ taught principles based upon the fact of God's Fatherhood, one of them being that the human body was to be honoured. This was taught not by a formulated rule, but by the fact of the Incarnation as soon as it was accepted. Hence, in the course of the history of Christianity, social customs have to be considered and modified in accordance with the underlying principle of reverence being due to our bodies made in the image of God. Thus the question of the kind of food that we eat arises naturally as the Incarnation is gradually being better understood.

Further, Christ's life on earth was an exhibition of divine power triumphing in and through the uttermost of created weakness. By His endurance of that weakness He manifested His personal strength, inherent and inalienable, as the Son of God.[1] Now that strength was the strength of a Redeemer, a Transformer, an Uplifter. Christ found mankind sunk in evil prejudices and evil customs. He took upon Himself our poisoned nature, as it was, that He might cleanse and reinvigorate it; what He did not do was to better the conditions so as to make His task easier. He took on Himself all the disabilities which resulted from human blundering, to show how, not so much in spite of them but by means of them, He could triumph over Satan. Hence the freedom from temporary restrictions and the universality of His teaching.

It is therefore strictly relevant to the main question to ask what kind of food best helps us in our endeavour to show reverence to our bodies, while at the same time we assert our mastery over them. There is no dispute as to the latter duty, but there is much haziness of mind in regard to the former, due to ignorance which can be dispelled only by experience of the effects of a reformed diet. Vegetarians learn them with surprise, yet they all seem naturally to result from nothing more than the relieving of the body and the mind from constant injection of poison. One that is discovered, but remains for obvious reasons unpublished, is that a 'simple' diet, consisting principally of fruit, lettuces, and 'unstarchy' foods, secures *cleanliness for the inside of our bodies*, in contrast to the noisome defilement which in flesh-eating societies has come to be taken as a matter of course. Here there is no room for dispute. If a certain diet promotes cleanliness while another causes dirt, that is enough reason by itself for preferring the former. It is then a question of fact which can only be tested by experience. Again, vegetarianism favours moderation in diet; and if —as seems to be the case, and has indeed been certified by the restriction of diet in time of war—most people clog their energies by needlessly taxing their digestions, it remains that a diet free from poison is to be preferred. True, elaborate cooking encourages excess, whatever the diet be; but, as the poison of meat is a stimulant which is followed as usual by a reaction, and as the reaction is a certain languor which feels like hunger but has nothing to do with it in reality, there is a peculiar danger in a diet of flesh which vegetarians for the most part escape. It will be noticed that it is here assumed that excessive eating is common. We need not give all the evidence for this assumption. Perhaps the most distinct indications were given during the ration-time in 1917 and 1918 that the prevalent fashion of excess had been mainly among men who could afford superfluous food, between the ages of 40 and 60, when advancing years dictate the wisdom of a gradually diminishing diet, but when also it is quite easy to maintain by skilful cooking the craving of a palate-appetite almost at the level that it kept at 30 years of age. Our social customs, our prejudices, and our cooking all make real moderation in eating difficult; and among the influences that favour excess, meat-eating followed by a nerve-reaction that is mistaken for hunger must be numbered.

In this connexion, however, the most serious indictment against flesh-eating has still to be mentioned. Meat is a stimulant, and its heating properties act upon the system by increasing the power of the animal in man. By meat-eating, in other words, the temptation to sensuality of all kinds is strengthened.

No sooner is this affirmation made than it is traversed as follows: either (*a*) it is flatly denied, and instances of vegetarian or quasi-vegetarian yet sensual peoples are adduced; or (*b*) it is contended that, if any immunity from animalism is secured, it is at the cost of diminished bodily vigour.

(*a*) No arguments are more fallacious than those which rest on a false induction. The whole question is far too complex to allow of certainty. We can guide our conduct by probability only, and probability admits of degrees. If we confine our attention to ourselves—the British people—the evidence, as already remarked, yields no scientifically certain results. It is nevertheless very weighty and cogent as a guide to conduct. We know something about the temperament of our own people, practically nothing about foreigners' temperament, such as that of the Hindus or the Japanese. That is to say, while it is very difficult

[1] R. M. Benson, *The War-Songs of the Prince of Peace*, London, 1901, i. 117.

to exclude other influences, such as heredity, religion, and social habits, even when we are considering ourselves alone, it is wholly impossible in the case of foreigners. In other words, evidence as to the physiological and spiritual effect of a certain diet in England is of some value for English people, but of less value for foreign white people, and practically of no value whatever for people so different from us as the yellow or the black races. The evidence, then, which it is worth while considering is that which is drawn from British people; and, further, it may be drawn from the experience of those who have made the experiment, while very little weight can be attached to the affirmations of those who have not. For, while a large majority of young men, all flesh-eaters, are troubled with strong sensual desires to which a huge proportion give way, the constant asseverations of those, the minority, who have made the change, to the effect that continence has forthwith become easier for them, remain uncontradicted in reality, no matter how often they are ridiculed.

Moreover, the benefit, it cannot be too often insisted on, is not only relief from certain troublesome physical sensations but a marked purification of thought and desire. 'Mali mores sunt mali amores,' said St. Augustine, and no cause of life-wreckage has been more fatally operative than the attempt to check bad actions without eradicating the desire. If, then, converts to vegetarianism who have tried both forms of diet are the only witnesses in possession of first-hand evidence, and if their testimony is practically unanimous and wholly unshakable in confidence as to the reform of their diet being to them an immense assistance to the higher life, we are bound to conclude that, in a difficult and complex question, we have here in good sooth a solid foundation on which to build, a real light in the darkness, a veritably guiding principle. Especially is this the case when we remember that the matter is far too personal to admit of publication. A little *a posteriori* evidence given confidentially outweighs all noisy *a priori* contradictions.

Nothing, however, is easier than that a principle admitted in theory should be denied in practice. If people meant what they say when they deplore the ravages of venereal disease, they would eagerly grasp at anything that held out any hope whatever of mitigating the power of the temptation, no matter if their personal convenience suffered thereby, or even if they themselves were called on to undergo real prolonged discomfort. No such excuse, however, is available. The only real obstacles to change are the most stubborn: hatred of change, positive dread of a new idea, both confirmed by deep and wide-spread misunderstanding.

(*b*) The objection that a non-flesh diet lowers the bodily vigour must be met with a flat contradiction, as very nearly all the evidence points to the contrary, except in abnormal cases. It is true that for a time a *sudden* change from a full meat diet to a régime of vegetables strictly so called may mean under-nourishment, if the foods are not carefully chosen. Or a still more disastrous blunder is made in substituting a huge amount of innutritious vegetables for beef and mutton—a sure way of inducing corpulence and lowering vitality. The right method is to make the change gradually and discover by experiment and counsel both the amount and quality of the nourishment required. Other benefits found in many cases to result from a non-flesh diet, especially if it avoids the danger of excess of starch and is diminished with advancing years, are as follows: (1) equability of spirits and immunity from depression, especially on waking in the morning—many would admit that this evil is due to heavy feeding over night, but it is not generally known that it is chiefly due to the meat poison; (2) immunity from rheumatism, lumbago, and gout; (3) reduced requirements of sleep; (4) comparative indifference to cold; (5) cure or mitigation of sea-sickness, mountain-sickness, headache, languor, etc. It is asserted by vegetarians that all of these may be expected after an interval of time varying in different cases, from the change of diet, and that so-called failures are either abnormal cases or due to want of perseverance.

Other objections are advanced not because of their cogency but as excuses for maintaining the *status quo*. It is urged that a vast industry would be destroyed and many thousands of caterers deprived of their livelihood. The whole force of this argument rests on the absurd assumption that all classes of the community would make the change suddenly. What is far more relevant is the prospect of a great stimulus to the wholesome cottage industry of fruit-growing, allotments, and agriculture generally. But it should be borne in mind that, granted the cogency of the ethical arguments, Christians ought not to be in a hesitation as to the results. Faith in God means that, in the long run anyhow, suffering is diminished by right action and never increased.

Summary.—For the sake of establishing principles which might serve to guide conduct, the history of vegetarianism is of little use. Nor can it be contended that the physiological effects can be stated with anything like scientific cogency. Numberless individual testimonies in its favour could be quoted against a comparatively small number adverse. But the induction is too narrow to allow of any conclusions being drawn which can be reckoned more than very probable. Once, however, so much as probability is conceded, the ethical argument becomes irresistible. Two considerations alone would establish this assertion: (1) the slaughter of animals being unjustifiable unless its necessity can be proved; (2) the practical certainty that flesh foods are stimulative to the animal passions, especially of the adolescent male, unless the consumption of them is restricted to a level hardly possible of attainment. Other benefits of a fruitarian and light farinaceous diet concern such exceedingly important departments of life as interior cleanliness and, of course, health of body, and therewith the paying of due reverence to it; equability of spirits, and increased capacity for sustained hard work, both bodily and mental. Where a fair trial of the reformed diet has been given, it must be conceded that in these respects the individual testimonies in its favour are very numerous and convincing. Against all this, however, are custom, prejudice, misunderstanding, ignorance, and social inconvenience, much exaggerated but sufficient to demand thought and care. These forces, though for the most part inert, will probably check any considerable advance in the direction of change for many years to come.

LITERATURE.—The literature is extensive; the following is a selection: Anna B. Kingsford, *The Perfect Way in Diet*², London, 1885; A. F. Hills, *Essays on Vegetarianism*, do. 1893; Howard Williams, *Ethics of Diet*², do. 1896; Eustace H. Miles, *Failures of Vegetarianism*, do. 1902; A. R. Kenney-Herbert, *Vegetarian and Simple Diet*, do. 1904; H. S. Salt, *The Logic of Vegetarianism*, do. 1906; Eustace H. Miles and Mariella John, *Builders of the Body, or Lessons on Food Values*, do. 1907; J. L. Buttner, *A Fleshless Diet: Vegetarianism as a National Dietary*, New York, 1910; Eustace H. Miles, *The Food Reformer's Companion*, London, 1910; H. Carrington, *The Natural Food of Man*, do. 1912; G. Krueger, *Man's Best Food*, Eng. tr., do. 1914; *The Law of God*, by a Vegetarian, do. 1915; M. A. White, *Why I do not eat Meat*, Zarephath, N.J., 1915; E. Bonnejoy, *Le Végétarisme et le régime végétarien rationnel*, Paris, 1891; R. Meunier, *Le Végétarisme*, do. 1911; A. Muñoz Ruiz de Pasanés, *Alimentacion y su influencia en la degeneracion de la raza latina: Ventajas del regimen vegetariano*, Madrid, 1907; A. Aderholdt, *Die* *naturgemässe Lebensweise* [*Vegetarianismus*], Frankfort, 1884; G. Bunge, *Der Vegetarianismus*, Berlin, 1885; A. Winckler, *Kritik des Vegetarianismus*, Neuwied, 1891; *The Vegetarian Messenger*, Manchester; *The Vegetarian Annual*, London; *The Vegetarian Directory and Food Reformer's Guide*.

E. LYTTELTON.

VENDĪDĀD.—See AVESTA.

VESTAL VIRGINS.—See HEARTH, HEARTH-GODS, PRIEST (Roman).

VESTMENTS.—See DRESS.

VICARIOUS SUFFERING.—See SUFFERING.

VIKRAMA ERA.—The era known by the name of Vikrama, or more fully Vikramāditya, or, according to the Jains, Vikramārka, is that commonly used by Hindus over all N. India, except in Bengal, where reckoning by the Śaka era (*q.v.*) is preferred. It is commonly called *Samvat*, an abbreviation of *Saṁvatsara*, 'year,' but that word is sometimes used in connexion with dates expressed in other eras. The Vikrama era is also current in Teliṅgāna, or the Telugu country, and in Gujarāt. Most authors place its initial point in 57 B.C., but, according to Fleet, 58 B.C. is correct. The year is luni-solar, consisting of twelve lunar months, harmonized with the apparent motion of the sun by an elaborate system of intercalation and omission, which may be studied in the technical chronological works by Jacobi, Sewell, and other scholars who are cited in some of the publications mentioned at the end of this article. In N. India the Vikrama year begins in the month Chaitra or Chait (March–April), but in Gujarāt it begins seven months later in Kārtika or Kārtik (Oct.–Nov.). We also hear of localities where the year began either in Āṣāḍha or Āṣārh (June–July), or in Mārgasiras, or Māgh (Jan.–Feb.). Another variation arises from the practice of sometimes reckoning the month to end with the full moon (*pūrṇimānta*), and sometimes taking it to end with the new moon (*amānta*). The year, in any case, never coincides exactly with a year A.D., so that no summary formula of conversion will give more than approximate results. Commonly the subtraction of 57 from a V.E. date gives the year A.D.; *e.g.*, 1857 V.E. is equivalent to the period from 27th March, 1800, to 15th March, 1801 A.D., according to Cunningham's tables for a year beginning with the month Chait. Another complication is caused by the use in Rājputāna of a variety of the era called A-nanda, 'without *nanda*,' the term *nanda* being taken as equivalent to 90. An A-nanda year V.E. is converted roughly into a year A.D. by adding (90–57) 33. Thus 1857 V.E. A-nanda would be approximately 1890 A.D. instead of 1800, as according to the ordinary (*sa-nanda*, or 'with *nanda*') reckoning. The bardic poet Chand, who habitually uses the A-nanda form, was unjustly accused of erroneous dating until his practice was understood.

A Hindu date may be expressed in an 'expired' year, as, when we say a man is 70 years of age, we mean that he has completed 70 years; or it may be expressed in a 'current' year, as when we say that an article was written in 1918, meaning the unfinished year at the time of writing. The causes mentioned above, besides others, make the exact conversion of V.E. into A.D. dates a difficult business. Tables must be consulted, but they do not always agree, and detailed calculation of the equivalent of a date requires an expert.

The name Vikrama or Vikramāditya appears not to have been applied to the era until quite a late date, in the 10th or 11th century A.D. In Gupta times (5th and 6th cent.) the era was known as that reckoned according to the practice of the Mālava tribe (*gaṇa*), who inhabited Mālwā, then including S. Rājputāna. Probably the era originated in that area, perhaps at Ujjain, the ancient capital, from which the Hindus reckoned longitude. At that period the years were sometimes called *kṛta* (lit. 'made'), apparently with reference to a Vedic 4-year cycle of which the first year was termed *kṛta*.[1] No record is known of any *rājā* Vikrama or Vikramāditya at Ujjain or elsewhere in 58 or 57 B.C., from whose accession the epoch of the era might be reckoned, as tradition affirms that it actually was reckoned. But it is possible that such a *rājā* may have existed, and the presumption is that the name Vikrama as applied to the era should be that of the king who established it. It is also possible that one of the later kings bearing the common title of Vikrama or Vikramāditya may have become associated with the era by erroneous tradition. The strongest candidate for the honour of being considered the original of the *rājā* Bikram (Vikrama) of popular legend is Chandragupta II. (*q.v.*), Vikramāditya (*c.* A.D. 375–413). Hoernle suggests Yaśodharman (*c.* A.D. 520), who may possibly have borne the same title. Both kings ruled over Mālwā. The origin of the era remains unknown, nor is there any clear evidence to show how, when, or why the name was changed from 'the era according to the practice of the Mālavas or the Mālava tribe' to 'the era of [King] Vikrama.' The subject has been much debated by archæologists without positive result.

LITERATURE.—The following list gives the more important references, but the subject has been discussed or mentioned in many other books and articles. J. Prinsep, 'Useful Tables,' in *Essays on Indian Antiquities*, ed. E. Thomas, London, 1858, vol. ii.; A. Cunningham, *Book of Indian Eras*, Calcutta, 1883; F. Kielhorn, in *IA* xix. [1890], and xx. [1891], esp. pp. 397–414; D. R. Bhandarkar, *ib.* xlii. [1913] 163, *ASWI Progress Report for 1915–16*, p. 56, and 'Vikrama Era,' in *Bhandarkar Commemoration Volume*, Poona, 1917; K. B. Pathak, 'New Light on Gupta Era and Mihirakula,' *ib.*; Sten Konow, 'Indoskythische Beiträge,' *Sitzungsber. der königl. Preuss. Akad. der Wissenschaften*, 1916; J. F. Fleet, *JRAS*, 1913, pp. 994–1000, and other artt. in *JRAS*, 1907, etc.; A. F. R. Hoernle, *JRAS*, 1909, p. 100; H. P. Śāstrī, *Epigraphia Indica*, xii. [1913–14] 119. The A-nanda variety is explained fully by Syam Sundar Das, in *Ann. Rep. on the Search for Hindi MSS for 1900*, Allahabad, 1903, pp. 5–10; and summarily by Hoernle, *JRAS*, 1906, p. 500.

VINCENT A. SMITH.

VIMUTTI.—See MOKṢA.

VINAYAS.—See LAW (Buddhist).

VIRGIN BIRTH.—I. **Ethnic.**—(1) A wonder birth or a supernatural birth is one of the commonest ideas in folk-tale and myth. In not all of these, however, is there what can strictly be called virgin birth. The latter certainly does not occur where ancient myths of the birth of heroes, great men, or kings are concerned. In spite of direct evidence of true human descent, myth told how a god was their real father. Plato and Augustus were said to be sons of Apollo, the kings of Egypt sons of a god and a human mother. In these myths also the mother is already wedded, and the divine parent is father in a purely physical sense and has a material form, in that form taking the place of the husband. In many folk-tales and sagas where the conception of the child is supernatural, and due to contact with or to swallowing some substance, or to the breath or glance of a man or divine being falling on the woman, or to many other causes, the woman is already married, and the birth is not, strictly speaking, a virgin birth. In this aspect these stories are parallel to ritual customs in which married women desirous of having children make use of certain substances, certain means, certain rites, to aid or perhaps to cause conception.

[1] *Epigraphia Indica*, xii. 319.

There are, however, a number of stories, both from the lower and from the higher culture, in which a virgin bears a child because she has swallowed a pebble, a blade of grass, or some other substance.

Poshaiyänne, a hero of the Sia of New Mexico, was born of a virgin who had eaten two nuts. Fo-hi, who founded the Chinese Empire, was the son of a virgin who ate a flower which had clung to her garment when bathing.

Sometimes pregnancy is caused by mere contact with an object, by bathing, or by the sun's rays. But, while such stories regarding virgins or at least unmarried girls (and this distinction is an important one, considering the commonness of prenuptial unions) are fairly numerous in the lower culture, it is certainly an exaggeration to say that 'the Virgin-Mother myth is universal in Paganism.'[1]

E. S. Hartland, in his work, *Primitive Paternity*, maintains that these stories, the corresponding rites to cause pregnancy, and many other factors have resulted from a former universal ignorance of the physical causes of conception, still alleged to exist among Australian tribes. While his arguments are weighty, it still remains doubtful whether this ignorance ever actually was so wide-spread. The universal existence of the couvade would seem to imply knowledge of fatherhood. Whether in supernatural or in virgin birth the child born is often the metamorphosed form of some substance swallowed by the woman, and that again is a man or hero who has taken the form of that substance, in order to be reborn. Yehl, the culture-hero of British Columbian tribes, frequently transformed himself into a small object which was swallowed by a woman, and he was then reborn. With the Arunta of Australia a spirit of a totemic ancestor enters a woman and is reborn from her. Conception, with the Arunta, is not supposed to result at all from intercourse, though that may prepare the way for it.[2] Perhaps, therefore, we may say (1) that it has been widely believed that sexual intercourse is a condition, rather than a cause, of birth or of conception;[3] or (2) that conception might be due to more than one cause. In any case, in the stories which tell of a supernatural birth the stress is more often upon the metamorphosis of the substance swallowed than upon the miraculous birth.

On the other hand, the theories of the Freudian school with regard to the relation of myths and folk-tales to dreams in which there is 'wish-fulfilment,' and in which the unconscious supplies a symbolism and various sets of transpositions, afford an explanation of such legends of supernatural and virgin birth without reference to this hypothetical ignorance of the cause of conception.[4] In support of this the mythical act of conception actually occurs in a dream in some of the stories in question—*e.g.*, that of Buddha's mother and the white elephant and that of the mother of St. Molasius.[5]

(2) Although virgin birth has been asserted of Zoroaster, this is hardly supported by the accounts in the sacred books. A substance called 'the Heavenly Glory,' created by Ahura Mazda, mingled with all the stages of birth in Zoroaster's ancestral line. The sacred books tell how his father ate a plant containing the *fravashi* of Zoroaster, and how both his parents ate food containing his substance. But this leads up to his actual physical generation. So, also, when myth tells how the future saviour Saoshyas would be born of a girl, this is because some of the *semen* of Zoroaster, preserved through long ages, will enter her womb.[6]

(3) The myths of Buddha's birth came into being long after his historic existence, while, in being based on transmigration, they expressly contradict his own teaching. Buddha, existing in heaven, decides to be born again on earth for the enlightenment of men. For this purpose he chooses his father and mother, and this puts his virgin birth (also commonly asserted of him) out of court. His mother dreamt that, in the shape of a white elephant, he entered her womb. Next day this dream was interpreted by several Brāhmans, who told Suddhana that he would have a son, the Buddha. The ordinary physical generation is implied, but to this is added the supernatural element of Buddha's pre-existence, as in the Arunta theory of birth. Later stories, however, alter the dream into an actual occurrence. It is nonsense to speak of his mother as 'Maya the virgin.'

[1] J. M. Robertson, *Christianity and Mythology*[2], London, 1910, p. 292.

[2] Spencer-Gillen[b], p. 150; Hartland, *Primitive Paternity*, ii. 274.

[3] Cf. art. INCARNATION (Buddhist), vol. vii. p. 186[b].

[4] See F. Ricklin, *Wish-fulfilment and Symbolism in Fairy Tales*, tr. W. A. White, New York, 1915, p. 52 and *passim*; I. H. Coriat, *The Meaning of Dreams*, London, 1916, p. 136 f.

[5] T. W. Rhys Davids, *Buddhist Birth Stories*, London, 1880, p. 63; S. H. O'Grady, *Silva Gadelica: A Collection of Tales in Irish*, do. 1892, ii. 19.

[6] *SBE* xxiii. [1883] 195.

2. The Virgin Birth of Christ.—The narrative of the Virgin Birth of Christ is found in Mt 1[19ff.] and Lk 1[26ff.], *i.e.* in the only Gospels which profess to record the event of the Birth. The alleged silence of the rest of the NT is no necessary proof of its non-acceptance—*e.g.*, by St. John or St. Paul. It was universally accepted without contradiction in the early Church, except among the Ebionites, even some Gnostic groups approving of it. Ignatius, soon after the death of St. John, witnesses to it most emphatically, and 'everything that we know of the dogmatics of the early part of the second century agrees with the belief that at that period the Virginity of Mary was a part of the formulated Christian belief.'[1] The first denials of it came mainly from Deistical writers in the 18th cent., and later objections come generally, though not wholly, from those who reject the 'supernatural' aspect of Christ's personality. The accounts in Matthew and Luke appear to be independent of each other, while they yet correspond as to the main fact. Matthew's narrative is written as if from Joseph's point of view, Luke's from that of Mary, and these, as the original repositories of the knowledge of the fact, have been regarded as the respective sources from whom the narratives were drawn. The story itself is apparently older than either of the accounts of it. The silence of Mark need not be viewed seriously, as it is no part of his purpose to relate the story of the Nativity, while he uses the significant phrase 'Son of God' (1[1]).[2] This applies equally to John, though his language regarding the Incarnation has been thought to presuppose the Virgin Birth—*e.g.*, 'the Word became flesh' (1[14])—while his reference to believers being born 'not of blood . . . but of God' (v.[13]) may presuppose the divine element in Christ's conception as the symbol of Christian regeneration. There is nothing to show that St. John repudiated the story.

The reading in some Patristic quotations which makes the passage itself refer to Christ, 'who was born . . .', has been accepted as the true one by some critics, but need not be pressed.

St. Paul's silence is regarded as weighty, yet he does not repudiate it, and, while its use might have added weight to his arguments for Christ's divinity and pre-existence, he does not formally refer to it, just as he makes scanty reference to any fact of Christ's earthly life, outside the Crucifixion and the Resurrection. Perhaps he wrote before it was generally known; certainly before it was known from the Gospels. Orr has argued with truth that St. Paul regarded Christ's entrance into the world as 'no ordinary act,' and his references to it have always 'some significant peculiarity of expression'—*e.g.*, Ro 1[3f.] 5[12ff.] 8[3] ('God sending his Son'), Ph 2[7] ('becoming [RVm] in the likeness of men'), Gal 4[4] (γενόμενον ἐκ γυναικός instead of the more usual γεννετός elsewhere used by him).[3] St. Paul's doctrines of Christ as the Second Man from heaven and of His freedom from the taint of Adam's sin almost imply belief in the Virgin Birth.

Orr also suggests a significant parallelism between the phraseology of Ro 1[3f.] and Lk 1[35].

The passages of Matthew and Luke are found in all the MSS and Versions, and cannot be regarded as interpolations. They do not differ in style from

[1] J. R. Harris, *The Apology of Aristides* = *TS* i. [1891] 25.

[2] 'The words are omitted in a few authorities, some of which are weighty; but they may be accepted as possibly genuine' (*The Gospel according to St. Mark*, ed. A. Plummer, Cambridge, 1915, p. 1).

[3] J. Orr, *The Virgin Birth of Christ*, London, 1907, p. 114 f.

the rest of the Gospels,[1] and probably always formed an integral part of these. It has been suggested, however, that, if Lk 1$^{34f.}$ be excised, as a later insertion, the narrative reads smoothly, and the Virgin Birth drops out.[2] In view of the facts, and also with regard to other changes which require then to be made (in 1^{27} 2^{5}; cf. also 1^{37}, which implies that the announcement is of something wonderful), this purely subjective criticism seems arbitrary. Generally the arguments based on the *form* of the phraseology in Lk 1$^{28-35}$ are grotesque;[3] and no critic has yet shown, by himself writing a Virgin Birth narrative, what precisely was most fitting for Mary and the angel respectively to have said.

It has been argued that Mary and Joseph showed no consciousness of Christ's supernatural personality, as they should have done, granting the Virgin Birth. That consciousness, however, is found in Jn (2$^{1f.}$), who does not mention the Birth. On the other hand, the verses Lk 2$^{33.\ 48f.}$ are alleged to contradict any such consciousness. But do they? What more natural than that One who to all outward appearance was an ordinary infant and youth should momentarily be so regarded in spite of any profounder consciousness? The argument takes no account of human nature.

In Lk 2^{33} the 'marvelling' may be a mere continuance of the wonder already excited. Note also the suggestion of Mary's consciousness of who her Son was in 2$^{19.\ 51}$. There is no evidence that she was one of the 'kinsmen' in Mk 3^{21} who thought Him 'beside Himself.'

The references to Joseph as father of Jesus in Mt 13^{55}, Lk 4^{22}, Jn 1^{45} 6^{42} represent current opinion (the Jews, Philip before becoming a disciple) which is merely reported, not endorsed. Legally Joseph was His father, and even Mary could so speak of him (Lk 2^{48}), as Luke (2$^{27.\ 41.\ 43}$) speaks of His 'parents.' How else could they speak colloquially of one who stood *in loco parentis*? On the other hand, that Joseph was not actually His father may have been known, and this popular knowledge in the form of an aspersion on Mary's character[4] (cf. Jn 8^{41}) may be the source of the slanders in Celsus and Rabbinic works. In the earliest Gospel Jesus is 'the carpenter, the Son of Mary' in popular view (Mk 6^{3}), and this was evidently a contemptuous reference, not as in the parallel passage in Mt 13^{55}, 'the carpenter's son' (cf. Lk 4^{22}, 'the son of Joseph'). The references to Rahab, Tamar, and Bathsheba in the genealogy of Matthew may have an apologetic aspect. Such women 'played an honoured rôle in the history of the Davidic lineage. Mary's character, he proceeds to argue, was not irregular. How much less, therefore (the inference is), are Jewish objections to her and to Jesus justified!'[5]

The genealogies are alleged to contradict the Virgin Birth as showing the Davidic descent of Jesus through Joseph. The two genealogies are independent and have been adopted by the evangelists from existing documents. Do they represent more than a legal connexion? The writers who tell of the Virgin Birth see no contradiction in giving this descent, and in any case modify the genealogy by the phrases used in Mt 1^{16}, Lk 3^{23}. Not impossibly Mary was also of Davidic descent and related to Joseph.[6]

Those who regard the Virgin Birth as mythical trace it to (*a*) Jewish, (*b*) pagan sources. (*a*) The Jewish source is found in Is 7^{14}. No Jew, however, ever applied this to the birth of the Messiah, though it was in accord with Matthew's method to use it as pointing to an event otherwise known to him. Other critics have conclusively proved that the myth of virgin birth was unknown to Jewish thought. (*b*) Many have therefore sought its origin in pagan mythology, some going so far as to assume an Oriental myth, for the existence of which there is no evidence whatever. The other mythical sources are those discussed in § 1, and it must be obvious that they have nothing whatever in common with the stories of Matthew and Luke: in these there is no idea of physical procreation as there is in Greek myths, and all such myths were regarded with abhorrence in Christian circles. Any comparison of Matthew and Luke with such pagan myths (notwithstanding that these show the human feeling that extraordinary personages should have an extraordinary origin) will prove that we are moving in a different atmosphere—in the one reticence, in the other lack of it and a piling up of mystery. Matthew and Luke give no explanation of the mystery. They feel that here is a fitting introduction to a life such as the world had never seen before, and to the events of that life they immediately pass on. With sublime simplicity they use no words but those of the angelic messenger (Mt 1^{20}, Lk 1^{35}). Divine power, the power of a spiritual God, causes the Incarnation through the Virgin Birth. The reticence is marked in comparison with the exuberant language of the Apocryphal Gospels, and, if the Virgin Birth narratives are mythical, no myth was ever expressed in such bald and restrained language. The comparison with pagan myths has been influenced by knowledge of the lack of reticence in later Christian art and theology, into which pagan elements have crept. What we find there is, however, quite foreign to the Gospels.

3. Doctrinal significance of the Virgin Birth.—Only the briefest statement is possible here. It has been held that belief in the divinity of Christ, in the Incarnation, is possible without a belief in the Virgin Birth. While this is not to be denied, the fact undoubtedly remains that those who reject the latter are generally those who in greater or less degree reject the former. It is impossible for any one to say, granting the Incarnation, that virgin birth may not have been necessary to it. An absolutely unique personality such as Christ's demands some new beginning, just as it was consummated on earth by the Resurrection. An Incarnation inaugurating a new humanity, itself to be creative in the lives of men, implies some new kind of birth, and the Virgin Birth is not out of harmony with this new step in development. The pre-existent Logos taking human flesh is a new event in history: the Virgin Birth adequately supplies the means to this, and no other method is even suggested in the NT. Such an Incarnation is itself so wonderful that the additional event of virgin birth hardly makes any further demand on faith.

While virgin birth is not the ground of Christ's sinlessness through the absence of human paternity—the handicap of a predisposition to sin being presumably as transmissible by motherhood alone—yet it is apparently connected with it through 'the power of the Holy Ghost,' in both Matthew and Luke. The miraculous conception is in direct relation to the subsequent personality and function—'It is he that shall save his people from their sins' (Mt 1^{21}); 'that which is to be born shall be called holy' (Lk 1^{35}). The assumption is that the unique birth coupled with the dynamic and ethical power of the Spirit excluded the natural disposition to sin. The sinlessness of Christ was that of a

[1] F. C. Burkitt, *Evangelion da-Mepharreshe*, Cambridge, 1904, ii. 258; A. Harnack, *Luke the Physician*, tr. J. R. Wilkinson, London, 1907, p. 96 f.

[2] P. W. Schmiedel, 'Mary,' *EBi*, col. 2956.

[3] *E.g.*, by Schmiedel, *loc. cit.*, and C. Clemen, *Primitive Christianity and its Non-Jewish Sources*, Eng. tr., p. 289.

[4] A. C. Headlam, *CQR* lxxix. [1914] 23.

[5] J. Moffatt, *Introd. to the Literature of the New Testament*, Edinburgh, 1911, p. 251. Cf. T. Zahn, *Introd. to the New Testament*, Eng. tr., ii. 537 ff.

[6] R. J. Knowling, *The Virgin Birth*, p. 32, quoted in Orr, p. 105.

new Personality, human and divine, and it was fitting that such a Personality should be embodied in One whose earthly existence was uniquely conditioned. Whatever the link between sinlessness and virgin birth may be, 'a sinless man is as much a miracle in the moral world as a virgin birth is a miracle in the physical world.'[1]

LITERATURE.—G. H. Box, *The Virgin Birth of Jesus*, London, 1916; C. Clemen, *Primitive Christianity and its Non-Jewish Sources*, Eng. tr., Edinburgh, 1912; C. Gore, *Dissertations on Subjects connected with the Incarnation*, London, 1895, *The Incarnation*, do. 1891; H. Gressman, *Das Weihnachts-Evangelium auf Ursprung und Geschichte untersucht*, Göttingen, 1914; A. Harnack, *Das apostolische Glaubensbekenntniss*, Berlin, 1896, *Lehrbuch der Dogmengeschichte*[4], Tübingen, 1909–10; E. S. Hartland, *The Legend of Perseus*, London, 1894–96, *Primitive Paternity*, do. 1909–10; A. C. Headlam, *The Miracles of the New Testament*, do. 1914, ch. 7; P. Lobstein, *The Virgin Birth of Christ*, Eng. tr., do. 1903; J. A. MacCulloch, 'Comparative Religion and the Historic Christ,' in *Religion and the Modern World: Lectures delivered before the University Society of St. Ninian*, London, 1909; H. R. Mackintosh, *The Doctrine of the Person of Jesus Christ*, Edinburgh, 1912 (Appendix: 'Jesus' Birth of a Virgin'); O. Pfleiderer, *The Early Christian Conception of Christ*, Eng. tr., London, 1905; W. Sanday, *Bishop Gore's Challenge to Criticism*, do. 1914; P. W. Schmiedel, 'Mary,' *EBi*, col. 2952 ff.; V. Taylor, *The Historical Evidence for the Virgin Birth*, Oxford, 1920; H. Usener, 'Nativity,' *EBi*, col. 3340 ff., *Das Weihnachtsfest*[2], Bonn, 1911; T. Zahn, *Introd. to the New Testament*, Eng. tr., Edinburgh, 1909.

J. A. MACCULLOCH.

VIRGIN MARY.—See MARY.

VIRTUE.—See ETHICS AND MORALITY.

VIRTUES.—See SEVEN VIRTUES.

VITALISM.—See ABIOGENESIS, BIOGENESIS.

VIVISECTION. — Etymologically the term 'vivisection' denotes the cutting of living animals under any conditions and for any purpose. But it has come to be associated with experiments made on the vertebrates below man for the advancement of medical science, whether with or without pain. To define vivisection, therefore, as 'the infliction of real and serious suffering on a vertebrate living animal for scientific purpose'[2] is misleading.

1. The justification of experiments on animals.—Experiments accompanied by pain were undoubtedly performed on animals before 1876 in this country, and in other countries more generally and perhaps less reservedly. Their ostensible object was to promote man's knowledge of physiology and pathology. A committee of the Royal Medical and Chirurgical Society, *e.g.*, made experiments before that date on a number of animals to discover some better means for the resuscitation of persons apparently drowned, in order to give assistance to the Royal Humane Society. In the course of these experiments animals were half-drowned and kept in water three, four, or five minutes.[3] As a matter of fact, from the time of Galen of Pergamos (born A.D. 131) painful experiments on animals were practised, and from them unquestionably knowledge of anatomy as well as of physiology and pathology was gained. Thus Harvey was enabled to establish the circulation of the blood; Hunter its collateral circulation; Claude Bernard discovered glycogen in the liver; Sir Charles Bell laid bare the intricacies of the nervous system, and the names of Pasteur and Koch will always be associated with the most far-reaching of all pathological discoveries—those connected with micrococci. That pain accompanied the experiments by which these and other steps in medical science were reached, that prolonged pain was frequently inflicted, that medical students were taught by experiments made before them by their professors, and that they not infrequently experimented on their own account—all these facts are generally admitted. And the admission justifies the determined attempts to put an end to experiments on animals made in the past by 'the Victoria Street Society for the Protection of Animals from Vivisection' and other anti-vivisection societies. It is, however, only fair to add that during the thirty years immediately preceding 1876 the 'torture' of animals under vivisection had been materially lessened by the discovery and use of anæsthetics.

But, apart from the cruelty which was practised, a principle of importance was involved, viz. whether medical science was to depend for its progress on the casual observations of the doctor or was to be promoted by experiment also. In the former case progress would be minimized owing to want of control over the phenomena; in the latter case the time, method, and subject-matter would be determined by the investigator. No responsible person contests the fact that science advances mainly by selective experiments, or that all knowledge shows sooner or later the way to practical utility. There is no sense in reviling winter sowing because in April there are no crops. Experiments on animals have enabled us to fight the causes of disease, instead of dealing with the symptoms. If, in the process of acquiring knowledge by experiment, pain is inflicted in some degree, this must be counter-balanced, in forming our judgment, by the greater pain we thereby learn to prevent. Unfortunately this fact has been overlooked as a rule in the controversy about vivisection, and so the remark of Lord Justice Fletcher Moulton before the Royal Commission of 1906 was to the point:

> 'If you want to do good in a particular way, and want to know how you can do it effectively, give your heart a rest, and your brain a chance.'[1]

2. Findings of the Royal Commission.—The year 1876 marks a turning-point in the history of vivisection. Since that year protests against the 'torture' of animals have become, in this country at least, an anachronism. A Royal Commission, consisting of Viscount Cardwell, Baron Winmarleigh, W. E. Forster, Sir John B. Karslake, T. H. Huxley, J. E. Erichsen, and R. H. Hutton, was appointed on 22nd June 1875 to 'inquire into the practice of subjecting live animals to experiments for scientific purposes, and to consider and report what measures, if any, it may be desirable to take in respect of any such practice.' The Commission issued its report on 8th Jan. 1876.

> Its conclusion was that it is 'impossible altogether to prevent the practice of making experiments upon living animals for the attainment of knowledge applicable to the mitigation of human suffering or the prolongation of human life; . . . that by the use of anæsthetics pain may in the great majority of cases be greatly mitigated; that the infliction upon animals of any unnecessary pain is justly abhorrent to the moral sense of Your Majesty's subjects generally.'

The Commission finally recommended that the practice of experiments on living animals should be regulated by law and placed under the control of the Home Secretary.

The first result of the findings of the Commission was the passing of the Cruelty to Animals Act, 1876 (39 and 40 Vict. c. 77). By it all experiments on animals by an unlicensed person were prohibited, and ordinarily experiments were confined to a registered place; all licences were to be vouched for by one or more of the presidents of six great scientific bodies and by a professor; the use of curari as an anæsthetic was disallowed; invertebrate animals were excluded from the operation of the Act; and a series of restrictions on

[1] A. B. Bruce, *Apologetics; or, Christianity defensively stated*, Edinburgh, 1892, p. 410.

[2] S. Coleridge, *Vivisection, a Heartless Science*, London, 1916, p. 3.

[3] *Vivisection: the Royal Soc. for Prevention of Cruelty to Animals, and the Royal Commission*, p. xix.

[1] *Evidence of Lord Justice Fletcher Moulton*, p. 70.

experiments were imposed, especially one which insisted that 'the animal must during the whole of the experiment be under the influence of some anæsthetic of sufficient power to prevent the animal feeling pain,' this being modified by a subsequent section which allowed one series of experiments without anæsthetics on a prescribed certificate and for given reasons. One important fact had not come to light at the passing of this Act. Bacteriology as a science was but beginning its career. Hence all the evidence given before the Royal Commission dealt with current physiology, and when the Act was passed it was soon found that it made no provision for experiments by inoculation, which are now 95 per cent of the whole. Accordingly, these had to be allowed for, and they are brought under certificate A and certificate B.

3. Legal regulation of experiments.—Under the powers conferred by the Act of 1876 on the Home Secretary, certificates marked A, B, C, E, EE, or F are granted to licensed persons.[1] Certificate A allows experiments to be made without anæsthetics when anæsthesia would necessarily frustrate the object of the permitted experiment. As a matter of fact, no cutting operations are performed under this certificate; it sanctions inoculations, feeding, and similar procedures only, which involve no cutting; and the animal has to be killed under anæsthetics, if it be in pain, as soon as the result of the operation is ascertained. In view of the somewhat grotesque statements which are frequently made about the prevalence of cruelty under the existing law, it will be advantageous to state the nature of the 'pain condition' now prevailing. Additional safeguards against the infliction of pain have been provided, in accordance with the recommendation of the Commission of 1906, by strengthening the special condition (known as the 'pain condition') which is endorsed on the licence in respect of all certificates which either dispense with the use of anæsthetics or allow the animal to recover from the anæsthetic (provisos 2 and 3 of sec. 3). The 'pain condition' now runs as follows:

'If an animal, after and by reason of any of the said experiments under the said Certificate . . . is found to be suffering pain which is either severe or is likely to endure, and if the main result of the experiment has been attained, the animal shall forthwith be painlessly killed.

If an animal, after and by reason of any of the said experiments, is found to be suffering severe pain which is likely to endure, such animal shall forthwith be painlessly killed, whether the main result of the experiment has been attained or not.

If any animal appears to an Inspector to be suffering considerable pain, and if the Inspector directs such animal to be destroyed, it shall forthwith be painlessly killed.'

Certificate B allows an animal to be kept alive after the initial operation, where a more or less prolonged observation is necessary to the scientific success of the experiment. Certificate C allows experiments to be made in illustration of lectures, but under anæsthesia. Certificates E and EE permit experiments on dogs or cats, and certificate F on horses, asses, or mules.

The best proof that the administration of the Act has been satisfactory is afforded by the findings of the second Royal Commission on Vivisection appointed in 1906, which published its report in 1912. The report was signed by all the Commissioners; it recommended no change in the text of the Act of 1876, but suggested, without recommending, a special certificate for all experiments on dogs; it recommended certain increased restrictions and safeguards, which were adopted by the Home Office. It may be added that an unsuccessful attempt to pass a Dogs' Protection Bill was made in 1919 in the House of Commons.

4. Practical conclusion.—Few questions have roused more embittered feeling than that engendered by the belief that lower animals were being callously and uselessly 'tortured' by medical men and others. Men felt that the humaneness inculcated by centuries of Christian teaching was being wantonly abandoned, and the outcry was in proportion to the nearness to man of the animals which were used for experiment. Invertebrate animals were passed over as being negligible, and it was with man's nearest friends, the dog, the cat, and the horse, that sympathy was most loudly expressed. Frequently, however, an adequate sympathy for the sufferings of man himself was wanting to supplement that felt for these lower animals. No sufficient recognition was made of the fact that without experiments on animals doctors would frequently have no option save to experiment on their patients, for want of the knowledge which experiments on animals could alone secure. And, as it is, much of the success attending treatment for diseases connected with the blood, with the alimentary canal and the digestion of food, and with the central nervous system, springs from knowledge gained by experiments on animals. Especially is this the case with diseases due to infection by microbes. As the Royal Commission of 1876 pointed out,

'It was by observation that Dr. Jenner discovered the immunity from small-pox of those who had contracted cow-pox. But it was by experiments upon cows that the origin of the cow-pox, a disease stated to be derived from "grease" in the horse, was ascertained.'

Pasteur's discovery of the activity of micro-organisms in fermentation was the beginning of antiseptic and aseptic treatment of wounds, by which thousands of human lives have been saved and indescribable suffering removed, and with which the name of Lord Lister will be always connected by a grateful world. The treatment of tuberculosis and diphtheria and the protective treatment against tetanus and rabies are dependent on knowledge gained by experiments on animals. In the same way the nature of cholera, bubonic plague, typhoid fever, epidemic meningitis, Malta fever, and other curses of mankind is now understood, and the road to their annihilation opened. When we weigh the suffering caused to hundreds of thousands of human beings by these plagues against that far less pain caused by inoculation to a comparatively small number of mice, rats, guinea-pigs, and rabbits, we realize how irrational it is to agitate for the total prohibition of vivisection. The method of regulation, not suppression, adopted in this country does justice at once to the unquestioned claims of the lower animals to kindly treatment and to the duty of man to his fellows—the duty of using his reason in the age-long task of diminishing and finally extinguishing that particular form of evil which goes by the name of disease.

LITERATURE.—Stephen Paget, *Experiments on Animals*, London, 1900; *The Vivisection Controversy: a Selection of Speeches and Articles* (published by The Victoria Street Society), do. 1883; *Evidence of Lord Justice Fletcher Moulton before the Royal Commission on Vivisection*, do. 1908; Publications (pamphlets and leaflets) of the Research Defence Society, do. 1908 ff.; *Vivisection: the Royal Society for the Prevention of Cruelty to Animals, and the Royal Commission*, do. 1876; R. J. S. Simpson, *The Medical History of the War in South Africa*, do. 1911.

W. F. GEIKIE-COBB.

VOLCANOES. — See PRODIGIES AND PORTENTS.

VOLITION.—See WILL.

VOLTAIRE.—François Marie Arouet, who is known to us as Voltaire, was born either at Chatenay or in Paris in November 1694. His father, François Arouet, had been treasurer to the Chambre des Comptes, and his mother, Marie-

[1] Certificate D, which was based on section iii. subsection b. 4 of the Act allowing experiments 'for the purpose of testing a particular former discovery,' is no longer issued.

Catherine Daumart, was born, we are told, of a noble family of Poitou. Voltaire afterwards took his name from a small property in his mother's family, though it has been maintained that it was derived from an anagram on his signature Arouet L. J. ('le jeune'); but the fact that in the dedication to his *Œdipe* he signed 'Arouet de Voltaire' proves that he did not take the second name in order to cast the other into oblivion. Voltaire was thus born in a state of moderate affluence, and he was sent to the Jesuit College Louis-le-Grand, which bore the high reputation for learning possessed by schools of that order. Here he was not only distinguished intellectually but was pointed out by his tutor as the future 'coryphæus of deism in France.' On leaving college, he came into touch with the Abbé de Châteauneuf, who had been a friend of his mother, and who was his godfather; he brought him into relation with Ninon de l'Enclos. That remarkable woman, who had had the courage to reject Madame de Maintenon's offer of an invitation to the court on condition that she should become *dévote*, was now very old, but she maintained her freshness of spirit, and she soon discerned the remarkable character of the boy and left him a legacy for the purchase of books. Already he deplored in verse 'his Jansenist of a brother' and declaimed a poem, called the *Moïsade*, by J. B. Rousseau[1] (though the author attributed it to Voltaire), which portrays Moses as an impostor. Perhaps it was from Ninon that Voltaire first learned the lesson whose influence pervaded all his life, that the spirit of man is free, and that men are entitled to form their judgments for themselves. The society into which young Voltaire was launched was indeed a dissolute one. It represented a reaction against the hypocrisy and intolerance of the court of Louis XIV., and its wit was frivolous and its literary efforts trifling. The Abbé Chaulieu, a versifier of some merit, exercised much influence on Voltaire and typified the outlook of the society in which he moved.

Naturally M. Arouet, the father, was shocked at the company kept by his son, and by the fact that he began to write a tragedy instead of learning law. He finally dispatched him to the Marquis de Châteauneuf, brother to the Abbé, and French ambassador in Holland; but the young man became entangled in a love affair and the ambassador sent him home. The love, if such it was, was soon forgotten, but Voltaire, to the despair of his father, was determined to live in the world in which he had got a footing, mingling with the nobles and more bent on versifying than occupying an office-stool, in spite of the fact that he had matriculated as a lawyer. A friend of his father took pity on him and brought him to a château near Fontainebleau, where he became engrossed in the study of history—a study which resulted later on in the production of *La Henriade* and *Le Siècle de Louis XIV*. Louis XIV. died in 1715, and there followed an outburst of satires on the memory of the monarch who had enjoyed such adoration. One of these was termed *Les j'ai vu* and concluded, after describing the evils which in his short life the writer had seen, the crowded prisons, the unjust taxes, with 'And I am but twenty years old.' Though Voltaire was actually twenty-two, he was falsely accused of being the author, and in May 1717 he was cast into the Bastille, where he remained till April 1718, being allowed to return to Paris in the following October. This was not his first detention; he had been sent out of Paris as early as 1716, owing to verses that he had written regarding certain distinguished personages.

[1] Not to be confused with Jean Jacques Rousseau.

Confinement in the Bastille, which was perhaps not very severe, had little effect on Voltaire's spirits, for here he sketched out the poem of *La Ligue*, corrected his tragedy *Œdipe*, and even wrote gay verses on his misfortune. *Œdipe* was performed in 1718 with great success, and this was the first of his dramatic works, which were to follow one another in such marvellous succession. Before this he had written only fugitive pieces, including an ode which had vainly contested for a prize given by the French Academy. Afterwards he went on with his great work, the *Henriade*, and also wrote the tragedy of *Artémire* (1720), which was much more severely criticized than was the *Œdipe*. Everywhere the young poet was welcomed, though he appears to have again been banished for a season from Paris for his intercourse with the enemies of the regent, and more especially with Richelieu and de Gortz. With Madame de Rupelmonde he visited Holland and saw J. B. Rousseau at Brussels. Voltaire read his *Épître à Uranie*, and Rousseau recited his works to him, but the two men separated as irreconcilable enemies. Voltaire returned to France in 1722 and in 1724 produced *Mariamne*, which was on the same lines as *Artémire* under new names and plot; then came the famous *Henriade* under the name of *La Ligue*. Voltaire as author of this wonderful trilogy—*La Henriade*, *Œdipe*, and *Mariamne*—may be said to have made his mark in literature. The idea of being the eulogizer of King Henry IV. had inflamed his imagination since his twenty-first year, and he had begun to write in the Bastille. His idea was to dedicate the work to the king of France (Louis XV.), and the dedication was written, but there were difficulties in regard to censorship, and it did not appear. The book was issued in 1723 at Rouen after an abortive effort to get it published by subscription at The Hague. An English edition (1726) was dedicated to the queen of England, consort of George II. The poem is often compared with the *Æneid*, and it has a place in French literature which brings it into comparison with the classics of ancient days. The subject was a great one, and, while it adheres to historic facts, there is in the work a fine sense of morality, and above all that deep love of humanity and liberty which characterizes its author's best writings. Condorcet says that the *Henriade* was born in the century of reason, and the more progress made by reason among men, the greater will be its circle of admirers. Unfortunately for the truth of this dictum, life and dramatic power are also necessary to make a work such as this immortal, and these are lacking in the poem. Perhaps it was not possible for Voltaire to write a great epic: it required a depth of thought and concentration that was not his. Also the age was possibly too critical and superficial.

In 1722 Arouet the elder died, implacable to the last as regards his gifted son, who was now definitely known by his famous name of Voltaire. The latter was living a life of social pleasure, visiting country-houses,—those of Sully, Villars, etc.—composing verses *d'occasion*, arranging theatricals, and writing all the while with set and definite purpose. He loved the country, but dreaded the loss of precious time spent in country-house pleasures. Change of scene seemed necessary to him; he was ever passing from one place to another in a way that was astonishing in those days of comparatively fixed abode. It was a life of quick impressions, but not entirely one of self-indulgence, for Voltaire never forgot that his work claimed his first endeavours, and he never hesitated to speak his mind with perfect vigour. One would have imagined that that work would have given him an established place in society and caused his person to be respected, but, if he himself might be tempted to think so, he got a rough awakening.

Voltaire was dining, as he often dined, with the Duke of Sully. There he met the Chevalier de Rohan, who took it amiss that Voltaire's sentiments did not agree with his own. 'Who is that young man,' he asked, 'who contradicts me in tones so loud?' 'My lord,' Voltaire replied, 'it is one who bears no great name but who wins respect for the name he bears.' A few days later the chevalier took revenge upon the young man by causing his lackeys to administer a caning to him at the duke's door. Sully refused to interfere, and, stung by rage, Voltaire obtained instruction in the use of the small sword and challenged de Rohan. The family of the latter prevented him from fighting, and Voltaire was thrown once more into the Bastille, where he was kept for sixteen days.

This was in April 1726, and on 2nd May he was allowed to leave for England, accompanied by an escort as far as Calais.

Voltaire's journey to England was not only a turning-point in his life, but a factor in the economic and intellectual history of France. One can imagine the spirit in which he went there, burning with indignation at the manner in which he had been treated by the laws or customs of his country. He passed into the country of Newton and Locke, of Shaftesbury and Bolingbroke, of Swift and Pope—a country which allowed men to speak without let or hindrance of what they had experienced or believed. Voltaire had become known as a writer of verse and tragedy; now he felt it to be his mission to become the liberator of his countrymen from bondage and false beliefs. 'Voltaire left France a poet, he returned to it a sage.'[1] Newton's careful examination of facts strongly appealed to the young man, and his mind was specially drawn towards the Newtonian theory of attraction as well as to Locke's appeal to experience as the basis of all knowledge. Metaphysics—even the metaphysics of Descartes—took on a new aspect to him. The *Lettres philosophiques, ou Lettres sur les Anglais* draw attention to the many matters in which the country in which he was living was in advance of that of his birth. He was but a refugee from the Bastille, and his country was still in a condition of feudalism with an aristocracy which was exempt from certain forms of taxation. In England, on the other hand, he saw intellectual eminence honoured and rewarded; even administrative posts were granted to distinguished men of letters, whilst the liberty of the press was absolute. We cannot wonder that the *Lettres* were publicly burned by decree of the French Parliament.

The tragedy of *Brutus* was the firstfruits of Voltaire's visit to England, expressing as it did the aspirations of an oppressed people. The next twenty years of Voltaire's life, between his leaving England and going to Berlin, were a prolific period. The dates of his most famous tragedies are as follows: *Brutus*, 1730, *Zaïre*, 1732, *Mort de César*, 1735, *Alzire*, 1736, *Mahomet*, 1741, *Mérope*, 1743, *Sémiramis*, 1748, *Tancrède*, 1760. The *Mort de César* was a brave venture, for not only did it deal with ground well trodden by a greater dramatist than Voltaire himself, but it was a play without love scenes or women, and in three acts only, and thereby a complete innovation. Its republicanism, too, was sufficient to cause its publication to be at first prohibited in those days of tyranny. Its author came into further contact with the authorities over an attack he made on the excommunication of a celebrated actress, who on her death was refused burial rites. But, though Voltaire was ever ready to take up real causes of oppression, he was far too susceptible to any vulgar calumny, and his time and talents were used in petty quarrels unworthy of a man of intellect and position. His struggle was by his writings to win for himself a place in public esteem which would secure for him the goodwill of the populace. *Ériphyle* was not a success, but *Zaïre* had the tender note that appealed to the sentiments of the human heart. *Adélaïde du Guesclin*, though on similar lines, did not take the public fancy. It was followed by the *Temple du Goût*, a criticism of past and living writers. The *Lettres philosophiques* had been burned in 1734. There appeared in them certain notes, now well known, in criticism of Pascal, which were specially resented, and the causes mentioned before made it thoroughly detested. The *Épître à Uranie* its author felt himself constrained to disavow and ascribe to Chaulieu, now dead—an action impossible to justify. In 1729 Voltaire began that poem which has made his name famous or infamous, and which was his amusement for many years of his life. *La Pucelle d'Orléans* is an indefensible attack on the memory of a great deliverer of the writer's country, and it cannot be justified from either a historical or a moral point of view. It was constantly being quoted to eager listeners, and the publication of it was a constant peril hanging over its writer's head. Voltaire all this time was in constant trouble with his many critics, one of the chief of whom in 1735 was Défontaine, who attacked him in *La Voltairomanie*. This was a reply to Voltaire's *Le Préservatif*. There was much personal abuse on Défontaine's part, in which Voltaire's private life and relationship to Madame du Châtelet were involved.

This was a time of persecution and humiliation for Voltaire, but it was also a time of happiness and prosperity, for the fortune which his enormous output, in addition to his speculations, brought him left him a liberty which he never before possessed. He wanted riches and independence, and he got them. Then between 1733 and 1749 he formed that connexion with Madame du Châtelet which proved such a strong influence on his life. It was a strange friendship—one of comradeship rather than passion. The 'divine Emily' was a student of a very serious type, and she made the kind of surroundings which Voltaire required for his very serious work, in the famous château of Cirey in the independent duchy of Lorraine. Here these two wonderful people—for Madame du Châtelet was a brilliant and accomplished woman—studied Newton, quarrelled sometimes, made friends again, worked literally day and night together, and even competed together for a prize offered by the Academy (on so uninspiring a topic as the propagation of fire), though taking, characteristically enough, opposite views on the subject. Voltaire wrote on the philosophy of Newton, and Madame du Châtelet co-operated with him. Voltaire was deeply interested in scientific questions, but he had no real aptitude for science; his mind was not that way inclined, and an enemy went so far as to say that he was the man who could 'best write down what other people have thought.'[1] Voltaire was therefore well advised to devote himself to poetry and philosophy rather than become a second-rate savant.[2] He followed this advice, and at Cirey produced *Alzire*, *Zulime*, *Mahomet*, and his *Discours en vers sur l'Homme*, whilst he also wrote the *Histoire de Charles XII.* and prepared the *Siècle de Louis XIV.*, and collected the materials for his *Essai sur l'hist. générale et sur les mœurs et l'esprit des nations*. All the while he was not stationary at the château, but moved about from place to place—Amsterdam, Brussels, Berlin, etc.—always glad to return to his settled home again. Paris was free to him after 1735. His

[1] John Morley, *Voltaire*, p. 58.

[1] Morley, p. 120.

[2] Condorcet, *Vie de Voltaire*, p. 166.

own sovereign, Louis XV., would have none of him, and Frederick, now king of Prussia (1740), took advantage of Voltaire's fear of how his writings might cause him trouble, and tried to secure his presence by an offer of protection. A constant correspondence took place between the two, as well as a *soi-disant* diplomatic visit on Voltaire's part to the king.

Voltaire's historical writings occupied him greatly at this period of his life. He is not remembered as, properly speaking, a historian, but his historical works are all written in reference to the times in which he himself lived, and hence their interest for us to this day. They are full of intelligence and good sense, with moralizings which are to the point and are yet combined with an irony which is characteristic of the author. His *Siècle de Louis XIV.* is specially interesting, inasmuch as he was able to make use of his own private information and of memoirs hitherto unpublished, like those of Saint-Simon. He gives a very full account of the government, commerce, and industry of the time. In fact, he had in view not only to write a history of the period with which he dealt, but also to relate the history of the human mind in that wonderful epoch of history. He worked with great diligence, passing the whole day at his desk, and, despite frequent ill-health, never seemed to tire.

Madame de Pompadour was Voltaire's first friend at court, and through her he was asked to celebrate the marriage of the dauphin in a court piece called the *Princesse de Navarre*. In view of this work, which he regarded very lightly, he was made in 1745 historiographer of France—a position once jointly held by Racine and Boileau—and given thereby a certain protection as well as a salary of 2000 livres. But above all he desired to obtain admission to the Academy, and before this was possible he wrote to Latour, head of his former school, professing his devotion not only to religion but also to the Jesuits. He achieved his end in 1746. But he did not long hold a place in royal favour, for libels poured upon him, worse even than before. Crébillon was given the pre-eminence as an author by Madame de Pompadour and others, and everything was done that could be done to humiliate and discourage him.

In 1749 Madame du Châtelet, the friend of sixteen years, died. Her companionship had meant much to Voltaire, and his life with her had been on the whole useful and not without dignity. Frederick of Prussia, who had for long corresponded with Voltaire and had formerly urged his migration to Prussia, came to the throne in 1740, and renewed his blandishments. The result was that in July 1750 Voltaire arrived at Potsdam. He was received with the greatest respect by his remarkable host and endowed with a pension; but the step was one which he had every cause to regret. By his action he even gave offence in his own country and to Louis XV., his king, little appreciated as he had been by him before. He thought he would find liberty and peace in his new abode, but he found on the intellectual side obscurantism only. The Academy of Sciences, founded by Sophie-Charlotte under the direction of Leibniz, had fallen on evil days. The king was mainly concerned about drill and orthodox theology, and Berlin was far behind Paris in civilization, being in many ways but a mediæval town. The association of these two, the greatest figures in Europe, will always be a matter of the profoundest interest to mankind. But actually the combination was disastrous. Frederick was Voltairean, it is true, but his interests were centred in the establishment of the Prussian ascendancy and the transformation of the face of Europe. Voltaire's task was a no less momentous one, for his aim and object were to change the intellectual outlook of the Continent and destroy the old spiritual ascendancy. But the two men moved in different planes—nothing could have made them agree—and during the two and a half years spent by Voltaire as Frederick's guest there were constant and undignified quarrels and stupid practical jokes of a spiteful sort. It was all unworthy, and we cannot wonder that the visit came to an untimely end. Voltaire was no easy guest, always looking out for insults, which were not hard to find. There is a famous and cruel saying which La Métrie quoted as having been applied to Voltaire by the king: 'I require him a year longer . . . one sucks the orange and casts away the skin.'[1] Voltaire was grasping, while Frederick was parsimonious; he quarrelled with Lessing and got into not too creditable financial transactions. But, despite all this, and the fact that he was asked to criticize and amend the king's verses, Voltaire made progress with the *Siècle de Louis XIV.*, and the famous *Dictionnaire philosophique*. There was doubtless a certain fellow-feeling between the two men, who were at one in their hatred of superstition and prejudice; but there was a strong disagreement too, and Maupertuis was the means of bringing this disagreement to a head. Maupertuis was an ancient rival of Voltaire, and a quarrel arose between the two. The one issued *Lettres*, the other the *Diatribe du Docteur Akakia*. The king was at first amused, but the *Diatribe* was proscribed and ordered to be burned. Voltaire had, however, according to his wont, sent copies away, which were printed, and the king was annoyed by this and placed him under arrest. After a sort of reconciliation Voltaire finally left Potsdam in 1753 and went to Leipzig, there to stay with the Duchess of Saxe-Gotha, for whom he commenced the *Annales de l'Empire*, a popular history of Germany, which he himself did not rate highly. Subsequently he journeyed to Frankfort, where he and his niece, Madame Denis, were arrested and kept for three weeks under guard. Frederick tried to put the blame on another, but the matter caused much resentment, and Voltaire told his friends that the king had 'a hundred times kissed the very hand which he had just caused to be enchained.'[2]

On leaving Frankfort Voltaire went to Colmar in Alsace, where he completed his *Annales* and spent nearly two years, and where he thought of settling. But France seemed impossible, as persecutions threatened; he happened on one occasion to go to Geneva to consult Tronchin, and its beauty, language, and liberty captivated him; consequently he settled in a country-house outside the town, named Les Délices. Even that resting-place did not seem perfectly secure, and, in order to have retreats from the persecution of the Catholics on the one hand and the extreme Reformed party on the other, he bought houses in the different territories and in turn inhabited Tournay, Ferney in France, and Les Délices close to Geneva. It was at the last place that he and Madame Denis, his widowed niece, made their home and set up a considerable establishment.

The year 1754 was, so to speak, a dividing time in Voltaire's life. After a stormy period of combat and fear he passed from dependence to independence and comparative freedom. He was wealthy—not from the proceeds of his works, but from speculations—and was able to set up a theatre and keep open house, whilst he could print as he wished in Geneva. He was no longer dependent on the great as formerly, but received them into his house on equal terms. It promised to be a

[1] Letter to Madame Denis, Berlin, 2nd Sept. 1755.
[2] Condorcet, p. 206.

peaceful life, but he meant to devote himself to political work, to obtaining a change in the constitution of European states such as would bring them more into line with that of England. He wished above all to procure economy of public money, to put an end to persecution and intolerance, and he carried on a vast correspondence with these ends in view. He was ambitious, desired to produce and to teach. He might indeed be compared to a great European instructor—one whose work was to enlighten nations which were not too favourably disposed to receive the instruction offered them. He was not an idealist perhaps, but he had the good of his fellow-countrymen at heart, and there was no better place from which to preach his gospel of the deliverance of mankind from the thraldom of the oppressor than the republics of Berne and Geneva.

His literary work went on apace. The first play to appear was *L'Orphelin de la Chine*, composed when he was in Alsace and performed in 1755. His peace was, however, disturbed by the piratical publication of *La Pucelle*, which forced him to finish and issue it himself. By its means there was plenty of reason given to the enemy to blaspheme, although it may be possible to argue that it aims at the destruction of hypocrisy and superstition. It is impossible, if so, not to wish that a better and less gross manner of bringing about that result had been adopted and that more respect had been shown for a famous woman and patriot. He also wrote at this time the poem entitled *La Loi naturelle* and the *Désastre de Lisbonne*. The first was burned by the parliament at Paris because of its attack on intolerance and the fear of where such opinion would lead. The second was in antagonism to the orthodox view of the origin of evil, and was condemned in consequence. In 1759 he published *Candide*, undoubtedly one of the best of all his works of the romantic and philosophic type. It is an ironical satire on the optimism of Leibniz, and is extremely amusing as well as full of a commonsense type of wisdom, so that it can be read in the present day with as much pleasure as when it was first published. At the end of it there is the famous injunction to himself and his readers to 'cultivate one's own garden.' Voltaire also made a free translation of Ecclesiastes and part of the Song of Solomon. In 1757 the first edition of his collected works appeared. This was published under his own supervision, and to this edition there was added the *Essai sur l'hist. générale et sur les mœurs et l'esprit des nations*, a work undertaken in order to influence Madame du Châtelet in favour of the study of history. This work involved an immense amount of research and labour that must have been irksome to a man of quick wit like Voltaire, who was neither an earnest student nor a metaphysician. But his historical writing was never dull. He grouped his facts and interpreted these in a wide way, giving them life and significance. His reflexions may not be very profound, but they are full of common sense and just. He obtained the best material available and put it to the best use in his power. On the whole he was scrupulous and critical in respect of the value of his evidence. Satire and wit were always at his command.

In 1765 Voltaire sold Les Délices and settled at Ferney, where he occupied the position of a country gentleman, and where he was visited by most of the celebrated men of the day in Europe. He corresponded voluminously and even came into touch with his former friend King Frederick. Diderot and d'Alembert launched their great project of the *Encyclopédie* while Voltaire was still at Berlin, and with their object, the free and open statement of the facts of science and philosophy, he was in the most intense sympathy. Hence from Ferney he wrote a number of articles for the work. That work had to be printed in secrecy, and, when it once became known, it was speedily proscribed. The writers were known as the *philosophes* and *encyclopédistes*, and among them the chief was often named 'the patriarch of Ferney.' The latter was as usual ready to make reply to the ignorant attacks made on the writers who numbered among them those most distinguished in the literary world; and a series of lampoons was the result. One of these is known by the name of *L'Écossaise*, a comedy in which a calumniating journalist is introduced.

At the age of sixty-six Voltaire wrote *Tancrède*, dedicated to Madame de Pompadour. This work was admired by Gibbon[1] and translated by Goethe, and it has always been considered one of the author's best dramas. But he was not only concerned with literature, for the human side of him was ever conspicuous.

His admiration for the great Corneille was profound, and his notes on some of Corneille's works are classic. Though he might criticize where he thought criticism due, none recognized more fully the greatness of this man of whom France was so justly proud. His grand-niece was, he heard, in distress, and at once Voltaire said that it 'was the duty of a soldier to succour the niece of his general.'[2] Consequently he brought her to Ferney and provided for her education, and with wonderful tact and good feeling he caused her to believe that she owed her support to the proceeds of her uncle's writings.

Another case, much more remarkable, is that of Calas. This old man, a Protestant, had been broken on the wheel because his son was found dead and he was accused of poisoning him, although there was not the slightest evidence of the fact. The accusation rested on the statement, quite unwarranted, that Calas feared his son's turning Catholic and therefore brought about his death; in consequence the son was regarded as a martyr. The father died, but Voltaire took enormous trouble to have the sentence annulled and to prevent the other members of the family from being convicted as accomplices; and, in the end, after years of work, he was successful. During the three years which were taken up with this matter Voltaire stated that 'not a smile passed over my face but that I reproached myself for it as though I had committed a crime.'[3] No wonder that when he came to Paris in triumph before his death he was acclaimed as the saviour of Calas.

Sirven's case was somewhat similar, but he had time to save himself and take refuge with the protector of the oppressed and persecuted, and he was consequently secure.

But it must not be assumed that it was only those of another faith than that in which he had been brought up whom Voltaire succoured. He was ready to help any one oppressed in whatever way, and whatever his professed religion. The Jesuits even, his old instructors, whose order was destroyed—'the friends of letters and enemies of reason,' as Condorcet calls them—enlisted his sympathy, and one of them, persecuted by the Jansenists, became his almoner at Ferney. Possibly he was not without his use when Voltaire's own enemies blasphemed. But free-thought was speeding apace, and persecution did little, if anything, to stem the tide. Jean Jacques Rousseau was writing, and his writings were being circulated abroad. Political feeling was strong against a privileged and effete aristocracy. And yet the most astonishing events occurred, like the case of a young soldier named La Barre, about seventeen years old, who was accused of defacing a crucifix placed on the bridge of Abbeville. The lad was executed with horrible barbarity, and this aroused a blaze of indignation in Voltaire's bosom, although he had some cause to fear for himself, seeing that the *Dictionnaire philosophique* was in a manner involved (it was burned with La Barre's body). No wonder that he exclaimed, 'I am tired of hearing that twelve men were able to establish Christianity; I should like to prove that one is capable of destroying it.' We cannot forget Voltaire's efforts on behalf of our own Admiral Byng, who retired before the French at Minorca and was

[1] *Decline and Fall*, ch. lii., note 98.
[2] Letter of 7th Nov. 1760. [3] Condorcet, p. 240.

shot in 1757. 'In this country,' says Voltaire of England in *Candide*, 'it is well to put an admiral to death now and then to encourage the others.'[1]

This side of Voltaire's character—his righteous indignation with injustice and indefatigable efforts after restitution when injustice had been inflicted—is the side which attracts us most. He, perhaps the greatest personality in Europe (for Frederick was his only rival till the star of Goethe rose), endowed with a power of sarcasm and of invective of the most incisive kind, had the power to act, and it is entirely to his honour that in those difficult times he did act without fear and without delay. His humour was the bitter humour of the man who felt that things were too desperately bad to be taken entirely seriously, but this sardonic merriment did not prevent his practical action. His correspondence, which forms in some ways the most interesting part of his voluminous writings, is full of expressions of his inmost feelings regarding the events that were occurring daily around him. The iron burned deep into his soul, and he was given the power to foresee what was wholly realized only later on and then was dealt with by the terrors of revolutionaries.

There is another side to Voltaire's character which is more difficult to fathom. When he built his new manor house, he also built a small church with the inscription on it 'Deo erexit Voltaire.' And his correspondence shows him to be apparently anxious to prove himself to be all things to all men. He was likewise always ready to shelter himself through anonymity, and even to ascribe his works to another, though the other was dead and unable to defend himself. No doubt the times were bad and men's lives had to be preserved; but, whatever the customs of the day, this action was far from heroic. Then there is the famous communion made on 1st April 1769, followed by a public protestation of respect for the Church. His impish delight in forcing the priest to administer the communion to him, though forbidden by his bishop, and his 'forgiveness' of the bishop, is not an edifying spectacle, any more than the fact that Voltaire had himself made temporal father of the order of Capuchins for the district of Gex—an act done probably to annoy the bishop of Annecy. Even his sympathizers were scandalized by these actions, and in regard to them and many others no real justification seems possible. Voltaire was a deist, but that he regarded orthodox Christianity in any other way than as a scoffer is unthinkable, and this is the rôle he played throughout. He scoffed at the ordinary optimistic point of view, whether it was that of the philosopher or that of the ordinary believer. He was always ready to criticize and show the errors incipient in any positive creed or system of philosophy, but he never reached a constructive system either of spiritual belief or of social theory. Indeed he did not appear to have constructive power any more than great originality, but his interest in theological matters is apparent from his constant references to them. His religion, though it partook of negation, was not of the wholly negative character of that of some of his contemporaries, nor did it partake of the nature of the beliefs of Rousseau. Voltaire denied what he believed to be false, and that included practically all that he had received as religious tradition from the past. But it left a sort of possibility for the future which seemed to satisfy many of his successors, bald and empty and unfruitful as it might seem to be. 'I shall always be convinced that a watch proves a watchmaker and that the universe proves a God.'[2] And Voltaire's attacks on religion were not philosophic. His was a mind of extreme lucidity, which took hold of detailed facts that he held to be false and on which he poured derision as well as argument. He tried to cover the teaching of the Church on miracles, *e.g.*, with ridicule. With Rousseau Voltaire had little in common. Rousseau's sentimentalism made but little appeal to the older man's reasoning mind. Rousseau had repelled Voltaire's offers of assistance and shelter, and that was one cause of their estrangement, but their writings were antipathetic to one another, and Rousseau's effusions seemed to Voltaire false and his conduct hypocritical.

Voltaire's long life at Ferney—it lasted almost twenty years—has made a deep impression on mankind. Here he was growing into an old man on whom the eyes of Europe were constantly set either in deep dislike and fear or in admiration. He was in continual controversy, whether with the republic of Geneva or with the clerics. His hospitality to every kind of man, whether from Russia, England, or Germany, was constant and ungrudging. His niece, Madame Denis, who was unattractive and not agreeable in temper, kept house for him on a lavish scale, and he became a sort of 'hotel-keeper for Europe.' The winters were cold, but the life suited one who was glad to evade the distractions and intrigues of Paris, and doubtless for a man who was constantly subject to illness it tended to the prolongation of life. He wrote perpetually, corresponding with every civilized court and with distinguished persons of every country. Not only did the great men of the earth write to the patriarch but also every one, young or old, who wished for advice on literary or speculative questions. Many thousands of Voltaire's letters are now in existence, and they are full of wit, if not always pleasant reading.

Paris, much as he hated its atmosphere and resented its treatment of him in the past, had the same attraction for Voltaire as it has for all its children, and in 1778 he set out for the metropolis. His departure was bemoaned by his tenants and the peasantry of the Pays de Gex, a district which by his wise management he had caused to prosper exceedingly. Voltaire, as we know, managed his own monetary matters to great advantage, and he also had the business faculty which is necessary to make a countryside prosperous. At the same time he took an acute interest in politics abroad, more especially in the war between Russia and Turkey and the partitioning of Poland. By this time Louis XV. had died (1774), and Turgot was in power, greatly to Voltaire's satisfaction. He hoped everything from the advent of this great minister, who worked hard to bring about the reforms in economics that Voltaire so keenly desired; and his fall in 1776 brought him near to despair. But he had conceived a desire to see his tragedy *Irène*, now completed, produced, and above all to revisit the city from which he had been absent for thirty years. Nothing could be more flattering than his reception. Admiring crowds pressed around him, and jealousy was silent before the great old man whose personality had so impressed itself on the nation. People threw themselves at his feet and kissed his garments, for he was greeted as the true vindicator of the cause of humanity against oppression, more even than as a great and famous writer. 'They will kill me with joy,' he said, and indeed this proved but too true. *Irène* was performed amidst tears of enthusiasm; the author's bust was crowned in the theatre, and it was difficult for him to pass through the surging masses of people. 'Long live Voltaire! Long live the *Henriade*, *Mahomet*, and *La Pucelle*!' they cried. The Academy, after all its coldness to him

[1] Condorcet, p. 245.
[2] *Corr.*, 1744, letter to M. M. Kahle.

in early days, lavished honours upon him. Franklin was in Paris, and Voltaire insisted on speaking to him in his own tongue and blessing his grandson in the simple words 'God and liberty.' And the great man was not idle. He was revising his *Essai sur les mœurs*, and he had a scheme for a new dictionary to be issued by the Academy, and he even himself undertook the first letter in it. But all this was too much for a man of 84. Sleep went from him, he took more opium than was good for him, and finally died on 30th May 1778. The Abbé Gaultier confessed him some time before his death, and it was declared by him that he died in the Catholic religion in which he was born. 'I am about to appear before God, the Creator of the universe,' he wrote. 'If you have anything to say to me, it will be my duty and privilege to receive you.'[1] When he was in the act of death, the curé of Saint-Sulpice tried to get him to give a more detailed statement of his beliefs, and, as he was frustrated in this, made difficulties about his burial. Finally, however, Voltaire was buried at the Monastery of Scellières in Champagne, where his nephew was abbé, in time to avoid the interdict of the bishop. There was also objection made to the usual service for one of the members of the Academy; the king of Prussia, however, held a service at Berlin in his memory and himself wrote his *éloge*. In 1791 the body was removed to the Panthéon, but later it was disturbed and taken away, like so many others.

Voltaire's personal appearance is perhaps better known than that of any literary man of his time. He was extremely thin, almost like a skeleton in old age, with bright piercing eyes and a 'mocking smile,' and he wore a wig. He had a great attraction for women and a certain devotion to them, but this was for the most part of a platonic kind, and in any case he did not, like so many of his contemporaries, allow himself to be carried off his feet by it. His life was never indecent, judged by the standards of his time, whatever his expressions may seem to us to be. His powers of work were prodigious, and, though not physically strong, he often worked for eighteen or twenty hours on end. He was interested in medicine and has the credit of recommending inoculation for smallpox when it was hardly thought of. His conclusion as to health matters is given in a letter to M. Bagieu, a well-known surgeon: 'I have come to the conclusion that every man must be his own doctor . . . above all he must know how to suffer, grow old, and die.'[2] Sometimes he is seen bargaining and quarrelling about sums of no importance, and then inordinately munificent on another occasion. From such contradictoriness of nature he may be painted black or white, as the sympathies or prejudices of the observer dictate. To many of his own and later generations he was the most sinister figure of his age, and his writings (excepting some of his historical works) the most harmful in the 18th century. Others regard him as the deliverer of the oppressed and the champion of liberty. He wrote with the utmost ease and lucidity. He was a prince among journalists, and his output was enormous, as the 80 volumes of his writings testify. What he wrote was written as from himself and not as the views of those who had written before, though he had a wonderful power of absorbing the work of others. Goethe, after enumerating all the gifts which great writers should have, denies him only two—depth and finish ('Tiefe und Vollendung').[3] He was no philosopher, but a child of the 'Illumination'; *i.e.*, he belonged to the school of those who saw facts so clearly that there seemed no possibility of error in them. It was the time of cataloguing and arranging, the heyday of encyclopædic knowledge. Yet all Voltaire's work was impressed with his own individuality. He seemed to have the power of seeing the truth that others were groping after, and, when he came upon a false belief, he ran atilt against it without hesitation. He could not be called a sceptic, for he had his own beliefs clearly defined and certain: his was no doubting spirit. 'My reason tells me that God exists; but it also tells me that I cannot know what He is.'[1] There were occasions on which he lied, but the lies were lies begotten of the circumstances of life which he was ready to justify. His vanity was apparent to all, but that again was the conscious vanity of the man who felt himself to be above his fellows. He was money-loving, but he loved money because it redeemed him from a position of subservience and gave him the power he required. He had another side which proved him ready to be generous and hospitable in the extreme, so that he cannot be truly called avaricious or miserly. He was by nature a politician, and, as entrance to the politics of his country was denied to him, he showed what could be done on a small scale in his own domains and passionately supported reforms, fiscal and political, in his country. He did not live to see that his teaching bore fruit in a manner none could foretell, though many must have anticipated it when they saw how vain the efforts after orderly reform had proved. Such men as Voltaire were never used, and never had a chance of being used, for the amelioration of the conditions of their country. Such as he, who had an intense love of humanity, and on whom the misery of the common people under their unjust taxation rested like a constant cloud, were set aside. His reception in Paris as a human benefactor might have enlightened the rulers of the time.

Voltaire loved the stage from his boyhood onwards, and among his works there are 50 or 60 *Théâtre* pieces of various merit. The interest in his tragedies is often said to be too purely intellectual; *i.e.*, love plays little part in them. This is characteristic of the writer on whom in manhood affection never seemed to take any passionate hold. His poetry is fluent, and the usual criticism is that its fluency is excessive. Hence the *Henriade*, great as is its theme (and the theme is one that specially appealed to Voltaire), is not the really great poem that he intended it to be. He wrote many comedies, but no one could say that real humour, such as we find in Sterne, was present in Voltaire's writings. Of wit he had an ever-ready store, and his subjects knew too well of his powers in caricature. But Voltaire had not the terrible bitterness of Swift. His romances and tales appeal to the largest section of readers, if we except his historical works. They are delightful to read to this day. *Candide* gives us an admirable specimen of his style. *Zadig* and others attack the orthodox view of Biblical events, though not the larger idea of Providence. The most numerous of his writings, however, if we except his *Correspondance*, are his historical works, of which the best known are *Charles XII.*, *Louis XIV.*, *Louis XV.*, and the *Histoire de l'Empire de Russie sous Pierre le Grand*. The first is celebrated for the attractive way in which it is written, the ease of its style, and clearness of its narrative. With his *Essai sur les mœurs* he breaks with the old forms, so unsatisfying, as he explains, to an intelligent reader like Madame du Châtelet, and he gives us a sense of proportion which was absent from the writings of those who had made sacred

[1] *Corr.*, 21st Feb. 1778, letter to the Abbé Gaultier.
[2] *Ib.*, 10th April 1752.
[3] Note on Voltaire in Goethe's translation of *Le Neveu de Rameau* by Diderot.

[1] *Corr.*, October 1737, letter to Mlle. Quinault.

history their pivot. Of course he runs to the opposite extreme, as always, and makes his work too much a polemic against the old prejudiced beliefs. As in the *Catéchisme de l'honnête homme*, Church and Bible history is either parodied or misrepresented in the way that was so common long after Voltaire's day. The history of the Church was to him for the most part a history of imposture and fraud. Voltaire was not a great scholar in the historical sense, despite his vast stores of knowledge. His merit was to have a large and comprehensive view of the subject with which he dealt. This largeness of vision is indeed the quality which most impresses itself upon us when we think of this great man. The mark he left on European thought will never be effaced.

LITERATURE.—Voltaire, *Œuvres complètes*, 70 vols., Paris, 1785–89 (includes correspondence), new ed., 52 vols., do. 1877–85; Marquis de Condorcet, *Vie de Voltaire*, do. 1789 (also given in the 1877–85 ed. of the *Œuvres complètes*); R. d'Argental, *Hist. complète de la vie de Voltaire*, Neuchâtel, 1878; G. Bengesco, *Voltaire: Bibliographie de ses œuvres*, 4 vols., Paris, 1882–90; F. Brunetière, *Études critiques sur l'hist. de la littérature française*, do. 1886–1907, ser. i., iii., and iv.; E. du Bois-Reymond, *Voltaire in seiner Beziehung zur Naturwissenschaft*, Berlin, 1868; J. Parton, *Life of Voltaire*, 2 vols., London, 1881; L. Perey [*i.e.* Luce Herpin] and G. Maugras, *La Vie intime de Voltaire aux Délices et à Ferney (1754–78)*, Paris, 1885; S. G. Tallentyre, *The Friends of Voltaire*, London, 1906, *Life of Voltaire*, 2 vols., do. 1903, *Voltaire in his Letters*, do. 1919; A. Vinet, *Hist. de la littérature française au 18e siècle*, 2 vols., Paris, 1853, Eng. tr., Edinburgh, 1854; Marquise du Deffand, *Correspondance inédite . . . suivie des lettres de M. de Voltaire*, 2 vols., Paris, 1809; F. Espinasse, *Life of Voltaire*, London, 1892; E. Faguet, *Dix-huitième siècle: Etudes littéraires*10, Paris, 1892, *La Politique comparée de Montesquieu, Rousseau, et Voltaire*, do. 1902; Mme. de Grafigny, *Vie privée de Voltaire et de Mme. du Châtelet à Cirey*, do. 1820; E. B. Hamley, *Voltaire*, Edinburgh, 1877; V. Hugo, *Centenaire de Voltaire, 1878: discours pour Voltaire*2, Paris, 1878; Arsène Houssaye, *Le Roi Voltaire*, do. 1853; John (Viscount) Morley, *Voltaire*, new ed., London, 1888; Sainte-Beuve, *Causeries de lundi*, Paris, 1851–62, ii., vii., xiii., xv.; T. Carlyle, 'Voltaire' in *Foreign Review*, iii. [1829] 419 ff., reprinted in his *Critical and Miscellaneous Essays*; G. Desnoiresterres, *Voltaire et la société française au xviiie siècle*, 8 vols., Paris, 1867–77; G. Lanson, *Voltaire*, do. 1906 ('Collection des grands Ecrivains français'), 'Voltaire et les Lettres philosophiques,' in *Revue de Paris* of 1st August 1908; J. Churton Collins, *Voltaire, Montesquieu, and Rousseau in England*, London, 1908; H. Sée, 'Les Idées politiques de Voltaire,' *Revue Historique*, xcviii. [1908] 254–293, *Voltaire philosophe*, Paris, 1908; E. Champion, *Voltaire: Etudes critiques*2, do. 1897; E. du Bois-Reymond, 'Voltaire physicien,' *Revue des Cours scientifiques de la France et de l'Étranger*, 25th July 1868, pp. 537–544; G. Pellissier, *Voltaire philosophe*, Paris, 1908; Leslie Stephen, *Hist. of English Thought in the 18th Century*3, 2 vols., London, 1902; Ernest Lavisse, *Hist. de France, jusqu'à la Révolution*, Paris, 1901–11, vol. viii. pt. ii.

E. S. HALDANE.

VOLUNTARISM.—See WILL.

VOLUNTARYISM.—I. Introductory.

—The historical illustrations of this article have been taken largely from Scottish Church history, for Scotland, in a special degree, has been the battle-ground of spiritual independence, and it is there that the theory of voluntaryism has been most fully developed and most clearly defined, but it is there also that it has never yet been realized.

Five different theories of the relation of Church and State may be distinguished and enumerated.

(1) *The Erastian.*—This is the view that the authority of the State is supreme in every department of the citizen's life, whether civil or spiritual. For the question of whether this view dates from and owes its origin to Erastus and whether Erastus himself was an Erastian see art. ERASTIANISM. The most notorious instance in British history of pure Erastianism, in the opinion of many, is the decisions of the Court of Session in Scotland and of the House of Lords in England that led to the Disruption of the Church of Scotland in 1843.

In the second Auchterarder case Lord President Hope said: 'What makes the Church of Scotland but the Law? They are the Church of Scotland only so far as the Law has established this Church.'[1] In the Stewarton case the same judge said: 'The spiritual authority of an establishment cannot exist in law, except in so far as the Legislature has allowed or sanctioned that authority'—an opinion which was corroborated by Lord Wood: 'The Church, as an establishment, is the creation of statute.'[2]

'The decisions as to all of them (in the Auchterarder, Lethendy, Strathbogie, Culsalmond, and Stewarton cases) were uniformly founded on the one general law, laid down with cumulative deliberation and emphasis, that the Kirk derives "all its powers" and "its whole authority" from Parliament and the laws of the realm . . . and that the jurisdiction of the church Courts is derived from and defined by the State.'[3]

It is only just, however, to note that the subordinate standard of the Church, the *Westminster Confession of Faith*, speaks with two voices on the relation of the Church and State. In one passage it enunciates the principle that 'God alone is lord of the conscience, and hath left it free';[4] in another the principle of spiritual independence is not less clearly enunciated: 'the Lord Jesus, as king and head of his Church, hath therein appointed a government in the hand of church officers, distinct from the civil magistrate';[5] but in other passages this document is as frankly Erastian as, if not more so than, the decisions of these judges and the reasons by which they are supported.

'The civil magistrate . . . hath authority, and *it is his duty*, to take order, that unity and peace be preserved in the Church, that the truth of God be kept pure and entire, that all blasphemies and heresies be suppressed, all corruptions and abuses in worship and discipline prevented or reformed, and all the ordinances of God duly settled, administered and observed. For the better effecting whereof *he hath power to call synods*, to be present at them, and to provide that whatsoever is transacted in them be according to the mind of God.'[6]

(2) *Hildebrandism.*—According to this theory, the Church's authority is final not only in things spiritual but in things civil as well. This theory takes its name from Hildebrand, the family name of Pope Gregory VII., and finds its most memorable illustration in the excommunication of Henry IV. and his pilgrimage to Canossa. For three days he stood in the courtyard of the castle, in midwinter, clothed only in the hair shirt of a penitent, till he was absolved and restored by the pope. Excommunication, by the civil law of the empire, involved deposition; no excommunicated person could sit on the throne. Indirectly, therefore, if not directly, the enthroning and the dethroning of monarchs was part of the authority to which the Vatican laid claim.

The claim of the Free Church of Scotland in 1843 has been described as Vaticanism or Hildebrandism, but the assertion is groundless. The core of the claim of the Free Church of Scotland and of those secessions by which it was preceded was the right to regulate their spiritual concerns, confession, worship, discipline, without interference from the State—a claim that differs in two essentials from that of Rome.

(*a*) The finality of the authority of the State in temporal matters, including Church property, was not questioned. The decisions of the Legislature and Law Courts might be unjust and oppressive, involving hardship even to persecution, but the right of the State to pass these laws and to enforce them was not disputed or resisted.

(*b*) The Free Church, unlike the Church of Rome, claimed no authority over the conscience of the individual.

(3) *Co-ordinate jurisdiction.*—Establishment in England and Scotland has been described by many under this conception. The Church, it is argued, existed before the State and still exists independently of it. She framed her own creed and constitution and adopted them: she organized her own courts and defined their sphere and jurisdiction. The State, recognizing that these things were in accordance with the teaching of revealed religion, or accepting them as such on the authority of the Church, inscribed the Creed in its statutes,

[1] *Reports of the Court of Session*, Dunlop, iii. p. 197.
[2] *Special Report on the Stewarton Case* (Bell and others), pp. 53, 72.
[3] A. Taylor Innes, *Church and State*, p. 227.
[4] Ch. xx. [5] Ch. xxx. [6] Ch. xxiii.

ratified the Church's claim to jurisdiction in her own sphere, and voted support from the nation's exchequer. If moreover, it is argued, Church and State would restrict themselves respectively to their own sphere, they need never come into conflict.

Co-ordinate jurisdiction is the ideal outlined and advocated by Thomas Chalmers in his *Lectures on the Use and Abuse of Literary and Ecclesiastical Establishments* (1827) and later in his *Lectures on the Establishment and Extension of National Churches* (1838), but Chalmers had to confess that his ideal had not been realized. The cause of establishment had been vindicated in argument, in his opinion, but his grief was that the cause had suffered defeat at the hands of those who believed in it, but stultified their convictions by submitting to the jurisdiction of the State in the sphere of the Church.

(4) *Nominal establishment with real and effective endowment.*—This theory is that the function of the State is only to furnish monetary support, and it is not for the State to intervene or to judge whether the creed and constitution on which the Church had been established had been departed from or not, an ideal which seems to be the objective of the articles declarative of the constitution of the Church of Scotland and the proposals for union with the United Free Church, but, as these articles and the question they involve are still *sub judice*, they will not be further referred to in this article.

(5) *Voluntaryism.*—The voluntary takes high ground and argues from first principles. The Church is the Bride of Christ, and the phrase is more than a figure. There is so much of reality in it that, if the Church enter into a wedded relation with any earthly institution, the loyalty and obedience which she owes to her King and Head are thereby imperilled.

The Church's sphere is faith and conduct; but these are questions of conscience, and conscience must not be forced. Liberty of conscience is one of the first principles of religion. The only weapons of the Church are moral and spiritual. The weapon of the State is force. The entry of the State into the sphere of conscience is thereby *de facto* debarred.

Liberty of conscience implies universal religious toleration. Religious toleration connotes religious equality. Each of these principles, argues the voluntary, is traversed by Church establishment. Not only is loyalty to Christ imperilled by alliance with the State, but history has proved that such alliances are impossible without situations arising often in which the Church must choose between the will and command of the State and the will and command of Christ.

Conscience is forced by establishment, for State support directly or indirectly comes from all classes and creeds, and people are compelled to support what they may or may not get benefit from, and in many cases for the propagation of doctrines which they do not believe.

Toleration is traversed, for the principle of intolerance is the same whether it be expressed in the form of active persecution or in that of passive disability. Equality and justice are traversed wherever one Church or one creed is favoured, privileged, provided for more than others.

Voluntaryism is thus reached by the path of deduction. The voluntary takes his stand on great *a priori* principles of justice, liberty, equality, and, in particular, spiritual independence, of which he holds that voluntaryism is the logical and indisputable corollary. It is reached equally by the path of induction. It is supported by masses of evidence accumulated from the history of the Church in every age. The Church was never so vital, so convincing, so fruitful as in the first three centuries before her alliance with the State. The spiritual activities of the Church in modern times in every field of service (Home Mission, Foreign Mission, Church Extension, liberality)—not to speak of the inward graces of the spirit—have been confessedly greater and more fruitful in voluntary churches than in those allied with the State.

Not less convincing are the testimonies of those who, previously to the disestablishment of the Church of which they were members, not only believed in the principle but believed also that the existence of religion in their country was bound up with the alliance of Church and State, but after their experience of disestablishment moved rapidly to the opposite pole of opinion. Lyman Beecher wrote:

> 'It was as dark a day as ever I saw. The injury done to the cause of Christ, as we then supposed, was irreparable. For several days I suffered what no tongue can tell. And yet it was the best thing that ever happened to the State of Connecticut. It cut the Churches from State-support: it threw them wholly on their own resources, and on God.'[1]

Colonel Sanderson, formerly M.P. for North Armagh, whose every sympathy was strongly biased against disestablishment, politically as well as religiously, declared that he voted against the disestablishment of the Irish Church, but he would undo that vote if he could: 'He believed the Irish Church at the present moment was stronger and more spiritual than it ever was before.'[2]

2. Voluntaryism and Scripture.—The argument against State support is often rested upon Scripture, but the argument is not final. The passages most frequently quoted and relied upon are:

1 Co 9[14]: 'Even so hath the Lord ordained that they which preach the gospel should live of the gospel'; Jn 18[36]: 'My kingdom is not of this world: if my kingdom were of this world, then would my servants fight, that I should not be delivered to the Jews'; 2 Co 10[4]: 'For the weapons of our warfare are not carnal, but [spiritual or] mighty through God to the pulling down of strong holds'; Gal 6[6]: 'Let him that is taught in the word communicate unto him that teacheth in all good things.'

Now it must be premised that the weight of the Scripture argument depends upon the interpretation and application of the passage. So convinced a voluntary as the late Principal Cairns acknowledged this frankly in a lecture delivered in the Synod Hall in 1882.[3]

> 'The voluntary principle is, in one sense, held by all Christians. They all admit the duty and privilege of giving for religious purposes, according to 2 Cor. ix. 7, "Every man according as he purposeth in his heart, so let him give; not grudgingly, or of necessity: for God loveth a cheerful giver." All Christians agree likewise that this principle in some way or other embraces the support of Christian ministers and ordinances and put their own construction on such passages as 1 Cor. ix. 11. 13. 14. . . . Even so hath the Lord ordained that they which preach the gospel should live of the gospel. *The peculiarity of the Voluntary Principle (so called) lies in giving such texts an exclusive interpretation so as not to take anything beyond the free-will offerings of the Church.*'[4]

Confessedly, then, the weight of the Scripture argument rests upon the interpretation of these passages. Scripture authority would be final only if one interpretation were possible. But that is not maintained.

1 Co 9[14], the great proof text of voluntaryism, may be correctly rendered: 'even so did the Lord give instructions or directions that they who preach the gospel should live of the gospel.' The instructions referred to, doubtless, were those given on the occasion of the mission of the twelve and the seventy, but most of these were local and temporary in their nature: some of them assumed the power of miracle; others inculcated a voluntary poverty and dependence on Providence ('no purse, no scrip') compatible only with a temporary and unique Providential dispensation, but abrogated afterwards by our Lord when He said: 'But now, he that hath a purse, let him take it, and likewise his scrip: and he that hath no sword,

---

1 *Disestablishment in Connecticut*, quoted in J. Barr, *Scottish Church Question*, p. 139.
2 *Glasgow Herald*, 21st June 1902, quoted in Barr, p. 140.
3 *Synod Hall Lectures*, Edinburgh, 1882.
4 The italics are the present writer's.

let him sell his garment, and buy one' (Lk 22[36]). Many of the apostle's instructions in his epistles were local and temporary, and the fact that he still considered this instruction valid for the Church in Corinth does not prove its validity for all time. To say that such an instruction debars the Church in every age from taking any help except from its own members is surely an irrelevance.

Jn 18[36] and 2 Co 10[4] enunciate the same principle that the Church as such will not resort to the weapons of force, but the inference that she will never in any circumstances accept help from a civil power as such is not a self-evident corollary from it. Gal 6[6] is an exhortation to liberality on the part of the individual Christian. To say that the Church as such is thereby forbidden to accept a contribution from the State is a *non sequitur*.

Isolated passages from the OT or the NT for or against disestablishment and disendowment are so differently interpreted and applied by different writers, and these interpretations are so coloured and biased by the writer's position, that definite conclusions cannot be rested upon them.

3. Voluntaryism in history.—The first quarter of the 4th cent. was signalized by three remarkable edicts: (1) an edict of Galerius signed also by Licinius and Constantine, a *venia indulgentia*, by which the last great persecution was brought to an end; (2) the edict of Milan (A.D. 313), a declaration of universal religious toleration; (3) proclamation by Constantine 'to the Peoples of the East' (A.D. 323), in which toleration is based on the principle of justice.

The logical issue of the edicts of Constantine was voluntaryism, but the practical issue of his action and influence was State-Churchism. His personal benefactions were very large, and the gifts of an imperial autocrat can hardly be distinguished from those of the State. The whole weight and wealth of the Byzantine Empire under Constantine and his sons in the middle of the 4th cent. were put in the scales on the side of Christianity, and it was established and endowed as the religion and the worship of the empire.

Space limits us to two or three great names in the voluntary succession.

(1) *Dante Alighieri.*—

'Ah, Constantine! to how much ill gave birth,
Not thy conversion, but that plenteous dower,
Which the first wealthy Father gain'd from thee.'[1]

(2) *John Milton.*—

'It concerns every man's conscience to what religion he contributes. The civil magistrate is entrusted with civil rights only, not with conscience. . . . That which each man gives to the minister, he gives either as to God or as to his own teacher. If as to God, no civil power can justly consecrate to religious uses any part either of civil revenue which is the people's and must save them from other taxes, or of any man's property, but God by special command as He did by Moses, or the owner himself by voluntary intention and the persuasion of his giving it to God. If he gives it as to his teacher, what justice or equity compels him to pay for that which religion leaves freely to his choice whether he will learn or no, whether of this teacher or another and especially to pay for what he never learned or approves not, whereby, besides the wound of his conscience, he becomes less able to recompense his true teacher . . . most of all are they to be reviled and shamed who cry out with the distinct voice of notorious hirelings that if ye settle not our maintenance by law, farewell the Gospel, than which nothing can be uttered more false nor ignominious, and I may say more blasphemous against our Saviour who hath promised without this condition both the Holy Spirit and His presence with the Church to the world's end.'[2]

No clearer or weightier exposition of the principle of voluntaryism and the sense of justice to which it appeals has anywhere been given.

(3) *John Locke.*—Locke's *First Letter on Toleration* is a powerful exposition of the motto from which it begins: 'Absolute liberty, just and true liberty, equal and impartial liberty is the thing that we stand in need of'—an exposition that would have been weightier still, had it been carried to its logical issue from the magistrate to the Government by which the magistrate is appointed.

(4) *A. R. Vinet.*—

'How will it be possible to persuade the state that it has no right to superintend services for which it pays . . . whoever pays is master: whoever accepts payment, accepts servitude.'[1]

(5) *Henry Alford.*—Coming, as it does, from one of the most scholarly and most spiritually-minded men in the Church of England, the thoroughgoing voluntaryism of Alford is remarkable.

'The next term is, the severance of the Church from the State. Whether years, or decades of years be taken for the accomplishment of this:—however it may be deprecated, and however opposed;—accomplished it will certainly be . . . God's arm is thrusting it on, and man's power cannot keep it back.'[2]

Voluntaryism as a principle was not professed by the founders of the Secession and Relief Churches in Scotland or by the Free Church of Scotland at the Disruption. In Scottish Church history it is a practical corollary rather than an *a priori* principle. The claim of spiritual independence, and the growing certainty that it could not be realized in a State Establishment; the conviction that State support for one branch of the Church was unjust and forced the conscience of those who did not belong to it or believe in it; the conviction, also, on the part of many that State alliance and support were contrary to the teaching of Scripture, led the former United Presbyterian Church almost unanimously, and a large majority of the former Free Church of Scotland, to adopt voluntaryism as the polity of the Church. The leaders in that movement were the Principals of four colleges—John Cairns, Robert Rainy, Thomas M. Lindsay, and George C. Hutton of Paisley.

The Church of Ireland was disestablished in 1869, the Welsh Church in 1909, the bill becoming operative in 1911, the Church in France in 1905. No Church is established in Canada, Australia, New Zealand, or South Africa; there is none in the United States. The only English-speaking nations in which establishment still exists are England and Scotland.

4. Questions.—(1) Is voluntaryism compatible with the conservation of endowment? James Barr, in his recently published *Scottish Church Question*, the most effective and comprehensive contribution to the subject yet produced, holds that it is not.

'What we on our part insist on is that none of the endowment shall go to ecclesiastical uses.'[3] 'It is a needless precaution so far as the main bodies of non-Presbyterian Protestant Dissenters in Scotland are concerned, for to their honour, they would not accept State endowments.'[4]

Some, however, have claimed for themselves the designation of 'pure voluntaries' who deprecated the alienation of the endowments. Speaking in the Assembly of the Free Church of Scotland in 1882, W. Robertson Smith said:

'I will stand here as a Free Churchman, but perfectly free to say as I do now, that while I am a loyal Free Churchman, recognizing the value of the act of 1843, I also stand here as a voluntary—a pure voluntary';

but Robertson Smith made it clear that he did not take exception to accepting relief from the State.

Objection to endowment rests on three grounds: (*a*) it is anti-Scriptural—to which it is replied that that is a matter of interpretation and of circumstances; (*b*) it is contrary to sound political economy that a State should give monetary help without determining and enforcing the conditions on which it is administered—to which it is replied that, if the State is satisfied with the wisdom and conscience of those to whom the money is given in trust, its duty to itself and to its citizens has been fulfilled; (*c*) it is incompatible with the principle of spiritual independence; it is not possible that a Church should be State-endowed and spiritually free. A distinction, however, may be drawn, and

[1] *Inferno*, tr. H. F. Cary, xix. 118.
[2] *Considerations*, etc., 1659.

[1] *An Essay on the Profession of Personal Religious Conviction, and upon the Separation of Church and State*, tr. C. T. Jones, p. 382 f.
[2] *Essays and Addresses by Henry Alford, D.D., Dean of Canterbury*, p. 166.
[3] P. 58.
[4] P. 159.

has been drawn, between an endowment and a donation.

'It is perhaps conceivable that the State should make *a donation* to the Church without imposing conditions, but that it should make permanent provision for the ministers of religion and impose no conditions is not for a moment to be thought of.'[1]

Furthermore, when it is remembered that many believe that morally as well as legally the endowments are the property of the Church, that the State has never really owned them, but only administered them, that the alienation and secularization of these endowments would be morally unjust and religiously harmful; when further it is remembered that centuries of undisturbed possession establish a prescriptive right in law as well as in equity, it seems clear that one may claim to be a voluntary and yet hold also that the endowments of the Church should not be secularized.

(2) Voluntaryism appeals so often to conscience that one is constrained to ask, Is it possible to be a State-Churchman and yet to be sincerely conscientious? Does voluntaryism claim a monopoly of conscience? Was Ebenezer Erskine not true to his conscience when in 1735 he wrote:

'Whenever it shall appear that the established Judicatories are heartily adopting the cause of Christ, purging and planting His house according to His will and the solemn covenant lying upon the land and giving justice to His oppressed members throughout Scotland, I hope not only to return to communion but to enter the gates of our Zion with praise'?[2]

Thomas Chalmers was loyal to his convictions and conscience when, in his opening address to the first Free Church Assembly, he declared, 'We are not voluntaries,' and when in 1827 and 1838 he bent the weight of his massive intellect and pure heart to the vindication of Church establishment as being right and expedient. The voluntary is conscientious according to his light; so also is the State-Churchman. To say otherwise would be a 'railing accusation' on one side or the other.

But, if both are equally convinced and equally conscientious, it follows that the conscience of a sincere State-Churchman is forced and wronged by disestablishment in the same measure as the conscience of a sincere voluntary is forced and offended by an existing establishment. The argument leads to a moral dilemma. Neither side could press its conviction if the conscience of another were thereby offended.

Solvitur ambulando. The question is one for men as citizens of the State more than as members of the Church; some convinced voluntaries have held that it should not be touched by the Church *qua* Church. In a democratic Government like our own the will of the State is the will of the majority of its people. If that majority believe that the best and wisest way in which national religion can be expressed is by a national Church, their right to establish such a Church cannot be impugned. If, on the other hand, the majority believe that a national Church is a public inequity and a wrong to religion, their right to disestablish and to disendow cannot be questioned.

The voluntary ideal is a Free Church in a Free State. The trend of public opinion everywhere is towards it; its realization is inevitable. The principle has been recognized and embodied in Queen Victoria's Proclamation to the native religions when she assumed empire in India.

'Firmly relying ourselves on the truth of Christianity, and acknowledging with gratitude the solace of religion, we disclaim alike the right and the desire to impose our convictions on any of our subjects. We declare it to be our royal will and pleasure that none be in any wise favoured, none molested or disquieted by reason of their religious faith or observance but that all shall alike enjoy the equal and impartial protection of the law: and we do strictly charge and enjoin all those who may be in authority under us that they abstain from all interference with the religious belief or worship of any of our subjects on pain of our highest displeasure.'

The justice of that Proclamation to many minds is self-evident; but what is just in India is just all the world over, and the day will come when justice shall be done.

By what path will it come? It may come by way of the State or by way of the Church. State-compelled voluntaryism sounds like a contradiction in terms. Voluntaryism for the individual is real only when it is spontaneous. Compulsory voluntaryism may force the conscience of the State-Churchman as really as State-Churchism forces the conscience of the voluntary. Let voluntaryism get its majority and power, and, on the ground of abstract justice, it is entirely justified in enforcing its convictions on the nation. The true voluntary will, however, hesitate to do it. He will rather suffer wrong than inflict it on the conscience of another.

Voluntaryism may come by way of the Church. Conviction in favour of it is growing rapidly not only in Free Churches but in those allied with States. The proposed union of the two great Presbyterian Churches in Scotland and the tentative approaches towards union on the part of the Church of England and Nonconformists are full of hope and promise. The voluntary conviction in each of these unions would leaven the whole lump, and voluntaryism would come by a great free-will surrender and sacrifice in which these Churches would denude themselves of every State-conferred privilege, prerogative, preferment, and prestige and take their place on the platform of toleration and equality with all the Churches of the land.

LITERATURE.—**Benjamin Martin**, Tract xxv. *Jubilee of the United Presbyterian Church*, Edinburgh, 1897, the best résumé of the testimonies of the Secession, Associate Synod, Relief, and United Presbyterian Churches; **John Milton**, *Considerations*, etc., pamphlet, London, 1659; **Dante**, *de Monarchia*, tr. F. J. Church, London, 1879; **Locke**, *Letters on Toleration* (*Works*, vi., London, 1823); **A. R. Vinet**, *An Essay on the Profession of Personal Religious Conviction, and upon the Separation of Church and State*, tr. C. T. Jones, London, 1843; **E. Miall**, *Views of the Voluntary Principle*, do. 1845; **J. MacKerrow**, *History of the Secession Church*, Glasgow, 1841; **R. Wardlaw**, *National Church Establishments Examined*, London, 1839; **W. Graham**, *A Review of Ecclesiastical Establishments in Europe*, Glasgow, 1792; **Baptist W. Noel**, *Essay on the Union of Church and State*, London, 1848; **H. Alford**, *Essays and Addresses*, do. 1869; **P. Schaff**, *The Creeds of Christendom*, 3 vols., London and New York, 1877, iii.; *Synod Lectures*, Edinburgh, 1882 and 1883; **A. Taylor Innes**, *Church and State*, do. 1890; **D. Woodside**, *The Soul of a Scottish Church*, do. 1918; **J. Barr**, *The Scottish Church Question*, London, 1920; **A. R. MacEwen**, *The Erskines*, Edinburgh and London, 1900; **H. Macpherson**, *Scotland's Battles for Spiritual Independence*, London, 1905; **A. Oliver**, *Life of George Clark Hutton*, Paisley, 1910; see also *Proceedings of British Voluntary Society*, do. 1834; *Liberation Society in Scotland*, Edinburgh, 1877; *Disestablishment Council for Scotland*, do. 1886; sermons and pamphlets, etc.

WILLIAM ROSS.

VONDEL.—1. Early life and writings.—Joost van den Vondel (1587–1679), the greatest of Dutch poets and one of the greatest religious poets of the Counter-Reformation, belonged by descent to the South Netherlands, his parents being natives of Antwerp, pious 'Doopsgezinde,' or Baptists, who were driven by religious persecution to settle at Cologne, where the poet was born in 1587. The lovely opening stanzas of his *Olyftack aen Gustaef Adolf*, written when that town was threatened by the Swedish army, recall his earliest experiences. While he was still a child, his parents migrated, first to Utrecht and later to Amsterdam, where his father soon acquired a considerable business in the hosiery trade. Vondel's younger brother was thus enabled to obtain a good classical and legal education, but the poet entered his father's business and was a self-educated man. As an exile from the south, he became early a member

[1] Andrew Henderson, *Synod Hall Lectures*, Edinburgh, 1883, p. 63.
[2] A. R. MacEwen, *The Erskines*, p. 85 f.

of the Chamber of Rhetoric, 't Wit Lavendel (White Lavender), to which most of the Brabanters in Amsterdam belonged; and his earliest plays and poems are written in the style of the *Rederijkers* and of the Bible plays which, under the influence of the Renaissance and the Reformation, had taken the place of the mediæval moralities. The poems show also, like some of Milton's first verses, traces of an admiring study of the French Protestant poet Du Bartas. His wife took over the management of the hosiery business, and Vondel set himself to the task of repairing the defects of his literary education. He took up the study of Latin, French, Italian, and ultimately Greek. Seneca and later Sophocles became his models in tragedy. Besides metrical versions of Sophocles' *Electra* and *Œdipus Rex*, he made complete translations, at one time or another, in prose or verse of Virgil's *Eclogues*, *Georgics*, and *Æneid*, of Ovid's *Metamorphoses*, and of Horace's *Odes* and *Epodes*. But classical influence in Vondel never repressed the spontaneously lyrical inspiration of his poetry or modified the passionately Christian temper of his mind. From first to last the poetry of Vondel has two great sources of inspiration—God and his native country; and, whatever form his poetry may take, its master-quality is always lyrical—ardour and sweetness, fertility and subtlety of thought, a music of verse which is at every turn the full and resonant counterpart of the changing moods of his exalted mind. He wrote few or no love poems. Only once or twice in his long life does the current of his private feelings of joy and sorrow rise to the surface in a lyric of joy or sorrow. His personal interests were merged in his passion for great causes, patriotic and religious.

The first conflict which evoked the full strength of Vondel's religious feeling and poetic genius was the critical struggle between the Remonstrant Arminians, supported by the magistrates and cultured circles, and the Calvinist Contra-Remonstrants with the common people behind them, which ended with the Synod of Dort and the execution of Oldenbarneveldt. Vondel's soul was moved to its depths, and about 1618 he attacked Prince Maurice and the preachers under the thin veil of a classical tragedy on the subject of Palamedes. He had to go into hiding and was fined for his boldness. Vondel found a more effective outlet for his feelings in a series of satires, begun about this time and continued at intervals throughout his life. The best of these, the fiery *Geuse Vesper of Sieckentroost*,

> 'Had hij Hollandt dan gedragen
> Onder zijn harte,'

and the *Rommelpot van Hanekot*, where the mutual amenities of the Calvinist clergy are portrayed under the figure of a roost full of gobbling, scratching, fighting cocks, are popular songs handled by a poet of genius. The *Decretum Horribile* is an impassioned denunciation in Alexandrines of the doctrine which consigned infants to eternal perdition. *Roskam* and *Harpoen*, in the same verse, are more quiet and argumentative expostulations against endless theological hatred and strife. The *Uitvaert van Apollo* and *Speelstrijdt van Apollo en Pan*, written when his *Lucifer* was driven from the stage, read like folk-songs into which a great poet has blown a music as winged and sweet as the *Hymn of Pan* by Shelley. None of Vondel's poems have preserved their popularity so entirely as the satires.

It would be out of place to give here any full account of the secular poems which flowed from Vondel's pen hereafter till the end of his long life. A large number of them are political and occasional pieces, descriptive and lyrical in character, written to celebrate the sea-power of Holland, the birth of a prince to the House of Orange, the victories of Frederick Henry by land or of van Tromp and de Ruijter by sea, the building of a new Stadthuis at Amsterdam, the visits of royal persons, the marriages and deaths of his friends. He was the laureate of Amsterdam when that city was the heart of the Netherlands, and the Netherlands almost the heart of Europe, responsive to every movement from Sweden to Spain, from England and France to Turkey, and looking out over the seas to the East and West Indies. Here we must confine ourselves to the history of his religious development and some of the chief poems in which his devout and ardent feeling found expression, dramatic, didactic, and lyrical.

2. Attractions of Roman Catholicism.—The steps which led Vondel into the Church of Rome have nowhere been clearly indicated by himself, but they are not difficult to trace. As a 'Doopsgezind' he had been brought up to reject the doctrine of predestination as formulated by the Calvinists.[1] That movement had its ultimate source in the desire to find in the Reformation not so much a new creed as a new life, a closer personal and spiritual communion with God; and for Vondel himself it is clear that Christianity was primarily a movement of the heart, a passionate love of God, a faith in God's love to man as revealed in Christ. To him Calvin's doctrine seemed an outrage on that faith and love. The bitter fanaticism of the Contra-Remonstrant preachers appeared equally hostile to the spirit of Christian love. Moreover, as a poet and lover of the culture of the Renaissance, he ranged himself with the poets, dramatists, and men of learning, like Grotius, the object of his warmest admiration, who found their chief friends and patrons in the magistrates and middle class who were also the supporters of the Arminian movement. In short his religious and artistic sympathies alike drew him to the side of the Remonstrants. But he had no sympathy with the somewhat Epicurean and sceptical spirit of some of the humanists, as Hooft, who took the same side. Religion was for him the first of interests. Further, within his own Baptist communion were differences that disturbed him and doctrines enunciated to which he could not subscribe. In the *Antidotum tegen het Vergift der Geestdrijvers* (1626) he ranges himself against the supporters of the doctrine that the private spirit is a source of inspiration and instruction equal or superior to the written Word. He does not go further in this poem. He does not ask whether the interpretation of Scripture may be left to the individual enlightened by the Spirit. But events showed that this was the question on which his mind was busy, that he was in search of an authority able to allay such storms of conflicting dogma as had swept over the Netherlands and brought to the scaffold one of the saviours of his country. The trend of Vondel's mind was diametrically opposed to that of Milton, who was a republican in politics, and became always more hostile to the recognition of any organized Church, any authoritative interpreter of Scripture, any mediator between the Scriptures and the individual conscience and reason.[2] An uncompromising adherent of authority in the State, Vondel could not rest till he found a centre of authority in religion.

It was not till the autumn of 1641 that he took the final step, but in the interval he was busy with Church history and legend. In the *Olyftack aen Gustaef Adolf* (1632), an appeal for the safety of Cologne, he recalls, like Milton, how

[1] See art. ANABAPTISM, II. I (2).
[2] See art. MILTON, vol. viii. p. 644[a].

> 'The great Emathian conqueror bid spare
> The house of Pindarus,'

but elaborates more fully the legend that Alexander the Great spared Jerusalem at the intercession of the high-priest. Like Milton also, Vondel was planning in these years a heroic poem, and the subject he selected was the conversion and victories of Constantine. He had reached the battle of Aquileia when his wife died, and the poem was never completed nor any part of it published. He turned to tragedy, and prepared for the new Amsterdam theatre a classical tragedy on the legendary history of Amsterdam, *Gijsbrecht van Aemstel,* supplying the details of his plot from the description of the destruction of Troy in the second and third books of the *Æneid.* The best things in the play are the beautiful choruses on married love and on the Massacre of the Innocents; but the sympathetic treatment of Roman Catholic rites and beliefs throughout the play warned his countrymen of the coming change which was consummated in the autumn of 1641. With the *Gijsbrecht,* too, Vondel began a long series of dramas on Biblical subjects or saints' legends, but including two patriotic plays—*De Batavische Gebroeders* and the beautiful pastoral *De Leeuwendaalers.* Vondel did what Milton in the same years would probably have done had he not turned from poetry to political and religious controversy. But Vondel had ready to his hand, what Milton would not have found in England,—a theatre to perform his religious plays.

The relations of the Protestant Reformation and the drama were complex, and differed in different countries.[1] In general Protestantism was antagonistic to the stage generally, on much the same grounds as the early Church, and especially to the realistic presentation of the great mysteries of the Christian faith in the miracle- and mystery-plays. But, on the other hand, the moralities lent themselves to polemical ends, Protestant as well as Roman Catholic; and the educational interest of the time found a useful instrument in dramas composed in Latin—*e.g.,* the *Jephthes* and *Baptistes* of Buchanan and the flourishing drama, Terentian and Senecan, on Scriptural subjects, of Germany, Switzerland, and the Low Countries. From both of these sources were descended the naive Biblical plays of the Chambers of Rhetoric, the kind of play with which Vondel had begun. But the Eglantine, the most famous of the Amsterdam Chambers, and its successor the Academy, founded by Coster, a minor dramatist, preferred secular plays, native farces, romantic plays of the English type, but without their poetry, and classical plays. The new Theatre which finally took the place of Coster's Academy was opened with Vondel's *Gijsbrecht,* and it was here that all his subsequent plays were presented with elaborate and gorgeous staging and scenery. These plays differ from his earliest experiments simply in their more classical form, as that was understood, their closer resemblance to the Latin plays of Grotius.

3. Vondel and Milton.—Vondel's genius was not dramatic, and his ardent piety still further limited his dramatic treatment of its themes. He was incapable of letting his artistic genius so far get the upper hand of his didactic purpose as to create a great figure like Milton's Satan. His favourite hero is the pious and submissive saint whose first virtue is unquestioning obedience to the will of God as revealed by God's priest. The result is sometimes even painful, as in *De Gebroeders,* a play on the subject of the expiatory murder of Saul's sons, in which David's piety is shown by his becoming accessory to a crime at the bidding of a pious and politic high-priest. Vondel's temper is more attractively expressed in plays whose hero is some young saint of pure and ardent piety, like Joseph in the two plays with which he followed up his translation of Grotius's drama on the subject of Joseph's temptation, *Joseph in Dothan* and *Joseph in Egypten,* or again in the beautiful character of Jephtha's daughter in *Jephtha.* The most famous of all his plays, the *Lucifer,* will not bear comparison dramatically with the great opening books of *Paradise Lost.* Vondel gives as the motive for the rebellion of Lucifer the announcement that Christ will take on Him the nature of man and thereby raise humanity to a higher level than the angels, following the tradition that the Incarnation was independent of the Fall. With his eye upon the Rebellion in England, to which he was passionately hostile, he presented the revolt more in the form of a mutiny among the angels, in which Lucifer allows himself to be pushed to the front, concealing his deeper ambitions under a veil of zeal for the rights and privileges of his order—a Cromwell, in short, as royalist sentiment interpreted Cromwell's policy and career. For Milton also disobedience to the absolute and unconditioning will of God is Satan's crime, but there was in Milton the temper that rebels, and he was on Cromwell's side, and the apologist of regicide. His feelings and imagination got the better of his theology and gave us the great dramatic and human figure of Satan as he is presented to us in the opening books. Vondel's strength did not show itself in dramatic creation, nor, any more than Milton's, in philosophical or mystical interpretation of the inexplicable episode; but in descriptive and lyrical poetry—the opening picture of Eden, the final conflict of angels in the air, a great naval battle as between angelic van Tromps and diabolic Blakes, and the choral odes—*e.g.,* that on God which closes the first act:

> 'Wie is het die zoo hoogh gezeten,
> Zoo diep in 't grondelooze licht.'

All Vondel's plays show the same weakness in the portrayal of heroic and dramatic characters, the same descriptive and lyrical qualities. Such a pious and complete acceptance of the Christian view of life as Vondel's leaves little room for tragedy such as that of the Greeks or Shakespeare; for it eliminates those conceptions of fate and chance and the enigma of human life of which such tragedy is an expression.

4. Teaching of the plays.—The teaching of the plays is in general simply Christian and Biblical; only latently is it specifically Roman Catholic, as in *Jephtha,* where Vondel makes Jephtha's sin his stubborn reliance on his own conscience rather than on the authority of the priest whom he consults. Vondel's more purely Roman Catholic sentiments found expression in lyrico-didactic poems such as the *Brieven der Heilige Maeghden* (1642), saints' letters modelled on the *Heroides* of Ovid: the *Altaer-geheimenissen* (1645), an impassioned didactic on the sacrament of the Mass, the Scriptural and ecclesiastical authority for the Roman Catholic view of the mystery, the worship of the Host, and the rites with which that worship is invested: *De Heerlijckheit der Kercke* (1663) on the glory of the Church; and the *Bespiegeling van Godt en Godtsdienst* (1662) on the attributes of God.

More interesting than these to the reader of to-day, especially the non-Catholic reader, are those poems in which Vondel pours forth, with no didactic purpose, his personal feelings in strains which reveal what a fullness of happiness the devotional richness of the Roman Catholic Church brought to him as to the English poet Crashaw. *De Koningklycke Harp,* a brimming river of song

[1] See art. DRAMA (Introductory), § 5.

in praise of David's Psalms, the *Opdraeght aen De Heilighe Maeght*, prefixed to the *Brieven* mentioned above, a white flame of adoration, are good examples; but perhaps most touching of all are the shorter, simpler lyrics evoked by the death of his wife, his little son 'Constantijntje 't zalig kijntje,' his daughter, and his granddaughter. The *Uitvaert van myn Dochterken*, written in 1633, is an unrelieved cry of sorrow, simple but perfect in form. The corresponding *Uitvaert van Maria van den Vondel* (1668) is a hymn of resignation to God's will that hardly breathes regret.

'When this our earthly life hath ended
Begins an endless life above,
A life of God and angels tended,
His gift to those that earn His love.

. . . .

What from that Unity is severed
Must here in weary exile roam,
On earth no resting-place discover,
In Heaven her fatherland and home.

. . . .

Her dying breath went out to God
Whither all hearts must turn at last,
The goal, the rest, the perfect portion;
And in that prayer all sorrow passed.'

The resignation which such poems breathe was displayed by Vondel in the heroic close of his life when the aged poet sacrificed his whole fortune to redeem the debts of a worthless son and spent ten years of his life in the service of his native city as an official in the public pawnshop—a very Dutch pound for Pegasus. He died in 1679 at the age of ninety-two.

5. Place as a religious poet.—The personal note of the last poems cited is even historically the most important; for the significance of such poets as Crashaw and Vondel, emphasized by the supreme place which the latter holds among the poets of a country which had been in the vanguard of the Reformation, is that it reveals the importance of the Counter-Reformation, where it was that the Protestant movement had miscarried, had ended, not as its leaders anticipated, in a victory of Christ's Church over Antichrist, but in a definite rending of the seamless garment, a division leaving truth and untruth, good and evil, on either side. In its eager quest of a purer and more Scriptural creed and simpler worship, its impatient desire to root out the tares of 'human' traditions and ceremonies, Protestantism had outrun the human heart, had ignored the depth and power of the instincts of which those beliefs and rites were the expression. The idea of a united Christian Church speaking with authority; the significance of the sacraments, above all of the Eucharist—the 'This is my body,' 'This is my blood'; the devotion to the person of Christ and its overflow in the cult of the Virgin and saints—there were in Protestant countries and churches of all denominations hearts to which these things had only to be presented to make immediate and irresistible appeal. Some of the most interesting movements in Protestantism since the 17th cent. have represented the effort of individuals to recover these sources of devotion without sacrificing Protestant loyalty to Scriptural and historical truth; and there have been corresponding movements in the Roman Catholic Church to secure a higher level of Scriptural and historical truth without any sacrifice of traditional devotion. Vondel is not a poet of the calibre of Dante or Milton; there is nothing striking and original in the content of his thought; but a poetry so resonant and harmonious, uttering with perfect sincerity the passionate ardours and exultations of a great Christian soul—a Roman Catholic poet in a Protestant country—can never be without significance for the student of religious thought and feeling in Western Europe since the Reformation.

For the student of the drama too there is an interest, corresponding to that of the religious drama of Calderon, in this last survival in a Protestant country of the drama of the Middle Ages.

'The Spanish drama,' says a recent writer, 'like the Greek but unlike the English, had not cut itself adrift from its religious origins, and so remained a far more truly national institution than the English drama ever became after the Reformation.'[1]

Vondel's drama is throughout religious and patriotic. If it is not completely national, it is because the religious spirit which it expresses is not that of the great body of the Dutch people and because it does not do full justice, as Shakespeare's did, to the secular interests of the nation as these had taken shape and colour under the quickening influence of the Renaissance.

LITERATURE.—The most complete bibliography, up to date, is **J. H. W. Unger**, *Catalogue of Writings, etc., by J. van den Vondel*, Amsterdam, 1907, *Bibliographie van Vondels Werken*, do. 1888. See also **G. Kalff**, *Geschiedenis der Nederlandsche Letterkunde*, Groningen, 1906–12, iv. 333–336. The best ed. of Vondel's works is that of J. van Lennep, in 25 vols., Leyden, 1888–94; **Geeraardt Brandt**, *Leven van Vondel*, Amsterdam, 1682, ed. Eelco Verwijs, 1866, is the classical biography. A complete list of Vondel's dramas, not including translations, in order of production is: *Het Pascha* (1612), *Palamedes* (1625), *Hierusalem verwoest* (1629), *Gijsbrecht van Aemstel* (1637), *Maeghden* (1639), *De Gebroeders* (1639), *Joseph in Dothan* (1640), *Joseph in Egypten* (1640), *Pieter en Pauwels* (1641), *Maria Stuart* (1646), *De Leeuwendaalers* (1647), *Lucifer* (1654), *Salmoneus* (1657), *Jephtha* (1659), *Koning David in ballingschap* (1660), *Koning David Herstelt* (1660), *Samson* (1660), *Adonias* (1661), *De Batavische Gebroeders* (1663), *Faëton* (1663), *Adam in ballingschap* (1664), *Zunchin* (1667), *Noah* (1667). *Joannes de Boetgezant* (1662) is a short didactic epic suggested in part by G. B. Marino's *La Strage degli Innocenti*. For the religious drama of the Reformation see art. DRAMA (Introductory), § 5; **C. H. Herford**, *Literary Relations of England and Germany in the 16th Century*, Cambridge, 1886; and **W. Creizenach**, *Gesch. des neueren Dramas*, Halle, 1893–1909, vol. ii. bk. i. and elsewhere. Note also **G. Edmunson**, *Milton and Vondel*, London, 1885; **H. J. C. Grierson**, *The First Half of the Seventeenth Century* (in 'Periods of European Literature' ser.), Edinburgh, 1906, p. 193; and Kalff, *op. cit.*; *Vondel's Lucifer*, tr. L. C. Van Noppen, New York, 1898.

H. J. C. GRIERSON.

VOODOO.—Voodoo is devil-worship and fetishism brought from the Gold Coast of Africa by negro captives to the United States and West Indies. Its chief sacrifice is a girl child, referred to by the initiates as 'the goat without horns.' When a child is not available, a white kid takes its place. Excepting at the great semi-annual festival when the 'goat' is drugged, killed, and eaten, black dogs, cocks, and hens are cruelly sacrificed by being slashed so that their bowels fall out. There is a regular priesthood to intimidate and rob the devotees. These sometimes have the name *papaloi* and *mamaloi*, more frequently *pappy* and *mammy*, used as a prefix to their given names. The head of the circle or association of priests and priestesses has the title of 'king'; *e.g.*, King Alexander was long the head of the cult in the south-western states. The entrance into the priesthood is won by many and difficult tests. The aspirant (man or woman) must endure hunger, thirst, extreme heat and cold; must go sleepless, unless commanded to have the dream-tormented sleep induced by drugs; must eat offal and drink the ooze of garbage. While enduring this, he must keep a calm mind and strong will, and memorize the power of various poisons, from rattlesnake venom, stramonium, and water-hemlock to putrid liver and earth from under carrion. Also he must acquaint himself with the properties of healing herbs, such as red clover for cancer, dock for liver trouble, boneset for fever, etc. He must learn to make luck-balls, tricken-bags, hands-of-love, fingers-of-death, and other fetishes, and lay up in his memory the incantations which he must mumble as he works and the number of times he must repeat them, for numbers are very important

[1] John Eglinton, *Anglo-Irish Essays*, 1917, p. 59.

in his magic.[1] He must, above all else, concentrate his will, so that, by the time he is considered a finished product of his school, he is a hypnotist of power. When he has satisfied his teachers as to his acquirements, he is set to lead a season's dances, these being fire-, snake-, and moon-dances. The fire-dance is the most important, and is called 'the dance of the Old Master' (meaning the devil). It is given at mid-summer and mid-winter in a lonely field or ravine, around a great fire of wood and tar. At a little distance is a sort of altar at which the 'goat without horns' is sacrificed. It has already been stupefied with some sort of narcotic. Each dancer gets a quivering fragment, and then hops and whirls and howls more frantically than ever. It is only justice to say that the priests swear that no child has been killed for a dance for fifty years. The moon-dances are the same unregulated caperings, indulged in when the moon is full. The performers start in a circle, clasping hands. At a signal from the leader, all start running round a big stone which is set in their midst, and, soon breaking away from one another, begin to caper and howl and yelp compliments to the moon, such as 'Pretty moon! Old Master's moon! Ho-ho! I love you, pretty moon.' The snake-dances are given by the owners of snakes at any time. The reptiles are brought out in their baskets and set down uncovered in the midst of a dancing circle. They are expected to be torpid, but occasionally one tries to escape and, being trodden on, bites a naked foot, but no serious consequences follow if the dancer is not too maddened to apply an embrocation of snakeweed (*liatris scariosa*), which is kept in readiness.

It is not really necessary for a voodoo to have great knowledge of poisons, for such is the power of suggestion on the ignorant and superstitious that, if a negro imagines that he has been 'hoodooed,' 'witched,' or 'cunjered,' he pines away and dies, unless some one can be found whom he considers a voodoo of greater powers, to minister to his mind diseased and root out death-compelling terrors by the tricks and baubles of his nefarious profession. Few white people realize the menace of voodoo due to its absolute power over a certain class of minds. MARY A. OWEN.

[1] Ten is so unlucky that it must never be said, four is the luckiest, and four times four times four is the devil's own number.

VOTIVE OFFERINGS (Greek).—**1. Definition and terms.**—The votive offering may be defined as a permanent memorial dedicated of free will to a supernatural being. It thus differs from the sacrifice (*q.v.*), which is not permanent, and from the tax, which is not given of free will. Tithes and firstfruits are properly not included, since they are neither; yet they must be considered, since a votive offering may be given in consequence of them.

The custom may safely be assumed for the whole history of worship on Greek soil. In the most ancient sanctuaries, such as those of Crete, Argos, Olympia, Sparta, Ephesus, these offerings are found in every stratum down to the earliest. At least small vessels that once held some kind of perishable offering are found in large numbers everywhere, and these also in the beehive tombs extend the practice to ancestor-worship. Such vessels, however, may be there by accident, simply because the sacrifice could not be presented without them; and the argument must be based on more significant things—human-like figures or animals which meet us in the sanctuaries just named. These are of course not the only offerings that may be assumed for the early age; other kinds that are found later may well have been found there, but, when the material was less lasting or more precious than clay, they had less chance of escaping destruction or theft. The custom seems, however, to have been extended and systematized in the time between Homer and Hesiod. In Homer the formula varies: we have no special word for act or thing (*ἄγαλμα, ἀνάψαι, κρεμάσαι*, and *θεῖναι, δῶρα* and *διδόναι* being used of other things as well); but in Hesiod we first meet with the technical *ἀναθεῖναι*, and inscriptions of about the same age have *ἔθηκεν, ἀνέθηκεν, ἔστησεν*, and *ἵσατο*. Shortly after this the terms used for the votive offering become generally fixed: *ἀνατίθημι* and, as its passive, *ἀνάκειμαι*, with the noun *ἀνάθημα* (*ἀνάθεμα, ἄνθεμα, ἄϝτημα*), being used to distinguish such things from gifts to human beings (*δῶρον, διδόναι*). These terms remained until in the 4th cent. and later they lose their force. These changes probably correspond to psychological changes,[1] the offering being considered at first as a gift to the god, then as a gift from the giver, and finally the religious feeling being swallowed up in self-glorification. The shifting centre of gravity changes the character of the gift, and at last robs it of its value.

2. Occasion.—The offerings might be given on any occasion, customary or special, public and private; but, whether state or person was the giver, the principle remained the same. Our classification therefore is only made for convenience.

(*a*) *Customary.*—There are many records of customary offerings at the recurrent feasts. Such are the dedication of a *πέπλος* to Athene every four years at the Great Panathenæa, and a *πέπλος* to Hera at Olympia every four years, and a *χιτών* to Apollo at Amyclæ;[2] Alcman's *Partheneion* seems to describe a similar gift to Artemis Orthia at Sparta.[3] We know that many other ancient images were clothed,[4] and it is not unreasonable to suppose that these customs did not stand alone. The periodical washing and dressing of images is common in the East, and its ancient character is obvious. Hecuba indeed gives a fine robe to Athene,[5] but the records of the public and customary dedications do not go beyond the 6th century. A *θεωρία* sent to an oracle carried with it votive offerings as well as sacrifice. Hyperides describes how one of them dressed and decorated the statue of Dione at Dodona,[6] and an oracle from the same place demanded sacrifice with the gift of a bronze table for the gift that the Athenian people had sent.[7] Other records show a silver *φιάλη* as the customary gift of a *θεωρία*; we find them year after year at Branchidæ, where fourteen cities dedicate in one year,[8] and at Delos.[9] So the Athenian colonies sometimes sent gifts to the great feasts of Athens.[10] It is reasonable to assume that the practice was customary at public feasts.

The private worshipper who took part in a festival was certainly expected to offer something. There are occasional allusions to this;[11] but it may be safely inferred from the preservation of thousands of little saucers of the same shape and make, and of anthropomorphic figures of certain types. These are found in most ancient shrines in regular series from the earliest strata; and, whatever they meant, we may assume them to have been sold by the priest to visitors for the purpose of dedication. The worshipper may very likely have taken the

[1] See Piepers, *Quæstiones Anathematicæ*, p. 20.
[2] Paus. v. xvi., VI. xxiv. 10, III. xvi. 2.
[3] T. Bergk, *Poetæ Lyrici Græci*, Leipzig, 1878, Alcman, 23; H. W. Smyth, *Greek Melic Poets*, London, 1900, p. 6.
[4] Rouse, *Greek Votive Offerings*, p. 275.
[5] *Il.* v. 87, vi. 301.
[6] Hyp. *Euxen.* 35.
[7] Dem. *Meid.* 531.
[8] Rouse, p. 278.
[9] *BCH* vi. 29 ff., 144, xiv. 408, xv. 125.
[10] *CIA* 339, 340 (5th cent.).
[11] *E.g.*, the Andanian inscription, H. Collitz, *Sammlung der griech. Dialekt-Inschriften*, iv. [Göttingen, 1899] 4689, 91, and at Delphi.

opportunity then to present some special petition; so that it is impossible to be certain of the occasion for any one.

But there are a large number of objects, common in the Archaic period and later, that can best be explained as memorials of the act of worship. Such are the well-known statue of Rhombus at Athens, bearing a calf over his shoulders, just as the modern Greek does still on Good Friday.[1] There are several similar figures known; and large numbers of little clay figures carry some offering, often representing a lamb or pig, cock, dove, or other bird, fruit, flower, or garland, which have been found in Athens, Calaurea, Corcyra, Crete, Cyprus, Dodona, Ephesus, Naucratis, Sparta, Tegea, Thebes. Others, again, are grouped in a ring-dance, and there are single figures who bear pipes or harp or play upon some musical instrument, who carry in the hand a bowl or jug or lustral spray or a jar of water on the head, who clap the hands or uplift them in the attitude of worship. A peculiar variety are the figures of Artemis found in Corcyra; the goddess stands facing, and a votary is seen in the act of dancing before her.[2] Others are depicted in ritual costume, and may be priests or priestesses. The most remarkable of these are those discovered in Crete and Ephesus. In a shrine at Cnossos were found figures elaborately painted, representing a female in ceremonial dress, holding and girt with snakes; similar figures, less elaborate, at Palaikastro and Gourmies;[3] at Ephesus, perhaps priestesses, and probably the eunuch priest.[4] Relief-carving reached its perfection in the 5th cent.; and then and later the sacrifice, the libation, and the feast are commemorated in reliefs. The worshipper may dedicate the clothes actually worn in doing the rite; even models of them have been found made in porcelain.[5]

(*b*) *Occasional.*—Here fall the great majority. State or person may return thanks thus for victory in war or deliverance from peril; and the person often marks by an offering the date of some event such as marriage and retirement from active life. Any supposed wrath of a deity may be met with a propitiatory offering, and the sin of the human being thus expiated.

3. Motive.—The motive may be thanksgiving, prayer, or propitiation, chiefly the two former. Help or deliverance from peril and success in some undertaking are the commonest occasions of the act. With a prayer the votive offering was sometimes given in anticipation, to keep the god in mind of the prayer; if we may draw a deduction from the customs of modern Greece, this would be common in cases of sickness. The crew of Odysseus, intending to steal the oxen of the sun, vow to build him a temple if they return to Ithaca;[6] and Crœsus appeased with rich gifts the oracles of Apollo and Amphiaraus, which had guessed his riddle and were angry with him for his unbelief.[7] For unbelief a worshipper at Epidaurus was ordered to offer a silver pig,[8] and other indications exist that small offerings were made for a breach of etiquette.[9] Fixed fines or confiscations differ from these in being compulsory. For bloodguilt propitiation was not uncommon. Temples are recorded as being built for this cause;[10] and after the murder of Pausanias the Delphic oracle commanded that

[1] *CIA* iv. 1. 372, 235; Rouse, p. 284 ff.; *BSA* viii. [1901–02] 96, fig. 55.
[2] *BCH* xv. pl. vii.
[3] *BSA* ix. [1902–03] 75 ff., figs. 54, 56; x. [1903–04] 217. Some are called the goddess and some the votary; but there is no reason why they should not all be votaries.
[4] D. G. Hogarth, *Excavations at Ephesus: the Archaic Artemisia*, 2 vols., London, 1908, pl. xxi. 2, xxiv. 7. 11.
[5] Rouse, p. 370; *BSA* ix. [1904–05] 81.
[6] *Od.* xii. 343.
[7] Herod. i. 50–52.
[8] *Cure Inscr. of Epidaurus*, 59. 39.
[9] Rouse, p. 312 f.
[10] *Ib.* p. 313 f.

his statue be dedicated in the Brazen House, whence he was dragged forth to die.[1] The nine archons at Athens swore to dedicate a golden statue (ἀνδριάς) if they should break the laws.[2] One inscription mentions as the motive of dedication 'fear of the wrath of the twin Tindarids.'[3]

4. Classification.—A certain number of the worshipper's gifts are of direct use in the god's service. Such are temples or shrines and the articles used in them. Temples dedicated on a special occasion are recorded in legend and in history. Danaus erects a temple to Apollo in Argos, in memory of an omen which encouraged him in seizing the kingdom;[4] Heracles and Theseus do the like. The temple of Apollo at Bassæ commemorates the deliverance of a city from pestilence, and that of Hera in Sparta deliverance from flood.[5] The murder of a tyrant was expiated by the temple of Artemis at Tegea.[6] A colonnade is built in some religious precinct with the spoils of war, as that of the Athenians at Delphi;[7] so with certain of the Treasuries at Delphi.[8] Parts of a temple might be specified, as the pillars of that in Ephesus dedicated by Crœsus;[9] this becomes very common in late times, when it often means no more than that some official paid for repairs or even arranged for them. Altars are a common dedication, especially late, some being apparently memorials of a ritual act.[10] Garments for the idol have already been mentioned. Many articles of intrinsic value, such as ornaments or coins, may have been given as valuables; but these are generally appropriate to the occasion, as we shall see.

Another class consists of what may properly be called ἀγάλματα, οἷς ἀγάλλεται ὁ θεός. The ἀκροθίνια, or choice pieces, are given from spoils of war—as the throne of Xerxes, the manger of Mardonios,[11] statues from the temples of a conquered foe.[12] So also any rarity—the stone swallowed by Cronus, the sceptre of Hephaistos, Dædalus's wings, mammoth bones.[13]

But in the great majority of things dedicated, even if they have material value, the ideal value predominates: they are in fact appropriate to the occasion. We may classify these: (*a*) image of the deity, (*b*) the act or process blessed by the deity, (*c*) the winnings, (*d*) the tool or means.

(*a*) *Image of the deity.*—In all the great shrines large numbers of clay figures are found that must represent the deity. These are sometimes not differentiated: the same seated type does duty for Athene in Athens or Demeter in Tegea. Others have attributes, as Artemis with a fawn or other animal, Athene armed cap-à-pie, Zeus with the thunderbolt. Probably the small figures reproduced the general aspect of the cult-image; anyhow it is impossible to say that the attributes suited the occasion. The naked male figures found in Bœotia, in the shrine of Apollo Ptoan, and many other places, were probably meant for the god;[14] and so also the κόραι of Athens and Delos were probably meant for the goddess.[15] Some in each class are dedicated as a tithe or firstfruit;[16] and the armed bronze Athene dedicated by a baker-woman[17] shows that there need be no connexion of the type and the occasion.

[1] Paus. III. xvii. 7, 9.
[2] Arist. *Const. Ath.* 7.
[3] *IGA* 62*a*.
[4] Paus. II. xix. 3.
[5] *Ib.* VIII. xli. 7, III. xviii. 8.
[6] *Ib.* VIII. xlvii. 6.
[7] *Ib.* x. xi. 6.
[8] *Ib.* x. xi. 5.
[9] Herod. i. 92; *Brit. Mus. Excavations at Ephesus*, i. 294.
[10] Rouse, p. 354.
[11] Herod. ix. 20–24, 70, viii. 121.
[12] Paus. VIII. xlvi. 3, v. xxv. 5; Rouse, p. 117.
[13] Paus. x. xxiv. 6, IX. xl. 11; Justin, *Parænet.* 34; Paus. VIII. xxxii. 5.
[14] Rouse, p. 307; those inscribed are dedicated to Apollo.
[15] *Ib.* p. 306.
[16] *Amer. Journ. of Arch.*, new ser., ii. 50; *GA* IV. i. 373. 9, p. 179.
[17] *Cat. Acrop. Mus. Bronzes*, 260; *JHS* xiii. [1893] 124.

Perhaps the figure of the nursing mother may be a goddess in her beneficent aspect; but these seem more likely to represent the devotee. Later, the god's benevolent activity is represented in a series of reliefs, which show Asklepios and his attendants curing the sick.[1] With less confidence, the same may be held for a few other classes of reliefs. These begin late in the 5th century.

(*b*) *Act or process blessed by the god.*—The earlier examples are simpler in conception. We would include here the warrior armed, a type that goes back to the 7th cent. at least, sailors rowing their galley, the victor in his car with Victory driving, the jockey on his courser, the athlete[2] with his proper attributes or in proper pose, the hunter with his game, the dairy-farmer milking his cow, perhaps the peasant in hat and cloak.[3] Here also we would place the common statuettes of the nursing mother and the various scenes of child-birth, which are becoming more common with the progress of excavation.[4] These must sometimes represent the devotee, and it is reasonable to assume that they always do, in the absence of direct proof that they represent the deity. A more summary representation is a bronze stone-ram from the Athenian acropolis, inscribed so as to leave no doubt as to its meaning: τὴν ὀκεἱαν (=ὀχεἱαν) με τάθεναίαι ἀνέθηκεν.[5] This may give the key to interpret other figures of rams, bulls, and horses, which are found everywhere.[6] A complete scene of animal life is not uncommon: brood-mare suckling a foal, stag attacked by hounds, or the hound alone, hawk gripping hare.[7] There are vast numbers of other animals, which more probably belong to the next class. In many cases the figure may be a simple reminder of a tale to which the key is lost, like the figure of an ass that prevented a surprise by his bray,[8] or that of a frog which directed a traveller to a spring.[9] An early series of painted tablets found at Corinth depicts every stage of the staple industry of the place, pottery-making, together with hunting and farming and vine-dressing; later, athletic contests were often commemorated by a relief.[10]

We may perhaps add the rather rare instance of a workman dedicating his first or chief piece of work, or a model of it. The most definite instance of the 'masterpiece' is Lycinus's pot, inscribed, Λυκῖνος ἀνέθηκεν τῆι Ἀθηνάιαι τὸ πρῶτον ἠργάστο. Mandrocles, who could not place his bridge over the Hellespont in the temple of Hera, placed a picture of it instead.[11] A summary memorial of healing was often a model of the part affected. These have now been discovered in very ancient deposits of Crete and Ephesus; hitherto they have been very common from the 4th cent. B.C. to our own day, and hardly known before.[12] In Ephesus was also a real human tooth, bound with gold wire (for hanging?).[1] Things outworn may be regarded as similar memorials of the act blessed. There is little record of this in early days: the earliest is an epigram of Simonides,[2] but there is enough to show that the thing might be. Later, its sentiment won favour for it, and it became common. So the lame man dedicates his crutch or the sick man his bandage; children dedicate their toys at puberty; and clothes worn in time of peril are dedicated by the survivors.

(*c*) *The winnings.* — The oldest and most important group of these are the spoils of war, which are found everywhere, dedicated to practically all gods, from the earliest times to far into the Christian era. The trophy itself is a war-dedication; and the warrior made his gift to the god whom he believed to have helped him, *i.e.* usually to the patron of his own city or tribe. It is rather mean to dedicate a small model of spoils, but it seems to have been done. In Olympia, Delos, Lusi, and Crete have been found useless or miniature models of shields, helmets, loinguards, cuirasses, and knives, besides others, such as axes, which may be memorials of war.[3] So with the athletic prize: from Hesiod's tripod in the 8th cent.[4] to the prize tripods at Athens and the Triopia, *stlengis*, vase, or crown here or there, and the iron sickle at Sparta,[5] there is plenty of evidence of the custom. Models in gold of corn-sheaves, silphium, olives, or vine doubtless display thanks for a good harvest; and perhaps some of the numerous animal models, which include every domestic kind and most game, are due to the hunter's gratitude.[6]

(*d*) *The tool or means.*—Sometimes the soldier dedicated the arms or weapons used in battle; sometimes the athlete dedicated his chariot or his quoit or leaping-weight. Later, we have models of sickles, wine-presses, and the like recorded in literature. There is not much evidence of this, but there is enough to show that the thing was done.[7]

It should be noted that, wherever the worshipper's figure appears, he is depicted as engaged in some significant act. His portrait, as such, is never dedicated by himself. The human being never appears except when something of the ideal is implied. There are some apparent exceptions; but in Greece they are only apparent, and, if not apparent, they are not Greek. Later, beginning in the 4th cent., all this changed; and the honorific statue came in just when the votive offering became a means of self-glorification. The old spirit hardly survived except in cases of dedications for relief from sickness and peril.

LITERATURE. — G. Piepers, *Quæstiones Anathematicæ*, Leyden, 1903; E. Reisch, 'Griechische Weihgeschenke,' *Abhandlungen des archäol.-epigraph. Seminares der Univ. Wien*, Vienna, 1890; W. H. D. Rouse, *Greek Votive Offerings*, Cambridge, 1902; F. Ziemann, *De Anathematis Græcis*, Königsberg, 1885.

W. H. D. ROUSE.

1 Rouse, p. 217 ff.
2 The athletes at Olympia appear to differ somewhat, as the right to erect a statue was an honour.
3 Rouse, p. 361 f.; *Athenische Mittheilungen*, xxx. [1905] 65 ff., pl. iv.; *BCH* xxvii. [1903] 300, pl. viii.; xxviii. 1904, p. 201, fig. 21. The last is in the attitude of worship. The first two are called Pan by their editors.
4 A very early series has been found in Crete; others at Ephesus (Hogarth, p. 313); Rouse, p. 255 ff.
5 *Cat. Acrop. Mus. Bronzes*, 527.
6 Rouse, p. 75 ff.
7 *Ib.* p. 76; Hogarth, p. 146.
8 Paus. x. xviii. 4.
9 *Anthol.* vi. 43.
10 Rouse, pp. 81 f., 175 ff.
11 *BCH* ii. 522, 547; Rouse, p. 367.
12 *BSA* ix. 374 ff., pl. xii.; Hogarth, pl. vii. 35, 36, 39–42, 47, 48, p. 196.

1 Hogarth, pl. xxix. 7.
2 *Anthol.* vi. 52.
3 Rouse, p. 116; *BSA* viii. 258, xi. 306. Possibly these were currency, as axes certainly were and are in some parts (Rouse, p. 389, pl. i., ii., fig. 63).
4 Hesiod, *Works and Days*, 654.
5 Rouse, p. 366; *BSA* xii. 361, 384.
6 Rouse, p. 368.
7 *Ib.*

VOWS.

VOWS (Buddhist).—**1. Vows at ordination.**—The primitive and most fundamental form of taking vows in Buddhism consisted in expressing one's confession of faith on the occasion of ordination (*upasampadā*). The words uttered at ordination before the master of the ceremony were the regular formula (*kamma-vāchā*) of taking refuge in the Buddha, in the Dharma, and in the Sangha, repeated three times as a rule.[1] This profession of faith was associated with other professions—of personal purity, of the determination to practise all the precepts and rules of conduct ordained by the Buddha—for the newly ordained was, after the regular profession, instructed in the rules of discipline, and therein was implied the vow to observe the rules. The procedure and methods of the ceremony differed among the schools of Buddhism, and various doctrines developed as to the efficacy of the ceremony, its influence upon the life of the ordained, its relationship with the other branches of Buddhist training, etc.[2] The more important aspect in the development of the practice and doctrine was the Mahāyāna conception of vow-taking, *i.e.* its significance in the ethics of the *bodhisattva*.

2. The vow of a bodhisattva.—As is seen in the art. PRAYER (Buddhist), prayer in Buddhism amounted to taking the vow to perfect oneself on the way to *bodhi* and thereby to save others. It takes, as a rule, the form of vows (*praṇidhāna* or *praṇidhi*) taken by a *bodhisattva* (or any other Buddhist) before a master Buddha, who gives assurance (*vyākaraṇa*) that the vow-taker shall finally attain full Buddhahood; the task of the vow-taker is then to dedicate all his good qualities and meritorious deeds for the realization of his high purpose. The specific methods and points in the acts of dedication (*pariṇāmanā*) are copied from the special vows attributed to the Buddhas and *bodhisattvas* of the past, recorded in various texts. As a specimen we cite here a passage from the 'Lotus' (*Saddharma-puṇḍarīka*) where Buddha Śākyamuni tells his all-saving power:

> 'There shall never be any being,
> Who, having heard the truth of Buddha, shall not attain Buddhahood;
> For the vow taken by all the Buddhas is this:—
> "Let me lead them to Bodhi, by accomplishing (my works)."
> Throughout future days Buddhas will expound
> Many billions of the threads of truth;
> They shall reveal this unique road (*eka-yāna*)
> And preach thereby the truth for the Tathāgataship.'[3]

The 'unique road' is explained as working out in life the stability of truth, the continuity of existence. Being is one throughout all existences, and therefore the ardent intention expressed in a *bodhisattva's* vow and his work of salvation can induce other beings to the same zeal and life, while the assurance given by his predecessor not only encourages him in the work of salvation but has a mysterious, or metaphysical, efficacy to help him in the progress of *bodhi*.[4]

3. The communion of the vow-takers.—The vows are destined to be fulfilled not only by means of earnest intention and ardent work on the part of the vow-taker but also in virtue of the assuring help rendered him by the master Buddha and of the mutual reaction between all the vow-takers. This is due to the metaphysical continuity of existences and to the consequent reciprocation among the vow-takers, *i.e. bodhisattvas*, of the works of dedication done in fulfilment of their vows. The realm of existence is likened, in a metaphor often used, to a net in which every knot is studded with a brilliant diamond and all those diamonds mutually reflect their lustre and figures. Every one in the realm does perpetually affect, more or less, all others by his or her ideas and deeds, good or bad, noble or mean. The intention and resolution (*chittotpāda*) are the preliminary to the vow, and the consequence is the dedicatory work; but these three phases are one in their essential nature, not only on the part of an individual vow-taker but in the communion of all the vow-takers, of the past, present, and future, because these phases and the individuals are but manifestations of the *bodhi-chitta*,[1] one and the same throughout all the realms of existence.[2]

Seen from this point of view, all the branches of Buddhist training are but accessories to, or methods of carrying out, the vows solemnly pledged. This is why in various texts a special emphasis is put on the practice of taking vows.

The Penitence of Manjuśri, *e.g.*, enumerates the six methods of practising faith, which are: (1) penitence, (2) invocation (of all the Buddhas), (3) entreatment (to reveal truths), (4) adoration, (5) dedication, and (6) taking vow.[3] Similarly the *bodhisattva* Samantabhadra vows to accomplish the following work: (1) reverence towards all the Buddhas, (2) adoration of the Buddhas, (3) the practice of offering and giving, (4) confession, penitence, and absolution, (5) emulation of meritorious deeds, (6) entreating the Buddhas to turn the wheel of truth, (7) entreating them to live among human beings for ever, (8) perpetually observing Buddhist discipline, (9) constantly adapting oneself to fellow-beings, and (10) the practice of universal dedication.[4]

4. Further examples.—The Buddhist ideal was to emulate the *bodhisattvas* of the past, and we have many records of vows taken by historical or imaginary personages. These were an expression of emulation as well as a source of inspiration, because in Mahāyāna Buddhism every one is a potential *bodhisattva*, and it is within the reach of a common mortal to emulate a *bodhisattva* and to pledge himself to similar tasks. We may cite here the vows taken, in the presence of the Buddha Śākyamuni and his great disciples, by Queen Śrīmālā, of Benares, the alleged daughter of King Prasenājit, of Kośalā. The vows consist of ten preliminaries and three great vows, wherein she says:

> 'I shall never cherish any thought of breaking the precepts which I have now accepted. From to-day up to the attainment of Buddhahood I shall never cherish any idea of pride toward the elders . . . I shall never arouse any angry thought toward any fellow-being . . . I shall never envy any others in their bodily excellence or beauty . . . I shall never arouse arrogant thought concerning all things, whether subjective or objective . . . I shall never accumulate wealth for my own sake but give out all that I shall receive for helping poor and suffering people

1 See *SBE* xiii. [1881] 115, etc.; *JRAS*, 1875, pp. 1–16.
2 See, *e.g.*, *Mahāvastu*, ed. E. Senart, Paris, 1882, i. 2; *SBE* xxxvi. [1894] 251–258.
3 *SBE* xxi. [1884] 53.
4 See D. T. Suzuki, *Outlines of Mahāyāna Buddhism*, p. 398, for a typical *bodhisattva* vow taken from a Chinese version of the *Suvarṇa-prabhā*.

1 See art. PRAYER (Buddhist).
2 For illustration of this point see *The Garland of the Bodhisattva's Previous Work*, in a Chinese tr., perhaps a Mahāyāna development of the *Jātaka-mālā*; see B. Nanjio, *Catalogue of the Chinese Translation of the Buddhist Tripiṭaka*, Oxford, 1883, no. 1092; cf. art. PRAYER (Buddhist), vol. x. p. 169.
3 *The Penitence of Manjuśri* (Nanjio, no. 1091).
4 In the *Bhadra-charī*, or *Samantabhadra-charī-praṇidhāna-gāthā*; see K. Watanabe, *Die Bhadracarī*, Leipzig, 1912, text and translation.

. . . I shall practise the four embracing methods (*sangraha*) not only for myself but for the sake of all beings, and thus, being free from attachment, never being weary (of my work), and being without any entanglement in the mind, shall embrace all fellow-beings into the same communion . . . Whenever I shall meet any unfortunate people, orphans, deserted, imprisoned, or suffering from various mishaps and tribulations, I shall never leave them unhelped nor stop until they will be saved and freed from sufferings, through righteous means . . . Whenever I shall see any people offending rules of decency or committing crimes, I shall never pass by them without trying to correct them but try to persuade or coerce them, according to the degree and nature of the offences. For persuasion and coercion are the methods of perpetuating righteousness; and when righteousness is perpetuated, the beings in the heavenly resorts grow in their number while those in the woeful resorts diminish, and thus the wheel of truth will perpetually be turned, to the benefit of all beings. . . . I shall never cease to embrace the perfect truths, since thus, and thus alone, we can remain mindful of the Buddha, the Communion and the Pāramitās.

Now, let me take the vow to save innumerable fellow-beings and to attain the perfectly right view of truth throughout all my coming lives. Let me take the vow to preach the truth to all without ceasing, on my having realized the perfect truth. Let me take the vow, for the sake of embracing the perfect truth, to dedicate my body, my life and my wealth for guarding the truth.'

Here ends the vow of the queen, and the book adds a comment:

'When Bhagavā listened to and accepted these vows taken by the Queen, all the innumerable vows taken by the *bodhisattvas* were caused by him to be embraced into and consummated in the three, just as all material existences are embraced in space.'[1]

We have here an instance of the vow intended for normal training in Buddhist morality.

In contrast to the peaceful intention of the queen's vow, we have another type of the vow to persevere in persecution and missionary activities. We are told in the 'Lotus' how the Buddha Śākyamuni, before entering the Great Decease, prepared his disciples, both human and superhuman, for the hard tasks to be achieved and the difficulties to be encountered by them after the Master's death. Then the *bodhisattvas* pledge themselves in the presence of the Buddha to remain faithful to his admonition and warning, even after he passes away, and to fight opponents and persecutors, even in remote countries. The ardent zeal and passionate tone of this vow sometimes aroused the fighting spirit in combative Buddhists and gave them a consoling assurance of the righteousness of their cause.[2] Apart from the question of the period and circumstances of the composition of the book, we have here a counterpart to the missionary charge and an extension of the story of Punna, the first missionary to the barbarous Sunās.[3]

5. The 'prime vow' of a Buddha as a redeeming power.—Just as the vow taken by a *bodhisattva* served as an inspiration and incentive to Buddhist morality, the vow accomplished by a Buddha furnished the occasion for adoration and devotion to the achiever of the wonderful vow. A *bodhisattva* is a being on the way to *bodhi*, while a Buddha is one who has reached the end of the way, where he has established a paradise to receive those who believe in his power. His vow is fulfilled, as shown in the glories of his paradise, and is called the 'prime' vow (*pūrva-praṇidhāna*), while its actual efficacy manifests itself in the saving power, more or less vicarious, of the Buddha. We see here a special stream of Buddhist faith developed out of the metaphysical conception of the power of vow-taking—a stream which was further divided into various branches according to the respective nature of the vows taken by several Buddhas.

Of the vows attributed to Buddhas who on that account became objects of specific worship we take two most important cases—that of the Buddha Bhaiṣajya-guru (the Medicine-Master), the lord of the eastern paradise Viśuddhi-vaidūrya, and that of the Buddha Amitābha (the Infinite Light), the lord of the western paradise Sukhāvatī, the Land of Bliss. Apart from the questions pertaining to the mythical origin of these Buddhas and their paradises, we note here an interesting contrast between their respective vows and between the streams of religious faith based on their worship. The lord of the eastern paradise pledges himself, among other things, to save the sick and other sufferers and to give them immediate comfort, while the lord of the Land of Bliss promises to take to his paradise all those who cherish a pious faith in his saving power. Thus the Medicine-Master was a supernatural medicine-man, and his worship became a religion of healing, while the Buddha of Infinite Light was almost a vicarious saviour, and the faith in his redemptive power developed into a pietism, a Christianity within Buddhism, so to speak.

Let us now see the vows taken by Bhaiṣajya-guru. The story is that, while he was still a *bodhisattva*, he pledged himself to the following twelve vows:

'(1) Let me, on attaining Buddahood, realize all the supernatural glories of a Buddha's body which illumines all the realms of existence, and induce all beings to the same glories.

(2) Let me realize all the luminous splendours and thus illumine all those who are shrouded in darkness.'

[(3)-(5) amount to vowing that all beings be induced to Buddhist perfection.]

'(6) Let me release all the crippled, mutilated, blind, deaf, lepers, sick of every description, from their sufferings and have them furnished with wholesome limbs or body.'

[(7) Saving of helpless and unfortunate.]

'(8) Let me save women suffering from the diseases peculiar to their sex and let them be transformed to men.'

[(9) Saving of those entangled in illusions.]

'(10) Let me release all those who would be imprisoned, punished, tortured or sentenced to death, if they should implore in my name.

(11) Let me release all those who, being starved, commit offences for getting food, by giving them, first, delicate food and then giving them a saturation in the taste of truths.

(12) Let me save all those who, being destitute of clothings, would be attacked by cold or heat, insects and worms, by giving them all kinds of fine clothings, decorations, perfumes.'[1]

Here we see a Buddhist counterpart of the Vedic Sūrya or Aśvins, and it is no wonder that Bhaiṣajya-guru was worshipped for the sake of immediate helpfulness.

In the myth of the western paradise the Buddha Amitābha was once a monk Dharmākara, who vowed to furnish a paradise for the pious souls and accomplished the task by a long and severe self-training and by supplying to his believers his name as the sole means of calling forth his saving power. The vow is taken before the Buddha Lokeśvararājā as the testimony, and consists of three parts. The first part is chiefly in praise of the Master Buddha and is an expression of the vow-taker's determination to imitate and emulate him.[2] The second part consists of the forty-six[3] specific terms of Dharmākara's intention and purpose in furnishing a paradise in the west and inducing all beings, without distinction of good and bad, of wise and fool, to share the glorious and blissful life in the paradise.[4] The last part is the consummation of the second and takes the form of a passionate committal to carry out the plan, and even of a compelling call to the universe to respond to his ardent intentions and to give an assurance of the final attainment.

Here we see the Buddhist conception and practice of taking a solemn vow developed to a faith in the saving and redeeming power of the vow.

Finally let us add a remark on a modification, or degeneration, of the vow to curse or magic formula — the case with the Tantric form of Buddhism. Here we see a circuit of the idea of *praṇidhāna*, starting from entreatment and petition and resulting in the use of the vow and prayer

[1] In the *Śrīmālā-devī-siṃhanāda* (Nanjio, no. 59).

[2] For the stanzas of the vow, called the 'Stanzas of Perseverance,' see *SBE* xx. [1885] 259–261; for a man who believed himself to have carried out the vows in his life see M. Anesaki, *Nichiren, the Buddhist Prophet*, Cambridge, Mass., 1916, esp. pp. 39–42.

[3] See *Saṃyutta-nikāya*, iv. 60–63.

[1] *The Prime Vows of the Tathāgata Bhaishajya-guru* (Nanjio, no. 170).

[2] *Sukhāvatī-vyūhā* (*SBE* xlix. pt. ii. [1894] pp. 7–9).

[3] Forty-eight in a Chinese version, a number which hence has become sacred among the Amita-Buddhists in China and Japan.

[4] *SBE* xlix. pt. ii. pp. 12–22.

for compelling the divine power to fulfil the demand expressed or implied in the formula.

LITERATURE.—Besides the works cited in the article see: artt. BODHISATTVA, ETHICS (Buddhist), PRAYER (Buddhist); L. de la Vallée Poussin, *Bouddhisme*, Paris, 1909, pp. 301-312; H. Kern, *Manual of Indian Buddhism*, Strassburg, 1896, p. 65; D. T. Suzuki, *Outlines of Mahāyāna Buddhism*, London, 1907, p. 307 f.; J. W. Inglis, 'The Vows of Amida,' *JRAS*, N. China Branch, xlviii. [1917], pp. 1-11; M. Anesaki, 'The Idea of Moral Heritage in the Japanese Family,' *The Open Court*, xxxi. [1917] 227-238.

M. ANESAKI.

VOWS (Chinese).—**1. Vows in ancient China.**—The earliest historical records of China, as of other countries, are mainly concerned with the activities of rulers and with internal and external warfare. It is not surprising, therefore, that the first vows or oaths mentioned in Chinese annals[1] were taken by the princes and great officers of the various feudal states of the empire, and that the occasion of such vows or oaths was usually the conclusion of a treaty of peace or alliance, or a similar event of public importance.

The customary term for the ceremonial taking of a vow or entering into a covenant was *mêng-shih*. The two characters comprising this ancient term are still in common use, though usually found in different combinations. They are explained thus. *Shih* is equivalent to *yüeh-hsin* and *mêng* to *li-shêng*. *Yüeh* signifies a bond or covenant, and is still used to denote an international treaty. *Hsin* means 'good faith' or 'sincerity.' The signification of *li-shêng* is less transparent. There is no difficulty about *shêng*, which means 'a sacrificial animal.' The character *li* is an unusual substitute for *lin*, which means 'to approach,' 'to draw near to,' and is a euphemism for 'to slaughter.' Hence the combination *li-shêng* signifies 'to slaughter a sacrificial animal.' Thus the term *mêng-shih* is a concise expression meaning 'a covenant entered into with sincere heart and confirmed by the slaughter of a sacrificial animal.'

The sacrificial animals chiefly used in ancient China on the occasions of a solemn oath-taking were oxen and pigs (by princes and great fiefs), dogs (by ministers and officials), and fowls (by the common people). The method of procedure was as follows.

A pit was prepared in the ground (called *k'an*), at the edge of which the animal was slaughtered. The victim's left ear was held by the master of ceremonies or by the person undertaking the vow; and immediately after the slaughter the ear was cut off and deposited in a dish called *chu-p'an*. Then blood was taken from the victim and poured into a goblet called *yü-tui*.[2] When this part of the ceremony had been carried out, the vow or oath was written in the blood collected in the *yü-tui*, and the oath-taker also used the blood to smear his own mouth.[3] The tablet on which the words were inscribed (called *tsai shu*) was placed on the carcass of the victim, which was then buried in the prepared pit.[4] The covering of the victim with soil was an essential part of the ceremony, as it was equivalent to calling upon the earth to be witness of the vow.

There was an officer known as *Ssŭ-mêng* ('Director of Covenants') whose special duty it was to superintend ceremonies of this kind. His functions were to some extent of a priestly character. He also made copies of the inscribed tablets, and either deposited them among the official archives or (in the case of covenants between private persons) became himself their custodian.[5] It was also this officer who administered the oath to persons who had revolted against the Government and had subsequently returned to their allegiance. Other officers who had certain duties to perform in connexion with these ceremonies were the Grand Minister of Justice (*Ta-Ssŭ-K'ou*) and the Guardian of the Imperial Ancestral Temple and Treasury (*T'ien-fu*), who were responsible for the safe-custody of certified copies of covenants made between the emperor and the great vassal princes.[6]

[1] See art. ORDEAL (Chinese).
[2] See *Le Tcheou-Li*, tr. E. Biot, Paris, 1851, ii. 247. *P'an* and *tui* are terms used for two kinds of sacrificial vessel. That they were supposed to be, and perhaps were, decorated or inlaid with pearl and jade respectively is indicated by the words *chu* and *yü*—the Chinese names for those substances.
[3] The technical term for smearing the mouth was *sha*. See *The Chinese Classics*, tr. J. Legge, Hongkong, 1861-72, ii.[2] 437.
[4] See Biot, ii. 359. [5] *Ib.* ii. 359-361. [6] *Ib.* ii. 314.

Numerous instances of vows and oaths taken by the princes of the Chinese states in the early historical period may be found in the famous narrative of Tso (*Tso Chuan*).[1] A good example of these early covenants is the following, which belongs to the eleventh year of Duke Hsiang (562 B.C.).

'All we who covenant together agree not to hoard up the produce of good years, not to shut one another out from advantages that we possess, not to protect traitors, not to shelter criminals. We agree to aid one another in disasters and calamities, to have compassion on one another in seasons of misfortune and disorder, to cherish the same likings and dislikings, to support and encourage the royal House. Should any prince break these engagements, may He who watches over men's sincerity and He who watches over covenants, [the Spirits of] the famous hills and [of] the famous streams, the kings and dukes our predecessors, the whole host of Spirits, and all who are sacrificed to, the ancestors of our 12 (13?) States with their 7 surnames:—may all these intelligent Spirits destroy him, so that he shall lose his people, his appointment pass from him, his family perish, and his State be utterly overthrown!'[2]

Some of the old commentators and moralists began at a very early period to complain that the frequency of sworn covenants and formal vows was detrimental to sound morals, because, when solemn engagements were lightly made, they were apt to be lightly violated. Cases were known, in Chou-dynasty China, of covenants that were broken 'before the blood smeared on the mouth was dry.' It was held that in the golden age of the 'holy kings' vows and covenants were unknown (*ku chê pu mêng yeh*), and that the simple spoken word required no vow or oath to make it binding. It was pointed out that the making of many solemn protestations fostered distrust between state and state and also between rulers and ruled. In the 'Classic of Poetry' (*Shih Ching*) we read of a king who added to the disorders of his kingdom by entering into frequent covenants with the vassal princes; for he showed thereby that he had no confidence in them and lived in fear of rebellion.[3] Commentators also observe that no formal covenants were known before the Yin dynasty (1766-1122 B.C.) and that this was precisely the time when the State began to be disturbed by rebellious movements. Oaths and vows were introduced only 'when loyalty and sincerity had worn thin and men's hearts were perplexed with doubts.'

It will have been noticed that these State covenants were really the ancient Chinese equivalents of modern treaties; and the vows or oaths that accompanied such engagements practically corresponded to the modern seals and signatures of plenipotentiaries. The violation of a covenant was therefore nothing more or less than what we should call the wilful breaking of a treaty.

2. Vows of friendship.—Chinese social life has for ages been characterized by five 'relationships,' each of which implies certain rights, privileges, and duties. These are the relationships between 'sovereign and minister' (this will probably be reinterpreted to mean 'citizen and State' if the Republican form of government proves permanent), 'husband and wife,' 'father and son,' 'elder brother and younger brother,' 'friend and friend.' Friendship thus often assumes the importance of a recognized social institution, with its appropriate rules, customs, and traditions. When two or more Chinese decide to become 'friends' in what may be called the institutional sense of the term, they become bound to one another by solemn vows which are sometimes accompanied by a ceremonial mingling of blood. This is supposed to create a bond identical for all practical purposes with that of blood-kinship. The following example of a vow

[1] Tr. J. Legge, *The Chinese Classics*, v.
[2] *Ib.* p. 453. It may be noted that there were instances of treaties with smearing of lips as late as the wars between the Chinese and the Tatars (*c.* 1131).
[3] See Legge, iv. 340 f.

of friendship is taken from the official annals of the Sung dynasty.

'We . . . will cling together like serpents and dragons inextricably coiled. When one of us attains riches and honour he will share his prosperity with the others. May he who breaks this vow receive divine chastisement.'

After uttering these words, the parties would prick their arms and let the blood flow into a goblet. Of the mingled blood each took a sip, thus becoming the 'blood-brother' of the other.[1] If 'sworn brothers' wish to terminate the relationship, they must do so in a formal manner. This is sometimes known as 'withdrawing the incense-stick' (*pa hsiang-t'ou-tzŭ*).[2]

A few foreigners have become the 'brothers' of Chinese officials and others, though probably in these cases the ceremony is abbreviated and simplified. H. A. Giles describes how, in 1868, he became the 'younger brother' of the influential court eunuch, An Tê-hai.[3] A similar relationship has also been entered into between various Chinese emperors and some of their chosen subjects; *e.g.*, Shêng Tsu (10th cent. A.D.) and Hsing Tsung (11th cent. A.D.) of the Liao dynasty both became 'bound brothers' (*chieh wei hsiung-ti*) of certain trusted friends. In modern times the Chinese Government (especially under the Manchu dynasty) has shown itself extremely hostile to this custom, and indeed made it a punishable offence.

Soon after the accession of the Manchus it was decreed that for persons of different surnames to salute each other as brothers (*chieh pai hsiung-ti*) was an offence punishable by a hundred blows. In 1661 the death-penalty was decreed against 'sworn brothers' who took part in the ceremonies of blood-smearing and the ritual burning of paper slips on which vows were written. A slightly less rigorous law was enacted in the seventeenth year of K'ang-hsi (1668), but membership of sworn brotherhoods was still an offence punishable by flogging and, in aggravated cases, by death. The death-penalty was reduced to 'a hundred blows' if there was no blood-drinking or smearing and no burning of vows. In 1671 a further law enacted that persons guilty of joining sworn brotherhoods were liable to three years' banishment to the frontiers; but in 1673 a new law made a clear distinction between harmless brotherhoods and those which were regarded as criminal. The blood-smearing and drinking, and the formal consignment of the written vows to the keeping of the gods by means of fire, constituted the decisive evidence of guilt in its most serious form.

Formal vows of friendship between women are not unknown. They salute each other as 'dry sisters' (*kan chieh*). One method of entering into this relationship is for each of the two women to hold the end of a straw over the village well and to call upon a divinity known as 'the Peach-Flower Maiden' to witness the compact.

3. Vows of secret brotherhoods and societies.—The reasons for the severity with which 'sworn brotherhoods' have been treated by the Chinese Government are not far to seek. Secret fraternities, all the members of which are bound by inviolable vows to be loyal to one another as against the whole world, are very apt to become a danger to almost any form of government, especially if that government is controlled by an alien dynasty that has supplanted a native one. In ancient times, nevertheless, it was considered a right and proper thing that men should take vows of co-operation and mutual aid. The *Chou Li* declares that 'by entering into mutual engagements accompanied by vows the people are taught to extend brotherly love to one another and to put away apathy.'[4] A commentator on this rather enigmatic statement is worth quoting.[5]

'There are different ways,' he says, 'in which people show their apathy and laziness. They do not hurry to give help to those who are in danger or suffering hardship, thus they are lacking in charity and sympathy. It is therefore a good thing that people should be stimulated by means of solemn vows to aid one another in distress, to support one another in sickness, to extend a friendly hand to those who need it, to help one another in times of anxiety or peril, and to be faithful to one's word as long as life lasts, setting aside all petty personal considerations[1] that might cause delay or give an excuse for laziness.'

This remarkable description of the social value of vows seems strangely modern; it might almost serve as a statement of the ethical basis of the Boy Scout movement. Chinese history affords innumerable instances of vows of this kind entered into and most faithfully carried out by bands of associates or members of social groups. Where the ethical ideal falls short is in the fact that the obligation to succour the distressed is not usually regarded as of general application, but concerns only fellow-members of the oath-bound fraternity. Yet this depends, of course, on the specific purposes for which the fraternity has been constituted; and sometimes they far transcend the individual or collective interests of the members, even if they do not go so far as to include all mankind within their purview.

The most famous and memorable Chinese example of a vow entered into for purposes that went far beyond the private interests of those concerned was 'the Vow of the Peach-garden,' whereby the three heroes Liu Lei, Kuan Yü, and Chang Fei (2nd and 3rd centuries A.D.) bound themselves to fight for the preservation of the reigning dynasty against the attacks of the Yellow-Turban rebels.[2] We are told that the ceremony (which took place in Chang Fei's peach-garden) consisted in the sacrifice of a black ox and a white horse and in the taking of a vow to the following effect:

'We swear to regard one another henceforth as brothers, to unite our abilities and our hearts, to bring succour to the miserable, to raise up the fallen. We will serve our country and give peace to the people. Though we were born on different dates we wish to die together on the same day. Our hearts are open to the inspection of the divine powers of Heaven and Earth. If any one of us proves false to his duty and forgetful of his obligations, may God and man unite to destroy him.'

This celebrated 'Vow of the Peach-garden' has been imitated countless times, especially by members of societies formed for purposes of mutual protection. Such societies, indeed, are still formed from time to time; several new ones sprang into existence among the tens of thousands of Chinese labourers who worked behind the fighting lines in France during the Great War.[3]

It is interesting to note that the Peach-garden Vow was 'often referred to by the Triad Society,' and that its members were 'exhorted to emulate the faithfulness to each other and loyalty to their cause of the heroes who took it.'[4] The vows of the Triad Society were thirty-six in number.[5] It is characteristic of China that the first of them is a vow of filial piety. After repeating the vows, each candidate is required to take a lighted incense-stick and dip it in a bowl of water. As the light is extinguished, he says, 'If I prove false to my vows, may my life go out like the fire of this stick of incense.' The master of ceremonies ('incense-master') then takes up a porcelain basin and dashes it on the ground, saying, 'May such be the fate of all traitors.' He proceeds to take up the paper on which the vows are written, and sets fire to it. By this means it is supposed that the vows pass from the material into the spiritual world and are received by the divine powers, who will register them in the archives of heaven and inflict punishment on traitors. The next part of the ceremony consists in cutting off the head of a cock, as an indication of the grim fate that will befall any one who betrays the cause. The incense-master then drops some of the dead cock's blood into the water in which the incense-sticks were extinguished; and each of the candidates pricks one of his fingers and lets the blood drop into the same vessel or (sometimes) into another bowl containing wine. The ashes of the burnt papers on which the vows were written are put into the bowl containing the mingled blood of

1 Cf. art. BROTHERHOOD (Artificial), § 2 ff.
2 Cf. L. Wieger, *Moral Tenets and Customs in China*, tr. L. Davrout, Ho-kien-fu and London, 1913, p. 519 f.
3 *Adversaria Sinica*, no. 9, p. 310.
4 Biot, i. 197.
5 This commentator, Chêng O, who belonged to the Sung dynasty, is not quoted by Biot.

1 Literally, 'even if one has to go with cap tied over one's unbound hair,' *i.e.* before one has completed one's toilet. The expression is taken from Mencius. See Legge, ii. 336.
2 Cf. Favre, in the *T'oung Pao*, vol. xix. [Leyden, 1919] no. 1, p. 1 ff. See also H. Doré, *Recherches sur les superstitions en Chine*, pt. i. vol. ii. [Paris, 1912], no. 4, p. 346.
3 For details see Favre. Cf. art. SECTS (Chinese).
4 William Stanton, *The Triad Society or Heaven and Earth Association*, Hongkong, 1900, p. 1.
5 *Ib.* pp. 61 f., 118 f.

the candidates, and the bowl is then handed round and sipped by each in turn. This concludes the ceremonies of initiation, after which the new members of the society are hailed by the old ones as 'brothers.'[1]

Sisterhoods are less common than brotherhoods, but by no means unknown. Detailed information regarding them is lacking, but mention must be made of the Golden Orchid Society (*Chin-Lan Hui*), which is described by H. A. Giles as 'a secret association of unmarried girls who bind themselves not to cohabit with their husbands after marriage (which they are unable to avoid) but to leave them and return to their old homes or go elsewhere.'[2] It has been said that members of this society would commit suicide rather than break their vow.[3]

4. Religious vows.—(*a*) *Buddhism.*—In China as in other Buddhist lands there are vows for both monks and laymen, those of the former being naturally much stricter and more comprehensive than those to which laymen subscribe. Sometimes, however, lay Buddhists of both sexes voluntarily bind themselves by one or more of the obligations which are ordinarily binding only on the monkhood. There is a society of lay vegetarians which is said to have been founded in the T'ang dynasty by the fifth and sixth 'patriarchs' of the Ch'an school of Buddhism. Members of this society are known as *chai kung* ('fasters'), a term which is also applied to those who take vows of temporary vegetarianism during their pilgrimage to a sacred mountain.

The fact that practically the whole of Chinese Buddhism[4] belongs to the Great Vehicle (Mahāyāna) explains the existence of religious vows of which little or no trace can be found in primitive Buddhism. The great models of all such vows are those which are supposed to have been taken by the *bodhisattvas*. These vows are numerous—in the *Wu-liang-shou-sūtra* they are forty-eight in number[5]—but they are practically all summed up in the formula, 'So long as there remains a single being who has not attained Buddhahood, I vow that I will not become Buddha.' The 'vows' of the *bodhisattvas* (*praṇidhāna*) may be described as expressions of will which, through the intensity of the selfless emotion that inspires them, are instrumental in bringing about a realization of the desired conditions.[6] The Mahāyāna, as J. J. M. de Groot has shown, 'admits the creative power of thought,'[7] and indeed this is insisted upon so frequently that it may be regarded as one of the fundamental principles of Buddhist psychology. This fact is apt to be ignored by those who dwell upon the 'vain repetitions' said to be characteristic of Buddhism in practice, and who do not understand that the repetitions are believed to reinforce the creative power of thought to which the spoken words give expression.

We have already seen that forty-eight *bodhisattva*-vows are preserved in a famous *sūtra*; but according to another classification only four are essential. These 'four great vows' (*ssŭ hung shih-yüan*) are as follows: (1) the vow to save the world, *i.e.* not to rest until all beings in the universe have been brought to salvation; (2) the vow to destroy in oneself all evil and the passions

[1] Stanton, *The Triad Society*, pp. 61–66.

[2] *A Glossary of Reference to Subjects Connected with the Far East*, Shanghai, 1900, p. 108.

[3] S. Couling, *Encyclopædia Sinica*, Shanghai, 1917, *s.v.* 'Secret Societies,' p. 501.

[4] See art. CHINA (Buddhism in).

[5] *SBE* xlix. [1894], *Buddhist Mahāyāna Texts*, pt. ii. (*The Larger Sukhāvatīvyūha*, § 8), pp. 12–22. Cf. R. F. Johnston, *Buddhist China*, London, 1913, pp. 96–98; J. W. Inglis, 'The Vows of Amida' in *JRAS*, North-China Branch, xlviii. [1917] 1 f.

[6] See D. T. Suzuki, *Outlines of Mahāyāna Buddhism*, London, 1907, pp. 238–241.

[7] De Groot, *Le Code du Mahāyāna en Chine*, Amsterdam, 1893, pp. 5 f., 95; cf. also p. 164 f.

that produce evil; (3) the vow to study and practise the *dharma*, *i.e.* the law of Buddha, with a view to the attainment of wisdom and virtue; (4) the vow to attain the perfection of Buddhahood. These vows are related to the *San Kuei*—the 'Three Refuges' (the Buddha, the Law, and the Church)—common to both Vehicles. The second and third (the destruction of evil and the cultivation of virtue) have reference to the Buddha and the Law, and to self-development (*tzŭ li*); the first (the helping of others and bringing them to salvation) has reference to the Church or community, which, in the Mahāyāna, includes all beings in the universe (*li t'a*).[1] The full accomplishment of the three first vows will lead automatically to the accomplishment of the fourth—the attainment of universal Buddhahood.

There are several other classifications of *bodhisattva*-vows, but we need not give a detailed analysis. It will be sufficient to refer to the ten vows set forth in the *sūtra* known as the *Ta-Pei-Hsin T'o-lo-ni Ching* (the Dharani '*Sūtra* of the all-Pitiful Heart').[2] In this *sūtra* Kwan-yin (Avalokiteśvara) is represented as being the inventor or teacher of these vows; hence the recital of each is followed by an invocation of the name of this *bodhisattva*. The vows are (1) to become acquainted with the true faith; (2) to attain spiritual vision; (3) to lead others to salvation; (4) to be charitable; (5) to embark on the ship of *prajña*, 'wisdom'; (6) to cross the ocean of bitterness (life and death); (7) to be steadfast; (8) to attain *nirvāṇa*; (9) to join the company of the saints; (10) to become one with the Dharmakaya (the mystical body of the eternal and universal Buddha).

The vows taken by Buddhist monks on their reception into the order, or on subsequent occasions, may be conveniently studied in the *Brahmajāla-sūtra*, called in Chinese the *Fan-wang-ching.*[3] The 35th and 36th sections of this popular *sūtra* deal with the vows which should be taken and constantly retaken by 'every son of Buddha' (*ko Fo tzŭ*). They bind him to regard his parents and religious teachers with respect and devotion, to associate only with virtuous companions, to study the scriptures and perform good works, and to obey the commandments of Buddha in all things. He must be ready to sacrifice life itself rather than allow himself to act or think in such a way as to hinder the realization of these ideals.[4] Similar vows should be taken by those who seek to attain mystical illumination by practising the rules of *dhyāna*.

In the *Tso-Ch'an-I*, written by the monk Tsê-Ch'an for the guidance of such aspirants, it is stated that the novice should begin by cultivating an attitude of love towards all beings, and should then make a 'great vow' (*fa hung shih-yüan*) to devote himself earnestly to the spiritual welfare of others and not to seek salvation or enlightenment for himself alone (*pu wei chi shên tu ch'iu chieh-t'o*).[5]

It will be seen from the foregoing that the Buddhist vow is practically a self-dedication to an ideal of conduct of which the central feature (in the Mahāyāna) is the service of others. But, apart from what may be described as the 'official'

[1] The terms *tzŭ-li* and *li-t'a* constitute a concise statement, from the Mahāyānist standpoint, of the essential difference between the Small and the Great Vehicles. *Tzŭ-li* (to benefit oneself) is regarded as the ideal of the Small Vehicle, and *li-t'a* (the helping of others) is regarded as the characteristic ideal of the Great Vehicle. The combination of the two (*erh li yüan man*) is aimed at by Mahāyānists.

[2] B. Nanjio, *A Catalogue of the Chinese Translation of the Buddhist Tripiṭaka*, Oxford, 1883, no. 320.

[3] *Ib.* no. 1087.

[4] For Chinese text and French tr. see De Groot, p. 66 f.; cf. pp. 160–168. See also L. Wieger, *Hist. des Croyances religieuses et des opinions philosophiques en Chine*, Ho-kien-fu, 1917, p. 483 ff.

[5] As far as the present writer is aware, there is no European translation of this work.

vows, there are others which have sole reference to the spiritual needs or personal aspirations of the individual who utters them.

One of the most remarkable and comprehensive is the vow which is said to have been taken by a monk of the Sung dynasty named Jui Chien, who dwelt as a hermit on the sacred mountain of Wu-t'ai. It was to the following effect: (1) that he would never allow his eyes to look upon forbidden sights; (2) that he would never allow his ears to listen to forbidden sounds; (3) that he would never allow his mouth to utter forbidden words; (4) that he would never allow his mind to be occupied by forbidden thoughts.

Of the numerous vows made for particular objects or in view of particular circumstances it is unnecessary to give a detailed account. Sometimes a Buddhist will make a vow to recite a certain number of *sūtras* or portions of *sūtras*, in which case beads are often used to count off each completed recital.[1] Sometimes he will register a vow to go on a pilgrimage, or to supply oil for keeping a lamp burning in some shrine for a term of years, or to burn a certain number of sticks of incense before the image of a *bodhisattva*.[2] Some, again, will undertake to print and circulate copies of a favourite *sūtra*.

One such person, *e.g.*, vowed that he would cause 1000 copies of the Diamond *Sūtra* to be printed and given away if his mother were cured of sickness. The emperor Yung-chêng (1723–35) vowed that he would feed a stated number of monks in return for seasonable weather.

Sometimes the vow is accompanied by some act of austerity or even self-mutilation, though the latter is contrary to Buddhist law.

A monk of the 12th cent. named Tsun-Shih, who belonged to the famous monastery of Kuo-ch'ing at the foot of the T'ien-t'ai mountain in Cheh-kiang, made a vow to devote himself to the propagation of the teachings of the T'ien-t'ai school, and in proof of his sincerity burned off one of his own fingers before an image of the *bodhisattva* P'u-hsien. A similar act, showing regrettable fanaticism but great fortitude and powers of endurance, was performed by a monk who died less than ten years ago. Having made a vow of self-dedication to religion, he burned off two of his fingers. Throughout the rest of his life he was known as Pa-chih-t'ou-t'o, 'the eight-fingered ascetic.' He rose to be abbot of one of the most prosperous monasteries now existing in China (the T'ien-t'ung Ssŭ, near Ningpo) and to be head of the newly-founded Association of Chinese Buddhists.

Various opprobrious epithets are bestowed on members of the monkhood who have broken their vows (especially the vows of chastity and vegetarianism) or have been expelled from their monasteries for misbehaviour. Among these are such terms as 'slanderer of the Three Holy Ones,' 'shameless one,' 'obstruction on the holy pathway,' 'bald-headed huntsman,' 'cassock-wearing robber.'

All the Buddhist or quasi-Buddhist sects which have played so prominent a part in the political as well as the religious life of China in the past have their characteristic rituals and vow-formulas.[3] But in many cases these societies have very little to do with religion and merely make use of religious formulas in order to inspire their members with a due sense of the binding nature of their vows. This is so in the case of the Tsai-Li Society, one of the most flourishing organizations of the kind in N. China. It professes to be associated with the cult of the *bodhisattva* Kwan-yin, but its activities are of a social and ethical rather than a religious nature, and in any case its slight religious basis is almost as much Taoist as Buddhist. It is said to have sprung from the dreaded White Lotus Society, and, though it has apparently long ceased to meddle in politics, it was dreaded by the authorities up to the time of the Boxer movement, if not later.[4] It flourishes in the leased territory of Wei-hai-wei, but has never given any trouble to the British authorities there. Its members take vows to abstain from strong drink, opium, and tobacco. When a member is known to have broken his vows, he is expelled from the society and is said to be *pu tsai*, a phrase meaning 'not present'—a common Chinese euphemism for 'dead.' The phrase implies that the disgraced member is 'dead' to the society. There is a play on the word *tsai*, which also forms part of the society's name.

[1] See De Groot, *Sectarianism and Religious Persecution in China*, Amsterdam, 1903, i. 225 f.

[2] For a short account of some of these vows see H. Doré, *Recherches sur les superstitions en Chine*, pt. i. vol. ii. no. 4, p. 342 f.

[3] Much useful information is contained in De Groot's *Sectarianism and Religious Persecution in China*, already cited; but allowance must be made for the author's strong prejudices, and especially for his antipathy to Confucianism.

[4] See Stanton, p. 6.

(*b*) *Taoism*.—(1) The vows of Taoists are similar to those of Buddhists. In this, as in many other respects, modern debased Taoism has merely adapted the usages of Buddhism. The *bodhisattvas* who are supposed to hear and register the vows made by pious Buddhists are of course replaced by Taoist divinities. The three goddesses (*Niang-niang*) whose worship flourishes on the sacred mountain of T'ai-shan in Shantung, on Miao-fêng-shan near Peking, and many other places, are among the divinities most often resorted to for the purpose. Several of the mountains consecrated to Taoist worship (such as T'ai-shan and Hua-shan) have been the scenes of pitiful tragedies enacted by those who have vowed to sacrifice their lives in return for favourable responses to prayers made on behalf of parents or others. These and other mountains possess 'suicide cliffs' (*shê-shên yai*), over which religious fanatics have hurled themselves to death in fulfilment of rashly-made vows; and, though this practice has always been discountenanced and even forbidden by the officials, it is not even yet quite extinct.[1] From such acts of fanaticism it may be gathered that a Chinese rarely fails to keep a vow that he has once made, provided that it is physically possible for him to fulfil it. The Chinese are, and always have been, too fond of making vows. They certainly do not act in accordance with the good advice of Ecclesiastes, 'Be not rash with thy mouth'; but it must be admitted that they would readily endorse the other principle laid down by the same Hebrew writer—'When thou vowest a vow unto God, defer not to pay it. . . . Better is it that thou shouldest not vow, than that thou shouldest vow and not pay.'[2]

LITERATURE.—This has been indicated in the footnotes.

R. F. JOHNSTON.

VOWS (Christian).—I. **New Testament.**—(*a*) *The word*.—The discussion starts naturally with a consideration of the data afforded by the earliest Christian books, the writings of NT, but these are scanty and to some extent irrelevant. The word 'vow' (εὐχή) occurs twice (Ac 18[18] 21[23]), but in both cases the atmosphere is Jewish rather than Christian. In the first instance Paul (or Aquila) has his hair cut at Cenchreæ, 'for he had a vow.' Whether the making or the redemption of the vow is meant is not clear; if the latter, it was probably in connexion with some escape from danger. The second passage is similarly connected with the hair-offering. To avert the reproach of anti-Judaism, Paul, at the request of the Jerusalem elders, associates himself with four men about to be 'purified' on the termination of a vow, and bears the expense of their hair-cutting and probably of their sacrifices—a custom not uncommon among rich Jews on behalf of their poorer brethren. On the Nazirite vow (Nu 6), of which these incidents, and the account given by Hegesippus[3] of James the Just, are illustrative, and the significance of the hair as the seat of the devotee's life, see artt. NAZIRITES, VOWS (Hebrew), and W. R. Smith, *The Religion of the Semites*², London, 1894, p. 483.

Two other NT passages may be glanced at. One is the vow made by forty Jews to fast until they had killed Paul (Ac 23[13f.]), but this is at least as much an oath as a vow. The other is the 'Korban' passage (Mk 7[9-13] = Mt 15[3-6]) in the teaching of Jesus, a reference to cases in which the keeping of a vow conflicted with duty to parents. The case of Ananias (Ac 5) has no pertinence, though Roman theologians find a precedent for vows in the community of goods supposed to have existed in the early Jerusalem Church.

[1] See art. SUICIDE (Chinese).

[2] Ec 5[2. 4. 5].

[3] Eus. *HE* ii. 23.

(*b*) *The thing.*—When, however, we consider the basal ideas of vows as solemn promises and engagements offered to a personal God, the NT has something vital to say. The service and gift here are nothing less than the whole personality and its powers (*e.g.*, Ro 6^{11-13} 12^1, Gal 2^{20}, 2 Co 5^{16}), dating from the hour of baptism and the entry on a consciously Christian life. The undertakings therein involved may be called a vow, though nothing is promised which is not obligatory. It is the natural response of the soul to the appeal of redemption, the expressed impulse of the new life. This impulse is partly a desire to show gratitude and devotion, partly a desire for increasing perfection by growing intimacy with the Saviour, and further involves a claim to continued and new blessings. Thus the vow has its approach to a covenant.

In the narrower sense a vow is the promise of something not generally regarded as already obligatory, not strictly owed to God. The starting-point here is to be found in passages of NT where, though the word is not used, the idea (of asceticism) is present — *e.g.*, in the references to fasting, poverty, and virginity. The most probable interpretation of the curious counsels given by Paul in 1 Co 7 is that he is dealing with cases of spiritual marriage in which man and woman united in taking a vow of continence. Parallel to this is the reference in Ignatius:

'If any one is able to abide in chastity to the honour of the flesh of the Lord, let him so abide without boasting. If he boast, he is lost, and if it be known beyond the bishop, he is polluted.'[1]

What one notices in this reference to a vow of celibacy or of continence is its privacy as opposed to the publicity which was of the essence of the Jewish vow. The Christian is not to parade his vow, but to realize that his chief danger is pride and vainglory.

2. The early Church and vows of virginity.—On early Christian asceticism, especially as regards celibacy, see artt. ASCETICISM (Christian) and CELIBACY (Christian). There are abundant evidences within NT that by the end of the 1st cent. virginity was often looked upon as superior to marriage and indicative of a higher spiritual life, and this opinion gained ground extensively and rapidly in the sub-apostolic and ancient Catholic ages, especially as regards the clergy. The latter half of the 3rd cent. was a period of increasing stringency, for, while Cyprian[2] had advised that young women who felt they could not maintain their virginal vows should marry, the 19th canon of Ancyra (A.D. 314) says that such vows are perpetually binding and that to break them is as bad as committing bigamy. By the 4th cent. the unmarried state had come to occupy the place that martyrdom had held during the persecutions, and is a favourite theme with such Fathers as Athanasius and the Cappadocians. Chrysostom rhapsodizes over the lustrous sanctity of virginity, though he has to bewail the reverse side of the picture, 'the broken vow, the frequent fall.' Fulgentius († 533) in his *de Fide* lays it down that vows of chastity are perpetually binding on both men and women. Those who vowed themselves to virginity had their names formally recorded, and the vow was made an impressive ceremony.[3] The 15th canon of the 2nd Council of Toledo (A.D. 567) is evidence that the secular arm was invoked to aid the ecclesiastical, by imposing divorce on a monk who had married; but in general the episcopal court was able to deal with such matters itself, and the bishop could modify the penalty according to circumstances.[4] For a statement of what was expected from virgins we may refer to Jerome's treatise on the subject and his letters to Eustochium (xxii.) and Demetrias (cxxx.). The thirty years' interval between these epistles may account for the milder and less fanatical tone of the second.

1 *Ad Polyc.* 5.
2 *Ep.* 4 (Oxford ed.), 61 (*PL*).
3 Chrys. *de Sacerd.* iii. 16 f.
4 Canons of Chalcedon, 16.

The subsequent history of vows of celibacy belongs mainly to the story of monasticism (*q.v.*). Poverty, chastity, and obedience are the triple cord of the monastic life. They had been required from its early days, and the great Benedict of Nursia, while making obedience still more absolute, added what was known as the 'vow of steadfastness.'

'Henceforth the door of the monastery opened only inwards. Formerly, if the monk forsook his cell and married he was liable to penance, but his marriage was not annulled. Now such marriages were declared, *ipso facto*, void, and the offender was compelled to return. The vow, written out, was laid upon the altar, those who could not write signing it with their mark.'[1]

The Trappist (Reformed Cistercian) 'vow' of silence seems rather an injunction and comes under the vow of obedience.

3. Patristic evidence. — A few examples of general references to vows in the Fathers may be given. Eusebius[2] says that it was customary for vows to be taken at the tombs of martyrs, and Hilary[3] says that they are effective and helped by the Holy Spirit only when taken in a church with due ceremonial. In his day the usual personal vows were those of abstinence, chastity, and fasting.

The opinion of Augustine is interesting:

'If in Scripture a vow is usually termed εὐχή, being called a prayer, we must understand particularly that kind of prayer which we offer when making a vow, *i.e.* πρὸς εὐχήν. But everything we offer to God is vowed, and above all the offering of the holy altar, in which is implied the greatest of all our vows that by which we vow to be in Christ, as members of His body.'[4]

Commenting on Ps 76, he encourages the taking of vows as an inspiration to otherwise unaided strength. Among the customary vows in his time were those between man and wife either to be faithful to each other or to abstain from intercourse with each other, and those on the part of the rich either to show hospitality to all 'religious' persons or to give their goods to the poor and embrace the 'religious' life.

Ambrose contributes something. In *de Off. Minist.* III. xii. he lays down the general proposition that we must make no promise that is wrong, and, if we have made an unjust oath, we may not keep it. He illustrates his contention from the familiar cases of Herod and Jephthah. In his funeral oration over his brother Satyrus he says:

'We now recognize that thy departure hence was obtained by thy vows to the holy martyr Lawrence.'[5]

There are other references to vows to martyrs,[6] but they seem to be of the nature of prayers for martyral intercession. In the Satyrus oration, § 35, he says:

'Not that I was ignorant of his condition, but a certain kind of prayers and vows had so clouded the sense of common frailty, that I knew not how to think anything concerning him except entire prosperity.'

Ambrose is also responsible for the clear distinction between *præcepta* and *consilia*, on which see below.

4. The mediæval doctrine; consilia evangelica.—In the theology of the mediæval and modern Roman Church the subject of vows occupies a large place. It is bound up with the concept of works of supererogation.[7] The doctrine of good works

1 E. Backhouse and C. Tylor, *Witnesses for Christ*³, London, 1899, p. 185.
2 *Præp. Evang.* xiii. 7.
3 *In Ps.* lv. 1.
4 *Ep.* cxlix. 'ad Paulinum,' § 16.
5 § 17.
6 *Exhort. Virg.* iii. 15, *de Viduis*, ix. 55.
7 See art. MERIT.

rests in the first place on the Augustinian doctrine of grace together with the idea of the universal working of God. Strictly speaking, a meritorious work is inconceivable, but, on the other hand, free man is bound to acquire merit before God and through it to make satisfaction for his sin — a notion compounded of Jewish legalism and Stoic moralism and found as early as Tertullian. The Stoics also supplied a distinction between *medium* and *perfectum*, and the Jews emphasized special and unusual virtues—*e.g.*, To 12^{8}. Certain NT passages (Mt 19^{16-22}, 1 Co 7^{25-40}) were regarded as similarly indicating a graded valuation of works. In time the doctrine of *consilia evangelica* ('evangelical counsels') was developed. The term is used in contrast with *præcepta* ('commands'), and the distinction, though traceable in Hermas,[1] Tertullian,[2] and Cyprian,[3] is first expressly formulated by Ambrose.[4] We find it in Augustine, though two tendencies are visible. For, while the external and literal observance of the counsels (*e.g.*, poverty, virginity) is commended as a higher standard of morality procuring greater merit, he sees the danger of measuring the ultra-moral by this standard, since all conduct is judged in the light of inward moral intention.

For many centuries, in the heyday of monasticism, the first consideration outweighed the second, but in Thomas Aquinas[5] the other tendency again appears. Commandments are given 'about those things which are necessary to attain the end of eternal felicity,' but the counsels 'about those things by which one may obtain this end better and sooner.' In general the counsels deal with poverty, chastity, and obedience, but there was an enumeration of twelve culled from the Sermon on the Mount, including, *e.g.*, the injunctions 'Love your enemies' and 'Resist not evil.' Aquinas[6] puts it that perfection consists *essentialiter* in the command of love, but *instrumentaliter* depends on the counsels. Generally speaking, the disregard or non-observance of the counsels is not sinful, though their observance entails greater perfection and greater reward. They are 'auxiliary norms toward the discernment of those obligatory commands which govern a Christian in his particular circumstances.'

5. Roman Catholic doctrine.—Roman theology classifies vows as personal (applying mainly to oneself) and real (applying to external objects and circumstances); also as perpetual or for a definite time; also as solemn (publicly pronounced before the Church like the monastic vows or the subdiaconate implicit vow of celibacy) or simple. The doctrine of works of supererogation drew vows of all kinds, even simple and private vows, within ecclesiastical jurisdiction. Dispensations can usually be granted by the bishop, but in five cases by the pope alone. Vows that prejudice the rights of a third person and vows made by minors without parental consent are inadmissible.

6. Protestant and evangelical views.—Half a century before Luther, Johann Pupper von Goch in the *de Libertate Christiana* and *Dialogus* maintained that God has given but one law and set before all Christian people one kind of perfection. Luther declared for the all-embracing nature of the baptismal vow and combated Aquinas's idea that the higher degrees of love are not commanded. He condemned all breaches of the law alike and would not allow 'inferior' perfection, though this sin God forgives on condition of faith with daily repentance. Monastic vows he declared not only invalid but sinful and idolatrous, and the *Augsburg Confession* and *Apology* and the *Schmalkald Articles* follow his lead. They also oppose the Roman doctrine of evangelical counsels as setting up works of supererogation, admitting private revenge, and casting doubt on the civil commonwealth.

With regard to special vows (promises made to God from motives of gratitude or devotion or as a means of deepening the spiritual life) he was tolerant, though not putting any stress on them. Calvin, however, while giving pride of place to the baptismal vow and championing Christian freedom against the Roman doctrine, was more convinced of the utility of particular vows by which a Christian might in some signal way express his gratitude, or strengthen his will-power. In this connexion it is worth recording the testimony of the *Westminster Confession of Faith*, ch. xxi. 5, where it is said that religious oaths and vows, solemn fastings, and thanksgivings upon special occasions are an addendum to the 'ordinary religious worship of God.' Ch. xxii. 'Of Lawful Oaths and Vows,' includes the following paragraphs:

'v. A vow is of the like nature with a promissory oath, and ought to be made with the like religious care, and to be performed with the like faithfulness.

vi. It is not to be made to any creature, but to God alone: and that it may be accepted, it is to be made voluntarily, out of faith, and conscience of duty, in way of thankfulness for mercy received, or for the obtaining of what we want; whereby we more strictly bind ourselves to necessary duties, or to other things, so far and so long as they may fitly conduce thereunto.

vii. No man may vow to do any thing forbidden in the word of God, or what would hinder any duty therein commanded, or which is not in his power, and for the performance whereof he hath no promise of ability from God. In which respects, popish monastical vows of perpetual single life, professed poverty, and regular obedience, are so far from being degrees of higher perfection, that they are superstitious and sinful snares, in which no Christian may entangle himself.'

The 'proof texts' adduced are as follows: (v.) Is 19^{21}, Ec 5^{4-6}, Ps 61^{8} $66^{13f.}$; (vi.) Ps 76^{11}, Jer $44^{25f.}$, Dt 23^{21-23}, Ps 50^{14}, Gn 28^{20-22}, 1 S 1^{11}, Ps $66^{13f.}$, Ps 132^{2-5}; (vii.) Ac $23^{12.\ 14}$, Mk 6^{26}, Nu $30^{5.\ 8.\ 12f.}$, Mt $19^{11f.}$, 1 Co $7^{2.\ 9}$, Eph 4^{28}, 1 P 4^{2}, 1 Co 7^{23}.

Modern Biblical criticism had not yet been born. Similarly in the *Larger Catechism* vowing unto God is included among the 'duties required in the Second Commandment,'[1] and sinful vows among the 'sins forbidden in the Third Commandment.'[2]

7. Conclusion.—There are certain ethical duties which the community, whether ecclesiastical, civil, or social, imposes upon the individual and which he accepts (marriage vows at least in part may be reckoned in here), and there are others of a more particular kind which the individual imposes on himself either to develop his spiritual life or to express his gratitude to God for some special mercy. It is quite legitimate to argue that these are implicit in the general vow taken at baptism or on conscious entrance into the Christian circle. It is also evident that all action is conditioned by circumstance, and circumstance may vary so that what seems to-day a clear and positive duty may to-morrow occupy quite a subordinate place. It is possible for a formally expressed vow to become a burden on the conscience, and it then exposes the soul to extra peril. In any case special and formal vows are best left to extraordinary circumstances, and normally it is well simply to lay one's impulses earnestly before God with a prayer for the grace of perseverance and constancy. A closing word may be said about the 'counsels.' Alongside the 'commandments,' whether 'of God' or 'of the Lord,' there are not only the 'commandments' of Paul, which hardly concern us here (1 Co 16^{1} 7^{17}), but also his 'judgments' (1 Co 7^{3-6}, 2 Co $8^{10.\ 8}$), counsels whose acceptance presupposes a divine *charisma* (1 Co 7^{7}). Making all allowance for time and place, the apostle's counsels still have pertinence, and 1 Co 7, like Mt $19^{11f.}$, furnishes a basis for distinguishing between an 'advisory

1 *Mand.* IV. iv. 2, *Sim.* v. iii. 3.
2 *De Exhort. Cast.* iv.
3 *De Habitu Virg.* xxiii.
4 *De Viduis*, xii.
5 *Summa*, II. i. qu. 108, art. 4.
6 *Ib.* II. ii. qu. 184, art. 3.

1 Qu. 108.
2 Qu. 113.

norm' and the absolute force of a command. This, however, is not to admit the whole Roman doctrine of *consilia evangelica*.

LITERATURE.—In addition to the references cited in the art. see J. Bingham, *Origines ecclesiasticæ*, London, 1840, VII. iii. 7 f., iv. 2, XVI. vii. 9; Thomas Aquinas, *Summa*, II. ii. qu. 88, qu. 184, art. 4, *In IV Sent.* d. 36, qu. 1, *Opusc.* 18 (al. 22) c. 24; F. Daab, *Die Zulässigkeit der Gelübde*, Gütersloh, 1896; art. 'Vows' in *CE* and appended bibliography; and sundry works on moral theology—*e.g.*, Simon and Paderborn (Roman Catholic) and Rothe and Hase (Protestant). A. J. GRIEVE.

VOWS (Greek and Roman).—I. Greek.

—We understand by a vow a conditional promise made by the worshipper to the divine power. The condition is the rendering of aid; and the vow, thus strictly regarded, is the proposal of a bargain that the recipient of the favour required shall make suitable recompense. Viewed in relation to prayer (*q.v.*),[1] the vow is intended to add cogency to the request and to help towards its fulfilment. The fulfilment of a contingent vow is often pledged by the security of an oath, as when the nine archons at Athens on entering office swore at the altar in the market-place that they would dedicate a golden statue, if they transgressed the laws during their term.[2] But, of course, a promise may be ratified by an oath which lacks the essential conditions of a vow, as when Odysseus undertook to bring Philoctetes to Troy, offering in the event of failure to yield his life to any one who might choose to take it.[3] Further, to the Greek conception a vow could not be merely negative; a definite offering must be promised as a return for the favour to be granted.[4] If therefore the Nazirite vow taken by St. Paul (Ac 18[18]) involved merely an act of abstinence or consecration promised by way of thanksgiving for escape from danger,[5] it would not be a vow in the full sense of the term as explained above. It frequently happens that, although we have reason to suppose that a vow has been made, evidence is lacking of the conditions imposed. Thus in the version of Iphigenia's sacrifice referred to by Euripides[6] and Cicero[7] we are simply told that Agamemnon vowed to Artemis the fairest thing born in his kingdom within a particular year. Among the very numerous examples of 'votive' offerings recorded in literature and inscriptions there are comparatively few where it can be determined with certainty whether the consecration was made by way of thanksgiving or in fulfilment of a vow.[8] The illustrations which we propose to give have been taken from sources where the evidence is unambiguous. It should be added that several inscriptions which have been preserved and were attached to votive offerings bear as a label the statement that the dedication is in consequence of a vow.[9]

(*a*) *Public vows.*—It may be stated generally that vows were made in times of fear and danger. Women especially, Plato[10] tells us, and men too when they are sick or in trouble, if alarmed by dreams or apparitions, are apt to consecrate the occasion by vowing sacrifices and promising the building of temples. Times of war, especially when the existence of the State was imperilled by hostile attack, often gave occasion for vows to be made in public on behalf of all.

Hector bade his mother Hecuba promise the sacrifice to Athene of twelve heifers, if she would have pity upon the city of Troy and its inhabitants.[11] In historical times the most famous of such public acts of intercession was the vow of the Athenians made before the battle of Marathon offering to sacrifice to Artemis a number of she-goats equal to that of the enemy who might be killed in the impending fight. But so many corpses of the enemy were found that it was impossible to procure the victims; and consequently it was resolved to compromise the liability and to sacrifice 500 every year. The custom was still maintained in the life-time of Xenophon.[1] This famous vow is parodied in Aristophanes,[2] where the sacrifice of 1000 goats is offered to Artemis so soon as the price of anchovies is down. Before Salamis a vow was taken by the Greeks to destroy the Medizing states and to consecrate their goods.[3] The oath said to have been taken before Platæa to found in that town a festival *Eleutheria* to be celebrated perpetually[4] is considered to be apocryphal. Herodotus, discussing the motive which impelled Cyrus to place Crœsus and fourteen Lydian youths on a pyre for sacrifice, recognizes the prevalence of human sacrifice among Oriental nations by suggesting that Cyrus may have so acted in fulfilment of a vow.[5] Heracles, before the capture of Œchalia, vowed the dedication to Zeus of altars and tributes of fruit-lands.[6]

Before entering upon a campaign, it was customary to offer to the gods a share in the spoils as a reward for their assistance.[7] Similar obligations were undertaken in the crises of civil war or when national interests were seriously endangered.

Cypselus offered, if he succeeded in his attempt to become master of Corinth, to dedicate all the property of the citizens to Zeus, and evaded the extremity of the hardship imposed upon them by exacting a tithe of their goods for ten successive years.[8] On the other hand, Moxus the Lydian, after he had freed his countrymen from the tyranny of Meles, ordered them to fulfil his vow by handing over a tithe of their possessions to the gods.[9] In the hope of freeing themselves from the horrible tribute of human lives exacted by Minos the Cretan king, the Athenians are said to have promised Apollo that they would every year dispatch a sacred embassy to Delos.[10]

(*b*) *Private vows.*—We may now pass to vows made by individuals in order to save lives dear to them on occasions of peril.

Peleus vowed that, if Achilles came back safe from Troy, he would dedicate a lock of his son's hair, together with rich sacrifices, to the river-god Spercheios.[11] Similarly Berenice vowed a lock of her hair to the gods on the occasion of her husband, Ptolemy Euergetes, starting on an expedition to ravage the Assyrian borders.[12] So long as the owner is exposed to a special peril, the hair remains uncut, but, when he has safely passed through the crisis or has reached a certain age unharmed,[13] a lock is rendered in thanksgiving to the protecting power. Hector, about to meet Ajax in single combat, promises that in the event of his success he will dedicate the spoils in the temple of Apollo.[14] Telemachus urges his mother Penelope to vow the sacrifice of hecatombs to the gods, if Zeus should grant retribution for the wrongs they have suffered.[15]

The successful completion of a sea-voyage was frequently celebrated by offerings to the gods.[16]

Eurylochus, on behalf of the companions of Odysseus, when they prepared to kill the oxen of the sun-god, offered to build a splendid temple in his honour, if he would grant them a safe return to Ithaca.[17] Diogenes, in peril on the Carpathian sea, vows to dedicate his cloak to the Bœotian Cabirus, if he escapes safe to land.[18] An epigram of Callimachus parodied these vows by describing the dedication to the Samothracian Cabiri of a salt-cellar which by providing its owner with frugal meals had enabled him to escape from the storms of debts.[19]

In the same way the traveller by land who has safely completed his journey dedicates his felt hat to Artemis in the due accomplishment of his vows.[20] We have a copious record of dedications by those who successfully competed in the ordeal of the great Games.[21] Many of these must have been made in consequence of previous vows such as that of Xenophon of Corinth, who, as a competitor for the Olympic crown in 464 B.C., vowed that, if successful, he would consecrate 100 ἱερόδουλοι for the service of the temple of Aphrodite in that city.[22]

Many examples of vows are connected with the ordinary incidents of family life. A mother makes and pays vows for the safety of her child.[23] The

1 εὐχή is used for 'vow' and 'prayer' alike; cf. the combination of *vota* and *preces*, which frequently occurs in Latin (*e.g.*, Stat. *Theb.* xi. 616, where of course *vota* has the wider sense).
2 Arist. *Ath. Pol.* vii. 1, lv. 5.
3 Soph. *Phil.* 618.
4 Headlam on Æsch. *Ag.* 924.
5 Jos. *BJ* II. xv. 1.
6 *Iph. Tauris*, 21.
7 *Off.* iii. 95.
8 Hor. *Od.* i. 5. 15, or *Anth. Pal.* vi. 164, as compared with Verg. *Æn.* xii. 769.
9 W. H. D. Rouse, *Greek Votive Offerings*, Cambridge, 1902, p. 328 f.
10 *Legg.* 909 E.
11 Hom. *Il.* vi. 274 ff.

1 Xen. *Anab.* iii. 2. 12.
2 *Eq.* 660 ff.
3 Herod. vii. 132, with the commentators' notes.
4 Diod. xi. 29.
5 Herod. i. 86.
6 Soph. *Trach.* 238 ff.
7 Dem. *Epist.* i. 16.
8 [Arist.] *Œcon.* 1346*a* 32.
9 Nicol. Damasc. frag. 24 (*FHG* iii. 371).
10 Plat. *Phæd.* 58 B.
11 Hom. *Il.* xxiii. 144 ff.
12 Catull. lxvi. 8 ff.
13 *Anth. Pal.* vi. 198.
14 Hom. *Il.* vii. 82 ff.
15 Hom. *Od.* xvii. 50.
16 Rouse, p. 228.
17 Hom. *Od.* xii. 345.
18 *Anth. Pal.* vi. 245.
19 *Ib.* vi. 301.
20 *Ib.* vi. 199.
21 Rouse, p. 149 ff.
22 Pindar, frag. 122.
23 Xen. *Mem.* ii. 2. 10.

dedication consequent upon the parent's vow is frequently in the form of a portrait-statue of the child,[1] which is offered to Æsculapius or Apollo on condition of the cure of sickness.[2] Or it may be the patient himself who makes the vow, as is indicated in parody by the tricky vow of a devotee of Bacchus to abstain from strong drink for 'a hundred suns' in the event of recovery from fever.[3] The Greek Anthology furnishes several examples of vows made to Ilithyia or Æsculapius if they will grant a safe release from the pains and dangers of child-birth.[4] The appropriate offerings in such cases were articles of dress or jewelry.[5] Sometimes the condition of the vow is the granting of a good harvest;[6] more often it is relief from the stress of poverty.[7] There is even on record the promise of a sacrifice, if the god will make a curse effective upon an enemy.[8]

(*c*) *Penalty for infraction.*—The infraction of a vow was visited with a suitable penalty;[9] and this might be directed against the community of which the transgressor was a member, as we have seen that, according to one form of the story, the Greeks were punished with adverse winds at Aulis for the default of their leader Agamemnon. It rarely happened that the favour of the gods was so confidently anticipated that offerings were made to them in advance; Polynices, who dedicated statues to Aphrodite and Ares before starting from Argos on his expedition against Thebes,[10] was not an encouraging example. But no doubt confidence was more frequent in the daily requirements of domestic need.[11]

2. Roman. — Whereas with the Greeks vows tended more and more to become a matter of individual concern, as being employed chiefly in the critical moments of domestic life, and the records of vows offered publicly on behalf of the whole community are comparatively scanty, at Rome the conditions were entirely different. It is true that we have sufficient evidence that here also individuals menaced with danger applied for the assistance of the gods with promises of offerings or sacrifice. The illustrations to be found in Vergil should not be set down to the influence of his Greek models.

Æneas, shipwrecked on a foreign coast, promises sacrificial victims as a reward to the disguised Venus, whom he recognizes as a goddess.[12] Ascanius calls upon Jupiter to direct his arrow, vowing gifts and the sacrifice of a bullock in the event of success.[13] Cloanthus promises a sacrifice to the sea-gods on condition of victory in the boat-race.[14]

Copious evidence will be found in inscriptions of the frequent occurrence of vows in the private life of the Romans. As an example we may mention the inscription from Sora[15] in which the two brothers Vertulei dedicate a tithe to Hercules in payment of their father's vows. From the time of Augustus onwards the formula *VSLM* ('votum solvit lubens merito') is regularly employed.[16] A collection of these private votive inscriptions has been made by A. de Marchi, *Il culto privato dei Romani*, i. 271 ff.

Nevertheless, the characteristic formalism of the Roman religion is chiefly apparent in the administration of the public vows. A regular contract is drawn up between the State and the deity concerned, and its conditions are publicly announced (*nuncupatio*); the form of words necessary in accordance with sacred law is prescribed by the priest (*concipere vota*); a solemn engagement (*suscipere vota*) is entered into by the official who

1 *Anth. Pal.* vi. 357. 2 Rouse, pp. 210, 329.
3 *Anth. Pal.* vi. 291. 4 *Ib.* vi. 146, 147, 148, 270.
5 Rouse, p. 252; *Anth. Pal.* vi. 270, 274.
6 *Anth. Pal.* vi. 41. 7 *Ib.* vi. 190, 231, 300.
8 Rouse, p. 339, note 9. 9 Hom. *Il.* i. 65.
10 Paus. ii. 25. 1. 11 *Anth. Pal.* vi. 209.
12 *Æn.* i. 334. 13 *Ib.* ix. 626.
14 *Ib.* v. 234. 15 *CIL* i. 1175.
16 *E.g.*, *ib.* i. 1462.

represents the State; in his public capacity he becomes liable to carry out the vow (*votum solvere, reddere*); and, if he fails, the breach in the sacred compact must be duly punished. The State representative is thus, during the period between the undertaking of the vow and its fulfilment, in the position of an accused person awaiting his trial (*voti reus*);[1] and, so soon as the condition was fulfilled, he was cast in the terms of his bond (*voti damnatus*).[2] Sometimes an estimate was made of the cost involved, and the sum required was entered in the public records. The cost of the celebration of *ludi magni* on a solemn occasion during the Second Punic War was assessed at the figure of 333333⅓ sesterces—a number evidently chosen for its magical potency.[3]

One of the usual occasions for the making of vows was at the opening of a war.

Thus Acilius Glabrio, at the commencement of the war against Antiochus, vowed a celebration of *ludi magni* for ten days with gifts laid on all the *pulvinaria*, if the war should be satisfactorily brought to an end.[4] Augustus, at the beginning of the campaign which was closed by the battle of Philippi, vowed a temple to Mars Ultor, which he dedicated forty years later.[5] App. Claudius, in the thick of a battle with the Samnites, exclaimed: 'Bellona, if thou givest victory to-day, I vow thee a temple.'[6] Marius before the battle of Vercellæ was said to have vowed a hecatomb as the price of victory.[7] Marcellus, having vowed a temple to Honos and Virtus, was met, when he proceeded to its execution, with a technical objection by the pontiffs that a single *cella* could not be dedicated to two deities.[8]

An outbreak of pestilence was another occasion on which extraordinary vows were usually made. On the occurrence of such a visitation, among the vows to be fulfilled on the cessation of the plague we find the dedication of a temple to Apollo,[9] the oblation of gifts and sacrifices to Apollo, Æsculapius, and Salus,[10] and the institution of public holidays (*feriæ*) and ceremonial processions (*supplicationes*).[11] These and similar rewards suitable to the particular occasion or to the functions of the god whose favour is to be enlisted meet us continually in the pages of Livy.

Thus the Pythian Apollo was offered a tithe of the booty for assistance rendered in the capture of Veii.[12] The most remarkable example of votive dedications was the consecration of a *ver sacrum*, *i.e.* the sacrifice of all living animals to be born within the limits of a particular spring. There is only one instance on record in historical times, that is to say, at the beginning of the Second Punic War in 217 B.C.[13] The vow was actually performed twenty-one years later.[14]

Sometimes the condition imposed upon the divine agent was the continuance of the commonwealth in its then present condition for a period of five[15] or ten years.[16] The specification of a definite time-limit forms a link between the extraordinary vows and those which were repeated regularly after the lapse of a certain period. Thus, every year on 1st January the consuls, suitably attended, climbed the Capitoline hill, made a solemn sacrifice of white oxen in fulfilment of the vow made the previous year, and entered into a new obligation for the year to come in order to secure the safety of the State.[17] From the year 30 B.C. onwards a special vow was made for the safety of the *princeps* and his house;[18] and at a later date the rite was fixed to be performed annually on 3rd January.[19] Similarly, when sacrifice was made at the opening of a new *lustrum*, a vow was made of a new offering to become due after the expiration of the quinquennial period.[20] In imperial times a custom grew up of making vows for periods of five, ten, fifteen, or twenty years.[21] This may have been

1 Verg. *Æn.* v. 237.
2 Verg. *Ecl.* v. 80; Liv. xxvii. 45.
3 Liv. xxii. 10. 4 *Ib.* xxxvi. 2. 5 Ov. *Fast.* v. 550 ff.
6 Liv. x. 19. 7 Plut. *Mar.* 26. 8 Liv. xxvii. 25.
9 *Ib.* iv. 25. 10 *Ib.* xl. 37. 11 *Ib.* xli. 21.
12 *Ib.* v. 21. 13 *Ib.* xxii. 10. 14 *Ib.* xxxiii. 44.
15 *Ib.* xxx. 27. 16 *Ib.* xlii. 28.
17 Ovid, *Pont.* iv. 4. 27 ff.; Liv. xxi. 63.
18 Dio Cass. li. 19. 19 Plut. *Cic.* 2.
20 Val. Max. iv. 1. 10; Sueton. *Aug.* 97.
21 *E.g.*, *CIL* iii. 8706.

partly due to their substitution for the old *lustra*, and partly to the periods of five and ten years for which Augustus assumed the imperial power, starting from the year 27 B.C.[1] The establishment of the empire not unnaturally gave rise to a multiplication of the vows offered on extraordinary occasions by courtiers anxious to testify their devotion to the reigning Cæsar and his household. Tacitus records vows made for the safe return of Tiberius from a campaign,[2] for the safety of the dying Claudius,[3] and for the safe delivery of Poppæa.[4]

We have seen that the choice of the god whose aid is invoked—*e.g.*, Æsculapius or Bellona—is determined by the occasion of the desired intervention. In the fierce struggle of a decisive battle, as a final effort to leave no possible means of victory untried, it was sometimes determined to appeal to the enemies' gods and to offer them an inducement to transfer their protection. The classical instance is the offer of the dictator A. Postumius at the battle of Lake Regillus to dedicate a temple to Castor, the patron deity of Tusculum.[5] A special application of this practice was the solemn rite of *evocatio*,[6] according to which, before the final assault was delivered against a beleaguered city, its gods were summoned to abandon it and to accept a new resting-place at Rome. In this way Juno was invited to leave her home at Veii and follow the fortunes of the conquerors.[7] An interesting account of the whole matter is given by Macrobius,[8] who remarks that the Romans endeavoured carefully to conceal the name of their protecting god, in order that others might not employ against them the device which they used against Corinth and Carthage as well as against Veii and other Italian towns. He records the *formulæ* which were employed at the siege of Carthage and points out that the *evocatio* of the gods must be carefully distinguished from the simultaneous *devotio* of the hostile garrison and citizens who were handed over to the dominion of the deities of the under world Dispater, Veiovis, Manes, and Tellus. To these powers a sacrifice of three black sheep was offered at the same time. The *devotio* of the enemy appears here as the consequence of the *evocatio*;[9] but the term was specifically employed when during the progress of a battle the Roman commander made a vow to the infernal powers that he was prepared to sacrifice either his own life or that of a Roman citizen serving under him on condition that in return for this surrender the annihilation of the enemy's forces was assured.[10] The peculiarity which distinguished the *devotio* from the offering of vows in general was that the forfeit was rendered in advance to the divine promiser in the assurance that the required service would be forthcoming. Our knowledge of the custom rests almost entirely upon Livy's account of the self-sacrifice of P. Decius Mus in the battle with the Latins in the neighbourhood of Vesuvius in 340 B.C.,[11] and of his son at Sentinum in 295 B.C. during the course of the war against the Etruscans and their allies.[12] Even if these events are not to be regarded as historically true,[13] the particulars of the ritual and formularies adopted are sufficient to prove the antiquity of the

1 Dio Cass. liii. 13. 2 *Ann.* iii. 47. 3 *Ib.* xii. 68.
4 *Ib.* xv. 23. 5 Liv. ii. 20.
6 For possible traces of the following of this custom by the Greeks see the present writer's *Fragments of Sophocles*, London, 1917, ii. 105 (frag. 452).
7 Liv. v. 21. 8 iii. 9.
9 Wissowa regards this as a case of *consecratio* rather than *devotio* (Pauly-Wissowa, iv. 901).
10 Liv. viii. 10. 11. 11 *Ib.* viii. 6–10.
12 *Ib.* x. 28.
13 T. Mommsen, *History of Rome*, Eng. tr., London, 1877, i. 366. The report of the *devotio* of a third Decius at the battle of Ausculum (Cic. *de Fin.* ii. 61) in 279 B.C. is certainly apocryphal (Pauly-Wissowa, iv. 2285).

custom. If the person whose life was pledged fell in battle forthwith, the sacrifice was considered acceptable and the result assured.[1] If the Roman general who made the vow did not meet with his death, he became *impius*, and was excluded from participation in public and private *sacra*;[2] but, if the vow was made for the self-immolation of a legionary soldier, and the sacrifice of his life was omitted or rejected, he could obtain expiation by the burying in the ground of a *signum* at least seven feet high and the offering of a piacular sacrifice, and the place where expiation was made became *locus religiosus*.[3] The development of *devotio* in later times as an act of self-sacrifice for the emperor[4] does not concern the present subject.

LITERATURE.—Besides works referred to above see I. Marquardt, *Römische Staatsverwaltung*², Leipzig, 1885, iii. 264 ff.; A. Pernice, *SBAW*, 1885, p. 1146 ff.; W. Warde Fowler, *The Religious Experience of the Roman People*, London, 1911, p. 204 ff.; G. Wissowa, *Religion und Kultus der Römer*, Munich, 1902, ²1912, p. 319 ff., and in Pauly-Wissowa, *s.v.* 'Devotio'; G. E. Marindin, in Smith's *Dict. Ant.*, London, 1890, ii. 981ᵇ.

A. C. PEARSON.

VOWS (Hebrew).—By a vow a person brings himself under a sacred obligation to God (or to some particular god) to do something or to refrain from something. The thing he vows to do is something which goes beyond the normal demands of his religion, and the thing he vows to refrain from is something permissible in normal circumstances—*e.g.*, the enjoyment of food, the fruit of the grape, sexual intercourse. The motive of the vow is usually desire to secure divine help, and its form is usually expressed conditionally: if God does something for the man, the man will do something for God, something with which He is believed to be well pleased.

In the OT a vow is unconditionally valid only when it is made by a person whose will is not subject to the challenge of another—*i.e.* by the head of a house (the father or husband), a widow, or a divorced woman (Nu 30). A wife (Nu 30^{6-8}) or an unmarried daughter (30^{3-5}) could of course make a vow; but the husband in the one case, and the father in the other, had the right of veto. If, however, this right of the husband was not immediately exercised, the vow of the wife was held to be valid: it could not properly be cancelled by a subsequent disavowal on the man's part; if he did so cancel it, the guilt of non-fulfilment attached to him, not to the woman. The 'strange' woman of Pr 7, who is married, is represented as making vows and inviting a paramour to the sacrificial feast (7^{14}) which is a frequent accompaniment of the vow (cf. 1 S 1^{21}, Ps 66^{13-15}). There are no extant regulations in the OT governing the vows of an unmarried son.

Vows must have been practised from immemorial antiquity; they are as old as the feeling for God and the experience of distress. They are attested for every period from the patriarchal to NT times (Ac $21^{23ff.}$ $23^{12.21}$), and they seem to have played a more prominent part in religious practice as time wore on. Early historians record vows, but there is no early legislation on the subject. This first appears in a simple form in Deut. (7th cent. B.C.); but in the later (post-Exilic) literature vows are the subject of minute legislation—a fact which indicates extensive indulgence in the practice. This is confirmed by numerous references in later books—Prophets and Psalms (Is 19^{21}, Jon 1^{16} 2^{9}, Job 22^{27}, Ps 22^{25} 50^{14} 56^{12} 65^{1} 76^{11}).

Illustrations of vows from the period of the judges and the early monarchy are as follows: (i.) Jephthah vows that, if Jahweh give him victory over the Ammonites, he will sacrifice to Him the first human being (this is the implication) that comes out of his house to meet him (Jg $11^{30f.}$); (ii.) Hannah

1 Liv. x. 28. 13. 2 *Ib.* viii. 10. 13. 3 *Ib.* viii. 10. 12.
4 τὸν τῶν Ἰβήρων τρόπον (Dio Cass. liii. 20).

vows that, if Jahweh give her a son, she will dedicate him to the life-long service of Jahweh, and no razor shall come upon his head (1 S 1^{11}); (iii.) Absalom, while in exile in Aram, vowed that, if Jahweh brought him back in safety to Jerusalem, he would serve Him (*i.e.* worship Him—with sacrifice) at Hebron (2 S 15^{8}). To these may be added—though not in the same sense historical—Jacob's vow to make the pillar at Bethel a sanctuary and to pay God tithes, if He furnished him with food and clothing and brought him safely back to the land he was leaving (Gn 28^{20-22}). As an illustration of vows of abstinence may be taken the curse which Saul invoked, in the course of a battle with the Philistines, upon any one (and, by implication, upon himself) who would eat any food before the evening (1 S $14^{24ff.}$), and the vow attributed to David—whether historical or not—that he would not enter his house, ascend his bed, or give sleep to his eyes, till he had found a place for Jahweh (Ps 132^{2-5}). The nazirites, according to the later law, abstained, while the vow was upon them, from wine, from contact with the dead, and from cutting the hair (Nu 6^{1-8}); the Rechabites not only abstained from wine, but refused to practise agriculture or to live in houses (Jer $35^{6f.}$). The abstinence, however, which accompanies such vows is to be interpreted not as arbitrary privation, but as a tabu 'incident to the state of consecration, the same taboos, in fact, which are imposed, without a vow, on everyone who is engaged in worship or priestly service in the sanctuary, or even everyone who is present in the holy place.'[1] Uriah's refusal to enter his house or deal with his wife (2 S 11^{11}) is explained by his being a warrior on campaign, and war is a sacred activity.

Most of the vows from the early period reveal the prominence with which at that time national interests bulked in the mind of the individual, whose chief duty and privilege was to promote the religious, military, or political welfare of his people, and thus to promote the interests of the national God, which were bound up with those of His people. Jephthah and Saul, *e.g.*, desire victory over the enemy of their nation and the nation's God; David is represented as passionately concerned with the suitable worship of that God. Even in that early period, however, the individual had a life and interests of his own: Jacob and Absalom long for a safe return, and Hannah for a son. As, through the collapse of the State, the individual came into ever-increasing prominence as a religious unit, vows affecting purely individual interests became increasingly common, and even the vicissitudes of ordinary life must have offered many occasions for them. The Psalms preserve some of the songs sung by grateful worshippers at the payment of their vows, *i.e.* when they brought their 'sacrifices of thanksgiving' (*e.g.*, Ps 22^{22-31} 66^{13-20} 116). In particular, the various stanzas of Ps 107, with its repeated appeal to the worshippers to give thanks to Jahweh (vv.$^{1. 8. 15. 21. 31}$), give us a glimpse of the sort of occasions on which anxious hearts made vows and grateful hearts paid them: in each stanza deliverance from some distress is contemplated—from the perils of a journey across the wilderness or on the sea, from sickness, prison, etc. Ps 116^{13} preserves for us the interesting custom (cf. Mt 26^{27}) of raising in the hand the 'cup of salvation' when invoking the divine name in connexion with the payment of vows. The Psalms abound in expressions of overflowing gratitude which are manifestly the sincere utterance of much happy experience of divine deliverance, and profound joy in the privilege of performing the vows (which would frequently take the form of sacrifice) made in the hour of distress.

The readiness to vow, however, had its dangers. Instinct and legislation alike (Lv 22^{17-23}) prescribed that nothing short of the best was good enough for Jahweh—a male without blemish, if the offering was an animal; but vows made in haste were often repented at leisure, and offerings of inferior worth (*e.g.*, a blind, lame, or sick animal) were made—a practice which evokes the fierce indignation of Malachi ($1^{8. 14}$). There is no obligation to make a vow (Dt 23^{22}); but, once made, there is a solemn obligation to keep it in the form in which it was made (Dt $23^{21. 23}$, Nu 30^{2}). It must cost the offerer something, whether in money, effort, or privation; and deliberately to evade or reduce the cost to which one has voluntarily and without compulsion committed oneself is to be guilty of a breach of faith which invites the divine vengeance. But many were willing to run the risk, as we may infer from Pr 20^{25}, Ec 5^{4-6}: the latter passage (v.^{6}) shows that men sought to evade their obligation with the plea that their vow was the result of an inadvertence. The inconsiderate levity with which vows were made and the specious religious pretexts on the basis of which men withdrew from moral obligations (cf. Mk 7^{11}) go to show the danger to which in certain circles religion was exposed of losing its ethical content. The excuse of inadvertence stigmatized in Ec 5^{6} is not contemplated by the Law, which peremptorily demands that a vow must be kept; probably therefore such cases were subsumed—at least in the mind of the worshipper—under the general provision for cases where an oath was subsequently found to involve consequences which the speaker had not contemplated when he made it; relief from a rash oath could be secured after confession and the presentation of a trespass-offering (Lv 5^{4-6}). The OT characteristically considers the vow rather as an external act than in its inner quality and implications: it does not, *e.g.*, discuss cases in which the fulfilment of a vow might be found to collide with some higher (*e.g.*, ethical) obligation. That was the problem by which Jephthah was confronted, but to him it was hardly a problem at all; his belief, on the one hand, in the sacredness and irrevocableness of the vow and, on the other, in the rightness—at least on unique occasions—of human sacrifice contributed to make his decision inevitable, with however sore a heart he reached it.

The thing vowed was very frequently an animal, but it might also be money, a house, land, or a person. When an animal was offered, the sacrifice was accompanied by an oblation, as in the case of the other sacrifices (Nu $15^{3ff.}$). Money given to sacred prostitutes could not be accepted at the sanctuary in payment of a vow (Dt 23^{18})—it was 'tainted' money. As the thing vowed must be something extra to normal demands, nothing could be vowed—such as firstlings—on which Jahweh already had a claim (Lv 27^{26}). If an animal technically unclean and therefore unfit for sacrifice had been vowed, it was sold at a price put upon it by the priest, and the money was given to the sanctuary. If the man who vowed the animal wished to retain it, he could do so by paying the estimated price with an addition of 20 per cent (Lv 27^{11-13}). The same procedure was followed in the case of a house that had been vowed ($27^{14f.}$), and, with certain modifications, in the case of land (27^{16-25}). The value of the land was determined by the distance of the next year of jubilee: for the complete period the basis of valuation was 50 shekels for an acreage seeded with a *homer* of barley, the value being reduced (apparently at the rate of a shekel a year) as the year of jubilee approached. If the land belonged by inheritance to the man who vowed it, he could secure the reversion of it in that year to himself by paying 20 per cent in addition to the price as ascertained on the above basis; if he failed to do this, it went to the priests. If, however, the land had not been originally his own but purchased, it reverted in the year of jubilee to the original owner.

In the older period human beings could be dedicated to the god by a vow in one of several ways—by actual sacrifice (Jg $11^{30ff.}$), by service at a sanctuary (1 S 1^{11}), or by the nazirite life (Jg 13^{5}). Since, however, in the post-Exilic period human sacrifice had passed away and the service of the sanctuary was exclusively in the hands of the Levites (Nu $3^{5ff.}$), only the nazirite vow—and

[1] W. R. Smith, *Rel. Sem.* p. 482.

that in a modified form (temporary, not now life-long)—remained (6[2ff.]). But, though the custom of vowing human beings was no longer possible, the shadow of it remained in the practice of substituting for the person a sum of money determined by the age and sex of the person, 50 shekels being payable for a man and 30 for a woman between the ages of twenty and sixty, when the powers were presumably at their highest, and smaller sums for those under twenty and over sixty (Lv 27[1-7]). These estimates doubtless often represented a substantial demand on the financial resources of the worshipper; the priests would have many motives of both a higher and a lower kind for insisting that he must not escape with an offering which had cost him little or nothing (cf. the noble words of David in 2 S 24[24]). They stood to gain heavily by the practice of vows, as what was vowed to God was as good as made over to them (Lv 27[21]). But the OT shows here its customary regard for the poor by providing that in their case these demands should be relaxed: they are only to pay according to their ability, as estimated by the priest (Lv 27[8]).

Persons devoted by the ban could not be redeemed; they must be put to death (Lv 27[29]). This law had doubtless chiefly in view the destruction of Canaanite idolaters: it could have been enforced, or applicable, only in early times (Jos 6[21]: cf. 1 S 15[3]); for the later age it would suggest little more than the obligation of uncompromising hostility to idolatry.

An examination of the vows recorded and of the laws regulating vows throws some light on the character both of the worshipper and of his God. The vow was born in a sense of need or an experience of distress (Ps 66[14]). The things that men desired were deliverance, prosperity, health, children, victory; and the God to whom the vows were offered was believed to be pleased with sacrifice (even—in the early period—with human sacrifice). The circle of ideas with which vows were associated is priestly rather than prophetic, and there is an externalism and a quasi-commercial conception of the relation between God and man which is alien to the higher prophetic spirit. But, though vows in the later period were sometimes lightly made and dexterously evaded, the manifest emotion with which many a singer in the Psalter records his gratitude to God as he pays his vows shows that they must often have represented a warm and genuine religious experience. They are an implicit confession of the speaker's recognized insufficiency, and their fulfilment is the expression of his gratitude for the experienced help of Jahweh (cf. Jer 33[11]). It is no accident, however, that vows play practically no rôle at all in the NT, where the demand is for a consecration not occasional but continuous, and for a consecration not of gifts but of the entire personality.

LITERATURE.—Artt. on 'Vows' in *HDB*, *EBi*, and *PRE*[3]; W. R. Smith, *Religion of the Semites*[2], London, 1894, p. 381 ff.; B. Stade, *Bibl. Theologie des AT*[2] (ed. A. Bertholet), Tübingen, 1911, pp. 60 f., 69 ff.

JOHN E. MCFADYEN.

VOWS (Hindu).—Vows are a highly important element in the Hindu religion. Thus, according to a Sanskrit lawbook, a Brāhman ascetic must keep the five vows (*vrata*) of abstention from injuring living beings, of truthfulness, of abstention from theft, of continence, and of liberality, besides five minor vows, such as abstention from anger, purity, etc. (Baudhāyana, ii. 18. 1, 3). Brāhmanical students were subject to restrictive rules of the same kind during their residence with a teacher, and they had to undertake, moreover, special vows when learning particular portions of the Veda, such as the *Sāvitrīvrata*, in connexion with the study of the sacred prayer called *Sāvitrī*. The five great *vratas* of the Jainas, 'I renounce all killing of living beings, lying, stealing, sexual pleasures, all attachments whether great or small,' are evidently formed upon the Brāhmanical model. Nor are the five commandments (*pañcaśīla*) of the Buddhist canonical books essentially different from the five Brāhman vows, especially as they are supplemented like the latter by five other vows which are binding on the Buddhist monk only. On his entrance into the Order, the would-be Buddhist had to raise his joined hands and to declare: 'I take refuge in the Buddha, in the Law, in the Congregation.' Many different Brāhmanical *vratas*, in the sense of self-imposed devout or ceremonial observances of any sort, are described in the Purāṇas, and have passed from them into the mediæval and modern Sanskrit Digests of Religious Usages, such as Hemādri's *Caturvargacintāmaṇi* (written *c.* 1300 A.D., printed in the *Bibliotheca Indica*), which devotes more than 2300 pages to the subject of *vratas*, most of them to be performed and repeated on certain stated days of the year. Thus the *puṣpadvitīyāvratam* (i. 382), to be performed on the second (*dvitīyā*) of the bright half of every month for a whole year, beginning with the month of Kārttika, consists of eating nothing but flowers or blossoms (*puṣpa*) during all those days, and presenting the Brāhmans at the close of the *vrata* with flowers made of gold and with a cow. As a recompense for performing this *vrata* a man obtains heavenly enjoyments and a metallic car. For seven consecutive re-births he will be imbued with a knowledge of the Vedas and of the Vedāṅgas, and will live in happiness for a long time, surrounded by his sons and grandsons. In the case of the 'bull-vow' (*vṛṣabhavratam*), which is undertaken on the eighth of the bright half, one bestows a bull clad in a white robe and decked with ornaments, the spiritual reward consisting in a long residence in the heaven of Śiva, followed by re-birth in the station of a king. One performing the 'river-vow' (*nadīvratam*) should, within certain intervals, worship seven different sacred streams, each for one day, offering milk in water, giving water-pots filled with milk to the Brāhmans, subsisting on nothing but milk himself, bathing far from the village, and taking food at night only. At the end of the year he should give a *pala* of silver to the Brāhmans. By so doing he will enjoy a long and prosperous life, and will in a future birth be free from disease, eminent, virtuous, and rich, enjoying the position of a king, or of a distinguished Brāhman (ii. 462). By the side of these comparatively simple rites, we find others with a more complicated ceremonial; but the ingredients of fasting, gifts to Brāhmans, offerings to deities, etc., recur in nearly all these endless *vratas*, which give a nice round of religious observances, entailing spiritual blessings and natural comforts for the whole of the Hindu year. The *Vratarāja*, which is considered the leading Sanskrit treatise on *vratas* in W. India at the present day, contains a description of no fewer than 205 *vratas*. The performance of *vratas* is nowadays specially common among women, and this may be an ancient custom, considering that in Kālidāsa's drama Urvaśī, the queen, when desirous of effecting a reconciliation with her husband, sends for the king, inviting him to undertake a certain *vrata* in common with her; and that the Sanskrit lawbooks exhort wives to perform their *vratas* together with their husbands. Speaking of modern *vratas*, R. C. Bose observes: 'When the boy is sent to the *Pātsālā* (school), the girl at the age of five has to begin her course of *vratas*.' The first *vrata* is the river Pūjā, instituted after the example of the goddess Durgā, who performed this ceremonial that she might obtain a good husband, Śiva being considered a model husband. On the last day of the Bengali year, two little earthen images of the goddess Durgā are made by the girl and worshipped by her. The next two *vratas* are those of Hari or Kṛṣṇa, and of the ten images. Then comes the *Sajāti vrata*, in performing which the girl repeats a volley of abuses against her *satīn*, or rival wife in the possible future, in order to avert the dreaded evils of polygamy. Of *vratas* to be practised by a married woman, the *Sāvitrīvrata* is made specially prominent by Bose. This *vrata* derives its name from the ancient legend of the faithful Sāvitrī, who through her devotion revived her deceased husband. It is annually celebrated in the Bengali month of Jyaiṣṭha both by women whose husbands are alive and by widows who are desirous of averting the evils of widowhood in a future birth. In the former case the husband is worshipped by his wife with sandal and flowers, and she cooks a good dinner for him. The prayers are read by the priest, who gets his usual fee and all the offerings. This *vrata* should be performed regularly for fourteen years, at the end of which the expense is tenfold more, in clothes, bedding, brass utensils, and an entertainment to Brāhmans and friends, than in the previous years. The *Sāvitrīvrata* has also been described by Ward, who mentions, besides, the *Adūrasiṁhāsanavrata*, at which 30 different wives of Brāhmans are entertained, one on each day, during the month of Vaiśākha; and the *Pañcamīvrata*, a *vrata* on a large scale extending over a period of six years, and including many partial or total fasts, and various gifts to Brāhmans on the part of the woman who is to perform this *vrata*, and various acts of worship on the part of the officiating Brāhmans, the whole ceremony closing with a grand dinner to Brāhmans and others. Ward calls the *vratas* a very lucrative source of profit to the Brāhmans. He defines them as unconditioned vows to perform religious ceremonies, distinguishing them from conditional vows consisting of a promise to present offerings on condition that the god bestow such or such a benefit. Vows of this kind are, *e.g.*, when a man promises to sacrifice a goat, or to present two loads of sweetmeats, or cloth, ornaments, money, a house, etc., if the god grant his request to have sickness removed, or to become the servant of some European, or for riches, a house, a wife, and son. Bose observes that vows made in times of sickness are fulfilled.

LITERATURE.—*The Laws of Manu*, tr. by G. Bühler, *SBE*, vol. xxv., Oxford, 1886; M. Williams, *Indian Wisdom*[4], London, 1893; H. Kern, *Manual of Indian Buddhism*, Strassburg, 1896; T. W. Rhys Davids, *Buddhism*; Mandlik, *Hindu Law*, Bombay, 1880; W. Ward, *A View of the History, Literature, and Religion of the Hindoos*[3], 2 vols., London, 1817; R. C. Bose, *The Hindoos as they are*, Calcutta, 1881.

J. JOLLY.

VOWS (Jewish).—As the OT amply indicates, vows were a familiar feature in the religious life of Israel in former days (see art. VOWS [Hebrew]).

In the Apocrypha the references to the subject are few.

'Let nothing hinder thee,' says Ben Sira, 'to pay thy vow in due time; and wait not until death to be justified [*i.e.* 'to pay thy debt']. Before thou makest a vow, prepare thyself, and be not as a man that tempteth the Lord.'[1]

Philo[2] has some interesting observations on vows.

The word of the good man, he says, should be his oath, firm and unchangeable, founded steadfastly on truth. Therefore vows and oaths should be superfluous.[3] If a man swear at all, he should swear not by the Divine Name, but by the sacred name of his parents or by some of the great objects of nature, which are ancient and, in accordance with the will of their Creator, never grow old.[4] Once made, a vow should be sacred, particularly if it were made 'with sober reason and deliberate purpose.' (Philo would thus seem to open the door to an annulment of vows made rashly and without due consideration of what they involved.) Some men, Philo continues, make vows 'out of wicked hatred of their species, swearing, for example, that they will not admit this or that man to sit at the same table with them, or to come under the same roof.'[1] And he adds impressively: 'Sometimes, even after the death of their enemy, they keep up their enmity. I would recommend such men to seek to propitiate the mercy of God that so they may find some cure for the diseases of their souls.' He then proceeds to explain the Mosaic laws concerning vows in his characteristic allegorical fashion.

All the invective of the religious teachers failed to kill the practice of vow-making. The Talmudic Rabbis were forced, accordingly, to legislate for the popular inclination to it in their turn, and, since that inclination survived long after the Talmudic age, the codifiers had to adapt the Talmudic enactments to the needs of their day, and even to amplify them. Two whole tractates of the Talmud—*Nedarim* ('The Laws on Vows') and *Nazir* ('The Laws on the Nazirite')—are devoted to this subject. The laws on vows are embodied in Joseph Qaro's *Shūlḥān 'Ārûkh* (16th cent.), the latest of the great codes, and a separate section, consisting of 33 chapters, each containing many paragraphs, is devoted to them. To give even a summary of this extensive and intricate legislation is obviously impossible here. Its magnitude and complexity are themselves an indication of the large place which vows occupied in Jewish life in former times, and of the importance attached to the subject by the Rabbinical mind. The contents of the first chapter of the treatise on vows in the *Shūlḥān 'Ārûkh* are, however, interesting as an illustration of the spirit in which the Talmudic and the later teachers approached the subject. The title of the chapter is: 'Which Vows are Praiseworthy and which Improper?' For, besides a desire to preserve the inviolability of the vow, the great anxiety of the Talmudic doctors and of their successors was the prevention of useless vows which failed to minister either to religion or to morality. Among such vows were those made hurriedly or frivolously. There were also vows imposing upon the persons taking them a needless austerity and self-mortification.

Thus, when a beautiful youth under a vow of Naziriteship presents himself to Simon the Just (3rd cent. B.C.), the sage asks him reprovingly, 'How couldst thou have consented to destroy thy fair locks?'[2]

The chapter in Qaro's work to which reference has just been made[3] opens with the following monition, borrowed, like most of the prescriptions of the codes, from the Talmud:

'Be not habituated to make vows;[4] he that makes a vow is called wicked.[5] This of ordinary vows; but, as to vows made for holy ends, it is a positive duty to fulfil them. Even vows for charitable purposes are not desirable; if one have the money, let him give it straightway without a vow, and if not, let him defer his vow until he have it [which obviously means that, in either case, a vow is undesirable]. It is "permissible" to make a vow in time of trouble. He that saith "I will study this or that chapter of the Torah, and, fearing lest he may be slothful, binds himself to study it by a vow, his vow is permissible, as is that of one who, fearing for his strength of purpose, fortifies by a vow his determination to fulfil a certain precept of the Law."[6] He that takes a vow in order to strengthen his good resolves, and to improve his way of life, is a man of energy, and worthy of praise. For example, if he be a glutton, and abstains by vow from meat for one year or two, or if he be a drunkard and denies himself wine for a time or for life, or if, proud of his comeliness, he becomes a Nazirite [as a penance]—all such acts are a service of God, and to them the Talmudic Sages refer when they say that "Vows are a protecting hedge to renunciation."'[7] And the concluding utterance is instructive: 'But, in spite of their being a service of God, it is well that a man should not make many vows of self-denial; rather let him abstain without a vow.'

The saying is typical of the Jewish spirit, which looks askance at vows, often made to be broken, and at asceticism, which makes for inefficiency in the great work of life. For, according to the

[1] Sir 18[22]; cf. Epistle of Jeremiah, 35.
[2] Ed. Bohn, iii. 255 ff.
[3] The Essenes gave practical effect to this opinion. See Jos. *BJ* II. viii. 6.
[4] Cf. Mt 5[34ff].

[1] Cf. the interesting parallels, or contrasts, in *Mishnāh Nedarim*, iii. 3, xi. 3.
[2] *Nedarim*, 9b.
[3] *Yorē Deāh*, 203
[4] Cf. *Nedarim*, 20a.
[5] Cf. *ib.* 22a.
[6] Cf. *ib.* 8b.
[7] Cf. Maimonides, *Hilc. Nedarim*, end; *Ābhōth*, iii. 13.

Jewish idea, the true servant of God, nay, the true man, is he who takes his full share of the activities of the world and harbours no scorn for its legitimate pleasures. Voluntary renunciation springing from an ennobling sense of freedom, not servitude to a despotic asceticism, is the Jewish ideal. The one is the mark of the strong; the other is the self-condemnation of the weak. For the rest, the following enactments may be cited:

All vows, to be valid, must be uttered aloud.[1] Boys of twelve and girls of eleven, provided they understand the meaning of their act, are capable of making vows;[2] on the other hand, in accordance with the Pentateuchal precept, a father may annul the vows of his daughter, and a husband those of his wife, if they involve hardship to the daughter or the wife.[3] A man, moreover, may impose some restriction upon himself by vow; he cannot so restrict others.[4] Moreover, vows the fulfilment of which is made impossible by *force majeure* are, *ipso facto*, null.[5] The formal annulment of vows can be effected only by an expert Rabbi or by three laymen specially indicated for the duty by repute and experience.[6]

It will have been seen that, like the Biblical teachers, the Rabbis were opposed to vows on principle. Simon the Just only once approved of the taking of a vow—when the youth, in the story above cited, explained that he had become a Nazirite as a penance for having fallen in love with his own beauty. 'Would that there were many such Nazirites in Israel!' he exclaimed. But his objection, generally speaking, held, and it was shared by later eminent teachers like Hillel and the first Gamaliel.[7] He that made a vow built an idolatrous altar, and he that fulfilled a vow offered sacrifice on it.[8] Jephthah is cited as the type of such transgressors; his vow was a worship of Baal.[9] The Nazirite is commanded in the Pentateuch (Nu 6^{11}) to bring a sin-offering. 'In what has he sinned?' the Talmud asks. 'In having abstained from wine,' is the answer.[10] On the other hand, a vow, duly made, must be scrupulously fulfilled; Heaven itself testifies against the man who breaks his word.[11] Further, the Supreme is pictured as thus exhorting Israel, 'Take heed that ye break not your vows, for he that does so will come to break his oaths, and that would be to deny Me, and so to commit mortal sin.'[12] 'He shall not break his word' (Nu 30^2)—the Scriptural utterance is the basis and starting-point of much of the Talmudic legislation concerning vows, and so sensitive was the Rabbinical mind to the sacredness of the vow, and to the danger of its being infringed by the common folk, that one Rabbi—Jehudah Gaon, of Sura (*c.* 750)—forbade even the study of tractate *Nedarim*.

Despite these facts the Rabbis have been accused of too readily 'opening the door,' to use their own phrase, to evasions or, more correctly, to annulment of vows. The prescriptions in *Mishnāh Nedarim*, ix., have been specially cited in support of this charge. But it is only necessary to read these enactments intelligently and fairly in order to vindicate their underlying motive. Far from being animated by a loose regard for morality, they have an ethical intent, that of saving persons who have made virtually impracticable vows from the guilt of breaking them, and of preventing the hardship and injustice which their fulfilment will entail upon others. Men would make vows in a fit of ill-humour, or in a morose and anti-social temper, from which it was only kind to them, and just to the members of their family or to their neighbours, to release them.[13] But even such undertakings were not lightly cancelled. They had to be annulled formally by recognized and competent authority. On the other hand, a vow made by order of the court could, under no circumstances, be set aside by any authority whatsoever.[1] A further charge of a different character has been brought, doubtless with reason, against ancient Jewish practice in regard to vows. In the Gospels the Pharisees are condemned for making vows under circumstances which involved a positive violation of the express commands of the Mosaic Law (Mt 15^4, Mk 7^{10}). That, in the Middle Ages, divergent practices, varying with the authorities immediately concerned, prevailed with regard to granting absolution from vows is unquestionable. Some Rabbis were more lenient in the matter than others. But this difference of practice was due to the varying importance attached to the two opposing considerations which have already been mentioned. One Rabbi would lay the greater stress upon the desirability of preventing the violation of vows, and so be inclined to grant dispensation from them; another would think more especially of the sanctity of the vow itself, however lightly made, and however trivial its character, and so refuse dispensation. A familiar instance is that of a man who vowed to give up gambling. The temptation to break such a vow was particularly strong. Should this consideration justify its annulment? Or should the man be held to his vow notwithstanding? So great was the dread of breaking the plighted word that we find a Jew of the 16th cent. swearing that he would never swear![2]

Here reference may appropriately be made to the formula for the annulment of vows which ushers in the service in orthodox synagogues on the Eve of the Day of Atonement. Deriving its name *Kol Nidrē* ('All Vows') from its initial words, it runs as follows:[3]

'All vows, bonds, oaths, etc., wherewith we have vowed . . . and bound ourselves, from this Day of Atonement unto the next . . . lo, we repent us in them. They shall be annulled, made void and of none effect. . . . Our vows shall not be vows; our bonds shall not be bonds; and our oaths shall not be oaths.'

And, since the congregation may have sinned by violating its vows in the past, the declaration is immediately followed by the verse (Nu 15^{26}):

'And all the congregation of the children of Israel shall be forgiven, . . . for in respect of all the people it was done unwittingly.'

This declaration has provided anti-Jewish writers with much welcome ammunition. Here, they have contended, is a proof that the word of a Jew cannot be trusted, seeing that he absolves himself from his vows and promises beforehand, in his very synagogue, and on the most solemn day in the year. The accusation is the fruit either of ignorance or malevolence or of both combined. The best answer to it is supplied by the unequivocal doctrine of the Rabbinical teachers in all ages, who warned their people that their very 'Yea' and 'Nay' must be truthful,[4] and that it is even more sinful to deceive a Gentile than a Jew.[5] The history of the declaration completes the defence. Owing its origin, at some unknown period not later than the early Gaonic age, to the dread of violating vows, it was nevertheless viewed with stern disapproval by the greatest authorities.

1 *Yorē Deāh*, 210; *Shebuōth*, 26*b*.
2 Maimonides, *Yad, Nedarim*, xi. 1; *Yorē Deāh*, 233.
3 *Mishnāh Nedarim*, x. 1 ff.
4 *Siphrē* to Nu 30^2.
5 *Mishnāh Nedarim*, iii. 1 ff.
6 *Yorē Deāh*, 228; *Beḥorōth*, 36*a* ff.
7 *Nedarim*, 9*b*, 22*a*.
8 *Ib.* 22*a*.
9 *Ta'anith*, 4*a*.
10 Jer. *Nedarim*, 36*d*.
11 *Ib.*
12 *Nedarim*, 20*a*; *Yalqut Shimeoni* to Nu 30^1.
13 See *Mishnāh Nedarim*, ii. 1, and cf. the passage from Philo, above.

1 For further information on this subject see S. Schechter, in C. G. Montefiore's *Hibbert Lectures* for 1892, p. 557 ff.
2 Abrahams, *Jewish Life in the Middle Ages*, pp. 392 ff., 109 ff.; for the ethical as well as the legal aspects of vows and oaths see I. Aboab, *Menorath Ha-maor* (14th cent.), II. ii. 2.
3 The formula exists in many variants; the version given in this article is taken from the *Service of the Synagogue*, London, 1904 (the authorized Festival Prayer Book of the Anglo-Jewish community), Day of Atonement, pt. i. p. 15.
4 *Bābhā Meṣī'ā*, 49*a*; *Siphra* to Lv 19^{36}; cf. Mt 5^{37}.
5 *Ḥūllīn*, 94*a*; *B. Qamma*, 113*b*; *Tosefta B. Qamma*, 10. 15; *Shūlḥān 'Ārūkh, Hoshen Mishpat*, 366 ff., and the mediæval moralists *passim*.

'I hear,' said one of them (R. Natronai [8th cent.]), 'that a formula called *Kol Nidrë* is used in certain congregations, but we have never received it from our fathers.'

'A stupid custom'—so others styled it, and the majority of their fellow-Gaonim shared their opposition.[1] Their condemnation would probably have been sterner still if they had known the declaration in its later form. In their time it had a retrospective effect only, and was, therefore, comparatively harmless. Nor, according to one weighty opinion, was it intended to apply to personal and private vows, but only to those made by the leaders of a congregation, in their official capacity, for congregational purposes, either without due forethought or under duress.[2] It certainly applied, at most, to such personal vows as affected only the individual making them; it could not possibly cover vows involving the rights of others, for absolution from them under such conditions was impossible under the Talmudic law.[3] But unfortunately a Rabbi (Meir ben Samuel [11th cent.]) took it into his head to change the wording of the declaration so as to give it a prospective meaning. The original phrase 'from the past Day of Atonement to this Day of Atonement' was altered into 'from this Day of Atonement to the next,' which is the existing version in some Prayer Books; and thus a weapon was placed in the hands of the enemy, which he was not slow to use. It need hardly be said that the Rabbi who made this ill-conceived alteration was actuated by innocent motives. Dispensation from vows already taken was, he held, impossible save at the hands of competent authority, which might not be available; better, then, he argued, to annul vows in advance. Thus, in both of its forms, the declaration owes its place in the Day of Atonement Prayer Book to that fear of the violation of vows to which repeated reference has been made, and to a natural desire to safeguard those who made them from the penalty for such violation. Certainly, ignorant persons may have been misled by the formula into making vows thoughtlessly; but they did so in spite of its real object, not in virtue of it, and their mistake was severely castigated by authority. Such persons were declared to be incapable of giving evidence in a court of justice.[4] But the ignorant malpractices and the unhappy misunderstandings that have resulted from the introduction of the formula sufficiently condemn it; and there are ancient congregations in which, owing possibly to these considerations, it has never been adopted. If it survives anywhere to-day, despite its crude and misleading phraseology, it is partly because of the force of old associations, especially powerful on an occasion so solemn as the Day of Atonement, and partly because of the moving and cherished melody to which it is sung. In modern Reform congregations it was expunged from the Prayer Book nearly a century ago. All that was of value in it—the tune—was retained; the declaration itself went the way of all unmeaning survivals.

Finally it may be pointed out that vows of a monastic character were almost unknown among the Jews, for the good and sufficient reason that the monastic idea made little or no way among them. The Essenes furnish the outstanding exception. After novitiate those desirous of being admitted into that order took a solemn vow—Josephus styles it 'tremendous oaths'—binding them to piety towards God, justice and forbearance towards men, obedience to authority, fidelity to truth, and secrecy as to the doctrines of the society. They seem also to have imposed chastity upon themselves; but since, as K. Kohler has pointed out, they joined the order, as a rule, after the prime of life, they must not be deemed, because of their submission to this restriction, to have necessarily set at naught the characteristically Jewish duty of procreation. They lived the ascetic life of the Nazirite; but whether they took the Nazirite vow is uncertain.[1] The Essenes, however, stand practically alone in Jewish history. From time to time religious associations came into existence, the rules of which bound the members (*ḥaberim*) to holy living—to devotional exercises, to scrupulous rectitude in the daily life, and to works of benevolence. But these societies were, at the very most, brotherhoods rather than orders. In some cases the offspring of the mystical temper, and intended to minister to the mystical life, they were, however, far from monastic. There was nothing of the cloister in them. The associates lived in their own homes and, in a greater or less degree, busied themselves in worldly affairs. The bond that united them was purely voluntary, and any member could free himself from it at will. In such cases a vow of initiation was out of the question.

LITERATURE.—I. Abrahams, *Jewish Life in the Middle Ages*, London, 1896; A. Büchler, *Der galiläische 'Am-ha 'Areṣ*, Vienna, 1906; I. Elbogen, *Der jüdische Gottesdienst*, Leipzig, 1913; H. Graetz, *Gesch. der Juden*, Leipzig, 1866–78; Hamburger's *RE*, artt. 'Gelübde,' 'Nasir,' 'Kol Nidre'; *JE*, artt. 'Essenes,' 'Nazarite,' 'Vows'; L. Löw, *Gesammelte Schriften*, iii., *Die Lebensalter in der jüdischen Literatur*, Szegedin, 1875; *MGWJ* liii. [1909] 269 ff.; C. G. Montefiore, *Hibbert Lectures*, London, 1892; Philo Judæus, ed. Bohn, London, 1854–55; S. Schechter, *Studies in Judaism*, 2nd ser., London and Philadelphia, 1908; I. H. Weiss, *Dor Dor we-Dorshaw*, Wilna, 1904.

MORRIS JOSEPH.

VOWS (Teutonic).—Vows were solemn promises which were made before some deity or superior power, and by which the person making the vow undertook within a given time or in the future to perform a particular act, to obtain a purpose, to bestow a gift, or to devote himself to some person or thing—as, *e.g.*, in a sworn brotherhood. Such vows were rather common among the Teutons both in the North and in Germany, and they were considered absolutely sacred and inviolable. A person not redeeming his vow or his promise was considered an out-caste, and no regard was paid to him. Among the ancient Teutons all offerings and sacrifices were carried out with great attention and seriousness. They were generally closed with much hilarity and drinking, and then all kinds of promises were made for the future while the goblets were drunk, each of them devoted to some special divinity or to the memory of some great name. The Braga-goblet was the most imposing of all. Of such an occasion we have a description in the *Heimskringla*:

'First Odin's goblet was emptied for victory and power to his king; thereafter, Njord's and Freya's goblets for peace and a good season. Then it was the custom of many to empty the Braga-goblet; and then the guests emptied a goblet to the memory of departed friends, called the remembrance-goblet.'[2]

This goblet was not drunk to Bragi himself, but was emptied before him to the honour of some great person or name, or before some great undertaking. At the larger festivals, such as the Jol (or Midwinter) festival, the vow was made while touching the golden-bristled boar of Frey, which was prepared for the common meal, so that the vow should be made sacred by all that is honourable and great.

Vows were made at funerals of earls, kings, and other great persons, as may be seen from the

1 Weiss, *Dor Dor*, 4. 17. 16; see art. 'Kol Nidre' in *JE* and Hamburger. It must, however, be pointed out that, influenced by the Talmudic permission (cf. *Nedarim*, 23*b*), it was the custom of some pious Jews privately to annul their vows at the advent of every New Year festival.

2 Weiss, *op. cit.*

3 *Tur Oraḥ Ḥayim*, i. 619; see also footnote to Hamburger's art., p. 97.

4 See the references in *JE* vii. 541.

1 See art. ESSENES; Jos. *BJ* II. viii. 2 ff.; Philo, ed. Bohn, iii. 523 ff., iv. 2 ff.; art. 'Essenes,' in *JE*, p. 228.

2 *Heimskringla*, i. 77 (*Saga of Hakon the Good*, ch. 16).

Ynglinga Saga, ch. 36, where we read that King Ingjald at the funeral festival of his father rose when the Braga-goblet was filled in order to offer his vow, promising that he would extend his kingdom one half in each quarter of the world or die.[1] At funeral occasions all sorts of promises were made which could in any manner be connected with the wish of the deceased.

A typical funeral vow or a series of such vows may be quoted from *King Olaf Trygvason's Saga* :

'King Svein made a magnificent feast, to which he invited all the chiefs in his dominions; for he would give the succession-feast, or the heirship-ale, after his father Harald. A short time before, Strut-Harald in Scania, and Vesete in Bornholm, father to Bue the Thick and to Sigurd, had died and King Svein sent word to the Jomsborg vikings that Earl Sigvalde and Bue, and their brothers, should come to him, and drink the funeral-ale for their fathers in the same feast which the king was giving. The Jomsborg vikings came to the festival with their bravest men, forty ships of them from Vendland, and twenty ships from Scania. Great was the multitude of people assembled. The first day of the feast, before King Svein went up into his father's high seat, he drank the bowl to his father's memory, and made the solemn vow, that before three winters were past he would go over with his army to England, and either kill King Adalred (Ethelred), or chase him out of the country. This heirship-bowl all who were at the feast drank. Thereafter for the chiefs of the Jomsborg vikings was filled and drunk the largest horn to be found, and of the strongest drink. When that bowl was emptied, all men drank Christ's health; and again the fullest measure and the strongest drink were handed to the Jomsborg vikings. The third bowl was to the memory of Saint Michael, which was drunk by all. Thereafter Earl Sigvalde emptied a remembrance-bowl to his father's honour, and made the solemn vow that before three winters came to an end, he would go to Norway, and either kill Earl Hakon, or chase him out of the country. Thereupon Thorkel the Tall, his brother, made a solemn vow to follow his brother Sigvalde to Norway, and not flinch from the battle so long as Sigvalde would fight there. Then Bue the Thick vowed to follow them to Norway, and not flinch so long as the Jomsborg vikings fought. At last Vagn Aakeson vowed that he would go with them to Norway, and not return until he had slain Thorkeld Leire, and gone to bed to his daughter Ingebord without her friends' consent. Many other chiefs made solemn vows about different things. Thus was the heirship-ale drunk that day, but the next morning, when the Jomsborg vikings had slept off their drink, they thought they had spoken more than enough. They held a meeting to consult how they should proceed with their undertaking, and they determined to fit out as speedily as possible for the expedition; and without delay ships and men-at-arms were prepared, and the news spread quickly.'[2]

Any vow or promise was made sacred by placing one's foot upon a stump or a stone and saying, 'Here I stand and promise that I shall accomplish this matter,' which was then mentioned and the conditions of the vow given.[1] Those promises were, no doubt, offered to make certain undertakings more sure—*e.g.*, to win such-and-such a woman, whom the maker of the vow wanted to secure for himself or for somebody else, to avenge a crime or an injury, to obtain an honour or any such thing which required honest personal effort—and they were often made in the interest of higher duties so as to render the act itself morally binding.

Sworn brotherhoods were mostly entered into by young men who had been brought up together or who had formed close friendships because of peculiar experiences. The ceremony was as follows.

The sod of a selected piece of ground was loosened and cut in three oblong slices, which were raised and held up by the spears of the covenanters, so as to form an arch under which they let drops of their blood from self-inflicted wounds freely flow in the fresh and open soil, vowing to be faithful to one another in life and death. Such men would afterwards be inseparable and never failed one another. The one would always avenge the injury done to the other, which meant in case of death that he had to take the life of the slayer, even though that one be a relative or a highly exalted person. In later times of ancient Teuton history sworn brotherhoods were the most sacred of all covenants, no one ever thinking of breaking a vow thus made or even considering such a thing possible.[2]

It is apparent that vows as sacred obligations entered into public life in various manners, and also that mutual behaviour thereby became more pregnant and dependable. Even to this day it is very common in countries of the North to demand, or at least to request, that certain promises be made sure by the oath, neither before the court nor in the way prescribed for judicial proceedings, but as a vow made to a friend or to the second party of the contract; for, where such a vow has been taken, one feels assured that the promise will hold.

LITERATURE.—*EBr*[11], *s.v.*; E. H. Meyer, *Germanische Mythologie*, Berlin, 1891, pp. 197–253; Paul Herrmann, *Nordische Mythologie*, Leipzig, 1903; G. O. Hyltén-Cavallius, *Wärend och Wirdarna*, Stockholm, 1863, i. 154–175; *Sveriges Hednatid af Oscar Montelius*, do. 1877 (in *Sveriges Historia fran äldsta tid till vara dagar*, p. 338 f.); A. M. Strinnholm, *Svenska Folkets Historia*, do. 1834–36, i. 122 f., ii. 600–602; J. Enander, *Förenta Staternas Historia*, Chicago, 1875, i. 122–130; Saxo Grammaticus, *Danish History*, bks. i.–ix., tr. O. Elton, London, 1894; Snorri Sturlason, *Heimskringla*, tr. Samuel Laing, and ed. R. B. Anderson, in the 'Norrœna Library,' 3 vols., New York, 1897; Vilhelm Grönbeck, *Menneskelivet og Guderne* (*Leg og Löfte*), Copenhagen, 1912, p. 64. Cf. also lists of literature under artt. SACRIFICE (Teutonic) and SALVATION (Teutonic).

S. G. YOUNGERT.

W

WAGES.—See ECONOMICS, EMPLOYMENT.

WAHHĀBĪS.

WAHHĀBĪS.—Named after 'Abd al-Wahhāb, this Muhammadan community has its headquarters in the part of Arabia called Nejd, but is also represented in Mesopotamia, India, and Africa.

1. Tenets.—The aim of the founders of the community appears to have been ostensibly to restore Islām to its original purity, as taught by Muhammad and practised by his converts. Hence, when their system was examined by Sunni experts in Cairo, it was found not to differ from the ordinary orthodoxy. Their pretext for branding all other Muslims as idolaters lay in the practice of visiting the tombs of saints and appealing to them in emergencies, which the Wahhābīs identified with the practice of the pre-Islāmic pagans that is repeatedly condemned in the Qur'ān. Hence they destroyed such tombs, when they got the opportunity, not even sparing that of Muhammad in Medīnah. One of their enemies summarizes the points wherein they differ from the orthodox under ten heads.

(1) They regard the Deity as having bodily form, with face, hands, etc.
(2) Reasoning has no place in religious questions, which must be settled solely by tradition.
(3) The source of law called 'Consensus' is rejected.
(4) The source called 'Analogy' is rejected.
(5) The opinions of the compilers of codes have no authority, and those who follow them are unbelievers.
(6) All Muslims who do not join their community are unbelievers.
(7) Neither the Prophet nor any saint may be employed as intercessor with the Deity.
(8) Visits to the tombs of saints, etc., are forbidden.
(9) Oaths by any one but God are forbidden.
(10) Vows to any one but God are forbidden, as is also the practice of sacrificing at the tombs of saints and prophets.

It is doubtful whether no. (5) is correct, as the Wahhābīs are said to be followers of the system of Aḥmad Ibn Ḥanbal († A.H. 241), the adherents of which were notorious in 'Abbasid days for their interference with pilgrimages to the tombs of

[1] Snorri Sturlason, *Kongesagaer*[2], Christiania, 1906.
[2] *Heimskringla*, i. 160 (*King Olaf Trygvason's Saga*, ch. 39).

[1] Cf. *Hardar Saga*, 14; *Hoensa Thoris Saga*, 12; *Fagrskinna*, 55.
[2] Strinnholm, *Svenska Folkets Historia*, ii. 511–515. Cf. also art. BROTHERHOOD (Artificial).

saints; in A.H. 323 the khalīfah Raḍi issued a rescript against them.[1] European travellers lay stress on their tabu of tobacco and all drugs that benumb or stupefy, and their objection to the use of silk in any part of the attire, and of ornaments of gold, silver, or gems. Practices of which their history gives evidence are the massacre of the women and children as well as the men of their Muslim enemies, and the mild treatment of the tolerated communities; these were characteristic of the early Khārijīs, whose revolts were brought about by deviations from the rigidity of Islām. If it be true, as has been asserted, that they suppose the Qur'ān to have been mutilated by the third khalīfah, they retain therein the notion which brought about the earliest Khārijī movements. Their iconoclasm bears some resemblance to the practice of the Khārijīs called Qarmaṭians, with whom they are not otherwise connected.[2]

2. History. — The history of the Wahhābīs appears to have been written exclusively by European travellers; there is therefore some uncertainty about the origins of the system. As early as 1764 it attracted the notice of Carsten Niebuhr, who brought the first mention of it to Europe. There are contradictory statements about both the birthplace and the tribe of that Muḥammad Ibn 'Abd al-Wahhāb from whose patronymic the sect derives its name. Born in Central Arabia about 1730, he is said to have travelled as a student and merchant, and to have attached himself to one Muḥammad b. Sa'ud, chief of Ḍira'iyyah (about 46·20 E. long. 25 N. lat.), who married his daughter and became his first disciple. To what extent these persons contemplated from the first the establishment of an independent state cannot now be ascertained; Palgrave,[3] whose account of this matter is more than ordinarily romantic, makes Ibn 'Abd al-Wahhāb allure Ibn Sa'ud with a definite promise of the sort. It is clear that the two made their resolve to restore Islām to its original purity a ground for attacking their neighbours, at first, it is said, with a force of seven men mounted on camels; but a little initial success carries such adventurers a long way where, as in Central Arabia at the time, there is no organized government. Muḥammad b. Sa'ud had before his death extended his authority over 'Ariḍ, Qasim, Ḥasa, Dowāsir, and Sulayyil, and become master of all the provinces situated between the Ḥijāz and the Persian Gulf, with the exception of Qaṭif.

Under the successor of Muḥammad b. Sa'ud, his son 'Abd al-'Azīz, the Wahhābīs came into collision with the outposts of the Ottoman Government, and attacked and plundered Imam Ḥusain, where they massacred the inhabitants. This was in 1801, and in the following year the Wahhābī chief, who had for some time been struggling with the then sharīf of Meccah, Ghalib, was able to wrest from him the important town of Ṭa'if. Owing to the supineness of the Ottoman Government and the incompetence of the pashas who attempted to oppose the Wahhābīs, the latter progressed with great rapidity; in 1803 Sa'ud, son of 'Abd al-'Azīz, took Meccah, where, however, Ghalib, having adopted Wahhābī tenets, was allowed to resume his government; and in 1804 Medīnah was also taken after its port, Yanbo, had fallen. The tomb of Muhammad was robbed of all its ornaments and treasures. By this time Sa'ud was chief of the community, his father 'Abd al-'Azīz having been assassinated in 1803. Raids were made by Wahhābī officers in the direction of the Yemen, which, however, was not permanently occupied. Though the new rulers of the Ḥijāz did not actually abolish the pilgrimage, fear of them kept away the pilgrim caravans from Persia, Syria, and Egypt.

Muḥammad Ali, on whom the government of Egypt had been conferred by the Porte in 1804, with an express injunction to reconquer the sanctuaries, took no serious step in that direction till 1809, not even prohibiting the export of food from Egypt to Arabia, though that measure would have rendered the position of the Wahhābīs in those cities difficult. After two years of preparation the pasha of Egypt sent his son Tuzun, a man famous for his personal courage, at the head of an expedition, which seized Yanbo in Oct. 1811. In the following year he succeeded in reconquering Medīnah; and in Jan. 1813 Meccah and Ṭa'if also were recovered. In this year Muḥammad Ali himself took the command in Arabia, and fought with varying results against Sa'ud till the death of the latter in the following year; he was succeeded by his son 'Abdallah, with whom peace was made by Muḥammad Ali in 1815, after each party had won some considerable victories. Muḥammad Ali returned to Egypt; but the terms of peace could not be carried out, and in the following year the pasha's son (or stepson), Ibrahim Pasha, was sent out to reduce what remained of Wahhābī power; in 1818 he took Ḍira'iyyah, the Wahhābī capital, and obtained possession of 'Abdallah's person; the latter was taken to Cairo and sent thence to Constantinople, where he was executed.

A Turkish governor was left in the Nejd by Ibrahim Pasha when he returned to Egypt; a son of 'Abdallah, named Turki, who had escaped when the capital was taken, succeeded in re-assembling the Wahhābī forces and expelling the governor. A new capital, Riyaḍ, was chosen by Turki for the renovated state; and under this chief, who reigned till 1830, several of the provinces which the Wahhābīs had formerly held were recovered. He was assassinated in that year by a cousin, but was succeeded by his son Faiṣal, who was greatly helped in securing his accession by one 'Abdallah Ibn Rashid, whom he rewarded with the hereditary possession of the province Shamr. Faiṣal, however, was attacked by an officer sent against him by Muḥammad Ali, captured and sent off to Egypt, where he remained a prisoner till he was released by 'Abbas, son of Muḥammad Ali. Returning to Arabia, he easily obtained recognition in Nejd, and his dynasty is still established in Riyaḍ, the dynastic name being Ibn Sa'ud. The province of Shamr became detached during Faiṣal's reign, and the dynastic name of the ruler is Ibn Rashid. His capital, Ḥaiel, has been visited by several European travellers, who have maintained a continuous history of these states.

From 1842 to 1872 the Wahhābī empire in Arabia was split up into the following communities: (1) dynasty of Ibn Sa'ud holding Riyaḍ and Ḥasa, (2) the emirate of Ḥaiel, (3) the city 'Unaizah with the tribe of the name and dependencies, (4) the city Buraidah, (5) the town Shakra, (6) the state and city Ḥariq-Hutah, (7) the tribe Ḥarb, (8) the tribe 'Utaibah, (9) the Mutair. From 1843 to 1870 the second of these was governed by two capable rulers, Ṭilal and Mat'ab; in 1872 the emirate was seized by one Muḥammad, who, after putting to death possible rivals in his own family, endeavoured to bring the remaining communities under his rule. Ultimately in the spring of 1891 most of the above-named communities formed a league against the emir of Ḥaiel, under the leadership of Zamil, ruler of 'Unaizah. On the side of Ibn Rashid there were, in addition to his own forces, the Ḥarb and the Mesopotamian Shamr. Ibn Rashid succeeded in inflicting on the league a crushing defeat, and became master of all their towns, including Riyaḍ,

[1] Miskawaihi, *Experiences of the Nations*, tr. D. S. Margoliouth (in the press [1920]), i. 364.

[2] Cf. artt. KHAWĀRIJ, CARMAṬIANS.

[3] *Personal Narrative of a Year's Journey through Central and Eastern Arabia*, i. 376.

where he installed one of the Ibn Sa'ud family as ruler, remembering that the founder of his own dynasty had been a creature of Ibn Sa'ud. Since this date the ruler of Riyaḍ has emancipated himself from Ibn Rashid's control, and in the intrigues which preceded the Great War of 1914–18 the latter favoured Germany, whereas the former favoured Britain.

3. Wahhābism in India.—Wahhābism was introduced into India by one Sayyid Aḥmad, who was born in 1786–87 in Rai Bareli, and started a revivalist movement among the Muslims of India, with headquarters at Patna, before he made the pilgrimage to Meccah which was the occasion of his conversion to the Wahhābī system. Returning to India in 1824, he gained a following in Peshawar, and in 1826 started military operations against the Sikhs, in which he had considerable success; national dissensions, however, broke out among his followers, and in 1831 he met his death at the hands of the Sikhs. The movement was continued by some of his disciples, who obtained dominion over a large extent of territory along the left bank of the Indus, which, however, they lost in 1847, when the Wahhābī troops surrendered to a British force. Patna continued to harbour a number of Wahhābīs, who are said to have taken part in the Indian Mutiny. For about twenty years after the mutiny had been quelled attempts were made by Wahhābī preachers to stir up risings against the British in different parts of the Peninsula and to found Wahhābī states.

The Indian Wahhābism is said to differ from that of Arabia in its identification of one or other of the founders of the system with the Mahdi of the Sunnis, whereas in Arabia this term was not used.

4. Literature.—It does not appear that the founders of the system in Arabia did more than issue letters and manifestos; and at this day there is no printing-press in Riyaḍ or (probably) in Ḥaiel. Such literature as the system has produced is mainly Indian, and in Persian or Urdu; but there is some anti-Wahhābī literature in Arabic, emanating from Mesopotamia—*e.g.*, *al-Fajr al-Sadiq fi'l-radd 'ala munkiri'-twassul wal-karamat wal-khawariq* by Jamil Efendi Sidqi Zahawi (Cairo, A.H. 1323).

5. Life and conduct.—The Wahhābīs appear from the commencement of the system till our time to have maintained the institutions of orthodox Islām with far greater rigidity than other Muslim communities. Like the early Muslim leaders, the first generations of Wahhābīs propagated their views mainly with the sword; with the introduction of Arabia into the Pax Britannica more peaceful methods are coming into vogue, and the following description by a recent visitor to Riyaḍ gives an idea of both the practices and the aims of the Arabian Wahhābīs at the present day:

'In this city men live for the next world. Hundreds are studying in the Mosques to go out as teachers among the Bedouin tribes. It is the center of a system of religious education that takes in every village of Central Arabia, and imparts the rudiments of an education to much the larger part of the male population of the various towns. Great efforts are being made now to educate the Bedouins. Men pray five times a day in Riyadh. In the winter the roll is called at early morning prayers, and also at the service in the late evening. Absentees are beaten with twenty strokes on the following day. In the summer duties in the date gardens and elsewhere are considered a valid excuse for praying at home. Only a few years ago a man absented himself some days from all prayers and was publicly executed for so doing. It is safe to say that there is one city on earth where men are more interested in the next world than they are in this one. Late dinners are unknown. The evening meal is eaten an hour before sundown so that there may be time for religious readings and exhortations before going to bed. That is the regular program in the house of the great chief himself.'[1]

LITERATURE.—J. L. Burckhardt, *Travels in Arabia*, 2 vols., London, 1829, French tr., Paris, 1835, ii. 253–470 (this tr. continues the history somewhat later than the original); W. G. Palgrave, *Personal Narrative of a Year's Journey through Central and Eastern Arabia*, 2 vols., London, 1865; E. Rehatsek, 'Hist. of the Wahhabis in Arabia and in India,' *JRASBo* xiv. [1880] 274–401; C. M. Doughty, *Travels in Arabia Deserta*, 2 vols., Cambridge, 1888; Eduard Nolde, *Reise nach Innerarabien, Kurdistan und Armenien*, Brunswick, 1895; *al-Manar*, xii. [Cairo, A.H. 1327] 390–396.

D. S. MARGOLIOUTH.

[1] P. W. Harrison, in *The Moslem World*, Oct. 1918, p. 418.

WAKANDA.—See MANITU, ORENDA, MANA, PLAINS INDIANS.

WAKASHAN.—The Wakashan linguistic family consists of two main branches: the Kwakiutl, extending from the Tsimshian country southward to the northern end of Vancouver Island, and the Nutka of the west coast of Vancouver Island and the extreme north-western corner of the State of Washington. The northernmost Kwakiutl, usually known as Heiltsuk, were divided into clans governed by mother-right, but the Kwakiutl divisions, while not true gentes, inclined to be patriarchal, although crests descended to a man's daughter's son rather than to his own son, thus showing a confused or mixed system of descent. The Nutka tribes were divided into a number of septs of varying rank, which were not, however, exogamic. If a man married outside of his sept, his children belonged to that which stood higher socially, but, if he married inside, the descent was patrilineal.

I. *KWAKIUTL.*—**1. Supernatural beings.**—The principal Kwakiutl deity was the sun, called Atā ('the one above'), Kanskīyi ('our brother'), Kansnōla ('our elder brother'), Amiaeket ('the one to whom we must be grateful'), Gyīkamae ('chief'), and Kautsōump ('our father'). The last of these names is said not to have been used until after the advent of Europeans, but this is not quite certain. He was frequently addressed in prayer in such words as 'O chief, take pity upon us'; and in bad weather the steersman of a canoe would say to him 'Take care of us, chief.' His son Kanikilak ('with outspread wings') largely takes the place of the northern transformer, Raven. He descended from heaven and wandered over the face of the whole earth, giving man his arts, customs, and institutions. He also was addressed in prayer. Raven, however, appears as well, and the stories told of him resemble those related by the Haida, Tlingit, and Tsimshian (*qq.v.*). Besides being partially displaced by the sun's son, he shared his functions of trickster with Mink, who was often even more prominent.

A host of lesser spirits were believed in, but they were not especially different from those found elsewhere in America, except the spirits concerned with the great winter ceremonials. Twins were believed to be transformed salmon and were supposed to have power over the winds and weather. When a salmon was killed, its soul was believed to return to the salmon country.

2. The dead.—After death a man's soul, which was thought to have its seat in the head, became a ghost, or *lâlenok*, the sight of which was deadly. These *lâlenok* either lived in a place under ground called Bebēnakaua ('the greatest depth') or roamed through the woods. They might not enter a house, but hovered round the villages, causing bad weather. The name Bebēnakaua is said not to have been used before the advent of the Whites, but the idea for which it stands was certainly aboriginal. Ultimately the *lâlenok* was reborn in the first child of a relative. Probably Bebēnakaua was not the only region of the dead, for one story speaks of a man whose soul went to live with the sun before it was reborn.

3. Shamanism.—The common name for a shaman among the Kwakiutl was *naualak*, but, when curing diseases, he was called *heilikya* or *pakala*. Disease was supposed to be caused either by some foreign object in the affected part, such as a stick, piece of skin, bone, or quartz, or by the absence of the soul from the body. In the former case the shaman moistened the place where the disease had its seat from a small dish of water, went through the usual incantations to the accompaniment of his rattle, and finally sucked out the disease and showed it to the bystanders. Sometimes he used whistles and blew the disease from the hollow of his hand into the air. When the soul had left the patient's body—a fact which the shaman discovered by feeling the patient's head and the root of his nose—the shaman caught it and replaced it in the head, its proper seat. Sometimes it was seen in his hand in the shape of a bird or mannikin. The shaman was also able to cause disease by throwing something into his victim's body. The secrets of the shaman proper or medicine-man were derived from Haialikyawe, the ancestor of the gens of that name. One of the secret societies, however, the Mamaka, conferred power to catch the invisible disease-spirit—which was supposed to be constantly flying through the air in the form of a worm—and throw it back upon one's enemies.

4. Witchcraft.—True witchcraft was of two kinds. In one the person was made sick by having a portion of his clothing buried with a corpse. The second, called *eka*, was more complicated:

A portion of a person's body, or clothing that had received perspiration from him, was obtained and roasted before the fire along with fragments of a corpse; then they were ground up together, sealed in a piece of skin or cloth, and placed in the hollow of a human bone. This in turn was placed inside a human skull and the whole deposited in a small box, which was afterwards buried in the ground so as to be barely covered with earth. Almost on the top of this a fire was built so as to warm the whole, and, while it burned, the wizard beat his head against a tree, naming and denouncing his enemy. This was done secretly and at night or in the early morning, and was repeated at frequent intervals until the enemy died. Such a spell might be removed, however, by finding and unearthing the box—carefully, lest a sudden jar prove fatal to the sick man—and then unwrapping the contents, covering them with feathers, and throwing them into the sea. It might also be removed by some one going over the bewitching ceremonies again, the second ceremony serving to undo the first.

5. Eclipses.—When an eclipse of the sun or moon took place, it was supposed that those bodies were being swallowed, and to liberate them the Kwakiutl burned blankets, boxes, and food. They also made noises to frighten away the enemy and sang 'Haukuä!' ('Throw it up!').

II. *NUTKA*.—The Nutka are treated in art. VANCOUVER ISLAND INDIANS.

III. *MAKAH*.—The Makah Indians around Cape Flattery in the State of Washington are merely a colony of Nutka from Vancouver Island, but their beliefs show certain points of divergence.

1. Supernatural beings and cosmology.—Like the other Nutka, they worshipped a supreme being, whose name was spoken only to those who had been initiated into the sacred rites and ceremonies. One name for this being was Chabatta Hatartstl, or Hatartstl Chabatta ('the great chief who resides above'). He was said to be called upon by individuals only when they were alone, and probably received very little actual attention, the worship of the people being paid as usual to a multitude of inferior deities residing in animals, plants, and other natural objects. Swan[1] cites only one case where to his personal knowledge the supreme deity was directly addressed, but he was told that a person who wished to talk to him retired into the mountains when the moon was full, washed in a pond, and rubbed his limbs with cedar boughs, which are liked by the deity on account of their fragrance. In the same way a man acquired his individual guardian-spirit. The sun (Kléseakarktl) was considered the representative of the supreme being, and it was the object to which the young were told to direct their prayers when they were awakened and made to bathe before daylight. They then called upon him to let them live. The north, south, south-east, east, west, and north-west winds were each supposed to be produced by the blowing of a certain spirit. Stars were believed to be the souls of individuals or of animals formerly existing on earth, and lunar eclipses were ascribed to a *tooshkow*, or 'cultus' cod, endeavouring to eat up the moon, which was believed to be composed of a jelly-like substance. The *aurora borealis* was caused by a small race of Indians in the far north who lived on ice-floes and were cooking seal and walrus meat. Comets and meteors were supposed to be spirits of departed chiefs, and the rainbow a malignant spirit connected with the thunder-bird and having powerful claws with which it seized any one coming near.

[1] 'The Indians of Cape Flattery,' in *Smithsonian Contributions to Knowledge*, xvi. 61f.

2. Shamanism.—Male shamans formerly went through a certain ceremony called *kahaip* in order to acquire supernatural powers. Sickness was believed to be occasioned by a demon, which entered the victim's mouth when drinking at a brook or pierced his skin when bathing in sea-water. It assumed the form of a little white worm, which the shaman knew how to extract. During the operation he washed his hands frequently and warmed them at the fire; finally he caught the demon, squeezed it, blew through his hands towards the roof of the house, and assured the patient that it was gone. An injured bone was renewed by binding over it the bone of a dead person. There were also female shamans or, rather, doctors, who knew the uses of herbs and acted as midwives. Still other individuals were supposed to have power over the winds and weather.

3. The dead.—After death the souls were supposed to reside in the earth, where they existed, deprived of their bones, and received flesh and skin only as fast as it decayed from their material bodies. The usual tales are told of persons who had been to this region and had returned. Little opportunity for such a return was given, however, since to look upon the face of a corpse was considered unlucky, and the Makah consequently bound the body at once tightly in a blanket and laid it away in the grave-box.

LITERATURE.—The Kwakiutl are treated in F. Boas, report v. 'On the North-Western Tribes of Canada,' in *Report of the British Association for the Advancement of Science*, 1889, p. 801 ff., report vi. *ib.* 1890, p. 562 ff., and their secret societies in Boas, 'The Social Organization and the Secret Societies of the Kwakiutl Indians,' in *Report of the United States National Museum* for 1895, Washington, 1897 (this also touches upon secret societies among other tribes in the same region). The Nutka are treated in report vi. 'On the N.W. Tribes of Canada,' and their Washington colony, the Makah, by J. G. Swan, 'The Indians of Cape Flattery,' in *Smithsonian Contributions to Knowledge*, xvi. [Washington, 1870]. Much valuable material may be had from J. R. Jewitt, *A Narr. of the Adventures and Sufferings of John R. Jewitt*, Middletown, Conn., 1815, and from G. M. Sproat, *Scenes and Studies of Savage Life*, London, 1868.

JOHN R. SWANTON.

WAKE.—See DEATH AND DISPOSAL OF THE DEAD.

WALDENSES.—The Waldenses are a Protestant Church, bearing among its own people the name of Vaudois, derived from the geographical situation of its origin and headquarters among the southern valleys of the Cottian Alps, through which run the tributaries of the Pellice and the Po, and which are approached from Turin across the plain of Piedmont. Thus situated as a community of hardy mountaineers far away from the town life of Italy, and with interior valleys still more remote into which to retreat in times of danger, this Church was able to develop and maintain its own individuality and to withstand the attacks of opponents in a way that has almost suggested the miraculous. We need to realize the physical geography of the area in which it grew up in order to understand its rare characteristics and account for its sturdy independence and heroic achievements. Legend has been busy weaving fanciful impossibilities into the fabric of its story. But a sufficient substratum of solid fact remains to account for the importance that has been attached to so small a group of people who have produced no thinkers, writers, or scholars sufficiently eminent to give them world-wide fame. It is the romance of their story that first calls attention to them. Then the frightful persecutions from which they suffered, appealing to the sympathy of the great Protestant Powers, connected them with the larger politics of Europe, especially when Cromwell interposed to champion their cause and Milton immortalized their sufferings in a great sonnet. Over and above these facts critical questions concerning their origin have attracted the attention of scholars and aroused the energies of controversialists, with the consequence that a literature has grown up round the Waldensian name quite out of proportion to the small number of simple folk to whom it has been attached.

I. *ORIGIN*.—The question of the origin of the Waldenses has been complicated by controversial considerations. While Roman Catholic writers have settled the matter by regarding these people as simply the followers of Peter Waldo of Lyons, they themselves repudiate this view and push back their beginnings to the age of primitive Christianity. Thus they deny that they first appeared as a sect of heretics breaking off from the historic Church, and claim to have preserved the purity of the faith through the ages, while all the rest of the Church was degenerating and accumulating the corruptions against which they protested from the first.

1. Claim to apostolic origin.—This claim is first met with in a Dominican monk at Passau in the year 1316,[1] who states that the Waldenses declare that they are the most ancient of all the sects, some even saying that this sect 'duravit a tempore patrum.' It was but a step from this position to add that the Waldensian Church was founded by St. Paul when on his way to Spain. A little later a woman under examination for heresy is said to have made a similar statement. It is not met with again earlier than a letter of Barbe[2] Morel written in 1530 and addressed to Œcolampadius.[3] But it was adopted by Robert Olivétan and published in the preface to his translation of the Bible in 1535, and from that time onwards it was universally adopted by the Protestants, who thus came to honour the Waldenses as the one Christian Church that had preserved the primitive faith of NT times. Its adoption by Beza, its appearance in the Confession of 1541, the assertion of it by Leger in the preface of his history, the encouragement it obtained from Samuel Morland, the British envoy in Savoy, all helped to confirm its popular acceptance. It even came to be regarded as the primary source of Calvinism, an ingenious way of accounting for its otherwise suspicious resemblance to that type of Reformation theology. But now it has been pointed out that no trace of this notion can be found in any of the early Waldensian writings. The inquisitor Moneta of Cremona, discussing the source of Waldo's heresy, makes no mention of the theory of apostolic origin. Nor is there any evidence of the existence of the Waldensian Church as a separate community maintaining primitive NT ideas for more than a thousand years from apostolic days till it emerged in the times of mediæval persecution. Its total seclusion as well as the maintenance of its purity uncorrupted throughout all these centuries would demand a double miracle, for which no evidence is forthcoming. Then this very purity of doctrine in conformity with the NT is exactly what the Protestants claimed to have recovered at the time of the Reformation. In so far as that claim cannot be entirely justified, since Protestantism is not merely a return to the apostolic type of Christianity, but, with all its effort to conform to the NT standard, still a historical development true to the spirit of its age, the same must be said of the Waldensian type of Christianity. Therefore, if we admitted the theory of apostolic origin, we should have the further marvel of a line of development in the solitude of the Alpine valleys leading to much the same results as were obtained by the Reformation theologians in their fresh studies of the NT, unless we were to conclude that Protestantism as a whole was an outgrowth of Waldensian teaching; and we are sufficiently well acquainted with its genesis in the minds of the German and Swiss reformers to know that this was not the case.

2. The time of Sylvester.—A second theory of the ancient origin of the Waldensian Church is that it arose at Rome in the time of the episcopate of Sylvester, when that bishop, after baptizing Constantine, put the Church under the power of the emperor; whereupon a colleague of the bishop protested, broke off communion with Rome, and retreated into the Vaudois valleys. Thus the Waldensian movement is represented as being a reaction against the corruption of the Church in the 4th century. This theory has been combined with the claims to apostolic origin, with the suggestion that the secluded Church, already some centuries old, now received an accession of refugees who found a welcome home in its primitive simplicity. It is given by the inquisitor Moneta,[1] as held by 'the Poor Men of Lyons.' But the want of evidence during the intermediate period, which is fatal to the claim to an apostolic origin, is also applicable to this theory, though the intermediate centuries are not quite so many. Moreover, Sylvester did not baptize Constantine. Nor had the Church preserved the primitive simplicity advocated by the Waldenses uncorrupted until the age of Sylvester, as the upholders of this theory have maintained. Thus its basal assumption is discredited by history.

3. The time of Claude of Turin.—Claude, bishop of Turin in the 8th cent., under Charlemagne and Louis the Pious, revived the Augustinian doctrine of predestination, but ignored the High Church side of Augustine's teaching, according to which the Church was the appointed medium of communication between God and man, resisting the papal claims, and denying that St. Peter had received power to bind and loose. He had crosses as well as images removed from his churches, in all these matters anticipating the Reformation. Accordingly Leger, Muston, and other Waldenses, understanding the churches of the Vaudois valleys to have been included in Claude's diocese, maintained that, if their separation from the Roman Catholic Church could not be traced back to primitive times, their distinctive movement should be attributed to the influence of this French bishop, who has been described as a Calvinist before the Reformation. That Claude may have had some

[1] *Contra Valdenses*, in *Maxima Bibliotheca veterum Patrum*, Lyons, 1677–1707, xxv. 262 ff.

[2] The title 'barbe' (Romance for 'uncle') was employed by the Waldenses for their clergy, perhaps as distinguished from the Roman Catholic title 'father' for a priest, and at the same time as suggestive of an affectionate relationship; also as a cryptic term, a 'commonplace' in times of persecution.

[3] See A. Scultetus, *Annalium Evangeli . . . decades duo*, Geneva, 1618, pp. 295, 306.

[1] Comba, p. 90.

influence among the mountaineers in leading them towards the freer, simpler type of religion, and so preparing for their subsequent breach with Rome, is likely enough. But there is no evidence that he was in any sense the founder of the Waldensian Church as a separate community or the originator of Protestantism in it. There is no indication of the existence of such a church for centuries later than the time of Claude. Besides, it is very improbable that this bishop should have succeeded in originating a vigorous, independent organization in a remote corner of his diocese while he did nothing of the kind at Turin or in the more civilized towns nearer his metropolis. Champions of the antiquity of the Waldensian Church as a distinct community in separation from Rome claim a mass of Romance literature in the libraries of Geneva, Zürich, Grenoble, Paris, Cambridge, and Dublin in support of this contention, maintaining that it is (1) representative of the views of that Church, and (2) of great antiquity. But a critical examination has made it clear (1) that much of this literature is of Roman Catholic origin and not marked by characteristics peculiar to the Waldenses, and that some of it is Hussite, and (2) that none of it gives evidence of coming from an earlier date than the 14th century.

One of these documents, entitled *Nobla Laiczon* ('Noble Reading'), is a poem setting forth Christian doctrine of the Waldensian type which Perrin, Leger, Muston, Monastier, and other writers declare contains a statement that 1100 years have passed since the origin of the New Testament. But in a copy of this work discovered in the Morland MSS it was seen that the tail of an Arabic 4 has left some traces, so that the original reading would have been 'mil e 4 cent anz.' Another MS in this collection has 'mil e CCCC anz.' Further, a MS of the NT at Zürich, which had been assigned to the 12th cent., is found to be dependent on Erasmus' Greek Testament. Lastly there is the 'Waldensian Confession of Faith,' for which a pre-Reformation origin had been claimed, as composed in the year 1120; but now it has been discovered that this date is not written by the original hand, and also that the MS 'copies almost word for word the utterances of the Reformer Bucer as given in Morel's report of his negotiations with that divine and Œcolampadius.'[1]

The statement of Muston[2] that in the year 1096 Urban II. described the Vaudois as 'infected with heresy' is founded on a mistake, since no such reference to these people is to be found among his bulls.[3]

4. Albigenses.—The Albigenses, or Catharists, were near neighbours, occupying the northern and French side of the mountains, the southern and Italian valleys of which were inhabited by the Waldenses. But there does not seem to have been much intercommunication across the great Alpine barrier. The national and racial distinction between the two populations would tend to keep them apart. Moreover, there is not the slightest trace of Catharist doctrines in the Waldensian Church. That this Church should not have received any infection of the Manichæan teaching, with which the Albigenses are said to have been imbued by an emigration from Eastern Europe, and yet have received their comparatively innocent Protestant principles from this tainted source, is not at all probable. On the other hand, we have little or no first-hand information about the tenets of the Albigenses, the reports of which come to us through the suspicious channel of their enemies' accounts of confessions under torture. We may well admit that a common spirit of resistance to the dominance of Rome, and similar efforts at realizing a more spiritual type of worship than was generally seen in mediæval Catholicism, may have led to mutual encouragement in these respects. What must be affirmed, however, is that certainly the Waldensian is not a direct offshoot of the Albigensian movement.

[1] J. H. Kurtz, *Church History*[10], Eng. tr., London, 1892, [2]ii. 471 f.
[2] *L'Israël des Alpes*, Paris, 1851, vol. i. p. xxxii, n. 2.
[3] Comba, p. 154.

The supposed connexion between the Waldenses and the Albigenses was championed in England by several writers, of whom the most notable was G. S. Faber, *An Enquiry into the History and the Theology of the ancient Vallenses and Albigenses* (1838). But in the same year the idea was completely demolished by S. R. Maitland in *Facts and Documents illustrative of the History, Doctrine, and Rites of the ancient Albigenses and Waldenses* (1838). Lastly, Charles Schmidt of Strassburg made an exhaustive examination of the question, giving the legend, as Comba says, its *coup de grâce*.[1] See, further, art. ALBIGENSES.

5. Various later influences. — It may well be that various influences tended to cut off the Vaudois from continuous close Roman influence. Their isolated geographical situation would minimize intercommunication, and at the same time their life as mountaineers would foster a spirit of independence and its simplicity keep them from the materializing influence of a sumptuous ritual. Then the Gothic and Lombard invasions would associate ecclesiastical with political aloofness. For a time these people came under the wave of Arian dominance. We cannot regard the Waldensian faith as in any sense a product of Arianism, and yet the local separation produced by the heresy would tend to engender a habit of independence. Arnold of Brescia, a disciple of Abelard, executed at Rome in 1155, was a strenuous opponent of the temporal claims of the papacy. He contended that sacraments administered by priests who were not living an apostolic life were invalid. Lucius III.'s bull of excommunication (1184) shows that he left followers behind him whose influence may well have lingered in Northern history till it was merged in that of the definitely anti-papal Waldenses. But Leger, in setting his name at the head of the list of barbes, was confusing it with that of another Arnold. Then, on both sides of the Alps, those parts of France and Italy respectively which were nearest to the Waldensian valleys witnessed during the Middle Ages repeated protests against the abuse of images and materialistic forms of worship. With greater probability Peter of Bruys (1104–25) is claimed by Comba, Gay, and others as one of the precursors and originating influences of the Waldenses.

Unfortunately our knowledge of Peter's tenets is almost confined to the statements of Peter the Venerable, abbot of Cluny.[2] It would appear that he ascribed the highest authority to the Gospels, especially the teachings of Jesus contained in them, finding a second and lower authority in the Epistles. It is not clear how he regarded the Old Testament. He taught believers' baptism and repudiated the efficacy of infant baptism, rejected the doctrine of transubstantiation and the Mass—perhaps even going so far as to give up the observance of the Lord's Supper as a rite of the Church—repudiated the custom of prayers for the dead, denied the sanctity of church buildings, and carried out an iconoclastic crusade against the use of crosses. Döllinger's association of the Petrobrusians with the Cathari has been shown to be erroneous.[3] Peter was twenty years combating what he regarded as the superstitions of the Church, especially the 'Roman idolatry.' Beginning in the obscure village of Bruys high up among the Alps, his influence spread through Narbonne, Guyenne, and Gascony, and was for a time centred at Toulouse, where he enjoyed great and growing popularity. Nevertheless, at the instigation of the monks of St. Gilles, he was seized by a mob and publicly burnt, without any legal trial, and also without any interference from the authorities. Peter of Bruys was followed as a reformer by Henry of Cluny, who was condemned at the Council of Pisa (1134), but escaped, and was again imprisoned in 1150 at Toulouse, where he died. His supposed connexion with the famous abbey of Cluny is a mistake; so is the claim that he was an Italian; he seems to have been a Swiss born at Lausanne. Henry followed Peter in protesting against corruptions in the Church, especially the degeneration of the clergy, whom he persuaded to marry their concubines. Unfortunately, as in the case of his predecessor, our knowledge of this reformer is chiefly dependent on information supplied by his enemies, according to which the result of his energetic activity was that the altars were abandoned and the sacraments of the Church despised.[4] Farther than this we cannot go. We have no record of Henry's

[1] *Hist. et doctrine de la secte des Cathares ou Albigeois*, Strassburg, 1849, ii. 267–270.
[2] *Adversus Petrobrusianos hæreticos*, *PL* clxxxix. 719–850.
[3] A. H. Newman, *American Soc. of Church Hist.* [New York, 1892] iv. 183–189.
[4] *Acta Epis. cenomanensium*, in J. Mabillon, *Vetera Analecta*, Paris, 1723.

specific doctrinal teaching and cannot say that he shared Peter of Bruys' primitive Protestantism. Apparently his protests were on moral rather than on theological grounds. Meanwhile there was a spirit of revolt in the air and a growing desire for a more spiritual religion than was commonly met with. On the other hand, the Council of Tours (1163) excommunicated both the Petrobrusians and the Henricians. The Humiliati have been claimed as precursors of the Waldenses; but they were simply workmen's gilds in Lombardy, many of whose members joined the new religious movements, but who were not themselves formative influences in them.

6. Waldo and the Poor Men of Lyons.—The Christian name Peter commonly attached to the reformer appears to be due to later tradition and usage. His name is given in French as Valdes, in Latin as Valdesius, Valdenius, Gualdensis, in Italian as Waldo. Again we have to turn to the prejudiced account of enemies for most of our information about this reformer. It is from an anonymous writer at Laon, however, that we obtain the story of his conversion.

He had been enriched by the practice of usury when in 1173, after being deeply impressed by the legend of St. Alexius, describing how the saint had given all his property to the poor and gone on a pilgrimage to the Holy Land, he was directed by a theologian to the words of Christ in Mt 19[21]. Thereupon, making over his landed possessions to his wife, and distributing the rest of his property among the poor, he first of all gave himself to the study of the Gospels, the Psalms, and other parts of Scripture as well as some patristic writings, which he got two friendly priests to translate for him into the Romance dialect.

After taking a formal vow of poverty and going through the streets begging his way and preaching his message of self-abnegation, he gathered about him a group of followers, who in turn went about with the same message and became known as the Poor Men of Lyons. They travelled in strict observance of Christ's directions to the Seventy (Lk 10[1-4]), going two and two, without staff or scrip, their feet only in wooden sabots, preaching repentance and exhorting people to return to the purity and simplicity of the primitive Christians. Forbidden to preach by the archbishop, they replied with the apostolic defence in Ac 5[29], and later (1179) appealed to the Third Lateran Council, under Alexander III., for recognition, only to have their request scornfully denied—although the pope himself had received Waldo kindly and he is said to have been secretly ordained by one of the cardinals. Daring to persist in their preaching, they were put under the ban at the Council of Verona (1184), presided over by Pope Lucius III. They had no wish to break off from the Church, nor did they imagine that they were opposing its doctrine, ritual, or government. They claimed to be loyal sons of the Church, called to lead their erring brethren back to the ways of their ancestors, and this entirely as a practical reformation of life and conduct. Nevertheless their refusal either to recant or to be silent and their condemnation by the ecclesiastical authorities forced them into a position tantamount to open rebellion. Then this condemnation, followed by an edict of Barbarossa, drove the Poor Men of Lyons out of the city and scattered them abroad, only however to spread the seed of their message the more effectually through Southern Europe. Thus they found their way into Provence, Dauphiné, the valleys of Piedmont, Lombardy, Lorraine, Flanders, Picardy, Germany, Spain, and even as far as England. Since Waldo and his followers had not been condemned for any doctrinal heresy, but only for a breach of discipline in preaching without ecclesiastical authority, strictly speaking they should have been prosecuted as schismatics rather than as heretics. Nevertheless the determined opposition with which they were met implies that their free handling of Scripture gave offence to the theologians, and in point of fact, like the followers of Peter and Henry, they were denounced as heretics. They had their own ministers (called *ministri*), chosen annually for the administration of the communion, which was only once a year. Waldo remained at the head of the community (*societas*) till his death, selected and ordained the ministers, and admitted the new members, though he did not claim to be a bishop. The conditions of membership, called 'conversion,' were renunciation of private property and an ascetic life, separation of husbands from wives, and three days' fast in the week. It is said that they repudiated indulgences, purgatory, and masses for the dead, and denied the efficacy of the sacraments administered by unworthy priests. If so, they certainly would be deemed heretics. But the question of the full contents of their preaching is obscure. A literal application of the teachings of Christ contained in the Gospels was its chief theme, as it had been that of their founder, and, they being for the most part simple folk, without any theological training, it would be pedantic to try to fix any definite theology upon them. We do not know much about the later days of Waldo; he died in Bohemia in the year 1217.

7. The fusion.—An inquiry into the origin of the Waldensian Church brings us to the result that it grew out of a fusion of the work of Waldo and the Poor Men of Lyons with the movements originated by Arnold of Brescia, Peter of Bruys, and Henry 'of Cluny.' It came to contain elements in the teaching of these four leaders, and it rounded into a definite form and ripened into a distinctly organized Church with its own specific teaching in parts where their fourfold influence had been felt, and this not till the latest and most vigorous of these movements, that of Waldo, came into contact with the earlier types. Thus, while the old Waldensian claim to primitive and even apostolic antiquity is abandoned, and it cannot be maintained that Waldo found a Church of evangelical teaching in the Vaudois valleys ready to welcome him and learnt more from it than he imparted to it, neither is it right to say that the Waldenses are simply the followers of Waldo of Lyons. It does not appear that he simply founded the community *de novo*, or that its evangelical and Protestant character is entirely due to his influence. The ideas were in the air, the spirit was alive and awake, when Waldo and his Poor Men came with apostolic fervour to embrace them and blend them with their own version of the teaching of Jesus. There were Arnoldists, Petrobrusians, and Henricians before Waldo, existing as scattered religionists. But it was his movement that gathered in the harvest of their lives and brought about the formation of a Waldensian Church.

II. *MEDIÆVAL PERIOD.* — Disputations in 1175–76 between the barbes Olivier and Sicard and their bishop Montpeyroux having alarmed the neighbouring clergy, two or three years later the pope, Alexander III., sent the cardinal of St. Chrysogone, Henry of Cîteaux, and Reginald, bishop of Bath, then on his way to the Lateran Council, accompanied by the monk Walter Mapes and the priest Raymond of Daventry, to Toulouse to inquire into the matter. Two barbes came there with safe conducts, Bernard of Raymond and Raymond of Baimiac, to be examined by John of Bellesmains, bishop of Poitiers, and then to Narbonne to be examined by Bernard of Fontcaude, under the presidentship of the English priest Raymond of Daventry. It is this Raymond who first uses the name 'Waldenses' (*Vallenses*)—as far as it can be traced back—in his sentence of condemnation, which must be dated 1179 at latest, because, as already said, Raymond was then on his way to the Lateran Council as an attendant of the bishop of Bath. The next year Bernard of Fontcaude wrote a book entitled *Adversus Vallenses et Arianos.*[1] It seems that these discussions arose out of the union of the Petrobrusians and Henricians with the Poor Men of Lyons in Provence. About the same time Waldo's followers united with the Arnauldists in Lombardy. Thus the Waldenses of France and Italy were united, and their union was cemented by persecution. A sentence of excommunication by the Council of Verona cleared the remaining followers of Waldo out of Lyons and drove them to Provence, Dauphiné, the valleys of Piedmont, Lombardy, and some even to Germany. So numerous had they become in Provence that Innocent III. sent his best legates to suppress them in the years 1198, 1201, and 1203, on the third occasion including in his embassy a Spanish bishop and the great St. Dominic, who conducted a succession of disputations with little result till 1207, when the legate Peter of Châteauneuf was killed. Two years later the pope had recourse to a crusade. In 1210 the emperor Otho ordered the archbishop of Turin to drive the Waldenses out of his diocese, and in 1220 the Statutes of Pignerol forbade the inhabitants to harbour them. Some fled to Picardy, and Philip Augustus drove them on to Flanders. Some came to Mayence and Bingen, where 50 were burnt in 1232. They were seen early in Spain, condemned by Church councils, and harried by three of the kings. In 1237 Pope Gregory IX. sent a bull to the archbishop of Tarragona which resulted in fifteen of the heretics being burnt, King Ferdinand himself casting wood on the fire. In course of time these Spanish Waldenses were exterminated. In this century Waldensian churches in Germany sent candidates for the ministry to study at a Waldensian college in Milan. Martyrs to their faith suffered death in Germany during the two following centuries. Bohemia, where Waldo died, became an important field of Waldensian activity. Forty years after the founder's death the inquisitor of Passau named 42 places as nests of the heresy. The king Otakar started persecution, which became most severe in 1335 under Pope Benedict XII. The rise of the Hussite movement led to a fusion of some of the two groups of reformers under the name of Taborites, the most famous of whom was the barbe Frederic Reiser, who spent 25 years in visitations among the Waldenses in Bohemia and Austria and was burnt at Strassburg in 1458. Austria had been reached as early as the 13th cent., and in 1315 the inquisitor of Krems denounced 36 localities as infected with the heresy and secured the burning of 130 martyrs, the most illustrious of whom was the bishop Neumeister, who was burnt at Vienna; he is said to have declared that there were more than 80,000 Waldenses in the duchy of Austria! The end of this century witnessed a terrible persecution in Styria. Meanwhile the movement was spreading in Italy under an organized itinerant mission, the missionaries travelling as pedlars and preaching over many districts. They prospered especially at Milan, where they had a college under John of Ronco, who was appointed to the headship for life, in spite of Waldo's disapproval, which resulted in a division into two groups, the French group and the Italian and German group. The Lombards appointed their own chief pastor (*præpositus*), and he, as well as their ministers (*ministri*), held office for life, while Waldo and the French Waldenses on his authority elected annual leaders to administer the Lord's Supper and serve as pastors. Another and more vital division between the two parties arose out of the teaching of the Italian Waldenses that the sacraments could not be efficacious if administered by priests of unworthy character, while the French Waldenses did not accept this view. Holding the Roman Catholic priests to be morally wrong in many of their practices, because unscriptural, the Italians repudiated all their sacraments. At the same time this branch of the Waldenses insisted most strongly on close adhesion to NT teaching and practice generally and on rejection of everything in the Church which lacked that authority. Thus they were the more thoroughgoing anti-Romanists. In May 1217 six members of the two parties met at Bergamo to draw up terms of agreement, but failed (1) on the question of the salvation of Waldo, which the Lombards made conditional only on his repentance of his wrong-doing in condemning their views, while the French regarded it as absolute; (2) on the question of the validity of sacraments administered by unworthy ministers, denied by the Italians, allowed by the French. Nevertheless fraternal intercourse came to be established in course of time between these two branches of Waldenses. In the 15th cent. there was a very influential number of the Waldenses in central Italy. The Inquisition records reveal the existence of groups throughout the whole of this region. In Calabria the Waldenses from Piedmont, who had been sent for to cultivate a great estate, proved themselves most effective missionaries, winning over most of the population of the district. These converts obtained exceptional privileges of religious liberty and flourished for 250 years, after which they were almost exterminated by a wholesale persecution.

While the French Waldenses seem to have developed the episcopal form of government with the three orders—bishops, priests, and deacons—in spite of Waldo's greater simplicity of ministerial functions, the Italians worked out more of a presbyterian type of church, each church being under a pastor with whom was associated in government a consistory of laymen, and a synod met once a year composed of an equal number of ministerial and lay members.

The valleys on the Italian side of the Cottian Alps now became the centre and chief home of these Waldenses, so that in course of time their very name (in French 'Vaudois') was regarded as geographical, and it was asserted that Waldo took his surname from that of the inhabitants of this district after joining their religious movement, whereas later researches have shown that there is no justification for this view, and it must be admitted that the name of the Church is derived from that of the founder of the society of the Poor Men of Lyons. In the 15th cent. these valleys came under the rule of the duke of Savoy. Then followed a time of severe persecution. In 1434 its violence drove numbers to emigrate. The inquisitor Acquapendente visited the valley of Luserna in 1475, and, disapproving of the religious views and practices of its inhabitants, roused their overlords to compel submission to his orders, with the result that a few years later there was a rebellion which led in 1484 to the interference of Duke Charles I., who was able to bring about a peaceful arrangement between the two parties. The first serious attack with armed forces took place under Philip II., who became regent of the duchy of Savoy in 1490, and duke in 1496. It was in 1494, during his regency, that Philip launched an expedition against the Waldenses of the Luserna valley, only to meet with so disastrous a defeat that he at once made peace with them, guaranteeing them liberty for 40 years. It is not easy to be clear as to the theological views of the Waldenses during this period. The notion that, when the Reformation broke out, the Protestants were surprised to find their ideas anticipated by the inhabitants of the Alpine valleys, who had pre-

[1] See Gay, *Hist. des Vaudois*, p. 16, n. 1.

served them from primitive times, proves to be a delusion. When we do meet with a Waldensian statement of belief, this is subsequent to the Reformation and characterized by doctrines and phrases distinctive of Swiss and German theologians of that movement. The earlier Protestantism was partly negative, in the rejection of Roman Catholic teachings and practices which could not be justified by the NT, and, in so far as it was positive, a return to the simplicity and spirituality of worship believed to have been characteristic of the primitive Church. Waldo and his immediate followers relied mainly on the Gospels. The ordinance of poverty thought to be required by the teachings of Christ was not universally adopted, nor did it long continue in operation. On the other hand, the Pauline theology, so emphatically and elaborately taught both by Luther and by Calvin, does not appear to have been brought forward by these earlier Protestants. There was no tendency among them to elaborate a system of theology. The barbes were drawn for the most part from the peasantry, and the college at Milan in which they were trained had to begin with the most elementary instruction in reading and writing. The great requisite was ability to read the Gospels and familiarity with their contents. Here we have the religious teaching of the mediæval Waldenses.

III. *Reformation Period.*—**1. First contact with the Protestants.**—When the Reformation broke out the only organized opponents of the papacy on the Continent were the Waldenses and the later Hussites, who were called the Bohemian Brethren, but whom the Protestants as well as Roman Catholics designated Waldenses. In 1522 these Bohemians sent two of their ministers on a visit to Martin Luther with a message of congratulation and encouragement, and ten years later they sent a confession of faith, entitled *Apologia veræ doctrinæ eorum qui vulgo appellantur Valdenses*, with a eulogistic preface. Subsequently communications were maintained by the missions of successive deputations. In 1540 the Bohemian Brethren sent a deputation to confer with Calvin in Strassburg. Driven out of their own country in 1548, they took refuge in Poland, where they united with the Protestant churches which they found there. Calvin then wrote to the Reformed churches of Poland, 'I hope for every kind of good from your union with the Waldenses (avec les Vaudois).'[1] Meanwhile the churches of the Alpine valleys took steps to come into contact with the new reforming movement, and in 1526 the synod of Laus (Pragela), in which 140 barbes took part, having received confusing reports, sent the barbes Martin Gonin and Guido of Calabria both to Switzerland and to Germany to make inquiries and bring back some of the Protestant writings.

Their report and the literature which they circulated among the churches helped to draw them into contact with the Reformers. Four years later the synod which met at Marindol decided to consult the principal Swiss Reformers on several points of doctrine, organization, and discipline, for which purpose they sent two barbes, George Morel and Peter Masson, who visited and conferred with Farel and Haller, and at Basel received a fine response to their questions from Œcolampadius, who then sent them on to Strassburg, where they were well received by Bucer, who gave them an equally full and explicit reply. Morel published the Waldensian questions and the Reformers' replies in a work now at Dublin.[2] The same year the two delegates returned by way of France, when Masson was put to death at Dijon; but Morel was able to bring back their report to the Waldensian churches. This was discussed at a synod in Piedmont, held apparently in 1531. The discussion resulted in a division of opinion, and the formation of two parties, known respectively as 'Conservators' and 'Innovators,' the former holding on to their old position, the latter accepting the new Protestant teaching. This indisputable fact affords clear evidence that the pre-Reformation Waldenses were not simply hidden Protestants, cherishing the doctrine subsequently held by the Swiss and German Reformers. On the other hand, like the Hussites, with whom they practically coalesced in Hungary, and the descendants of the Lollards still in hiding from persecution in England, they were ready to fraternize with the new opponents of the papacy, though some did not adopt all their views. Liberation from the yoke of Rome, the abandonment of mediæval ritual which was regarded as idolatrous, spirituality of worship, and the popular use of the Scriptures in the vernacular as the authoritative standard of faith and discipline were Waldensian characteristics, which found welcome support from the powerful new Protestantism that was making so great a stir in the world.

2. Association with the Swiss Reformation.—The differences of opinion among the Waldenses of the valleys and their division into two parties on the question of accepting the Protestant views which their delegates reported to them led to the desire for fuller knowledge and conference with leading Reformers. With this end in view a general synod was convoked in 1532 under the chestnuts of Chamforans at Angrogna, in which the Reformers Farel, Saunier, and Olivétan met a large assembly containing laymen as well as barbes. Three recommendations, which rose out of the previous consultations with Œcolampadius and Farel, were then read: viz. (1) the adoption of public worship by the Waldensian churches instead of secret meetings, (2) an absolute condemnation of the custom of some of the Waldenses in attending Roman Catholic services, (3) an acceptance of the Reformers' views on predestination, good works, oaths, the denial of obligatory confession, Sunday fasts, marriage of the clergy, and the two sacraments. Farel's enthusiastic eloquence carried the great majority of the assembly with him in a vote for adopting these propositions, though some of the barbes protested against them on two grounds, (1) as unnecessary, (2) as casting a reflexion on those who had hitherto led the churches happily. Olivétan remained for three years travelling among the valleys and setting up schools. Meanwhile—the next year after the synod of Chamforans—two barbes who had been conferring with their brethren in Bohemia returned with a long letter conjuring the Waldenses of the valleys to weigh well the question of adhesion to the proposals of the foreign teachers. Accordingly a synod was at once called at Prali to reconsider the question; but it adhered to the previous decision, with only a handful of dissentients. The chief differences between the Waldenses and the Swiss Protestants had been based on the question of the degree in which everything must be determined by the authority of Scripture. Both parties held, as against the Catholic position, that this was the one supreme authority; but, while the Swiss theologians would allow of nothing which was not expressly taught in the Bible, the Waldenses had held that only those tenets and practices of Catholicism which were expressly contrary to Scripture need be condemned. But now the closer adhesion to the Swiss Reformed Church tended to assimilation of views and practices and subsequently to the adoption of Calvinism.

3. Olivétan's Bible.—One important and lasting outcome of the friendly intercourse between the Waldenses and the Swiss Reformers was the production of the first Protestant French translation of the Bible. Waldo had translated some portions into the Romance vernacular dialect; but most of his publications had been destroyed by the Roman Catholic authorities. In the conference at Chamforans, Farel and Saunier urged the Waldensian barbes to bring out a new translation of the whole Bible in the French language. This work the barbes persuaded Olivétan to undertake. Olivétan was a cousin of Calvin; he had been educated at the university of Paris and at Orleans; on accepting Protestantism he had escaped to Strassburg, and later he had come to Geneva. He accepted the task, and completed it in 1535. Considered better in the OT portion than in the NT, Olivétan's version is the basis of the later French versions, or rather revisions.

4. The new order.—In course of time the Waldenses on the French side of the Alps, who for the most part consisted of Conservators, were fused into French Protestantism. Then persecu-

[1] Gay, p. 49.

[2] J. H. Todd, *Books of the Vaudois preserved in Trinity College, Dublin.*

tion in Bohemia and also in Southern Italy nearly exterminated the churches of this communion in those parts, leaving Piedmont and the Italian valleys of the Cottian Alps, the Vaudois country, as its only important habitat, though this very persecution scattered many of its victims among the Swiss and German Protestant states. It took some 20 or 30 years to supply adequately trained ministers and organize the worship, discipline, and teaching of the Waldensian Church in the valleys on the lines agreed upon in the conference with the Swiss Reformers. The linguistic difficulty was one cause of delay. The Swiss theologians could preach only in French, the Italian ministers, educated in the college at Milan, only in Italian. Neither knew the Romance dialect which was used in the villages of the valleys. Instead of taking the course usually adopted by missionaries and themselves learning the provincial dialect, the French- and Italian-speaking teachers induced the peasants to learn the languages of these teachers, so that they could be used in the church services. Until this curious change had been effectively completed, the movement could not make much progress. Meanwhile Piedmont came under the power of France. This was in 1536 — under Francis I.; and the French domination lasted till 1559. The first governor appointed by the French king (1537) was William of Fürstenberg, a resolute Protestant, who proved friendly to the Waldenses, and, on being sent into Germany, left his secretary Farel, a brother of the Reformer, in charge of the valley of Luserna. This man set to work vigorously furthering the Reformation and abolishing the Mass which the Catholics were still celebrating at Angrogna — an act of violence which provoked reprisals on the part of René of Montejean, the governor of Turin, who sent soldiers into the valley, sacked its villages, and imprisoned the barbes. The governor, returning to the province in 1539, released them, and Francis then left the Waldenses of Piedmont in peace for seven years, while he was persecuting those on the French side of the Alps. Henry II., succeeding to the throne of France in 1547, was also severe on the northern Waldenses; but Caraciolo, his governor of Piedmont, was friendly to them, and persecution did not break out in this district till 1550, when the inquisitor Giacomelli sent for the syndic of Angrogna and imprisoned him at Turin. War put a stop to further proceedings. In 1555 a number of fully trained ministers came from Switzerland to take charge of the congregations in the valleys, together with some Swiss pastors who travelled about inducting them and regulating the new order of worship in the French language, also a colporteur who distributed the service books among the villages. Many 'temples' were built, and by 1556 the new form of worship was being conducted in all the parishes. Thereupon two commissioners were dispatched from Turin with directions to stop these services. The villagers disobeyed the edict, and an arrest of the pastors was ordered. But proceedings were stopped owing to the influence of Swiss and German authorities with the French Government. Thus another respite was secured, during which the Waldensian Church was being fully organized and equipped with capable ministers. This is a significant fact, in view of the terrible times that were to follow. The discipline and leadership now secured proved to be invaluable in arming the Waldenses to make one of the most magnificent stands for religious liberty ever recorded in the annals of history.

IV. *PERIOD OF GREAT PERSECUTIONS* (*1540–1690*). — **I. Persecution of early Protestants.** — Although the Waldenses had been liable to persecution as heretics from the first and had suffered from some severe outbreaks previous to the Reformation, there were times of lenient treatment—a fact which, if not logical, was indicative of the absence of rigorous lines of demarcation. But now their open co-operation with the Swiss and German Protestants allowed of no ambiguity as to their quarrel with Rome, and consequently stern measures of oppression were taken against them. The political arrangement formally adopted in Germany as a refuge from civil war and practically operative in other countries left the religion of each state to be that of its prince or other ruling authority. In democratic and republican Switzerland this worked smoothly, since it meant the dominance of the faith of the majority. But it was otherwise with a country such as France under an autocratic ruler, and accordingly in 1534 there was a wholesale destruction of the Waldensian churches of Provence. Piedmont was subject to the rule of the duke of Savoy, and therefore it depended on the will of that prince, or sometimes rather on that of his overlord, whether the practices of the Waldensian Church in that province should be sanctioned or measures taken to suppress them. Another feature of the consequent contest is the fact that it was by no means one-sided. Those sturdy mountaineers were not meek martyrs led as lambs to the slaughter. They carried the war into the enemy's camp, and the first outbreak of persecution directed against them was an act of reprisal for the suppression of the Mass at Angrogna. Then the Waldenses became in a literal sense a Church militant, taking to the field in arms and fighting valiantly for their liberty of worship, with hardy heroism and at times with brilliant success. The outstanding personality of this period is Scipione Lentolo, born at Naples, but said to have come from a Roman patrician family, who became a priest, a doctor of theology, and preacher at Venice and Ferrara, at the latter of which places he was converted to Protestantism. Accused of heresy for his preaching at Lucca, he was imprisoned and sent to Rome. Escaping first to Sicily and then to Geneva, he there came in contact with Calvin, who appointed him pastor of St. Jean in the Waldensian country. Not confining his activity to this parish, he visited other valleys, and even went down to the plain of Piedmont on an evangelizing tour. When persecution broke out, he got refuge for fugitives in the valleys and encouraged the people everywhere to stand true to their faith. Lentolo is the author of the earliest history of the Waldenses and the chief authority for that of the persecution of his own times. This history was virtually unknown till in 1897 Comba called attention to a copy of it in the Berne Library; eight years later it was reprinted and published, and thus a flood of light was thrown on the persecution with which the author was so closely connected. Expelled from the valleys in 1566, he ministered in the Engadine and carried on literary work till his death in 1599.

The principal persecution with which Lentolo was brought into contact led to 'the war of della Trinità.' Philibert, the duke of Savoy at this time, though personally averse to the molestation of his mountaineer subjects, was compelled by the papal nuncio, backed up by France and Spain, to issue an edict requiring them to attend the Mass and forbidding their holding Waldensian services. On their disobeying this order, he sent an army under the command of della Trinità to enforce it. This commander, arriving in November 1560, met with such strenuous opposition that he consented to allow a deputation of barbes to go to the duke and present their plea for religious liberty, while he went into winter quarters at La Tour. The deputation was treacherously treated at Turin, in order to compel them to abjure their faith. Accordingly, on their return in the spring, the indignant mountaineers rose in a mass and repulsed every attack of della Trinità at Luserna, at Angrogna, at Prali, with the result that Philibert was glad to come to terms with the heretics, leaving them at peace to carry on their Protestant services (5th June 1561). At the same time a persecution to the extent of extermination was carried out by Spanish troops at the instigation of the grand inquisitor, Michele Ghislieri (later Pope Pius V.), in Calabria, where, in spite of wholesale slaughter in the 13th cent., some representatives of the early Waldenses had persisted in maintaining the faith of their fathers, and had now welcomed the new Protestant movement. Two thousand were put to death and 1600 imprisoned. In Piedmont, after this, attempts were made successively by missions of Jesuits and by Capuchin friars, sometimes with the aid of soldiers, to bring the mountain villagers back into the fold of the Church; there followed several local persecutions, exactions of fines for supposed offences, and violent seizures of churches and even a sanguinary war in the year 1624, in which both sides suffered severely. The most important Waldensian leader of this time was Peter Gilles, an inspiring preacher and vigorous polemical writer, who died in 1644.

2. The great persecution under Louis XIV.—The determined loyalty of the Waldenses to their faith, combined with their amazing military prowess and the reluctance of the duke of Savoy to harass his mountaineer subjects—a policy rarely undertaken excepting under pressure from France—had secured them treaties of peace with liberty of worship. For a quarter of a century they were very little molested. In 1650 Charles Emmanuel II., the young duke of Savoy (only 15 years old), came to the throne. Behind him was the real power, his mother the duchess, daughter of Henry IV. and Mary de Medici, granddaughter of the notorious Catherine de Medici, the author of the Massacre of St. Bartholomew. Thereupon a 'Council of the Propagation of the Faith,' consisting of the chief councillors of State and Church dignitaries, was established in Turin. Five years later there was issued the 'Decree of Gastado,' ordering all Waldensian families in the plain back into the mountains and the sale of their lands within 20 days, unless they would renounce their Protestantism. This was in the depth of winter, and much suffering was involved, which they endured courageously. A little later (17th April 1655) the marquis of Pianezza was dispatched with an army of 15,000 men to La Torre—the key of the valleys—although at this very time there were deputies in Turin attempting to negotiate terms of settlement. The Waldenses first retreated to the mountains. But, on their assailants offering to treat with them, they opened the passes, and some of them fraternized with the soldiers, eating at the same tables. This was the prelude to wholesale massacre throughout the valleys of Luserna and Angrogna. Jean Leger, the author of the monumental history of the Waldenses, is the leading barbe of this period and the inspirer of his people. He enumerates 1712 martyrs. A great number who had hidden in a cave at Castelluzzo, the castle-like mountain above La Torre which dominates the entrance to the valleys, were dragged out and flung down the precipice. These were the

> 'slaughtered saints, whose bones
> Lie scattered on the Alpine mountains cold . . .
> Slain by the bloody Piemontese, that rolled
> Mother with infant down the rocks'

of Milton's famous sonnet. This was before the revocation of the Edict of Nantes, and it sent a shock of horror through Europe. Cromwell proclaimed a fast and got Milton to draw up a letter to the king of France and the Protestant princes. He also sent Sir Samuel Morland to the duke of Savoy to convey his vigorous protest by word of mouth. Morland visited the valleys and brought back information together with some Waldensian books which are now deposited at Cambridge. His published results of investigations on the spot are one of our historical sources for this period.

The interference of so powerful a ruler as Cromwell had an immediate effect. Mazarin directed the duke to put an end to the persecution and grant an amnesty to the Protestants. This was settled on 18th August in the 'Patentes de grâce' of Pignerol. But it did not result in a real or lasting peace inasmuch as the Piedmontese did not respect its terms, and accordingly in 1663 they rose in rebellion. Contrary to the treaty stipulations, the duke's authorities began to restore the fort at La Torre, ordered all foreign pastors out of the province, commanded the principal heads of families to answer charges of disloyalty, and, on their failing to appear, condemned them to death in their absence, and compelled Leger to escape out of the country by ordering his execution. The governor of the fortress of La Torre, Count Burbolorneo di Bagnolo, repeatedly sent troops into the valley of Luserna, and their devastations drove the inhabitants into the mountains. Janavel and a body of outlaws, called banditti by the Piedmontese, took up the cause of the persecuted villagers and repeatedly attacked the duke's soldiers. On 6th August the duke issued an edict condemning all the Waldenses to death as rebels. The war continued till the end of the year, by which time Janavel had 2000 followers, who occupied a number of advantageous positions. Meanwhile the persecuted people sent messengers to Switzerland and Holland begging for help, and their great leader Leger made good use of his enforced absence from home in travelling about to urge the plea. The duke got little satisfaction from the war. At Angrogna, after his soldiers had been ravaging the neighbouring villages, he lost 600 men and the two captains Sanfront and della Trinità. This had been a dishonourable expedition, because at the very time he was pledged to a truce while conducting negotiations with some Waldensian deputies, aided by an embassy of Swiss mediators at Turin. The public conferences with these emissaries from Switzerland were followed by a month of private discussion, till at length, on 14th Feb. 1664, the ducal government issued the 'Patente of Turin.' This covenant granted an amnesty to all the Waldenses except their victorious leader Janavel, who was ordered out of the country, and liberty of worship in their own way without molestation, except at St. Jean (Leger's parish), where the Protestant worship was prohibited. It is much to the credit of Janavel that this hero of the war consented to his own exile without protest for the sake of a peaceful settlement of his people. Twenty years of liberty now followed.

3. The exile.—In the year after the revocation of the Edict of Nantes (*i.e.* 1686) Louis XIV. sent a demand to his cousin Victor Amadeus II., the duke of Savoy, that he would treat his Protestant subjects as the French king was treating the Huguenots. He found some ground for this interference with a foreign government in the fact that fugitives from his terrible persecution were taking refuge in the Waldensian valleys. The result was that the duke ordered the Waldenses to discontinue their religious meetings on pain of death and the confiscation of their property; their churches were to be razed to the ground; their pastors and schoolmasters to leave within fifteen days under pain of death and confiscation, and to renounce all claim on a pension; and all their children to be educated as Roman Catholics. The Waldenses, assembling at Angrogna, dispatched two envoys to Turin to plead for their pledged rights; but they were refused an audience. On hearing of the terrible plight of their co-religionists, the Swiss Protestants held a conference at Baden, which decided to send envoys to Turin on behalf of the Waldenses. Accordingly the brothers De Muralt, selected for this mission, went to that city and obtained an audience with the duke on 13th March. The result was a proposal of Victor that his Protestant subjects should be allowed to emigrate to Switzerland. It was with the utmost difficulty that the De Muralts persuaded the mountaineers to accept this suggestion of voluntary exile (in an assembly at Serre, 4th April). On 9th April the duke signed a decree permitting the emigration. In spite of this fact, some of the Waldenses who had agreed to accept it were arrested and imprisoned. Not believing that the decree was being adhered to, the people prepared to resist the authorities to the last. Then, with the aid of soldiers sent by Louis XIV. as well as his own men, Victor sent expeditions up the Luserna and Perosa valleys. By the end of the year 9000 had been killed and 12,000 carried off as prisoners, many of them to perish in the dungeons of Piedmont. 'The valleys are deserted,' wrote Catinat, the leader of the invading troops, at the completion of his work. Among those who escaped to Switzerland was Henri Arnaud, who was to be the leader of the return from exile and whose narrative is our principal authority for this period. Victor declared all the property of the Waldenses confiscated, and he reckoned the heretics to be extirpated. But there were 200 fugitives lurking in the mountain caves, who afterwards descended at times to the terror of the immigrants from the plain who had taken possession of their homes. The duke sent messengers bidding them escape to Switzerland, but after sending these to consult Janavel and Arnaud they declared that they would resist till death. Victor had no mind to keep up the war with these brave mountaineers, and he agreed to let them go to Switzerland with their arms and baggage, to allow their imprisoned relatives to accompany them, and on their arrival there to permit all the imprisoned Waldenses, for whose liberation they had been holding out, when offered an earlier opportunity of escape, to follow them. The persistent guerilla warfare of this handful had secured the release of all the surviving Waldenses. Early in 1687 the prisons were opened, and the prisoners, now reduced to 3000, set off on their terrible journey across the Alps for Geneva, by the Mont Cenis route, a journey which occupied on an average twelve days, during which many perished in the snow. But, in spite of the protest of the Swiss against the flagrant breach of treaty, children under twelve years of age were detained to be educated as Roman Catholics. The fugitives came in driblets, and the last detachment did not arrive till the end of August. Their reception at Geneva was very hospitable, and by degrees they were settled in various Swiss towns and generously supported by Holland, England, and Germany. But they were anxious to return to their valleys, and the duke of Savoy was so much annoyed at one or two futile attempts that he induced the Swiss authorities to have them removed farther away, and arrangements were made by which they were received in Brandenburg, Prussia, Württemberg, and the Palatinate.

4. The return.—In spite of their scattered condition in the centre and north of Europe, the Waldenses were able to creep back and gather in Noyon on the Lake of Geneva to the number of nearly 1000 fighting men with their wives and families; and on the evening of 16th Aug. 1689, eluding the vigilance of the Swiss authorities, they embarked in boats hired for the purpose and crossed to Savoy, led by Turel de Die, in the unexplained absence of their appointed captain Bourgeois, and accompanied by Arnaud and two other pastors, one of whom, however, Cyrus Chyon, was arrested at the moment of departure. Six days' travel by mountain paths brought them to Mont Cenis, and four more over and down to the valley of the Jaillon. There—to quote Arnaud's figures—they were met by 2500 French soldiers under the command of the Marquis of Larry, whom they defeated with the loss of 600 men, while the Waldenses only lost 15 killed and had 12 wounded in the battle, after as many as 116 lives had been sacrificed to the hardships of the journey. They entrenched themselves at La Balsiglia at the back of the valley of San Martino for the winter. Arnaud was now both their pastor and their commander in the field. Mountain warfare was carried on throughout the spring of 1690, and the returned exiles gradually succeeded in regaining possession of their valleys. Then a combination of England, Holland, Germany, and Spain so crippled the power of France that the duke of Savoy was glad to make overtures to the Waldenses. But no satisfactory arrangement was reached as yet. Meanwhile fresh detachments were still returning from the more remote parts of their exile, and by the end of 1690 Arnaud had succeeded in settling them in their valleys. They had to wait four years for a definite edict regularizing their position and with it recognizing their religious liberty. This was issued by Victor on 23rd May 1694. The pope, Innocent XII., denounced the edict, whereupon the senate in Turin repudiated the papal decree and forbade publication of it in the duchy under penalty of death. Though now enjoying freedom in their valleys, the returned exiles would have been in sore straits if it had not been for the relief which was sent to them from Holland and England. William and Mary, and later on Queen Anne, interested themselves warmly in their heroic fellow-Protestants, as Cromwell had done in a previous generation.

V. *LATER HISTORY.* — **I. Policy of Victor Amadeus (1694–1730).**—Although the Waldenses now had their homes and religious liberty guaranteed by a decree of the duke, they were still often tyrannically dealt with. Victor had broken with Louis XIV. and become allied with William III. of England by the treaty of the Hague. The Waldenses had then contributed soldiers to a joint military expedition, one result of which was that Val Perosa was taken over from France and incorporated in the duchy. During the war the Waldenses had enjoyed religious liberty and had been able to hold their synods without any hindrance from the Government; in 1697 they petitioned the duke to allow their co-religionists of Val Perosa to be incorporated in their Church. This was refused, and these people had to leave the country in order to obtain freedom for their religion, going to Germany, where they founded a colony at Gochsheim. The next year the duke ordered all French Protestants in his dominions to leave the country within two months under penalty of death. The consequence was the exile of 2883 persons, including seven pastors. Changeable as a weather-cock, on the outbreak of the war of the Spanish succession, Victor wrote personal letters to the Waldensian pastors urging them to encourage recruiting in his service and even appealed to the Camisards and other French Protestants, whom he had banished five years before, to return and join his army. When the war was over, those French Protestants who had responded to his invitation were again expelled, and in 1707 he even sent back the Swiss parsons whom he had welcomed only eight years earlier. In 1708 Victor took possession of the valley of Pragela, whereupon its Protestant inhabitants were delighted to have the duke's permission for a visitation of Waldensian pastors; but he soon changed his policy and ordered these people to observe the Roman Catholic festivals. His policy all along was opportunist, with a strong leaning to the Roman Catholic side when he was free from the necessity of conciliating his Protestant subjects. There was no depending on his word. When the people of Pragela protested against his later treatment of them, the leading Waldenses in the valley were arrested and imprisoned; in 1716 the Protestant schools were closed; in 1720 the Reformed worship was absolutely forbidden in the valley. From time to time there was imprisonment of recalcitrants till the climax was reached in 1730, when, in spite of the intercession of Frederic William I. of Prussia, all the Waldenses in the valley were ordered to abjure their faith or leave the country. They elected the second course, and by the end of the year 800 exiles had gone over into Switzerland.

2. The 18th century.—During the remainder of the century, until Piedmont felt the effect of the French Revolution, the Waldenses had no eventful experiences. Though guaranteed rights of religious liberty, they suffered from time to time from exactions and restrictions by the Government, which showed that they were only allowed to exist on sufferance; and, when they complained against local acts of injustice, their complaints met with little consideration. Thus in 1733 a decree was issued forbidding them to leave their valleys; in 1740 a hospice was founded at Pignerol for the education of Waldensian children; in 1748 a bishop was appointed there to work for their conversion to Rome, and the *Opera dei prestiti* which exists in the present day was then founded, in order to assist Roman Catholics to buy land from the Waldenses; in 1756 they were forbidden to hold meetings outside the temples; kidnapping of children was a common and growing practice. Gay reprints an elaborate document entitled *Compendio degli edditti concernenti i Valdesi*, containing a host of vexations, enactions, and restrictions which emanated from the senate.[1] Meanwhile, in common with Protestantism throughout the rest of Europe, the religion of the Waldenses now suffered from decline of spiritual vigour. The Arian movement in England affected some of the pastors, and after that the Continental 'rationalism.' During this period they received pecuniary help from Holland and from England under encouragement from George II. and George III.

3. Period of the Revolution.—The Revolution brought an interval of complete religious liberty to the Waldenses owing to the French Republic being established in Piedmont in 1798. On 19th December all civil government authority over the Church was abolished; on 31st December liberty and equality were proclaimed for all kinds of religion, and early in the new year absolute liberty of the press and the abolition of the Inquisition. The Waldenses were unavoidably mixed up with the war of the Revolution when the absence of Napoleon in Egypt enabled the Russians and Austrians to invade Piedmont. After at first siding with the French, to whom

[1] *Hist. des Vaudois*, pp. 152–155.

they owed their liberty, the Protestant mountaineers, driven into a corner, gave the allies a pledge of neutrality. In spite of this agreement, the Austrians availed themselves of the military opportunity to involve the Waldenses in trouble on charges of plotting and collusion with the French and on other accusations. These vexatious proceedings, however, do not justify Gay in describing the action of the Austrians as 'a crusade' against them.[1] During the three and a half years when Lombardy and Piedmont were governed as a republic the chief grievance of the Waldenses was their pastors' loss of pecuniary aid from England owing to their association with the French. But, on receiving a petition from 'the Table'—their central governing body—for assistance, the executive commission issued a decree reducing the Roman Catholic parishes from 28 to 13 and granting the revenues of the suppressed parishes to the Waldensian pastors, and by this means half their salaries were secured. Thus the Church now obtained support from State funds. The valleys had taken over the administration of national property. But, after the establishment of the French Empire, Napoleon issued a decree sequestrating this property and so depriving the pastors of the contributions which they had received from them during four years (25th March 1805). The following May, however, when the emperor was at Turin, he granted 'the Table' an audience, when he treated its members very graciously and invited them to present to him a statement of their wishes. Accordingly an open-air meeting was held at St. Jean, which drew up a petition on three points: (1) the grievance of the sequestration of the State funds out of which the pastors' salaries had been made up after the loss of aid from abroad; (2) a request for the application of the Organic law of the Reformed Churches of France to the valleys; (3) a plan or organization for grouping the parishes in five consistorials.[2] In reply Napoleon agreed to restore the sequestrated funds and to allow three consistorials in the valleys. The cringing flattery with which the emperor was approached in this matter, and the painful anxiety shown about the recovery of money grants, do not reflect much credit on the representatives of the heroic Church of Leger and Arnauld and its stand for religious liberty. A further mark of Government favour is seen in the grant of land for the erection of the temple at St. Jean, the Waldensian cathedral, which was dedicated with great *éclat* on 1st Nov. 1806.

4. 19th cent. vicissitudes.—During the first half of the 19th cent. the Waldensian Church passed through great vicissitudes of fortune. For 34 years, from the fall of Napoleon in 1814 till the Revolution of 1848, it was oppressed under the rule of the king of Sardinia, who actively espoused the papal cause. On Victor Emmanuel I. coming to the throne, the Waldenses of Piedmont sent to Turin a deputation, which had an audience with the king, but obtained no response at the time. Meanwhile the Jesuits had been put in charge of education. The State funds which Napoleon had allowed the pastors to resume were again withdrawn; the only mitigation of the hardship against which the Table protested was a partial remission of dues from the valleys. Charles Felix (1821–31) was much more severe. When the Table asked for an audience at his accession, he insolently answered that all they needed was to become Catholics. It was only after repeated appeals that they were allowed to hold a synod. When the Waldenses reopened their college at La Torre, they were peremptorily ordered to close it again. Charles Albert (1831–48) was also severely re-

[1] P. 164. [2] Gay, p. 171.

pressive with the Waldenses till near the end of his reign. Charvay, whom the king appointed bishop of Pignerol in 1835, announced that all the old laws against them should be enforced. When the English ambassador interceded on their behalf, the king ordered them not to appeal to foreigners and forbade the coming of alien visitors among them. All along they were excluded from the universities, the learned professions, and commissions in the army. But at length, even before the Revolution of 1848, the current of European opinion was running so strongly in favour of religious liberty that Charles Albert abandoned his harsh treatment of the Waldenses. On 5th January of that year he granted an audience to the Table, which gratefully acknowledged the legislative reforms and removal of hard enactments he was granting to all his subjects, but which at the same time appealed for relief from the laws especially adverse to their Church. They were well received, and on 17th February the king issued an edict of emancipation, granting the Waldenses the full civil and religious rites enjoyed by other subjects, including access to the public schools and universities, and allowing them to give their Protestant religious teaching in their own schools. The good news was welcomed in the valleys with illuminations and bonfires. A Waldensian congregation was now formed at Turin, and it became a home for refugee Protestants from all parts of Italy. In 1854 there was a division owing to the objection of these refugees to come under the government of the Table and its old rigorous rules. The use of the French language in the services was another ground of complaint. The division spread to other congregations, in which we may regard the malcontents as liberalizers and progressives, and also as protestant Italian patriots in their desire for the use of the Italian language just when a new spirit of a united Italian patriotism was sweeping the country. The result was a split, and the formation of the 'Free Church' (Chiesa Libera) of which Luigi Desanctis, a learned and eloquent priest and theologian of the Inquisition at Malta, who had become a convert to Protestantism, was leader. After serving as pastor of this church for ten years he left it, owing to its adoption of J. N. Darby's views—the Plymouth Brethren position, which allows of no stated ministry—rejoined the Waldenses, and became their professor of theology at Florence and the editor of their journal, *Eco della Verita*, till his death in 1869. The chief leader of the Free Church, after Desanctis had left it, was Alessandro Gavazzi, an ex-Barnabite father from Naples, who subsequently became an eloquent hero of Italian emancipation, accompanying Garibaldi as his chaplain and also enthusiastically supporting Victor Emmanuel as 'the only saviour of Italy as Jesus Christ is the only Saviour of sinners.' In 1870 a general assembly of the Free Church was held at Milan, when a simple Biblical confession of faith was drawn up, and the next year another assembly at Florence adopted rules of a constitution recognizing the pastoral office—as against the Plymouth Brethren idea—arranging for annual assemblies, and appointing an evangelization committee. It now took the title 'Unione della chiesa libera in Italia.' Some of the congregations, still adhering to Darby's views, broke off from this body and formed themselves into a community, which they ventured to designate simply 'Chiesa Christiana.' On 1st May 1884, with the exception of these people, the various evangelical congregations in Italy inaugurated an annual evangelical conference with a view to Church unification. Owing to the Baptists and the Methodists not altogether agreeing with the position taken up by the Waldenses and the Free Church, the two latter bodies took their own course for coming together on condition that the Free Church adopted the confession and Church order of the Waldenses.

5. Present condition.—The following facts concerning the present condition of the Waldensian Church have been supplied by the Moderator, Signor Ernesto Giampiccoli.

This Church holds its old position in the Alpine valleys, and since 1848 (the year of liberation) it has spread throughout the Peninsula and the Islands. There are now more than 200 towns and villages outside the original valleys where congregations, large or small, have been formed. The full membership of the whole Church amounts to about 25,000; but there is a much larger number of adherents. For their training the ministers spend three years in the theological college at Florence (which is soon to be transferred to Rome) and at least one more year in a foreign university. They are ordained at the annual Synod in Torre Pellice. The Waldensian Church is in the Alliance of Reformed Churches of the Presbyterian order. Besides its mission work in Italy, it has missionaries working in Africa in connexion with the Missions évangéliques de Paris, and also in connexion with the Swedish missions. It maintains four high schools for boys and girls—the only Protestant high schools recognized by the Government — also hospitals, orphanages, and other benevolent institutions. The Waldensian Church is absolutely independent of the State, and it enjoys complete liberty in all branches of its activity. The worship is in the main the same as in the kindred Evangelical Churches of France and Switzerland, the liturgies being almost identical; but there is a tendency to introduce congregational responses in the morning service. Neither the narrower type of Calvinism nor advanced liberalism is to be found in the present teaching of the Church, which is what is commonly known as 'Evangelical.' This Church is still progressing, though slowly. It always has been and still is hampered with financial difficulties, although it receives assistance from abroad and the contributions of its own members are increasing.

LITERATURE.—Among original sources the principal are A. Muston, *Israël des Alpes*, Paris, 1851; J. H. Todd, *The Books of the Vaudois preserved in Trinity College, Dublin*, London, 1865; J. P. Perrin, *Hist. des chrestiens Albigeois*, Geneva, 1618, *Hist. des Vaudois*, do. 1619; J. Leger, *Hist. générale des églises évangéliques de Piémont, ou Vaudoises*, Leyden, 1669; S. Morland, *The Hist. of the Evangelical Churches of the Valleys of Piedmont*, London, 1658; H. Arnaud, *Hist. de la glorieuse rentrée des Vaudois dans leur vallées*, Paris, 1710, Eng. tr., London, 1827. Among later works are W. S. Gilly, *Waldensian Researches during a Second Visit to the Vaudois of Piemont*, London, 1831; A. Blair, *A Hist. of the Waldenses*, 2 vols., Edinburgh, 1833; W. Beattie, *The Waldenses*, London, 1838; A. Monastier, *Hist. de l'église vaudois . . . jusqu'à nos jours*, 2 vols., Paris, 1847, Eng. tr., London, 1848; J. A. Wylie, *Hist. of the Waldenses*, London, 1880 (a good popular account). But all these books belong to the precritical period. The critical history begins with Döllinger and Comba: J. J. I. von Döllinger, *Beiträge zur Sektengeschichte des Mittelalters*, ii., Munich, 1890; Émile Comba, *Hist. des Vaudois*, new ed., Paris, 1898; T. Gay, *Hist. des Vaudois, refaite d'après les plus récentes recherches*, do. 1912; T. de Cauzons, *Les Vaudois et l'Inquisition*, do. 1908.

WALTER F. ADENEY.

WANG YANG-MING. — Wang Yang-ming (A.D. 1472–1529), known also as Wang Shou-jen, Wang-shen, Wang Peh-an, and Wang Wen-ch'eng, was a Chinese statesman, strategist, reformer, and scholar of note during the Ming dynasty, specifically during the reigns of Hung Chih, Cheng Te, and Chia Ching. Like many other Orientals who had posthumous honours conferred upon them, Wang has had hero-stories associated with his career. In early youth he began to exhibit unusual ability as a student. At twelve he is reported to have made inquiry of his teacher concerning the most important thing in life. When the latter said, 'Study to become a Chinshih' (an academic degree of about the same rank as the Ph.D.), Wang replied, 'Study to become a sage: that is the first and greatest occupation.' At twenty-one he was decorated with the degree of Chüjen; at twenty-eight he was made Chinshih; and a little later he received the highest academic honour the Government could bestow, the degree of Hanlin.

Having unjustly incurred the hostility of the eunuch Liu Tsing when he was thirty-five, he was sent as a disgraced official into the Government dispatch service in the province of Kweichow. His biographer describes Lungch'ang, where he was stationed, as a resort of venomous snakes and poisonous worms, inhabited by babbling barbarians with whom he could not converse. It was a critical situation: in suspense over his own fate, realizing that at any moment a decree from the capital might order his death, he found his followers one by one falling ill. Nothing daunted, he chopped wood, carried water, and made soft-boiled rice for them, cheering them with songs and stories of home. In view of his own precarious position, he had a sarcophagus made for himself. In the midst of these adversities the chief subject of his meditation was the conduct of a sage under similar circumstances. One night at midnight the great enlightenment came, and suddenly he realized what the sage meant by 'investigating things for the sake of extending knowledge to the utmost.' Overjoyed, he unconsciously called out, and, arising from his couch, paced the floor. 'I was wrong,' he said, 'in looking for fundamental principles in things and affairs. My nature is sufficient to solve all the problems of existence.' From that time on he was a faithful defender of idealism in opposition to the realism of the philosopher Chu, whose commentaries, then as now, were esteemed the final authority.[1]

At the age of thirty-nine Wang was restored to honour and promoted to the magistracy in Lulinghsien in Shansi. As time passed he held numerous positions of trust and honour in the Government. He was President of the Court of Ceremonies, Military Governor of Kiangsi, first assistant to the President of the Censorate, President of the Board of War at Nanking, Viceroy of Kwangtung, Kwangsi, Kiangsi, Hunan, and Hupeh, and was made Earl of Hsinchien with the title of 'Master of the Banqueting Office and Pillar of the Government.'

His greatest military campaign was undoubtedly conducted while he was Military Governor of Kiangsi, against the rebellious Prince Ch'en Hao (Prince Ning), who, it was feared, might utilize the down-river current and invade the capital. Wang first sent up several memorials advising the emperor of the rebellion; then by a series of subterfuges he misled the rebellious prince, finally engaging him in battle near Poyang Lake at Huangchiatu and Patzunao, and taking him prisoner of war. His success aroused the jealousy of several officials, to which we may ascribe the fact that his philosophic point of view was attacked and branded as heterodox.

It was not, however, as strategist and statesman that Wang made his largest contribution to human welfare, but rather as a great moral reformer, who may justly be ranked with Socrates in his appreciation of moral values and his emphasis upon fullness of life and moral integrity as of far more worth than fame or gain. He found himself intellectually fettered by a conventional interpretation of classic literature which was just as firmly fixed and as rigidly observed as the most hallowed religious traditions of any other Oriental civilization. He insisted upon a rationalization of the interpretation of the Four Books and the Five Classics that would give room for progressive adjustment. The highest values of life, he held, are realized only through development; apart from development life must prove a miserable failure. That he lacked the modern scientific approach to the problem does not detract from the fact that he had a glimpse of the developmental character of human institutions, and that this standpoint will invariably result in moral progress, if it is thoroughly assimilated.

[1] See art. PHILOSOPHY (Chinese), § 4.

When, at the time of his enlightenment, he gave utterance to the dictum, 'My nature is sufficient,' he laid the foundation upon which the entire structure of his philosophy and ethics rests: man's mind holds the key to all the problems of the universe. Nature—or experience, as we would call it—is the stuff out of which the universe is made. If nature at large is the macrocosm, then human nature is the microcosm; and for Wang human nature was the human mind.

Pointing to the flowers and trees on a cliff, a friend one day said to him: 'You hold that there is nothing under heaven outside the mind. What relation exists between my mind and these flowers and trees on the high mountain?' Wang replied: 'When you cease regarding these flowers, they become quiet with your mind, and when you see them, their colours at once become clear. From this you may know that these flowers are not external to your mind.'

This is undisguised idealism in which the microcosm creates as truly as the macrocosm. In the great all-pervading unity of nature the most differentiated and highly specialized portion is the human mind. It manifests the only creative ability within the reach of man's knowledge. Wang asserted again and again that the mind is natural law, and as such is the embodiment of the principles of Heaven.

The ground-pattern of his philosophy may be summarized as follows.

(1) Every individual may understand the fundamental principles of life and of things, including moral laws, by learning to understand his own mind, and by developing his own nature. This means that it is not necessary to use the criteria of the past as present-day standards. Each individual has the solution of the problems of the universe within himself.

(2) On the practical side, every one is under obligation to keep knowledge and action, theory and practice together; for the former is so intimately related to the latter that its very existence is involved. There can be no real knowledge without action. The individual has the spring of accurate knowledge within his own nature, and should constantly carry into practice the things that his intuitive knowledge of good gives him opportunity to do.

(3) Heaven, earth, man, all things, are an all-pervading unity. The universe is the macrocosm, and each human mind is a microcosm. This naturally leads to the conceptions liberty and equality of opportunity, and serves well as the fundamental principle of social activity and reform.

Wang's philosophy is to-day held in high esteem by Japanese students and is being extensively read by the Chinese. His system is a direct product of the Oriental mind; as a rationalizing and socializing force it strikes a sympathetic chord in China and Japan.

During the last days of his life the charge of heterodoxy was frequently brought against him. At his death no hereditary honours were conferred upon him, but instead an order from the emperor prohibited the dissemination of the 'false doctrine.' However, in the first year of the emperor Lung Ch'in he was by imperial order made Marquis of Hsinchien and given the posthumous title of Wench'eng ('Perfect Learning'). In the twelfth year of the emperor Wan Li an imperial order was issued to sacrifice to Wang in the Confucian temple, after sacrificing to Confucius. In the city of Yüyao, Chekiang, Wang's ancestral home, an image of the great teacher has been erected in a small temple on a hill.

LITERATURE.—The chief Chinese sources are the works of Wang Yang-ming, which may be secured from the Commercial

Press, Shanghai. See also F. G. Henke, *The Philosophy of Wang Yang-ming* (tr. from the Chinese). Chicago, 1916, 'The Philosophy of Wang Yang-ming,' *JRAS, North China Branch*, xliv. [1913] 46-64, 'The Moral Development of the Chinese,' *The Popular Science Monthly*, lxxxvii. [1915] 78-89, 'Wang Yang-ming, a Chinese Idealist,' *The Monist*, xxiv. [1914] 17-34; Paul S. Reinsch, *Intellectual and Political Currents in the Far East*, New York, 1911, Index.

FREDERICK G. HENKE.

WAR.—Human warfare is not merely the climax and the symbol of the strife which pervades the realm of nature: it is itself an institution which has been involved in the struggle for existence, and which has had to adapt itself to a changing environment. The institution is rooted in a deep instinct and an inveterate habit of the race; but it has also come into conflict with powerful forces, emanating from the intellectual, the moral, and the religious life of mankind, which have been bold enough to summon it to judgment, have had considerable success in regulating its violence, and have proposed and attempted various methods for its abolition. The present article will trace the impression made upon war by morality and religion, examine the spiritual issues to which it gives rise, and discuss the desirability and the possibility of the cessation of armed conflict among the nations.

I. *NAME AND DEFINITION.*—The term 'war' is popularly applied to any conflict between nations, communities, or other large social groups in which violence is used for the settlement of a quarrel. Cicero defines it as 'genus decertandi per vim' in distinction from the method of argumentation (*disceptatio*).[1] In ethical discussion it has been defined as 'conflictus multorum contra multos extraneos': it is not a state of general antagonism, but a conflict in which matters are forced to an issue; it is the affair of many or of masses, and the name may not lightly be used to dignify sedition.[2] In legal definitions the term has been limited to conflicts in which the belligerents are states, or at least combinations which can reasonably claim a higher status than bands of rioters or brigands.

'War is a contest carried on by public force between states, or between states and communities having with regard to the contest the rights of states.'[3]

The aspects of war on which the genius of language fixed in its coinage of words may still to some extent be recognized.

(*a*) *Approach and assault.*—Πόλεμος, from root *pel*, akin to πέλας, πλησίον (perh. *pello*), seems to express the idea of going at, or 'going for.'[4] πλήσσω, *plango*, may be from the same root. 'Battle,' O.Fr. *bataille*, L.L. *battualia*, from root *bhâ*, 'to smite,' with Celtic cognates, recalls the blows and the clash of arms.[5]

(*b*) *A contest between two adversaries.*—*Bellum* is commonly explained from the alternative form *duellium* as the quarrel which it takes two to make—'quod duabus partibus de victoria contendentibus dimicatur.'[6]

(*c*) *An intense effort.*—*Krieg*, O.H.G. *Kreg*, *Kric*, *Kriec*, laid stress on the excited and strenuous exertion, and later on the gain which resulted.[7] O.H.G. *Wic*, with derivatives, seems to have had the same primary and secondary meanings.

(*d*) *Confusion and tumult.*—The word 'war,' late A.S. *werre*, O.H.G. *Werra*, L.L. *werra*, Fr. *guerre*, if connected (as commonly) with *wirr*, *verwirren*, may have sprung from the observation that 'every battle of the warrior is with confused noise' (Is 9[5] AV), or that war upsets the general order of things. The root may, however, be *ver*, preserved in *Wehr*, *wehren*, weir, beware, guard (cf. *vereor*), when the term would be an illustration of the habitual apologetic tendency to attribute to all wars the character of self-defence.

(*e*) *Organized movement.*—Heb. מִלְחָמָה, from root לחם, 'to set in order,' draws attention to the ordered action of the battle array.

(*f*) *The fateful plight.*—A.S. *or-lege*, O.H.G. *Or-loge*, Dan. *or-log*, may reflect the fatalistic mood which is fostered in war, or the common experience that nowhere else is man so surely in the hand of God and so little certain that he can himself control the issue. This interpretation has been supported by connecting the verbal group with the Norns, the Moirai or Parcæ of the North.[1]

II. *THE PREVALENCE OF WAR.*—War has been one of the most constant and distinctive features of human history, and it may even be thought to be a sinister peculiarity of the human species that hordes should pursue hordes of the same kind with a persistent purpose of rapine and destruction.

The pre-historic age, which extends over tens of thousands of years down to about 5000 B.C., enjoys a fairly pacific reputation. If it was usually raining, as Ratzel puts it, the age was at least free from the thunderstorm and the devastating floods of war.[2] Man being the *animal inerme*, furnished by nature with no more formidable weapons than fists and teeth, he was too much preoccupied by his designs on the beasts, and by theirs against himself, to meddle much with his own species except when rival claims emerged over a hunting-ground, or at a later stage over pastures and wells (Gn 13[7f.] 26[19f.]).

'Pastoral man,' it is observed, 'hardly needs tools, or weapons either, for it is to the common interest of pastorals to range apart, and on the steppe there is room enough for all.'[3] 'It is doubtful,' it is added, 'if serious war was known in Europe until the Bronze Age was established.'[4]

Historic times have their landmarks in the rise, the conquests, and the fall of great military states. In the period of Oriental antiquity martial races moulded the history of China and India. Further west, and in the central current of history, arose the powers of Egypt and Mesopotamia, which during thousands of years engaged in an ever-renewed struggle for supremacy, while in the intervals Mesopotamia was the scene of a fierce and prolonged conflict, waged with alternating success, between the rival peoples of Babylonia and Assyria. From these centres of empire there also proceeded frequent campaigns against sedentary or migratory peoples which raised a threatening front in Western Asia, or which tempted warlike kings by prospects of sovereignty and spoils. In the end Assyria was overthrown by Babylonia, Babylonia by the Persians, and a Persian empire entered on its course with a similar programme of conquest and tribute that brought it into collision with Greece.

In the age of classical antiquity, when the scene shifted to the Mediterranean, and the Greeks and Romans assumed the chief rôle, war continued, notwithstanding the growing culture, to be regarded as the most honourable and almost the most urgent of human pursuits. Men had now iron weapons in their hands, and the Aryans had arrived on the central European stage to show how effectively they could be used. The Greeks made their advent as barbarian conquerors from the north, who served themselves heirs to an older civilization that had developed its powers and accumulated its treasures in the Levant. Thereafter they went on fighting with little intermission —against the Trojans, as they said, for Helen of the glorious tresses and for honour, but doubtless also with an eye to dominion and the wealth of Anatolia, against the Persians in maintenance of their racial independence, against one another from cupidity, ambition, or jealousy; while even in their exhaustion they could claim for Greek arms a considerable share in the conquests of Alexander the Great, and in the creation of his grandiose but short-lived empire. In the meantime the Romans, dug from the same pit, and similarly equipped, gradually made themselves masters of Italy, settled the long-drawn and hard-

---

[1] *De Offic.* i. 11.
[2] E. Elbel, *Theologia Moralis*, Paderborn, 1891, ii. 50.
[3] T. J. Lawrence, *The Principles of International Law*[4], London, 1910, p. 331.
[4] G. Curtius, *Grundzüge der griech. Etymologie*[4], Leipzig, 1873.
[5] A. Fick, *Vergleichendes Wörterbuch der indogerman. Sprachen*, Göttingen, 1890-1909.
[6] Festus the Grammarian. [7] Fick, art. 'Kreiga.'

[1] J. Grimm, *Deutsche Mythologie*, Göttingen, 1841.
[2] *Die Erde und das Leben*, Leipzig, 1902, ii. 672.
[3] J. L. Myres, *The Dawn of History*, London, 1911, p. 18.
[4] C. F. Scott Elliot, *Prehistoric Man and his Story*, London, 1915, ch. xxvi. 'War and Iron.'

fought issue between the Semites and the Aryans through their victory over Carthage in the Punic Wars; and by the beginning of our era, notwithstanding the distractions of civil broils, they had subjugated and embraced within their empire a great part of the known territories of the three continents. Under the Roman emperors it seemed for two or three centuries as if the curse of war had wrought its own cure, and the world had been saved by the sword from the sword, but the hope was short-lived, and the Pax Romana proved to be only a lull that heralded more furious storms.

The period of antiquity came to a catastrophic end, and the Middle Ages were ushered in by the Teutonic migrations, which reduced the Roman empire to ruins, and gave new masters, with a fresh deposit of population, to its richest and fairest provinces. The outcome was that for the next ten centuries Europe was afflicted by wars of every known kind—between imperial dynasties like the Carolingian and peoples which repudiated their sway; between the new-born nations as in the Hundred Years' War of England and France; between rival claimants to a throne, as in the English Wars of the Roses; between the central authority as represented by a king and feudal aristocracies which magnified regional and particular interests; between the governing classes and oppressed populations which sought redress or revenge in social war. Religion supplied additional motives and occasions. In the early Middle Ages the armies of Islām penetrated into the heart of Europe, and at a later date Christendom retaliated in prolonged and sanguinary Crusades for the recovery of the Holy Sepulchre.

The modern age, dating from the beginning of the 16th cent., has perhaps had more intervals of repose, but it has found evil compensation in the magnitude of the struggles and the destructiveness of the operations. Instinct and tradition disposed the European rulers to seek an extension of their dominions whenever opportunity arose, while the discovery of the new world offered to the possessors of sea-power the prospect of unlimited aggrandisement and wealth. The possibilities of effective warfare were also enormously increased, in the centuries that followed the invention of gunpowder, by the enlistment of science in the improvement of the instruments of destruction. During the last four hundred years the outstanding fact in the political history of Europe was that one great power after another—Austria, Spain, France, Germany—sought to become the master of the Continent, while at each stage the nations which felt themselves threatened formed combinations which should be strong enough to frustrate, and which also deemed it prudent to anticipate, the development of ambitious and aggressive schemes. The programme of Britain was to rule the seas, and to avert a European hegemony. The result was that almost every generation witnessed a European war of the first magnitude—among them the Thirty Years' War, the War of the Spanish Succession, the War of the Austrian Succession, the Napoleonic Wars, and finally the World War of 1914–18, which has cost Europe the lives of 10,000,000 picked men, decimated wide areas of Europe by famine and disease, swallowed up one-third of the accumulated wealth, and shaken to its foundations the moral order no less than the economic fabric of society. The peace of the modern world has also been disturbed by the ferment due to the assertion of the ideals of democracy and nationality in opposition to the arrangements of an existing order. The democratic cause has its military monuments in the English Civil War of the 17th cent., and in campaigns of the French Revolution, but for the most part it has pursued its triumphant progress without the necessity of sanguinary, or at least of prolonged, fighting. The spirit of nationality, which developed in the 19th cent. with extraordinary fervour, promoted war in several ways. On the one hand, it claimed independent sovereignty for populations which could establish a claim to nationhood on physical or historical grounds, and thus came into collision with existing imperial structures, giving rise to wars of emancipation such as those which liberated the Greeks and the Balkan peoples from the rule of the Turks, and the convulsions which have dissolved the heterogeneous Austrian empire. On the other hand, the national spirit fosters the ideal of the consolidation of separated kinsfolk in a single state, and this aspiration dictated the mid-century policy of Prussia which achieved the desired unification of the German people through the Austro-Prussian campaign of 1866 and the Franco-German War of 1870. Imperial ambitions also proved to be a natural sequel to the fulfilment of national aspirations. Within the great realms trouble has arisen, apart from any racial antithesis, in connexion with the respective rights of a central authority and of the subordinate members: in the 18th cent. the American colonies, in assertion of colonial rights against imperial claims, fought the American War of Independence; in the 19th cent. the Southern States of the Union affirmed the indestructible rights of particular states in opposition to the prerogatives of an indestructible Federation, and the matter was brought to an arbitrament in the American Civil War. Finally, the modern world has had grave warning that, if the religious war is obsolete, religious enthusiasm has been replaced by a more violent fanaticism rooted in political and social ideals, as was evidenced in some of the phases of the French Revolution and most recently in the spirit and the efforts of Soviet Russia.

III. *The causes of war.*—War is traceable to elemental desires and passions of human nature. According to Hobbes, its threefold root is the desire of gain, the fear of injury, and the love of glory.

> 'In the nature of man, we find three principal causes of quarrel. First, competition; secondly, diffidence; thirdly, glory.
>
> The first, maketh men invade for gain; the second, for safety; and the third, for reputation. The first use violence, to make themselves masters of other men's persons, wives, children, and cattle; the second, to defend them; the third, . . . for any sign of undervalue, either direct in their persons, or by reflection in their kindred, their friends, their nation, their profession, or their name.'[1]

This analysis is useful, but it unduly simplifies the psychological problem.

(1) The desire for gain, in the narrower sense intended by Hobbes, has doubtless supplied the principal impulse to warlike aggression. Territory, with the attendant booty of various kinds, has been the usual stake in war, coveted alike by peoples and by dynasties. At the same time cupidity in the matter of territory has often been associated with other motives involving lesser degrees of culpability, and even trenching on the realm of the virtues. Account has justly to be taken of the frequent play of fairly reputable reasons—as the pressure of famine or scarcity, resulting from drought or the increase of population, the defence and development of trading interests as vital to the subsistence of a commercial nation, the migratory impulse, the spirit of adventure, and also the consciousness of a mission to develop waste or neglected regions of the globe, and to conquer and take charge of people for their own good.

(2) The fear of injury, as well as the resentment due to actual injury, has unfailingly prompted to defensive war when resistance was possible, and

[1] *Works*, London, 1839, iii. 'Leviathan,' p. 112.

often when it might well be deemed hopeless. The interests which nations have usually been prepared to defend at all costs are, in addition to their territory, their jurisdiction and their honour. It has also been commonly accepted that a palpable and growing threat to these interests justifies a nation in seizing a propitious opportunity for an anticipatory or preventive war.

(3) The desire of glory has in the main been a dominant motive of the great conquerors and of their armies, but it has also taken possession of peoples. Apart from such ambition, indignation at a national insult has proved to be capable of evoking the utmost effort and self-sacrifice.

(4) The desire of power is an additional motive which cannot be entirely resolved into cupidity. It is true that power may be sought as the means of appropriating territory and increasing the wealth of a people, but nations as well as individuals find satisfaction in the exercise of power as an end in itself. This desire manifests itself positively in the attempt of a nation or class to acquire dominion over others. The love of power for its own sake has been an important factor in the movements which established the great empires of history, and it has been not less conspicuous in struggles for the supremacy among allied states—as illustrated in the ancient rivalry of Athens and Sparta, and in the modern contest of the German principalities which issued in the hegemony of Prussia. It has also supplied much of its energy to civil strife, and on occasion has kindled the flames of civil war. The desire of power comes into collision with the spirit of liberty. The demand for liberation is the natural response to the policy of domination, being rooted in the same appreciation of power; and, as the assertion and extension of the power of one nation or class presupposes the abridgment of the power of another, a system of imperial rule or of autocratic government involves the permanent possibility of wars directed to the achievement of national independence or of political revolution.

(5) The passions of hatred and revenge have also furnished a relatively independent motive. A nation can take up an attitude that is on a still lower plane than brutal selfishness; it can become inspired by a hatred of the diabolic kind which makes it disregard even the counsels of self-interest for the satisfaction of inflicting deadly injury on a loathed enemy. The spirit of hatred has sometimes been engendered by centuries of conflict or oppression, sometimes it has had its spring in deep-seated differences of racial character and culture.

(6) Finally, a religious zeal which can no more be resolved into self-interest than hatred has been the cause, and not merely the pretext, of many wars. Zeal for the glory of God at least co-operated with lust of booty to inspire the onslaughts of Islām, and it blended with the spirit of adventure in the Christian Crusades.

IV. *THE REACTION AGAINST WAR.*—The most general explanation of war is that men and nations have a legitimate desire for the goods of wealth, honour, and power, and that they are tempted to grasp them by force instead of earning wealth by labour, and honour and power by service. Human nature, however, embodies other principles to which this peculiar method of acquisition, with its inevitably cruel accompaniments, has constituted a challenge, and which have reacted against it in varying degrees of criticism and opposition. The complex constitution of man exhibits along with his ingrained selfishness a vigorous sense of justice and a lively capacity of sympathy; and at least one of the belligerents must usually have been conscious of a gross violation of his sense of justice, while the butchery and the atrocities attending the stricken field and the sack of a city, when reviewed in cold blood, must often have excited the commiseration even of the conquerors. The general conscience, accordingly, from an early date, pressed for a certain ethical regulation of the occasions and of the practices of war. The great religions strongly supported the ethical plea. At the animistic stage, it is true, religion was practically indifferent to moral considerations, but the faiths which captured the mind of Asia and Europe were agreed in representing it as normally a part of religion to do justly and to love mercy even in the waging of war. Philosophy, with its distinctive appeal to rational considerations, has also contributed to foster and diffuse critical and reforming opinion through its disciplines of Moral Philosophy and Jurisprudence. The theoretical work was followed up in the 19th cent. by international conventions and conferences which established a fairly authoritative code of International Law.

The moral reaction against war has culminated from time to time in the assertion that war is essentially immoral, and in the repudiation of any traffic with it, in any cause whatsoever, as an unworthy compromise. It will be convenient to deal first with this radical position, which is supported by a considerable show of moral authority, before proceeding to trace the influence of religion and morality in the discrimination of just and unjust wars and in the humanization of the conduct of war.

V. *THE LAWFULNESS OF WAR.*—There have doubtless been men in all ages who have objected to war, and refused to have any hand in fighting. They could be determined to this attitude either by sheer cowardice, or by counsels of prudence natural to a difficult or desperate situation, or again by the conviction that the shedding of human blood was a criminal outrage, and in any case a futile way of attempting to oppose and prevent wrong-doing. At the risk of their principle being mistaken for cowardice, voices have been raised on the heights of moral idealism in absolute condemnation of war and all its works.

i. THE RELIGIOUS JUDGMENT.—1. **The older religions.**—While the Vedas are sufficiently warlike, and Brāhmanism gives a consecration to the military caste, the mild spirit of Hindu religion tended to view war under the repugnant aspect of murder.

> 'Alas! we are engaged in committing a heinous sin, seeing that we are making efforts for killing our own kinsmen out of greed of the pleasures of sovereignty. If the sons of Dhritarâshtra, weapon in hand, should kill me in battle, me weaponless and not defending (myself), that would be better for me.' [1]

The influence of Buddhism was cast on the same side.

> 'If you desire to honour Buddha,' said a Brāhman who successfully mediated between two belligerents, 'follow the example of his patience and long-suffering.' 'Conquer your foe by force, you increase his enmity; conquer by love, and you will reap no after-sorrow.' [2]

The teaching of the OT prophets contains a decided pacifist strain. They condemned wars of aggression as magnified schemes of murder and plunder, and they were disposed to think defensive wars useless or unnecessary—useless, since a wicked nation would not escape punishment; unnecessary, since a righteous or repentant nation might safely dispense with armaments, and look for protection to the omnipotent Ruler of history (Is 31$^{1.\,5.\,8}$). It may, however, be questioned whether the prophetic attitude meant more than that non-resistance was the duty of Israel in the special circumstances of the situation and time (Jer 28$^{12ff.}$). The great prophets lived at a period when it was a manifest inference from the providential order of the world

1 *Bhagavad-Gītā*, *SBE* viii. [1882] 42.
2 *Life of Buddha*, *SBE* xix. [1883] 328 f.

that a pacific and submissive policy was the duty of their little border-state, and they might well have judged differently of the duty of a nation to which had been providentially entrusted a larger and more promising political mission than was open to Israel under the conditions of the 8th and 7th centuries before the Christian era.

2. The bearings of the Christian ethic.—The teaching of our Lord and of His apostles includes precepts which on a first impression appear to rule out all traffic with war as inconsistent with the moral ideal. Not only is there a law of love, which condemns the passions that incite to aggression, but there is a law of meekness, expressed in non-resistance, which suffers the aggressor to work his evil will.

'Ye have heard that it was said, An eye for an eye, and a tooth for a tooth: but I say unto you, Resist not him that is evil: but whosoever smiteth thee on thy right cheek, turn to him the other also. And if any man would go to law with thee, and take away thy coat, let him have thy cloke also' (Mt 5^{38-40} RV). 'Ye have heard that it was said, Thou shalt love thy neighbour, and hate thine enemy. But I say unto you, Love your enemies, bless them that curse you, do good to them that hate you, and pray for them which despitefully use you and persecute you' (v.$^{43ff.}$).

'Avenge not yourselves, beloved, but give place unto wrath: for it is written, Vengeance belongeth unto me, I will recompense, saith the Lord' (Ro 12^{19}).

The precepts were enforced by the example of Jesus, who 'left an example that ye should follow his steps,' and who, 'when he was reviled, reviled not again; when he suffered, he threatened not; but committed himself to him that judgeth righteously' (1 P $2^{21.\ 23}$).

As to the bearing of this teaching on the lawfulness of war, there have been two schools of Christian opinion.

(*a*) *The literalist interpretation.*—The view was widely prevalent in the early Church that war is an organized iniquity with which the Church and the followers of Christ can have nothing to do. This sentiment was expressed, though with varying degrees of lucidity and emphasis, by Justin Martyr, Tatian, Irenæus, Tertullian, Origen, Athanasius, Cyprian, and Lactantius.[1] The allusions to the subject are often casual, and the pacifist testimony sometimes does no more than affirm the undeniable position that the Church differed from the kingdoms of this world in that it cherished no schemes of conquest, equipped no military forces, and did not dream of propagating the faith, or even of resisting persecution, by armed rebellion. But the position was also definitely taken up that war as such was an institution of the realm of darkness, and some were quite emphatic that a professed Christian should not be mixed up with the foul and devilish thing.

'It is not lawful,' says Lactantius, 'for a just man to engage in warfare, since his warfare is justice itself.'[2]

The prohibition of military service was partly due to the consideration that the soldier was required to compromise his faith by participation in the pagan rites associated with Roman warfare, and to jeopardize his character by association with brutal and licentious comrades, but objection was also taken on principle to the military profession, and was supported by arguments such as these—that the military oath was inconsistent with the pledge of loyalty to Christ, that Christ had warned His disciples against taking the sword (Mt 26^{52}), that, if the lesser strife of litigation be forbidden, much more is the greater (1 Co 6^{7}), that, if it be unlawful to fight on our own behalf, it is also unlawful to fight in the quarrels of others,[3] and especially that in war men fight to kill, and that intentional killing is murder.[4] The last consideration so impressed the general ecclesiastical mind that certain canons of the period excluded a soldier from the Lord's Table till penance had been done for the blood that had been shed.[1]

The literalist view, which had its exponents throughout the Middle Ages and at the Reformation, was made a cardinal tenet of 'the people called in scorn Quakers.'

'Whoever can reconcile this, Resist not evil,' says R. Barclay, 'with, Resist evil by force; again, Give also thy other cheek, with, strike again; also, Love thine enemies, with spoil them, make a prey of them, pursue them with fire and sword; or, Pray for those that persecute you, with, persecute them by fines, imprisonment and death itself; whoever can find a means to reconcile these things, may be supposed also to have found a way to reconcile God with the Devil, Christ with Antichrist, Light with Darkness, and good with evil.'[2]

The doctrine has recently been popularized by Tolstoi, who developed it in the thoroughgoing fashion which would also sweep away the whole of the machinery by which civilized states repress and punish crime. The justification offered for war, he says, is that it seeks to repair or avert injury, while the command of Christ is that we offer no resistance to injury. The practice of war is no less inconsistent with the injunction to love our enemies. It may be objected that Jesus does not prohibit war in set terms. But 'a father who exhorts his son to live honestly, never to wrong any person, and to give all that he has to others, would not forbid his son to kill people on the highway.'[3]

(*b*) *The reasoned judgment of the Church.*—The mind of the primitive Church, so far as reflected in the NT, does not join in the unqualified condemnation of war. The Church of the apostolic age found solace in apocalyptic dreams which presupposed that the final redemption of humanity would follow upon appalling conflicts between the powers of heaven and hell, of which the Christian saints, who would be collected in a camp, would at least be sympathetic spectators (Rev 20^{9}). In any case the Epistle to the Hebrews pronounces a glowing panegyric on warrior saints of the Old Dispensation ($11^{32ff.}$), while the book of Acts welcomes Cornelius the centurion to the Christian society ($10^{1ff.}$). During the succeeding four centuries, as has been exhaustively shown by Moffatt in the article cited, the Church as a whole declined to be committed to the extreme position. From Tertullian himself we learn that there were numerous Christians in the Roman army by their own choice, and that the Church did not condemn them. Clement of Alexandria taught that the position of a soldier was governed by the Pauline principle that a man should 'abide in that calling wherein he was called.'[4] Diocletian found so many Christians in the army that he deemed it a danger to the State, and Constantine was impressed by their importance as a military asset no less than as a political influence. When Christianity became the religion of the empire, the general tendency, exemplified by Eusebius, was to support the civil power by the benediction of military service. The Council of Arles in one of its canons appears to have visited ecclesiastical censure on those who abandoned the army even in time of peace from conscientious scruples.[5] Some even thought that the sword might be drawn in a holy war for the extirpation of idolatry.[6] Ambrose eulogized the warlike courage which prefers death to bondage and disgrace, and claimed the OT

[1] For particular utterances and shades of opinion see J. Moffatt, art. 'War' in *DAC*, Edinburgh, 1918.
[2] *Div. Inst.* vi. 20.
[3] Tertullian, *de Corona*, *de Idololatria*.
[4] Basil of Cæsarea, *Ep.* 188.

[1] *Canons of Hippolytus*, 13, 14.
[2] *Theologiæ vere Christianæ Apologia*, Amsterdam, 1676, Eng. version, 1678, ch. xv.
[3] *My Religion*, Eng. tr., London, 1889, p. 101.
[4] *Protrept.* x. 100.
[5] 'De his qui arma projiciunt in pace, placuit abstineri eos a communione' (J. D. Mansi, *Sacrorum Conciliorum Collectio*, Paris, 1801 ff., ii. 471).
[6] Firmicus Maternus, *de Errore profanarum Religionum*, Migne, *PL*, xii. 1048.

warriors as spiritual ancestors. He even adopted the classical maxim that one who does not defend a friend from injury is as much at fault as he who commits the injury.[1] Augustine was forced to face the question by the havoc of the Teutonic migrations and the peril of the empire, and his active mind fully explored the subject and laid down the lines on which in the main the thought of the Churches has subsequently moved.

That war is sometimes lawful on Christian principles is maintained by Augustine on these and other grounds: (*a*) that it has been and may be waged by appointment of God;[2] (*b*) that the case of a wanton and rapacious attack by one nation on another falls under the same category as the crimes of murder and burglary, and should presumably be similarly dealt with;[3] (*c*) that John the Baptist did not require the soldiers to abandon the service, but only exhorted them to do violence to no man and be content with their wages.[4] The implications of the Sermon on the Mount are most fully discussed in the Epistle to Marcellinus, which was called forth by the pagan objection that the precepts of non-resistance were inconsistent with public policy, and would prove ruinous to the State.[5] The precept to turn the other cheek to the smiter, Augustine says, cannot be taken literally. What it requires is an inward disposition of patient good-will towards the aggressor, and it does not prescribe any uniform manifestation of the disposition in act, as appears from the fact that Jesus Himself at least protested against violence (Jn 18[23]; cf. Ac 23[3]). We ought always to cherish the spirit of clemency, and be willing to render good for evil, but 'many things have to be done in which we have to pay regard not to our own kindly inclinations but to the real interests of others, and their interests may require that they should be treated, much as they may dislike it, with a certain benignant asperity': 'Cui licentia iniquitatis eripitur, feliciter vincitur, quoniam nihil infelicius est felicitate peccantium, qua poenalis nutritur immunitas, et mala voluntas velut hostis interior roboratur.'[6] At the same time war is merely a means to the end of peace.[7] It is better and more glorious to achieve peace by peaceable means than by war.[8]

Thomas Aquinas replies as follows to objections founded on the teaching of Jesus.

(*a*) 'Jesus said that he who takes the sword shall perish by the sword.' But 'to take' means 'to use without warrant,' and the words only prohibit unauthorized or private persons from drawing the sword. (*b*) 'War is inconsistent with the command that we "resist not evil" (Matt. 5: 38) and "avenge not ourselves."' But these injunctions are fulfilled by the cultivation of a placable spirit, and cannot require us to do mischief by allowing wickedness to go unpunished. (*c*) 'If the peacemakers are blessed, war-makers are accursed.' But war may be the best or the only means of attaining the end of peace.[9]

Luther held that the gospel presupposes natural rights and duties, and vigorously defended the Christian soldier.[10] Calvin argued that war is a branch of the work of retributive justice which has been entrusted by God to the civil magistrate, and that it has the same moral justification as the police measures which protect the citizens against the criminal population.

Whether it be a king who does it on a big scale, or a scoundrel who does it on a small scale, he is equally to be regarded and punished as a robber. It is no breach of the command, 'Thou shalt not kill': the slaying of the authors of the unjust war is an execution, the judge is God, and the fighting men who defend the right are merely God's instruments. If it be objected that the NT does not expressly permit Christians to fight, it is to be observed that the NT does not undertake to legislate about civil polity, and that it presupposes the OT, in which the greatest men of God, like Moses and David, were mighty men of valour in the service of God.[11]

The topic received prominence in the leading Protestant Confessions, which found it desirable to allay any misgivings that might be felt by princes as to the political implications of evangelical religion. The modern Protestant literature of Christian Ethics[12] is in general agreement with the Roman Catholic moralists.[13]

1 *De Officiis Ministrorum*, i. 35, 40.
2 The reff. are to the Benedictine ed., *Opera*, Venice, 1729-35, *Contra Faustum*, viii. 405*e*.
3 *De Civ.* vii. 92*d*.
4 *Ep.* 138, ii. 410*b*.
5 *Ib.*
6 ii. 415*g*.
7 *Ep.* 189, 'ad Bonifacium,' ii. 699*b*.
8 *Ib.* 229, 'ad Darium,' ii. 836*d*.
9 *Summa Theol.* II. ii. qu. xl. art. i., 'Utrum bellare semper sit peccatum.'
10 *Ob Kriegsleute auch im seligen Stande sein können*, 1526.
11 *Inst. Rel. Christ.*, 1559, bk. iv. ch. xx. 10-12.
12 See esp. R. Rothe, *Theologische Ethik*[2], Wittenberg, 1867-71; H. Martensen, *Christian Ethics*, Edinburgh, 1892, div. ii.
13 Cf. Elbel, *Theol. Moralis*, ii. 'de Bello.'

The ultra-pacifist interpretation of Christian duty, while plausible, really rests on a superficial view of the ethical system of Christianity. It ignores an observation which is now a commonplace of the science of Comparative Religion, viz. that, in distinction from the nomistic religions which attempt to lay down hard-and-fast precepts prescribing the action to be taken or avoided in particular situations, the ethical scheme of Christianity consists essentially of a stock of principles, accompanied by some illustrations of how they are to be applied in practice. Had Christianity been a nomistic religion, it would have distinctly enacted that 'war is always sin,' or would have enumerated all the cases in which it is lawful; being a religion of the spirit, it bequeathed to the Christian Church, and to all others that claim the Christian name, the task of forming a Christian judgment upon a diversity of concrete questions and situations as they may arise. Again, the original Christian ethic, so far as elucidated in detail, was chiefly illustrated from the individual sphere. While the OT is mainly concerned with the nation, the NT is mainly concerned with God and the soul; and the consequence is that little was done to illustrate the application of Christian principles in the political departments of thought and action, which for the most part lay outside the purview of the primitive Church.

There are, now, besides non-resistance, two other principles, deeply embedded in the teaching of Jesus, which demand to be carefully weighed before a judgment is formed as to the lawfulness of war in the abstract or the sufficiency of a particular occasion of war. The doctrine of retributive justice, to begin with—that wickedness ought to be and will be punished—filled at least as large a space as the doctrine of non-resistance in the circle of Christ's thought. He pronounced upon Jerusalem an inevitable doom because of its obdurate blindness and disobedience (Mt 23[37ff.]), and He drew the picture of a last judgment in which the wicked and impenitent would be punished according to their works (Mt 25[31ff.]). The idea of penal retribution, moreover, is the central and inspiring thought of the apocalyptic sections of the NT, represented by eschatological discourses of Jesus (Mt 24), the Pauline Apocalypse (2 Th 2), and the book of Revelation. And, if it be a law of the universe that wickedness ought to be restrained and punished, if God Himself, while ready to forgive on condition of repentance and submission, and ever taking the initiative towards reconciliation, fights against the obdurate rebels of His dominions with all the resources of His providential order, not to speak of the menaces of apocalyptic prediction, it may well be thought incredible that Christianity has made it criminal for a nation to be a fellow-worker with God in restraining the powers of wickedness and in seeing justice done upon the earth. The ultra-pacifist school thinks fit to impose upon the nations a code of morality and a plan of procedure which, if absolutely binding, would entail grave censure on God Himself and give ground for an indictment of the methods of His government of the universe.

Further, in forming a Christian judgment as to the lawfulness of war, respect must be chiefly paid to the master-principle of the Christian ethic, which is love of man as man. It is of course evident that, if Christian charity were universal, there would be no more war, and also that, if war took place, a belligerent animated by Christian love at its highest reach would differ in vital respects from any pattern shown in history. But the essential feature of love is that it seeks the welfare of its objects, not necessarily that it seeks it by the measures suggested by easy good nature

—as is sufficiently familiar in the discipline of the family and in the social provisions of the penitentiary and the gaol. The law of love, now, has three main applications for a nation—in reference to the race as a whole, in reference to a particular enemy, and in reference to its own population; and in the face of unjust aggression the law of love may actually urge a demand for forcible resistance on a threefold ground. The interests of the race may require it: a nation is no benefactor of mankind if it does nothing to support, and even contributes to undermine, the general arrangement that the world is a realm of moral order. That the nation which checks and chastises another in a criminal enterprise is in a real sense its benefactor is supported by the contention of Plato in the *Gorgias* that it is a greater evil to commit injustice with impunity than to be punished for it, inasmuch as the wicked who go scot-free are deprived of the valuable remedial discipline of merited chastisement. Again, the Christian law of love lays special stress on what may be called duties of guardianship, which were exemplified in the attitude of Jesus towards the house of Israel, towards Jerusalem, towards little children, and towards those who were called 'his own.' And in considering the duty of a state in regard to war, it has to be remembered that, while in one point of view it is a collective personality which has to think and act as one, in another point of view it consists of those who rule and of those whose interests are committed to the trust of the rulers. It is therefore absurd to maintain that it can be a postulate of Christian morality that the rulers of a nation are under obligation, not merely to sacrifice themselves, but to take the responsibility of sacrificing others who instinctively look to them for protection, and of abandoning old men, women, and children to privations, sufferings, and moral perils. The Christian spirit was surely better interpreted in the mediæval code of chivalry.

The literalist view also overlooks a serious difficulty as to the possibility of rendering an act of national self-sacrifice of unquestionable sacrificial value. The suggestion is that, even as Christ suffered Himself to be led as a lamb to the slaughter, so a Christian people might dutifully, and with similar profit, suffer a national crucifixion; but it is forgotten that for a sacrifice there is needed a stainless as well as a willing victim, and no nation that is or has been has remotely possessed the spotless perfection, not to speak of the willing mind, which would qualify it for a literal imitation of Christ in this regard, or give promise that if attempted it would produce effects in any degree comparable with the effects of the sacrifice once offered on Calvary.

Christian thinkers have, then, to take their orders from the whole Christ and not a fragmentary Christ—from the Christ who is the expression of the complete moral purpose of God, the revelation of justice and love as well as meekness. And from this standpoint it may be maintained with a good conscience that Christianity makes room for warfare in co-operation with God in a world which teems with violence and injustice, breaks His laws, and challenges His righteous authority. But, while the principles of meekness and clemency have no title to be the sole determinant of the international relations of a Christian state, they ought to make their influence effectively felt as maxims of co-ordinate dignity and authority: they ought to have such recognition that every concession short of the impossible should be made to avert war, hatred and revenge should be ruled out from deliberation as the most dangerous and short-sighted of counsellors, magnanimity should prevail in the day of victory, and after the struggle everything should be attempted to obliterate the evil memories and to promote sincere and lasting reconciliation.

The question as to whether a Christian may lawfully bear arms is governed by the decision as to whether a nation may lawfully engage in war. Clearly it cannot be wrong to give personal assistance towards the execution of a necessary and righteous task. The debt which a man owes to the State is even greater than that which he owes to his parents, and the desertion of parents in sickness or old age is not more discreditable than the refusal by a citizen of such service as it is in his power to render to his fatherland in its time of distress or peril. It is less easy to define his duty in the case of a war which he thinks unjust, and in which he is compelled to fight; and all that can be said is that, except in a case of manifestly flagrant injustice, the average person has reason to credit the chosen rulers of a civilized state with possessing more knowledge and wisdom than himself, and at least as great a sense of responsibility. Those who refuse to fight from a genuine conviction that it is unlawful to shed blood are wisely treated with consideration in the modern world, inasmuch as conscience, even when uninstructed, is an asset which a nation cannot disparage and flout without grave injury to its higher life.

Recent events have revived interest in the relation of ministers of religion to military service. The claim to immunity was very generally made for heathen priesthoods, and allowed by the secular power.[1] The question did not arise in the circumstances of the Christian Church in the early centuries.[2] The popes and bishops of the mediæval Church were often involved in war, and could even foment it in support of their worldly interests, but the official teaching was that it was unlawful for all clerics who belonged to the *ordines majores* to take a direct part in the shedding of blood. The conclusion of Thomas Aquinas is to this effect:

> 'Cum bellica exercitia hominem maxime a divinorum contemplatione avertant, et ad humani sanguinis effusionem tendant, minime clericis ac spiritualibus personis bellare licet, nisi in necessitatis articulo.'[3]

Military service, it is added, is inconsistent with the clerical office on two grounds—it is inconsistent with the cultivation of a spiritual temper and the discharge of pastoral duties, and in particular those who are ordained to minister at the altar should rather be eager themselves to suffer as martyrs than think it seemly to spill the blood of others.[4] The Lutheran Church has followed this tradition,[5] and the Anglican Church re-affirmed its adherence to it during the recent war by forbidding the clergy to offer themselves for combatant service. The Reformed Churches, narrowly so called, while agreeing that in ordinary circumstances ministers have an all-important spiritual function to perform in war and should abide in their calling, have taken a broader view of what is covered by the accepted condition 'in articulo necessitatis,' and have occasionally left it to ministers, as was lately done by the Church of Scotland, to judge for themselves as to whether the necessity was such as to require them to offer their services as fighting men to the State. On the question of principle it may be observed that it is difficult to maintain the view that the clergy as representatives of Jesus Christ ought to refrain

1 'Druides . . . militiae vacationem, omniumque rerum habent immunitatem' (Cæsar, *de Bell. Gall.* vi. 14).
2 'Nec ad arma jam spectat usus noster' (Ambrose, *de Offic. Ministrorum*, i. 35).
3 II. ii. qu. xl. art. 2.
4 Cf. Elbel, ii. 54: 'an liceat etiam clericis pugnare.'
5 H. Martensen, *Christian Ethics*, Eng. tr., Edinburgh, 1892, div. ii. p. 236.

from all violence and the shedding of blood, and at the same time to resist the Quaker contention that the same prohibition extends to persons of every class who profess and call themselves Christians. Further, while it is generally admitted that the clergy may and ought to encourage the soldiery to fight in a just cause, in the ordinary judgment of mankind a person who thinks it wrong or degrading to do a thing himself ought not to aid and abet others in doing it. The argument based on 2 Ti 2[4] can be used with equal force in support of the view that the clergy should not be distracted from their spiritual work by the cares of married life or by the discharge of the duties of any civic office. It may be added that the traditional attitude of the Church seems to have been largely determined by the interest felt in magnifying the distinction of priesthood and laity, and by the reflex influence of the mediæval sacramental doctrine.

ii. THE PHILOSOPHICAL VINDICATION. — The verdict of ethical philosophy, ancient and modern, has been that under certain conditions war is justifiable, and non-resistance blameworthy and even immoral. The Greek view was summarily expressed by the inclusion of courage among the four cardinal virtues. Justice, according to Cicero, involves for nations as for individuals the duty of preventing injury and of exacting punishment and reparation. The modern schools have their varying conceptions of the ground of obligation and of the nature and basis of natural rights,[1] but there has been practical unanimity as to the moral justification of self-defence when one nation is assailed by the ambition and cupidity of another. From the intuitionist point of view there is an eternal and immutable moral law attested by conscience, which includes the requirement that nations shall render to all their due, and, in the absence of other machinery for making the law effective, it is held to be the duty of the particular nation to do what lies in its power to enforce and safeguard this obligation. From the utilitarian standpoint repressive and punitive action is held to be called for in view of the disastrous effects which unrestrained injustice would produce for particular nations and the general life of the race. The doctrine of non-resistance, Herbert Spencer argues, is anti-social, as it involves the non-assertion, not only of one's own rights, but of those of others, while it holds out no prospect of leading to the desirable end of international peace.[2]

The findings of the jurists, while reflecting the varieties of ethical theory, are at one in giving an affirmative answer to the question, 'an bellare unquam justum sit.' Grotius argues that recourse to war is permitted and approved by the law of nature, by the consent of the many and of the wise, and by the law of nations, as well as by the divine law which was promulgated and attested in the Scriptures. The law of nature has two branches—the course dictated by natural instincts, and the principles approved by reason. This law intimates its permission of war through the universal instinct of self-preservation, accompanied as it is by nature's disclosure of purpose in the provision of means of defence to all creatures, and also by the voice of reason which makes it clear that the well-being of society is incompatible with the unchecked reign of violence.[3]

By the law of nature, says E. de Vattel, the nations are under an obligation to do justice and also have the right to be treated with justice; and 'it would be in vain that nature gave us the right of not suffering injustice, and required others to be just towards us, if we could not legitimately use compulsion when they refuse to acquit themselves of this duty.'[1]

Some recent treatises find it sufficient for their purpose that the practice of war is a human custom, and they prefer to leave to philosophy the treatment of the question of the ultimate justification.

VI. *THE DISTINCTION OF JUST AND UNJUST WARS.*—The primitive view was that fighting was as natural and proper as any other means of acquiring wealth and servants, and the only matter needing careful consideration was the prospect and the cost of success in a particular venture. From a comparatively early period, however, the moral consciousness drew a distinction between just and unjust wars, and procured for the distinction such recognition that almost every belligerent has been anxiously concerned to make out that he had the sanctions of morality and religion on his side.

1. The distinction in the non-Christian religions.—The distinction of just and unjust wars was impressed on the princes of China and India by the higher religions of the East. Greek religion did something to develop a conscience in regard to occasions of war, at least as carried on among the Hellenic tribes. The Romans understood that it was the will of the gods, not merely that wars should begin and end with solemn ceremonies, but that they should be waged only with a view to redress or security, and they were taught that their piety in these respects had been rewarded by the series of victories which safeguarded and extended their empire.

The general view represented in the OT was that wars of aggression, such as were waged by the insatiable and arrogant Asiatic empires, were wicked and criminal, and that wars waged for the defence or liberation of a people, like those organized by the Judges and the good kings, were in accordance with justice and the known will of God. The criminality of the heathen wars of conquest was not held to be inconsistent with the observation that they were sometimes used for the merited chastisement of other peoples: the guilt was the aggressor's, God's were the wisdom and the power that made the wrath of man to praise Him, and that in the end over-ruled the evil for good. The prohibition of the war of conquest was, however, subject to exceptions—even from the point of view of the prophetic idealism. It was an axiom of the historical writers, even of those of the prophetic school, that the conquest of Canaan by their fathers had been abundantly justified, partly on the ground of an ancient promise and of the provisional occupation by the patriarchs, partly because the conquest and even the extermination of the Canaanites had been richly deserved by their impiety, their corruption, and their cruelties (Jg 1[5], 1 S 15[2]; cf. Jos 10[40]). For the expedition of Cyrus against Babylon a similar moral and religious sanction was asserted (Is 45[1]). The contribution of Islām was to elevate into a rule the commission given in the OT in the war against the Canaanites, and to glorify as most just and necessary the war of conquest which is waged for the conversion or the punishment of unbelievers. 'They who believe fight for the religion of God.' 'Give to those who misbelieve glad tidings of grievous woe.'[2] The Qur'ān is full of exhortations to fight against misbelievers and hypocrites,[3] with promises of Paradise to those who should fall in the holy warfare.[4]

2. The standard of the classical moralists.—The argument of Plato in the *Laws* is to the effect that rulers should organize their realms with a view to virtue and peaceful prosperity as the chief

[1] D. G. Ritchie, *Natural Rights*, London, 1894, pt. i.
[2] *Social Statics*, new ed., London, 1902, p. 116.
[3] *De Jure Belli ac Pacis*, 1646, Cambridge, 3 vols., 1853, Washington, 1913.

[1] *Le Droit des gens*, 1758, Washington, 1916, ii. 5.
[2] *SBE* vi. 173 ff.
[3] *Ib.* pp. 176–180, 183–186, etc.
[4] *Ib.* pp. 27 ff., 31 ff., 37 ff., ix. 63, etc.

end, and that military provisions should be relegated to a quite secondary place. At the same time he accepted the view that Greeks and barbarians were natural enemies, and that the code of justice was barely relevant to their relations. For Aristotle it was the self-evident duty of a state to defend itself, and to enrich itself by war as a legitimate way of acquiring property; and he also justified the war of conquest against outside nations on the ground that there are peoples which are destined by nature to servitude, and which are properly coerced if they do not voluntarily accept their destiny.[1] The discussion of the subject by Cicero is important as a summary of the ethical reflexions of classical antiquity which was also to serve as a useful legacy to the later guides of the Christian Church.

He condemns the common view that the use of peace was to prepare for war: peace is to be kept in view as the end, and war regarded as a means which is sometimes unhappily necessary to secure a satisfactory peace.[2] It is the irrational and brutal way of ending disputes. Unjust wars are those which are prompted by covetousness of the possessions of others. Just wars are of different types, according as they are required for the safety of the State, when measures are taken to ward off injury, and to secure reparation and punishment, or are prompted by the honourable motive of succouring those who have a claim to assistance on the ground of natural ties or of treaty-obligations. To fulfil the requirements of justice it was further necessary that the demand for satisfaction, and an eventual declaration of war, should be made in due religious forms.[3]

These principles, it may be added, made it possible to offer a tolerable moral apologia for the proceedings of the Roman empire: when a war could not be plausibly represented as defensive, it could at least be conceived as partaking to some extent of the character of a war of honour on behalf of allies, or of a war of chivalry on behalf of an oppressed and wronged population.

3. The judgment of the Church.—The need of an official Christian criterion emerged with the union of Church and Empire, and guidance was given by Augustine with considerable obligation to Cicero.

He had no difficulty in deciding that there are unjust and just wars—the unjust represented by the contemporary barbarian onslaughts on the Empire, the just by the efforts of the Empire to defend itself and the cause of civilization. 'Inferre autem bella finitimis, et inde in caetera procedere, ac populos sibi non molestos sola regni cupiditate conterere et subdere, quid aliud quam grande latrocinium nominandum est?'[4] Such wars have their spring in the worst of passions—'nocendi cupiditas, ulciscendi crudelitas, impacatus atque implacabilis animus, feritas rebellandi, libido dominandi, et si qua similia.'[5] Just wars are those which are waged to inflict punishment, or to secure reparation for injury, or (as in OT) by express commandment of God.[6] So terrible, however, are the calamities of war—veritable games in honour of the devils[7]—that it should only be entered on under stress of the direst necessity.[8] He also laid it down that war may only be lawfully undertaken by a prince and carried on by a regular soldiery.[9] The caveat is put in that victory in war is not necessarily to be ascribed to the deserts of a belligerent.[10]

Thomas Aquinas laid down three criteria of a just war: it must be waged by a prince invested with legitimate authority, against an enemy who has deserved punishment, and with the intention that good shall be promoted and evil removed.[11]

Following on the Decrees of Gratian the subject was elaborately treated by Suarez, Ayala, Gentilis, and other Canonists. They were agreed in vindicating defensive and punitive warfare, but developed some differences of opinion in regard to the ethics of conquest, the powers of the pope in sanctioning wars and annexations, and the lawfulness of war against infidels and heretics.[1]

Protestantism generally reproduced the Augustinian criterion of just and unjust wars. The representatives of the Lutheran and Anglican schools were peculiarly emphatic in branding rebellion as one of the most criminal types of unjust war. According to Luther, the worst tyranny ought to be submissively and patiently endured, inasmuch as every nation richly deserves chastisement, and on the other hand tyrants will be adequately punished in the future state of retribution.[2] With still greater solemnity, even ferocity of language, is the iniquity of rebellion established in the Anglican *Homily against Disobedience and Wilful Rebellion*. The reasons given include the following in addition to the two mentioned above:

Rebellion had its prototype in the apostasy of Lucifer; monarchy is of divine right, being a copy of the divine rule; rebels will be punished with eternal damnation; history abundantly proves that it is as foolish and futile as it is wicked; subjects are no fit judges of the goodness or badness of a prince; rebellion is not a single sin, but 'the puddle and sink of all sins against God and man.'

The unjust war, according to Calvin, is one inspired by cupidity, and the just war is one in which a prince, as vice-regent of God, undertakes to coerce another nation which has embarked on a murderous and marauding enterprise.[3] He urged the usual arguments against rebellion, but with a significant addition:

'When misgovernment becomes intolerable,' he says, 'deliverance may be expected from God, whose way it is either to raise up avengers from among his servants, or to use for his purpose agents who may be pursuing different purposes of their own.'

On this principle it could be contended by the Puritans that rebellion against Charles I. became lawful when God raised up a deliverer in the person of Oliver Cromwell. The Scottish Church emphasized another qualifying doctrine, that obedience to kings ceases to be a duty when they make demands inconsistent with the laws of God, and in the National Covenant the subscribers accordingly bound themselves to maintain their sacred cause with 'their best counsel, bodies, means, and whole power against all sorts of persons whatsoever.'

The modern literature of Christian ethics has in the main reproduced the ideas of Augustine, Luther, and Calvin. One of the most interesting discussions is contributed by Rothe, who justifies aggressive war against a nation whose lusts may have made it a chronic disturber of the peace, and also defends the war of conquest, at least in extraordinary times, as legitimate in order to the replacement of a lower by a higher civilization, or for the correction and improvement of a nation which has become effete and degenerate.[4]

4. Jurisprudence and philosophy.—The classic treatises on international law deal elaborately with justificatory causes and unjust occasions of war. To Hugo Grotius more than any other it was due that political realism was called to account in the name of justice and humanity, though in some matters he applied the ethical principles with a measure of timidity.

Grotius recognizes three forms of just war—in the maintenance by a nation of its own interests, in interposition on behalf of others, and in duty towards God. A nation is entitled and even bound to maintain its own interests by the defence of the life, honour, and property of the citizens, by the exaction of reparation for injuries and insistence on the fulfilment of obligations, and by the punishment of the aggressors.[5] War may be lawfully undertaken by a nation on behalf, not only of its own subjects, but also of its allies, its friends, and of fellow-men as such.[6] The impious creed which denies the two

[1] *Politics*, i. 8.
[2] 'Quare suscipienda quidem bella sunt ob eam causam, ut sine injuria in pace vivatur' (*de Offic.* i. 35).
[3] 'Nullum bellum esse justum, nisi quod aut rebus repetitis geratur, aut denuntiatum ante sit et indictum' (i. 36).
[4] *De Civ.* vii. 92*d*.
[5] *Contra Faustum*, XXII. viii. 405*a*.
[6] *Quæst. in Josue*, iii.[2], 584 f.
[7] *De Civ.* vii. 76 f.
[8] 'Pacem habere debet voluntas, bellum necessitas' (*Ep.* 189, ii. 699*b*).
[9] *Contra Faustum*, XXII. viii. 405*a*.
[10] *De Civ.* vii. 454*d*.
[11] *Summa*, II. ii. qu. xl. art. 1.

[1] For a review of the literature cf. E. Nys, *Le Droit de la guerre*, Brussels, 1883, sect. iv.
[2] *Op. cit.*
[3] *Inst. Rel. Christ.* iv. 20.
[4] *Theologische Ethik*, 5 vols., Wittenberg, 1867–71, § 1160.
[5] *De Jure Belli ac Pacis*, bk. ii. ch. ix.
[6] ii. 25. 3–6.

fundamental articles that there is a Deity, and that He cares for human affairs, is a doctrine so dangerous to the world as well as dishonouring to God that it may well be forcibly repressed in the name of human society.[1] War may not be entered on through blind fear of another nation, or a supposed utility that is not supported by absolute necessity. It is a monstrous doctrine that war is justifiable against a neighbour on the mere ground that his power is increasing and may continue to grow.[2] Other insufficient pretexts are the refusal of women in marriage, the desire of better lands, the purpose of imposing a more beneficent government, and imperial and ecclesiastical projects.[3] Again, while atheism may justly be suppressed, war is not justified against nations on the mere ground that they refuse to embrace the Christian religion, unless the unbelievers cruelly persecute Christians on account of their faith.[4] Rebellion is generally to be condemned although it may be justified by necessity—as when a prince invades the privileges of a free people, or abdicates, or betrays the cause of his subjects, or generally acts as their enemy.[5] On the other hand, the fact that a population does not enjoy liberty is not sufficient ground for rebellion. If they have come into servitude in a legitimate way, they should be content with their condition.[6]

The subject is also minutely treated by Vattel, and on similar lines—the shade of difference being that he allows more justification for the anticipatory war, and that he feels less hesitancy in apologizing for rebellion in justification of natural rights.[7]

The Scottish School of Jurisprudence is so far identified with the view that 'aggression is a natural right, the extent of which is measured by the power which God has bestowed on the aggressor,' and that 'the right of aggression justifies an application of force.'[8]

The criterion of justice has likewise been applied to wars in the schools of Moral Philosophy. Kant emphatically affirmed the lawfulness of defensive wars, and specified as criminal types the war for dominion (*bellum subjugatorium*) and the war of extermination (*bellum internecinum*). He refused to concede the moral title of one state to attack another on the mere ground of its iniquities (*bellum punitivum*).[9] Hegel affirms the paramount duty of a nation to preserve and develop its individuality, and holds that this may give a title to a great nation, as the best representative of the world-spirit for the time being, to embark upon wars of conquest. As against such an elect member of the human family, other peoples can assert no natural rights.[10] W. R. Sorley has criticized the 'defensive selfish' theory no less than the 'offensive selfish' theory as unethical, and makes the criterion to be whether a war contributes to the establishment of a higher civilization.[11]

The distinctive features of the public opinion of the 19th cent. were that the religious war is an anachronism, that a war of conquest against civilized nations is criminal, that oppressed nationalities have a sacred right of rebellion, and that there is a moral privilege, if not a duty, of chivalrous interposition on behalf of the wronged. On the other hand, the jurists were increasingly disposed to disclaim the office of directors of conscience to the nations in the matter.

'It is not possible,' says Hall, 'to frame general rules which shall be of any practical value, and the attempts in this direction which jurists are in the habit of making result in mere abstract statements of principles or perhaps of truisms, which it is unnecessary to reproduce.'[12]

What is the value of this chapter of the history of thought? It must be admitted that a review of the subject is calculated to raise misgivings as to the judicial capacity of the human mind, if not even to foster moral scepticism. The general result was that, while it was agreed both by the many and by the wise that morality should regulate the occasions of war, there was serious difference of opinion as to the prohibitions actually involved in the moral law, the parties who had to judge of its application to particular situations were so biassed by their interests and passions as to be incapable of equitable judgment, and the enforcement of ethical demands practically depended on whether it happened to coincide with the advantage of a state or states to lend its support to a righteous cause. The lesson to be drawn is that, if the demands of morality are to be properly expounded and enforced in this sphere, the task must be proceeded with under different conditions, and the problem must be formulated in a different way. If the chaotic situation of the past were replaced by a society of nations, the problem of just and unjust wars would be simplified, inasmuch as the typical form of unlawful war would be an act of rebellion against the general body in which a particular state broke the law that prohibits aggressive military action, and defied the authority supporting the law. Under these conditions the great question for ethical reflexion would be, not what wars were just or the reverse, but what were the rights which particular nations were entitled to assert or to have safeguarded. This subject is no doubt a difficult one; and it is probable that much would have to be adjudicated upon from the point of view of equity rather than in accordance with the provisions of a cast-iron statutory code. There would, however, be a good guarantee for just judgment in the fact that the elaboration of the code of rights would be undertaken by representatives of the general mind of the race, for whom the criterion would be the greatest good of the whole, and that in the application and enforcement of the recognized law the parties directly interested would play a subordinate part.

VII. *HUMANIZATION OF THE CONDUCT OF WAR*.—The ancient tradition was 'Væ Victis!' The penalty of defeat was the extremity of ruin and humiliation. The invaded country was ruthlessly devastated, the captured city was commonly sacked and destroyed, neither age nor sex could count on immunity, and a whole population might be put to the sword. If the practice was commonly less thorough than the theory, this was probably due not so much to clemency as to the reflexion that a ruined and depopulated country could pay no tribute, and that the services or the ransom of slaves gave more permanent satisfaction than the slaughter of captives. Such was the general spirit of warfare at the advent of certain of the great religions, and they vindicated their claim to the title of ethical by embodying provisions which represented a real advance on the primitive ferocity of mankind.

1. The curb of the religions.—The *Laws of Manu*, while showing no scruples about aggressive and acquisitive war, make a strong plea for humane fighting.

'What the King has not (yet) gained, let him seek (to gain) by (his) army.'[1] 'Let him plan his undertakings (patiently meditating) like a heron; like a lion, let him put forth his strength; like a wolf, let him snatch (his prey); like a hare, let him double in retreat.'[2] At the same time he is to conduct war mercifully and even chivalrously. 'When he fights with his foes in battle, let him not strike with weapons concealed (in wood), nor with (such as are) barbed, poisoned, or the points of which are blazing with fire.' 'Let him not strike one who (in flight) has climbed on an eminence, nor a eunuch, nor one who joins the palms of his hands (in supplication), nor one who (flees) with flying hair, . . . nor one who is naked, . . . nor one who looks on without taking part in the fight, nor one who is fighting with another (foe). Nor one whose weapons are broken, nor one afflicted (with sorrow), nor one who has been grievously wounded, nor one who is in fear, nor one who has turned to flight, (but in all these cases let him) remember the duty (of honourable warriors).'[3]

The ethical inspiration of the religion of Israel left its mark on the regulations for the conduct of war. Israel was familiar with the ferocity of Oriental warfare, to which a religious consecration

[1] ii. 20. 44-46. [2] ii. 22. 5-6, 1. 5, 7.
[3] ii. 22. 7-14. [4] ii. 20. 48 f.
[5] i. 4. [6] ii. 22. 11.
[7] *Le Droit des gens*, i. 4.
[8] J. Lorimer, *The Institutes of Law*², Edinburgh, 1880, pp. 414-419.
[9] *Gesammelte Schriften*, 1902-12, i. 4, *Rechtslehre*, vi. 347.
[10] *Werke*, Berlin, 1832-40, *Philosophie des Rechts*, viii. 433.
[11] 'The Ethics of Conquest,' *Blackwood's Magazine*, Edinburgh, Dec. 1898.
[12] W. E. Hall, *International Law*⁶, p. 60.

[1] *SBE* xxv. [1886] 232. [2] *Ib.* p. 233. [3] *Ib.* p. 231.

was sometimes given by the application of the doctrine of the *herem*, or ban (Nu 21^{24}, Jos 6$^{17f.}$ etc.). It could imitate its neighbours in the ruthless devastation of territory (2 K 3$^{19-25}$), the massacre of conquered communities (1 K 11^{16}), the mutilation of captives (Jg 1^{6}), and the murder of pregnant women (2 K 15^{16}). It would appear, however, that Israel had a general reputation for clemency (1 K 20^{31}), and that the treatment meted out to their enemies was 'not to be compared to the Assyrian devilries.'[1] The subject of atrocities bulks largely in the prophetic invective.

Amos thunders against the nations for the cruelty and perfidy that marked their methods of warfare, and judgment is denounced against Damascus because it has threshed Gilead with threshing-instruments of iron; against Gaza because it has sold Israelites into captivity; against Tyre because it has violated a treaty; against Edom because of its pitiless vendetta against Israel; against Ammon because it ripped up the woman with child that it might enlarge its border; against Moab because it burned the bones of the king of Edom with lime (chs. 1–2).

The Deuteronomic legislation did something in this field to sustain its general character for humanity. It provides that the inhabitants of a city which capitulates are to be treated with clemency, and that, if it be carried by assault, the non-fighting population is only to forfeit its liberty (20$^{11f.}$ 21^{10}). It was also forbidden to cut down fruit trees during the siege of a city 'since the tree of the field is man's life' (20$^{19f.}$).

Among the great religions Islām alone upheld the ruthless traditions of Oriental warfare. As it was a religious duty to fight for the faith, so the worst excesses of war were given the character of a righteous judgment on the infidel, and the forfeits demanded of the vanquished by the law of the savage were passed on to the faithful as their natural rights.

'O thou prophet, fight thou strenuously against the misbelievers and hypocrites, and be stern towards them, for their resort is Hell, and an evil journey shall it be.'[2] 'The reward of those who make war against God and His Apostle and strive after violence in the earth, is only that they shall be slaughtered or crucified, or their hands cut off and their feet on alternate sides, or that they shall be banished from the land.'[3]

It should be added that some Muhammadan peoples have their share of human kindness, and that they have also found it necessary to compromise with their exterminating doctrine as a condition of being allowed to retain political power and even to occupy the planet.

2. The Græco-Roman period and its spirit.—During the classical period the traditional usages of war were somewhat softened. Although vengeance was pitilessly wreaked on an enemy who had inspired deadly fear or hatred, and although the principle still held that a victorious soldiery was entitled to the compensations of pillage and outrage, there was a milder strain in the Aryan constitution, which re-asserted itself in cold blood. While the Greeks did not evolve a code of international law, there was a minimum of common morality which a common religion enjoined on all Greeks alike. The chief elements of the code were the rights of the alien (ξενός), the sacred immunity of the herald, pious treatment of the slain (whose corpses might not be mutilated and should not be left unburied), and merciful treatment of prisoners. Unconditional surrender, if voluntary, carried with it a right to mercy; conditional surrender, if confirmed by an oath, was to be respected; and a captive had a title to be liberated (though it was doubtful if the captor was compelled to accept it) on payment of a fixed sum. These rules were believed to be sanctioned by divine authority, and the Amphictyonic Councils, which represented unions of tribes and cities, also lent their influence to mitigate the rancour of war.[1]

[1] A. R. S. Kennedy, art. 'War' in *SDB*.
[2] *Qur'ān*, lxvi. 9. [3] *Ib.* v. 39.

Roman warfare retained enough of the old ruthlessness and savagery, as appears from the detailed records of massacre and pillage in the campaigns of conquest. The claims of mercy, however, are stated by Cicero in terms which probably do not greatly overstate the working theory of the later period.

A distinction is drawn between wars in which a state fights for its existence and those in which it contends for power and glory, and he observes that, while the former inevitably take on a merciless and murderous character, the latter may be and often are fought out with comparative clemency. The treatment of an enemy depended on what manner of enemy he was. Those who were of evil character—arrogant, cruel, and perfidious—were properly scourged without mercy, while it was a dictate of nobility as well as of prudence to deal magnanimously with those who were decisively beaten, and who were no longer a source of danger. He lays stress on the duty of acting honourably towards the enemy, and enlarges on the magnanimity of Pyrrhus, who declined to hold his prisoners to ransom, on the ground that, if fortune had granted them their lives, the conqueror might well grant them liberty.[2]

3. The mediæval period.—In the fighting of the early Middle Ages there was some relapse into primitive ferocity due to the fact that the conflict was between civilization and barbarism, and the stakes were the material foundations of existence. Writing in the very throes of the world-struggle, Augustine recalls that the tradition even of heathen Rome recommended clemency and magnanimity, and urges that war be conducted in accordance with the merciful precepts of the gospel.[3] When the outline of a cosmos re-emerged, Christianity was already generally professed, and it contributed, in conjunction with the nobler elements of the European character, to the formation of a chivalrous ideal, which in some particulars toned down the hideousness of war. The Church, as the moral guide of the nations, took the matter into consideration, and in its canon law framed rules which were leavened by the Christian spirit.

4. The modern advance.—In modern times regulations for the conduct of war have been humanized to an extent that has been a welcome offset to the multiplication and intensification of the horrors due to modern inventions. The forces making for this improvement were the Christian leaven working in European society and the developing moral reflexion of the civilized world, and those happily met in the personality and equipment of Hugo Grotius, theologian, moralist, and lawyer, and became widely operative through the influence of the treatise *de Jure Belli ac Pacis*.

After expounding the general theory and practice of the conduct of war, he proposes in the name of humanity a list of amendments and mitigations (*temperamenta*) in regard to the treatment of the persons and the property of the enemy.[4] The general principle insisted on is that the right to slay, enslave, confiscate, etc., is not absolute, but is limited by consideration of what is necessary to break an enemy's resistance or to obtain reparation for injury inflicted.

During the 18th and 19th centuries there was a marked development of the cosmopolitan and humanitarian spirit, accompanied by much ethical reflexion in the departments of International Law, Moral Philosophy, and Christian Ethics. The common-sense benevolence of the 18th cent., as voiced by Benjamin Franklin, saw no reason why the law of nations, which had already discarded something of the old savagery, should not go on improving; and Franklin proposed that, when nations were at war, immunity should be granted to cultivators of the earth, fishermen, merchants and traders in unarmed ships, artists, and mechanics working in open towns, also that rapine and privateering should be abolished and that hospitals

[1] A. H. J. Greenidge, *A Handbook of Greek Constitutional History*, London, 1896, pp. 16–18.
[2] *De Offic.* i. [3] ii. 415*g*, 416*c*.
[4] Bk. iii. chs. xi.–xxiv.: 'Circa jus interficiendi, vastationem, res captas, captos,' etc.

should be respected. In the treatises on International Law, which was sedulously cultivated during the period, the humane trend was strongly accentuated, and the doctrine was even ardently developed by some continental writers that war ought to remain a conflict of states as such, in which the non-combatant citizens might rank as neutrals. While the Roman Catholic Church brought its canon law up to date, Protestant theology was prolific in systems of Christian Ethics, which at least made it clear that the spirit of Christian morality required radical reform of the usages of war. Definite and valuable practical results were achieved by the Geneva Convention of 1864 which dealt with the treatment of the wounded, the sick, and prisoners.[1] The Hague Tribunal covered practically the whole ground, except that it was only permitted to glance at the topics of arbitration and disarmament.[2] The chief provisions illustrating the ethical progress were as follows.

(A) *Methods and weapons of war.*—(*a*) In re-affirming the principle that the right to injure the enemy is not unlimited, the Hague tribunal prohibited poisoning, treacherous wounding and killing, declarations that no quarter will be given, and the improper use of flags of truce. (*b*) It prohibited attacks on and bombardment of defenceless towns, and unnecessary destruction of edifices devoted to religion, art, science, and charity. (*c*) It prohibited the sack of captured cities. (*d*) It laid down that prisoners are entitled to be provided for and relieved. (*e*) The treatment of the sick and wounded was put on a much better footing. It was provided that ambulances and military hospitals are to be respected; that persons employed in this work are to be protected and returned to their posts, that wounded and sick soldiers are to be cared for and treated, to whatever nation they belong.

(B) *Treatment of the enemy's country when occupied and of property therein.*—The rights of private property were asserted—both as against pillage by individuals and as against confiscation by the enemy state. Wanton destruction of property was forbidden. Requisitions in kind or in services were only to be demanded from communes or inhabitants for the necessities of the armies of occupation. The inhabitants could not be compelled to take part in military operations against their own country.

The two other main subjects dealt with are commerce with the enemy during hostilities, and the law of reprisals.

During the recent war there were doubtless grievous violations of these humane regulations—notably in the use of poisonous gases, the wanton destruction of property, and the occasional refusal of quarter—but that the modern world had reached a higher level of morality than antiquity was still in evidence in the fact that, in the most gigantic and desperate struggle in history, law and order were to a large extent maintained in occupied territories, prisoners were not as of old callously butchered or reserved for the slave mart or the gladiatorial spectacle, and the sick and wounded found themselves under the shelter of the Cross and tended by the ministrations of the Good Samaritan.

VIII. *THE DESIRABILITY OF ENDING WAR.*—The general judgment of mankind upon war is that it is a scourge of the nations which, along with famine and pestilence, makes up the dread trinity of human woes. This estimate rests on considerations which have certainly not lost in force in modern times.

(1) War is organized destruction of the harvest of civilization and of those who produce it. It impoverishes a country in two ways—by diverting labour from productive to unproductive tasks, and by annihilating wealth which had previously been accumulated by peaceful industry. It also sets at naught the civilized doctrine of the sanctity of human life, and replaces the beneficent efforts of science to save and husband life by measures which directly or indirectly sweep away whole masses of population. The ever-increasing efficiency of the instruments and methods of destruction has still more decidedly given to modern warfare an aspect of folly and clothed it with a suicidal character. The conquerors, hardly less than the vanquished, have emerged from the World War bleeding, dazed, exhausted, and doomed to shoulder almost intolerable burdens.

(2) The tragedy of the waste of life is aggravated by the circumstance that the victims are the *élite* of the nations. War, as Æschylus says, is a gold-merchant, with whom his customers do most unprofitable business.

> 'From each home once there went
> A man forth: him it sent
> Each knows; but what are these return?
> A little dust, an urn.'[1]

A Greek epitaph puts the point pithily: Ἄρης οὐκ ἀγαθῶν φείδεται ἀλλὰ κακῶν.[2] While the machinery of nature works for the survival of the fittest, the winnowing of war results in the elimination of the fittest, and the more so in latter-day warfare, which gives little advantage to the strong, the skilful, and the wise, in the carnage of the frontal attack and of the fire-swept zone.[3]

(3) In fighting man reverts to the sub-human plane. The badge of humanity is the possession of reason, which at least suggests that man ought to try to settle his disputes by rational methods.[4]

(4) War makes an appalling addition to the miseries of the human lot. A whole world of cruel suffering is compressed by Sallust into his list of the horrors of ancient war:

> 'Rapi virgines, pueros; divelli liberos a parentum complexu; matres familiarum pati quae victoribus collibuissent, fana atque domos exspoliari; caedem, incendia fieri, postremo armis, cadaveribus, cruore, atque luctu omnia compleri.'[5]

With more detail and colour but hardly more impressiveness, a great preacher depicts the horrors of the battle-field, the agonies of the occupied country, the ravages of want and sickness, the desolated lives, and the broken hearts.[6] It is a service rendered by realistic fiction that it has shown how dearly purchased even by the fighting man is 'the one crowded hour of glorious life' which itself under modern conditions may be like nothing so much as the death of a poisoned rat in a hole.[7]

(5) War, when looked at as a whole, is a gigantic moral evil. The aggression which sets in motion and sustains the strife has its dynamic in lusts and passions that defy and reverse the recognized maxims of morality. Even a just war sets the heart of a nation aflame with hatred, malice, and revenge. War turns the moral world upside down and sanctions a temporary suspension of respect for life and property and truth. It is therefore probably inevitable that it should be waged with some grim accompaniment of unlicensed outrage and of unchained vice. Experience also shows that the moral chaos of war makes its influence felt later on in a certain hardening of a people's heart, and a perversion of their moral sentiments, and also in a ground-swell of unrest, licentiousness, and crime which continues to surge after the actual tempest has subsided.

To this indictment there has been opposed a eulogy of war, which has some basis in facts, but fails to establish that the blessings traced to the experiences could not otherwise be obtained, much less that it is desirable to perpetuate war

1 Text in L. Oppenheim, *International Law*, London, 1906, ii. app. iii.

2 *The Hague Conventions and Declarations of 1899 and 1907*, Carnegie Endowment, 1918.

1 *Agam.* 441 f., tr. W. Headlam, Cambridge, 1910.

2 J. W. Mackail, *Select Epigrams from the Greek Anthology*, London, 1891.

3 D. Starr Jordan, *The Human Harvest*, London, 1907.

4 Cicero, *de Offic.*; cf. Ennius, 'Pellitur e medio sapientia, vi geritur res, Spernitur orator bonus, horridus miles amatur' (*Carminum Reliquiæ*, ed. L. Mueller, Petropolis, 1884).

5 *De Catilinæ Conjuratione*, § 51.

6 Robert Hall, *Miscellaneous Works*, London, 1839, 'Reflections on War.'

7 Tolstoi, *War and Peace*; E. Zola, *La Débâcle*, Paris, 1892; B. Suttner, *Die Waffen Nieder!*, 2 vols., Dresden, 1891; Bairnsfather's cartoons.

as the condition of like benefits accruing in the future.

(1) The progress of human civilization, it is said, has been due to nations which came to the front in war, were organized and steeled by war, and won through war their power and title to guide or serve the world. 'If progress stops war on one side, it makes it on another, and war is its instrument.'[1] Few indeed would so far venture to criticize the course of history as to deplore that, *e.g.*, Rome made herself mistress of the world, or that the Anglo-Saxons conquered and settled Britain, and that their descendants took forcible possession of the greater part of North America, as well as of Australia and New Zealand. Such events have a certain ethical justification, since self-realization is a right if not a duty of nations, while under former conditions a people was practically thrown back on war as the one form of enterprise by which to supply its vital wants and in which to find scope for great native powers. At the same time it may not be forgotten that the after-world owes the most valuable elements in its spiritual heritage to the culture of the Greeks and the religion of the Jews, both of which peoples went down in the military struggle, and it is not unreasonable to expect that in the future great races will find it possible to come to their own in the leadership and service of the world without the necessity of proving their superiority and claiming their opportunities by the exercise of brute force.

(2) War is necessary, it is said, to preserve the vitality of a state and avert degeneracy. 'No Body can be healthfull,' says Bacon, 'without *Exercise*, neither Natural Body, nor Politique: And certainly, to a Kingdome or Estate, a Just and Honourable Warre is the true *Exercise*.'[2] One might reply that it gets sufficient exercise, if it has a mind to work, in subduing the earth and developing industry and commerce, and that in any case there are more healthful forms of exercise than gashing the body and spilling its life-blood. Probably what Bacon meant was to give discreet utterance to the maxim of statecraft that a foreign war is the best recipe for grave domestic dissensions, but to this assertion the reply is that sedition is more sanely and humanely treated by measures of political and social reform. That nations become effeminate and degenerate in peace, and because of peace, has been often asserted, and no doubt it has sometimes happened that a nation, on being guaranteed peaceful security, has become idle and vicious. But the charge often amounts to no more than that a people, as the result of a long period of peace, has become unskilled in the use of the soldier's tools, and the experience of the recent war showed that peoples which according to theory should have become weak and spiritless had preserved unimpaired throughout a commercial era the strongest ancestral qualities of their stock.

(3) War, it is said, has not its equal as a school of the virtues. The modern militarists are able to collect opinions in support of this tenet from eminent moralists of all ages. And undoubtedly there are qualities, distinctive of the soldier as such, which contrast impressively with the unbridled egotism that runs rampant in times of peace and prosperity—as courage, obedience, self-discipline, endurance, comradeship, self-sacrifice. It is, however, incredible from the point of view of the moral order that the only way in which individuals can be given the opportunity to reach the heights of virtue is that nations should continue to plan and perpetrate crimes against one another. Fortunately the facts do not warrant the inference of the moral indispensableness of war. For one thing the virtues in question to a great extent are merely brought to light, not engendered, by the experiences of war. In so far as they are created and developed by war, the same end could be achieved by other means, since the world contains enough of peril, adventure, and opportunities of sacrifice to provide material for a training of youth that would yield similar ethical results, while it might guard more effectively against such concessions as are made in the school of warfare to the evil forces which are summarily comprehended under the names of the Devil and the flesh.[3] German Social Democracy has undertaken to provide a disciplinary equivalent in the economic field for the advantages of military training.

(4) War, it is said, has supplied much of the inspiration and impetus which have promoted the higher developments of the life of the race. The great achievements of the nations in war have usually been followed by a golden age of spiritual achievement—in literature, in philosophic thought, and in art.[4] Even great religions in their origins, and subsequent religious revivals, have been closely connected with the throes of the nations incident to the deadly struggles of war. It appears that the tension and excitement of war stimulate the human spirit to put forth its utmost powers, quicken its interest in the capital problems of existence, and also deepen its insight and increase its receptiveness. But it is also a tenable view that the spiritual achievements of the race would have been greater, not less, had not war made its appalling drafts from generation to generation on the best energies and material of the race, and that the gains credited to war are really due to the alchemy of the over-ruling Providence which is able to do something to turn a curse into a blessing. That religion on the whole has profited by war is more than doubtful: the religious revival is a lesser fact in the midst of most wars than the bewilderment or eclipse of faith, the unsettlement of moral maxims, and the diffusion of a pessimistic philosophy.

1 J. B. Mozley, *Sermons*, Oxford and Cambridge, 1876, p. 125 f.

2 'Of the true Greatnesse of Kingdomes and Estates' (*Essays*, ed. W. A. Wright, London, 1865, p. 127).

3 Cf. William James, *Memories and Studies*, London, 1911, ch. xi. 'The Moral Equivalent of War.'

4 Ruskin, *Crown of Wild Olive*.

IX. *THE POSSIBILITY OF THE CESSATION OF WAR.*—The belief that war will eventually cease has been entertained on various grounds.

(*a*) It is held that God's purpose with the world is to establish in it a Kingdom which will be a realm of peace, as well as of righteousness and love, and that the omnipotent and all-wise God may be depended on to carry His purpose into execution. This confidence was the ground of the OT prediction that in the Messianic age 'they shall beat their swords into plowshares, and their spears into pruninghooks; nation shall not lift up the sword against nation, neither shall they learn war any more' (Is 2^4). The prediction has naturally been accepted by the Church as a promise of God vouched for by inspired prophets, but apart from the authority of the prophets it is inevitable that those who share their faith in the divine government of the world should share their conviction that universal peace is an end worthy of God which He will eventually attain in spite of human perversity and opposition.

(*b*) The hope of permanent peace has been based on a belief in the essential goodness of human nature, which it is supposed has sufficient idealism to respond in the long run to the message of justice and the appeal of brotherhood. Short of this it is held that as the human race grows more humane and refined, it will turn in disgust from the wild and brutal work of war. The hope is based on thus much of fact, that human nature has deep unrecognized and unrealized possibilities of an ethical kind, but the optimism resting on this foundation is happily reinforced by other considerations.

(*c*) The self-interest of the nations as a whole requires them to take measures for the abolition of war. The great difficulty, says Rousseau, is not even so much the wickedness as the stupidity of the rulers of states, who would be pacifists if they understood their own interests.

'They do not need to be good, generous, disinterested, public-spirited, humane. They may be unjust, greedy, putting their own interest above everything else; we only ask that they shall not be fools, and to this they will come.'[1]

The same view is taken by Kant, who says that even a race of devils, provided only they were intelligent, would be forced to find a solution other than war for their disputes. 'Nature guarantees the final establishment of peace through the mechanism of human inclinations.'[2] The view that the nations will eventually be driven by considerations of interest to protect themselves against war has been urged with renewed force in recent times on the ground that the civilized nations are now so intimately interdependent through trade and finance that in fighting one another they infallibly injure themselves, that as a fact the victors suffer hardly less than the vanquished,[3] and that the destructiveness, not to speak of the cost, of modern armaments is so terrible that persistence in war will imperil the very existence of civilization.[4] These arguments have been powerfully reinforced by the latest chapter of history.

(*d*) The eventual cessation of war, further, has been expected as the culmination of the process which has already annulled the right of the individual to take into his own hands the redress of his private wrongs. The civilized states have all succeeded in instituting machinery which checks and punishes individual wrong-doers who

1 *Œuvres*, Paris, 1839, iv. 280.

2 *Werke*, 'Zum ewigen Frieden,' viii. 366.

3 Norman Angell, *The Great Illusion*, London, 1910.

4 I. S. Bloch, *Is War now Impossible?*, Eng. tr., London, 1899.

may be minded to rob or murder, and it seems to be essentially the same problem with which the race has to deal in repressing crimes attempted by particular nations against other members of the human family. The same necessity, as Kant points out, 'which forced men to take steps to insure the security of individuals within the particular state will compel the nations to take similar measures for their protection against violence and robbery.'[1] In opposition to this view it has been maintained that the nations have not the same reasons for instituting a system for the maintenance of international law and order that a nation has for repressing crime within its own borders. It is not so necessary, it is said, to regulate the reciprocal relations of states as the reciprocal relations of fellow-citizens, since the former are not so inextricably bound up together as the latter, and, further, a state has no right to limit its independence to the same extent to which the individual consents when he submits to the laws of his country.[2] But those objections have been weakened since the 18th cent.—the first by the ever-increasing economic solidarity of the nations, the second by the demonstration afforded by the British Empire and the United States of the possibility of reconciling the rights of a central authority with the enjoyment of a satisfactory regional autonomy.

(*e*) An optimistic attitude is justified in view of the progress that has been made towards the pacific organization of areas and populations within which war formerly raged as part of the order of things. There has been a steady expansion of the areas within which war is regarded as illicit and even impossible. The history of Britain illustrates the evolutionary process. Time was when there were seven kingdoms in England, and at least three in Scotland, which were chronically at war among themselves; later, war between England and Scotland had the aspect of a natural necessity, while the situation was further complicated by a chronic feud between Scottish Highlands and Lowlands, and by struggles between king and barons. But the stage was eventually reached at which the interests of each part of the country and all sections of the population were entrusted to the wisdom and equity of the representatives of the whole body, and the notion of a war between north and south, or other sections of the population, would be scouted as insane and unthinkable. Similarly the territorial conflicts of former days are no longer possible between the Departments of modern France or the provinces of unified Italy. It is reasonable to believe that at no distant date the problem which was solved by particular nations will be solved by Europe as a whole, and that to future generations European war, if not impossible, will be stamped with the criminal character of civil or fratricidal war.

Some of the counter-arguments are weighty, but not unanswerable.

(1) It is said that, as war has prevailed from the beginning, so it will prevail to the end. But it has been the destiny of man to grapple with the most dire and formidable evils, and the marvellous progress he has made in knowledge, power, and skill seems to presage that he will master all ills in his domain save the menace of death.

'Æons rolled behind him with thunder of far retreat,
And still as he went he conquered and laid his foes at his feet.'[3]

(2) The law of the world, we are reminded, has been progress through struggle, and the nations may not expect to escape from it. But it is not necessary that the struggle should continue to be carried on by the method of violence, and it is quite conceivable—and indeed in accordance with analogies—that it should come to be confined to rational forms of emulation and competition.

(3) Human nature, it is also said, contains within itself the permanent possibility, nay, the guarantee of war—in its ingrained selfishness, its cupidity, its ambition, and its passions of hatred and revenge. But, even if we grant a root of wickedness in human nature, it is also true that it contains traits of divine nobility, which might be mobilized with success in support of altruistic and chivalrous ideals. Moreover, as already pointed out, nations may be expected to find out, as individuals have done, that fighting is at least bad and may even be ruinous policy.

(4) Religion has contributed the arguments that the permanence of war may be expected from the justice, and even from the goodness, of God. The argument from the divine justice is that God has ever punished guilty nations, and that, racial sin being inveterate, He will needs continue to employ the scourge of war as the necessary and appropriate method of the expression of His holy wrath. It is true that national sins entail punishment, and that wars have often been used as the means of chastisement, but God has ample resources of other kinds in the providential order by which to reveal His anger against national corruptions. It has also been argued that God's goodness moves Him to send wars upon the earth to prevent mankind from fixing their affections on earthly things. 'There is hardly to be found a child of fortune,' says Campanella, 'who would desire to exchange his terrestrial paradise for a celestial one; and so God applies a salutary remedy by sending upon us wars and persecutions.'[1] Similarly Hegel observes that hussars and sabres discourse much more impressively than preachers on the edifying text of the instability and vanity of earthly things.[2] But surely there is enough of irremediable misery in human life to undertake the work of weaning our affections from this world. Another branch of the religious argument founds on NT predictions of the persistence of wars and rumours of wars. These, however, belong to the apocalyptic stratum, which is concerned with events expected at the end of the world, and have nothing to do with the period during which the human race is appointed to work out its destiny under the conditions of a natural development.

The immediate outlook.—While there is reason to hope for the eventual abolition of war, it is not to be forgotten that each successive generation is disposed to military adventure by its fresh energies and its youthful inexperience. Although no generation wants two great wars, every generation seems pleased to have one. Moreover, our world is full of tension which involves the possibility of manifold future conflicts. There are many antitheses which, in addition to the legacies of hatred from the past, disturb the present and menace the future. The antitheses are (*a*) between the unreconciled forces of autocracy and democracy, (*b*) between nationalities and empires, (*c*) between nationality and nationality, (*d*) between parties representing individualistic and communistic theories of social organization, while in the distance there even loom possible conflicts (*e*) between continent and continent and (*f*) between the dominant white race and the coloured races which it has taken under its tutelage. It was therefore vitally urgent that the world should take advantage of the present revulsion of feeling to place things on a better footing, and to secure that war shall be rendered, if not impossible, at least more difficult and odious, and more dangerous to those who play with the fire.

X. *METHODS OF SECURING PERPETUAL PEACE.*—There are three ways in which war might cease: (1) there might be no more aggression; (2) there might be no more resistance; (3) there might be a political organization whose function was to preserve peace. The first and second methods have been the dreams of prophets and idealists. The third has entered in different ways into history and practical politics.

(1) Clearly there would be no more war if all nations refrained from anything of the nature of aggression. This implies, however, a moral transformation of the race such as may not be looked for in the present dispensation, and the hope of such radical conversion has chiefly been cherished as a sequel to the Second Coming and a visible reign of Christ on earth.

(2) The end, also, would obviously be attained if those whose interests were assailed consistently agreed to offer no opposition, but to show forgive-

[1] *Op. cit.* [2] E. de Vattel, *Le Droit des gens*, preface.
[3] William Watson, 'The Dream of Man,' *Poems*, London, 1905.

[1] *De monarchia Hispanica*, Amsterdam, 1640, p. 349.
[2] *Loc. cit.*

ness and goodwill. It is possible that, if this could be tried, it would have the effect of shaming hatred and aggression out of the world.[1] But it seems even more probable that, if a nation could confidently depend on immunity in wrongdoing, this would give a fresh impetus to criminal impulses. In any case the method is not practicable, as there is nothing about which human nature feels more strongly than injustice, and nothing in which men in the mass are less disposed tamely to acquiesce.

(3) Political organization might attain the end by one nation conquering the rest and compelling them to keep the peace, by nations forming themselves into two or more groups to hold one another in check, or by all the nations, or the great majority, forming a society of nations for the maintenance of peace on the basis of a recognized code of law. The last arrangement, finally, might develop into a world republic with particular countries as its provinces.

(a) *The imperialistic method.*—While the empires in one point of view have been centres of aggressive warfare, in another point of view they have made for peace within the area embraced in their dominion, and have compensated for loss of liberty by according protection and ensuring tranquillity. The great conquerors have usually quieted any compunctions of conscience by the reflexion that the end of their fighting would be peace, and that peace would be the more widely extended and the better assured the greater and more thorough their conquests. Rome gave a practical demonstration that the power strong enough to master the nations of the civilized world was able to solve the problem of preserving a general peace. The Middle Ages inherited the Roman tradition, and inclined to believe that the ideal was the unification of the world under emperor and pope as representatives of the divine sovereignty.

'Dante imagined a single authority, unselfish, inflexible, irresistible, which could make all smaller tyrannies to cease, and enable every man to live in peace and liberty, so that he lived in justice. He could conceive of its accomplishment only in one form, as grand as it was impossible—a universal monarchy.'[2]

The Holy Roman Empire was seldom, if ever, the effective master of Europe; during modern times there has been no acknowledged master; and the struggle for the hegemony among the European nations which has formed so large a part of modern history was doubtless prompted, not only by ambition and cupidity, but by the desire to give to Europe the ruler that it needed to bring its miseries, including the bloodshed, to an end. Napoleon has left it on record that he sought to conquer Europe, not only for glory, but to bless it with lasting peace. The Holy Alliance, formed after 1815, undertook to keep the peace, but unfortunately attached even more importance to its futile policy of stemming the rising tide of democracy. It was at least a tenable theory, favoured by some German historians, that, if Germany made itself master of Europe by the might of its sword, it would serve itself heir to the pacific mission of Rome. But this programme came into collision with deep-seated prepossessions —the prediction of Rousseau was twice fulfilled that no nation is strong enough to contend with the rest of Europe, and the course of events has happily shut up the world to attempting a co-operative solution.

(b) *Defensive alliances.*—For the last 400 years Europe has witnessed combinations of nearly equal strength which made it hazardous to itself for any single state, however powerful, to develop aggressive designs. The system of the balance of power was no doubt better than none in a world that was unceasingly threatened by dreams of ambition and cupidity, but it had too little of an ethical basis—naked interest being palpably dominant on both sides—and as it was deemed proper to guard against the growing strength of a possible enemy as well as to repel actual injury, the general result was, not to avert war, but to make war almost the chronic experience of Europe, and, when it occurred, to extend the area of the convulsion and to increase the horrors of the struggle.

(c) *The League of Nations.*—The third method is that the nations, and at least as a beginning the civilized nations, should form themselves into a confederation for maintaining peace on the basis of an accepted code of rights and obligations. Such an organization was adumbrated in Greek and Germanic confederations, but the idea is modern of working out a scheme to embrace the whole of Europe and the rest of the civilized world, accompanied by a recognition of moral relations with the other divisions of mankind.

The idea of a European League of Nations was conceived by Henri IV. of France, who imagined that the great powers might be persuaded by the offer of certain adjustments and compensations to renounce their special aspirations, and to bind themselves to resist any attempts to disturb the agreed settlement.[1] To the Abbé of St. Pierre belongs the honour of having opened the modern discussion in his *Projet de la paix universelle.* As fundamental articles of the League he proposed the following:

(1) 'There shall exist henceforth between the European sovereigns signing the five articles a perpetual alliance.'

(2) 'Each of the Allies shall contribute, in proportion to his actual revenues, and the charges of his state, to the expenses of the Grand Alliance.'

(3) 'The Grand Allies, for the termination of their present and future differences, have renounced and renounce for ever, for themselves and their successors, the method of arms and are agreed always to adopt henceforth the method of conciliation, through the mediation of the rest of the Allies at the meeting-place of the General Assembly, and in case of mediation being unsuccessful they agree to submit to the judgment of the Plenipotentiaries of the other Allies, a majority of votes to determine the matter provisionally, three-fourths finally after the lapse of five years.'

(4) 'If any one of the Grand Allies refuse to execute the findings and the regulations of the Grand Alliance, negotiate contrary treaties, or make warlike preparations, the Grand Alliance shall arm, and take offensive action against the power in question, until it shall have complied with the said findings and regulations, or given security for the reparation of the injuries caused by its hostile measures, and made good the military expenses as estimated by Commissioners of the Grand Alliance.'

(5) 'The Allies agree that the Plenipotentiaries, by a majority of votes, shall definitely regulate in their permanent Assembly all the articles which shall be judged necessary and important, in order to procure for the Grand Alliance more stability, security and other advantages, but the fundamental articles shall be unalterable save by unanimous consent of the Allies.'[2]

As regards the basis of the Concordat, it was proposed that the *status quo* should be accepted and maintained.

'To facilitate the formation of this Alliance, it is agreed to adopt as fundamental actual possession and the execution of the latest treaties, and to guarantee to each Sovereign jointly, and to his house, all the territory and the rights which he actually possesses.'[3]

The main features of the project were reproduced in an influential essay by Rousseau, who laid stress on the following points as essential—that such a League must include all considerable states, that it must have a judicial tribunal and an executive, and that it must have at its disposal sufficient force to prevent secession. In his final

[1] 'Hatred does not cease by hatred at any time; hatred ceases by love, this is an old rule' (*Dhammapada*, *SBE* x. 5). 'Odium reciproco odio augetur et amore contra deleri potest' (Spinoza, *Ethica*, iii. 43).

[2] R. W. Church, *Dante, an Essay, and tr. of De Monarchia*, by F. J. Church, London, 1878, p. 90.

[1] M. de B. Sully, *Mémoires*, 10 vols., Liége, 1788, Eng. tr., Edinburgh, 1805, iv. 406 ff.

[2] *Œuvres de politique et de morale*, 15 vols., Rotterdam, 1738, i. 21-31 (Eng. tr., London, 1814).

[3] P. 23.

judgment on the scheme Rousseau declared it to be hopeless to expect to convince autocratic sovereigns and self-seeking ministers that they would find it to their interests to fall in with the project. The presupposition of its success was to get rid of autocracy, and this operation might prove too painful and costly.

'A Federative League,' he concludes, 'can only be established by revolution, and who then would venture to say that its coming is more to be desired or feared?'[1]

The subject was advanced by Kant, who, while owing much to St. Pierre and Rousseau, went somewhat deeper into the conditions of lasting peace.

'The greatest problem set to the human race,' he says, 'is the formation of a political organisation under which justice will be dispensed to all, and a branch of this is the subordination to law of the external relations of the particular states.'[2]

The goal of the development on the international side is a *Völkerbund*, in which every state, even the smallest, may expect the maintenance of its security and its rights, not from the exercise of its own power or from its own decisions, but from the collective power of the League, and from judicial decisions of its collective will.[3] He lays down the following among other conditions of enduring peace:

(1) A treaty of peace should not contain matter provocative of future wars. (2) No existing state should be annexed by another through inheritance, barter, sale, or gift. (3) Standing armies should be abolished. (4) National debt should not be accumulated in support of foreign policy. (5) No state should interfere in another's domestic concerns.

Kant also expresses the opinion that perpetual peace has the best chance of being achieved under republican institutions, although he is careful to point out that a republic may exist in substance without democratic forms.[4]

No recent writer has done so much to commend the scheme as Léon Bourgeois, who played a leading part in the judicial discussions of the Hague Conferences.[5] His definition of the essence of the scheme is that the nations should agree upon a code of national rights and bind themselves as a whole to enforce it. This would correspond to the conditions under which internal order is maintained by civilized states. The other presupposition of the preservation of peace is effective machinery for enforcing decisions.

(1) 'There can be no veritable peace save under the reign of justice. To have material peace it is necessary to have first realised moral peace, and there can be no moral peace if the rights of any are felt to be, or really are menaced. Rights must be determined before they can be guaranteed.'

(2) 'The organisation of a jurisdiction which guarantees these rights is the essential condition of the establishment and the maintenance of peace.'[6]

The project was translated into a political institution by the Treaty of Versailles, which, incorporating the Covenant of the League of Nations, came into force on its ratification by Germany and Austria, and by three of the principal Allied and Associated Powers.[7]

General Scope.—(*a*) *Ends.*—Promotion of international cooperation and achievement of international peace and security. (*b*) *Means.*—Acceptance by contracting parties of obligations not to resort to war, prescription of open, just, and honourable relations between nations for the establishment of understandings of international law as rules of conduct, maintenance of justice and respect for treaty obligations (Preface).

A. *Membership.* — (1) *Original members*—those named as signatories and those named who shall sign within two months. (2) *Later adherents*—any named self-governing state or colony on the strength of a two-thirds vote of the Assembly, and on acceptance of the obligations of the League and special regulations of the Assembly (art. i.).

B. *Organization.* — *Assembly and Council* (art. ii.). 1. *Assembly.* — *Membership* — representatives of the members of the League. *Time and place of meetings*—stated and occasional. *Competent business*—any matter within its sphere of action and affecting the peace of the world. *Voting strength*—each member to have one vote, and not more than three representatives (art. iii.).

2. *Council.*—*Membership* — representatives of the principal allied and associated Powers, and of four other members to be selected by the Assembly—in the first instance Belgium, Brazil, Greece, and Spain. Representatives of other members may have a permanent seat, and selective representation may also be increased. *Time and place of meetings*—stated and occasional. *Competent business*, as before. Occasional representation of members of the League when their interests are affected. *Voting power*—one member one representative only and one vote (art. iv.).

Decisions of Assembly and Council, unless otherwise provided for, to be unanimous. First meeting to be summoned by President of the United States (art. v.). A permanent Secretariat at the seat of the League. Expenses to be shared by the members and officials (art. vi.). *Seat of the League*—Geneva in the first instance. No sex disqualification for offices (art. vii.).

C. *Reduction of armaments.*—General aim — reduction of national armaments to the lowest point consistent with national safety and the enforcement of international obligations. Plans for reduction to be submitted by the Council to the Powers, and adhered to after acceptance. Private manufacture of munitions to be discouraged and in any case reported on (art. viii.).

D. A Watching Commission to report on diligence in the execution of provisions of artt. i.–viii. (art. ix.).

E. *Basis of action.* — Guarantee of existing rights against external force. 'The Members of the League undertake to respect and preserve against external aggression the territorial integrity and existing political independence of all Members of the League' (art. x.).[1] The Council to advise upon the means of fulfilling this obligation (art. xi.).

F. *Peaceful settlement of disputes.*—Disputes likely to lead to a rupture to be submitted either to arbitration or to inquiry by the Council (art. xii.).

(1) *Arbitration.* —(*a*) Suitable matters—interpretation of a treaty, alleged facts constituting breach of an international obligation, extent and nature of reparation for injury, (*b*) court to be specially agreed on, (*c*) undertaking to abide by award, (*d*) Council to propose steps for carrying out award (art. xiii.). Court of International Justice a permanent institution. Its functions—to arbitrate as requested, and to advise the Council (art. xiv.).

(2) *Inquiry.*—(*a*) Failing agreement to arbitrate, members agree to submit dangerous disputes to the Council for investigation. (*b*) One party may effect the submission to the Council. (*c*) The Council will endeavour to effect a settlement. (*d*) If the Council does not succeed, it will publish a report of its findings (whether unanimous or by a majority); if the award is unanimous, the members agree not to go to war with the power complying with the recommendations; if there is no unanimity, members are free to take such action as they deem necessary to maintain right and justice. No report shall be made on a matter which by international law falls within the domestic jurisdiction of a party (art. xv.).

G. *Sanctions.*—Penalties for a resort to war in breach of artt. xii., xiii., xv. (*a*) Economic boycott. (*b*) Employment of armed force contributed by the governments on the recommendation of the Council. (*c*) Material support, financial, economic, and military. (*d*) Expulsion by the covenant-keeping powers of a covenant-breaking member (art. xvi.).

H. *Disputes between Powers outside the League.* — Such Powers are invited to act as if subject to the obligations of members, and to be dealt with accordingly. If both parties refuse, the Council to make such recommendations as will prevent hostilities (art. xvii.).

I. *Open diplomacy.*—All future treaties and international agreements to be registered and published (art. xviii.).

J. *Advisory and precautionary function of Council.*—Advises members to reconsider inapplicable treaties and to consider threatening international conditions (art. xix.).

K. *Inconsistent obligations and understandings.*—Abrogation and release therefrom to be sought (art. xx.).

L. *Treaties* of arbitration and regional understandings directed to peace *unaffected* — especially Monroe Doctrine (art. xxi.).

M. *The mandate.*—(*a*) Application—to territories released by the war and to backward or immature races. (*b*) Mandatories —advanced nations who can best undertake the responsibility, and are willing to accept it. (*c*) Types of mandate—to give administrative advice and assistance (*e.g.*, to former portions of the Turkish empire); to administer territory, subject to consideration for order and morals, and the grant to other nations of equal opportunities of trade and commerce (*e.g.*, in S. Africa), to administer territory as an integral portion of an empire (S.W. Africa, Oceania). The mandatories to make an annual report to the Council (art. xxii.).

N. *Wider aims of the League.*—Improvement in the conditions of labour, just treatment of natives, control of slavery and the opium and liquor traffic, and of trade in arms, secure freedom of communication, the prevention and control of disease (art. xxiii.).

International Bureau and matters of kindred concern to be placed under the direction of the League (art. xxiv.).

[1] *Œuvres*, ed. 1839, iv. 256–288.

[2] *Idee zu einer allgemeinen Geschichte in weltbürgerlicher Absicht* (*Gesammelte Schriften*, Berlin, 1902, viii. 24).

[3] *Zum ewigen Frieden*, viii. 341; Eng. tr., *Perpetual Peace*, London, 1903.

[4] P. 349 ff.

[5] *Pour la Société des nations*, Paris, 1910.

[6] P. 10 ff.

[7] *The Covenant of the League of Nations with a Commentary thereon presented to Parliament*, June 1919.

[1] But cf. xi. and xix. on possible development.

Humanitarian agencies to be encouraged and promoted (art. xxv.).

O. *Amendments to the Covenant*—to take effect when ratified, a member dissenting having the remedy of withdrawing from the League (art. xxv.).

The Covenant of the League of Nations is founded on a skilful compromise between the dictates of ethico-political theory and considerations of political expediency. Of the two elements of the combination, the lower was necessary if it was to come into existence, and the development of the higher may safely be left to the future as its custodian and trustee.

The Covenant embodies provisions and regulations which involve a notable advance in the moralization of international relations. That the leading nations should form themselves into a confederation whose object is the preservation of the peace of the world on the basis of justice and right; that they should pledge themselves to refer their differences to arbitration, or at least take advice about them, and renounce the resort to arms until the resources of reason and conciliation have been exhausted; that they should agree in principle to the limitation of their armaments, and be willing to discuss with one another concrete proposals for a reduction; that they should consent to keep one another informed as to treaties and military preparations; and finally that they should arrange to call to account and punish any disturber of the peace—these provisions mark an enormous improvement upon the principles of foreign policy which have made and coloured tragic centuries of European history and which issued in the catastrophe of the World War. On the other hand, the Covenant, recognizing that a new system must gradually evolve out of the pre-existent order, adapts itself as far as possible to the conditions of the world in the first quarter of the 20th century. The states retain unchallenged possession of their sovereign rights. It is not suggested that they should resolve themselves into the constituent provinces of a world-republic.[1] Deference is shown to the natural sensibilities of sovereign states by making the functions of Council and Assembly advisory, except in cases where the action of a particular state involves a violation of the terms of the League, or involves a menace to the peace of the world. Again, it is arranged that the great Powers shall wield authority and influence in the affairs of the League in a degree that reflects their economic and military strength, since the Council consists in the main of the representatives of a group of first-class states, instead of being made to rest on the popular Assembly. The constitution in short is not democratic, but aristocratic or oligarchical. Further, possession of territory and rights as from the date of the European settlement is recognized as constituting a foundation of right which is on the whole defensible from the point of view of justice as well as of national aspirations; and an undertaking is given that possession will be defended by the League at least against the aggression of external powers. This undertaking is, however, qualified by the provision that developments threatening the peace of the world—which might well arise from internal disorder, or the uprising of a subject population against an existing fabric of empire—would be held to be a matter on which the League would properly make more or less forcible representations to the state immediately concerned. Finally, the foreign dominions embraced in empires are regarded as lawful possessions, and the title is even strengthened on the ethical side by the doctrine of the mandate which exhibits imperial rule under the ideal aspect of friendly protection, civilizing tutelage, and moral guardianship.

The tasks assigned to the League of Nations will be of no ordinary difficulty. It will have to play the part of an impartial arbiter among the nations, and the representatives of the various powers in Council and Assembly will be predisposed to work primarily for the interests of their respective countries. It will have to give decisions in accordance with justice, and it is not easy to define justice, and to work out its implications in a world occupied by peoples which differ so widely, not merely in numbers and power, but in their capacities, their deserts, and their ability to be of service to the rest of mankind. It will require sanctions—in the last resort it must be able to compel respect for its authority and to coerce covenant-breaking nations by force of arms, and, while nations will readily go to war in defence of patriotic interests, it will be less easy to procure popular support for mere police measures which are dictated by far-seeing and disinterested international policy. These difficulties, however, are not altogether novel; they have already been experienced in other spheres of political action and development, and, as the League of Nations is an institution which the world requires, there is good reason to hope that the intelligence, the public spirit, and the resolution of mankind will prove able to cope with the essential problems of the situation.

The League of Nations, founded to protect the peace of the world, will itself no doubt breed new occasions of strife. It represents the first stage of a political development; and the analogous history of other forms of political organization suggests the probability of manifold conflicts on questions of its constitution and its powers. It starts, as has been observed, with the concession of oligarchical privileges to a minority, and the commonalty of the nations—now represented, as it were, by an Assembly and tribunes—may be expected to agitate for a more democratic constitution which would give equal voting rights to each state, and arrange that the Council should grow out of and depend upon the collective will of the whole body. The League, again, will naturally develop an increasing sense of its own importance, and will be ambitious to claim for itself the larger powers which are felt to befit a central authority, while the particular states will be jealously on their guard against action which savours of encroachment upon their independence and sovereignty. It may be added that the law which forms the basis of the judgments of the League will also afford occasion for controversy, as the League starts with a somewhat meagre outfit of moral precepts in its doctrines of non-aggression and self-determination, and it will be found necessary to do further thinking in regard to the chief good of the human race and the equitable application of an accepted moral ideal to particular peoples and to concrete historical situations. But if experience leads us to anticipate such struggles, the analogies of political history, and not least of the history of Britain and of the United States, justify the hope that working solutions will be found which will be a practical satisfaction of what is legitimate in the conflicting claims of the whole and the parts. It may somewhat confidently be predicted that the constitution will become increasingly democratic, and also that the League, while treating as sacred the domestic autonomy of the peoples, will acquire a steadily-extending authority and influence over the relations of particular states to one another and to the whole.

The endeavour to end war is only the negative side of the task of the League of Nations. The

[1] On the different ideal of the Federal World State and reasons for thinking it Utopian see L. Oppenheim, *The League of Nations and its Problems*, London, 1919, p. 18 f.

positive side is to persuade the nations to do more to bear one another's burdens, and to enrich one another's lives by reciprocal service.

'Of the constructive work we have an augury in the earnest thought which has already been given to the conditions of labour in the covenanting countries, and to the principles which have been laid down for the amelioration of the common lot. It will, moreover, obviously be the duty of the League to encourage, by every means in its power, the chief form, and one of the most beneficent forms of national co-operation, viz. the freest and fullest interchange in honest commerce of the products of the fields and the workshops of every continent and clime. Imagination may even take a wider flight, and picture a time when nation will seek to serve nation by imparting what the other may lack out of the manifold riches of a higher civilization.'[1]

In its spiritual aspect this idea is not novel: it is an ancient possession of the Christian Church, underlying its enterprise of Foreign Missions, but little has been done to act on the idea in other fields. There is room for philanthropic schemes through which each civilized people as such will make an adequate contribution towards the provision of the rudiments of rational knowledge, and especially of modern medical skill, for the benefit of the savage and semi-civilized races of mankind. A great philanthropic opportunity was lost in the two years following the war, when the peoples of Great Britain and America might have agreed to ration themselves so that they might be in a position to release the necessaries of life and some comforts for the starving populations of Europe. The response to the call of the Russian famine is, however, of good omen for the future. One very practical service would be to arrange that all manufacturing nations got an adequate supply of raw materials. It may be added that the success of the League in developing the positive and constructive activities will be an important factor in determining the success of its efforts to avert armed conflicts. It is a law of human nature that an evil habit is best overcome through the expulsive power of a new affection, and, if the nations are to cease to have the desire to devour and plunder one another, it is imperative that, through reciprocal offices of service, they should learn to think of one another with kindly and grateful feelings, and respect one another as fellow-workers in the common cause of humanity.

LITERATURE.—i. *Military history.*—G. Maspero, *The Dawn of Civilization*[4], Eng. tr., London, 1901, p. 305 ff. (Egyptian army), p. 722 ff. (Chaldæan army); H. Delbrück, *Gesch. der Kriegskunst im Rahmen der politischen Geschichte*, Berlin, 1900–02; C. W. C. Oman, *A Hist. of the Art of War; the Middle Ages from the 4th to the 14th Century*, London, 1898; J. W. Fortescue, *Military History*, do. 1914; C. von Clausewitz, *Hinterlassene Werke über Krieg und Kriegführung*, 10 vols., Berlin, 1857–63, containing 'Vom Kriege,' Eng. tr., *On War*, London, 1873; F. von Bernhardi, *On War of To-day*, Eng. tr., do. 1912; A. T. Mahan, *Influence of Sea-Power upon History*, do. 1889, *The Influence of Sea-Power upon the French Revolution and Empire*, 2 vols., do. 1892, *Sea-Power in its Relation to the War of 1812*, 2 vols., do. 1905; Herbert Spencer, *Principles of Sociology*[3], do. 1885, pt. v. *Political Institutions*, ch. 12, 'Military Systems.'

ii. *Christianity and war.*—R. H. Charles, *Eschatology, Hebrew, Jewish, and Christian*, London, 1913; A. Harnack, *Militia Christi: die christliche Religion und der Soldatenstand in den ersten drei Jahrhunderten*, Tübingen, 1905; S. J. Case, 'Religion and War in the Græco-Roman World,' *AJTh* xix. [1915] 179; C. J. Cadoux, *The Early Christian Attitude to War*, London, 1919; C. W. Emmet, 'War and the Ethics of the NT,' in *The Faith and the War*, do. 1915; P. T. Forsyth, *The Christian Ethic of War*, do. 1916; F. Laurent, *Etudes sur l'histoire de l'humanité*, 18 vols., Brussels, 1860–70; W. E. H. Lecky, *Hist. of European Morals*, 2 vols., London, 1888; J. F. Bethune-Baker, *Influence of Christianity on War*, do. 1888.

iii. *International law.*—H. Wheaton, *Hist. of the Law of Nations in Europe and America*, New York, 1845, *Elements of International Law*, ed. J. B. Atlay, London, 1904, pt. iv. 'International Rights of States in their Hostile Relations'; T. Twiss, *The Law of Nations*, do. 1861–63; W. E. Hall, *A Treatise on International Law*[7], ed. A. P. Higgins, Oxford, 1917; T. E. Holland, *The Elements of Jurisprudence*[12], do. 1916, *The Laws of War on Land*, do. 1908; Frederick Pollock, 'The Modern Law of Nations and the Prevention of War,' in *Cambridge Modern History*, xii., Cambridge, 1910, p. 703; H. Bonfils, *Manuel de droit internat. public*[7], Paris, 1914; G. Heffter, *Europäisches Völkerrecht*[8], Berlin, 1888; F. von Liszt, *Das Völkerrecht*[11], Berlin, 1918; K. von Martens, *Causes célèbres du droit des gens*, Leipzig, 1827; F. W. Holls, *The Peace Conference at the Hague*, New York, 1900; J. H. Choate, *The Two Hague Conferences*, Princeton, 1913.

iv. *Political science.*—J. Bentham, *Principles of International Law* (*Works*, London, 1843, ii.); W. Bagehot, *Physics and Politics*, do. 1872; J. K. Bluntschli, *Theory of the State*, Eng. tr., Oxford, 1885; H. Sidgwick, *The Elements of Politics*, London, 1891; Benjamin Kidd, *Social Evolution*, do. 1894; B. Bosanquet, *The Philosophical Theory of the State*, do. 1899; D. G. Ritchie, *Studies in Political and Social Ethics*, do. 1902; D. P. Heatley, *Diplomacy and the Study of International Relations*, Oxford, 1919.

v. *Arbitration.*—Gaston Moch, *Hist. sommaire de l'arbitrage permanent*, Paris, 1905; R. L. Jones, *International Arbitration as a Substitute for War between Nations*, London, 1908; M. N. Tod, *International Arbitration among the Greeks*, Oxford, 1913; H. Erle Richards, *The Progress of International Law and Arbitration*, do. 1911.

vi. *Latter-day conditions.*—*The International Crisis in its Ethical and Psychological Aspects*, by various writers, Oxford, 1915; J. L. Garvin, *The Economic Foundation of Peace*, do. 1919; J. M. Keynes, *The Economic Consequences of the Peace*, do. 1919; Lord Bryce, *The Relations of Advanced and Backward Races of Mankind*, do. 1902.

vii. *The League of Nations.*—*Bulletin de l'Association française pour la Société des Nations*, Paris, since 1918; *The Covenant, A Quarterly Journal of the League of Nations*, since 1919; General Smuts, *The British Commonwealth of Nations*, London, 1917; H. N. Brailsford, *A League of Nations*[2], do. 1917; Lord Robert Cecil, *The New Outlook*, do. 1919; Viscount Grey and others, *The League of Nations*, do. 1919; A. F. Pollard, *The League of Nations*, do. 1919; C. Sarolea, *The Peace Treaty and the League of Nations*, do. 1919.

W. P. PATERSON.

WAR, WAR-GODS.

WAR-GODS (Celtic).—At the time of the migrations of the Celts a war-god, whom the Greeks identified with Ares and the Romans with Mars, seems to have been the chief god worshipped by the Celtic tribes.[2] Gods guide their migration and bring the army to a stop on the territory destined for it;[3] to the gods they dedicate all or part of the booty in victory;[4] to them they sacrifice victims before the combat[5] and prisoners after victory;[6] in their honour they raise the war-cry.[7]

1 W. P. Paterson, *Recent History and the Call to Brotherhood*, Edinburgh, 1919.
2 Callim. iv. 173; Florus, ii. 4; Sil. Ital. iv. 200–202; Amm. Marc. xxvii. 4. 4.
3 Justin, xxiv. 4. 3; Livy, v. 34.
4 Florus, i. 20. 4.
5 Justin, xxvi. 2. 1.
6 Diod. Sic. xxxi. 13; Paus. x. 22. 3.
7 Livy, v. 38.

The war-god to whom the Celts dedicated Roman arms in 223 B.C. is called Vulcan by Florus;[1] the one to whom the Gauls sacrificed men is called Saturn by Varro.[2] The ancient Celts probably had a goddess of war; this goddess has been identified by the Greeks with Athene,[3] and by the Romans with Minerva.[4] It was in the temple of this goddess that the Insubres kept their ensigns of war.[5]

Cæsar gives us no more definite information; he mentions Mars third among the five chief gods of Gaul, and adds that Mars directs wars, and, after the issue is decided, the spoils are usually dedicated

1 ii. 4.
2 Aug. *de Civ. Dei*, vii. 19; cf. Dion. Hal. i. 38. 2.
3 Polyb. ii. 32. 6.
4 Justin, xliii. 5. 5.
5 Polyb. ii. 32. 6.

to him; when the Gauls have carried off the victory, they sacrifice all the living beings that they have taken and gather the booty to one place; in many of the tribes heaps of war booty may be seen in the sacred places.[1] We must come to the Gallo-Roman inscriptions of Gaul, Great Britain, and Central Europe—with the Celtic epithets which there accompany the name of the god Mars—to get an idea of the variety of the war-deities of the Celts. Whereas 18 epithets of Mercury have been found, 15 of Apollo, 7 of Juppiter, and 3 of Minerva, we can count 50 of Mars; and these epithets of Mars are particularly numerous in Great Britain. Some of them have a local meaning, in which cases it is not certain that we have to do with a Celtic god; we may be in presence of local cults of the Roman god Mars. But of the 40 epithets that remain after the local epithets have been deducted 8 are used alone as well as along with the name of Mars—*e.g.*, Toutatis, which is probably a variant of the name Teutates,[2] which scholiasts of Lucan elsewhere identify with Mars, and the god Esus, also mentioned by Lucan. They are probably, therefore, the very names of the indigenous gods assimilated to Mars. As regards the others, it is probable that at least a number of them also indicate Gaulish deities. And it is impossible to ascertain whether some epithets of Minerva do not denote war-goddesses. Further, Mars Loucetius is associated in two inscriptions with Nemetona, who is undoubtedly a war-goddess, and Mars Cicolluis is associated with Litavis, whose bellicose character is undoubted, since in an inscription she is replaced by Bellona as the consort of Mars. Dio Cassius[3] mentions among the Britons of the time of Boudicca the worship of a goddess of victory, Andata or Andrasta, to whom human sacrifices are offered, and whose name presents a close resemblance to that of Andarta, a goddess of the Vocontii, on whose territory have been discovered the majority of the altars of Victory that belong to Southern Gaul.

The information that has come down to us from antiquity is so imperfect that we can merely state that the ancient Celts had numerous gods and goddesses of war, and it indicates several details of their worship. But we have no figured representations of war-deities among the numerous Gallo-Roman bas-reliefs, unless we regard as such the wheel-bearing horseman who tramples under his horse's feet the monster dragon. The characteristic symbols of the Gaulish gods—the wheel, the hammer, and the cup—can hardly be interpreted as warlike. As for the attempts to explain by means of Celtic languages the names and epithets of the Gaulish gods assimilated to Mars, they supply only vague characteristics—Albiorix, 'the king of the world,' Belatucadros, 'comely in slaughter,' Caturix, 'the king of combat,' Leucetius or Loucetius, 'the brilliant.' We have no reason to believe that the Mars of Gaul had, like the Mercurys, many famous temples in Gaul. Doubtless the Roman pacification allowed as few as possible of their cults to subsist. Nevertheless we find in an inscription of the Rhine valley mention of a temple of Mars Camulus.[4]

From the text of the Irish epic, which has preserved some details of ancient Celtic mythology, we may glean some notions of war-gods and goddesses, and etymology helps us to recover others. In Cormac's *Glossary* Nét is described as 'a battle-god of the heathen Gael.' The king of the Tuatha Dé Danann, Nuada, has been identified with the Deus M[ars] Nodons known from inscriptions from Great Britain. Neman, the name of Nét's wife, has been connected with Nemetona, the Gallo-Roman goddess, consort of Mars; and the name of Nét has been compared to the first part of the name Nantosuelta, associated in a Gallo-Roman inscription with the god Sucellus, 'the good striker.' In the mythological cycle and in the Cúchulainn cycle three fairy warriors appear—a kind of valkyries with the power of changing into animals—the first Morrígan, wife or granddaughter of Nét, or wife of Dagda, the second Macha, granddaughter of Nét, the third Badb, wife or granddaughter of Nét, all three daughters of Ernmas, one of the Tuatha Dé Danann. The name Badb, which in Irish means a scald-crow, and which has a variant Bodb, has been compared to the second part of the name of a Gallo-Roman goddess [C]athu-bodvæ, in Irish Badb-catha, 'battle-crow.'[1]

It is much more difficult to discover traces of the ancient Celtic gods in the tradition and literature of Wales than in the Irish literature of the Middle Ages. Nevertheless scholars are probably right in identifying Nudd, the father of Gwyn, in whom was 'the force of the demons of Annwfn,' with the god Nodons of Romanized Great Britain.

This, then, as far as the evidence of the ancients and the epics of the Celts of the British Isles enable us to reconstruct it, is the fragmentary pantheon of the war-gods of one of the most warlike races of ancient Europe.

LITERATURE.—W. M. Hennessy, 'The ancient Irish Goddess of War' in *RCel* i. [1870–72] 32–57; J. Rhys, *Lectures on the Origin and Growth of Religion, as illustrated by Celtic Heathendom (HL)*, London, 1888; H. d'Arbois de Jubainville, *Cours de littérature celtique*, 12 vols., Paris, 1883–1902; C. Jullian, *Recherches sur la religion gauloise*, Bordeaux, 1903, *Hist. de la Gaule*, vols. i.–ii., Paris, 1908–09; G. Dottin, *Manuel pour servir à l'étude de l'antiquité celtique*², do. 1915.

G. DOTTIN.

WAR-GODS (Chinese).—China has no god of war, if by that term we imply a belief in the existence of a divine being similar in functions, characteristics, or divine attributes to Ares or Mars. This, however, is not inconsistent with the fact that war, in China as elsewhere, has usually kept itself in close touch with religion. We read in Tso's famous Commentary on the *Ch'un-Ch'iu* of Confucius that 'the great affairs of a State are sacrifice and war';[2] and the latter unaccompanied by the former was a thing unheard of. A Chinese writer has recently remarked that from the earliest historic times up to the date of the Boxers (and he need not have drawn the line there) his countrymen have never ceased to regard supernatural or spiritual agencies as constituting an essential portion of the national military equipment.[3]

It is not surprising, then, that among the most ancient ceremonial rites mentioned in Chinese classical literature are those which were carried out during warfare by rulers of states and leaders of armies with the direct object of invoking the aid of the unseen powers and impressing the troops with the belief that those powers would protect and help them in the hour of battle. The two most solemn ceremonies in ancient China connected with war were known as the *lei* and the *ma* sacrifices.

Very few details regarding them have come down to us, and we cannot always be sure that the records we possess are altogether worthy of trust. It is clear, however, that the *lei* was a sacrifice to God (T'ien or Shang-Ti) and that it was offered on many solemn state occasions. The ceremony could be performed only by the sovereign himself, because it was the 'Son of Heaven' alone who had the prerogative of offering

1 Cæsar, vi. 17; cf. Livy, v. 39. 1.
2 Lucan, i. 444.
3 lxii. 6 f.
4 *CIL* xii. 2571.

1 See art. CELTS, § VI. f.
2 J. Legge, *The Chinese Classics*, Hongkong, 1861–72, vol. v. pt. ii. p. 382 (Chinese text on p. 379).
3 Yi Pai-sha, in the Chinese monthly journal *Hsin Ch'ing-nien*, vol. v. no. 1, p. 17.

sacrifices to Heaven.[1] It was not exclusively associated with war, but it was always offered when an army was about to be set in motion and seems to have been regarded as pre-eminently a military sacrifice.[2]

The *ma* was offered on the field of battle or at the army's halting-places. There is great uncertainty with regard to this sacrifice; the most probable view is that it was offered to T'ien or Shang-Ti, but that certain minor divinities were also invoked or associated with that high deity—namely, the local tutelary powers who might be expected to object to the intrusion of armed forces into their private spheres of activity or who might feel outraged by the shedding of blood on soil that was under their special protection.

It is highly improbable that the early Chinese ever regarded warfare abstractly, as a quasi-institution, or that they ever felt the need of nominating a deity to preside over it as 'god of war.'

1. Kuan Yü or Kuan Ti, 'god of war.'—Although it is not correct to say that the Chinese pantheon contains a Mars, there are several famous warriors who, having shown themselves to be stout fighters and unselfish patriots during their earthly lives, have been deemed worthy of having their names and 'spirit-tablets' enshrined in a kind of national Valhalla or 'Temple of Military Heroes,' just as the names and tablets of great sages and philosophers and other public benefactors have been enshrined in the 'Hall of Worthies' or the 'Temple of Confucius.' It is the most celebrated of these national heroes who has been so often described as 'god of war' and as 'the Chinese Mars';[3] and, although neither term is strictly applicable, and the latter is certainly inadmissible, the former may be retained if only because it has passed into common usage among Western writers on China and because there is no very suitable term in our language by which it could be replaced. We should be careful to remember, however, that the Chinese have never lost sight of the fact that their god of war was once a man like themselves and lived at an epoch which Chinese annalists do not consider very remote. Even now his manhood is by no means altogether merged in his divinity; and, though he is regarded as a worker of miracles and has certainly been the object of much superstitious devotion, this seems hardly sufficient to justify us in regarding him as more than a very potent saint.

Though dead heroes have always been honoured in China, and the custom of 'canonizing' those who deserved well of their country either in peace or in war is a very ancient one,[4] it was not till China had fallen into a state of military decadence that a distinct cult of great soldiers began to take a conspicuous place in the religious life of the Chinese people. Kuan Yü had been dead about eight hundred years when the Sung emperors set him up as the central figure in a national cult that has lasted to this day.

Kuan Yü, a native of the village of Ch'ang-p'ing in Hsieh-chou (Shansi province), was born A.D. 162 and died in 219. He lived during the time of disunion and strife that is commonly known as the period of the Three Kingdoms, and he is regarded as the most romantic figure in one of the most romantic epochs of Chinese history. Of abnormal size and strength, he distinguished himself above all his contemporaries by his prowess and courage and by his chivalrous sense of honour. The influence of the drama, coupled with that of a great novel known as the *San Kuo*—both full of fantastic details which can have had little or no foundation in fact—have raised him to a pitch of popularity which is really independent of his position in the official roll of divinities or saints and would hardly be affected by the total withdrawal of official recognition. His surname is unknown; for Kuan was merely adopted by him in order to conceal his identity during his flight from his native place after he had entered upon his career of glory by slaying a tyrannical magistrate. Later he accidentally made the acquaintance of two other celebrated characters of the period—Liu Pei and Chang Fei. The three became devoted and lifelong friends and entered into a relationship of sworn-brotherhood by taking the famous 'oath of the peach-orchard.'[1] The leader of the three was Liu Pei, who was or declared himself to be a descendant of the founder of the Han dynasty and eventually carved his way to the throne of one of the Three Kingdoms—that of Shu—largely through the devotion and generalship of Kuan Yü. After a brilliant career which was not too uniformly successful to be monotonous, he was captured by the forces of Sun Ch'üan and executed.[2] Ten years or (according to another authority) forty-one years after his death he was given the posthumous title of *Chuang Mu Hou*, 'Marquis of Martial Dignity,' and various other titles were added throughout the centuries.

There is some doubt as to the exact date upon which Kuan Yü first acquired the high-sounding title of *Ti*—a term which is usually translated 'god,' but for which the word 'emperor' is, in this and many similar cases, a more fitting equivalent. The generally accepted date is 1594, when the emperor Wan-Li bestowed the title of *Hsieh-T'ien Hu-Kuo Chung-I Ta Ti*, 'In-harmony-with-Heaven Protector-of-the-State Loyal-and-Righteous Great Emperor.' For some reason not much notice seems to have been taken at first of this addition to Kuan Yü's honours, for he continued to be designated by his old title of 'Marquis.' This was brought to the notice of the emperor Hsi Tsung (T'ien-ch'i), who in 1624 issued an edict declaring that the commands of his late majesty Shên Tsung (Wan-Li) were to be carried out, and confirming the titles, including that of *Ti*, conferred upon Kuan Yü by that monarch. From that time to the present the 'god of war' has been generally known as Kuan Ti.

2. Yo Fei, hero of the Sung dynasty.—The figure of Kuan Ti looms far larger than life-size through a mist of romance created by the popular drama and by the great novel of *The Three Kingdoms*. Were it not for this fact, his place in the affections of the Chinese people might long ago have been disputed by another great national hero—Yo Fei. This high-souled patriot lived nearly a thousand years after Kuan Ti; there has been much less time, therefore, for the growth of legends. As a historical figure, however, it may be questioned whether Yo Fei should be regarded as in any way inferior to Kuan Ti either as soldier or as patriot.

Yo Fei was a native of the province of Honan. As a boy he was studious, but the natural bent of his mind soon showed itself in the fact that his favourite books were those which discussed warfare and military tactics, such as the *Ping Fa* of Sun Tzŭ, described by its recent English translator as 'the oldest military treatise in the world.'[3] As he grew up, Yo Fei became a noted archer, and soon distinguished himself in martial exploits against the Golden Tatars, who were at that time engaged in gradually driving the Sung dynasty from the plains of Northern China. Had Yo Fei been adequately supported by the Court and Government, it is possible that the invaders would have been expelled from China. Unfortunately he incurred the active hostility of the powerful Ch'in Kuei, the emperor Kao Tsung's trusted minister.[4] It was this minister who was mainly responsible for the cession of Northern China to the Tatars. At any rate he appears to have entered into a treasonable agreement with Wu Shu, a Tatar prince, to bring about a peace advantageous to the invaders. Yo Fei earnestly desired to continue the struggle, and stoutly opposed the purchase of peace by a disgraceful cession of territory. When compelled to retire and leave the enemy in possession of territory that he felt quite competent to defend, he made bitter complaints that the fruits of his ten years of strenuous labour had been destroyed in a single day. As a vigorous opponent of the peace policy, Yo Fei was regarded by Ch'in Kuei as a dangerous enemy. He caused charges of treachery to be trumped up against him and in 1141 succeeded in having him arrested. Shortly afterwards Ch'in Kuei personally issued a secret order for his summary execution, which was duly carried into effect; and it was falsely reported to the throne that Yo Fei had died a natural death in prison. As time went on, the true history of the events that led to Yo Fei's betrayal and death gradually came to be known among the people, and, though Ch'in Kuei lived fourteen years longer, loaded with honours and high in the good graces of his sovereign, he has earned an immortality of infamy in his country's annals. On the other hand, the name of the warrior whom he defamed and slew has gathered fame and honour with the passing of the centuries, and his temple, which is situated near the margin of the beautiful Western Lake, outside the walls of Hangchow, is

1 Cf. the *Li Chi* (*SBE* xxvii. [1885] 116, 225; xxviii. [1885] 212).
2 *SBE* xxvii. 218.
3 *E.g.*, by H. C. Du Bose, *The Dragon, Image and Demon*, New York, 1886, p. 128; W. E. Soothill, *The Three Religions of China*, London, 1913, p. 288; H. Doré, *Recherches sur les superstitions en Chine*, Shanghai, 1911–15 (*Variétés sinologiques*, no. 39), vi. 59.
4 Cf. *SBE* xxviii. 207 f.

1 See art. Vows (Chinese).
2 For accounts of Kuan Yü see H. A. Giles, *A Chinese Biographical Dictionary*, London, 1898, nos. 1009 and 1803; and Doré, vi. 54 f.
3 *Sun Tzŭ on the Art of War*, tr. L. Giles, London, 1910.
4 H. A. Giles, *A Chinese Biographical Dictionary*, no. 392.

a place of pilgrimage for all Chinese who love their country and wish to show their reverence for the memory of a national hero.

The gradual elevation of Yo Fei to a place among China's patron-saints and divinities began in the reign of Hsiao Tsung (1163–1189), who succeeded the weak and vacillating Kao Tsung on the throne of the Sung empire. That ruler restored the honours and titles of which Yo Fei had been deprived after his impeachment. He also ordered a re-burial of his body, and gave a large sum of money to defray the cost of an official funeral. It was further decreed that a temple should be built and dedicated to the hero, and funds were provided for the performance of periodical sacrificial rites.

3. The cult of military heroes or 'war-gods' under the Republic.—As Kuan Ti was specially venerated by the late Manchu dynasty, it would not have been surprising if the victorious revolutionaries had decided to treat that divinity with cold disdain and to abolish the official rites connected with his cult. The establishment of a nominal Republic has not had this result; but Kuan Ti's position is not precisely what it was before 1911. In the third year of the Republic (1914) it was decreed by the President (Yüan Shih-k'ai) that the 'Military Temple' was to be devoted to the cult not of Kuan Ti alone but of Kuan Ti and Yo Fei and twenty-four other celebrated military leaders and patriots. Kuan Ti and Yo Fei were to share the highest honours equally, and the twenty-four others were to be regarded as their spiritual 'associates.' Nothing was done to interfere with the existing Kuan Ti temples or their rituals; but a new temple was dedicated to Kuan Ti and Yo Fei and their associates. The temple chosen for the purpose comprises a large group of buildings immediately to the north of the palace of Prince Ch'un, ex-prince regent and father of the young emperor Hsüan T'ung. It was erected by the imperial government about a quarter of a century ago and was intended for use as an ancestral temple for Prince Ch'un, but had never actually been used as such when the dynasty was deposed. When it was taken over by the Republican Government, it was speedily converted into what might be described as the 'mother-church' of the reorganized cult of military heroes. The main buildings of this temple are covered with beautiful coloured tiles and stand in spacious courtyards. The principal hall or chapel is called the *Wu Ch'êng Tien*, 'Hall of Military Perfection,' in contradistinction to the *Ta Ch'êng Tien*, or 'Hall of Great Perfection,' the principal sanctuary in the Temple of Confucius. The interior, with its magnificent timber pillars and its richly-decorated roof, is impressive in the stately simplicity of its arrangements. There are no images. The canonized heroes are represented by their 'spirit-tablets' only—*i.e.* plain oblong pieces of wood, each bearing the name of the person whom it represents. In the place of honour at the north side of the hall, facing the entrance, stand two tablets side by side, somewhat larger than the others. These are the tablets of Kuan Ti and Yo Fei. It is to be noted that Kuan Ti's tablet does not bear all his titles or the highest of them. He is merely *Kuan Chuang Mu Hou*, 'Kuan the Marquis of Martial Dignity,' the earliest of his posthumous titles. The designation on Yo Fei's tablet also consists of four characters—*Yo Chung Wu Wang*, 'Yo the Prince of Loyalty and Martial Prowess.' On the east and west sides of the hall stand the tablets of the twenty-four 'associates,' twelve on each side, all well-known historical characters.

The reorganization of the cult of heroes was based on sound considerations of practical statecraft and national expediency. The main objects were to encourage patriotic ideals among the people, to raise the public estimation of the profession of arms, and to inspire the soldiers themselves with military zeal and professional pride. On the occasions of the periodical ceremonies appointed to be carried out in honour of the twenty-six heroes army commanders are enjoined to bring their troops to the local 'Military Temple,' so that they may be spectators of the rites and have an opportunity of showing their reverence for the memory of the great soldiers of past days. The troops are also expected to take oaths of allegiance and good conduct. The first ceremony at Peking took place in January 1915. General Yin Ch'ang, as deputy for Yüan Shih-k'ai, led his officers and soldiers to the newly-established temple, and there they took the military oaths, which may be summarized as follows: (1) to be loyal; (2) to be obedient; (3) to protect the people of China from enemies; (4) to be ready to die for their country; (5) to be diligent and zealous in their duties, to respect their superiors and comrades, and to be true and upright in speech and action; (6) to abstain from taking part in political movements and from joining political societies or parties.

The ceremony is as simple as it is impressive, and, though Christian missionaries have asserted that it fosters superstition and 'shows in a painful manner the backward strides that are being taken by the Government,'[1] such complaints show a curious lack of sympathy and understanding. The religious significance of the cult is, indeed, very slight. The soldiers are not called upon to subscribe to any dogmas or beliefs regarding the powers or functions supposed to belong to the objects of the cult, nor do they prostrate themselves before any idol. They are merely expected to bow the head as they file past a row of wooden tablets bearing the honoured names of those who fought and in many cases died for their country.[2] Surely no more fitting place could be chosen for administering the military oaths of loyalty, obedience, and self-sacrifice than a building which has been dedicated to the memory of the heroes who are believed to have been the highest Chinese embodiments of those ideals.

LITERATURE.—This has been indicated in the footnotes. A large proportion of the material has, however, been taken from untranslated Chinese sources.

R. F. JOHNSTON.

WAR, WAR-GODS (Greek and Roman).—**1. Greek.**—The importance of war in early communities must always have been such as to bring it into close relation with the worship of the gods. In fact we usually find that it is one of the chief functions of any god to help and protect his people in war; and that they regard it as a matter of the highest importance to secure his approval for any such enterprise. In civilized warfare the conventions and rules generally observed, such as the sanctity of heralds and other envoys, or the inviolability of a truce, were also under the protection of the gods. But the ritual of declaration and conclusion of war was not so highly developed among the Greeks as among the Romans.

A curious instance is recorded by the scholiast on Eur. *Phœn.* 1377, who states that before trumpets were invented torches were used as a signal at the beginning of a battle; these were borne by two priests of Ares, one from each army, who were alone inviolable.

Here we seem to see some approach to an international sanction under divine authority; another custom is the truce always allowed by the victors

[1] This sentence occurs in an account of the ceremony as held in a provincial city. See *North China Daily News* (Shanghai), 7th Oct. 1915.

[2] A short account of the proceedings at Peking appeared in the *North China Daily News*, 26th Jan. 1915. Similar ceremonies have been regularly carried out ever since, both in Peking and in the Provinces. The spring ceremony in 1920 took place on 31st March, and in Peking the President (Hsü Shih-ch'ang) was represented by the general who had attended the proceedings on behalf of Yüan Shih-k'ai.

to the defeated army for collecting and burying the dead.

A typical example of a truce between combatant armies occurs in the *Iliad*, where a solemn sacrifice is made, and over it a curse is invoked from the gods on whoever may break the oath; but the gods are those who preside over the oath rather than over war.

In these cases both parties alike appeal to the same gods; in them we see merely a particular application of the principle that the gods, and Zeus as the chief god, enforce honour and mutual faith in all relations between strangers.

Examples like these are not, however, concerned with gods of war as such. The function of a war-god was above all to give victory to his own people, and to preside over such preparations as were likely to lead to it. These functions are sometimes attributed to a special deity, but more often to the chief god, or to the god who takes any town or people under his particular protection. Conversely, it might be an effective measure to withdraw from the enemy the protection of their own special divinity.

A good example is the secret expedition made by Odysseus and Diomed to carry off the Palladium, or sacred image of the war-goddess of Troy, because its presence prevented the capture of the town. A clear and instructive example of the gods to whom victory is ascribed occurs in an inscription found at Delphi, in which the Selinuntians say 'they are victors by the aid of the following gods—Zeus and Phobos (Fear) and Herakles and Apollo and Poseidon and the Tyndarids (Dioscuri) and Athene and Malophoros (Demeter) and Pasikrateia (Persephone) and the other gods—but above all of Zeus.'[1]

Here are to be noted the reiterated insistence on the predominance of Zeus in this capacity, and the placing next to him on the list of Phobos—here probably to be regarded, like other epithets of gods in the list, as a name for Ares himself rather than as a satellite of his. Some of the other divinities in the list are elsewhere regarded as especially givers of victory to their devotees; but the whole is probably to be regarded rather as an enumeration of the chief deities of the State cultus.

In the Homeric poems we constantly find the gods not only as givers of victory and as strong partisans of one side or the other, but also as actually mingling in the fray among mortal combatants. This, however, though it applies to all the other gods, is not true of Zeus, who decides the issue by his will and imposes it by his emissaries. So in all great national crises or deliverances due to a successful war the victory is ascribed to **Zeus**, especially under his title of Eleutherios ('the Liberator'). Thus at Platæa, in commemoration of the decisive victory over the Persians, games called Eleutheria were celebrated at the altar of Zeus Eleutherios, and a race between men in armour was the chief event. An emblem of this power of Zeus is the ægis (*q.v.*), which he lends to **Apollo**[2] to turn the battle against the Greeks, and which is constantly worn by **Athene**. It has the power of causing terror and flight among those against whom it is shaken, and is used only by these three deities. All three have a specifically warlike side. Apollo was honoured in the festival of the Boedromia at Athens and of the Karneia at Sparta, both of a warlike character; he was especially the leader and giver of victory to the Dorians. After the Persian wars all the Greeks who had participated in the struggle set up a common thank-offering to him at Delphi. The same victory was attributed by the Athenians to their patron goddess, and commemorated in offerings or statues on the Acropolis; and the Platæans who shared in the battle of Marathon set up, from their share of the spoils, a temple and statue at Platæa to Athene Areia as goddess of war. Another epithet of

[1] C. Michel, *Recueil d'inscript. grecques*, Brussels, 1900, no. 1240.
[2] *Il.* xv. 229.

Athene which was probably of a warlike character was Nike, goddess of victory. Athene Nike had an altar and shrine on the bastion south of the entrance to the Akropolis and guarding its approach; on this bastion was erected, in the time of Perikles, the little temple which commemorated in its reliefs the victories of the Greeks over the Persians. The goddess is sometimes called 'Wingless Victory' by a misconception; as a form of Athene she was distinct from the winged figure of Victory so common in Greek art of all periods. This latter Nike is a mere impersonation of victory, whether in the games or in war. She has no separate cultus before the time of Alexander, and no place in mythology. She is placed on the hand of Zeus or of Athene in their great statues, and so is regarded as their satellite. Winged victories are often to be seen crowning victors—but usually athletic, not martial ones—making sacrifices, and decking trophies. Famous statues of Nike are set up to commemorate victories in war—the best known are that by Pæonius dedicated to Zeus by the Messenians at Olympia, and that from Samothrace, now in the Louvre, placed on a ship to record a naval victory of Demetrios Poliorketes. It has been rightly observed that she is in each case represented as the messenger rather than the giver of victory. Trophies, set up on the field of battle, were regarded as dedications—presumably to the god to whom the victory was ascribed. They were protected thus by a religious sanction, for they appear usually to have been respected even when set up in enemy territory.

The deities so far mentioned preside over war only as one side of their activities, and as a necessary part of their protection and help to their chosen people. In **Ares**, on the other hand, we recognize a specialized god of war. It has indeed been suggested that his functions were once of a wider character, perhaps among the Thracians or some other foreign people; but there is little trace of any such character in Greek mythology or ritual.[1] Some confusion has arisen in this matter from the misleading identification of Ares with the Roman Mars. Ares fares but poorly at the hands of the poets from Homer down. In the *Iliad* he is wounded by a mortal and overthrown by Athene; Sophocles actually calls him 'the god unhonoured among gods,'[2] and the aid of other deities is implored against him; and this not as the war-god of an adversary, but as representing the horror and evils of war and pestilence. He is thus essentially the destructive god, delighting in slaughter; yet his worship, so far as we can judge, does not appear to have any connexion with the ritual and belief associated with terrible 'chthonic' powers or the possible spiritual influence which could arise from such belief. On the other hand, the name of Ares often occurs in conventional expressions and epithets applied to warriors implying military prowess; but in such cases it seems to be used as an impersonation of war rather than with any mythological reference. So too in expressions like 'Ares destroyed him' in an epitaph or, in a hymn to Apollo, 'He stayed the Ares of the Gauls,' it even seems as if the name of Ares was used by preference for the power of the enemy. One of the earliest and best attested shrines of Ares in Greece, that on the Areopagus at Athens, was said to have been founded by the Amazons, terrible women warriors of foreign origin who were defeated by Theseus. Whatever the origin of Ares, he seems in all these cases to represent the brutal and barbarous or 'barbarian' side of war, which is overcome by the Greeks with the help of their gods of civilized warfare. Such an impression is confirmed by the legend that tells how Herakles,

[1] Cf. art. THRACE.
[2] *Œd. Tyr.* 215.

the typical Greek hero, by the aid of Athene, slew Kyknos, the son of Ares, in spite of Ares' attempt to support him. Ares indeed takes his place among the gods in their usual assemblies, and in such common exploits as the battle against the Giants; but even here he does not perform a leading rôle.

Ares is associated with a goddess Enyo (cf. his epithet or by-name Enyalios), who, however, has little mythological personality. His association with Aphrodite (which was given a scandalous turn by the poets from Homer down) is probably due to his having in some places a warrior-goddess as consort, who was identified, *e.g.*, with the armed Aphrodite worshipped at Corinth—very probably a survival from primitive worship. Phobos, or 'Fear,' is either his satellite or another name for himself, rather in the sense of Terror, but is a mere impersonation, though sometimes represented on shields and similar objects—possibly originally with the magic intention of inspiring terror in the enemy. There are also dæmons of battle or strife who delight in slaughter, Eris (Strife) and the like; and Keres, dæmons of death, who drag away the corpses of warriors; but these belong to poetical imagination, at least in their artistic form. A curious myth about Ares is that he was bound in a pot for twelve months by the Aloadæ.[1] Similar stories of the binding and hiding of a malevolent spirit are known to folk-lore; a similar notion is found in the binding of Satan for a thousand years (Rev 20^2).

To sum up, the gods who presided over war in Greece fall into two classes: those who gave 'the civilized art of war' and 'the tempered civic courage exalted by Aristotle and other Greek moralists,' and Ares, who inspired 'the brute battle-rage,' with which 'the Greeks had little sympathy.'[2] With the advance of ethical feeling in religion, the latter became the representative of the spirit of destruction and of barbarian rather than Hellenic warfare, though his cult still survived in many cities.

2. Roman.—In the religious usages of war, and in the beliefs as to war-gods and the practice of their ritual, Rome differs from Greece in two respects: (1) Mars, the specialized war-god, was also in many ways the chief national god, and so differs widely from Ares, with whom the Romans identified him; and (2) the ritual and observances of war were far more elaborate and more definitely prescribed, and were to a great extent under the charge of special priestly officials.

In addition to Mars, Janus, Jupiter, and Quirinus are concerned with war, though not as their special function. **Janus**, as the spirit of doorways, is usually first among gods to be invoked, in connexion with every going out and coming in. His temple in Rome appears to have consisted of two doorways, with a kind of court between them. Here an image of Janus, with a head facing each way, was set up as guardian of the threshold. But this statue probably belongs to a later stratum of belief and ritual; originally the doors themselves were the symbol or even the habitation of the god. This temple was open in time of war and closed in time of peace—a custom which has puzzled mythological speculators alike in ancient and in modern times. Virgil[3] seems to regard war as being shut up within the doors and released when they are opened; Horace[4] speaks of the bars that shut in Janus, the guardian of peace. Virgil at least records the custom, common to other Latin towns as well as Rome, that the king or the consul should formally open the doors as a declaration of war. An explanation that has appeared probable to modern mythologists, as to Ovid,[1] is that the door was left open during an expedition so that there might be no obstacle to the return of those who had gone forth. The gates are said to have been closed during the reign of Augustus for the first time but one since the reign of Numa.

[1] *Il.* v. 385 ff.
[2] *CGS* v. 407.
[3] *Æn.* vii. 607 ff.; cf. i. 294.
[4] *Ep.* II. i. 255.

The worship of **Jupiter** was also in many ways associated with war. The most conspicuous example is in the case of the *spolia opima*, which consisted of the spoils of an enemy leader slain in single combat by the leader of a Roman army. These are said to have been first dedicated by Romulus in a temple to Jupiter Feretrius which he established for the purpose. In this temple was kept the sacred stone, Jupiter Lapis, which was taken with them by the *fetiales* when they went out to ratify a treaty, and by which they swore on other solemn occasions. The god was probably in primitive times thought of as immanent in this stone and in the oak-tree on which Romulus hung the spoils. The rites of war connected with this primitive temple were later eclipsed by those of the great temple of Jupiter Capitolinus. This temple is especially associated with the celebration of the triumph which was the highest honour that could be given to a victorious general. The most remarkable feature of the triumph was that the general was actually invested with the insignia of the god, borrowed from the temple for the purpose, and had his face painted with vermilion, in imitation of the image of the god. He proceeded from the Campus Martius through the Forum to the temple of Jupiter Capitolinus, and there deposited the laurels from his *fasces* and the laurel branch which he carried on the knees of the god, thus assigning to him the glory.

The worship of Jupiter Latiaris on the Alban Mount belonged to the Latins generally rather than to Rome in particular; but it was adopted into the Roman State cultus. The celebration of the Feriæ Latinæ in his honour was the first duty of the consuls on their assuming office; and military disasters were attributed to its omission. A triumph was celebrated on certain occasions on the Alban Mount in honour of Jupiter Latiaris, especially by generals who had not obtained the Senate's sanction for a triumph in Rome. Other epithets of Jupiter which are obviously of a military character are Victor and Stator. There appear to have been three temples of Jupiter Victor in Rome, dedicated on various occasions; that of Jupiter Stator on the Palatine, on the spot where the flight of the Romans before the Sabines was stayed, was attributed to Romulus; it was renewed in consequence of a vow in battle against the Samnites. Jupiter was also worshipped in various forms as protector and giver of victory to the emperors on their military expeditions; and in the later imperial age the *imperator* is often portrayed with the attributes of Jupiter—an extension of the practice followed earlier in the case of a triumphing general.

The most important priestly college connected with the military side of the worship of Jupiter was that of the *fetiales*, who were concerned with questions of international faith and the sanctity of solemn pledges made in the name of the god. Their special functions were the demands for reparation in cases of international offences, the declaration of war, and the conclusion of peace and of treaties. They had the inviolable character of sacred envoys, and carried with them on their expeditions the sacred stone and the sceptre from the temple of Jupiter Feretrius, and the sacred vervain gathered on the Arx (*sagmina*). Their spokesman was the *pater patratus*. In demands for reparation (*clarigatio*) three intervals of ten days were allowed. If by the thirty-third day satisfaction was not given, war was declared. This was done by the *pater patratus* hurling a spear over the enemy's frontier. When this in later times became impracticable owing to the distance of some military expeditions, a parcel of land near the temple of Bellona in Rome was ficti-

[1] *Fasti*, i. 279 f.

tiously converted into enemy soil, its boundary being marked by the *columna bellica*; and the spear was cast into this instead. A war declared by these formalities was called a *iustum piumque bellum*, not in any moral sense, but simply in that all the ritual had been correctly followed out so as to secure divine sanction. At the conclusion of a treaty or truce at the end of a war the consul could only make a *sponsio*, or agreement, which did not become binding upon the people until it was ratified by the *fetiales* with a special form of sacrifice. In all these observances Jupiter is appealed to rather as the guardian of international faith and honour than specifically as a war-god; but they are closely associated with war as supplying the religious sanction without which success could not be expected. The *fetiales* naturally acquired some knowledge of international law, and were sometimes appealed to on a question of procedure.

It has been much disputed among mythologists whether **Mars** should be regarded as specifically a war-god; the opinion appears now to prevail that, although this side of his functions was prominent in early times and predominant in later, it was not the most primitive or the most important. Mars appears to have been a god of the land, not only in Rome, but also in many other Italian states. It is noteworthy that he had no temple within the *pomœrium* at Rome. This is explained by some authorities as indicating a notion that his presence was undesirable or a desire that civil strife should not exist within the city; but it is more probably connected by others with the notion that he was god, not of the town, but of the country both cultivated and wild, especially the latter. For this reason he was able to protect his worshippers when they ventured out on warlike expeditions. Similarly the spring and autumn ceremonies in his honour, such as the dances of the Salii with the sacred shields (*ancilia*), are by some associated with the beginning and end of the campaigning season, and so with the activity of the war-god. But it has been pointed out that similar dances occur among many peoples in connexion with the cult of the powers of vegetation or the processes of agriculture at the most critical seasons of the year, and were intended to arouse the sleeping forces of such powers, or to avert or exorcize malignant influences. This may well have been the original meaning of these dances in honour of Mars, though they doubtless acquired a warlike meaning in quite early times. Though Mars had no temple within the city of Rome, sacred objects connected with his worship were preserved in some of the most ancient shrines in the city. The spears of Mars (*hastæ Martis*) were kept in the *sacrarium* in the Regia, at the foot of the Palatine, and were shaken by a consul before entering on a campaign with the words: 'Mars, vigila'; these were evidently regarded as the symbol of the god, who was in early times probably thought to be immanent in them; their spontaneous shaking was regarded as a portent. In the Hall of the Salii on the Palatine were kept the sacred shields. These were of a very ancient pattern similar to those used in the Mycenæan age in Greece. One of them was believed to have fallen from heaven in the time of Numa; and the safety of the city was thought to be dependent on its preservation, as in the case of the Palladium at Troy. Numa had eleven other shields made to match it; and these were annually carried round various altars in the city by the Salii in the month of March; they were ceremonially purified and put away by the Salii in October. The Salii on their way executed a kind of war-dance and beat the shields with sticks. Another ceremony in honour of Mars which was given in later times a warlike significance was that of the October horse; the winning horse in a race was sacrificed, and his head fixed up on the Regia, though here too later investigators see a rite originally agricultural in intention. The sacrifice took place at the altar of Mars in the Campus Martius.

The identification or contamination of Mars with the Greek Ares, and the universal tendency of poetical mythology, led to Mars being more and more regarded as the god of war, the protector of Roman armies and of soldiers in general; and he has come to be thought of only in this aspect in mediæval and modern times. His association with the first month of the year in the old Roman calendar is probably due to agricultural rather than to military influences. A remarkable custom in connexion with Mars was the *ver sacrum*, which was decreed to him in times of pestilence or disaster. In accordance with this all animals and human beings born within the succeeding spring were to be sacrificed or devoted to the service of the god. In the case of human beings this devotion took the form of being sent forth beyond the boundaries of the State. Hence arose colonies of a military character, with Mars as their leader and founder. The foundation of many Italian cities was attributed to Mars; but legends like that of Romulus, who was said to have been borne to the god by Rhea Silvia, show an anthropomorphism alien to primitive Italian religion, and are probably of Greek origin.

Another Roman or rather Italian war-god is **Quirinus**, who was later identified with Romulus. He seems to belong to the Sabine settlement on the Quirinal Hill, though he came to be adopted as one of the chief divinities of Rome, and even to represent the peaceful or citizen side of the god, as Mars Gradivus represents the warlike side; but he is expressly identified with Enyalios or Ares. It is significant that the three classes of *spolia opima* were offered, the first to Jupiter Feretrius, the second to Mars, and the third to Quirinus.

Other minor divinities connected with war have little mythological significance. **Bellona** had a temple in the Campus Martius, which was dedicated after a vow made in battle in 296 B.C.; close to it was the *columna bellica* mentioned in connexion with the *fetiales*. She seems, however, to have been little more than a personification, and her cult is of no great importance. She was later identified with an Asiatic warrior-goddess, or with the old Sabine Nerio. Nerio is by some writers regarded as the consort of Mars, but Nerio Martis is more probably to be explained as the strength or courage of Mars—an aspect, so to speak, of the god's manifestation. In later times Victoria, Virtus, and other impersonations were frequent, especially in art.

It is obvious that, in important undertakings such as military expeditions, sacrifice and divination would play a prominent part, especially among a people who, like the Romans, showed extreme anxiety to keep in right relations with divine powers. These, however, need not be more than mentioned here, since they are fully treated under their proper headings. A remarkable instance of *devotio* is that in which, at a critical moment of the battle, a general 'devotes' himself and the enemy's forces.

A well-known example is the case of P. Decius Mus in 340 B.C. Here the devotion was said to be due to a dream; but the rites and formula provided by the *pontifex maximus* seem to show that the act had official precedents. The case of Codrus at Athens is similar. Decius Mus was instructed to address in his *devotio* 'Janus, Jupiter, Mars, Quirinus, Bellona, the Lares, the gods Novensiles and Indigetes, the gods of his own people and the enemy, and the Manes.'

The formula is instructive, as giving in accepted order the divinities to whom the result of war is ascribed; it confirms what we learn from other sources as to the order assigned to war-gods in Roman religion. It is noteworthy also that the national gods both of Rome and of the enemy are invoked. The custom of *evocatio* is thus recalled, by which, as after the capture of Veii and of Carthage, the national gods of the enemy were invited to desert his city and transfer themselves to Rome.

In all these matters, as in all other Roman religion, we find an elaborate and highly developed ritual, with every possible safeguard against unintentional oversights. The personal character of the gods concerned comes to be realized only gradually and in later times under Greek influence, but is so strongly developed in later literature that it is by no means easy to recover the primitive meaning of the various rites and of the divine powers who were invoked.

The ensigns (*signa*) of Roman troops and the eagles (*aquilæ*) of the legions 'were objects of religious worship to the Roman soldier.'

'The "birthday of the eagle" was celebrated as that of the legion; the "genius of the signa" is mentioned in inscriptions. We read in Livy of an oath "by the signa and the eagles," and in Tacitus of a commander who saved himself from the fury of a mutinous legion by "embracing the signa and the eagle and putting himself under the protection of their sanctity."'[1]

In camp they were placed in a kind of small chapel. At Rome they were kept in the *ærarium*; hence it would seem that their sanctity was due rather to military feeling than to any official recognition or early sanction.

LITERATURE.—i. *Greek.*—L. R. Farnell, *CGS*; Roscher; Pauly-Wissowa; O. Gruppe, *Griechische Mythologie und Religionsgeschichte* (in Iwan von Müller's *Handbuch der klass. Altertumswissenschaft*, v. ii. 1, 2), 2 vols., Munich, 1897–1906; Daremberg-Saglio.

ii. *Roman.*—W. Warde Fowler, *The Religious Experience of the Roman People*, London, 1911, *The Roman Festivals*, do. 1899; H. Stuart Jones, *Companion to Roman History*, Oxford, 1912; Roscher; Pauly-Wissowa; G. Wissowa, *Religion und Kultus der Römer*[2] (in I. von Müller's *Handbuch*, v. iv.), Munich, 1912; Preller; Daremberg-Saglio.

E. A. GARDNER.

WAR, WAR-GODS (Semitic).—The earliest extant Semitic inscriptions, whether on stone, baked clay, papyrus, or parchment, whether Babylonian, Egyptian, or Hebrew, tell of wars between tribes and nations. From the time of Mesilim, before 3000 B.C., through that of Eannatum, the military genius of Lagash, of Lugal-zaggisi of Erech, the conqueror of the whole of Mesopotamia, of Sargon I., of Gudea, or of Ḫammurabi, to that of Ašurbanipal or of Nabonidus, wars and rumours of wars never ceased; from the time of the earliest Egyptian inscriptions to that of the latest the kings and rulers of Egypt are pictured smiting their foes; and from the time of the Exodus to the final fall of Jerusalem the Hebrews as a nation were warriors, and long before they became a nation—if tradition be trusted—they were subject to the same condition. The Babylonians, Assyrians, and Hebrews were warlike peoples, especially the Assyrians. But, although Egypt had her great military pharaohs at all periods of her history, such as Sesostris III., Thutmose III., Amenhotep II., Seti I., and Rameses II., she was not a great military nation.

I. *BABYLONIAN.*—**1. War.**—The quarrels and feuds between rulers of early Babylonian city-states were the beginnings of strife which later developed into the elaborate warfare of the Assyrians. The king or head of the city, originally the patriarch of the clan, was the centre of all public life. As priest he was the *šangu*, as representative of the god he was the *patesi*, and as war lord he was the *šarru*. Wars were begun by him and were carried on under his direction. But all wars were really the affair of the gods.[2]

Warlike operations were usually of a military nature. But as early as the time of Samsu-iluna wars were carried on at the head of the Persian Gulf partly on land and partly by the use of boats. The Assyrians, indeed, although not seamen themselves, built a navy with the aid of Phœnician boat-builders, and Sennacherib employed Phœnician sailors in the pursuit of Merodach-baladan across the Persian Gulf. But the Neo-Babylonians not only had developed a great merchant fleet, but also had become a considerable naval power.

[1] H. Stuart Jones, *Companion to Roman History*, p. 215.
[2] See below, 2.

From the earliest times in Babylonia the support of warfare was considered a public obligation, and those who were unfit for actual fighting were expected to furnish money to pay for a fighting unit. The army was recruited by conscription, each district being responsible for its quota. This militia, called the *ṣābē* or *ummanâte*, were subject to immediate call by the king. The levy (*dikutu*) was under the direction of a special officer, called the *nâgiru*, who saw to it that no liable person escaped, and, if a man so far forgot himself as to harbour a defaulter from the levy, he was put to death.[1] All estates had to furnish troops at the command of the king, who could even impress the produce of the land and could also commandeer labourers for civilian purposes. By the time of the Ist Babylonian dynasty there is evidence of a regular standing army of professional soldiers, recruited partly from natives, but mostly from Amorites and from the inhabitants of other conquered territories. The body-guard of the king consisted of most trustworthy native soldiers. In the absence of the king the troops were led by the *tartannu*, or commander-in-chief, who often conducted the military campaigns. The armies of the Assyrians were well officered. These officers formed a semi-caste of a military character, were paid with land, a house, and a garden, were assigned sheep and cattle, and received in addition a regular salary. But they were always at the service of the king, conducting especially the works of mobilization. In case of capture every effort was made to procure their ransom. Soldiers were well paid, were rewarded with land and a cow, and good discipline was observed among them. They were divided into cavalry and foot-soldiers, and a careful register of them was kept. The whole army was divided into companies of thousands, hundreds, fifties, and sometimes tens. In Assyria the army was still more highly developed until the time of Ašurnaṣirpal, who had created a fighting machine such as the ancient world had never seen before. The military unit in Assyrian times was the bowman, who was accompanied by his pikeman and shield-bearer. According as Assyria became more and more a conqueror of foreign peoples, she condemned forced labour at home, as in the case of Sargon II., exempted certain cities from the obligation of the levy, as in the case of Ašurbanipal, and depended upon her vast numbers of mercenaries, hired from conquered countries. The Neo-Babylonian army was modelled on that of Assyria, making extensive use of hired troops.

The Stela of Vultures, which depicts the successful war of Eannatum of Lagash, in the name of his god Ningirsu, against Umma, gives an excellent idea of some of the materials of war in that early period. In one battle, in which 6600 (or perhaps 3600) men were slain, the troops were drawn up in a solid phalanx with long spears, protected by huge shields. The lance-bearers carried an axe, and were protected by shields which were borne by the soldiers in the front rank. Each shield protected two soldiers. The shields were probably of leather with bosses of metal, as were also the conical helmets, which extended down the neck, and were furnished with ear-pieces. A chariot is represented on the stela, but it was undoubtedly drawn by asses, for the use of the horse was not known till the Kassite period. Military standards were common in early Babylonian times. The royal weapons consisted of a long lance or spear, wielded in the left hand, and a curved mace or throwing-stick. Naram-Sin is represented armed with battle-axe, bow, and helmet. In his chariot the king carried a flat-headed axe and a number of light darts, some fitted with double points. It was Dungi of Ur who adopted the bow as a national weapon.

[1] *Code of Ḫammurabi* (hereafter cited as *CḪ*), ed. R. F. Harper, Chicago, 1894, § 16.

After the introduction of the horse by the Kassites[1] cavalry took the place of chariots. Chariots were still used, but only on comparatively level terrain, and even then they were more ornamental than useful. The cavalry at first used only the bow and arrow, but later the spear was used and the horseman was furnished with a complete coat-of-mail. In Assyrian times infantry was divided into light- and heavy-armed troops. The light-armed troops wore little clothing—usually only a kilt and a fillet round the head—and were armed with spears. The heavy-armed wore sandals, a coat-of-mail over the tunic, a long fringed robe (over which was a cuirass), and a peaked helmet; they carried a short sword, and were furnished with a long rectangular shield of wicker-work covered with leather. Infantry were usually divided into archers and spearmen. Sennacherib abolished the long robe of the heavy-armed infantry and substituted leather greaves and boots. He also established a corps of slingers clad in helmet and breastplate, leather drawers, and short boots; and also a company of engineers or pioneers, furnished with double-headed axes, conical helmets, greaves, and boots. The Assyrians fought with metal weapons. Their spear-heads and arrows were usually of bronze, more rarely of iron; their coat-of-mail consisted of bronze scales sewn to a leather shirt; and many shields were of metal, though others were of wicker-work covered with metal. The army was supplied with abundant wagons for transportation of baggage, food, furniture, tents, ladders, and battering-rams; and much skill was expended upon the building of canals and fortifications.

Wars were waged very often for the sake of booty and spoils, and the usual demand made by the victor of the vanquished was payment of tribute. The favourite method of attack was by surprise, but, when that was impossible, a frontal assault was made. Many inducements were offered the foe to surrender, none being more common than the proclamation of the prowess of the reigning king; but very often a third party intervened to bring about peace and conclude a treaty, as in the case of Mesilim of Kish, who was instrumental in settling a dispute between the kings of Umma and Lagash. Peace was declared and a treaty made.

2. War-gods. — The early Babylonians, like other primitive folk, peopled their world with gods. Every mysterious phenomenon—sun, moon, vegetation, storms, water, and all the forces with which men were brought into frequent contact—was the abode of gods or demons, and usually the latter were shunned and the former propitiated. Around the abode of the gods men gathered and formed a settlement, which was often called after the god, just as Shuruppak was named from the god Shuruppak. Such a deity was always a war-god, for his people depended upon him for defence. War was not incompatible with the character of a god, for did not Ea and Apsu, Enlil and Tiamat, Marduk and Tiamat, engage in deadly warfare? So, when one city made war upon another, it was because their gods were at feud, and because their gods had ordered the strife.

The war between Umma and Lagash, as told on the Stela of the Vultures, was waged by the command of the god of Umma upon the territory of Ningirsu, god of Lagash, and Ningirsu, backed up by Enlil, joined battle. It was Zamama, god of Kish, who achieved victory over the land of Khamazi, just as it was Ašur, the great Assyrian war-god, who won military fame for Assyria.

And, when peace was declared and treaties were made, it was the gods who did it, for Mesilim records the treaty of peace which the gods of Umma and Lagash themselves had drawn up. The city-gods were thus the real kings and rulers, and so the very title *patesi*, borne by early rulers of Babylonian states, designated them as representatives of their state-god, for it was a religious title. This explains how it happened that certain Babylonian kings, desiring to enhance their own power, assumed the title of *ilu*, 'god'; and, when a *patesi* felt himself powerful enough to risk the displeasure of his own god, he would appeal to the god of a city other than his own, when the petition was for something which the foreign god alone could procure.[2]

[1] The earliest mention of a horse in Babylonia is found on a tablet of the Ist Babylonian dynasty (*OLZ* x. [1907] 638 f.).

[2] *E.g.*, Ur-Nina appealed to Enki (Ea) for a favourable oracle, when planning to build the temple of E-ninnu.

Whenever, as often happened, two or more settlements amalgamated into one city or state, the various gods sometimes amalgamated, transferring the attributes of all the gods to the strongest god, with whom all the others were identified. But sometimes the various gods remained independent, the most warlike retaining the title of war-god. Hence, while every city- or state-god was originally a war-god, yet when, by amalgamation, a state acquired a pantheon, only one of the members of that pantheon, as a rule, retained the title of war-god. Then all wars were carried on in the name of that particular god. And so it was that, while the Babylonians of the period of Ḫammurabi recognized many gods, Marduk was the war-god[1] *par excellence*, although Nabu was also recognized as a war-god. The following are the Babylonian and Assyrian deities who retained more or less of their warlike characteristics.

Enlil, son of Anu and chief god of Nippur, whose temple was the mighty E-kur, was primarily a storm-god, and he had his origin and home in a mountain. Although he is most commonly known as a storm- and vegetation-god, he was also, as patron deity of the mighty city of Nippur and head of an early Babylonian pantheon, 'king of the gods,' 'father of the gods,' and husband of the great goddess Ninlil. But he never lost that attribute which was ascribed to all early Babylonian gods, viz. 'warrior.' He was the 'mighty warrior,' and, as such, retained his place as supreme war-god when Nippur, his own city, became mighty. Among all the other cities that came under the sway of Nippur no one possessed a war-god as powerful as Enlil, and so Enlil, the son of Anu, and consequently solar deity, became the official war-god of Nippur. No one could hope to fight victoriously against Enlil;[2] hence his fame as a great warrior-god.[3] As all gods were represented by symbols, as seen on the numerous *kuddurus*, or boundary-stones, so Enlil was symbolized by his weapon, an 'ensnaring net which encircles the hostile land,'[4] and is pictured carrying away his enemies who are entangled in his net.

Ištar, or, according to the Sumerians, Ninni or Innina, was daughter of Enzu, and 'mistress of the lands.' She was also 'mistress of heaven and earth,' and had her home in Uruk. The word 'Ištar' is Semitic, and perhaps indicates that she was a vegetation-goddess, if *iš* be from *giš*, 'tree,' 'wood.' She was considered a solar deity at a very early period, and is referred to as the 'light of heaven and earth.' But with the passage of time she assumed other attributes. She was the mother-goddess *par excellence* and the goddess of love; she was identified with Venus as the 'queen of heaven'; she was the patroness of law and order; she was the raging storm that devastates heaven and earth; and she and Tammuz were associated in a way suggesting the female and male principles of life. But more than all else she was 'mistress of battles'[5] and 'mistress of war and battle.'[6] She is the *muttabbilat kakkê*, 'the bearer of arms,' the 'goddess of battle and warfare, who goes by the side of the king, favourite one, the terrible one of his enemies.'[7] Her warlike

[1] After Ḫammurabi's conquest of Rim-Sin, and his control of Nippur, Enlil, the chief Sumerian deity, lord of many city-states, surrendered his chief attributes to Marduk.

[2] *Cuneiform Texts from Babylonian Texts, etc., in the British Museum* (hereafter cited as *CT*), xv. 11. 22.

[3] T. Paffrath, *Zur Götterlehre in den altbabylonischen Königsinschriften*, Paderborn, 1913, pp. 112–123, 218–220.

[4] *WAI* iv.[2] 27, no. 4, 58.

[5] F. Thureau-Dangin, *Die sumerischen und akkadischen Königsinschriften*, Leipzig, 1907, p. 74 (hereafter cited as *SAK*).

[6] *CḤ* xxvii. *a*, 92 f.

[7] A. T. Clay, *Miscellaneous Inscriptions in the Yale Babylonian Collection*, New Haven, 1915, p. 58.

character is excellently brought out in Ašurbanipal's dream.[1] As a war-goddess she is frequently (and as early as 3000 B.C.) depicted on seals, where she is usually represented with clubs, scimitars, bows, and other weapons, leading captives to the king.[2] In the Gilgamesh epic Ištar is a war-goddess, and in the time of Ḫammurabi, and more especially in Assyrian times, she was 'mistress of war and of battle.' As Assyrian war-goddess she became the consort of Ašur and was the special war-protector of Assyrian kings. Ašurbanipal's description of the warlike Ištar is famous,[3] and, when he founded his capital at Nineveh, he established there the cult of Ištar of battles. In fact, the goddess became so popular in warlike Assyria that she was identified with three great shrines, Nineveh, Arbela, and Kidmuru, and became sometimes three separate goddesses, although usually only two, because of the comparative unimportance of Kidmuru. There was an Ištar of the north as well as of the south —a differentiation which resulted in the belief in a male and female Ištar.[4] As a male Ištar was the morning star, and as a female she was the evening star. To the very end of the Neo-Babylonian dynasty she was the war-goddess, who carried quiver and bow and flew to battle like a swallow.[5] Her symbol as war-goddess was the lion and the five- or eight-pointed star Sirius, but sometimes she was symbolized by a bow.[6]

Ištar, as goddess of war, was identified with several other goddesses of war, especially **Isḫara**,[7] who was 'lady of conquest'[8] and 'lady of victory over the lands';[9] **Innini**, who, originally a goddess of light and the star Venus, because of warlike qualities ascribed to the stars, was regarded by the Sumerians as a conquering deity,[10] the 'lady of battle,'[11] and was represented in a standing position leading a captive by a string inserted in his nose,[12] her symbol being the bow;[13] **Anunit**, who was worshipped as a goddess of battle at Agade and Sippar, of whom Nabonidus said that he built a temple

> 'to Anunit the lady of battle, she that bears bow and quiver, who executes perfectly the command of Enlil her father, who exterminates the foe, who annihilates the evil, who walks before the gods, who at sunrise and sunset renders favourable my omens.'[14]

She is also identified with **Antu**, a heavenly deity, whom Ḫammurabi calls the Aštar of Agade,[15] and with **Ajā**, a goddess of light and of war; with the warlike **Ninni**, to whom Eannatum on the Stela of Vultures ascribes his victory; and with **Nana**.

Marduk, 'the first-born son of Ea,' was originally a solar deity, but his warlike character became prominent in the time of the Ḫammurabi dynasty, when his city, Babylon, became great. When the creation legends were recast, during this same dynasty, Ḫammurabi's war-god (often addressed as such in hymns[1]), Marduk, was the warrior-hero who slew Tiamāt, the spirit of chaos. He became so great that a (shortlived) custom arose of identifying all gods with him.[2] His greatness outlived the Assyrian empire, when he was called Bel-Marduk, having absorbed the characteristics of the old god Bel, second person of the triad, Anu, Bel, and Ea, and lived on till the end of the Neo-Babylonian period. He is often pictured as a warrior with scimitar,[3] and his symbol was the flaming sun.

Nergal, son of Enlil, was originally god of the midday or scorching sun, and was often identified with Šamaš. He then was associated with disease and death, and from that he developed into a war-god. As such he was called *Marduk ša ḳabli*,[4] 'Marduk of war,' 'the lord of spears and bows,'[5] *ur-sag karradu*, 'the warrior,' the great sword-god,[6] and, as destruction that accompanies war, he was identified with the planet Mars. He first became known as a war-god during the Ḫammurabi dynasty, and continued so throughout the Assyrian and Neo-Babylonian periods.

Ninib,[7] son of Enlil and god of Nippur, was originally a solar deity, and, as first-born of Ea, was a vegetation- and water-god. As early as the Ḫammurabi dynasty he was called *Marduk ša âlli*, 'Marduk of strength,'[8] and in Samsuiluna's reign he was called 'the great warrior.'[9] He is addressed as 'mighty god, warrior, ruler of the Anunnaki, controller of the Igigi.'[10] In a text translated and discussed by Pinches in *PSBA* xxviii. [1906] 203–218, 270–283, Ninib is fully described as a war-god of the mountains. He is called 'the lord, the destroyer of the mountains, who hath no rival,' 'the warrior who is like a steer'; and he is said to collect his army in order to spoil the land of the enemy. In Assyrian and Neo-Babylonian times, especially the former, Ninib continued to be 'the destroyer of the king's enemies' and 'the mighty one of the gods.' He was symbolized as a wild bull, as a double-headed raven, and later as an eagle.

Nin-dar-a, husband of Išḫara, was called 'the warlike king,'[11] and **Nin-dub** was compared to a warrior.[12] **Ningirsu**, chief god of Lagash and son of Enlil, is called the 'warrior of Enlil,'[13] and is identified in this rôle with Ninib. On the Stela of the Vultures he is shown clubbing the enemies of Lagash, whom he has bound in a net; and he is symbolized by the divine storm-bird. **Nin-giš-zida**, son of Ninazu, prototype of Ninib and protective god of Gudea, was perhaps also a war-god, although no reference to him as such has been found. **Nin-šakh**, prototype of Ninib, and **Nin-si-a**, called also Nin-du-a, are also thought to have been war-deities. **Ramman**, whose ideogram is IM, and who is identified with Adad, Mer, and Iškur, was known as early as the time of Ḫammurabi as a 'warrior,'[14] although he is the storm-god *par excellence*. From the time of Ḫammurabi, however, he was recognized as a war-god, except

1 E. Schrader, *Keilinschriftliche Bibliothek*, ii. [1890] 249 ff. (hereafter cited as *KB*).
2 W. H. Ward, *Seal Cylinders of Western Asia*, Washington, 1910, pp. 155 ff., 248 ff., *Cylinders and Other Ancient Oriental Seals*, New York, 1909, nos. 90, 91; J. de Morgan, *Mission scientifique en Perse*, Paris, 1894–96, vol. iv., pl. x. and p. 161 ff.
3 S. Langdon, *Tammuz and Ishtar*, Oxford, 1914, p. 106.
4 M. Jastrow, *Die Religion Babyloniens und Assyriens*, Giessen, 1905–12, i. 539.
5 *KB* iii. 1. 113, 2. 105; G. A. Reisner, *Sumerisch-babylonische Hymnen*, Berlin, 1896, pp. 108, 44.
6 Langdon, pl. i. no. 1.
7 *CT* xxiv. 18 rev. 7; S. A. B. Mercer, *The Oath in Babylonian and Assyrian Literature*, Paris, 1912, p. 43 ff.
8 *KB* iv. 72, 28.
9 L. W. King, *Babylonian Boundary-Stones and Memorial Tablets in the British Museum*, London, 1912, p. 47.
10 A king of Erech addressed her as 'lioness of battle' (*RA* ix. 114, 27).
11 *SAK*, p. 74 f.
12 Ward, *Seal Cylinders of W. Asia*, p. 157; *SAK*, p. 172.
13 K. Frank, *Bilder und Symbole babylonisch-assyrischer Götter* (*LSSt* ii. 2), Leipzig, 1906, p. 19.
14 *Vorderasiatische Bibliothek*, iv. 228, 22–26.
15 *CḪ* iv. 48; *i.e.* the Ašdar of early Semites. She is the 'Anat, queen of heaven, mistress of the gods, who was goddess of war in Egypt.

1 *Beiträge zur Assyriologie*, v. 281.
2 M. Jastrow, *Aspects of Religious Belief and Practice in Babylonia and Assyria*, New York and London, 1911, p. 102.
3 Ward, *opp. citt.* p. 163 ff., and nos. 92–94.
4 Jastrow, *Aspects of Relig. Belief*, p. 102.
5 King, *Babylonian Boundary-Stones*, p. 47.
6 *LSSt* i. 6.
7 Properly transcribed Nin-Ib, perhaps 'lord of Ib' (*CT* xxiv. 1, 5; xx. 4*b*), sometimes transcribed Ninip, Nirig, Ninrag, Enu-rêštû, En-maštu, Anušat, Ninurta, and finally Nin-uraša.
8 Jastrow, *Aspects of Relig. Belief*, p. 103, *CT* xxiv. 50.
9 A. Poebel, *Babylonian Legal and Business Documents*, Philadelphia, 1909, p. 79.
10 P. Jensen, *Die Kosmologie der Babylonier*, Strassburg, 1890, pp. 470–472.
11 *SAK*, p. 74.
12 *Ib.* p. 94.
13 *Ib.* pp. 26, 90, 98. See Paffrath for many references to him as war-god.
14 *CḪ* xxvii. *a*, 64.

in Assyria, where he played just one rôle, that of god of storms. In Babylonia he was associated—*e.g.*, by Nebuchadrezzar I.—with Ištar, as war-deity, and was pictured with a club.[1] **Samaš** (Sumerian Babbar), although the sun-god *par excellence*, was known as 'the conqueror of foreign lands,'[2] and as such was a war-god, whose weapon was 'the great net.'[3] **Sukamuna** was a Kassite god of war, whose symbol was the midday sun, and, therefore, a destructive power like Nergal. **Tur-lil-en**, a Neo-Babylonian deity, was described as 'breaking the weapons of the enemies.' **Zamama**, patron deity of Kish, was early associated with Ištar as a war-god,[4] and was called *Marduk ša taḫazi*, 'Marduk of battle,'[5] as well as 'the king of battle.'[6]

Ašur, the great god, Assyria's war-god *par excellence*, was originally a solar deity, his symbol representing a sun-disk with protruding rays. Then he developed into a god of fertility—a corn- and water-god—and finally became a war-god. According as Assyria became more and more militaristic, so Ašur's attribute as war-god became more and more all-absorbing, until he became the dominating character in Assyrian religion. His divine city depended upon the location of the royal residence, and from there all warfare was carried on in his name. His popularity was due to Assyria's military prowess. He is always associated with mighty weapons (*kakka danna*), and is he 'who protects the troops.' The disk as his symbol was surmounted by the figure of a warrior.[7]

II. *EGYPTIAN*.—I. **War.**—While some classical writers say that Egypt was divided among the king, priests, and warriors, others assert that from the beginning Egypt was a peaceful country. At any rate it can truly be said that the Egyptians never admired a military career, nor were the conditions under which they lived favourable to the development of a military nature; *e.g.*, Egypt was shut in geographically from the rest of the world; there were no great peoples in her neighbourhood to contend with, and no fertile lands within her reach to covet. Nevertheless, from the very first Egypt was called upon to wage war. Her literature attests this, and her earliest nome standards are, in all probability, military in character. Pre-dynastic and proto-dynastic monuments, such as the Palette of Nar-Mer, preserve evidence of warlike conflict, and Uni, a nobleman of the VIth dynasty, tells of important wars (although they are the only known important ones of the Old Kingdom) carried on against the Bedawīn in the time of Pepi I.[8] There were other military expeditions during this early period, and by the time of Sesostris III. of the XIIth dynasty rather formidable armies were mustered. Yet, when compared with the wars of later periods or with those of Assyria, these military expeditions of the Old and Middle Kingdoms must be pronounced mere razzias—raids for loot, slaves, cattle, gold, etc.

Nor was the period of disintegration which followed the XIIth dynasty conducive to the growth of militarism. But the conquest of Egypt by the Hyksos (*q.v.*) breathed a new spirit into the land. The foreigners must be ejected, and Egypt proved herself, under Ahmose I., equal to the occasion. Thenceforth she began her career of conquest under the empire-builders, Thutmose III., Seti I., Rameses II., and Rameses III. She became a great military power, and took up the offensive against her erstwhile Asiatic masters. Rameses II. even developed a military caste, and for a while the military profession ranked high. Her military character, however, was not enduring; the Egyptians lacked that gallantry and chivalry which are essential to a truly military character. There is evidence that the Egyptians were as destructive to the living and as savage to the dead—whose corpses they often mutilated—as other peoples, although Diodorus[1] seeks to excuse their conduct.

Nor were the Egyptians a naval people, although they possessed considerable fleets of merchant ships, which navigated the Mediterranean, the Red Sea, and the Nile. But the same great national crisis which developed a strong army and a shortlived liking for conquest developed also a navy. When Ahmose I. attacked the Hyksos, he did so by sea as well as by land. Of course there were warships before his time. Uni escorted his flotilla of merchantmen from Elephantinē down the Nile to Memphis; Kheti II. of the IXth dynasty had ships; and Sesostris III. re-made a canal in the First Cataract through which his warships could pass. By the time of the XVIIIth dynasty a real navy had developed, and was employed in connexion with the campaigns in Syria. Although Rameses II. had a considerable fleet, the first king to recognize the true importance of the navy was Rameses III., who established a fleet in the Mediterranean and another in the Red Sea. The naval battles of this king are splendidly pictured at Medinet Habu. With the exception of the battle with the Hyksos,[2] the battles of Rameses III. are the only real naval conflicts known to Egyptian history. The navy, like the army, soon deteriorated, and never more played any important part in Egypt, not even in the time of Cleopatra, who is credited by Orosius[3] with a fleet of 170 large ships.

Egyptian religion never condemned war. The most ancient of Egyptian wars were among the gods themselves or between gods and men; and so Egyptian kings in making war claimed divine example. The Egyptians named all wars revolt, because they were presumed to be against the Egyptian gods. The duty of the king was to avenge the gods of impiety, the word for 'impiety' (*aaditiw*) being the same as for 'enemy.'[4] In short, all war was moral, ideal, supernatural, and sanctioned by divine precedent.

In earliest Egypt there were soldiers who were selected from all parts of the political district, and, as early as Pepi I., conquered territories were compelled to contribute men in case of war. But there did not exist an army in the modern sense of the term. In the Middle Kingdom there were professional soldiers who were called 'followers of his majesty.' They were divided into companies of 100 men, and they garrisoned the palace and the strongholds of the royal house from Nubia to the Asiatic frontier. They were the nucleus of a standing army. In case of actual war the great nobles, or nomarchs, sent their quota of men, whom they had carefully trained, armed with bows and arrows. Then there were contingents supplied by the estates of the great temples, besides mercenaries of friendly chiefs. These armies were often called upon to do guard duty, as in the case of the army of Sesostris I., which was employed in the defence of labourers. With the rise of the Empire, and as a result of the Hyksos overlordship, a regular army was gradually developed. It had

1 Ward, *Seal Cylinders*, p. 176 ff.
2 *SAK*, p. 206. 3 *Ib.* p. 16 f.
4 *CH* xxiv. *a*, 23 f.
5 Jastrow, *Aspects of Relig. Belief*, p. 103.
6 King, p. 47.
7 See, further, J. Hehn, *Die biblische und die babylonische Gottesidee*, Leipzig, 1913, pp. 89–96.
8 J. H. Breasted, *Ancient Records of Egypt*, Chicago, 1905–07, i. 311–315.

1 i. 78.
2 C. R. Lepsius, *Denkmäler*, 12 vols., Berlin, 1849–60, iii. 12*d*.
3 vi. 19.
4 K. Sethe, *Urkunden der 18. Dynastie*, Leipzig, 1905–09, iv. 5 f.

two grand divisions, composed of experienced troops who had learned tactics in Syria. These two grand armies were divided into divisions, each division named after a god—*e.g.*, Amen, Rā, Ptah, etc. Military schools were established and barracks abounded. In fact, military training began in childhood, when gymnastics, archery, and the use of the battle-axe and javelin were taught. The trained and disciplined troops of Egypt were often the subject of artists and sculptors, and the drilling of recruits, racing, jumping, war-dances, and sieges were often depicted.[1] Rameses II. held regular councils of war,[2] and Diodorus[3] preserves a tradition that the military formed one of the three classes into which Egyptian society was divided. In spite of all, however, Egypt never possessed an army equal in discipline and equipment to those of Assyria.

During the height of Egypt's military power the soldier was well treated. He was allowed, free of all charge, eight acres of land, he was free from forced labour when on active service, he could not be cast into prison for debt, and he was expected to provide himself with the necessary arms and everything requisite for a campaign. If he were brave, distinctions and other signs of honour were showered upon him. As early as the VIth dynasty mercenaries were employed, and these were allowed to retain their own arms and customs. The peoples most commonly engaged to fight the wars of Egypt were the 'Nine-bow Barbarians' from Nubia, the 'Shardana' from Europe, the Libyans, and the Syrians. The last-named were so frequently employed that the term *ḫarw-srj*, 'young Syrian,' became a common word for soldier. Most of the army of Rameses III. were mercenaries, and after his reign these men were so much accustomed to the country that they in turn as foreigners conquered and dominated Egypt—such were the Libyans, the Sudanese, the Persians, the Greeks, and the Romans.

In early Egypt some soldiers carried a large bow, had one or two ostrich feathers on their head, and a narrow band around the upper part of their body; others carried a large shield and a spear, or a small shield, over which skin was stretched, and a battle-axe; still others carried no shield but had a large axe, a lance, and a sling. During the Empire regiments of light infantry carried a javelin, a lance, and a dagger, or a short straight sword; the heavy infantry bore spears and a curved sword. The cavalry were armed with the battle-axe, and most of them carried shields made of bull's hide, while bronze helmets were worn, although a more common head-dress was a thick quilted cap, the colour of which varied with the regiment, some with fringes, others with tassels. The archers were the most important soldiers in the army. They were divided into companies of foot- and chariot-archers. They wore quilted helmets with coloured tassels. The arrows were about 34 inches long, and were of wood or reed tipped with metal. They sometimes carried an axe or boomerang.[4] Cavalry was not known till the Hyksos period, for it was these Semites who introduced the horse into Egypt. Thenceforth chariots drawn by horses and cavalry became very popular. Sheshonk I. is reported to have had 60,000 horsemen in his army which marched into Palestine.

The weapons of the earliest Egyptians were very simple. At first they consisted of large stout sticks. But later the offensive weapons were bow, spear, javelin, sling, sword, dagger, knife, falchion, axe, and club; defensive arms were metal helmet or quilted head-piece, coat of armour, and shield.

The Egyptians fought best behind walls, and many forts were therefore built in Egypt, especially at the Second Cataract and on the north-eastern boundary of Egypt. Towns were fortified, such as Pelusium, Syene, Elephantinē, Semneh in Nubia; and Thutmose I. fortified the island of Tombos at the Third Cataract. In the great campaigns of the Empire materials of all kinds for siege, such as scaling ladders and battering-rams, for transportation, such as wagons and baggage-trucks, and for convenience, such as chairs, tables, and elaborate tents, were provided. Each company had its own standard, which was held in admiration; and each regiment was furnished with musical instruments, usually trumpets and drums.

The only Egyptian campaign conducted on any definite plan was that of Rameses II. against the Hittites. But there is evidence of the use of a great deal of strategy in the manœuvres of the soldiers of Thutmose III., and especially in the way in which Joppa was taken by Thutiyi. Armies were drawn up in well-arranged battle-array, with due regard to the wings, centre, and flanks. The many Egyptian inscriptions afford an excellent idea of the way in which Egyptian battles were fought, such as those at Megiddo, Kadesh, and the early wars in the time of Pepi I. A favourite company-formation with the Egyptian was the phalanx, with the heavy infantry in the centre and light infantry and archers disposed round them. Light-armed regiments were also left free for skirmishing and for flanking movements, such as those which were so well carried out at Kadesh by Rameses II. The Egyptian phalanx became so famous that Crœsus used it most effectively against Cyrus.

War at all times and especially under the Theban monarchs was a means of procuring slaves and booty. The demand for tribute does not appear before the Asiatic conquests, although ransom seems to appear as early as the civil wars which preceded the XIIth dynasty. In order to prove to the king the completeness of victory, warriors were in the habit of cutting off the hands and sometimes the heads[1] of the vanquished and placing them in heaps before him. But the Egyptian was always glad when peace came and a treaty was drawn up. The most famous treaty in Egyptian history, and the most detailed known to the ancient world, was that drawn up between Rameses II. and Hattusil II. the Hittite king.[2]

2. War-gods.—Originally every social group had its god, and every god was, in a sense, a war-god. When smaller groups amalgamated into larger cities and nomes, the gods of the constituent groups amalgamated into the god of the most powerful unit in the group, just as Sekhet and Hathor were absorbed into Amon of Thebes, and to him were ascribed the characteristics of the absorbed gods. If the age was warlike, one of the attributes of such a deity would be that of war-god. Whenever the age and location were not warlike, the war attribute of the deity receded into the background. Thus it is that previous to the Hyksos period there are no prominent Egyptian war-gods. As a matter of fact, the Egyptians never of themselves developed great war-gods; those deities in their pantheon who retain their warlike attributes are Asiatic, and were introduced during the Empire. Yet the idea of war-deities was well known in Egypt from earliest times. Did not Horus battle with Set, and did not every king, as son of Horus, have to fight the god's enemies? The fierceness of the wars with the Hyksos was due to the fact that Egypt's gods were at war with the hated gods of the Asiatics.

The following deities, almost all of whom are foreign, are the war-deities known to Egyptian literature. **Āasīth** is usually represented as a woman armed with shield and club, riding a horse into the battle-field. She is a war-goddess of Semitic origin in whom W. Max Müller sees the counterpart of Esau. A stela set up by Seti I. at Redesiyeh, on the road to the gold-mines of Mt. Zābārā, connects her with the desert. **Amon-Rā**, one of the primeval deities of Egypt, whose chief seat of worship was at Thebes, became very prominent as a war-god in the XVIIIth dynasty as a result of the victories of that period. **An-hôret**, or Anhur, local god of Abydos, was god of the dead, but was also represented as a man standing with a spear in his raised hand. He was a warrior-

[1] See, *e.g.*, J. G. Wilkinson, *The Ancient Egyptians*, London, 1878, *passim*, esp. i. 192.

[2] *RTr* viii. 128 f.

[3] i. 54.

[4] Excellent illustrations of Egyptian soldiery are to be seen in Lepsius, iii., and in Wilkinson.

[1] Lepsius, iii. 128.

[2] W. M. Müller, *Der Bündnisvertrag Rameses' II. und des Chetiterkönigs* (*MVG* vii. 5), Berlin, 1902.

god, and as such became identified in the Greek period with Ares. **'Anat**, 'queen of heaven, mistress of the gods,' was an Asiatic goddess of war. She was the same as the Sumerian An, with Semitic feminine termination, Antu. She is represented as sitting with a spear in one hand and swinging a battle-axe. She is probably the same as the goddess referred to by Ḫammurabi.[1] **Anthyt** was a Syro-Phœnician war-goddess, represented with shield and spear in the right hand and club in the left. Her cult was associated with N. and S. Syria, where cities were named after her—*e.g.*, Bath-Ānth. **Antæus**, probably another name of the same goddess, is known only in late sources. She was worshipped at Antaiopolis, and was represented as a warrior or hunter with a high feather on her head and clad in Roman armour. **Āsthyrthet** of Apollinopolis was introduced into Egypt in the XVIIIth dynasty. She is the same as Astarte, a Syrian war-goddess, and was depicted as a lion-headed human figure, driving a chariot drawn by four horses over her prostrate foe. **'Asît** may be another form of Āsthyrthet. **Bār**, or Pa-Bār, was a Syro-Phœnician war-god, the Baal of the OT. He was introduced into Egypt in the XVIIIth dynasty. Originally he was the personification of the burning and destroying heat of the sun and of the blazing desert wind. He was worshipped in the neighbourhood of Tanis, and was a favourite of Rameses II., who compared himself with Bār. **Bast**, 'lady of the East,' as well as Sekhet, was a personification of heat and light, and was renowned as a destroyer of the enemies of the sun-god and of the deceased. **Bes**, of 'the land of Punt,' was a god of complex character, but as a god of war and slaughter he carried two knives in his hands. As a warrior he was represented wearing a short military tunic, and holding in his left hand a shield, and a short sword in his right hand. As a war-god he appears in the XVIIIth dynasty. **Ḥeru-Beḥuṭet** is a form of Horus, under which he waged war with Set or Typhon. His symbol is the Sphinx at Gizeh. Another form of Horus is **Ḥeru-Sept**, the smiter of the Menti, and god of battle; and still another form of Horus, who 'loved an hour of fighting more than a day of rejoicing,' is **Ḥeru-Themā**, the piercer, and, as such, a god of war. **Mafiet** is a war-goddess, whose symbol is the sign 'to follow,' *šems*. **Menthu** was an ancient Egyptian war-god, whose seat was at Thebes. He is represented in human form with a bull's tail and head of a hawk. His head is surmounted by a sun-disk between double plumes. Sometimes he is depicted as a hawk-headed sphinx. He is represented with bow and arrows, a club, and a knife. He is seen on the prow of the sun-boat and slays the demon with his lance. He was an old local god, a personification of the destructive heat of the sun, but in later times he became Mentu-Rā. He was Rameses II.'s patron war-god. **Neith** was worshipped in the Delta in pre-dynastic times. While she was, at an early period, a personification of a form of the great inert primeval watery mass, she was later represented with bow and arrows, and as such was considered a war-goddess as well as a goddess of the chase. **Nephebet** and her twin-sister **Uatchet** were destroyers of the enemies of the gods. **Reshpu**, or Resheph, had his centre of worship at Ḥet-Reshep in the Delta, but was an imported Syrian deity. In Egyptian texts he is called 'lord of the two-fold strength among the company of the gods.' He is represented as a warrior with spear and shield in the left hand, and club in the right hand. As his Semitic name shows, he was a personification of the burning and destruction of fire and lightning. **Sekhmet**, or Sekhet, 'the powerful,' is represented wearing a solar disk on her head, symbolizing the warlike attributes of the sun. She was called 'the fiery one emitting flames against the enemies' of the god, and her duty was to scorch and consume the enemies of her father. **Up-Uaut**, 'the opener of the way,' was originally a war-god, who opened the way for troops through the enemies' land. He is sometimes represented in the prow of the boat of Rā.

[1] *CḤ* iv. 48. To the same cycle of divine beings belong Ištar of Nineveh and Astarte, mistress of horses, who was confused with the warlike Sekhmet, all of whom were known and recognized as war-goddesses in Egypt.

III. *HEBREW*.—I. **War.**—Although the ideal of the great prophets of the 8th and 7th centuries was peace, war was approved by the prophets of early Israel. The Hebrew people were not unwarlike, and with them, as with other Oriental peoples, war was sanctioned by the deity. From the earliest to the latest times in the history of Israel Jahweh fought for His people, and they followed Him to battle. Before battle oracles were consulted to learn Jahweh's will;[1] prophets of Jahweh were appealed to for guidance;[2] and prayer was offered up to Him before the attack.[3] Jahweh Himself called His consecrated one to battle;[4] priests of Jahweh sounded the alarm with trumpets;[5] and campaigns were begun with sacrificial rites.[6] In fact, warfare was a holy calling, with which tabu was associated,[7] for to 'prepare' or to 'sanctify' war was to carry out initiatory religious rites.[8] The camp was a holy place because Jahweh was there,[9] and there were the sacred ephod[10] and the ark of Jahweh.[11]

The Hebrews did not possess an army worthy of the name till the time of the monarchy. Gideon's band numbered 300, and the Danites had a force of 600. At this early period warfare consisted of raids and forays. All males were collected by the recognized leader,[12] to whom friendly tribes allied themselves.[13] But, besides a bodyguard,[14] Saul had a standing army of 3000 men.[15] Israel's army was divided into thousands, hundreds, fifties, and tens.[16] As early as the time of David steps were taken to recruit a regular army, and it was placed under the command of Joab as commander-in-chief. Besides that, David himself had his own bodyguard of from 400 to 600 men. Mobilization was announced by sound of the trumpet throughout the land.[17] An interesting picture of mobilization in Israel can be seen in Is 22^{6-8} and in Ezk $21^{3ff.}$. It is described as the drawing of the sword from the sheath. Sometimes a formal declaration of war was made, as in the case of Amaziah of Judah against Jehoash of Israel,[18] but more often spies were sent out,[19] and hostilities began in spring.[20] In later times regular mercenaries were employed,[21] and under Herod soldiers were trained in Roman fashion.

Hebrew armies up to Solomon's time consisted only of infantry, light and heavy. Heavy arms consisted of a round helmet of bronze, a coat of mail, bronze greaves, a sword of iron, a spear, and a lance. Light arms comprised bow and arrows and a small shield. Solomon introduced cavalry and chariots, and had 12,000 cavalry, 1400 chariots, and 40,000 chariot horses. The troops had ensigns, banners, and standards, and were furnished with tents or booths, but each soldier was obliged to provide his own food, though sometimes regular provision was made for him.[22] Guards were placed round the

[1] Jg $20^{18ff.}$, 1 S 14^{37} 23^{2} 28^{6} 30^{8}.
[2] 1 K 22^{5}, 2 K 3^{11}.
[3] 1 Mac 3^{53} 4^{30} $5^{32f.}$.
[4] Is 13^{3}.
[5] 2 Ch 13^{12-16}.
[6] 1 S 7^{8-10} 13^{9}.
[7] 2 11^{11}, Dt 20^{7} 23^{10}.
[8] Jer 6^{4} 22^{7} $51^{27f.}$, Mic 3^{5}, Jl 3^{9}.
[9] Dt 23^{9-14}.
[10] 1 S 14^{18}; see W. R. Arnold, *Ephod and Ark* (*Harvard Theol. Studies*, iii.), Cambridge, Mass., 1917.
[11] 1 S 4^{3}.
[12] Jg $11^{1ff.}$.
[13] 1 S $11^{3ff.}$.
[14] 1 S 22^{14}.
[15] 1 S $13^{1ff.}$.
[16] 1 S 8^{12} 17^{18} 18^{13}, 2 S 18^{1}, 2 K 1^{9} $11^{4.19}$, 1 Mac 3^{55}.
[17] Jg 3^{27}, 1 S 13^{3}, 2 S 15^{10}.
[18] 2 K 14^{8}.
[19] Jos 2^{1}, 1 S 26^{4}, Nu 13^{17}.
[20] 2 S 11^{1}, 1 K $20^{22.26}$.
[21] Jos. *Ant.* XIII. viii. 4, xiii. 5.
[22] Jg 20^{10}.

camps,[1] which were changed three times during the night.[2] The Hebrews inherited the fortresses of the Canaanites, but Solomon built his own, such as that at Hazor, Megiddo, etc. They usually stood on hills. Special battering-rams and catapults were constructed for siege work.[3]

Hebrew forces were drawn up either in line or in three divisions, a centre and two wings. There was also a rearguard for protection during the march and to take care of stragglers.[4] Sometimes, instead of a general conflict between two opposing forces, a decision was left to two opposing groups of equal but limited number,[5] or even to two opposing individuals.[6] There was a battle-cry to inspire courage,[7] and the order to retreat was given by sound of the trumpet.

Strategy was not unknown to the Hebrews: Joshua made a night attack after a rapid night march to relieve Gibeon;[8] circumvention was practised by David;[9] Joshua surprised the Canaanites at the waters of Merom;[10] David executed a flank movement against the Philistines;[11] the men of Israel made a successful feint against the Benjamites at Gibeah;[12] and Joshua captured Ai by ambush.[13]

The victor was hailed with song,[14] and victory was celebrated with public thanksgiving;[15] but prisoners were sold as slaves[16] and often treated in a savage manner.[17] The spoil was divided equally between those in battle and those in camp;[18] a portion was reserved for the Levites and as a tribute to Jahweh;[19] part was reserved for the king;[20] and sometimes armour was dedicated as a trophy.[21]

The ideal in prophetic Israel was peace[22] brought about by Jahweh.[23] The end of hostilities was signified by the blowing of the war-horn,[24] and ambassadors negotiated terms.[25] Treaties were drawn up and signed,[26] and defensive and offensive alliances were made.[27]

2. War-god. — Pre-historic Hebrews were undoubtedly polytheists, or at any rate henotheists; they recognized the existence of other gods and worshipped them; but, so far as we know, they never developed a pantheon such as we see in Babylonia and Egypt. In historic times the Hebrew people tended more and more towards monotheism, and, although they recognized the existence of other gods even as late as the 7th cent. B.C., yet they never recognized any other deity than Jahweh as their national god. So to Jahweh were ascribed all the characteristics which belonged to a pantheon. The derivation of His name is uncertain, but as good a guess as any is that it is derived from the verb *hawa*, 'to fall,' and, in the causative, 'to prostrate.' Whether this be so or not, there is abundant evidence to prove the warlike character of Jahweh. He it was, as a warrior, who brought His people out of Egypt, and who drove out the nations before Israel; He revealed Himself to Joshua as the captain of His hosts; His angels led the hosts of Joshua and Barak, and gave David victories over Aram and the peoples round about. It is true that He was considered a mountain-god, being associated with Sinai-Horeb, and, as such, a storm-god, controlling and regulating the weather; He was *baal* of the land, and therefore a vegetation-god; He was perhaps a lion-god,[1] and an ox-god;[2] and He was god of heaven and of earth; but He was pre-eminently 'a man of war,'[3] whose peoples' victories were His 'righteous acts,'[4] whose exploits were recorded in the 'Book of the Wars of Jahweh,'[5] and whose favourite servant was the warrior David, a man after Jahweh's own heart;[6] Israel's battle-cry was 'the sword of Jahweh and of Gideon';[7] and Meroz was cursed because it did not come to battle, 'to the help of Jahweh.'[8]

The title 'Jahweh Ṣebāōth,' whatever its original meaning, designates Jahweh as god of battles.[9] The term *Ṣebāōth* may have referred sometimes to the hosts of heaven. But warlike qualities were ascribed to the stars not only by the Hebrews,[10] but also by the Babylonians. It may have referred sometimes to Israel as a people.[11] But it certainly had reference to the title of Jahweh as leader of the armies of His people Israel.[12] The term as used in the OT regularly denotes armies of men, and it formed the title of Jahweh as war-god. A similar title is found applied to the Babylonian Tišpak, who is called *Marduk ša ummani*, 'Marduk of hosts,' and Tišpak was a war-god.

Jahweh's emblem, as war-god, was an ark. Eleven of the occurrences of Jahweh Ṣebāōth in the books of Samuel are connected with the ark. It was the symbol of the presence of Jahweh,[13] and was perhaps a throne upon which Jahweh sat,[14] when He was carried into war, just as the Babylonians carried their gods on thrones in processions. In fact, the ark was so closely associated with Jahweh, as war-god, that it was identified with Him,[15] and was greeted as if it were Jahweh Himself.[16]

LITERATURE.—With the exception of T. G. Pinches, 'The Babylonian Gods of War and their Legends,' *PSBA* xxviii. [1906] 203–218, 270–283, a discussion of Ninib, there is no separate article, monograph, or book on this subject. Besides E. A. W. Budge, *The Gods of the Egyptians*, 2 vols., London and Chicago, 1904, and literature referred to in this article, the author has made full use of the original inscriptions. In the case of the Hebrews, the standard Dictionaries of the Bible have been consulted, besides Nowack and Benzinger.

S. A. B. MERCER.

1 1 S 25^{13} 30^{10}. 2 Jg 7^{19}, 1 Mac 12^{27}.
3 Ezk 4^{2} 21^{22}, 2 Ch 26^{15}.
4 Jg 7^{16}, 1 S 11^{11}, 2 S 18^{2}, 1 Mac 5^{33}.
5 2 S 2. 6 1 S 17. 7 Jg 7^{20}, Am 1^{14}.
8 Jos 10^{9}. 9 2 S 5^{23}. 10 Jos 11^{7}.
11 2 S 5$^{22f.}$. 12 Jg 20$^{20ff.}$. 13 Jos 8$^{3ff.}$.
14 1 S 18^{6}. 15 Ex 15$^{1ff.}$, Jg 5$^{1ff.}$, 1 Mac 4^{24}.
16 2 K 5^{2}, 1 Mac 3^{41}. 17 2 S 8^{2} 12^{31}, 2 K 15^{16}.
18 Jos 22^{8}, 1 S 30$^{24f.}$, Nu 31^{27}.
19 Nu 31$^{28.\ 30}$. 20 2 K 14^{14}, 1 Ch 18$^{7.\ 11}$.
21 1 S 21^{9} 31^{9}. 22 Hos 2^{18}, Is 2^{4}, Mic 4^{3}.
23 Ps 46^{9}. 24 2 S 2^{28}. 25 Is 33^{7}.
26 1 K 20$^{30f.\ 34}$. 27 1 K 22$^{2ff.}$.

1 Hos 5^{14} 11^{10} 13$^{7f.}$.
2 1 K 12^{28}, Am 4^{4} 5^{5} 7$^{9ff.}$.
3 Ex 15^{3}. 4 Jg 5^{11}. 5 Nu 21^{14}.
6 1 S 13^{14}. 7 Jg 7^{18}. 8 Jg 5^{23}.
9 1 S 17^{45}. 10 Jg 5^{20}.
11 Ex 7^{4} 12^{41}, Jer 3^{19}, Ps 44^{10} 60^{12} 108^{12}. 12 1 K 2^{5}.
13 Jos 6$^{4f.}$, 1 S 4$^{3ff.}$, Nu 10$^{35f.}$ 14$^{44f.}$. 14 Jer 3$^{16f.}$.
15 1 S 4$^{7f.}$ 6$^{8f.}$. 16 Nu 10$^{35f.}$.

WATER, WATER-GODS.

WATER, WATER-GODS (Primitive and Savage).—Since water is a first need of man in a primitive state of culture, it is little wonder that it is regarded as possessed of *mana* (*q.v.*), and that, in consequence, it figures prominently in magico-religious cult.

1. Water in seasonal rites.—J. G. Frazer is undoubtedly correct when he says:

'At a remote period similar modes of thought, based on similar needs, led men independently in many distant lands, from the North Sea to the Euphrates, to celebrate the summer solstice with rites which, while they differed in some things, yet agreed closely in others; that in historical times a wave of Oriental influence, starting perhaps from Babylonia, carried the Tammuz or Adonis form of the (midsummer) festival westward till it met with native forms of a similar festival; and that under pressure of the Roman civilization these different yet kindred festivals fused with each other and crystallized into a variety of shapes, which subsisted more or less separately side by side, till the Church, unable to suppress them altogether, stripped them so far as it could of their grosser features, and dexterously changing the names allowed them to pass muster as Christian.'[1]

In Mesopotamia the year is divided into two seasons—the rainy and the dry. The welfare of the country depends upon the abundant rains which continue uninterruptedly for several months. In the earliest period to which the history of the Euphrates valley can be traced, a system of canals existed, serving the purpose both of irrigation and of avoiding disastrous floods. It is not surprising, therefore, that the early Babylonians regarded water as possessed of *mana*, and in later times that it became for them the abode of spirits and gods. Similarly, commerce, following in the wake of agriculture, would lend an additional importance to water as a means of transportation, which again would find expression in a cult of water-spirits. As notions of departmental deities arose, these spirits would assume the rôle of gods ruling over the various functions formerly controlled by lesser spirits.[2]

Now, we know that Tammuz was an ancient personification of the sun of the springtime, his name consisting of a Sumerian phrase *Dumu-Zi*, 'true (or faithful) son of the deep,'[3] and that he was the first lover of Ishtar, the great mother-goddess. He became her consort, was slain by the goddess, and descended into the under world, whither Ishtar went in quest of him. The promise made to her by Gilgamesh to present him with a chariot of lapis-lazuli, and to shelter him in a palace of plenty, unmistakably points to the triumph of the sun when vegetation is at its height. Tammuz and Ishtar, like Gilgamesh and Ishtar, thus represent the combination of the two principles which bring about life, and upon their separation follow death and decay. It appears from the fragmentary documentary evidence that the early Babylonians supposed that every year the goddess went to 'the land of No-return,' and that during her absence man and beast alike could not discharge their sexual functions, so intimately was Ishtar associated with fertility. If Tammuz was a personification of the springtime sun, and if his return from the under world bore a direct relationship to the revivification of nature, he must have been intimately connected with fertility. But the close relation that existed between vegetation and the water supply in the Euphrates valley would inevitably lead to his association with a water cult, and to his rites being performed about midsummer.[4]

At the festival of Tammuz in Babylon the image of the god was washed with pure water, just as in the summer festival the image of Adonis was thrown into the sea at Alexandria, and in Greece 'the gardens of Adonis' were similarly treated, to secure a due supply of fertilizing rain.[5] But originally it must have been the *mana* in the water, and not the deity, that was regarded as the means by which the desert in the springtime was suddenly made to blossom as the rose. It was not that primeval man was so overawed by the miracle of spring, the radiance of the flowers, and the singing of the birds; it was not that his heart went out in gratitude to the High God who was the giver of all good things. Rather it was his will to live that he uttered and represented in his elaborate spring and summer ceremonies—the promotion of life and fertility in plants, animals, and man. Since water is one of the essential factors in the preservation of life and the growth of the crops, it naturally plays a conspicuous part in rain-making ceremonies and other seasonal rites among primitive people.

1 *GB*3, pt. iv., *Adonis, Attis, Osiris*, London, 1914, i. 250.
2 Cf. art. TUTELARY GODS AND SPIRITS.
3 H. Zimmern, *Der babylonische Gott Tamuz*, p. 6 (in the *Abhand. der Konigl. sächs. Gesellschaft der Wiss.* xx. [Leipzig, 1909] 701, 722).
4 M. Jastrow, *The Religion of Babylonia and Assyria*, Boston, 1898, pp. 547, 682.
5 R. Rochette, *RA* viii. [1851] 97–123.

2. Water as a rain-charm.—Water is widely used in ceremonies for bringing rain.

In Australia, among the Arunta, a group of people have water for their totem, and the men of the totem are assembled from time to time by their *alatunja*, or leader (a celebrated rain-maker residing in the Rain Country), to make rain.[1] In the rites that ensue water does not play a part, the ceremonies, according to Frazer, representing a rising storm.[2] Among the Kaitish tribe of Central Australia, on the other hand, rain is made by the head man of the water totem pouring water over stones out of which the rainbow was supposed to have arisen, and over himself,[3] just as in Russia a man called the 'rain-maker' sprinkled water from a vessel on all sides to produce rain.[4] The Torajas of Central Celebes pour water over the grave of a famous chief to procure rain. After that they hang a bamboo full of water over the grave, a small hole having been pierced in the lower end of the bamboo, so that the water drips from it continually. The bamboo is kept refilled with water until rain drenches the ground. Conversely, if dry weather is desired, the rain-doctor (*sando*) assiduously avoids touching water during the performance of his functions. He does not bathe or wash himself, he drinks nothing but palm-oil, and, when crossing a stream, he is careful not to step in the water. Should rain afterwards be wanted, he has only to pour water on his fire, and immediately the rain will descend in sheets.[5] In India the Brāhman rain-maker had to bring himself into union with water by touching it three times a day as well as on various special occasions, to make himself, as it were, an ally of the water-powers, and to guard himself against their hostility.[6] The Ba-thonga, a Bantu tribe in S. Africa, think that droughts are the result of the concealment of miscarriages by women. To procure rain they bury a pot in the ground and cause it to be filled with water by girls who have not attained the age of puberty, till it overflows into four channels which run in the direction of the cardinal points of the compass. The women then hold a rain-dance, and pour water on the graves of prematurely born infants and of twins to 'extinguish' (*timula*) them, thereby removing the cause of the drought.[7]

In S.E. Europe, at the present day, rain is made by pouring a pail of water over a boy or girl clothed from head to foot in grass, flowers, or corn.[8] H. S. Moore records a similar practice at Poona (India). When rain is needed, the boys dress up one of their number in nothing but leaves and call him 'king of the rain' (*mrūj raja*). They then visit all the houses in the village, the householder sprinkles the rain-king with water, and makes offerings of food to the party.[9] In Rumania a clay figure is substituted for a living person in the rain-making rites. The image, which represents Drought, is placed in a coffin and carried by children in a funeral procession, with a burning candle before it. Finally, the coffin and candle are thrown into a stream or well.[10] In France images of saints until recently were dipped in water to procure rain, just as the Shans drench statues of Buddha with water when the rice is perishing from drought.[11] In Arcadia, in the classical period, the priest of Zeus dipped an oak branch into a certain spring on Mount Lycæus in times of drought, to cause the water to send up a misty cloud, from which rain would soon fall.[12] The Athenians sacrificed boiled, not roast, meat to the season because they imagined that the water in the pot would be transmitted to the gods, and return to them as rain.[13]

That the use of water as a rain-charm was directly connected with fertility is shown in the custom of clothing the person (or image), apparently the personification of vegetation, in leaves, corn, vines, etc., before water is poured on him. In support of this view may be quoted the European spring celebrations of St. George's Day.[14] It is

1 Spencer-Gillen[a], p. 189 ff.; cf. art. RAIN.
2 *GB*3, pt. i., *The Magic Art*, London, 1911, i. 261.
3 Spencer-Gillen[b], p. 294 ff.
4 W. Mannhardt, *Antike Wald- und Feldkulte*, Berlin, 1877, p. 342.
5 A. C. Kruijt, in *Tijdschrift voor Indische Taal- Land- en Volkenkunde*, xliv. [1901] 6, 8 ff.
6 H. Oldenberg, *The Grihya-Sûtras*, ii. (*SBE* xxx. [1892]) 72 ff.
7 H. A. Junod, *REth* i. [1910] 139.
8 *GB*3, pt. i., *The Magic Art*, i. 272 f.
9 *The Cowley Evangelist*, May 1908, p. 111 ff.
10 *GB*3, pt. i., *The Magic Art*, i. 273 f.
11 *Ib.* p. 307 f.
12 Pausanias, VIII. xxxviii. 4.
13 Athenæus, xiv. 72, p. 656 A.
14 *GB*3, pt. i., *The Magic Art*, ii. 75.

difficult to avoid the conclusion that originally these rites were performed to promote vegetation, and secure an abundant food supply, just as, until quite recently, water was thrown on the last corn cut at harvest in this country to procure rain for next year's crops.

3. Water in purification ceremonies.—Just as water naturally suggests to the primitive mind the process of fertilization, so it appears to the savage as the normal means of washing away material or spiritual pollution. As this subject has been treated separately,[1] we shall here confine our attention to the ceremonial use of water, the universal cleanser, in ritual purification.

After childbirth and menstruation, and in fact after sickness generally, the contagion is removed by a bath, while the contagion of death and the sins of the penitent are often got rid of in the same way. It is a common belief that the effect of contact with a sacred object must be removed by washing before a man may freely mix with his fellows.

Thus the high-priest was required by the Jewish Law to wash himself and put off the garments which he had worn in the holy place before coming forth from the sanctuary after offering his burnt offering (Lv 16²³ᶠ·). Likewise Greek ritual decreed that, after offering an expiatory sacrifice, the offerer must wash his body and his clothes in a river or spring before he entered a city or his own house.[2] In like manner, among the Jews the contact with the book of the Law or a phylactery 'defiled the hands,' and called for an ablution.[3] Among the Matabele of S. Africa, before the people ate of the new fruits they went down to the river to wash,[4] and before changing from one food to another the Eskimos must wash themselves,[5] as a kind of 'rite de passage.'

(*a*) *Childbirth.*—Birth, the attainment of puberty, marriage, death are great personal events associated with the mysteries of life, and at these times the individual is especially exposed to mystic and dangerous sacred forces. A pregnant woman is, in consequence of her condition, a dangerous person and one to be avoided until all traces of her 'sacredness' have been removed. Similarly, a newly-born infant is in fullest contact with the sacred world, and, therefore, he is subject to attacks from malignant influences, from which he must be guarded by rites. Like his parents, he is unclean, and, in consequence, some form of regeneration is necessary to remove this original taint.

The mother and child among the Koragars of West India are ceremonially unclean for five days, when both are restored to purity by a tepid bath.[6] The Hottentots considered a mother and child unclean till they had been washed and their bodies smeared with other purifying agents. Lustrations with water are common in W. Africa. The Mantras of the Malay Peninsula require their women to bathe after childbirth, and among the indigenes of India the custom also prevails.[7] The Aztec midwife washed the infant with the prayer, 'May this water purify and whiten thy heart: may it wash away all that is evil.'[8] The lustration speedily took definite form in the Mediterranean religions, and passed from the idea of washing away of defilement and sin to that of spiritual new birth. In the Isis rites the baptism with water was thought to raise the mortal to the divinity, although it is not clear that there was any ceremonial purification of the new-born infant with water in Greece. It appears that the rite called ἀμφιδρόμια, in which the infant was carried round the domestic hearth, took the place of a baptism by water.[9]

(*b*) *Initiation and marriage.*—Water is sometimes substituted for other purificatory rites (such as tatuing, setting the novice on a smoking fire, scourging, etc.) in initiation ceremonies.[10]

(*c*) *The shedding of blood.*—To the primitive mind nothing is more uncanny than blood. Life and death are the great primeval mysteries, and all the substances that are associated with the inner principle of either partake of this sacredness. For the savage what is sacred is also dangerous and a source of contagious impurity. Therefore, when a man has shed blood, he is tabu until the 'miasma' has been removed by purification rites.

In New Guinea warriors are secluded for about a week after their return from battle, during which time they may not come in contact with their wives, and they may not touch food with their hands. On the fifth day of his seclusion a man who has taken life walks solemnly down to the nearest water, after having been smeared with the spleen and liver of a kangaroo, and, standing straddle-legs in it, washes himself.[1] Among the Basutos warriors go straight from battle to a stream, where they purify themselves and their implements of war by washing away the tabu in the water, and putting themselves out of reach of the revenge of the slain.[2] Similar rites are performed by the Akikuyu, in which the final ablutions consist in cleansing with water.[3] In the Pelew Islands the young warriors, on their return from their first fight, are shut up for three days, and then, after smearing their bodies with charmed leaves and betel, bathe together as near as possible to the spot where the killing took place.[4] When a Pima Indian killed an enemy, he was tabu for sixteen days, and retired to the groves along the river bottom, or wandered about the adjoining hills. During this period he was forbidden to touch his head or his face, and before he might go to his home he had to bathe in the river, no matter how cold the temperature.[5]

(*d*) *Death.*—Contact with death and the spirit-world is a strong source of impurity in primitive society and, therefore, is the cause of tabus and purification rites. Bathing and fumigation are the most usual methods of purification. See art. DEATH AND DISPOSAL OF THE DEAD (Introductory), vol. iv. p. 434, § XIV.

(*e*) *Disease.*—Water is frequently regarded by primitive people as having the power to wash away sickness, especially if the disease is in the nature of skin eruption. The miraculous cure of Naaman (2 K 5¹⁰) reflects an ancient Semitic belief in the efficacy of water as a cure of leprosy. Of all inanimate things that which has the most marked supernatural virtues among the Semites is running (or, as the Hebrews said, 'living') water (cf. Nu 21¹⁷ᶠ·, Ezk 47⁹· ¹²). It is, therefore, not surprising that certain wells and rivers were credited with the power of healing.

In Babylonia a sick person was sprinkled with water while the priest pronounced certain sacred formulæ, having the power of 'cleansing' a patient from sickness. The water was specially sanctified for this purpose, and drawn from such sacred streams as the Tigris and Euphrates. One or more springs, and a *bît rimqi*, or 'bath-house,' were attached to every large temple, where purification rites were performed. Details of the rites varied in different cities, and there are indications that, even in later times, they were performed on the banks of running streams—perhaps a survival of the period when the incantation ritual did not form part of the official cult.[6] To this day a 'bath-house' is sometimes attached to synagogues, whither women resort monthly to cleanse themselves—a reminiscence, perhaps, of the old Semitic purification ritual, now restricted to women.[7]

The importance of water as a means of healing must have been greatly reinforced by the growth of Baal-worship, in which the deity as the giver of life was specially connected with life-giving waters. The indignation of Naaman when he was told to wash in Jordan, and his confidence that the rivers of Damascus were better than all the waters of Israel, probably arose from the idea that the Jordan was a sacred healing stream of the Hebrews, just as Abana and Pharpar were the sacred rivers of the Syrians, and not from any astonishment at being asked to perform a purification rite with which he must have been well acquainted. In the time of Antoninus Martyr[8] patients frequently bathed ceremonially by night

1 See art. PURIFICATION (Introductory and Primitive).
2 Porphyry, *de Abst.* ii. 44.
3 W. Robertson Smith, *Religion of the Semites*, new ed., London, 1907, p. 452.
4 *GB*³, pt. v., *Spirits of the Corn and of the Wild*, London, 1912, ii. 70 f.
5 *6 RBEW* [1884–85], p. 595.
6 *JAI* iv. [1874–75] 375.
7 E. B. Tylor, *PC*³, ii. 432 f.
8 B. de Sahagun, *Hist. general de las cosas de Nueva España*, Mexico, 1829, vi. 37.
9 Schol. Plato, *Theæt.* 160 E.
10 See examples in art. PURIFICATION (Introductory and Primitive), vol. x. p. 463 f.

1 *JAI* xxviii. [1899] 213 f.
2 E. Casalis, *The Basutos*, Eng. tr., London, 1861, p. 258.
3 *JAI* xxxiv. [1904] 264.
4 J. Kubary, *Die socialen Einrichtungen der Pelauer*, Berlin, 1885, pp. 126 ff., 130.
5 *26 RBEW* [1904–05], p. 204 f.
6 M. Jastrow, *Aspects of Religious Belief and Practice in Babylonia and Assyria*, New York and London, 1911, p. 312 f.
7 *JE* viii. 588.
8 *De Locis Sanctis*, vii.; cf. Jn 5²⁻⁴ 9¹¹.

in the thermal waters of Gadara, and in the Middle Ages it was still believed that he who bathed in the springtime in the source of the Euphrates would be free from sickness for the whole year.[1]

In Europe water figures conspicuously in folk-lore as a means of preventing and curing disease.

Thus at Vitrolles in the south of France, during the Mid-summer rites, the young people bathed in a pond in order that they might not suffer from fever during the year, and at Saintes-Maries they watered the horses to protect them from the itch.[2] Similarly, in Sweden, certain holy springs are supposed to be endowed with wonderful medicinal virtues on St. John's Eve, and many sick people resort to them for the healing of their infirmities.[3] At Stoole, near Downpatrick, in Ireland, on Midsummer Eve three wells, to which extraordinary virtues are attributed, are 'thronged by crowds of halt, maimed and blind, pressing to wash away their infirmities with water consecrated by their patron saint, and so powerful is its efficacy on their minds, that many of those who go to be healed, and who are not totally blind, or altogether crippled, really believe for a time that they are by means of its miraculous virtues perfectly restored.'[4] At Marsala in Sicily the sick resort to a spring in a subterranean grotto, called the Grotto of the Sibyl, to be cured of their diseases by bathing in the water,[5] just as on the same day the people of Copenhagen used to go on a pilgrimage to a neighbouring spring to heal and strengthen themselves in the water.[6] The famous grotto at Lourdes, which has been the reputed source of so many miracles since the alleged appearance of the Blessed Virgin to Bernadette Soubirous on 11th Feb. 1858, belongs, perhaps, to a different category, since the existence of the spring was unknown to the inhabitants prior to the apparitions.[7]

4. Water as a means of divination.—The use of water in divination has been common both in ancient and in modern times among people in a primitive state of culture.

Thus the Tahiti seek to discover the identity of a thief by digging a hole in the floor of the house in which the robbery occurred, and filling it with water; a priest then invokes the aid of his god to conduct the spirit of the thief to the water, so that his image may be reflected in it and perceived by the diviner.[8] In S.E. New Guinea a criminal's face is thought to be seen in a pool of water into which coco-nut oil has been squeezed.[9] The Malays discover a thief by two people holding a bowl of water between their fingers and presenting to it in writing the names of the suspected persons; at that of the guilty man it twists around and falls to the ground.[10] Among the Bahima of Central Africa a medicine-man puts herbs and coffee-berries into a pot of water and ascertains the wishes of the gods according to the direction in which the berries lie.[11] The Eskimos determine the fate of a man who has not returned from a voyage by causing a wizard to gaze into a tub of water.[12] In Greece the favourable or unfavourable disposition of the gods was declared by casting offerings into holy wells. If the gift was accepted, it sank; if it was unacceptable, it was cast forth.[13] At Delphi, to the east of Apollo's temple, there was a sacred spring which proceeded from a narrow gorge shut in by rocky walls, the waters of which were supposed to be oracular. The priestess of Apollo therefore drank of the sacred spring and chewed the sacred laurel before she prophesied.[14]

In Babylonia as early as the reign of Urukagina, king of Lagash (*c.* 2800 B.C.), there is evidence of divination by oil, and from the texts of a later period (*c.* 2000 B.C.) it appears that the method adopted consisted in pouring oil on the surface of water in a bowl, and determining future events by the behaviour of the bubbles when the water was struck.[15] In one of the texts the method is traced back to the legendary founder of the *bârû* priesthood.[16] Two of the texts, dating from the Ḫammurabi period, describe the signs to be observed in the mingling of oil and water, together with the interpretation thereof.[17] On the early monuments there is also an interesting allusion to the use of this method of divination by a ruler of the Cassite period (*c.* 1700 B.C.), before undertaking an expedition to a distant land to bring back the statues of Marduk and his consort, which had been carried off by an enemy.[1] In ancient Egypt divination did not play so conspicuous a part as in Babylonia and in the Hellenic world. The Egyptian texts do not mention hydro-mancy, although we know from the classics that Anubis was invoked by a vase full of liquid or a flame.[2] In the story of the homeward journey of Joseph's brethren (Gn 44[1-15]) from Egypt to Palestine mention is made of a divining cup (vv.[5. 15]), the purpose of which would seem to have been that of detecting a thief. 'Know ye not that such a man as I can indeed divine?' There is good reason to believe, however, that the episode connected with Joseph belongs to the Hyksos period,[3] and that the custom of divination by water was introduced into the valley of the Nile from the east by the invading 'shepherd kings.'

In modern times among the Slavs at Ceklinj, in Crnagora, maidens gaze into a well at daybreak on St. George's Day, till their eyes fill with tears and they think they see the image of their future husbands reflected in the water.[4] In the Highlands of Scotland apples and a sixpence were put in a tub of water at Hallowe'en for oracular purposes. The person who could extract either of these articles from the water with his mouth without using his teeth was regarded as likely to be very lucky. Similarly three plates were placed on the hearth, one filled with clean water, another with dirty water, and the third empty. A blindfold youth then knelt in front of the hearth and groped about till he put his finger in one of them. 'If he lighted on the plate with the clean water, he would wed a maid; if on the plate with the dirty water, he would marry a widow; and if on the empty plate, he would remain a bachelor. For a girl the answer of the oracle was analogous. . . . But to make sure, the operation had to be repeated thrice, the position of the plates being changed each time. If the enquirer put his or her finger into the same plate thrice or even twice, it was quite conclusive.'[5]

An oracle may very readily pass into an ordeal, where the person accused of a crime is tested by being subjected to a process which would normally prove fatal, or at least injurious to him. People accused of witchcraft and other offences are frequently tested by being compelled to drink water into which a poisonous substance has been placed. If the stomach rejects the draught, the accused is declared innocent and released; if, on the other hand, it is retained or evacuated by purging, he is pronounced guilty.[6]

5. Water-spirits and water-gods.—To say with Tylor that a 'belief in the existence of spiritual beings' constitutes the 'minimum definition of religion' is to forget that the outlook of primitive man is towards the sacred and mysterious rather than in the direction of the spiritual. Psychologically the religious sense manifests itself on the emotional side before the mind is capable of forming definite notions like spirits or gods. Primitive man sees around him certain phenomena which puzzle him, and, long before he has evolved a 'belief in spiritual beings,' he has come to explain mysterious objects in terms of the supernatural. Now, water is most certainly calculated to arouse in the primeval consciousness the animatistic attitude of mind dictated by awe of the mysterious. Upon it man depends for his very existence, through its agency he sees the desert made to blossom as the rose, and in it he beholds the manifestation of life and movement, and even the power of death and destruction. He regards it therefore as possessed of *mana*, and, in consequence, sacred. But there is always a tendency to personify the sacred. The mysterious roll of thunder becomes associated with the voice of the tribal All-Father, and the magic downfall of rain is explained as the work of spirits or gods. So with water. Originally the Trojans regarded their sacred river, Skamandros, as containing *mana*, and by way of oblations cast live bulls and horses into its depths. In later times, when they had reached an animistic or theistic stage, Homer speaks of altars or shrines being erected on the river-bank, on which a bull was sacrificed, the belief being that the spirit in

1 W. R. Smith, p. 183.
2 *GB*³, pt. vii., *Balder the Beautiful*, i. 194.
3 L. Lloyd, *Peasant Life in Sweden*, London, 1870, p. 261.
4 Quoted from *Hibernian Magazine*, July 1817, by Frazer, *GB*³, pt. vii., *Balder the Beautiful*, i. 205 f.
5 *GB*³, pt. v., *Adonis*, i. 247.
6 *Ib.* p. 248; cf. Grimm, *Deutsche Mythologie*⁴, Berlin, 1875–78, i. 489.
7 Cf. art. LOURDES.
8 W. Ellis, *Polyn. Researches*, London, 1830, ii. 240.
9 H. Newton, *In Far New Guinea*, London, 1914, p. 89 f.
10 Skeat, *Malay Magic*, p. 540 f.
11 J. Roscoe, *The Northern Bantu*, Cambridge, 1915, p. 135.
12 D. Crantz, *Hist. of Greenland*, London, 1767, i. 214.
13 W. R. Smith, p. 178.
14 Lucian, *Bis accusatus*, i.; cf. Pliny, *HN* ii. 232; Paus. IX. x. 5; *CGS* iv. 188 f.
15 *Cuneiform Texts from Babylonian Tablets in the British Museum*, London, 1906, iii. pl. 2 ff., v. pl. 4 ff.
16 H. Zimmern, *Ritualtafeln für den Wahrsager, Beschwörer und Sänger*, in *Beiträge*, Leipzig, 1896–1901, ii. 82 ff.
17 *Cun. Texts*, iii. pl. 2–5.

1 H. C. Rawlinson, *WAI* v. pl. 33, col. ii. 8.
2 Pliny, *HN* xxxiii. 46; Plutarch, *de Iside*, lxi., lxiv.
3 E. A. W. Budge, *A History of Egypt*, London, 1902, iii. 133 ff.; W. M. Flinders Petrie, *A History of Egypt*, do. 1894, i. 233 ff., *Egypt and Israel*, do. 1911, p. 27.
4 *GB*³, pt. i., *The Magic Art*, ii. 345.
5 *Ib.* pt. vii., *Balder the Beautiful*, i. 237 f.
6 See art. ORDEAL (Introductory and Primitive).

the water, or the god of the stream, was capable of departing from his element to consume the essence of the offerings in the holy place on the shore.[1] We do not suggest, in quoting this example, that a stratigraphical evolution took place in early times. On the contrary, we regard the assumption of strata in the evolution of religion as the fundamental error in the universalistic form of the comparative method as adopted by Frazer.[2] The conception of the sacred river is undoubtedly psychologically a more rudimentary notion than the more complex animistic and theistic beliefs. But it can hardly be said that there was a pre-animistic era in the history of religion, when animism was not and nevertheless religion of a kind existed.[3] Some sort of animism may have been a primary condition of the most primitive religion of mankind, but it would seem that the vaguer and more comprehensive animatistic conception surrounded such objects as water from the beginning.

Among people in a more developed state of culture water-spirits and water-gods are of frequent occurrence. Stories of the Perseus and Andromeda type have been found from Japan and Annam to Scandinavia and Scotland, and, although the details vary with the locality, the central feature is always connected with the sacrifice of a human victim (generally a virgin) to a water-demon. It is, therefore, highly probable that these legends reflect a real custom of sacrificing girls to be the wives of water-spirits, since we know that girls are frequently married to river-gods, etc., in primitive society.[4] The custom may have arisen from the belief that water-spirits are the bestowers of life and fertility, whose kindly gifts of rain from above and springs from below produce pasture for the cattle and fruits for the service of man. In Syria the life-giving operation of Baal was connected with springs, streams, and underground water, and therefore the Baalim had their seats on the banks of rivers and by deep water-courses, in spots of natural fertility.[5] As authors of fertility in general, it is in accordance with the working of the primitive mind that these water-spirits should come to be regarded as the bestowers of offspring. Accordingly we find that barren women frequently betake themselves to a stream known to be inhabited by a water-spirit, and bathe in the waters.[6] Down to classical times girls bathed in the Skamandros before their marriage, praying as they did so, 'Skamander, take my virginity.'[7]

Sometimes, however, human beings are cast into water simply as a propitiatory sacrifice to appease the wrath of the indwelling spirit. The frequency with which maritime people are reminded of the dangers of the sea would naturally lead to a belief that water-spirits are dangerous and malignant beings capable of assuming monstrous forms.

Thus the Warramunga of Central Australia perform elaborate ceremonies to coerce a gigantic but purely mythical water-snake who is said to have destroyed a number of people.[8] The Tarahumares place their houses at a distance from the water, and never sleep near it when on a journey lest they should be molested by the indwelling spirit. Whenever they make weirs to catch fish, they are careful to offer fish to the water-serpent of the river.[9] To ensure a good catch of fish the fishermen of Efiat throw a human victim into the water at the mouth of the river,[1] and in the St. George's Day rites in England the Green George was thrown into the water to secure the favour of the water-spirits, as well as to make the meadows green in summer.[2] The idea of propitiating a malignant water-spirit is undoubtedly the underlying motive in the legend of Perseus and Andromeda, and in its mediæval counterpart of St. George and the Dragon.

LITERATURE.—Authorities have been given in the footnotes.

E. O. JAMES.

WATER, WATER-GODS (Babylonian).—**1. Water.**—The Babylonians divided their universe into three parts—the heavens, the earth, and the sea—which they personified as the gods Anu, Enlil, and Ea respectively. Each element was considered divine. But more emphasis was placed upon the divinity of the sea, because the water of 'the great deep' was considered the element out of which all things were generated. This 'great deep,' or Apsu, encircled the earth, was the source of all irrigation, and was the home of Ea, the god of waters. The Euphrates and the Tigris as children of the great deep were 'the soul of the land' and 'the bestower of blessings' respectively. But there was a sense in which the waters were regarded as an agent of destruction, viz. in their appearance in the form of violent rains and floods. Under this aspect they were personified as Tiamāt, the Tēhōm of Gn 1, an aspect which is much emphasized in the Old Testament. There Tēhōm is opposed to Jahweh, and is the cause of much dread to the people.[3] In Babylonia, however, the beneficent aspect of water comes more to the front. It was not only one of the commonest of natural phenomena, appearing as rivers, streams, seas, lakes, ponds, brooks, springs, fountains, wells, mist, dew, rain, hail, snow, ice, vapour, fog, and clouds, but also indispensable to men, animals, and vegetables. Water was divine and holy, and as such was worshipped as a god. It played a very important part in omens and oracles and all kinds of magic. It could dispel demons, wash away disease, and purge from sin. It acted as a divine power in decisions by ordeal, and in it flowed the blood of the gods.

The Babylonians believed that all waters were peopled by living creatures, actual and mythical, some of which were beneficent and others harmful. The *anunnaki* (*a*, 'water,' and *nun*, 'strength') were probably beneficent water-spirits, and the seven[4] *utukku* were demons of the sea. Both spirits and demons were controlled by Ea, or by the ferryman who kept watch over the river of death, who was called Arad-Ea, 'servant of Ea.' Water, being thus associated with divine beings, was usually considered the source of life, and at Eridu there was a sacred spring which figured in early Babylonian mythology and incantation rituals.

Because of its sacred properties, water played the chief rôle in incantations. Ea, by virtue of his being a water-god, was the most prominent figure in the ritual of incantations, being called the great physician. But Marduk, in later times, usurped much of his power, and always acted as mediator between the patient and Ea. The Ea-ritual in incantations involved washing and sprinkling of the body of the patient with water from the Euphrates or Tigris or from some bubbling source coming directly out of the earth. Then an image was made of the demon or sorcerer who controlled the victim, and it was placed in a boat. The image was drowned in sacred water, and the patient was relieved.[5]

2. Water-gods.—Babylonia was always sorely dependent upon her streams and canals, and this partly accounts for her numerous water-gods. But

1 *Il.* xx. 4, v. 7, xxi. 130.
2 E. O. James, *Primitive Ritual and Belief*, London, 1917, pp. 2, 153 f.
3 R. R. Marett, *The Threshold of Religion*², London, 1914, p. ix.
4 *GB*³, pt. i., *The Magic Art*, ii. 150, 152 f.
5 W. R. Smith, pp. 100, 102.
6 S. I. Curtiss, *Primitive Semitic Religion To-day*, Chicago and London, 1902, p. 117 ff.; cf. Paus. II. xv. 5, v. vii. 2 ff.; J. E. Harrison, *Prolegomena to the Study of Greek Religion*², Cambridge, 1908, p. 434.
7 Æschines, *Epist.* x.
8 Spencer-Gillen^b, p. 226 ff.
9 C. Lumholtz, *Unknown Mexico*, London, 1903, i. 402.

1 H. Goldie, *Calabar and its Mission*, Edinburgh and London, 1901, p. 43.
2 *GB*³, pt. i., *The Magic Art*, ii. 76.
3 Ps 93⁴ 104⁶ 135⁶ 18⁴.
4 Rawlinson, *WAI* iv. 2, col. v.
5 For details see M. Jastrow, *Die Religion Babyloniens und Assyriens*, Giessen, 1905, i. 273 ff.

more important in the minds of the people were the waters of the Euphrates and the Tigris and the Persian Gulf. Being mysterious, often beneficent, frequently destructive, never subject to control, they were considered from the very earliest times as manifestations of divine beings. They were worshipped, propitiated, and supplicated. All things, good and bad, came from them, and from them was no escape.

The source of all water was thought to be situated at the head of the Persian Gulf, or to *be* the head of the Persian Gulf. At a very early period this was personified and called **Ea**,[1] 'the house of water.'[2] Ea's home was at Eridu on the shore of the Persian Gulf. He was called *šar apsi*, 'king of the abyss,' but more especially, perhaps, he was god of the sweet waters which were believed to be under the earth and to fill streams, canals, and rivers. Tiamāt personified the salt waters. Ea and his consort, Damkina, are often represented as dwelling in the great deep, and hence it is that he was often worshipped as Dagan, the fish-god. As a water-god, all fountains and streams were sacred to him. Water, being a sacred, healing, and fertilizing agency, became the symbol of life, and Ea was the great physician. Because of the universal utility of water, Ea was claimed by all Babylonia as its champion, and, according to the Legend of Creation, when the gods decided to destroy mankind, Ea interceded. He befriended the Babylonian Noah, Ut-napištim, advising him to build a vessel so as to be prepared for the approaching deluge. He thus became the wise one, who taught men all the arts, and who even created mankind. Ea's consort was sometimes called Dam-gal-nun-na, 'great wife of the deep,' her Sumerian name being Nin-ki, 'lady of the earth'; but she was also called 'queen of the deep.' The god himself sometimes appeared under the name Nin-a-gal, 'god of great strength.' Ea is represented on a seal cylinder as sitting on his throne, while Damkina is leading a worshipper into his presence. The great fish or capricorn under the seat is the symbol of the god.[3] Sometimes he is seen carrying a vase of water with flowing streams and fish, and standing on a capricorn.[4] He is very often represented in the form of a fish, or of a man covered by the skin of a fish. In Assyria Ea appears as 'king of the ocean,' 'opener of fountains,' 'creator,' and god of wisdom. He is described by Berosus, under the name Oannes, as 'a creature endowed with reason, with a body like that of a fish, with feet below like those of a man, with a fish's tail.' When Babylon became prominent in the time of Ḫammurabi, Marduk was classified as son of Ea, and collaborated with him in incantations, being associated, as Ea was, with waters of life.

Adad (Sumerian, [d]Im), or **Ramman**, was a god of rain and lord of subterranean waters. He was never associated with any particular city, nor was he a very early Sumerian deity. He came from the west-lands, where he was a solar deity. In Babylonia he was usually associated with the destructive aspect of rain when accompanied by thunder and lightning, although sometimes he was considered a vegetation-god. Ḫammurabi, in the epilogue to his Code, calls upon Adad to deprive his enemy 'of the rain from heaven and the water-floods from the springs.' Nebuchadrezzar I. calls him 'the lord of springs and rains,'[5] and Meli-Shipak beseeches him to bestow 'abundant streams.'[1] Adad was symbolized by a thunderbolt, was associated with the sky-god, Anu, at Ašur, and often appeared under the name Numušda. Although **Enlil** was known as a rain-god[2] and was supposed to have brought on the flood, he was not very prominent as a water-deity. In like manner **Ašur**, the great Assyrian war-god, was associated with water as a corn- and water-deity and as a god of fertility, but his rôle as such was not very important. **Innini**, primarily the heavenly queen, was a water-goddess. She is represented with serpents and blades of grass, which in Oriental art are associated with water and vegetation. She bore the title *azag-sug*, 'sacred libator,' and, like Ašnan, a grain-goddess, was described as goddess of the 'holy meal water.'[3] **Ištar**, the great mother-goddess and goddess of love, was also prominently associated with water. She referred to herself as 'daughter of the ocean stream';[4] she was connected with the cleansing power of water; she was patroness of streams and canals, without whom 'no stream is opened, no stream is closed, which brings life,' without whom 'no canal is opened, no canal is closed, which gives the wide-dwelling peoples to drink';[5] and she is addressed as 'thou that rulest over springs and mountains and seas.'[6] She is represented in art with a vase of water. Besides being identified with Kir-gi-lu, or Nin-kir-gi-lu, a rain-goddess,[7] she appears as Ninā, Ea's daughter, who was originally a water-deity, and quite distinct from Ištar. But from time to time the goddesses Ištar, Ninā, Innini, and Anunit were confused one with another. **Ninā** was the goddess who rode upon the sea in a boat, was at one time known as Geštinanna, 'queen of waters,' and was a fish-goddess. In fact, her name is written with the ideogram which means 'goddess of the fish-house.' In time she became sister of Ningirsu, lord of the freshets. She was also called Nin-en and Nin-en-na-ge, 'lady of incantation.'[8] Ninā was also identified with **Išḫara**, goddess of water-animals, whose symbol was the scorpion,[9] and who bore the title, *tiamāt* (dragon) of the primeval waters (*[ilat]iš-ḫa-ra ti-amat*).[10] Išḫara appeared at an earlier period as Išḫana, 'heavenly goddess of the fish-house,' and daughter of Ea, and still earlier as Esḫa. Ur-Bau built a temple to **KU-anna** in Girsu. He says that she deluges the land with water, and it would thus seem that she was a storm-goddess. **Marduk**, who became the mighty god of Babylon, absorbed the attributes of many inferior deities. He succeeded Ninā as god of incantation by water; he was made a water-god, being Ea's son; and his consort was **Zer-panitum**, 'the lady of the abyss.' He became all-powerful, and was called 'king of the abyss.' A hymn says of him: 'Command the sea and the sea obeyeth';[11] he was addressed as 'lord of the mountain stream and of water, opener of sources and cisterns, controller of streams';[12] and he is represented in company with a water-dragon, and standing above the watery deep. His cult has been traced to Eridu. **Nabu**, a patron deity of Borsippa and son of Marduk, was a

1 His Sumerian name was En-ki, 'lord of the earth.'
2 *Cuneiform Texts from Babylonian Tablets in the British Museum*, xxiv. 15, 50, xlix. 5.
3 J. Menant, *Catalogue méthodique et raisonné de la Collection de Clercq*, Paris, 1886–90, no. 106.
4 W. H. Ward, *Cylinders and Other Ancient Oriental Seals*, New York, 1909, no. 95.
5 L. W. King, *Babylonian Boundary-Stones and Memorial Tablets in the British Museum*, London, 1912, p. 36.

1 King, *Babylonian Boundary-Stones*, p. 20.
2 *CT* xv. 11. 13–16.
3 S. Langdon, *Sumerian and Babylonian Psalms*, Paris, 1909, p. 158. 64.
4 S. Langdon, *Tammuz and Ishtar*, Oxford, 1914, p. 138.
5 J. A. Craig, *Assyrian and Babylonian Religious Texts*, 2 vols., Leipzig, 1895–97, vol. i. pl. 15, ll. 15–17.
6 Langdon, *Tammuz and Ishtar*, p. 57.
7 *CT* xv. 23.
8 F. Thureau-Dangin, *Die sumerischen und akkadischen Königsinschriften* (hereafter cited as *SAK*), Leipzig, 1907, p. 263.
9 S. A. B. Mercer, *Oath in Babylonian and Assyrian Literature*, Paris, 1912, *passim*.
10 *CT* xxvi. 42. 10.
11 *WAI* iv. 26, no. 4, l. 5 f.
12 See J. Hehn, *Hymnen und Gebete an Marduk* (*BASS* v.), p. 325.

counterpart of Ea. He was therefore a water-god and god of vegetation. He was also a god of wisdom, and as such was associated with the watery deep. In later times his character as a water-god was overshadowed by that of wisdom, and he became secretary of the gods and inspirer of mankind. His symbol was the stylus with which he recorded the decisions of fate. **Nâru** was a water-deity, but his or her character is otherwise unknown. Langdon says he was 'probably a male deity,'[1] although he also refers to her as a river-goddess.[2] **Nidaba**, a grain-goddess, was closely connected with the water-goddess Ninā-Išhara, one of her titles being *nu-maš-še-gún-nu*, which Langdon connects with *numašše*, a title of Ninā. J. Krauss[3] likewise identifies Lugal-ki-sī-a, a consort of Ninā, with Lugul-ki-sa-a, a consort of Nidaba. Ninā refers to Nidaba as her sister,[4] and is called the 'holy reed-Nidaba';[5] and, on a seal dedicated to Naram-Sin, Nidaba is connected with the water-goddess Ninā.[6] **Nin-akha-kuddu**, also known as **Nin-karrak** and **Gula**, was a goddess of purification, and was connected with Ea and Eridu. In incantation texts she is associated with Ea and is called 'the lady of incantation.' In like manner **Ninhabursildu**, goddess of pure fountain-water, was queen of incantations. She was symbolized by a jar of holy water (*egubbû*). The war-god **Ninib** preserved water attributes. As the first-born of Ea, he was known as 'lord of wells and of the sea' and 'opener of wells.' He was therefore also a vegetation-god. According to a hymn to Enmešarra,[7] **Ningirsu**, brother of Ninā, was connected with irrigation. It is there said, 'Great lord, without whom Ningirsu does not direct the water-course and canal.' He was also associated with Scorpio and the scorpion of Išhara. The Sumerian name of **Tammuz** is Dumu-zi-abzu, 'the faithful child of the deep.'[8] Tammuz was called 'the real son of the deep,' and belonged to the family of Ea.[9] Of course he is well known as the Babylonian corn-spirit, who dies and comes to life again every year. He was one of Sumeria's oldest gods, and, when the Sumerians moved into the Tigris-Euphrates valley, Tammuz became a god of the fertilizing waters. He was then called *bêl girsū*, 'lord of the flood,'[10] and under this name or its equivalent, Nin-girsu, he became the local lord of Lagash. Belonging to the Eridu circle, he employed the holy water of the great basin, *pašiš apsī*, in incantations, and as the youthful god *par excellence* he represented the beneficent waters which flooded the valley of the Tigris and Euphrates in winter and which died away in summer. He bore the title ᵈNiba-alam, 'image of Ea.' Many hymns were sung to Tammuz as vegetation-god, but in them there is frequent reference to his water attributes. The death of Tammuz was said to have been marked by the cessation of libating the waters of Eridu, but drowning in the waters was meant to induce Tammuz to send refreshing floods.[11]

LITERATURE.—See the works cited in the footnotes.

S. A. B. MERCER.

1 *Babylonian Liturgies*, Paris, 1913, p. 140.

2 *PSBA* xl. [1918] p. 45, n. 47.

3 *Die Götternamen in den babylonischen Siegelcylinder-legenden*, Leipzig, 1911, p. 7.

4 *SAK*, p. 94, col. 5, l. 25. 5 *RAssyr* vii. [1910] 107.

6 W. H. Ward, *Seal Cylinders of Western Asia*, Washington, 1910, p. 136.

7 Craig, *Assyr. and Bab. Relig. Texts*, vol. i. pl. 13.

8 In the great theological list in *CT* xxiv. pl. 16, l. 30, Tammuz is called 'the faithful son of the fresh waters which come forth from the earth.'

9 Ur-Bau erected a temple to him in Girsu (*SAK*, p. 60, col. 6, ll. 9–12).

10 Langdon, *Sumerian and Babylonian Psalms*, p. 160, l. 14, note 9, *Babylonian Liturgies*, p. 96.

11 *RAssyr* viii. [1911] 161, col. i. 12; Langdon, *Tammuz and Ishtar*, passim.

WATER, WATER-GODS (Egyptian).

— 1. **Water.**—The Egyptians believed in a primeval watery mass, deep and boundless, out of which had come into existence the heavens, the earth, and everything that is in them. The germs of all life, human and divine, were in the watery mass, which was personified and received the name Nu. It was eternal, and part male and part female. The lowest circle of the watery mass was described as 'Osiris who encircles the under world'; but the whole watery realm was frequently identified or summarized as the ocean or the Nile. It was believed that the Nile sprang from the great watery abyss and divided into two rivers—the one the Nile of Egypt, and the other that of which it was said, 'Great and mighty is the river of the sky, flowing across the heavens and through the Duat, the world of night and thick darkness, and on that river floats the boat of Rā.' In other words, there were two rivers which sprang out of the watery abyss—an earthly and a heavenly. Water was sacred to the Egyptians and possessed all the qualities of a divine being. In all lakes, rivers, fountains, wells, and streams the divine essence was resident. For this reason all fish[1] were sacred, and were venerated from the earliest to the latest dynastic times. Those fish venerated at Latopolis and Oxyrhynchus were eaten sacramentally on the ninth day of the month Thoth. Some water-animals were even given names as deities—*e.g.*, the hippopotamus (Taurt) and the crocodile (Sebek). Fish were thus considered the abode of the gods.

Because of the divine character of water, it was considered fortunate to be drowned, a drowned person being sometimes regarded as a deity. Osiris was drowned,[2] just as Ino of Greece and Bhairwanand in India. The greatest service one could render a god was to be drowned, and thus be united with him. The word for 'drown,' *ḥsy*, originally meant 'praise.'[3] Gods and great men loved to be associated with sacred water; thus the 'mother of Mendes' is depicted carrying a fish upon her head, and Rameses II. was credited with powers as a rain-maker. To control divine water was greatly desired. Chapters lvii. and lviii. of the *Book of the Dead* are called 'The Chapter . . . of having the Mastery over the Water in the Underworld,' and the suppliant prays: 'Grant that I may have dominion over the water.' Water is not only a fertilizing and destroying force, to which offerings are made, but also a means of warding off demons. It played a great rôle in lustrations and incantations.

As a deity water was worshipped. The water-worship of Canopus and its cult in Egypt are well known.[4] There were many instances of sacrifice to water, the victims being usually bulls, horses, or human beings. Even as men were sacrificed to the Tiber in Rome, and to the Ganges in India, so in Egypt human beings, especially girls, were sacrificed to the Nile. A favourite place for an altar, therefore, was on the banks of the Nile. But all streams and fountains, lakes and rivers, were the abode of spirits, which had to be propitiated.[5]

Even as Egypt was the gift of the Nile, so all life was sustained by the Nile, and the Nile was the water of life; and, as the inhabitants of Egypt depended upon the waters of the Nile for daily life, so the departed are represented as drinking the water of life from the celestial Nile. In this world sacred water was used for purification, and in pre-

1 E. Mahler, 'Das Fischsymbol auf ägyp. Denkmälern,' *ZDMG* lxvii. [1913] 37–48.

2 *ZA* xxxix. [1903] 41, pls. i., ii.

3 *Ib.* xlvi. [1910] 132 ff.

4 *Ib.* l. [1914] 132; Athanasius, *in Gent.* 24 (*PG* xxv. 48).

5 *GB*³, pt. i., *The Magic Art*, London, 1911, ii 155 ff.

paration for the next world it was used in an interesting ceremony called the 'Opening of the Mouth,' which consisted of sprinkling or pouring water over the statue of the departed to make it a pure abode for the *ka*. This ceremony not only purified and sanctified the person represented by the statue, but also removed from him all possibility of decay and death in the world to come.[1]

2. Water-gods.—At a time which antedates the earliest records Egyptians had deified the Nile and worshipped it under the name **Ḥāpi.**[2] In the Pyramid Texts his name occurs[3] as that of a well-established god. It was natural that such should be the case, for Egypt's welfare depended more upon the Nile than upon any other one thing. Because of the two great divisions of Egypt, Ḥāpi was worshipped with some distinctions in both north and south. In the north he was Ḥāp-Meḥt and in the south he was Ḥāp-Reset. But there were not two gods, for Ḥāpi is represented holding two plants, the papyrus and the lotus, or two vases from which the North and South Nile poured. He is usually depicted in the form of a man, with hanging breasts from which water streams, wearing the sign of water and holding lotus-flowers. Ḥāpi was at an early time identified with the primeval watery mass, personified as the god Nu, or, at least, he absorbed Nu's attributes. Because of the mystery to the Egyptians of the cause of the Nile's inundations, Ḥāpi's being was always shrouded in mystery.

In a hymn to the Nile it is said of him that he 'cannot be figured in stone, he is not to be seen in the image on which are set the crown of the South and the North with their uraei, offerings cannot be made to him, he cannot be brought forth from his secret places, his dwelling-place is not to be found out, he is not to be found in the shrines which are inscribed with texts, there is no habitation which is sufficiently large for him to dwell in, and the heart [of man] is unable to depict him.'[4]

Because of his great reputation, he was called 'father of the gods,' 'creator of things which exist,' 'vivifier,' 'the lord of fishes,' was identified with Osiris, Amon, and Ptaḥ, and was considered greater than Rā. In later times a festival of the annual rise of the Nile was celebrated with great solemnity throughout Egypt—an event mentioned by Heliodorus.[5] Hekatæus[6] speaks of a sanctuary of the Nile, and the early Church Fathers bear witness to his worship.[7] During the Nile festivals[8] hymns were sung to Ḥāpi in which the worshippers said:

'Offerings are made, oxen are slain to thee, great festivals are kept for thee, fowls are sacrificed to thee, beasts of the field are caught for thee, pure flames are offered to thee.'

Even the Nile's inundations were personified and called **Bāḥ**, and the waters of the Nile were sometimes deified as **Ānḳet**, a goddess, usually represented in the form of a woman with a crown of feathers on her head, arranged in such a way as to suggest a savage origin. Originally she was a goddess of some island in the First Cataract, but she was later identified with Nephthys. She personified the waters of the Nile which embrace and fructify the fields. She is sometimes pictured in a boat, seated in a shrine, with a table of offerings before her. Set, the personification of the forces of water which were supposed to resist light and order, was symbolized by the serpent **Āpep**, the great monster of the deep, whose four heads represent the four sources of the Nile. **Ageb** is mentioned in the Pyramid Texts as a god of the deep. **Hathor**, the cow-goddess and personification of the house in which Horus dwelt, was one of the oldest of Egypt's goddesses. She was the principal counterpart of Rā, and became the great mother-goddess. She was identified astronomically with the star Sepṭ, and was thereby connected with the rise of the Nile preparatory to its inundation. Being the mother of all, she was easily identified with phases of the Nile. There were supposed to be seven Hathors, but this is not surprising, since her popularity as mother-goddess caused many secondary deities to be identified with her and gave rise to a Hathor cult in many localities. She is represented in many forms and attitudes, but none is more interesting than a picture in a Theban tomb which depicts her in a persea-tree giving drink to a soul in Amentet. **Hekes**, 'lord of the mouth of the rivers,' is a rarely met god with stellar characteristics.[1] **Isis**, or **Ast**, was in pre-dynastic times a water-spirit or river-goddess, probably Libyan in origin. From the earliest to the latest times she was Egypt's greatest goddess, the beneficent goddess and mother, the highest type of the faithful, a loving wife and mother, the mother of Horus, the giver of food and life to the dead, 'wife of the lord of the abyss,' 'wife of the lord of the inundation,' and 'creatrix of the Nile flood.' As the power of the Nile, she was called Sati and Sepṭ, and, as the embracer of the land and producer of fertility by means of water, she was called Ānḳet. She was the female counterpart of the primeval abyss from which all life sprang, and she was so popular that at an early period she absorbed all characteristics of other goddesses. She was not only a water-deity, but also an earth-, corn-, and star-goddess. She is usually depicted as a woman with vulture head-dress and with a papyrus-sceptre in her hand. Sometimes she is crowned with a pair of horns, between which is a solar disk, surmounted by the sign for 'seat,' the symbol of her name. With the horns and disk are often two plumes; and sometimes she wears the double crown of Egypt, to the back of which is attached the feather *maāt*. Her symbol was the star Sepṭ, which announced the inundation of the Nile. In the Roman period elaborate ceremonies, related by Apuleius and Pausanias, were conducted in connexion with the use of a vessel of Nile water in the Isis festival, which took place at the time of the Nile's inundation. **Khnemu**, the first member of the great triad, Khnemu, Satet, and Anḳet, at Ābu, or Elephantinē, was originally a river- or water-god, as were the other members of the triad. He was often identified with Nu and Ḥāpi. He was one of the oldest of Egypt's gods, being mentioned in the text of Uni. He was without doubt a pre-dynastic god, symbolized by the flat-horned ram from the East. At a very early period he became god of the Nile and of the annual Nile flood, and as such bore the name Ḳebḥ. He was called 'maker of heaven and earth, and Duat, the waters, and the mountains.' He says of himself, 'I am the primeval watery abyss, and I am the Nile who riseth at his will.' As a water-god, he became almost universal in Egypt, uniting in himself the attributes of Rā, Geb, and Osiris, and with his four rams' heads represented the four elements—earth, air, fire, and water—and perhaps also the four sources of the Nile. He is depicted in the form of a ram-headed man, and, as a water-god, he is seen with outstretched hands over which

[1] E. A. W. Budge, *The Book of Opening the Mouth*, 2 vols., London, 1909, *passim*.

[2] A. Erman holds that the original form of the name was *ḥāpr* (*ZĀ* xliv. [1908] 114), but A. H. Gardiner suggests the possibility of *hyrp* or *ḥrp* (*ZĀ* xlv. [1909] 140 f.).

[3] *E.g.*, K. Sethe, *Die altägyptischen Pyramidentexte*, Leipzig, 1908, § 149.

[4] E. A. W. Budge, *The Gods of the Egyptians*, i. 147. Yet there are statues of him in the British Museum, in the Museum in Florence, in Turin, in the Cairo Museum, and in the Isis temple at Philæ.

[5] *Æthiop*. ix. 9.

[6] Stephen of Byz. *FHG* i. 277.

[7] F. Zimmermann, *Die ägyp. Religion nach der Darstellung der Kirchenschriftsteller und der ägyp. Denkmäler*, Paderborn, 1912, p. 72.

[8] An excellent description of two Nile festivals instituted by Rameses II. is to be seen in Lepsius, iii. 175*a*, 200*d*, 218*d*.

[1] *RTr* xxi. [1899] 3; cf. Sethe, § 452.

flows water. He is sometimes represented with a jug above his horns. His worship was especially common in that part of Egypt extending from Philæ to Thebes. **Meḥt-wrt,** the emblem of the primeval female creative principle, and the name of the celestial cow, was originally a female personification of the watery matter which formed the substance out of which the world proceeded. She is a pre-dynastic goddess, and is mentioned in the texts of Uni. **Meret,** depicted with an aquatic plant on her head, and therefore a water-goddess, was associated with Mut. Her name occurs in a dual form, Merti, and as such represented the Southern and Northern Nile. **Mut,** the great mother-goddess, 'who giveth birth, but was herself not born of any,' was an ancient water-goddess. She was called 'the watery one,' 'the watery flood,' and as such was called the wife of the Nile. Her principal temple was in Asher, a quarter of Thebes, which probably derived its name from the sacred lake which existed there. **Neit,** one of the oldest of Egyptian goddesses, was the personification of a form of the great primeval watery mass. At a later period she was represented with bow and arrows as a goddess of war and of the chase. **Nu,** in pre-dynastic Egypt, was the personification of the watery mass of heaven, whose counterpart was Nut. He was called 'the great god whose dwelling is in the waters of the sky,' and was sometimes identified with Kheper, the self-created one. He was ordinarily represented as an obese man, like the Nile, with whom he was often identified. **Nut** was the personification of the female aspect of the great watery mass out of which all things came. She was the daughter of Shu and Tefnut, the wife of Geb, and mother of Osiris, Isis, Nephthys, and Set. She is usually represented as a woman with a vase of water on her head. She sometimes wears the horns and disk of Hathor, and holds a papyrus-sceptre and sign of life in her hand. She is also depicted as a woman standing in a sycamore-tree pouring out water from a vase. In the *Book of the Dead* a suppliant prays, 'Grant thou to me of the water and of the air which dwell in thee.' Her attributes were many, because, like all water-deities, she absorbed the characteristics of many minor deities, and was recognized and worshipped in many different places in Egypt. **Osiris** was the god of the dead *par excellence.* He may have originally been a human being who was deified. When such transformation was made cannot be decided. But from the earliest dynastic period till the latest he was worshipped. He became the most popular, best known, and most powerful Egyptian deity. But what interests us is that he was originally a water-spirit or god of some portion of the waters of the Nile, and with the passage of time he became a great water-god, representing in general the creative and nutritive powers of the Nile, and particularly the inundation.[1] As a Nile-god he naturally became a creative and generative power. And, just as the Nile sank and rose, so Osiris died and rose again, becoming thus the god of resurrection. Osiris was depicted in many forms, the most usual being that of a mummy with a beard and wearing the white crown and a *menat.* He was from time to time identified with most of the greatest gods until he attained a position which made him appear as the natural god of Egypt. As a water-deity he was identified with Ḥāpi, and later with Nu, representing water as a life-giving element. As there were thought to be four sources of the Nile, so Osiris had four birth-genii, for he was the Nile personified. Plutarch records the belief of the Egypt of his day when he says that Osiris was looked upon as not only the Nile but also the ocean. Osorkon II., as an embodiment of Osiris, was represented with streams of water pouring from his hands.[1] In the Nebseni papyrus of the *Book of the Dead* Osiris himself says, 'I flood the land with water and Great Black One is my name'; and in the papyrus of Nu he says, 'I am the god of inundation and Great Black One of the Lake is my name'; and in a hymn to Osiris it is said of him, 'Thou drawest thy waters from the abyss of heaven.' **Ptaḥ,** sometimes considered the oldest of gods, was a co-worker with Khnemu in creation. He was identified with many other gods as well as with Nu, the primeval abyss, and with Ḥāpi, and he was called 'lord of fish.' **Rem** was perhaps the personification of Rā's tears. He may have been the same as **Remi,**[2] who was probably a fish-god, and associated with Sebek, a personification of Nu. **Sati,** originally connected with the chase, was worshipped at the First Cataract, where she was associated with Khnemu. Her name probably refers to the falling waters of the Cataract. She thus became a goddess of inundation, who pours out and spreads over the land the life-giving waters of the Nile. She is usually represented in human form with a high conical crown. **Sebek,** as lord of the Fayyum and deified crocodile, was most probably a water-god. **Selḥet** was a scorpion-deity, and one of the four goddesses who assisted Nu and protected the four sources of the Nile. **Teṭenen** was usually identified with Ptaḥ, and sometimes with Nu. **Tefnut** was a rain-goddess whose male counterpart was Shu. She was the personification of the moisture of the sky. They were both born of the great watery mass. The cult of Tefnut does not seem to have been associated with any special city.

LITERATURE.—On this subject there exist no separate articles, monographs, or books. Besides original texts, the literature used has been mentioned in the course of the article. Special mention should be made of E. A. W. Budge's great work, *The Gods of the Egyptians*, 2 vols., London and Chicago, 1904.

S. A. B. MERCER.

WATER, WATER-GODS (Greek and Roman).—**I. Greek.**—The account given in art. NATURE (Greek) includes much information on this subject which need not be repeated here, especially as to the cult of river-gods, nymphs, and similar divinities. There are, however, certain aspects of the subject which require some addition.

The worship of rivers or of water generally as the origin of life was one expression of a belief which is also found in early speculation and philosophy. Thus Homer[3] speaks of Ὠκεανόν τε, θεῶν γένεσιν, καὶ μητέρα Τηθύν, and says[4] that Ocean is the origin of all things. Hesiod fits Oceanus and Tethys into his *Theogony*[5] as children of Earth and Heaven. Ocean, according to the Homeric conception, was regarded as a river flowing round and bounding the earth; thus it was set around the rim of the shield of Achilles.[6] It is personified in art as an elderly man with flowing locks and beard, but has little importance in religious cult.

The gods of the sea may be divided into two classes: (1) the elemental beings who constantly occur in folk-lore and popular belief, and (2) the clearly defined and personal Olympian gods who rule over the sea. The former had as a rule little importance in the official worship, though we hear of a public cult of the Old Man of the Sea (Ἅλιος Γέρων) at Byzantium. Triton, Proteus, Glaucus, Nereus, and the Nereids have many of the qualities attributed to sea-divinities or dæmons

[1] E. A. W. Budge, *ad loc.*

[1] E. Naville, *The Festival-Hall of Osorkon II. in the Great Temple of Bubastis* (*EEFM* x.), London, 1892, pl. xi.

[2] E. A. W. Budge, *The Book of the Dead*, London, 1898, clxxxviii. 13.

[3] *Il.* xiv. 201.

[4] *Ib.* 246.

[5] 133–136.

[6] *Il.* xviii. 607.

in the folk-lore of various nations, such as the gift of soothsaying or foretelling the future, and the power of transforming themselves into various shapes. Thus Proteus, when seized by Menelaus, changed into various beasts, and into water, and could change into fire; but, if bound, he could be compelled to impart his knowledge. Similarly Thetis, the Nereid, changed into various forms when seized by the mortal Peleus. In the systematized religion of Greece all these were regarded as subordinate to Poseidon as supreme god of the sea. In this capacity Poseidon was associated with Amphitrite, possibly an old goddess or impersonation of the sea, though in later mythology sometimes regarded as one of the Nereids. She is often represented in art as the consort of Poseidon, both in the assembly of the gods on Olympus and in her bridal procession, which is escorted by Tritons and Nereids on hippocamps and other sea-monsters; but she has no important place in official worship. Poseidon, on the other hand, is one of the chief gods of the State worship of many Greek cities, and was regarded as the ancestor of many leading families, especially among the Ionians and Minyans. The tale of his contest with Athene for the land of Attica is familiar, and was the subject of the western pediment of the Parthenon. The Isthmian games at Corinth were celebrated in his honour. As god of the sea, Poseidon can arouse and pacify storms, and so is appealed to by seafarers; but it is noteworthy that, in the greatest of sea-poems, the *Odyssey*, he appears as a malignant, rather than a beneficent, god. He has little or nothing to do with ships. The Argo was built under the direction of Athene, and mariners often attribute their safety to Aphrodite Euploia or to the Dioscuri rather than to him. Odysseus owed his safety to Ino Leucothea, who was often appealed to by sailors.

As sea-god Poseidon is the sender of earthquakes (Ἐννοσίγαιος). He split the mountains to make the ravine of Tempe, and hurled about or submerged islands. Salt springs inland are also attributed to him. By a symbolism which is common and easy to understand, waves are often compared to sea-horses; and either the origin of the horse or its training to human service is attributed to Poseidon Hippios. Horses were sacrificed to him, sometimes by being thrown into the sea. The bull also was especially sacred to him, and bull-taming exhibitions were held in his honour. In connexion with this we are reminded of the mixed human and bull form often taken by river-gods.

We might naturally expect Poseidon, as the chief sea-god, to give victory in sea-fights; and in fact Persian galleys were dedicated to him at the Isthmus and at Sunium after the great naval victory at Salamis. But other gods often received thank-offerings for such victories.

A characteristic of all water-divinities and dæmons, from Poseidon down, in later Greek art is an expression of restless and passionate yearning, which is attributed to them as impersonating the restlessness of their element and its desire to embrace and engulf the land and its creatures. Apart from representations of sea-gods, the sea itself is often represented in art by conventional wave-patterns and by dolphins, fishes, and other sea-creatures.

2. Roman.—Here also the art. NATURE (Roman) gives most of the information required. The Romans were not a seafaring people, and their god Neptunus was not originally a sea-god, though he came later to be identified with the Greek Poseidon; but he may have been a *numen* associated with water, though very little is known as to his primitive worship. He appears, however, to be a god of springs, and so associated in worship with the nymphs. The worship of the nymphs in connexion with springs was very widespread in Italy and throughout the Roman empire, though it is not easy to distinguish how much was merely borrowed from Greece. Their frequent representations in art, like those of river-gods, evidently follow Greek models. The Camenæ, associated with soothsaying and poetry, appear to have been spring-goddesses in origin; and the nymph Egeria, Numa's counsellor, also had a similar character. River-gods, nymphs (often holding shells), and similar representations of water-deities are very common in Græco-Roman art, but they do not, as a rule, bear any distinctively Italian character. A more original conception is that of the famous figure of Jupiter Pluvius, the rain-god, on the Antonine Column,[1] who is represented hovering over the armies with outspread wings, and pouring down rain in torrents from his beard and outstretched arms. Such a naturalistic personification is alien to Greek anthropomorphism, and much more akin to mediæval and modern symbolism.

LITERATURE.—In addition to works quoted in artt. NATURE (Greek) and (Roman), articles in Roscher on 'Okeanos,' 'Poseidon,' 'Neptunus,' etc.; O. Gruppe, *Griechische Mythologie und Religionsgeschichte*, 2 vols., Munich, 1897–1906; G. Wissowa, *Religion und Cultus der Römer*, do. 1902, ²1912; L. R. Farnell, *Cults of the Greek States*, 5 vols., Oxford, 1896–1910, iv. 1–97.

E. A. GARDNER.

WATER (Hebrew and Jewish).—The importance attached to water in Jewish belief and practice is so great that it embraces almost every manifestation of life, and can best be studied in the following subdivisions: (1) cosmogony, in its widest sense, (2) lustration, (3) rain.

1. Cosmogony.—According to the record of the Bible, the primordial element of creation was water. Only by the separation between the waters above and the waters below could the earth appear, but the waters above the firmament were not entirely separated from those that were gathering below, first into a great sea and then into rivers and fountains of the deep. On the contrary, an intimate connexion between the two was continually kept up.[2] A connexion was believed to exist between the upper and lower waters in the form of pipes which led from the heavens above to the sea below, and through the medium of such pipes the waters that had come down from above, and which slowly gathered into the sea, were sucked up into the heavens, thence to descend again upon earth.[3]

The primeval sea surrounds the earth like a snake; so it is seen by Alexander the Great in his attempted ascent to heaven.[4] This view is found often repeated in Rabbinical writings. The sea stands under the rule of a special prince or spirit (Sar), who opposes Moses when he tries to cleave the waters of the Red Sea. He refuses to obey a being created on the sixth day, whilst the sea was created on the second.[5] He is conjured by the sages to cast up the strength of a man thrown into the sea by a witch.[6]

The sea is the counterpart of the earth, and it contains every creature that is found upon the earth, save the fox, which by a stratagem escapes the fate of being cast into the sea.[7] The waves of the sea can be appeased by magical formulas.[8] On the other hand, the waves and storm are messengers sent to carry out divine ordinances, and cast up on land a man from a foundered boat whom divine providence wishes to save. Thus Aqiba is saved.[9] But ever since the flood, which in a supreme

1 Mrs. Eugénie Strong, *Roman Sculpture, from Augustus to Constantine*, London, 1907, pl. lxxxvii.

2 See below, § 3.

3 *Pirqê R. Eliezer*, ch. 3.

4 *The Exempla of the Rabbis*, ed. M. Gaster, London, 1896, no. 5.

5 *Midrash Vayosha*, in *Oṣar Midrashim*, ed. J. D. Eisenstein, New York, 1915, p. 148.

6 Jerus. *Sanhedrin*, vii. 25*d*; see *Maase Buch*, Amsterdam, 1725, no. 225.

7 *Alphabetum Siracidicum*, ed. M. Steinschneider, Berlin, 1858, fol. 27*a* and *b*.

8 *The Sword of Moses*, ed. M. Gaster, London, 1896, and Sepher Raziel.

9 *Exempla of the Rabbis*, ed. Gaster, no. 262.

form carried out the divine decree of universal destruction, boundaries have been set to the sea which it cannot overthrow, especially the boundary of sand (Jer 5[22]).[1] The waters of the deep are also part of the cosmogonous process. They are kept under ground; and, since they broke out in the time of the flood, they are now kept in check by the Eben Shetiyah, or 'the stone of foundation,' which, according to legend, is the centre of the earth and the corner-stone of the Temple in Jerusalem, or the stone upon which the Ark of the Covenant rested. When digging the foundations of the Temple, David came upon the floods of the deep; they started surging up, threatening to flood the world. David receded slowly step by step, and, whilst receding, he recited the seventeen Songs of Degrees (or Steps), until at last, writing the ineffable name of God upon a stone, he closed with it the mouth of the abyss, and, when the waters saw the divine name, they withdrew in terror, and thus the world was saved from a second flood.[2]

The waters under ground are flowing close to the fires of hell, hence the hot springs; and the waters of the flood which surged up from the deep were boiling and helped in the destruction of the wicked world, from which Og, king of Bashan, alone escaped through his gigantic stature. (He had boasted that he and the other giants could stop up with their heels the openings of the fountains.)

There are also miraculous wells and rivers. The well in the desert, created on the sixth day, accompanied the Israelites in their wanderings through the desert and ceased to flow with the death of Miriam.[3] There is then the famous Sabbath river Sambatyon (*q.v.*), which plays a great rôle in the history of the portents previous to the advent of the Messiah.

Just as Moses, Joshua, and Elijah divided the waters, so did also sages of a later period. Jesus walked upon the waters, and in another connexion we are told that the waters of the river flowed backwards when appealed to by a sage as a proof of the correctness of his interpretation of the Law.[4]

On the other hand, wells and rain-pipes were considered to be haunted by demons.

On one occasion a man who rested on one of the gutters was hurt by a demon because he trod upon his toe. Abbaye helped one demon to fight another who was trying to drive him from his own habitation. At the end of the fight some drops of blood of the slain demon were seen floating on the surface of the water in the well. On another occasion a many-headed monster came out from the well and was slain by Abbaye.

It was therefore forbidden to drink water from any vessel that was left open overnight, more especially over Wednesday or Saturday night,[5] for it might have become defiled or poisoned by a demon; and the only protection in such cases was to blow upon the water and to pour a few drops of it on the ground before drinking—a kind of libation. During the winter solstice (Tekufa) it is said that three drops of blood fall from heaven and contaminate all the water found in vessels in houses, and that water must be poured away.[6] This, by the way, is of a purely Egyptian origin, and belongs to the cycle of the Isis legends. The Angel of Death is said to dip the sword by which he has taken the life of man in the water found in the house. All the vessels must therefore be emptied. This, however, is a popular interpretation of the ancient law of purity, according to which death defiles all food and drink found under the same roof as a dead body.

2. Lustration.—Water is the great purifier and cleanser.[7] Practically and symbolically, just as water is identified with the spirit and the Law is described as the water of life, water cleanses man from all kinds of physical contaminations, mostly after contact either with dead bodies or with anything described by the Law as impure.[8] The degree of levitical purity claimed for service in the Temple was sometimes transferred to private life,

[1] So also in *Enoch*, lxxxix. 3 ff.; and, as shown by the present writer, the same chapter is incorporated into the Greek magical papyrus of Paris under the name of *Logos Ebraicos*, *i.e.* 'Jewish conjuration,' *JRAS*, 1901, p. 109 ff.

[2] *Midrash Tehillim*, ed. S. Buber, Wilna, 1891, Ps 93[6].

[3] *Pirqē Ābhōth*, v. 9.

[4] *Bābā Meṣia*, 59*b*; *Yebhāmōth*, 121*a*.

[5] *Pesāḥim*, 112; *'Abōdah Zārāh*, 12.

[6] *Shulḥan 'Ārûkh, Yorē De'ah*, ch. 116, § 4.

[7] Cf. art. PURIFICATION (Hebrew).

[8] S. Krauss, *Talmudische Archäologie*, Leipzig, 1910, i. 208 ff., where also is full bibliography; and J. Döller, *Die Reinheits- und Speisegesetze des AT*, Münster, 1917.

and the sect of the Essenes obtained their name in all probability from their habit of constant lustration and purification, refraining as they did from mixing with the common people or touching any food or object not properly purified. The only means for such purification were bathing and ablution—complete immersion in a sufficient quantity of water, more especially running water, or the pouring of a quantity of water over the naked body. The spiritual significance attached to a ritual bath is of later origin; for bathing was never understood in Judaism to mean also washing of the soul. Physical contamination could be eliminated by immersion or by ablution, but the spiritual contamination remained the same; for, as one of the sages puts it, 'a man who sins and confesses his sin and yet continues to live in sin is like a man who takes the bath of purification and holds an unclean animal in his hand.'[1]

The question whether both immersion and ablution were required for purification from defilement seems to have been interpreted differently by Jews, Samaritans, and Ḳaraites. The two last hold that ablution (pouring of the water over the body without immersion) is sufficient. How far this practice has prevailed in pre-Christian times is a question which lies outside the scope of this article and may have some importance for the history of baptism.[2] In later times the washing of hands alone was considered sufficient to eliminate the charge of defilement,[3] although, as no ashes of the red heifer are to be found—which were an indispensable adjunct to religious purification—all the people in modern times must be considered as living in a state of levitical impurity attenuated by this constant washing of hands and by occasional immersions in properly constructed baths. The priests, the descendants of the *kōhanîm*, even now have their hands washed by the Levites present in the synagogue before they ascend the rostrum to recite in a special cantilation the priestly benediction. Moreover, no dead person is shriven without being specially washed,[4] and the mourners when leaving the cemetery are also expected to wash their hands, for they have been in a place considered impure by the Law.

Water, again, was used for purification or as a token of innocence by the elders when a dead body was found and the murderer could not be traced; they went to the banks of a roaring stream and, washing their hands, declared publicly and solemnly their innocence of the murder (Dt 21[6ff.]). In the ceremony for testing the purity of a suspected wife she had to drink bitter waters (or rather 'waters of curse'), prepared by the priest.[5]

It is not unimportant to explain the words used in connexion with this kind of water. It is called 'holy water' (Nu 5[17]), whilst in connexion with the purification of the leprous the priest used 'living water' or, according to the RV, 'running water' (Lv 14[5. 50]), but the same word occurs in Genesis to denote the well digged by Isaac's servants where they found 'living water.' It is difficult to imagine how running water could be in a vessel. The operation in each case is of a symbolical and magical character, and the designation of the water as 'holy' can best be understood by comparing the use of water in other mystical processes. The vessel or the bowl must be filled with water which no one else has touched, and of which no one else has drunk. It is kept intact and sanctified for the purpose to which it is to be put. The moment it has been touched or some of it drunk, it becomes defiled or dead.

Bowls for water with magical inscriptions have

[1] *Ta'anith*, 16*a*.

[2] See art. BAPTISM (Jewish), and W. Brandt, *Die jüdischen Baptismen* (*ZATW* xviii.), Giessen, 1910. Adam's spending 100 years in the waters of Gihon is an act of self-chastisement and repentance, not of purification. See *The Books of Adam and Eve*, ed. L. S. A. Wells, in R. H. Charles, *Apocrypha and Pseudepigrapha of the OT*, Oxford, 1913, ii. 134 ff.; and L. Ginsberg, *Legends of the Jews*, Philadelphia, 1909, i. 86 ff.

[3] *Ṭur* and *Shulḥan 'Ārûkh, Oraḥ Ḥayyim*, ch. 181.

[4] *Shulḥan 'Ārûkh, Yorē De'ah*.

[5] See art. ORDEAL (Hebrew).

often been used for such purposes in the well-known Lekanomaty.[1]

3. **Rain.**—It was natural that in an agricultural land like Palestine rain should be considered a blessing and drought a curse. In Dt 11[14] the early and the latter rains are promised as a blessing for obedience to God's commandments. Palestine does not depend, like Egypt, on the water supplied by the overflow from the river, but 'drinketh water of the rain of heaven' (Dt 11[11]).[2] The sources of rain were believed to be treasuries in the heavens. The 'waters above' are mentioned in Gn 1[7], and at the flood the 'windows of heaven were opened' (7[11]). They are described in greater detail in *Enoch*, xli. 4, and in the *Revelation of Moses*.[3] According to the legend, the key which locks and unlocks this treasury was one of the three keys which God kept, and He only once delivered it up to man when He handed it over to the prophet Elijah, upon whose 'word' alone depended the drought or rainfall (1 K 17[1]). The rainfall was therefore regarded as a divine gift and a blessing which followed the fulfilment of the Law, and drought was caused by sin; a moral connexion was established between the phenomena of nature and man's moral actions. It was thus natural that the action of the pious and the sinner should have a direct bearing upon obtaining rain or causing the withholding of it, and, furthermore, that the intercession of the pious could under certain conditions counteract the consequences of evil deeds.

According to the teaching of the Rabbis, rain fell only for the sake of the righteous, and was withheld when the Israelites deserved punishment. Drought was the consequence of remissness in paying tithes and heave-offerings, or of slander, impudence, and neglect of study of the Law.[4] Collective action no less than individual intercession would also have the desired effect of breaking up the drought. Prayers for rain and symbolical ceremonies would then become efficacious. The prophet, through his action on Mt. Carmel, brings back rain (1 K 18[42ff.]). In later times the high-priest prayed especially for rain on the Day of Atonement, when he performed the service in the Temple. He not only prayed for rain in due season, but went out of his way to pray that God should not heed the prayers of the wayfarers who might be greatly inconvenienced through the rain.

There was a special festival held in the Temple, the Day of the Water-Libation, which was the occasion of rather boisterous rejoicings. The Mishnāh[5] and Talmud[6] contain a graphic description of it. It was called *Simhath beth hashoebah*, 'the rejoicing at the place of the drawing' (*i.e.* of the water), and was kept on the 21st day of Tishri, the 7th day of the Feast of Tabernacles, the day of the Great Hosha-a-na. No explanation has hitherto been given for the use of water as a libation on that day instead of the regular wine-libation. It is, no doubt, of a propitiatory and symbolical character. It is an offering of the element which the people prayed to be blessed with during the year at the threshold of which they were standing. There may have been another reason for the libation as well as for the season chosen. According to the Bible narrative (Gn 7[11]), the flood began and terminated about this time (it began on the 17th and ended on the 27th of the second month). There is now a difference of about a month between the two dates. Probably the coincidence of time was considered sufficient to celebrate the anniversary of the flood by a water-libation, and by such an act to obviate the recurrence of a flood and to show gratitude for the promise that henceforth the rain would come only as a blessing. There may also have been a closer correspondence of the time in the intercalary year, if the intercalation was made at the close of the civil year, at the end of what is now reckoned as the sixth month, but is really the twelfth month. Thus the seventh would become the eighth (second) and on the 17th of the second (eighth) the sluices of the heavens were opened (Gn 7[11]). With the destruction of the Temple a special prayer for rain had been added to the service of the eighth day of Tabernacles.[1] Though the ceremony ceased in the Temple, the remembrance has been kept in the service of the seventh day of the Great Hosha-a-na, which is modelled on the service arranged for the occasion of drought.[2] A special significance has been given in later times to the service of the seventh day, for people seem to have forgotten the real meaning and origin of these supplementary prayers and ceremonies. Moreover, since Temple times special prayers are recited in the additional (*mūsāf*) '*amīdhah* for the Day of Festive Assembly. Corresponding to the change of season, similar prayers for dew form an integral part of the liturgy for the first day of Passover.[3] The month of Tishri was also considered most propitious for prognosticating the weather.[4]

A most elaborate description has been preserved of the ceremonies instituted and the service arranged for the occasion of drought. It is, in fact, the most complete description found in the Talmud. The solemnity was increased by the strewing of ashes on the head, the blowing of trumpets, the insertion of supplicatory prayers, and the extension of a rigorous fast for young and old, strong and infirm, male and female. It was made the occasion of general mourning also by performing that service in the open market-place. The severity of the penance and the multiplication of prayers increased with the fear that the rain might fail. Such a service could not be performed anywhere except in the Holy Land.[5] Great men enjoyed the reputation of having obtained rain by their own merits.

Outside of Palestine no special service could be arranged on the lines of the Talmudic prescription. As far as possible, fasting and special prayers were used on the occasion of severe drought, but there is no fixed form. Each community may arrange it in its own way, and either use older compositions or compose its own prayers. They do not form part of the regular service, and are not included in the recognized standard forms of the Prayer-Book. Such prayers may be met with in collections of Occasional Prayers both in MS and in print.

The most important feature of that service has been introduced in a reduced form into that of the seventh day of Tabernacles, the exact day of the water-libation. It has been invested with the solemnity and character of a second Day of Atonement. In order to explain the supplicatory prayers and the other ceremonies which now form part of the additional service, it must also be remembered that the trumpets are blown exactly as prescribed in the Talmud for the day of solemn prayer for rain. The attributes of God are recited;

1 See J. A. Montgomery, *Aramaic Incantations*, Philadelphia, 1913.
2 Cf. Dt 32[2], Is 55[10].
3 See Gaster, *JRAS*, 1893, p. 574, etc.
4 *Ta'anith*, 8a, 24a. 5 *Sukk.* v. 1-4. 6 *Sukk.* 50a.

1 *Book of Prayer and Order of Service according to the Custom of the Spanish and Portuguese Jews*, ed. Gaster, London, 1901-06, iv. 176.
2 See below. 3 *Book of Prayer*, v. 106.
4 *Bābhā Bathrā*, 147a; see Gaster, 'Jewish Weather Lore,' in jubilee number of the *Jewish Chronicle*, 1891.
5 This ceremony is described in the first chapter of the *Mishnāh Ta'anith* and the treatise of that name. It is still more fully described afterwards by Asheri (1250-1328) in his *Ṭur Oraḥ Ḥayyim*. A fuller, though not complete, MS of this service, with the poems and supplicatory prayers, etc., has come from the Holy Land into the possession of the present writer. It must be anterior to the 16th century.

the procession of the palm-leaf and the willow takes place, just as in the time of the Temple; and prayers are offered up almost exclusively for rain in its due season. They are, in fact, the very prayers found in the Mishnāh and the treatise *Ta'anîth*, and also in the description of Asheri. Curiously enough, similar prayers have also been arranged for the cessation of rain. In fact, all the supplicatory services for grave occasions like plague, etc., follow the lines of this liturgy for rain.[1] In addition to these special services, a regular change takes place in the form of the daily prayer (*'amīdhah*), or eighteen benedictions, in the special blessing for rain and dew. It is connected with the change of the equinox. It begins approximately sixty days after the winter solstice. This is also a season which is not free from superstitious beliefs and practices.[2]

A Talmudic legend[3] tells of a certain Nicodemus (Nakdimon), son of Gorion, who had obtained from the Hegemon a number of pits filled with water, which he distributed among the poor at the time of a great drought. He promised to pay a heavy fine if before a certain date the rain did not fill the pits. In the afternoon of the appointed day the sun was still shining brightly, and no sign of rain was visible. Nicodemus went up to the Temple and prayed, and the sun, which was sinking, rose up again and thus prolonged the day, before the close of which a heavy downpour of rain freed Nicodemus from his obligation. Honi,[4] another pious man, drew a circle, and, standing within it, prayed to God, and the rain came down in heavy drops. In another legend it is through the merit of the wife that drought is broken, the clouds gathering first in the corner where she was praying.[5]

The drought, according to a legend, is also broken up by the cry of the raven. It is said that it was granted to him as his reward for showing Adam how to bury Abel, by digging a grave and burying a dead raven.[6]

A new element has been added to these prayers for rain, in the processions to the cemetery and in the prayers to the pious and illustrious dead for their intercession. No man is found in the later generations so worthy of appealing to God as were those of old times; they therefore pray that those who 'slumber in the dust' may intercede with God in favour of the suffering people. Such processions are headed, as a rule, by the Rabbi, who is accompanied by the elders and the children. Sometimes—but rarely—the scrolls of the Law are carried in the procession. Litanies are sung and recited, and prayers are said over the graves.[7] It is the Jewish counterpart to the Christian procession, notably of the Eastern Church, in times of severe drought, when the relics of a saint are carried on the shoulders of the clergy in a solemn procession through the town, headed by the bishop or the metropolitan of the place.[8]

A local legend in Salonica heard by the present writer tells that the Jews who fled from the Inquisition in Spain at the end of the 15th cent. were admitted into Turkey on condition that they would bring rain in time of drought. The people of that town, especially the children, used to gather under the window of the *Haham* asking for rain. It is told that on such an occasion the late *Haham* Kovo, going out in procession to the cemetery, warned his people to prepare themselves with coverings for the rain, and they returned under such a downpour that the streets were turned into rivers.

The rain thus plays a very important part in the Jewish service. The prayer which is recited daily, and the introduction of special prayers on important occasions into the liturgy, as well as other ceremonies and practices, testify to the belief that a divine gift such as rain can be obtained only through piety and uprightness and by means of supplication and self-chastisement.

LITERATURE.—The bibliographical references are given in the footnotes. No special study exists anywhere on the subject.

M. GASTER.

[1] See Asheri, ch. 580. [2] *Book of Prayer*, i. 31 f., 232.
[3] *Ta'anîth*, 19*b*–20*a*; see Gaster, *Exempla*, no. 85.
[4] *Ta'anîth*, 23*a*; see Gaster, 'Beiträge zur vergleichenden Sagen und Märchenkunden,' in *MGWJ* xxix. [1882] 79 f.
[5] *Ta'anîth*, 23*a*; see Gaster, 'Beiträge,' p. 79 f.
[6] *Pirqē R. Eliezer*, ch. xxi. [7] See Asheri, *loc. cit.*
[8] The present writer has seen such processions in Bukharest, when the relics of St. Demetrius were carried through the streets of the city.

WATER, WATER-GODS (Indian).

—The special conditions of the Indian climate, producing, as in the western desert, a scanty and irregular rainfall, in other places excessive downpour resulting in loss of life and property from inundations, and the constant risk of failure or irregularity of the monsoon, promote the popular animistic beliefs and that of special deities ruling the ocean, rivers, tanks, and wells.

'Water runs up this whole gamut or scale of religious expression. The honours paid to the running brook, a hot spring or to a river that alternately floods and falls—causing famine or abundance, bringing riches or ruin—are intended for the living water itself by a large class of votaries; and this notion of material identity seems preserved by the custom of bathing in sacred streams, of self-drowning, and of witch-dipping, which last custom resembles exactly that of England. Suicide and witch-dipping in rivers present both sides of the same conception, acceptance or rejection by the divine element. Further on, the water-power is no longer deified Nature, but controlled by a supernatural spirit we have the kelpie who inhabits rivers under the form of a buffalo, and personifies their effects. His name is *Mahisoba*; he has no image, but a buffalo's head is cut off and deposited on his altar. After this we ascend to mythologic fictions about the origin and descent of the greater rivers from the Hindu heaven, and to legends of streams turned, stopped, or otherwise engineered by interposition of the divine energy incarnate.'[1]

In Mirzapur a pool in which some buffaloes were once drowned is now inhabited by the buffalo demon, Bhainsāsura, who in company with the *nāgās*, or serpent deities, is so malignant that no one dares to fish there until he has propitiated these powers by an offering; another form of demon attacks fishermen, appearing in the shape of a turban which fixes itself to his hook and increases in length as he tries to drag it ashore.[2] Sometimes the demon, as in the case of the Zalgur of Kashmīr, takes the shape of a horse, the foam-crested waves breaking on the bank naturally assuming this shape in the popular fancy.[3] Such sea-horses in the Hindu legend are provided by Varuṇa, the sea-god.[4] The custom of taking oaths on water conceived as a spirit is common among the Karens and other primitive tribes.[5]

1. Water-gods in the Veda and later literature.—Much controversy has arisen on the question of the amount of knowledge of the sea possessed by the Indo-Aryans. On the one hand, writers like H. H. Wilson[6] assert that they were a maritime and mercantile people, familiar with the ocean and its phenomena; and references in the Veda are quoted of merchants making expeditions to some foreign continent or island. Other writers represent them as living far from the coast and unfamiliar with the sea. The evidence quoted by Bühler of voyages in the Indian Ocean seems inadequate, and the use of the word Samudra for the ocean implies a knowledge of the sea which needs not to be confined to the estuary of the Indus.

'This is to circumscribe too narrowly the Vedic knowledge of the ocean which was almost inevitable to people who knew the Indus.'[7]

In later times this knowledge gradually increased. There seems to be no proof of sea trade with Babylon in Vedic times; this probably developed about A.D. 700.[8]

'The extensive and long-continued emigration from India to the East—including Pegu, Siam and Cambodia on the main-

[1] A. C. Lyall, *Asiatic Studies*, London, 1899, i. 14.
[2] Crooke, *PR*[2] i. 44.
[3] J. H. Knowles, *Folk Tales of Kashmīr*, London, 1888, p. 313; J. G. Frazer, *Pausanias's Description of Greece*, do. 1898, iv. 291; *ERE* i. 501.
[4] J. Dowson, *A Classical Dictionary of Hindu Mythology and Religion*, etc., London, 1879, p. 267.
[5] *JASB* xxxvii. [1868], pt. ii. p. 160 f.; cf. Frazer, p. 253 ff.
[6] *Rig-veda Sanhitá*, London, 1850–58, i. p. xli.; cf. P. T. Srinivas Iyengar, *Life in Ancient India in the Age of the Mantras*, Madras, 1912, p. 39 ff.
[7] A. A. Macdonell and A. B. Keith, *Vedic Index of Names and Subjects*, London, 1912, ii. 106 f.; E. W. Hopkins, *The Religions of India*, Boston, 1895, and London, 1896, p. 34 ff.
[8] J. Kennedy, *JRAS*, 1898, pp. 241–288; V. A. Smith, *Early History of India*[3], Oxford, 1914, p. 28 n.

land, with Java, Sumatra, Bali and Borneo among the islands of the Malay Peninsula—and the consequent establishment of Indian institutions and art in the countries named, constitute one of the darkest mysteries of history.'[1]

The deification of the great rivers by the Vedic Indo-Aryans was highly developed.[2]

2. Varuṇa.—The imperfect knowledge of the ocean possessed by the Indo-Aryans explains why Varuṇa, whose name probably corresponds with the Greek Οὐρανός, 'though the identification presents some phonetic difficulties,'[3] does not clearly rank as a sea-god in the Veda.

'Though Varuṇa is not generally regarded in the Rig-veda as the god of the ocean, he is yet in the following passages (i. 161. 14, vii. 49. 2, viii. 64. 2) connected with the element of water, both in the atmosphere and on the earth, in such a way as may have led to the conception of his character and functions which is fully established in the later mythology.'[4] 'With the growth of the conception of Prajāpati as a supreme deity, the characteristics of Varuṇa as a sovereign god naturally faded away, and the domain of the waters, only a part of his original sphere, alone remained to him. Thus he ultimately became in post-Vedic mythology an Indian Neptune, god of the sea.'[5]

In more recent times Varuṇa has lost the dignified position which he once occupied,[6] but he still retains some of the functions of a sea- or water-deity. The most famous festival in E. Bengal is held in his honour at the full moon of the month Kārttik (Oct.–Nov.), when devout Hindus bathe at a famous bathing-place.[7] In other parts of Bengal no image of Varuṇa is made, nor is he honoured at any festival or temple; but he is worshipped as one of the guardian-deities of the earth, and by fishermen before they start their work, or in time of drought to secure the needed rain.[8] In Gujarāt he is believed to live in the waters, or, by another account, he has five abodes—the sea, the river, the pond, the spring, and the well.[9] In ancient times he received human sacrifices, as in the story of Śunaśepa, the prototype of the offering of infants to the water-goddess Gangā at the confluence of that river with the sea.[10] He is invoked in daily worship as 'king of waters, who curbs the wicked, who made a road in the heavens to receive the rays of the Sun. I therefore follow that route.'[11] Like many water-gods, he is commemorated as a fertility-deity at marriages.[12]

3. Kṛṣṇa and Śiva; the Apsaras.—The place of Varuṇa as a sea-god was at a later period to some extent assumed by Kṛṣṇa and Śiva.

'Kṛṣṇa, a god who is the hero of many solar myths, the slayer of the demons, who dives under the sea and slays Kaṃsa and Kesi and Madhu, this semi-agricultural, semi-solar or atmospheric god is evidently connected with the dark sun and the storms of the rainy season, and his shrine is at Dwārkā on the sea shore, where the sun dips into the boundless western ocean.'[13]

During the 5th and 6th centuries A.D., on the arrival of the white Hūṇas in Gujarāt and Kāthiāwār, the sea began to influence these new-comers, as is shown by the fame which gathered round the new or revived gods, Śiva in his form as Somanātha or Someśvara ('lord of the moon'), with his shrine at Somnāth (*q.v.*), and Kṛṣṇa, the Apollo or St. Nicholas of Dwārkā (*q.v.*), to whom sailors pray to save them from shipwreck. Śiva, an inland god, is worshipped at river junctions.[1] But the place of the primitive rain-gods has been gradually assumed by figures drawn from the local animism. In Madras in time of drought, instead of worshipping Varuṇa, men pray to the spirit Kodumpāvi ('the wicked one'), or to some other local spirit, to send the rain.[2] The Apsaras (Skr. *ap*, *āpas*, 'water,' *sṛi*, 'going,' in the sense of moving in the waters or between the waters of the clouds), a kind of nymphs who even in the *Rigveda* appear completely separated from any physical basis, in the *Atharvaveda* have their abode in the waters, and in post-Vedic literature frequent lakes and rivers, especially the Ganges, were in later times believed by the Rājputs to convey the souls of dead warriors from the battlefield to the mansion of the sun, and have now little influence over the waters or on the rain.[3]

4. Modern ocean-worship.—The sea, known to modern Hindus as Ratnagarbha ('filled with jewels'), is revered by the pious, and at the Amāvas, or new moon, a sea bath is considered cleansing, as on that day the waters of 999 rivers are supposed to be brought into the sea by the spring tides. Bathing is also efficacious during the whole of the Laund, or intercalary month, and in parts of Kāthiāwār on the bright second of every month people light a fire on the shore, throw butter into the fire, and on the day when the fleet puts to sea fishermen pour milk, sugar, and liquor into the water and throw in flowers and coco-nuts.[4] In W. India Coconut Day (*nāriyal* or *nāral purnimā*) is held at the full moon of the month Śrāvan (July–August) in the height of the annual monsoon, when flowers and coco-nuts are thrown into the water to secure the favour of the sea, or as a thank-offering, because by this time the most serious storms are supposed to have ceased; and even as far inland as Poona clerks go to the riverside and fling coco-nuts into the water, and, when they return, the women of the house wave lighted lamps round their heads to disperse evil influences.[5] The Vāda fishermen on the east coast worship the sea-goddess Orusandiammā, who roams over the sea at night with a male deity, her brother Rāmasondi, and is worshipped with special rites.[6] On the west coast Kolī fisherwomen wear glass bangles only on the left wrist, because on their wedding-day the right arm bangles are thrown into the sea to win its favour.[7] In the *Purāṇas* we find a belief, which still survives, that the seven continents of the world are surrounded by seven great seas: Lavaṇa, or salt water; Ikshu, sugar-cane juice; Sura, wine; Ghrita, clarified butter; Dadhi, curds; Dugdha, milk; Jala, fresh water; and this idea also appears in Musalmān traditions.[8]

5. Muhammadan sea-saints.—The objection felt by Hindus to travelling by sea resulted in the Arabs and Persians monopolizing the trade of India. Hence Musalmān saints became the guardians of the sea. One of the most important of these sea- or river-saints is Khwāja Khidr.

1 V. A. Smith, *A Hist. of Fine Art in India and Ceylon*, Oxford, 1911, p. 259; *BG* i. pt. i. [1896] p. 487.
2 A. A. Macdonell, *Vedic Mythology* (=*GIAP* III. i.), Strassburg, 1897, p. 86 ff.
3 Macdonell, *Hist. of Sanskrit Literature*, London, 1900, p. 75; F. Max Müller, *Contributions to the Science of Mythology*, do. 1897, i. 416 ff.
4 J. Muir, *Original Sanskrit Texts*, London, 1858–72, v. 72 ff.
5 Macdonell, *Vedic Mythology*, p. 28; Muir, v. 72 ff.
6 *ERE* vi. 690.
7 J. Wise, *Notes on the Races, Castes, and Trades of Eastern Bengal*, London, 1883, p. 139.
8 W. Ward, *View of the Hist., Lit., and Relig. of the Hindoos*², Serampore, 1815–18, ii. 57 ff.
9 R. E. Enthoven, *Folklore Notes*, i., *Gujarāt*, Bombay, 1914, p. 40.
10 Macdonell-Keith, ii. 385 f.; Rājendralala Mitra, *The Indo-Aryans*, London and Calcutta, 1881, i. 79.
11 H. T. Colebrooke, *Essays on the Religion and Philosophy of the Hindus*, new ed., London, 1858, p. 86.
12 Colebrooke, p. 134; E. Thurston, *Castes and Tribes of Southern India*, Madras, 1909, i. 280.
13 Kennedy, p. 962.

1 J. Tod, *Annals of Rajasthan*, new ed., Oxford, 1920, i. 18, ii. 704.
2 Thurston, iii. 5, vii. 393.
3 Macdonell, *Vedic Mythology*, p. 134 f.; Muir, v. 309, 345, 409, 430; Tod, ii. 675, 696, 864, 991.
4 *BG* ix. pt. i. [1901] p. 349.
5 J. Murray Mitchell, *Hinduism Past and Present*, London, 1885, p. 205; *BG* xviii. pt. i. [1885] p. 245 f. See the account of sea propitiation in the Maldive Islands, F. Pyrard, *Voyages to the East Indies*, etc., tr. A. Gray (Hakluyt Society Publications, lxxvi., lxxvii., lxxx.), London, 1887–90, i. 175, with many references.
6 Thurston, vii. 261 f.
7 *BG* xi. [1883] 69, xiii. pt. i. [1882] p. 149.
8 *Vishṇu Purāṇa*, tr. H. H. Wilson, London, 1840, p. 166; R. F. Burton, *The Book of a Thousand Nights and a Night*, London, 1893, iv. 255.

'Abd al-Qādir al-Jīlānī (*q.v.*), who takes his name from Gīlān or Jīlān in W. Persia (A.D. 1078–1166), rules the Arabian Sea, as Māmā Salmā watches the Persian Gulf and Zulaimah the Red Sea.[1] Qādirwalī Sāhib on the Coromandel coast helps sailors, and he is said to have done many strange miracles.[2] Daryā Pīr, the 'sea-saint,' sometimes identified with Khwāja Khiḍr, is in Gujarāt patron of the Lavānā merchants and lives in the sea, and offerings are made to him by pouring a little water on the ground through a sieve dedicated to him.[3]

6. Water-sprites or spirits.—Besides the greater water-gods a host of spirits or sprites are worshipped. This cult is specially prominent in the Buddhist *Jātaka*. Some of them are malevolent; in a bas-relief at the *stūpa* of Bharhut a sea-monster devours a ship and its crew.[4] Others, again, are kindly and are worshipped in conjunction with the *nāgās*, or serpent-gods.[5] Among spirits of this class at the present day in the Konkan, Bombay, the *asarās*, or *asrās*, are ghosts of young women who, after giving birth to one or more children, committed suicide by drowning; they live in the water, attack any one who approaches them, and go about in groups of seven; their victims are young women, and, when a girl is attacked, an exorcist is summoned, who makes an offering of food, red powder, and green clothes to the sprites.[6] Another Konkan sprite of the same kind is Hadal, the ghost of a drowned woman, who wears yellow clothes, lets her hair flow loose, and is plump in front and a skeleton behind; when women are attacked by her, they let their hair flow loose, shake all over, and scream.[7] The *girhā* entices men into deep water.[8] In Gujarāt the *mātā*, or 'mother,' and the *śankhinī*, or 'ogress,' haunt springs and pools and drown or enter the persons of those who venture near their haunts; an exorcist effects a cure by giving a charmed thread to the patient.[9] In Mysore the *akkagāru*, or 'seven sisters,' attack women, and in such cases the village washerman performs a rite of propitiation by setting up seven stones near the water and making an offering.[10] In the Salem District, Madras, the *āāsakanigal* are female sprites who occupy tanks and cause the embankments to burst as they tread on them while they are quarrelling.[11] In N. India the *ghātbhāī*, or 'ferry brother,' must be propitiated in rites of black magic.[12] In the United Provinces within the bed of the Jumnā 'was the fearful pool of the serpent Kālīya ("the black one") boiling with the fires of poison, from the fumes of which large trees on the bank were blighted, and by whose waters, when raised by a gale into the air, birds were scorched'; the demon was conquered by Kṛṣṇa and driven into the ocean.[13] In the Panjāb District of Kulu the *jalparī*, or water-fairy, can be conciliated by offering a lamb and flowers on the bank of a watercourse; if she catches a man, she compels him to cohabit with her, and kills him if he refuses.[1] In the Panjāb plains the *yoginī*, or *joginī*, haunts waterfalls, while the *jaljoginī* occupies wells and streams and casts spells on women and children, causing sickness and even death.[2] In Assam the Garos believe that still pools in rivers are the abode of the *bugarik*, a lovely siren, whose hair floats on the current; she has the body and arms of a woman, but no legs; some say that she is well disposed, but others allege that she kills women to add their lives to her own, and will kill men if she can catch them.[3]

Among the Mikirs 'localities of an impressive kind, such as mountains, waterfalls, great boulders, have each their Ārnam, who is concerned in the affairs of men, and has to be placated by sacrifices; all waterfalls, in particular, are haunted by them.'[4]

Sometimes these sprites demand human sacrifice, like that of the Pennār river, who, when the Mālas were escaping from their Musalmān enemies, demanded the sacrifice of a first-born child before she would allow them to cross.[5] The Kaivarta fishermen of Bengal at the rite for guarding their nets fling a live kid into the water.[6] The Gaddī shepherds of the Panjāb offer food, water, or a sheep made of flour to the Batal water-spirits.[7] The Khasis of Assam offer a goat to the river-goddess before a fisherman can cast his net; in old days she used to block the passage in the form of a crocodile until she was appeased.[8] In Burma a Kachin boy was accidentally drowned in a river, and for some years after the parents and other villagers used to come and hack the water with their knives.[9] The floods in the Pin river are so violent that it is said to eat people every three years.[10] Persons drowned being thus regarded as victims offered to the flood-spirit, the saving of a life from drowning is fraught with danger.[11] In Gujarāt and the Konkan the water-nymphs drown a person who tries to save a drowning man.[12]

The presence of such malignant water-spirits renders it dangerous to cross rivers, especially in the case of those who are unclean or under tabu.

The Nāyars and Vellālas of Madras impose stringent rules against crossing certain streams; for fear of arousing the wrath of the water-god, a Toda woman will not cross the sacred river of the tribe, the men will not use the water for any purpose; they will not touch it unless they are obliged to ford it, and then they make a bow when they reach the opposite bank.[13] The Nayādis, the lowest caste in Malabar, are not allowed to cross a bridge, and in the Central Provinces Pardhī women in their menses must not cross a river or sit on its bank, and the bar of pregnancy is also recognized.[14] At a wedding in the Magh tribe of Bengal the pair 'eat some curry and rice from the same dish, and what they leave is kept in a covered earthen vessel for seven days, during which time the married couple may not leave the village or cross running water'; at a wedding among the Kandhs there is a mock fight between the clans of bride and bridegroom, and, 'after the struggle is over, the priest attends the bride and bridegroom home, in order to avert by a charm the evil which would threaten their married life in case their path should cross a running brook.'[15]

---

1 R. C. Temple, *Legends of the Panjāb*, Bombay, 1884–86, ii. 153; T. W. Beale, *An Oriental Biographical Dictionary*, new ed., London, 1894, p. 5; Wise, p. 13; J. J. Morier, *Journey through Persia, Armenia, and Asia Minor*, London, 1812, p. 6; Burton, *Narrative of a Pilgrimage to Al-Madinah and Meccah*, ed. 1893, i. 199 f.

2 Jaffur Shureef, *Qanoon-e-Islam*², Eng. tr., Madras, 1863, p. 160 ff.

3 Enthoven, *Folklore Notes, Gujarāt*, p. 40.

4 *Jātaka*, Cambridge, 1895–1913, i. 25 f., 54 ff.; A. Cunningham, *The Stūpa of Bharhut*, London, 1879, p. 106, pl. v. fig. 2.

5 *Jātaka*, ii. 77 f., i. 311.

6 J. S. Campbell, *Notes on the Spirit Basis of Belief and Custom*, Bombay, 1885, p. 149 f.; Enthoven, *Folklore Notes, Konkan*, 13; *ERE* iii. 314.

7 Campbell, p. 150.

8 Enthoven, *Folklore Notes, Konkan*, p. 15.

9 Enthoven, *Folklore Notes, Gujarāt*, p. 40.

10 *Ethnographic Survey Reports, Mysore*, no. 4, Bangalore, 1906, p. 17, no. 12, do. 1907, p. 16.

11 F. J. Richards, *Salem Gazetteer*, Madras, 1918, i. 120.

12 *NINQ* i. [1891] 46 f.

13 *Vishṇu Purāṇa*, bk. v. ch. vii., tr. H. H. Wilson, London, 1840, p. 512.

1 H. A. Rose, *A Glossary of the Tribes and Castes of the Punjab*, Lahore, 1911–14, i. 216.

2 *Ib.* 215.

3 A. Playfair, *The Garos*, London, 1909, p. 116.

4 E. Stack, *The Mikirs*, London, 1908, p. 33.

5 Thurston, i. 139, iv. 344, v. 74 f.

6 Wise, p. 299.

7 *Census of India, 1901*, xvii., *N.W. Provinces and Oudh*, pt. ii. p. 120.

8 P. R. T. Gurdon, *The Khasis*², London, 1914, p. 114 f.

9 J. G. Scott and J. P. Hardiman, *Gazetteer Upper Burma and the Shan States*, Rangoon, 1901, pt. i. vol. i. p. 416.

10 *Ib.* pt. ii. vol. ii. p. 107; cf. the Scottish rhyme of the Tweed and Till (E. B. Tylor, *PC*² ii. 209).

11 *PR*² i. 46.

12 Enthoven, *Folklore Notes, Gujarāt*, i. 41, *Konkan*, ii. 14.

13 Thurston, v. 303 f., vii. 377 f., 135; W. H. R. Rivers, *The Todas*, London, 1906, pp. 418 f., 501.

14 Thurston, v. 274; R. V. Russell, *The Tribes and Castes of the Central Provinces of India*, London, 1916, ii. 208, iv. 362, 551.

15 H. H. Risley, *The Tribes and Castes of Bengal*, Calcutta, 1891, ii. 32; W. W. Hunter, *Orissa*, London, 1872, ii. 83.

The wide-spread belief that a ghost cannot cross running water prevails in India;[1] a thread is passed over a stream to help the soul to return to its home, a belief developing into the Bridge of Death and Charon, the ferryman.[2]

7. Wells, tanks, lakes.—All over the country sacred wells, tanks, and lakes, and their indwelling spirits are reverenced. Their sanctity arises in various ways: they have been made, discovered, or occupied by some god or saint; hot water flows in them, a special mark of divine power;[3] their waters periodically increase or decrease; they possess curative power (especially in cases of leprosy); bathing in them may cause a change of sex.[4] No well is considered lucky until its spirit is solemnly wedded to that of the garden which it is intended to water, the former being represented by the *sālagrāma*, or ammonite, sacred to Viṣṇu, and the latter by the holy *tulasī*, or basil plant (*ocymum sanctum*).[5] In the same way, every tank should have a wooden pole in its centre to which the water-spirit is married; until this is done, the water will increase and not allay thirst and may cause disease; the pole also protects the tank-spirit from the attacks of demons.[6] The prince of Jaisalmer goes annually in state to the lake Gharsīsar to perform the sacred act of cleansing it from the accumulated mud and sand; first he takes out a handful, and then rich and poor follow his example.[7]

LITERATURE.—This is quoted in the footnotes.

W. CROOKE.

WEALTH.—Wealth is variously defined according to the standpoint from which it is regarded. But, in whatever aspect it may be viewed, its significance lies in its relation to life as a whole, and it can only be adequately understood when treated as a part of the larger study of man. It cannot be dissociated from the social and moral development of the race. It obtains its ultimate meaning from its place in the scale of values which determine the worth of life. Ethical considerations must therefore be dominant throughout the entire treatment of the subject. 'It is man's "good," or rather his goodness, that endows wealth with all its value.'[8] While the various phases of the question shade into each other, for the purposes of this article it will be convenient to consider the theme under three aspects—economic, ethical, and Christian.

I. *ECONOMIC ASPECT.*—**1. Historical sketch of the rise and progress of the science of wealth.**—Man alone among the denizens of the earth is the conscious possessor of its resources. Though he has many primary instincts in common with the lower animals, he differs from the brute creation in that he has the faculty of unifying his desires, postponing the present to the future, and making the accumulations of past labour the basis of fresh endeavour. In the growth of his needs and the methods of satisfying them we can trace the economic development of the human race. Very early in history questions of the right of property arose. In the patriarchate period, as depicted in the OT, there is evidence of the existence of private possessions. In early Greek philosophy investigations into the nature and extent of economic law occur. By Plato and Aristotle the industrial aspect of social life is treated as a part of politics. The Roman jurists, while recognizing the sacredness of property, direct their attention chiefly to questions of its tenure and transmission. The asceticism of the early and mediæval Church cast suspicion upon all forms of wealth and tended to check individual enterprise and private possession. The Renaissance gradually broke down the feudal system; and, with the enfranchisement of spirit which the Reformation brought, trade and adventure awoke and the possibilities of the physical world came within the vision of man. The search for unity and law underlying economic facts was greatly stimulated by the researches of Bacon and Newton, while the investigations of Grotius and Leibniz on the Continent and of Hobbes, Locke, and Hume in England aroused the thinking world to the bearing of industrial questions upon the progress of mankind. With the exception of the writings of French physiocrats, of whom Quesnay was the leader,[1] there was no really scientific treatment of the nature and functions of wealth till the appearance of Adam Smith's treatise on *The Wealth of Nations* in 1776.

This book marks an epoch in industrial thought and enterprise. Political economy for the first time becomes a science. Following Smith's work there appeared in quick succession Malthus's *Essay on Population* (1778), Ricardo's *Principles of Political Economy and Taxation* (1817), and J. S. Mill's *Principles of Political Economy* (1848). Smith dealt with the causes of wealth, Malthus with the causes of poverty, while Ricardo and Mill treated mainly of the ways and means of distribution. *The Wealth of Nations* appeared at a propitious hour.

During the Middle Ages the successive phases of social disability which feudalism and serfdom had bequeathed tended to hinder the free life and development of man; and it was not till the individualistic gospel of Rousseau found a response among thinkers that a new sense of human right and freedom awoke. Adam Smith claimed to be the champion of popular liberties. He exposed several traditional fallacies in regard to property and its rights and uses. He showed that the progress of society depended upon individual initiative, division of labour, freedom of contract, and unrestricted interchange of goods. Money, he maintained, was not in itself wealth, but only a medium of exchanging commodities which constitute wealth; and the riches of a nation consisted not in the amount of gold hoarded in its coffers, but in the quantity, variety, and facility of its exports and imports. Unrestrained and widely distributed industry, he held, was the prime and dominant factor of a country's prosperity.

The historical treatment of economics generally adopted in recent years by French and German writers owes its inception largely to the historical insight and philosophical grasp of Adam Smith. But, though he was in advance of his times, many facts have emerged since his day which necessitate a reconstruction of economic science. The new historical instinct which was just awakening and has since been applied so effectively to many departments of inquiry; the general acceptance of the 'evolution theory,' with the light it has thrown upon the conflict and co-operation of man in the development of the race; the industrial reaction caused by the progress of science and the substitution of machinery for hand labour; the growth of democracy, with the spread of new ideas of liberty following in the wake of the French Revolution—these are among the factors which have greatly

[1] *ERE* ii. 368, iv. 604; J. G. Frazer, *The Belief in Immortality*, London, 1913, i. 152.
[2] T. H. Lewin, *Wild Races of South-Eastern India*, London, 1870, p. 209 f.; Playfair, p. 108.
[3] Crooke, *PR*² i. 53; L. A. Waddell, *Among the Himalayas*, Westminster, 1899, p. 203; *Census of India, 1901*, xviii., *Baroda*, p. 16; *BG* vii. [1883] 582 f., viii. [1884] 91.
[4] Crooke, *PR*² i. 48 ff.; *BG* ix. pt. i. [1901] 350 f.; Enthoven, *Folklore Notes, Gujarāt*, p. 38 ff., *Konkan*, p. 13 ff.
[5] Crooke, *PR*² i. 49.
[6] *NINQ* iii. [1893] 160.
[7] J. Tod, ii. 1228; *NINQ* ii. [1892] 111; Thurston, ii. 360 f.
[8] Henry Jones, *The Principles of Citizenship*, p. 162.

[1] See Adam Smith, *Wealth of Nations*, bk. iv. ch. 9.

modified economic study and made the problem of wealth a theme of vastly wider implication than its early investigators dreamt. Later writers, such as Spencer, Fawcett, Bagehot, Toynbee, and Marshall, have shown that political economy must be subservient to human progress in the highest sense and that the moral element cannot be eliminated.

2. Meaning of wealth.—We are now in a position to state generally what economists mean by wealth. The 'good' in the economic sense is every natural product which serves the satisfaction of man. By universal consent the word is applied to things which are material and exchangeable. Four attributes are usually comprehended in its definition: (1) materiality, (2) transferability, (3) limitation in quantity, (4) utility.[1] Of these the first is now regarded as doubtful, since wealth may embrace things not entirely material, such as some forms of service. The last is essential, but a larger meaning must be given to 'utility.' Shortly, wealth is said to consist of things that can be bought and sold, the amount they represent being measured by the quantity of money that they would fetch in the market. The definition, however, is defective on the side of both inclusion and exclusion. On the one hand, a large trade exists in supplying certain satisfactions of a sensual nature which cannot be regarded as economically good or useful; and traffic of this kind, though involving exchange of money, does not contribute in any sense to the weal of man. On the other hand, light, air, even water, unless involving conveyance, have apparently no exchange value; but indirectly they are considerable elements in the wealth of nations. Further, 'potentiality of being bought and sold' excludes many goods, such as health, integrity of character, parental affection, which, though not saleable, have undoubted value, since they render their possessors more fit for the battle of life and more capable members of the national organism.

In protesting against the crude conception that wealth consists in the amount of gold or silver a nation possesses, Adam Smith deliberately describes the wealth of a country as 'the annual produce of its land and labour,' or 'the necessaries and conveniences of life which it annually consumes.' The important point in this statement is that wealth is not land, cattle, machinery, etc., possessed at *a particular point of time*, but rather the annual produce or fruits derived from these *in active use*. The English statisticians of the 17th cent. regarded the wealth of the country with the eyes of a farmer, and, like the French physiocratic school, denied the quality of productivity to all labour not employed immediately on the land. Hence a second important point to be noted is that Adam Smith rightly included in 'productive labour' not only labour employed on the land, but all kinds of work which improved material objects. The French economist, J. B. Say, extended the idea of productive labour to cover 'non-material products.' And from his time the annual produce has been conceived as including 'services' as well as commodities. Economically, wealth may be summed up as the product of what in modern life is termed 'the economic or industrial system,' meaning by industry 'all those articles which go to make any sort of wealth including the services of the judge, the clergyman, the acrobat';[2] not material goods alone, but 'the work of government, the learned professions, the fine arts, all gainful recreations, must be brought under the "industrial system."'

3. The factors of wealth.—In the production of wealth economists enumerate three factors: land, labour, capital. Land and labour are obviously requisite at all times and places; and, though in primitive societies capital existed only in very rudimentary forms, it also becomes essential in any community which is organized on a large scale.

(*a*) *Land.*—The two primary sources of wealth are material for work and work for material—Nature and man. The starting-point is found in the original needs which stimulate men to engage in labour for their satisfaction. But labour of itself produces nothing. It can exercise itself only upon the given. In one sense Nature is the mother of all wealth. We are rich when she gives, poor when she withholds. Yet Nature yields nothing for nothing. Her gifts are available only as man brings the toil of hand and brain to bear upon them. As economists put it (though not quite accurately), it is the land—including not its surface fruits only, but all that is contained in the bowels of the earth, coal, iron ore, minerals of all kinds, and even the sea with its manifold treasures—that is the prime source or factor of potential wealth.

(*b*) *Labour.*—It is the function of labour not to create but to extract, transform, and shape to the uses of man the potencies and raw material of the earth. The supreme service which labour renders to society is defined by J. S. Mill as 'putting things in fit places.'

'Labour in the physical world,' he says, 'is always and solely employed in putting objects in motion; the properties of matter, the laws of nature, do the rest.'[1]

Though no wealth can be produced without labour, there are some kinds of labour which may be very useful though not actually productive of material wealth. Hence a distinction has been drawn between 'productive' and 'non-productive' labour. But this distinction can hardly be sustained. Can it be said, *e.g.*, that the work of a miner is productive, that of a teacher, a poet, or a statesman unproductive? Men who do not work with their hands may be really contributing to the material well-being of man. And what seems at first sight to be fruitless or even wasted activity may in the highest sense be conducive to life. Indeed there are some things which, though not computable in money, greatly tend to increase the productive power of even physical labour. Three elements at least may be mentioned: division of labour, combination in effort, invention and application of tools and machinery. 'All tools and engines of the earth,' says Emerson, 'are only extensions of man's limbs and senses.'[2] But machines can only second; they cannot supply his unaided faculties. To these means must be added what, after all, is of most importance—the moral and intellectual elements — the skill, intelligence, character, and fidelity of the worker himself. A man is more than a machine; and, without the personality behind, physical and mechanical appliances, however complete, would fail of their results. In the production of wealth the economist is apt to overlook spiritual values. Education, the discipline and training of the home, the school, the college, the hardships and hazards of life, and all the moulding and informing institutions of society may appear to have no immediate monetary worth, but they are inestimable forces in the making of the workman, rendering him to himself and the community a more fit and effective agent of productive service.

(*c*) *Capital.*—It is difficult to define this element or designate precisely its functions. The term has become the storm-centre of modern industrial con-

[1] See *Dict. of Political Economy*, *s.v.* 'Wealth.'
[2] J. A. Hobson, *Science of Wealth*, p. 13.

[1] *Principles of Political Economy*, bk. i. ch. i. § 2.
[2] R. W. Emerson, *Society and Solitude*, 'Works and Days,' p. 1.

flict. Capital has unfortunately been regarded by labour as the instrument by which owners of property and possessors of money can make their own terms and manipulate work in their own interests. Capitalism has undoubtedly been a stern taskmaster in the past. The owners of capital may be said to have been, and to be still, the controlling power of our industrial system. They have taken the place formerly held by the landed aristocracy as the pivot of the social and industrial order. As the holders of power they have offered a stubborn opposition to all encroachments upon their privileges; and during the last quarter of a century all advancement of wages and improvement of environment on behalf of labour have been secured only by the pressure of trade unionism and the employment of the strike weapon. Hence the interests of employers and workmen have come to be regarded as inimical; and embitterment and class hatred have ensued which have led to conflicts costly alike to masters and to men. An impartial judgment is bound to recognize faults on both sides. At bottom of the perversity there has prevailed a materialistic philosophy involving a false exaltation of money and a vulgar conception of life which, as a result of the spell of commercial prosperity at the close of last century, has pervaded all classes of society. It is the pride of riches, the indifference, the cruelty, and the vulgarity—in a word, the selfishness of wealth that has roused jealousy and suspicion and become a danger to the community. The working classes have been too apt pupils of their masters and have indulged in habits of laxity and improvidence which are a menace to the true weal of the nation. But, whatever may have been its abuses, and however it may have tended to exploit labour for its own ends, absorbing within itself the legitimate fruits of toil, capital is an indispensable element in the production of wealth and an instrument of incalculable service in the development of the resources of civilization. In the economic sense, capital is wealth appropriated to productive employment. It may be defined as the aggregation of the surplus which has been saved from immediate use and is available for the further development of industry. It is of two kinds, circulating and fixed. Circulating capital consists of the wages paid to the workmen and of the raw material which is being actually used in the process of work. Fixed capital consists of buildings, machinery, tools, railway plant, shipping, etc. Circulating capital is being constantly used up, while fixed capital is permanent, more or less. Capital generally is the result of the industry of past generations used to promote and facilitate the industry of the present and the future. In every form of capital we trace the labour, ingenuity, and foresight of men who have built up the trade of the present. For the development of capital it is necessary that production should exceed consumption, leaving a margin for future increase and development of trade. It cannot be denied that labour has contributed to the making of capital and ought to have a share in its possession and employment. It is the duty and task of the capitalist to organize, direct, and supervise the labour of the country, so that it shall adequately meet the needs of the community. These services have been rendered in the past principally by private individuals. It has been argued that they might be equally well, if not better, supplied by the State, in which all have a stake and in the prosperity of which all have a claim to participate. But, whatever may be said in favour of collectivism, it must be noted that, whether controlled by the nation and supervised by State officials or possessed by private individuals, capital in the form of liquid assets is absolutely necessary for the organization and development of commerce; and without it labour would be practically incapable of producing its maximum results or obtaining for itself an assured or adequate return for its efforts. It is evident that the interests of capital and labour are mutual, and the success of their common enterprise depends upon their harmonious co-agency. But, to attain this unity of aim, both labour and capital will have to revise their ideas. Instead of an unending strife, by which each tries to secure as much and give as little as possible, a wider outlook must be sought in which each party shall realize that industry is only a means to an end and that life has more to offer than the things which can be estimated in terms of money alone.

II. *ETHICAL ASPECT.* — From the foregoing sketch of the economic aspects of wealth it will be seen that all industrial questions lead up inevitably to ethical issues. Economic proposals for the re-adjustment of society assert a principle the neglect of which was the great failure of the 19th century and is still the source of much of our avoidable social unrest.

'That principle is simply that industrial prosperity is not to be measured solely in terms of material wealth; or, in other words, that industry must be regulated by reference to supra-economic ends. Its profit and loss account must show human as well as material values; and that industry is neither prosperous nor healthy which shows a great output of material goods at the cost of a great deterioration of health, the character and the human capacity of the worker.' [1]

1. Relation of economics and ethics.—If economic science is designed for the advancement of life itself (and this is its tacit claim), then human considerations cannot be ignored. Work must serve man, not man work. Our starting-point must be that life is the principal thing and that every human being has a right to live and work; and that in giving his services to the good of the community he ought to have some share in the common weal. Even if a living wage be conceded, a living wage must be interpreted not as that which gives a mere subsistence, but as that which affords to each the opportunity of human self-expression.

It has been truly said that 'life without the means of living, personal gifts or skill that have no outlet, liberty that is only an inner consciousness and has no sphere of exercise, are all alike meaningless.' [2]

Considerations like these have led many to be suspicious of the doctrines of political economy and especially doubtful whether the conception of wealth as usually assumed in scientific works can be accepted as ultimate. The common fallacy of confounding wealth and money is not yet obsolete. The idea that wealth consists solely in material things of utility dies hard and continues to exert considerable influence upon economic thought.

'Property is meaningless, not wealth at all, apart from its purpose, or apart from its possible or actual practical use. . . . We have fallen into the error of regarding material wealth as having intrinsic value, and we tend not uncommonly to devote our energies to gaining possession of it, irrespective, or with the slightest consideration, of what is to be done with it. . . . Wealth is not wealth, but only its unrealized possibility, apart from the spending of it.' [3]

Hoarded wealth is not really wealth; and even less is misused or wasted wealth. Even the phrase 'satisfaction of wants' is ambiguous. 'What we want' may mean either what a particular individual or class desires at the moment or what is an essential need of our whole nature as men. In other words, in order to decide what constitutes wealth in its largest sense, it is necessary to know what is the true good of man—an inquiry with which political economy must reckon if its results are to be of vital import for mankind. But, while the

[1] H. J. W. Hetherington and J. H. Muirhead, *Social Purpose*, London, 1918, p. 191.
[2] H. Jones, *Principles of Citizenship*, p. 165.
[3] *Ib.* p. 161.

economist defines his subject as one of 'the sciences of man,' the conception of the human value of wealth does not rule either his thought or our practice in dealing with it. But it is only from this point of view that the problems of capital and labour, profit and wages, free trade and protection, or the respective rights and limits of production by the State and the individual are to be considered. It is the personal element that brings the science of economics into closest touch with ethics. Both have to do with the 'good'; but the economic 'good' is mostly regarded as material, whereas the 'goods' with which ethics is concerned are those acts which are the conditions of the attainment of the highest end of life. While it is perfectly legitimate to consider what will increase or diminish the material side of human happiness, it must never be forgotten that neither an individual's nor a nation's life consists in the abundance of the things which it possesses. If we are rightly to estimate the worth of economic goods, we must consider them ultimately in their relation to the highest good—the good of life itself. Social reform has been not a little retarded by writers who so exalt material prosperity as to encourage the belief that the possession of riches is the secret of happiness and the only reasonable motive of human endeavour.

2. **Doctrine of values.**—The conception of values, which has become a dominant idea of modern thought, has been applied with considerable effect by some recent writers to economic subjects. A distinction is drawn between 'intrinsic' and 'instrumental' values. A thing has intrinsic value when it is an end in itself or is valued for its own sake apart from anything else to which it leads. A thing has instrumental value when it is merely a means to something else that follows from it as an effect, when it does not exist for itself but only for the sake of a further good. The value of any economic good is determined by its relation to other things which can be got in exchange for it. Thus, to use the technical phrase of economists, 'a thing's price is its value.' It is its 'value in exchange.' Its worth depends on what at the moment it can bring. It is relative, not absolute. It may be said that nearly everything in the world, the whole apparatus of living, has, in this sense, merely an instrumental or relative value. Things are nothing in themselves and would be useless in other conditions. Money, jewels, etc., would mean nothing on a desert island. But there are some things that must always retain their value in every world. If life has any meaning at all, there are objects, ideals, such as honour, purity, truth, belonging to life itself, and of the essence of man, which cannot be bought or sold, and are incomparable, unexchangeable, absolute. In the last resort it may be said that intrinsic value belongs to personalities rather than things—to things of the soul rather than things of the sense. All other values are relative and obtain such worth as they have from their power to minister to the highest enrichment of man.[1]

3. **Real wealth.**—Along this line of thought we are led to the absolute and all-inclusive conception of wealth as embracing everything that contributes to the fullness of life. 'There is no wealth but life,' says Ruskin, 'including all its powers of love, joy, and admiration.'[2] It is true that merely instrumental objects may be transmuted by their use into more than means and may partake of the character of the values to which they contribute. Objects of natural beauty, works of art, the affections and sympathies of life, intellectual knowledge and pursuits—everything, in short, that enlarges human vision and enriches heart and mind—are more than instruments: they are the constituents of real wealth. Things even that might be regarded as of themselves worthless, mean, or trivial may be elevated by becoming the vehicles of higher ends. The material world is the environment of the spiritual. Ideals require for their realization physical things. The soul must build its city of God of earthly materials, and the ordinary experiences and facts of life—man's common toil and trial, his instincts and passions—may be elevated and transfigured into assets of the spirit. Thus we see that money and all material possessions, like every other gift, may be consecrated to the highest service and be made a channel of enrichment and blessing to mankind.

The question of the place of luxury in life and the justification of expenditure upon things which go beyond the mere necessaries of existence naturally arises here. The manner of spending wealth from both an economic and an ethical point of view is not less important than the method of acquiring it. Yet it is hardly an injustice to say that the modern world is more given to the production of riches than the art of using them. But obviously the object for which an individual or a people uses its wealth is a decisive test of character and an index of worth. Before calling a man rich or poor, therefore, we must know to what uses he puts his possessions, whether they be broad or narrow. Are luxuries justifiable? Or must money be expended only on such objects as contribute to the bare support of life and the attainment of the simple decencies and moderate comforts of existence? Are we, as moral beings, to be ruled by the strictly ascetic view of life? Or can we vindicate a place for desires which, though not immediately useful or necessary, do in an indirect way help to enrich life and raise it to a higher level? It has been truly said that some objects, such as pictures, books, and even recreations, are so essential to the higher development of mankind that it may be fairly affirmed of them that 'the necessaries of life could be better spared than the superfluities.' Many objects which seem at first only to yield a momentary gratification are yet of considerable importance in so far as they 'serve to oil the wheels of existence and add a bloom to life.'[1]

If we take the word 'wealth' in its strictly etymological sense, as allied to 'weal' (as 'health' is related to 'heal' and means 'wholeness' or soundness of body), things which can be used as a means of contributing to a man's or nation's true well-being, to the fullest development and expression of the intellectual and spiritual life, are, in the last resort, the elements of wealth in its highest sense. That country is richest which nourishes the greatest number of efficient and happy human beings; that man is richest who uses his gifts to the utmost in perfecting the functions of his own life and in exerting his influence for the enrichment of the lives of others.[2]

III. *THE CHRISTIAN ASPECT.*—It does not lie within the scope of this article to discuss the remedies which have been proposed to overcome the most prominent evils accompanying a highly industrial state. In general the most radical of these proposals fall under the head of what may be described as a form of socialism (*q.v.*), or at least State control or collective ownership of all monopolies. It is urged by many, on the other hand, that the ultimate hope of a better order

[1] See W. R. Sorley, *Moral Values and the Idea of God* (*Gifford Lectures*), Cambridge, 1918, pp. 37 ff., 75 ff., 124 ff., 134 ff., 508 ff.
[2] *Unto this Last*, § 77.

[1] J. S. Mackenzie, *Introd. to Social Philosophy*, Glasgow, 1890, p. 305; see also some remarks on this subject, in Marshall, *Economics*, pp. 124, 181.
[2] See Ruskin, *op. cit.*

rests not in change of outward condition, but in the regeneration of inward character. And an honest application of the teaching of Christ to the practical affairs of life is, it is held, the secret of social and industrial betterment. It seems fitting here to give a rapid review of Christ's teaching in reference to wealth.

Jesus has much to say concerning wealth. The subject bulks largely in His teaching and enters prominently into the frame-work of nearly all His parables.

1. The teaching of Jesus.—Though Jesus dwells frequently on the perils of wealth, He does not condemn the possession of property or denounce ownership in land, goods, or money. There is no depreciation of riches in themselves. He lays emphasis on their deceitfulness (Mt 13^{22}); He warns His disciples against covetousness (Lk 12^{13-15}); and especially does He point out the danger of accumulating earthly treasures (Mt 6^{19}) and the impossibility of serving God and mammon (6^{24}). He lays down the principle that 'a man's life consisteth not in the abundance of the things which he possesseth' (Lk 12^{15}). Yet these sayings and warnings, so far from implying disapproval, imply rather that property and trading are the indispensable bases upon which the outward fabric of the social order is built. He shows no trace of belief that temporal possessions are evils in themselves. His parables constantly assume the right, and indeed the responsibility, of the individual to hold and administer wealth (Mt 25^{14}, Lk 19^{12} 16^{1}). Many of His sayings would be devoid of meaning if His attitude to the industrial system of His day had been one of uncompromising hostility. He could not, *e.g.*, have justly advised the young ruler to sell what was not really his, or have suggested that he should induce another to accept for money what it was unlawful for him to retain. Many of His parables deal with the use of money, without indicating a single reproof on account of its possession (Mt 25^{14-30}, Lk 19^{13-27} 16^{1-13} 12^{16-21}). Christ does not demand withdrawal from the activities of the world. The asceticism of the early Church and the renunciation practised by those sects which make a profession of poverty find no countenance in the Gospels. Jesus and His disciples honour work and recognize trade. Christ acknowledges the rights of the wage-earner. Within the circle of His followers were men and women who were possessed of worldly substance (Mt 27^{57}, Lk 8^{3} 19^{8}). His disciples had a common purse, and one of their number acted as treasurer.

2. Wealth and the supreme end of life.—The one and only aim of our Lord was the establishment of the rule of God in the hearts of men.[1] The Kingdom of God is first; all else is secondary and subsidiary. This is the test of all earthly things. Possessions and occupations have validity only in relation to the supreme end of life. His calls to renunciation were made not because He deemed wealth to be inherently evil, but because in each case the required act of denial would remove the special hindrance to the realization of the spiritual life (Mt 19^{24}, Mk 4^{19}, Lk 6^{24}). In Mk 10^{21} it is to be noticed that it is a deficiency of character that necessitates the repudiation of earthly possessions. Christ thus raises the whole question of material wealth to a spiritual plane. What He really condemns in connexion with riches is the spirit which holds them falsely, by non-use, misuse, or abuse.

3. Wealth a trust and a test.—Finally, wealth is everywhere regarded in reference to man's relation to God. It has thus a twofold significance. It is a trust and a test. There is no such thing as absolute ownership. All things belong to God our Father. We are but the pensioners on His bounty and the trustees for what He lends to us. No one can say, 'I can do what I like with my own' (Mt 20^{15}, Lk 12^{19}). The Gospels indicate three ways in which the stewardship of wealth may be exercised.

(*a*) *Almsgiving* (Lk 18^{22}).—The beauty of charity may be marred by ostentation (Mt 6^{2-4}) or consciousness of merit. A man's gift of money has no value except as the expression of himself (Lk 11^{41} 21^{3}, Mk 12^{43}).

(*b*) *Fidelity to one's daily work.*—Those who receive Christ's severest condemnation are the persons who have been unfaithful in the task entrusted to them (Mk 12^{1-11}, Mt 25^{24}, Mk 13^{34}, Lk 19^{20-24}); while those most highly commended are such as conscientiously discharge their duties in the appointed spheres of life.

(*c*) *Ministry of joy and beauty.*—A third form of stewardship is indicated in the employment of gifts in ministering to the joy and beauty of life. The most impressive instance of this use of private means is exhibited in the story of the woman who anointed the head and feet of Jesus with precious ointment. In answer to the reproachful question, 'To what purpose is this waste?' Jesus defends the act and appreciates the beauty and symbolism which it embodied. Here is the charter of all undertakings which propose in the name of Christ to feed the mind, to stir the imagination, to make life less meagre and dull, and more rich, beautiful, and spiritual.[1] Expenditure of wealth on art and music, on the graces which enrich the emotional and intellectual life, is justified not only by its elevating and enlarging effect, but also by the explicit authority of Christ's example and teaching.

From the standpoint of Christian ethics possessions of all kinds are subject to the law of conscience. What makes them right or wrong is their influence on character, and thus they become a test of life. Every gift is bestowed for purposes of service. God has no room for parasites or idlers. Every one, be he rich or poor, is a trustee for the Creator. There is no such thing as mere money. It is always a symbol or a measure. Property is but the expression and instrument of personality. We have only what we use. Hoarded wealth is barren. And only as we give forth our life in service and sacrifice is it fruitful.

LITERATURE.—All the larger works on political economy deal with the subject on its economic side. Alfred Marshall, *Principles of Political Economy*⁵, London, 1907, and the older works of Adam Smith and J. S. Mill ought to be consulted. Edwin Cannon, *Wealth: a Brief Explanation of the Causes of Economic Welfare*, London, 1914; J. A. Hobson, *The Science of Wealth* (Home University Library), do. 1911; D. H. Macgregor, *The Evolution of Industry*, do. 1911, and S. J. Chapman, *Elements of Political Economy* (in same series), do. 1912, deserve mention.

On the ethical and religious side see T. von Haering, *The Ethics of the Christian Life*, Eng. tr., London, 1909; F. G. Peabody, *Jesus Christ and the Social Question*, New York, 1901; Oliver Lodge, *Modern Problems*, London, 1912; J. MacCunn, *The Ethics of Citizenship*, Glasgow, 1894, and *The Making of Character*, Cambridge, 1900; Henry Jones, *The Principles of Citizenship*, London, 1919; J. Clark Murray, *A Handbook of Christian Ethics*, Edinburgh, 1908; J. Wilson Harper, *Christian Ethics and Social Progress*, London, 1912; Walter Rauschenbusch, *Christianity and the Social Crisis*, New York, 1907; W. N. Clarke, *The Ideal of Jesus*, Edinburgh, 1911; R. L. Ottley, *Christian Ideas and Ideals*, London, 1909; H. C. King, *The Ethics of Jesus*, New York, 1910; J. Stalker, *The Ethic of Jesus*, London, 1909; A. B. D. Alexander, *Ethics of St. Paul*, Glasgow, 1910, *Christianity and Ethics*, London, 1914. See also relevant articles in *ERE*; *Dictionary of Political Economy*, 3 vols., ed. R. H. Inglis Palgrave, London, 1894–1908; L. L. Price, *Political Economy in England from Adam Smith to Arnold Toynbee*, do. 1891.

A. B. D. ALEXANDER.

WELFARE.—(1) By the ethical term 'welfare' is meant the highest human good, the faring well or properly, the desirable human experience. In this formal use of the term nothing is implied as to the nature or constituents of this good. Aristotle notes this as the accepted usage in his day of the term εὐδαιμονία.[2]

(2) The term usually implies the highest human good conceived as consisting in certain objective conditions rather than in subjective feelings. In this sense it is opposed to pleasure as the supreme good. The term 'perfection' is nearly its equiva-

[1] See W. M. Clow, *Christ and the Social Order*, London, 1913, p. 81.

[1] F. G. Peabody, *Jesus Christ and the Social Question*, p. 218 ff.

[2] *Nicom. Ethics*, i.

lent, but has usually a somewhat narrower significance, exclusion of pleasure, whereas welfare, though not in its essence pleasure, involves pleasure as its completion. As the supreme end perfection and happiness are usually conjoined, while welfare involves this conjunction.

Aristotle's usage is typical, but not without difficulties of interpretation. Human welfare is not pleasure, or practical activity, or the scientific life, but is the activity proper to man as man. This is reason, and human welfare consists in the excellence of rational activity. This rational activity is both theoretic and practical; in the former man is akin to the divine, but in the latter he is more specifically human. Outward goods, wealth, health, children, fame—these are good in so far as they are conditions of, or illustrations of, man's rational activity, but have no independent value. They exist for the sake of the rational life and not the life for them.[1] The position of pleasure relative to welfare is not wholly clear in the details of Aristotle's treatment, yet his fundamental principles seem certain. Pleasure is not the end of human action;[2] yet it is the universal concomitant of perfect activity and that which serves to mark and consummate this perfection.[3] If the two could be separated, the wise man would choose the activity without the pleasure rather than the pleasure without the activity,[4] but, as a matter of fact, this separation is not possible.[5] Yet, in all cases, it is the objective nature of the activity that determines the value of a pleasure, and not the amount of the pleasure itself. The emphasis in Aristotle's treatment is upon the idea of welfare as the right condition of the *whole* man. It consists in rational activity because this is not a specific and exclusive form of activity, but is one which includes and harmonizes all others. In reason all human activities find their interpretation and completion and hence their well-being.

So also Paulsen:

'The goal at which the will of every living creature aims [welfare] is the normal exercise of the vital functions which constitute its nature.' Man 'desires to live a human life and all that is implied in it; that is, a mental, historical life, in which there is room for the exercise of all human, mental powers and virtues.'[6]

LITERATURE.—J. A. Stewart, *Notes on the Nicomachean Ethics*, 2 vols., Oxford, 1892; E. Zeller, *Aristotle and the Earlier Peripatetics*, Eng. tr., London, 1897, ii.; J. H. Muirhead, *Chapters from Aristotle's Ethics*, do. 1900; F. Paulsen, *System of Ethics*, Eng. tr., do. 1899, bk. ii. ch. ii.; James Seth, *A Study of Ethical Principles*, do. 1894; S. G. Mezes, *Ethics, Descriptive and Explanatory*, New York, 1901, ch. xv.

NORMAN WILDE.

WELLS.—See WATER, WATER-GODS.

WERWOLF.—See LYCANTHROPY.

WESLEY.—I. Early life.—John Wesley was born on 17th June (O.S.) 1703, at the rectory of Epworth, being the son of Samuel and Susannah Wesley. Both his grandfathers were among the ejected ministers of 1662, so there was a strong Puritan strain in him. His father, Samuel, was rector, poet, scholar: he spent ten years in preparing his work on the *Book of Job*. The mother, Susannah, trained her children in the great truths of the Christian faith. There is something singularly beautiful in the way in which this mother brought her many children into the audience chamber of God. On 28th Jan. 1714, John Wesley was nominated a pupil at Charterhouse, London. The treatment meted out to the boys of those days was Spartan, but Wesley always felt a true love for his school. As we read his *Journal*, and see him lovingly wander each year about the grounds, we note that Wesley never forgot his boyhood, and that age could not wither his affection for Charterhouse. On 24th June, 1720, he was elected to Christ Church, Oxford, and remained there until 1725, when he was ordained deacon by Bishop Potter. About this time the *Imitatio Christi* and *The Rules for Holy Living and Dying* became his frequent companions. The *Imitatio* taught him that 'true religion was seated in the heart, and that God's law extended to all our thoughts as well as words and actions.'[1] It is of the *Rules* that Wesley writes:

'In reading several parts of this book, I was exceedingly affected with that part in particular which relates to purity of intention. Instantly I resolved to dedicate all my life to God: all my thoughts, and words, and actions.'[2]

Wesley was now a determined seeker, there was a great hunger within him for something beyond the experience which he had—for thirteen years he sought peace by prayer, tears, and through difficult and tragic experience, and on 24th May, 1738, entered into a true evangelical experience of Divine love.

In March, 1726, he was elected Fellow of Lincoln College, Oxford. It is with this College, rather than Christ Church, that Wesley's name is so closely linked; for, though the great hall of Christ Church is adorned by the Romney painting of Wesley, Lincoln College has a greater treasure in the room in which the Holy Club met, and where the movement began which was to give new life to the Churches of this and other lands.

Much help came to Wesley by the reading of William Law's *Serious Call* and his *Christian Perfection*. Although some parts of Law's work offended him, he tells us: 'The light flowed in so mightily upon my soul, that everything appeared in a new view.'[3] Readers of the *Journal*, and especially of the diary, remember the strenuous efforts of Wesley to be accounted worthy; his early rising, his mastery over himself, his methodically planned day, with a task for every hour, his thoughtful care for his pupils, his ejaculations which sob forth even now after the lapse of so many years, his passionate and unceasing quest for a deeper experience—all these things are clearly recorded there. The Castle and the Bocardo at Oxford were both visited by him; for to the prisoners he must preach the message of Divine grace—even though he had not yet entered consciously into it. In August, 1727, Samuel Wesley being infirm, John Wesley went to his help, and remained in his parish for about two years. He then returned to Oxford. Later (1734) his father pleaded with great insistence that he should take his work and rectory. The reply of Wesley is elaborately wrought, and is a strong plea that his sphere is in Oxford, and not in Epworth. There is in it no splendid disregard of self such as we see in his later days; he seems more anxious to have circumstances conducive to his own soul's culture than to save the souls of others. On his return to Oxford he found that his brother Charles, who was then at Christ Church, had gathered round him a small group of men to read the New Testament. John Wesley joined this company, and soon became its leader. It is well to remember that the Holy Club showed a much greater diligence with regard to Holy Communion than the Church of those times, a tendency to guide their life by early Church practice, a passion for prisoners and outcasts, and a diligent and careful apportionment of time. As the members went with regularity to take the sacrament, they received much taunting from the undergraduates. It was at this time that they were called 'Sacramentarians,'

[1] *Nicom. Ethics*, vii. 14. [2] *Ib.* i. 3, x. 2.
[3] *Ib.* x. 3. [4] *Ib.* x. 2. [5] *Ib.* i. 9.
[6] *System of Ethics*, bk. ii. ch. ii. § 5.

[1] *The Journal of John Wesley*, standard ed., 8 vols., London, 1909-16, i. 466.
[2] Wesley's *Works*, 14 vols., London, 1829-31, xi. 366.
[3] *Journal*, i. 467.

'Bible Moths,' and Methodists (a double reference—both to a medical sect and to their 'method' in all religious practices). John Wesley was now, it seems, rooted in Oxford. A band of keen undergraduates gathered round him; he believed that he had found his work. Owing to the insistence of his family, however, he applied for the living of Epworth, but without success. His dying father spoke prophetic words; to John he said: 'The inward witness, son—the inward witness, that is the proof, the strongest proof of Christianity'; to Charles he said: 'Be steady. The Christian faith will surely revive in this Kingdom; you shall see it, though I shall not.'

2. The Georgia ministry.—In 1735 Wesley was invited to go on a mission to the colony of Georgia. His father now being dead, he with some diffidence mentioned the fact of the offer to his mother, who said: 'If I had twenty sons, I should rejoice if they were all so employed, though I should never see them more.' John and Charles Wesley embarked at Gravesend on 14th Oct. 1735. He tells a friend the motives which sent him forth as a missionary.

'My chief motive is to save my own soul . . . I hope to learn the true sense of the Gospel of Christ by preaching it to the heathen.'[1]

In later years he was not so anxious about his own salvation, but rather about that of others.[2] On the voyage, as at Oxford, he showed meticulous strictness in the apportioning of time: he learned German and studied his Greek Testament, and held services even amidst the storms. He was greatly impressed by a party of Moravians on board, especially by their conduct in the tempest. Amidst the storm they were quite unalarmed and went on singing. Wesley asked one of them, 'Were you not afraid?' He replied, 'I thank God, no.' 'But were not your women and children?' 'No, our women and children are not afraid to die.' Wesley landed at Savannah on 6th Feb. 1736. He soon met Spangenberg, the Moravian, who asked him, 'Do you know Jesus Christ?' 'I know He is the Saviour of the world.' 'True, but do you know that He has saved you?' 'I hope He has died to save me.' Spangenberg then asked, 'Do you know yourself?' Wesley answered, 'I do,' but, in telling the story of this conversation, says, 'I fear they were vain words.' Wesley's main purpose in going to Georgia was to become a missionary to the Indians. This was frustrated by the governor of the colony, General Oglethorpe, who desired his presence in the European settlement. Denied his chief end in coming, he nevertheless found work for each moment in the day; he taught the children, visited the sick, reproved the sinner, and gathered a few folk together for mutual conversation. He encouraged, he rebuked, he prepared communicants, and repelled those whom he thought not worthy. He was a rigorous High Churchman, and a most earnest seeker of the Light. In summing up the matter in his *Journal* Wesley tells us that he 'was a child of wrath, an heir of hell,' but in later years, when he revised his writings, he says, 'I believe not. . . . I had even then the faith of a servant, though not of a son.'[3] Grave misunderstandings arose between Oglethorpe and the Wesleys; but they were later reconciled. Suspicions and misunderstandings grew like weeds in the garden of this colony. As we now know from the standard edition of the *Journal*, Wesley fell in love with Sophy Hopkey, the niece of the chief magistrate of Savannah, Mr. Causton. A change, however, came in her affection, and she swiftly married Mr. Williamson. Soon after Wesley repelled her from Holy Communion—no doubt because he thought that she was not in a fit state of heart to receive it; but on the surface it appeared like the act of a disappointed man. Her uncle brought a charge against John Wesley, who refused to acknowledge the power of a civil court in ecclesiastical affairs. Wesley, realizing that no further good would come from his ministry there, left the colony, and sailed for England on 22nd Dec. 1737.

[1] *Works*, xii. 38.

[2] Cf. 'The Twelve Rules of a Helper,' rule xi.: 'You have nothing to do but to save souls. Therefore spend and be spent in this work. And go always, not only to those who want you, but to those who want you most.'

[3] *Journal*, i. 421.

3. His evangelical conversion.—Wesley's comment on his Georgia ministry was:

'I went to America to convert the Indians; but oh, who shall convert me? . . . I have a fair summer religion. I can talk well; nay, and believe myself, while no danger is near. But let death look me in the face, and my spirit is troubled. . . . Oh, who will deliver me from this fear of death?'[1]

Eager and hungry, on his return to England he met Peter Böhler, who told him, 'My brother, my brother, that philosophy of yours must be purged away.' 'Preach faith till you have it, and then because you have it you will preach faith.' He gathered with the members of the little society in Fetter Lane. On 24th May, 1738, there came to Wesley his *Magna Dies*—the day of his evangelical conversion. No one had ever sought the haven of peace with more passionate devotion—it was a day never to be forgotten. He describes every part of it:

'I think,' he says, 'it was about five this morning, that I opened my Testament on those words, "There are given unto us exceeding great and precious promises."' He writes that, just as he went out, he opened the New Testament again on those words, 'Thou art not far from the kingdom of God.' He tells of his afternoon visit to St. Paul's, and notes that the anthem was 'Out of the deep have I called unto Thee, O Lord.' We now come to the *locus classicus* of the life of Wesley. 'In the evening I went very unwillingly to a society in Aldersgate Street, where one was reading Luther's preface to the *Epistle to the Romans*. About a quarter before nine, while he was describing the change which God works in the heart through faith in Christ, I felt my heart strangely warmed. I felt I did trust in Christ, Christ alone for salvation; and an assurance was given me that He had taken away *my* sins, even *mine*, and saved *me* from the law of sin and death. I began to pray with all my might for those who had in a more especial manner despitefully used me and persecuted me. I then testified openly to all there what I now first felt in my heart.'[2]

Wesley had now received the gift of life; and what he did in Aldersgate Street—'I then testified openly to all there what I now first felt in my heart'—he continued to do until the end of his life. It was with him an appeal no longer to the practices and customs of the early Church, but to the experience of the Living Christ within his own heart. For fifty-two years he offered to all through Christ the grace of forgiving love. For the wonder of Wesley's life is not to be found in the fact that on a certain evening about a quarter before nine he felt his heart strangely warmed, but that the fires of that love never died down. His eye was indeed single, and thus his whole body was full of light.

4. The great offensive.—From 1738 to 1791 Wesley led the great offensive—he attacked sin in its strongholds, and everywhere proclaimed the free grace of Christ. He seized every opportunity: if he were in a coach, he spoke to his fellow-travellers; if he were staying at an inn, he told his fellow-guests of the love of Jesus; even when crossing to Ireland, when the ship was tossed by the storm, he held a service for the passengers. Driven out of the Churches, he, through necessity and quite against his taste, followed the example of Whitefield, and took his stand in the open air, and preached to the crowds at Kingswood, Bristol, and Moorfields. His greatest help came from his brother Charles, whose hymns were sung by the miners of Kingswood, the labourers of Lincoln-

[1] *Journal*, i. 418. [2] *Ib.* i. 475.

shire and Cornwall and throughout the land. The Evangelical Revival spread by song as well as by sermon. There was much of the great military commander about Wesley; he chose three main strategic points—London, Bristol, and Newcastle-on-Tyne—and for the conquest of Ireland he made Dublin his base. When others were deaf to the calls of America he sent out a band of preachers to capture that continent for Christ. He moved constantly from place to place, riding on horseback until his later years, a sort of *avant-courier* of the Kingdom, the tireless rider, the invincible fighter, and the herald of the grace of God. J. Hampson, one of Wesley's preachers, who left with a grudge against him, published in 1791 a Life of Wesley. In its admissions it is of immense value, for he writes critically, and is a contemporary of the man of whom he writes. He thus sums up Wesley's life of toil:

'His public administrations were but a part of his labours, but from these we may form some conception of the rest. During fifty-two years he generally preached two sermons a day: very frequently four or five. Calculating, therefore, at twice a day, and allowing fifty sermons annually for extraordinary occasions, which is the lowest computation that can be made, the whole number in fifty-two years will be 40,462. To these may be added an infinite number of exhortations to societies. Of his travels, the lowest calculation we can make is 4000 miles annually, which, in fifty-two years, will give 208,000 miles. An almost incredible degree of labour: and which nothing but the best constitution, informed by the most active spirit, could have enabled him to support.'[1]

Augustine Birrell epitomizes his labours, and mingles with the telling of them his peculiar piquancy:

'John Wesley contested the whole kingdom in the cause of Christ during a campaign which lasted forty years. He did it for the most part on horseback. He paid more turnpikes than any man who ever bestrode a beast. Had he but preserved his scores at all the inns where he lodged, they would have made by themselves a history of prices. And throughout it all he never knew what depression of spirits meant, though he had much to try him—suits in Chancery and a jealous wife.'[2]

There is no other story of a life so crowded with toil, yet over which there broods so steadily the spirit of rest.[3] This man, like the Apostle Paul, could have drawn up his catalogue of sufferings; for he was stoned, enemies rose up against him on all sides, and besides there rested upon him the care of all his societies which were stationed from Land's End to Newcastle-on-Tyne, beyond the border, and across the Irish Sea. All this is written in Wesley's *Journal*.

'From which we can learn better than from anywhere else what manner of man he was, and the character of the times during which he lived and moved, and had his being.'[4]

This leads us to one of the most wonderful of his gifts. For fifty-two years he preached, visited his societies, entered prisons, galloped along the highways of England, the programme varying but little, and yet he never became stale; each day called him to a new adventure and was a fresh gift from God. His work never became to him a commonplace; he thrilled to it, he hailed it ever with a song. A comparison of the early years after his evangelical conversion and the later years of his life reveals that his enthusiasm never waned, but rather waxed stronger and stronger. Here is the record of 11th Sept. 1789.

'I went over to Kingswood. Sweet recess! where everything is now just as I wish. But—
"Man was not born in shades to lie!"
Let us work now; we shall rest by-and-by.'[5]

In March, 1790, he began a great preaching tour through England and Scotland, which lasted five months. Here is another entry—1st Jan. 1790:

'I am now an old man, decayed from head to foot. My eyes are dim; my right hand shakes much; my mouth is hot and dry every morning. I have a lingering fever almost every day. . . . However, blessed be God, I do not slack my labour. I can preach and write still.'[1]

He died on 2nd March, 1791.

5. His controversies.—As we have seen, Wesley owed a great deal to the Moravians. He was for a short time a great admirer of Zinzendorf. At first he hailed Herrnhut as a new city of God. But the breach between Wesley and the Moravians came soon after Wesley launched his great offensive. A section of them had a tendency towards a mistaken kind of pietism; they preached that there was no need for Bible or sacraments, that there was nothing to be done, and that the soul must wait in silence. These 'still-men,' as they were styled, roused his ire, and the break between the Methodist Societies and the Moravians was soon complete. The indictment of Wesley could only have referred to a small section, for in that Moravian band there were men and women of real saintliness. It was, however, an unfortunate happening, for it gave Wesley a somewhat violent antipathy to mysticism.

He speaks of 'the poison of mysticism,' and refers to 'Ralph Mather, a devoted young man, but almost driven out of his senses by Mystic Divinity. If he escapes out of this specious snare of the devil he will be an instrument of much good.'[2]

Wesley was right in speaking strongly against that which was mysticism falsely so called, but he was a mystic himself. The man who translated with such passion Tersteegen's hymn, 'Thou hidden love of God,' could not have been anything else. His controversy with William Law is surely due to a misunderstanding on the part of Wesley. Wesley wrote when he was perplexed, and his soul was strangely restless, and the honours are chiefly on the side of his teacher, Law. His greater and most fundamental controversy was with the Calvinists—and with logic and passionate love he claimed that Christ died for all. The battle was fought and won, but the victory came not through the strident notes of controversy, but rather through the rousing strains of song—

'For all, my Lord was crucified,
For all, for all my Saviour died.'[3]

One of the most beautiful things in the history of this controversy is the fact that such vital theological disagreements as there were between Wesley and Whitefield never broke their friendship, but seemed rather to deepen and strengthen it.

6. Wesley and the Church of England.—The Church of England never had a more loving son than John Wesley, and never one who strove more strenuously to be loyal to her. He was driven out of the Church, yet in 1789 he wrote:

'I declare once more that I live and die a member of the Church of England; and that none who regard my judgment or advice will separate from it.'[4]

But he did things which show that in another sense he did not belong to her. He believed in her, but he saw with his quick eye the needs of his age, and the organization of the Church of England was not flexible enough to meet the changing conditions of the time. He saw the great needs of America, and, realizing the urgency of its claims, in 1784 consecrated Coke as bishop and Whatcoat and Vasey as presbyters for that continent. In 1786 Wesley ordained preachers for Scotland. His loyalty was of that higher kind which would not allow rules to interfere with the advance to which he believed Christ was calling His people. This is seen early in the encounter with Joseph Butler, when bishop of Bristol. The great writer of *The Analogy* said that Wesley had no right to preach in that diocese. Wesley said, 'I can do

1 *Memoirs of John Wesley*, 3 vols., Sunderland, 1791, iii. 190.
2 Augustine Birrell, *Miscellanies*, London, 1901, 'Essay on John Wesley,' p. 12.
3 'By the grace of God I never fret. I repine at nothing. I am discontented with nothing' (*Journal*, iv. 131, note).
4 Birrell, *Miscellanies*, p. 35.
5 *Journal*, viii. 10.

1 *Journal*, viii. 35.
2 *Ib.* vi. 10.
3 For the theology of Methodism see art. METHODISM.
4 'Farther Thoughts on Separation from the Church' (written 11th Dec. 1789), *Works*, xiii. 240.

most good here, so here I stay.' That was his one test. He was at heart a Catholic and like the scribe who brought out of his treasure things new and old. We see this in his 'Christian Library,' in which he included writings from men of all Christian communities, the only requirement being that each reprint should give spiritual strength to its readers.

7. Wesley and humanism.—It was the boast of Wesley that he was 'homo unius libri,' and so he was, though few men of his age read more books. His final appeal was to the Scriptures illumined by the living spirit. The variety and amount of his reading leaves us breathless. It was Hampson who wrote: 'With a book in his hand, he frequently rode from fifty to sixty or seventy miles a day.'[1] His *Primitive Physic* shows his quaint and practical knowledge: and the quotation he places at the beginning, 'Homo sum: humani nihil a me alienum puto,' reveals his keen interest in human affairs. The *Journal* could have been written only by a man who had read enthusiastically the book of life. There may be little charm of style, but there is a conciseness, a forthrightness of writing, a perspicuity, that is hard to excel. He had not studied his Addison for nothing; the references in his early diary—'Read Addison'—are illuminating. He had much humour,[2] and we must not forget that Alexander Knox writes that his 'sportive sallies of innocent mirth delighted even the young and the thoughtless,' and Thomas Walsh writes of his 'witty proverbs.'[3] Hampson says: 'It was impossible to be long in his company without partaking his hilarity.'[4] This man, who could have chosen the company of the great, lived and loved to live with the unknown. There are many parallels between St. Francis and Wesley, and one is to be found in this, that both went to the people—what the Little Brothers were to Francis that wonderful band of men, the early Methodist preachers, were to Wesley. It is interesting to note that two men command the 18th cent., and one (Dr. Johnson) said of the other, 'He can talk well on any subject.' Johnson would fain have seen more of Wesley.

'John Wesley's conversation is good, but he is never at leisure. He is always obliged to go at a certain hour. This is very disagreeable to a man who loves to fold his legs, and have out his talk as I do.'[5]

Southey says:

'His manners were always irresistibly winning, and his cheerfulness was like perpetual sunshine.'[6]

It is true that his printed sermons do not best reveal his humanism; but they are treatises. A study of the *Journal* teaches us that the texts upon which he preached most were those which reveal his tenderness and his love of the doctrines of grace. The text 'When they had nothing to pay, he frankly forgave them both' is met again and again in the *Journal*, and is the *motif* of his ministry. Horace Walpole informs us of his vivid way of preaching.

'I have been at one opera—Mr. Wesley's. . . . Wondrous clever, but as evidently an actor as Garrick . . . he told stories like Latimer, of the fool of his college who said "I *thanks* God for everything."'[7]

John Nelson, one of his early helpers, describes the power of Wesley's preaching:

'But I was like a wandering bird, cast out of the nest, till John Wesley came to preach his first sermon in Moorfields. O that was a blessed morning to my soul! He stroked back his hair, and turned his face towards where I stood, and I thought fixed his eyes upon me. When he had done I said, "This man can tell the secrets of my heart; he hath not left me there; he hath shewed me the remedy, even the blood of Jesus."'[1]

Sir Walter Scott tells us that he heard Wesley preach more than once in the churchyard at Kelso.

'He was a most venerable figure, but his sermons were vastly too colloquial for the taste of Saunders. He told many excellent stories.'[2]

This man, of five feet three inches, of weight eight stone ten, 'an eye the brightest and most piercing that can be conceived,'[3] with his finely chiselled face which came to view again in that of the Iron Duke,[4] loved men and women not for what they were but for what they might be: he loved colliers, drunkards, cock-fighters, prisoners, because he saw in them the children of the One Father. He gave first his love to God, and that exalted his love for men—that is why it never grew cold. He commands the 18th cent. on the religious side as much as Johnson on the literary. Lecky has told us that Wesley saved England from a revolution, but we must remember that he brought about another revolution which has done more to break down social barriers than men realize—for he taught men and women the essential oneness of us all, that One is our Father and we are all brethren. His doctrine of faith stripped off the superficial disguises of life and revealed the divine possibilities of all men. Wesley was always ahead of his century; he was a great forerunner with regard to social reform; he lived on as little as possible, and gave the rest away. Hampson says, 'Perhaps the most liberal man in England was Mr. Wesley. His liberality to the poor knew no bounds.'[5] He gave the people cheap literature, founded schools and orphanages, wrote numerous pamphlets on public questions, and his last letter was one in which he encouraged Wilberforce in his great fight against slavery—that traffic which he termed 'that execrable villainy, which is the scandal of England, of religion, and of human nature.' This 'brand plucked from the burning' broke up the frost of the 18th cent. by the glow of his flaming message. He formed a society which has become a world-wide Church; he brought inspiration to all the Churches, and his message still rings down the years—'The best of all is God is with us.'

LITERATURE.—See the literature under METHODISM.

W. BARDSLEY BRASH.

WESLEYAN METHODISM.—See METHODISM.

WEST AFRICA.—See NEGROES AND W. AFRICA.

WESTERN CHURCH.—The epithet 'Western' differentiates the Church of the West, or Roman Catholic Church, from that of the East, known as the Holy Orthodox Church.[6] The dis-

[1] iii. 191.

[2] For illustrations of his humour see W. Bardsley Brash, 'Wesley's Wit and Humour,' in *London Quarterly Review*, January, 1921.

[3] For Alexander Knox see J. Whitehead, *Life of John Wesley*, Dublin, 1805, ii. 486. For Walsh see Wesley's *Journal*, vi. 10, footnote.

[4] iii. 178.

[5] Boswell's *Life of Johnson*, ed. Birkbeck Hill, Oxford, 1887, iii. 230.

[6] *Life of Wesley*, 2 vols., London, 1846, i. 409.

[7] Walpole's *Letters*, ed. Mrs. Paget Toynbee, 16 vols., Oxford, 1904, vii. 47, Letter 1143, dated 10th Oct. 1766.

[1] *The Lives of Early Methodist Preachers*, London, 1865, i. 14; cf. testimony of another, 'But when John Wesley began to speak, his words made me tremble. I thought he spoke to no one but me, and I durst not look up; for I imagined all the people were looking at me' (*ib.* p. 16).

[2] J. G. Lockhart, *Life of Sir Walter Scott*, Edinburgh, 1848, vi. 46.

[3] Hampson, iii. 167.

[4] The following is a most interesting reminiscence of Dr. George Osborn: 'Henry Moore, in whose house at City Road, as a young preacher, I lived, once took me to see a review by the Duke of Wellington in Hyde Park. During an interval the Duke, dismounting, stood by his horse near Mr. Moore and myself. Pointing to the Duke (for he was short of stature), Henry Moore said, "That is John Wesley as I knew him"' (*Journal*, vii. 462, footnote). Wesley and the Duke of Wellington sprang from collateral branches of the same family.

[5] iii. 185.

[6] See artt. EASTERN CHURCH, GREEK ORTHODOX CHURCH, RUSSIAN CHURCH.

tinction between these two branches of the Holy Catholic Church arose from the interaction of many causes, geographical, political, and theological, but ultimately it may be traced to an event of supreme importance in the historic evolution of the Christian faith.

1. Introduction: schism of East and West.—Up to A.D. 330, when Constantine the Great chose the ancient Byzantium as the new capital of the Roman Empire and gave it the name of Constantinople, the Catholic Church of Christendom had remained one and undivided; and, though the final schism was to be delayed for centuries, the rivalry between the old and the new Rome at once introduced a divisive factor into the ecclesiastical relationships of the empire. Constantinople, already a Greek city with a large Greek population, was destined to become a second metropolis of the faith, representing Christian life and thought of a distinctively Greek type. Indeed, it may be said that imperial Christianity had shifted its centre of gravity to the Ægean world of Hellenistic culture, intellectual and spiritual. It is significant that, when it was found necessary to formulate the terms of the orthodox creed in order to finish the desolating heresy of Arius,[1] Nicæa and not Rome had been chosen in A.D. 325 as the place of assembly for the historic council which, so far from pacifying the Christian world, was the forerunner of other councils—Ephesus, Chalcedon, and Constantinople[2]—where the various phases of the seemingly perpetual Christological problem received discussion and authoritative settlement. Christianity had spread with a relatively greater rapidity over the Eastern empire than in the provinces of the West. The Greek language known as 'common' Greek—the *lingua franca* in which the early records of the faith were written—was naturally the medium by which the symbols of the Christian faith found their most logical and accurate expression. It is true that the patriarch of Constantinople, who was always under the control of the emperor, was never to achieve a position like that of the pope, who, left free from civil control, became the undisputed pontiff and vicar of Christ upon earth; but by the 5th and 6th centuries he had secured a commanding influence and bore the title of 'œcumenical patriarch'—a designation which, in spite of papal protests, has continued till to-day. The relations of emperor and pope were severely strained during the period of the Christological heresies, and in 680 the Council of Constantinople, when it condemned the Monothelete position, did not hesitate to anathematize the memory of Pope Honorius I. In A.D. 725 the opposition of Pope Gregory II. to Leo the Isaurian, who on the outbreak of the Iconoclastic controversy[3] had vehemently condemned, and commended a crusade against, the use of images, led to a fatal separation between East and West; for Leo transferred Sicily, Southern Italy, and Illyricum from the ecclesiastical jurisdiction of the pope to that of Constantinople. A reaction in favour of images took place in the reign of Constantine VI., and in 786 the so-called Second Council of Nicæa gave a decision in favour of image-worship, which the pope approved. But this reconciliation was temporary and in effect was nullified in 800 on the coronation of Charlemagne by the pope; for, while in the West the pope became the religious head and the emperor the secular head of the Church, the process was reversed in the East, the emperor becoming head of the same Christian Church with a patriarch subordinate to him. Still, though the separation between East and West was complete in secular matters, the final breach did not occur for two centuries. The rejection of the *Filioque* clause,[1] which had been added by the Spanish Church to the Nicene creed in the 5th cent., and which was subsequently inserted in the Roman creed, was definitely decreed by the Council of Constantinople (A.D. 867), which excommunicated the pope. But, though this was significant of the steadily widening breach between the two sections of Catholicism, it was not till a century and a half later that the last blow was struck. The patriarch of Constantinople, Michael Cerularius, closed the Latin churches and convents of the city in 1054, and this drastic act was followed by the written attacks of his clergy on the Latin religion and its observances, and especially the practice of celibacy on the part of its clergy. The pope's legate, Cardinal Humbert, entered St. Sophia on 16th July during divine service and laid on the altar a decree of excommunication against the patriarch and his adherents. This act rent the Catholic world in twain, and it was the climax of the long-continued and deep-rooted misunderstanding between the two great geographical sections of Christendom. The massacre of the Latins by the Greek populace in 1182 and the sack and capture of the city by the forces (chiefly Venetian) of the Fourth Crusade in 1204 were events which revealed and confirmed the hopeless fissure in the unity of the Church and led up to the fateful capture of Constantinople by Muhammad II. in 1453. Western Europe had left the Christian capital of the East to its fate: divided Christendom had enabled Muhammadanism to enshrine itself in Europe, and a sultan sat on the throne which Christian emperors had occupied since the days of Constantine.

The following survey is limited (1) to the general development in history of the polity, organization, and secular relationships of the Western Church, and (2) to its dogmatic history and its position in Christian thought, leaving the reader to study in other articles (to which reference is made) the more specialized treatment of the inner life of the Church, its observances and sacraments, its ritual and its liturgies, its canon law and discipline, its orders and congregations, the history of its movements in their religious, intellectual, and social aspects, and finally the biographies of its outstanding personalities in the annals of its government, sainthood, and scholarship.

Both sections of the survey are conveniently treated in chronological order under the following heads: (*a*) the early period (from Constantine to Charlemagne [A.D. 312–800]); (*b*) the mediæval period (from Charlemagne to Boniface VIII. [A.D. 800–1303]); (*c*) the modern period (from the later Middle Ages to the present time [A.D. 1303–1920]).

In the first period, the period of *expansion*, we have the rise of the papacy[2] with the conversion of the Teutonic races to Christianity; in the second, the period of *consolidation*, we have the papacy supreme in Europe, having attained the zenith of its influence and prosperity; in the third period—the period of *decline*—we have the waning power of the papacy and the rise of Protestantism, which eventually led up to the distinction between religions of authority and a religion of the spirit, and their conflicting ideals of ecclesiastical unity and catholicism.

2. Ecclesiastical polity and organization.—(*a*) *Early period.*—With the accession of Constantine in 323, Christianity became the imperial religion, and henceforth its destiny was to be closely associated with that of the empire. The vicissitudes through which the empire passed during the three

[1] See art. ARIANISM.
[2] See artt. COUNCILS AND SYNODS (Christian), CREEDS (Ecumenical), and CONFESSIONS.
[3] See art. ICONOCLASM.

[1] See artt. CONFESSIONS, CREEDS (Ecumenical).
[2] See art. PAPACY.

succeeding centuries under the attacks of the barbarians of Northern and Eastern Europe left an enduring mark on the constitution and organization of the Church. The monarchical episcopate, which was recognized by Ignatius and accepted by Cyprian as the basis of Church government, was the germ from which the primacy of the bishop of Rome was evolved. The doctrine of apostolic succession (*q.v.*) laid down by Irenæus ascribed a spiritual pre-eminence to the Church of Rome as founded by the two greatest apostles, St. Peter and St. Paul, and Tertullian in his early pre-Montanist treatise, the *Prescription of Heresy*—always a favourite with the Roman Church—eloquently adopted the same line of argument, proclaiming the transmission of the apostolic 'deposit' through the succession of bishops. Established in 'the Eternal City,' which was the visible focus of imperial greatness and might, the bishopric of Rome was invested with a dignity which far surpassed that of the rival sees of Alexandria and Antioch. Moreover, the Latin conception of the Church as an external institution, moulded indeed on the type of the empire, but controlled by bishops who were the vicars of an absent Christ and depositaries of saving grace, led up to the papacy as a logical conclusion. No salvation outside the Church, the Church built on St. Peter as chief of the apostolic college, a hierarchy which traced its lineal descent by due succession from the first of apostles—these are the principles upon which the supremacy of the Roman see was established by Augustine, the greatest of the Latin theologians. In the 4th and 5th centuries the Church as it developed its organization on the new political divisions of the empire—especially Gaul and Spain, following the conquest by Christianity of the nations of the Franks and the Spaniards or Iberians — rose, by its beauty of ritual, its succession of distinguished Christian leaders, bishops, and kings, and its moral influence, to a position of great splendour. A generation after Augustine, Leo the Great, bishop of Rome (440–461), put forth a claim[1] for the authority of the Roman see which was never afterwards relaxed, and which saw its realization in the imperial authority over Christendom wielded by Hildebrand and Innocent III.

In 445 the emperor Valentinian III. issued a law declaring the bishop of Rome the supreme head of the Western Church on the three grounds of the primacy of St. Peter, the dignity of the city, and the decree of a holy synod. Resistance to the authority of St. Peter's successors in the Roman see was thus constituted a State offence.

The title 'papa' (pope), which was applied in the West to all the bishops, became in the 6th cent. the exclusive designation of the bishop of Rome. Gregory VII. was responsible for the decree which thenceforth limited the title to the occupant of the Roman see.[2]

Although for a short time Justinian the Great (527–565) held sway over Italy and placed the Roman bishops on a level with those of Constantinople, the Lombards finally broke the power of the Byzantine emperor in Italy and by their conquest practically assured the independence of the bishops of Rome. The decretals of the popes were codified in the year 500 by Dionysius Exiguus, who included in his collection the decrees of the councils and the chief canons of the provincial synods. The Donatist position,[3] which made holiness of life the test of catholicity, was defeated by the influence of Augustine, and the Donatists were in the end repressed by force of arms. The supremacy of the hierarchy and the efficacy of baptism and the Lord's Supper were maintained to be independent of the personal character of individual officials and members of a Church which was founded on the 'rock' Peter and owed its catholic authority as a visible holy community to its apostolic descent. On the other hand, the rise of monasticism in this period[1]—first in the form of hermit colonies under the inspiration of St. Antony, then in the form of religious communities with a *regula*, or rule, of common-life discipline under Cassian at Marseilles, Benedict of Nursia (480–545) at Monte Cassino, and his disciple Maurus (St. Maur) in Gaul and Sicily—was a movement within the Church towards a higher type of spirituality, though it tended to fix the orthodox separation between things sacred and profane or secular. From 590 to 800 Christianity spread over Western Europe, Anglo-Saxon England, Germany, and the new nations along the Danube, the missionary movement owing much to the inspiring zeal of Gregory I., known as 'the Great.' That the papal power not only survived the political and ecclesiastical fluctuations and unrest of the times, but emerged with added prestige, is due to the personality of this powerful leader who founded the Church in England, consolidated the Church in Spain, brought the Church of Gaul into close connexion with Rome, and checked the abuses which had crept into his own diocese. In contradistinction to the Eastern title of œcumenical patriarch, he assumed as pope (590–604) the title of 'servus servorum,' which his successors have always maintained. After Gregory's death the outstanding event is the anointing of Pepin, king of the Franks, in 751, probably by Boniface, Archbishop of Maintz, with the sanction of Pope Zacharias. A second coronation by Stephen II. of the same king at St. Denys in 754 was the price which a grateful papacy paid to him for his help against the Lombards and his presentation of the lost lands to the Roman Church. Here is a sequence of events which marks a beginning of the long-coveted temporal dominion of the papacy. But the political troubles were not at an end, and Pope Leo III., owing to the disaffection of the Roman nobles, had to flee for his life to the court of Charlemagne, king of the Franks. The result was that, when Charlemagne came to Rome to re-establish order, Leo crowned him at St. Peter's on Christmas Day 800 as emperor of Rome. This event, the significance of which can be paralleled only by Constantine's establishment of Christianity as the religion of the Roman Empire, revealed the fact that the majestic traditions of that empire—for three centuries merely *magni nominis umbra* in the West—still swayed the minds of men. Church and State were once more united, and the Holy Roman Empire became a compelling ideal, if not as yet a historic reality.

(*b*) *Mediæval period.*—In this period the papacy held undisputed sway over Western Europe. Missionary enterprise widened the scope of its influence. If to Eastern Christianity is due the credit of the conversion of Russia under Vladimir, Scandinavia, the Slavic nations, the Moravians, Bohemia and Hungary, the Wends of the north and east of Germany were Christianized by the Church of the West. When warring factions broke up the empire on the death of Charlemagne, the popes took advantage of political changes to secure greater independence and strove to establish the ascendancy of the papal see over the State as the one solution of the European problem. The pseudo-Isidorian decretals (*c.* 850) proclaimed the

[1] Cf. *Serm.* iv. 2: 'De toto mundo unus Petrus eligitur, qui et universarum gentium vocationi, et omnibus apostolis, cunctisque ecclesiæ patribus præponatur: ut quamvis in populo Dei multi sacerdotes sint multique pastores, omnes tamen proprie regat Petrus, quos principaliter regit et Christus.'

[2] See *EBr*[11], *s.v.* 'Pope'; Ducange, *Gloss. Mediæ et Infimæ Latinitatis*, *s.v.* 'Papa.'

[3] See art. DONATISTS.

[1] See art. MONASTICISM.

inviolability of the hierarchy and the pope as the fountainhead of justice, while the *Donation of Constantine*, concocted on even more audacious lines, asserted that no earthly potentate may rule where God's anointed has his throne. In 962 Otto was crowned as the emperor of what is known as the Holy Roman Empire. Otto owed his crown to the chair of St. Peter, but had the power of deposing Christ's vicar and determining his successors; nevertheless this union of two world-rulers—one supreme in secular matters, the other in the spiritual realm—was a fact of transcendent historical moment. Hildebrand, a native of Tuscany, educated in the Cluny monastery at Rome though not himself a monk, was gifted with the instincts of leadership and a genius for statesmanship, and under the name of Gregory VII. ascended the throne of St. Peter in the year 1073 to claim absolute power in the affairs of the Church, the right to depose kings and to sit in judgment on their sins. On a memorable occasion during the year 1077 he proved his strength by reducing the defiant Henry IV. to penitence at Canossa, and his humiliation of the king of Germany had been preceded by threatening Philip I., king of France, with deposition, if he did not mend his ways. The policy of State domination was carried on by his successors Urban II., and, more notably, Innocent III. The protest of Arnold of Brescia, a pupil of Abelard, who advocated a return to apostolic simplicity and the abandonment of secular pretensions, was unavailing. The answer of the papacy was the destruction of the heresy of the Cathari and the Albigenses and the establishment of the Inquisition, while the policy of asserting independent control over the kings of France, Germany, and England was continued until 'Innocent III. had as his vassals the majority of the princes of Christendom.'[1] On the other hand, this struggle weakened the moral influence of the papacy. The Latin Empire in the East fell, and the Crusades (*q.v.*) came to an end in 1272. Monasticism under Bernard (*q.v.*) of Clairvaux (1090–1153) and the Cistercians assumed a more rigid tone and discipline, and the mendicant orders of St. Francis and St. Dominic aroused the conscience of the Church to the needs of the common people, social and spiritual. The Fratres Minores in particular enshrined in their labours and their lives of frugality and simplicity an ideal of self-renunciation joyous rather than austere, and by their care for the poor and their own self-imposed poverty leavened the decadence and corruption of the age with the true spirit of the Christian gospel.[2]

(*c*) *Modern period.*—The two and a half centuries which constitute the later Middle Ages (from the death of Boniface VIII. to the beginning of the Reformation—1303 to 1517) may be conveniently included under this head as bringing to a climax the tendencies prophetic of and preparatory to the rise of Protestantism. The famous papal bull *Unam Sanctam*, issued by Boniface VIII. in 1302, had declared that the belief that every human creature is subject to the pope was necessary to salvation. It was burnt by Philip IV. 'the Fair' of France in Notre Dame, and its author, when about to excommunicate Philip, was made a prisoner in a rising instigated by Philip and a month later died of a broken heart. Such was the tragic end of the papal claim to a world-leadership. The *de Monarchia* (*c.* 1314) of Dante expressed the sentiment of hostility to the papal ambition for temporal power and was significant of the growing reaction against papal pretensions. The 'Babylonian captivity' of the papacy at Avignon was a further blow to the prestige of the holy see. While William of Occam (1280–1347) placed the emperor and the general council above the pope as his judges, and Marsilius of Padua in his *Defensor Pacis* assumed the rôle of higher critic in the matter of the supremacy of St. Peter and the primacy of the Roman see, France reduced the pope to complete submission and Germany disregarded his anathemas. When Wyclif protested that the papal office was poisonous to the Church, the great schism which had resulted in the election of two popes in 1378 was the basis of his argument —an argument which became irresistible when, on the failure of the Council of Pisa in 1409 to solve the problem, three popes instead of two widened the schism. Five years later the Council of Constance condemned John Hus to death.[1] Stimulated by the writings of Wyclif, he had inaugurated a new religious movement in Bohemia and had been invited to the council under a safe-conduct granted by the Holy Roman Emperor Sigismund. There he expounded his views and was called upon to retract what were considered to be erroneous teachings subversive of the authority of the pope. He refused on the grounds of fidelity to conscience, was condemned and on 6th July 1415 burned. A year later his friend and disciple, Jerome of Prague, suffered the same fate. The essence of the Hussite movement was its insistence on the rights of conscience and its appeal to a higher tribunal than that of pope and council. On the other hand, the Council of Constance had ended the schism by asserting its supreme authority over pope and Church. It had established its right to regulate the action of the pope and 'had secured the transformation of the papacy from an absolute into a constitutional monarchy'[2]—an event of great significance for the future history of the papacy. Constantinople fell in 1453, and in the latter half of this century the popes sought to restore their waning supremacy by invoking crusades against the Muslim. Savonarola ([*q.v.*] 1452–98), a Dominican monk of Florence under the rule of the Medici, became alarmed by the prevailing decadence of morals, and owing to his zeal for the purification of society was excommunicated by Pope Alexander VI., who after failing to bribe him into silence secured his death by working on the hostility of the Florentines to their noblest fellow-citizen. Such movements as those of Hus and Savonarola, who were both martyrs in the cause of a higher morality, and the exemplification of an inward and spiritual religion in the lives of mystics like Tauler and Thomas à Kempis,[3] were signs of the coming change. It was in vain that Pope Leo X. (1513–21) secured the repeal of the 'pragmatic sanction'—by which Louis IX. of France had in 1269 asserted the right of the State to refuse papal taxation—and in vain that his imitation of the warlike policy of his predecessor Julius II. and his successful diplomacy had enabled him to recover something of the old papal prestige. It was but a momentary rekindling of the embers of a dying cause. The Reformation had arrived. It is true that the Protestant movement,[4] triumphant in Northern and Central Europe, was checked in Italy, though even in the native land of the papacy hatred of the vices and corruptions of the papal régime rallied many adherents to the new movement. The traditional greatness of an institution which had brought wealth and influence to the Italian

[1] A. Lagarde, *The Latin Church in the Middle Ages*, Eng. tr., Edinburgh, 1915, p. 243.

[2] See, besides art. MONASTICISM, art. RELIGIOUS ORDERS (Christian).

[1] See art. HUSSITES.

[2] Williston Walker, *A Hist. of the Christian Church*, p. 310.

[3] See art. MYSTICISM (Christian, Roman Catholic).

[4] See art. PROTESTANTISM, and esp. art. REFORMATION.

people evoked a patriotic response to the forces of the Counter-Reformation. Moreover, the foundation of the Society of Jesus by Loyola (1491-1556),[1] with its régime of unquestioning obedience to the will of its general and its unswerving devotion to the papal see, was a powerful factor in withstanding the advance of Protestantism, while by its missionary zeal it carried Roman Catholic influence into new lands and reconquered lost territory. The Council of Trent met in 1545 and after two interruptions produced in 1563 under Pius IV. the famous *Professio Fidei*, to which all teachers and ecclesiastics were required to assent. The Catholic theologian Bellarmine with uncompromising dogmatism expounded the Tridentine symbol and the Roman Catechism, which even more rigidly supported the papal supremacy, and his labours for orthodoxy were continued by the Jesuit theologians Suarez and Petavius, while the mysticism of Francis of Sales, Molinos, and Fénelon wielded a powerful influence in favour of the Roman type of piety. The publication of the Catechism, the Breviary, and the Missal, together with an authorized edition of the Vulgate, aided the work of the Counter-Reformation by providing standards of Catholic orthodoxy. The Inquisition[2] was re-organized and carried on in Italy, though not with the fanatical excesses which in Spain under Torquemada had covered the holy office with lasting infamy. The *Index Expurgatorius* pronounced its ban on all anti-Roman books and particular passages of books. In 1685 the repeal of the Edict of Nantes, which was the great charter of Huguenot rights in France, marked the climax of a half-century of persecution and political ostracism. In the 18th cent. the efforts of the Western Church to withstand the Protestant movement had spent their vigour, just as Protestantism had lost its earlier glow and enthusiasm. A spiritual and intellectual lassitude prevailed—a reaction partly from the theological strife of the previous generations and partly from the dynastic struggles caused by the ambitions of Louis XIV. and Frederick the Great. The Society of Jesus was temporarily extinguished. Where religious reforms were attempted—*e.g.*, by Joseph II. in Austria—they proved abortive, probably because they were inspired by the free-thinking spirit rather than by genuine religious earnestness.

Under the French revolution the Church shared the fate of all the privileged classes, and the Catholic religion was formally abolished as being hostile to the new republic. The Goddess of Reason was enthroned in Notre Dame, and Robespierre's attempt to restore religion by enforcing a belief in God only checked for a moment the torrent of infidelity. In 1801 Napoleon concluded a concordat with Pius VII., in which the Catholic religion was declared to be the religion of the majority of the French people; but he provoked the pope's hostility by demanding the right to appoint a patriarch of France, the abolition of clerical celibacy, and the support of the pope against England. Excommunication of Napoleon was followed by a protracted struggle with the pope, which was only ended in 1814 by the fall of Napoleon. In Germany the ecclesiastical states were secularized and subjected to civil rule. In Spain the Inquisition was abolished. The pope espoused the cause of absolutism which the formation of the Holy Alliance of European Powers was intended to uphold, in order to prevent revolutionary and democratic movements aimed at the authority of kings. In 1814 the Jesuit order was revived. Lamennais's attempt in France to associate ultramontane ideas of the pope's spiritual supremacy[1] with the advocacy of freedom of worship and liberty of conscience was repudiated by Pope Gregory XVI. On the other hand, in England Catholic emancipation released Roman Catholics from the political disabilities imposed at the Restoration. In 1846 Pope Pius IX. began his policy of liberalism by providing for his kingdom a constitutional system and cherished a scheme for the unifying of Italy under his control. A quarter of a century later, on the capture of Rome by Victor Emmanuel (1870), Italy was unified under one kingdom with Rome as its capital, and the pope's temporal authority was finally lost. In 1854 Pius IX. had promulgated on his own authority without any conciliar sanction the dogma of the immaculate conception (*q.v.*), and in 1870 at the Vatican Council the dogma of papal infallibility[2] was decreed in spite of the opposition of the 'Old Catholics'[3] of Germany, who held that the concurrence of pope and council was required for the validity of a doctrinal definition. Some of these, like Hefele, submitted, but Döllinger and his associates seceded and formed a confederation of English, Americans, Swiss, Russians, and Greeks, while in Paris Père Hyacinthe Loyson formed an Old Catholic congregation. But the movement never captured the people. Both England and Germany were alarmed by the ultramontane policy of the papacy, and Germany under Bismarck gave political protection to the Old Catholics. In France the National Assembly in 1871 was possessed with the ultramontane ideals, and the Government four years later authorized the foundation of Catholic universities. The inevitable reaction followed, and under Ferry and Gambetta (1880-81) the 'March decrees,' breaking up the Jesuit Society and congregations not recognized by the State and requiring Catholic students to be enrolled in State universities, were carried. During the last generation the secularist movement in France advanced stage by stage—until in 1905 the separation of Church and State was decreed by the French government and all churches and church property became the possession of the State. A situation was thus created for both Catholics and Protestants which called for voluntary generosity on the part of their adherents, with the result that the cause of religion in France has not lost but rather gained in public esteem.

Even from this rapid survey, which has selected what may be called decisive events illustrative of the political aims of the papacy and the development of ecclesiastical life and order within the Roman Church, we may infer what the Western Church has stood for in European history since the days of Constantine. Its aim has been to include humanity within its spiritual fold, while exerting a dominating control over the secular fabric of the State, its kings and governing authorities. This fundamental dualism of spiritual authority and temporal domination, which reached its climax in the Holy Roman Empire, was held to be the secret of progress religious and social, and none can deny the splendour of the conception which inspired Hildebrand and lifted the Mediæval Church to a position of majestic influence and striking prosperity. But it was a glorious dream destined to vanish at the touch of reality, a harmony of incompatible opposites which could not endure, a service of two masters which was to end in disillusion and disaster. The interpenetration of Catholicism with political ambitions and with worldly aims of kingly power tended to weaken its spiritual life. History has but recorded its verdict on the unreality of the Western claim to catholicity by adopting the

[1] See artt. JESUITS and LOYOLA.
[2] See artt. INQUISITION and OFFICE, THE HOLY.

[1] See art. ULTRAMONTANISM.
[2] See art. INFALLIBILITY.
[3] See art. OLD CATHOLICISM.

limiting epithet 'Roman' in its designation of the Catholic Church of the West.[1] The narrowness of its conception of what constitutes catholicity abides, even when we take into account its splendid annals of saintliness, piety, missionary zeal, its strength and compactness of organization—a bulwark in dark and barbaric ages conserving spiritual truth and light against the powers of evil—its enduring services in the task of redeeming the world from atheism and saving it from sin, and further in its self-renouncing ministries to the poor, the sufferers and outcasts of mankind. From age to age it has received warnings and calls to forsake the path of earthly domination and to seek only the unity and freedom of the spirit; but its answer is the dogma of papal infallibility, which is the admission of a fatal weakness—a bold but despairing attempt to enforce an authority which cannot endure the light of reason and spiritual liberty. Paganism and traditionalism are the perils of most forms of faith—the one, according to Sabatier,[2] finding 'its most obvious and crudest expression in Catholicism, in the constitution of its priestly hierarchy, in the *opus operatum* of its sacraments, and all the superstitious practices with which Catholic devotion persists in overlaying itself'; the other revealing itself in the Catholic apotheosis of the past—whether the history of a period or the body of custom, tradition, and dogma—which in the course of time becomes a hindrance and a despotism fatal to spiritual progress. And the view that the Western Church has been materialized and narrowed by its persistent policy of confining the Spirit within forms and rites and hierarchical authority, and by its fatal distrust of reason and conscience, is confirmed as we trace the attitude of Rome to the developments of Christian thought in the ages under review.

3. Development of theology and religious thought in the Church of the West.—(*a*) *Early period: Augustinianism and influence of Greek theology.*—The evolution of the Christian Church into the unity of Catholicism was not entirely a development of organization necessitated by its progress over the Roman Empire and moulded by its imperial environment and its secular relationships. The external and institutional form of the Latin Church cannot be explained if the influence of its theological standpoint and its fundamental dogmas is ignored. Its claim to authority over the soul and conscience of mankind was based on a type of theology to which the distinguishing epithet 'Latin' has invariably been applied. From this point of view Augustine is more palpably the founder of the Western Church than St. Peter. This remarkable thinker[3] is reverenced by the Catholic and the Protestant alike: by the former because of his emphasis on the authority of the Church and the impossibility of salvation outside the Church, by the latter because of his assertion of the divine sovereignty and of predestination (*q.v.*) and his interpretation and practice of evangelical and experimental piety. But, though it is true that his personal witness to Christianity lifts him beyond all the divisions of Christianity, the fact remains that he devoted all the resources of his intellect and spiritual zeal to the service of the Catholic Church, which he believed to be the only possible medium of salvation to the world. The grace (*q.v.*) which saved came indeed from above, but it was deposited with the succession of bishops who alone were empowered to administer it to the elect. His God was essentially a deistic or transcendent Deity dwelling apart from mankind and regulating human affairs by His commissioned agents, the hierarchy of the Catholic Church. Original sin (*q.v.*) was an effectual barrier to man's reconciliation with God; and Augustine placed a greater emphasis on the external rite of baptism (*q.v.*) as a mode of regeneration than on the merits of Christ. The power of sin which is seated in the will could be broken only by the agency of the Church as the appointed channel of grace. In fact, 'grace' takes the place of Christ in Augustinian theology: on the one hand, it is the sovereign will of God who decrees the salvation of the elect, and, on the other, 'a kind of spiritual potency' deposited in the hierarchy and mediated by the priesthood in the sacraments to the people. Only a portion of the race could be generated in baptism; the residue were doomed to eternal punishment. It was by these views that Augustine made possible the development of the Church of the 5th cent. into the papal empire of the Middle Ages. There is hardly a distinctively Roman doctrine or practice—purgatory, the intermediate state, the celibacy of the clergy, the invocation of saints, reverence for relics and images, the distinction between mortal and venial sins, the loss of unbaptized children—which cannot be found at least in germ among his opinions. With all its defects, however, this can be said in favour of the Augustinian theology, that it consolidated the Western Church, its thinking and its discipline, and saved it from the wave of Muhammadanism which overwhelmed the Church of the East. Augustine was powerfully influenced by the Platonism of the Alexandrian teachers, especially in his earlier life; but his mature treatises show but scanty traces of sympathy with the standpoint of the Greek theologians and are obsessed by his theory of the Church, which in its rigidity and narrowness reveals the mind of a great ecclesiastic rather than of a profound philosopher.

It has often been asked if the principles of Greek theology influenced the thought of the West. While it is universally agreed that the Latin Church borrowed freely from the customs and ritual of paganism, to what extent was its dogmatic teaching affected by the views of Clement of Alexandria, who proclaimed the continuity between Christianity and the higher thought of the Greek philosophers? The Platonists of Alexandria derived this idea of continuity from the truth of the divine immanence (*q.v.*) in human nature, taught that the Incarnation revealed the organic union between God and man and was the real atonement for sin, asserted that there was no opposition between reason and faith, regarded the Church as a community whose spiritual life was that of the Logos (*q.v.*) and its sacraments as symbols of inner processes, and proclaimed that heresy was an aid to the discovery of truth. Origen[1] followed with a profounder learning and philosophic insight to lay the foundation of the doctrine of the Trinity in his teaching respecting the 'eternal generation of the Son.' Athanasius (*q.v.*) shaped in an atmosphere of controversy the orthodox Trinitarian formula against the deistic interpretation of Arius, and secured the insertion of the vital term ὁμοούσιος in the Nicene symbol. His triumph is for ever significant, and the creeds of Christendom show that Greek thought fulfilled a providential task in the reconciliation of Christianity with reason, while the genius of Latin Christianity built up on the model of the empire the government, law, and constitution of the Church. In other words, the Western Church, while in the

[1] Cf. A. V. G. Allen, *Continuity of Christian Thought*, London, 1885, p. 387.

[2] *The Religions of Authority and the Religion of the Spirit*, Eng. tr., London, 1904, p. 338.

[3] See artt. AUGUSTINE; CHURCH, DOCTRINE OF THE (Roman Catholic), and cf. 'Ego . . . evangelio non crederem, nisi me catholicae ecclesiae commoveret auctoritas' (*Contra Ep. Manich.* v. 6).

[1] See art. ALEXANDRIAN THEOLOGY and Allen, ch. i.

spirit of Tertullian's *Prescription of Heresy* always hostile to heretical thought[1] and the independent activities of reason, owed to Greek theology the intellectual gift, the philosophic insight and accuracy of definition, the logical subtlety and lucidity by which alone the truth could be established on a firm basis. It owed its symbols and the power of defending them, its doctrine, and its apologetic to Greek theology; but the findings of Greek theology were held to be valid only when enforced by its authority. Without the benediction of the hierarchy, no truth, no new conception of truth, could be tolerated. Indeed, there were certain principles of Greek thought, such as the essential kinship of man with God, which the Western Church has never regarded with complete conviction; rather it has clung to the conception of the infinite distance between the human and the divine which was characteristic of the theology of Antioch. It has to be remembered that, when Greek theology passed into the Western Church, new peoples and races were coming to the front and were eventually to be won to Christianity; hence the method of presenting the simpler type of Christian thought based on Church authority, rather than the more intellectual and philosophic aspects of the truth, might be justified on grounds of expediency. It remains true, however, that the earlier Greek theology of the Alexandrian type has never really rooted itself in the consciousness of the Latin Church; its breadth and universality of vision, its synthesis of the human and divine, has illuminated but not transformed the dogmatic teaching of Catholicism. With Clement and Origen Rome has shown less affinity than with the pseudo-Dionysius. The *Celestial Hierarchy* (translated by John Scotus Erigena), with its ranges of angelic intermediaries between God on the one hand and the bishops and deacons of the Church and finally common humanity on the other, and with its path to God by the practice of Oriental asceticism, was the very negation of the sane and logical teaching of the Christian Platonists of Alexandria.

(*b*) *Mediæval period: scholasticism.*—The age of Charlemagne marked a low stage of religious thought, although the culture of John Scotus Erigena,[2] based on his knowledge of Greek and in particular of Plato and Origen, enabled him to produce a philosophy of religion far ahead of his times. Alcuin of York was a popular teacher, but he was not an original theologian and has a larger place in the history of the Roman liturgy as a compiler of the Lectionary and works of private devotion. It is significant that in the 9th cent. the dogma of transubstantiation[3] first became the subject of formal discussion. Neither Cyprian nor Tertullian was an exponent of a materialistic conception of the Lord's Supper, while Augustine held that its benefits were available only for the elect. To the monk Paschasius Radbertus, who wrote about 831 a treatise *De Corpore et Sanguine Domini*, belongs the credit of introducing the view that the presence of Christ was not in the soul of the worshipper but in the eucharistic elements. On the other hand, the early Middle Ages had rejected the image-worship of the degenerate East, and it was at a later period, when society was in the state of confusion and unrest caused by the invasions of Huns and Northmen, Danes and Saxons, that a reaction in favour of the Church as the one stable institution and refuge in a world of chaos took place: the great cathedrals were built; gifts of nobles and people were lavished on majestic Gothic temples; art ministered to religious devotion in music, in the impressive ritual and fair pageantries of worship, in the composition of hymns like the *Dies Iræ* and the *Stabat Mater*,[1] which broke with the classic models of poetry, and in the mysteries and miracle-plays staged within the sacred walls. Above all, the scholastic theology of which Anselm[2] was the intellectual offspring expressed the wide-spread feeling that the dogma and ritual of the Church must be harmonized with the intellect and adjusted to the conscience of mankind. If monasticism fostered piety and devotion, scholasticism in schools and universities endeavoured to establish the Christian Church and its doctrine on an intellectual basis. Abelard (*q.v.*) resisted the blind acceptance of traditional dogmas, while sects like the Cathari and Waldenses (*q.v.*) upheld the principle that the Spirit of God was not limited in its operations to the Church but illuminated the soul of man. The supporters of the authority of the Church became alarmed by the prevalence of such teaching. The condemnation of Abelard at the instance of the saintly Bernard of Clairvaux was upheld by the Council of the Lateran (1215), which formally decreed the dogma of transubstantiation. Fourteen years later the Council of Toulouse declared it a sin for the laity to possess a Bible or to read the Psalter or the Breviary in the vernacular. *The Book of Sentences* by Peter the Lombard became the accepted standard of orthodoxy. And finally Thomas Aquinas (*q.v.*) took up the task of reconciling faith and reason and, as a counterblast to the Platonism of Scotus Erigena and Abelard, called to his aid the *a posteriori* method of Aristotle.[3] Rejecting the philosophy which had always produced rationalism—so he believed—by its search for reality in an ideal realm, he based his argument on the views of a thinker to whom reality lay in the actual physical universe. To Thomas Aquinas the ground of truth was in the visible Church, the sole channel of salvation, and in its dogmatic system with its corollaries of transubstantiation, purgatory, and indulgences.[4] The Roman Church has never abandoned the Thomist theology; and whenever, as in this generation, the human reason, curious of the secrets of the universe and enlightened by new discoveries and new aspects of truth, strives to relate traditional dogmas to the larger knowledge won by science and historical research, the papal authority bases its defence of accepted truth on the conclusions of the *Summa Theologiæ*.[5]

(*c*) *The Reformation Age to modern times: Protestantism, Rationalism, Modernism.* — The attempt of Aquinas to compromise with reason came too late. Reason, which had been flouted and repressed, took its revenge. The papacy had flourished on the ignorance of the masses. It had built itself up on a distrust of humanity, which was believed to be unequal to self-government and to stand in need of a controlling visible authority. In the dark ages, let it be admitted, there were grounds for this view of mankind. The world was in the melting-pot. The Church ministered to a great need. By the Crusades it introduced men to new lands and gave them knowledge of other nations than their own; by the worship of relics it cherished a vivid consciousness of the past; by the veneration of the saints it contributed to human reverence; by its art and ritual it ennobled and enlightened personality; by monasticism it ministered to the soul of the individual and recognized its claims; and by scholasticism it quickened the processes of the human mind. But a new order had arisen, and the Church, which had

1 See art. HERESY (Christian). 2 See art. SCHOLASTICISM.
3 See artt. EUCHARIST, SACRAMENTS (Christian, Western), and SACRAMENTS (Christian, Lutheran).

1 See art. HYMNS (Latin Christian).
2 See art. ANSELM OF CANTERBURY.
3 See artt. REALISM, ARISTOTLE, ARISTOTELIANISM.
4 See art. PENANCE (Roman Catholic).
5 Cf. the encyclical *Pascendi* of 1907.

conferred indisputable benefits on the world, was found unequal to the opportunity. The world had widened; new nations and new languages had appeared. Latin was no longer a medium of communication for the Western world. Wyclif's translation of the Scriptures into homely English had opened the way to a new authority. The Bible, not the Church, was the source of revelation. Mysticism, whether of the Frankish saints belonging to the order of St. Victor, who used the tender and almost voluptuous imagery of love, or of the German saints like Eckhart and Tauler, whose expositions were cast in a sterner and more ethical mould, impressed on the world the truths of the immediate intuition of God by the soul and the divine immanence. The air of Europe was alive with new currents of spiritual and intellectual power. Even prior to the fall of Constantinople in 1453, when Greek scholarship and learning sought a fresh habitation in the cities of Europe, the Renaissance had inaugurated in Italy under Petrarch and Boccaccio the cult of beauty and classical literature and evoked a new sense of the many-sided interest of the present life—in a word, the humanism which was henceforth not only to transform the intellectual and ethical life of society as a whole but also to modify the Christian outlook on the world and the course of Christian thought and theology. It was on the intellectual side an expression of the individualism which within the realm of the spirit ecclesiasticism had failed to quench. By the work of Wyclif and Hus, by evangelical movements like that of the Waldensians, by the mysticism of the cloister and the pulpit and lay-societies such as the 'Friends of God' in Germany,[1] the individual soul had expressed its spiritual conviction and ideals and the way had been prepared for a revolution in Christian thought. Luther[2] entered into the heritage won for spiritual freedom by Wyclif and Hus, the latter of whom had died for the rights of conscience. The Reformation was not a break but a fresh stage in the evolution of Christianity. It was the re-assertion of vital principles of faith which had found expression from time to time in the history of the Church from the days of St. Paul onwards. In essence, the position taken up by Luther was not the negative conviction that certain abuses which called for destruction had crept into the Church: he declared afresh the positive conditions of human salvation. He began with the people, not the cloister, nor the hierarchy. It is true that he rejected the claims of Rome as the primal and absolute authority upon whose will depended the destiny of the soul; but his rejection arose from his broad and clear conception of the value of the individual soul. His emphasis on justification by faith was in effect a plea for human rights—the right of access to God and the right of communion with Him as the condition of ultimate salvation. In other words, Luther came into conflict with the Latin Church because it was founded on ideas repugnant to the Christian conscience. The practice of selling indulgences by which the sinner obtained remission of the 'temporal' penalties of his offence was to him only one among many results of the false assumptions on which Rome based her claims, viz. the supreme authority of the episcopate as constituting the Church and the denial of spiritual privilege to the laity (*q.v.*). He opposed the fatal distinction which the Mediæval Church had emphasized between things divine and human as inherently incompatible with each other —the distinction which had created the opposites, Church and State, clergy and people, nature and grace. It followed, if this dualism was erroneous, that a layman had the power to interpret the written revelation which hitherto had been claimed as a priestly prerogative. Finally, from these premisses flowed the truth of private judgment (*q.v.*)—a position upon which Melanchthon temporized when he appealed for the retention of a visible authority while admitting its human origin. In Switzerland Zwingli (*q.v.*) and Calvin[1] were the outstanding personalities of the new movement. The former by his emphasis on the divine immanence re-affirmed the standpoint of Greek theology, and he was Greek in his denial of original sin, in his assertion of the salvability of the heathen, and in his doctrine of the sacraments as symbolic and memorial. Calvin stood for order and discipline, and founded a Church the polity of which took root in Scotland, the Netherlands, in Germany, in Switzerland, in France among the Huguenots, and in England among the Puritans. He held that the Church consisted of the elect and that the clergy were endowed by the Holy Spirit in ordination with powers which gave them authority over the people. It was, however, less as an ecclesiastical administrator than as a theologian that he left his mark upon the world. His rigid insistence on the verbal inspiration of Scripture, his theory of the fall and election, his rejection of the doctrine of immanence, his assertion of the divine sovereignty which rendered God remote from nature and humanity and made progress depend on His arbitrary will, are the familiar elements of his theology. As compared with Zwingli, he continued the Latin tradition, but, on the other hand, he was essentially Protestant in his doctrine of the individual who, though his conscience was controlled by the clergy, yet owed his ultimate destiny to the sovereign majesty of God—a theory which made for human freedom and was destructive of clerical tyranny, while it disposed at once of the customs of image-worship and Mariolatry and brought to the profession of the Christian a robust ethical standard based on the teaching and example of Christ. As Thomism was wrought into the texture of Dante's *Divina Commedia*, Calvinism received a majestic setting in the epic of Milton, while Bunyan made an appeal alike to the humblest and to the most enlightened intellects by his immortal delineation of the Reformed theology in the *Pilgrim's Progress*.[2]

Protestantism left its mark on Catholicism by producing the kindred movements of Jansenism (*q.v.*) and Gallicanism (*q.v.*), the former for ever to be associated with Pascal as the latter was thenceforth to be distinguished by the great name of Bossuet. Pascal (*q.v.*) opposed the Jesuits with much of the Calvinistic fighting spirit and stands in the line of Augustine and Calvin as a theologian, though at heart a melancholy sceptic who never succeeded in harmonizing his beliefs with the dictates of reason and conscience. Calvinistic Protestantism had left to Christian thought the necessity of defending the Scriptures in an age of cold and unsparing rationalism. The *Augsburg Confession* (1530) and the *Institutes* of Calvin had proclaimed Scripture to be the very word of God —in fact it was the infallible external authority by which Protestantism had superseded the authority of Rome. The 18th century, the age of Voltaire and Rousseau in France and of the English deists,[3] notwithstanding its opposing tendencies—Cambridge Platonism (*q.v.*) upholding the divinity of reason, natural theology contesting the supremacy of revealed religion, new scientific discoveries revealing the reign of law in nature, the attack on the miraculous elements of Christian truth—was not wholly the barren and unspiritual

[1] See artt. Friends of God, Deutsch-Katholicismus.
[2] See artt. Luther, Reformation, Protestantism.

[1] See art. Calvinism, and Allen, *op. cit.* p. 287 f.
[2] See art. Bunyan.
[3] See art. Deism and Allen, p. 287 f.

epoch which it is often supposed to have been. The controversy aided the progress of vital Christianity in the sense that the deists were really preparing the ground for a sounder and more rational conception of the divine nature and government, while their opponents remained loyal to the truth of a divine revelation which had been made directly to the human soul. In fact, the evangelical revival under Whitefield and Wesley[1] provided a memorable and impressive demonstration of the truth which the orthodox apologists had propounded, by bringing to the soul of the 'common people' a divine salvation and assurance of pardon which were declared to be available for simple faith. The 'saving faith,' which enabled the sinner by immediate contact with God to find peace and the strength for a new life of ethical holiness, was the mighty note upon which a renascence of spiritual religion sounded abroad its message of hope for a world in transition.

The Illuminism of Germany[2] may also be claimed as a renascence of the spirit, if on intellectual lines, by virtue of its proclamation of the gospel that the moral consciousness is divinely inspired, and that the Divine Spirit, acting through the letter of Scripture but not bound to it, is universally revealing Himself in history. But the witness of Lessing (1729–81) was of less value as an exposition of the Christian view of history than that of a greater thinker, Schleiermacher (*q.v.*), to whom belongs the credit of originating the critical method as applied to Scripture and religion. His clear grasp of the solidarity of the race, his disbelief in the individualism of Protestant and Catholic as expressed in the doctrines of election and probation, his loyalty to the Church as an institution which expressed the idea that man is saved as the member of a redeemed family, and his conception of the progressiveness of revelation place him in the succession of Greek theologians as they make him the most formative of the Christian thinkers of the last century. His firm conviction of the immanence of God powerfully affected the art, literature, philosophy, and science of the 19th century. Romanticism, the poetry of Wordsworth and Shelley, the truth of evolution as expounded by Darwin, the art of Turner and his interpreter Ruskin, the Christian socialism of Maurice (*q.v.*) and Kingsley, Hegelianism,[3] and the Neo-Hegelianism (*q.v.*) of the Cairds and T. H. Green (*q.v.*)—all these phases and movements indicate the prevalence of a new spirit. The Victorian Age was in effect a period of revolt. The triumph of the critical and scientific method was not less marked in the realm of theology than in other fields of knowledge. De Maistre[4] (1754–1821) in France and John Henry Newman (*q.v.*), from quite different standpoints, opposed what appeared to them the deadly liberalism of Christian thought. Tractarianism resulted in a revival of mediæval practice and ritual in the worship of the Church of England; but Anglo-Catholicism has never, like Roman Catholicism, repudiated the methods and results of modern criticism. Mediævalism in the Anglican Church has shown itself in ecclesiastical observance and in a revival of the Catholic view of the continuity of orders and ecclesiastical tradition, but the Erastianism of the English Church has been a safeguard against the triumph of a narrow orthodoxy and has in fact aided the forces of liberal thought. As we have already seen, the Roman Church under Pius IX. and his successors has shown itself impervious to the newer currents of theological thought. The critical method is anathema to Rome. Science, comparative religion, psychology, have their place in the world, but are banned by the infallible fiat of the Church, whenever Catholic dogma is subjected to the test of their new light.

Newman paved the way to Modernism (*q.v.*)—the name given by Pope Leo XIII. (1878–1903) to the liberalizing movement within the Roman Church—by his famous *Essay on the Development of Christian Doctrine* (1845, new ed. 1878), but the logical issues of his attempt to bridge the chasm between Protestantism and Catholicism were repudiated by the papal see when they were expounded by Alfred Loisy and George Tyrrell. Pius X. (1903–14) in his decree *Lamentabili* (July 1907) condemned the 60 propositions in which he summed up the Modernist doctrine, and by his encyclical *Pascendi* shortly afterwards reasserted the scholastic dogmas of the Middle Ages as the necessary faith of a true Catholic.

The drift to Rome of individual mediævalists within the Anglican pale will continue, but there are no signs of any approach to reunion between Rome and Anglicanism, the validity of whose orders received contemptuous rejection in the bull *Apostolicæ Curæ* (1906). Roman Catholicism and the Holy Orthodox Church remain disjoined, apparently without the slightest sign of a possible reconciliation. In the Reformed and Protestant Churches the cause of intellectual and religious freedom has triumphed beyond the reach of reaction, while there are symptoms both in England and in Scotland of a growing movement towards reunion—in England taking the form of a proposed federation of the Free Churches, which inherit the Protestant tradition, while in Scotland the union of the Established Church and the United Free Church is widely desired and anticipated. Generally speaking, among such Churches the necessary re-adjustments of religious thought and restatements of doctrine are likely to be carried through without any controversial strain, while the authority of the Scriptures will be associated with a more profound and broader view of the Spirit of Truth as 'the Lord and Giver of Life,' not only to the writers and 'holy men' of the Scripture dispensations, but to all the saints of Christ in all ages and in the future. Already with this larger conception of revelation as the perpetual work of a controlling Spirit who is the eternal source of light amidst the fluctuations of dogmas, institutions, and forms, the religious outlook of Western Christendom has tended to a clearer vision of the social and spiritual needs of humanity. The reaction of the European War, which has affected nearly every country in the world, has deepened the sense of international solidarity and has created the ideal of a League of Nations. Whether this new vision of brotherhood will result in a new synthesis of the rival ideals of Catholic and Protestant remains to be seen. For the moment the vision of a new Catholicism of Christendom appears to be both less convincing and less capable of realization than that of a political League of Nations. The old Catholicism, in the sense of ecclesiasticism, is dead or dying. So long as Rome claims absorption into her fold as the price of Christian reunion and so long as she asserts her mediæval standard of authority, she will stand outside the progressive movements of social and spiritual thought. The trend of the modern mind is against any external authority, whether of pope or priesthood or sacred book; and this is in effect a reaction against the extravagant claims which both Catholic and Protestant have put forth on behalf of their respective standards of authority—claims which offend the moral consciousness and intellect of mankind. Nevertheless, the Holy Catholic Church and the written Word

1 See artt. EVANGELICALISM, METHODISM.
2 See artt. ENCYCLOPÆDISTS, ENLIGHTENMENT, LESSING.
3 See art. HEGEL.
4 Cf. his work *Du Pape*², Lyons, 1819.

alike reveal the directing and controlling authority of the Spirit of Truth: the one proclaims the reality of the *consensus sanctorum*—the community of experience and witness—in the life of Christendom; the other declares the reality of God's perpetual self-revelation in the history of the race. In this corporate and individual response to the Spirit of God, of which both the Scriptures and the Church as an institution are witnesses, is to be found the ground of our hope for mankind. The future lies with the religion of the Spirit of Christ which under many forms of worship, systems of discipline and organization, with interpretations and settings suited to the various peoples of the world, will yet embody the Christian idea. The essence of Christianity is not to be confined to this or that dogma, creed, or institution, but is at once a spiritual experience and an activity of love—a kingdom of heaven within—inspired by the unifying control of the Spirit of Truth over the individual and collective consciousness of mankind. However desirable the consummation of an organic union of Christendom may be to many minds, a review of the history of the Church affords but scanty support to the idea that this result is attainable, or that, granting the possibility of its attainment, it would minister to the highest welfare of humanity. On the other hand there is a wide-spread and growing assent to the interpretation of both Scripture and history which favours a unity that will be not less real because it will co-exist with diversity —the ἑνότης πνεύματος for which St. Paul intercedes —the oneness given by the Divine Spirit who at once overrules and is immanent within the whole body of the faithful upon earth.

LITERATURE.—The leading authorities have already been given under articles referred to above. For the general history of the Western Church the reader should consult lists under artt. CHRISTIANITY, PAPACY, CHURCH; for doctrine CHURCH, DOCTRINE OF (Roman Catholic), CREEDS, CONFESSIONS, and special phases under their own heading—*e.g.*, ARIANISM, NESTORIANISM, etc.; for worship SACRAMENTS (Christian, Western), EUCHARIST, etc.; for law LAW (Christian, Western). In a useful chapter entitled 'Bibliographical Suggestions' in Williston Walker, *A Hist. of the Christian Church*, Edinburgh, 1919, the reader will find the most recent literature in Church History indicated and classified.

R. MARTIN POPE.

WHEEL.—See JEWEL (Buddhist), PRAYER-WHEELS.

WHEEL OF THE LAW.—This Buddhist expression is derived from the earlier Buddhist legend of the Mystic Wheel. This legend, or edifying fairy tale, is told in almost identical terms in several of the most ancient Buddhist documents.[1] It is none the less essentially Buddhist because several details (the ethical, not the essential ones) can be traced back to details in one or other of the pre-Buddhistic sun-myths. The Wheel is said to be one of the treasures of a righteous king who rules in righteousness; and it is because of that righteousness that the Wheel appears. The legend says:

'When he [*i.e.* the king; the names of course differ] had gone up on to the upper storey of his palace on the sacred day, the day of the full moon, and had purified himself to keep the sacred day, there then appeared to him the heavenly treasure of the Wheel, with its nave, its tire, and all its thousand spokes complete.

Then the king arose from his seat, and reverently uncovering his robe from his right shoulder, he held in his left hand a pitcher and with his right he sprinkled water over the Wheel, as he said: "Roll onward, O my lord the Wheel! O my Lord, go forth and overcome."

Then the wondrous Wheel rolled onward toward the region of the East. And, after it, went the king with his fourfold army (cavalry and chariots, war-elephants and men). And wheresoever the Wheel stopped, there too the king stayed, and with him all his army in its fourfold array.

Then all the rival kings in the region of the East came to the king and said: "Come on, O mighty king! Welcome, O mighty king! All is thine, O mighty king! Do thou, O mighty king, be a Teacher to us!"

And the king said: "Ye shall slay no living thing. Ye shall not take that which has not been given. Ye shall not act wrongly touching the bodily desires. Ye shall speak no lie. Ye shall drink no maddening drink. And ye may still enjoy such privileges as ye have had of yore."[1]

Then all the rival kings in the region of the East became subject to the king. And the wondrous Wheel having plunged down into the great waters in the East, rose up out again, and rolled onward to the South . . . and to the West . . . and to the North [and all happened in each region as had happened in the region of the East].

Now when the wondrous Wheel had gone forth conquering and to conquer over the whole earth to its very ocean boundary, it returned back again to the royal city and remained fixed on the open terrace in front of the entrance to the inner apartments of the great king, shedding glory over them all.'[2]

So far the appearance and work of the Wheel. In another passage we are told that on the approach of the death of the righteous king the Wheel falls from its place, and on his death or abdication disappears. Should the successor carry on the Law of the Wheel, it will reappear and act as before, and this may continue for generations. But, should any successor fail in righteous rule, then the country will fall gradually into utter ruin, and remain so for generations till the Law of the Wheel has been revived. Then only will the Wheel reappear and with it wealth and power and the happiness of the people. All this is set out at length in the *Chakka-vatti Sīha-nada Suttanta.*

The *Chakka-vatti*, literally the 'Wheel-turner,' and by implication the ruler who conducts himself (and whose subjects therefore conduct themselves) according to the Law of the Wheel, is the technical term for the righteous king or over-lord. It has not been found in any pre-Buddhistic literature; and, though it is so frequent in later books, it has, in Hindu works, lost its ethical connotation, and simply means a war-lord, a mighty emperor, 'one who unhindered drives the wheels of his chariot over all lands.' But it should be noticed that the wondrous Wheel of the Buddhist legend is not really a chariot wheel. The idea of sovereignty is no doubt linked up with it. The Wheel, however, is a single disk, not one of a pair. And it is very clear that it is really a reminiscence, not of a chariot wheel, but of the disk of the sun, which travels over all lands from sea to sea and sheds glory over all. By the pouring of new wine into the old bottles, it is the sun-god himself, transmuted into a forerunner of the king of righteousness, whose rule of life brings happiness to all.

This is the legend made use of to give a title to the doctrine of the reign of law, the basis of the reformation we call Buddhism and which the leaders of that reformation called 'the Law.' The discourse summarizing this doctrine, the first discourse delivered by the founder of the new movement, is entitled 'The Setting in Motion onwards of the Wheel of Law' (*Dhamma-chakkappavattana*). The allusion is to the action of the king of righteousness in the foregoing legend when he baptizes the Wheel, and exhorts it to roll onward, to go forth and overcome. The allusion is apt; and it gains both in poetry and in its appeal to the mental attitude of the time by the irony with which it enlists the service of the ancient and repudiated sun-god in the propagation of the Buddha's doctrine that the gods too are under the domain of law. Just so was Brahmā made into a convert to the new teaching, and the old god of war and drink, the mighty Indra, had been transmuted into the peace-loving and sober Sakka, devoted to the doctrine of the reign, not of divine whim, but of law.

Very naturally the early European writers on Buddhism, ignorant of the legend of the Wheel,

[1] *E.g.*, the *Mahā Sudassana Suttanta, Dīgha*, ii. 172; the *Chakka-vatti Sīha-nāda Suttanta, Dīgha*, iii. 61.

[1] On this phrase see *Dialogues of the Buddha*, ii. 203; *Kindred Sayings*, i. 15.

[2] *Dialogues of the Buddha*, ii. 202–204.

and ignorant also of the doctrine of the reign of law, completely failed to understand this curious title of the oldest summary of the new teaching. It would be wearisome to point out all their mistakes. Perhaps the worst of the many blunders is the identification of the Wheel with what Anglo-Indian writers call, quite erroneously, the praying-wheels of Tibet. They are not so called by any authority, Tibetan or Buddhist. They are not praying-wheels, but wheels of good luck, containing an invocation to some deity—the contrary therefore to the old doctrine of the Wheel. We may learn some day what the original meaning in Tibetan of *Oṁ maṇi padme Hūm* really was. The phrase is not likely to be less than about 1400 years later than the time of the Buddha. And it is most unlikely that, after that long lapse of time, any memory of the legend of the Wheel or of its adoption to the title of the First Discourse had still survived. To judge from what we know of Lāmaism, the Tibetans had quite forgotten that, in early Buddhism, the reign of gods had been superseded by the reign of law (or, to express the same fact in modern technical terms, that animism had given way to normalism).

It remains to add that some centuries after the canon had closed we find also another use of the figure or simile of the wheel. Only the wheel is here, not the disk of the sun, but a chariot wheel. The figure is used of the circle or cycle of rebirths. Mrs. Rhys Davids has pointed out the use of this simile in Greek and Sanskrit,[1] and it has since then been discovered in Pāli.[2] This is in harmony with the doctrine of the Wheel of Law in early Buddhism, but it is a supplementary idea, and has a different origin, and is never called the Wheel of the Law. It is *samsāra-chakka*, not *dhamma-chakka.*

LITERATURE.—*Dīgha Nikāya*, ed. T. W. Rhys Davids and J. E. Carpenter (*PTS*), Oxford, 1890–1911; T. W. Rhys Davids, *Dialogues of the Buddha*, do. 1899–1910; C. A. F. Rhys Davids, *Kindred Sayings (PTS)*, do. 1917, *Buddhism*, London (Home University Library, no date); *Visuddhi Magga*, ed. Mrs. Rhys Davids (*PTS*), 1920.

T. W. RHYS DAVIDS.

WIDOW.—See MARRIAGE, SATĪ.

WIFE.—See MARRIAGE.

WILL.—The word 'will' (Gr. βούλησις, Lat. *voluntas*, Germ. *Wille*, *Wollen*, Fr. *volonté*) is used in a wide variety of senses by philosophical and psychological writers. In the widest sense it means all the 'active powers' which the Aristotelian bipartite division in psychology contrasted with the 'intellectual,' and so includes all striving, appetition, and interest, even at an infraconscious level. In the narrowest sense it is taken to mean, or at least to imply, deliberate and responsible choice.

1. Physiological basis.—The analysis of will in the widest sense requires the analysis of the physiology of movement. Physiologists base their conceptions upon reflex action, and then discuss the integration of reflexes in the brain and spinal cord. The unit of this explanation is the simple reflex. The stimulation of an end-organ *must* issue in movement, and a simple reflex is the simplest possible response of an organism to stimulation. The simplicity of a simple reflex, however, is the result of analysis rather than a fact of observation. What we find in fact is a combination of reflexes into reflex patterns of various kinds.

All reflexes take place through a chain or arc of neurons which passes through the central nervous system, and it is important to notice the differences between the stimulation of a bare nerve-trunk and of a reflex arc. The latter shows slower speed, a marked 'after-discharge,' irreversibility of direction, greater liability to fatigue, notable inhibition, and 'refractory phase,' together with a very marked response to cumulative stimulation where the stimuli are too weak to lead to movement severally. These differences, taken conjointly, show that reflex action, so far from being a mere conduit of nervous discharge, is, even in its simplest form, a kind of response in which the organism counts for more than the stimulus.

Simple reflexes are allied when two or more work together. They alternate, *e.g.*, in the rhythmic contraction of the flexor and extensor muscles in walking. They compensate one another, inhibit one another, and form reflex patterns of great variety. The main points to notice about them, however, are (1) the way in which they reinforce one another in their conjoint eventual discharge through a final common path, and (2) the co-ordination of them in time. The first phenomenon is so marked that some observers believe that reflex patterns work on the 'all or nothing' principle. The second appears in its primary form in the successive stimulation of antagonistic reflexes, and many physiologists suppose this temporal co-ordination to be the principal office of the central nervous system.

This general conception applies to all reflex movements, and its connexion with will becomes manifest when we consider the relation between the nerve-endings specially adapted to the reception of distant stimuli and the muscles of the skeletal system. These skeletal muscles (with unimportant exceptions) are the voluntary ones, and they are intimately connected with senses like sight or hearing which are affected by stimuli from a relatively distant point of origin. It is easy to interpret these facts in a way that has great significance for the economy of organic behaviour. To use Sherrington's terms, while some reflexes are 'consummatory,' those connected with the skeletal muscles are for the most part 'precurrent.' They do not enjoy, but anticipate. The union between sight and the skeletal muscles enables the animal to adapt itself in advance. The end of its action, to be sure, is consummatory, swallowing or being swallowed; but the means to this end is a preparation in the way of movement —crouching, stalking, running, leaping. It is significant in this regard that the head is the organ of the 'distant' senses and of balance. For the head is the rudder of the body, and it steers the quicker in proportion as the path of the nervous impulse to the brain is shorter.

Psychology is concerned with consciousness, first and foremost, and the reasonable inference from this evidence is that consciousness continues the work of the nervous system. Pleasure gives an added zest to action; pain is the body's spur to release from its distress. Consciousness, again, implies a certain 'togetherness' of experiencing. A certain minimum of memory is held together in our consciousness, and this acquired experience is at the behest of action. Consciousness, once again, is most acute in connexion with the organs of exploration, and the connexion between eye or ear or finger-tip and the skeletal or voluntary muscles indicates that consciousness widens the range of precurrent adjustments especially in point of time.

2. Instinctive action.—The theory of impulse and instinct is the natural corollary to this account of neural integration. The connexion between reflexes and impulses or appetites is plainly very close indeed, and instincts are the great racial patterns of co-ordinated action. The moor-hen has a diving 'set' in its muscles when it is little

[1] *Visuddhi Magga* (*PTS*), 1920, p. 198.

[2] *JRAS*, 1894, p. 388; cf. also Mrs. Rhys Davids, *Buddhism*, p. 98, and art. PAṬICCA-SAMUPPĀDA, vol. ix. p. 674.

more than a fledgling, and it dives as soon as cause and opportunity offer.

The question how far human action or the action of the higher animals is fundamentally instinctive is still hotly debated, but the debate tends to become verbal since the partisans of the instincts insist upon the indefinite pliability of these responses, while their opponents try to narrow instincts down to mere racial routine. The other point in the dispute is the relation of nature to nurture, and this also is a thorny topic which a wise man leaves alone. It is clear, however, that most human activities, whether or not they have become habitual, are acquired in individual experience (even if they are grafted upon a primitive instinctive root), and all these problems are highly speculative in comparison with the fact of the reflective adaptation of human beings to their circumstances. Again, there is another reason why the analysis of will suffers when psychologists devote themselves exclusively to speculative theories concerning the instincts. However important the instincts may be, and however closely allied with normal human perception and action, the consciousness in instinctive behaviour does not differ in kind from acquired or from reflective consciousness, and its principal features cannot be discerned so readily at the instinctive level of consciousness as at others. It is best, therefore, to try to give a direct psychological analysis of the consciousness in ordinary human action.

3. Ideo-motor theory.—Probably the simplest type of conscious action is that which is called ideo-motor. This occurs when the thought of a movement leads directly (so far as consciousness is concerned) to the execution of the movement. A great many movements need no other explanation. Those who take the injunction 'Kill that fly!' seriously begin hostilities as soon as they see the fly; and 'Eight o'clock and time to get up' is frequently a sufficient and the only mental prelude to getting out of bed in the morning.

These instances show that the idea of a movement tends of itself to the execution of the movement, and some psychologists, generalizing somewhat hastily, have concluded that all voluntary action is ideo-motor and nothing else. According to this theory, we learn from impulse, instinct, imitation, and random muscular play what movements can be executed. The immediate antecedent of any movement which is consciously directed, however, is the temporary dominance in our consciousness of the idea of that movement; and this idea is always the cause of the movement.

This theory is plausible because the idea of a future action is a *sine qua non* of voluntary action of any kind, but there are serious objections to it. (1) Our ideas of movement are usually suffused with feeling and tense with conscious endeavour. It is a mistake, therefore, to suppose that these feelings, desires, and strivings do not play their part as directly and as effectually as the bare idea of movement. (2) There is universal testimony to prove that much of our action does not seem to be merely ideo-motor. The bare idea of movement is sometimes merely an idea. We may have to strive most resolutely to bring ourselves to the point of acting—*i.e.*, we may have to reinforce the idea by endeavouring after its end. And sometimes we have to choose between several conflicting ideas of movement simultaneously present to minds.

Since the ideo-motor theory does not dispute these facts (it would not be worth considering if it did), it has to provide an alternative explanation, and so it maintains that striving or choice in these cases secures the temporary dominance of some particular idea of movement. The only possible cause of conscious action, according to this way of it, is a man's temporary single-mindedness towards the idea of the action, and his temporary oblivion of all else. Choice or striving influences the action at second remove, and causes the temporary dominance of the idea of the action.

This theory is unnecessarily complicated. We seem to ourselves to choose this or that, and not merely to attend to some idea of movement exclusively; and there is no good reason why this seeming should not be actuality. Again, the idea of our chosen course of action often does not seem to be the only alternative before the mind either at the time of choosing or afterwards, even granting that we ought to stick to our plan, after we have adopted it, on pain of inefficiency or Hamlet-like vacillation. It is false in fact, therefore, that conscious action is always preceded by this exclusive possession of consciousness. Moreover, this theory is just an attempt to save the 'strongest motive' theory with as little violence as may be. It is assumed that action must be due to the 'strongest motive'; and therefore the motive which immediately precedes the action is assumed to be either predominant or else the only one present; but this argument is circular, since there is no way of telling which motive is the strongest except by saying, *après coup*, that it was *the* motive of the action which followed in fact. Again, even if this theory could account for most specific voluntary movements, it would still be too narrow for voluntary choice as a whole. When a barrister resolves to make out a case for his client, or a journalist tries to discover the gist of Einstein's theory or of Ludendorff's influence, the movements they make in the way of speaking, writing, or travel are quite subsidiary in importance. And the ideo-motor theory simply omits these cases. Movements are seldom chosen for their own sakes. They are usually chosen because they are means to an end, and the ideo-motor theory is so preoccupied with the means that it neglects the end altogether.

This theory, indeed, is too intellectual; for it resolves action into the automatic effect of mere thinking, and rejects the primary and direct influence of interest, passion, and striving. This mistake is not uncommon; it permeates, *e.g.*, the Benthamite theory of psychological hedonism (*q.v.*). To say, with Mill,[1] that 'happiness is the sole end of human action' may mean many things. It might mean, *e.g.*, that no one, on reflexion, judges anything to be good except his own happiness; and in that case the theory would have no bearing on unreflective action. It might also mean that the anticipation of pleasure is the only possible motive for action. This form of the argument is required as a premiss in many of the utilitarian arguments, and it is preposterously false. In impulsive or instinctive action, *e.g.*, the impulse comes first, and the gratification follows; and the baulked dispositions which are the root of psychasthenia (in nine cases out of ten) must exist before there is pain in the baulking of them.

4. Reason and will.—On the other hand, many theories are not intellectual enough, for they take volition to be an affair of impulse or desire, and they leave no place for reflexion, except the recognition of means and the discovery of bad reasons for some sentimental or impulsive *parti pris*. Most of the modern theories of this type, it is

[1] Bentham's argument (*Introd. to the Principles of Morals and Legislation*, ch. i. § 1) is even more explicitly fallacious. 'Nature,' he says, 'has placed mankind under the governance of two sovereign masters, pain and pleasure. It is for them alone to point out what we ought to do, as well as to determine what we shall do. On the one hand the standard of right and wrong, on the other the chain of causes and effects are fastened to their throne. They govern us in all we do, in all we say, in all we think: every effort we can make to throw off our subjection, will serve but to demonstrate and confirm it.'

true, do not seem to have descended *in linea recta* from Hume, but Hume gave what is still the clearest and the most concise expression of them.

Reason, he says, can have no original influence on the will, for reason is either the abstract demonstration of relationships or else the discovery of causes and effects. The will, however, has to do with sensible realities and not with abstract relationships; and the discovery of causes and effects cannot concern us in the least if we are indifferent to them. Hume assumes in the next place that the difference between interest and indifference is wholly identical with the presence or absence of passion, and then he argues with perfect logic that 'since reason alone can never produce any action, or give rise to volition, I infer, that the same faculty is as incapable of preventing volition, or of disputing the preference with any action or emotion.'[1] He concludes that the so-called contrast between reason and passion is really the battle between calm emotions and sudden, tempestuous ones.

There is a double fallacy in this argument. (1) Even if reason were restricted to the means to action, and if the knowledge of these causes and effects were indifferent without emotion, it would not follow that reason was ineffective when allied with emotion. (2) Reason (unless it is robbed of this function by an arbitrary definition) can discriminate the values of ends as well as ascertain the means to them. The values that are important for action, to be sure, are those which are felt with emotion and followed with conviction, but this fact does not imply that the intellectual recognition of these values is of no account.

This consequence would not follow even if all these values were themselves emotions. That, however, is not the case. The principal values which we admit to be intrinsically good are happiness, social intercourse, knowledge, beauty, and righteousness; and perhaps also the bearers of these values—Plato, who had the knowledge, Keats, who was touched with the beauty, Cato, who did what was right, and the greyhound which leaps with the joy of coursing. Most of these values are not emotions, though all are felt with emotion. And there is another point. A man's emotion is his own; and, if nothing but emotion could touch his will, the happiness of others or the honour of his country could not influence him directly. In fact, however, we do not merely judge intellectually that another's good is worth as much as ours, but we frequently choose to sacrifice our own good to his. This personal sacrifice, it is true, is sometimes superficial only. That occurs when we choose a less obvious instead of a more commonplace personal satisfaction; and the existence of non-rational but altruistic impulses and emotions certainly lessens the gap between this theory and the facts. But often we have to accept the truth that a man may sacrifice ease, culture, and leisure to undertake work which he loathes, though he knows that his own loss is certain. For the good, he thinks, constrains him.

5. Analysis of voluntary action.—We may now analyse deliberate voluntary action. Action of this kind implies knowledge of the means which are needed, choice between alternative ends, and the belief that *we* can achieve, or help to achieve, the end by adopting the means. The end, to be sure, may not be wholly attainable by us, but we believe, in that case, that we can contribute towards its attainment; and, for the rest, the thought of *will* implies the thought of *can*. No one deliberately chooses anything which he knows to be utterly out of his reach. We choose between alternatives which we believe are within our power, and our choice, in the end, is a choice between conflicting values.

The difficulties of voluntary choice are due to the false perspective which nearer values may have in comparison with more remote ones, to preoccupation with our own personal welfare and our consequent blindness towards the claims of other people, to our lack of acquaintance with many attainable values, to our ignorance concerning the means which are necessary in fact, to the difficulty of knowing for certain which consequences are most probable, to the doubt whether some means could ever justify some ends, and so on. This subject is too wide to be treated adequately here, even in outline. And there are other complications.

(1) We usually have too little time for mature reflexion. Most of our deliberations are cut short because life is brief and the need for action clamant. We have to distinguish, therefore, between voluntary action and deliberate reflective action. Voluntary action is the genus of which deliberate choice is the species. It implies the adoption of an end (the fact of 'consent') together with belief in the possibility of attaining the end; but there need not be choice between alternatives, since we may be too much pressed for time to take account of more than the first expedient that occurs to us, and our belief may be little more than a vague expectation that something may be done on the lines we have adopted.

(2) The analysis given above was restricted to the deliberate choice of a single course of action, but will is a subtler thing than this, with a wider net. When we speak of a formed will, we mean the whole character of a man so far as it can be expressed in action. A man's habits of choice pertain to his will as well as his choice on this or the other occasion, and so do his capacities and his general aims. The formed or stable will, therefore, has to be examined very carefully in connexion with physiological and instinctive dispositions on the one hand and with conscious personality on the other, and the ramifications extend very far. On the other hand, there are limits set to it through the fact of personality and its 'tunicle' the body (to use Berkeley's phrase). We have no acquaintance with any will that is superpersonal, and, in particular, we are not acquainted with any *volonté générale*. The will of society is not *a* will any more than the spirit of the times is *a* mind. The general will, so called, means (*a*) that the majority of the members of a community may resolve, or act as if they had resolved, to pursue a common end which each of them furthers in his own way; and (*b*) that each member must take account of the other members in considering the ends to be attained and the means of attaining them. More than that it should not mean.

6. Voluntarism.—The most interesting questions arising out of the theory of will are voluntarism, or the metaphysical theory that the will is sovereign over the self or the world, and the perennial problem of the freedom of the will.[1] While voluntarism has many varieties, its main contention is either that knowledge is a phase of willing (or, perhaps, subordinate to it) or else that will is the *causa essendi* of all existing things. Knowing, we are told, must be only a phase of willing, because all speculative activities are either virtual actions or else merely delayed reactions. The psychology of development, *e.g.*, shows that knowledge is a kind of virtual action. *Am Anfang war die That.* Man's earliest and most fundamental business is just to adapt himself to his environment, and so his earliest and most important knowledge is only a retainer to this fundamental need. And it is claimed that knowledge never outgrows its small-clothes. The life of nations, broadly speaking, is the application of their knowledge in the way of machinery, armaments, navigation, and government for the ultimate purpose of maintaining human subsistence as

[1] *Treatise of Human Nature*, bk. ii. pt. iii. § 3.

[1] See art. Free Will.

agreeably as possible on a large social scale. The theoretical adventures of the intellect are practical in their germ and in their fruit, and belief is either action or readiness for action.

This line of argument is obviously inconclusive. Even if it be granted that man, at the beginning, had to use all his wits to keep alive, and that most of the able-bodied members of a community have still, in a way, to co-operate for this purpose, there is plainly a huge lacuna between the premisses of this argument and its conclusion. For, even if much knowledge has to be given to the necessities of action, it does not follow that all must be given. The argument, indeed, is quite consistent with the belief that knowledge, originally a servant, may become a master and reign in its own right, or that it is possible, in an ordinary human community, for many people to spend their lives in the pursuit of knowledge for its own sake, and for all members of the community to do so at some times. And the facts seem to support this hypothesis. Those who maintain that all knowledge is only a preparation for action may be invited to say what preparation for action is implied in my knowledge that Bolingbroke wore a wig, or that Sophocles was a greater poet than Dryden, and to explain why gossipy reminiscences or intellectual curiosity concerning Chinese puzzles (to mention trivial instances only) must be 'virtual actions.' They may also be reminded that practical men need not act the worse because their information is accurate. True belief is the most useful guide to action, but some truths do not concern action directly, and it is only a quibble to say that any connexion with action, however remote, is the same thing as 'virtual action.'

Similar arguments apply to the theory that all speculation is delayed reaction and nothing else. It is true, no doubt, that there cannot be deliberate reflective choice without delay in reaction, and that deliberation is a speculative activity. But controversies with circle-squarers, *e.g.*, are not merely delayed reactions; and it is a fallacy to argue either that all speculation is only delayed reaction because some speculations imply delayed reactions, or that the speculative activities which may occur during certain delayed reactions are themselves *only* delayed reactions.

The theory that knowledge is subordinate to will is based either on psychological description or on metaphysical grounds. In the former case it is argued, as a matter of psychological fact, that knowledge is only the attempt to discover ways and means for satisfying impulses. It is sufficient to reply to this argument that these impulses may include curiosity and disinterested impulses towards knowledge for its own sake, and that, even if impulses are always the primary *causes* of knowledge, it does not follow that the effect is subordinate to the cause.

The metaphysical argument is a *non sequitur* of the same type. It maintains that effects are always subordinate to their conditions, and that will is the cause of all mental process including every piece of knowing. This principle, as we have seen, is false, and, apart from that, the premiss of the argument is highly dubious. Will, in the sense of striving or of deliberate choice, is not the sole cause of mental process in any intelligible sense. We have no right to exclude any antecedent from the list of causes of any effect if this antecedent is always present in fact, and if it always seems to play its part along with the other antecedents. And knowledge and feeling are antecedents of any mental process just as plainly as will is. This metaphysical argument, in a word, finds no support in the psychological phenomenon of will.

It may be argued, to be sure, that the scholastic maxim *Operari sequitur esse* is false, or that 'function always determines structure'; and views of this kind (usually with more enthusiasm than knowledge) may even claim kinship with certain modern theories of physics. These arguments are irrelevant, however, because voluntarism is meaningless unless it is based on the psychological phenomenon of willing. The will, as we experience it, is at best only a useful analogy for such theories; and those pluralisms which maintain that the *conatus* (or the desires and appetitions) of every existing thing is its *causa essendi* cannot claim more than a metaphorical support from the facts of will, as we find them. A spiritualistic pluralism of this kind[1] may be true in fact; and voluntarism, possibly, may be the least inept name for it, but it is not a logical consequence from the relation of willing to personality, and it becomes nothing but conjecture when this vague psychological analogy is extended to unconscious things.

LITERATURE.—On the physiology of willing: C. S. Sherrington, *The Integrative Action of the Nervous System*, London, 1906.

On ideo-motor action: W. James, *The Principles of Psychology*, London, 1891, many subsequent edd., vol. ii. ch. xxvi.; G. F. Stout, *A Manual of Psychology*³, do. 1913, bk. i. ch. ii. § 2.

On psychological hedonism: Bentham, *Introd. to the Principles of Morals and Legislation*, London, 1789 (*Works*, ed. J. Bowring, Edinburgh, 1838–43, vol. i. ch. i.); J. S. Mill, *Utilitarianism*, ch. iv. (any ed.).

On the influence of reason and emotion in willing: Hume, *Treatise of Human Nature* (ed. T. H. Green and T. H. Grose, new ed., 2 vols., London, 1888, or T. Selby-Bigge, Oxford, 1888), bk. ii. pt. iii. § 3; W. McDougall, *An Introd. to Social Psychology*⁷, London, 1913, ch. i. f.; Bertrand Russell, *Principles of Social Reconstruction*, do. 1916, ch. i.; Graham Wallas, *The Great Society: a Psychological Analysis*, do. 1914, ch. iii.

On the analysis of choice: Aristotle, *Nicomachean Ethics*, bk. iii. ch. ii.

On voluntarism: Schopenhauer, *Die Welt als Wille und Vorstellung* (any ed.), and the works, *e.g.*, of Fichte or Bergson.

On freedom of the will: art. FREE WILL.

JOHN LAIRD.

WIND, WIND-GODS.—See AIR AND GODS OF THE AIR.

WINGS (Greek and Roman).—Wings, as an attribute of animals to whom they do not properly belong, were borrowed by the Greeks from Oriental art, mostly that of Mesopotamia.[2] They probably appeared first on composite animals into which the bird form entered as an element, such as the gryphon; but they seem to have been applied almost indiscriminately to quadruped and even human forms as symbolic of divine strength and swiftness. It is doubtful, however, whether this symbolism was what attracted the early Greeks; more probably it was the decorative value of wings, as seen in Oriental carvings and woven stuffs, that first appealed to the Greek artistic sense, though they doubtless were given a symbolic meaning in later Greek art.

In the art of Crete and Mycenæ we find both gryphons and sphinxes with wings, but we have no means of judging whether these had any meaning or were merely borrowed as elements of decoration; the fact that the sphinx is female and winged suffices to show that it came from Mesopotamia and not from Egypt. But the frequent appearance of winged creatures is conspicuous in the great influx of Eastern influence, at first through the medium of the Phœnicians and later, more directly, in the 'Orientalizing' Greek vases and in decorative carvings and reliefs of a similar period. On the sub-Mycenæan vases of Cyprus are various winged animals, including centaurs (a winged centaur appears in Mesopotamia about 1200 B.C.). On the later Orientalizing pottery from Rhodes, Asia Minor, and Corinth

[1] See art. PLURALISM, § 2.
[2] See art. ART (Greek and Roman), § 3 f.

the commonest winged forms, other than birds, are the gryphon, the sphinx, human-headed birds, and human beings; winged horses are also found, especially in chariots of the gods, on Melian and other vases, and winged horses, sea-horses, boars, and other animals, such as the gryphon and sphinx, are common on the so-called 'island gems' and on early coins.

In many of these cases it is evident that the decorative value of the wings, as helping the design to fill a given field, has been paramount; but there are other examples, in which a symbolic meaning may be inferred, and where such winged forms have become the accepted type of characteristic creations of Greek myth. In most of these instances, however, the types were not invented or composed by the Greek artist to express the idea of the myth, but were adopted from foreign or borrowed forms. Thus there is no evidence that the Sirens (*q.v.*) were thought of by Homer and his contemporaries in the form assigned to them by later art; either a fancied appropriateness or a chance coincidence may sometimes have led to such identifications. The type of the human-headed bird was not, however, used only for the Sirens; it occurs constantly on tombs or in connexion with them, and appears to represent a death-dæmon. The best known instance is on the misnamed 'Harpy monument,' which, though not Greek but Lycian, shows evident affinity with Greek ideas. Here the figures in question have not only human heads and breasts, but also human arms, as well as birds' legs and talons, both of which they use to carry off the souls of the dead. Thus they show the same unnatural reduplication of limbs which we find in other winged creatures, and which the human-headed bird sometimes escapes. The wings, here as in human or quadruped winged forms, appear to grow from the shoulder-blades, and yet to work independently of the arms. Such an inorganic composition seems to confirm the view that the wings, except where they belong properly to the bird form, are borrowed from an art in which they were purely symbolic. The funereal connexion in the case of the Siren may perhaps be explained by Egyptian influence, since the human-headed bird is used in Egypt as a symbol of the soul. It is often found as the crown of a tombstone in Athens.

It is not certain that the wonder-horse, Pegasus, was at first thought of as having wings; he appears without them on an early relief; but he early adopted the winged form in which he has been familiar to all later art. Gryphons have a place in myth, since they fought with the Arimaspi in the far North; though they have beaks, their body is that of a quadruped rather than a bird, and their wings are consequently as much out of place as on a horse or lion.

What is, however, most characteristic of the Greek application of wings is their addition to the human form. This also appears first in borrowed forms, such as that of the Oriental Artemis; a similar form is that of the Gorgon, whose hideous grimacing face is set in a human body with wings; here again we have no evidence that the 'head of the terrible monster, the Gorgon,'[1] was thought of in this form by the poet of the *Odyssey*. Another shape akin to the Gorgon is the Harpy. This sometimes seems to be a death-dæmon, though the bird-like figures on the Harpy tomb are probably wrongly named. On early vases Harpies appear in completely human form, winged, and sometimes with talons or claw-like hands; there is no doubt as to identification, since the name is written beside them. These Harpies are sometimes interpreted as maleficent wind-dæmons; and this is consistent with the tale of their being chased away by the Boreads, the sons of the North Wind. Wind-gods generally appear as winged human figures, and the small winged figures that are common on early vases—*e.g.*, those of Cyrene—are probably to be interpreted thus. Boreas himself, who is represented on Attic vases and elsewhere as carrying off Oreithyia, appears as a winged, bearded man, sometimes with a mane of feathers for hair and beard.

[1] *Od.* xi. 634.

It is probable that in early Greek art such winged figures are used with many different meanings; but they come to be differentiated into two main types of constant occurrence—the winged nude male figure or Eros, and the winged draped female figure or Nike. The sculptor Archermos of Chios is said to have been the first to represent Nike with wings, and the statue in which he did this has been discovered in Delos; it represents a female figure in rapid flight, with wings not only on the shoulders, but also on the ankles. Floating figures of winged Victories, as symbolical of victory either in war or in athletic contests, are extremely common throughout Greek and Roman art. Nike was placed on the outstretched right hand of the colossal gold and ivory statues of Zeus and Athene at Olympia and Athens, by Phidias. Eros in earlier Greek art always appears as a youth of fully-grown proportions, though sometimes of diminutive size. In the Hellenistic and Roman ages he becomes the baby Cupid familiar to Renaissance and modern art, and his wings are correspondingly small. Iris, as the messenger of the gods, is usually winged, and so is hardly to be distinguished from Nike, apart from her attribute of the rainbow.

A different series of winged figures, usually diminutive, represent the souls of the dead; as such they are sometimes depicted on Attic vases as hovering about the tomb. Similarly, in the weighing of the Keres of two warriors by the gods—as of Achilles and Hector in the *Iliad*—the usual representation is of two minute winged figures placed in the scales. Homer describes them as δύο κῆρε . . . θανάτοιο,[1] and hence it seems doubtful whether the two figures are to be regarded as the souls or lives of the heroes or rather their fates of death. But the resemblance to the little souls on the vases is striking. Keres (*q.v.*) seems to vary in meaning between death-dæmons, who seem usually thought of as horrible, though not necessarily winged, and ghosts or souls of the dead, who almost always are winged. But the Psyche of later times, who is associated with Eros and has butterfly wings—sometimes even takes the shape of a butterfly—is a creation of later allegory. Death (Thanatos) often appears as a winged figure in art; on Attic funeral vases he, with his brother Sleep, often bears the deceased to the tomb. Sleep is similar to him, but beardless, while he is bearded; and both usually have similar wings growing from their shoulders. But in the beautiful figure of Sleep of the Praxitelean age the god has only a small pair of wings growing from his temples: a similar position for the wings is seen in later sentimental versions of Medusa, who has exchanged the horror of the Gorgon for a death-like beauty, and occasionally in other figures.

A variation on wings actually growing from a part of the body, head, or limbs is seen in wings that can be attached to some article of dress, and so put on and off. The most familiar example is offered by the winged sandals of Hermes, which he lends to Perseus; the notion of lending wings to the feet is also seen in the earliest Nike, and in later allegorical figures such as Kairos (Occasion). Hermes sometimes wears also wings attached to

[1] *Il.* xxii. 210.

his cap; the resemblance to wings on Scandinavian helmets is probably accidental. Wings are sometimes attached to other objects—*e.g.*, to the tripod of Apollo when he travels on it,[1] or to the chariot on which Triptolemus carries the gift of corn over the earth, or to that in which Medea escapes after her revenge on Jason. Other gods also have means of swift flight, as exemplified by Athene, when she describes how she came *πτερῶν ἄτερ ῥοιβδοῦσα κόλπον αἰγίδος*.[2]

It is with much the same associations that gods are often described as coming like birds or even taking the shape of birds. The fatal attempt of Dædalus and Icarus to fly with mechanical wings is probably to be regarded as similar magic. The desires of mankind in this direction are wittily parodied in Aristophanes' *Birds*.

In Roman art the types handed down from the Greek and Hellenistic periods frequently recur, but without any essential additions or difference. Victories, both in the round and in relief, are especially common, and are chiefly interesting as supplying the type which was later to be adopted—with change or rather absence of sex—for the angel of Christian art.

So far, though the position of wings has been noted, nothing has been said as to their shape. The wings of early decorative types are almost always curved back at the end, in a manner which, if not quite unnatural, is at least greatly exaggerated. This is a characteristic which is also found among the winged creatures of Oriental art, and is borrowed from them, but is emphasized for decorative reasons in archaic Greek art. When wings came to be applied freely by Greek artists to various figures, human and other, they naturally supplemented and corrected the conventional forms by their own observation, using especially the wings of large birds as their models, often probably those of the eagle. The wings are frequently outstretched as in flight; when lowered, they do not lie folded close to the body, as in the case of a bird, but usually project at right angles behind the back of the figure. Smaller wings show many varieties; thus, according to H. Brunn,[3] the wings on the temples of the head of Sleep are those of a night-hawk. Such variety of imagination was readily suggested by the subjects themselves.

LITERATURE.—J. Langbehn, *Flügelgestalten der ältesten griech. Kunst*, Munich, 1881; G. Weicker, *Der Seelenvogel in der alten Litt. und Kunst*, Leipzig, 1902; articles on subjects quoted above in Roscher and Daremberg-Saglio—*e.g.*, 'Sphinx,' 'Harpyia,' 'Nike,' 'Eros,' 'Keres.'

E. A. GARDNER.

WISDOM.—As distinguished from the reasoned, systematic view of the world and man which is the conscious aim of philosophy (*q.v.*), wisdom may be defined as the direct, practical insight into the meaning and purpose of things that comes to 'shrewd, penetrating, and observant minds, from their own experience of life, and their daily commerce with the world.'[4] It is the fruit not so much of speculation as of native sagacity and wit. Consequently, while philosophy appeals only to the intellectual *élites*, wisdom appeals to all who are interested in life and have understanding enough to appreciate a word of truth well spoken. In spite of this distinction, however, the two are closely allied. The knowledge of life reached intuitively by wisdom is the raw material out of which philosophical systems are evolved. And in its bolder flights wisdom moves in the atmosphere of philosophy.

1. Proverbial wisdom.—The beginnings of wisdom are found embodied in the terse, sententious sayings known as proverbs (*q.v.*). The art of proverb-making is universal. It flourishes among the rudest of tribes as well as among the more brilliantly endowed peoples of India, Greece, and Palestine. Collections of high value—in substance often much alike—come to us from such widely separated sources as the North American Indians and Negroes and the natives of Australasia and West Africa. But among the most interesting, not only for their intrinsic merit, but also for the light they shed on the development of Semitic wisdom, are those of the Arabs, as they are preserved for us in the great thesaurus of al-Maidānī († A.D. 1124) and still thrown out with astonishing ease by the sharp-edged Bedouin tongue. The simplest are brief similitudes (*amthâl*), like 'bolder in onset than 'Amr b. Kulthûm,' 'faster friends than the two palm-trees of Ḥulwan,' and 'more unlucky than the hamstringer of the she-camel' (*Qudar al-Aḥmar*). But many are finely-polished epigrams on human life, distinguished alike for their literary grace and for the keenness of their moral perception. Though in general the motive is enlightened self-interest, they are by no means forgetful of the nobler qualities of character. Especially do they delight in extolling the virtues of contentment, cheerfulness, truth, self-respect, restraint in word and action, perseverance, kindness, friendship, neighbourliness, hospitality, and love of home and country. In all this they are a mirror of Arabian life at its best.

2. Egyptian wisdom.—While the proverbial lore of Arabia brings us close to the running fountain of Semitic wisdom, the Egyptian sages had at a far earlier date evolved a gnomic literature, in the shape of books of moral precept or instruction (*seb'oyet*), full of sound sense, and sometimes even high moral excellence. The earliest of these books, the *Wisdom of Imhotep*, chief architect of Zoser, founder of the IIIrd dynasty, is known to us only from allusions in later literature; but two products of the IIIrd and Vth dynasties, the *Wisdom of Kegemne* and the *Wisdom of Ptah-hotep*, not only enjoyed wide popularity in their own day, but have been preserved in MSS of the Middle Kingdom. The former is a simple treatise on deportment; the latter covers a much wider range, offering 'maxims of beautiful speech' (as the author himself phrases it) on such subjects as diligence, courtesy, faithfulness to trusts, humility, self-restraint, purity, loyalty to friends, love of wife and family, kindness to dependents. Of similar tenor, though richer in content, and fresher and more artistic in expression, are the later *Maxims of Ani* (from the XXIst dynasty), urging not merely the moral virtues of purity, temperance, modesty of speech, a gracious demeanour alike at home, in the street, and in social fellowship, kindness, consideration for the poor and aged, reverence towards parents, but also the strictly religious obligations of chaste and loving worship, prayer, praise, and sacrifice.

'Celebrate thou the festival of thy God, and repeat the celebration thereof in its appointed season. Bear testimony [to Him] after thy offering.'

'The sanctuary of God abhorreth noisy demonstrations. Pray thou with a loving heart, and let thy words be secret. Do this, and He will do thy business for thee. He will hearken unto thy words, and He will receive thy offering.'

'Devote thyself to God, take heed to thyself daily for the sake of God, and let to-morrow be as to-day. Work thou [for Him]. God seeth him that worketh for Him, and He esteemeth lightly the man who esteemeth Him lightly.'[1]

Couched in a more cynical vein is the *Wisdom of Amenemhet I.*, founder of the XIIth dynasty, written shortly before his death (*c.* 1980 B.C.). Embittered by the rebellion of his subjects, he warns his son Sesostris against putting any con-

[1] *Mon. dell' Inst. di Corr. Arch.* i. [1832] 46.

[2] *Æsch. Eum.* 404.

[3] *Griechische Götterideale in ihren Formen erläutert*, Munich, 1893, p. 31.

[4] J. Morley, *Studies in Literature*, London, 1891, p. 57.

[1] Tr. from E. A. Wallis Budge, *The Literature of the Ancient Egyptians*, p. 228 ff.

fidence in those around him. The only influence that really appeals to men is terror; so let him 'harden himself against all subordinates,' know neither friends nor intimates, 'wherein there is no end,' and guard himself well as he sleeps, 'for a man has no people in the day of evil.' Equally depressing are the *Lament of Khekheperre-Sonbu*, priest of Heliopolis under Sesostris II. (1906–1887 B.C.), with its dismal picture of the corruptions of the time, the *Dialogue of a Misanthrope with his Soul*, ending in a wistful longing for death as the only release from evil, and the *Admonitions of Ipuwer*, the gloom of which, however, is relieved at the end by the vision of a righteous ruler, 'with no evil in his heart,' who goes about like a 'shepherd,' gathering together his scattered and 'fevered' herds. On a different key are the *Precepts of Duauf*, urging his son Pepi to diligence in learning, as the most 'beautiful' and honourable of callings, and the remarkable *Song of the Harper*, which finds the only consolation against the vanity and transience of life in the frank pursuit of pleasure.

'Give comfort to thy heart,
And let thy heart forget these things;
What is best for thee to do is
To follow thy heart's desire as long as thou livest.
Anoint thy head with scented unguents,
Let thine apparel be of byssus
Dipped in costly [perfumes],
In the veritable products (?) of the gods.

Enjoy thyself more than thou hast ever done before,
And let not thy heart pine for lack of pleasure.
. . . .
Pursue thy heart's desire and thine own happiness.
Order thy surroundings on earth in such a way
That they may minister to the desire of thy heart;
[For] at length that day of lamentation shall come,
Wherein he whose heart is still shall not hear the lamentation.
Never shall cries of grief cause
To beat [again] the heart of a man who is in the grave.'[1]

3. Babylonian wisdom.—Thus far the cuneiform records have yielded little in the way of wisdom literature. In Rawlinson, II. p. 16, however, there is found an interesting bilingual tablet (Sumerian and Assyrian), containing a number of riddles, proverbs, and gnomic maxims, apparently but specimens of a class (selected for the training of scholars in 'the grammatical construction of short phrases'), and therefore evidence that in Babylonia also proverbial wisdom was the basis of more conscious reflexion on life and conduct. The following may be quoted as typical:

'The life of yesterday goeth on daily the same.'[2]
'Thou goest and takest the field [*i.e.* property] of thine enemy; The enemy hath come and taken thy field.'[3]
'If the seed be not good, the stalk will not grow, nor will grain be produced.'[4]
'I am a young heifer, yoked with a mule; On the wagon to which we are harnessed . . . I bear the yoke.'[5]
'What man eateth when he is dead? Why then should he toil when he is alive?'[6]
'In the case of incurable sickness and insatiable hunger, a box full of silver and a chest full of gold are powerless to restore the health and to satisfy the hunger.'[7]
'He who says, "O that I might have revenge, and more so!" draws from a well without water, pours from a skin that is empty.'[8]

The Epicurean tendency revealed in the Egyptian *Song of the Harper* finds expression also in a remarkable fragment from the Gilgameš epic;[9] while the high ethical and religious note we have heard in *Ptah-hotep* and *Ani* rings through the Wisdom Tablet[10] deciphered and translated by K. D. Macmillan.

'Their freedom [?] thou shalt not take away,
Thou shalt not tyrannically oppress them.
For this [or, he who acts thus], his god is angry with him:
It is not pleasing to Šamaš, he will requite him with evil.

Give food to eat, give wine to drink,
Seek the right, provide for and . . .
For this [or, he who acts thus], his god is pleased with him:
It is pleasing to Šamaš, he will requite him [with good].
. . . .
Thou shalt not slander, but speak kindly,
Thou shalt not speak evil, but show mercy.
Him who slanders and speaks evil,
With its recompense will Šamaš visit (?) his head.

Thou shalt not make large thy mouth, but guard thy lip;
In the time of thine anger thou shalt not speak at once.
If thou speakest quickly, thou wilt repent (?) afterward,
And in silence wilt thou sadden thy mind.

Daily present to thy god
Offering and prayer, appropriate to incense.
Before thy god mayest thou have a pure heart,
For that is appropriate to the deity.'[1]

Akin to the more pessimistic wisdom literature of Egypt is the *Lament of Ṭâbi-utul-ellil*,[2] in which the old king grieves over his own misfortunes and the general evil in the world. As for himself, he has sought consistently to honour God's name and follow His righteous ways.

'I myself took thought only for prayers and supplication.
Prayer was my rule, sacrifice my order,
The day of God's honouring was my heart's joy,
The day of following after the goddess was for me gain and riches. . . .
I taught my land to keep God's name;
To honour the name of the goddess I cautioned my people.'[3]

But how very differently from his deserts has God treated him.

'My house is become a prison for me,
In the chains of my flesh are my arms laid,
In my own bonds [?] are my feet cast.
. . . .
With a whip he has beaten me, not . . .
With a staff he has pierced me, the point was strong.
All day long doth follow the avenger,
In the middle of the night he lets me not breathe for a moment.'[4]

Both theme and language remind one of Job. But the *dénouement* is different. Whereas Job returns to a deeper, more personal faith in God, the Babylonian sage finds no help in god or goddess. God's ways are too inscrutable for man to rely on Him. The only hope is in the mercy of one's 'guardian angel'—the ancestral spirit of the family.

'But I knew the time, of all my family,
When among the guardian angels their divinity had mercy.'[5]

4. Chinese wisdom.—Passing eastward to China, we enter upon a larger field. The grave, practical temperament of the Chinese predisposed them to ethical reflexion. And the logical sharpness and balanced harmony of their speech made it a happy medium for sententious expression. The old classics, especially the *Shu King*, are rich in proverbial lore. Confucius and his grandson Tse-sse, Mencius (*q.v.*), and the Confucian school generally[6] are distinguished, not for originality or depth of thought, but for the terseness and point of their sayings as well as for the attractive grace of their personalities. Even the mystical and sceptical writers, like Lao-tse, Yang Chu, and Hui Shih, make their impression not so much by the reasoned compactness of their systems as by the beauty and force of their aphorisms. Chinese literature as a whole is 'seasoned with the salt' of proverbs. And the common people are not far inferior to their masters in the art. 'Chinamen may be almost said to think in proverbs.'[7] And instruc-

[1] Budge, p. 243.
[2] Lines 7 f.; cf. Ec 1[9ff].
[3] Lines 14–17.
[4] Lines 30–33.
[5] Lines 34–38.
[6] Lines 42–45; cf. Ec 2[18ff].
[7] Lines 46–53.
[8] Lines 53–57 (tr. based on M. Jäger, *BASS* ii. 274 ff. and J. A. Craig [written communication]).
[9] iii. 3 f.; cited by A. Jeremias in the art. ETHICS AND MORALITY (Babylonian), vol. v. p. 447b.
[10] Brit. Mus. K. 7897.

[1] Translation from K. D. Macmillan, *BASS* v. 557 ff.
[2] Rawlinson, IV.[2] p. 60.
[3] *Ib.* II. line 23 ff.
[4] Reverse, line 1 ff.
[5] Line 24 f. (Translations from R. W. Rogers, *Cuneiform Parallels to the OT*, New York, 1912, p. 164 ff.)
[6] See art. CONFUCIAN RELIGION.
[7] H. A. Giles, *A Hist. of Chinese Literature*, p. 437; see art. LITERATURE (Chinese).

tion in proverbs is a main element in the education of the young.

The centre of interest throughout is the *Tao*—the true or normal way of life. Various qualities are singled out by the classical writers as essential to an all-round moral character. But these are reduced by Confucius to the five cardinal virtues of benevolence, righteousness, propriety, wisdom, and sincerity.[1] As a virtue, therefore, wisdom (*chih*) is moral rather than intellectual. It includes, no doubt, knowledge of men and their affairs, acquaintance with the rules of propriety, and the command of language, as the key to success in the world; but its chief concern is with matters of ethical conduct. The wise man (*tse*) is he who knows the principles of right living and is able to instruct his fellows in them. Still higher stands the sage or holy man (*shêng jên*), who not merely knows these principles, but conducts his life in perfect harmony with them and thus becomes the moral teacher and guide of the ages. Such a man is the constant subject of praise in the Chinese classics:

'Perfection of nature is characteristic of Heaven. To attain to that perfection belongs to man. He who possesses that perfection hits what is right without any effort, and apprehends what is true without any exercise of thought;—he is the sage who naturally and easily embodies the right way. He who attains to perfection is he who chooses what is good, and firmly holds it fast.'[2] 'Therefore the movements of the superior man [sage] mark out for ages the path for all under heaven; his actions are the law for ages for all under heaven; and his words are the pattern for ages for all under heaven. Those who are far from him look longingly for him, and those who are near are never weary of him.'[3]

'The superior man [sage] does not, even for the space of a single meal, act contrary to virtue. In moments of haste, he cleaves to it. In seasons of danger, he cleaves to it.'[4] He fulfils completely the rules of a virtuous life: 'when you go abroad, to behave to every one as if you were receiving a great guest; to employ the people as if you were assisting at a great sacrifice; not to do to others as you would not wish done to yourself; to have no murmuring against you in the country, and none in the family.'[5]

As the personal embodiment of the mean—*i.e.* the harmony of all the virtues—'he is all-embracing like heaven, deep and active as a fountain.' 'He is seen, and the people all reverence him; he speaks, and the people all believe him; he acts, and the people are all pleased with him.'[6]

'A man who commands our liking is what is called good. He whose goodness is part of himself is what is called a real man. He whose goodness is accumulated in full measure is called a beautiful man. He whose completed goodness is brightly displayed is called a great man. When this great man exercises a transforming influence [over others], he is what is called a sage.'[7]

On the more philosophical developments of Chinese wisdom see artt. MYSTICISM (Chinese), PHILOSOPHY (Chinese).

5. Indian wisdom.—The wisdom of the Semitic and Turanian races we have found to be predominantly practical; that of the higher Indo-European peoples is as distinctively intellectual. This underlying quality of Indian wisdom is suggested from the outset in the name Veda, 'knowledge,' applied to its classical literature; and bright foregleams of its future triumphs in speculative thought appear even in the *Rigveda*, with its questionings as to the 'wood' and the 'tree' from which were fashioned 'the earth and the heaven,'[8] and its bold theories of the evolution of *sat*, the existent, from *asat*, the non-existent.[9] At the same time, the poets of the *Rigveda* are not lost in the empyrean. They have a true feeling for human life, both in its dignity and in its weakness, and clothe this in sententious sayings which are worthy of comparison with the best in other literatures. Some are mildly humorous, such as the song on the pursuit of gain,[1] others pathetic, like the fine *Lament of the Gambler*,[2] still others cynical, especially those that moralize on women and their ways.[3] But others strike a high note—*e.g.*, the hymn in praise of wise speech,[4] and that on generosity:

'Who has the power should give unto the needy,
Regarding well the course of life hereafter:
Fortune, like the chariot wheels revolving,
Now to one man comes nigh, now to another.

Ploughing the soil, the share produces nurture;
He who bestirs his feet performs his journey;
A priest who speaks earns more than one who's silent;
A friend who gives is better than the niggard.'[5]

In the *Upaniṣads* and the fully developed Vedantic system[6] the incipient gnosticism of the Vedic poets reaches its climax. The *summum bonum* is union with Brahman, attained by the *jñāna-mārga*, 'way of knowledge,' though on the higher planes even knowledge is dispensed with, and the individual soul with all its activities is merged in the tideless ocean of the unknown and unknowable. The same intellectualism pervades the other orthodox systems[7] as well as the heresies of Jainism and Buddhism. Salvation is won by *vidyā* (Pāli *vijja*), *jñāna*, or *prajña* (Pāli *pañña*), knowledge of the real, *bodhi*, enlightenment (as distinguished from *avidyā*, ignorance, *i.e.* mere empirical knowledge, *māyā*, illusion, delusion). But for the ordinary man this way of salvation is too high to attain to. Thus we find a lower way offered him—the *karma-mārga*, 'way of works,' or salvation through sacrifice and moral conduct. The choicest expression is given to this 'way' in the later dramas and epics, notably the *Mahābhārata* and the *Rāmāyana* (*qq.v.*), the former of which is 'an inexhaustible mine of proverbial philosophy'[8]—and in the *nīti*, or wisdom literature, which corresponds very closely to the gnomic poetry of Greece. The outstanding examples of *nīti*—the *Pañchatantra* and *Hitopadeśa*—are manuals of instruction for rulers. But others, both Sanskrit and vernacular, are written for the people. With these may be classed the ethical sections of the *Bhagavad-Gītā* (*q.v.*), and the beautiful catena of Buddhist aphorisms entitled the *Dhammapada*, 'Pathway of Virtue.' A few examples of this wisdom may be given:

'To injure none, by thought or word or deed,
To give to others, and be kind to all—
This is the constant duty of the good.'[9]

'High-minded men delight in doing good,
Without a thought of their own interest;
When they confer a benefit on others,
They reckon not on favours in return.'[10]

'Hear thou a summary of righteousness,
And ponder well the maxim: Never do
To other persons what would pain thyself.'[11]

'A man of truest wisdom will resign
His wealth, and e'en his life, for good of others;
Better abandon life in a good cause,
When death in any case is sure to happen.'[12]

'The good show pity even to the worthless,
[As] the moon irradiates the meanest hovel.'[13]

'Act then and do thine own appointed task,
In every action my [*i.e.* Kṛṣṇa's] assistance ask;
Do all with heart and soul absorbed in me,
So shalt thou gain thine end and be from trouble free.'[14]

'Like a beautiful flower, full of colour but without scent, are the fine but fruitless words of him who does not act accord-

1 See ETHICS AND MORALITY (Chinese).
2 *Lî Ḳî*, XXVIII. ii. 19 (*SBE* xxviii. [1885] 317 f.).
3 *Ib.* 50 (*SBE* xxviii. 325).
4 *Confucian Analects*, IV. v. 3.
5 *Ib.* XII. ii.
6 *Doctrine of the Mean*, xxxi. 3.
7 *Mencius*, VII. pt. II. xxv. 3–8 (trr. from J. Legge, *Chinese Classics*, *passim*).
8 x. 81.
9 x. 72, 121, 129.

1 ix. 112.
2 x. 34.
3 viii. 33, x. 27, 95.
4 x. 71.
5 x. 117 (tr. from A. A. Macdonell, *A Hist. of Sanskrit Literature*, p. 129).
6 See art. BRĀHMANISM.
7 See artt. NYĀYA, SĀNKHYA, YOGA.
8 Macdonell, p. 378.
9 *Mahābh.* iii. 16782.
10 *Ib.* 16796.
11 *Pañchatantra*, iii. 104.
12 *Hitopadeśa*, i. 45.
13 i. 63.
14 *Bhag.* xiii. 29 (tr. from M. Monier-Williams, *Indian Wisdom*[4], pp. 152, 442 ff.).

ingly. But like a beautiful flower, full of colour and full of scent, are the fine and fruitful words of him who acts accordingly.'[1]

'Do not have evil-doers for friends, do not have low people for friends: have virtuous people for friends, have for friends the best of men.'[2]

'Let no man forget his own duty for the sake of another's, however great; let a man, after he has discerned his own duty, be always attentive to his duty.'[3]

'If anything is to be done, let a man do it, let him attack it vigorously! A careless pilgrim only scatters the dust of his passions more widely.'[4]

6. Greek wisdom.—Intellectualism is as definitely the quality of Greek wisdom as of Indian. Σοφία (from root *sap*, 'to know') is primarily 'cleverness' or 'skill' in any of the arts or professions of life—*e.g.*, carpentry,[5] medicine or surgery,[6] poetry,[7] music and singing.[8] Thence it comes to mean 'sagacity,' 'soundness of judgment,' 'intelligence,' 'prudence,' 'political tact,' and general 'knowledge of life,' sometimes with the sinister suggestion of 'shrewdness,' 'cunning,' 'craft.' Finally, it is applied to knowledge in the pure sense of the term—'learning,' 'science,' and 'philosophy' (as the harmony of all the sciences).

The beginnings of Greek wisdom are found in the outcrop of gnomic poetry associated with the names of Hesiod (*q.v.*), Mimnermus, Solon, Phocylides, and especially Theognis (*q.v.*), who crystallized the current morality in lucid phrases and thus became the favourite teachers of their people. As a whole, their wisdom is trite and prosaic, the key-notes being moderation (μηδὲν ἄγαν) and fitness of act to time and situation (καιρὸν γνῶθι), though they have all an instinct for justice as the fundamental element in every true life. Through most of them, also, runs the strain of melancholy which reaches such tragic depths in later Greek literature.[9] The Seven Wise Men did little more than point the maxims of the poets. Chilon's γνῶθι σεαυτόν, 'Know thyself,' however, lent the initial impulse to the great philosophical movement in Greece. Its first efforts, no doubt, were spent in rather futile cosmogonic speculations; but Pythagoras held fast to the idea 'that philosophy was above all "a way of life,"'[10] while the fragments of Heraclitus and Democritus (*qq.v.*) abound in moral maxims of considerable insight and aptness of expression. With the Sophists ([*q.v.*] σοφισταί, 'masters of wisdom') the interest reverted once for all to the problems of human life and conduct. In their persons the pursuit of wisdom—practically equivalent to intellectual culture as a preparation for private and public life[11]—became a conscious profession. The love of money, so often associated with professionalism, the critical and sceptical tendency of their teaching, the charge that they subordinated moral issues to expediency—that in fact they identified right with might[12]—all conspired to bring the later Sophists into disrepute as subverters of the popular faith and jugglers with the great spiritual realities of life. As a school, however, they deserve credit for having broken the crust of dead tradition, and cleared the way for the intellectual renaissance under Socrates and his disciples.

Socrates (*q.v.*) refused to be called either a σοφός or a σοφιστής. For him God alone was wise; and the man who claimed actual possession of wisdom was guilty of presumption, if not blasphemy.[13] Taking up, then, a term already used by Pythagoras, he described himself as φιλόσοφος, 'a lover of wisdom.' The wisdom he thus sought was essentially ethical: it turned on the principles of virtuous conduct. But with Socrates virtue was identical with knowledge. The enlightened understanding was *ipso facto* morally good character. On this basis Plato (*q.v.*) built up his majestic system of ethical idealism, with its four cardinal virtues—wisdom, courage, temperance, and justice. Of these, wisdom, or rationality, is the highest phase of virtue, for it inspires and regulates the whole inner life.[1] Though he recognizes the rationality of virtue in all men, Plato was conscious of a distinction between the virtue of the work-a-day world and that of the philosopher, who spends his days in the disinterested pursuit of truth.[2] The distinction thus vaguely apprehended by Plato was sharply drawn by Aristotle (*q.v.*). Practical wisdom, prudence, or good sense (φρόνησις) deals with matters of ordinary human interest; speculative wisdom, which is wisdom *par excellence* (σοφία), with the first principles of things. The former enables a man to apply the 'right rule' to every line of activity, whether professional, civic, or strictly moral; the latter leads, by a union of science and intuitive apprehension, to a knowledge of 'those things which are most precious in their nature.'[3]

The later schools also honoured wisdom as the root of all the virtues. For only through wisdom was man able either to know or to pursue the true end of life. Naturally their conceptions of wisdom differed according to their different ideals. For the Sceptics (*q.v.*) it meant the wholesome sense of the relativity of knowledge that permitted a man to suspend judgment where it was impossible to be certain; for the Epicureans (*q.v.*) the insight into life's conflicting motives and desires that set him free from false opinion and helped him to choose the sweetest and most lasting pleasures; for the Stoics (*q.v.*) the grasp of truth, both human and divine, that made him possessor of all virtue, freedom, and inward happiness. In their delineations of the 'wise man' the Stoic writers reach their highest level. He knows all there is to know, for he alone maintains that serenity of soul which is the spiritual presupposition of knowledge. He is thus fitted for every sphere of life. He is likewise free from fault or failing, weakness or passion. He is lord of his actions, as being responsible only to himself. He is truly rich, for he has all he needs. He is also happy at all times and under all circumstances, for the springs of his happiness are in himself.[4]

7. Hebrew wisdom.—In Israel we pass once more to the practical side of wisdom. חָכְמָה is used in a general sense of 'skill' in the ordinary affairs of life—*e.g.*, technical work (Ex 28^{3} etc.), spinning (Ex 35^{25}), war (Is 10^{13}), seamanship (Ps 107^{27}), and often of 'sound judgment' in administration (Gn $41^{33f.}$, Dt 34^{9}, 1 K 3^{12} etc.)—but it comes to be applied peculiarly to 'moral principle.' The wise man is he who directs his life worthily and well. His wisdom is thus virtually equivalent to 'goodness.' And the root of this wisdom lies in religion. The fool says in his heart, 'There is no God' (Ps 14^{1}); the wise man makes God the centre of all his thoughts, hopes, and endeavours. For him 'the fear of the Lord' is not only 'the beginning' (Pr 1^{7}), but also 'the crown' and 'the perfect fulness' of wisdom (Sir $1^{14ff.}$).

As elsewhere, the simplest expressions of Israelite wisdom are in the shape of proverbs. Originally pointed similes (*m^eshālîm*), like the Arabic *amthâl*—*e.g.*, 'Like Nimrod a mighty hunter before the

1 *Dhammapada*, iv. 51 f.
2 vi. 78.
3 xii. 166.
4 xxii. 313 (tr. from F. Max Müller, *SBE* x. [²1898] 18 ff.).
5 Hom. *Il.* xv. 412.
6 Pind. *Pyth.* iii. 96.
7 Pind. *Ol.* i. 187.
8 Hom. Hymns, *Hermes*, 483.
9 Cf. especially Theognis, 425–428.
10 J. Burnet, *Early Greek Philosophy*², p. 89.
11 Plato, *Prot.* 318 E, 319 A.
12 So Thrasymachus in Plato, *Rep.* 338 C ff., Callicles in *Gorgias*, 482 E ff.
13 Cf. Plato, *Apol.* 20 ff.

1 Cf. *Rep.* 441 C ff.
2 *Phædo*, 82 B, *Meno*, 100 A.
3 *Nic. Eth.* VI. v. 2, VII. i. 5.
4 See also artt. ETHICS AND MORALITY (Greek), PHILOSOPHY (Greek).

Lord' (Gn 10[9]), or 'Like mother, like daughter' (Ezk 16[44])—they gradually assume the perfect balance of thought and literary finish which we find in the couplets of Proverbs and Ben Sira. These two collections are a compendium of Hebrew wisdom at its purest. In clear-cut vignettes they portray the good man at his various tasks—as workman, citizen, neighbour, friend, husband, and father—and unveil the principles by which he conducts his life. The general motive may be eudæmonistic. Both collections show an undisguised appreciation of the good things of this world—its prizes, honours, riches, and pleasures—and direct men to the best way of winning these. Nevertheless, the moral tone is throughout honest and true. Righteousness is the first concern. Only as men follow after righteousness do they reach prosperity. In the emphasis thus laid on righteousness the proverbs of Israel outshine all other prudential literature. And at their higher levels they draw very near to the standard of Christ.

With this growing refinement in the art of proverbs there developed in Israel also a more professional interest in wisdom. On the pages of the greater prophets 'the wise' appear as a separate gild of spiritual advisers, whose 'counsel' ranked in influence with the *tôrāh* of the priests and the 'word' of the prophets (Is 29[14], Jer 18[18] etc.). In the post-Exilic period the 'wise men' practically replaced the prophets as moral guides and teachers. Gaining wisdom from the study of the older Scriptures, or through prayer and supplication, or in the school of experience, as they wandered about the world, 'travelling through strange countries,' mingling with kings and princes, and 'testing the good and evil among men' (Sir 39[1ff.]), they took their stand in the market-place, or at the corners of bustling streets, or by the gates where people congregated, and appealed to the simple ones to embrace wisdom and to fools to turn from their folly and live (Pr 1[20ff.] 8[2ff.]), or in their homes and lecture-halls instructed their pupils in the ways of wisdom (Sir 51[23]). Out of this formal discipline arose not merely the gnomic wisdom of the *Pirḳē Ābōth*, 'Sayings of the Fathers,' but also the wisdom-speculation which we find in later elements of Proverbs, in the Apocryphal books of Sirach, Wisdom of Solomon, Enoch, Baruch, and 4 Maccabees, and in outside sources like Philo and the Odes of Solomon.

In Pr 8[22ff.] Wisdom appears as the first creation of God, the 'foster-child' who played beside Him as He wrought His mighty works and now moves among men as His mouth-piece and representative on earth. It seems hardly possible here to deny the fertilizing influence of Greek thought. Yet the picture is Hebrew in its essence. Wisdom is no archetypal hypostasis emanating from the divine. She is still the impersonation of a moral quality, endowed with life by Jahweh, whose place in creation she nowhere usurps. The ethical character of Wisdom is equally evident in the great Song of Praise, Sir 24[3ff.], where Wisdom is ultimately identified with 'the law that Moses commanded,' which found its resting-place and seat of authority in Israel. A similar linking of Wisdom with the Law appears in Bar 4[1ff.] and 4 Mac 1[17]. Following out the more ethical line, Enoch 42[1] 49[1] etc. pictures her as descending from heaven to earth, being rejected by men, returning to heaven, and there awaiting the Messianic age, when she will be poured out in her fullness on the elect. A much bolder attitude is assumed in Wis 7[22ff.], where she is celebrated as the spiritual 'artificer of all things,' an 'effulgence of the everlasting light, and an unstained mirror of the power of God,' which by her purity and mobility 'penetrates and permeates all things.' Here the concrete imagination of Israel has been caught up in the full sweep of Greek influence, and we seem to be actually moving within the inner circle of Neo-Platonic speculation. But the most systematic attempt to blend Hebrew wisdom with Greek idealism is met with in Philo (*q.v.*), whose doctrine of the Logos finds poetical reflexion in certain of the Odes of Solomon (12[9ff.] 13[1ff.] 16[9ff.] etc.).

In other phases of Hebrew literature there is a decided protest against the current ideas of wisdom. The book of Job challenges the whole theory that outward prosperity is the reward of righteousness, while Ḳoheleth leaves us with the cynical conclusion that 'all is vanity.' Elsewhere the speculations of the wise are traversed by a species of agnosticism which insists that Wisdom is undiscoverable by man. The most brilliant poetic expression is given to this tendency in the Song of Wisdom incorporated in Job 28. The poet has sought wisdom in the depths of the earth, where miners dig for gold and silver, in the heights of heaven, whither the eagles soar in flight, and in the desert places, where the beasts roam in solitary majesty. But nowhere can he find the object of his quest. A still more depressing view is expressed in 'the words of Agur, the son of Jakeh,' incorporated in Proverbs:

'I am wearied, O God, I am wearied;
  I am altogether spent.
I am but a brute, and no man:
  I have nought of human intelligence.
No wisdom have I learned,
  No knowledge I have of the Holy One.
Who is He that hath mounted to heaven, and come down.
  That hath gathered the wind in His fists,
The waters hath wrapped in His cloak,
  And established all ends of the earth?
What is His name, and His son's name,
  If thou dost know?'[1]

It is significant, however, that Hebrew scepticism never touches the being of God. The beginning of wisdom was 'the fear of the Lord'; and, even when wisdom was despaired of, the fear of the Lord remained the sheet-anchor of faith and hope. However perplexed he was with the mysteries of Providence, Job still clung to God; and at the end he rose beyond himself and his questionings to a new sense of God's wisdom, power, and grace in the boundless universe of nature. Even Ḳoheleth's pessimism is quickened by the fear of God into a certain sanctified common sense. The poet of Job 28 has failed to reach wisdom. But 'God knoweth the place thereof'; He hath 'established and searched it out' (v.[23ff.]). And for Agur, too, God is the great energizing Force behind all the phenomena of nature. He may not be able to 'name' Him; yet he feels His presence all about him. And to Him he addresses his prayer:

'Give me neither poverty nor riches,
  Feed me with food sufficient for my wants;
Lest I be full, and deny thee,
  And say, Who is Jahweh?
Or be poor, and steal,
  And profane the name of my God.'[2]

8. Christian wisdom.—Early Christianity is a return from speculation to the simple realities of faith and life, which are 'hid from the wise and prudent,' but 'revealed unto babes' (Mt 11[25], Lk 10[21]). In preaching the gospel of the Kingdom Jesus avoided the idiom of the schools and addressed men in that concrete, parabolic style which we have found to be of the essence of the popular proverb. But those who listened to His preaching found in it a 'wisdom' beyond that of all their teachers (Mt 13[54], Mk 6[2]). He Himself claimed to be 'greater than Solomon,' to hear whose wisdom the queen of Sheba came 'from the uttermost parts of the earth' (Mt 12[42], Lk 11[31]). And this because He had been supremely endowed

[1] 30[1-4]. [2] 30[8f.].

with 'the grace of God' (Lk 2^{40}), so that the words He uttered were the very wisdom of God (Mt 11^{27}, Lk 10^{22}). To Jesus 'wisdom' was that practical understanding of the mind of God, that entire sympathy with His will and purpose, which enabled men to walk in His ways and do His will 'on earth as in heaven' (cf. Mt $6^{10f.}$ 7^{21} etc.). The same idea is set forth in Ja $3^{13ff.}$, where 'the wisdom that is from above' is contrasted with the wisdom that is 'earthly, sensual, devilish' by the fruit it yields in purity, meekness, gentleness, mercy, and 'a good conversation.' The Pauline Epistles and the Fourth Gospel show a much closer affinity with the Wisdom literature. The apostle, it is true, renounces the 'wisdom of the wise,' which leads to no real knowledge of God, and even obscures the gospel of 'Christ crucified' (1 Co $1^{20ff.}$). But in Him he finds a wisdom higher than that of men, even 'the power of God, and the wisdom of God' (v.^{24}). In the sacred quaternion of graces personally manifested in Christ—wisdom, righteousness, sanctification, and redemption—wisdom takes the foremost place (v.^{30}). But the pursuit of wisdom is reserved for the full-grown in Christ (τέλειοι), who alone have minds to comprehend the hidden mysteries of God (2^{6}). Himself increasingly filled with the spirit of heavenly wisdom, St. Paul elaborates in the Epistles to the Colossians and Ephesians a real speculative philosophy, based on Him 'in whom are hid all the treasures of wisdom and knowledge' (Col 2^{3}). Adapting ideas and phrases from the Wisdom of Solomon, he worships Christ as 'the image of the invisible God, the firstborn of the whole creation,' by whom all things were created—'that are in heaven, and that are in earth, visible and invisible'—in whom all subsist, and through whom all are destined in the fullness of time to be 'gathered into one' (Col $1^{15ff.}$, Eph $1^{9ff.}$). Yet the apostle does not lose sight of the practical aspects of the case. For him true Christian wisdom is still that which consists in 'the knowledge of God's will' (Col 1^{9}) and leads to a consistent 'walk' before those both without and within the fold (4^{5}). Similarly, the Logos philosophy of the Fourth Gospel is valuable only for its results in character. The Logos became flesh and dwelt among us, that we might behold His glory—'glory as of the only begotten of the Father'—and be progressively transformed into the image of that glory (Jn $1^{14ff.}$).

LITERATURE.—On proverbial wisdom see the literature cited under art. PROVERBS; ancient Arabian: G. W. Freytag, *Arabum Proverbia* (based on al-Maidānī), 3 vols., Bonn, 1831–43; modern Arabian: J. L. Burckhardt, *Arabic Proverbs*, London, 1830; C. M. Doughty, *Travels in Arabia Deserta*, 2 vols., Cambridge, 1888; J. Wortabet, *Arabian Wisdom*, London, 1907; G. M. Mackie, 'Proverbs of Oriental Wisdom,' *ExpT* xxviii. [1917] 346 ff.

On Egyptian: J. H. Breasted, *Development of Religion and Thought in Ancient Egypt*, New York, 1912; E. A. Wallis Budge, *The Literature of the Ancient Egyptians*, London, 1914; A. Erman, *Ägypten und ägyptisches Leben im Altertum*, 2 vols., Tübingen, 1887, *Gespräch eines Lebensmüden mit seiner Seele*, do. 1896; B. G. Gunn, *The Instruction of Ptah-hotep*, London, 1906; A. H. Gardiner, *The Admonitions of an Egyptian Sage*, Leipzig, 1909.

On Babylonian: H. Gressmann, *Altoriental. Texte und Bilder*, 2 vols., Tübingen, 1909; R. W. Rogers, *Cuneiform Parallels to the Old Testament*, New York, 1912; M. Jäger, 'Assyrische Rätsel und Sprüchwörter,' in *BASS* ii. [1891–94] 274 ff.; K. D. Macmillan, 'Some Cuneiform Tablets bearing on the Religion of Babylonia and Assyria,' in *BASS* v. [1903–06] 531 ff.

On Chinese: H. A. Giles, *A Hist. of Chinese Literature*, London, 1901; A. H. Smith, *Proverbs and Common Sayings from the Chinese*, do. 1902; D. T. Suzuki, *A Brief Hist. of Early Chinese Philosophy*, do. 1914; and literature cited under artt. ETHICS AND MORALITY (Chinese), PHILOSOPHY (Chinese), esp. J. Legge, *The Chinese Classics*³, 3 vols., Oxford, 1893–95.

On Indian: A. A. Macdonell, *A Hist. of Sanskrit Literature*², London, 1905; H. Oldenberg, *Die Literatur der alten Indien*, Stuttgart, 1903; O. von Böhtlingk, *Indische Sprüche*, 3 pts., Leipzig, 1870–74; M. Monier-Williams, *Indian Wisdom*⁴, London, 1893; and literature cited under artt. ETHICS AND MORALITY (Buddhist), NYĀYA, SĀNKHYA, YOGA, etc.

On Greek: J. Burnet, *Early Greek Philosophy*², London, 1908, *Ethics of Aristotle*, do. 1900; J. Marshall, *Aristotle's Theory of Conduct*, do. 1906; W. L. Davidson, *The Stoic Creed*, Edinburgh, 1907; and literature cited under artt. ETHICS AND MORALITY (Greek), PHILOSOPHY (Greek).

On Hebrew: J. F. Bruch, *Weisheitslehre der Hebräer*, Strassburg, 1851; H. Bois, *La Poésie gnomique chez les Hébreux et chez les Grecs*, Toulouse, 1886; T. K. Cheyne, *Job and Solomon*, London, 1887; W. T. Davison, *Wisdom Literature of the Old Testament*³, do. 1900; W. R. Harvey-Jellie, *The Wisdom of God and the Word of God*, do. 1911; W. Fairweather, *The Background of the Gospels*, Edinburgh, 1908; J. Meinhold, *Die Weisheit Israels*, Leipzig, 1908; A. R. Gordon, *The Poets of the Old Testament*, London, 1912; J. Abelson, *Jewish Mysticism*, do. 1913; A. B. Davidson, *Biblical and Literary Essays*, do. 1902, ch. ii. 'The Wisdom of the Hebrews'; artt. 'Wisdom,' in *HDB*, *DCG*, and *DAC*, 'Wisdom Literature,' in *EBi*.

A. R. GORDON.

WISDOM TREE.—The venerable *Bo*-tree at Anurādhapura is the oldest historical tree in the world. The planting of the *Bo*-, or *Bodhi*-, tree (the Sinhalese *Bo* is merely a contraction of the Pali *Bodhi*, both meaning wisdom) is recorded at length in the Chronicles of Ceylon as having taken place in about 245 B.C.[1] Incidental references, in later centuries, to repairs to the enclosure, or to gifts of staircases or statues or ornaments by subsequent kings, show how great was the care that was continually devoted to it.[2] It is now (1920) 2165 years old.

Its botanical name is *ficus religiosa* (the Anglo-Indian *pipal*), and trees of this kind can put out fresh roots if a branch be planted, or if soil be heaped up near the base of the trunk. The soil has been thus so often raised that the tree now appears as three distinct trees (three branches of the old tree), growing from different points of an enclosed plateau about 25 ft. above the level of the spot where the tree was originally planted. A winding staircase of stone leads up to the enclosure of this plateau. Wherever the branches threaten to become too long they have been propped up by rough supports of wood or masonry. A stone slab, a *malāsana*, or flower-stand, has been provided for the memorial presentation of the white blossoms of the *champaka*. Everything about the spot gives the impression of a hoary antiquity. But we could not be sure of the identity of the tree without the long chain of documentary evidence.[3] The trees are somewhat like elms in size and shape; but the tapering leaves, about six inches long and four inches across the broadest part, are lighter in colour underneath, and the never-ceasing rustling of the leaves causes a constant flash of vanishing and reappearing light and colour curiously suggestive of one of the main doctrines both of the ancient Buddhist and of much modern philosophy.

Anurādhapura (*q.v.*) and the country round had been for nearly seven centuries, from the middle of the 12th to the middle of the 19th cent., almost abandoned. The Tamils, after centuries of intermittent attempts to take it, had been driven back to the north of the island. The Sinhalese, outnumbered ten to one, had retired to the fastnesses of the mountains to the south. East to west the jungle stretched from shore to shore, and north to south for a hundred miles. In what had been the most populous and prosperous part of Ceylon there were left a few far-scattered peasantry and woodmen; and the great capital had become a few mud huts. But there were always devoted *bhikkhus* to tend the *Bodhi*, the Wisdom Tree. A railway now runs through the jungle, and roads have been made. The magnificent reservoir, 50 miles in circumference, which had supplied half the country-side with water, has been restored to working order; and population and prosperity are slowly being restored. One consequence is

[1] *Dīpavaṃsa*, ch. xvi.; *Mahāvaṃsa*, ch. xix.

[2] See the appendix to vol. ii. of J. E. Tennent's *Ceylon* for a long list of such references.

[3] Much of this is given in an appendix to the second volume of Tennent's *Ceylon*.

that a constant stream of pilgrims comes from all parts of the world to pay reverence to the tree.

Various different, and indeed contradictory, explanations have been given of this reverence paid to the *Bodhi*-tree. The oldest explanation is that given in Ceylon itself. This can be gathered from different passages in the Chronicles and in the Commentaries on the canon, and is best summarized in a book called the *Mahābodhivaṃsa* ('Story of the great Wisdom Tree'), probably written about A.D. 950. It is an amplified version in bombastic Sanskritized Pali prose of what had been already said in the older authorities just referred to; and, however interesting as a literary work, the oldest to show that acquaintance with Sanskrit then just beginning in Ceylon, it really adds nothing to the historical details contained in the older documents. The Ceylon view is that the tree is held in so much affectionate esteem and awe because it was grown from a branch of the original *Bodhi*-tree at Gayā (*q.v.*) in India (often distinguished as Bodh-Gayā, 'Gayā of the Wisdom Tree') under which the Buddha had actually sat when he passed through the intense mental crisis, the turning-point of his career, which led to his coming forward as the teacher of a new religion. The 'wisdom' is the wisdom, not of the tree, but of the teacher. It is derived not from the tree, or from any fruit of the tree, but from the mental struggles and the victory won by the founder of their faith. They adore the tree, not because of the power of any spirit or dryad within the tree, but because the outward form of it is a constant reminder of what they hold to have been the most important event in the history of the world. In other words, their attitude towards the tree is much the same as that of many Christians towards the Cross. And, just as opponents of Christianity have thought, quite illogically, that they could score a point against it by showing that the cross was a religious symbol (with quite different associations) before the rise of Christianity, so opponents of Buddhism have sought, and quite successfully, to show that the tree was a religious symbol (with quite different associations) before the rise of Buddhism. They fail to see that that is not the point. Granted that other people had previously used the same (or a similar) symbol in a different sense, the question is: In what sense did the Buddhists use it? We shall deal with only the more important of these theories of the tree.

James Fergusson, the eminent historian of Indian architecture, held that the main features of 'Turanian' belief were tree- and serpent-worship, that the despatch of a branch of the *Bodhi*-tree by Aśoka to Ceylon is a proof of the Turanian tree-worship practised by that Buddhist emperor of India, and that the monuments show that early Buddhism was a 'Turanian' faith. What exactly he means by Turanian he does not state. The conclusions put forward in his massive volume, entitled *Tree and Serpent Worship*, have not been accepted by any other scholar who has written on the subject.

E. Senart, the editor of the *Mahāvastu* and the interpreter of Aśoka's inscriptions, will have none of this. He holds that Buddhism was, in its origin, Aryan; that it was derived almost entirely from the Brāhman mythology contained in the Vedic records; that the legend of the Buddha is almost a myth; that in that myth the tree is almost, if not quite, as important as the teacher; and that the tree is the cloud-tree of the famous atmospheric struggle for the rain when the god with his thunderbolt defeats the demon who keeps back the rain in the clouds. The wisdom of the tree is the ambrosial rain, for is not their *nibbāna* sometimes called by the Buddhists 'ambrosia'?[1] All the author's literary skill, poetic imagination, and great learning have not availed to secure acceptance for this theory. For no attempt is made to explain how or why or when or where the transmutation of the one set of ideas into the other can have taken place.

Heinrich Kern, the late professor of Sanskrit at Leyden, was of yet another opinion. In his view the Buddhist accounts of their teacher's life are a euhemerized sun-myth. The Buddha is really the sun, and his disciples are the stars. He regards the tree, not (with Senart) as the cloud-tree, but as 'the world tree, the tree of life.' This is obscure, as the two are quite different; and he refers only to a post-Buddhistic *Upaniṣad* (*Kaṭha*, vi. 1) which does not clearly speak of either.[1] Even if it did, what evidence could that be of Buddhist belief?

[1] Senart, *Légende du Buddha*, Index, *s.v.* 'Bodhi.'

It should be pointed out, firstly, that these theories are mutually exclusive, and cannot be combined. If any one of them is right, then each of the others is wrong. Secondly, they are all almost exclusively based, so far as the Buddhist side of the question is concerned, on late records—records eight hundred years or more later than the events they purport to describe. To the present writer it seems indisputable that, if a historian wishes to ascertain the genesis of a 'legend,' the only scientific method is, first of all, to ascertain what is the earliest form in which the legend is recorded. The earliest form of the legend about the original tree is as follows.

It is well known that there is no consecutive life (or legend) of the Buddha in the canon. But there are incidental references to certain episodes in his career. Of these at least twelve refer to the episode of the Wisdom Tree. But only two of them even mention the tree; and then it is merely to say that when seated under the tree the Teacher thought such and such things. This simple fact is enough to dispose of the theory that the tree was nearly, if not quite, as important as the teacher.[2] In one of the longer composite Suttantas contained in the *Dīgha* there is a short account of six previous Buddhas with a sketch of the life of Vipassi, the first of the six. This is so evidently drawn up as a mere imitation of the life of the historical Buddha that it is suggestive to find that the sketch contains no reference to a wisdom tree. This is the more remarkable since in the tabular paragraphs giving certain details about each of the six the name of the tree under which each attained to enlightenment is also given. In none of the cases is the tree called a wisdom tree.

If the above statements of fact are correct, it follows that the expression 'wisdom tree' or 'tree of enlightenment' does not occur at all in any of the oldest of those canonical works which deal with the Dhamma (the law or religion), that it occurs once in all the other canonical works on the Dhamma, that it occurs only once in those that deal with the regulations of the order (the *Vinaya*), that that single reference is in the very latest portion of the *Vinaya*,[3] and that the expression is then used merely to distinguish from other trees of the same kind and name that particular one under which the teacher was seated when he obtained enlightenment.

For the later history of the original 'wisdom tree' at Bodh-Gayā in India see art. GAYĀ.

LITERATURE. — J. E. Tennent, *Ceylon*², London, 1859; *Dīpavaṃsa*, ed. H. Oldenberg, do. 1879; *Mahāvaṃsa*, ed. W. Geiger (*PTS*, do. 1908); *Mahā-bodhivaṃsa*, ed. S. A. Strong (*PTS*, do. 1891); James Fergusson, *Tree and Serpent Worship*, do. 1868; E. Senart, *La Légende du Buddha*², Paris, 1882; H. Kern, *Der Buddhismus*, Germ. tr. H. Jacobi, 2 vols., Leipzig, 1882–84; *Katha Upaniṣad*, tr. Max Müller, *SBE* xv. [Oxford, 1884]; *Vinaya*, ed. H. Oldenberg, London, 1879–83, tr. in *Vinaya Texts, Mahāvagga and Chulavagga*, tr. from the Pali by T. W. Rhys Davids and H. Oldenberg, *SBE* vols. xiii., xvii., xx. [Oxford, 1881–85]; *Saṃyutta*, ed. Léon Feer (*PTS*, London, 1884); *Majjhima*, ed. V. Trenckner and R. Chalmers (*PTS*, do. 1888–99); *Udāna*, ed. Paul Steinthal (*PTS*, do. 1885); *Dīgha*, ed. T. W. Rhys Davids and J. E. Carpenter (*PTS*, do. 1899–1903), tr. T. W. Rhys Davids in *Dialogues of the Buddha*, Oxford, 1899–1910; A. Cunningham, *The Stūpa of Bharhut*, London, 1879; J. Legge, *Travels of Fa-hien*, Oxford,

[1] Kern, *Buddhismus*, ii. 224. For the world-tree and the tree of life see J. H. Philpot, *The Sacred Tree*, London, 1897, chs. iv. and vi.

[2] The mention of the tree is at the opening page of the *Vinaya* (translated in *Vinaya Texts*, i. 2 = *Udāna*, i. 4, and in *Udāna*, iii. 10). The other passages, which do not refer to the tree, are *Saṃyutta*, i. 105, 136 (tr. in *Kindred Sayings*, i. 128, 171 ff.); *Majjhima*, i. 22, 167 ff., 240 ff., ii. 93–96; *Udāna*, i. 4, ii. 1, iii. 10.

[3] On the chronological relations of the various portions of the Vinaya to one another see the Introduction to *Vinaya Texts*.

1886; T. Watters, *On Yuan Chwang's Travels in India*, ed. T. W. Rhys Davids and S. W. Bushell, 2 vols., London, 1904–05; T. W. Rhys Davids, *Buddhist India*, do. 1903.

T. W. RHYS DAVIDS.

WITCHCRAFT.—See DIVINATION, MAGIC.

WOMAN.—See BIRTH, EDUCATION, EMANCIPATION, ETHICS, FAMILY, MARRIAGE, and other articles.

WONDERS.—See MIRACLES, PRODIGIES AND PORTENTS.

WORD (Sumerian and Babylonian).—**1. Original ideas.**—The Sumerian vocable for 'word,' or formal expression of command, is *inim*, deflected early to *enem*, and it was carefully distinguished from the noun *dug*, 'discourse,' 'speech,' and the verb *dug*, 'to speak.' *Inim, enem*, is always a noun and was translated into Semitic by *amātu*. Both *enem* and *amātu* obtained the secondary meanings 'affair,' 'matter' (Latin *res*). The Sumerian word also developed the sense 'incantation,' *i.e.* the formal words of the magician, and hence the reduplicated form *inim-inim-ma* (pronounced *inim-nim-ma*) became the ordinary rubric in the magic literature for 'incantation' (Semitic *šiptu*). The present writer derives the noun *inim* from the verbal root *nim*, 'utter a decision,' 'issue a formal word,' whence is also derived the noun *nam*, 'fate,' 'decision.' The Semitic noun *amātu* is derived from a root *wamû* (אמא), 'speak,' 'curse,' found otherwise only in Aramaic in the forms *iāmā'*, *'āmā'*. The Sumerians and consequently the Semites regarded a formally spoken 'word,' containing the force of a command or promise, as a definite and real thing. It possessed magical and terrible power if it issued from a deity, from a priest, or from a human being under formal circumstances. Hence witnesses who were present at a legal transaction which ordinarily involved an oath were called *galu inim-inim-ma*, 'men of the words,' or men who were present when formal 'words' or matters were arranged. A witness is sometimes called *inim-zu*, 'one who knows the word,' *i.e.* one who knows what formal words were stated in a transaction.

The formally spoken word of any of the great gods was regarded by the Sumerians as a real divine entity. For the early period we have only the personal names of Sumerians as a source for our study, but undoubtedly the conception of the word as an agent of god's wrath, which became in later times one of the principal features of Sumero-Babylonian religion, arose long before the liturgical texts in which alone this doctrine has been preserved. This is the aspect of the word which was chiefly developed in Sumerian theology, but they also held that the *enem*, or word, of a great god might be a good and kind agent of deity when not uttered in wrath to punish the sins of men. Before 2900 B.C. occur such personal names as the following: *Enem-ma-ni-zid*, 'His word is true,' *i.e.* the god's word is a faithful support;[1] *Enem-azag-zu-da-ri*, 'The word of the wise one is eternal.'[2] In the period of Ur (25th cent.) occur the names *Enem-dug-ga-(ni)*, 'His good word,'[3] and *Enim-ᵈBau-ni-gi*, 'The word of the goddess Bau is true.'[4] Even in a passage to the destructive word of the gods Anu, Enlil, Marduk, and Nebo from a liturgy of the 21st cent. a line runs, 'His word has no evil,' *i.e.* does no wrong.[1] It is, therefore, certain that the Sumerian conception of the word of the gods was not necessarily that of an avenging messenger. Nor is the idea of a curse inherent in the original use of the term. They simply attributed to the formally spoken word of a great god a semi-personality; they thought of it as a divine agent.[2]

2. The 'word of wrath.'—The Sumerian liturgies in all periods of their evolution chant at great length the destructive work of the avenging word which is sent by the angered gods to chastise mankind for their sins.[3] In the earliest known liturgical fragment (period of Gudea, *c.* 2650) a passage to the *Verbum Iræ* occurs.

'Thy Word upon the sea has been projected and returns not.'[4]

But passages on the 'word of wrath' must have been employed in public choral services in pre-Sargonic times, *i.e.* before 2800 B.C. The name *Enem-dúg-dúg-ga-ni an-dūb*, 'The word which he spoke shakes the heavens,' is found on a temple record of Lugalanda (*c.* 2850),[5] and an abbreviated form of it, *Enem-du-du*, occurs in the period of Ur.[6] This name, like so many Sumerian personal names, has been taken from the liturgies, and the line which supplied it recurs frequently in passages to the destructive word.

'The Word which on high shaketh the heavens,
The Word which beneath causes the earth to tremble.'[7]

That alone is conclusive evidence for the existence of this theological conception and for these doleful descriptions of the destructive word in public song services at the very beginning of Sumerian civilization.

In the earlier stages of Sumerian liturgical worship, when only single song melodies or lamentations were employed, we find references to this idea. A long lament of the Weeping Mother, who is represented, as so frequently in later compositions, in the rôle of a mother-goddess wailing for her people, has in the very opening lines a passage which attributes all the woes of humanity to the words of Anu and Enlil. Sin invariably provokes the anger of the gods and they send the 'word of wrath' to hasten forth and afflict mankind. Hence the great earth-mother, who loves men and shares their sorrows, is also afflicted by the word.

'In the home it causes life to cease, in the flocks (?) it causes life to cease,
To the wedded ones it causes life to cease, among children it causes life to cease.
It has taken them as prey, it has caused them to disappear.

His Word speeds me, speeds me forth, as oft as it comes to me my face is prostrated.

. . . .

When the Word of Anu came to me,
When the Word of Enlil came to me,
When to my temple he came,
When by the mountain road he entered.'[8]

. . . .

A liturgy of the compiled type, which preceded in order of evolution the canonical compositions of the Isin period,[9] has a remarkable melody of the Weeping Mother, in which she thus describes the misery of the city Ur:

'May Anu prevent his Word.
May Enlil order kindness.

. . . .

[1] M. V. Nikolski, *Documents de la plus ancienne époque chaldéenne de la collection Likhatcheff*, St. Petersburg, 1908, no. 3, col. vii. 3, and see p. 100; also Maurice Allotte de la Fuye, *Documents présargoniques*, Paris, 1908–13, no. 87, ii. 1 and *passim*; also frequent in the later period; E. Chiera, *A Syllabary of Personal Names*, Philadelphia, 1916, p. 69.

[2] Unpublished. 'The wise one' refers to a deity.

[3] E. Huber, *Die Personennamen in den Keilschrifturkunden aus der Zeit der Könige von Ur und Nisin*, Leipzig, 1907, p. 125.

[4] *Ib.*

[1] S. Langdon, *Sumerian and Babylonian Psalms* (hereafter cited as *SBP*), p. 76, 22.

[2] See, on both propitious and hostile views of the Word, § 3 below, *ud, udde*, the angry spirit.

[3] See art. PRAYER (Babylonian), vol. x. p. 165 f.

[4] *PSBA* xxxiv. [1912] 156.

[5] Allotte de la Fuye, no. 234, iii. 3.

[6] Huber, p. 125.

[7] Langdon, *SBP*, p. 78, 13–14, see also pp. 98, 44; 38, 11; 100, 49. On personal names which refer to the hymns on the Word see *ERE* ix. 172.

[8] S. Langdon, 'Liturgy to Innini,' *RA* ix. [1912] 5–11.

[9] See the Introduction to Langdon, *Sumerian Liturgies and Psalms* (hereafter cited as *SLP*), Philadelphia, 1919.

Its foundations it has annihilated and reduced to the misery of silence.
Unto Anu I cry, "How long?"
Unto Enlil I myself do pray.
"My city has been destroyed," will I tell them.
"Ur has been destroyed," will I tell them.'[1]

The fifth melody of this early liturgy is the *Verbum Iræ*, and henceforth all the canonical Sumerian liturgies contain one song to the 'word of wrath.' Before giving a selection from this most notable song to the word, let us note that the idea of *enem*, 'word,' had become so fully associated with divine wrath that it was called *ud*, *udde*, 'storm,' 'angry spirit.' Portions of this melody to the word of Enlil follow:

'Enlil utters the angry spirit and the people wail.
The angry spirit has destroyed prosperity in the land and the people wail.
The angry spirit has taken peace from Sumer and the people wail.
He sent the woeful spirit of wrath and the people wail.
Ḳingaludda and Uddagubba into his hand he entrusted.
He has spoken the angry spirit which exterminates the Land and the nation wails.
Enlil sent the fire-god as his helper.
The mighty wrathful spirit of Anu was spoken and the people wail.
The city Ur like a garment thou hast destroyed, like . . . thou hast scattered.'[2]

The above is the most important passage in Sumerian literature for the personification of the word. Enlil sends two messengers, Ḳingaludda and Uddagubba, to attend the word as he goes forth to execute vengeance upon mankind for their sins. The name Ḳingaludda means 'messenger of the angry spirit,' and Uddagubba means 'he who stands by the angry spirit.' Both of these are minor deities, and the former became a well-known demon.[3] Here also the fire-god is sent forth by the earth-god Enlil as an attendant of the angry spirit—an idea which survived in post-Exilic Hebrew in connexion with the visitation of the *rūaḥ*, or spirit, of Jahweh among men. Joel describes the visitation of God's spirit in the words:

'I will place marvels in heaven and earth, blood, and fire, and pillars of smoke.'[4]

And the idea appears notably in the gift of tongues at Pentecost in NT times:

'And there came suddenly from heaven a sound as of a rushing mighty wind, and it filled the whole place in which they were sitting, and there appeared unto them cloven tongues as of fire.'[5]

In all the canonical Sumerian liturgies which were borrowed by the Semites and continued in use down to the age of Alexander the Great, and even into the era of the Seleucidæ, is found at least one song to the spirit of wrath. Since the word (*enem*) or spirit (*ud*) of Anu, the heaven-god and father of all gods, almost invariably comes first, we infer that the spoken word issued from heaven is the original idea, and then the same power was attributed to Enlil, the earth-god, and to a few others of the great deities. The following list of partially restored liturgies in which the song to the word or spirit has been preserved is in the present stage of Sumerology exhaustive:

(1) Enlil series: *babbar-ri babbar-ri-gim te-ga-bi zal*, 'Like the sun, like the sun his approach illuminates'; inserted in the first melody.[6] Here *ud* and *enem* are both employed.

'Spirit (*ud*) that brings the youth to extremity, spirit that brings the maid to extremity.
Spirit that destroys the stalls, spirit that desolates the folds.
Possessor of *wisdom*, spirit whose intentions are not discerned.
. . . .
Spirit that reduces all things to obedience.
The word of Enlil rushes forth and eye beholds it not.'

(2) Enlil series: *elum gudsun-e mu-zu kurkurra*, 'Mighty one that overwhelms, thy name is upon all lands'; fourth song.[1]

'A tempest it is, shattering the mountains.
As for the lord his word is a tempest.
The heart of the mighty one is a tempest.
The heart of Enlil is a tempest.'

(3) Enlil (?) series: *uddam gù-de-de-dš*, 'When like a storm he cries'; first song on tablet 2 of the Assyrian edition; song to the *enem* of Anu, Enlil, and Adad.[2]

(4) Weeping Mother series: *nimalla gu-dé-dúg ki-bi ba-da-nad*, 'The cow wailed and in her place lay down'; song to the word inserted in the first melody, lines 11–15.[3] An extremely long hymn to the word of Anu and Enlil of this series occupies two tablets.[3]

(5) Nergal series: a long hymn to the word of Nergal; the last song of the series, followed by the *eršemma*, or recessional.[4]

(6) Nergal series: two long hymns to the word of Nergal, the first of which is a duplicate of the one cited in no. 5; the last two songs of a liturgy to Nergal followed by the *eršemma*.[5]

(7) Nebo series: two songs to the word of Nebo in the third tablet of the series *ukkin-ta eš-bar-ra til-la*, 'In the assembly wisdom is departed.'[6]

(8) Weeping Mother series: contains two passages to the word of Anu and Enlil inserted into two songs.[7]

(9) A liturgy of songs, all devoted to the word. Particular attention is given to the word of Marduk, and the Weeping Mother is represented in two songs as afflicted by the word:

'The exalted one like a wind, like a wind,
The exalted one like a wind has cast me down, even me.
The exalted one, the lord of lands,
He of intangible thoughts, whose word is true,
Against whose command there is no turning back,
The exalted Enlil, the utterance of whose mouth is unalterable.
This angry spirit destroys the folds, rends the stalls.
My roots are rent, my forests are despoiled of leaves.
. . . .
Like a lone *willow*-tree by the river's bank he has made me,
Like a *cedar* in the desert he has made me.
Like a lone tamarisk in the storm he has made me.
Behold the mighty one like a lone rush-reed has brought me low.'

An exceedingly difficult passage attributes the following expression to the mother-goddess:

'I am the word of the lord, because of its misery wailing I sit.'[8]

The first half of the line is interpreted to mean that the mother-goddess is possessed by the wrathful word, she is completely in its power.[9]

(10) Nergal series: *agalgalla šel-susu*, 'Flood that drowns the harvest'; a song to the word of Nergal is inserted into the first litany, and it was followed by a second hymn to the word which has not yet been recovered.[10]

(11) A liturgy to the word of Anu arranged to commemorate the destruction of the city Ur: *anna elume ū-a enemmani*, 'Of exalted heaven lofty is his word.' The first two tablets only are preserved. They include hymns to the words of the moon-god, the sun-god, and the thunder-god. The second song of the liturgy, following upon the hymn to the word of Anu and Enlil, is devoted to the Weeping Mother.[11]

(12) Selection from an unknown series containing two hymns to the word. The first hymn begins, 'His word hastens forth from Ekur, his word is the burden of the storm.' It is an old hymn to the word of Enlil, the earth-god. The litany includes references to the word of Ea, of Damkina his spouse, of Marduk, of Nebo and of Sakkut, all of which are said to proceed from Ekur, the temple of Enlil in Nippur.[12] The second hymn on this tablet is among the most remarkable of all the songs to the word. Fifteen

[1] Selections from the fourth melody of Nippur 7080, published in *SLP*, no. 11.
[2] Selection from the fifth melody of Nippur 7080.
[3] See the note in *SLP*, p. 283.
[4] Jl 2[30].
[5] Ac 2[2f.].
[6] Langdon, *Sumerian Liturgical Texts*, 158, 16–159, 25. It is probable that this liturgy contained a section entirely devoted to the word. A Weeping Mother series employs the same hymn; see below, no. 16.

[1] The text (after Zimmern) is ed. in *SLP*, pp. 292–308; see, for the song to the word, p. 299.
[2] See Langdon, *Babylonian Liturgies* (hereafter cited as *BL*), p. 25.
[3] Published in *BL*, p. 43, and *SBP*, pp. 18–35.
[4] Published in *BL*, no. 73, pp. 47–49, to be restored from the duplicate, *SBP*, p. 76.
[5] Text in G. Reisner, *Sumerisch-babylonische Hymnen*, Berlin, 1896, no. 7; ed. in *SBP*, pp. 76–78.
[6] *BL*, pp. 65–68.
[7] For the text see *BL*, plates lxix.–lxx. For a tr. of the first passage see p. 74. For the second passage see pp. 107 f. and 74 f.
[8] That is clearly the meaning of the line (see *SBP*, p. 46, 15, where the end of the line should be read *še-ám-du ám-dù*).
[9] The series was called *uddam ki-ám-(mu)-uš*, 'Like the wrathful spirit (his word) has been established.' Six songs of tablets 1 and 2 are edited in *SBP*, pp. 38–55. The remainder of the series, *i.e.* tablets 3–6, are supposed to contain similar material.
[10] K. 69, ed. in J. Böllenrücher, *Gebete und Hymnen an Nergal*, Leipzig, 1904, pp. 32, 40–35, 35. See also for variant of a part of this song to the word, *SBP*, 43, 49–47, 18.
[11] Ed. in *SBP*, pp. 58–67.
[12] This remarkable hymn to the word is ed. in *SBP*, pp. 72–74 (lines 1–30), and the remainder of the hymn will be found on pp. 76–78, lines 16–reverse 4.

lines from the end of the composition have been preserved, but the opening lines are lost. It reads:

. . . .

'Its *flail* (*ḫuluppu*) distresses small and great.
Small and great it crushes and pours into a heap.
When on the river it rushes, a deluge it causes.
When on the Tigris it rushes, a deluge it causes.
When on the Euphrates it rushes, a deluge it causes.
[When on the . . . it rushes, a deluge it causes].[1]
When it hastens in the ravines of the hills a deluge it causes.
When the Lord[2] speaks, then it hastens and a deluge it brings.
The child-bearing mother wailed, "Behold my son doth send (the word)."
The mother Damkina wailed, "Behold my son doth send."
Unto her chamber she entered, she hastened (wailing), "Behold my son doth send."
Son whom in the sacred bowl I baptized, "Behold my son doth send."
Son who from the stone bowl has eaten, "Behold my son doth send."
He who ate has of himself grown great, "Behold my son doth send."
Him that with a measuring-rod I proved, "Behold my son doth send."'[3]

We have here an interesting situation. Damkina, a mother-goddess, wife of Ea the water-god, laments the ruin caused by the word of her own son Marduk.

(13) Nergal series, second tablet: a long hymn to the word of Nergal occupies nearly the entire tablet; it is followed by a short song in which Nergal is imprecated to send his destructive word upon all wicked lands.[4]

(14) Enlil series: title unknown. Only one tablet of the series has been recovered. The liturgy contained two short hymns to the word of Enlil at the end of this tablet.[5]

(15) Enlil series: *ame barana-ra*, 'The hero to his sanctuary.' Four of the six tablets of this liturgy are known.[6] The liturgy contained at least one song to the word of Enlil.[7]

(16) Weeping Mother series: *uru ḫulage*, 'She whose city was destroyed.' Four of the six tablets of this liturgy are known. Tablet 5 has a song to the word of Enlil, identical with the one employed in the first tablet of the Enlil series, no. 1 above.[8]

3. The spirit (ud).—In the preceding discussion some attention is necessarily given to the identification of the word of a god with his breath or spirit. As in the case of the 'word' (*enem*, *inim*), the term for 'spirit' or 'breath' (*ud*) of a god had not originally a destructive and violent sense, but its use in that sense became almost universal and consequently should be rendered in most passages by 'angry spirit,' 'spirit of wrath.' In all of the present writer's translations 'angry spirit' renders the Sumerian *ud*=Semitic *ûmu*. The Sumerian *ud* is the ordinary word for 'day,' and so is the Semitic *ûmu*. The Sumerians, and after them the Semites, conceived the breath of a god as a warm flood of light. When a god's anger was aroused, his breath went forth as a storm, and consequently both *ud* and *ûmu* came to mean 'storm.' But the original idea of the divine spirit or breath must be defined. A passage on the wrathful word of Enlil is introduced by the remarkable statement, 'The utterance of thy mouth is a beneficent wind, the breath of life of the lands.' The soul of the god is here defined as a kindly wind[9] which gives life to mankind.[10] A proper name of a man in the period of the Ur dynasty was *Udde-nigšag*, 'the spirit (of god) is a blessing,' and another is *Udde-nigšig*, 'the spirit is goodness.'[11] A name in the pre-Sargonic period is *Ud-mukuš*, 'the spirit has become reconciled,' *i.e.* the wrath of god is appeased.[1] It is said of the mother-goddess Ishtar, *ud-de-da ba-e-sig*, 'by the spirit thou art filled,' *i.e.*, the spirit of one of the great gods was given unto her.[2] She is thus endowed with supreme power. In the same manner kings are given the divine 'word.' Ur-Ninā is called the man *inim-sig* *ᵈNinā*, 'unto whom was given the word of the goddess Ninā.'[3] Ur-Bau is described as the man *inim-ma-sig-ga* *ᵈInnini*, 'unto whom was given the word of Ishtar.'[4] It is obvious, therefore, that the spirit or breath of a god was practically identical with his word, and it was personified as an agent of good works. This phase of its activity as a *verbum creator*, a spirit of wisdom and cosmic reason, appears only in Semitic texts where the Semitic word *mummu* is employed. In Sumerian texts the beneficent and philosophic aspect of the word is wholly overshadowed by its activity as an agent of wrath.

'The spirit (*ud*) of the heart of Anu which has become evilly disposed,' says a line of a hymn to the word, and the *ud* is called the messenger of the lord of the lands (*i.e.* Enlil).[5] Another passage states explicitly, 'The spirit is the word of Enlil.'[6] The expression, 'the merciless spirit,' was so common that it appears in grammatical texts.[7] And, when the wrathful word had executed judgment on the earth, the god who sent him forth recalled him. 'When Anu spoke, the word returned to its place.'[8]

4. The 'word of wrath' in Hebrew.—The Sumerian belief in the wrathful word of the gods passed into late Hebrew theological beliefs. The description of Jahweh's word by an Alexandrian Jew in the Greek book, the *Wisdom of Solomon*, is obviously under the influence of Sumerian liturgies which were being sung everywhere in Babylonia at that time:

'Thine all-powerful Word leaped from heaven down from the royal throne,
A stern warrior, into the midst of the doomed land,
Bearing as a sharp sword thine unfeigned commandment,
And standing filled all things with death.'[9]

A post-Exilic Psalm reflects clearly the Sumerian idea:

'He sendeth his commandment upon the earth;
His Word runneth very swiftly.'[10]

Even more direct is the evidence of the post-Exilic Isaiah, for here we have words written by a prophet who almost certainly lived in Babylonia.

'So shall my word be which goeth up from my mouth; it shall not return unto me void,
For it shall have done that which I desired,
And shall have accomplished that for which I sent it.'[11]

5. The word as creative wisdom.—The Sumerians and Babylonians invariably regarded water as the uncreated first principle and source of all things created. The creative form or principle resided in the primordial watery chaos. Since we do not have any Sumerian sources for the doctrine of the cosmic word, but only a syllabar which gave the term, now unfortunately broken away, it is impossible to state exactly what it was. Evidence deduced above for the beneficent activity of a god's word and breath induces the conjecture that the Sumerians employed the term *inim*, 'word,' for cosmic creative form or reason. At any rate we know that the term *mummu*[12] was said to mean 'loud voice,' apparently because the roar of the thunder- or rain-god was adopted as a term for the indwelling wisdom of water. We know that *ud*,

[1] This line is omitted on the variants.
[2] Marduk is referred to here.
[3] The text of this hymn has been reconstructed from Reisner, plate 14=*SBP*, p. 74; *BL*, no. 41, and a small fragment published by Bruno Meissner, *Assyriolog. Studien* (*MVG* xv. 5), Leipzig, 1912, no. 3, p. 79.
[4] Ed. in *SBP*, pp. 80–88.
[5] See *SBP*, p. 92, 8–13, for the first hymn to the word in this liturgy; and for the second hymn which followed here, see H. Zimmern, *Sumer. Kultlieder aus alt-babylon. Zeit*, Leipzig, 1913, no. 195, obv. 6 ff.
[6] Reisner, no. 26, tablet 3; no. 33, tablet 6. Nos. 14 and 15 belong to the series, but cannot be fixed in order.
[7] See *SBP*, pp. 99, 36–100, 59.
[8] Tr. in *SBP*, pp. 187, 19–188, 37.
[9] With this aspect of the divine breath is to be compared the Hebrew *rûaḥ* of Gn 6³, 'Not shall my spirit abide in man.'
[10] *SBP*, p. 124, 17–18.
[11] L. Legrain, *Le Temps des rois d'Ur*, Paris, 1912, p. 105. See also Huber, *Personennamen*, p. 55, where read *Udde-nigšagga* for the *Utu-bil-gar-šagga*.

[1] Nikolski, 16, I. 11.
[2] *SLP*, no. 3, line 17.
[3] F. Thureau-Dangin, *Die sumer. und akkad. Königsinschriften*, Leipzig, 1907, p. 4 c. col. v. 5.
[4] *Ib.* p. 60, II. 1.
[5] *SBP*, p. 18, lines 10 and 28.
[6] Or 'the spirit of the word of Enlil,' the storm-breath of the word of Enlil (*SBP*, p. 98, 38; see also *BL*, p. 107, 16).
[7] *Ûmu la padû*.
[8] *PSBA* xl. [1918] 70, line 15.
[9] See S. Holmes in R. H. Charles, *Apocrypha and Pseudepigrapha of the Old Testament*, Oxford, 1913, i. 565.
[10] Ps 147¹⁵.
[11] Is 55¹¹.
[12] Commonly supposed to be Semitic. *Mummu* may be, however, Sumerian and a word for 'form.' See Thureau-Dangin in *RAssyr* xvi. [1920] 166, II. 3. The Semitic interpretation of

'breath,' 'storm,' was also identified with the thunder-god.[1] *Mummu* at any rate was the accepted Semitic[2] term, and means 'voice.' It was personified and survived in the writings of the Greek historian Damascius as Mōymis. According to Damascius, Mummu was the intelligible world and the only-begotten son of Apsū, the nether sea of fresh water, and Tiamat, the salt water sea. Since all things descended from water and wisdom resided in water, Enki, god of water, was called *mummu bān kala*, 'Mummu (creative reason) which creates all things.' Also Nebo, god of writing and son of Enki, was identified with *mummu*, 'who fashions the things created.' When Marduk, at the hands of the Babylonian priests, became the son of Enki and creator of the world, he also was identified with *mummu*.

According to Sumero-Babylonian philosophy, the reality of anything consists in its 'form' (*ḫar*; Semitic *uṣurtu*), *i.e.* the divine mental concept which is revealed to mankind by its name. For example, the word 'bowl' is a name by means of which its 'form' or the divine concept is revealed to man. All knowledge is revelation, and the reality of things is not their tangibleness but the mental concept, and things cannot exist until a god has this mental concept. Fundamentally all things, material and immaterial, rest upon the mental activity of the water-god, which is *mummu* and was personified cosmic reason. Hence the universe was conceived to be held together by a band or cord, *riksu*, *markasu*, a divine creative reason. Such was the philosophic and mystic concept of the word in Babylonia.[3]

6. The Greeks borrow the Babylonian idea of creative reason.—There can be little doubt but that Thales, founder of the Ionian school of hylozoism, who regarded water as the first principle, borrowed his ideas from Babylonia. Here in the Ionian school of Thales, Anaximander, and Anaximenes, all of Miletus, cosmic substance itself is reason, wisdom, and harmony.[1] That strikingly corresponds to the activity of the Babylonian Logos or Mummu. Heraclitus (*q.v.*) of Ephesus, who developed the ideas of his predecessors at Miletus at the end of the 6th cent. shortly after the fall of Babylonia, adopted fire as the universal element, sometimes defined as hot breath in his writings. He is the originator of the cosmic philosophy of 'becoming,' the ceaseless transformation of all things from fire or heat through various stages back again to fire. And the cosmic law or reason working beneath all this process of becoming is λόγος, or the word. We do not know whether the earlier Ionian philosophers employed λόγος in this sense, but there seems to be an apparent connexion between the creative wisdom or word of the Babylonians and the law of eternal becoming or the 'word' of Heraclitus.[2]

7. Influence of Babylonian creative word in Hebrew.—The Hebrew employs both 'word' (דָּבָר) and 'spirit' (רוּחַ) in much the same way as the Babylonians employed *mummu*. We have seen that the Sumerians and Babylonians regarded the spoken word and the breath of the god as intimately connected and originally as beneficent agents. Although Hebrew has not the profound mystic and cosmic philosophy of the Babylonian, there is an obvious connexion between the two cultures at this point. We may not infer borrowing here, but the similarity must be noted. A passage of an Exilic Psalm confirms the suspicion that the writer knew Babylonian theological ideas:

> 'By the word of Jahweh were the heavens created,
> And by the breath of his mouth all their host.'[3]

LITERATURE. — S. Langdon, *Sumerian and Babylonian Psalms*, Paris, 1909, *Babylonian Liturgies*, do. 1913, *Sumerian Liturgical Texts*, Philadelphia, 1917, *Sumerian Liturgies and Psalms*, do. 1909, 'The Babylonian Conception of the Logos,' *JRAS*, 1918, pp. 433–449. Other texts and literature are cited in the footnotes.

S. LANGDON.

WORLD.—See COSMOGONY AND COSMOLOGY.

WORSHIP.

WORSHIP (Primitive).—What is worship? The word itself is English, and almost untranslatable into other languages. Originally it implied acts prompted by veneration, but with stress of time and weight of usage it has come to be applied to the whole range of religious behaviour, so that one might well say that worship is the active side of religion. Even so, the meaning does not stop with the notion of act; it is also the attitude which prompts the act; it is the belief which stays the attitude; it is the faculty which empowers the belief. In each of these guises it is multiform: *qua* act it includes cult and tabu, rites sacramental and rites ascetic, indulgence and devotion, feast and penance; *qua* attitude it pairs off fear and love, dread and adoration, or it mingles them in the sense of awe; *qua* belief it ranges from myth to philosophy, from creed to science, from passion for ideas to respect for truth; and *qua* faculty it is said to be absent in some men. Nor can it be defined by its objects; for in the context of worship is included not only communion with deity, but also traffic with the devil, while it cannot be

mummu as 'voice' would then be based upon a false etymology or be influenced by their use of the term *amātu*, 'word,' as a *verbum creator*.

[1] R. E. Brünnow, *A Classified List of . . . Cuneiform Ideographs*, pt. i., Leyden, 1887, no. 7791. It should be noted also that the Hebrews often spoke of the breath (רוּחַ) of Jahweh as a storm-wind (Ex 15^{8}, Is 59^{19}, Ps 18^{15}) and as his wrath (Job 4^{9} 15^{30}).

[2] Perhaps a Semiticized Sumerian word *mumma*, 'form' (?).

[3] See, on this section, Langdon, 'The Babylonian Conception of the Logos,' *JRAS*, 1918, pp. 433–449.

[1] See art. IONIC PHILOSOPHY.

[2] For a definition of the metaphysical use of λόγος (word) in Heraclitus see H. Diels, *Herakleitos von Ephesos*^{2}, Berlin, 1909, p. ix. Diels translates λόγος in Heraclitus by 'world-law'; see also Diels, *Die Fragmente der Vorsokratiker*^{2}, Berlin, 1912, p. 77. This interpretation is generally adopted by all historians of philosophy. See P. Tannery, *Pour l'histoire de la science hellène*, Paris, 1887, pp. 172, 186–189, and *passim*; E. Zeller, *Grundriss der Gesch. der griech. Philosophie*^{7}, Leipzig, 1905, p. 60, where λόγος in Heraclitus is rendered by 'universal intelligence'; Max Heinze's ed. of F. Ueberweg, *Grundriss der Gesch. der Philosophie*^{8}, Berlin, 1894, pt. i., p. 55 and *passim*; also art. LOGOS, vol. viii. pp. 133–138.

[3] Ps 33^{6}.

separated from the intercourse of man with man. If we were to judge by phrase alone, its comprehensive complexity would be apparent: along with 'divine worship,' the 'house of worship,' etc., come 'ancestor-worship,' 'devil-worship,' 'idol-worship,' 'nature-worship,' 'snake-worship,' 'tree-worship,' and what not? The residual fact seems to be that the word is catholic of all activities—physical, psychical, social—to which the adjective 'religious' can be applied; while, by discourtesy, it passes on to every other kind of pursuit that may be regarded as governed by a sufficiently intense interest, as 'dollar-worship,' 'woman-worship.'

Probably no readier mode of suggesting the range of meaning embraced in the conception of worship is at hand than the presenting of a list of the principal articles in this Encyclopædia which portray its phases (and along with them should be taken the general art. RELIGION). They include ANOINTING, ASCETICISM, AUSTERITIES, BAPTISM, CELIBACY, CHASTITY, COMMUNION WITH THE DEAD, COMMUNION WITH DEITY, CONFESSION, CONSECRATION, DEIFICATION, DEVOTION AND DEVOTIONAL LITERATURE, EXPIATION AND ATONEMENT, FASTING, FEASTING, HUMAN SACRIFICE, HYMNS, IMAGES AND IDOLS, INITIATION, MYSTERIES, OATH, ORDEAL, PENANCE, PILGRIMAGE, PRAYER, PRIEST AND PRIESTHOOD, PROCESSIONS AND DANCES, PROPHECY, PROPITIATION, PURIFICATION, SACRAMENTS, SACRIFICE, SECRET SOCIETIES, TABU, TOTEMISM. All these refer to modes or ideals of worship which are nearly universal among the races of men, while a multitude of special titles indicate particulars of rite and cult developed from these major forms. Along with these designations of ritual forms, constituting the acts of worship, should be considered those having to do with its occasions: BIRTH, DEATH, MARRIAGE, PUBERTY, or, in a social mode, seed-time (cf. PHALLISM), HARVEST, SABBATH, WAR; and again those designating its objects: ANCESTOR-WORSHIP, DEMONS AND SPIRITS, GOD, RELICS, SAINTS; while, finally, the psychical states induced by rites or regarded as their foundation cannot be excluded from the meaning of the term: ANIMISM (which is really a state of mind, not a system of thought), HOLINESS, LOVE (in its theological sense), MYSTICISM, POSSESSION, REVERENCE, SANCTIFICATION are examples. The whole idea is complex beyond definition, and, although it is undoubtedly primarily a designation of the active side of religion, especially of cult and rite, yet the activities are of such a nature as to be beyond characterization except when taken in connexion with their objects, their occasions, and their psychical effects.

1. Cult and culture.—Worship, broadly defined, is the active phase of religion, as made manifest in rite and cult. What, then, is its 'primitive' character? The question has been often debated and is really important: Are we to identify as the primitive (1) modes of worship found among contemporary or recent savage peoples, or (2) the historically and biologically first evidences of religious cult, or (3) the logically prior factors—*i.e.* the psychologically significant and the philosophically essential elements of human nature displayed throughout the whole course of the religious development of mankind? The first of these three is without question the current usage, and the second is commonly aligned with it; *i.e.*, contemporaneous savage cults are regarded as typical of historically primitive ideas by a majority of writers. Nevertheless, there has been in the past, and there is still, a vigorous current of opinion which maintains that savagery shows quite as much degeneration as it does conservation of religion, in its primitive value; and this opinion derives explicit support from the observed facts, for grossness and decadence in rite and cult belong not to the most utter savages, but frequently to peoples well advanced in material civilization, while an enormous amount of superstitious lumber is obvious survival from what was once significant custom or intelligible belief. In short, in the matter of religion, as in all other matters showing the form of evolution, the law of development seems to be that of the central and healthy type, following a true norm of nature, while over against it are all manner of fantastic outgrowths and by-plays, alike degenerative and destructive. Religious cult, formal worship, is, in fact, no direct variable of culture; it possesses a type and significance of its own which must be dissected out from the accompanying contexts of economic, political, æsthetic, and intellectual life, before it can be properly comprehended.

It is at this point that the third mode of consideration, the psychological and the philosophical, becomes important. Recent years have seen the rapid growth of a very considerable literature devoted to the psychology of religion, its effort being (1) to describe the particular states and processes of mind which lead to worship and define it, and (2) to explain their relationship to the whole context of human nature and the world which has created it. If there is a religious 'instinct,' the definition of its forms and occasions is the patent key to the interpretation of all religious phenomena, and from it the 'primitive' in religion must be trued to type. This is the task of the psychologist, while on the side of the philosopher there remain to be put the great problems of the truth and value of religion. The philosophic task, too, is receiving yearly more attention, with the 'philosophy of values' as the central controversy.

A broad observation of the whole range of facts connected with the relation of cult to culture fortifies the significance of the psychologico-philosophical view-point. Shamanism (*q.v.*), in one form or another, with its accompaniments of trance and ecstasy, is the most universal of the ritual forms known to the least cultured peoples; that it is primarily the development of a psychical aptitude is evident. In the higher societies by far the greater number of cults trace their foundation to an 'inspired' founder, be he ancestor or prophet. The great syncretistic religions hark directly back to the life of a master as their source and explanation. In every level of civilization the origin of religious forms and beliefs goes straight to the individual experiences of individual men for foundation and guidance; nowhere is there evidence of an original religious 'compact' (unless totemism may be regarded as such), although, of course, there are plenty of instances of the application of religious forms to social and state interests. On the whole, the type of cult development, in high civilization and low, is (1) the moral or mystical teacher; (2) the ritualization of the original ceremonies, songs, or prayers, accompanied by social recognition; (3) their corruption, partial or whole, through syncretism (*q.v.*); and (4) not infrequently an effort, through a subsequent prophet or reformer, to purify the cult and bring it back to norm. This is obviously the Hebrew development as represented by the OT; it may fairly be applied to Christianity, to Buddhism, to Brāhmanism; and it finds signal illustration in the more backward regions of the world; *e.g.*, the majority opinion of Americanists is that in the Aztec cults, with their horrible rites, we have a clear-cut case of degradation from what had once been a religion (probably Maya in origin) containing much that was clean and noble, while in Peru there is evidence of several successive purifications and degradations of worship; and in neither centre was the highest religious development invariably concomitant with the greatest material power. Finally, in modern society, the Protestant tendency to identify 'personal' religion with 'primitive' Christianity is clearly a reaction towards a psychical valuation of worship; and, indeed, it is altogether pertinent to note that the three Christian virtues, faith, hope, and love, are essentially and exclusively personal and psychical: here the primitive in religion is clearly individual experience.

2. Ritualism.—However founded, worship inevitably passes over into ritual forms. Rites are variously classified, usually under a broad initial dichotomy, as magical and religious, positive and negative, attractive and avertive, participative and ascetic, etc., though nowhere are these divisions sharp and fast; there are always intermediate classes looking in both directions. Thus imitative magic passes insensibly into devotional prayer; propitiation and praise are directed to the same deity and in the same ceremony; asceticism terminates in its own ecstatic indulgence, hardly to be distinguished from vinal enthusiasm. Furthermore, even where the division is clear, such classifications over-simplify the facts. Similar magical rites may be employed to bind a lover or to destroy an enemy; sacrificial rites, indistinguishable in form, may be designed for propitiation of divine anger or the expression of gratitude for divine protection. Acts of worship no doubt all express desire, but the desires may vary *toto cœlo* in the matter of conscious definition; they may be wholly specific or utterly vague, and their psychical backgrounds as complex as are human moods. The customary classifications afford convenient heads for the arrangement of the facts, but they become dangerous fictions when states of mind or theories of origin are inferred from them.

There are, of course, definable levels in the use of ritual expedients, and these correspond in a general way with cultural development. (1) At the simplest level of life the few rites employed are so nearly *instinctive* in character, and their occasions so spontaneous, that it is hardly necessary even to call upon tradition as an explanation of their presence. Perils which command propitiation, hours of plenty which invite feasting and song, the pains of disease calling for 'medicine' and vision-caught assuagement—all these have obvious, even if psychologically complex, human motives. It is but a step beyond this to the formation of tropaic and apotropaic rituals having to do with the changes which mark the normal lives of men and women: *rites de passage*, with birth, puberty, marriage, parentage, eldership, death, as their posts. Finally, just as there are seasons in the arc of a man's days, so there are the seasons of the natural year which men must observe: rites of seed-time and harvest are doubtless as ancient as is agriculture, while immemorially more ancient still are the simple reactions to the changes of the living world which all known men, at least, make articulate. The fetish, the burial, the primitive calendar, may be taken as symbols respectively of these three elemental directions of ritual life.

(2) Above this first level comes the cultural grade, wherein ritualism is modified to reflect and sustain *social* organization. Already with initiation and marriage rites, with sowing and harvest ceremonies, the social factor enters into the ritual occasion. As community life becomes complex, its enterprises are surrounded and emphasized by prohibitions and commands, tabus and sanctities, which serve as its bond and fixative. This is true not only of the internal life of a community, based on the instincts and the seasons, but also of its external relations: the making of war and the making of peace; and, as time passes, it becomes true in a third dimension, the historical, for the momentous events of tribal and national life inevitably appear to acquire a sanction from nature itself, and their commemoration becomes as seasonal and cyclic. It is worth noting, too, that morality finds its most cogent support in ritual emphasis. The virtues are all in the nature of inhibitions set upon the more animal instincts; they are all in the nature of conscious habits, and are, therefore, subject to deliberate education. It is therefore quite in the order of reason that communal ritualism should become marked by the presence of a definite class of men—the priesthoods—whose special province is the preservation of traditional wisdom and the enforcement of the moral sanctions. Here society becomes specialized, and the religious, as a man apart, answers as it were for the conscience of the group. Worship is no longer governed by the 'inner light' of the elemental instincts, but is established as a moral law.

(3) Still more complex, although by no means rare even among savage peoples, is the level marked by motives which govern *proselytizing*. Cults pass readily from people to people, along with other customs, but there is an especial impulse fathering the desire to convert which is certainly other than instinctive and more than moral. It may be accompanied by motives wholly sordid; it may be utilized by calculating leaders for entirely secular ends; but, whether its character be that of intolerance, of benevolence, or the two admixed, it comes finally to gather to itself the essential zeal of religion. Then it is that the State sheers off from a Church which outgrows it; then it is that religion and morality become divided in consciousness; and then it is, finally, that there arises a problem of reason *versus* faith, of intellectual as against spiritual interests.

(4) Doubtless, a last level should be added—that in which the secular life is felt to be lived in more or less separation from the religious, and in which the motives of the latter become matter of critical and sceptical interest. Conscious study of religion, conscious philosophizing about it, mark this finality; but it is to the point to observe that even here the essential experience maintains itself in the Protestant seclusion of the individual soul. The final rite, the ultimate worship, is retirement into the closet in the hour of spiritual need; and this, after all, is not radically different from the elemental act of instinctive worship, in propitiation or thanksgiving.

3. Objects of worship.—As the occasions of worship give only a partial key to its forms, so the forms afford but a partial clue to its objects. Not all ritual observances are regarded as worship; magical rites are usually placed in another class, and many rites having obvious social values—marriage rites, chief-making rites, the 'potlatch,' are examples—are connected with worship only incidentally, if at all. In order that the ritual form may be recognized as true worship, it must be accompanied by some evidence of a religious sanction; *i.e.*, it must in some sense be directed to powers superhuman, if not supernatural. This means recognition of deity. Ordinarily gods are defined as the objects of worship; the better mode would be to say that the act of worship is the definition of the god. Wherever the religious sanction is present, the conception of God is being created.

Such a reversal in the order of definition would clear the atmosphere of much controversial dust. Many a missionary has accused the heathen of atheism because of his failure to find belief in a Supreme Being with Christian attributes (not infrequently among people incapable of thinking either 'being' or 'attribute'), and many a field anthropologist has described his savages as totally irreligious in one sentence and in the next has gone forward to describe rites which were obviously directed to superhuman powers. Nor need these be personified: personification is itself an act of some intellectual subtlety, and it appears to be the prime token of animism, as distinct from polytheism, just that the animist has failed of achieving this subtlety; but that animism is in the nature of religion, and its placations and reverences in the nature of true worship, few would care to deny. Again, magic: magical ends are usually clearly definable, but the means employed invariably rest upon an implied recognition of unseen or unfelt forces; and it is at least significant that, when gods come to be formulated in thought, their powers are of a piece with all magic potency: the Great Medicine is another name for the Great Mystery. Wherever men placate unseen foes or make offerings to hidden friends—and there are no human tribes so low in mind that these customs are not found among them — there worship is present and divinity recognized.

Above such formless minima the objects of worship build themselves up hierarchically. The definition of a 'thing' becomes the recognition of a 'power,' and the treatment of the power—if the thing be of any importance—becomes the symptom of a cult. Fetishes, 'medicine,' talismans, belong here; they are cherished, they are tended, they are regarded as vehicles of grace; there is no psychological gulf between the fetish and the idol, between the 'medicine' and the sacrament, between the talisman and the holy relic, or even the holy word. Worship is present even in gross superstition—perverted, no doubt, as to its object, but clear in the mode of its regard. As intelligence grows, the purification of human sentiments is accompanied by the elevation of the objects of regard; the near and trivial objects which attract the feebler animist or fetishist give place to the more inspiring or more august forces of nature, which become the spirits that move in wind and wave, that rise as luminous heavenly orbs, or circle through the year on the swift feet of the seasons. Nature-worship is, even to the last, the great fount of the imagery by which we represent to ourselves the augustness and sublimity of divinity, and if, in the end, we feast our imagination of things spiritual with celestial rather than terrestrial phenomena, this is surely but the natural projection of that recognition of the beneficence of light which makes us also liken our most intimate spiritual inward gift to an 'illumination'; the metaphor of light is equally inevitable when applied to wisdom and to grace.

There are, of course, other images which define the objects of adoration. Foremost among them are kinship terms, which, even among the least tutored of men, are the natural titles of gods. 'Father Heaven' and 'Mother Earth' have each a double title to reverence, for the kinship expressed adds to the sublimity and beauty of nature the whole context of humanity in its most winning character, while behind this is also that prophecy of life which parenthood and the whole mystery of procreation have made central in all religious veneration. Indeed, these two factors (natural sublimity and human kinship) are so powerful in appeal that the remaining imaginal mode, which utilizes the likenesses of human society to picture divinity, has never more than passingly and accessorily aided the picture: gods have been likened to warriors, judges, lords, kings, but in their supremacies the light of heaven and the love of the parent have always been their final attributes.

At the foundation, in the mind of the most beclouded savage, the object of worship is a power in strength transcending his own. Whether in his rite-making he goes forward, timidly, to active adoration and a sense of comradeship with his divinity, or, panic-stricken, strives to exorcize the presence and escape its dooms, may well turn upon the colour of his personal fortunes: the Power will be good or evil according to its effects. But, if good, what more inevitable than that very address by a kinship term which is so often enjoined in mythic teachings and which so naturally adds to the sense of power that of benevolence? The third step is that natural association of wisdom with solicitude which is represented by the idea of Providence and imaged by the idea of illumination. Thus the gods, even of dark-minded men, are conceived as more or less strong and good and wise; and it is only a metaphysical theology which universalizes these attributes into omnipotence, omnibenevolence, omniscience. The presence of all three attributes is, of course, not necessary for the existence of worship, though all three are present where the deity is truly adored. But in many cases strength and knowledge are not known or thought to be accompanied by goodness, and out of the terror of evil appetites, immeasurable in power, have grown most of the cruelties and horrors of superstitious worship. If one may so put it, where there is deformity in cult, there will be found deformity in the conception of God.

4. Psychical factors.—Before the conception of worship can be fully developed, to its occasions and its objects must be added the consideration of the distinctive psychical values associated with rite and cult. Here again the problem of the primitive is not easily disengaged. More than any other objects of thought psychical values are dependent upon the associations of words for their designation; and consequently more than any other objects they are subject to the ambiguities and tricks of transference which verbal meanings further. Especially must this be true where the differences in linguistic level are great: words such as 'adoration,' 'communion,' 'reverence,' 'conscience' have no equivalents in untutored tongues, and it is difficult to make certain the presence of analogous experiences. The first problem, therefore, which presents itself to the psychologist is to endeavour to infer from the ritual forms and the imagery involved what modes of experience prompt them, and in particular to separate the symbolical from the literal interpretation.

For it should be borne in mind (and it is too often forgotten) that religious ideas are images or they are nothing. The great elementary psychical fact which makes ritualism ritual is that the act of worship is never realistic: it moves and lives in an atmosphere of double meaning; the feather, the pebble, the geometrical sign, the chanted word, the sacramental bread, and the sacrificial flesh are never what in the bald reality of the senses they appear to be; their sanctities are derived from supersensible modes of experience. That such modes of experience should for their expression resort to every type of the imagery of sensible experience is in the order of nature. That the most intimate of these images should be those most deeply founded in our own organic life, as physical human beings, and in our conscious relations, as social human beings, is equally intelligible. And it is not, therefore, unintelligible that religious meanings should be peculiarly easy to pervert; the very difficulties which make their communication to be symbolical call for a subtlety of response that frequently fails. Thus it is that many rites, conceived in spiritual purity, if their symbolism is lost, become gross because the images in which they are conveyed are bound to be gross.

In particular this is the peril of images of sex: the procreation of life is the most inevitable of human experiences, because of the social as well as the emotional significance, to stand as a religious emblem, and nearly all the noblest modes of religious expression rely upon it for their source (the fatherhood of God, divine love, eternal life); but in the course of religious change no imagery has given rise to more perversion.

Possibly this very fact of ready perversion—'spiritual blindness,' as it is called—may have something to do with the second great source of worship: the sense of a need of salvation. Literal fear and literal desire, sensible ends coupled with sensible means, are the emotions most dealt with as explanations of ritual acts. Bionomically, they are no explanations at all, for the phenomena of worship show little or nothing that can be interpreted as furthering a physical salvation; the irreligious is as healthy and safe as the religious. It is here once more that the images are full of deceit: paradise and hell are painted in the pigments of sensation, whereas the thing meant is supersensible. The fact that calls for a real accounting is just the fact that men (of high culture and of low) feel a need for a salvation which is as a matter of fact inexpressible, just as they feel reverence for a divinity which is indefinable. The quest of this salvation is bound up, on the emotional side, with the group of words ('awe,' 'adoration,' 'communion') whose contextual meaning harks back to the very roots of human life.

One may say, then, that, on the intellectual side, the great factor that is fundamental in the experience of worship is the sense of double-meaning, and therefore of the duality of nature. On the emotional side the key is the feeling of need for salvation (which might be negatively described as a conviction of sin). These two come as near to defining the religious 'instinct' as any broad partition is likely to come. In any case, they give the major forms under which the experiences defining worship are to be subsumed.

The psychology of worship, however, must advance a step beyond this, even to lay its foundations. The human mind, the human being, moves as a unit, as a person; and the act of worship is in some sense so complete an act that it characteristically creates the reciprocal figure in the worshipper of the image of his salvation. Religion in the long run tends to define man, not as an individual, but in his type and form. Animism, in ascribing souls to things, personifies them; personification is the first step towards anthropomorphism, which in itself is but the sensible rendering of a psycho-eidism that is both more elemental and more significant. It is more significant because it defines for us, inwardly, the traits which we regard as ideal, and therefore as divine; and it is thus that the whole psychic play of religious experience takes final form as the depiction of an ideal man, a pattern man, who becomes a saviour, if only through the fact of his recognition. Whether the pattern man be given an incarnation and a story as a human individual, or whether he be read as a man-like God, or whether, in the third place,[1] he be composed through the union of all active ideals, as an *anima mundi*, is accident of tradition. The psychical fundamental is that all forms of worship figure him forth, as in a true theophany.

5. Philosophical implications.—Portrayal and analysis of the facts of worship constitute the science of comparative religion. But, when all its labours are completed, there still remains for consideration the thinker's most profound problem, viz., that of the truth upon which it rests, the demand of nature to which it responds. Modes of thinking are as correspondent with their cosmic context as are modes of perceiving; the eye of the mind is as truly adapted to its formative forces as is the physical eye; in the end, no beliefs come into being save in orientation to some truth, and superstition is assigned its character from some measuring rectitude. The facts of worship and the facts of faith spring up in response to some spontaneous impulse of human nature, and, like all other human impulses, this becomes a ground of philosophy. In its first form philosophy of religion is theology: the reason's apology for the man's traditional beliefs. But in its sophistications the philosophy of religion assumes at least the form of utter detachment and sits in judgment not upon the article but upon the fact of faith, as a mode of cosmic intuition.

What the philosophic solution must be, in type, can be answered only by appeal to the whole history of thought. Philosophy is reflexion upon the whole range of human experience; this experience grows in variety and in implication with the continuance of life; philosophies, therefore, form and reform with the changing generations of men. Nevertheless, even as there is a generic human nature which defines the kind through the course of time, so there is a generic form which shapes and limits philosophic thinking; its sources are, after all, as few as are our gifts and aptitudes. Occasionally an anthropologist, with a gesture of impatience, would clean the slate of old significances. Reinach proposes as a definition of religion, 'un ensemble de scrupules qui font obstacle au libre exercice de nos facultés';[1] but this is literature, not science or philosophy. The very question that is most profound is that of the reality to which those scruples correspond: What, in the nature of the world, is their foundation and bearing? If men have prayed and sacrificed for naught, how is this to be accounted for? If their rites have suffered perversion, whence is the evil? and what good does it violate? If the symbolism and *double entente* which pertain to all worship is wholly fictive, what power has written so strange a gloss into the constitution of man? If conviction of sin and yearning for salvation are prompted by no truth, whence is the lie to which they give life? In its pragmatic way the fact of worship is ever rehabilitating the ontological argument. There is something in the old Stoic inference: 'If altars, then gods'; and the philosophy of religion is the exposition of what man may perceive in his own deeply impulsive belief in divinity.

LITERATURE.—Landmarks in the comparative and sociological study of religious forms, indicating both the spirit of the investigation and the content of the science, are: David Hume, *The Natural History of Religion*, London, 1757; E. B. Tylor, *PC*[4], do. 1903; and Herbert Spencer, *Principles of Sociology*, 3 vols., do. 1876–96. J. G. Frazer, *The Golden Bough*, 2 vols., do. 1890, of which the third edition (1907–12) has been expanded into a veritable encyclopædia of religious rite, is doubtless the most important, as it is the most massive, collection of information. With it should be reckoned the numerous writings of Andrew Lang in this field, first in significance, *Myth, Ritual, and Religion*[2], London, 1899; Salomon Reinach, *Cultes, Mythes, et Religions*, 4 vols., Paris, 1905–13; Goblet d'Alviella, *Croyances, Rites, Institutions*, 3 vols., do. 1911; A. van Gennep, *Religions, Mœurs, et Légendes*, 5 vols., do. 1908–14; and *The Mythology of All Races*, ed. L. H. Gray (Boston, U.S.A., 1915 ff.), of which the following have been published: i. W. S. Fox, *Greek and Roman*; iii. J. A. MacCulloch, *Celtic*; J. Máchal, *Slavic*; vi. A. Berriedale Keith, *Indian*; A. J. Carnoy, *Iranian*; ix. R. P. Dixon, *Oceanic*; x. H. B. Alexander, *North American*; xi. H. B. Alexander, *Latin American*; xii. W. Max Müller, *Egyptian*; J. G. Scott, *Indo-Chinese*. Books of an earlier date of value and importance include: P. D. Chantepie de la Saussaye, *Lehrbuch der Religionsgeschichte*[3], 2 vols., Tübingen, 1905; H. Bois, *La Valeur de*

[1] A most interesting and enlightening example of this subtler form of anthropomorphic thinking, in a primitive community, is the account of 'The Symbolic Man of the Osage Tribe,' by Francis La Flesche, *Art and Archæology*, vol. ix. no. 2 [Feb. 1920].

[1] *Orpheus*, p. 4.

l'expérience religieuse[12], Paris, 1908; F. B. Jevons, *Introd. to the Hist. of Religion*[4], London, 1908; Charles Letourneau, *L'Evolution religieuse dans les diverses races humaines*, Paris, 1892; Conrad von Orelli, *Allgemeine Religionsgeschichte*, Bonn, 1899; A. Réville, *Les Religions des peuples non civilisés*, Paris, 1883; Raoul de La Grasserie, *Des Religions comparées au point de vue sociologique*, do. 1899; C. P. Tiele, *Kompendium der Religionsgeschichte*[3], Breslau, 1903. Among the more significant works of the past dozen years are G. A. Barton, *The Religions of the World*, Chicago and London, 1917; Karl Beth, *Religion und Magie bei den Naturvölkern*, Leipzig, 1914; A. Bros, *La Religion des peuples non civilisés*, Paris, 1907; S. A. Cook, *The Study of Religions*, London, 1914; E. Doutté, *Magie et religion dans l'Afrique du Nord*, Paris, 1909; Emile Durkheim, *Les Formes élémentaires de la vie religieuse*, do. 1912 (doubtless the most important sociological interpretation since Spencer's *Principles of Sociology*); René Dussaud, *Introd. à l'hist. des religions*, do. 1914; R. Eisler, *Weltenmantel und Himmelszelt*, 2 vols., Munich, 1910; L. R. Farnell, *The Evolution of Religion*, London, 1905; G. B. Foster, *The Function of Religion in Man's Struggle for Existence*, Chicago and London, 1909; George Foucart, *Hist. des religions et méthode comparative*, Paris, 1912; Frederic Harrison, *The Positive Evolution of Religion*, London, 1913; E. S. Hartland, *Ritual and Belief*, do. 1914; Marcel Hébert, *La 'Forme idéaliste' du sentiment religieuse*, Paris, 1909, *Le Divin*, do. 1907; Irving King, *The Development of Religion*, New York and London, 1910; A. Le Roy, *La Religion des primitifs*, Paris, 1909; R. R. Marett, *The Threshold of Religion*[2], London, 1914; S. Reinach, *Orpheus*, Paris, 1909. Two recent American books, systematic in character, are G. Foot Moore, *Hist. of Religions*, 2 vols., New York and Edinburgh, 1914–20; C. H. Toy, *Introd. to the Hist. of Religions*, Boston and New York, 1913; while a book which undertakes a critical survey of methods of approach to religious phenomena is Frederick Schleiter, *Religion and Culture*, New York, 1919. For the psychology of religion the fountain-head is W. James, *Varieties of Religious Experience*, New York and London, 1902, which has already proved the inspiration of a large special literature.

H. B. ALEXANDER.

WORSHIP (Babylonian).—Form and content of Babylonian worship are almost entirely borrowed from the Sumerians. This is particularly true of the principles of formal worship or the gestures employed in religious devotion. As to the content of worship or the words spoken therein, the Babylonian public service or daily liturgies are without exception Sumerian. But the prayers of private devotion and all the intricate rituals of the magic cults are largely of Semitic Babylonian origin. The Assyrian religion and worship were thoroughly Babylonian, but here a distinct tendency to preserve the Semitic principle of gesture in private devotion is everywhere noticeable. The Assyrian religion likewise owed much to the Sumerians, and their liturgical offices were borrowed entirely from the old canonical Sumerian breviaries of the 23rd century.

I. *GESTURE IN SUMERIAN PRAYER.*—**1. Pre-historic period.**—Very early Sumerian seals which belong to the pre-historic period (*c.* 3500 B.C.) reveal three orthodox poses in private devotion, or in the gesture assumed by a Sumerian layman when he came before a seated deity to say his prayers.

(1) He is represented in the so-called processional scene, where his own protecting god[1] leads him by the hand and presents him to a seated deity. In the early pre-Sargonic period the posture of the adorant's free arm is not yet fixed. Occasionally the disengaged arm is employed to carry a lamb or kid as an offering. On one very early seal the unoccupied arm is folded across the waist.[2] It is remarkable that this idea is characteristic of both Sumerian and Egyptian religions and of these only—a fact which seems to reinforce much other evidence for an original pre-historic contact between Sumer and Egypt. Naturally the figure of a deity who conducts the worshipper is a pure fantasy. In reality a priest led the layman by the hand in this form of adoration, as we can see from a few scenes which depict the processional form of worship as it really was.[3] (2) The worshipper stands with one hand raised parallel to the breast, palm inward and fingers touching the lips; the other arm is folded across the waist. This is the very ancient salutation by throwing a kiss and is the most common gesture in the private devotions of Sumerians and Babylonians down to the Neo-Babylonian period.[1] (3) The worshipper stands with both hands folded at the waist; from statuettes in the round in all periods it can be seen that this gesture imposed a fixed custom of clasping the hands. The right hand is clasped by the left hand in an extraordinary manner so that the right thumb lies against the body and the fingers of the right hand lie almost horizontal. The position is physically impossible and only an exaggeration of the natural clasp seen in bas-reliefs of Assyria. The gesture seems to belong to the religion of pre-historic Sumer and is as ancient as the kissing hand gesture.

Such were the three positions assumed under various circumstances in private devotion by the Sumerians from pre-historic times down to the period of Agade, when the great Semitic dynasty of Sargon the Ancient seized the hegemony of all southern Mesopotamia for 197 years. Sargon may be dated about 2850.

2. Sargonic period.—The Semites of this period as well as those who had lived in close contact with and among the Sumerians in the pre-Sargonic age adopted the Sumerian principles of gesture. A seal dedicated to Narām-Sin, fifth king of the Sargonic dynasty, represents the worshipper in the kissing hand position. Although the Sumerians recognized this attitude as consisting in throwing a kiss to a deity by the pictograph for the word 'to pray,' yet they commonly designated it, at any rate in later stages, by the term 'lifting of the hand.' In subsequent discussion, when the expression 'lifting of the hand' is employed, the attitude of the kiss hand is always implied. Archæological evidence for religious gesture in this period is meagre, but a few seals seem to indicate that the folded hands position was also common. The old processional scene with intercessory priest disappears entirely in this age.

3. Period of Gudea and Ur dynasty (2650–2358).—In the age of the great Sumerian revival which terminated in the powerful dynasty of Ur we have first of all a return to the old processional scene. But now the disengaged arm, henceforth always the right arm, is held in the attitude of saluting with a kiss. In the time of the Ur dynasty the folded hand gesture becomes extremely common. The present writer has assumed that this gesture was employed in the penitential psalms or prayers of contrition and sorrow, later known as *eršaḫunga* prayers. The kiss hand gesture he takes to be the one adopted in prayers of the magic rituals whose principal motif is praise of the deities. The ancient independent kiss hand gesture, *i.e.* without an interceding figure who leads the suppliant by the hand, appears rarely in this period.[2] In other words, the prayers of the lifting of the hand in the last great age of Sumerian civilization always imply a processional scene and a priest.

4. Period of Isin, Larsa, and Babylonian (Ist) dynasty (2357–1926).—Archæological evidence furnished by a great number of seals in this period leads to the inference that the processional scene with kiss hand gesture was abandoned for the independent attitude. The suppliant now stands with right hand raised and fingers touching the lips, the left arm folded at the waist. On the older seals of the period the priest still performs the act of intercession, but he stands before the seated deity in the folded hand pose.[3] The inference from the evidence of seals alone that the ancient custom of approaching a deity through

[1] The Sumero-Babylonian doctrine concerning man's relation to his own god and goddess is discussed in *ERE* v. 637 f.; see esp. Langdon, 'Religious Interpretation of Babylonian Seals,' in *RAssyr* xvi. [1919] 49–68.

[2] Langdon, 'Gesture in Sumerian and Babylonian Prayer,' *JRAS*, 1919, pp. 531–556, fig. 4.

[3] Stone tablet of Nabuapaliddin (890–854) published in Rawlinson, *WAI* v. 60, a copy of tablet of the Ist dynasty. Engraved memorial deed of Melishipak (end of 13th cent.) (V. Scheil, *Textes élamites-sémitiques*, Paris, 1908, x. pl. 13).

[1] For pre-historic examples see the seals cited in Langdon, 'Gesture in Sumerian and Babylonian Prayer,' p. 533 f., from the publications of Delaporte and Ward.

[2] Cf. a seal dedicated to Dungi (J. Menant, *Recherches sur la glyptique orientale*, Paris, 1883, fig. 86).

[3] See, *e.g.*, L. Delaporte, *Catalogue du Musée Guimet, Cylindres orientaux*, Paris, 1909, no. 45; also *Catalogue des Cylindres orienatux de la Bibliothèque Nationale*, do. 1910, nos. 124–128.

the offices of a priest was abandoned after the Ur dynasty is clearly misleading; for two clear examples of this custom are illustrated on monuments of the Cassite period and on the stone tablet of Nabuapaliddin.[1] Moreover, in prayers of private devotion frequent reference is made to the priest who recites portions of the prayer.[2] But from this period onward until the rise of the Neo-Babylonian empire at the end of the 7th cent. the pose of the kiss hand with left arm folded at the waist is the ordinary gesture in Babylonia.

II. *GESTURE IN ASSYRIAN RELIGION.*—The Assyrians retained the old open hand Semitic pose in prayer, although the kiss hand was also adopted by them from the Sumerians. Since they also borrowed all the prayers and liturgies of the official cults from Sumer and Akkad, the retention of the Semitic gesture emphasizes the tenacity with which they adhered to racial customs. The open hand gesture, which was also the principal one used by the Hebrews, is made by extending both hands upward towards heaven, palms inward. In art the suppliant is always represented standing as in Sumer and Babylonia.[3] But the pose in taking up the gesture of the kiss hand in Assyria was ordinarily modified in two respects. The right arm is now thrown forward and the hand turned outward, the index finger pointing at the god or sacred object. The thumb is closed over the three remaining fingers. This attitude is similar to one seen on Greek monuments and represents the adorant in the later stages of the act of throwing a kiss. But under influence of the Assyrians and Aramæans the old Semitic spirit reasserted itself in Babylonia; seals of the Neo-Babylonian, Persian, Seleucid, and Parthian periods almost invariably represent the worshipper in the open hand pose.

Kneeling and prostration do not appear to have been admitted in the orthodox forms of Sumerian religion, but there is evidence for their use among the Babylonians and the Assyrians. Prostration and kneeling were certainly acts of worship at certain points in the recitation of prayers and penitential psalms among the Semites, and on the whole it seems probable that they are of Semitic origin. In Sumerian literature almost no prayers of the private cults have been preserved. We possess extensive catalogues of the titles of such prayers, and the seals show that they approached their deities in private devotion from the very earliest period. But the spirit of their religion asserted itself rather in communal or public worship, and the liturgies of their various cults are extensive. In the Ur and Isin periods liturgies became canonical and extremely intricate. They were accompanied by music, and in fact the names of instruments were employed as technical terms to describe kinds of songs; *e.g.*, the recessional or final song of a liturgy was sung to the double flute and called the flute song. The canonical liturgies of the Sumerians were borrowed by the Babylonians and the Assyrians and were always said in Sumerian. The greater portion of each liturgy was provided with an interlinear Semitic translation for laymen. No changes in the old Sumerian liturgies were ever permitted, and even in Assyria the national god Ašur is excluded from the deities mentioned in the litanies because his cult arose after the canon of sacred prayer books was closed.

[1] See above, p. 757a, note 3.

[2] So, *e.g.*, in the *eršagḫunga* prayer, iv. Rawlinson, no. 2= Zimmern, *Babylonische Busspsalmen*, Leipzig, 1885, no. 6. And a number of prayers of the 'lifting of the hand' end with the phrase 'I will sing thy praise and I the priest of magic thy servant will sing thy praise' (see E. Ebeling, *Keilschrifttexte aus Assur*, Leipzig, 1919, no. 25, rev. III. 10; C. D. Gray, *Shamash Religious Texts*, Chicago, 1901, K. 3394 rev. 14; L. W. King, *Babylonian Magic and Sorcery*, London, 1896, no. 12, 94).

[3] See Langdon, 'Gesture in Sumerian and Babylonian Prayer,' figs. 16, 18–20, and p. 539.

The Babylonians usually employed Semitic prayers in the private rituals of purification, and these were known as the 'prayers of the lifting of the hand.' They were of course modelled on the Sumerian prayers of the kiss hand ceremonies, and a very great number of prayers of this kind have survived in Semitic. They form almost invariably part of the magic ceremonies of purification.[1] A considerable number of the prayers said by the priests in these services of healing and atonement have been recovered, and these were written and recited in Sumerian, and were known by the rubric (*kišub*). Prayers of penance which are pure religious prayers of great spiritual power and unconnected with magic rituals were not popular, and of these comparatively few have survived. They are all composed in Sumerian and probably represented the prayers said in the old Sumerian processional scene. Obviously they could not be employed by the ordinary layman, who knew no Sumerian. They represent the exclusive and aristocratic side of Sumerian and Babylonian religion. In them the priest takes a leading part, and they are usually provided with a Semitic translation.

LITERATURE.—*On gesture in worship.*—S. Langdon, 'Gesture in Sumerian and Babylonian Prayer,' *JRAS*, 1919, pp. 531–556; Friedrich Heiler, 'Die Körperhaltung beim Gebet,' *Orientalische Studien Fritz Hommel zum sechzigsten Geburtstag gewidmet*, Leipzig, 1918, ii. 168–177.

Liturgical worship.—S. Langdon, *Babylonian Liturgies*, Paris, 1913 (esp. the Introduction concerning the use of musical instruments, the origin and development of the breviaries and their theological content), *Sumerian Liturgical Texts from Nippur*, Philadelphia, 1917, and *Sumerian Liturgies and Psalms*, do. 1919 (Introduction has a résumé of most recent knowledge on liturgical worship), *Sumerian and Babylonian Psalms*, Paris, 1909. For the liturgies of the Tammuz cult, whose festival was probably celebrated at mid-summer, see H. Zimmern, *Der babylonische Gott Tamūz*, Leipzig, 1909, and *Sumerisch-babylonische Tamūzlieder*, do. 1907; S. Langdon, *Tammuz and Ishtar*, Oxford, 1914. Liturgical worship in the cults of deified kings of the late Sumerian period is discussed in 'Sumerian Liturgies and Psalms,' and in 'Notes on the Deification of Kings,' by T. G. Pinches, *PSBA*, 1915, pp. 87–95, 126–134, and in 'Three New Hymns in the Cults of Deified Kings,' by S. Langdon, *PSBA*, 1918, pp. 30–40, 45–56.

Prayers of the lifting of the hand and penitential psalms are discussed and full literature given under PRAYER (Babylonian). In addition to the literature there see Erich Ebeling, *Quellen zur Kenntnis der babylonischen Religion*, Leipzig, 1918–19. What is known concerning the great New Year festival at the spring equinox will be found in H. Zimmern, *Zum babylonischen Neujahrfest*, Leipzig, 1903, 21918; S. Langdon, *Exp* VII. viii. [1909] 143–158. Benno Landsberger, *Der kultische Kalendar der Babylonier und Assyrer*, Leipzig, 1915, has begun a series of monographs upon the Sumerian and Semitic monthly festivals.

S. LANGDON.

WORSHIP (Buddhist).[2]—**1.** Worship (*pūjā*, *vandana*, *māna*, etc.) is no part of the Path (*mārga*). Path is insight into and meditation on the four truths (the four *nirvedhabhāgīya*, *satyadarśana*, *satyabhāvanā*); but worship is an important part of what is styled *mokṣabhāgīya* ('acts connected with or leading to deliverance'). No man can in this life enter into the Path, if he has not, in a previous existence, 'planted' some 'root of merit' (*kuśalamūla*). Among the 'roots of merit' worship is the best.

2. Worship is the best *dāna*, or giving. A man gives material gifts (*āmiṣadāna*) or security (*abhayadāna*) to his fellow-men, to animals, to *pretas*, for their benefit and also for his own benefit. He shall give to the Buddha, to the

[1] See artt. EXPIATION AND ATONEMENT (Babylonian), MAGIC (Babylonian), and PRAYER (Babylonian).

[2] Details concerning Buddhist worship are to be found in all books dealing with Buddhism. Some of the sources are indicated below. But the principles that command the Buddhist Hīnayāna doctrine of worship have never been elucidated, and there is the justification of the present short note.

Dharma, to the Church, for his own advantage, because they are 'fields of merit' (*puṇyakṣetra*) *par excellence*. The better the field, the better the fruit. Now the merit of giving is either *tyāgānvaya* or *paribhogānvaya*; *i.e.*, a merit accrues to the giver either because he gives away (*tyāga*) something or because the recipient enjoys (*paribhoga*) the thing that has been given away. Buddha does not enjoy the flowers, etc., that are offered to *chaityas*. The merit is not weaker for that. The point is discussed in Pali and Sanskrit sources.

LITERATURE.—*Abhidharmakośa*, iv. 32 (on the *triśaraṇagamana*), 112 (on the merit accruing to the future Śākyamuni on account of his worshipping Puṣya), 121 (on the worship of *chaityas*; why actual acts of worship are useful), vii. 34 (paradises and *nirvāṇa* obtained owing to a single thought of faith in the qualities of a Buddha), iii. 99 (avoiding *antarakalpas* by giving to the Saṅgha); *Milinda* (*SBE* xxxv. [1890]) 144–154, 246–248; *Kathāvatthu*, ed. A. C. Taylor (*PTS*), London, 1897, vii. 5 f. (*Points of Controversy*, tr. C. A. F. Rhys Davids and S. Z. Aung [*PTS*], London, 1915, p. 200); Śāntideva, *Bodhicharyāvatāra*, ix. 39–40 (*Introduction à la pratique des futurs Boudhas*, tr. and ed. L. de la Vallée Poussin, Paris, 1907, p. 119); *Madhyamakavṛtti* (*Bibl. Buddh.* v. [Petrograd, 1909]) xvii. 4 f.; *Śikṣāsamuchchaya* (*ib.* 1902), *kārikā* 5 f.; I-tsing, *A Record of the Buddhist Religion*, Eng. tr., Oxford, 1896, p. 115 and *passim*; R. Spence Hardy, *Eastern Monachism*, do. 1860, p. 196; J. P. Minayeff, *Recherches sur le bouddhisme*, French tr., Paris, 1894, p. 155; H. Kern, *Manual of Indian Buddhism* (=*GIAP* III. viii.), Strassburg, 1896, p. 88; W. Wassilieff, *Der Buddhismus*, Petrograd, 1860, p. 244 (whether giving to the Saṅgha is useful); A. Foucher, *The Beginnings of Buddhist Art*, Eng. tr., London, 1918, *L'Art gréco-bouddhique du Gandhāra*, 2 vols., Paris, 1905–17, *passim*.

L. DE LA VALLÉE POUSSIN.

WORSHIP (Chinese).—I. *INTRODUCTORY*.—It is not easy to find any Chinese word or phrase which conveys identically the same meaning as that which the word 'worship' conveys to one who has been brought up in a Christian environment. Probably the first word which would occur to most students of Chinese is *chi*. It consists of three parts—the symbols for 'spiritual beings,' 'flesh,' and 'the right hand,' giving the meaning, 'to hold a piece of flesh in the right hand and offer it to the spirits.' One of the pioneer Anglo-Chinese lexicographers, Morrison, gives as one of the meanings of the character *chi* 'to offer flesh in the rites of worship, to sacrifice with worship.' J. Legge criticizes this interpretation by pointing out that it is not countenanced by the compilers of the standard native dictionary, *K'ang Hsi*. He adds, 'The general idea symbolised by the character *chi* is—an offering whereby communication and communion with spiritual beings is effected.'[1] The importance of this criticism will be manifest when we remember that the symbol *chi* is the one which is commonly used to denote the religious side of the cult of ancestors. If *chi* does not mean 'worship,' a doubt at once suggests itself as to whether we are technically correct in describing that cult as the 'worship' of ancestors. This doubt is fully justified if to the word 'worship' in this phrase we attribute a meaning identical or nearly identical with that which it bears in Christianity. If we assume that 'worship' can only be offered to a god or gods (real or imagined), and we insist upon describing the Chinese ancestral cult as the 'worship' of ancestors, it follows that the ancestors so 'worshipped' are regarded as gods. And this is precisely the principal ground on which the cult in question has been attacked by Christian missionaries. Obviously the process of translation from one language into another can give rise to a great deal of misunderstanding and question-begging.

There are, of course, many other Chinese words and phrases which correspond, more or less roughly, to the word 'worship'; but no one of them can be regarded as strictly equivalent. *Pai* means merely 'to bow' or 'to salute'; when *ch'ung* is prefixed, the term acquires a religious meaning and may be translated 'to salute with reverence.' *Li-pai*, much used by Christian missionaries, does not necessarily mean more than to salute in accordance with the appropriate rites. *Ching-yang* means 'to respect and look up to.' There are several other terms which give the idea of ritual sacrifice. It may be urged that these and similar Chinese terms are, after all, just as satisfactory as the English term, which can hardly be said to contain within itself an adequate indication of what it has come to mean in Christian thought and ritual. If we are careful to remember that there are some not readily definable differences in spiritual content between the European and Chinese terms, not much harm will be done by regarding the two sets of terms as roughly equivalent.

In this article it is unnecessary to attempt to make any such subdivisions or differentiations as are used by the Church of Rome to distinguish the varieties of Christian worship. Such differences as those between λατρεία, ὑπερδουλεία, and δουλεία do not exist in China—simply because they have never been called into existence by the exigencies of religious controversy.

II. *CONFUCIANISM*.[1] — **1. Introductory.** — The clearest expression of the Confucian notions of worship is found in that remarkable collection of religious treatises which goes under the name of the *Li Chi* (*Record of Rites*). 'More may be learned,' says Legge, 'about the religion of the ancient Chinese from this classic than from all the others together.'[2] And it should be added that, as the *Record of Rites* forms one of the Five Classics of the orthodox Confucian learning, it still remains[3] what it has been for many centuries—the principal source of Chinese ideas regarding not only the ritual but also the inner significance of religious observances.

The reader must be warned, however, that, when we give the name of Confucianism to the religious beliefs and rites described in the *Li Chi* and other 'Confucian' classics, we are using the term in a somewhat vague sense as including all that Confucius and his school sanctioned, eulogized, or tacitly accepted. Confucius insisted that he was only 'a transmitter and not a maker,' and in any case he never posed as a religious prophet or as an inspired teacher of religious truth. Much that has come down to us as Confucianism is pre-Confucian in origin; and this we find to be specially true when we enter upon the sphere of religious thought. In the sections that follow it must be understood that 'Confucianism' is used in the looser sense here indicated.

2. Nature of true worship as understood in Confucianism. — (*a*) *Reverence.* — The *Record of Rites* opens with the striking words 'Always and in everything let there be reverence.'[4] In many parts of this classic (which came from many different hands and belongs to many different dates) the supreme necessity of reverence is emphasized, especially in connexion with all ceremonies which regulate the intercourse between the seen and the unseen worlds. Commenting on one of its subdivisions, Legge remarks:

> 'Throughout the Book it is mostly religious rites that are spoken of; especially as culminating in the worship of God. And nothing is more fully brought out than that all rites are valueless without truth and reverence.'[5]

The *Record* quotes Confucius as saying that in the ceremonial rites of mourning the most important thing is reverence,[6] and in another passage he is

---

[1] *SBE* xxviii. [1885] 201.

[1] Cf. artt. CONFUCIAN RELIGION, CONFUCIUS.
[2] *SBE* xxvii. [1885] 13.
[3] Or rather remained up to 1911. The whole Confucian system has been more or less on the defensive since that date.
[4] *SBE* xxvii. 61. Cf. Legge's comment on p. 12.
[5] *Ib.* p. 25.
[6] *Ib.* xxviii. 153.

credited with the following remarkable utterance: 'With the ancients in their practice of government the love of men was the great point; in their regulation of this love of men, the rules of ceremony was the great point; in their regulation of those rules, reverence was the great point.'[1] It is an oft-reiterated Confucian theory that reverence in the performance of the prescribed rites and good conduct in the ordinary relations of man with man were inseparable.

'When one has mastered (the principle of) ceremonies, and regulates his person accordingly, he becomes grave and reverential. Grave and reverential, he is regarded with awe. If the heart be for a moment without the feeling of harmony and joy, meanness and deceitfulness enter it. If the outward demeanour be for a moment without gravity and reverentialness, indifference and rudeness show themselves.'[2]

It is evident that Confucius thoroughly approved of the strong emphasis laid by the ancients on the necessity of reverence. 'Authority without mercy, *ceremonial without reverence*, mourning without sorrow—what have I to do with these?'[3] The same lesson of reverence is inculcated in the Classics of Poetry and History.

'From of old, before our time, the former men set us the example;—How to be mild and humble from morning to night, and to be reverent in discharging the service.'[4] In the *Shu Ching* (Classic of History) there is a description of how the emperor Shun (23rd cent. B.C.), when appointing a high-priest or director of religious ceremonies, addressed the newly-appointed officer thus: 'You must be the Arranger of the ancestral temple. Morning and night you must be respectful. Be upright, be pure.' The officer did obeisance and suggested that one worthier than he should be appointed; but the emperor adhered to his decision and said, 'Do you go and undertake the duties. Be reverential.'[5] Similar exhortations are to be found in the *Tso Chuan.*[6]

Irreligion or irreverence is frequently declared to be the cause of the withdrawal of God's support from a reigning house.[7]

(*b*) *Sincerity.*—A fair acquaintance with Confucian thought shows that the true Confucianist is far from exaggerating the importance of ceremonies and ritual as such. He constantly insists that it is the spirit, not the letter, that really matters, and that rites in themselves are worthless without sincerity. A recent writer has said that the earlier types of 'commercialized' religion were displaced by 'faiths like those of Jesus and Mahomet which make God's favor depend on the *heart* of the worshipper rather than on his *sacrifice.*'[8] But this was precisely the teaching of classical Confucianism several centuries B.C. In one of the books of the *Record of Rites* we are told that the 'superior man' is not only extremely reverential in all ceremonial matters but is also absolutely sincere.[9]

'Sacrifice [which in this passage is practically synonymous with religion] is not a thing coming to a man from without; it issues from within him, and has its birth in his heart. When the heart is deeply moved, expression is given to it by ceremonies; and hence, only men of ability and virtue can give complete exhibition to the idea of sacrifice. The sacrifices of such men have their own blessing;—not indeed what the world calls blessing. Blessing here means perfection;—it is the name given to the complete and natural discharge of all duties. When nothing is left incomplete or improperly discharged;—this is what we call perfection, implying the doing everything that should be done in one's internal self, and externally the performance of everything according to the proper method.'[10]

In the *Tso Chuan* we are told that, when 'intelligence and sincerity' are present, almost any offerings, however common and easily obtained, may be 'presented to the spirits and set before kings and dukes.'[11] An English writer has commented on this in the following words:

'The idea that *intelligence* and *sincerity* are prerequisites to *sacrifice* indicates an advanced stage of religious culture on the part of the writer.'[1]

The testimony of the other classical books is to the same effect.

'God has no partialities,' the *Shu Ching* tells us, 'only to those who are reverent does He show favour. The people are not constant in their affections, except to those (rulers) who have charity of heart. The spirits do not necessarily enjoy sacrifices; what they enjoy is the sincerity.'[2]

(*c*) *Simplicity and dignity.*—Next to reverence and sincerity in prayers and sacrifices nothing is more earnestly insisted upon than simplicity and dignified restraint—something very near to the Greek σωφροσύνη. Ostentation and a lavish display of costly temple furniture is strongly discouraged; plain water is better than wine, coarse cloth is to be preferred to gorgeous embroideries, expensive mats of fine rushes and bamboo are no better than mats of coarse reeds and straw. The soup which formed part of the sacrificial offerings should be unseasoned, to denote simplicity; the grand symbols of jade should be left plain instead of being carved. The king, when about to take part in sacrificial rites, should not ride in a carved and lacquered state-carriage but in a plain one. 'In all these things it is simply the idea of the simplicity that is the occasion of the preference and honour.'[3] Sacrificial offerings should be chosen not from rare and expensive products, but from what is seasonable and abundant.[4] Self-restraint—a moral quality which manifests itself outwardly in simplicity—is one of the principal Confucian virtues. Without self-restraint there is necessarily a lack of dignity; and without dignity the rites of worship cannot be properly performed. It was not only the actual sacrificial rites that had to be conducted with quiet dignity and solemnity; the temple-dances, too, 'displayed the gravity of the performers, but did not awaken the emotion of delight.'[5] Similarly, 'the ancestral temple produced the impression of majesty, but did not dispose one to rest in it.'[6] This is because 'the idea which leads to intercourse with spiritual Beings is not interchangeable with that which finds its realisation in rest and pleasure.'[7]

3. Godward and manward aspects of Confucian worship.—There is another feature of Chinese religion which is perhaps more characteristically Chinese than any of those yet mentioned—a moral attitude which may be briefly summed up in the formula 'Look after the human and the divine will look after itself.' This 'manwardness,' if it may be so termed, does not necessarily imply a neglect of or contempt for the 'Godward' side of religion. It is based on a reasoned conviction that whatever is good for man will satisfy God; that God does not desire and will not accept any offerings or sacrifices that will hamper or impoverish His worshippers in their necessary mundane activities or human relationships; and that in the last resort divine and human interests are identical. To quote the words of Mencius—

'He who brings all his intellect to bear on the subject, will come to understand his own nature; he who understands his own nature will understand God. To preserve one's intellect, and to nourish one's nature—that is how to serve God. To waste no thoughts upon length of life, but to cultivate rectitude—that is to do the will of God.'[8]

Doubtless this view, or something like it, is one to which all evolving religions tend to approximate; what is remarkable is the very early date at which it was reached by the Chinese and the consistency with which it has been maintained.

1 *SBE* xxviii. 264. 2 *Ib.* p. 224.
3 H. A. Giles, *Confucianism and its Rivals* (*HL*, 2nd ser.), London, 1915, p. 80 f.
4 *SBE* iii.2 [1899] 305.
5 J. Legge, *The Chinese Classics*, Hongkong, 1861–72, vol. iii. pt. i. p. 47.
6 *Ib.* vol. v. pt. ii. p. 846.
7 *SBE* iii. 131 f., 177 f., 185, 187.
8 E. A. Ross, in *IJE* xxx. [1920] 292.
9 *SBE* xxvii. 404. 10 *Ib.* xxviii. 236.
11 Legge, vol. v. pt. i. p. 13.

1 H. K. Wright, in *JRAS*, *N. China Branch*, xlviii. [1917] 172 f. See also *SBE* xxvii. 448, xxviii. 211; and art. PURIFICATION (Chinese), vol. x. p. 472a.
2 Giles, p. 15 f., and *SBE* iii. 99. See also *SBE* iii. 176, and Legge, vol. v. pt. i. p. 146.
3 *SBE* xxvii. 435 f. 4 *Ib.* p. 395.
5 *Ib.* p. 435. 6 *Ib.* 7 *Ib.*
8 Tr. by Giles, p. 95.

It may have hampered Chinese religion in its attempts to soar heavenward, but it has undoubtedly had the excellent result of enhancing the honour and prestige of moral values. Nor are these moral values confined to earth. Chinese religious speculation extends them to the spiritual world as well, and this is why we have no capricious or irresponsible despot in the Chinese pantheon, no acts or utterances ascribed to divine beings which are incompatible with the highest moral ideals known to Chinese humanity. In this we have a sufficient explanation of another remarkable fact that has often extorted the admiration of European students: the high moral tone of the whole body of the classical and sacred literature of China and the absence of all expressions suggestive of licentious thought.

A modern writer on Eastern religions remarks that in his opinion Confucius laid 'unnecessary emphasis upon social and political duties, and may not have been sufficiently interested in the honour to be paid to Shang-Ti or God. He practically ignored the Godward side of men's duties.'[1] More just are H. A. Giles's observations on Confucius's general attitude:

'In regard to the relative importance of serving God and serving man Confucius has often been blamed for setting man before God; but it should be remembered that his interpretation of true service to God was embodied in right and proper performance of duty to one's neighbour. The idea of personal service to God Himself, as understood by the Jewish patriarchs, is entirely foreign to the Chinese conception of a Supreme Being.'[2]

In one of the books of the Historical Classic we are told of the eight branches of administration which ought to engage the attention of good rulers. The first is agriculture—the most important of all, because it provides the people with the means of subsistence; the second, commerce, which regulates the distribution of commodities; the third, religious ceremonies. With the fourth, fifth, and sixth we need not concern ourselves; the eighth and last is preparation for war.[3] It is characteristic of China that the rites of religious worship should occupy only the third place; for religion, the Chinese would say, has small practical importance for men who have nothing to eat; and spiritual beings, if they deserve human homage at all, are not likely to demand sacrificial offerings from men who cannot find the wherewithal to feed themselves. The doctrine which is implicit in this ancient passage from the *Shu Ching* reappears in an explicit form in the teachings of Mencius: 'The most important element in the State is the people; next come the altars of the gods; least in importance is the king';[4] and is repeated in the utterances of the first emperor of the Ming dynasty:

'God puts the sovereign in charge of his people, and the sovereign who wishes to serve God properly must first show that he loves the people. To show love for the people—that is the way to serve God. . . . He who would be a true sovereign should regard Heaven as his father, Earth as his mother, and the people as his children, and must carry out his duties to each with the utmost devotion. He does not perform the sacrifice to Heaven and Earth in order to bring prosperity upon himself, he does it to promote the welfare of the whole realm.'[5]

4. The motives of worship.—What, then, is the principal motive of religious worship, according to Chinese theory? Confucius and the majority of thinking Chinese since his day would have assumed that the object of religious rites is a double one—to do honour to spiritual beings and to benefit living men. The benefits anticipated by the living are moral and spiritual as well as material. It cannot be disputed that a great deal of the ceremonial connected with the cult of ancestors has direct reference to purely worldly considerations. It is assumed that the ancestors, if approached with the proper rites and offerings, will maintain the family in a state of prosperity and save it from disaster or extinction. Nevertheless this is not the reason why Confucian orthodoxy sanctions the cult of ancestors. The truly filial son, we are told, should offer his sacrifices 'without seeking for anything to be gained by them.'[1] Further, it should be remembered that there is, and long has been, a very large number of people in China who have been more or less sceptical on the question of the continued existence of human individuals after death, and who have nevertheless been among the most zealous supporters of the ancestral cult. Those who study the cult not merely in books (whether Chinese or foreign) but as it is actually practised by the people will soon realize that the practical if not the theoretical basis of the cult is social and moral rather than religious. As the present writer has said elsewhere, Confucianism has insisted on 'the importance of keeping up the cult of ancestors not so much for the sake of the dead as because it fostered among living men feelings of love, respect, reverence, and duty towards family and state. The souls of the dead might or might not be conscious of what was done for them, but it was in the interests of social harmony and political stability that the traditional religious and commemorative ceremonies should be jealously preserved and handed down to posterity, and that during the performance of such ceremonies the presence of the ancestral spirits should at least be tacitly assumed.'[2] Filial piety is, of course, the principal virtue which the ancestral cult is expected to strengthen and confirm; and it should be remembered that filial piety in China has a much wider and deeper signification than it has elsewhere. We are told that it is the root of all virtue, and the stem which produces all moral teaching; that it is an all-embracing rule of conduct, by the practice of which the people are brought to live in peace and harmony, and ill-will between superiors and inferiors is extinguished; that it commences with the service of parents, proceeds to the service of the king, and is completed by the consolidation of the character.[3]

A well-known Christian missionary in China, J. Edkins, drew attention to what he conceived to be a serious defect in the Chinese attitude towards religion when he said:

'An ethical test is the only one they know. When the evidence of a new religion is presented to them, they at once refer it to a moral standard, and give their approval with the utmost readiness if it passes the test. They do not ask whether it is divine, but whether it is good.'[4]

It is not strictly accurate to say that an ethical test is the only one they know, but it is certainly the test which they show the greatest readiness to apply. Probably the most religiously-minded Chinese would cheerfully admit the truth of Edkins's observation that when confronted with a new religion they 'do not ask whether it is divine but whether it is good,' not because they are contemptuous or oblivious of the divine, but because they feel or believe that the direct and exclusive search for the divine may lead them into swamps and wildernesses, whereas the search for the good is in itself a great good, even if only partially successful; and that, although few glimpses of the divine may be vouchsafed during the arduous ascent of the mountain of good, it will be found, when the summit is reached, if not

[1] W. E. Griffis, *The Religions of Japan*[4], New York, 1901, p. 104. For observations on this statement see the present writer's *Lion and Dragon in Northern China*, London, 1910, p. 322.

[2] Giles, p. 73 f.

[3] Legge, vol. iii. pt. ii. p. 327.

[4] For Chinese text see Legge, vol. ii. (rev. ed.), p. 483.

[5] This passage occurs in the official history of the Ming dynasty, under the date of the 20th year of Hung Wu (1387).

[1] *SBE* xxviii. 237.

[2] *Lion and Dragon in Northern China*, p. 347.

[3] See *SBE* iii. 465 f.; and cf. xxviii. 222.

[4] *Religion of China*, rev. ed., London, 1893, p. 74 f.

sooner, that the good and the divine are twin peaks joined by a level pathway over which men and gods may come and go at will, greeting one another as they pass with the friendly recognition of spiritual kinship.

III. *TAOISM.*[1]—It is unnecessary to deal at length with Taoist notions of worship, because, regarded as a religion, Taoism is almost wholly imitative. Primitive Taoism was not a religion, and, though the mysterious *Tao* was regarded as ineffable, wonderful, omnipotent, immanent in all the universe, infinitely great and infinitesimally small, it cannot be said to have been an object of worship. After the introduction of Buddhism, Taoism found it necessary to go through a process of reinterpretation and reconstruction in order to maintain its position in an environment that was becoming increasingly Confucian on its ethical, increasingly Buddhist on its religious, side; it therefore adapted to its own uses some of the religious formulations and rituals of its Indian rival, borrowed moral teachings from both Confucianism and Buddhism, and turned itself into an institutional religion by adopting monasticism and establishing temples for the worship of the numerous and ever-multiplying deities who began to throng its pantheon. It apotheosized its legendary founder, Lao-tse, and made him one of a divine triad which would certainly never have come into existence had a model not existed in the San Pao, the 'Three Precious Ones,' of Buddhism. As time went on, it also drew into its own system some of the divine beings of the pre-Confucian state religion of China; and so the Shang-Ti, or Supreme God, became (in comparatively recent times) the Yü Huang Shang-Ti, the 'Jade Imperial God,' who is one of the most prominent objects of worship in the debased Taoism of to-day. In spite of all its bare-faced borrowings, its crudely-artificial methods of turning dead men and women and shadowy abstractions into gods and goddesses, and its haphazard deification of animals, real and mythical, there is no doubt that even in these degenerate days the deities of Taoism are capable of inspiring religious devotion and that some of them at least are objects of real worship.

IV. *BUDDHISM.*[2]—It is often said that Buddhism is atheistic and therefore offers the believer no object of worship. However true this may be of Buddhism as a metaphysical system, and of the Hīnayāna (*q.v.*), in its primitive form, it is certainly not true of the Mahāyāna (*q.v.*), which claims the allegiance of practically all Chinese Buddhists. For all but a small minority of Buddhist scholars and mystics the Buddhas and *bodhisattvas* cannot be fitly described as other than objects of worship. The cult of these beings has reached its greatest development in one subdivision of the Mahāyāna, which is known to Chinese as the 'Pure Land' and to Western students as the Amidist school. For adherents of this school the figure of Amitābha has practically taken the place of Śākyamuni, the historical Buddha; and the worship of which he is the object can hardly be described as anything less than λατρεία. For ordinary believers he is the sublime deity who rules over Sukhāvatī, the Western Paradise, and who, with the assistance of the great *bodhisattvas* Avalokiteśvara (Kuan-yin) and Mahāsthama (Ta-shih-chih), brings to salvation all those who invoke his name with sincerity. That Amitābha evokes feelings of deep and sincere devotion is often doubted or thought impossible by those who cannot understand how the contemplation of a non-existing being (for Amitābha is entirely a product of the religious imagination) can give rise to a really devotional attitude. Yet a close observation of the religious beliefs and practices of Amidists will certainly dispel any doubts. Perhaps no more conclusive testimony on this subject could be obtained than that of L. Wieger, whose evidence is all the more important and valuable from the fact that, as a loyal Catholic missionary, he may be regarded as incapable of unduly emphasizing the spiritual fervour that a pagan cult is capable of inspiring.

'The Amidist temples in China and Japan are the only ones in which the people pray—pray truly and from the bottom of their hearts, where they repent and implore, with attitudes so natural and so touching that no suspicion of make-believe is admissible. As long as I live I shall never forget the feelings that I experienced when I saw a young Amidist mother making her devotions before the lighted and empty throne.[1] She began by closing her eyes and concentrating her thoughts, her lips murmuring the words of repentance and petition. Then she brought two little children before the throne. The second could scarcely walk, but both did exactly as their mother had done, correctly and most gravely. Finally she took from her breast a third child, newly-born, and pressing his head very delicately between her thumb and forefinger, made him bow towards the throne.'[2]

In recent years some rather crude attempts have been made by a small school of English writers to prove that the beliefs and rites of Amidism, or some of their most striking features, were borrowed from or inspired by Christianity. Wieger, whose learning, conscientiousness, and comparative freedom from bias make him almost unique among Western missionaries who have studied Chinese religion, unreservedly rejects the theory. He believes, on the contrary, that all the characteristic features of the Mahāyāna—including the 'altruisme exubérant' and the 'fièvre salvifique' associated with the activities of the *bodhisattvas*—are a logical development of primitive Buddhist theory.[3] He sees nothing mysterious in the gradual expansion of the so-called egoism of the Hīnayāna into the altruism of the Mahāyāna; indeed he regards it as necessary and inevitable. He traces Mahāyānist origins to the centuries immediately succeeding the death of Gautama Buddha. The Mahāyāna 'serait donc antérieur de plusieurs siècles au Christianisme.'[4] These views appear to the present writer to be entirely just. The worship of Buddha, or of Amitābha, or of Kuan-yin is, at its best, as true and sincere as the worship of God, of Christ, or of the Virgin in Christendom; and its roots are planted very deep in Buddhist soil.

LITERATURE.—This has been indicated in the footnotes.

R. F. JOHNSTON.

WORSHIP (Christian). — Religious worship being the expression of that sense of 'worth,' or title to honour, which man feels due to the Divine nature, its idea and forms will vary with the notion of God and man and of their mutual relations. Christian worship, moreover, as distinct from the other historic types, has a definite character due to the teaching and example of the Church's Founder Himself. This remains regulative for the whole history of Christian worship, deciding between true and false developments, and forming the standard by which reform or progress is to be judged.

The gospel of Christ itself emerged out of the religion of Israel, and accordingly its genius or distinctive nature defined itself largely in relation to Judaism, both as faith and as worship. In both Jesus claimed to 'fulfil' the religion of the Hebrew prophets, whose emphasis was on the heart or inward attitude, as determinative of real devotion to God and His will; 'obedience' of life was the truest 'sacrifice,' and moral relations, rather than

[1] Cf. art. TAOISM.

[2] Cf. artt. CHINA, CHINA (Buddhism in).

[1] That is, the canopied dais usually occupied by an image, but which is sometimes purposely left empty, to indicate that the real Buddha is not to be found in stone or clay but in the heart of man and of the universe (cf. R. F. Johnston, *Buddhist China*, London, 1913, pp. 111, 303).

[2] *Hist. des croyances religieuses et des opinions philosophiques en Chine*, Paris, 1917, p. 567 f.

[3] P. 561.

[4] P. 563.

ritual or formal acts of worship, were the primary form and means of communion with God. Love to God as Father, and to all men as brethren in virtue of their relation to Him—this constitutes essential worship; to it all forms of specific worship are subordinate, and have value only as expressive of this and all it implies, according to Christ's idea of God's character. Where known moral relations are at fault, worship is inacceptable; the 'gift' of homage is to be left unoffered until it can be offered with a good conscience (Mt $5^{23f.}$).

Spirituality, then, in this sense, is the touchstone of Christian worship; and those forms of worship are most entitled to the term 'Christian' which conform most to the simplicity and naturalness which marked Jesus' own devotional practice, or are most analogous to these. This does not fix beforehand how far other modes of expressing the same ideas and emotions, under other conditions of culture and particularly of art, may or may not be allowable. But it does fix where the emphasis which determines the spirit of worship must lie, if worship is to be true to 'the mind of Christ.'

Worship has two senses, a wider and a stricter. The wider, expressing a man's devoutness in all his living, is equivalent to piety; the narrower, denoting specific forms of devotion, personal or social, is nearly synonymous with cultus. It is with the latter that this article has chiefly to do. Yet, since the relation between the two senses of worship, the inward or inclusive and the external and particular, is so intimate in Christianity, it is needful constantly to bear in mind the context of 'holy' or devout life in which worship is set, in so far as it is Christian at all. This we shall find to be very manifest in primitive Christianity, when 'holy' was *the* epithet of the Church, and when participation in its worship, as pure and loving—with the Kiss of Peace as its seal—was conditioned by serious moral Church discipline.

1. The NT idea of worship.—(*a*) Religion, according to Jesus, consists in filial trust and love towards God, and loyalty to His will for His Kingdom 'on earth as it is in heaven.' Thus the Christian norm of worship is the Lord's Prayer. In keeping with this, the effect of Jesus' whole teaching, alike by its emphasis and by its silence, is to change the relative importance attaching to heart religion and to outward expression in worship. He never treated ritual or cultus as determinative of man's real relation to God, as did current Judaism—a fact revolutionary in the history of ancient religion. Nor did He, while creating a new religious bond between His disciples and constituting them a new Israel within Israel spiritually, make them a new community for purposes of worship or prescribe new forms of worship proper.[1] 'Pray without ceasing: in everything give thanks' (1 Th $5^{17f.}$; cf. Eph 6^{18}), rightly became a watchword of the Christian life. Worship thus becomes relatively independent of any given forms of expression, so far as these are not bound up with normal human life, the fulfilment of all relations 'as unto God and not (merely) unto men.'

This comes out clearly in Paul's attitude to special seasons in Ro 14. 'One man esteemeth one day above another: another esteemeth every day alike' (v.^{5}). 'He that regardeth the day, regardeth it unto the Lord' (v.^{6}), and *vice versa*. Here we have a principle of all-embracing range, since it turns on the very nature of 'faith,' as Paul is using the term, viz. personal conviction before God. 'Whatever is not of faith is sin' to him who does or abstains. 'For the kingdom of God is not eating or drinking (as religious observance), but righteousness and peace and joy in the Holy Spirit. For he that herein serveth Christ is well-pleasing to God.' There can, then, be no absolute rules or laws of worship in Christianity. This principle of relativity is implied too in the great maxim which sums up the distinctive advance of Christian worship—because of the Christian idea of God—upon that of all previous religion, including Judaism. 'The hour . . . now is, when the true worshippers shall worship the Father in spirit and truth [full reality]: for such doth the Father seek to be his worshippers. God is Spirit: and they that worship him must worship in spirit and truth' (Jn $4^{23f.}$). As J. B. Lightfoot puts it,[1] 'The Kingdom of Christ . . . has no sacred days or seasons, no special sanctuaries, because every time and every place alike are holy. Above all it has no sacerdotal system. It interposes no sacrificial tribe or class between God and man, by whose intervention alone God is reconciled and man forgiven. Each individual member holds personal communion with the Divine Head.' The conception is indeed, as he adds, 'strictly an *ideal*,' which cannot be applied rigorously in the practical life either of individuals or of the Christian society, the Church. But it remains the regulative principle behind all Christian institutions of worship, as of organization generally, giving them only a conventional value, as expediencies tested by much experience, yet as such to be treated reverently, especially for the sake of others, *i.e.* in love as well as faith.

(*b*) *Forms of worship in the NT.*—Here the main fact is that Jesus' own example and teaching are associated with the synagogal type of worship rather than with the Temple, the seat of the sacrificial and priestly system of worship. For to Him the Temple was primarily 'a house of prayer,' and that private (Lk 18^{10}) rather than public prayer. Indeed the latter hardly seems to be alluded to by Jesus at all (not even in Mt 18^{19}). His teaching on worship is mainly on genuine prayer, as opposed to formal prayers, 'vain repetitions' (Mt $6^{5ff.}$; cf. Lk 18^{10-14}); and even 'the Lord's Prayer' is given as an example of prayer of the right sort rather than as a form for regular repetition. Such a valuation of forms of worship, in proportion as they express simply and directly the spirit of worship, is not only continuous with that of the prophets, as of parts of the Psalter and the Jewish Apocrypha; it appears also in some Rabbinic utterances, such as that of R. Menaḥem of Galilee (about the Christian era):

'One day all sacrifices will cease, only the Thankoffering will not cease; all prayers will cease, only the Thanksgiving prayers will not cease.' Compare the spirit of Ecclus 35^{1-3}.

This Rabbinic saying seems relative to the Messianic era of perfected worship, when sacrifices for sin should no longer be needful; and that is just the position in which the first followers of Jesus felt themselves to be, as spiritually united to Messiah. Thus their relation to God was now conditioned solely by the representative self-oblation of Jesus. This was at first conceived on the lines of 'the Suffering Servant' of Is 53, but was later worked out, as in the Epistle to Hebrews, in terms of the Mosaic sacrificial system, regarded as 'the shadow' of the perfected spiritual reality of purely personal relations, those of the devoted will (He 10^{1-18}). Thus the Christ, as God's sinless Son, is the abiding objective basis of His people's holiness ($2^{10f.}$ 10^{14}). All Christians, then, are in fact made priests to God, as united in spirit with the 'Great Priest,' and as such have access for communion with God of the most intimately spiritual kind (10^{19-22}).

This conception conditions the whole of primitive Christian worship. Its normal character is thanksgiving, at once praise and prayer, which, as Menaḥem said, remains after other kinds of 'prayers' have ceased. Christians 'offer up' through Jesus 'sacrifice of praise to God continually, that is, the fruit of lips which make confession to His Name' (He 13^{15}; cf. 1 P 2^{5}, Rev 1^{6} 5^{8} $8^{3f.}$). As for outward sacrifices, only the thankoffering remains, viz. deeds of beneficence and fellowship, 'for with such sacrifices God is well pleased'[2] (He

[1] Mt 18^{17}, the language of which is probably secondary, is no real exception, while our evidence is divided in the case of even the Lord's Supper (see art. Eucharist [to end of Middle Ages], I.). But in any case the words 'This do in remembrance of me' would mean only the investing of a Jewish form of worship, the 'breaking of bread' with blessing of God or thanksgiving, with specific Christian associations, in fulfilment of the domestic Paschal meal.

[1] *The Christian Ministry*, London, 1901, *ad init.*

[2] Probably echoing the most striking OT anticipation of this conception of worship, found in Ecclus 35^{1-3}; 'He that keepeth

13[16]). Here the word 'continually' shows that the abiding attitude of a worshipful spirit is what is chiefly in view, as in Paul's 'praying always,' and this on the part of Christians severally. And in fact the bulk of NT references to worship have this personal rather than corporate reference.

Such, *e.g.*, is the nature of another passage which affords striking illustration of the new conception of spirituality of life as itself worship. 'Pure religion and undefiled before our God and Father is this, to visit the fatherless and widows in their affliction and to keep himself unspotted from the world' (Ja 1[27]), where the word rendered 'religion' (θρησκεία) means 'devotion' expressed in devout acts.

Once we enter upon the history of Christian worship through the centuries, we shall have to confine ourselves in the main to the corporate or common worship of the Church, with only occasional glimpses at the forms of private devotion, though this all along exists in the background.[1] But here we may note that in the NT itself the relation between personal and corporate worship is peculiarly intimate, the former overflowing into the latter and constituting much of its contents, under the lead of individual members of the Spirit-filled Body of Christ's 'saints.' This meets us particularly in Paul's Gentile churches, *e.g.*, in his advice to the Church at Corinth (1 Co 11–14). 'What is it, then, brethren? When ye come together, each one hath a psalm, hath a teaching, hath a revelation, hath a tongue, hath an interpretation. Let all things be done unto edifying' (14[26], also 15–17, where praying, singing, blessing of God or 'eucharist,' all 'by the Spirit' on the part of individuals in Church worship, are specified; cf. Col 3[16], Eph 5[18-21]).

Evidently the forms of worship in the Apostolic Age were not fixed or uniform. The new Christian spirit brought a fresh element of spontaneity (2 Co 3[17]) into the forms of common worship, which otherwise followed in the main synagogal usage. To this the earliest converts, both Jews and proselytes, were accustomed; and it would naturally be adhered to, save for any feature distinctive of the new Messianic form of their faith, such as 'the breaking of bread' with thanksgiving to God for the Messianic redemption in Christ and in His Name. This note of *adoring gratitude* to God for His goodness in creation and redemption, which explains the term 'eucharist' as used for the central act of Christian worship, remains through all changes its abiding characteristic.

The blending here of old and new would be similar to the use of the Sabbath alongside the Lord's Day, as both special days of worship, though in different modes. But, as time went on and conditions changed, the need was felt (*e.g.*, in 'Barnabas' and Ignatius) to distinguish sharply between the two, as relative to different 'economies' in God's relation to man; and for the most part the Sabbath ceased, especially in the West, to have positive religious significance for Christians.

2. Worship, particularly eucharistic, in the ancient Church.—(*a*) *Worship in the sub-Apostolic Church.*—The forms of Sunday worship were still determined mainly by those of the Synagogue, as modified by the 'prophetic' spirit in the primitive Church. Synagogal worship included recitation of psalms, set prayers, Scripture lessons, address, benediction. Our first glimpse of Christian worship, as reported by Pliny *c.* A.D. 112, shows us, at the Christian assembly before dawn on a stated day (Sunday), 'a hymn (*carmen*) to Christ as to a God' (cf. 1 Ti 3[16], Eph 5[14], 2 Ti 2[12f.] for snatches of such hymns), sung responsively, and a pledging of each and all in solemn form (*sacramento*) against theft, adultery, and other prevalent social wrongs. With the former we may compare the *Odes of Solomon*, and with the latter 2 Ti 2[19], for moral

the law (*ipso facto*) multiplieth offerings . . . and he that giveth alms sacrificeth a thankoffering. To depart from wickedness is a thing pleasing to the Lord; and to depart from unrighteousness is a propitiation.'

[1] See Christian sections of artt. PRAYER, FASTING, FESTIVALS AND FASTS.

fealty as felt to be part of Christian religious allegiance, and as not only made explicit in baptismal vows—witness *Did.* vii. 1 and the *renuntiatio diaboli* found later—but perhaps also reaffirmed week by week in some solemn form during divine service. No doubt there were other less distinctive elements in the morning worship besides the two Pliny names, *e.g.* prayer, Scripture lessons, address, and benediction, as in the synagogal worship familiar to the Romans.

The essential atmosphere of Christian worship, as we see most clearly from the Ignatian Letters, was loving unity.

'For if the prayer of one and another hath so great strength, how much more that of the bishop and of the whole church. Whosoever therefore cometh not to fellowship' [lit. 'together,' as in Ac 2[1. 44. 47]] stands apart from 'the altar' or 'the sanctuary' (θυσιαστήριον), the holy place where the assemblage of God's people [which Methodius also later styles 'a bloodless altar'] offers up the sacrifice of prayer, and particularly that of the eucharist.[1]

For a similar reason, viz. as specially devoted to the sacrifice of prayer, widows are called by Polycarp 'God's altar.'[2] The very boldness of these metaphorical uses of 'altar' for persons, in relation to their 'sacrifice' of prayer, shows how intense was the early Christians' sense of the sacredness of prayer as the supreme form of worship, and how spiritual and personal was their idea of the Christian sacrifice. Of this genus the eucharistic prayer of the whole Church corporately was the supreme species; and to this we must now turn.

It was perhaps the association of 'sacrifices' of 'beneficence,' for the service of God in His people (according to He 13[16]), with the offering in prayer of part of such oblations (or 'gifts') for the special purpose of Holy Communion in 'the breaking of bread,' that led in time to the elements so used being also called the Christian 'sacrifice.'[3] But, before this occurred, the bread and the wine over which thanksgiving prayer (*eucharistia*, like the Jewish *Kiddûsh*, or 'hallowing') was uttered themselves came to be styled 'thanksgiving' (eucharist). In Ignatius 'eucharist' as a rule still denotes the communion service, the whole act of eucharistic worship associated with the memorial bread. This act seems also in *Did.* xiv.[4] to be called the Christians' 'pure sacrifice' of praise to God's Name (after Mal 1[11. 14]); and its profoundly spiritual nature is shown by the warning that the Church's 'sacrifice' will not be 'pure' if unbrotherly feeling be present even between two of the worshippers. Beyond this, for the time, the use of 'sacrifice' in this connexion does not go.

So far, then, Christian worship is the fulfilment, general or special, of Paul's exhortation, 'Present your bodies a living sacrifice, holy, well-pleasing to God—your spiritual [lit. rational, as distinct from material] service.' It is the kind of worship which Justin sets over against the pagan type, as worship of 'the Creator of this Universe,' One 'in no need of blood-offerings and libations and incense,' who is worthily to be honoured only by praise, 'in word of prayer and thanksgiving over all our food.'[5] Such worship, generally, does not differ in idea from that of the corporate Eucharist of the Church:[6] each is a form of the 'unbloody sacrifice' which befits the God Christians worship, viz. 'the service of the mind' (τὴν λογικὴν λατρείαν; so Athenagoras, xiii. *fin.*; cf. Ro 12[1]; so too Irenæus a little later).

Accordingly the prayer of 'eucharist' or thanksgiving was the heart of primitive Christian worship

[1] *Ad Eph.* 5, *Magn.* 7, *Trall.* 7, *Philad.* 4, *Smyrn.* 6 f.
[2] *Ad Phil.* iv.
[3] Ignatius, *ad Smyrn.* 6; *Didache*, ix. 5; Justin Martyr, *Apol.* i. 66; Iren. iv. 18; Orig. *c. Cels.* viii. 57.
[4] Cf. *de Aleatoribus*, 4.
[5] *Apol.* i. 13; see *Apost. Const.* vii. 49.
[6] *Ib.* i. 65.

(as of that of Judaism, which it modifies),[1] and this as co-extensive with life, in that 'it is very meet, right and our bounden duty, that we should at all times and in all places give thanks' unto God (ancient opening of the Eucharistic Prayer, adopted in the Anglican Prayer Book). But such worship attained special expression in all corporate meetings for Christian fellowship, of which '*the* Eucharist' of the whole local Church was the climax. To these principles striking witness is afforded by that 'missing link,' the Agape (*q.v.*).

This was, even after its separation from the eucharist proper (*c.* A.D. 100 in some, though not all, churches), a corporate meeting of the church, of a more family and informal nature than the liturgical eucharist (now the climax of a Sunday morning service). Such the love-feast still appears not only in the N. Africa of Tertullian's day but in that of Cyprian's,[2] as also in the Ancient Church Order commonly known as Hippolytean, though in this part it may rather reflect Syrian usage *c.* 300. There 'at the Supper of the congregation,' at the 'bringing in of lamps,' the bishop 'gives the Salutation' usual before eucharistic prayer, ending, 'Let us thanks-give to the Lord.' The people reply, 'Right and just,' as before the Anaphora proper; but it is added, 'And he shall not[3] say: Lift up your hearts' (the *sursum corda* formula), because that shall be said at the Oblation alone. Otherwise the prayer of 'eucharist' which follows is obviously regarded as a solemn one, and the fragments from the bread thus consecrated by prayer are taken from the hand of the bishop as *eulogia* (*i.e.* blessed bread), though 'not *eucharist*, as the body of our Lord.'

As regards the Eucharist, what has just been said prepares us for changes due to its separation from the associations of a social meal, and its inclusion in a morning service of the synagogue type, as its central element. Thus it took on a more liturgical and ere long (under the influence of current sacramental ideas other than Jewish) a mysteriously realistic character, alien to the original Jewish notion of a meal of religious fellowship with blessing or eucharist of God. The former of these developments, the liturgical, was fostered by the ancient notion of worship outside prophetic Judaism, that some material offering was essential to worship. Hence the self-oblation of the loyal heart came in time to appear to most Gentile Christians to fall short of perfect worship; and this led to a new meaning being attached to the eucharistic prayer over the bread and wine used for the purposes of Communion (originally as a meal of Christian fellowship), viz. as offering the elements to God, in worship of homage, *as a gift to the Giver of all* (a sanction in Scripture being seen in Mal 1$^{11.\ 14}$). To this there was insensibly added, by a natural reaction of old associations as to such worship—particularly in connexion with the mysteries (the superficial likeness of which to the Christian Eucharist Justin feels and apologizes for)—the notion that God met the earthly gift with a divine gift in return, by filling it with a new and mysterious quality. The way in which this came about was probably in the first instance purely religious, arising out of the very intensity of the soul's experience of a special quickening in the act of corporate worship, while contemplating and partaking of the symbols of Christ's dying love. This is strongly suggested by the experimental atmosphere and language of the devotional utterances, including eucharistic prayers, in the earliest Apocryphal Acts, the basis of which, if semi-gnostic in type, yet probably reflects the general Christian devotional feeling at Holy Communion both before and after the middle of the 2nd century.

[1] See for full details F. E. Warren, *The Liturgy and Ritual of the Ante-Nicene Church*², London, 1912, ch. iv.

[2] In *Ep.* 62 (63) he says that at it 'we cannot convoke the people (the whole Church) to our banquet, so as to celebrate the truth of the sacrament [*i.e.* with 'the mingled cup' for which he is arguing] in the presence of *all* the brotherhood' (ch. 16).

[3] This caution suggests that an older usage to the contrary was in view. If so, the parallel to full eucharistic worship becomes yet more complete.

In the *Acts of Thomas* we have what seems a sample of the more enthusiastic and prophetic type of eucharistic invocation.

'And the Apostle, standing by it ("the bread of blessing"), said: Jesus, who hast deemed us worthy to have communion of the Eucharist of Thy holy body and blood, lo, we make bold with the eucharist and invocation of Thy holy name. Come now and commune with us. And he began to say, Come perfect Compassion; come, Communion of the male (=Christ); come, that [feminine, like 'communion,' the substantive preceding] knowest the mysteries of the Chosen one; come, that hast communion in all the contests of the noble Athlete [against the powers of Evil]; . . . come, Hidden Mother; come, that is manifest in her activities and affords joy and rest to those united to her; come and have communion with us in this Eucharist which we perform in [on the basis of] Thy name and in the love wherein we are assembled in [on the basis of] Thy calling.'[1]

Here what is specially noteworthy is the experimental nature of the grace of Christ's eucharistic presence thus invoked. Added to this, however, we find, first in Justin and then in Irenæus, the belief that the words of institution, cited in the Church's eucharistic prayer, were a formula of Divine power, producing in the elements themselves the presence of the *body and blood* of Christ, the Incarnate Logos; and therewith was laid the foundation of what came to be the specifically 'Catholic' doctrine of the Eucharist, and of the corresponding devotional attitude towards the elements themselves. In Justin and Irenæus it appears only as the belief that the worshippers' bodies are prepared for resurrection by participation in Christ's resurrection body and blood. That such presence of Christ's 'body and blood' was of benefit to the *soul* there is no suggestion. Such a realistic conception (present already in some sense[2] in Ignatius's mystical view of the Eucharist as 'medicine of immortality'[3]) fostered first the habit of taking portions home for private use (already in Tertullian), and then devotional anxiety as to what became of all parts of the consecrated elements. Adoration of Christ as present in the elements, and the notion that He in them was being offered as the Christian sacrifice —and that with propitiatory intent and effect—represent forms of devout thought and feeling of which we have no trace until after Cyprian's day, or indeed until the 4th century.

(*b*) *Justin Martyr's witness.*—At this point we must quote from the famous passages of Justin's *Apology*[4] which afford our one connected picture of Christian corporate Sunday worship in the 2nd century.

On Sundays 'there is a gathering together' of the local church, 'and the memoirs of the Apostles or the writings of the Prophets are read, as long as time allows. Then the president gives by way of discourse admonition and exhortation to copy these noble lessons. Next we all rise together and send up prayers,' 'making common prayers for ourselves . . . and for all others everywhere, earnestly, that we may be deemed worthy . . . by our deeds also to be found good livers and keepers of the commandments, that so we may be saved with the eternal salvation. When we cease from the prayers, we salute each other with a kiss.' 'Next, bread is brought and wine and water, and the president, taking them, sends up (ἀναπέμπει) as best he can prayers in like manner and thanksgivings,' 'sends up praise and glory to the Father of the Universe through the Name of the Son and the Holy Spirit, and makes thanksgiving (eucharist) at length for our having been deemed worthy of these (blessings) at His hands' . . . 'and the people chimes in with the Amen. Then takes place the distribution to each, and the partaking from the elements for which thanks were given; and to the absent portions are sent by the hand of the deacons.'

One or two aspects of the eucharistic prayer of the Church, through the lips of its president, are made clearer by the more general language already cited from ch. xiii. in describing the reasonable nature of Christian worship. But the main point is that in both connexions its essence lay in 'sending (πέμπειν) by reasonable word,' 'to the Creator of this Universe,' 'processions of homage (πομπάς) and hymns (as if on their way to the divine pres-

[1] Ch. 50; cf. ch. 27, for both text and sense.

[2] See art. EUCHARIST. [3] *Eph.* 20; cf. *Smyrn.* 7.

[4] 65, 67.

ence), in acknowledgment of being and all the means of well-being,' as well as in 'sending requests to be once more in incorruption, on the ground of faith in Him';[1] or, as expressed in the later passages, 'sending up (ἀναπέμπειν) prayers and thanksgivings.'

If we have not here the very origin[2] of the term 'mass' (*missa*=*missio*=Gr. ἀναφορά=ἀναπομπή, which was not used in a special religious sense) and its original meaning, namely 'the oblation' of worship to God on high (cf. the Liturgy of St. Mark, just before offering of incense and a prayer of oblation, σοὶ τὴν δόξαν καὶ τὴν εὐχαριστίαν ἀναπέμπομεν), at any rate this, and nothing else, was *the primitive conception of the Christian sacrifice.* It is one continuous with the later Jewish notion of prayer, in the Dispersion in particular, and is quite distinct from any notion of the body and blood of Christ as 'the sacrifice of the altar'—a notion which had not yet arisen, even where realistic theories existed of the relation of the Incarnate Logos to the elements, as the Christian bread of life or 'food of immortality.' Another and closely connected aspect of the same contrast is the fact that eucharistic worship in Justin, as in Irenæus and during the 3rd cent. for the most part, has no relation to sin in the worshippers. Christians as such are consecrated by union with Christ,[3] and as such are 'counted worthy' of the high function of offering as priests their prayers and giving-of-thanks, as acceptable sacrifices to God.[4] Thus far, then, the Eucharist has no propitiatory aspect even for the living, let alone the dead, although on the anniversary of martyrs, from Polycarp (about the same date as Justin's *Apology*) onwards, eucharist was offered in their name also (as having *par excellence* 'offered their bodies as a living sacrifice'), 'the communion of saints' being conceived to include also the Church triumphant.

(*c*) *Justin and later 'Catholic' worship.*—The full significance of Justin's witness to the simple spirituality of Christian worship in his day becomes most apparent when we compare it, especially as to order, with extant liturgies from the latter part of the 3rd cent. onwards.[5] To the variations and changes of order in these he gives us the true key, as showing that they reflect a change in religious ideas and emphasis at different stages. The above table of the chief known types will exhibit this.

Justin.	Gallican Liturgy.	Egyptian.	Syrian.	Roman.
1. Common intercessions.	1. 'Preces.' Offertory. Intercessions for dead and living.	1. Common intercessions.	1. Common intercessions. Offertory.	1. ('Oremus.') Offertory.
2. Kiss of peace or unity. The elements brought. (Offertory)	2. *Pax.*	2. *Pax.*	2. *Pax.*	2. 'Pax' (simply a formula of peace).
3. Eucharistic prayer(s).	3. Eucharistic prayers.	3. Intercession for dead and living in preface of the eucharist prayers before consecration.	3. Eucharistic prayers. Intercessions for dead and living.	3. Eucharistic prayers. Intercessions for dead and living.
4. Communion.	4. Communion.	4. Communion.	4. Communion.	4. Communion.

The changes of order here visible, a progressive series from Justin to the Roman Mass, receive their one adequate explanation in change in the idea of the eucharistic 'sacrifice,' from the people's self-oblation, in thanksgiving and thankofferings 'in memory of' Christ's thanksgiving at the Last Supper and self-oblation on the Cross, to that of the body and blood of Christ (thought of as present in the elements), as the Church's own sacrifice, presented and pleaded anew as propitiation for sins of dead and living Christians. It was natural that to the eucharistic sacrifice so conceived should gravitate the prayers of intercession (now for the sins of dead and living) which originally came before the eucharistic oblation (ἀναφορά, *missa*), in order to give them more efficacy with God. In the Gallican and Alexandrian liturgies, indeed, we see that the sacrifice with which these intercessions are associated is still the Christian people's own oblations, prior to what later was called 'consecration' with the sacred words of institution[1] (without or with invocation of the Holy Spirit to change the elements into body and blood of Christ). In the Roman Mass, however, as it is known to us, the process of change is complete. It has dropped the *Pax* proper, the kiss of brotherly unity which seals the people's fitness to offer their 'sacrifice' as 'pure' (according to early Christian ideas) and acceptable to God; and has only a formal trace of it in the words, 'The Lord's Peace be ever with you,' between the Mass proper and the Communion. It has also gone further than the other liturgies cited in effacing the idea of the service in Justin, by suppressing intercessions (without specific reference to sins) for Christians and all men before the eucharistic worship, retaining only the empty injunction, 'Let us pray.'

(*d*) *Irenæus on the Christian sacrifice.*—We are now prepared to appreciate to the full Irenæus's emphatic witness to the older idea of the Christian sacrifice, before passing on to refer to some intermediate stages in the change just indicated, as witnessed from the 3rd cent. onwards.

According to Irenæus, 'Our Lord gave counsel to His own disciples to offer firstfruits to God from His creatures, not as to one who stands in need, but so that they themselves may be neither unfruitful nor unthankful.' And so 'the Church offers to God, to Him who affords us food, firstfruits of His own gifts,' as Malachi prefigured.[2] This oblation 'is with God reckoned a pure sacrifice and one accepted of Him, . . . because he who offers is himself glorified in the offering, if his gift be accepted.' 'Accordingly *sacrifices do not sanctify a man*, for God needs not a sacrifice, but *the conscience of him who offers sanctifies the sacrifice*, if it be already pure, and causes God to accept it as from a friend.' It is 'because the Church offers with singleheartedness' (*simplicitas*) that 'her gift is rightly accounted with God a pure sacrifice,' like the gift of the Philippians sent to Paul through Epaphroditus. 'For we ought to make oblation to God, and in all things to be found thankful to God the Creator, offering in a pure mind and faith without pretence, in firm hope and fervent love, firstfruits of those creatures which are His. And this oblation the Church alone offers in purity, offering to Him with thanksgiving from his creation.' The purpose of this is that we may

1 Ch. 13.

2 Most authorities favour another, connected with the 'dismission' of the worshippers (see Rietschel, *Liturgik*, i. 347 f.).

3 *Dial.* 41.

4 *Ib.* 116 *fin.*, 117.

5 See artt. EUCHARIST and PRAYER (Christian, Liturgical) for details.

1 'All liturgies of every type agree in bearing witness to the fact that the original form of consecration was a thanksgiving' (W. C. Bishop, *CQR* lxvi. 388).

2 IV. xvii. 4 f.

thereby be fruitful, and so God 'may render to us the recompense of His benefits,' on the principle of Mt 25[34-36]. As 'the Word enjoined on the People (of the OT) the making of oblations, . . . that it might learn to do service to God; so and for that reason He wills us also to offer a gift at the altar often, without intermission. There is, then, an altar in heaven, for thither our prayers and oblations are directed; and a temple, as John in the Apocalypse says, And the temple of God was opened.'

(*e*) *Irenæus and certain 'Catholic' developments.*—Here we have several ideas characteristic of the Christian 'sacrifice' in worship towards the end of the 2nd century. Some are wholly primitive and rooted in the NT; *e.g.*, 'sacrifices do not sanctify a man,' but the worshipper's pure conscience the sacrifice; God's acceptance of a sacrificial gift 'as from a friend' honours the giver;[1] the real, *i.e.* the spiritual, gift is the thanksgiving of the heart, and is offered at the heavenly altar, to which 'prayers and oblations are directed.'[2] The last is implied in the call 'Hearts on high' (*sursum corda*), which prefaces ancient eucharistic prayers generally. But in time the idea lost its pure spirituality, as the notion arose that the material gifts themselves were received by God on His altar on high by the hands of His angels. This notion occurs already in the eucharistic prayer of the 4th cent. North Italian *de Sacramentis*, in several Eastern liturgies, and in the traditional Roman Canon of the Mass. The earlier of these, however, preserve in the main Irenæus's notion of an oblation of bread and wine which Christians were privileged to offer—with clear reference to Ro 12[1]—as expressing their self-oblation, in sacramental commemoration of the self-oblation of their Lord. But the Roman Canon, by substituting for 'since it is *figura* of the body and blood of our Lord' 'that it may become to us the body and blood of . . . our Lord,' and by a good deal else in the context, brings in another train of thought altogether, that of Christ's body being present on the Church's 'altar' on earth and partaken of by the communicants. This is the full realistic form assumed by the secondary and non-primitive element in Irenæus's principles set forth above, viz. that God gives *in this way*, in recompense for the Church's thanksgiving, a certain unique benefit in return. This, in extant liturgies generally, is conceived as communicated first to the consecrated elements themselves and through them to the communicants. In some early Eastern liturgies the Word or Spirit is thought to become present in the elements, so making them, in a metaphorical sense, His sacramental 'body and blood'; but in Irenæus's discussion of this aspect of the Eucharist, as in the Roman Canon and some later Eastern Anaphoras, the above realistic conception appears of Christ's human body as present in the elements. And with this added notion a fresh phase of worship begins to enter into the eucharistic service, viz. the adoration of the Incarnate Saviour in the elements of the oblation, conceived now as effecting afresh, in some sense (that of *re presentare*, 'really presenting'), the offering of His body, once for all offered on the Cross but perpetually presented in heaven with atoning efficacy.

(*f*) *Cyprian transitional.*—'Cyprian is here, as generally, transitional between the second century and the fourth. His eucharistic theory is in the main Tertullian's, as regards the sacramental rather than the proper body of Christ' being present in the elements after consecration. But

[1] So Justin, *Dial.* 28. The idea lies at the root of the gift-theory of sacrifice in much Greek religion, the gift being to an Iamblichus's mind, as to Irenæus, 'a symbol of friendship between the mortal and the deity'; see art. SACRIFICE (Greek).

[2] The fullest and still the truest discussion of 'the Christian sacrifice' in the ancient Church is in Bunsen's *Hippolytus and his Age*, 4 vols., London, 1852, iii. 253 ff., iv. 135 ff., where also much bearing on worship at large is well said.

as regards the prior *offering* of the elements in eucharistic *worship*, Cyprian insists that 'the priest' 'performs his office in Christ's place' (*i.e.* with His authority for the sacramental efficacy of his act) when he 'imitates that which Christ did.'[1] And, though he has in mind what Christ did at the Last Supper,[2] not on the Cross, yet his broad language elsewhere gave a footing for another and less experimental[3] sense being read into his words. So he says, 'The Lord's passion is the sacrifice which we offer,' sacramentally or commemoratively, as 'we make mention' of it in our 'sacrifices' of bread and wine, and speaks of 'offering the blood of Christ' in 'the sacrifice of the Lord,' as commemoratively observed by use of the sacred words of institution in the prayer of consecration.[4] 'Thus in time "the blood of Christ" and His body were thought of as actually present and offered in the wine and bread, and that not only as the prototype of His people's self-oblation, but as a propitiatory sacrifice "for the sins of living and dead."'[5]

(*g*) '*Catholic' eucharistic worship and survivals in it.*—From Cyprian's day the whole nature of eucharistic worship insensibly underwent profound alteration in the Church's thought and in the growingly elaborate ritual which expressed it, until in the course of the 4th cent. it attained in most localities that form which is known as 'Catholic.'[6] Yet down to the 5th cent. there remained clear traces of the older order in certain phrases not really of a piece with the conceptions then prevalent. Thus, in addition to those already alluded to, in the Anaphora of Serapion in Egypt, *c.* 350, before the words of institution we read:

'Full is heaven, full also is earth of thy excellent glory, Lord of Powers: fill also this sacrifice (θυσίαν) with thy power and participation: for to Thee have we offered this "living sacrifice" (θυσίαν, Ro 12[1]), this bloodless oblation (cf. Eph 5[2]): to thee we have offered this bread, the likeness (ὁμοίωμα) of the body of the Only-begotten.' Then comes the reference to Christ's example in the institution, followed by: 'Wherefore we also, making the likeness of His death, *have offered* the bread, and beseech Thee through *this sacrifice*, be reconciled to all of us and be propitious, O God of Truth.' Only after this do we get the invocation which is conceived to make the bread 'body of the Word' and the cup 'blood of the Truth,' and so 'medicine of life' for body and soul to those partaking.

Here there seems to be a blending of primitive and later elements.

(*h*) *Retrospect of eucharistic worship to the end of the 4th century.*—In idea it at first corresponded simply to its name, 'thanksgiving' to God for His benefits in nature and grace, as rooted in His adorable being or Name. As *1 Clem.* xxxviii. 4 puts it, 'Seeing, then, that we have all these things from Him, we ought in all things to render thanks [Eucharist] to Him, to whom be the glory for ever and ever, Amen.' Of such a life of thanksgiving the solemn corporate worship in full Church gathering is the climax, being the earthly imitation of the worship in heaven,[7] where (as pictured in Dn 7[10]) 'the whole company of His angels standing near Him do sacred service (λειτουργία) to Him,' the adoration attributed to the Seraphim in Is 6[3], 'Holy, holy, holy is the Lord of hosts: the whole earth is full of His glory.' As visible, concrete expression of this homage of thanksgiving, the Church's 'offerings' or 'gifts' in kind from the Creator's own gifts were presented in sacred service or *liturgy*, in the prayer

[1] *Epist.* 63. 14. [2] *Ib.* 4.

[3] For his real meaning cf. ch. 11, where he dwells on *wine* as by natural and scriptural symbolism, or sacramental value, able to 'express (*exprimere*) the blood of Christ' as water could not, and so to produce the sense of newness and joy suggested by the blood or passion of Christ, which the wine 'shows forth' (*ostendit* [ch. 4]).

[4] *Ib.* 9. 14. 17.

[5] J. V. Bartlet and A. J. Carlyle, *Christianity in History*, London, 1917, p. 171 f., where also are quoted the chief liturgical types illustrating the developments here in question.

[6] See art. EUCHARIST. [7] *1 Clem.* xxxiv.

of uplifting (ἀναφορά), directed to God's spiritual altar on high (cf. the imagery of the Apocalypse), where Christ the High-priest presents the Church 'sacrifice' of praise—if pure from defilement by sin, such as enmity between any of its members.[1] This prayer was led up to by 'common prayers' of intercession, as Justin says, 'for ourselves . . . and for all other men everywhere,' in urgent petition (εὐτόνως) 'that we may be counted worthy, after having learned the Truth, by our deeds also to be found, finally, good in conduct and keepers of the commandments, that we may be saved with the eternal salvation.' After these intercessions the kiss of peace sealed the spirit of unity which was specially asked for, and was the condition of the 'purity' and acceptableness of the coming eucharistic prayer, the Church's 'sacrifice' of praise to God's Name[2] or revealed nature. Of such intercessions as offered in Rome *c.* A.D. 95 we probably have the substance, and largely the very words, in the Epistle of Clement (lix.–lxi.); and we find them strikingly continuous with those of the OT and of contemporary Jewish public worship (cf. 'The Eighteen' Petitions)—a feature also common in the earliest extant Christian hymns. The changes which passed over Christian worship, especially the eucharistic part, show a steady decrease in this Biblical or Hebraic spirit (as distinct from Biblical quotations adapted to new uses), and a corresponding infusion of a non-Biblical or Hellenistic element of thought in the interpretation of the Eucharist as worship and means of grace, together with a transposition of traditional elements in the service generally, in keeping with the new ideas (*e.g.*, the place of the intercessions). This is the most momentous fact in the development of ancient Catholic worship out of primitive Christian forms, and has its parallels in other aspects of Catholic Christianity.[3] The change is associated, too, with a growing sense of sin in 'the saints' or 'the holy Church,' especially from the 4th cent., when Christian wholeheartedness on the average rapidly declined, owing largely to the new relations of State and Church tempting worldly people to join the latter. The eucharistic 'sacrifice' is more and more conceived in a propitiatory sense, which had its roots in the newer view of the elements, as literally made by consecration 'the body and blood' of Christ's passion, though as existing now in resurrection glory. Along with such changes of thought went those of form. The eucharistic prayer became more stereotyped, not only as the habitual usage of a given bishop but also as the fixed tradition from bishop to bishop; and what had once been a single prayer was broken up into specialized moments or phases, marking stages in the sacred drama of the Liturgy. This gave the service a 'hieratic' or formally sacred[4] effect, alien to the genius of primitive Christian worship, but quite congenial to the non-Christian cults around it. To these innovations was now added yet another characteristic of later Catholic worship generally, viz. the notion that the intercession of saints is a factor in the divine pardon provided in the Head Himself.

(*i*) *Persons to whom worship is addressed.*—The practice of direct invocation of saints as distinct from the earlier veneration, especially on a martyr's 'birthday,' itself appears in Catholic piety about the latter half of the 4th cent.;[5] but there is no invocation of this sort in eucharistic prayers, where Saints are 'commemorated,' 'that by their prayers and mediations God may receive our petition.'[1] The Church's prayers are addressed only to God the Father, in keeping with the strict theory of Christian prayer, as expounded by Origen.[2] According to this, the Father was the ultimate, the Son or Word the proximate, object of prayer, as of adoration and thanksgiving. Thus the Divine Word is 'to be petitioned as High-priest to offer up our prayer, that has first reached Him, unto His God and our God.' In practice, however, at least in individual devotions, Christ was directly addressed, all along, in prayer of invocation and petition in particular. In solemn doxologies, on the other hand, a gradual change is visible, both in eucharistic and in other connexions. There Christ, as God's historic Son (originally 'Child' or 'Servant,' παῖς, as in Acts), appears originally as the medium through whom glory is offered to the Father; and only from the latter part of the 3rd cent. (as it seems) becomes gradually associated, as the Logos-son, with the Father as also the object of such worship. Similarly the Holy Spirit, which earlier had been thought of as the element 'in' which worship was rendered to God,[3] came to be associated with the Father and the Son as co-equal object of praise. In many MSS the modification of the older form by later feeling gave rise to an awkward blend, like that in the 'Hippolytean' Church Order as current *c.* 350–400, viz. 'through Thy Child Jesus Christ, through (*or* with) whom to Thee (be) glory, dominion, honour — Father and Son, with Holy Spirit' (*or* 'with Holy Spirit,' only). Basil[4] says that 'with' is most fitting in relation to the Son in doxology, 'through' in thanksgiving; but this, while true enough, does not apply to the history of the matter.

3. Special forms of Catholic cultus.—(*a*) *The cult of 'saints.'*—It is needless here[5] to go into this subject further than to notice that both in its ritual forms, like so much other fresh ritual (in which the Gnostics often led the way) from the middle of the 2nd cent. onwards,[6] and in its origins this cultus owed much to the funeral and commemorative customs of pagan society, in which Christians lived and from which many of them passed into the Church. 'Prayers and appeals to the dead' were familiar ideas in the one sphere before they appeared in the other—in the case of 'saints,' from Basil's day († 379) onwards. 'Hence it seems probable that the prevalent atmosphere of paganism exercised some vague influence upon Christian feeling, especially in the case of the ruder populace. The strongly marked desire to be buried near the martyrs is no doubt to be attributed to a similar hope of protection. It was a matter not so much of logic as of a deep and primitive instinct—the same which in pagan times had led to the development of hero-worship.' These frank words of a modern Roman Catholic[7] deserve attention as pointing to a principle of wide possibilities of application in the history of 'Christian' worship, especially in view of his later statement that 'the ceremonial of Christianity and that of paganism include many identical elements—*e.g.*, the use of ablutions, lights, incense, prostrations, unctions, linen vestures, *ex votos*, etc.'[8] Few can doubt that they represent a kind of development which the NT writers, particularly St. Paul—not to name Paul's Master—would have found foreign, to say the least, to the genius of 'the Gospel,' as

1 1 *Clem.* xxxvi. 1; *Didache*, xiv.
2 Cf. *Did.* xiv. 3.
3 See *Christianity in History*, bk. ii., *passim*, and E. Hatch, *The Influence of Greek Ideas and Usages upon the Christian Church*, London, 1890.
4 There was a corresponding change in the form and appointments of the place of worship.
5 See art. SAINTS AND MARTYRS (Christian).

1 Cyril of Jerusalem, *Myst. Cat.* v. 9.
2 *C. Cels.*, v. 4, viii. 26; see C. Bigg, *The Christian Platonists of Alexandria*, Oxford, 1886, p. 185 ff.
3 *E.g.*, Serapion's Prayer Book, 1A, 1C, 2, 7; cf. 'in the holy Church' in the 'Hippolytean' Church Order.
4 *On the Spirit*, 16.
5 See art. SAINTS AND MARTYRS (Christian).
6 Cf. Hatch, *op. cit.*
7 *ERE* xi. 54b.
8 *Ib.* 58b.

'worship in spirit.' And, when one reads the words of St. Melania, in 438, at a shrine of the martyrs, 'O ye, who have always free speech with God that loves mankind, be my ambassadors (πρεσβεύσατε) with Him that He may receive my soul in peace'—along with the comment, 'It is just this παρρησία,' or free speech, 'attributed to the martyrs, that is put forward again and again in patristic writers as the motive for having recourse to their help'—one cannot but feel the distance, not so much of time but of spirit, between such worship and that of the NT.[1] For there the same 'free speech,' as of child with parent, is claimed as the glory of all sons of God in Jesus Christ, and particularly right of entry in this spirit into the Holy Place in heaven, as of priests in union with the 'Great Priest over the family of God' (He 10^{19}). As by a lightning-flash, such a comparison reveals the enormous change of attitude which has come about, by insensible stages, in the worship of Christians.

The cult of the relics of saints, as aids to devotion, especially in connexion with the celebration of the anniversary of martyrdom or spiritual birthday (*natalicia*), goes back in its simplest form to a relatively early date, as witness the contemporary *Acts of Polycarp* (*c.* 155). But its developments, both in the Catacombs, where martyrs' remains abounded, and elsewhere, later assumed extravagant and superstitious forms, especially in the 4th cent. and onwards, calling forth the scorn of Julian and many other cultured pagans.[2]

(*b*) *Artistic aids to devotion.*—The place of art in the expression of Christian thought and feeling, and the function of images (*eikons*) or representations of sacred persons to the eye, usually in paint or mosaic work, are dealt with in special articles.[3] There was at first great shyness of such things, on account both of the Jewish and other feeling against all that could be construed as idolatry and of the tainted nature of so much pagan art. Hence the earliest use of art (*e.g.*, in the Catacombs) was symbolic in character; and it was only in the 4th cent., when so many changes, especially in the way of coming to terms with pagan culture, first came about, that such restraint was largely thrown aside. One of the earliest forms in which art was used to assist devotion was in the form of Church buildings, which even from the end of the 3rd cent. begin to be more specially designed to suit the developing ritual of the worship carried on within them.[4] The veneration of 'images' of sacred persons, as manifestations of the divine in creaturely form, was probably stimulated in part by the preoccupation of Christian thought in the 4th and 5th centuries with the idea of the Incarnation.[5]

(*c*) *The Christian Year.*[6]—As the central service of Church worship, the offering of the eucharistic sacrifice came to represent dramatically, or in a series of sacred acts and words, the Christian redemption wrought by the Incarnate Son of God, so the Gospel story of the Incarnate Saviour was set forth ever more fully in the yearly festivals and holy seasons commemorative of the same. Naturally the week first felt the touch of Christ. The Lord's Day, the Christian's day of resurrection joy, took the place of the Sabbath, the Jewish day of grateful gladness. To this were soon added[7] Wednesday and Friday, as fast days, in remembrance of the sin that occasioned the Saving Cross. But what the Lord's Day was to the week, that the anniversary of the central act of redemption was to the year. Thus Easter, with its associated Friday, became the first season in the Christian devotional year; how early we cannot say. Then followed Pentecost, and gradually the other great 'moments' of the Redeemer's life, until each year became a time-sacrament of the divine drama of human salvation. The fact that the birthday of the Saviour came relatively late into the calendar points to the practical rather than theoretic nature of the Church's apprehension of its own salvation, in which the Cross, the final act of Redemption, is more central for Christian experience than His birth.[1] Into the calendar of the Christian salvation, in terms of Christ's history and its sequel in the gift of His Spirit, the Church's birthday, were fitted the 'birthdays' of martyrs into the heavenly realm of life eternal. Such, then, was the Christian Year in idea and as an aid to worship. The festivals in honour of the Virgin Mother of Jesus appeared only late in the calendar.

(*d*) *Devotional 'hours,' in private and corporate worship.*—From the Church Year we turn to the day as a unit of devotion.[2] 'Hours' of worship, other than the Sunday worship centring in the eucharist, came to be of two chief types: (*a*) those for special classes within the Church, particularly ascetics ('virgins' of both sexes), later known as monks and nuns; (*b*) Church services proper. The former type grew out of an earlier kind, namely individual devotions continuous with the three hours of prayer in later Judaism (Ps 55^{17}, Dn $6^{10f.}$), which from apostolic precedents in Acts (3^{1} 10^{9}; cf. *Did.* viii.) came to be called 'the apostolic hours.'[3] Clement of Alexandria refers to Christians who set apart certain hours, viz. the third, sixth, and ninth.[4] Already in Cyprian's day[5] piety had found mystical reasons for the use of the apostolic hours, connecting them generally with the Trinity, and severally with two stages of Christ's Passion and the descent of the Spirit at Pentecost (the third hour). So far, however, such day-time hours were purely private devotions. The earliest Church service other than the Sunday one was the 'vigil,' a night service suggested by the NT calls for vigilance. But it was never of daily occurrence, only on the eve of a holy day—first Easter, then the Lord's Day, the weekly fasts (*stationes*) of Wednesday and Friday, and the yearly festivals of local martyrs.

The night hours proper were, like the day hours, the outcome of private devotions, to judge from Cyprian,[6] who writes:

> 'Besides the hours observed from ancient times [the 'apostolic' day hours], both seasons and mystical reasons for prayer have now grown upon us. At morn, to celebrate the Lord's Resurrection . . . At sunset, when day ceases, prayer must needs again be offered,' alike for the return of the light and for the advent of Christ, the true sun and true day, with the grace of eternal light. 'Let us, however, who are ever in Christ, *i.e.* in the light, not cease from prayer even in the hours of night,' any more than Anna in the temple.

Here we find an hour of early morning prayer on rising, before the first of the 'apostolic hours,' ere putting hand to work, and also a vesper hour. These five hours mostly reappear in the East in the 'Hippolytean' Church Order—the last part of which reflects some circle of piety in Syria about A.D. 300—each with its mystical reference, though a different one from Cyprian's;[7] but there is no vesper hour in the old Eastern Order, possibly

1 Eph 3^{12}, He 3^{6} 4^{16} $10^{19.\,35}$, 1 Jn 2^{28} 3^{21} 4^{17} 5^{14}.
2 See art. RELICS (Primitive and Western).
3 See Christian sections of artt. ART, IMAGES, SYMBOLISM.
4 See art. ARCHITECTURE (Christian).
5 See, further, art. ICONOCLASM.
6 See Christian sections of artt. CALENDAR and FESTIVALS AND FASTS.
7 Cf. *Did.* viii.

1 For Christmas Day, and the problems connected with it, see art. *s.v.*, and J. Wordsworth, *The Ministry of Grace*, p. 392 ff., and for the calendar as a whole, chs. vii., viii.
2 Cf. Wordsworth, ch. vi.
3 Tert. *de Orat. Dom.* 24, *de Jejun.* 10.
4 *Strom.* vii. 7. 4.
5 *De Orat. Dom.* 34 f.
6 *Ib.* 35 f.
7 Ps. Athan. *de Virg.* xii., xvi., and *Apost. Const.* viii. 33, have still later modifications.

because it was already set apart for more social worship. On the other hand, there are not in Cyprian any night hours, only prayer in the night seasons (*noctibus*). Thus our earliest witness for night hours proper is Syrian, viz. this 'Hippolytean' Church Order.

There, after passing reference to prayer before lying down, solemn prayer (with hand-washing) at midnight is enjoined, 'inasmuch as the fathers have handed down that at that hour all creation pauses for a moment to praise God, and all the angelic host does Him service (λειτουργία)—along with the souls of the righteous, hymning God (almighty) at that hour.' Prayer, too, at this hour fulfils the Lord's words, 'At midnight a cry arose . . . Therefore watch, for ye know not at what hour he (the Bridegroom) cometh.' 'Cock-crowing' is the last of its series of hours, the second of the night hours, when the believer rises to pray in memory of Christ's resurrection and 'in hope of eternal Light in the resurrection of the dead.' About a century later, namely in *de Virg.* 20, the midnight hour seems to last on till 'towards dawn' when come Ps 62[2], the *Benedicite opera omnia*, and *Gloria in excelsis*.

Here we see how the regular hours of those under vows, 'virgins' or 'religious' (in later Latin parlance), grew out of the more informal devotions of earnest Christians living in society or 'the world,' by increasing severity of requirement, which demanded first a midnight hour (a daily, rather than occasional, vigil) and then an hour when the cock heralded the approach of a new day. Such ascetic vigilance of worship was as a rule possible, physically as well as otherwise, only to those who were at leisure (from daily labours) to cultivate a professional and more individualistic life of piety. There is, however, no sign of distinct night hours (even for ascetics) before A.D. 300. Even in Egypt, where asceticism appeared earliest, as late as the end of the 4th cent. there were only two corporate daily seasons of worship, evening and morning. At Antioch we hear that *c.* 350 Bishop Leontius 'brought the congregations collected by the ascetics Flavian and Diodorus in the cemetery chapels, into the city churches,' and so introduced antiphonal singing, by two opposite choirs, into wider use. Here we seem to have a clear case of the transition from the daily corporate worship of ascetics, as a special class, to that of the Church under its clergy, of which Etheria, the female pilgrim to Eastern centres of devotion *c.* 385, affords us evidence at a rather later stage. Describing the public services in Jerusalem, she mentions matin hymns at dawn (=hour of rising, in the foregoing), the sixth (*sext*), and ninth (*none*) hours, vespers ('lighting-up' hour); to which the third (*terce*) was added in Lent. There was also an early vigil from cock-crow to dawn kept by 'all monks and virgins,' and by some lay-folk also. Of course the devotions at the central holy place of Christendom were more generally attended than elsewhere and more elaborate in form, including already four daily services at least. But the account gives us clear insight into the way in which worship became more specialized and developed. And by a good deal of evidence from the last quarter of the century we can 'fix the period A.D. 350–375 as that of the introduction of daily public evening and morning prayers into the Eastern Church, followed a few years later by that of Milan.'[1]

As regards *forms of devotion* dating from the 4th cent., neither the morning hymn (*Gloria in excelsis*) nor the evening one,[2] for instance, seems then to belong to public service. The former appears in varied contexts (*e.g.*, after the Biblical Canticles or 'Odes' in the *Codex Alex.*); and in the Eastern Church it is part of the Daily Office (Lauds), while in the Western it is in the Mass—whither most prized forms tended to gravitate. Once, however, both perhaps were part of the worship of an ascetic community. The evening hymn, like another vesper hymn, 'Hail, gladdening light' (φῶς ἱλαρὸν), referred to by St. Basil[1] as already ancient, may originally have been a thanksgiving 'at the lighting of the lamps' either in the home or at an Agape,[2] passing later into use among ascetics, like the table-prayers of the *Didache* into *de Virg.* xii f. In this last the *Gloria* is part of the virgin's praise 'towards dawn.'[3] Closely connected in feeling and ideas with the *Gloria*, and perhaps with its fellow vesper hymn (*Te decet laus*), is the best known Latin hymn, the *Te Deum*, now traced to Nicetas of Remesiana, who as living on the road between the East and West would naturally feel the influence of Greek models. Nicetas in his works 'On Vigils' and 'On the good of Psalmody' illustrates further the similarity of ideals of private and corporate devotional hours in East and West *c.* A.D. 400;[4] and he was one of the pioneers of the newer feeling which allowed hymns other than those in Scripture, the Psalter above all, to form part of corporate Christian worship, though the prejudice against this died hard.[5] The authority of St. Ambrose, who himself wrote hymns for public worship, had no doubt great influence. The musical difficulty to their more general use was a real one. It was in monastic circles, then, that hymns proper took real root, and from their daily offices passed in the later Middle Ages into the Breviary of the ordinary clergy. The early Celtic monks in particular were active in the use and production of hymns; and from the 12th cent. onwards we can trace the periods of fresh revival in monastic religion by this spontaneous form of devotional expression—*e.g.*, in 'Jesus, the very thought of Thee,' *Dies Iræ* (by the Franciscan, Thomas of Celano), and the eucharistic hymns of St. Thomas Aquinas.[6] The Church of Rome did not adopt daily services so early as the N. Italian and Gallican Churches, under the influence of Eastern monastic practice, carried thither by a number of pilgrims and others from those regions, such as Hilary in the middle of the 4th cent. and Cassian of South Gaul towards its end. Rome was always conservative in usages, as appears most clearly in its manner of reciting the Psalms, which were the staple of worship other than prayer. The Eastern form was antiphonal singing between two choirs, a method which took definite shape at Antioch about 350, and spread westwards rapidly—through Cappadocia, Constantinople, Milan. In Rome, as also in Africa, the old 'plain song'—with its simpler style of music—continued longer to prevail, probably seeming to the Roman mind, as to Augustine, to be 'better adapted to the sober gravity of Divine worship.'[7] Yet the practical advantages of the new system, especially as 'winning weaker brethren to devotion by the delight which it ministered to the ear,' were manifest; and ere Augustine's death in 430 the change in Rome had begun to act, though it took effect only gradually.[8] Similarly as regards daily church services 'the recitation of the Cockcrow and Matins office does not appear to have been binding on the clergy, as distinct from monks and nuns, till the sixth century (perhaps under Pope Hormisdas, 514–523); and Vespers was made an obligation still later.'[9] In Gaul and Spain matins and vespers had taken general root rather earlier; while a civil law of Justinian also decreed that all clergy attached to

1 J. Wordsworth, *The Ministry of Grace*, p. 347.
2 Both in *Apost. Const.* vii. 47 f.

1 *De Spir.* 73.
2 Cf. Tert. *Apol.* 39 and the Ancient Church Order as extant in Ethiopic, 47.
3 Ch. xx.
4 Cf. A. E. Burn, *Niceta of Remesiana*, Cambridge, 1905.
5 Cf. the Council of Laodicea, *c.* 360, of Braga, in 561.
6 See art. HYMNS (Christian).
7 Swete, *Services*, etc., p. 41.
8 *Ib.* p. 41.
9 Wordsworth, p. 350 f.

a church should sing Vespers, Matins, and Lauds themselves, and not leave the duty to others. Almost contemporary with it was the issue of the famous Rule of St. Benedict (*c.* A.D. 528), which prescribed the use of 'the complete circle of eight "hours" for monks which is the foundation of the Breviary.' These hours were much the same as the six of Syrian ascetics in the 4th cent., completed at its close in Jerome's Bethlehem monastery by a supplemental matins, between lauds at dawn and the third hour (to which prime in the West came to correspond), together with compline (*completorium*) before retiring to rest. The last was added by Benedict himself, who dropped the midnight hour, so as to give his monks a longer period of unbroken sleep, and placed matins about 2 a.m.[1]

4. Mediæval worship.—In the main mediæval worship, alike as piety and as cultus, shows simply the working out and adaptation of the traditional cultus to new conditions, created by the break-up of the Roman Empire and its civilization. This meant the flooding of the Church with crude fresh types of humanity, each with its religious bias and customs, largely superstitious, and so fostered those elements in the Church of the Empire which were farthest from primitive piety and cultus, as fundamentally Hebraic. Hence it is the element which Catholic worship owed to other sources than the Biblical—as already described or alluded to—that increasingly distinguishes its mediæval phase, both in the East and in the West.

In the East the hieratic and mystic tendencies, the latter parallel to and influenced by the rise and spread of Neo-Platonism, as a religion as well as a philosophy, are most marked. Particularly was this so in what we may call 'Byzantine' piety, as distinct from various national types of Oriental Christianity, comparatively unaffected by Greek influence. But in all the eucharistic service was essentially a divine drama or 'mystery,' appealing to the emotions through the senses, with the idea of the mystic sacrifice at its heart. The notion of the parallelism between the worship of heaven and of earth, of the celestial hierarchy and the terrestrial, was worked out elaborately and with surprising literalism. It finds its typical expression in the pseudo-Dionysius, through whom it also exercised a deep influence on the more practical and ethical genius of Western, particularly Latin, worship. In both, too, worship, so far as expressed in cultus, becomes more vicarious and sacerdotal, less congregational, in character. The connexion between priest and people, especially in the East —where the cultus went on in the sanctuary or altar-area, largely out of the people's sight— becomes a more formal one; worship is less corporate, less an active participation of all, with mind and voice, in common acts of spiritual and moral communion with the Christ of the Gospels, and through Him with the God unto whom and with whom all life is to be lived in harmony of will.

A special note of mediæval worship, inherited from this later patristic age, was the sense of sins calling for the constant 'propitiation' of God. This was to be achieved partly through special good works (such as alms of all sorts, and various mortifying exercises of penance), often prescribed by the priest through whom absolution was looked for, and partly by private eucharistic oblations or 'votive masses' offered in the donor's name in special services. Parallel with this went a development of purely clerical masses, without lay participants, which in the 7th cent. produced that contradiction in terms, according to primitive ideas of eucharistic worship, 'private masses.' In these the priest administered communion to himself alone. No doubt this unsocial type of cultus was condoned as being ideally corporate in spirit, the priest acting in intention as a member of the whole Church, in its name and as pleading for its welfare. But one result at least of such purely vicarious masses, together with the celebration of several masses by the same priest on the same day (10th cent. onwards), was natural; viz. a concomitant decrease in lay participation. The Church had to be content with two or three communions a year on the part of ordinary Christians; and many communicated once only in the year.[1]

As regards 'hours' services, the new impulse given by Benedict led to 'the erection of monastic communities in connexion with the parishes (*tituli*) of Rome,' which 'supplied the parish churches with clergy at liberty to conduct the daily offices, and qualified by their training in music to do so.'[2] Thus, soon, terce, sext, and none were sung in the Roman churches, and before 800 prime and vespers also. These early Roman offices became, through the abbot Augustine and others, the basis of English mediæval breviaries. Attempts were made, too, as time went on, to extend the 'hours' services to parish churches and get the laity to attend (witness the English names of such services). But for the most part the 'hours' proper remained a monastic or at least clerical form of service throughout the Middle Ages; and in England, owing to historical conditions which effaced the older type of non-Roman Christianity, they were virtually Roman 'offices' or dutiful acts of divine worship. Yet they contained some Gallican elements, especially before the Norman Conquest; and after it these survived in the distinct Uses of the great dioceses, of which that of Salisbury (Sarum) was the chief. Through its influence, in particular, there set in also in the latter part of the Middle Ages a tendency towards a uniform English Use.

Rise of the 'Breviary.'—Ever since the 'hours' services had been adopted, the mass of fixed forms of devotion—psalms, prayer, lessons (not only Biblical, but also *Legenda* from patristic sermons and expositions and from the Acts of the Saints)— had grown to ever greater dimensions. The process of its simplification and unification in one service-book, instead of several, first appears in England about the 11th cent., in the Breviary (*Brev. sive Ordo Officiorum*) or *Portiforium*, i.e. the book 'carried' by the priest when he went 'abroad,' the latter being a smaller and more portable form of the former. It was the Breviary, then, that formed the basis of the first efforts of those who early in the Protestant reformation of worship, as of Christian religion generally, tried to bring back its public forms to primitive and purer models. But an experiment in the way of a reformed Breviary on Catholic lines was also made in 1535 by Cardinal Quignon, general of the Franciscan Order in Spain. Much was omitted as superfluous, and a simplification all round, amounting to a revolution in effect, was carried out. It and its preface greatly influenced Cranmer's first Book of Common Prayer. But Cranmer's purpose was far more radical, viz. 'to produce not merely a good manual of devotion for the clergy, but a Book of Common Prayer'[3] for all Christians, learned and unlearned, if only they could read their mother tongue.

Transition to the new order.—The old service-books were for the use of the clergy and 'the religious': the layman had only the 'little Office,'

[1] For the Benedictine Rule, as for types of monastic piety generally, see art. MONASTICISM.

[1] Funk, *Manual of Church History*, i. 315.
[2] Swete, p. 43. [3] *Ib.* p. 69.

whether the Latin *Horæ*[1] or the English *Prymer* based on it in the late Middle Ages. But the English Prayer Book became the layman's manual, as well as the clergy's, alike in church and in private use. Cranmer compiled it on the basis of the Sarum Breviary in particular, but in the light of principles of religion and worship drawn direct from the NT itself, with the aid of patristic precedent. Thus 'Whitsunday, June 9, 1549, witnessed the beginning of a new era in the public worship of the English Church,'[2] an era already inaugurated in most of the other countries which had gained a new sense of what the Christian 'gospel' was, and what sort of worship best befitted its nature.

In all of these the vital change took place that forms of worship were in a language 'understanded of the people.' This meant an enormous gain in spiritual reality, especially as their Biblical language and allusions could now be interpreted by and fitted into the regular reading of Scripture. The poverty of Scriptural background, and indeed the scarcity of 'the Word' of God in piety and worship, even in the later Middle Ages, when a certain amount of preaching existed in parts of the Church, is hard for us to realize to-day.

Cultus rites and ceremonies, as such, so predominated over the inward element or meaning, or 'faith' in the NT sense (esp. Ro 14[22f.]), that average mediæval worship was psychologically legal rather than filial in type. It was in fact such as Christ criticized in current Judaism, and Paul censured as persisting among Christians at Colosse (Col 2[16] 3[3]). Religion was statutory in nature and spirit, a being 'subject to ordinances' in daily life and in church, 'after the precepts and instructions of men.' Men were 'judged in meat or drink, or in respect of a feast day'—or a fast day or a saint's day—'which are a shadow of things to come.' Of course the mass alike of clergy and laity were not fit, as things were, for a NT type of worship, because those 'ages of Faith' had not the type of faith to which that belonged. This fact had historic causes, some of which have been indicated. But none the less such cultus, and such spiritually passive and unenlightened worship, represented no normal advance, save in the education of æsthetic and emotional sensibility to the divine, as majestic and mysterious in its nature and ways, with which it affected certain souls. Nor on these lines, from which the official Church through the papacy refused to depart, was there any promise of return to truer continuity with principles and methods of spiritual worship at the first.

It was small wonder, then, if, worshipping with but little direct aid from the NT and its distinctive spirit, mediæval piety was full of 'the spirit of bondage again unto fear,' and sadly devoid of 'the spirit of adoption whereby we cry Abba, Father.' This appears most vividly from many examples of the religious art which was used as an aid to worship.[3] But it was implied also in the elaborate system of mediators, both on earth and in the invisible world—patron saints and the saints at large, with the Mother of Jesus at their head—whose aid was felt needful to supplement the too exalted or remote help, or even to placate the too severe judgment, not only of God the Father but also of Jesus, the 'One mediator of God and man, himself man.' Nor was the element of fear—the fear of mystified minds, as well as of consciences not fully appeased by the Church's rites of penance and absolution that were a large part of the mediæval sacramental system—absent from the sense of mystery with which the central sacrament of worship, Christ's very Body and Blood, present in an inconceivably real sense[4] in the transubstantiated bread offered to God anew as 'the Host,' and eaten for the benefit of body and soul, was regarded by all mediæval Christians.

Finally, participation in the Church's cultus was largely viewed as of value *per se*, like sacraments on the *opus operatum* theory, and as a meritorious work before God, rather than a specially direct and effective mode of attaining spiritual fellowship with God, as the soul's supreme good. A radical revival of the original Christian spirit of faith was vitally needful to a new birth of worship, on lines which could lead to the development of a cultus more suited to the growing spiritual maturity of humanity at large. This needed a system of worship which could first stimulate and educate it in certain directions, and then by gradual modification of the traditional forms make available (for the adherents both of the old and of the new types of Christian piety) the elements of positive value latent in the historical forms of continuous Catholicism.

5. Protestant worship.—(i.) IN GENERAL.—The intimate connexion between the kind of religious faith and the worship which expresses it is nowhere clearer than in the change which passed over cultus as a result of the Protestant Reformation. The new experience of saving faith, with its correlative doctrine of grace (*q.v.*), summed up in the twin ideas, justification by faith and the priesthood of all believers, made itself manifest in the sphere of religious feeling to which worship belongs. The sense of assured access to God on the part of Christians, as children reconciled and accepted in His beloved Son, Jesus Christ, brought into worship a fresh note of glad thanksgiving. This ran through all, at first even the confession of sins (as of children in a family, rather than of debtors or lawbreakers before a judge—the prevalent mediæval conception), and particularly the Communion of the Lord's Supper. This was now viewed primarily as a memorial but efficacious pledge, both on God's part and on man's, of the abiding covenant relation of forgiveness and grace brought about by Christ crucified, which it 'sealed' anew by a sacramental or sensibly expressed act, and at the same time strengthened. There was generally no thought of this most sacred act of worship being a 'bare sign' of the spiritual relations which its forms suggested, those of vital communion with God in Christ, and with fellow-members of His mystical Body, the Church. But there was a definite setting aside of the notions specially marking the 'old religion' (as mediæval Catholicism was often called). These were (1) that consecration effected change in the elements themselves (transubstantiation); and (2) that the changed elements were 'offered' as a 'propitiatory sacrifice for living and dead' by the action of the celebrant, viewed as having a supernatural power as 'priest' in virtue of the sacrament of 'orders.' Thus the ritual of the Mass was generally felt by Protestants of all types to involve non-Scriptural, and therefore un-evangelic, ideas of the nature and means of the Christian salvation.

Accordingly, after attempts to retain some of the forms and formulas still dear to many by use and sentiment, both in Lutheranism and in Anglicanism (here the contrast between the First and Second Prayer Books of Edward VI. is most significant), the ritual effects of the new conscience about making NT teaching and precedent sovereign at any cost were accepted in all Protestant communions. The Holy Communion of the Lord's Table replaced the Mass and its distinctive worship.

The retention of old forms for the expression of the new type of faith was pushed to the furthest point of compromise in the Elizabethan Prayer Book, particularly in its juxtaposition of the formulas of administration characteristic of each of the two

[1] 'Besides the canonical hours the mediæval Church observed hours in honour of the Blessed Virgin Mary, known as the "little office."' Originally 'a monastic devotion,' in 1098 it was made binding on the secular clergy, and eventually became popular with the laity. 'Other devotional matter gathered round the Hours of the Virgin,' and the Sarum *Horæ B.V.M.* had its calendar of saints, its penitential psalms, litany, and especially vigils of the dead. 'In this fuller form the Horæ became the prayer-book of the educated laity' (Swete, p. 212 f.).

[2] Swete, p. 7.

[3] See, *e.g.*, T. M. Lindsay's study of Luther's early training in the *Cambridge Modern History*, ii. [1903] 106 f.

[4] See passages in Darwell Stone, *A History of the Doctrine of the Holy Eucharist*, 2 vols., London, 1909, i. 277 ff., cited also in *Christianity in History*, p. 444 ff.

Edwardine editions. But the Articles of Religion, which define the distinctive beliefs of the Anglican Communion, as the Augsburg and other Confessions do those of other Protestant types, make plain the official sense in which these and other formulas were to be taken. See Article xxii. in particular.

Here the experimental cast of the new Anglican formula of administration, framed in 1552, is noteworthy, as well as the declaratory form of the words of absolution. Further the preaching of the Word now held a central place, if not the central one, in the whole service among Protestants. This brings us to the chief difference between Catholic and Protestant worship, viz. their respective emphasis on Word and Sacrament. For Catholicism, with its notion of grace as secretly infused participation in the divine nature, particularly as embodied in Christ's flesh and blood, emphasis falls on the sacrament of the Mass. For Protestantism, which conceives grace as the working of the Holy Spirit mediated primarily through the Word or uttered mind and will of God—the proper object of faith—it falls rather on preaching (*q.v.*); it is the means of grace which conditions the efficacy of all others, and prompts the worship that faith is helped by them to render to God. Even as regards the sacrament of the Lord's Supper, its Protestant form places the rite in a setting of the Word, partly by appropriate Scripture reading, partly by the communion address usual in non-Episcopal communions. Through the latter it is brought in idea within the scope of the 'prophetic' ministry of the Word, to which belongs also the prayer of thanksgiving where there is no fixed liturgy but it is left, as at the beginning, to the prophet 'to give thanks as much as he will.'[1] The Holy Communion being in fact, like other sacraments, 'a visible word' (to use Augustine's phrase), it speaks to the heart by the inward working of the Holy Spirit—the real agent in all grace, and especially in that faith of which other forms of grace are modes—whether mystically, by direct personal appeal through its symbolism, or by reflective unfolding of its meaning by ministry of the Word.

Protestantism, besides its emphasis on Word rather than Sacrament as means of communion with God, and in keeping with its idea of salvation by faith and not by deeds of 'merit' (rendered possible by sacramental grace), regards worship not as a meritorious action or 'service' (λειτουργία) to God, but rather in the light of realized fellowship with God through Christ, as of children with a father.

In worship God's perfections, especially His goodness, are simply answered by the homage of the heart's adoring and grateful recognition, and increasing conformity of man's will and personality to the divine character is sought after. The genius of Protestant religion, then, being to emphasize the filial consciousness, as making 'all things new' in man's outlook on life, all life becomes in idea a prolonged act of worship, because of filial trust and loyalty. Hence the line between such general worship 'in spirit and in truth,' and special acts of worship or cultus, whether private or corporate, is less marked than on the Catholic view—in virtue largely of the latter's sacerdotal and sacramental conception of the Church and its authoritative rites. Docile performance of the divinely appointed forms of cultus, in implicit reliance on Church authority, apart from personal consciousness of their effects in edification, is on the latter view 'meritorious' and will have its reward in divine blessing.

Another feature characteristic of the Protestant form of worship,[2] one expressive of its concern for

1 Cf. *Didache*, x. *fin.*

2 The hymn-singing of the 'Lollards' was personal rather than in public worship, but illustrates the tendency of fresh personal religion to break into song.

the active participation of the whole congregation, with a faith fully conscious of its proper objects of adoration, is vernacular singing, whether of psalms or of other forms of devotion. Here a mode of worship which in mediæval Catholicism had been confined to the few, particularly those separated by vows to a specialized 'religious' life, was made part of common worship for all.[1] In this Luther and Lutheranism[2] took the lead, using every form of singing, and all available musical aids, while the Calvinistic branch of reformed religion for long held strictly to Scriptural models, the Psalter in particular. This leads to the consideration of the several species within the common Protestant or Evangelical genus of worship.

(ii.) SPECIFIC TYPES.—The difference, especially in emphasis, between Catholic and Protestant worship is great, as was fully realized by the early Protestants, who had themselves lived first under the one and then under the other. But the degree to which the forms of cultus developed under the one were set aside as alien to the genius of the other, which took as its model the type reflected in the NT, varied with different species of Protestantism (*q.v.*). Among Protestant types Lutheranism and Anglicanism were the most retentive of traditional forms, each in its own way.

(*a*) *Lutheranism.*—Lutheranism (*q.v.*), in keeping with Luther's personal genius,[3] was conservative of the old forms rather than of their informing spirit (which had failed him religiously), save as regards the Holy Communion, where his doctrine of consubstantiation shows much the same mode of conceiving the Real Presence as the traditional Catholic one. Naturally, however, as time went on, the spirit of Lutheran worship prevailed over its forms (even as Melanchthon's sacramental doctrine approximated to Calvin's), save in certain local varieties of High Lutheranism. This inherent tendency is reflected in various ways throughout its history, particularly in the eras of Pietism and the Enlightenment (*Aufklärung*), and under the influence of Schleiermacher's recoil from the latter in the direction of giving feeling its proper place in religion. The most concrete instance of this emphasis on the Evangelical core of Lutheran worship was the union between the Lutheran and 'Reformed' (Calvinistic) communions in the Prussian State Church in 1822, with a revised order of worship (the *Agenda*). It is true that the Romantic movement as a whole led to a certain reaction towards older traditional forms (*e.g.*, a revision of the Church Order of 1650 was adopted by Mecklenburg-Schwerin in 1867), but this meant a break with the mind and feeling of the people at large; and more recently Schleiermacher's ideas of cultus as a corporate representation and expression of the religious life of communion with God in Christ, its exact forms being only of relative moment, have gained ground in thoughtful circles.

1 See art. HYMNS (Modern Christian).

2 F. C. Burkitt, in an address on 'The Growth of Christian Hymns' (*Proceedings of the Oxford Soc. of Hist. Theology*, 1907–08), points out that Luther's own part in this matter was less than is commonly supposed. German mediæval Christianity was specially rich in vernacular hymns (both original and from the Latin), and 'all he had to do was to select, to revise, and here and there to recast.' Even his own *Ein' feste Burg* is a paraphrase of Ps 46. 'It was the great merit of Luther to recognize the religious value' of vernacular hymnody and to give an impulse to its use and imitation. Conditions were different outside Germany.

3 For Luther's varying attitudes on varying occasions towards cultus in Christian worship 'in spirit and in truth,' and his steady rejection of the statutory notion of cultus, see P. Drews' art. 'Gottesdienst,' in *RGG*, on which also is based what follows on the development of Lutheran worship. For the Lutheran order of Sunday worship see Bersier's art. 'Culte,' in Lichtenberger's *Encyclopédie des Sciences religieuses*, iii.; and, for extracts from Luther himself on cultus, Daniel, *Codex Liturgicus*.

(*b*) '*Reformed*' *or Calvinist worship.*—The germ of this type is seen already in Zwingli (*q.v.*), who made the Protestant emphasis on the Word of the gospel rather than its Sacraments determine the order and forms of public worship: such worship, too, was to him only a special mode of the worship of the whole Christian life, and here 'obedience is better than sacrifice' or any formal act of worship. Simplicity, then, in cultus was his practical rule, in the interests of worship 'in spirit and in truth.' Zwingli's influence, however, was soon withdrawn, and was confined to Switzerland save in so far as it was taken up into that of others. Of these Bucer of Strassburg[1] was the chief link in the development between him and Calvin, in whom the 'Reformed,' as distinct from the 'Lutheran,' type of worship took classic shape. Calvin shared his predecessor's suspicion of 'Catholic' cultus as too sensuous in form, leaving the worshippers too purely the subjects of passive impressions and transient emotions, for lack of the interpretative message of the Word, whether of Scripture read in their own tongue or of Scriptural preaching, conceived as a 'prophetic' and expository ministry for adapting and applying, through personal appeal to the conscience and reason, the gospel in all its range to the worshipping people. The traditional cultus, then, failed at the point of spiritual reality, which was the test of true religion for Calvin. Yet there was a true place for the symbolism of cultus and its action on man's complex nature, but one defined and limited by divine gospel ordinance and precedent in Scripture. This alone was binding; what went beyond it could only be justified by strict analogy, and related to minor details such as 'did not matter' in principle (ἀδιάφορα), but were only seemly or convenient in changing times and places.

In keeping with these principles, Calvin insisted on the value of congregational singing, as helping the soul to rise into the atmosphere of worship; but he limited the contents of sacred song to the inspired Scriptural models, the Psalter in particular, adapted only verbally to musical melody. Prayer, by the same canons, in order to be as real and close to personal life as possible, both for the minister and for the people, should include prophetic or unprescribed prayer (analogous to the preaching of the Word), as in the primitive Church, as well as forms familiar to all—the people expressing their co-operation in both by the Amen. The preaching of the Word became a central part of public worship on the Lord's Day, while once a month (not oftener, lest it should lose something of its sacredness and preparation of soul by self-examination [1 Co 11[28]]) the sacrament of the Lord's Supper was added. Before it a confession of faith was made, in the Apostles' Creed, at first sung by the people (in 1545 ed. of *La Forme des prières*, etc.), later as recited by the minister. The simplicity and ceremonial bareness of Calvin's order of worship, deliberately based as it was on Scripture, with its Hebraic forms, was at first made up for by the new realism of the vernacular as used in worship and the new warmth of congregational singing.

In the sphere of private devotion—which dispensed in the main with fixed forms of prayer (save over food)—fasting, for chastening of soul but not as a 'meritorious' work, was practised both on appointed fast days (not the traditional ones of unreformed religion) and at times chosen for personal reasons. The Church Year was set aside, as lacking Scriptural warrant and as having superstitious associations (here Luther's different attitude determined the more conservative practice of Lutheranism as to Church festivals, also as to the crucifix, images, and pictures as devotional aids). The Calvinistic type, with minor variations, came to prevail not only in Switzerland and France but also in parts of Germany, in Holland, in Scotland, and in England among the chief Nonconformist bodies, both Presbyterian and Congregational (including Baptists), while it contributed not a little to the ethos and forms of the Church of England as established by law. Before, however, dealing further with English Christianity, as specially rich in varieties of Church life and worship, reference must be made to the non-established or minority type of worship as represented on the Continent.

1 See P. Drews, as above.

(*c*) *Independent or* '*Anabaptist*' *worship.*—From the nature of the case, the worship of these proscribed groups of radical reformers is hard to describe save in general terms.[1] As based on Scripture, read with strong emphasis on the illumination of the individual believer, it was very simple in form and spontaneous in method, having affinity with and aiming at reproducing the Spirit-prompted fervour and freedom reflected in parts of the Pauline Epistles, at which official religion everywhere looked askance. Free prayer, personal witnessing to God's working in religious experience, 'prophetic' exposition of Scripture in the light of this—in fact the features which marked the early 'Quakers' in England—were its chief characteristics. But, unlike the Quakers, the Continental Anabaptists practised both sacraments, in their own simple way and sense, and (so far as persecution allowed) the singing of praise to God in hymns expressive of their new-found and often deep religious feeling. Among them Luther's principle of 'the freedom of the Christian man,' along with love of the brethren, led to a thoroughgoing exercise of 'the priesthood of all believers,' on the lines of the autonomy of the local group or church —to the great scandal of all legally regulated types of State Church in the various lands—much as was the case later with the 'Separatists' under Elizabeth's system of uniformity in worship in England.[2]

(*d*) *Anglicanism.*—While the Elizabethan settlement, no less than Lutheranism, banished mediæval forms savouring of Roman doctrine, especially as to the Mass (not only transubstantiation but also consubstantiation was set aside), there was not the same check upon the return of the older associations of the ritual retained by the conservative and comprehensive policy of the Crown and its advisers that there was in Luther's own influence in Lutheranism. There was besides the extra influence in the same direction of the retention in the one case, and not in the other, of the Catholic order of the episcopate, and that in its mediæval form. Accordingly, although the type and forms of worship in the Elizabethan Prayer Book[3] were fundamentally Protestant rather than Catholic (in the opinion of a 'central' Churchman like Jewell, as of Calvin and other 'Reformed' rather than Lutheran Protestants), yet there were in it, as in Luther's Church order of worship, features proper to the standpoint and tone of 'Catholic' rather than 'Evangelical' religion, which were dropped by the types of Protestantism most careful to conform everything to the NT model and ethos.

Among such features was the litany, which, though it marks a great advance on the mediæval examples, and in its form 'is perhaps Cranmer's greatest liturgical triumph,' yet falls decidedly below the filial type of consciousness. This was partly due to its origin. It was not compiled by Cranmer for the Prayer Book at all, but in 1544 for use in a special season of

1 See art. ANABAPTISM.
2 See below, and cf. C. Burrage, *The Early English Dissenters*, 2 vols., Cambridge, 1912.
3 As also in that of 1662; see art. PRAYER, BOOK OF COMMON.

public calamities (like the earliest Western litanies),[1] yet 'was printed also in the Prymer of 1545,' which, like those of the 15th cent., was a book of devotion for lay-people. Thence it passed into the Prayer Book of 1549, with omission of the invocation of the saints. It is natural, then, that its tone is not the normal one for ordinary Christian prayers. It is significant that Luther's litany of 1529, the revision of a mediæval one, and itself a source of Cranmer's, was never part of normal Lutheran worship, but was used only on special occasions; and that the litany was one of the parts of the English rite which the Puritans most objected to as unfitting.

On the whole, then, the amount of traditional language retained in the Prayer Book—particularly its special offices of Baptism, Orders, Visitation of the Sick, etc.—gives no little warrant to those who in later times have gone on a view of its intention not in fact consonant with the Articles, which are of a piece with common Protestant doctrine, *e.g.*, on justification by faith, and with the experiential, rather than *ex opere operato* or Catholic, conception of sacramental grace which went with it. The result of the divergent readings of the Anglican cultus has been a diversity in ritual practice peculiar to Anglicanism among Protestant communions.[2]

(*e*) *The Puritans.*—Divergences began with those who, starting from the belief, probably a correct one, that the doctrinal affinities of the Elizabethan settlement of religion were with the Calvinistic type of Protestantism rather than the Lutheran, pressed for greater conformity to its form of worship as more Scriptural. Aiming at making the cultus yet more 'pure' from 'papal' or traditional Catholic ideas, usages, and especially vestments, the English 'Puritans' (*q.v.*) went further even than their foreign friends, who themselves lived under the Presbyterian system, thought necessary. When repressed by the Crown, using the bishops as its agents, many 'Puritans,' like Cartwright and Travers, worked for a Presbyterian Church polity, and issued in 1572 an 'Admonition to Parliament' to this effect.[3] Their objections to the rigid and exclusive use of fixed forms of prayer in public worship, their emphasis on 'preaching' of the Word, as distinct from mere fixed Scripture lections (with or without printed homilies), and their rejection of the traditional fasts and festivals of the Church Year, called forth from Richard Hooker (*q.v.*), a 'central' Anglican of the end of Elizabeth's reign, as Jewell had been in its earlier half, a classic defence of the worship of the Prayer Book as then understood. He writes, however, on the basis of essential agreement between the Reformed Churches, including the Anglican, as 'Sacramentarian,' not papal or Lutheran, in their view of the Lord's Supper.[4] In this he stands in contrast to those who in the next century went to the other extreme from the Puritan tendency in their views of Prayer Book worship, Laud and the High Church or Catholicizing divines often styled 'Caroline.'

(*f*) *Congregationalism.*—But, while the Puritans as a body remained inside the National Church, until after the Act of Uniformity in 1662, a minority among them gave up, under Elizabeth's coercive policy of ritual uniformity, all hope of further reform and began perforce to worship in semi-private church meetings or congregations. Their ideal of worship appears in R. Browne's *Booke which sheweth the Life and Manners of all True Christians* (1582), in a form which keeps remarkably close in spirit as well as idea to the NT picture of church fellowship in worship. This consists in (1) 'communion of the graces and offices in the Head of the Church, which is Christ,' (2) 'communion of the graces and offices in the Body, which is the Church of Christ,' and (3) 'using the Sacrament of the Lord's Supper, as a seal of this communion.' In such worship on a definitely Congregational basis,[1] whether their baptismal practice was that of Protestantism at large or that of Anabaptism (*q.v.*), two highly primitive features were recovered, namely, the intimate union in idea of Christian worship and Christian walk, and the place assigned to personal graces of the Spirit in fitting each particular church for corporate fellowship in both spheres of its life of union with God in Christ. These were connected with the Separatists' idea of church membership proper, as conditional on a personal act of 'covenant' with God and His people, whereas in national Churches it was determined merely by infant baptism and catechizing,[2] supplemented in Calvinism and English Puritanism by 'a godly discipline' meant to ensure a reasonable loyalty in life and worship. When Congregational ideals and forms of worship had lost something of their original reality, they were more than revived in the Society of Friends (*q.v.*), with its characteristic emphasis on 'the inner light' and its reliance on the promptings of the Spirit of God, alike in life and in corporate worship. Here new traits were fellowship in silent adoration and meditation, waiting for the 'moving of the Spirit,' and complete spontaneity of utterance for mutual edification, whether in the reading or quoting of Scripture, exhortation based on it, or in the form of a more direct message of the Spirit or 'inner light.' Negatively Quakerism dispensed with sacraments and even singing in worship. But the latter received an important extension among Nonconformists at large (with whom adherence to the psalms in one form or another had been stricter than among Anglicans) early in the next century, through the hymns of Isaac Watts, written specially for public worship.

(*g*) *The Evangelical Revival.* — Thereafter in connexion with the Evangelical Revival, both Wesleyan and Calvinist, a greater outburst of hymns and hymn-singing in worship marked the fresh spirit of praise to God which filled men's newly inspired experience of His grace and goodness in Christ. And the like has been true of all revivals of religion, including the Tractarian, down to the revivalism of the latter half of the 19th century.

6. The present situation.—In the Evangelical Revival and the succeeding Romantic movement, within both Romanism and Protestantism, religious feeling came again to its rights after the chilling era of rationalism. In Evangelical circles, both in Germany and in England, it appeared mainly in the forms of hymnody and enhanced spontaneity in prayer and preaching; in Catholic and Catholicizing circles it infused fresh earnestness and reality into the ritual and ceremonial aspects of cultus. In Anglicanism in particular it created a zeal for the restoration of 'historic' and 'Catholic' forms, both those allowed by the Prayer Book but fallen into disuse, and others disallowed by it. During the last half-century, moreover, the taste for a 'richer' and more æsthetically suggestive cultus has spread to almost all religious circles in England, and even Scotland, as also in all English-speaking lands. But it remains unassociated for the most part with the specific Catholic and sacerdotal ideas for which ritual was chiefly valued by the leaders of the Oxford Movement and their followers. The fact is that the strong

1 See art. LITANY, §§ 5, 8.
2 Cf. art. PROTESTANTISM.
3 See art. PURITANISM, 2 (*b*).
4 *Ib.*

1 See artt. BROWNISM, CONGREGATIONALISM.
2 In the Prayer Book by confirmation also, though it fell into wide disuse (Hooker, *Eccl. Pol.* v. lxvi. 8) for a time. No reformed Church treated this 'rite or ceremony' (Hooker) as a sacrament, since it lacked Christ's own authority, and Calvinism disallowed it even as a 'profitable ceremony.' Lutheranism, after a period of disuse, like that in England, restored it in a simpler form as a result of Pietism (see art. SACRAMENTS [Lutheran]).

recoil from those ideas, especially in their extreme forms, at the eve of the Protestant Reformation led to an undue suspicion of not a few natural forms of symbolism, fitted to express the poetry of the feelings and give appropriate vent and exercise to the mystical side of religious faith, where the reflective expression of the same faith through the spoken word cannot equally secure this, especially for certain temperaments and even for certain moods of most men and women. That recoil has now spent itself, and to-day many are feeling after the proper redressing of the balance of worship long disturbed by historical causes, and are seeking a synthesis of the Protestant or Evangelical emphasis and ethos, on the one hand, and of the Catholic or sacramental, on the other.

The ruling tendency, then, in present-day worship is towards a harmony of the various historic types. These in the past have existed too much as rivals or at least in one-sided self-sufficiency, each as if alone legitimate. Now they are being felt to be all of them but partial embodiments of the possibilities of Christian worship, complementary rather than hostile to one another. They are seen to be methods of meeting the instinctive needs of different types of our manifold human nature, while yet each of us requires, for perfected communion with God and his fellows, a fulfilling on all sides of that nature; and to this end each needs also the help of modes of worship which do not at first come natural to him, but are suited to educate undeveloped capacity. Thus there is abroad a movement towards unity in and through diversity, not only in Church fellowship generally as needful to full Christian unity (cf. the Lambeth Appeal of 1920), but also in the sphere of worship. It is strongest in the younger generation, especially among University and College students, largely through the co-operative, 'interdenominational' spirit of the Student Christian Movement. In the 'give and take' of student life, where personal relationships at close quarters and on the same mental level favour the observation of the similarity of the Christian character fostered by varying modes of cultus, inherited bias least hinders the frank recognition of the strength as well as the limitations of each of these distinct types. Persons are not, as so often in the past, seen through their forms of worship, but these through the persons who practise them. Hence a new and more hopeful, indeed a more reverent, attitude to all such expressions of Christian life.

The result is an ideal of Catholicity in worship that is due, not to lack of personal conviction or preference, but to faith in God and love to all His sincere worshippers. Men conceive of a Catholic worship, within a reunited Church communion, that shall be inclusive of the genius and the more essential methods of 'Catholicism' and 'Evangelicalism,' whether in Orthodox, Roman, or Protestant circles. Historic approximations to a synthesis of such tendencies exist already in Anglican, Old Catholic, Catholic Apostolic (Irvingite) worship, while recently a League of Free Catholics has been formed to work out experiments in this direction. No doubt sure progress will also be gradual. Meantime for all who seek this ideal the master-thought must be, 'Pure worship under the Gospel stands neither in forms nor in the formal disuse of forms,'[1] but in spiritual reality of devotion, evidenced by the fruits of the Spirit in life and character.

LITERATURE.—A. (i.) *General idea and principles.* — R. Hooker, *The Laws of Ecclesiastical Polity*, bk. v.; C. J. Bunsen, *Hippolytus and his Age*, 4 vols., London, 1852, 2nd ed., 2 vols., do. 1854 (a work of real insight); E. Bersier, art. 'Culte,' § viii. in F. Lichtenberger's *Encyclopédie des Sciences religieuses*, Paris, 1877–82, vol. iii.; sections in the *Christian Institutions* of A. P. Stanley, London, 1881, and A. V. G. Allen, Edinburgh, 1898; G. Rietschel, *Lehrbuch der Liturgik*, Berlin, 1900, 1908, i., where also full literature is given; H. Hering, 'Gottesdienst, Begriff,' in *PRE* vii. 1–7 (where, too, terms like 'service' and 'cultus' are traced); F. Cabrol, art. 'Worship (Christian),' in *CE* xv. (1912), and reff. there.

(ii.) *Christian worship in history.*—H. Leclercq, 'De rei liturgicæ in synagogis Ecclesiaque analogia,' in *Monumenta Ecclesiæ Liturgica*, Paris, 1900–02, I. xi. f.; E. Bersier, art. 'Culte,' as above (one of the best general surveys of the subject); A. A. Pelliccia, *The Polity of the Christian Church*, Eng. tr., London, 1883; H. B. Swete, *Church Services and Service-books before the Reformation*, do. 1896 (very useful); J. Wordsworth, *The Ministry of Grace*, do. 1901, chs. vi.–viii.; W. H. Frere, *Principles of Religious Ceremonial*, do. 1906; P. Drews, 'Gottesdienst, Geschichte des christlichen,' in *RGG* ii. (1910).

B. (i.) *The Ancient Church.*—(*a*) *Generally.*—Chief original source, *Didascalia et Constitutiones Apostolorum* (with related documents), ed. F. X. Funk, Paderborn, 1906; cf. C. C. J. Bunsen, *Analecta Ante-Nicæna*, 3 vols., London, 1854, iii. (see also A. (i.) above); C. E. Hammond, *Liturgies Eastern and Western*, Oxford, 1878, new ed. by F. E. Brightman, vol. i., do. 1896; E. Martène, *De antiquis Ecclesiæ Ritibus*, Rouen, 1700; J. Bingham, *Antiquities of the Christian Church*, 10 vols., London, 1708–22, bks. xii.–xv.; R. Rothe, *Comm. de primordiis cultus sacri Christianorum*, Bonn, 1851; T. Harnack, *Die christl. Gemeindegottesdienst*, Erlangen, 1854 (full and still valuable); F. Probst, *Die ältesten römischen Sacramentarien und Ordines erklärt*, Münster, 1892; P. Batiffol, *History of the Roman Breviary*, Eng. tr., London, 1912; L. Duchesne, *Christian Worship*², 'A Study of the Latin Liturgy up to the Time of Charlemagne,' Eng. tr., do. 1904 and later; F. Cabrol, *Le Livre de la prière antique*³, Paris, 1903, and *Les Origines liturgiques*, do. 1906; A. Fortescue, *The Mass, a Study of the Roman Liturgy*, London, 1912; also Allen, Swete, Wordsworth, and particularly Rietschel (where further literature), as above.

(*b*) *Special aspects.*—See Christian sections of artt. BAPTISM, CALENDAR, CONFIRMATION, EUCHARIST, FASTING, FESTIVALS AND FASTS, HYMNS, INCENSE, KNEELING, LITANY, PENANCE, PILGRIMAGE, PRAYER, SACRAMENTS, SAINTS AND MARTYRS; further E. von der Goltz, *Das Gebet in der ältesten Christenheit*, Leipzig, 1901, *Tischgebete und Abendmahlsgebete*, do. 1905; F. Leitner, *Der gottesdienstliche Volksgesang im jüd. und christl. Altertum*, Freiburg i. Br., 1906; and W. Caspari, 'Unters. zur Kirchengesang im Altertum,' in *ZKG* xxvii., xxix.

(ii.) *The Mediæval Church.*—See Bersier, 'Culte,' as in A. (i.), §§ v.–vi., Batiffol, Frere, Rietschel, and Swete, as above; also artt. cited in (*b*) above. Further F. E. Brightman, *The English Rite*, London, 1915, and literature on its mediæval sources cited at end of art. PRAYER, BOOK OF COMMON; and for details C. Wordsworth, *Notes on Mediæval Services in England*, do. 1898, and (with H. L. Littlehales) *The Old Service-books of the English Church*, do. 1904.

(iii.) *The Reformation and since.*—Bersier, 'Culte' (as above), § vii.; Drews, in *RGG*, §§ 3–5; Rietschel, with H. A. Daniel, *Codex Liturgicus*, 4 vols., London, 1847–53. For worship in England, in particular, see W. Palmer, *Origines Liturgicæ*, 2 vols., Oxford, 1832 and later, and artt. PRAYER, BOOK OF COMMON, PURITANISM, and reff. in text above *ad loc.*; also artt. EUCHARIST, HYMNS (Chr.), PIETISM, PRAYER (Chr.), PREACHING, QUIETISM, SACRAMENTS (Chr.).

J. VERNON BARTLET.

WORSHIP (Egyptian). — I. *THE DAILY TEMPLE LITURGY.*—**1. Its Heliopolitan origin.**— A striking feature of Egyptian temple worship is the fact that the same daily liturgy was celebrated on behalf of every god and goddess throughout the length and breadth of the land.[1] The reason for this uniformity, which seems to have prevailed as far back as the Old Kingdom, is as follows. The daily temple liturgy, as we know it, seems to be derived from that celebrated on behalf of the sun-god at Heliopolis, which city exercised in early times a very far-reaching religious and political influence. To enhance their prestige, therefore, a number of local gods were identified by their priests with the sun-god, of whom the king was regarded as the son. The king was thus also regarded as the son of the gods identified with the sun-god. As pointed out in the art. PRIEST, PRIESTHOOD (Egyptian), II. 2, this idea of sonship would have soon affected the relationship of the king with all divinities, whether male or female. The king was likewise high-priest of the sun-god, and he became high-priest of all the local divinities of Egypt by the same process as that by which he came to be regarded as their son. The local high-

[1] Printed Epistle of the Society of Friends in 1885.

[1] A. Erman, *A Handbook of Egyptian Religion*, Eng. tr., p. 47 f.

priesthoods also, of course, devolved upon the Pharaoh as representative of the centralized government of Egypt, all political and religious functions, which once belonged to the local chiefs, being united in him. Accordingly, as their son and high-priest, the Pharaoh, or his priestly deputy, celebrated the same liturgy on behalf of the local divinities as on behalf of the Heliopolitan sun-god.[1]

Heliopolitan influence on Egyptian worship is to be recognized not only in the uniform cult of all divinities, but also in numerous cult-accessaries and in the very constitution of the priesthood; furthermore, in the temple structures themselves and the views which the Egyptians entertained about them.

(*a*) Egyptian temples, certainly in early times[2] and often later, looked east, so that the rising sun might light up their dark interiors.[3] Thus in an inscription on the shrine found by Griffith at El-'Arish we read that 'the face of this temple (*i.e.* of the god Shu) is towards the east wherein Rē' rises.'[4] The Egyptians, indeed, pictured to themselves the sun-god, before all other divinities, as dwelling in every temple, which they accordingly regarded as a miniature heaven.[5] In texts of the Ptolemaic age, though the idea is probably far older, the two pylon-towers are equated with the two sisters Isis and Nephthys, who, according to one conception, lifted up the sun-god into the sky every morning.[6] The sanctuary or naos, in which the cultus-image was kept, was not infrequently designated 'heaven' or 'the horizon,'[7] and a title often borne by the high-priests of Amūn of Thebes was 'Opener of the doors of heaven in Elect-of-Places (Karnak).'[8]

(*b*) Every temple in historic times seems, like the Heliopolitan sun-temple, to have possessed its House of the Morning (*pr-dw;t*), in which the Pharaoh underwent lustration before celebrating the daily liturgy.[9]

(*c*) The sacred pool for purification, a feature of all temples, was associated not with the presiding deity of the temple but with the sun-god.[10]

(*d*) The obelisk which generally stood in front of the pylon was closely associated with the sun-cult.[11]

(*e*) The boat-shrine was also probably in the first instance a feature of the sun-cult.[12]

(*f*) The practice of offering to a divinity the figure of Mē'et, righteousness personified, in the daily temple liturgy[13] must have grown up at Heliopolis;[14] the formula recited at the presentation of the figure is clearly of solar origin.[15]

(*g*) The historic priesthood also displays marks of Heliopolitan influence. The four watches (*s;w*), or phylæ, of priests bear the names of the four quarters of a ship, which names were also assigned to the four watches into which the crew of the sun-god's heavenly ship were divided.[16] It was evidently the sun-god's priests who were first divided into four watches bearing these names, the sun-god being supposed to traverse the sky in a ship and his priests being therefore regarded as his crew. Even the general term for a priest, *we'eb*, may be Heliopolitan, for *we'eb* means 'pure person,' and purity is a very marked feature of the sun-cult.[17]

(*h*) In many temples the high-priestess was identified with Ḥathor, the wife of the Heliopolitan sun-god, and in this capacity figured as the wife of the god to whom the temple in which she was high-priestess was dedicated.[18]

(*i*) The sistrum-shaking musician-priestesses,[19] who were attached to every Egyptian temple, and the human concubines, who were assigned to several divinities,[20] seem also originally to have been Heliopolitan institutions.[21]

[1] See A. M. Blackman, *Journ. of Egyp. Archæology*, v. [1918] 156, 162 f., *RTr* xxxix. [1920] 44 ff.
[2] L. Borchardt, *ZÄ* xxxviii. [1900] 13, note 4.
[3] Blackman, *Journ. Egyp. Arch.* v. 154.
[4] E. Naville and F. Ll. Griffith, *The Mound of the Jew . . . and the Antiquities of Tell el Yahûdiyeh*, London, 1890, pl. xxiv., line 12.
[5] W. Spiegelberg, *ZÄ* liii. [1917] 99.
[6] *Ib.* p. 100.
[7] K. Sethe, *Urkunden des ägyp. Altertums*, iv. [Leipzig, 1906] 159.
[8] Spiegelberg, p. 99, note 4.
[9] Blackman, *Journ. Egyp. Arch.* v. 148 ff., 156, *RTr* xxxix. 44 ff., 65 ff., 75 ff.
[10] Blackman, *PSBA* xl. [1918] 88, with note 97.
[11] See J. H. Breasted, *Development of Religion and Thought in Ancient Egypt*, London, 1912, p. 70 ff.
[12] Blackman, *Journ. Egyp. Arch.* v. 156, with note 7.
[13] Blackman, *Journ. of the Manchester Egyp. and Oriental Society*, 1918–19, pp. 49, 52.
[14] See art. Righteousness (Egyptian), 6.
[15] A. Moret, *Le Rituel du culte divin journalier en Égypte*, Paris, 1902, p. 138 ff.
[16] Sethe, *ZÄ* liv. [1918] 3, note 5.
[17] See artt. Priest, Priesthood (Egyptian), VIII. 1; Purification (Egyptian), V. 2; Blackman, *PSBA* xl. 57.
[18] Blackman, *Journ. Egyp. Arch.* vii. [1919] 11 ff.
[19] Art. Priest, Priesthood (Egyptian), VIII. 3 (*d*).
[20] *Ib.* VII.
[21] Blackman, *Journ. Egyp. Arch.* vii. 14 ff.

2. Its Osirianization.—As pointed out in the art. Priest, Priesthood (Egyptian), II. 2, the relationship of the king with any god or goddess was, owing to the influence of the Osiris myth, conceived of as that of Horus with Osiris. Accordingly for cult-purposes every divinity came to be regarded as an Osiris, while the king, or his deputy the priest, played the part of Horus. The formulæ, therefore, pronounced during the celebration of the originally solar temple liturgy constantly attempt to equate the various episodes composing it with events connected both with the death and resuscitation of Osiris and with the successful conflict of Horus with Sēth.[1] But, despite this Osirianization of the rite, many of the formulæ still retain clear traces of its solar origin.[2] Indeed, the Egyptian priests with their characteristic disregard for logic often employed both earlier solar and later Osirian formulæ side by side.[3] The Osirianization of the daily temple liturgy did not affect its outward form, which remained unchanged and in its main features is clearly solar.[4]

3. The chief officiants.—(1) *Pharaoh.*—With comparatively few exceptions the temple reliefs represent the Pharaoh not only in the capacity of high-priest in the temple services but as sole officiant. In historic times he could seldom have officiated in person, his place of course being taken by one of the priests who were his deputies.[5]

On the occasions when the Pharaoh actually did exercise his high-priestly functions he was conducted to the temple in procession.[6] At the head of the procession walked the 'pillar of his mother' (*Iwn-mwt-f*),[7] burning incense. Immediately in front of the Pharaoh were carried a number of sacred standards, which are said to 'clear the way'[8] to the temple or to 'drive away what is evil.'[9] A chief lector might also walk in the procession, 'adoring the god,' *i.e.* reciting hymns in his honour, and thereby 'warding off those hostile to the king.'[10] On reaching the temple precincts the Pharaoh straightway proceeded to the House of the Morning (*i.e.* the temple vestry). Reliefs at Edfu[11] and Abydos[12] represent him as being welcomed by the souls of Buto and Nekhen[13] (the dead predynastic kings of Lower and Upper Egypt), who conduct him into the House of the Morning for the performance of his ceremonial toilet. Here he underwent lustration,[14] and then he was robed, anointed, decked with ornaments, crowned, and invested with royal insignia, and possibly also presented with a repast. He was then ready to enter the temple to officiate.[15]

(2) *Priest.*—The ordinary chief officiant at the daily temple liturgy was a prophet[16] (*ḥm-nṯr*), *i.e.* a member of the higher class of the priesthood,[17] or else a great *we'eb*-priest[18] (*w'b '*;). All priests and priestesses had to purify themselves before entering upon their course, and while serving had to adopt various precautions in order to avoid ceremonial impurity. They had also, like the

[1] See, *e.g.*, Erman, *Handbook*, p. 45; Blackman, *RTr* xxxix. 63 f.
[2] See, *e.g.*, Moret, *Rituel*, pp. 16, 20 f., 26, 49, 79, 96, 105 108, 138 ff.
[3] Cf. Blackman, *RTr* xxxix. 66.
[4] Blackman, *Journ. Egyp. Arch.* v. 162.
[5] See art. Priest, Priesthood (Egyptian), II.
[6] A. Mariette, *Denderah*, Paris, 1869–80, i. pl. 9; C. R. Lepsius, *Denkmäler aus Aegypten und Aethiopien*, Berlin, 1849–59, iv. pl. 71*a*; A. M. Blackman, *Temple of Bigeh*, Cairo, 1915, pl. xxvi.
[7] See art. Priest, Priesthood (Egyptian), VI. 1; Blackman, *Journ. Egyp. Arch.* v. 122, note 7.
[8] H. Brugsch, *Hieroglyph.-demot. Wörterbuch*, 6 vols., Leipzig, 1867–82, vol. ii. p. 430.
[9] J. Dümichen, *Altägyp. Kalenderinschriften*, Leipzig, 1866, pl. cxiii.
[10] *Piankhi Stele*, line 103=Schäfer, *Urkunden*, iii. 38.
[11] Kees, *RTr* xxxvi. 6 f.
[12] A. Mariette, *Abydos*, Paris, 1869–80, i. pl. 29.
[13] The Edfu relief figures the souls of Buto and Nekhen, but the accompanying inscription speaks only of the souls of Heliopolis, an indication of the solar origin of the rite of the House of the Morning (Kees, *loc. cit.*).
[14] For particulars see art. Purification (Egyptian), V. 1.
[15] Blackman, *Journ. Egyp. Arch.* v. 161, note 10, *RTr* xxxix. 45 f.
[16] Moret, *Rituel*, pp. 42, 105.
[17] See art. Priest, Priesthood (Egyptian), VIII. 2.
[18] Moret, p. 7. Cf. *Canopus Decree*, hieroglyphic text, l. 30= Sethe, *Urkunden*, ii. 147.

Pharaoh, to undergo purification before entering the temple to officiate.[1]

4. The resemblance of the daily temple liturgy to the Pharaoh's ceremonial toilet.—A large part of the daily temple liturgy consists of a series of toilet episodes and closely resembles the ceremonial toilet of the Pharaoh in the House of the Morning. This resemblance is due to the fact that both are based upon the same performance, the supposed daily matutinal lustration of the sun-god—the cultus-image of the sun-god undergoing lustration every day at dawn in the Heliopolitan sun-temple, as the god himself was conceived of as doing in the horizon. That the other toilet episodes of the rite of the House of the Morning, viz. robing, anointing, crowning, etc., had their equivalents in the daily temple liturgy is due to the sun-god being regarded as a king.[2]

5. The three divisions of the daily temple liturgy.—There are three main divisions of the daily temple liturgy; (1) a series of episodes preliminary to the performance of the divinity's toilet, (2) the actual toilet, and (3) the presentation of food- and drink-offerings.

We know of two editions of the first two divisions of the liturgy. The one, an illustrated edition, is carved on the walls of the chapels of Horsiēse, Isis, Osiris-Onnophris, Amūn, Atum, and Ptaḥ, in the temple of Sēthos I. at Abydos. It consists of a series of reliefs representing the liturgy being performed, each relief being accompanied by the formula pronounced by the priest while the particular episode depicted was being enacted. The other edition, written for the temple of Amunrē' of Karnak,[3] is preserved on papyrus no. 3055 of the Berlin Museum and dates from the XXIInd dynasty.

The Abydos and Karnak liturgies are merely different editions of the same portions of the service-book. The formulæ for the toilet episodes are practically identical in both cases, and, when the pre-toilet episodes of the one correspond to those of the other edition, the accompanying formulæ are often either the same or have points in common.[4]

Both these editions are incomplete, but combined they no doubt supply us with a very adequate representation of the pre-toilet and toilet episodes of the daily liturgy in an Egyptian temple (originally the sun-temple), when the ceremonial was fully carried out.[5]

The third division of the liturgy can be fairly satisfactorily reconstructed from numerous representations and formulæ occurring among the reliefs which decorate the walls of the various temples.

There are numerous indications that the temple service-book assumed the form in which we possess it at a very early date, probably not later than the Old Kingdom.[6]

(1) *The pre-toilet episodes.*—Having undergone purification in the water of the sacred pool or tank, the priest entered the temple, reciting a formula as he did so. His first act after entering the temple was to kindle a fire, a bow-drill being used for that purpose, or perhaps only a spindle and 'hearth.'[7] The priest then picked up the principal part of the censer, which was of metal, usually bronze, and in the form of an outstretched arm with the hand open palm upwards.[8] Taking hold of the rest of the censer, the little brazier in which the incense was burned, he fixed it in its place, namely in the open hand at the end of the arm. Having filled the brazier with burning charcoal from the fire he had previously kindled, he set incense thereon, and, holding the smoking censer in one hand, proceeded to the sanctuary, the double doors of which were bolted and the bolts secured with a clay seal. The bolts seem often to have been tied with a strip of papyrus to which the clay seal was affixed. The priest broke the seal, drew back the bolts, and opened the doors of the sanctuary, whereupon the sacred boat was disclosed with the cultus-image enshrined therein.[1]

After the unfastening of the seal, and presumably the opening of the doors, the priest sometimes burned incense in honour of the uræus goddess. On beholding the image, the priest made a profound obeisance, 'kissing the ground prone,' as it was said, or 'placing himself upon the belly stretched out flat.' Then, standing or kneeling, he chanted first a hymn in honour of the divinity—lifting up both his hands as he did so in the attitude of worship, or else burning incense—and after that a second hymn in honour of *R'yt*, the female counterpart of the sun-god and identified with Ḥatḥor. The priest next offered the image scented honey, or a figure of the goddess Me'et, and then burned more incense. Having swept the floor of the sanctuary with a cloth, he was now ready to 'lay his hands upon the god,' *i.e.* take the image out of the boat or naos in order to perform its toilet.

(2) *The toilet.*—The priest's first act after 'laying hands upon the god' was apparently to divest the image of the clothing and ornaments in which it had been arrayed the previous day and to remove the pat of scented grease that had been placed on its forehead.[2] Then, placing the image on a little heap of sand, which he had previously poured out for that purpose, and having fumigated it with incense, he proceeded to sprinkle it with water, first from four *nmst-* and then from four *dšrt*-vessels, or else with water from one so-called '-vessel. He then censed the image again, cleansed its mouth with different kinds of natron, and yet again censed it. Having thus purified the image, he began to dress it, putting on it the white headcloth and arraying it in white, green, red, and dark red cloths in succession. After decking it with ornaments, he anointed it with unguents and then painted its eyelids with green and black cosmetic. Either immediately before or immediately after this application of unguent and cosmetics the priest invested the image with royal insignia—a diadem, *w3s*-sceptre, crook, and whip. The toilet episodes were probably brought to a close with a final burning of incense.[3]

(3) *The presentation of food- and drink-offerings.*—The procedure observed at the presentation of food- and drink-offerings in the temple liturgy seems to have been practically identical with that observed at the corresponding part of the funerary liturgy. This is indicated among other things by the fact that in the temple reliefs depicting a divinity being fed there is sometimes inserted above the altar or offering-table, and between the divinity and the chief officiant, a so-called list of offerings identical to all intents and purposes with the lists occurring in the tomb reliefs and paintings.[4] This is only to be expected, since every divinity was regarded for cult-purposes as an Osiris.

Before the offerings could be laid upon it, the table or altar had to be purified.[5] The act of placing the offerings on the altar or table, or else on mats spread upon the ground, was variously

[1] See art. PURIFICATION (Egyptian), V. 7.

[2] Blackman, *Journ. Manchester Egyp. and Oriental Soc.*, 1918–19, p. 30, *RTr* xxxix. 44 ff.

[3] On the same papyrus is a duplicate version for Mut, the consort of Amunrē'.

[4] Blackman, *Journ. Manchester Egyp. and Oriental Soc.*, p. 30 f.

[5] *Ib.* p. 51.

[6] See also Erman, *Handbook*, p. 46.

[7] See W. S. Blackman, 'The Magical and Ceremonial Uses of Fire,' in *FL* xxvii. [1916] 355–358.

[8] For a picture of a censer see Erman, *Handbook*, p. 46.

[1] See H. Schäfer, *Urkunden des ägyp. Altertums*, iii. [Leipzig, 1908] 39. When a stone naos took the place of a boat-shrine, the ceremonies of breaking the seal and withdrawing the bolts would have been performed in connexion with the opening of its doors and not of those of the sanctuary.

[2] See Blackman, *Journ. Egyp. Arch.* vi. 58 ff.

[3] For this and the preceding paragraph see Blackman, *Journ. Manchester Egyp. and Oriental Soc.*, 1918–19, p. 51 ff.

[4] Lepsius, *Denkmäler*, iii. 48, *b*, 244, *b*, 245, *a*; Mariette, *Denderah*, i. pl. 32; A. Gayet, *Le Temple de Louxor*, Paris, 1894, pl. xxvi. fig. 85.

[5] See art. PURIFICATION (Egyptian), V. 5 (*b*); see also Mariette, *Abydos*, i. pl. 21; E. Naville, *The Temple of Deir el-Bahari*, London, 1895–1908, ii. pl. xxviii.; Lepsius, *Denkmäler*, iii. 66*b*.

termed 'setting out the repast upon the altar,' 'setting down the divine offering,' 'setting down the repast.'[1] While thus engaged the officiant either stood or knelt.[2]

The god's meal having been laid before him, two closely connected ceremonies were performed, apparently in immediate succession, the one being variously designated 'presenting the repast,' 'presenting the divine offering,' 'performing the presentation of [or 'causing to be produced'] the divine offering,' and 'performing the presentation to, causing to be produced a great oblation for, NN,'[3] and the other being termed 'bringing the god to his repast.'[4]

At the former ceremony the officiant extended his right arm and bent the hand upwards in the prescribed manner[5] and pronounced the formula beginning with the words 'an offering which the king gives.'[6] When the king is depicted performing this ceremony, he is often shown holding a mace and staff in his left hand.[7] The recitation of the formula 'An offering which the king gives, etc.,' was closely associated with, and, on the analogy of the funerary liturgy, was doubtless preceded by, the burning of incense and the pouring out of a libation of water.[8] At the ceremony of bringing the god to his repast the officiant recited a formula calling (*dwi*)[9] upon the god to come to his bread, beer, roast flesh, etc.[10]

Various attitudes might be adopted by the officiant, whether king or priest, while he pronounced the summons. He might stand with right arm and hand extended in the prescribed manner and with left hand hanging at his side, or he might kneel with both hands, palms downwards, held above or beside the knees. Again he might kneel with left hand held in the attitude just mentioned or holding a censer, while with his right hand and arm he made the ritual gesture.[11]

The act of consecration, by which each item of food and drink was finally[12] made over to the god, was termed 'stretching out the arm four times.' According to the temple reliefs, it was performed in the following manner. The king, standing before what was to be offered, stretched out over or towards it four times the so-called *ḫrp*-baton, which he grasped in his right hand; in his left hand he held staff and mace, or else this hand hung at his side holding the symbol of life.[13]

In the series of temple reliefs depicting the god being fed is one representing the king in the act of 'elevating' (*fꜣ*) a tray of offerings 'before the face' of the divinity.[14] Does this scene represent one special episode in this part of the liturgy; *i.e.*, after the pronouncement of 'An offering which the king gives, etc.' was a specimen of the offering elevated in the presence of the cultus-image? More probably the scene is a summarization of a series of elevations; for doubtless, as in the funerary liturgy, each particular item of food mentioned in the list of food- and drink-offerings was elevated at its presentation to the accompaniment of a special formula. In the funerary liturgy, according to Utterances 108–171 of the *Pyramid Texts*,[1] each item was elevated four times.

In addition to the meal laid out before the image of the principal divinity in the sanctuary and before the images of the co-templar divinities in the adjacent chambers, offerings were also laid, of course, upon the great altar in the forecourt. If the procedure in the temple of the Aton at El-Amarna prevailed also in other Egyptian temples,[2] it was upon this altar that the Pharaoh mostly laid his oblations.

(4) *The removal of the footprints.*—The final act of the chief officiant before leaving the sanctuary, shutting the doors, and affixing the clay seal to the bolts, was to obliterate all traces of his own and his assistant's footprints. This he did by sweeping the floor with a cloth or with a besom made of twigs of the *ḥꜣdn*-plant.[3] In the sanctuary of the temple of Derr, on either side of the door, is a representation of Ramesses II. holding a cloth for sweeping the floor in one hand and a vase (for sprinkling it?) in the other.[4]

6. The functions of the assistant officiants.—The ordinary schematic representations of the various episodes convey the impression that only one officiant, the king, or a priest acting as his deputy, took part in the celebration of the daily temple liturgy. Inscriptions and a few quite exceptionally detailed reliefs, however, show that in addition to the celebrant a number of other officiants participated in all these ceremonies. The ritual was no doubt particularly elaborate when the Pharaoh himself was celebrant.

(1) A scene in the temple of Luxor depicts in some detail the presentation of the cloths used for Amunrē''s ceremonial toilet. After the burning of incense, the episode immediately preceding the arraying of the image in the royal head-cloth (*nms*), there enters the sanctuary a long procession of priests bearing chests containing the cloths in question, with members of the higher class of the priesthood, the fathers of the god, walking at their head. Some of the latter carry smoking censers and libation- or lustration-vessels, while others clap their hands and sing, one of them rattling a sistrum. Bringing up the rear of the procession is the king, with 'the god's adorer, the god's hand' (the high-priestess of Amunrē')[5] walking in front of him. The king holds out the *ḫrp*-baton and is said to be 'extending the arm four times,' *i.e.* consecrating the offering. But he also forms part of the procession, for between him and the high-priestess are the words 'bringing clothing.' We have here, pictorially combined in one, what were really two distinct actions, namely the procession of priests, accompanied by the king and high-priestess, conveying the clothing into the sanctuary, and the consecration of that clothing by the king assisted by the high-priestess, who either sang a hymn or chanted some formula.[6]

(2) A number of jars of unguent, which another Luxor[7] relief represents the king as consecrating, have been solemnly brought in procession by ten priests.

(3) Another relief in the same temple[8] shows a procession of twenty-eight priests bearing a number of ewers of water, to be used for such purposes as the washing of the altar, the pouring out of the libation before the bringing of the food-offering,[9] and for various drink-offerings.[10] At the end of the procession walks the king. The theory of the ritual demanded that the king should draw the water himself, come running[11] with it into the sanctuary, as he is depicted doing in the adjacent

1 *E.g.*, Mariette, *Abydos*, i. pls. 38*c*, 40*c*, 50; Lepsius, iii. 67*a*; Naville, i. pl. xxi.

2 *Locc. citt.*

3 *E.g.*, Mariette, *Denderah*, i. pl. 60*a*, *Abydos*, i. pls. 40*a*, 44; Naville, i. pls. xiv., xxiv., ii. pl. xxxvi., iv. pls. xcv., xcviii., v. pl. cxxxvii.; D. Randall-MacIver and C. R. Woolley, *Buhen*, Philadelphia, 1911, p. 49.

4 *E.g.*, Mariette, *Abydos*, i. pls. 37*b*, 40*a*.

5 Sethe, *Urkunden*, iv. 28, line 17.

6 That this suggestion is correct is indicated by the scene at Luxor described below, 6 (4), and also by the fact that the formula is closely associated with the ritual stretching out of the arm and the bending upwards of the hand (see Sethe, *loc. cit.*).

7 *E.g.*, Naville, *Deir el-Bahari*, iv. pl. xcv.

8 *E.g.*, Mariette, *Abydos*, i. pls. 42*a*, 44.

9 Naville, ii. pl. xxviii.; Gayet, *Temple de Louxor*, pl. xxxv., fig. 138.

10 Mariette, *Abydos*, i. pl. 37*b*.

11 *E.g.*, *ib.* i. pls. 37*b*, 40*a*, *b*, 51*b*; Naville and Gayet, *locc. citt.*

12 H. Brugsch-Bey, *Drei Fest-Kalender des Tempels von Apollinopolis Magna*, Leipzig, 1877, pl. x. line 6 ff.

13 See, *e.g.*, H. Kees, *Der Opfertanz des ägyp. Königs*, Leipzig, 1912, p. 59; Gayet, pls. xxxiv., xlv.; G. Legrain and E. Naville, *L'Aile nord du Pylône d'Aménophis III. à Karnak*, Paris, 1902, pl. xi. A; Mariette, *Denderah*, iii. pls. 54*y*, 56*d*.

14 *E.g.*, Mariette, *Abydos*, i. pl. 47*a*, *Denderah*, i. pl. 65*b*, ii. pl. 13*a*.

1 K. Sethe, *Die altägyp. Pyramidentexte*, Leipzig, 1908–10, §§ 72–100.

2 See below, IV. I (ii.).

3 See Mariette, *Abydos*, i. p. 56; A. M. Blackman, *The Rock Tombs of Meir*, London, 1914–15, i. 27 with note 4; ii. 17a, pp. 20 and 21 with note 1, *Journ. Manchester Egyp. and Oriental Soc.*, 1918–19, pp. 36, 39; N. de G. Davies and A. H. Gardiner, *The Tomb of Amenemhēt*, London, 1914, p. 93 f.

4 A. M. Blackman, *The Temple of Derr*, Cairo, 1913, pl. lxiv.

5 The statement in art. PRIEST, PRIESTHOOD (Egyptian), VII. 4, that 'the god's hand' was distinct from 'the god's adorer' is a mistake; see *Journ. Egyp. Arch.* vii. p. 10, note 3, p. 13.

6 Gayet, pl. li. fig. 104.

7 *Ib.* pl. xxxviii. f.

8 *Ib.* pl. l. fig. 106.

9 Lepsius, iii. 48*b*.

10 See list of offerings in Lepsius, *loc. cit.*

11 Cf. H. Junker, *Die Stundenwachen in den Osirismysterien*, Vienna, 1910, p. 102; Blackman, *RTr* xxxix. 68.

relief,[1] and then pour it out as a libation.[2] The two vessels which ancient custom prescribed the king should bear did not, of course, contain sufficient water for the elaborate rites of the historic periods. Accordingly the king's running with the water was in practice merely a symbolic act whereby he secured to himself the rôle of sole offerer of the water, whereas nearly the whole of the water actually used was brought in by the priests in a large number of vessels.[3]

(4) Yet another relief at Luxor,[4] depicting the presentation of food-offerings to Amūn and the co-templar divinities, gives one a good idea of the important rôles played by priests even when the king was celebrant. The king appears merely to be presiding during a considerable part of the performance. He stands holding a staff in his left and a mace in his right hand and is said to be 'viewing the presentation' of offerings. Facing the king and at some distance from him are four officiants, one of whom holds some indefinable object (perhaps a libation-vessel?). The other three with right arm extended and hand bent upwards are 'making the offering which the king gives.' Immediately in front of and facing the same way as the king stands another priest—a *sem*, or 'pillar of his mother'—accompanied by the high-priestess of Amūn, 'the god's adorer and god's hand.' This priest, whose right arm and hand are held out like those of the three above-mentioned officiants, is engaged in summoning the divinities to their repast: 'Come ye to this your bread, to your roast meat of the evening meal, which your son Amenōphis . . . has given you.' The high-priestess's hand is raised in adoration, palm outwards, and she is doubtless repeating simultaneously with her companion the formula of summoning the gods. In an adjacent relief[5] the king is seen with uplifted baton consecrating—'extending his arm four times' towards—the repast to which the gods had just been bidden.

7. Music.—Musician priestesses were attached to every temple, and male musicians and dancers also took part in the temple services.[6] The temple musicians of both sexes played a particularly important rôle in festival services and in the processions which were a special feature of these celebrations.[7] There is some reason for supposing that at Thebes and elsewhere, on the occasion of the annual festival of Ḥatḥor, that goddess's priestesses, when the temple service and the subsequent procession were ended, paraded the streets and, in company with the *iḥwey*-priests, stopped at one house after another in order to bestow Ḥatḥor's blessing upon the inmates. This they did by dancing and singing and holding out to their audience—perhaps that they might touch them—the emblems of their goddess, the sistra and *mnit*-necklaces.[8]

It should be pointed out here that the rattling of the sistrum was supposed to keep at a distance what was evil or inimical to the gods.[9]

8. The object of official worship.—The whole object of official worship, as represented in the temple reliefs, was to obtain the favour of the divinities for the Pharaoh. In return for the offerings which he presents to them they promise him victory, gladness, life, stability, health, good fortune, abundance, millions of years, the duration of Rē, an eternity of jubilees, etc. The very temples of the gods were erected by the king that he might receive in return the 'duration of heaven,'[10] 'hundreds of thousands of years,'[11] and that he might 'be granted eternity as king.'[12] Thus the designation of every ritual act, 'giving [var. doing] this or that to [for] his father [var. mother] NN.' is followed by the words 'in order that he may make an "Endowed-with-life"[13] like Rē forever,' the 'Endowed-with-life' being of course the king himself.

1 Gayet, pl. li. fig. 105. 2 Kees, *ZÄ* lii. 66, fig. 2.
3 See Kees, *Opfertanz*, p. 60 ff.
4 Gayet, pl. xxxv. fig. 138. 5 *Ib.* pl. xxxiv. fig. 140.
6 See art. PRIEST, PRIESTHOOD (Egyptian), VIII. 3 (*d*) (musician priestesses), III. 2 (*iḥy*-priests), XIII. 2 (*c*) (male dancers and musicians).
7 Blackman, *Rock Tombs of Meir*, i. 23 f.; ii. 25, *Journ. Egyp. Arch.* vii. 21 f.; Davies-Gardiner, *Tomb of Amenemhēt*, 94 f.; Maspero, *Études de mythologie et d'archéologie égyptiennes*, Paris, 1893–1916, viii. 313; Sethe, *Urkunden*, ii. 151 f.; Kees, *Opfertanz*, pp. 105, 226 f.
8 Blackman, *Journ. Egyp. Arch.* vii. 22.
9 *Ib.* 21 f.
10 H. Gauthier, *La grande Inscription dédicatoire d'Abydos*, Cairo, 1912, p. 1, l. 4.
11 *Ib.* p. 1, l. 6. 12 *Ib.* p. 2, l. 20 *ter*.
13 See T. E. Peet, *Journ. Egyp. Arch.* iii. [1916] 63.

II. *PRIVATE WORSHIP.*—We know very little about private worship. The individual citizen, we are told, refrained from what his local god hated,[1] avoided his wrath by joining in the celebration of his festivals,[2] and cared for the local sacred animals.[3] In some houses, if Mariette's account of excavations at Abydos is to be trusted, the innermost room served as a private chapel, in which was kept the image of a divinity, offering being made to it on a stone offering-table placed before it. Here, Erman supposes, the householder made his daily adoration.[4] A man would erect a shrine to Ernūtet, the harvest-goddess, in the yard of his granary,[5] or near his wine-press,[6] or he might, it would seem, set aside for his god a portion of his meal, placing it on an offering-stand prepared for that purpose.[7] To prosper his work the scribe, before he began to write, poured out from his water-bowl a libation to Imhotpe, the patron-divinity of scribes.[8] The ordinary citizen might be seen praying outside the great pylon of a temple, after having, perhaps, placed a gift for the god on an offering-table set up there to receive the contributions of humble folk.[9] The middle Kingdom citizens of Asyūt offered the first-fruits of the harvest to their local god Upwawet.[10] Theban landowners, or officials responsible for the harvest on temple- or crown-property, and no doubt the ordinary peasants as well, made offering to Amūn and the harvest-goddess Ernūtet on the twenty-seventh day of the fourth month of Prōyet, *i.e.* the first day of the harvest festival. Also on the last day of that festival, the first day of the first month of Shōmu, the day the corn was winnowed, offering was made to Ernūtet.[11] On the last-named day the winnowers, ere they began their work, set up on the edge of the threshing-floor a rude figure of a harvest-divinity, apparently made out of a bundle of corn furnished with mud hands which grasp ears of corn. Before it they laid an offering consisting of dishes of food and a pot of water or beer.[12] On the analogy of harvest practices in other lands, may we not suppose that this 'divinity' is the first or last sheaf, the embodiment of the corn-spirit?[13]

III. *UNUSUAL POPULAR CONCEPTIONS OF WORSHIP.*—Remarkable ideas about worship and man's relation to the gods were current among the middle and lower classes during the latter part of the New Kingdom—ideas which do not seem to have existed hitherto among the Egyptians and are not met with again till Christian times.

'To the sanctuary of God,' we are told, 'clamour is abhorrent. Pray to him with a loving heart whose words are all hidden; so will he grant thy request, hear what thou sayest, and accept thine offering.'[14] Similarly a hymn to Thōth of this date likens that god to a well in the desert which is 'closed for those who

1 Erman, *Life*, p. 272. 2 *Ib.*
3 *Ib.*; see also N. de G. Davies, *The Rock Tombs of Deir el-Gebrâwi*, London, 1902, ii. 30.
4 Erman, p. 272 f.; A. Mariette, *Catalogue général des monuments d'Abydos*, Paris, 1880, p. 1.
5 Erman, p. 273; cf. Maspero, *Dawn of Civilization*, Eng. tr., London, 1894, p. 120, and Davies, *El-Amarna*, i. pl. xxxi.
6 Erman, *loc. cit.*; J. G. Wilkinson, *Manners and Customs of the Ancient Egyptians*, 3 vols., London, 1878, i. 385.
7 Davies, iii. pl. iv. p. 5b.
8 Gardiner, *ZÄ* xl. [1902–03] 146.
9 Erman, *SBAW* xlix. [1911] pl. xvi.
10 J. H. Breasted, *Ancient Records*, 5 vols., Chicago, 1906–07, i. § 546.
11 N. de G. Davies, *The Tomb of Nakht at Thebes*, New York, 1917, p. 64 f.
12 Davies, pl. xx. p. 63 f.
13 For the purification of the lay-folk before entering a temple see art. PURIFICATION (Egyptian), V. 8. For the participation of the populace in the dramatic performances, at Abydos and elsewhere, illustrating the death, burial, and resuscitation of Osiris, see J. H. Breasted, *Development of Religion and Thought in Ancient Egypt*, New York and London, 1912, pp. 287–290.
14 F. Chabas, *Les Maximes du scribe Ani*, Paris, 1876, p. 91= Erman, *Handbook*, p. 84.

speak there and open for those who keep silence there. When the silent man cometh he findeth the spring.'[1]

IV. *THE ATON-CULT OF KING AMENŌPHIS IV. ('ŌKHNATŌN)*.—The liturgy celebrated in the temple or temples[2] erected by the heretic king 'Ōkhnatōn at El-Amarna differs in so many ways from the temple liturgy of the preceding and succeeding periods that it must receive separate treatment. For the beliefs responsible for these differences see Erman, *Handbook*, p. 62 ff.; Breasted, *Development of Religion and Thought*, pp. 319–345.

1. The daily liturgy in the temple of the Aton.—There was no cultus-image of the Aton, and so all the toilet and pre-toilet ceremonies of the old temple liturgy were done away with. The worship of the Aton consisted mainly in the singing of hymns and presentation of food- and drink-offerings, of perfumes and flowers. The ritual acts, however, accompanying the presentation of these offerings were those of the old worship, the only difference visible in the representations of the various ceremonies being that the queen is shown acting in exactly the same capacity as the king.

As in the case of the old temple liturgy, the presentation of food- and drink-offerings was closely associated with the burning of incense and the pouring out of libation,[3] and the offerings were consecrated by the stretching out of the *ḫrp*-baton.[4] The practice of elevating trays of offerings was also continued.[5] As there was no cultus-image to anoint, unguent was held up to the Aton in alabaster jars and then placed on the altar.[6] The offering of unguent was evidently preceded by the burning of incense.[7]

It is possible that the offering of flowers was a more important feature in the Aton-cult than in the worship of the old Egyptian divinities, though they are constantly depicted as receiving a bouquet from the Pharaoh,[8] while their heaped-up food-offerings were regularly surmounted by a bunch of flowers.[9]

The El-Amarna reliefs permit us to reconstruct to some extent the sequence of episodes in the liturgy celebrated in the larger or outer temple.

(i.) When the king and queen came to this temple, their first act, according to a scene in the tomb-chapel of the high-priest Merirēʿ,[10] was to make each an oblation at offering-stands set up in front of the pylon. After the burning of incense and the pouring out of a libation—the attendant high-priest is depicted bowing low and holding the censer and vase that have just been used for that purpose—the king and queen consecrated their gifts by extending over them the *ḫrp*-baton. During this performance the royal daughters rattled their sistra, and the attendant courtiers stood at a respectful distance bowing low with hands on knees.

(ii.) Having passed through the pylon, the king and queen, as we learn from a relief in the tomb-chapel of Paneḥesi,[11] proceeded to mount the steps to the high altar in the first court. On this altar a great oblation of joints of meat, poultry, vegetables, and bouquets of flowers was laid, and there was set on top of all three open pans of burning incense. The relief in question depicts the royal officiants in the act of scattering incense into these pans. One of their daughters stands near and holds out two bowls of incense to her parents, and the other two daughters rattle sistra. In front of the altar, facing the king and making profound obeisance, are the high-priest and the 'chief servitor of Aton.' The former, and probably the latter also, holds a bouquet of flowers—perhaps for the king to present after he has burned incense. Behind these two priests are four other priests in the same respectful attitude, each holding a round vessel containing liquid of some kind. Beside these again are four chanters, also bowing low and accompanying their singing with hand-clapping. The rest of the royal retinue remains in the entrance or outer court, or else altogether outside the temple precincts.

(iii.) While the king and queen were thus officiating at the high altar, priests placed offerings upon the altars in the outer court.[1] A relief in the tomb-chapel of Aḥmōse[2] also shows priests attending to the offering-tables, in this case in the outer court of the smaller temple, just before the arrival of the royal party.

(iv.) A visit of 'Ōkhnatōn to the temple was the occasion for the sacrifice of numerous oxen. The victims, beplumed and garlanded, were led straight to the slaughter-house,[3] or else to meet the royal cortège as it drew up at the temple-entrance.[4]

2. The functions of musicians in the Aton-cult.—(*a*) *Sistrum-players*.—While the king and queen burned incense, poured out libation, presented unguent, flowers, food- and drink-offerings, raised their hands in adoration before the altar, or performed the ceremony of consecration with outstretched *ḫrp*-baton, the royal daughters rattled their sistra.[5]

(*b*) *Temple choir*.—A body of blind vocalists accompanied by a blind harpist and sometimes by a lute-player, also blind, performed in the outer court or enclosure of the smaller temple.[6] An inscription in the tomb-chapel of Merirēʿ speaks of 'the singers and musicians . . . in the court of the House of the Benben . . . in Ikhtaton.'[7] The choir evidently sang and played off and on during the whole day, for they are depicted thus engaged both during and outside of the performance of the liturgy.[8]

(*c*) *Male chanters*.—Four chanters also figured in the Aton-worship. They are twice depicted singing and clapping their hands while the king and queen burn incense in the pans placed on the top of the food-offerings, in the one case in the great court of the larger temple,[9] and in the other apparently in the outer court of the smaller temple, where they are seen in close proximity to the blind vocalists and harpist who simultaneously make music.[10] They also ran in front of the royal procession to the temple,[11] thus, perhaps, performing the same functions as the lector of the old religion, who walked in front of the Pharaoh, when he went to the temple, and dispelled inimical powers by his recitations.[12]

(*d*) *Female musicians*.—According to the relief in the tomb-chapel of Paneḥesi discussed above, among those of the royal retinue who remained ontside the entrance to the enclosure or outer court of the larger temple, while the king and queen officiated at the high altar, were a number

[1] *Sallier Papyrus*, I. 8, 2 ff.; Erman, *Handbook*, p. 84. For a full account of this particular phase of Egyptian thought see B. Gunn, *Journ. of Egyp. Archæology*, iii. 81 ff.; Erman, *Handbook*, p. 78 f.; Breasted, *Development of Religion and Thought in Ancient Egypt*, p. 344 ff.; see also art. SIN (Egyptian), 6.

[2] For the temple structure see Davies, *El-Amarna*, i. pls. x. A, xi. f., xxvi. ff., xxxiii., ii. pls. xviii. f. p. 20 ff., iii. pls. viii. ff., xxx., p. 19 ff., iv. pls. v. ff., xviii., xx., vi. pl. xx.

[3] Davies, ii. pl. v., v. pl. iii., vi. pl. xvi.

[4] *Ib.* i. pl. xxvii., ii. pl. vii., iv. pl. xv., vi. pl. xxvi.

[5] *Ib.* i. pl. xx.

[6] *Ib.* ii. pl. vi.

[7] *Ib.* iv. pl. xxxv.

[8] *E.g.*, Lepsius, iii. 141*a*.

[9] *E.g.*, Mariette, *Abydos*, i. pls. 32, 42*a*.

[10] Davies, i. pl. xxvii.

[11] *Ib.* ii. pl. xviii.

[1] Davies, ii. pl. xviii.

[2] *Ib.* iii. pl. xxv.

[3] *Ib.*

[4] *Ib.* i. pl. x. A.

[5] *Ib.* i. pls. xxvi. f., ii. pls. v., vii. f., xviii., iv. pl. xv., v. pls. iii., xxviii.

[6] *Ib.* i. pls. xi., xxii., xxxiii., iii. pl. xxx

[7] *Ib.* i. pl. xxxvii., ii. p. 26[b].

[8] *Ib.* i. pls. xi., xxii. f., iii. pl. xxx.

[9] *Ib.* ii. pl. xviii.

[10] *Ib.* i. pl. xxii.

[11] *Ib.* i. pls. x. A, xiv.

[12] *Piankhi Stele*, 1. 104; Schäfer, *Urkunden*, iii. 38.

of female musicians. These are depicted singing to the accompaniment of hand-clapping, waving of palm-branches, and the beating of tambourines, or else lifting their hands in worship.[1] These female musicians likewise greeted the king on his arrival at the temple.[2] It was apparently also the same women who participated in the rejoicings at the decoration of courtiers.[3] It is to be noted that the female musicians are never shown performing inside the temple precincts.

3. Private worshippers in the temple of the Aton.—It seems to have been customary for a subject, after he had been decorated by 'Ōkhnatōn, to make a food- and drink-offering outside the pylon of the larger temple and to pray at the same time for the king's life, prosperity, and health, and that the Aton would 'vouchsafe him for ever.'[4]

In the top register of a scene in Merirē''s tomb-chapel depicting 'Ōkhnatōn's visit to the temple[5] two men wearing wigs, and carrying each a bouquet, lead along a beplumed and garlanded cow and a calf. Accompanying them, and also carrying bouquets, is a man with a shaven head, *i.e.* a priest. Possibly the two laymen are offering these victims themselves on the occasion of a royal visit, the presence of the priest being required in order that he might superintend the slaughter of the victims and make certain that they were pure.[6] In the same scene, bottom register, lay-folk are carrying bouquets and duck, while four priests follow, two leading oxen and two carrying bouquets. Both victims and duck are quite possibly private offerings. Davies[7] suggests, indeed, that the offerings placed on the altars in the outer or enclosing court of either temple were those of private people. This would account for priests serving these altars before the arrival of the king,[8] or while the royal party and chief priests were officiating at the high altar.[9]

LITERATURE.—See the works cited in the text and footnotes.

A. M. BLACKMAN.

WORSHIP (Greek).—I. *DEFINITION, ETC.*—Worship, in the widest sense, may be defined as the acknowledgment by man of his dependence on a power or powers beyond himself. And these powers, in whatever form they may be conceived, are believed by the worshipper to be more potent than himself; and, in whatever visible semblance or sign they are worshipped, they are imagined to be normally invisible.

At the outset of our study of Greek worship we are met by a consideration which it is important to realize. The central meaning of worship as we conceive it is the endeavour after a higher and better life. Whether as individuals or on stated occasions with our fellow-men we perform an act of worship, while we do indeed render thanks for blessings received and pray for blessings to come, yet the paramount intention of our worship is that we may be reminded, amid the clash and din of things temporal and fleeting, of the things which are unseen and eternal, to attune our hearts and minds to higher ideals of life. And, while we consider it right and seemly to bring to God offerings of a temporal kind, to beautify His sanctuary, to lay before Him tithes and firstfruits, and in His name to give our goods to feed the poor, yet we count it a better thing to bring the sacrifice of a contrite heart, which He will not despise.

Now, if we leave out of account some rare and sporadic utterances of the more advanced and enlightened thinkers and confine ourselves to the typical Greek conception of worship, we find that the motive and intention is of a wholly different kind. Man worships his god or gods not because he has any lively feeling of gratitude for blessings experienced, still less because he desires to live a better life, but because he has an overwhelming conviction of his dependence on his god or gods for all temporal blessings. H. Usener[1] perhaps rather overstates this point of view, but in general it is true.

> 'Pray now, O stranger, to the Lord Poseidon: for his feast it is on which you have happened in coming here. And when thou hast made libation and hast prayed, as is right (θέμις), then give to this man also a cup of honey-sweet wine to make libation, since I deem that he too prays to the immortals. All men have need of Zeus.'[2] 'From the gods come all means of mortal excellence—from the gods are men wise and mighty of hand and eloquent of tongue.'[3] 'Always we all have need of Zeus.'[4]

If our definition of worship is open to the objection that it would include magic, the defence must be that it is impossible to frame a definition of worship which would be at once sufficiently wide and yet exclude magic. The acts of worship and the acts of magic are in origin at least inseparable. If we so define worship as to distinguish it from magic, it will be by a definition applicable only to the higher kinds of worship. It is no more possible to distinguish worship and magic by absolute and generally valid *criteria* than it is to distinguish religion from superstition.

Essentially magic is the performance of an act accompanied by verbal incantations which invoke objects of worship not known or not recognized by ordinary society. And just so far the modern view may be justified which makes the prime distinction between religion and magic to be that religion is social and promotes the good of the community, while magic is anti-social and tends to exalt the individual to the detriment of the community.

II. *THE RELATION OF RITUAL TO RELIGION.*—It used to be the fashion to regard the practices of ritual as later than the religious ideas of which they were the expression. The religious theory was regarded as primitive and essential; the religious ritual was regarded as the reasoned form in which the theory found expression. But modern investigation suggests that the reverse is the case. A festival which in historical times is definitely religious in character and is accompanied by a theory which professes to account for the various practices of the ritual may easily have been in its origin of an entirely secular character. The wide-spread practice of seasonal festivals, particularly those of mid-winter and of spring, can hardly be accounted for on any supposition that they were originally religious in character. Their origin is much more reasonably explained and their universality is much more easily understood if we regard them as having been at first purely secular, the natural reaction to the character of the season. The tribe meet at mid-winter and in spring to hold their festival with song and story. The character of the season will naturally influence the character of the festival. But, save in so far as mere ecstasy is religious in character, there is nothing religious in the celebration until a theory is evolved. When at mid-winter all nature is asleep—ἐνιαυτός[5] can hardly mean anything else than the sleeping season—the tribal festival may be explained as intended to celebrate the passing of a god who is asleep or is slain. When in spring all nature awakes to life, the festival may be explained as the awakening or the resurrection of

[1] Davies, ii. pl. XVIII. [2] *Ib.* i. pls. x. f., XIII.
[3] *Ib.* i. pl. VI., ii. pls. XI., XXXIII.
[4] *Ib.* iv. pl. XVIII. p. 15. [5] *Ib.* i. pls. x. A, XIV.
[6] See artt. PURIFICATION (Egyptian), V. 5, PRIEST, PRIESTHOOD (Egyptian), XVI.
[7] ii. 22a. [8] *Ib.* iii. pl. XXX.
[9] *Ib.* ii. pl. XVIII.

[1] *ARW* [1904]. [2] Hom. *Od.* iii. 45.
[3] Pind. *Pyth.* i. 41 f. [4] Aratus, *Phæn.* 4.
[5] The old derivation from ἐνὶ τῷ αὐτῷ ('Here we are again!'), though revived in recent times, is of course absurd.

the god. But the ritual in its main outlines precedes the theory. Indeed it is only with the utmost difficulty that the theory will produce any innovation in the ritual. Many of the ritual usages are probably in their origin purely accidental. When on a memorable occasion something happens to be done in a particular way, the tendency will be to do it in the same way again. The usage becomes stereotyped, and the theory will try to account for it: thenceforth it is held to be the only way that is valid and effective. Even if no convincing explanation is found in theory, ancestral custom will be sufficient to perpetuate it. This ancestral custom is what the Greeks call *ὁ πάτριος νόμος*.[1] This *νόμος* (or *νόμοι*) is believed to be of immemorial antiquity, with all the superior sanction that attaches to the unwritten as opposed to the written law, and is held to regulate all the fundamental sanctities of life. The point of view is beautifully expressed in the words of Antigone: *οὐδὲ σθένειν τοσοῦτον ᾠόμην τὰ σὰ | κηρύγμαθ' ὥστ' ἄγραπτα κἀσφαλῆ θεῶν | νόμιμα δύνασθαι θνητὸν ὄνθ' ὑπερδραμεῖν. | οὐ γάρ τι νῦν γε κἀχθές, ἀλλ' ἀεί ποτε | ζῇ ταῦτα, κοὐδεὶς οἶδεν ἐξ ὅτου 'φάνη.*[2]

Hence in the *Politicus*, 290 E, we find custom almost equated with sanctity: *τὰ σεμνότατα καὶ μάλιστα πάτρια τῶν ἀρχαιῶν θυσιῶν*. So the solemn supplication of Himilkas is carried out *κατὰ τὸ πάτριον ἔθος*.[3]

III. *OBJECTS OF WORSHIP.*—We may conveniently divide the objects of worship into primitive or non-anthropomorphic and later or anthropomorphic.

A. NON-ANTHROPOMORPHIC.[4]—The evidence for non-anthropomorphic worship cannot occupy much space in a brief sketch like the present, and there is the less need to discuss it in detail because in general the lower strata of Greek religious ideas resemble those found in the earlier stages of development of other peoples or among primitive peoples of the present day. As among these, so among the Greeks we find traces of the worship of inanimate things and of animals. But before we glance at the evidence it is desirable that we should represent clearly to ourselves what exactly such worship means.

The ultimate root of religion is to be found in the instinctive sense of the mysterious, the uncanny. This sense is not equally strong in all men any more than all men are equally religious, and the things by which it is excited vary indefinitely, from the uttermost of beauty to the uttermost of loathing. In the street and under the garish sun all experience is immediate and commonplace. But if, for instance, one make his way to some lonely glen high among the hills—'per loca pastorum deserta atque otia dia'—where only the moorfowl call and only the whaups are crying, then even the most commonplace feels an instinctive awe, a sense of mystery which he cannot express even to himself. This is what the Romans call 'religio loci.' The origin of the word *religio* is a matter of dispute to-day as it was among the Roman antiquaries themselves. But even through the perplexities of the Roman discussions[5] there shines some perception of what we believe to be the right idea of the word, which corresponds very closely to 'reflexion,' *ἀναλογισμός*, the 'sense of something far more deeply interfused,' the 'misgiving of a creature moving about in worlds not realized'—in a word, the sense of the uncanny. This sense may be awakened merely by the loathly, as, *e.g.*, the toad, to which the rustic mind ascribes all manner of strange powers,[1] or by the merely curious—a stone or tree of fantastic shape. Objects which in whatever form have power to excite such emotions are regarded with awe. They must be approached with circumspection. They are looked upon as things apart: they are *ἱερά*. When then we find it said that a certain Greek tribe worship a particular animal or a particular object, often no more is meant than this. Their worship is predominantly fear.

But there are higher mysteries than these: the mystery of death and birth, of growth and adolescence, of the regular recurrence of the seasons, of mother-love and self-sacrifice, of instincts which 'aspire to immortality and seem to promise it.' It is by way of such mysteries that the religion of fear becomes transformed and transfigured into something higher: if not into a religion of love, which is essentially a Christian idea, at least into a religion in which reverence is more prominent than fear, in which the gods are no longer imagined as the jealous enemies of mankind but as their protectors. Swift to punish transgression, yet they do not will that any should perish. They are givers of good things,[2] if they are also givers of evil. Even if they 'deal to men two evils for one good,' only the foolish murmur. Good men loyally accept the conditions of mortality, turning the bright side out.[3]

1. Holy places.—Among non-anthropomorphic things to which sanctity, in the sense we have described, attaches we have first of all holy places. The Mucklestane Moor was felt by Hobbie Elliot to be 'an unco bogilly bit.'[4] The same sort of feeling was perfectly familiar to the Greeks. A bush-clad hill in Arcadia was fabled to be the place where Rhea gave birth to Zeus:

> 'In Parrhasia (Arcadia) it was that Rhea bare thee, where was a hill sheltered with thickest brush. Thence is the place holy and no four-footed thing that hath need of Eileithyia nor any woman approacheth thereto, but the Apidanians call it the primeval childbed of Rhea.'[5]

As a typical case we have the cave sanctuaries all over Crete, particularly those on Mount Ida and Mount Dictæum associated with the worship of the Cretan Zeus.

2. Holy animals.—The same kind of sanctity attached to various animals in different localities: storks and ants in Thessaly; weasels in Thebes; especially the snake—*e.g.*, in connexion with Asklepios, Sopolis, Cychreus. Best known of all is the *οἰκουρὸς ὄφις* on the acropolis at Athens which every month received honey-cakes.[6] Other familiar cases are the mice in the temple of Apollo Smintheus, the owl of Athene, etc.

3. Holy trees.—Among proofs of the cult of living trees we have the familiar idea of the tree-nymphs under their various names—Dryads, Hamadryads, Meliæ, etc.—who live in the life and die with the death of the holy tree. Where myth gives an ætiological legend to explain just why a tree is sacred, we may quite confidently neglect the legend and infer that the holiness attached to the tree before myth gave the alleged reason.

Thus the Delian palm was sacred. Myth gave as the reason that this was the palm which supported Leto at the birth of Apollo. So the laurel in the vale of Tempe, from which crowns were made for the victor at the Pythian games, derived its sanctity, according to myth, from the purification of Apollo at Tempe after he had slain the Python. Similarly the stump of the wild strawberry-tree at Tanagra was held sacred for the alleged reason that Hermes had been reared under it.[7]

1 Plato, *Laws*, 959 B; Thuc. ii. 34.
2 Soph. *Ant.* 453 ff.; cf. Plato, *Laws*, 793 A, 680 A.
3 Diodor. xiii. 86. See also E. Monseur, 'La Proscription religieuse de l'usage récent,' *RHR* liii. [1906].
4 See M. W. de Wisser, *Die nicht menschengestaltigen Götter der Griechen*, Leyden, 1903.
5 Esp. Aulus Gellius, iv. 9. 1; Cic. *de Nat. Deor.* ii. 28, 72; Cato, *ap.* Fest. *s.v.* 'Repulsior.'

1 Hence the magic potency of 'Eye of newt, and toe of frog (Shakespeare, *Macbeth*, IV. i. 14).
2 *θεοὶ δωτῆρες ἑάων*, Hom. *Od.* viii. 325.
3 Pind. *Pyth.* iii. 81 ff.
4 Scott, *The Black Dwarf*, ch. ii.
5 Callim. *Hymn.* i. 10 ff.
6 Herod. viii. 41.
7 Paus. ix. 22. 2.

In these and in numberless other cases we must recognize now that the holiness is a much earlier thing than the myth—which merely attempts to explain an existent fact.

4. Holy stones.—Stones to which a special sanctity attaches form one of the most common features of early legend everywhere. Greece is no exception.

Thus Phemios, king of the Ainianes, fought a duel with Hyperochos, king of the Inachians, for their land and guilefully slew him by hurling a stone, which was thenceforward regarded by the Ainianes as holy.[1]

There are a number of references in Pausanias to 'undressed stones,' *λίθοι ἀργοί*, which were the object of veneration.

Thus in vii. 22. 3 he tells us that at Pharai in Achaia certain square stones (*τετράγωνοι λίθοι*), about thirty in number, were worshipped by the people of Pharai, who applied to each of them the name of a god: and he adds an important remark: *τὰ δὲ ἔτι παλαιότερα καὶ τοῖς πᾶσι Ἕλλησι, τινὰς θεῶν ἀντὶ ἀγαλμάτων εἶχον ἀργοὶ λίθοι.* In ix. 24. 3 Pausanias mentions at Hyettos in Bœotia a shrine of Herakles where the image was 'not artistic but an undressed stone in the ancient fashion.' On the acropolis at Athens Pausanias, i. 28. 5, mentions two *λίθοι ἀργοί*: *τοὺς δὲ ἀργοὺς λίθους, ἐφ' ὧν ἑστᾶσιν ὅσοι δίκας ὑπέχουσι καὶ οἱ διώκοντες, τὸν μὲν Ὕβρεως, τὸν δὲ Ἀναιδείας αὐτῶν ὀνομάζουσι.*

The typical case of the holy stone is the *βαίτυλος*, which legend explained to be the stone which Rhea gave to Cronus in place of the infant Zeus.[2] Pausanias, x. 24. 5, speaking of Delphi, says:

ἐπαναβάντι δὲ ἀπὸ τοῦ μνήματος (of Neoptolemus), *λίθος ἐστὶν οὐ μέγας· τούτου καὶ ἔλαιον ὁσημέραι καταχέουσι, καὶ κατὰ ἑορτὴν ἑκάστην ἔρια ἐπιτιθέασι τὰ ἀργά· ἔστι δὲ καὶ δόξα ἐς αὐτόν, δοθῆναι Κρόνῳ τὸν λίθον ἀντὶ τοῦ παιδὸς, καὶ ὡς αὖθις ἤμεσεν αὐτὸν ὁ Κρόνος.*

This brings us to the question of the place in Greek worship of the holy pillar. Every one is familiar with the passage in Gn 28[18ff.] which tells how 'Jacob rose up early in the morning and took the stone that he had put under his head and set it up for a pillar (מַצֵּבָה), and poured oil upon the top of it [as the Delphians did with the *βαίτυλος* in Pausanias, *loc. cit.*]. And he called the name of that place Bethel [House of God], . . . and Jacob vowed a vow,' etc. It is an old suggestion that *βαίτυλος* is nothing else than a Greek transliteration of the Hebrew בֵּית־אֵל. But, in any case, the important thing to realize is that there are two kinds of sanctity attaching to such things as we have been discussing: natural sanctity and derivative sanctity. There is what may be called the natural sanctity which everywhere attaches to the uncanny. To this class belongs the *λίθος καππώτας* which is mentioned by Pausanias, iii. 22. 1:

Γυθείου δὲ τρεῖς μάλιστα ἀπέχει σταδίους ἀργὸς λίθος· Ὀρέστην λέγουσι καθεσθέντα ἐπ' αὐτοῦ παύσασθαι τῆς μανίας· διὰ τοῦτο ὁ λίθος ὠνομάσθη Ζεὺς Καππώτας κατὰ γλῶσσαν τὴν Δωρίδα.

That is to say, there was something which seemed uncanny about this stone, and so an ætiological legend arose to explain it. But in the case of Jacob there is no hint that the stone which he selected for his pillow possessed in itself any unusual virtue, and, familiar as we are with the potency of, say, a bit of wedding-cake as a provoker of auspicious dreams, we seem to have no right to read any such meaning into Jacob's use of the stone. Indeed in Gn 28[22] it is rather emphasized that its particular meaning derives from the voluntary act of Jacob and not from any natural quality.

We hold, then, that the holy pillar in worship is originally purely symbolical. That this is the case and that we have here to do with no original sanctity is already obvious when we consider that the pillar is rather an artificial than a natural form. It seems to be generally assumed that the *ἀργὸς λίθος* of Pausanias is merely an 'undressed stone,' of no particular shape. We think there is better reason to suppose that it was a stone dressed to a quadrangular shape but not carved into a definite anthropomorphic type. The quadrangular block seems quite well established as a half-way stage to the fully developed image. There is a very significant passage in Pausanias, viii. 48. 6, where, speaking of Tegea in Arcadia, the natural home of 'pre-lunar' customs, he says:

'There is also erected an altar of Zeus Teleios and a square image (*ἄγαλμα τετράγωνον*): *for this is a type in which*, it seems to me, *the Arcadians particularly delight.*'

The two most familiar Greek forms of this type are the pillars of Hermes and the pillars of Apollo Agyieus. For the shape of the Hermai we have the very definite testimony of Thucydides, vi. 27:

ὅσοι Ἑρμαῖ ἦσαν λίθινοι ἐν τῇ πόλει τῇ Ἀθηναίων· εἰσὶ δὲ κατὰ τὸ ἐπιχώριον ἡ τετράγωνος ἐργασία,

where, with Sir Richard Jebb (against Hude), we regard the last three words as thoroughly genuine. The shape of the Apollo pillars is perhaps not quite so clearly established by the ancient authorities. But it is quite clear that they had an artificial shape, and therefore an artificial, and not a natural, sanctity.[1]

But it is to be clearly understood that this is a question of origins only. Derivative sanctity may be quite as valid and quite as potent as natural sanctity. The landmark of my neighbour or the coffin in which he obtains his last landtenure may be made of common wood, but just because the timber is employed for this solemn purpose it acquires extraordinary virtues. And in the same way the symbolic pillar may easily acquire unnatural virtues, and may indeed, as seems well attested, be regarded as the abode, at least temporarily of the godhead. And the pillar may, of course, survive as a symbol even in a fully developed anthropomorphic worship—*e.g.*, the obelisk as the *βαιτύλιον* of Apollo Agyieus on coins of Ambracia.[2]

B. ANTHROPOMORPHIC CULTS.—It is characteristic of the objects of anthropomorphic cult that they are all, in greater or less degree, worshipped in the higher sense: that is to say, they are invoked with prayer and offerings. A rigid classification is difficult, because there is a continual transference of the members of one class into another, from higher to lower, no less than from lower to higher. But the classes of cults may be conveniently arranged as follows.

1. The dead.—We find in Homer that the funeral of a great prince is accompanied by funeral games. Thus in *Il.* xxiii. we have the ἆθλα ἐπὶ Πατρόκλῳ, in Hesiod, *Works and Days*, 654, the ἆθλα Ἀμφιδάμαντος. In the case of a private individual doubtless the ceremonies were less elaborate, consisting of the offerings at the grave and the funeral feast,[3] with which we used to be familiar in Scotland, and which might be of decent proportions or might rise to the extravagance of Lord Ravenswood's funeral, when, according to Caleb Balderstone, 'there was as much wine drunk in this house as would have floated a pinnace.'[4] But in any case the funeral feast did not terminate the dues of the dead (*γέρα θανόντων*). In historical

[1] Plut. *Qu. Gr.* 13.

[2] Cf. Hesych. *s.v.* *βαίτυλος· οὕτως ἐκαλεῖτο ὁ δοθεὶς λίθος τῷ Κρόνῳ ἀντὶ Διός.*

[1] Cf. Harpocrat. *s.v.* *ἀγυιᾶς . . . ἀγυιεὺς δέ ἐστι κιὼν εἰς ὀξὺ λήγων* (*i.e.* terminating in a cone) *ὃν ἱστᾶσι πρὸ τῶν θυρῶν ὡς σαφὲς ποιοῦσιν Ἀριστοφάνης τε ἐν Σφηξί* (875) *καὶ Εὔπολις*=Suid. =schol. Aristoph. *Vesp.* 870; cf. Hellad. *ap.* Phot. 535^b 33 ff.; Æsch. *Ag.* 1081; Eur. *Ph.* 631; Pherecr. frag. 87; Plaut. *Bacch.* 170.

[2] B. V. Head, *Hist. Numorum*, Oxford, 1887, p. 319 f. Into the details of pillar cult we cannot here enter. For a somewhat extreme view the reader should consult the important paper by Arthur J. Evans in *JHS* xxi. [1901] 99–204, on 'Mycenæan Tree and Pillar Cult and its Mediterranean Relations,' and in the same volume, p. 268 ff., the reply by W. H. D. Rouse, and for a *via media* L. Ziehen, in *Bursian's Jahresbericht*, 1908, who thinks that both Evans and Rouse have rushed to extremes which the evidence does not justify.

[3] *περίδειπνον* (Dem. xviii. 288).

[4] Scott, *The Bride of Lammermoor*, ch. vii.

times we hear of a further celebration on the third, ninth, and thirtieth days after the funeral.[1] The character of these celebrations, attended by the friends and relatives of the dead, is sufficiently attested.[2] The ceremonial on the thirtieth day, which apparently marked the end of the normal period of mourning,[3] was noteworthy for the fact that the company who met to banquet together in honour of the deceased (ἐπὶ τῷ ἀποθανόντι) did not *recline* but *sat*, in accordance with ancient custom; hence the ceremonial was called καθέδρα.[4] Still further there was the annual festival called γενέσια. It is disputed whether this celebration was held on the anniversary of the birthday of the deceased or on the anniversary of the day of his death.[5]

The generic term for offerings to the dead is ἐναγίσματα,[6] which is precisely the Latin *sacra* and implies that the offerings were 'consecrated' to the dead: that the living did not partake of them. The corresponding verb is ἐναγίζειν. These offerings (called also χοαί, because normally they were 'poured' into the grave) consisted of milk, honey, water, wine, oil.[7] The schol. on Eur. *Hec.* 527 adds ἄλευρον (wheaten-flour).[8] Eustath. *Hom. Od.* 519, says the μελίκρατον, as the offering was called, was honey and milk in Homeric times, but honey and water in historical times. Stengel holds that milk was always an ingredient.

The libation was poured upon the grave and was accompanied by prayer.[9] The tomb was sometimes so constructed that the liquid could easily reach to the bones or ashes below.

Besides the libation there were other offerings constituting the δεῖπνον of the dead.[10] Naturally the constitution of this would be fairly constant, but would vary to some extent with individual taste or with the locality of the offerer.

The meal presented to the dead was not one which the living could share and was therefore wholly burnt.[11] The lexicographers define ἐναγισμοί as ὁλοκαυτώματα.[12] In other words, they belong to that class of sacrifices which were called θυσίαι ἄγευστοι.[13] It is sometimes said that these offerings to the dead were made at night, but there is no evidence of this; and, since funerals took place by day, there seems no reason why offerings to the dead should not also take place by day. In classical times they certainly did so.[14] Hom. *Il.* xxiii. 217 ff. certainly does not prove the contrary for Homeric times.

[1] Cf. Poll. viii. 146: τρίτα, ἔνατα, τριακάδες; Aristoph. *Lys.* 611 ff.; Isæus, ii. 36, viii. 39.

[2] Æschin. iii. 225: τελευτήσαντος δὲ ἐλθὼν εἰς τὰ ἔνατα διεξίοι πρὸς τοὺς οἰκείους; Dem. xviii. 243: ἐπειδὴ δὲ τελευτήσειέ τις καὶ τὰ νομιζόμενα αὐτῷ φέροιτο, ἀκολουθῶν ἐπὶ τὸ μνῆμα διεξίοι.

[3] Lysias, i. 14: ἔδοξε δέ μοι, ὦ ἄνδρες, τὸ πρόσωπον ἐψιμυθιῶσθαι, τοῦ ἀδελφοῦ τεθνεῶτος οὔπω τριάκονθ' ἡμέρας.

[4] Cf. Phot.: ἐκαλεῖτο δὲ καθέδρα ὅτι καθεζόμενοι ἐδείπνουν καὶ τὰ νομιζόμενα ἐπλήρουν.

[5] This question is fully discussed by W. Schmidt, *Geburtstag im Altertum*, Giessen, 1908, p. 37 ff. who reaches the conclusion that, while γενέθλια denotes the celebration of the birthday of the living, γενέσια is the anniversary celebration of the death-day of the dead: cf. Herod. iv. 26. The γενέσια thus correspond precisely to the Roman *parentalia*.

[6] Poll. viii. 146.

[7] Æsch. *Pers.* 609 ff.; Soph. *El.* 894; Eur. *Or.* 114, *Iph. in Taur.* 158, *El.* 511.

[8] Cf. Æsch. *Ch.* 91, πέλανον (for discussion of the meaning of this word cf. P. Stengel, *Hermes*, xxix. [1894] 281, Herzog, *ib.* p. 625, Stengel, *Hermes*, xxxi. [1896] 477); Ovid, *Fast.* ii. 539: 'inque mero mollita Ceres.'

[9] *Com. Att. Fr.*, ed. T. Kock, i. 517; Aristoph. n. 488, 12: καὶ θύομεν αὐτοῖσι τοῖς ἐναγίσμασιν | ὥσπερ θεοῖσι καὶ χοάς γε χεόμενοι | αἰτούμεθ' αὐτοὺς δεῦρ' ἀνεῖναι τἀγαθά; Æsch. *Ch.* 91 ff.: ἢ τοῦτο φάσκω τοὔπος, ὡς νόμος βροτοῖς, | ἔσθλ' ἀντιδοῦναι τοῖσι πέμπουσιν τάδε.

[10] ἐν νεκρῶν δείπνοις (Artemid. *Oneirocr.* i. 4); δαῖτες ἔννομοι . . . χοάς (Æsch. *Ch.* 483 ff.).

[11] G. Kaibel, *Ep. Gr.*, Berlin, 1878, 646.

[12] Hesych., Suid., etc.; cf. Lucian, *Char.* 22.

[13] Cf. Plut. *Mor.* 124 B: ἄν τέ τις παρέχων ἑστίασιν ὥσπερ θυσίαν ἄγευστον αὐτὸς ἀπέχηται.

[14] Æsch. *Pers.* 609 f., *Ch.*, *ad init.* and 149; Soph. *El.* 326 f., 405, 431, 883; Eur. *Hec.* 521 f., *Or.* 1114 f.

Mourning dress was worn.[1] No garlands apparently were worn; the music (it is sometimes said there was none), if any, was provided not by the cithara but by the flute or pipe.[2] The usual statement that there were no ὀλαί[3] is highly disputable.

To sum up, the essential features of the ritual of the dead are: (1) the ritual is restricted to the tomb; (2) liquids are poured into the tomb; (3) foods are burnt entirely and are not partaken of by the offerer; (4) prayer is, or at any rate may be, made to the dead, at least by members of their family.

2. The heroes.—Greece, like other countries, was full of legends of an earlier race of men upon the earth, who were mightier than their degenerate successors.[4] It was natural to imagine those heroes as the offspring of gods and human beings. It is precisely the idea of Gn 6[4]: 'There were giants in the earth in those days; and also after that, when the sons of God came in unto the daughters of men, and they bare children to them, the same became mighty men which were of old, men of renown.' Hence ἥρως was identified with ἡμίθεος. The idea was perfectly familiar to Homer. Every one admits that Hesiod equated ἥρως with ἡμίθεος. But equally in Hesiod and in Homer this express identification is confined to a single passage: Hom. *Il.* xii. 23; Hesiod, *Works and Days*, 160; cf. Hom. *Hymn.* xxxi. 19, xxxii. 19.

From these imagined heroes the great families of Greece traced their descent. It is easy enough to understand that this canonization or 'heroization' was extended to contemporaries: thus Brasidas, the famous Spartan who fell at Amphipolis in 422 B.C., received heroic honours.

The terms used in heroic worship are closely akin to those which are used in the worship of the dead.

ἐναγίζειν, ἐναγίσματα. Herod. ii. 44 f.: δοκέουσι δέ μοι οὗτοι ὀρθότατα Ἑλλήνων ποιέειν, οἳ διξὰ Ἡράκλεια ἱδρυσάμενοι ἔκτηνται, καὶ τῷ μὲν ὡς ἀθανάτῳ Ὀλυμπίῳ δὲ ἐπωνυμίην θύουσι, τῷ δ' ἑτέρῳ ὡς ἥρωι ἐναγίζουσι; i. 167: καὶ γὰρ ἐναγίζουσί (*sc.* the people of Agylla) σφι (*sc.* the Phoceans whom they had stoned to death) μεγάλως καὶ ἀγῶνα γυμνικὸν καὶ ἱππικὸν ἐπιστᾶσι.

The offerings, or χοαί, in the case of heroes consisted of blood, and the more strict term for those was αἱμακουρίαι.[5] It was the custom to kill the victims[6] over an ἐσχάρα (hearth) or over a trench (βόθρος), so that the blood flowed into the earth.[7] But other things than blood were offered. Thuc. iii. 58 speaks of firstfruits of the crops: ὅσα ἡ γῆ ἡμῶν ἀνεδίδου ὡραῖα, πάντων ἀπαρχὰς ἐπιφέροντες. This refers to the annual offerings made to those who fell at Platæa (479 B.C.). They received also ἐσθήματα καὶ τὰ ἄλλα νόμιμα.[8] There is here no mention of blood-offerings. But Plutarch[9] very clearly recognizes blood-offerings.[10]

The testimony is uniformly that hero-worship was performed by night.[11]

In the case of the hero the place of the tomb was taken by the Heroum (Ἡρῷον).

A very important feature was the solemn procession.[12]

The essential features of heroic worship are thus: (1) the offerings belong to the class of θυσίαι ἄγευστοι: they are ὁλοκαυτώματα, wholly burnt, and the offerer does not partake; (2) the place of offering is a trench (βόθρος) or at any rate an ἐσχάρα (hearth);[13] (3) normally these offerings are performed at night (this statement can be taken only

[1] Æsch. *Ch.* 11; Eur. *Hel.* 1038.

[2] Heliodor. *Æth.* 3. 1; cf. Æsch. *Ch.* 151 f.; Eur. *Iph. in Taur.* 145.

[3] For meaning cf. Keil, *Hermes*, xxxi. [1896] 472.

[4] See art. HEROES AND HERO-GODS (Greek and Roman).

[5] Pind. *Ol.* i. 90; Bacchyl. vi. 5.

[6] Thuc. v. 11; Plut. *Sol.* 9; Sertor. 9.

[7] Cf. Paus. x. 4. 7; Plut. *Arist.* 21; Eur. *Tr.* 381, *El.* 92; Plut. *Thes.* 4.

[8] Thuc. *loc. cit.*

[9] *Arist.* 21.

[10] So Plut. *Sol.* 21, *Arist.* 58, *Cat. Maj.* 15.

[11] Proclus, on Hes. *Works and Days*, 763; Diog. Laert. vii. 33; schol. Pind. *Isthm.* iv. 110, etc.; schol. Ap. Rh. i. 587; schol. *Il.* viii. 66.

[12] Pind. *Nem.* vii. 46 ff.; Hel. *Æth.* iii.

[13] Cf. Paus. ii. 10. 1.

of the firstfruits of thy ground thou shalt bring into the house of the Lord thy God' (Ex 23^{19} 34^{26}). These gifts formed part of the revenue of the priesthood, and were destined to be stored in the Temple. Great importance was attached to this offering, which alone among the offerings that were given to the priests by the people had to be brought by them directly to the Temple. It was of great antiquity and naturally lapsed with the destruction of the sanctuary. The description of the scene by Franz Delitzsch[1] is well known and need not be repeated.

(2) The daily routine of the Temple-worship, including the weekly Sabbath celebrations, was interrupted only by the great festivals, the most important of which were kept with special ceremonial, for several days. The characteristic features of the worship, however, are well illustrated by the ceremonial of the morning and evening sacrifice (*Tāmîd*). Delitzsch as before gives a good reconstruction.[2]

In the Temple itself the opening of the sanctuary gates was the signal for the actual slaughter of the sacrifice, the sprinkling of its blood upon the altar, and the flaying of the victim. The pieces into which the sacrifice was divided were carried by the six allotted priests (each taking one piece) to the altar, while a seventh carried the offering of flour, an eighth the baked meal-offering (of the high-priest), and a ninth the wine of the drink-offering. These were all laid at the foot of the altar-ascent and salted: and then all the priests assembled once more in the Hall of Polished Stones, there to celebrate, first of all, a service of prayer. It is highly significant that the sacrificial service should have been interrupted at this point and temporarily suspended. This can only have grown up as a concession to the overwhelming popular feeling in favour of the recital of the prescribed sections of the Law, with the appropriate accompaniment of prayer. The priests retired for this purpose to the Hall of Polished Stones, which was sufficiently near the court to allow of their quick withdrawal to it and rapid return to the sanctuary. It will be remembered that they had already assembled at early dawn in this chamber to cast the first lots for determining the distribution of certain priestly duties. The passage in the Mishnah[3] which speaks of this meeting and its purpose runs as follows:

(1) And they descended and entered the Hall of Polished Stones to read the *Shema*.
(2) The president said to them: 'Give one blessing'; and they blessed,
(3) And recited the Ten Commandments and the *Shema* (in its three sections)
(4) And they blessed the people with three blessings; viz. (the blessing) 'True and firm' (אמת ויציב), that of 'service' (עבודה), and 'the blessing of the priests' (ברכת כהנים).

This brief account is extraordinarily interesting, but not free from difficulty. The purpose for which the priests forgathered is described as 'to read (or recite) the Shema.' This is a summary way of describing the reading of certain portions of Scripture the most important of which was the *Shema* (Dt 6^{4-9}), and certain accompanying liturgical Blessings. The leader or 'president' is to be regarded, not as the minister who recites the prayers on behalf of the congregation, but as the leader who leads in the recitation, the assembled priests all joining in. Possibly 'Bless' here means merely 'Begin the liturgical service.'

It is explicitly stated in line three that the Decalogue was recited in close connexion with the *Shema*. This was the ancient practice, later discontinued because the *Minim* were wont to allege that the moral law, summed up in the Decalogue, was more important than all the rest.[1] Possibly the first two sections only of the *Shema* were recited in the ancient liturgy, and the addition of the third may be due to a gloss, reflecting the later practice. The recital of the *Shema* was *preceded* by a Benediction; but the Mishnah here gives no clue as to what it was, though, according to the Babylonian Talmud,[2] the question was early disputed by the Rabbinical schools. Probably the form used was that known as *Ahabah rabbah* ('with abounding love'), which is still chanted in the synagogue service.[3]

In the fourth line of the Mishnah passage the present text runs: 'And they blessed *the people* with three blessings.' As I. Elbogen has pointed out,[4] the words *the people* are probably an incorrect gloss. The priests were engaged in a service of prayer within a semi-private room, outside the Temple proper. There could be no question of blessing the people, which would naturally form part of the *public* service within the sanctuary. The three blessings that followed coincide partly with well-known liturgical forms: 'true and firm' is the name still given to the Blessing recited after the *Shema*—as used in the Temple its form was doubtless much shorter than the recension now current in the Prayer Books. 'Service' (עבודה) was probably an earlier form of the 17th paragraph of the *Shemōnĕh 'Esrēh*,[5] and expressed gratitude for the splendid Temple-worship. The last 'Blessing of the Priests' was probably a petition uttered *for* the priests.

This liturgical service of prayer for the priests is noteworthy. It shows how high a place prayer had come to assume, even in the sacrificial worship. The high place accorded to the liturgical recitation of the Scriptures is also a remarkable feature, and serves, perhaps, to show how far-reaching the influence of Pharisaic and synagogal piety really was.

After the conclusion of this priestly liturgy the assembled priests again drew lots—the third and fourth—to determine who should offer the incense in the sanctuary, and who should lay the various parts of the victim upon the altar. Those on whom no lot had fallen were now free to go away, after divesting themselves of the priestly dress. Then followed the sacrifice proper—the offering of incense and of sacrifice, accompanied by prayer. At the solemn moment when the chief officiating priest, alone within the sanctuary, offered the incense, which became visible in clouds of smoke, the people withdrew from the inner court and prostrated themselves, spreading out their hands in silent prayer (cf. Rev $8^{13f.}$). The incensing priest, after prostrating himself for worship, also withdrew from the sanctuary. A period of silent prayer followed, and the people were then blessed by the priests, the five priests who had been engaged in the offering of the incense standing on the steps in front of the Temple proper, and, led by the principal officiant, pronouncing the blessing on the people with uplifted hands.

The offering of the burnt-offering now went forward, together with the appropriate accompaniments (meal-offerings and drink-offering), and then followed the musical part of the service. The Levitical choir, to the accompaniment of instrumental music, sang the psalm of the day. The psalm was sung in three sections, the end of each

[1] *Jewish Artisan Life*, London, 1902, ch. iv. ('A June Day in ancient Jerusalem during last Decade before Christ'). The firstfruits had to be presented annually between Pentecost and the Feast of Dedication.

[2] *Ib.* Cf. also the art. 'Temple-Service' in *EBi* (by the present writer), esp. cols. 4951–4956.

[3] *Tāmîd*, v. 1.

[1] See C. Taylor, *Sayings of the Jewish Fathers*², Cambridge, 1897, *Exc.* 4. 119.

[2] *Berāk.* 11*b*.

[3] See Singer, p. 39 f. For the much shorter form recited in the Temple see *JE*, *s.v.* 'Ahabah Rabbah,' i. 281.

[4] *Studies in Jewish Literature*, Berlin, 1913, p. 80 f. There is some evidence that the text was read without the suspected words in earlier times.

[5] Cf. Singer, *The Authorised Daily Prayer Book (Hebrew and English)*, p. 50 f.

(*b*) *Sacrifice.*—The general features of ritual sacrifice are sufficiently well known to us, and a comparison of Hom. *Od.* iii. 417 ff., *Il.* 410 ff.; Ap. Rh. i. 402 ff. with Aristophanes, *Peace*, 937 ff., where Trygaios sacrifices to the goddess of Peace, shows that, as we should expect, the ritual remained very conservative. The procedure is outlined in art. SACRIFICE (Greek), where also the oath-sacrifice is discussed. See also art. PROPITIATION (Greek) for expiatory sacrifice, and art. VOTIVE OFFERINGS (Greek).

LITERATURE.—P. Stengel, *Die Griechischen Kultusaltertümer: Opferbräuche*, Berlin, 1910; L. Ziehen, 'Bericht über griechische Sakralaltertümer,' in *Bursian's Jahresbericht*, Leipzig, 1908; S. Reinach, *Cults, Myths, and Religions*, London, 1912; C. C. J. Webb, *Group Theories of Religion and the Individual*, do. 1916; J. B. Carter, *The Religious Life of Ancient Rome*, Boston and New York, 1911; E. Durkheim, *The Elementary Forms of the Religious Life*, London, 1915.

A. W. MAIR.

WORSHIP (Hebrew).—**I. Introductory.**—(*a*) *Terms and underlying conceptions.*—The fundamental idea of worship, as conceived by the Hebrews, was expressed by the term 'service' (*'abôdāh*), the corresponding Greek term being λατρεία ('servitus religionis quam λατρείαν Graeci vocant').[1] 'To perform the service of God (or the Lord)' means, in the Pentateuch, to carry out the worship of God in accordance with the requirements of the Levitical Law (Nu 8^{11}, Ex 12^{25}). While such 'service' is, on its external side, elaborated in a series of ceremonial and liturgical acts, its inward and spiritual side is also emphasized; it is essentially a 'service' of heart and soul (Dt 11^{13}: 'And it shall come to pass, if ye shall hearken diligently unto my commandments which I command you this day, *to love the Lord your God*, and to serve him with *all your heart and with all your soul*,' etc.).

From the time when worship at one central shrine was established (*i.e.* the 18th year of Josiah, 621 B.C.) down to the destruction of the Jerusalem Temple in A.D. 70 the worship of God was regarded as finding its only complete and adequate expression in the Temple service, with its elaborate cultus of priesthood and sacrifice (cf. Jn 4^{20}).

'The immense and manifold religious activities that concentrated themselves in the temple worship, can only be adequately realized when it is remembered how unique was the position occupied [for nearly seven centuries] by Judaism's central shrine. It was absolutely the one and only sanctuary where the highest expressions of the religious life of a whole people could be offered. Judaism possessed but one sanctuary, and that was in Jerusalem.'[2]

Jerusalem was for a long period visited by pilgrims from all over the ancient world, who appeared in the Holy City laden with gifts for the Temple. They came to Jerusalem 'for to worship' (Ac 8^{27}; cf. 24^{11}), and it was a pious duty for every faithful Jew to visit in this way the sanctuary at least once in a lifetime. This happened more particularly at the great feasts.[3]

The term *'abôdāh*, while it primarily had reference to the worship of the Temple, and more particularly to the ministry of the officiating priesthood therein, received further an extended application, and is used in the sense of divine worship generally, and especially prayer. A famous dictum ascribed to the high-priest Simeon the Just (*c.* 200 B.C.) runs: 'On three things the world stands: On the Torah, on the 'Abôdāh (*i.e.* the Temple-service), and on acts of love.'[4] It was after the destruction of the Temple that the term was applied specifically to prayer; cf. *Ta'anith*, 2*a* (with ref. to Dt 11^{13}): What is meant by the 'service of the heart? Prayer'; and (with ref. to Dt 28^{47} and Nu 4^{47}) *'Arak*, 11*a*: 'What is meant by service (worship) in joy and cheerfulness of the heart? It is song . . . What service is that which accompanies sacrificial service (worship)? It is song.' This spiritualizing of the idea of sacrificial worship had already made progress within Judaism (cf. *e.g.*, Ps 51^{17}), and is strongly emphasized in the NT. St. Paul speaks of 'your reasonable service' (τὴν λογικὴν λατρείαν ὑμῶν, Ro 12^{1}), which means 'a service to God such as befits the reason' (λόγος), *i.e.* a spiritual sacrifice and not the offering of an irrational animal; cf. 1 Pet. ii. 5.[1]

The other general term for 'worship' is in Hebrew *hishtaḥawāh* (השׁתחוה), the Greek προσκυνεῖν. This means 'prostrate oneself,' the most characteristic form of which action was among Orientals to fall upon the knees and touch the ground with the forehead as a mark of supreme reverence (the 'salaam'). This was one of the attitudes of prayer—prostration for prayer—which is defined in the Talmud[2] as 'spreading out the hands and feet.' It is related in the Rabbinical sources that, when the Temple was thronged with pilgrims, assembled to worship at the great feasts, though the congregation was wedged together so tightly as to be unable to move freely, when the moment arrived for prostration, in some unexplained and miraculous manner every member was able to prostrate himself.[3] The term (השׁתחוה) is often employed in Scripture in the sense of 'worship,' though it is not confined to acts of worship directed to God. Thus it is used to express supplication or reverence towards men.[4] But it is applied to acts of public worship in the Temple, especially in the Psalms and Chronicles. Such characteristic phrases occur as 'O worship the Lord in the beauty of holiness' (*i.e.* in festal attire); Ps 29^{2} 96^{9} (cf. 1 Ch 16^{29}, 2 Ch 20^{21}). Perhaps the idea of worship is most fully expressed in Psalms 93 and 95–100, especially in such verses as the following:

'O come, let us worship and bow down:
Let us kneel before the Lord our Maker' (95^{6}).

The other great element in the fully developed worship was that of praise, or thanksgiving. One of the keynotes of the Psalms is 'give thanks' (*hôdû*)—cf., *e.g.*, Pss 118, 105–107—or 'praise' (*Hallel*); cf. Pss 111–113, etc. 'Praise ye the Lord' (*Hallelu-jah*).

A good illustration of the acts of worship which were typical of Jewish piety is contained in the following passages:

'Sing unto the Lord, all the earth;
Shew forth his salvation from day to day.
. . . .
Give unto the Lord the glory due unto his name:
Bring an offering, and come before him:
Worship the Lord in the beauty of holiness' (1 Ch $16^{23.29}$).

'And Ezra opened the book in the sight of all the people; . . . and when he opened it, all the people stood up: and Ezra blessed the Lord, the great God. And all the people answered, Amen, Amen, with the lifting up of their hands: and they bowed their heads, and worshipped the Lord with their faces to the ground' (Neh $8^{5f.}$).

(*b*) *The ancient cultus.*—Before the centralization of the cultus in the Jerusalem Temple, worship was carried out at various local shrines or altars, which were numerous throughout the land. Probably every city or village had its *bāmāh*, or 'high place' (cf. 2 K 17^{9} 23^{8}, Ezk 6^{6}), and in some cases the seat of the local worship was of more than local importance. There were famous shrines at Dan, Bethel, Gilgal, Beersheba, Shechem, Gibeon, and Samaria, some (but by no means all) of which figure in the patriarchal history (cf., *e.g.*, for Bethel Gn 28^{19}, Am 5^{5}, etc., and for Beersheba Gn 26^{23-25}, Am 5^{5}).

That Jahweh could be worshipped at the local *bāmāh* in a perfectly legitimate way is clear from 1 S 9, 10, where Samuel the seer is represented as going up to the *bāmāh* to worship, and where his arrival to bless the sacrifice is awaited by the people. To this a room or hall (Heb. *lishkāh*) is attached, where the sacrificial meal is eaten by the assembled guests. In the time of David, and during the early years of Solomon, Gibeon was the great 'high place,' to which the king himself resorted for sacrifice (1 K $3^{3.4}$, 2 Ch $1^{3.13}$). In the earlier period (of the Judges) a special importance seems to have been attached to the place where the ark was located, and during the period of its existence Shiloh may be regarded as the principal sanctuary. Here a special building (a 'temple,' *hekal*) was erected for the greater safety of the sacred symbol; a local priesthood, the house of Eli, was attached to it; and its annual festival was much frequented (cf. Jg 21^{19}, 1 S $1^{3.21}$). This sanctuary, which R. H. Kennett regards as a genuinely Israelitish sanctuary, not taken over from the Canaanites, and possibly the original sanctuary of the Levites, was probably destroyed by the Philistines after the battle of Ebenezer (1 S 4^{11}), a catastrophe to which Jeremiah, apparently, alludes (Jer 7^{12}). Subsequently the family of Eli was established at Nob, which thus became a sacred shrine.

[1] Augustine, *de Civ. Dei.* v. 15.
[2] G. H. Box, in *EBi*, col. 4948 (*s.v.* 'Temple-Service').
[3] 'The normal population [of Jerusalem] cannot possibly have ever exceeded 50,000, but at the great feasts more than a million were frequently gathered around the Temple' (*The Beginnings of Christianity*, ed. by F. J. Foakes Jackson and K. Lake, London, 1920, pt. i. vol. i. p. 1).
[4] *Pirqē Âbôth*, i. 2.

[1] Sanday-Headlam, *Romans*[5] (*ICC*), Edinburgh, 1902, *ad loc.* For the transformation of sacrificial ideas in the synagogue liturgy see below, p. 794, § 4.
[2] *T.B. Berāk.* 34*b*, *Meg.* 22*b*.
[3] *Ber. Rab.* v. on Gn 1^{9} and parallels.
[4] Cf. 1 S 25^{24}, 2 K 4^{37}, Est 8^{3}, Mt 18^{29}, Lk 8^{41}, Ac 10^{25}.

What became, however, the most important of all the Israelite sanctuaries was that of Jerusalem, which was held by the Jebusites till the time of David (cf. Jg 1[21] 19[11f.], 2 S 5[6-9]). Here the sacred rock and cave, which have played so conspicuous a part in Hebrew, Christian, and Muhammadan worship, may already have been the seat of an earlier Jebusite shrine. When Solomon built on this site his splendid Temple and royal palace, the former (as in the case of Shiloh) was sanctified by the presence of the ark.

An interesting survival of the earlier Israelite shrines is probably to be seen in the institution of Levitical cities. This is a feature of the late priestly legislation, and is probably to be accounted for by the fact that the Levites, who in the post-Exilic period occupied a position subordinate to the priesthood proper, were the descendants of the old local priestly families, which ministered at the local sanctuaries or 'high places.' The Levites possessed large estates at such places as Shechem, Gezer, Hebron, Beth-shemesh, Kedesh, Taanach Ashtaroth, Ramoth-Gilead, Bezer, Gibeon (cf. Jos 21[1-42]). These priestly estates existed in the various localities where there had been a 'high place.' 'Could the complete history of these Levitical cities be written it seems probable that in each case it would be found that each had been the centre of an independent shrine in the days before Josiah's reform.'[1]

Recent excavation in Palestine has brought to light many remains of ancient 'high places' and altars.[2] It was around these shrines that the worship of the ancient Hebrews was concentrated. To these spots they flocked as the annual festivals came round, and at the recurring new moons and sabbaths, to offer their tithes, their firstfruits, and their sacrifices (cf. 2 K 4[23], Am 8[5], etc.). The character of this worship was essentially joyous, music, dancing, and revelry being marked features (cf. Am 6[5f.]). Unfortunately it is impossible for us to reconstruct fully and adequately the ceremonies that accompanied the ancient worship. All we can say with certainty is that its centre was the local altar—in some cases the local shrine being of more than local importance (Shiloh, later Dan, Bethel, and Jerusalem). The altar had as its practically indispensable adjuncts the sacred pillar (*maṣṣēbāh*) and *ăshērāh*, or sacred pole, which was the symbol, apparently, of a goddess.[3] Another adjunct was the sacrificial hall or room (Heb. *lishkāh*) where the sacrificial feast was held.

The local sanctuaries were served by a local priesthood, though it is improbable that, as a rule, more than one family exercised the priestly office at any smaller particular locality. The story of Micah given in the appendix to the book of Judges (ch. 17 f.) shows how a shrine could be set up by the head of a household, who could appoint one of his sons (an Ephraimite) to act as his priest. It is only later that a wandering Levite is appointed in his place, who subsequently was carried off by the Danites and became the founder of the long line of priests who ministered at the famous sanctuary of Dan in the far north. Similarly David made his sons priests (2 S 8[18]), although the principal priest at the time was Abiathar, a descendant of Eli. It was natural that the priests who were attached to the more important shrines should themselves increase in importance and wealth, in course of time. 'The wealth thus acquired was in many instances invested in land in the vicinity of the city in which the priests officiated. In course of time, therefore, there were large priestly estates in and about the cities where temples or high places were situated.'[4] According to Ezk 44[7], in the pre-Exilic period the manual labour connected with the shrines and sacrifices had (doubtless only after wealth had increased) been performed by foreign slaves, who were kept by the more wealthy priests.

The character of the old simple worship of Jahweh was fundamentally transformed when the Israelites passed from the nomadic stage and became a settled agricultural community. Jahweh, who had at first been regarded as essentially a war-god, who led His chosen people to victory against enemies—though this was not the only aspect of His character—now became the God (Baal) of the land, and as such the God of agricultural law. The body of agricultural laws which gradually grew up under these conditions came to be looked upon as an essential part of the original covenant by which Jahweh became the God of the Hebrews (Ex 21–23). Another result was that the great festivals were placed upon an agricultural basis.

'To the simple Passover feast, which commemorated the yeaning time of domestic animals, an agricultural offering of first fruits in the form of unleavened bread was added. This occurred because the first ripe grain was gathered at the very season in which the old nomadic feast fell. Seven weeks later a new agricultural festival, commemorative of the completion of the harvest, was added, while the old autumn festival of the date harvest became the festival of the grape-gathering.'[1]

The local sanctuaries were the centres at which this worship was carried out, and it was at these shrines that for several centuries Jahweh was worshipped with the full sanction of the religious leaders (cf. 1 S 7[17], 1 K 3[4] 18[30], etc.). 'Such local worship is alone contemplated in the oldest Hebrew legislation ("in every place where I record my name I will come unto thee and I will bless thee" [Ex 20[24]]).'[2] But by this very fact it was exposed to serious dangers. The admixture of heathen Canaanitish elements threatened seriously to imperil the purity of the old simple tribal religion, and it was against this, the mixed cultus, that the 8th cent. prophets, especially Hosea, raised their powerful opposition. The great prophetic movement marked the conflict of Israel in strife with its own paganism. It is clear from the language of the prophets that in the 8th cent. B.C. during the prosperous reigns of Jeroboam II. and Uzziah public worship, both in the Northern and in the Southern Kingdom, was carried out, especially at the great central shrines (Bethel, Jerusalem), with great zeal, elaboration, and pomp. The ceremonial was splendid, wealth was lavished on the sanctuaries, and these were thronged with zealous worshippers. And all this, it must be remembered, was ostensibly worship of Jahweh. What Amos inveighs against is not open disloyalty to the national God, but a wrong conception of the kind of service acceptable to Him. The worship is Jahweh-worship, but inspired by heathenish ideas.[3] Doubtless this worship was, on the whole, purer in Judah than in N. Israel. But in Judah heathen tendencies, though submerged, were powerful, and asserted themselves in violent reactions, such as occurred, in the 7th cent., in the reign of Manasseh.

Perhaps the general character of the old worship at the local shrines, or *bāmôth*, may be illustrated from similar festivals that take place in Syria and the neighbouring lands to-day. S. I. Curtiss has illustrated this aspect of the matter in his *Primitive Semitic Religion To-day*,[4] where the results of considerable and extensive research are gathered together. He shows that many sacred spots, probably in some cases the very sites of ancient 'high places,' are still venerated and resorted to by the peasantry. At many of these time-honoured spots 'there is virtually a priesthood in existence. . . . They do not have the designation of priests; they are known rather as sheiks of certain shrines, or as servants of certain saints. But their duties and emoluments correspond in some degree to those about which we read in the Old Testament.' Usually one priest or priestly family is connected with such a shrine, though cases occur where several priestly families live together at one shrine, as at Nebi Daud (outside the wall of Jerusalem). Sacrifices are still, apparently, offered at some of these shrines, especially in connexion with vows, and dues in the shape of the hide of the animal, and one of the quarters, are paid to the minister of the shrine, who in ordinary life is an orthodox Muslim.[5]

Vows at such spots play a considerable part in modern popular religion in Syria. 'During the year, at a popular makam [sacred spot or shrine], many sheep and goats, and sometimes larger animals, are killed in payment of vows. Besides there are vows of grain, which are promised on condition of good harvests. These vows are collected by a servant of a shrine.' According to a native authority,[6] 'if the sheik, that is, the minister of the shrine, is present, he kills the victim, otherwise any one who can read the first sura of the Koran. He uses the formula, "This is from thee and for thee." The *dahhiyeh* sacrifice is slaughtered by the one who brings it. If, however, it is brought by a woman, she puts her hand on that of the man who kills it.' The minister of the shrine is not

[1] G. A. Barton, *The Religion of Israel*, New York, 1918, p. 167.
[2] See art. HIGH PLACE. For a full discussion see S. R. Driver, *Modern Research as illustrating the Bible* (Schweich Lectures), London, 1909, p. 60 ff.
[3] See C. F. Burney, *Judges*, London, 1918, p. 195 ff.
[4] Barton, p. 162 f.

[1] Barton, p. 79 f.
[2] A. R. S. Kennedy, in *HDB* iv. 396[b].
[3] See G. A. Smith, *The Book of the Twelve Prophets*, London, 1896, i. ch. ix.
[4] London, 1902.
[5] Curtiss, p. 144 ff.
[6] *Ib.* p. 148 f.

only its guardian, but also the repository of the legends connected with its origin and the life of the saint whose name and deeds are commemorated. Not all the modern shrines have annual festivals. Where such a festival occurs it is in some cases attended by thousands of people.

The festivals referred to by Amos (5^{21-23}) must have borne a strong general resemblance to these present-day celebrations, which are probably their lineal descendants. Reference may also be made in this connexion to the annual feast of Jahweh at Shiloh (Jg $21^{19. 21}$), where dancing by the maidens of the locality was a feature (cf. also Ex $32^{5. 6. 19}$).

For the use of images by the early Hebrews, and the prevalence of idolatrous tendencies among them, see art. IMAGES AND IDOLS (Hebrew and Canaanite), vol. vii. pp. 138–142. It was by the 8th cent. prophets Hosea (8^{4-6} $13^{1f.}$; cf. 3^4) and Isaiah ($2^{8. 20}$) that the first effective protest was made, apparently, against the use of idolatrous emblems in Jahweh-worship. It was probably at Isaiah's instigation that Hezekiah was moved to destroy the brazen serpent (*neḥushtan*) which had long been an object of worship (2 K 18^4). Such serpent-worship was widespread in antiquity, and appears to have prevailed, as a popular superstitious practice, among the Hebrews, if we may judge from the results of the Gezer excavations.[1]

(*c*) *The effects of Josiah's reformation.*—The remarkable and far-reaching movement of reform which expressed itself in the Deuteronomic legislation and was inaugurated in practice by the drastic action of King Josiah in 621 B.C. was the outcome of an alliance between the prophetic party and the priesthood. We have already noted that the possibilities of such an alliance had always been greater in Judah than in the Northern Kingdom. It now became an accomplished fact, and the results were momentous. The two great elements in the religious life of the community now united in a sustained and sincere effort to translate the lessons of the teaching of the great 8th cent. prophets into practice, by fundamental reforms in the religious institutions of the nation. The aim was to make public worship a more fitting and adequate instrument for expressing the prophetic religion. It was essential that the rites of worship should be purified, and divorced from the heathen accompaniments and associations in which they were involved. To effect this end the reformers insisted on two things, the nationalization of the worship and its centralization in Jerusalem. The old time-honoured, local sacrifices of clan and family were to be suppressed, and all the worship (including the private sacrifices) was to be concentrated in one central sanctuary in Jerusalem.

It was only by such a drastic reform that the necessary break with age-long traditions and associations could be effected. We are expressly told that the Passover celebrated as a result of the reform movement was unprecedented (2 K $23^{21f.}$). This was because it was kept, on this occasion, not as in the past by the people in their own homes, but by the united nation in Jerusalem.

The suppression of the local shrines and the centralization of the worship mark a revolution. With the publication and national acceptance of the Deuteronomic code the beginnings of the Canon were formed which was to grow into the Hebrew Bible; and with the centralization of the worship the first stone of the edifice was laid which was later to develop into the post-Exilic Jewish Church. The foundations of Judaism were laid.

The aim of the reformers was to gather up the local sacrificial rites into a truly national worship.

Deuteronomy 'cuts at the roots of the family and tribal sacrifices when it forbids the offering of sacrifice elsewhere than at the central sanctuary ($12^{13-19. 27}$). But it does more than merely forbid. It provides the great festivals, which had their close association with the spring sowing and the harvest, and which, being common to all men, brought the people into contact with their heathen neighbours, with motives taken from the history of Jahveh's dealings with His people. The people, when they come together to worship their God, are to come to a shrine which has associations with their national life and with that alone; and they are to worship through forms which continually impress upon them the unity of their historic life as a people. Even when the private man comes to offer his personal recognition of Jahveh's bounty to him, he does it through a ritual in which he recounts how he belongs to a nation with a past which is great because it is full of God's grace (xxvi. 1–11).'[1]

This national impress upon the character of the worship was never lost. The old agricultural feasts, though their primitive features were not eliminated, acquired a new significance. The Passover became the festival of national redemption; Pentecost (the 'feast of weeks') was transformed into a commemoration of the giving of the Law—the festival of Revelation; and Tabernacles was invested with the associations of the wilderness life. The old unity of the nation, which had expressed itself in the nomadic period by the gathering of the clans at a central shrine, was recovered, and henceforth remains a permanent feature of the cultus.

Another momentous result was the disestablishment of the local priesthood. The legislation of Deuteronomy provides no complete law of the priesthood. It merely deals with the practical consequences of the centralization of the worship as these affected the old order of priests. The members of this order, who are referred to as 'Levites,' are still priests *de jure*. They are all 'levitical priests,' and are so styled in the Code ('the priests the Levites' [Dt 18^1 etc.]). But in consequence of the new legislation the exercise of priestly functions can only be carried out legitimately in the central sanctuary. The rural priest ('the Levite within thy gates') can only secure the name and rights of a priest when he removes to Jerusalem (Dt $18^{6f.}$).

It was only in the later legislation of P that the distinction between priests and Levites grew up. The Levites, who were the descendants of the old local order of priests, were then degraded to an inferior rank, and the priesthood proper was confined to the family of Aaron.

The immediate results of the Deuteronomic reform seem to have proved disappointing. So drastic a break with age-long tradition could not at once be absolutely successful. In the dark days that preceded the final extinction of the Southern Kingdom there were lapses to older practices, and even to idolatry. But a real step forward had been taken and the way had been prepared for the later reconstruction of the Jewish community who survived the Exile as a Church-nation with one holy sanctuary served by an official priesthood which is set apart for the performance of holy functions. The central idea of Ezekiel and his successors is that of a holy God, worshipped in the holy land in one holy sanctuary by a holy people whose sacrifices are offered by a sacred order of ministers, who constitute a holy priesthood.

2. The worship of the second Temple.—The erection of the second Temple was not improbably the work of the remnant of the old Israelites who had been left behind in the land; but the leaders seem to have been Babylonian Jews. It was from the exiles in Babylonia that the enthusiasm and energy were drawn which impelled the somewhat weary and sluggish Palestinians to move forward. But it was, at first, a 'day of small things.' The new structure appeared mean and despicable in the eyes of those who remembered 'this house in its former glory' (Hag 2^3). But Haggai's bold prophecy of future glory (2^7) was destined ultimately to be fulfilled.

It is important to realize that the worship of the restored Temple, though influenced to some extent by Ezekiel's ideas, did not at first conform to the elaborate prescriptions of P. It was based upon the Deuteronomic law, which was still the only written form of the Tôrāh of Moses. Even in Malachi (? *c.* 450 B.C.) the conception of the

[1] See R. A. S. Macalister, *The Excavation of Gezer*, ii. 399.

[1] A. C. Welch, *The Religion of Israel under the Kingdom*, London, 1912, p. 209.

priesthood is still essentially that of Deuteronomy; it belongs to the House of Levi (Mal $2^{4ff.}$). It is true that the distinction between priests and Levites had been recognized already at the time of the Return, if we may judge by the list of those who came up with Zerubbabel (Neh 7). But the relatively small number of Levites there given may be explained, perhaps, by supposing that most of those tabulated as priests were originally Levites whose claim to the priesthood had been recognized. Ezekiel's influence was obviously at work. A clear indication of this appears in Zec 3^7, where one of the principal functions of the high-priest is to keep God's courts.

'Here we have an unmistakable indication,' says Robertson Smith, 'that Ezekiel's conception of holiness, and his jealousy of profane contact with holy things, had been taken up by the spiritual leaders of the new Jerusalem. There is, therefore, a strong presumption that from the first the arrangements and ritual of the second Temple were more closely conformed to the principle of concentric circles of holiness than those of the first Temple had been.'[1]

The ideas of Ezekiel were potent—in particular the conception of the service offered as a stated and regular ceremonial; but the ceremonial had not yet attained the elaborateness of the Priestly Code. That was only realized later, when Ezra promulgated his edition of the Tôrāh.

The date for this event usually given (444 B.C.) is by no means certain. Ezra's mission may plausibly be assigned to the reign of the second Artaxerxes, in which case some date between 400 and 390 B.C. is more probable.

'That the stated services of the first ninety years of the new Jerusalem were much less elaborate and costly than the Priestly Code prescribes seems to follow from Ezr 9^5, where we learn that [at the time when Ezra arrived in Jerusalem] the evening oblation was still only a *minḥa* or cereal offering. The same thing follows still more clearly from Neh 10^{32}, where we see that a new voluntary tax became necessary when the full Pentateuchal ritual was introduced. Before that time the stated service appears to have been maintained, with much grumbling and in an imperfect way, at the expense of the priests (Mal 1^{6-13}).'[2]

With the promulgation and public acceptance of the full priestly law in Jerusalem by Ezra the services in the Temple became more elaborate and the priesthood more fully organized. This process, perhaps, did not begin till after 400 B.C. Unfortunately the history of the period 400–200 B.C. is very obscure. That Ezra encountered much opposition from the old conservative party in Jerusalem is clear; and this ultimately culminated in the Samaritan schism and the erection of a rival Temple on Mount Gerizim (probably about 330 B.C.). After this event the strict hierarchical party within the Jewish community held undisputed sway. The elaboration of the Temple worship proceeded, it would seem, without a check; and its effects are visible in the work of the chronicler (*c.* 300–250 B.C.). The elaborate organization of the Levitical arrangements in the Temple described in 1 Ch 23 ff. no doubt reflects the realities of the writer's own time. Here the duties of priests and Levites (now two completely distinct orders), with those of the subordinate classes of doorkeepers and singers, are fully set forth. The *teaching* of the Law to the people had now, apparently, become a recognized part of the functions of the priestly class. The priest was also a teacher (2 Ch 15^3). Possibly a system of schools for such teaching had been established (cf. 2 Ch 17^{7-9}). The priestly class was also in control of the courts of justice (2 Ch 19^{4-11}), and this function descended from them later to the Rabbinical doctors of the Law (scribes). The care for public worship and its elaborate organization which the chronicler ascribes to such kings as David, Solomon, Hezekiah, and Josiah illuminate the actual state of affairs as he knew them.

[1] *The Old Testament in the Jewish Church*[2], London, 1892, p. 443.
[2] *Ib.* p. 444.

In these acts praise, supplication, and thanksgiving are a prominent feature. The old abuses of worship denounced by Isaiah and Jeremiah have passed away. We are confronted with a pious community that finds in the great services of the Temple its highest satisfaction and constant care. The ancient ritual of animal sacrifice was celebrated with pomp and impressive ceremonial. But it was no mere empty formality, devoid of spiritual significance and appeal. It was hallowed by true spiritual fervour, by the sense of sin forgiven and by unstinting recognition of the goodness of the Giver of all good things. Especially significant in this connexion is the large place given to prayer. 'It is hardly possible to read the prayers of the great kings in Chronicles and not feel that they echo a liturgy of prayer—for the individual and for the nation.'[1] It is indeed highly probable that some of the older liturgical prayers, embodied in the Prayer Book of the synagogue, were already, in an earlier form, in existence at the time of the chronicler. The service of music and praise was especially rich, and is dwelt upon with loving minuteness by the chronicler, who was himself, perhaps, a member of one of the Levitical choirs (cf., *e.g.*, 2 Ch $5^{12f.}$). The Psalter was the book of praise (cf. 1 Ch $16^{8ff.}$).

That the service of prayer and praise was liturgical in character is clear from the fact that the people were expected to respond: 'And all the people said, Amen, and praised the Lord' (1 Ch 16^{36}). It is probable also that the Law was read in public worship. At any rate, the recital of the *Shᵉmaʿ* ('Hear, O Israel') is almost certainly as old as this period, as can be shown by the antiquity of the present (synagogue) Benedictions that accompany it.

As Elmslie remarks: 'Even if it be thought that this picture represents rather the ideals of the Levites than the actual attainments of the community, it is still important that such a standard of worship was conceived by the priests and set before the people. One recalls the words of the great prophet of exilic or post-exilic times who wrote: "for mine house shall be called an house of prayer for all peoples" (Is 56^7). His was a vision of the Temple as the centre of the whole world's worship. To the Chronicler it had at least become a true "house of prayer" for Israel.'[2]

How deep and real the devotional spirit could be that underlay the imposing ceremonial of the Temple worship can be seen from the Psalter, which may be regarded as the hymn-book (and also, to some extent, as the prayer-book) of the second Temple.

Here the worshipful spirit, which lingers so lovingly on the services and devotions of the House of God (cf. Ps 84, 27^4 42^2 100^4, 122, 15), which finds in that House the focus of its devotion (Ps 5^7 138^2 $99^{5.9}$ 132^7), which delights to celebrate the pomp ('the beauty of holiness'=holy adornment or vestments: Ps 29^2 96^9; cf. 1 Ch 16^{29}), and the stately processions (Ps 68^{25-29} $24^{3f.7-10}$) of the Temple, has yet no narrow conception of worship. To the Psalmists the God of Israel is also the God of nature, and is celebrated as such in the splendid nature-psalms (8, 19^{2-6}, 29, 104, 107, 139, 147, 148); and the transition from one aspect to the other is easy (Ps $29^{3ff.}$). Thus in the composite Ps 19 the psalmist passes from extolling the wonders of nature (the light of nature) to praise of the Law (the light of revelation). But in truth the range of the Psalter is as wide as the outlook and experience of man; the Psalmists touch the height and depth of the human spirit; and the universality of their appeal reveals how an intense and particularistic religion can expand and deepen when it is founded upon a genuine and profound spiritual experience.

The feeling excited in the breast of a pious Jew by the splendid ceremonial of the Temple worship as it could be witnessed at the end of the century (about 200 B.C.) during which the Chronicler flourished, is fervently expressed by Ben Sira in his striking tribute to the high-priest Simon (II.), surnamed 'the Just.' He is pictured as he appeared in the Temple on the Day of Atonement, where 'clothed in his glorious robes' and surrounded by 'all the sons of Aaron in their glory' he 'went up to the altar of majesty and made glorious the court of the sanctuary.' The crowded court and

[1] W. A. L. Elmslie, *The Books of Chronicles*, Cambridge, 1916, p. lii.
[2] *Ib.* p. lii f.

the worship of the people who receive the high-priestly blessing are vividly described:

'Then the sons of Aaron sounded
With the trumpets of beaten work;
Yea, they sounded and caused a mighty blast to be heard
For a remembrance before the Most High.
(Then) all flesh hasted together
And fell upon their faces to the earth,
To worship before the Most High,
Before the Holy One of Israel,' etc.[1]

The upheaval produced by the attempted suppression of Judaism at the hands of Antiochus Epiphanes, and the consequent Maccabean revolt, was fruitful in momentous consequences. Judaism was rooted more firmly than ever in the hearts of true believers by the persecution. Affection for the Law was deepened, and the study and knowledge of its ordinances was more widely diffused and more actively pursued among laymen. When the fury of the storm had spent itself, Judaism emerged profoundly modified in many important ways. New parties—the Pharisees and Sadducees—came into existence; a new literature, which found its classical example in the book of Daniel, emerged. A new native dynasty ruled, and communal life was re-organized. A new Temple-feast, commemorating the re-dedication of the sanctuary (164 B.C.) after its defilement by the Syrian tyrant, was added to the sacred calendar. This is known as the Feast of Dedication (cf. Jn 10[22]), or *Chanukkah*, and is celebrated in the winter for eight days. It was inaugurated in the circumstances described in 1 Mac 4[36ff.]: 'After the Temple had been purified, a new altar of burnt-offering built, and new holy vessels made, the fire was kindled on the altar, the lamps of the candlestick lit, and the re-dedication of the altar celebrated for eight days.'[2] According to Josephus, its popular name was the 'Festival of lights.'[3] But during the period that followed the establishment of the new Jewish state a profound change in the whole character of Jewish piety manifested itself in the rise of the Pharisaic party and wide extension of the synagogue as a religious institution. The monopoly of religious leadership, which had hitherto been enjoyed by the priests, was now, perforce, shared by the popular party of the Pharisees, who represented the pious laymen, the old priestly party, which was still all-powerful in the Temple, being represented by the Sadducees.[4] The synagogues were under the control of the Pharisees.

The origin of the synagogue as a religious institution is enveloped in obscurity. The Jewish scholar Moriz Friedländer[5] regards it as a product of the Diaspora, which came in to Judæa from outside. If the synagogue had already become an institution in Judæa at the time of the Maccabean revolt, the silence of the books of Maccabees regarding it would be inexplicable. On the other hand, the existence of synagogues in Egypt during the second half of the 3rd cent. B.C. (during the reign of Ptolemy Euergetes, 247–222 B.C.) seems to be demonstrable;[6] while a famous synagogue was certainly in existence at Antioch in the reign of Antiochus Epiphanes. The circumstances of the Diaspora would naturally promote the growth of such an institution.

Friedländer insists that the synagogues of the Diaspora were pervaded by a much freer atmosphere than those of Palestine, which were under Pharisaic influence. The former, he thinks, were in reality places of teaching and instruction (*Lehrhäuser*). They were thus far more than houses of prayer; while the Pharisaic synagogues, which arose later, were more of the latter character. Though sections from Scripture were read, and edifying discourses were given in them, prayer still remained the principal element, and had many points of contact and relation with the sacrificial cultus, as the existing prayers of the synagogue liturgy, which originated from the time both before and after the Roman destruction of the Temple, testify. The Sabbath worship of the Diaspora was, according to Friedländer, of a different character; it consisted not merely of lections from Moses and the Prophets, and of prayer, but principally in the exposition of Holy Scripture, which was allegorical in character, which saw 'in the words [of the text] symbols of a secret nature revealed in allegories,' and deduced from them the loftiest philosophical ideas. The Diaspora synagogue also, according to Friedländer, had as a distinguishing feature that it did not derive its instruction from the authoritative oral teaching of the priest, but that whoever possessed knowledge in the Scriptures was here at liberty to come forward in order to expound God's word. This was still the case in the Diaspora synagogues in the times of the Apostles (Ac 13[15]).

Friedländer in these contentions seems to exaggerate the difference between the orthodox synagogues of Palestine and those of the Diaspora. In both the element of instruction—the reading and exposition of the Law and the Prophets—was the main element. In both, also, prayer occupied an important place. Indeed, the most frequent designation of 'synagogue' in Philo is προσευχή—a term which also occurs in Josephus.[1] One principal difference there was: in the synagogues of the Diaspora the Scriptures, and probably the prayers, were recited in Greek. The allegorical method of expounding the Scriptures was more freely employed in the Dispersion—though it was by no means absent from the ancient homiletic discourses given in the synagogues of Palestine. Pharisaic restrictions only became marked after the close of the 1st century A.D. Up to that time a greater freedom prevailed, probably, in the synagogues of Palestine as well as in those of the Diaspora. A trace of the survival of such a spirit in certain Hellenistic synagogues may be seen in the fact that in the time of Origen the book of Baruch was still publicly read (in Greek).[2]

3. The later Temple service.—It has already been pointed out that the system of worship which was developed by the Jewish community in Palestine found its most elaborate expression in the services of the Temple of Herod. How elaborate the organization of these services was can be seen from the details that have been preserved regarding the priestly arrangements,[3] which need not be repeated here. Reference may also be made to such Rabbinical evidence as is contained in the Mishnah Tractates *Middôth* and *Yōmā*—to cite only the most obvious sources. In the former minute details are given regarding the Temple structure and arrangements; while in the latter a full account is set forth of the elaborate Temple services and ceremonial on the Day of Atonement.[4]

It should be remembered that for the purposes of the national worship the land of Palestine was divided up into 24 districts (corresponding to the 24 'courses'), and one 'course' from each district (consisting of priests, Levites, and lay Israelites) was on duty in the Temple for a week at a time. Not all the priests belonging to a particular course could do duty at the same time at the sacrifice; the 'course' was therefore divided into 'father's houses.' In the same way not all the laymen belonging to a particular 'course' could be present during the whole week when its course was on duty in the Temple. It was consequently represented by a deputation at the sanctuary; the others, who had been left behind, assembled in the local synagogues (at the time when the sacrifice was actually being offered in the Temple) and engaged in prayer and the reading of Scripture.[5] To illustrate the character of the worship which was focused in the later Temple, it will suffice here (1) to describe the ceremonies associated with one of the more popular occasions for such service, outside the three great national festivals of Passover, Pentecost, and Tabernacles; and (2) to summarize briefly the ceremonial of the daily service.

(1) The presentation of the firstfruits (*bikkurim*) was one of the occasions which gave opportunity for pompous pilgrimage to the Holy City outside the cycle of the great festivals. It was concerned with the fulfilment of the command: 'The first

[1] The text is cited in the translation given in the Oxford Corpus, *The Apocrypha and Pseudepigrapha of the Old Testament*, i. 510.
[2] W. O. E. Oesterley and G. H. Box, *The Religion and Worship of the Synagogue*[2], p. 404.
[3] For the present-day celebration of the festival in the synagogues cf. Oesterley and Box, p. 404 ff.
[4] See artt. PHARISEES, SADDUCEES.
[5] *Synagoge und Kirche in ihren Anfängen*, Berlin, 1908.
[6] Cf. W. Bousset, *Rel. des Judentums*, p. 72.

[1] *Vita*, 277.
[2] For the synagogue forms of worship, see, further, the end of this article.
[3] See art. PRIEST, PRIESTHOOD (Jewish).
[4] Cf. also the Tractate *Tāmîd* ('continual'), which describes the Daily Service of the sanctuary.
[5] Cf. Mishnah, *Ta'anith*, iv. 2.

being marked by three blasts on silver trumpets (blown by a body of priests), at the sound of which the people once more prostrated themselves for worship. This terminated the morning service, and private sacrifices were then proceeded with. The evening service (about 3 o'clock in the afternoon) was practically a repetition of the morning, the same priests officiating—except in the case of the incensing priest, for whom a fresh lot was taken. On the Sabbaths and great festivals the essential features of the services were the same. There was more elaboration, and a larger number of sacrifices were offered, but the character of the worship was substantially identical.

There are, of course, to be noted special ceremonies in connexion with particular occasions. The most remarkable of these, perhaps, was the Water-Feast held in connexion with the Feast of Tabernacles. It began at nightfall on Tishri 15 (first day of Tabernacles) and lasted till the following morning; and was repeated on other nights of the festival (except Friday). This was the only celebration in the Temple that took place by night. The place was the court of the women, which was specially illuminated for the occasion, the women looking on from their galleries. A torchlight procession, dances, and singing followed. Towards morning a more solemn note was introduced by the chanting of the fifteen 'songs of Degrees' (Pss 120–134) led by the Levitical choir to the accompaniment of various musical instruments. During the day the great feature was the procession which accompanied the priest who had been allotted the duty of drawing water for the libation from the pool of Siloam.[1] A relic of these processions still survives in the worship of the synagogue.

4. The synagogue worship.—For the transition, which had been gradually prepared for, between the sacrificial cultus and the form of worship which found expression in the synagogue, as well as for the rivalry between synagogue and Temple, the momentous consequences of the destruction of the Temple, and the character of the synagogue prayers, reference may be made to the article PRAYER (Jewish).[2] Here it must suffice to make a few general observations on the characteristic features of the synagogue worship. (1) In harmony with its origin the synagogue worship is essentially of a popular and democratic type. It has no organic connexion with the priesthood; its ministers are essentially laymen—at first it had no professional ministers at all, the Rabbis whom it singled out for special honour being simply learned laymen; its services, though liturgical in character, and provided with (in many cases) interesting and dignified ceremonial, are essentially simple in character; their tendency is to emphasize the element of instruction and edification (the reading and exposition of Scripture), with which is combined the service of praise and prayer.

(2) As has already been pointed out, the synagogue, as a religious institution, had already come into existence long before the destruction of the Temple and the consequent cessation of the sacrificial worship. It met a widespread religious need, owing to the centralization of the sacrificial worship in Jerusalem. While only a limited number of Jews could be present at any one time in the central sanctuary, and assist in the offering of the sacrifice, no such disability would apply to the services of the synagogue. To a certain, though limited, extent the synagogue was affiliated to the Temple worship.[3] It will be remembered that, for purposes of the daily sacrificial worship, not only the priests and Levites, but also the lay Israelites generally were divided into twenty-four courses of service, each of which had to take its turn in coming before God (in the Temple) every day for a whole week by way of representing the whole body of the people, while the daily sacrifice was being offered to Jahweh. But it appears that not the whole division of Israelites on duty but only a deputation from it was actually present at any given time in the Temple; the others, who had been left behind, assembled in the local synagogues (at the time when the sacrifice was actually offered in the Temple) and engaged in prayer and the reading of Scripture.[1] But in spite of this affiliation the synagogue was entirely free from the limitations applying to a centralized worship and a sacerdotal system. 'Hence, when the latter disappeared in the great catastrophe of 70 A.D., the synagogue was the one institution exactly fitted to be the instrument for the reconstruction of Judaism.'[2]

(3) At the same time it is important to remember that the Temple-worship has profoundly influenced not only the structure of the synagogue liturgy, but also the form and substance of its prayers.

The disappearance of the old sacrificial cultus was felt by pious Jews at the time as a real catastrophe. But the way had already been prepared by Rabbinical teaching (not to speak of that of the great prophets and some of the psalmists) for a spiritualizing of the sacrificial idea; and this tendency received a strong impulse from the exigencies of the situation which left the synagogue as the sole religious institution in which the Jewish religious consciousness could express itself. A real satisfaction of the instincts and cravings which had been, to some extent, met by the splendid Temple-worship was provided by the traditional liturgy of the synagogue, which could be regarded as a sort of parabolic and metaphorical fulfilment of sacrifice in the following ways:

(*a*) It furnished forms of prayer for daily worship which corresponded to the original daily sacrifice. In accordance with this principle those days for which additional sacrifices had been appointed (Sabbaths, new moons and Festivals) were provided with additional forms of prayer, called *musaf* (='additional').

(*b*) In the synagogue Liturgy special sections from the Law and the Mishnah, which contain the original enactments about the daily and Sabbath offerings, occupy a place at the beginning of the service:[3] and on high days and festivals it is the rule to supplement the Pentateuch lesson by the paragraph from the Law which prescribes the sacrifices appropriate to the day. For instance, during the Feast of Tabernacles the paragraph Nu 29^{12-39} is read in addition from a second scroll.

The principle underlying all this is stated in a haggadic passage in the Talmud. Abraham is represented to have anxiously asked God 'how the sins of Israel would be forgiven when their Temple was destroyed, and they should have nowhere to bring their sacrifices, and he was told that to read the duty of these sacrifices from the *Torah* would be accepted as a full equivalent.'

(*c*) Further, various petitions have been introduced into the prayers for the restoration of the Temple services and sacrifices. In some cases an older prayer has been amplified in this sense.

In these various ways the sacrificial idea has been largely spiritualized. 'The daily offering of prayer, praise, and thanksgiving morning and afternoon in the Synagogue is a spiritual counterpart and fulfilment of the old daily sacrifice in the Temple. In this way the words of the prophet Hosea are in spirit fulfilled: *We shall render as bullocks (the offering of) our lips* (Hos 14^2).'[4]

(4) The language employed in the synagogue liturgy is Hebrew, with a slight admixture of Aramaic. As has already been pointed out, the older elements in the prayers go back to a considerable antiquity (long before the Christian era)—possibly, in some cases, to the late Persian period. In such cases the prayers very probably

[1] See W. O. E. Oesterley and G. H. Box, *The Religion and Worship of the Synagogue*², p. 401.

[2] I. 3ff.

[3] During the latter years of the Temple's existence there was, apparently, a synagogue within the Temple precincts.

[1] *Ta'anith*, iv. 2; Oesterley and Box, *The Religion and Worship of the Synagogue*², p. 360.

[2] Oesterley and Box, *loc. cit.*

[3] Cf. Singer, *The Authorised Daily Prayer Book* (*Hebrew and English*), p. 9ff.

[4] Oesterley and Box, *The Religion and Worship of the Synagogue*², p. 362. It may be added that in the Talmudic period the synagogue building seems to have been modelled, to some extent, on the Temple. The entrance was from the east, and the ark, containing the scrolls of the Law, was in the west. In the modern synagogue the position is exactly reversed, the ark being placed in the east end, and the reader, while on the *bema*, facing east.

grew up in connexion with the Temple liturgy and were afterwards transferred to the liturgy of the synagogue.

The language in the fixed parts of the liturgy is not only Hebrew, but largely Biblical Hebrew—in fact a Scriptural character is deeply impressed upon the prayers generally. Whole passages (Psalms and other sections) are taken from the Bible, and Biblical language is interwoven into the texture of the prayers.

Outside Palestine among the Jews of the Dispersion in Greek-speaking countries the case was different. There Greek was largely, if not exclusively, used. It seems that not only the Scriptures, but also the most important parts (if not all) of the Liturgy—such as the *Shema* and *Shemōnēh 'Esrēh*—were regularly recited in the Hellenistic synagogues in Greek, and not in Hebrew at all.[1] In the vast synagogue at Alexandria, where the Jews who attended the services were ranged according to their trades, this was the case. We are told that the signal for the vast audience to join in the Amen response was given by the reader waving a cloth from the *bema*.[2] Even in the Mishnah sanction is given to the use of any language whatever in repeating the *Shema*, the *Shemōnēh 'Esrēh* ('Eighteen Blessings'), and the grace at meals.[3] In later practice, however, Hebrew has been the only language recognized as legitimate for prayer and worship in the orthodox synagogue.

(5) In studying the synagogue liturgy it is all-important to realize the central position of the Law. The recitation of the *Shema* (which may be regarded as a summary of the Law) is invested with great solemnity, and is preceded and followed by special Benedictions, as we have seen. But the Sabbath morning service—which is the principal one—culminates in the chanting of the lesson from the Law. The reading of the sections is the occasion of much ceremony—the carrying of the scrolls to and from the 'ark' is invested with great solemnity, not to speak of the scrolls themselves, which are prepared with the most elaborate care, according to minute rules, and are treasured in gorgeous and valuable vestments. The Law itself, *i.e.* the Pentateuch, is regarded as the supreme and final revelation of God. It stands at the head of the canonical books, and by the side of it the other two divisions of the Hebrew Scriptures, the Prophets and the 'writings' (Hagiographa), occupy quite a subordinate place. They but serve to illustrate and enforce its precepts, and are interpreted accordingly. All this is but the expression of a profound conviction that God has chosen to make a supreme revelation of Himself and His requirements in the divine Law; and that man is sanctified by the divine Law, which is the very principle of his perfection.[4]

Jewish piety thus exhausts and expresses itself in the minute and punctilious performance of the divine Law as elaborately codified and defined by the Rabbis. The performance of these duties is regarded as exercising a sanctifying influence on the worshipper; he feels that he is, by so doing, obeying the divine voice; and in this utter obedience he finds a real spiritual satisfaction; the practice of it evokes in the breast of a pious Jew a genuine devotional spirit which finds expression in constant and regular acts of praise and thanksgiving. A characteristic feature deeply impressed upon the liturgy is the regular recurrence of formulas of blessing or benediction (Heb. *berākāh*); something like a hundred are extant in Rabbinical literature. As a Jewish writer well says: 'Every manifestation of divine protection and help became an opportunity for the pious Israelite to offer up thanksgiving in the usual form of a benediction.'[5] In the liturgy proper the set Benediction plays an important part. One of the most famous of its constituent elements—the so-called 'Eighteen Blessings' (*Shemōnēh 'Esrēh*='Eighteen')—consists of a number of Benedictions constructed in regular form, which are strung together, and invariably end with the formula: 'Blessed art Thou, O Lord our God, King of the Universe, Who,' etc. Here remarkably the element of petition is mingled with that of blessing. The *Shemōnēh 'Esrēh*[1] is one of the central parts of the Prayer Book of the synagogue; it recurs in various forms in all the services, and, moreover, is recited in double form, first silently and then audibly, by the congregation. It is the Prayer (*Tephillah*) *par excellence* (*Tephillah* is one of its designations), and is recited by the congregation standing (*'Amidah*='standing' is another designation), the most solemn attitude for worship recognized in the synagogue service.

Special benedictions are also recited before and after the recitation of the Law, being introduced by the formula 'Bless ye.' This is in accordance with Biblical precedent (Neh 8⁶). The element of praise is also, of course, represented by the recitation of certain psalms, especially the Hallel (Pss 113–118). Another element of great importance is represented by various forms of confession of sin (Heb. *widduy*). The two great forms of this are the *Abînû malkēnû*, 'Our Father, our King,'[2] and the *'Al Ḥet*, 'for the sin.'[3] The latter is appended to the *'Amidah* prayer for each service of the Day of Atonement.[4]

LITERATURE.—For the ancient cultus: much new light has been thrown on this department of knowledge by excavation and discovery. For a good summary of these results see S. R. Driver, *Modern Research as illustrating the Bible* (*Schweich Lectures*), London, 1909; cf. also, H. Vincent, *Canaan d'après l'exploration récente*, Paris, 1907. For the discoveries at Gezer and elsewhere, the *PEFSt* of recent years, and R. A. S. Macalister's full summary in his *Excavation of Gezer*, 2 vols., London, 1912. All-important, too, are such studies as those of W. Robertson Smith, *Religion of the Semites*², London, 1894; W. W. Baudissin, *Studien zur semitischen Religionsgeschichte*, Leipzig, 1876–78; and the researches of S. Ives Curtiss, *Primitive Semitic Religion To-day*, London, 1902. See also the Hebrew, Jewish, and Semitic sections of artt. ALTAR, HIGH PLACE, IMAGES AND IDOLS, PRAYER, PRIEST, PROPITIATION, SACRIFICE (with the literature cited), and the corresponding artt. in the Bible Dictionaries; and the art. 'Kultus (Gottesdienst)' in Hamburger, ii. 658 ff.

For the later Temple-service, Hamburger as just cited; the elder Lightfoot (J. Lightfoot), *The Temple-Service* (*Works*, ix.), London, 1823; A. Edersheim, *The Temple: its Ministry and Services*, do., n.d. (still useful); art. 'Temple-Service' in *EBi*, cols. 4948–4956; A. Büchler, *Die Priester und der Cultus*, Vienna, 1895; J. Hochman, *Jerusalem Temple Festivities*, London, 1908 (important for sources). See also G. H. Box, *Virgin Birth of Jesus*, do. 1916, where various ceremonial usages of the later Temple are described. For the synagogue worship see the art. 'Gottesdienst, synagogalen,' by G. Dalman, in Herzog-Hauck (with the literature cited). The various works of L. Zunz are important in this connexion; also I. Elbogen, *Der jüdische Gottesdienst in seiner geschichtlichen Entwickelung*, Leipzig, 1913 (indispensable); I. Abrahams, *Annotated Edition of the Authorised Daily Prayer Book*, London, 1914, *Festival Studies*, do. 1906; cf. also W. O. E. Oesterley and G. H. Box, *A Short Survey of the Literature of Rabbinical and Mediæval Judaism*, London, 1920, pt. iii., *The Jewish Liturgy*; cf. also Lewis N. Dembitz, *Jewish Services in Synagogue and Home*, Philadelphia, 1898; and W. Rosenau, *Jewish Ceremonial*, Baltimore, 1903.

The following works of a general character deal with the worship both of the Temple and of the synagogue: Schürer, *GJV*³, § 24; W. Bousset, *Die Religion des Judentums im neutestamentlichen Zeitalter*², Berlin, 1906; W. O. E. Oesterley and G. H. Box, *The Religion and Worship of the Synagogue*², London, 1911. Other works have been cited in the body of the article.

G. H. BOX.

WORSHIP (Hindu).—Worship springs from the inward feeling of dependence upon other powers, from the awe caused in man's mind by the perception of supernatural agents which influence his or others' welfare. The desire to gain their favour or propitiate them, to call forth their sympathy, to appease or inflame their wrath, has led men to invent that instrument of rite and spell which is thought to ensure and even to enforce

[1] See Schürer, *Hist. of the Jewish People*, iv. 283 ff.; also iii. p. 10.

[2] Cf. *Tosephta Sukkāh* (ed. Zukermandel), p. 198.

[3] Cf. *Sota*, vii. 1 (exceptions 2).

[4] A lesson is also read (from a separate scroll) from the Prophets (*Haphtara*).

[5] K. Kohler, in *JE* iii. 10.

[1] It can be read in full in Singer, pp. 44–54.

[2] Singer, pp. 55–57. [3] *Ib.* pp. 259–262.

[4] See, further, art. PRAYER (Jewish).

their assistance. Rite and spell form the centre of primitive belief and of institutions of religious or social character in ancient times. The hypothesis advanced by R. Karsten 'that strange and dangerous objects and phenomena as well as fatal events of every kind have suggested to primitive man the existence of invisible spiritual powers in the universe,' 'that at first only the cruel and destructive aspect attracted man's attention, whereas the fruitful and beneficial one almost entirely escaped him,'[1] is, though well founded otherwise, not in accordance with the facts to be gathered from Sanskrit texts and needs reconsideration in that respect, or the Indian sacrifice must be assumed to have already passed this supposed stage of primitive belief.

Hindu writers divide the various kinds of sacrifice into two principal classes: *nitya* ('regular') and *naimittika* ('accidental') *karmāṇi*, one following the course of the year or the duties imposed upon man during life, the other comprising incidental offerings occasioned by special wishes of the sacrificer. This is, of course, a distinction more of practice than of principle, but it seems better than the modern distinction into thanksgiving, suppliant, and expiatory sacrifices, which to the student of Indian rituals will not appear sufficient; *e.g.*, the series of regular periodical offerings cannot be subsumed under any of these three classes. On the other hand, some scholars (*e.g.*, Wundt)[2] seem to overestimate the importance of expiatory ceremonies. The *prāyaśchitta*, though often mentioned, is more an accessory than a constructive element and mostly intended to rectify blunders committed against the ritual. We do meet with expiatory rites in Indian ritual,[3] but on the whole the idea of expiation, as far as sin is concerned, plays no prominent part; it is more a juridical than a ritual subject and is elaborately discussed in the lawbooks. We do not hear of thanksgiving sacrifice; even the term 'suppliant sacrifice' we cannot accept without restriction. Gods are invoked to come and take their share in offering, but there is no deep emotion, no uplifting of the heart or stirring of the soul; there always lingers the old idea that the god is ensnared by sacrifice and bound to render his assistance.

India thus testifies to the results arrived at by ethnographical writers 'that primitive worship, being prompted merely by the instinct of self-preservation or by interested motives, has no ethical character.'[4] It must, however, be added that in the *puruṣamedha* and the *sarvamedha* we find examples of the 'self-denying sacrifice'; for they enjoin abandonment of all property and renunciation of the world;[5] but it is to be remembered that the general tendency of these sacrifices has grown on Indian soil and seems to be somehow connected with the later idea of the *parivrājaka*, or 'religious mendicant.' Of the three purposes of sacrifice distinguished by La Grasserie[6] only the first can, in fact, be said to hold true of the Vedic sacrifice.

Every sacrifice forms an intrinsic unity, the special character of which throughout is dictated by the particular wishes for the fulfilment of which the sacrificer sets in motion the ritualistic apparatus. If the sacrificer aims at the life of an adversary, the priests offering the *śyena*-sacrifice must wear a red frontlet, sacrificial butter is made

[1] *Origin of Worship*, p. 40 ff.
[2] *Völkerpsychologie*, ii. 2, 330: 'der Ursprung des Opfers.'
[3] See art. EXPIATION AND ATONEMENT (Hindu); J. Jolly, *GIAP* ii. 8, § 36.
[4] Karsten, p. 97.
[5] A. Hillebrandt, *GIAP* iii. 2, § 77 f.
[6] *RHR* xliv. 35: 'Alimentaire pour les dieux, social et cosmosocial pour l'homme, expiatoire pour l'individu et pour le genre humain, dans ce dernier cas altruiste.'

from the milk of a sick cow, and the skin necessary for *soma*-pressing is taken from a cow used as *anustaraṇī* during the burial ceremonies. Subjects who wish to prosper their king offer the *gosava*-sacrifice, in which he is anointed on a levelled piece of ground (*sthaṇḍila*) and addressed as '*sthapati*.'[1] Of still more interest are the *vrātyastomas*[2] and the *mahāvrata*, or solstice-sacrifice, where drums are beaten in order to dispel the demons and assist the sun, and obscene rites symbolize the desired fertility. *Similia similibus* is the principle which permeates the whole cult.

The sacrifices of the domestic ritual, which are described in the *gṛhyasūtras*, are very simple; they are as a rule performed by the householder and his wife, but they often call in a *brāhmaṇa* or *pūjāri* to function in their stead or to assist. Persons of high rank, especially kings, had their spiritual adviser, the *purohita*; for the gods, it is said, do not eat the food of a king who has no *purohita*.[3] The sacrifices of the *śrauta* ritual, the complicated system of which is taught with the utmost care, all need priestly help, and the number of Brāhmanical functionaries increases up to sixteen in the *soma*-sacrifice, with its intricate ceremonial, its many hymns and chants.[4] Nearly all functions are left to this band of scholarly priests, with whom rests the power even to destroy the life of him who has entrusted them with their office. The *yajamāna* had to select the priests from the families of the Brāhmanical caste, and particular care had to be taken that they should be without bodily defects and well instructed; for any blunder in the strict observation of rules, in the proper wording or pronunciation of the sacred *mantras*, might annihilate the result of the sacrifice and even endanger the health and life of priests and *yajamāna*. It is comparatively little that the sacrificer and his wife can do themselves. Their part gradually became restricted to personal preparation or points of minor consequence.[5] An exception is found only in great *sattras*, or sacrificial sessions, where none but Brāhmans are admitted and the priestly duties devolve on the partakers. In India, therefore, more than elsewhere sacrifice has lost its social aspect, and, except in a few cases like the *rājasūya*, the *aśvamedha*, the aforesaid *sattras*, and a few traces of *sacra publica* in the *Rigveda*,[6] it can be regarded only as a private institution.

Particular care was bestowed on selecting the day fit for sacrifices and the place where the *tantra*, the sacrificial 'tissue,' was to be woven; there were no temples as in later times, but the special character of the sacrifice and priestly knowledge determined the spot where the holy grass had to be strewn as carpet for the gods and the fires had to be made. All *śrauta* sacrifices require three fires: the *āhavanīya*, the *dakṣiṇa*, and the *gārhapatya* fire, corresponding to heaven, antariksa, and earth, and dedicated to the world of gods, ancestors, and men.[7] No doubt, this way of selecting and preparing the sacred ground had its origin in the custom of pastoral tribes[8] pitching their tents anywhere, and had been retained by the conservative mechanism of sacrificial rules. Between the three fires (of which the *dakṣiṇa* serves also for conjuring purposes and is probably the successor of the old magic fire) the *vedi* is traced, a place of special sanctity, where the gods

[1] *Kāt.* xxii. 11. 11.
[2] *GIAP* iii. 2, p. 139, § 72.
[3] Oldenberg, *Rel. des Veda*², p. 375.
[4] See art. PRIEST, PRIESTHOOD (Hindu); J. Eggeling, *SBE* xii. [1882], xxi.; *Yajñeśvarasarman Vidyāsudhākara*, p. 61; A. Weber, *Indische Studien*, x. [Leipzig, 1868] 141 ff.; W. Caland and V. Henry, *L'Agniṣṭoma*, 2 vols., Paris, 1905–07; Oldenberg², p. 758 and *passim*.
[5] Cf. Oltramare, 'Le Rôle du Yajamāna,' *Muséon* IV. i. [1903].
[6] Hillebrandt, *Vedic Myth.*, ii. 121 ff.
[7] *Ib.* 90.
[8] Oldenberg², p. 345.

are supposed to sit down and take their meal, and every precaution is taken by word and action to ward off the demons and destroy their evil influences.

In the objects of sacrifice there is little variety. Different kinds of milk, cakes made of rice or barley, flour, etc., form the materials for the oblations of the new and full moon sacrifice and its almost endless modifications; the cakes are offered on potsherds or tablets, the number of which depends upon the character of the god to whom they are given. The ordinary *paśubandha*, or animal-sacrifice, requires goats, rams, bulls, which are offered almost indiscriminately to all gods, the difference generally being expressed by the shape, colour, and other bodily characteristics of the animal.[1] Horse-sacrifices (*aśvamedha* [*q.v.*]), which are regarded as an act of state and are of great importance, are of course an exception. There were in ancient India even human sacrifices, celebrated with the same pomp and following nearly the same ritual as the horse-sacrifice, till they were gradually replaced by the milder practice of an ordinary *paśubandha*.[2] Of other materials we find in a few cases *surā*, an intoxicating drink, sometimes in the *Rigveda* honey; the liquor the gods like best is the juice of the *soma*-plant, pressed and offered in the *agniṣṭoma* (a spring festival), and its numerous varieties. More than other sacrifices the *soma*-sacrifice is an imitation and representation of heavenly proceedings. As Soma, the moon, contains the heavenly ambrosia, so the yellow shoot of an unknown (and probably often changed) plant is supposed to yield that costly drink enjoyed by *devas* and *pitaras*. If an analogy to the 'sacrifice of the God,' so well treated by J. G. Frazer, ever existed in India, it cannot be looked for anywhere else than in the sacrifice of the plant representing a ray of the lunary god.

The norm of all sacrifices belonging to the *śrauta* ritual is given by the *darśa-pūrṇamāsaiṣṭi* (the new and full moon sacrifice), the *paśubandha* (animal-sacrifice), and the *agniṣṭoma* (the *soma*-offering); all other sacrifices follow these, with variations required by the special case. The whole series of ceremonies forms a *tantra*, 'tissue,' the framework, into which the *āvāpa* is inserted. The *tantra* remains the same for almost every sacrifice; the *āvāpa* consists of the chief offerings and invocations (verses, etc.) and varies according to circumstances. All ceremonies, unctions, libations, spells, etc., converge to the one point, to bring about that religious potency, 'the magical soul of the sacrifice,' as it may be called, which forms the spiritual instrument that ensures success. Hubert and Mauss[3] have well illustrated the metamorphosis which takes place in the persons as well as in the implements needed for sacrifice. All that concerns gods must be of divine character; the *yajamāna* must be prepared by certain rites in order to be worthy to approach the precincts of the supernatural. This is done by various penances, by shaving, bathing, abstaining from food and sexual intercourse, etc. Different substances are used to impart their mystic power, are poured over him, inhaled by him, etc. The implements are consecrated with *mantras* or *yajus*; *e.g.*, the rice is thrown into the winnowing basket with the words, 'I take you at the impulse of God Savitṛ, with the arms of the Aśvins,' etc. If they bring an animal-sacrifice, the sacrificial post erected on the *vedi* is sanctified by unctions and *mantras* and looked upon as a thing of superior holiness. The oblations are consecrated by various ceremonies, among which the *paryagnikaraṇa* deserves special mention.

The priest takes a firebrand and carries it three times round the oblation or the animal, describing thus a magic circle in order to keep off the demons and make the victim appropriate to the gods. Several libations precede the main offering. In an animal-sacrifice the divine essence, which permeates the animal when it is on the point of being immolated and sent along the path of gods, communicates itself to the *yajamāna*, who touches it on its way to the slaughtering place by means of the *vapāśrapaṇī*, the two spits upon which the *vapā* (the omentum) is later to be roasted. After the recitation of expiatory *mantras*, apologizing for the crime to be committed, the animal is 'quieted' by strangulation. Those performers who are not immediately concerned in this act step back and sit down, turning their face towards the *āhavanīya* fire in order to avoid being eye-witnesses of the act. The religious drama has then reached its climax. Among the parts of the animal assigned to the gods the omentum is most conspicuous; the blood is poured out for the demons, who later receive also the husks of the grain. Special parts of the principal oblations form the *iḍā*, which is the portion of the priests and the sacrificer and is regarded as a mystic deity who is invoked with great solemnity to come together with other mystic powers of the universe and bestow prosperity on the *yajamāna*. The ceremony then gradually relaxes: the 'tissue' has been woven, it must be dissolved again. As the drama after the peripetia, so the sacrifice must descend from the summit which it has reached and dismiss the performer from its magic circle to his worldly atmosphere. Various libations follow the *pradhānas*. The butter or fat that is left over is thrown into the fire; so are some of the implements, while others, especially those penetrated by some magic substance imparted to them by the purpose which they served, are concealed in the ground. The sacrificer finishes his vow by repeating the same *mantras* which he said at the beginning, of course with the modifications required by the different situation: he 'loosens' the sacrifice (*vimuñchati*). A bath in some cases concludes the sacrifice.

A good many accessory practices serve to enforce the general purpose of the sacrifice: the heads of certain animals, immured in the *agniciti*, give the altar strength and solidity; an *avakā* plant laid in the holes dug for the pillars or posts of the house prevents the house from breaking into a blaze. These accretions are like small rivulets which feed the main stream of sacrificial effectiveness. But secondary designs may also be fulfilled.

He who stands in need of rain has to fasten the rope by means of which the animal is tied to the sacrificial post, round the bottom; if the priest's intentions are friendly towards the sacrificer, he holds himself straight while offering; if his intentions are inimical, he stoops; if he wants somebody to be his friend, he turns the press-stones one towards the other. It is possible to foretell the future from single occurrences, to expiate certain blunders or faults, etc.—practices accompanying the sacrifice which crept into the ritual from an older stratum, from times when the ritual was less developed and mere symbolic actions sufficed to work man's will. But the difference is only one of degree. It is usual to draw a sharp line between magic and sacrifice (or, rather, religion; for sacrifice formed part of ancient religion). But the present writer fails to discover the line in the face of facts. Magic is the lowest stratum in the development of religion. The limits between magic and sacrifice are constantly shifting, in consequence not of change of system, of inward dissimilarity, but of intellectual progress and growing enlightenment.

'To the operator the magical act,' say R. R. Marett, 'is generally a projection of imperative will, and specifically one that moves on a supernormal plane.'[1]

If that will has become less imperative, a little more subdued by the feeling of being subjected to supernatural powers independent of itself, magical art has changed into religion. As the genius of Greek art lies concealed under the awkward attempts of antecedent times and awaits its release by the progress of intellect, so the genius of religion in order to be freed from the entangling net of magical superstition awaits the progress of civilization. If to a symbolic action the performer prefers a sacrifice, the instrument becomes some-

1 Oldenberg², p. 356; Hillebrandt, *Tiere und Götter im ved. Ritual*, Breslau, 1905.

2 Cf. artt. HUMAN SACRIFICE (Indian), SUICIDE (Hindu).

3 'Essai sur la nature et la fonction du sacrifice,' *ASoc* ii. [1897–98] 48, 51, 56 ff.

1 'From Spell to Prayer,' *FL* xv. 148.

what loftier, more refined by the invocation of higher powers, but remains altogether akin to the lower art of the magician. The god receives his share in order that he may grant the request; but he stands in need of the oblation as much as the sacrificer stands in need of his assistance. In the Indian sacrifice the mutuality begins to give way to the conception of the god's grace, but is not yet vanished. The mind of the ancient poets and ritualists is perfectly aware of the mystic power of sacrifice; we see it personified in the Vedic hymns and considered as a magical element by means of which the gods produced the world[1] and the ancestors achieved their wonderful deeds; to the ancient ritualists who invented countless legends in order to account for its origin, its disappearance and its single practices and variations,[2] it is still more; to them it appears as creator and creation, as centre of life and universe, even as a living being that is created and killed and reborn again in innumerable alternations. The present writer therefore agrees with Haug,[3] who was the first to define Indian sacrifice as 'a kind of witchcraft,' with Wundt,[4] who defines sacrifice as 'an outgrowth of magic art,' with Marett, who, though conceding that from one point of view magic and religion must be held apart in thought, yet thinks that from another point of view they may legitimately be brought together.[5] Sylvain Lévi is also of the same opinion:

'Le sacrifice qui règle les rapports de l'homme avec les divinités est une opération mécanique qui agit par son énergie intime; caché au sein de la nature, il ne s'en dégage que sous l'action magique du prêtre. Les dieux inquiets et malveillants se voient obligés de capituler, vaincus et soumis par la force même qui leur a donné la grandeur. . . . Le sacrifice a donc tous les caractères d'une opération magique.'[6]

The Indian sacrifice has, it is true, partly passed beyond this first stage and ascended a higher step; the very word *yajna*, equal to Iranian *yasna*, already betrays a loftier conception, and with still more reason this may be said of a great part of the Vedic hymns; but the ceremonial itself leaves no doubt that it is deeply rooted in magical art.

Inseparable from the sacrifice is the word.[7] With a few exceptions, which are met in ancestor-worship and offerings to malign deities and are easily accounted for,[8] the word, be it prose or verse, is the constant companion of ritual action, a kind of spiritual agent directing it to its goal.

'The spell or uttered "must,"' Marett says, 'will tend, I conceive, to embody the very life and soul of the affair. Nothing initiates an imperative more cleanly, cutting it away from the formative matrix of thought and launching it on its free career, than the spoken word. . . . It is the very type of a spiritual projectile.'[9]

The mystery of human speech has led to many speculations in India as well as elsewhere;[10] but it becomes, even according to Indian notions, especially important by association with sacrifice:[11] *vāg devebhyo yajñaṃ vahati* ('speech leads the sacrifice to the gods'), says *Śat. Brāhm.* i. 4.4.2. Corresponding with the tendency to make everything subordinate to the general character of the sacrifice, the ritual tries not only by different modulations (low, loud, mezzo, very frequent stoppings) to accommodate speech to the different situations, but also to distinguish from the formulas and prayers of the ordinary sacrifice the imprecations aiming at the destruction of the foe and his prosperity. The person who utters the malediction has to use 'rudenesses of speech,' *i.e.* words distinguished by hard consonants or otherwise expressive of its inward tendency.[1] A hymn having this imprecatory character, which may have once accompanied an act of sorcery, is met with in the collection of the *Rigveda.*[2] It is worth mentioning that also in other cases verses or formulas try to indicate, by choosing adequate expressions, the action they are intended to accomplish; a conciliatory spell, *e.g.*, repeats the preposition *sam* ('together' or 'with'), the plant *arundhatī*, healing broken limbs, is addressed in a *mantra* that often makes use of derivations from the root *ruh*, 'to grow.' The magical art often presses verses or formulas of the higher descent into its low service; prayers addressed to Artemis, Helios, or Christian saints sometimes appear auxiliary to witchcraft practices. The question has as yet not been answered—and probably remains unanswerable—whether this abuse is not comparatively modern and the texts may not have replaced older wordings more in keeping with the stratum to which the practices they are alluding to belong. It is a long way from spell to prayer, as long as from magic to sacrifice. The word ceases to be spell and turns into prayer as soon as it is felt to be depending in its effect, not upon the imperative will of the speaker, but upon the good will or the grace of a superhuman power. The modern notion of prayer, fashioned under the influence of Jewish and Christian creed, as lifting the heart to God and abiding in His will and law has not yet sprung up in Indian sacrifice. Even the prayer which we find at the end of the new and full moon sacrifice[3] seems more a conclusive recapitulation of the principal wishes than a prayer in our sense. The only exception in the ritual seems to occur in the sacrificial atmosphere of Varuṇa, where devotion of heart and forgiveness of sin form a characteristic feature. But it must be owned that there are prayers, at least in the Vedic collections of hymns and also in India, that testify to the universal existence of prayer in primitive times.[4] The 'salvum fac regem' of India[5] is by no means inferior to national anthems of modern nations, and there are other hymns of still higher type in the *Rigveda.* It seems probable that they represent, though earlier in time, a higher state of civilization than the sacrificial practices, which, though later recorded, nevertheless were inherited from remote antiquity.

[1] Bergaigne, *La Rel. véd.* (cf. Index, *s.v.* 'Sacrifice'); Ludwig, *Der Rigveda*, iii. 299 ff.; Oldenberg², p. 320.
[2] Sylvain Lévi, *La Doctrine du sacrifice*, Paris, 1898, *passim.*
[3] 'Ueber die ursprüngliche Bedeutung des Wortes *brahma*,' *SBAW*, 1868, p. 16.
[4] *Völkerpsychologie*, ii. 2, 339, 342, 447.
[5] *FL* xv. 165; cf. also M. Winternitz, 'Witchcraft in Ancient India,' *New World*, vii. [1898] 523.
[6] *La Doctrine du sacrifice*, pp. 9 f., 129. The views of Oldenberg² (p. 313 ff.), Oltramare ('Le Rôle du Yajamāna,' p. 3 ff.), and Lyall (*Asiatic Studies*², ii. 75 ff.) are somewhat different.
[7] Bergaigne, i. 296, ii. 267.
[8] Cf. also Oldenberg², p. 431.
[9] *FL* xv. 150. See also Hubert's excellent treatise on 'Magie,' *Dictionnaire des antiquités*, v. 31, p. 25 f.; Hubert and Mauss, 'Esquisse d'une théorie générale de la magie,' *ASoc* [1902–03] 51 ff.; V. Henry, *La Magie*, *passim.*
[10] D. G. Brinton, *Religions of Primitive Peoples*, London, 1898, p. 86; Bergaigne, Index, *s.v.* 'Prière.'
[11] Bergaigne, i. 296.

LITERATURE.—A. Bergaigne, *La Religion védique*, 3 vols., Paris, 1878–83, i.–iii. *passim* (cf. Index, *s.vv.* 'Sacrificateur,' 'Sacrifice,' 'Prière'); W. Caland, 'Over de "Wenschoffers"' (*Verslagen en Mededeelingen der Koninklijke Akad. van Wetenschappen, Afdeeling Letterkunde*, IV. 4), Amsterdam, 1902; J. G. Frazer, *GB*³, pt. i., *The Magic Art*, London, 1911, p. 52 ff.; V. Henry, *La Magie dans l'Inde antique*, Paris, 1904; A. Hillebrandt, *Rituallitteratur* (=*GIAP* iii. 2), Strassburg, 1897; E. W. Hopkins, 'Theories of Sacrifice as applied to the RV,' *PAOS* ccxxxix. [1895]; H. Hubert and M. Mauss, 'Essai sur la nature et la fonction du sacrifice' (*ASoc* ii. [1897–98]), Paris, 1899; R. Karsten, *The Origin of Worship*, Wasa, 1905 (Diss. of Helsingfors); Raoul La Grasserie, 'Du Rôle sociale du sacrifice religieux,' *RHR* xliv. [1901] 16 ff.; Sylvain Lévi, *La Doctrine du sacrifice dans les Brāhmana*⁵, Paris, 1898; Alfred Ludwig, *Der Ṛgveda*, 5 vols., Prague, 1876–88, iii. 296 ff., 353 ff.; R. R. Marett, 'From Spell to Prayer,' *FL* xv. [1904]

[1] Hillebrandt, *GIAP*, § 88, p. 170.
[2] vi. 53; *Ved. Myth.*, iii. 366.
[3] Hillebrandt, *Das altindische Neu- und Vollmondsopfer*, Jena, 1880.
[4] M. Müller, 'On Ancient Prayers,' *Semitic Studies in Memory of Alex. Kohut*, p. 1 ff.
[5] *Atharvaveda*, iv. 22.

132 ff.; F. Max Müller, 'On Ancient Prayers,' *Sem. Studies in Memory of Alex. Kohut*, Berlin, 1897, pp. 1–41; H. Oldenberg, *Religion der Veda*, do. 1894, p. 302 ff., 2p. 307 ff.; A. Réville, *Des Religions des peuples non-civilisés*, Paris, 1883; W. Robertson Smith, *Lectures on the Religion of the Semites*2, London, 1894, p. 414 ff., art. 'Sacrifice' in *EBr*; E. B. Tylor, *PC*, London, 1871, ch. xviii.; W. Wundt, *Völkerpsychologie*, Leipzig, 1906–09, ii. 2, 330 ff.

A. F. ALFRED HILLEBRANDT.

WORSHIP (Jain). — **I. Śvetāmbara.**[1] — (*a*) *Morning worship.*—The hour of the morning and more elaborate worship in a Śvetāmbara temple is 7.30. Leaving their shoes at the gateway that guards the temple courtyard, the worshippers come to a room where the more devout and more leisured exchange their secular dress for the two freshly-washed cloths[2] (a loin-cloth and a shoulder-scarf) in which alone they may enter the inner shrine. They also leave in this room any money they have brought and desire to keep, for the *tīrthaṅkara* must have everything on which his eye 'lights,' and those two cloths admit of no pockets for concealment. The worshippers now ascend the steps to the temple proper, at the doorway of which are two carved beasts supporting the threshold.[3] These are said to represent Yakṣa and Yakṣaṇī, the servants of the *tīrthaṅkara* to whom the temple is dedicated. It is left to the temple-servants to worship these beasts, the ordinary devotees having, so they say, no time to spend on them. The ritual acts of the lay-worshipper are our best guide in investigating this worship, for the temple-officiant, usually a Brāhman, or even a gardener by caste, can give no reliable instruction.[4]

In the open porch (*maṇḍapa*) outside the temple-door the devotee marks his own forehead with the auspicious saffron-mark (or *chandana*), using, of course, his third finger to make the mark, and then circumambulates the temple outside three times in the auspicious way, *i.e.* with his right hand nearest to the building. Still standing outside the temple, the worshipper joins his hands together in the attitude of prayer immortalized in Dürer's 'Praying Hands,' and says for the first time '*Nissahi.*' An instructed devout worshipper uses this expression not once (as is the common wont), but three times:[5] (1) he says it outside, in the temple-porch, asking that he may be cut off and freed from all worldly cares; (2) crossing the threshold and standing just inside, he again says it, asking that he may be cut off and freed from all thought of the temple-servants or his fellow-worshippers; (3) when he comes to the great spiritual point of his worship, he repeats the word once more, asking that he may be cut off from all thought of the worship he himself has offered, and enabled to concentrate all his thoughts on the qualities of the *tīrthaṅkara*.

As the worshipper crosses the raised threshold, it is interesting to see that he does not hesitate to put his foot on the plain boss of it—a thing no Brāhman would do, believing it to be the seat of Gaṇeśa.[6] The worshipper is now in the Hall of Assembly, or *sabhā maṇḍapa*, a hall supported by a circle of pillars and at the present day generally disfigured by the crudest colourings, terrible blues and reds and yellows mingled together on a plaster background; but in the older temples on Mount Abu (Rajputānā) or Śatruñjaya Hill (State of Palitāṇā) the delicate tracery in stone or marble of the struts between the pillars in this hall and the carved work surrounding the doorway leading to the inner shrine make the whole resemble a veritable ivory palace in fragility and delicacy. The worshipper proceeds at once to cross the threshold and enter the inner shrine (*gabhāro*). Visitors, however, must advance only up to the doorway; but, standing there, they can gain a view not only of the big image of the principal *tīrthaṅkara* (*muḷa nāyaka*) of that particular shrine,[1] perhaps Mahāvīra, to whom the whole temple is dedicated, and the two servants (Yakṣa and Yakṣaṇī) that flank the big image, but also of the rows of twenty-four smaller *tīrthaṅkara* that, arranged on a long altar-shelf, stretch on either side of the main image for the whole length of the inner shrine. There are very often two smaller doors leading from the Hall of Assembly to this inner shrine, and opposite each of these on the altar-shelf are arranged large images of some other *tīrthaṅkara*, perhaps Ādinātha and Ṛiṣabhadeva respectively. All the *tīrthaṅkara* in a Śvetāmbara temple are represented with staring glass eyes, and with carved stone loin-cloths. They are nearly always, too, seated figures, the larger images being adorned with jewels and flowers. Below the big central statue of Mahāvīra (let us say) may be seen a gleaming image of some *tīrthaṅkara* (perhaps Pārśvanātha) fashioned out of five metals.

On a lower altar-shelf there may or may not be a folding brass lotus-flower with some *tīrthaṅkara* in the centre and twenty-three smaller images of *tīrthaṅkara* in bas-relief on the petals; or a little tray with the eight good omens that always precede a *tīrthaṅkara*; or a copper plate (the *mantra* of Vijaya) covered with mystic symbols; or twenty-four two-inch brass plates, each bearing outline pictures of the *tīrthaṅkara*. All of these may or may not be present, but there must be at least one *Siddha chakra*, for no temple is complete unless it contains this crystallized creed of Jainism. The *Siddha chakra* resembles a little tray; in the centre is a raised figure of an Arihanta, and around it the figures of Sādhu, Upādhyāya, Āchārya, and Siddha, and between the encircling figures are written the names of the Three Jewels of the Jain faith: Right Knowledge, Right Faith, and Right Conduct, and *tapa* (austerity), the key-word to the Jain system.[2]

In a Śvetāmbara temple the worshipper bids for the right to win merit by performing the worship under the form of 'auctioning the *ghī*.' Any number of worshippers may purchase the right for sums varying from five annas to one rupee or more, and each successful bidder starts the morning worship again from the very beginning as soon as his predecessor has finished. The first worshipper enters the inner shrine and, removing the jewels and old flowers, performs *jaḷa pūjā*, *i.e.* washes the idol with water and milk and the five nectars, drying it afterwards most carefully with different cloths (*aṅgaluñchchanā pūjā*). As soon as the idol is dry, the worshipper rubs a little *barāsa*[3] all over it with his second and third fingers, and then marks it with liquid saffron (*chandana pūjā*) in fourteen different places in the following order:

[1] The worship of the non-idolatrous Sthānakavāsī sect has already been described in art. PRAYER (Jain).

[2] These two cloths the worshipper keeps in this room and pays the temple-servant to wash for him after every act of worship.

[3] These strange animals are also seen in every Hindu temple-threshold; for other explanations of them see the present writer's *Rites of the Twice-Born*, Oxford, 1920, p. 372.

[4] Śvetāmbara Jains can never in a Śvetāmbara temple receive money for worshipping; indeed they cannot even act as head clerk to the temple, so that those responsible for temple worship necessarily belong to an alien faith; hence the difficulty of gaining accurate knowledge of Śvetāmbara worship. Many Jains have private shrines in their own houses (there are said to be 360 in Ahmadābād alone); if they have, they worship there first in private before coming on to public temple worship.

[5] So far the writer has found no trace of this custom in a Hindu temple.

[6] See the present writer's *Rites of the Twice-Born*, p. 373.

[1] Recognizable at once by the differing symbols at the base of the idols.

[2] See the present writer's *Heart of Jainism*, p. 262.

[3] This *barāsa* is so expensive that it can only be applied to the chief image. A very rich worshipper might also case the image all over with gold- or silver-leaf.

right toe, left toe, right knee, left knee, right wrist, left wrist, right shoulder, left shoulder, top of skull, forehead, throat, heart, navel, and centre of right palm; and, as he marks it, he sings ten separate verses in its praise.

If the worshipper is a very rich man, he may now offer fifty rupees, in return for which he or (if he be indolent as well as rich) the temple-officiant will put on the idol its very best jewellery[1]—crown, necklace, ear-rings, bracelets, armlets, girdle, sandals, all of gold—and give it a gold or silver coco-nut to hold in its hands. (The best jewellery may also include ropes of pearls.) If the worshipper cannot afford more than twenty-five rupees, the second-best jewellery only will be brought out. Except when a wealthy client is present or on great festivals, the ordinary worshipper proceeds at once to decorate the statue with flowers and garlands (*puṣpa pūjā*). He then steps outside[2] the inner shrine to perform the remaining ritual acts; he waves a stick of incense (*dhūpa pūjā*) and a lamp (*dīpa pūjā*) at the threshold of the shrine, and places on the table in the Hall of Assembly before the doorway of the inner shrine rice (*akṣata pūjā*), the only grain which (unlike Hindu ritual) can ever be offered in a Jain temple, sugar (*naivedya pūjā*), and fruit (*phaḷa pūjā*), such as coco-nut, plantains, mangoes, or almonds.[3] It is important to notice how the last three offerings are made.

The worshipper arranges the rice in the following form:

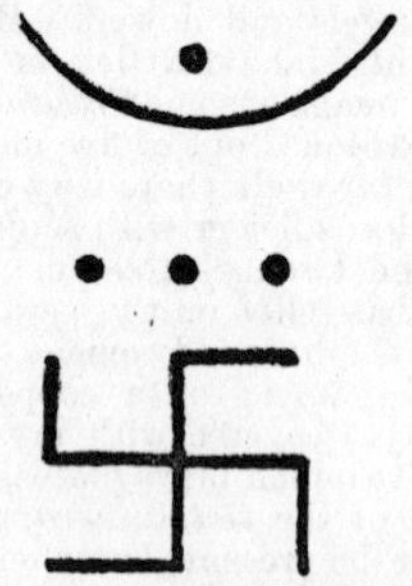
(c)

(b)

(a)

On the centre of (*a*), if a rich man, he places a coin of varying value, and beside it or on it he places the sugar and the fruit. This *swastika* sign (*a*) symbolizes the *gati* in which a man may be born according to his accumulated hoards of past *karma*, either as a dweller in heaven or in hell, as a man or a beast. The three little heaps (*b*) represent the Three Jewels of the Jain faith which lead a man to *mokṣa* (*c*), symbolized by the sign of one dot in the segment of a circle.

In studying the worship in a Jain or a Hindu temple special attention must always be paid to four points:

(1) Who is allowed to go into the inner shrine. It was surprising to be told that in a Śvetāmbara temple any devout Jain lady of position who had bathed and came wearing clean clothes might enter the inner shrine and indeed perform every ritual act that a layman is allowed to do.[4]

(2) What change the offering undergoes by being offered to a god. In a Jain temple the deeply interesting change from *naivedya* to *prasāda*[5] is unknown, and the word *prasāda* is never used, but in a Śvetāmbara or Digambara temple, once food has been offered to the *tīrthaṅkara*, it is called *deva dravya*, or, very often by the ignorant, *nirmalya*.[1]

(3) What may and may not be offered. In a Digambara temple no fresh fruit may be offered, and in a Śvetāmbara temple no over-ripe fruit may be given.

(4) Perhaps most illuminating of all, who eats the offering. In a temple of Viṣṇu all can take communion with their god and eat the food, which is known as *prasāda*; in a temple of Śiva only a fallen and despised set of *pujāris* known as *atita*[2] can eat the food, which, once it has been offered, is called *nirmalya*; but in some Śvetāmbara temples, as a mark of special honour, Bhāṭas are given the fruit and the sugar, the rice being sold to 'menial people' in open market, for no Jain of position would knowingly buy and eat *deva dravya*.

To account for the honour paid to the Bhāṭas, the legend is told of how, when Muhammad Ghazni was in power, two Bhāṭas laid their living bodies on the burning pyre at Pālitāṇā day after day and were burnt to death, to ransom the images on the sacred Hill of Śatruñjaya from desecration. In commemoration of their heroism, the whole offering (fruit, sugar, and rice) is given to Bhāṭas in the State of Pālitāṇā; elsewhere they are sometimes given the fruit and sugar only.

If there be no Bhāṭa, the head-clerk of the temple distributes the fruit and sugar among the temple-servants and their children.

As a rule, cooked food is not offered in a Śvetāmbara temple, but on the occasion of a marriage in his family some wealthy client might send down a specially dainty dish. This would be put on the open table in the Hall of Assembly, and not offered behind a curtain, as in a temple of Viṣṇu,[3] and would afterwards be eaten by a Bhāṭa or, failing him, by a temple-servant.

When these offerings have been duly made and arranged, all is ready for the great act of spiritual worship. 'As bread is flavourless without salt,' runs the proverb, 'so worship is without savour and useless, unless *bhāva pūjā* be performed.' The worshipper first prostrates himself three times (*chaityavandana pūjā*) before the main idol (the *mula nāyaka*), which gazes out from its shelf in the inner shrine into the Hall of Assembly, and then says the third *Nissahi*, asking to be cut off from all remembrance of his own acts of worship and offerings. He proceeds to perform *bhāva pūjā*; but neither then nor at any other time does he offer petitions for any spiritual or material boon; rather he encourages himself by remembering the virtues of the *tīrthaṅkara*, 'like a soldier before the tomb of Napoleon,' and devotes himself to singing the saint's praises. Finally he walks backwards, as though in the presence of royalty, to the main door, towards which the chief image is looking ('only a "fool-man" walks out by a side door'), and, arrived at the threshold, repeats the word *Avissahi*, thereby asking to be allowed to follow his necessary avocations every day. As he says it, he bows with joined hands to the idol. A devout Jain will say this word again as he leaves the porch of the temple, and a third time before he passes out into the street from the gateway of the temple courtyard; but the uninstructed generally content themselves with saying it once.

'It is "compulsory" on us to do part of this worship in the early morning, and part of it at noon,' said a leading Jain official to the writer, 'but, as we are in Government offices at mid-day, we do it all together in the morning.'

On the great festivals, and at places of pilgrimage like Śatruñjaya, Abu, and Girnār, the writer has witnessed more elaborate worship. Sometimes royal worship is offered, when a brush of Tibetan cow's hair (*chamarī pūjā*) is waved in front of the main image, and three silver umbrellas are placed

[1] Note that, unlike a Vaiṣṇava idol, the images of the male *tīrthaṅkara* are never draped in actual clothes.

[2] A worshipper in ordinary dress can perform the remaining acts, as they are done outside the inner shrine.

[3] If a child, *e.g.*, comes into a temple accidentally bringing with it a plantain, or some sugar, or a copper coin in its open hand, these must be added to the offering, for 'the eye of the god has lighted on them.'

[4] The present writer, however, has never actually seen a woman enter the inner shrine.

[5] For the change the offering undergoes in a Hindu temple see the present writer's *Rites of the Twice-Born*, p. 385.

[1] This word properly belongs to food offered to Śiva.

[2] See *Rites of the Twice-Born*, p. 320.

[3] *Ib.* p. 402.

over it. At other times a silver image of some *tīrthaṅkara* is placed on a silver throne in the Hall of Assembly. The men all sit on one side and the women on the other and offer *snātra pūjā*, by singing songs in its honour. Or a pilgrim may purchase the privilege of sitting in a silver chariot, holding a little silver image in his lap, and being thus dragged three times round outside the temple —a sort of circumambulation *de luxe*. On Śatruñjaya Hill a special pilgrimage is performed, known as 'the Ninety-nine,' when daily for over three months the pilgrim must toil up the stone stairway to the top of the hill, circumambulate the most famous temple, and tramp down again in honour of the ninety-nine thousand times that a *tīrthaṅkara* visited Śatruñjaya. 'But, as life is short, we only do it ninety-nine times, and leave out the thousands!' On the last day of the ninety-nine the pilgrim offers the eightfold worship with more than the usual 'harmony-barmony,'[1] as an English-speaking Jain once called it.

In a big Śvetāmbara temple there is often a map of Mount Abu, a plan of Sameta Śikhara (in Bengal), or a model of the great temple of Śatruñjaya. On the special days when merit is gained by going to these pilgrim resorts a man who is too poor or too busy to undertake the journey may yet gain merit by offering to the map or plan or model the fourfold *pūjā* of lamp, incense, rice, and fruit. In the same way, if a man is too ill to get out of bed and come to the temple, he may offer worship to a picture of the twenty-four *tīrthaṅkara* at home,[2] for the Indian proverb runs prettily: 'If you cannot offer a flower, offer a petal.'

All through the day worshippers can come and do *bhāva pūjā*, for the god is never put down for a siesta as among the Hindus in a temple of Viṣṇu, though the wired doors of the inner shrine are often locked to keep off thieves.

(*b*) *Evening worship*.—In the evening, as a rule, only the paid temple-officiant enters the inner shrine, for no layman wants the trouble of bathing and donning the special dress so late in the day. At sunset the hanging lamps in the Hall of Assembly are lighted, as are also two or more lamps of clarified butter in the inner shrine; and, before beginning the evening service, the officiant lights some incense and places it in front of the chief idol of the temple. Then the right to perform the evening worship is auctioned (it can be sold to five successive worshippers), and the officiant from inside the shrine hands to the highest bidder the little *āratī* lamp. This consists of two tiers of lamps; in the upper tier is only one lamp, and in the lower there are five; in each of these six lamps a little wick is floating in clarified butter.[3] Five times the worshipper waves this from left to right, singing, as he does so, the special *āratī* hymn, whilst all the other worshippers bang gongs, beat drums, and make as much noise as possible. Each successful bidder follows suit. When the *āratī pūjā* is complete, the waving of the *maṅgala-dīpaka* is performed. A *maṅgala* lamp consists of a lamp in a saucer; it burns camphor in the saucer and *ghī* in the lamp itself; it has only one wick and can be auctioned to only one worshipper. As the worshipper waves it from left to right three times, he sings the *maṅgala-dīpaka* hymn, and again all the instruments, musical and unmusical, are played. The object of the *āratī*-waving is said to be to protect the worshippers themselves from all molestation by evil powers of darkness during the night. The *maṅgala-dīpaka* is waved for the welfare of the whole world. The incense is allowed to burn itself out, which it does by about 8.30 p.m., when all the shrine doors are locked by the officiant and (since the jewels are left on the idol all night) inspected by the temple watchman before the final shutting up of the temple about 9 o'clock. It is noticeable that (unlike the evening ritual in a temple of Viṣṇu), there is no stretching out of the hands by the worshippers to either *āratī* or *maṅgala-dīpaka*.

2. Digambara.—(*a*) *Morning worship*.—It is easier to obtain information in a Digambara temple, since the officiant there is himself a Jain. The main lines of the worship are the same as in the Śvetāmbara temple (washing, drying, offering rice, dry fruit, incense, and lamp); but between the worship in a Digambara temple which belongs to the Terāpanthī and that in one belonging to the Visapanthī there are many minor differences. In any Digambara temple the idols on the long shelf in the inner shrine have no eyes, no carved loin-cloths, and wear no jewels or flowers. Fresh fruit cannot be offered to them, and no woman on any consideration is allowed to enter the inner shrine (for with the Digambara no woman as such can obtain salvation). The privilege of performing worship is not put up to auction, and the *jaḷa pūjā* can be performed only at one time, not at intervals of thirty minutes or an hour, as in a Śvetāmbara temple. The idol is washed with plain water (not water mixed with milk or nectars), and it has seemed to the writer, as she watched, that even greater care is shown by Digambara that not one drop of water should fall to the ground. Among the Visapanthī the idol is marked with *chandana* on both toes; but the Terāpanthī do not mark the idol itself when performing *chandana pūjā*, but mix the saffron with the rice on the table.

One main difference that strikes every visitor is that, whereas in a Śvetāmbara temple the whole Hall of Assembly is dotted with worshippers, who (having done at any time they chose as many of the ritual acts of washing, drying, marking, and offering as they had leisure for) are now seated each before a separate little stool, arranging the rice in the mystic way and offering coin and fruit, then telling their beads, and doing their *bhāva pūjā*, in a Digambara temple there is one united act of worship.[1] The rice and dried fruit are all arranged in separate little heaps on one tray on one table, and are removed by the priests from that tray to form a large mound on another tray. In front of the main idol on a table in the Hall of Assembly the officiant arranges a tall vase like an upturned chalice, two brass tumblers of water, a full tray containing rice, almonds, and sugar arranged in separate heaps, and an empty tray marked with a *swastika*. He then stands behind the table on a little stool and to the accompaniment of elaborate genuflexions and intonings transfers the contents of the full tray to the empty one[2] and the upturned chalice. The food thus ceremonially transferred in the presence of the idol changes from *naivedya* to *deva dravya*. But here again the most important part of the worship is the mental *bhāva pūjā*, when the officiant stands silent, then bows, and finally kneels, touching the floor with his head, mentally repeating *mantras* all the time. So essential do they count this that an officiant in a Digambara temple said to the writer: 'If any one spent a lakh of rupees on performing the eight-fold worship, it would all be worthless without *bhāva pūjā*.'

[1] See *Heart of Jainism*, p. 254.

[2] In this case, instead of marking it with freshly ground and moistened saffron, he scatters over the picture dried saffron (*vaskepa*) brought from the temple.

[3] No lamp may be burnt in the inner shrine, unless it contains *ghī* or camphor. Oil is never allowed there.

[1] At least in the writer's part of India.

[2] For full details of the transference see *Notes on Modern Jainism*, p. 91.

(*b*) *Evening worship.*—All sects of the Śvetāmbara that the writer has met perform *āratī*; but, though among the Digambara it is performed by the Visapanthī, the Terāpanthī perform neither *āratī* nor *maṅgala-dīpaka*, contenting themselves with lighting a lamp, carefully protected by glass, in the inner shrine and burning incense there. But, though Terāpanthī have no lamps, they sing songs and read some of their scriptures aloud in the temples at their evening worship.

It is interesting to notice that (unlike the ritual in a Viṣṇu temple) neither among the Śvetāmbara nor among any sect of the Digambara is food ever offered to the gods at night.

'We account it a sin to eat after the lamps are lit, for inadvertently we might eat some insect; how could we then offer food in the temples after sunset and so force our *tīrthaṅkara* to sin?'

LITERATURE. — The writer has confined herself to temple worship, as other forms of worship have been dealt with under PRAYER (Jain), FESTIVALS AND FASTS (Jain). The researcher should notice local differences; *e.g.*, temple worship on Mt. Abu is described in the present writer's *Notes on Modern Jainism*, Oxford, 1910, while for temple worship in Rājkot and Pālītāṇā reference may be made to *The Heart of Jainism*, Oxford, 1915. In addition to these, new material for the present article has been derived mainly from the worship in the temples at Junāgadh at the foot of Girnār, the famous Jain pilgrim resort. MARGARET STEVENSON.

WORSHIP (Japanese). — I. *SHINTŌ CULT DESCRIBED IN THE ECLIPSE-MYTH.*—The various component parts of Shintō worship have already been treated in separate articles. The best way to gather them into a complete whole, and to picture the actual worship, will be to give the old account of the eclipse-myth, and by simple references connect with it the details already examined. For this story is not only the nucleus of Japanese mythology, but also the most primitive and most authentic description of Shintō worship, since it was written expressly for the purpose of giving the legendary origin of the chief ceremonies of this worship, as officially practised at the court of the mikado in the most ancient times, and of explaining the ascendancy of the great priestly families who officiated in them. We therefore have in this text, which is more than 1200 years old, a brief account of all that is essential in the rites of Shintō worship and its priests.[1]

First of all, let us recall how, by reason of certain offences committed by the terrible god Susa-no-wo,[2] the sun-goddess, Amaterasu, shut herself up in the rocky cavern of heaven, and left the world in darkness (*toko-yo*, 'eternal night'); how the eight hundred myriad gods in dismay then assembled in the dried-up bed of the Tranquil River of Heaven (the Milky Way), to take counsel as to how they might induce the goddess to come forth from her retreat; and how for this purpose their usual counsellor, the god of artifice, Omohikane, conceived a plan, which was nothing else than the transference to the sky of the terrestrial rites of Shintō, but which, naturally, is given us as having been, on the contrary, their prototype. The plan was as follows:

'Assembling the long-singing birds of eternal night and making them sing; taking the hard rocks of heaven from the river-bed of the Tranquil River of Heaven, and taking the iron from the heavenly Metal-Mountains; calling in the smith Amatsu-mara; charging His Augustness Ishi-kori-dome to make a mirror, and charging His Augustness Tama-no-ya to make an augustly complete string of curved jewels eight feet long, of five hundred jewels; and summoning His Augustness Ame-no-Koyane and His Augustness Futo-dama, and causing them to pull out with a complete pulling the shoulder of a true stag from the heavenly Mount Kagu, and take heavenly *haha-ka*[1] from the heavenly Mount Kagu, and perform divination; and pulling up by pulling its roots a true *sakaki* with five hundred branches from the heavenly Mount Kagu; and taking and putting upon its upper branches the augustly complete string of curved jewels eight feet long, of five hundred jewels, and taking and tying to the middle branches the mirror eight feet long, and taking and hanging upon its lower branches the white soft offerings and the blue soft offerings; His Augustness Futo-dama taking these divers things and holding them together with the grand august offerings; and His Augustness Ame-no-Koyane prayerfully reciting a grand ritual; and the deity Ame-no-Tajikara-wo standing hidden beside the door; and Her Augustness Ame-no-Uzume hanging round her the heavenly *hikage* of the heavenly Mount Kagu as a sash, and making the heavenly *masaki-no-kazura* her head-dress, and binding the leaves of the *sasa* of the heavenly Mount Kagu in a posy for her hands, and laying a sounding-board before the door of the heavenly Rock-Dwelling, and stamping till she made it resound, and doing divine possession, and pulling out the nipples of her breasts, and pushing down her skirt-string *usque ad privatas partes.*'[2]

Thereupon, as the *Kojiki* says, 'the Plain of High Heaven shook and the eight hundred myriad Deities laughed together.' Amazed at this Homeric laughter, the sun-goddess slightly opens the door of the heavenly cavern. To entice her further, the artful Uzume explains to her that the gods are rejoicing 'because there is a Deity more illustrious than Thine Augustness,' and at the same time Ame-no-Koyane and Futo-dama push the mirror towards her, which induces her to come out still farther from the door. At this moment Ame-no-Tajikara-wo seizes her by the hand and drags her out, while Futo-dama immediately stretches behind her a *shiri-kume-naha* ('bottom-tied-rope,' *i.e.* a rope made of straw drawn up by the roots, which stick out from the end of the rope), saying to her, 'Thou must not go back farther in than this.'[3] From this moment the universe is illuminated anew, to the great joy of gods and men.

II. *ANALYSIS OF THE VARIOUS ELEMENTS OF CULT EMBODIED IN THIS MYTH.*—In this famous episode we observe certain rites which are more especially connected with the special object of the story, *i.e.* with the magical means to be employed to cause light to reappear when, for some reason or other (eclipse, typhoon, heavy clouds), the sun hides for such a long time that primitive man becomes afraid. These means are the 'long-singing birds of eternal night,'[4] *i.e.* cocks, which were made to utter their long cry in front of the cavern, and which are found symbolically represented in the old temple of the sun-goddess at Ise by dancers called *tona-ko* ('bird-cry'); with the roosts of those sacred birds (kept for the ordinary purpose of heralding the dawn, but also, when need arises, for evoking daylight by magical means) native philologists connect the origin of *tori-i*,[5] the well-known gateway of Shintō temples, although it seems rather to be a continental importation.[6] It is in the same spirit that, in another version of this myth,[7] it is stated that the goddess Uzume, in the midst of her dance, 'kindled a fire,' the aim of which was likewise to evoke the solar light by imitative magic, and which represents the legendary prototype of the *nihabi* ('courtyard fire'), practised in certain ceremonies of Shintō worship, especially in the nocturnal rite of the *nihi-name* ('new tasting'). But, besides those rites which belong more specially to eclipse-ceremonial, this episode also describes rites of a more general character.

1. The solar mirror, central point of the national worship.—First of all, we see the celestial gods

[1] The original text in Chinese characters, with reading in *kana* and transcription, is published in M. Revon, *Le Shinntoïsme*, pt. i., Paris, 1907, pp. 414–428. An English tr. will be found in B. H. Chamberlain, *Kojiki*[2] (*TASJ*, vol. x., suppl.), Tōkyō, 1906, p. 63 ff., and a French tr. in M. Revon, *Anthologie de la littérature japonaise*[4], Paris, 1919, p. 46 ff.

[2] See the enumeration of those *ama-tsu-tsumi* ('heavenly sins') in art. SIN (Japanese), § 2.

[1] The words not translated are explained below, p. 803[b].

[2] *Kojiki*[2], tr. Chamberlain, *loc. cit.*, into which, however, the present writer has introduced some modifications; cf. his *Anthologie, loc. cit.*

[3] *Kojiki*[2], p. 65.

[4] Or, perhaps, here, 'eternal land,' the continent of Asia, from which those animals were said to have been imported.

[5] *Tori*, 'bird,' 'fowl'; *i*, from *iru*, 'dwelling.'

[6] On this question of *tori-i* see B. H. Chamberlain, 'A Preliminary Notice of the Luchuan Language,' in *JAI* xxvi. [1897] 47 ff., and *Things Japanese*[3], London, 1898, p. 407; S. Tuke, 'Notes on the Japanese Tori-i,' in *Trans. Japan Soc. of London*, iv. [1898] pt. ii. p. 81 ff.; W. G. Aston, 'Tori-wi, its Derivation,' in *TASJ* xxvii. [1899] pt. iv. p. 153 ff.; Eugène Goblet d'Alviella, *La Voie des Dieux*, Brussels, 1906, p. 22.

[7] *Nihongi: Chronicles of Japan . . . to A.D. 697*, tr. W. G. Aston, London, 1896, i. 44.

taking rocks from the River of Heaven and iron from the Metal Mountains, *i.e.* the iron mines of primitive Japan, for the purpose of manufacturing a mirror under the superintendence of the gods Ama-tsu-mara (the Cyclops of Japanese mythology, also with a single eye, whose name, meaning *cœlestis penis*, is evidently connected with the old phallic cult)[1] and Ishi-kori-dome (the mythical ancestor of the manufacturers of mirrors, whose obscure name may mean 'stone-cutter,' and consequently call up the idea of stone moulds in which certain metal objects were cast). This 'mirror of eight feet' (*ya-ta-kagami*) is still a magical means of recalling the star whose form and brilliance it imitates, in the same way as other 'mirrors of the sun' (*hi-kagami*) which are discussed elsewhere.[2] But, besides the special function which it is called upon to perform in this episode, the solar mirror fills a much larger rôle in Shintō worship in general, in which, in the temple of Ise, it represents the sun-goddess herself, and therefore forms the very centre of the national worship.

The fact that the present mirror at Ise is, in the imagination of the Japanese, the same as was forged at the time of the eclipse is due both to the *Kojiki*[3] and to the *Nihongi*.[4] The latter says that the mirror of the eclipse 'is the great deity who is worshipped at Ise'; and, as this sacred object shows a slight flaw, it is explained quite naturally by the hypothesis of a blow which it received against the door of the cavern.[5] It is therefore a case of a primitive talisman which afterwards became the greatest national fetish. For before long the sun-goddess herself bestows it upon her grandson, Ninigi-no-mikoto, in terms which clearly show that her soul is united with it, by the application of a conception, wide-spread among primitive races, of the mysterious relations that may exist between a mirror and a soul.

'Regard it,' she said, 'as my august spirit, and worship it as if thou wert worshipping in my presence.'[6] And again: 'Let it be with thee in thy home, on thy mat; let it be sacred to thee!'[7] And, when she deputes two other gods to accompany her grandson on the earth, viz. Ame-no-Koyane and Futo-dama, who are precisely the ancestors of the great national sorcerers, 'Watch over me,' she commands them; 'take care, both of you, of this mirror and guard it well.'[8]

From that time the solar mirror becomes the most important and most precious of the three regalia (mirror, sword, and jewel) of the sovereign house. Later, however, a timid emperor, worried with his responsibilities in a time of public disorders, was uncomfortable at the thought that he was living with such a formidable deity; he broke the tradition which had been observed up to this time and entrusted the mirror to an imperial priestess, who kept it in a neighbouring village; she, in her turn, transferred it to the princess of Yamato, the famous vestal who, after various religious travels, stopped finally at Ise according to the instructions of the goddess.[9] There, in the bosom of the 'inner temple' (*naïku*), the mirror will henceforward rest, invisible in its precious tabernacle.

This supreme object of Shintō worship is, as a matter of fact, enclosed in a brocade bag, which is never opened; when the old material shows signs of giving way, the whole is put into a new bag: so that to-day the mirror is enfolded in several layers of silk. Thus protected, it is in addition enclosed in a box of *hi-no-ki*,[10] provided with eight handles, placed on a slightly raised stand, and covered with a piece of white silk. Lastly, above all this there

[1] See art. NATURE (Japanese), vol. ix. p. 239a.
[2] See Revon, *Shinntoïsme*, pt. i. p. 212, note.
[3] P. 130.
[4] i. 48.
[5] *Ib.*
[6] *Kojiki*², p. 130.
[7] *Nihongi*, i. 83.
[8] *Ib.*; cf. i. 76.
[9] *Ib.* pp. 151 f., 176 f.
[10] *Chamæcyparis obtusa*, a sort of *Thuya*.

is a sort of cage of white wood, with ornaments of pure gold, itself enveloped in a rough silk curtain, which reaches to the ground on every side. These coverings of the box are all that the people are allowed to see on the festivals on which the sanctuary is opened.

Viscount Mori, the Minister of Public Instruction, who dared to raise a corner of an outer curtain of the sanctuary at Ise, was soon after, on the very day on which the new constitution of Japan was proclaimed in 1889, assassinated by a fanatic Shintōist, whose tomb became a place of pilgrimage.

Although the sun-goddess was the only one in the mythology who assumed the particular form of a mirror, other deities are represented by the same object; *e.g.*, it is said that in the other great temple of Ise, the 'outer temple' (*geku*), the *mi-tama-shiro* (substitute for the august spirit) of the goddess of food is likewise a mirror, as well as the fetishes of the *ahi-dono no kami* (deities of a joint shrine), which are also worshipped in those two great temples. This is simply a natural generalization of the material side of the cult. The mirror of the sun has gradually become multiplied, and, under Buddhist influence, it has ended in being exhibited in all the temples, though the sacred fetish of Ise remained hidden from human eyes.

2. The sacred jewel.—The eclipse-myth relates further that the god Tama-no-ya ('jewel-ancestor'), from whom the hereditary corporation of jewellers claims to be descended, makes a necklace of numerous jewels. The name of this necklace is very difficult to interpret,[1] and its history throughout the centuries is no less uncertain.[2] The imperial jewel, at first identified with the necklace of the eclipse,[3] was gradually reduced to the single sacred stone, two or three inches in diameter, which is carefully preserved to this day in the palace of Tōkyō. But, in spite of the religious character of the mikados, this jewel is evidently of little cult importance compared with the sacred mirror.

3. Priests.—Later in the text there appear two gods who are important from the point of view of worship—Ame-no-Koyane (etymology uncertain), the ancestor of the *nakatomi*, the high priests, 'mediators' between the gods and the mikado, who recited the ritual in name of the latter, and Futo-dama (perhaps 'great jewel,' but more probably 'great gift'), the ancestor of the *imibe*, those 'abstaining' priests who were specially charged with preparing the offerings.[4]

4. Divination.—Those two gods pull out the shoulder of a stag from Mount Kagu (mountain of heaven, which quite naturally has its homonym in Yamato), and take from the same mountain the bark of a certain tree (*haha-ka* [cherry? or birch?]) in order to light a fire to roast the shoulder-blade, the cracks in which they will then examine for divinatory signs. The ancient Japanese, as a matter of fact, always practised divination when they found themselves in presence of any unusual phenomenon, and their gods naturally did the same, for they were by no means conceived as omniscient.[5] Omoplatoscopy was the favourite form of divination—the official 'greater divination.'[6]

5. Sacred tree of Shintō.—The gods then uproot a *sakaki*[7] with five hundred (*i.e.* countless) branches. This tree, which is evergreen, is the sacred tree of Shintō, and is usually found planted in the precincts of the temples; it furnishes wands

[1] See Revon, *Shinntoïsme*, p. 224, note 5.
[2] *Ib.* p. 225.
[3] *Kojiki*², p. 130.
[4] See, for the *nakatomi*, art. PRAYER (Japanese), vol. x. p. 189b, and, for the *imibe*, art. SACRIFICE (Japanese), vol. xi. p. 22a.
[5] See art. DIVINATION (Japanese), vol. iv. p. 801b.
[6] *Ib.* p. 802a.
[7] *Cleyera japonica*; a fairly good idea of this tree may be got from the fact that the family of *Ternstrœmiaceæ*, to which it belongs, includes also the camellia and the tea-plant.

for the *oho-nusa* and the *tama-gushi*,[1] and its branches, which are always carried in funeral processions, make it possible to distinguish at a glance a Shintōist funeral from a Buddhist one. The use of evergreen trees, especially cypress, in ancient times in the West and also in China is analogous.

6. Offerings.—The gods now hang the necklace on the higher branches, the mirror midway, and the offerings of soft materials on the lower branches. The natives of Banks Islands have a similar rite to obtain sunlight; they employ a circular stone, called 'the stone of the sun,' which they decorate with ribbons and fix in a high tree.[2] The offerings of white and blue materials made on this occasion are the general type of Shintōist offerings which play the chief part in the worship,[3] and which have already been exhaustively treated.[4]

7. Recitation of the ritual.—While Futo-dama presents these offerings, Ame-no-Koyane fervently pronounces a ritual whose powerful words (*futo-norito-goto*) are to force the will of the goddess. The character of these Shintō liturgies has already been treated.[5] It should be noted that, besides the magical effect of the recited formula, those old Shintō prayers had also the intention of charming the gods by their literary beauty, as a sort of offering.[6] The respectful gestures accompanying them have also been described.[7]

8. Sacred dance of priestesses and divine possession.—Lastly there appears upon the scene Ame-no-Uzume ('heaven's dread female'), the legendary ancestress of the Sarume-no-kimi ('princesses of Saru,' from *saru*, 'monkey,' and *me* 'woman'), a priestly corporation of court dancers, so called by reason of another myth.[8] With some *hikage* she makes an arm-support (*tasuki*, 'hand-helper'), *i.e.* a kind of cord like that which the imperial stewards, referred to in this connexion in the Ritual of the Great Purification (*Oho-harahi*), had round their necks; the ends were fastened to their wrists to enable them to carry heavy things more easily; she makes a garland for her head (*kazura*) with *masaki-no-kazura*,[9] and a bouquet (*ta-gusa*) with leaves of *sasa*[10] (generic name of various small bamboos). Then she places in front of the cavern the sounding-board on which she is to perform her dance, the prototype of the sacred pantomime (*kagura*) which is still one of the regular rites of Shintō worship—an æsthetic offering to the gods—and which may be seen danced at the present day by young priestesses wearing masks and damask draperies, on the platform of a special building in the precincts of certain temples, like those of Ise and Nara.[11] Uzume soon reaches a state of ecstasy (*kamugakari-* or *kangakari-shite*), 'doing divine possession,' the real or simulated character of which may be disputed,[12] but which in any case corresponds exactly with what we know of the important rôle of nervous phenomena in the ancient practices of Shintō, as they may be observed even at the present day.[13]

[1] Cf. art. SACRIFICE (Japanese), vol. xi. p. 22^b.
[2] See Revon, *Shinntoïsme*, p. 212, note; and cf. *Nihongi*, i. 46, which shows clearly that the 'sun mirror' of the Japanese myth is likewise an imitation star.
[3] See art. SACRIFICE (Japanese), vol. xi. p. 21^a.
[4] *Ib.* p. 22^a, and p. 22^b specially for the offerings of soft materials, the origin of the *gohei*, which has remained an essential cult-object, and the sight of which in a temple devoid of ornaments at once indicates a Shintō temple.
[5] See art. MAGIC (Japanese), vol. viii. p. 296 ff.
[6] See artt. PRAYER (Japanese), vol. x. p. 190^b, and SACRIFICE (Japanese), vol. xi. p. 24^a.
[7] Art. PRAYER (Japanese), vol. x. p. 190^b.
[8] See *Kojiki*², pp. 129 f. and 138.
[9] Club-moss (*Lycopodium*).
[10] *Euonymus radicans*, a Japanese species, parent of our spindle-tree.
[11] See art. SACRIFICE (Japanese), vol. xi. p. 24^a.
[12] See art. POSSESSION (Japanese), vol. x. p. 131^a.
[13] *Ib.* p. 132^a.

As regards the indecent gesture with which this scene ends, and which the *Nihongi*, which appeared only eight years after the *Kojiki*, thought right to omit in the corresponding account,[1] but whose reproduction even the *Nihongi* mentions in another connexion,[2] it gives a good idea of the naively bold character of this goddess, whose sportive naturalness the mythology associates with that of the monkey-god Saruta—an interesting point for phallic worship.[3]

9. Magic cords.—All these rites having been performed, the sun-goddess is gradually attracted outside, first by the clamorous mirth of the gods, then by the mirror which, in the *Kojiki* account, seems mainly to have a psychological action, exciting the curiosity of the goddess, but which, in the original form of the myth, must have been regarded as having rather the action of imitative magic. The god Ame-no-Tajikara-wo ('hand-strength-male'), who is hiding near the door, seizes this moment to drag the sun-goddess forcibly outside, and Futo-dama immediately prevents her from stepping back by means of a magic cord, just as, in the Fiji Islands, they tie grasses to stop the sun.[4] This cord is the prototype of the *shime-naha* ('close-rope'), the cords of rice-straw which are usually to be seen in front of Shintō temples. At Ise a huge *shime-naha* unites two rocks between which one gets an admirable view of Fuji-yama, and which are regarded as the best point of view in the archipelago for admiring and worshipping the rising sun. In a more popular form of the cult these cords are hung in front of the houses at the New Year to ward off evil influences—a custom whose origin local legend of smaller importance attributes to an adventure of the god Susa-no-wo.[5]

10. Other cult-forms.—Thus the eclipse-myth is the central point towards which all the paths of Shintō converge, and it is only necessary to start from this centre to see radiating in all directions, not only the essential rites of this worship, but also branches which end in secondary practices. The only cult-forms of any importance which are not found here are those which naturally could not figure in a story of this kind, such as the custom of pilgrimages to distant sacred places—*e.g.*, to the ancient temples of Ise or to the top of Fuji-yama, to which thousands of worshippers flock every year—or, as a substitute for such pilgrimages, the custom of worship from a distance (*em-paï*) by going to some neighbouring temple easier of access. But, although these customs are highly developed in Japan, they are found in other religions also, and there is nothing specially Shintōist about them.

LITERATURE.—This is cited in the foot-notes.

MICHEL REVON.

WORSHIP (Jewish).—The Hebrew term for 'worship' is עֲבוֹדָה and in the famous saying of Simon the Just (*c.* 300 B.C.) with which the Tractate *Ethics of the Fathers* opens[6] '*abhōdah* is the second of the 'foundations of the world.' At that period, no doubt, the word '*abhōdah* primarily implied the sacrificial system of the Temple, though this system was also accompanied by prayers, but the meaning was not necessarily restricted to the altar. This term[7] has developed, but the saying

[1] *Nihongi*, i. 45. [2] *Ib.* i. 77.
[3] Cf. art. NATURE (Japanese), vol. ix. p. 239^b.
[4] See Revon, *Shinntoïsme*, p. 212, note.
[5] See art. HOSPITALITY (Japanese and Korean), vol. vi. p. 814^b.
[6] See Singer's *Prayer Book*, p. 184 (2). (The pagination is identical in all edd.)
[7] The literal meaning is 'work,' 'service,' and, like the English equivalent, it may be used in various senses. Thus '*Abhōdah Zārāh*, 'strange worship,' is idolatry. It can refer to song or gladness, *e.g.*, איזו היא עבודה שבשמחה ובניוב לבב הוי אמר לו שירה ('*Erekhin*, 11*a*), or to prayer, *e.g.*, איזו היא עבודה שבלב הוי אמר זו תפלה (*Ta'anîth*, 2*a*). With the article, it is sometimes used as an asseveration, 'By religion!' (see

of Simon remains none the less characteristic of Jewish theology, which lays more stress on *'abhōdah* (works) than on *'emūnāh* (faith).[1]

With the destruction of the Temple, worship naturally concentrated on the synagogues.[2] Had the altar system been the exclusive means of divine access available to the Israelite, the cessation of sacrifices would have marked a much greater liturgical disturbance than actually took place. As a fact, continuity was preserved; the keynote of the transition was Hos 14^{3} (Heb. $=14^{2}$, RV), 'Let our prayers make up for the bullocks of our sacrifices.'[3] Even to-day the services, in particular those relating to atonement, re-echo this sentiment,[4] and, in almost every rite, the portion from the Pentateuch which ordains the morning, afternoon, or additional sacrifice is recited, at the appropriate occasion. This is done to show the correspondence between the particular service and the sacrifice instead of which it is offered. Nor must this feature be regarded as, *eo ipso*, a prayer for the restoration of sacrifices in their old form. It has often been shown that a belief in the restoration of the Temple, as a Messianic event, to be a centre of universal worship, may not necessarily be linked with the re-institution of the altar, and it cannot be demonstrated beyond doubt that this re-institution is an axiom of Jewish belief, for it has been repudiated by some orthodox Jewish authorities (as well as upheld by others; thus it is not included in the Thirteen Articles of Creed and Maimonides).[5]

In the synagogue worship subsequent to the Destruction the service developed on three lines: (1) prayers of repentance and penitence; (2) thanksgiving and praise; (3) petitions. Study and the recital of didactic passages of post-Biblical literature were a later institution.[6]

In (1), *i.e.* penitential worship, asceticism and fasting naturally find a place. But the limits of this asceticism were strictly defined. Fasting (*ta'anîth*, which really means 'affliction') was, generally speaking, restricted to prescribed occasions and rites. This element should be studied in connexion with FEASTING (Hebrew and Jewish). Indiscriminate and exaggerated asceticism was rather the mark of sects, such as the Essenes, Zadokites, or certain Qabbālists; it was not general. Confession, expiation, and atonement constituted acts of worship in connexion with penitence.[7]

(2) Thanksgiving in worship centred in the festivals, with the ceremonial appropriate to each, such as the palm branch,[1] tabernacle,[2] the *Hallel*[3] Psalms, the *Qiddush*,[4] etc. There is a special benediction of thanksgiving for joyous occasions and anniversaries, 'Blessed art Thou, O Lord our God, King of the universe, who hast kept us in life, and hast preserved us, and hast enabled us to reach this season.'[5]

(3) Petitions, the outpourings of the heart in supplication for the private needs of the individual, have their proper place in the Jewish system of prayer.[6] Some of these needs are specifically mentioned, when they are objects for which every individual will necessarily pray, such as health, in the *'Amīdah*,[7] or sustenance, in the grace after meals.[8] But in most cases these petitions are formulated in the plural number; cf. 'Give *us* this day *our* daily bread' (*lĕḥĕm ḥŭqqênū*). There are opportunities accorded for the individual to offer his own special prayers. But the service represents rather a corporate act of worship on the part of the community. Hence in the confessions the plural number is always used.[9] On the other hand, 'ancient formulæ, written for individual prayer, were often adapted to public worship.'[10] The needs of the individual might come under the heading of תחנונים, though this word is used in *Mishnāh Berākhôth*, iv. 4,[11] in the sense of prayer in a proper spirit. For the necessity of devotion, and of praying when in a fitting mood, is over and over again prescribed in the *Mishnāh*. Early saints, we are told, used to spend a preliminary hour in attuning their minds,[12] and, when under the stress of strong emotion, such as deep sorrow or supreme joy,[13] or when in situations of difficulty,[14] the regular prayers were postponed or abrogated.

It is an axiom of worship that praise and thanksgiving should precede petition, as being more disinterested in quality.[15] For this reason the morning service opens with *Pesuqe de Zimra*, psalms and versicles of this description. After the recital of the sacrificial descriptions[16] the 'blessing of praise' (ברוך שאמר) introduces the thanksgiving of 1 Ch 16^{8-36}, Pss 100, 145–150, and the following doxologies: 1 Ch 29^{10-13}, Neh 9^{6-11}, and the Song of Moses (Ex 14^{30}–15^{18}). These passages are brought to an end by the formula of praise ישתבח,[17] and the first portion of the service is concluded. Then follows the שמע[18] (with its blessings) or, as this section is termed, 'the assumption of the yoke of the kingdom of heaven,'[19] and then, in the תפלה (*'Amīdah*), opportunity is given for private devotions. This order shows the Jewish scheme of worship. For this reason it was considered proper to 'join Redemption to the Prayer' (סומכין גאלה לתפלה),[20] *i.e.* to proceed without interruption from the daily

Levy's *Lexicon*, *s.v.*). In the daily *'Amīdah* the term is applied to the 16–17th benediction of the ש״ע, in which the restoration of the *'abhōdah* is the subject of prayer (see Singer, p. 50, par. 2). In the *Muṣaf* service for the Day of Atonement, the *'Abhōdah* is the recital of the expiation ritual of the high priest in the Temple on that day, in the Holy of Holies (see M. Gaster, *Book of Prayer*, London, 1904, iii. 167 f., or H. M. Adler and H. Davis, *Service of the Synagogue Festivals*, etc., 'Atonement,' pt. ii. p. 159 f., London, 1904–08). Finally, see also the opening words of the concluding blessing after the reading of the prophetical lessons (Singer, p. 149, last line).

1 See *JE* ii. 148b.

2 See art. JUDAISM, vol. vii. p. 586a foot; see, however, art. PRAYER (Jewish), vol. x. p. 192b foot, for another view.

3 See *JE* viii. 132a, x. 166b, 622a, 625a.

4 See, *e.g.*, Adler and Davis, p. 169.

5 Singer, p. 89; see art. SACRIFICE (Jewish), but see also *JE* x. 628b.

6 After such passages a special *Qaddish* was pronounced (see Singer, p. 86). Such passages may be found in Singer, p. 167 f. Yemenite Jews more frequently do not read a set passage, but insert in their daily service a portion of the book they happen to be studying. The Mesopotamian rite assigns a greater place to study as an act of worship than do others. Not only are the first night of Pentecost and the night of *Hosha'ana Rabba* kept as vigils and devoted to study, as in Europe, but the custom called חֲתִימָה ('Sealing') on account of *Hosha'ana Rabba* associations prevails at other times.

7 See artt. ASCETICISM (Jewish), FASTING, FEASTING (Hebrew and Jewish), CONFESSION (Hebrew), EXPIATION AND ATONEMENT (Jewish).

1 Singer, p. 218. 2 *Ib.* p. 232.

3 *Ib.* p. 219 f. 4 *Ib.* pp. 124, 174, 230, 243.

5 *Ib.* p. 292. See art. FESTIVALS AND FASTS (Jewish).

6 *Berākhôth*, 31*a*, tr. Cohen, Cambridge, 1921, p. 206.

7 Singer, p. 47. 8 *Ib.* p. 281.

9 See *Ber.* 30*a* (=Cohen, p. 196); Singer, pp. 258–263.

10 See Abrahams, *Annotated Edition of Singer's Prayer Book*, p. xix.

11 העושה תפלתו קבע אין תפלתו תחנונים. The meaning of קבע is disputed; here, according to Bartinoro and others, it means 'that his prayer is burdensome, as much as to say that he has a fixed, distasteful task, which has to be accomplished.' See *Gemara*, f. 29*b*, p. 194 of Cohen's tr. But קבע usually is found in a good sense, *i.e.* regularity; cf. the *fixing* (קביעת) of the calendar, or תפלת הערב אין לו קבע (*Ber.* iv. 1), or עשה תורתך קבע (*Abhôth*, i. 16; see Taylor).

12 *Ber.* viii. 1.

13 The *Gemara* discusses, *e.g.*, the cases of bridegrooms and mourners.

14 *E.g.*, when riding (30*a* [Cohen, p. 197]), sailing, or in perilous surroundings. See also 31*a* (Cohen, p. 203 f.).

15 *Ber.* 32*a* foot (Cohen, p. 214), 34*a* (Cohen, p. 228)

16 Singer, pp. 9–13. 17 *Ib.* p. 36.

18 See art. GOD (Jewish), vol. vi. p. 298.

19 Singer, p. 37 f.

20 *Ber.* 30*a* (Cohen, p. 198).

thanksgiving for the deliverance from Egypt to the recital of the '*Amīdah*.[1]

Practically every item of Jewish ritual, synagogal or domestic, is an act of worship, for in Judaism the secular sphere has very little independent existence, and thus many acts, not in themselves religious, are associated with blessings and become acts of ceremonial. In order that these blessings should not be forgotten, or to give opportunity to an individual who might have omitted to say them, or to enable the congregation to respond 'Amen,' some of these blessings have been incorporated in the liturgy itself.[2] Others that have not been thus incorporated, because they were not likely to be needed every day, may be seen in Singer, p. 287 f. The ideal of the pious Jew was to pronounce a blessing on the name of God one hundred times a day;[3] 'in all thy ways know Him.'

'For every enjoyment and *in* every enjoyment he is to render thanks to God the Giver. He is to smell the rose, and to rejoice in its perfume. And he is to say and to feel: "Blessed art Thou, O Lord, who createst fragrant plants."'[4]

The Sabbath, with all its domestic ceremonies, has become practically a day of acts of worship; the three meals are preceded by sanctification and followed by hymns and carols. But such a day, far from being a burden to an orthodox Jew, is to him a day of spiritual happiness, for the highest bliss in the world to come is poetically described as a period 'wholly a Sabbath,' which 'will bring rest in life everlasting.'[5]

The term 'worship,' therefore, logically includes many more operations, besides prayer, by which the Jew seeks to serve God, in addition to numerous acts of his daily life and his private and public devotions. A specific act of charity may become an adjunct of worship, if not worship itself. Thus, in the East, Jews sometimes make use of *tsedaqah* (charity) boxes containing eighteen apertures, each devoted to a different philanthropic institution. As each of the eighteen blessings of the '*Amīdah* is recited, a coin is placed in one of the slots.[6]

The scheme of synagogal worship may thus be analyzed.[7] The normal daily services, associated with the statutory Temple offerings,[8] and also ascribed by tradition to patriarchal institution,[9] are three—morning, afternoon, and evening. On Sabbaths, festivals, and new moons, and on the Day of Atonement, but not on the other fasts, there is an 'additional service,' called *Muṣaf*.[10] There is no *Muṣaf* on Ḥanuca (the Maccabæan Feast of Dedication, Encœnia), or on Purim, the Feast of Esther, because the ordinances for these days are post-Biblical and no special offering was brought. Every service includes an '*Amīdah*[11] as its essential element, other features being thanksgiving Psalms, *Shᵉma'*, *Hallel*, reading of the Law and Prophets. Propitiatory prayers, hymns (*pĭyyûṭim*),[12] study, and sermons are not original statutory components, though antiquity and popularity have often endowed them with an importance which their origin does not altogether warrant. The recital of the Ten Commandments in public worship was discontinued,[13] and the doxology was altered,[14] on account of the Minim, but the private reading both of the Decalogue and of the Maimonidean Creeds is regarded as desirable after the morning service.[1] The essential features of Jewish worship may thus be summarized:

At every morning service throughout the year.—(1) *Pesuqe de Zimra*, or introductory Psalms and versicles of thanksgiving; (2) *Shᵉma'* and blessings; (3) '*Amīdah*; (4) the *Hallel* Psalms on new moon, festivals, and Ḥanuca; (5) reading of the Law on Mondays and Thursdays, Sabbaths, fasts, festivals, New Year, Day of Atonement, new moon, Ḥanuca, Purim; (6) reading from the Prophets on Sabbaths, festivals, New Year, and Atonement, ninth of Ab; (7) *Muṣaf*, or 'additional' service, on Sabbaths, festivals, new moon, New Year, and Atonement; additional items where appropriate, such as *Seliḥoth*, blowing of *Shofar*, prayer for rain, *Hosha'anôth*, etc.

At every afternoon service throughout the year.—Passages reminiscent of sacrifices and incense, Ps 145, '*Amīdah*; reading of the Law on Sabbaths and Day of Atonement and on certain fasts; *hafṭarah* on Atonement and certain fasts; Canticles, Ruth, Ecclesiastes on the Three Festivals.

At every evening service throughout the year.—*Shᵉma'* with blessings, '*Amīdah*, introductory Psalms on Friday night; special Psalms or poems for festivals in some rites; Lamentations on ninth of Ab, Esther on Purim, etc.

The two main divisions into which the present liturgy may be divided are the Ashkenazic and Sefardic rites. These correspond, to some extent, with the early Palestinian and Babylonian uses,[2] but there are other uses—*e.g.*, Italian, N. African, Turkish, Mesopotamian and Indian, Cochini, Persian, etc.—being modifications of the main Sefardic use, and certain Ḥassidic, Qabbālistic, and other rites in Russia and E. Europe, which are Ashkenazic variants. Among extinct rites may be mentioned the *Seder Amram* (use of Amram Gaon, 870 C.E.), Maḥzor Vitry, Maimonides, Isaac Lurya, and C. Vital, Castile, etc. Little is known of the ritual of the Falashas or of that current among the Chinese Jews. Qaraites and Samaritans have their own worship, which has been printed.[3] Modern Reform rites, generally speaking, contain vernacular translations and sometimes additions, and modify certain references to the restoration of sacrifices. The *pĭyyûṭim*, or hymns, are of two main types, Kalirian and Spanish;[4] they do not form a statutory constituent and are often shortened or omitted. The divergencies of rites are due to the circumstance that the liturgy was originally not stereotyped. 'Those who write down blessings' were considered as reprehensible.[5] The reader was told the subjects to be mentioned by him and their order; hence the variety of prayers arose. The whole of the tractate *Bᵉrākhôth* is an indication of this method. The reader was 'free.'[6]

The underlying theory of the Jewish conception of worship can best be studied in chs. l. and li. of pt. iii. of the *Guide* of Maimonides.[7] Maimonides calls worship 'the highest aim man can attain.' He insists that worship must be based on the intellect, if it is to have real value. 'The intellect which emanates from God unto us is the link that joins us to Him.' The chapters should be carefully studied.

Pilgrimage as an act of worship occurs only sporadically in Judaism.

Other information may be found in artt. CONFESSION (Hebrew), FEASTING (Hebrew and Jewish), FESTIVALS AND FASTS (Jewish), GOD (Jewish), for *Shᵉma'* and '*Alenu*, vol. vi. p. 298, HYMNS (Hebrew and Jewish), MUSIC (Jewish), SABBATH (Jewish), PREACHING (Jewish), PRIESTHOOD (Jewish), PRAYER (Jewish), SACRIFICE (Jewish), and *JE*, *s.v.* 'Prayer,' 'Liturgy,' etc.

LITERATURE.—M. Duschak, *Gesch. und Darstellung des jüd. Cultus*, Mannheim, 1866; W. O. E. Oesterley and G. H. Box,

[1] See Singer, p. 44; and Abrahams, note on p. liv.
[2] See Singer, pp. 4–6; Abrahams, p. xviii.
[3] *Menaḥôth*, iv.
[4] C. G. Montefiore, *Judaism and St. Paul*, London, 1914, p. 46.
[5] Singer, p. 168.
[6] For the association of almsgiving and prayer see art. EXPIATION AND ATONEMENT (Jewish), vol. v. p. 662ᵇ.
[7] For the 'external form of the Service' see vol. x. p. 194ᵃ.
[8] *Bᵉr.* 24*a*.
[9] See *JE* x. 166ᵃ.
[10] See *ib.*, *s.v.*
[11] See *ib.*, *s.v.* 'Shemoneh Esreh.'
[12] See *ERE* x. 195ᵃ, § 4.
[13] *Mishnāh Tāmīd*, v. 1; see Feibus' commentary *in loc.* given in Berlin ed. of 1833; see also *JE* viii. 133ᵃ.
[14] *Mishnāh Bᵉr.* ix. 5.

[1] *JE* x. 170ᵃ.
[2] Abrahams, p. i f.
[3] See art. PRAYER (Jewish), bibliography.
[4] See Abrahams, p. ii.
[5] See vol. x. p. 193ᵇ.
[6] See 'The Freedom of the Synagogue,' I. Abrahams, *Studies in Pharisaism*, Cambridge, 1917, p. 1 ff.
[7] P. 380 ff. in M. Friedländer's tr.², London, 1910.

The Religion and Worship of the Synagogue[2], London, 1911; artt. by L. Blau, I. Elbogen, A. Büchler, in *JQR* and *REJ*; a new translation, with full notes, of T.B. *Berākhôth*, by A. Cohen, is in course of being issued by the Cambridge Press; the annotated Singer's *Prayer Book*, by I. Abrahams, London, 1914, is invaluable.

HERBERT LOEWE.

WORSHIP (Parsi).

1. Pre-Zarathushtrian period.—That the attitude of the early Iranians towards those whom they conceived as the Supreme Powers was one of adoration and worship is practically certain.[1] In what precise outward forms that attitude expressed itself during the earlier period is a question which can be only partially answered. We may safely assume, however, that Herodotus's description[2] of Persian habits and modes of worship was, in its essential features, applicable to the Iranians generally centuries before his own time, and probably more generally and truly applicable to the Persians of that period than it was to those who were his contemporaries. In the Greek historian's account of Persian worship the whole ceremony centres in an act of animal sacrifice.[3] It was accompanied by prayer on the part of the offerer and the intoning of some form of liturgy on the part of the priest. When this 'theogony' ceased to be a mere form of incantation or magic formula, which originally and for a long period it undoubtedly was, we have no means of determining. The sacrifice was individual in its presentation—there is no hint of a united offering—but the sacrificer was expected to be imbued with a sense of solidarity; for, in its main character and content, his prayer must needs be intercessory—embracing the welfare of the king and the whole Persian people. It is to do violence to the text of Herodotus, however, to make him say that the bringer of the sacrifice could ask nothing for himself. The natural inference from Herodotus's narrative is that, so far as the outward and visible forms of Persian worship were concerned, they consisted of merely an occasional act of animal sacrifice performed on a mountain top or beside a stream of water. We can scarcely imagine that all their religious impulses and beliefs found their full and only expression in such forms. Still, the small value the Persians placed upon architectural aids to outward worship prepares us to find among them a very simple ritual and perhaps a not very multiform mode of religious expression. Regard must also be had for the early period that we are treating—perhaps more than a millennium before our era.

2. Zarathushtra's time.—Like the founder of Christianity, Zarathushtra, so far as the records enable us to judge, made no provision whatever for ceremonial or outward forms of worship. The *Gāthas*, which are the truest reflexion of his teaching and spirit, contain not the remotest hint[4] of such matters. There we have an intensely earnest soul seeking to learn the truth and to get into the right inward relationship to its God. The outward expression and symbolization of that relationship receives no consideration at all. Spirit and conduct are the all-absorbing subjects of the *Gāthas*. *Vohumano*, best thought; *Asha*, right; and *Aramaiti*, piety, are the ever-recurring objects of the prophet's desire. It is hardly too much to say that Zarathushtra's ideal of worship is best expressed in Christ's great and final saying that 'they that worship him must worship in spirit and truth.' How far this high ideal was appreciated and accepted by his contemporaries, and to what extent his influence availed to ensure its persistence after his death cannot be ascertained. Certainly some of the divinities invoked and praised in the *Yasna haptaṇhaiti*, which, on linguistic grounds, cannot be assigned to a very much later date than the *Gāthas*, clearly indicate that at that early time there was a distinct descent from Zarathushtra's high spiritual conception of worship.

3. Late Avestan period.—By the time of the Later Avesta Mazdaism had developed an elaborate system of ceremonial worship. Animal sacrifices on the largest scale prevailed. *Haoma* had regained more than its pristine veneration in the new order; and henceforth the preparation of its juice (*parahaoma*) becomes the central point of the Mazdæan ritual[1]—a position from which, to this day, it has never receded.[2] The return of the old Iranian gods as angels (*yazatas*, beings meet to be worshipped) in the new pantheon increased enormously the ritual of Mazdaism and the acts of worship devolving upon the followers of the faith. Every day of every month was devoted to some special divinity, who was specially invoked, praised, and sacrificed to in addition to the regular worship of that day. Thus the 1st, 8th, 15th, and 23rd of each month were consecrated to Ahuramazda; the 3rd and 5th to the *ameshaspentas*; and in a similar manner the remaining days to other genii.[3] Over and above these were the special feasts, such as New Year in honour of Mazda. Prayers, hymns, and liturgies befitting all these occasions were utilized.[4] Each day was divided into five parts, and at each division a special prayer, one of the so-called *Gâhs*, was uttered. For the elaborate ritual associated with the rites of initiation and the disposal of the dead see under those headings. What worship gained in extent and elaborateness during this period it seems to have largely lost in inwardness and spirituality. The value of the prayers came to be regarded as consisting mainly in the words and their correct utterance. We get the impression that they came to be employed as mere charms and magic formulæ.[5]

4. Present time.—If animal sacrifices are excepted, Parsi worship is to-day, outwardly, practically what it has been from late Avestan days. Before the sacred fire of their temples the same Avestan liturgy is recited, accompanied by the priestly performance of the same ceremonies. The same divinities are invoked and praised by the orthodox Parsi to-day in the same prayers and hymns as were used two millennia earlier. But it should be noted that a strong reform movement has set in among many educated Parsis, the tendency of which seems to be not so much to work radical changes in the outward form of their worship as to change the whole emphasis from outward forms to the moral and spiritual ideas symbolized in the ceremonies. In one or two instances lately, it is true, the priest has gone to the length of introducing a sermon or address into the service. But this is exceptional.

5. Collective and individual worship.—Although devout Parsis often frequent the fire-temples, as, we gather from *Visparad*, iii., their ancestors also did, especially on sacred days, such as those consecrated to Atar (3rd, 9th, 17th, and 20th), yet the Parsi does not consider attendance at the temple

---

1 Cf. Skr. *yaz*, 'worship,' 'dedicate,' 'offer'; Av. *yaz*, Gr. ἅζομαι; indicating that, before the separation, the habit of worship obtained among the Indo-Europeans.

2 i. 131 f.

3 See art. SACRIFICE (Iranian).

4 The occurrence of the word *zaotar*, 'priest,' in one passage in the *Gāthas* (*Ys.* xxxiii. 6) cannot be held to require the modification of the above statement. See J. H. Moulton, *Early Zoroastrianism*, London, 1913, p. 116.

1 For a detailed account of that ceremony and of the successive steps by which ritual and liturgy alternate in the preparation of the *haoma* juice see M. Haug, *Essays on the Sacred Language, Writings, and Religion of the Parsis*, ed. E. W. West, London, 1907, p. 393 ff.; and art. HAOMA.

2 See art. SACRIFICE (Iranian).

3 See art. CALENDAR (Persian).

4 See art. FESTIVALS AND FASTS (Parsi).

5 See art. PRAYER (Iranian).

indispensable to worship, and places far less store upon it than the faithful Christian does upon church-going.[1] One reason for that fact is that much of the priestly worship at the temple is without special reference to any laity that may be present—the long *Yasna* ceremony is a conspicuous example. But, even when assembled in large numbers at the temples, their worship seems to be almost if not quite entirely individual and separate, not collective and united. These two facts are surely very significant. We noted them in Herodotus's description of early Persian worship—slight regard for religious edifices as aids to worship, and absence of united action in public worship. But they are in perfect keeping with the highly individual and independent character with which Zarathushtrianism imbues its adherents. Moreover, the private and individual devotions of a faithful Parsi are as numerous as those of the devotees of most religions. We give the following quotation to substantiate this fact:

'For the modern Parsees the precise forms of prayer are strictly laid down; a brief survey of them will be sufficient. On rising, washing, and dressing, especially on tying the sacred string, a series of prayers are to be repeated. Next follows the special morning-prayer. Before and after each meal, likewise, prayers are said; and in the evening, before the Parsee goes to sleep, he has, further, to reflect upon and examine what he has done in the course of the day, and then only, after reciting certain prayers, he retires to rest. To the prayers which form part of the order of the day are added a number of others which must be said on certain occurrences, viz. after sneezing, after connubial intercourse, after satisfying natural purposes, after pollutions during sleep, after the cutting of nails and hair, as well as after the lighting of candles.'[2]

LITERATURE.—In addition to the works already referred to see Anquetil du Perron, *Zend-Avesta, Ouvrage de Zoroastre*, 2 vols., Paris, 1771, 'Usages civils et religieux des Parses,' pp. 527–591, and 'Système théologique cérémonial et moral,' pp. 592–618; Dosabhai Framji Karaka, *Hist. of the Parsis*, London, 1884; Maneckji Nusservanji Dhalla, *Zoroastrian Theology*, New York, 1914; J. H. Moulton, *The Treasure of the Magi*, Oxford, 1917. The reader will find much relevant material in the two last-mentioned works.
E. EDWARDS.

WORSHIP (Roman).—**1. General principles.**—The term 'worship' may be treated as comprising all modes of giving expression to the various feelings entertained towards the divine powers—feelings of awe, reverence, obligation, deprecation, gratitude, hope, and others. The forms given to the expression varied, first, according to the conceptions entertained about the nature and functions of the beings who swayed the destinies of men and women, next, with the development of civilization among the people. The limitations of certain kinds of worship to certain classes of people, public and private, also fall to be considered.

2. Worship as related to conceptions of divinity.—In the earliest known forms of Roman religion men's conceptions were vague, and the divine influences were not supposed to pertain to definite personal gods, being described by the shadowy phrase *numina*. Observances of worship were therefore naturally far more simple than they afterwards became. The early Roman did indeed regard divine power as perceptible in every portion of the world, and in every department of life. In a sense he may be said to have entertained the opinion of the Greek philosopher, Heraclitus, who said that 'all things are full of gods' (πάντα πλήρη θεῶν). Every stage in human life was passed in contact with superhuman powers. The Roman nursery was haunted by a host of divinities, whom the fathers of the early Church were given to ridicule. The earliest religious observances reflect the life, mainly, of an agricultural community, and aimed at securing the safety of men and animals, and of the boundaries of the farm. In many cases the actual implements used in life, or accessory to it, were regarded as in some way the seats of the superhuman influences. Thus each *terminus*, or boundary-stone, was regarded as the seat of a *numen*, and this idea seems to be anterior to that of a god Terminus protecting all boundary-stones.[1] Another primitive notion which influenced the forms of worship was that each community had its own protecting divinities, who belonged to it and no other. Gods were generally supposed to confine their interest to particular tribes, clans, or civic organizations or to groups of persons within them. There were therefore in Italy infinite diversities of local religious usage, many of which, when Rome became the governing power, affected and complicated the religious practice of the dominant city.

Political and religious obligation were never held asunder in the ancient world. It was in theory the duty of every citizen to maintain intact the religious observances which had been handed down to him from his ancestors. But no such theory has ever prevented change. At most it has restrained changes not sanctioned by political authority. The literary Romans regarded all the institutions of religion as owing their existence to a single lawgiver, King Numa. Later rulers were only imitating him when they adapted religious practice to the changed needs of their times.

3. Rigorousness of ancient forms.—At all times the Roman was deeply impressed by the importance of ascertaining precisely the forms of the words, actions, and offerings which he should use in doing honour to divine personages. First, the proper divine title must be ascertained if possible. To the latest times expressions were introduced into formulæ which might obviate the evil effects of a slip. Thus, if there was a doubt as to the sex of the divinity, the words 'siue tu deus, siue dea es,' were added. Precise accuracy in the words of which the petition or salutation consisted was of the highest consequence. This rigorousness applied also to the secular formulæ of the law, to which, indeed, in early days, a certain sacredness attached. This strict formalism led to the publication by the priestly authorities of a religious document which bore the name of *Indigitamenta*, and preserved for later times names of divinities and lists of usages which would otherwise have died out of memory.[2] Down to the latest times the simple offerings which had satisfied the old *numina* were preserved side by side with the more elaborate dedications. At the family shrine the *far pium* and *saliens mica* of Horace continued to be presented, and the *mola salsa*, prepared according to a very primitive method, was placed before Vesta three times a year by her priestesses, the Vestals, who performed for the great State-family at the State altar the functions which belonged to the unmarried daughters of the private family. Similar offerings, prominent in the worship of different divinities, were bean-meal, lard, milk, wine, and honey.

As to animal sacrifices, their oldest form of which record is preserved was the peculiar ceremonial offering called *suovetaurilia*, in which a bull, a sheep, and a pig were led three times in procession round the farm, and then the victims were sacrificed, and a prayer couched in Latin of ancient form was pronounced, which is preserved by Cato.[3]

[1] See A. V. Williams Jackson, *Persia Past and Present*, New York, 1906, p. 368.

[2] W. Geiger, *Civilization of the Eastern Irānians in Ancient Times*, tr. Dārāb Dastur Peshotan Sanjānā, London, 1885, i. 71 f.

[1] W. Warde Fowler, *The Roman Festivals*, London, 1899, p. 326.

[2] See the articles on 'Indigitamenta' in Pauly-Wissowa and in Roscher.

[3] *De Re Rustica*, 141; see Warde Fowler, p. 126.

4. Changes in worship due to external influences.—The Roman pantheon and Roman worship had doubtless gone through a number of changes before the earliest time which has left traces in historical practice of religion. Many attempts have been made by modern scholars to pierce the dense pre-historic darkness in which the state of early Italy is enveloped. The material, however, which has come down to us from ancient days is so completely untrustworthy that the efforts of scholars have chiefly testified to their power of imagination. This material indeed, if it deserves the name, was produced mainly by the unbridled imagination of poets, genealogists, annalists, grammarians, and antiquaries of the late Republic and early Empire. To correlate even the results of modern archæological research with this heterogeneous mass of statements, so as to produce any solid results, is a hopeless task. The earliest safe source of information about Roman cults is to be found in the inscriptions which have preserved the remains of the ancient Roman calendar. When ancient Roman scholars, like Varro and Verrius Flaccus, drew from the actual records of the cults illustrations of the ceremonies mentioned in the earliest calendar, they preserved actual religious history. And religious usage was so tenacious in Rome that the light thus obtained carries us back a long way.

Conservative as the early Roman State was with regard to religion, the recurring desire for novelties in cults was from a very early time satisfied in a remarkable way. When the demand became clamorous, in times marked by great public disasters, such as severe defeats at the hands of enemies or sore famines or pestilences, the Senate would order the mysterious *Sibylline Books* to be consulted, so that the proper mode of meeting the religious emergency might be discovered. It was felt that conjunctures occurred when the aid to be drawn from the gods who ordinarily protected the country was insufficient. It dawned upon the consciousness of the citizens that perhaps divinities who presided over foreign communities might be able to come to the rescue. At a very early time the Greeks were recognized as masters of divine lore, and the *Sibylline Books* were believed to enshrine precious results of their experience. An inquiry therefore into the proper mode of expiating disasters, which were naturally supposed to indicate divine wrath, almost invariably resulted in an injunction to adopt into the ceremonial of the State religion some rite derived from Greece. The *Sibylline Books* therefore constituted a sort of open door through which entered such a mass of new religious usage that the Roman religion was extensively Hellenized. Sometimes the new usage was connected with a divinity not previously worshipped by Romans, at other times the new practice was grafted on the cult of an old Roman divinity. For one great feature of the movement was the identification of Roman divinities with Greek, the divine beings concerned being supposed to differ only in names.

This process of Hellenization began very early, and the legend which attributed the introduction of these books to the period of the monarchy enshrined a particle of historic truth. But the religious revolution was much accelerated by the advance of Rome to world power, when important crises, giving rise oftentimes to superstitious fears, were multiplied. Some of the most archaic forms of Roman ritual survived in the late Republican time as popular festivals with disorderly accompaniments. Such were the Saturnalia and the *Festum geniale* of Anna Perenna,[1] the Floralia in April,[2] the festival of Fors Fortuna in June,[3] the

[1] Ovid, *Fasti*, v. 523 ff. [2] *Ib.* v. 331 ff. [3] *Ib.* vi. 775 ff.

Ancillarum feriæ in July (mentioned in late literature), and others. Many, however, of the most venerable survivals in Roman religious practice of the later time were maintained by the appointed administrators merely from a conservative sense, and were forms that excited little interest except among scholars and antiquarians. Such ceremonies were, *e.g.*, the driving of the nail into the wall of the temple of Fortuna, the Fordicidia,[1] and many others. The influence of Augustus led to an archaistic religious revival, which re-established many primitive rites that were all but forgotten, and prevented many others from sinking into complete oblivion, under the weight of indifference induced by many influences, especially the sceptical tendencies stimulated by the Hellenization of culture, and the manifold new impressions produced by contact with various peoples during the process of world conquest.

The Oriental religions came more and more to attract the Italic and Western populations after the establishment of the Empire. During the Republican age, the government had opposed barriers to the advancing tide of Orientalism in religion. The first Eastern cult to find a place in the official framework of Roman religion was that of the Magna Mater, adopted in 204 B.C. It is not easy to explain the official acceptance of a form of worship of such a frenzied character at so early a date, even when one takes into account the enormous strengthening of superstition by the tremendous experiences of the Hannibalic war: the old feeling reasserted itself in 186 B.C. when the so-called 'Bacchic conspiracy' was ruthlessly suppressed by the Senate, with whom rested the final authority in such matters. In the later days of the Republic many private attempts to establish at Rome Egyptian forms of worship, especially those of Isis and Serapis, were frustrated. These cults naturally tended to find a refuge in the seaports to which fleets from Egypt came, especially the Campanian maritime towns. At Puteoli, for instance, there was a temple of Serapis as early as 105 B.C., and near the coast, at Pompeii, a shrine of Isis existed even before the Roman conquest of the town. Three times in the ten years between 58 and 48 B.C. shrines of Isis were destroyed in Rome. Under Augustus the pressure produced by the popularity among the masses of Egyptian rites became very great, but naturally the ruler could not favour divinities who had allied themselves with his enemy Mark Antony. In 19 B.C. Tiberius, in consequence of a gross scandal, destroyed a shrine of Isis, and caused her image to be cast into the Tiber. Nevertheless private dedications of temples continued to be increasingly common. The government did attempt to prevent them from being erected within the *pomœrium*, but in vain; for in A.D. 69, when the army of Vitellius beset the city, Domitian assumed the garb of a devotee of Isis and sought safety among the servants of her temple.[2] The full tolerance of this divinity at Rome took place before the death of Lucan in A.D. 65, as we see from a scornful reference in his poem.[3] The actual formal inclusion of Egyptian deities in the Roman pantheon, whereby they were thoroughly naturalized and no longer restricted by authority to the space outside the *pomœrium*, came in the time of Caracalla. This emperor built a sumptuous temple of Serapis on the Quirinal. The attraction of the public to the ritual of the Egyptian deities was largely due to the mysteries which were connected with them. Brotherhoods and initiations, whereby these 'saviour' gods (σωτῆρες) rescued the

[1] Ovid, *Fasti*, iv. 631 ff. [2] Suet. *Domit.* i.
[3] viii. 831 ff.

devotee from evil, exercised a powerful fascination. The Roman soldiers who had served in the East brought with them on their return, from the time of Sulla onwards, many Oriental cults, which tended to flourish greatly in the time of the Severi, whose origin was in the East. Some of these divinities assumed Roman names, such as Jupiter Dolichenus, Invictus Sol Elagabal (from whom the emperor Elagabalus took his name). The worship of Mithras reached its height in the West in the 3rd and 4th centuries A.D.

The divinization of the Roman emperors changed in many respects the whole face of Roman religion. Their cult became the strongest bond of union between the different populations of the Empire, and it became, from another point of view, an important element in the scheme of provincial government.

5. Important public rituals. — The different rituals under which the gods were officially venerated may be distinguished. At Rome the State priests came to bring together under the title of *ius sacrum* all the principles and practices of Roman religion, just as the secular law was comprised under the *ius publicum.* The severance between sacred and secular law was indeed not completed until a comparatively late date. Survivals in late Rome indicate that in early days a kind of religious sanctity attached to the formulæ of the civil law, and the great exponents of the two systems were often the same. The *pontifices maximi* were in primitive times generally distinguished lawyers also. And Roman religion was at all times under the final control of secular authorities, the magistrates and the Senate. When a colony was founded, the fundamental charter always required the first magistrates to consult their Senate as to the divinities whom the colonists were to serve, and the modes of their service. These divinities were naturally, as a rule, taken from the Roman pantheon, because, according to a common saying, a Roman colony was 'quasi effigies parua simulacrumque populi Romani';[1] but, like the parent city, the new community had full autonomy in the arrangement of its public worships.

Whenever the State undertook a new duty towards the divine power, it was expressed in the form first of a *uotum.* The conditions which constituted the validity of the *uotum* of the magistrate were well understood; but in important cases the magistrate would be careful to obtain a preliminary understanding with the Senate. The recorded cases in which a question was raised whether the *uotum* was binding on the community are few in number. The contents of the *uotum* might be of many descriptions, as its objects might vary from the perfectly general *uota pro rei publicæ salute* which the principal magistrates pronounced each New Year's Day to some specific thing. Sometimes the *uota pro salute* mentioned a particular number of years; the *decennalia uota* of the emperors asked for the safety of the empire during a period of ten years. There were also *quindecennalia* and *uicennalia.* The fulfilment of the *uota* was carried out by the secular magistrates, though the precise forms which had to be employed (concerning which usage was extremely conservative) were prescribed and supervised by the experts in the *ius sacrum,* the *pontifices.*

The fulfilment of the *uota* would generally issue in the dedication to sacred uses of some material thing — often a *templum.* This thing became technically *res sacra,* and was protected against secular encroachments by the *ius sacrum.* On the whole, the Roman government watched rather jealously the transference of rights in property from the secular to the sacred sphere, but when the transference was accomplished, it was rigidly maintained by law.

In the case of the *uota* the community, through its magistrates, approaches the divinity and practically enters into a legal compact with the god. Not only the community, but the god also is bound, and the procedure had a distinctly legal aspect.

There were other ways in which the community might be bound. Certain occurrences showed that in some way the gods were offended, and it was the duty of the public officers to find a way of averting the divine wrath. Thus *prodigia,* portents which seemed to interrupt the order of nature, called for *piacula,* offerings or services intended to secure appeasement of the offended deity. Thus Livy says:[1] 'C. Servilius pontifex maximus piacula irae Deum conquirere iussus.' In times of stress and public peril, *prodigia* (or *ostenta*) would be reported to the authorities in great numbers. The information was carefully sifted and often some of it was rejected; the signs of divine wrath which were accepted as real were then expiated (*procurata*). Signs which occurred 'in privato loco' or 'in loco peregrino' were not admitted.[2] The *haruspices* had a great part in these expiations.

It was also foreseen that, apart from such special indications, the community would continually contract pollution from the imperfect or erroneous performance of religious duties, so that provision was made for a general clearance of offences at regular intervals. The *lustrum* (literally 'washing') with which the proceedings of the census concluded was a clearance of this kind. The annual perambulation of the city (*amburbium*) was another. An ancient body of priests, the *Fratres Arvales,* annually performed a *segetum lustratio* at Rome. Similar, though not regular, was the *lustratio* of the army, when it was overcome by some superstitious dread. Scipio had to pause before crossing into Asia, in order to free his force from the sense of pollution. Similar was in part the purpose of the *supplicatio* which after a victory was held in honour of the whole body of divinities, in order to get rid of the taint of blood-shedding. The procession took place round all shrines ('circa omnia pulvinaria') and provided the population with an enjoyable holiday. The ancient temple was not freely open to be seen; there were no recurring services such as take place in a modern church. In most instances there was but one festival in a year at a temple. Therefore, as many contained wonderful monuments and precious treasures dedicated by Roman heroes of former times, there was great eagerness to survey them. The *supplicatio* took place in early times on one day only. Later, generals pressed to have the importance of a victory emphasized by repeating the *supplicatio* on succeeding days, and in the age of Cæsar the number of days might extend to forty or fifty. The triumphal procession also doubtless belonged to the same class. Both it and the *supplicatio* were probably of Hellenic origin. Similar was the procession of twenty-seven virgins, round the city, singing a sacred hymn, which was sometimes ordained.[3] All *ludi* were in one aspect religious performances, offered to some divinity. The gladiatorial *ludi* came from Etruria, and were intended to appease the partly divine spirits of the dead, which were reinvigorated by the blood which was shed. Even at the end of the Republic, these *ludi* were always, as a matter of form, declared to be held in honour of some deceased person con-

1 Gellius, XVI. xiii. 9.

1 XL. xxxvii. 5. 2 XLIII. xiii. 23. 25.
3 Livy, XXVII. xxxvii. 7.

nected with the exhibitor. It is in connexion with the *ludi* in general that we hear most of the practice called *instauratio*, the repetition of a ceremony because of the discovery of some flaw which vitiated its effect. In the time of the later Republic, when men ambitious to obtain high office paved their way to it by vast expenditure on *ludi*, these flaws were artificially created in order to justify additional lavishness.

Rules relating to sacrifice were elaborate. Particular deities called for particular offerings, and the accompaniments of sacrifice were very various. The separation between the divinities of the under and the upper world was in this respect specially important. Thus to Varro is attributed the view that *altaria* were appropriate to the *di superi*, *aræ* to the *di terrestres*, and *foci* to the *di inferi*.[1]

Public and private cults to some extent were parallel. For example, the worship of Vesta was as important for the family circle as for the State, which, like the family, had its own *lares* and *penates*. Many cults were indeed adopted from patrician families by the community. Rites in honour of the dead were extensively rendered by private persons as well as by the magistrates and priests of the community. Almost every regularly constituted group within the State had its own special cults. Thus every *collegium*, whatever might be the principal bond of union between its members, had its own special form of worship. Some groups within the city of Rome, which had survived from very primitive times, such as those called *pagani* and *montani*, maintained down to a late date their special religious usages. The *sacra* attached to families occupied an important place in the *ius sacrum*, the policy of the religious lawyers having been to prevent, so far as possible, the extinction of these *sacra* by the dying out of the families. To the *gens* as well as the *familia* also appertained its own *sacra*.[2]

Among important public ceremonies to which reference has not been made above may be mentioned the *lectisternium*, certainly borrowed from the Greeks, and the *ludi sæculares*, which originated from the *ludi terentini*, a ceremony connected with departed spirits, celebrated at an altar of Dis pater. These *ludi* and the *ludi sæculares* which succeeded them were supposed to occur at the end of a *sæculum*, which was first assumed to comprise a hundred years, but in later times the period was fixed at 110 years. The ceremony is best known from the records of the celebration ordered by Augustus in 17 B.C., for which Horace wrote his *Carmen Sæculare*. This series of celebrations went on until A.D. 314, and another series, theoretically to celebrate the end of each century from the foundation of Rome, ran parallel with it.

The observances due annually to the gods were prescribed at settled dates on the calendar, published yearly under the supervision of the college of *pontifices*.

6. Ritual proper to groups.—Among celebrations (*feriæ*) connected with groups of men may be noted the *Quinquatrus*, observed by the *artifices* in honour of their patron divinity Minerva, and the *Quinquatrus minusculæ*, held by the flute-players (*tibicines*). There were many similar festivals. One was carried out by the *mercatores*, on the foundation-day of the temple of Mercurius by the Circus, another by the workmen where trade depended on the use of water (*aquatores*). The date for this was 11th Jan., a day sacred to Iuturna, a goddess of springs and fountains, fabled by Virgil to have been sister of Turnus, king of the Rutuli. Not all persons were qualified to be present at all services; from some women were excluded, and men from others.

[1] Servius on Virgil, *Ecl.* v. 66.

[2] Cf. G. Wissowa, *Religion und Kultus der Römer*, p. 337.

7. Religious officers.—Along with the *pontifices*, the *augures*, and the keepers of the Sibylline oracles (*Quindecimviri sacris faciundis*) were the great priestly colleges; membership of these was a great object of ambition to men engaged in public life. The *haruspices* had not the same distinction; they did not really constitute a college, like the other bodies. Until a late date they were Etruscans, summoned by the Senate from time to time as occasion required, to expound the peculiarly Etruscan lore of means of expiation, chiefly for the evil sign of the thunderbolt. Later, *haruspices* trained in Etruria were settled in Rome and employed publicly and privately.

8. Minor collegia.—Real standing *collegia* of minor importance, but great antiquity, were those of the *fetiales*, the Salii, the Luperci. In order to assure itself that a war was correct in the eyes of heaven, the early State employed the *fetiales* to make a demand on the opposing power, according to a certain fixed form, and if the demand was not conceded, instructed the same priests to announce in another fixed ceremonial fashion to the opposing power that peace had been replaced by war. On the conclusion of the war, the same *fetiales* supervised ceremonially the conclusion of a treaty (*fœdus*). No compact was a *fœdus* unless its conclusion had been so carried out by the *fetiales*. The *ius fetiale* has often erroneously been regarded as a sort of international law. But the *fetiales* were not concerned with policy, or with questions of right and wrong. A *iustum piumque bellum* was not one which was morally correct, but one which was ceremonially flawless, having been opened with some forms on which the gods had looked with favour from immemorial time. The Salii were priests who specially served Mars. Priests bearing that name existed in a number of ancient Italic cities besides Rome. At Rome itself these priests were, even in late time, patricians. There were really two *collegia* which bore the name, one with a sanctuary on the Palatine hill, the other on the Quirinal. Each of the colleges must have originally represented a separate independent community, and both survived after the two had coalesced. The ceremonies, supposed to have been instituted by King Numa, were of the most archaic description. They sang hymns in honour of Mars as war-god, and danced in armour, in procession round the city, twice in the year, in March and October. They bore lances and the sacred *ancilia* (shields), preserved in shrines, from which they were taken on these occasions with great solemnity. The purification of the holy weapons (*armilustrium*) was performed with minute ceremony. Virgil[1] speaks with reverence of the ceremonial, but Seneca[2] allows himself to deal lightly with the *saltus saliaris*. The Luperci also had two distinct forms, like the Salii. One was connected with the Palatine hill, the other with the Quirinal. As in many other instances, it is clear that the State at an early time took the services out of the hands of particular families, for the two bore the names respectively of *Luperci Quinctiales* (from the Quinctii) and *Luperci Fabiani* (from the Fabii). In 44 B.C. Cæsar's memory was honoured by the creation of a third *collegium*, the *Luperci Iulii*, but its duration was brief. The ritual of the Luperci (evidently connected with a primitive pastoral community) was directed to purification and reconciliation with the divinity honoured (Faunus or Silvanus). The Luperci ran round the foot of the Palatine hill, on

[1] *Æn.* viii. 285. [2] *Ep.* xv. 4.

the north-west side of which lay the sacred cave called Lupercal. The priests sacrificed goats, and ran their ceremonial course with the skins of the sacrificed animals round their hips, their bodies being otherwise unclad. They bore whips in their hands, made of strips of goatskin; with these they struck women who ran in their way, desirous to escape from the reproach of barrenness. The thongs bore the name of *februa*, a word connected (as in the name *mensis Februarius*) with purificatory ritual. It is no wonder that, as Plutarch says, the Luperci themselves were constrained to laugh at portions of the ceremonial.[1] The Lupercalia continued to be performed down to A.D. 494, when Pope Gelasius I. appointed the day for the ritual of the Purification of the Virgin. The worship of Faunus, the deity with whom the festival was concerned, was a cult almost peculiar to Rome and the country immediately round it.

Although the *Fratres Arvales* are only once mentioned in extant Latin literature[2] they are well known to us from inscriptions discovered on the site of the shrine of the brotherhood, a few miles from Rome on the right bank of the Tiber, in the direction of its mouth. The first discovery was made in 1570; afterwards fragments which had been removed from the site came to light, and then in the years 1867–71 excavations on the site greatly increased the number of fragments. The whole were carefully studied by a succession of scholars, especially by W. Henzen, who published the whole with a commentary (Rome, 1868, and Berlin, 1874); also (without commentary) in *CIL* vi. (1876). The inscriptions proved to be an important source for the earlier imperial history. They embody minutes of proceedings of the brotherhood from A.D. 14, when it was refounded by Augustus, to A.D. 238. The fact of the connexion of Augustus with the shrine seems to have given the brotherhood a special interest in events and anniversaries connected with the emperors and their families; on the suitable days offerings were made and recorded in the minutes. The inscriptions have preserved (in an entry relating to A.D. 218) a hymn in Saturnian metre which is the most ancient monument of the Latin language.[3]

One college of importance, that of the Vestal Virgins, was composed of women. The early Romans were conscious of a parallelism between the religion of the family, whose centre was the family hearth, and that of the great State family, for which the hearth was in the temple of Vesta. There, as in the separate families, the unmarried daughters had a great share in the family cults. The *rex sacrorum* stood in the same relation to the Vestals as the *paterfamilias* held with the maidens of his family; and this *rex* succeeded to some of the duties which had belonged to the old *reges* before the institution of the Republic.

Other brotherhoods subsisted, some from primitive days, like the *sodales Titii*, who traced their origin to King Titus Tatius, and were supposed to maintain a ritual borrowed from the old Sabines.[4] Others were of late creation, such as the *sodales Augustales*, devoted to the imperial cult, that of the *diui imperatores*, the divinized emperors. The brotherhood consisted of twenty-one ordinary members, chosen (Tacitus says) from the very highest ranks, with four members of the imperial family. The first of these representatives were Tiberius, Germanicus, Drusus, and Claudius. Similar brotherhoods were established in honour of later emperors, Claudius, Vespasian, Titus, Hadrian, Antoninus Pius, and others; but these never attained to the same importance.

Many separate priesthoods, to which the name *flamen* was attached, also existed; some, like the *flamen* of Jupiter (*flamen Dialis*), of Mars (*Martialis*), Quirinus (*Quirinalis*), from time immemorial, others of later creation and less consequence. The three just mentioned were *flamines par excellence*, sometimes called *maiores* in contrast to all others. The *flamines minores* were attached to the service of a great many divinities, and in later time were all of plebeian quality. The really ancient offices were concerned with ritual of a remarkably archaic type. The rigorous restrictions under which the *flamen Dialis* lived are well known. He and his wife (the *flaminica*) must be married by the very ancient form of *confarreatio*. If the *flaminica* died, the *flamen ipso facto* lost his office; he could originally undertake no civil duties, though he wore the distinctive robe of civil office, the *toga prætexta*, and sat on the chair of office (the *sella curulis*); could look on no armed array; could not absent himself from his house (the *regia*, attached to the temple of Vesta) without leave from the *pontifex maximus*. He was hemmed in by many minute rules of the nature of 'tabus'; for example, it was not permissible for him to have a knot anywhere in his clothing. The office of *flamen*, generally speaking, involved personal participation in certain definite sacrifices.

LITERATURE.—The course run by Roman religion during the time of the empire is brilliantly sketched by G. Boissier, *Religion romaine d'Auguste aux Antonins*[4], Paris, 1892, and *La Fin du paganisme*[2], do. 1894. For all the subjects mentioned in this article, the best work in English is W. Warde Fowler, *Roman Festivals*, London, 1899; in German the most useful are J. Marquardt, *Römische Staatsverwaltung*, vol. v. 'Das Sacralwesen,' Leipzig, 1878, and G. Wissowa, *Religion und Kultus der Römer*, Munich, 1902 (vol. v. pt. 4 of *Handbuch der klassischen Alterthumswissenschaft*, by Iwan Müller). Many valuable articles on separate topics are in Pauly-Wissowa, and also in Roscher.

J. S. REID.

WRATH.—See ANGER.

WREATH.—See CROWN.

WRONG.—See ETHICS AND MORALITY.

WYCLIF.—I. *LIFE*.—1. **Early years and parentage.**—John Wyclif, or Wycliffe, 'drew his origin'[1] from the village of that name in Yorkshire on the southern banks of the Tees. The name of this village, the first syllable of which is *wy*, 'water,'[2] determines the spelling; the German form 'Wiclif' should be avoided. The manor of Wyclif was in the honour of Richmondshire, and the Wyclif family were undertenants of the Earl of Richmond. We first hear of the Wyclif family in 1253, when a certain Robert de Wyclif was granted a messuage in the manor; in 1263 he obtained the advowson of the church,[3] and in 1287 held of the mesne lord, William de Kirkton, twelve carucates of land in Wyclif, Girlington, and half of Thorpe.[4] In 1316 a Robert de Wyclif was lord of the manor.[5] His son or nephew Roger[6] married in 1319 Katherine, the Reformer's mother. At that time Roger's father or uncle, Robert, the lord of the manor, was still alive, and this may account for the uncertainty as to the birthplace of their

1 *Quæst. Rom.* 21.
2 Varro, *de Ling. Lat.* v. 85.
3 See Mommsen's text and comments on *CIL*, n. 28.
4 Tacitus, *Annals*, i. 54.

1 J. Leland, *De rebus Britannicis collectanea*, ed. T. Hearne, 6 vols., Oxford, 1715, ii. 329.
2 F. D. Matthew, in *Academy*, June 1884.
3 C. W. Foster, *Final Concords of the County of Lincoln*, 1920, ii. 289.
4 *J. de Kirkby's Inquest* (Surtees Soc.), London, 1867, p. 167 f.; *Vict. Co. Hist. Yorks. N.R.* i. 139, 142; R. Gale, *Registrum Honoris de Richmond*, London, 1722, p. 50.
5 *Kirkby's Inquest*, p. 334.
6 T. D. Whitaker, *Richmondshire*, 2 vols., London, 1823, i. 200; or better *Genealogist*, xx. 133–136, xxi. 95–99, for the Wyclif pedigree.

son. According to Leland,[1] he was born at 'Ipreswell, a poor village, a good mile from Richmond.' But Hipswell is at a considerable distance from Wyclif village, nor is there any proof that the Wyclifs owned land there.[2] On his marriage Roger Wyclif would be assigned one of the smaller houses on the estate, possibly Thorpe, close to Wycliffe, for which he paid the relief in 1319 of 25s. for three carucates of land that he held.[3] At what date Robert Wyclif died is unknown, but the Reformer's father Roger paid the subsidy for the whole estate in 1332–33[4] and was still alive in 1347–49.[5] The year of his death is also unknown, except that it was before 1362, for unfortunately the black letter inscription in the church at Wyclif over the tomb of Roger and Katherine gives no date.[6]

The date of birth of the son of Roger and Katherine is unknown. He is usually assumed to have been the eldest son, born shortly after the marriage.[7] But it is probable that there was an elder brother William.[8] Moreover, the date at which John Wyclif took his doctorate, in or about 1372, points to a later date of birth, nearer 1330 than 1320. Before 1362 Wyclif's father Roger died, and the Reformer became the lord of the manor. His mother was still alive in Oct. 1369, when John associated her with himself in a presentation to the living.[9] The only other connexion of Wyclif with his family estate was his nomination on 17th May 1367 on a commission issued to seven Yorkshire gentlemen to see to the keeping of the statute recently passed prohibiting the taking of salmon in certain seasons in the Tees and other rivers.[10] After Wyclif's death the estate passed to a Robert Wyclif, probably his brother, an energetic ecclesiastic who from 1390 to 1405 acted as chancellor to Walter Skirlaw, bishop of Durham. As such he took a prominent part in the trial at Bishop Auckland of the famous Lollard, Richard Wyche.[11] In 1412 Robert settled the estates on a John de Ellerton, who assumed the name of Wyclif[12] and from whom the later lords of the manor were descended. They were noted for their intense fidelity to Rome after the Reformation.

2. Early Oxford career.—At what date Wyclif went to Oxford is unknown. If he was born in 1330, it would be in or about 1345. Three colleges claim him. The claim of Queen's[13] may be dismissed as due to a confusion with a John Wyclif, possibly the Reformer's nephew, an 'almonry boy' in the Queen's grammar schools for whom in 1371 we find the college buying Latin grammars, etc.[14] The claim of Merton rests upon a catalogue of Fellows made in 1395 by Thomas Robert, still in the possession of Merton.[15] This John Wyclif, a steward or seneschal,[16] may be John Whitclif of

1 *Itinerary*², 9 vols., ed. T. Hearne, Oxford, 1744, v. 112.
2 The clerical blunder in Hearne's ed. of Leland, *Collect.* of 'Spreswell' has deceived many—*e.g.*, G. V. Lechler, *John Wyclif and his English Precursors*, ed. 1884, p. 81. For this work (hereafter known as Lechler, *JW*) see Literature below, and for Hearne's blunder R. L. Poole, *Illustrations of the Hist. of Medieval Thought*, p. 285, n. 3. No such village ever existed (Whitaker, ii. 41).
3 Gale, p. 73.
4 *Lay Subsidy Rec.* 211, no. 7*a*.
5 *Ib.* no. 23.
6 For this inscription see Whitaker, i. 198.
7 The current date, 1324, is a guess of John Lewis, *The Life and Sufferings of John Wicliffe*, 1720, p. 1 (hereafter cited as Lewis, *JW*).
8 Whitaker, *loc. cit.*
9 *Ib.* i. 200.
10 *Cal. Pat. Rolls Ed. III.*, xiii. 439. The Reformer was also returned as lord of the manor in 1375 (*Vict. Co. Hist. Yorks. N.R.* i. 139).
11 *Eng. Hist. Rev.* v. [1890] 530–544.
12 *Vict. Co. Hist. Yorks. N.R.* i. 139.
13 A. Wood, *History and Antiquities of the Colleges and Halls in the University of Oxford*, Oxford, 1786, p. 82.
14 *Hist. MSS Commission*, ii. App. 141.
15 G. C. Brodrick, *Memorials of Merton*, Oxford, 1885, p. viii.
16 Wood, p. 82.

Mayfield († Nov. 1383).[1] Possibly John Wyclif was the rare exception, a northerner in a southern college, and a recent writer claims that he had 'been worked into Merton to pacify the Northerners,'[2] and was thus the seneschal of the week expelled in 1356, as the result of a college struggle.

Wyclif's connexion with Balliol is certain. That he was Master of Balliol in the spring of 1360 (and therefore presumably previously a Fellow) is clear from a document citing his taking possession as such of a property in Gresham St. E.C.[3] His predecessor Robert Derby[4] still acted in 1356.[5] This gives the earliest possible date of Wyclif's Mastership. On 9th April 1361 Wyclif was still Master and took possession for the college of the living of Abbotsley.[6] But on 14th May 1361 he was instituted to the college living of Fillingham, near Lincoln, value 'thirty marks,' and by the then statutes was forced to resign his Mastership. Some delay, however, occurred, for in the following July he still signed himself 'Master' in a legal document connected with the transfer to the college of Abbotsley.[7] The restriction of the Fellowships at Balliol founded in 1340 by Sir Philip Somervile for those proceeding to a degree in theology to six in all will account for Wyclif leaving.

After his presentation to Fillingham Wyclif vanishes for a while from clear vision. But on 29th Aug. 1363 he obtained from his bishop, John Buckingham of Lincoln, a licence for non-residence at Fillingham 'that he might devote himself to the study of letters in the university.'[8] In consequence he paid a short visit to Oxford in Oct. 1363, living in rooms in Queen's, and a longer visit between 21st March 1365 and 26th Sept. 1366, paying 40s. 'for the rent of his room for two years.'[9] Meanwhile on 24th Nov. 1362 the University in presenting its annual 'roll of Masters' had petitioned Urban V. to provide Wyclif with 'a canonry and prebend in York, notwithstanding that he holds the church of Fillingham.' Urban granted instead the prebend of Aust in the ancient collegiate church of Westbury-on-Trim, near Bristol, worth £6, 13s. 4d. *p.a.*[10] Wyclif accepted the prebend[11] but did not reside. He was, as we have seen, reading for his doctorate at Oxford. In the spring of 1366 William Wittlesey, bishop of Worcester,[12] visited Westbury. He found that all the five canons were non-resident, and that only one had provided a vicar to discharge his duties. 'Master John Wynkele' (for thus the bishop spells the name) is expressly mentioned among the delinquents; and on 28th June 1366 Wyclif was cited to appear before the bishop on 18th July. Meanwhile his 'fruits' were sequestrated. Of any further action by Wittlesey there is no record. Wyclif continued to hold the prebend to the day of his death,[13]

1 A view strenuously maintained by W. Shirley, in *Fasciculi Zizaniorum* (1858), Rolls Series, p. 513 f. (hereafter cited as *FZ*); following Courthope in *Gent. Mag.* ii. [1842] 146–180, and extensively adopted.
2 H. S. Cronin, in *Trans. Royal Hist. Soc.*, 1914, p. 73 n.
3 *Hist. MSS Com.* iv. 448.
4 Not William Kingston, as Lechler, *JW*, p. 101, following *FZ*, p. xiv.
5 *FZ*, p. xiv n.
6 *Hist. MSS Com.* iv. 447 f.
7 *Reg. Ep. Gynwell*, f. 123, modern pagination ix f. 172; *FZ*, p. xiv.
8 Cronin, p. 74 n. This earlier licence is usually overlooked.
9 *Hist. MSS Com.*, *loc. cit.*
10 *Cal. Papal Petitions* (Rolls Ser.), i. 390; *Eng. Hist. Rev.* xv. [1900] 529, where the documents are given in full.
11 Rashdall's doubts in *DNB* lxiii. 205 are contrary to the evidence.
12 *DNB* lxi. 158.
13 In most lives of Wyclif (*e.g.*, *DNB* lxiii. 205) it is assumed that he resigned Aust in Nov. 1375. On 6th Nov., for reasons that are not clear, he was confirmed in this prebend, which on 18th Nov. was given by the king to Robert de Farrington. On 22nd Dec. 1376 this grant to Farrington was revoked on the 'information' of John of Gaunt as given in error under the

but of any discharge of duty there is no evidence.[1]

One other matter in connexion with Aust should be mentioned. By the constitution *Horribilis* of Urban V., 3rd May 1366, a return was demanded of all pluralities. Wyclif's return, which should have been made to Bishop Buckingham, does not exist, whether through his neglect or because now lost cannot be determined.[2]

While these matters were in dispute at Aust, Wyclif was nominated by Archbishop Islip[3] in a deed dated at Mayfield, 9th Dec. 1365, to be the warden of Canterbury College, Oxford, founded by Islip in 1361. Islip intended it to be a joint college of eight seculars and of four regulars from Christ Church, Canterbury. The college was started on 13th March 1363, Islip selecting as head Henry Wodehull, a monk of Abingdon. On 9th Dec. 1365 Islip dismissed Wodehull and substituted 'John de Wyclyve.' The regulars were driven out and three seculars from Merton introduced. Not content with this, Islip furthermore changed the statutes and altered the whole character of the college. While accepting the position, Wyclif did not choose to give up the rooms at Queen's. Wyclif's tenure of the office was brief. On the death of Islip (26th April 1366) the monks of Canterbury lodged an appeal. Islip's successor, Simon Langham,[4] deprived Wyclif of his office (30th March 1367), sequestrated the revenues, and finally expelled Wyclif and his three secular colleagues. Wyclif thereupon appealed to Urban V., but meanwhile for two years, if his opponents may be trusted, still lived on at Canterbury, spending freely the college goods. Wyclif's proctor, Richard Benger, one of his associates at Canterbury, failed to put in an appearance when summoned at Viterbo, and on 23rd July 1369 Cardinal Androin de la Roche, to whom Urban had referred the case, gave his decision at Monte Fiascone, though, owing to his death, it was not published until 15th May 1370. The action of Langham was upheld in every detail and Wyclif's appeal dismissed. The costs, however, were thrown upon the estate. There is no doubt that this decision was right. Islip had acted illegally in altering the trusts, upon which the royal licence in mortmain had been secured,[5] and for the condonation of this offence the monks of Canterbury were condemned on 8th April 1372 to pay a fine of 200 marks.[6] Urban evidently had some sympathy for Wyclif, for in 1369 he reserved for him a prebend in Lincoln, which, however, Wyclif never obtained or, if he obtained it, soon resigned.[1]

While the controversy over Canterbury College was still unsettled, Wyclif's licence for five years for absence from his cure expired. So on 13th April 1368 he obtained an extension 'for two years.'[2] In the following autumn he exchanged Fillingham for Ludgershall in Buckinghamshire, where he was instituted on 12th Nov. 1368. The nearness to Oxford would compensate for loss of income (10 marks instead of 30).[3] In Nov. 1371 Wyclif was one of the executors of the will of William de Askeby, archdeacon of Northampton, who in 1369 had been appointed chancellor of the exchequer.[4] Towards the close of 1372 Wyclif completed the long course of nine years and a term after Mastership necessary for taking his doctorate[5] and shortly afterwards entered the king's service.

3. In the king's service.—We date Wyclif's entrance into the civil service as about 1372. Possibly it may have been a little earlier, for Wyclif gives us a report of a speech which he himself 'heard' in the parliament which met in Westminster on 24th Feb. 1371.[6] At once he seems to have allied himself with John of Gaunt and his faction, altogether unconscious of the unscrupulous ambition and selfishness which underlay the duke's politics. But Wyclif's first appearance as a publicist was as the representative of the nation in resistance to papal exactions. On 6th June 1365[7] Urban V. had demanded the payment of the King John's annual tribute of 1000 marks together with arrears since the last payment made on 7th July 1333. Edward laid the matter before the parliament of May 1366, which indignantly refused.[8] Until recently it was believed that 'this solemn declaration set the question at rest for ever,'[9] and the older historians have all dated Wyclif's public life from 1366.[10] But there is evidence that the question of tribute was reopened by Gregory XI. in 1374, and it is in connexion with this later event that we would date Wyclif's first political tract. To consider this and other demands of Gregory a council was held at Westminster on 21st May 1374,[11] at which a prominent part in defence of papal claims was taken by a monk, John Ughtred of Boldon,[12] assisted later by William Binham, a monk of St. Albans. The debate and consequent controversy led to the publication by Wyclif,

belief that 'the prebend was vacant' (see H. J. Wilkins, *Was John Wyclif a Negligent Pluralist?*, Bristol, 1915, p. 33; *Cal. Pat. Rolls Ed. III.*, xvi. 121, 195).

[1] For Wyclif and Aust reference should be made to the researches of H. J. Wilkins, *op. cit.*, and *An Appendix to John Wycliffe*, London, 1916.

[2] A. H. Thompson's note in Wilkins, *Negligent Pluralist*, p. 86.

[3] *DNB* xxix. 74.

[4] *Ib.* xxxii. 99.

[5] *Cal. Pat. Rolls Ed. III.*, xii. 139.

[6] The identification of the warden of Canterbury with the Reformer has been a matter of much controversy. It was accepted by N. Harpsfield in his *Historia Wiclefiana*, printed in his *Historia Anglicana ecclesiastica*, London, 1622, p. 668; then by A. Wood, Lewis, Vaughan, Lechler, Poole (*Med. Thought*, p. 287 n.), Milman, Matthew. The best arguments in defence are by Canon Wilkinson in *Church Quart. Rev.* v. [1877–78] 119–141; and Cronin, pp. 55–76. The main documents have been printed by Pratt in his ed. of Foxe, *Acts and Monuments*, 1870, ii. App. 922 ff. (hereafter cited as Foxe, *AM*). Doubts were first cast by W. Courthope in *Gent. Mag.* xvi. [1841] 146, followed by Shirley, *FZ*, pp. 513–528, H. Rashdall (*DNB* lxiii. 203 f., *Universities of Europe in the Middle Ages*, London, 1895, ii. 498 n.), and others (*e.g.*, *Vict. Co. Hist. Oxford*, ii. 68), who identify the warden with John Whitclif, vicar of Mayfield, for whom see above. This identification should be rejected, for the scanty arguments in its favour cannot outweigh the evidence of contemporaries—*e.g.*, William Woodford in his *Septuaginta Questiones de sacramento altaris* (in *FZ*, p. 517), of the *Chronicon Angliæ* (Rolls Ser., 1874), p. 115. The present writer suspects also a reference in Netter, *Doctrinale*, ed. F. B. Blanciotti, Venice, 1757, iii. 485. In his *de Ecclesia*, p. 371, Wyclif makes a singularly impersonal reference to the matter.

[1] *Cal. Pap. Letters*, iv. 193.

[2] *Mem. Ep. Buckingham*, f. 56 d.

[3] *Reg. Buckingham Instit.* x. f. 419; cf. f. 130 d.

[4] A. W. Gibbons, *Early Lincoln Wills*, Lincoln, 1888, p. 25 f.; also in *Gent. Mag.* xxii. [1844] 136; Foxe, *AM* ii. 946.

[5] Knowledge of this important date, usually given, *e.g.*, by Shirley in *FZ*, p. 527, F. D. Matthew, *Eng. Works of Wyclif*, p. vi (hereafter cited as *EWW*), as 1366, can now be inferred from *Cal. Papal Letters*, iv. 193, from which we learn that Gregory XI. in a provision dated 26th Dec. 1373 (not Jan. 1373, as *DNB* lxiii. 206, copied by many) states that Wyclif recently became 'master of theology.' The date given by Bishop Bale, in the margin of *FZ*, p. 2, of 1372 is thus accurate. This date is of fundamental importance for the chronology of Wyclif's life and works, the earlier date leading to disastrous results. Unfortunately in many of the prefaces to the works of Wyclif printed by the Wyclif Society this earlier date is taken as a basis.

[6] *De Civ. Dom.* ii. c. 1. The idea of Lechler (*JW*, p. 130 f.) that Wyclif was a member of parliament either at this time or later should be dismissed. The speech in question is merely a tale taken from the contemporary *Vade mecum in tribulatione* written in 1349 by the Spiritual Franciscan, Jean de la Rochetaillade, and will be found in E. Brown's ed. of Ortuin Gratius' *Fasciculus rerum expetendarum*, London, 1690, ii. 496–507.

[7] *Cal. Pap. Lett.* iv. 16; not 13th June, as Raynaldus, xxvi. 116, followed by most historians.

[8] *Rotuli Parliamentorum*, London, 1783, ii. 289 f.

[9] J. Lingard, *Hist.*[5], London, 1849, iii. 253.

[10] *E.g.*, R. L. Poole, who is thus led as editor to date Wyclif's *de Dominio Divino* as shortly after 1366 (pp. xxiii–xxiv), following Shirley in *FZ*, pp. xvii, xxi n.; Lechler, *JW*. But see below, p. 819.

[11] Reported only in *Eulogium Historiarum*, iii. 337–339; in *DNB* lxi. 159 treated as fiction.

[12] For whom see *DNB* lviii. 17, or J. Loserth, 'Die ältesten Streitschriften Wiclifs,' in *SWAW*, 1908, pp. 7–23.

though possibly not until two years later, of his *Determinatio contra unum monachum* (*i.e.* Binham).[1] Special reference is made in the tract to the question of the tribute. Wyclif replies to Binham by giving the answer 'which I heard recently was given by secular lords in a secular council,' and reports seven so-called speeches. On analysis the speeches resolve themselves into the various 'conclusions' of Wyclif condemned by Gregory XI. in 1377, while the sixth lord gives us a brief outline of Wyclif's views of 'lordship.' To suppose that we have in them 'the earliest instance of a report of a parliamentary debate'[2] is absurd. They are all reflexions of Wyclif's own views, written, probably, eighteen months after the council.

Wyclif's services had already been rewarded by his presentation by the Crown to the rectory of Lutterworth (7th April 1374).[3] On 26th July 1374 he was appointed a member of a small commission, with John Gilbert, bishop of Bangor, as the head, to meet at Bruges a commission from Gregory.[4] For his travelling expenses Wyclif received 42s. 3d., and for his other expenses 20s. a day.[5] On the day before his departure Wyclif took some legal steps on behalf of his former proctor Richard Benger. Along with Ralph Strode, the Common Sergeant of London,[6] he went bail for him that Benger would not at Avignon attempt to obtain any papal provisions, etc.[7]

The conference at Bruges effected nothing, and by the middle of September Wyclif was back in Oxford, living in rooms at Queen's, which needed much repair, in that month.[8] In Aug. 1375 another deputation was appointed to go to Bruges to confer with Gregory's nuncio. In this deputation, though most of his former associates were retained, Wyclif was left out.[9] This omission (usually overlooked by historians, who have in consequence exaggerated his influence at Bruges) probably shows that he was too unbending for Edward's purpose. As a result on 1st Sept. 1375 a concordat between Gregory and Edward was struck.[10] Wyclif had thus no complicity in a great sham, in its main provisions a victory for the papacy.

As a result of the conference several of the actors in it received preferments. In after years Wyclif's enemies invented the story that he expected to obtain the bishopric of Worcester.[11] The story is worthless. Months before Wyclif sailed to Bruges a nomination had been made to the vacant see by Edward III.[12] That Wyclif, however, expected to receive the prebend of Caistor in Lincoln has more basis.[13] Wyclif returned from Bruges a disillusioned man. He formed the idea of writing a *Summa* of his doctrines, the introduction to which should deal with the philosophical positions which underlay the recent dispute. For the two years, Sept. 1374–Sept. 1376, he probably resided at Lutterworth, but with frequent visits to Oxford (Queen's). During those two years he developed his theory of 'lordship,' expanding his tracts against Ughtred and Binham into the two great political treatises *de Dominio Divino* and *de Civili Dominio*. He was probably engaged upon these writings during the meeting of the 'Good Parliament' (28th April 1376–6th July 1376). It is difficult to explain Wyclif's action in the autumn of 1376. John of Gaunt packed a parliament, which met on 27th Jan. 1377, with his followers, who at once proceeded to annul all the acts of the Good Parliament, while Wyclif, 'running about from church to church' in London, denounced the episcopate, who under the lead of Courtenay and Wykeham were the duke's chief opponents.[1] Wyclif's protest against the wealth, luxury, and worldliness of the clergy fell on willing ears; but nevertheless he unconsciously played the duke's reactionary game. The parliament of Jan. 1377, with its iniquitous poll-tax,[2] its restoration of Alice Perrers, and the aggrandisement of the duke by the creation of Lancashire into a county palatine,[3] is one of the worst on record.

The bishops, powerless in parliament, struck at the duke through Wyclif, and summoned the latter to appear before Convocation in St. Paul's on Thursday, 19th Feb. 1377.[4] The duke took up the challenge and, together with Earl Percy, the king's marshal, accompanied Wyclif to the trial. The proceedings ended in a riot. Wyclif was carried off by his supporters, while the London mob, on the following day, burned the duke's palace of Savoy.

Meanwhile some of Wyclif's old opponents at Oxford had accused him at the papal court. On 22nd May 1377[5] in S. Maria Maggiore in Rome Gregory issued a series of bulls directed against the Reformer.[6] With these bulls Gregory forwarded a schedule of nineteen erroneous 'propositions and conclusions,' culled from Wyclif's political and politico-ecclesiastical writings. These Gregory identified with the 'opinions and ignorant doctrine of Marsiglio of Padua and John of Jandun' condemned by John XXII.[7] An examination of the pope's schedule shows that the theses concern the status or polity rather than the doctrines of the Church.[8]

Before Edward could receive the bulls, he had passed away at Sheen (21st June 1377). His death caused delay, and the bulls were kept back until after the meeting of parliament on 13th October. This parliament was in no mood to truckle to Rome. By a writ dated 12th Dec. 1377 the bishops were ordered to make a return of all aliens, including cardinals, who held benefices.[9] To stop the drain the Council asked Wyclif for his advice 'whether the kingdom of England may lawfully . . . keep back the treasure of the kingdom.' Wyclif replied in a state-paper,[10] in which he advocated not only the stopping of all the drain to Rome but the 'prudent distribution to the glory

1 For this tract, first imperfectly printed in Lewis, *JW*, pp. 363–371, we have now Loserth's ed. in *Op. Minora*, p. 415 f. The tract should be distinguished from the *Determinatio ad argumenta Outredi*, published at the same time (*Op. Minora*, p. 405 f.).

2 Shirley, *FZ*, p. xix; Lechler, *JW*, p. 129.

3 *Cal. Pat. Rolls Ed. III.*, xv. 424.

4 T. Rymer, *Fœdera*, Record ed. iii. 1007, or ed. 1704, vii. 41; *Cal. Pat. Rolls Ed. III.*, xv. 462.

5 F. Devon, *Issues of the Exchequer*, London, 1837, p. 197.

6 For whom see *DNB* lv. 57 and the doubtful plea of J. Gollancz in his introduction to *The Pearl*, London, 1891. For Wyclif's debates with Strode see *Op. Minora*, pp. 175 f., 398 f.

7 *Cal. Close Rolls Ed. III.*, xiv. 94.

8 *Hist. MSS Com.* ii. App. 141.

9 *Cal. Pap. Lett.* iv. 144.

10 Rymer, iii. 1037–1039.

11 Netter, *Doctrinale*, i. 560, 934; the story was repeated at Basel in 1433; see P. Zatacensis, 'Lib. Diurnus,' in *Monumenta Conciliorum Generalium sec.* xv., Vienna, 1857, i. 317.

12 7th Dec. 1373; see *Reg. Sede Vacante* (Worcester Hist. Soc.), 1897, pp. 283, 290 f.

13 See references in *de Civ. Dom.* iii. 17; *Cal. Pap. Reg.* iv. 193; H. S. Cronin, in *Eng. Hist. Review*, xxxv. [1920] 564 f.

1 *Chron. Angliæ*, 116.

2 *Rotuli Parl.* ii. 364.

3 Rymer, iii. 1073.

4 For the events that follow the chief authority is the full *Chron. Angliæ*, 117–134, copied by Foxe, who had access to it, in *AM* ii. 800 f. Narratives written before the publication in 1874 of this long-lost *Chron. Angliæ* often go sadly astray.

5 Not 30th May, as *FZ*, p. xxviii.

6 For these bulls see Walsingham, *Hist. Ang.* i. 345–353; Wilkins, *Conc.* iii. 116–118, who omits those to Oxford and to Edward III.; Lewis, *JW*, pp. 46–49, 254–264, or Foxe, *AM* iii. 4–7.

7 From a study of Wyclif's works the present writer is of opinion that Wyclif knew nothing of Marsiglio first hand.

8 The schedule is best studied in Wyclif's *Protestatio* (see below), or in *FZ*, pp. 245–257. The first eight theses are taken almost verbally from Wyclif's *de Civ. Dom.*

9 *Rotuli Parl.* iii. 19; E. Powell and G. M. Trevelyan, *The Peasants' Rising and the Lollards*, London, 1899, p. 57 f., gives the return.

10 For this see *FZ*, pp. 258–271; partly translated in Foxe, *AM* iii. 54–56.

of God' of the goods of the Church. At this point 'silence was imposed upon him by the king.' Wyclif had probably been consulted by the Crown because of a paper recently published by him on the question of the oath sworn by the papal nuncio, Arnauld Garnier, on 13th Feb. 1372 that he would do nothing to the hurt of the kingdom.[1] Wyclif printed the oath and asked whether there was not a contradiction between its terms and the permission to collect monies for Rome.[2]

No steps had yet been taken to publish the bulls, though Thomas Brunton, bishop of Rochester,[3] told Wyclif in the hearing of many members of parliament that he had been condemned.[4] About this time Wyclif entered into controversy with a 'motley doctor' of Oxford, probably his accuser at Rome. This tract[5] is remarkably bold in tone. Wyclif calls upon 'the soldiers of Christ, especially the professors of evangelical poverty,' to rouse themselves against the claims of the papacy. On 28th Nov. parliament was dismissed,[6] and probably Wyclif returned to Oxford.[7] On 18th Dec. a mandate was issued to the chancellor of Oxford enclosing one of Gregory's bulls. The mandate ordered the chancellor to ascertain whether Wyclif had taught the theses in question, and to cite him to appear within thirty days at St. Paul's.[8] As the pope's bull demanded that Wyclif should be arrested,[9] the Oxford authorities were in a dilemma, for to obey 'would seem to give the pope lordship and regal authority in England.' So the vice-chancellor contented himself with ordering Wyclif 'to stay in Blackhall and not to go out.' Wyclif's theses were sent to the masters regent in theology, who 'all handed to the chancellor their conclusions.' They 'declared publicly in the schools that Wyclif's theses were true, though they sounded badly to the ear.' Wyclif replied that catholic truth should not be condemned because of its sound.[10] A few months later, on the occasion of a student-row, the vice-chancellor, who was a monk, was thrown into prison on the pretext 'that he had imprisoned John Wyclif at the mandate of the pope.'[11] About this time Wyclif published an edition of his *Protestatio* in a shortened, popular form.[12] The tract is really an appeal to the educated public against the pope's decisions. He also published an appeal to the nobility, in defence of disendowment, entitled *Speculum Secularium Dominorum.*[13]

The imprisonment by the Crown of the vice-chancellor of Oxford seems to have been intended as a warning to the papal commissioners that the Crown would not recognize papal penal jurisdiction. About the same time Wyclif appeared at Lambeth. The date is fixed by a statement of Walsingham[14] that it was shortly before the death of Gregory XI., *i.e.* before 27th March 1378, probably at the end of February, which would fit in with the summons given to Wyclif at Oxford to appear at St. Paul's. The queen-mother, Joan of Kent, sent a message to the bishops ordering them to abstain from pronouncing any final judgment. But the trial proceeded, and Wyclif put in a paper that he called a *Protestatio*[1] in which he expanded more fully the meaning of his theses. At the same time the citizens broke into the archbishop's chapel and tried to stop the trial. So the bishops contented themselves with prohibiting Wyclif 'from canvassing such theses in schools or sermons because of the scandal thereby given to the laity.'[2] Wyclif replied by publishing *Conclusiones Triginta tres de Paupertate Christi,* dealing with his idea of poverty and disendowment.[3]

In the autumn of 1378 Wyclif was seen, for the last time, in alliance with the Crown. On 11th Aug. 1378 by the order of the Government the sanctuary of Westminster was violated in order to capture two English knights between whom and the Government there had been a struggle over a Spanish captive, the count of Denia, and his ransom. One knight, Shakyl, was arrested—he had been enticed outside; the other, Haulay, was chased twice round the chancel and killed 'beside St. Edward's shrine.' Excommunications followed; and, as the outrage was popularly attributed to the hated John of Gaunt, London seethed with excitement. On 20th Oct. 1378 parliament met at Gloucester, and Archbishop Sudbury at once demanded satisfaction. The court retorted by claiming the right of arrest. The privilege of the Church was not denied, but the matter, it was pleaded, was one of debt, for which there were no rights of sanctuary. 'And on this there came into parliament doctors of theology and civil law who made argument against the prelates by many colourable and strong reasons.'[4] Among the doctors was John Wyclif, who interrupted the writing of his *de Ecclesia* to lay before parliament a defence of the Crown's action.[5] He claimed for the Crown a right to absolute obedience in all matters not contrary to God's law and, while admitting sanctuary for accidental homicide, subjects the right in general and of Westminster Abbey in particular to severe criticism. Shortly after this incident Wyclif finished his great treatise *de Ecclesia.* This was followed by a companion work, *de Officio Regis,* the two forming a complete exposition of his views on the relations of Church and State.

4. Break with the Mediæval Church.—The Great Schism in the autumn of 1378 flung Wyclif into complete antagonism to the papacy. Hitherto Wyclif had not disputed the spiritual primacy of the popes, though ready enough to attack papal pretensions and to speak ill of individual popes.[6] His position had been this: we must obey the pope as the vicar of Christ, but the vicar of Christ, who could have no temporal sovereignty, must be the holiest, the most God-enlightened man in Christendom. Moreover, 'no pope is to be believed unless he is teaching by the inspiration of God, or founding his utterances on Scripture.'[7] The whole authority of the office was thus determined by the pope's character as one of the elect, and, inasmuch as this knowledge was beyond human ken, could only be judged from his deeds. Obedience to the papacy was thus a matter of convenience and church order—a position in which Wyclif unconsciously closely followed Marsiglio in his *Defensor Pacis.*

The schism drew Wyclif from this standpoint. He had hailed the election of Urban VI. (8th April

1 Rymer, iii. 933; and cf. *Cal. Close Rolls Ed. III.*, xiii. 424.
2 For this paper, which is preserved in two Vienna MSS, see Lechler, *JW* (German ed.), App.
3 *DNB* vi. 350.
4 Wyclif, *de Ecclesia*, p. 354.
5 *FZ*, pp. 481-492.
6 *Rotuli Parl.* iii. 29.
7 *Eulog. Hist.* iii. 348.
8 Lewis, *JW*, p. 264 f.; also Wilkins, *Conc.* iii. 123 f., with wrong date of 28th Dec.
9 Walsingham, *Hist. Ang.* i. 351.
10 *Eulog. Hist.* iii. 348
11 *Ib.* iii. 349; Rymer, iv. 32; Wilkins, iii. 137; and cf. Wyclif, *de Eccl.* p. 355; the tract, *de Incarcerandis Fidelibus* in *Op. Minora*, p. 92 f., should be assigned to this date.
12 *FZ*, pp. 245-257.
13 *Op. Minora*, p. 74 f.
14 *Hist. Ang.* i. 358.

1 Found in Walsingham, i. 357-363; *Chron. Angliæ*, 184-189, tr. in Foxe, *AM* iii. 13 f.
2 Walsingham, i. 363; *Chron. Angliæ*, 183.
3 *Op. Minora*, p. 19 f.
4 *Rotuli Parl.* iii. 37.
5 Wyclif's defence of the Crown and his general attack on sanctuary was expanded by him into six chapters which he incorporated in his *de Ecclesia*, pp. 142-274.
6 *De Eccl.* p. 358; cf. *ib.* p. 366.
7 *De Apostasia*, pp. 65, 173. Wyclif's middle views on the papacy can best be studied in his *de Potestate Pape*, ed. J. Loserth, 1907.

1378) and had 'thanked God for providing our mother church with a catholic head, an evangelical man.'[1] But the tactlessness of the new pope, the breaking out of the schism by the election at Fondi on 20th Sept. of the French pope, Clement VII., and the subsequent conduct of Urban drew Wyclif into a fierce antagonism, the more bitter because he acknowledged that Urban had been lawfully chosen. This antagonism became complete when on 6th Dec. 1382 Richard II. authorized Bishop Despenser[2] to proclaim a crusade on Urban's behalf against the antipope.[3] The later development of this crusade,[4] its disgraceful attack upon Dunkirk, its defeat at Ypres, and the return to England in Oct. 1383 of the discredited host infused into all Wyclif's later writings a deadly hatred to the papacy itself. At first he attempted to save his position by maintaining that 'our Urban' was innocent of this 'crime,' which was really the work of the friars.[5] But, when this argument was cut away by Urban's deeds, he averred that the cardinals had no right to choose a man who acted contrary to God's will.[6] All his theories were wrecked by the spectacle of two popes each claiming to be the sole head of the Church, each labelling the other as antichrist 'like dogs quarrelling for a bone,' 'like crows resting on their carrion,'[7] each seeking to bring about a general Armageddon for the destruction of his rival. The writings of his last years, especially in 1383, are full of this theme.

Wyclif's break with the papacy might have been passed over as an extreme form of the Gallicanism of the age which culminated in the Council of Constance. But his anti-papalism developed side by side with his attack upon the central doctrine of the mediæval Church, transubstantiation. Wyclif's attack flung Oxford into an uproar, and the new chancellor, William de Berton,[8] in the autumn of 1379 or early in 1380,[9] called a council of twelve doctors, of whom six were friars, to consider Wyclif's heresies. Their verdict, published late in 1380, was a foregone conclusion.[10] It was read unexpectedly in Wyclif's presence while he was sitting in the schools of the Augustinians and 'determining the contrary.' On hearing the condemnation Wyclif was 'confused,' but he recovered himself sufficiently to say that 'neither the chancellor nor any of his accomplices could alter his convictions.'[11] He might have appealed to the Congregation of Regent Masters and from their decision to the Great Congregation of the University;[12] characteristically he appealed instead to the king. John of Gaunt hurried down and urged him to be silent.[13] Wyclif refused. He had done with his entanglement in the Lancastrian alliance, and on 10th May 1381 published a Latin defence of his views called the *Confessio*.[14] This was followed at Oxford by a series of determinations against him, three of which have come down to us.[1]

After the publication of his *Confessio* Wyclif left Oxford for ever, and retired to Lutterworth. To those last months at Oxford must be assigned the familiar tale of his illness and of his declaring to certain friars who came to counsel him: 'I shall not die, but I shall live and declare the works of the Lord.'[2] To this period also we assign the commencement by Wyclif and his assistants of his translation of the Bible, and the full organization of his Poor Priests, who, however, had already been at work for some years.[3] The Poor Priests were not laymen, as is so often assumed, but 'unauthorised preachers,' *i.e.* without a bishop's licence, who moved from place to place, carrying Wyclif's tracts and sermons with them. Clad in russet robes of undressed wool, without sandals, purse, or scrip, for a few years they became a power in the land until crushed out by the legislation of Archbishop Arundel and Henry V.

Meanwhile at Oxford on 30th May 1381 Berton was turned out of the chancellorship, and Robert Rigg[4] took his place. Rigg allowed full liberty to teach the condemned doctrines, and during the winter of 1381-82 feeling ran high. The flames were fanned by the Peasant Insurrection of the summer of 1381. Both parties sought to fasten upon the other the opprobrium of this revolt. The regulars accused Wyclif and brought forward alleged confessions of John Ball.[5] Nicholas of Hereford[6] and the Lollards retorted by accusing the friars. On 18th Feb. 1382 the friars appealed to John of Gaunt through Stephen Patrington.[7] As the duke returned no answer, the friars appealed to Courtenay. On 7th May 1382, when parliament assembled,[8] Wyclif laid before it a memorial. He claimed that England should obey no prelate unless such obedience agreed with Christ's law, that money should not be sent to Rome unless it could be proved from Scripture to be due, that the Commonwealth 'should not be burdened with new tallages' until the endowments of the clergy be exhausted, that the king should employ neither 'bishop nor curate' in secular business, that the temporalities of any bishop 'living notoriously in contempt of God' should be confiscated, and that no one should be excommunicated until it is proved that the sentence is according to 'God's law.'[9]

Along with this formal petition Wyclif prepared an English *Complaint*, which has come down to us in an incomplete form.[10] In this *Complaint* he deals with four only of the seven matters of his petition, but includes the request that 'Christ's

[1] *De Eccl.* p. 37.
[2] *DNB* xiv. 416.
[3] Rymer, iv. 157; Knighton, *Chron.* ii. 201-203; Wyclif, *Polem. Works*, 2 vols., London, 1883, ii. 600.
[4] There is a sketch in English by G. M. Wrong, *The Crusade of 1383*, London, 1892; for the Flemish account see J. Meyer, *Commentarii sive Annales rerum Flandricarum*, Antwerp, 1561, p. 193 f.
[5] *Polem. Works*, ii. 574, 593.
[6] *Ib.* ii. 613.
[7] *Ib.* ii. 591.
[8] *DNB* iv. 411.
[9] The date of Wyclif's attack is usually placed later (Matthew, *Eng. Hist. Rev.* v. 328-330, in the summer of 1380, and most writers later still), following *FZ*, p. 104. The date will depend upon that of the Council of Twelve, usually placed (*e.g.*, *DNB* lx. 229) as early in 1382. But this date is too late (see *DNB* iv. 412). Berton was chancellor from 1379 to 1381 (*Eng. Hist. Rev.* v. 329), and the council must have been held within these limits and before the publication of Wyclif's *Confessio*. According to a note on the MS of *FZ*, p. 115, this was published on 10th May 1381.
[10] *FZ*, pp. 110-113.
[11] *Ib.* p. 113.
[12] *Munimenta Academica Oxon.*, in Rolls Series, 2 vols., London, 1868, i. 231.
[13] Wilkins, *Conc.* iii. 171; *FZ*, p. 114.
[14] In *FZ*, pp. 115-132. There is a brief English abstract in *Select English Works of Wyclif*, ed. T. Arnold, Oxford, 1869 (hereafter quoted as *SEW*), iii. 500, which Knighton, *Chron.* ii. 157, avers was by Wyclif, put in by him as a disavowal at the Blackfriars Synod (see below).

[1] *FZ*, pp. 133-241.
[2] Foxe, *AM* iii. 20.
[3] The Poor Priests undoubtedly preceded the Peasants' Rising, in the organization of which they were accused of playing a part. See T. Wright, *Political Poems*, in Rolls Series, 2 vols., London, 1859-61, ii. 23-56; *Rotuli Parl.* iii. 124 f.; *Eulog. Hist.* iii. 351; Matthew, *EWW*, p. 444; Walsingham, i. 324.
[4] *DNB* l. 53.
[5] *FZ*, p. 273 f.; repeated in J. Stow, *Annales*, London, 1615, p. 294. For Ball see *DNB* iii. 73.
[6] *DNB* xl. 418.
[7] *FZ*, pp. 292-295; for Patrington see *DNB* xliv. 47; J. H. Wylie, *The Reign of Henry the Fifth*, Cambridge, 1914, i. 236 f.
[8] *Rotuli Parl.* iii. 122.
[9] For this petition, which Wyclif called *Imprecationes*, see Wyclif, *de Blasphemia*, p. 270 f. It is also found in Walsingham, ii. 51 f. where no. 4 really forms the last clause of no. 3. Walsingham or his editor, H. T. Riley, mistakenly calls it *Interpretationes*. Lechler, *JW*, p. 405, following R. Vaughan, *John de Wycliffe*, London, 1853, p. 289, wrongly dates as presented after the Blackfriars Synod to the parliament which met 6th-26th Oct. (*Rotuli Parl.* iii. 132). There is no mention of the Petition in the records of parliament.
[10] Printed by T. James in 1608; also very imperfectly by Lewis, *JW*, p. 83 f., and with rectification of the order of the text by Arnold, *SEW* iii. 507-523.

teaching concerning the Eucharist, that this sacrament is very bread and also very Christ's body,' 'may be taught only in churches.'

To these attacks the new archbishop, William Courtenay, replied by summoning a committee to meet on 17th May in the Blackfriars. Nine bishops, sixteen doctors of theology, eleven doctors of laws, seven bachelors of theology, and two bachelors of laws were selected by Courtenay.[1] Of the sixteen doctors of theology all but one, and he a monk, were friars, several of them noted opponents of Wyclif.[2] Wyclif himself was not summoned to appear,[3] nor was his name mentioned. Twenty-four conclusions from his writings were produced which were deemed 'heretical' or 'erroneous.'[4]

On Wednesday 21st May the Committee met again. Between two and three in the afternoon a terrific earthquake shook the city. Courtenay pointed out that it was the effort of the earth to purge itself, 'though not without violence,' of heresy. Courtenay's happy interpretation saved the Committee, and Wyclif found it necessary to publish an interpretation in an opposite sense. 'The earth-din,' he maintained, was the outcry of the world against the heretic prelates and friars.[5] Henceforth Wyclif always called it in contempt 'the Earthquake council,'[6] so much so that Netter complained that Wyclif treated the earthquake as a miracle wrought for his benefit.[7]

On the day after the Earthquake Synod Courtenay persuaded Richard to admit into the final statute of parliament a chapter ordering sheriffs, upon certification from the bishops, to arrest and imprison all itinerant preachers. The ordinance had never received the consent of the Commons.[8] This was followed on 26th June by letters patent from Richard directed against the itinerant preachers.[9] When parliament reassembled on 6th Oct., protest was at once made against the pretended statute,[10] but to no avail, for in after years it was treated as still valid.[11] Action more constitutional was taken by Courtenay when on 30th May, a week after the Blackfriars Synod, he forwarded a mandate to the bishops bidding them publish Wyclif's condemnation 'with all possible speed.'[12]

5. Last years.—After the Blackfriars Synod Wyclif took no further public part in controversy at Oxford. On 30th July 1382 his followers, Nicholas of Hereford and Repingdon,[13] were excommunicated, but Wyclif's name was not inserted.[14] Possibly he owed his immunity to John of Gaunt. The idea that Wyclif, when summoned in Nov. 1382 before a Synod at Oxford, made a recantation[15] may be dismissed. In the minutes of the Synod[16] there is no such record. The whole story

1 Wilkins, *Conc.* iii. 157.
2 Lists in *FZ*, pp. 286–288, and less completely in *FZ*, p. 498; also in Wilkins, *Conc.* iii. 158. In all lists the names are inaccurate.
3 Knighton, *Chron.* ii. 157, is an error.
4 No direct record of this committee has come down to us. But we have copies of its conclusions in Wilkins, *Conc.* iii. 157 f., carefully copied into the *Register of Wykeham*, ed. T. F. Kirby, 2 vols., London, 1896, 1899, ii. 338–342; also in *FZ*, pp. 277–282; Walsingham, ii. 58 f.; Knighton, *Chron.* ii. 158 f.
5 Arnold, *SEW* iii. 503; Knighton, *Chron.* ii. 162; cf. Wyclif, *Trialogus*, p. 376.
6 *Trial.* p. 374, *Sermones*, iii. 292, 370, and *passim*.
7 *Doctrinale*, iii. 770.
8 For this see *Rotuli Parl.* iii. 124 f., *Statutes of the Realm*, Record Com. ed. ii. 25, carefully entered into *Reg. Wykeham*, ii. 343.
9 *Cal. Pat. Ric. II.*, ii. 150; Wilkins, iii. 156, wrongly dated as 12th July; *Register of Thomas de Brantyngham*, ed. F. C. Hingeston-Randolph, London, 1901, i. 466 f.
10 *Rotuli Parl.* iii. 141.
11 *Statutes*, iii. 454, iv. 244.
12 Wilkins, *Conc.* iii. 157 f.
13 *DNB* xlviii. 26.
14 Wilkins, iii. 167–168.
15 A. Wood, *Hist. and Antiquities of the University of Oxford*, ed. J. Gutch, 2 vols., Oxford, 1792, i. 500.
16 Wilkins, iii. 172.

rests upon a blunder of Knighton,[1] who has confused an uncompromising defence by Wyclif of his views[2] with a recantation.

Nothing in fact more emphatically marks the hold that Wyclif still had upon the nation than the reluctance of Courtenay to push matters to the extreme. Wyclif was left to close his days in peace at Lutterworth. In the autumn of 1382 he was stricken with paralysis[3] and thereafter was largely dependent on his curates, John Horn and Purvey. But his pen was never more prolific than in these latter days. He published polemic after polemic, as well as finishing the *Summa* of his doctrines in thirteen volumes. With tireless energy he repeated all his old attacks, dwelling especially on the need of disendowment—this he carried to the extreme of demanding even the confiscation of the revenues of Oxford colleges[4]—holding up to ridicule the misdeeds of the friars and the unapostolic character of the papacy, and defending at length his views of the Eucharist, to the need of which sacrament he attached less importance than formerly.[5] In matters of Church organization he became completely critical and destructive. He seems to have been occupied with many works at once, dictating the main lines of thought and leaving to his disciples the necessary copying of material, a method which led to repetition and frequent inconsistency. In two of his *Sermons* on the same Gospel we have a totally different translation.[6] Several of his works, including the important *Trialogus* and his *Opus Evangelicum*, were still unfinished when the end came.

Wyclif's English writings form one of the special features of these last years. Abandoning Oxford and the appeal to the Schoolmen, he became a popular pamphleteer, trusting to his Poor Preachers to scatter the tracts broadcast. To this period also we must ascribe the publication of his English *Sermons*. Wyclif's last works are also marked by an extreme bitterness of tone, especially in his attacks against the friars.[7] To this he was aroused by the part they had taken in 1383 in Bishop Despenser's blundering crusade in Flanders, and by their attacks upon his Poor Preachers. Despenser's crusade also completed the break between Wyclif and the papacy. No words became too strong with which to express his detestation of the whole institution.

There are grounds for believing that the friars in their anger appealed to Rome and that Urban replied by citing Wyclif to appear before his court. All we know, however, is deduction from a reply or letter of excuse which Wyclif addressed to Urban VI., in reality a keenly ironical statement of his attitude towards the papacy. He excuses himself from obeying 'this unskilful summoning' because of his physical infirmities, for the 'king of kings has willed it that he should not go.' The reference is to a stroke of paralysis from which he suffered 'for two years before his death.'[8]

The account of Wyclif's death has been handed down by John Horn, his curate at Lutterworth after his stroke. In 1441 Horn gave his evidence to Dr. Thomas Gascoigne. He stated on oath that on 28th Dec. 1384 'as Wyclif was hearing mass

1 *Chron.* ii. 156–158, 160–162.
2 Printed also in *SEW* iii. 502–503; very imperfectly in Lewis, *JW*, p. 87.
3 Lewis, *JW*, p. 286.
4 *Polem. Works*, i. 271 f.; cf. *Serm.* ii. 18.
5 *Polem. Works*, ii. 620; cf. i. 257.
6 *SEW* i. 235, ii. 393; a proof, probably, that the translation was by his followers.
7 See especially his *Polem. Works*.
8 For this incident see *Polem. Works*, ii. 556; *Op. Minora*, p. 159; *Op. Evang.* i. 20, 434; *FZ*, p. 341 f. The letter is also printed by J. Loserth, in *Op. Minora*, London, 1913, p. 1, who dates it 1378, for reasons that do not convince.

in his church at the time of the elevation of the host he fell down, smitten by a severe paralysis especially in the tongue so that neither then nor afterwards could he speak to the moment of his death.'[1] Three days later, Saturday, 31st Dec. 1384, he passed away.[2]

On 4th May 1415 the Council of Constance, acting on the request of an English Synod under Arundel held in the early spring of 1411,[3] condemned 260 propositions in Wyclif's writings and ordered 'his bones to be dug up and cast out of the consecrated ground, provided they could be identified from those of Christians buried near.'[4] After some years of delay the decree was carried out by the ex-Lollard Richard Fleming, bishop of Lincoln,[5] acting on the peremptory orders of Martin V. (9th Dec. 1427).[6] On 16th Dec. letters were sent by Martin V. to various mayors to assist.[7] So shortly after 25th March 1428 'his vile corpse they consigned to hell and the river (Swift) absorbed his ashes.'[8]

II. *Teaching and writings.* — **1. Philosophical.**—Wyclif's philosophical writings were written in his earlier Oxford career, when he was the 'flower of Oxford' Scholasticism. At a later date they were collected into a *Summa*. Some of the works have come down to us—*e.g.*, *de Compositione Hominis*—rather as notes for lectures or disputations than as mature treatises. All his works abound in quotations, often vague and inaccurate, from the accepted authorities of his day, including the great Arabians.

Judged as a Schoolman, Wyclif belonged to the moderate realists. He had learned much from the criticisms of Ockham,[9] of whom he speaks with respect. But the Platonism to which he leaned he had derived from St. Augustine, though in his method he bowed, as did all Schoolmen, to the authority of Aristotle. To Wyclif nominalism in any form was an impossible creed. He held that names stand for realities.[10] He therefore held, as his many writings on the subject show, that the most important question in metaphysics was that of universals.[11] As with all realists, Wyclif was at times in danger of pantheism. When he states that body and soul are united eternally, it is because he considers man as *materia prima*, 'in consequence created in the beginning of the world,' whose individuality therefore as distinct from the common 'form' of humanity becomes unreal and phenomenal, or at any rate hard to explain.[12]

2. Political and social. —(*a*) *His theory of 'dominion.'*—Shortly after his return from Bruges Wyclif commenced the expansion of his *Determinatio* into two large treatises, the *de Dominio Divino*—which work was intended to serve as an introduction to the *Summa*—and the *de Civili Dominio*. In both we note the influence upon Wyclif of Richard Fitzralph, archbishop of Armagh.[13] Wyclif 'has added no essential element to the doctrine which he read in the work of his predecessor.'[1] Wyclif commences his *de Dominio Divino* with a distinction between 'lordship' and 'use,' in which he followed, through Fitzralph, the views of William Ockham, and the Spiritual Franciscans to whom the distinction had been fundamental in their struggle with John XXII. 'Lordship' is the prerogative of God and is never separated from possession. The possession of the creature is always held subject to due service to the lord in chief; it is but the possession of a steward. Thus Wyclif works out by use of feudal ideas the same belief in the duties of property which modern reformers attempt to reach by other means. From this fundamental position it is an easy transition to the corollary that dominion is founded on grace and that mortal sin is a breach of tenure and so 'incurs forfeiture.'[2]

Wyclif's doctrine would have led to anarchical consequences, as indeed was pointed out to Hus at Constance,[3] had it not been for Wyclif's careful distinction between 'dominion,' which belongs to the righteous man alone, and power, which the wicked may have by God's permission. From this main thesis 'that every righteous man is lord over the whole sensible world' it was an easy step to Wyclif's doctrine of communism.[4] But Wyclif always insists that the righteous must in nowise attempt to acquire their inalienable rights by force. He had yet to learn, through the Peasants' Revolt, that a smouldering fire and a powder magazine are dangerous neighbours. When the blaze came, he was, in consequence, charged with being responsible. The charge was unjust; the two movements were coincident.[5] The confessions of John Ball were fictitious; nevertheless the Peasants' Revolt (1381) was but the rude translation into the world of practice of a theory of 'dominion' that destroyed the 'lordship' of the wicked. 'It is to Wyclif's credit that, when the Peasants were defeated, he dared to own his sympathy with their wrongs and to put in a plea for mercy.'[6] But sorrow for the woes of the poor runs through all his English writings like a wail of love and redeems his fiercest denunciations, his most impossible dreams. 'Poor men,' he cries, 'have naked sides, and dead walls have great plenty of waste gold.'[7]

(*b*) *Church and State.*—His theory of 'dominion' drew Wyclif into an examination of the limits of obedience[8] and of the prerogatives and duties of the kingly office in his *de Officio Regis*, in reality his most complete treatise on the relations of Church and State. The dignity of the king, he held, was derived immediately from God. The king represents the glorified and therefore ruling Christ, the priest the suffering and submissive Christ; the king represents the will, the priest the love of God.[9] As God's vicar the king has supremacy over the clergy.[10] Episcopal jurisdiction is derived from the king,[11] and the king may inquire into all sins[12] and must withdraw temporalities from those in sin—a duty which Wyclif soon widens into that of general disendowment. By His obedience to Pilate Christ has shown that even tyrants must be obeyed.[13] Henry VIII. could have asked no more thoroughgoing defence of Erastianism or of the divine right of kings against

1 Leland, *Collect.* ii. 409. In Lewis, *JW*, p. 286, there is a slightly different version from *Cotton MSS* A. 14, said to be in Gascoigne's own handwriting.

2 The date is given in Walsingham, ii. 119, and in Gascoigne, *Loci e libro veritatum* (ed. J. E. T. Rogers, Oxford, 1881), p. 116, as also in the official statement in the Lincoln registers recording the institution of his successor, John Morhouse, on 25th Jan. 1385 (H. J. Wilkins, *Chapters in the Ecclesiastical History of Westbury on Trim*, Bristol, 1909, p. 81).

3 Wilkins, *Conc.* iii. 350.

4 H. von der Hardt, *Magnum œcumenicum Constantiense concilium*, iv. 149–157; F. Palacky, *Documenta J. Hus vitam, doctrinam, etc., illustrantia*, Prague, 1869, p. 569.

5 *DNB* xix. 282.

6 O. Raynaldus, *Annales*, ed. J. D. Mansi, Lucca, 1752, vol. xxviii. ann. 1427, § 14.

7 *Cal. Pap. Letters*, vii. 23.

8 Netter, *Doctrinale*, iii. 830; and for the date J. Bale, *Script. illust. Maj. Bryt. Catalogus*, i. 456.

9 *DNB* xli. 357.

10 Cf. *de Apost.* pp. 136, 141, 142.

11 Treated fully in *Miscell. Philosoph.* ii.

12 *De Comp. Hom.* pp. 19 f., 33, 35.

13 *DNB* xix. 194.

1 R. L. Poole, in *de Dom. Div.* p. xlviii.

2 *De Civ. Dom.* i. chs. 1–6.

3 Palacky, *Doc.* p. 299.

4 *De Civ. Dom.* i. chs. 7, 14.

5 So admitted in *Chron. Ang.* pp. 310–312.

6 *EWW*, p. 233 f.; *de Blasphemia*, pp. 188–203.

7 *SEW* iii. 170; *EWW*, p. 91.

8 *De Civ. Dom.* i. ch. 28.

9 *EWW*, p. 362; cf. *Eng. Hist. Rev.* xix. [1904] 333.

10 *De Off. Reg.* p. 66 f.; cf. *de Eccl.* p. 322; *SEW* ii. 88.

11 *De Off. Reg.* ch. 6.

12 *Ib.* p. 119.

13 This is the origin of Wyclif's famous fatal contention that 'God must obey the devil,' Walsingham, pp. 52, 58.

Church and pope than this treatise, with its claim that it is lawful to pull down a church to build a (military) town, or to melt chalices to pay for soldiers.[1]

3. Theological.—(*a*) *Doctrine of the Church.*—Wyclif's realism lay at the root of all his views of the Church and its sacraments. It led him to warn his hearers against the nominalist heresy that there was no Church before the incarnation of Christ.[2] It drew him into an extreme determinism. Above all it brought him into collision with the prevailing nominalist heresies concerning the Sacrament. For the nominalist, who held that the universal name was but a mere *flatus vocis,* found it easy to believe in the Scotist doctrine of the annihilation of the substance of the elements. To Wyclif such an idea was an absurdity; his whole philosophical system fell to the ground with its mere possibility. If in one case accidents can exist without substance, why postulate substance at all?[3] Hence his realism is a protest against any doctrine of illusion. So, in the interpretation of his ideas, we must remember that, when Wyclif speaks, as he sometimes does, of the host as a 'sign,'[4] he does not use the word in any Zwinglian sense. With him every figure is a reality, with its own real though ideal existence, while every real is also of necessity universal. To this philosophic basis we may also attribute Wyclif's complete repudiation of the nihilianism as to the humanity of Jesus which through Peter Lombard's *Sentences* had infected the mediæval Church. He identifies Christ, especially in his early scholastic treatise, *de Benedicta Incarnatione,* with the *communis homo,* or universal man, who is identical with all His brethren.

Wyclif's views on the Church are best studied in his *de Ecclesia,* written about Easter 1378.[5] The key to the whole is his rigid predestinarianism, in which he shows the influence upon himself of Archbishop Thomas Bradwardine's *de Causa Dei.*[6] Like Bradwardine, he bases everything upon the all-conditioning absolute will of God. The Church Militant he defines as the whole number of the elect, containing 'only men that shall be saved,' and who cannot as predestinate cease to be such even by mortal sin, for theirs is the grace of final perseverance.[7] He adds that no man, not even a pope, 'wots whether he be of the church or whether he be a limb of the fiend,'[8] nor will he allow that 'the church can ever be called the whole body (*universitas*) of faithful travellers.' In this narrower view Wyclif shows a marked contrast to Marsiglio. He refuses therefore to allow that 'Christ is the head of all men, both of the faithful and unfaithful,' but claims that this is restricted to the predestinate.[9] Nevertheless he guards his doctrine from some of its dangers by his warning that, 'as each man shall hope that he is safe in bliss, so he should suppose that he be a limb of holy Church.'[10]

From this basis of the Church certain conclusions followed. The pope is not necessarily the head of the Church, for it is not certain that he is a member of it. His position is therefore determined not by his institutional status but by his conformity with the tests of the predestinate, especially harmony with the teachings of the Bible.[1] Much also of the Catholic system as then believed was swept away as needless for the predestinate and useless for the foreknown—*e.g.*, prayers for the dead, the cult of saints, absolution—nor is he clear as to the value of the priesthood, the sacraments, or even of prayer which 'standeth in good life' and 'holy desire to do God's will.'[2] We may note that Wyclif's theory of spiritual values grounded in worthiness, resting on the absolute Divine Will, was logically one with his theory of dominion grounded on grace, and led to a sweeping doctrine of disendowment.

(*b*) *Doctrine of the Eucharist.*[3]—In the mediæval theory of the Eucharist there was at consecration a twofold movement: the cessation of the bread and the creation of the Body. Wyclif's difficulties lay with the former of these. It was acknowledged that as regards the cessation of the bread the movement was not complete, for it did not extend to the accidents. The *noumenon* was changed, but the *phenomena* remained. Explanations of this mystery varied. Thomas Aquinas answered the question by his conception of *quantitas*—or, as we should now term it, 'subsistence' as distinct from 'substance.' 'Quantity' is not extension or a mere abstraction or a mere mode of being. It may be defined as the force which makes extension, *vis extensiva materie.* At the words of consecration 'quantity' takes the place of the substance of the bread and upholds the accidents, and therefore whatever the bread can do, even to feeding the body, is performed by the 'quantity' that remains.

The same question was answered by Duns Scotus, following Ægidius Romanus,[4] by his doctrine of absolute accidents, maintained, on the annihilation of the substance, by the unconditioned will of God. The Eucharist is thus the constant repetition of a stupendous miracle. To Wyclif as a realist the annihilation of anything was inconceivable.[5] At first he fell back in his defence of the Real Presence upon the Thomist idea of 'quantity,' then prevalent in Oxford, though he subjected it later to considerable criticism.

It is not possible out of Wyclif's later writings to deduce a consistent system. Of the Real Presence he had no doubt, and looked upon its denial as a renewal of the heresy of Berengarius,[6] but he lost himself in trying to explain his position. He was driven by his nominalist opponents from position to position until he put forth a theory practically identical with consubstantiation, full of hair-splitting distinctions. He regarded as

1 *De Off. Reg.* p. 185; cf. *de Eccl.* p. 376 f.
2 *De Eccl.* chs. 17, 18, also p. 123 f.
3 *De Euch.* p. 69 f.
4 *Ib.* p. 16, *de Apost.* p. 223.
5 Wyclif published in 1383 a compressed version which he called *de Fide Catholica* in *Op. Minora,* p. 98 f. This was widely disseminated in Bohemia.
6 For Bradwardine, who is not mentioned by Ueberweg, see *DNB* vi. 188, and the preface by H. Savile in his ed. of T. Bradwardine's *de Causa Dei,* London, 1618. Wyclif differed considerably from Bradwardine in his definition of free will (*de Ente,* p. 152 ff.).
7 *SEW* iii. 447; *de Eccl.* pp. 74, 111, 140.
8 *De Eccl.* pp. 3, 5, 29, 130, 464; cf. *SEW* iii. 339.
9 *De Eccl.* p. 57 f.; cf. *SEW* iii. 395; *EWW,* p. 198.
10 *EWW,* p. 350.

1 *De Eccl.* pp. 34, 88; *de Apost.* p. 200; *SEW* iii. 505.
2 *EWW,* pp. 76, 274; *SEW* iii. 219, 425.
3 Wyclif's earlier views are best summed up in *FZ,* pp. 104–109, 115–132. The last is of special importance, and should be studied by all. His later and larger Latin works add little but expansion and repetition to the above, and may be passed by save by the specialist. But the reader should not neglect Loserth's Introduction to the *de Eucharistia,* London, 1892, or M. H. Dziewicki's Introduction to the *de Apostasia,* do. 1889. (Of the body of the *de Apost.* chs. xv. and xvi. are the most valuable; of the *de Euch.* pp. 15, 16, 18, 53, 83, 84, 85, 90, 93, 99, 111, 113, 123.) Cf. also Dziewicki's Introduction, *de Simonia,* London, 1898, xvi–xxi. His views in English are best summed up in *SEW* iii. 426, 403–410, 502. This last is practically identical with the *Wycket,* which, if written by Wyclif, represents a very late phase, almost Zwinglian in outlook. The present writer inclines to ascribe it to his followers. For other important passages of Wyclif dealing with the Eucharist, see *EWW,* p. 465, *SEW* ii. 358, 386, 404, iii. 484, 500, *de Blas.* 26–30, 287, *Trial.* iv. 247–255, *Serm.* ii. 453 f., 458 f., 461–463. For the relation of Wyclif's doctrines of space and time to his doctrine of transubstantiation see M. H. Dziewicki, *Johannis Wyclif Tractatus de Logica,* London, 1893–96, iii. Introd. vii–viii. The withholding of the cup from the laity, which played so important a part in Bohemia, did not trouble Wyclif.
4 *Theoremata de Corpore Christi,* Venice, 1502, prop. v. 38 f.
5 *De Ente,* p. 288 f.
6 *De Apost.* p. 79.

beyond question 'that Christ lies hidden in the elements,' that we can 'see' Him there 'by faith,' and receive Him in the host as the sun's fire is received through a sphere of crystal, and that Christ is in every part of the host, as when you break a glass and in every part 'thou mayest see thy face, and thy face not parted' or 'as a man may light many candles at one candle.' But the words of consecration 'make the occasion only' of Christ's presence, who is there 'not identically according to substance,' but 'really and truly according to His whole humanity.' On the logical side Wyclif never wearied of pouring scorn upon the idea of 'accidents without subject.' Such a doctrine seemed to him to strike at the root of all being, including that of the saints, and by throwing a doubt on the testimony of our senses to discredit all science.[1] Unfortunately in his abhorrence of all Scotist annihilations he used language that easily became twisted, especially by his more ignorant followers. That which is not or which is mere phantasm is necessarily less perfect than that which is, especially that which has life. Hence the unfortunate comparisons of the host to 'rat's bread,' 'spiders,' and the like,[2] especially by the later Lollards—*e.g.*, John Badby.

Along with this main position Wyclif advocated other doctrines that seemed to him corollaries. In his earlier years he insisted on the sacramental function of the priest,[3] though regarding it as inferior to the duty of preaching, in Wyclif's view the highest duty of all clerics.[4] In his later developments he allowed that under certain circumstances the Eucharist might be consecrated even by a layman.[5] Nor did he always make clear even to himself the relation of sacramental grace to character and to foreknowledge. At one time he maintained that the foreknown even when in actual sin can administer the sacrament with profit to the faithful, though to his own damnation, Christ supplying all the defects of the priest;[6] but later that the value depended on the character of the priest and the nature of his prayers—in a word, on the priest 'being consecrated by God.'[7] But he is careful to redeem this last conclusion from perilous uncertainty by pointing out that the sanctity, which comes from Christ's presence, is always the same.[8]

4. Wyclif and the Bible.[9]—Even in his earlier days Wyclif, following Ockham, appealed to the Bible as the primary, unconditional, and absolute authority, of universal range and entire sufficiency. He differed from Ockham in distinguishing between the Bible and the teaching of the Church, which Ockham had regarded as in harmony. He further asserted the right of every man to examine the Bible for himself. This was a corollary from his theory of 'dominion.' Every man was God's tenant in chief holding direct under 'God's law,' Wyclif's usual title for the Scriptures. He had a right therefore to know on what conditions he held. Nor would he allow that the tradition of the Church is the standard of interpretation. He sweeps away therefore the whole mass of tradition, doctrine, and ordinance, whether papal or conciliar, which had claimed to be of equal or superior value to Scripture. Nor has he any place for a doctrine of development.

Wyclif's appeal to the Scriptures was followed by the translation under his inspiration of the whole Bible from the Vulgate into English.[1] The first form of this translation would seem to have been a translation of the Sunday Gospels, still extant in his English *Sermons*. Independently of this his followers brought out a version of the whole Bible. The exact share that Wyclif took is uncertain, and probably was slight. But the fact of this translation is beyond doubt, though recent research has shown that the so-called Wyclif version, the first of the complete Bible, had been preceded by other partial versions. Translation of the Bible was in the air. Wyclif's first version, a large part in whose production was taken by Nicholas of Hereford, was very unsatisfactory—a verbal, almost gloss-like, rendering into a midland dialect, without clearness of expression or idiomatic use of language. Accordingly before 1388 the revision of Wyclif's version was begun by John Purvey, Wyclif's secretary at Lutterworth, who smoothed out the harsh literalness of the original, changed its dialect to the uninflected type common at that time at Oxford, and contributed, about 1395, a notable General Prologue.[2] The two versions of Wyclif and Purvey have often been confused, and the influence of Wyclif's translation upon the development of the English language has been exaggerated. In later years the existence of Wyclif's version became almost forgotten, and its authorship unknown, though the translation of Purvey's version into Scots by Murdoch Nisbet, about 1520, proves the latter's continued influence.[3]

III. *INFLUENCE*.—**1. In England.**—During his lifetime Wyclif's influence passed through marked changes. At Oxford there was a time when he was acknowledged by his enemies to be supreme,[4] and in 1378 he bade fair to lead the nation in his own direction. But after that year, with the promulgation of his doctrine of the Eucharist, his influence rapidly waned both at Oxford and in the nation at large. Men woke up to find whither he was leading them, while the growing violence of his views estranged his more moderate adherents. Moreover, his influence was local rather than national. South of the Thames and north of the Trent it scarcely existed. Scholasticism also proved fatal to him. His prestige as a Schoolman, which first secured him a hearing and gave weight to the movement he started in Bohemia, ultimately reacted against the success of his reforms. When driven out of Oxford, he found no suitable environment for the spread of his ideas, and his intellectual type of piety lacked that

1 *De Euch.* pp. 78, 124, 132, 195.

2 *De Apost.* pp. 172, 205.

3 *De Euch.* p. 99, *de Eccl.* p. 457 f.

4 *SEW* i. 288, iii. 143; *EWW*, pp. 111, 189, 441; *Serm.* iv. 47; *Polem. Works*, i. 261.

5 *Trial.* p. 280.

6 *De Eccl.* pp. 448, 456 f.

7 *De Euch.* p. 113; *SEW* iii. 426. But in *SEW* iii. 227 the opposite is held.

8 *De Euch.* p. 114.

9 Wyclif's views on the authority of the Bible can be briefly studied in his *de Veritate Sacræ Scripturæ*, 3 vols., ed. R. Buddensieg, London, 1905, *Op. Evang.* i. 79, 368, *Trial.* p. 64, or, in English, *SEW* i. 225, ii. 343, iii. 186, 362.

1 The older views on Wyclif's version are set forth in Forshall and Madden's great ed. (1850) of Wyclif and Purvey's versions. For recent research on the partial versions of R. Rolle of Hampole and others see *Camb. Hist. Eng. Lit.*, Cambridge, 1908–16, ii. 43–48; A. C. Paues, *Fourteenth-Century English Version*, Cambridge, 1902; a less valuable reprint in 1904; H. R. Bramley, *Rolle's Psalter*, Oxford, 1884; M. J. Powell, *The Pauline Epistles contained in MS Parker 32* (E.E.T.S.), London, 1917, and, above all, M. Deanesly, *The Lollard Bible and other Medieval Biblical Versions*, Cambridge, 1920. Cardinal Gasquet's scepticism (*The Old English Bible*, London, 1897) has been answered by F. Matthew, *Eng. Hist. Rev.* x. 91–99, *Church Quart. Review*, li. [1900–1901] 138, 265, and Miss Deanesly. For early references to Wyclif's version see Knighton, *Chron.* ii. 152; Wilkins, *Conc.* iii. 350, 498; Lyndwood, *Provinciale*, ed., Oxford, 1679, p. 286; and *Hist. et Monumenta J. Hus*, Nuremberg, 1558, i. 108. Gasquet's scepticism originated with Sir T. More, *Dialogus* (*Works*, London, 1557), i. 233, 241.

2 Deanesly, p. 275 f.; and for the proofs of Purvey's authorship, *ib.* pp. 260–267, 376 f. Gasquet's arguments were founded on failure to note the Lollardy of this General Prologue.

3 *The New Testament in Scots*, ed. T. G. Law, 2 vols., Edinburgh, 1901.

4 Knighton, *Chron.* ii. 151; *Eulog. Hist.* iii. 345: 'flos Oxioniæ.'

personal magnetism which might have drawn the people to him.

To the end of his life Wyclif 'stammered out many things which he was unable clearly to make good.' He wanders about in worlds not realized. Like other men who have ventured on the great task of forming a scheme of religion for themselves, Wyclif often is and must be inconsistent. All attempts to hammer out of his writings a symmetrical body of doctrine must fail because they ignore the successive, contradictory stages of his own development.

Considered as a statesman, Wyclif was unfortunate in that there was no deep national movement with which he could ally himself. If he could have had in England the same conditions as in Bohemia, his success might have been equal. But in England the national movement lost itself in the follies of the Hundred Years War with France, and Wyclif mistook the selfish John of Gaunt for a leader. If in this Wyclif showed an unfortunate opportunism, at other times he lost much by mental detachment. In his idealism he even regarded the loss of Oxford with indifference, fatal though it proved to his cause. Like most Schoolmen, he trusted too much in his logic, and allowed it to lead him too far. We see this in his proposal to include the universities in his scheme of disendowment, and in his advocacy of a system of voluntaryism which would have reduced the clergy to beggars, to the level, in fact, of the mendicant friars whom in his last years he ceaselessly denounced, but with the spirit of whose founder he was always in more sympathy than he knew. Another illustration will be found in his demand that the life of the priests should be purely spiritual. He wished to narrow down their studies at the university to theology merely; 'the lore that Christ taught us is enough for this life; other lore,' even mathematical studies, should be 'suspended.'[1] Thus Wyclif destroyed his influence among the educated and reduced his movement to an illiterate sect[2] which in the hundred years after his death slowly lost balance and influence, though surviving, in spite of persecution, to the dawn of the Reformation. Nor did he know how to gain the reform that lay next to hand by keeping back ideas not immediately practicable. He failed also to see the injury he did his cause by mixing himself up with doubtful transactions, as in the affair of Shakyl and Haulay. He allowed his hatred of the false to get the better of his judgment, while by the violence of his language he estranged many. But the vehemence of his temper was not without its advantages. A calmer spirit would have counted the cost or awaited the future; Wyclif, who felt deeply the needs of the present, placed himself at the head of a forlorn hope.

We believe that the failure of Wyclif's premature reformation was, on the whole, for the good of the Church. His conception of the Church was too Erastian, his claim for the royal supremacy too absolute, and would have made the Church a mere department of the State. The unscrupulous pillage of the Church by Henry VIII. and Edward VI. was but slight compared with the disaster that would have followed an immediate acceptance of Wyclif's schemes and theories.

Finally, Wyclif's revolt was too negative. He swept away rather than established, though in his assertion of the supreme authority of Scripture he laid the foundation upon which a later age should build. But his teaching, though containing the principles of the 16th cent. Protestants, lacked the definiteness of their theological reconstruction.

1 *Op. Minora*, pp. 324 f., 439 f.
2 *SEW* ii. 71, iii. 122; cf. i. 225, 310, iii. 326.

He abolished existing forms of Church government without devising, like Calvin, any scheme that should take their place. As his crude views on the marriage of brothers and sisters show, he was an individualist without the social instinct.[1] Viewed as an evangelist, he lacks the consciousness of the reality of sin. His doctrine that sin is a negation, 'that it has no idea,' linked on Wyclif the realist with the philosophers and St. Augustine, but proved a poor substitute for conversion. He identifies knowing and being, and in consequence his theology is intellectual and ethical and, unlike St. Augustine's, lacks a sufficient foundation in grace.[2]

2. In Bohemia.—It was in Bohemia that Wyclif's influence was greatest and, if the Moravians be included, most abiding. The marriage of Anne, the sister of Wenzel, king of Bohemia, to Richard II. of England on 14th Jan. 1382 led to much Czech intercourse.[3] On 4th March 1388 Adalbert Ranco founded in his will scholarships at Oxford for Czech students.[4] By these students the philosophical works of Wyclif were introduced into Prague shortly after Wyclif's death. In 1401 Jerome of Prague brought back from Oxford Wyclif's *Dialogue* and *Trialogus* together with some lesser works,[5] and introduced the writings to Hus, who had previously known only the philosophical works, five of which, written out in his own hand in 1398, are now at Stockholm.[6] Under the influence of Hus the influence of Wyclif soon became a dominant force in Bohemia, and large sums were given for corrected copies of the works of the English doctor.[7] Hence often the only MSS of works of Wyclif are now in Prague or Vienna, whither they were carried after the Thirty Years War. Of Wyclif's *de Ecclesia*, for instance, only one small fragment is found in Dublin; the MS at Vienna was 'corrected' at Oxford on 1st Feb. 1407 by two Czechs, and the only other MS of any value is at Prague.[8] The Vienna MS of his *de Officio Regis* belonged to a Czech student who took his degree in 1395. Other illustrations of the intercourse between English Lollards and Bohemia are found in the correspondence between Sir John Oldcastle, the most prominent Lollard of the generation after Wyclif,[9] and the Czech leaders in 1410, and Hus and Richard Wyche.[10] Hus's dependence on Wyclif is very complete. His *de Ecclesia* is taken almost word for word from that of Wyclif—with the omission of the incident of Haulay and Shakyl. By a strange historical injustice the doctrine of the Plagiarist, because linked with a national consciousness, came to be regarded as almost the original, while Wyclif, from whom Hus had borrowed, receded into obscurity, especially after the failure of Oldcastle's rebellion. No doubt this may be explained by the troublous wars and crusades which the doctrines caused in Bohemia.[11]

1 *Trial.* p. 318.
2 *SEW* i. 21, iii. 183, 219; *de Ente*, p. 221 f.
3 See the list of Czechs whom Richard II. on 1st May 1381, when the marriage was settled, 'retained to stay with him for life,' in *Cal. Pat. Rolls Ric. II.*, ii. 4; Rymer, iv. 110.
4 J. Loserth, *Wiclif and Hus*, London, 1884, p. 41; Count Lützow, *Life and Times of Master John Hus*, London, 1909, p. 43 f.
5 Von der Hardt, *Cons. Con.* iv. 634, 650-652; F. Palacky, *Die Verläufer des Hussenthums*, Leipzig, 1845, pp. 113-116; *Eng. Hist. Rev.* vii. 306-311.
6 Wyclif, *Miscell. Phil.* i. Introd. p. 47 ff.
7 Palacky, *Documenta*, p. 389.
8 Wyclif, *de Eccl.* p. xvii; and Poole's note in *de Dom. Div* p. xii.
9 For Oldcastle the only complete study is in Wylie, *The Reign of Henry V.*, i.
10 *Eng. Hist. Rev.* v. 530-544; H. B. Workman, *Letters of John Hus*, London, 1904, pp. 32-38.
11 For Hus and the Hussites, and the dependence on Wyclif, see *ERE* vi. 886 f. This dependence is often exaggerated. See Workman, *The Letters of Hus*, pref. p. ix, who points out that both Wyclif and Hus were alike copying from Gratian's *Decretum*.

LITERATURE.—(*a*) *Contemporary records.* — The most important of these is the collection of documents bearing on Lollardism made by the famous Carmelite, **Thomas Netter** of Walden or possibly by Stephen Patrington (*FZ*, pref. p. lxxvi), with additions by Netter, about the year 1428. Of this work, entitled *Fasciculi Zizaniorum*, the only existing MS, now in the Bodleian, bearing date 1439, was freely annotated by Bishop Bale, and from Bale was borrowed by Foxe. In 1858 it was published by W. Shirley in the Rolls Series. Another work by **Netter** of great value for the study of Wyclif's doctrines is his *Doctrinale Antiquitatum Fidei Ecclesiæ Catholicæ* (best ed. by F. B. Blanciotti, 3 vols., Venice, 1757, with valuable introduction and life of Netter), written by him in 1426–28. Other records published in the Rolls Series of great importance are the *Chronicon Angliæ*, ed. E. M. Thompson, London, 1874; **Thomas Walsingham**, *Historia Anglicana*, ed. H. T. Riley, 2 vols., do. 1869; **Henry Knighton**, *Chronicon*, ed. J. R. Lumby, 2 vols., do. 1889–95 (the last is of special value for matters connected with Leicester, of whose abbey Knighton and his unknown continuator were inmates); also, in the same series, the continuation of the *Eulogium Historiarum*, ed. F. S. Haydon, 3 vols., London, 1858–63. The usual sources of history, *Calendars of Patent Rolls*, *Calendars of Close Rolls*, *Calendars of Entries in Papal Registers*, *Rotuli Parliamentorum*, must not be neglected, while *Piers Plowman* (ed. W. W. Skeat for the E.E.T.S.) is indispensable for the knowledge of the age. **D. Wilkins**, *Concilia Magna Britanniæ et Hiberniæ*, 4 vols., London, 1737, iii., though badly edited, is of great value. The bishops' registers, which might throw much light, for the most part have not yet been printed—*e.g.*, the registers of Lincoln. For extracts from those of Courtenay we are still dependent on Wilkins. Wyclif's own writings are strangely impersonal and give little assistance to his biographer.

(*b*) *Wyclif's writings.*—Wyclif's voluminous writings have only recently become accessible in print, and some are still unpublished. The MSS of the Latin works for the most part were in Prague or Vienna, while the English works in British libraries, especially at Dublin and in Corpus Christi, Cambridge, were neglected. The earliest work of Wyclif to be printed was his *Trialogus* (under the title *Dialogorum libri quattuor*) at Basel on 7th March 1525, probably by Frobenius, reprinted in 1752 by J. G. Vierling, Frankfort and Leipzig, under the inspiration of P. W. Wirth. An English tract on the Eucharist, *The Wycket*, usually ascribed to Wyclif, was printed at Nuremberg in 1546, reprinted by Coverdale, London, 1548, 1550. In 1608 Bodley's first librarian, Thomas James, published at Oxford Wyclif's *Two Short Treatises against the Orders of the Begging Friars*, and in 1612 the *Wycket* was reprinted at Oxford. Apart from the publication in his appendix of a few short pieces by J. Lewis in 1720 and of Purvey's *New Testament* by J. Lewis in 1731 no other original work of Wyclif either in Latin or in English was printed for over two centuries, unless we may count the reprint of Purvey's *New Testament* by H. Baber, London, 1810, and S. Bagster, do. 1841. With his customary ill-luck, the first sign of revived interest was the publication of a spurious fanatical tract, probably the work of some Spiritual Franciscan, entitled *The Last Age of the Church*, and attributed by its editor, J. H. Todd, to Wyclif (Dublin, 1840; republished by Wilmot Marsh, *Biblical Versions of Divine Hymns*, London, 1845, p. 221 f.). This work deceived many and did not conduce to a higher estimate of the Reformer. In the same work Wilmot Marsh also published one of Wyclif's sermons on the Annunciation (pp. 91–93). The long neglect of Wyclif and Purvey's English versions of the Bible was broken by Lea Wilson's ed. of Wyclif's *New Testament*, London, 1848, and by the publication at Oxford in 1850 of the fine edition of the whole by J. Forshall and F. Madden in 4 vols. Of the Old Testament no part had hitherto been printed except Purvey's tr. of the Song of Songs, by Adam Clark in his *Commentary*, London, 1808. In 1851 Todd printed at Dublin *Three Treatises of John Wyclif*, namely, 'Of the Church and her Members,' 'Of the Apostacy of the Church,' and 'Of Antichrist and his Meynee.' In 1863 G. V. Lechler published at Leipzig Wyclif's *de Officio Pastorali*, and in 1869, at Oxford, his *Trialogus*. In 1865 W. Shirley pointed out what had yet to be done by his *Catalogue of the Original Works of John Wyclif*, Oxford. Though many of its details need correction, it is still of great value and superseded the inaccurate lists in J. Bale, *Scriptorum illustrium Majoris Brytanniæ Catalogus*, 2 vols., Basel, 1557, i. 451 f.; J. Bale, *Index Britanniæ Scriptorum*, ed. R. H. Poole and M. Bateson, Oxford, 1902; or T. Tanner, *de Scriptoribus*, London, 1748, p. 761 f. Between 1869 and 1871 Thomas Arnold edited for the Oxford University Press *The Select English Works of John Wyclif* in 3 vols. Several of the works included are by disciples and not by Wyclif himself.

On this matter of authorship no decisive opinion is yet possible. The student should note the able paper of **E. D. Jones** in *Anglia*, Halle, xxx. [1906] 261 f., and **J. E. Wells**, *Manual of the Writings in Middle English*, Yale, 1916, ch. 12. The approach of the fifth centenary of Wyclif's death brought home to English scholars the disgrace of their continued neglect. In 1880 F. D. Matthew brought out for the Early English Text Society *The English Works of Wyclif hitherto unprinted*, but much that is here included should be rejected. In the same year R. Buddensieg published at Gotha Wyclif's *Tractatus de Christo et suo adversario Antichristo*. At last in 1883 the foundation of the Wyclif Society led to the publication of Wyclif's more important Latin works. With but indifferent support from the public the society has brought out some 30 volumes of Wyclif's Latin works. To the more important of these reference has been made in our text. Their various prefaces are of great value, though often the works are dated too early owing to ignorance of the date of Wyclif's doctorate.

For the literature and views of the later Lollards reference should be made to the *Twelve Conclusions* presented to parliament in 1394. For this document, probably the work of J. Purvey, see *FZ*, pp. 360–369; **Wilkins**, *Concilia*, iii. 221–223; and **H. S. Cronin**, in *Eng. Hist. Rev.* xxii. [1907] 292–304. For the reprobation by Boniface IX. see *Cal. Papal Letters*, iv. 515. To Purvey has also been assigned the *Ecclesiæ Regimen*, published in 1851 by J. Forshall with the title *Remonstrance against Romish Corruptions . . . in 1395*, London, 1851. The work is really of composite origin, its kernel consisting of the *Thirty-Seven Conclusions* of earlier date, the authorship of which is assigned in the flyleaf of the only existing MS to Wyclif. For this work see *Eng. Hist. Rev.* xxvi. [1911] 738–749. A work of considerable interest is *The Lantern of Light*, written after 1408, ed. 1917 by L. M. Swinburne for the E.E.T.S. This work is far more restrained in its judgments than Wyclif. About the same time there was brought out *An Apology for Lollard Doctrines*, ed. J. H. Todd, Dublin, 1842, and assigned to Wyclif. But the most interesting Lollard document is the *Examination of Master William Thorpe*, written by himself in 1407. This valuable autobiography was first edited 'from a text copied out and corrected by Master William Tyndale' by **Foxe** (*AM* iii. 249–285). It is also found in *The Select Works of John Bale* (Parker Soc.), Cambridge, 1849, pp. 62–133; in E. Arber's *English Garner*, 8 vols., London, 1895, vi.; and in **A. W. Pollard**, *Fifteenth Century Prose and Verse*, do. 1903, pp. 97–167.

(*c*) *Lives of Wyclif.*—The first life of Wyclif was that of **Foxe** in his well-known *Acts and Monuments* (best ed. by J. Pratt, 8 vols., London, 1877). Though the work of a partisan, it is still of value for its many official documents. From Foxe and Bale all other 'lives' were compiled, including that of T. James, *An Apologie for John Wicklyfe*, Oxford, 1608. The prejudiced references of Anthony Wood and T. Hearne culminated in the publication of *The Pretended Reformers*, by **Matthias Earbery**, London, 1717. This scurrilous work was really a translation of **A. Varillas**, *Histoire du Wiclefianisme*, Lyons, 1682. Its only importance lay in its leading **John Lewis**, 'minister of Margate' (for whom see *DNB* xxxiii. 186 f.), to write his valuable *History of the Life and Sufferings of the Reverend and Learned John Wicliffe*, Oxford, 1720, 1723, and 1820. Its collection of documents made it for over a century the only life of Wyclif of value. In 1754 the first German biography of Wyclif, *D. Johannes* (*sic*) *Wiclefi wahrhafte und gegründete Nachrichten von seinem Leben, Nachsaetzen und Schriften*, was published by **P. W. Wirth**. In 1828 **Robert Vaughan** brought out *The Life and Opinions of John de Wycliffe* in 2 vols., London, a work superseded by the writer's more mature judgments in *John de Wycliffe, D.D.: a Monograph*, do. 1853. Vaughan's work showed industry and sympathy, but suffered from his limited acquaintance with Wyclif's writings and with English history. Passing by as of little value **C. W. Le Bas**, *Life of Wiclif*, London, 1832; **S. A. J. de Ruever Gronemann**, *Diatribe in Johannis Wicliff reformationis prodromi, vitam, ingenium, scripta*, Utrecht, 1837; **O. Jäger**, *John Wycliffe*, Halle, 1854; **A. Jeep**, *Gerson, Wiclefus, Hussus inter se comparati*, Göttingen, 1857, we come in 1858 to **W. W. Shirley**'s valuable study in his introduction to his *Fasciculi Zizaniorum*. In the same year **G. V. Lechler** published at Leipzig an inauguration thesis, *Wiclif, als Vorläufer der Reformation*. This was followed by his *Johann von Wiclif und die Vorgeschichte der Reformation*, 2 vols., do. 1873. Lechler's knowledge of English mediæval life and history is very imperfect, and much has come to light since he wrote. But no student, except possibly J. Loserth, has ever surpassed Lechler in his intimate knowledge of Wyclif's writings and theological system. Though in many places misleading, Lechler's is still the only authoritative life of Wyclif (tr. into English, abridged, by P. Lorimer, *John Wiclif and his English Precursors*, 2 vols., London, 1878, new ed. 1 vol. in 1881, 1884; to this ed. the references in the art. have been made). The following, some written with a view to the quincentenary, should also be mentioned: the excellent introduction by **F. D. Matthew** in his *English Works of Wyclif hitherto unprinted*, London, 1880; **M. Burrows**, *Wyclif's Place in History*, do. 1882–84; **R. Buddensieg**, *J. Wiclif und seine Zeit*, Halle, 1883, 1885, Eng. tr., *John Wyclif, Patriot and Reformer*, London, 1884; **V. Vattier**, *J. Wyclyff, sa vie, ses œuvres, sa doctrine*, Paris, 1886, with good catalogue of Wyclif's writings; **R. L. Poole**, *Wycliffe and Movements for Reform*, London, 1889. **Poole** has also given a valuable study of Wyclif's doctrine of 'dominion' in his *Illustrations of the Hist. of Medieval Thought*, London, 1884, ch. 10. **L. Sergeant**, *John Wyclif*, New York, 1893, is popular and often inaccurate. Its first chapter on the birthplace of Wyclif contains some material of value, previously printed in *Athenæum*, 1892, pp. 344, 405. The opposition views were given by **J. Stevenson**, a Jesuit, in his *The Truth about Wyclif*, London, 1885. The best sketch of Wyclif is undoubtedly **H. Rashdall**'s in *DNB* lxiii. 202–223, especially if read with **G. M. Trevelyan**'s study of Wyclif's environment in his *England in the Age of Wycliffe*, London, 1899, or **J. H. Wylie**'s valuable *History of England under Henry IV.*, 4 vols., do. 1884–98. A short work by the present writer, *The Dawn of the Reformation*, 2 vols., vol. i., 'The Age of Wyclif' (London, 1901), will shortly be brought out as a comprehensive study.

H. B. WORKMAN.

X

XAVIER.—St. Francis Xavier was the son of Juan de Jassu, a hidalgo and formerly a high official at the court of the last kings of Navarre. The name Xavier was that of the castle (*castillo*), some thirty miles from Pampeluna, which belonged to the family of his mother, Maria de Azpilcueta, and in which he himself was born (7th April 1506). Francis apparently counted himself a Basque, for he said that Basque was his native tongue, but the language is now no longer spoken so close to the borders of Aragon. Whilst his brothers followed the career of arms, Francis, as the youngest son of an impoverished family, was driven to seek a livelihood in the profession of letters. His abilities were remarkable, and, on coming to the University of Paris in 1525, he seems to have been regarded as a student of exceptional promise. He took his degree of licentiate in 1530 from the Collège Ste. Barbe, and was then made reader in philosophy at another college of the University, known as the Dormans-Beauvais. While still at Ste. Barbe, he fell under the influence of Ignatius Loyola (*q.v.*), a man some fifteen years his senior. Ignatius (who was then feeling his way towards the organizing of a band of followers pledged to labour for the greater glory of God in whatsoever form the summons might come to them), discerning a conflict in Xavier's heart between worldly ambition and the call of grace, plied him again and again with the gospel warning: 'What is a man profited if he shall gain the whole world and lose his own soul?' In the end Xavier surrendered, and he was one of the seven who, on 15th Aug. 1534, took vows of poverty and chastity at Montmartre, thus laying the foundations of the Company of Jesus or Jesuit Order.[1] Their original intention was that, after completing their theological studies and receiving ordination, they should all make their way to Palestine and take up the preaching of the gospel in the very spot where Christ Himself had lived. However, it was foreseen that it might be difficult to execute this plan, and they decided that, if after waiting a year in Venice, where they expected to arrive in Jan. 1537, it was found impossible to obtain a passage to the Holy Land, they should go to Rome and place themselves at the disposition of the pope. It was the latter alternative that was forced upon them. They were ordained priests at Venice in June 1537, spending their time in preaching and serving the sick in the hospitals; but in 1538 they all met in Rome and offered their services to Pope Paul III. It seems that already at this time Xavier had some strange presentiment of what his future career was to be, for in his dreams he thought he was carrying an Indian on his shoulders under whose overwhelming weight he cried out so loudly that he awakened his companions. It was not, however, Xavier who was first nominated when King John III. of Portugal in 1539 instructed his ambassador at Rome to obtain some of Loyola's followers from the pope to serve as missionaries in the Indies. The choice fell upon Rodriguez and Bobadilla, but the latter became ill, and his place was taken by Xavier.

During a long delay at Lisbon such wonderful results followed from the preaching and example of the fathers that the king wished to retain both in Portugal. Finally, by the decision of Loyola, Xavier alone set sail (7th April 1541), bearing with him briefs from the pope appointing him apostolic nuncio in the Indies. The voyage occupied more than a year. He reached Goa on 6th May 1542, and it was not until October that he began missionary work in a strict sense by preaching to the natives of the Fishery coast in the extreme south of the Indian peninsula. In this region, including Ceylon, he remained for over two years, interrupted only by one visit to Goa. The continuous strain of the work was almost beyond human endurance, but its manifold consolations buoyed him up. His letters to Europe give a most vivid picture of his methods, more particularly of his care to have the elements of Christian doctrine translated into the vernacular, so that they could be learned by heart and even sung by young and old alike. It was always characteristic of him to take immense pains with the children. He went about ringing his bell and apparently had a wonderful power of attracting and impressing the little ones. No doubt a large proportion of those whom he baptized were quite young children, the families of adult converts.

> 'Often,' he wrote on 15th Jan. 1544, 'my arms are weary from baptizing and I cannot speak another word from having so repeatedly recited the prayers to the people, one after another, and given instruction in Christian doctrine to them in their native tongue.'[1]

So again in a letter, written a year later from Cochin (27th Jan. 1545), in which he supplies much detail regarding his methods of instruction, he states that in the space of one month he had baptized more than 10,000 persons. The *Exposition of the Creed*, of which a good English translation is provided by Edith A. Stewart,[2] and which is by her rightly stated to be 'more characteristic of Xavier than anything else he has left except the letters,' may probably be accepted as representative of all the elementary instruction, to whomsoever addressed, which he made the foundation of his missionary efforts.

A contemporary letter from Portugal (dated 22nd Oct. 1545) reproduces the description of Xavier brought back by one who had known him well in the Indies:

> 'Father Xavier goes about with bare feet; his garments are shabby and torn. He is called the "great father," and all love him well. A rajah has given orders throughout his kingdom that all are to show obedience to his brother the "great father," as though it were to himself; all who wish are free to become Christians. He also gave him much money, but Xavier distributed it all among the poor. Along the coast he has built 44 or 45 churches. He has four native-born Indians with him whom he has had ordained as priests. Six other Indians from the College of Goa are on the point of taking Orders. He carries with him two, three, four, yea six thousand men into the open country, climbs a tree and then preaches to them.'[3]

The creation of the College of Goa, here referred to, was one of the most far-seeing of the measures adopted by Francis to secure the permanency of his conquests. By his influence with the Portuguese authorities, he obtained ample means of support for this foundation, and here he was able to train a considerable number of natives, many of whom persevered and after ordination did excellent work in the missions which Xavier himself had started.

The three years from 1545 to 1548 were almost entirely spent in the Eastern archipelago, Malacca, Amboyna, and the Moluccas. He was shipwrecked three times, lost his slender possessions, was attacked by the Muhammadans, and was always cut off from all human sympathy and congenial companionship, and yet he could write of his stay at Moretai:

[1] See art. JESUITS.

[1] *Monumenta Xaveriana*, i. 286.

[2] *Life of St. Francis Xavier*, pp. 242–251.

[3] *Monumenta Historica Societatis Jesu* [Madrid, 1894], 'Epistolæ Mixtæ,' i. 231 f.

'I cannot remember having so much spiritual consolation anywhere else, nor more continuously. . . . These islands ought to be called the "Isles of Hope in God."'[1]

By the middle of January 1548 he was at Cochin, from which as a centre he revisited the Fishery coast. Thence he returned to Goa, but this was only to make preparations for a yet more adventurous expedition, with the idea of which he had been inspired by a meeting with a Portuguese merchant at Malacca who had brought in his company a native Japanese. This young man, called after his conversion Pablo de Santa Fé, was afterwards of great use. Even as early as 1547 Francis was convinced that in these newly discovered islands of Japan

'our holy faith might be spread with great success, and that there, more than any other country of the Indies, were great things to be hoped for, since the people of those islands were quick-witted and eager to learn.'[2]

Further intercourse with merchants returning from Japan seems only to have deepened the impression, and from that time forth Xavier's heart was set upon this new conquest, although it was not until April 1549 that he was able to carry out his purpose. He went by way of Malacca, making provision from there for the needs of his recent converts in the Moluccas. There seems, however, no ground for the assertion, which has sometimes been made, that Xavier ever landed in the Philippines. After many delays and inconceivable vexations Xavier eventually reached the port of Kagoshima in a Chinese junk on 15th Aug. 1549, accompanied by Father Cosmo de Torres, a lay brother named Juan Fernandez, and the Japanese convert Pablo de Santa Fé. As Kagoshima was the native place of the last-named, a kindly welcome was accorded to the missionaries by his relatives, and a breathing-space was found during which it was possible to learn something of the people and the language. Progress was at first slow, but three months after his arrival Xavier wrote most enthusiastically of the natural qualities of the Japanese, and two years later his admiration had not evaporated.

'This is the only country yet discovered in these regions,' he wrote to Ignatius on 29th Jan. 1552, 'where there is hope of Christianity permanently taking root.'

He planned an expedition to Meaco (the modern Kioto), then the residence of the mikado. The journey to and fro entailed terrible sufferings from cold and other causes. Owing to political disturbances, the visit was ill-timed and almost fruitless of results. But at Yamaguchi, and particularly in Bungo, many conversions were made, and there is good evidence of the steadfastness of these Christian communities.[3] In Yamaguchi a formal document[4] records the conveyance to the missionaries in 1552 of a former Buddhist monastery. The church founded in Japan by Xavier spread and prospered. Thirty years afterwards Father Coelho estimated the number of Christians there at 150,000, and James Murdoch, an unfriendly critic, while admitting that the estimate is reliable, remarks that this constituted a wonderful record for thirty years, when we consider the small number of missionaries engaged in the work.

It is Murdoch who informs us that 'in Hideyoshi's famous invasion of the Corea in 1592 the first and third divisions of the invading army totalling nearly 30,000 men were almost entirely composed of Christians,' while the great *daimyos* who commanded those divisions—Konishi, Kuroda, Otomo, Arima, Ōmura, and Sō—were also all converts with the single exception of Ōmura.[5]

Some thirty years after this Christianity in Japan was exterminated literally by fire and sword; but even so, when Japan was again opened up to the missionaries in the middle of last century, some village communities were still found who retained the Christian beliefs and practices taught to their forefathers in the 17th century.

After two and a half years spent in Japan Xavier thought it necessary to return to his base at Goa, both to look after things there and to make better provision for a succession of suitable missionaries in the Far East. In a letter addressed to his brethren in Europe from Cochin in Jan. 1552 we find that a new field of labour had already attracted his attention. He had met a number of Chinese in Japan and had heard much of their country from merchants and others.

'Like the Japanese,' he wrote, 'they are acute and eager to learn. In intellect they are superior even to the Japanese.' 'I hope,' he added, 'to go there during this year, 1552, and penetrate even to the Emperor himself.'[1]

In intermediate letters he refers to this great design again and again, being full of courage and hope. Before the end of April he was well on his way. After overcoming interminable opposition from the Portuguese at Malacca and Singapore he reached the little island of San Cian, opposite the mouths of the Si-kiang, on which Canton is situated, before the end of August. He could find no one who would take the responsibility of conveying him across to the mainland. The trading ships began to sail away. Xavier, prostrate with illness, was left with only a Malabar servant and a Chinese boy. After endless alternations of hope and disappointment he himself began to lose heart. On 13th Nov. he wrote, 'Shall I reach China? I cannot tell . . . everything is against it.' To the last, however, he strained every nerve to accomplish his purpose, but his illness grew upon him, and on 27th Nov. 1552 (not 2nd Dec., as often stated) he died, in sight of the land which he had fought so hard to reach.

If Xavier has found many indiscreet panegyrists, he has also been much criticized. Many of these criticisms will be found effectively answered in the brilliant pen sketch of the great missionary by C. C. Martindale.[2] Others are discussed in *The Month* for Feb. and March 1905 and Dec. 1912. A good deal of the criticism turns upon the miraculous incidents with which the life has been overlaid by later biographers. As Astrain remarks:

'In the case of a life so extraordinary as that of Xavier, a life spent in such far distant lands, the presence of a legendary element was inevitable, and, in point of fact, it manifested itself at an early date. Already in the second half of the 16th century Fathers Teixeira and Valignano, in passing judgment upon the Life of St. Ignatius written by Ribadeneira, protested against various miracles falsely attributed to Xavier, and reduced to their just proportions the magnitude of certain of his missions and apostolic undertakings.'[3]

Again, Xavier has been accused of 'restlessness,' but is it sufficiently remembered that his charge embraced the whole mission field of the Indies, and that it was his duty to look after the base at Goa as well as to establish those advanced posts for which he, more than any other man, had the necessary enterprise and capacity? Shall we blame him because in many cases he was content, like the great *conquistadores* of the New World, to take possession of a vast province, to hoist a standard and leave a tiny garrison, knowing well that years must elapse before the full tide of Christian life could pulsate through its arteries? Nor can we admit, as is often alleged, that the conversions effected by him were 'mainly nominal.' The evidence of the Calvinist Dutch *predikant* Baldæus, who spent many years on the Malabar

1 *Monumenta Xaveriana*, i. 427.
2 *Ib.* pp. 433 f. and 444 f.
3 See *The Month*, Feb. and March 1905.
4 The text of this has been restored by Ernest Satow, *TASJ* vii. [1880] 140.
5 *A Hist. of Japan, 1542–1651*, Kobe, 1903, p. 362.

1 *Monumenta Xaveriana*, i. 694 f.
2 *In God's Army*, vol. i. 'Commanders in Chief.'
3 *Historia de la Compañia de Jesús*, p. 492, note.

coast and in Ceylon, a century after Xavier's time, goes far to prove the contrary, as does also the whole history of Japanese Christianity. Nor was the saint so fanatically intolerant as has sometimes been pretended. Xavier undoubtedly in his letters of Jan. 1548 to King John III. and to Simon Rodriguez speaks of forcing the governor to give the gospel to India. But, as E. A. Stewart remarks:

'The force, we have in fairness to observe, was not to be used towards the converts—he knew well enough that, with these southern tribes of which he was thinking, the Gospel had only to be preached in order to be received—it was the authorities who were to be forced to give opportunities of hearing the Word.'[1]

And Xavier himself adds:

'In this way the injustices and robberies towards the poor Christians will cease, and those who are ready to become Christians will get good courage to do so.'[2]

If Xavier can in any sense be described as fanatical, it is only in the heroic self-denial and austerity of his life. No missionary has realized more perfectly than he the counsel of becoming all things to all men, resolute to see and develop in every lawful way all the elements of good in those with whom he was brought into contact.

LITERATURE.—The sources, the most important of which are Xavier's own letters, are all, practically speaking, contained in the two volumes of *Monumenta Xaveriana ex autographis vel ex antiquioribus exemplis collecta* (forming vols. vi. and vii. of the *Monumenta Historica Societatis Jesu*), Madrid, 1899–1912. For English readers the most reliable biography is that of Edith A. Stewart, *The Life of St. Francis Xavier, Evangelist, Explorer, Mystic*, London, 1917; the most complete is that of A. Brou, *Saint François Xavier*, 2 vols., Paris, 1912. Other useful books are J. M. Cros, *Saint François de Xavier, sa vie et ses lettres*, 2 vols., Toulouse, 1900, *Saint François de Xavier de la Compagnie de Jésus, son pays, sa famille, sa vie*, do. 1894; H. J. Coleridge, *Life and Letters of St. Francis Xavier*, new ed., 2 vols., London, 1886; C. C. Martindale, *In God's Army*, vol. i. 'Commanders in Chief,' do. 1915; A. Astrain, *Hist. de la Compañia de Jesús*, vol. i.2, Madrid, 1912; H. Haas, *Gesch. des Christenthums in Japan*, 2 vols., Tokyo, 1902–04; J. Stephen, *Essays in Ecclesiastical Biography*, 2 vols., London, 1849, and many subsequent edd., Essay no. 3, 'The Founders of Jesuitism'; A. Dickson White, *A Hist. of the Warfare of Science with Theology in Christendom*, 2 vols., do. 1896; H. Thurston, in *The Month*, Feb. and March 1905, and Dec. 1912.

HERBERT THURSTON.

XENOCRATES.—See ACADEMY.

XENOPHANES.—See IONIC PHILOSOPHY.

Y

YAKUT.—1. Distribution.—The northernmost branch of the Turkish race, the Yakut, live in the Yakutsk district, along the Lena as far south as the Amur and the Island of Sakhalin and to the north-west as far as the Yenisei.[3] The region between the Lena and the Aldan is especially densely populated. This region was formerly occupied by the Tungus (*q.v.*), with whom the Yakut, who came from the south, had many fights before they succeeded in obtaining the best pastures. From their metropolis, the district of Yakutsk, the Yakut went to Olekminsk, down the Lena to its mouth, and spread along the Vilui, Yana, and Indigirka, and a very few reached Kolima. Meanwhile another immigration to the north went along the Yenisei as far as the Lower Tunguska, thence to Lake Chirinda, where they met the Yakut who migrated north through the Lena. Their original home may have been in Central Asia between the sources of the Yenisei and the Amur. N. A. Aristoff[4] thinks that the Yakut are the remnant of a Turkic nation called the Sakha (Saka?). The Saka, who in the 2nd cent. B.C. were expelled from their home in the north of Syr Darya southwards by the Yuechi, migrated to India. Towards the end of the 2nd cent. A.D. they seem to have been driven northward again. On their way back they left one branch, now called the Kara-Kirgis, in West Tian-Shan. The Kara-Kirgis have a clan called Saka.[5] Recently noticed linguistic evidence (tribal and clan names) makes the two routes of Yakut migration from Central Asia to the north something more than a hypothesis.

In 1897 the Yakut numbered 225,772; in 1911, 245,406.

2. Physical type.—The Yakut are now much mixed, first with the Neo-Siberians, *i.e.* Tungus, Mongols, and Manchu, and then with the Russians. They seldom have any moustache or beard, their hair and eyes are dark, and their heads round. All these characters are Mongolian, but the setting of their eyes is not Mongolian. The Russian anthropologist A. A. Ivanovsky[1] thinks that he can distinguish a special Yakut group, but this group has more in common with the Northern Tungus and Astrakhan-Kalmuk than with other Turkish nations. They are of medium size with many tall individuals, broad-headed, but not pre-eminently so, and long-faced.

3. Technique.—Originally horse-breeders, the Yakut are now horse-breeders where the climate permits, and in the north reindeer-breeders; but, as far north as they can, they keep the horse for its meat and *kumys* (mare's milk). How highly the Yakut values his horse is shown by the fact that to the good gods he will sacrifice a horse, but to the bad gods only cattle. In matchmaking, to compare the girl to a mare and the youth to a colt is the greatest compliment that can be paid them. In their mythology the horse always appears as the adviser and friend of man, often wiser than man himself. The Yakut, many of whom have never seen a horse, trace the origin of man to a being half-horse and half-man. A horse must not be struck, nor even must unkind words be said to it. While cattle are used for heavy work, the horse is kept for riding. In the region where there are horses no longer, reindeer bucks are trained for riding—a custom known also to the Tungus, but not to the old inhabitants of the Tundra, as the Samoyed or Eskimo.

Where possible, the Yakut become seasonal nomads. Only the people south of Vilui, the agriculturists, are quite sedentary, and even these have a winter house (*balagan*) and a summer house (*urasa*, sometimes called *yurta*). The *urasa* is often covered with birch-bark beautifully engraved and painted, but the *balagan*, made of logs of wood and covered with earth and snow, is pre-

1 *Life of St. Francis Xavier*, p. 259.
2 *Monumenta Xaveriana*, i. 459; cf. p. 452.
3 See art. TURKS.
4 *Attempt at an Explanation of the Ethnic Composition of the Kirghis-Kaizak living in Ancient Times*, St. Petersburg, 1894, i.
5 Leon Sternberg, 'Turks,' *Encyc. Andreevsky*, St. Petersburg, 1902, xxxiv. 344.

1 *Anthr. Composition of the Population of Russia*, Moscow, 1904.

ferable in winter. Their most strenuous time is the hay-making season.

The Northern Yakut are hunters, fishermen, and reindeer-breeders. As net- and trap-makers they are much superior to the other natives. They are also known as iron-smelters. They place their ore in the fire hole and pile coal round it, then they keep the fire blazing by means of hand-bellows. When the coal is used up, they dig out the metal and hammer it into implements. They used the iron ore of the Aldan near Yakutsk long before it was known to the Russians.

Like the Azarbaijan Tatars in the Caucasus, the Yakut are the cleverest traders in Northern Siberia; their language became a *lingua franca* and till recently had to be known even by Russian fur-traders. As reindeer-breeders, however, they are not so clever as the Palæo-Siberians or even as the Tungus. They are people of the Iron Age with all the characteristics which this age implies in Asia, pre-eminently horse-breeding. Since the clan crests are usually used as *tamga* (cattle or horse brands), it is possible to trace the Yakut's emigration and contact with other peoples by tracing the distribution of some particular *tamga*. The *tamga* usually represent an animal, but it would be an exaggeration to see in that any totemistic notions. Certain animals—*e.g.*, the bear, wolf, eagle, white crane, and goose—appear as the shaman's spirit assistants, but they are never called high gods.

4. Sociology.—The Yakut of to-day are grouped in clans (*aga-usa*), *naslegs*, and *uluses*. A clan is composed sometimes of only a few individuals, and sometimes of several hundred. A *nasleg* comprises from one to more than thirty clans. The *ulus* often includes several *naslegs*. The Yakut reckon as descendants of a clan only as far as the ninth generation. Of course at the present time the blood-relationship within the clan is hardly more than a tradition. When the Russians first came into contact with the Yakut, their clan system was quite highly developed, and the head of a clan had his power limited to that of a judge and leader in war.

All economic questions were decided by a council of elders, *i.e.* fathers, uncles, and elder brothers. Thus *aga* ('elder'; fem. *agas*) is the name for the father, *abaga* for other of his relatives older than himself, *ini* (fem. *balys*) for a father's younger brother and any other younger relative who was not his son. Relatives in the third degree are called *sïan*. The name for mother is *yä* (literally 'embryo'), for wife *oyokh*, while there is no specific name for the husband, who must be called by his wife *är*, 'man,' or *ogonior*, 'old man.' The term *aga* used for the father really means 'older'; thus one asks about a person, 'Is he *aga* or *balys* ['younger'] than yourself?' There are special terms for the wife to use when addressing her husband's relatives (*e.g.*, *toyon*, 'chief,' for the husband's father), and for the husband addressing his wife's relatives (*e.g.*, *aga-kylyn*, 'wife's father'). The terminology of relationship takes into consideration primarily sex and degrees of age. Thus the Yakut clan is divided into two main groups: (*a*) men and women of the paternal and maternal line born earlier, and (*b*) men and women of the paternal and maternal line born later.

Clans sometimes made alliances. All the traditions testify to the great solidarity of these alliances between the chiefs of clans and also to their independent attitude to one another. Superior to them all was the council of the confederation.

(*a*) *Marriage.*—The Yakut are exogamous, so the wife must be taken from another clan (*aga-usa*) and another settlement (*ulus*). In their marriage ceremonies several stages may be distinguished: (1) the matchmaking, (2) the compact, (3) the betrothal, (4) the bringing home of the bride. Children are betrothed when only one or two years old, but the bride cannot leave her father's house till all the *kalym* (bride-price, called by the Yakut *suwu*) has been paid. Serving for a wife is often met with instead of the *suwu*. The young man has the rights of a husband after he has paid the first instalment of the *kalym*. After the betrothal the young man remains in the bride's house. At the head of the bed the first night a meal consisting of flour and melted butter is placed. If the bridegroom is not pleased with the bride, the meal is left untouched, and this is considered a great disgrace to the girl. This points to the fact that chastity is required of the bride.

The custom of avoidance is especially strictly observed in relations called *kinitti*—*i.e.* the bride to her father-in-law and all other older male relatives. Thus she must not show her hair or her bare feet, step in front of them, address them directly, or call objects of common use by their real names (a paraphrase must be used).

(*b*) *Birth.*—According to W. Sieroszewski,[1] Yakut marriages are generally fruitful, averaging ten children to a woman, but becoming less so in the northern districts, although the Yakut are everywhere more prolific than the Tungus. Lack of children they attribute entirely to the woman, as their proverb says, 'If there are no children, the woman is to blame.' According to Jochelson, the women of the north have very difficult deliveries. The Yakut regard the pains of childbirth as a sickness caused by evil spirits, and therefore, if the assistance of a midwife or the goddess of fertility, Ayisit, is of no avail, a shaman is called in to fight the evil spirits. No consideration is shown to either mother or child, for women possessed of evil spirits are regarded by the Yakut as no less perilous to society than those infected with germs of an epidemic. This accounts for the entire absence of compassion and for the cruelty manifested towards women suffering from the pains of labour. When a child is born, the Yakut make holiday on the first and after the third day. On the first day they prepare a large quantity of fat which they melt and drink, sacrificing a portion to the fire. After the third day the friends and relatives visit the mother and child, and it is customary for the former to serve the guests herself. Nowadays it is not fat but meat that forms the principal dish. The birth of a foal is accompanied by ceremonies slightly less important.

(*c*) *Burial.*—The only thing that the Yakut really cares for before death is to be certain that an animal will be slain directly after he dies in order that, accompanied by this animal, his soul may make its journey to the abode of the departed. On the death of a man a bullock or a horse is killed, on the death of a woman a cow or a calf. If the deceased is rich, the animal is fat and able to be ridden, otherwise the soul must drive it in front of him or drag it by the horns. The flesh of the dead animal is eaten by the gravediggers and all the funeral company. When a man dies, the body is clothed in a rich garment and placed in a corner of the dwelling, where it lies for three days; on the third day it is placed in a wooden coffin, which is drawn to the grave by a horse or bullock. No one accompanies it but the gravediggers, and even they hasten to complete their work and return home; on their way back they do not stop or look behind, and, when they enter the gate of the village, they and the animal must pass through a fire made from

[1] *The Yakut*, St. Petersburg, 1896

the straw on which the dead man lay and the wood left from the making of the coffin. Other things which have been in contact with the dead, such as the shovel, are also broken and burnt. On the death of a child its cradle is left on the grave and its toys hanging on the nearest tree. The Yakut have great fear of a corpse (especially that of a shaman) before it is buried; it is supposed to be able to disturb the forces of nature, producing great storms. A great wind is held to be favourable, as it will smooth out the tracks on the way to the place of the funeral; otherwise many of the living will follow the dead. There is another form of burial among the Yakut, which consists in abandoning the dead in the house with all the utensils belonging to him.

The custom formerly existed that an old or very weak person should request his relatives to bury him. All the villagers were invited to a three days' feast, at which the old man, attired in his finest garments, occupied the chief position. On the third day his relatives took him to the forest, where a grave had been prepared, and one of them would suddenly strike him down. Food and his weapons were placed with him in the grave. Until the corpse is buried the soul remains near the house and endeavours to remind the relatives of its existence.

Some souls never leave the earth and are never quiet; such souls are called *yor*. The souls of those who have died an untimely or a violent death, or who were buried without ceremonies, and those of shamans and great people become *yor*.

5. Soul.—Like other Turks, the Yakut believe in the existence of several souls all more or less material. *Kut* seems to be one of the most important of these. Thus they think that the *buor-kut*, 'earth soul,' is communicated to the infant at the moment of birth from the earth; *salyn-kut*, 'air soul,' it receives from the air shortly afterwards; while the third element, *yä-kut*, 'mother soul,' comes to the child from the mother. *Kut* is a physical conception of the soul, while *sür*, although in some degree a material conception, has a more psychical character. After death *kut* is devoured by the *abassylar*, though there is a belief also that the *kut* remains for some days near the body of the deceased, and then departs to the other world. *Sür* is a kind of 'soul shadow' common to men and animals; it is even possessed by fishes.

6. Gods and spirits.—Although most of the Yakut are now officially reckoned as Christians, belief in the good old gods and shamanistic ceremonies is still alive. The gods are divided into nine *agas* (clans) or *bis*, and the malicious gods into eight. The natives are quite ready to give information about the clan arrangement of the kind gods, but it is very difficult to get similar information about the gods of the under world west and north, since few of the ordinary people know anything about them and the shamans are afraid of betraying the secrets of these formidable beings.

According to Sieroszewski, the chief of the sky-gods is Art-Toyon-Aga, the powerful ruler of light and life, speaking in the storm and thunder, somewhat indifferent to human affairs, and appealed to only in exceptional circumstances. In his honour are celebrated the great clan ceremonies, *ysakh*, in which the sacrifice of *kumys* is made to him. The *kumys* festival is a ceremony performed very regularly. Its object is to secure fertility for the family and for the herd. Lads and girls are placed opposite one another and sprinkle the *kumys* on one another as a sacrifice to the god. In the north, where horses cannot live, reindeer milk is used, though it is still called *kumys*.

The chief of the dark spirits is called Ulutuyer-Ulu-Toyon, 'omnipotent lord.' He is always described as living in the western sky, and, in contrast to the indolent Art-Toyon-Aga, he is the personification of action and of the passions. Ulu-Toyon is not always harmful to men, for he gives to them one of their souls, *sür*, and defends them from the attacks of *abassylar*. The *abassylar* are divided into 'upper,' living in the western sky, 'middle,' living on the earth, and 'lower,' inhabiting the subterranean world; but, wherever they live, they are all harmful to man.

Ichchi, literally 'owner,' signifies the 'owner-spirit' of various objects. Every river, lake, stone—and even parts of these sometimes—has its own *ichchi* controlling it. Movable objects and those which can produce sounds also have their *ichchi*.

The Yakut divide the universe into seventeen stories. They have also a horizontal division comprising two parts—east and south, the habitation of good spirits, and west and north, that of evil spirits. The great evil spirit, Allara-Ogonür, 'underground-old-man,' lives in the far north.

7. Shamanism.—The study of Yakut shamanism, which is one of the most developed forms of northern shamanism, can be limited to the study of the shaman (*oiun*), his ceremonial coat (*tanara*; same word for 'sky') and ceremonial drum (*tünür*). The preparation of his official garment is accompanied by ceremonies no less important than the shamanizing itself. Even those who, like the smith, prepare the metal symbolical adornments attached to the shaman's leather coat occupy a half-magical position, being credited with 'peculiar fingers.' The smith is often approached for assistance if there is no shaman to be found in the neighbourhood. The smith in the ninth generation acquires certain supernatural powers and can without harm to himself prepare the iron symbols of the shaman's costume and especially the *ämyägat* (a metal plate representing a human figure sewn on the ceremonial coat over the heart and symbolizing the special shaman's ancestor, *i.e.* the spirit of some dead shaman).

There are 'black' shamans and 'white' shamans; the duties of the latter are not clearly defined, for in cases of great urgency, as in sickness, it is the black shaman who is called in to fight the spirits of disease. At the spring festivals, however, performed in daylight and called *aïy-ysyakh*, it seems that white shamans always officiate, while the autumn festivals, *abassy-ysyakh*, performed in the darkness, are conducted by black shamans. Troshchanski,[1] who made an exhaustive study of Yakut shamanism, believes that the duties of the black shaman were originally in the hands of women, and that the Yakut black shaman even now assumes some women's characteristics: (*a*) two iron circles on his apron represent women's breasts; (*b*) he braids his long hair like a woman; (*c*) the place on the right side of the tent, covered with horseskins, is forbidden to shamans and women; (*d*) when he does not use the ceremonial dress, he wears that of a young girl; (*e*) he is allowed to visit a woman after childbirth before the three days are over and men are allowed to approach her. As the office of hereditary smiths became powerful, the duties of the black shamans passed to them. Seeing that the family among the Yakuts, as among the other Turks, is patriarchal, this theory seems very improbable. The women's characteristics adopted by the shaman point to something else, viz. that, being a person with supernatural powers, the black shaman is supposed to have both female and male qualities; whether sexual abuses follow this conception it is difficult to ascertain.[2] Generally speaking, women, being more nervous and suffering more often from the Arctic forms of hysteria (*menerik* and *amürakh*)

[1] *The Evolution of the 'Black' Faith*, Kazan, 1912.

[2] See M. A. Czaplicka, 'Shamanism and Sex,' in *Aboriginal Siberia*, London, 1914.

than men, are more successful as shamans.[1] The shamans, especially the black shamans, form a professional class, and a period of preparation under the guidance of an old shaman is necessary. The initiation into the shamanistic office is finally accomplished by the clothing of the novice in the ceremonial coat and presenting him with the drum and stick.

The shamanistic ceremony, as elsewhere,[2] is divided into the following parts: (*a*) preparations for the shaman's journey, (*b*) songs, which among the Yakut are unusually rhythmical and are answered by the chorus, beating the drums and dancing, (*c*) the going out of the fire, when the shaman is supposed to have gone away, (*d*) a period of silence, after which he comes back and relates his experiences.

8. Ceremonies.—There are among the Yakut two kinds of sacrificial ceremonies, bloody (to the *abassy*) and bloodless (to the *aïy* and *ichchi*). Although bloody sacrifices are not made to Urun-Aïy-Toyon, yet it is customary to dedicate certain animals to him; *i.e.*, such animals are not to be used for work, and mares so dedicated are not to be milked. Formerly it was the custom to dedicate in this manner all mares which had foals; they were let loose to wander on the tundra. The offerings to *abassylar* have the character of a compromise or bargain. The evil spirit wishes to have the *kut* (one of the souls) of a man, and the shaman gives instead the *kut* of an animal.

There are two tribal festivals: a spring festival, *aïy-ysyakh*, and an autumn festival, *abassy-ysyakh*. As the name shows, the first is celebrated for the good spirits in general, and for Urun-Aïy-Toyon in particular. After the sacrifice, which is followed by certain sports and games, a dramatic representation of the struggle between spring and winter is given. One man, called the *aïy-uola*, is dressed in white and mounted on a white horse to represent spring, while another, *abassy-uola*, represents winter, being dressed in black or reddish garments and mounted on a horse of corresponding colour. The *abassy-ysyakh* is held in autumn, and in the open air like the first festival, but at night. It is dedicated to the black spirits, and especially to Ulu-Toyon. While the first festival is conducted by the clan-father, the second is under the direction of nine shamans and nine shamanesses.[3]

9. Legends.—The Yakut possess the richest mythology, in both form and conception, of all the natives of Siberia. The richness of imagination shown in their oral compositions is only comparable to that of the Iranians, and one can indeed find some traces of Iranian mythology, probably brought from Central Asia. They are not lacking in the humour for which the Tungus legends are justly famed. The legend of creation bears witness.

> The evil spirit wished to show the good spirit that he had the greatest power, so he dived into the water and came up with a mouthful of clay. From this the good spirit created the earth, but, not having sufficient clay, he made it flat. He then noticed that the evil spirit had not given him all the clay; therefore he struck him on the neck so that he had to spit it all out. It fell on the earth and so mountains were formed.

The origin of grass is explained by a more romantic legend.

> The god Yassagai-Toyon directs the movements of all migratory birds. His seven daughters, in the form of seven white cranes, also often come down to the earth. Once Yassagai-Toyon commanded his most beautiful daughter to help and serve the Yakut. (The crane is always considered a sacred bird by these people.) The girl begged to be excused, and as a punishment the father cut off her wings and she became a blade of grass to feed the animals of the Yakut.[4]

These ætiological myths form but a small part of their literature, for it is the heroic stories that are the longest and the most elaborate.

The Yakut do not possess a written character, but the few who have been educated in Russian schools write in Russian.

Literature.—In addition to the works quoted in the footnotes, see N. N. Agapitoff and N. M. Khangaloff, 'Materials for the Study of Shamanism in Siberia' (Russ.), *E. Sib. Sect. Imp. Russ. Geog. Soc.* [Irkutsk, 1883], p. 169 ff.; M. A. Czaplicka, *My Siberian Year*, London, 1916, *The Turks of Central Asia*, Oxford, 1918; W. Jochelson, 'Kumiss Festivals of the Yakut,' *Boas Anniversary Volume*, New York, 1906; P. Klark, 'Viluisk and its District' (Russ.), *Mem. Sib. Sect. Imp. Russ. Geog. Soc.* vii. pt. 1 [St. Petersburg, 1864] pp. 91–165; F. Y. Kohn, *Physiological and Biological Data concerning the Yakut* (Russ.), Minusinsk, 1899; R. Maak, *The Vilui District of the Yakutsk Territory*, St. Petersburg, 1887; A. T. von Middendorff, *Reise in den äussersten Norden und Osten Sibiriens während der Jahre 1843–4*, do. 1847–74; V. A. Priklonski, 'Materials for the Ethnography of the Yakut of the Yakutsk Territory' (Russ.), *Bull. E. Sib. Sect. Imp. Russ. Geog. Soc.* xviii. [Irkutsk, 1887] 143; E. Piekarski and P. Vasilyeff, 'The Coat and Drum of the Yakut Shaman' (Russ.), *Mat. for the Ethn. of Russia*, i. [St. Petersburg, 1910] 93–116.

M. A. Czaplicka.

YASHTS.—See Avesta.

YASNA.—See Avesta.

YAWNING.

1. The primitive conception of the soul.—The conception of the soul among the lower races has been described as follows:

> 'It is a thin unsubstantial human image, in its nature a sort of vapour, film, or shadow; the cause of life and thought in the individual it animates; independently possessing the personal consciousness and volition of its corporeal owner, past or present; capable of leaving the body far behind, to flash swiftly from place to place; mostly impalpable and invisible, yet also manifesting physical power, and especially appearing to men waking or asleep as a phantasm separate from the body of which it bears the likeness; continuing to exist and appear to men after the death of that body; able to enter into, possess, and act in the bodies of other men, of animals, and even of things.'[1]

J. G. Frazer likewise maintains that the savage explains the phenomena of life by supposing the living body to be animated by some power within.

> 'If an animal lives and moves, it can only be, he thinks, because there is a little animal inside which moves it: if a man lives and moves, it can only be because he has a little man or animal inside who moves him. The animal inside the animal, the man inside the man, is the soul. And as the activity of an animal or man is explained by the presence of the soul, so the repose of sleep or death is explained by its absence; sleep or trance being the temporary, death being the permanent absence of the soul. Hence if death be the permanent absence of the soul, the way to guard against it is either to prevent the soul from leaving the body, or, if it does depart, to ensure that it shall return.'[2]

2. The escape of the soul through the mouth.—The soul is commonly supposed to escape by apertures of the body, especially the mouth and nose.

> 'The Marquesans used to hold the mouth and nose of a dying man, in order to prevent his soul from escaping; the same custom is reported of the New Caledonians. . . . The Itonamas in South America seal up the eyes, nose, and mouth of a dying person in case his ghost should get out and carry off others'; and the people of Nias, who identify the spirit of the deceased with the breath, tie up the jaws of the corpse to confine the vagrant soul.[3] The Hindus always snap their thumb and finger and repeat the name of some god, as Rāma, when a man yawns in their presence, believing that by so doing they prevent the soul from escaping through the open mouth. To neglect this is a sin as great as the murder of a Brāhman.[4]

Great care is taken at the time of a birth lest the soul of the child should escape and be swallowed by a gaping mouth.

> To prevent this calamity, the Alfoors of Celebes, when a woman is about to be delivered, 'tie up the mouths of all animals inside and outside the house'; and 'all persons present in the house, even the mother herself, are obliged to keep their mouths shut the whole time the birth is taking place.' Noses are not similarly secured because the breath is exhaled through the nostrils, and therefore 'the soul would be expelled before it could have time to settle down.'[5]

---

[1] Czaplicka, *Aboriginal Siberia*, pp. 307–326.
[2] See artt. Shamanism, Ostyaks, Samoyed, Tungus.
[3] Czaplicka, *Aboriginal Siberia*, p. 297 f.
[4] I. W. Shklovsky, *In Far North-east Siberia*, London, 1916, pp. 43, 227.

[1] *PC*[3] i. 429.
[2] *GB*[3], pt. ii., *Taboo and the Perils of the Soul*, London, 1911, p. 26 f.
[3] *GB*[3], pt. ii., *Taboo*, p. 31.
[4] W. Ward, *View of the Lit., Hist., and Mythol. of the Hindoos*[4], London, 1822, i. 142.
[5] *GB*[3], pt. ii., *Taboo*, p. 33.

Even in sleep it is possible for the soul to escape through the sleeper's mouth if it is not kept tightly closed, its departure being sometimes indicated by snoring.[1]

Mary H. Kingsley tells of a Kruman who 'for several nights had smelt in his dreams the savoury smell of smoked crawfish seasoned with red peppers. He became anxious, and the headman decided some witch had set a trap baited with this dainty for his dream-soul, with intent to do him grievous bodily harm.' For the next few nights, to prevent his soul from straying abroad, he lay in the heat of a tropical night under a blanket, his nose and mouth tied up with a handkerchief.[2]

The legend of King Gunthram shows that this belief long survived in Europe. As the king lay asleep in the wood with his head in his henchman's lap, his servant saw as it were a snake issue from his mouth and run to the brook. His progress being hindered, the servant laid his sword across the water and the creature ran along it and up into a mountain; after a while it came back, and returned into the mouth of the reposing king, who, upon waking, told him how he had dreamt that he went over an iron bridge, and into a mountain full of gold.[3]

3. Possession through the open mouth.—As the human soul is considered to enter and leave the body by the mouth, so it is with other spiritual beings, particularly such as possess people with evil intentions.

According to the Ewe-speaking peoples of the Slave Coast, when the indwelling spirit has left the body, 'it behoves a man to be careful about opening his mouth, lest a homeless spirit should take advantage of the opportunity and enter his body. This, it appears, is considered most likely to take place while the man is eating.'[4] The Zulus, like the Persians, regard repeated yawning and sneezing as a sign of approaching spiritual possession,[5] and in N. Africa men constantly keep the lower part of their face veiled, even while eating and sleeping, in order to protect themselves against evil spirits.[6] The same reason may explain the custom observed among Arab women of muffling their faces.[7] In Samoa a man whose family god was the turtle was obliged to wear a bandage tied over his mouth if he were taking any part in the cutting up or cooking of the animal, lest an embryo turtle should enter his mouth and grow up within him.[8] In S.E. Australia a newly-initiated youth must always cover his mouth with a rug in the presence of a woman,[9] just as in W. Timor 'a man holds his right hand before his mouth in speaking lest a demon should enter his body,' and lest the person to whom he is speaking should harm his soul by magic.[10] To prevent the soul of a fox killed in the chase from escaping and revenging itself on the hunters or warning its fellows of their approach, the Ainus, in former days, took care to tie up the mouth of the animal tightly.[11]

From this brief survey of the part played by the open mouth in primitive cult it will readily be understood how the act of yawning has come to be associated with the exit of the soul and the entrance of evil spirits. This ancient belief still survives in the polite custom of putting the hand before the gaping mouth, thereby (it was originally supposed) impeding the flight of the soul, and barring the way to a spiritual foe. Even to this day, when a man yawns, the Muslim puts the back of his left hand to his mouth saying, 'I seek refuge with Allah from Satan the accursed,' just as in the Tyrol the sign of the cross is made to prevent the entrance of an evil spirit when a person gapes. The Jewish proverb, 'Open not thy mouth to Satan!' shows that the Hebrews associated the devil with a gaping mouth—a conclusion supported by the story narrated by Josephus,[12] describing how Eleazer, a Jew, cured demoniacs in Vespasian's time by drawing out demons through their nostrils by means of a ring containing a root of mystic virtue mentioned by Solomon. It was probably supposed that the evil spirits entered through the mouth and were exhaled through the nose, much in the same way as the Alfoors regard the wandering soul of a child as expelled with the exhaled breath, after having entered the body of a bystander through the mouth.

It will thus be seen that the folk-lore of yawning has arisen from the primitive doctrine of the separable soul and the notion of possession by spiritual beings. It is not surprising that the uncultured races should thus think of the relation of the human body to the spiritual world, since they are ignorant of the very rudiments of science and can only explain the phenomena of life, consciousness, disease, and death by what the senses seem to tell. In sleep, trance, and death the soul appears to leave the body. To the rude philosopher this is the only possible interpretation of the facts which his senses can give. The most natural means by which these exits and entrances are made is through the mouth, and therefore the opening and closing of this organ—especially in an involuntary act like that of yawning—is beset with no small danger. If the soul were to escape, it might never return, and, in consequence, death to the body would ensue. Likewise, when the mouth is open, a homeless spirit is liable to take up his abode in the body. To prevent this calamity, the entrance has to be carefully guarded.

LITERATURE.—The literature has been given in the footnotes.

E. O. JAMES.

1 E. H. Man, *On the Aboriginal Inhabitants of the Andaman Islands*, London, 1883, p. 94; *GB*³, pt. ii., *Taboo*, p. 37.
2 *Travels in West Africa*, London, 1897, p. 315.
3 J. Grimm, *Deutsche Mythologie*, Göttingen, 1854, p. 1036.
4 A. B. Ellis, *The Ewe-Speaking Peoples of the Slave Coast*, London, 1890, p. 107.
5 H. Callaway, *Religious System of the Amazulu*, Natal, 1868–70, p. 263.
6 *GB*³, pt. ii., *Taboo*, p. 122.
7 Tertullian, *de Virginibus velandis*, 17.
8 G. Turner, *Samoa*, London, 1884, p. 67 f.
9 A. W. Howitt, *JAI* xiii. [1884] 456.
10 *GB*³, pt. ii., *Taboo*, p. 122.
11 H. Batchelor, *The Ainu and their Folk-lore*, London, 1901, p. 504.
12 *Ant.* VIII. ii. 5.

YEAR.—See CALENDAR.

YEMENITES.—See ARABIANS.

YENISEIANS.—See OSTYAKS.

YEZIDĪS.—The name of Yezidīs has been given to a religious sect numbering about 50,000 persons, scattered from Mossul to the Caucasic region (districts of Mossul, Van, Diarbekr, Bitlis). They call themselves Dasni and speak a Kurdish dialect.

At the head of the community is a *khalīfah*, who is a descendant of Shaikh Adi. Under him are *shaikhs*, *kavvals*, and *faqīrs*. Priesthood is hereditary. Morality is above the average in that part of the world. They are brave and shrewd. Their temperament is cheerful but calm. They have cleanly habits. Their women are not veiled and may receive strangers. They feel great repulsion for the colour blue. Being completely illiterate, they handed down their traditions orally. Their greatest festival is on 10th Aug., when a procession of flagellants takes place in the village of Ba'adri. There is the grave of their great saint, Shaikh Adi ben Musafir, who died in A.D. 1155. All around fires of naphtha and bitumen are kept burning.

The Yezidīs have been often persecuted by the Turks. During the 19th cent. efforts were made repeatedly to force them into the Turkish army. They have stubbornly resisted that pressure.

The origin of the word Yezidī has been much discussed. Most probably it is related to Av. *Yazata*, 'deity,' Pers. *Yazdān*, 'God.' It was given to them in contrast either to the Zoroastrians or to the Muhammadans. Although their priesthood is of the Muhammadan type and they recognize Muhammad and Abraham as prophets, they are far from being a Muhammadan sect. Nor are they Nestorians, although they have baptism and regard Christ as an angel in human form. In fact, they perpetuate with various admixtures a doctrine of the Magian type, combining Iranian and Assyrian elements. Their cult of fire is Iranian. They profess that the devil is a creative agent of the supreme God, inasmuch as he produced evil. Hence he deserves our adoration.

These ideas resemble closely Mazdæan cosmogony.[1] Zoroastrianism regarded the worship of the evil spirit (Ahriman) as an abomination, but this did not apply to all Iranian sects. The Mithraists used to offer sacrifices 'deo Arimanio,' and Plutarch[2] reports that the Magians invoked Hades and Darkness in a sombre place, with libations of the *haoma*-plant juice and of the blood of a wolf. No doubt, the devil-worship of the Yezidīs is a survival of the Magian sects who in those districts could resist orthodox Mazdæism.

The doctrine is supposed to be contained in a sacred book called *Yalvah*. It is said to be hidden on a mountain-top where nobody can go and see it. In fact, the real book, in the form in which it exists at present, is written in an obsolete dialect of Kurdish that apparently was in use in the time of Shaikh Adi. Particulars about the Yezidī books, their authenticity, and their contents are given by Bittner,[3] Mingana,[4] and Horten.[5]

Although the publication of these books has been on the whole disappointing, it has made more certain that Yezidism is an offshoot of Mazdæism. It is, in fact, simply an effort to bring unity in dualism. It secures that result through presenting darkness as a mere absence of light, and evil as imperfection the positive element of which is good in the eyes of God, whose plan it serves although, to our insufficient knowledge, it seems to be bad. The book literally says: "I [the Spirit of Good] am active in all events which the outsiders regard as bad because they do not answer to their wishes while they answer to mine." Sin therefore can only be a deficit which is to be made good through the wandering of the soul. The Good Spirit or First Principle is conceived in a pantheistic way as the light radiating from God and a kind of λόγος. It is compared to a white pearl in the sea of Chaos out of which everything has arisen. In this conception we recognize the White Hōm of Pahlavi books, a sacred plant growing in the sea Vourukasha and in which the creative power of God is contained. This white pearl is also a bird, a peacock, the most revered symbol of the Yezidīs (Malak-Tāus). It is also an old Iranian symbol. On the Gaokerna (another name of the White Hōm) growing in the cosmic sea roosts the marvellous bird Simūrgh (Av. *saēna*), who, under the name of Vāregha, is said to have seized the godly glory (Old Pers. *farnah*) that rested on Yima, the primeval king (also on Zoroaster). The λόγος-bird of the Yezidīs was also supposed to incorporate himself in prophets. They believe him to have manifested himself both in Christ and in Shaikh Adi. The Aryans often compared the sun to a bird. Preference is given to the peacock on account of its way of spreading out its tail like a wheel (the wheel is a still better known symbol of the sun). The same symbol has been found on a Coptic coffin, and in the sacred books of the Mandaites. To what extent the Yezidi doctrine is permeated by that old symbolism can be shown by a quotation from their books: "Before heaven and earth arose, God rested on the seas. He had made for Himself a boat and was sailing on the waves, glorifying Himself alone. Then emanated out of Him a white pearl, and He reigned upon it forty thousand years till He threw it off out of anger." This mysterious language is very much in the manner of the Iranian Bundahishn. It is clear only to those who know that the Iranians compared the sun not only to a bird but also to a ship.

1 Cf. art. ZOROASTRIANISM. 2 *De Is. et Osir.* 4.
3 'Die heiligen Bücher der Jeziden oder Teufelsanbeter,' *DWAW*, 1913.
4 *JRAS*, 1916, p. 505 ff.
5 *Der Neue Orient*, iii. [1918] 105–107.

LITERATURE.—J. Menant, *Les Yézidis*, Paris, 1892; J. B. Chabot, *Notice sur les Yézidis*, do. 1896; H. Lammens, *Le Massif du Gebel Simm*, Beirut, 1906; R. Frank, *Scheich 'Adī, der grosse Heilige der Jezidis*, Berlin, 1911; A. Mingana, 'Devil-worshippers: their Beliefs and their Sacred Books,' *JRAS*, 1916, pp. 505–526; M. Bittner, 'Die heiligen Bücher der Jeziden oder Teufelsanbeter,' *DWAW*, 1913; W. B. Heard, 'Notes on the Yezidis,' *JAI* xli. [1911] 200–219; M. Horten, 'Die Geheimlehre der Yezidi, der sogenannten Teufelsanbeter,' *Der Neue Orient*, iii. [1918] 105–107.

A. J. CARNOY.

YGGDRASIL.—See NATURE (Teutonic).

YOGA.—The word *yoga* has two meanings in India: (1) contemplation raised to a formal art, and (2) the system to be treated below, which is entirely taken up with it, gives it a philosophical basis, and ranks as one of the six systems of Brāhmanic philosophy. Contemplation exercises for the attainment of higher states of consciousness and faculties are very old in India. It has been shown, especially by Hermann Beckh (*Buddhismus*[2], 2 vols., Berlin and Leipzig, 1916), that they were of great influence at the foundation of Buddhism. The Yoga system had its rise at a later period, which cannot be determined with certainty. Nor is there absolute certainty yet about the age of the Yogasūtras, *i.e.* the text-book in which the system was first set forth by Patañjali. The Hindus unanimously regard Patañjali as the founder of the system and as identical with Patañjali, the grammarian, the author of the *Mahābhāṣya*, who lived in the 2nd cent. B.C. But Hermann Jacobi (*JAOS*, xxxi. [1911] 24 ff.) has made it probable on philosophic-historical grounds that the Yogasūtras were composed after A.D. 450 by another man of the same name. On the other hand, Bruno Liebich (*Zur Einführung in die indische einheimische Sprachwissenschaft*, i. 'Das Kātantra,' Heidelberg, 1919, p. 7 ff.) has asserted noteworthy philological-critical grounds *for* the identity of the two Patañjalis. The question therefore still awaits the final solution. But in any case the Yoga system is in the main essentially older than the Yogasūtras of Patañjali. We find almost completely developed in the *Maitrī Upaniṣad* the technique prescribed in the Yogasūtras.

In Indian literature the Yoga system is rightly regarded as a branch of the Sāṅkhya (*q.v.*). For all the doctrines of the Sāṅkhya on cosmology, physiology, and psychology have been simply adopted by the Yoga. So, too, the doctrine of emancipation is the same—not merely the conception of emancipation itself as a complete separation of the soul from matter, but also the theory that this emancipation is effected solely by means of the clear distinction drawn between matter and spirit. The characteristics of the Yoga philosophy, apart from points of less importance, are—(1) the rejection of the atheistic views of the Sāṅkhya, and (2) the treatment of the doctrine of absorption as the most effectual means for the attainment of the knowledge that secures emancipation. The technical detail of the theory of absorption forms the proper contents of the Yoga system, and has given to it its own name; for *yoga* signifies originally 'yoking,' then 'diversion of the senses from the external world, and concentration of thought within.'

The object of the Yoga system in inserting the conception of a personal God into the Sāṅkhya is merely to satisfy the theists, and to facilitate the propagation of the theory of the universe expounded in the Sāṅkhya. The idea of God, far from being organically interwoven in the Yoga system, is only loosely inserted. In the Yogasūtras the passages that treat of God stand disconnected, and are, indeed, in direct contradiction to the contents and aim of the system. God neither creates the universe, nor does He rule it. He does not reward or punish the actions of men, and the latter do not regard union with Him (at least according to the older doctrine of the Yoga) as the supreme object of their endeavour. God is only a 'particular soul,' not essentially different from the other individual souls which are coeternal with Him; the distinction consists solely in the manner of His connexion with matter. God cannot in this philosophy be conceived as existing unrelated to matter like an emancipated soul, for then He would be without consciousness. It is assumed, therefore, in the Yoga doctrine that the divine soul stands in an eternal and indissoluble connexion with the noblest and most refined constituent of matter, *sattva*, which is completely purified from the lower material elements; and that this soul is in consequence from and to all eternity endowed with supreme power, wisdom, and goodness. Being free from entanglement in worldly existence, which is full of misery, or in the cycle of births, God lives in eternal bliss, without merit or guilt, unaffected by all the impulses and fatal dispositions with which all other living beings are burdened.

It is evident that this is no God in our sense of the term, and that we have to do with perplexing speculations the aim of which is to conceal the originally atheistic character of the system, and to bring the assumption of God into bare accord with its fundamental teaching. Assuredly these speculations prove, were there any need at all for proof, that in the real Sāṅkhya-Yoga there is no room for a personal God. The two systems are frequently thus joined together in India, in order to emphasize their unity. The idea of God, however, once having been received into the Yoga system, it became necessary to establish a connexion between God and the world of mankind, for God could not continue to exist for His own sake alone. A relation between God and man was found in the fact that, while God does not bestow earthly or heavenly felicity (for this is to be obtained only by individual merit and springs necessarily from it), He in His mercy aids the man who is entirely devoted to Him to remove the hindrances which stand in the way of the attainment of deliverance. But even this slight relation dependent on human devotion to God and on divine favour is with difficulty intelligible as combined with the doctrine of the Yoga.

Nevertheless, in the later Yoga literature, especially in the numerous more recent Upaniṣads which are founded upon and develop the Yoga doctrine, the conception of God takes a much more definite place. God gradually becomes more personal, and the relation between God and man closer. Here also, therefore, the universal need of the human heart has proved stronger than the logical reasonings of philosophy.

The true subject of the Yoga is the doctrine, discussed at great length in the text-books, of *yoga*, or concentration of thought. These texts describe how the senses may be withdrawn from the objects of sense and reduced to inactivity, so that their natural tendency is reversed, and they assume altogether the character of the inner central organ, whose emanations they are; how, in the next place, the activity of the organ of thought, in which all the functions that are dependent upon the influence of the external world are suppressed, is wholly centred upon the *ātman* (the self, the soul); and how, finally, in the last stage of absorption, thought and its object completely coincide. By regular observance of the Yoga praxis the hindrances arising from our natural disposition, which make the attainment of saving knowledge so difficult, are most successfully overcome. When absorption has risen to such a height, or rather has penetrated so deep, that no wandering of thought towards other objects is any longer possible, when that disposition of our organ of thought which is prone to go astray can no longer manifest itself, the knowledge of the essential difference of soul and matter is revealed in the form of an intuitive perception, and therewith the final goal of human endeavour is reached.

The Yoga praxis consists in a series of stages which have to be traversed, in which external aids play a large part. Various bodily attitudes, named *āsana*, are prescribed, the counting of the inhalations and exhalations, but especially the holding of the breath, and the concentration of the gaze on a definite point—on the tip of the nose, the navel, etc. One result of these external Yoga practices is the loss of consciousness, the so-called Yoga-sleep (*yoganidrā*), which is considered to be a stage preceding emancipation, in those cases especially in which during the Yoga-sleep the life becomes extinct. That this Yoga-sleep, which naturally among Indians is regarded as a supremely marvellous phenomenon, is none other than the hypnotic sleep scarcely needs formal demonstration. In fact, the Yoga texts describe a whole series of hypnotic devices which have been effective at all times. Under the name of *trāṭaka*, for instance, Yoga texts which are themselves late, but rest upon an older tradition, enjoin the concentration of a steadfast gaze upon a small object until the eyes begin to shed tears. The result of such practices is declared to be that the body becomes as stiff as a piece of wood, *i.e.* becomes cataleptic. One method, which is especially significant in view of the artificial production of apparent death by the Yogins (see art. YOGĪS, and cf. James Braid, *Observations on Trance or Human Hybernation*, London and Edinburgh, 1850), is the so-called *khecharī*. This consists in artificially extending the tongue, bending it round and inserting the tip in the hollow of the throat, while at the same time the gaze is steadfastly directed on the spot between the eyebrows. Even among ourselves in recent times it has been noticed that the persistent turning upwards of the eyeball at a certain angle induces the hypnotic sleep.

When employing these methods the Yogī, according to the *Haṭhayogapradīpikā* and other texts, before completely losing consciousness hears within his body (in the heart and throat, between the eyebrows, and in other parts) various sounds, viz. those of a drum, the roaring sea, the thunder, a bell, a shell, a reed, a lyre, and a bee. There can be no doubt that as a result of self-suggestion such sounds were actually heard.

The Yoga praxis when correctly and perseveringly observed has, according to the Indian view, therapeutic effects, and other consequences of various kinds. In particular, according to the belief universally held in India, the practice of Yoga procures for a man the miraculous powers often mentioned in Indian literature. When the authors of the Yoga texts hold out the promise of these supernatural powers, it must not be forgotten that these authors were men who regarded very seriously their task of expediting the final attainment of the supreme goal. They certainly did not intend consciously to deceive. They have simply given expression to the conviction of the Yogīs, who believed themselves by means of suggestion in the hypnotic state to be in possession of such powers. These alleged miraculous powers are, in fact, partly the same as our mesmerists think that they possess. Only a few of the many powers that are enumerated can here be named. Among them was the ability to become infinitely small or invisible; to swell to an immense size, so as to reach even to the most distant objects—*e.g.*, to the moon with the tip of the finger—or to be transported anywhere by the simple act of will. There is mentioned also such an intensification of the perceptions that the most remote things, even though separated by intervening walls or the like, come under the cognizance of the senses, and the processes going on in the minds of other men become known in the same way (thought-reading). Other faculties obtainable are the knowledge of the past and future, especially of the hour of one's own death; or the ability to make the dead appear, and to hold converse with them. Many more are cited. That these miraculous powers may be gained by means of the Yoga praxis the most enlightened Brāhmans of the present day are themselves immovably convinced. The reason why such powers of the Yogī are not openly exercised is attributed to the preliminary condition of their attainment, viz. to the absolute indifference of the Yogī to the things of this world.

The conditions of ascetic contemplation practised in the Yoga are the final result of a long development, which takes us back to primitive times, to the ecstatic rites of savage peoples, of which we find traces also in the Veda. Following the analogy of primitive peoples of the present day, we may confidently ascribe to that early period the belief that it was possible by ascetic practices to win the power to hold intercourse with the spirit world, and in a marvellous way to change the ordinary course of nature. In ancient India the name for asceticism was *tapas*. This word signified in the first instance 'warmth,' 'heat,' 'fervour,' in the literal sense; then, 'the sweat generated by self-mortification,' and 'the condition of internal heat thus caused,' *i.e.* 'ecstasy.' As at the present day the conjurers among the Indians of America and among the Negro peoples are wont to proceed in a similar way, so according to the ancient Indian ritual the offerers of the Soma juice prepared themselves for their task by prolonged fastings, while, clad in dark skins of wild animals, and 'speaking in a stammering voice,' they tarried by the magic fire. The fact that the word *tapas* in its metaphorical meaning is found first in the later hymns of the Rigveda proves nothing against the extreme antiquity of the above-mentioned ideas or their practical application; for the circle in which the thought of the Rigveda moves has few points of contact with ascetic practices. *Tapas* meets us more frequently in the Yajur- and Atharvavedas, and very often in the literature of the Brāhmaṇas and Upaniṣads. Since *tapas* occupies here the position of a cosmogonic power, by means of which the creator of the universe produces living beings and inanimate objects, it is evident that already at that period no less influence was ascribed to asceticism than in classical Sanskrit literature, in which the ascetics appear as all-powerful magicians. While, then, originally the ecstatic condition, in which man believes himself capable of rising to higher spheres, was sought mainly by fasting and other self-mortification, in India, owing to the increasingly introspective character of the spiritual life, stress was laid more and more on meditation and absorption. The conception of *yoga*, therefore, was developed out of that of *tapas*. In this meaning the word *yoga* is first met with considerably later than *tapas*. But the existence of the peculiar Yoga doctrine is certified already, as stated above, as early as pre-Buddhist times.

The attempt was made by A. E. Gough [1] to trace the origin of the Yoga praxis back to the influence of the dark-skinned races with whom the incoming Aryans mingled. For proof he relies upon Tylor's *Primitive Culture*,[1] where it is shown that the ecstatic conditions excited by meditation, fastings, narcotics, stimulants, or disease are held in high esteem among savage peoples. According to what has been stated above, there is no need to subject Gough's opinion to a more searching examination; for what he regards as a borrowing in historical times is, in fact, an inheritance from the most hoary antiquity of the Indo-Germanic race.

Mention must be made finally of a subordinate doctrine, which had its origin among the grammarians, but which then came to form a subject of discussion in the text-books of the Yoga system. This was a philosophical and philological theory on the relation of word and meaning. We read of a 'supersensible word' (*sphoṭa*), which is said to inhere in the word as formed by the letters, but to be distinct from it. That which thus conveys the meaning contained in the word as apprehended by the senses is explained to be an indivisible imperishable element which 'breaks forth,' *i.e.* manifests itself on the articulation of the sounds that form the word. It will be seen that a true thought is here presented, though obscurely expressed. This obscurity, however, will not appear strange to any one who considers that here for the first time a difficult problem is touched which since then has occupied many minds; for that 'supersensible word' is, of course, no other than the idea which is expressed by the combination of the letters.

LITERATURE.—R. Garbe, *GIAP* iii. 4B; cf. also A. Barth, *Religions of India*[3], London, 1891; Sir Monier Monier-Williams, *Indian Wisdom*[4], London, 1893; F. Max Müller, *Six Systems of Indian Philosophy*, ch. vii., London, 1899; P. Deussen, *Philosophie der Upanishads*, ch. xvi., tr. Edinburgh, 1905; J. C. Oman, *Mystics, Ascetics, and Saints of India*, London, 1903; *Sarva-darśana-saṅgraha*[2], tr. Cowell and Gough, ch. xv., London, 1894; P. Tuxen, *Yoga*, Copenhagen, 1911; F. H. Woods, *The Yoga-System of Patañjali*, Cambridge, Mass., 1914; T. W. Boissevain, *Yoga-Sootra's door Patanjali*, Haarlem, 1918; Emil Abegg, 'Die Lehre vom Sphoṭa,' in *Festschrift Windisch*, Leipzig, 1914. R. GARBE.

YOGĪS.—*Yogī* is a term denoting in India a follower of the Yoga system (*q.v.*). The word is used especially as a name of the Brāhman ascetics, who devote themselves to the practice of *yoga* as laid down in the rules of the system, and seek thus to gain in the first instance the possession of miraculous powers, and finally deliverance from the cycle of existence. The *yogīs* in India are frequently, in consequence of the *yoga* exercises, plunged in hypnotic slumber, the so-called *yoga*-sleep; and several have been able to remain for a lengthened period in a cataleptic condition without any indication of life, thereby acquiring a reputation for sanctity. A few individuals, by virtue of peculiar disposition and constant training, have succeeded in so prolonging the cataleptic state that they have been able to allow themselves to be buried alive for several weeks without suffering any immediate injury to life and health.[2] In Indian story *yogīs* appear as wizards and all-powerful magicians. The feminine *yoginī* denotes a kind of witch in the train of Śiva and his wife Durgā. The most important of the Yogī sects are the Kānphaṭā Yogīs. See the following article.

LITERATURE.—J. C. Oman, *Mystics, Ascetics, and Saints of India*, London, 1903; R. Schmidt, *Fakire und Fakirtum im alten und modernen Indien*, Berlin, 1908. R. GARBE.

YOGĪS (KĀNPHAṬĀ).—The Kānphaṭā Yogīs are a sub-sect of Śaiva ascetics, so called from their

1 *Philosophy of the Upanishads*[2], London, 1891, p. 18 f.

1 Vol. i. p. 277.

2 Cf. James Braid, *Observations on Trance or Human Hybernation*, London and Edinburgh, 1850; Ernst Kuhn, as quoted in R. Garbe, 'Sāṅkhya und Yoga,' in *GIAP* iii. 4; R. Garbe, 'Über den willkürlichen Scheintod indischer Fakirs,' in his *Beiträge zur indischen Kulturgeschichte*, Berlin, 1903, p. 199 ff.

peculiar custom of slitting their ears (*kān*, 'ear,' and *phaṭā*, 'slit') and inserting huge earrings in the holes. They are also known under the names of Darśanīs from their earrings (see below), and Gorakhpanthīs or Gorakhnāthis from their founder Gorakhnāth (*q.v.*).

Their origin is involved in great obscurity. They trace their tenets to a much earlier period than Gorakhnāth's, and consider the latter as merely the reorganizer of the doctrine and the founder of the sub-sect. Gorakhnāth himself is said to have been a pupil of Machchhendarnāth (Skr. Matsyendranāth)—the Nepalese local deity[1]—who in his turn is represented as the pupil of Ādināth, and in some accounts the list is still more prolonged. A tradition current in N.E. Bengal (Rangpur District) identifies the Kānphaṭās with Sankarāchārya's disciples, who, having taken to drinking, were consequently disowned by their teacher.[2] In the Tibetan tradition Gorakhnāth is recorded as a Buddhist thaumaturgus, and his Yogīs are accused of having passed from Buddhism to Śaivism simply to please their heretic rulers and to gain political favours.[3] What seems to be most likely, amidst the general confusion of the various accounts, is that the Kānphaṭā sect came from the north of India, where it was probably already in existence during the prevalence of Buddhism, but it grew to power only when the latter religion began to lose ground and Brāhmanism to make its reconquest. It is possible that, while Buddhism prevailed, the Yogīs could not help being in some way attracted into its sphere, and that Gorakhnāth was the man who rallied them out from the ranks of the Buddhists and brought their principles into harmony with the philosophy of the *Upaniṣads*; and he was not much posterior to Sankara; at least he certainly acted under the influence of the Brāhmanic renaissance.

The particular tenets of the Kānphaṭās are also clad in darkness, not only for us, but even for their present adepts, who seem to have long forgotten them. Little light can be derived from the *Haṭhayogapradīpikā*, a Yoga treatise,[4] which is said to be one of the books of the sect,[5] or from the *Gorakhnāth-kī Goṣṭhī*, a kind of controversial dialogue between Gorakhnāth and Kabīr concerning their respective doctrines.[6] All that can be gathered from the above sources is that the Kānphaṭās recognize Śiva as Supreme God, and hold that emancipation from worldly existence lies in the union of the individual soul with him, and recommend Yoga as the means of achieving this end. A short poetical composition, bearing the title *Gorakhnāth-ke Vacan*, is included among the works of Banārsī Dās,[7] a Digambara Jain poet, who flourished in the first half of the 17th cent., and who for some time in his youth had also been a follower of Śaivism (probably of the Lingāyat sect); but that too is of little help. The most important source of information, which has remained unedited to the present day, is, therefore, the *Gorakhbodh*, a work written in an old form of Hindī and reported to date from the 14th century.[8] The work is in rhymed prose, sixty stanzas in all, and is in the form of a conversation between Gorakhnāth and his *guru* Machchhendarnāth, the stanzas being a question and an answer alternately. Unfortunately the extreme conciseness and difficulty of the text and the particular character of the exposition make this source only partially utilizable; yet there seems to be sufficient ground in it for concluding that the system here expounded is a combination of Śaivism with the Yoga philosophy, and apparently closely related to the Śaivism comprehended by Mādhavāchārya under the name of *Śaiva*,[1] though different from it. The close alliance of the Kānphaṭā system to the Yoga both of Patañjali and of the *Upaniṣads* is visible from the prominent part given to the Yoga praxis as well as to the mystical theory of the circles in the body (*chakra*, *kausala*), arteries (*nāla*), vital air (*pavana*), and breaths (*haṃsa*).

According to the authority of the *Gorakhbodh*, the vital air resides in the circle of the navel (*nābhi*), and is supportod by the void (*śūnya*), which is spread everywhere. In its turn, the vital air vivifies the *manas*, which resides in the heart. The *manas* is open to the influence of the moon (*chandra*), which resides in the sky, the vital air to the influence of the sun (*sūrya*), and the void to that of the time (*kāla*). There is, further, another element, the word (*śabda*), which resides in form (*rūpa*). Before the coming into existence of heart, navel, form, and sky, the *manas* was contained in the void, the vital air was shapeless (*nirākāra*), the word was unformed, and the moon resided in the intermediate space between heaven and earth. The void is of four kinds: *sahaja-*, *anubhava-*, *parama-*, and *atīta-śūnya*, and it is to it that the vital spirits (*prāṇa*) resort during sleep or death. There are five principles (*tattva*), one of which seems to be *nirvāṇa*, and ten *dvāras*, or means of attaining perfection, which are not named.

From this it would seem that Gorakhnāth too resorted to a symbolism of the kind found in many of the *Upaniṣads*, especially the later ones,[2] to account for such metaphysical problems as cannot be solved by reason. The phrase *yato vācho nivartante*, occurring in the *Taittirīya* and *Brahma Upaniṣads* to signify incapability of definition, is also found in the *Gorakhbodh*, 50–51 (*vācha nivaiṭai*). Contrarily to what had been asserted on the authority of the *Haṭhayogapradīpikā*,[3] a Kānphaṭā Yogī is not necessarily obliged to remain within a monastery, the second stanza in the *Gorakhbodh* allowing him to live in market-places and roads, and under the shade of trees. One of the most important features of the doctrine of Gorakhnāth is, no doubt, its universality, it being open to all castes and being not very particular in regard to food, in both respects bearing an analogy to the Vaiṣṇava system of Rāmānanda. The affinity between the two systems is increased by the adoption of the same term *avadhūta* for the designation of their respective ascetics.[4]

The present Kānphaṭās are more or less spread all over India, and their customs are substantially the same in all places. They have no caste prejudices and freely eat flesh, with the exception of beef and pork, and indulge in spirits and opium, whenever they can afford it. They bury the dead. Those who take to secular callings are mostly money-lenders, weavers, cultivators, peddlers, or soldiers. They are said to be good soldiers, and

1 S. Lévi, *Le Népal*, Paris, 1905, i. 347 ff.

2 F. Buchanan, in R. Montgomery Martin's *Eastern India*, 3 vols., London, 1838, iii. 535 f.; G. A. Grierson, 'The Song of Mánik Chandra,' *JASBe* xlvii. pt. i. p. 139.

3 Lévi, i. 355 f.; Tāranātha, *Gesch. des Buddhismus in Indien*, tr. A. Schiefner, St. Petersburg, 1869, p. 255.

4 See art. YOGA.

5 H. H. Wilson, *Select Works*, ed. R. Rost, 2 vols., London, 1861–62, i. 214.

6 W. Price, *Hindu and Hindustani Selections*, i. 140; Wilson, i. 213 f.

7 See *Banārsī Vitas*, ed. Nāthū Rām Premi, Bombay, 1905, p. 209 f.

8 The present writer was made acquainted with it through the kindness of Sir George Grierson, who lent him his own copy of the original MS, which is in the Darbār Library of Jodhpur.

1 *Sarva-darśana-saṃgraha*, vii.

2 Cf. P. Deussen, *Sechzig Upanishad's des Veda*[2], Leipzig, 1905, p. 542.

3 Wilson, p. 216 n.; G. S. Leonard, 'Notes on the Kānphaṭā Yogīs,' *IA* vii. [1878] 300.

4 Throughout the *Gorakhbodh* Gorakhnāth is addressed by Machchhendarnāth as *avadhu*, a corruption of *avadhūta*, and in the *Gorakhnāth-kī Goṣṭhī* he calls himself *Yogī Gorakha avadhūta*.

their military fame seems to be of an ancient date.[1] In some parts of India they live by singing cyclic poems[2] or religious songs.[3] They are generally believed to be soothsayers and sorcerers, and to have the power of curing children and protecting them from the evil eye.[4] Marriage is common among them.[5] Those who live by begging smear their bodies with ashes and wear a waist-cloth and an upper-sheet dyed in ochre, a woollen string (*jāneu*, *sailī*) round their neck with a horn-whistle (*nād*) attached to it, a wallet (*jholī*) hanging from their left shoulder, and a hollow gourd, in which to receive alms, in their right hand. But the great characteristic of the Kānphaṭās is the huge ear-rings (*darśana*, *mudra*) which they wear in their slit ears. These earrings are generally made of agate, horn, or glass, about 2¼ ounces in weight, and are conferred on the Kānphaṭās at the time of their initiation. They are worn as a kind of fetish and are regarded by them as the symbol of their faith.[6] The initiation takes place as follows:

First there is a preparatory ceremony, in which the neophyte, after having been shaved and smeared with ashes, is invested with the woollen string and horn-whistle and is appointed to serve his *guru*. After a period of six to eight months, during which his conduct is strictly watched, the novice is admitted to the ear-slitting ceremony, which is performed before the head *guru* or the god Bhairava, with the novice sitting with his face turned to the north. The slit is made with a double-edged knife and is about three-fourths of an inch to an inch in length; in the wound a *nimb* stick is inserted and the cure is made by a treatment of *nimb* oil and daily bathings with pure water.[7] When the ear is well again, the earrings are conferred on the neophyte, and he has his name changed into a new one ending in *-nāth* and becomes a regular Yogī.

Of all Kānphaṭās of India the best known to us from trustworthy accounts are those of the west. These generally trace their origin to Dharamnāth, who is said to be one of Gorakhnāth's disciples, who went from Peśāwar to Kāṭhiāwāṛ and Kachchh to perform penance and turned the sea between the two peninsulas into the present Raṇ. The Western Kānphaṭās live in monasteries, the most celebrated of which are that of Dhīnodhar in Kachchh on the edge of the Raṇ, which claims to have been founded by Dharamnāth himself on the spot of his penance,[8] and that of Gorakhmaḍhi in Kāṭhiāwāṛ.[9] The characteristic of the Western Kānphaṭās is charity; they make it a rule to distribute provisions, twice every day, to any who ask for them;[10] they can well afford to do this, as they are rich and have been endowed with lands by more than one of the former Rāos. The monastery (*maṭh*) of Dhīnodhar Hill is the most important; it is a large fenced and turreted establishment, comprising dwelling-houses, temples, tombs of the former *pīrs*, halls for the treating of guests, etc. The *pīr*, or abbot, is held in great honour by the Rāo himself, who after his election invests him with a dress and instals him on his seat. Both the Yogīs and the *pīr* of Dhīnodhar are said to observe the strictest celibacy, but in the case of other monasteries the abbot (who takes also the name of *mahant* or *bāvā*) is allowed to marry and, failing issue, to adopt one of his disciples.[1] The chief object of worship of the Dhīnodhar Kānphaṭās is Dharamnāth, whom they habitually call by the term *dādā*, 'father.'

1 See. J. Tod, *Annals and Antiquities of Rajast'han*, 2 vols., London, 1829–32, i. 445 f.; K. Raghunāthjī, 'Bombay Beggars and Criers,' *IA* x. [1881] 145.
2 Martin, *Eastern India*, iii. 407, 534; Grierson, *op. cit.*
3 *IA* x. 146.
4 W. Crooke, *TC*, Calcutta, 1896, iii. 158.
5 *BG* xxi. [1884] 183; *PNQ* ii. [1884–85] 964.
6 *BG* viii. [1884] 155; Crooke, iii. 156. According to George Le Grand Jacob's authority, a Kānphaṭā whose earring had been cut off did not allow his ear to be sewn up and a new earring provided, but chose to die instead.
7 *BG* v. [1880] 87, viii. [1884] 447; Crooke, iii. 156 f.
8 For a complete account of this monastery as well as of the Kachchhī le[illegible]nd of Dharamnāth see Dalpatrām Prāṇjīvan Khakhar, in *I*[illegible] vii. [1878] 47–53; cf. also T. Postans, in *JRAS* v. 268–271.
9 *BG* viii. 1[illegible] 446 f.
10 According to the Kachchhī legend, this liberal distribution of food was enjoined on the monks of Dhīnodhar by Dharamnāth himself, as a reaction against the uncharitable character of the inhabitants of Kachchh.

The Kānphaṭās of Bombay and Belgaum are peculiar in so far as they carry a trident (*triśūl*)—the emblem of the god Śiva—when they go for alms.[2] In Bombay they also carry a drum (*daur*), whence their name of Daurī Gosāīns. These marry freely and are said to bury their dead in a sitting position. In most of Northern and Eastern India the Kānphaṭās still appear to perform some sort of sacerdotal functions, to officiate as priests in the temples of Bhairava, and even to offer sacrifices to the village-gods.[3] In Gorakhpur, where Gorakhnāth is said to be buried, they worship, besides Bhairava, a goddess called Bālā Sundarī,[4] which is probably another form of the Tripurasundarī of the Sāktas.[5] The Kānphaṭās of Benares have the temple of Kāl Bhairo as their headquarters and bury their dead in their own houses. The most depraved of all the Kānphaṭās of India seem to be those of the hills, who are said to follow the ritual of the *Tantras* and to indulge in the orgies of the left-hand Sākta cult.[6] These too, like the Kānphaṭās of Kachchh, trace their origin to Dharamnāth.

LITERATURE.—This is given in the footnotes.

L. P. TESSITORI.

YOUNG MEN'S CHRISTIAN ASSOCIATION.—The Young Men's Christian Association (Y.M.C.A.) was founded on 6th June, 1844, by George Williams. Twelve young men were present at the first meeting, which was held in his bedroom in St. Paul's Churchyard, London. Years afterwards it was discovered that of the twelve gathered in that upper room three belonged to the Established Church of England, three were Congregationalists, three Baptists, and three Methodists. It was the day of small things, and half a crown only was the weekly rent of the first headquarters of the movement. Organized Bible Classes became an important feature of the work in 1847, and in the following year the famous series of Exeter Hall Lectures was inaugurated. In 1851 Lord Shaftesbury became President, and in the following year a Y.M.C.A. was formed in Paris and another in Holland, whilst farther afield the movement took root in Adelaide, Calcutta, Montreal, and Boston, U.S.A. An epoch-making World Conference was held in Paris in 1855, when what is known as the Paris Basis was adopted, and on this simple statement of faith the Associations of the world, through their national organizations, are still affiliated. It reads:

'The Young Men's Christian Associations seek to unite those young men, who, regarding the Lord Jesus Christ as their God and Saviour according to the Holy Scriptures, desire to be His disciples in their doctrine and in their life, and to associate their efforts for the extension of His Kingdom amongst young men.'

In 1863 the aims of the British movement were defined in the following words:

'The one great aim of the Association is to win young men for the Saviour,'

and that note has been dominant ever since. Educational features were adopted in 1864, and the Central International Committee as the executive of the World's Alliance was formed in 1878 with headquarters in Geneva. The jubilee of the movement was celebrated in London in 1894, and on that occasion the founder, George

1 *BG* viii. 155; Crooke, iii. 156.
2 *BG* xxi. 185; *PNQ* ii. 964.
3 Martin, *Eastern India*, iii. 536; Crooke, iii. 159.
4 Crooke, iii. 157.
5 Cf. R. G. Bhandarkar, *Vaiṣṇavism, Śaivism, and Minor Religious Systems* (=*GIAP* III. vi.), Strassburg, 1913, p. 146.
6 Crooke, iii. 158 f.

Williams, received the honour of knighthood from Queen Victoria. The official figures issued by the World's Committee show that on 1st Jan. 1920 the Y.M.C.A. was represented in 8789 centres, of which 6250 were in Europe, 32 in Africa, 2098 in America, 386 in Asia, and 23 in Australasia.

The Association has thus been in existence for three-quarters of a century, and in all parts of the world has proved the friend particularly of the young man away from home. The exceptional conditions of the Great War have brought it into the limelight and gathered round the Y.M.C.A. a host of new friends and naturally not a few critics. On the one hand, it has been urged by many that there is no need for the Y.M.C.A., and that the Churches can do all that is necessary as far as Christian work among young men is concerned. Many Christian people have gone even further and said, 'Drop the "Christian" out of your title and confine your efforts to social service, and you can count on our cordial support.' In like manner it was often said, even during the Great War, by certain Army people who had no sympathy with the higher aims of the Association: 'We have our own canteens, and, therefore, we do not need the Y.M.C.A.'—forgetting that the Association is something far more than a canteen and seeks to introduce through its programme that inspiration and uplift which men so greatly need.

Many have accused the Association of being too broad, and others have withheld sympathy and support because in their judgment it is administered on too narrow lines. Then, again, during the War many have accused the Y.M.C.A. of being too much commercialized, though, on the other hand, they insist on the work being self-supporting. The fact is that, if it was to meet the real need of the men during the War, it was compelled to trade, though never for trading's sake or for private profit, and indeed all the profits were spent for the direct and immediate benefit of the men.

The Y.M.C.A. commenced its work on somewhat narrow lines. It had a definite objective which it kept always before its members—to win men for Christ and to enlist them in His service. The story of the movement has been a story of gradual but steady and constant evolution. It has gradually extended, and to-day it stands for a broad progressive programme of Christian and social service. To appreciate the importance of the service it has rendered during the past seventy-five years, and the programme it is gradually evolving for the future, certain facts must be borne in mind concerning the Association.

1. Its functions are those of the pioneer.—It does not seek so much to build upon the foundations laid by others as to find new methods of serving and enlisting men. As an emergency organization it appealed to the imagination of the public in August, 1914, when, through its mobile machinery, it was able to meet a definite national emergency with unexpected rapidity. Long before the adaptation of the Labour Exchanges to meet the needs of discharged men, the Y.M.C.A. in London had its own employment agency, through which it found work for more than 20,000 ex-soldiers and sailors. Before the Armistice it had its own training workshops in London, Manchester, and other centres, and the little farm colony it has established in Dorset for tubercular ex-service men has been regarded by the authorities as one of the best things of the kind, though to meet the need fully the machinery of no private organization would be adequate. The Y.M.C.A. was the pioneer of the present Army system of education, and more than £140,000 was spent by the British movement on educational work among the soldiers in France. As the War went on, many other societies and private individuals organized recreation huts and tents on the lines mapped out by the Y.M.C.A., but it was the pioneering work in the early days of the century in volunteer and territorial camps that provided the experience upon which all this work in war-time has been built up.

2. It is essentially an auxiliary movement.—It does not profess to be an educational authority, but in a hundred ways it supplements the work of school, university, and educational committee. On the battlefield it supplemented the work of the official R.A.M.C., attending to the needs of the walking wounded, and in the base camps caring for the relatives who visited their loved ones when dangerously ill in hospital. So in like manner it seeks to supplement the work of the Churches, and has always resisted the temptation to develop into another denomination, whatever it may be called, or to take to itself functions that rightly belong to the Churches, or to supplant or in any way supersede their work.

3. It is interdenominational rather than undenominational.—It holds that the first duty of the member is to his Church. A recent official declaration states:

'(1) The Y.M.C.A. does not come on the scene to teach the Churches how to do their work, much less to supplant them. It desires to help and serve the Church as the permanent Divine Institution designed by God to help and save the world.

(2) It believes it is called of God to serve our soldiers, sailors, and airmen until demobilisation is complete, and then to continue to serve them when demobilised or disabled, and, as far as possible, all the young men and boys of the Nation in town and city, camp and barracks, village and hamlet, East End and West End, guiding and befriending them as they move from place to place, and looking after their interests when in response to the call of commerce or vocation they travel in search of health or wealth to the most distant parts of the British Empire, or to the utmost parts of the earth.

(3) It regards the whole world as its parish, believing that the work done during the war has demonstrated that the Red Triangle has a message for the men of every creed and nation. It believes it can help the Churches to find the key to the solution of one aspect of the Missionary problem, and that the "Hut" will prove as helpful to the young men of missionary lands as to those of our own country.

(4) It believes that the very success of its war service constitutes a challenge to undertake work on an adequate scale for the men and boys of every class.

(5) It holds that it is of more importance that the need should be met, and the work done, than that any particular society or organisation—even the Y.M.C.A.—should do it. It recognises that the field is so wide that there is ample scope for the activities of all societies that have the same end in view, and it earnestly desires that over-lapping and consequent waste of energy should be avoided, and all such work co-ordinated.

(6) It seeks to provide a rallying centre for those who, irrespective of distinctions of creed or party, desire to engage in social service and to work for the extension of the Kingdom of God.

(7) It would state definitely and categorically that, whilst fully recognising its position as an agency of the Christian Church, it regards as the primary aim of the movement the winning of young men for our Lord Jesus Christ, and the leading of them into the fellowship and service of the Churches.'

4. It is missionary in its outlook.—The mission of the Y.M.C.A. is to the man outside, and it seeks to touch him at every point and, as far as possible, in every place. It seeks to form a half-way house, a kind of communication trench, between the men of the nation and the Churches. It has always placed emphasis upon the work of the member in the sphere of his daily calling. Meetings for prayer and for the study of the Bible have ever held a prominent place in the programme of the Y.M.C.A., and it seeks through its members to proclaim the message of the Evangel in the language of the times. It has always made a feature of meetings in the open-air and in unexpected places. It counts more upon atmosphere than meetings, and depends, more than upon any other single factor, on the personality of its workers.

As may be inferred from the foregoing, the

Association has spread to non-Christian lands, where it has speedily become an indigenous movement. In India, China, and Japan it has been proved that the countries of the Orient can themselves provide leadership that will compare favourably with the best that the Western nations can produce.

5. It is essentially a layman's movement.—Possibly the greatest service the Association has rendered to the cause of Christianity has been in winning men when young for Christian discipleship and providing them with their first training in Christian service. Such training must often have been crude, but it has been practical and effective, and has provided the incentive to further study and an earnest longing for fuller knowledge. It will probably be conceded that the greatest weakness of many of the Churches to-day is to be found in their failure to fire the imagination of their male members and to enlist their co-operation in the work of winning men. This lack, to a certain extent, has been supplied by the Y.M.C.A. —to how large an extent has not been fully realized. Leading ministers of every denomination have told the story of the help and training the Association gave them at a critical period of their careers. It is true that many a branch of the Y.M.C.A. does not live up to the high ideals of the movement, but no Association is regarded as really efficient from the Y.M.C.A. standpoint unless it aims at keeping first things first and inspires young men to help their fellows in the daily fight against temptation. Emphasis is placed, too, on the importance of the voluntary worker. In the great city Association the General Secretary is the key to the situation. The work must be built up largely around his personality, but his business is to inspire men and work through his members. The very last thing to be desired is the development of a professional class of men, however able, who will do the work themselves rather than through others.

In the early days of the Great War the Y.M.C.A. had to face a serious crisis with regard to personnel. Hitherto it had been regarded as 'a work for young men by young men.' The very men on whom it relied for its ever-expanding war work were needed for the Army and Navy, and their places had to be taken by men who, through age or health, were disqualified for active service. It was soon found, however, that there were many things women could do even in the work of a Young Men's Christian Association, and, as a matter of fact, later on there were in the war service of the British Y.M.C.A. alone more than 40,000 women workers as compared with less than 4000 men. There can be no doubt that the Y.M.C.A. woman worker has come to stay, and that to the great advantage of the movement.

6. Emphasis is laid on practical service.—In the early days of the War some people spoke sneeringly of what they termed 'canteen religion.' As the War years passed slowly by, the vast majority saw its utility and learned that it was not incompatible with the teaching and example of our Lord. He spoke of the 'cup of cold water' given in His name, and many a war-weary soldier saw the Master's hand in the hand that gave him a cup of hot coffee or cocoa when he was 'up against things' in the trenches. The Y.M.C.A. believes that the most effective way of combating intemperance is by providing an effective counter-attraction. Given the 'Hut' run by the right people and with a strong constructive programme, there will be little need to fear the wet canteen, the public-house, or the far more deadly drinking club. The Association seeks to promote purity of life, not only by education and precept, but also by making provision for the sexes to meet amidst wholesome surroundings and by catering for the leisure of young people. A well-equipped hostel is an important feature of most of the large city Associations at home and overseas, and in a hundred practical ways the all-round needs of young men and boys are being looked after. It is the conviction of the leaders of the movement that it is possible to serve God acceptably in any one of the many activities of the Association. The Hut, or the Red Triangle Club, as it is usually called, with its big lounge or common room, is regarded as a centre to work from, and an object lesson in practical Christianity. It is recognized that

> 'Where Truth in closest words may fail,
> Then Truth embodied in a tale
> Shall enter in by lowly doors.'

7. It is a unifying force.—Sir George Williams always regarded the prayer of the Master—'That they all may be one'—as a call and a challenge to the Association which he founded and with which his name will for ever be identified. Through the whole period of its existence the Y.M.C.A. has been a unifying force, though it has talked little about unity. It has provided a common platform for Christians of all denominations, and has actually succeeded in bringing together and uniting in Christian service those who never otherwise found opportunity to move beyond their denominational barriers. We believe it is destined to play an important part in years to come in bringing together class and class, party and party, creed and creed, nation and nation. None will be asked to give up their special beliefs or convictions, but all will be invited to co-operate in the service of the Kingdom of God. In the War the Association was allowed to serve the Indian troops only on condition that there should be no religious work as men commonly call work religious. There were to be no hymns, no prayers, no addresses, no distribution of Bibles or Testaments. The leaders of the movement gave their promise and carried it out to the letter. It is doubtful if anything that has ever been done will have more effect upon the future of Christianity in India than the unselfish Christian social service carried out by consecrated men under the sign of the Red Triangle. Not only during the War, but before and since, the Association has had the privilege of serving men of every nation and creed.

8. It begins with the boy.—The hope of the future of the Y.M.C.A. is to be found in the fact that it begins with the boy, and it seeks to get him at the age when he begins to feel too big for the Sunday School. If we can only reach and influence the boy during the crisis of adolescence, the future is assured.

9. The significance of the Red Triangle.—During the War the Red Triangle had become almost as familiar as the Red Cross itself. It typifies the service the Association seeks to render. Its very colour signifies sacrifice, and its three sides speak to the Association man of the needs of body, mind, and spirit, all of which may be consecrated to the service of the living God. Nothing that can be used to the glory of God is regarded by the Association as common or unclean. Its programme is ever widening and its roots getting deeper down. For years the leaders of the Y.M.C.A. set their faces steadily against even the most innocent of games, and, when these were included, another running fight, which lasted for years, took place over the proposed inclusion of smoking rooms and billiard tables. These have now become almost universal in Britain, though there are still many of the great Association buildings in the United States where smoking is not permitted. More recent agitation has been in favour of cards, dancing, and the drama, and almost imperceptibly the Association has seemed to modify its position to meet the new needs of a new generation. Emphasis is placed on proper supervision, right company and hours, a programme that is clean and elevating and in connexion with which there is no gambling. It is urged that these innovations can only be included as part of a well-considered constructive programme. In these days, when there is a more or less general tendency to kill time, everything that can be done is being done to build up in every Association centre a programme that will lead the members on to aspiration and achievement.

Critics have accused the Y.M.C.A. of attempting the impossible, of building on the apex of the Triangle. They gladly accept the criticism. They *have* attempted the impossible, and by God's grace the impossible has been achieved, for the secret of the Red Triangle is that it is upheld by invisible hands.

LITERATURE.—i. *Historical.*—E. W. Shipton, 'The History of the Y.M.C.A. in London,' *Exeter Hall Lectures for 1845–1846*, London, 1864, i.; G. J. Stevenson, *Historical Records of the Y.M.C.A. 1844–1884*, do. 1884; *The Jubilee of the Y.M.C.A. 1894*, do. 1894; *History of the Y.M.C.A.*, vol. i. (only vol. issued) deals with 'The Founding of the Association' (L. L. Doggett), New York, 1916; *Fifty Years' Work among Young Men* (a world survey), London, 1894; *The Association Handbook*, New York, 1892 (gives a chapter on 'The History of the Y.M.C.A.'); *Work for Young Men in N. America*, do. 1901; *History of the North American Y.M.C.A.*, do. 1913. A history of the whole movement is in preparation.

ii. *Biographical.*—J. E. Hodder Williams, *The Life of Sir George Williams*, London, 1906, re-issued as *The Father of the Red Triangle*, do. 1918; H. Begbie, *The Ordinary Man and the Extraordinary Thing*, do. n.d. (*c.* 1912) (a study of the founder and the movement); J. Kellett, *That Friend of Mine* (the Life of Miss M. McArthur, a pioneer of educational work with the Army in France), do. 1920; *Betty Stevenson, Y.M.C.A., Croix de Guerre avec Palme*, do. 1920 (the life of a lady transport driver); L. L. Doggett, *The Life of Robert R. McBurney*, Cleveland, U.S.A., 1902; R. C. Morse, *My Life with Young Men*, New York, 1918.

iii. *General and descriptive.*—*Handbook of the History, Organisation and Methods of Work of Y.M.C.A.*, New York, 1892; *The Army and Religion*, ed. D. S. Cairns, London, 1919, pt. ii. ch. 8; A. K. Yapp, *The Romance of the Red Triangle*, London, n.d.; E. W. Hornung, *Notes of a Camp-Follower on the Western Front*, do. 1919 (gives an account of the work of a Y.M.C.A. Librarian at Arras); G. Henderson, *The Experiences of a Hut Leader at the Front*, Paisley, 1918; J. W. Barrett, *The War-Work of the Y.M.C.A. in Egypt*, London, 1919; H. Boas, *The Australian Y.M.C.A. with the Jewish Soldier of the Australian Imperial Force*, do. 1919; K. Mayo, *That Damn Y*, Boston, U.S.A., 1920 (gives a racy account of the American Association's War-Work); Sherwood Eddy, *Everybody's World*, London, 1920; Conrad Hoffmann, *In the Prison Camps of Germany*, New York, 1920 (describes the work among prisoners right through the War); S. H. Baker, *Character Building Clubs for Boys*, London, 1919 (the text-book for the Boys' Department of the Y.M.C.A.); see also year-books and pamphlets issued by various departments, 13 Russell Square, London.

iv. *Periodicals.*—Every country has its own publications; for English readers the chief periodicals are: *The Red Triangle Magazine*, monthly, London; *Red Triangle News*, Scotland; *Young Men of India*, monthly, Calcutta; *Association Men*, monthly, New York; the trilingual quarterly, *The Sphere*, Geneva.

A. K. YAPP.

YOUNG WOMEN'S CHRISTIAN ASSOCIATION.

—I. *IN GREAT BRITAIN.*—The Young Women's Christian Association (Y.W.C.A.) has been a growth, not an organization, a creation rather than a manufacture; its very nomenclature denotes this. Quite naturally and gradually branches have grown up all over the world. A branch involves a living organism, so that the Y.W.C.A. has sometimes been compared to a tree with its central stem and spreading branches whose leaves have been for the healing of the nations. As in all human activities, the spirit has been too often lost in the letter, and life cramped by form and substance; there have in consequence been many failures, but its motto, 'Not by might, nor by power, but by my Spirit, saith the Lord of hosts,' still binds the Y.W.C.A. together as an international federation; the British Y.W.C.A. was one of the first to join it.

1. History.—The history of the Association circles round three great events in the spiritual, social, and political realms which have in a special way affected women.

(1) First in 1855 began the spiritual movement which culminated in the revival of 1859–60 in Great Britain and Ireland, on the Continent, and in U.S.A. The idea that 'thy sons and thy daughters shall prophesy' was revived at this time, and it was then that women shared in the blessings which accrue from a fully developed spiritual ideal. To a daughter came the idea of forming a Y.W.C.A. worked as a prayer union for young women. Girls became anxious for the welfare of their friends, and, as the new tide of life began to flow, they were caught into it and began to realize their responsibilities. Up to that time it was not considered proper for a woman to attend even a missionary meeting, much less to go out as a missionary, or to take part in evangelistic work. The present writer remembers attending a meeting where no hymn could be sung, for it was not considered proper or right for a woman to raise the tune at a religious meeting, even when no man could do so. Emma Robarts asked ten friends to join her in intercession—a prayer union, as it was then called—and these women, filled with the spirit of revival, began to bring the names of others to be prayed for. A list of the first 27 members still remains in a tiny book, and a quarto sheet, of a few years later date, is in the writer's possession, containing a list of some 140 names, each undertaking some small piece of religious and social service. Gradually the list grew until 10,000 members were enrolled in different branches, each member being taught to realize her corporate as well as her individual responsibility. Thus the foundation of the Y.W.C.A. as a fellowship of service and prayer was laid.

(2) In 1887 came the social upheaval which followed the revelations of W. T. Stead. Wages boards were unknown, and few girls earned a living wage. The consequence was grave moral danger, and many indications of evil were discovered and made public at that time. It was an appeal to a Christian association of women. The London Y.W.C.A. made an appeal to the public which for the first time brought the Association into national prominence, and set it on its path of social as well as definitely religious work. Hostels were opened all over London and in other towns; the Travellers' Aid Society was inaugurated; the Park Mission for visiting in the London parks; and the Factory Helpers' Union, which has since developed into the Federation of Working Girls' Clubs, began its useful work under the Y.W.C.A., while the Association gathered educated girls into a 'Time and Talents' movement, quickly followed by the Guild of Helpers.

An association which belongs to the British Empire and has its part in the life of a nation which has ever offered hospitality to the people of all nations could not fail to extend beyond its own borders. The Y.W.C.A. was carried to India, with Bombay as its first centre, to S. Africa at Cape Town, to the Continent, and to Australia. The Provincial Council (as the South of England Council was then called) had its links in many lands. The Y.W.C.A. became the office in England for the 'International Union of the Friends of Young Women,' an organization which had spread all over Europe. 'Prevention and Protection' was its watchword, and its motto 'By love serve one another.' A visit of the then president, the present Lord Kinnaird, with his sisters Gertrude and Emily Kinnaird, to the U.S.A. brought the British Association into touch with a similar movement among students, which was organized along the lines of the Y.M.C.A., and formed the student department of the Y.W.C.A., which has been adopted in many lands as an integral part of the national Y.W.C.A. work of the country. This led to frequent communication and intervisitation until finally an entirely new policy was adopted. All the branches which had been started by the British Association and linked to it, but which were not in Great Britain or Ireland, were cut off gradually and formed into national groups under national committees; each could make its own rules and affiliate to the World's Y.W.C.A. office.

(3) The third national movement which brought a call to the British Y.W.C.A. was the Great War of 1914–18. On the first day of war, 4th August, some of the workers met, and within a week called together the National Council to consider the responsibility of a women's association in time of war; it established a War Emergency Committee in the first month, which eventually developed into a War Department with six different committees. The Association put itself at the disposal of Government for anything that might concern women. It was found that London had become a cosmopolitan city, and girls of all lands were working in it. Immediately they were anxious to get back to their own country, the Y.W.C.A. provided the necessary links, and thousands of girls found that the Association Directory could guide them and that its membership meant friendship and fellowship above national or denominational ties. The Blue Triangle, similarly to the Red Triangle of the Y.M.C.A., became the symbol of Y.W.C.A. activities. It was evident to the nation that a Christian association could be looked to to provide for the physical and social well-being of the soldier boy and the girl war-worker. The War Department gradually became responsible for establishing and expanding work along two lines—those of providing for the mental and for the physical needs of girls—and on a third line to carry on the religious work of the Association, thereby completing the triangle symbol. The three—physical, mental, religious—are equally dependent on the spiritual force which energizes and binds them together. The Blue Triangle is now seen in Government enclosures and controlled factories, in the centre of busy cities and in the lonely countryside wherever munition and aerodrome settlements were established. It denotes to the girl of to-day, as the letters Y.W.C.A. denoted to the girl of yesterday, that family life, community life, and the life of the State are better if animated by the spirit of Jesus Christ their Lord, which is the animating spirit of the Y.W.C.A. The Association also makes its contribution to the Kingdom of God on earth by remaining in close relation to all the Christian Churches; it is strictly interdenominational, and its service is rendered to all women irrespective of creed.

2. Organization.—(*a*) *National.*—The activities of the Association are carried out on certain well-defined lines under the direction of: (1) the National Biennial Conference elected by the membership, thus aiming at the development of democratic management; (2) a National Council appointed at the Conference and composed largely of national and divisional office-bearers, with co-opted members, representative of labour and Church, meeting at least once a year; (3) a National Executive, meeting monthly to direct and evolve any activities necessary for the growing needs of the girls of the land. The work is directed by a president, four acting vice-presidents, a treasurer, a general secretary, and a staff of national secretaries.

(*b*) *Departmental.*—National, departmental, and sectional committees, meeting every month or in alternate months, are appointed for studying problems affecting girls, and thus a large body of women take part in and guide the activities of the Association. The Overseas and Foreign Committee seeks to interest members in Association work in non-Christian lands; secretaries are sent out to all parts of the world.

(*c*) *Basis and aims.*—All women taking up active work, salaried or honorary, on these councils and committees must agree with the basis and aims:

'Faith in God the Father as Creator, and in Jesus Christ, His only Son, as Lord and Saviour, and in the Holy Spirit as Revealer of Truth and Source of Power for life and service, according to the teaching of Holy Scripture.'

'The aim of the Young Women's Christian Association is:—
To call young women and girls to the allegiance of Our Lord Jesus Christ, the fellowship of His Church and the service of His Kingdom.
To unite them in a fellowship of prayer, Bible study and service, through which they may make their contribution to the spiritual, moral and social progress of the world.
To make available for them all that will minister to character, mental capacity and physical health.'

(*d*) *Training of secretaries.*—The aim is to have a well-staffed training centre where students offering for home or overseas work can receive a year or more of training, so that the Association secretaryship may be looked on as a vocation as important as teaching.

(*e*) *Headquarters.*—The Headquarters of the British Y.W.C.A. are at 22, 25, and 26 George Street, Hanover Square, London, W.1.

(*f*) *Membership.*—Membership in the Association is open to women who desire, in fulfilment of the motto, to serve one another and the world by love in the spirit of Jesus Christ. There are also associate membership and club membership which do not involve membership of the Association.

(*g*) *Magazines.*—By its literature the Association seeks to carry its ideals to all sections of the community. Its magazines are: *Woman's Outlook* (monthly), *Our Own Gazette* (monthly, for younger members), *Home and Overseas Bulletin*, *The World's Quarterly*, *The Y.W.C.A. Almanack and Motto Card*, *The Monthly Letter*.

(*h*) *Territorial work.*—The activities are carried on through divisions, embracing a given number of counties: London, East of England, Midlands, North of England, South of England, West of England, Scotland, Wales. Each has its president, general secretary, and council, and directs the work of the local branches by grouping them into district councils.

3. Methods.—Along the lines of the physical, intellectual, and religious development of the young women of the land, and through its departments, the Association moves forward. The most important methods are:

(*a*) *Canteens.*—The Y.W.C.A. has the honour of starting the first women's restaurant, which is still feeding hundreds of working girls at 'Ames House,' Mortimer Street, London, W.

(*b*) *Hostels.*—The largest of these is Bedford House, London. Others are Ashley House, London; 4 Saville Place, Newcastle; 116 George Street, Edinburgh; Sherbrook House, Bristol, etc.

(*c*) *Clubs.*—Clubs are carried on under the direction of a club-leader, who organizes their operations with the help of committees consisting of members, and encourages Y.W.C.A. membership, so that club-membership may lead to national and international interest in all that concerns young women.

(*d*) *Branches.*—Groups in any locality where there are a sufficient number of girls needing Y.W.C.A. fellowship and protection are called branches.

(*e*) *Holiday Homes.*—In Holiday Homes and Holiday Camps (with Convalescent and Holiday Club Department) recreation, fellowship, and comradeship are promoted, and all classes meet together.

(*f*) *The Social Question Department* is continually watching the needs of working girls and spreading information as to legislation on questions affecting women.

(*g*) *The International and Emigration Department* works in co-operation with the Immigration Departments of other lands and the Employment Bureau (foreign), and seeks to solve some of the problems of household work by establishing training hostels and rewards for long service. The Blue Triangle Household Orderly Corps is the newest development.

(*h*) *The Educational Department*, with its libraries and a growing staff of secretaries, seeks to fit the girl of labour for her future life, and to induce the girl of education and leisure to share her opportunities with those who have fewer advantages. In clubs, though they are mainly recreational and social, it encourages study by means of circles and lectures. Co-operation with the Y.M.C.A. is being arranged. A Working Women's College has recently been established.

(*i*) *The Reception Hostel and Moral Question Department* has for its aim to maintain a Christian attitude towards all moral questions, and by practical work to help every girl to attain it.

(*j*) *The Religious Work Committee* touches the very centre of Y.W.C.A. work. Its aims are to promote the spiritual life of workers and members by Quiet Days, Retreat conferences, Camps, and Summer Schools. There are special secretaries for promoting Bible study, evangelistic efforts, prayer and fellowship, home study, and co-operation with the Church.

II. *THE WORLD'S Y.W.C.A.*—At first looked on as undenominational, the Y.W.C.A. has proved itself to be interdenominational. In its earliest years avoided by some sections of the Church, and its position misunderstood, it held to its principles, which have been formulated into a truly catholic basis, and with a truly world-wide aim—the winning of the girls of the world to recognize the claims of Jesus Christ as a personal Saviour and Lord.

The basis was at first that of the British Association, but at the Stockholm Conference the following was adopted:

'Faith in God the Father as Creator, and in Jesus Christ His only Son as Lord and Saviour, and in the Holy Spirit as revealer of truth and source of power for life and service, according to the teaching of the Holy Scriptures.'

The first World's Committee met in London in 1894; Mrs. J. H. Tritton was appointed president and Mary Morley treasurer. A sum of £800 was guaranteed by the United States and Canada, which were then united, and by Great Britain and Ireland, also united at that time. It was agreed that the general secretary of the World's Association should be from another country than that in which the World's Office was located, and therefore Annie M. Reynolds, the first general secretary, came from the U.S.A. An executive committee was chosen, composed of women resident at Headquarters, to which is committed the work for the period between one World's Conference and another. On this committee women of several nationalities have served during residence in London. The office was located first at 26 George Street, Hanover Square, and has since been removed to 22 York Place, W. 1. Although at present in London, there is no rule as to which country the office of the World's Y.W.C.A. should be located in. It is at the choice of the Quadrennial Conference. Two other national Associations were sharers equally with Great Britain and the United States in their moral earnestness and desire to form a World's Association—those of Norway and Sweden.

In the two years which intervened between the conference held in London, 8th–11th April 1892, and the formation of the World's Committee in 1894 the committee appointed had been carefully drawing up a constitution, which, while it should leave entire freedom of control and direction to each national organization, should guarantee federation on the basis of the voting membership of all branches according to each national membership. The object of the new body is threefold: (1) to bring into closer mutual knowledge the national associations already existing that they may be more practically helpful to those of their members who go out from their own country; (2) to help countries having only scattered Associations to form such into self-reliant national committees; (3) to develop a greater spirit of responsibility among the young women of Christian countries towards the young women of non-Christian countries.

The first four years—November 1894 to June 1898—had naturally to be spent in striving to attain the first object of the World's Association and in becoming mutually acquainted. The second object of the World's Association also had its place in the first year, when in May 1895 the Canadian Associations, through accredited representative and honorary secretary, made formal application for admittance. The American committee, under whose direction they had formerly been, appreciated their spirit of self-reliance and bade them God-speed. The year 1895 also saw a closer union established between the S. African as well as the Australian Associations. At the fifth regular meeting of the Executive Committee (9th March 1895), the third object, of greater interest in non-Christian countries, was foreshadowed by a note from Madras, India, recording that Agnes Hill 'has made a splendid start here and been greatly blessed in all her work since her arrival in India.' At the meeting of 18th Feb. 1897, formal notice was given of the organization of the National Committee of India, Burma, and Ceylon, with headquarters at Calcutta. Agnes Hill was asked to take the position of national secretary. China and Japan were not long in developing more purely Chinese and Japanese National Committees.

The first World's Y.W.C.A. Conference was held in London, 14th–18th June 1898. The basis of representation adopted was that each national committee should have the right to send ten voting delegates to the World's Conference, provided each national committee represented 100 or more branches; if it represented less than 100 branches it should have power to send only five voting delegates. Every five branches after that should have the right to send one delegate to the conference. It was recommended that a 'quarterly' from October 1898, called *The Women's International Quarterly*, be regarded as the official organ of the World's Y.W.C.A., that the second Sunday in November and the week following be considered as the International Week of Prayer for the World's Y.W.C.A., and that the Executive Committee be empowered to select a suitable international badge, which is now the Blue Triangle.

The first event of active importance after the conference was the application of the German national council for affiliation with the World's Association.

At the London conference eighteen countries were represented, at Geneva (1902) nineteen. At the London conference English had been the only language; in Geneva French was the prevailing language. The Geneva conference was privileged to welcome the Danish national committee to active membership in the World's Association.

All through the Great War, although no international work could be undertaken, there was no breach in the World's alliance, and most national associations developed on very similar lines. In June 1920 representatives of 28 countries met at Champeri, Switzerland, for a World Y.W.C.A. Commission to inquire into the social and industrial conditions which affect women so largely. It was followed by a meeting of the World's Y.W.C.A. Committee, the meeting of which had been suspended during hostilities. No affiliated country held aloof, and there were added representatives of South America and Central Europe, on which continents Associations are rapidly developing.

LITERATURE.—The work which the Y.W.C.A. is doing is recorded in its magazines. The chief of these are (1) *Our*

Own Gazette, (2) *The Y.W.C.A. Monthly Letter*, and (3) *The Y.W.C.A. Bulletin of Home and Overseas News*.

For further information the following publications may be consulted: *The Y.W.C.A. Overseas; The Y.W.C.A. in China; The Y.W.C.A. in Africa; The Woman's Movement in India; Social Service in South Africa: The Y.W.C.A. and Reconstruction; The Y.W.C.A. and Education; The Y.W.C.A. in the Twentieth Century*. These publications are all issued at the offices of the Y.W.C.A. in London and New York.

EMILY KINNAIRD.

YUAN-CHWANG, FA-HIAN, and I-TSING.—Yuan-chwang (Hiuen-tsiang), the greatest Chinese traveller in India (A.D. 629–645), is also one of the most important figures in the history of the development of Chinese Buddhism. There were three pilgrims before him, among whom Fa-hian was the first to penetrate (A.D. 399–413) into the holy land of the Buddhists, and his return marks a step in the progress of the study of Buddhist literature, while the two others, Sun-yun and Hui-seng (A.D. 418) by name, left only a short narrative of their travel[1] and do not seem to have done any important work at home, though they brought back with them some 170 Buddhist texts. After Yuan-chwang in the T'ang dynasty there were so many travellers in India that those recorded by I-tsing alone amount to 56.[2] The recorder himself, who stayed for a prolonged period (A.D. 671–695) in India and the Malay islands, was by far the most prominent among them and the only scholar who could in any way be compared with Yuan-chwang himself.

The three, Fa-hian, Yuan-chwang, and I-tsing, are styled in Japan the 'three mirrors that reflect Indian Buddhism.' They are therefore treated together in the present article.

1. The routes.—There were from of old four principal routes into India, two through Central Asia, the northern and the southern. On his journey out Yuan-chwang took the northern road through Turfan, Kucha, Issik-kul, Tashkend, Samarkand, Kunduz, Kabul, and Peshawār, while on his way home he preferred the southern road, turning eastward from Kunduz and passing Pamir Kul, Kashgar, Yarkand, Khotan, and Nainshe (Ansi).[3] The southern road is much shorter and the most direct way to India, and corresponds roughly with the route of Fa-hian and other predecessors. The third route to India was through Tibet, leading either to Bhutan or Sikkim or sometimes to Nepal. During the T'ang dynasty there were many who took this road, especially after the marriage of a Chinese princess to the Tibetan king Srong-tsan-gampo, who sent envoys to India in A.D. 632.

The fourth route was the over-sea one which was chosen by I-tsing, who embarked in a Persian ship from Kwang-tung to Sumatra, where he changed to a Malay boat, sailing through the strait to Tāmralipti near Calcutta. Fa-hian as early as A.D. 413 embarked in a Brāhman ship to cross the Indian ocean to Java, there taking another merchant ship for China. Thus the journey to India of the earliest traveller Fa-hian was over-land, and his return journey over-sea *via* Ceylon and Java. Yuan-chwang, on the other hand, confined himself to the over-land route, not even crossing over to Ceylon, while the last pilgrim I-tsing took the sea route both ways.

2. Records.—(*a*) *Fa-hian.*—As he himself says towards the end of his record, Fa-hian started in A.D. 399 from Ch'ang-an, the western capital of China, reached India after six years, and, staying there another six years, returned in A.D. 413, spending three years on the way. His record, which was finally revised in A.D. 414, was called sometimes *Fo-kwo-ki*, 'Record of the Buddhist Countries,' or simply *Fa-hian-chüan*, 'Record of Fa-hian.'[1] The word 'high priest' is often added before the title *Fa-hian-chüan*, so it is certain that this designation was not given by the author himself. At the beginning of the record we find a note, 'Fa-hien's own record of his travels in India,' which is in all probability the writer's original title. The work was rendered into French by A. Rémusat in 1836, into English by S. Beal in 1869 and 1884, and again by J. Legge in 1886, the last with the Chinese text as well.

His six years' travel, beginning from Peshawār and ending at Tāmralipti, covers almost all parts of India, 30 countries in all, except the Dekkan, which he himself says that he could not visit. From Tāmralipti he crossed to Ceylon, thence to return to China.

When he left China, he was accompanied by some ten priests, but a party of three went to Turfan in the second year with the intention of getting the royal patronage there, and another party of three retraced their steps from Peshawār to China in the fourth year for a reason not stated, while two others died in Peshawār and on the Hindu Kush. Fa-hian with his sole companion Tao-chêng visited Mathurā, Kanauj, Śrāvastī, Kapilavastu, Vaiśālī, and Kuśinagara, and, having made a pilgrimage to all the sacred spots of the Buddha, came to Pāṭaliputra, whence they visited Rājagṛha, Gayā, Kukkuṭapadā, and Benares. They returned to Pāṭaliputra, where they sojourned three years and collected and copied the sacred texts of various schools. Tao-chêng was charmed with the fine discipline of the Buddhist order there, and, having been disgusted with the ill-regulated manners of the Chinese Buddhists, he decided to live in India and never to return home. Fa-hian, whose desire was to enlighten China by his newly-acquired knowledge, took leave of his companion and travelled alone farther down the Gangā to Campā and Tāmralipti on his way home. He seems to have found Buddhism in general in a very flourishing state, as it was in the imperial Gupta period. Though the Mahāyāna and the Hīnayāna are mentioned now and again, there are as yet no traces of a dispute between the two schools nor signs (such as we find in Yuan-chwang's record) of either being much more influential than the other.

(*b*) *Yuan-chwang.*—The record of the great traveller is handed down to us in three forms. The first is of course his own work, *Hsi-yü-chi*, 'Record of the Western Region,' in 12 volumes, translated by Yuan-chwang and compiled by Pien-chi, his pupil, A.D. 646.[2] The travels cover 138 countries in all—110 which he himself visited and 28 of which he gathered news from his informants, as we are told in an introduction by Ching-po.[3] The characters and usages of the people and the state of Buddhist learning and practices are minutely described. The book is unique and in-

1 Samuel Beal, *Fô-kwô-ki by Fâ-hien*, London, 1869 and 1884, pp. 174–208.

2 Edouard Chavannes, *Voyage des pèlerins bouddhistes, mémoire composé à l'époque de la grande dynastie T'ang sur les religieux éminents qui allèrent chercher la loi dans les pays d'occident, par I-tsing*, Paris, 1894.

3 Tao-hsüan, in his geography of the region of the Sākya (Bunyu Nanjio, *Catalogue of the Chinese Translation of the Buddhist Tripitaka*, Oxford, 1883, no. 1470), calls this route the 'middle' and the Tibetan road the 'southern.' Hui-lin, in his *In-i* (vol. 81), describes the Tibetan route rather minutely (Tokyo ed., case 39, vol. x. fol. 45a).

1 Nanjio, no. 1496. 2 *Ib.* no. 1503.

3 This introduction was not translated by Julien. The separate edition of Kyoto University has it. In the postscript of the record it is expressly said that the use of the word *hing* ('gone') indicates a country which was visited by Yuan-chwang himself, while the word *chih* ('arrive') shows a place which was described from hearsay. Thus we can easily distinguish the countries which the traveller did not visit, *i.e.* 21 countries in Central Asia (vol. i.), Nepal in the Himālayan district (vol. vii.), Ceylon and Persia (vol. xi.), and 4 countries again in Central Asia (vol. xii.), 28 altogether. It is strange that no scholar has hitherto called attention to this fact.

dispensable for the study of Indian history and the geography of the Buddhist period. In 1857 Stanislas Julien published his French translation with the title *Mémoires sur les contrées occidentales traduits du sanscrit en chinois, en l'an 648*[1] *par Hiouen-thsang*,[2] *et du chinois en français par St. Julien.* An English translation by S. Beal followed in 1884 with the title *Si-yu-ki, Buddhist Records of the Western World, translated from the Chinese of Hiuen-tsiang*, 2 vols., London.

The second is a résumé of Yuan-chwang's travels contained in the *Record of the Region of the Sākya* in 8 books by Tao-hsüan.[3] It is interesting to note that the author was Yuan-chwang's pupil and one of his assistant translators, and that the work was compiled during Yuan-chwang's lifetime, *i.e.* A.D. 650.

There seems to have been another work in 10 books entitled *Hsi-yü-chüan*, 'Record of the Western Region,' by Yen-ts'ung, another pupil of the traveller. This record, it is said, treated more of the Indian life than the religion itself, whereas the traveller's own *Mémoires* paid more attention to the religion than the life. Tao-hsüan says in his own preface that both of these were too minute and copious for general information and that this very fact led him to a fresh compilation of his own work. No European translation of it has as yet appeared.

The third is a curtailed form of the *Mémoires* given in the life of Yuan-chwang in 10 volumes, compiled by Hui-li and annotated by Yen-ts'ung, A.D. 665.[4] Julien published it, at the same time as the *Mémoires*, in an abstract under the title *Histoire de la vie de Hiouen-Thsang et ses voyages dans l'Inde, 629–645*, London, 1853, and Beal has also given us a similar abstract.

So far as Yuan-chwang's routes and geographical names are concerned, Thomas Watters, a great Chinese scholar, did a great deal, and the result of his studies was published in 1904–05 by T. W. Rhys Davids and S. W. Bushell with the title *On Yuan Chwang's Travels in India, 629–645, by Thomas Watters.* His researches are accurate as usual, and, if he could have made more use of the results of the Indian and Central-Asian excavations and several old MSS of the record discovered in Japan, nothing would remain to be desired.

Yuan-chwang's record can be divided roughly into five parts: (1) a general introduction to Jambudvīpa and a description of Central-Asian countries along the northern route, *i.e.* Agni to Kapiśa (vol. i.); (2) a detailed introduction to India (name, geography, calendar, life, language, customs, religion, castes, products, etc.) and a description of countries in the Panjāb and in the north of the Gangā as far down as the valley of the Gandakī, *i.e.* Lampā to Nepal (vols. ii.–vii.); (3) a detailed description of Magadha, including Nālanda (vols. viii.–ix.); (4) the lower region of the Gangā, countries on the south sea coast, in the Dekkan and on the lower Indus, *i.e.* Iraṇa to Varaṇa (vols. x.–xi.); (5) Central-Asian states along the southern route, *i.e.* Jāguda to Khotan (vol. xii.).

A résumé of the contents can be obtained best from Watters' work, which gives the travels in their shortest possible form. Further, a lengthy note on the itinerary was added by Vincent A. Smith at the end of the work.

When Yuan-chwang, as a young and brilliant scholar, expressed his desire to visit India, there seem to have been some willing to accompany him in his journey, but when he came near to the Desert he had only two companions, of whom one was sent back to China as he was thought unfit for the hardships of the journey, while the other started in advance to T'un-hwang and was heard of no more. Finally, when he took leave of his patron the king of Turfan, four novices were allotted to him as his attendants. The king helped him with brotherly care and introduced him to many of the Central-Asian chieftains; consequently he was welcomed everywhere and travelled with great facility. In India too he was patronized by King Harśa of Kanauj and had opportunities of meeting many worthies and savants of his time. At Nālanda, the then centre of the Mahāyāna learning, he found an able teacher in Śīla-bhadra, the president of the university, and there he spent several years[1] learning Sanskrit and chiefly Buddhist idealism, occasionally discussing or disputing with sectarian teachers. The interest of the Buddhists of his time seems to have centred in the Mahāyāna, though the Hīnayānistic schools too were followed in all India.[2]

(*c*) *I-tsing.*[3]—I-tsing's record was called *Nan-hai-chi-Kuei-nei-fa-chüan*, 'Record of the Buddhist Practices sent home from the Southern Sea,' in four volumes.[4] The 'Southern Sea' means in Chinese the Malay islands (Sumatra, Java, and the neighbouring places). It is so called because he sent his record home while he was sojourning in Palembang (Bhuje), Sumatra, collecting and copying Sanskrit Buddhist texts. The record was translated into English by the present writer in 1896 and published at Oxford with the title *A Record of the Buddhist Religion in India and Malay Archipelago* (*A.D. 671–695*) *by I-tsing.* The text is entirely different from the two preceding ones, inasmuch as it records only the religious life and practices, especially discussing minute points of the Vinaya rules. The author does not describe his travels at all. The record will prove indispensable, however, when research into the Vinaya branch of Buddhist literature is seriously taken up. Further, it is very interesting that he limits his discussions of the Buddhist practices to the Sarvāstivāda (realistic) school. For it is a very difficult task definitely to class Vinaya practices of that epoch in various schools.

There is another record by I-tsing giving biographical notices of 56 Chinese priests who travelled in India before or during his stay abroad.[5] This is practically a book of travels, and it is in this that he describes the incidents which happened on his journey to India, the chance return to China, and the second sailing to Sumatra to copy the sacred texts.[6] E. Chavannes published his French translation of it in 1894, with the title *Voyages des pèlerins bouddhistes, mémoire composé à l'époque de la grande dynastie T'ang sur les religieux éminents qui allèrent chercher la loi dans les pays d'occident, par I-tsing.* The two records of I-tsing should always be consulted together, for the whole of his life and work cannot be known without either one.

The biographer[7] tells us that I-tsing was 25 years (A.D. 671–695) abroad and travelled in more than 30 countries. That he made a pilgrimage to all the sacred spots of the Buddha can be seen from his own narratives, but we cannot state with certainty that he travelled in so many countries as the biographer asserts.

As was the case with Fa-hian and Yuan-chwang, he had some five or six followers at the outset, but finally started with only a young priest, Shan-hing by name. In India he himself says that he lived ten years in the University of Nālanda (probably A.D. 675–685), chiefly studying the Vinaya. On his way home he stayed in Palembang, Sumatra, to collect and copy more of the Sanskrit texts.

1 This date must be a mistake. Yuan-chwang's own memorial to the emperor T'ai-tsung on the presentation of the record is dated the 13th of the 7th moon in the 20th year of the Chêng-kuan period, *i.e.* 646. Julien's Chinese text probably did not include this memorial.

2 Hiouen-thsang = Yuan-chwang. Seven different ways of spelling the name have been discussed by Rhys Davids (see T. Watters, *On Yuan Chwang's Travels in India, 629–645*, 2 vols., London, 1904–05, i. 17).

3 Nanjio, no. 1470.

4 *Ib.* no. 1494.

1 According to the life of Yuan-chwang (vol. iii.), he stayed there five years. Vincent Smith makes it two years (see Watters, ii. 325).

2 *JRAS*, 1891, p. 420.

3 Otherwise spelt I-ching.

4 Nanjio, no. 1492.

5 *Ib.* no. 1491.

6 These facts are summed up in the present writer's introduction to *Life and Travels of I-tsing*, p. xxv.

7 Nanjio, no. 1495.

One day he wanted to send letters home and went on board a merchant ship, when a favourable wind began to blow and the ship set sail at once. He thus came back by chance to Kuang-tung, and, meeting his old friends, tried to obtain some new companions for his work abroad. At last he succeeded in finding four able assistants, Chêng-ku, Tao-hung, etc., with whom he set out once again in A.D. 689, when he was fifty-five years of age. He finally returned in midsummer A.D. 695.

3. Their work at home.—Buddhism was introduced into China in A.D. 67. The emperor Min-ti sent envoys to India and invited two Buddhist priests, Kāśyapa Mātaṅga and Fa-lan [1] by name, to come to China. They were stationed in a specially built monastery called the 'White Horse' and were kept busy translating. The following three centuries were a period of translation by foreign priests. This we can call the first period of translation (A.D. 67–414). Those foreign priests who came from India itself were surnamed 'Chu,' a curtailed form of 'Tien-chu' (=Sindhu, *i.e.* Indian),[2] while those from Yue-chi (Kuṣana) were styled 'Chi.'[3] Those surnamed 'An' are from An-hsi (=Arsak, Parthian),[4] 'K'ang' from K'ang-chü (=Samarkand)[5] and 'Po' from Kucha (for the royal family was so named).[6] There were practically no Chinese priests who carried out translations by themselves, though there were a few who assisted in the work as subordinates.

The second period of translation (A.D. 414–645) was inaugurated by Fa-hian's return. He brought home the Vinaya texts of the Mahāsaṅghika and the Sarvāstivāda schools, the *Mahāparinirvāṇa Sūtra* of the Mahāyānists, and also the *Abhidharma-hṛdaya Śāstra*; and he himself did the work of translating some of these texts [7] with the assistance of Buddha-bhadra, an Indian priest. Almost at the same time Chi-yen [8] and Pao-yun,[9] his companions half-way to India, and Chi-mang [10] and Tao-tai,[11] both of whom went to India soon after Fa-hian, followed the latter's brilliant example in independent translations. Many priests seem to have done the same, though some of their works are lost.[12]

This period of translation, though conducted by Chinese priests, was not without brilliant works achieved by gifted foreigners, such as Kumārajīva,[13] who is said to have had 3000 pupils, Gunabhadra,[14] Paramārtha,[15] Bodhiruchi,[16] and Jñānagupta.[17]

The above two periods are generally designated the old era of translation. The following period opens the new era of translation (A.D. 646–1127), which was begun by the epoch-making work of Yuan-chwang [18] and was continued by I-tsing,[19] the two being the most prominent figures in the Buddhist culture of the T'ang dynasty. Yuan-chwang brought home the Mahāyāna *Sūtras* (224 texts), the Mahāyāna *Śāstras* (192 texts), the works of the Sthavira school (14), those of the Mahāsaṅghika school (15), those of the Sammitīya school (15), those of the Mahīśāsaka school (22), the Kāśyakīya texts (17), the Dharmaguptīya texts (42), the Sarvāstivāda texts (67), the Hetuvidyā (Logic) (36), and the Śabdavidyā (Grammar) (13), altogether amounting to 520 bundles and 657 different texts. What he specially laid stress on was the Vijñānamātra doctrine (idealism), and he may be deemed the founder of the Buddhist idealism in China.

The catalogue of I-tsing's collections is not given so minutely as his predecessor's. The Sanskrit texts of the *Tripiṭaka* collected by him during his stay of ten years at Nālanda were nearly 400 in number, amounting to 500,000 *ślokas*, which he himself says he had in hand whilst in Palembang.[1] What he considered most important was the Vinaya literature, and his translations in this branch of study are very full and minute, especially in the Vinaya of the Sarvāstivāda (realistic) school, which amounts to 19 texts in 209 volumes out of 56 texts in 256 volumes in all. His works in this line are generally called the 'New Vinaya,' while those of Tao-hsüan, a pupil of Yuan-chwang, and of the other predecessors are styled the 'Old Vinaya.'

Thus he founded a new school in the study of this branch of Buddhist literature and made his own school the most influential of all. The work of translation in the T'ang dynasty was on a grand scale. All had to be done by the imperial sanction, so many officials and assistants being specially appointed. The completed texts had to be presented to the imperial court to be authorized for publication or to be incorporated into the Buddhist library.

This new era was further enriched by the works of Amoghavajra,[2] Dharma-deva,[3] Dāna-pāla,[4] etc., but their translations, numerous as they are, cannot be compared in nature and bulk with those of Yuan-chwang and I-tsing, for almost all of them are *dhāraṇīs*, *stotras*, or mystic texts of the kind.

With the Sung dynasty (A.D. 960–1127) the periods of translation which were so ably represented by the three travellers practically came to an end, Indian Buddhism gradually giving its place to Tibetan Lamaism.

LITERATURE.—All the translations of the records referred to have been indicated in the article. For reference the following may be recommended: J. Legge, *A Record of Buddhistic Kingdoms, being an Account by the Chinese Monk Fâ-hien of his Travels in India and Ceylon (A.D. 399–414)*, Oxford, 1886; S. Beal, *Si-yu-ki, Buddhist Records of the Western World: translated from the Chinese of Hiuen Tsiang (A.D. 629)*, 2 vols., London, 1884; T. Watters, *On Yuan Chwang's Travels in India, 629–645*, 2 vols., do. 1904–05; E. Chavannes, *Voyage des pèlerins bouddhistes, mémoire composé à l'époque de la grande dynastie T'ang sur les religieux éminents . . . dans les pays d'occident, par I-tsing*, Paris, 1894; J. Takakusu, *Record of the Buddhist Religion in India and Malay Archipelago (A.D. 671–695) by I-tsing*, Oxford, 1896; E. Chavannes, *Voyage de Song-yun dans l'Udyāna et le Gandhāra* (518–522), Hanoi, 1903; E. Chavannes and S. Lévi, *L'Itinéraire d'Ou-Kong (751–790)*, Paris, 1895.

J. TAKAKUSU.

1 Nanjio, appendix ii. 1–2.
2 *Ib.* 2, 5, 11, 20, 23, 27, 38, 47, 48.
3 *Ib.* 3, 7, 18, 22, 33, 35, 37.
4 *Ib.* 4, 6, 17, 25.
5 *Ib.* 8, 14, 21, 41.
6 *Ib.* 16, 28(?), 36; see Sylvain Lévi, 'Le "Tokharien B," langue de Koutcha,' *JA*, Sept.–Oct. 1913, pp. 371, 377, 378.
7 *Ib.* 45 and *Cat.* nos. 118, 120, 676, 1150.
8 *Ib.* 76.
9 *Ib.* 77.
10 *Ib.* 70.
11 *Ib.* 71.
12 *Ib.* 49, 50, 51, 82, 84, 87–91.
13 *Ib.* 50 (he translated 50 texts).
14 *Ib.* 81 (he translated 27 texts).
15 *Ib.* 104–5 (42 translations).
16 *Ib.* 114 (30 translations).
17 *Ib.* 129 (36 translations).
18 *Ib.* 133 (76 translations).
19 *Ib.* 149 (56 translations).

1 Chavannes, *Mémoire d'I-tsing*, p. 125.
2 Nanjio, appendix ii. 155 (108 translations).
3 *Ib.* 159 (118 translations).
4 *Ib.* 161 (111 translations).

YUCATANS.—See MEXICANS.

YUGRA.—See OSTYAKS.

YULE.—See CALENDAR (Teutonic), CHRISTMAS CUSTOMS.

Z

ZAIDI.—Zaidi (Zaidiyyah; in Arabia Zuyud) is the name of a Muhammadan sect, called after Zaid, son of ʻAlī, son of Ḥusain, son of ʻAlī, cousin and son-in-law of the Prophet Muhammad. This person came forward as a pretender in the reign of the Umayyad Hisham (121–122 A.H.) in Kufah, was defeated, and was put to death. His story is told with unnecessary prolixity by Ṭabari.[1] His sect survived, though doubtless in secret, in Kufah, where they were concerned in various risings of ʻAlid pretenders, such as those of 151, 250, and 251 A.H.;[2] on the last occasion they are called 'men of wool,' *i.e.* ascetics, and the same historian casually mentions them after this time among heretical sects.[3] If it be true that Harun al-Rashid employed one of the community to assassinate Idris, founder of the Idrisi dynasty of Fez,[4] it is likely that they were tolerated by the legitimate khalīfahs to the same extent and for the same services as were afterwards the Assassins by the Egyptian sultans.

1. History.—The first dynasty founded by a member of the sect was that of the Idrisids (172–362 A.H. = A.D. 788–973), called after Idris b. ʻAbdallah, a descendant of Ḥasan, who, after a rising organized by a nephew of his in the Hijaz in the time of the ʻAbbāsid Mahdī had been suppressed, escaped into Africa and gained a following among the Berbers of Ulili (Volubilis) near one of the sources of the Sebou. After winning over or subduing a great number of tribes, he took the title khalīfah, and was, as has been seen, assassinated by an emissary from Baghdād in A.D. 793. He was succeeded by his infant son, called by the same name, who founded in 808 the city of Fez, which became the capital of the dynasty. Its population was supplemented in 814 by some 8000 families exiled by al-Ḥakam from Cordova, but welcomed by Idris II., 'whose subjects, being for the most part nomads, showed an invincible repugnance to becoming citizens.'[5] At the time of his death, in 828, his kingdom comprised the whole of the Farthest Maghrib and reached Mina in the Central Maghrib. His successor Muhammad divided his territories (other than Fez itself and its neighbourhood) between eight of his relatives, reserving the capital and the suzerainty for himself; this act led to the permanent break up of the kingdom, which was left in a state of civil war at his death in 836. The princes who succeeded him in Fez were involved in wars with other sects, such as the Khārijis and the Faṭimids of Africa, the latter of whom took Fez in 959. In 973 it fell into the hands of the Spanish Umayyads, and the last of the Idrisi monarchs, named Ḥasan, was compelled to abandon his fortress, 'The Vulture's Nest,' somewhere in the neighbourhood of Ceuta, on condition of his life being spared.[6]

The next and most important dynasty of Zaidites was that founded in S. Arabia by a descendant of ʻAlī, Yaḥyā b. Ḥusain b. Qāsim Rassi; his grandfather Qāsim was a son of one Ibrahim Ṭabāṭabā, and brother of a Muhammad whose abortive rising at Kufah about 200 A.H. is described at length by Ibn Khaldūn.[7] This Yaḥyā established a khalifate at Ṣaʻdah in Yemen, taking as his imperial title al-Hādī ila al-ḥaqq (280 A.H. = A.D. 893). The story of this dynasty, as told by Ibn Khaldūn,[8] is translated by H. C. Kay,[9] who corrects some mistakes. The name Rassi, whereby this dynasty is known, is said to come from Rass, a mountain in Najd, where Yaḥya's grandfather Qāsim took refuge. Yaḥya was himself the author of numerous works, among them refutations of the Shīʻah sect called the Imamiyyah, and of the views of the contemporary historian Ṭabari. The capital of the dynasty was sometimes Ṣaʻdah, sometimes Ṣanʻa, and the territory included within its dominions varied greatly at different times; the earlier geographers (of the 3rd and 4th Islāmic centuries), so far as they allude to these princes, call them 'resident in Ṣaʻdah.' In the 6th Islāmic cent. they were driven out of Ṣaʻdah by the Meccan Sulaimanis, but towards the end of that century a Rassi monarch resumed possession of the place with the title Manṣūr. He is said to have dispatched missionaries to remote parts of the ʻAbbāsid empire, such as Jilan, and to have attracted the notice of the ʻAbbāsid Nāṣir (1180–1225), who, however, did not succeed in securing his person. In the year 1258 (about the same time as the fall of Baghdād) their imām Yaḥya b. Ḥusain was killed in battle.[1] Their political power was for the time broken; but imāms continued to be appointed, and to maintain themselves in some regions till the date at which Ibn Khaldūn's narrative closes, 793 A.H. Probably this condition was maintained till 945 A.H. (A.D. 1538), when the Yemen fell under the domination of the Ottomans; but in 1597 one Qāsim, who claimed to be a descendant of the Rassi family, assumed the imāmate at a place called Ḥadīd-qara, and found numerous adherents; after a long series of struggles with the Turkish pashas, with varying success, in 1619 he obtained recognition from the Ottoman authorities as ruler of a considerable portion of Yemen; he died the next year (1620), and was succeeded by his son the imām Muhammad the Muayyad. In 1626 this person, owing to the execution of an agent of his by the Turkish governor Ḥaidar Pasha, started a fresh revolt, and with the aid of his brothers conducted it so successfully that before the end of the year few places, besides Ṣanʻa, Aden, and the ports, remained in Ottoman hands; everywhere else the Zaidi power was recognized in Yemen. In 1629 Ṣanʻa, after a siege of two years, was surrendered to the Muayyad; and in 1635 Yemen was definitely evacuated by the Ottomans, and the Zaidi ritual established in the mosques. These details are taken from the Turkish *History of Yemen and Ṣanʻā*, by Aḥmad Rashīd,[2] who attributes the expulsion of the Ottomans chiefly to the incompetence, laziness, and corruption of the governor Ḥaidar Pasha, who was exiled in consequence. The new Zaidi ruler, as has been seen, took a title in the style of the khalīfahs, and similar titles were taken by his successors, of whom the first was his brother Ismāʻīl, called the Mutawakkil, who captured Aden in 1640, and extended his rule into Ḥadramaut and other regions neighbouring Yemen. From this time till 1750, though there were numerous wars of succession and local revolts and insurrections, the Zaidi realm remained intact; after 1750 it split up into numerous petty governments, of which the most important continued to be that of Ṣanʻa. To the list of imāms given by Stanley Lane-Poole,[3] after Niebuhr, we should add Mutawakkil, who ascended the throne on the death of his father Manṣūr in 1814, and Mutawakkil's son Mahdī, who succeeded in 1820–21, and after whose demise in 1830–31 there was a period of anarchy, which ended in 1846 with the restoration of the Ottomans, one Tewfiq Pasha being installed as governor in that year at Ṣanʻa. Since that time, however, there have been numerous revolts and internal dissensions.[4]

Besides the Zaidites of Fez and Yemen there were in the 3rd and 4th Islāmic centuries those of Tabaristān and Jilan. Various pretenders of the family of ʻAlī, entertaining the Zaidi system, established themselves, though ephemerally, in these regions, where they are thought to have made converts among the till then pagan populations.[5]

2. Characteristics.—In the Diplomatic Encyclopædia of Qalqashandī called *Ṣubḥ al-Aʻshā*[6] some notices of the Zaidi court are collected from various authors. According to these, the imām lived in Arab simplicity with no attempt at magnificence or display. He claimed, however, to be the supreme sovereign, the usurpers of whose rank (such as the ʻAbbāsid khalīfahs) would be punished in the next world for their rebellion. His followers looked forward to the time when his supremacy would be generally acknowledged, and expected that his family would produce the Mahdī who is to appear at the end of the world. His prayers were regarded as intercessory; his hand was laid on the sick; and at times of drought it was his business to procure rain. The emirs of Meccah (in the 6th Islāmic cent.) were supposed to favour his claims secretly. The imām was thought to possess a secret store of knowledge, handed down from his predecessors, and going back ultimately to ʻAlī and

[1] *Chronicle*, ed. M. J. de Goeje, Leyden, 1879–1901, ii. 1267–1298.
[2] Ṭabari, iii. 360 f., 1515, 1617 f. [3] *Ib.* 1684.
[4] E. Mercier, *Hist. de l'Afrique septentrionale*, Paris, 1888, i. 260.
[5] R. Dozy, *Spanish Islam*, tr. F. G. Stokes, London, 1913, p. 254.
[6] See Mercier, i. 372.
[7] *Kitāb al ʻIbar*, Būlāq, 1867, iii. 242.
[8] iv. 111–113.
[9] In ʻOmārah, *Yaman, its Mediæval History*, London, 1892, p. 184 ff.

[1] Khazraji, *The Pearl-Strings: a Hist. of the Rasúli Dynasty of Yaman*, tr. J. W. Redhouse (E. J. W. Gibb Memorial Series, III. i.–v.), Leyden, 1906–13, i. 150.
[2] Constantinople, 1290.
[3] *The Muhammadan Dynasties*, London, 1894.
[4] An account of the period commencing with that of the recovery of independence by the imāms is to be found in W. B. Harris, *Journey through the Yemen*, Edinburgh, 1893, chiefly after R. L. Playfair, *History of Arabia Felix*, Bombay, 1859.
[5] Some account of these persons is given in Ibn Isfandiyār's *History of Tabaristān* and by H. L. Rabino, 'Les Provinces caspiennes de la Perse,' *RMM* xxxii. [1915–16]. An abridged translation of the *History*, by E. G. Browne, was published as vol. ii. of the Gibb Memorial Series, London, 1905.
[6] Cairo, 1915, v. 51–54.

the Prophet (a common Shīʽah notion). He maintained agents who travelled over all Islāmic countries, associating with those who were already adherents and winning others. These were all on the look-out for the collapse of the khalīfate (in 732 A.H. that maintained by the Egyptian sultans) and the exaltation of the imām. In the effects of a man who had died in Aleppo (somewhat before this time) letters had been found addressed to him and to his ancestors from the imāms soliciting information about the Shīʽah in that country and also aid. There were different accounts of the number of the imām's armed followers, but there was no question of their valour. The Rasulids, who from 1229 to 1451 A.H. were the chief power in Yemen, ordinarily treated the imām with respect; during the reign of Nāṣir in Egypt (1293–1340) an imām had sent a proposal to form an alliance for the purpose of ousting the Rasulids, which had been rejected.

3. Doctrine.—The Zaidis in doctrine come between the Shīʽah (*q.v.*), to whom they technically belong, and the Sunnah (see SUNNITES). They maintain that the imāmate is inherent in the house of ʽAlī and Fāṭimah; but they revere the memory of the first two khalīfahs, holding that, though ʽAlī had a right to the office, there were political reasons which rendered his appointment undesirable. Their theory is known as *tafḍīl*, meaning the legitimacy of the appointment of the *mafḍūl*, *i.e.* the person whose claims are inferior, while the *fāḍil*, or person with superior qualifications, is accessible. Copious extracts from their literature on this subject are given by R. Strothmann.[1] The imām Hādi, as has been seen, compiled a treatise on the subject. In normal times the imāmate in their system belongs to the fittest person among the descendants of either Ḥasan or Ḥusain, the grandson of the Prophet whose duty it is to 'come out.' To rebel against an iniquitous ruler (*al-bāghī*) is in their opinion a duty. This, according to the author of *al-ʽAlam al-shāmikh* (Sālih b. Mahdī, † 1108 A.H.), is their most distinctive tenet and that which separates them from the other schools.

'Otherwise,' he says, 'there is little that is distinctive about them; in the articles of religion they agree with the Muʽtazils, whereas with respect to the Branches (*i.e.* the religious and civil code) they differ; with some of them the system of Abu Ḥanifah prevails, whereas with others that of Shafiʽi, though this is not a case of following, but of agreement; some however are not of this sort, but are like other independent enquirers (*mujtahidūn*); only fanaticism makes people anxious to differ from others. Thus the Expiatory Prostration (*sujūd al-sahw*) has become a kind of badge of the Zaidites; the followers of the four Sunni systems are abandoning it altogether, indeed we have never seen them practise it; the reason being the anxiety of the Zaidites about it, which is like their caution in other matters, *e.g.* the Minor Ablution. Damaghani [perhaps Muhammad b. ʽAlī Dāmaghānī, † 478 A.H.] found fault with them for over-ablution, which he rightly said is contrary to the Sunnah.'[2]

Of their law-books the first part of one called *Muntazaʽ al-Mukhtār* ('The Abstract of the Select'), based on the *Kitāb al-Azhār* of the imām al-Muhdi li-din Allah Aḥmad b. Yaḥya (775–840 A.H.), was published at Cairo in 1328, but has up to the present date remained unfinished. It deals only with ceremonies, and differs in minute points from the law-books of the Sunni schools. Many other law-books of the Zaidis are contained in MSS. A *Corpus Juris* of Zaid b. ʽAlī, edited by E. Griffini, Milan, has been issued.

4. Divisions.—The classical heresiologists, ʽAbd al-Qāhir[3] and Shahrastani,[4] divide the Zaidis into three sub-sects—the Jārūdiyyah, the Sulaimāniyyah or Jarīriyyah, and the Butriyyah, with whom the latter of these writers couples the Ṣālihiyyah. The three names Jārūdiyyah, Sulaimāniyyah, and Butriyyah are given in the *Mawāqif* of ʽAḍud al-Din Iji († A.D. 1355).[1] The second are called after one Sulaimān b. Jarīr; the third, according to this work, after Butair al-Thūmī, but, according to the *Firaq*, after Kuthayyir called Abtar and Ḥasan b. Ṣaliḥ b. Ḥayy. In the *Ghunyah*[2] of ʽAbd al-Qādir al-Jīlānī, who is but slightly later, they are divided into six sub-sects—Jārūdiyyah, Sulaimāniyyah, Butriyyah, Nuʽaimiyyah, Yaʽqūbiyyah, and a sixth. In the Persian *Bayān al-adyān*,[3] which is about a century earlier (A.D. 1092), the number of sub-sects is said to be five—Jārūdiyyah, Dhākiriyyah, Khashabiyyah (the followers of Ṣarḥāt Ṭabarī, who used wooden weapons at the time of their rising), and the Khalafiyyah. The questions about which they differed were mostly concerned with the imāmate, or aspects of it—*e.g.*, whether Muhammad had appointed ʽAlī as his successor or not; whether he had also appointed his grandsons or not; it is asserted that the Jārūdiyyah (called after one Abu'l-Jārūd Ziyād) denied the death of Muḥammad b. ʽAbdallah, a pretender of the time of the ʽAbbāsid Manṣūr, and looked forward to his return as Mahdī (though some of them looked forward to the return of some other pretender); further, that they call the first two khalīfahs 'unbelievers,' and in consequence are execrated by the rest of the Zaidis, who in turn execrate them. The only claim of this sub-sect to be called Zaidis would then lie in their recognizing the imāmate of the Zaid after whom the sect is named. The doctrine mentioned above is usually regarded as characteristic—*e.g.*, by the Spanish traveller Ibn Jubair, who indeed does not expect his readers to have heard of the sect.[4] A traveller of a century earlier (1035–1042), Nāṣir-i-Khusrau, who found them in Yemamah, apparently expects his readers to know their name, but not to know that they were of the Shīʽah.[5] It is probable that the names of the sub-sects were little known.

LITERATURE.—A few works emanating from Zaidi theologians are mentioned in the *Kitāb al-Fihrist*, ed. G. Flügel, Leipzig, 1871–72, i. 193. Their literature is, however, very copious, and there is a large MS collection of it lodged in the Ambrosiana of Milan, of which notices have been given by E. Griffini, in *Rivista degli Studi Orientali*, i.–iii., Rome, 1908–10; many Zaidi MSS are also to be found in the Berlin Library. A treatise on rhetoric called *al-Ṭirāz*, by the Zaidi khalīfah Yaḥya b. Ḥamzah (729–749 A.H.), was published in Cairo in 1914.

D. S. MARGOLIOUTH.

ZANZIBAR AND THE SWAHILI PEOPLE.—The name Zanzibar, now applied only to the town of that name and the island in which it is situated (both called in Swahili *Unguja*), anciently designated the whole coast, from the Juba River to Sofala.[6] Originally Zangibar (Zengibar, Zanguebar), from the Persian زنگی; 'negro' and بر, 'region,' it was modified by Arab and Portuguese pronunciation into Zanjibar and Zanzibar. The town is said to have been founded by settlers from Shiraz, in the 8th or 9th cent.,[7] but there is less definite information available as to its early history than in the case of Kilwa, Lamu, and Pate. Sacleux[8] suggests that the Wahadimu (the early inhabitants, whose chief, the *Mwinyi mkuu*, ruled the island up to the time of Sayyid Barghash) may have been a colony from Kilwa. The coast

1 *Das Staatsrecht der Zaiditen*, Strassburg, 1912.
2 P. 319.
3 *Al-Farq bain al-firaq*, Cairo, 1910, pp. 22–26.
4 *Kitāb al-milal wa'l-niḥal*, tr. T. Haarbrücker, Halle, 1850, i. 174–184.

1 Ed. T. Soerensen, Leipzig, 1848, p. 353.
2 Cairo, 1208, i. 77.
3 C. Schefer, *Chrestomathie persane*, 2 vols., Paris, 1883.
4 *The Travels of Ibn Jubayr*, ed. M. J. de Goeje (Gibb Memorial Series, v.), London, 1907.
5 *Safarnāmah*, ed. C. Schefer, Paris, 1881, p. 224.
6 Masʽudi, quoted by Yule and Burnell, *Hobson-Jobson*, p. 746.
7 Sacleux, *Grammaire des dialectes swahilis*, pp. xiv, xv.
8 *Ib.* p. xv n.

is also known by its Arabic designation of ساحل (*sahil*, 'coast'—hence the term 'Swahili coast' is a pleonasm, like 'Lake Nyasa,' etc.), and its inhabitants as سواحل, 'coast-people'—in African pronunciation 'Swahili.' (They are spoken of in their own vernacular as Waswahili, pl. of Mswahili; the language as Kiswahili.) They are called by the 'Nyika' tribes Adzomba (Wajomba), by the Pokomo Watsawaa or Wadzawaa, and by the Galla Hamara.

The name 'Swahili'[1] does not belong to any one indigenous African race: it connotes the descendants of Arab settlers by native women of various tribes, chiefly Bantu. There are also traces of Persian descent, and possibly their pedigree includes other ethnic elements.

1. Distribution of the Swahili.—The territory inhabited by the Swahili is the strip of coast defined in 1886 as the Sayyid of Zanzibar's dominions—viz. from Warsheikh on the Somali coast to Cape Delgado. This, however, does not include all, as distinct dialects of Swahili are recognized for Ibo and the Kirimba Islands, nearly two degrees south of Cape Delgado, and for the Angoshi Islands, half-way between Mozambique and the mouth of the Zambesi. The people themselves—at any rate those of the northern parts—limit the expression 'Swahilini' (=the Swahili country) to the coast north-east of the Tana mouth, though some extend it as far south as Malindi. This fits in with the assertion made by various writers that the dialects of Lamu and the adjacent coast are reckoned the purest,[2] or, as Krapf says,[3] that 'the real home of the Swahili language is considered to be in the islands of Patta [Pate], Lamu, and in the country opposite to those islands.' Swahili, however, is spoken and understood far beyond the confines of its proper home: it has been carried half-way across the continent by traders and caravan porters and is current, in debased forms, both on the Congo and in Sindh.[4]

2. Physical characteristics.—There is probably no uniform Swahili type, and this is scarcely surprising when we consider, not only the composite origin of the people and the various sources whence their race has from time to time been recruited, but the fact that there are many persons calling themselves Swahili who have not the slightest claim to Arab descent. These may be the descendants of imported slaves, or they may be members of inland tribes who have adopted Islām and settled on the coast. Consequently shades of complexion (the darker and lighter being broadly distinguished by the people themselves as 'black' and 'red') and types of feature vary indefinitely; and we must remember that the compound factors are not merely the Oman Arab (with the possible, or indeed probable, Persian) and the Bantu native, but the tribes of Hamitic or 'Helot' stock, of whom the Wasanye and Dorobo are present-day representatives, and the various Galla, Abyssinian, Somali, and even Georgian or Circassian women who have at different times found their way into the harems of wealthy Arabs. Characteristics are apt to vary greatly, even within one and the same family; *e.g.*, a member of the 'l Batawi (Arab) clan, living at Mombasa, has decidedly negroid features and woolly hair, while his sister, as dark as himself in complexion, has fine, silky, and perfectly straight hair. As Baumann says:

> 'Gar leicht kann man schliesslich zur Ansicht gelangen, dass es überhaupt einen Swahili-*Stamm* nicht gebe, dass das Wort keine andere als die ursprüngliche arabische Bedeutung "Küstenbewohner" habe.'[1]

Burton's description[2] is too sweeping, as regards both appearance and character, though he appears to have chiefly in view the island of Zanzibar—perhaps the least favourable ground for observation.

3. Origin.—It is uncertain at present whether there were any Arab or Persian settlements in pre-Islāmic times; and the vexed question of the Zimbabwe mines cannot be discussed here; but it is worth noticing that the Karanga language of Rhodesia has some words in common with Swahili, which do not seem to occur in languages geographically intermediate.[3] There was, however, commercial intercourse at a very early period. The first Arab settlement to which a definite date is assigned is that of Pate, in A.D. 689;[4] the colonists are said to have been Syrians. Native tradition says they found Waboni and Waemezi hunters living in the island.[5] They intermarried with these people, though their descendants have tried to suppress the fact. Vague traditions (which the present writer has never been able to verify) of pre-Islāmic people worshipping a golden idol (a calf or bull?) at Kau may point to some early Persian or Hindu settlement of which no other record survives. Contact with the Bantu was probably, in the first instance, with the Pokomo, who, according to native tradition, were settled in the Tana valley long before the southward migration of the 'Nyika' peoples in the 16th century. The Pate colonists are said to have come from Syria; and some ascribe the same origin to Malindi, Zanzibar, Mombasa, Lamu, and Kilwa;[6] though the Kilwa Chronicle states that the founder of this city came from Shiraz. The settlement of the 'Emozeids' (Ummu Zayd), somewhat later than that of Pate,[7] seems to have introduced a considerable Persian element. Baumann says:

> 'Der Name Swahili ist bei den Angehörigen des Stammes selbst nicht sehr verbreitet; am liebsten hören sie sich *Schirazi* nennen und leiten ihre Abkunft von Schiraz her.'[8]

This probably applies to Tanga and neighbourhood: it is certainly not true of Mombasa or the coast north of it, where the present writer has never heard of the slightest objection to the name Swahili—not even on the part of some men at Jomvu who said their ancestors came from 'Shirazi.' In fact, the people of Jomvu are known to have emigrated thither, not more than three or four generations back, from Shirazi, near Vumba, which was originally a colony from the Persian Shiraz. Shaka, near Kipini (celebrated in connexion with Liongo Fumo, and possibly the 'Jaca' of the Portuguese inscription on the Mombasa fort), was also a Persian colony.

4. History.—The sources are: native tradition, Portuguese records and historians, and Arabic documents, of which only two have been published, viz. the Chronicle of Mombasa, printed in Owen[9] and also as an appendix to Guillain's first volume, and the *History of Kilwa*, edited by S. Arthur Strong.[10] This seems not to be quite identical with the *Chronica dos Reys*

1 This is the commonly accepted spelling, though some French writers still cling to 'Souahéli'; and 'Suaheli' is the form current in Germany. Salt has 'Sowauli' and 'Sowaiel,' Owen, 'Sowhylese'; see Cust, *Modern Languages of Africa*, ii. 345.

2 Sacleux, p. ix.

3 *Vocabulary of Six East African Languages*, p. iv.

4 Burton, *Sindh, and the Races that inhabit the Valley of the Indus*, p. 233.

1 *Usambara und seine Nachbargebiete*, p. 22.

2 *Zanzibar City, Island and Coast*, i. 414–420.

3 These are not Arabic loan-words, such as *ndarama* and *mali*, which might have been derived from the later Arab settlements at Sena and Sofala.

4 MS information, and Stigand, *The Land of Zinj*, p. 29.

5 MS information, and Stigand, p. 160.

6 Stigand, p. 29.

7 Guillain, *Documents sur l'histoire, la géographie, et le commerce de l'Afrique orientale*, i. 140; Stigand, p. 6.

8 P. 22.

9 Owen, *Narrative of Voyages, etc.*, i. 414–422.

10 'The History of Kilwa,' *JRAS*, 1895, pp. 385–430.

de Quiloa, of which the substance has been fortunately preserved by Barros.[1] Another Arabic MS, known as the *Book of the Kings of Pate*, after being preserved at Pate for some time, was carried to Witu when Ahmad Simba fled thither (about 1856) and was finally destroyed in the bombardment of 1890; no other copy is known to be in existence. Some Swahili MSS, written down in recent times at Lamu, preserve what has hitherto been handed down orally; one of these was published in the *Journal of the African Society*, 1913–14. Similarly, the second chapter of Stigand's *Land of Zinj* embodies the result of conversations with the oldest living authority, 'Bwana Kitini' (Muhammad bin Fumo Umari) of Lamu. The scattered notices of E. Africa in the works of Greek and Roman geographers and other ancient writers, as well as in those of the mediæval Arabs, have been well summarized by Guillain in his first volume. The Arab geographers have also been carefully studied from this point of view by Gabriel Ferrand.

Intercourse between Arabia and the east coast of Africa seems to have taken place from very early times. Indonesian influence is also probable, and by Stuhlmann[2] is made responsible for the introduction of the coco-nut palm and the outrigger canoe; he assigns a similar origin to the curious kitchen implement (*mbuzi*) used for scraping coco-nuts. One of the Lamu MSS above referred to says that seedlings of coco-palms (*mite ya minazi*) were brought by certain Arabs from 'Kalhindi'—but there is no clue as to what is meant by this name. Ferrand[3] places the Indonesian colonization of Madagascar (which has notable Malayo-Polynesian affinities) not earlier than the Christian era; but it by no means follows that this was the earliest contact.

Pate was founded (A.H. 69, A.D. 689) by colonists of the il-Batawi tribe (or clan?)—hence, say some, the name (Ar. Bata or Batta). The royal house of these Batawi continued in power till A.D. 1204 (A.H. 600), when a fugitive from Maskat, Suliman b. Suliman of the house of Nabhan, landed there, was hospitably received, and ultimately married the daughter of the last Batawi chief. The Nabhans remained sultans of Pate till 1866.

About 740 the followers of Zaid, great-grandson of the 4th khālif, 'Alī, escaping from the persecution of the Umayyads, fled to E. Africa and became the ancestors of the people now called Wagunya (or Watikuu) who inhabit the mainland north of Lamu, speak a peculiar dialect of Swahili, and are regarded as in some respects a distinct people by their southern congeners. They are known in history as 'Emozeids' (Ummu Zaid). Makdishu and Barawa are said to have been founded about A.D. 909 and Kilwa in A.D. 975; but the Kilwa Chronicle quoted by De Barros and that published by Strong show some discrepancy with regard to these two migrations. Both agree in saying that Kilwa was founded by 'Alī ibn Hasan of Shiraz. One of his brothers is said by the latter authority to be the founder of Mombasa; but elsewhere[4] its origin is ascribed to Muhammad, son of 'Alī ibn Hasan. Zanzibar does not figure conspicuously in the early records; it was long tributary to Mombasa, though by some said to be equally ancient. The various small city-states were originally independent of one another, and, though one might, for a time, establish a sort of precarious hegemony—as was the case, in turn, with Kilwa, Mombasa, and Pate—no empire or permanent confederacy was ever established. Lamu differed from the rest in being ruled, not by a sultan, but by a council of elders (*wazee*).

The Portuguese arrived at Malindi in 1498 on their way to India, and established friendly relations with its ruler, who asked for help against his rival, the shaikh of Mombasa. Mombasa was burnt by Nuno da Cunha in 1529[5] (it had been previously in 1505 sacked and burnt by Almeida, who took Kilwa in the same year). By 1530 the whole coast, from Barawa to Cape Corrientes, was under Portuguese dominion, and this continued intermittently (one town or another being usually in a more or less successful state of revolt) until 1652. In that year an Arab fleet arrived from Oman, the Swahili towns having some time previously entreated the help of the *imām* in order to drive out the Portuguese, and the war thus begun culminated in the fall of Mombasa, 12th Dec. 1698, which was followed by the occupation of Kilwa, Zanzibar, and Pemba. Thenceforward, except for the short time during which they held Mombasa and Pate, retaken in 1728, the Portuguese were restricted to their present possessions, south of the Rovuma. It is curious that Pate, where their rule was far less continuous than at Mombasa, seems to keep the most vivid traditional memories of them. 'Violent [or 'proud'] as a Portuguese' is still a proverbial saying; and the townsmen of Pate point out, in the bed of the tidal creek, the remains of the causeway by which, as they affirm, the invaders dragged their cannon up from the anchorage at Shindakazi. It is impossible to assign a date for the destruction of the towns whose ruined sites occur almost every few miles between the Juba and Mombasa. Some may be accounted for by the invasion of the Zimbas, a warring people not yet certainly identified, in 1586–89.[1] Later came the Galla raids which (probably during the 18th cent.) reduced Malindi from a flourishing city to the heap of ruins found by Krapf in 1846.[2]

From 1729 onward the coast was supposed to be under the suzerainty of Maskat, and the *imām* placed governors in Mombasa and Zanzibar, but apparently not at Pate, which was frequently at war with both Lamu and Mombasa. The reigning family of Maskat, in the early part of the 18th cent., was that of Ya'arubi, and the first Liwali who administered Mombasa under him was Muhammad b. Said 'l Maamiri;[3] but in 1739 the appointment was given to Muhammad ibn 'Athman of the Mazrui clan, afterwards so famous. Shortly after this, in 1741, the imāmate was transferred from the Ya'arubi to the house of 'l Bu Said (Albunseyidi), from which the present sultan of Zanzibar is descended. One result of this change was the virtual independence of Mombasa under the Mazrui, which lasted till 1837. The Mazrui attempted, in 1823–24, to place themselves under British protection;[4] but their request was refused, owing to the representations of the Indian Government, who considered it important to keep on good terms with Maskat; and Mombasa was ultimately reconquered by Sayyid Said, who had, in 1832, removed from Maskat to Zanzibar and thenceforth made the latter his principal residence. Details of events subsequent to that date will be found in some of the works already referred to; also in those of Charles Eliot, Lyne, Craster, and the Blue Books.

5. Religion.—The Swahili are, almost without exception, Muslims and of the Shafi'i sect.[5] The Sayyid's family and most of the Oman Arabs are Ibadis.[6] The people in general, especially the women—so far as the present writer came in contact with them—seem better instructed than some writers admit.

E.g., Burton says: 'The Wasawahili calling themselves Moslems know little beyond the Kalmah, rarely pray, and fast only by compulsion';[7] and Baumann: 'besonders jüngere Leute stehen dem ganzen Islam auffallend gleichgiltig gegenüber und können oft nicht einmal die Fatha hersagen. Noch mehr ist diese Indifferenz bei Weibern zu beobachten.'[8]

This did not seem to be the case at Jomvu, Mambrui, or Lamu, where there is comparatively little contact with Europeans. It is quite true, however, that there is a marked absence of fanaticism. Strangers are admitted, even invited, into their mosques. Women do not as a rule go to the mosques, though 'some of them are as well or better read in the Koran than the men.'[9] Each town—even small ones of a few hundred inhabitants—has one or more schools, where boys are taught to read (and sometimes to write) the Arabic character, and learn the Qur'ān by heart. More advanced instruction is occasionally given by *mu'allims*, who hold evening classes at the mosque and explain the sacred text in the vernacular. The writer heard of schools for girls, both at Lamu and at Mambrui, though none were actually in existence at the time of her visit, and well-to-do parents, at least, engaged visiting teachers for their daughters.

'Among the pure Swahilis many of the women are well educated in reading and writing, while in the Lamu Archipelago they are often better than the men in versifying.'[10]

A feature which has hardly attracted the attention it deserves is the wide diffusion of a considerable body of religious poetry in the vernacular. MS copies are handed down in families, and many men and women who cannot read know long passages by heart. Among the most popular are: a poem of 264 stanzas, relating the death of the Prophet, another on the history of Job, the *Utenzi wa Shufaka* published by Büttner, and *Qissat Sayyidinâ Isa*, which relates the life of Christ according to Muslim tradition and the Apocryphal

1 See Burton, *Zanzibar*, i. 411.
2 *Handwerk und Industrie in Ostafrika* (vol. i. of *Abhandlungen des hamburgischen Kolonialinstituts*), pp. 82, 85, 113, 135.
3 *Le K'ouen-louen*, p. 228.
4 Strandes, *Die Portugiesenzeit von Deutsch- und Englisch-Ostafrika*, p. 84.
5 Barros says the assault began on 17th Nov. 1528—no date is given for the actual taking, and the operations do not seem to have occupied more than a few days. Da Cunha stayed till the end of the monsoon allowed him to sail for India, which he did (from Malindi) 3rd April 1529—having previously burnt Mombasa—evidently towards the end of March (see J. Barros and D. de Couto, *Da Asia*, dec. iv. pt. i. bk. iii. vol. 7, chs. v.–viii. [pp. 276–305]).

1 Strandes, p. 153 f.; Stigand, p. 17 f.
2 *Reisen in Ost-Afrika, ausgeführt in den Jahren 1837–55*, i. 287–290.
3 Owen, i. 418.
4 *Ib.* i. 403.
5 Baumann, p. 56; Burton, i. 421.
6 Burton, i. 396 ff.: he calls them 'Abazi' and 'Bayazi'; see Eliot, p. 43, which seems to show that the sect is on the decline, and Badger, *Hist. of the Imâms and Seyyids of Oman*, p. 385 ff.
7 *Loc. cit.*
8 P. 56.
9 Stigand, p. 114.
10 *Ib.*

Gospels. A didactic and devotional poem known as the *Utendi wa Mwana Kupona*, composed by a Lamu woman, some 60 or 70 years ago, was published in 1917, in the *Harvard African Studies*.

As in other cases where the Muslim religion has been superimposed upon a system of primitive beliefs, it has absorbed all sorts of extraneous elements. The Bantu cult of the ancestral ghost has passed into something like saint-worship at the graves of noted shaikhs—*e.g.*, the shrine known as Pa Shehe Jundani at Mombasa. The diviner, instead of casting lots by means of the 'bones' or analogous objects (a practice still in vogue among the Giryama, etc.), uses the sand-board (*kupiga ramli*) or writes texts from the Qur'ān and the names of the four angels (Gabriel, Michael, Azrael, Israfil), on paper or parchment, to be used as charms.

'Descended from "devil-worshippers"'—a designation based on a misapprehension—'the Waswahili rather fear the "Shaytani" than love Allah, and to the malignant powers of preternatural beings they attribute sickness and all the evils of human life.'[1]

The word *shaitan* has been borrowed from the Arabs and is applied to the spirits haunting rocks, trees (more especially baobabs), etc., for which the genuine Swahili word is *wazimu* or *wazuka*. These are originally, in all probability, ghosts of the dead, but imported notions, such as that of the Arab *jinn*, have introduced some confusion. In Krapf's time every boatman who passed 'Makame's Rock' (on the landward side of Mombasa Island, almost opposite Frere Town) threw a lime into the sea; the custom is still remembered, but reduced to a mere symbolic act, like the throwing of a pin into a holy well in this country. Probably offerings were once made to propitiate the ghost of a man drowned there, but the story told to Krapf was that Makame was a fisherman who had been turned into a rock because he followed his occupation on a holy day.[2] Similarly, there are lonely spots in the bush, known as *kwa kibibi* ('the place of the little lady')—probably forgotten graves—where passing travellers are wont to lay down a stick, stone, leaf, or other trifle. Spirits haunting trees may at any time seize and possess passers-by; they are then known as *pepo*, and there are recognized and usually very elaborate formulas for exorcizing them. In fact, there is a whole hagiology of these *pepo*, and each one has his special *ngoma*, or 'dance.'[3]

6. Customs.—As may be inferred from what has already been said with regard to religion, we meet here with an interesting blend of imported and indigenous ideas. The reckoning of kinship in the male line cannot be counted as one of the former, as the transition from mother-right to father-right has already taken place in many Bantu tribes. But the prohibited degrees enumerated by Velten[4] are those recognized by Muslim law, and the clan system, still in full vigour among Giryama, Pokomo, Digo, etc., who may not marry inside their clan, has fallen into oblivion. (The so-called twelve 'clans' [*kabila*] of Mombasa, seem to be local associations, *i.e.* the Wapate, Wapaza, etc., are immigrants from the places denoted by their names.) The tabus (*miiko*) observed in families[5] would probably give a clue to former clan-relationships. All persons who have any claim to Arab descent keep the records of their genealogy with the greatest care, adding the clan name to their own—*e.g.*, 'Alī ibn Muhammad ibn

[1] Burton, i. 423. [2] Krapf, *Reisen*, i. 242.
[3] See Velten, *Sitten und Gebräuche der Suaheli*, pp. 176–206; also R. R. Skene, in *JRAI* xlvii. [1917] 413–434; and M. Klamroth, in *Zeitschrift für Kolonialsprachen*, i. [1910–11] 37, 118, 189: 'Religiöse Vorstellungen der Saramo' (the Wazaramo, whose home is near Dar-es-Salaam, are probably among the tribes who have contributed most largely to the Swahili stock); also Baumann, pp. 142–144.
[4] P. 396. [5] *Ib.* p. 93 n.

'Umar 'l Batawi, or 'l Mandhiri, or 'l Auzii, etc., as the case may be. The Muslim rite of circumcision has been blended with the Bantu initiation-ceremonies (*kumbi, manyago*) and consequently takes place earlier than it would, as a rule, among the Bantu.[1] Girls are not operated on by the Swahili, though they are by some of the Arabs. Much valuable information, derived from native sources, is given by Velten; but it is by no means exhaustive and applies chiefly to the Mrima, the coast-land opposite Zanzibar. A native authority[2] says that, in all essentials, Swahili customs are the same from Lamu to Lindi—but this possibly needs some little qualification.

7. Language and literature.—Swahili is not, as some have thought, a mere composite jargon, comparable to 'Pidgin-English' or 'Kitchen Kafir'; but it is not the language of any indigenous African tribe—*i.e.*, it did not exist before the Arab colonization. The Bantu groundwork may, as Krapf thought,[3] have been Pokomo; certainly it seems to have taken shape in the Lamu archipelago and adjacent mainland, including the Tana delta. But other tribes may have exercised a modifying influence, especially in the southern dialects, where intervocalic *l*, elsewhere consistently dropped out, has a tendency to reappear (*fungula* for *fungua*, etc.). Arabic has contributed largely to the vocabulary (about to the same extent as Latin in English), but has not influenced the grammar to any appreciable degree. A few Persian and a few Portuguese words have been incorporated with the language—in the latter case, not nearly so many as might have been expected. It has been written (probably for some centuries, but at present it is difficult to procure evidence on this point) by means of the Arabic character, which, however, is by no means well adapted for the purpose; and even with the help of additional symbols such as are used in Persian—*e.g.*, for *p* and *v*—a Swahili MS may be very difficult to read, even for a native. It is obvious that the vowel points are indispensable; they are only omitted in Arabic words which are easily recognized, such as the conventional phrases at the beginning of a letter. The oldest MSS examined by European scholars may go back to the 18th or possibly the late 17th century; perhaps some still older ones may exist in the archives of the mosques. The poems (there are no ancient Swahili prose-writings)—if not the actual copies—may be of considerable antiquity, but we have no certain data on this point. W. E. Taylor thinks that the *Inkishafi* (a religious poem edited by him and published as the appendix to Stigand's *Dialect in Swahili*) may have been written before Vasco de Gama's arrival in Africa (1498), and, if the poems assigned to Liongo Fumo are genuine, they must go back at least to the 16th, and possibly to the 12th cent., or earlier. Very few of these poems have found their way into print. Büttner, in his *Anthologie*, published three long poems, all of a religious character, and a charming selection of recent lyrics and folk-songs and a large body of minor verse has been collected by Velten, while the *Chuo cha Herkal* ('Book of the Emperor Heraclius'), of which a MS was brought to Europe by Krapf, was published by Meinhof in the *Zeitschrift für Kolonialsprachen* for 1912–13. With the exception of the *Utendi wa Mwana Kupona* mentioned above, and the gnomic stanzas attributed to Liongo, in Steere's *Swahili Tales* (there is a MS of this poem in the British Museum), this is all that has been done so far in this direction. Swahili has eminent possibilities as a literary language, and some attempts recently made—notably the traditions of the Wakilindi (Usambara), written down by the late Abdallah ibn Hemedi Liajjemi—promise well for the development of prose writing.

LITERATURE.—Salil ibn Ruzaik, *Hist. of the Imâms and Seyyids of 'Oman*, tr. G. P. Badger [Hakluyt Soc., 44], London, 1871; Oscar Baumann, *Usambara und seine Nachbargebiete*, Berlin, 1891; M. W. H. Beech, *Aids to the Study of Ki Swahili*, London, 1918; *Blue Books: Africa*, no. 7 (1897): Report by Sir A. Hardinge on the Condition and Progress of the E. Africa Protectorate from its Establishment to the 20th July 1897 [C. 8683]; *Africa*, no. 3 (1899): Report . . . for the Year 1897–98 [C. 9125]; R. F. Burton, *Zanzibar City, Island and Coast*, 2 vols., London, 1872, *Sindh, and the Races that inhabit the Valley of the Indus*, do. 1851; C. G. Büttner, *Anthologie aus der Suaheli-Litteratur (Gedichte und Geschichten der Suaheli)*, Berlin, 1894; J. E. E. Craster, *Pemba, the Spice Island of Zanzibar*, London, 1913; R. N. Cust, *Modern Languages of Africa*, 2 vols., do. 1883; C. Eliot, *East Africa Protectorate*, do. 1905; G. Ferrand, *Le K'ouen-louen et les anciennes navigations interocéaniques dans les mers du Sud*, Paris, 1919, *Relations de voyages et textes géographiques arabes, persans et turcs*, 2 vols., do. 1913–14, and numerous papers in the *JA*, esp. 'L'Origine africaine des Malgaches' [1908], and 'Les Voyages des Javanais à Madagascar' [1910]; W. W. A. Fitzgerald, *Travels in the Coastlands of British East Africa and the Islands of Zanzibar and Pemba*, London, 1898; C. Guillain, *Documents sur l'histoire, la géographie, et le commerce de l'Afrique orientale*, 3 vols., Paris [1856]; J. L. Krapf, *A Dictionary of the Suahili Language*, London, 1882, *Reisen in Ost-Afrika, ausgeführt in den Jahren*

[1] Velten, pp. 75–100. [2] *Ib.* p. 1.
[3] *Vocabulary of Six East African Languages*, p. vii.

1837–55, Kornthal, 1859, *Vocabulary of Six East African Languages*, Tübingen, 1850; **R. N. Lyne**, *Zanzibar in Contemporary Times*, London, 1905; **W. F. W. Owen**, *Narrative of Voyages, to explore the Shores of Africa, Arabia, and Madagascar*, 2 vols., do. 1833; **C. Sacleux**, *Grammaire des dialectes swahilis*, Paris, 1909; **H. Salt**, *A Voyage to Abyssinia . . . [including] some Particulars respecting the Aboriginal African Tribes extending from Mosambique to the borders of Egypt*, London, 1814; **E. Steere**, *Swahili Tales as told by Natives of Zanzibar*, do. 1869 (reprinted 1889, 1916), *Handbook of the Swahili Language*, do. 1884, 'East African Tribes and Languages,' *JAI* i. [1871] p. cxliii; **C. H. Stigand**, *The Land of Zinj*, London, 1913; *A Grammar of the Dialectic Changes in the Kiswahili Language*, Cambridge, 1915; **S. A. Strong**, 'The History of Kilwa,' *JRAS*, 1895, p. 381; **J. Strandes**, *Die Portugiesenzeit von Deutsch- und Englisch-Ostafrika*, Berlin, 1899; **F. Stuhlmann**, *Handwerk und Industrie in Ostafrika* (vol. i. of *Abhandlungen des hamburgischen Kolonialinstituts*), Hamburg, 1910; **W. E. Taylor**, *African Aphorisms, or Saws from Swahililand*, London, 1891; **C. Velten**, *Märchen und Erzählungen der Suaheli*, Berlin, 1898 (Swahili text published as vol. xviii. of *Lehrbücher des Seminars für orientalische Sprachen*), *Reiseschilderungen der Suaheli*, Göttingen, 1901, *Sitten und Gebräuche der Suaheli*, do. 1903 (Swahili text of this and the preceding entry published simultaneously), *Prosa und Poesie der Suaheli* (Swahili text with German notes), Berlin, 1907; **H. Yule** and **A. C. Burnell**, *Hobson-Jobson*, London, 1886; **F. B. Pearce**, *Zanzibar, the Island Metropolis of Eastern Africa*, do. 1920; **J. de Barros** and **D. de Couto**, *Da Asia*, 24 vols., Lisbon, 1778.

A. WERNER.

ZAPOTECS.—See MEXICANS.

ZARATHUSHTRA.—See ZOROASTRIANISM.

ZEALOTS.—**I. Name.**—The term 'Zealots' (*i.e.* 'the zealous') is derived from ζηλωτής, the Greek equivalent of the Hebrew קַנָּא, *Qannā*, pl. *Qanna'im* and the Aramaic *Qannāi*, pl. *Qannā'in*.[1] The terms both in Hebrew and in Greek have a general and a specific usage. The former is naturally of most frequent occurrence in Scripture and Jewish literature.[2] The latter usage as a designation of the fanatic Jewish nationalists and opponents of Roman domination is rare. *Qanna'im* is not found in the Targum Onḳelos.[3]

The adjectives קַנָּא, קַנְּאָן, קוּנְיוֹן, and קַנָּאִי are found in the Talmud and Midrashim, but the plural in a technical or quasi-technical sense occurs only twice: *Sanh.* ix. 11, 'Whoever steals a libation-cup, or curses one by the Holy Name, or has intercourse with a Syrian woman shall be struck down by the *Qanna'in*' (קנאין, Zealots, apparently in a religious sense only); and *Ābôth de R. Nathan*, vi.: 'And when the emperor Vespasian came to destroy Jerusalem the *Qanna'im*[4] attempted to burn everything with fire'—the only Talmudic passage mentioning the political Zealots.

How early the title *Qanna'im* was applied to the extreme anti-Roman political party is uncertain. According to Josephus,[5] it was a self-designation. If this is so, it is impossible to determine whether 'Zealots' was a self-designation from the beginning of the movement under Judas the Galilæan and became generally known and recognized as their title under Gessius Florus because of their remarkable activity and increase then, or, on the other hand, whether these 'fanatics of Roman hate' had no definite appellation for the first sixty years (A.D. 6–66) of their history until the time of Florus, under whom Josephus first employs the term.[6]

The epithet 'the Cananæan' in Mk 3^{18}, Mt 10^{4} (for which 'the Zealot' is given in Lk 6^{15}, Ac 1^{13}), has been variously interpreted. The AV reads Κανανίτης, 'the Canaanite' (which is given in Mk by A and other second-rate uncials and later versions, and in Mt by א and later authorities), but that would require χαναναῖος=כְּנַעֲנִי. Jerome interpreted it as *de vico Chana Galileæ*, and Holtzmann[1] as קַנְאָנִי='a man from (an unknown) Kanan,' both of which interpretations would require the Greek Καναῖος. Dalman[2] considers Καναναῖος an error for Καναῖος by assimilation to the more familiar 'Canaanite.' These explanations are superfluous. Καναναῖος is simply the Greek transliteration of קַנְאָנָא, *i.e.* קנאן, with the post-positive article א—and so='the *Qanna*' (Zealot), just as in Aramaic מלכא='the king.' Luke has therefore rightly and literally translated it ὁ ζηλωτής.[3] Whether Simon was an adherent of the Zealot party before he joined the company of Jesus, or the term was won subsequently through zeal in Jesus' service (as the brother of Andrew won the surname Peter, and the Zebedaides that of Boanerges) may not be quite certain, but the probabilities point to the former view.

2. Origin.—As the oppression and Hellenizing policy of the Seleucids caused the Maccabæan revolt and the rise of the Ḥasîdîm, the policy of Rome, especially from A.D. 6, caused the rise of the Zealots. The genealogical descent of the Zealots may be traced from the Ḥasîdîm through the Perûshîm (Pharisees), who appeared in opposition to the Hellenizing sympathies of the aristocratic Sadducees about the time of John Hyrcanus (135–105 B.C.). The Zealots thus combined the policy of the Ḥasîdîm (against foreign domination) with that of the original Pharisees (against liberalism towards foreign thought and manners and laxity towards the Law).

Although the Zealot movement dates from A.D. 6, there had been for years previous a growing discontent against both Idumæan and Roman rule. The statement of Rabbi Kohler that 'the reign of the Idumæan Herod gave the impetus to the organization of the Zealots as a political party' seems to go beyond our evidence. But the Zealots had forerunners in the 'robber' bands of Herod's reign. Ezekias 'the arch-robber' (ὁ ἀρχιληστής) at the head of a strong 'robber' force caused great trouble to Herod, by whom he was finally captured and executed.[4] His son Judas, after the death of Herod, made an insurrection in Sepphoris in 4 B.C.[5] Even conspirators with concealed daggers banded together against Herod,[6] the forerunners of the later Sicarii.

The Jews had come into contact with Rome in the days of the Maccabees. If Pompey captured Jerusalem in 63 B.C., and abolished the Hasmonæan kingship, he left the Jews in the enjoyment of a considerable independence and respected their nationhood. In A.D. 6 Archelaus, who for ten years as ethnarch had ruled Judæa, Idumæa, and Samaria, was accused before Augustus by a joint commission of Jews and Samaritans of intolerable cruelties, for which the emperor recalled and banished him. Judæa was then loosely annexed to the Roman province of Syria, to be administered under a procurator.[7] From this date the Jews began to discover—what they learned better on the extinction of the Herodian dynasty in A.D. 44—that the sly half-Jewish Herods understood and respected their peculiarities and religious customs better than did the Romans. The Jews found the Roman administrators to be other than they had imagined. There was to be no return to the 'honours and alliances of the Romans and their emperors with our nation'[8] of Maccabæan days, nor to the δόγματα of the great Julius in the years 47 B.C. and following, which bestowed upon the Jews all the privileges of Roman protection together with religious toleration and political home rule. These Julian decrees were regarded later by the Jews as their Magna Charta, and by them all subsequent Roman administration was appraised.

[1] קַנָּאִי, קַנְּאָן; not *Kenaim*, as given in *PRE*³ xxi. 655; cf. J. Levy, *Neuheb. und chald. Wörterbuch*, Leipzig, 1876–89, and M. Jastrow, *Dictionary of the Targumin*, etc., London and New York, 1886–1903.

[2] It is found, *e.g.*, in Ex 20^{5} 34^{14}, Dt 4^{24}, Ac 21^{20}, Gal 1^{14}, 1 Co 14^{12}, and in Talmud; cf. Levy, *op. cit.*

[3] E. Brederek, *Konkordanz zum Targum Onkelos* (*ZATW* ix.), Giessen, 1906.

[4] קנּנים, but סקרין, in S. Schechter's second version, London, 1887, p. 31 f.

[5] *BJ* IV. iii. 9: ζηλωταῖς· τοῦτο γὰρ αὐτοὺς ἐκάλεσαν.

[6] See § 4 below.

[1] *Hand-Kommentar zum NT*, Freiburg, 1889–91, *ad loc.*

[2] *Grammatik der jüd.-palästin. Aramaisch*, Leipzig, 1894, p. 174.

[3] Wellhausen and Schürer also interpret Καναναῖος as 'the Zealot,' but arrive at their interpretation in a way different from each other and from the above. Wellhausen (*Das Evang. Marci*, Berlin, 1903, p. 25) evidently regards the Greek as the equivalent of קנאי, while Schürer (*GJV*⁴ i. 487 f.) prefers to regard it as a Greek formation from קַנְאָנָא, plur. of קַנְּאָן.

[4] *Ant.* XIV. ix. 2, *BJ* I. x. 5.

[5] *Ant.* XVII. x. 5, *BJ* II. iv. 1.

[6] *Ant.* XV. viii. 3 f.

[7] *Ib.* XVII. xiii.

[8] *Ib.* XIV. x. 1.

Roman interference had never been palatable to the masses of the people, and it was among the lower classes that the hatred of Rome now became intensified, though, as often in popular upheavals, many of the leaders were supplied from the aristocratic classes. The conflict began with the resentment caused by the census of Quirinius (A.D. 6–7) to which Judæa as a procuratorial province was subjected. The Jews at first resented the taxation, but were persuaded to submit by the high-priest Joazar. The Zealot movement began as a protest against this census when Coponius was procurator of Judæa.[1] The outbreak did not occur in Judæa, but in Galilee, which was not directly affected by the census. The insurrection was headed by Judas,[2] a Gaulonite of the city of Gamala (better known as 'the Galilæan'), who allied himself with a prominent Pharisee, named Sadduk, probably a member of the more nationalistic school of Shammai. Though Josephus speaks of Judas and Sadduk as joint authors of the Zealot movement,[3] he more frequently represents Judas as the prime mover.[4] Judas the Galilæan became leader of the fourth of these sects.[5] The motives of the party were partly political and partly religious, but the political and the religious were always conjoined in Jewish history. In the closing scenes the political and secular far overshadowed the religious. The Roman taxation meant 'nothing else than downright slavery';[6] it was a breach against the theocracy.[7] The census was a sign to the people that the Romans designed to destroy the last trace of their liberties: it was a gross insult both to them and to Jahweh. The object of the Zealots was to preserve intact Jewish nationalism and cult-traditions, and, by force if necessary, to throw off the Roman yoke and restore the theocracy. Thus they would hasten the Kingdom of God. The Zealot party was a 'combination of noble and base elements; superstitious enthusiasts, and political assassins, the so-called sicarii, were conjoined with honest but fanatical patriots.'[8]

3. Subsequent history.—The history of Zealotism extends from A.D. 6–7 to the fall of Jerusalem, Sept. A.D. 70, or to the capture of Masada, April 73. The slighting reference of the Pharisee, Gamaliel, in Ac 5[37ff.] might give the impression that the insurrection of Judas did not assume grave proportions, being suppressed immediately by the Roman authorities by the death of the leader and the scattering of his followers. Josephus does not chronicle either the fate of Judas or the history of the revolt, but affirms that it was the beginning of the end for the Jews.

'The daring plot made great headway. There is no evil that did not spring from these men [Judas and Sadduk], and the nation was filled with it to an incredible extent . . . whence seditions were engendered and as a result political bloodshed . . . and famine reducing us to extreme shamelessness, and the capture and sacking of cities, until finally this insurrection consumed the temple of God in the fire of the enemy.'[9]

Another proof of the importance of Judas's rebellion is the fact that his sons and descendants inherited his fanatical hate of Rome and became outstanding exponents of Zealotism until it was extinguished at Masada. Two sons of Judas, Jacob and Simon, were crucified by Tiberius Alexander.[10] Another son, Menahem, was a protagonist in the rising of A.D. 66.[11] A descendant, named Eleazar, was commander of the garrison of Masada and perished there, probably by his own hand.[1] The Roman question became the test question in political life and led to a fatal split in the Jewish nation. This internal division affected to a greater extent the Pharisaic party which had first resented the direct interference of Rome in the affairs of Palestine. The majority of Pharisees, however, were pacifists and fatalists; only a minority became extremists anxious to appeal to the arbitrament of the sword, and, under Sadduk, seceded to the Zealots.

After the first challenge of the Zealots to Rome was crushed, the Roman government seriously attempted to understand their Jewish subjects and in many ways humoured them. For a time the Zealot movement lost in numbers and influence, for lack of matters of complaint. Quirinius deposed the unpopular high-priest Joazar, who counselled compliance with the census.[2] The Jews were excused from Roman military levies: the auxiliary troops under the procurator were recruited from among the non-Jewish populations of Palestine.[3] The first four procurators were friendly disposed towards the Jews. Roman authority, most tolerant of Jewish customs and religious beliefs, placed the Jewish cult on the status of a *religio licita*. The cult of the Cæsars, elsewhere established and even welcomed in the empire, was not forced upon the Jews except during the mad attempt of Caligula which led to fearful massacres in Alexandria and caused much heart-searching in Judæa. On this occasion the holy city was spared desecration, through the tactful and generous management of P. Petronius, the legate of Syria, who pleaded the cause of the Jews at the risk of his own life, for Caligula, offended at Petronius's hesitation, ordered him to commit suicide—a command which fortunately did not arrive until after the assassination of Caligula. King Agrippa I., a special favourite with Caligula, likewise used all his influence to secure the withdrawal of the offensive decree.[4] The Romans, out of regard for Jewish scruples concerning the imperial image on coins, granted Judæa a copper coinage which bore only the name of the emperor and inoffensive symbols. When from time to time Roman troops marched into Jerusalem, they did so without the usual military banners which bore the image of the emperor—a considerable condescension on the part of the conquerors.[5] Unfortunately, between Jewish demands and scrupulosity on the one side and Roman arrogance and ignorance of their subjects on the other, even this *modus vivendi* was not destined to succeed or to reconcile Palestine to accept the Roman yoke. Moreover, Roman practice did not always harmonize with Roman theory. The result was an ever-widening cleft between the pro-Roman and the anti-Roman parties in the nation, with increasing bitterness and recklessness among the latter. The pro-Roman or pacifist party was represented by the Sadducees and the Herodian rulers and the aristocracy generally, together with the more prudent of the Pharisees; the anti-Roman party was composed chiefly of the Zealots and the populace. The Pharisees, at first decidedly anti-Roman, after A.D. 66 generally sided with the Sadducæan aristocracy and the party of law and order against the extremists.

Under the first four procurators (Coponius, A.D. 6–9; Marcus Ambibulus, A.D. 9–12; Annius Rufus, A.D. 12–15; Valerius Gratus, A.D. 15–26) Judæa seems on the whole to have been equitably

[1] *Ant.* XVIII. i. 1, XX. v. 2, *BJ* II. viii. 1.
[2] This Judas the Galilæan and Gaulonite cannot consistently with the language of Josephus be identified with Judas, son of Ezekias, as is done by Grätz and Schürer (*GJV* i. 486).
[3] *Ant.* XVIII. i. 1: εἴ γε καὶ Ἰούδας καὶ Σάδδουκος τετάρτην φιλοσοφίαν ἐπεισάκτως ἡμῖν ἐγείραντες.
[4] *Ib.* XVIII. i. 6.
[5] *Ib.* XX. v. 2, *BJ* II. viii. 1.
[6] *Ant.* XVIII. i. 1.
[7] *Ib.* XVIII. i. 6, *BJ* II. viii. 1.
[8] Wellhausen, *Proleg. to Hist. of Israel*, Eng. tr., p. 535.
[9] *Ant.* XVIII. i. 1.
[10] *Ib.* XX. v. 2.
[11] *BJ* II. xvii. 8 f.

[1] *BJ* II. xvii. 9, VII. viii. 1.
[2] *Ant.* XVIII. ii. 1.
[3] Cf. Schürer, *GJV*[4] i. 459.
[4] Philo, *ad Gaium*, xxix ff. (Mangey, ii. 573); Jos. *Ant.* XVIII. viii.
[5] *Ant.* XVIII. iii. 1; cf. also the enumeration of Roman favours towards the Jews in the speech of Titus (*BJ* VI. vi. 2).

administered, and there was little disaffection to further the Zealot party. But the fifth procurator (Pontius Pilatus, A.D. 26–36) was a man of a different mind. He was, according to a letter of Agrippa I. to Caligula,[1] 'naturally inflexible and stubbornly relentless,' and guilty of 'acts of corruption, insults, rapine, outrages on the people, arrogance, repeated murders of innocent victims, and constant and most galling savagery'—a description quite in keeping with the impression given of him in the Gospels.[2] He defied Jewish religious prejudices by introducing a Roman garrison with the imperial ensigns into the city by night—an act which met with such opposition that Pilate was obliged to yield.[3] Another offence was his confiscation of part of the Temple treasury (the Corban) to build an aqueduct for Jerusalem. To the Jewish protests against this sacrilege Pilate replied by commanding the soldiery to punish the mob, which they did so thoroughly that many lives were lost.[4] Again, he set up gilt shields without the imperial image, but bearing his own and the emperor's name, in the palace of Herod within the city, 'not so much for the honour of Tiberius as to annoy the people.' He was ordered by the emperor to transfer them to the Augusteum at Cæsarea.[5] His last act of carnage was committed against the Samaritans, who laid their complaint before Vitellius, legate of Syria, by whom Pilate was sent to Rome to answer for his conduct, and Marcellus was appointed in his place.[6] All Vitellius's conciliatory acts could not undo the anti-Roman feelings engendered by the late procurator. It was under this Pilate, when the spirit of the dead Judas of Galilee again inspired the people with a desire for liberty, that Jesus taught and suffered. One of His disciples was probably a Zealot. In Galilee especially Jesus came in contact with Zealot propaganda which, in its advocacy of violence, ran counter to His preaching concerning the Kingdom of God, and against which He raised His protests.[7] Our Lord's death is also, possibly, linked with the history of Zealotism. It was the plots and violence of the Zealots which aggravated Pilate's apprehensions upon which the Jewish authorities played. At Jesus' trial before Pilate the multitude was granted the option between 'Jesus Barabbas' (Mt $27^{16f.}$) and 'Jesus called Christ.' This Barabbas was a 'robber' (Jn 18^{40}) who had been 'imprisoned with the insurrectionists who in the insurrection had been guilty of murder' (Mk 15^{7}). The word found in the Fourth Gospel (18^{40}), λῃστής, is the word most frequently used by our chief historian of Zealotism (Josephus) as synonymous with Zealot; and Mark's account indicates that Barabbas was no ordinary highwayman, but one who had headed one of the numerous revolts (στάσις) against Roman authority. Barabbas was, therefore, probably a Zealot leader.

The objection urged against this interpretation is that as a Zealot leader Barabbas would be in favour with the masses and likely to be preferred by the people, whereas Pilate hoped, by permitting the choice, that the multitude would ask for the release of Jesus. But (1) the accounts are somewhat confused. According to the Fourth Gospel and Matthew, Pilate proposed the choice as a possible means of acquitting Jesus, while, according to the oldest account (Mark), the people reminded Pilate of his customary clemency at the feast. (2) The alternative was not between a popular Zealot and an unpopular Messiah. Both Barabbas and Jesus were popular. Pilate knew that Jesus was in such favour with the people as to be called 'King of the Jews' (cf. Jn 6^{15}), but that by the authorities He was regarded with jealousy. Of these two popular prisoners Pilate was convinced that Jesus would be preferred by the multitude, which, however, partly under the influence of the high-priest, demanded Barabbas. It was not the first time that a procurator misunderstood Jewish feelings, nor the first occasion on which a ruler was misled by the psychology of the mob.

Little is known of the next two procurators—Marcellus (A.D. 36–37) and Marullus (A.D. 37–41).[1] Such was the Jewish national consciousness that the news of the bloody persecutions to which their brethren in Alexandria were subjected towards the close of A.D. 38 (and which continued fitfully until the close of Caligula's reign because of their opposition to the erection of the imperial image in the synagogues) would intensify the fanatical hate against Rome. The same demand for the recognition of the imperial cult was made upon Judæa the next year as a punishment for the act of the Jews of Jamnia in overthrowing an altar erected to Caligula.[2] After much hesitation the emperor yielded to the entreaties of the Syrian legate, Petronius, and Agrippa I. and withdrew the edict. The act of Claudius immediately on his accession, whereby he restored to Agrippa I. (the Herod of Ac 12) the dominions of his grandfather, Herod the Great, by adding Judæa and Samaria to his kingdom, was intended to placate Jewish nationalism. This arrangement continued in force till A.D. 44, when, on the death of Agrippa I., Rome passed over his twelve-year-old son and incorporated all Palestine with Syria under a procurator.[3] This disappearance of the semi-Jewish Herodian dynasty, which had stood as a buffer between Rome and the Jews, formed a crisis in Jewish history and caused a renewed outbreak of Zealotism. The social peace and material prosperity of the few years under Agrippa I., together with bitter memories of Roman procurators, made a return under direct Roman administration repugnant to the masses. Fuel was added to the fires of fanaticism. From this important date till A.D. 66 seven procurators administered Palestine.

'If the history of the Roman procurators, to whom Palestine was now entrusted, is reviewed, one might imagine that all, as if by some secret compact, systematically aimed at driving the people into revolt. Even the best of them—not to mention the others who trod all right under foot—had no idea that a people like the Jews desired above everything else tolerance toward their distinctive customs. Instead of practising mildness and caution, they opposed all the vital agitations (*Lebensregungen*) of the people with a pitiless severity.'[4]

The régime of the first two procurators after A.D. 44 (Fadus from 44, and Tiberius Alexander, nephew of Philo, till 48) was mild compared with that of the subsequent five: 'by making no innovations in our ancestral customs they kept the nation quiet.'[5] The misdeeds of Fadus recorded by Josephus are (1) his demand that the high-priest's vestment should be restored to Roman custody, which Claudius rescinded,[6] and (2) his suppression of the 'magician' or prophet Theudas, an idol of the people.[7] That Zealotism broke out with fresh vigour under Fadus's administration we may infer from the words of Josephus about the death of Tholomaios 'the arch-brigand'[8] and the clearance of all Judæa of 'robberies.'[9] We are

[1] Philo, *ad Gaium*, xxxviii. (Mangey, ii. 590).

[2] Cf. Lk 13^{1}: 'the Galilæans, whose blood Pilate mingled with their sacrifices.' It is quite possible that these Galilæans were Zealots whose opposition would be aroused by the cruel régime of Pilate. In the list of heresies in Justin Martyr, *Dial.* 80, and in Hegesippus (Eusebius, *HE* iv. 6) the Zealots are called Galilæans. The Zealot followers of John of Gischala are referred to as Galilæans in *BJ* IV. ix. 10.

[3] *Ant.* XVIII. iii. 1.

[4] *Ib.* XVIII. iii. 2, *BJ* II. ix. 4.

[5] Philo, *ad Gaium*, xxxviii. (Mangey, ii. 590).

[6] *Ant.* XVIII. iv.

[7] Cf. J. Weiss, *Die Predigt Jesu vom Reiche Gottes*, Göttingen, 1893, p. 24; and A. M. Hughes, 'Anti-Zealotism in the Gospels,' *ExpT* xxvii. [1915–16] 152. The words in Mt 11^{12} (from the Logia)—ἡ βασιλεία τῶν οὐρανῶν βιάζεται καὶ βιασταὶ ἁρπάζουσιν αὐτήν—may quite well be aimed against the Zealots. So Bousset, *Die Relig. des Judentums*², p. 101; K. Kohler, art. 'Zealots,' in *JE*.

[1] *Ant.* XVIII. iv. 2, vi. 10.

[2] Philo, *ad Gaium*, xxx f. (Mangey, ii. 575 ff.); Jos. *Ant.* XVIII. viii., *BJ* ii. 10.

[3] *Ant.* XIX. ix.

[4] Schürer, i. 565.

[5] *BJ* II. xi. 6.

[6] *Ant.* XX. i. 1.

[7] *Ib.* XX. v. 1; Ac $5^{36ff.}$.

[8] ὁ ἀρχιλῃστής—οἱ λῃσταί being practically synonymous in Josephus for ζηλωταί.

[9] *Ant.* XX. i. 1.

not informed whether the motive of Fadus was an insight into the nationalist danger or merely to keep order. The fact that the next procurator, Tiberius Alexander, deemed it necessary to crucify the Zealot leaders, Jacob and Simon, sons of Judas, shows that there was an alarming recrudescence of Zealot agitation such as to require summary treatment.[1] Under Ventidius Cumanus (A.D. 48–52) the people were in a constant state of insurrection.[2] Their resentment was embittered by (1) an indecent act of a Roman soldier at the Passover leading to a tumult, in which 30,000[3] Jews perished; (2) an order of Cumanus that whole villages be plundered in retaliation for the robbery of an imperial official by 'robbers' (probably Zealots): in the execution of this command a Roman soldier tore a copy of the Law to shreds with obscene language, upon which the people became so threatening that Cumanus beheaded the guilty soldier to placate them.[4] (3) As a result of the refusal of Cumanus to do justice to the Jews in a quarrel with the Samaritans, the people, against the advice of their elders, called in the help of the Zealot leader, 'Eleazar, son of Dinæus, a robber,' and Alexander, doubtless also a Zealot chief. Cumanus fell upon them and slew many. An appeal was carried to Ummidius Quadratus, legate of Syria, who referred the matter to Rome. Claudius, well-disposed through the offices of Agrippa ii., condemned the Samaritans and banished Cumanus.[5] The administration of Felix (A.D. 52–60) formed 'the turning-point in the drama which commenced in 44 and reached its bloody issue in 70.'[6] 'The affairs of Judæa continued to grow steadily worse.'[7] Felix intensified the revolutionary spirit by (1) his offensive marriage with Drusilla; (2) his treacherous capture of the Zealot leader, Eleazar; (3) the murder of the high-priest, Jonathan, which he perpetrated by means of the Sicarii; (4) the slaughter of 400 followers of the Egyptian prophet who led 30,000 men[8] into the wilderness; (5) unfair treatment of the Jews of Cæsarea in their quarrel with their Syrian townsmen.[9] He endeavoured to exterminate the 'robbers' (Zealots), who, nevertheless, became increasingly numerous and influential among the masses. His conduct rendered the nationalist party eager to bring the matter to the issue of arms. The sympathies of the people, now driven to desperation, were alienated from the pacifist leaders to the side of the Zealot party. Further, alongside, or within, the Zealot movement appeared a more extreme faction known as Sicarii, or 'dagger-men,'[10] who from then till the end of the siege struck down indifferently pro-Roman and Roman. Under Porcius Festus (A.D. 60–62) the cancellation of the Jewish *isopoliteia* in Cæsarea roused bitter resentment. The imperial letter relative thereto 'furnished the causes of all the subsequent evils to our nation.' Another popular movement led by an 'impostor' (probably a would-be Messiah or a Zealot) was suppressed by Festus. The opposition of Agrippa ii. and Festus to the erection by the Jews of the wall to prevent the Temple sacrifices from being overlooked from Agrippa's palace was another instance of blind neglect of Jewish sentiment.[11] Though Festus did not stain his office by the cruelties of his predecessor, the national party grew apace. The Sicarii who appeared under Felix became numerous. Festus

[1] *Ant.* xx. v. 2. [2] *BJ* ii. xii. 1.
[3] Josephus, *Opera*, ed. B. Niese, Berlin, 1887–95, vi. 98 (ὑπὲρ τρισμυρίους), *BJ* ii. xii. 1, *Ant.* xx. v. 3.
[4] *Ant.* xx. v. 4, *BJ* ii. xii. 2.
[5] *Ant.* xx. vi., *BJ* ii. xii. 3 ff.
[6] Schürer, i. 571. [7] Jos. *Ant.* xx. viii. 5.
[8] *BJ* ii. xiii. 5, but 4000, according to Ac 21[38].
[9] *Ant.* xx. vii., *BJ* ii. xii. 8.
[10] *Ant.* xx. viii. 5, 10, *BJ* ii. xiii. 3.
[11] *Ant.* xx. viii. 9 ff.

attempted to exterminate the Zealots: 'he captured the majority of the "robbers" and destroyed many.'[1] The last two procurators, Albinus (A.D. 62–64) and Gessius Florus (A.D. 64–66), acted as if they were resolved to provoke the Jews to rebellion. They reduced the country to anarchy. Josephus relates of Albinus: 'There was no species of wickedness which he left undone.'[2] He levied oppressive taxes, plundered privately and publicly, sold justice, and released all prisoners who could pay. He alternately connived at and punished the actions of the Sicarii and Zealots. Hearing that Florus was coming as his successor, he executed his most dangerous prisoners and released the others. As the released prisoners belonged mostly to the Zealot faction, 'the land was filled with robbers.'[3] Josephus has left a terrible account of the villainies of the last procurator, Florus,[4] by comparison with whom Albinus was upright. He flaunted his crimes publicly, took bribes, and wrung all he could out of the miserable people. On the one hand Bernice interceded, but in vain, for a more humane treatment of the Jews, while Agrippa ii. attempted to appease the people. Florus desired war to cover his misdeeds, and the younger men, mostly Zealots, were likewise eager for war. The provocation was furnished on Florus's part by his seizure of part of the Temple treasury and by his brutal attack on the people when they resented the insolence of the two cohorts which they were ordered to welcome from Cæsarea; and on the part of the Jews by a jest of some Jewish wags who pretended to beg for the destitute Florus, by the seizure of Masada and the slaughter of the Roman garrison by the Zealots, and by the discontinuance of the daily sacrifice for the emperor. Even now the peace party—the Sadducæan high-priests and the chiefs of the Pharisees—advocated conciliatory measures with the seditious Zealots, who refused to hearken.[5]

The insurgents under Eleazar, son of Ananias, allied with the Sicarii, attacked Agrippa's troops, upon whom the peace party relied.[6] Menahem, son of Judas the Galilæan, armed the Zealots, entered the city, and forced the capitulation of the soldiery of Agrippa and the citizens of the peace party. The war party further celebrated their victory by murdering the high-priest Ananias. Menahem's cruelty led to a quarrel with the other Zealot leader, Eleazar, which resulted in the death of Menahem. Eleazar celebrated his uncontested leadership by a shameful butchery of the Roman garrison under Metilius, which had capitulated on terms.[7] The successful defence of the capital against Cestius Gallus, governor of Syria, and his defeat at Beth-horon inspired enthusiasm in the Zealot and war party.[8] Many pro-Romans and moderates now abandoned the holy city. The war party came into control by violence or persuasion,[9] and the moderates were much disheartened.[10] As the die was now cast and an attack expected from Rome, the authorities proceeded to organize for war and appointed generals for Jerusalem and the provinces.[11] It should be noted that at this early stage those in authority were mostly members of the aristocracy—Sadducees and Pharisees—who considered it prudent to put themselves at the head of the popular revolution. The position of affairs was reversed after the misfortunes of the first year of the war, as fortress after fortress fell before the Romans. The revolution which unseated the native authorities and put provincial

[1] *BJ* ii. xiv. 1. [2] *Ib.*
[3] *Ant.* xx. ix. 5. [4] *Ib.* xx. ix., *BJ* ii. xiv. 2 ff.
[5] *BJ* ii. xvii. 3. [6] *Ib.* xvii. 6 ff.
[7] *Ib.* 10. [8] *Ib.* xix.
[9] *Ib.* xx. 1, 3. [10] *Ib.* xxii. 1.
[11] *Ib.* xx. 3, *Vita*, 7.

radicals in power was brought about by the Zealot, John of Gischala, the enemy of Josephus, in the winter A.D. 67–68. On the fall of Gischala (Nov. A.D. 67) John fled to Jerusalem, gained over the youth of the city, and was abetted by the increasing numbers of provincial refugees entering the city.[1] The authorities were, with some truth, accused of lack of energy in the prosecution of the war and even of Roman sympathies. The Zealots believed that the safety of the nation lay in ousting the aristocratic native leaders and in taking control themselves. They began by imprisoning Antipas (one of the royal lineage and public treasurer) and other persons of rank, and elected a new high-priest from the proletariat. The native party of order strenuously opposed the provincials and their Zealot supporters. The former was led by Gorion, son of Joseph, Simon, son of Gamaliel, and the high-priests Ananus and Jesus, son of Gamaliel. A speech of Ananus roused a majority of the inhabitants against the Zealots, who, in self-defence, summoned the Idumæans on the pretext that the authorities of Jerusalem had made common cause with the Romans. The Idumæans on arrival were refused admission by the inhabitants, but were secretly introduced at night by the Zealots. The Idumæans signalized their entrance by the perpetration of intolerable cruelties, in which the Zealots heartily joined, against the bourgeoisie and the aristocracy. This reign of terror accomplished the utter collapse of the native party of order and ended in a victory for the Zealots and reactionaries. The high-priests, Ananus and Jesus, and a prominent citizen, Zecharias, son of Baruch, were put out of the way. When the Idumæans, satiated with the blood of the citizens, realized the falsity of the pretence upon which they were introduced by the Zealots, they withdrew, but assassination and *sabotage* were continued by the Zealots. John, at the head of the Zealots, now became undisputed dictator of the city, while the Sicarii and Zealots carried on their brigandage and murders throughout the country. The Roman civil wars delayed military operations for a time. Meanwhile Simon, son of Giora, at the head of a mixed following of slaves and Zealots, overran a large portion of S. Palestine (A.D. 68–69) and came into conflict with the Zealots under John. The Romans, under Cerealis, put an end to Simon's marauding by conquering all Palestine outside the capital, except the three fortresses of Herodeion, Machærus, and Masada, held by the Zealots (summer of A.D. 69). Simon now appeared with his army before the walls of Jerusalem, the inhabitants of which, groaning under the tyranny of John, invited, at the suggestion of the high-priest Matthias, Simon 'as a second tyrant' within the city. There were now two factions, each distinguished by the same Zealot hatred of Rome and the same indifference to the rights of the citizens. Vespasian had meantime ascended the throne and commissioned Titus with the reduction of the Jewish rebellion. While the Romans were preparing to invest the city, there appeared a third faction headed by Eleazar, son of Simon, who, with a large following of priestly Zealots, revolted from John's party.[2] The incessant bickerings of these three tyrants, John, Simon, and Eleazar, caused terrible misery to the city and led to the disastrous burning of vast stores of grain sufficient to withstand a siege of many years.[1] A bloody riot occurred at the Passover of A.D. 70, in which John vanquished Eleazar's party and thus reduced the three Zealot factions to two.[2] As the Romans commenced to beleaguer the city, party faction was stilled. Eleazar with 2400 Zealots again united with John and his Zealots, while the Idumæans united with Simon.[3] The two leaders, John and Simon, made such an heroic and strategically planned defence against the Roman beleaguering forces that, had it not been for the previous internecine strife, which lessened the defenders, and the mad destruction of the ample supplies of grain, it is improbable that the Romans would have succeeded. In spite of Titus's desire to shorten the campaign and spare the city, the appeals of Josephus to his countrymen, and the famine prevailing within, the peace party was silenced by the Zealots. On the capture of the city (Sept. A.D. 70) John and Simon fell into the hands of the Romans; the former was condemned to life imprisonment, the latter was spared to grace the triumph and then executed. Herodeion, Machærus, and Masada still remained in the hands of the insurgents, chiefly Zealots and Sicarii. Lucilius Bassus captured Herodeion, and compelled Machærus to surrender. The last stronghold of the Zealots was Masada, occupied by the Sicarii and Zealots early in the war under Eleazar, a descendant of Judas the Galilæan.[4] This place fell in April, A.D. 73, before Flavius Silva, who discovered to his chagrin that the defenders had by agreement slain each other and the last survivor had committed suicide, only two women and five children surviving. With the fall of Masada the history of the Zealots as a party ends. The Jews had ceased to be a nation: it was, however, the spirit of the Zealots that inspired the sanguinary insurrections in the reigns of Trajan and Hadrian.

There is much in the history of Zealotism which recalls the Highland devotion to hopeless causes. Zealot enthusiasm was doomed to failure because it was not guided by prudence. Their indiscretions, their separatist spirit, their disregard of the other parties in the nation, and their enormities led to the defeat of the cause to which they devoted themselves with such indefatigable heroism in a life-and-death struggle with the imperial might of Rome.

4. Relation to other Jewish parties.—The chief questions are those of the relation of the Zealots to the Pharisees and to the Sicarii.[5] Josephus speaks of the Zealots as a fourth party alongside of the Sadducees, Pharisees, and Essenes.[6] His description of the Zealot sect is:

> 'Of the fourth of these philosophies Judas, the Galilæan, became leader. In all other respects they agree with the opinions of the Pharisees, but they are distinguished by an unshakable devotion to liberty, holding that God alone is Ruler and Lord (ἡγέμονα καὶ δεσπότην). They consider it a trifling matter to endure extraordinary deaths and the tortures of relatives and dear ones, in their refusal to address any mortal as "Lord." And since multitudes have witnessed their immovable courage under such circumstances I do not dwell upon it in detail. For I am not afraid that anything related of them should be disbelieved, but on the contrary I fear lest the narrative may do less than justice to their contempt in enduring the misery of pain. The nation commenced to suffer from the malady of this madness through the reckless insolence of Gessius Florus, the procurator, in driving the people to revolt from Rome.'[7]

The Zealot movement arose in the bosom of Pharisaism and retained throughout its brief

1 *BJ* IV. iii.

2 Ewald (*Hist. of Israel*, Eng. tr., vii. 559 ff.) classifies these three Zealot factions into the learned Zealots (who came into power under John in spring of A.D. 68), the popular Zealots (admitted under Simon, April, A.D. 69), and the priestly Zealots (who seceded under Eleazar early in A.D. 70); *per contra* Jackson and Lake, *Beginnings of Christianity*, i. 423, who contend that the name 'Zealot' applies to John of Gischala's following and to no other.

1 Tacitus, *Hist.* v. 12.
2 *Ib.*; Jos. *BJ* v. iii. 1.
3 *BJ* v. vi. 1.
4 *Ib.* II. xvii. 9, VII. viii. 1.

5 Hippolytus in his *Ref. of all Heresies*, ix. 21, represents the Zealots or Sicarii as an extreme sect of the Essenes. His account disagrees with all the other accounts of Essenism given by Philo, Josephus, Pliny, Hegesippus, Porphyry, and Epiphanius, and with that of Zealotism given by Josephus.

6 See *Ant.* XVIII. i. 3 f., *BJ* II. viii. 2. In *Vita*, 2, he mentions only three parties.

7 *Ant.* XVIII. i. 6.

history a striking resemblance to Pharisaism. The Pharisees represented generally the popular party, distinguished by their dislike of Roman overlordship and their zeal for the Law and the theocracy. The Roman question caused a split among the Pharisees into the majority of moderates and the minority of extremists or war party. The former were fatalists,[1] who viewed Roman domination as due to an act of the inscrutable will of God or as a punishment for the people's infidelity. While their ideal was national independence, their policy was passive resistance. The other party favoured war *à outrance*. The one party valued the liberal measure of tolerance granted by Rome for the exercise of their religion: the other believed that autonomous nationalism was requisite for the very existence of the theocracy. These extremists, led by Sadduk, gladly attached themselves to a nationalist like Judas. The Herodians[2] were probably not strictly a separate party, but belonged to, or for political purposes allied themselves with, the most pacific section of the Pharisees. Herodians and Pharisees would agree (1) in discountenancing everything which threatened to disturb the political *status quo*, while (2) preferring the Herodian dynasty (instead of a Roman procuratorship), which some Pharisees would view as a compromise for the fuller theocracy. The Zealots occupied, therefore, the extreme right of the Pharisees, and the Herodians the extreme left, on the question of the *status quo*.

Unfortunately our chief source for the history of Zealotism is Josephus—a moderate Pharisee and pro-Roman, with a decided penchant against the Zealots,[3] probably due to the fact that he wished in the minds of the Romans to throw the blame of the rebellion upon a party which became extinct with the Roman victories, and partly to screen his own sect, which after the end of the Jewish nation became the guardian of its traditions. The excesses of which the Zealots were guilty furnished him a feasible excuse. The Zealot movement not only arose within Pharisaism, but throughout its course really stood for the ideals of the Pharisees, though adopting different means.

> 'The latter [Zealot party] only drew the last practical conclusions out of the hate of the Pharisees against heathen domination. The Pharisees therefore never disapproved of their conduct until it degenerated into absolutely unlawful proceedings. Where this happened [*BJ* IV. v. 9], the doctors of the Pharisees broke loose from the Zealots, who now betrayed their connexion with the Pharisees by immediately falling upon the Sadducean aristocracy.'[4]

The Zealots did not scruple to accomplish the death of Sadducean high-priests. Even Josephus cannot conceal the close relations between Zealots and Pharisees, the Zealots being distinguished only by their marked devotion to independence,[5] though elsewhere[6] he speaks of Judas as *σοφιστὴς ἰδίας αἱρέσεως οὐδὲν τοῖς ἄλλοις προσεοικώς*. But from A.D. 66 the Pharisees, foreseeing the issue of a conflict with imperial Rome, withdrew more and more from the Zealots and joined the Sadducees in advocating conciliatory measures.[7] Josephus generally speaks of the Zealots as 'brigands' (*λῃσταί*). This nomenclature was due to (1) the absence for some time of any definite party name for these radicals, the title 'Zealot' being a self-designation of the party,[8] and perhaps not definitely

[1] Cf. *Ant.* XVIII. i. 3, *BJ* II. viii. 14.
[2] *τοὺς τὰ Ἡρώδου φρονοῦντας* (*Ant.* XIV. xv. 10).
[3] Cf. *Ant.* XVIII. i. 1, *BJ* IV. iii. 3, 9, V. i. 1, VII. viii. 1, etc.
[4] Sieffert, *PRE*^{3} xv. 287.
[5] *Ant.* XVIII. i. 6. Zealotism 'was the philosophy which had the strongest influence on everyday life, and which maintained its principles with the greatest obstinacy: it was indeed, which is not mentioned by the politic Pharisee Josephus, simply and unreservedly Pharisaism' (Keim, *Jesus of Nazara*, Eng. tr., i. 257). 'Zealotism was ultimately only thoroughgoing and logical Pharisaism' (Ewald, *Hist. of Israel*, Eng. tr., vii. 567).
[6] *BJ* II. viii. 1. [7] *Ib.* II. xvii. 3.
[8] *Ib.* VII. viii. 1.

chosen till the days of Florus, under whom Josephus first employs the term,[1] his ordinary designation up to this point being 'robbers' or 'assassins'; and (2) the fact that, being outlawed by the Romans and hated by and hating the pro-Romans, the Zealots in self-defence organized into bands and lived in troublous times by brigandage.

The Sicarii are thus described by Josephus:

> 'The Sicarii, as they are called (they are robbers), then grew very numerous. They use swords similar in length to the Persian *acinacæ*, but curved and very like what the Romans call *sicæ*, from which the robbers received their appellation because they destroyed with this weapon many victims. They mingled themselves at the festivals, as described elsewhere, in the multitude of those who had assembled from all quarters for worship and easily murdered whom they chose. And often they proceeded armed against the villages of their enemies pillaging and burning.'[2]

Josephus seemingly identifies the Sicarii and the Zealots.[3] (1) He also indirectly identifies them by assigning to the Sicarii the same policy as that pursued by the Zealots[4] and their refusal to acknowledge the emperor as *δεσπότης*;[5] and (2) the Sicarii became prominent under Felix and Festus when the Zealots were a source of annoyance to the procurators.[6] Elsewhere[7] Josephus says that the Sicarii first appeared on the scene in the days of Quirinius synchronous with the rebellion of Judas the Galilæan, the father of all Zealotism; he apparently regards the agents in that rebellion indifferently as Sicarii or Zealots. But Josephus sometimes uses language which would also suggest some distinction in his mind between Zealots and Sicarii.[8] Originally the Sicarii were perhaps a separate group from the Zealots. As the Zealots were an extremist offshoot of the Pharisees, the Sicarii were originally an extremist offshoot from the Zealots. The Zealots were the soldiers of the theocracy and the Sicarii the *francs tirailleurs* of the Zealots. In the confused years following A.D. 66 the Sicarii increased in numbers and in frightfulness, and the line of demarcation between them and the Zealots, if remaining, became very faint. Whether the Sicarii remained the extremists of the Zealots or whether Zealots and Sicarii became ultimately synonyms (so Renan and Kohler) our sources do not determine with certainty.[9]

LITERATURE.—(1) *Ancient*. — The chief ancient source is Josephus, esp. *Ant.* XVIII. i. 1, *BJ* II. viii. 1 ff., and IV. Cf. Tacitus, *Hist.* v. 1–13; Philo, *Leg. ad Gaium*; Dio Cassius, *Hist. Rom.* lxvi. 4 ff.; Hippolytus, *Ref. Omn. Hær.* ix. 21.

(2) *Modern*.—Artt. 'Zeloten' in *PRE*^{3} (F. Sieffert), and 'Zealots' in *JE* (K. Kohler); J. Hamburger, *Real-Encyclopädie für Bibel und Talmud*, Leipzig, 1866–1900, ii. 1286 ff.; also artt. 'Judas Galiläus' in *PRE*^{3} (K. Schmidt), and 'Pharisäer und Sadducäer,' *ib.* (Sieffert); J. Wellhausen, *Die Pharisäer und die Sadducäer*, Greifswald, 1874, and *Prolegomena to the Hist. of Israel*, Eng. tr., London, 1885, pp. 533–538; Schürer, *GJV*^{4}, Leipzig, 1901–11, i. 453–544 (a good account with detailed bibliography); T. Keim, *Jesus of Nazara*, Eng. tr., London, 1873–83, i. 255 ff.; A. Edersheim, *Life and Times of Jesus*, do. 1883, i. 237 ff.; J. Derenbourg, *Essai sur l'hist. et la géographie de la Palestine d'après les Thalmuds*, Paris, 1867, p. 237 ff.; W. Bousset, *Die Religion des Judentums*^{2}, Berlin, 1906, pp. 99–103; A. M. Hughes, 'Anti-Zealotism in the Gospels,' *ExpT* xxvii. [1915–16] 151–154; H. Ewald,

[1] *BJ* IV. iii. 9.
[2] *Ant.* XX. viii. 10; cf. *ib.* viii. 5, *BJ* II. xiii. 3, 6, xvii. 6, IV. vii. 2, VII. x. 1; Ac 21^{38}.
[3] In *Ant.* XX. viii. 10: *οἱ σικάριοι δὲ καλούμενοι, λῃσταὶ δὲ εἰσιν οὗτοι*, *λῃσταί* being a common term in Josephus for 'Zealots'; and in *BJ* II. xvii. 6: 'the Sicarii—for so they called robbers carrying swords in their bosoms.'
[4] Cf. *BJ* II. xiii. 4, and esp. VII. viii. 1.
[5] *Ib.* VII. viii. 1; cf. with *Ant.* XVIII. i. 6.
[6] *Ant.* XX. viii. 5, *BJ* II. xiii. 3. [7] *BJ* VII. viii. 1.
[8] *E.g.*, after describing the Sicarii and really assigning to them the policy of the Zealots in *BJ* VII. viii. 1, he adds *ἐν ᾗ τὸ τῶν ζηλωτῶν κληθέντων γένος ἤκμασεν*, as if a different class from the Sicarii. Again, having related the policy of extermination of the 'brigands' (*i.e.* Zealots) pursued by Felix (II. xiii. 2), he proceeds *καθαρείσης δὲ τῆς χώρας* (of the Zealots) *ἕτερον εἶδος λῃστῶν ἐν Ἱεροσολύμοις ὑπεφύετο, οἱ καλούμενοι σικάριοι* (*ib.* 3).
[9] Schechter's second version of the Talmud in *Ābôth de Rabbi Nathan*, 6, reads סיקרין, where the first reads *Qanna'im* (pp. 31–32).

The Hist. of Israel[4], Eng. tr., London, 1883-86, vi. 48-54, vii. 486-616 ('The Seven Years from 66 to 73 A.D.'—very readable); B. Stade, *Gesch. des Volkes Israel*, Berlin, 1887-88, ii. 628-654; J. E. H. Thomson, *Books which influenced our Lord and His Apostles*, Edinburgh, 1891, p. 66ff.; F. J. Foakes Jackson and K. Lake, *The Beginnings of Christianity*, i., London, 1920, pp. 421-425.

S. ANGUS.

ZENANA.—See FAMILY (Hindu).

ZEND AVESTA.—See AVESTA.

ZENO.—See ETHICS (Greek), STOICISM.

ZINZENDORF.—See MORAVIANS.

ZIONISM.—1. Title and object.—Zionism is the designation of a modern nationalist movement among the Jews, the programme of which was definitely formulated at an international congress held in Basel, Switzerland, on 29th-31st Aug. 1897, in the following terms: 'The object of Zionism is to establish for the Jewish people a publicly recognized, legally secured home in Palestine.'[1]

2. The basis.—The aim of Zionism, the re-establishment of the Jewish people in the land promised to the patriarchs as an eternal inheritance of the people of Israel, is a fundamental conception inherent in the religion of the Jews, and has actively asserted itself at various epochs since the destruction of Jerusalem by Nebuchadrezzar.

הארץ, the land *par excellence*, became to Israel a symbol of God's grace. The possession of the land was a sign of Israel's faith, as its loss was to be the result of disobedience. In the Tôrāh this is a recurring theme, and the prophetic utterances ring its changes in every key. Concurrently with this idea the religious ordinances took shape in accordance with political circumstances—first in close attachment to the land, and then by reason of exile from it. Psalms 137 and 126 mirror the despair of those who were driven away from, and the joy of those who returned to, Zion. A special virtue or sanctity was ascribed to its very soil: 'For thy servants take pleasure in her stones, and have pity upon her dust' (Ps 102[14]). The Talmudic ritual and other legislation, which declares mere residence in Palestine, *Yishub Ereṣ Israel*, to be of the utmost merit, observes this standpoint throughout and contains special religious precepts, *Miṣvoth ha-teluyoth ha-areṣ*, applicable only to those living in *Ereṣ Israel*, as Palestine came to be called in the language and literature of the Jews.

Of essential importance to the religious mentality of the Jews became the yearning for the departed glory of Israel, of which the sanctuary on Mount Zion was the sacred symbol, and the prayer for the restoration of the kingdom of the house of David, which was synonymous with the Messianic age, is a *Leitmotiv* in the Jewish liturgy that is repeated in almost endless variety. The prophecies and incidents which accompanied the return of the exiles from the Babylonian captivity were applied to the ages and circumstances following the destruction of the Second Temple (A.D. 70). Even though in the course of time life proved stronger than ritual and the universalist aspirations of Judaism inspired a prophetic vision which turned the restoration of Israel into a far-off spiritual ideal, it nevertheless assumed concrete appearance at the first favourable opportunity.

The patriarchate and academies which maintained a Jewish spiritual centre in Palestine for centuries after the fall of the Jewish State, the pilgrimages to Judæa from all parts of the Diaspora, and the continuous attempt to create Jewish settlements on what was always regarded as Jewish soil, testified throughout the ages to the intense desire of the Jews to regain a footing in their ancestral country. The succession of pseudo-Messiahs, from Bar Kokhba († A.D. 135) to Shabbethai Ṣebi (1626-76), always appealed successfully to this Jewish passion.[1]

Even non-Jews (such as Napoleon, in his manifesto to the Jews of Asia and Africa to re-establish themselves under his auspices in Palestine [1799]; Henry Dunant, the founder of the Red Cross, in his efforts to organize Jewish colonization there; Lord Shaftesbury, Lord Palmerston, and other Englishmen, in their sympathetic support; and Laurence Oliphant in his scheme in Gilead [1890]) realized the hold which the idea of a Jewish State in Palestine had on the Jews.

3. The revival of Jewish nationalism.—But it was only towards the middle of the 19th cent. that the sense of a national and political revival of the Jewish people assumed reality. The national resurrection of ancient Hellas, and the resurgence of national sentiment in Europe generally, proved a stimulus to Jewish hopes. The wave of Jewish solidarity that followed in the wake of the Damascus affair (1840) was a symptom, as the establishment of the Alliance Israélite Universelle (1860) was the first organized embodiment, of the re-awakened Jewish collective consciousness. Foremost in this direction was Sir Moses Montefiore (1784-1885), who, since his first visit to Palestine (1827), proved the forerunner in Western Europe of a keen, though none the less discriminating, interest in the Jewish future of Palestine. This inter-relation between Palestine and the Diaspora acted and reacted upon the general course of Jewish life, and eventually proved a measure of its vitality.

This was, however, the period of Jewish history when all the energies and resources of the Jews were wholly directed to their civil and political emancipation. This tendency, which derived its spiritual conception from the ideas of enlightenment and reform emanating from Moses Mendelssohn (1729-86) and his followers, received its most striking manifestation in the promulgation of the principles of the French Revolution, which, by the Napoleonic conquests, spread over Central Europe. The so-called Sanhedrin convened at the behest of Napoleon (1806) gave to the new orientation of Jewish life a formal sanction. It became an axiom of Jewish thought, at first in Western lands and then among the upper strata in the great communities in Eastern Europe and the Orient, that the Jews were no longer a nation but a faith, that the *beau idéal* of the Jewish future was a complete social and political adaptation to the dominant surroundings. Even in the religious sphere this process of 'assimilation,' as it is technically termed, came to be applied in an ever-widening measure. The national or particularist elements of Judaism were put into the background, and the universalist aspects emphasized. In the liturgy the references to the restoration and the rebuilding of the Temple were toned down, and in some prayer-books the words 'Zion' and 'Jerusalem' even eliminated; the vernacular began to rival, and gradually to supersede, the original Hebrew, and, while avoiding schismatic tendencies, this reform of Judaism assumed distinctive colourings adapted to the circumstances of time and place.

4. The Chovevé Zion.—While traditional and modernist conceptions of Judaism as a religion struggled for mastery on the question of the validity of ancient dogmas, forms, and ordinances, there set in a fermentation in the racial consciousness of the Jews that gave a new direction to their aspirations. True, in the West, the devoted efforts of Sir Moses Montefiore to bring his English co-religionists to a realization of Jewish potentialities in Palestine met with no effective response. The publication in 1862 by Moses Hess of *Rom und Jerusalem*, advocating the recognition of a distinctive Jewish nationality and a Jewish re-settlement in Palestine, also found no favour among the Jews of Germany, where it appeared. The publication of a pamphlet, *Auto-Emanzipation*, by Leo Pinsker, of Odessa (1881), definitely proclaiming the necessity for the establishment by the Jews of a country of their own marked, however, a definite stage in the emergence of a movement which was to captivate the imagination of the mass of the Jewish people.

The consequent rise of the movement of the Chovevé (Ḥobébé) Zion ('Lovers of Zion') broke

[1] The title 'Zionism' is said to have been used first in 1886 by Nathan Birnbaum (*nom de plume*, Matthias Acher) in his art. 'Selbst-Emanzipation,' *Ost und West*, 1902, p. 576. He subsequently, however, expressed his preference for the designation, 'Jewish Renaissance Movement,' as more comprehensive (cf. *Ost und West*, 1902, p. 526).

[1] See art. MESSIAHS (Pseudo-).

with the ideology of assimilation that had been taking hold of ever-increasing numbers of the Jewish people.[1]

5. Jewish nationalist aspirations.—The outward events detailed in art. ANTI-SEMITISM[2] reinforced the trend of sentiment and thought that was proceeding within Jewry. A complete spiritual transformation took place, particularly in the outlook of the younger generation. The effort to turn the Jews into a mere religious denomination, distinguished from their neighbours only by their religion, and even in this approximating to the ideas and customs of time and place, was opposed by the affirmation that the people of Israel, though dispersed over the whole earth, was still one people, not only bound together by a common past, but consecrated by the hopes and aspirations of a common future. It was put forward that the Jews had indeed a distinctive mission in the economy of the world—as was claimed by those who would insist upon the universality of Judaism as a world-religion—but, while recognizing that only a part of the Jewish people would settle in Palestine, it was asserted that the spiritual purpose of Israel could be worthily accomplished only in its hallowed homeland, whence, as in the days of old, it would draw inspiration from its native soil, and give again of its own genius, unaffected by alien influences, its distinctive contribution to the religion and civilization of the world. It was particularly in the cultivation of the specific Hebraic spirit of righteousness and social justice that the Jewish nationalists saw the Messianic fulfilment of the destiny of the Jew in history.

6. Modern Hebrew literature.—The nationalist conception of Jewish life found in time a host of advocates in the Jewish literature of all languages, so that it is now, particularly in the press, the most potent intellectual force in Jewry. In particular the Hebrew language, hitherto confined to prayer and study as well as to religious and literary correspondence, proved both a means and an end in nationalist propaganda. Hebrew, adapted to modern needs, became the vehicle for the issue of original works and translations, and a Hebrew press fashioned the ancient tongue for everyday use. It became the medium of instruction in schools, and finally in Palestine the vernacular of the younger generation. In the course of a few decades modern Hebrew literature revealed an intellectual individuality of a high order. Perez Smolenskin (1842–85), by his Hebrew periodical *Ha-shaḥar* ('The Dawn'), was a nationalist pioneer among the intellectuals of his time. Aḥad Ha-'am (Asher Ginzberg) (born 1856) is a thinker of profound depth and endowed with extraordinary clarity of judgment and diction. He has given a philosophical content to Jewish nationalism, and the idea of a Jewish spiritual centre in Palestine is emphasized by him in contradistinction to an exclusively politico-economic conception of the movement. Ḥaim Naḥman Bialik (b. 1873) and Saul Tchernichowsky (b. 1875) stand out among those who in these latter days have revived the inspiration of Hebrew poetic expression. Nahum Sokolow (b. 1859) wields the Hebrew language with a versatility and grace reminiscent of the wealth of classical Greek and the elegance of French literature. The new Hebrew University in Jerusalem will give modern Hebrew the definite scientific canons of which it is still in need.

Modern Hebrew is based on the Bible, with its developments in the Mishnāh, Talmud, and mediæval literature. A complete lexicon, with the latest terminology, is the מילון (*Thesaurus Totius Hebraitatis*) of Eliezer ben Yehudah, now in course of publication.

7. Jewish colonization in Palestine.—In its practical development the movement assumed the form of colonization in Palestine with the aspiration for the ultimate revival of the Jewish people, not only in its homeland but in the whole Diaspora. The work of agricultural colonization was initiated by Sir Moses Montefiore in 1854 by the settlement on the land of 35 families from Safed, and by Charles Netter in 1870 in the foundation of the still existing training farm Miqveh Israel, near Jaffa. There followed the establishment of the agricultural colony Petaḥ Tiqvah in 1878 and of Rishon le-Zion and Zikhron Ya'acob in 1882. The movement of the Chovevé Zion had by then gathered sufficient force to hold in 1884 an international conference at Kattowitz, Silesia. The idea of the colonization of Palestine, which, amid exceptional difficulties, has been put into effect by men of high ideals but no practical experience (notably, in 1882, by the so-called 'Bilu' group, composed mainly of Russo-Jewish students), enlisted the sympathies of the Western Jews more out of philanthropic than nationalist motives, while in Eastern Europe the imagination of enthusiasts was stirred by visions of a Jewish national revival. Baron Edmond de Rothschild, of Paris (b. 1845), with an idealism equalled only by his princely generosity, provided the financial means by which alone the colonies could have been maintained. In 1889 the Russian Jews established the Odessa Committee for the colonization of Jews in Syria and Palestine, while in Western Europe benevolent efforts were made to further this object. But the disappointingly slow progress in Palestine and the gradual restriction of the horizon of the Chovevé Zion led to general disillusionment and apathy.

8. Herzl and Political Zionism.—It was in 1896 that the Jewish world was aroused by the appearance of Theodor Herzl, of Vienna (1860–1904), who, in his *Judenstaat*, promulgated the view that Jews should leave the inhospitable lands inhabited by them, and set out in detail a scheme for the creation of a Jewish commonwealth. Though this publication may be said to have been distinguished by its boldness and lucidity, it was only the magnetic personality of Herzl that made of this apparently utopian project a living reality to the great masses of his people. In other ages he might have been invested with Messianic claims. In the authority he wielded and the extraordinary fascination he exercised over those who came under his sway he stands beyond compare among the Jews since Moses Maimonides (1135–1204), and time has confirmed his position in modern Jewry as that of judge and prophet in Israel. He found many notable adherents, such as Max Nordau (b. 1849), who, though holding no office, enjoys the moral leadership of the movement, and Israel Zangwill (b. 1864), who, since his secession, has become the 'candid friend' of Zionism. A congress of Jews from various parts of the Diaspora took place in Basel, 29th–31st Aug. 1897, at which there was established the Zionist Organization with its fundamental programme:

'The object of Zionism is to establish for the Jewish people a publicly recognized, legally secured home (öffentlich-rechtlich gesicherte Heimstätte) in Palestine. In order to attain this object, the Congress adopts the following measures:—

1. To promote, in so far as it serves the above purpose, the settlement in Palestine of Jewish agriculturists, craftsand tradesmen;
2. To select and organize the whole Jewish people in appropriate local and general bodies in conformity with the laws of the land;
3. To strengthen Jewish national sentiment and self-consciousness;
4. Preparatory measures to obtain the sanction of governments required for attaining the object of Zionism.'

[1] But see art. ANTI-SEMITISM.
[2] *ERE* i. 598 f.

From the fact that this new development of the nationalist movement laid special stress on the thesis that the Jewish question could not be solved in the Diaspora by the prevailing methods of philanthropy, but only in Palestine on political lines, the adherents of the Basel programme came to be known as Political Zionists, in contradistinction to the former Chovevé Zion and those who claimed that all faithful Jews are Zionists in the spiritual sense. The Zionist Organization further assumed a definite nationalist attitude on Jewish public matters, as, indeed, it developed a Jewish *Weltanschauung* generally, and thereby aroused fierce and wide-spread opposition from the leading ecclesiastical and lay heads of the Jewish communities. Zionism, however, continued to gather force in most parts of the Jewish Diaspora, and became the largest organized body of Jews since the days of Jewish independence. Altogether it exercised an ever-increasing influence on Jewish life. In Jewish communal politics, in literature, art, and education, it endeavoured to create a specific national Jewish note. The hold which it has obtained over the numerous Jewish university students, particularly on the European continent, has secured for Zionism the intellectual leadership of the Jewish people.

The immediate object of Zionism, which was to obtain from the sultan of Turkey a legal concession or charter for the settlement of large numbers of Jews on a basis of local self-government, failed. Three personal interviews of Herzl with Sultan Abdul Hamid (1901 and 1902) proved fruitless. Impelled by the pressure of urgent circumstances in the general condition of the Jews, Herzl considered the advisability of acquiring from the Anglo-Egyptian Government the region of El Arish, on the Sinai peninsula, for a Jewish autonomous settlement (1901); but, owing to the lack of water for irrigation, the scheme was found impracticable. This was followed in 1903 by an offer to the Zionists by Joseph Chamberlain (then Secretary of State for the Colonies) of the Guas Ngishu plateau in the East Africa Protectorate, which was submitted to a Zionist congress, but the mere suggestion of any project outside Palestine aroused violent opposition. A commission of exploration was sent out, but on its report to a subsequent congress this so-called Uganda scheme was definitely rejected. The secession of a number of Zionists followed and led to the establishment of the Jewish Territorial Organization (colloquially termed 'ITO') in order 'to procure a territory upon an autonomous basis for the Jews who cannot or will not remain in the lands in which they already live.' After unsuccessful attempts to find a suitable territory, in Cyrenaica, Canada, Australia, Mesopotamia, and Angola, the Jewish Territorial Organization has ceased to function.

The death of Herzl (who, in 1905, was followed in the office of president of the Zionist 'Actions Comité' [central executive] by David Wolffsohn, of Cologne, and in 1911 by Otto Warburg, of Berlin) created a profound depression in the movement, which, in the absence of political success, attempted to develop the existing institutions in Palestine and—with a hope for better prospects—to cultivate as *Gegenwartsarbeit* the nationalist idea in the Diaspora.

9. Organization and finance.—The membership of the Zionist Organization consists of those who pay annually the shekel (one shilling [raised in 1919 to 2/6], or its nominal equivalent in other coinage), which gives the right to a vote in the election of delegates to the congress, the highest Zionist forum. Women have the franchise on the same terms as men. About 800,000 persons paid the shekel in 5681 (1919–21).

The Zionist Organization is composed of national federations of Zionist societies or other bodies all over the world (*e.g.*, the English Zionist Federation, the Federation of American Zionists, etc.), and, in addition, there are recognized international federations representing specific principles, as, *e.g.*, the Misrahi, which endeavours to promote Zionism on an 'orthodox' religious basis, or the Poalé Zion, which professes Socialist doctrines.

As a general rule, Zionism is in favour of traditional Judaism, at least in a spiritual sense, but recognizes complete liberty of conscience for the individual, in accordance with the official declaration at the second congress (1898):

'Zionism does not only aim at the economic and political but also at the spiritual regeneration of the Jewish people, and in this respect stands on the basis of modern civilization, with the achievements of which it identifies itself. Zionism does not undertake anything which conflicts with the religious law of Judaism.'

In 1899 there was established, as the financial institution of the Organization, the Jewish Colonial Trust Ltd., with an authorized capital of £2,000,000, of which about £380,000 was subscribed by December 1920. Over 100,000 persons were holders of single £1 shares, the largest number of shareholders of any joint-stock company. In 1903 the Trust established a subsidiary body, the Anglo-Palestine Co. Ltd., for the special purpose of transacting banking business in Palestine. The Jewish National Fund was created in 1897 for the purchase of land in Palestine as the inalienable possession of the Jewish people. The principle regarding the nationalization of the land and the co-operative experiments undertaken by the Fund will render it not only one of the most useful agencies in the Jewish colonization of Palestine, but, from the general economic and sociological point of view, valuable and interesting in its practical application. During the Great War (1914–18), and even more since its conclusion, the Jewish National Fund has received wide-spread support all over the world.

10. Zionism since 1914.—The outbreak of the Great War necessarily created a cleavage in the international Zionist Organization, which, for geographical reasons, had its central office in Berlin. The political, and, later on, the administrative, headquarters were transferred to London, which, by the registration of its financial institutions, was already the legal *locale* of the movement.

Zionism received its most powerful impetus by the recognition on the part of the British Government of the historical connexion of the Jewish people with Palestine and the claim which this gives them to reconstruct Palestine as their national home.

There are in England traditions, dating back to Puritan times, which favour the restoration of the Jews to their ancient country. It was also in England that the first society for the Jewish colonization of Palestine was formed by George Gawler in 1845. George Eliot's *Daniel Deronda* (1876) was in those days a remarkable revelation of the Jewish nationalist aspirations of a Gentile, while the romanticism of Benjamin Disraeli, with his strong Jewish sympathies, gave a glamour to the idea of the restoration of Israel, with which the English-speaking world is familiar through the Bible.

Since 1915 the diplomatic activities of the Organization have been centred in England and the United States. In the latter country the movement received its greatest impetus by the accession of Louis D. Brandeis, Justice of the Supreme Court (since 1920 President of the Organization). In England Chaim Weizmann, whose extraordinary gifts of eloquence and statesmanship have raised him to the leadership of the movement, and Nahum Sokolow (Chairman of the Executive), who combines the philosophical serenity of a man of letters with a keen judgment of men and affairs, were able to enlist the sympathies of British public opinion and ultimately the support of the British Government. Herbert Samuel (subsequently the first British High Commissioner for Palestine) ranged his Jewish influence, while in the Cabinet as well as out of it, definitely on the side of Zionism, which found also convinced advocates among other British statesmen, notably Lloyd George, Arthur J. Balfour, and Lord Robert Cecil. Sir Mark Sykes (who in 1916 had acted for Great Britain in the Sykes-Picot Agreement with France) became the champion of Zionist interests in the settlement of the Palestine question.

On 2nd November 1917 Arthur J. Balfour, as Secretary of State for Foreign Affairs, addressed to Lord Rothschild a communication in the following terms:

'His Majesty's Government view with favour the establishment in Palestine of a national home for the Jewish people, and will use their best endeavours to facilitate the achievement of this object, it being clearly understood that nothing shall be done which may prejudice the civil and religious rights of existing non-Jewish communities in Palestine or the rights and political status enjoyed by Jews in any other country.'

This declaration, which was hailed in the Jewish world as a counterpart to the edict of Cyrus, was followed in 1918 by similar statements from the Governments of France and Italy, as well as by the support of President Wilson, and the friendly acquiescence of the pope.

On 3rd February 1919 a delegation, headed by Sokolow and Weizmann, and including the Russian Zionist leader M. Ussishkin, who spoke in Hebrew, submitted to the Peace Conference in Paris the Zionist claims in Palestine with these proposals:

'The sovereign possession of Palestine shall be vested in the League of Nations, and the government entrusted to Great Britain as the mandatory of the League, it being a special condition of the mandate that Palestine shall be placed under such political, administrative and economic conditions as will secure the establishment there of the Jewish National Home and ultimately render possible the creation of an autonomous commonwealth.'

Following the conquest of Palestine by the British under Lord Allenby, in which officially designated 'Jewish troops' took part, the above Zionist proposals to the Peace Conference were on 25th April 1920 adopted at San Remo by the principal Allied Powers and incorporated in the British Mandate for Palestine under the League of Nations, as was also the Balfour Declaration in the Treaty of Sèvres. With this solemn international recognition of the Jewish title to Palestine there emerges after a millennial struggle the national revival of a people comparatively small in numbers but incomparable in endurance and faith.

LITERATURE.—There is an extensive Zionist literature in almost all the languages spoken by Jews, notably in Hebrew, Russian, German, and English. *Die Welt*, the official organ of the movement from its inception in 1897 till 1914, contains all official statements and current topics, while the Reports of the Congresses (in German) give a full reproduction of their deliberations. Among authoritative works on Zionism are **Theodor Herzl**, *Zionistische Schriften*, ed. Leon Kellner, Berlin, 1905; **Leon Kellner**, *Theodor Herzls Lehrjahre*, Vienna, 1920; **Adolf Friedemann**, *Das Leben Theodor Herzls*, Berlin, 1914; **Max Nordau**, *Zionistische Schriften*, Cologne, 1909; **Marcel Bernfeld**, *Le Sionisme*, Paris, 1920; **N. Sokolow**, *History of Zionism: 1600–1918*, 2 vols., London, 1919; **Richard J. H. Gottheil**, *Zionism*, Philadelphia, 1914; **Aḥad Ha-'am**, *Selected Essays*, tr. Leon Simon, do. 1912; *Zionism and the Jewish Future*, by various writers, ed. H. Sacher, London, 1916; *Zionism: Problems and Views*, by various writers, ed. Paul Goodman and Arthur D. Lewis, with an Introduction by Max Nordau, do. 1916; *Zionist Work in Palestine*, by various writers, ed. Israel Cohen, do. 1911; **Frank G. Jannaway**, *Palestine and the Powers*, do. 1914; **H. Sidebotham**, *England and Palestine*, do. 1919; **Albert M. Hyamson**, *Palestine: The Rebirth of an Ancient People*, do. 1917; **Norman Bentwich**, *Palestine of the Jews*, do. 1919; **Leon Simon**, *Studies in Jewish Nationalism*, do. 1920; *Reports of the Executive of the Zionist Organisation to the XII. Zionist Congress*, do. 1921. There are numerous pamphlets published by the English Zionist Federation (official organ, *The Zionist Review*) and the Federation of American Zionists (official organ, *The Maccabæan*, and, since 1921, *The New Palestine*). Views opposed to Jewish nationalism are to be found in the writings of **Claude G. Montefiore**, the leader of Liberal Judaism in England, and in America the Central Conference of American Rabbis (representing Reform Judaism) has repeatedly expressed itself in its *Year Book* and other publications against Zionism. Cf. also **Laurie Magnus**, *Aspects of the Jewish Question*, London, 1902; **Morris Jastrow, Jr.**, *Zionism and the Future of Palestine: The Fallacies and Dangers of Political Zionism*, New York, 1919; **Lucien Wolf**, art. 'Zionism' in *EBr*[11], and 'The Zionist Peril,' *JQR* xvii. [1905] 1 ff. On special subjects cf. *JE*.

PAUL GOODMAN.

ZÔHĀR. — From the 14th cent. the *Zôhār* ('Splendour') has been the fundamental book of Jewish Ḳabbālā (*q.v.*), the fountainhead of all mystical inspiration. It has exercised a deep influence upon the spiritual and religious life of the Jews, and has extended its influence beyond the borders of Judaism. An ever-increasing literature has gathered round it; for from its first appearance it excited the curiosity of the scholar and the mystical philosopher. Its origin seemed wrapt in mystery, and to this day the problem presented by the *Zôhār* has not been solved. It is a curious fact that only one manuscript prior to the first edition seems to exist. All the researches therefore start from the printed edition. And even then they have been limited to the *Zôhār* alone, instead of being extended over the whole range of the Ḳabbālistic literature, of which this book forms only one, though a very prominent, portion.

1. Problem of origin.—The most widely accepted theory as to the origin of this book is the somewhat legendary report of the investigation which a certain Rabbi Isaac made in Spain immediately after the book became known.

Rabbi Isaac belonged to a school of mystics which had made its headquarters in Acco, and was one of the foremost representatives of the Ḳabbālistic interpretation of the Law in accordance with the system of Naḥmanides; he himself composed a supercommentary on Naḥmanides, *Meirat Enayim*, hitherto still in MS, a veritable mine of information on the pre-Zôhārite phase of the Jewish Ḳabbālā. He is said to have travelled to Granada in Spain, and to have inquired of the widow of a certain Rabbi Moses de Leon what she knew about her husband's activity in connexion with the book which he for the first time had circulated among the scholars. He offered her a very high price for the original MS, from which Rabbi Moses said that he had made the copies which he sold. The woman declared that she knew of no such copy and that Rabbi Moses used to write the things himself. On the strength of this curious report modern scholars have not hesitated to declare that this book was a deliberate forgery made by Rabbi Moses and palmed off on his contemporaries as the work of Rabbi Simeon ben Yoḥai, and that it was thus quite a modern fabrication by this obscure scholar of the 13th century. The reason assigned for ascribing this book to Rabbi Simeon ben Yoḥai (2nd cent.) was that, according to an ancient legend found in the Talmud, he and his son had taken refuge in a cave from the Roman persecution, and that he dwelt in it for thirteen years, giving himself up entirely to solitary meditation and mystical speculations. Proofs were then adduced to show the improbability of early origin, as the book teems with anachronisms. References made in it also to Talmudic laws and ceremonies of a later origin, and the author's knowledge of the system of vowels and accents, also precluded the possibility of such high antiquity.

But the whole investigation was vitiated by the fact that it rested exclusively on the printed text, which, as will be shown, was of a composite character. But even in this form the *Zôhār* is only a portion of a much larger mystical literature which has been preserved in part to this very day under various names. The relation of these independent treatises and works to the larger compilation commonly known as the *Zôhār* has not yet been investigated, and thus the true character of the *Zôhār* has remained obscure, and the legendary origin which ascribes it to an almost unknown scholar of the 13th cent. has most uncritically been accepted. It is utterly impossible to conceive that such a vast literature, containing elements of the most diverse and often contradictory character, should be the work of a single man. It is much more probable that the real *Zôhār* was only one out of many treatises of a similar kind, which by fortunate accident had come into the hands of a diligent scribe, who could easily make copies of it and profit by the sale.

(*a*) *Evidence from contents.*—The mystical speculations contained in these writings can often be traced back to those of the Hellenistic period, intermingled with later developments, but all centring in the word of the Bible. We find in them almost every system—new Platonism, the teachings of the Stoa in its later form, the allegorical interpretation so prominent in Philo, the gnostic theories—and very often in a distorted form. No less prominent are the apocalyptic visions of heavenly halls and heavenly glories of the temple in heaven, and of the terrors of hell. The ineffable name of God forms another centre of speculation, and the mystical value of letters and vowels, just as in the ancient magical papyri according to the school of the new Pythagoreans. The theories of dualism are not wanting in these schools, and often develop into a kind of trinity, consisting of father, mother, and son. The demiurgos, the syzygies, and the archons have also found a place in them. They often dissolve the literal meaning of the words and rest upon fantastical etymologies, and apparent similarities in sound and form are often the only basis for these extraordinary speculations which never lead to a logical conclusion. Almost every principle or law or even every name in the Bible is subjected to this peculiar process of sublimation, and all the thoughts float and run into one another as so many nebulæ which change their shape and form constantly, and which elude the grasp. It is all a world of mystical and fantastic imagery, in which only one principle is constant, viz. that the harmony of this world, and especially that of the celestial world, is dependent on carrying out these laws, and that Israel has the merit of being chosen to be the foremost representative of the Law, charged with its fulfilment, and thus guaranteeing not only the stability of the world, but its ultimate perfection.

The conception of God is just as vague as all the rest, for each school seems to have had its own theory, and these are all hopelessly blended. God is the *Ên Sôf* ('Infinite'), the Hoary Head, the Long Face (or, rather, the Long Suffering), Erech Appaim. He is the centre of various emanations, or rather manifestations. He is depicted as the head of the divine college, and very numerous are the anthropomorphic representations of the Shekinah, and just as vague and contradictory are the systems of creation and the many conceptions concerning the evil power (the other, or left, side) with its hosts of demons male and female, all wishing to join man for his destruction, to cover him, as it were, with so many *keliphin*, like invisible skins. There is also to be found the Platonic theory of Ideas, or divine prototypes for every earthly creature. In one separate treatise, also embodied in the *Zôhār*, the theory of metempsychosis is taught, the existence of which can be traced back to very early times in Syria and Palestine no less than in Egypt, and which later became one of the new principles carried by the Gnostic and Manichæan sects into Europe. Two physiognomic treatises called 'The Secret of Secrets' have also found a place in this compilation.

It is obvious from this brief sketch that a work of such complexity cannot be the result of a single man's activity. The utmost that can be said is that Moses de Leon either pieced some of these treatises together or copied them from older MSS in a haphazard manner.

Interspersed throughout the book there are numerous tales and legends, some of which have parallels in the other Rabbinical literature, but a large number are quite independent and cannot be found anywhere else. Some apocalyptic visions are also recorded which have a character of their own, and the whole setting reminds one strongly of the literature of the monks and cenobites, or ascetics, in Egypt and Palestine—*e.g.*, the *Lausiaca* of Palladius and others. The sages are represented as walking together in the open, discoursing on metaphysical problems, when they are joined by an aged man, the Saba, almost equal to the Abba in the *Lausiaca*, a Ta'yya, a travelling Arab, who explains the questions put and who afterwards disappears, being either the prophet Elijah or some other heavenly personage, even God Himself. The whole picture is one which can only be conceived as drawn by one of these ascetics, given up to his meditations in the wilds of Galilee or in some part east of Jordan.

Some beautiful hymns of a very exalted type, almost pantheistic, have enriched this compilation and, together with these tales, have largely contributed to its great popularity among those who were unable to follow the mystical speculation contained in its pages.

(*b*) *Evidence from language.*—The book, as printed, is not uniform. The largest part of it is written in a peculiar Aramaic dialect, which is unquestionably Palestinian. It is not the classical form, but a popularly corrupted form, such as would be the living language of the people of Galilee between the Hellenistic and Arabic periods. It approximates partly to the language of the Palestinian Talmud, which is also of Galilæan origin, and in many ways reminds one of the Targum to Ecclesiastes. It is evidently the language spoken by the Jews in Galilee, who refused to adopt Greek and to whom this was the only language. Some parts are written more correctly, others show greater corruption, and a few of the technical terms the present writer believes to be of Greek origin. Other sections of the book are in Hebrew, also of a popular form. Corruptions in either portion, especially in the Aramaic, are probably due to a large extent to the fault of copyists not fully conversant with the Aramaic, to whom these new words appeared strange. No forgery was intended, and even the association with the name of Moses de Leon as author is out of the question, and, even as copyist, should perhaps be limited to that portion of the compilation which is specifically called the *Zôhār* (for it must be made definitely clear that only a portion of the book has a right to claim this title).

The problem thus presented can now be more easily solved. It must be once for all established that the book is a compilation of a large number of independent treatises which belong to a wider circle; out of them a certain number have been selected in a haphazard manner and pieced together not by any author who endeavoured to write what it appears now to be, viz. a commentary to the five books of the Pentateuch, but by the enterprising publishers and printers of the first editions. These men have collected and selected a certain number of books, one of which—the largest one—was the *Zôhār*, or, as it was called, the *Midrash Ha-Zôhār*, or the Midrash of Rabbi Simeon b. Yoḥai. They have deliberately and arbitrarily arranged these writings together, like a chain or *catena patrum*, as a continuous commentary to the Pentateuch in the same manner as an unknown author has pieced together various other Midrashim of a Haggadic character and made out of them the well-known *Yalḳut*. These writings were not intended to form continuous commentaries, and the largest portion deals almost exclusively with the first part of Genesis, whilst originally there was no commentary at all to Deuteronomy. In order to obtain such a commentary the publishers and printers transferred wholesale portions from one section to another, and, whenever this was found impossible as the text had already been allocated to another section, they contented themselves with inserting a note to the effect that an appropriate commentary to these passages would be found in some of the preceding sections. They did not even keep the various portions carefully separated; but, when the fragments were too small, they printed them one after the other, often omitting even the name, sometimes, however, inserting in the text the title, such as *Raza* ('Mystery'), which a reader could not now easily understand, being unaware of the fact that it was an interpolation. Thus it confuses still more the already difficult text.

The printers, however, endeavoured to make it clear that the book published by them was a compilation of various treatises pieced together by them, for they stated on the title-page that in addition to the *Sepher Ha-Zôhār* they had included in this publication the following: *Sitre Tôrāh* ('Mysteries of the *Tôrāh*'), *Midrash Hane'lam* ('The Hidden Midrash'), *Tosefta* (additions to some sections), *Ra'ya Mehemna* ('*Pastor fides*,' 'The True Shepherd')—thus far in the Mantua edition, and in the Cremona edition the following are also added: the *Bahir*, *Midrash Ruth*, *Midrash Ḥazita* (on Songs), the section *Ta Hazi* ('Come and Behold'), *Hekhalot* ('The Halls of Heaven and Hell'), and again other additions, such as *Pikkudîm* ('Ordinances'). This fact, hitherto entirely ignored, is of decisive importance for the history of the *Zôhār*, inasmuch as it proves that in the very first editions both of Mantua and of Cremona we have only a compilation before us, and not a homogeneous work. All the investigators who have taken the *Zôhār* to be a homogeneous compilation, the skilful forgery of an ingenious author, have been led completely astray.

Moreover, no notice was taken by the scholars of the other books belonging to the same cycle. Nor have the two editions, which appeared almost simultaneously, been compared—the folio edition of Cremona (1558), which already contains various texts printed side by side, and the other edition at Mantua (1558–60) with the introduction by Rabbi Isaac de Lattes, in three quarto volumes, which has since become the authorized edition, all subsequent editions being faithful reprints page for page of this edition. The Cremona edition has only been reprinted twice, once in Lublin (1623) and a second time in Sulzbach with the help of the famous Knorr von Rosenroth (1684). In all the other (quarto) editions Genesis and Exodus form each a separate volume. The third volume contains the *Zôhār*, etc., of the remaining three books of the Pentateuch. Curiously enough, even before the *Zôhār* appeared in Mantua, the *Tikkune ha-Zôhār*, or 'Additions and Improvements to *ha-Zôhār*,' appeared in Mantua in 1557. It consists of 70 chapters, all dealing practically with the cosmogony and with the first verse of Genesis. They are all written in the same style (except that they are arranged in a more systematic order) and show the same peculiarities as the chief portion of the *Zôhār*. The language is also Aramaic, and there is scarcely anything to distinguish one from another. The same holds good of the *Zôhār Ḥadash*, 'the *New Zôhār*,' which appeared for the first time in Salonica (1597), compiled from MSS brought from Palestine. It contains, in addition to the new Zôhāric matter on the Pentateuch, similiar mystical commentaries to the five scrolls or *Megilloth*, *i.e.* Lamentations, Song, Esther, Ruth, and Ecclesiastes.

In addition it may now be mentioned that the present writer possesses separate MSS of those writings which have been incorporated in the *Zôhār*, such as *Sitre Tôrāh* and fragments of *Ra'ya Mehemna*, all corroborating the view that the book in its printed form is a compilation made in modern times of older material. A further and more decisive proof is now found in the MS of the *Zôhār* (*Codex Gaster*, no. 747) in the present writer's possession, older than the print and of Spanish Oriental origin. It differs very considerably from the printed edition. It contains only parts of what is now called the *Zôhār*, but none of the other texts which have been joined on to it in that edition. With the help of this MS also one of the chief problems connected with the *Zôhār* can now be satisfactorily solved. It is well known that the book is ascribed to Rabbi Simeon b. Yoḥai of the 2nd cent., and it was not very difficult for the critics to prove this claim untenable, inasmuch as the book in its entirety not only contains unquestionable anachronisms but also refers in sundry passages to and quotes from the Talmud and even from later forms of liturgy. But this wrong assumption of Simeon b. Yoḥai's authorship rests upon a mistake or a neglect on the part of the printers. The opening formula has been omitted, and this made all the difference, for it is a well-known fact in the Midrashic literature that many an ancient book is quoted by the first name which is mentioned at the opening of the book; it does not mean, *e.g.*, that R. Kahana is the author of the Pesiḳta or R. Tanhuma of the Midrash which go under their names. The title is derived from the opening sentence where these two scholars are mentioned. There are other books of a similar character, such as *Midrash Ḥazita*, mentioned on the title-page of the *Zôhār* and forming part of the compilation. It is the initial word of the book, and it is the same with the *Midrash Tadeshe*, etc., and the very title of the *Zôhār* is probably derived from that name occurring in the opening sentence. In the MS, similarly, the opening formula is thus 'Pataḥ R. Simeon b. Yoḥai,' which would thus explain absolutely the origin of the title *Midrash of R. Simeon b. Yoḥai*, by which this Midrash was quoted almost on its first appearance by the oldest authorities. This does not mean that R. Simeon was the author, but only that the book began with the mention of his name. Unfortunately the printers left out these initial words, for no obvious reason except perhaps in order to give prominence to that weighty mystical pronouncement which stands as a fitting introduction to this mystical book. Now there can no longer be any question of connecting this book with R. Simeon and considering him as the author. The anachronisms, on the other hand, are not general. The treatises embodied in the book may and probably do all belong to different periods. They represent a constant development which has been going on for a long time in various schools of Palestine. Each of these component elements must henceforth be studied separately, for we are dealing with a mass of material accumulated during centuries, much of which is evidently of high antiquity.

2. History and influence.—The history of Jewish mysticism has still to be written, for much of it which is very old has for some reason or other been declared to be of more recent origin. The *argumentum ex silentio* has been too often used to prove the non-existence of mystic speculations in olden times in spite of the apocalyptic and magical literature which flourished already in the early centuries before and after the destruction of the Temple. The mystics had very little in common with the scholars; they very seldom committed their speculations to writing—it was all secret lore; even that which they wrote down they hid away carefully. Yet the continuity was not broken, and the secret doctrine was handed down from generation to generation as Ḳabbālā, *i.e.* oral mystic tradition. Thus old and new were constantly blended; to old systems of theosophic speculations newer were added, until it was found necessary to fix them in writing, and in this Ḳabbālistic activity must be found the origin and the explanation of the *Zôhār* and the Zôhāric literature. In it we find embedded, side by side, those old speculations from the time of Philo downwards, on to probably the 5th and 6th cent., when they were the object of concentrated meditations in Galilee and there preserved until the time when they became the common property of scholars and mystics alike. It would be easy to trace almost every phase and aspect of older mysticism which flourished in Syria, Palestine, and Egypt in one page or another of the books referred to; they will often stand together on one page. It is therefore futile to draw up the system of the Ḳabbālā contained in the *Zôhār*, and those systems that have hitherto been evolved out of that book are only partial representations of one section or another, far from exhausting even one of the many writings embedded in the *Zôhār*. Mystical commentators have felt this, and have therefore often singled out one portion as the object of their interpretation. Such has been the case with the so-called *Idra Rabba*, 'The Big Hall,' and *Idra Zutta*, 'The Small Hall,' in Num. and Deut., or again the *Siphra de Seniuta*, 'The Book of the Veiled Mystery,' in Exodus. These were treated either together with other treatises or published and commented upon separately.

The philosophic movement which found its highest expression in Maimonides' († 1204) *Guide of the Perplexed* led to a rationalistic interpretation of the Law, which by its very extravagance called forth the mystical reaction which succeeded in practically extinguishing it.

The Ḳabbālistic doctrine then received a great impetus through the works of Naḥmanides (1263), especially through his widely read and highly appreciated commentary to the Pentateuch.

Mysticism flourished then. There were other great scholars who had been deeply impressed by the older Ḳabbālistic speculations by Naḥmanides, Solomon b. Adrat, and others who had formed a school of mystics in Palestine, and especially in Acco. These schools were probably revivals of older schools and mystic circles which continued to flourish unobserved in the mountains and caverns of Galilee, and also on the banks of the Jordan, where from immemorial times schools of prophets, of ascetics and recluses, of Essenes and Ḥasîdîm, have continued their mystical speculations and contemplative life. The storm of the Crusade swept over those parts, destroyed the schools, and drove the adepts into other countries. The remnants of their literature were also carried far and wide, and that is, to the present writer's mind, the only explanation of the sudden appearance in the 12th and 13th centuries of such a large number of mystical writings; it is probable that some of these fell into the hands of Moses de Leon, if he is at all to be connected with it. They represent often divergent tendencies, and are the outcome of various schools of thought.

The Ḳabbālā entered into ever-widening circles, especially as men of the highest authority in Rabbinical learning confessed themselves to be students of it. No wonder, therefore, that the new mass of Ḳabbālistic material should overflow its narrower borders and cover practically the whole field of Jewish learning. The political persecutions to which they were exposed also drove the Jews more and more to an inner contemplative life. Soon after their appearance these mystical writings spread far and wide, and within a short space of time had conquered the mind of the people.

Menaḥem Recanati (1290–1330) already makes full use of this *Midrash of R. Simeon b. Yoḥai* in his commentary to the Pentateuch, in which he gives large abstracts—a few years only, as it were, after the death of Moses de Leon. And, if it could be proved that the author of the *Libnat Hasappir* (Jerusalem) had lived before that period, that would at once destroy the legend of de Leon's authorship, for he also quotes large portions from the *Zôhār*. Be that as it may, the *Zôhār* henceforth held undisputed sway, and it was universally accepted in the form of the Mantua edition which had the 'imprimatur' of R. Isaac de Lattes. All the other mystical writings, some of which, as shown, were of equal antiquity and of equal importance, were none the less considered of less value.

The influence of the *Zôhār* became still greater when a new mystical school rose again in Galilee in the middle of the 16th century. There R. Isaac Luria (1534–72) evolved a new system of Ḳabbālā, a further development of some of the leading principles found in the *Zôhār*, and founded a school in Safed. It became the ruling system, being further developed by his colleagues and pupils, Ḥayim Vital Calabreze († 1620), Moses Cordovero († 1570), and Meir Popers († 1662). The Jews became then so deeply immersed in the study of the Ḳabbālā, and so much intoxicated by the fumes of these mystical speculations, that they easily fell a prey to the Messianic claims of Shabbethai Ṣebi. The pseudo-Messiah, his prophet Nathan of Gaza, and most of his followers were deeply versed in the study of the *Zôhār*, and were able to manipulate its obscure wordings to further their own purposes. Real learning was sapped by this mystic teaching of the *Zôhār*, which superseded the study of the Talmud and of Rabbinical literature. A prominent place having been given to the efficacy of prayers and their mystical meaning, the whole character of the Prayer Book became almost totally changed by the introduction of mystical formulas, and by the interpolation of mystical names and symbols which almost entirely destroyed the sublime simplicity of the original diction. Through the influence of the *Zôhār* and the Ḳabbālā, a new mystical force was developed among the Jews. A spiritual love, an immersion in the Divine, was taught by the founder of the Ḥasîdîm to be of higher value, if possible, than the strict observance of the letter of the Law. Thus light and shadow, action and reaction, have succeeded one another with the spread of the Ḳabbālā, and notably of the *Zôhār* and the Zôhāric literature. Its influence is now greatly on the wane, and the time has therefore come when all the problems connected with that literature can again be taken up and studied in the light of independent scholarship.

The study of the Ḳabbālā and subsequently of the *Zôhār* was not limited to Jews alone. One has only to mention Pico della Mirandola, Reuchlin, Paracelsus, and even Luther to show the keen interest Christian scholars have taken in it. Many a Christian scholar found in the *Zôhār* proof of the dogmas of the Trinity, hence a large number of pamphlets *c.* 1650–1800. Especially meritorious was the work of Knorr von Rosenroth, whose *Kabbala Denudata* (i., Sulzbach, 1677–78, ii., Frankfort, 1684) has remained the most reliable source for subsequent Christian scholars, down to the latest translation in *The Kabbala Unveiled*, by S. L. Macgregor Mathers (London, 1887).

Jewish commentators ever since the appearance of the *Zôhār* have been busy drawing up glossaries of its rare and technical expressions, and then explaining the text itself, or laying down rules of exegetical interpretation. Some attempted to draw up a system of the Ḳabbālistic teaching of the *Zôhār*, but these stood already under the influence of Luria and his school. Towards the middle of the 18th cent., and in Italy before that time, doubts began to be raised as to the genuineness of the authorship, and practically the whole controversy turned round the one question as to whether the *Zôhār* was written by R. Simeon b. Yoḥai or not. A commentary to the whole of the

Zôhār, consisting of twelve folio volumes, the work of a modern scholar in Morocco, was seen by the present writer many years ago, in MS, but so far all traces of its whereabouts seem to have been lost.

LITERATURE.—The fullest bibliography on the *Zôhār* and Zôhāric literature down to 1863 is that given by J. Furst, *Bibliotheca Judaica*, iii. [Leipzig, 1863] 329–335. For additional bibliography see *JE*, *s.v.* 'Zohar,' xii. 693, to which may be added the French translation by Pavly. M. GASTER.

ZOROASTRIANISM.—Zoroastrianism is the religious doctrine attributed to Zoroaster which gradually became the prevalent religion of Īrān and notably was the State religion under the Sasanian dynasty (A.D. 211–640). It is still professed by the Parsis of Bombay and by some sporadic communities in Persia. Zoroastrianism is one of the most interesting religions of the world. Its doctrines and rites are well known either in their present form or as they are to be found in the Pahlavi books and in the Avesta (*q.v.*).

1. Zoroaster (Zarathushtra).—There is much obscurity concerning the person of the founder and the time and place of his preaching. Although the Avesta is the Zoroastrian Bible, it is quite certain that only a small portion of the book can with probability be regarded as the work of the prophet. That portion is the *Gāthās*, or versified preachings, written in a dialect slightly different from the language of the rest of the Avesta. The Gāthic dialect, the late Avestan dialect, and the language of the inscriptions of the Achæmenids are three closely related forms of Old Iranian.

In the *Gāthās* Zoroaster appears as a very real and human personality, devoid of all the marvellous features which surround him in later literature. He is presented there as the son of Pourushaspa of the Spitama family. For ten years he had only one disciple, Maidhyoimaoṅha, his cousin. At last he converted to his doctrine Vīshtāspa, a local prince; but the *Gāthās* show that much resistance still was offered to the prophet, who, in some places, exhibits signs of anxiety. He had undertaken to reform not only the beliefs but also the social habits of the tribes of Eastern Īrān among which he had settled. His desire was to deter them from nomadic life and to induce them to devote themselves to husbandry. According to tradition, Zoroaster had come from Western Īrān (he is represented as a native of Raghæ in Media), a region which was more advanced in civilization. He was, so it seems, trying to introduce the Western customs into the wilder districts of the East. The names of Zoroaster and all the persons of his and Vīshtāspa's families have nothing mythical about them, but refer to horses, camels, etc. In later tradition Zoroaster's birth has been surrounded with marvels. He was supposed to have inherited the *xvarenaṅh* (=O. Pers. *farnah*), or 'glory,' of Yima, the law-giver of ancient ages. The *daēvas* repeatedly sought to kill him. Ahura Mazdāh and the *amesha spentas* entered into communication with him and revealed to him the tenets of the new faith. He is represented as having subsequently travelled in Bactria and in Seistan.

Vīshtāspa's conversion took place after the prophet had given miraculous signs of his power. It was followed by a long series of wars against the unbelievers. During those battles Zoroaster was killed near an altar with a group of priests. There was all the time a conflict going on between the sage and sorcerers—a feature which is probably truer to the facts than most of the other elements of the legend. Zoroaster was a Magian who, no doubt, rebelled against the practices of the majority of the members of his corporation. As will be shown later, Zoroaster's doctrine is a reform and an epuration.

The Magi (*q.v.*) are mentioned by Herodotus as a Median tribe along with the 'Αριζαντοί ('the nobles') and a few other names which may have referred to groups of the population more or less similar to the Indian castes. In *Museon*, new ser., ix. 121, the present writer has interpreted the name 'Magi' as meaning 'the helpful, the curers or the averters of evil spirits' (cf. Gr. Μαχάων, μῆχαρ, μηχάνη). This is quite consistent with what is known of their activities through the statements of the ancients. Astyages consulted them as oneiromancers.[1] They were astrologers, physicians, magicians. While there is little trace of those functions in the Avesta, two of their most characteristic customs have crept into Zoroastrianism—probably after Zoroaster's time: the giving over of dead bodies to the vultures and the next-of-kin marriages. The former of those practices is apparently borrowed from the populations of Central Asia, whose shamans are a kind of prototype of the Magians.

Although Zoroaster occupies a very special position among those Magians, he has been regarded by the Greeks as the Magian *par excellence*. Folk-etymology has connected Ζωροάστρης with ἀστήρ and has contributed in associating Chaldæan astrology with the Iranian sage. The Magi of Persia gradually adopted a form of Zoroastrianism combined with less exalted beliefs (cf. below). In this way the name of Zoroaster was attached to Magians and magic by the Greeks, who do not seem to have had—at an ancient period—any clear idea of the prophet's own teaching and real personality. In ancient as well as in modern times Persia was a country of religious thought. Moreover, the Aryans there were in contact with the ideas of Semites, Sumerians, Caucasians.[2] The unity of faith as it is found in Sasanian times is the final stage of an evolution and has resulted in the suppression of the records concerning the other forms of Mazdæism which existed in Media and Persia and of which some scanty trace seems to have been preserved in Armenian literature.[3] Zoroastrianism ignores the Achæmenians. On the other hand, neither these kings nor Herodotus, their contemporary, mention the name of the prophet. This circumstance, of course, is not in favour of the opinion often given that Darius and his successors were faithful Zoroastrians.[4]

2. His reform.—Herodotus gives a description of the religion of the Persians which applies admirably to what we know of primitive Aryan religion.

> 'The Persians ascend the highest peaks of the mountains and offer sacrifice to Zeus, calling the whole vault of the sky Zeus, and they also sacrifice to Sun, Moon, Earth, Fire, Water and Winds. . . .'[5]

For many Persians this sky-god may still have been called Dyāus pitar. The Achæmenian inscriptions, however, show that Darius called his supreme god Auramazda, like the Zoroastrians, and this deity appears there with the lofty features which he possesses in the Avesta. He has an omnipotent will (*vashna*) and an absolute power (*xshathra*). There are representations of the 'confessions' (*fravarti*=Av. *fravashi*) or *genii* of the Mazdæans, an expression preserved also in the name of the Median king Phraortes. Names like Artaxerxes, Artaphernes, etc., show reverence both for *arta* (Av.=*asha*), 'truth,' 'justice,' and for *farnah* (Av.=*xvarenaṅh*), 'supernatural glory of the kings.' Moreover, there is a solemn con-

1 Herod. i. 107.

2 The Massagetæ and Caspii are reported as exposing their corpses (Moulton, *Early Zoroastrianism*, p. 192).

3 A. Meillet, *JA* vii. 127.

4 Most recently in Dhalla's *Zoroastrian Theology*.

5 Herod. i. 13; cf. art. ARYAN RELIGION.

demnation of *drauga*, 'lie,' which recalls the hatred of the Zoroastrian for the *druj*. On the other hand, the specific name of the spirit of lie, Angra Mainyu, is not mentioned, while much emphasis is laid on other gods (*aniyā bagāha*), and especially on Mithra and Anāhita.

Now, it is precisely the originality of Zoroaster's reform to have rejected all the 'other gods,' including those two prominent deities who later found their way back into Zoroastrianism. The use of representations for the gods and the practice of burial are other un-Zoroastrian features, so that one is impressed equally by the striking resemblances and the essential differences between the two creeds. Darius's Mazdæism represents precisely the kind of *milieu* in which Zoroastrianism could have arisen as a special sect, under the influence of a reformer inspired by an exalted religious ideal. It is probable that Zoroaster's school, although it had not yet taken hold of Īrān at large, had already existed for some time at that period. The name of Darius's supreme god, Auramazda, is a crystallization of Mazdāh Ahura, 'Wisdom, the Lord,' as it appears in the *Gāthās*. The language of those hymns is much more archaic than Darius's language. Both versification and expression in Zoroaster's sermons have a flavour of antiquity quite familiar to a reader of the Veda. The fact that the dialect is different from the normal form of the sacred language of the Avesta makes it almost certain that it was the vernacular actually spoken by the prophet. This obliges us to push the date of his publication back at least two centuries before Darius's reign. This impression can only be confirmed by the great phonetic adulteration in the names of the Mazdæan religious terms as they appear in Pahlavi, the vernacular of Persia from 300 B.C. onwards.[1] While the Pahlavi translation of the later parts of the Avesta is not too far from the original, it gives a very poor rendering of the *Gāthās*, which have been misunderstood both in their expression and in their spirit. The translation of those hymns by J. Darmesteter, based mainly on the Pahlavi rendering, is a demonstration *ab absurdo* of the impossibility of understanding the *Gāthās* in the atmosphere of the 2nd cent. A.D. Darmesteter's great effort to place the composition of the whole Avesta in that period is no less of a failure. His argument is only secondarily based on a few passages of the latest parts of the Avesta which may show traces of Judaic or Buddhistic literature. His main reason for placing the Avesta in Neo-Platonic times is derived from resemblances between the religious allegories of the *Gāthās* and the δυνάμεις of Philo, and especially between Vohu Manah and the Logos. This circumstance has also struck Lagrange.[2] 'To suppose the gāthic system old,' he says, 'is to suppose the development of philosophy before the Greeks.' The fault of those scholars is that they have mistaken ethical abstractions or allegories for philosophical concepts and have ignored the fact that the antiquity of most of those very conceptions is vouchsafed by their presence both in the proper names of ancient Persia and in the Veda.

Asha (*arta*), 'justice,' 'truth,' the law of men, gods, and the universe is the Vedic *ṛta*. It appears in Artatama, the name of a Mittani king, and later in Artaxerxes, Artaphernes, Artachæes, etc. *Ārmaiti*, 'prudence,' 'wisdom,' is the Vedic Aramati, 'prudence,' 'piety'; *Haurvatāt*, 'salvation,' 'health,' is Ved. *saurvatātī*; *Xshathra Vairya*, 'wished-for kingdom,' recalls the *kṣatra* of Varuṇa, the great moral god of India, protector of the *ṛta*, in the same way as Mazdāh is the god of the *asha* (=*arta*). Varuṇa is called 'Wise Asura,' just as Mazdāh is 'Asura-Wisdom.'

[1] Οσλαγνο=Verethraghna, Μιορο=Mithra, Φαρρο=Xvarenaṅh, Σαορηοαρ=Xshathra Vairya, on the Indo-Scythian coins—Vohu Manah is rendered in Strabo by Ὠμανός.

[2] *RB*, 1904, pp. 42, 199.

The very name of Ahura Mazdāh, often regarded as characteristic of Zoroastrianism, has been found in a list of Assyrian gods published by Scheil[1] in the form of Assara Mazaash. It is immediately followed by the seven *igigi*, or 'good spirits,' which suggests that the association of Ahura Mazdāh with the *amesha spentas*, 'immortal holy spirits,' may be an old one like that of Varuṇa with the *ādityas* in India.[2] There are many abstractions in the Veda. It is clear that Zoroaster has combined in a coherent ethical system data which he found around him, transmitted in the teachings of the sages of Īrān as well as of India. By comparing the religion of the *Gāthās* with that of the oldest Vedic hymns and with what is known of the current beliefs of ancient Īrān one can form an idea of Zoroaster's originality. The Vedas knew of two series of gods, (1) the *devas*: sky, light, storm, etc., *i.e.* gods as powers of nature (sensuous deities—θεοί), and (2) the *asuras*, or gods in their relation to men as protectors of morality, inspiring awe, reverence, and fear (δαίμονες). Varuṇa, the great *asura*, was the ethical god *par excellence*. In later times the term *asura* came to be used of dreaded deities and evil spirits (the moral aspect of divinity with the Aryans was mostly associated with the cult of the souls—*e.g.*, in the Great Erinyes), while the *devas* became the real gods. The exaltation of Ahura Mazdāh in Īrān, which is certainly older than Zoroaster, shows that there was a school there promoting the ethical side of religion. As Herodotus shows, however, the people remained attached to the *daēvas* (=*devas*). Darius's religion is a combination in which the Magian ethical system is predominating. The same compromise eventually prevailed in later matured Zoroastrianism, which accepted Mithra (god of light, etc.), Anāhita (goddess of water, great mother), and the sacrifice of the *haoma* (=Ved. *soma*, 'the drink of life'). The old mythical apparel came back in the *yashts*, or hymns, addressed to the moon, Sirius, the god of victory, etc. But Zoroaster carefully avoids alluding to any of those deities and condemns the sacrifice of *haoma duraosha*[3] practised by the *kavis*. This very name, execrated in the *Gāthās*, is applied to the devotees of the *devas* in India and reappears in late Mazdæism as the name of a dynasty of legendary heroes. Zoroaster is evidently a radical reformer wishing to extricate the strict monotheism which existed potentially around him from all the concessions which it was making to tradition, and to rid man completely from all allegiance to deities implicated in magic.

The systematic character of his reform is even more clearly seen in his way of handling the moral abstractions. Much older than himself, they had had time to receive a materialization in the religion of the people, while their abstract meaning had not been lost by the priests. In Zoroaster's writings their moral meaning is always the real one, unmistakable for the initiated devotee, but at the same time there is in many passages an allusion to the material aspect of the hypostasis, so that sometimes the text has both an esoteric and an exoteric meaning.

So in *Ys.* xxxi. 10 the 'cattle-tending husbandman' is called 'the man that furthers Vohu-Manah,' 'Good Mind,' while for a simple devotee this would apply to Vohu Manah as the protecting genius of cattle. Xshathra Vairya is the 'Kingdom to be wished for,' the 'reign of justice and of Mazdāh,' but it is also 'the genius of metals.' In *Ys.* xxx. 7 one sees how both conceptions are reconciled: 'By thy retributions through the metal, man may gain the prize.' That prize is often called *xshathra savanham* ('kingdom of blessings'). It is paradise, the kingdom of the righteous, which will follow the universal ordeal through the molten metal. Asha (=Arta) 'Law,' 'Right' is the genius of fire, and, in *Ys.* xxxiv. 4, it is easy to

[1] *Rec.* xiv. 100.

[2] Cf. art. ORMAZD.

[3] *Yasna*, xxxii. 14.

find that the connexion existed in Zoroaster's times, although Asha in his writings always means 'Law': 'Of thy Fire, O Ahura, that is mighty through Law (Asha), we desire that it may be for the faithful (*ashavan*) delight . . .' And, indeed, the relation of fire to the great law of the universe is much older, since it already transpires in the Vedas in which *agni*, 'fire,' is called *prathamajas ṛtasya*,[1] 'primogenitus Legis,' *ṛtaprajāta*,[2] 'natus de Lege,' and very often *ṛtavan*, 'the faithful of Law.'

Ārmaiti, 'Good Purpose,' 'Prudence,' 'Devotion,' was at the same time a name of the earth, as shown, *e.g.*, in a passage like *Ys.* xlvii. 3, which literally reads: 'Thou art, O Mazdāh, the Holy Father of that Spirit (Vohu Manah) that has created for us the Ox, bringer of blessings. Good Purpose (Ārmaiti) is his pasture giving him peace.'

Comparison with parallel passages shows that Xshathra, 'the Kingdom,' is compared to a meadow,[3] that the Ox, bringer of blessings, is another name of the paradise.[4] The passage, therefore, was quite spiritual, but, no doubt, the uninitiated were likely to find in it an invocation to obtain from Mazdāh, through the genius of cattle, that he bestow cattle, while earth would provide meadows and peace would reign. Similarly Haurvatāt, 'Perfect Happiness,' and Ameretāt, 'Immortality,' may express the blessings of future life, but they are also water and plants, and in *Ys.* li. 7 both meanings are present together: 'Give me, O Thou, the creator of cattle, water and plants, give me immortality and perfect happiness.'

In everything, thus, the reform of Zoroaster appears to us as a purification, a spiritualization of the beliefs current at the time among both the sages and the people. It is also a systematization. The preacher has built up a coherent religious doctrine out of elements provided by a tradition in which the ethical element was predominating.

3. His doctrine.—The substance of Zoroaster's doctrine is to be found in this sentence of *Ys.* xxx.:

'The two primal spirits who revealed themselves in vision as twins are the Better and the Bad in thought, word and action. And between these two the wise knew to choose aright, the foolish not so.'

This is the essence of Zoroaster's morals which developed later into a large cosmogonic system. By his right choice the man who obeys law (*ashavan*) helps in the final victory of the good spirit, the spirit of the wise lord (Ahura Mazdāh), over the spirit of deceit and treachery (*druj*, Angra Mainyu). Inspired by a right mind (Vohu Manah), he takes his stand against the whole world of the *druj*, its satellites (*daēva*), its priests (*kavi*, *karapan*), its sorcerers (*yatu*) and fairies (*pairikā*), and its cult (sacrifices of living creatures and of the intoxicating drink, *haoma*). He repudiates with special emphasis nomadic life with brigandage and strife, the life of infidels (*dregvant*) and Turks. He leads with wisdom of purpose (*ārmaiti*) an orderly existence, according to law (*asha*), in obedience (*sraosha*) to the good spirit represented by a moral adviser (*ratu*). In this way he will realize in this world and hereafter the 'wished-for kingdom' (Xshathra Vairya), the kingdom of blessings, the kingdom of the best (Vahista manah), the good reward (*ashi, adā*) with perfect happiness (Haurvatāt) and immortality (Ameretāt), that will follow the last ordeal (*yāh mazishta*) and the renovation of the world (*frashō-kereti*).

4. Mazdæism matured.—Although pure Zoroastrianism was not very mystical, it was fairly abstract and was very radical in its rejection of some essential elements of traditional Persian religion. The profound impression which the prophet made on some elements of the Iranian population has gradually secured the victory to the doctrine bearing his name, but only at the price of a compromise with the current beliefs. Dualism loses its strictly moral character. It is interpreted in terms derived from the old mythical contest found among both Babylonians (Marduk and Tiamat, Zu and Enlil,[5] etc.) and Aryans (storm-myths in which some god of light or sky kills a dragon).

There were from the beginning two principles, independent, hostile, and essentially opposed to one another. The evil spirit (Pahl. Ahriman), spirit of darkness, having arisen from the abyss, has rushed to destroy the light and the creatures of Ormazd (=Ahura Mazdāh). The latter hits him with the *Ahuna-vairya* prayer as a weapon, but the fight is not concluded. There will be a period during which there will be some kind of equilibrium between the power of the two spirits. The good spirit will finally conquer. There are pure and helpful creatures in the service of Ormazd, and impure ones constituting the host of his opponent. The whole world is divided in that way. Any defilement of a good being by an impure one helps Ahriman, but the moral contest of Zoroaster is introduced into this system also, and by his 'right choice,' his good deeds, good words, and good thoughts, man is fighting for the victory of Ormazd.

Mazdæan dualism approaches monotheism closely, since Ormazd is to prevail ultimately and since the evil spirit is a mere negative entity. Moreover, serious efforts were made in Īrān to reduce dualism to unity. The Zervanites placed *zervan akarana*, 'unlimited time,' at the beginning of things. Others presented *bakht*, 'fate,' as the ruler of everything. In that dualistic division of the universe the *daēvas* as a whole have remained the servants of Ahriman, and among them are even Indra and Nāsatya (=Aśvins), who are among the most revered gods of the Indo-Iranians. Yet, under the name of *yazatas*, a few have been admitted into the host of Ormazd. Among them in particular is Mithra, god of contracts and oaths, eye of Mazdāh, the god that gives victory to the armies. His association with the sun, his part as a mediator, as a benefactor of mankind by his killing of the primeval bull, etc., are explained in art. MITHRAISM. The longest hymn of the Late Avesta (*Yasht* x.) is addressed to Mithra. It is one of the finest, with *Yasht* v., devoted to Ardvī Sūra Anāhitā (Y+5), the female member of the great Persian triad: Mazdāh—Mithra—Anāhitā. She is 'lady of waters' and 'lady of birth,' the Iranian equivalent of Ishtar and of the Sumerian Nin-Ellā.[1] She is sometimes identified with a mythical source on Mount Hara, from which all waters flow down in a thousand outlets, fertilizing the earth.

Another *yazata* enjoying a very special position is Ātar, 'fire.' For Indo-Iranians fire was the most essential part of the cult. Their priests were *ātharvan*, 'fire-priests.' Fire was conceived as a representative of divine essence on earth. It was the great source of life, burning in the bodies of men and animals (as *vohu fryana*, 'good friend'), in the stems of plants (*urvazishta*), in air and ether, in paradise itself. As *berezisavaṅh*, 'very useful,' it shoots up before Ahura Mazdāh and is kept with great care in the fire temples. The fire that represents the emanation of divine essence in kings is the famous *xvarenaṅh* (=O. Pers. *farnah*) mentioned above. It decides the fate of the kings. The Avesta preserves a curious myth in which Frangrasyan (Pers. Afrāsiyāb), a fiend, in a series of onrushes endeavours to catch hold of the *xvarenaṅh*, just in the same way as Zu on high battles for the tablets of fate in Chaldæan mythology.[2]

As to Verethraghna, the genius of victory, he was destined to a brilliant destiny in some quarters —*e.g.*, in Armenia, where, under the name of Vahakan, he usurped all the Herculean exploits of a dragon-killer attributed in turn in Īrān to Thraētaona (Pers. Faridūn), Keresāspa, and Rustam.

The *amesha spentas*, 'holy immortal beings,'

[1] *Rigveda*, x. v. 7. [2] *Ib.* II. xxiii. 15.
[3] *Ys.* xlviii. 11. [4] *Ib.* xliv. 6–12.
[5] M. Jastrow, *The Rel. of Bab. and Assyr.*, Boston, 1898, pp. 538 ff.

[1] Cf. *JAOS* xxxvi. 301. [2] Jastrow, p. 537.

however, officially remain at the head of the Zoroastrian pantheon of good gods.[1] They form the court of Ormazd, and, although their moral aspect is not forgotten, their material functions have become paramount. Ahriman is able to neutralize those archangels with a host of arch-demons which incarnate the opposites of the virtues represented by the *amesha spentas*. Among them is Aka Manah, 'bad spirit,' opposed to Vohu Manah, Aēshma daēva, 'violence' (the Asmodeus of Tobit's story), etc.

If the *amesha spentas* may be considered as archangels, protectors of the most important portions of creation, the *fravashi* (Pahl. *fravarti*) are like the guardian-angels of all individual persons.[2] They are a duplicate of the soul, existing before birth and uniting themselves to the soul after death. The name seems to mean 'confession,' 'conscience,' and may be an equivalent of *daēnā*, 'conscience,' 'religion,' which survives a man and is shaped after his conduct during life. In origin, however, the *fravashi* probably are *dii manes*, and their festival among the Parsis has all the characters of an all-souls' day. *Gēush urvan*, 'the soul of the ox,' is to be considered as the *fravashi*, the deified soul, of the ox, and as such the protector of cattle and of all the good things of which it is the symbol. The *fravashi* of all creatures existed already before creation proper. Moreover, the creation of all living things was dependent upon the production of a prototype. The 'tree of all seeds' and the *gaokerena*, 'ox-horn,' 'tree of life,' growing in the sea Vourukasha, are causing all plants to grow and thrive. The primeval bull contained the germs of all animals, and, as mentioned above, its soul nourishes and protects the animal world. The first man, Gaya Maretan, born from the sweat of Ormazd, perished, but his seed brought forth the first pair, Mashya and Mashyoi, from whom all mankind has descended. The soul of Gaya is invoked with that of the bull.

Against all those prototypes of good creation Ahriman spent his rage. Against the *gaokerena*-tree he formed a lizard in the deep water of Vourukasha, that it might injure the tree, but the marvellous *kar*-fish protected it. The primeval ox was also killed by Ahriman, according to the *Bundahishn*, while another myth represents Mithra as the slayer of the animal. Gaya Maretan was a victim of the demons. His seed only escaped, preserved by Ārmaiti as goddess of the earth.

The cosmogonic struggle is thus found in all aspects of the Zoroastrian creed. As said before, it is also the leading feature in the moral and religious life of the faithful. By the practice of virtue man places himself on the side of Mazdāh. By sin he makes himself a prey to evil spirits. The duties of the righteous are the upkeep of the worship of Ormazd and the *yazatas*, the preservation of the sacred fire, and the veneration of the dead.

Of personal virtues it is honesty and straightforwardness that are most highly valued. Scrupulous purity is demanded, and this consists not only in abstinence from adultery, rape, unnatural vice, and the like, but also in all manner of ritual performances relating to sexual relations and to all contact with ceremonially unclean persons or objects, especially corpses.[3] Charity towards the poor and hospitality towards the stranger are likewise preached as virtues. In the sphere of social virtues, down from Zoroaster's time, the duty of the tillage of the soil and of cattle-breeding is exalted to the rank of a primary virtue. The tenderest care surrounds the ox and the dog.

[1] Cf. art. Amesha Spentas. [2] Cf. art. Fravashi.
[3] Cf. art. Purification (Iranian).

This extremely moral code is marred to a certain extent by the childish character of some minute observances for which, in the *Vendīdād*, sanctions are provided as grave as those which refer to genuinely criminal actions. Thus it is as grave an offence, *e.g.*, to refuse food to a dog as to allow a priest to die of starvation.[1] For a Western conscience the code is also disfigured by the canonization as a virtue in the Pahlavi books of the *khvetukh-dāh*, 'incestuous marriage.' This curious aberration was probably due to a custom of the nobility desirous to preserve purity of blood and breeding. Parsis to-day deny that the word in question is to be translated in this way at all.[2]

The penances imposed for the expiation of sins or the removal of pollution are manifold. They are indicated at length in the *Vendīdād*, which enlarges especially on the number of blows with an ox-goad. Offerings later replaced those bodily penances. Certain crimes, such as cremation and sins against nature, cannot be expiated and make the guilty *pesho-tanu*, 'lost body,' *i.e.* irretrievably the prey of the *druj*. This should be understood to mean that no good acts could make up for those great sins, since Zoroastrianism in its doctrine of merits accepts the principle of compensation.

5. Zoroastrian worship. — The Zoroastrian temples contain the urn in which the holy fire burns. Over it perfumes are sprinkled from time to time. Five times a day a *mobed*, 'priest,' enters the room. The lower part of his face is covered with a veil (Av. *paitidāna*), preventing his breath from polluting the sacred fire, and his hands are gloved. He lays down a log of sandal-wood and recites three times the words *duzhmata, duzhukhta, duzhvarshta*, to repel 'evil thoughts, evil words, evil deeds.' Every Zoroastrian has, moreover, a sacred fire in his own house.

The liturgy includes the daily recitation of a few verses of the Avesta. For this purpose the sacred book has been divided into short portions which are arranged according to the date on which they must be recited, not according to their natural interrelation, exactly like the Gospels in a Missal. While he recites the prayers, the priest holds in his hands the *baresman*, or bundle of twigs.

Each month and each day has its patron. The chief feasts are the New Year (Pers. *naurōz*), the equinoxes consecrated to Mithra, the *gahanbars* at the change from one season to another, the days of the dead at the end of the year, the days of full moon and new moon. The sacrifice consists of an oblation of bread and *myazda* (this term, applied originally to solid offerings, was later applied to milk). Besides this there was, despite Zoroaster's ban upon it, the sacrifice of the *haoma* (=Skr. *soma*), an intoxicating plant of which the stems were crushed in a mortar and the juice strained off; this was presented before the fire and drunk by the officiating priest (Av. *zaotar*, Pers. *zōt*) and his acolytes (*raspi*).

A child at birth has his lips steeped in *haoma*, but he does not become a full Zoroastrian until, between the ages of twelve and fifteen years, he receives the girdle (*kushtī*), which he will always wear thenceforward except at night. The presentation of this girdle forms the centre of a ceremony which lasts nine days.[3] On this occasion the young man makes choice of a director of conscience (*ratu*).

Marriage is a duty for the Zoroastrian, and its ritual, as celebrated to-day, is borrowed from Hindu customs. The customs and rites connected with death and the exposure of the corpse on *dakhmas*, 'towers of silence,' are described in artt. Death and Disposal of the Dead (Parsi) and

[1] *Vend.* xiii. 59 f. [2] Cf. art. Marriage (Iranian).
[3] See art. Initiation (Parsi).

PURIFICATION (Iranian). For three days the soul of the Mazdæan haunts his home, and then takes wing for the judgment tribunal (*ākā*), where it presents itself before Mithra, Sraosha, and Rashnu. Its merits and demerits are weighed in the balance. If neither scale sinks, the soul proceeds to the *hamēstakān*, 'equilibrium.' Otherwise it must take its way to the abode of bliss (Pers. Behesht = Av. *vahishta*, 'best,' or *garōnmāna*, 'house of songs,' home of eternal light, lovely dwelling of Vohu Manah, where the souls rest upon the rugs of gold), or, if it is to be damned, it falls from the bridge of Chinvat into the abyss of darkness with its great variety of torments described in the vision of Arṭa i-Virāf, the Persian Dante. But that hell is not eternal. There will be a general resurrection when the molten metal will have purified everything and everybody.[1]

6. Influence of Zoroastrianism.—The teaching of Zoroaster, after having spread among the Magians, eventually took hold of the whole of Īrān. Did it extend beyond the borders of the Persian world? There is still surprisingly great uncertainty on this point, due not only to the fact that few persons have a real knowledge of Mazdæism but also to the difficulty of drawing a line between direct borrowing from Zoroastrianism proper and the more subtle penetration of ancient thought by Iranian (or Magian) conceptions in general. As said above, the probabilities are that Zoroaster preached in Eastern Īrān and that the ideas especially associated with him can hardly have reached either Jews or Greeks in a pure form. In the question of the relation of Judaism to Mazdæism one must distinguish between Gāthism, late Zoroastrianism, the doctrines which are transmitted only through Pahlavi books of Sasanian times, and the doctrines which are common to Magism and to the various sects of Īrān. As Gaster, after Söderblom, Böklen, etc., shows, there is little in Judaism that can be shown to have been actually borrowed from Zoroastrianism.[2] Yet this does not exclude a mutual interpenetration—especially in exilic times—between the ideas of Jews who had gone far into the Persian empire and those of the Persians with whom they appear to have felt themselves in real sympathy. It is, however, impossible in our present state of knowledge to obtain any certainty on any particular detail. An important angelology and the idea of a resurrection and of a kingdom of God are found at an earlier period in Īrān than in Israel, but the development of those conceptions among the Jews, according to most Semitic scholars, can be accounted for without Persian influence. It is, however, hardly doubtful that this cause acted at least as a ferment.

The only part of the Bible which is directly inspired by Mazdæan (not Zoroastrian) ideas is the book of Tobit.[3]

As to the similarities of all kinds existing between Christian or late Jewish eschatology and cosmogony and the Mazdæan accounts as found in Pahlavi books, they of course are explainable by the interpenetration of all religious ideas in the near East at the beginning of our era. The Jews here have probably given much to the Zoroastrians, while, in other cases, both may have been submitted to the same influences.

Greek philosophy offers an analogy. Here also up to Hellenistic times one is confronted with an evolution which does not seem to be dependent upon any external factors. Yet, although the originality of Greek thought—as a whole—can hardly be questioned, it is probable that, if we knew more about the movement of ideas in Asia at that time, we should be able to discover various connexions which do not appear at present. As things are, one can only suspect the influence of the East in a general way on the old philosophers of the Ionian coast. Did Heraclitus, *e.g.*, who was born in Ephesus, hear indirectly of some Magian conceptions? There is in any case a curious resemblance between the conception of *asha* (=*arta*), 'law of the universe,' 'moral law, which manifests itself in fire,' and Heraclitus's first principle, which is a fire, a law of order (λόγος), a moral law (man's perfection is in his conformity to the law of the universe), and a manifestation of the godhead, opposed to darkness. He, moreover, believed in a world-conflict tending to greater order (πόλεμος πάντων μὲν πατήρ ἐστι, πάντων δὲ βασιλεύς). It is not without interest to point out the fact that Heraclitus's conceptions are recognizable in the complex system of the Stoics. It is admitted by all historians of philosophy that, although this doctrine has to a large extent been derived from the teachings of Greek sages, it has been seriously influenced by Eastern thought. Now the founders of the school, with very few exceptions, came from Cilicia (Chrysippus of Soli, Zeno of Tarsus, Antipater of Tarsus) or Cyprus (Zeno of Citium). Tarsus, a great commercial and intellectual centre, was perhaps the most cosmopolitan city of the Mediterranean. With Hittite and Assyrian antecedents, it became for centuries the capital of a province of the Persian empire. It had a Greek and a Jewish colony. In common with Iranian thought (although one can hardly speak of real borrowing), Stoicism has a prevalent ethical preoccupation, a striving for submission to the law of nature (*asha*=*arta*). Φύσις for the Stoics is identical with λόγος. This cosmic law is identified with fire, which is God. Men are either wise and good (σπουδαῖοι) or fools and bad (φαῦλοι), just as Zoroastrianism only knows of *ashavan* and *dregvan*. Fire will finally consume the whole world in an ἐκπύρωσις, which is the exact equivalent of the *mazē yāh* of the Mazdæans. The ethical dualism of the Stoics is in contradiction with their cosmic pantheism, a fact that could be accounted for only by admitting that it has been imitated from an Eastern (Magian?) doctrine.

At Alexandria Hellenistic philosophy was in closer contact with Jewish than with Iranian conceptions. Philo, however, certainly heard of the Magian system. His δυνάμεις, or potencies, intermediary between God and the world, in spite of their Greek colouring, are reproducing the idea of the *amesha spentas*. Just as *asha*, 'law of the world,' is the greatest of the latter, the λόγος, who at the same time is a σοφία, is at the head of the δυνάμεις. In man the νοῦς, 'spirit,' works in the flesh to raise him through virtue to identify him with the pure spirit of God, just as Vohu Manah, the spirit of Mazdāh, brings man to salvation. This Iranian aspect of conceptions that were mostly Greek has struck Darmesteter to the extent of making him think that Zoroastrianism had developed out of Philonian philosophy. This, we have shown, is impossible, but there is some connexion in the reverse order.

The Neo-Pythagoreans have been most directly under Magian influence, although the fact does not seem to have sufficiently attracted the attention of the historians of philosophy. The fact had probably already struck the ancients, and this may be the origin of the tradition that represents Pythagoras as receiving at Babylon the teaching of the Magians. Although it would be impossible to verify this statement, the case is very different with those who in the 1st cent. B.C. tried to revive his teachings. They were Orientals, and the best

[1] Cf. art. STATE OF THE DEAD (Iranian).
[2] See art. PARSIISM IN JUDAISM.
[3] Moulton, p. 332 ff.

known of them, Apollonius, was from Tyana, in that province of Cappadocia which received a peculiarly strong Iranian influence. A sharp dualism of spirit and matter was the fundamental postulate of their theory in the sense that the former was the good principle in life and the latter the bad, unholy principle. God is the πνεῦμα (cf. Spenta Mainyu).[1] Between Him and the world there are mediating dæmons. In substance they are Plato's ἰδέαι, but they are regarded as 'thoughts of the divine mind,' which makes them the equivalent of the *amesha spentas*. Man's spirit is in a corporeal prison and has to free itself through purification. It is immortal. Neo-Pythagoreanism is the first Greek system which expressed the principle of authority in the form of divine revelation,[2] and in this especially it is inspired by Zoroastrianism. Its saints are divinely favoured men who have had the intuition of the divine good mind (cf. Vohu Manah), like Zoroaster and in general all the *ratu*.

Gnosticism with its syncretic tendencies could hardly have escaped absorbing Zoroastrian ideas. There are many systems of γνῶσις[3] which have a dualistic theory of the world in which matter is eventually bad. They all have mediating potencies between God and the world (αἰῶνες). Σοφία, one of the æons, attempts a union with God. Now in Plutarch's enumeration of the *amesha spentas*[4] σοφία is the translation of Ārmaiti, the genius of wisdom and the earth. There is a tradition of Ārmaiti as the spouse (or daughter) of Ahura Mazdāh and the mother of all creatures,[5] which is nothing but a Magian interpretation of the old mythical marriage of 'heaven and earth.' Christ's 'æon' has joined corporal Christ in the manner of a *fravashi*.[6] Christ saves the world through science (γνῶσις) from ignorance and deception (cf. *druj*).

As to Manichæism (*q.v.*), its relation to Iranian religion has never been doubted. The recent discovery of an important Manichæan literature in Eastern Turkestan, no doubt, will throw much light on the problems connected with that sect which had such a hold on the ancient world. Manichæan dualism is as radical and as cosmological as that of Mazdæism. It recognizes two principles eternally contiguous, distinct and separate. The kingdom of light is guarded by the æons (=good angels=*amesha spentas*). The good spirit has a series of virtues. The equilibrium is broken by an attack of the evil spirit, just as in Zoroastrian cosmogony. Man has to fight for the kingdom of God (cf. Xshathra Vairya). A great catastrophe (cf. *mazē yāh*) will restore the cosmic order. Jesus 'patibilis' is like a light diffused in the world (cf. Mithra). He is accompanied by a Jesus 'impatibilis' (*fravashi*). Salvation, as for the Gnostics, is operated by knowledge. In the ascetic rule of the Manichæan there is a threefold seal of mouth, hands, and bosom, corresponding to the Zoroastrian triad of good words, good works, and good thoughts. There is the same emphasis on purity as in Zoroastrianism, and the head of the society is supposed to represent Mani, just as the head of the *mobeds* was Zarathushtrotema. Manichæism, in fact, should be considered as a Mazdæan sect contaminated with Christian ideas. Mithraism (*q.v.*) is another scion from the Iranian religious stem. It should be considered, however, as a rival to Zoroastrianism—even to Mazdæism—rather than to one of its aspects.

[1] Windelband, tr. Cushman, p. 344 ff.
[2] *Ib.* p. 345.
[3] The word γνῶσις is the exact translation of Avesta and of Zend interpretation.
[4] *De Is. et Os.* 47.
[5] Cf. West, *SBE* xviii. [1882] 417, app.
[6] The Gnostics, like the Mazdæans, gave two souls to man.

As to the doctrine of Mazdak (*q.v.*), which was presented in the 6th cent., it was more social than religious. It advocated State socialism with a communism extending even to women. These theories were associated with asceticism.

Although this review of the influence of Mazdæism is necessarily superficial, and in some parts only tentative, it shows how important has been the part played by that doctrine in the elaboration of the syncretic religious mentality of the near East. The seduction exerted by the Iranian conceptions is to be found in the simple solution which they give to the problem of evil. While the philosopher finds himself almost invariably attracted by some form of a more or less radical monism, the ethical man will find a simple and inspiring background sufficient for practical purposes in the doctrine of the conflict between the good principle and the powers of darkness. Iranian religion is ethical and pragmatic. It furthers activity, productivity, industry. It is decidedly unfanatical. It stands in sharp contrast to Indian faith, which out of the very same original data developed in a metaphysical direction towards pantheism and mysticism.

On both sides popular polytheism has been absorbed into a much more exalted doctrine, which is for the wise men. The Mazdæan system is much less profound, but much more intelligible. It makes for piety and good conduct, while the other is better adapted to meditation and asceticism. The aim of the former is the 'righteous man.' The ideal of the latter is the 'holy man.' The principle of revelation and of spiritual direction, so essential in Zoroastrianism (Zoroaster calls himself *ratu*, 'spiritual director,' or *saoshyant*, 'the coming helper'), is another aspect of its practical nature. The Zoroastrian not only has a clear vision of life after death, and of the means of reaching eternal happiness, but he is striving for the immediate realization in this world of a social, ethical, and religious organization of a very concrete character. This explains both why his religion extended by proselytism and why it gradually became closely associated with one nationality. All the characteristics had prepared it to be a State religion, and so it was under the Sasanian dynasty.

Its religious literature during that period is extensive, but not very appealing. There is no philosophy in it, no poetry, no religious transport, no sentiment. It is a collection of didactic, moralizing, interpretative considerations in which some myths, genealogies, and cosmological and eschatological considerations are enclosed. The translations and commentaries to the Avesta form a large part of it.

On account of its simplicity of cult and doctrine, its lack of mysticism, its belief in a revelation made by a prophet and preserved in a book, Zoroastrianism did not differ enough from Muhammadanism to be able to offer to it the long resistance displayed during so many centuries by Christians in Turkish and Arabic lands. The history of the conversion of Persia is not very well known, because it is to a large extent the story of an adaptation of a religious mentality to new forms without giving up any essential elements of the previous creed. All the traditions of Irān were preserved in Persia under a thin cover of Muhammadanism. Moreover, Zoroastrianism never completely disappeared from Persia, where it is still practised by the Gabars around Yazd. Other orthodox Zoroastrians resorted to emigration and formed in Western India, especially at Bombay, the community of the Parsis which has survived up to the present time.[1]

[1] Cf. artt. GABARS and PARSIS.

LITERATURE.—A. V. W. Jackson, 'Die iranische Religion,' in *GIrP* ii. [1904] 612 ff.; K. F. Geldner, art. 'Zoroaster,' in *EBr*[11]; J. Darmesteter, *Le Zend-Avesta*, i., Introd., Paris, 1892–93, Introd. to *SBE* iv.[2] [1895]; C. P. Tiele, *Geschiedenis van den Godsdienst in de Oudheid*, Amsterdam, 1895–1901, ii.; H. Oldenberg, 'Die iranische Religion,' in *Die Kultur der Gegenwart*, London, 1906, i. 31; C. de Harlez, *Avesta: Livre sacré des sectateurs de Zoroastre*, Paris, 1875, Introd.; M. Haug, *Essays on the Parsis*[4], London, 1907; M. N. Dhalla, *Zoroastrian Theology*, New York, 1914; L. C. Casartelli, *La Philosophie religieuse du Mazdéisme sous les Sassanides*, Louvain, 1884; L. H. Mills, *Zarathushtra, Philo, the Achæmenids and Israel*, Chicago, 1906; J. H. Moulton, *Early Zoroastrianism*, London, 1913; N. Söderblom, *La Vie future d'après le Mazdéisme*, Angers, 1901; E. W. West, *Pahlavi Texts* (*SBE* v. [1880], xviii. [1882], xxiv. [1885], xxxvii. [1892], xlvii. [1897]); C. Bartholomæ, *Die Gāthās des Awesta*, Strassburg, 1905, *Altiranisches Wörterbuch* (definition of the Zoroastrian religious terms, etc.), Strassburg, 1904; A. J. Carnoy, *Iranian Mythology* (=*Mythology of all Races*, vi.) 2 f.; see also artt. ACHÆMENIANS, AVESTA, GABARS, ORMAZD, PARSIS, PARSIISM IN JUDAISM, etc.

A. J. CARNOY.

ZULUS.—See BANTUS.

ZUÑI.—The religion of the Zuñi in the town of that name in western New Mexico is, like the religion of the other Pueblos, a highly ritualized structure elaborated upon the primitively animistic religion of the American Indians generally. This Pueblo religion is perhaps the most complex and also most closely welded system of native cults north of central Mexico. Within its compass the Zuñi have evolved an organization even more intricate at some points than that of the Hopi, Keres, and Tanoan groups. Being nearer the heart of Pueblo civilization on the Rio Grande, their religion is more representatively Pueblo in its forms, and more sharply crystallized, than that of the peripheral Hopi. Less exposed, on account of comparative remoteness, to the pervading competition of Roman Catholicism and the inevitably disintegrating influences of Caucasian civilization, than the Keres and Tanoans, the Zuñi have preserved their cults in greater intactness. And their concentration under Spanish influence for over two centuries in a single large town has provided the occasion or stimulus for a special set of elaborations that would not have been feasible while they lived, as the other Pueblos still do, in smaller settlements.

This religion may be examined as to the beliefs upon which it rests, as to the ritual apparatus which it uses, and as to its machinery for relating individuals to the national cults.

I. *BELIEFS*.—**1. Maize.**—The most pervading concept in Zuñi religion is a group of ideas connected with the fertilization and growth of maize. This lends a strong symbolic value to all parts of the plant, but especially the pollen, the ripe ear, and the meal; to water, springs, streams, lakes, which promote the growth of maize; to animals associated with water, such as frogs, tadpoles, turtles, dragon-flies; to the mythical horned serpent, inhabitant of waters; to the squash blossom, as the most conspicuous of the fertilizing mechanisms of cultivated plants; to rain, mist, clouds, and therefore to their accompaniments thunder, lightning, rainbow; to the sun as germinator and vivifier; and to the genital parts and functions and indications of the two sexes. A few random examples must suffice out of the thousands that might be cited.

The rooms where maize is stored are entered only after prayer and barefoot. Corn meal is sprinkled on altars, on dancers who impersonate gods, and as an offering generally; pollen enters as an ingredient into fetishes and medicines. Most flowing springs are shrines; the *kokko* gods and the Zuñi dead live in a lake; ceremonial objects are destroyed by burial in the Zuñi river. Yucca suds are raised by priests to denote and bring foam and clouds; their bowls bear tadpole and dragonfly symbols. A whole series of summer dances, and of penitential retreats by the priests, is designed to bring rain. The squash blossom, lightning, and rainbow appear on masks and dancers' accoutrements. The *Ololowishkya* dance is a frankly phallic, though decent, representation referring to maize.

This wealth of symbolic ideas and acts, being organized into a definitely centred system, differs from the equally magical but much more miscellaneous beliefs and practices of most non-Pueblo Indians. The coherence goes far to indicate the developmental antiquity of Zuñi and Pueblo religion; for an unsystematized condition must have preceded the existing interconnected one.

2. Ancestor-worship.—The dead, at least those of them who were Zuñi and tribally initiated, are thought to become *kokko* gods; the first of these originated, long ago, from Zuñi children that fell from their migrating mothers' backs. The *kokko* are the *kachina* or *katsuna* of the other Pueblos—a large and varied class of gods impersonated by masked dancers, whose appearance is thought to bring rain and other benefits. The Zuñi therefore are ancestor-worshippers; but in general it is the undifferentiated mass of the dead that is prayed to or honoured, and there exist no cults of family and lineage.

3. Animal-gods. — The practice of deifying animals the Zuñi share with all other Indians, but work out in peculiar Pueblo form. Since they possess no true shamans, they do not as individuals dream of animals or pretend to receive supernatural potence directly from them. They do, however, associate animals with medicine. The curative fraternities are thought to have been instituted with the help of animal-gods. The fetishes which these societies employ on their altars comprise figures of beasts, especially beasts of prey.

4. Witchcraft.—The belief in black magic and witches is very deeply rooted in the Pueblo and Zuñi mind. Witches are members of the community, often whole families, who practise in secret to the harm and death of other Zuñi or even the entire community. There is some idea that they constitute a society parallel to the recognized curative societies, but of course meeting only in the deepest secrecy. Besides producing epidemics and individual sickness, they cause accidents, blast crops, and neutralize the efforts of the constituted priests to bring rain-clouds. Public sentiment often runs mutteringly against a witch for many years and then suddenly crystallizes. Once an open charge has been made, the victim is tried and often executed by the Bow Priests of the Warrior society. Usually an attempt is first made to extort a confession by suspension by the thumbs or other torture. Until the suspect is accused, he is avoided as much as possible without any open giving of offence, and takes part in public and ritualistic acts as if he were not under the most threatening of clouds. No non-Pueblo Indians possess beliefs as to witchcraft that are so standardized or that so enter into daily life as those of the Zuñi. Among other tribes the evil wizard and the beneficent shaman are often not seriously differentiated. An individual is believed to use the identical spirit or magical power according to circumstances: every shaman is a potential witch and every witch *ipso facto* possesses shamanistic power. This is the attitude of the Pacific Coast tribes. For the central and eastern portions of the continent there does not seem to be so complete a merging of the two sets of powers as this, but the antithetical differentiation which the Pueblos make is also lacking. The causes of the anomalous specialization of Pueblo witchcraft beliefs appear to be twofold: (1) they have outgrown the normal American belief in the shaman, medicine being practised by the heads of highly organized and ritualistic societies, whose leaders enjoy their faculties by virtue of election to their offices instead of receiving them in personal communication with the spirit world; as the beneficent shaman has been replaced by these society heads, so the evilly-minded shaman has crystallized among the Pueblos into the more or less professional although concealed witch; (2) influence of Spanish civilization must be reckoned with. The whole cast of Zuñi witchcraft suggests that of Europe a few centuries ago—the innate and persistent malignity of the witches, the complete secrecy of their operations, the legalized system of accusation, torture, and punishment. As yet there has been no demonstration of derivation from European sources. At the same time it is probable that, when the Spaniard settled among the Pueblos more than three hundred years ago, he was able to strengthen and solidify their beliefs as to witchcraft precisely because these beliefs were already tending towards a status more nearly resembling that of contemporary Europe than that of the other American Indians.

5. Supreme being. — Awonawilona has been described as 'the supreme life-giving bisexual power, the symbol and initiator of life pervading all space.'[1] The Zuñi do seem to regard Awonawilona as a sort of ultimate power, but the word appears to mean 'those who hold the roads'—'of life' being understood. Awonawilona is therefore not so much a defined single chief deity as a group or class of vague powers.

6. Origin beliefs.—The Zuñi have a long origin story. In the beginning of things there existed Awonawilona, Sun father and Moon mother, and Shiwani and his wife. *Shiwani* is the Zuñi word for 'priest,' but in other Pueblo languages the word denotes 'lightning' or 'thunder,' and in the present connexion it appears to express a deification of the power of priests. Shiwani and his female counterpart are said to have been the parents of the Zuñi, who were born in the lowermost of four subterranean worlds, called the fourth or Soot World. They were led out of this by a ladder cut from a pine-tree by two sons of the sun, Kowituma and Watsusi. From the third or Watermoss World they climbed by a spruce to the second or Mud World, and from this up an aspen to the first or highest of the subterranean levels, the Feather or Sunray World, where they first saw faint light. The two guides then led them by a silver-spruce to this world, the place of light of day, the spot of emergence, Chimikyanapkyatea, being located by the Zuñi in the west or northwest. They already had priests and fetishes in the lower world and brought with them witches and maize. In fact it was the witches who carried the seeds of things with them, and the Zuñi were forced to accept the death-bringers in order not to be deprived of maize. Kowituma and Watsusi appointed Yanowuluha as *pekwine*, or deputy of the sun—the spiritual leader of the nation. The people at first were human but with tails, long ears, webbed hands and feet, and a body-covering of moss. They travelled in a general easterly direction through a long series of places, staying in each four years (time periods), and were closely followed from the lower worlds by the Hopi, Havasupai, and Navaho tribes. Their first stop was at Awisho ('moss'), where their leaders cut their webbed hands and feet and organized the earliest of the ritual societies.

After long wanderings, the head priest sent out his son and daughter Siwulutsiwa and Siwulutsitsa to look for a new abode. The pair, however, committed incest, with the result that ten children of deformed appearance were born, nine of whom, together with their father, are impersonated by the Zuñi of to-day as the *koyemshi*, clowns who wear knobbed masks, act as attendants on the other masked dancers, and perform interludes of buffoonery. Siwulutsiwa also made the Little Colorado and Zuñi rivers, and near their junction a lake and in its depths a town, Kotluwalawa ('god-town'), which became the home of the *kokko* gods and the Zuñi dead.

In their farther journeyings, as the people crossed the river, the members of the *Tlewekwe*, or Staff society, preceding, the children scratched and bit their mothers' backs until the frightened women dropped them into the water. The children were transformed into tadpoles, turtles, frogs, and watersnakes, and then, swimming to Kotluwalawa, took on human form again and became the first of the *kokko*. The two divine leaders visited Kotluwalawa, found the children adult and masked, and returned to report that they had not really died.

Next Hantlipinkya was reached, where Kowituma and Watsusi assigned clan names to groups of the people. Their place as guides and directors now began to be taken by the diminutive war-god twins, Uyuyewi and Matsailema, sons of the sun and the waterfall. The war-gods soon led the Zuñi and allied *kokko* into battle against a group of hostile gods known as the Kyanakwe, the conflict with whom is dramatized in a quadrennial ritual of the same name. Two survivors of the Kyanakwe who possessed fetishes and maize-seeds were adopted into the Zuñi maize clan. Still continuing their search for the spot which was to be their ultimate home, the people finally reached the vicinity of modern Zuñi, and, after several tentative settlements, found the sought-for middle-place when Waterskate stretched his legs to the ends of the four directions and declared the centre of the world to be beneath his heart. Here Zuñi was built, which the Zuñi still call indifferently Itiwanna, 'the middle,' or Halonawa, 'ant place,' or Shiwanakwe, 'Zuñi place.'

The settlement of the people in this town was followed by the gradual completion of their religious institutions. The *kokko* came from God-town to organize the performance of the masked dances, including the great *shalako* ritual. Then the corn maidens—divinities who had brought maize with them from the lower world—were discovered, frightened and driven away, found again after witches had reduced the Zuñi to famine, brought to the town, and induced to institute the *Tlahewe* ceremonial and leave their seed treasures. Kowituma and Watsusi visited Shipapolima, where lived Poshayanki, the great juggler. From him the existing societies received additional powers, and new ones were founded by him. The divine beings who had accompanied Poshayanki in his emergence from the lower worlds were converted into animals to preside over the six directions and to serve as fetishes in the society rituals. The twin war-gods, having taken the first scalp, instituted the victory dance and Warrior society.

Finally a flood drove the people to the summit of the mountain Towayalana until it was stayed by the sacrifice of the son and daughter of the high-priest. Redescending, the Zuñi lived in a number of villages (as the Spaniards found them in the 16th cent.); but one after the other these were destroyed by divine anger, until only Zuñi proper remained.

The striking elements and traits of this origin story are (1) the ideas of birth from the earth and wandering in search of a final abode; (2) the pseudo-historical cast of the entire myth; (3) the centring of its interest in the tribe as such, balanced by an indifference to speculations on the origin of mankind or animal life; (4) the fullness with which ritual institutions are explained and the contrasting lack of interest in non-ritualized divinities.

II. *APPARATUS.*—The concrete apparatus of Zuñi religion, both physical and intangible, is exceedingly elaborate, and only a few of the more striking developments can be touched upon. The

[1] M. C. Stevenson, *23 RBEW* [1904], p. 22.

content of their religion is essentially that of the other Pueblos, but is modified in many details.

1. Numbers, colours, directions.—Number symbolism is introduced into every aspect of ritual with monotonous insistence, but is enriched by linkage with reference to colour and direction. The directions are always thought of in a fixed order: north, west, south, east, above, below, to which the middle or whole is sometimes (although usually by implication rather than explicitly) added as the seventh. The corresponding colours are yellow, blue, red, white, variegated, and black. There are prey animals, birds, trees, and a variety of other classifiable natural objects identified with these directions and colours. Maize is actually grown in an astounding variety of colours of the grain, but these are reduced in the Zuñi mind and religious practice to the standard six varieties. Where six is not used, the ritual number is four, the above and below being in this case omitted. Periods of time are usually grouped by fours or multiples thereof. Thus certain ceremonials are performed quadrennially, and the number of days for which the priesthoods go into retreat is either four or eight.

2. Prayers.—Highly formalized prayers are much used by the Zuñi. They are definitely standardized, couched in a language which may be more or less archaic and is certainly ritualized, and are recited in a rapid muttering drone. Certain prayers belong to the constituted priests alone, others are spoken by religious officials or laymen. The tenor is understood even when many of the words are difficult of explanation by the speaker.

3. Feather sticks.—The visible embodiment of prayer, and at the same time the most important form of offering, is prayer sticks (*telikyinawe*), short rods to which feathers are tied according to exact rules and which are then set out in shrines or buried in the ground. These feather sticks are 'planted' by every priesthood before every ceremony, by the officials of all societies, for the dead, and on regular occasions such as the recurrent year or moon. They have many slightly differing forms according to their purpose. They are always deposited privately.

4. Altars.—Altars of some sort enter into all major rituals. The most elaborate are those of the curing societies. These consist of a painting made on the floor in coloured earths, behind which is set up an elaborate screen of slats which is carved or painted with symbols; and of animal images, stone concretions, sacred corn ears, offerings in bowls, and similar paraphernalia deposited on or about the ground painting. Priests' altars are simpler: the screen is wanting and the sand painting is replaced by one of coloured maize meal. In general, altars are set up indoors for esoteric portions of ceremonies, and put away at their conclusion. Allied to altars are shrines—nearly always out of doors—at which offerings, especially of prayer sticks, are made. These shrines may be springs, clefts in the rocks, or small stone cysts on the summit of knolls. They are visited by priests, by society officials, and by dance impersonators.

5. Masks.—The most spectacular apparatus of Zuñi ritual is the mask, which is made in enormous variety of elaborate and standardized forms. There are probably a hundred kinds, each with a name and definite place in cult. With a mask go a specific costume and style of body paint, although these are not as diversified as the masks. Every mask represents a deity, and the dancer who has donned one is himself called *kokko*, or god. These *kokko* being the *kachina* of the other Pueblos, many Zuñi masks recur among the Hopi or on the Rio Grande. The names are sometimes the same in towns of different stock; at other times they are as different as the masks themselves are similar. In some instances importation of a mask from one Pueblo to another can be traced by indirect evidence, or is admitted by the natives themselves. In this interchange the Zuñi seem to have given and received about equally. Most of the masks are monstrous, some animal-like. This does not argue that the Zuñi look upon their gods as terrifying rather than beneficent. It seems that limitations of technical skill prevented the Pueblos from making their masks representatively beautiful, but did not prevent their attaining effects that are grotesquely interesting and decoratively pleasing. In other words, their conceptions of the *kokko* are the result of the masks which it was within the powers of the Zuñi to make. Manual ability directed beliefs more than the reverse. This comes out clearly in the fact that many of the masks representing goddesses are bearded. The beard simplifies the construction and allows the wearer's song to issue unimpaired while effectually concealing his identity. It may be added that masks are regarded as extremely sacred, and that the uninitiated children and younger women seem to believe the wearers to be true gods.

6. Fetishes.—The most sacred of all material objects in the Zuñi religion are certain fetishes called *ettonne* (plural *ettowe*), and these they have developed to a greater extent than the other Pueblos. The *ettonne* shows a fundamental relationship to another class of fetishes called *mi'le* (plural *miwe*), 'maize ear,' which is the form more current elsewhere in the region. The *mi'le* is an ear of maize sheathed in feathers and otherwise specially prepared. It is the badge of membership in the curing orders of the societies. These *miwe* are individual property and are buried at the owner's death. The *ettowe*, on the contrary, are supposed to have been brought up in their present physical form from the lower world, and appertain to groups—priesthoods, societies, clans, etc. They are guarded with extreme care, 'fed' with offerings, never exposed except when ritual definitely provides; and even the room in which they are kept is tabu. They seem to consist of several reeds bundled together and filled with materials that are either precious in themselves or symbolic of the precious things of life: meal, pollen, seeds, turquoise, and the like. The *ettowe* are enclosed in native cotton and kept in wrappings. They number about fifteen each for the priesthoods, the societies, and the clans, besides a few of more special reference.

III. *ORGANIZATION.*—On the side of organization or hierarchy of functioning individuals, Zuñi religion has developed in three principal directions: (1) there is a series of thirteen societies or fraternities whose most distinctive function is the religious curing of disease; (2) there is a communal organization which conducts the dances in which the *kokko* are impersonated; (3) there is a series of priests, or rather priesthoods, devoted to the spiritual welfare of the nation. The communal society and the priesthoods are linked by the fact that their objectives, such as rainfall for the crops and other general blessings, are the same. This does not of course imply that they are the historical result of the same impetus. They share, however, in native theory a devotion to the interests of the community at large, whereas the factor of individual benefit enters more definitely into the scheme of the fraternities.

1. The fraternities.—The fraternities are thirteen in number and are treated by the Zuñi as full equivalents of one another. They are all organized on the same pattern, with membership by initiation, secret meetings, and esoteric rites; and in general they are open to men, women, and children alike. The only exception is that one Hunters' and two Warriors' societies are entered by men only. These three bodies nevertheless are very similar in organization, rites, and paraphernalia to the curative bodies, thus evidencing the strong tendency of the Zuñi to equate all societies, irrespective of differences in their origin or avowed purpose. For instance, the Cholla-cactus people are a Warrior society secondary to that of the Bow Priests. They admit men who have not yet scalped an enemy and thereby attained to membership among the Bow Priests, but who have fought in battle or been wounded. At the same time they resemble the curing societies in that they heal wounds.

(*a*) *Warrior societies.*—The most unique of all the societies is that of the Bow Priests, not only on account of the limitation of membership, but especially because the members are looked upon as the guardians and physical executors of the decisions of other religious officials. They are the soldiers, as it were, who enforce the decrees of the paramount theocracy and guard the masked dancers. At least one of their number—and if possible two—is chosen as a member by each of the other fraternities to protect the altar and keep out intruders. This is the only case of an individual being an active member of more than one society. The Bow Priest fraternity is also unique in that it alone possesses two heads. These two are the representatives of the twin war-gods, and in this capacity sit with the supreme council of priests as watchers and administrators. It is to them that the execution of witches, *e.g.*, or the taking away of his staff of office from a deposed governor would be delegated.

A Warrior society corresponding to the Zuñi Bow Priests appears to have existed in every Pueblo, the development of the institution among the Tanoans and Keresans being very similar to that of the Zuñi, whereas among the Hopi the organization was less important, probably because Hopi religion was less centralized.

(*b*) *Hunters' society.*—The *Saniakyakwe*, or Coyote society, spiritually fosters the hunting interests of the tribe and supervises the rabbit hunts which are a conspicuous feature of the *kokko* worship. It does not treat illness, but its organization and ritual are wholly of a pattern with that of the curing societies.

(*c*) *Curing societies.*—The remaining societies all heal. They are, however, diverse in origin, according both to Zuñi belief and to comparative analysis. The oldest societies, according to native tradition, are the *Ne'wekwe* and *Shi'wanakwe*, which correspond to the Clown and Dancing societies of the Rio Grande, the *Koshairi* and *Kwirana*. The *Ne'wekwe* have kept the clown features of the *Koshairi*, and sometimes appear in public dances. They also cure, however; and the *Shi'wanakwe* have become purely a curing society, scarcely to be distinguished from any other. The *Tlewekwe*, or 'Wood' (*i.e.* Staff-swallowing) society, with the two foregoing, and the Hunters, are the four earliest fraternities in native belief. The *Tlewekwe* is given a special position in mythology (see above), and has particular rain-making functions. The Little Fire-brand and the Great Fire-brand societies are said to have originated later, the former being derived from the Hopi and the latter instituted in the period after the mythical Poshayanki began to instruct the societies in medicine. The *Uhuhu*, *Ant*, and *Shuma'* groups are also thought to owe their origin at least in part to Poshayanki. The first of these has no known equivalents among other Pueblos. The second seems to be a local equivalent of the Rio Grande Knife societies; and the *Shuma'* is the equivalent of a *Sayapa* or *Shumaikoli* society elsewhere, which is distinguished by the possession of masks. The last two Zuñi fraternities, the Rattlesnake-medicine-water and Bedbug, must be of comparatively recent origin, since tradition recalls that they arose as the result of splits within the *Uhuhu* and the Little Fire-brand bodies. A close parallelism of ritual confirms tradition on this point.

Each of these fraternities has a head or chief, a speaker or deputy to the chief, a medicine chief, and usually other functionaries. They are divided into orders, the most important distinction being between members who know medicine mystery and those who do not; in most societies only the former possess *mi'le* fetishes. There are special orders for fire-eating, staff-swallowing, and feats of jugglery which vary from society to society. Yet the orders recur: it is not only the Fire-brand societies that eat fire, and not only the Staff society that swallows.

Initiation into the societies takes several forms. The commonest is by sickness. A person seriously ill is 'given' to one of the officials and after cure by him remains almost in the position of an adopted child. If he can afford the necessary payments, he becomes a member. This idea that the purpose of the societies is to cure and that it is curing that constitutes membership is deeply impressed on Zuñi consciousness. Another method of admission is by trespass: a man breaks into an esoteric ritual, has seen what he should not see, and can expiate the offence, in fact save himself from the consequences, only by learning the remainder of the mysteries. In practice admission by trespass seems to be a means of legal fiction through which adults can quickly enter a society while in good health. It is also a rule that a member of any society can transfer from one to the other with only a nominal re-initiation. Such transfers are numerous as a result of personal disagreements.

2. The communal Dancing society.—Dances, or, it would be better to say, ritualistic exhibitions by masked performers representing *kokko*, are very numerous, and there is scarcely a month when they cannot be witnessed in the streets and plazas of the town. An elaborate set of exhibitions begins at the winter solstice, when a sequence of gods not seen at other times appears. Shortly after follows a series of rites known as the 'cleansing the earth.' Thereupon comes a series of dances called *koyupchunawe*, in which the members of the six estufas synchronously dance on six occasions for one to eight nights. A sort of aftermath are the 'little dances,' which continue irregularly for a couple of months. At about the same period, during spring, occurs the quadrennial initiation with the image of the sacred horned serpent. Towards the end of spring comes the rabbit hunt, participated in by masked performers and the people at large. At the summer solstice a visit is made to the sacred lake of the dead. The return from this is in masks and initiates the series of summer dances, six in number. In late summer and early autumn there fall three ceremonies: the *Owinawe*, a harvest festival under the direction of the Bow Priests, the *Tlahewe*, a maize ceremony performed quadrennially without masks, and the *Kyanakwe*, also quadrennial, which is an elaborate dramatization of a myth and introduces masks not worn on other occasions. The year is brought to a close in the month preceding the winter solstice by the *Shalako*, which from the exoteric aspect is the most sumptuous and elaborate of all Zuñi rituals.

These ceremonies are performed by the adult, *i.e.* initiated, males of the Zuñi nation, as constituted into the *Ko-tikyili*, or '*kokko* fraternity,' *i.e.* God society. It is interesting that the Zuñi name this organization as if it were a restricted curing society. Boys are initiated twice, in what may be described as the involuntary and the voluntary initiations. After the second they wear masks in ceremonies. Women become members only under very exceptional circumstances. The membership is grouped into six sub-organizations about equal in numerical strength, each of which has its own *kiwitsine*, or 'estufa,' *i.e.* ceremonial chamber. Membership in these estufas is arranged on a criss-crossing plan. A man after initiation joins that estufa to which belongs the husband of the woman who first touched him at birth. This brings it about that estufa affiliation does not follow the lines of cleavage formed by clans, curing societies, or other groups, and normally puts father and son in different estufas. Each estufa makes its dances separately; and, even in what may be called strongly communal rituals, the mask allotment and other functions are on an estufa basis. The entire God society is under the direction of a 'god chief' and a 'god speaker' who must be members of certain clans. The whole organization is intricate, as is necessary for the continuous practice of so elaborate a ritual. At the same time it obviously is closely knit, as if designed to prevent its breaking apart into conflicting units. Even the competitive rivalry which the six estufas evince tends to make them feel themselves parts of a whole.

3. Priests.—Above and apart from the societies and the communal God society stand the 'rain priests,' *shiwani* (plural *ashiwani*), to whom is entrusted the spiritual welfare of the nation. They take as little part as possible in mundane affairs, do not dance, go into fixed retreats for fasting, penitence, and meditation, and by the blamelessness of their conduct, concentration of mind, and sacredness of office, are thought to keep peace, cause the community to prosper, and above all bring the rains upon which the crops and sustenance of the people depend. In Zuñi theory public ceremonies are largely only an exoteric accompaniment to the still more important esoteric activities of these priests. They are organized into fifteen sets, each of which consists in theory of a priest proper, his associate and prospective successor, two assistants, and a female associate. The last, in spite of her venerability, is not properly a priest, but has special duties connected with the care of the fetish which is the vehicle of continuity of each priesthood through the generations. In practice the constituted membership of each priesthood is sometimes greater or less than this scheme demands.

The first four of these fifteen priesthoods, those which 'go in' first in the series of penitential retreats, and represent the north, east, south, and west, are the most sacred. Among these the first, the 'house-chiefs,' again have the primacy. The fifth priesthood is anomalous in consisting only of the *pekwine*, or 'speaker,' of the sun, who is the regulator of the calendar and the guardian of public sanctity, and is expected to be the individual removed above all others from worldly affairs. He typifies the 'above,' whereas the 'below' is represented by the two head Bow Priests, representatives of the war-gods. Strictly, neither *pekwine* nor the Bow Priests are priests like the others; but they are so reckoned by the Zuñi, and, on occasions such as the retreats spoken of, function like them.

The source of government in Zuñi is theocratic. There are a governor and other civil officials; the priests do not interfere in the affairs of men. The civil officials, however, are chosen or nominated and can be deposed by a supreme council of six priests—the 'daylight people,' as they are called. These consist of the chief priests of the four first sets, with two additional priests from the first priesthood. The Bow Priests sit with the council as guardians and execute all its decisions. The head of the council, and in fact of the entire Zuñi hierarchy, is the *kyakwemosi*, or house-chief proper, whose power is almost that of a pope.

4. Origin of the hierarchical system.—This intricate hierarchical organization has parallels among other Pueblos, but has nowhere else attained the same degree of elaboration. Its power and sanctity are so great as to leave a first impression that the hierarchy is the basis of all Zuñi religious organization. Analysis and comparison, however, reveal that it is of secondary and probably rather late origin. The 50 or 60 priests represent an elaboration of a smaller number; probably this nucleus was the six 'daylight people,' since such a body functions on the Rio Grande without the accompaniment of additional priesthoods. The kernel of this group of six appears to be its primate, the house-chief, who in authority and sanctity corresponds to the *tiamoni*, or 'cacique,' of the Rio Grande Pueblos. There too he always has a speaker or deputy, has his decisions executed, if need be, by the heads of the Warrior society, and is aided in council by associates, who are normally the heads of the leading fraternal societies. This simpler organization of the Rio Grande obviously makes a less sharp distinction than the Zuñi one between priests, curing societies, and the communal dance organization. The course of development at Zuñi seems to have been that the concept of the cacique, or of the cacique *plus* deputy, was reduplicated first into a group of four or six priests; that then these were given associates and assistants; and that finally still other priests and associates were added, until the present large number had been attained. The luxuriance of this development led to such abundance of material for specific priestly purposes that the curing society heads became unnecessary in this connexion and came to withdraw from the hierarchical organization, restricting themselves almost exclusively to the functioning of their respective societies. The same process carried further probably led to a more complete separation of the communal, or *kokko*, society. As this grew in independence, it came to need more organization of its own. One result of this process of differentiations seems to have been the limitation of the estufas to the communal society—a condition which occurs only at Zuñi. In general, then, the special traits of Zuñi ritual organization are a greater functional differentiation and consequent greater elaborateness than elsewhere, but without loss of coherence.

The principal cause in this development is likely to have been the size of Zuñi Pueblo. It may be suspected that, while this people lived scattered in half-a-dozen independent towns, the organization of each was more similar to that of the Keresans and Tanoans. When, however, under the influence of the Spaniards and perhaps of Navaho and Apache raids, the Zuñi more than two centuries ago assembled in a single town, the concentration in numbers may have forced, and certainly stimulated, a tendency towards systematization. Where half-a-dozen ill-defined priests had sufficed for a population of a few hundreds, a larger number with more specialized functions would be called for in a closely compacted community of two or three thousand. It is also possible that the example of the ever-present Roman Catholic priest may have aided in this development, especially as regards the rain-priest as distinguished from the society heads and dance directors. It does not appear, however, that this influence was more than secondary at best. Both the nature of the priestly office in the Zuñi mind and the fact that a similar development failed to take place on the Rio Grande, where Roman Catholic influence was even stronger, point in this direction.

LITERATURE. — M. C. Stevenson, 'The Zuñi Indians,' *23 RBEW* [1904], p. 13, 'The Religious Life of the Zuñi Child,' *5 RBEW* [1887], p. 539; F. H. Cushing, 'Zuñi Fetishes,' *2 RBEW* [1883], p. 9, 'Outlines of Zuñi Creation Myths,' *13 RBEW* [1896], p. 325, *Zuñi Folk Tales*, New York, 1901; E. C. Parsons, 'Notes on Zuñi,' pts. i. and ii., *Mem. Am. Anthr. Ass.*, iv. [1917] 149, 227, 'Zuñi Winter and Summer Dance Series in 1918,' *Univ. Calif. Publ. in Am. Arch. Ethn.* (in press); A. L. Kroeber, 'Zuñi Kin and Clan,' *Anthr. Pap. Am. Mus. Nat. Hist.*, xviii. [1917] 39. There are dozens of brief studies, most of which are referred to in one or the other of the foregoing works.

A. L. KROEBER.

ZWINGLI.—1. Early years.—Ulrich (Huldreich) Zwingli was born on 1st Jan. 1484, in the little township of Wildhaus—the highest village in the Toggenburg valley. He sprang from its most prominent family. His father was a leading farmer and the chief magistrate. His uncle Bartholomew was the parish priest, and afterwards (1487) dean of Wesen. The clerical traditions of the family on both sides determined the boy's career. His education, begun at Wesen with his uncle, was continued at Basel and Bern. In his school-days his progress in learning seems to have been less conspicuous than his proficiency in music. In fact, his musical gifts nearly made him a monk. At fourteen he was sent to the University of Vienna, apparently because it was a centre of the Humanists. He may have spent at least one term in the University of Paris.[1] But neither Vienna nor Paris was to be his real Alma Mater. In 1502 he returned to Basel. For four years he studied there, supporting himself by teaching, and graduated in 1504 as Bachelor and in 1506 as Master. So ended his school and university career, spent in Humanist schools and universities, but following the familiar Scholastic routine, for which there was as yet no substitute. It was not till later, during his first cure of souls, that the Humanist impulse was to become so strong that it burst the old bottles.

2. Early ministry.—Immediately on graduation he was appointed parish priest of Glarus, where he remained for ten years (1506–16). There his effective education began. He seems at first to have been absorbed in classical studies, in music, and in the history of his native land. Typical of those days is the *Fable of the Ox*, his first literary effort, a somewhat crude warning against the dangers that lurked in the popular mercenary service. But that his opposition was not irreconcilable is manifest from the fact that in the campaigns of 1513 and 1515 he served as chaplain with his own men from Glarus, being with them both at Novara and at Marignano. His experiences in Italy undermined some of his accepted tenets about the authority of the Church, and just at the moment when doubts and questions were jostling in his mind he came into contact with a whole new world of thought through Erasmus. Erasmus's programme of a 'restitution of Christianity' through the *philosophia Christi* fired his imagination. He caught at once his contempt for Scholasticism and his conviction that the true Christian philosophy was to be found only in the moral teaching of Jesus and of His great disciple, Paul. '*Ad fontes*' became his motto. So in 1516, when Erasmus published his Greek New Testament, Zwingli was an early reader, and very soon most of it was transcribed into note-books to be learned by heart. Acquaintance with it revealed how far the Church which he had so lately imagined unchanged and unchangeable had really fallen away from the NT standard. With an alert and critical mind he began to study what traces he could find of the stages of this decline in Christian history.

[1] So W. Köhler, *Zwingliana*, Gedenknummer auf Neujahr 1919, p. 7.

Meanwhile his hostility to the mercenary service had been growing, and a second poem called *The Labyrinth* proved unacceptable to the warlike parish of Glarus. Zwingli, therefore, accepted the position of preacher at Einsiedeln, the great pilgrimage resort of Switzerland. Here he came to know at first hand superstition, saint-worship, relic-worship, and the abuse of indulgences. During his two years at Einsiedeln Zwingli was advancing steadily towards the Reformed position. Can we say further, with some of the early historians of the Reformed Church, and as Zwingli himself more than once asserted, that in those days at Einsiedeln he had already reached his full Reformed position, and that, in consequence, he anticipated Luther? We cannot. The papal pension (continued till 1520) and the pilgrimage to Aachen (1517) are conclusive. But it is clear that, if his conscience was not yet touched, his mind was awake, and the amount of Scriptural and Patristic knowledge he acquired during those two years is a real matter for wonder. Alike in moral life and in teaching he was still Humanist rather than Reformer.

3. Work in Zürich.—On 27th Dec. 1518 Zwingli removed to Zürich, which was to be henceforward the centre of his activities. He went as people's priest in the Great Minster. At the beginning of the year he announced his programme from the pulpit. He was going to expound the Scriptures, book by book and chapter by chapter. He began with St. Matthew's Gospel, the favourite book of the Humanists because it contained the Sermon on the Mount, the basis of the *philosophia Christi*. Then came the Acts of the Apostles, that in the primitive Church men might see after what pattern the Church ought to be. Then followed Galatians and 1 and 2 Timothy, to make Paul's teaching familiar; then the two Epistles of Peter, to show how Peter agreed with Paul. By 1525 Zwingli had preached through the whole of the NT. Long before that, however, the Reformation had been established. From the first his preaching was so fresh, so full of new ideas, that the services were thronged. Very soon he had to begin a market-day series, on Fridays, on the Psalms. One of the strongest proofs of his popularity and influence is that, in the very first year of his preaching (1519), a bookseller came to Zürich and placed his printing-press at the service of the new movement. This was Christopher Froschauer; round Zwingli and him there gathered at Zürich a literary circle comparable to that already assembled at Basel round Erasmus and Froben.

The year 1519 saw a deepening of Zwingli's convictions. This was due partly to the early works of Luther and partly to the coming of the plague, with which Zwingli, who had fearlessly returned to duty after its outbreak, was attacked. These two together seem to have hastened him along the road he was unconsciously travelling, from Erasmian to Reformer. Simplification of the liturgy and drastic action in regard to mercenary service were premonitory symptoms of the breach that was coming. The first definite move in the religious revolution came in the Lent of 1522, as a result of Zwingli's preaching, though he himself took no part in it. The form it assumed was a revolt against the law of the Lenten fast. Zwingli was not slow in justifying the action of his friends. In their defence he published his first Reformation tract *Von Erkiesen und Freiheit der Speisen* ('Concerning Selection and Liberty in Foods'). The City Council incurred the anger of the bishop of Constance by dealing, and dealing leniently, with the offenders. In August 1522 Zwingli issued his first Reformation treatise of any length, the *Archeteles*, which did in Latin and for the learned what his next works, the *67 Articles*, and their *Exposition*, did in German and for the common people. In the beginning of 1523 took place the first Zürich disputation, of which the *67 Articles* formed the programme. It was a triumph for the party of reform, and a great personal triumph for Zwingli. At its close the Great Council pronounced its decision that the accusations of heresy against Zwingli were unfounded, and that he was 'to continue as before to proclaim the Holy Gospel, and the true, Divine Scriptures.' Further it declared that all other preachers and pastors in the city and the country were 'not to preach anything which they could not establish by the Holy Gospel, and the pure, Divine Scriptures'; and that they were to refrain from personal controversy and bitter names. The victory of the Reformation in Zürich was thus assured. But the practical steps remained to be taken, and these involved divisions of policy and further disputations. The monasteries began to empty. Better uses were at once found for them as hospitals and academies. The Great Minster was transformed into something not unlike a Theological College. The energy spent in the performance of innumerable masses was transferred to Biblical and Biblico-theological instruction. A vernacular ritual came into use, first in the Sacrament of Baptism. Change in the Lord's Supper was much slower. The old service held its place in Zwingli's own Church till April 1525.

Sporadic and unauthorized removal of images and the imprisonment of the offenders led to the second disputation in Oct. 1523. The programme of removal and the gradual change of ritual were put into the hands of a committee of laymen and ministers whose business was to devise means 'for moving forward the work of Christ.' The line along which they moved forward proved unacceptable to the few remaining adherents of traditionalism in Zürich, and their protest was the occasion of the third disputation, in Jan. 1524. Its decision was an order to these Scholastics to carry out loyally the line of action of the Council. The breach with the old order was complete, and the new order rapidly took shape. The temporary committee gave place, in 1525, to church courts for discipline and for marriage cases. By 1527 a synodical organization was complete. During all these revolutionary actions the pope pronounced no anathema. He was still not without hope of military help from Zürich. Zürich, in turn, encouraged the hope, for it was waiting for arrears of military pay. The Swiss mercenary service had made the path of Reformation much smoother than in Saxony.

4. **His varied activities.**—During the third decade of the 16th cent. there can have been few busier men in Europe than Zwingli. One might thus catalogue his manifold labours.

A. He had to think out his plan of Reformation, and to communicate the conclusions he had reached to a great host of active sympathizers in other centres by letter and to the general public in book and pamphlet.

In addition to the works referred to above, mention should be made of the *Short Christian Introduction*, the nature and intention of which are fully indicated in its extended title, 'A short Christian introduction which the honourable Council of the city of Zürich has sent to the pastors and preachers, living in its cities, lands, and wherever its authority extends, so that they may in unison henceforth announce and preach the true Gospel to their dependants'; *Der Hirt* (1524), or, as it is called in the English translation of 1550, *The Image of Both Pastors*, an expansion of a sermon preached to the pastors present at the second disputation; the *Commentary on the True and False Religion*, the most comprehensive summary of his mature teaching; the treatise *On Divine Providence*; and the *Confession of Faith* presented to the Diet of Augsburg (1530), generally known as *Ratio Fidei*.

B. From the pulpit and by private interview he had so to educate the people of Zürich and, in particular, the members of its governing bodies, that they would be prepared to take action along the line of Reformation, no matter what it should cost.

Although Zwingli's official position from 1525 was that of head of the Carolinum, the theological college of Zürich, he continued his public expositions of Scripture, passing to the OT—especially the Prophets—when he had run through most of the NT.

C. In order that the Evangelical reforms might be firmly rooted in the intelligent sympathy of the people, it was necessary that the Bible should be put into their hands in the vernacular.

Here his task was lightened by the industry of Luther. Luther's NT, finished in the Wartburg in 1522, was being printed in Zürich in 1524. This was speedily followed by the historical books of the OT. But Zwingli could not wait for Luther's translation of the Prophets. So an independent translation was begun, and finished in 1529. A complete German Bible appeared in Zürich in 6 volumes by 1529, and a single-volume edition in 1530. Switzerland, therefore, had the Bible complete several years before Germany. Though the main burden of translation fell on his friend and colleague, Leo Jud, Zwingli's share in it is by no means negligible.

D. He had to defend his Reformation against radicals who thought that Zürich had not gone half far enough.

This radical element, which was to develop into Anabaptism, made its first public appearance at the second disputation. Conrad Grebel was their leader, and their point of view was that a clean sweep ought to be made at once of images and ritual and all the disastrous accumulations of fifteen centuries, and that this was Zwingli's esoteric teaching. In particular, they challenged Zwingli to produce any Scriptural warrant for tithes or infant baptism. In 1524 these dissidents were confirmed in their positions by two visitors from the Anabaptists of Germany, Thomas Münzer and Andreas Carlstadt. This widened the breach. Zwingli saw the Reformation movement slowly disintegrating into two, and saw some of his friends taken captive by what they felt to be the purer Biblicism of the new movement. He appealed to them not to form a separate body. The appeal was in vain. The separation took place. For the healing of the breach Zwingli proposed the inevitable public disputation. The first took place in Jan. 1525. The decision was against the Anabaptists. And it was followed by a decree that all unbaptized children must be baptized within a week, or their parents would be banished from Zürich. The council soon proceeded to severer measures. One of the leaders suffered death by drowning, and others were banished.

No movement could have given more trouble to Zwingli. As they took their stand on Scripture, and as Zwingli claimed to do the same, the controversy was the fiercest he was ever called upon to face. The impression left by his numerous treatises is that, to find grounds for condemning them and their practices, he was driven to exaggerate the non-essential peculiarities of the movement. It was not these writings, but the fate of the Peasants' Revolt in Germany, that eased the strain.

E. At the same time as he was called upon to encounter radicals within the movement he had to deal with champions of the old order. The most prominent phase of this was the disputation which, after long negotiation, took place at Baden in 1526. Œcolampadius of Basel and John Eck were the protagonists. Zwingli was not present. But much of the work fell on him. Messengers were constantly coming and going. Thomas Platter's autobiography gives a vivid picture of the extent of his assistance. The disputation served Eck's purpose, in increasing Lutheran suspicion of the unsoundness of the Zwinglians in regard to the Lord's Supper. We note here also the more important of the relevant controversial works: the *Antibolon* (1524) against Jerome Emser, 'defender of the canon of the Mass'; and the *Answer to Valentin Compar* (1525).

F. He had to take a large part in the first phase of the prolonged controversy between Lutherans and Reformed concerning the Lord's Supper. For details see art. EUCHARIST (Reformation and post-Reformation period).

G. During those years Zwingli was drawn more and more into the main stream of federal politics. The rival confessions within the confederacy and their rival leagues created a situation which demanded the constant vigilance of a statesman. And it was on Zwingli that Zürich leaned.[1]

H. In the midst of all these labours Zwingli maintained his Humanist studies. In 1526 there was published in Basel Ceporin's edition of the poems of Pindar, with a preface and a conclusion by Huldrychus Geminius.

I. But the main concern of Zwingli during the later 20's was to secure the Reformation in Zürich by introducing Reformation teaching and practice into every city and canton of the confederacy.

In Bern the value of the preparatory work of Berthold Haller was revealed by the thoroughness of the Reformed victory in its disputation in Jan. 1528, in which Zwingli took the leading part. This same disputation brought to a head the new movement in Basel, where Œcolampadius had long been actively at work. Vadianus was his correspondent in St. Gall, which, with Glarus, Schaffhausen, and Appenzell, followed Zürich's example in Zwingli's lifetime. A certain measure of success was attained in the allied Graubund, but elsewhere the results were meagre.

5. The last years.—Certain of the cantons were untouched by the Reformation, and were as keen to retain the 'common lands' as Zwingli was to win them. A cleavage within the confederacy appeared, and deepened into uncompromising hostility. The League of the Forest Cantons, formed at Beckenried in 1524, was soon faced by a counter-alliance. Both parties made a strong bid for outside help, but, before any effective assistance had been secured by either, the first Civil War broke out. It was short and bloodless. There was no battle. The two armies which came face to face at Cappel (1529), instead of fighting, negotiated terms of peace. The terms were a triumph for Zürich, but it speedily appeared that there were more than one possible interpretation of them. The civil war had only been postponed. The feverish search for outside alliances continued. The Marburg Colloquy, in Zwingli's mind, was no unimportant part of this quest. More time was spent by Zürich and by Zwingli in fruitless foreign negotiations than in independent preparation. Amid all this talk of help from outside it ceased to manifest the old self-help. The war began by a blockade of the Forest Cantons, which only served to rouse them to more vigorous action. They took the field in force. Zürich's improvised resistance was a failure. For Zürich the battle of Cappel (1531) was a veritable Flodden. Zwingli was among the slain. In his forty-eighth year this great pacifist and patriot fell on the field of battle. The second treaty of Cappel reversed the first. But under Henry Bullinger and his associates the work of reformation continued, though the leadership of the Swiss Reformation soon passed into the hands of Geneva.

[1] For these political movements see an excellent brief account in *Cambridge Modern History*, ii. 326 ff.

6. Appreciation.—Very diverse judgments have been passed on Zwingli's doctrine and work. Apart altogether from those who know him only from some inadequate statement of his doctrine of the Lord's Supper and who, in consequence, use the name Zwinglian almost as equivalent to rationalist, among those who are professed students of his teaching there is a sharp division of opinion. On the one hand it is said: 'His world of thought, as a whole, and also in its inner component parts, is more mediæval' [than Luther's].[1] The opposite is just as confidently maintained: 'Luther took up his station on the ground already occupied by the Latin church: his desire was only to purify; to put an end to the contradictions between the doctrines of the church and the gospel. Zwingli, on the other hand, thought it necessary to restore, as far as possible, the primitive and simplest condition of the Christian church: he aimed at a complete revolution.'[2] Now, without doubt, in the collected works of Zwingli, written at different times, out of the heart of widely different controversies, it would be easy to find material for justifying either of these conclusions, but not much progress is made by bandying about the word 'mediæval' as a term of reproach. In essentials Zwingli and Luther were nearer each other than they let themselves believe, as Martin Bucer saw. Having regard to its purpose, one must call the Marburg Colloquy a failure, but it did reveal how much at one the protagonists were. There was, certainly, a difference of emphasis. Zwingli had not the same all-transforming, world-renewing experience to drive him onwards. His theology was more Biblical than experimental. Even when he had caught the thrill of Luther's protest, it came to deepen rather than to change the direction of the impulse he had received from Erasmus, the desire to explore the sources, to get back to the simplicities of primitive Christianity, to the pure, untainted Church of the NT. It is significant that the Zürich Reformation followed hard after Zwingli's exposition of the Acts of the Apostles, interpreted as historically as the knowledge of that day would permit. It is significant also that the full programme of the *67 Articles* has this preface:

> 'The articles and opinions below, I, Ulrich Zwingli, confess to have preached in the worthy city of Zürich *as based upon the Scriptures* which are called inspired by God, and I offer to protect and conquer with the said articles, and where I have not now correctly understood said Scriptures I shall allow myself to be taught better, but only from said Scriptures.'[3]

Further, largely in consequence of this Biblicism, the reformation he directed was more radical. What Zwingli specially detested in the later growths which had buried this early Christianity was anything that could be called 'the worship of the creature.' Worship belonged to God alone, 'the God and Father of our Lord and Saviour Jesus Christ.' He did not undervalue art or music in themselves—far from it—but, when they were so employed as to hinder an intelligent approach to the Creator, then to him they were anathema. The most conspicuous feature of Luther's protest against mediævalism was its anti-Judaic side—his hostility to its conception of work-righteousness; in Zwingli's it was the anti-pagan—his hostility to its idolatrous corruptions.

This note was dominant at the beginning, and, despite all alterations and deepenings, it remained dominant to the end.

[1] R. Seeberg, *Dogmengeschichte*², Leipzig, 1917, IV. i. 357.

[2] L. von Ranke, *Hist. of the Reformation in Germany*, London, 1905, p. 521.

[3] S. M. Jackson, *Selections from Zwingli*, Philadelphia, 1901 p. 111.

'Eight or nine years ago,' he wrote in 1523, 'I read a comfortable fiction written on the Lord Jesus by the learned Erasmus of Rotterdam: in which Jesus complains that men do not seek all good things from Him, whereas He is the fountain of all good. Then I thought if this be the case, why do we seek help from the creature? I began to search in Scripture, and the works of the fathers: whether I could find there any certain information with regard to prayer to Saints. In short I found nothing of it in the Bible at all; amongst the ancients I found it in some, and not in others. However, it did not much move if *they* did teach prayer to saints. For they always stood on testimony alone. And when I read the Scriptures which they quoted for this purpose, in the original, they had no such meaning as they wished thrust upon them; and the more I considered this doctrine of opinion, the less authority I found for it in Scripture, but rather more and more against it.'[1]

This and similar autobiographic reminiscences can be too strongly stressed. We must ever remember that most of them are influenced by his claim to independence of, and priority to, Luther. But in them all there appears, undesignedly, this anti-pagan interest.

Zwingli's radicalism is perhaps most apparent in his keen eye for, and his strong detestation of, what the Scottish Reformers were accustomed to call the 'dregs of papistry.'

Still further, this difference of emphasis is apparent in the doctrine of God, not so much in its content as in the place it occupies in the system. Though Zwingli doubtless owed here something both to Seneca and to Pico della Mirandola, his doctrine, like Luther's, is accurately enough described as Pauline and Augustinian. No one, however, would be likely to seek in his doctrine of God Luther's fundamental conception: it is otherwise with Zwingli.

'While Lutheran Protestantism protested against the Judaising righteousness by works, it asked the question, What is it in man that wins salvation? and gave the answer, Not works but faith, whereas the Reformed Protestantism asked, Who is it that saves, the creature or God?, and answered, God alone, salvation being referred to its ultimate source in the fore-ordaining and determining will of God.'[2]

This trend of Reformed Protestantism is not to be traced to Calvin alone; it goes back to Zwingli. Though not so evident in his earliest Reformation treatises, it began to be increasingly evident in the controversies with the Anabaptists. One of their strongest arguments against baptism as practised by the Reformers was that the infant was incapable of the faith which alone could give it meaning; to which Zwingli replied that baptism might easily precede faith, for election does: 'antecedit igitur electio fidem';[3] indeed, 'ii qui electi sunt, filii dei sunt anteaquam credant.'[4]

From all this, leaving out of account their great divergence on the doctrine of the Lord's Supper,[5] it is evident that Zwingli was no mere echo of Luther from the mountains of Switzerland, but that he evolved a type of reformation, pursuing a parallel path, which was determined largely before ever the news of Luther's heroic stand at Wittenberg gave it the momentum which carried it to victory. What Zwingli contributed to it was the Humanist training and the Humanist outlook.

1 *Werke*, Zürich, 1828 ff., i. 298.
2 W. Hastie, *Theology of the Reformed Church*, Edinburgh, 1904, p. 145 (expounding Schweizer).
3 *Werke*, Zürich, 1828 ff., iii. 426.
4 iii. 426.
5 For which see art. EUCHARIST (Reformation and post-Reformation).

Nor did he ever forget them. One of the things which made Luther doubtful if Zwingli were a fellow-worker or, indeed, a fellow-Christian was his continued regard for the heroes of classical antiquity, whom, in his very last writing, the *Fidei Expositio* (1531), addressed to Francis I., he placed along with the OT worthies and the saints and fathers of the Church in the heaven he hoped to reach.

'Denique non fuit vir bonus, non erit mens sancta, non est fidelis anima, ab ipso mundi exordio usque ad ejus consummationem, quem non sis isthic cum deo visurus.'[1]

Humanist, Biblical scholar, protestant, liberal, patriot as he was, Zwingli could never have been the main agent in carrying through an epoch-making reformation, even with the conditions to help him: he lacked the passionate earnestness and driving force of Luther; but, with the aid of Luther's work, he did accomplish a reformation to which many in our generation feel more strongly attracted than to either its great German counterpart or even its Genevan completion.

LITERATURE.—The best guide to all but the most recent Zwingli literature is to be found in G. Finsler, *Zwingli-Bibliographie*, Zürich, 1897. Later studies are fully dealt with in *Zwingliana*, do. 1897 ff.

i. *Works*.—The earliest collected ed. was that of R. Gualther, Zürich, 1545, which was superseded by the excellent ed. of M. Schuler and J. Schulthess, 8 vols., do. 1828–42 (Supplement, 1861), which in turn is now giving way to the ed. in progress in the *Corpus Reformatorum*, vol. 88 ff., ed. E. Egli, G. Finsler, and W. Köhler, Berlin, 1905 ff. An English tr. was begun under the editorship of S. M. Jackson, vol. i., New York, 1912, to whom also we are indebted for *Selections from Zwingli*, Philadelphia, 1901. An admirable summary of the contents of Zwingli's writings is that of P. Wernle, *Der evangelische Glaube nach den Hauptschriften der Reformatoren*, vol. ii. 'Zwingli,' Tübingen, 1919. A popular ed. in modern German of Zwingli's main writings is that of G. Finsler, W. Köhler, and A. Rüegg, Zürich, 1918. Mention should be made, too, of O. Farner's similar ed. of Zwingli's letters, Zürich, 1918.

ii. *Life and teaching*.—Among the older biographies and the more recent treatments the most valuable are: J. C. Mörikofer, *Ulrich Zwingli nach den urkundlichen Quellen*, 2 vols., Leipzig, 1867–69; A. Baur, *Zwinglis Theologie*, 2 vols., Halle, 1888–89; R. Stähelin, *Huldreich Zwingli; sein Leben und Wirken nach den Quellen dargestellt*, 2 vols., Basel, 1895–97; S. M. Jackson, *Huldreich Zwingli, 1484–1531*, New York, 1901; S. Simpson, *Life of Ulrich Zwingli*, London, 1903; T. M. Lindsay, *A Hist. of the Reformation*, vol. ii., Edinburgh, 1907; E. Egli, *Schweizerische Reformationsgeschichte*, ed. G. Finsler, vol. i., Zürich, 1910; A. Lang, *Zwingli und Calvin*, Bielefeld, 1913; W. Köhler, in *Unsere religiösen Erzieher*[2], Leipzig, 1917; O. Farner, *Huldreich Zwingli*, Zürich, 1917; P. Burckhardt, *Huldreich Zwingli, eine Darstellung seiner Persönlichkeit und seines Lebenswerkes*, do. 1918; W. Köhler, *Ulrich Zwingli und die Reformation in der Schweiz*, Tübingen, 1919, *Die Geisteswelt Ulrich Zwinglis*, Gotha, 1920.

iii. *Discussions on special points*.—W. Cunningham, *The Reformers and the Theology of the Reformation*[2], Edinburgh, 1866; A. Schweizer, *Zwinglis Bedeutung neben Luther*, Zürich, 1884; J. M. Usteri, *Zwingli und Erasmus*, do. 1885; E. Nagel, *Zwinglis Stellung zur Schrift*, Freiburg, 1896; C. von Kügelgen, *Zwinglis Ethik*, Leipzig, 1902; W. Hastie, *The Theology of the Reformed Church in its Fundamental Principles*, Edinburgh, 1904; J. Kreutzer, *Zwinglis Lehre von der Obrigkeit*, Stuttgart, 1909; G. von Schulthess-Rechberg, *Luther, Zwingli, und Calvin in ihren Ansichten über das Verhältnis von Staat und Kirche*, Aarau, 1909; J. I. Good, *The Reformed Reformation*, Philadelphia, 1916; E. Vischer, in *Zum Gedächtnis der Reformation*, Basel, 1917; P. Wernle, *Das Verhältnis der schweizerischen zur deutschen Reformation*, do. 1918; T. Pestalozzi, *Die Gegner Zwinglis am Grossmünsterstift in Zürich*, Zürich, 1918; O. Farner, *Zwinglis Bedeutung für die Gegenwart*, do. 1919; A. Lang, *Reformation und Gegenwart*, Detmold, 1918; and the special studies in the memorial volume, *Ulrich Zwingli, 1519–1919, Zum Gedächtnis der Züricher Reformation*, Zürich, 1919.

HUGH WATT.

1 *Werke*, iv. 65.

THE END OF VOL. XII.

Printed by MORRISON & GIBB LIMITED, *Edinburgh*

T